世界交通运输工程技术论坛（WTC2021）论文集

（上册）

世界交通运输大会执委会　编

人民交通出版社股份有限公司
北京

内 容 提 要

本书为世界交通运输工程技术论坛（WTC2021）论文集，是由中国公路学会、世界交通运输大会执委会精选的378篇论文汇编而成。此论文集重点收录了交通运输工程领域的前沿研究及创新成果，分为公路工程、桥梁工程、隧道工程、交通工程、运输规划、水上运输、轨道交通、航空运输、交叉学科9个方向。

本书可供从事交通运输工程等领域的人员参考，也可供院校相关师生学习。

图书在版编目（CIP）数据

世界交通运输工程技术论坛（WTC2021）论文集：上中下册 / 世界交通运输大会执委会编. — 北京：人民交通出版社股份有限公司，2021.6

ISBN 978-7-114-17355-4

Ⅰ. ①世… Ⅱ. ①世… Ⅲ. ①交通工程—文集 Ⅳ. ①U491-53

中国版本图书馆 CIP 数据核字（2021）第 095758 号

Shijie Jiaotong Yunshu Gongcheng Jishu Luntan（WTC2021）Lunwenji（Shangce）

书　　名：	世界交通运输工程技术论坛（WTC2021）论文集（上册）
著 作 者：	世界交通运输大会执委会
责任编辑：	韩亚楠　郭晓旭
责任校对：	赵媛媛　卢　弦
责任印制：	张　凯
出版发行：	人民交通出版社股份有限公司
地　　址：	（100011）北京市朝阳区安定门外外馆斜街3号
网　　址：	http://www.ccpcl.com.cn
销售电话：	（010）59757973
总 经 销：	人民交通出版社股份有限公司发行部
经　　销：	各地新华书店
印　　刷：	北京交通印务有限公司
开　　本：	880×1230　1/16
印　　张：	163
字　　数：	4900千
版　　次：	2021年6月　第1版
印　　次：	2021年6月　第1次印刷
书　　号：	ISBN 978-7-114-17355-4
定　　价：	600.00元（含上、中、下册）

（有印刷、装订质量问题的图书由本公司负责调换）

世界交通运输大会执委会学部委员会

编 委 会

主　　席　　沙爱民　张占民

副 主 席　　龙奋杰　陈春阳　安　实　顾祥林
　　　　　　王云鹏　刘　攀　赵　鹏　何　川
　　　　　　杜修力　严　伟　王小勇　谈传生
　　　　　　吴超仲　周建庭　巨荣云

编辑委员会

主　　任　　刘文杰

委　　员　　汪海年　陈艾荣　陈建勋　陈　峻
　　　　　　姚恩建　葛颖恩　张卫华　曹先彬
　　　　　　王兴举　等

本 册 目 录

第一篇 公 路 工 程

地下防洪墙对半刚性沥青路面受力特性影响分析 …… 尹祖超 蔡 鹏 汪鹏福 袁卢均 郑 璐(3)

Investigation on the Self-healing Behavior of Asphalt Binder Based on the Molecular Dynamics
　　Simulation ……………………………………………………… Yan Li　Bowei Sun　Jingwen Liu(8)

基于随机细观模型的沥青混合料劈裂行为研究 ……………… 马 迪 汤 文 王 欢 吕悦晶(17)

移动荷载作用下沥青路面反射裂缝影响因素分析 …………………… 宋 帅 何 帅 杨茂林(26)

Flame Resistance and Pavement Performance of Asphalt Mixture Incorporating Composite Flame Retardant
　　……………………… Yao Tengfei　Han Sen　Men Changpeng　Zhang Zhuang　Dong Shihao　Li Yang(32)

基于旧路分层铣刨的沥青老化规律及老化程度分级
　　……………………………………………… 郝 林 陈 钊 吴建灵 王选仓 李燕军(46)

Preliminary Study on the Problem of Improving the Interfacial Properties of Fiber and Asphalt Binder
　　…………………………… Junxian Huang　Zhibin Su　Susu Xing　Jing Li　Canyun Mao(52)

矿料分异型沥青混合料路用性能及力学参数研究 ……………………… 吴喜荣 郑南翔 雷俊安(58)

层间黏结状态对沥青路面结构使用寿命的影响分析 …………… 孙 强 李 夏 江照伟 韦金城(68)

半刚性基层沥青路面横向裂缝发展规律及影响因素研究 ……… 朱玉琴 倪富健 周 岚 丛 菱(73)

平交口抗车辙沥青路面结构与材料一体化设计研究
　　……………………………………………… 蒋应军 倪辰秧 张 宇 易 勇 邓长清(79)

万州大跨度悬索桥 LUHPC 钢桥面铺装组合方案分析
　　……………………………………………… 李鸿盛 胡凤明 宋 健 丁庆军 付 军(89)

全温域条件下沥青路面加速加载响应规律分析 …… 徐希忠 韦金城 张晓萌 符东绪 李作钰(94)

温度和剪切速率对沥青-集料试件剪切力学特性的影响 ……… 汪忠明 王永春 董满生 吴大帅(101)

基于力学响应的沥青面层改性分级标准研究 ……… 罗耀芦 王选仓 张 义 邓玉缘 宋丽萍(107)

高速公路隧道路面抗滑性能分布规律及养护关键技术研究 …………………… 徐志祥 吁新华(112)

基于胎路耦合的沥青路面摩擦行为数值仿真 ……… 余 苗 罗延生 童铈尧 陈海峰 孔令云(118)

冰-沥青路面黏结特征分析 …………………………… 胡新悦 冷滨滨 王中俊 吕廷军(127)

某山区干线公路灾害恢复重建对策及实践 ………………… 陈俞嘉 康孝先 周子豪 陈祥斌(134)

水性环氧超薄磨耗层抗滑耐久性试验研究 ……………………………………… 李晶晶 张 擎(138)

既有桥梁水下基础防冲刷措施与关键技术分析 …………… 周子豪 康孝先 陈俞嘉 陈祥斌(144)

The Anti-stripping Performance of the Anti-skid Wear Layer of Highway Tunnel Cement Concrete Pavement
　　………………………… Qing Zhang　Wenbo Ding　Tong Shi　Hongchang Guo　Yakun Liu(148)

正负变温条件下引气水泥混凝土强度增长规律研究 …………………………………… 梁 磊(156)

Research on Low Temperature Performance of SBS Modified Asphalt under the Action of Different Regenerants ………………………………… Yanan Cui　Maorong Li　Lidian Guo　Lu Liu(159)

沥青材料分析研究技术进展 ……………………………………………… 高润杰　陈　玉(170)

冻融循环下冷拌环氧沥青的韧性衰减规律 ……………… 王俊彦　于　新　丁功瀛　阮　伟(175)

基于 DSR 流变学测试的老化 SBS 改性沥青性能变化规律
　　…………………………………………… 田周义　李福林　寇小舟　吴祥海　张　壮(182)

一种常温黏稠乳化沥青胶结料的研究 ………… 吴玉辉　蒋明伟　吴耀东　赵冬明　邱百万(189)

融雪盐化物掺量对沥青胶浆性能影响研究 ……………………………… 温钰婷　郭鸿晨(194)

SBS 改性沥青热储存稳定性试验方法研究 ……………………… 彭　煜　从艳丽　杨克红(199)

基于沥青性能快速检测方法的胶粉改性沥青的蠕变变形恢复研究
　　…………………………………………… 蔡凤杰　冯振刚　姚冬冬　陈婷婷　韦金城(204)

冷补沥青混合料材料设计及其性能研究 ……… 孙垚垚　刘安述　吴双全　郑　斌　郭艳明(210)

Evaluating the Relationship between Internal Structure and Moisture Damage of Fiber-reinforced Steel Slag Asphalt Mixture ………… Wenzhen Wang　Aiqin Shen　Ziming He　Lusheng Wang(216)

温度及老化时间对沥青混合料抗疲劳性能影响的试验研究
　　…………………………………………… 张金喜　张阳光　韩丁丁　禚永昌　郭旺达(225)

Experimental Study on Optimum Asphalt Content of Basalt Fiber Asphalt Mixtures Considering Fine Aggregates Reduction …… Yao Zhang　Yuhao Wu　Bangwei Wu　Peng Xiao　Haochen Wu(231)

乳化沥青冷再生混合料动态模量影响因素研究 …………………………………… 李洪祥(240)

Study on the Influence of Benign Temperature Induced Admixture on Thermal Induced Performance of Cement Concrete ………………………… Lv Jiaoyng　Tian Bo　Quan Lei　Li Sili(244)

Research on Freeze-thaw Durability of Porous Concrete based on the Pore Characteristics and Supplementary Cementitious Materials ………………… Li Zhang　Hui Li　Hanbing Wang(251)

Influence of Fluidity of Cement Paste, Cement Dosage and Vibration Forming Mode on the Anti-segregation Performance of Pervious Concrete ……………… Yong Feng　Hui Li　Haonan Zhou(257)

纤维用量对砂浆的工作性和强度影响研究 ………… 郝　运　曹阳森　张　帆　胡鑫康　张　进(270)

Application Evaluation of Steel Slag in Road Base
　　……………………………………………… Wuju Wei　Jinyu Xu　Bingfeng Zheng　Chao Han(274)

基于微观角度废橡胶复合材料性能研究进展 …………………………… 高润杰　陈　玉(281)

Effect of Humidity and Oxygen on the Weathering Aging Process of High Viscosity Modified Asphalt Using a Coupled Rheology-Morphology-Chemistry Characterization Approach
　　……………………………………………… Mingjun Hu　Weiwei Zhou　Daquan Sun　Jianmin Ma(288)

Improving Rheological and Mechanical Performance of Epoxy Asphalt Modified with Graphene Oxide
　　……………………………………… Jingjing Si　Yang Li　Junyan Wang　Xiaoyong Zou　Xin Yu(301)

基于果脯废糖液的公路用液态融雪剂试验研究 ………………… 向　豪　弥海晨　陈华鑫(307)

Research on the Carbon Materials/Polymer Self-sensing Composites for Pavement Micro-strain Detection …………………… Xue Xin　Ming Liang　Linping Su　Zhengmei Qiu　Zhanyong Yao(314)

碱激发矿渣—硅酸盐水泥复合胶凝材料性能与微观结构试验研究

.... 丁 博 张金喜 王建刚 党海笑（326）

建筑垃圾在道路工程中的应用综述 .... 李 想 毛雪松（332）

基于通行能力和安全性分析的集散一级公路硬路肩宽度研究 .... 张方哲 赵一飞 杨思杰（335）

Study on Inspection of Highway Three-dimension Sight Distance Method Based on Civil 3D

.... Zhibo Liu　Tao Wu　Yuhua Peng（341）

高速公路连续下坡路段货车追尾风险研究 .... 马如鹏 胡 涛 王亚楠（350）

公路隧道路段静态行车风险指标体系构建与评估 .... 杨榕玮 靳敏达 张昆仑（357）

高速公路连续下坡路段货车运行速度模型适用性分析 .... 吕 博 罗昱伟 任士鹏（367）

道路行车风险评估模型综述 .... 谢永淑 任晓玮 向宇杰 唐忠泽 杨雅钧（373）

高速公路同向曲线路段车辆行驶轨迹研究 .... 李永春 李 枭 刘 斌 杨榕玮 靳敏达（382）

高速公路分路段横净距评价方法与改善措施 .... 向宇杰 李丙烨 谢永淑 唐忠泽 胡瑞来（392）

高速公路隧道与主线出入口小净距路段行驶特征分析

.... 唐忠泽 翟艺阳 张昆仑 杨雅钧 谢永淑（399）

A New Method of Safety Evaluation for Sharp Bend and Steep Slope Sections of Highway

　Based on Braking Behavior ...... Yajun Yang　Hong Zhang　Bo Wang　Yongshu Xie　Yijing Zhao（408）

公路运行速度模型研究综述 .... 黄春富 魏东东 王亚楠 马如鹏 白 杰（426）

Study on the Influence Factors of Point Load Test by Flat Joint Model of PFC3D

.... Zhi He　Wuchao Yang　Peijie Yin　Changgen Yan（435）

不同击实功下黄土回弹模量变化规律分析 .... 刘贤旺 杜秦文 赵伟杰 程灿灿 魏 进（445）

颗粒圆度对路基填料振动压实影响的离散元分析 .... 方传峰 聂志红 刘维正 刘顺凯（450）

Influence of Relative Humidity on Physical Properties of Bound Water Adsorbed by Loess

.... Hao Zhou　Xuesong Mao（459）

有关硅藻土及地基处理方法研究现状分析 .... 谢锦倩 张宏光 杨婷婷（470）

结合水对黄土抗剪强度的影响研究 .... 周 豪 毛雪松（474）

Stability Analysis of Cracked Loess Slope Based on Upper-bound Method

.... Linxuan Zhu（479）

Analysis of the Influence of Pipe Pile Composite Foundation on the Earth Pressure and

　Deformation Characteristics of Circular Pipe Culvert

.... Zhenyu Song　Weifeng Zhao　Zhongju Feng　Siqi Wang　Yumeng Hao（487）

路面状态对水泥磷石膏稳定土路基模量的影响研究

.... 彭 波 王振生 宋云峰 李奕娜 刘 帅（496）

滨海地区地下水位动态变化对土体影响研究 .... 程马遥 曾 洋 魏 永 杨 虹（502）

某高速公路顺层路堑高边坡病害处治 .... 张 魁（508）

沿海地区岩溶发育区路基处治技术数值分析 .... 伊力夏提·奥斯曼（512）

地下水位变化对基坑非稳定渗流的影响研究 .... 程马遥 魏 永 曾 洋 杨 虹（520）

不同击实功对黄土压实特性影响试验研究 .... 黄鑫中 杜秦文 李宝江 石 磊 魏 进（527）

蒸发条件下非饱和砂性土水汽迁移试验研究 ················· 张建勋　毛雪松(535)

Experimental Study on Strength Degradation Characteristics of Cement-improved Loess under Wetting-drying Cycles ················ Jiangtao Fan　Yingjun Jiang　Tian Tian　Yong Yi(541)

TX-B 型固化剂复配无机材料改良黄土强度特性研究
················· 梁　燕　陈　晨　刘　霜　吴仁悠　张　婧(550)

混凝土结构裂缝检测系统的设计 ················· 龚　涛　苏时玲　廖丽琼(554)

青藏公路路基不均匀变形对路面病害的影响分析 ················· 李　铭　支喜兰(558)

基于惩罚型变权物元理论模型的路面使用性能评价 ················· 黄卫国　张　硕　胡　勇(563)

ECA-10 在预防性养护中的应用及跟踪 ················· 顾艳静(570)

盲沟在泡沫沥青冷再生路面中的应用 ················· 顾艳静(576)

基于红外光谱的老化沥青转移率研究 ················· 唐　伟　李　宁　于　新　詹　贺　张　宇(579)

Research on the Remaining Service Life and Rutting Deformation of Highway Pavements
················· Longsong Jiang　Shujie Wang　Huiyong Wang(586)

道路非开挖注浆加固材料性能研究 ················· 李　亚　张　瑜　陈先勇(593)

Study on Multi-Scale Finite Element Model for Bridge Load Test ················· Wei Wang(596)

基于 RAP 精细化分离技术的全比例冷再生微表处技术在高速公路中的应用
················· 高立波　周健楠　戴康瑜　张　伟　齐盛涛(603)

氯盐类融雪剂性能影响因素及评价方法 ················· 夏金平　韩　森　张秋瑞(610)

A Mechanical Approach to Restore Road Friction Coefficient under Various Snowpack Conditions
················· Weixin Yang　Jinrui Shi　Xiaochen Zhang　Sirui Zhang(614)

绿色理念在昌九高速公路改扩建工程中的应用实践 ················· 付凯敏　黄智华　曹林辉(621)

第二篇　桥 梁 工 程

基于文化、生态、体验的桥梁设计实践初探——以唐岛海湾大桥为例 ················· 李　敏(629)

Effects of Complex Temperature Actions on the Dynamic Response of High-Speed Railway Trains
················· Hongye Gou　Tianqi Zhao　Rui Yang　Liang Li(633)

装配式箱涵在公路中的应用实践及思考 ················· 付凯敏　黄智华　聂建春　曹林辉(640)

Disease Mechanism and Influence Analysis on Force-bearing Members of Composite Beam Cable-stayed Bridge ················· Chi Wang　Hanhao Zhang　Linhao Zhu(644)

A New Model for Slender Columns Retrofitted with CFRP
················· Zhengpu Yang　Peiwen He　Peng Wang(653)

Force Analysis of T-beam from Simple Support to Continuous
················· Liuyu Zhang　Qichen Wang　Xinyue Chen　Peiqi He　Zhiguo Wang　Guitong Zhang(662)

Analysis of Mechanical Capacity of Continuous Rigid Frame Bridge under the Climate of Chloride Erosion ················· Lei Hao　Feng Chen　Bin Zha(672)

基于海外设计实践的桥梁汽车荷载对比研究 ················· 商雪枫　潘竺兰(681)

系杆拱桥吊杆更换关键技术研究 ··· 商雪枫(686)

曲线钢箱组合梁桥空间受力特征及简化设计方法研究
·· 朱 钊　贺拴海　宋一凡　李 源　沈传东(694)

Modal Frequency Analysis of Suspension Bridge under the Action of Temperature
·· Qichen Wang　Xiaoyue Gao(700)

钢筋混凝土桥梁用融雪剂的探讨 ·· 吴玉辉　蒋明伟(714)

基于机器视觉技术和深度学习算法的桥梁荷载时空分布识别系统 ······ 易雨时　乔可鑫　张 路(718)

Safety Evaluation of Continuous Beam Bridges under Heavy Load ············ Yushi Yi　Lu Zhang(730)

Research on Non-stationary Characteristics of Wind Field at Bridge Site Based on Multiresolution
　　Analysis ·· Huan Zhang　Zufeng Liu　Cong Li　Yang Wang (738)

基于有限元的钢围堰施工阶段分析 ··················· 朱豪杰　张谢东　汪 威　李志锋　潘靖勃(748)

The Effect of Ernst Equation on the Dynamic Characteristics of Double-Tower Cable-Stayed Bridge
　　with Different Heights of Towers ·· Lu Wang(754)

Shear Behavior of Joints in Precast Concrete Segmental Bridges
　　············· Hao Chen　Liang Xie　Gao Cheng　Zhiheng Zhang　Kaiqiang Wang(760)

Study on Boundaries Between Straight Bridges and Curved Bridges with Box Section in Cantilever
　　Construction ············· Liang Xie　Hao Chen　Gao Cheng　Zhiheng Zhang　Bohua Wen(767)

桩径变化对不同剥落厚度下桩基横轴向承载特性影响 ········ 冯忠居　全超文　李 铁　白少奋(773)

Construction Technology of Pile Foundation of Bridge passing through Extra-large Karst Cave
　　············· Shaofen Bai　Junhua Cai　Zhongju Feng　Chenming Xia　Huiyun Chen(781)

V形峡谷地区空间Y形钢箱拱桥缆索吊装系统设计 ········ 黄 骞　邬晓光　胡科坚　徐 宁(788)

Automatic Modal Identification Based on Graph Clustering and Outlier Detection
　　··· Shengyu Liu　Xin Sun(799)

不同中小跨径梁桥动态称重算法对比研究 ················ 乔可鑫　韩万水　陈适之　易雨时(808)

Structural Safety Assessment of Steel-concrete Composite Girder Cable-stayed Bridge Exposed
　　to Fires on Deck ············· Linhao Zhu　Haoyun Yuan　Chi Wang　Zhi Liu(816)

刚构-连续结构体系梁桥组合式桥墩力学性能分析 ·· 杨 光　徐 岳(825)

高墩超多跨连续刚构桥合龙方案与顶推控制研究 ············ 朱军生　陆泽磊　牛六喜　王少鹏(830)

Component Importance Analysis of Composite Girder Cable-stayed Bridge Based on Generalized
　　Structural Stiffness ············· Binxian Wang　Hanhao Zhang　Zhi Liu　Huishuang Xiao(835)

Study on Construction Control Parameters of Pile Foundation of Highway Bridge passing through
　　Beaded Karst Cave ············· Junhua Cai　Zhongju Feng　Jie Cai　Huiyun Chen　Shaofen Bai(843)

Analysis of Long-term Deformation Sensitive Parameters of Extradosed Cable-stayed Bridge
　　··· Guang Yang　Lingzhu Yang　Yue Zhao(850)

连续刚构桥施工中大悬臂停工的分析研究 ················· 陆泽磊　张永飞　朱军生(857)

Research on Preventive Maintenance Timing of Steel-Concrete Composite Beam Cable-stayed
　　Bridge ············· Zhi Liu　Hanhao Zhang　Binxin Wang　Linhao Zhu(861)

Finite Element Analysis of Pile-Soil Interaction under Scouring
·· Haofei Guo　Wenliang Hu　Huishuang Xiao　Haoyun Yuan(868)

中等跨径钢-混凝土组合箱梁桥负弯矩区力学性能研究
·· 姬子田　张之恒　程　高　谢　亮　王鹏琪(876)

Study on Shrinkage of Concrete with Multi Row Stud Connectors in Steel-concrete
　　Composite Beams ············· Shuaishuai Zhang　Laijun Liu　Changjiang Yu　Peiqi He(882)

Research on Slender Column with Circular Cross-section Considering Boundary Condition
　　and Imperfection ············ Peng Wang　Zhengpu Yang　Peiwen He　Jiawei Niu　Runxiang He(893)

小半径曲线简支叠合梁桥设计分析 ·· 张　茜(898)

Prediction of Effective Width of Varying Depth Box-girder Bridge Using Artificial Neural
　　Network ··· Kejian Hu　Xiaoguang Wu(902)

箱形截面独柱墩连续弯桥倾覆稳定性分析 ············ 肖慧双　李　源　宋一凡　边旭辉(912)

Force Analysis of Frame Abutment ············· Kunkun Jiang　Huishuang Xiao　Fujun Li(918)

大跨度斜交框架式地道桥空间有限元分析研究 ········ 范香艳　刘来君　丁　昊　王　鑫(927)

矩形空心钢筋混凝土高墩延性抗震性能分析 ······························ 廖泳华　张谢东(931)

Research on the Technology of Lag Pouring of Wet-joint Used in Composite Girder Cable-stayed
　　Bridge ······································· Tianrui Gao　Zhenbei Liu　Haijing Ning(937)

双向压弯下空心矩形截面桥墩承载力分析 ······································ 孟宪聪　张谢东(948)

基于挠度影响线导数的连续梁桥损伤识别 ······································ 王康迪　生尧文(953)

Performance Evaluation of Bridge with Cracks under Heavy Load ········· Yushi Yi　Kexin Qiao(958)

Dynamic Analysis for Hanger Fracture of Network Arch Bridge
·· Ruixuan Li　Xianwu Hao　Teng Xu　Xinke Cao(968)

基于CFD数值模拟研究扁平流线型钢箱梁流场和三分力系数 ···················· 王　路(976)

中承式钢桁架拱桥设计参数敏感性分析 ············ 许汉铮　任浪博　韦　辉　唐署博(980)

大跨径桥梁风致振动和抗风措施研究 ··· 王　路(986)

高强钢丝及缆索体抗火性能研究进展 ···························· 厉　萱　沈锐利　陈　巍(989)

The Formulation of the Error Control Range of Composite Beam Section Size Based on Monte
　　Carlo Method ·············· Liuyu Zhang　Xingyue Chen　Xiaochuan Shi　Qichen Wang(993)

Study on Shrinkage Properties of Stud Connectors for Steel-composite Beams
·· Changjiang Yu　Laijun Liu　Jie Zhang(1002)

单向流及往复流作用下桩基局部冲刷研究 ···················· 翁博文　郭　健　吴继熠(1012)

准设计状态下简支梁桥冲击系数研究 ·· 赵　洋　曹　群(1021)

基于模糊综合评价法的桥梁火灾脆弱性评价 ·································· 李　洁　徐　峰(1028)

承托设置对钢混组合箱梁桥面板横向预应力效应的影响 ················ 杨领柱　杨　光(1035)

弹性支承压杆承载力数值分析 ············ 何培文　杨正朴　王　鹏　贺润祥　牛家伟(1040)

提高铁路悬索桥竖向刚度的结构措施研究 ···················· 陈　鑫　沈锐利　童登国(1045)

变权理论在桥梁评定中的应用 ············ 张亚博　陈　峰　彭文锋　曹黎明　查　斌(1049)

Seismic Hazard Analysis Study for the Panama Canal Fourth Bridge
……………………………………………… Jun Wu　Jun Ji　Yun Liao　Jiaer Wu　Penglin Li(1054)
纵向约束体系对公铁两用三塔斜拉桥静力特性影响的分析 ………… 刘　喆　沈锐利　马政辉(1065)
Two-Dimensional Site Response Analysis for the Panama Canal Forth Bridge
……………………………………………… Yun Liao　Jiaer Wu　Jun Ji　JunWu　Han Xiao(1070)
不同高宽比下钢箱梁三分力系数变化规律研究 …………………………………… 王　路(1080)
独柱墩微弯梁桥横向抗倾覆稳定性研究 ………………………… 王业路　闫　强　郑　东(1087)
循环荷载下高强螺栓受剪连接状态声发射监测 ………………… 吕世文　李　丹　任伟新(1095)
疲劳裂纹止裂孔与高强螺栓复合止裂方法研究
……………………………………… 杨　羿　刘　朵　陈春霖　王贤强　张建东(1102)
循环荷载下高强螺栓抗剪模型 …………………………………… 曹燕飞　李　丹　任伟新(1105)
基于LSTM的子结构试验模型更新方法 ………………………………… 于长江　郑艺炜(1111)
基于锁相红外热成像的钢桥涂层厚度检测 ………………… 王贤强　杨　羿　刘　朵　张建东(1118)

第一篇 公路工程

地下防洪墙对半刚性沥青路面受力特性影响分析

尹祖超[1] 蔡鹏[1] 汪鹏福[1] 袁卢均[2] 郑璐[1]

(1. 长江勘测规划设计研究有限责任公司；2. 中交第三航务工程局有限公司宁波分公司)

摘 要 为了研究地下防洪墙对半刚性沥青路面结构受力特性的影响，采用数值模拟手段建立了力学计算模型，分析了防洪墙位置、格栅设置情况对沥青路面设计指标包括无机结合料稳定层层底拉应力、路基顶压应变、沥青层底竖向压应力的影响。计算结果表明，防洪墙位于路床范围内时，将改变无机结合料稳定层层底应力情况，使应力变化更复杂；路基顶压应变较正常情况增大约4倍；对沥青层底竖向压应力影响不大，均为0.35~0.4MPa。设计时应将防洪墙置于路床以下，否则应做破除处理，以利沥青路面结构受力。

关键词 防洪墙 半刚性沥青路面 受力特性

0 引 言

随着经济社会的发展，堤防的功能越来越多元化，从单一的防洪功能逐渐转向集防洪、交通、景观、休闲等多重功能于一体，堤防与道路结合建设的工程实践也越来越多[1]。由于道路与堤防分属不同的学科领域，目前堤防道路改造设计一般采用水利行业规范、交通行业规范或城市道路规范相结合的做法。例如，现状堤防为防洪墙而改造成道路时，防洪墙需位于路面结构下，一般参照《公路水泥混凝土路面设计规范》(JTG D40—2011)对路面进行补强处理。

国内外研究方面，目前针对构造物对路面结构力学影响研究方面主要集中在管道、涵洞、通道等构造物方面[2-5]，而针对路面结构下存在墙体结构情况的研究很少。

本文对沥青路面结构下存在墙体(如防洪墙、挡土墙等)的情况开展研究，在选取合适的路面设计力学指标基础上，分析了防洪墙位置、格栅设置情况、材料模量对沥青路面的受力影响，并基于此研发了一种与防洪墙结合的沥青路面结构，研发成果可为类似堤防道路改造设计提供参考。

1 有限元模型

1.1 模型建立

为简化计算并参考文献[6]的研究成果，本文采用二维有限元模型进行模拟，并假设土工格栅仅受拉，防洪墙与土体间考虑接触处理，路面双圆荷载简化为矩形，大小为0.7MPa。考虑最不利情况，荷载位于墙体正上方。考虑尺寸效应的影响及计算精度的需要，二维模型尺寸为5m(宽)×6.6m(深)。边界条件为：土基底部固定，各层间设置为连续，各侧面约束其法向位移，如图1所示。

路面结构材料参数参照《公路沥青路面设计规范》(JTG D50—2017)并结合实际进行选取，土工格栅模量参照文献[7]选取，通过非线性弹性材料模型设置土工格栅仅能受拉，长度取4m，见表1。

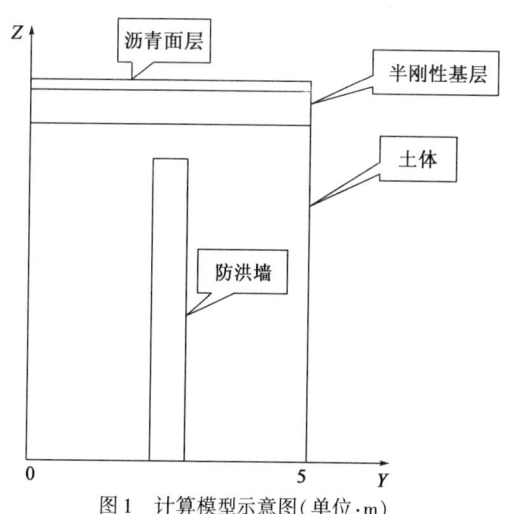

图1 计算模型示意图(单位:m)

基金项目：企业自主创新基金(CX2019Z08)。

路面结构材料参数表 表1

结构层	厚度(cm)	弹性模量(MPa)	泊松比	备注
沥青面层	18	9000	0.25	—
水泥稳定碎石基层	60	7000	0.25	—
土基	—	60	0.4	摩擦系数0.3
混凝土防洪墙	60	25000	0.2	
土工格栅(仅受拉)	0.5	2500	0.3	长4m

1.2 计算指标选取

根据《公路沥青路面设计规范》(JTG D50—2017)，对于无机结合料稳定类基层类型，设计指标包括无机结合料稳定层层底拉应力及沥青混合料层永久变形量，力学响应为无机结合料稳定层层底沿行车方向的水平拉应力及沥青混合料层各分层顶面竖向压应力。参照长寿命沥青路面[8]设计指标，本次研究同时考虑将路基顶面竖向压应变作为力学指标。

1.3 计算工况

计算工况见表2。

计算工况一览表 表2

工况1	正常工况，无防洪墙
工况2	防洪墙顶位于路面结构底以下0.3m
工况3	防洪墙顶位于路面结构底以下0.3m，墙顶设置1层土工格栅
工况4	防洪墙顶位于路面结构底以下0.9m
工况5	防洪墙顶位于路面结构底以下0.9m，墙顶设置3层土工格栅

计算模型分别如图2~图6所示。

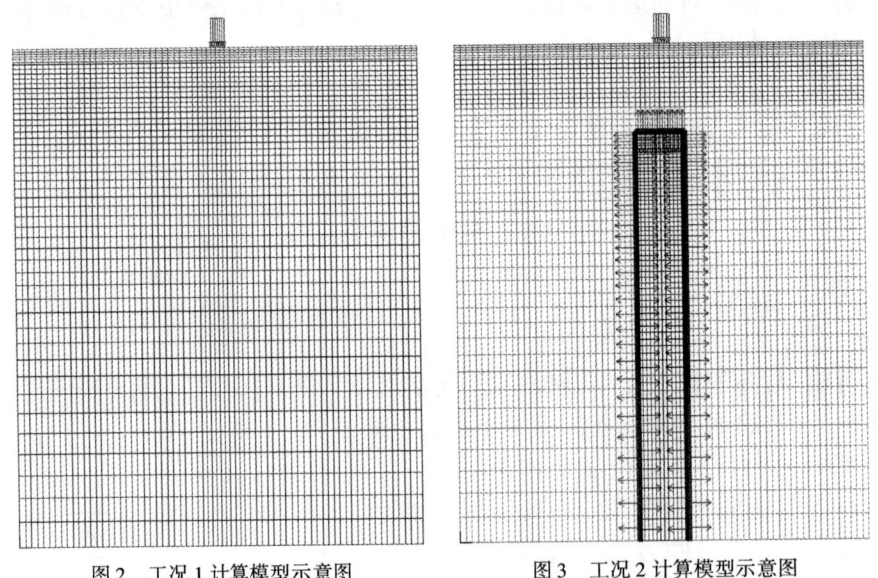

图2 工况1计算模型示意图　　图3 工况2计算模型示意图

2 力学响应分析

本次研究针对上述5种工况有限元模型的计算结果沿Y轴方向变化情况进行分析。

2.1 无机结合料稳定层层底拉应力

从图7中可以看出，随深度增加，X轴方向正应力由压应力逐渐变为拉应力再变为压应力，拉应力主要位于无机结合料稳定层，最大值位于无机结合料稳定层层底。

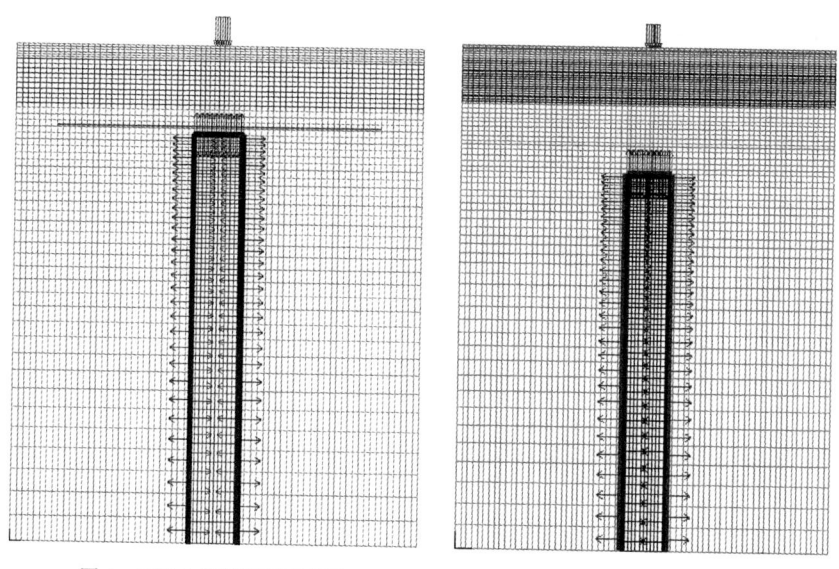

图 4　工况 3 计算模型示意图　　　　图 5　工况 4 计算模型示意图

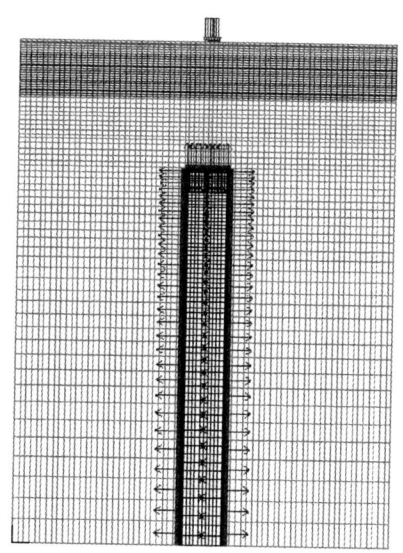

图 6　工况 5 计算模型示意图

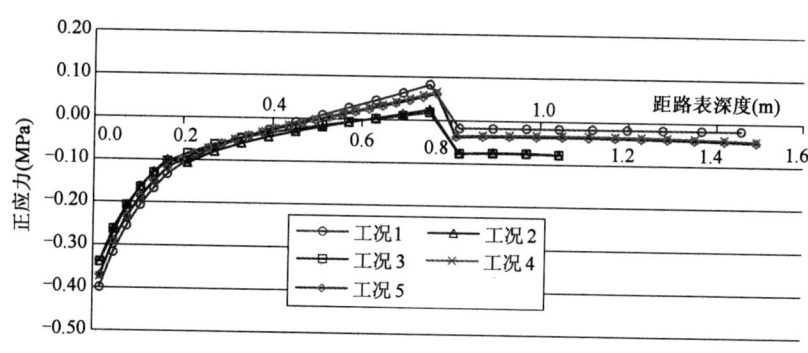

图 7　行车荷载中心下 X 轴方向正应力沿深度变化图

从图 8 中可以看出,层底拉应力由大到小为:工况 1＞工况 4＞工况 5＞工况 2＞工况 3,最大处位于荷载中心下方。表明防洪墙位于路床范围内时将较大程度改变水稳层底应力情况,使得水稳层应力变化复杂。工况 5 比工况 4 拉应力减少约 8％,即设置土工格栅将有利于减小水稳层的疲劳应力。

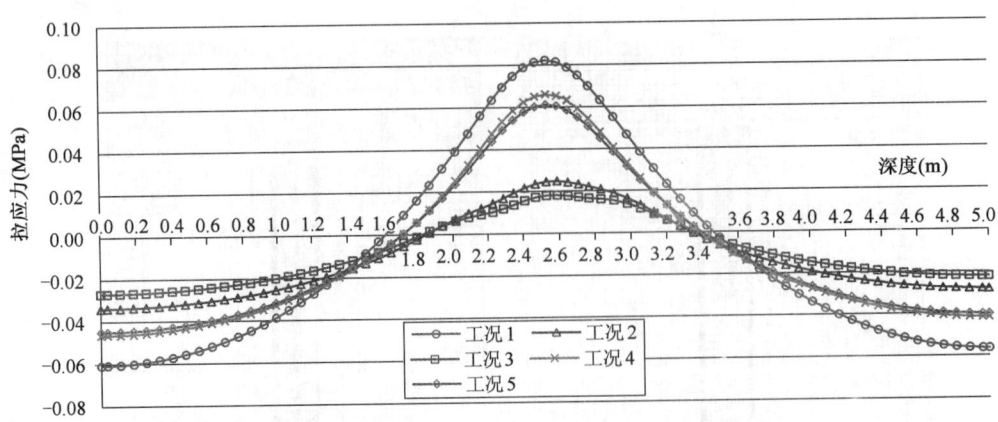

图8　无机结合料稳定层层底拉应力沿 Y 轴变化图

2.2　路基顶压应变

从图9中可以看出,路基顶压应变由大到小为:工况3＞工况2＞工况5＞工况4＞工况1。防洪墙位于路床范围内(工况2和工况3)时将显著增大路基顶压应变,较正常值增大约4倍。防洪墙位于路床范围以下(工况4和工况5)时有利于减少路基顶压应变,设置格栅对路基顶压应变影响不大。

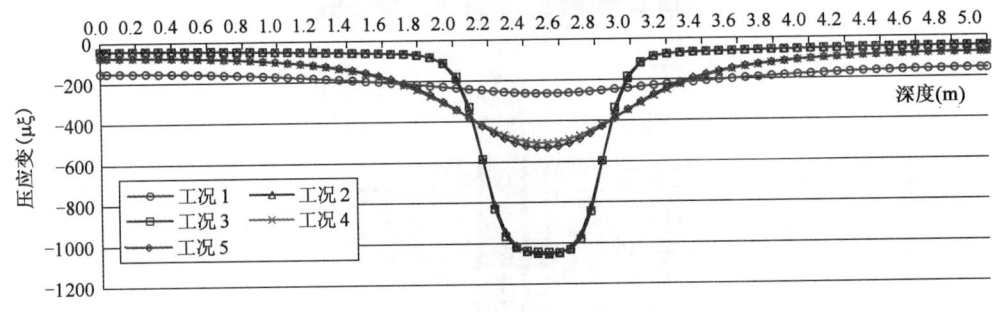

图9　路基顶压应变沿 Y 轴变化图

2.3　沥青层底竖向压应力

从图10中可以看出,由于沥青面层离防洪墙距离较远,防洪墙位于路床范围内(工况2和工况3)时和防洪墙位于路床范围以下(工况4和工况5)时对沥青层底竖向压应力影响不大,均为0.35～0.4MPa。

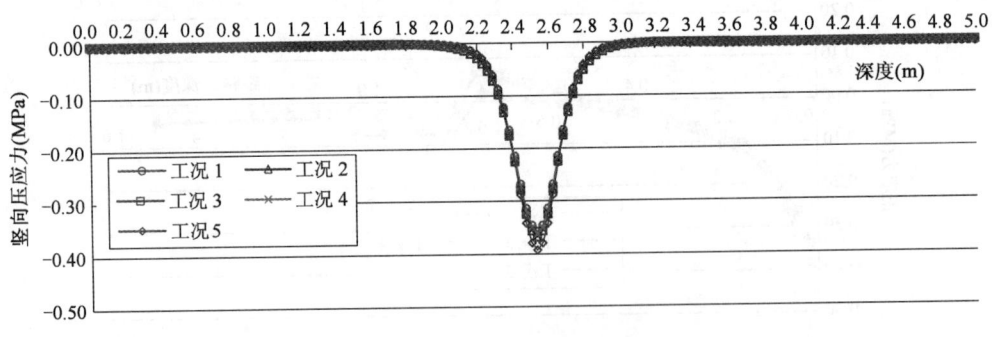

图10　沥青层底竖向压应力沿 Y 轴变化图

3　一种位于防洪墙上的沥青路面结构

结合上述计算分析结果及堤防防渗要求,提出一种位于防洪墙顶上的沥青路面结构,如图11所示。

路面设计高程在设计水位加堤顶超高以上,现状防洪墙位于路床以下,若位于路床范围则需进行破除处理。路堤采用黏性土分层填筑压实,现状防洪墙背水侧路堤底部设置50cm厚碎石垫层,以利堤防背水侧的导渗。上路床及下路床采用水泥土分层填筑压实,土工格栅铺设在现状防洪墙顶路床范围内,共3层,分别铺设在上路床顶面、下路床顶面和下路床底面,宽度为2~4m。防洪墙顶至路床顶范围内可设置垂向防渗土工膜。通过上述综合措施降低防洪墙对路面结构的受力影响,改善路面结构的受力状况,同时确保了堤防的防渗效果。

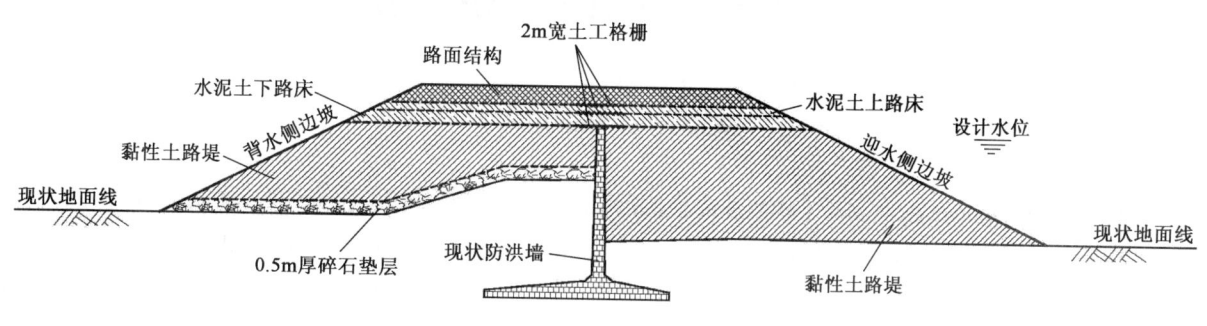

图11 防洪墙顶上的沥青路面结构示意图

4 结　语

针对半刚性沥青路面结构下存在墙体(如防洪墙、挡土墙等线状墙体)的情况开展路面受力研究,采用数值模拟手段建立了各种工况下的力学计算模型,分析了防洪墙位置、格栅设置情况、材料模量对沥青路面设计指标包括无机结合料稳定层层底拉应力、路基顶压应变、沥青层底竖向压应力的影响。分析认为,设计时应将防洪墙置于路床以下,否则应做破除处理,以利沥青路面结构受力。研究结果对于改善地下存在线状墙体的路面结构受力状况、提高其路用性能具有重要意义。下一步工作可考虑对刚性路面、柔性路面下存在墙体的情况进行研究,同时考虑动载情况,以便更好地分析各种路面及工况下的受力特性。

参考文献

[1] 郝伟,樊恒辉,张争奇.我国堤防道路研究与技术进展[J].长江科学院院报,2018,35(10):58-62.
[2] 许海亮,覃吉宁,任和欢,等.行车荷载作用下含埋地管道沥青路面结构受力状况分析[J].国防交通工程与技术,2019,17(5):24-28.
[3] 张锋.城市地下综合管廊路段沥青路面力学响应分析及其工程应用[D].哈尔滨:哈尔滨工业大学,2018.
[4] LI Y,SONG G,CAI J. Mechanical Response Analysis of Airport Flexible Pavement Above Underground Infrastructure Under Moving Wheel Loa[J]. Geotechnical and geological engineering,2017,35(5):2269-2275.
[5] Justin F Lundvall,John P Turner. Miligation of roadway settlement above buried culverts and pipes[R]. FHWA-97/01(Final Report),June,1997.
[6] 王威娜,李小飞,徐青杰,等.沥青路面二维和三维结构分析模型的比较[J].深圳大学学报理工版,2018,35(1):39-47.
[7] 马驰,朱亚林,彭雪峰.地震作用下土工格栅加筋高土石坝的稳定性分析[J].长江科学院院报,2019,36(11):125-131.
[8] 薛忠军,王春明,张伟,等.半刚性基层长寿命路面结构和材料设计研究[J].公路交通科技,2015,32(10):37-42.

Investigation on the Self-healing Behavior of Asphalt Binder Based on the Molecular Dynamics Simulation

Yan Li　Bowei Sun　Jingwen Liu

(Chang'an University)

Abstract　Molecular dynamics (MD) simulation is an effective way to explore the self-healing behavior of asphalt binder. In this study, the four-component molecular models of neat and aged asphalt binder are established, and then verified by the density and solubility respectively. The self-healing models with different damage levels are developed by introducing a vacuum pad between two layers filled with asphalt molecular models. The simulation of self-healing behavior is performed at different temperatures under NPT ensemble. Results show that the self-healing process mainly contains two stages: the density healing stage where the density increases rapidly with time, and the intrinsic healing stage where the molecules diffuse across the closed crack surfaces to reach a more equilibrium and randomization state. Raising the healing temperature and time provides a favorable condition for the thermal movement of asphalt molecules, leading to the greater diffusion coefficient. The larger damage level increases the difficulties in self-healing process of crack because of the extended travel distance and the weakened molecular interaction force. The aged asphalt binder has a higher value of cohesive energy density (CED), making the molecular chains more tightly bonded and hindering the self-healing of asphalt binder.

Keywords　Asphalt binder　Self-healing behavior　Molecular dynamics simulation　Damage level　Diffusion coefficient

0　Introduction

Cracking is one of the major distresses of asphalt pavement, seriously decreasing the driving comfort and service life. It has been found that the cracks in asphalt can be healed automatically after resting for a period of time under suitable temperature conditions, and the mechanical property of asphalt can be restored to a certain extent simultaneously (García, 2012). This phenomenon is called the intrinsic self-healing property of asphalt, contributing to the delay of crack development and the extension of pavement lifetime (Kim et al., 2003; Qiu, 2012). An enormous amount of research has been done on this issue, aiming to comprehensively reveal its mechanism and characteristics. In essence, the formation, expansion and healing process of cracks in asphalt material are fundamentally determined by the molecular behavior of asphalt binder, which is difficult to be observed by traditional test methods (Sun et al., 2018). In recent years, the development of molecular simulation technology provides a new solution to the in-depth study of asphalt self-healing phenomenon at the molecular scale. Molecular simulation technology is a general term for computer virtual simulation experiment on the molecular structures of materials, which greatly saves time and economic costs (Wang, 2017). It can be used to theoretically explain and predict the molecular behaviors of materials, providing strong support for the study of structure-performance relationship. MD simulation is one of the molecular simulation methods, which is widely used in the field of asphalt materials to investigate the dynamic motion law and macro characteristics of the asphalt molecular system.

The basic of asphalt molecular behavior simulation is the construction of a reasonable and reliable asphalt molecular model that can reflect the asphalt microstructure and ensure the accuracy of the simulation results. It is widely known that the chemical compositions and structures of asphalt binder are extremely complex because there are millions of molecular species, and thus it is very difficult to put forward a clear molecular structure of asphalt binder (Wang et al., 2016). Up to now, the average molecular structure model and the multi-component molecular structure model are the two main construction methods for asphalt molecular system. The average molecular structure model has a high consistency with the real element composition of asphalt binder (Jennings et al., 1993). However, it is incapable to reflect the various chemical components and their interactions. To solve this problem, the multi-component molecular model is built by constructing the representative molecular structure of each asphalt chemical component, and then assembling them according to the mass ratio of each component. It can better show the diversity of asphalt molecular structure and the interaction between the components, but consumes more computational resources. Zhang and Greenfield proposed a three-component asphalt model, and further investigated the correlation between molecular structure and physicochemical properties of asphalt binder (Zhang and Greenfield, 2010, 2007a, 2007b). Hansen et al. and Li et al. built the four-component molecular models of asphalt binder, and the simulation results had good consistency with the measured values.

In 2011, Bhasin et al. (Bhasin et al., 2011) first used MD simulation method to analyze the self-healing property of asphalt binder, and investigated the effect of chain length and chain branching on the self-diffusivity behavior of asphalt binder. They found that the longer molecular chain with less branching had faster self-diffusion rate and better self-healing performance. Sun et al. adopted MD simulation to evaluate the self-healing capacity of neat and SBS modified asphalt binders (Sun et al., 2016). They also studied the effect of chemical composition and microstructure of asphalt binder on self-healing ability (Sun et al., 2017). Gao and Liu (Gao and Liu, 2019) revealed the self-healing mechanism of bio-oil recycled asphalt (BRA) by MD simulation, and put forward that the self-healing process of BRA was dominated by the viscous flow at higher temperatures and the elastic recovery at lower temperatures. Yu et al. reported that the crack width had a significant influence on asphalt self-healing property, and further explained the laboratory test results by MD simulation (Yu et al., 2020). Xu et al. found that the aging of asphalt binder is unfavorable to the self-healing process (Xu and Wang, 2017). He et al. investigated the self-healing property of different asphalt molecular models, and proposed that the volume compression and molecule stretching led to the disappearance of the crack (He et al., 2020). All the practice showed that MD simulation serves as an effective method for exploring the self-healing process of asphalt binder. However, the self-healing behavior is quite complex, whose characterization and evaluation methods are still unclear, and needs further investigations.

In this paper, the self-healing behavior of asphalt binder is investigated by MD simulation using Materials Studio (MS) 7.0 software of Accelrys. The four-component molecular models of neat and aged asphalt binders are established and verified respectively, and then the self-healing models with different damage levels are developed by introducing a vacuum pad between two layers filled with asphalt molecular models. The self-healing process is simulated at different temperatures under NPT ensemble. Finally, the characteristics, influencing factors and evaluation of asphalt self-healing behavior are investigated according to the simulation results.

1 Simulation Models and Methods

1.1 Construction of Asphalt Molecular Model

The representative molecular structures selected for the four chemical components (asphaltene, resin, saturates, aromatics) of neat asphalt binder are illustrated in Fig. 1. The aging process of asphalt binder is mainly dominated by the oxidation reaction, and thus the molecular model of aged asphalt binder is constructed by introducing oxygen atoms to the possible oxidizable sites in the neat asphalt binder molecules (Xu and Wang, 2017). It has been identified that carbon and sulfur compounds in asphalt binder are susceptible to oxidation, and their oxidation productions are respectively ketone and sulfoxide (Pan and Tarefder, 2016). The benzylic carbon, defined as the first carbon connected with the aromatic ring, is found to be a readily oxidizable site. Hence, the oxygen atom is introduced by replacing the hydrogen atom bonded to the benzylic carbon atom, leading to the formation of ketones. In the asphalt chemical components, asphaltene is the most polar component, followed by resin, aromatics and saturates (Xu and Wang, 2017). It is difficult to oxidize the saturates because it has no polar atoms or aromatic rings. In this study, the saturates of the aged asphalt binder is assumed to be the same with that of the neat asphalt binder. The other three chemical components are all added with oxygen atoms at the possible oxidizable sites, as shown in Fig. 2.

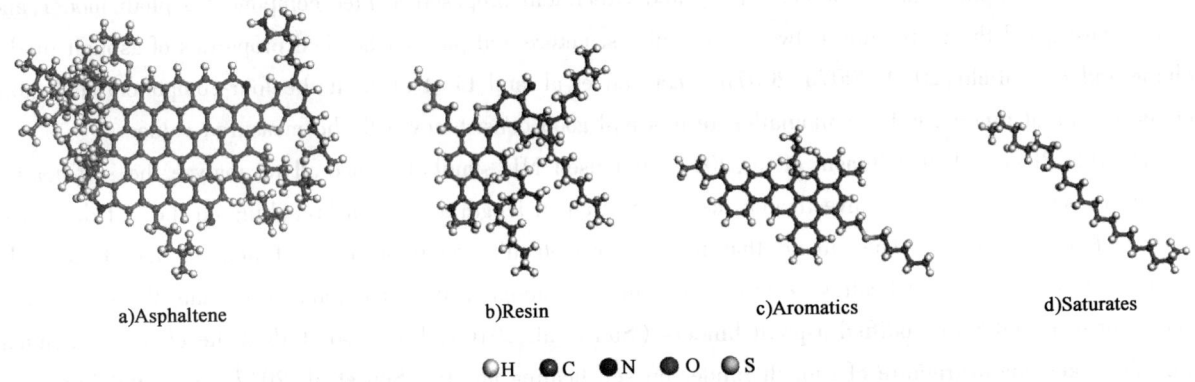

Fig. 1 Molecular Structures of the Chemical Compositions in the Neat Asphalt Binder

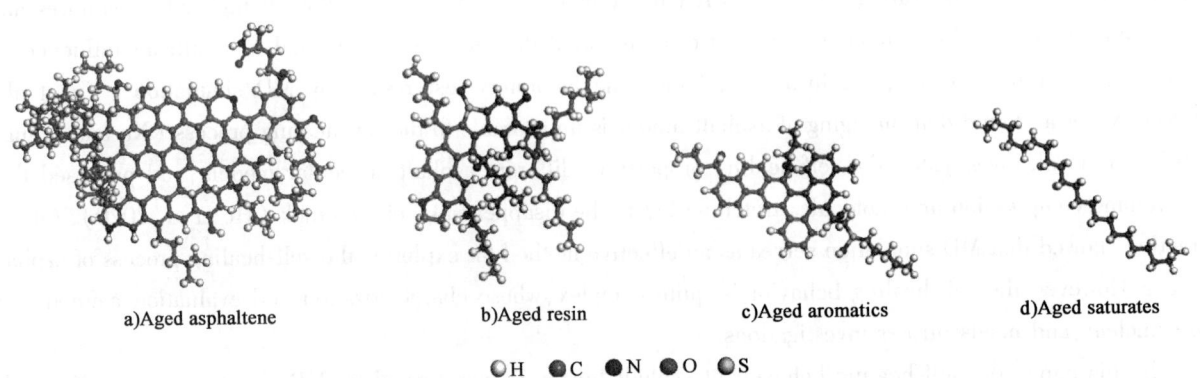

Fig. 2 Molecular Structures of the Chemical Compositions in the Aged Asphalt Binder

In the Amorphous Cell module embedded in MS7.0 software, the moleculesare put into a cubic box with an initial density of 0.5g/cm^3 to establish the neat and aged asphalt molecular model with periodic boundary conditions. According to previous research results (Guo, 2015), the detailed constituent contents of the models are determined and listed in Tab. 1. Then, the geometry optimization is performed on the model to bring it to a situation with the lowest energy. Subsequently, the dynamic simulation is carried out under NPT ensemble at 1 standard atmosphere pressure and different temperatures for 100ps, aiming to make the asphalt molecular model reach a more equilibrium state. The last frame of the model is depicted in Fig. 3. The force field used in this simulation is COMPASS II (Condensed-phase Optimized Molecular Potentials for Atomistic Simulation Studies), which is an extension and optimization of COMPASS force field.

Chemical Composition Content of the Neat and Aged Asphalt Binder				Tab. 1
Chemical composition	Asphaltene	Resin	Aromatics	Saturates
Neat asphalt binder(%)	19.8	24.1	41.6	14.5
Aged asphalt binder(%)	26.2	29.9	32.9	11.0

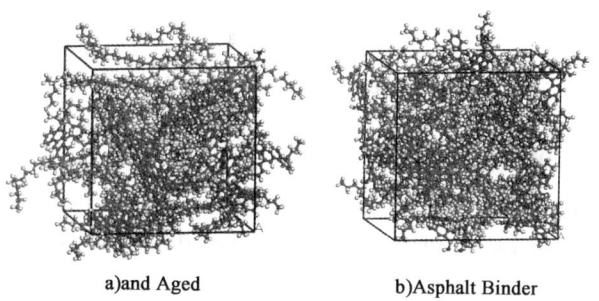

Fig. 3 Amorphous Cell of the Neat a) and Aged b) Asphalt Binder

1.2 Self-healing Model Development and Simulation Details

The self-healing model of asphaltbinder is built in the Build Layer module embedded in MS7.0 software. It is consisted of three parts, namely two layers filled with asphalt molecular model and a vacuum pad (crack) with a certain width between the layers. The self-healing models of neat asphalt binder with different damage levels (crack widths) are illustrated in Fig. 4. The crack self-healing process is simulated on the model under NPT ensemble at various temperatures (298.15K, 318.15K, 338.15K) for 100ps in the Forcite-dynamics module.

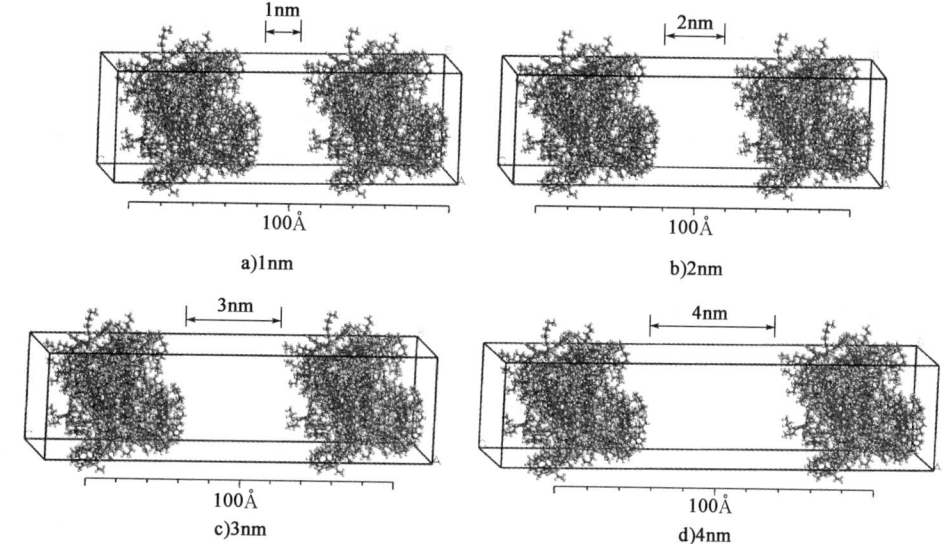

Fig. 4 Self-healing Model of the Neat Asphalt Binder with Different Crack Widths

1.3 Calculation Method of Molecular Diffusion Coefficient

Diffusion coefficient is adopted to characterize the molecular diffusion ability, which can be calculated by equation (1) and (2).

$$D = \frac{1}{6} \lim_{t \to \infty} \frac{d}{dt} \sum_{i=1}^{N} (|r_i(t) - r_i(0)|^2) \tag{1}$$

$$\text{MSD}(t) = (|r_i(t) - r_i(0)|^2) \tag{2}$$

Where, D is the diffusion coefficient of particles in the molecular system; N is the number of particles in the molecular system; MSD is defined as the mean square of particle displacement referenced to its initial position; $r_i(0)$ is the initial displacement of the mass center of particle i at time 0; $r_i(t)$ is the displacement of the mass center of particle i at time t; the angle bracket means the overall average of all particles during the simulation time.

By substituting equation (2) in equation (1), the diffusion coefficient D is expressed as equation (3).

$$D = \frac{a}{6} \quad (3)$$

Where, a is the slope of the MSD-time curve.

2 Results and Discussions

2.1 Verification of Asphalt Molecular Model

It is important to ensure that the asphalt molecular model is rational and applicable so that it can provide accurate simulation results. The thermodynamic parameters, including density and solubility, are used to verify the accuracy of the asphalt molecular model. The density is simulated in Forcite-dynamics module under 1 standard atmosphere pressure for 100ps at different temperatures, namely 298.15K, 318.15K and 338.15K. The solubility simulation is performed in Forcite-cohesive energy density module to judge the stability of asphalt molecular model. The simulated values of density and solubility are listed in Tab. 2. During the simulation process, the density increases with time, and stabilizes at 1.00 g/cm^3 at 298.15K, which is in good agreement with the density values reported previously. As expected, the density of aged asphalt binder is slightly higher than that of the neat asphalt binder. The simulated solubility value of neat asphalt binder is 17.19 (J/cm^3)$^{1/2}$, which is consistent with previous values 13.3 – 22.5 (J/cm^3)$^{1/2}$ (Sun et al., 2018). For the aged asphalt binder, it is 18.29 (J/cm^3)$^{1/2}$. In a word, the simulated values of density and solubility are all in a reasonable range. Thus, the asphalt molecular model can reflect the macro properties of normal asphalt binder, providing reliable results in the following simulations.

Density and Solubility of Asphalt Molecular Model   Tab. 2

Asphalt Type	Density (g/cm^3)	Reference Value (g/cm^3)	Solubility (J/cm^3)$^{1/2}$	Reference Value (J/cm^3)$^{1/2}$
Neat asphalt binder	1.00	1.01 – 1.04 (He et al., 2020)	17.19	13.3 – 22.5 (Sun et al., 2018)
Aged asphalt binder	1.04		18.29	

2.2 Self-healing Process Analysis

The temperature and density variation of the self-healing model with 1nm crack width at 298.15K is plotted in Fig. 5. It can be seen from Fig. 5a) that the temperature fluctuates greatly in the first 10ps, and gradually becomes stable around the target value since 10ps. In Fig. 5b), the initial density is lower than the normal density of asphalt binder due to the introduction of crack. In the first 10ps, the system is being heated to reach the target temperature, and thus the density is unstable. This stage is a unique phenomenon of the molecular simulation, which is not caused by the crack healing process. The self-healing process of crack at the target temperature (298.15K) occurs during 10ps – 100ps, which is divided into two stages: the density healing stage (stage 1: 10 – 40ps) and the intrinsic healing stage (stage 2: 40 – 100ps). At the density healing stage, the density increases stably with the simulation time, indicating that the crack is gradually closed at the given condition. At the intrinsic healing stage, the slope of density curve is close to zero, and it converges at 1.0 g/cm^3 for neat asphalt binder, which is close to the macroscopic density of undamaged asphalt binder. At this stage, the molecules further diffuse across the closed crack surfaces to reach a more equilibrium and randomization situation, contributing a lot to the strength recovery of the asphalt binder. It should be noticed that the strength recovery mainly happens at stage 2, and 100ps may not be enough for a complete strength recovery. The images of the crack self-healing model in different states are illustrated in Fig. 6. It can be seen that the asphalt molecules gradually diffuse into the crack and finally fill the crack, leading to the disappearance of crack at the end of the simulation.

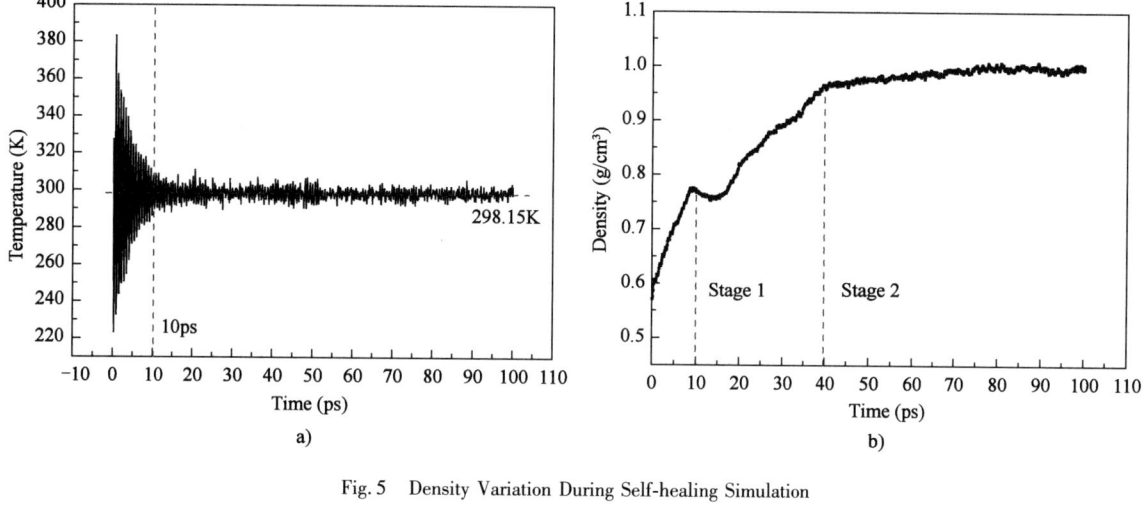

Fig. 5 Density Variation During Self-healing Simulation

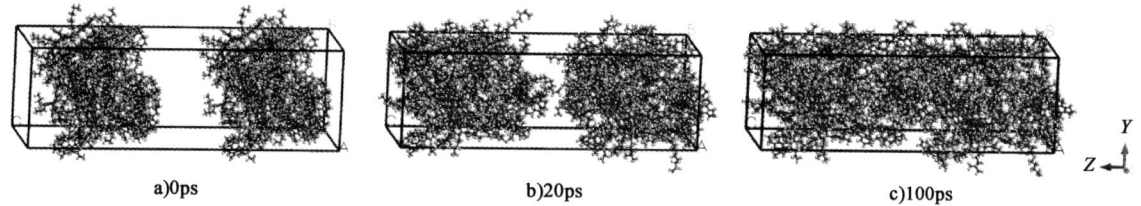

Fig. 6 Self-healing Process of the Neat Asphalt Binder

2.3 Influence of Temperature and Time

The density variation of the self-healing model with a crack width of 1nm at different healing temperatures is illustrated in Fig. 7. As can be seen, the temperature and time have great effects on the density variation during the self-healing process. At stage 1, the density shows a consistent growth with time, and the platform phenomenon is more obvious with rising temperature. At the platform, the density keeps at a relatively stable value, indicating that the compression of model volume almost stops. This may be explained by the acute molecular movement, causing difficulties in compressing the molecule model to a rational volume. The higher the temperature is, the greater the compression difficulty is, and the longer period the platform exists. At stage 2, the density is close to the real value of asphalt binder, and only has a small fluctuation with time. Under different temperatures, the asphalt molecular model has different density values, which is consistent with reality.

The variation of MSD with time is shown in Fig. 8. It can be found that MSD grows up with the increasing simulation time and temperature. The diffusion coefficient is calculated by fitting the MSD-time curve during 10ps-70ps combined with equation (3). As shown in Tab. 3, the diffusion coefficient is gradually improved by raising the temperature, indicating that the higher temperature is conducive to the molecular thermal movement and diffusion.

Diffusion Coefficient of the Molecules in the Model Tab. 3

Temperature	Fitting Formula	Diffusion Coefficient
298.15K	$y = 1.18x - 4.83, R^2 = 0.99$	$0.197 Å^2/ps$
318.15k	$y = 1.34x - 7.28, R^2 = 0.99$	$0.223 Å^2/ps$
338.15K	$y = 1.49x - 9.71, R^2 = 0.99$	$0.248 Å^2/ps$

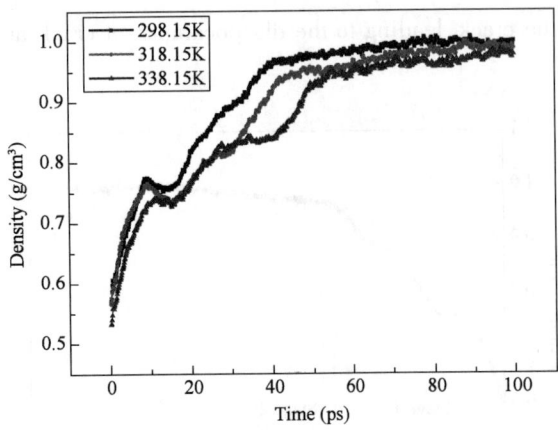
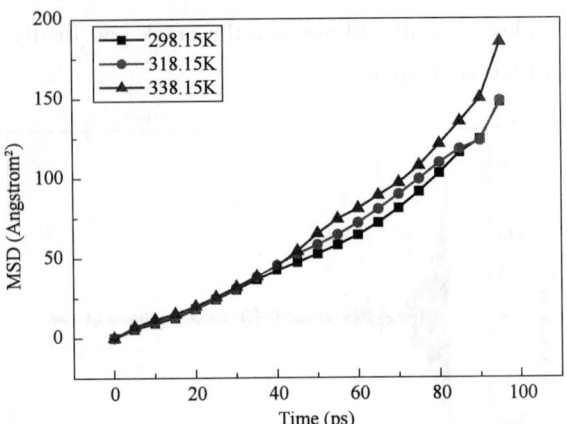

Fig. 7 Density Variation of the Self-healing Model under Different Temperatures

Fig. 8 MSD Variation of the Self-healing Model under Different Temperatures

2.4 Influence of Damage Level

The damage level is represented by the crack width in the self-healing model. Larger crack width means higher damage level. Fig. 9 shows the density variation of neat asphalt self-healing model with different crack widths (1nm, 2nm, 3nm, 4nm) at 298.15K. During the simulation period, the model with 1nm crack has completed the density healing stage (stage 1), and steps into the intrinsic healing stage. But the models with 2 - 4nm cracks are still at stage 1 even at the end of simulation. This can also be verified by the relative concentration distribution of the model along z axis, as shown in Fig. 10. It can be found that at the starting point of the simulation, the molecular distribution is a bimodal shape, with higher concentration at peaks and lower concentration at the edge. There is no molecules in the middle of the model, which is a vacuum space representing the crack. During the healing process, the molecules on the two sides of the crack gradually diffuse into the crack and contact with each other. The molecular concentration distribution tends to obtain an average value

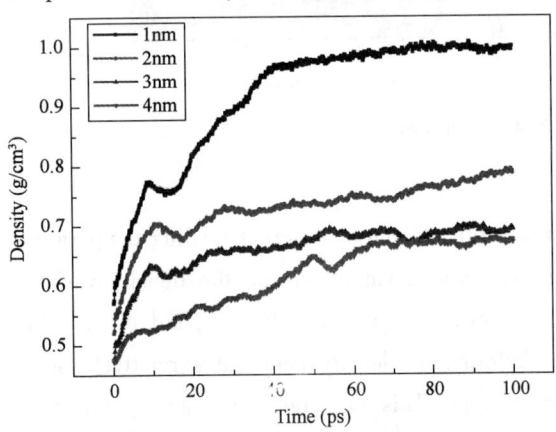

Fig. 9 Influence of Damage Level on Density Variation of the Self-healing Model

along the z axis, meaning a more uniform distribution in the model. With the increasing of crack width, the time required for a complete healing is obviously prolonged. The 100ps running time is enough for the density healing of the model with 1nm crack, but is inadequate for the models with 2 - 4 nm cracks. It is inferred that the increased crack width not only extends the distance for the particles to travel, but also reduces the molecular interaction force, finally resulting in the longer healing time for the higher damage level (wider crack).

2.5 Influence of Aging

The MSD-time curves of neat and aged asphalt molecular model at 298.15K are illustrated in Fig. 11. The aging of asphalt seriously reduces the MSD value of asphalt molecules. The diffusion coefficient is calculated using the fitting curve during 10ps - 70ps. It is 0.20 $Å^2$/ps and 0.09 $Å^2$/ps for the neat and aged asphalt binder respectively, demonstrating that the diffusion behavior of the aged asphalt binder is seriously weakened. This can be explained by their difference in cohesive energy density (CED) defined as the intermolecular force per unit volume, which is usually adopted to evaluate the molecular interaction in the model by measuring the mutual attraction of molecules. As illustrated in Fig. 12, the aging process increases the CED of asphalt binder, making the molecular chains more tightly bonded. This hinders the free stretch and rotation of molecules in aged asphalt binder, resulting in the slowdown of diffusion behavior.

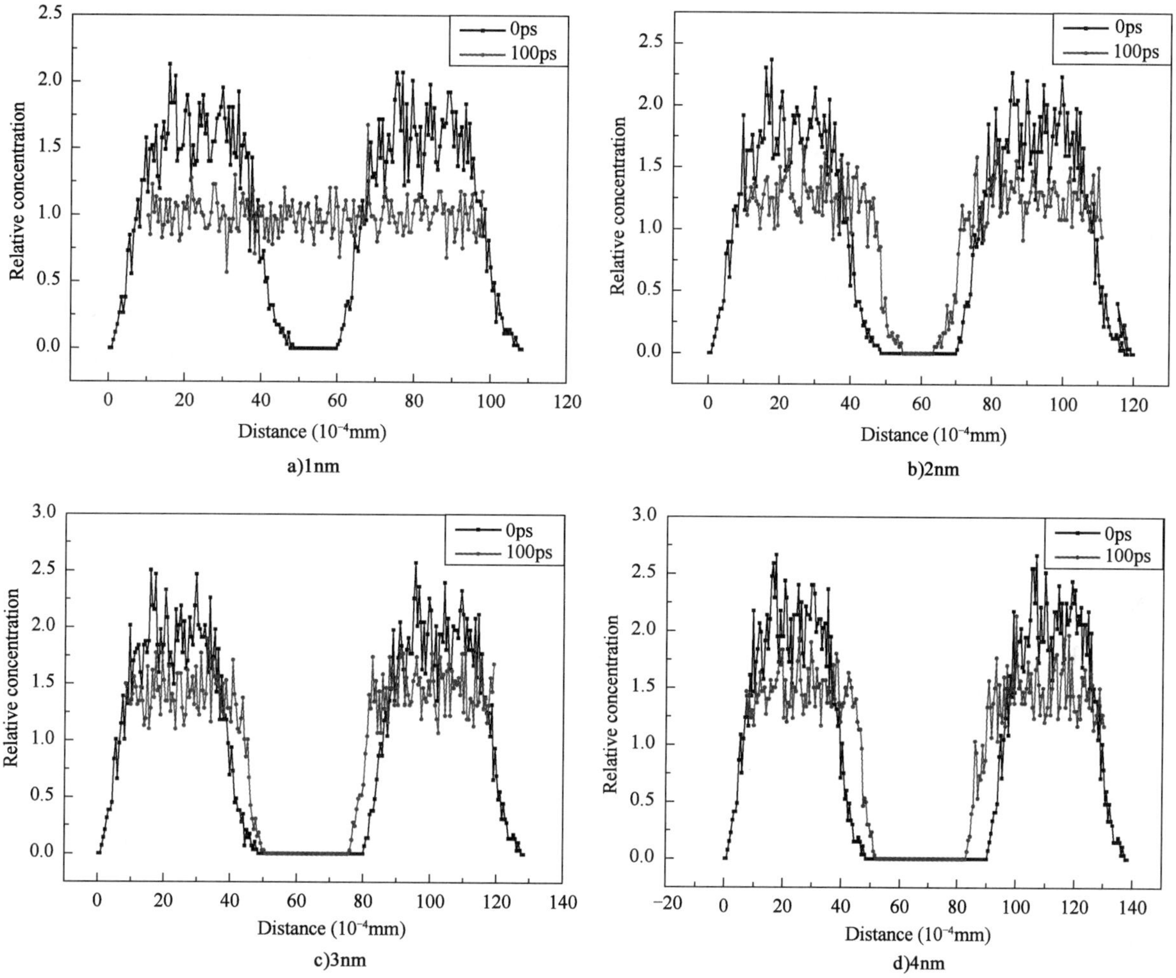

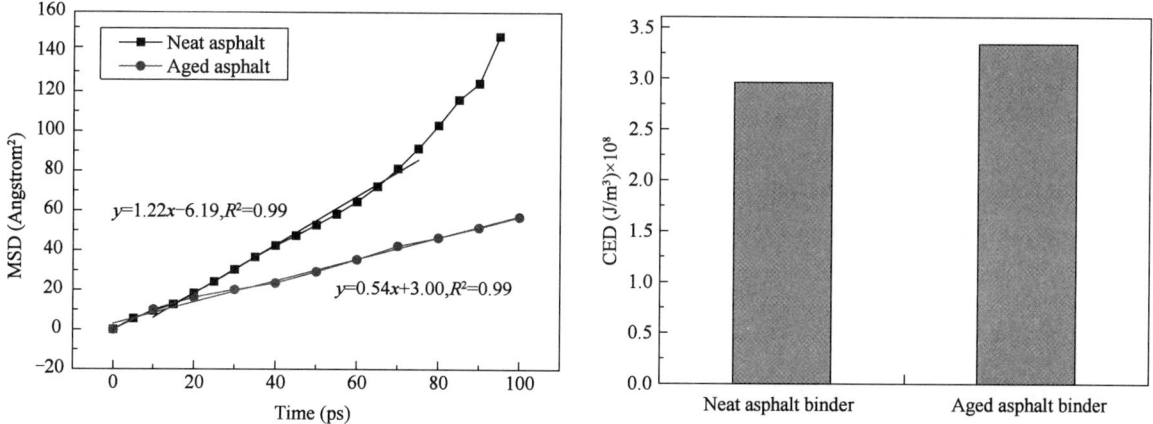

Fig. 10 Relative Concentration Distribution Along z Axis of the Self-healing Model with Different Crack Widths

Fig. 11 MSD Curve of Molecules in the Self-healing Model

Fig. 12 CED of the Neat and Aged Asphalt Binder

3 Conclusions

(1) Both the neat and aged asphalt molecular models are established and verified. Their simulated values of density and solubility are all in a reasonable range. Thus, theestablished molecular model can reflect the macro properties of normal asphalt binder, and provide reliable results in the simulation.

(2) The self-healing process of crack at the set temperatureis divided into two stages: the density healing stage (stage 1) and the intrinsic healing stage (stage 2). At stage 1, the density increases rapidly with the simulation time, indicating that the crack is closed at the given condition. At stage 2, the slope of density curve is close to zero, and it converges at the normal density value, which is close to the macroscopic density of undamaged asphalt binder. At this stage, the molecules further diffuse across the closed crack surfaces to reach a more equilibrium and randomization situation.

(3) Healing temperature and time have great effects on the density variation during the self-healing process. The rising temperature makes the platform phenomenon of density curve more obvious, which may be caused by the increasing difficulties in compressing the molecule model to a rational volume due to the acute molecular movement. MSD and the diffusion coefficient grow up with the increasing simulation time and temperature, indicating that the higher temperature and longer time are conducive to the molecular thermal movement and diffusion.

(4) The higher damage level and aging all have negative effects on asphalt self-healing behavior. It is inferred that the increased crack width not only extends the distance for the particles to travel, but also reduces the molecular interaction force. The aging of asphalt binder reduces the MSD value and diffusion coefficient of asphalt molecules. It is deduced that the increased CED of aged asphalt binder makes the molecular chains more tightly bonded and hinders the free stretch and rotation of molecules.

References

[1] Bhasin, A., Bommavaram, R., Greenfield, M. L., Little, D. N. Use of Molecular Dynamics to Investigate Self-healing Mechanisms in Asphalt Binders[J]. J. Mater. Civ. Eng, 2011, 23:485-492.

[2] Gao, X. W., Liu, Z. H. Self-healing Mechanism of Bio-oil Recycled Asphalt[J]. China J. Highw. Transp, 2019, 32:235-242.

[3] García, Á. Self-healing of Open Cracks in Asphalt Mastic[J]. Fuel, 2012, 93:264-272.

[4] Guo, M. Study on Mechanism and Multiscale Evaluation Method of Interfacial Interaction between Asphalt Binder and Mineral Aggregate[J]. Harbin Institure of Technology, 2015.

[5] Hansen, J. S., Lemarchand, C. A., Nielsen, E., Dyre, J. C., Schrøder, T. Four-component united-atom Model of Bitumen[J]. J. Chem. Phys, 2013, 138:94508.

[6] He, L., Li, G. N., Lv, S. T., Gao, J., Kowalski, K. J., Valentin, J., Alexiadis, A. Self-healing Behavior of Asphalt System Based on Molecular Dynamics Simulation[J]. Constr. Build. Mater, 2020, 254, 119225.

[7] Jennings, P. W., Pribanic, J. A., Desando, M. A., Raub, M. F. Binder Characterization and Evaluation by Nuclear Magnetic Resonance Spectroscopy[J]. Washington, DC, 1993.

[8] Kim, Y. R., Little, D. N., Lytton, R. L. Fatigue and Healing Characterization of Asphalt Mixtures[J]. J. Mater. Civ. Eng, 2003, 15, 75-83.

[9] Li, D. D., Greenfield, M. L, Chemical Compositions of Improved Model Asphalt Systems for Molecular Simulations[J]. Fuel, 2014, 115:347-356.

[10] Pan, J., Tarefder, R. A. Investigation of Asphalt Aging Behaviour due to Oxidation Using Molecular Dynamics Simulation[J]. Mol. Simul, 2016, 42:667-678.

[11] Qiu, J. Self healing of Asphalt Mixtures: Towards a Better Understanding of the Mechanism[J]. Delft Univ. Technol. Delft University of Technology.

[12] Sun, D. Q., Lin, T. B., Zhu, X. Y., Tian, Y., Liu, F. L. Indices for Self-healing Performance Assessments Based on Molecular Dynamics Simulation of Asphalt Binders[J]. Comput. Mater. Sci, 2016, 114: 86-93.

[13] Sun, D. Q., Sun, G. Q., Zhu, X. Y., Ye, F. Y., Xu, J. Y. Intrinsic Temperature Sensitive Self-healing Character of Asphalt Binders Based on Molecular Dynamics Simulations[J]. Fuel, 2018, 211: 609-620.

[14] Sun, D. Q., Yu, F., Li, L. H., Lin, T. B., Zhu, X. Y. Effect of Chemical Composition and Structure of Asphalt Binders on Self-healing[J]. Constr. Build. Mater, 2017, 133: 495-501.

[15] Wang, P. Interfacial Enhancement Mechanism and Rheological Properties of Composited Polymer Modified Asphalt with Carbon Nanotubes[J]. Harbin Institute of Technology, 2017.

[16] Wang, P., Dong, Z. J., Tan, Y. Q., Liu, Z. Y. Research on the Formation Mechanism of Bee-like Structures in Asphalt Binders Based on Molecular Simulations[J]. China J. Highw. Transp, 2016, 29: 9-16.

[17] Xu, G. J., Wang, H. Molecular Dynamics Study of Oxidative Aging Effect on Asphalt Binder Properties[J]. Fuel, 2017, 188: 1-10.

[18] Yu, T. J., Zhang, H. T., Wang, Y. Multi-gradient Analysis of Temperature Self-healing of Asphalt Nanocracks Based on Molecular Simulation[J]. Constr. Build. Mater, 2020, 250: 118859.

[19] Zhang, L., Greenfield, M. L. Rotational Relaxation Times of Individual Compounds within Simulations of Molecular Asphalt Models[J]. Chem. Phys, 2010, 132: 184502.

[20] Zhang, L. Q., Greenfield, M. L. Molecular Orientation in Model Asphalts Using Molecular Simulation[J]. Energy and Fuels, 2007, 21: 1102-1111.

[21] Zhang, L. Q., Greenfield, M. L. Analyzing Properties of Model Asphalts Using Molecular Simulation[J]. Energy & Fuels, 2007, 21: 1712-1716.

基于随机细观模型的沥青混合料劈裂行为研究

马 迪[1] 汤 文[1] 王 欢[1] 吕悦晶[1,2]

(1. 武汉科技大学汽车与交通工程学院;2. 青海省公路局)

摘 要 为了从细观层次研究沥青混合料内部结构劈裂行为,利用CCD高清相机获取集料的真实二维图像,构建二维集料图像库,提出新的干涉判断算法建立沥青混合料的随机细观模型,采用内聚力模型表征沥青胶结料内部以及沥青-集料塑性区的裂纹发展。利用随机细观模型构建AC-13虚拟试件进行虚拟劈裂试验,探讨温度和加载位置对劈裂性能的影响。结果表明:该随机细观模型可以准确地模拟沥青混合料的劈裂行为;沥青混合料劈裂强度随着温度上升而降低,加载位置也影响劈裂强度;主裂纹往往发生于粗集料周围,加载位置对裂纹的产生和发展过程有明显影响,温度不影响主裂纹的轨迹。

关键词 沥青混合料 细观模型 劈裂试验 内聚力模型 温度

0 引 言

沥青混合料是由集料、沥青砂浆和沥青-集料界面三相组成的非均质复合材料。在不同尺度上,增强相离散地分布于基体材料中,增强相的几何尺寸、空间方位等结构特性具有随机分布的特征。这种随机特性造成了沥青混合料的劈裂强度、劈裂能等宏观力学参数具有较大的变异性与尺寸效应,仅从宏观尺度上利用宏观力学试验对沥青混合料的力学特性进行现象学研究存在明显缺陷。随着计算机模拟与仿真技术的发展,利用随机方法构建细观模型,通过材料参数反映微观结构的随机特征,采用数值模拟方法研究沥青混合料的力学行为逐渐成为一种研究沥青混合料损伤行为的有效手段。

国内外学者在沥青混合料细观模型构建、细观力学模拟等方面开展了广泛研究[1-4]。张富强等[5]建立了一种考虑集料的棱角性、粗集料占比和混合料空隙率的随机集料投放模型。Li 等[6]基于数字图像处理技术,研究了细观模型的劈裂行为,发现仿真结果的裂纹扩展路径与实际的裂纹路径非常相似。郑得标等[7]构建具有细观特征的离散元沥青混合料模型,分析不同开裂类型的裂缝扩展角度和断裂过程。Li 等[8]通过蒙特卡洛随机集料数值模拟方法对混凝土的Ⅰ-Ⅱ混合模式中尺度劈裂行为进行了研究。Yong Peng 等[9]通过不同方向加载沥青混合料的水平截面,模拟 IDT 试验中集料分布对劈裂强度和最大水平应力的影响。

多位学者研究发现温度变化以及集料分布对沥青混合料的劈裂行为影响显著。然而,现有的细观模型多采用圆形、椭圆形或凸多边形集料,且得到的模型填充率低于实际混合料。此外,模拟裂纹扩展通常采用人为的预设裂纹扩展路径,只能模拟单一方向的简单裂纹扩展情况。因此本文利用 CCD 高清相机获取集料的真实二维图像,建立基于真实集料特性的二维集料图像库,改进现有的随机集料建模方法得到更加真实的细观模型。采用内聚力模型表征沥青胶结料内部以及沥青–集料塑性区的裂纹发展。利用随机细观模型构建 AC-13 虚拟试件进行虚拟劈裂试验,探讨不同温度和加载位置条件下沥青混合料的劈裂行为。

1 沥青混合料随机细观模型

1.1 基于数字图像技术的2D集料库

利用高清 CCD 相机扫描获取马歇尔试件二维截面图像,采用图像处理技术自主编程算法识别分离集料颗粒,形成基础集料库。并根据标准马歇尔试件尺寸(截面直径为101.6mm)对集料大小进行标定,集料尺寸大小以像素为单位计,即100个像素代表实际1mm。

研究对象为粒径2.36mm及以上的集料颗粒,故将粒径小于2.36mm的细集料颗粒,视作沥青砂浆的一部分。集料粒径划分为4个档次,即[2.36mm,4.75mm)、[4.75mm,9.5mm)、[9.5mm,13.2mm)和[13.2mm,16mm]。对集料颗粒粒径进行划分,通过编程算法,读取集料库中集料颗料图像,按一个方向以1°为步长旋转集料图像,并计算每旋转1°时集料在水平轴上的最大投影长度,直至累计旋转到180°,从这180个最大投影长度中找出最小值,即为该集料颗粒粒径。并与上述4个粒档比较,可确定该集料所属粒档。图1为粒径划分粒档后部分集料示意图。

图1 各档粒径部分集料示意图

基金项目:国家自然科学基金青年项目——基于分子动力学的沥青胶结料自愈合机理研究(51508428);胎-路交互作用下的沥青路面细观损伤多尺度表征及演化机理研究(51778509);青海省重点研发与转化计划项目(2021-QY-207)。

1.2 基于蒙特卡洛方法的细观模型构建

相较于使用圆形、椭圆形或凸多边形集料,利用真实形状集料生成的沥青混合料细观结构更接近于真实情况。运用建立的2D集料库,使用蒙特卡洛方法生成随机细观结构模型。主要流程如下:

(1)获取沥青混合料二维图像,阈值分割提取集料颗粒,建立集料库。
(2)设定填充率、级配,计算各档粒径理论投放面积。
(3)从集料库中随机选取代表性的集料在指定区域进行随机投放。
(4)检测集料间是否存在干涉重叠。若是,重新执行;反之,继续下一步。
(5)判断投放填充率是否满足要求。若是,执行下一步;反之,继续投放。
(6)生成满足要求的随机细观模型。

为了得到符合实际沥青混合料的高填充率模型,提出了一种新的判断干涉算法,解决细观结构中集料随机分布的重叠问题。其主要原理:在特定区域中,选择各粒径范围内具有代表性的集料颗粒进行投放。当随机投放完第1颗后,继续随机投放第2颗。由于区域背景和集料颗粒分别为0和255像素代表的数字图像,当检测到某部分区域像素值大于255时,说明有重叠,则重新执行上述步骤(3);反之,继续投放,直至该档集料填充率大于理论投放填充率,投放完成。

其中涉及一种重要的统计模拟方法,即蒙特卡洛法。在应用方面主要是指借助计算机,通过科学合理的统计建模,将复杂的研究转化成对随机数及其数字特征的模拟和计算[10]。在细观结构中,集料的填充率可表征级配,是一种表明算法有生成密集填料的能力[11]。由于集料形成与投放过程相互独立,集料的级配与填充率也得到保证,因此集料形状适应性强。通过上述算法实现沥青混合料高填充率模型建立,生成不同集料填充率的数字模型如图2所示。

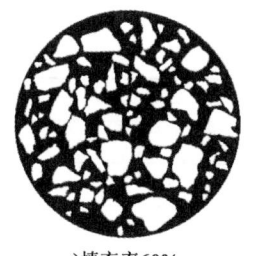 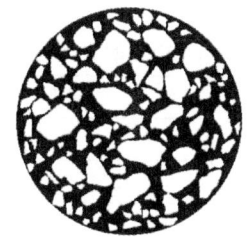 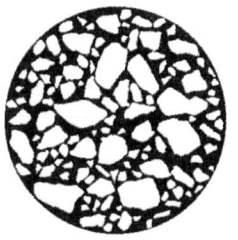

a)填充率60%　　　　b)填充率70%　　　　c)填充率85%

图2　不同填充率的细观模型

2　沥青混合料的虚拟劈裂试验方法及验证

2.1　虚拟劈裂试验方法

以《公路沥青路面施工技术规范》(JTG F40—2004)中AC-13级配范围中值为设计级配,基于随机细观模型建模方法建立AC-13细观模型,见表1。细观模型采用的集料填充率为85%。

AC-13级配参数表　　　　表1

级配类型	质量百分率(%)			
	筛孔13.2mm	筛孔9.5mm	筛孔4.75mm	筛孔2.36mm
细粒式AC-13	90~100	68~85	38~68	24~50
中值	95	76.5	53	37

虚拟劈裂试验步骤:通过对生成的数字细观模型进行预处理,利用自主编程算法获取集料边界坐标,导出单元编号、节点坐标、边界节点等信息,程序实现了直接与有限元软件接口互通,建立沥青混合料有

限元模型。设置集料杨氏模量为55000MPa,泊松比为0.2[12],采用50mm/min速率的位移加载作用于顶部,约束底部,两侧不加约束,模拟沥青混合料劈裂试验。

2.2 黏弹性材料模型

沥青混合料表现出随时间和温度变化的特性,是一种典型的黏弹性材料。其中广义Max-well模型是国内外使用较为广泛的一种黏弹性模型,该模型由许多相互平行的Max-well单位以及一个弹簧组成,可以表征瞬时弹性、延迟弹性、应力松弛和黏性流动[13]。模型的应力应变遗传积分可采用式(1)描述:

$$\partial = E_\infty \varepsilon + \int_0^t E_t \frac{d\varepsilon^{(t)}}{d\tau} d\tau \tag{1}$$

式中:∂——应力;

E_∞——松弛弹性模量;

ε——应变;

E_t——延时模量关于时间的函数;

τ——延迟时间。

E_t用式(2)Prony级数来表示:

$$E_t = \sum_{m=1}^{M} E_m \exp[-(t-\tau)/\rho_m]$$
$$\rho_m = \frac{\eta_m}{E_m} \tag{2}$$

式中:E_m、η_m、ρ_m——表示第m个Max-well模型的弹性模量、黏度、松弛时间。

本文运用广义Max-well模型表征沥青混合料的黏弹性行为,采用文献中广义Max-well模型Prony级数系数[14],见表2。

广义Max-well模型的Prony级数系数　　表2

m	温度(℃)					
	-10		0		10	
	ρ_m	E_m	ρ_m	E_m	ρ_m	E_m
1	3.97E-03	2.45E-07	1.91E-04	2.73E-07	1.39E-05	2.62E-07
2	1.82E-01	3.45E-06	8.61E-03	3.44E-06	6.31E-04	3.44E-06
3	1.63E+00	1.83E-06	7.82E-02	1.84E-06	5.69E-03	1.84E-06
4	3.84E+00	1.94E-06	1.83E-01	1.91E-06	1.33E-02	1.92E-06
5	1.07E+01	1.00E-06	5.12E-01	1.01E-06	3.73E-02	1.01E-06
6	2.62E+01	8.59E-07	1.25E+00	8.48E-07	9.12E-02	8.52E-07
7	6.60E+01	5.55E-07	3.15E+00	5.55E-07	2.30E-01	5.56E-07
8	2.16E+03	1.15E-07	1.03E+02	1.15E-07	7.49E+00	1.15E-07
E_0(MPa)	5.22E+03		5.25E+03		5.24E+03	

2.3 二维内聚力模型

为模拟沥青混合料复杂的劈裂行为,运用二维内聚力模型表征沥青混合料内部微裂纹的产生和扩展。在有限元模型的材料内部,包括所有沥青砂浆单元之间、沥青砂浆与集料单元的界面处插入具有双线性牵引分离定律的内聚力单元,以允许任意随机裂缝路径的出现。裂纹面上各向应力定义为与裂纹面上位移之间的关系,即开裂界面上的张力位移函数[15]可采用式(3)描述:

$$\sigma = f(\delta) \tag{3}$$

式中:σ——裂缝上的张开应力;

δ——开裂界面上的张开位移。

材料在形成新裂纹时,将开裂过程中所需释放的能量称之为断裂能 G,计算通式为式(4):

$$G = \int \sigma d\delta = \int f(\delta) d\delta \qquad (4)$$

式中:G——断裂能。

张力位移函数一般表现为:在内聚力区承载的初始阶段,裂缝上的张开应力 σ 值随着开裂界面上的张开位移 δ 的增加而增加,直至达到材料可以承受的最大值 δ_0,此时张开应力 σ 也达到最大,意味着材料出现初始损伤。应力达到最大值 σ_{max} 后开始下降,该阶段为材料的损伤扩展阶段,直到张开应力减小为零,材料完全失效破坏,内聚力区在该处发生完全开裂并向前扩展形成新的宏观裂缝。此阶段所释放的断裂能是其最大的临界断裂能 G,为张力-位移曲线下所围成的面积。因此在内聚力模型中,有两个主要参数 σ_{max} 和 G[16]。

假定沥青砂浆单元以及砂浆与集料之间的界面发生劈裂,沥青砂浆-集料连接界面是常见的损伤起始点,对法向、切向断裂能进行独立的表征,劈裂在法线方向和切向方向上是相同的。不同温度下断裂能通过三点弯曲试验确定[17]。不同温度下 CZM 参数见表3。

不同温度下 CZM 参数 表3

项目	沥青主体部分			沥青-集料界面		
	−10℃	0℃	10℃	−10℃	0℃	10℃
抗拉强度 T_0 (MPa)	4.7	2.7	2.5	4.5	2.5	2.3
劈裂能 G (Nmm/mm²)	0.314	0.76	1.631	0.314	0.76	1.631

由于内聚力单元的植入会引入虚假的刚度,从而造成材料的软化和收敛困难等问题。为减少其影响,本文采用双线型内聚力模型并运用黏性正则化稳定界面分层,使计算过程流畅且不易出现收敛错误。双线型内聚力模型张力-位移关系如图3所示。

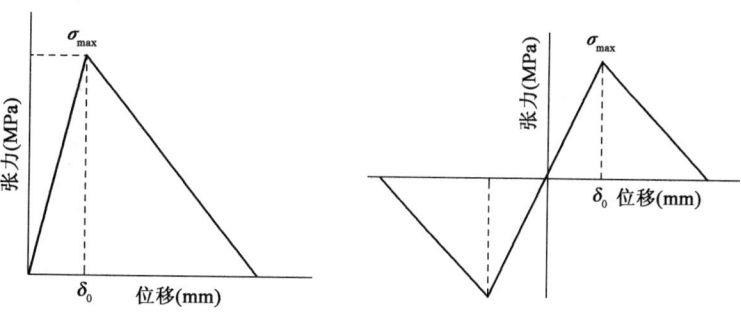

图3 双线性 CZM 张力-位移关系

完成虚拟劈裂试验步骤,生成集料填充率为 85% 的 AC-13 沥青混合料圆柱体试件(直径为 101.6mm,高 63.5mm)二维有限元模型,如图4所示。

2.4 模型验证

为了验证模型的合理性,通过虚拟劈裂试验与室内劈裂试验进行比较。室内劈裂试验按《公路工程沥青及沥青混合料试验规程》(JTG E20—2011)设计,采用壳牌70号基质石油沥青,辉绿岩为粗集料,石灰岩矿粉为填料。在最佳沥青用量下成型 AC-13 级配的马歇尔试件,试件直径为 101.6mm,高度为 63.5mm。分别在 −10℃、0℃、10℃ 条件下进行劈裂试验,计算得到沥青混合料劈裂强度。运用生成的 AC-13 细观模型在与室内试验相同的温度条件下进行虚拟劈裂试验,计算得到劈裂强度,比较不同温度条件下虚拟试验与室内试验劈裂强度平均值,如图5所示。对比室内试验和虚拟试验结果,0℃ 条件下,虚拟试验劈裂强度的平均值与室内试验更加接近,不同温度下虚拟试验劈裂强度平均值大于室内试验。虚拟试验与室内试验的劈裂强度相对误差较小,造成这种差异的原因是三维样本投影到二维几何图形上[18]。对比结果说明该模型模拟沥青混合料的劈裂行为具有较高的准确性。

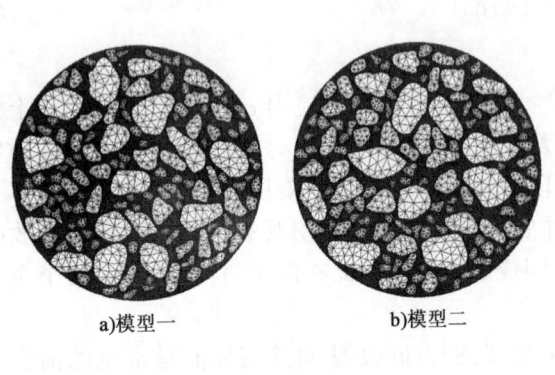

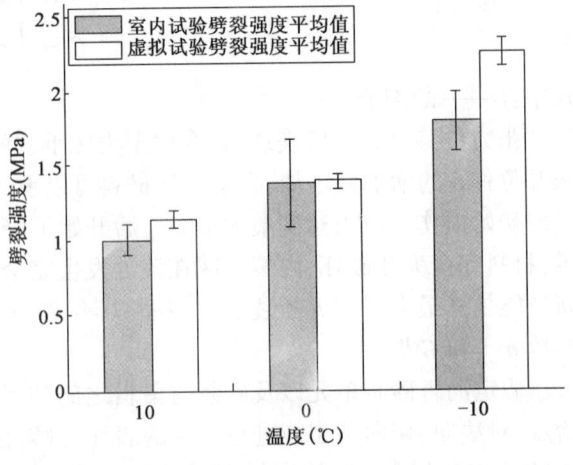

图4 二维有限元模型

图5 不同温度条件下虚拟试验与室内试验劈裂强度平均值

3 沥青混合料的劈裂行为分析

3.1 加载位置对劈裂行为的影响

沥青混合料是由集料、沥青砂浆和沥青-集料界面构成的非均质复合材料,沥青混合料各成分的随机分布状态必然会对劈裂行为产生影响[19]。本文将对同一个虚拟试件的不同位置加载,以研究不同加载位置对劈裂行为的影响。加载位置分别为垂直方向呈 0°、45°、90°以及 135°,分别在 -10℃、0℃、10℃ 3 种温度条件下进行虚拟劈裂试验。加载位置如图 6 所示,在 0℃ 环境中不同加载位置的裂纹轨迹发展如图 7 所示,不同温度条件下加载反力随时间的变化如图 8 所示。

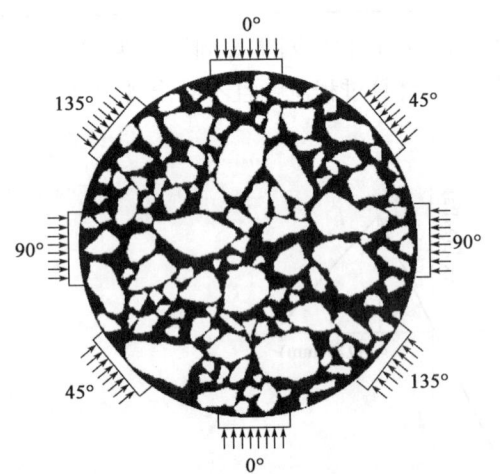

图6 劈裂试验4种不同加载位置

对比不同加载位置的劈裂试验中裂纹的产生和发展过程,显然各裂纹轨迹在开始位置、裂纹长度、裂纹走向等方面均存在明显差异。分析可知,裂缝产生的初始位置通常为粗集料的边界处,且沿着粗集料的边界逐渐发展直至试件破坏,三种温度条件下均呈现这种规律。

在细观层面上沥青混合料的结构模型呈现出显著的不均匀特性,不同的位置加载必然导致试件内部应力、应变状态的显著差异。劈裂试验的时间-反力曲线清楚地呈现了加载位置对试件劈裂强度的影响,不同的加载位置下试件的劈裂强度表现出明显差异。

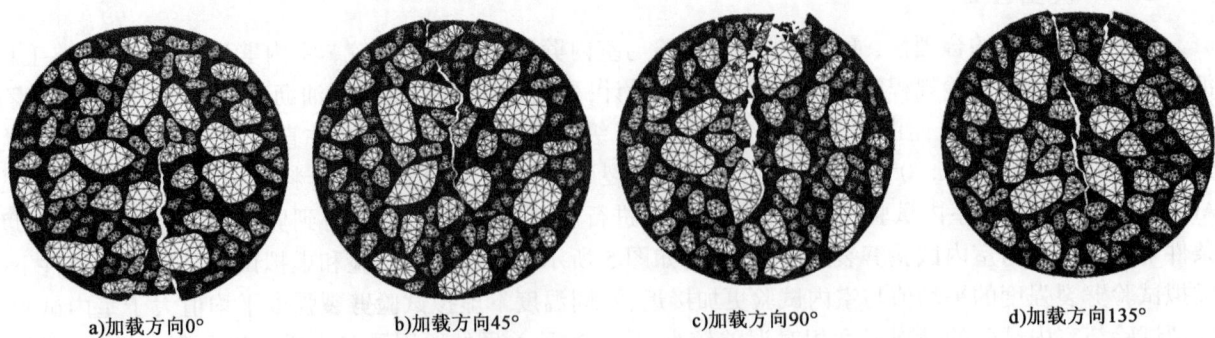

a)加载方向0°　　　b)加载方向45°　　　c)加载方向90°　　　d)加载方向135°

图7 一个试件在0℃环境中4个不同位置加载时的最终裂纹轨迹

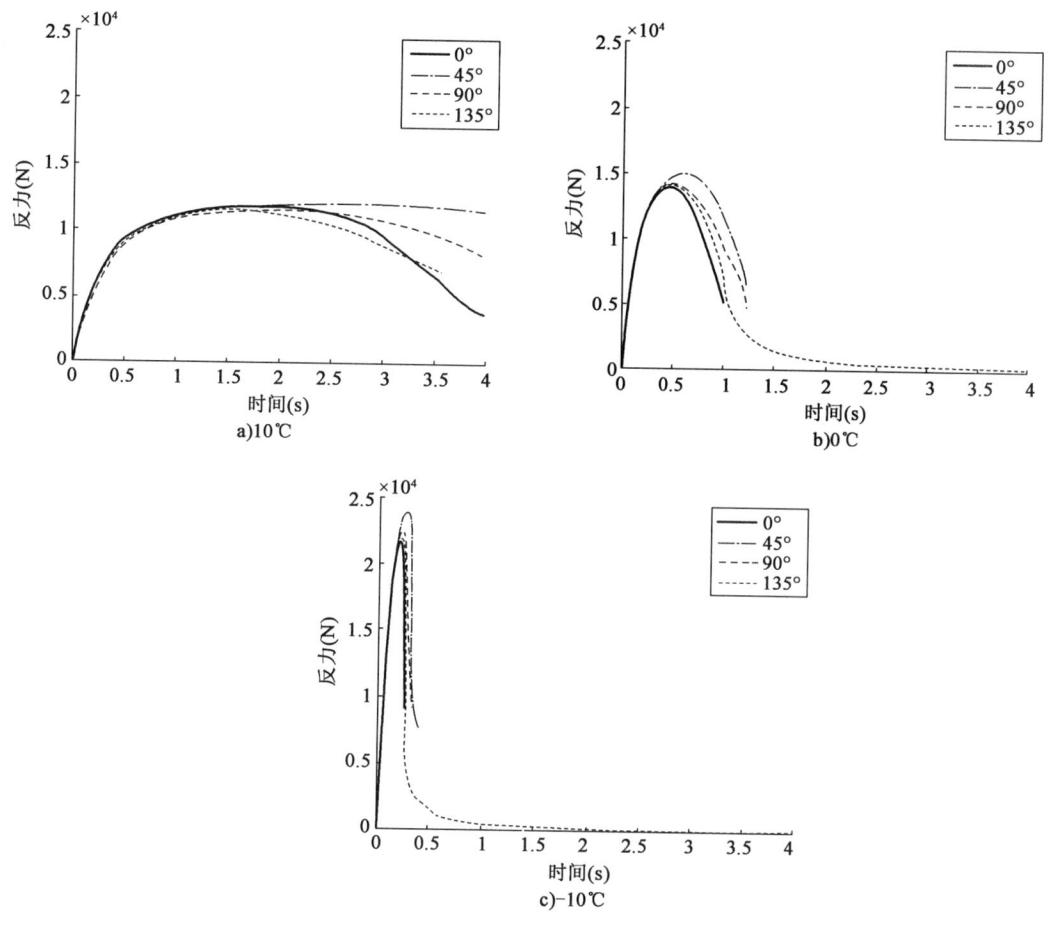

图8 不同温度下4个不同方向加载时间—反力曲线图

3种温度条件下均表现为45°加载方向的最大反力最大，这表明该虚拟试件在45°方向上集料的排列和嵌挤方式可承受更高的载荷。其他3个方向显示出相似的最大反力结果，最大反作用力的变异系数在3%以内。这种一致性表明，在这些方向上观察到的沥青混合料劈裂行为，符合这种沥青混合料在统计学上最可能的劈裂行为。试件模拟结果表现出沥青混合料的不均匀性，一个试件的加载方向影响着试件的劈裂强度，因此劈裂试验中应包括多个样本，以平衡沥青混合料内部细观结构的方差和统计特征，足够大的样本数量对于识别实验异常值，分析沥青混合料的力学性能具有重要的意义。

3.2 温度对劈裂行为的影响

沥青混合料表现出随温度变化的特性，温度变化必然会对试件的劈裂行为产生影响。本文将对同一个虚拟试件在不同温度条件（-10℃、0℃、10℃）下进行加载，研究温度对劈裂行为的影响。代表模型如图6所示，不同温度下代表模型裂纹轨迹发展如图9所示，不同温度下加载反力随时间的变化如图10所示。

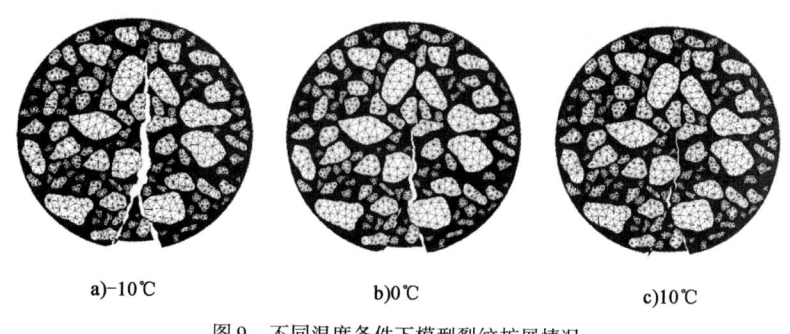

图9 不同温度条件下模型裂纹扩展情况

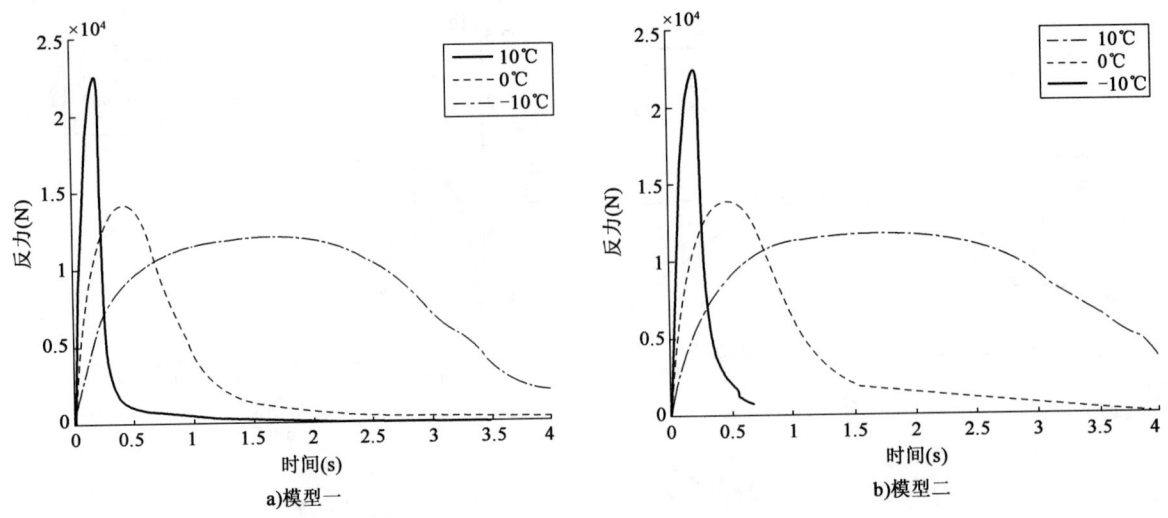

图10 不同温度条件下同一模型时间反力曲线图

对比多组模型的劈裂试验中裂纹的产生和发展过程,可以发现温度变化不影响劈裂发生时主裂纹的轨迹,主裂纹往往发生在粗集料周围,且沿着粗集料的边界逐渐发展直至试件破坏,而局部裂纹在不同温度下出现差异。分析可知:在-10℃环境中,沥青混合料表现出脆性材料性质,脆性劈裂行为在应力重新分布之前会导致明显的局部破坏,这导致了更明显的损伤发展路径。损伤分布表明,集料-砂浆界面单元与砂浆单元比较更加容易损伤。

在细观层面上沥青混合料的黏弹性行为受温度影响显著,在不同温度环境下加载必然导致试件内部应力、应变状态的显著差异。劈裂试验的时间—反力曲线清楚地呈现了温度对试件劈裂强度的影响。时间-反力曲线描述试件从开始加载到损伤破坏的整个过程中反力随时间的变化情况。裂纹尖端内聚力区域中应力在外载荷的作用下,最初阶段随着位移的增加而增加;在应力达到最大值后,该处材料点损伤开始萌生,刚度出现软化;此后应力值随着位移的增加下降,该处承受载荷能力减小,该处损伤逐渐累积;当应力完全减小至零,该处裂纹完全扩展,界面在该处开裂失效,失去承载能力。

在10℃环境中,沥青的黏度降低,沥青混合料的黏结力也随之降低,沥青混合料在该环境温度下表现出黏性材料性质,延展性增强,黏性降低,沥青混合料劈裂强度降低,材料损伤破坏的时间变长。在-10℃环境下,沥青的黏度增强,沥青混合料的黏结力也随之增强,沥青混合料在该环境温度下表现出脆性材料性质,延展性降低,黏性增强,沥青混合料劈裂强度增大,材料在比较短的时间内破坏失效。

4 结 语

(1)采用CCD高清相机获取集料的真实二维图像并构建二维集料图像库,基于蒙特卡洛方法建立沥青混合料的随机细观模型,可将集料填充率提高到85%,得到的随机细观模型更加接近实际沥青混合料试件。

(2)利用内聚力模型模拟微裂纹的开展,采用随机细观模型建立了虚拟劈裂试验方法,并采用室内试验验证了虚拟试验准确性。

(3)试件的加载位置对劈裂强度和裂纹生成及扩展过程存在明显影响;主裂纹往往发生于粗集料周围,且沿着粗集料的边界逐渐发展直至试件破坏,温度不影响主裂纹的轨迹,集料-砂浆界面单元的损伤比砂浆单元损伤更为严重。随着温度升高,沥青混合料劈裂强度降低,材料损伤破坏需要的时间变长。

参考文献

[1] 付军,刘洁,雷力,等.沥青混合料劈裂试验的细观有限元模拟与测试[J].实验力学,2018,33(03):

419-427.
[2] Kuang D, Wang X, Jiao Y, et al. Influence of Angularity and Roughness of Coarse Aggregates on Asphalt Mixture Performance[J]. Construction and Building Materials, 2019, 200: 681-686.
[3] Kollmann J, Liu P, Lu G, et al. Investigation of the microstructural fracture behaviour of asphalt mixtures using the finite element method[J]. Construction and Building Materials, 2019, 227: 117078.
[4] Gao J, Wang H, Bu Y, et al. Effects of Coarse Aggregate Angularity on the Microstructure of Asphalt Mixture[J]. Construction and Building Materials, 2018, 183: 472-484.
[5] 张富强, 滕旭秋, 李斌斌. 基于随机集料投放的沥青混凝土细观模型研究[J]. 铁道科学与工程学报, 2019(5): 1217-1223.
[6] Li C, Guo J. Cracking Simulation of Asphalt Concrete Beam Specimen Using Cohesive Zone Model[J]. Construction and Building Materials, 2019, 214: 49-60.
[7] 郑得标, 倪富健, 蒋继望, 等. 基于离散元法的沥青混合料复合断裂行为研究[J]. 江苏大学学报(自然科学版), 2020, 41(1): 87-92.
[8] Li G, Yu J, Cao P, et al. Experimental and Numerical Investigation on I-II Mixed-mode Fracture of Concrete Based on the Monte Carlo Random Aggregate Distribution[J]. Construction and Building Materials, 2018, 191: 523-534.
[9] Yong Peng, Li jun Sun. Aggregate Distribution Influence on the Indirect Tensile Test of Asphalt Mixtures Using the Discrete Element Method[J]. International Journal of Pavement Engineering, 2015, 18(8).
[10] 朱陆陆. 蒙特卡洛方法及应用[D]. 武汉: 华中师范大学, 2014.
[11] Salemi M, Wang H. Image-aided Random Aggregate Packing for Computational Modeling of Asphalt Concrete Microstructure[J]. Construction and Building Materials, 2018, 177: 467-476.
[12] Z. You, S. Adhikari, Q. Dai, Three-dimensional Discrete Element Models for Asphalt Mixtures, J. Eng. Mech. 134(12)(2008)1053-1063.
[13] J. Baek, Modeling Reflective Cracking Development in Hot-mix Asphalt Overlays and Quantification of Control Techniques(Doctoral dissertation), University of Illinois, Urbana-Champaign, 2010.
[14] Kollmann, Jonas, Lu, Guoyang, Liu, Pengfei, et al. Parameter Optimisation of a 2D Finite Element Model to Investigate the Microstructural Fracture Behaviour of Asphalt Mixtures[J]. Theoretical and Applied Fracture Mechanics, 2019, 103.
[15] 熊学玉, 肖启晟. 基于内聚力模型的混凝土细观拉压统一数值模拟方法[J]. 水利学报, 2019, 50(4): 448-462.
[16] 梁何浩, 王端宜, 邓志刚, 等. 内聚力模型在泡沫沥青混合料离散元模拟中的应用[J]. 湖南大学学报(自然科学版), 2019, 46(5): 115-123.
[17] Biao Ding, Xiaolong Zou, Zixin Peng, Xiang Liu, Hiroshi Noguchi. Evaluation of Fracture Resistance of Asphalt Mixtures Using the Single-Edge Notched Beams[J]. Advances in Materials Science and Engineering, 2018.
[18] Jonas Kollmann, Pengfei Liu, Guoyang Lu, Dawei Wang, Markus Oeser, Sabine Leischner. Investigation of the microstructural fracture behaviour of asphalt mixtures using the finite element method[J]. Construction and Building Materials, 2019, 227.
[19] H. Wang, P. Hao, Numerical Simulation of Indirect Tensile Test Based on the Mi-crostructure of Asphalt Mixture, J. Mater. Civ. Eng. 23 (1)(2010)21-29.

移动荷载作用下沥青路面反射裂缝影响因素分析

宋 帅 何 帅 杨茂林

（长安大学公路学院）

摘 要 为探究沥青路面反射裂缝形成的影响因素，本文利用有限元软件构建三维道路结构模型，采用沥青路面面层层底最大水平应力 σ_{max} 和剪应力 τ_{max} 表征反射裂缝发育能力，研究温度、基层裂缝间距、基层底基层模量和厚度对 σ_{max} 和 τ_{max} 的影响。结果表明：基层的裂缝间距越小，σ_{max} 和 τ_{max} 越大；从 0℃ 到 60℃ 时，σ_{max} 由受拉变为受压，40℃ 时 τ_{max} 最大；基层、底基层模量对 σ_{max} 和 τ_{max} 的影响均较小，基层、底基层厚度对 τ_{max} 的影响较小，但对 σ_{max} 的影响较大，随基层、底基层厚度增加而减小；增加应力吸收层后，σ_{max} 和 τ_{max} 降低明显。

关键词 沥青路面 有限元 半刚性基层 反射裂缝

0 引 言

反射裂缝是水泥路面加铺沥青面层和半刚性基层沥青路面的常见病害，主要是基层或者旧水泥路面板贯穿裂缝在道路温度变化和行车荷载的共同作用下导致的。通常用室内试验、解析法和软件仿真的方法研究反射裂缝的发育和防治，其中 ABAQUS 通用有限元软件因其灵活性在路面反射裂缝的研究中得到了广泛的应用。

论文用 ABAQUS 建立三维模型，并施加移动荷载，考虑基层裂缝间距、温度、基层底基层模量、厚度等因素，计算移动荷载作用下沥青面层底部应力状态，使用沥青面层层底最大水平应力 σ_{max} 和剪应力 τ_{max} 分别表征半刚性基层裂缝对沥青路面拉裂型裂缝和撕裂型裂缝反射能力，从而分析影响半刚性基层反射裂缝的影响因素，希望能给工程应用提供借鉴。

1 有限元模型建立

1.1 模型建立和基本假定

参照文献[1]建立半刚性基层沥青路面有限元模型，模型尺寸为 6m×6m×6m，道路结构如图 1a)所示。研究中变化半刚性基层、底基层厚度时，变化土基厚度使模型总尺寸不变。裂缝贯穿基层，裂缝之间无传荷能力。模型基本假定：各层之间连续；不考虑重力作用；路面结构各材料为弹性材料，且各向同性。边界条件参照文献[2]选取，底部完全固定，垂直于 X 轴的两个面关于 X 轴对称约束，垂直于 Z 轴的两个面自由，行车方向沿 Z 轴向。

对模型进行网格划分时全局尺寸控制取 0.3，进行局部加密布种，沿 Y 轴方向上面层、中面层、下面层布种 3~4 个，基层、底基层布种 8 个，对基层裂缝处的布种进行适当加密。网格的划分采用结构网格划分技术，全部划分为六面体单元。网格划分结果如图 1b)所示。

1.2 材料属性

根据国内外相关研究[3]，当汽车以 70km/h 的速度行驶时对路面的作用时间为约为 0.1s，因此论文中选取荷载移动速度为 70km/h，以 10Hz 频率下沥青混合料动态回弹模量作为沥青混合料的材料参数，沥青混合料动态回弹模量参考《公路沥青路面设计规范》（JTG D50—2017）选取。参照文献[3]的沥青混合料在不同温度下的动态模量预估公式,以及参照文献[4]计算不同动态回弹模量下沥青混合料的泊松比,最终确定沥青混合料的材料参数见表1,其中式(1)、式(2)分别为AC-13、AC-20在不同温度下的动态回弹模量预估公式。式(3)为不同动态回弹模量时泊松比的计算公式。

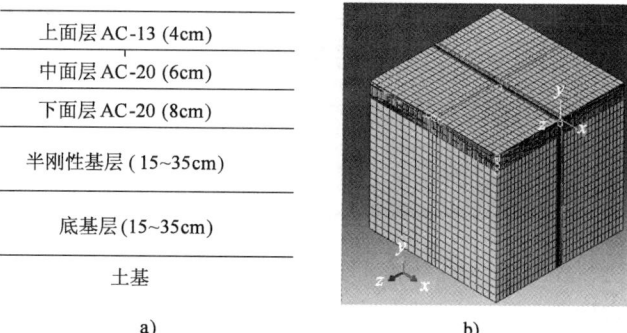

图1 道路结构及网格划分示意图

$$\frac{E_{20}}{E_T} = e^{-0.0464(20-T)} \quad (R^2 = 0.9950) \tag{1}$$

$$\frac{E_{20}}{E_T} = e^{-0.0517(20-T)} \quad (R^2 = 0.9865) \tag{2}$$

$$\mu = (-7 \times 10^{-15})|E^*|^3 + (8 \times 10^{-10})|E^*|^2 - (3 \times 10^{-5})|E^*| + 0.483 \tag{3}$$

沥青混合料动态回弹模量及泊松比　　　　表1

温度(℃)	AC-13		AC-20	
	E^*(MPa)	μ	E^*(MPa)	μ
0	26559	0.12	31638	0.11
20	10500	0.25	11250	0.24
40	4151	0.37	4000	0.38
60	1641	0.44	1422	0.44

半刚性基层的动态回弹模量是静态回弹模量的1.2~1.5倍,受动态荷载影响较小,而且随深度增加,道路结构及材料受动荷载的影响较小,因此除面层外,均采用静态回弹模量。参照文献[3-7],土基、基层、底基层、等材料参数见表2。

路面各结构材料参数及单元类型　　　　表2

材料类别	弹性模量(MPa)	泊松比	密度(kg/m³)	阻尼	厚度(cm)	单元类型
AC-13	—	—	2400	0.9	4	C3D8R
AC-20	—	—	2400	0.9	14	C3D8R
基层、底基层	1300~1700	0.25	2300	0.8	15~35	C3D8R
土基	40	0.4	1800	0.4	—	C3D8R
应力吸收层	400~800	0.35	2400	0.9	3	C3D8R

1.3 荷载施加

(1)荷载施加参数确定

论文考虑一侧双轮对路面施加荷载,荷载采用移动荷载,通过用户子程序 VDLOAD 来实现,荷载作用时间 0.15s,荷载速度为 70km/h,荷载移动距离 3m,荷载大小为 0.7MPa。根据文献[8]的研究结果,接地压强 $p=0.7$Pa,轮胎接地面积示意图如图 2 所示。

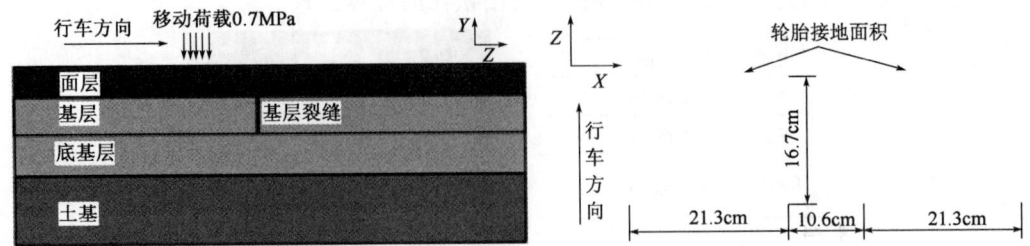

图 2　荷载施加示意图

(2)模型中荷载添加方法

将模型的上表面进行分区,如图 3 所示。小方块沿 Z 向的长度为 16.7cm,沿 X 轴方向的长度为 21.3cm。方块沿 X 轴方向间隔为 10.6cm。对处于中间的 18×2 个长方形表面施加压力。定义荷载时,Edit Load 中 Distribution 选择 User-defined,Magnitude 输入 1。荷载子程序在创建任务时添加,动荷载分布子程序(vdload)编写方法参照文献[2]。荷载和边界条件施加后模型如图 3 所示。

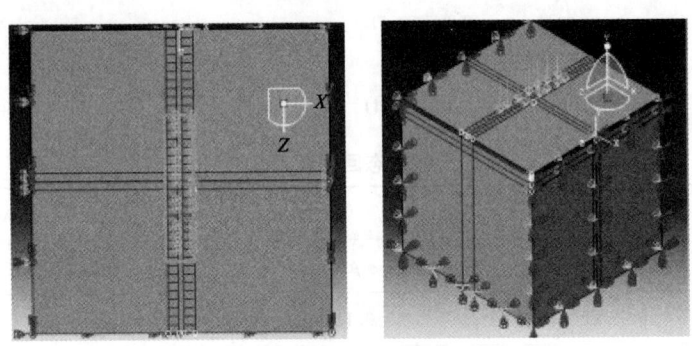

图 3　模型分区及荷载添加示意图

2　半刚性基层反射裂缝发育影响因素分析

论文使用半刚性基层裂缝处沥青面层层底最大拉应力 σ_{max} 和剪应力 τ_{max} 分别表征半刚性基层裂缝对沥青面层层底拉裂型裂缝和撕裂型裂缝的反射能力,采集数据的单元如图 4 所示。

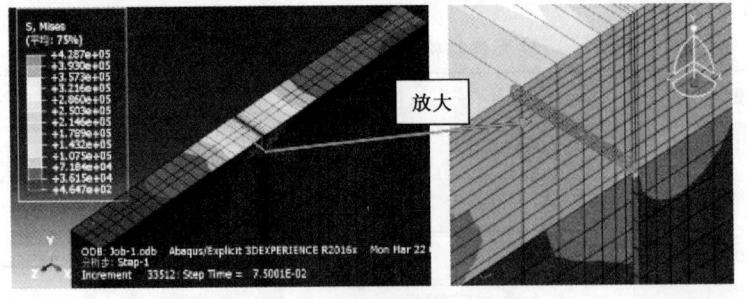

图 4　10mm 基层裂缝时模型应力云图

此处特别说明:基层、底基层模量和厚度不为变量时,分别默认为 1500MPa 和 25cm;当温度为不变量时,面层材料属性取 20℃时对应值。

2.1　裂缝间距

由图 5 可知,当荷载最接近基层裂缝时(0.075s),剪应力和水平拉应力达到最大值。当基层不存在裂缝时,沥青面层层底最大剪应力 τ_{max} 和最大拉应力 σ_{max} 均较小。当基层裂缝宽度为5mm时,沥青面层层底最大剪应力 τ_{max} 和最大拉应力 σ_{max} 分别增大1.9倍和3.4倍。随着裂缝间距的增大,沥青面层层底最大剪应力 τ_{max} 和最大水平应力 σ_{max} 逐渐减小。间距20mm时,沥青面层层底最大剪应力 τ_{max} 和最大水平应力 σ_{max} 降低33.9%和13.9%。这是因为基层裂缝的间距变小,沥青面层底部应力集中导致。

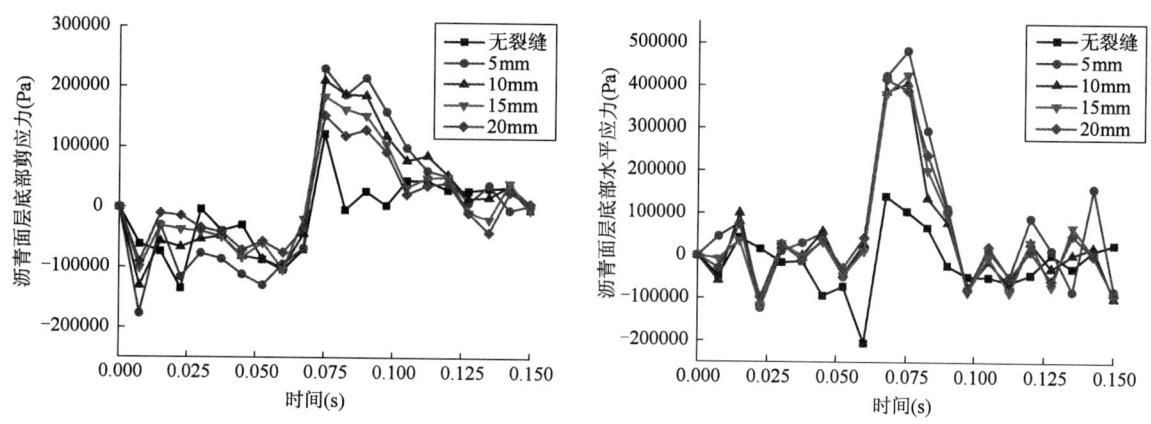

图5 不同裂缝间距沥青面层底部应力关系

2.2 温度

由图6可知,随着温度的增加,沥青面层底部最大水平应力 σ_{max} 由0℃时的0.61MPa的拉应力变化为0.23MPa的压应力。因为温度升高,泊松比增大,在荷载作用下侧向变形变大,导致沥青面层底部最大水平应力 σ_{max} 减小,甚至变为压应力。与水平应力不同,沥青面层底部最大剪应力 τ_{max} 随着温度的升高先升高后降低,温度由0℃到40℃,沥青面层底部最大剪应力 τ_{max} 增加了34.3%。

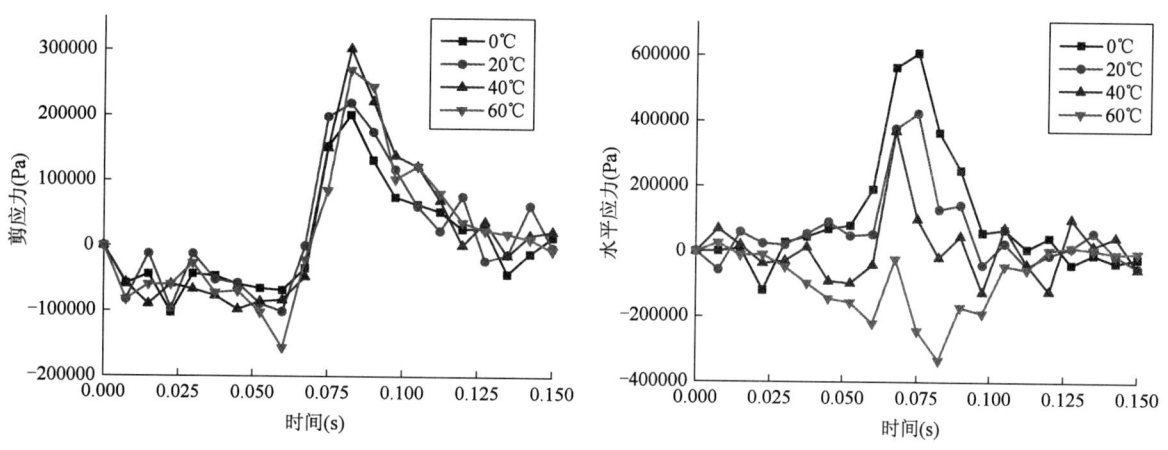

图6 不同温度下沥青面层底部应力关系

2.3 基层模量和厚度

由图7可知,沥青面层层底最大剪应力 τ_{max} 和最大拉应力 σ_{max} 随基层模量的变化趋势不明显,且变化幅度较小,不超过0.021MPa和0.019MPa;由图8可知,沥青面层层底应力受基层厚度的影响大,沥青面层层底最大剪应力 τ_{max} 随厚度的增加而提升,厚度由15cm增加到35cm,沥青面层底部最大剪应力 τ_{max} 增加110%,而沥青面层底部最大水平应力 σ_{max} 随基层厚度的变化较小。

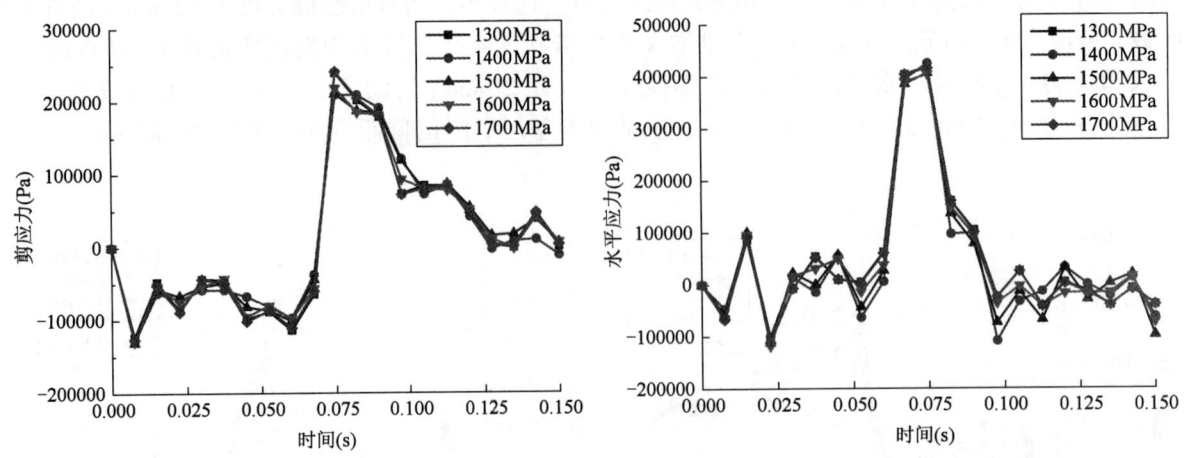

图7 基层模量和沥青面层底部应力关系

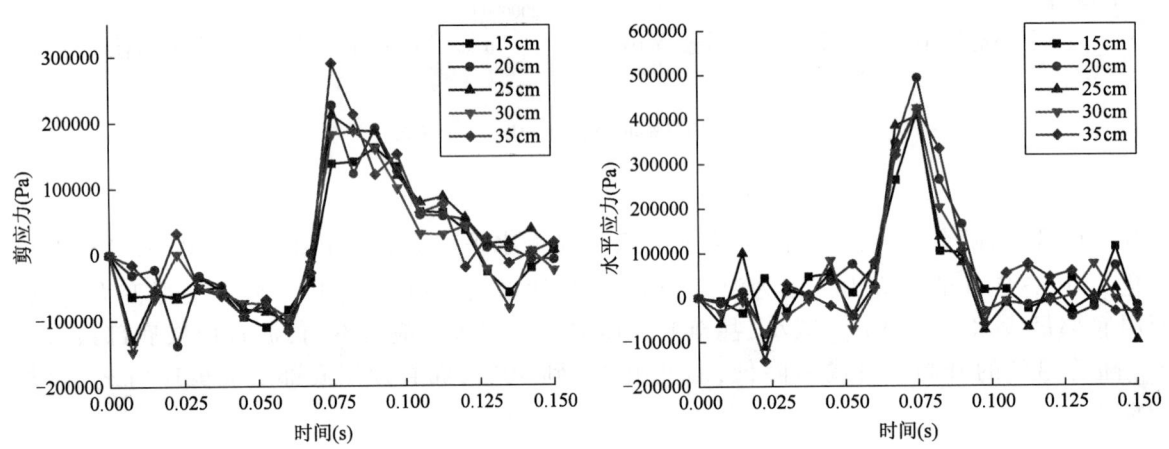

图8 基层厚度和沥青面层底部应力关系

2.4 底基层模量和厚度

由图9、图10可知,沥青面层底部最大剪应力 τ_{max} 随底基层厚度的增加,变化并不明显,变化幅度不超过0.026MPa;沥青面层底部最大水平应力 σ_{max} 随底基层厚度的增加而降低,底基层厚度由15cm增加到35cm,沥青面层底部最大水平应力 σ_{max} 降低37.1%。沥青面层底部最大剪应力 τ_{max} 随底基层模量的增加变大,但幅度小,底基层模量从1300MPa增加到1700MPa,τ_{max} 提升18.5%;沥青面层底部最大水平应力 σ_{max} 随底基层模量的增加减小,但幅度较小,底基层模量从1300MPa增加到1700MPa,沥青面层底部最大水平应力 σ_{max} 降低11.4%。

2.5 应力吸收层模量

由图11可知,应力吸收层可大大降低沥青面层层底最大剪应力 τ_{max} 和最大拉应力 σ_{max}。在应力吸收层模量为900MPa时,沥青面层层底最大剪应力 τ_{max} 和最大拉应力 σ_{max} 分别降低了74.3%、24.3%。沥青面层层底最大拉应力 σ_{max} 随应力吸收层模量的增加而先减小后增大,如应力吸收层模量从600MPa到800MPa,沥青面层层底最大拉应力 σ_{max} 降低11.0%,从800MPa到900MPa,沥青面层层底最大拉应力 σ_{max} 提升2.1%;沥青面层层底最大剪应力 τ_{max} 随应力吸收层模量的增加而先减小后增大,如应力吸收层模量从600MPa到800MPa,沥青面层层底最大剪应力 τ_{max} 降低13.2%,从800MPa到900MPa,沥青面层层底最大剪应力 τ_{max} 提升4.8%。

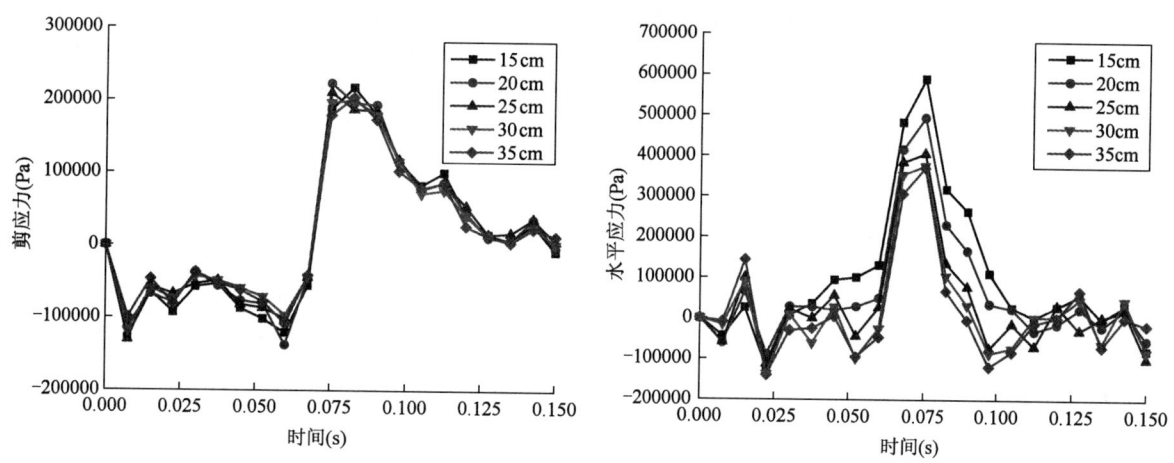

图9　底基层厚度与沥青面层层底应力关系

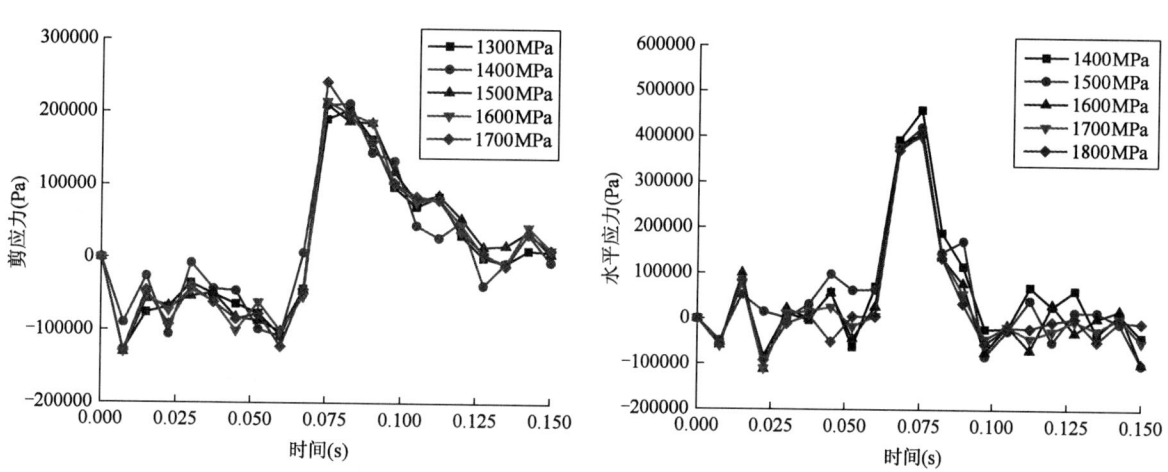

图10　底基层模量与沥青面层层底应力关系

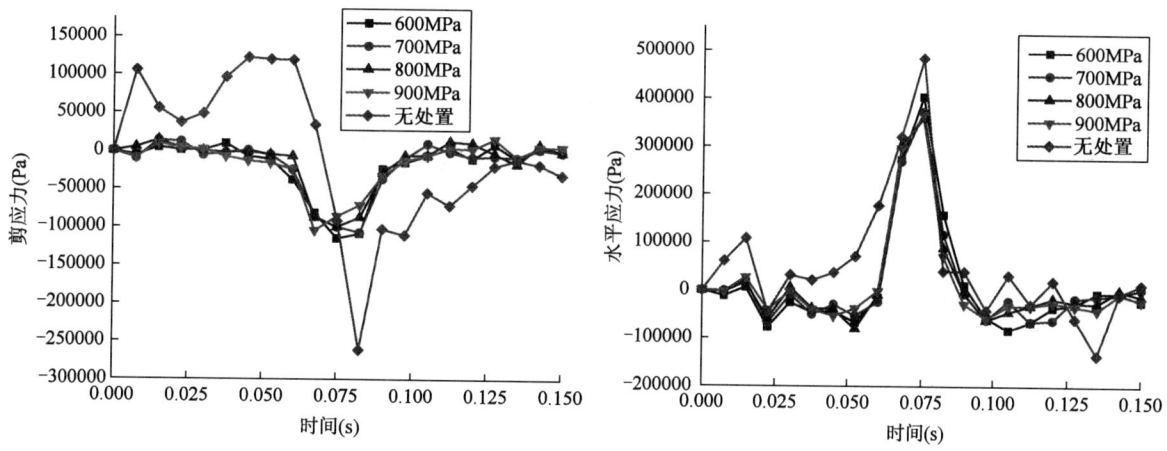

图11　应力吸收层模量与沥青面层层底应力关系

3　结　语

(1)随着移动荷载的接近,半刚性基层裂缝上方的沥青面层底部的剪应力和水平应力逐渐增大。

(2)半刚性基层的裂缝间距越小,沥青面层层底最大剪应力 τ_{max} 和最大拉应力 σ_{max} 越大,这是因为应力集中导致的;不存在裂缝时,沥青面层层底最大剪应力 τ_{max} 和最大拉应力 σ_{max} 最小,裂缝宽度为 5～20mm 时,沥青面层层底最大剪应力 τ_{max} 是无裂缝情况的 1.25～1.9 倍,沥青面层层底最大拉应力 σ_{max} 是无裂缝情况的 2.7～3.4 倍;路面温度越高,沥青面层层底最大剪应力 τ_{max} 先增加后降低,40℃时沥青面层层底最大剪应力 τ_{max} 最大,水平应力由拉应力减小,并且转化为压应力。

(3)基层模量对沥青面层层底最大剪应力 τ_{max} 和最大拉应力 σ_{max} 的影响均较小,模量值由 1300～1700MPa,沥青面层层底最大剪应力 τ_{max} 和最大拉应力 σ_{max} 变化值不超过 0.021MPa;沥青面层层底最大剪应力 τ_{max} 随基层厚度增加而增加,厚度由 15cm 增加到 35cm,沥青面层层底最大剪应力 τ_{max} 提升了 110%,沥青面层层底最大拉应力 σ_{max} 随厚度的增加变化较小;底基层厚度对沥青面层层底最大剪应力 τ_{max} 的影响小,对沥青面层层底最大拉应力 σ_{max} 的影响大,厚度由 15cm 增加到 35cm,沥青面层层底最大拉应力 σ_{max} 降低了 37.1%;底基层模量增加,沥青面层层底最大剪应力 τ_{max} 增加,沥青面层层底最大拉应力 σ_{max} 减小,但是影响小。

(4)应力吸收层可有效阻止反射裂缝的发展,添加应力吸收层后,当其材料的回弹模量为 700～800MPa 时,可更好阻止反射裂缝发育。

参考文献

[1] 李辉.沥青路面车辙形成规律与温度场关系研究[D].南京:东南大学,2007.
[2] 廖公云,黄晓明.ABAQUS 有限元软件在道路工程中的应用[M].南京:东南大学出版社,2008.
[3] 王月峰,王传沛,庄传仪.沥青混合料动态模量温度修正研究[J].中外公路,2012,32(02):210-214.
[4] 刘涛,唐佑绵,范海琪,等.基于间接拉伸动态模量试验的沥青混合料泊松比研究[J].广东公路交通,2018,44(02):1-6.
[5] 吕松涛,陈杰东,张晖.水泥稳定碎石拉压弯静态模量与动态模量比较分析[J].公路交通科技,2016,33(10):39-43,59.
[6] 程箭,许志鸿,李淑明,等.水泥稳定碎石静态模量与动态模量比较[J].建筑材料学报,2009,12(01):63-66+75.
[7] 肖川.典型沥青路面动力行为及其结构组合优化研究[D].成都:西南交通大学,2014.
[8] 胡小弟.轮胎接地压力实测及沥青路面力学响应分析[D].上海:同济大学,2003.

Flame Resistance and Pavement Performance of Asphalt Mixture Incorporating Composite Flame Retardant

Yao Tengfei[1]　　Han Sen[1]　　Men Changpeng[1]　　Zhang Zhuang[1]　　Dong Shihao[1]　　Li Yang[2]

(1. Key Laboratory for Special Area Highway Engineering of Ministry of Education, Chang'an University;
2. Shaanxi Provincial Transport Planning Design and Research Institute)

Abstract　With wide application of asphalt mixture on tunnel pavement, this study aims to evaluate the flame resistance of asphalt binders incorporating a composite flame retardant (CFR) and the pavement performance of flame retardant asphalt mixtures in the laboratory. 70# matrix asphalt and SBS modified asphalt were selected. The basic technical characteristics of asphalt binders with different dosages of CFR were determined, and the resistance of flame retardant asphalt was determined by Limit oxygen index (LOI) test and Combustion Test. It was found that the blending amount of the matrix asphalt should not exceed 6%, and the blending amount of the SBS modified asphalt should be 8% – 10%. Finally, the pavement performance of the asphalt mixture blended with the CFR was verified by determining the high – temperature performance, low – temperature performance and water stability of the flame retardant asphalt mixture. The results show that the addition of a CTR could improve the high temperature performance of the asphalt mixture, and may reduce the low temperature performance and water stability. Therefore, the amount of CTR should be strictly controlled to ensure good flame retardant performance and pavement performance requirements.

Keywords　　Flame retardant (FR)　　Flame resistance　　Limiting oxygen index　　Combustion test　　Pavement performance

0　Introduction

Recently, more and longer tunnels are constructed, through mountainous ranges or in urban areas, to develop new road networks. Meanwhile, in the construction of tunnel pavement, asphalt pavement tends to replace cement concrete pavement because of its low noise, comfortable driving, good skid resistance, convenience of maintenance, etc.[1-4] Then, due to the relatively closed space in the tunnel and the flammable asphalt material, accidental fires in the asphalt pavement tunnel may cause greater casualties and property damage.[5-8] Therefore, the fire safety of asphalt pavements in tunnels is very important.

Flame retardant, a functional additive that imparts flameresistance to flammable polymers, mainly for flame retardant design of polymer materials. At present, flame retardants could be mainly classified into organic flame retardants and inorganic flame retardants, halogen flame retardants (organic chlorides and organic bromides). Organic flame retardants are some flame retardants represented by bromine, phosphorus and nitrogen, nitrogen and red phosphorus and compounds. Inorganic flame retardants are mainly antimony trioxide, magnesium hydroxide, aluminum hydroxide, silicon, etc.[9-10]. The chemical principles of flame retardant have been developed since the early 19th century. The pioneering research of flame retardant asphalt was initially completed in the 1950s. Common flame retardants mainly include halogen and phosphorus flame retardants for roofing felts and asphalt coatings.[11-13] The study of flame-retardant (FR) asphalt can be traced back to 1980s. The research of flame retardant asphalt in China began in the 1990s, mainly concentrated on asphalt felt and waterproof materials.[14-15] Yu[16] et al. investigated the effect of aluminum hydroxide (ATH) on the thermal properties of asphalt binder by Differential Scanning Calorimetry (DSC) and Thermogravimetry (TG), and verified the feasibility to prepare asphalt mixture with the excellent flame resistance and pavement performance using ATH modified asphalt binders. Therefore, the combination of various flame retardants may achieve better flame retardant effect. In addition, there are only several tests used to evaluate properties of FR asphalt mixtures. Currently, there is no standard method or evaluation index for the FR mixtures.

This study aims to evaluate the flame retardancy of asphalt binders incorporating a composite flame retardant (CFR) and the pavement performance of flame retardant asphalt mixtures in the laboratory. The CFR is prepared by mixing three different types of flame retardants in a certain proportion. Two kinds of asphalt, 70# matrix asphalt and SBS modified asphalt were selected. The basic technical characteristics of asphalt binders with different dosages of CFR were determined, and the resistance of flame retardant asphalt was determined by Limit oxygen index (LOI) test and Combustion Test. Combined with the technical properties and flame retardant properties of flame retardant asphalt, a comprehensive analysis gives a reasonable range of use of CFR. Finally, the pavement performance of the asphalt mixture incorporating CFR was verified by determining the high and low-temperature performance and water stability of the flame retardant asphalt mixture.

1 Materials and Testing Program

1.1 Experimental Materials

1.1.1 Asphalt

In this study, two kinds of asphalt were selected for experimental research, one is 70# matrix asphalt and the other is SBS modified asphalt. Softening point, ductility, and penetration tests were conducted to test the basic properties of the asphalt according to the specification used in China [JTG E20—2011(JTG 2011)][17], The results of the general technical properties for the two asphalt binders, are shown in Tab. 1 and Tab. 2.

The Technical Properties of 70# Matrix Asphalt   Tab. 1

Properties		Technical Requirement[18]	Results
Penetration(25℃,100g,5s)(0.1mm)		60-80	76
Penetration index(PI)		−1.0 ~ +1.0	0.8
Ductility(10℃,5cm/min)		≥25	51.8
Softening Point (Ring ball)(℃)		≥46	48.1
Flash Point(℃)		≥260	273
Dynamic Viscosity(60℃)(Pa·s)		≥180	182
Wax Content(Distillation)(%)		≤2	1.4
Density(15℃)(g/cm^3)		Measured Record	1.023
Solubility(Trichloroethylene)(%)		≥99.5	99.8
TFOT (or RTFOT)	Quality Change(%)	±0.8	+0.3
	Penetration Ratio(25℃)(%)	≥61	69.2
	Residual Ductility(10℃)(cm)	≥6	7.6

The Technical Properties of SBS Modified Asphalt   Tab. 2

Properties		Technical Requirement	Results
			I-C
Penetration(25℃,100g,5s)(0.1mm)		60 – 80	66
Penetration index(PI)		≥ −0.4	−0.0662
Ductility(5℃,5cm/min)		≥30	34.7
Softening point (Ring ball)(℃)		≥55	>90
Kinematic viscosity(135℃)		≤3	2.469
Flash point(℃)		≥230	337
Solubility(%)		≥99	99.8
Elastic recovery(25℃)(%)		≥65	86
Density(15℃)(g/cm^3)		Measured record	1.026
Segregation,48h softening point difference(℃)		≤2.5	1.1
TFOT (or RTFOT)	Quality Change(%)	≤1	0.01
	Penetration Ratio(25℃)(%)	≥60	74
	Residual Ductility(5℃)(cm)	≥20	28

1.1.2 Composite flame retardant

The composite flame retardant(CFR) used in this paper is compounded by three flame retardants according to a certain ratio. As shown in Fig. 1, FR-A (Decabromodiphenyl Ether) is a highly effective flame retardant with good thermal stability, non-corrosiveness and high flame retardant efficiency. FR-B (zinc borate) is an environmentally friendly non-halogen flame retardant. It is not used as a flame retardant alone, but plays a synergistic role in the CFR system. It can effectively improve the flame retardancy and reduce the smoke generation during combustion. FR-C (antimony trioxide), white powder, slightly soluble in water, belongs to inorganic flame retardant. The proportion of the three flame retardants is A:B:C = 3:1:1. In the test process, the CFR should be uniformly mixed, otherwise, the proportion of the flame retardant will be uneven. Therefore, the CFR should be used after 3 minutes of mixing with a Micro-mixer shown in Fig. 2.

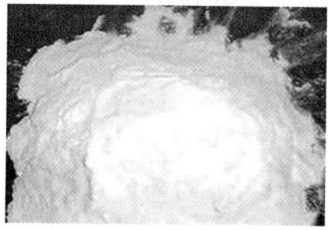
a) decabromodiphenyl ether

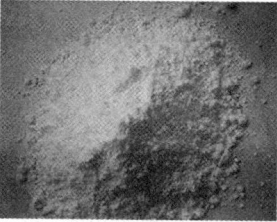
b) zinc borate

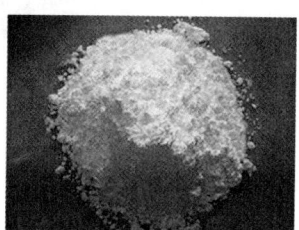
c) antimony trioxide

Fig. 1 Flame Retardant

Fig. 2 Micro-mixer

1.2 Aggregate and Gradation

The coarse aggregates are diabase materials, and fine aggregates and fillers are limestone materials. According to JTG F40—2004, the gradation of AC-13 mixture was selected medium value of gradation shown in Tab. 3. The maximum size of the aggregates is 13.2mm. The asphalt-aggregate ratio is 4.8%.

Gradation Range of Asphalt Mixture AC-13 Tab. 3

Mesh size(mm)	Mass percentage through the mesh(%)								
	16	13.2	9.5	4.75	2.36	1.18	0.6	0.3	0.15	0.075
Upper limit	100	100	85	68	50	38	28	20	15	8
Lower limit	100	90	68	38	24	15	10	7	5	4
Medium value	100	95	76.5	53	37	26.5	19	13.5	10	6

1.3 Basic Performance Test of Asphalt Mixed with Composite Flame Retardant

High-speed Shearing Machineis required in the preparation of flame-retardant asphalt to ensure that CFR can be uniformly dispersed in the asphalt during the addition process. The asphalt was heated to a melting state, and then the flame retardant was slowly added to the asphalt to make it fully immersed in it. Then started the high-speed shearing machine, the shear rate was 4000r/min, and the high-speed shearing time was 30~45min, then the desired asphalt binder could be prepared. The preparation process is shown in Fig. 3. The penetration, softening point and ductility of prepared flame retardant asphalt were tested.

Fig. 3 Flame Retardant Asphalt Preparation Process

1.4 Flame Retardant Performance Test

1.4.1 Limit Oxygen Index (LOI) Test

The oxygen test method, used to detect the flammability of plastics, was used in this study to assess the continued burning capacity of the modified binders in accordance with ASTM D-2863[19]. The specimen size was 10cm × 1cm × 0.4cm, shown in Fig. 4. The minimum oxygen concentration, required to just support a candle-like burning of the sample, was maintained in a flowing gas mixture of oxygen and nitrogen[20]. The limit oxygen index (LOI) is calculated as shown in Equation 1.

$$\text{LOI} = \frac{[O_2]}{[O_2] + [N_2]} \times 100\% \tag{1}$$

Where, $[O_2]$ indicates the volume flow of oxygen in mixed airflow at critical oxygen concentration; $[N_2]$ indicates the volume flow of nitrogen in mixed airflow at critical oxygen concentration.

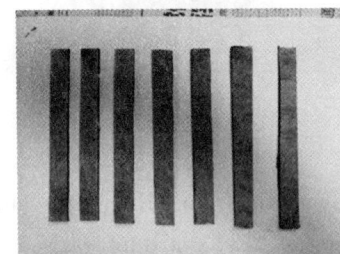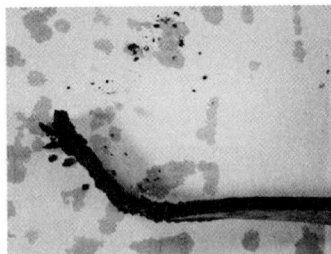

a) oxygen index apparatus b) standard samples c) burned sample

Fig. 4 Limit Oxygen Index (LOI) Test

1.4.2 Combustion Test

The asphalt binders and the compacted mixtures were subjected to a combustion test to evaluate the flame retardant properties of the asphalt binders and the compacted concrete, respectively. The combustion test of asphalt binder could reflect the flame resistance of the mixture. The combustion test of the compacted mixture could simulate the flame resistance of the asphalt pavement in tunnels.

1) Asphalt Binder

During the test, the same quality asphalt was weighed and placed in two different pallets, then 25 mL gasoline was poured into the pallets. every sample was ignited with a long steel pipe. Record the burning time of asphalt, then weigh the quality of burned asphalt and pallet, and calculate the quality change of samples before and after burning.

2) Compacted Mixture

The combustion test of asphalt binder could reflect indirect flame retardant properties of asphalt. However, the asphalt pavement in tunnels is compacted concrete, so the combustion tests of compacted Marshall samples and specimen plates were carried out in this study. The Marshall specimens were immersed in gasoline for 5 seconds and ignited immediately. The burning time and quality of the specimens were tested. The test piece burning performance test is to better simulate the situation of on-site gasoline leak combustion. Pour 25ml of gasoline into the center of the plate and ignite immediately to test its burning time.

1.5 Pavement Performance Test of Asphalt Mixture Incorporating Composite Flame Retardant

1.5.1 High-temperature Performance

In this study, the Rutting depth at 45min and 60min and dynamic stability of test plates were tested to reflect the high-temperature stability of asphalt mixture incorporating CFR.

1.5.2 Low-temperature Performance

In this study, the low-temperature performance of flame retardant asphalt mixture was studied by low temperature bending test. The formed specimen plates were cut into prismatic specimens, 250mm ± 2mm in length, 30mm ± 2mm in width and 35mm ± 2mm in height. The specimens were placed in a constant temperature flume at a specified temperature for not less than 45 minutes until the internal temperature reached the experimental temperature (Error, ± 0.5℃). The press was started to load at a rate of 50 mm/min until the specimen was broken. Calculating the bending strength RB, the maximum bending strain εB at the bottom of the beam and the bending progress modulus SB at failure

1.5.3 Water Stability

In this study, the water stability of the flame retardant asphalt mixture was reflected by the water immersion Marshall test and the freeze-thaw split test. The residual stability of the water immersion in the test piece was calculated by measuring the stability of the test piece after 48 hours of water immersion and the stability of the test piece. The freeze-thaw split test is a measure of the strength ratio of the splitting damage of the test piece before and after water damage. According to the test method of JTG E20—2011 T0729(2011), the Tensile Strength Ratio was calculated.

2 Results and Discussions

2.1 Basic Technical Properties of Flame Retardant Asphalt

From Tab. 4 and Tab. 5, the basic technical properties of matrix asphalt and SBS modified asphalt at different flame retardant dosages are listed. From Fig. 5a), the addition of the CFR increases the consistency of the matrix asphalt, and the penetration decreases significantly in the CFR content at 6%. With the increase of flame retardant content, the penetration decreases gradually. The penetration of SBS modified asphalt with the addition of flame retardant also shows a downward trend. Under 6% - 10% of the flame retardant dosage, the penetration degree decreases significantly. This may be due to the high self-consistency of SBS modified asphalt, and the effect of adding a small amount of flame retardant on its consistency may be small. When the flame retardant increases to a certain amount, SBS modified asphalt hardens and penetration decreases significantly.

From Fig. 5c), the softening point of the matrix asphalt increases with the increase of the flame retardant content, and the softening point increases significantly when the dosage is 6%. Then, as the flame retardant content increases, the softening point increases tend to be gentle. From Fig. 5d), the incorporation of a flame retardant reduces the softening point of the SBS modified asphalt. It may be due to the high consistency of SBS modified asphalt itself. In the process of adding flame retardant, agglomeration and agglomeration may occur, and it may not be uniformly dispersed in the asphalt, resulting in a decrease in high-temperature stability performance, which is manifested by a decrease in the softening point of the asphalt binder.

Technical Properties of Matrix Asphalt with Flame Retardant Tab. 4

Sample	Penetration(25℃,100g,5s)(0.1mm)	Softening point(℃)	Ductility(10℃,5cm/min)(cm)
Matrix asphalt	76	48.1	51.8
Matrix asphalt +2% CFR	74	48.9	19.6
Matrix asphalt +4% CFR	62	49.8	16.8
Matrix asphalt +6% CFR	56	50.3	14.8
Matrix asphalt +8% CFR	55	50.4	10.2
Matrix asphalt +10% CFR	52	50.5	10.0

Technical Properties of SBS Modified Asphalt with Flame Retardant Tab. 5

Sample	Penetration(25℃,100g,5s)(0.1mm)	Softening point(℃)	Ductility(5℃,5cm/min)(cm)
SBS modified asphalt	66	91.0	34.7
SBS modified asphalt +2% CFR	65	90.7	35.1
SBS modified asphalt +4% CFR	63	89.2	27.4
SBS modified asphalt +6% CFR	62	88.0	26.3
SBS modified asphalt +8% CFR	58	87.0	26.9
SBS modified asphalt +10% CFR	45	85.0	18.4

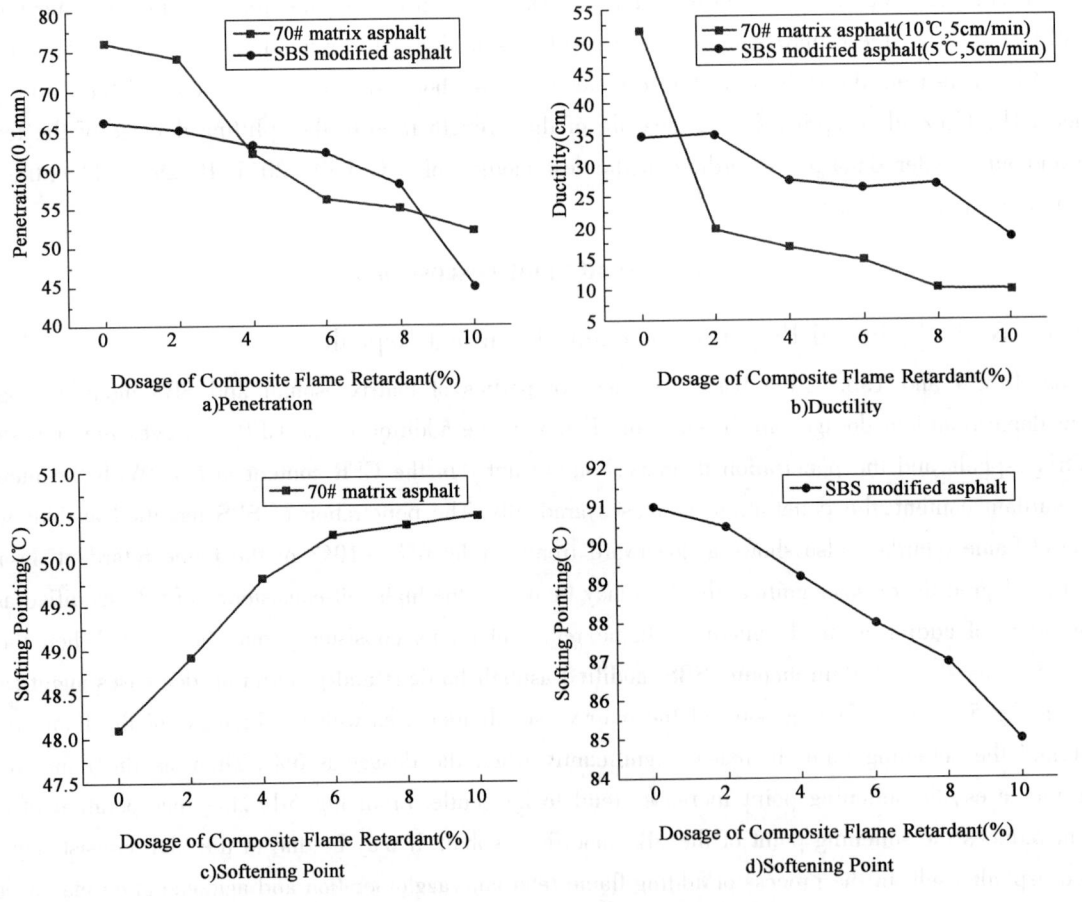

Fig. 5 Basic Technical Properties of Flame Retardant Asphalt

From Fig. 5b), when the matrix asphalt was initially added with a flame retardant, its 10℃ ductility decreased significantly. When the flame retardant content is 2%, the ductility decreases by about 62.2%. Then, with the increase of the content of flame retardant, the ductility decreases gradually. When flame retardant is added to SBS modified asphalt, the ductility increases slightly when 2% flame retardant is added. This is due to the mutual cross-linking between the internal components of the asphalt binder after the addition of a small amount of the CFR. The network structure is gradually developed to increase the resistance to deformation, and the low-temperature ductility is slightly increased. As the amount of addition increases, this network structure reduces the ability of the SBS segment to move freely, making the asphalt cement hard and the ductility reduced. The abrupt change of 5℃ ductility occurs when the content of flame retardant is 8%. When the content of flame retardant is 10%, the ductility value is less than the minimum value of 20 cm of SBS (Class I) modified asphalt specified in the technical requirements of flame retardant modified asphalt.

Adding CFR to base asphalt, through the analysis of its influence on the basic properties of asphalt, it can be seen that when the content of CFR reaches 6%, the ductility at 10℃ is 14.8cm, which is less than the minimum value of base asphalt specified in the code 15 cm. Therefore, in order not to affect the pavement performance of matrix asphalt mixture, the maximum content of CFR should not exceed 6%. According to the technical requirements of flame retardant modified asphalt, the ductility of SBS modified asphalt should not be less than 20 cm. When the content of CFR is 8%, the ductility value at 5℃ is more than 20 cm. When the content of flame retardant is 10%, the ductility at 5℃ decreases to 18.4 cm, and the decrease is 31.6%. Therefore, for SBS modified asphalt, the content of flame retardant should be 8%, and the maximum content should not exceed 10%. Otherwise, the low-temperature performance of the asphalt binder would be seriously affected.

2.2 Flame Retardant Performance Test

2.2.1 Limit Oxygen Index (LOI) Test Results

From Tab. 6 and Tab. 7, after adding the flame retardant to the matrix asphalt and SBS modified asphalt, the limit oxygen index LOI value of the asphalt binder is significantly increased. This also shows that the flame retardant can effectively prevent the burning of the asphalt, and the flame retarding effect is continuously enhanced as the amount of the flame retardant added. The SBS modified asphalt obtained by adding SBS modifier is easier to burn. This may be because the base asphalt contains not only C, H, O, but also a small amount of N, P. These N and P elements have a little flame retardancy. However, SBS modifier only contains C and H elements, so when SBS modifier is added to the base asphalt, the LOI value of SBS modified asphalt is less than that of the matrix asphalt, that is, SBS modified asphalt is easier to burn. The CFR component has a great influence on the oxygen index of the asphalt, in which the FR-A is decomposed by heat and absorbs part of the heat, and at the same time releases the effect of the non-combustible gas to the gas phase shielding. Moreover, the non-combustible gas also cuts off the chain reaction of the radicals, so that the burning rate of the asphalt is greatly reduced. On the other hand, the CFR forms a stable carbon layer on the surface of the combustion material to achieve a self-extinguishing effect.

Matrix Asphalt LOI Test Results Tab. 6

Sample	Limit Oxygen Index (LOI) (%)
Matrix asphalt	23.3
Matrix asphalt +2% CFR	23.9
Matrix asphalt +4% CFR	24.2
Matrix asphalt +6% CFR	24.8
Matrix asphalt +8% CFR	25.4
Matrix asphalt +10% CFR	26.1

SBS Modified Asphalt LOI Test Results Tab. 7

Sample	Limit Oxygen Index (LOI)(%)
SBS modified asphalt	22.3
SBS modified asphalt +2% CFR	22.8
SBS modified asphalt +4% CFR	23.6
SBS modified asphalt +6% CFR	24.8
SBS modified asphalt +8% CFR	25.4
SBS modified asphalt +10% CFR	27.3

2.2.2 Combustion Test Results

Fig. 6 is a photograph of the asphalt binder at the beginning and end of combustion. From Tab. 8, the quality of the matrix asphalt after combustion is increased compared to that before combustion, and the quality of the asphalt added with the flame retardant is reduced after combustion than before combustion. From the experimental phenomenon, the degree of combustion of the matrix asphalt is more severe than that of the matrix asphalt with the flame retardant added, accompanied by sporadic splashing and a large amount of concentrated smoke; while the asphalt of the matrix blended with the flame retardant is relatively stable. There is basically no obvious flame in the late combustion, only accompanied by the smoldering process. Combined with the actual combustion test process, SBS modified asphalt is easier to burn, and the combustion process also produces a lot of smoke and burns longer than the matrix asphalt. This may be due to the fact that SBS modified asphalt contains more SBS modifier, which makes the combustion components more and burns for a longer time. From the analysis of the properties of asphalt with flame retardant, the quality of SBS modified asphalt increased before and after combustion, and the quality of SBS modified asphalt decreased after combustion, which is similar to the trend of base asphalt before and after combustion.

Fig. 6 Pictures of Initial and Final Burning Stages of Asphalt Binder

Asphalt is a high molecular organic material containing a large amount of C and H elements. During the combustion of matrix asphalt and SBS modified asphalt, many light substance components are carbonized, so the quality of the asphalt is slightly increased. However, the burning process of flame retardant asphalt prepared by adding flame retardant in matrix asphalt and SBS modified asphalt is relatively fierce in the early stage, and the temperature has reached the volatilization decomposition point of CFR components, so some flame retardants are decomposed into gaseous phase by heat, which delays the burning intensity. At the end of the combustion process, the smoldering process makes the burning time relatively long. After burning, the asphalt surface without flame retardant has been burned out with only residual ash, while the asphalt with flame retardant has formed a hard carbon layer on the surface after burning, and the asphalt below the carbon layer has not been burned down. This indicates that it is because of the protective effect of the carbon layer that it isolates the contact of the lower asphalt with oxygen so that the asphalt is not ignited. It can be inferred that the addition of CFR in asphalt can prevent combustion to a certain extent.

Weight Change of Asphalt before and after Combustion   Tab. 8

Sample	Pre-combustion weight (g)			Weight after burning (g)	Burning time (s)	Percentage of weight change(%)
	plate	asphalt	Plate + asphalt	Plate + asphalt		
Matrix asphalt	37.13	100.33	137.46	138.23	141	0.56
Matrix asphalt +6% CFR	51.44	100.00	151.44	148.77	116	-1.76
SBS modified asphalt	58.43	100.06	158.49	159.04	160	0.35
SBS modified asphalt +8% CFR	40.65	100.00	140.65	136.82	121	-2.72

As shown in Fig. 7, the combustion process diagram of the compacted Marshall specimens is presented. Fig. 8 shows the combustion process on the surface of the specimen plate. The burning time and weight change of Marshall specimens before and after burning are shown in Tab. 9. Combining Tab. 9 and Fig. 9, the burning time of Marshall specimens decreased significantly when the matrix asphalt and SBS modified asphalt were mixed with CFR. The burning time of SBS modified asphalt is slightly longer than that of matrix asphalt. The weight after combustion increases slightly compared with that before combustion. The burning time of the test plate with flame retardant is also significantly reduced, which indicates that the asphalt mixture with CFR has an effective flame retardant ability on its surface after compaction, and plays a role in inhibiting asphalt combustion.

 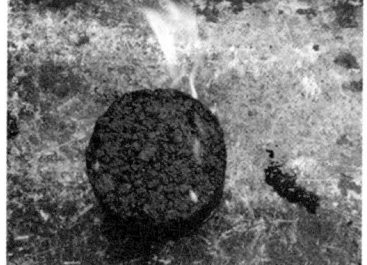 

Fig. 7 Combustion Pictures of Marshall Specimen

Fig. 8 Surface Combustion Pictures of Test Plate

Burning Time and Weight Change of Marshall Specimens Tab.9

Sample	Burning Time (s)	Average (s)	Standard Error	Percentage of Weight Change(%)	Average (s)	Standard Error
Matrix asphalt	101	100	1.29	0.20	0.16	0.02
	96			0.19		
	103			0.13		
	99			0.10		
Matrix asphalt +6% CFR	50	61	4.52	0.06	0.06	0.01
	58			0.02		
	60			0.05		
	75			0.10		
SBS modified asphalt	115	111	4.22	0.09	0.08	0.03
	111			0.04		
	121			0.02		
	98			0.15		
SBS modified asphalt +8% CFR	64	73	3.65	0.04	0.06	0.01
	77			0.03		
	83			0.10		
	69			0.08		

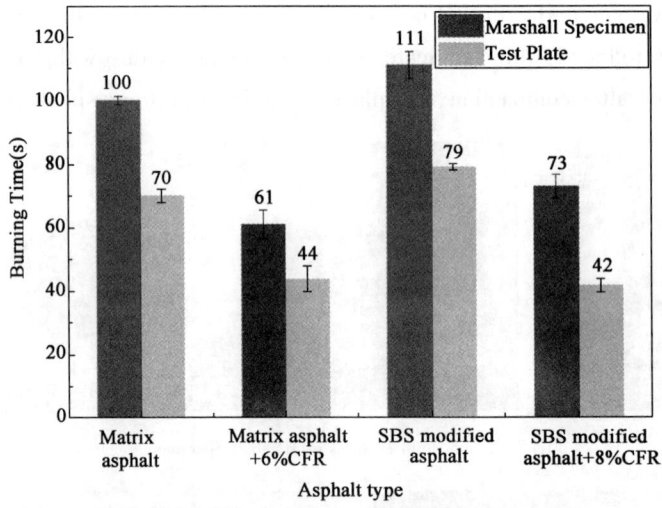

Fig.9 Burning Time of Different Specimens

2.3 Pavement Performance Test of Asphalt Mixture Incorporating Composite Flame Retardant

2.3.1 High-temperature Performance Test Results

As shown in Fig. 10, the rutting depth of the asphalt mixture test piece when the 6% flame retardant was incorporated into the matrix asphalt was reduced at 45 min and 60 min. And the same trend appeared in the addition of 7% of the CFR to the SBS modified asphalt. After adding the CFR to the matrix asphalt, the dynamic stability of the asphalt mixture increased by 29.70%, and the dynamic stability of the mixture added with the flame retardant in the SBS modified asphalt increased by 32.21% compared with the unadded. It shows that the high-temperature performance of asphalt mixtures can be enhanced by adding CFRs, because the addition of flame retardants in a sense plays a role in increasing the proportion of mineral powder, thus enhancing the high-temperature performance and rutting resistance of asphalt mixtures.

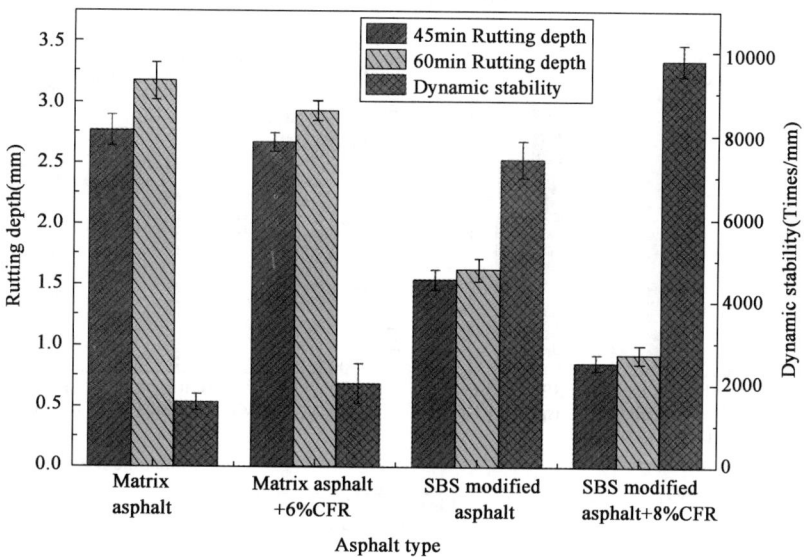

Fig. 10　Rutting Depth and Dynamic Stability of Different Specimen Plates

2.3.2　Low-temperature Performance Test Results

As shown in Fig. 11, the flexural tensile strength, the maximum bending strain, and the bending stiffness modulus of the matrix asphalt and the SBS modified asphalt mixture after the addition of the CFR are somewhat reduced. The flexural strength of matrix asphalt at low-temperature bending is reduced by 29.8% compared with unmixed flame retardant, and the maximum bending strain is reduced by 12.2%. The flexural tensile strength of SBS modified asphalt was 6.8% lower than that of unmixed CFR and the maximum bending strain was reduced by 4.5%. This indicates that the incorporation of the CFR would affect the low-temperature performance of the asphalt mixture, and this effect is more significant for matrix asphalt mixture. This may be due to the insufficient viscosity of the matrix asphalt itself, and its ductility is drastically reduced after the incorporation of the CFR, which is reflected in the asphalt mixture being a significant reduction in the flexural tensile strength and the maximum bending strain. In the comparison before and after the sample burning test, the low-temperature performance of the asphalt mixture in the combustion process is reduced. In summary, the blending of the CFR would reduce the low-temperature performance of the asphalt mixture, mainly because the flame retardant increases the viscosity of the asphalt binder formed by the asphalt and the mineral powder, resulting in the asphalt mixture. Low temperature crack resistance is reduced. In addition, the CFR has a great influence on the low temperature performance of the matrix asphalt. To ensure the flame resistance performance and pavement performance of the asphalt mixture, the blending amount of the CFR for the matrix asphalt should not exceed 6%.

2.3.3　Moisture Susceptibility Test Results

From Tab. 10, after adding the CFR to the matrix asphalt, the water stability of the asphalt mixture decreased, which shows that the residual stability decreases by 4.03% and the Tensile Strength Ratio decreases by 4.94%. The addition of flame retardant in SBS modified asphalt mixture reduced the residual stability of asphalt mixture by 0.53% and the Tensile Strength Ratio by 6.05%. The results show that the CFR has some influence on the water stability of asphalt mixture, but the extent of the reduction is not obvious. It may be because the addition of the flame retardant reduces the thickness of the asphalt film, but the addition amount is relatively small, and thus the thickness reduction of the asphalt film is limited. And the water stability of the asphalt mixture after adding the CFR can still meet the requirements of the specification.

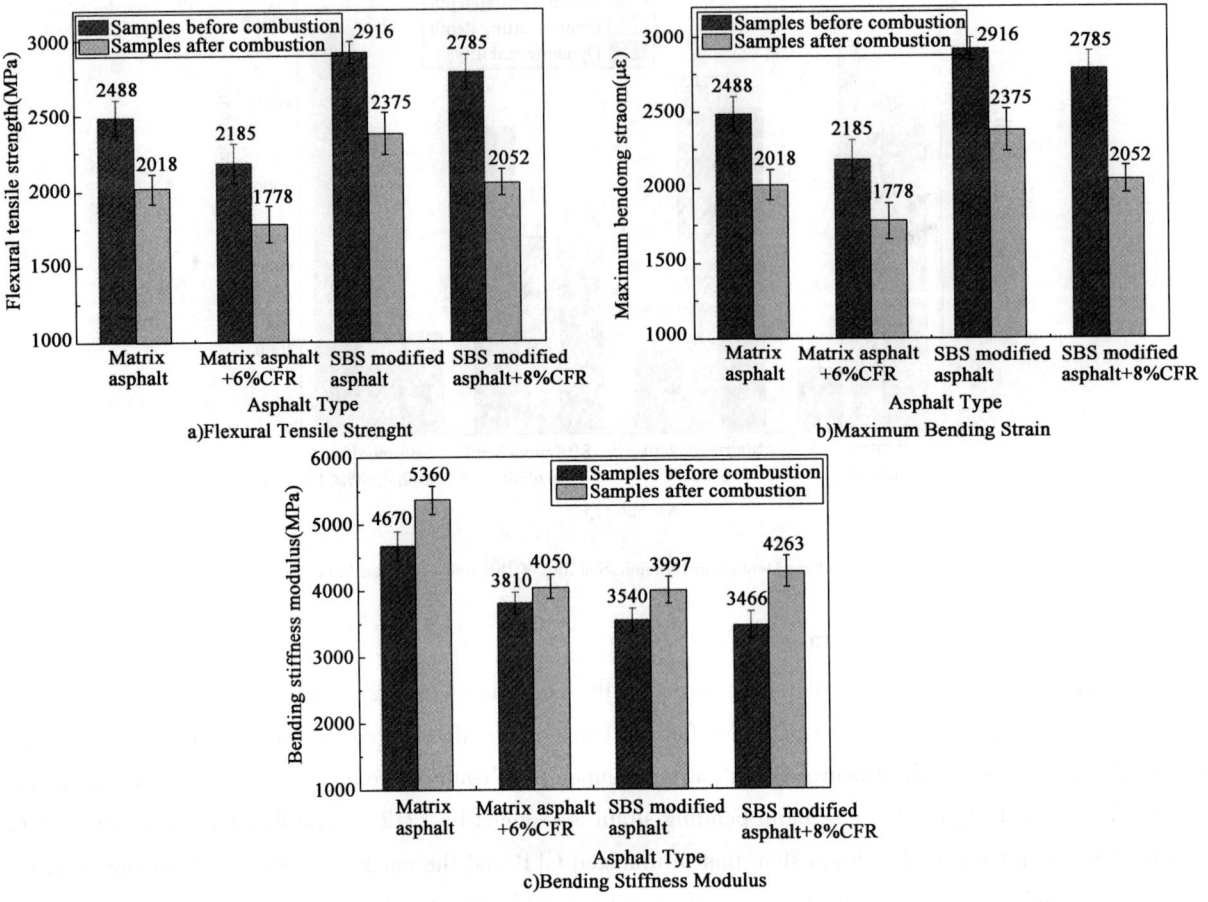

Fig. 11 Low Temperature of before and after Combustion of the Specimens

Tab. 10 Moisture Susceptibility Test Results

Asphalt type	MS_1 (kN)	MS (kN)	MS_0 (%)	TSR (%)
Matrix asphalt	9.5	11.6	81.9	74.9
Matrix asphalt + 6% CFR	6.6	8.4	78.6	71.2
SBS modified asphalt	11.51	12.10	95.2	87.6
SBS modified asphalt + 8% CFR	10.61	11.2	94.7	82.3

Note: MS1 = Marshall Stability (Soaked for 48h), MS = Marshall Stability, MS0 = Residual Stability of Immersion, TSR = Tensile Strength Ratio.

3 Conclusions

According to the results tested in laboratory, the basic technical properties and flame retardant properties of 70# matrix asphalt and SBS modified asphalt incorporating CFR and pavement performance of flame retardant asphalt mixture were mainly researched, and the main conclusions and recommendations are summarized as follows.

The incorporation of CFR has a significant effect on the low-temperature performance of 70# matrix asphalt and SBS modified asphalt. In order to ensure the low-temperature performance of asphalt binder and the pavement performance of asphalt mixture, the blending amount of the matrix asphalt should not exceed 6%, and the blending amount of the SBS modified asphalt should be 8% – 10%.

According to the Limit oxygen index (LOI) test, as the amount of CFR increases, the LOI value of the asphalt oxygen index increases gradually, which means that the flame retardant effect is also more obvious; The combustion test (include asphalt binders and compacted asphalt mixture samples) could directly reflect the obvious flame retardant effect of the CFR.

The high-temperature performance of asphalt mixture could be improved by adding CFR which is equivalent to increasing the proportion of mineral powder; the blending of the CFR would reduce the low-temperature performance of the asphalt mixture, and the effect on the low-temperature performance of the matrix asphalt mixture is more significant.

In the matrix asphalt mixed with 6% CFR and SBS modified asphalt with 8% CFR, the water stability of the asphalt mixture is not obvious compared with the unmixed CFR, and can still meet the requirements of specifications.

In short, the successful utilization of CFR in pavement construction can provide a new and safer road material, especially in tunnel engineering. Future research will focus on technical performance testing of asphalt binders incorporating CFR after aging and application of CFR in warm-mixed asphalt mixture. Meanwhile, the test data in the lab should be further examined in field.

4 Acknowledgment

This research was supported by the Shaanxi Provincial Department of Transportation Project (KY19 – 07, 19 – 33K). These supports are gratefully acknowledged.

References

[1] Liu, M., Huang, X., & Xue, G. Effects of Double Layer Porous Asphalt Pavement of Urban Streets on Noise Reduction[J]. International Journal of Sustainable Built Environment, 2016, 5(1):183-196.

[2] Hu, S., Huang, S., Ding, Q. Porous Flame-retarded Asphalt Pavement for Highway Tunnel. J. Wuhan Univ. Technol., Mater. Sci. Ed., 2008, 23(5):750-754.

[3] Dan, H.-C., He, L.-H., & Xu, B. Experimental Investigation on Skid Resistance of Asphalt Pavement under Various Slippery Conditions[J]. International Journal of Pavement Engineering, 2017, 18(6):485-499.

[4] Yu, H., Yan, X., Bobet, A., Yuan, Y., Xu, G., & Su, Q. Multi-point Shaking Table Test of a Long Tunnel Subjected to Non-uniform Seismic Loadings[J]. Bulletin of Earthquake Engineering, 2018, 16(2):1041-1059.

[5] Zheng, C., Li, R., & Lv, D. Study on Performance of Composite Flame-retardant Asphalt Material in Tunel[J]. IOP Conference Series: Materials Science and Engineering, 2018, 392:022030.

[6] Puente, E., Lázaro, D., & Alvear, D. Study of Tunnel Pavements Behaviour in Fire by Using Coupled Cone Calorimeter-FTIR Analysis[J]. Fire Safety Journal, 2016, 81:1-7.

[7] Zhao, J., Huang, X., & Xu, T. Combustion Mechanism of Asphalt Binder with TG-MS Technique Based on Components Separation[J]. Construction and Building Materials, 2015, 80:125-131.

[8] Shi, H., Xu, T., Zhou, P., & Jiang, R. Combustion Properties of Saturates, Aromatics, Resins, and Asphaltenes in Asphalt Binder[J]. Construction and Building Materials, 2017, 136:515-523.

[9] Qiu, J., Yang, T., Wang, X., Wang, L., & Zhang, G. Review of the Flame Retardancy on Highway Tunnel Asphalt Pavement[J]. Construction and Building Materials, 2019, 195:468-482.

[10] Xiao, F., Guo, R., & Wang, J. Flame Retardant and its Influence on the Performance of Asphalt -A Review. Construction and Building Materials, 2019, 212:841-861.

[11] Levchik, S. V., & Weil, E. D. A Review of Recent Progress in Phosphorus-based Flame Retardants[J].

[12] Lu, S.-Y., & Hamerton, I. Recent Developments in the Chemistry of Halogen-free Flame Retardant Polymers[J]. Progress in Polymer Science, 2002, 27(8): 1661-1712.

[13] Green, J. A Review of Phosphorus-Containing Flame Retardants[J]. Journal of Fire Sciences, 1992, 10(6): 470-487.

[14] Chen, L., & Wang, Y.-Z. A Review on Flame Retardant Technology in China. Part I: Development of Flame Retardants[J]. Polymers for Advanced Technologies, 2010, 21(1): 1-26.

[15] Lu, H., Song, L., & Hu, Y. A Review on Flame Retardant Technology in China. Part II: Flame Retardant Polymeric Nanocomposites and Coatings[J]. Polymers for Advanced Technologies, 2011, 22(4): 379-394.

[16] Jianying, Y., Peiliang, C., & Shaopeng, W. Investigation of the Properties of Asphalt and its Mixtures Containing Flame Retardant Modifier[J]. Construction and Building Materials, 2009, 23(6): 2277-2282.

[17] JTJ E20—2011. Standard Test Methods of Bitumen and Bituminous Mixtures For Highway Engineering[J]. Ministry of Transport of China, Beijing (in Chinese), 2011.

[18] JTG F40—2004. Technical Specification for Construction of Highway Asphalt Pavements[J]. Ministry of Transport of China, Beijing (in Chinese), 2004.

[19] ASTM D2863. Standard Test Method for Measuring the Minimum Oxygen Concentration to Support Candle-like Combustion of Plastics (Oxygen Index)[J]. West Conshohocken, PA, 2013.

基于旧路分层铣刨的沥青老化规律及老化程度分级

郝 林[2]　陈 钊[1]　吴建灵[2]　王选仓[1]　李燕军[2]

(1. 长安大学；2. 兴泰建设集团有限公司)

摘　要　为研究旧路沥青的老化规律及老化分级，通过室内老化试验及现场实测数据确定沥青短期老化、长期老化及老化速率预估方程，通过三指标、四组分分析回收料沥青老化程度，得到旧路上、中、下面层老化规律，提出沥青老化程度分级。结果表明，沥青长期老化方程比短期老化方程的 a、r 参数值偏大，但均呈现为开始老化速率最快，后期随时间增加，老化速率逐渐降低，老化程度趋于平缓；基于三指标与四组分试验及得出不同层位老化规律不同，总体呈现上面层老化程度最大；最终建立以针入度、软化点、延度为一级指标，沥青质为二级指标的沥青老化程度分级方法。

关键词　道路工程　沥青老化规律　老化分级　三指标四组分

0 引　言

高速公路改扩建旧路材料再生利用工程中，不同老化程度的旧料宜分开使用，以充分利用旧料性能，因此旧沥青老化分级研究显得极为重要。目前少数学者对沥青老化规律进行了研究，且取得了一些成果。

常琨通过延时RTFOT试验模拟沥青的老化，对不同老化程度的改性沥青与集料黏附性进行量化分析，为老化沥青黏附性量化评价提供理论和试验依据[1]；丁婕等利用红外光谱对基质沥青和不同程度的

基金项目：内蒙古兴泰建设集团科技项目(X-SZ-20171209-02-15-0001)。

老化沥青进行试验,从微观方面分析了沥青的微观结构及老化的成分变化[2];刘苹等利用 RTFOT 对重交 70 号道路沥青来模拟沥青老化试验,测得老化前后 70 号沥青的 3 大指标及 4 组分组成[3]。

本文通过分析沥青老化的影响因素,采用 RTFOT 试验进行老化模拟及现场实测数据建立短期及长期老化方程;通过三指标、四组分试验提出沥青老化程度分级方法。

1 沥青老化机理

沥青路面由于其长期受到环境及荷载的反复作用,往往出现松散、开裂等病害,其原因主要是面层沥青的老化。通常认为面层沥青受环境作用,内部组分及官能团发生变化,导致沥青硬化,这种不可逆转的过程即为沥青老化[4-5]。

目前沥青老化的微观理论主要有组分迁移和溶液相容性两种理论。组分迁移理论认为老化是芳香分-胶质-沥青质的单向转变过程。而相容性理论假设沥青为高浓度溶液,沥青质为溶质,老化后相容性变差,性能衰变[5]。

2 短期及长期老化方程建立

2.1 短期老化方程建立

2.1.1 室内老化试验

研究证明,延时 RTFOT 老化也可以表征沥青路面实际过程中的长期老化[6]。为分析实际沥青老化规律,本文采用 RTFOT 试验对 90 号沥青进行老化模拟,测其针入度、软化点及 15℃延度。

由图 1 可得,90 号沥青的三大指标 85min 前老化较快,之后速率下降,最终趋于 0。这说明 85min 之前代表的施工过程中沥青老化较快。

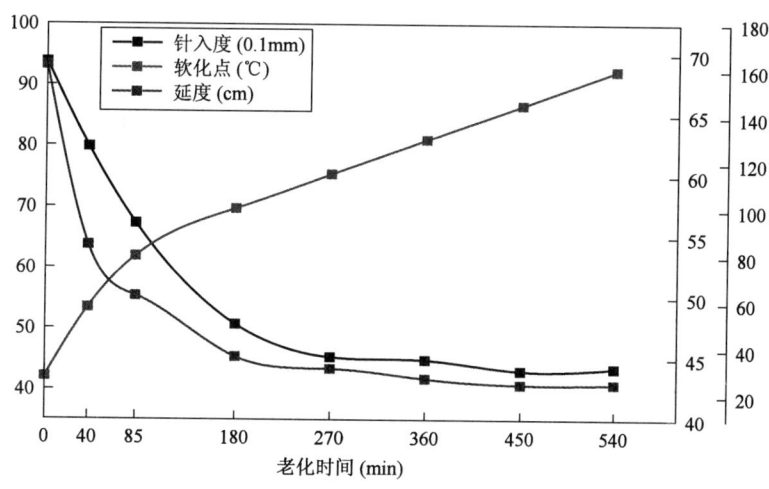

图 1 RTFOT 老化试验结果

2.1.2 短期老化方程的建立

针对沥青老化,Peter 提出非线性模拟性能指标的变化,见式(1)。

$$y'(t) = my(t) - ny^2(t) \tag{1}$$

式中:$y(t)$——t 时刻指标值;

$y'(t)$——t 时刻指标变化率;

m, n——常数。

令 $m = r, m/n = k$,则式(1)可表示为:

$$y'(t) = ry(t)\frac{k - y(t)}{k} \tag{2}$$

得微分方程解见式(3)：

$$y(t) = \frac{k}{1 + Ce^{-rt}} \quad (3)$$

式中：C、k、r——常数。

若沥青初始时刻$t=0$时其指标值为y_0，则$C = \frac{k}{y_0} - 1$，代入式(3)得：

$$y(t) = \frac{k}{1 + \left(\frac{k}{y_0} - 1\right)e^{-rt}} \quad (4)$$

取$a = k/y_0$则式(4)简化为：

$$y(t) = \frac{ay_0}{1 + (a-1)e^{-rt}} \quad (5)$$

当$t \to +\infty$时，$a = \lim_{t \to \infty} \frac{y(t)}{y_0}$。

对式(5)求导得老化速率：

$$v(t) = \frac{be^{-rt}}{[1 + (a-1)e^{-rt}]^2} \quad (6)$$

式中：b——常数，$b = ray_0 - ra^2y_0$。

以未老化的沥青指标为初始性能。通过RTFOT沥青指标拟合确定老化方程，并计算相关系数，见表1。

RTFOT老化沥青指标老化参数及方程　　　　表1

指标	r	a	老化方程	老化速率	相关系数
软化点	0.0081	1.3992	$T = \dfrac{61.1450}{1 + 0.3992 e^{-0.0081t}}$	$T' = \dfrac{0.4913 e^{-0.0081t}}{(1 + 0.3992 e^{-0.0081t})^2}$	0.90
针入度	0.0047	0.4351	$P = \dfrac{40.5513}{1 - 0.5649 e^{-0.0047t}}$	$P' = \dfrac{0.1897 e^{-0.0047t}}{(1 - 0.5649 e^{-0.0047t})^2}$	0.95
15℃延度	0.0053	0.1540	$\eta = \dfrac{24.8556}{1 - 0.846 e^{-0.0053t}}$	$\eta' = \dfrac{0.1310 e^{-0.0053t}}{(1 - 0.846 e^{-0.0053t})^2}$	0.91

2.2 现场实测及长期老化方程建立

依托工程路面不同年限的抽提老化结果见表2。用式(5)、式(6)拟合得长期老化方程，见表3。

不同年限路面抽提试验结果　　　　表2

服役时间(月)	0	24	36	72	90
软化点(℃)	54.1	55.9	57.2	62.7	64.6
针入度(0.1mm)	65.9	59.8	51	44.5	42.2
延度(cm)	63.7	47.1	37	27.2	25.7

长期老化及老化速率预估方程　　　　表3

指标	r	a	老化方程	老化速率	相关系数
软化点	0.0079	1.45	$T = \dfrac{77.575}{1 + 0.45 e^{-0.0079t}}$	$T' = \dfrac{0.6081 e^{-0.0079t}}{(1 + 0.3992 e^{-0.0079t})^2}$	0.97
针入度	0.0091	0.4921	$P = \dfrac{32.6754}{1 - 0.5079 e^{-0.0091t}}$	$P' = \dfrac{0.2946 e^{-0.0091t}}{(1 - 0.5079 e^{-0.0091t})^2}$	0.88
15℃延度	0.0109	0.2917	$\eta = \dfrac{18.4938}{1 - 0.8083 e^{-0.0109t}}$	$\eta' = \dfrac{0.1994 e^{-0.0109t}}{(1 - 0.8083 e^{-0.0109t})^2}$	0.91

通过室内老化及长期老化结果分析,长期老化方程比短期老化方程的 a、r 参数值偏大,但均呈现为开始老化速率最快,后期老化速率逐渐降低,老化程度趋于平缓。总体3年、6年与RTFOT的270min、360min结果相当,初始老化程度与85min老化程度接近。

3 基于三指标及四组分的旧路老化程度评价

对旧路材料进行分层铣刨,分别对上、中、下三层分层铣刨及整体铣刨进行抽提,试验步骤如下:

铣刨料破碎后,用三氯乙烯浸泡30min,之后对溶液进行抽提试验,转速8000r/min,提取上层清液,进行旋转蒸发,三氯乙酸回收,抽提出沥青放入60℃烘箱30min,取出后成型试件进行针入度、软化点、延度试验,并测试其四组分。试验过程如图2、图3所示。

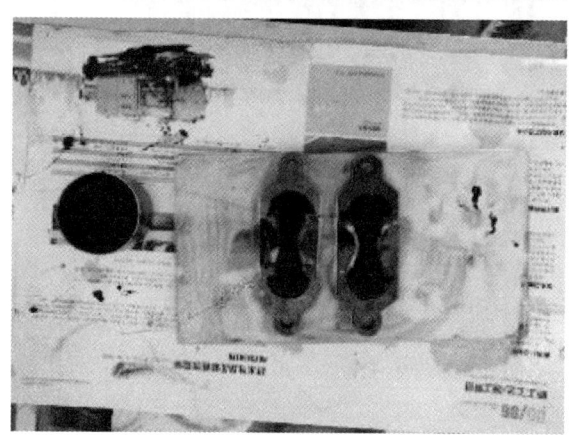

图2 沥青抽提试验并成型试样

由图4可知:

(1)施工期老化是整体老化的关键部分,相比90号沥青,施工期老化后针入度下降20%以上,而延度下降了60%。

(2)回收沥青与施工期结束刚开始服役的沥青相比,针入度减少20~30(0.1mm),软化点提高10~20℃,15℃延度减小30cm以上。从上面层到下面层,针入度增大,软化点与延度降低,说明上面层老化程度最大,下面层老化程度最轻。

(3)与90号沥青相比,芳香分减少了6%~10%,而沥青质增加了5%以上,说明老化是由芳香分向沥青质转变的过程,与沥青老化机理相吻合。

(4)将各层的各指标代入表3长期老化方程计算,中、下面层老化程度分别与服役5年、4年结果相同,上面层老化程度与使用13年结果相同。

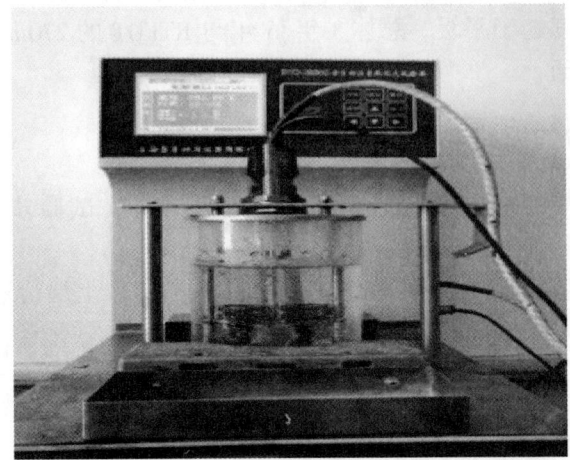

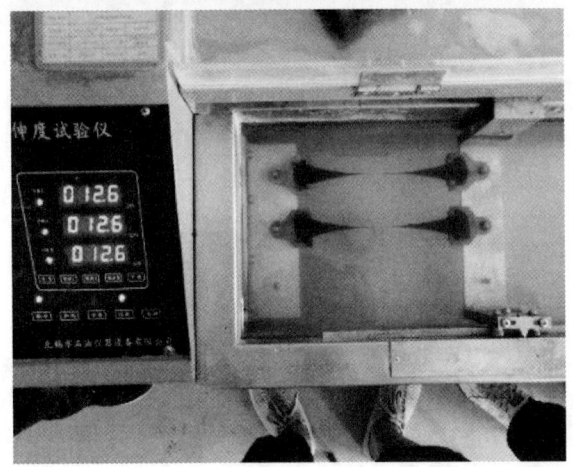

图 3 三指标及四组分试验

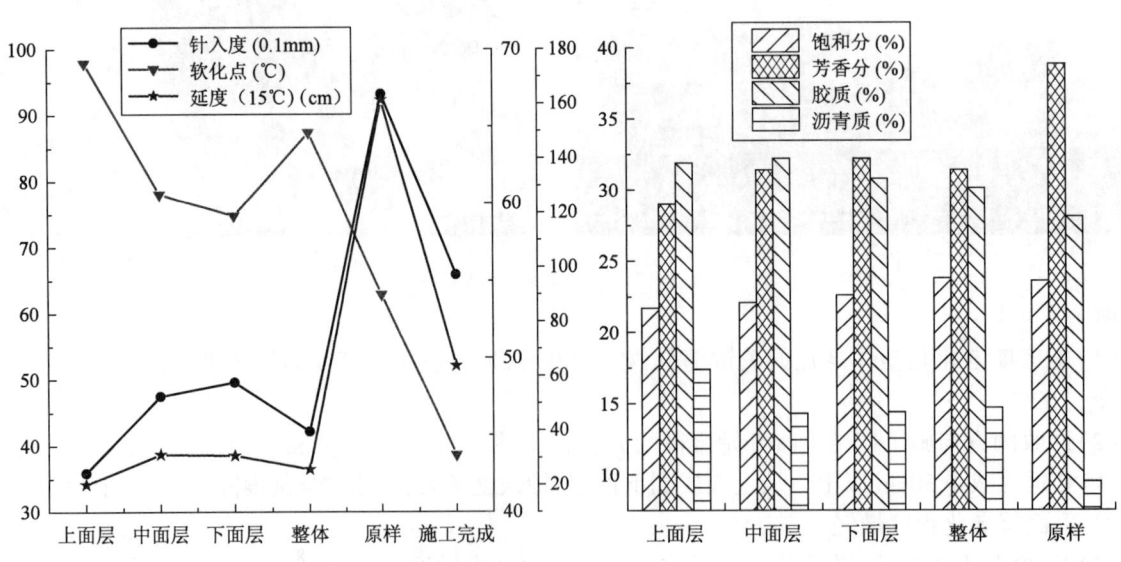

图 4 不同层位三指标、四组分试验结果

综上,三指标结果更加精确。而四组分受仪器、操作影响大,规律不明显。故旧路沥青老化评价分级应以三指标为主,四组分为辅。

4 基于分层铣刨的沥青老化程度分级

不论短期老化或长期老化,其老化程度随时间的增加,老化速率先增加后减小,老化程度最终趋于稳定。即老化程度存在拐点,拐点对应的老化时间可以认为是临界值[7]。

因此,沥青老化的拐点可以作为沥青老化程度的分级标准[8]。结合前文可知,沥青85min(对应施工期结束)出现第一个拐点。在第一拐点之前,沥青各指标变化快,但性能影响小。在360min(对应服役6年)时,老化程度出现第二拐点,老化速度变缓,但沥青中芳香分仍然在向沥青质转变。在360min之后,沥青指标下降趋于平缓。

基于上述分析得到的两个老化拐点,结合旧路铣刨后的三指标、四组分试验,参考我国再生设计规范和相关研究,考虑回收沥青三指标中针入度和延度降低,软化点升高百分率,四组分中芳香分减少、沥青质增加百分率,以针入度、软化点、延度为一级指标,沥青质为二级指标,将沥青的老化程度分为轻、中、重三级,见表4。

基于沥青三指标、沥青质的沥青老化分级 表4

项 目	老化分级	轻	中	重
一级指标	老化模拟(min)	0~85	85~360	>360
	路面长期服役(年)	施工阶段	0~6	>6
	针入度降低(%)①	<40	40~50	50~70
	软化点增加(%)②			
	延度降低(%)③	<50	50~70	>70
二级指标	沥青质增加百分率(%)	<5	5~15	>15

注:①针入度降低百分率=(基质针入度−老化后针入度)/基质针入度。
②软化点增加百分率=(老化后软化点−基质软化点)/基质软化点。
③延度降低百分率=(基质延度−老化后延度)/基质延度。

根据上述分级可以看出,铣刨料上面层材料为重度老化,中下面层材料为中度老化。总体为中度老化。这也与上面层沥青受污染较为严重、老化程度大的实际情况相吻合。

5 结 语

(1)通过室内老化模拟及现场实测结果,建立了短期及长期老化预估模型与老化速率模型;长期及短期老化方程均呈现为开始老化速率最快,后期老化速率逐渐降低,老化程度趋于平缓。

(2)基于三指标与四组分试验可知,三指标试验结果更加精确。而四组分受仪器、人为操作影响较大,规律相对不明显;因此旧路抽提沥青老化评价与分级应以三指标为主,四组分为辅。

(3)结合旧路铣刨后的三指标、四组分验,参考我国再生设计规范、相关研究,提出了以针入度、软化点、延度为一级指标,沥青质为二级指标的分级方法。

参考文献

[1] 常琨,王选仓.SBS改性沥青RTFOT老化黏附性量化评价方法研究[J].公路交通科技,2019,36(12):29-36.

[2] 丁婕,聂忆华,陈龙,等.道路沥青不同时间老化规律红外光谱微观分析[J].湖南交通科技,2014,40(02):10-12.

[3] 刘苹,聂忆华,张云龙,等.重交70号道路沥青不同老化时间的性能变化规律[J].湖南科技大学学报(自然科学版),2013,28(02):56-59.

[4] 宋家乐,何璐,王欣,等.SBS改性沥青的RTFOT微观老化机理[J].公路交通科技,2020,37(02):1-7.

[5] 梁志豪,邢明亮,李祖仲,等.短期老化方法对沥青性能评价的适用性[J].筑路机械与施工机械化,2019,36(09):23-29.

[6] 黄旭,姚晓光.沥青老化行为及其机理研究[J].公路工程,2018,43(06):228-235.

[7] Yu T J.,Zhang H Y.,Wang Y. Interaction of asphalt and water between porous asphalt pavement voids with different aging stage and its significance to drainage[J]. Construction and Building Materials,2020,252:119085.

[8] 汪莹.沥青老化评价指标分析及老化程度研究[J].路基工程,2014(06):63-68.

Preliminary Study on the Problem of Improving the Interfacial Properties of Fiber and Asphalt Binder

Junxian Huang Zhibin Su Susu Xing Jing Li Canyun Mao

(College of Chemistry and Chemical Engineering, Guangxi University)

Abstract In this paper, the modified fibers were prepared and their effects on the properties of modified bitumen were investigated by grafting silica onto the surface of poly(acrylonitrile) fibers (PAN) through the adhesion of poly(dopamine) coating on the surface of PAN by the self-polymerization reaction of dopamine, and by using the poly(dopamine) coating to provide reactive groups. The microstructure and morphology of the fibers before and after modification were observed by scanning electron microscopy (SEM) and atomic force microscopy (AFM), and the results confirmed the successful grafting of silica on PAN, which effectively improved its surface inertness. Dynamic shear rheometer (DSR) tests further confirmed that the viscoelasticity and deformation resistance of the asphalt were effectively improved, the complex modulus of 3% SiO_2/PDA-PAN modified asphalt being 10.4% higher than that of 3% PAN modified asphalt at 46℃.

Keywords Dopamine Polyacrylonitrile Adhesion Scanning electron microscopy Atomic force microscopy DAynamic shear rheometry testing

0 Introduction

Asphalt, which is widely used in road construction materials, is mainly derived fromparaffin-based crude oil, so asphalt is more sensitive to temperature, in the process of road use, prone to oil flooding, deformation and other problems(Tapkın,2008), and fiber has a strong adsorption, adhesion, stabilization, reinforcement and crack resistance of asphalt, can make up for the asphalt mixture of low temperature brittleness and poor tensile properties, while improving the high temperature stability of asphalt mixture, so the problem of adding fibers to asphalt mixtures to improve asphalt pavement damage has become a hot topic of research in this field(Baaj et al.,2005).

According to the composition, fibers applied to asphalt pavements are mainly divided into inorganic fibers, natural fibers and synthetic polymer fibers, inorganic fibers, such as basalt fibers, can effectively enhance the stress relaxation capacity of asphalt (Qin et al.,2018), but because their main components are inorganic, they are less compatible with asphalt (Celauro and Praticò,2018), and natural fibers such as lignin fibers can also enhance their high-temperature rutting resistance and low-temperature crack resistance, but their thermal stability is poor, and the enhancement mechanism for asphalt is mainly based on adsorption, so the lignin fiber modified asphalt is less resistant to external forces (Batista et al., 2018). Polyacrylonitrile fibers, a synthetic polymer fiber, are widely used in asphalt pavements because of their high strength, high modulus, corrosion resistance, chemical stability, and good dispersion, which can significantly enhance asphalt pavement performance. Carlos et al (Slebi-Acevedo et al., 2020) found that the incorporation of polyacrylonitrile fibers into asphalt mastic helped to improve the low-temperature fracture performance of asphalt mastic through indirect tensile tests. Yao et al (Yao et al., 2011) conducted rheological performance tests on polyacrylonitrile fiber modified asphalt and mixes and found that the incorporation of polyacrylonitrile fiber could fiber improve the high temperature stability of asphalt and asphalt mixes. However, the road performance of asphalt pavement needs to consider not only low-temperature fracture performance and high-temperature stability, but also water stability. Bu et al (Song et al., 2011) found that the incorporation of polyacrylonitrile fibers into the mixes significantly improved the water damage resistance of the mixes through residual Marshall stability and splitting strength tests.

The construction of durable asphalt roads is the focus of research today, and many researchers have extended the service life of roads by designing road structures and modifying road materials (Vyrozhemskyi et al., 2017). The disadvantages of synthetic polymer fibers such as polyacrylonitrile fibers have also been exposed, as their chemical inertness makes it difficult to perform surface modification work to enhance the performance of their composite asphalt without destroying the structure of the fibers themselves (Abtahi et al., 2010). To solve this problem, many researchers have conducted extensive investigations and found that polydopamine has a similar adhesion mechanism to that of mussels and can be deposited on most inorganic and organic inert substrates and is durable and stable (Ryu et al., 2010), and the adhesion of polydopamine has different modes of action on different substrates, forming coordination bonds for metal ions and metal oxides such as Fe_3O_4 (Palladino et al., 2019), and for SiO_2 non-metallic oxides are dominated by hydrogen bonding (Jones et al., 2013). For materials with amino or sulfhydryl groups, polydopamine will react with them to form chemical bonds (Feng et al., 2020). For nonpolar materials such as polyacrylonitrile, the indole structure of polydopamine forms hydrophobic interactions or stacking interactions with it (Li et al., 2015). For polar materials, the phenolic hydroxyl groups of polydopamine will form electrostatic interactions and hydrogen bonds with them.

In this paper, nanosilica was deposited and adhered to the PAN surface in one step to improve its interfacial interaction with asphalt using the bidirectional adhesion of polydopamine. The modified fibers were characterized by scanning electron microscopy (SEM) and atomic force microscopy (AFM) for microscopic morphology. The mechanical properties of functionalized fiber-reinforced asphalt binders were evaluated by dynamic shear rheometry (DSR) and preliminary results are presented.

1 Materials and Methods

1.1 Materials

The asphalt used in this experiment is ESSO AH-70. Dopamine hydrochloride and silicon dioxide were provided by Shanghai McLean Biochemical Technology Co., Ltd. China. Trimethylaminomethane was provided by Sinopharm group chemical reagent Co., Ltd. China. Concentrated hydrochloric acid provided by Linyi Mao Xing Chemical Co., Ltd. China. Poly-acrylonitrile fiber with a length of 6mm was purchased from Chengdu Keliang Building Materials Co., Ltd. China.

1.2 Experiment Process of Modified Fiber

Configure 50mM Tris solution, adjust pH to 8.5 with 1 g/L hydrochloric acid, add 2g/L dopamine hydrochloride and 2g/L nano-silica, stir well, and finally add polyacrylonitrile fiber and react at constant temperature for 24h to obtain modified fiber SiO$_2$/PDA-PAN.

1.3 Preparation Process of Modified Asphalt

After placing 1.2kg of asphalt in an oven at 135℃ for 3h to remove excess water, 5% SBS was added to the asphalt and shear emulsified at 170℃ for 1 h at 5000rpm, after shear completion, the SBS in the asphalt was dispersed by a high-speed disperser at 500rpm. The finished SBS modified bitumen was obtained after 2h of swelling development at a constant temperature of 170℃.

The fiber/SBS modified asphalt was prepared by weighing 150 g of SBS modified asphalt and adding fibers (1,2,3 % PAN or SiO$_2$-PAN, depending on the mass of asphalt) to it for 2h at 170℃ and 500r/min for uniform dispersion.

1.4 Microscopic Characterization and Performance Testing

The microstructure and morphology of PAN before and after modification were characterized by scanning electron microscopy and atomic force microscopy. The mechanical properties of the different modified asphalts were investigated by DSR tests. The samples of different asphalts were mounted on a sample table, set at a sample thickness of 1000μm, and tested in the temperature range of 46℃ to 64℃ using a 25.0mm diameter rotary axis compression mold in the frequency range of 0.1 Hz to 10 Hz.

2 Results and Discussion

2.1 SEM & AFM

Fig. 1 shows the 5000x SEM images of PAN and SiO2/PDA-PAN, respectively. Fig. 1a) shows the regular cylindrical shape and smooth surface of PAN. While the modified PAN in Fig. 1b) has a rough surface with many obvious particles on the surface, indicating that PDA and SiO$_2$ substances have been successfully deposited on the fiber surface.

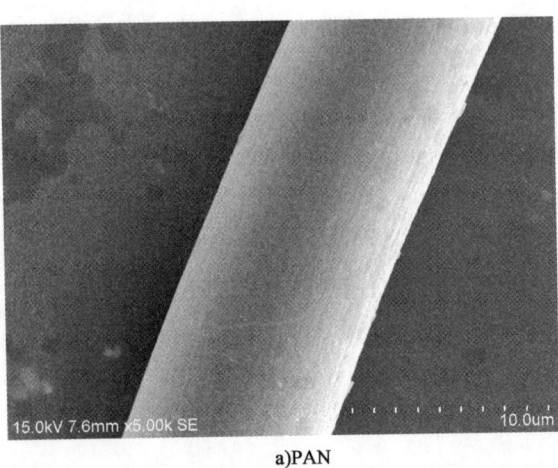

a)PAN b)SiO$_2$/PDA-PAN

Fig. 1 SEM Images of PAN and SiO$_2$/PDA-PAN

Fig. 2 shows the 3D maps of PAN and SiO$_2$/PDA-PAN. It can be seen from the AFM image that the PAN surface is relatively smooth, which is consistent with the SEM image, while the SiO$_2$/PDA-PAN surface has obvious particles with large surface undulations. This indicates that the PDA and SiO$_2$ substances successfully adhere to the fiber surface, which remains consistent with the SEM findings.

2.2 Complex Modulus

As can be seen from Fig. 3, the complex modulus of the two modified asphalts with different fiber dose always decreases with the increase of temperature, and the complex modulusof SiO_2/PDA-PAN modified asphalt with the same fiber dose is always higher than that of PAN modified asphalt in the whole test temperature range. When the fiber dose is 1%, the complex modulus of SiO_2/PDA-PAN composite SBS modified asphalt is not significantly higher than that of PAN composite SBS modified asphalt, which is due to the fact that when the fiber dose is small, the mesh structure formed in the asphalt is not obvious, and the mechanical engagement of the asphalt is weak. The modified fiber/SBS-modified asphalt enhancement becomes more and more pronounced when the admixture is increased, with the complex modulus of 3% SiO_2/PDA-PAN modified asphalt being 10.4% higher than that of 3% PAN modified asphalt at 46℃. This can be attributed to the bi-directional adhesion of polydopamine, which makes SiO_2 adhere to the fiber surface (obtained from SEM and AFM plots) and play a mechanical engagement role on the SBS modified asphalt, enhancing the interfacial interaction between the fiber and SBS modified bitumen to improve the deformation resistance of the modified asphalt.

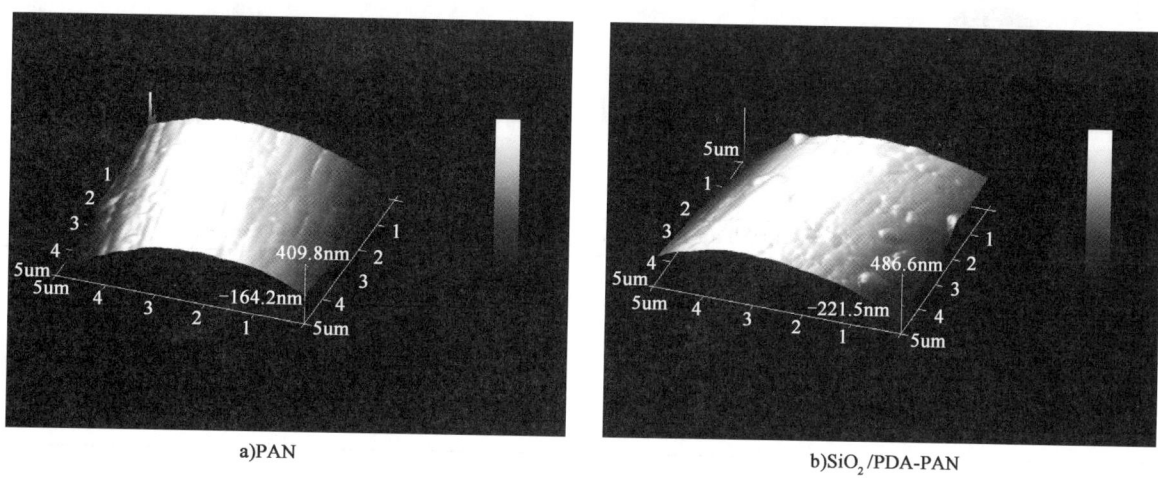

Fig. 2 AFM mages of PAN and SiO_2/PDA-PAN

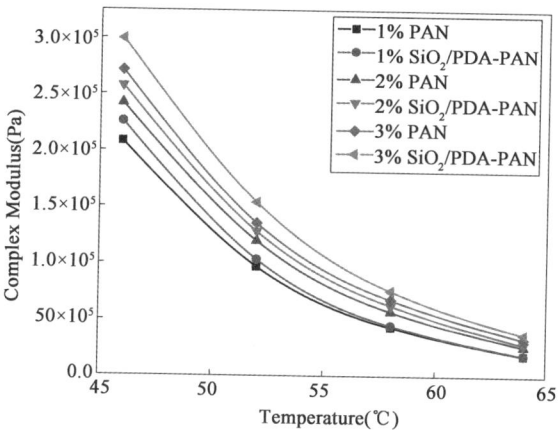

Fig. 3 Effect of Temperature on Complex Modulus at 0.1-10 Hz for Modified Asphalt with Different Fiber Dose

2.3 The Adhesion Work of Fiber and Asphalt

In order to study the adhesion between modified fiber and asphalt, the surface free energy of modified asphalt was calculated by Owens Wendt rabel kaelble (owrk geometric average method) (equation 1), and the adhesion work of asphalt was further calculated by equation 2.

$$\gamma_L(1+\cos\theta) = 2(\sqrt{\gamma_S^d \gamma_L^d} + \sqrt{\gamma_S^{nd}\gamma_L^{nd}}) \quad (1)$$

$$W_{sl} = \gamma_L(\cos\theta + 1) \quad (2)$$

Where, γ_S^d and γ_L^d represent the dispersion force components of solid and liquid respectively; γ_S^{nd} and γ_L^{nd} respectively represent the polar components of solid and liquid; W_{sl} and θ respectively represent adhesion work and contact angle between asphalt and aggregate (Fig. 4 and Tab. 1).

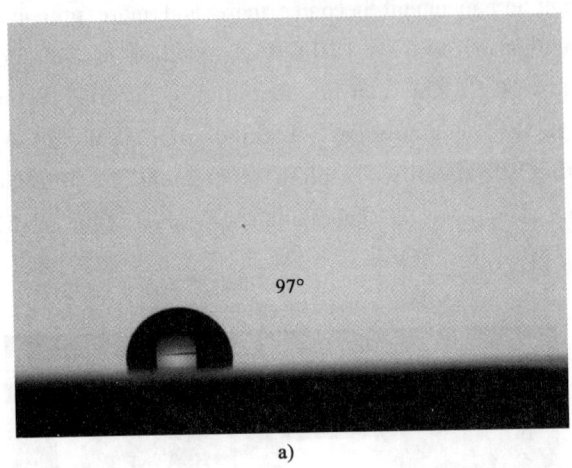 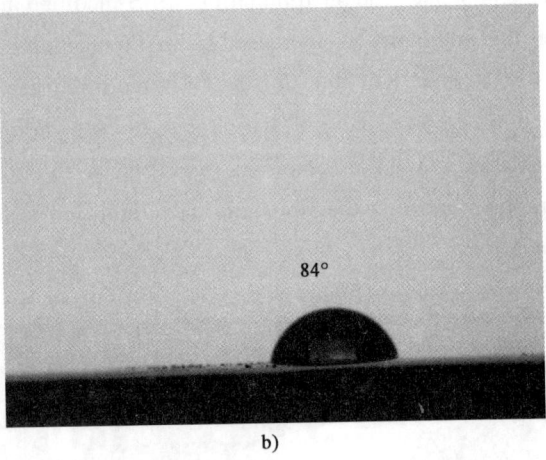

Fig. 4 Contact angles of asphalt with water and formamide

Surface Free Energy and Parameters (mJ/m^2) of Water, Formamide and Asphalt Tab. 1

Reagent	γ^d	γ^{nd}	Surface Free Energ
Water	29.1	43.7	72.8
Formamide	35.1	23.1	58.2
Asphalt	19.8	1.5	21.2

It can be seen from Tab. 2 that the adhesion of pan is obviously lower than that of SiO_2/PDA-PAN. It may be due to the multilayer structure of SiO_2 with large specific surface area, and the grafting of SiO_2 onto the fiber surface will make the fiber surface rougher (discussed in the previous SEM and AFM analysis), this helps to make the asphalt adhere to the fiber surface better. The contact angle of the modified fiber increases from 100.5° (Fig. 5a) to 112°[Fig. 5b] which indicates that the hydrophobicity of the fiber is improved. The test results show that the modified fiber SiO_2/PDA-PAN not only improves the adhesion between the fiber and asphalt, but also effectively improves the water resistance of asphalt.

Adhesion Work Between Two Kinds of Fibers and Asphalt (mJ/m^2) Tab. 2

Fiber Category	Adhesion Work (mJ/m^2)
PAN	13.27
SiO_2/PDA-PAN	17.35

3 Conclusions

This study reports the modification of SiO_2 on the PAN surface by the bi-directional adhesion of polydopamine. SEM and TEM analysis results confirmed that polydopamine and SiO_2 successfully adhered to the fiber surface with increased roughness. DSR tests showed that the complex modulus of 3% SiO_2/PDA-PAN modified asphalt was 10.4% higher than that of 3% PAN modified asphalt at 46℃, and the resistance to deformation of the modified asphalt was effectively improved, which could be attributed to the fiber surface This may be attributed to the mechanical engagement of the SBS modified asphalt by the SiO_2 adhered to the fiber surface, which enhances the interfacial interaction between the fiber and the SBS modified asphalt, thus improving the performance of the modified fiber-bound asphalt.

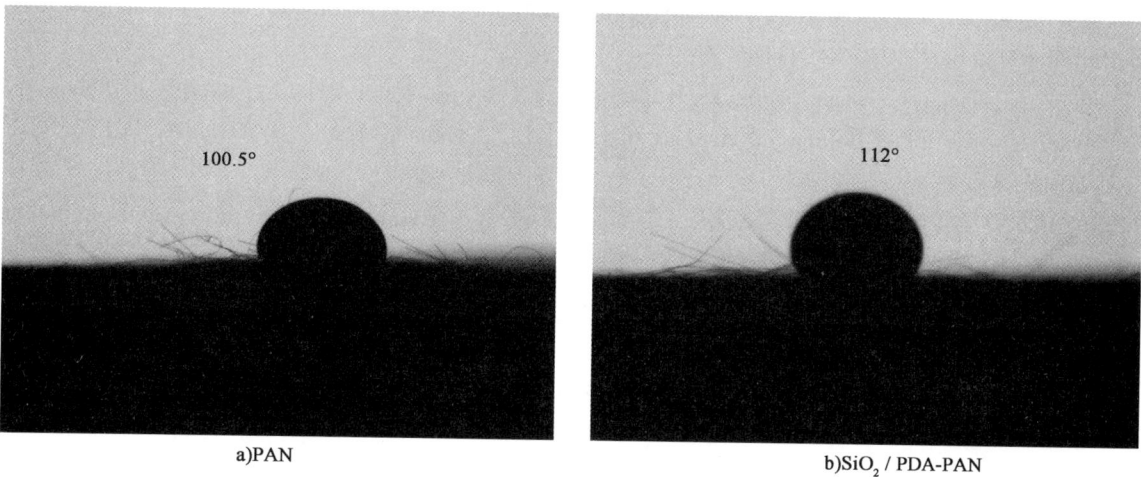

Fig. 5 Contact angle between PAN, SiO_2/PDA-PAN and asphalt

4 Acknowledgements

The authors thank the Guangxi Science and Technology Department (2018GXNSFAA281118) and the National Natural Science Foundation of China (Grant Nos. 51768007) for providing financial surrport.

References

[1] Abtahi, S. M., Sheikhzadeh, M., and Hejazi, S. M. Fiber-reinforced Asphalt Concretea Review[J],2010,24: 871-877.

[2] Baaj, H., Di Benedetto, H., and Chaverot, P. Effect of Binder Characteristics on Fatigue of Asphalt Pavement Using an Intrinsic Damage Approach[J]. Road Materials and Pavement Design,2005,6:147-174.

[3] Batista, K. B., Padilha, R. P. L., Castro, T. O., Silva, C., Araújo, M., Leite, L. F. M., Pasa, V. M. D., and Lins, V. F. C. High-temperature, Low-temperature and Weathering Aging Performance of Lignin Modified Asphalt Binders[J]. Industrial crops and products,2018,111:107-116.

[4] Celauro, C., and Praticò, F. G. Asphalt Mixtures Modified with Basalt Fibres for Surface Courses[J]. Construction and Building Materials,2018,170:245-253.

[5] Feng, M., Li, W., Liu, X., Huang, M., and Yang, J. Copper-polydopamine Composite Coating Decorating UHMWPE Fibers for Enhancing the Strength and Toughness of Rigid Polyurethane Composites-ScienceDirect[J]. Polymer Testing,2020,93.

[6] Jones, J. E. P., Kaye, A. B., Haglund, R. F., Cliffel, D. E., and Wright, D. Optical Sensors Including Surface Modified Phase-change Materials for Detection of Chemical, Biological and Explosive Compounds[J]. US.

[7] Li, Z., Wu, C., Zhao, K., Peng, B., and Deng, Z. Polydopamine-assisted Synthesis of Raspberry-like Nanocomposite Particles for Superhydrophobic and Superoleophilic Surfaces[J]. Colloids & Surfaces A Physicochemical & Engineering Aspects,2015,470:80-91.

[8] Palladino, P., Bettazzi, F., and Scarano, S. Polydopamine: Surface Coating, Molecular Imprinting, and Electrochemistry-successful Applications and Future Perspectives in (bio) Analysis[J]. Analytical and bioanalytical chemistry,2019,411:4327-4338.

[9] Qin, X., Shen, A., Guo, Y., Li, Z., and Lv, Z. Characterization of Asphalt Mastics Reinforced with Basalt Fibers[J]. Construction and Building Materials,2018,159:508-516.

[10] Ryu, J., Ku, S. H., Lee, H., and Park, C. B. Mussel-inspired Polydopamine Coating as a Universal Route to Hydroxyapatite Crystallization[J]. Advanced Functional Materials, 2010, 20: 2132-2139.

[11] Slebi-Acevedo, C. J., Pedro, L.-G., Castro-Fresno, D., and Bueno, M. An Experimental Laboratory Study of Fiber-reinforced Asphalt Mortars with Polyolefin-aramid and Polyacrylonitrile Fibers[J]. Construction and Building Materials, 2020, 248: 118622.

[12] Song, J. X., Chang, C. L., and Yang, H. R. Comparing Tests on Water Relating Stability of Polyester and Polyacrylonitrile Fiber Reinforced Asphalt Mixture[J]. Advanced Materials Research, 2011, 287-290: 742-746.

[13] Tapkın, S. The Effect of Polypropylene Fibers on Asphalt Performance[J]. Building and environment, 2008, 43: 1065-1071.

[14] Vyrozhemskyi, V., Krayushkina, K., and Bidnenko, N. Durable High Strength Cement Concrete Topping for Asphalt Roads[J], 2017.

[15] Yao, L. Y., Hu, Y. P., Ma, Q., and Ma, X. W. Stability of Asphalt Binder and Asphalt Mixture Modified by Polyacrylonitrile Fibers[J]. Advanced Materials Research, 2011, 228-229: 242-247.

矿料分异型沥青混合料路用性能及力学参数研究

吴喜荣[1,2] 郑南翔[1] 雷俊安[1]

(1. 长安大学; 2. 山西省交通科技研发有限公司)

摘 要 矿料分异可以提升沥青混合料的抗滑性能,但矿料分异后对路用性能和力学参数的影响还不明确。本文采用石灰岩取代相同粒径的铝矾土熟料作为分异方案,分析不同粒径集料的取代对沥青混合料的抗裂性能、水温性能、动态模量和单轴静态蠕变的影响。结果表明:铝矾土熟料中掺入石灰岩后的抗裂性能相对要好,石灰岩的掺入增加了沥青用量,界面黏附功增大,不易在界面处开裂;铝矾土熟料沥青混合料中掺入一定比例的石灰岩,沥青混合料水稳性能比单一采用铝矾土熟料集料、石灰岩或玄武岩集料所表现的水温性能要高;在矿料级配确定的情况下,沥青用量和矿料类型特别是2.36mm粒径的矿料类型对于沥青混合料动态模量有很大的影响;当温度大于45℃时,矿料分异型沥青混合料的蠕变变形变大。本文综合分析了矿料分异型沥青混合料路用性能的变化规律,为矿料分异型沥青混合料的工程适用性提供依据和参考。

关键词 沥青混合料 路用性能 矿料分异 铝矾土熟料集料 力学参数

0 引 言

集料的抗滑磨耗性能对沥青混合料抗滑性能有重要影响。目前,基于矿料资源的相对缺乏和提升路面抗滑性能的紧迫需要,研究者们提出了分异型沥青混合料的概念,利用集料之间耐磨性能的差异,使用不同材质的集料制备沥青混合料,从而使路面在使用过程中可以长期保持良好的构造特性[1]。王元元等对玄武岩和石灰岩分异处理后沥青混合料抗滑性能的影响进行了分析,认为以分异配比值(除了矿粉以外,混合料每一粒径所对应的集料中石灰岩集料与玄武岩集料的比值)为30%,能够改善混合料抗滑性能的衰减速率[2]。S. Shaban 等[1]研究指出,路面抗滑性能的维持能力主要由集料中的硬质矿物成分和软质矿物成分的组合决定,硬度值为6级的硬质矿物和硬度值为3~5级的软质矿物组合而成的粗集料的抗滑性能最为理想,并且硬质矿物和软质矿物的合理分异配比值得确定能够改善抗滑性能的衰减速率。李菁若等[3]研究了不同岩性集料互掺之后的抗滑性能衰减规律,认为互掺后集料的抗滑耐磨性能得到了提升。

综上所述,矿料分异性沥青混合料能够改善沥青混合料的抗滑性能,但是矿料分异后对沥青混合料的路用性能和力学参数等指标有什么影响还不明确。根据国内外已有研究结果表明,铝矾土熟料具有优良的抗滑性能,并且铝矾土熟料与石灰岩分异后的抗滑性能仍优于常规集料,如玄武岩。因此,本文利用石灰岩取代等粒径的铝矾土熟料作为分异方案,在此基础上,开展矿料分异性沥青混合料的抗裂性能、水稳性能、动态模量和单轴静态蠕变等相关试验,分析研究矿料分异型沥青混合料对沥青混合料路用性能及力学参数的影响。研究结果表明,矿料分异型沥青混合料在温度低于45℃时,其路用性能比单纯使用铝矾土熟料有一定的优势,但当温度高于45℃,分异性沥青混合料的蠕变变形变大。在工程应用中,需要综合衡量矿料分异型沥青混合料的适用条件及其优劣势。

1 原材料及矿料分异方案

1.1 沥青技术指标

本节采用的沥青是SBSI-D改性沥青,其技术性能见表1。

壳牌SBSI-D改性沥青的技术性能　　　表1

分析项目	单位	质量指标	检验结果	试验方法
针入度(15℃,5s,100g)	1/10mm	—	21.7	T 0604
针入度(25℃,5s,100g)	1/10mm	30~60	52	T 0604
针入度(30℃,5s,100g)	1/10mm	—	77.1	T 0604
针入度指数PI	—	≥0	0.54	
延度(5cm/min,5℃)	cm	≥20	34	T 0605
密度(25℃)	g/cm³	实测记录	1.028	T 0603
软化点(环球法)	℃	≥60	91	T 0606
RTFOT				
质量损失	%	≤±1.0	0.01	T 0610
针入度比(25℃)	1/10mm	≥65	87	T 0604
延度(5cm/min,5℃)	cm	≥15	39	T 0605

1.2 集料的技术指标

集料为铝矾土熟料、玄武岩和石灰岩,三种集料的常规技术性能见表2。

集料的技术性能　　　表2

集料类型	压碎值(%)	磨耗值(%)	吸水率(%)	密度(g/cm³)
铝矾土熟料	6.5	7.9	1.35	3.382
玄武岩	11.5	10.8	0.68	2.864
石灰岩	18.6	21.1	1.17	2.794

1.3 矿料级配及矿料分异方案

以骨架密实型级配SMA-13和悬浮密实性级配类型AC-13的混合料为基础进行分异化处理,混合料的级配组成构成见表3。

沥青混合料试样的级配组成 表3

项目	对应筛孔(mm)的质量通过率(%)								
级配类型	13.2	9.5	4.75	2.36	1.18	0.6	0.3	0.15	0.075
SMA-13	94.7	66	25.4	19.7	16	14.4	12.2	11.6	10.4
AC-13	95.5	80.5	52.8	35.5	24.1	19.8	12.1	9.6	7.1

以铝矾土熟料、石灰岩、玄武岩和混合矿料(铝矾土熟料中的13.2mm、9.5mm、4.75mm、2.36mm分别用等体积的石灰岩替换)为基础配制10种矿料级配,10种矿料级配的掺配方式见表4,沥青混合料试样的最佳沥青用量见表5。用AC-13(铝)、AC-13(石)、AC-13(玄)、SMA-13(铝)、SMA-13(石)、SMA-13(铝)代表不同级配及所采用的集料类型,用SMA-13(石代铝13.2)、SMA-13(石代铝9.5)、SMA-13(石代铝4.75)、SMA-13(石代铝2.36)表示级配中所采用的集料为铝矾土熟料,铝矾土集料中13.2mm、9.5mm、4.75mm、2.36mm部分被同粒径的石灰岩所取代。

沥青混合料试样矿料级配类型及矿料分异方案 表4

项目	对应筛孔(mm)的质量通过率(%)								
级配类型	13.2	9.5	4.75	2.36	1.18	0.6	0.3	0.15	0.075
SMA-13	94.7	66	25.4	19.7	16	14.4	12.2	11.6	10.4
AC-13	95.5	80.5	52.8	35.5	24.1	19.8	12.1	9.6	7.1
级配类型	集料类型								
SMA-13(铝)	全部铝矾土熟料 E								
SMA-13(石代铝13.2)	石灰岩	铝矾土熟料 E							
SMA-13(石代铝9.5)	铝矾土熟料	石灰岩	铝矾土熟料 E						
SMA-13(石代铝4.75)	铝矾土熟料 E	石灰岩	铝矾土熟料 E						
SMA-13(石代铝2.36)	铝矾土熟料 E	石灰岩	铝矾土熟料 E						
SMA-13(石)	全部石灰岩								
SMA-13(玄)	全部玄武岩								
AC-13(铝)	全部铝矾土熟料 E								
AC-13(石)	全部石灰岩								
AC-13(玄)	全部玄武岩								

1.4 最佳沥青用量

采用马歇尔设计方法确定配合比设计,确定10个级配类型的最佳沥青用量见表5。

矿料级配类型的最佳沥青用量 表5

级配类型	油石比(%)	级配类型	油石比(%)
SMA-13(铝)	4.7	SMA-13(石)	6.0
SMA-13(石代铝13.2)	4.8	SMA-13(玄)	6.3
SMA-13(石代铝9.5)	5.7	AC-13(铝)	4.2
SMA-13(石代铝4.75)	6.0	AC-13(石)	5.3
SMA-13(石代铝2.36)	4.8	AC-13(玄)	5.2

集料类型不同,集料的密度、集料的孔分布、集料的表面纹理的粗糙度会有所差异,沥青混合料的最佳沥青用量会有较大的差异,进而对沥青混合料的路用性能会产生较大的影响。

2 矿料分异型沥青混合料的路用性能研究

2.1 矿料分异型沥青混合料的抗裂性能

2.1.1 试验前准备工作

成型旋转压实试件,按照图1的方式切割试件,采用环氧树脂胶将切割好的试件粘在试验仪器的两块铁板上。试验仪器采用路面抗裂仪OT(Overlay Tester)如图2所示。其中,一块是固定在仪器里,另一块是活动块(重复加载块),如图3所示。养护时间根据环氧树脂胶的固结时间决定。试件养护好以后,将仪器温控箱的温度设置为25℃。待温度稳定后,将试件放入,保持2～4h,待试件内外温度保持均匀时就开始试验,试验自动停止为止。

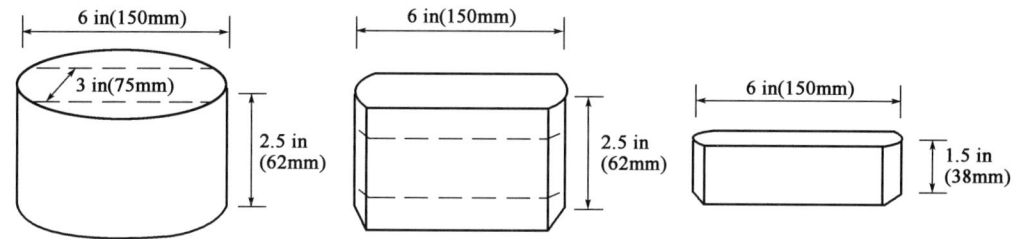

图1 试件成型方式

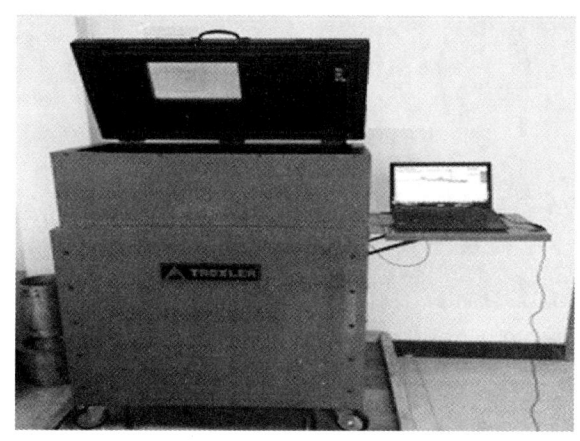

图2 路面抗裂仪

图3 试件黏附在固定板与活动板上

2.1.2 试验结果分析

采用重复加载方式,对四种混合料类型进行OT试验,测试结果见表6。

铝矾土熟料沥青混合料的OT测试结果　　　　表6

级配类型	最佳沥青用量(%)	空隙率(%)	峰值荷载(kN)	循环周期(次)
SMA-13$_{(铝)}$	4.7	3.5	2.6	247
SMA-13$_{(石代铝9.5)}$	5.7	3.4	3.7	367
SMA-13$_{(石代铝4.75)}$	6.0	3.4	3.5	458
SMA-13$_{(石代铝3.26)}$	4.8	3.4	3.3	310
SMA-13$_{(石)}$	6.0	3.4	2.1	507
SMA-13$_{(玄)}$	6.3	3.4	3.75	514

注:表中每种级配的测试结果是5个测试数据的均值。

从表6可知,对应于荷载循环次数最多集料类型是玄武岩,荷载循环次数最少的铝矾土熟料。沥青混合料的荷载峰值的大小与破坏荷载循环周期没有明显的关系,荷载循环周期并不依赖荷载峰值,因此,荷载峰值的大小也不能作为沥青混合料抗裂性能大小的指标。在沥青种类和集料种类和粒径大小确定的情况下,影响沥青混合料抗裂性能的主要影响因素有混合料类型、沥青用量、混合料孔隙率的大小等[7]。

在混合料类型 SMA-13 一致的情况下,玄武岩的沥青用量最大,其次是石灰岩,铝矾土熟料的沥青用量最小,这是铝矾土熟料抗裂性能较差的主要原因。相对铝矾土熟料来说,铝矾土熟料中掺入石灰岩后的抗裂性能相对要好,石灰岩的掺入增加了沥青用量,并且石灰岩与沥青的黏附性好,黏附性越好,界面黏附功也越大,也不容易在界面处开裂。为了提升铝矾土熟料的抗裂性能,可以适当地提高沥青的用量以及掺加抗剥落剂提高黏附性。

2.2 矿料分异型沥青混合料的水稳性能

采用级配类型 SMA-13$_{(铝)}$、SMA-13$_{(石代铝9.5)}$、SMA-13$_{(石代铝4.75)}$、SMA-13$_{(石代铝3.26)}$、SMA-13$_{(石)}$、SMA-13$_{(玄)}$ 成型两组马歇尔试件。一组测定水损害前的劈裂强度,另一组测定经过水损害后的劈裂强度,采用劈裂强度比来评价沥青混合料的水稳性能。水损害采用水损坏敏感性测试仪(MIST)来模拟。试验仪器如图4所示。试验仪器默认的压力值40PSI,试验温度为60℃。在60℃试验温度下,待测试件在样品仓内保持的时间为20h,孔隙水压力循环次数默认值为3500次。将两组试件在25℃保持2h,利用劈裂强度比值来评价沥青混合料的水稳定性,试验结果图5所示。

图4 水损坏敏感性测试仪(MIST)

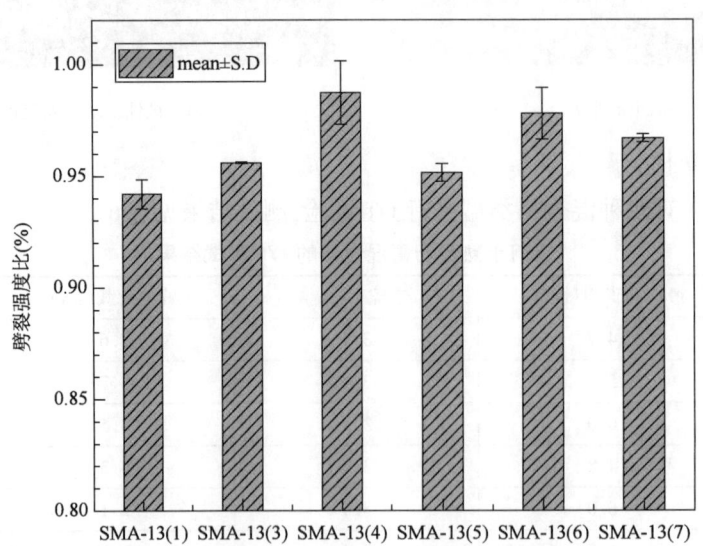

图5 铝矾土熟料沥青混合料的水稳定性测试结果

注:SMA-13(1)、SMA-13(3)、SMA-13(4)、SMA-13(5)、SMA-13(6)、SMA-13(7)分别代表级配 SMA-13(铝)、SMA-13(石代铝9.5)、SMA-13(石代铝4.75)、SMA-13(石代铝3.26)、SMA-13(石)、SMA-13(玄)

从图5可知,6个级配TSR值均大于80%,铝矾土熟料沥青混合料的抗剥落性能满足要求,SMA-13级配中4.75mm档的集料用量最大,采用同体积法用石灰岩取代相同粒径铝矾土熟料集料时,4.75mm这一档粒径被取代的用量最大,所以SMA-13(石代铝4.75)的石灰岩用量最多,劈裂强度也提升最大。SMA-13(石代铝4.75)的水稳定性比SMA-13(石)和SMA-13(玄)的水稳定性好,即沥青混合料中铝矾土熟料中掺入一定比例的石灰岩,沥青混合料水稳性能比单一采用铝矾土熟料集料、石灰岩或玄武岩集料所表现的水稳性能要高。

3 矿料分异型沥青混合料的力学参数分析

3.1 铝矾土熟料沥青混合料动态模量

为了评价铝矾土熟料、石灰岩、玄武岩以及矿料分异后沥青混合料力学参数变化规律,本文采用单轴压缩动态模量试验来评价沥青混合料试件可恢复的轴向应变。

3.1.1 动态模量主曲线

动态模量主曲线是将不同测试温度下的黏弹性材料动态模量曲线按照时间-温度换算方法进行位置平移,合成在某一温度下的光滑特征函数曲线,通常称之为主曲线[8-9]。

绘制动态模量主曲线,首先要确定各个温度下的平移因子,平移因子代表了各温度下动态模量主曲线到参考温度下主曲线的平移距离,平移因子a_T的计算公式为:

$$\lg f_r = \lg f - \lg a_T \tag{1}$$

式中:a_T——温度为T时的移位因子;

f——试验时的加载频率,Hz;

f_r——参考温度下的缩减频率,Hz。

使用Sigmoidal数学模型对动态模量主曲线进行描述,其数学模型如式(2):

$$\lg(|E^*|) = \delta + \frac{\alpha}{1+e^{\beta+\gamma(\lg f_r)}} \tag{2}$$

式中:δ、α、β、γ——回归系数;

δ——动态模量最小值;

$\delta+\alpha$——动态模量最大值;

β、γ——Sigmoidal函数形状参数。

3.1.2 试验方案

采用SMA-13(铝)、SMA-13(石代铝13.2)、SMA-13(石代铝9.5)、SMA-13(石代铝4.75)、SMA-13(石代铝3.26)、SMA-13(石)、SMA-13(玄)、AC-13(铝)、AC-13(石)和AC-13(玄)10个级配成型旋转压实试件,从旋转压实试件钻芯获得直径为100mm的圆柱形试件,将两头切掉降低试验误差。动态模量试验的测试仪器采用UTM-310,如图6所示。设备对试件施加半正弦荷载,加载频率分别为0.01Hz、0.01Hz、0.01Hz、0.01Hz、0.01Hz,试验温度设置为25℃、35℃、45℃和55℃。

3.1.3 试验结果分析

本试验结果如图7~图9所示。通过本试验主要分析试验温度、荷载频率及集料类型对沥青混合料动态模量的影响。

(1)矿料类型对动态模量的影响。

从图7可知,不同温度下,动态模量随着频率的提

图6 多功能试验机UTM-130

高而增大,随着温度的提高,动态模量逐渐降低,并且在同温度下,10个级配的变化趋势有明显区别:①在25℃时,SMA-13级配比AC-13型级配的动态模量要高,温度高于25℃时,AC-13型级配的动态模量要比SMA-13型级配的动态模量要高。25℃以后,级配类型的选取对于动态模量的影响较大。

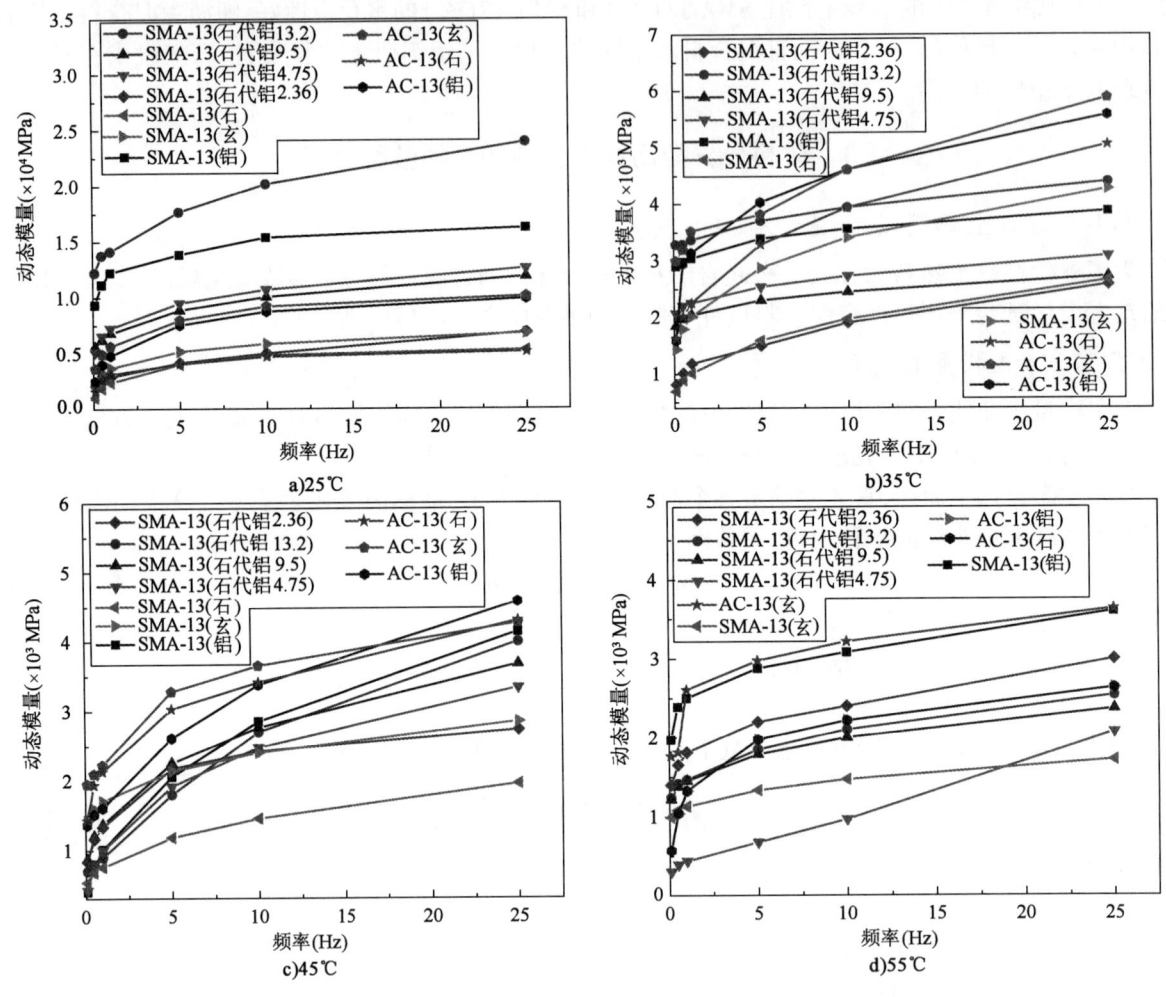

图7 不同温度下动态模量与频率的关系

②图7显示,SMA-13的7个级配中,铝矾土熟料以及铝矾土熟料与石灰岩掺合料的沥青混合料动态模量要比玄武岩沥青混合料和石灰岩沥青混合料的动态模量要大,AC-13型级配类型的试验结果也显示铝矾土熟料沥青混合料和玄武岩沥青混合料的动态模量要比石灰岩沥青混合料的动态模量要大。因此,温度低于25℃时,矿料类型对于动态模量的影响较大。Christensen等在2015年在沥青混合料改进动态模量预估模型Hirsch中首次引入了集料密度因子,并且认为在低温状态下,通过集料密度来反应集料的模量,能够很好地提升动态模量预估模型的准确度[10];SMA-13(铝)和SMA-13(石代铝13.2)所采用沥青种类、用量以及级配一致,唯一的差别是SMA-13(铝)中的13.2mm粒径的矿料全部由石灰岩取代,模量试验结果表明,矿料种类的变化对动态模量也有较大的影响。温度越高,硬度越大的集料,动态模量值越大。

③从7b)可知,温度高于35℃时,SMA-13(玄)玄武岩沥青混合料的动态模量相比SMA-13型的其他级配有明显的提高,SMA-13(石)石灰岩沥青混合料的动态模量也有所提高。这两个级配的沥青用量是SMA-13型7个级配中最大的,35℃以后,沥青用量的变化会对动弹模量的影响较为明显;④图7c)显示,温度高于45℃时,矿料类型对动态模量的影响又开始变大;⑤图7d)显示,当温度高于55℃,从曲线变化趋势可以看出矿料类型对动态模量的影响作用明显,并且SMA-13(石代铝2.36)级配的动态模量相比其他级配有增大的趋势,即此级配中2.36mm粒径的铝矾土熟料被石灰岩取代,因此,2.36mm粒径的矿料类型对于提升沥青的动态模量有重要作用。

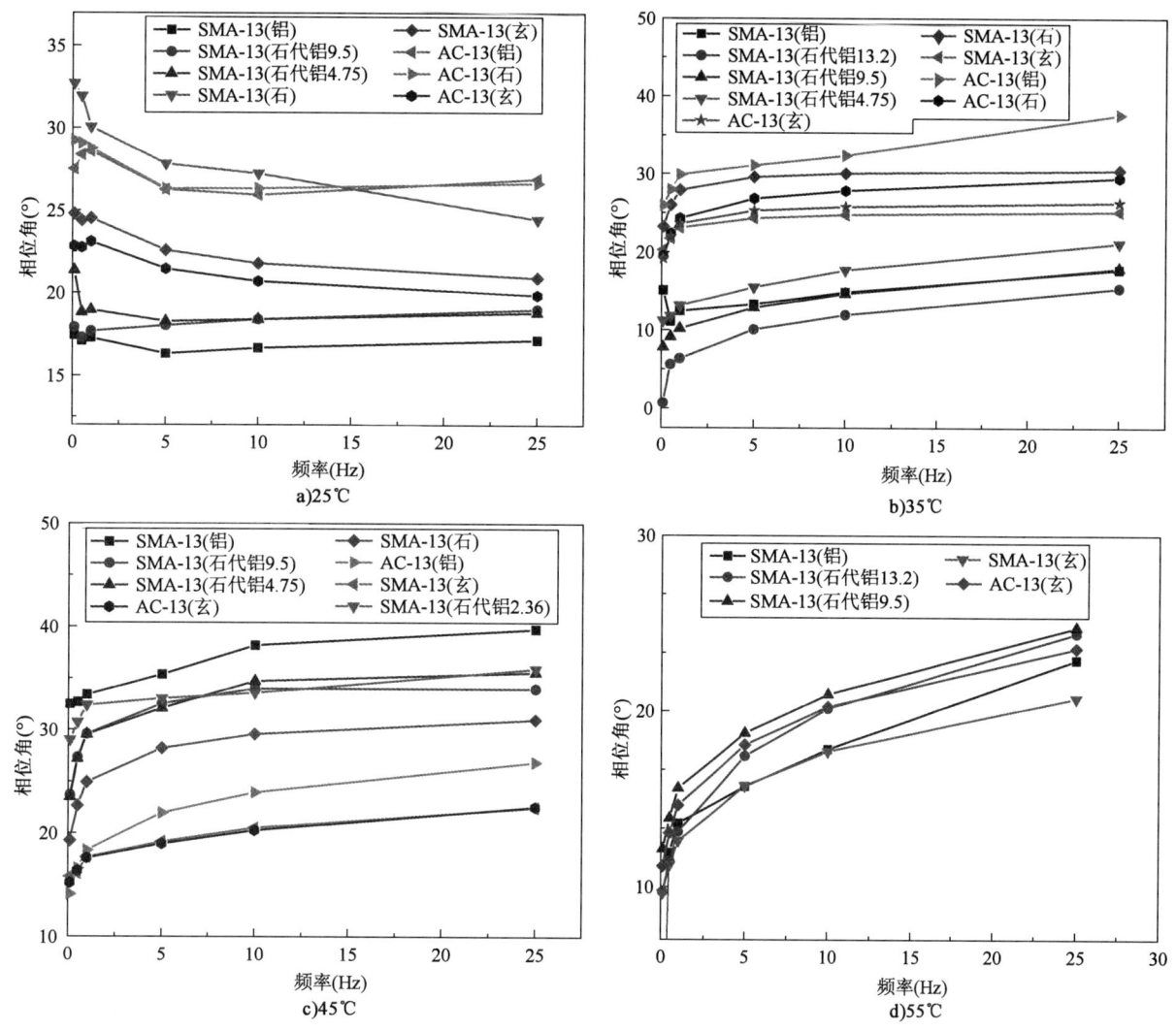

图8 不同温度下相位角与频率的关系

根据动弹模量试验结果定性分析得出:在矿料级配确定的情况下,沥青用量和矿料类型特别是2.36mm粒径的矿料类型对于沥青混合料动态模量有很大的影响。

(2)矿料分异对相位角的影响。

一般来说,随着温度的增加和荷载频率的减少,沥青混合料的黏性性质会增加,相位角会增大。本研究中当试验温度小于25℃时,从图8a)中的分析结果表明相位角随频率的增大而减小。当温度大于25℃时,从图8b)、c)、d)的试验结果可知,相位角随着的温度的升高会逐渐增大,并且随着频率的增大相位角也有所增大,所以当温度大于25℃时,温度对于相位角的影响更大,温度对于沥青混合料的流变特性产生更大的影响。有相关文献指出[10],当沥青混合料在高温时,相位角有所下降,其主要原因是沥青混合料矿料骨架的影响超过了沥青黏性的影响,因为矿料是弹性材料,相位角为零,所以沥青混合料的相位角会下降。从本试验的研究结果可知,沥青混合料的相位角的变化主要受沥青黏弹性性质的变化引起的。

(3)动态模量主曲线。

利用数学软件1stopt对式(1)的参数进行拟合,确定参考温度(25℃)下Sigmoidal函数中的各个参数的拟合值。绘制动态模量主曲线,如图9所示。

图9显示了铝矾土熟料E、石灰岩以及玄武岩三种集料在两种级配类型SMA-13和AC-13下的动态模量主曲线,反映了不同类型沥青混合料在温度与频率的综合作用下的动态模量值变化规律。但级配SMA-13(石代铝13.2)、SMA-13(石代铝9.5)、SMA-13(石代铝4.75)、SMA-13(石代铝3.26)的动态模量

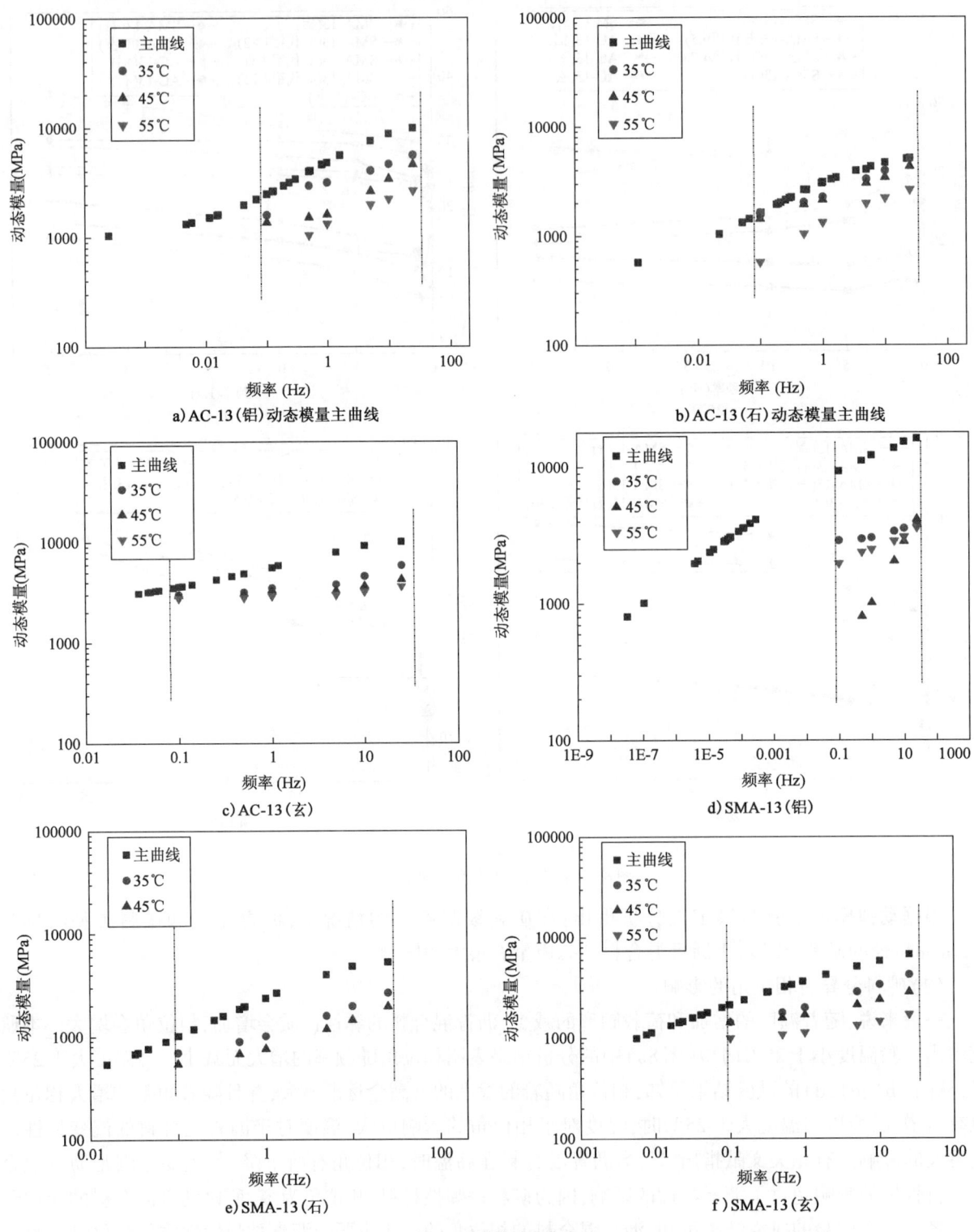

图9 动态模量主曲线

主曲线采用公式(2)无法拟合。可能原因：一方面是由于试验误差造成试验结果偏差较大，拟合结果不理想；另一方面是由于这4个级配的动态模量在参考温度下的变化趋势不符合 Sigmoidal 数学模型所反映的变化趋势。因为这4个级配中采用的矿料是由铝矾土熟料和石灰岩按照不同比例混合而成，铝矾土熟料与石灰岩之间的硬度和密度存在较大差异。在低温状态下，沥青混合料接近弹性材料，沥青混合料中各组分相对位移变化小，动态模量不会产生大的变化。当温度升高后，沥青变软，混合料中各组分，特别是集料之间的相对位移会变大，不同硬度的集料位置会发生重新分布，对动态模量产生较大的影响。

此时,用 Sigmoidal 数学模型在拟合矿料分异沥青混合料动态模量主曲线时就存在一定的局限性。

因此,在动态模量变化趋势的拟合及动态模量预估时,需要考虑集料的特性。Christensen 等[11]于 2015 年提出了改进的 Hirstch 模型,初次引入集料密度以及应力水平等因素,在模型中初次考虑了这些因素对动态模量的影响。上述研究结果表明,混合料中集料类型的变化对动态模量产生较大的影响,特别是当不同种类集料混合使用时。

3.2 铝矾土熟料沥青混合料蠕变性能

为了分析铝矾土熟料与普通集料沥青混合料黏弹性的差异,开展了单轴静态蠕变试验,测试了不同温度下混合料的蠕变变形与时间的关系,对不同类型沥青混合料的黏弹性进行评价。

3.2.1 单轴静态蠕变试验

采用 SMA-13(铝)、SMA-13(石代铝9.5)、SMA-13(石代铝4.75)、SMA-13(石代铝2.36)和 SMA-13(石)5 个级配类型成型马歇尔试件,每种级配类型成型 10 个试件,分为两组,一组试件的测试温度为 25℃,另外一组试件的测试温度为 45℃。试验数据取测试结果的平均值。采用多功能试验机 UTM-130(图6)对 5 个级配的沥青混合料进行蠕变试验研究。以 0.3MPa 作为蠕变加载应力水平。

3.2.2 试验结果分析

单轴静态蠕变试验结果如图 10 和图 11 所示。

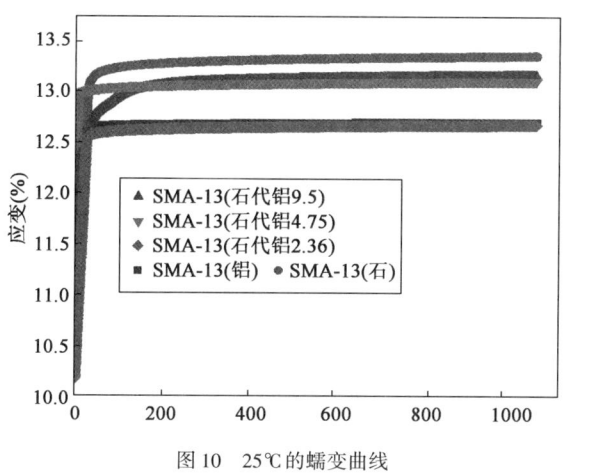

图 10　25℃的蠕变曲线

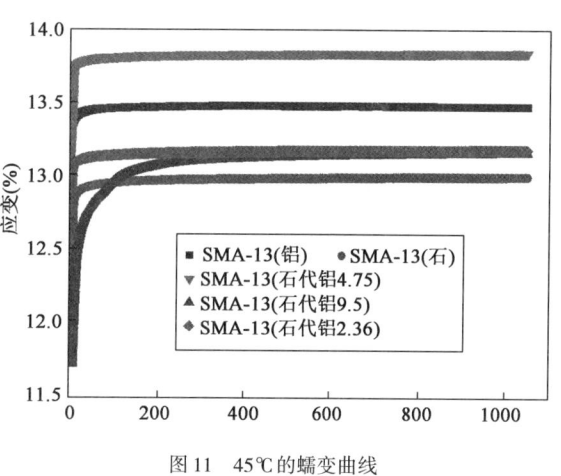

图 11　45℃的蠕变曲线

从图 10 和图 11 对比看出,沥青混合料在不同温度下的蠕变会发生很大的变化。在 25℃时,5 种级配的蠕变曲线较为集中,在 45℃时,5 种级配的蠕变曲线较为分散。温度对混合料的蠕变会产生很大的影响。在 25℃时,相比其他矿料,石灰岩沥青混合料 SMA-13(石)的变形最大,SMA-13(铝)和 SMA-13(石代铝2.36)的变形相对较小,在常温条件下,铝矾土熟料及其分异矿料沥青混合料具有较好的抗蠕变性能。在 45℃时,石灰岩沥青混合料的蠕变变形较小,而铝矾土熟料和分异矿料沥青混合料的蠕变变形变大。同单纯使用劣质集料相比,矿料分异尽管可以在一定程度上提升沥青混合料的抗滑性能,但同时也需要深入分析矿料分异后对沥青混合料力学特性的影响,综合衡量矿料分异型沥青混合料的适用条件及其优劣势。

4　结　语

(1)本文主要对矿料分异型沥青混合料的路用性能和力学参数特性进行了分析,同单独使用铝矾土熟料集料的沥青混合料而言,石灰岩的掺入在一定程度上提升了矿料分异型沥青混合料的路用性能,但在高温时,矿料分异型沥青混合料的蠕变变形会变大。

(2)后续不断完善不同矿料分异型沥青混合料路用性能的研究,可为矿料分异型沥青混合料在抗滑性能和路用性能上的提升做出最优化的分异方案,为矿料分异型沥青混合料在实体工程的应用提供理论依据。

受试验条件和时间的限制,本文采用石灰岩取代相同粒径的铝矾土熟料作为分异方案,没有对其他矿料分异方案的路用性能做对比分析。研究结论只针对本矿料分异方案。

参考文献

[1] Shabani, S., M. Ahmadinejad, M. Ameri. *Developing a Model for Estimation of Polished Stone Value (PSV) of Road Surface Aggregates Based on Petrographic Parameters* [J]. International Journal of Pavement Engineering, 2013. 14(3):242-255.

[2] 王元元,何亮,孙璐.矿料分异处理对沥青混合料抗滑性能的影响[J].东南大学学报(自然科学版),2017,47(06):1216-1220.

[3] 李菁若,张东长,谭巍.粗集料的抗滑耐磨性能评价新方法[J].公路交通科技,2016,33(12):76-82.

[4] Wu, X., N. Zhen, F. Kong. *Effect of Characteristics of Different Types of Bauxite Clinker on Adhesion* [J]. Applied Sciences, 2019, 9(22):4746.

[5] Wu, X., N. Zhen, F. Kong. *Evaluation of the Factors Affecting the Wear Resistance of Calcined Bauxite Aggregates* [J]. Coatings, 2019, 9(11):761.

[6] Wu, X., N. Zhen, F. Kong. *The analysis of the factors affecting the macrotexture of bauxite clinker aggregate gradation* [J]. Construction and Building Materials, 2020(244):118334.

[7] 吴喜荣.基于灰关联熵分析法的沥青混合料抗裂性能影响因素分析[J].水利与建筑工程学报,2017,15(02):92-97.

[8] 梁俊龙.沥青路面动态模量及裂缝扩展研究[D].西安:长安大学,2016.

[9] 薛羽,栗培龙,高朋,等.沥青混合料动态模量主曲线方法对比分析[J].广西大学学报(自然科学版),202.45(1):1-8.

[10] 赵延庆,吴剑,文健.沥青混合料动态模量及其主曲线的确定与分析[J].公路,2006(8):163-168.

[11] Christensen D W, R Bonaquist. *Improved Hirsch Model for Estimating the Modulus of Hot-mix Asphalt* [J]. Road Materials and Pavement Design, 2015, 16(sup2):254-274.

层间黏结状态对沥青路面结构使用寿命的影响分析

孙 强 李 夏 江照伟 韦金城

(山东省交通科学研究院)

摘 要 针对通过层间黏结状态评价沥青路面结构使用寿命的问题,以抗剪强度和抗拉强度作为沥青路面层间黏结状态的评价指标,分析乳化沥青用量和黏层污染对沥青路面层间黏结性能的影响,并使用法国Alize路面结构设计程序计算出了不同层间黏结状态下的路面结构使用寿命。结果表明:乳化沥青用量和层间污染物用量对层间抗剪强度和抗拉强度的影响显著,存在最佳沥青用量使层间黏结性能达到最佳,层间污染物的增加能急剧降低层间黏结性能;层间抗剪强度和抗拉强度之间具有较好的相关性,均可作为评价沥青路面结构层间黏结性能的有效方法;并且随层间黏结性能下降,路面结构使用寿命明显缩短,可拟合出不同乳化沥青用量和污染物用量下的沥青路面结构使用寿命。

关键词 层间黏结状态 抗剪强度 抗拉强度 Alize 使用寿命

国家重点研发计划项目(18YFB1600103)和山东省重点研发计划项目(2019GSF109020)资助。

0 引言

沥青路面是一种性能优良的路面结构,采用层状弹性体理论进行设计,认为各层材料均匀连续。良好的黏层能够使沥青路面结构长时间具备或接近理论设计状态,也是路面结构使用寿命的重要保证,一旦路面结构层间黏结效果降低,层间处于半连续或接近完全光滑状态时,将严重影响路面整体的耐久性。层间黏结状态是沥青路面结构使用寿命的重要影响因素。

近年来,大量学者对评价路面结构层间黏结性能的原材料、破坏机理、试验方法等进行了大量的研究。已有研究成果主要针对影响沥青路面层间黏结性能的单个因素。在此基础上,本文采用室内剪切试验和拉拔试验的评价方法,选用 4cmSMA-13 + 乳化沥青黏层 + 6cmAC-20 的路面结构、改性乳化沥青作为黏层材料,研究乳化沥青用量和污染物对沥青路面层间黏结性能的影响,并分析剪应力与拉应力的相关性,最后采用法国 Alize 路面结构设计程序,研究层间黏结状态对沥青路面结构使用寿命的影响。

1 试验方案

1.1 路面结构组合

在考虑道路表面磨耗等因素的情况下,目前大部分高速公路路面面层采用 SMA + AC 类沥青混合料的组合形式,因此本文采用"4cmSMA-13 + 乳化沥青黏层 + 6cmAC-20"的路面结构组合进行试验,如图 1 所示。

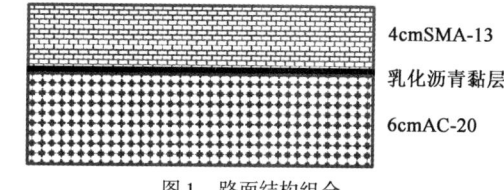

图 1　路面结构组合

1.2 试验方法

剪切试验是目前评价沥青路面结构层间黏结性能的主要方法,但该试验方法不能反映路面结构在车辆竖向荷载作用下的抗拉拔性能,因此本文选择斜面剪切试验和拉拔试验,并对沥青路面结构在受力状态下的剪应力和拉应力进行相关性分析,综合评价路面结构层间黏结性能。

剪切试验采用 40°斜面夹角,加载速度为 2mm/min,试验数据通过应力和位移传感器采集和记录,剪应力通过最大荷载值计算,计算公式如下:

$$\tau = \sin(40°) \times F/S \tag{1}$$

式中:S——试件剪切截面积,为 $7.85 \times 10^{-3} \mathrm{m}^2$。

拉拔试验采用环氧树脂作为黏结材料,采用万能试验机进行拉拔试验,加载速度为 20mm/min。

1.3 影响因素

研究表明,乳化沥青用量和层间污染是影响沥青路面层间黏结状态的两个主要因素。本文选用 5 个乳化沥青用量(表 1)和 4 个污染物用量(表 2)分别进行剪切试验和拉拔试验,研究其对层间剪应力和拉应力的影响程度。

乳化沥青用量　　　　　　　　　　　　　　　　表 1

纯沥青用量(kg/m^2)	0	0.2	0.4	0.6	0.8
乳化沥青用量(kg/m^2)	0	0.37	0.74	1.12	1.49

污染物用量　　　　　　　　　　　　　　　　表 2

污染物用量(g/m^2)	0	100	200	400

2 试验数据分析

2.1 层间黏结性能试验

2.1.1 乳化沥青用量对层间黏结状态的影响

乳化沥青作为沥青路面层间黏结的主要材料,乳化沥青用量的大小是路面层间黏结性能的直接影响因素,不同乳化沥青用量下的试验结果如图2和图3所示。

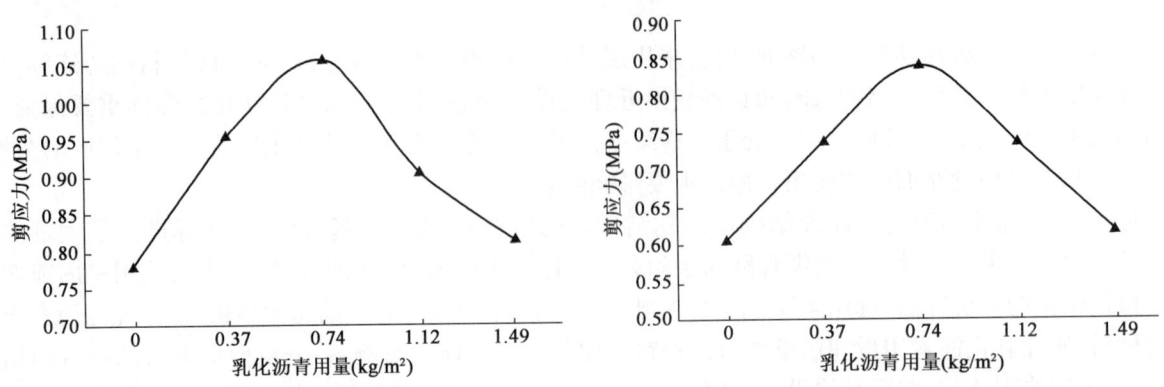

图2 剪应力与乳化沥青用量的关系曲线　　　　图3 拉应力与乳化沥青用量的关系曲线

由试验结果可知,随着乳化沥青用量的增大,在其他实验条件不变的情况下,层间剪应力和拉应力先增大后减小;在乳化沥青用量为$0.74kg/m^2$时达到峰值,故$0.74kg/m^2$为最佳乳化沥青用量,此时明路面结构层间黏结性能最优。在乳化沥青用量达到峰值前,沥青路面结构层接触面未达到完全黏结状态;在乳化沥青用量达到峰值后,沥青路面结构层间存在多余的乳化沥青,形成富油润滑层,降低沥青路面结构层间黏结效果。因此在施工过程中,应确定最佳乳化沥青洒布量,在节约建设成本的基础上保证沥青路面结构层间层间黏结效果。

2.1.2 污染物用量对层间黏结状态的影响

根据乳化沥青用量层间黏结试验结果,选取$0.74kg/m^2$作为乳化沥青用量,研究层间污染物对层间黏结效果的影响。根据相关文献研究和工程实践经验,在上承层施工前,施工环境、设备及人员会对下承层路面有一定的污染,本文采用土作为污染物模拟实际工程中层间污染。不同污染物用量下的试验结果如图4和图5所示。

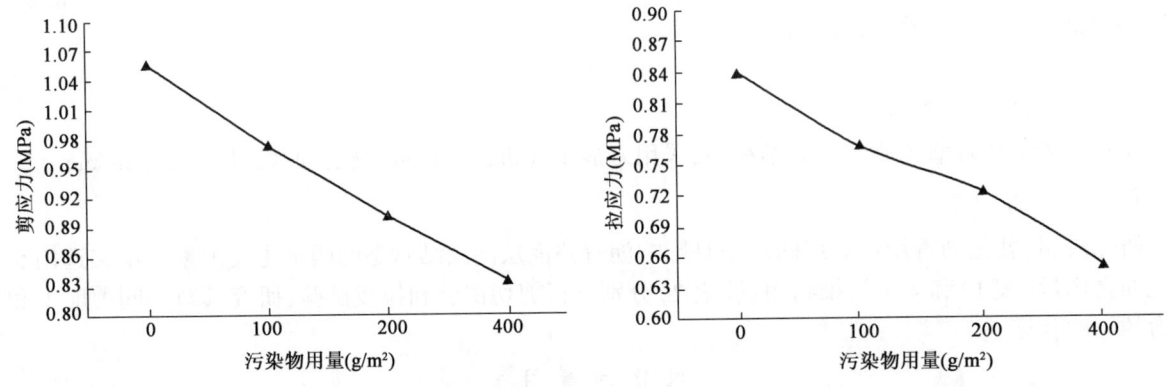

图4 剪应力与污染物用量的关系曲线　　　　图5 拉应力与污染物用量的关系曲线

由试验结果可知,污染物用量与拉应力线性相关,随着污染物用量的增大,在其他实验条件不变的情况下,层间剪应力和拉应力逐渐减小;当污染物用量增大到$400g/m^2$时,层间剪应力和拉应力分别为$0.836MPa$和$0.652MPa$,相比无污染状态时分别降低了20.8%和22.3%。土颗粒的增加减少了乳化沥青与结构层间的接触面积,导致沥青路面结构层架黏结效果降低,因此在实际施工过程中,应尽量减少层间污染,最大限度地保证层间黏结效果。

2.2 剪应力与拉应力的相关性分析

在路面使用过程中沥青路面结构层间黏结性能下降,将导致路面结构失稳、防水性能下降等情况,并引发车辙、坑槽等一系列道路结构病害。据相关研究和实践经验发现,抗剪强度值是室内试验评价层间黏结性能的关键指标,而施工现场多采用拉拔试验进行检测评价。

目前剪切试验和拉拔试验都可作为评价路面结构层间黏结性能的方法,但两种试验方法在加载类型、破坏机理等方面存在明显的区别。本文采用SPSS统计分析软件,对不同乳化沥青用量条件下两种试验数据进行相关性分析,试验数据见表3,分析结果见表4。

不同乳化沥青用量下层间剪应力和拉应力 表3

乳化沥青用量(kg/m²)	0	0.37	0.74	1.12	1.49
剪应力(MPa)	0.782	0.956	1.056	0.906	0.813
拉应力(MPa)	0.607	0.738	0.839	0.735	0.619

抗剪强度和抗拉强度相关性分析结果 表4

分类	指标	抗剪强度	抗拉强度
抗剪强度	Pearson相关性	1	0.987**
	显著性(双侧)		0.002
	N	5	5
抗拉强度	Pearson相关性	0.987**	1
	显著性(双侧)	0.002	
	N	5	5

注:**为在0.01水平(双侧)上显著相关。

由表4可知,由SPSS软件分析结果可知,Pearson相关系数为0.987、显著水平为0.002(双侧),表明两种试验方法的试验数据呈显著正相关关系,即室内剪切试验和现场拉拔试验的试验结果可相互验证,均可作为评价沥青路面结构层间黏结性能的有效方法。

3 层间黏结状态对沥青路面结构使用寿命的影响

法国在路面结构计算方面的研究从第二次世界大战之后广泛开展,如今已形成一套完善的沥青路面结构设计体系,并在全世界广泛应用。近几年,国内越来越多的学者开始研究法国沥青混合料设计方法,并尝试将其优点融入我国沥青混合料设计方法当中。在此背景下,本文采用法国Alize路面结构计算程序进行数值模拟计算。

本文以某工程实例为参考研究层间黏结状态对沥青路面使用寿命的影响,采用法国路面结构设计程序LCPC Alize中inverse compute模块反演了不同层间结合状态对沥青路面使用寿命的影响,计算基本参数见表5,计算结果见表6。

基本计算参数 表5

日平均当量轴次	平均增长率(%)	基准等效温度	设计车道
3192	6	22℃	双向六车道
层位	材料及厚度	模量(MPa)	泊松比
上面层	4cmSMA-13	9000	0.35
中面层	6cmAC-20	9000	0.35
下面层	18cmCTB	9000	0.35
上基层	18cmCTB	18000	0.2
下基层	18cmCTB	18000	0.2
底基层	15cmGB	18000	0.2
土基		90	0.4

计 算 结 果 表6

层间结合状态	完全连续	半连续	完全光滑
使用寿命(年)	14.59	8.39	2.18

由表6可知,相对于完全连续,层间半连续、完全光滑状态下路面使用寿命降幅分别为42.5%和85.1%,表明随层间黏结性能下降,路面结构使用寿命明显缩短。

为了直观地分析乳化沥青用量和污染物用量对沥青路面结构使用寿命的影响,以抗剪强度作为层间黏结状态评价指标,假设剪应力最大时为完全连续状态,剪应力为零时为完全光滑状态,由此可拟合出不同乳化沥青用量和污染物用量下的沥青路面结构使用寿命,具体数据如表7和表8所示。

不同乳化沥青用量下路面结构使用寿命 表7

乳化沥青用量(kg/m²)	0	0.37	0.74	1.12	1.49
剪应力(MPa)	0.782	0.956	1.056	0.906	0.813
使用寿命(年)	11.37	13.42	14.59	12.83	11.74

不同污染物用量下路面结构使用寿命 表8

污染物用量(g/m²)	0	100	200	400
剪应力(MPa)	1.056	0.973	0.902	0.836
使用寿命(年)	14.59	13.62	12.78	12.01

4 结 语

主要结论如下:

(1)层间黏结影响因素试验结果表明,存在最佳乳化沥青用量,乳化沥青用量在0.74kg/m²左右时,抗剪和抗拉拔性能达到最优;层间污染物的增加能急剧降低层间黏结状态。因此在具体施工时应选择最佳乳化沥青洒布量,并尽量减少层间污染。

(2)通过SPSS软件统计分析表明,剪切试验和拉拔试验数据呈显著正相关关系,均可作为评价沥青路面结构层间黏结性能的有效方法。

(3)通过路面结构数值模拟试验表明,相对于层间黏结完全连续状态,层间半连续、完全光滑状态下路面使用寿命降幅分别为42.5%和85.1%,并拟合出不同乳化沥青用量和污染物用量下的沥青路面结构使用寿命,随层间黏结性能下降,路面结构使用寿命明显减少。

参考文献

[1] 靳庆霞,彭斌,田亚磊,等.SBR改性乳化沥青对路面层间粘结效果的影响[J].河北工业大学学报,2019,48(05):55-58.

[2] 田俊壮,孙增智,武书华,等.基于模拟试验的沥青路面层间粘结性能研究[J].公路,2016,61(04):1-6.

[3] 苏新国,颜赫,鲁圣弟,等.沥青路面层间粘结效果影响因素[J].长安大学学报(自然科学版),2013,33(03):21-26+68.

[4] 孙强,胡腾飞,王光勇.沥青路面层间粘结性能试验研究[J].石油沥青,2015,29(03):46-50.

[5] 王磊,王树杰.层间粘结对沥青路面剪切强度及疲劳性能影响研究[J].石油沥青,2017,31(05):27-32.

[6] 杜永安.层间粘结性能对沥青路面抗剪强度的影响[J].交通科技,2012(01):75-78.

[7] 常艳婷,陈忠达,张震,等.沥青路面环氧乳化沥青粘层性能研究[J].武汉大学学报(工学版),2017,50(04):576-582.
[8] 黄开宇.高速公路沥青路面结构层层间粘接状态的研究[J].公路工程,2010,35(02):35-39.
[9] 莫雄,吴昌霞,吴冬兰.基层间接触状态对沥青路面结构受力的影响分析[J].西部交通科技,2014(03):23-28.
[10] 张成志.沥青路面层间抗剪强度影响因素试验研究[J].交通科技,2017(04):146-148.

半刚性基层沥青路面横向裂缝发展规律及影响因素研究

朱玉琴[1]　倪富健[2]　周岚[3]　丛菱[1]

(1.南京工程学院经济与管理学院;2.东南大学交通学院;3.南京道润交通科技有限公司)

摘　要　以反射裂缝为主的横向裂缝是我国高速公路最常见的病害之一。本研究依托江苏省路面养护管理系统中的各项数据,深入分析了半刚性基层沥青路面横向裂缝的发展规律和影响因素。提出了"节点型"和"发展型"两种评价指标类型,并分别计算和分析了这两项评价指标的评价结果。采用JMP软件中的拟合模型功能统计分析了路面结构材料和交通量这两类因素对发展型指标的影响程度,从而识别出显著影响因素。本次研究结果显示,当前未养护路段的横缝间距均值为91.6m,处于"中"等级和"差"等级的各占40%左右。85%的路段在通车3~9年之间首次开裂,影响横缝产生和发展的主要因素为路面各层位混合料类型、交通量以及基层材料类型。

关键词　道路检测与养护　横向裂缝影响因素　拟合模型　半刚性基层沥青路面　评价指标　发展规律

0　引　言

以反射裂缝为主的横向裂缝是半刚性基层沥青路面最常见的病害之一,然而目前该病害对半刚性基层沥青路面结构及功能方面的影响仍没有合理的分析和评价方法[1]。江苏省高速公路的发展历程,与我国高速公路的发展历程十分一致,具有很强的代表性;由东南大学倪富健教授团队开发的路面养护管理系统(PMS)已推广应用近20年,该PMS系统中存储的江苏省内超过4000km的半刚性基层沥青路面的各项信息,其中横向裂缝历年检测结果、路面原始结构信息,交通量信息以及路面养护历史为解决上述问题提供了重要的数据支撑。本研究即基于江苏省PMS系统中的大数据,分析研究半刚性基层沥青路面横向裂缝的发展规律及主要影响因素。

1　半刚性基层沥青路面横向裂缝评价

1.1　评价方法和评价指标

本研究定义了两种类型的评价指标,即节点型指标和发展型指标。节点型指标沿用东南大学周岚博士针对半刚性基层沥青路面横缝状况而提出横缝间距TCS[1,2],对于TCS的分级标准,朱玉琴在周岚的研究基础上,根据TCS的评价结果将横向裂缝状况分为了优、中、差三个级别[3]。

为了本次研究目标,拟定了出现横向开裂的路龄和每公里横缝数量增长速率(条/年)这两项发展型评价指标,评价半刚性基层沥青路面横向裂缝的发展规律,进而深入分析其影响因素[3]。

基金信息:南京工程学院人才引进基金"高速公路服役状态评价及病害预测研究"(YK201988)。

1.2 评价结果

1.2.1 节点型指标评价结果

为了反映未经养护的原始路面结构的横向裂缝状况,从江苏省高速公路网中整理出291段从通车至今未养护路段,总里程为854.18km,来自江苏省的15条高速公路。截至2019年横缝间距频率分布图如图1所示,横缝间距等级分布图如图2所示。

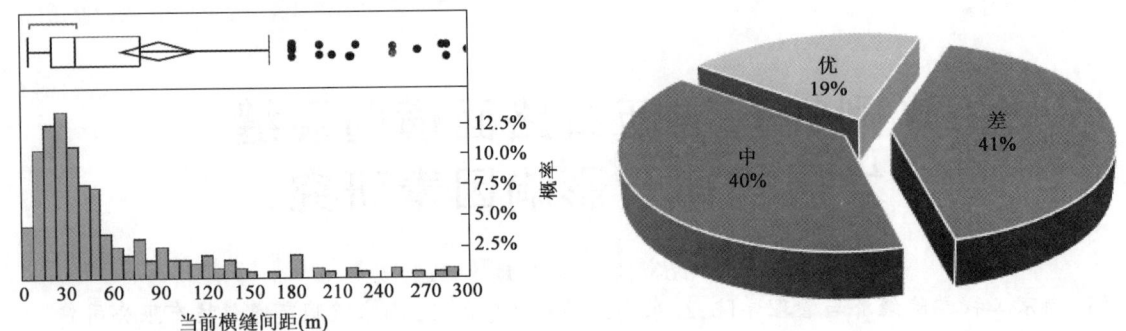

图1 当前未养护路段横缝间距频率分布图　　　　图2 当前未养护路段横缝间距等级分布图

根据统计结果,截至2019年统计路段的横缝间距均值为91.6m,标准差为207.32m,变异系数为226.34%。横缝间距的变异系数较大,表明横缝间距的分布状况比较分散,波动水平较大。统计路段中横缝间距处于"优"等级的不足20%,而处于"差"等级的超过40%,表明这些路段中的横缝状况不算良好。主要原因是大部分运营至今路龄较长,且均未经养护。

1.2.2 发展型指标评价结果

随着通车时间的增长,各路段逐渐开始出现横向开裂。图3为统计路段首次出现横向裂缝的路龄分布图。

从图中可以看出,累计约50%的路段与通车4年后出现横向开裂,通车9年后,超过85%的路段已产生横向裂缝。所有统计的未养护路段首次开裂的路龄均值为5.14年。统计路段总里程中约21%比例的路段在通车4至5年后产生横向开裂,约18%比例的路段在通车6至7年后产生横向开裂。

统计路段每公里横缝数量增长速率频率分布如图4所示。由统计可知,每公里横缝数量增长速率均值是4.42条/年。约25%里程的路段每年每公里横缝增加低于2条;约32%里程的统计路段每年每公里横缝增加[2,4)条/年;分布在[4,8)条/年的路段里程占比31%;约12%里程的路段每年每公里横向裂缝增加数量不低于8条,该比例的路段横向裂缝增长较快。结合其他统计数据分析,横向裂缝增长速度较快的时段集中在通车后5~10年期间。

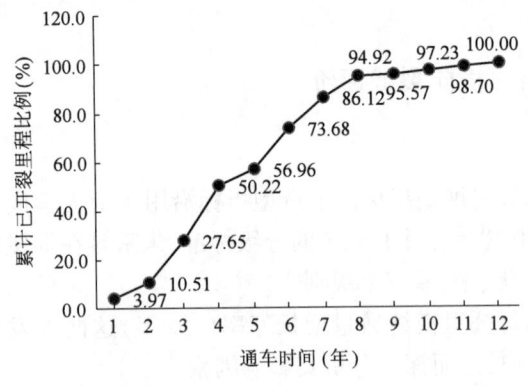

图3 随路龄发展已开裂路段里程累计比例状况

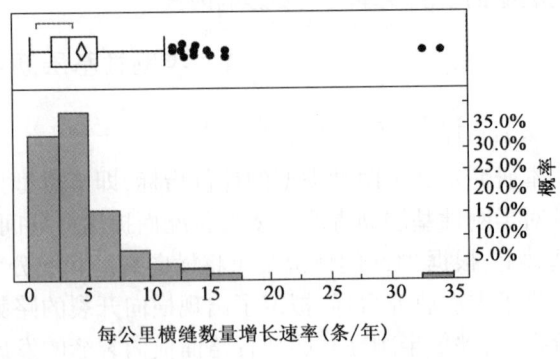

图4 每公里横缝数量增长速率

2 横向裂缝发展型指标影响因素

本研究筛选的可能影响横向裂缝发展的各类因素及对应水平如表1所示。采用JMP软件中的拟合模型功能分析各因素对发展型指标的影响显著性。概率 $>F$ 的结果小于 α 水平 0.05 即表明因素的影响显著。

横向裂缝评价指标影响因素　　表1

影响因素类型	影响因素名称	水　平
路面结构类因素	路面结构总厚度(cm)	71,73,74,75,76,77,78,80
	面层改性沥青层厚度(cm)	4,10,18
	级配类型-上面层	AK-13,SMA-13,AK-16,SUP-13,OGFC-13
	级配类型-中面层	SUP-20,AC-20,AC-25
	级配类型-下面层	SUP-25,AC-25
	基层材料类型	水泥稳定基层,二灰稳定基层,复合基层
交通量类因素	交通荷载等级	轻、中、重、特重
	年均车道累计轴载作用次数 YESAL(万次)	实际检测水平
	年均车道日交通量 AADT(辆)	
	货车比例(%)	

2.1 路面横向开裂路龄的影响因素

各显著因素的均值比较结果如图5所示,目标因素 X 是否对评价指标 Y 产生显著影响结果如表2所示(表中 <0.05 的 P 值用 * 号标出)。

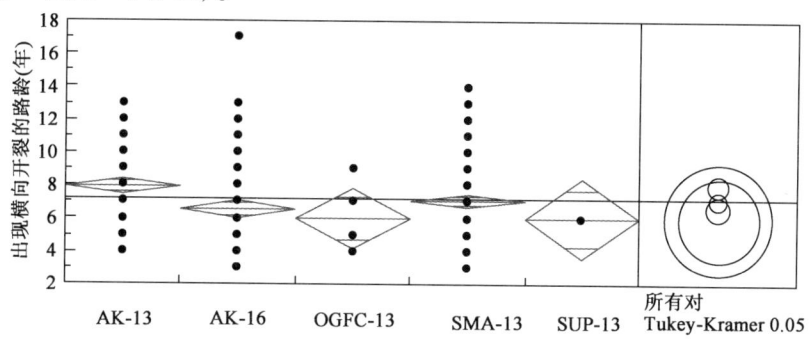

a) 级配类型-上面层

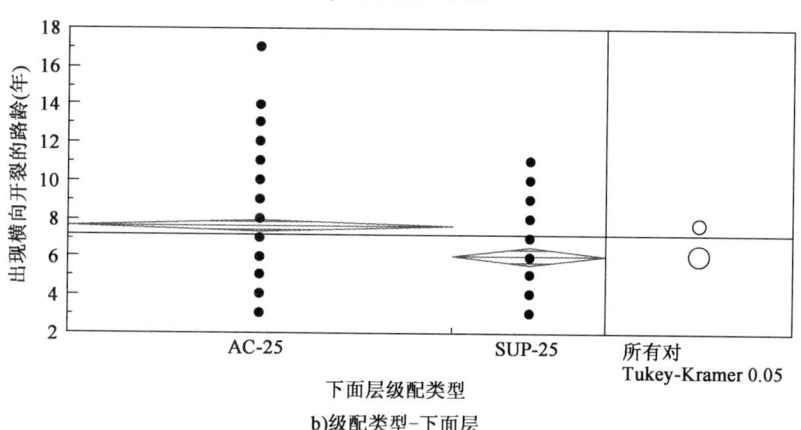

b) 级配类型-下面层

图　5

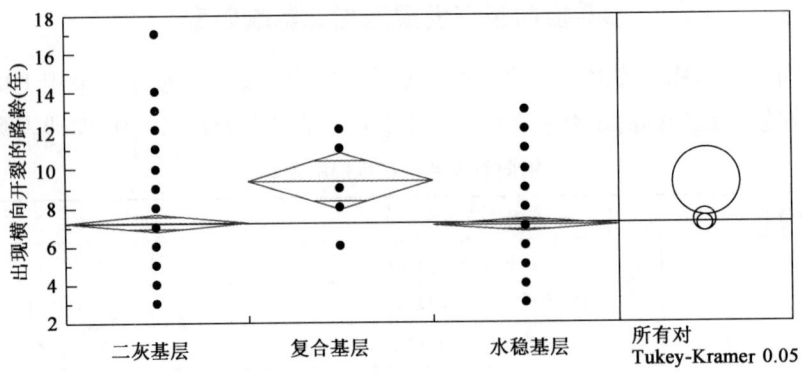

c) 基层材料类型

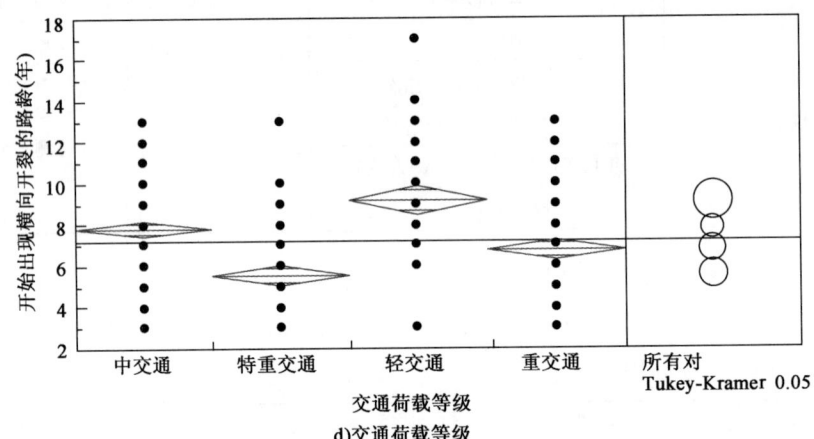

d) 交通荷载等级

图 5 影响首次出现横向裂缝路龄的显著因素均值比较结果

出现横向开裂的路龄(Y)的影响因素显著性分析结果　　　　表 2

影响因素(X)	参数数目	自由度	平方和	F 比	P
级配类型-上面层	4	4	44.99	3.23	0.0128*
级配类型-中面层	2	2	11.47	1.65	0.1942
级配类型-下面层	1	1	24.87	7.14	0.0079*
基层材料类型	2	2	51.67	7.42	0.0007*
面层改性沥青层厚度	1	1	12.03	2.94	0.0875
路面结构总厚度(cm)	1	1	0.80	0.23	0.6321
交通荷载等级	3	3	214.37	20.52	<.0001*
年均车道累计轴载作用次数 YESAL(万次)	1	1	2.59	0.74	0.3891
年均车道日交通量 AADT(辆/日)	1	1	94.90	27.25	<.0001*
货车比例(%)	1	1	49.18	14.12	0.0002*

由分析结果可知，上面层级配类型、下面层级配类型、基层类型、车道日均交通量及交通荷载等级这几项因素对路面首次横向开裂的路龄具有显著影响。

对于级配类型-上面层因素，采用 OGFC-13 开级配的路段及采用 SUP-13 级配的路段首次出现横向开裂的路龄最早，均值为 6.00 年；采用 AK-13 级配及 SMA-13 级配的路段均约在通车后 7 年左右首次出现横向裂缝。

级配类型-下面层因素同样是影响首次横向开裂路龄的显著因素,采用SUP-25级配的路段首次开裂路龄早于采用AC-25级配的路段,前者均值为6.05年,后者均值为7.64年,二者相差1.6年左右。

面层沥青材料方面,改性沥青层厚度较为显著地影响出现横向开裂的路龄。

基层材料类型同样显著影响路面首次出现横向裂缝的路龄。在统计路段中复合基层的结构形式由下而上依次为:20cm水泥稳定碎石的、9cm水泥稳定碎石、9cm沥青稳定碎石,基层总厚度为38cm。采用该复合基层的路段路面首次出现横向开裂的路龄显著晚于二灰基层及水稳基层,均值达到9.36年。

从交通荷载等级方面来看,属特重交通的统计路段首次出现横向开裂的路龄均值为5.54年,属轻交通的统计路段首次出现横向开裂的路龄均值为9.18年,二者差异显著。

2.2 每公里横缝数量增长速率及影响因素

目标因素X是否对评价指标Y产生显著影响结果如表3(表中<0.05的P值用*号标出)所示。每公里横缝数量增长速率显著因素的均值比较结果如图6所示。

每公里横缝数量发展速率(Y)的影响因素显著性分析结果 表3

影响因素(X)	参数数目	自由度	平方和	F比	P
级配类型-上面层	4	4	184.34	3.52	0.0078*
级配类型-中面层	2	2	10.93	0.42	0.6593
级配类型-下面层	1	1	3.92	0.30	0.5845
基层材料类型	2	2	115.22	4.40	0.0130*
改性沥青层厚度(cm)	1	1	24.06	1.84	0.1763
路面结构总厚度(cm)	1	1	11.46	0.87	0.3503
交通荷载等级	3	3	113.35	2.88	0.0358*
年均车道累计轴载作用次数YESALS	1	1	6.26	0.48	0.4899
车道年均AADT(辆/日)	1	1	22.00	1.68	0.1958
货车比例(%)	1	1	446.14	34.05	<.0001*

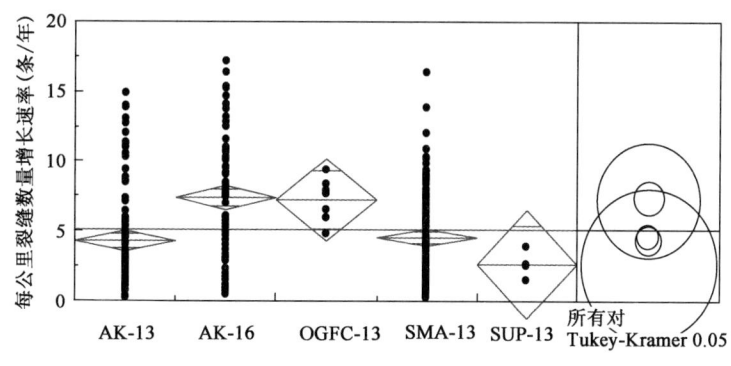

a)级配类型-上面层

图 6

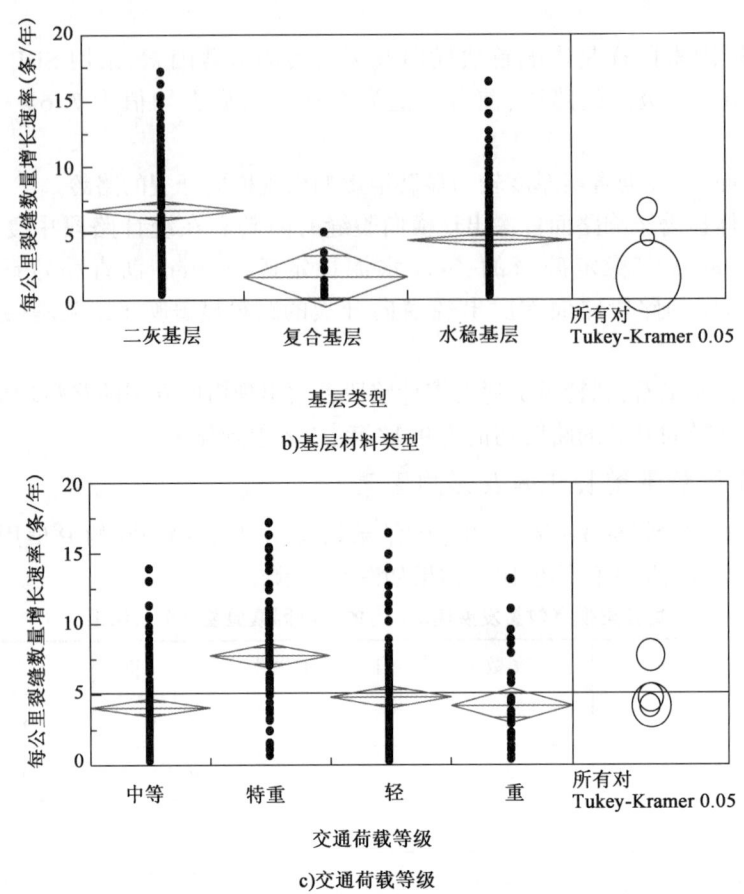

图6 每公里横缝数量增长速率显著影响因素均值比较结果

由统计分析结果可看出,上面层级配类型、基层类型、货车比例及交通荷载等级这几项因素均对每公里裂缝数量发展速率具有显著影响。

上面层各级配类型的影响方面,采用 SUP-13 级配的路段里程较少,已有 SUP-13 路段每公里裂缝数量发展速率较采用其他级配类型的路段慢。采用 AK-13 级配与采用 SMA-13 路段的裂缝发展速率相差不大,每年每公里均增加 4 条左右;在延迟开裂方面,采用 SMA-13 级配的路段略优于采用 AK-13 级配的路段;采用 AK-16 级配与采用 OGFC-13 开级配的路段横向裂缝发展速率均较快,每年每公里增加约 7 条横向裂缝。参考这两类级配类型路段的交通量等级,采用 AK-16 的路段均为重交通和特重交通荷载等级的路段,但采用 OGFC-13 的路段为中交通等级。因此在相似外部条件下,采用 OGFC-13 开级配类型路面开裂路龄最早,发展速率最快,抗裂性能比其他各级配类型路面差。

基层材料类型的影响方面,采用二灰基层路段的裂缝发展速率比采用水稳基层的路段要快:前者均值为 6.72 条/年,后者均值为 4.46 条/年,二者差异显著。

交通荷载等级的影响方面,属特重交通的统计路段每公里横缝数量发展速率均值为 7.75 条/年,属轻交通的统计路段每公里横缝数量发展速率均值为 4.06 条/年,二者差异显著。

3 结　语

根据超过 800km 未经养护的半刚性基层沥青路面路段的近 20 年内横向裂缝检测数据、交通量数据以及路面结构信息的综合统计分析,针对横向裂缝的发展规律和影响因素的研究可以得出如下几点主要结论:

(1)目前半刚性基层沥青路面的 TCS 分布较为离散,处于"中"等级和"差"等级的各占 40% 左右;85% 的路段首次开裂路龄在 3~9 年,均值为 5.14 年。

(2) 路面结构类型方面：上面层级配、下面层级配和基层类型均显著影响出现横向开裂的路龄；上面层材料级配类型显著影响每公里横缝数量发展速率。基层类型对横向裂缝的发展影响显著主要体现在复合基层与传统的半刚性基层的性能差异上。

(3) 沥青材料方面，改性沥青层厚度较为显著地影响出现横向开裂的路龄。

(4) 交通荷载等级显著影响横向裂缝起裂路龄和发展速率，但结合其他数据分析结果，交通荷载等级对横向裂缝开裂过程的影响程度随着基层开裂的能量逐步释放而逐渐减弱。

参考文献

[1] 周岚. 高速公路沥青路面使用性能评价及预测研究[D]. 南京：东南大学，2015.

[2] Zhou Lan, Ni Fujian, Zhao Yan-jing. Evaluation Method for Transverse Cracking in Asphalt Pavements on Freeways[J]. Transportation Research Record, 2010, 2153, 97-105.

[3] 朱玉琴. 半刚性基层沥青路面设计控制指标研究[D]. 南京：东南大学，2019.

[4] Alaswadko N, Hassan R, Meyer D, et al. Probabilistic Prediction Models for Crack Initiation and Progression of spray Sealed Pavements[J]. International Journal of Pavement Engineering, 2016:1-11.

[5] Dave E V, Hoplin C. Flexible Pavement Thermal Cracking Performance Sensitivity to Fracture Energy Variation of Asphalt Mixtures[J]. Road Materials and Pavement Design, 2015, 16(sup1):423-441.

平交口抗车辙沥青路面结构与材料一体化设计研究

蒋应军　倪辰秧　张　宇　易　勇　邓长清

（长安大学）

摘　要　为了提高平交口沥青路面抗车辙性能，通过分析平交口路面力学特征，确定了平交口沥青路面结构层材料，提出了平交口抗车辙路面结构并进行了力学验算。结果表明：沥青路面上面层厚度宜为4cm，推荐采用骨架密实型AC-13或AC-16普通沥青混合料，亦可采用SMA-13或SMA-16；中面层厚度宜取6cm，采用骨架密实型AC-25高模量沥青混合料；下面层厚度宜为5cm，采用骨架密实型AC-20普通沥青混合料。与传统路面结构受力特征相比，本文推荐的抗车辙沥青路面结构面层最大剪应力降低9%~13%，面层层底拉应力降低60%；不同水平荷载作用下，抗车辙路面结构面层最大剪应力降低9%~11%。

关键词　平交口　抗车辙沥青路面　路面结构　力学响应

0　引　言

车辆常在道路平交口附近制动停驻和起动，导致路面车辙、推移、拥包等病害问题频发。研究认为平交口沥青路面损坏的主要原因是路面承受的荷载作用时间较长和加速减速、制动起动产生的附加水平力[1-2]。平交口抗车辙技术措施主要包括路面结构的优化[3-6]、沥青的改性和级配的改进[7-9]以及施工工艺的改良[10-11]等。这些研究对于道路平交口沥青路面的车辙防治起到了推动作用，但没有将平交口受力特征与平交口路面结构组合及材料设计有机结合起来，且我国沥青路面设计仍采用静态竖向荷载，忽略了平交口由于加减速引起的剪应力对路面力学响应的影响，导致所设计的路面结构抗剪强度与抗车辙能力不足。

基金项目：河南省交通运输厅科技项目（2020J-2-2）。

基于非平交口路段沥青路面的面层结构与材料研究较多[12-13]，但与非平交口沥青路面相比，平交口沥青路面在交通特性、受力特征等方面差异较大，传统的面层结构与材料研究无法直接应用于平交口路面，因此本文根据平交口路面力学特征，对各结构层材料进行优化设计，实现平交口路面结构与材料一体化设计，提升平交口沥青路面抗车辙性能。

1 沥青路面各结构层力学行为

1.1 沥青路面力学行为分析模型

1.1.1 路面结构及计算参数

选用平交口沥青路面的基本结构及计算参数如图1所示。括号内为计算拉应力用模量，土基回弹模量均取60MPa，土基泊松比为0.35，其余材料泊松比为0.25。

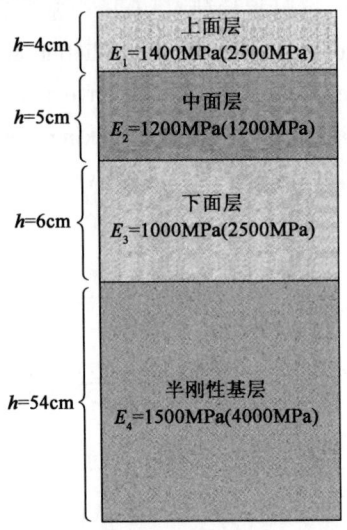

图1 沥青路面基本结构及计算参数

1.1.2 荷载及计算点

采用双圆均布竖向荷载作为计算荷载，取为0.7MPa；水平力系数取0、0.2、0.3、0.5[14]。计算点简化模型如图2所示，计算圆半径$R=106.5$mm，O_1、O_2点坐标为$(-159.75,0)$和$(159.75,0)$，B、C分别为AO_2、DO_2中点。

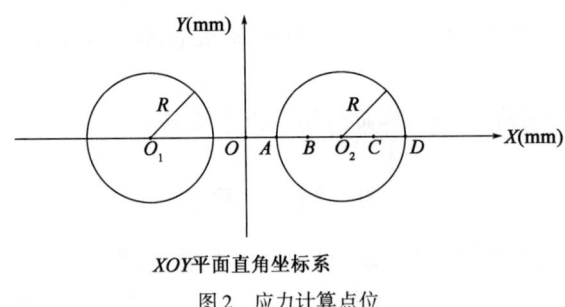

图2 应力计算点位

1.2 沥青路面力学行为

1.2.1 沥青面层剪应力

0.7MPa荷载作用下沥青面层剪应力分布规律如图3所示。C点和D点沥青面层剪应力分布规律如图4所示。

图3表明，沥青路面剪应力较大区域在中上面层内，深度3~9cm范围。其中，D点深度3cm处为沥青上面层最大剪应力位置，C点深度6cm处为中面层最大剪应力位置，因此，不同水平荷载上面层剪应力

研究点位确定为 D 点,不同水平荷载中面层剪应力研究点位确定为 C 点。

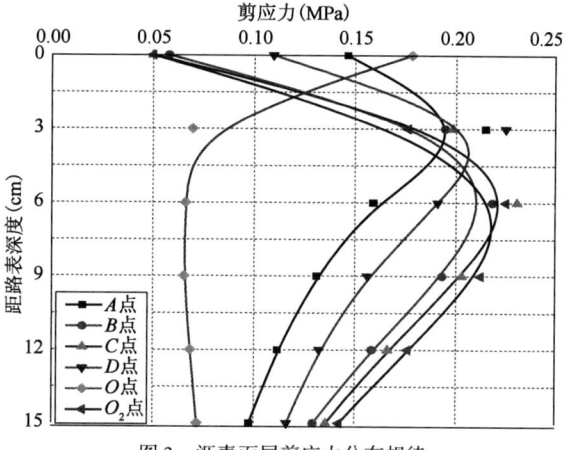

图3　沥青面层剪应力分布规律

图4表明,沥青路面上面层(D点)、中面层(C点)的剪应力随水平荷载的增加而增大,上面层最大剪应力位置出现在路表,同时在0～3cm路面深度范围,剪应力急剧下降,路面深度超过3cm后,水平荷载对剪应力几乎没有影响。0.14MPa、0.21MPa水平荷载作用时中面层最大剪应力位置依然在距路表深度6cm处,0.35MPa水平荷载时中面层最大剪应力位置出现在路表。

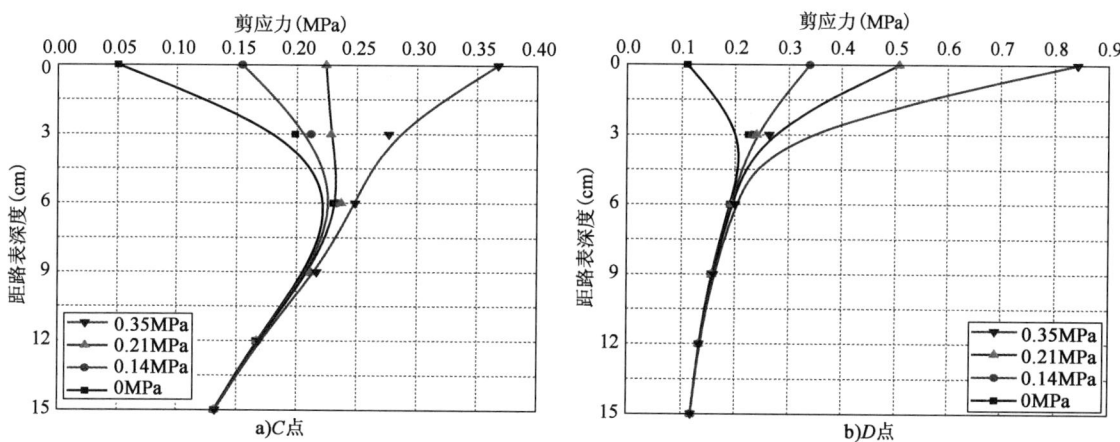

图4　沥青路面不同水平荷载对 C 点和 D 点剪应力的影响

1.2.2 沥青面层拉应力

0.7MPa荷载作用下沥青面层拉应力分布规律如图5所示。不同荷载作用下 O 点和 D 点沥青面层拉应力分布规律如图6所示。

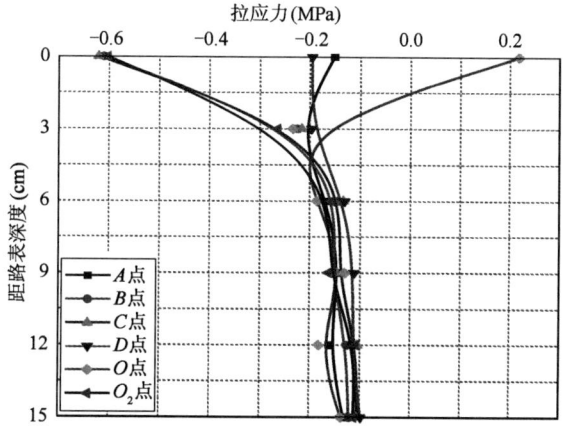

图5　沥青面层拉应力分布规律

图 5 表明,沥青路面路表 O 点受拉应力作用,而沥青面层深度 1.5cm 以下,计算特征点位均受压应力作用,沥青层底 D 点最接近受拉状态,因此,沥青路表拉应力研究点位确定为 O 点,沥青面层层底拉应力研究点位确定为 D 点。

图 6 表明,水平荷载对沥青面层 O 点、D 点拉应力没有影响。

a)O点 b)D点

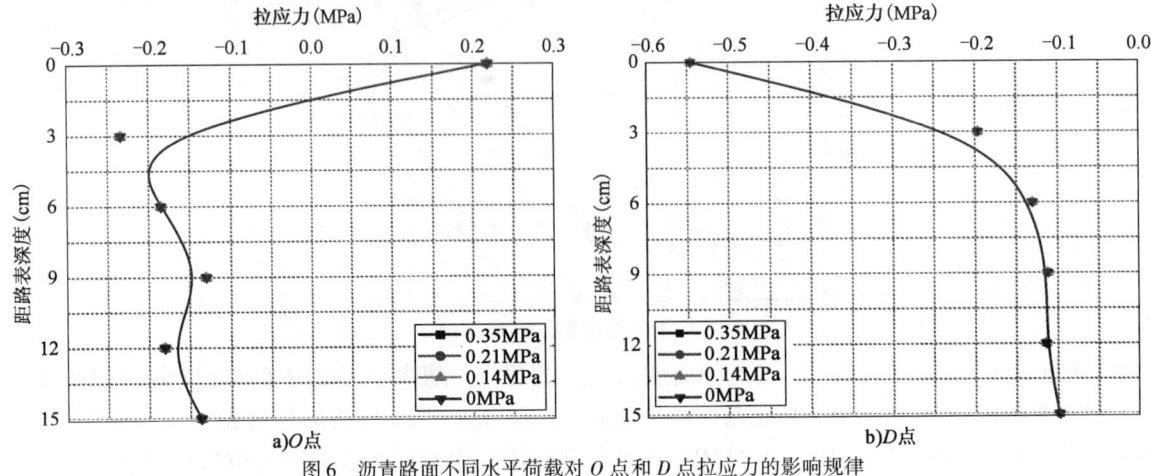

图 6 沥青路面不同水平荷载对 O 点和 D 点拉应力的影响规律

2 平交口抗车辙沥青路面结构与材料一体化设计

2.1 上面层

各结构层剪应力及拉应力受上面层厚度及模量变化的影响规律如图 7 所示。

a)C点深度6cm剪应力

b)D点深度3cm剪应力

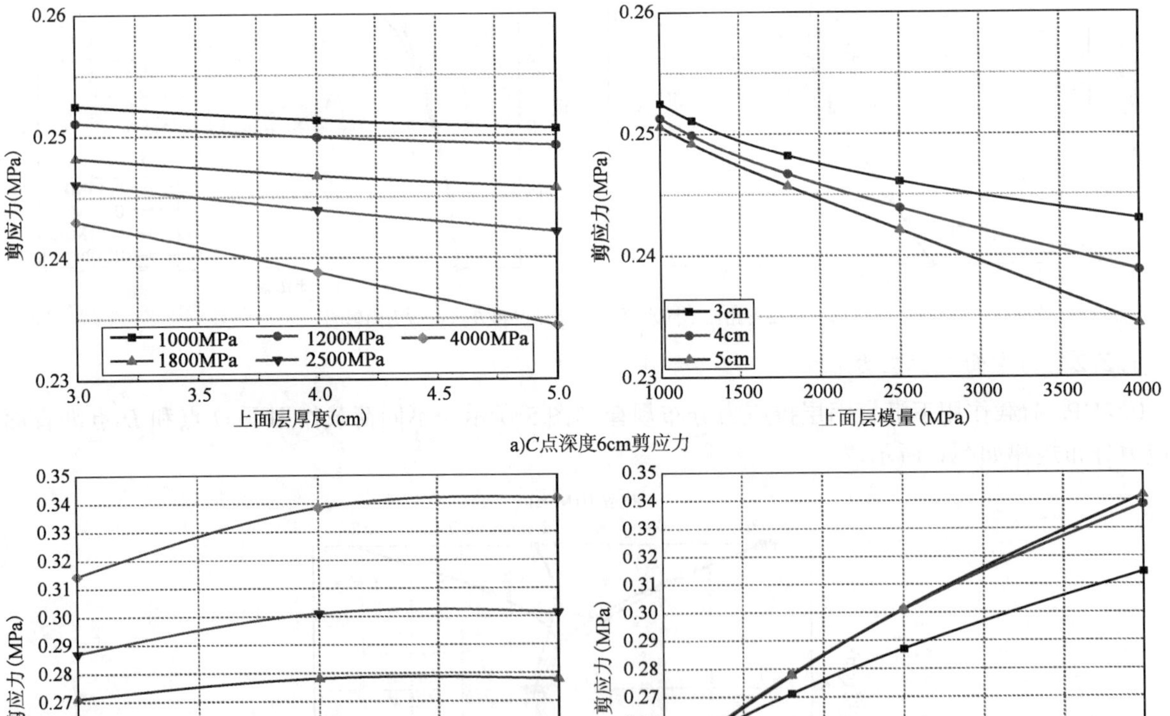

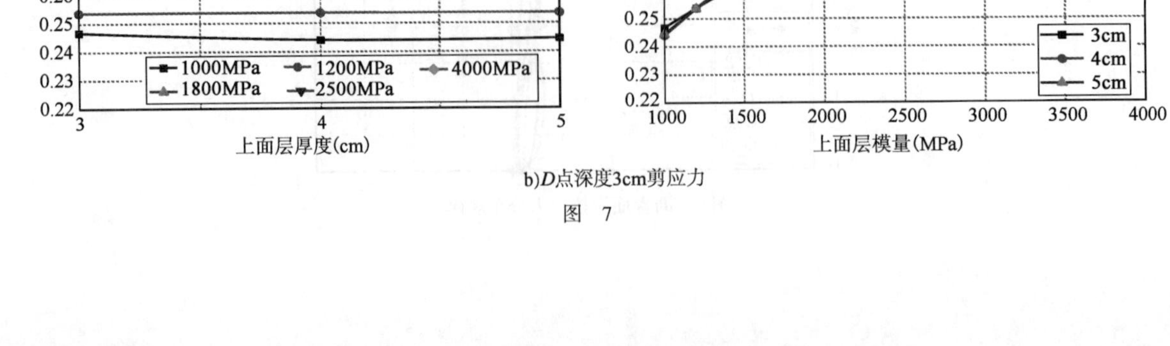

图 7

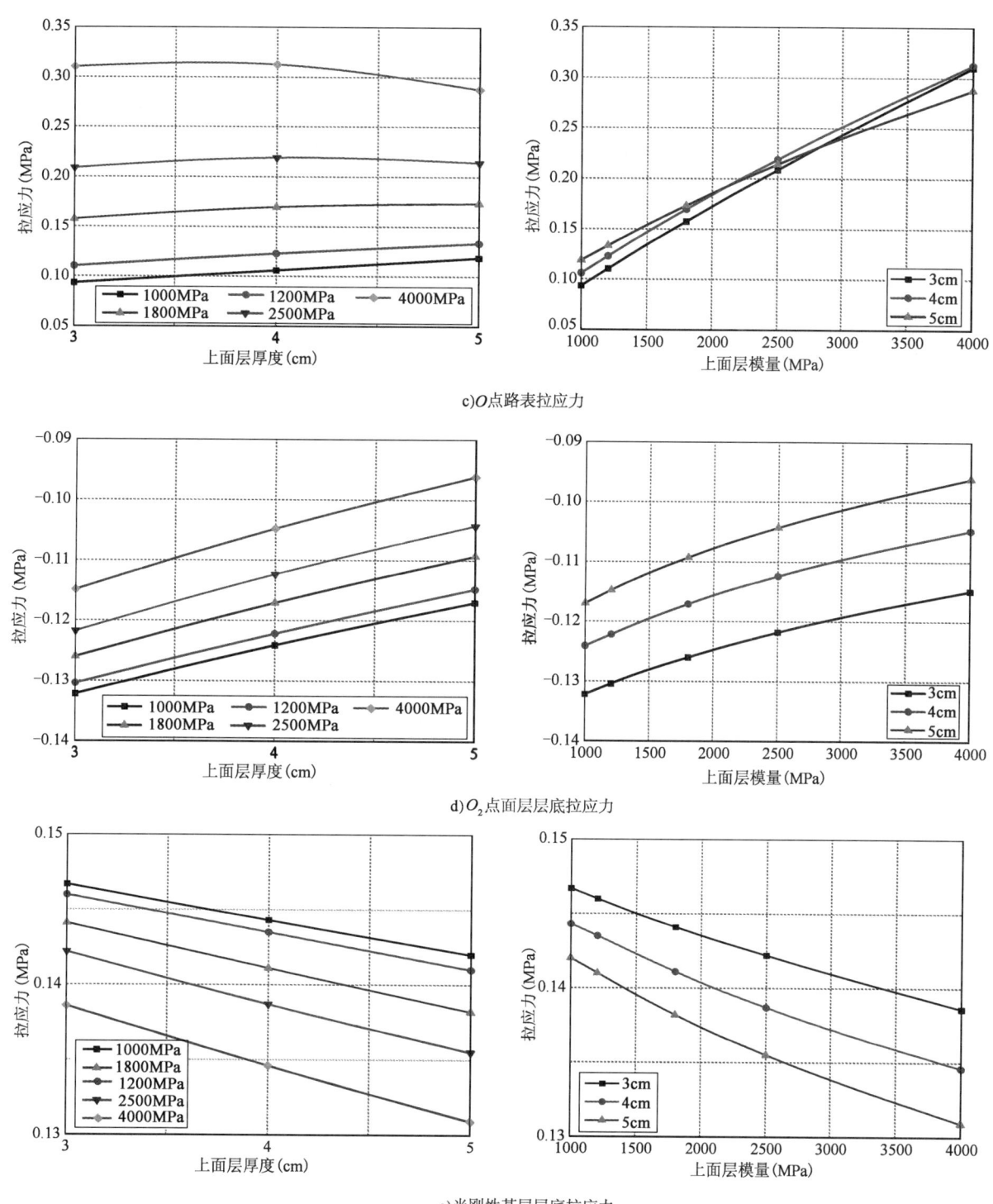

c) O 点路表拉应力

d) O_2 点面层层底拉应力

e) 半刚性基层层底拉应力

图 7 路面各结构层应力的变化情况

图 7 表明：

① 上面层厚度由 3cm 增大到 5cm 时，上面层模量为 1000~2500MPa，路表拉应力约增大 12%；上面层模量为 4000MPa 时，路表拉应力约降低 8%，沥青面层剪应力变化不足 5%，基层层底拉应力降低 5%~10%；

② 上面层模量由 1000MPa 增大到 4000MPa 时，C 点深度 6cm 剪应力约降低 5%，D 点深度 3cm 剪应力约增加 35%，路表拉应力增加 200%，基层层底拉应力变化不超过 7%。

综上，上面层剪应力和路表拉应力最大剪应力多位于路面深度 0~3cm 或 5~7cm 处。因此，上面层厚度建议值取为4cm,宜选用AC-13或AC-16,亦可采用SMA-13或SMA-16。

2.2 中面层

路面各结构层剪应力及拉应力受中面层厚度及模量变化的影响规律如图8所示。

图8表明:

①中面层模量由1000MPa增至4000MPa,D点深度3cm剪应力约降低11%,且随中面层厚度增大剪应力降低幅度增加,中面层厚度较大时C点深度6cm剪应力约降低10%,沥青路表拉应力约降低82%,基层拉应力约降低5%;

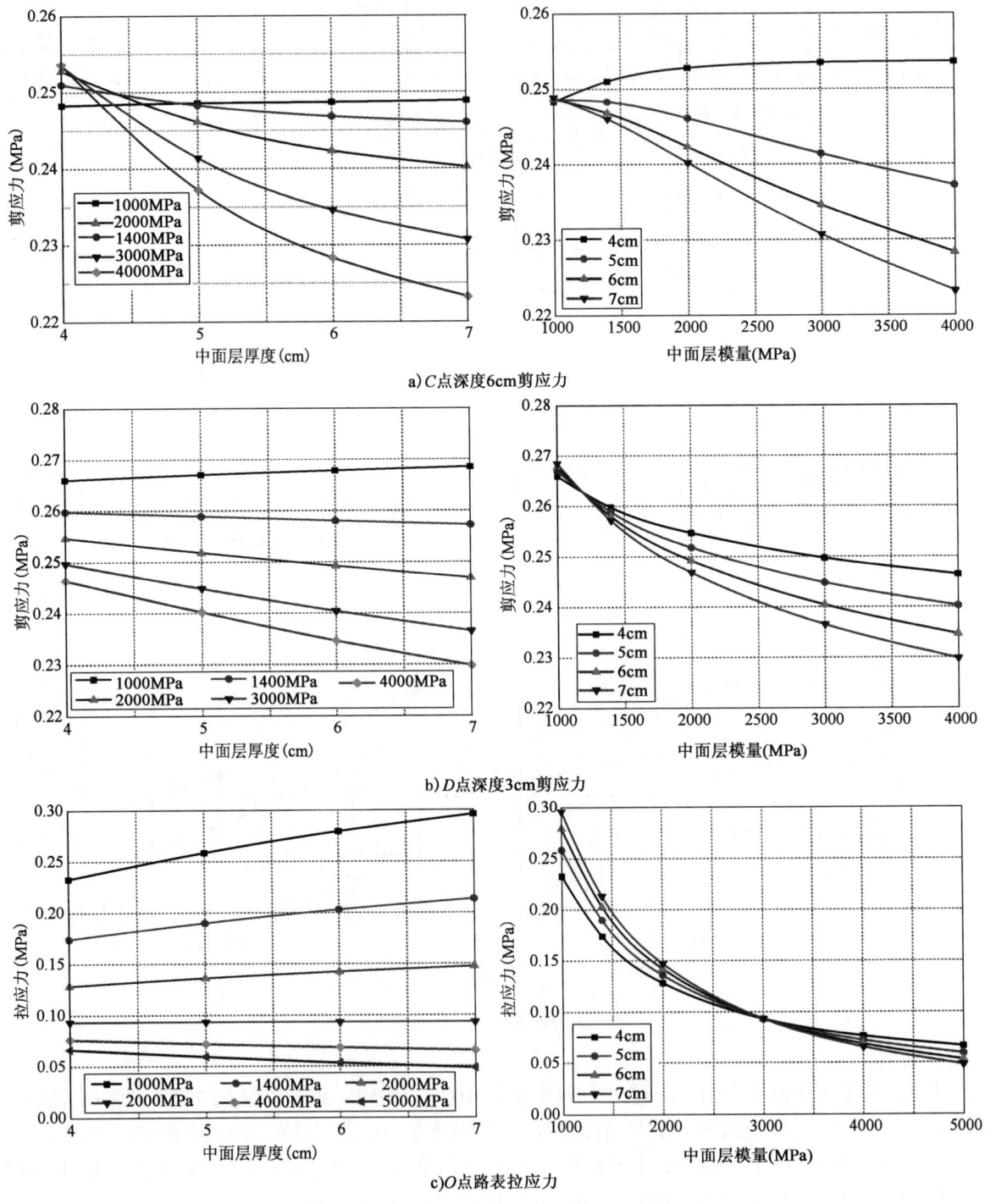

图 8

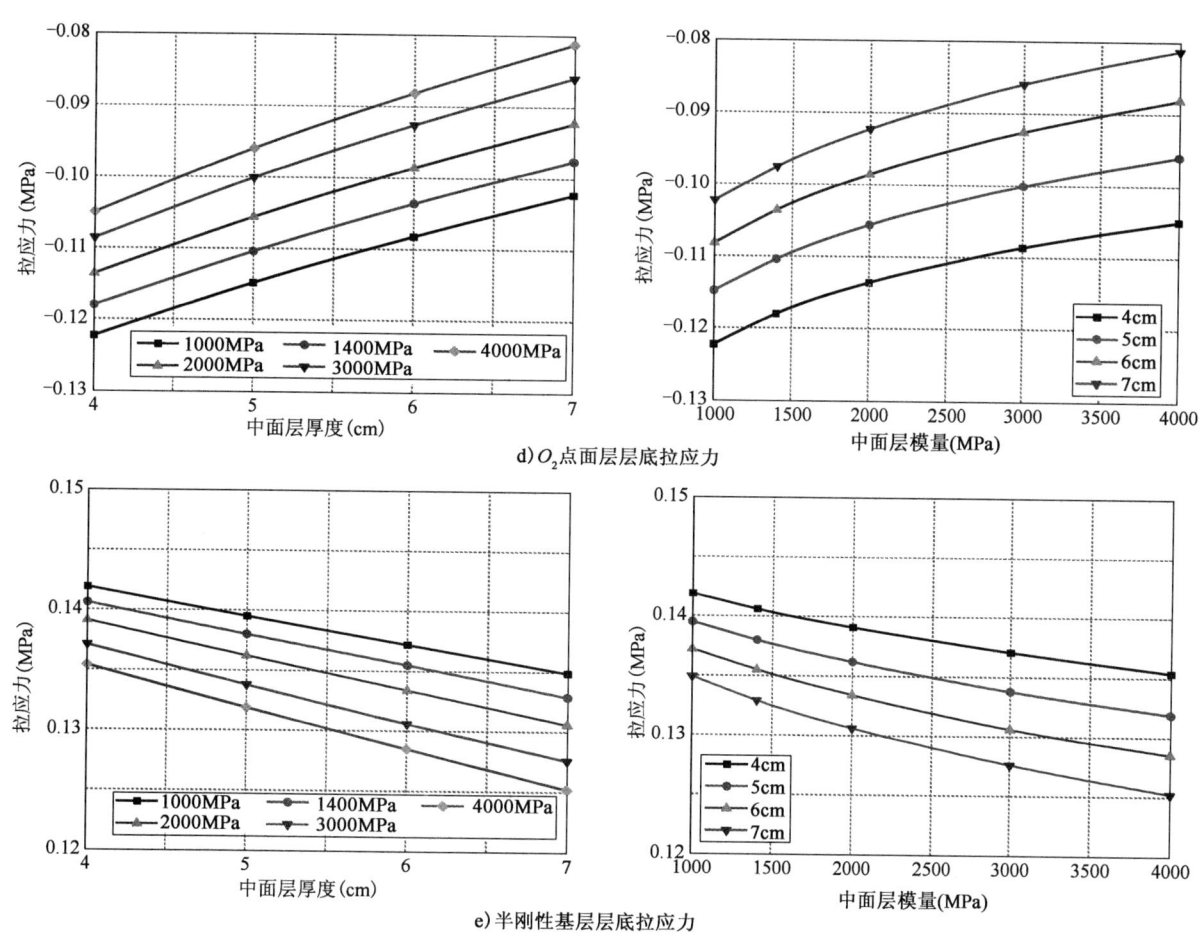

图8 路面各结构层应力的变化情况

②中面层厚度由 4cm 增加到 7cm 时,中面层模量较高时路表拉应力约降低 17%,基层拉应力约降低 7%,中面层模量较高时中面层剪应力约降低 10%,上面层剪应力变化不足 6%。

综上,平交口沥青路面结构层的剪应力和拉应力随中面层厚度、模量增加而显著下降,但中面层厚度超过 6cm 后,路表拉应力和面层剪应力变化不大。因此,中面层材料应具有较高的模量,厚度宜为 6cm。

沥青混合料抗剪强度和回弹模量随集料粒径增大而增大,其动态模量与集料粒径也是正相关关系[15-16]。因而,AC-25 型沥青混合料适用于中面层。

2.3 下面层

路面各结构层剪应力及拉应力受下面层厚度及模量变化的影响规律如图9所示。

图9表明:

①下面层模量由 1000MPa 增至 4000MPa,路表拉应力约降低 27%,基层层底拉应力降低不超过 7%,面层剪应力降低不足 8%;

②下面层厚度从 4cm 增加到 7cm 时,下面层模量较大时路表拉应力约增加 8%,基层层底拉应力变化不超过 7%,面层剪应力变化不超过 2%。

综上,沥青路面面层剪应力、拉应力及基层拉应力几乎不受下面层厚度的影响,但下面层厚度增加导致面层层底由受压急速向受拉转变。综合考虑,下面层宜采用 AC-20 型沥青混合料,厚度建议值为 5cm。

2.4 平交口抗车辙沥青路面结构

基于平交口沥青路面结构组合理论,提出路面结构组合形式见表1。

平交口抗车辙结构组合形式　　　　　表1

路面结构层	结构层厚度(cm)	各结构层材料选取
上面层	4	AC-13/16 或 SMA-13/16（禁用高模量沥青混合料）
中面层	6~7	AC-25（宜掺加高模量剂、抗车辙剂）
下面层	5~6	AC-20（普通沥青混合料）

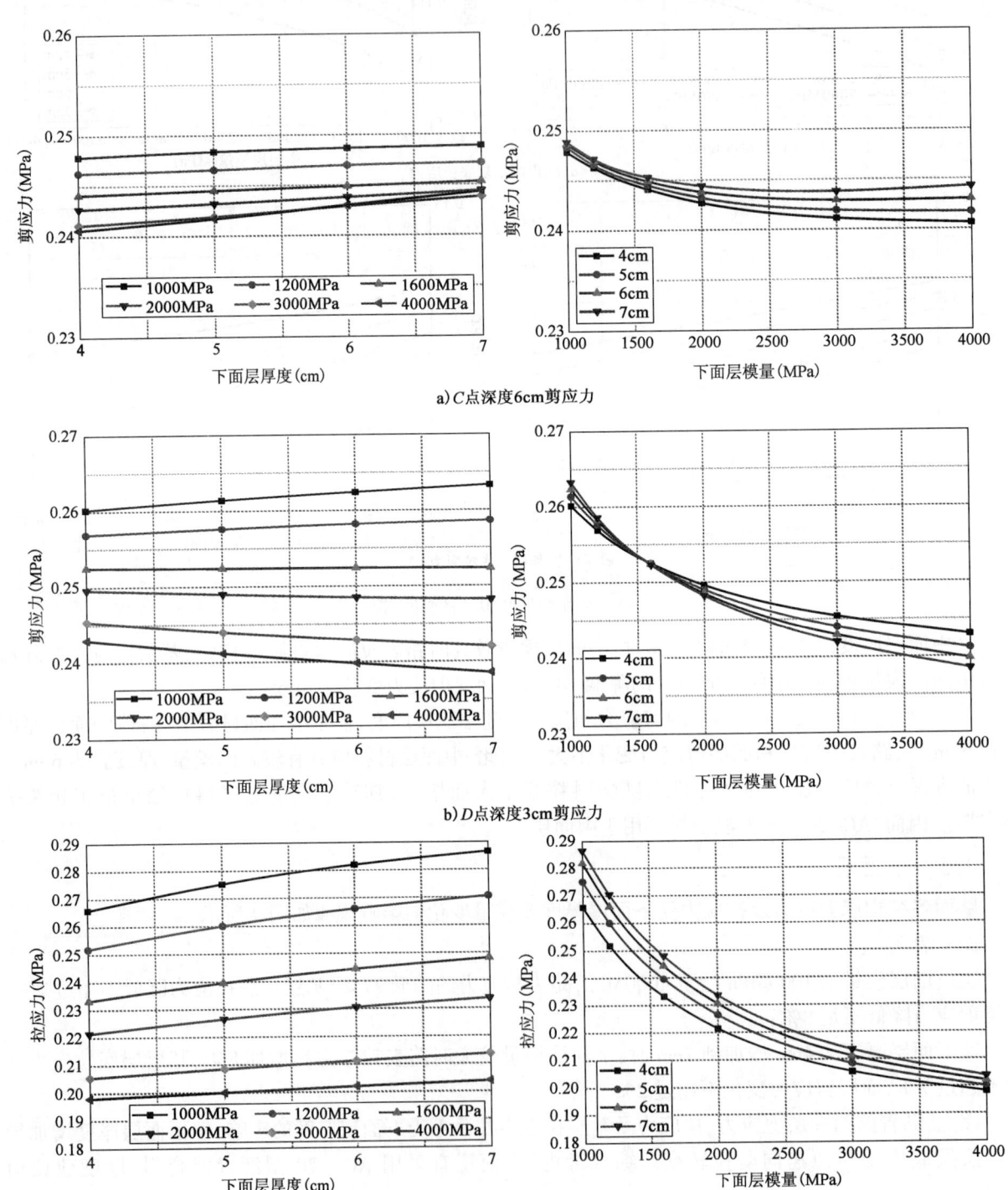

a) C 点深度6cm剪应力

b) D 点深度3cm剪应力

c) O 点路表拉应力

图 9

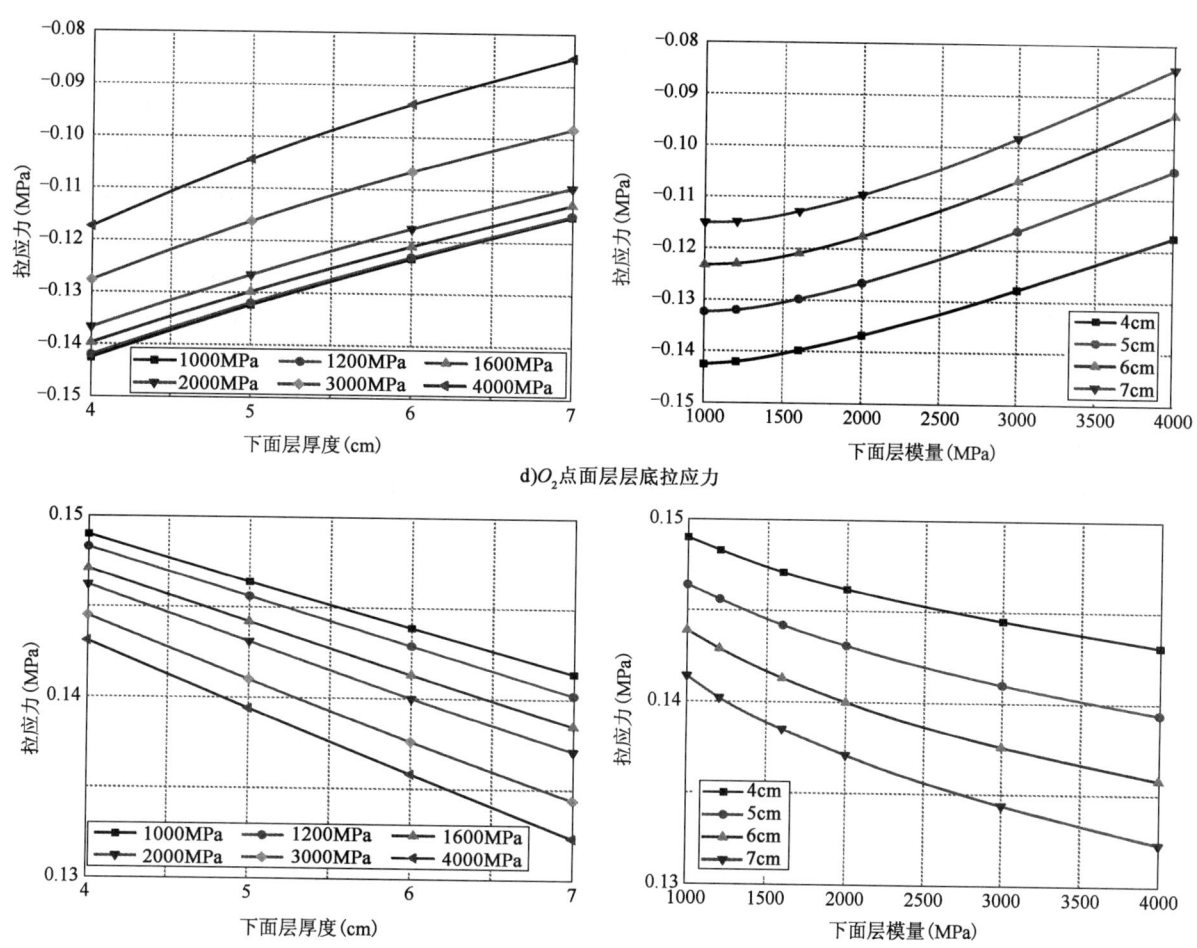

d) O_2 点面层层底拉应力

e) 半刚性基层层底拉应力

图9 路面各结构层应力的变化情况

对抗车辙沥青路面进行力学验证,结果见表2~表3。

传统路面结构与抗车辙路面结构力学行为比较 表2

应力指标	下列路面结构应力计算值(MPa)		应力比
	传统路面结构	抗车辙路面结构	
上面层剪应力	0.225	0.204	0.91
中面层剪应力	0.23	0.2	0.87
路表拉应力	0.219	0.087	0.40

不同水平荷载面层剪应力 表3

水平荷载(MPa)	下列路面结构剪应力值(MPa)		应力比
	传统路面结构	抗车辙路面结构	
0.14	0.232	0.212	0.91
0.21	0.239	0.218	0.91
0.35	0.263	0.234	0.89

表2~表3表明,本文推荐的抗车辙路面应力水平明显小于传统路面,与传统路面结构受力特征相比:

(1)抗车辙沥青路面结构面层最大剪应力降低9%~13%,面层层底拉应力降低60%;

(2)不同水平荷载作用下,抗车辙路面结构面层最大剪应力降低9%~11%。

3 结 语

(1) 沥青路面剪应力较大区域在中上面层内,深度 3~9cm 范围;其中,D 点深度 3cm 处为沥青上面层最大剪应力位置,C 点深度 6cm 处为中面层剪应力最大位置,随水平荷载的增大剪应力峰值增大且位置上移,路表轮系中心承受一定拉应力,半刚性基层层底承受的拉应力最大,水平荷载对路面拉应力几乎没有影响。

(2) 沥青路面上面层材料的模量应较低,厚度建议取 4cm,推荐采用骨架密实型 AC-13 或 AC-16 普通沥青混合料,亦可采用 SMA-13 或 SMA-16;中面层材料应具有较高的模量,厚度建议取 6cm,采用骨架密实型 AC-25 高模量沥青混合料;下面层材料模量适中,厚度建议取 5cm,采用骨架密实型 AC-20 普通沥青混合料。

(3) 与传统路面结构受力特征相比,本文推荐的抗车辙沥青路面结构面层最大剪应力降低 9%~13%,面层层底拉应力降低 60%;不同水平荷载作用下,抗车辙路面结构面层最大剪应力降低 9%~11%。

参考文献

[1] Huang X, Wang L, Li C. Integrated Experimental and Numerical Study on Permanent Deformation of Asphalt Pavement at Intersections[J]. Journal of Materials in Civil Engineering, 2013.

[2] Dong Z J, Sun Z J, Gong X B, et al. Mechanism Analysis of Rutting at Urban Intersections Based on Numerical Simulation of Moving Loads[J]. Advanced Materials Research, 2010, 152-153: 1192-1198.

[3] 刘阳. 交叉口区域沥青路面结构设计研究[D]. 长沙:长沙理工大学,2014.

[4] 马慧旭. 城市道路交叉口沥青路面荷载特征分析与车辙防治研究[D]. 南京:东南大学,2015.

[5] 孙晓刚. 城市化公路交叉口"白加黑"路面技术研究[D]. 西安:长安大学,2012.

[6] 康怀树. 城市道路交叉口[D]. 合肥:合肥工业大学,2011.

[7] 倪富健,郭咏梅,刘斌,等. 城市道路交叉口沥青混合料路用性能试验研究[J]. 东南大学学报(自然科学版),2003(06):777-781.

[8] Uesugi N, Mizuno M, Okasaki S. Study on Measure for Aggregate Stripping of Porous Asphalt Pavement at Intersection[J]. Doboku Gakkai Ronbunshuu E, 2006, 11: 81-88.

[9] Bao L S, Zhang X F, Yu L, et al. Study on Preventing from Deformation Diseases of Dolanit Fiber Asphalt Concrete at Road Intersection[J]. Advanced Materials Research, 2011, 243-249: 4131-4138.

[10] 최준성,이강훈,권수안, et al. 교차로 포장 소성변형 저감을 위한 해석적 연구 [J]. International Journal of Highway Engineering, 2012, 14(4): 29-36.

[11] 高莉,尤广华. 江苏省干线公路交叉口车辙处治方案研究[J]. 筑路机械与施工机械化,2017(6).

[12] 吕文江. 沥青路面结构与材料设计一体化研究[D]. 西安:长安大学,2006.

[13] 纪小平. 基于足尺 ALF 车辙预估模型的甘肃地区沥青混合料高温性能标准研究[D]. 西安:长安大学,2011.

[14] 谢水友,郑传超. 水平荷载对沥青路面结构的影响[J]. 长安大学学报(自然科学版),2004(02):14-17.

[15] 梁俊龙. 沥青路面动态模量及裂缝扩展研究[D]. 西安:长安大学,2016.

[16] 栗培龙,李建阁,邹鹏,等. 沥青混合料的动态响应影响因素分析[J]. 公路,2017(05):1-7.

万州大跨度悬索桥 LUHPC 钢桥面铺装组合方案分析

李鸿盛[1] 胡风明[1] 宋健[1] 丁庆军[2,3] 付军[2,3]

(1. 中交一公局重庆万州高速公路有限公司;2. 武汉理工大学;3. 硅酸盐建筑材料国家重点实验室)

摘　要　大跨径钢箱梁桥面铺装技术是该类工程的研究热点和难点。本文以万州新田大桥为研究背景,考虑千米级钢箱梁悬索桥的整体受力特征,提出了轻质低收缩超高性能混凝土(LUHPC)组合式铺装结构方案。建立整体桥梁与局部铺装有限元模型,研究其主要设计参数影响,并结合 LUHPC 组合疲劳试验进行分析。全桥模型考虑耦合荷载效应与不利曲率影响,其钢箱梁铺装层最大拉应变约 $145\mu\varepsilon$,仍小于 LUHPC 的开裂应变 $300\mu\varepsilon$;对主缆应力储备影响很小,与浇筑式沥青混凝土铺装方案相比仅减小约 1%。考虑剪力钉因素建模后,局部模型中 LUHPC 最大拉应力、层间剪应力与局部挠跨比均满足设计要求。LUHPC 组合结构疲劳试验次数超过 1000 万次。计算与试验结果表明,万州大桥 LUHPC 钢桥面铺装组合方案能够满足设计要求。本方案可为相关大跨径钢箱梁桥面铺装组合的研究与实践提供参考。

关键词　大跨度悬索桥　LUHPC 组合式钢桥面铺装　有限元分析　疲劳试验

0　引　言

钢箱梁桥具有自重轻、跨越能力大、架设方便、施工周期短等优点[1],被广泛应用于跨江越海的大型桥梁和城市立交桥工程。但钢箱梁桥面传统铺装材料与正交异性钢板性能差异明显,变形不协调,在行车荷载、风载、温度变化及钢桥面局部变形等因素的综合影响下,易导致桥面铺装出现层间滑移、疲劳破坏等病害,影响交通顺畅带来不可估量的经济损失;另外,现有铺装方案在如何应对安全服役周期短、性价比欠佳、养护维修难度大的问题上仍存在不足之处。

刘阳、钱振东等[2]研究发现,重载和恶劣温度条件下,钢桥面铺装因铺装表面拉应力较大而容易发生开裂破坏;万尧方、付军等[3]针对钢箱梁桥面的轻质混凝土剪力钉铺装方案,提出了相应的设计参数;徐菁、张磊等[4]指出,钢桥面铺装设置界面黏结层之后,铺装层的纵、横向最大拉应力(变)以及层间剪应力均有明显减小;薛昕等[5]研究表明,在桥面铺装中,复合改性沥青可以既满足混合料高温时的施工性,又能保证混合料结构的高温性能;邵旭东等[6]研究表明,由正交异性钢桥面板与薄层超高韧性混凝土 STC 组合而成的轻型组合桥面板结构,有较好的疲劳和静力性能;唐细彪[7]以厦门某桥为工程背景,对正交异性板桥面复合铺装进行试验研究,结果表明桥面铺装结构影响面分布具有强烈的局部效应。

新田长江大桥位于万州主城区长江上游 19km 处,采用双塔单跨 1020m 的钢箱梁悬索桥方案(图1),其钢箱梁标准节段长 18m,高 3m,宽 30.5m。万州新田长江大桥地处亚热带季风气候区,夏季炎热多雨,极端最高气温 44.5℃,极端最低气温 -10℃,夏季平均相对湿度 80% 以上,年平均降水量 1273mm,其服役环境为典型高温、高湿与重载交通流量区域。针对万州新田长江大桥,本文提出一种轻质低收缩(Light Ultra-High Performance Concrete,LUHPC)组合式铺装,其中 LUHPC 重度小于 $2100kg/m^3$,360d 收缩小于 $300\mu\varepsilon$。该铺装方案能较好地适应其特定交通特点与地理环境,对提高大跨度钢箱梁悬索桥的行车安全性、舒适性、经济性与耐久性具有重要意义。

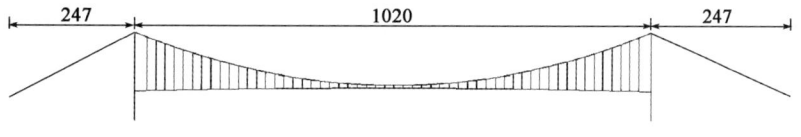

图1　万州新田长江大桥立面图(尺寸单位:m)

1 方案设计

设计采用铺装方案：正交异性钢板+钢筋网+剪力键+LUHPC+高黏高弹SMA。桥面铺装设计总厚度85mm，结构组成为50mmLUHPC+防水黏结应力吸收界面强化层+35mm高黏高弹改性沥青SMA。

LUHPC层内横桥向钢筋在上，纵桥向钢筋在下，纵、横桥向钢筋间距均为100mm，形成紧密的钢筋网并绑扎或焊接在剪力钉上，纵、横桥向钢筋均采用直径为10mm的HRB400钢筋。

剪力键采用ML15剪力钉，高度为40mm，直径为13mm，纵、横向间距均为200mm呈梅花状分布，如图2所示。

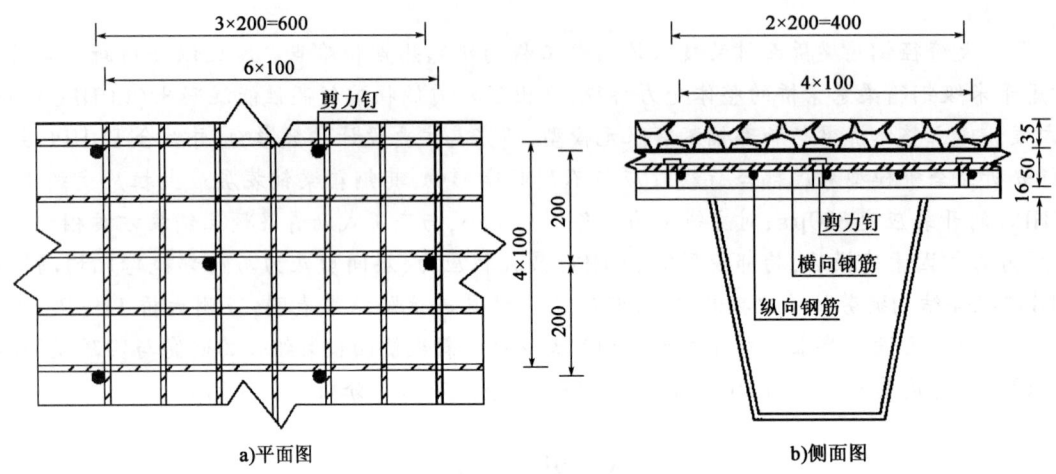

图2 LUHPC组合式铺装结构（尺寸单位：mm）

防水黏结应力吸收界面强化层采用高黏高弹改性沥青制成，它使得混凝土与沥青混凝土层间黏结强度达到0.4MPa，在0.7MPa水压力下1h不透水，并能够有效阻止混凝土板的裂缝反射，保证桥面铺装层整体的服役耐久性。

2 计算及试验分析

钢箱梁桥面铺装的受力与普通桥面铺装的受力有很大区别，铺装层与正交异性钢桥面板共同工作、协调变形，其受力受到整桥结构与桥面板局部正交异性板体系的双重影响，因此进行钢桥面铺装层的受力分析时需要综合以下3个层次进行考虑[8]：整桥受力分析、局部梁段受力分析、铺装层和正交异性板体系，即将从整桥模型中得到的力和变形进行等效作为边界条件约束局部结构模型，再从局部结构中分离出正交异性板体系进行精细分析。

由于采用正交异性板体系的钢箱梁表现出很强的局部效应，根据圣维南原理，在轮载作用下铺装层的受力状态主要与正交异性板局部有关，而受整桥结构的影响较小[9]。因此，在本文中，将建立整体二维模型和局部三维模型对铺装结构进行单独分析。

2.1 全桥效应初步分析

整体模型利用Midas Civil有限元软件建立鱼骨梁模型，不考虑施工过程，只对成桥状态进行分析。全桥共计645个节点，642个单元，如图3所示。

主要计算结果如下：

（1）钢主梁应力。成桥状态下LUHPC组合式铺装结构钢箱梁的应力分布如图4所示，其中主梁上翼缘最大压应力约为18.6MPa，最大拉应力约为28.7MPa，与原浇注式沥青混凝土铺装方案相比变化不大。在荷载组合作用下，全桥效应引起的铺装层最大拉应变约为145με，而LUHPC的开裂应变通常超过300με，满足设计要求。

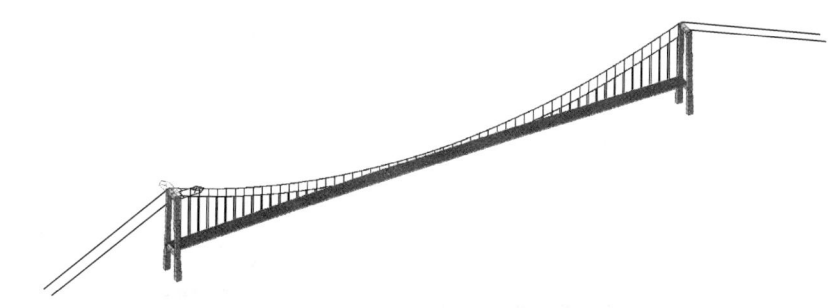

图3 整桥有限元模型

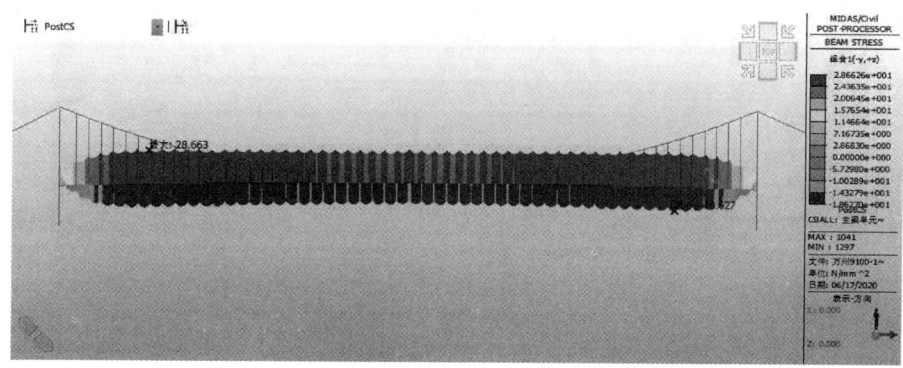

图4 钢主梁上翼缘应力云图(恒载+活载+温度作用)(单位:MPa)

(2)主梁挠曲线曲率。作为千米级柔性体系桥梁,在各种荷载/作用下,主梁容易发生较大挠曲,如果主梁挠曲程度过大而超过铺装层材料所能承担的应变限值,那必然造成铺装层开裂。现将主梁在最不利荷载作用下变形最严重处的挠曲线进行拟合,如图5所示,得到的拟合曲线为 $y = 5.2829 \times 10^{-9} x^3 + 6.0842 \times 10^5 x^2 - 0.01802 x + 0.34285$。根据拟合曲线求得最小曲率半径,现有试验证明LUHPC组合式铺装层完全可以满足此类桥梁对铺装层材料的变形匹配需求。

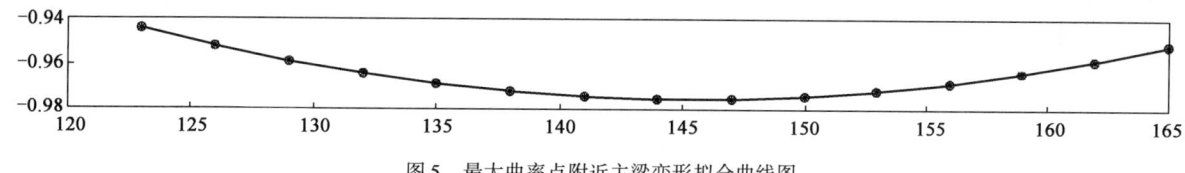

图5 最大曲率点附近主梁变形拟合曲线图

(3)不同铺装方案对比。本设计方案铺装层较75mm厚浇注式沥青混凝土铺装层增重约16%;本设计方案铺装层作用下较75mm厚浇注式沥青混凝土铺装层主缆应力储备量减少约1%。可见,与浇注式沥青混凝土铺装方案相比,本方案对大桥的受力情况影响不大。

2.2 梁段局部分析

(1)模型参数信息。利用ABAQUS有限元软件建立局部梁段模型,该模型纵桥向取12m标准梁段(4跨横隔板长度),横桥向取8.4m(14个U肋宽度),模型参数见表1。模型中各部件均采用八结点线性六面体单元C3D8R进行模拟,如图6所示。

局部模型计算参数 表1

项 目	参 数	项 目	参 数
顶板厚度(mm)	16	U肋间距(mm)	600
横隔板厚度(mm)	14	钢材弹性模量(MPa)	210000
横隔板间距(mm)	3000	钢材泊松比	0.3
横隔板高度(mm)	1000	LUHPC弹性模量(MPa)	28000

续上表

项　目	参　数	项　目	参　数
剪力钉高度(mm)	40	LUHPC 泊松比	0.25
剪力钉钉身直径(mm)	13	SMA 弹性模量(MPa)	1000
U 肋厚度(mm)	8	SMA 泊松比	0.25
U 肋高度(mm)	300		

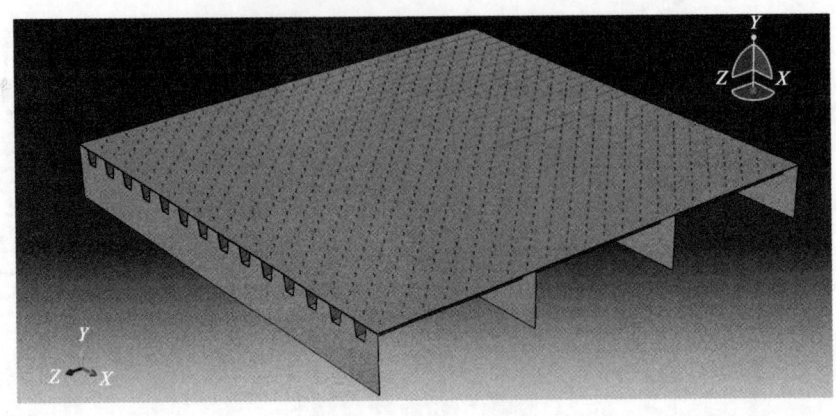

图 6　梁段局部有限元模型

局部模型的边界条件为:横隔板底部固端约束,顶板和铺装层纵横向平动自由度和三向转动自由度约束。

(2)主要计算结果。模型分析关键性指标:SMA 上面层横向最大拉应力、LUHPC 下面层横向最大拉应力、LUHPC 与钢板层间最大剪应力、加劲肋局部挠跨比。计算云图如图 7 所示。

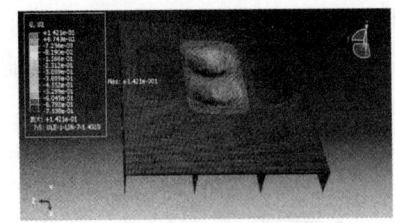
a)最大局部挠度变形

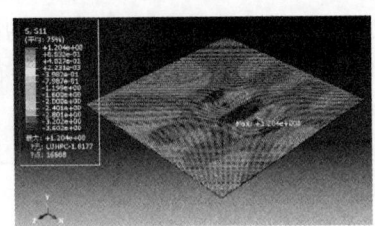
b)LUHPC层最大正应力

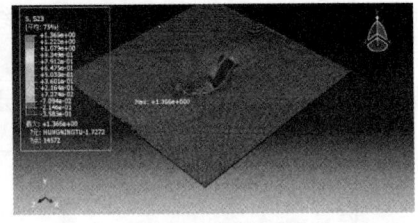
c)LUHPC层间最大剪应力

图 7　局部梁段模型分析云图

从图 7 的计算云图可以看出,桥面铺装体系应力应变局部效应明显,在以车轮为中心的局部范围内,铺装层应力应变波动明显。在车轮荷载作用中心附近,应力应变达到极值,而在该范围以外,应力应变趋近于零,这也说明了模型计算范围的选择是合理的,见表 2,相关计算数值均满足设计要求。

局部模型分析结果(单位:MPa)　　　　　　　　　　　表 2

项　目	SMA 上面层横向最大拉应力	LUHPC 下面层横向最大拉应力	LUHPC 与钢板间最大剪应力	加劲肋局部挠跨比
计算值	0.11	1.20	1.36	1/425
允许值	0.8	7.6	12.0	1/300

2.3　铺装组合疲劳试验

试验试件根据第 2 节中的设计方案进行制作。试验时采取控制应力加载,加载波形利用 MTS 自行控制的无间歇正弦波。选取应力水平 0.7,循环应力比 0.1,加载频率 10Hz,加载至 1000 万次后自动停止。试验采取四分点加载方式,如图 8 所示。浇筑成型 LUHPC 抗弯拉疲劳试件,测试钢-LUHPC 组合结构的疲劳寿命,并与常见浇注式沥青和环氧沥青的疲劳寿命研究成果进行对比,结果见表 3。

由上表可知,本研究设计的铺装层组合结构疲劳性能优异,达到1000万次以上,与环氧沥青混凝土及浇注式沥青混凝土的抗弯拉疲劳性能相当。

不同铺装结构疲劳试验指标对比　　表3

指　　标	本设计铺装层组合结构	浇注式沥青混凝土	环氧沥青混凝土
试验温度(℃)	20	20	20
加载频率(Hz)	10	10	10
加载方式	4点加载	5点加载	3点加载
加载点距支点(mm)	300	125	150
钢板平面尺寸(mm)	1100×600	700×200	380×100
钢板厚度(mm)	16	14	14
疲劳寿命(万次)	大于1000	大于1000	大于1000

图8　试验装置示意图

3　结　语

由该实例可知:

(1)与浇注式沥青混凝土铺装方案相比,LUHPC组合式铺装方案对大桥的受力情况影响不大,方案具有可施工性、高经济性。

(2)在局部梁段模型计算中,SMA上面层横向最大拉应力为0.11MPa、LUHPC下面层横向最大拉应力为1.2MPa、LUHPC与钢板层间最大剪应力为1.36MPa等关键性指标均远小于允许值,满足设计要求。

(3)抗弯拉疲劳试验应力循环次数达到1000万次以上,铺装方案具有高耐久性。

参考文献

[1] 黄卫.大跨径桥梁钢桥面铺装设计[J].土木工程学报,2007(09):65-77.

[2] 刘阳,钱振东,张勍.重载和温度耦合作用下钢桥面环氧沥青铺装结构疲劳损伤分析[J].东南大学学报(英文版),2017,33(4):478-483.

[3] 万尧方,付军,向念,等.钢箱梁桥面轻质混凝土剪力钉铺装方案有限元分析及参数确定[J].交通科技,2015(03):1-4.

[4] 徐菁,张磊,丁建明.黏结层特性对正交异性钢桥面铺装受力的影响[J].黑龙江交通科技,2013,(6):81-83.

[5] 薛昕,王民,高博,等.复合改性沥青浇筑式混凝土性能研究[J].重庆交通大学学报(自然科学版),2010,29(3):387-390,429.

[6] 邵旭东,曲宛桐,曹君辉,等.带大U肋的轻型组合桥面板基本力学性能[J].中国公路学报,2018,31(08):94-103.

[7] 唐细彪.正交异性板及桥面复合铺装影响面测试试验研究[J].铁道工程学报,2015,32(3):37-40,56.

[8] 黄成造.钢箱梁桥面铺装力学行为与结构优化研究[D].长安大学,2010.

[9] 万俊,丁庆军,胡方杰,等.钢箱梁桥面铺装优化设计[J].土木工程与管理学报,2016,33(05):6-13.

[10] 中华人民交通运输部.公路桥涵设计通用规范:JTG D60—2015[S].北京:人民交通出版社股份有限公司,2015.

全温域条件下沥青路面加速加载响应规律分析

徐希忠[1,2] 韦金城[1,2] 张晓萌[1,2] 符东绪[1,2] 李作钰[1,2]

(1.山东省交通科学研究院;2.高速公路养护技术交通行业重点实验室(济南))

摘 要 为了明确全温域条件下沥青路面实测响应规律,基于足尺试验加速加载直道试验,选择双轮轴载和FWD两种加载方式,以两种柔性基层和一种半刚性基层沥青路面为研究对象,对三种路面结构全温域条件下的加速加载响应进行测试分析,得到了温度与弯沉、温度与应力和应变之间的关系。结果表明:轮载作用下,沥青层底应变响应呈现出拉压交替状态,且温度越低,动力响应信号持续时间越短;全温域条件下,温度对结构弯沉、应力及应变响应有重要影响,随着温度升高,各响应明显增大,温度与弯沉、应力及应变响应可应用指数模型进行拟合分析,拟合优度均为0.9以上,具有良好的相关性。由此建议在进行沥青路面结构性能分析时,应当基于全温域力学响应,仅仅考虑代表温度是不全面的。

关键词 沥青路面 足尺试验 全温度域 力学响应 规律分析

0 引 言

在自然环境与交通荷载耦合作用下,沥青路面结构内部会产生应力、应变场,基于足尺加速加载实测可获取最接近实际的力学响应[1]。当前国内外专家学者围绕加速加载条件下沥青路面响应开展了大量的研究工作,国外加速加载设备应用有代表性的为法国LCPC环道、美国HVS试验装置[2]、澳大利亚ALF加载装置[3]及南非生产的MLS[4]系列加速加载设备等,国内有代表性的为交通运输部公路科学研究院的ALF[5]与MLS[6]、招商局重庆交通科研设计院有限公司加速加载环道[7]、东南大学环道[8]、长沙理工大学直道[9]、山东交通学院ALT加速加载设备[10]等。现有加速加载研究动力响应研究过多集中于轮载大小对动力响应的影响,主要分析轴载[11-12]、速度[13]、胎压[14]及FWD锤重[15]等对动力响应的影响,而对于全温域条件下沥青路面动力响应的研究还鲜有报道。

事实上,不同地区的气候差异,季节性变化下,路面不同层位的温度差异,路面结构内部各温度出现的时间频率等都会导致路面结构动力响应产生差异。同时,沥青混凝土作为一种温度敏感性材料,温度差异会引起沥青层模量的变化,这直接将影响沥青路面在行车荷载作用下的应力、应变响应,进而影响路面结构使役性能。因此,研究荷载、温度耦合效应下沥青路面动力响应是十分必要的。

为此,本文基于室内足尺加速加载直道试验,以两种柔性基层和一种半刚性基层沥青路面为研究对象,将实测温度分为高温、低温和常温3个工况,在此基础上增加两个中间间隔温度工况,研究五种温度工况条件下沥青路面结构响应特征,分析沥青路面全温度域条件下动力响应规律,并建立温度与弯沉、应力和应变的关系,可较全面描述沥青路面结构服役条件下动力响应行为。

1 加速加载试验概况

1.1 加速加载试验结构

考虑到较厚的沥青层较难产生疲劳破坏,因此设置了较薄的沥青层,用于分析柔性基层沥青路面结构行为,验证半刚性基层沥青路面疲劳模型。最终拟定结构如下:柔性基层结构—由7cm沥青混凝土面

基金项目:国家重点研发计划(2018YFB1600100)、山东省自然科学基金(ZR2020QE271、ZR2020KE024)山东省重点研发计划(2019GSF109020、2019GGX101042)。

层和40cm级配碎石基层、80cm水泥改善土和土基构成,柔性基层结构一除沥青混凝土层为9cm外,其余结构与结构一相同,半刚性基层则由4cm沥青混凝土面层、2层CTB基层、30cm水泥改善土组成。3种结构组合及层位厚度如图1所示。

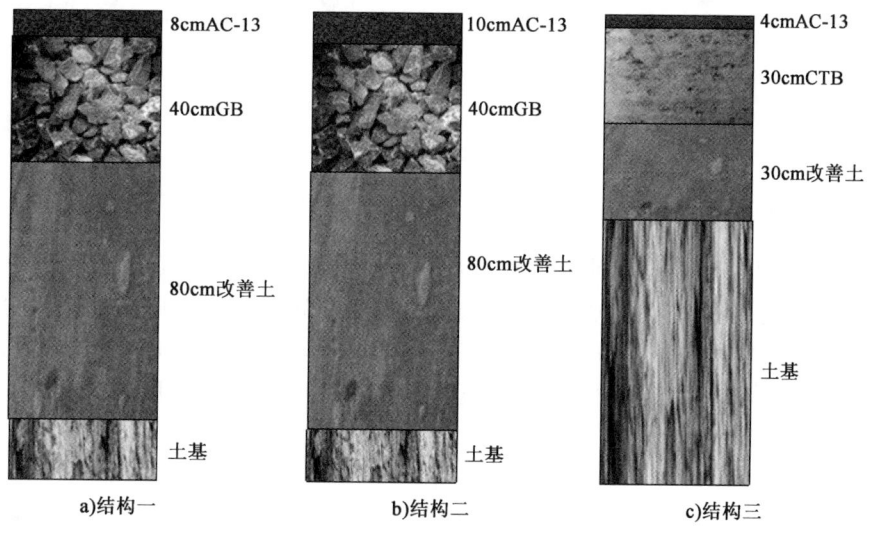

图1 路面结构及材料组成

1.2 传感器类型及埋设方案

本研究以传感器的灵敏度、响应速度快、适应性强及使用经济等为原则,比选分析了多种路面响应监测传感器。最终确定沥青应变计采用美国ASG生产的TCL应变传感器,温度传感器采用新型数字DS18B20温度传感器,土压力盒采用美国基康公司生产的Geokon3500传感器,如图2所示。传感器埋设方案如图3和图4所示,每种结构沥青层层底各布置4个,横向、纵向各2个,土基顶部各埋设一个土压力计,温度传感器分别埋设于结构一距路面2cm、5cm、7cm处,实时采集传输路面结构内部温度。

a)ASG应变传感器

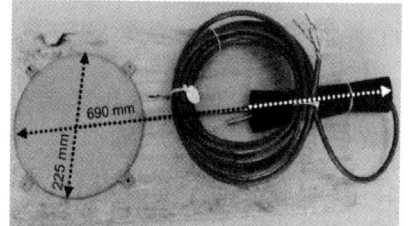
b)Geokon 3500型土压力计

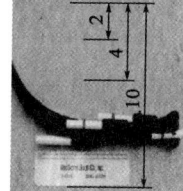
c)温度传感器

图2 应力、应变传感器

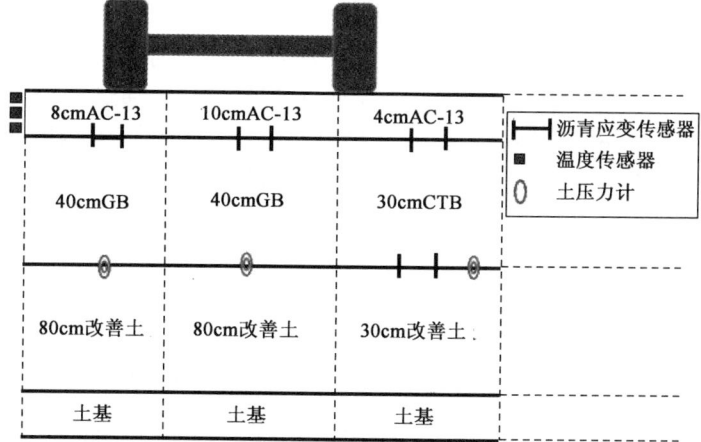

图3 传感器布设立面图

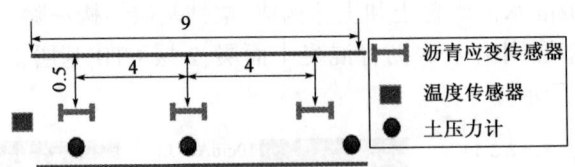

图 4 传感器布设平面图(尺寸单位:m)

2 加速加载试验

2.1 试验装备

本次加速加载采用山东交通学院研制的直道足尺加速加载试验装置 ALT,可实现单轴、双联轴切换加载,单轴、双联轴最大轴载分别为 280kN 和 400kN,双联轴轴距为 1.4m,可实现轮载的横向移动,能够较好地模拟实际车辆荷载,可在 10~26km/h 速度范围内运行,具体如图 5 所示。试验直道位于山东交通学院加速加载试验专用实验室内,试验槽有效长度为 10m,每种结构铺设长度 3m。

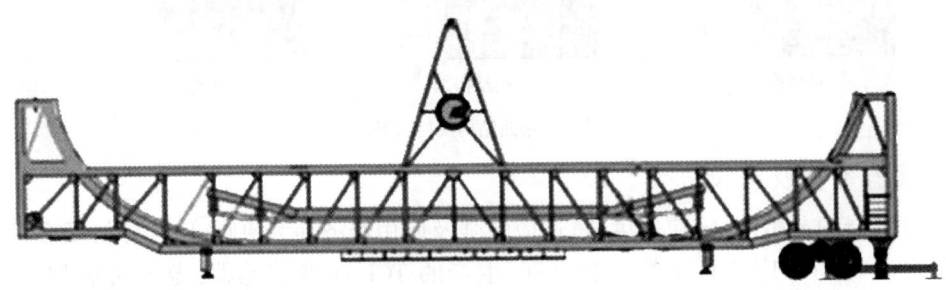

图 5 ALT 加速加载装置

2.2 试验方案

为分析全温域条件下沥青路面动力响应规律,将实测温度进行统计分析,得出高温、低温、常温 3 种工况,并在相应的时间段下测试沥青路面加速加载响应及 FWD 荷载响应,分析全温域条件下沥青路面动力响应规律。

3 典型温度工况确定及响应信号特征分析

3.1 典型温度工况确定

目前在进行沥青路面实测动力响应分析时,一般都未考虑温度的影响,而实际上沥青路面温度场会使沥青材料的力学性质变化,同时,温度差异会引起沥青层模量的变化,这会导致沥青路面荷载应变发生变化。因此,在分析沥青路面荷载响应时,应考虑温度影响。

为了对沥青路面实际温度场进行分析,本文在试验直道铺设完成后,通过取芯回填的方式,在沥青路面结构内部埋设了温度传感器,测试了整年的路面结构温度场,分别选取 8 月 20 日、2 月 10 日、5 月 15 日的数据作为高温、低温及平均温度进行分析,如图 6 ~ 图 8 所示。

由图 6 可知,3 种温度工况下,温度场日变化规律基本一致,一天中路表最高温度出现在 14:00 左右,最低温度出现在 5:00 左右。在 8:00 左右整个结构层温度场达到平衡稳定状态,之后离路表距离越近温度升高越快,到 18:00 左右温度场再次达到平衡。由此可

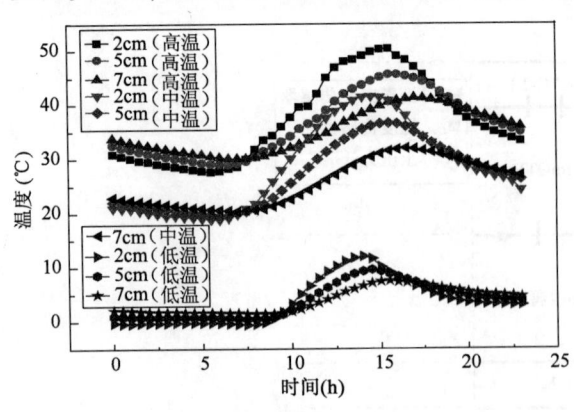

图 6 三种温度工况下日温度分布

见在一天 24h 中,8:00 至 18:00 和 18:00 至 8:00 两个时段内,温度场完全不同,在相同荷载作用下,结构层内部的应变状态也将差别较大,考虑到加载响应测试的可操作性及准确性,确定典型温度工况见表1。

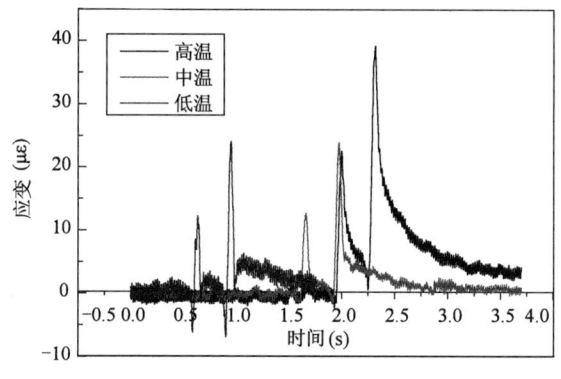

图 7　结构一全温域应变响应时程曲线

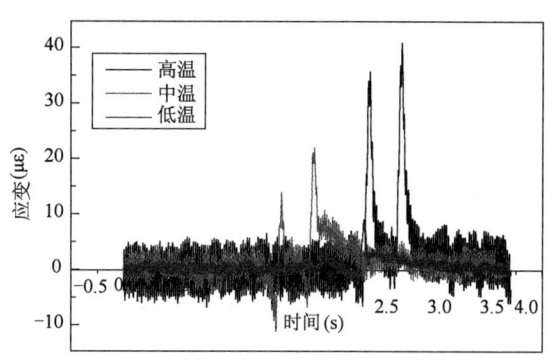

图 8　结构二全温域应变响应时程曲线

典型温度工况　　　　　　　　　　　　　　　　　　　　　　　　　　　　　　　　　表 1

典型温度工况	温度数据来源及描述
工况一	山东省 5 月 15 日 10:00 实测
工况二	山东省 8 月 20 日 14:00 实测
工况三	山东省 2 月 10 日 18:00 实测

3.2　响应信号特征分析

以 25t 轴重,20km/h 速度为例,在 3 种典型温度工况下实测 3 次动力响应,并取实测响应均值,3 种路面结构的纵向应变响应时程曲线分别如图 7 ~ 图 9 所示。

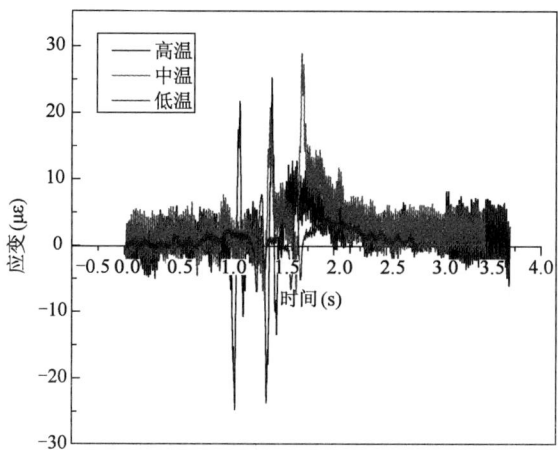

图 9　结构三全温域应变响应时程曲线

由图 7 ~ 图 9 可知,

(1)在轮载作用下,沥青混凝土层层底动应变呈现出拉、压交替的状态,其中,结构三的响应高温状态下压应变响应最大;

(2)对于动应变曲线形态,可以看出,3 种结构均表现出明显的黏滞作用,且应变响应持续时间随着温度的降低而减小;

(3)当加载轮载接触及离开传感器所在位置时,层底应变为压应变,且高温、中温状态比低温状态明显,当轮载作用于传感器正上方时,层底应变为拉应变,且出现峰值。

4 全温域沥青路面结构响应规律

4.1 温度与弯沉关系

弯沉主要表征路面结构的整体刚度,按照测试的荷载状态分为静态弯沉与动态弯沉,本研究采用FWD测试的动态弯沉进行分析。在选定沥青层结构7cm处高温、中温及低温工况前提下,又在高温与中温,低温与中温之间选定(6月10日)及(3月20日)2个温度工况,设定了5个温度工况,可基本代表全温域条件下路面温度,测试了5个温度工况下路面结构弯沉响应,每次测试3次,3种结构路面D_0均值与温度T的关系如图10所示。

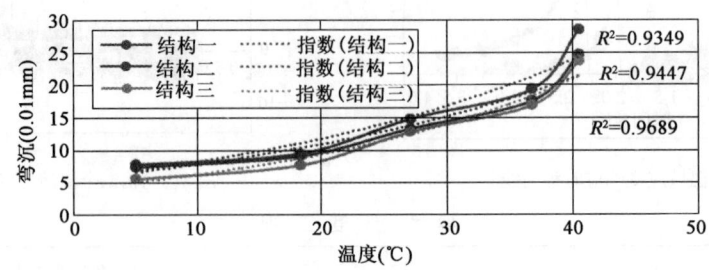

图10 温度与弯沉响应关系

由图9可知,温度对路面结构弯沉响应影响显著,弯沉响应随着温度的升高而增大,这是由于沥青混凝土是典型的温度敏感性材料,温度的变化会引起沥青混凝土刚度场的变化,进而影响沥青路面的弯沉响应。从图9还可看出,弯沉D_0与随温度T增大呈现单调增加的规律,参照文献[16],采用下式对温度-弯沉关系进行拟合分析。

$$l_0 = k_1 e^{k_2 \cdot T} \tag{1}$$

式中:l_0——弯沉响应D_0,0.01mm;

T——弯沉响应测试时对应的温度,℃;

k_1、k_2——拟合参数。

应用式(1)对图9中温度与弯沉响应关系进行回归,拟合优度均为0.9以上,拟合效果较好,回归参数见表2。

温度-弯沉响应回归模型系数 表2

回归参数	结 构 一	结 构 二	结 构 三
k_1	5.7998	5.6555	4.2157
k_2	0.0354	0.0375	0.04
R^2	0.9349	0.9447	0.9689

4.2 温度与应变关系

由于季节交替及自然环境的变化,路面结构温度场也随之变化。为充分保障温度取值的合理性,在进行FWD测试后,马上进行路面结构沥青层底动应变响应的测试,每个温度测试3次动力响应。各温度条件下路面结构内部动应变响应均值随温度变化的规律如图11所示。

由图11可知,3种路面结构沥青层层底动应变响应均随着温度的升高逐渐增大,这是由于温度的变化会引起沥青层模量的变化,温度场的变化将导致沥青层模量梯度的变化,这将直接影响路面结构在轮载作用下动应变响应。在低温状态下,沥青混凝土较多地表现出弹性性质,且材料刚度较大,有利于结构抵抗行车荷载作用,沥青层层底动应变较小;在高温状态下,沥青混凝土较多地表现出黏性,且材料刚度明显降低,导致沥青层层底动应变较大。根据图11温度应变曲线特征可知,可采用指数模型对温度-应变关系进行描述,建立如下的温度-动应变关系模型:

$$\varepsilon = k_3 e^{k_4 T} \tag{2}$$

式中:ε——沥青层层底动应变,$\mu\varepsilon$;

T——动应变测试时对应的温度,℃;

k_3、k_4——拟合参数。

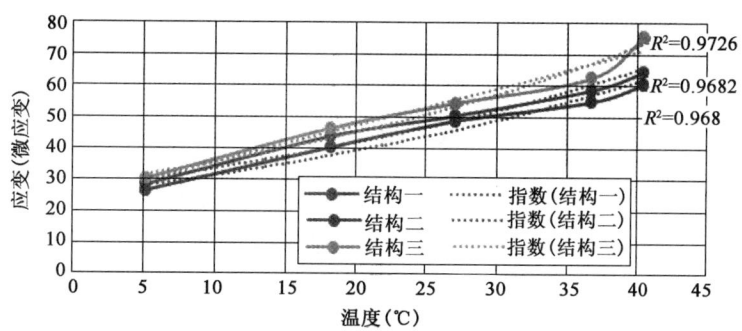

图11 温度与应变关系

模型拟合参数见表3。

温度-动应变回归模型系数　　　　　　表3

回归参数	结 构 一	结 构 二	结 构 三
k_3	27.92	24.995	26.875
k_4	0.0238	0.0241	0.022
R^2	0.9726	0.9682	0.968

4.3 温度与应力关系

为研究全温域条件下路面结构温度与结构层动应力关系,在测试动应变的同时,通过预埋设的土压力计实测了路基顶面动应力数据,每个温度测试3次。温度-应力关系如图12所示。由图12可见,结构层动应力随温度升高而逐渐增大,呈现出单调递增的规律,由于结构类型不同,增幅稍有差异。在温度较低时,半刚性基层压应力与柔性基层差别不大,随着温度的升高,应力差逐渐增大。图12中,温度-应力关系也可采用指数模型进行描述,具体模型如下:

$$\sigma = k_5 e^{k_6 T} \tag{3}$$

式中:σ——沥青层层底动应变,kPa;

T——动应力测试时对应的温度,℃;

k_5、k_6——拟合参数。

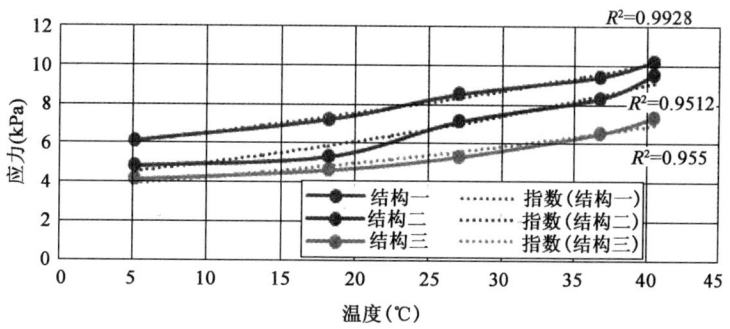

图12 温度与应力关系

模型拟合参数见表4。

温度-动应变回归模型系数　　　　表4

回归参数	结构一	结构二	结构三
k_5	4.0903	5.6363	3.5899
k_4	0.0197	0.014	0.162
R^2	0.9928	0.9512	0.955

5 结语

(1) 实测了足尺加速加载试验道路的整年度温度场数据,遴选出代表性高温、低温及平均温度进行分析,可知路面结构内部实时温度变化为 1.4~41.3℃,能够代表沥青路面服役周期内全温域温度范围。

(2) 在轮载作用下,沥青混凝土层层底动应变呈现出拉、压交替的状态,动应变曲线形态的黏滞性及应变响应持续时间均温度降低而减小。

(3) 在全温域条件下,沥青路面弯沉、应变及应力均随温度升高而增大,可采用指数模型进行描述,拟合优度均为 0.9 以上,具有良好的相关性。

(4) 在进行沥青路面性能分析时,应考虑全温域条件下沥青路面结构响应,仅仅采用代表性温度是明显不足的,温度轴载耦合作用下力学响应的分布更能贴近路面实际。

参考文献

[1] 陈静云,刘佳音,刘云全.加速加载条件下沥青路面结构动力响应[J].哈尔滨工业大学学报,2014, 35(6):771-776.

[2] 孙旭峰.路面加速加载试验设备装配与使用技术[D].西安:长安大学.2011.

[3] 董忠红,徐全亮,吕彭民.基于加速加载试验的半刚性基层沥青路面动力响应[J].中国公路学报, 2011,24(2):1-6.

[4] 冉武平,凌建明,赵鸿铎.环氧沥青道面高温足尺加速加载动力响应[J].同济大学学报,2015,43(12):1823-1830.

[5] 孟书涛,魏道新.SMA沥青路面抗车辙性能研究[J].公路交通科技,2005,22(12):5-9.

[6] 陈飞,孟书涛.沥青路面抗车辙加速加载试验研究[J].中外公路,2011,31(3):77-82.

[7] 苏凯,王春晖,周刚,等.基于加速加载试验的沥青路面车辙预估研究[J].同济大学学报,2008,36(4):493-497.

[8] 黄晓明,张晓冰,邓学钧.沥青路面车辙形成规律环道试验研究[J].东南大学学报,2000,30(5):96-101.

[9] 吕松涛,陈杰.基于加速加载试验的沥青混合料刚度衰变规律研究[J].公路交通科技,2016,33(5):5-9.

[10] 胡朋,张小宁.基于双轴加速加载试验的沥青路面车辙预测模型[J].重庆交通大学学报(自然科学版),2017,36(7):1-7.

[11] 肖川,邱延峻,黄兵.基于车辆加载试验的沥青路面动力响应分析[J].公路交通科技,2014,31(12):12-19.

[12] 吴玉,蒋鑫,梁雪娇,等.轮载作用下典型沥青路面结构力学行为分析[J].西南交通大学学报,2017,52(3):563-570.

[13] 董忠红,吕彭民.轴载与速度对半刚性沥青路面动力响应的影响[J].长安大学学报,2008,28(1)32-36.

[14] 肖川,邱延峻.胎压对半刚性沥青路面实测动应变的影响[J].筑路机械与施工机械化,2017,34(5)59-63.

[15] 肖川,邱延峻,曾杰.FWD荷载作用下的沥青路面实测动力响应研究[J].公路交通科技,2014,31(2):1-8.
[16] 周兴业,王旭东,关伟,等.宽温度域内沥青路面结构响应规律分析[J].哈尔滨工业大学学报,2020,52(9):63-39.

温度和剪切速率对沥青-集料试件剪切力学特性的影响

汪忠明 王永春[1] 董满生[2] 吴大帅[2]

(1.合肥工业大学土木与水利工程学院;2.合肥工业大学汽车与交通工程学院)

摘 要 本文研究了温度和剪切速率对沥青-集料界面剪切力学特性的影响。通过自制的成型设备放置砝码来施加荷载,试验选取的成型砝码质量为200g,并制作出集料—沥青—集料三明治试件。然后,通过剪切试验,得到应力-位移曲线,表征沥青—集料界面剪切力学性能。最后,分析了温度和剪切速率对峰值应力和峰值位移的影响。采用回归拟合研究沥青—集料界面峰值应力和峰值位移随温度和剪切速率的变化规律。结果表明:随着温度的升高,沥青—集料界面的破坏由黏附破坏为主转变为黏聚破坏为主,沥青—集料界面剪切强度呈现下降趋势,而剪切速率对峰值应力的影响越来越小。

关键词 道路工程 沥青—集料 剪切试验 黏附 黏聚

0 引 言

沥青混合料是由沥青相、集料相及沥青-集料之间的界面相组成的三相复合材料,其中沥青—集料界面相相对薄弱,是影响沥青路面耐久性的关键因素。沥青混合料的力学性能和破坏强度等界面缺陷特性对复合材料的路用性能有显著影响,因此,沥青混合料的许多性能中普遍存在沥青集料界面性能的表征[1-4]。

近年来,沥青-集料界面研究集中在沥青-集料界面的黏附性研究上。延西利等[5]设计剪切黏附试验,给出了沥青与石料间黏附性强弱的定量评价方法。Ling等[6]对沥青和石料进行了黏结试验,分析了黏附性随温度和剪切速率的变化。Kim等[7-10]利用动力学、热力学和表面物理化学等多种方法深入研究了沥青混合料的黏附性能。Xu等[3]利用分子动力学(MD)模拟研究沥青-集料界面的变形和破坏行为,发现界面破坏强度和峰值后变形受加载速率和温度的影响。Dong[11]等采用试验方法,研究沥青薄膜厚度对沥青-集料界面剪切力学性能的影响,建立沥青膜厚度与成型载荷的关系,发现沥青膜厚度会直接影响沥青-集料界面的剪切破坏形式。当沥青膜厚度小于等于23μm或大于等于219μm时,应力位移曲线均为单波峰曲线,在23~219μm范围内时,单波峰曲线和双波峰曲线均存在。沥青膜越厚,自由沥青占比越高,黏聚失效占比越高;沥青膜越薄,自由沥青占比越低,黏附失效占比越高。而沥青作为温度敏感性材料,其自身的黏聚力和与集料之间的黏附力受环境影响,因此,研究温度和加载速率对沥青-集料界面力学行为的影响,对沥青路面的合理铺设和养护有重要意义。

本文开展剪切试验,采用回归拟合的方式,建立了应力-位移曲线关系,研究了温度和剪切速率对沥青-集料界面相的力学性能的影响,并建立了沥青-集料界面的峰值应力以及峰值位移随温度、剪切速率的变化关系。

基金项目:国家自然科学基金项目(51978229)。

1 剪切试验

成型三明治试件(下石柱 φ19mm×40mm,上石柱 φ19mm×20mm)如图1所示,在室温下养护24h后在 WDW-1000 型电子万能试验机中进行剪切,如图2所示。

图1 三明治试件

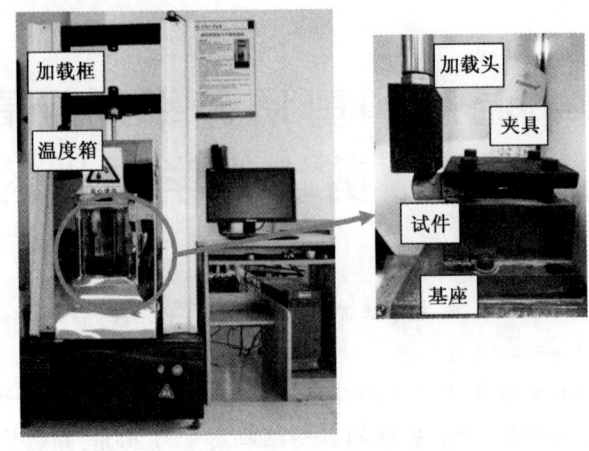

图2 剪切试验设备

1.1 试验材料

试验采用SBS改性沥青,沥青的各项性能指标见表1。采用的集料为石灰岩,集料的各项性能指标见表2。

SBS改性沥青性能指标 表1

SBS改性沥青性能指标	试验结果	技术参考
针入度(100g,5s,25℃)(0.1mm)	50	35~60
软化点(环与球法)(℃)	81	≥60
延度(5mm/min)(cm)	24	≥20
密度(15℃)(g·cm^{-3})	1.027	—

集料技术指标 表2

集料技术指标	吸水率(%)	表观相对密度(g·cm^{-3})	洛杉矶磨耗(%)	石料压碎值(%)
试验结果	0.84	2.473	12.1	11.9

1.2 试件制备

(1)为更好地获得试验数据,将石灰石切割成厚度为40mm和20mm的薄片。由于原材料粗糙度差异较大,故将薄片的一面统一使用120级SIC颗粒的磨料打磨处理,打磨后的薄片表面粗糙度为37.8μm,可用表面粗糙度仪进行检测[12]。

(2)将薄片打磨处理后的表面朝上,放在ZS-50B型取芯机上固定,钻取圆柱形石柱。将钻取后的石柱放在沸水中煮15min,去除表面灰尘。然后将清洗后的石柱放在温度控制为80℃温度箱中干燥4h后取出冷却至室温。

(3)将石柱和沥青放置在160℃的烘箱中预热1h,取处理好的高度为40mm的石柱,将软化后的沥青均匀涂抹在打磨面,并迅速与高度为20mm的石柱打磨面对齐合并成三明治试件,冷却至室温后养护1h[12]。三明治试件结构为集料-沥青-集料,用以模拟沥青混合料系统的组成单元。

(4)用砝码在加载平台施加8.07kPa的压力,同时加载平台自重提供2.3kPa的压力,三明治试件承受压力为 10.37kPa。

（5）将带有夹具的三明治试件放至烘箱，控制温度在80℃后开始计时，3min 后取出夹具与试件，冷却至室温后试件成型。成型后的试件放在温度25℃的环境下养护24h，试件边缘溢出的沥青应用加热的刀刮去[12]。

1.3 试验

将三明治试件安放 WDW-1000 型电子万能试验机温控室，保温40min 后进行剪切试验。当剪切载荷下降到相对较小的残余载荷时，剪切试验停止。

2 结果分析

2.1 应力-位移曲线

2.1.1 试验工况

本研究分析温度和剪切速率对应力的影响，试验工况：温度取15℃、20℃、25℃、30℃、35℃和45℃，剪切速率取5mm/min、10mm/min 和 15mm/min，共18 种工况。Dong[11]等用扫描电镜对所有被测样品的沥青膜厚度进行了测量，得到了沥青膜厚度与荷载水平的定量拟合关系如下：

$$y = 273.94e^{-x/30.609} + 22.66$$

式中：y——沥青膜厚度，μm；

x——荷载水平，kPa。

代入公式知本试验的沥青膜厚度为219.00μm。在相同的试验条件下，进行3组有效平行试验，得到的应力-位移曲线如图6所示。

2.1.2 应力-位移曲线图

所有试件的应力-位移曲线均有一个峰值，称为单波峰曲线，如图3a)所示，单波峰曲线可分为上升区 Ⅰ，下降区 Ⅱ 和残余区 Ⅲ 三部分[13]。荷载施加的初始阶段，试件的剪切应力迅速增大，剪切应力增长的速率逐渐减小，直至达到零。此时，应力达到峰值，即界面的剪切强度。随后曲线进入下降区 Ⅱ，应力降低的速度先缓慢，后变快，直到出现拐点。然后应力下降速率逐渐减小，最终过渡到残余区 Ⅲ，剪切应力值逐渐接近零。

本文在每种试验工况下选取一组具有代表性的数据绘制而成，图3b)、c)、d) 依次为5mm/min、10mm/min 和 15mm/min 时剪应力与剪切位移之间的关系曲线。由图可知：随着温度的升高，曲线变得陡峭，应力变化迅速，剪切强度增大，峰值位移整体越来越小。温度降低时，曲线变得平缓，剪切位移也变长。

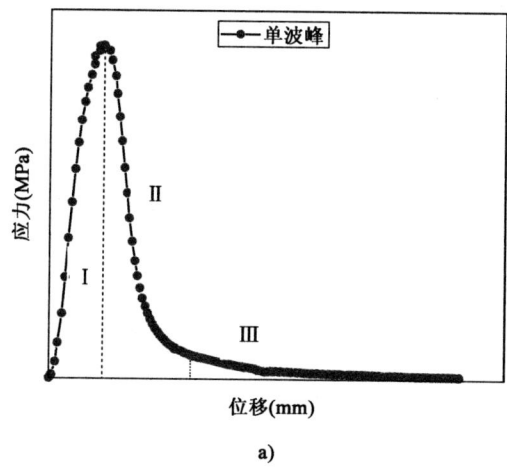
a)

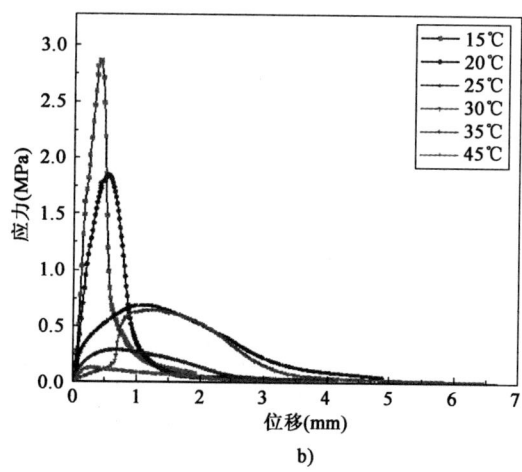
b)

图 3

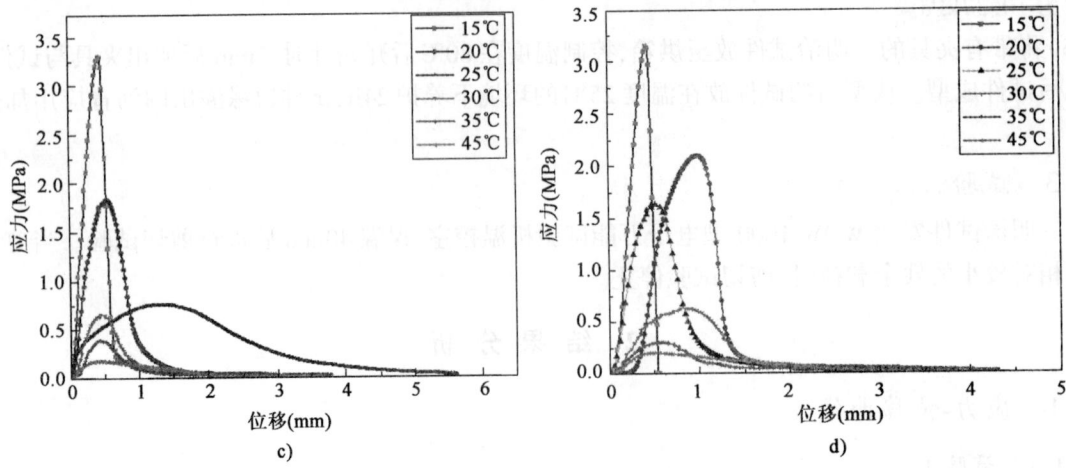

图3 应力-位移关系

2.2 温度对峰值应力和峰值位移的影响

相同的剪切速率下,沥青-集料界面的峰值应力和峰值位移随温度的变化情况如图4所示。从图4a)中可以明显地看出,相同的温度条件下,剪切速率越大,峰值位移越小。对于温度-峰值应力关系、温度-峰值位移关系分别进行回归分析。图4b)、c)、d)分别对应剪切速率为5mm/min、10mm/min和15mm/min时峰值应力随温度变化的关系。从图中可以看出,相同的剪切速率条件下,随着温度的上升,由于沥青的黏滞度减弱而导致流动性即变形能力增强,从而削弱了集料与集料之间的黏结力,即沥青-集料界面的峰值应力下降。

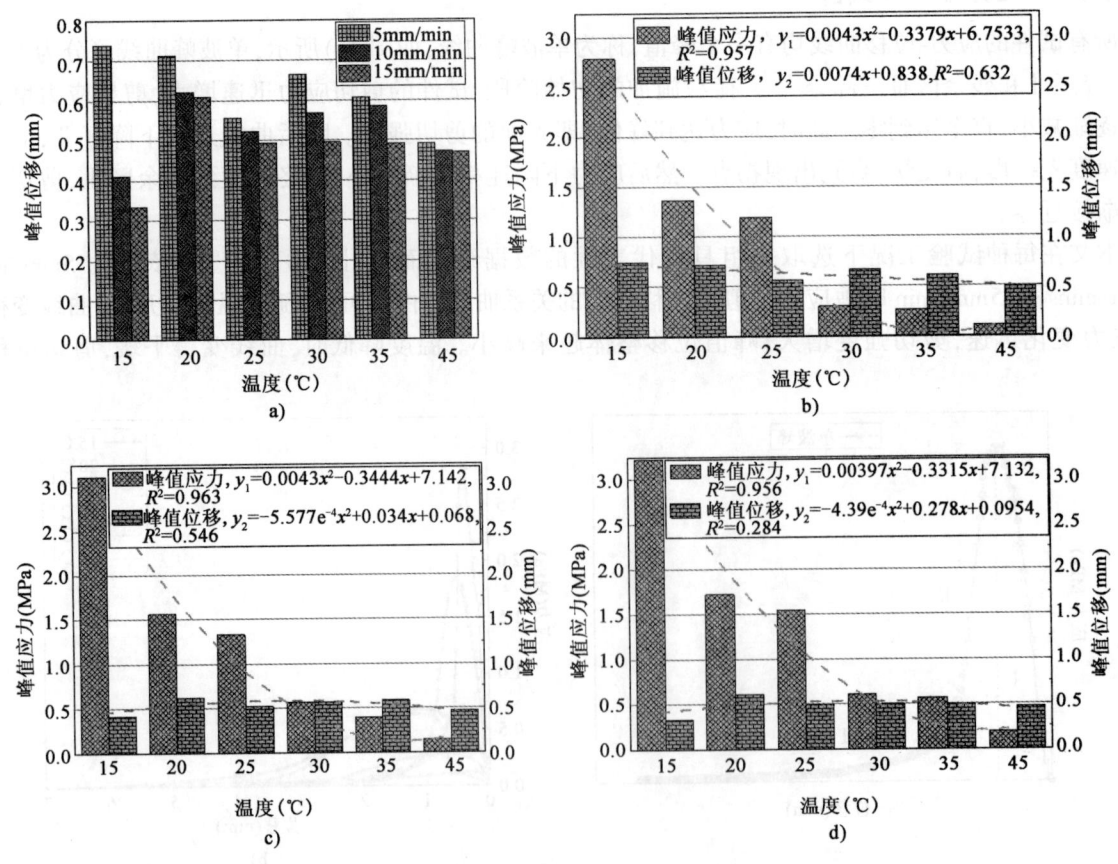

图4 峰值应力-温度、峰值位移-温度关系

2.3 剪切速率对峰值应力和峰值位移的影响

图5a)是三种不同剪切速率对应的峰值应力-温度曲线,采用指数型函数拟合,拟合优度均大于0.95,具有良好的相关性。由图5a)可知,随着温度的升高,峰值应力整体呈下降趋势,下降逐渐趋于平缓,且剪切速率对峰值应力的影响较小,在45℃时3条曲线几乎汇交于一点。这是由于沥青属于黏弹性材料,温度升高使得沥青趋近黏性流体状态,黏性增大,峰值应力减小,在45℃时,沥青的黏性十分明显,故此时剪切速率对峰值应力几乎没有影响。在温度较低时,沥青-集料剪切失效模式主要为黏附失效,此时界面失效主要发生在沥青与集料接触面;在温度较高时,界面剪切失效模式主要为黏聚失效,主要发生在沥青内部。

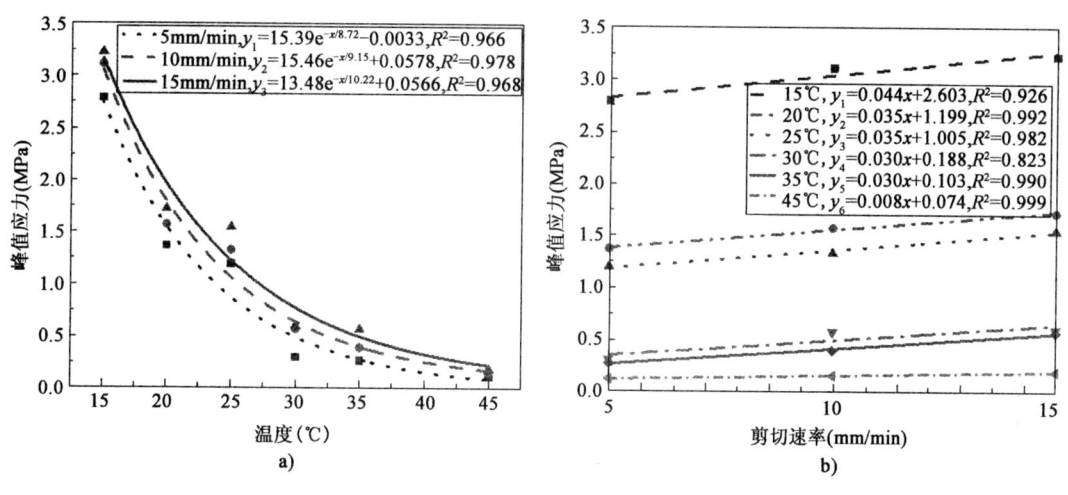

图5 峰值应力-温度、峰值应力-剪切速率关系

沥青-集料界面的峰值应力与剪切速率拟合关系如图5b)所示,二者之间呈现良好的线性关系,斜率 K 可以用来表征沥青-集料界面峰值应力的时间稳定性,K 越大,沥青-集料界面的峰值应力随剪切速率变化的增长显著,即时间稳定性越差。从图5b)中可以明显看出,相同的温度条件下,剪切速率越大,峰值应力越大。随着温度的升高,直线的斜率 K 整体呈现降低趋势,在温度为15℃时,K 值最大为0.044,当温度上升到45℃时,K 值最小,只有0.008。沥青是黏弹性材料,在低温环境下主要表现弹性体的特性,剪应力随剪切速率的增大快速升高,表现出较差的时间稳定性。反之,当处于高温的试验环境下,更多地表现出黏性体的特性,随着剪切速率的增大,剪应力缓慢升高,表现出较好的时间稳定性。

从图6中可以发现,相同温度下,剪切速率越大,峰值位移越小,在15~25℃温度范围内,线性拟合的斜率越来越小;在25~45℃温度范围内,线性拟合的斜率也越来越小。可见无论是温度较低(15~25℃)时,还是温度较高时(25~45℃),峰值位移均随着剪切速率的加快而减小。

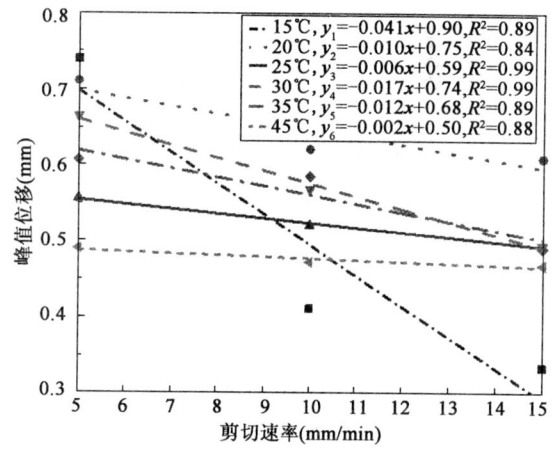

图6 峰值位移-剪切速率关系

3 结 语

(1)通过观察沥青-集料界面的断面发现:在温度变化时,断面中毛刺状的沥青区域面积和裸露的集料区域面积会随之变化,温度越高,带沥青的区域越多,界面越容易发生黏聚破坏,导致峰值应力下降;温

度越低,裸露集料的区域越大,界面越容易发生黏附破坏,峰值应力也越大。

(2)当环境温度改变时,沥青呈现明显的温度敏感性,温度升高使得沥青的黏性提升,弹性下降,表现为峰值应力随着温度的升高而下降,并且下降趋势逐渐趋向于平缓。相同剪切速率下,随着温度的升高,应力-位移曲线变得平缓,峰值位移随之增大,而剪切速率对峰值应力的影响越来越小。

(3)相同的温度条件下,沥青-集料界面的峰值应力均随着剪切速率的升高而增大,峰值位移随着剪切速率的增大而减小。剪切速率对于峰值应力的影响,反映了剪切时间对界面力学行为的影响,剪切速率大,时间就短促,材料变形小,应力变化快;相反,剪切速率小,时间相应延长,材料变形大,应力变化缓慢。

参考文献

[1] Poulikakos L D, Tiwari M K, Parti M N. Analysis of Failure Mechanism of Bitumen Films[J]. Fuel, 2013, 106(apr.):437-447.

[2] Zhang J, Airey G D, Grenfell J R A. Experimental Evaluation of Cohesive and Adhesive Bond Strength and Fracture Energy of Bitumen-aggregate Systems[J]. Materials and Structures, 2016, 49(7):2653-2667.

[3] Xu G J, Wang H. Molecular Dynamics Study of Interfacial Mechanical Behavior between Asphalt Binder and Mineral Aggregate[J]. Construction and Building Materials. 2016, 121: 246-254.

[4] L L, Huang X, Wang L, et al. Integrated Experimental and Numerical Study on Permanent Deformation of Asphalt Pavement at Intersections[J]. Journal of Materials in Civil Engineering, 2013, 25(7):907-912.

[5] 延西利,梁春雨.沥青与石料间的剪切黏附性研究[J].中国公路学报,2001,14(04):25-27.

[6] Ling T Q, Wang Y Y, Shi C H. Phased Evaluation Theory and Study on Adhesion between Asphalt and Stone Based on Surface Energy Theory[J]. Advanced Materials Research, 2013, 723:459-465.

[7] Kim S M, Darabi M K, Little D N, et al. Effect of the Realistic Tire Contact Pressure on the Rutting Performance of Asphaltic Concrete Pavements[J]. KSCE Journal of Civil Engineering, 2018. 22, 2138-2146.

[8] 张浩,张欣雨,龙红明.弱酸改性钢渣微粉的光谱学分析[J].光谱学与光谱分析,2018,38(11):188-192.

[9] Huh J D, Mun S H, Huang S C. New Unified Viscoelastic Constitutive Equation for Asphalt Binders and Asphalt Aggregate Mixtures[J]. Journal of Materials in Civil Engineering, 2011, 23(4):473-484.

[10] Erdem S, Blankson M A. Environmental Performance and Mechanical Analysis of Concrete Containing Recycled Asphalt Pavement (RAP) and Waste Precast Concrete as Aggregate[J]. Journal of Hazardous Materials, 2014, 264(jan.15):403-410.

[11] Dong MS, Sun W, Li LL, et al. Effect of Asphalt Film Thickness on Shear Mechanical Properties of Asphalt-aggregate Interface[J]. Construction and Building Materials, 2020, 263, 120208.

[12] Dong M S, Hao Y H, Zhang C, et al. Failure Mechanism Analysis of Asphalt-aggregate Systems Subjected to Direct Shear Loading[J]. Materials and Structures, 2017, 50:218.

[13] 董满生,孙炜,李凌林,等.沥青-集料剪切力学特性分析[J].武汉理工大学学报(交通科学与工程版),2019,43(16):67-72.

基于力学响应的沥青面层改性分级标准研究

罗耀芦[1,2] 王选仓[1] 张义[1] 邓玉缘[1] 宋丽萍[1]

(1.长安大学;2.中交第二公路工程局有限公司)

摘　要　改性沥青在我国高等级公路中的应用越来越广,但国内外对高等级公路沥青路面改性合理性及改性标准研究相对匮乏。针对相关规范缺乏对改性沥青路面及其改性标准的深入研究,通过分析不同工况因素对沥青路面的影响,利用有限元软件建立路面三维模型计算不同因素作用下沥青路面各层结构受力情况,最终提出沥青路面工作状况影响分级标准。

关键词　沥青路面　面层　改性　工况分级

0　引　言

改性沥青在我国高等级公路工程中扮演着重要的角色。近些年,采用改性沥青的高等级公路受到了越来越多的关注[1-2]。三层改性沥青路面的使用相对较少,仅适用于特殊地区道路,而双层路面改性使用的较为普遍。国内外对于高等级路面的沥青合理改性没有明确的标准,而沥青改性的不合理性会造成工程造价增加。本文分析沥青路面各项工作状态影响因素,建立有限元模型[3-5],计算不同因素作用下面层结构应力响应与分布[6-10],为后续研究沥青路面工作状态与改性效果提供理论支持。

1　路面工况影响因素分析

路面工作状况和路用性能受路面结构和材料、交通荷载、纵坡以及温度等多种因素影响,而这些因素又对沥青路面结构及其层间受力状况有影响。

1.1　路面结构

在路面设计中结构组合形式的选择至关重要,直接影响到路面的使用性能和极限荷载强度。目前应用最多的沥青高等级路面面层结构组合为三层结构,本文模拟仿真计算也采用三层沥青面层的不同组合结构。

1.2　路面纵坡

当车辆行驶在纵坡路段时,通常会频繁制动以达到减速效果,但增加了各层间的应力,应力过大会导致路面出现车辙、磨光、推移等各种病害。根据《公路工程技术标准》(JTG B01—2014)[11]规定,高速公路最大纵坡受设计速度限制(表1),而本文考虑高等级公路,设计速度均在80km/h以上,因此最大纵坡范围为2%~5%。

最大纵坡　　　　　　　　　　　　　　　　　　表1

设计速度(km/h)	120	100	80	60	40	30	20
最大纵坡(%)	3	4	5	6	7	8	9

1.3　交通荷载

根据《公路沥青路面设计规范》(JTG D50—2017)[12],公路交通等级划分主要依据于交通量以及交通荷载。我国部分公路超载现象较为严重[13],超载超限现象以及重交通量会对路面产生破坏损伤,如车辙病害。

1.4　路面环境

根据所处不同的自然条件,路面昼夜存在较大温差,而沥青路面性能对温度非常敏感,温度影响各层位受力情况。当温度梯度很大时,路面结构层间产生温度应力,当沥青材料本身极限抗拉强度不足时,路面就会产生裂缝。

2 计算模型建立

建立三轴空间直角坐标系,结构模型尺寸为5m×6m×5m。为模拟车轮接触地面时轮胎压力的真实情况,现将圆形接地面积进行等效,最终以矩形荷载作用在模型上。路面两端基本上没有力学约束,因此将其边界条件设置为自由端,并且约束纵向的水平方向位移和路基底面所有位移,采用8节点等参立方体单元C3D8R作为计算单元[14]并将路面模型划分网格如图1和图2所示。

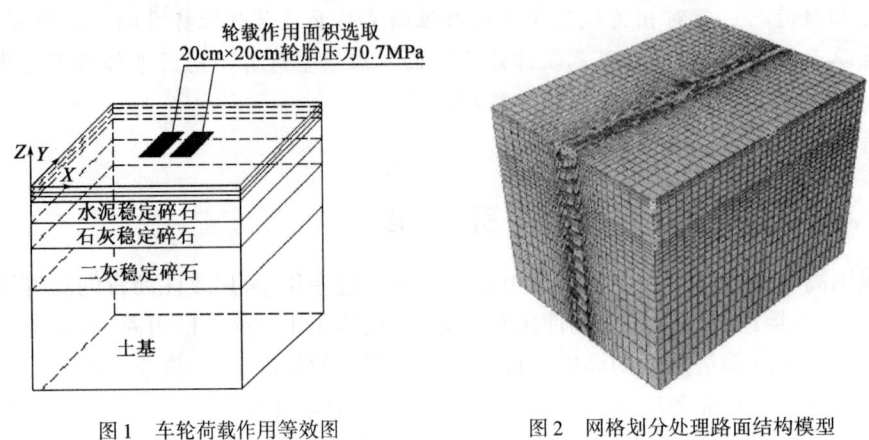

图1 车轮荷载作用等效图　　图2 网格划分处理路面结构模型

3 不同因素作用下力学响应分析

3.1 面层厚度对路面面层受力情况影响

根据我国高等级沥青路面面层的六种典型结构形式[15],在不同厚度组合条件下,各面层的最大竖向压应力、最大纵向和横向剪应力计算结果如图3所示。

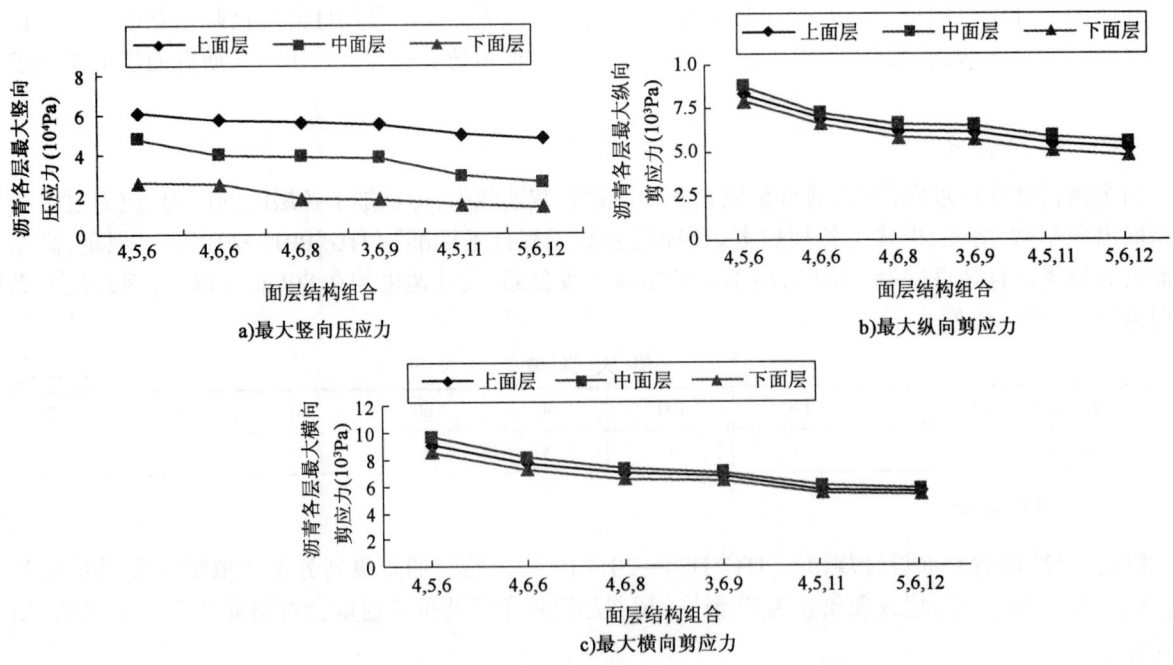

图3 面层各层受力情况随面层厚度变化规律

面层的各应力计算值,见表2。

不同面层厚度组合下应力值情况 表2

面层结构层厚度组合类型	下面层最大竖向压应力计算值(Pa)	中面层最大纵向剪应力计算值(Pa)	中面层最大横向剪应力计算值(Pa)
4cm+5cm+6cm	26030	8817	9717
4cm+6cm+6cm	25320	7263	8189
4cm+6cm+8cm	18000	6638	7360
3cm+6cm+9cm	17600	6569	7051
4cm+5cm+11cm	14700	5931	6011
5cm+6cm+12cm	13600	5609	5804

（1）由图3a)可知，上、中、下面层的最大竖向压应力下降幅度较大。由图3b)、c)可知，中面层所承受的最大纵向、横向剪应力最大。

（2）各层位的最大纵向、横向剪应力随组合厚度的递增而出现下降趋向，但下降百分比相差不大。

3.2 路面纵坡对路面面层受力情况影响

通过不同纵坡分析各层受力情况，得出不同坡度对面层结构的影响，坡度范围为0%～5%，每间隔1%。对面层各层位所受应力进行模拟计算，结果如图4所示。

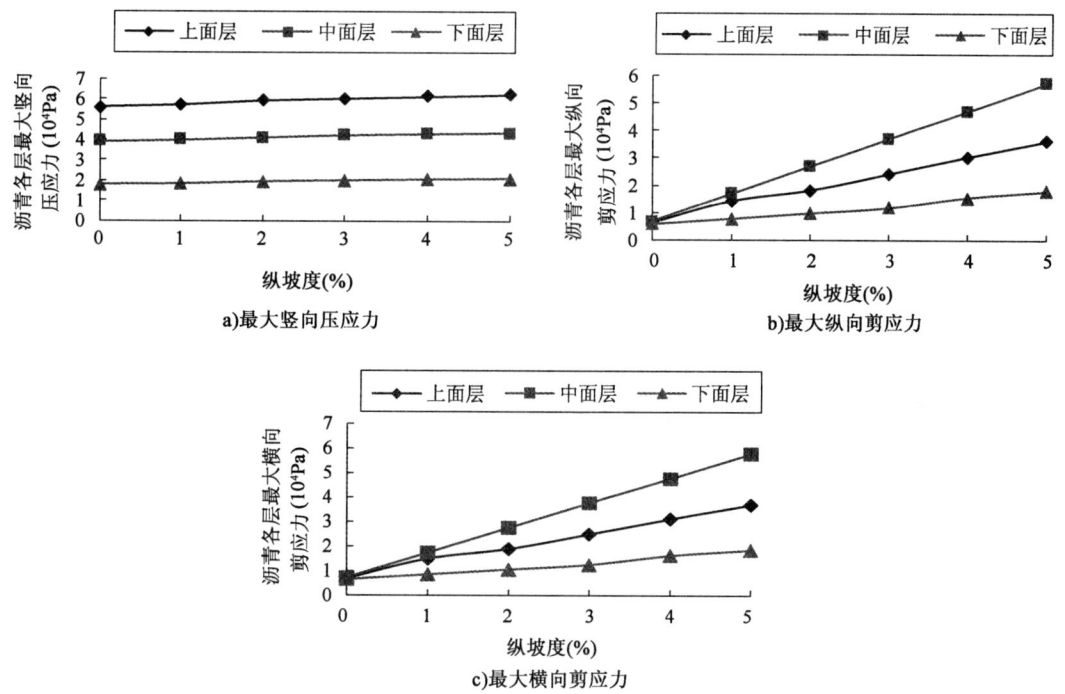

图4 路面各层位受力情况随纵坡度变化规律

面层的各应力计算值如表3所示。

不同纵坡坡度下各层位应力值情况 表3

路面纵坡(%)	0	1	2	3	4	5
下面层最大竖向压应力值(Pa)	18000	18323	19335	19945	20457	20858
中面层最大纵向剪应力值(Pa)	6638	16738	26838	36938	46937	57138
中面层最大横向剪应力值(Pa)	7360	17459	27559	37563	47670	57891

（1）路面面层结构由于坡度的逐渐递增而出现各项应力也随之增加现象。

（2）路面面层结构的各项应力与纵坡坡度大致呈线性正相关关系。

3.3 交通荷载对路面面层受力情况影响

结合道路的交通量和交通等级来综合考虑交通荷载对路面结构受力情况的影响,《公路沥青路面设计规范》(JTG D50—2017)规定各交通等级的交通量,如表4所示。

交通等级 表4

设计交通荷载等级	极重	特重	重	中等	轻
设计使用年限内设计车道累计大型客车和货车交通量($\times 10^6$辆)	≥50.0	50.0~19.0	19.0~8.0	8.0~4.0	<4.0

通过改变路面结构模型中的超载程度,算得各层位的应力值,研究交通荷载对各层位应力状态的作用,如图5所示。

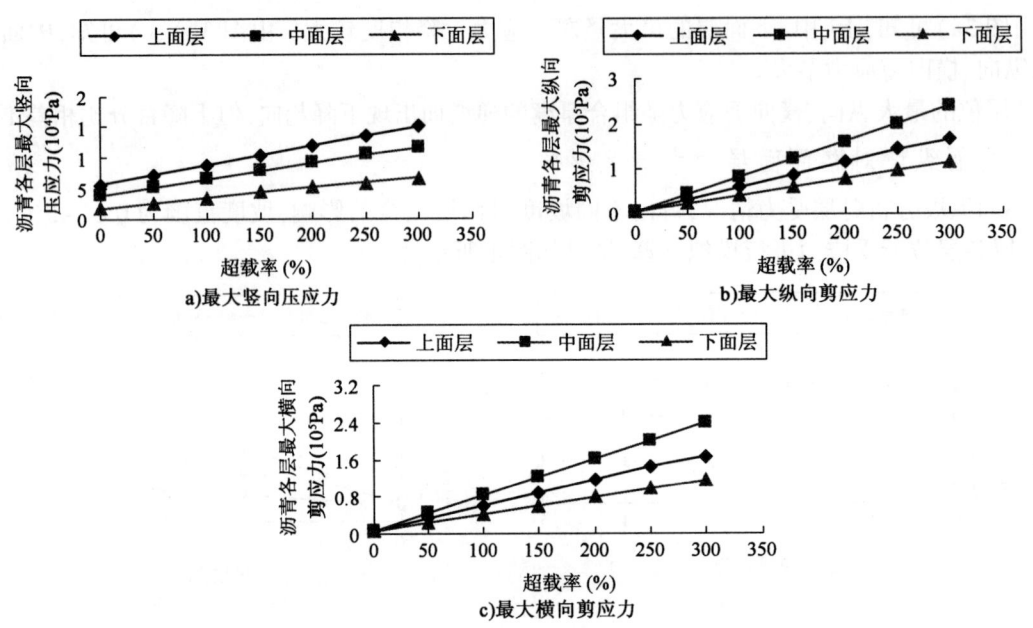

图5 路面各层位受力情况随荷载大小变化规律

面层的各应力计算值如表5所示。从表5可知:
(1)路面面层的各项应力值随超载率增加而出现增加现象。
(2)路面面层的各项应力与超载程度呈线性相关关系。

不同荷载程度下各层位应力值情况 表5

超载程度(%)	0	50	100	150	200	250	300
下面层最大竖向压应力值(Pa)	18000	26646	35292	43938	51765	59231	66312
中面层最大纵向剪应力值(Pa)	6638	45338	83938	122438	161038	199638	239638
中面层最大横向剪应力值(Pa)	7360	46060	84659	123159	161758	200354	240359

3.4 路面温度对路面面层受力情况影响

考虑路面温度对面层各层位间受力情况的作用,选取不同的路面温度,计算分析温度对路面各面层力学性能的影响,结果如图6所示。

(1)在不同温度条件下,上面层所受到的竖向压应力最大。在路面温度升高过程中,各层位的最大竖向压应力都急剧下降。看出温度因素对竖向压应力的影响非常显著。

(2)由图6b)、c)可知,中面层的最大纵向、横向剪应力最大。在温度升高过程中,各层位受到的最大纵向、横向剪应力迅速下降,可以看出温度对纵向、横向剪应力的影响也十分显著。

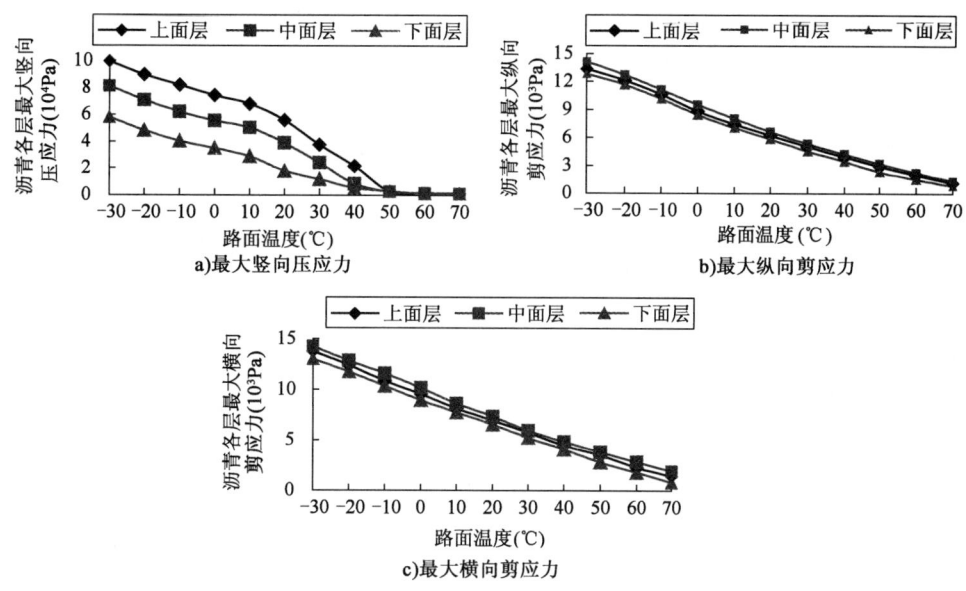

图 6　面层各层受力情况随路面温度变化规律

4　沥青路面面层工作状态分级

通过模拟系统计算沥青面层的不同厚度、模量组合以及纵坡坡度、交通荷载大小和路面温度等因素对各层受力情况的影响,根据上述多种因素对面层各层的受力情况进行分级,其指标根据路面温度与大气温度的关系,为了便于统计分析将其转化为大气温度,分别得出以下工况分级,如表 6 所示。

沥青路面面层工况分级　　　　　表 6

工况	纵坡坡度（%）	高温（℃）	低温（℃）一	低温（℃）二	超载程度（%）	各种货车交通量[辆/(天·车道)]
Ⅰ	[4,5)	>40	<-30	<-20	>150	>3000
Ⅱ	[2,4)	[30,40]	[-30,-10]	[-20,-10]	[50,150]	[1000,3000]
Ⅲ	(0,2)	<30	>-10	>-10	<50	<1000

注：当工作状态不同单一因素有多个工况分级时,以最不利的工况等级为准。

当路面结构处于工况Ⅰ时,其面层结构对抗剪强度和抗拉强度要求很高,建议对面层结构的上、中、下面层均进行改性;当路面结构处于工况Ⅱ时,其面层各层结构间对抗剪强度和抗拉强度要求比较高,建议对面层结构的上、中面层进行适当改性处理;当路面结构处于工况Ⅲ时,其面层结构对抗剪强度和抗拉强度要求比较高,建议必要时对面层结构进行改性,至少保证上面层进行改性。

5　结　语

本文通过建立路面面层各层的有限元模型,分析沥青路面工作状态影响因素对路面结构层受力的影响,计算不同因素条件下路面面层的竖向压应力和横向、纵向剪应力,总结提出沥青路面面层工作状况分级标准,为推进高等级公路面层结构的合理改性奠定基础。具体研究结论如下：

(1)对比分析交通荷载、纵坡及温度对沥青路面工作状况的影响,建立有限元模型计算路面各层间应力状况,确定路面结构的各项参数。

(2)计算分析在不同面层结构厚度、面层模量、纵坡坡度、荷载大小、路面温度条件下,沥青路面面层各层的最大竖向压应力和最大剪应力的分布,得到各项参数对面层各层受力情况的作用效果。

(3)通过研究沥青路面面层在各因素作用下的应力状态,并最终提出了影响沥青路面各层工作状态的三级改性等级指标,用于指导高等级公路路面的合理改性。

参考文献

[1] 肖凤,邓星鹤.沥青改性剂研究进展[J].中国胶黏剂,2020,29(09):61-66.

[2] 罗玉.改性沥青新材料在公路道路中的应用探讨[J].商品与质量,2020,000(008):114.

[3] 李铁洪,李春晓.半刚性路面层间实际结合状态的有限元模拟与分析[J].公路交通技术,2010,1:1-5.

[4] Ogoubi Cyriaque Assogba, Zhiqi Sun, Yiqiu Tan, et al. Finite-Element Simulation of Instrumented Asphalt Pavement Response under Moving Vehicular Load[J]. International Journal of Geomechanics, 2020, 20(3).

[5] Fanlong Tang, Tao Ma, Yongsheng Guan, et al. Parametric Modeling and Structure Verification of Asphalt Pavement Based on BIM-ABAQUS[J]. Automation in Construction, 2020, 111.

[6] 李浩,王选仓,房娜仁,等.基于敏感度的沥青路面结构应力传递行为[J].重庆交通大学学报(自然科学版),2021,40(01):119-126.

[7] 宋丽萍.高速公路沥青路面面层合理改性研究[D].西安:长安大学,2012.

[8] Imad L. Al-Qadi, Hao Wang, Pyeong Jun Yoo, et al. Dynamic Analysis and in Situ Validation of Perpetual Pavement Response to Vehicular Loading[J]. Transportation Research Record, 2008, 2087(1).

[9] Ogoubi Cyriaque Assogba, Yiqiu Tan, Xingye Zhou, et al. Numerical Investigation of the Mechanical Response of Semi-rigid Base Asphalt Pavement Under Traffic Load and Nonlinear Temperature Gradient Effect[J]. 2020, 235.

[10] 李彦伟,穆柯,石鑫,等.基面层间接触状态对沥青路面力学响应影响[J].长安大学学报(自然科学版),2014,34(02):38-44.

[11] 中华人民共和国交通运输部.公路工程技术标准:JTG B01—2014[S].北京:人民交通出版社,2014.

[12] 中华人民共和国交通运输部.公路沥青路面设计规范:JTG B50—2017[S].北京:人民交通出版社股份有限公司,2017.

[13] 张卫华.重载交通条件下高速公路沥青路面设计[J].山西交通科技,2010(02):8-9.

[14] Bassem Ali, Marwan Sadek, Isam Shahrour. Finite-Element Model for Urban Pavement Rutting: Analysis of Pavement Rehabilitation Methods[J]. Journal of Transportation Engineering, 2009, 135(4).

[15] 陈东鹏.不同沥青路面结构组合层间工作状态研究[D].西安:西安建筑科技大学,2010.

高速公路隧道路面抗滑性能分布规律及养护关键技术研究

徐志祥　吁新华

(江西省交通投资集团路网运营管理公司养护技术中心)

摘要 为掌握高速公路隧道路面抗滑性能的分布规律,对江西省14条高速公路共计113座单洞隧道的长度、路面类型以及通车年份进行统计,并对其路面抗滑性能进行了检测和分析。结果表明:无论是水泥路面还是沥青路面,隧道内路面抗滑性能均低于隧道外部,且随着隧道长度的增加,隧道内部路面抗滑性能指标越低,隧道内外路面抗滑性能差距越大。整体来看,隧道路面的抗滑性能曲线呈"碗形"分布,进入隧道入口后路面抗滑性能急剧下降,而后趋于稳定,在到达隧道出口前慢慢回升。最后,根据国内外相关文献和现场调查,分析了隧道路面抗滑性能述衰减过快的原因,并结合多年养护经验,总结了隧道路面养护决策关键技术点。

关键词 公路工程 隧道工程 抗滑性能 分布规律 关键技术

0 引言

目前,江西省高速公路桥隧比为15.5%,且随着路网的完善,未来建设将逐步向山区丘陵地带延伸,隧道所占比例将越来越高。然而,隧道路面在设计时大都参照普通路基路面,未考虑到隧道内部特殊环境及其对安全的特殊要求,在服役过程中出现不同程度的病害。江西省高速公路路况检测数据表明:隧道路面普遍存在抗滑不足且衰减过快问题,极大影响了隧道内行车安全性和舒适性。根据相关研究[1],隧道路段的交通事故率和严重程度要远高于普通路段,且交通事故率偏高与路面抗滑性能不足有明显的相关性[2]。基于此,本文对江西省高速公路典型路段隧道的基础信息进行统计,并对其路面抗滑性能进行检测和分析,得到分布规律,为后续新建高速公路隧道路面设计和养护决策提供参考。

1 隧道基础信息统计分析

本文选取江西省14条高速公路的113座单洞隧道作为研究对象。其中,113座隧道单洞长度共计154.68km。根据隧道分类标准,113座隧道类型分布和比例如表1和图1所示。路面类型以沥青路面为主,水泥路面隧道仅9座,占比8%,全部为2005年以前开通的隧道,路面类型和通车年份分布情况如图2和图3所示。

隧道类型分布情况 表1

隧道分类	特长隧道	长隧道	中隧道	短隧道
隧道长度 L(m)	$L>3000$	$3000 \geqslant L>1000$	$1000 \geqslant L>500$	$L \leqslant 500$
隧道数量(座)	12	41	27	33

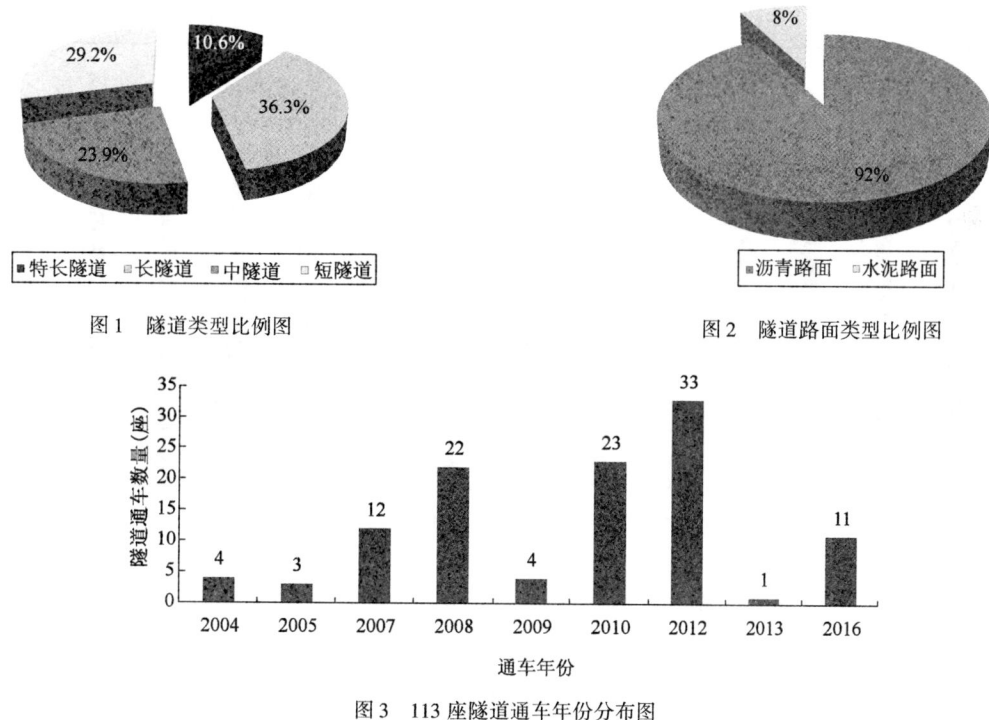

图1 隧道类型比例图　　图2 隧道路面类型比例图

图3 113座隧道通车年份分布图

2 隧道路面抗滑性能分布规律

为分析隧道路面抗滑性能分布规律,对上述113座隧道入口前400m至出口后400m区间范围的路面抗滑性能指标(SRI百米值)进行了检测。

2.1 空间分布规律

为分析隧道内外路面抗滑性能的差异,同时排除通车时间、路面类型以及交通量等因素的影响,本文对同一路段隧道内外路面抗滑性能指标进行纵向比较,结果见表2和图4。可以得出:

(1)隧道内外路面抗滑性能差距较大,隧道内路面抗滑性能指标主要分布在良、中等级,部分甚至在差等级,隧道外路面抗滑性能指标主要分布在优、良等级;

(2)无论是水泥路面还是沥青路面,所有路段的隧道内路面抗滑性能均低于隧道外部。

表2 各个路段隧道内外路面抗滑性能指标对比

序号	路段名称	路面类型	隧道入口外	隧道内	隧道出口外
1	TG高速	水泥路面	81.6	78.1	81.7
2	TJ高速	水泥路面	95.4	78.1	95.4
3	JY高速	沥青路面	89.8	82.5	88.7
4	WJ高速	沥青路面	91.4	80.9	91.4
5	RG高速	沥青路面	82.2	75.0	83.1
6	YR高速	沥青路面	90.3	80.6	88.7
7	SJ高速	沥青路面	90.5	84.5	90.8
8	DS高速	沥青路面	94.0	85.1	95.1
9	FJ高速	沥青路面	91.3	85.7	93.1
10	GC高速	沥青路面	91.0	84.2	91.4
11	JL高速	沥青路面	93.8	91.0	94.5
12	JM高速	沥青路面	96.5	60.1	95.1
13	CN高速	沥青路面	89.1	78.8	90.6
14	ND高速	沥青路面	87.7	78.1	83.7

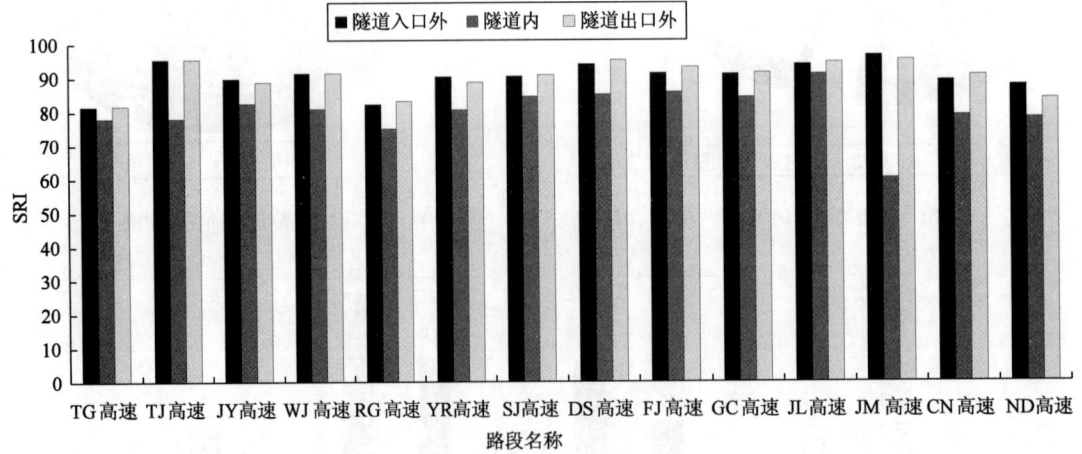

图4 各个路段隧道内外路面抗滑性能指标对比

为深入分析隧道内外路面抗滑性能空间分布规律,本文对隧道入口前400m至出口后400m的区间范围进行分段,示意图如图5所示。然后分别统计短隧道、中隧道、长隧道和特长隧道各百米段落SRI平均值,并进行曲线描绘,结果如图6所示。结果表明:

(1)随着隧道长度的增加,隧道内外路面抗滑性能的差距越来越大;

(2)整体来看,隧道内外路面的抗滑性能曲线呈"碗形"分布,在进入隧道入口后路面抗滑性能急剧下降,而后趋于稳定,在到达隧道出口前慢慢回升。

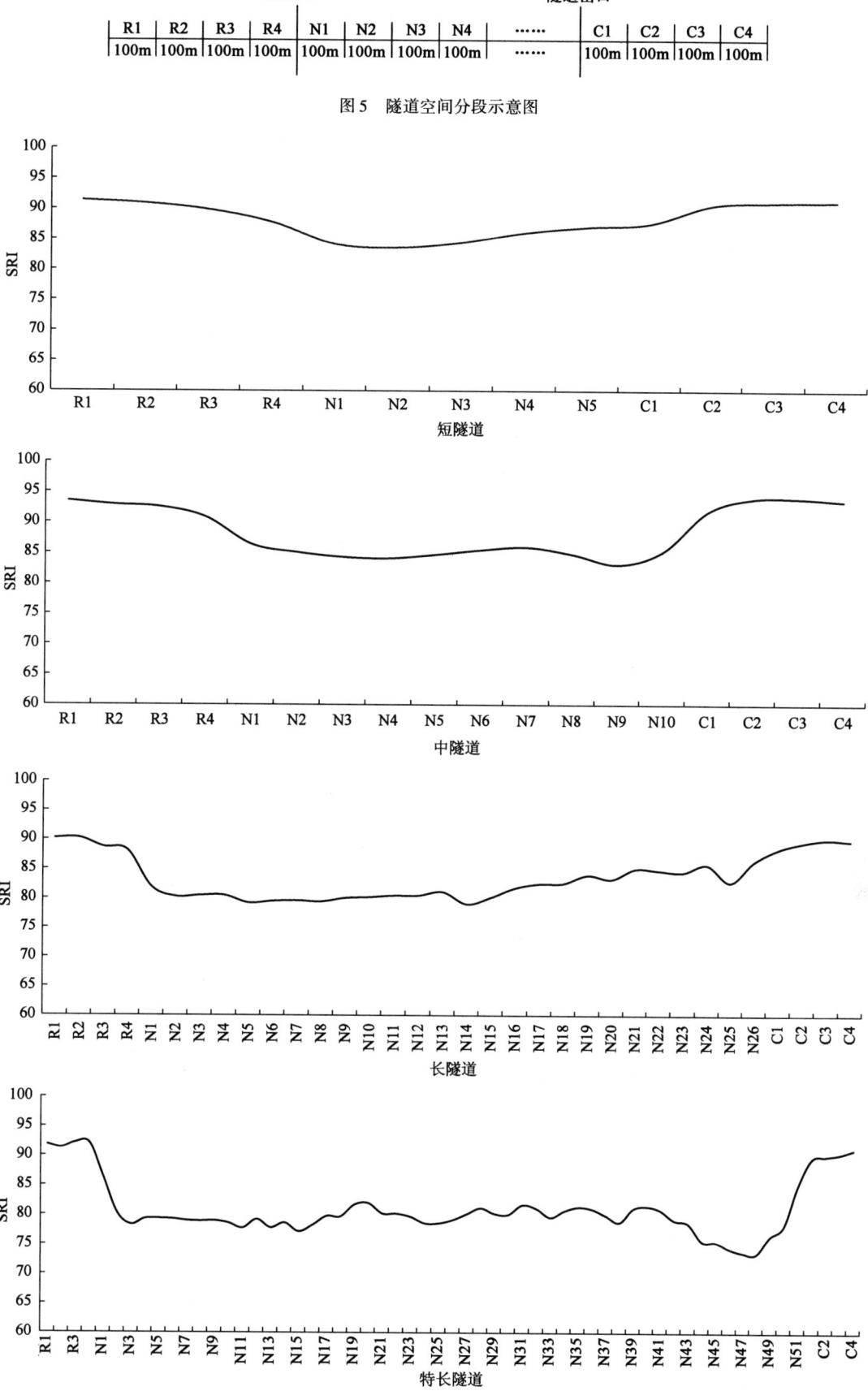

图 5　隧道空间分段示意图

图 6　各类型隧道路面抗滑性能(SRI)空间分布规律

为分析隧道长度对路面抗滑性能的影响,本文选取含有不同类型隧道(隧道总量大于10)的3个路段进行纵向比较,以排除其他影响因素(通车时间、路面类型、交通量以及施工质量等)的影响,不同类型隧道路面抗滑性能指标均值见表3和图7。3个路段的结果均表明:隧道越长,隧道内部路面抗滑性能指标越低。

3个路段不同类型隧道路面抗滑性能指标(SRI)均值　　　　表3

隧道类型	WJ 高速	DS 高速	GC 高速
短隧道	88.4	90.8	88.8
中隧道	86.5	87.8	86.1
长隧道	79.8	85.9	84.3
特长隧道	78.3	79.9	83.0

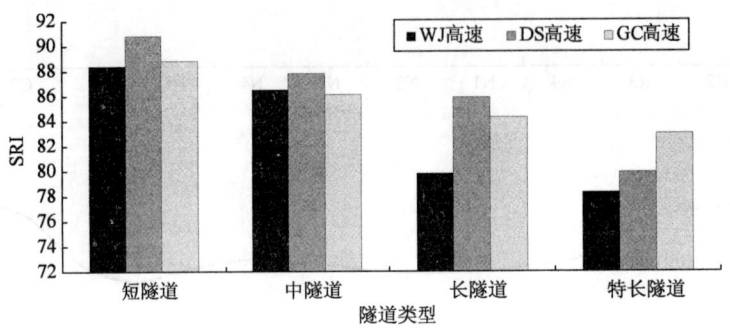

图7　3个路段不同类型隧道路面抗滑性能

2.2 时间分布规律

为分析隧道通车时间对隧道路面抗滑性能的影响,本文计算了历年通车的隧道路面抗滑性能均值,见表4和图8。可以看出隧道路面抗滑性能与通车时间长短无明显相关性,可见通车时间非主要影响因素。

历年通车隧道路面抗滑性能指标平均值　　　　表4

通车年份	2004	2005	2007	2008	2010	2012	2013	2016
隧道数量	4	3	12	22	23	33	1	11
SRI 平均值	78.1	78.1	84.5	80.9	83.6	85.8	60.1	79.0

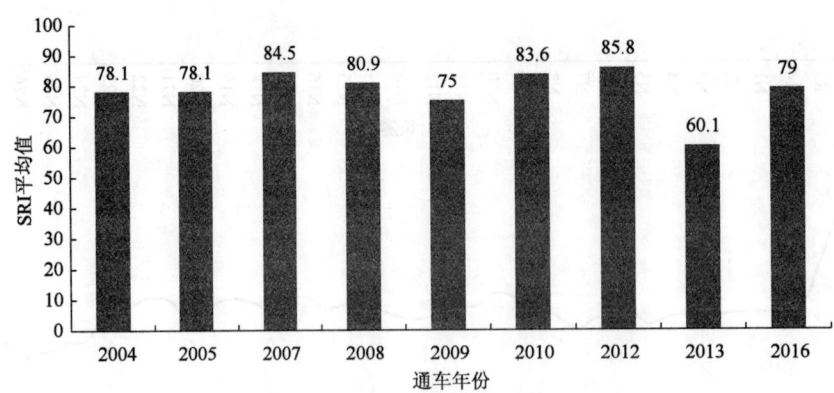

图8　历年通车隧道路面抗滑性能指标对比图

3　隧道路面抗滑性能衰减原因分析

综上所述,隧道内路面的抗滑性能明显低于隧道外路面,而在通车初期两者的抗滑性能处同一水平,可见隧道内路面的抗滑性能衰减更快。通过现场调查，并结合国内外相关文献[3-5]，本文将隧道路面抗滑性能衰减过快的原因总结为以下4个方面：

（1）隧道内环境相对封闭，湿度大，地下水丰富，这些条件导致路面长期处于潮湿环境中，导致路面结晶形成光滑表面。

（2）隧道内空气流动性小，汽车尾气、油烟、粉尘等在潮湿条件下易覆盖在路表形成油腻性膜层，降低轮胎和路面间的摩擦力，导致路面抗滑能力减小。

（3）隧道内车速慢、制动多，加上长期处于潮湿环境，易于磨损路面的宏观和微观构造，加速路面的磨光。

（4）隧道内部空间的限制，加上通风、照明等条件差，路面施工机械和施工人员的工作质量都会有一定程度的下降，使得隧道内部路面实体工程质量较隧道外部差。

4 隧道路面养护决策关键技术研究

隧道内路面养护作业受空间、时间等限制，隧道路面抗滑不足修复措施应选择施工和易性好、开放交通快、效果持续久以及经济效益好的技术。根据隧道内的限制条件，结合隧道抗滑性能衰减原因，总结隧道路面养护决策技术关键点包括性能和工艺两大方面。

4.1 性能要求

（1）抗滑性及其耐久性。由于隧道路面服役环境的复杂及对安全的特殊要求，隧道路面养护技术要有良好的抗滑性及耐久性，避免短时间内进行二次养护。

（2）抗水损害性能。由于隧道内湿度大，地下水丰富，导致隧道路面长期处在潮湿的环境中，隧道路面养护技术要有良好的抗水损害性能。

（3）耐腐蚀性能。隧道内空气流动性小，汽车尾气、油烟、粉尘等化学物质易覆盖在路面，隧道路面养护技术要有良好的化学惰性。

（4）阻燃性能。隧道内部一旦发生交通事故极易引发火灾，要求隧道路面养护技术具有阻燃性能。

4.2 工艺要求

（1）超薄。隧道内部通风条件差，加上空间限制，铣刨作业在隧道内难以实施，在进行加铺时要考虑到隧道净空需求。

（2）温拌。隧道内空气流通困难，尤其是长隧道或特长隧道，热拌沥青摊铺作业时会导致隧道内有害气体含量剧增，而温拌技术可有效减少作业过程烟气排放量，减少对施工人员身体的伤害。

（3）快速。隧道是高速公路交通咽喉要道，其施工作业会带来严重的交通拥堵甚至是中断交通，要求隧道路面养护技术施工过程快速且能在较短的时间内开放交通。

5 结 语

（1）无论是水泥路面，还是沥青路面，隧道内路面抗滑性能均低于隧道外部，且随着隧道长度的增加，隧道内路面抗滑性能越低，隧道内外路面抗滑性能的差距越来越大。整体来看，隧道内外路面的抗滑性能曲线呈"碗形"分布，在进入隧道入口后路面抗滑性能急剧下降，而后趋于稳定，在到达隧道出口前慢慢回升。

（2）隧道内部环境相对封闭，长期处于潮湿环境，空气流动性小，汽车尾气等易附着于沥青路表面，且隧道内车速慢，制动多，加速面的磨光，加上隧道路面先天施工质量难以保障，导致其抗滑性能衰减较快。

（3）在选择隧道路面养护技术时，应选择抗滑性及其耐久性、抗水损害性能好、具有耐腐蚀性能和阻燃性，且厚度超薄、施工快速、温拌的技术。

参考文献

[1] 许新权,吴传海,李善强,等.基于大样本数据的广东省公路隧道路面安全性能调查研究[J].武汉理

工大学学报:交通科学与工程版本,2016(6):1116-1119.
[2] 傅永强.高速公路隧道路面抗滑性能分析及改善方法比较[J].公路交通科技:应用技术版,2019,000(007):242-243.
[3] 杨小龙,李波,李晓辉.甘肃省公路隧道混凝土路面抗滑特性测试与分析[J].公路工程,2015,040(003):105-108.
[4] 许新权,吴传海,李善强.湿热地区隧道路面抗滑性能衰减原因分析及对策研究[J].广东公路交通,2016(5):1-6.
[5] 刘志胜.隧道路面设计影响因素综述[J].公路,2017(09):131-135.

基于胎路耦合的沥青路面摩擦行为数值仿真

余苗[1,2] 罗延生[1] 童铈尧[3] 陈海峰[4] 孔令云[1]

(1.重庆交通大学土木工程学院,交通土建工程材料国家地方联合工程实验室;
2.长安大学公路学院;3.重庆市彭水县交通局;4.绍兴市公路与运输管理中心)

摘 要 为进一步研究轮胎与纹理路面之间的耦合摩擦行为,明确沥青路面抗滑机理,本文在充分考虑路表纹理构造的基础上,借助ABAQUS有限元软件进行了轮胎-沥青路面动力学模型的构建。首先,分析了车辆在静载作用、制动情况下的轮胎与路面接触区域的接触面积及压强,发现相较于动态荷载作用,静载作用下的胎路接触更加充分;接下来,基于不同速度、滑移率,进行了指数摩擦模型与传统库仑模型的对比,并在此基础上研究了不同工况(路面、荷载、速度、滑移率)下的胎路耦合摩擦作用。结果表明:传统的库仑模型,并不适用于多因素耦合作用下的胎路摩擦行为研究,而指数模型更能反映实际情况下行车制动时胎路摩擦系数的变化,适用于全面评价多因素耦合作用下的胎路摩擦行为;对轮胎进行有效制动时,随着荷载的增大,胎路剪应力逐渐从胎冠往胎侧转移,且随着荷载的不断增大,剪应力呈现先减小后增大的趋势;而速度的增大会引起剪应力的不断减小,从而导致胎路摩擦系数减小;胎路作用存在最佳滑移率10%~15%,使得胎路摩擦系数达到最大值。

关键词 沥青路面 胎路耦合 路表纹理 摩擦系数 有限元 指数摩擦模型

0 引 言

轮胎与沥青路面接触在车辆稳定控制中起着重要作用,因为在车辆行驶过程中,地面摩擦力通过轮胎传递给车辆[1]。然而,轮胎与地面接触情况(路面类型、荷载、速度、滑移率等)复杂,会导致胎路摩擦力发生变化,从而影响车辆行驶稳定[2-3]。因此,在考虑各种工况的同时,对轮胎-沥青路面进行建模分析,对于车辆行驶安全分析具有重要研究意义[4]。

Henry[5]通过对现场的测量,得出橡胶轮胎与路面之间的摩擦力取决于轮胎的速度,但胎路相对运动过程中的接触行为并不明确:由于轮胎与沥青路面的接触区域的复杂性(荷载、沥青路面类型、接触面积等)会引起最大摩擦力发生变化,同样会导致现场测量情况与实际情况并不完全符合。而有限元能充分考虑轮胎与路面滚动接触的许多重要方面,如复合轮胎结构、轮胎的非线性行为、路面材料、复杂的边界条件及温度影响等[6]。因此,通过有限元数值方法来模拟实际情况是十分必要的(Laursen 和 Stanciulescu[7])。

基金项目:国家自然科学基金(51608085);中国博士后科研项目资助(2018M633444);陕西省博士后科研项目(2018BSHEDZZ123);长安大学中央高校基本科研道路结构与材料交通运输行业重点实验室业务费专项资金资助项目(300102210506);广东省交通科技创新平台研究项目(No.2018B020207003)

国内外的许多学者通过有限元对轮胎与路面接触情况进行了模拟,如 Ebbott T. G. 等[8]在轮胎的有限元建模中对轮胎材料的本构模型进行改进,研究了温度对轮胎运动的影响。采用热力耦合法,进一步预测瞬态温度场的分布,有效计算了轮胎的滚动阻力。该模型更多关注温度对轮胎材料的力学性能作用,未提及轮胎的不同运动工况对其运动阻力的影响。韩秀枝[9]在 ANSYS 软件中建立的轮胎与路面有限元模型,主要通过热力耦合方法讨论在不同速度、荷载、轮胎胎压等因素作用下,轮胎滚动阻力的变化。通过以前的研究[10]建立胎路耦合有限元模型,评价了含不同胶粉含量的干法橡胶沥青路面在可变荷载、不同轮胎胎压及滑移率作用下的抗滑性能。但都未能充分考虑胎路间接触的影响因素。因此,需要建立一个充分考虑各种胎路接触情况的胎路接触模型来准确地反映轮胎与路面之间的真实接触情况,以此来模拟在不同工况下的胎路耦合摩擦作用。

1 轮胎-路面接触作用有限元模型

1.1 胎路有限元模型的建立

利用有限元 ABAQUS 软件建立轮胎-路面有限元模型,并依赖于 Newton-Raphson 理论进行不断迭代。其中,轮胎模型采用 PIARC 光圆试验轮胎,由橡胶-帘线复合材料组成,材料参数见表1。并采用 rebar 单元和实体单元来模拟具有加强筋的帘线材料及橡胶材料[11]。

橡胶-帘线复合材料参数[11]　　　　　　　　　　　　　　　　表1

帘线材料	密度 (kg/m³)	杨氏模量 (MPa)	泊松比	横截面积 (mm²)	加强筋间距 (mm)	与子午面的夹角 (°)
钢丝带束第一层	5900	172200	0.3	0.212	1.16	70
钢丝带束第二层	5900	172200	0.3	0.212	1.16	110
尼龙帘布层	1500	9870	0.3	0.421	1	0

选用 SMA、AC、OGFC 三种常用的路面面层级配并在实验室内制备玄武岩、石灰岩、花岗岩的沥青混合料车辙试件,试件尺寸为 300mm×300mm×30mm,共计9块车辙试件,再利用激光轮廓扫描仪[12]对沥青路面进行信息重构。

在进行轮胎-路面模型建模时,由于轮胎与路面的接触过程较为复杂,需要考虑其约束条件,在 ABAQUS 中对参考点 RIM 和轮毂设置刚体约束,具体约束条件如下:

(1)对轮胎内表面施加均布荷载,模拟轮胎充气内压作用;

(2)由于所建轮胎与路面的距离很近,可限制参考点的自由度,以实现轮胎与路面的预接触。建立后的三维有限元模型如图1所示。

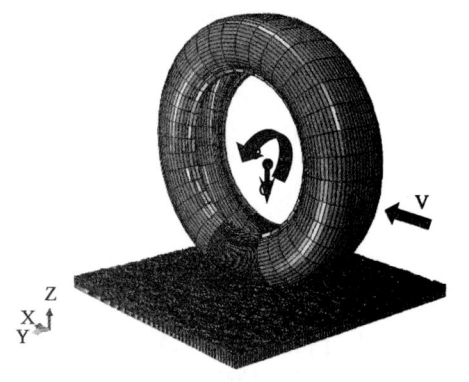

图1 胎路有限元模型

1.2 轮胎接地作用模型的有效性验证

为了验证胎路模型的实用性,需对轮胎的径向变形与接地面积以及轮胎在与接触状态进行验证。验证时路面模型选择平面,将胎压设置为 0.25MPa,荷载分别设置为 1500N、2000N、2500N、3000N,进行轮胎接地模型在静载作用下的有限元计算。

首先对轮胎的径向变形与接地面积进行了分析,如图2及图3所示。随着静载作用的增大,轮胎径向变形与接地面积都逐渐增大。当荷载为 3000N 时,轮胎的径向变形 Δr 约17.3mm,接触面积约为 103.5cm²,与实际情况[13]较为接近。

其次,分析了在不同荷载作用下轮胎与平面接触状态的变化。由图4可知,在固定胎压下,随着荷载的增大,胎路接触状态呈以下变化规律:最初,接触压强主要集中于接触区域中心;而荷载的增大,引起接触区域不断扩大,接触压强整体呈现增长的趋势;当荷载达到一定值后,轮胎与平面的应力集中区域从接触区域的中央过渡到接触区域的两侧,且接触区域逐渐趋于矩形。

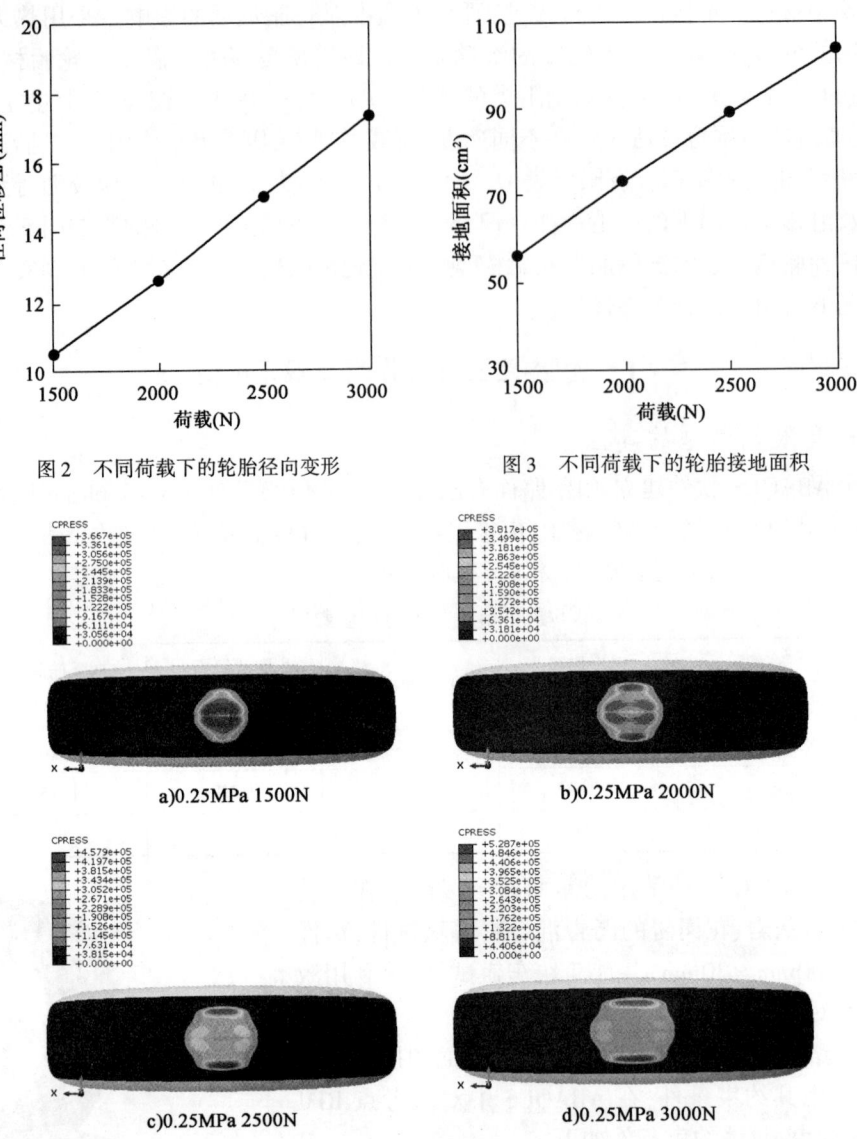

图2 不同荷载下的轮胎径向变形　　图3 不同荷载下的轮胎接地面积

a)0.25MPa 1500N　　b)0.25MPa 2000N

c)0.25MPa 2500N　　d)0.25MPa 3000N

图4 不同荷载下的胎路接触压强云图

以上分析结果表明,轮胎在荷载作用下的力学响应与实际情况相符。因此,三维轮胎有限元模型分析力学性能具有较强的可靠性。

2 胎路耦合摩擦行为研究

2.1 胎路接触动力学原理

在利用ABAQUS对胎路接触问题进行动力学求解的过程中,通过ABAQUS/Standard求解器对胎路的摩擦行为进行稳态分析。其中,主要涉及轮胎动力学原理。其方程如式(1)所示[14]。

$$MU + F_{int} = F_{ext} \tag{1}$$

式中:M——轮胎模型质量矩阵;
　　　U——轮胎模型节点的位移向量;
　　　F_{int}——轮胎内部的荷载向量;
　　　F_{ext}——轮胎外部的荷载向量。

$$M = \int_{\Omega^0} \rho^0 \phi^T \phi d\Omega^0 \tag{2}$$

$$F_{int} = \int_{\Omega^0} B_0^T S d\Omega^0 + \int_{\partial\Omega_c^0} k_p (n\phi)^T n\phi ds^0 \tag{3}$$

$$F_{ext} = \int_{\Omega^0} \rho^0 \phi^T f d\Omega^0 + \int_{\partial\Omega_N^0} \phi^T \hat{t}^0 ds^0 + \int_{\partial\Omega_c^0} [\phi^T \hat{t}_T^0 + k_p g(n\phi)^T] ds^0 \tag{4}$$

式中：Ω——轮胎空间域；

ϕ——包含基本函数的矩阵；

n——轮胎与刚体路面接触界面的法向向量；

ρ——轮胎密度；

k_p——轮胎切向弹性模量；

f——轮胎体力；

g——间隙函数；

t_T——轮胎与路面接触面的切向应力。

对应力向量 S、矩阵 B_0 的定义如下：

$$S = \{S_{xx}, S_{yy}, S_{zz}, S_{xy}, S_{yz}, S_{xz}\}^T \tag{5}$$

$$B_0 = \{B_0^1, \cdots, B_0^i, \cdots, B_0^n\} \tag{6}$$

$$B_0^i = \partial\phi_i/\partial X_i F_{jk} \tag{7}$$

$$F_{jk} = \partial x_i/\partial x_k \tag{8}$$

式中：S_{ij}——第二类 Piola-Kirchhoff 应力；

F_{jk}——变形梯度；

x_i——模型原始坐标；

x_k——变形向量。

2.2 摩擦模型选择

2.2.1 指数摩擦模型与库仑模型的对比分析

采用库仑摩擦模型与指数形式的抗滑模型来研究胎路的摩擦行为时，都需通过胎路有限元模型进行计算，从而得到不同速度、滑移率下的摩擦系数。研究前，均考虑轮胎胎压为 0.25MPa，荷载为 2500N。以玄武岩 AC 路面为例，将结果进行整理，同时将库仑模型与指数模型的抗滑数据进行对比。图 5a)~图 5d)均反映了相应速度下不同滑移率对摩擦系数的影响。从库仑摩擦模型计算得到的抗滑数据来看，速度的变化未对胎路的摩擦行为造成影响。此外，当轮胎的滑移率大于临界滑移率 10% 时，摩擦系数也不再发生任何变化。而现实车辆在制动情况下的胎路摩擦系数会受速度、轮胎滑移率等因素的影响[15-16]。因此，常数形式的库仑摩擦模型并不适用于多因素耦合作用下的胎路摩擦行为研究。反观指数模型计算得到的摩擦系数，其变化规律更符合实际情况。

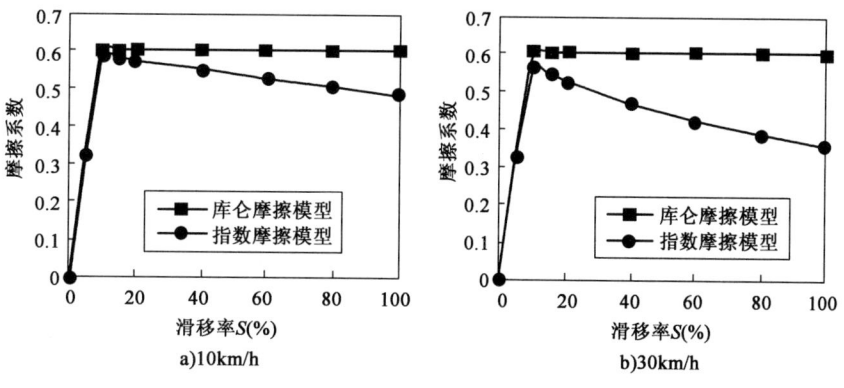

图 5

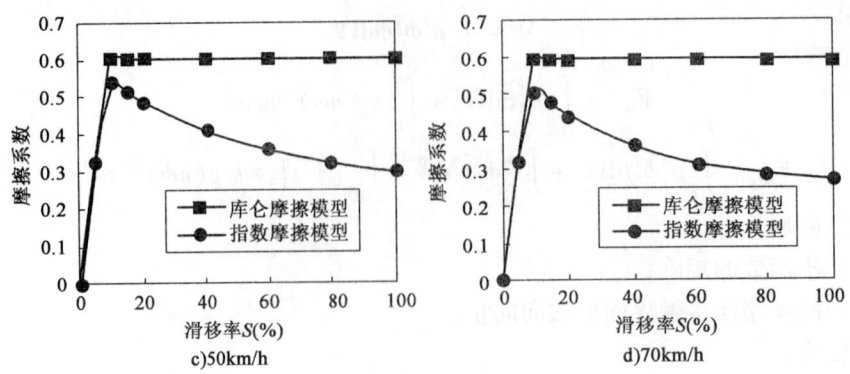

图5 基于库仑摩擦模型与指数形式抗滑模型的路面摩擦系数对比

综上所述，与库仑摩擦模型相比，指数摩擦模型更能反映实际情况下行车制动时胎路摩擦系数的变化，适用于全面评价多因素耦合作用下的胎路摩擦行为。因此，本文采用指数形式的摩擦模型定义轮胎与路面的摩擦行为，并结合有限元法进行胎路动态接触的稳态分析（式9）。

$$\mu = \mu_k + (\mu_s - \mu_k)e^{-d_c \Delta v} \tag{9}$$

式中：μ_k——最高滑移速度对应的动摩擦因数；

μ_s——临界状态的静摩擦系数；

d_c——路面状况衰减系数；

Δv——滑动速度。

2.2.2 指数摩擦模型的确定

轮胎与路面的摩擦性能与胎路接触状态密不可分，摩擦系数的预估模型可考虑断面构造深度 MPD、荷载 F、轮胎运动速度 v、滑移率 S、接触压强 P 等变量。对于同一类型的路面而言，速度对路面抗滑的影响较大。通常摩擦系数与速度的关系可通过幂函数或指数函数的形式进行表达[15,17-19]。

在 ABAQUS 中分别定义位移、荷载等边界条件，同时定义胎路平均接触压强 P、断面构造深度 MPD 等多个参数。由于真轮胎与试验轮胎的结构、尺寸存在差异，需要将有限元计算所得的胎路平均接触压强进行仿真值与实验值的相关性分析，构建转换关系（式14）再将转换后的压强带入摩擦模型，从而进行有限元模型的稳态计算。指数形式的摩擦模型如下：

$$\mu = Ae^{B \cdot \Delta v} + C \tag{10}$$

$$A = 0.208MPD - 0.341P + 0.546 \tag{11}$$

$$B = 0.023MPD + 0.028 \tag{12}$$

$$C = 0.341P - 0.057 \tag{13}$$

$$P = 3.703P^* - 0.203 \tag{14}$$

式中：μ——动摩擦系数；

P——转化后的压强，MPa；

Δv——轮胎的滑动速度，km/h；

MPD——平均断面构造深度，mm；

P^*——基于仿真研究所得的胎路平均接触压强，MPa。

3 仿真结果分析

在得到胎路耦合的指数摩擦模型后，将胎路接触时不同路面、荷载、速度、滑移率等工况下的影响因素代入指数摩擦模型进行胎路间的摩擦系数分析。

3.1 胎路静态接触状态研究

当轮胎在承受静载及处于制动工况时，胎路接触状态各异。首先在不同荷载（1500N、2000N、2500N、

3000N）下，对 SMA、AC、OGFC 路面开展静态接触工况进行研究。如图 6 所示，各图反映了轮胎与各类型路面在不同荷载下的接触面积与平均接触压强。

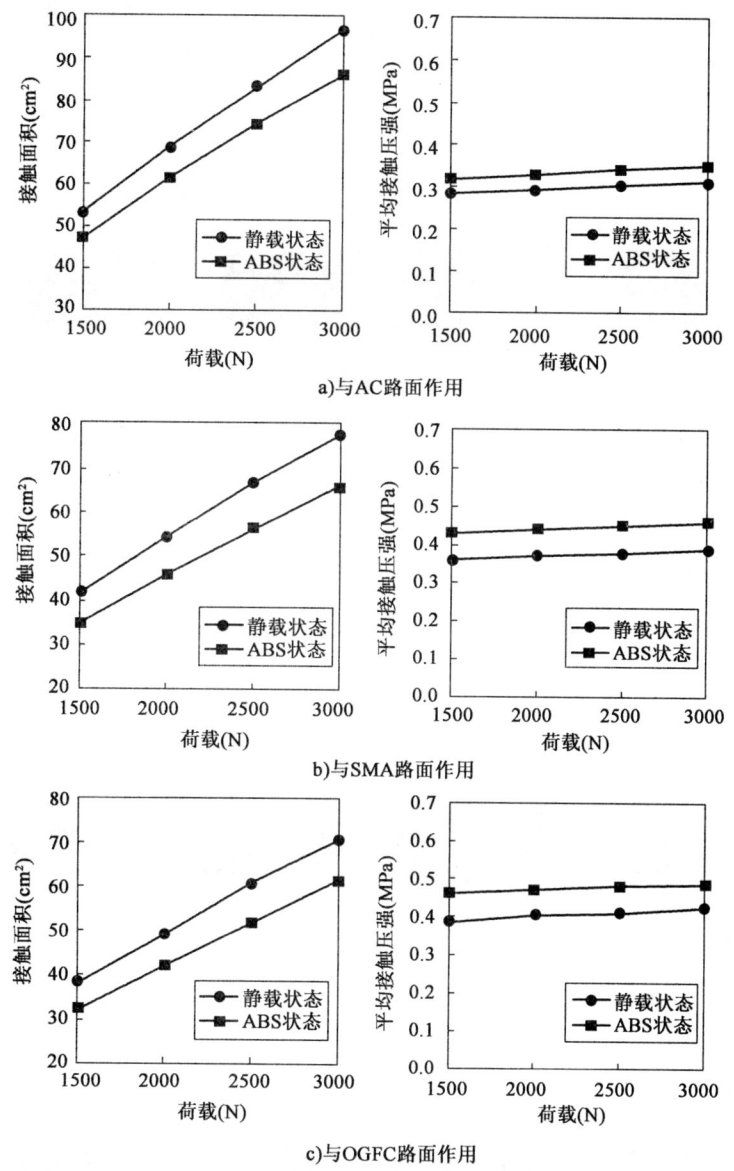

图 6　在静载、ABS 制动作用的轮胎与各类型路面的接触参数对比

从图中荷载与胎路接触参数的关系可看出，ABS 状态下的轮胎接地面积、平均接触压强的变化趋势与静载作用下的变化规律一致，即胎路接触面积与平均接触压强均随荷载增大而增大。此外，对比了静载状态与 ABS 状态的胎路接触参数。发现受 ABS 制动作用的轮胎接地面积比受静载作用的轮胎接地面积有一定减小，平均接触压强有所增大。由此表明，相较于动态荷载作用，静载作用下的胎路接触更加充分。

3.2　胎路动态摩擦行为研究

在进行轮胎与沥青路面摩擦行为研究时，通过有限元方法综合研究了多因素耦合作用下轮胎与路面摩擦作用的动力学响应。进而分析路面类型、轮胎所受荷载、运动速度、滑移率等因素对胎路摩擦行为的具体影响。

3.2.1　路面类型对胎路摩擦行为的影响

图 7 反映了荷载 3000N、速度 30km/h、滑移率为 15% 时不同类型的路面对轮胎胎面的剪切作用。从

图中可看出,因纹理的差异,不同路面对轮胎胎面的剪切效果也会明显不同。相比与SMA、OGFC两种路面,AC路面对轮胎的剪切作用偏小,而剪应力的大小会影响轮胎与路面的摩擦系数,剪应力越大,说明制动状态下轮胎与路面的摩擦作用越大。从剪应力的分布状态来看,在制动过程中,剪应力更多集中于轮胎运动方向(见图中 v 标注)的前端及胎肩。由此也可说明,轮胎在这些区域更容易受到磨损。

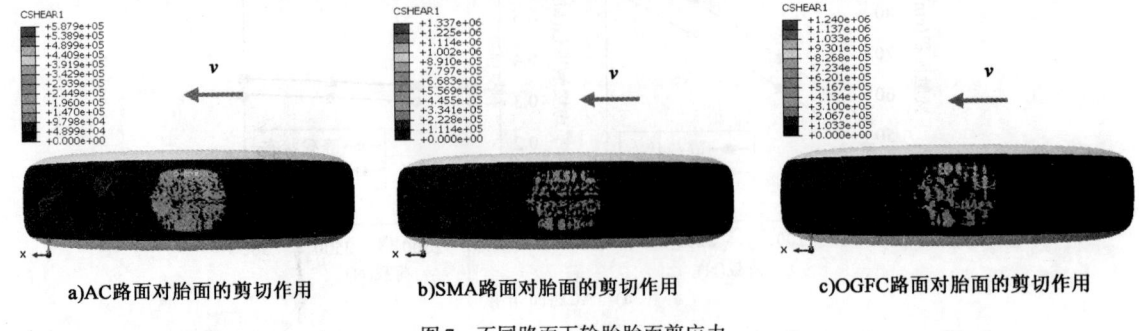

a)AC路面对胎面的剪切作用　　b)SMA路面对胎面的剪切作用　　c)OGFC路面对胎面的剪切作用

图7　不同路面下轮胎胎面剪应力

3.2.2 荷载对胎路摩擦行为的影响

在考虑最不利抗滑情况下,路面模型选用AC路面,保持轮胎运动速度为30km/h,轮胎滑移率15%,通过改变荷载(1500N、2000N、2500N、3000N),利用ABAQUS研究不同荷载对轮胎胎面的剪切作用,如图8所示。

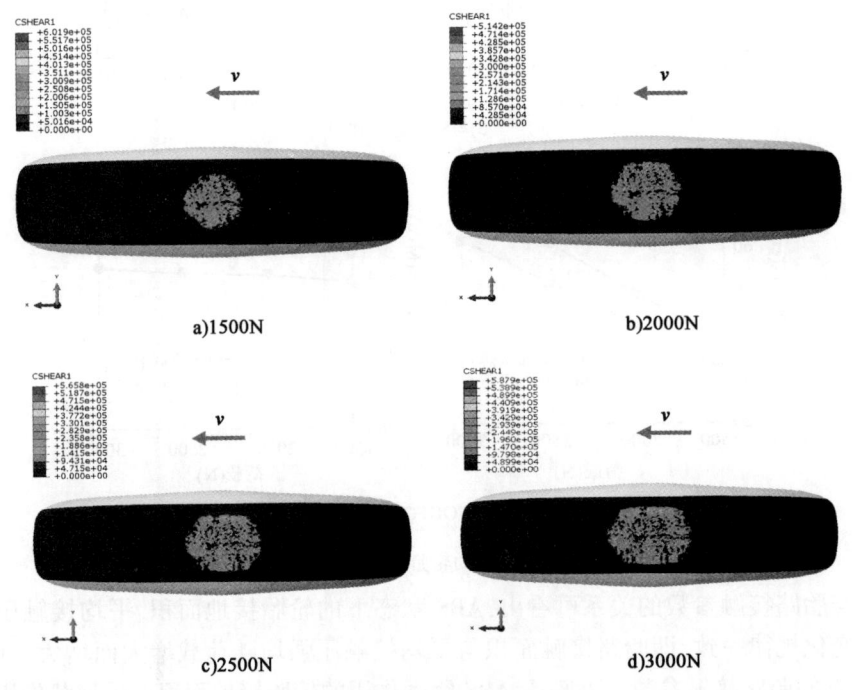

a)1500N　　b)2000N

c)2500N　　d)3000N

图8　不同荷载下的轮胎胎面剪应力

从图中不难看出,压力较小时,轮胎胎面主要由胎冠与路面接触,因此剪应力主要集中在沿轮胎运动方向的中心部分,随着荷载的不断增大,胎面剪应力逐渐由胎面中心往胎侧扩展;可以很明显地看出当荷载到达3000N时,剪应力集中胎侧。由于轮胎采用的是非线性复合材料,荷载的增大会导致胎路接触面积发生变化,导致胎面的剪切作用先减小后增大。表明了在一定荷载范围内,有效增大荷载可以提高轮胎与路面的抗滑水平。

3.2.3 速度对胎路摩擦行为的影响

保持AC路面、轮胎荷载2500N、滑移率15%不变,研究不同轮胎运动速度对轮胎胎面剪切力影响,将轮胎运动速度分别设为10km/h、30km/h、50km/h、70km/h,如图9所示。从图中可以看出剪应力更多集中在胎侧上,且随着速度的不断增大,接触面间的剪应力也呈明显下降趋势,因此,为保证行车安全,应将车速控制在一定范围内。

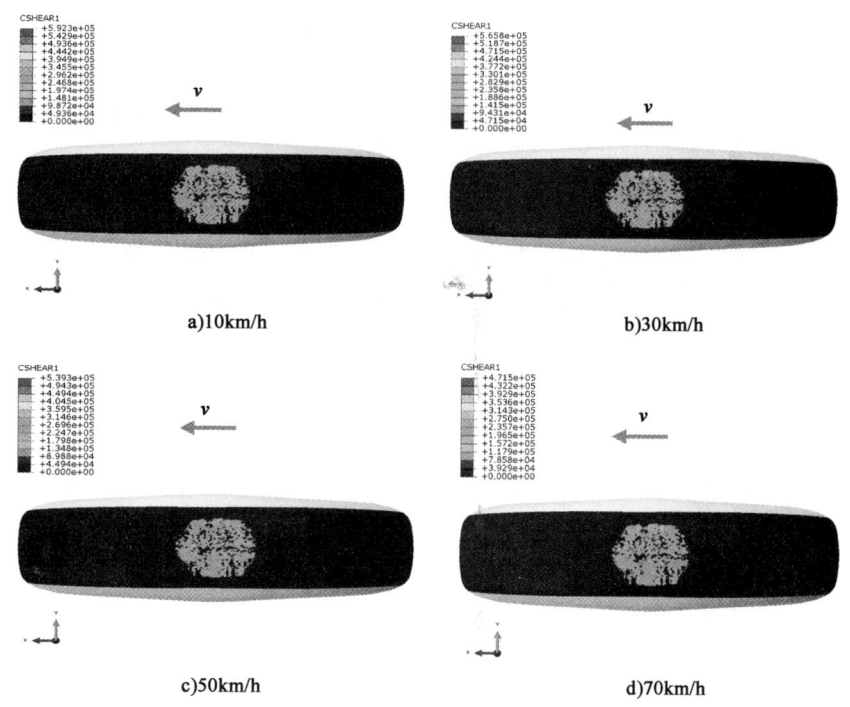

图9 不同速度下的轮胎胎面剪应力

同时考虑 ABS 与抱死两种情况的制动作用,对三种级配路面与轮胎胎面的摩擦行为进行有限元分析。速度与胎路摩擦系数的关系如图10所示。该图可反映出胎滑动速度的增大,会减小胎路摩擦作用的现象。由图10b)可看出,OGFC 与 SMA 路面在高速作用下,其抗滑性能的衰减速度比 AC 路面更加趋于平缓。主要原因在于,路面的构造深度越大,越有利于削弱速度对路面抗滑的影响。

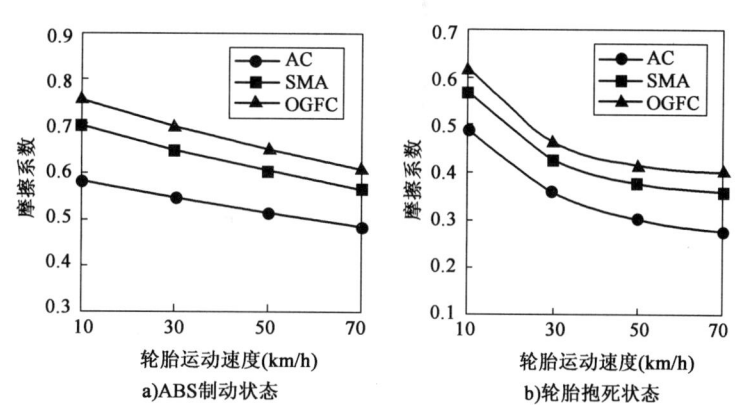

图10 轮胎速度对胎路摩擦系数的影响

3.2.4 滑移率对胎路摩擦行为的影响

保持轮胎荷载2500N不变,改变轮胎滑移率(0%、5%、10%、15%、20%、40%、60%、80%、100%),同时分别计算了轮胎在运动速度为30km/h、70km/h 时与三种路面的摩擦作用系数。如图11所示,随着滑移率的增大,胎路摩擦系数最开始会明显增大。在滑移率10%~15%时,胎路摩擦系数达到最大值。之后,胎路摩擦系数随着滑移率的增大会有所减小。同时对比图11a)、b)两图,可看出:随着滑移率的增大,在高速运动状态下,胎路摩擦系数会更快到达稳定值。

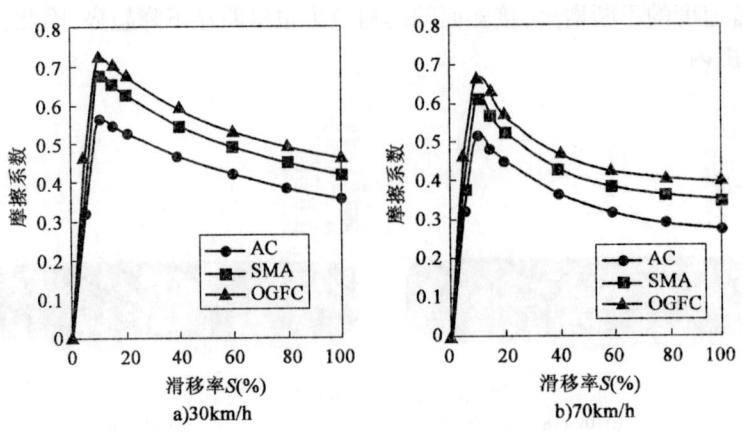

图11 轮胎滑移率对胎路摩擦系数的影响

4 结 语

本文通过ABAQUS有限元软件建立了轮胎-路面接触模型,并开发摩擦用户子程序,在胎路摩擦作用模型中计算胎路动摩擦系数,分析各因素对路面抗滑系数的影响,同时对指数摩擦模型的合理性进行验证。此外,重构了轮胎模型,对轮胎制动过程中与路面接触行为进行稳态分析,分析轮胎制动效率对路面抗滑性能的影响。基于以上研究,结果发现:

(1)对胎路胎路静态接触状态和ABS状态进行了对比,结果发现:相较于动态荷载作用,静载作用下的胎路接触更加充分。

(2)针对荷载、速度及滑移率等轮胎运动状态,进行了胎路接触状态单因素研究。结论为:①对轮胎进行有效制动时,可以明显地看出:随着荷载的增大,胎路剪应力从胎冠往胎侧转移,且随着荷载的不断增大,剪应力有着先减小后增大的趋势;②速度的增大会引起剪应力的不断减小,从而导致胎路摩擦系数减小;③随着滑移率的增大,摩擦系数先显著增大,但存在最佳滑移率10%~15%,随后摩擦系数会随着速度增大而缓慢降低。

(3)将指数摩擦模型与常数形式的库仑摩擦模型摩擦模型进行了对比,发现指数模型不仅可用于试验抗滑值的预估,还可结合有限元对胎路摩擦行为进行评价。因此,在未来的胎路摩擦行为研究中,可选择指数摩擦模型进行分析。

参考文献

[1] Wong J Y. Theory of Ground Vehicles[M]. Wiley, New York, 1993.

[2] Wang H, Al-Qadi I L. Combined effect of moving wheel loading and three–dimensional contact stresses on perpetual pavement responses[J]. Transp. Res. Rec., 2009, 2095:53-61.

[3] Wang H, Al-Qadi I L. Evaluation of surface-related pavement damage due to tire braking[J]. Road Mater. Pavement Des., 2010, 11(1):101-121.

[4] 郑双彬,朱晟泽,程永振,等.基于轮胎滑水模型的轮胎-沥青路面附着特性影响因素分析[J].东南大学学报(自然科学版),2018,48(4):719-725.

[5] Henry J J. Evaluation of Pavement Friction Characteristics: A synthesis of Highway Practice[J]. National Academy Press, 2000, Washington, DC, NCHRP Synthesis 291.

[6] Hao Wang, Imad L. Al-Qadi. Effect of Surface Friction on Tire-Pavement Contact Stresses during Vehicle Maneuvering. American Society of Civil Engineers, 2014, 140(1):001-008.

[7] Laursen A, StanciulescuI. An Algorithm for Incorporation of Frictional Sliding Conditions within a Steady State Rolling Framework[J]. Commun. Numer. Methods Eng., 2006, 22(4):301-318.

[8] Ebbott T G, Hohman R L, Jeusette J P, et al. Tire Temperature and Rolling Resistance Prediction with

Finite Element Analysis[J]. Tire Science and Technology,1999,27(1):2-21.
[9] 韩秀枝.子午线轮胎稳态滚动阻力及水滑特性的研究[D].北京：北京化工大学,2009.
[10] 余苗.基于轮胎-路面耦合的干法CRM抗滑面层研究[D].重庆：重庆交通大学,2014.
[11] Hibbit,Karlsson,Sorensen. ABAQUS/Standard User's Manual. Version 6.4,[M]. USA:Inc,2004.
[12] 徐自生.基于沥青路面表观纹理特征的路面摩擦抗滑机理研究[D].重庆：重庆交通大学,2019.
[13] 朱晟泽.基于路面宏观纹理的轮胎抗滑行为数值模拟研究[D].南京：东南大学,2017.
[14] Cho J R,Lee H W,Yoo W S. A Wet-Road Braking Distance Estimate Utilizing The Hydroplaning Analysis of Patterned Tire[J]. International Journal for Numerical Methods in Engineering, 2007, 69(7): 1423-1445.
[15] Wang H,AL-Qadi I L,Stanciulescu I. Effect of Surface Friction on Tire-Pavement Contact Stresses During Vehicle Maneuvering[J]. Journal ofEngineering Mechanics,2014,140(4):04014001.
[16] Srirangam S K,Anupam K,Kasbergen C,et al. Study of Influence of Operating Parameters on Braking Friction and Rolling Resistance[J]. Transportation Research Record,2015,2525(1):79-90.
[17] Dorsch V,Becker A,Vossen L. Enhanced Rubber Friction Model for Finite Element Simulations of Rolling Tyres. Plast. Rubbers Compos.,2002,31(10):458-464.
[18] Savkoor A R. Mechanics of Sliding Friction of Elastomers. Wear,1986,113(1):37-60.
[19] Oden J T,Martins J A C. Models and Computational Methods for Dynamic Friction Phenomena. Comput. Meth. Appl. Mech. Eng.,1985,52(1-3):527-634.

冰-沥青路面黏结特征分析

胡新悦[1]　冷滨滨[2]　王中俊[2]　吕廷军[2]

(1.哈尔滨工业大学交通科学与工程学院；2.青岛冠通市政建设有限公司)

摘要　路面积冰给行车安全带来了巨大的危害，因此除冰技术成为冬季行车安全的重要保障，而路表冰层与路面之间的黏结特征与除冰效率密切相关。为了探究冰与沥青路面的黏结特征及影响因素，本文采用自主开发的多角度测量冰与沥青路面黏结力的试验设备，测定了冰-沥青路面界面破坏过程中二者间拉力的变化，分析了冰层形变特征；采用温度、拉拔角度、级配类型分别表征外界环境、冰路界面与外荷载间的角度、路面粗糙度并研究其对黏结力的影响，设计正交试验，对3种影响因素进行显著性分析。结果表明：冰层在破坏时会经历弹性、塑性变形阶段，最终发生脆性破坏；冰与沥青混合料间的黏结力随着温度的升高而降低；当拉拔角度为45°时，黏结力最小；开级配沥青混合料与冰之间的黏结力小于间断级配小于连续密级配；在3个影响因素中，温度对冰与沥青混合料之间的黏结力影响最大，其次为级配类型和拉拔角度。因此采用合适的路面级配类型，并在除冰雪过程中改变温度和施荷角度可以大大提高除冰效率。

关键词　道路工程　冰-沥青路面界面黏结　试验研究　影响因素

0　引　言

在我国北方地区冬季多雨雪天气，路表积水在温度、风速、湿度等多因素作用下[1]极易凝结成冰并黏附在路表，导致轮胎与路面间附着系数降低[2]，车辆易发生侧翻、追尾等事故，给交通安全带来了巨大危

基金项目：国家重点研发计划(2018YFB1600203)；国家自然科学基金优秀青年项目(51922035)；黑龙江省优秀青年项目(YQ2019E019)。

害。因此,除冰雪技术成为了冬季行车安全的重要保障,而冰与路面之间的黏结机理及黏结力大小影响着除冰雪效率,因而研究冰与路面之间的黏结特征是十分必要的。

关于冰与路面的黏结特征的研究,各国学者从化学的角度解释了冰与路面的附着机理[3-5],通过有限元分析[6]或力学模型的建立得出冰层的破坏是荷载反复作用下冰层裂缝逐渐扩展失稳导致的脆性破坏[7],研发了多种测试冰与路面间黏结力的试验设备,探究了沥青种类[8-9]、冰层冻结时间[10-11]、集料的化学组成[12]、路表粗糙度[13-15]与除冰雪时破冰铲切入角度[16]等因素对冰与路面间黏结力的影响,这些研究都具有很好的理论价值与实际意义。但这些研究还存在以下不足:

(1) 目前对冰与沥青路面的黏结界面破坏时二者间黏结力的变化缺少试验论证及唯象分析;

(2) 车辆对路面产生的压力、真空吸力、水平作用力经过冰层的传输变为斜拉或斜剪作用,其与冰路黏结界面的角度也会随车速发生变化,而目前鲜有考虑车辆荷载角度的研究。因此,本文基于自主开发的一种多角度测量冰与沥青路面黏结力的试验设备及方法[17],对冰-沥青路面破坏过程中二者间的拉力变化进行了测定和分析,并研究了温度、荷载角度、沥青路面类型对冰路黏结力的影响,最终得出各个因素与冰路黏结极限拉力的关系,并对其进行了显著性研究,为除冰雪技术提供一定的理论支撑。

1 试验材料与配合比

1.1 原材料

本文采用 SBS 改性沥青制备 AC-16 和 SMA-16 试件,采用高黏高弹改性沥青制备 OGFC-16 试件,其物理性质见表 1 和表 2;所用粗集料为黑龙江地产安山岩,填料采用矿粉。

SBS 改性沥青物理性质　　　　　　　　　　表1

参　数	试验结果	技术要求	试验方法
针入度(25℃,100g,5s)(0.1mm)	68.7	60~80	T 0604
延度(5℃,5cm/min)(cm)	33.4	≥30	T 0605
软化点(℃)	85.2	≥55	T 0606

高黏高弹改性沥青物理性质　　　　　　　　表2

参　数	试验结果	技术要求	试验方法
针入度(25℃,100g,5s)(0.1mm)	88	80~100	T 0604
延度(5℃,5cm/min)(cm)	48.3	≥40	T 0605
软化点(℃)	87	≥50	T 0606
运动黏度(135℃)(Pa·s)	2.9	≤3	T 0625 T 0619
弹性恢复(25℃,5cm/min,1h)(%)	95	≥90	T 0662

1.2 配合比设计

本试验选用 3 种级配类型:AC-16,SMA-16,OGFC-16;级配采用《公路沥青路面施工技术规范》(JTG F40—2004)中的级配范围中值,见表3,SMA-16 与 OGFC-16 沥青混合料中木质素纤维掺量为总质量的 0.3%。

沥青混凝土混合料级配　　　　　　　　　　表3

级配类型	筛孔尺寸(mm)										
	19	16	13.2	9.5	4.75	2.36	1.18	0.6	0.3	0.15	0.075
AC-16	100	95	84	71	50	37	26.5	18.5	12.5	9.5	6.5
SMA-16	100	95	70	55	26	19.5	18	15	12.5	11.5	10
OGFC-16	100	95	80	57.5	21	16	12	9.5	7.5	5.5	4

1.3 试件成型

为了使沥青混合料试件达到更大的密实度并减少集料的破碎程度,本试验中沥青混合料试件采用旋转压实成型的方式,试件尺寸为 $\phi 100\text{mm} \times 63.5\text{mm}$。

2 试验方案

2.1 多角度黏结力测试系统

为了实现荷载角度对冰与沥青混合料黏结力的影响探究,本文自主开发了多角度黏结力测试系统。测试设备如图1所示。

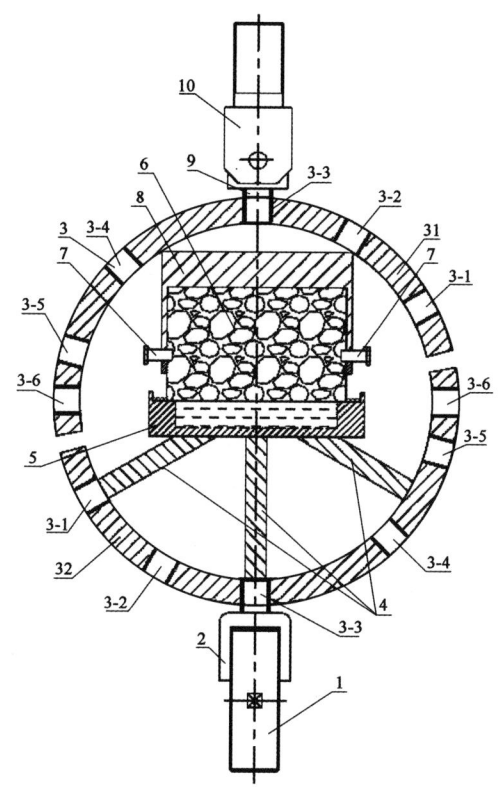

图1 黏结力测试设备结构示意图

该试验装置的基本原理为:试验装置上下两个环托尺寸相同,共同组成中心与冰-混合料界面中心重合的圆环,上下环托的圆心对称位置上分布有相同尺寸的螺孔,通过上下部连接组合件连接圆环上的螺孔与MTS液压式加载系统的工作台,可对冰-混合料界面中心施加竖直轴向力,直至冰面破坏,上下托环分开,MTS液压式加载系统读出破坏时的极限荷载,即为冰路之间的黏结力,而通过选择圆环上螺孔的位置,可以实现施荷角度的变化。图2为施加荷载与冰-沥青混合料试件界面的夹角为45°时的情景。试验过程中由MTS的集中冷源来控制环境的温度,确保空心槽内的冰不会融化。多角度测量冰与沥青路面黏结力系统的工作流程如图3所示。

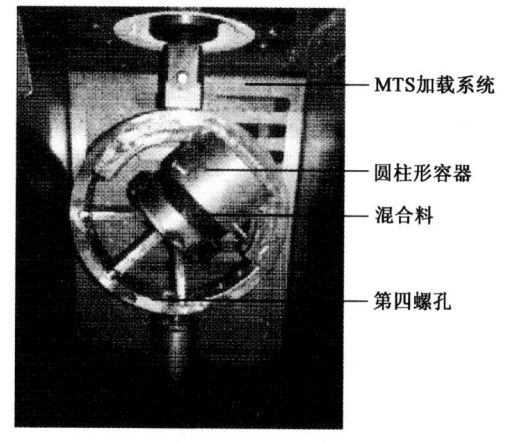

图2 黏结力测试设备实物照片示意图

2.2 试验方案设计

本文中试验分为3大组进行,试验方案见表4。每组试验取3个试件做平行试验,取其平均值作为最终结果记录。

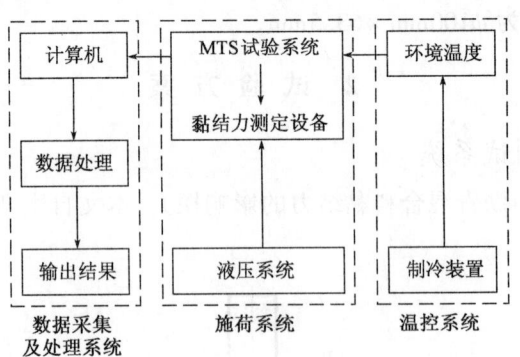

图3 黏结力测试系统工作流程图

试 验 方 案 设 计　　　　　　　　表4

项目	组别	温度(℃)	拉拔角度(°)	级配类型
试验一	1	−5	90	AC-16
	2	−10		
	3	−15		
	4	−5	90	SMA-16
	5	−10		
	6	−15		
	7	−5	90	OGFC-16
	8	−10		
	9	−15		
试验二	1	−15	30	AC-16
	2		45	
	3		60	
	4		90	
	5	−15	30	SMA-16
	6		45	
	7		60	
	8		90	
	9	−15	30	OGFC-16
	10		45	
	11		60	
	12		90	

3 试验结果及分析

3.1 冰与路面的黏结特征

在外荷载作用下,随着荷载的增大,冰层与沥青路面发生分离。为了探究界面破坏特征,本文利用多角度测量冰与沥青路面黏结力测试设备,测得了 AC-16 试件在 −15℃ 直拉状态下系统拉力的变化,如图4所示。

在试验过程中,由于 MTS 液压式加载系统匀速加载,因此图4反映了冰-沥青混合料试件界面处拉力与冰层形变的关系。在 0~4s 期间,随着施加载荷的增大,冰-沥青试件界面处拉力与冰层的形变呈线性关系,冰层发生弹性变形,在 4~10.3s,拉力与冰层变形呈非线性,冰层开始发生塑性形变。在 10.3s 时荷载达到最大值 2.15kN,随后冰层未发生显著形变而界面处拉力迅速降低,冰层发生脆性破坏,此时的拉力即为冰与试件之间的黏结力。由此可见,冰-沥青路面界面破坏过程中冰层经历了弹性、塑性变形过程,最终发生脆性断裂,这与周纯秀[7]研究的冰的破坏机理一致。

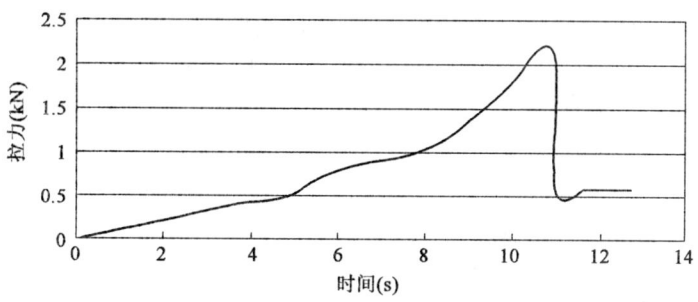

图 4　-15℃下系统拉力随时间的变化

3.2　温度对冰-沥青路面黏结力的影响

温度是路面结冰的重要因素,本文采用黏结力测试系统,在拉拔角度为 90°的条件下分别测试 -5℃、-10℃、-15℃时 AC-16、SMA-16 与 OGFC-16 三种沥青混合料试件与冰之间的黏结力,试验结果如图 5 所示。

从图 5 中可以看出,采用 90°直拉时,随着温度的降低,AC-16、SMA-16 与 OGFC-16 试件与冰之间的黏结力逐渐增强,其中 -10℃时较 -5℃时的黏结力增幅均可达 130% 以上,-15℃较 -10℃时的黏结力增幅可达 50% 以上,由此可见,温度对冰与沥青混合料之间的黏结有着显著的影响,温度降低,二者之间的黏结更加牢固。因此,温度的下降对于除冰雪具有不利影响,需要更大的外力来去除路面的积冰。

3.3　拉拔角度对冰-沥青路面黏结力的影响

采用拉拔角度表征车辆荷载的作用角度或除冰雪时的施荷角度。根据 3.1 中的试验结果,温度越低,冰与沥青混合料之间的黏结力越大,因此采用黏结力测试装置测定在 -15℃条件下,拉拔角度分别为 30°、45°、60°、90°时 AC-16,SMA-16 与 OGFC-16 三种试件与冰之间的黏结力。试验结果如图 6 所示。

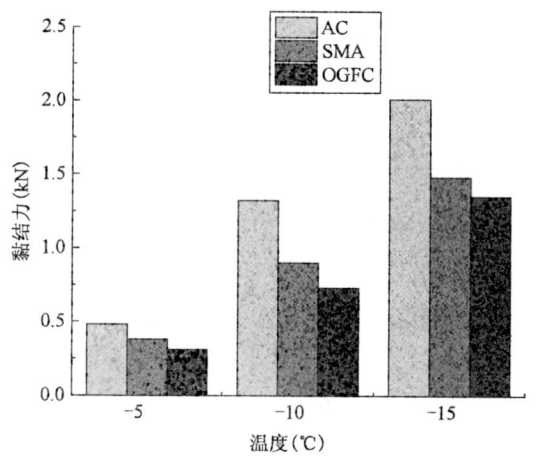

图 5　黏结力与温度的关系

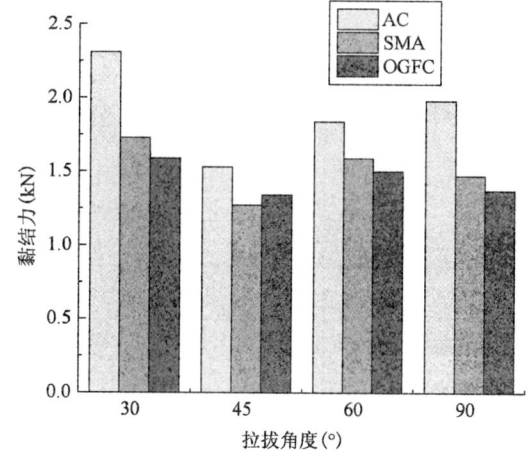

图 6　黏结力与拉拔角度的关系

由图 6 可见,在温度、级配类型相同时,冰与沥青混合料间的黏结力随角度的变化而变化,但不同级配间呈现不同的规律,AC-16 试件与冰之间的极限拉力随角度的变化关系为 30°>90°>60°>45°;而 SMA 与 OGFC 试件与冰之间的黏结力随角度的变化关系为 30°>60°>90°>45°。分析此现象,可能是因为集中力方向变化时,冰作为晶体受力较为复杂且无规律。但 45°时冰与试件的黏结力最小,推测其原因为黏结界面45°方向剪应力最大,破坏时冰层发生剪切破坏,因此在道路除冰时可考虑除冰角度接近45°以提高除雪效率。

3.4 级配类型对冰-沥青路面黏结力的影响

级配类型反映了路面的粗糙程度及空隙率,影响着冰与路面的接触面积,与冰-路黏结力密切相关。采用黏结力测试装置测定了在 −5℃、−10℃ 与 −15℃ 时,AC-16、SMA-16 与 OGFC-16 三种试件与冰间的黏结力,由于拉拔角度为90°时试验数据的离散性较小,因此采用直拉试验。结果如图7所示。

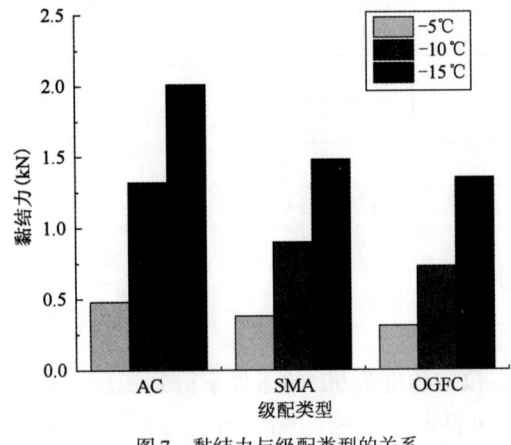

图7 黏结力与级配类型的关系

由图7可知,在温度、作用力角度相同的情况下,AC-16、SMA-16 与 OGFC-16 与冰间的黏结力大小关系为 AC > SMA > OGFC。分析此现象,可能是 AC 结构空隙较小,比表面积大,与冰之间的接触面积较大,因此黏结较牢固,而 OGFC 空隙最大,比表面积小,与冰的接触面积小,因此黏结力最小。由此可见,采用 SMA 或 OGFC 沥青路面对于降低冰-沥青路面黏结力较为有利。

4 冰-沥青路面黏结力影响因素显著性分析

为了明确温度、拉拔角度和级配类型对冰与沥青路面间黏结力的影响的主次顺序,设计三因素三水平正交试验进行探究,因素水平确定表和正交试验结果如表5和表6所示。

因 素 水 平 表　　　表5

项目	因素		
	温度(℃)	拉拔角度(°)	级配类型
水平	1	−5	30	AC-16
	2	−10	45	SMA-16
	3	−15	60	OGFC-16

正 交 试 验 表　　　表6

项目		因素			试验结果(kN)
		温度(℃)	拉拔角度(°)	级配类型	
水平	1	−5	30	AC-16	0.79
	2	−5	45	SMA-16	0.31
	3	−5	60	OGFC-16	0.27
	4	−10	30	SMA-16	1.03
	5	−10	45	OGFC-16	0.70
	6	−10	60	AC-16	1.25
	7	−15	30	OGFC-16	1.54
	8	−15	45	AC-16	1.52
	9	−15	60	SMA-16	1.57

对正交试验数据进行方差分析,如表7所示。在试验水平 $\alpha=0.01$ 的情况下,分别检验各因素的显著性。令 f_1、f_2、f_3 分别表示温度、拉拔角度、级配类型的自由度,则 $f_1=f_2=f_3=2$,总自由度为 $f_{总}=26$,若 $F_i>F_{0.01}(f_i,f_{总})$,则认为第 i 个因素对试验指标有显著影响,反之没有。

方差分析表　　　　　　　　　　　　　　　　　表7

因　素	偏差平方和 S	自由度 f	均方差	F	显著性 $F_{0.01}(f_i,f_{总})=5.53$
温度(℃)	1.77	2	0.89	1158.59	1158.59
拉拔角度(°)	0.12	2	0.06	78.15	78.15
级配类型	0.19	2	0.09	122.46	122.46
误差	0.02	21	0.00		

由表7可知,温度、拉拔角度与级配类型的 F 值分别为1158.59、78.15与122.46,均大于显著性水平为0.01时的 F 值5.53,因此可以认为三者均对冰-沥青路面黏结力有显著的影响,且温度为显著性最大的影响因素,其次为级配类型,拉拔角度的显著性最小。由此可见,在除冰雪时可以考虑改变温度、施荷角度来达到降低施荷大小、提高除冰效率的目的,在路面设计时,也可以考虑采用合适的级配类型以减少冰对路面行车的危害。

5　结　语

(1)本文自主开发了多角度测量冰与沥青路面黏结力的试验设备,并采用此设备测试了冰-沥青路面黏结力在荷载开始作用至界面破坏时的变化过程。结果表明,在冰-沥青路面界面破坏时,冰层发生脆性断裂。

(2)外界温度、荷载作用角度与级配类型对沥青混合料与冰之间的黏结力均有显著的影响,其中温度的影响要显著于路面级配类型,施加荷载的角度影响最小。

(3)冰与沥青路面之间的黏结力随着温度升高而降低,且当外荷载与冰-沥青路面界面夹角为45°时,黏结力最小。在相同的外界环境下,OGFC沥青混合料与冰之间的黏结力最小,其次为SMA沥青混合料,AC沥青混合料与冰之间的黏结力最大。因此,可以采用不同温度、荷载角度、级配类型的组合降低冰与沥青路面之间的黏结力,提高除冰效率。

(4)本文采用的黏结力测试设备对冰层有侧向约束作用,与实际路面有所差异,并且在试验过程中,没有对冰层厚度加以控制,在今后的研究中有待改进。

参考文献

[1] 但汉成,李亮,刘扬,等.潮湿山区路面凝冰机理及路面抗滑性研究综述[J].武汉理工大学学报(交通科学与工程版).2014,38(04):719-724.

[2] 谭忆秋,张驰,徐慧宁,等.主动除冰雪路面融雪化冰特性及路用性能研究综述[J].中国公路学报.2019,32(04):1-17.

[3] Chen Hua-xin, Wu Yong-chang, Xia Huiyun, et al. Review of Ice-Pavement Adhesion Study and Development of Hydrophobic Surface in Pavement Deicing [J]. Journal of Traffic and Transportation Engineering (English Edition),2018.5(3):224-238.

[4] Chen Hua-xin, Wu Yong-chang, Xia Huiyun, et al. Anti-Freezing Asphalt Concrete: Ice-Adhesion Performance[J]. Journal of materials science,2018.53(7):4781-4795.

[5] Guerin Frederic, Laforte Carolineet, Farinas Marie-Isabelle, et al. Analytical Model Based on Experimental Data of Centrifuge Ice Adhesion Tests With Different Substrates [J]. Cold Regions Science and Technology,2016.121:93-99.

[6] 徐岩,张弼强,王长棋.橡胶颗粒沥青混合料除冰机理及效果[J].大连工业大学学报.2020,39(05):359-364.

[7] 周纯秀.冰雪地区橡胶颗粒沥青混合料应用技术的研究[D].哈尔滨工业大学,2006.

[8] 瞿翔.沥青路面冻黏特性的试验研究[D].长沙:长沙理工大学,2017.

[9] 唐珊,丁云飞,吴会军.表面浸润性对冰黏附强度的影响研究[J].制冷.2014,33(03):16-20.

[10] 吴琴,曹林涛,张杰.不同因素对路表冰层冻黏强度的影响分析[J].交通科技.2014(02):74-76.

[11] 王国刚,穆静静,周红伟,等.覆冰垂直黏结强度的测试研究[J].工程热物理学报.2012,33(02):282-284.

[12] Perez A P,Wåhlin J,Klein-Paste A. Effect of Surface Roughness and Chemistry on Ice Bonding to Asphalt Aggregates[J]. Cold Regions Science and Technology. 2015,120:108-114.

[13] Dan Han-cheng,He Lin-hua,Zou Jin-feng,et al. Laboratory Study on the Adhesive Properties of Ice to the Asphalt Pavement of Highway[J]. Cold Regions Science and Technology,2014:104-105,7-13.

[14] 丁云飞,唐珊,吴会军.表面微结构对冰黏附强度的影响[J].表面技术.2015,44(04):74-78.

[15] 郭琦,申晓斌,林贵平,等.积冰黏附力试验及影响因素分析[J].飞机设计.2019,39(04):33-37.

[16] 王雪莹.道路冰雪与路面黏附特性及除雪机理研究[D].吉林:吉林大学,2019.

[17] 谭忆秋,王潇婷,徐慧宁,等.一种多角度测量冰与沥青路面黏结力的试验设备及方法[P].2014-12-03.

某山区干线公路灾害恢复重建对策及实践

陈俞嘉[1] 康孝先[1,2] 周子豪[1] 陈祥斌[1]

(1.西南科技大学;2.绵阳市交通运输局)

摘 要 针对山区国省干道公路选线困难、工程改扩建造价高、地质灾害多、河流冲刷严重等问题,对已产生的灾后恢复重建方式、改扩建方案进行总结。以四川省绵阳市平武县国道G247平武县响岩镇至江油大康镇段整治工程为例,对历年洪水冲毁、滑坡、泥石流等自然灾害造成的公路路基和边坡破坏的处置方式进行分析,并详细介绍特殊路基和边坡段的加固设计与施工,为类似的山区干线公路灾害恢复重建具有参考意义。

关键词 山区干线 地质灾害 恢复重建 冲刷

0 引 言

山区公路路基多高填、深挖,特殊困难地点以隧道或高架桥穿越,易发生滑坡、坍方等,修建费和养护费较高。山间盆地河流,水文条件比较复杂,且无水文资料,一般季节流量小、水位低,但暴雨往往造成短时间内水位暴涨、流量剧增,漫过河堤散流。暴雨来势凶猛,历时短,又因河床、河岸地表植被稀少,河岸相对较浅,河岸对水流的约束力有限,土体黏聚力差,地表径流汇流快,其洪水破坏力极强。公路本身即是受灾害作用的客体,同时也承担为抢险救灾提供交通支持的任务,因此开展山区国省干线公路灾害恢复研究有重要意义[1-2]。

1 山区公路存在的问题及常见地质灾害

1.1 山区公路存在的问题

设计方面。山区公路相对于普通公路几何线性复杂,路况重复率低,对于工程施工技术要求更高,所以山区国省干路公路的设计相比平原公路设计需要考虑的因素更多[3]。大量工程实例表明,山区地理环境勘探不全面是山区公路路线设计时最大的安全隐患,会增加施工意外的发生概率,而且会影响公路建设的稳定性和耐久性。除此之外,公路路线、地形地貌选择不恰当,也会增加公路建设的安全隐患[4]。同时,很多山区公路路基设计单位为追求设计进度,在公路路线设计前,并没有进行深入调研,忽略了山区公路真正的用途。

管理养护方面。我国国省干道养护意识薄弱,相关部门常重视道路建设而忽略了道路养护,致使山区国省道路养护不到位而对公路造成损伤[6-7]。首先,养护设备不全。目前我国的国省干道养护主要依靠人力养护,相应机械设施配置较低,这造成大量的人员浪费,并且工作效率较低。其次,养护人员的专业水平不高。国省干道养护的范围较广,专业性较强,所以对养护人员的技术要求也较高。最后,养护管理制度不完善。目前,国省干道的管理部门对道路的养护工作认识不够,只重建设而忽略养护,所以没有建立完善的干道养护管理制度。

1.2 山区公路常见地质灾害

山区公路工程地质灾害原因包含滑坡危害、崩塌危害、泥石流等,同时在分析相关危害原因基础上,针对性地给出地质灾害的防治措施,采取有效的防治方式,能够提高山区公路工程的施工稳定性[9]。

滑坡。滑坡主要是松散岩所组成的斜坡破坏形式,对于斜坡岩石的种类不同,尤其是上层组成为松散堆积层,而下层为坚硬岩石结构的时候,就容易出现滑坡的灾害。

崩塌。地形地貌是造成山体崩塌的直接原因。自然降水会大量浸入岩体与山体中,使得山体负荷逐渐增大,再加之岩体内部结构的作用从而产生了严重的崩塌问题。

泥石流。根据泥石流所形成的不同区域,一般可以分为上游形成区、中游流通区、下游堆积区。公路路线穿越泥石流沟口时,一般应布设桥梁跨越。为减小泥石流对桥跨下部结构施加的冲击力、剥蚀力,确保桥梁结构安全,满足耐久性要求,除在桥墩周围做必要的导流、防冲击、剥蚀构造外,路线应尽可能与泥石流沟口保持一定的距离,见图1。

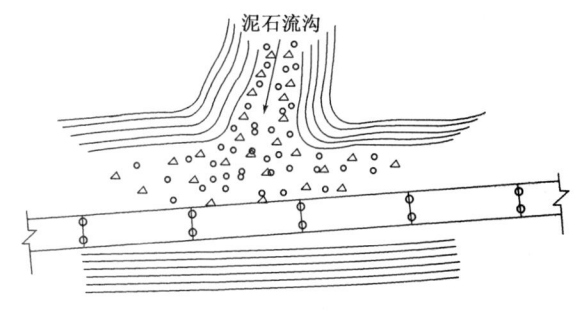

图1 泥石流沟前桥梁布置图

路基冲刷。沿河及水库地区由于地形地质条件及工程设置要求的限制,大多依山傍水顺着河谷或水库岸边行进。

2 工程案例

2.1 工程背景

项目为国道247线。由于临近龙门山中央断裂带,本段国道247线沿线地形地质条件极为复杂,岩性变化、山体破碎、降雨集中、沟壑纵横。在历次改建中,主要以拓宽路基宽度、提高线形标准、降低纵坡、改善路面舒适度等功能性目标为主,对路基边坡防护、临河路基的防冲刷等考虑较少。"5.12"汶川地震以来,沿线多次出现山体崩塌、滑坡、泥石流和暴雨山洪水毁等灾害致使公路中断,而该路段是绵阳至平武的主通道,也是九寨沟旅游环线的一部分,旅游旺季十分拥堵。整改项目设计起点为平武县响岩镇,止点为江油市大康镇。

场区位于龙门山中央断裂带与前山断裂带之间,且距离中央断裂带仅1.5~2.5km,同时也位于唐王寨向斜北翼,受断层影响,区内还发育多条次级断层,区内地层由志留系页岩与石英砂岩、泥盆系灰岩构成。通过地表调查,目前原路地质病害主要为:土质边坡溜坍440m/9处、崩塌落石段落2340m/24处、高位危岩830m/3处、泥石流130m/4处、临河坍塌380m/2处、临河冲刷210m/1处、滑坡290m/2处。

2.2 主要病害及处理措施

2.2.1 上边坡病害

(1)土质边坡溜坍处置。沿线多处土质边坡溜坍,较为松散。主要采取仰斜式路堑挡土墙进行处置。因土质边坡溜坍,原路内侧边沟有部分淤积、损坏现象,故在挡墙设计区段均进行了边沟的拆除恢复重建,边沟采用盖板边沟形式,考虑到部分工点挡墙基础开挖困难,对边沟形式设计中提供了两种不同宽度的盖板边沟,以满足施工需求。部分挡墙工点涉及与排水结构物交叉的问题,施工中因充分考虑两者的衔接,挡墙基础与涵洞排水底面高差不得小于30 cm。挡墙背回填预留部分碎落槽。

GK11+190-GK11+270段为土质边坡溜坍。可采用加固方案如图2所示。

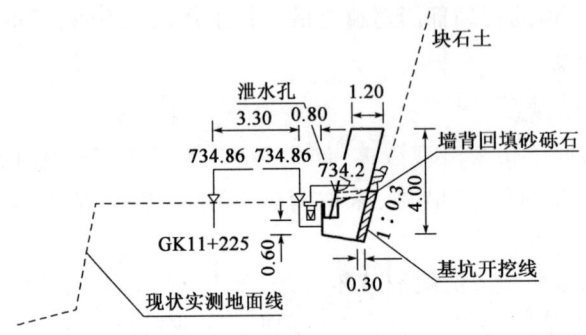

图2 土质边坡溜坍加固(尺寸单位:m)

(2)崩塌、危岩。路线上边坡大面积分布着灰岩、砂岩、页岩或砂岩、页岩互层,灰岩、砂岩性硬节理裂隙发育,地形上多为陡崖(坎),临空面大。页岩性软,抗风化能力弱,易发生碎落,特别是砂岩与页岩叠置形态时,页岩碎落致砂岩悬空,易失去平衡,在重力作用下沿着裂隙崩落形成岩堆和孤岩块。视坡高与岩体破碎情况采取导石网、主动网、垫墩锚杆方式进行处置。

GK0+340-GK0+575为崩塌落石段。原路右侧页岩边坡,最大坡高50m,边坡较陡,节理发育,落石。产状:2420、L420,节理:490、L710;1570、L790。块径0.1m~0.5m。采用加固方案如图3所示。

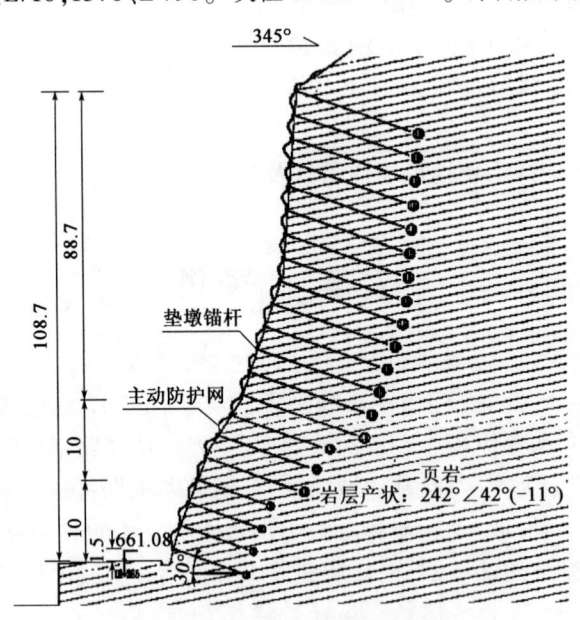

图3 崩塌落石段加固(尺寸单位:m)

(3)泥石流、碎石流。沿线发育泥石流4处。其中一处泥石流沟底纵坡较大,且沟槽前后缘较高,另外两处规模较小,但爆发频率较高,对公路运营安全均存在威胁。采取桩板墙、泥石流拦挡墙进行处置。

GK29+880-GK29+941.5为坡面泥石流段。原路左侧上边坡坡面泥石流,泥石流堆积物以块石为主,爆发频率较高,影响宽度60m。加固方案为GK29+880~GK29+941.5段左侧路堑处设桩板墙,且桩基采用圆截面桩体,桩体截面尺寸为直径 1.5m,桩间距 6m,桩长为 16m;桩间内挂挡板防止桩间填土挤出,挡板板厚 0.5m,施工时与抗滑桩整体现浇。桩体的受拉钢筋必须布于受推力侧。桩后最大一次可满足泥石流堆积方量约 500m³,当桩后堆积高度达到桩后可填高度的 2/3 高度时,后期养护时需及时清除。采用加固方案如图 4 所示。

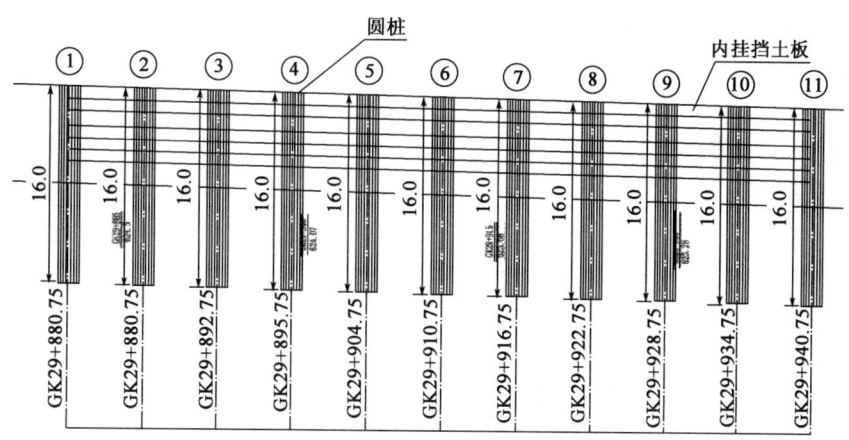

图 4 坡面泥石流段加固方案(尺寸单位:m)

2.2.2 下边坡病害

(1)临河坍塌。沿线临河坍塌共 2 处。主要位于河流弯道处,上覆盖第四纪冲洪积砂卵石层,由于河流冲刷导致,目前原路挡墙基础已被掏噬,路基开裂。采取桩基托梁挡土墙进行处置。

GK16+895-GK17+195 为临河坍塌段。临河冲刷严重,长度 330m,原路挡墙基础已被掏噬,路基开裂。采用加固方案如图 5 所示。

(2)滑坡、坍塌。沿线发育滑坡(坍塌)2 处,其中滑坡路段右侧下边坡受河流冲刷,造成滑坡,滑坡前后缘高差 15m,宽度 210m,目前原路路基已开裂。主要采取抗滑桩进行处置。

GK32+800-GK33+016 为滑坡病害。原路右侧下边坡受河流冲刷,造成滑坡,滑坡后缘高度 15m,宽度 210m,目前原路路基已开裂,需进行处置。采用加固方案如图 6 所示。

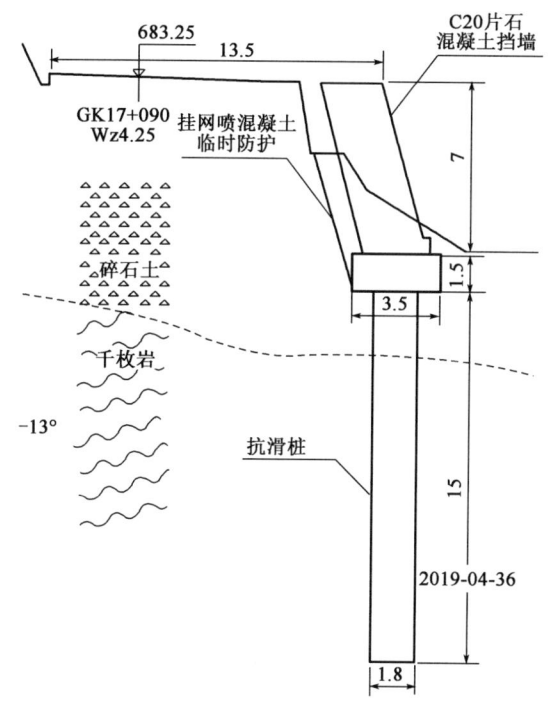

图 5 临河坍塌加固方案(尺寸单位:m)

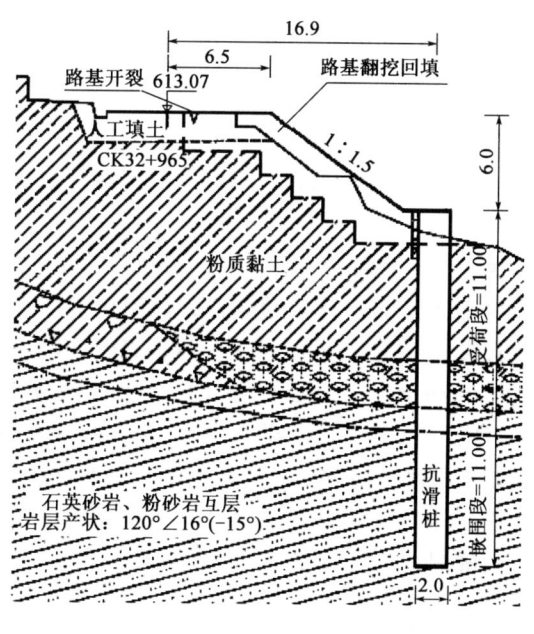

图 6 滑坡坍塌加固方案(尺寸单位:m)

3 结语

山区干线公路作为重要的交通道路,是不可或缺的部分,做好道路的设计、施工、养护可大大提高公路寿命并减少灾害发生频率。将供给侧改革理念应用于道路修复中去,改善质量,避免年年修复,年年破坏现象;同时增加科研投入,强调用科技提升质量,降低成本,解决实际问题;最后,有关部门应当针对山区国省干线提出新的措施和政策。

(1)应针对存在的问题进行计划改造提升,研究山洪的冲刷和防护,对原设计的临时线位进行分布、分阶段改造或改扩建,对地质灾害点进行完善的整治,必要时根据全造价的理念进行线位优化或改线。

(2)理顺管养并重的新理念。供给侧改革的提示就是改善质量,不能年年修,年年坏;增加科研的投入,强调用科技提升质量,降低造价,解决实际问题;强调既有道路经验对新建、改扩建山区公路的指导作用,同时国家应针对山区国省干线提出新的措施和政策。

参考文献

[1] 杨逊,刘双林.山区公路设计中应注意的问题[J].工程技术研究,2018(07):199-200.
[2] 叶春娲.山区公路设计分析[J].工程技术研究,2020,5(07):224-225.
[3] 杨艳岗.山区高速公路桥梁施工技术及其特点分析[J].工程技术研究,2019,4(16):90-91.
[4] 李龙骄,陈龙.山区高速公路线路设计的常见问题及解决对策研究[J].工程建设与设计,2020(09):73-74+77.
[5] 张海宁.山区高速公路施工特点与施工技术要求[J].建筑技术开发,2019,46(10):38-39.
[6] 熊玲.国省干道养护问题及对策研究[J].黑龙江交通科技,2014,37(04):190.
[7] 王礼特.国省干道养护问题及对策的应用研究[J].黑龙江交通科技,2019,42(11):203-204.
[8] 范琪,蒋浩鹏.基于灰色关联理论的山区公路线形影响因素分析[J].公路,2020,65(05):51-54.
[9] 李惠民,任光明,李源亮,范荣全,李畅.山区公路沿线地质灾害分布与环境影响关系研究——以汶川-茂县公路为例[J].人民长江,2017,48(19):66-71.
[10] 蓝宇聘.新时期公路工程施工中常见地质灾害防治处理探析[J].科技创新与应用,2013(29):221.

水性环氧超薄磨耗层抗滑耐久性试验研究

李晶晶[1,2] 张擎[2]

(1.陕西交通职业技术学院公路与铁道工程学院;2.长安大学公路学院)

摘 要 针对水性环氧超薄磨耗层抗滑耐久性能缺乏定量评价这一问题,成型超薄磨耗层试验板,借助加速磨耗仪和DFT动摩擦系数测试仪检测其抗滑性能,分析五大因素对抗滑耐久性能的影响规律。结果表明:随着抗滑骨料用量的增加,DFT20和DFT60均逐渐减小;随着水性环氧黏结材料用量的增加,DFT20和DFT60呈先增大后减小的趋势;随着骨料粒径的增大,DFT20和DFT60初值逐渐增大,但终值却逐渐减小;随着轮胎压力的增加,DFT20和DFT60初值呈减小趋势,并推荐水性环氧黏结材料的用量和玄武岩抗滑骨料的用量。基于试验分析,建立DFT20和DFT60的抗滑耐久性模型,并利用工程实例对预估模型进行验证,发现误差小于5%,表明抗滑耐久性模型具有良好的适用性。

关键词 道路工程 抗滑耐久性 水性环氧树脂 超薄磨耗层

基金项目:2019年度陕西省高等教育教学改革研究项目(19GG011);陕西高校第四批青年杰出人才支持计划(陕教工[2020]150号)。

0 引言

水性环氧树脂是指环氧树脂以微粒或液滴的形式分散在以水为连续相的分散介质中而配得的稳定分散体系,因其具有适应能力强、环保性能好和操作性佳等优点而被广泛应用[1-4]。近年来,水性环氧树脂在道路工程中的应用越来越广泛,常作为超薄磨耗层铺筑于桥面、水泥路面、沥青路面、收费站等工程,以提高结构的使用性能和安全性能。

随着通车时间和汽车荷载的增加,水性环氧超薄磨耗层表面的骨料会脱落,进而影响整个结构的抗滑耐久性。因此,研究水性环氧超薄磨耗层的抗滑耐久性能对于提高行车安全显得尤为重要。国内外研究学者对水性环氧超薄磨耗层抗滑及其耐久性能进行了一系列深入研究[4-7]。刘奕对湿热环境超薄磨耗层抗滑影响因素进行研究,指出超薄磨耗层的抗滑性能主要通过表面构造来提供[1]。何圳等人设计一种油性聚氨酯类超薄磨耗层,利用加速加载试验测试其国际摩擦指数,综合评价3种不同防滑骨料的抗滑耐久性能[2]。Spenser G W 等人对桥面铺装薄层磨耗材料进行理论计算与试验分析,结果表明磨耗层出现裂缝的原因是温度荷载和车辆荷载耦合作用下的疲劳开裂,进而影响其耐久性能[3]。张擎等人对隧道路面改性环氧树脂磨耗层抗滑性能进行试验研究,并利用数值分析软件研究潮湿状况下不同参数对其抗滑性能的影响[4-6]。综合分析这些文献,发现对环氧超薄磨耗层的研究主要集中在环氧沥青混合料的路用性能、桥面铺装、水泥路面和沥青路面抗滑性能的快速恢复等方面,对于水性环氧超薄磨耗层抗滑耐久性缺乏系统研究。因此,有必要对水性环氧超薄磨耗层抗滑耐久性能进行室内试验研究,分析各因素对抗滑性能的衰变特性,建立其抗滑耐久性衰变模型,以指导超薄磨耗层的养护工作。

1 试验

1.1 原材料

1.1.1 水性环氧黏结材料

本试验采用双酚A环氧树脂E51,其环氧当量为$184\sim194/g\cdot mol^{-1}$。固化剂选用乙二胺,其25℃的比重为1.104,25℃的黏度为$300/Pa\cdot s$。增韧剂为具有高度支化的三维球状CYH-277-S超支化聚酯,黄色液体,其分子量为279。选用淡黄色的稀释剂,其环氧值为0.70。水为洁净的普通水。水性环氧黏结材料的配比为环氧树脂:固化剂:增韧剂:稀释剂:水 = 100:25:25:5:15,如图1所示。

图1 水性环氧黏结材料

1.1.2 抗滑集料

抗滑集料选用商州区兴达石料厂生产的3~5mm玄武岩,各项指标满足规范要求。

1.1.3 水泥混凝土

制作水泥混凝土底板,每立方米混凝土所用量的材料见配合比见表1。

水泥混凝土配合比　　表1

每立方米材料用量(kg)				减水剂(%)
水泥	粗集料	细集料	水	
280	1166	714	171	1.0

1.2 试验仪器与过程

1.2.1 试验仪器

抗滑耐久性试验用到加速磨耗仪和DFT动摩擦系数测试仪,如图2和图3所示。试验板的平面尺寸为600mm×600mm。

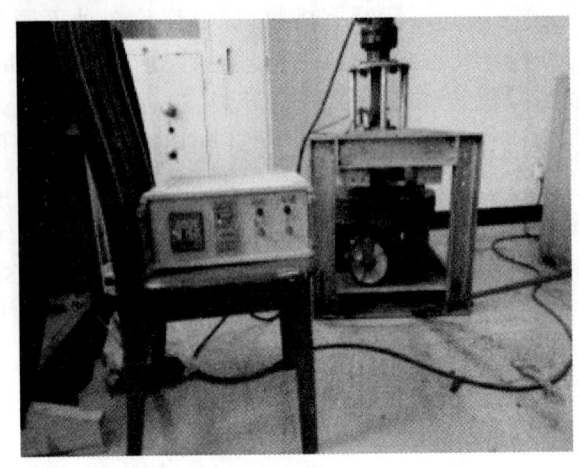 

图2　加速磨耗仪　　　　　　　　　　　　图3　DFT测试仪

1.2.2 试验过程

试验过程为:成型水泥混凝土底板,其尺寸为600mm×600mm×50mm;涂抹水性环氧树脂黏结材料;均匀撒布抗滑集料;室温固化,清除表面浮粒;进行加速磨耗试验。

2　水性环氧超薄磨耗层抗滑耐久性的影响规律

水性环氧黏结材料为1000g,3～5mm集料为2800～4400g,依据前述方法进行水性环氧超薄磨耗层抗滑性能试验,发现:随着汽车行驶速度的提高,摩擦系数在不断降低。20km/h是一个分界点,当行驶速度低于20km/h时,摩擦系数衰减很快,当行驶速度超过20km/h时,摩擦系数衰变缓慢。在汽车实际行驶过程中,存在低速与高速,为减少测试工作量,分别选取DFT20和DFT60作为水性环氧超薄磨耗层在低速和高速下的抗滑指标。

2.1 集料用量

玄武岩抗滑骨料的用量为2800～4400g,进行加速磨耗试验,测试结果如图4所示。分析可知:当抗滑集料一定时,随着荷载作用次数的增加,DFT20和DFT60均逐渐减小,20万次是一个分界点,当作用次数小于20万次时,DFT20和DFT60均衰变很快。这说明适当提高玄武岩抗滑骨料的用量能够增大环氧抗滑磨耗薄层的摩擦系数。

2.2 水性环氧黏结材料用量

水性环氧黏结材料为800～1000g,进行加速磨耗试验,测试结果如图5所示。分析可知:随着磨耗次数的增加,DFT20和DFT60均逐渐降低。随着磨耗次数的增加,DFT20和DFT60均随着水性环氧黏结材料用量的增加呈先增大后减小的趋势。

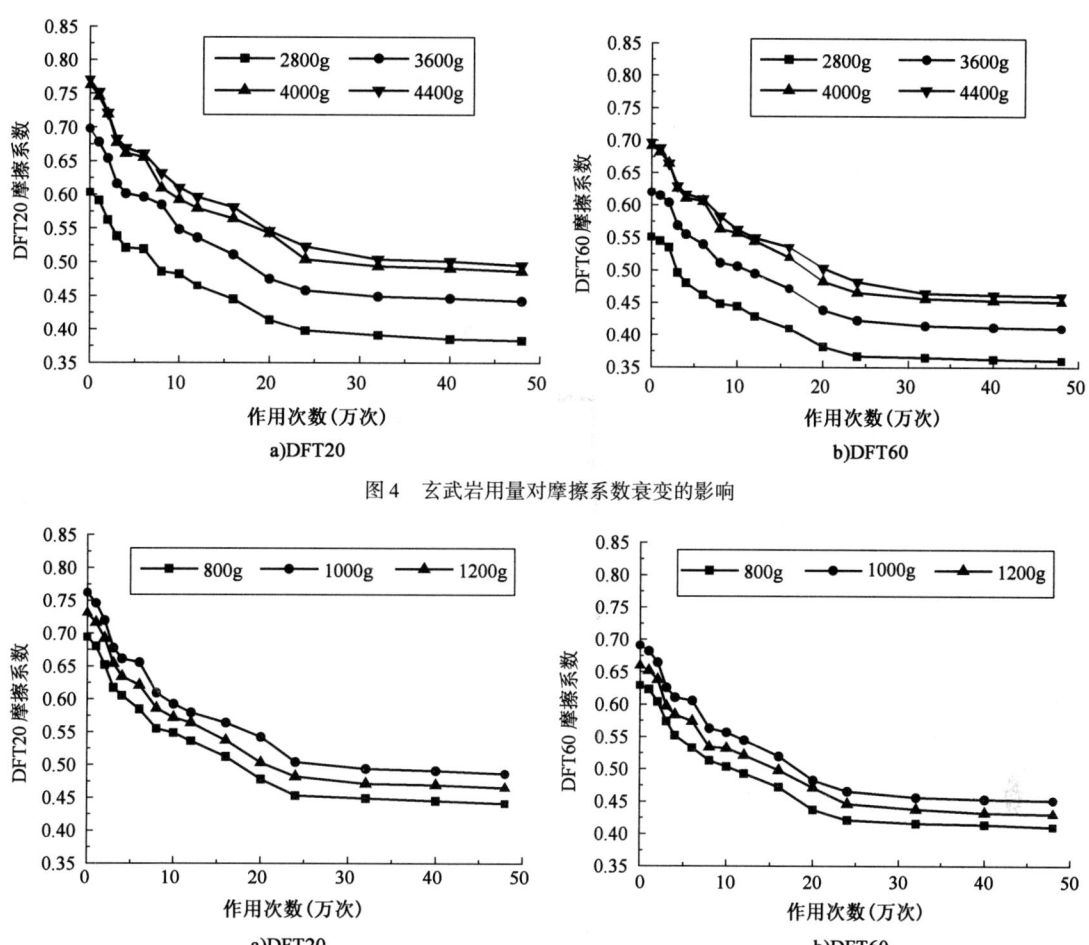

图4 玄武岩用量对摩擦系数衰变的影响

图5 环氧黏结材料用量对摩擦系数衰变的影响

通过对不同抗滑集料和黏结材料用量的 DFT20 和 DFT60 抗滑衰变规律进行分析,可知:水性环氧黏结材料用量与玄武岩用量比值为 0.25,抗滑性能最佳。按照此配比计算,水性环氧黏结材料用量控制在 2.5~2.8kg/m², 玄武岩抗滑集料用量控制在 9~11kg/m² 较好。

2.3 玄武岩粒径

两种玄武岩粒径进行加速磨耗试验,测试结果如图6所示。分析可知:DFT20 和 DFT60 初值随着骨料粒径的增大而增大,但是 DFT20 和 DFT60 终值却变小。这说明抗滑骨料粒径存在最优粒径。结合调研,玄武岩粒径 3~5mm 铺筑的环氧磨耗层抗滑耐久性能稍好。

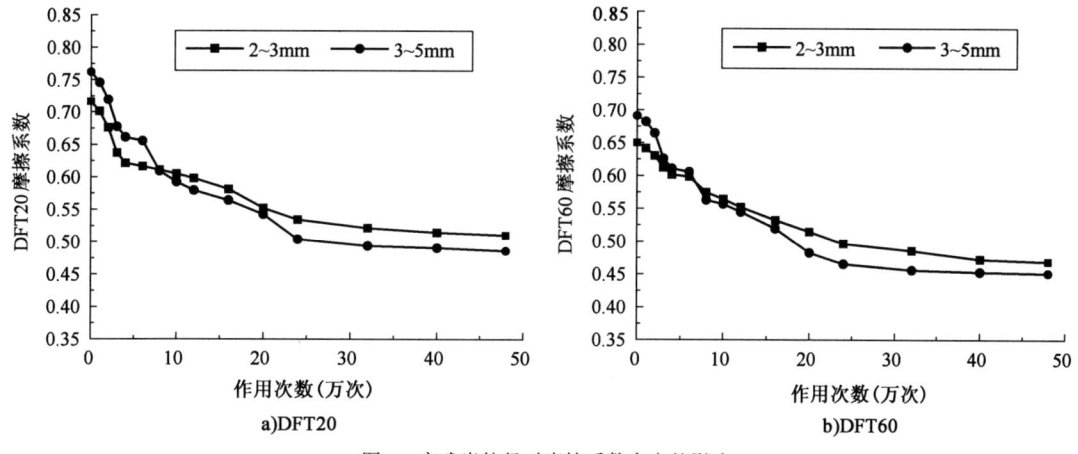

图6 玄武岩粒径对摩擦系数衰变的影响

2.4 轮胎压力

轮胎压力为0.5~1.0MPa,进行加速磨耗试验,测试结果如图7所示。分析可知:随着轮胎压力的增加,DFT20和DFT60初值呈减小趋势,0.5MPa、0.7MPa和1.0MPa轮胎压力下DFT20分别衰减了37.64%、36.19%和38.54%。

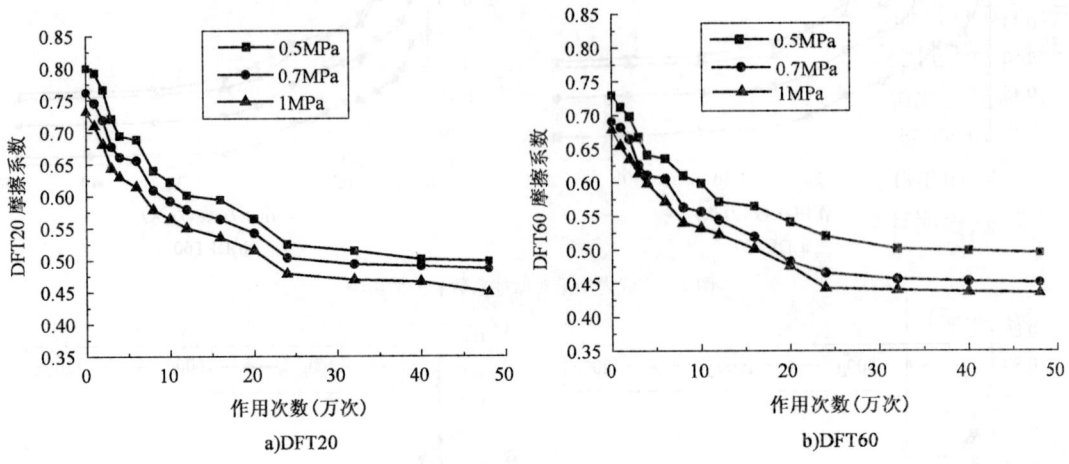

图7 轮胎压力对摩擦系数衰变的影响

2.5 路面结构类型

制作3种试验板,进行加速磨耗试验,测试结果如图8所示。分析可知:3种路面结构的抗滑性能在低速下的衰变程度要大于高速,且DFT20与DFT60衰变曲线有相同的变化趋势,均随着作用次数的增加而降低。在试验中发现沥青混凝土板上出现了车辙,水泥混凝土板出现了磨光现象,而水性环氧磨耗层却无病害。

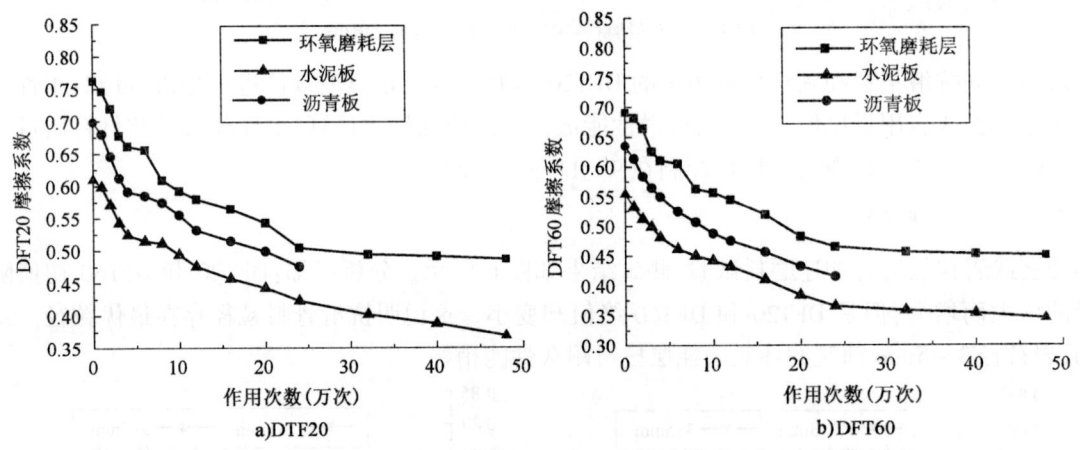

图8 路面结构类型对摩擦系数衰变的影响

3 水性环氧超薄磨耗层抗滑耐久性模型

3.1 抗滑耐久性模型的建立

通过分析五大因素对抗滑性能的影响,发现抗滑骨料用量、环氧黏结材料用量和轮胎压力是其主要影响因素。基于试验分析,建立抗滑耐久性模型。

$$\varphi_{20} = -1.086\omega + 0.264e^{-0.086N} + 0.798e^{-4.973p_0} + 0.716 \quad (1)$$

$$\varphi_{60} = -0.992\omega + 0.232e^{-0.084N} + 9.708e^{-10.103p_0} + 0.678 \quad (2)$$

式中:φ_{20}、φ_{60}——分别为20km/h和60km/h下的摩擦系数;

ω——胶石比；

N——荷载作用次数，万次；

p_0——轮胎压力，MPa。

3.2 抗滑衰变模型的验证

2017年6月在福银高速山阳县某隧道进行路用性能检测，发现构造深度和摆值均在中等以下，需对其进行养护。经过比较，采用水性环氧超薄磨耗层进行施工，单层撒布法铺筑，胶石比分为0.25，3~5mm玄武岩，按前述配比配制水性环氧黏结材料，通车三年后，其荷载作用效果相当于室内抗滑耐久性试验作用25万次，用DFT动摩擦系数测定仪检测，测试结果见表2。分析表2可知：通车3年后，环氧超薄磨耗层的DFT20和DFT60的现场测试值与预估计算值间误差均小于5%，且具有较好的摩擦系数，满足抗滑性能的要求，这表明环氧超薄磨耗层是一种可快速回复路表抗滑性能的养护措施。

环氧超薄磨耗层摩擦系数测试结果　　　　表2

环氧黏结材料(kg/m²)	DFT20现场测试值	DFT20预估计算值	DFT60现场测试值	DFT60预估计算值
2.8	0.57	0.56	0.54	0.52
	0.56	0.55	0.54	0.51
	0.56	0.54	0.52	0.50

4 结　　语

（1）随着作用次数的增加，DFT20和DFT60均逐渐减小，且在加载磨耗试验中，随着抗滑骨料用量的增加，DFT20和DFT60均逐渐减小；随着水性环氧黏结材料用量的增加，DFT20和DFT60呈先增大后减小的趋势。进一步分析发现，胶石比为0.25时抗滑性能最佳，经计算，水性环氧黏结材料的用量建议为2.5~2.8kg/m²，玄武岩抗滑集料的用量建议为9~11kg/m²。

（2）当作用次数一定时，随着骨料粒径的增大，DFT20和DFT60初值逐渐增大，但终值却逐渐减小；随着轮胎压力的增加，DFT20和DFT60初值呈减小趋势；3种路面结构的抗滑性能在低速下的衰变程度要大于高速下的衰变程度，且DFT20与DFT60衰变曲线有相同的变化趋势。

（3）基于试验分析，建立水性环氧超薄磨耗层在胶石比、轮胎压力和作用次数影响下的抗滑耐久性模型，并利用工程实例通车3年后的摩擦系数数据与理论计算值进行对比，发现误差较小，在5%以内。

参考文献

[1] 刘奕.湿热环境超薄磨耗层抗滑影响因素研究[J].中国科技信息,2016(12):48+50.

[2] 何圳,魏琳,杨孝思,等.聚氨酯类超薄磨耗层设计与抗滑性能研究[J].当代化工,2020,49(12):2702-2707.

[3] Spenser G W, Nelsen T, Ross L A. Performance of Concrete Bridge Deck Surface Treatments[J]. Brigham Young University, 2005, 5-22.

[4] BEYENE M A, RICHARD C M, NWLSON H G, et al. Forensic Investigation of the Cause(s) of Slippery Ultra-Thin Bonded Wearing Course of an Asphalt Pavement: Influence of Aggregate Mineralogical Compositions[J]. International Journal of Pavement Engineering, 2015(4):136-149.

[5] Readul M I, Shams A, Nazimuddin M, et al. Quantification of Reduction in Hydraulic Conductivity and Skid Resistance Caused by Fog Seal in Low-Volume Roads. 2017, 2657(1):99-108.

[6] 李晶晶,张擎,王占锋.潮湿状况下轮胎与环氧磨耗层抗滑性能研究[J].河北工业大学学报,2020,49(04):69-76.

既有桥梁水下基础防冲刷措施与关键技术分析

周子豪[1] 康孝先[1,2] 陈俞嘉[1] 陈祥斌[1]

(1.西南科技大学;2.绵阳市交通运输局)

摘要 大量理论研究与实例表明,跨江跨河的大型桥梁基础冲刷是导致桥梁损毁事故的最主要原因之一,若不及时采取措施有效应对,将会严重影响桥梁使用的安全性,甚至造成巨大的经济损失和人员伤亡。在总结大量常见基础冲刷病害及其应对措施的基础上,以成绵复线高速公路石亭江大桥为例,详细介绍近十多年来,"5.12"汶川大地震造成的地质灾害加剧河床的冲刷和2009—2013年间无节制的采砂导致涉河桥梁基础冲刷的严重病害及历次加固方案,并对常见的3类处治方案:维修加固、基础托换和重建进行对比分析,为以后类似桥梁水下基础冲刷防护工程维修加固提供参考。

关键词 桥梁 水下基础 基础冲 处治措施

0 引言

在众多桥梁损毁事故当中,基础冲刷往往是最主要的原因之一[1]。2010年8月7日,震后舟曲特大山洪泥石流造成1434人遇难331人失踪。8月12日四川汶川、什邡、都江堰等地连降暴雨引发泥石流、塌方灾害,有近80人死亡或失踪,2万多人被紧急转移,2000多间房屋受损,整个映秀新城浸泡在洪水中。在四川2013年"7.9"第一轮暴雨洪涝灾害发生时,江油市盘江大桥垮塌,6辆汽车坠河,12人死亡或失踪。同日,绵竹市境内有两座大桥垮塌,在第一轮暴雨洪涝灾害之后,四川省至少有19座桥梁垮塌。

本文以成绵复线高速公路石亭江大桥为例,对常见的3类处治方案:维修加固、基础托换和重建进行了对比分析,为以后类似桥梁水下基础冲刷防护工程维修加固提供参考。

1 常见基础冲刷病害及其应对措施

通常来说,冲刷造成的病害可以分为一般冲刷病害和局部冲刷病害[2](图1~图3)。

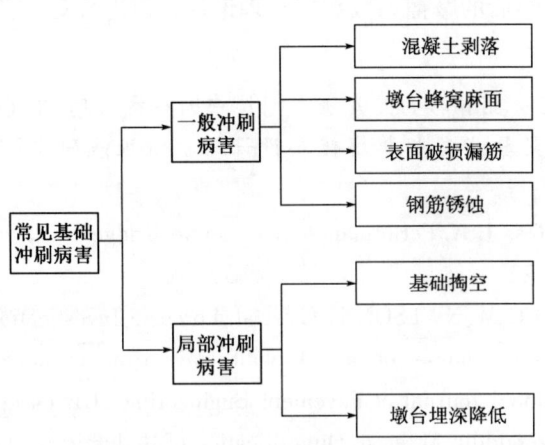

图1 常见基础冲刷病害

目前,国内外研究人员对桥梁基础冲刷防护已经做了大量的研究[2],具体而言,针对处于不同环境不同类型的桥梁基础冲刷病害,结合大量工程实例,通常可采取以下三类措施加以应对[4-9]:

(1)第1类:维修加固法。一般可采用基底压注水泥浆法、抛石防护法减小冲刷。
当现场条件不满足抛石防护或有环保美观要求时,会采取其他方法替代或改进抛石防护。

(2)第2类,采取水下基础托换技术。提高桩基的承载力、减小冲刷对桩基础影响等。

(3)第3类,拆除重建。在无法有效保障桥梁水下基础的冲刷防护和桥梁的承载力要求的情况下,可以改变桥型;或对上部结构进行更换,减少桥梁的跨数。

图2 表面破损漏筋

图3 基础掏空(局部沉降)

2 石亭江大桥加固方案

成绵复线石亭江大桥为跨越石亭江、串联地方公路而设。全桥采用29~30m预应力混凝土简支T梁,全桥长878.1m,河堤内共12跨(3号~14号墩)。桥梁下部结构采用钢筋混凝土双柱式桥墩,钻孔摩擦桩基础,按左、右幅分幅设计。大桥于2009年4月开工建设,建设时桥址下游100m范围内河道在开采砂石,施工时对原设计方案采取了加长桩基、降低系梁标高、加长墩柱长度等设计变更处理措施。2010年5月,河床内下部构造全部施工完成。

2.1 现存问题

2018年汛后,桥基河床7号、8号、9号桩基之间回填的砂卵石仍被冲走一部分,8号、9号桩基的外露长度比2017年减少,桥梁的安全暂时得以保证。

第一排抗冲桩下游右侧设置的钢筋石笼+六面体受到不同程度的破坏,右侧河床形成局部深沟,与现有河床面高差3~4m不等。右侧河堤护岸基本全部被冲毁,护岸垮塌10m深,加大了河道的过流断面。

第二排抗冲桩上下游河床2018年洪水后下切3~4m左右,抗冲桩下游右侧河道形成宽8~10m深沟,下游设置的钢筋石笼全部被冲走。图4为冲刷后的情况。

图4 船型承台完全暴露

2.2 处置方案设计(图5)

2.2.1 桥梁8号、9号桩基承台冲沟处铺设格宾石笼处置

为减小洪水对已经外露的桩基局部冲刷,从而达到保护外露桩基有效长度的目的,考虑从桥梁投影平面上游10m至下游第一排抗冲桩上游的铺填六面体的冲沟范围内均铺设一层1m厚的格宾石笼。

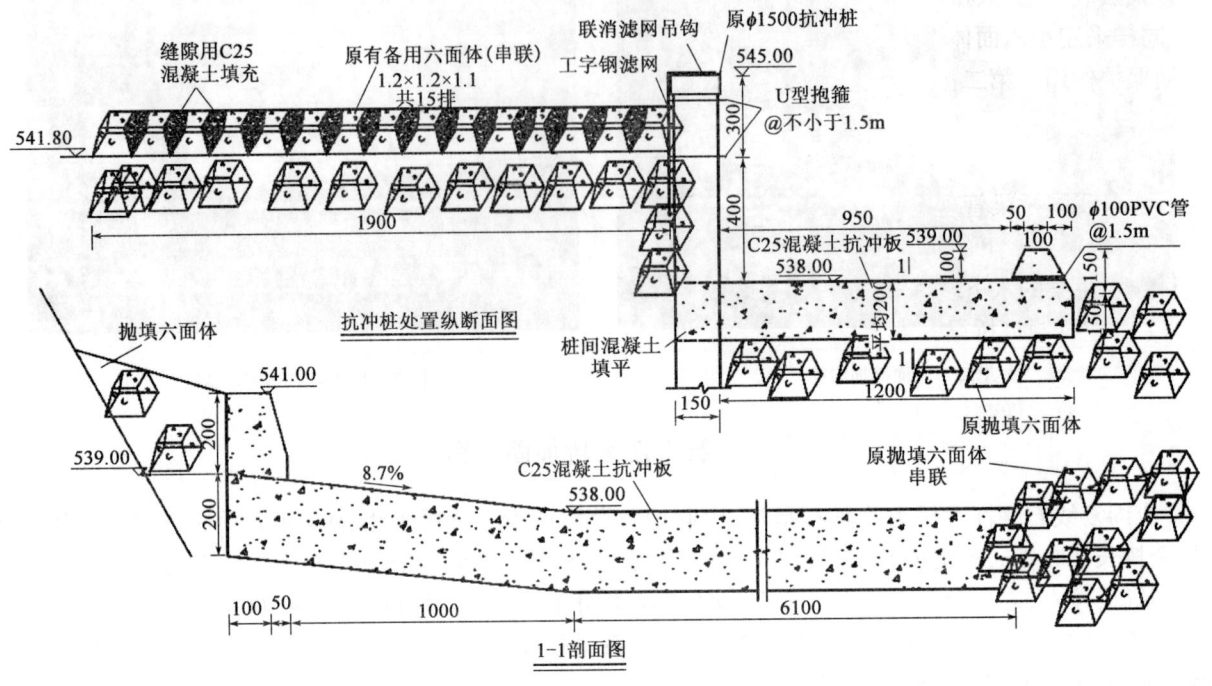

图5 抗冲桩处置设计图(尺寸单位:cm)

2.2.2 第一排抗冲桩上游

为加宽河道的过流断面,减小河道局部冲刷的进一步加深,先将8号、9号桩基承台下游冲沟河床基本整平,河床高程中间为541.80m,两侧河床可根据现场逐渐变高,但高差不应大于1m,并利用河岸现有六面体按照梅花形布置方式摆放一层,共摆放15排。其宽度范围,河道左侧延伸至左侧护坡,右侧延伸至河床既有六面体处,并将重新摆放的六面体和河床上既有六面体全部采用$\phi22$钢丝绳进行串联形成整体,增强抗冲能力。串联完成后六面体基本在一个高程,两侧根据地形变化串联六面体,不对现有河床大挖,六面体摆放完成后在其之间的间隙填满C25混凝土,以形成一个整体。同时纵横每隔10~15m设置一道沉降缝,缝内采用2cm泡沫板隔离。

为防止河床面继续下切导致既有的工字钢滤网与六面体分离,导致抗冲桩上游的推移装置从桩间缝带走的可能,将悬挂的工字钢网改造成附着在桩上的方式,同时将工字钢滤网和横工字钢与邻近六面体拴牢。具体方式如下:去掉悬挂水平段部分的工字钢,将既有两根6m长工字钢网焊接连接一根12m的工字钢网,每隔一根桩设置两个1.7×1.8m的$\phi25$U型抱箍,两个抱箍之间间距不小于1.5m,相邻两个工字钢网进行错位搭接且不小于20cm,两个12m工字钢网不得焊接。

2.2.3 第一排抗冲桩下游

河道右侧抗冲桩上下游形成6m左右的高差,防止大高差处的跌水直接冲洗并带走抗冲桩周边的土层,在低洼区域铺设一层平均厚度为2m的混凝土抗冲板,抗冲板的顶面高程按照438.0m控制,河道右侧抗冲板顶面高程略高,设置2m高的素混凝土垂直挡墙,垂直挡墙后铺设六面体护脚。抗冲板的水流方向长度为12m,尾部设置1m长,宽度为1.5m的齿坎,以解决小水量的河床平均分流和减缓流速的作用。因河床抛填较多六面体,抗冲板采用C25混凝土。同时在齿坎上每隔1.5m预埋一个100PVC管,以备后期连接抛填六面体使用。同时第一排抗冲桩下游露出水面的六面体应采用钢丝绳串

联成整体。

2.2.4 第二排抗冲桩上游

由于该排桩的现过流宽度仅有70m,再加上抗冲桩的外露,严重压缩了河道的过流断面,洪水期会加大对河床或两侧的边坡的冲刷。考虑在该排桩的上游河床进行整平,利用河岸现有六面体按照梅花形布置方式摆放一层,共摆放9排,两侧延伸至既有边坡的坡脚。同时全部采用φ22钢丝绳进行串联形成整体,同样采用小六面体填缝并串联形成整体,并在该排桩坡脚处抛填一定数量的六面体,以起到对边坡一定的保护作用。第二排抗冲桩上悬挂的工字钢网的改造方式与第一排抗冲桩一致。

3 结 语

随着我国桥梁管理的重心从新建为主向建养并重的方向转移,道路桥梁的养护管理工作也有了长足的发展,但桥梁水下的基础安全防护工作仍然处于粗放化管理阶段,不符合未来桥梁管养工作要求,特别是对涉水桥梁的水下基础的检查难度大,检测手段少,造成的安全隐患极大。

(1)建议制订桥梁管理和监测的标准或规范,加强管理和采用合理有效的监测手段对桥梁的情况及时了解并处理,最大限度地减少事故,预防和避免桥梁坍塌造成的人员和财产的损失。

(2)在地震后跨河桥梁设计中,要调查上游流域内的滑坡、淤积、泥石流、错落等不良地质情况;调查上下游水工建筑失效对冲刷的影响,如上下游是否有水库、滚水坝、挡水坝等;调查上下游人为因素的影响,如挖砂取石、桥址范围内弃渣等对桥梁的影响。

(3)认真执行桥梁水下基础的养护规范。新建水利设施时,加强对既有桥梁水下基础的影响评估和审批。

(4)应运用科学的手段和方法合理论证、正确判断桥梁基础病害成因,对旧桥基础病害的加固。不可能有一个固定模式,必须根据桥位所处地质、水文条件、桥型结构、施工技术条件等综合考虑,确定出符合实际的加固方案。

(5)桥位上、下游河道的乱采乱挖是造成河床不断冲刷的主要原因,如不禁止,即使花大量的经费防护,也难确保安全。应采取有力措施,在相关河流全河段内严禁采挖砂石。

参考文献

[1] 戴荣尧,卢金利,王群.桥墩冲刷防护计算[J].泥沙研究,1982(01):53-58.
[2] 陈稳.河流冲刷对既有桥梁墩台承载力影响的研究[D].长沙:中南大学,2013.
[3] 向琪芪,李亚东,魏凯,等.桥梁基础冲刷研究综述[J].西南交通大学学报,2019,54(02):235-248.
[4] 米居正.库区下游桥梁基础冲刷与防护[J].中国公路学报,1993(02):75-83.
[5] 胡江,康孝先,姜山.大跨度连拱桥震后大修关键技术研究与施工[C].中国公路学会养护与管理分会第八届学术年会论文集中国公路学会养护与管理分会会议论文集,2018:70-75.
[6] 康孝先,胡江,姜山.大跨度既有拱桥水下基础应急处治与加固[C].第4届世界交通大会论文集.
[7] 王安邦,张磊强,陈权,等.增补桩基法在石亭江大桥加固中的应用[J].甘肃科技,30(12),2014,06,106-108.
[8] 王之晗,夏叶,于合理,等.侵蚀基准面对石亭江双盛段河床演变的影响[J].工程科学与技术,49(增2),2017,06,67-73.
[9] 李海涛.广汉金鱼石亭江大桥桩基冲刷病害加固设计研讨[J].西南公路.2011年第2期,34-36.

The Anti-stripping Performance of the Anti-skid Wear Layer of Highway Tunnel Cement Concrete Pavement

Qing Zhang   Wenbo Ding   Tong Shi   Hongchang Guo   Yakun Liu

(Chang'an University)

Abstract   From the three aspects of Modified Resin bonding material (MRT) dosage, aggregate particle size, and aggregate material, through indoor pull-out test, shear test and pull-out strain test, the effect of the anti-slip wear layer anti-stripping durability was studied, and the enhancement was proposed. The anti-skid wear layer of highway tunnel cement concrete pavement is based on the material design optimization plan of anti-stripping durability.

Keywords   Highway Tunnel   Cement Concrete Pavement   Anti-skid Wear Layer   Anti-stripping Durability

0   Introduction

At present, the methods for restoring the anti-skid performance of cement concrete pavement mainly include the old road groove method and the overlay method. The first type of pavement notching method can quickly increase the depth of the road surface structure and increase the friction coefficient. The disadvantage is that the pavement notch structure is not durable. After a period of time, the anti-skid performance of the vehicle is significantly reduced. Grooving will reduce the thickness of the cement pavement structure layer and reduce the bearing capacity and service life of the pavement. The pavement groove method is not suitable for the repair of the cement pavement of highway tunnels. In addition, the road groove can only increase the friction coefficient of the road surface, but not Solve the problem of reduced road surface smoothness. The second type of pavement overlay is a new structural layer, subject to construction conditions. Under the conditions of meeting environmental protection and fire protection requirements, the tunnel pavement overlay can only use cement concrete overlay, that is, white + white. From the analysis of pavement working conditions and structural mechanics, the thickness of the new cement concrete overlay must be very large. On the one hand, it will reduce the clearance height in the tunnel; on the other hand, the cement pavement overlay construction process is complicated, the construction period is long, and traffic needs to be interrupted. It takes a long time and is not suitable for repairing the surface of highway tunnels[1].

Existing studies have shown that epoxy resin paving materials have high bonding strength, good water stability, good crack resistance at low temperatures, high wear resistance, good corrosion resistance, good flameretardancy, and can be compatible with cement concrete materials. And aggregates form a strong bonding structure, which is very suitable for super-thin wear layer overlay materials of tunnel cement pavement. However, epoxy resin paving materials are more sensitive to temperature changes. After the temperature rises, the bonding performance and the anti-aggregate peeling ability decrease significantly. In addition, the material is brittle in mechanical properties, and has poor peeling resistance, cracking resistance, and impact resistance. When the pavement construction and use are used for super-thin anti-skid surface layer of tunnel pavement, the anti-stripping durability still needs further research.[2,3]

Based on the characteristics of the traffic and tunnel environment of the long and large highway tunnels, this paper takes theFuyin Expressway from Shangzhou to Manchuanguan as the supporting project, and develops the cement concrete pavement epoxy resin ultra-thin anti-skid wear layer material of the long highway tunnel. Technical research on mix design method, construction technology, quality control technology and post-maintenance.

1 Durability Test of Anti-stripping and Anti-stripping of Cement Pavement in Highway Tunnel

The spalling resistance of the anti-skid wear layer of the tunnel pavement includes the spalling resistance between the aggregate and the bonding material in the abrasion layer structure, and the spalling resistance between the abrasion layer structure and the tunnel cement concrete pavement. In order to evaluate the anti-stripping performance of the anti-skid wear layer, this paper mainly conducts research through indoor pull-out test, shear test and pull-out strain test.

1.1 Shear Test

The pavement of the long highway tunnel is made of cement concrete, and the shear test specimen is made of cement concrete. First, a cement concrete slab with a thickness of 10cm is made, and after curing for 28 days to reach a flexural strength of 5.0MPa, a core drill is used to cut concrete test blocks with a diameter of 10cm and a height of 10cm. Then make an anti-slip wear layer test block with a diameter of 10cm and a thickness of 10cm, smear the prepared (MRT) bonding material on the bottom circular surface of the cylindrical test block, and bond the bonding surfaces of the two test blocks together. After curing for 2 days in an environment of about 25℃, shear specimens can be produced. The prepared shear specimen is shown in Fig. 1[5]. In the shear test, the lower part of the shearing specimen is fixed by the shearing jig, the upper half of the specimen is fixed to the tensile end, and the horizontal force is applied through the tensile end to place the upper and lower parts of the specimen. Shear stress is generated on the bonding interface of the test block. During the tensioning process, the applied load keeps increasing uniformly and steadily until shear failure occurs on the bonding interface of the upper and lower test blocks of the test piece. By measuring the load at the time of failure, the interface between the upper and lower test blocks of the test piece can be obtained. The bonding strength of the upper bonding material.

Fig. 1 Shear Test Specimen

1.2 Pull Test

First, make the cement concrete pavement slab or stone slab for the pull-out test specimen, the size of which is 30cm × 30cm × 10cm. The test board material is road cement concrete. The test results of the 28d flexural strength test of the cement concrete show that the compressive strength of the cement concrete for the test board reaches 5.1MPa. Then mark the bonding area with a diameter of 10cm on the test board, apply different thickness (MRT) bonding materials, and bond the drawing head of the puller to the test board, and the drawing can be made after 2 days of curing Specimen. Fig. 2 and Fig. 3 are schematic diagrams of the drawing apparatus and the specimens made by the drawing test.

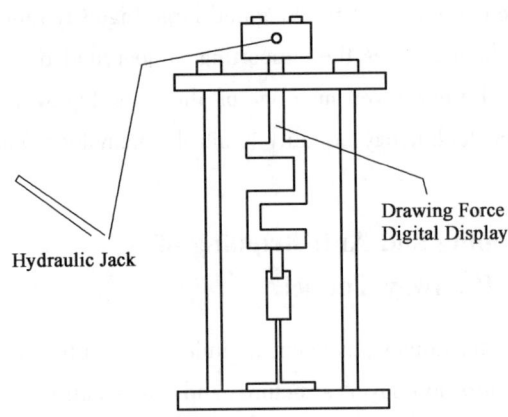

Fig. 2　Schematic Diagram of Drawing Instrument

Fig. 3　Pull Test Specimen

1.3　Strain Energy Test

In order to evaluate the durability of the anti-slip wear layer against peeling, the research team developed a pull-out strain energy tester. The tester adds a displacement measuring device to the original pull-out tester, and evaluates the durability of the wear layer against peeling off by measuring the pull-out stress and pull-out strain in the pull-out test. The amount of displacement in the process of the pull test is extremely small, and the displacement can be measured with high accuracy. The displacement measuring device used in this device is a photoelectric measurement, and its accuracy can reach 1μm. For accurate measurement, the connection of the drawing head of the drawing instrument also adopts a flexible connection. This connection method can ensure the verticality and avoid errors caused by the eccentric drawing force. The drawing strain gauge is shown in Fig. 4.

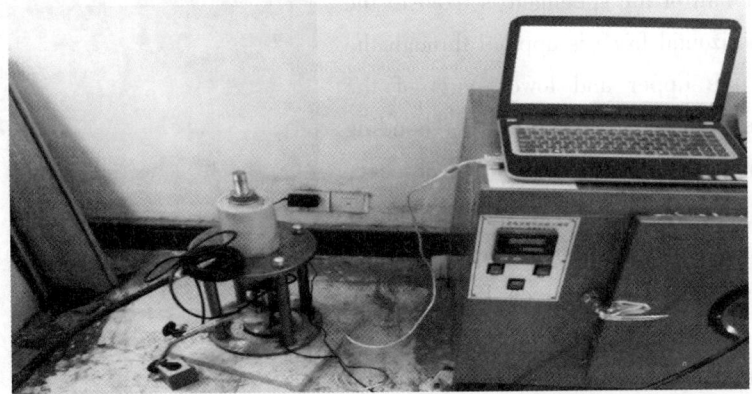

Fig. 4　Pull Strain Gauge

2　Study on the Anti-stripping Durability of Anti-slip Wear Layer

2.1　(MRT) Dosage to Resist the Effect of Peeling Performance

(MRT) The amount of bonding material has a greater impact on the anti-stripping performance of the anti-slip wear layer. During the construction of the anti-skid wear layer(MRT) bonding material is first painted on the surface of the tunnel cement pavement, and then the anti-skid aggregate is spread. If the amount of (MRT) is too small, the wearing layer bonding material will be brushed The thickness is small. After the aggregate is spread on the (MRT) coating, only a small part of the aggregate particles can contact with the (MRT). The area where the (MRT) and the aggregate particles are bonded is small, so the entire wear layer and the tunnel pavement The formed interlayer bonding strength is low, and the wear layer has poor peeling resistance. From the perspective of improving the interlayer bonding strength, the amount of (MRT) material should be increased. If the amount of (MRT) brushing is too large and the brushing thickness is too large, the (MRT) material will wrap the entire aggregate particles, reduce the exposed part of the aggregate, reduce the depth of the anti-skid structure on the surface of the wear layer, and lack the anti-skid performance. The depth angle of the sliding structure should be reduced (MRT) material coating thickness. Therefore, choosing the right amount of (MRT) material has an important effect on improving the durability of the anti-skid wear layer and controlling the depth of the anti-skid structure.

In the experiment, basalt was used as the aggregate, the particle size of the aggregate was controlled at 2.36-4.75mm, and the amount of aggregate was controlled at 10kg/m². (MRT) The amount of material is expressed in terms of its weight ratio to basalt aggregate. The drawing and shear test results of different (MRT) dosage tests are shown in Fig. 5.

The test results show that the two bonding strengths basically maintain linear growth before the amount of (MRT) is less than 0.25- 0.3. The fitted correlation coefficient R^2 can reach more than 0.92, and the tensile strength and shear strength can be increased to 2.3MPa and respectively. 1.95MPa. After the oil-stone ratio is higher than 0.3, the amount of (MRT) is increased, and

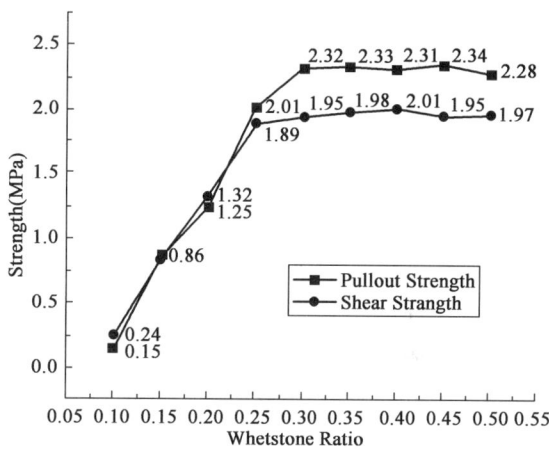

Fig. 5 (MRT) dosage affects the bond strength between layers

the two bonding strengths remain basically unchanged, which indicates that (MRT) has reached the maximum contact area with aggregates, and increasing (MRT) has little contribution to improving the viscosity. The larger the oil-stone ratio, the excessive (MRT) bonding material will increase the aggregate wrapping area, and the anti-slip structure on the surface of the anti-slip wear layer will decrease. Therefore, in order to improve the bonding strength between the anti-slip wear layers, (MRT) The bonding material and the wear layer aggregate have enough bonding area, and the oil-stone ratio can be controlled in the range of 0.25-0.3[6].

2.2 Influence of Aggregate Particle Size on Anti-flaking Performance

The aggregate particle size also has an important influence on the anti-stripping performance of the anti-slip wear layer. The smaller the aggregate particle size, the larger the specific surface area per unit volume, and the larger the bonding area with the (MRT), so the bonding strength between layers is higher; on the contrary, the larger the aggregate particle, the greater the specific surface area. Smaller, the smaller the bonding area per unit volume, the lower the bonding strength. Considering that the thickness of the wear layer does not exceed 1 cm, the range of available particle sizes is limited, and two aggregate sizes are selected for this experiment. The coarse aggregate particle size is between 4.75mm and 9.5mm, and the fine aggregate particle size is between 2.35mm and 4.75mm. The aggregates in the test can use three types of gradation. The first gradation uses only a single fine aggregate, the second gradation uses only a single coarse aggregate, and the third gradation combines fine aggregate and coarse aggregate. The aggregate is mixed in proportion. The oil-stone ratio was controlled at 0.1~0.28. The three graded aggregates were subjected to pull-out tests under different oil-stone ratios. The results of the bond strength test are shown in Tab. 1.

Bonding Strength of Different Grades Tab. 1

Whetstone Ratio	Single Fine	Single Coarse	Coarse and Fine
0.1	1.31	1.12	1.33
0.12	1.45	1.34	1.48
0.14	1.52	1.48	1.57
0.16	1.63	1.64	1.59
0.18	1.78	1.75	1.75
0.2	1.95	1.81	1.94
0.22	2.03	1.91	1.92
0.24	2.08	1.95	2.15
0.26	2.10	2.05	2.14
0.28	2.08	1.96	2.05

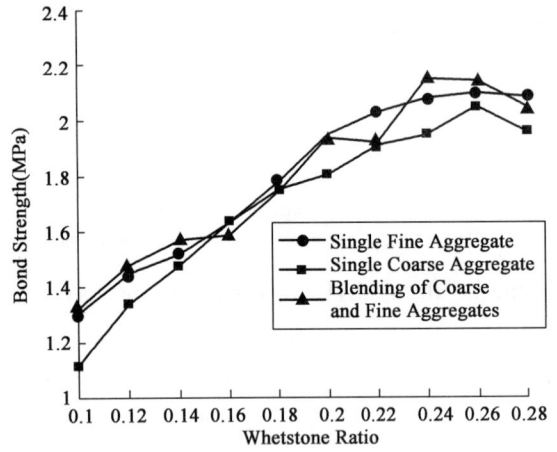

Fig. 6 Bonding Strength of Different Grades

The pull-out bond strength test of the wear layer with three grades of aggregates shows that the pull-out bond strength between the wear layers of the three grades of aggregates increases with the increase of the oil-stone ratio. When the ratio is 0.24 ~ 0.26, the pull-out bond strength reaches the highest. The smaller the aggregate size, the higher the bond strength between layers; the larger the aggregate size, the lower the bond strength. The test results are basically consistent with the aforementioned analysis, that is, the smaller the aggregate particle size, the larger the specific surface area per unit volume, the larger the bonding area with (MRT), and the higher the bonding strength between the layers; on the contrary, the bone The larger the material particles, the smaller the specific surface area, the smaller the bonding area per unit volume, and the lower the bonding strength. In addition, the blending of coarse and fine aggregates can also provide high bonding strength. The analysis reason is that the fine aggregate fills the voids of the coarse aggregate, increases the bonding area with the (MRT) material, and increases the bonding strength.

Further analysis shows that when a single aggregate with a smaller particle size is used in the wear layer, a dense skeleton structure can be formed, and the anti-slip wear layer with a single particle size fine aggregate has a small void ratio, which can save (MRT) material consumption; When only coarse aggregates of a single particle size are used for the slip wear layer, the porosity of the overlay anti-slip wear layer is large. If the porosity of the wear layer is to be reduced, the amount of (MRT) material needs to be increased; The aggregate is blended in an appropriate proportion. As the anti-skid wear layer aggregate, it can provide an anti-skid surface layer with better anti-skid and wear resistance, and can also achieve the minimum (MRT) dosage, but in this case, the coarse and fine aggregates need to be layered Spreading, the construction process is more complicated.

2.3 Aggregate Material Anti-flaking Performance

Aggregate is an important part of structural strength. Different aggregates will have an impact on strain energy. In this paper, 4 material aggregates of diabase, basalt, granite and limestone are selected for experiments to study the anti-slip wear layer resistance of the aggregate material Performance impact. The test results are shown in Tab. 2.

Strain Energy Test Results of Aggregate Tab. 2

Deformation δ(mm)	Basalt	Diabase	Granite	Limestone
0.02	0.07	0.06	0.08	0.07
0.04	0.19	0.17	0.21	0.29
0.06	0.33	0.30	0.38	0.44
0.08	0.45	0.48	0.53	0.58
0.1	0.68	0.65	0.65	0.75
0.12	0.89	0.85	0.79	0.88
0.14	1.12	1.02	0.98	1.01
0.16	1.32	1.15	1.13	1.22
0.18	1.44	1.33	1.45	1.58
0.2	1.55	1.46	1.77	1.85
0.22	1.59	1.50	1.93	Fracture
0.24	1.68	1.61	Fracture	
0.26	1.75	1.69		
0.28	1.88	1.75		
0.3	1.96	1.82		
0.32	2.03	1.90		
0.34	2.15	1.98		
0.36	2.23	2.07		
0.38	Fracture	2.15		
0.4		2.19		

The results show that diabase and basalt can form greater bonding strength with the bonding material, while the bonding strength of granite and limestone is lower. In addition, the deformation of the abrasion layer of basalt and diabase is close to or reaches 0.4mm. The variable is close to twice the wear layer of granite and limestone. Calculate the strain energy of basalt, granite and limestone at the fracture strain and the strain energy of diabase at 0.4mm, as shown in Tab. 3.

The Influence of Several Toughening Agents on the Strain Energy of the Wear Layer Tab. 3

Toughener Types	Basalt	Diabase	Granite	Limestone
Strain Energy (J/m^2)	443.2	500	178	154.4

The results show that when basalt and diabase are used as aggregates, the strain energy of the pull-out test is higher, and the peeling resistance of the wear layer is better.

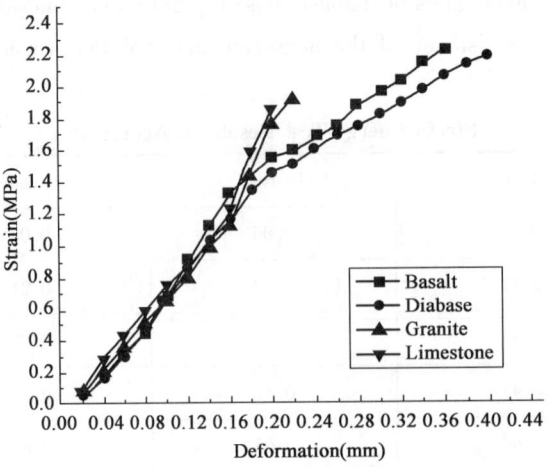

Fig. 7 Deformation-stress Curves of Different Aggregates

3 Design Optimization of Anti-wear Layer Material Based on Anti-stripping Performance

3.1 Ratio

According to the (MRT) material anti-stripping, abrasion resistance and flame-retardant test results, the ratio of the bonding material of the anti-slip wear layer based on the (MRT) material is:(MRT):Curing agent: Thinner = 100:20:6 ~ 100:40:9

3.2 Amount of bonding material

The amount of bonding material for the anti-skid wear layer is determined by the amount of brushing per unit area. The amount of bonding material is based on the treatment method of the tunnel pavement and the type of anti-skid aggregate, which is controlled in the range of 1.8 ~ 2.5 kg/m². Refer to Tab. 4 for the amount of bonding material.

Amount of Bonding Material   Tab. 4

Aggregate Size(mm)	Treatment Process	Shot blasting(kg/m²)
	Milling(kg/m²)	
2 ~ 4	2.0 ~ 2.2	1.8 ~ 2.1
3 ~ 5	2.1 ~ 2.3	2.0 ~ 2.3
4 ~ 6	2.2 ~ 2.7	2.2 ~ 2.5

3.3 Anti-sliding Aggregate Dosage

The amount of anti-skid aggregate is controlled within the range of 7.3 kg to 11 kg/m² according to the use condition of the tunnel pavement, the degree of disease and treatment methods, and the design requirements of the anti-skid wear layer. Refer to Tab. 5 for the amount of anti-skid aggregate.

Anti-sliding Aggregate Dosage   Tab. 5

Aggregate Size(mm)	Applicable Conditions	Dosage(kg/m²)
2 ~ 4	It is suitable for road sections with good road surface smoothness, small road surface diseases, manual cleaning or shot blasting treatment, and small longitudinal slope of tunnel road surface	8 ~ 10

Aggregate Size(mm)	Applicable Conditions	Dosage(kg/m²)
3~5	It is suitable for road sections where the road surface is relatively smooth, the road surface disease is relatively light, the road surface is treated by micro milling or shot blasting, and the longitudinal slope of the tunnel road surface is not large	9~11
4~6	It is suitable for road sections with poor flatness, staggered pavement, severe cracks, road surface treatment by milling or shot blasting, and large longitudinal slope of tunnel road surface	10~12

4 Conclusions

(1) In order to improve the bonding strength between the anti-slip wear layers, the bonding area between the bonding material and the anti-slip aggregate should be increased, and the oil-stone ratio can be controlled within 0.25~0.3.

(2) The smaller the aggregate particle size, the larger the specific surface area per unit volume, and the larger the bonding area with the bonding material, the higher the bonding strength of the abrasion layer added; the larger the aggregate particle, the lower the bondingstrength. The blending of fine aggregate and thickness can also provide high bonding strength, but it needs to be spread in layers and the construction process is more complicated.

(3) Diabase and basalt can form greater bonding strength with bonding materials, while granite and limestone have lower bonding strength.

(4) The design optimization plan of the anti-stripping layer material based on the anti-stripping performance is proposed, and the reference ratio, the amount of anti-sliding aggregate, and the range of the amount of bonding material are given.

References

[1] Chen Ting guang. The Application of Ultra-thin Wear Layer in Tunnel Pavement Overlay[J]. Guangdong Highway Transportation,2019,45(06):50-55.

[2] Santanu Pathak, Rajan Choudhary, Abhinay Kumar. Investigation of Moisture Damage in Open Graded Asphalt Friction Course Mixtures with Basic Oxygen Furnace Steel Slag as Coarse Aggregate under Acidic and Neutral pH Environments[J]. Transportation Research Record,2020,2674(8):887-901.

[3] Kong Tao. Application of Ultra-thin Wear Layer in Highway Maintenance Construction[J]. Green Building Materials,2019(12):111+113.

[4] Gao Wei, Shi Hongxing, Lu Shanfeng, et al. Comparison of Anti-skid Performance Between SMA and Very Thin Wear Layer[J]. Municipal Technology,2016,34(03):28-30.

[5] Fang Xing, WangXingchang, Lian Tong. Experimental Study on Accelerated Loading of Thin Epoxy Anti-skid Paving Material[J]. Highway,2010(10):214-219.

[6] Wu Juan. The application of Open-graded Anti-skid Wear Layer Pavement in Expressway[J]. West China Transportation Science and Technology,2015(10):38-40.

正负变温条件下引气水泥混凝土强度增长规律研究

梁 磊

(山西省长治市潞城区交通运输局)

摘 要 引气混凝土在正负变温环境条件下的强度增长规律与恒温养生研究得出的结论明显不同，本文通过开展模拟实际温度变化过程的强度特性试验研究，分析水泥混凝土材料的低温强度增长规律。通过试验分析发现混凝土在野外正负变温养生环境下的强度均小于标准养生强度，随着龄期的延长，混凝土的强度还会缓慢上升。提高水泥用量、适度降低水灰比可以提高混凝土的负温早期强度。

关键词 引气混凝土　正负变温环境　强度增长

0 引 言

青藏高原地区水泥混凝土路面的施工工期较短，在最佳的施工季节(5~9月)里，最高日平均气温为10℃~15℃，而夜晚却接近负温环境，这明显的低于一般地区的施工温度和现行规范的标准养生温度(20℃)，使得水泥混凝土的实际强度形成规律与一般地区的不同。同时，水泥混凝土的实际强度是在高低温交替变化甚至正负温交替变化过程中形成的，与恒温养生研究得出的结论明显不同。这样交替变化的温度条件也对水泥混凝土养护措施的要求很高。因此，为保证水泥混凝土路面的强度增长，有必要开展模拟实际温度变化过程的强度特性试验研究，分析水泥混凝土材料的低温强度增长规律。

1 引气混凝土变温养护试验研究

1.1 试验配比及方案

试验研究野外正负变温养生、室内标准养生两种不同养生方式下混凝土的强度发展规律。野外正负变温养生以青藏高原花石峡冻土气象观测站的六月份实际日温度变化观测值为基准(图1)，采用环境试验箱进行模拟，为了剔除湿度的影响，采用塑料袋密闭包裹保湿。最长养生龄期为56d，并分别在3d、7d、14d、28d、56d时测试试件的强度，与室内标准养生的混凝土进行比较。

试验混凝土的配合比见表1，每种试样均采用此两种不同养生方式，分别研究不同水泥用量、不同水灰比、矿物掺合料等因素下混凝土在不同养生方式下抗弯拉强度发展规律。

试验混凝土配合比　　　　　　　表1

试样号	混凝土用原材料(kg)				水灰(胶)比	外加剂(%)	
	细集料	粗集料	水泥	水		引气剂	高效减水剂
C1	661	1342	320	128	0.40	0.06	0.6
C2	651	1323	340	136	0.40	0.06	0.6
C3	642	1304	360	144	0.40	0.06	0.6
C4	633	1285	380	152.0	0.40	0.06	0.6
C5	649	1318	340	142.8	0.42	0.06	0.6
C6	647	1314	340	149.6	0.44	0.06	0.6
C7	651	1323	340 + 10% FA	136.0	0.40	0.06	0.7

续上表

试 样 号	混凝土用原材料(kg)				水灰(胶)比	外加剂(%)	
	细集料	粗集料	水泥	水		引气剂	高效减水剂
C8	651	1323	340 + 15% FA	136.0	0.40	0.06	0.7
C9	651	1323	340 + 20% FA	136.0	0.40	0.06	0.7
C10	651	1323	340(5% SF)	136.0	0.40	0.06	0.7
C11	651	1323	340(8% SF)	136.0	0.40	0.06	0.7
C12	651	1323	340(5% SF) + 10% FA	136.0	0.40	0.06	0.7

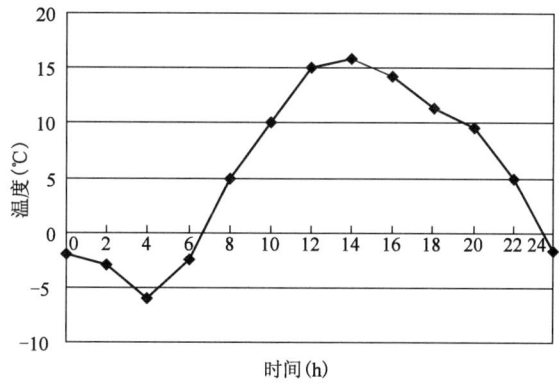

图1 青藏高原花石峡地区六月份实际温度日变化曲线

1.2 试验结果及分析

抗弯拉强度是道路混凝土的第一力学指标，试验主要分析了表2中各因素在两种养生方式下的抗弯拉强度发展规律。试验结果如图2~图5所示。

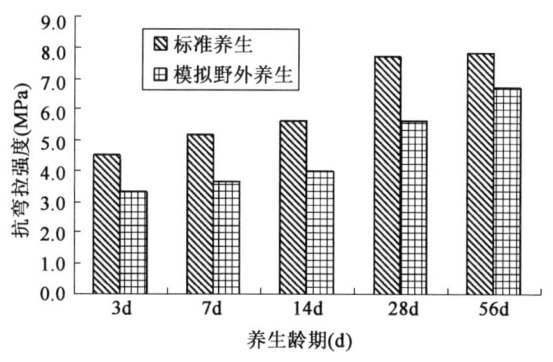

图2 C2试件不同养生方式下抗弯拉强度发展规律

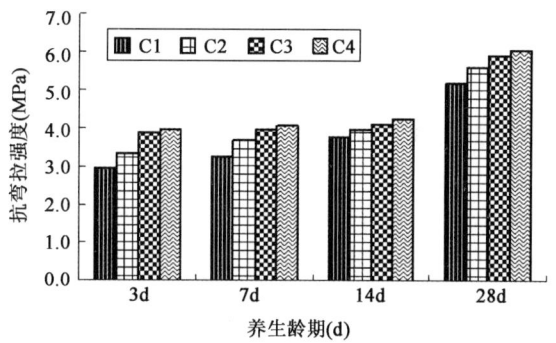

图3 模拟野外温度养生条件下不同水泥用量试件抗弯拉强度发展规律

表2为C2试件不同养生方式下各龄期抗弯拉强度，图2为C2试件在两种养生方式下抗弯拉强度的发展规律，其他试件在不同养生方式下的强度发展规律均与此类似。由图可以看出，相同龄期下，混凝土在模拟野外养生条件下的强度均小于标准养生强度，且在28d以前随龄期增长，强度降低越大。龄期为56d时两者强度差别有变小的趋势。从抗弯拉强度的增长趋势而言，模拟野外温度养生与标准养生是相近的，但其强度低于同龄期标准养生，表明养生过程中的高低温交替变化并没有限制混合料强度的形成，仅是延缓强度的增长速度。随着龄期的延长，混凝土的强度还会慢慢上升，因此，对于该地区的混凝土施工而言，早期强度低、受冻破坏是值得注意的问题，应采取措施提高混凝土负温下养生的早期强度。

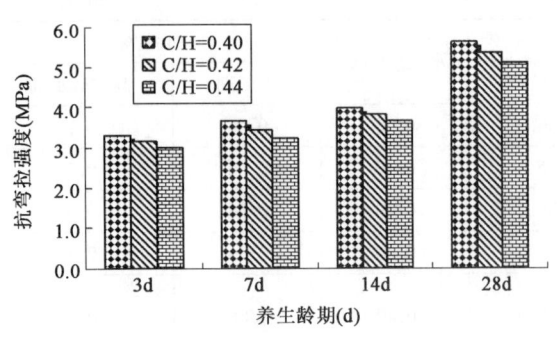

图4 模拟野外温度养生条件下不同水灰比试件抗弯拉强度发展规律

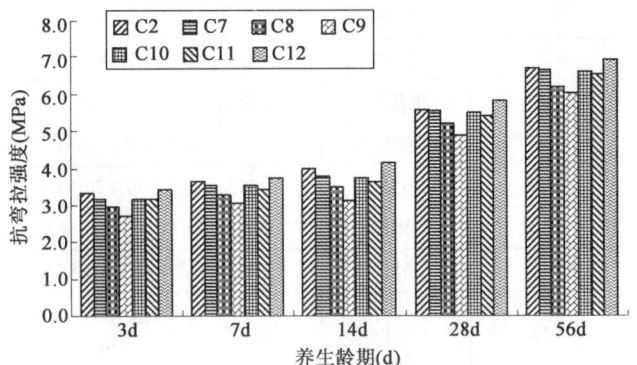

图5 模拟野外养生方式下矿物掺合料对混凝土强度发展的影响

C2试件不同养生方式下各龄期抗弯拉强度　　　　表2

养生方式	各龄期抗弯拉强度(MPa)				
	3d	7d	14d	28d	56d
标准养生	4.49	5.19	5.64	7.7	7.8
实际温度养生	3.32	3.66	3.98	5.6	6.7

从混凝土强度形成机理可以解释这种现象,在模拟养生早期,实际温度中的负温使混合料中的部分自由水冻结,参与水解和水化反应的水分减少,影响了水化产物的初期形成,也进一步延缓了水化物结晶析出过程;同时,低温又降低了水化反应速度,使强度形成缓慢,降低明显。随着龄期的延长和高低温的交替变化,水泥石骨架不断形成,溶液浓度不断提高,负温下自由水的冻结现象逐渐减少以至于消失,而且水泥水化水解和水化反应逐渐减弱,对强度形成的影响越来越弱,此时混凝土达到了抗冻临界强度,负温对混凝土强度增长的影响逐渐减小,使得负温和低温同时作用延缓强度增长,逐渐转变为以低温影响为主,因此强度降低幅度又逐渐减小。

图3为不同水泥用量条件下混凝土试件在模拟野外养生条件下的抗弯拉强度发展规律,由图可以看出,随着水泥用量的提高,混凝土试件的抗弯拉强度均有所增长,且在强度发展早期,在一定范围内,水泥用量提高可以显著提高混凝土的早期强度,水泥用量为380kg/m³试件的3d抗弯拉强度相比水泥用量320kg/m³试件的3d抗弯拉强度提高了35%,因此适度提高水泥用量对受冻环境下混凝土的早期抗冻有利。

图4为不同水灰比试件在模拟野外养生条件下的抗弯拉强度发展规律,其与图3有相似的规律,适度降低水灰比也可以同样提高混凝土的负温早期强度。水灰比为0.40的3d抗弯拉强度比水灰比为0.44的3d抗弯拉强度提高了11%,因此,在高原多年冻土区混凝土路面施工中,建议适当提高水泥用量及降低水灰比。

图5为模拟野外养生条件下矿物掺合料掺量对混凝土试件抗弯拉强度的影响曲线,由图可以看出,在模拟野外养生条件下,随着粉煤灰掺量的增加,各龄期强度均呈降低趋势,当掺量超过15%时,降低明显,早期强度发展缓慢,后期强度增长的优势也未体现出来。粉煤灰掺量小于15%时,虽然早期强度发展较不掺任何矿物掺合料的混凝土慢,但并不是很明显,强度发展能够满足低温施工的要求,7d强度可以达到设计强度的70%,且后期强度逐渐赶上未掺矿物掺合料的混凝土。掺入硅灰的混凝土在正负变温条件下强度发展较快,后期强度也较高,但掺量超过5%时,各龄期强度均有所降低。双掺粉煤灰和硅灰的混凝土强度无论在早期还是后期,在野外养生条件下强度的增长都最好,7d强度达到设计强度的80%,28d强度超过设计强度。

试验结果表明,单掺粉煤灰由于早期水化缓慢,会影响混凝土强度增长,但掺量较低时影响并不大,而且由于其形态、微集料效应,低掺量时使混凝土空隙细化,孔径分布均匀,形成合理的内部孔结构,密实度得以提高,从而降低混凝土中可冻水的冰点,增强混凝土在低温条件下的抗冻能力,使早期强度能够持续发展,但掺量不宜过高,试验结果表明:10%~15%为适宜掺量。单掺硅灰超过5%时,由于硅灰需水量大,拌合物变得黏稠,影响工作性及内部结构。双掺粉煤灰和硅灰,两者相互补充,能够更有效发挥两者的填充效应和微集料效应,结构更加致密,减少孔的数量和缩小了孔缝尺寸,尤其是降低了有害孔的数量,从而增强了早期抗冻能力。在后期,由于其二次水化反应,对后期强度及耐久性也非常有利。

因此,多年冻土区混凝土中矿物掺合料的掺量不宜过高,单掺时粉煤灰掺量应小于15%,硅灰掺量应小于5%。双掺时以粉煤灰10%及硅灰5%为宜。

2 结　语

通过以上的试验研究,可以得出以下主要结论:

(1)混凝土在野外正负变温养生环境下的强度均小于标准养生强度,28d以前随龄期增长,强度降低越大。龄期为56d时两者强度差别有变小的趋势。从抗弯拉强度的增长趋势而言,模拟野外温度养生与标准养生是相近的,但其强度低于同龄期的标准养生强度,表明养生过程中的高低温交替变化并没有限制混合料强度的形成,仅是延缓强度的增长速度。随着龄期的延长,混凝土的强度还会缓慢上升。

(2)提高水泥用量、适度降低水灰比可以提高混凝土的负温早期强度。为发挥矿物掺和料后期强度大的优势同时避免早期强度过低影响抗冻性能,试验发现在多年冻土区混凝土中的矿物掺合料粉煤灰掺量应小于15%,硅灰掺量应小于5%,双掺时以粉煤灰10%及硅灰5%为宜。

参考文献

[1] 武憼民,汪双杰,章金钊.多年冻土地区公路工程[M].北京:人民交通出版社,2005.
[2] 周幼吾,郭东信,邱国庆,等.中国冻土[M].北京:科学出版社,2000.
[3] C260-06 Standard Specification for Air-Entraining Admixtures for Concrete[S]. ASTM Standard.
[4] C229-96 Standard Specification for Air-Entraining Additions for Use in the Manufacture of Air-Entraining Hydraulic Cement[S]. ASTM Standard.
[5] 黄士元.从日本预拌混凝土的一条标准说起[J].混凝土,2000(1):29-30,23.
[6] 王超,杨全兵.水泥混凝土路面现场撒盐破坏试验研究[J].低温建筑技术,1999(3):14-17.
[7] 桥梁结构高耐久性混凝土设计与施工规程[S].黑龙江省地方标准　DB23/T 087—2002.

Research on Low Temperature Performance of SBS Modified Asphalt under the Action of Different Regenerants

Yanan Cui　Maorong Li　Lidian Guo　Lu Liu

(Inner Mongolia University of Technology)

Abstract　In order to study the low temperature performance of SBS modified asphalt under the action of different regenerants, this paper conducts a bending beam rheological test on matrix asphalt and SBS modified asphalt with different aging methods after mixing XT-1 regenerant and waste engine oil, and compares and analyzes the creep stiffness models of two regenerated asphalts under different aging methods. The change law of the amount and creep rate of the recycled SBS modified asphalt is studied, the type of regenerant, the amount of regenerant, the temperature and the change of low temperature performance of recycled SBS modified asphalt under different aging methods. The dissipated energy ratio is calculated based on the Burgers model, and the influence of temperature and regenerant content on the low temperature performance of recycled SBS modified asphalt is considered. The test results show: test temperature, aging method, regenerant content and type can affect the creep parameters of recycled SBS modified asphalt; the low-temperature deformation resistance of recycled SBS modified asphalt is better than that of recycled matrix asphalt; compared with XT-1 regenerant, a lower amount of waste engine oil will affect SBS modified asphalt and the regeneration effect of the recycled asphalt is more significant; the temperature has a greater influence on the low-temperature deformation ability of the recycled asphalt than the aging method.

Keyworks SBS modified asphalt Regenerant Bending beam rheological test Creep stiffness modulus Creep rate Dissipated energy ratio

0 Introduction

With the increase in the service life of roads in my country, functional and structural diseases have appeared on asphalt pavements. A large amount ofReclaimed Asphalt Pavement (RAP) are produced every year in maintenance and reconstruction operations. If they are abandoned, not only will they occupy land, but also will cause more serious environmental problems. SBS modified asphalt is the most widely used on highway pavements in my country, and it will inevitably age under the influence of atmospheric conditions and traffic loads. In order to make the waste pavement materials recycled, it is imperative to study the regeneration of SBS modified asphalt.

Asphalt regeneration is the reverse process of aging. At present, many scholars have studied the regeneration of aging SBS modified asphalt. Ranyan[1] has regenerated aging SBS modified asphalt many times, and studied the regeneration of SBS modified asphalt. The viscoelastic properties, rheological properties of asphalt mortar, and the aging and regeneration mechanism of SBS modified asphalt were explored through the fluorescence microscopic images of the asphalt, and the regeneration effect of multiple regenerations was evaluated. Xiaoming Huang [2] and others have developed Type A and Type B regenerants, that is, light oil is mixed with copolymer resin butadiene and acrylate, and then a tackifier is added as a regenerating agent. The study found that a certain proportion of regenerating agent was added. The performance of recycled asphalt can be restored to the initial level of use, and the recommended blending rate is 5% to 15%. H. A. Tabatabaee[3] found that the use of colloidal instability index (CII) to evaluate the impact of aging on regenerated asphalt, indicating that the regenerant can improve the glass transition of aged asphalt. Guilian Zou[4] used the dynamic mechanical analysis method (DMA method) to study the viscoelastic properties of SBS modified asphalt before and after multiple regenerations, and found that with the increase of aging and regeneration times, the regeneration agent has an effect on the viscoelastic properties of SBS modified asphalt. The regeneration effect is getting worse and worse, and the unique viscoelastic properties of SBS modified asphalt are gradually lost. Longfei Ran[5] used infrared spectroscopy, DSC and other methods to compare the performance of self-made ZZ regenerant and DN100, RA-2 and DN101. The results show that ZZ regenerant has superior ability to restore the rheological properties of aged SBS modified asphalt and resist cracking at low temperature. Hasan H[6] et al. studied the feasibility of waste vegetable oil (WVO) and waste engine oil (WEO) as regenerants to restore the performance of aged asphalt. Zhilong Cao[7] et al. used corn oil, waste engine oil, vacuum flow oil and cashew nut shell liquid to regenerate the aged SBS modified asphalt, and studied the composition and structure of the regenerating agent on the physical and rheological properties of the recycled SBS modified asphalt. The influence of the thermal oxygen stability of the regenerant on the aging behavior of the regenerated adhesive. Peiliang Cong[8] extracted old SBS modified asphalt from recycled asphalt mixtures, and used Rejuvenating agent I, Rejuvenating agent II and new SBS modified asphalt as regenerating agents to restore the performance of old asphalt. Ali Mansourkhaki [9] studied the changes in rheological parameters and chemical structure of recycled asphalt. By comparing the

$G^* \cdot \sin\delta$ curves of recycled asphalt, it can be seen that the regenerant can improve the performance of recycled asphalt. The FTIR test shows that the carbonyl and sulfoxide index of recycled asphalt increase with the increase of the old asphalt content. The use of softer asphalt and regenerant has a great impact on reducing the carbonyl index and sulfoxide index of recycled asphalt.

From a comprehensive analysis, there are few studies on the low-temperature performance of SBS modified asphalt after regeneration at home and abroad. Therefore, in this paper, through the bending beam rheological test, the recycled base asphalt and SBS modified asphalt are tested at different temperatures, the performance changes of the recycled asphalt under different low temperature conditions are studied, and combined with the complex environmental conditions in Inner Mongolia, the impact of other factors on recycled asphalt is analyzed. In addition, based on the Burgers model, the dissipated energy ratio is calculated to study the influence of different influencing factors on its low-temperature performance, and the mechanism of the low-temperature performance change of SBS modified asphalt after regeneration is studied from many aspects.

1 Test Materials and Methods

The raw materials used in this paper are base asphalt and SBS modified asphalt. The basic indicators are shown in Tab. 1 and Tab. 2. The regenerant adopts XT-1 asphalt regenerant produced by ChangzhouXintuo Pavement Modified Material Co., Ltd. Its basic properties are shown in Tab. 3. Waste engine oil is used in Volkswagen Jetta family cars. The waste engine oil is replaced after a new car has traveled for about 5000-6000 kilometers. Its engine oil brand is Shell OW-40 SN grade synthetic technology engine oil. Its basic performance is shown in Tab. 4.

Basic indicators of Matrix asphalt   Tab. 1

Technical Indicators of Matrix Asphalt	Results	Technical Requirements
Penetration(25℃,5s,100g)(0.1mm)	87.3	80~100
Penetration PI	-1.74	-1.8~+1.0
Softening Point (℃)	44.4	>42
Ductility(10℃,5cm/min)(cm)	>100	>20
Kinematic viscosity(60℃)(Pa·s)	175	>140

Basic Indicators of SBS Asphalt   Tab. 2

Technical Indicators of SBS Modified Asphalt	Results	Technical Requirements
Penetration(25℃,5s,100g,(0.1mm)	64	60~80
Penetration PI	0.05	>-0.4
Softening Point(℃)	71.8	>55
Ductility(5℃,5cm/min)(cm)	44	>30
Kinematic viscosity(135℃)(Pa·s)	2.21	<3

Basic performance of XT-1 asphalt regenerant   Tab. 3

Test Items	Performance Index			Measured Value
	XT-1	XT-2	XT-3	XT-1
Viscosity,(60℃)(cSt)	50~200	90~4500	37500~60000	195
Saturate,(%),≤	30	25	20	28.5
Aromatics,(%),>	60	70	75	70
Flash Point,(℃),>	160			226
Density,(15℃,g/cm³)	0.95~1.1			0.97

Basic Performance of Waste Engine Oil Tab. 4

Test Item	Technical Requirements
Kinematic Viscosity(60℃)(cSt)	37.2
Flash Point(℃)	230
Quality Ratio Before and after Film Oven Test(%)	−2.408
Viscosity ratio before and after film oven test(%)	0.815
Density/(20℃)(g·cm^{-3})	0.782

1.1 Preparation of Aged Asphalt

In this paper, heat aging, ultraviolet aging and water aging asphalt are prepared by simulating aging equipment in the laboratory. Heat-aged asphalt is operated in accordance with the method of RTFOT + PAV (20h) in T0630-2011 in "Standard Test methods of Bitumen and Bituminous Mixture for Highway Engineering" (JTG E20—2011)[10]. The water-aged asphalt is prepared by adding water to the surface of the sample on the basis of the pressure aging (PAV) test. The aging time is 300 minutes and the water required for the test is 8.5ml. UV aging asphalt adopts composite aging (PAV + UV) to carry out indoor UV accelerated aging of asphalt samples after long-term thermal aging. The RGT-UVAH-365F ultraviolet aging test box is selected and aged for 233h at a temperature of 50℃.

1.2 Preparation of Recycled Asphalt

Based on the preliminary test preparation, and with reference to the research results of Chuyu Sun[11], Yanzhang[12] and others, it is determined that 4%, 8%, 12%, 16% of XT-1 type regenerant are added to the aged asphalt, and 3%, 5%, 7%, 9% of waste engine oil. Use 300WJJ-1A precision booster electric mixer to uniformly mix the regenerated asphalt at a rate of 2000r/min, and the mixing temperature is controlled at about 135℃. After stirring for 15-20 minutes, place it in an oven at 110℃ and let it stand for 10 minutes, repeat the above process 4 to 5 times, and then let it stand for 24 hours to fully integrate the regenerant and waste engine oil with the aged asphalt. After the above test steps, the regenerant and waste engine oil can be uniformly mixed with the aged asphalt, so that the performance of the aged asphalt can be better restored.

1.3 Bending Beam Rheological Test

The low-temperature bending beam rheological test (BBR) was used to test the original asphalt, aged asphalt and recycled asphalt. With reference to the research results of scholars such as Jiuguang Geng[13] and Kunwang[14], the measurement temperature of BBR was selected to be −18℃, −24℃ and −30℃ respectively. The sample preparation steps and test operation procedures are strictly in accordance with T 0627—2011 in "Standard Test methods of Bitumen and Bituminous Mixture for Highway Engineering" (JTG E20—2011).

Aiming at the low temperature performance of asphalt, the BBR test mainly takes the creep stiffness S and creep rate m at the test temperature as technical indicators for evaluation. The calculation formula of creep stiffness and creep rate are shown below.

$$S(t) = \frac{Pl^3}{4bh^3 v(t)} \quad (1)$$

$$m = \frac{d\log S(t)}{d\log(t)} \quad (2)$$

In the above equation, $v(t)$, b, h and l respectively represent the deflection of the mid-span, the width of the asphalt beam, the height of the beam and the length of the beam span, in millimeters, and P is the constant load, in cattle N. $S(t)$ and m represent creep stiffness and creep rate respectively.

1.4 Dissipated Energy Ercentage Based on Burgers Model

Burgers model was first applied to study the viscoelastic properties of asphalt concrete in the 1960s, and it can better reflect the viscoelastic properties of asphalt concrete. After continuous research by scholars from various countries, the Burgers model, as a typical viscoelastic model, has been widely used in the quantitative description and prediction of asphalt mechanical deformation characteristics. Therefore, based on the Burgers model, the low-temperature performance of recycled SBS modified asphalt is calculated and studied.

In the Fig. 1, E_1 is the instantaneous elastic deformation of the elastic element affected by the load; E_2 is equivalent to the slow viscoelastic deformation of the object under long-term load; η_1 is the viscosity index that characterizes the unrecoverable residual deformation; η_2 is the object under long-term load deformation. σ and ε are stress and strain respectively.

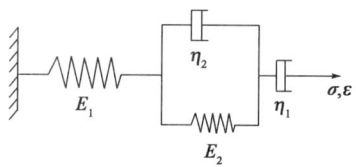

Fig. 1 Burgers Model

The expression of the creep equation of the Burgers model is below.

$$J(t) = \frac{\varepsilon(t)}{\sigma_0} = \frac{1}{E_1} + \frac{1}{\eta_1}t + \frac{1}{E_2}(1-e^{-\frac{t}{\tau}}) \qquad (3)$$

Where: $J(t)$——the creep compliance/(1/MPa);

$\tau = \eta_2/E_2$——the lag time of the system;

$\lambda = \eta_1/E_1$——the relaxation time of the system.

Dissipated energy ratio is a parameter that reflects the stress relaxation ability of a material, and is the ratio of dissipated energy to stored energy, namely $W_d(t)/W_s(t)$. The ratio of dissipated energy can be calculated by equation (4). For the low temperature performance of asphalt, the larger the dissipated energy, the smaller the stored energy. That is, the larger the value of the dissipation energy ratio, the better the asphalt has better stress relaxation ability and better low temperature performance. The dissipation energy ratio changes with time. In the Superpave design system and asphalt binder road performance specifications, the creep stiffness S and creep rate m are required to be 60s, so the calculation is at $t = 60s$. The dissipation energy ratio is analyzed, and the dissipation energy ratio of various modified asphalt before and after aging at different temperatures.

$$W_d(t)/W_s(t) = \left[\frac{t}{\eta_1} + \frac{1}{2E_2}(1-e^{-\frac{2E_2}{\eta_2}t})\right] / \left[\frac{1}{E_1} + \frac{1}{2E_2}(1-2e^{-\frac{E_2}{\eta_2}t} + e^{-\frac{2E_2}{\eta_2}t})\right] \qquad (4)$$

Where: $W_d(t)$——the storage energy of the system;

$W_s(t)$——the dissipated energy of the system [15].

2 Experimental Results and Analysis

2.1 S and Mchange Law of Recycled Asphalt

The change of creep stiffness $S(t)$ and creep rate m of asphalt at low temperature in winter reflects the quality of low-temperature cracking performance of road surface. The smaller the creep stiffness, the better the low-temperature deformation performance of the asphalt, and the greater the rate m of the creep stiffness changes with time, the better the ability to dissipate temperature stress. Therefore, the use of creep stiffness and creep rate can better reflect the low temperature recovery of recycled asphalt. In the Fig. 2 below, PAV, Water and UV represent long-term aging, water aging and ultraviolet light aging, respectively.

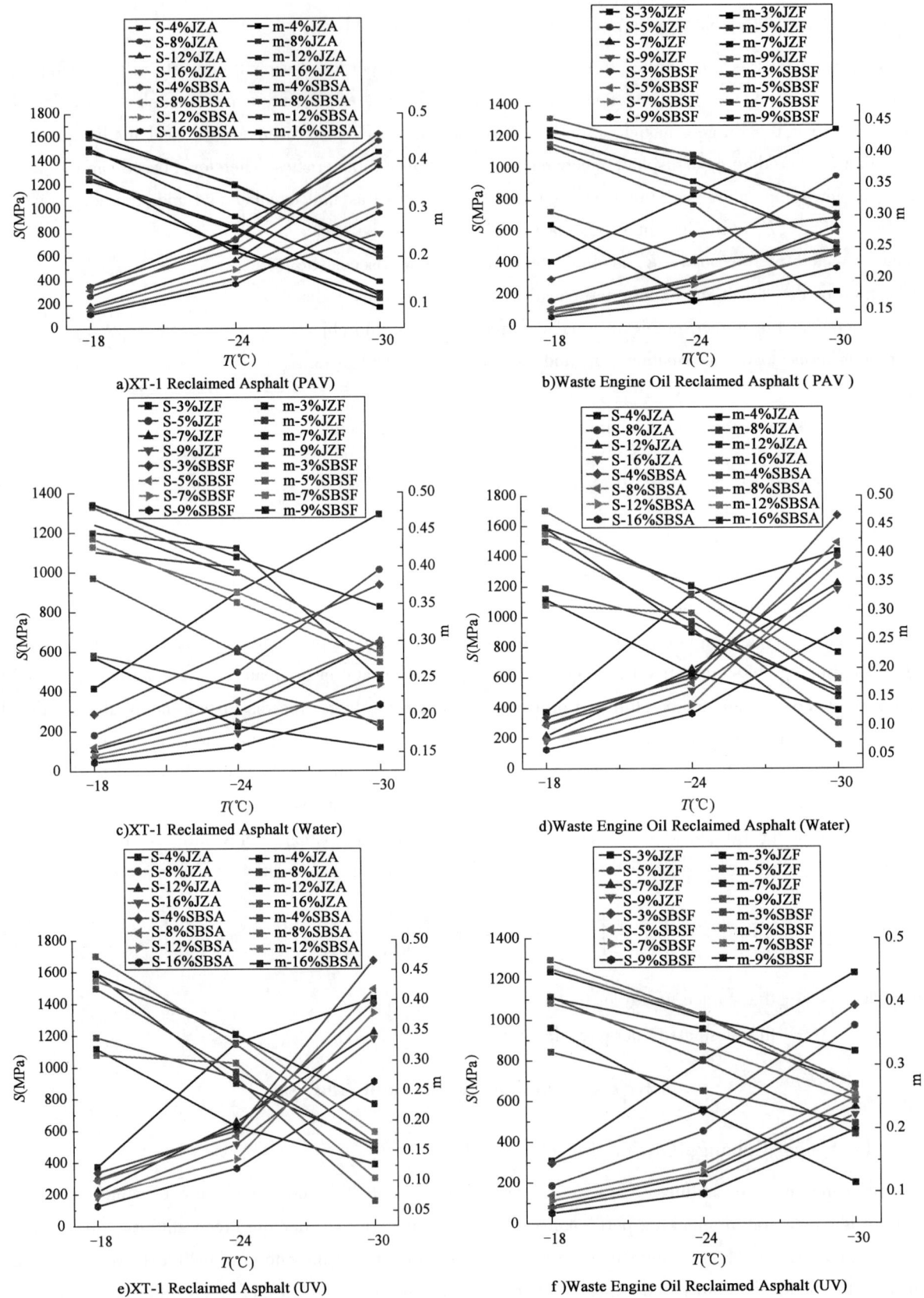

Fig. 2 S&m of XT-1 Regenerant and Waste Engine Oil Reclaimed Asphalt after Different Aging Methods

2.2 The Influence of Regenerant Agent Content on Flexural Creep Parameters of Recycled Asphalt

It can be seen from Figure 2 that with the increase in the content of XT-1 regenerant and waste engine oil, the stiffness modulus of the regenerated asphalt gradually decreases under the three temperature conditions, and the creep rate continues to rise, indicating that the regenerant and waste engine oil make the asphalt aged. As the elasticity decreases, the viscosity increases. As the stress relaxation capacity increases, the low temperature deformation capacity also increases. The aging of asphalt leads to the volatilization of some light components, and physical and chemical reactions such as small molecule polymerization increase the number of large molecules in the asphalt and the decrease of small molecules. In terms of low temperature performance, the S value increases and the m value decreases. The use of XT-1 regenerant and waste engine oil in the test can supplement the small molecular components lost in the asphalt aging process, improve the relative molecular mass distribution of the aging asphalt, and effectively improve its low-temperature resistance to cracking.

2.3 The Influence of Temperature on the Bending Creep Parameters of Recycled Asphalt

It can be seen from Figures 2 that as the test temperature decreases, the S value of the recycled asphalt increases, and the m value decreases, indicating that as the temperature decreases, the low temperature flexibility and crack resistance of the recycled asphalt deteriorate. Under the condition of -30℃, the stiffness modulus of the UV-aged base asphalt regenerated by XT-1 does not change significantly with the content of the regenerant, while under the same conditions, the stiffness modulus of the recycled SBS modified asphalt still maintains obvious change.

2.4 The Influence of Aging Methods on Bending Creep Parameters of Recycled Asphalt

From Figures 2(a),2(c) and 2(e), it can be seen that under the same temperature conditions, the regenerated asphalt with the same regenerant content increases with the deepening of the aging degree, and the stiffness modulus continues to increase, and its S value is UV > Water > PAV > Original indicates that the deeper the aging degree, the larger the amount of regenerant is needed to restore its low temperature performance. Compared with recycled base asphalt, recycled SBS modified asphalt shows better stress relaxation ability under the same aging method.

2.5 The Influence of Regenerant Agent Types on Bending Creep Parameters of Recycled Asphalt

The curves in Fig. 2a)、c)、e) change uniformly, while the curves in Fig. 2b),2d),f) have abrupt changes. This shows that the XT-1 regenerant has an excellent effect on the low-temperature performance of aged asphalt. The recovery is more even and stable. It can be seen from Fig. 2a)、b) that for base asphalt and SBS modified asphalt, when the amount of waste engine oil reaches the maximum 9%, the stiffness modulus of recycled asphalt is much lower than the 16% XT-1 of recycled asphalt. We can see that the waste engine oil has a good dispersing and dissolving ability for the asphaltenes in the aged base asphalt, thereby alleviating the degradation of the low-temperature rheological properties of the asphalt due to aging. When the amount of waste engine oil reaches 7%, the stiffness modulus of the recycled base asphalt and recycled SBS modified asphalt is much lower than that of the original asphalt, and the creep rate is much higher than that of the original asphalt. There is excessive "softening" in the recycled asphalt. Therefore, it is reflected as a sudden change in Figures.

2.6 Analysis of Dissipated Energy Percentage Based on Burgers Model of Recycled Asphalt

For the low-temperature performance of asphalt, the greater the dissipated energy, the better, and the smaller the storage energy, the better. That is, the larger the value of the dissipated energy percentage, it indicates that the asphalt has better stress relaxation ability and better low-temperature performance.

As can be seen from Fig. 3 that with the increase in the amount of regenerant and waste engine oil, the dissipated energy ratio of recycled SBS modified asphalt increases significantly. It can be seen from Fig. 3e) that at -18℃, the energy dissipation ratio increases rapidly with the increase of the blending amount. Therefore, the addition of regenerating agent improves the internal fluidity of the recycled SBS modified asphalt and increases the dissipation energy in the asphalt. Reduce energy storage, thereby improving stress relaxation ability. At the same time, it can be seen that the softening effect of the regenerant on the aging asphalt is not linearly increased, and it decreases first and then increases in some cases. Compared with Fig. 3a)、c), the curve of the dissipation energy ratio fluctuates more obviously, which also reflects the UV aging. The impact on SBS modified asphalt is more significant. With the decrease of temperature, at -24℃ to 30℃, the rate of energy dissipation of regenerated asphalt slows down with the increase of regenerant content. This shows that as the temperature decreases, the proportion of elasticity in the regenerated asphalt increases. When the temperature is lower than a certain temperature, the regenerated asphalt exhibits elastic characteristics, the brittleness increases, the energy dissipation in the regenerated asphalt decreases, and the storage energy increases and decreases. The flexibility of asphalt affects the relaxation ability of recycled asphalt at low temperatures.

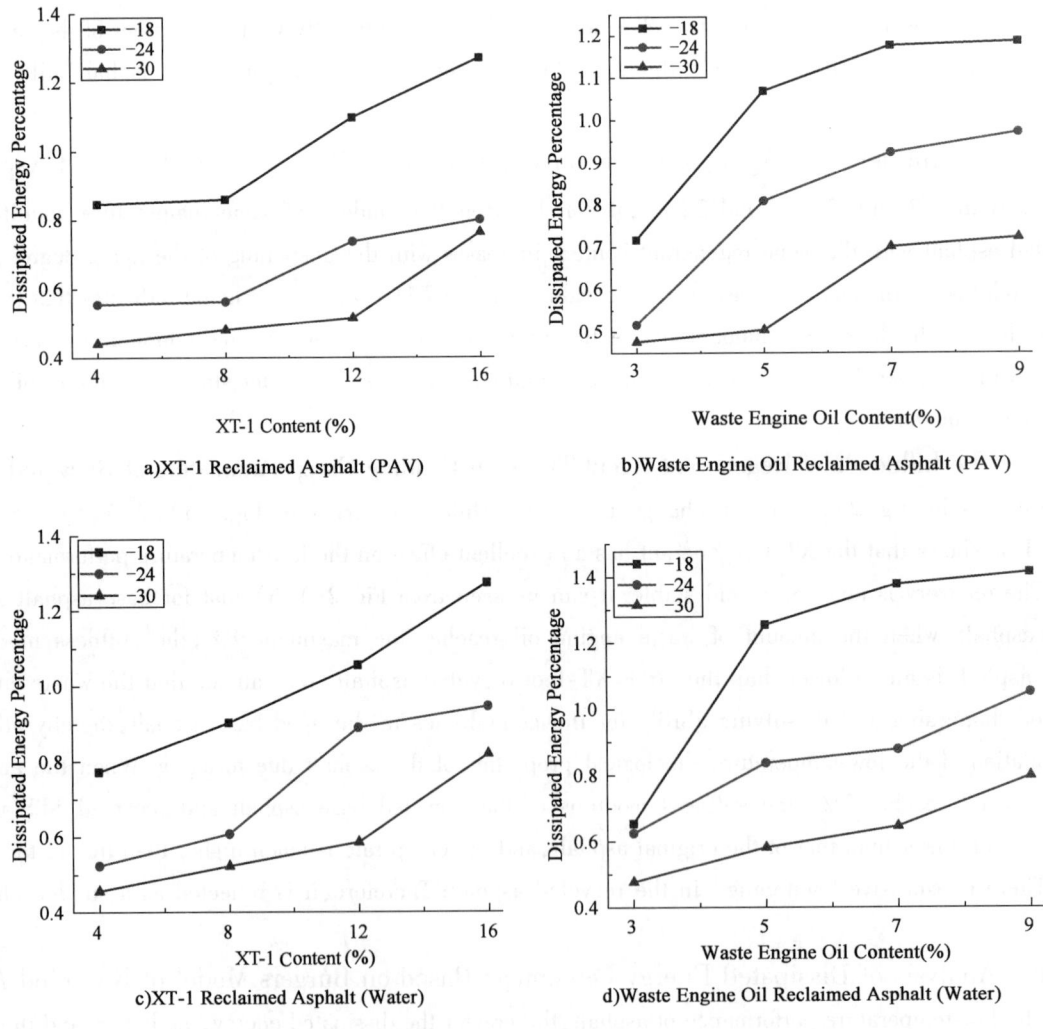

Fig. 3

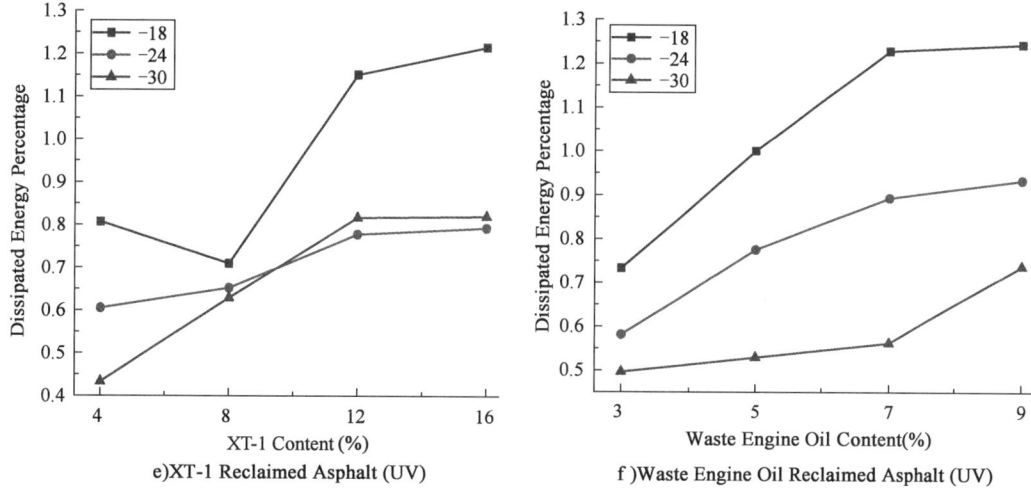

Fig. 3 Dissipated Energy Percentage of XT-1 Regenerant and Waste Engine Oil Recycled Asphalt Under Different Aging Methods

It can be seen from Fig. 3e) that waste engine oil can also increase the dissipated energy percentage of recycled asphalt. When the amount of waste engine oil is 3% to 7%, the dissipated energy percentage of recycled SBS modified asphalt by waste engine oil increases rapidly. when the amount reaches 9%, the curve of dissipated energy ratio-dosage tends to be flat, and the influence of different dosages of waste engine oil on the dissipated energy ratio gradually decreases. The aging method has little effect on the dissipated energy ratio of the recycled SBS modified asphalt, which also proves that the recycled SBS modified asphalt has better anti-aging performance, and the waste engine oil has a good effect and reconciliation on the recycled SBS modified asphalt after UV aging.

2.7 Dissipated Energy Ratio of Recycled SBS Modified Asphalt Under Different Aging Methods

It can be seen from Fig. 4a) that as the temperature decreases, the dissipated energy ratio of recycled asphalt has a downward trend, and the decrease is more obvious at -18℃ to -24℃, and the decrease at -24℃ to -30℃ is more gentle. This is because the decrease of temperature leads to the continuous increase of the elastic ratio in the asphalt material. When the temperature drops to -24℃, the aging asphalt is close to the elastomer, the internal dissipation energy of the asphalt material decreases, the storage energy increases, and dissipated energy ratio decreases. The low temperature crack resistance of the material has a negative effect [16].

The low-temperature recovery of recycled asphalt regenerated after different aging methods is also different under different temperature conditions. It can be seen from the dissipation energy percentage that the change curve of the dissipated energy percentage of the regenerated asphalt after PAV aging is between water aging and UV aging, while the regenerated asphalt after water aging and UV aging alternately rises with the decrease of temperature. And the situation of decline, which shows that the influence of temperature on the low-temperature deformation ability of recycled asphalt is greater than the influence of aging methods on it. This is because as the temperature decreases, the energy consumption rate becomes slower, and the time for the internal stress to become smaller becomes longer, resulting in an increase in the relaxation time, which is numerically expressed as a decrease in the dissipated energy ratio.

We can see from Fig. 4b) that the basic law of recycled asphalt from waste engine oil is basically the same as that of XT-1 recycled asphalt. Different from XT-1 regenerated asphalt, the difference in dissipated energy percentage between regenerated SBS modified asphalt under different aging conditions decreases as the temperature decreases, and reaches the minimum at -30℃. It shows that due to the decrease in temperature, the elastic ratio in recycled SBS modified asphalt is getting higher and higher. When the temperature is extremely low, the asphalt material tends to be elastomer, the dissipated energy becomes smaller and smaller, and the internal storage energy of the material becomes larger. At the same time, the influence of temperature on the energy dissipation ratio of waste oil regenerated asphalt is greater than the effect of aging on its dissipated energy ratio.

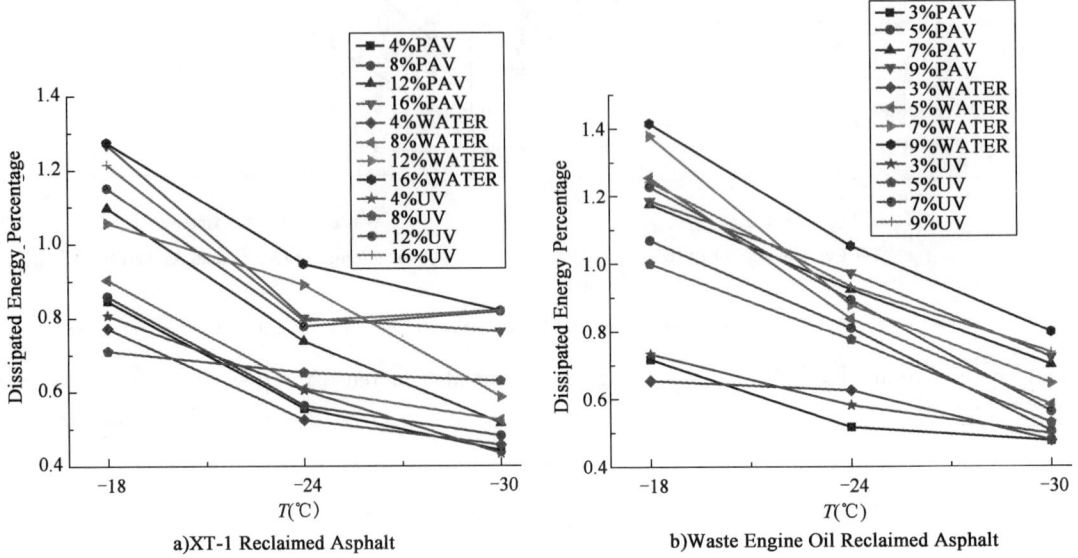

Fig. 4 Ratio of Dissipated Energy of Reclaimed SBS Modified Asphalt under Different Aging Methods

3 Conclusions

(1) The creep stiffness modulus S value of base asphalt and SBS modified asphalt increases as the aging degree deepens or the temperature decreases, and the creep rate m value decreases as the aging degree deepens or the temperature decreases. That is, aging reduces the low temperature performance of asphalt.

(2) Test temperature, aging method, dosage and type of regenerant can all affect the creep parameters of recycled SBS modified asphalt. With the addition of XT-1 regenerant and waste engine oil, its stiffness modulus decreases and creep rate increases. Among them, SBS modified asphalt requires a larger amount of XT-1 regenerant to restore its low-temperature deformation ability. The deeper the aging degree, the harder it is to recover its low-temperature performance. At extremely low temperatures, recycled SBS modified asphalt can still maintain a certain relaxation characteristic, which is better than recycled matrix asphalt.

(3) The dissipated energy percentage based on the Burgers model can better analyze the influence of different influencing factors on the low-temperature performance of recycled asphalt.

(4) The above analysis results show that the reasonable selection of regenerant agent and content has important influence on the regeneration effect of SBS modified asphalt and improving its low temperature performance.

4 Acknowledgment

This research was supported by Inner Mongolia Natural Science Foundation (2018MS05053) and Inner Mongolia Autonomous Region Higher Education School "Youth Technology Talents Program" (NJYT-19-A19).

References

[1] Ran Yan. Research on the Performance and Mechanism of Multiple Regeneration of SBS Modified Asphalt[D]. Guangzhou: South China University of Technology, 2018.

[2] Shaopeng Wu, Xiaoming Huang, Yongli Zhao. Research on Asphalt Recycling Agent for Road[J]. Science and Technology of Overseas Building Materials, 2001, 22(4): 47-50.

[3] H. A. Tabatabaee, T. L. Kurth. Analytical Investigation of the Impact of a Novel Bio-based Recycling Agent on the Colloidal Stability of Aged Bitumen Road Mater[J]. Pavement Des., 18(2017), pp. 131-140.

[4] Guilian Zou, Huan Qin, Ran Yan. Evaluation of Multiple Regeneration Effects of SBS Modified Asphalt based on Viscoelastic Properties[J]. Journal of South China University of Technology (Natural Science Edition), 2019, 47(07): 75-82.

[5] Longfei Ran, Zhaoyi He, Qingxia Cao. Study on the Performance of SBS Modified Asphalt Regenerant[J]. Journal of Building Materials, 2015, 18(04): 578-583 + 595.

[6] Hasan H. Joni, Rasha H. A. Al-Rubaee, et al. Al-zerkani. Rejuvenation of Aged Asphalt Binder Extracted from Reclaimed Asphalt Pavement Using Waste Vegetable and Engine oils[J]. Case Studies in Construction Materials, 2019, 11.

[7] Zhilong Cao, Meizhu Chen, Xiaobin Han, et al. Influence of Characteristics of Recycling Agent on the Early and Long-term Performance of Regenerated SBS Modified Bitumen[J]. Construction and Building Materials, 2019.

[8] Peiliang Cong, Weihua Luo, Peijun Xu, et al. Investigation on Recycling of SBS Modified Asphalt Binders Containing Fresh Asphalt and Rejuvenating Agents[J]. Construction and Building Materials, 2015(91).

[9] Ali Mansourkhaki, Mahmoud Ameri, Daryoosh Daryaee. Application of Different Modifiers for Improvement of Chemical Characterization and Physical-rheological Parameters of Reclaimed Asphalt Binder[J]. Construction and Building Materials, 2019(203).

[10] Industrial Standard of the People's Republic of China 'Standard Test methods of Bitumen and Bituminous Mixture for Highway Engineering' JTG E20—2011[S]. Beijing: China's Communications Press, 2011.

[11] Chuyu Sun. Research on the Performance of Recycled Asphalt and Asphalt Mixture from Waste Engine Oil[D]. Wuhan: Wuhan University of Technology, 2017.

[12] Yan Zhang, Meizhu Chen, Shaopeng Wu, et al. Study on the Physical Properties and Structure of Recycled Asphalt with Different Waste Grease[J]. Journal of Wuhan University of Technology (Transportation Science and Engineering Edition), 2017, 41(01): 104-108.

[13] Jiuguang Geng. Research on Asphalt Aging Mechanism and Recycling Technology[D]. Xi'an: Chang'an University, 2009.

[14] KunWang, Peiwen Hao. Asphalt Low-temperature Performance and Viscoelastic Analysis of BBR Test[J]. Journal of Liaoning Technical University (Natural Science Edition), 2016, 35(10): 1138-1143.

[15] LanWang, Zihao Wang, Chao Li. Low Temperature Performance of Polyphosphoric Acid Modified Asphalt based on Viscoelastic Theory[J]. Journal of Composite Materials, 2017, 34(2): 322-328.

[16] Jiang Yu, Qun Zhao, Fen Ye, et al. Low-temperature Rheological Properties of Natural Asphalt Composite Modified Asphalt Based on Viscoelastic Theory[J]. Science Technology and Engineering, 2018, 18(32): 217-225.

沥青材料分析研究技术进展

高润杰 陈 玉

(长安大学公路学院)

摘 要 沥青作为沥青路面的重要组成部分,其物理化学性质对沥青路面的使用性能表现具有重要的影响。由于沥青材料是由大小各异和极性不同的分子构成的复杂混合物,其微观结构组成复杂,并且沥青的物理化学性质在很大程度上取决于这种微观结构,因此,深入研究沥青材料结构性能具有重要意义。通过总结目前高新仪器分析沥青材料的试验方法,主要包括热分析技术、傅立叶红外光谱技术、凝胶色谱技术、核磁共振分析技术以及原子力显微镜技术,能够从不同角度对沥青材料结构组分进行分析。本文总结已有的沥青结构组成对性能表现研究,提出后续研究参考建议,有助于更好地使用沥青材料,设计出高质量的沥青路面。

关键词 道路工程 沥青材料 微观结构 分析检测 性能表现

0 引 言

目前,沥青路面病害日益增多,路面性能面临严峻考验[1]。沥青作为重要组成部分,其结构组成及性质对路面性能具有重大影响。在材料结构分析中,热分析技术、傅立叶红外光谱技术、凝胶色谱技术、核磁共振分析技术以及原子力显微镜技术正在投入使用[2]。选择合适的方法对沥青材料进行表征,有助于深入探讨沥青相关机理,了解路面使用过程中沥青结构与性能的变化规律,对于评价沥青性能和提高沥青路面使用性能具有重要的意义。

1 热分析技术

在沥青材料热分析技术中多使用差示扫描量热法(DSC)以及热重分析(TG)[3]。通过差示扫描量热法能够研究沥青材料随温度的变化情况。在沥青材料内发生的物理化学变化的热量改变在 DSC 曲线上得以表现,如图 1 所示。当材料吸收热量越多,表明此温度范围中出现相态改变越多,材料结构改变程度也越大,从而宏观表现产生改变[4]。

TG 是在设定温度下,通过热天平测量温度变化时材料的质量改变[5]。由 TG 得到的数据可以绘制热重曲线图,同时将热重曲线图进行温度或时间的数学求导,就可以得到 DTG 曲线,它能表征热重曲线变化的快慢,如图 2 所示。沥青材料受热会导致轻质组分挥发分解,因此 TG 是根据受热过程材料的质量改变来对材料的组成和性能进行研究[6]。

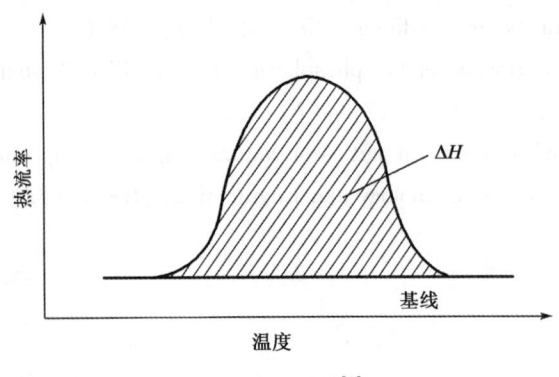

图 1 DSC 曲线[3]

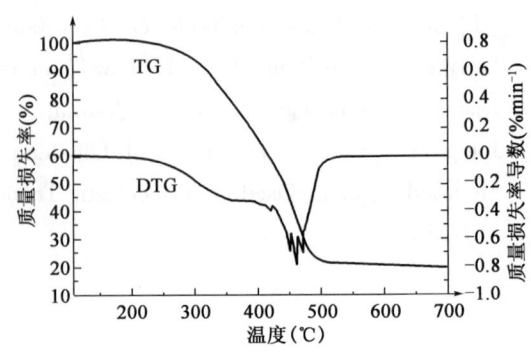

图 2 TG、DTG 曲线[6]

TG可研究成分对沥青热稳定性的影响,通过测量沥青材料质量变化与温度或时间关系,获取有关材料特性及成分信息。DSC测定沥青的吸热值、温度变化对沥青温度稳定性进行研究,TG试验能对沥青材料、老化沥青的热分解过程中质量损失的温度范围与速率进行评价。

2 傅立叶红外光谱技术

傅立叶红外光谱(FTIR)是沥青材料研究的重要方法,能够提供有关脂族、芳香族和氧合速率的信息。红外光谱是沥青中官能团在特定波长处吸收的能量图,每种化学键通过吸收光谱中的特征带来识别。表1中列出代表官能团FTIR吸收最大值。

沥青代表官能团的FTIR吸收最大值[7]　　　　　表1

官 能 团	波数(cm^{-1})	种　类	来　源
—OH	3300	酒精/苯酚	自然物质
—CH	3000	芳香分	自然物质
—CH_2	2920 2850	脂肪族	自然物质
—C(=O)—O—C(=O)	1780	酐	氧化产物
—C=O	1700	酮	氧化产物
—C=O(OH)	1650	羧酸	氧化产物
—C=C—	1600	芳香环	自然物质
—CH_2	1460	脂肪族	自然物质
—CH_3	1375	脂肪族	自然物质
—S—	690	硫化物	自然物质
—S=O	1030	亚砜	氧化产物
—(CH_2)n	745	脂肪链	自然物质

FTIR光谱可用谱带面积比计算官能团浓度。

脂肪族官能团指数:
$$I_B = \frac{A1375}{A1460 + A1375}$$

芳香官能团指数:
$$I_{Ar} = \frac{A1600}{\sum A}$$

羰基官能团指数:
$$I_{C=O} = \frac{A1700}{\sum A}$$

亚砜基官能团指数:
$$I_{S=O} = \frac{A1030}{\sum A}$$

沥青各官能团随老化的变化率:
$$W = \frac{I(老化-未老化)}{I 未老化}$$

上式中,A为沥青材料不同官能团峰面积,$\sum A$为范围内各种峰面积总和,可以依据不同官能团指数的变化推测相关物质在沥青材料中的变化[7]。

2.1 沥青老化分析

分析表明老化时氧的增加主要是由羰基和亚砜基引起的,FTIR还表明出从含硫原油中提取的沥青中芳基烷基酮的含量较高,可氧化硫化合物的含量较高[8]。除了极性化学官能团的氧化形成外,可逆的分子结构会改变老化的沥青的物理性能。在路面的使用寿命期间与氧化老化协同进行,并推测是沥青路面使用后期阶段导致路面脆化的主要原因。

2.2 沥青添加剂分析

Sun[9]进行了定量研究改性沥青中聚合物含量的活性测定,红外光谱法是确定几种类型的聚合物和改性沥青中的聚合物含量的最合适的试验方法。例如EVA材料的典型FTIR光谱表现出几个独特的吸收峰,聚乙烯链的特征是在2920 cm^{-1}、2850 cm^{-1}和724cm^{-1}处有尖峰,在1735cm^{-1}处的羰基峰与在1240至1270cm^{-1}处的双峰共同代表了EVA中的乙酸酯组分,在~1640cm^{-1}和~1560cm^{-1}处的两个峰与乙烯基有关。当添加到沥青中时,可用于对该添加剂的鉴定。

3 凝胶色谱技术

凝胶色谱技术(GPC)主要用来分离材料中不同分子量组分,通过分子量大小和含量多少结果来确定材料的分子量分布。沥青材料分子的差异使研究人员尝试使用凝胶渗透色谱法来分离这些组分[10]。GPC能够通过分子大小分离混合物的能力是一大优势。因此,GPC可用于检测沥青变化,每个沥青色谱图都显示其特征形状,可以反映沥青材料的变化。

3.1 沥青分子大小分级

GPC响应表观分子大小,因此是获得沥青分子量分布的简单方法。GPC在分子大小分布测量中不是获得分子量绝对值,而是确定表观分子大小,测量不同性质组成的沥青缔合度。溶剂功率对表观分子大小变化的影响可能带有沥青内部稳定性的信息。表2汇总了部分使用的色谱柱的型号及溶液配制浓度。

GPC试验设置参数及载体溶液[11]   表2

作 者	溶 液	浓度分数	体积(mL)	流速(mL·min^{-1})
Wahhab	四氢呋喃	0.05	0.1	1
Kim	四氢呋喃	0.0025	0.1	1
Lee	四氢呋喃	0.0025	—	1
Han	四氢呋喃	0.0025	0.05	1
Shen	四氢呋喃	—	—	1

利用GPC能够检测沥青的最值分子量、平均分子量及分子量分布。当沥青发生老化后,内部小分子会发生聚合等反应变为大分子,在沥青凝胶色谱GPC图上峰出现左移;而当向老化沥青中使用再生剂后,沥青中的小分子含量会增加,在沥青凝胶色谱图上峰出现右移;当沥青采用聚合物改性后,其分子量分布也会相应发生改变[11]。

3.2 沥青物理性质联系

沥青分子量分布是沥青性质差异的内在原因。Elseifi[12]研究了沥青在中低温下的变形性能,探讨分子组成与混合料之间的关系。努尔古丽[13]通过GPC证明硬质沥青的分子量大小、分布宽度与其高温性能具有良好的相关性。Churchill[14]利用HP-GPC研究了沥青老化前后分子量分布变化,并分析了利用GPC预测沥青性能的可行性。利用沥青的GPC色谱图可预测沥青针入度、运动黏度等特性。现有研究关注针入度、软化点、黏度及车辙因子与沥青GPC结果之间的关系,以及老化与分子变化之间相关性。

4 核磁共振技术

核磁共振(NMR)目前已用于有机化合物研究,能准确分析和芳香碳连接的氢与与饱和碳连接的氢。由谱峰可推导官能团的相对含量,因而用NMR来研究沥青材料化学结构的关键在能够区别和定量不同种类的C和H。表3及表4列出了常见的核磁共振^{1}H和^{13}C谱的质子化学位移。

常见的核磁共振^{1}H谱的质子化学位移[18]   表3

符 号	化学位移(ppm)	质子类型
H_γ	0.5~1.0	芳环的γ氢、环烷甲基氢
H_β	1.0~1.9	芳环的β-氢、环烷氢
H_α	1.9~4.5	芳环的α-亚甲基、α-甲基
$H_{\alpha 1}$	1.9~2.6	芳环的α-亚甲基
$H_{\alpha 2}$	2.6~4.5	α-甲基
H_A	6.3~9.0	芳环氢

常见的核磁共振^{13}C 谱的质子化学位移[18]　　　　表4

化学位移(ppm)	质子类型
170~150	被 OH 或烷氢基取代的芳碳原子
145~110	芳环碳原子
40~80	取代 C—O 的碳原子
58~8	饱和碳原子

4.1 沥青分子结构表征

Ramsey[15]通过^{1}H 核磁共振(^{1}H NMR)首次提出沥青的结构表征。此后 Hasan[16]提出结构化的分析方法来表征石油真空蒸馏残渣,Siddiqui[17]对方法进行补充修改,在获取 NMR 光谱之前先对沥青进行了分馏。随着技术改进,开始扩大使用^{1}H NMR 光谱(有时用^{13}C NMR 光谱)和元素分析对沥青馏分或类似材料的结构进行表征,目的在于定义沥青的特性与道路工程中的沥青路面使用性能相关的指标。

4.2 沥青老化分析

贺孟霜[18]选取老化沥青进行 NMR 试验,根据芳环氢含量差异提出将7.25ppm 附近的峰值看作沥青老化特征表现。Siddiqui[19]结合 NMR 和 GPC 信息,提出沥青的可能结构和老化机理。冉龙飞[20]采用基质沥青和 SBS 改性沥青进行多条件老化,发现老化会发生苯环氢取代反应,同时脂肪侧链的长度会变大。通过分析 NMR 图谱能得到沥青分子的结构参数、建立沥青分子微小单元,有助于进一步了解沥青化学成分结构。

5 原子力显微镜技术

原子力显微镜(AFM)作为新兴研究技术,是一种拥有原子级分辨率的实验设备。AFM 可以用于探究各种不同的样品表面,用于分析样品表面在纳米级上的化学、物理或热力学性质[21]。图3 为原子力显微镜扫描沥青的表面示意图。AFM 图像是基于高度的模拟图像,颜色变化反映表面形貌的相对高度。

5.1 沥青微观结构分析

沥青表面的 AFM 图像是一种独特的"蜂"结构,最初仅用于"凝胶"沥青。其中一种相图如图4所示,连续相用白色表示。研究表明,沥青具有与其化学成分和热历史有关的独特微观结构[23]。蜂结构变化会影响沥青力学性质,进而影响其宏观性能[24]。

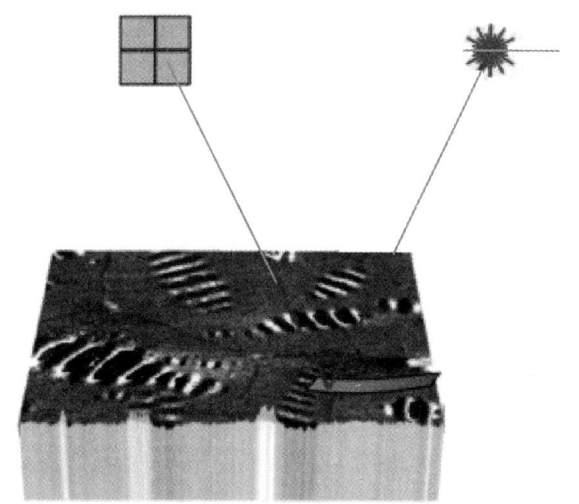

图3　AFM 扫描沥青表面示意图[22]

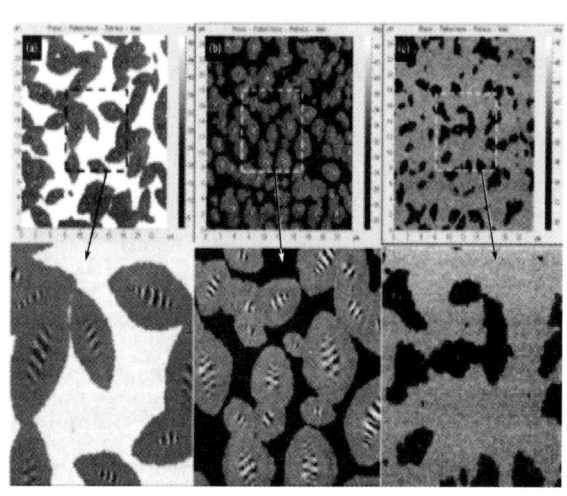

图4　沥青相图示意图[22]

5.2 沥青微观性能分析

杨震[25]使用 AFM 分析老化沥青性能,老化导致空间变化。Tarefder[26]使用 AFM 进行纳米级实验,测试基质沥青和聚合物(SB 和 SBS)改性的沥青内聚力的影响,聚合物改性沥青使沥青不易受水分损害。将 AFM 与其他高分辨率分析工具相结合,将为沥青的化学性质与其微观形态和性能联系起来提供一条途径,有利于开发不同的沥青材料的结构相关模型[27-30]。

6 结 语

随着各种沥青产品种类不断研发及使用,关于沥青材料结构、性能、老化等问题的认识慢慢深入,并且现代测试技术方法的快速变化与发展大趋势,后续相关研究可以从以下几个方面进行展开:

(1)现代高新试验技术具有其本身的研究优势,可以结合不同试验技术共同展开。

(2)由不同试验得到的结果进行联合分析论证,可以对沥青材料组分分子的研究更加全面。

(3)将沥青材料微观测试方法与计算机仿真技术和统计算法相结合,可能为将微观结构与沥青材料的宏观性能联系起来提供一种方式。

(4)将实验室研究结果与实际路面使用性能进行对比,加强沥青材料微观结构和宏观物理性能及路面使用性能的结合。

参考文献

[1] 彭东黎,张霞晖.改性沥青混合料的抗剪性能研究[J].交通标准化,2011,01:132-134.

[2] 洪浩凯,张恒龙,黄立葵.核磁共振、热分析和扫描电镜用于沥青材料表征的研究进展[J].公路交通科技,2019,36(12):15-28.

[3] 王君.SBS 改性沥青的技术性能和评价指标研究[D].重庆:重庆交通大学,2017.

[4] Wang S,Cheng D,Xiao F. Recent Developments in the Application of Chemical Approaches to Rubberized Asphalt[J]. Construction and Building Materials,2017,131:101-113.

[5] 曾凡奇,黄晓明,李海军.沥青性能的 DSC 评价方法[J].交通运输工程学报,2005(4):37-42.

[6] Moth M G,Lelte L F M,Moth C G.. Thermal characterization of asphalt mixtures by TG/DTG..DTA and FTIR[J]. Journal of Thermal Analysis and Calorimetry,2008,93(1):105-109.

[7] 张葆琳.基于红外光谱的沥青结构表征研究[D].武汉:武汉理工大学,2014.

[8] Michalica P,Daucik P,Zanzotto L. Monitoring of compositional changes occurring during the oxidative aging of two selected asphalts from different sources[J]. Petroleum and Coal,2008,50.

[9] Sun D Q,Zhang L W. A Quantitative Determination of Polymer Content in SBS Modified Asphalt. Part I:State of the Art[J]. Petroleum Science and Technology,2013,31(24):2636-2642.

[10] 张晓.蒸汽爆破预处理对红麻纤维性能影响及微观机理研究[D].青岛:青岛大学,2016.

[11] 周维鼎.凝胶渗透色谱法在沥青研究中的应用[J].筑路机械与施工机械化,2019(10):34-45.

[12] Elseifi M A,Mohammad L N,Glover L,et al. Relationship between Molecular Compositions and Rheological Properties of Neat Asphalt Binder at Low and Intermediate Temperatures[J]. Journal of Materials in Civil Engineering,2010,22(12):1288-1294.

[13] 努尔古丽,唐新忠,冉竹叶.高效凝胶色谱法快速测定硬质沥青分子量和分子量分布方法及其物理性能的相关性研究[J].石油沥青,2017,31(1):45-50.

[14] Eleni Vassiliadou Churchill,Serji N. Amirkhanian,James L. Burati Jr. HP-GPC Characterization of Asphalt Aging and Selected Properties[J]. journal of materials in civil engineering,1995,7(1):41-49.

[15] Ramsey J W,Mcdonald F R,Petersen J C. Structural Study of Asphalts by Nuclear Magnetic Resonance[J]. Industrial & Engineering Chemistry Product Research and Development,1967,6(4):231-236.

[16] Hasan M U, Bukhari A, Ali M F. Structural Characterization of Saudi Arabian Medium Crude Oil by N. M. R. spectroscopy[J]. Fuel, 1985, 64(6):839-841.

[17] Siddiqui, Mohammad Nahid, Ali, Mohammad F. Investigation of Chemical Transformations by NMR and GPC During the Laboratory Aging of Arabian asphalts[J]. fuel, 1999, 78(12):1407-1416.

[18] 贺孟霜. 道路石油沥青结构行为与性能表征[D]. 西安:长安大学, 2013.

[19] Siddiqui. NMR Fingerprinting of Chemical Changes in Asphalt Fractions on Oxidation[J]. Petroleum ence and Technology, 2010, 28(4):401-411.

[20] 冉龙飞. 热、光、水耦合条件下 SBS 改性沥青老化机理研究及高性能再生剂开发[D]. 重庆:重庆交通大学, 2016.

[21] 郭书翊. 原子力学显微镜 AFM 图像沥青蜂状结构特性研究综述[J]. 路基工程, 2019, 2:32-38.

[22] R. Grover A, Dallas N. L, Amit B, et al. The Effects of Chemical Composition on Asphalt Microstructure and Their Association to Pavement Performance[J]. International Journal of Pavement Engineering, 2014, 15(1-2):9-22.

[23] Menapace I, Masad E, Bhasin A. Microstructural Properties of Warm Mix Asphalt Before and after Laboratory-simulated Long-term Ageing[J]. Road Materials & Pavement Design, 2015, 16(1):2-20.

[24] Jahangir, R., D. Little, A. Bhasin. Evolution of Asphalt Binder Microstructure Due to Tensile Loading Determined Using AFM and Image Analysis Techniques[J]. International Journal of Pavement Engineering, 2015, 16(4):337-349.

[25] 杨震, 张肖宁, 虞将苗. 沥青老化前后微观与宏观力学性能的对比研究[J]. 建筑材料学报, 2018, 21(002):335-339.

[26] Tarefder R A, Zaman A M. Nanoscale Evaluation of Moisture Damage in Polymer Modified Asphalts[J]. Journal of Materials in Civil Engineering, 2010, 22(7):714-725.

[27] Zhang M, Hao P, Dong S, et al. Asphalt Binder Micro-characterization and Testing Approaches: A Review[J]. Measurement, 2019, 151:107255.

[28] Yuan Y, Zhu X, Lee K, et al. Correlation between the Characterization of Bee Structures and Chemical Composition/nano-scale Mechanical Property of Bitumens[J]. Construction and Building Materials, 2020, 237:117562.

[29] Li Z, Fa C, Zhao H, et al. Investigation on Evolution of Bitumen Composition and Micro-structure During Aging[J]. Construction and Building Materials, 2020, 244:118322.

[30] Yu X, Burnham N A, Granados-Focil S, et al. Bitumen's Microstructures are Correlated with its Bulk Thermal and Rheological Properties[J]. Fuel, 2019, 254(OCT.15):115509.

冻融循环下冷拌环氧沥青的韧性衰减规律

王俊彦 于 新 丁功瀛 阮 伟
(河海大学土木与交通学院)

摘 要 冷拌环氧沥青(CMEA)是一种"绿色"的桥面铺装材料。为了明确 CMEA 在冻融循环下的韧性衰减规律和机理,本文通过拉伸测试和动态力学测试研究了 CMEA 的衰减规律,并用扫描电子显微镜和红外光谱仪探究了韧性的衰减机理。结果表明:CMEA 的拉伸强度、断裂伸长率、断裂能等韧性性能表征整体上呈现下降趋势,其中第 1 个循环对于 CMEA 的韧性影响最大。此外,CMEA 的储能模量和玻璃化转化温度均呈现变大的趋势。CMEA 的韧性衰减机理可以解释为环氧树脂和沥青韧性共同衰减的结果。在衰减过程中，CMEA 内的部分交联网络发生破坏，体系内的"海岛"结构发生破坏，沥青颗粒直径变大，同时发生老化，使得 CMEA 受力后发生脆性破坏。

关键词 冷拌环氧沥青 韧性衰减 断裂能 衰减机理

0 引言

环氧沥青是一种钢桥面铺装所采用的重要材料之一。近年来，冷拌环氧沥青（CMEA）因其常温施工，能耗低，固化养生时间短等特点受到越来越多的关注。然而，在低温环境下，环氧沥青的韧性（拉伸强度、断裂伸长率、模量等）往往较差，易发生开裂等病害。同时，随着服役年限的增加，环氧沥青在冬季受到低温、雨雪等多种环境因素的影响导致其受到冻融循环作用，韧性逐渐衰减，从而引发更大的病害。因此，明确 CMEA 韧性衰减规律就显得十分必要。

CMEA 的韧性衰减是一个多种环境条件综合的过程。然而，目前关于 CMEA 韧性衰减规律的研究还比较少[1]，当前研究主要集中在环氧树脂和沥青的老化规律的研究。Yin 等人研究了在极端气候条件下，环氧沥青的开裂机理和修复手段[2]。Zhang 等人以高压汞灯模拟紫外老化条件，并研究了紫外线吸收剂对冷拌高韧性树脂的拉伸性能影响[3]。Wang 等人对环氧树脂进行了不同周期的湿热老化，结果表明老化过程中发生了物理吸湿和化学吸湿[4]。Xiao 等人的研究表明水与树脂在高温下发生不可逆作用水可以导致 C 和 O 的结合并切断环氧主链[5]。Apostolidis 等人研究了热氧条件下环氧沥青老化的机理，结果表明环氧沥青的老化是缓慢的，并且环氧化合物缓慢渗入沥青中，产生了抗氧化的物质，并且使得环氧沥青材料变得硬脆，模量变大[6]。Delor-Jestin 等人研究了环氧树脂的热老化和光老化过程，结果表明固化剂对环氧树脂的降解和稳定性起着重要的作用[7]。

由上述文献可知，目前研究者对 CMEA 的韧性影响及衰减规律认识并不明确。此外，冬季是一个冰雪冻融、水、温度多种因素综合作用的环境，并且环氧树脂在低温下韧性明显减小，故冬季条件对 CMEA 的韧性破坏更大。而当前的研究并没有考虑冬季多种因素长期作用下 CMEA 韧性衰减规律。基于上述不足，本文对 CMEA 在室内进行模拟冻融循环老化试验，通过拉伸测试、动态力学测试（DMA）等研究冻融循环对其韧性的影响，并通过扫描电子显微镜（SEM）和红外光谱（FTIR）探究 CMEA 的韧性衰减机理。

1 材料及试验方法

1.1 原材料

本文使用的 70 号基质沥青由通沙沥青科技有限公司提供，基本性质见表 1。双酚 A 环氧树脂（E51）由南亚公司提供，基本性质见表 2。固化剂为实验室自制的改性胺固化剂。沥青稀释剂为生物柴油。其他助剂为环氧化大豆油（化学纯）和 γ-(2,3-环氧丙氧基)丙基三甲氧基硅烷（KH560，化学提纯，97%），均由美国阿拉丁公司提供。

70 号基质沥青的基本性质 表 1

性　能	值	测试方法
针入度（25℃）（0.1mm）	81.7	ASTM D 5
软化点（℃）	49.0	ASTM D 36
延度（5℃）（cm）	7.01	ASTM D 100

基金项目：国家自然科学基金项目面上项目（52078191）。

E51 的基本性质 表2

指标	测试结果	测试方法
黏度(23℃)(Pa·s)	13.5	ASTM D445
环氧当量	185	ASTM D1652
闪点(℃)	218	ASTM D92
含水量(%)	0.01	ASTM D6304
比重(23℃)	1.165	ASTM D1475
外观	透明琥珀状	目测

1.2 冷拌环氧沥青样品的制备方法

CMEA 由 A、B 两种组分组成,其中 A 组为 E51,B 组分为 70 号基质沥青、生物柴油、固化剂、环氧大豆油和 KH560 的混合物。B 组分的制备过程如下:首先,将基质沥青加热至 120℃并保持 30 分钟,然后停止加热。随后,将生物柴油按与沥青的质量比 100:30 倒入沥青中,并以 600~800 rad/min 的速度均匀搅拌混合物。当混合料搅拌冷却至 40℃时,将固化剂,环氧大豆油和 KH560 添加到混合物中。最后,将共混物以 1000 rad/min 的速度搅拌 1h 后即可获得组分 B。

CMEA 固化物的制备方法为:在室温下以 43:57 的质量比混合 CMEA 的组分 A 和 B。将混合物均匀搅拌,倒入模具中,并在烘箱中按照以下步骤固化:25℃/24 h + 60℃/48h。

1.3 冷拌环氧沥青冻融循环试验方案

本文对 CMEA 固化物进行冻融循环试验,并定义一个循环的过程为:首先将 CMEA 固化物 25℃浸水 30 min,其次将测试材料置于-40℃冰柜中冷冻 16h,然后将其置于 60℃水浴中 24h,最后将其在 25℃下浸水 2h 完成一个冻融循环。本部分对 CMEA 固化物分别进行 0、1、2、3、4、5 次循环,共 6 组。对于冻融循环过后的 CMEA 固化物,分别进行拉伸测试、DMA、SEM、FTIR 等测试。

1.4 测试方法

1.4.1 拉伸测试

为了获得 CMEA 的拉伸强度、断裂伸长率和断裂能等力学性能,本文通过万能试验机(HG-MF501,中国)对 CMEA 进行拉伸测试。测试方法参考 ASTM D638—2014,哑铃试件采用 IV 型,测试温度为室温,拉伸速率为 10mm/min。断裂能通过计算拉伸测试获得的"应力-应变"曲线中,CMEA 固化物从开始到屈服破坏的面积来获得,单位为 N·m。每个样品进行 5 次有效测试。

1.4.2 动态热机械测试

为了获得 CMEA 的动态力学性能,根据 ASTM D4065,采用动态热机械仪器(DMA/SDTA861e,Mettler Toledo,Switzerland)对 CMEA 固化物进行测试。测试采用单悬臂梁模式,样品尺寸为 30mm × 10 mm × 2 mm,频率为 1 Hz,温度测试范围为-25~75℃,升温速率为 3℃/min。

1.4.3 扫描电子显微镜测试

为了获得 CMEA 的断裂面形貌,本文采用扫描电子显微镜(X650 型,日本日立公司)对拉伸拉伸试验结束后的 CMEA 哑铃试件断裂面进行观察,扫描放大倍数为 1000 倍,试验前在断面涂上金/钯合金。

1.4.4 红外光谱测试

为了研究冻融循环对 CMEA 官能团变化的影响,本文采用傅立叶衰减全反射红外光谱仪(ATR-FTIR,Nicolet IS20,ThermoFisher,USA)对经过不同冻融循环周期后 CMEA 固化物进行测试。波数扫描范围为 500~4000cm^{-1},分辨率为 4cm^{-1}。

2 结果与讨论

2.1 拉伸性能

图 1 为不同冻融循环下 CMEA 的力学性能。CMEA 经过冻融循环后拉伸强度和断裂伸长率均显著

下降。经过 1 个冻融循环后,CMEA 的强度为 1.57MPa,仅为原样状态下的 32.8%,强度明显下降。然后强度呈现波动下降趋势,最终在 5 循环时达到 1.22MPa,较 1 循环时下降 22.3%。从断裂伸长率的角度来看,经过 1 循环后,CMEA 的断裂伸长率值为 57.5%,较原样状态下降比例为 10.9%,然后与拉伸强度一样呈现波动下降趋势,最终在 5 循环时降为 42.0%,较 1 循环下降比例为 27.0%。这是因为冻融循环初期对环氧树脂和沥青的损害较大,因此 1 循环 CMEA 的拉伸强度、断裂伸长率显著下降。CMEA 拉伸性能的显著下降可能是因为随着冻融和 60℃水浴循环过程的增加,CMEA 中的部分交联网络发生破坏和沥青的老化有关。与热拌环氧沥青相比,CMEA 在冻融循环下拉伸强度和断裂伸长率下降幅度较小[8],这可能是与 CMEA 和热拌环氧沥青的固化剂不同有关。

2.2 断裂能分析

图 2 为不同冻融循环下 CMEA 的断裂能。断裂能(W)是指试样承受拉伸载荷,裂缝扩展单位面积所需要的能量,是材料韧性的一种体现,计算公式如式(1)所示[9]:

$$W = \int_0^\infty \sigma d\varepsilon \tag{1}$$

CMEA 的断裂能整体呈现下降的趋势,这表明 CMEA 的韧性随着冻融循环的进行,逐渐变差,低温状态下更易开裂。1 循环后 CMEA 的韧性值(80.58N·m)下降为原样状态(181.77N·m)下的 44.3%,2 循环(39.19N·m)较 1 循环又下降了 51.4%,随后断裂能衰减速度变慢,5 循环时达到最小值(30.95N·m)。这再次印证了冻融循环初期对环氧树脂和沥青的损害较大的结论。这可能是因为经历过冻融循环后,环氧树脂和沥青均发生了不同程度的水损坏。水在环氧树脂中具有较强的吸收和扩散能力,水分子不断被环氧树脂所吸收,并且以小分子形式存在减少了环氧树脂交联体系的网络作用力,使其强度发生一定损失。此时,沥青和环氧树脂均受热后发生了分子链断裂,破坏了体系原有的柔性[8]。

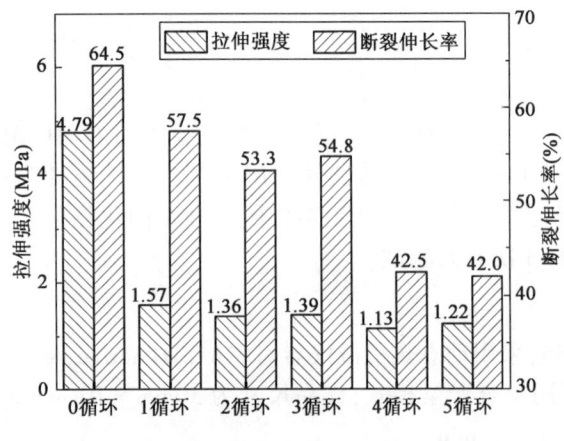

图 1　不同冻融循环周期下 CMEA 的拉伸性能

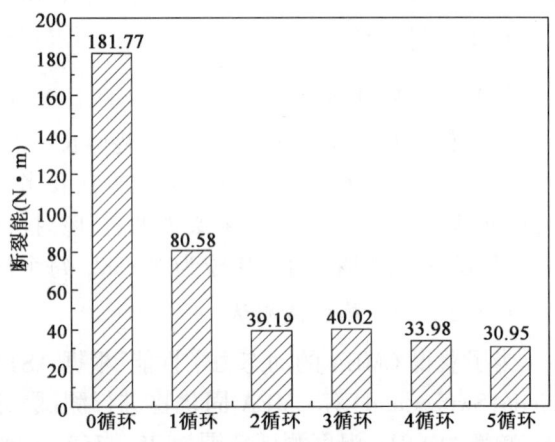

图 2　不同冻融循环周期下 CMEA 的断裂能

2.3 动态力学性能

图 3 为 CMEA 在动态力学条件下的力学响应。储能模量的大小反映了材料的受力后回弹的能力。由图 3a)可知,经过冻融循环后,CMEA 的储能模量整体上变大。-25℃时,3 循环组储能模量最大(834.8MPa),5 循环组储能模量最小(795.0MPa),最小值较未冻融循环组增大了 12% 以上。然而,在高温区域(>60℃),冻融循环之后的 CMEA 和原样的储能模量相近。这表明冻融循环未明显改变 CMEA 的高温韧性,而在较低温度下 CMEA 变硬,韧性变差,不易变形,容易发生开裂。

玻璃化转化温度(T_g)是材料脆性和弹性的转变温度。温度在 T_g 以上时,材料呈现高弹态;温度在 T_g 以下时,材料呈现玻璃态,表现出脆性[10]。本文以相位角的峰值对应的温度作为 CMEA 的 T_g。由图 3b)可知,随着冻融循环的进行,CMEA 的 T_g 不断变大。0 循环时 T_g 为 54.9℃,1 循环时 T_g 为 56.7℃,3 循环和 5 循环的 T_g(预计 70℃以上)则超出了试验温度范围,并仍呈上升趋势。这可能因为冻融循环中的高温条件使得 CMEA 中的环氧树脂发生了后固化,导致 CMEA 中的交联度进一步提高。这可能因为冻融循环中的高温条件使得 CMEA 中的环氧树脂发生了后固化,导致 CMEA 中的交联度进一步提高。这与 Yang 等人的研究结果是类似的[11]。T_g 上升表明 CMEA 在较低温度下处于玻璃态,韧性较差,易发生开裂,这与储能模量得出的结论是一致的。

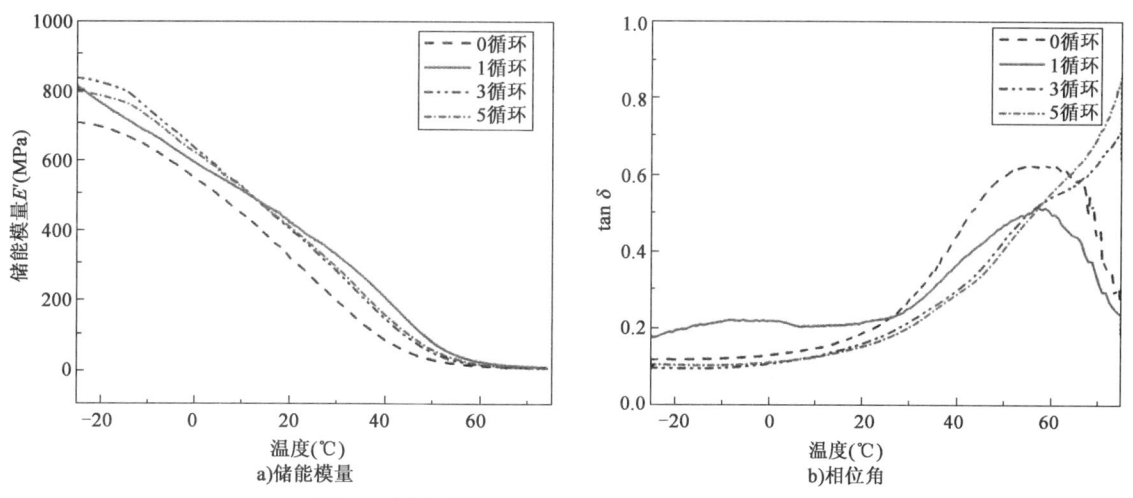

图3　不同冻融循环周期下 CMEA 的储能模量和相位角

2.4　韧性衰减机理分析

2.4.1　断裂面形貌

图 4 为不同冻融循环后 CMEA 的 SEM,可以发现随着冻融循环的进行,CMEA 的断裂面变得光滑,沥青颗粒直径变大,韧窝数量减少,说明材料的韧性变差。未经过冻融循环时,断面有较多的沥青颗粒,并且直径较小,这说明 CMEA 在发生断裂的时候,应力可以较好地被沥青颗粒吸收,使其具有较好的韧性[12]。随着冻融循环次数的增加,CMEA 体系的部分交联结构发生破坏,导致其对沥青颗粒的约束能力下降,从而导致沥青颗粒直径变大,体系的强度下降[13]。同时,环氧树脂在老化之后变脆,使 CMEA 的断裂伸长率和韧性等性能发生衰减。

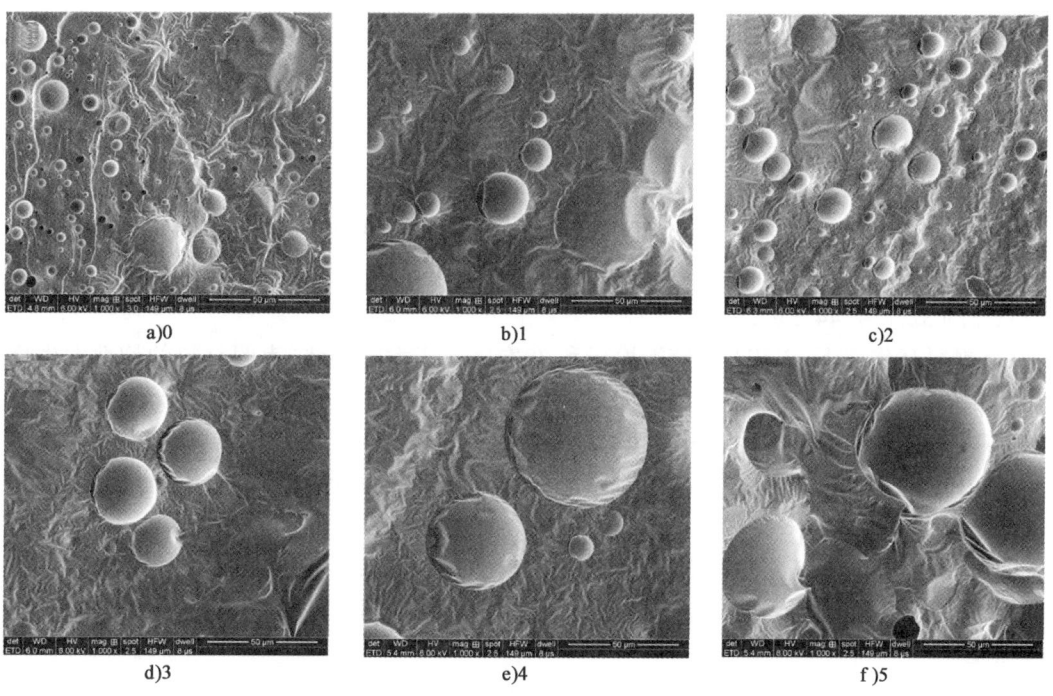

图4　不同冻融循环周期下 CMEA 的断裂面形貌

2.4.2 环氧沥青的官能团变化

图 5 为不同冻融循环周期下 CMEA 的红外光谱图。从图中可以看到 1 循环之后 CMEA 在 3355cm^{-1} 和 1604cm^{-1} 的峰变强。3355cm^{-1} 和 1604cm^{-1} 分别对应 O-H 伸缩振动以及 C=C 伸缩振动[14-15]。这可能是因为沥青中存在对水敏感的羧酸、酰胺等官能团,使得沥青有结合和运输水的能力,一定数量的水通过扩散并留在沥青或沥青胶浆膜中[16]。沥青质的分子结构使沥青和水分之间的界面结构膜随时间的增长而产生硬化,最终使沥青变质[17]。另一方面,环氧树脂的交联网络在冻融循环的作用下被破坏,并与游离 O 发生反应,从而使得 O-H 键和 C=C 出现[18]。

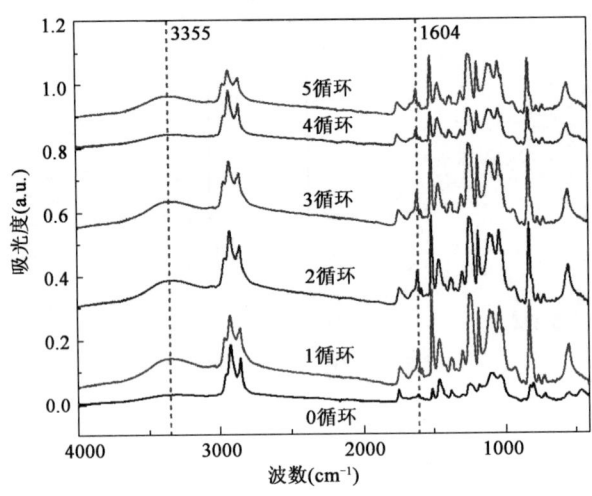

图 5 不同冻融循环周期下 CMEA 的红外光谱图

因此,CMEA 的冻融循环下韧性的衰减机理可以看作是环氧树脂和沥青共同作用的结果,其中环氧树脂对于 CMEA 的韧性衰减作用更大。在冻融循环过程中,环氧树脂受热和水的作用下部分交联网络被破坏,导致环氧树脂本身强度下降。另一方面,交联网络的破坏导致部分"海岛"结构发生破坏,环氧树脂对于沥青的约束作用下降,使得沥青的直径变大。当受到外力作用时,在沥青处发生了应力集中,导致局部应力过大,从而发生脆性断裂。同时,沥青在热和水的作用下发生氧化,重质组分不断转化为轻质组分,使其变硬、变脆。由于环氧树脂和沥青的韧性均发生衰减,导致 CMEA 的韧性呈现显著下降的趋势。

3 结 语

本文通过拉伸测试和 DMA 研究了冻融循环下 CMEA 的衰减规律,并用 SEM 和 FTIR 探究了 CMEA 的韧性衰减机理,得到主要结论如下:

(1)在冻融循环作用下,CMEA 的拉伸强度、断裂伸长率、断裂能等韧性性能表征整体上呈现下降趋势,并且下降速度呈现先快后慢的趋势。其中,第 1 个循环对于 CMEA 的韧性影响最大,拉伸强度、断裂能分别为原样的 32.8%、44.3%。

(2)在冻融循环作用下,CMEA 的储能模量和 T_g 均呈现变大的趋势,表明材料的韧性发生衰减,易发生开裂。其中,-25℃时储能模量至少增大 12% 以上,T_g 上升至 70℃以上。

(3)CMEA 的冻融循环下韧性衰减机理可以看成是环氧树脂和沥青韧性共同衰减的结果。在衰减过程中,CMEA 内的部分交联网络发生破坏,"海岛"结构发生破坏,沥青也发生老化,使得 CMEA 受力后发生脆性破坏。

本文的研究是对冻融循环下 CMEA 的韧性衰减的一次积极探索,将对日后改善 CMEA 的韧性及该材料的推广应用产生积极意义。后续的研究可以从元素分析、固化动力学角度对 CMEA 的韧性衰减机理进行深入探究。

参考文献

[1] Zhai Z,Feng L J,Li G Z,et al. The Anti-Ultraviolet Light (UV) Aging Property of Aluminium Particles/Epoxy Composite[J]. Progress in Organic Coatings,2016,101:305-308.

[2] Yin C E,Zhang H,Pan Y Q. Cracking Mechanism and Repair Techniques of Epoxy Asphalt on Steel Bridge Deck Pavement[J]. Transportation Research Record,2016,(2550):123-130.

[3] Zhang H,Gao P W,Pan Y Q,et al. Development of Cold-Mix High-Toughness Resin and Experimental Research into Its Performance in a Steel Deck Pavement[J]. Construction and Building Materials,2020,235.

[4] Wang Y Y,Liu Y,Xiao K,et al. The Effect of Hygrothermal Aging on the Properties of Epoxy Resin[J]. Journal of Electrical Engineering & Technology,2018,13(2):892-901.

[5] Xiao G Z,Delamar M,Shanahan M E R. Irreversible Interactions Between Water and DGEBA/DDA Epoxy Resin During Hydrothermal Aging[J]. Journal of Applied Polymer Science,1997,65(3):449-458.

[6] Apostolidis P,Liu X Y,Erkens S,et al. Oxidative Aging of Epoxy Asphalt[J]. International Journal of Pavement Engineering,2020.

[7] Delor-Jestin F,Drouin D,Cheval P Y,et al. Thermal and Photochemical Ageing of Epoxy Resin-Influence of Curing Agents[J]. Polymer Degradation and Stability,2006,91(6):1247-1255.

[8] 周威,赵辉,文俊,等.环氧沥青混凝土的水损坏机理研究[J].重庆交通大学学报(自然科学版),2015,34(01):54-59.

[9] Seira,Morimune,Masaru,et al. Poly(vinyl alcohol) Nanocomposites with Nanodiamond[J]. Macromolecules,2011,44(11):4415-4421.

[10] Yu X,Wang J,Si J,et al. Research on Compatibility Mechanism of Biobased Cold Mixed Epoxy Asphalt Binder[J]. Construction and Building Materials,2020,250:118868.

[11] Yang Y M,Xian G J,Li H,et al. Thermal Aging of an Anhydride-Cured Epoxy Resin[J]. Polymer Degradation and Stability,2015,118:111-119.

[12] 周威.环氧沥青材料的制备及性能研究[D].武汉:湖北大学,2016.

[13] 周威,文俊,蔡芳昌,等.环氧沥青在模拟自然条件下的老化机理研究[J].胶体与聚合物,2016,34(03):122-124+128.

[14] Si J,Li Y,Yu X. Curing Behavior and Mechanical Properties of an Eco-Friendly Cold-Mixed Epoxy Asphalt[J]. Materials and Structures,2019,52(4).

[15] Si J J,Li Y,Wang J Y,et al. Improving the Compatibility of Cold-Mixed Epoxy Asphalt Based on the Epoxidized Soybean oil[J]. Construction and Building Materials,2020,243:118235.

[16] 念腾飞,李萍,林梅,等.冻融循环下沥青特征官能团含量与流变参数灰熵分析及微观形貌[J].吉林大学学报(工学版),2018,48(4):1045-1054.

[17] 杨震,张肖宁,虞将苗,等.基质沥青老化前后多尺度特性研究[J].建筑材料学报,2018,21(03):420-425.

[18] 刘玉.湿热环境中环氧树脂的老化特性研究[D].重庆:重庆大学,2018.

基于DSR流变学测试的老化SBS改性沥青性能变化规律

田周义[1]　李福林[1]　寇小舟[1]　吴祥海[1]　张　壮[2]

(1.甘肃省公路局;2.长安大学公路学院)

摘　要　本文的目的是通过自研室内沥青老化设备SAT(Simple Aging Test),补充沥青在RTFOT和PAV之间的老化历程,并探索老化SBS改性沥青在此期间的流变行为。选用了两种SBS改性沥青,通过改变老化条件得到了16种老化沥青,使用DSR测试了老化后沥青样品的流变特性。研究发现,随着老化过程的深入,沥青高温性能逐渐增强,抗疲劳性能和低温抗裂能力逐渐减弱。RTFOT与PAV之间老化历程的沥青性能测试结果,为沥青路面再生过程中确定沥青老化阶段提供了参考,也有助于预测沥青路面使用过程中沥青性能的变化规律。

关键词　SBS改性沥青　动态剪切流变仪　流变特性　简单老化试验　路用性能

0　引　言

沥青路面在铺筑和服役过程中,沥青老化会导致沥青路面服务质量和寿命下降[1-4]。事实上,沥青的老化是其中轻质组分挥发和部分有机物氧化的结果[5-6]。SBS改性沥青是目前世界上应用在沥青路面上最多的改性沥青[7-8],了解SBS改性沥青不同阶段的老化行为,有助于针对旧沥青混合料的再生给出合理的解决方法。

在室内老化试验与现场老化对应关系方面,一般认为RTFOT老化85min可以模拟沥青拌和、运输阶段的老化,PAV老化20h近似于路面服役8年的水平[9]。马翔[10]对室内老化SBS改性沥青和实际回收的旧SBS改性沥青进行再生,并对再生沥青的性能进行测试。N.Dehouche[11]等通过对不同SBS掺量的改性沥青进行热氧老化并研究其性能变化。WOO[12]等通过动态剪切流变试验、凝胶渗透色谱试验、延度和测力延度试验研究老化SBS改性沥青。Wu[13]采用傅立叶变换红外光谱,原子力显微镜和动态剪切流变仪分别研究了老化对基质沥青和SBS改性沥青结构、形态和流变性能的影响。他们的研究结果表明,老化降低了沥青中芳香烃含量,同时增加了胶质和沥青质的含量。

实际工程应用时PAV设备更换气瓶、RTFOT和PAV设备得到的老化沥青样品较少、规范老化方法不能细化且完全对应实际路面老化历程等缺点,使得沥青路面再生应用过程中在匹配再生剂类型和掺量时存在不合理的地方。因此,本研究通过自研室内沥青胶结料老化设备,补充沥青在RTFOT和PAV老化水平之间的老化历程,并探索老化沥青的流变行为,为实际沥青路面再生过程中判断沥青老化水平提供依据。

1　试　验

1.1　试验材料

本研究选用来自中石化I-C类的成品SBS改性沥青,SBS掺量分别为3.0%(S3)、4.0%(S4),其技术性质见表1。

沥青胶结料技术性质　　　　　表1

沥青种类	技术指标			
	25℃针入度(0.1mm)	软化点(TR&B)(℃)	5℃延度(cm)	135℃旋转黏度(Pa·s)
S3	65	62.5	34.5	1.57
S4	60	68.0	39.7	1.90

1.2 试验仪器

本文进行沥青胶结料流变试验所用的设备动态剪切流变仪(DSR)。同时采用规范推荐的旋转薄膜烘箱(RTFOT)、压力老化试验仪(PAV)以及课题组自行研制的室内简单老化设备 SAT 进行室内老化模拟,如图 1 所示。SAT 主体为空气浴加热烘箱,最高温度可达 200℃。32 块调平托盘中有 500mm(长) × 250mm(宽) × 3mm(深)凹槽,浇入 125g 沥青后经过流动可以刚好形成 1mm 厚的沥青薄膜,从而进行后续老化试验。

a)SAT外部

b)SAT内部结构

c)SAT老化托盘

图 1 SAT 设备

采用 RTFOT 老化改性沥青时较难形成均匀薄膜,且沥青容易从老化瓶中溢出,研究人员开始关注旋转气瓶老化法(RCAT)[14]和室内简单老化法 SAT[15](Simple Aging Test)。众多学者的研究推荐沥青老化条件为:沥青膜厚 1mm,短期老化温度 163℃,长期老化温度 100℃[16-21],本文试验过程采用的长期老化(Long-Term Aging,LTA)温度为 95℃。短期老化(Short-term Aging,STA)温度与 RTFOT 保持一致,为 163℃。

经初步试验,STA 老化 180min 与 RTFOT 老化 85min 较为接近,而 STA 老化 7d 与 PAV 老化 20h 相近。为了探究沥青路面在整个施工与服役过程中(如热存储过程、加热过程、压实后的使用过程)的老化特征,故选择 120min、150min、180min 作为短期老化时间,3d、5d、7d 作为长期老化时间。

2 试验方法

采用动态剪切流变试验仪(DSR)对不同老化阶段的 SBS 改性沥青试样进行温度扫描试验,测试得到相位角 δ 及复合剪切模量 G^* 两个参数,根据它们的变化规律判断沥青老化程度。采用多应力蠕变恢复试验(Multiple Stress Creep Recover,MSCR)测试沥青高温性能,以线性振幅扫描 LAS 试验评价沥青的疲劳特性,评价沥青低温性能时采用 4mm-DSR 频率扫描试验替代弯曲流变梁 BBR 试验。

3 试验结果与讨论

选用不同的 SBS 改性沥青进行 RTFOT、PAV 和 SAT 老化试验,并将 SAT 老化试验进行扩展,测试不同条件下 SBS 改性沥青的动态流变性能。老化沥青命名按照"原样沥青-老化方式-老化时间"进行,如"S3-LTA-3d"表示 SBS 掺量为 3% 的 SBS 改性沥青在 SAT 设备中长期老化 3d,其他命名以此类推。

3.1 动态流变性能

采用动态剪切流变试验仪(DSR)对 S3 与 S4 两种沥青不同老化阶段的试样进行温度扫描试验,试验结果如图 2 和图 3 所示。

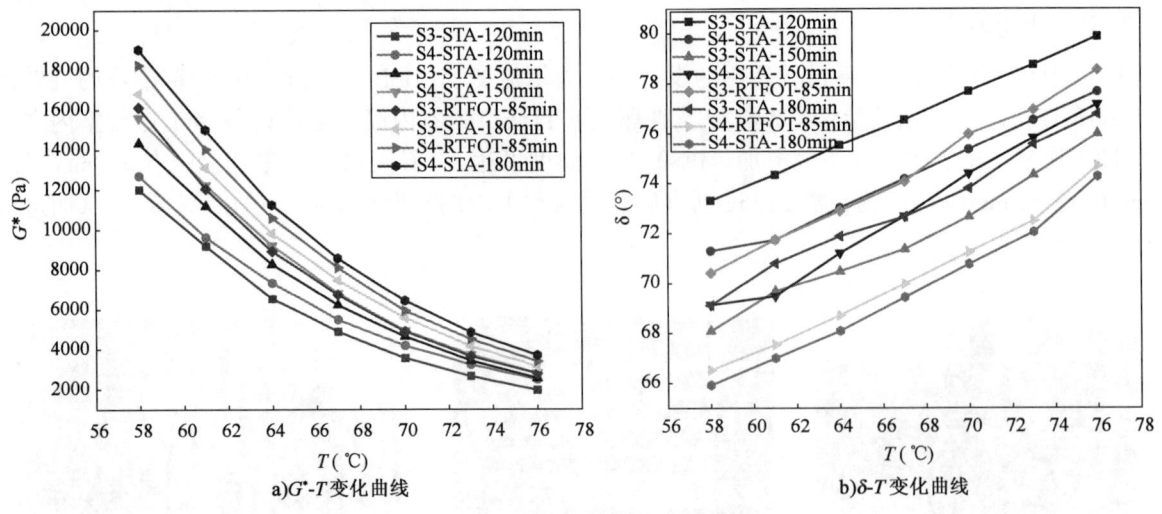

图2 SBS改性沥青短期老化温度扫描结果

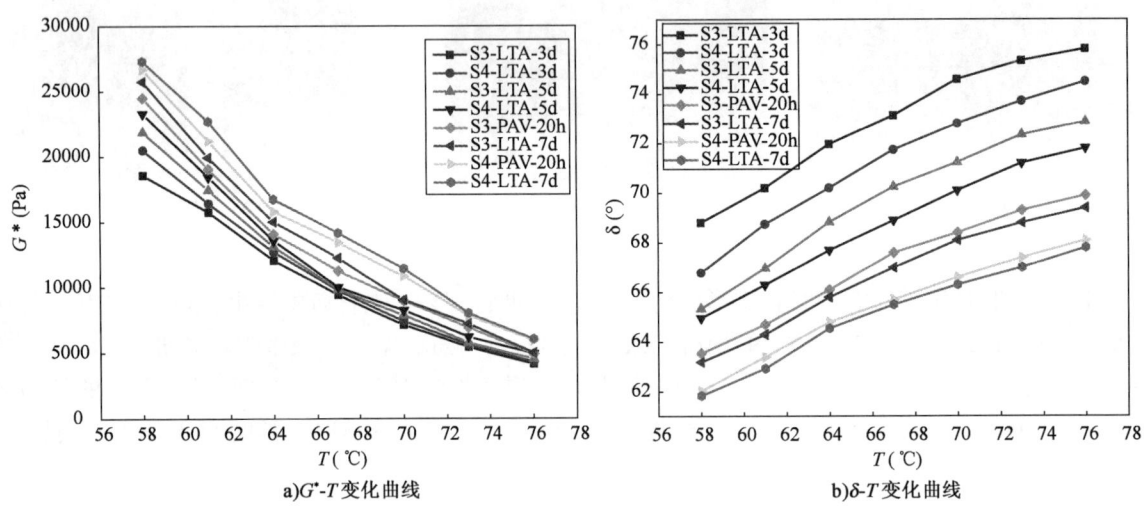

图3 SBS改性沥青长期老化温度扫描结果

可以发现,随着老化时间延长,使得沥青复合剪切模量 G^* 逐渐增大、相位角 δ 逐渐降低。当扫描温度为 58~70℃时,G^* 随温度变化较为明显,当扫描温度为 70~76℃时,G^* 变化较为缓慢。这说明,70℃是 SBS 改性沥青黏弹性成分比例转变的关键温度节点。

3.2 高温蠕变性能

选用多重应力蠕变恢复 MSCR 试验测试不同老化阶段沥青高温蠕变性能,试验温度为 64℃。不同老化程度的沥青胶结料 MSCR 试验结果如图4和图5所示。

从图4和图5可以看出,随着老化程度增加,沥青 R 逐渐增大,J_{nr} 逐渐降低,表明沥青高温性能提高。基于上述高、低两种应力水平对沥青不可恢复蠕变柔量 J_{nr} 产生不同的响应,将试验数据按式(1)进行处理(采自 AASHTO TP 70-09),分析老化对沥青应力敏感性的影响,试验结果如图6所示。

$$J_{nr\text{-diff}} = \frac{J_{nr\text{-}3.2} - J_{nr\text{-}0.1}}{J_{nr\text{-}0.1}} \times 100\% \tag{1}$$

由图6可知,老化均使得沥青应力敏感性 $J_{nr\text{-diff}}$ 增加,且老化程度越大 $J_{nr\text{-diff}}$ 越高,表明老化使沥青受荷载作用变化影响大,稳定性差。LTA-5d、LTA-7d 和 PAV-20h 的 $J_{nr\text{-diff}}$ 均超过 AASHTO MP19-10 分级标准 $J_{nr\text{-diff}} \leq 75\%$ 的要求,老化沥青可能达到了蠕变破坏。

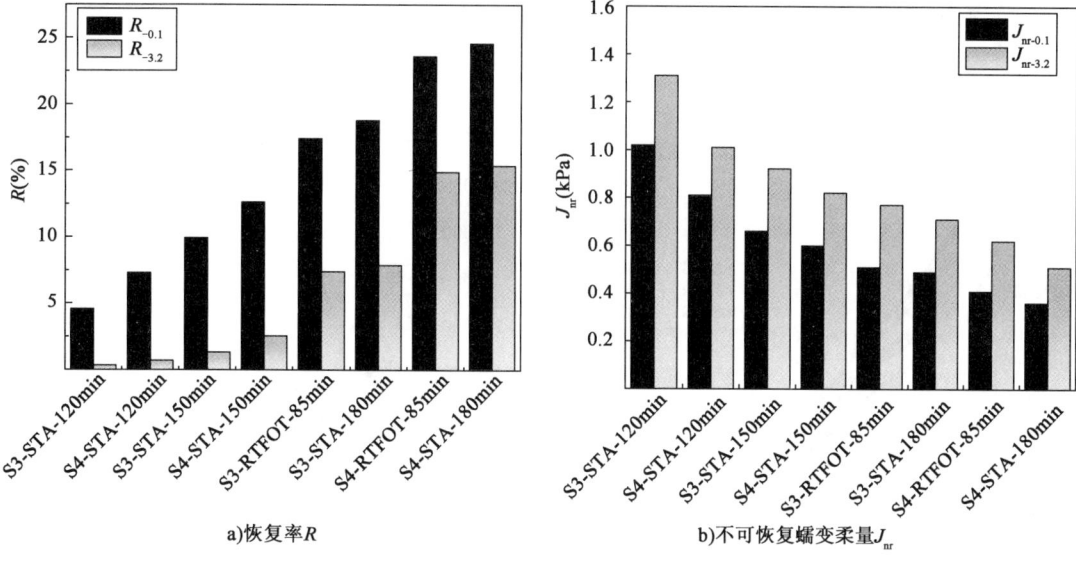

图4 SBS改性沥青短期老化MSCR试验结果

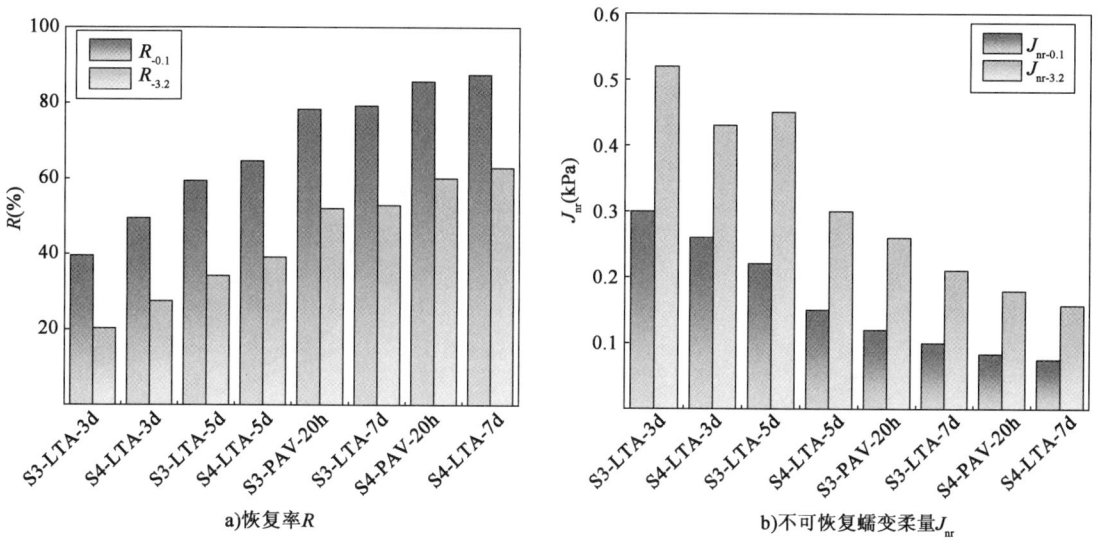

图5 SBS改性沥青长期老化MSCR试验结果

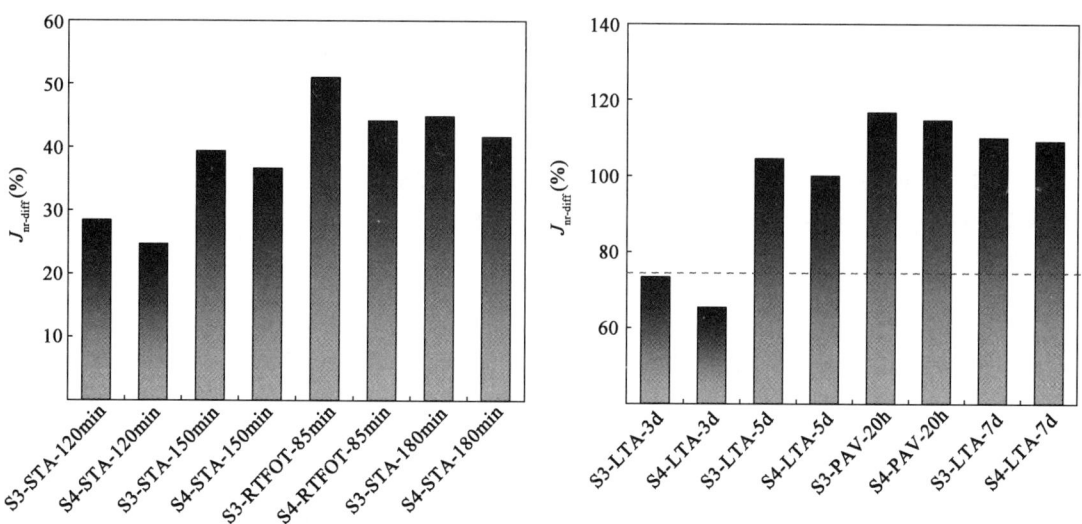

图6 老化沥青应力敏感性分析结果

3.3 中温疲劳性能

本文采用 LAS 试验研究不同老化阶段沥青疲劳性能的演变规律,试验温度为 25℃,结果如图 7 和图 8 所示。

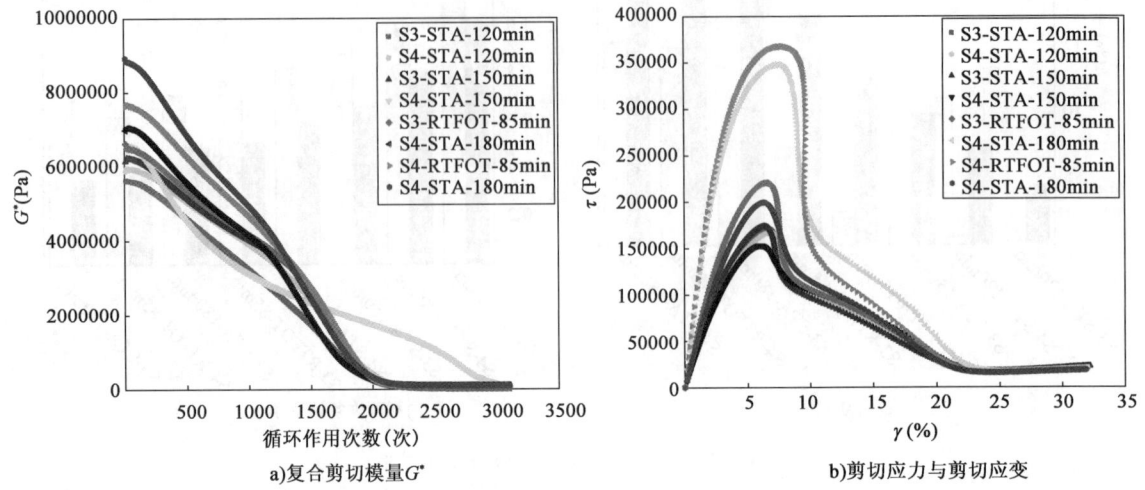

图 7 SBS 改性沥青短期老化 G^*、τ 变化曲线

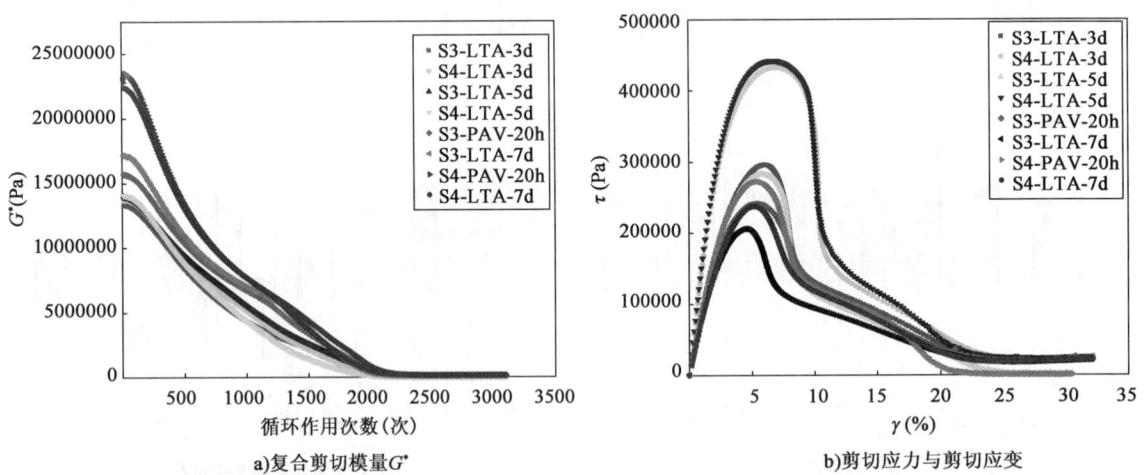

图 8 SBS 改性沥青长期老化 G^*、τ 变化曲线

由图 7 和图 8 可以看出,随着加载次数增加,沥青 G^* 逐渐降低,而剪切应力则出现一个峰值,呈现先增加后减小的趋势,随着荷载对沥青产生的损伤累积,沥青弹性增强、剪切应力增加至峰值后疲劳破坏,然后剪切应力逐渐减小。将复合剪切模量 G^* 衰减至初始值的 50% 和剪切应力 τ 峰值分别对应的作用次数记为 N_p 和 N_f,以此作为不同老化阶段沥青胶结料疲劳性能评价指标,结果如图 9 所示。

随着老化时间延长,沥青疲劳寿命 N_p 和 N_f 均逐步降低。N_f 总是滞后于 N_p 出现,这主要是沥青材料初始模量衰减至 50% 时产生了应力屈服,而后随着荷载作用的损伤累积,沥青材料在剪切应力达到峰值时出现疲劳失效破坏。

3.4 低温松弛性能

本文采用 4mm-DSR 频率扫描试验评价不同老化阶段沥青胶结料低温松弛性能。试验过程所用温度为 -12℃,利用式(2)转化得到复合松弛模量主曲线如图 10 和图 11 所示[22]。

$$G(t) \approx G'(\omega) \mid \omega = 2/\pi t \tag{2}$$

转化得到的应力松弛主曲线是一条松弛模量对数随时间对数变化的曲线,将其进行拟合,拟合方程记为 $y = ax^2 + bx + c$(a、b、c 均为拟合参数),并将 $\lg(60) = 1.78$ 代入式(3)、式(4)即可得到 60s 时的松

弛模量 $G(60s)$ 和松弛速率 $m(60s)$。

$$\text{Lg } G(60s) = ax^2 + bx + c \mid x = 1.78 \quad (3)$$
$$m(60s) = 2ax + b \mid x = 1.78 \quad (4)$$

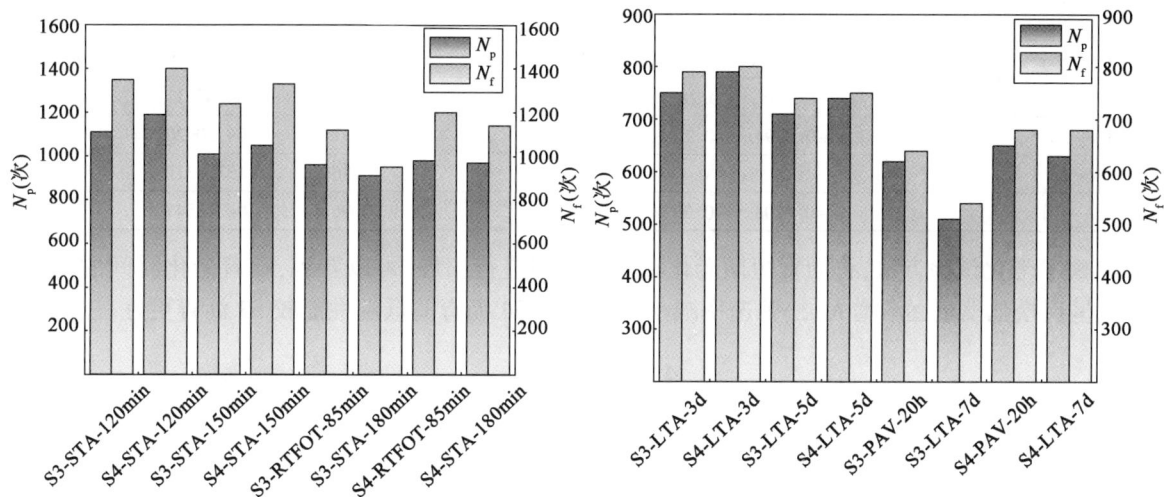

图 9　不同老化阶段沥青疲劳性能演化

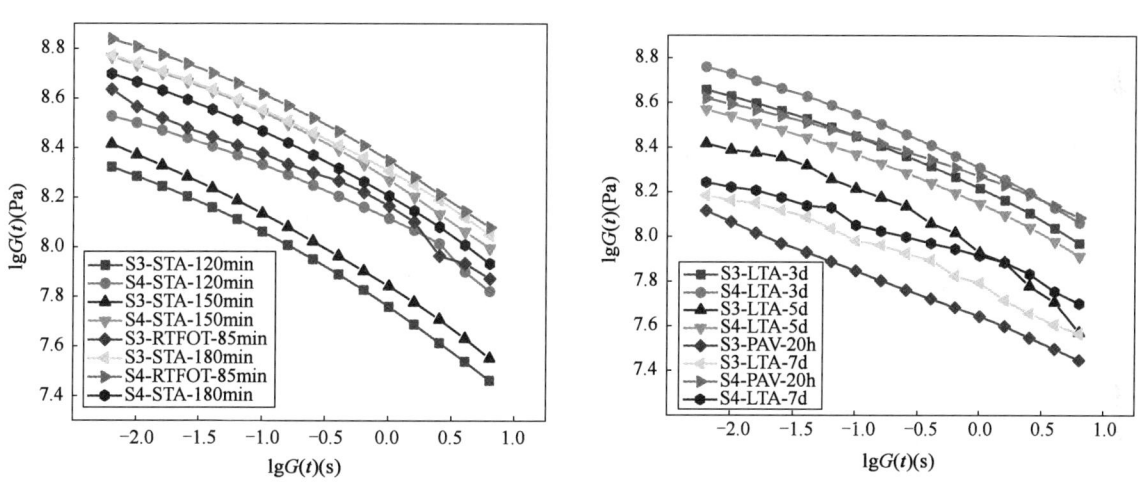

图 10　短期老化沥青松弛模量 $G(t)$ 主曲线　　图 11　长期老化沥青松弛模量 $G(t)$ 主曲线

将老化沥青松弛模量主曲线进行拟合,并计算出松弛模量 $G(60s)$ 和松弛速率 $m_r(60s)$ 两个低温性能评价指标,结果见表 2。

不同老化阶段沥青松弛模量拟合结果　　表 2

老化水平	回归方程 $\lg G(t) = ax^2 + bx + c$	R^2	$G(60s)$ (MPa)	$m_r(60s)$
S3-RTFOT-85min	$y = -0.0364x^2 - 0.2891x + 8.304$	0.99	47.21416	-0.353892
S4-RTFOT-85min	$y = -0.0395x^2 - 0.3089x + 8.2583$	0.99	38.30947	-0.37921
S3-PAV-20h	$y = -0.0018x^2 - 0.2148x + 8.4836$	0.97	124.61	-0.218004
S4-PAV-20h	$y = -0.0207x^2 - 0.2041x + 8.3682$	1.00	86.95932	-0.240946
S3-STA-120min	$y = -0.0394x^2 - 0.3418x + 8.0499$	0.99	20.73295	-0.411932
S4-STA-120min	$y = -0.0669x^2 - 0.3363x + 8.0846$	0.99	18.79404	-0.455382
S3-STA-150min	$y = -0.0305x^2 - 0.3271x + 8.1831$	0.99	31.93198	-0.38139
S4-STA-150min	$y = -0.0411x^2 - 0.3148x + 8.1287$	0.99	27.42425	-0.387958
S3-STA-180min	$y = -0.0327x^2 - 0.2838x + 8.3242$	1.00	51.93132	-0.342006

续上表

老化水平	回归方程 $\lg G(t) = ax^2 + bx + c$	R^2	$G(60s)$(MPa)	$m_r(60s)$
S4-STA-180min	$y = -0.0349x^2 - 0.3007x + 8.2589$	0.99	41.02767	-0.362822
S3-LTA-3d	$y = -0.0313x^2 - 0.27x + 8.3829$	0.99	63.55198	-0.325714
S4-LTA-3d	$y = -0.0314x^2 - 0.274x + 8.3718$	0.99	60.89649	-0.329892
S3-LTA-5d	$y = -0.008x^2 - 0.2877x + 8.4621$	0.99	84.07111	-0.30194
S4-LTA-5d	$y = -0.0294x^2 - 0.2608x + 8.4284$	0.97	74.30620	-0.313132
S3-LTA-7d	$y = -0.0338x^2 - 0.1436x + 8.486$	0.96	132.8312	-0.203764
S4-LTA-7d	$y = -0.0203x^2 - 0.2024x + 8.4077$	0.96	96.18547	-0.238534

采用 SAT 老化试验方法，将沥青短期老化和长期时间进行拓展，可以看到，随着老化时间的推移，沥青总体上呈现松弛模量逐渐增大、松弛速率减小现象。且 S4 沥青的低温性能较 S3 沥青更好。

4 结　语

本文研究了不同老化条件对 SBS 改性沥青流变性能的影响。选用两种 SBS 改性沥青，经过 DSR 测试，研究了不同时间 SAT 老化、RTFOT 老化和 PAV 老化后沥青的流变性能变化规律，得出以下具体结论：

（1）针对 S3 和 S4 沥青，采用 SAT 设备，沥青膜厚为 1mm，SAT 试验 163℃短期老化 180min 等效于 RTFOT 老化 85min，SAT 试验 95℃长期老化 7d 相当于 PAV 老化 20h。

（2）随着老化水平提高，沥青复合剪切模量 G^*、蠕变恢复率 R 和不可恢复蠕变柔量差 $J_{nr\text{-}diff}$ 增大，相位角 δ、不可恢复蠕变柔量 J_{nr} 减小，表明老化使得沥青弹性成分增加，温度敏感性降低、应力敏感性提高，高温抗变形能力增强。

（3）在 LAS 试验中，发现 50% G_0^* 时对应的屈服寿命 N_p 和剪切应力 τ 峰值对应的失效寿命 N_f 能较好地评价沥青疲劳性能。随着老化水平提高，沥青疲劳寿命 N_p 和 N_f 均逐步降低。

（4）最新发展的 4mm-DSR 频率扫描试验能测试沥青低温状态下的松弛行为，松弛模量 $G(60s)$、松弛速率 $m_r(60s)$ 指标能较好反映路面内部温度应力累积与释放速率。随着老化时间推移，沥青 $G(60s)$ 逐渐增大、$m_r(60s)$ 减小，低温松弛能力下降。

参考文献

[1] Xu O, Xiao F, Amirkhanian S N, et al. Long-term Aging Effect on Rheological Properties of Combined Binders from Various Polymers with Ground Tire Rubber[J]. Canadian Journal of Civil Engineering, 2016, 43(5):165-174.

[2] 查旭东,闵斌,宋微. RAP 掺量对热再生沥青混合料性能影响分析[J]. 长沙理工大学学报自然科学版, 2013, 10(4):1-8.

[3] Baghaee Moghaddam T, Baaj H. The Use of Rejuvenating Agents in Production of Recycled Hot Mix Asphalt:A Systematic Review[J]. Construction and Building Materials, 2016, 114:805-816.

[4] 祝谭雍. 基于再生沥青混合料性能特点的再生路面设计研究[D]. 南京:东南大学, 2017.

[5] Sun L, Wang Y, Zhang Y. Aging Mechanism and Effective Recycling Ratio of SBS Modified Asphalt[J]. Construction & Building Materials, 2014, 70:26-35.

[6] 庞凌. 沥青紫外光老化特性研究[D]. 武汉:武汉理工大学, 2008.

[7] Wen G, Zhang Y, Zhang Y. Rheological Characterization of Storage-Stable SBS-Modified Asphalts[J]. Polymer Testing, 2002, 21(3):295-302.

[8] 王岚,陈刚,刑永明,等. 老化对胶粉和 SBS 改性沥青流变性能的影响[J]. 建筑材料学报, 2015, 18(3):499-504.

[9] 耿九光. 沥青老化机理及再生技术研究[D]. 西安:长安大学, 2009.

[10] 马翔,倪富健,李强.SBS改性沥青的回收与评价[J].公路工程,2014(6):250-253.
[11] Jérôme Lamontagne, Françoise Durrieu, Planche J P, et al. Direct and Continuous Methodological Approach to Study the Ageing of Fossil Organic Material by Infrared Microspectrometry Imaging: Application to Polymer Modified Bitumen[J]. Analytica Chimica Acta,2001.
[12] Woo W, Hilbrich J, Glover C. Loss of Polymer-Modified Binder Durability with Oxidative Aging: Base Binder Stiffening Versus Polymer Degradation[J]. Transportation Research Record Journal of the Transportation Research Board,2007,1998:38-46.
[13] Shao-peng Wu, Ling Pang, Lian-tong Mo, et al. Influence of Aging on the Evolution of Structure, Morphology and Rheology of Base and SBS Modified Bitumen[J]. Construction & Building Materials, 2009,23(2):1005-1010.
[14] Lu X,Talon Y,Redelius P. 406-001 Aging of Bituminous Binders-Laboratory Tests and Field Data[C]// E&E Congress. 2008.
[15] Michael J Farrar. Recovery and Laboratory Testing of Asphalt Emulsion Residue: Application of Simple Aging Test and 4-mm Dynamic Shear Rheometer Test[J]. Transportation Research Record,2018.
[16] Glover,Charles J,Davison,Richard R,et al. Development of a New Method for Assessing Asphalt Binder Durability with Field Validation[J]. Bituminous Binders,2005.
[17] Zhao X,Wang S,Wang Q,et al. Rheological and Structural Evolution of SBS Modified Asphalts Under Natural Weathering[J]. Fuel,2016(184):242-247.
[18] 张霞,黄刚,刘昭,等.热、光、水耦合老化条件对温拌沥青性能的影响[J].公路交通科技,2019,36(7):10-19.
[19] 丛玉凤,廖克俭,翟玉春.道路沥青老化动力学的研究——以软化点为参数建立沥青老化动力学模型[J].石油炼制与化工,2005,36(5):23-26.
[20] 贾彦丽,栗威,魏建国.基于力学流变特性的高模量沥青老化性能研究[J].材料导报.2016(30):406-415.
[21] Elwardany M. D., Rad F. Y., Castorena C, et al. Evaluation of Asphalt Mixture Laboratory Long-Term Ageing Methods for Performance Testing and Prediction[J]. Road Materials & Pavement Design,2017.
[22] 王超.沥青结合料路用性能的流变学研究[D].北京:北京工业大学,2015.

一种常温黏稠乳化沥青胶结料的研究

吴玉辉[1] 蒋明伟[2] 吴耀东[1] 赵冬明[1] 邱百万[3]

(1.辽宁省交通科学研究院有限责任公司高速公路养护技术交通运输行业重点实验室;
2.辽宁省沈阳市第十中学;3.辽宁信诚人才服务有限责任公司)

摘 要 工程上使用的沥青或改性沥青胶结料通常需要加热至高温使其达到一定的黏度才能保证施工和易性,耗能大、不安全、不环保。而乳化沥青虽然可以实现常温、环保、安全施工应用,但是黏度小,极易流淌,与工程基面或界面附着不良,涂布或裹持性差而流失,达不到预期使用效果,影响工程质量和使用寿命,因而极大地限制应用范围并影响使用性能。鉴于常用热沥青及乳化沥青胶结料的不足,本文阐述了通过对乳化沥青进行改性增黏处理后,制得一种常温黏稠乳化沥青的过程,并对其性质进行了测试研究。研究表明,通过在乳化沥青中掺入适宜的增稠剂,根据不同工程需要,可调制出不同黏度的黏稠乳化沥青,具有常温施工、节能减排、安全环保、性能可靠的优点。

关键词 黏稠乳化沥青 黏度 胶结料 常温

0 引言

沥青是由不同分子量的碳氢化合物及其衍生物等有机物组成的黑褐色复杂混合物，常温时多呈半固态，高温时呈高黏度液态，是应用广泛的胶凝材料、防水材料、防腐材料，可用于建筑、道路、防水、防腐工程等。工程应用往往需要在加热的高温条件下，降低沥青流淌性和黏度到适当范围才易于施工，自然冷却后才能很好地发挥其黏结作用，不仅耗能，而且高温时也会释放大量的有害物质，污染环境、有害健康、操作不安全。乳化沥青主要由沥青、水和乳化剂组成，有时也含有某些添加剂，是一种水包油型乳状液体。乳化沥青是一种常温下被广泛使用的工程胶结材料，与使用热沥青相比，具有节能减排、减轻沥青老化、经济环保等优势。但在实际工程应用中，因普通乳化沥青液体黏度太低，流动性太高，流淌性极强，其与工程基面或界面附着不好，涂布或裹持性差而流失，达不到预期使用效果，影响工程质量和使用寿命，因而大大限制应用范围并影响使用性能。

无论是普通沥青还是乳化沥青，在不同需求的工程上应用时，为了施工和易性和输送可行性，保证其在施工与输送过程中应具有与之相适宜的黏度和流变性、控制黏度在合理的范围内是十分关键和重要的[1]。综合考虑常用沥青和乳化沥青的优缺点，本文研究开发一种在常温条件下黏稠度适宜的乳化沥青，提高乳化沥青的黏度，改善其与工程基面或界面的流动性、黏附性、涂覆裹持性、匀布性，以满足不同工程使用的要求，经济、环境、社会效益明显，具有广阔的应用前景[2-3]。

1 原材料的性能

1.1 道路石油沥青

本研究采用的道路石油沥青为 A 级 90 号沥青，技术指标见表 1。

道路石油沥青技术指标　　　　　　　　　　表1

序号	测试项目		A 级 90 号道路石油沥青
1	针入度(0.1mm),25℃、100g、5s		86
2	针入度指数 PI		-0.50
3	软化点(℃)		45.0
4	延度(cm),10℃,5cm/min		95
5	延度(cm),15℃,5cm/min		大于 100
6	60℃动力黏度(Pa·s)		174
7	135℃旋转黏度(Pa·s)		0.390
8	蜡含量(%)		1.9
9	闪点(℃)		289
10	溶解度(%)		99.70
11	TFOT 老化后	质量变化(%)	0.20
12		残留针入度比(%)	66.0
13		10℃残留延度(cm)	10

1.2 乳化剂

本研究选用的乳化剂是非离子型乳化剂 ASPHALAK 7TX，常温下是一种浅黄色澄清液体，其理化性质见表2。

ASPHALAK 7TX 乳化剂主要技术指标　　　　　　表2

项　目	指　标	项　目	指　标
密度(kg/m³),25℃	1.138	闪点(℃)	>100

续上表

项　目	指　标	项　目	指　标
浊点(℃)	-9	黏度(mPa·s),25℃	30

1.3 高吸水性树脂

本研究选用高吸水性树脂(LQ)作为增加黏稠度的外加剂,其是一种浅黄色固体粉末,其技术指标见表3。

LQ 技 术 指 标　　表3

项　目	指　标
密度(kg/m^3),25℃	1.25~1.40
溶解性	极易溶于水,不溶于乙醇、丙酮等有机溶剂
黏度(2%水溶液)(mPa·s),25℃	>10000

1.4 水

水是分散介质,本研究采用的是符合饮用要求的自来水。

2 乳化沥青的制备和性质

本研究设计制备蒸发残留物含量(以下简称"固含量")为50%、55%、60%,乳化剂用量为1.5%(乳化剂质量占乳化沥青总质量的百分比)的乳化沥青备用。乳化沥青的技术指标见表4。

乳化沥青主要技术指标测试结果　　表4

测试指标		样　号			
		乳化沥青1-0号	乳化沥青2-0号	乳化沥青3-0号	A级90号道路石油沥青
蒸发残留物	设计固含量(%)	50	55	60	—
	实测固含量(%)	49.8	55	59.9	—
	针入度(0.1mm),25℃	89	87	87	86
	延度(cm),15℃	>100	>100	>100	>100
	延度(cm),10℃	95	96	96	95
	软化点(℃)	45.1	45.1	45.2	45.0
	60℃动力黏度①(Pa·s)	175	175	176	174
	闪点(℃)	288	288	289	289
	溶解度(%)	99.82	99.80	99.81	99.80
TFOT①老化后	质量变化(%)	0.20	0.20	0.20	0.20
	残留针入度比(%)	66.1	66.2	66.2	66.0
	10℃残留延度(cm)	10.2	10.0	10.1	10
筛上剩余量(%)		0.15	0.14	0.16	—
粒子电荷		非离子	非离子	非离子	—
30天储存稳定性(%)		0	0	0	—
旋转黏度②(mPa·s)		50	75	95	390

注:①表中乳化沥青的60℃动力黏度、TFOT老化后的测试指标是针对乳化沥青残留蒸发物测试结果。
②旋转黏度测试条件:乳化沥青:30℃；A级90号道路石油沥青:135℃。

对制备的以上3种乳化沥青的测试结果表明:

(1)蒸发残留物的性质与基质沥青的主要测试指标几乎没有变化,乳化对沥青性质没有影响;

(2)筛上剩余量基本相同,表明黏稠乳化沥青满足质量要求;

(3)乳化沥青储存稳定性良好。

3 LQ对水的黏度的影响

将LQ粉末易溶于水,按设计用量缓慢均匀加入水中,边加入LQ边搅拌10min后,成透明黏稠胶状物,采用旋转黏度计进行LQ不同掺量下的水溶液的黏度测试,如图1所示。LQ对水的黏稠度影响显著,随着增黏剂掺量的增加,水的黏度是上升的。当增黏剂掺量小于0.2%时黏度增加比较缓慢,大于0.2%后黏度迅速升高,表明此种高吸水性树脂在较低掺量条件下便可实现增稠效果。

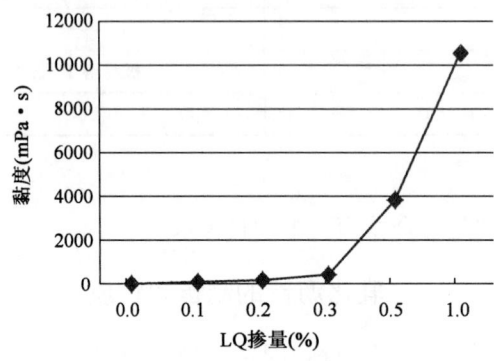

图1 LQ对水的黏度影响

4 黏稠乳化沥青的研究

本研究开展了LQ掺加量(LQ质量占乳化沥青质量百分比)为0%、0.1%、0.2%、0.3%、0.5%、1.0%对乳化沥青黏度及相关性质的影响研究。在常温下,物理搅拌,转数为30~50rpm,边搅拌边加入LQ粉末,搅拌速度至20~30r/min,持续搅拌10min,即制得黏稠乳化沥青。LQ对乳化沥青的增稠作用实质上是LQ对水包油乳状液微小液滴外围的水分子作用,内部沥青微粒不受影响而形成的黏稠乳化沥青。

分析LQ不同掺量下对不同固含量乳化沥青黏度的影响,试验设计与测试结果见表5。

不同黏稠乳化沥青黏度测试结果 表5

样 品	设计固含量(%)	实测固含量(%)	黏稠剂掺量(%)	黏度(mPa·s)
1-0号	50	49.8	0	50
1号			0.1	155
2号			0.2	380
3号			0.3	685
4号			0.5	4880
5号			1.0	12500
2-0号	55	55.0	0	75
6号			0.2	490
7号			0.3	860
3-0号	60	59.9	0	95
8号			0.1	265
9号			0.2	675
10号			0.3	960
11号			0.5	6680
12号			1.0	15550

注:Brookfield旋转黏度测试条件:30℃。

(1)设计固含量为50%、55%、60%的1-0号、2-0号、3-0号三种乳化沥青是未掺入LQ的乳化沥青固含量越高,相对黏度越大,但总体上是水包油的乳液体系,黏度基本在同一数量级。

(2)从图2可以看出:LQ掺入量越大,相同固含量的乳化沥青的黏度越高,但不是线性增长的趋势;LQ小于0.3%低掺入量时,黏度增加缓慢;当LQ掺入量大于0.3%后,黏度出出陡增;根据工程需要确定LQ合理掺入量,控制乳化沥青的黏度在科学范围内,保证施工和易性和施工质量。

(3)从图3可以看出,乳化沥青固含量越大,掺入LQ后形成的黏稠乳化沥青黏度越大,且相同固含量的乳化沥青,LQ掺入量越高,其黏度越大。

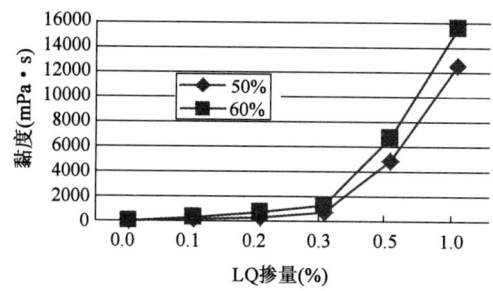

图2 LQ掺入量对乳化沥青黏度的影响

(4)60%固含量乳化沥青3-0号加入0.3% LQ加工制作乳黏稠乳化沥青,测试了20℃、30℃、60℃时黏稠乳化沥青的黏度,并绘制了黏度—温度的曲线,从图4可以看出,随着温度的升高,黏稠乳化沥青黏度降低。温度对黏稠乳化沥青黏度的影响比较大。在使用黏稠乳化沥青时,应注意工程所在地气温的影响,控制增稠外加剂的用量,达到满意的效果。

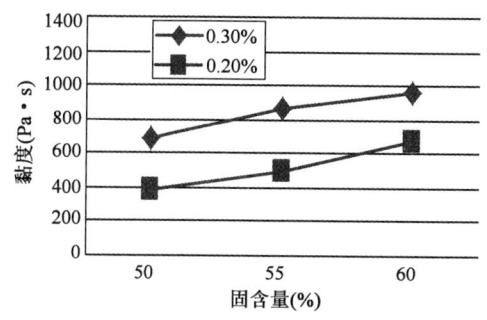

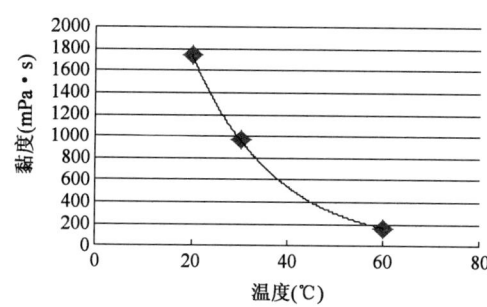

图3 乳化沥青固含量增稠乳液黏度的影响   图4 温度对黏度的影响

(5)黏稠乳化沥青技术指标测试。参照《公路工程沥青及沥青混合料试验规程》(JTG E 20—2011)中相应的试验方法,评价黏稠乳化沥青的技术性能,试验数据见表6。

表6 黏稠乳化沥青技术指标测试结果

样 品		蒸发残留物					筛上剩余量 (%)	30d稳定性 (%)	黏度 (mPa·s)
		固含量 (%)	针入度25℃ (0.1mm)	延度10℃ (cm)	软化点 (℃)	溶解度 (%)			
1-0号	1天	49.8	89	95	45.1	99.82	0.15	0	50
	30天	49.9	89	96	45.2	99.80	0.17	0	50
1号	1天	49.8	87	96	45.0	99.81	0.16	0	155
	30天	50.0	86	96	45.0	99.81	0.15	0	155
2-0号	1天	55.0	87	96	45.1	99.82	0.14	0	75
	30天	55.1	87	96	45.1	99.81	0.15	0	75
6号	1天	55.0	87	96	45.1	99.80	0.15	0	490
	30天	55.0	86	96	45.2	99.82	0.16	0	485
3-0号	1天	59.9	87	96	45.2	99.82	0.16	0	95
	30天	60.0	87	96	45.2	99.81	0.15	0	95
11号	1天	60.0	88	97	45.2	99.82	0.16	0	6680
	30天	60.1	87	96	45.2	99.80	0.16	0	6720

综上所述,黏稠乳化沥青中 LQ 掺入量很小,其技术指标的微小差异在测试误差范围内。储存稳定性数据显示。LQ 的掺入对黏稠乳化沥青储存稳定性无不良影响。总的来说,黏稠乳化沥青性质相对稳定,施工性能可控。

5　结　语

通过在乳化沥青中掺入外加剂,改变其乳化沥青黏度和流变性,以克服普通乳化沥青黏稠度小、易流失、与材料基面分布裹敷不匀的不足,技术可行,效果可靠。此技术在冷拌再生、冷拌冷铺及防水等领域将有广阔的应用前景。

参考文献

[1] 田志红,吴叶兵.乳液增稠技术的研究进展[J].化学与黏合,2012(5):72-74.
[2] 莫美忠,骆介禹.高吸水性树脂增稠体系流变学性能的研究[J].广西师院学报:自然科学版,1994(1):27-31.
[3] 杨东科,王志超.羧甲基纤维素纳对阴离子乳化沥青稳定性的影响机理研究[J].石油沥青,2014(2):15-19.

融雪盐化物掺量对沥青胶浆性能影响研究

温钰婷[1]　郭鸿晨[2]

(1.长沙理工大学;2.长安大学)

摘　要　路表面积雪结冰对车辆行驶安全危害极大,如何有效防止路面结冰是道路设计与安全营运亟待解决的一大难题,盐化物自融雪沥青路面是道路积雪结冰的一个可行的解决方案。本文把矿粉用相同体积自主研发的融雪盐化物取代,应用总结的盐化物沥青胶浆制备工艺分别制备 5 个掺量(0%、25%、50%、75%和100%)的盐化物沥青胶浆,通过布氏黏度、低温弯曲梁流变等试验分析不同掺量下盐化物沥青胶浆的常规性能、黏度、温度敏感性等,确定自研融雪盐化物最大的掺量。

关键词　沥青及其他胶结料加工表征与性能　沥青路面　等体积替换法　沥青胶浆　盐化物

0　引　言

季节性冰冻地区在我国国土面积中超过一半以上,有 14 个省份处于季冻区[1]。冬天下雪,导致车辆在路面行驶时轮胎附着系数下降并且制动需要更长的距离才能停止[2],很容易发生交通事故,其中包括车辆失控无法停止而连续追尾、车辆侧翻等[8-11]。本文的研究从融雪盐的掺入量对沥青胶浆性质的影响出发,创新采用自主研发的融雪盐化物对沥青胶浆性能影响。把矿粉用相同体积自主研发的融雪盐化物进行取代,分别制备 5 个掺量(0%、25%、50%、75%和100%)的盐化物沥青胶浆采用归纳总结出的融雪盐化物沥青胶浆制备工艺,通过布氏黏度、低温弯曲梁流变等试验分析不同掺量下盐化物沥青胶浆的常规性能、黏度、温度敏感性等,确定自研融雪盐化物最大的掺量。

1　盐化物沥青胶浆制备

本文选用的自制融雪盐化物的密度为 $1.914 g/cm^3$,矿粉的密度为 $2.724 g/cm^3$,SBS 改性沥青的25℃密度为 $1.022 g/cm^3$。在搅拌沥青和填料时应该采用搅拌机,必要时使用剪切机进行剪切。

制备融雪盐沥青胶浆具体步骤如下:

(1)由沥青混合料配合比试验得到最佳沥青用量求算出粉胶比为 0.85。自制融雪盐化物和矿粉质量可由按式(1)和式(2)计算得出。

$$m_1 = 0.85 \times \frac{\rho_2}{\rho_1} \times m_0 \times p \tag{1}$$

$$m_2 = 0.85 \times m_0 \times (1-p) \tag{2}$$

式中：m_0——沥青质量，g；

m_1——盐化物质量，g；

m_2——矿粉质量，g；

ρ_1——矿粉密度，g/cm³；

ρ_2——盐化物密度，g/cm³；

p——盐化物掺量。

（2）将矿粉和自制融雪盐化物分别都通过0.075mm筛，在制备前，应将矿粉和自制融雪盐化物在烘箱中烘干，烘箱温度宜为105℃左右，矿粉和盐化物质量至恒重后保温1h。保证填料和沥青在搅拌过程中尽可能更充分。

（3）当SBS改性沥青温度加热至175℃时，即可开始少量多次地加入相应质量盐化物和矿粉进行拌和，直至混合均匀。

2 盐化物沥青胶浆的常规试验

2.1 盐化物沥青胶浆常规试验分析

研究盐化物掺量对沥青胶浆在低温时的延展度、稠度和回弹能力的影响，按相关标准测定融雪盐化物不同掺量下沥青胶浆的5℃延度、25℃针入度和弹性恢复试验，试验结果如图1～图3所示。

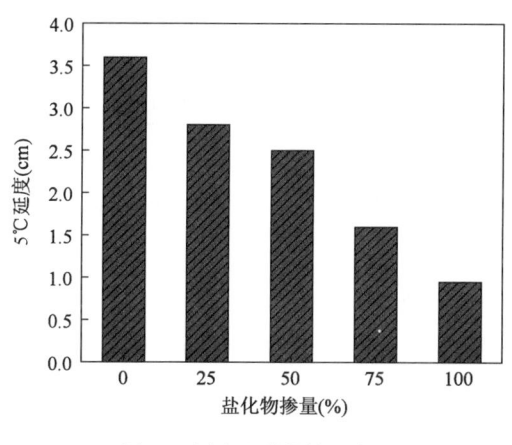
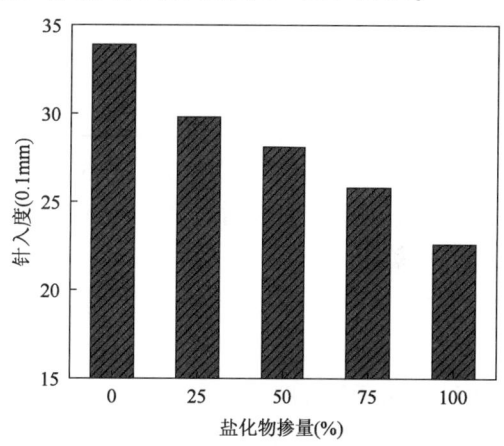

图1　延度与盐化物掺量关系　　　　　　　　图2　针入度与盐化物掺量关系

由图1、图2可以看出，当盐化物掺量大于75%时，盐化物沥青胶浆的塑性开始剧烈降低，盐化物沥青胶浆迅速变硬，稠度迅速增加，从5℃延度和25℃针入度角度来说，融雪盐化物掺量应控制在75%以下。由图3可知，在加入盐化物后，沥青胶浆的弹性恢复出现了明显的增长。所以推荐盐化物沥青胶浆的盐化物掺量宜控制在25%～75%。

2.2 盐化物沥青胶浆黏温特性

2.2.1 盐化物掺量对布氏黏度的影响

本文所用黏度测试装置为NDJ-1F布氏旋转黏度计，选用27号转子。

由图4可知，在135℃、150℃、165℃、180℃时，伴随盐化物的掺量持续增加，沥青胶浆的黏度均呈现向上的趋势。这就表明伴随盐化物掺量增加，盐化物吸附自由沥青的数量也会持续增加，结构沥青数量很大程度的增加，矿粉与盐化物的相互作用变大，内摩阻力和模量也变大。

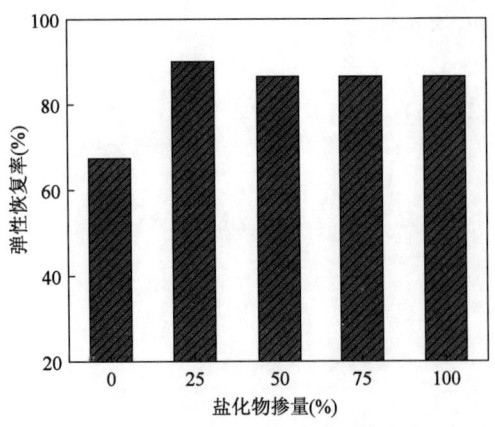

图3 恢复率与盐化物掺量关系

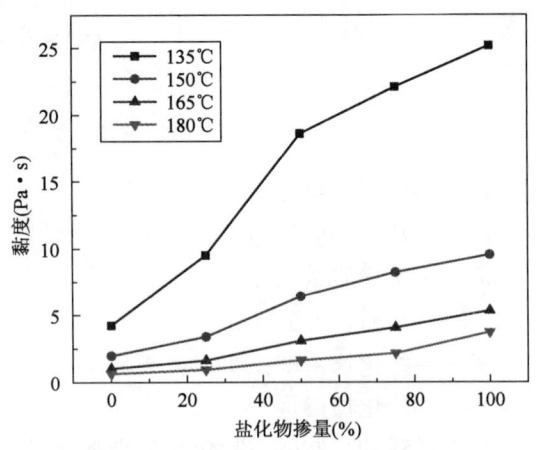

图4 盐化物掺量对黏度的影响

为了使沥青胶浆的黏度与盐化物掺量的相互关系更加直观明了,用式(3)回归各温度下黏度随盐化物掺量的变化趋势,结果分别如表1和图5所示。

$$\lg(\eta) = AC + B \tag{3}$$

式中：η——黏度,Pa·s;

C——盐化物掺量,%;

A、B——回归系数。

沥青胶浆黏度与盐化物掺量在135℃、150℃、165℃、180℃的回归结果　　　　表1

温度(℃)	回归方程	相关系数 R^2
135	$\lg(\eta) = 0.0077C + 0.7409$	0.8841
150	$\lg(\eta) = 0.0070C + 0.3542$	0.9363
165	$\lg(\eta) = 0.0074C + 0.0390$	0.9689
180	$\lg(\eta) = 0.0077C - 0.2069$	0.9917

表1和图5表明,温度在150℃、165℃、180℃时,沥青胶浆的黏度和融雪盐化物之间都存在着很好的相关性。回归系数随温度增大呈现逐渐增大的趋势。这表明温度越高,沥青胶浆黏度对融雪盐化物的掺量的敏感度越大。

2.2.2 盐化物沥青胶浆的温度敏感性

沥青的温度敏感性可以表示为黏度对沥青温度变化的敏感程度。沥青是典型的感温性材料。盐化物沥青胶浆黏度随温度的变化如图6所示。

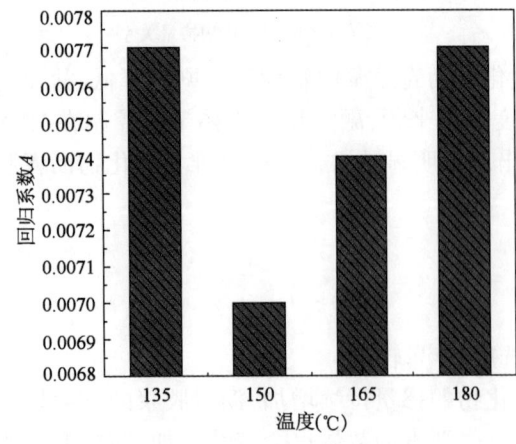

图5 回归系数A随温度的变化

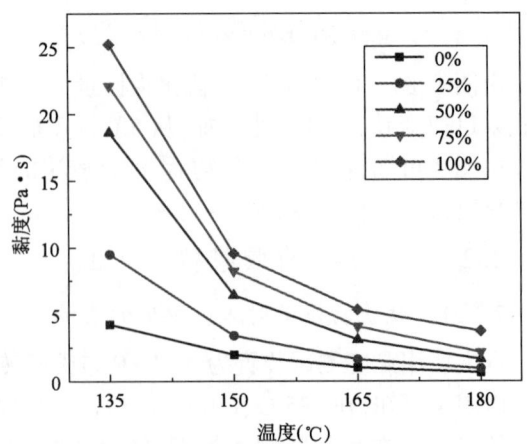

图6 温度对盐化物沥青胶浆黏度的影响

图6表明,各掺量下盐化物沥青胶浆的黏度均随着温度升高而变小,但是减小速率有所不同。135～150℃时,各掺量下盐化物沥青胶浆的黏度随着温度的增大而减小的速率很快;150～180℃时,沥青逐渐向牛顿流体转变,所以各掺量下盐化物沥青胶浆黏度随着温度的增大而减小的速率逐渐变缓。

融雪盐化物沥青胶浆,期望它具有较低的温度敏感性,根据Saal试验式(4)计算不同温度区间沥青胶浆的黏温指数 V_{TS}。具体结果如图7所示。

$$V_{TS} = \frac{\lg}{\lg} \frac{\lg(\eta_1 \times 10^3) - \lg}{(T_1 + 273.13) - \lg} \frac{\lg(\eta_2 \times 10^3)}{(T_2 + 273.13)} \quad (4)$$

式中:η_1、η_2——不同温度 T_1、T_2(℃)时的黏度,Pa·s。

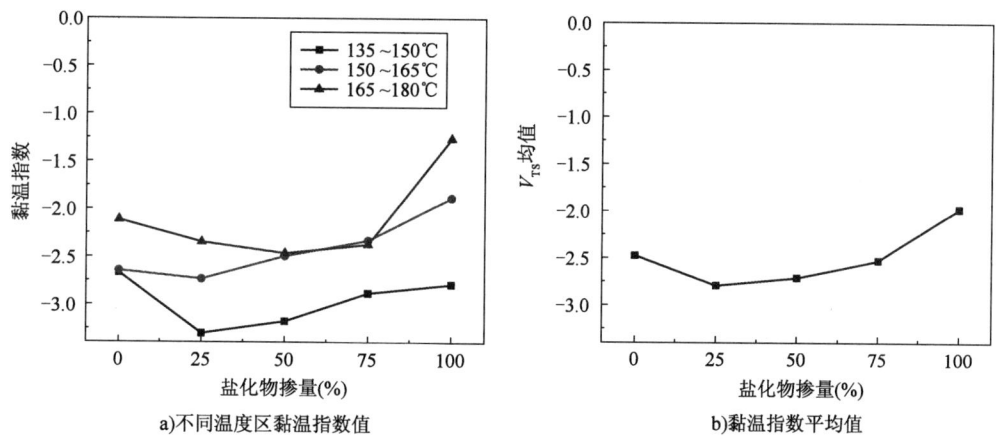

图7 融雪沥青胶浆黏温指数与盐化物掺量的变化曲线

图7a)表明当盐化物掺量大于25%时,V_{TS}呈上升趋势;在165～180℃温度区间内,当融雪盐化物的掺量小于75%时,V_{TS}呈下降趋势,当盐化物掺量大于75%时,V_{TS}增大。

黏温指数平均值 V_{TS} 越大表征盐化物沥青胶浆的温度敏感性越大。图7b)表明了 V_{TS} 与融雪盐化物掺量之间的关系。当盐化物掺量大于25%时,V_{TS}呈下降趋势。且盐化物掺量为25%时,V_{TS}达到最大值,为2.795。

综上所述,综合考虑盐化物沥青胶浆弹性恢复和沥青胶浆的针入度和延度降低情况,在推荐的盐化物掺量范围25%～75%之间,最终选择融雪盐化物的掺量为75%。

2.3 盐化物沥青胶浆低温性能

低温弯曲梁流变试验测试结果如图8、图9所示。

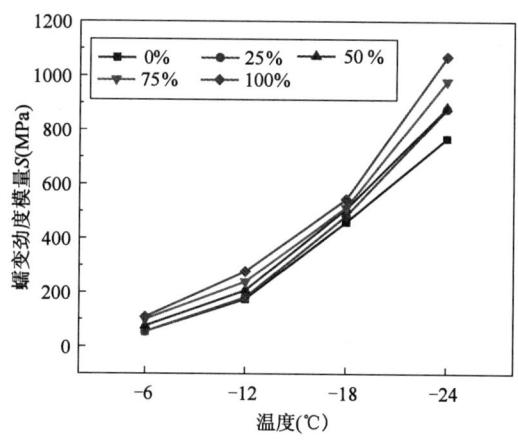

图8 五种沥青胶浆在不同试验温度下的 S 值

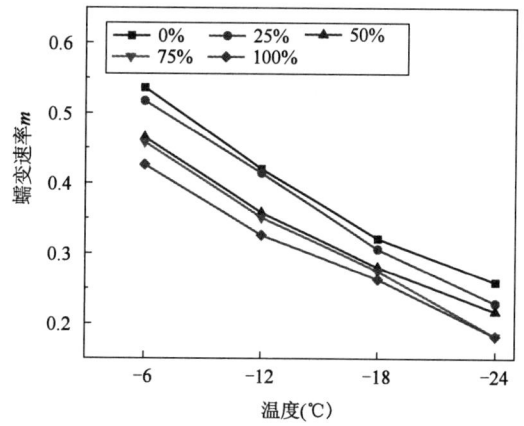

图9 五种沥青胶浆在不同试验温度下的 m 值

图8、图9表明:随着温度持续下降,沥青胶浆的蠕变劲度模量 S 在0%、25%、50%、75%、100%的盐化物掺量下均为增大,说明因温度应力增大,盐化物沥青胶浆的低温性能越差,而蠕变速率 m 在0%、25%、50%、75%、100%的盐化物掺量下均为降低,表明应力随时间减小得慢,路面发生低温开裂的可能性增大。

由图10、图11可知,随着盐化物掺量增大,因为盐化物沥青胶浆在低温下变硬变脆,蠕变劲度模量 S 基本呈线性增大,蠕变速率 m 基本呈线性减小。温度较高时,S 和 m 的变化趋势均不明显,随着温度降低,这种增大或减小趋势愈发明显。这表明温度是影响沥青胶浆低温性能的最重要因素。

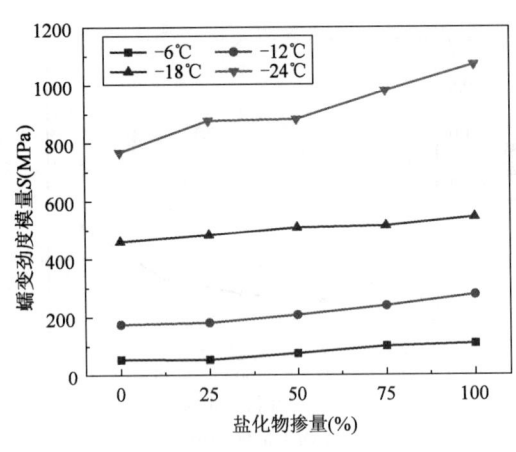

图10 不同温度下不同盐化物掺量下的 S 值　　图11 不同温度下不同盐化物掺量下的 m 值

3 结　语

(1)盐化物掺量持续增加,会导致沥青胶浆延度与针入度下降,但对其弹性恢复有利。当盐化物掺量大于75%时,沥青胶浆的弹性恢复保持在较高水平,但针入度和延度下降较快,所以推荐盐化物掺量范围在25%~75%之间。

(2)在温度一定的条件下,盐化物沥青胶浆的黏度与盐化物掺量呈正相关;温度提高,黏度对盐化物掺量越敏感。从盐化物掺量为25%时起,随着盐化物掺量增大,温度敏感性逐渐降低,为了让盐化物沥青胶浆保持较低水平的温度敏感性,并且结合盐化物沥青胶浆延度与针入度下降的情况,在推荐的盐化物掺量范围25%~75%之间,最终选择融雪盐化物的掺量为75%。

(3)伴随温度的下降,沥青胶浆蠕变劲度模量 S 增大,蠕变速率 m 降低。沥青的蠕变劲度和蠕变速率随着盐化物替代比的增加基本呈线性改变,但趋势并不明显,伴随温度的下降,沥青胶浆低温性能受到盐化物掺量的影响越发显著。对沥青胶浆低温性能产生影响的最重要因素是温度。

参考文献

[1] 徐慧宁,张锐,谭忆秋,等.季节性冰冻地区冬季冰冻路面温度分布规律[J].中国公路学报,2013,26(2):135-139.
[2] 刘状壮.沥青路面盐化物的研发与应用[D].西安:长安大学,2013.
[3] 庞请楠.太阳能-土壤蓄热融雪系统应用软件开发[D].大连:大连理工大学,2013.
[4] 豆怀兵.超薄罩面盐化物自融雪沥青混合料组成与性能研究[D].西安:长安大学,2015.
[5] 陈杰.盐化物融雪沥青路面耐久性及其融雪持久性研究[D].西安:长安大学,2013.
[6] 卜小明,田静.除雪机械现状及发展趋势[J].黑龙江科技信息,2006,32(8):98-102.
[7] 洪乃丰.氯盐融雪剂是把"双刃剑"——浅议国外使用化冰盐的教训与经验[J].城市减灾,2005(4):

[8] 傅广文.融雪剂对沥青及沥青混合料性能影响研究[D].长沙:长沙理工大学,2010.
[9] 赵丽丽.基于微波加热和机械冲击的道路除冰车[J].黑龙江科技信息,2015,35(4):102-103.
[10] Liu X,Wu S. Research on the conductive asphalt concrete,s piezoresistivity effect and its mechanism[J]. Constr Build Mater,2009,23(8):2752-2756.
[11] 张忠,刘红莹,李云霞,等.盐化物融雪剂在高速公路建设中的应用研究[J].公路工程,2012,37(6):203-207.

SBS改性沥青热储存稳定性试验方法研究

彭煜 从艳丽 杨克红

(中石油克拉玛依石化有限责任公司炼油化工研究院)

摘 要 鉴于聚合物改性沥青离析试验(T 0661—2011)评价SBS改性沥青的热储存稳定性的不足。对比研究了SBS改性沥青在163℃条件下经离析管热储存48h后上层、下层试样的软化点差$\Delta T_{R\&B}$、黏度差、延度差和多应力不可恢复蠕变柔量变化率J_{nrdiff}。提出采用多应力重复蠕变恢复试验评价SBS改性沥青的热储存稳定性,定义了评价指标离析率R_S,并推荐离析率R_S小于或等于20%为合格,离析率R_S大于20%为不合格。最后评价了该试验方法和评价指标的合理性。

关键词 SBS 改性沥青 稳定性 评价方法 MSCR试验

0 引 言

现行聚合物改性沥青离析试验(T 0661—2011)评价SBS改性沥青热储存稳定性,操作简便,设备成本低,在一定程度上能较好地控制SBS改性沥青的产品质量,因此在世界各国得到了广泛应用。研究发现,在实际工程应用中,新疆市场上大量存在一类SBS改性沥青,虽然其离析软化点差$\Delta T_{R\&B}$可以达到小于2.5℃的指标要求,但是该类SBS改性沥青在163℃条件下经离析管热储存48h后,上层、下层试样却存在较大的延度差、黏度差。这说明该类SBS改性沥青在热储存过程中已经明显离析分层,稳定性是不合格的,可聚合物改性沥青离析试验(T 0661—2011)方法却误判其热储存稳定性"合格"。

鉴于此,本研究采用多应力重复蠕变恢复试验,深入研究了SBS改性沥青经离析管163℃热储存48h后,上层、下层试样的多应力不可恢复蠕变柔量变化率J_{nrdiff}。提出采用多应力重复蠕变恢复试验方法评价SBS改性沥青的热储存稳定性,定义并给定了参考评价指标,为SBS改性沥青的质量检测提供依据。

1 试 验

1.1 试验样品

A-1和A-2、B-1和B-2、D-1和D-2、E-1和E-2、F-1和F-2、G-1和G-2、H-1和H-2分别为7组相同配方而不同反应时间的实验室试样,C-1和C-2为新疆市场上收集的相同配方而不同出厂时间的SBS改性沥青。

1.2 试验原理

SBS改性沥青是一种热力学不稳定体系,经热储存后,SBS改性剂往往会逐渐上浮并富集于上层,下层则因SBS改性剂逐渐游离而导致其含量降低,最终使得上层、下层试样在流变性能上对应力变化具有不同的敏感性。根据此原理,通过多应力重复蠕变恢复试验,检测SBS改性沥青经离析管163℃储存48h后,上层、下层试样在两个不同应力水平(0.1kPa、3.2kPa)下经受10个蠕变和恢复循环后所产生的不可恢复蠕变柔量,得到两应力水平的不可恢复蠕变柔量变化率,进而计算出离析率,根据离析率的大小判断SBS改性沥青的离析程度。

1.3 试验方法

将16种SBS改性沥青经0.3mm筛过筛,称量质量约为50g的试样浇灌于直径约为25mm,长为140mm的铝管中,待冷却至室温后密封开口端,在163℃±5℃烘箱中竖直放置48h±1h,将盛样管连同试管架取出,放入冰箱的冷柜中,竖直放置不少于4h,经骤冷固化后把试样均分为上、中、下3部分,分别取得上部和下部试样,测定其环球法软化点、黏度、延度和多应力不可恢复蠕变柔量变化率J_{nrdiff}。其中多应力不可恢复蠕变柔量变化率$J_{nr\ diff}$是通过动态剪切流变仪,在70℃和0.1kPa、3.2kPa应力作用下,进行多应力重复蠕变恢复试验[1],分别得到0.1kPa、3.2kPa应力作用下的不可恢复蠕变柔量变化率J_{nrdiff},并按式(1)计算不同SBS改性沥青的离析率R_S。

$$R_S = \left| \frac{J_{\text{nrdiff}\perp}}{J_{\text{nrdiff}\top}} - 1 \right| \times 100\% \tag{1}$$

2 结果与讨论

2.1 常规性质

分别对8组SBS改性沥青进行离析管163℃热储存48h,经冰箱冷柜骤冷固化4h,把试样均分为上、中、下3部分,分别取得上部和下部试样。参照聚合物改性沥青离析试验T 0661、沥青旋转黏度试验T 0625和沥青延度试验T 0605,检测各试样上层、下层试样的软化点、黏度、延度,试验结果见表1。

结果表明:采用聚合物改性沥青离析试验方法T 0661检测八组16种SBS改性沥青各上层、下层试样的环球法软化点差$\Delta T_{R\&B}$,虽然C-2号样品的离析软化点差$\Delta T_{R\&B}$满足《公路沥青路面施工技术规范》(JTG F40—2004)中对SBS改性沥青离析指标不大于2.5℃的技术要求,但实际上该试样已明显分层,上层试样较软,富有弹性,而下层试样较硬,表现为脆性易断。再通过沥青旋转黏度试验方法T 0625和沥青延度试验方法T 0605检测C-2号样品的上层、下层试样的黏度和延度,都存在较大差别。由此可见,采用聚合物改性沥青离析试验T 0661判断SBS改性沥青的热储存稳定性具有一定局限性,甚至还会产生误判。

基于新疆X沥青的黏度大、芳香分少、硫含量小、沥青质低等特殊的理化性质,以至于难以被SBS改性,并直接影响其加工、储存、运输和应用。故不少厂家和施工单位采用40%~60%的新疆Y沥青与之调和制备改性沥青的基质沥青,以降低其改性难度和生产成本,由此出现了类似于上述C组的SBS改性沥青。研究发现,新疆Y沥青的沥青质高(19.96%)、60℃黏度大(392Pa·s)、软化点高(52℃),而且密度也比新疆X沥青大,因此两者调和而制备的基质沥青经SBS改性后,其密度较大的沥青质在热储存过程中沉降于下层,使得下层SBS改性沥青的黏性和软化点增大,而密度较小的高分子聚合物SBS则上浮,使得上层富含高分子聚合物的SBS改性沥青的弹性和韧性增强,同样表现为软化点增大,由此减小了上、下层试样的软化点差$\Delta T_{R\&B}$,最终导致得出离析"合格"这一错误结论。

2.2 多应力重复蠕变试验

采用多应力重复蠕变恢复试验,在70℃条件下,分别对经离析管163℃储存48h后的8组16种SBS改性沥青的上、下层试样,在0.1kPa、3.2kPa应力作用下测得其不可恢复蠕变柔量及其变化率,并按1.3中的式(1)计算得到不同SBS改性沥青的离析率。试验结果见表2。

表1 离析管163℃储存48h后上下层性质

样品编号	软化点 上层(℃)	软化点 下层(℃)	软化点 差值(℃)	$\|\frac{软化点_上}{软化点_下}-1\|$(%)	黏度 上层(Pa·s)	黏度 下层(Pa·s)	黏度 差值(Pa·s)	$\|\frac{黏度_上}{黏度_下}-1\|$(%)	延度 上层(mm)	延度 下层(mm)	延度 差值(mm)	$\|\frac{延度_上}{延度_下}-1\|$(%)
A-1	78.7	69.5	9.2	13.2	4.056	2.438	1.618	66.4	45.0	38.2	6.8	17.80
A-2	76.4	72.2	4.2	5.8	4.371	4.183	0.188	4.5	53.1	46.4	6.7	14.44
B-1	82.8	65.2	17.6	27.0	4.537	2.368	2.169	91.6	49.0	32.7	16.3	49.85
B-2	74.1	73.1	1.0	1.4	4.440	4.225	0.215	5.1	45.0	44.1	0.9	2.04
C-1	79.8	71.5	8.3	11.6	1.603	2.959	-1.356	45.8	92.0	7.0	85.0	1214.29
C-2	78.4	76.5	1.9	2.5	1.386	5.716	-4.330	75.8	80.2	7.8	72.4	928.21
D-1	75.8	53.3	22.5	42.2	1.699	0.920	0.779	84.6	71.1	13.3	57.8	434.59
D-2	68.9	66.5	2.4	3.6	1.864	1.773	0.091	5.1	21.0	18.0	3.0	16.67
E-1	66.1	58.3	7.8	13.4	1.849	1.563	0.286	18.3	44.2	45.5	-1.3	2.86
E-2	61.1	60.7	0.4	0.7	1.690	1.663	0.027	1.6	41.5	41.2	0.3	0.73
F-1	73.5	63.9	9.6	15.0	3.125	1.835	1.290	70.3	40.0	30.0	10.0	33.33
F-2	73.8	71.2	2.6	3.7	3.312	3.100	0.012	6.8	30.0	28.0	2.0	7.14
G-1	75.2	75.0	0.2	0.3	2.894	2.791	0.103	3.7	33.5	31.8	1.7	5.3
G-2	74.8	74.7	0.1	0.1	2.605	2.563	0.042	1.6	29.4	25.8	1.6	5.8
H-1	70.6	68.1	2.5	3.7	3.026	2.681	0.345	12.9	30.7	26.9	3.8	14.1
H-2	71.3	68.9	2.4	3.5	3.343	2.836	0.507	17.9	24.6	20.7	3.9	18.8

不同 SBS 改性沥青上层、下层试样的多应力重复蠕变恢复试验结果 表2

样品编号		多应力重复蠕变恢复试验参数			
		$Jn_{r0.1}$ (kPa^{-1})	$Jn_{r3.2}$ (kPa^{-1})	$Jn_{r_{diff}}$ (%)	$\left\| \dfrac{J_{nrdiff上}}{J_{nrdiff下}} - 1 \right\| \times 100$ (%)
A-1	上层	0.3797	1.082	184.90	91.67
	下层	0.7334	1.441	96.47	
A-2	上层	0.3396	0.7119	109.60	59.28
	下层	0.2989	0.5045	68.81	
B-1	上层	0.2906	1.257	332.55	248.57
	下层	0.8444	1.65	95.41	
B-2	上层	0.2013	0.3032	50.65	9.30
	下层	0.1948	0.285	46.34	
C-1	上层	0.1222	0.4855	297.30	720.14
	下层	0.1675	0.2283	36.25	
C-2	上层	0.1474	0.4449	201.80	522.46
	下层	0.0665	0.0881	32.42	
D-1	上层	0.2232	1.5480	593.55	684.89
	下层	1.165	2.0460	75.62	
D-2	上层	0.5544	0.7005	26.34	18.30
	下层	0.5193	0.6310	21.52	
E-1	上层	1.3600	3.2500	138.97	47.70
	下层	2.2000	4.2700	94.09	
E-2	上层	1.1350	2.4520	116.04	3.88
	下层	1.3250	2.8050	111.70	
F-1	上层	0.6245	1.3440	115.30	41.57
	下层	0.9226	1.6740	81.44	
F-2	上层	0.3617	0.5991	65.62	20.74
	下层	0.3518	0.5430	54.35	
G-1	上层	0.0662	0.0786	18.73	5.64
	下层	0.0849	0.1017	19.79	
G-2	上层	0.7395	0.8173	10.52	2.23
	下层	0.8461	0.9371	10.76	
H-1	上层	0.3842	0.6428	67.31	20.24
	下层	0.4534	0.6968	53.68	
H-2	上层	0.8871	1.3705	54.49	19.72
	下层	0.7669	1.1024	43.75	

结果表明：8 组 16 种相同配方不同反应时间的 SBS 改性沥青经离析管 163℃储存 48h 后，上层、下层试样对应力的变化具有不同的敏感性，这是因上层、下层试样的 SBS 改性剂含量的不同而引起。对于离析分层严重的样品，上层试样因高分子聚合物 SBS 含量较高，在 0.1kPa、3.2kPa 应力作用下，其不可恢复蠕变柔量变化率 J_{nrdiff} 较大。而下层试样因高分子聚合物 SBS 含量较小，在 0.1kPa、3.2kPa 应力作用下，其不可恢复蠕变柔量变化率 J_{nrdiff} 较小。根据上述 1.3 中的式(1)计算得到不同 SBS 改性沥青的离析率见表 2。从结果可以看出，通过不可恢复蠕变柔量变化率 J_{nrdiff} 计算得到的离析率 S_R 能有效地鉴别不同

SBS改性沥青的热储存稳定性,尤其能准确判断类似于C组的SBS改性沥青的热储存稳定性。

3 合理性评价

采用聚合物改性沥青离析试验(T 0661—2011)评价SBS改性沥青的热储存稳定性,关键在于测定其离析管上、下层试样的软化点。但是在软化点测定过程中,因人为因素和仪器误差影响较大,往往难以精确测定其软化点。同时,在测定诸如C-1和C-2这类SBS改性沥青的离析指标时,甚至还会出现误判现象。因此,采用聚合物改性沥青离析试验(T 0661—2011)评价SBS改性沥青的热储存稳定性具有一定局限性。

采用沥青延度试验(T 0605—2011)评价SBS改性沥青的热储存稳定性,同样因人为因素和仪器误差影响较大,而难以鉴别诸如A组、E组这类相同配方不同反应时间的试样在离析程度上的差异性。相比于聚合物改性沥青离析试验(T 0661—2011)和沥青延度试验(T 0605—2011),采用沥青旋转黏度试验(T 0625—2011)评价SBS改性沥青的热储存稳定性,其试验环节较少,人为因素影响较小。同时,仪器的精密度也相对较高,因此更能有效地鉴别SBS改性沥青的离析状态。但是,对于离析严重的SBS改性沥青,因上层试样不仅含有较多的SBS改性剂,而且交联成团,难以准确测定其上层试样的黏度,故该检测方法仍然不具有较好的通用性。

多应力重复蠕变恢复试验的开发,旨在解决以往SHRP评价体系不能真实反映SBS改性沥青的延迟弹性恢复性能这一问题。它能很好地反映SBS改性沥青在恒定应力作用下的受力变形特性,撤去应力作用后,部分蠕变变形恢复,而不可恢复的变形将会累加到下一个载荷循环中,能真实模拟路面车辆载荷反复加载与卸载过程[2]。从仪器精密度来看,动态剪切流变仪的控温精度可以达到0.1℃,试验频率精确到0.1rad/s,应变振幅精确到0.1%,作用应力精确到0.01N[3],具有较高的精密度。从试验过程来看,该方法试验步骤少,受人为因素影响的只有试模的处理过程,因此,试验的可靠性更高。从试验结果来看,因SBS高分子聚合物对作用应力的变化具有较高的敏感性,从而能够准确区分SBS改性沥青在163℃条件下经离析管热储存48h后的上层、下层试样的差异性,而且还能准确测定通过聚合物改性沥青离析试验(T 0661—2011)难以鉴别的类似于C组的SBS改性沥青的热储存稳定性。

根据离析软化点差$\Delta T_{R\&B}$与式(1)计算得到的离析率的对应关系,离析率越小,说明其热储存稳定性就越好,反之则越差。其中D-2、F-2、H-1、H-2试样的上层、下层离析软化点差$\Delta T_{R\&B}$分别为2.4℃、2.6℃、2.5℃、2.4℃,与之对应的多应力重复蠕变恢复试验测得的离析率分别为18.30%、20.74%、20.24%、19.72%。因此,当多应力重复蠕变恢复试验测得的离析率小于或等于20.00%时,可以认定其热储存稳定性合格,反之则认定其热储存稳定性不合格。

4 结　语

通过聚合物改性沥青离析试验(T 0661—2011)、沥青延度试验(T 0605—2011)、沥青旋转黏度试验(T 0625—2011)和多应力重复蠕变恢复试验(AASHTO TP 70-10)对SBS改性沥青热储存稳定性的对比研究,初步得出以下结论:采用多应力重复蠕变恢复试验(AASHTO TP 70-10)评价SBS改性沥青的热储存稳定性,其准确率、精密度、可靠性都高于前三种试验方法。根据离析软化点差$\Delta T_{R\&B}$与式(1)计算得到的离析率的对应关系,推荐当离析率R_S小于或等于20%时,待测试样的热储存稳定性合格,当离析率R_S大于20%时,待测试样的热储存稳定性不合格。

参考文献

[1] American Association of State Highway and Transportation Officials (AASHTO). Standard Method of Test for Multiple Stress Creep Recovery (MSCR) Test of Asphalt Binder Using a Dynamic Shear Rheometer (DSR), AASHTO TP 70-10 [S]. Washington DC: AASHTO, 2010.

[2] 蔡莉莉. 利用多应力重复蠕变恢复(MSCR)方法评价改性沥青胶结料高温性能[J]. 石油沥青, 2013,

12,27(6):21-24.
[3] 熊萍,郝培文.SBS改性沥青储存稳定性试验方法和评价指标的研究[J].中国公路学报,2005,1,18(1):1-6.

基于沥青性能快速检测方法的胶粉改性沥青的蠕变变形恢复研究

蔡凤杰[1]　冯振刚[1]　姚冬冬[2]　陈婷婷[3]　韦金城[3]

(1.长安大学公路学院;2.吉林省交通科学研究所;3.山东省交通科学研究院)

摘　要　沥青性能快速检测方法使用空气(氮气)压力使沥青材料产生压痕,并使用激光探测系统测量和记录由此产生的变形和变形恢复。利用沥青性能快速检测设备,对基质沥青和不同掺量的胶粉改性沥青分别进行不同温度下的空气压力加载试验。试验结果表明,随着胶粉掺量的增加和温度的降低,沥青的最大蠕变变形减小,变形恢复率增大,同时沥青的最大蠕变变形绝对值和变形恢复率与针入度具有很好的相关性。

关键词　胶粉改性沥青　快速检测　最大蠕变变形　变形恢复率

0　引　言

近年来聚合物改性沥青逐渐成为国内外研究的重点,而且随着我国经济的发展,日益增加的废旧轮胎造成的"黑色污染"正威胁着全人类的生存环境。因此充分、有效地利用这些废旧轮胎,消除"黑色污染"已经刻不容缓。其中将废旧轮胎加工成不同粒径的胶粉是废旧轮胎再生利用的主要途径,利用胶粉制备胶粉改性沥青也逐渐成为再生胶粉主要的应用方法[1-3]。

目前国内外对于沥青性能的评价体系分为针入度分级、黏度分级、性能等级(Performance Grade,PG)分级[4-8]。对于针入度和黏度分级,该评价体系操作简单,分析方法易懂,但其试验具有一定的经验性,试验结果与工作人员的操作有很大的关系,而且对于改性剂颗粒比较大的胶粉改性沥青的试验结果具有一定的离散型[9-11]。对于PG分级,该评价体系可以对基质沥青和胶粉改性沥青的性能进行评价,而且试验结果离散型小,结论准确率高,但其操作、分析复杂,对工作人员的专业性要求比较高[12-14]。因此,有必要开发一种操作简单、快速、准确的适合于基质沥青和改性沥青的性能检测方法。

沥青性能快速检测方法是一种新型的沥青性能评价方法,该方法是在一定的时间内通过给沥青材料加载一定的空气压力,然后用激光探测系统记录和测量沥青的蠕变变形和空气压力卸载后的变形恢复来对沥青的性能进行快速的评价[15-16]。沥青性能快速检测方法不仅适用于基质沥青,而且适用于改性沥青,操作简单、迅速,整个过程分为3个阶段:预加载阶段、加载阶段、变形恢复阶段。

本文利用沥青性能快速检测方法对基质沥青和掺量为5%、10%、15%、20%、25%的胶粉改性沥青分别在20℃、25℃、30℃温度下进行了空气压力加载试验,研究了在25℃时不同掺量胶粉的胶粉改性沥青和胶粉掺量为20%的胶粉改性沥青在20℃、25℃、30℃的变形规律,同时分析了在20℃、25℃、30℃时沥青的最大蠕变变形绝对值和变形恢复率随胶粉掺量的变化,最后建立沥青的最大蠕变变形绝对值和变形恢复率与针入度之间的关系。

基金项目:国家自然科学基金项目(51508032);吉林省交通运输科技计划项目(2018-1-4);山东省交通运输厅科技计划项目(2020B38);山西省公路局科技项目(2019-1-2)。

1 试验部分

1.1 原材料

本文选择东海-70基质沥青、细度为60目的废旧轮胎胶粉。沥青和胶粉的性能指标见表1、表2。

沥青的性能指标　　　　　表1

项　目	东海-70	测试方法
针入度(25℃)(0.1mm)	73.8	JTG E20—2011 T0604
软化点(℃)	45.9	JTG E20—2011 T0606
延度(15℃)(cm)	>100	JTG E20—2011 T0605

胶粉的性能指标　　　　　表2

胶粉	密度(g/cm^3)	金属含量(%)	灰分(%)	丙酮抽取物(%)	炭黑(%)	胶粉烃含量(%)
60目	0.297	0.02	3.4	2.5	32.6	53.2

1.2 试样制备

将一定质量的东海-70基质沥青加热至150℃，加热80min，然后将基质沥青倒入温度为180℃的油浴锅，保温20min。将转速调到300r/min，同时缓慢加入占沥青质量分数为5%、10%、15%、20%、25%的胶粉。随后将转速调到500r/min，搅拌1.5h，胶粉改性沥青制备完成。

1.3 性能测试

1.3.1 针入度

采用SYD-2801F型沥青针入度试验仪，按照JTG E20-2011/T0604-2011规定对沥青针入度进行测试，试验温度分别为(20±0.1)℃、(25±0.1)℃、(30±0.1)℃，贯入时间为5s，单位以0.1mm表示。

1.3.2 沥青性能快速检测方法

沥青性能快速检测设备的工作原理示意图如图1所示，沥青性能快速检测设备图如图2所示。沥青性能快速检测系统由硬件系统和软件系统组成。平台上面放置沥青样品，沥青样品放在直径为5.5cm，高度为4.3cm的圆形铝盒里，质量为(70±5)g。试件上方是激光测量系统和空气加载系统。系统的左边是一套小型触摸屏计算机，外部连接着键盘和鼠标；计算机软件系统包括Windows操作系统、快速检测操作系统以及数据处理软件。

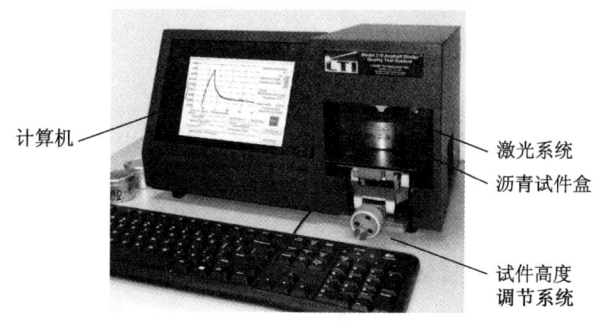

图1　沥青性能快速检测设备图

沥青性能快速检测设备原理图如图3所示。该方法采用空气加载的方式对常温条件下的沥青试件在一个圆形区域进行一段时间的加载，加载开始的同时系统的激光测量系统会测量并记录加载中心的变形(位移)。当加载结束后，沥青材料的变形开始恢复。激光测量系统不仅测量加载时的变形，也测量并记录卸载后材料的变形从而得到材料一定时间内随时间的变形恢复率。

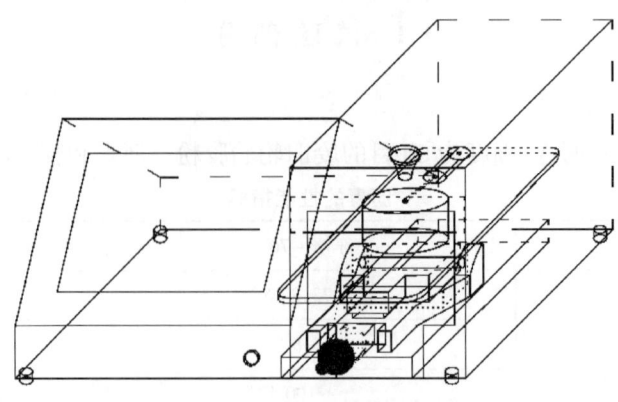

图2 沥青性能快速检测设备结构图

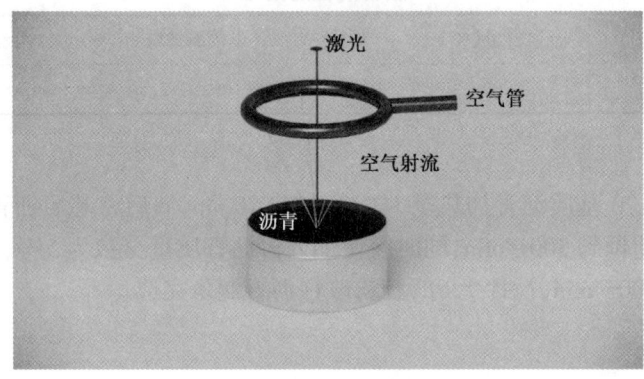

图3 沥青性能快速检测设备原理图

本文的空气压力预加载时间、加载时间、卸载时间分别为10s、20s、10s,空气加载压力为0.062MPa。预加载阶段、通过调节阀门和稳定气压、确保加载开始后的加载压力达到并维持在目标值容许范围内;加载阶段、沥青材料产生蠕变变形;变形恢复阶段、压力卸载后沥青变形恢复。试验前,将填充的样品罐放置在温度保持在(20±0.1)℃、(25±0.1)℃、(30±0.1)℃的环境室中1h±10min,以控制样品温度。随后从试验箱中取出铝盒,并将其放入装置中,测试在两分钟内完成。测试期间,使用安装在装置内的红外线温度计监测样品温度。

2 结果与讨论

2.1 沥青性能快速检测试验结果分析

2.1.1 胶粉掺量的影响

图4为25℃时不同掺量胶粉改性沥青的快速检测试验结果。由图4可知,在0~10s时,沥青没有发生明显变形;在10s时开始施加压力,沥青开始变形产生,到30s时停止释放空气压力,沥青的变形达到最大,随后开始变形恢复。同时从图中可知,随着胶粉掺量的增大,沥青的变形变小,这是因为胶粉颗粒对压力的穿透起到了阻碍的作用,胶粉掺量越多,阻碍作用越强。由此可知,胶粉的加入增大了沥青的硬度,提高沥青的抗变形能力,而且掺量越大,性能越好。

不同掺量胶粉改性沥青在25℃时的变形速度随时间的变化如图5所示。图中0~10s为空气压力预加载阶段,沥青的变形速度没有明显的变化,保持在0mm·s^{-1}附近,沥青没有明显的变形。在10s时开始加载空气压力,变形速度变为负值,变形速率突然增大,随着时间的增加大致呈减小的趋势,这是因为空气压力随着穿透的沥青越来越多,受到沥青的阻力越来越大,变形速率也就越来越小。同时在20~30s阶段,随着胶粉掺量的增加,沥青的变形速率减小,这是因为胶粉改性沥青中的胶粉颗粒阻止了沥青的变形,而且胶粉含量越高,沥青越硬,变形越慢。在 30s 时,沥青的变形速度变成正值,这是因为空气加载压力卸载后,沥青开始恢复变形,并且随着时间的增加,沥青的变形速率逐渐变小,最后变为 $0\ mm\cdot s^{-1}$。在 30~40s 时,这 6 种沥青的变形速度差别不大,只有略微的区别,随着胶粉掺量的增大,变形速率大致呈减小的趋势,这是因为沥青中胶粉颗粒阻止了沥青的变形恢复。

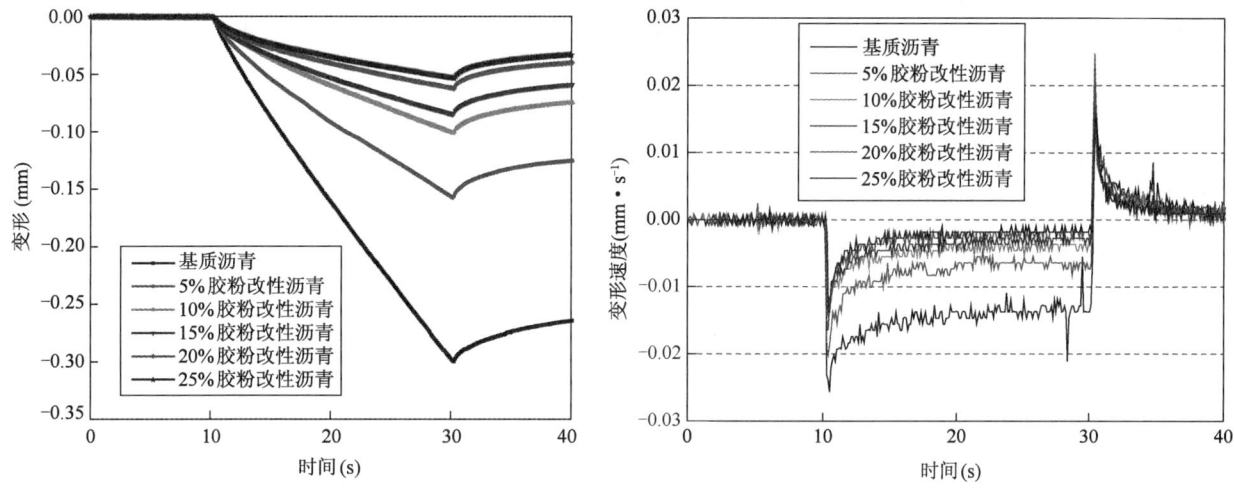

图 4　不同掺量胶粉改性沥青的变形随时间的变化　　　　图 5　不同掺量胶粉改性沥青的变形速度随时间的变化

2.1.2　温度的影响

图 6 为胶粉掺量为 20% 的胶粉改性沥青在 20℃、25℃、30℃ 时的快速检测试验结果。由图 6 可知,胶粉改性沥青的变形在 10s 前基本上没有变化,到 10s 时,胶粉改性沥青在空气加载压力的作用下随着时间的变化逐渐产生变形。在 30s 时,卸载空气压力,沥青的变形开始恢复。由图 6 可知,随着温度的升高,沥青的变形增大,这是因为温度越高,沥青越软,沥青的变形能力增强。

胶粉掺量为 20% 的胶粉改性沥青在 20℃、25℃、30℃ 时变形速度随时间的变化如图 7 所示。图中 0~10s 沥青的变形速度变化不明显,基本上保持在 $0\ mm\cdot s^{-1}$ 附近。在 10s 时变形速度变为负值,变形速率急剧增大,到达最大后随时间变化减小。同时在 10~30s 阶段,随着温度的升高,沥青的变形速率增大,这是因为温度越高,沥青越容易变形,而且变形速率越快。在 30s 时,沥青的变形速度变成正值,沥青开始恢复变形,然后逐渐减小,最后变为 $0\ mm\cdot s^{-1}$。在 30~40s 时,温度越高,胶粉改性沥青的变形恢复速率越大,这是因为温度升高导致沥青的可恢复变形部分减少,不可恢复变形部分增加,导致 30℃ 时胶粉改性沥青的可恢复部分的变形恢复速率最大。

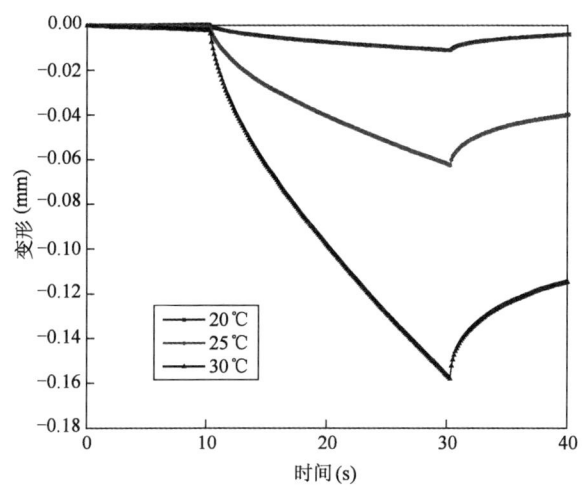
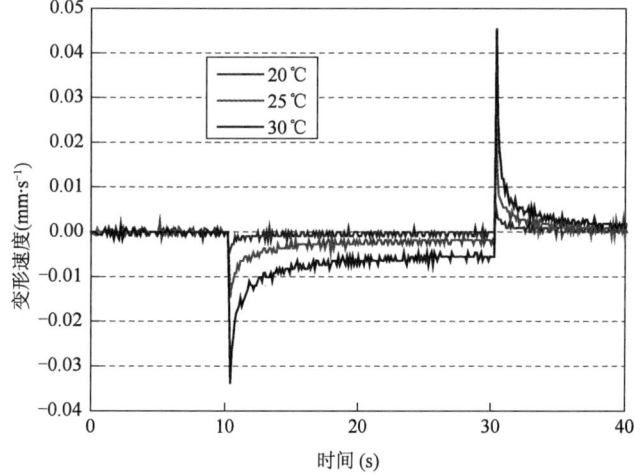

图 6　不同温度下胶粉改性沥青的变形随时间的变化　　　　图 7　不同温度下胶粉改性沥青的变形速度随时间的变化

2.2 沥青性能快速检测评价指标随胶粉掺量和温度的变化结果分析

图 8 为在 20℃、25℃、30℃时沥青的最大蠕变变形绝对值随胶粉掺量变化的曲线图。由图 8 可知,在 3 种温度下,沥青的最大蠕变变形随胶粉掺量的变化趋势保持一致,都是随着胶粉掺量的增加而减小,这是因为胶粉颗粒阻碍了沥青的变形,颗粒越多,阻碍作用越强,从而提高了沥青的抗变形能力。从图 8 还可看出,随着温度的升高,沥青的最大蠕变变形增大,这是因为温度的升高导致沥青变软,沥青的弹性成分减少,黏性成分增加,沥青的抗变形能力减弱。

图 9 为在 20℃、25℃、30℃时沥青的变形恢复率随胶粉掺量变化的曲线图。由图 9 可知,在 3 种温度下,沥青的最大蠕变变形和变形恢复率随胶粉掺量的变化趋势保持一致,沥青的变形恢复率均随着胶粉掺量的增加而增大,这是因为胶粉颗粒从而提高了沥青的弹性恢复能力。由图 9 还可看出,随着温度的升高,沥青的变形恢复率减小,这是因为温度越高,沥青黏性成分越多,可恢复变形部分减少,沥青的抗永久变形能力和弹性恢复性能下降。

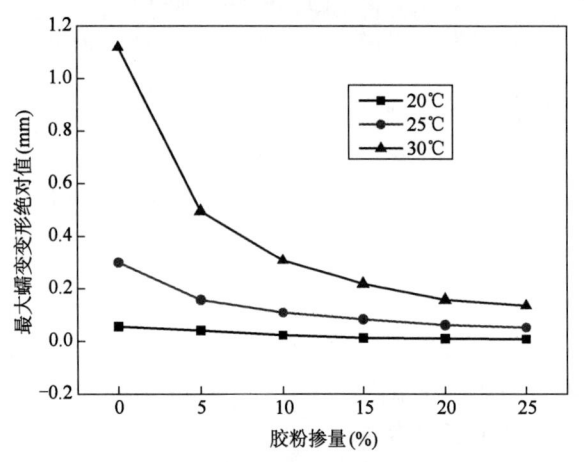
图 8 不同温度下沥青的最大蠕变变形绝对值随胶粉掺量的变化

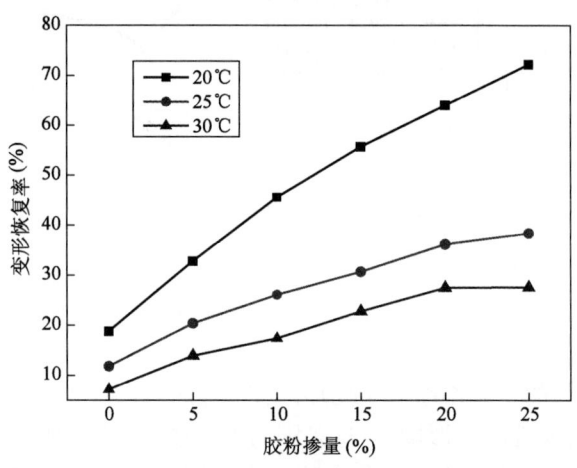
图 9 不同温度下沥青的变形恢复率随胶粉掺量的变化

2.3 沥青性能快速检测评价指标与针入度的关系

图 10 是 20℃、25℃和 30℃温度下基质沥青和掺量分别为 5%、10%、15%、20%、25%的胶粉改性沥青的最大蠕变变形绝对值与针入度的关系图。由图 10 可知,沥青的最大蠕变变形随着针入度的增加而增大。通过拟合,沥青的最大蠕变变形绝对值和针入度的关系式为 $Y = 1.06 \times 10^7 X^{3.65}$,呈正相关关系,沥青的针入度越大,沥青的最大蠕变变形绝对值越大,这是因为针入度越大,沥青越软,在压力作用下容量产生变形。同时沥青的最大蠕变变形绝对值和针入度的相关系数高达 0.98,表明沥青的最大蠕变变形和针入度具有很好的相关性。

图 11 是在 20℃、25℃和 30℃下基质沥青和掺量分别为 5%、10%、15%、20%、25%的胶粉改性沥青的变形恢复率与针入度的关系图。由图 11 可知,沥青的变形恢复率随着针入度的增加而减小。通过拟合,沥青的变形恢复率和针入度的关系式为 $Y = 2067.12 X^{-1.20}$,呈负相关关系,即沥青的针入度越大,变形恢复率越小,这是由于沥青越软,弹性成分越少,沥青的变形越难恢复。再由沥青的变形恢复率和针入度的相关系数为 0.95 可知,沥青的变形恢复率和针入度的相关性很高。

由以上分析可知,沥青性能快速检测方法指标(最大蠕变变形绝对值和变形恢复率)与针入度的相关系数都很高,都具有很好的相关性,所以可以使用沥青性能快速检测方法指标代替针入度对沥青性能进行评价。

3 结 语

(1)随着胶粉掺量的增加,沥青的变形减小,最大蠕变变形绝对值减小,弹性恢复率增大,沥青的抗永久变形能力和弹性恢复性能增强。

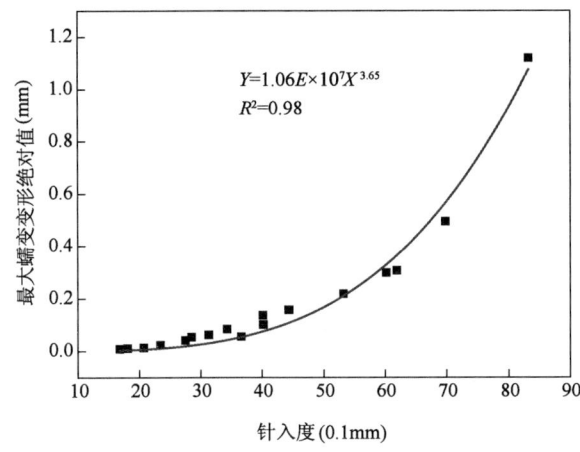
图10 沥青的最大蠕变变形绝对值和针入度的关系

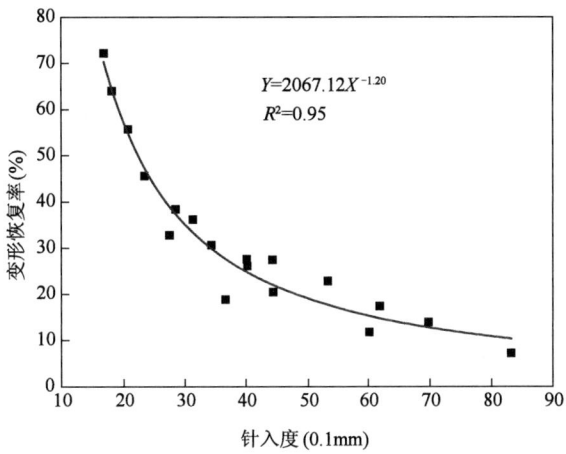
图11 沥青的变形恢复率和针入度的关系

(2)温度升高使沥青变软,沥青的弹性成分减少,黏性成分增加,从而降低沥青的抗永久变形能力和弹性恢复率。

(3)沥青性能快速检测评价指标与针入度之间具有很好的相关关系,可以采用沥青性能快速检测方法代替针入度方法对沥青性能进行快速评价。

参考文献

[1] 王志刚.橡胶粉改性沥青重复蠕变恢复试验研究[J].河南城建学院学报,2018,27(05):57-60.

[2] 董瑞琨,戚昌鹏,郑凯军,等.高温裂解胶粉改性沥青的低温性能试验[J].中国公路学报,2017,30(10):32-38.

[3] 孙建刚.废胶粉改性沥青的性能及机理研究[D].武汉:武汉科技大学,2014.

[4] 文龙,李凯,吴涛.基于针入度等级与PG等级的改性沥青性能评价指标相关性研究[J].施工技术,2019,48(17):59-61.

[5] 孙艳娜,李立寒.基于流变性能试验的沥青高温性能评价指标研究[J].建筑材料学报,2019,22(05):750-755.

[6] 马翔,倪富健,陈荣生,等.沥青感温性能评价指标[J].交通运输工程学报,2008,(01):31-35.

[7] The American Association of State Highway and Transportation Officials, Standard Method of Test for Multiple Stress Creep Recovery (MSCR) Test of Asphalt Binder Using a Dynamic Shear Rheometer (DSR), AASHTO TP70,2013.

[8] 段周洋.沥青性能综合分析与优选方法研究[D].西安:长安大学,2015.

[9] 何立平.基于DMA方法的橡胶沥青粘弹特性和高温性能研究[D].西安:长安大学,2014.

[10] 李纯,时敬涛,王体宏,等.不同外加剂对沥青PG分级影响研究进展[J].石油沥青,2020,34(02):1-4.

[11] 张凌波,时敬涛,康剑翘,等.沥青常规指标与PG分级指标的关联关系研究[J].公路,2016,61(02):172-176.

[12] CAO Z L,HUANG X Q,YU J Y,et al. Laboratory Evaluation of the Effect of Rejuvenators on the Interface performance of Rejuvenated SBS Modified Bitumen Mixture by Surface Free Energy Method[J]. Construction and Building Materials,2021,271:121866.

[13] 王岚,崔世超,常春清.基于流变学与黏弹性理论的温拌胶粉改性沥青的高温性能研究[J].材料导报,2019,33(14):2386-2391.

[14] 张广泰,方烁,叶奋. 双螺杆挤出胶粉改性沥青流变性能研究[J]. 中国公路学报,2019,32(05):57-63.

[15] Raj D, John S Y, John N. New Bitumen Quality Control Test (QCT) for Europe[C]. Prague: 6th Eurasphalt & Eurobitume Congress. 2016.

[16] Raj D, John S Y, John N. Development of a Quality Control Test (QCT) for Asphalt Binders[C]. Canada: Canadian Technical Asphalt Association (CTAA). 2014: 173-193.

冷补沥青混合料材料设计及其性能研究

孙垚垚[1] 刘安述[1] 吴双全[3] 郑斌[1] 郭艳明[2]

(1. 长安大学;2. 衢州市公路管理局;3. 河南省交通规划设计研究院股份有限公司)

摘 要 为提高冷补沥青混合料性能,优化冷补沥青液制备工艺。以 0 号柴油为稀释剂,加入自主合成添加剂 α,通过加热溶解,制得液态冷补沥青液。通过试验确定了冷补液的配方和最佳掺配比例为 14%;并以 AC-13 型和 LB-13 型级配验证冷补沥青混合料的路用性能,提出冷补沥青混合料马歇尔初始稳定度不小于 2.5kN、马歇尔成型稳定度不小于 4.5kN、残留稳定度应不小于 75% 及冻融劈裂强度比不小于 70%、破坏应变不小于 2000$\mu\varepsilon$、破损率不大于 15% 的要求。

关键词 冷补沥青混合料 冷补沥青液 马歇尔稳定度 评价标准

0 引 言

沥青路面在外界环境作用下会产生车辙、裂缝及坑槽等危害,严重影响行车安全性与舒适性[1-2]。目前,热拌沥青混合料修补坑槽过程中存在能耗高、污染大等缺点;且沥青作为一种黏弹性材料,施工受到温度与季节等限制[3-5],因此冷补沥青混合料的应用便应运而生。

目前国内外学者针对冷补沥青混合料的研究主要集中在添加剂的研发和工艺优化方面[6],自 Cho Young S 等[7]提出以煤油、柴油和汽油作为沥青稀释剂以来,英国 Emcol 公司以石油为稀释剂,制备了冷补沥青,该产品的优点包括修补速度快、可存储、成本低、施工温度范围为 -45~54℃[8]等;耿立涛等[6]基于当前冷补沥青混合料黏附性及黏聚性差的缺陷,以柴油为稀释剂通过化学合成的方式研制出一种溶剂型冷补沥青。但大多数冷补沥青制备工艺复杂,且没有完善的评价体系,限制了其推广使用。

本文将所有添加剂制成一种液态制剂,在一定温度下与基质沥青混合制成冷补沥青,简化了冷补沥青制备工艺,提出一些适用于冷补沥青混合料的评价方法和评价标准。

1 原 材 料

1.1 沥青

冷补沥青主要是由基质沥青、稀释剂、添加剂等按照一定的比例配制而成[9]。冷补沥青一般根据当地气候条件选择选取"70~110 号"A 级道路石油沥青。本文选择 70 号基质沥青,基本指标见表 1。

基金项目:高温多雨区公路沥青路面早期水损坏精细化评价与快速预养护技术(2018H37)。

基质沥青技术指标　　　　　　　　　　　　　　　表1

试验项目	单位	试验结果	标准要求	试验方法
针入度(25℃,100g,5s)	0.1mm	68.5	60~80	T 0604
针入度指数	—	-1.15	-1.5~+1.0	T 0604
软化点(环球法)	℃	48.5	≥46	T 0606
延度(5cm/min,15℃)	cm	>100	≥100	T 0605
密度(15℃)	g/cm³	1.032	≥1.01	T 0603

1.2 稀释剂

通常将汽油、煤油、柴油和无水乙醇等有机溶剂加入沥青种降低其黏度,保证沥青混合料的施工和易性。本文选择挥发性慢,闪点高,易储存的0号柴油作为稀释剂,提高基质沥青的流动性,促进界面融合[9]。

1.3 添加剂

添加剂的实质是对沥青进行改性,改善冷补沥青混合料与原有路面的结合,使混合料强度达到路用要求[10]。目前添加剂主要以橡胶、树脂、矿质黏土为主。本文采用实验室自主合成添加剂α。

1.4 集料与级配

本文采用AC-13和LB-13类型进行冷补沥青混合料级配设计(图1、图2)。

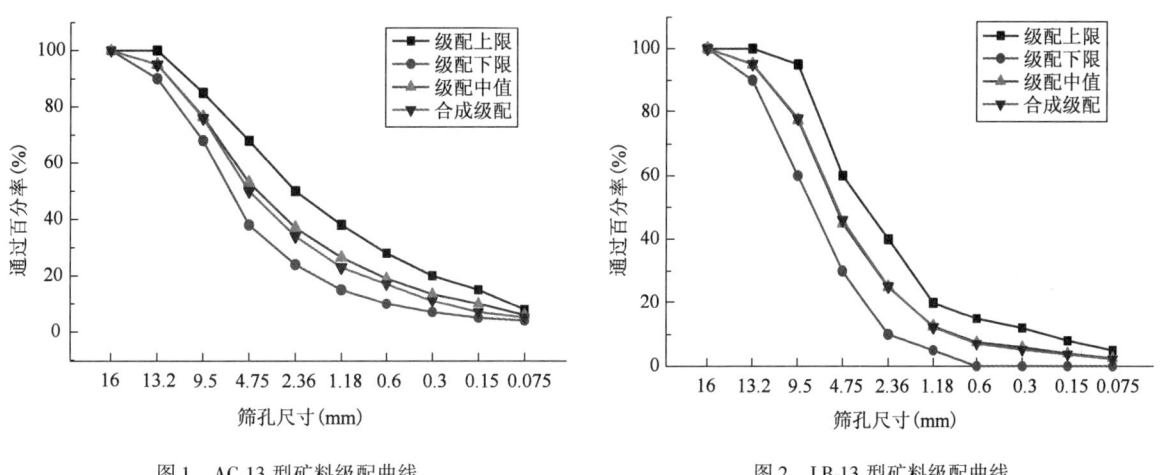

图1　AC-13型矿料级配曲线　　　　　　　　图2　LB-13型矿料级配曲线

2 试验方法

2.1 冷补沥青及混合料的制备

将装有100g柴油的圆底烧瓶置于40℃磁力搅拌器中以120r/min对其加热搅拌,边搅拌边加入称量好的添加剂α,添加完成后继续搅拌1h。同时利用直流冷凝管对其冷却回流,最后制得一种液态制剂。

冷补沥青制备:将基质沥青加热到140~150℃后加入定量的冷补剂,并用玻璃棒搅拌均匀,制得冷补沥青,保温待用。冷补沥青混合料的制备:在"热油冷料"的条件下利用自动拌和机拌和冷补沥青混合料,首先将粗集料和冷补沥青加入拌和机中拌和90s,再将细集料与矿粉一起加入拌和机中拌和300s。

2.2 冷补沥青性能测试

为获得柴油和添加剂α的最佳掺量,设计并制备多组冷补沥青,根据《公路工程沥青及沥青混合料试验规程》(JTG E20—2011)进行60℃旋转黏度和黏附性测试。

2.3 冷补沥青混合料的性能测试

AC-13和LB-13最佳沥青用量分别为5.58%的5.3%为基础,进行50℃时沥青混合料的水稳定性能测试,参考文献[11,13]进行了沥青混合料的初始强度,成型强度、低温性能和黏聚性能测试。

3 试验结果与分析

3.1 旋转黏度试验

采用60℃旋转黏度计对冷补沥青黏度测试,以3种类型配比和5种掺量研究其黏附性变化规律,探究其最佳掺量。试验方案见表2,试验结果如图3所示。

液态制剂类型表 表2

液态制剂类型	A型	B型	C型
柴油与添加剂α质量比	20∶3	20∶4	20∶5

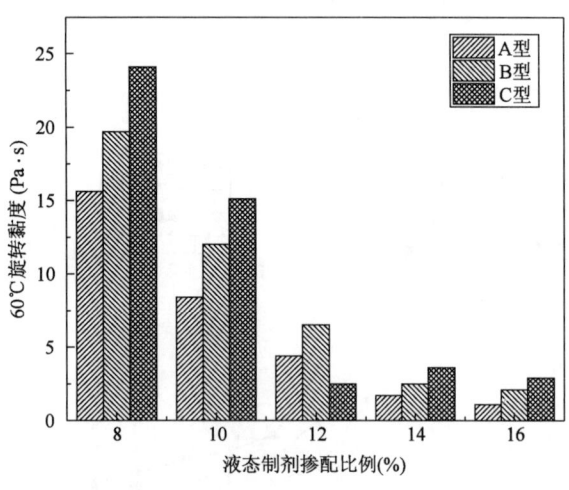

图3 不同掺配比例的冷补沥青黏度测试结果

从图3中可以看出不同类型的液态制剂和掺量对冷补沥青黏度具有一定影响,60℃黏度都随着液态制剂掺配比例的增大而降低;在相同掺加比例的情况下,3种类型冷补沥青的黏度大小为A型<B型<C型。当液态制剂掺配比例为14%~16%时,3种类型的冷补沥青黏度变化均较小。SHRP沥青结合料规范中提出对沥青135℃的黏度不得超过3Pa·s[15],考虑到冷补沥青混合料的施工条件较热拌沥青更为严苛,因此本文建议冷补沥青60℃黏度不得超过2.5 Pa·s。

3.2 黏附性试验

沥青混合料性能的提升很大程度上取决于黏附性的影响。采用水煮法评价冷补沥青与集料的黏附性,试验结果见表3。

不同掺配比例的冷补沥青黏附性测试结果 表3

液态制剂类型	不同掺配比例液态制剂的冷补沥青黏附等级(级)				
	8%	10%	12%	14%	16%
A型	4	5	5	4	4
B型	5	5	5	5	4
C型	5	5	5	5	5

由表3可知,3种类型的冷补沥青黏附性等级均满足沥青与矿料黏附等级不低于4级的要求。在冷补沥青黏附性试验中,由于柴油作为稀释剂,在试验过程中柴油会有一定溢出和挥发,对沥青的黏附性起到了一定的降低作用,因此本文建议冷补沥青混合料的黏附性等级不低于5级。

3.3 初始马歇尔稳定度试验

冷补沥青路面须具备一定的强度来抵抗车辆荷载作用,保证路面不被破坏[16]。本文以初始稳定度作为早期开放交通提供依据,选用级配为规范中LB-13级配,试验结果如图4所示。

由图4可知,随着液态制剂掺配比例的增加,冷补沥青混合料的初始稳定度呈现先增加后减小的趋势。主要是因为,矿粉与沥青发生交互作用时形成结构沥青,使得沥青混合料初始强度增加;但当沥青增加到一定程度时转换为自由沥青,促使马歇尔稳定度下降。综合上述试验,当液态制剂添加比例较低时,冷补沥青黏度较大易出现结团,难以拌和;A型液态制剂掺配比例为12%时,B型、C型在掺配比例为14%时,沥青黏度较低,最大初始稳定度分别为2.65kN、3.15kN、3.07kN。通过对比发现,当加入14%的B型液态制剂时冷补沥青和易性较好,初始稳定度最大。

综合考虑冷补沥青60℃布氏黏度、黏附性和初始马歇尔稳定度试验结果,最终确定液态制剂为B型,在沥青中的掺配比例为14%。

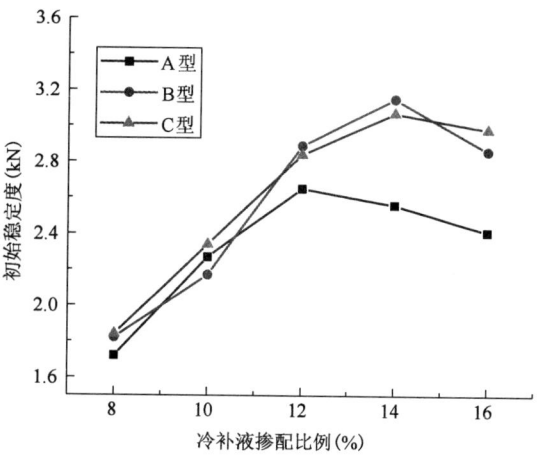

图4 不同掺配比例的冷补沥青初始马歇尔稳定度

3.4 沥青混合料试验

3.4.1 冷补沥青混合料强度试验

同济大学吕伟民提出冷补沥青混合料初期稳定度应不小于2kN[17],在《公路沥青路面施工技术规范》(JTG F40—2004)中规定成型稳强度不小于3kN。本文采用前述两种级配,在最佳油石比和液态制剂的作用下制备了沥青混合料并研究了马歇尔初始稳定度和成型稳定度。

由表4可知,LB-13型冷补沥青混合料成型稳定度相比于初始稳定度增长了98.4%,AC-13型仅提升75.9%。本文建议冷补沥青初始稳定度不小于2.5kN,成型稳定度不小于4.5kN。

两种级配沥青混合料马歇尔稳定度试验结果表 表4

级配类型	马歇尔初始稳定度(kN)	马歇尔成型稳定度(kN)
AC-13	3.20	5.63
LB-13	2.46	4.88

3.4.2 水稳定性试验

现有规范中并无对冷补沥青混合料水稳定性评价要求,但较多研究人员提出残留稳定度应不小于75%及冻融劈裂强度比不小于70%[19],本文也参照该要求评价冷补沥青混合料的水稳定性。

(1)浸水马歇尔试验

浸水马歇尔试验方法参照《公路工程沥青及沥青混合料试验规程》(JTG E20—2011)。试验结果见表5。

浸水马歇尔残留稳定度 表5

级配类型	未浸水马歇尔稳定度(kN)	浸水48h后马歇尔稳定度(kN)	浸水残留稳定度(%)	规范规定浸水残留稳定度(%)
AC-13	6.44	5.23	81.2	≥75
LB-13	5.36	4.05	75.6	

由表5知,两种级配的沥青混合料的残留稳定都大于75%的要求,且AC-13型马歇尔强度大于LB-13型。本文建议冷补沥青混合料的残留稳定度应不小于75%。

(2)冻融劈裂试验

冻融劈裂试验方法参照《公路工程沥青及沥青混合料试验规程》(JTG E20—2011)。试验结果见

表6。

冻融劈裂试验结果 表6

级配类型	劈裂强度(MPa)	冻融劈裂强度(MPa)	劈裂强度比(%)	规范规定劈裂强度比(%)
AC-13	0.58	0.46	79.3	≥70
LB-13	0.44	0.32	72.7	

由表6知,两种级配的沥青混合料的劈裂强度比都大于70%,达到了普通热拌沥青混合料的要求。同残留稳定度结果一样,AC-13型比B-13型混合料劈裂强度比大,满足水稳定性要求。本文建议冷补沥青混合料的劈裂强度比应不小于70%。

3.4.3 低温性能

在低温环境下,沥青逐渐变脆,沥青混合料易出现裂缝。本文按照《公路工程沥青及沥青混合料试验规程》试验,加载速率为50mm/min。试验结果见表7。

小梁弯曲试验结果 表7

级配类型	抗弯拉强度(MPa)	破坏应变($\mu\varepsilon$)	劲度模量(MPa)
AC-13	5.34	2515	2123
LB-13	4.51	2342	1926

由表7知,两种类型的冷补沥青混合料动稳定度都达到了2000$\mu\varepsilon$。AC-13型冷补沥青混合料的破坏应变大于LB-13型,说明其低温性能优于LB-13型。本文建议冷补沥青混合料的破坏应变应不小于2000$\mu\varepsilon$。

3.4.4 黏聚性

防止新旧路面接缝处在雨水和荷载的作用下发生剥离脱落,冷补沥青混合料应具有一定的黏聚性。按照《公路沥青路面施工技术规范》(JTG F40—2004)进行,同时参照李峰[12]的试验方法进行部分改进。试验结果见表8。

冷补沥青黏聚性试验结果 表8

级配类型	混合料破损率(%)	规范规定破损率(%)
AC-13	2.2	≤40
LB-13	4.4	

两种级配的冷补沥青混合料破损率均小于试验规程。从满足使用性能要求及实现的技术难度两方面均衡出发,建议冷补沥青与集料之间的黏聚性试验评价指标为破损率不大于15%。

4 结 语

本文将0号柴油与自主合成的添加剂α制成一种液态制剂,与一定温度的基质沥青混合,制得新型的冷补沥青,简化了制备工艺。并与两种级配拌合得到两种类型冷补沥青混合料,对其初始强度、成型强度、水稳定性、低温性能和黏聚性试验,试验结果均大于规范要求,并根据实验结果提出了相应指标要求。

(1)根据旋转黏度试验、黏附性和初始马歇尔稳定度试验,确定液态制剂类型为B型,最佳掺量为14%;得出冷补沥青旋转黏度不大于2.5Pa·s,建议以柴油为稀释剂的冷补沥青黏附性等级不低于5级。

(2)AC-13型冷补沥青混合料比LB-13型冷补沥青混合料的性能较好。AC-13型和LB-13型冷补沥青混合料的马歇尔初始稳定度分别达到3.24kN和2.46kN,马歇尔成型稳定度分别为5.63kN和4.88kN,建议冷补沥青初始稳定度不小于2.5kN,成型稳定度不小于4.5kN;残留稳定度分别为81.2%和75.6%,建议冷补沥青混合料的残留稳定度应不小于75%;破坏应变分别为2515$\mu\varepsilon$和2342$\mu\varepsilon$,破坏应变应不小于2000με；黏聚性试验破损率仅为2.2%和4.4%，建议冷补沥青与集料之间的黏聚性试验评价指标为破损率不大于15%。

参考文献

［1］ H. O, B. G, A. G. A Fast Pothole Repair Method Using Asphalt Tiles and Induction Heating［J］. Construction and Building Materials,2017,131:269-274.
［2］ 刘凯迪.冷补沥青混合料与旧路面界面黏结特性研究［D］.哈尔滨:哈尔滨工业大学,2019.
［3］ Litao G, Qian X, Xiaoxia Y, et al. Laboratory performance evaluation of a cold patching asphalt material containing cooking waste oil［J］. Construction and Building Materials,2020,246.
［4］ 刘晓文.冷补沥青混合料研究［D］.广州:华南理工大学,2010.
［5］ 张新天,高金歧.沥青路面冷补材料与应用技术的研究［J］.北京建筑工程学院学报,2004(01):22-27.
［6］ 耿立涛,王丽艳,姜成岭,等.溶剂型冷补沥青及冷补沥青混合料的性能评价［J］.建筑材料学报,2019:1-11.
［7］ Cho Y S, Lin F B. Integrity Analysis of Single and Multi-layer Thin Cement Mortar Slab Structures Using the Spectral Analysis of Surface Wave NDT Method［J］. Construction & Building Materials,2000,14(8):387-395.
［8］ L. E C, A. M, E. A, et al. Modelling of the Performance of Asphalt Pavement Using Response Surface Methodology—the Kinetics of the Aging［J］. Building and Environment,2005,42(2).
［9］ 张争奇,王素青,路国栋,等.水性环氧冷补沥青的性能与制备工艺［J］.建筑材料学报,2018,21(05):848-854.
［10］ 谭忆秋,周水文,单丽岩,等.抗冻型冷补沥青混合料优化设计及性能研究［J］.建筑材料学报,2014,17(01):89-94.
［11］ 张争奇,许铖,成高立,等.溶剂型冷补沥青液研制及其沥青混合料路用性能研究［J］.铁道科学与工程学报,2016,13(09):1728-1736.
［12］ 李峰,黄颂昌,徐剑,等.冷补沥青混合料性能评价及技术要求［J］.同济大学学报(自然科学版),2010,38(10):1463-1467.
［13］ 林科杰,弥海晨,向豪,等.沥青路面快速修复用单组分树脂冷补料性能研究［J］.硅酸盐通报,2020,39(05):1585-1593.
［14］ 孟文专,杨亮,夏智,等.冷补沥青混合料的制备及其性能［J］.武汉工程大学学报,2011,33(10):49-53.
［15］ 徐文,汪美慧,罗蓉,等.冷补沥青的材料设计及其混合料性能研究［J］.武汉理工大学学报(交通科学与工程版),2018,42(06):1049-1054.
［16］ Saadoon T, Garcia A, Gomez-Meijide B. Dynamics of water evaporation in cold asphalt mixtures［J］. Materials & Design,2017,134(nov.):196-206.
［17］ 宋建生,吕伟民.储存式沥青混合料组成设计的研究［J］.同济大学学报(自然科学版),1998(06):3-5.
［18］ 段炎红.高寒区缓粘型沥青缓粘特点及机理研究［D］.西安:长安大学,2013.
［19］ 陈新,丁立.双指标评价沥青混合料抗水损害性能［J］.公路,2005:18-29.

Evaluating the Relationship between Internal Structure and Moisture Damage of Fiber-reinforced Steel Slag Asphalt Mixture

Wenzhen Wang   Aiqin Shen   Ziming He   Lusheng Wang

(Chang'an University)

Abstract   To improve the early-age moisture susceptibility, three fibers (Basalt Fiber, Polyester Fiber, and Lignin Fiber) were blended to the steel slag asphalt mixture (SSAM). X-ray computed tomography was employed to obtain images on the Marshall specimen and image processing technology was used to identify the internal pore structure. Then, an indirect tensile strength ratio (TSR) of wet-to dry-conditioned core samples was determined in the laboratory and used as a moisture damage potential parameter. Additionally, the inherent correlations among the pore structure and moisture stability were analyzed. Based on the research, the addition of fiber, as well as steel slag improve the moisture damage resistance of the SSAM. Besieds, linear regression analysis indicates that air voids had a significant correlation with the moisture damage. Furthermore, SEM analysis validates the improvement of fiber and steel slag on moisture damage of asphalt mixture.

Keywords   Steel slag asphalt mixture   Moisture stability   X-ray computed tomography   Internal pore structure

0 Introduction

In recent years, researchers have begun to consider the application of steel slag to asphalt pavement[1]. Some scholars hold the opinions that steel slag asphalt mixture is a good pavement material with good resistance to permanent deformation[2], and fatigue cracking[3], excellent wear resistance[4] and anti-slip performance[5]. However, steel slag is different from ordinary aggregates, and its surface is rich in pores, thus water is more likely to invade especially when the asphalt concrete pavement is in service in harsh weather[6]. Fiber-reinforced asphalt mixture technology is currently the effective material technology for improving mechanical properties[7]. Currently, the fibers commonly used in pavement construction are Basalt Fiber[8], Polyester Fiber[9], and Lignin Fiber[10]. Some scholars[11,12] compared and summarized the reinforcing principle and preparation method of conventional fiber. Although several studies have indicated that fiber palys an important role in moisture stability, but little attention has been paid to the interaction between fiber and steel slag on moisture stability.

Air voids play a significant role in influencing the performance of asphalt mixtures[13,14]. At present, some scholars used X-ray computed tomography technology to obtain the three-dimensional digital images[15,16], and the digital image analysis technology was used to capture the air void structure of asphalt mixture[17], while Banadaki et al.[18] based on the finite element and numerical modeling to explore the distribution of air voids. Zhao et al.[19] distinguished the valid and invalid interconnected pores and evaluate the interconnectivity of porous asphalt concrete. However, there are few studies focused on the effect of fiber to improve the air void structure of SSAM, and most of the previous studies do not take in account the effect of internal structure on moisture stability.

The objective of this study is to elucidate the correlations among internal structure and moisture susceptibility of fiber-reinforced steel slag asphalt mixture (FRSSAM). Internal structures were captured based on the X-ray CT and image recognition and processing technology. Moisture susceptibility was measured through the Freeze-thaw test, and the TSR value was performed to assess it. The data were analyzed and the damage changes in air void structure with freeze-thaw cycle have been investigated, the interaction of fiber and steel slag on moisture resistance has been revealed and the relationships between internal structure and moisture susceptibility have been established. The scanning electron microscope (SEM) test technology was used to elaborate the effect of steel slag and fiber on moisture damage of asphalt mixture.

1 Experimentali Materials and Methods

1.1 Materials

In this study, rubber asphalt was used to prepare FRSSAM. The rubber asphalt was prepared by SK A-90# matrix asphalt with 20% rubber powder (30 mesh). The physical properties of rubber asphalt are shown in Tab. 1. Two different aggregates (steel slag and diabase) were used as coarse aggregate. The swelling rate of steel slag after immersion in water reached 1.7%. The physical and mechanical properties of the two aggregates are shown in Tab. 2. In this study, three kinds of fibers commonly used in asphalt mixture were selected for comparative analysis, which were basalt fiber (BF), polyester fiber (PF) and lignin fiber (LF). The physical properties of different fiber are shown in Tab. 3.

Physical Properties of Rubber Asphalt   Tab. 1

Test	Unit	Value	Standard
Penetration (100 g, 5 s, 25°C)	0.1 mm	51.9	ASTM D5/D5M-19
Ductility (5cm/min, 5°C)	cm	13.6	ASTM D113-17
Softening Point	°C	64.7	ASTM D36-14
Brookfield Viscosity (180°C)	Pa·s	2.8	JTG E20 T0625
Elastic Recovery (25°C)	%	80	JTG E20 T0662
Density (15°C)	g/cm^3	1.047	JTG E20 T0603

Physical Properties of Fine and Coarse Aggregate   Tab. 2

Test	Steel Slag		Diabase		Specif-ication Limit	Standard
	9.5~16 (mm)	4.75~9.5 (mm)	9.5~16 (mm)	4.75~9.5 (mm)		
Bulk Specific Gravity (g/m^3)	3.226	3.273	2.925	2.840	—	ASTM C127
Apparent Specific Gravity	3.366	3.437	2.940	2.878	≥2.60	ASTM C127
Crushed Value (%)	11.5		15.3		≤26	JTG F40
Los Angeles Abrasion (%)	12.2		16.7		≤28	ASTM C131
Water Absorption (%)	2.05	1.83	0.6	0.6	≤2	ASTM C127
Flat and Elongated Particle content (%)	7.3	4.7	4.2	5.7	≤12(18)	JTG F40 T0312
Diabase 0~2.36 (mm)						
Apparent Density (g/m^3)	2.756				≥2.50	JTG F40

Note: when particle size > 9.5 mm, the specification limit of flat and elongated particle content is no greater than 12%, otherwise the specification limit is no greater than 18%.

Physical Properties of Different Fibers Tab. 3

Test	Unit	Basalt Fiber (BF)	Polyester Fiber (PF)	Lignin Fiber (LF)
Length	mm	6	6	1
Diameter	μm	13 – 15	13 – 21	—
Color	—	Gold brown or dark brown	White	Gray
Specific Gravity	g/cm^3	2.63 ~ 2.65	1.18	0.8
Melting Point	℃	1050	169	—
Water Absorption	%	< 0.1	2	12 ~ 15
Tensile Strength	MPa	3000	900	< 300
Elastic Modulus	GPa	105	46.3	3.5
Elongation at Break	%	3.1	10 ~ 20	15 ~ 25

Four different asphalt mixtures of the incorporating of steel slag as a partial substitute of coarse aggregate with replacement levels of 30%. While three kinds of fibers was added at 0.4% (BF), 0.2% (PF), and 0.3% (LF), respectively by weight. The SMA-13 type skeleton compact structure was selected and designed according to the specification JTG F40—2004[20]. Fig. 1 shows the aggregate gradations used in this study. All specimens were fabricated with the Marshall compactor by applying 50 blows per side. The properties of FRSSAM are shown in Tab. 4.

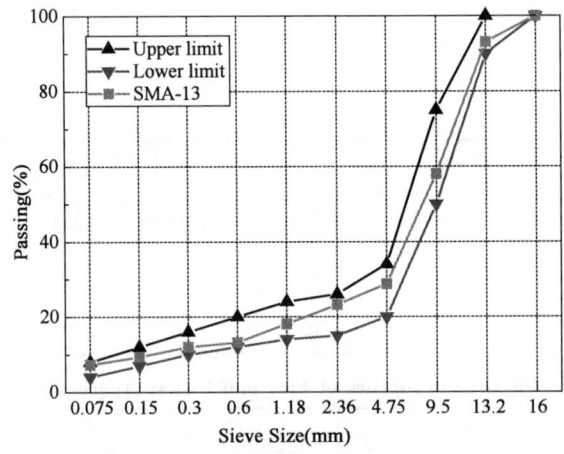

Fig. 1 Aggregates Gradations

Properties of Fiber-reinforced Steel Slag Asphalt Mixture Tab. 4

Fiber Type	OBC (%)	VV (%)	Bulk Specific Gravity (g/cm^3)	VMA (%)	VFA (%)	Stability (kN)
Base	6.40	3.624	2.588	17.30	79.05	9.53
BF	6.62	3.562	2.581	17.69	79.87	12.72
PF	6.53	3.577	2.581	17.65	79.73	12.38
LF	6.67	3.660	2.559	18.45	80.17	11.29

Notes: OBC = Optimal bituminous content, VV = percent air voids in bituminous mixtures, VMA = percent voids in mineral aggregate in bituminous mixtures, VFA = percent voids in mineral aggregate that are filled with asphalt in bituminous mixtures.

1.2 Test Procedure

In this paper, the X-CT spiral cone-beam is used to scan common SSAM and FRSSAM, which can clearly and intuitively display the internal structure of the specimen. After the test is completed, the specimen is subjected to the freeze-thaw damage test and permeability test.

The specimen is scanned every 3 mm from top to bottom using the X-CT technology, and the microstructure parameters of each layer, such as volume content and air voids number, are extracted by the MATLAB program. Fig. 2 shows the process of capturing the air void distribution in an asphalt concrete specimen empolying the X-CT technology and the MATLAB program.

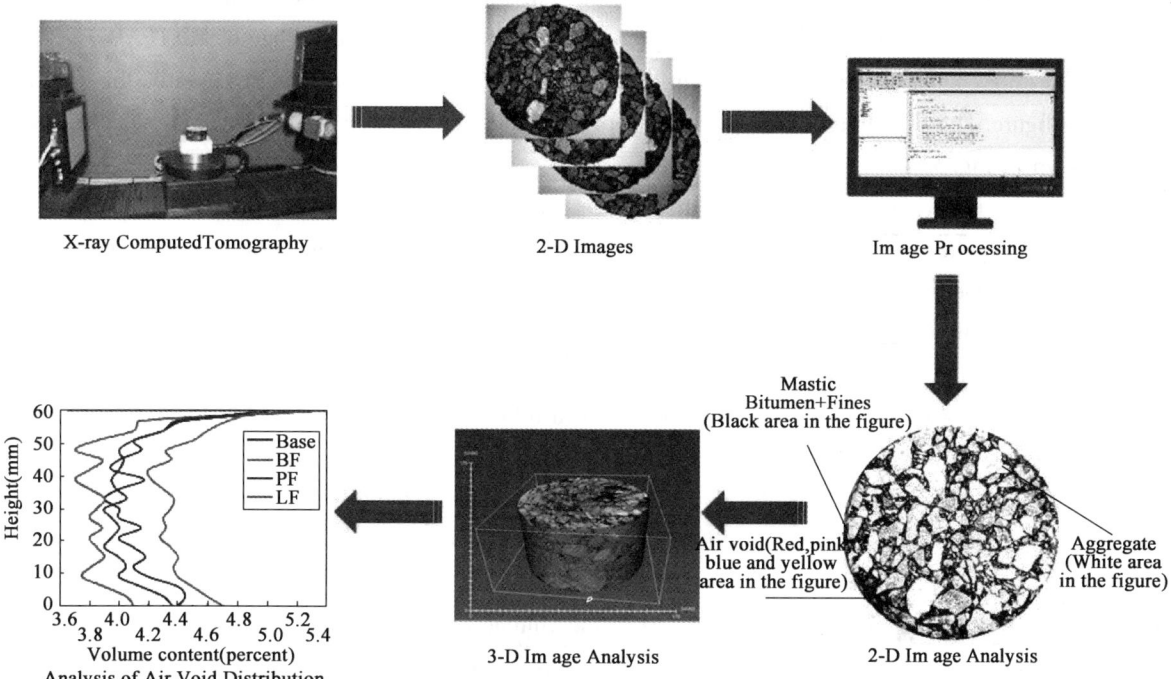

Fig. 2 The Process of Capturing the Air Void Distribution in Asphalt Concrete Specimen

The effect of steel slag and the fiber type on the moisture damage resistance of the asphalt mixture was characterized by the freeze-thaw splitting strength ratio (TSR). The freeze-thaw splitting test was carry out according to the specification JTG E20—2011[21]. Specifically, the dry-and wet-conditioned specimens were loaded to fail diametrically. The load was applied at 50 mm/min rate, and the peak value of load was recorded. Then, the indirect tensile strength was determined from Eq. (1).

$$\text{IDT} = \frac{2P}{\pi D h} \tag{1}$$

Where, IDT is the indirect tensile strength (kPa); P is the peak force needed to break the sample diagonally, recorded from the compression testing device (kN); D is the diameter of the specimen (m); h is the height of the speciemn (m). The TSR was calculated by using Eq. (2)

$$\text{TSR} = \frac{IDT_{\text{wet}}}{IDT_{\text{dry}}} \times 100 \tag{2}$$

where, TSR is the freeze-thaw split test strength ratio (%); IDT_{wet} is the average IDT of wet-conditioned specimens after freeze-thaw cycles (MPa); IDT_{dry} is the average IDT of dry-conditioned specimens (MPa).

2 Results and Discussion

2.1 Air Void Parameter of Asphalt Mixture

The volume content is an essential parameter for evaluating the compactness degree of the internal structure of asphalt mixture, and it was usually used to characterize the distribution of air voids inside the mixture. In the study, the wet-conditioned specimens after freeze – thaw cycles were employed to calculate the volume content.

The calculation of volume content is shown in Eq. (3).

$$(VC)_i = \frac{(A_V)_i}{(A_T)_i} \tag{3}$$

Where, VC represent the volume content, %; $i = 1,2,\cdots,N$, N represent the total number of scanned cross-sections; A_v represent the air void area of the image; and A_T are the cross-sectional area of the image. A_v and A_T were obtained based on the digital image processing and analysising technology of MATLAB.

Since the differenceof the volume content in the height range of 60 – 63.5mm varies greatly, this part is not shown in the figure. The distribution of the volume content in a different layer of the specimen after freeze-thaw cycles is shown in Fig. 3.

As shown in Fig. 3, the volume content in different bituminous mixtures exhibit similar distribution characteristics along the height direction. This means the volume content in the middle of the height (10 ~ 50mm) of the specimen is relatively small, while the volume content at both ends of the specimen is large. The volume content of asphalt mixture with basalt fiber is the smallest, while the LF-SSAM obtain a relatively high volume content, which is in corresponding with the design air voids (see Tab. 4). However, after freezing and thawing, the volume content of asphalt mixture increased in different degrees compared to the air voids.

Obviously, the volume content in different bituminous mixtures shows quite difference while volume content of each FRSSAM in different height is also quite different. Among them, the average volume content of LF-SSAM is 12.95% larger than BF-SSAM, but the difference of the air voids in bituminous mixtures between the two is only 2.75%. Moreover, the numerical difference between the air voids in bituminous mixtures and volume content is large. Besides, the addition of BF and PF made volume content as well as the air voids in bituminous mixtures decrease, but the addition of LF made the air voids in bituminous mixtures increase. This many result from the inherent physical properties of BF and PF, namely long length and high tensile strength. In contrast, LF is short and soft, thus there are a large number of fibers in the Marshall specimen, which caused the compaction is not dense.

The void number is a parameter of how much air voids are inside the asphalt mixture. To some extent, it can reflect the process of generating new air voids or interconnected the original air voids inside the asphalt mixture. In the study, the void number was calculated by digital image processing software MATLAB. The distribution of the voids number in a different layer of the specimen is shown in Fig. 4.

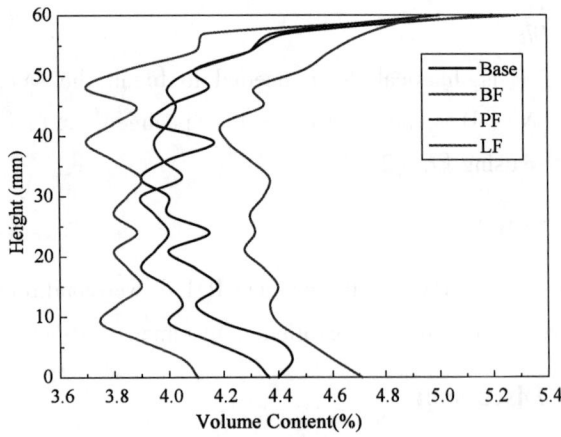

Fig. 3 Vertical Volume Content Distribution of FRSSAM

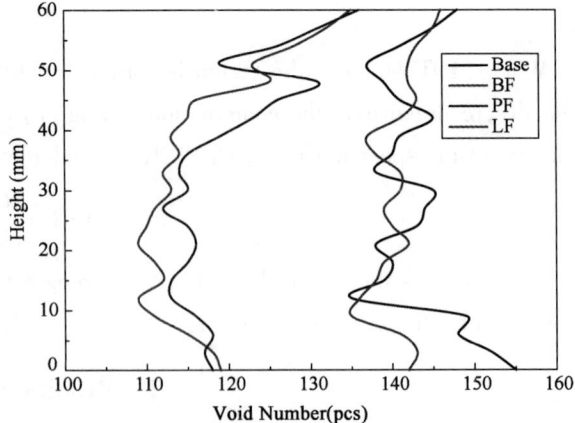

Fig. 4 Vertical Void Mumber Distribution of FRSSAM

Fig. 4 shows the distribution of the voids number in the thickness direction from top to bottom. On the one hand, the distribution of the void number seems chaotic, especially for the base group. On the other hand, it can be seen that the void number of different FRSSAM has a similar pattern along the height direction. Additionally, the asphalt mixture with basalt fiber and polyester fiber presented the less void number than base asphalt mixture. The average void number was 108.65 pcs, 97.7 pcs, 101.85 pcs and 107.23 pcs, respectively, which means that the addition of fibers reduced the number of air voids. This may be because that some small pores are extended under the guidance of the fibers to form large pores.

The average void radius is a parameter that characterizes the size of the air void. In order to evaluate the size of the air voids in the FRSSAM, the concept of the equivalent void radius was introduced [19]. In the study, the air void in the two-dimensional image was approximated as a circle, and the equivalent void radius was obtained by the Eq. (4).

$$\bar{r}_i = \sqrt{\frac{(VC)_i}{M_i}} \times R \qquad (4)$$

Where, r_i is the average void radius of each image (mm); M_i represent the void number of each image (pcs); and the R is the radius of Marshall specimen (mm). The average void radius of the scanned cross-sections is shown in Fig. 5.

As shown in Fig. 5, the equivalent void radius distribution from top to bottom in the thickness direction is somewhat confusing. The overall trend is that the equivalent void radius within the specimen height range of 10~50 mm is relatively small, however the equivalent void radius of the mixture at both ends (0~10 mm, 50~60 mm) was significantly larger, and the equivalent void radius of the four mixtures was 0.943mm, 0.942mm, 0.946mm and 0.925mm, respectively. In addition, there are some convex and concave points in the distribution of void radius, as shown in the Fig. 5, it is clear that there are different protruding parts around 50mm, 42mm, and 10mm. These parts will be the weak points of durability performance of asphalt concrete.

2.2 Moisture Stability of Asphalt Mixture

The tensile strength ratio (TSR) was used to evaluate the moisture stability of the asphalt mixture, the TSR of asphalt mixture with different fiber types are shown in Fig. 6.

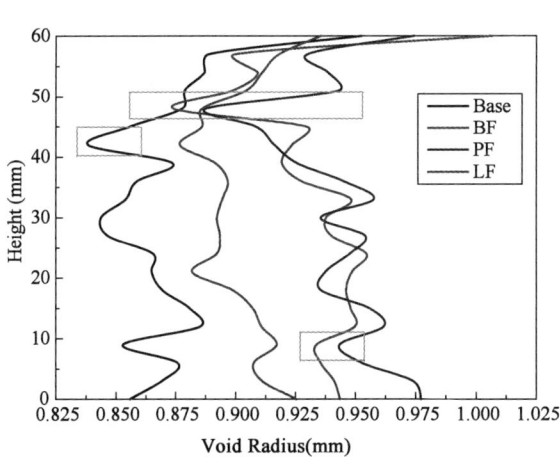
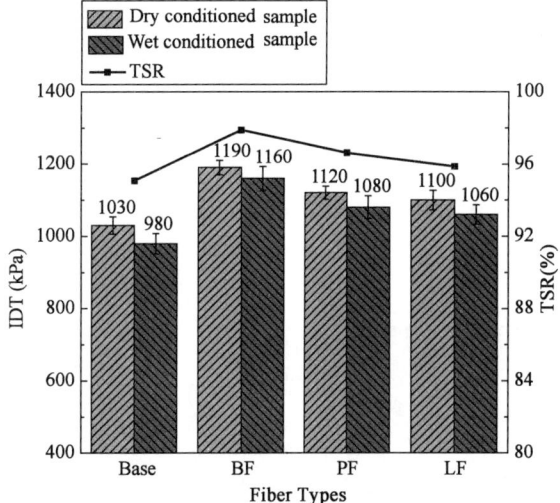

Fig. 5 Vertical Equivalent Void Radius Distribution of FRSSAM

Fig. 6 The TSR Value of FRSSAM

Fig. 6 shows the variation of the indirect tensile strength (IDT) and freeze-thaw splitting tensile strength (TSR) of FRSSAM. It can be seen from the figure that with the addition of fibers, the IDT and TSR of the FRSSAM have different degrees of increase. Taking TSR as an example, the FRSSAM with three fibers increased by 2.96%, 1.62%, and 0.83%, respectively, compared to the unfibered SSAM. This indicated that the addition of fiber has improved the moisture stability of the FRSSAM, and the improvement effect of different fibers has obvious differences. Regardless of the perspective of IDT value or TSR value, the improvement effect of basalt fiber is obviously better than that of polyester fiber and lignin fiber.

2.3 Effect of Internal Structure on Moisture Stability

The area composed of volume content and void number at a different height were calculated to obtain the area of volume content (AVC) and area of void number (AVN), then their effects on moisture damage were discussed. The inherent correlations among the pore structure and moisture stability are shown in Fig. 7.

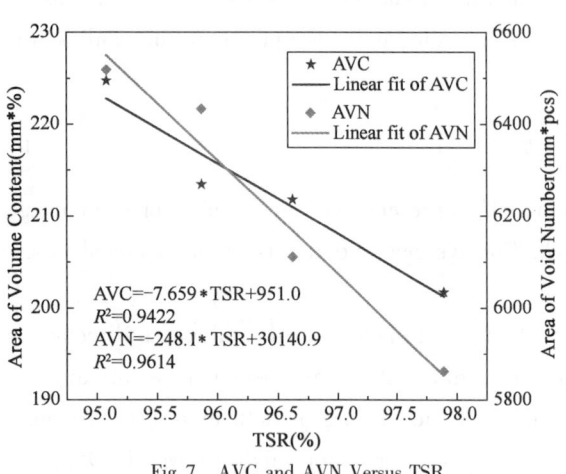

Fig. 7　AVC and AVN Versus TSR

Fig. 7 shows a significant correlation between the area of volume content, the area of void number and the moisture damage, with correlation coefficients of 0.9422 and 0.9614, respectively. For dense-graded asphalt concrete, the effect of water flowing in the void is minimal, but this does not affect the further expansion of some surface existing individual voids, coalescing of two separated air voids, as well as formation of new voids under the action of freeze-thaw cycles. Therefore, to some certain extent, the moisture damage performance of asphalt concrete can be illustrated through the distribution of internal structure.

2.4 Mechanism Analysis

The scanning electron microscope (SEM) test technology was used to obtain the microstructure of steel slag and fiber on asphalt mixture. The adhesion interface between steel slag and fiber asphalt mortar are shown in Fig. 8, and the SEM image of fiber distributed in asphalt mortar are shown in Fig. 9.

Fig. 8　Adhesion Interface Between Steel Slag and Fiber Asphalt Mortar

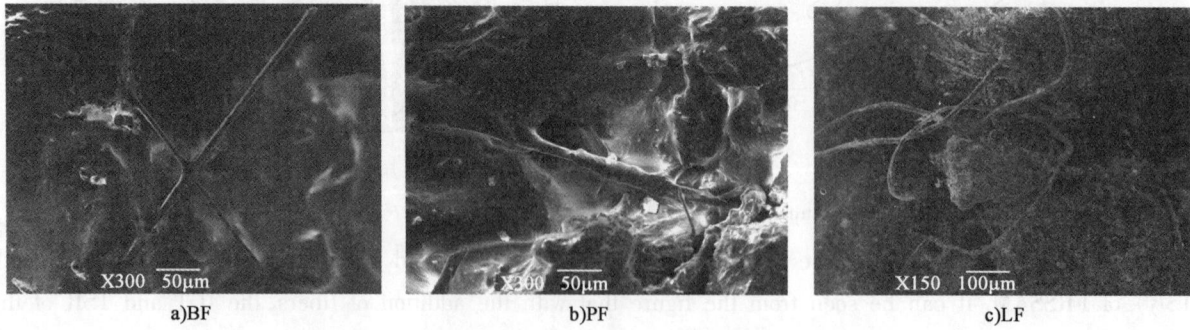

Fig. 9　SEM Image of Fiber Distributed in Asphalt Mortar

Fig. 8 shows that all three types of fiber asphalt mortar reflect great contact with steel slag. As is well known, the steel slag has a complex microstructure and pore structure, thus it form a large contact area with the asphalt. Further, the different fibers will produce a better mechanical interaction force between the asphalt and aggregate. There are obvious interface transition area between steel slag and fiber asphalt mortar, and the contact area are multilateral. The fiber asphalt mortar is evenly wrapped on the surface of steel slag, besides, the deep asphalt embeds in the surface of steel slag can be found which reflect a large effective contact area between asphalt and steel slag. This also indicates that the steel slag have a good adhesion with fiber asphalt mortar.

Fig. 9 shows that fibers are criss-crossed in the asphalt mortar, they form a three – dimensional network structure and the steel slag acts as a filler inside the network. Then the combined effect of fiber and steel slag increases the integrity of the mixture. By comparison, the basalt fiber has a good distribution orientation, and it is pulled in all directions when there is an external force. While the lignin fibers are curved, thus the reinforcement effect of it in the asphalt mortar is relatively weak.

The fiber has a large specific surface area thus many small molecular substances in asphalt are easily absorbed to the fiber surface. Thus the stresses area between asphalt and steel slag is enlarged, improving the ability to resist the destruction from external forces. Meanwhile, asphalt is adsorbed on the surface of the steel slag, thereby the interface bonding performance between the asphalt mortar and the steel slag was improved, and the high cohesion and adhesion is conducive to the reinforcing effect of the fibers. Thus the addition of fiber improves moisture stability of SSAM.

3 Consulations

In this paper, the void structure of FRSSAM was measured through X-CT scanning technology. Based on image processing technology, the volume content and the void number in the specimens were identified and calculated. Subsequently, a freeze-thaw cycle test was carried out to evaluate the moisture damage performance, the correlation between moisture damage and the internal structure were obtained, the following conclusions can be drawn:

(1) The pore structure of different asphalt concretes exhibit the same regularity with the height of the specimen, that is, the middle is generally small and the two sides are large. The addition of fibers significantly improved the air void structure, resulting in different degrees of reduction on volume content and void number, but the effect on the equivalent void radius was not significant.

(2) The incorporation of fibers significantly enhanced the moisture damage performance of the FRSSAM. Although the TSR value of the unfibered SSAM reaches 95.08%, the moisture damage performance of the FRSSAM is enhanced by 2.96%, 1.62%, and 0.83%, respectively after the three types of fiber are incorporated.

(3) According to the correlation analysis, the area composed of the void parameters, ANC and AVN showed a good correlation with the TSR, respectively. Finally, it is recommended that internal structure can be used to characterize the moisture damage performance.

(4) Steel slag have a good adhesion with fiber asphalt mortar and fibers improve the interfacial adhesion property between asphalt and steel slag. The addition of fiber improves moisture stability of SSAM, and the BF has the most significant effect while the curved LF do not work well.

4 Data Availability Statements

All data, models, and code generated or used during the study appear in the submitted article.

5 Conflicts of Interest

No conflict of interest exists in the submission of this manuscript.

6 Acknowledgments

The authors would like to acknowledge the financial support from the Natural Science Basic Research

Project of Shaanxi Province (Grant No. 2017JQ5085).

References

[1] Ma L, Xu D, Wang S, et al[J]. Expansion Inhibition of Steel Slag in Asphalt Mixture by a Surface Water Isolation Structure[J]. Road Materials & Pavement Design, 2019:1-15.

[2] Oluwasola EA, Hainin MR, Aziz MMA. Comparative Evaluation of Dense-graded and Gap-graded Asphalt Mix Incorporating Electric Arc Furnace Steel Slag and Copper Mine Tailings[J]. Journal of Cleaner Production, 2016, 122:315-325.

[3] Jens Groenniger, Augusto, Cannone, et al. Experimental Investigation of Asphalt Mixture Containing Linz-Donawitz Steel Slag[J]. Journal of Traffic and Transportation Engineering, 2017, 4(4):64-71.

[4] Qazizadeh MJ, Farhad H, Kavussi A, et al. Evaluating the Fatigue Behavior of Asphalt Mixtures Containing Electric Arc Furnace and Basic Oxygen Furnace Slags Using Surface Free Energy Estimation[J]. Journal of Cleaner Production, 2018, 188:355-361.

[5] Chen Z, Wu S, Pang L, et al. Function Investigation of Stone Mastic Asphalt (SMA) Mixture Partly Containing basic Oxygen Furnace (BOF) Slag[J]. Journal of Applied Biomaterials and Fundamental Materials, 2016, 14:68-72.

[6] Kyungnam K, Shin HJ, Nakseok K, et al. Characteristics of Hot Mix Asphalt Containing Steel Slag Aggregate According to Temperature and Void Percentage[J]. Construction and Building Materials, 2018, 188:1128-1136.

[7] Klinsky Lmg, Kaloush Ke, Faria Vc, et al. Performance Characteristics of Fiber Modified Hot Mix Asphalt[J]. Construction and Building Materials, 2018, 176:747-752.

[8] Liu Zh, Chen Cy, Qin Rj, et al. Research to Performance of Basalt Fibre Strengthen SBS Modified Asphalt Mixture[J]. Advanced Materials Research, 2012:446-449, 191-195.

[9] Xiong R, Fang JH, Xu AH, Guan BW, et al. Laboratory Investigation on the Brucite Fiber Reinforced Asphalt Binder and Asphalt Concrete[J]. Construction and Building Materials, 2015, 83:44-52.

[10] Zhen F, Shen W, Yue H, et al. Laboratory Evaluation of Pavement Performance Using Modified Asphalt Mixture with a New Composite Reinforcing Material[J]. International Journal of Pavement Research & Technology, 2017, 10(6):507-516.

[11] Abtahi SM, Sheikhzadeh M, Hejazi SM. Fiber-reinforced Asphalt-concrete-A Review. Construction and Building Materials, 2010, 24(6):871-877.

[12] Slebi-Acevedo CJ, Lastra-Gonzalez P, Pascual-Munoz P, et al. Mechanical Performance of Fibers in Hot Mix Asphalt: A Review[J]. Construction and Building Materials, 2019, 200:756-769.

[13] Wang H, Li H, Liang X, et al. Investigation on the Mechanical Properties and Environmental Impacts of Pervious Concrete Containing Fly Ash Based on the Cement-aggregate Ratio[J]. Construction and Building Materials, 2019, 202:387-95.

[14] Tarefder RA, Ahmad M. Evaluating the Relationship between Permeability and Moisture Damage of Asphalt Concrete Pavements[J]. Journal of Materials in Civil Engineering, 2015, 27(5).

[15] Zhang Y, Verwaal W, Ven MFCVD, et al. Using High-resolution Industrial CT Scan to Detect the Distribution of Rejuvenation Products in Porous Asphalt Concrete[J]. Construction and Building Materials, 2015, 100:1-10.

[16] Zhou H, Li H, Abdelhady A, Liang X, et al. Experimental Investigation on the Effect of Pore Characteristics on Clogging Risk of Pervious Concrete based on CT Scanning[J]. Construction and Building Materials, 2019, 212:130-139.

[17] Zelelew HM, Almuntashri A, Agaian S, et al. An Improved Image Processing Technique for Asphalt

Concrete X-ray CT Images[J]. Road Materials & Pavement Design,2013,14(2):341-359.
[18] Banadaki AD, Guddati MN, Kim YR. An Algorithm for Virtual Fabrication of Air Voids in Asphalt Concrete[J]. International Journal of Pavement Engineering,2016,17(3):225-232.
[19] Zhao Y,Wang X,Jiang J,et al. Characterization of Interconnectivity, Size Distribution and Uniformity of Air Voids in Porous Asphalt Concrete Using X-ray CT Scanning Images[J]. Construction and Building Materials,2019,213:182-193.
[20] Ministry of Transport of the People's Republic of China. Technical Specifi Cations for Construction Highway Asphalt Pavements:JTG F40—2004[S]. Beijing:China Communications Press,2004.
[21] Ministry of Transport of the People's Republic of China. Standard Test Methods of Bitumen and Bituminous Mixtures for Highway Engineering:JTG E20—2011[S]. Beijing:China Communications Press,2011.

温度及老化时间对沥青混合料抗疲劳性能影响的试验研究

张金喜[1] 张阳光[2] 韩丁丁[3] 褚永昌[2] 郭旺达[2]

(1.北京市城市交通运行保障工程技术研究中心(北京工业大学);2.北京工业大学城市交通学院;
3.交通运输部公路科学研究院)

摘 要 沥青路面在寿命周期内需要经历多次不同温度场的作用,温度是影响沥青混合料抗疲劳性能的重要因素之一。本次研究通过采用SBS改性沥青的AC-25沥青混合料分别在-10℃、15℃以及25℃三种温度条件与0d、3d以及5d三种老化时间下进行间接拉伸疲劳试验,研究温度与老化程度对沥青混合料抗疲劳性能的影响。试验结果表明在相同的小应力水平下,随着温度的降低,两种沥青混合料受应力的敏感性随之增加,疲劳寿命亦随之增加;在相同的试验温度与较小的应力水平下,随着老化程度的加深,两种沥青混合料的疲劳寿命均随着老化程度的加深而呈现出一定的增长趋势。

关键词 沥青混合料 疲劳寿命 温度 老化时间

0 引 言

沥青路面与水泥混凝土路面结构相比,具有施工工艺简单,施工速度快,质量容易控制,平整度好,抗滑性能好和行车噪声低等优点[1],因此沥青路面也成为我国高等级公路及城市道路的主要路面形式。截至2018年底,我国公路养护里程达475.78万km,占公路总里程98.2%[2]。沥青路面在投入使用之后,经过一段时间行车荷载及自然因素的双重作用,路面抗疲劳性能下降,路面往往会出现裂缝、车辙、坑槽、拥包等路面病害,使得路面的路用性能降低,使用寿命减少,不仅严重影响行车安全,而且增加养护维修的费用[3-4]。因此,提升沥青路面的抗疲劳性能,对提高沥青路面的使用年限和路用性能,提高行车安全具有重要的意义。

有研究显示,沥青路面抗疲劳性能的降低主要是由于长期行车荷载的反复加载以及恶劣环境对沥青混合料各组分性能的影响[5-6]。环境是影响沥青混合料疲劳性能的最大不确定因素,不同的温度以及不同的老化时间下沥青混合料的各组分性能以及整体抗疲劳性能都会有巨大的差别。瞿鑫等人通过直接拉伸疲劳试验得到随着温度的升高,沥青混合料模量降低,在应力控制条件下,疲劳寿命会减小[7]。葛折圣等人通过正交设计的方法得出试验温度对沥青混合料的疲劳寿命影响较显著,仅次于荷载间歇时间的影响程度[8]。吕松涛、刘晓彤等人的研究表明,老化越严重,在相同的应力比下其疲劳寿命越短,且其疲劳寿命对应力比变化的敏感程度也越显著[9-10]。秦旻等人的研究表明,温度升高会使沥青混合料的抗疲劳特性减弱[11]。陈瑞璞、王海燕等人研究发现老化作用显著削弱了沥青混合料的抗疲劳性能[12-13]。

本文在前人沥青混合料抗疲劳性能研究的基础上,通过控制试验温度以及老化时间,分别研究温度或者老化时间单一因素作用下对沥青混合料疲劳特性的影响,得到沥青混合料疲劳曲线,得到不同因素下沥青混合料的抗疲劳性能。

1 试验材料及方法

本次研究采用间接拉伸疲劳试验方法,将制备好的沥青混合料在三种试验温度以及不同老化时间条件下测量其疲劳寿命,通过对比,研究不同温度条件及老化时间下沥青混合料的抗疲劳性能,分析温度和老化时间对沥青混合料疲劳寿命的影响。

1.1 试验材料及设备

试验中所用到的试验材料见表1。由于在目前道路的养护过程中使用改性沥青的较多,因此选用SBS改性沥青为研究种类。试验设备采用UTM-100伺服试验机。AC-25沥青混合料采用Superpave配合比设计方法,级配曲线如图1所示。

试 验 材 料　　　　　　　　　　　　　　　　表1

编　号	沥青种类	级配类型	矿料来源	添加剂类型
①	SBS改性沥青	AC-25	河北三河石灰岩	木质素纤维

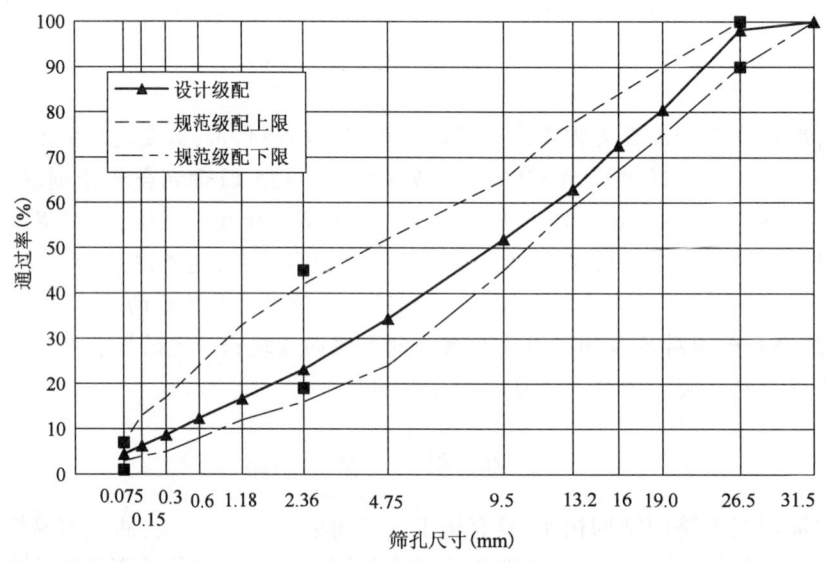

图1　AC-25级配曲线

经检测本次研究所采用各项原材料以及各项技术指标均符合《公路沥青路面施工技术规范》(JTG E20—2011)的技术要求。根据试验要求和技术规范,制备AC-25沥青混合料,最佳油石比为3.9%。

1.2 试验方法

本文对不同沥青混合料的抗疲劳特性的研究采用的方法是间接拉伸疲劳试验法。主要通过两部分试验来研究不同温度以及不同老化时间对沥青混合料疲劳性能的影响。具体试验方案如下:

(1)老化试验:沥青混合料的老化试验,本文依据JTG E20—2011试验规程中T0734—2000热拌沥青混合料加速老化试验方法完成。此方法用于模拟沥青混合料的短期老化及长期老化过程,试件的长期老化前必须先经过松散混合料的短期老化,短期老化在135℃±3℃的烘箱中进行,在强制通风条件下加热4h±5min。结合本文的研究内容,本次试验长期老化时间采用0d、3d以及5d三个时间。

(2)间接拉伸疲劳试验:疲劳试验采用UTM-100伺服试验机进行。疲劳试验前需进行劈裂试验,试验方法参照 JTG E20—2011 试验规程进行操作。疲劳试验过程中设定试验参数分别为:选择试验温度为 $-10℃$、$15℃$、$25℃$；试验荷载加载时间为 100ms；加载波形为半正弦波，相邻波形间歇时间为 100ms。控制模式为应力控制，确定应力水平分别为 0.3、0.5、0.7。

2 沥青混合料间接拉伸疲劳试验结果

2.1 沥青混合料劈裂试验

按照试验流程，在进行间接拉伸疲劳试验前需要先进行劈裂实验，将 AC-25 沥青混合料在 $-10℃$、$15℃$、$25℃$ 三种试验温度以及 0d、3d、5d 三种老化时间下进行劈裂实验，试验结果见表 2。

沥青混合料劈裂试验结果汇总　　　　表 2

温　　度	混合料类型	P_{Tmax}(kN)	Y_T(mm)	P_T(kN)	Y_{Tmax}(mm)	R_{Tmax}(kPa)	X_T(mm)
25℃	AC-25 0d	7.2	3.15	5.23	3.96	700.5	0.74
	AC-25 3d	7.6	3.09	4.70	4.11	736.4	0.77
	AC-25 5d	7.8	2.72	4.46	4.23	755.8	0.80
15℃	AC-25 0d	11.7	2.79	8.52	4.47	1133.2	0.71
	AC-25 3d	12.6	2.52	7.87	4.78	1220.5	0.76
	AC-25 5d	13.4	2.37	7.34	4.46	1304.0	0.71
-10℃	AC-25 0d	28.8	2.40	3.09	3.15	2795.8	0.46
	AC-25 3d	29.0	2.37	3.15	2.81	2812.3	0.41
	AC-25 5d	33.3	2.32	3.02	2.55	2934.4	0.37

劈裂试验中，劈裂强度 R_T、水平方向位移 X_T 等参数计算公式如下：

$$R_T = \frac{0.006287 P_T}{h} \tag{1}$$

$$X_T = \frac{Y_T \times (0.135 + 0.5\mu)}{1.794 - 0.0314\mu} \tag{2}$$

式中：R_T——劈裂抗拉强度，MPa；
　　　μ——泊松比，根据试验温度于表 3 中选用；
　　　h——试件高度，mm；
　　　P_T——试验结束时荷载值，N；
　　　Y_T——试验荷载的最大值对应的位移，mm。

不同温度下劈裂试验泊松比取值　　　　表 3

试验温度(℃)	30	25	20	15	≤10
泊松比 μ 值	0.45	0.40	0.35	0.30	0.25

2.2 沥青混合料疲劳试验

沥青混合料的疲劳试验以 AC-25 在 3d 老化时间下 25℃ 时的劈裂强度为基准，对应三种温度下选择的泊松比由低温到高温分别为 0.3、0.5、0.7，应力水平分别为 221kPa、368kPa、515kPa。同理，可以得到沥青混合料在三种温度不同老化程度下的应力水平。沥青混合料的疲劳寿命结果见表 4 与表 5。

在试验温度为 $-10℃$ 时，AC-25 沥青混合料对应应力为 844kPa，此时的疲劳寿命大于 150000，则认为在该应力水平下沥青混合料不发生疲劳破坏，增加沥青混合料在 1266kPa（对应泊松比为 0.45）应力水平下的疲劳试验，记录试验结果见表 5。

25℃与15℃时沥青混合料不同老化时间下的疲劳寿命　　　　　　　　　　　　　　　　　　　　　表4

项　　目		25℃		15℃	
混合料类型	老化时间	应力水平(kPa)	平均N_f值	应力水平(kPa)	N_f均值
改性AC-25	0d	221	14601	366	24321
		368	1321	610	2161
		515	281	854	341
	3d	221	34281	366	48841
		368	2681	610	3201
		515	501	854	581
	5d	221	47441	366	62481
		368	3281	610	5041
		515	761	854	801

-10℃时沥青混合料在不同老化时间下的疲劳寿命　　　　　　　　　　　　　　　　　　　　　表5

混合料类型	老化时间	应力水平(kPa)	均　　值
改性AC-25	0d	844	>150000
		1266	46241
		1406	27281
		1969	2481
	3d	844	>150000
		1266	68141
		1406	30561
		1969	3021
	5d	844	>150000
		1266	139001
		1406	47601
		1969	6881

3　试验结果分析

温度与老化程度是影响沥青混合料的重要外界因素,分别固定试验结果中的温度与老化时间,结合沥青混合料疲劳寿命绘制疲劳曲线,分析不同温度与老化时间对沥青混合料疲劳寿命的影响。

3.1　老化时间对沥青混合料疲劳性能的影响

固定试验中温度因素,仅考虑老化时间对AC-25沥青混合料疲劳性能的影响,根据试验结果将三种温度下的AC-25疲劳寿命汇总,绘制疲劳寿命曲线如图2所示。

由图2可知,在三种温度下,随着老化时间的增加,AC-25的疲劳曲线均呈现出不同程度的向上侧偏移的趋势,其中老化3d时疲劳曲线偏移量最大,说明在试验中,在同一温度下随着老化程度的增加,AC-25的疲劳寿命亦随之增加。

在图2中,每张图中三条疲劳曲线分别为沥青混合料在老化时间0d、3d以及5d状态下试验得到的。在25℃与-10℃条件下,不同老化时间下的疲劳曲线斜率随着老化时间的增加而增大,表明AC-25对应力的敏感性随着老化程度的增加而增加。同时,随着老化程度的加深,疲劳曲线的截距也随之增加,表明AC-25疲劳寿命有所增加。在15℃疲劳曲线中,随着应力比的增大,老化时间分别为3d与5d的疲劳曲线出现相交,最后与老化时间0d也相交。表明在较大的应力比下,老化5d的沥青混合料疲劳寿命小于老化3d的。在25℃与-10℃疲劳曲线中随着应力比的增大,不同老化程度下的AC-25疲劳曲线也呈现出相交趋势。表明在短期老化的情况下,沥青混合料的抗疲劳性能会有所增加。但是随着老化程度的加剧,AC-25 不但对应力的敏感性增加,而且越深的老化程度下,在高应力水平下,其抗疲劳性能急剧下降。从疲劳曲线中可看出在三个温度下老化 3d 与未老化的曲线相比向上偏移量比老化 5d 与老化 3d 的偏移量要大,说明在老化过程中,前期的老化对于疲劳寿命的增加效果要好于后期的老化,随着老化时间的增加,疲劳寿命的增加将会越来越少,到最后甚至会出现抗疲劳性能的急剧下降。

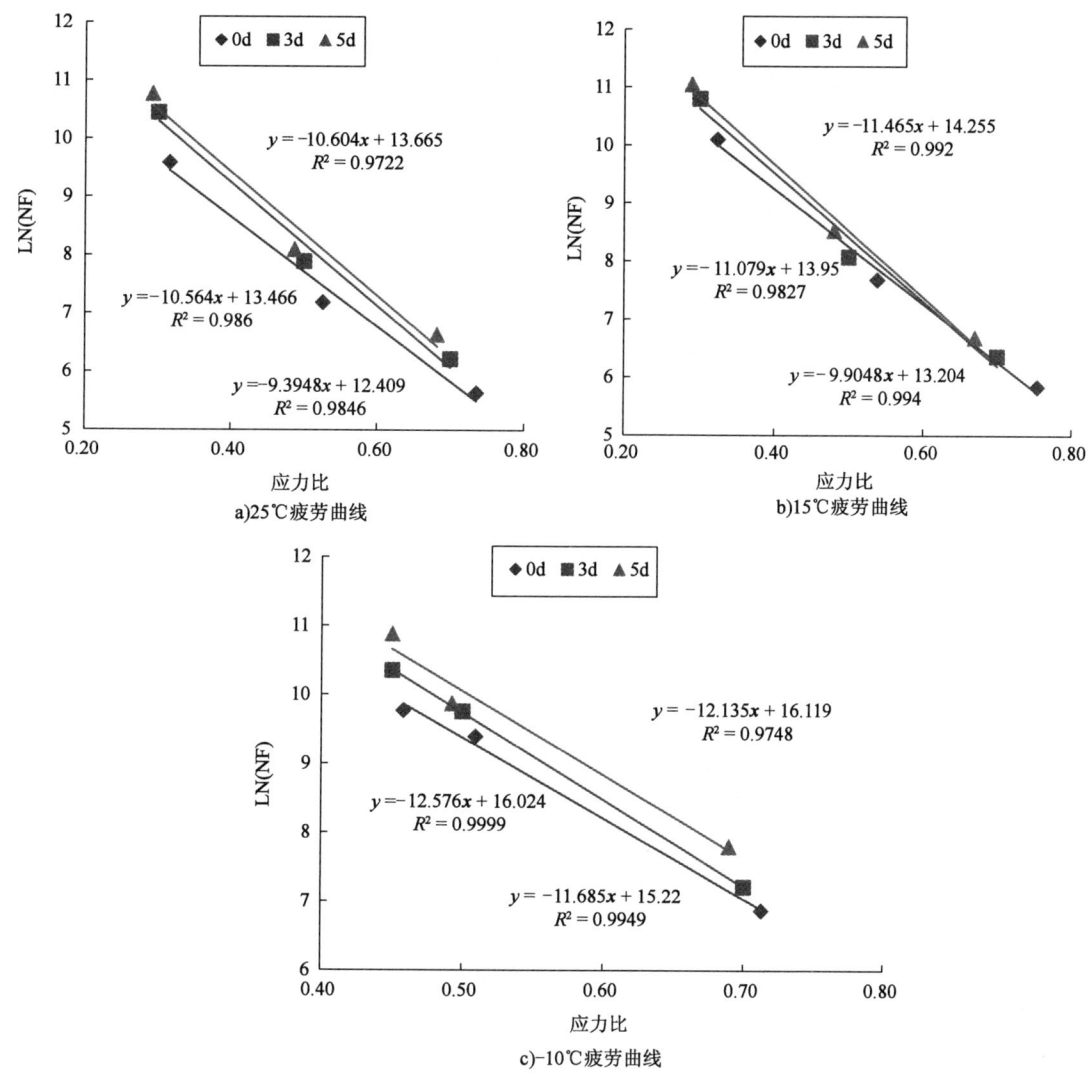

图 2 不同老化时间下 AC-25 疲劳曲线

3.2 温度对沥青混合料疲劳性能的影响

固定试验中老化时间因素,仅考虑温度对 AC-25 沥青混合料疲劳性能的影响,将三种老化程度下的 AC-25 疲劳寿命汇总,绘制疲劳寿命曲线如图 3 所示。

由图 3 可知,在相同的老化程度下,随着温度的降低,AC-25 沥青混合料的疲劳曲线向上侧偏移,表明随着温度的降低,AC-25 抗疲劳性能有一定增加的趋势。在图 3 中可以看出在相同老化程度下,随着温度的降低,疲劳曲线的斜率 K 逐渐增大,表明随着温度的降低,沥青混合料对应力的敏感性增加,同时疲劳曲线的截距亦随之增加,说明 AC-25 在小应力比条件下随着温度的降低,疲劳寿命有所增加。在图 3b)与图 3c)中可以看出随着应力比的增加,25℃与 15℃条件下的疲劳曲线有相交的趋势,-10℃下的疲劳曲线亦有较大的下降幅度。表明在较高的应力比下,AC-25 对应力的敏感性随着温度的增加而降低,抗疲劳性能也有增加的趋势。

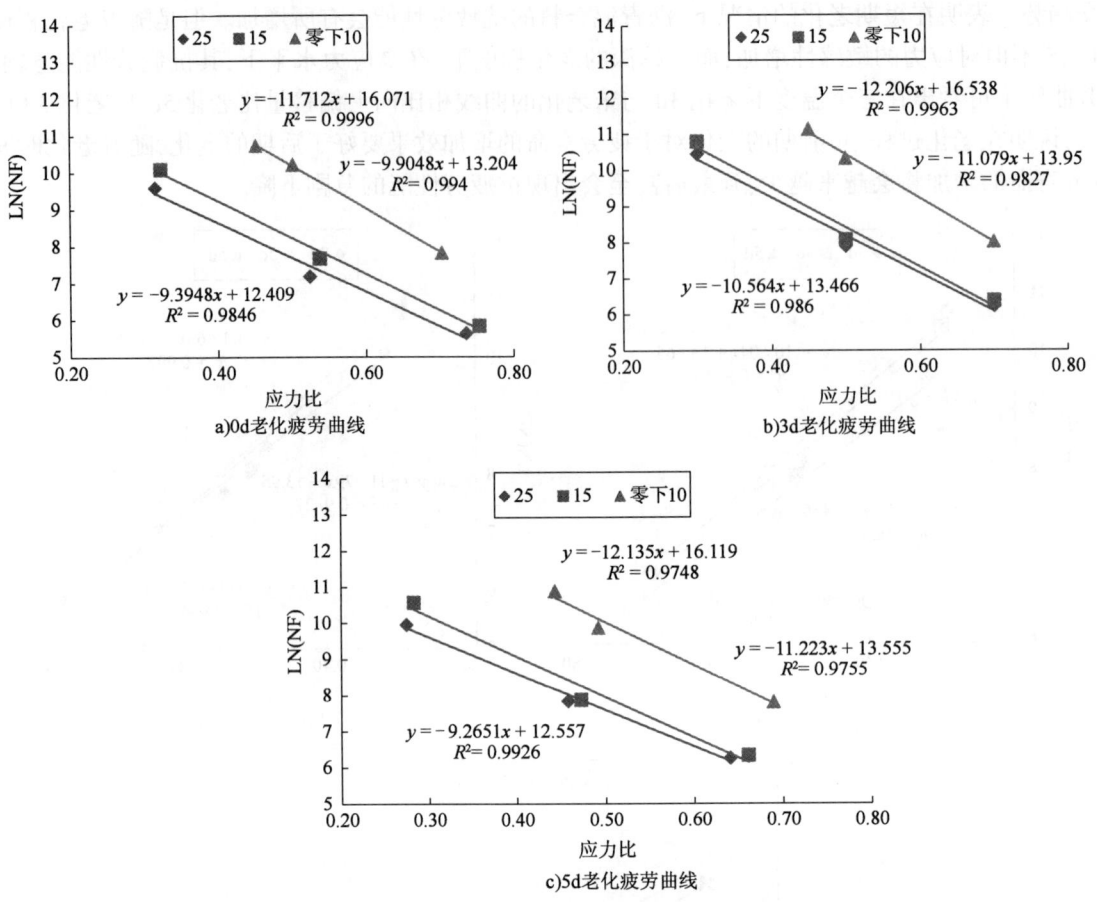

图3 不同温度条件下 AC-25 疲劳曲线

4 结　语

沥青路面的耐久性除了受自身材料因素的影响外,温度与老化程度也是影响沥青混合料抗疲劳性能的重要因素,本文以 AC-25 为试验对象,分别研究温度与老化程度对沥青混合料抗疲劳性能的影响,本次试验研究表明：

(1)在小应力比条件下,AC-25 沥青混合料在相同的温度环境中,随着老化程度的加深,其对应力的敏感性增加,抗疲劳性能有所增加;老化时间越长,沥青混合料受应力水平影响越大。

(2)在小应力比条件下,AC-25 沥青混合料在相同的老化时间里,随着温度的降低,其对应力的敏感性增加,抗疲劳性能有所增加;低温环境中,沥青混合料的疲劳性能受应力水平的影响较大。

(3)在较大的应力比条件下,相同的温度环境下 AC-25 的抗疲劳性能随着老化程度的增加而降低;在相同的老化时间下 AC-25 的抗疲劳性能随着温度的降低而降低。

参考文献

[1] 郝宝峰.高速公路沥青路面常见病害成因与防治分析[J].山西建筑,2019,45(2):127-128.
[2] 中华人民共和国交通运输部门户网站.2017年交通运输行业发展统计公报[2018-03-30]http://zizhan.mot.gov.cn/zfxxgk/bnssj/zhghs/201803/t20180329_3005087.html.
[3] 尹蕊,王治,王连伟.公路路面病害成因分析及防治措施[J].南建材,2018(5):73-76.
[4] 安建霞.城市道路沥青路面病害防治方法[J].交通世界,2018,463(13):8-9.
[5] 周亮,凌建明,林小平.考虑环境因素的沥青路面疲劳开裂预估模型[J].中国公路学报,2013,26(006):47-52.
[6] Jiangmiao Y. Evaluation of Environmental Factors to Fatigue Performance of Asphalt Mixes[J]. 东南大学

学报(英文版),2005.
[7] 瞿鑫,田小革,栾利强,等.沥青混合料疲劳寿命及其影响因素研究[J].中外公路,2010(5):266-269.
[8] 葛折圣,黄朝晖,黄晓明.沥青混合料疲劳性能的影响因素分析[J].公路交通科技,2002,19(6):1-4.
[9] 吕松涛.老化对沥青混合料疲劳性能的影响[J].科技信息,2012,000(001):67-68.
[10] 刘晓彤,李翔,徐洋,等.不同老化方式下沥青混合料疲劳性能研究[J].石油沥青,2018,32(05):42-48.
[11] 秦旻,梁乃兴,陆兆峰.水-温作用下沥青混合料疲劳性能分析[J].中南大学学报(自然科学版),2011,42(4):1126-1132.
[12] 陈瑞璞,崔亚楠,冯蕾.老化作用下沥青混合料的疲劳及自愈合性能[J/OL].建筑材料学报. http://kns.cnki.net/kcms/detail/31.1764.TU.20181025.1619.002.html.
[13] 王海燕,王延海.老化对沥青路面疲劳性能的影响[J].华东公路,2016(4):65-67.

Experimental Study on Optimum Asphalt Content of Basalt Fiber Asphalt Mixtures Considering Fine Aggregates Reduction

Yao Zhang　Yuhao Wu　Bangwei Wu　Peng Xiao　Haochen Wu

(Yangzhou University, College of Civil Science and Engineering)

Abstract　The use of basalt fiber can effectively improve the pavement performance of asphalt mixtures, but the asphalt content will be increased with the addition of basalt fiber. This may make a higher cost of pavement construction, which seriously impacts the application of basalt fiber asphalt mixture. This study aims to reduce the optimum asphalt content of basalt fiber asphalt mixture by optimizing the gradation design. The fine aggregate content in the basalt fiber asphalt mixture is adjusted based on the calculation of the average asphalt film thickness. After adjustment, the high-temperature stability, low-temperature crack resistance and moisture stability of basalt fiber asphalt mixtures are performed. The result shows that the best asphalt-aggregate ratio of asphalt mixture with a maximum nominal sieve size of 13 mm is 4.7%, and the best asphalt-aggregate ratio is 4.9% after adding 0.3% basalt fiber with a length of 6 mm. Comparative test results indicate that the optimum asphalt content of basalt fiber asphalt mixtures with less fine aggregate content can be reduced by 0.2% to 0.4%. And the penetration strength is slightly reduced by 2.42% compared with the original basalt fiber asphalt mixture. The low-temperature crack resistance and moisture stability performance also have a small decrease. But compared with the asphalt mixture without basalt fiber, the performance still improves significantly. Based on a slight influence on the performance of basalt fiber asphalt mixture, the optimum asphalt content is reduced through optimized gradation design, which greatly saves the pavement construction cost. This will be of great significance to the promotion of using basalt fiber asphalt mixture.

Keywords　Basalt fiber asphalt mixture　Optimum asphalt content　Gradation design　Average asphalt film thickness　Pavement performance

0　Introduction

At present, Chinese investment in road construction is increasing, and the requirements for its performance are getting higher and higher. Since the addition of basalt fiber can effectively improve the road performance of asphalt mixture (Huang et al., 2020), the basalt fiber has been vigorously promoted in road and pavement construction. Li et al. (2020) found that by adding 0.4% and 0.3% basalt fibers to AC-13 and AC-20, the low-temperature performance of asphalt-mixtures can be significantly improved. Lou et al. (2020) added different lengths of basalt fiber to the asphalt mixture and found that the crack resistance and high-temperature performance of the asphalt mixture has been enhanced.

In addition to the improvement of road performance, domestic and foreign scholars have also investigated the influence of basalt fiber on the optimal asphalt aggregate ratio of asphalt mixture (Hu, 2015). The addition of basalt fiber will greatly affect the size of the optimal asphalt-aggregate ratio (Cheng et al., 2019). Wang et al. (2018) established a mathematical model of basalt fiber reinforced SBS modified asphalt mixture. It was confirmed that the blending of basalt fiber and the asphalt-aggregate ratio increased simultaneously. Cheng (2018) found that as the content of basalt fiber in the asphalt mixture increases from 0% to 0.5%, the optimal asphalt aggregate ratio corresponding to the asphalt mixture also increases from 5.03% to 5.42%. With the incorporation of basalt fiber, the fiber itself will be coated with a certain amount of asphalt, resulting in a larger area where the asphalt needs to be in contact with the package, and ultimately increasing the optimal asphalt aggregate ratio. This greatly increases the cost of road construction and seriously affects the popularization and use of basalt fiber in the asphalt mixture.

At present, scholars have researched the influence of the thickness of the gradation and the ratio of coarse and fine aggregate in the gradation (Li et al., 2005) on the optimal asphalt aggregate ratio (Chen et al., 2020). Esmaeili (2019) et al. used 3 different materials in of aggregate to design the mix ratio of two different asphalt mixtures. The result show that any change in the gradation and aggregate material would affect the optimal asphalt dosage of asphalt mixture. Zhao (2010) et al. conducted a study on LSPM large-particle porous asphalt mixtures and found that aggregates with a particle size greater than 4.75 mm in the asphalt mixture have little effect on the specific surface area of the aggregates. This leads to the insignificance variation of the asphalt-aggregate ratio. Currently, there are limited studies on adjusting the optimal asphalt-aggregate ratio of basalt fiber asphalt mixture by changing the amount of coarse and fine aggregates in the gradation.

This experimental study aims to propose an adjustment method for fine aggregate content to reduce the optimal asphalt-aggregate ratio without changing the content of basalt fiber. The adjustment needs to meet the requirements of road performance and optimize the design of asphalt mixture gradation. By doing this, the goal of reducing the production and use the cost of basalt fiber asphalt mixture is achieved, and its large-scale promotion has great economic benefits and research value.

1 MATERIALS AND MIX DESIGN

1.1 Asphalt

Styrene-butadiene-styrene (SBS) modified asphalt was used in this study, and its related performance is shown in Tab. 1.

Testing results of SBS modified asphalt Tab. 1

Characteristic	Penetration (25℃)/0.1mm	Penetration Index	Softening point (℃)	Softening point variation(℃)	Ductility (5cm/min, 5℃)(cm)
Requirements	60~80	-0.4~1.0	≥55	≤2.5	≥30
Test results	72	0.5	63	1.5	48

1.2 Aggregate and Mineral Powder

Basalt, limestone aggregate and limestone powder were used in thisstudy. The corresponding performance is shown in Tab. 2 and Tab. 3.

Testing results of aggregate Tab. 2

Aggregate types		Apparent relative density	Gross volume relative density
Basalt	1#(10~15mm)	2.953	2.908
	2#(5~10mm)	2.962	2.902
	3#(3~5mm)	2.902	2.853
Limestone	4#(0~3mm)	2.704	—

Testing results of mineral powder Tab. 3

Technical indicators	Apparent density ($g \cdot cm^{-3}$)	Water content (%)	Hydrophilic coefficient	Granularity range(%)		
				<0.6mm	<0.15mm	<0.075mm
Test results	2.704	0.38	0.60	100	100	92.2
Requirements	≥2.50	≤1.0	<1	100	90~100	75~100

1.3 Basalt Fiber

Chopped 6mm basalt fiber produced by Jiangsu Tianlong Company was used in thisstudy. The performance is shown in Tab. 4.

Testing results of basalt fiber's characteristics Tab. 4

Project	Elongation at break (%)	Breaking strength (MPa)	Heat resistance, fracture strength retention rate(%)	Alkali resistance, fracture strength retention rate(%)
Test results	2.71	2218	93	89
Requirements	≤3.1	≥1200	≥85	≥75

1.4 Mixture Design of AC-13

The asphalt mixturewith nominal maximum sieve size of 13 mm (AC-13) was use in this study, and the grading design results were shown in Tab. 5. The optimal asphalt-aggregate ratio was determined according to the Marshall standard test method. The optimal asphalt-aggregate ratio of the original AC-13 asphalt mixture was 4.7%, and that of a basalt fiber asphalt mixture (BF-AC-13) was 4.9%. In this study, 6mm basalt fiber was used, and the mixing amount was 0.3% of the mass of the asphalt mixture.

Gradation design of AC-13 Tab. 5

Gradation range	Percentage of passing quality(%)									
	16.0	13.2	9.5	4.75	2.36	1.18	0.6	0.3	0.15	0.075
Upper limit	100	100	85	68	50	38	28	20	15	8
Lower limit	100	90	68	38	24	15	10	7	5	4
Median	100	95	76.5	53	37	26.5	19	13.5	10	6
AC-13 (19:33:15:28:5)	100	97.1	83.4	52.2	30.9	23.0	15.7	10.0	8.1	6.3
BF-AC-13 (19:33:15:28:5)	100	97.1	83.4	52.2	30.9	23.0	15.7	10.0	8.1	6.3

2 Adjustment of Fine Materials Dosage Based on Asphalt Film Thickness

2.1 Fine aggregates Dosage Adjustment Methods

Comparing the above-mentioned optimal asphalt-aggregate ratio of AC-13 with and without basalt fiber. Under the same molding conditions, the asphalt mixture incorporation of basalt fiber increases the optimal asphalt-aggregate ratio from 4.7% to 4.9%.

The test reduces the number of fine aggregates in the original gradation to decrease the passing ratio of the sieve size below 2.36mm in the gradation, which makes the aggregate coarser. Thereby the specific surface area of the mineral aggregate is decreased, and finally the optimal asphalt-aggregate ratio is reduced. By doing this, the optimal asphalt-aggregate ratio of BF-AC-13 can be maintained at 4.7% with and without the addition of basalt fiber. Hence, two types of mixtures of BF-AC-13-1 and BF-AC-13-2 are defined after adjusting the amount of fine aggregates. The corresponding gradation is shown in Tab.6.

Gradation design of asphalt mixture with adjustable fine material consumption Tab.6

Gradation range	Percentage of passed quality(%)									
	16.0	13.2	9.5	4.75	2.36	1.18	0.6	0.3	0.15	0.075
Upper limit	100	100	85	68	50	38	28	20	15	8
Lower limit	100	90	68	38	24	15	10	7	5	4
Median	100	95	76.5	53	37	26.5	19	13.5	10	6
BF-AC-13-1 (19:33.5:15:28:4.5)	100	97.1	83.4	51.7	30.4	22.5	15.2	9.5	7.6	5.9
BF-AC-13-2 (19:34:15:28:4)	100	97.1	83.4	51.3	29.9	22.0	14.8	9.0	7.1	5.5

At the same time, the average asphalt film thickness is introduced as a reference factor. When the target asphalt-aggregate ratio is controlled at 4.7%, calculating the asphalt film thickness of BF-AC-13-1 and BF-AC-13-2, and compared them with the asphalt film thickness of BF-AC-13. Finally, the method for adjusting the amount of fine material in this experimental study is built.

2.2 Calculation of Asphalt Film Thickness

The calculation formula of asphalt film thickness can refer to JTG F40—2004, and the specific calculation formulas are shown in Eqs. (1) ~ (10).

The asphalt film thickness DA is given as,

$$DA = \frac{P_{be}}{\gamma_b \times SA} \times 10 \tag{1}$$

The effective asphalt content P_{be} is presented as,

$$P_{be} = P_b - \frac{P_{ba}}{100} \times P_S \tag{2}$$

$$P_S = 100 - P_b \tag{3}$$

Aggregate specific surface SA is expressed as,

$$SA = \sum (P_i \times FA_i) \tag{4}$$

FA_i is the aggregate surface area coefficient corresponding to each particle size, as shown in Tab.7.

Aggregate surface area coefficients Tab. 7

Mesh size(mm)	19	16.0	13.2	9.5	4.75	2.36	1.18	0.6	0.3	0.15	0.075
Surface area coefficient FA_i	0.0041	0.0041	0.0041	0.0041	0.0041	0.0082	0.0164	0.0287	0.0614	0.1229	0.3277

The calculation formula of P_{ba}, which is the proportion of asphalt binder absorbed by the aggregate in the asphalt mixture, is shown below.

$$P_{ba} = \frac{\gamma_{se} - \gamma_b}{\gamma_{se} \times \gamma_{sb}} \times \gamma_b \times 100 \tag{5}$$

The calculation of the effective relative density of mineral aggregates will vary with different asphalts. Since this experimental study uses SBS modified asphalt, the calculation of γ_{se} is as follows:

$$\gamma_{se} = C \times \gamma_{sa} + (1 - C) \times \gamma_{sb} \tag{6}$$

The asphalt absorption coefficient C isgiven as,

$$C = 0.033 w_x^2 - 0.2936 w_x + 0.9339 \tag{7}$$

The calculation of the synthetic mineral water absorption rate w_x is calculated according to Eq. (8).

$$w_x = \left(\frac{1}{\gamma_{sb}} - \frac{1}{\gamma_{sa}}\right) \times 100 \tag{8}$$

The calculation of Relative Density of Mineral Material Synthetic Gross Volume is calculated according to Eq. (9).

$$\gamma_{sb} = \frac{100}{\dfrac{P_1}{\gamma_1} + \dfrac{P_2}{\gamma_2} + \cdots + \dfrac{P_n}{\gamma_n}} \tag{9}$$

The calculation of the apparent relative density of mineral aggregate is calculated according to Eq. (10).

$$\gamma_{sa} = \frac{100}{\dfrac{P_1}{\gamma'_1} + \dfrac{P_2}{\gamma'_2} + \cdots + \dfrac{P_n}{\gamma'_n}} \tag{10}$$

This experimental study uses SBS modified asphalt, and its relative density γ_b is 1.013.

Calculating the asphalt film thickness of BF-AC-13, theoptimal asphalt-aggregate ratio is 4.9%. In this study, the target asphalt-aggregate ratio of the asphalt mixture which was adjusted by the amount of fine aggregates is 4.7%. Therefore, the asphalt film thickness of BF-AC-13-1 and BF-AC-13-2 is calculated when the asphalt-aggregate ratio is 4.7%. The calculation results of the asphalt film thickness corresponding to three asphalt mixtures are shown in Tab. 8.

Calculation result of asphalt film thickness Tab. 8

Asphalt mixture types	BF-AC-13	BF-AC-13-1	BF-AC-13-2
Asphalt film thickness of asphalt mixture DA (μm)	8.17	8.21	8.61

By comparing the calculation results of the asphalt film thickness of the two adjusted basalt fiber asphalt mixtures, it can be found that with the same asphalt-aggregate ratio, as the amount of fines decreases, the aggregate specific surface area decreases and the asphalt film thickness becomes thicker. The asphalt film thickness of BF-AC-13 at the optimal asphalt-aggregate ratio of 4.9% is 8.17μm, which is very close to the asphalt film thickness of BF-AC-13-1 at 4.7% asphalt-aggregate ratio. When the asphalt-aggregate ratio of BF-AC-13-1 is 4.7%, the asphalt film thickness is 8.61μm. So we have also calculated the asphalt film thickness of BF-AC-13-2 when its asphalt-aggregate ratio is 4.4% to 4.6%. The calculated results are shown in Tab. 9.

Tab. 9 Calculation results of asphalt film thickness of BF-AC-13-2

Asphalt aggregate-ratio(%)	4.6	4.5	4.4
Asphalt film thickness of asphalt mixture $DA/\mu m$	8.45	8.26	8.08

According to the calculation results, the asphalt film thickness of BF-AC-13-2 when the asphalt-aggregate ratio is 4.5% and 4.4% are respectively 8.26 μm and 8.08 μm.

The same method as above was used to determine the optimal-asphalt-aggregate ratios of BF-AC-13-1 and BF-AC-13-2, which were respectively 4.7% and 4.5%.

Since the target asphalt-aggregate ratio of 4.7% is the optimal asphalt-aggregate ratio of BF-AC-13-1, BF-AC-13-1 is selected as the research object for the performance comparison in the following research.

3 Study on the Influence of Fine Material Dosage Adjustement on the Road Performance of Basalt Fiber Asphalt Mixture

3.1 High-Temperature Stability

High-temperature stability reflects the ability of asphalt mixtures to resist deformation at high temperatures. Insufficient high-temperature stability is a key factor in the appearance of rusting disease. The uniaxial penetration test was used to measure the peak load of AC-13, BF-AC-13 and BF-AC-13-1 specimens. The penetration strength of the asphalt mixture is calculated by Eq. (11) and Eq. (12), and the penetration strength is used as the standard for evaluating the high-temperature stability of the asphalt mixture. The test equipment is shown in Fig. 1, and the test data is shown in Fig. 2.

$$R_r = f_\tau \times \sigma_p \quad (11)$$

$$\sigma_p = \frac{P}{A} \quad (12)$$

Wherer: R_r——penetration strength;

σ_p——penetration stress;

P——ultimate load when the specimen fails;

A——cross-sectional area of indenter;

f_τ——penetration stress coefficient, 150mm diameter specimen, $f_\tau = 0.35$.

Fig. 1 Uniaxial Penetration Test Equipment

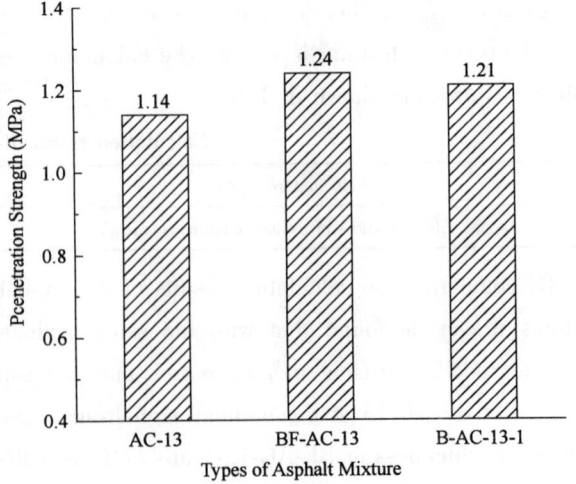

Fig. 2 Uniaxial Penetration Test Results

It can be seen from Figure 2 that the penetration strength is increased significantly after adding basalt fiber to the asphalt mixture, and the increasing rate is 8.77%. Comparing the penetration strength of BF-AC-13 and BF-AC-13-1 with AC-13, the penetration strength is slightly reduced after the amount of fine aggregates is reduced, but the reduction is not worthy of mention, only 2.42%. Therefore, from the analysis of the uniaxial penetration test results, the reduction in the amount of fine aggregates in this test only slightly decreases the high-temperature stability of the asphalt mixture, this effect is much smaller than the increase in high-temperature performance brought about by the addition of basalt fiber.

3.2 Low-Temperature Crack Resistance

The crack resistance of asphalt mixtures characterizes their ability to resist cracking diseases in low-temperature environments. The test temperature is -10°C. The calculation formulas for flexural tensile strength and maximum flexural strain are shown in Eq. (13) and Eq. (14). The data obtained from the test is shown in Fig. 3.

$$R_\text{B} = \frac{3LP_\text{B}}{2bh^2} \tag{13}$$

$$\varepsilon_\text{B} = \frac{6hd}{L^2} \tag{14}$$

Where: b——the interruption of the width of the interview piece;

h——the height of the cross-interruption interview;

L——the span of the test piece;

P_B——the maximum load when the specimen fails;

d——the mid-span deflection when the specimen is broken.

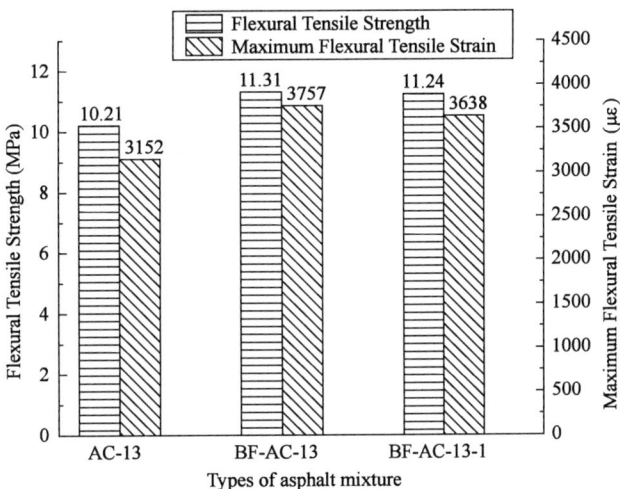

Fig. 3 Flexural Tensile Strength and Maximum Flexural Tensile Strain

Analyzing the data in the figure shows that the maximum flexural strain of the three asphalt mixtures in this test can meet the requirements of the specification. The flexural tensile strength and maximum flexural tensile strain exhibited by the asphalt mixture mixed with basalt fiber have been significantly improved, and the increase rates are 10.77% and 19.19%, respectively. Compared with BF-AC-13-1 and BF-AC-13 with AC-13, the amount of fine aggregates in BF-AC-13-1 has been reduced, the flexural tensile strength and maximum flexural tensile strain have a small decrease, the magnitude is 0.62% and 3.17% respectively. The degree of reduction is not obvious.

3.3 Water Stability

Water is a major factor that causes damage to asphalt pavements. The water immersion Marshall test is used to evaluate the water stability of asphalt mixtures. The water immersion Marshall test results of the three asphalt mixtures are shown in Fig. 4 and Fig. 5.

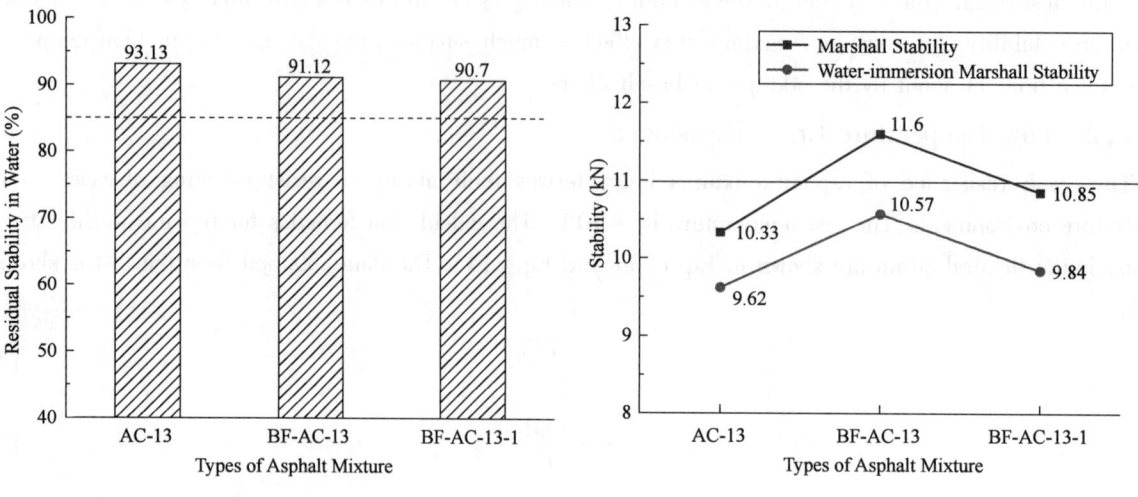

Fig. 4 Residual stability in water   Fig. 5 Marshall stability

Comparing and analyzing the data in the figure, as a whole, the stability of the three kinds of asphalt mixtures meets the requirements. Analyzed from the water-immersion Marshall stability, the addition of basalt fiber in the asphalt mixture increases the stability by 12.29%. The immersion Marshall stability of BF-AC-13-1 is 6.46% lower than that of BF-AC-13, but it still increase by 5.03% compared to the original AC-13 asphalt mixture.

4 Conclusions

This study uses an optimizing the gradation design method to reduce the optimum asphalt content of basalt fiber asphalt mixture. The fine aggregate content in the basalt fiber asphalt mixture is adjusted to conduct the performance of high-temperature stability, low-temperature crack resistance and moisture stability. The detailed conclusions are shown below.

(1) The optimal asphalt-aggregate ratio of original AC-13 is 4.7%, and the optimal asphalt aggregate-ratio of BF-AC-13 increase to 4.9% after adding 0.3% of basalt fiber with a length of 6mm.

(2) The average asphalt film thickness of BF-AC-13 at the optimal asphalt-aggregate ratio of 4.9% is close to that of BF-AC-13-1 at target asphalt-aggregate ratio of 4.7%. When the asphalt-aggregate ratio is 4.7%, the average asphalt film thickness of BF-AC-13-2 is increased by 0.4μm compared with BF-AC-13-1. When the asphalt-aggregate ratio of BF-AC-13-2 is reduced from 4.7% to 4.5% and 4.4%, the average asphalt film thickness is respectively decreased by 0.35μm and 0.53μm.

(3) By adjusting the amount of fine aggregate content, it is determined that the optimal asphalt-aggregate ratios of BF-AC-13-1 and BF-AC-13-2 are 4.7% and 4.5%, respectively. The optimum asphalt content of basalt fiber asphalt mixtures with less fine aggregate content is reduced by 0.2% to 0.4%.

(4) Compared with original AC-13, BF-AC-13 has greatly improved high-temperature stability, low-temperature cracking resistance and water stability. The performance of the BF-AC-13-1 is lower than that without adjustment, but the performance improvement is still significant compared with the original AC-13. On the basis of minor influence on the performance of basalt fiber asphalt mixture, the optimum asphalt dosage is reduced through optimized gradation design, which greatly saves the pavement construction cost. This is great

significance to the popularization and application of using basalt fiber asphalt mixture.

References

[1] You Huang, Zhaohui Liu, Li Liu, Yunbao Zhang, et al. Hybrid Modification of Stone Mastic Asphalt with Cellulose and Basalt Fiber[J]. Advances in Materials Science and Engineering, 2020, 1-11.

[2] Jiangang Yang, Yan Liu, Tianfa Liu. Study on road performance of basalt fiber Tarmac[J]. Road Machinery and Construction Mechanization, 2015, 01: 53-57.

[3] Xiangjie Liu. Research on Road Performance of Basalt Fiber Asphalt Mixture[J]. Journal of China and Foreign Highway, 2018, 38(05), 242-245.

[4] Zhennan Li, Aiqin Shen, Han Wang, et al. Effect of Basalt Fiber on the Low-temperature Performance of an Asphalt Mixture in a Heavily Frozen Area[J]. Construction and Building Materials, 2020, 253, 119080.

[5] Keke Lou, Peng Xiao, Aihong Kang, et al. Suitability of Fiber Lengths for Hot Mix Asphalt with Different Nominal Maximum Aggregate Size: a Pilot Experimental Investigation[J]. Materials, 2020, 13, 3685.

[6] Xiaoyu Hu. Study on the Performance and Characteristics of Basalt Fiber Reinforced High-Viscosity Asphalt and Mixture[D]. Zhejiang University, 2015.

[7] Dong Luo, Ahmed Khater, Yanchao Yue, et al. The Performance of Asphalt Mixtures Modified with Lignin Fiber and Glass Fiber: A Review[J]. Construction and Building Materials, 2019, 209. 377-387.

[8] Guozhou Qiu, Jianhong Fang, Anhua Xu, et al. Research on High-Temperature Performance of Basalt Fiber Asphalt Concrete[J]. Bulletin of the Chinese Ceramic Society, 2019, 38, 3890-3896.

[9] Yuxiao Zhao. Experimental Study on Crack Resistance of Basalt Fiber Reinforced Asphalt Concrete[J]. Highway Engineering, 2014, 39, 48-51.

[10] Yongchun Cheng, Liding Li, Peilei Zhou, et al. Multi-objective Optimization Design and Test of Compound Diatomite and Basalt Fiber Asphalt Mixture[J]. Materials, 2019, 12, 1461.

[11] Wensheng Wang, Yongchun Cheng, Guojin Tan. Design Optimization of SBS-modified Asphalt Mixture Reinforced with Eco-friendly Basalt Fiber Based on Response Surface Methodology[J]. Materials, 2018, 11, 1311.

[12] Yongchun Cheng, Wensheng Wang, Yafeng Gong, et al. Comparative Study on the Damage Characteristics of Asphalt Mixtures Reinforced with an Eco-Friendly Basalt Fiber under Freeze-thaw Cycles[J]. Materials (Basel, Switzerland), 2018, 11(12): 2488.

[13] Peiwen Hao, Hui Wu, Dengliang Zhang. Influence of Different Asphalt Amount and Gradation Composition on Anti-rutting Performance of Asphalt Mixture[J]. Journal of Chang'an University, 1998(S1), 59-62.

[14] Lihan Li, Yabing Guo, Hang Zheng, et al. Relationship between Gradation Composition and Volume Parameters of Asphalt Mixture[J]. Journal of Building Materials, 2005(06): 625-631.

[15] Yu Chen, Shibing Xu, Gabriele Tebaldi, et al. Role of Mineral Filler in Asphalt Mixture[J]. Road Materials and Pavement Design, 2020, 1-40, doi:10.1080/14680629.2020.1826351.

[16] Wending Wei, Decheng Feng, Yin Zhao, et al. Analysis of the Influence of Fine Aggregate Properties on the Volume Characteristics of Asphalt Mixture[J]. Journal of China and Foreign Highway, 2011, 31, 241-244.

[17] Naisheng Guo, Zhanping You, Yiqiu Tan, et al. A Method for Determining Optimal Asphalt Consumption of Asphalt Mixture Considering Uniformity[J]. Journal of Traffic and Transportation Engineering, 2017, 17(01), 1-10.

[18] Niloofar Esmaeili, Gholam Hossein Hamedi, Mojtaba Khodadadi. Determination of the Stripping Process of Asphalt Mixtures and the Effective Mix Design and sfe Parameters on its Different Phases. Construction and Building Materials, 2019, 213, 167-181.

[19] Yongli Zhao, Xiaoming Huang. Design Method and Performance for Large Stone Porous Asphalt Mixtures [J]. Journal of Wuhan University of Technology-Materials Science Edition, 2010, 25(5): 871-876.

乳化沥青冷再生混合料动态模量影响因素研究

李洪祥

(长安大学公路学院)

摘要 动态模量更能准确地体现出混合料的真实受荷状况,是再生沥青混合料路面结构设计的重要参数。本文从级配类型、乳化沥青用量、水泥掺量、旧料掺量四种因素出发,分析其对乳化沥青冷再生混合料动态模量指标的影响。结果表明:乳化沥青冷再生混合料的动态模量随级配的变粗、旧料掺量、水泥掺量的增加而增大,随乳化沥青用量的增加先增大后减小。

关键词 公路工程 动态模量 乳化沥青冷再生混合料 影响因素

0 引言

近年来乳化沥青冷再生混合料以其经济环保的优势已广泛应用于公路的大中修及改扩建工程中[1]。现行路面再生技术规范种路面结构设计考虑的参数为静态抗压回弹模量,但其与再生路面的实际受力之间存在较大差异。美国 MEPDG 设计法、法国沥青路面设计方法中均采用动态模量指标[2-4],它更能真实地反应路面在车辆动荷载作用下的受力状况,较为准确的预测再生路面的力学响应[5]。因此应开展再生沥青混合料动态力学性能研究,为其在道路中的应用提供新的理论支持。

李敏[6]等研究发现乳化沥青及泡沫沥青冷再生混合料动态模量随温度、加载频率的增加而增大,在频率相同时前者略大于后者。户桂灵[7]等研究得出冷再生混合料的动态模量及相位角随温度及频率的变化具有与普通热拌沥青混合料相似的规律,前者受温度与频率的影响较小。汪德才[8]等研究发现,冷再生混合料的动态模量随再生剂掺量的增加呈现出先增大后减小的趋势,动稳定度随再生剂掺量的增大逐渐减小,推荐最佳再生剂用量为8%。李禹铮等[9]在分析不同因素对再生沥青混合料动、静态模量影响的基础上建立了二者之间的联系。朱玉等[10]研究发现热再生沥青混合料的车辙性能与动态模量指标表现出相类似的变化规律。杨小龙等[11]对沥青混合料的动态模量预估模型展开研究,为其在我国沥青路面设计中的研究和应用提供了坚实的基础。

影响乳化沥青冷再生混合料动态模量的因素主要包括外因和内因两个方面,目前的研究大多集中于外因,即温度、围压、加载频率等,对内因即混合料的材料组成研究较少,因此本文从混合料的级配类型、水泥用量、乳化沥青用量、RAP 旧料掺量 4 个方面出发,分析其对动态模量的影响。

1 试验材料及方法

1.1 原材料

1.1.1 回收沥青混合料(RAP)、集料

首先将 RAP 旧料放在自然条件下风干,对其逐档筛分,在进行级配设计时逐档回配并通过添加碎石及机制砂来调整。其基本技术指标见表1、表2。

RAP 及碎石性能指标　　表1

RAP		碎 石		
试验项目	沥青含量(%)	砂当量(%)	压碎值(%)	磨耗值(%)	表观相对密度(g/cm³)
试验结果	4.95	68.06	19.10	16.21	2.7

机制砂技术指标　　表2

试验项目	表观相对密度(g/cm³)	砂当量(%)	坚固性(>0.3mm 部分)(%)
实验结果	2.73	60.8	4.5
技术要求	≥2.50	≥60	≤12

1.1.2　乳化沥青

本文选择阳离子乳化剂、双龙90号沥青与自来水制备冷再生用乳化沥青。将乳化剂、水按照一定剂量配置成乳化剂水溶液，添加盐酸调节 pH 值，后与基质沥青制备乳化沥青。乳化沥青在制备完成后放在容器中冷却，冷却过程中及使用前应进行适当搅拌。制备的乳化沥青性能指标见表3。

乳化沥青性能指标　　表3

试验项目		试 验 结 果	技 术 指 标
恩格拉黏度 E_{25}		15.7	2~30
粒子电荷		阳离子	阳离子
破乳速度		慢裂	中裂或慢裂
筛上剩余量(1.18mm)(%)		0.02	≤0.1
与粗集料的黏附性，裹覆面积		>2/3	>2/3
蒸发残留物性质	残留物含量(%)	64.9	≥60
	针入度(100g,25℃,5s)(0.1mm)	92.9	50~130
	延度(15℃)(cm)	>100	≥40
	溶解度(%)	98.7	≥97.5
常温储存稳定性	1d(%)	0.35	≤1
	5d(%)	3.30	≤5

1.2　试验方案

按照《公路沥青路面再生技术规范》(JTG F41—2008)[12]中乳化沥青冷再生混合料级配推荐选用三种粗细不同的级配，筛孔通过率如表4所示，选择0%、0.5%、1%、1.5%、2%五种水泥掺量，2.5%、3%、3.5%、4%四种乳化沥青用量，30%、40%、50%、60%四种RAP旧料掺量。

试验级配　　表4

级配类型	筛孔尺寸(mm)											
	26.5	19	16	13.2	9.5	4.75	2.36	1.18	0.6	0.3	0.15	0.075
JP-1	100	100	97.8	94.1	75.4	60.8	44.3	31.4	19.8	10.5	6.8	5.6
JP-2	100	97.5	94.4	87.1	72.3	52.2	38.4	25.3	15.4	8.3	6.3	5.1
JP-3	100	93.5	88.6	78.4	66.3	43.6	27.3	18.4	10.7	7.7	5.9	4.8

通过旋转压实法制成直径150mm、高170mm试件，按要求钻芯切割去除试件表面的空隙不均匀层，得到直径100mm,高150mm的圆柱体试样。固定试验条件：温度为20℃，频率为10Hz正弦波加载，无围压状态。试验采用AMPT试验机，具体方案见表5。

动态模量试验方案　　　　　　　　　　　　　　　　表5

影响因素	影响因素用量	其他因素用量
级配	JP-1、JP-2、JP-3	水泥用量1.5%,乳化沥青用量3.5%,旧料掺量60%
乳化沥青用量	2.5%、3.0%、3.5%、4.0%	级配为JP-3,水泥掺量1.5%,旧料掺量60%
水泥掺量	0、0.5%、1%、1.5%、2%	级配为JP-3,乳化沥青用量3.5%,旧料掺量60%
旧料掺量	30%、40%、50%、60%	级配为JP-3,水泥掺量1.5%,乳化沥青用量3.5%
试验结果	每一条件下测试两个试件,最终取二者平均值作为最终结果,若二者差值较大则重新测试	

2 动态模量试验结果分析

2.1 级配类型的影响

如图1所示,在固定水泥用量为1.5%,乳化沥青用量为3.5%,旧料掺量为60%的情况下,动态模量随着级配的变粗而逐渐增大,从大到小依次为:JP-3＞JP-2＞JP-1。其中JP-1的最大粒径为16mm,在公路沥青路面再生技术规范所推荐的级配范围中属于细粒式范畴,而JP-2和JP-3最大粒径为19mm,属于中粒式冷再生沥青混合料,但JP-3中各筛孔的通过率均大于JP-2,级配相对较粗,因而其动态模量最大,比JP-2的动态模量值增加了17%。

2.2 水泥掺量的影响

如图2所示,在固定级配为JP-3,乳化沥青用量为3.5%,旧料掺量为60%的情况下,动态模量随水泥掺量的增加而增大后趋于平缓,掺量由1.5%增大至2%时动态模量的增幅,与掺量由0%增大至0.5%相比大大减小。相较于未掺加水泥的乳化沥青冷再生混合料,掺加1.5%的水泥使得其动态模量增加137%,掺加2%水泥使得其动态模量增加146%,原因可能是水泥会与乳化沥青中的水发生水化反应,其水化产物可提高乳化沥青冷再生混合料黏弹性特质,增强混合料的抗变形能力。因此从提高动态模量的角度来说,乳化沥青冷再生混合料中应添加少量的水泥。

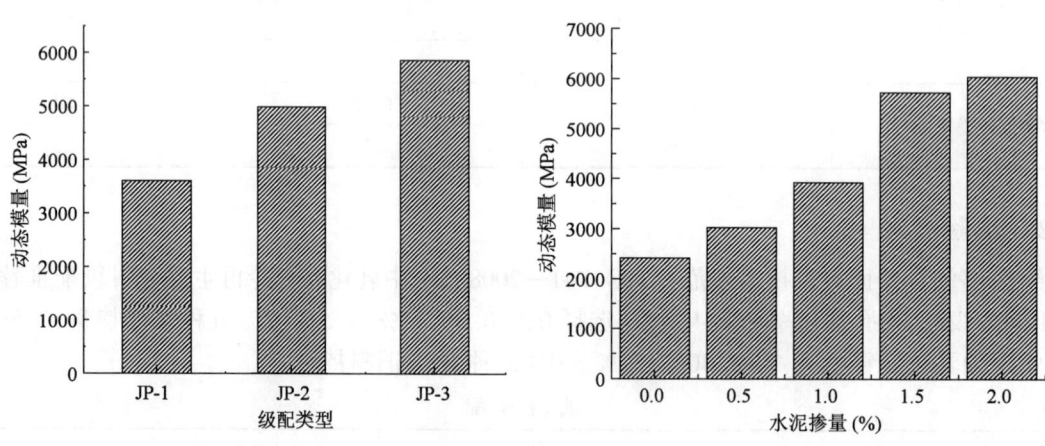

图1　不同级配类型下混合料动态模量　　　　图2　不同水泥掺量下混合料动态模量

2.3 乳化沥青用量的影响

如图3所示,在固定级配为JP-3,水泥掺量为1.5%,旧料掺量为60%的情况下,动态模量随着乳化沥青用量的增加呈现出先增大后减小的变化趋势,在3.5%用量时达到最大值,动态模量从大到小依次为:3.5%＞4%＞3%＞2.5%。这是由于乳化沥青用量的增加使得沥青与矿料颗粒之间的黏结力增大,因此混合料在外力作用下抗变形能力得到增强,动态模量增加。但过多的乳化沥青会在混合料中形成自由沥青,使得集料颗粒间的摩擦力减小,相对位移变得容易,混合料抗变形能力降低,动态模量减小。因此,为提高冷再生混合料的动态模量,其乳化沥青用量不宜过大。

2.4 RAP 掺量的影响

由图 4 可知,在固定级配为 JP-3,水泥掺量为 1.5%,乳化沥青用量为 3.5% 的情况下,混合料的动态模量随 RAP 掺量的增加而逐渐增大,不同旧料掺量条件下的动态模量从大到小依次为:60% > 50% > 40% > 30%,相较于 30% RAP 掺量,40% RAP 掺量的混合料动态模量增加 4%,50% RAP 掺量的混合料动态模量增加 17%,60% RAP 掺量的混合料动态模量增加 34%。分析其原因可能是 RAP 旧料中的沥青结合料已经发生老化,相比于新沥青而言会变硬,旧料掺量越高,其中所含的旧沥青结合料越多,混合料的动态模量相应增大。

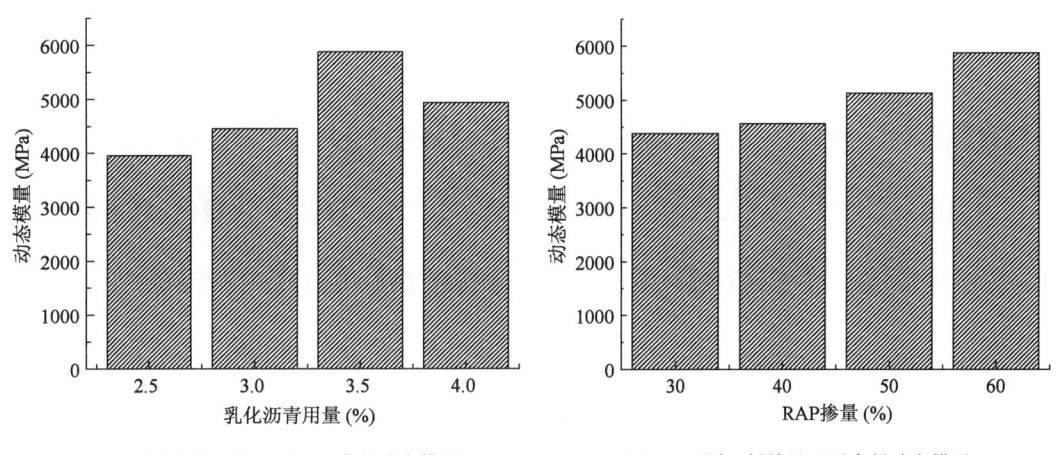

图 3 不同乳化沥青用量下混合料动态模量　　图 4 不同旧料掺量下混合料动态模量

3 结 语

本文从乳化沥青冷再生混合料的材料组成出发,分析了动态模量随级配类型、水泥掺量、乳化沥青用量、旧料掺量的变化规律,具体结论如下:

(1)乳化沥青冷再生混合料的动态模量随级配变粗、RAP 旧料掺量的增加而增大。

(2)掺加少量水泥可以改善乳化沥青冷再生混合料的动态模量,尤其是水泥掺量由 0% 增加至 1.5%,其动态模量值显著增长,此时继续增大水泥掺量动态模量值趋于平缓。

(3)乳化沥青冷再生混合料的动态模量随乳化沥青用量的增加而先增大后减小,在最佳乳化沥青用量条件下混合料模量达到最大值。

本文主要在固定温度、频率等条件下,从混合料的组成材料方面入手分析其对动态模量的影响,而对于组成材料与温度、频率等因素之间的交互作用尚未展开研究。

参考文献

[1] 付涛.旧沥青路面冷再生混合料性能研究[J].中外公路,2018,38(6):263-269.

[2] 刘伟,严金海,李锋,等.乳化沥青冷再生混合料动静模量相关性[J].公路交通科技,2015,32(05):1-6,24.

[3] 王宏,刘锋,张葆永,等.不同养生温度乳化沥青冷再生混合料空隙分布特征[J].武汉理工大学学报:交通科学与工程版,2015,39(2):392-388.

[4] 严金海.沥青路面冷再生设计方法及性能评价[D].南京:东南大学,2006.

[5] 孙立辉,吕骄阳.基于动态模量试验影响因素的灰关联熵分析[J].公路交通科技(应用技术版),2017,13(12):179-182.

[6] 李敏.泡沫(乳化)沥青冷再生混合料动态模量特性及其主曲线研究[J].公路工程,2016,41(3):8-16.

[7] 户桂灵,韩文扬,余四新.乳化沥青冷再生混合料动态模量的试验研究[J].科学技术与工程,2018,18(4):339-343.

[8] 汪德才,常昊雷,郝培文,等.改性乳化沥青冷再生混合料动态模量特性[J].长安大学学报:自然科学版,2020,40(6):35-46.
[9] 李禹铮.寒冷地区再生沥青混合料动态模量的研究[D].长春:吉林建筑大学,2019.
[10] 朱玉.基于动态模量试验的热再生沥青混合料性能评价[J].公路交通科技(应用技术版),2017,13(05):143-144.
[11] 杨小龙,申爱琴,郭寅川,等.沥青混合料动态模量预估模型研究进展[J].材料导报,2018,32(13):2230-2240.
[12] JTG F41—2008,公路沥青路面再生技术规范[S].北京:人民交通出版社,2008.

Study on the Influence of Benign Temperature Induced Admixture on Thermal Induced Performance of Cement Concrete

Lv Jiaoyng[1] Tian Bo[1] Quan Lei[2] Li Sili[2]

(1. University of Harbin Institute of Technology;2. Research Institute of Highway Ministr)

Abstract To study the effect of benign temperature conduction of this material on the heat-sensitive characteristics of the concrete itself, this paper analyzes the thermal conductivity of the most benign temperature material, develops a heating test after the preparation of concrete and finds that the heat-sensitive capacity of the concrete itself is enhanced by the addition of graphene material. And with the help of test analysis, it is concluded that when the single-dark phase of doping of steel fibers, graphite and steel velvet is low, the thermal capacity of the concrete is very small, because the cement suspension of the poor thermal conductor is wrapped so that the temperature chain formed by benign temperature-conducting material is in an isolated state, and the heat cannot be transmitted smoothly. Graphene composite steel fiber, this multi-phasic composite can get single-phase composite material, can't achieve the effect of temperature-oriented, some compounds of benign temperature diversion outside doped in the concrete to form a number of continuous heat channels, improve the heat of the concrete itself.

Keywords Cement concrete Graphene Temperature conduction characteristics Temperature conduction material

0 Introduction

High-speed railway cement concrete pavement, airport pavement, slag-free track slab and other concrete surface slabs bear the fatigue of moving goods (vehicles or planes) and environment (temperature, humidity, etc.). At the same time, due to the difference in heat conduction of concrete, solar radiation and temperature difference between day and night will form a temperature gradient along the slab thickness, causing warpage deformation of the slab. Among them, the thermal conductivity and structural thermodynamic performance of concrete during thermal induction are the key issues related to the durability of cement concrete pavement structure[1-2].

Sponsored by the National Key R&D Program of China (Grant Number:2018YFB1600100), and the National Natural Science Foundation of China Youth Fund Project (51908260)。

Over the years, many experts and scholars have done a lot of research on improving the thermal conductivity of concrete. Xiao Jianzhuang and others[3] studied the influence of the replacement rate of recycled coarse aggregate on the thermal conductivity of recycled concrete, and found that the thermal conductivity of high aggregate concrete is also higher, and the thermal conductivity of concrete increases with the increase of the steel bar volume fraction. Liu Kai and others[4] studied the generalized grey correlation method used to analyze the factors affecting the thermal conductivity of concrete, and it is concluded that the thermal conductivity of concrete test blocks with the same water-cement ratio increases linearly with the increase of aggregate volume fraction, and the thermal conductivity of concrete also increases obviously with the increase of admixture content. Zhao Xing and others[5] used basalt fiber to improve the performance of foam concrete, and pointed out that the thermal conductivity of foam concrete with basalt fiber is slightly higher than that without fiber. The change of fiber content has a great influence on the thermal conductivity of foam concrete. Cement concrete has low thermal conductivity. In the mentioned methods, the increase of aggregate content will reduce the bonding force between slurry and aggregate, thus weakening the integrity of concrete and reducing the strength of concrete. While the additive increases the thermal conductivity of steel fiber, adding too much steel fiber will increase the iron oxide content in the casting, reduce its corrosion resistance and make the durability unable to meet the relevant requirements. Therefore, a method must be found to ensure thermal conductivity. The larger the concrete, the higher the thermal sensing capacity, which can meet certain bearing capacity and good strength requirements. The method of adding graphene[6,7] isothermal phase with high thermal conductivity material is adopted to improve the thermal conductivity of concrete so as to improve heat transfer. The influence of alloying technology of harmless thermal conductivity materials such as steel fiber and graphene on the thermal induction performance of cement concrete is also studied, which provides a certain experimental basis for the research of high temperature cement concrete in the future.

1 Review

The cement concrete pavement structure is completely in the atmospheric environment and is affected by the changing environment. Therefore, the temperature field of the pavement structure changes with the change of the environment. The energy carried away by the road surface in the process of solar energy collection will inevitably cause changes in road surface temperature. Cement concrete has poor thermal conductivity, and the temperature gradient caused by hydration heat or changes in the external environment in concrete structures generally has adverse effects on its performance. In view of the poor electrical conductivity of cement concrete, the thermal conductivity phase filler is added to cement concrete through various additives prepared by cement concrete to study its thermal induction effect and the change of temperature transfer rate.

2 Experimental Method

2.1 Raw materials and mix proportion

The conventional benchmark index of Portland cement conforms to GB175—85 "Portland Cement, Ordinary Portland Cement". The fine aggregate consists of quartz sand with a bulk density of $1520kg/m^3$. And the content of drilling fluid is less than or equal to 3%, and the fine elastic modulus ratio is 2.65. The coarse aggregate consists of granite with a particle size of 5 ~ 20mm and a solid granular gravel of 20 ~ 40mm, with an apparent density of $2450kg/m^3$. And the drilling fluid content is 0.8%. Graphene is made by the redox method of Dongxu Guangxuan Co., Ltd. The sheet diameter is 1 ~ 5 microns, the resistivity is 1.8 cm · cm, the conductivity is 555cm/cm, and the thermal conductivity is 4000W/m. As shown in Tab. 1, when graphene is mixed, a certain amount of dispersant 303 is added at the same time. After evenly stirring with a high-speed mixer, ultrasonic dispersion is carried out for 1h with an ultrasonic cleaning machine with a power of 360W, and then the concrete is mixed.

Concrete Test Calculation Mix Proportion   Tab. 1

Title	Quantity Unit	Title	Quantity Unit
Cement	330 kg	Supplementary dose	6.6 kg
Water	132 kg	Sand rate SP	31 %
River sand	630kg	Water cement ratio	0.42
Gravel 5~20mm	561 kg	Air content of fresh concrete	2.5%~3.5 %
Gravel 20~40mm	841 kg	Decline	10~20mm

2.2 Pilot programme

During the experiment, specimens of different benign thermal conductivity materials (Tab. 2) and control specimens were made, and the specimens were numbered A1, A2, A3, A4, A5, A6, A7, A8, A9 and A10. When making the test piece, the temperature sensor probe is embedded according to the position shown in Fig. 1. The index number of the temperature sensor is Pt100, the measurement range is −50 ℃ ~ 200 ℃, and the measurement accuracy is 0.1. Place the test piece in the curing box and leave it for 24 ± 0.25h (counting from the beginning of adding water), then take it out. After being taken out of the mold, the sample is immediately put into the water at 20℃~1℃ for curing. There should be gaps between the samples, and the water surface should be not less than 20mm higher than the samples. It is naturally dried in air for 24h, then dried in an oven at 60 ℃ ~ 5 ℃ for 4h, and then cooled to room temperature. Take the dried sample and cover it with an insulating layer composed of benzene board and aerogel felt. One end of the test sample is close to the heating plate, connect the equipment and tools, as shown in Fig. 2, and turn on the paperless recorder. Turn on the paperless recorder (the data collector shall adopt the paperless recorder, and the real-time display accuracy shall not exceed ± 0.2% F. S. The cold end error of the instrument shall be eliminated during the test). The laboratory test conditions shall not be less than 50% relative humidity and temperature, keep at 20 ℃ ± 5 ℃, and let stand for 30 minutes. After the above operation is completed, the heating plate is opened, the temperature is adjusted to 60 ℃ and heated, and the thermal induction effect and heating rate of different groups of test blocks of different materials with good thermal conductivity are compared.

Amount of soft temperature control material   Tab. 2

Group	Graphene	Steel Fiber	Steel wool
A1	1% W_{Cement}	—	—
A2	—	—	—
A3	—	0.5% W	—
A4	—	1% W	—
A5	—	—	0.5% W
A6	—	—	1% W
A7	—	—	1.5% W
A8	1% W_{Cement}	1% W	—
A9	1% W_{Cement}	—	1.5% W
A10	—	—	—

Fig. 3 is the photo of test section.

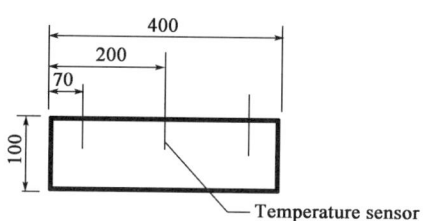

Fig. 1 Sensor Layout (Unit Dimension: mm)

Fig. 2 Schematic Diagram of Composition of Thermal Conductivity Tester

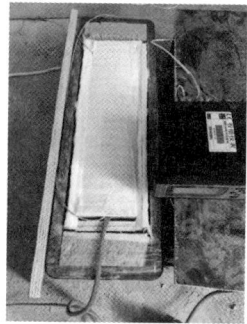 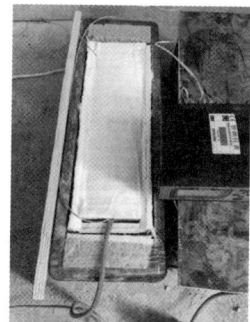 

Fig. 3 Actual thermal conductivity test section

3 Analysis of Heat Transfer Mechanism

3.1 Theoretical Calculation

Heat conduction is based on the heat transfer of electronic molecules, atoms and microscopic particles. The higher the temperature, the higher the energy of the particles. When adjacent particles collide with each other, the particles with larger energy will inevitably want to transmit smaller energy. Similarly, when the concrete has a temperature gradient, the energy obtained by heat transfer must flow to the place where the temperature is lower. This situation can be accelerated by improving the internal thermal conductivity of concrete, adding benign thermal conductivity materials and building thermal conductivity passages.

In the process of linear heat conduction, there is no relative displacement and no energy form conversion inside the concrete. The steady - state heat transfer and energy transfer rate equation without heat source can be expressed by Fourier law as follows:

$$q' = -k \nabla T = -k\left(i\frac{\partial T}{\partial x} + j\frac{\partial T}{\partial y} + k\frac{\partial T}{\partial z}\right) \tag{1}$$

Where: q'——the heat flux density of cement concrete, which means the heat transfer per unit area of concrete (W/m^2);

k——thermal conductivity of concrete [$W/(m\ ℃)$];

∇——three-dimensional inverted triangle operator;

$\frac{\partial T}{\partial x}$——X-direction temperature gradient.

Fourier's law means that the heat flow is a vector, and the heat flow is always perpendicular to the isothermal surface. Therefore, another expression of Fourier's law is:

$$q'_n = -k\frac{\partial T}{\partial n} \tag{2}$$

Where: q'_n——n direction cement concrete heat flux density.

The main purpose of heat conduction analysis is to determine the temperature field formed in the medium under the given boundary conditions, i.e. to find the functional relation t = f (x,y,z,t). After determining the internal temperature field, the heat conduction density of any point on the surface of the medium or object can be calculated according to Fourier's law. By solving the differential equation describing the temperature distribution in the rectangular coordinate system, the expression of Fourier differential heat conduction equation in the rectangular coordinate system can be obtained:

$$\frac{\partial T}{\partial t} = \frac{k}{c_p\rho}\left(\frac{\partial^2 T}{\partial x^2} + \frac{\partial^2 T}{\partial y^2} + \frac{\partial^2 T}{\partial z^2}\right) + \frac{q'_g}{c_p\rho} = \alpha \nabla^2 T + \frac{q'_g}{c_p\rho} \tag{3}$$

where: ∇^2——Laplace operator on T.

α——thermal conductivity (m^2/c).

Formula (3) is applicable to concrete. The Laplace operator in the equation has clear physical meaning. When it is positive, it means that the object is heated, otherwise it is cooled. Thus, thermal conductivity k and specific heat capacity are important physical properties of materials, and are also important parameters that characterize the thermal induction of cement concrete and affect the thermal conductivity of concrete.

3.2 The mechanism of improving heat induction of cement concrete by multi-phase composite temperature control system

Multi-phase connection can obtain heat conduction effect that single-phase connection cannot obtain. In the temperature induced composite system, the mixing law can be used to explain the combined effect of thermal characteristics, as shown in the following formula

$$A_c = \sum A_i^n V_i \tag{4}$$

In the formula, the volume fraction and thermal conductivity of component i in the system are respectively expressed, $n = -1 \sim 1$.

It can be seen from formula (4) that the temperature conductivity and the volume content of the heat conducting phase are parameters that significantly affect the thermal conductivity of the composite system. The electrical conductivity can be improved by selecting high thermal conductivity phase materials and increasing their volume content, and the temperature performance is preferred. At the same time, the shape, dispersion state, the surface energy of components and structural arrangement direction of the temperature-induced phase materials in the system should be considered. Among the three thermal phase materials selected in this study, graphene can be used as the main thermal phase material in thermal conductivity cement concrete due to its high thermal conductivity and more uniform dispersion state due to the addition of dispersant and ultrasonic stirring technology. The conductivity of optical fiber ranks second, and the dispersion is limited by the mixing amount, but its large size ratio provides a better enhancement effect per unit volume. Steel wool is second in conductivity, but in cement mixture. Compared with steel fiber, the volume content of steel that is easy to be mixed is higher, and the coverage rate inside the concrete is larger.

In the graphene/steel fiber/steel wool partial composite thermal conductivity system, aggregates with higher thermal conductivity compared with cement stone form a thermal conductivity network structure, graphene is filled to form a main chain of thermal conductivity particles, and steel fibers or steel wool dispersed in the middle form an auxiliary conductive bridge, thus greatly improving the thermal conductivity of the substrate. Therefore, the multi-phase composite temperature conductivity system prepared by the composite material can overcome the limit temperature conductivity of the single-phase thermal conductivity system, give full play to the thermal conductivity of each phase thermal conductivity material, and significantly improve the thermal conductivity of the cement mixture.

The size of graphene is much smaller than that of mineral aggregates. However, the "insulating" cement stone has an obvious blocking effect on the contact of graphene conductive particles. More hot particles are needed to form conductive paths through cement stone. These hot particles should be distributed on the surface of cement stone, and aggregate participates in the formation of a heat chain (Fig. 4). which inevitably requires a certain amount of graphene. The capture of cement dough makes the heat conduction chain formed by graphite particles become isolated, reducing the possibility of graphite particles forming a heat network. As shown in Fig. 4 and Fig. 5, adding steel fibers with large aspect ratio or steel wool with a certain aspect ratio and wide distribution can break through the barrier of some cement stones to conductive chains and connect heat chains through cement stones. At the same time, it can act as a bridge, forming a thermal bridge between adjacent insulation thermal chains, promoting the formation of a three-dimensional thermal network, shortening some curved multi-section thermal chains, shortening the thermal path, and improving the thermal conductivity of cement concrete.

Fig. 4 Heat Chain Formation Process of Graphene Particles

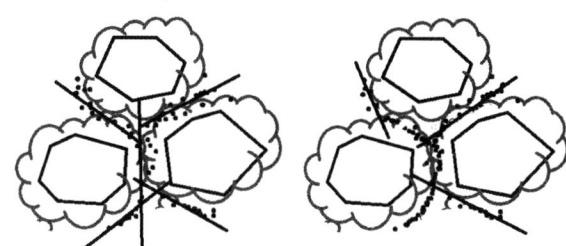

Fig. 5 Function of Steel Fiber Lintel (Left) Steel Fiber Short Circuit Temperature Detection Function (Right)

4 Results and Analysis

4.1 Effect of Graphene Admixture on Thermal Induction of Concrete

Aerogel felt and benzene board are coated to prevent loss of ambient temperature. One side of specimen A1 ~ A10 is heated for nearly 8 hours, and the change of the internal temperature of the specimen is recorded by a data acquisition instrument, as shown in Fig. 6.

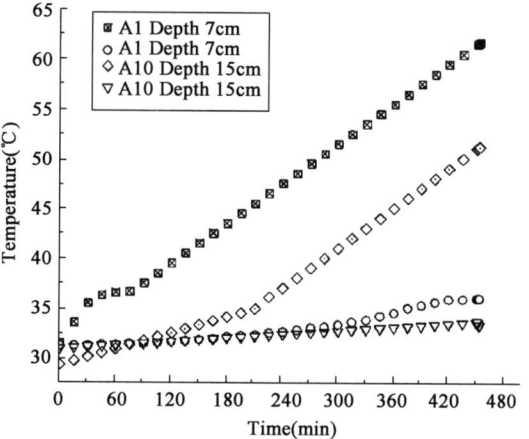

Fig. 6 Temperature Changes at Different Points of Test Blocks A1, A2 and A10

As can be seen from Fig. 6, graphene doped test blocks A1 and A2 have faster pre-heating rates than undoped test blocks A10. Under the same heat source temperature, the total temperature superscalar of specimens A1 and A2 is higher than that of specimen A10. It is proved that the addition of graphene increases the thermal conductivity of the concrete itself and can make the concrete transfer more heat energy. The thermal induction coefficient A2 is bigger than the thermal induction coefficient A1, and the temperature is higher at the same depth after the same time, which proves that the increase of graphene content makes the formation of thermal conduction chain more obvious and the test block becomes more sensitive to temperature.

4.2 Influence of Graphene Addition on Thermal Conductivity of Concrete

The measurement results of concrete graphene thermal conductivity are shown in Fig. 7. With the increase of graphite content, the thermal conductivity of concrete tends to increase obviously. In order to find out whether there is a linear relationship between graphite content and thermal conductivity, the thermal conductivity relationship curves under different graphite content are drawn.

$$\lambda = 20.259x + 0.9253 \qquad R^2 = 0.9946 \qquad (5)$$

Where: λ——thermal conductivity;

x——X Graphite volume fraction.

As can be clearly seen from Fig. 7, the amount of graphite is positively correlated with the thermal conductivity.

4.3 Effect of Graphene Adding Steel Fiber or Steel Wool on Thermal Induction of Concrete

As can be clearly seen from Fig. 8, in the unidirectional heating process, the distance between the heating surface and the temperature sensor can overlap with graphene to form a heat conduction path by adding steel fiber or steel wool, thus increasing the temperature.

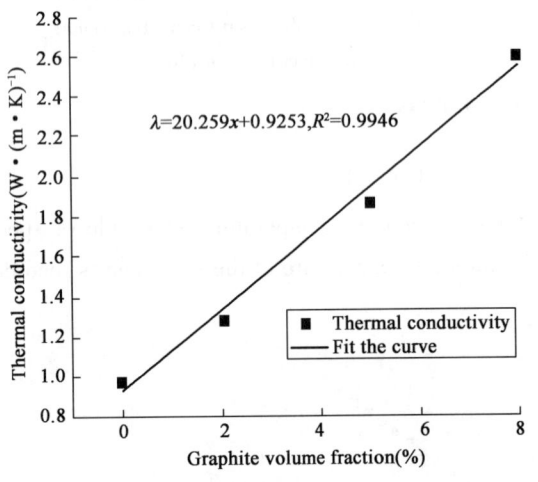

Fig. 7   Relationship Diagram between Graphene Content and Thermal Conductivity

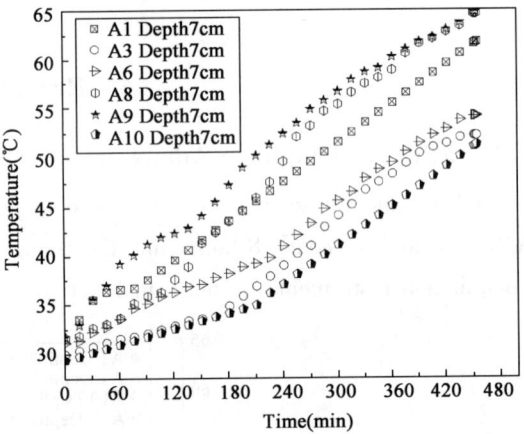

Fig. 8   Temperature Changes at Different Points of Test Blocks A1, A3, A6, A8, A9 and A10

5 Conclusions

(1) With the increase of graphene content, the heat induction ability of cement concrete increases and the heating rate increases. However, when the graphene content is 10%, the thermal conductivity of the concrete is relatively high and the slump during the experiment is relatively large. Graphene agglomeration and agglomeration are easy to occur in concrete mixing.

(2) Graphene can improve the thermal conductivity of concrete. The more graphite is added, the higher the

thermal conductivity of concrete, because with the increase of specific gravity of graphite, thermal conductivity channels will be formed.

(3) Graphene and steel fiber or steel wool can improve the thermal conductivity of concrete, because multi-phase composite can obtain thermal conductivity that single-phase composite cannot achieve, forming a plurality of continuous thermal conductivity channels.

(4) The low content of the single temperature phase has little effect on the heat induction ability of concrete. The reason is that the cement dough with poor thermal conductivity makes the heat chain formed by the material with good thermal conductivity in an insulated state and the heat cannot be transferred smoothly.

(5) Temperature-induced soft admixture has a certain degree of influence on the thermal induction performance of cement concrete, but its optimal content still needs to be further determined by other mechanical properties of cement concrete.

References

[1] Yao Zukang. Theory and Method of Designing Cement Concrete[M]. Sidewalk Public Transport Press, 2003.
[2] Tian B, Li S, Yin F, et al. Experimental Evaluation of the Consolidation Behavior of SlipformPaving Concrete Materials [C].//Transport Research Council Meeting. 2014.
[3] Xiao Zhuangjian, Song Zhiwen, Zhang Feng. Testing and analysis of thermal conductivity of concrete [J]. Building Materials Journal 2010, 13 (1): 17-21.
[4] Liu Kai, Wang Fang, Wang Xuancang. Study of influencing factors and a model for predicting the thermal conductivity of cement concrete [J]. Journal of BuildingMaterials, 2012, 15 (6): 771-777.
[5] Zho Xing, Huo Yaji, Gao Ya, et al. Study the properties of basalt fibers to enhance aerated concrete[C]. // 9th National Fiber Cement Products Academic, Standard and Technical Information Exchange Conference and China Silicate Society of Concrete and Cement Products Branch of Fiber Cement Products Professional Committee three sessions, Chinese Silicate Society of Housing Materials Branch of Three Sessions of Paper Compilation, 2014: 4.
[6] Shen, Jianfeng, et al. Comparison of the thermal properties of silicone reinforced with different nanocarbon materials[J]. Soft Materials 11.3 (2013): 326-333.
[7] K Sobolev, M Ferrada-Gutierrez. How Nanotechnology Can Change the Specific World: Part I, Am. Ceram [J]. The juice. Bull. 84 (2005) 14-17.

Research on Freeze-thaw Durability of Porous Concrete based on the Pore Characteristics and Supplementary Cementitious Materials

Li Zhang Hui Li Hanbing Wang

(Tongji University)

Abstract It is well known that the Portland cement porous concrete (PCCP) has lower strength and durability due to its more inter-aggregate voids compared to dense concrete. In this study, Computerized Tomography (CT) technology was used to obtain the pore characteristics of porous concrete with different freeze-thaw cycles. Flexural strength, compressive strength and weight loss were tested to analyze the freeze-thaw cycle durability of porous concrete. Also, the effects of four kinds of supplementary cementitious materials (SCMs), they are fly ash, slag, silica fume and nano silica, on porous concrete freeze – thaw cycle durability and pore characteristics were studied. Results show that gradual cumulative damage and sudden fracture damage are the two failure modes of porous concrete in the freeze – thaw cycle. With the increase of the number of cycles, the flexural and compressive strength of porous concrete decreased significantly, accompanied by a decrease in the number of pores and an increase in the average pore area. This reveals the expansion and merger of pores during the freeze – thaw cycle. Additionally, the four SCMs can all reduce the weight loss rate of porous concrete during the freeze – thaw cycle among which silica fume has the strongest effect on suppressing weight loss (Improve 47.6%). However, the addition of SCMs can also reduce the porosity of porous concrete to varying degrees, which will cause the decrease of its water permeability.

Keywords Porous concrete Freeze-thaw durability Pore Supplementary cementitious material

0 Introduction

Insufficient strength and durability have always been the main difficulties that limit the application of porous concrete on permeable pavements[1]. Existing research has been clear about the failure mechanism and porosity effects of dense concrete under freeze – thaw cycles. However, for porous concrete, its more opening and large diameter pores will make its frost resistance drop significantly[2]. For the pore characteristics researching, Yang explored the relationship between the pore characteristics and ecological performance of pervious asphalt concrete by processing CT scan slices[3], and Zhou studied the effect of the size of the clogging particles and holes on the clogging through CT scanning and image processing. The experimental results show that the size of the holes determines whether the clogging particles can block or pass through the holes[4]. Therefore, CT technology has been proven to be an effective means to explore the characteristics of concrete meso – pores.

Supplementary cementitious materials (SCMs) are a kind of admixtures that can effectively promote the hardening process of cement, optimize the bonding interface and improve concrete density, which makes them widely used in dense concrete[5-7]. Hu Liguo used a single blend of silica fume and fly ash, added polycarboxylate water-reducing agent to improve frost resistance, and used compressive strength loss and weight loss to evaluate frost resistance[8]. And it shows that both silica fume and fly ash can effectively improve the anti-destructive ability of concrete under freezing and thawing conditions. However, the addition of SCMs will reduce the porosity of porous concrete, thereby affecting its water permeability[9]. Therefore, while SCMs are being utilized, its adverse effects on PC water permeability should be considered.

In general, most of the previous studies focused on improving the freeze – thaw cycle durability of porous concrete by adding new materials or changing the mix ratio, but the observations on the changes in pore characteristics during this process are lacked. The main objective of this study is to explore the change law of pore characteristics of PC during freeze-thaw cycles, and evaluate the influence of SCMs on its porosity.

1 Laboratory Testing

1.1 Materials

This study evaluated four common supplementary cementitious materials, namely fly ash (FA), slag, silica fume (SF) and nano silica (NS). Tab. 1 shows the type and dosage of SCMs used in each group. Three repeated test pieces were set for each group to reduce accidental errors in the test. The particle size range of the aggregate in this study was 4.75mm ~ 9.5mm, which is the most common for porous concrete. The Water-cement ratio (W/C) between 0.26 ~ 0.34 is recommended by the relevant technical specification[10]. Therefore, the water-cement ratio of 0.31 and the cement – aggregate ratio (C/A) of 0.19 were selected in this study. Two size specimens of 100mm * 100mm * 400mm and 100mm * 100mm * 100mm were made and used for flexural strength test and compressive strength test respectively.

Types and Dosage of SCMs Addition   Tab. 1

No.	1	2	3	4	5	6	7	8	9	10	11	12	13
Type	Control	FA	FA	FA	Slay	Slay	Slay	SF	SF	SF	NS	NS	NS
Dosage (%)	0	10	15	20	15	20	25	3	6	9	1.0	1.5	2.0

1.2 CT Scanning Technology

Computerized Tomography (CT) is a technology that uses precisely collimated X-ray beams, together with a highly sensitive detector to scan each section of the object one by one, which can be used to quickly and accurately understand the internal structure of the object. In this study, obtaining 2D images of different sections (1mm apart) of the specimen by CT technology was the first step. Then the acquired image was performed image preprocessing. Some processed CT images are shown in Fig. 1. Finally, MATLAB was used to extract a number of pore parameters from the image to characterize the pore characteristics of the specimen. The acquired original parameters of the pores include the number of pores, the inner diameter of the pores and the pore area. On this basis, more pore parameters can be obtained through data statistics.

1.3 Freeze-thaw Cycle Test

The numbers of freeze-thaw cycles designed in this study were 25, 50, and 75. Then, CT scanning, weight measurement, open porosity measurement and mechanical test (including flexural strength and compressive strength) were carried out on the specimens of each cycle group. A few pictures of specimens after freeze-thaw cycles are shown in Fig. 1.

2 Resualts and Discussion

2.1 Macroscopic Damage Characteristics

Gradual cumulative damage and sudden fracture damage are the two failure modes of porous concrete in the freeze-thaw cycle, as shown in Fig. 1. Gradual cumulative damage means that during the freeze-thaw cycle, due to the capillary water pressure, the cement and aggregate barriers between the pores loose and fall off. And the pores merge at the same time. It must be pointed out that this condition tends to only increase the porosity of the porous concrete, which can lead to the strength reduction, while the fracture failure does not occur. However, if many cement and aggregate failures unfortunately occur at the same section, it is easy to cause sudden fracture damage.

Fig. 1 Specimen Pictures and CT Scan Images of Gradual Cumulative Damage and Sudden Fracture Damage

2.2 Strength and Pore Characteristics Analysis

Fig. 2a) shows that the 28day's flexural strength and shear strength of porous concrete decrease as the number of freeze-thaw cycles increases. Fig. 2b) reveals the changes in the internal pore structure of porous concrete during the freeze-thaw cycle. It can be seen that as the number of cycles increases, the number of pores in the porous concrete continues to decrease, while the average pore area continues to increase, which is crucial to prove that pore expansion and pore merging are occurring inside. Compared with dense concrete, porous concrete obviously has more voids between aggregates, which causes an easier water penetration. Therefore, the freeze-thaw cycle has a great influence on the mechanical properties of porous concrete. It is very difficult to apply in cold regions without enhancing measures.

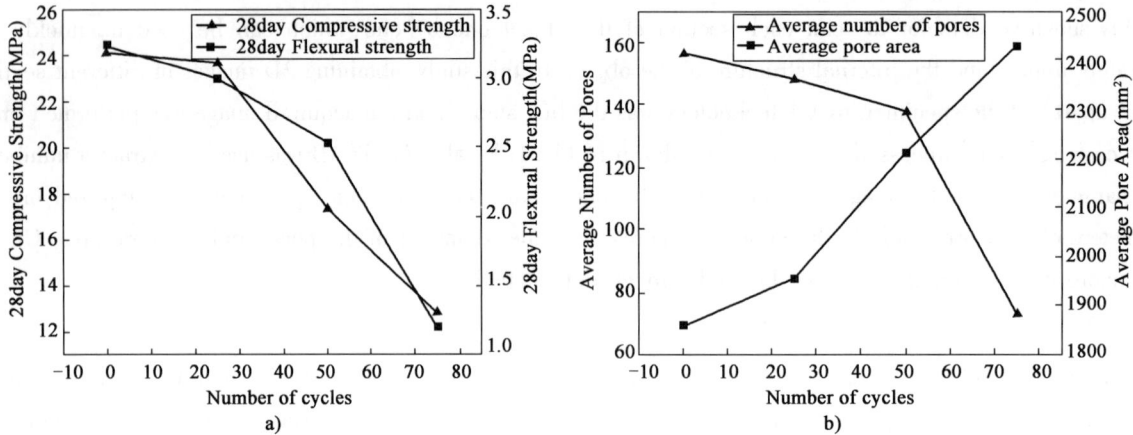

Fig. 2 Changes in Bending Resistance, Compressive Strength, the Average Number and Area of Pores Under Freeze-thaw Cycles

Fig. 3 shows the changing trend of pore diameters in different quantiles with the increase in the number of freeze-thaw cycles of the specimen. It shows that from 0 to 50 cycles, the maximum pore diameter increases the fastest. As mentioned above, the freeze-thaw cycle of porous concrete is accompanied by an increase in the average pore area and a decrease in the number of pores, which reveals the merging process between pores. Therefore, Fig. 3 indicates that during the freeze-thaw cycle of porous concrete, the existence of small–diameter pores may be more stable than large-pore pores, which explains that the degradation of the mechanical properties of porous concrete during freeze-thaw cycles is much higher than that of the dense concrete.

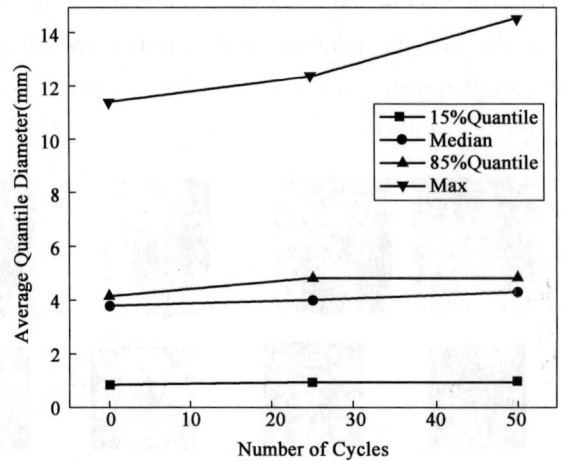

Fig. 3 Changes in Bending Resistance, Compressive Strength, the Average Number and Area of Pores Under Freeze-thaw Cycles

2.3 The Influence of SCMs

This study explored the effect of SCMs on the pore characteristics and freeze – thaw cycle durability of porous concrete. Fig. 4a) shows that the addition of SCMs will reduce the porosity of porous concrete, and it decreases with the increase of SCMs dosage. The weight loss rate is an index that can be used to measure the durability of concrete freeze-thaw cycles. Under the same number of freeze-thaw cycles, the lower the weight loss rate, the better the durability. It can be seen from Fig. 4b) that SCMs can reduce the weight loss rate and improve the durability of freeze-thaw cycles. Among them, the effect of adding silica fume is the most significant. It can be observed that part of the optimization of freeze-thaw cycle durability by SCMs is due to the reduction of its porosity. Therefore, it is necessary to find a balance point between water permeability and freeze-thaw cycle durability of porous concrete.

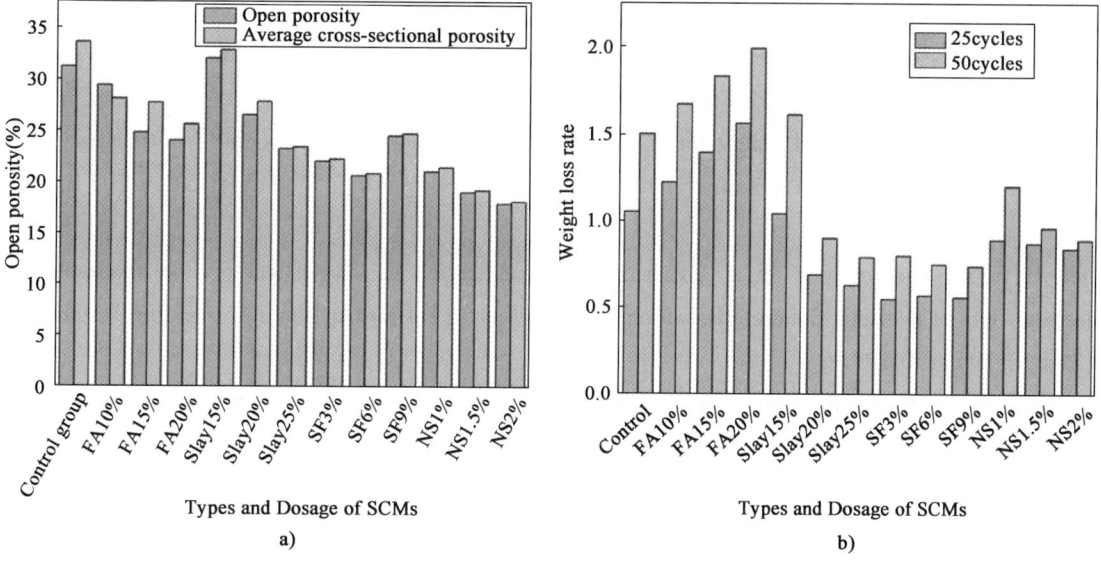

Fig. 4 The Influence of SCMs on the Pore Characteristics and the Weight Loss Rate During Freeze-thaw Cycles of Porous Concrete

3 Conclusions

The variation of strength and void characteristics of porous concrete under freeze-thaw cycles was researched in this study. The influence of four kinds of SCMs on its frost resistance and water permeability was also studied. It was seen that there is a strong relationship between the freeze-thaw resistance and porosity and pore size distribution for porous concrete. The following conclusions were determined from the laboratory tests:

(1) Gradual cumulative damage and sudden fracture damage are the two failure modes of porous concrete in the freeze-thaw cycle. During the freeze-thaw cycle of porous concrete, the cement and aggregate between the pores are destroyed, resulting in expansion and merger of pores. which shows strength attenuation or even fracture failure macroscopically.

(2) The four SCMs will reduce the weight loss rate of porous concrete. Among them, the effect of silica fume is the most significant, with a maximum reduction of 46.7%. However, SCMs will slightly reduce the porosity, indicating that part of the improvement in frost resistance is due to the improvement of compactness.

(3) The reaction and change of porous concrete pores with different diameters during the freeze – thaw cycle are still worthy of further study. And controlling the diameter distribution of porous concrete pores may be an effective way to improve its frost resistance.

4 Acknowledgements

The research was supported by grants from the National Key R&D Program of China (No. 2018YFB1600100), National Key Research and Development Program of China (No. 2016YFE0108200), National Natural Science Foundation of China (Grant No. 5150080567), the Science and Technology Commission of Shanghai Municipality of China (No. 17230711300), and the Fundamental Research Funds for the Central Universities (No. 22120200129). The sponsorships are gratefully acknowledged. The contents of this paper only reflect the views of the authors and do not reflect the official views or policies of the sponsors.

Referances

[1] ACI committee 522, Report on Pervious Concrete, American Concrete Institute Farmington Hills [R], MI, Farmington Hills, Michigan, USA, 2010.

[2] National Ready Mixed Concrete Association (NRMCA), Freeze-Thaw Resistance of Pervious Concrete [R], NRMCA, Silver Spring, MD, USA, 2004.

[3] Yang B, Li H, Zhang H, et al. Laboratorial Investigation on Effects of Microscopic Void Characteristics on Properties of Porous Asphalt Mixture [J]. Construction and Building Materials, 2019, 213 (JUL. 20): 434-446.

[4] Zhou H, Li H, Abdelhady A, et al. Experimental Investigation on The Effect of Pore Characteristics on Clogging Risk of Pervious Concrete Based on CT Scanning [J]. Construction and Building Materials, 2019, 212 (JUL. 10): 130-139.

[5] Lothenbach B. Thermodynamic Equilibrium Calculations in Cementitious Systems [J]. Materials & Structures, 2010, 43(10): 1413-1433.

[6] Geng Jiahui, Yu Chunrong, Liu Zhijie. Commercial Concrete Production and Application technology [M]. Beijing: China Building Materials Industry Press, 2015.

[7] Xu Zhihui, Wei Jiangxiong, Li Fangxian, et al. The Influence of the Amount of Cementitious Material on the Chloride Ion Diffusion Coefficient of Self-compacting Concrete [J]. Concrete, 2014, 000(007): 73-75.

[8] Hu Liguo. Research on the Frost Resistance of Permeable Concrete [D]. Dalian: Dalian Jiaotong University, 2013.

[9] Huang Yangcheng, Luo Lu, Zeng Guanbo. The Influence of Mineral Powder, Silica Fume and Latex Powder on the Performance of Pervious Concrete [J]. Shanxi Architecture, 2010, 36(032): 154-155.

[10] Ministry of Housing and Urban-Rural Development of the people's Republic of China. Technical Specification for Permeable Cement Concrete Pavement: CJJ/T 135—2009 [S]. Beijing: China Architecture K Building Press, 2009.

Influence of Fluidity of Cement Paste, Cement Dosage and Vibration Forming Mode on the Anti-segregation Performance of Pervious Concrete

Yong Feng　Hui Li　Haonan Zhou

(Tongji University)

Abstract　Pervious concrete pavement is one of the important parts of sponge city. As binder, cement paste plays a vital role in determining the performance of pervious concrete. The fluidity of paste and the amount of cement are the most important factors for the segregation of pervious concrete. And the main forming method of pervious concrete is vibration mode. This study investigated the effect of cement paste fluidity, cement dosage, and vibration forming mode on the segregation resistance performance of two kinds of pervious concrete mixtures with different particle sizes. The results show that the greater the fluidity of paste or the greater the amount of cement, the greater the degree of segregation of pervious concrete. The increase of segregation degree with the increase of cement dosage is positively related to the fluidity of cement paste. The segregation index of pervious concrete is in the range of 1 - 5% when the aggregate particle size is large. When the aggregate particle size is small, the segregation index is also small, generally between 0 - 3%. Vibration forming mode aggravates the segregation of pervious concrete, especially in the case of high cement-aggregate ratio and high fluidity of paste. The segregation index can be used to represent the segregation degree of pervious concrete when the vibration time is 10s.

Keywords　Road engineering　Pervious concrete　Cement paste　Fluidity　Vibration forming　Segregation

0　Introduction

Due to the acceleration of urbanization, a large amount of green space was occupied by various buildings and impervious pavements, which contribute mainly to road runoff. More and more attention has been paid to the problem of stormwater. Therefore, China is committed to the construction of sponge cities. Sponge city is a new concept related to urban stormwater management, which can be achieved using pervious pavements, achieving water storage, cooling, noise reduction, and traffic safety improvement [1].

Pervious concrete is a kind of special concrete with cement paste. The paste wraps the aggregate so that the bonding surface and bonding point between aggregate form the strength. In other words, pervious concrete is a kind of porous concrete mixed by aggregate and cement paste.

Cement paste is one of the main components of pervious concrete. Given the high requirements for the performance of raw materials, various modifiers are often added, so the properties of cement paste are complex. The bond strength and other properties of cement paste are generally determined by the cement grade, additives, water-cement ratio, etc., and the addition of additives, water, and other materials will affect the fluidity of cement mortar [2-7].

Aggregate is also one of the main components of pervious concrete. Coarse aggregate is generally used in pervious concrete, and less or no fine aggregate is used. Two kinds of aggregate, 2.36 ~ 4.75mm and 4.75 ~ 9.5mm, are generally used for single particle size pervious concrete pavement surface [4,8-10].

It is one of the most common and effective means to improve the strength of pervious concrete by adding admixtures to enhance the performance of cement mortar. At present, there are many kinds of admixtures used in the preparation of pervious concrete around the world, and the most commonly used and most economical admixtures are powder admixtures [11-14]. Among them, silica fume and polycarboxylic acid water reducer are two kinds of powder admixtures that can obviously improve the performance of pervious concrete.

Admixtures can optimize the strength, freeze-thaw resistance, and other properties of pervious concrete. After adding various admixtures, the performance of cement paste often changes, and the change of paste performance may cause the change of pervious concrete performance. At present, most of the researches on pervious concrete ignore the study of cement mortar. When studying the influence of admixtures on the performance of pervious concrete, most researchers only used the simple method of adding admixtures or adding admixtures, then studied the influence of admixtures on the properties of pervious concrete directly. They did not deeply study the change of cement paste properties after adding admixtures and the effect of cement paste on the performance of pervious concrete [2,15-17]. In particular, little attention has been paid to the segregation of the mixture caused by the change of the fluidity of cement paste after the addition of admixtures in pervious concrete, which undoubtedly increases the risk of segregation of pervious concrete.

In addition to the differences in material design, the molding mode also affects the performance of pervious concrete. At present, the main molding mode of pervious concrete is vibration forming mode. Given the large pores in pervious concrete, the cement paste and aggregate will be separated due to the excessive fluidity of cement paste during the vibration molding process. Excessive cement dosage or too long process time, which makes the cement paste deposit to the lower part of the concrete along with the pore structures, and finally block the pores to make the permeability of pervious concrete decrease or lose [18,19]. Li Bin, Ma Yufang, and other researchers believed that the strength of pervious concrete prepared by vibration forming mode is higher than that of concrete prepared by other molding methods [20-22]. However, at the same time, Chen Xiao et al. prepared pervious concrete with different rheological properties through vibration molding mode and concluded that pervious concrete is more likely to segregate [23]. Therefore, it is necessary to pay attention to the influence of vibration forming mode on the anti-segregation performance of pervious concrete.

According to those mentioned above, existing research aimed to improve the performance of pervious concrete is inadequate. Previous studies paid more attention to the concrete itself and ignored the study of cement paste. The relationship between paste fluidity and anti-segregation performance of pervious concrete is uncertain. Simultaneously, the influence of vibration forming mode on the anti-segregation performance of pervious concrete is also ignored.

Therefore, based on the characteristics of silica fume and polycarboxylic acid water reducer, this study investigated the effect of cement paste fluidity, cement dosage, and vibration forming mode on the segregation resistance performance of two kinds of pervious concrete mixtures with different particle sizes.

1 Materials and Test Methods

1.1 Materials Used

Cement, water, additive, and aggregate were used in this study. The cement is portland cement with a strength grade of 42.5. The specific indexes are shown in Tab. 1. Basalt aggregate with a single particle size of 4.75~9.5mm and limestone aggregate with a single particle size of 2.36~4.75mm were used in the research. The specific parameters are shown in Tab. 2. Silica fume and polycarboxylate water reducer were used as additives, and tap water was used as mixing water.

Parameters of Cement Tab. 1

Grade	Dry Density ($g \cdot cm^{-3}$)	Fineness (%)	Initial Setting Time (min)	Final Setting Time (min)	Compressive Strength (MPa)	Flexural Strength (MPa)
P.O.42.5	3.1	1.1	120	220	40.3	8.2

Parameters of Aggregate Tab. 2

Type	Particle Size (mm)	Apparent Relative Density ($g \cdot cm^{-3}$)	Dry Density ($g \cdot cm^{-3}$)	Relative Density of Gross Volume ($g \cdot cm^{-3}$)	Water Absorption (%)
Basalt	4.75~9.5	2.94	2.83	2.78	2.0
Limestone	2.36~4.75	2.86	2.66	2.55	4.2

1.2 Mixtures Design

1.2.1 Influence of paste fluidity on segregation resistance of 4.75-9.5mm pervious concrete

This section explored the change of anti-segregation performance of pervious concrete mixture when the fluidity of cement paste changes. Pervious concrete mixtures with different paste fluidity were prepared by changing the content of silica fume, water reducing agent, and water-cement ratio. The mix proportion is shown in Tab. 3. The cement-aggregate ratio was fixed at 0.24.

Mix Proportion in the Experiment of the Influence of Paste Fluidity on Anti-segregation Performance of Pervious Concrete Tab. 3

Group	W/C	Aggregate (g)	Cement (g)	Silica Fume (g)	Proportion of Silica Fume (%)	Polycarboxylate Water Reducer (g)	Proportion of Reducer (%)	Fluidity of Paste (mm)
Control Group		5300	1272	—	—	—	—	219.5
1-1	0.325	5300	1235	37	3	—	—	200.3
1-2	0.325	5300	1200	72	6	—	—	179.6
1-3	0.325	5300	1167	105	9	—	—	162.4
2-1	0.3	5300	1272	—	—	—	—	210.9
2-2	0.35	5300	1272	—	—	—	—	232.8
2-3	0.375	5300	1272	—	—	—	—	245.3
2-4	0.4	5300	1272	—	—	—	—	258.4
3-1	0.225	5300	1272	—	—	2.5	0.20	210.6
3-2	0.225	5300	1272	—	—	3.2	0.25	232.1
3-3	0.225	5300	1272	—	—	3.8	0.30	243.5
3-4	0.225	5300	1272	—	—	4.4	0.35	255.4

Note: W/C stands for water-cement ratio.

1.2.2 Effect of Cement Dosage on Segregation Resistance of 4.75~9.5 mm Pervious Concrete

The influence of cement content on the segregation index of the mixture was studied, and the cement content was expressed by cement-aggregate ratio. Three kinds of paste with different fluidity were prepared in three proportions and divided into three groups. The specific test proportion is shown in Tab. 4.

Mix Proportion in the Anti-segregation Test Tab. 4

Group	W/C	C/A	Aggregate (g)	Cement (g)	Silica Fume (g)	Polycarboxylate Water Reducer (g)	Fluidity of Paste (mm)
1-1	0.3	0.22	5300	1100	66	—	171.2
1-2		0.24		1200	72		
1-3		0.26		1300	78		
1-4		0.28		1400	84		
2-1	0.325	0.22		1132	34	—	200.3
2-2		0.24		1235.2	37.1		
2-3		0.26		1338.3	40.2		
2-4		0.28		1441.4	43.3		
3-1	0.225	0.22		1166.0	—	2.9	232.1
3-2		0.24		1272.2		3.2	
3-3		0.26		1378.4		3.4	
3-4		0.28		1484.7		3.7	

Note: W/C stands for water-cement ratio, C/A stands for cement-aggregate ratio.

1.2.3 Influence of Fluidity and Dosage of Paste on Segregation Resistance of Pervious Concrete with a Particle Size of 2.36-4.75mm

Limestone aggregate with small particle size was used, which has small particle size, high density and requires more cement. The specific test proportion is shown in Tab. 5.

Mix Proportion in the Experiment of the Influence of Fluidity and Dosage of Paste on Anti-segregation Performance of Pervious Concrete with Particle Size of 2.36-4.75 mm Tab. 5

Group	W/C	C/A	Cement (g)	Aggregate (g)	Silica Fume (g)	Proportion of Silica Fume (%)	Polycarboxylate Water Reducer (g)	Proportion of Reducer (%)	Fluidity of Paste (mm)
1-1	0.3	0.24	1267.9	5600	76.1	6	—	—	171.2
1-2		0.26	1373.6		82.4				
1-3		0.28	1479.2		88.8				
1-4		0.30	1584.9		95.1				
2-1	0.325	0.24	1304.9		39.1	3	—	—	200.3
2-2		0.26	1413.6		42.4				
2-3		0.28	1522.3		45.7				
2-4		0.30	1631.1		48.9				
3-1	0.225	0.24	1344.0		—	—	3.4	2.5	232.1
3-2		0.26	1456.0				3.6		
3-3		0.28	1568.0				3.9		
3-4		0.30	1680.0				4.2		

Note: W/C stands for water-cement ratio, C/A stands for cement-aggregate ratio.

1.2.4 Influence of Fluidity and Dosage of Paste on the Anti-segregation Performance of Pervious Concrete under Vibration Condition

To explore the influence of vibration and vibration time on the anti-segregation performance of the mixture, the proportion is shown in Tab. 6. In terms of vibration time, the general vibration time of ordinary concrete is in the range of 10-30 s, and the specific vibration time depends on the situation of the mixture on site. To comprehensively study the influence of vibration time on the anti-segregation performance of the mixture, the vibration time was 0s, 5s, 10s, 20s and 30s.

Mix Proportion in the Experiment of Segregation Index under Vibration Condition Tab.6

Group	W/C	C/A	Cement (g)	Aggregate (g)	Silica Fume (g)	Proportion of Silica Fume (%)	Fluidity of Paste (mm)	Vibration Time (s)
1	0.3	0.24	1200	5300	72	6	171.2	0、5、10、20、30
2		0.28	1400		84			
3	0.35	0.24	1272.2		—	—	232.8	
4		0.28	1484.7					

Note: W/C stands for water-cement ratio, C/A stands for cement-aggregate ratio.

1.3 Methods

1.3.1 Sample Preparation

The fresh pervious concrete mixture was made of a single shaft horizontal HJW-60 mixer, with a rotation speed of 45R/min ±2R/min and mixing time of 45-60 seconds.

1.3.2 Anti-segregation Performance Test

The segregation degree of the fresh mixture is expressed by the segregation index. The segregation index mainly reflects the difficulty of cement paste peeling off from the aggregate surface and depositing downward. The segregation index is twice of the ratio of the difference between the top and bottom mixture and the total mass after the test. The larger the segregation index is, the more serious the segregation is. The equation of the segregation index is shown in Equation 1.

$$I_{seg} = 2 \times \frac{m_{bot} - m_{top}}{m_{bot} + m_{top}} \times 100 \tag{1}$$

I_{seg} is the segregation index, m_{bot} is the mass of the bottom mixture, m_{top} is the mass of the top mixture.

The test method of anti-segregation performance mainly referred to the 《"Technical Specification for Application of Self-compacting Concrete》(JGJ/T 283—2012) and method of anti-segregation performance of self-compacting concrete in ASTM C 1610—2006. Then this test method was modified to study the segregation resistance of fresh pervious concrete mixture.

As shown in Fig. 1, the anti-segregation performance test device is mainly composed of a detachable threelayer steel tube cylinder, in which each layer is 100 mm, the inner diameter is 115 mm, and the outer diameter is 135 mm.

The mixed pervious concrete mixture was first put into the anti-segregation performance test device in three layers during the test. After the first two layers were installed, a manual tamping operation was carried out from the edge to the middle to fill the test device. When installing the third layer, the mixture's height should be 3 cm ± 1 cm higher than that of the test device.

After filling the mixture, the test group without vibration was allowed to stand for 120 seconds. The test group that needs to be vibrated was quickly

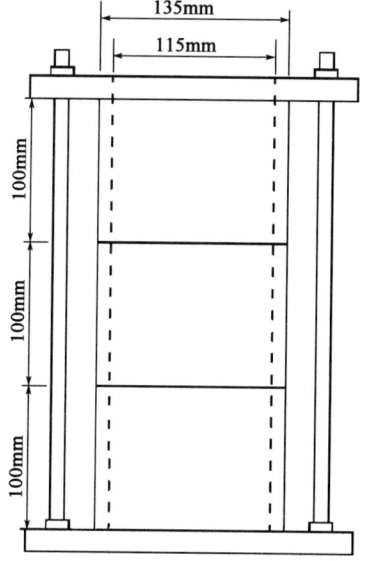

Fig. 1 Experimental Device of Segregation Index

placed on the vibration testbed. After the vibration testbed was turned on, the time required for the vibration test was t seconds, and then the mixture was allowed to stand for 120 − t seconds.

When the above workwas completed, the surplus concrete mixture on the test device was scraped off with a spatula and smoothed. After each layer was removed, the surface and bottom of each layer were smoothed to keep the mixture in a full state. The mass of each layer was weighed, and the data was recorded.

2 Results and Discussion

2.1 Influence of Fluidity of Cement Paste on Anti-segregation Performance of Pervious Concrete with Particle Size of 4.75-9.5mm

The fluidity of the paste was changed in different ways, and the samples were prepared according to the date in Tab. 3. The segregation index of the mixture with different paste fluidity was measured without vibration. The data are shown in Tab. 7.

Experimental Data of Anti-segregation Performance of Pervious Concrete Mixture Tab. 7

Group		Weight of each part (g)			Segregation Index (%)	Density (g·cm^{-3})
		Top	Middle	Bottom		
Control Group		1945	1939	1982	1.9	1.883
Adding Silica Fume	1-1	1949	1942	1982	1.7	1.886
	1-2	1946	1943	1980	1.7	1.884
	1-3	1946	1940	1977	1.6	1.882
Changing W/C	2-1	1942	1940	1980	1.9	1.882
	2-2	1936	1942	1986	2.5	1.883
	2-3	1930	1950	1993	3.2	1.886
	2-4	1908	1963	2006	5.0	1.887
Adding Water Reducer	3-1	1939	1946	1979	2.0	1.883
	3-2	1938	1945	1983	2.3	1.883
	3-3	1932	1948	1990	3.0	1.885
	3-4	1912	1960	2001	4.5	1.886

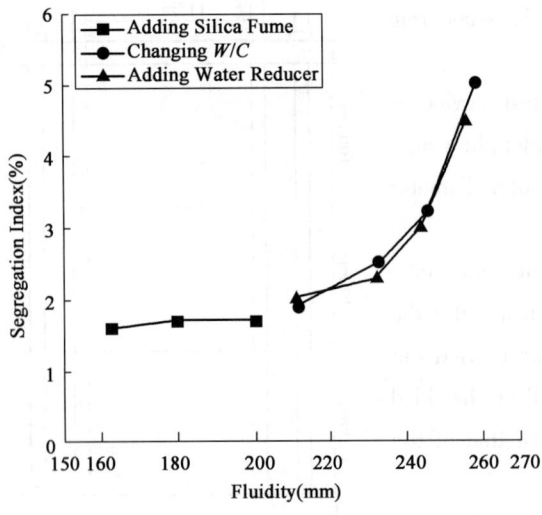

Fig. 2　Segregation Index of Pervious Concrete with Different Paste Fluidity

The curve was drawn according to the segregation index data in Tab. 7 and the cement paste fluidity data in Tab. 3. The relationship between segregation index and fluidity is shown in Fig. 2.

It can be seen from Fig. 2 that the segregation index increases with the increase of the fluidity of paste no matter how the fluidity is changed. Secondly, based on the previous conclusion, it can be seen from the slope changes of several curves that the segregation index is almost not affected by the paste fluidity when the fluidity is small. The segregation index is about 1%-2%, and the reason for a small amount of cement deposition is caused by manual tamping and compaction. With the increase of fluidity, the segregation degree of the mixture increases rapidly when the fluidity exceeds 220 mm. That is to say, under the influence of gravity, the cement paste deposit to the lower part through the pores between the mixture.

The segregation test equipment can be disassembled into upper, middle and bottom parts. Fig. 3 shows the cement accumulation on the surface of each part of the samples after the segregation test. It can be seen from Fig. 3 that in the upper part of the mixture, the amount of cement paste on the aggregate surface is less, and the pores between adjacent aggregates are larger. Compared with the upper part of the mixture, the amount of cement paste on the surface of the aggregate increases obviously, and some pores between the aggregates have been blocked by the cement paste. At the bottom of the mixture, there is too much cement paste on the surface of the aggregate, most of which have been connected into one piece. Almost all the macropores are blocked by the paste. And it can be seen that this part of the cement mortar is relatively thin and has a large fluidity before solidification. It can be seen that the cement paste in this part is relatively thin and has larger fluidity before solidification. From the side view of the mixture at the bottom of the sample, it is evident that there are layers. Only cement paste can be seen at the bottom, and aggregate and pores can be seen at the top. All these show that the segregation of mixture makes the pores in the middle and bottom parts of concrete blocked by paste after forming, which reduce the connected porosity and significantly reduce or lose the permeability of concrete.

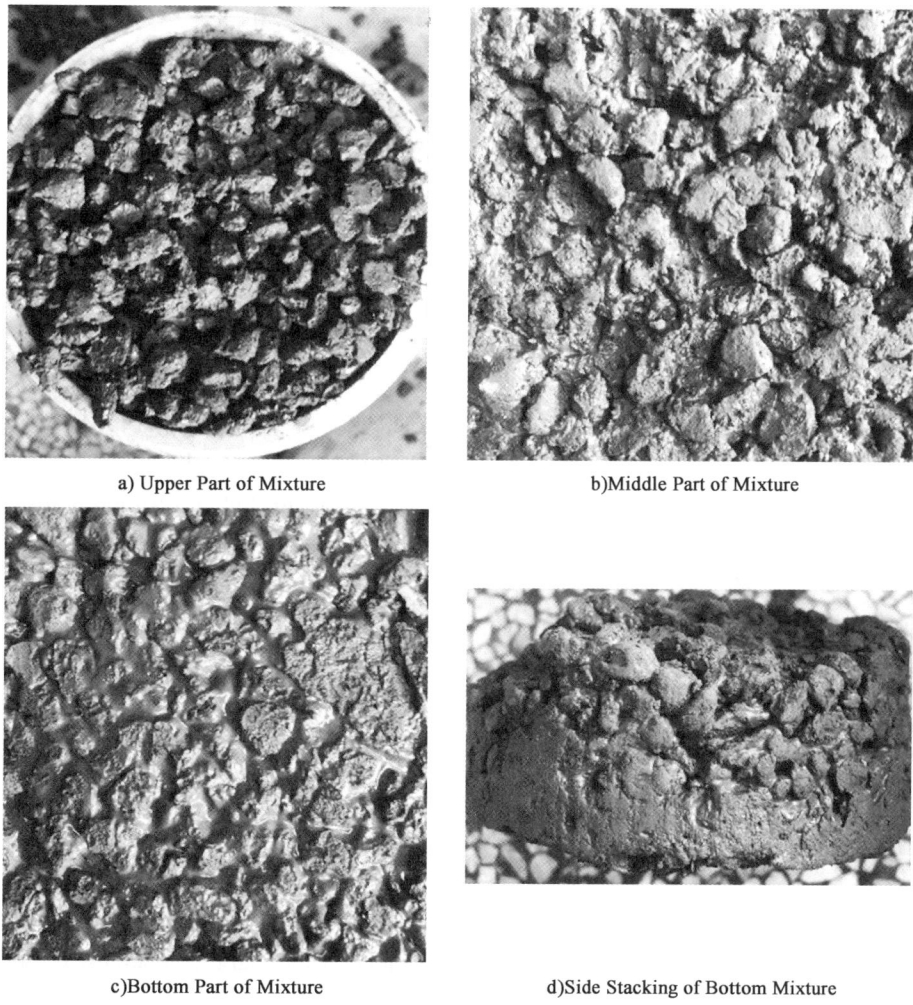

a) Upper Part of Mixture   b) Middle Part of Mixture

c) Bottom Part of Mixture   d) Side Stacking of Bottom Mixture

Fig. 3 Condition of Each Part of Mixture after Segregation Test

2.2 Influence of Cement Dosage on Segregation Resistance of Pervious Concrete with Particle Size of 4.75-9.5mm

The samples were prepared according to the data in Tab. 4, and the anti-segregation test results of each experimental group are shown in Tab. 8. According to the results in the table, the sample with a large cement-aggregate ratio has a higher density, which is caused by more cement filling in the pores between the mixture. In each test group, the segregation index is increasing, reflecting that the segregation index of the mixture increases with the increase of cement-aggregate ratio.

Influence of Cement-Aggregate Ratio on Segregation Index of Mixture Tab. 8

Group	C/A	Fluidity of paste (mm)	Weight of Each Part(g)			Segregation Index (%)	Density (g·cm^{-3})
			Top	Middle	Bottom		
1-1	0.22	171.2	1935	1938	1954	1.0	1.871
1-2	0.24		1950	1948	1976	1.3	1.886
1-3	0.26		1973	1975	2005	1.6	1.911
1-4	0.28		1994	2004	2035	2.0	1.937
2-1	0.22	200.3	1933	1940	1960	1.4	1.873
2-2	0.24		1948	1949	1982	1.7	1.888
2-3	0.26		1970	1958	2018	2.4	1.909
2-4	0.28		1986	1987	2061	3.7	1.937
3-1	0.22	232.1	1930	1933	1970	2.1	1.873
3-2	0.24		1936	1942	1986	2.5	1.883
3-3	0.26		1952	1985	2024	3.6	1.914
3-4	0.28		1977	2010	2081	5.1	1.948

In order to further analyze the relationship between the segregation index and the cement-aggregate ratio of the mixture, the relationship between the segregation index and the cement-aggregate ratio can be drawn according to the data in Tab. 8, as shown in Fig. 4.

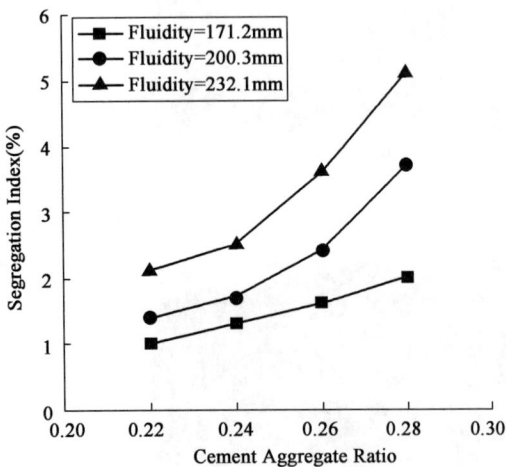

Fig. 4 Influence of Cement-Aggregate Ratio on Segregation Index of Mixture

It can be seen from the figure that when the fluidity of paste is small, the change of segregation index of the mixture is small, which can be regarded as a linear change. When the fluidity is above 200 mm, the slope of the broken line increases, which indicates that the change rate increases obviously. Also, in Fig. 4, the spacing between two adjacent broken lines gradually increases with the increase of the cement-aggregate ratio, which indicates that the greater the fluidity is, the greater the influence of the cement-aggregate ratio on the segregation index of the mixture is. The reason for these results is that when the fluidity of the paste is small, the aggregate can be wrapped by more cement paste, so the cement-aggregate ratio can not affect the segregation performance of the mixture too much. When the fluidity of cement paste is large, the adhesive property of paste to aggregate becomes weak. When too much cement is added, the excess cement will be affected by gravity, and deposit to the lower part through the pores between aggregates, so the degree of segregation increase rapidly.

2.3 Influence of Fluidity of Cement Paste on Anti-segregation Performance of Pervious Concrete with Particle Size of 2.36-4.75mm

The samples were made according to the mix proportion in Tab. 5, and the segregation index data of each test group are shown in Tab. 9.

Segregation Index of Small Size Mixture   Tab. 9

Group	C/A	Fluidity of Paste (mm)	Weight of Each Part/g			Segregation Index (%)	Density (g·cm^{-3})
			Top	Middle	Bottom		
1-1	0.24	171.2	2089	2109	2089	0.0	2.019
1-2	0.26		2112	2133	2118	0.3	2.043
1-3	0.28		2136	2169	2150	0.7	2.073
1-4	0.30		2170	2205	2196	1.2	2.110
2-1	0.24	200.3	2082	2120	2095	0.6	2.022
2-2	0.26		2106	2151	2122	0.8	2.048
2-3	0.28		2134	2180	2168	1.6	2.081
2-4	0.30		2163	2211	2206	2.0	2.113
3-1	0.24	232.1	2080	2125	2103	1.1	2.025
3-2	0.26		2106	2160	2154	2.3	2.061
3-3	0.28		2135	2191	2200	3.0	2.095
3-4	0.30		2170	2223	2219	2.2	2.123

According to the data in Tab. 9, although the fluidity of cement paste is consistent with that in 2.2 and a higher cement-aggregate ratio is adopted, the overall segregation index is obviously smaller than that of the mixture with a particle size of 4.75-9.5mm, and the maximum segregation index is 3%.

According to the data in Tab. 9, the influence curve of cement-aggregate ratio on segregation index of the small-size mixture was drawn, as shown in Fig. 5. It can be seen from the figure that when the cement-aggregate ratio is small, the segregation index of the small particle size mixture is low. For example, when the fluidity of paste is 171.2mm and the cement-aggregate ratio is 0.24, the mixture hardly segregates. Even because of the mixing uniformity, the segregation index is negative in some parallel experimental groups. The segregation index almost increases with the increase of cement-aggregate ratio. But there is an exception, when the fluidity is 231.2mm and the cement-aggregate ratio is large, the segregation index decreases with the increase of cement-aggregate ratio. The weight difference between the upper and bottom parts of the two samples with the C/A of 0.28 and 0.3 was analyzed. When the C/A is 0.28, the upper mass of the sample is 2135g and the bottom mass is 2200g, while when the C/A is 0.3, the upper mass of the sample is 2170g and the bottom mass is 2219g. That is to

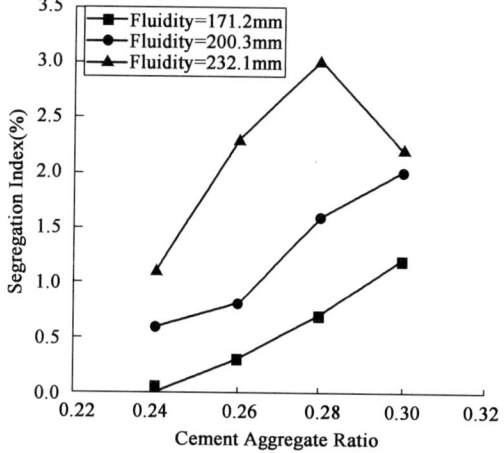

Fig. 5 Influence of Cement-Aggregate Ratio on Segregation Index of Small Size Mixture

say, the mass of the upper part and the lower part increased by 35g and 19g respectively because of the increase of the C/A. While in most cases, the mass growth of the upper part was less than or equal to the mass growth of the bottom part. There are two main reasons. First, when the aggregate particle size is small, the internal porosity and pore size of the mixture are not large. In the case of a high cement-aggregate ratio, it is difficult for cement paste to flow from the upper and middle part of the mixture to the bottom part. In addition, after a certain degree of segregation has occurred in the mixture, the pores in the bottom part can not accommodate more cement paste, more paste will be concentrated in the middle part. And the smaller the aperture of the middle and bottom parts make segregation more difficult. Therefore, when the particle size of the mixture is small, the segregation index is generally small.

2.4 Influence of Fluidity and Dosage of Paste on the Anti-segregation Performance of Pervious Concrete under Vibration Forming Mode

According to the mix proportion and vibration time in Table 6, the final segregation index data is shown in Tab. 10. Compared with the data when the vibration time is 0, the density of the sample increases significantly after 30 s vibration. This shows that the vibration makes the mixture sample sink as a whole, making the concrete denser. In addition, according to the data in the table, the segregation index of the mixture increases significantly after vibration. Comparing the segregation index of 30 s vibration with that of no vibration, the segregation index of each experimental group increased by 2-5 percentage points respectively, and the increase ratio was more than double. This shows that vibration has a great influence on the segregation of mixture. This is mainly due to the cement paste itself has a specific viscosity. It needs a certain external force to produce deformation and displacement. When the mixture is vibrated, it is equivalent to exerting external force on the paste, and there is enough force to make it move. Therefore, the segregation degree of the mixture is increased.

Influence of Paste Fluidity and Cement-Aggregate Ratio on Segregation Index of Mixture under Different Vibration Time Tab. 10

Vibration time (s)	Group		1	2	3	4
0	Weight (g)	Top	1950	1994	1936	1977
		Middle	1948	2004	1942	2010
		Bottom	1976	2035	1986	2081
	Segregation Index (%)		1.3	2	2.5	5.1
	Density (g·cm^{-3})		1.871	1.937	1.883	1.948
5	Weight (g)	Top	1970	2013	1963	2017
		Middle	2034	2039	1976	2046
		Bottom	2015	2089	2061	2156
	Segregation Index (%)		2.3	3.7	4.9	6.7
	Density (g·cm^{-3})		1.933	1.972	1.926	1.997
10	Weight (g)	Top	1985	2027	1986	2023
		Middle	2060	2069	2000	2091
		Bottom	2044	2120	2104	2199
	Segregation Index (%)		2.9	4.5	5.8	8.3
	Density (g·cm^{-3})		1.955	1.996	1.955	2.027

Vibration time (s)	Group		1	2	3	4
20	Weight (g)	Top	1989	2045	2001	2027
		Middle	2075	2099	2011	2098
		Bottom	2056	2158	2142	2245
	Segregation Index (%)		3.3	5.4	6.8	10.2
	Density (g·cm^{-3})		1.965	2.023	1.976	2.045
30	Weight (g)	Top	1992	2048	2009	2031
		Middle	2086	2104	2014	2103
		Bottom	2060	2167	2144	2250
	Segregation Index (%)		3.4	5.6	6.5	10.2
	Density (g·cm^{-3})		1.971	2.029	1.980	2.050

Fig. 6 is the curve of the segregation index of samples changing with vibration time.

From the trend of the curve, it can be seen that in general, when the vibration time is 0~10s, the segregation index changes greatly. And with the increase of the vibration time, the change amplitude also gradually decreases.

The analysis of each test group shows that when the fluidity of cement paste is low and the cement-aggregate ratio is low, the segregation index of the mixture is less affected by the vibration, and it will not change with the vibration time soon. It is similar in the case of high cement-aggregate ratio, but the overall segregation index is higher than that in the case of low cement-aggregate ratio. This is mainly due to the fact that when the water-cement ratio is low, the viscosity of cement paste is generally high, the yield stress is large, and a larger external force is needed to make the cement paste move. Therefore, the paste shows a strong binding ability to the aggregate at this time.

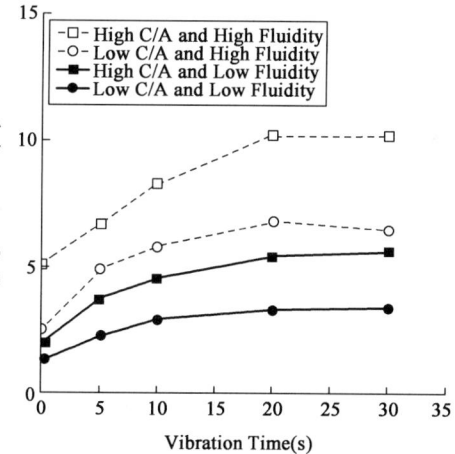

Fig. 6 Influence of Fluidity and Dosage of Paste on Segregation Index under Different Vibration Time

In the case of the high fluidity of cementpaste, the influence of vibration on the segregation index is more apparent, and the influence time is longer. Within 10-20 s, the segregation index is still in the apparent rising stage. However, it changes slowly in 20-30s, and even has a downward trend. On the one hand, during the test, the pores are more and more blocked by the paste. That is, space for the paste to flow is smaller and smaller, so the change of segregation index is slowed down. On the other hand, with the increasing of segregation index, the bottom part of the mixture can not hold more paste, while the mass of the middle and upper parts is still growing, so the segregation index decrease. In addition, with the increase of time, the decrease of the fluidity also has an impact on this.

As a standard molding method of pervious concrete, vibration forming mode will reduce the segregation resistance of mixture, especially in the case of high fluidity and high cement-aggregate ratio.

3 Conclusions

This paper mainly studied the influence of fluidity of cement paste, cement dosage, aggregate particle size and vibration time on the anti-segregation performance of fresh pervious concrete mixture. The main conclusions are as follows:

(1) Generally, the segregation degree of the mixture increases with the increase of fluidity of cement paste. Moreover, this effect has no great relationship with what factors lead to the change of cement paste fluidity.

(2) In the design of mix proportion of pervious concrete, too much cement lead to the segregation of the mixture. The increase of the segregation degree caused by the increase of the cement-aggregate ratio is positively related to the fluidity of the cement paste.

(3) When the particle size of the mixture is large, the segregation index is generally large, which is in the range of 1-5%. And when the cement-aggregate ratio changes, the segregation index changes significantly. When the particle size of aggregate is small, the segregation index is also small, generally between 0-3%. The segregation index may decrease with the increase of cement-aggregate ratio.

(4) Vibration forming mode aggravates the segregation of pervious concrete mixture, especially in the case of high cement-aggregate ratio and high fluidity of paste. When designing pervious concrete, on the one hand, the influence of cement-aggregate ratio and paste fluidity should be considered; on the other hand, vibration time should also be considered when molding. When the vibration time is 10s, it is close to the vibration time of the actual molding specimen. At this time, the paste is most affected by vibration, and the segregation index is not too high. Therefore, the segregation index when the vibration time is 10s could be considered to represent the segregation degree of pervious concrete.

(5) Segregation index is a parameter to judge the uniformity of concrete, which is not directly related to a specific performance of concrete. When the aggregate particle size is 2.36-4.75mm, the segregation index is relatively small, generally lower than 3%. That is, the uniformity of concrete is better. But whether it means that its mechanical properties must be better than that of concrete with a larger segregation index needs further study.

4 Acknowledgements

The research was supported by grants from the National Key Research and Development Program of China (No. 2016YFE0108200), the Science and Technology Commission of Shanghai Municipality of China (No. 17230711300), and the Fundamental Research Funds for the Central Universities (No. 22120200129). The sponsorships are gratefully acknowledged. The contents of this paper only reflect the views of the authors and do not reflect the official views or policies of the sponsors.

References

[1] Song Z, Shi Y. Pervious Concrete and Its Application Technology[M]. Beijing: China Architecture and Building Press, 2011.

[2] Chen Y, et al. Mechanical Properties of Pervious Cement Concrete[J]. Journal of Central South University, 2012, 19(11): 3329-3334.

[3] Kong S. Summary of Performance and Influence Factors of Pervious Concrete[J]. Ready-mixed Concrete, 2017(Z1): 46-50.

[4] Yu C, et al. Strength, Fracture and Fatigue of Pervious Concrete[J]. Construction and Building Materials, 2013, 42(5): 97-104.

[5] Li J, et al. Preparation and Performance Evaluation of an Innovative Pervious Concrete Pavement[J]. Construction and Building Materials, 2017, 138(5): 479-485.

[6] Zhang Z, et al. Influence Factors of Compressive Strength and Permeability of Pervious Concrete[J]. Concrete, 2008, (3): 7-9.

[7] Li J. Experimental Study on Influence Factors of Permeable Concrete Properties[D]. Nanchang: Jiangxi

University of Science and Technology.

[8] Kasemchaisiri R, Tangtermsirikul S. A Method to Determine Water Retainability of Porous Fine Aggregate for Design and Quality Control of Fresh Concrete[J]. Construction & Building Materials, 2007, 21(6): 1322-1334.

[9] Neithalath N, et al. Characterizing Pore Volume, Sizes, and Connectivity in Pervious Concrete for Permeability Prediction[J]. Materials Characterization, 2010, 61(8): 802-813.

[10] Wang Y, Wang D. Effects of Aggregate Species and Quality on the Properties of Pervious Concrete: a Review[J]. Materials Reports, 2017, 31(17): 98-105, 121.

[11] He J, et al. Research on the Performance of Pervious Concrete with Admixtures[J]. Shanxi Architecture, 2019, 45(14): 74-76.

[12] Koehler E P, et al. Chemical Admixture System for Pervious Concrete[J]. American Concrete Institute ACI Special Publication, 2009, 44(6): 978-981.

[13] Tran T T, et al. Effect of Pre-compressive Stress on Chloride Permeability of Concrete Used anti-permeable Admixture[C]// in Proceedings of the 4th Congrès International de Géotechnique-Ouvrages-Structures, Vietnam, 2018: 442-447.

[14] Chen B, et al. Experimental Study of Lightweight Expanded Polystyrene Aggregate Concrete Containing Silica Fume and Polypropylene Fibers[J]. Journal of Shanghai Jiaotong University (Science), 2010, 15(2): 129-137.

[15] Jing Y, Jiang G. Experimental Study on Properties of Pervious Concrete Pavement Materials[J]. Cement and Concrete Research, 2003, 33(3): 381-386.

[16] Huang B, et al. Laboratory Evaluation of Permeability and Strength of Polymer-modified Pervious Concrete[J]. Construction and Building Materials, 2010, 24(5): 818-823.

[17] Li Z, et al. Effect of Mineral Active Ultrafine Powder on the Interface Performance of Pervious Concrete[J]. Highway Engineering, 2017, (5): 311-314.

[18] Sibay J, Tulsontai. Rheological Analysis of Concrete Segregation and Bleeding in Highway Bridge Construction[J]. West-China Exploration Engineering, 2006, 18(S1): 388-389.

[19] Zhao G. Rheological Analysis of Concrete Segregation and Bleeding[J]. China Water Transport, 2007, (05): 30-31.

[20] Xu R, et al. Impact of Different Molding Methods on Pervious Concrete performance[J]. Concrete, 2011, (11): 136-138.

[21] Hao J. Technical Requirements, Forming Methods and Aggregate Gradation Design of Porous Concrete[J]. Journal of Highway and Transportation Research and Development, 2007, (2): 46-47, 50.

[22] Ma Y. Study on Indoor Molding Method of Porous Concrete for Road[J]. Highway, 2007, (12): 176-180.

[23] Chen X, et al. Effect of the Cement Paste Rheological Characteristics on the Properties of Pervious Concrete[J]. China Journal of Highway and Transport, 2019, 32(4): 177-186.

纤维用量对砂浆的工作性和强度影响研究

郝 运 曹阳森 张 帆 胡鑫康 张 进

(长安大学公路学院)

摘 要 为了研究纤维用量对于水泥砂浆工作性和力学强度的影响,选取聚丙烯纤维、耐碱玻璃纤维,以水泥砂浆的流动度、吸水率、抗压强度、抗折强度为评价指标,分析纤维对于砂浆的工作性和力学性能的影响。纤维在最佳掺量附近,流动度和吸水率下降速度较快,抗折强度和抗压强度增强效果明显。水泥水化早期,纤维对砂浆的锚固作用小于应力集中,抗折强度增加幅度较小,抗压强度降低。水泥水化后期,纤维对砂浆的锚固作用增强,砂浆的抗折和抗压强度均有提高,随纤维掺量的增加呈现先增大后减小的趋势。

关键词 水泥砂浆 聚丙烯纤维 玻璃纤维 工作性 力学性能

0 引 言

水泥基材料是一种常用的建筑材料,其抗压强度较高,但是抗变形能力较差,在使用过程中加入纤维可以很好地提高水泥基材料的耐久性[1-6]。常用的纤维有聚丙烯纤维、耐碱玻璃纤维、玄武岩纤维、钢纤维等。李英丁[7]、王来贵[8]等人对于聚丙烯纤维对砂浆强度影响进行研究,聚丙烯纤维可以明显改善砂浆的抗折强度。Yan Wang[9]对于不同掺量聚丙烯纤维对于砂浆破坏的影响进行了研究。方圆[10]等人对于玻璃纤维增强砂浆强度进行了研究,玻璃纤维掺量过多,会将部分水泥包裹,形成未反应基材。刘竞怡[11]等人对玻璃纤维加入煤矸石水泥砂浆性能的影响进行分析,加入玻璃纤维后砂浆的流动性明显下降。高妮[12]等人研究发现,玻璃纤维可以提高砂浆的抗压强度和抗折强度。目前,单一纤维对于砂浆的强度影响研究成果较多,而纤维对于砂浆的工作性和强度系统性研究存在不足。

本文采用聚丙烯纤维和玻璃纤维两种常用纤维,制备纤维砂浆,对纤维砂浆的流动度、吸水率、抗压强度、抗折强度进行试验研究,较为系统地分析了纤维对于砂浆的工作性能和力学强度的影响。

1 实验材料及方法

1.1 实验材料

针对玻璃纤维易受水泥侵蚀的问题,采用复合硅酸盐水泥可以减少对玻璃纤维的侵蚀损害,由冀东水泥厂生产,C32.5复合硅酸盐水泥,主要成分见表1。细集料采用河沙,细度模数为1.922。选用聚丙烯纤维和耐碱玻璃纤维,其参数指标见表2。

复合硅酸盐水泥的组成　　　　表1

成分	Na_2O	MgO	Al_2O_3	SiO_2	SO_3	K_2O	CaO	Fe_2O_3	其他
质量百分率(%)	0.4	1.5	5.4	22.2	0.4	0.8	63.8	3.3	2.2

纤维物理性能　　　　表2

纤维种类	直径(μm)	长度(mm)	密度(g/cm³)	抗拉强度(MPa)	杨氏模量(MPa)	耐 碱 性
玻璃纤维	12	10	2.46	2000	70000	良好
聚丙烯纤维	48	12	0.91	276	3800	优秀

1.2 试验方法

为了分析纤维的空间分布对水泥砂浆工作性和强度的影响,聚丙烯纤维、玻璃纤维采用相同的体积掺量,按照0.06%、0.08%、0.1%、0.2%加入水泥砂浆中。水灰比0.55,水泥450g,砂浆1350g,按照规定成型水泥砂浆试件,试件尺寸为160mm×40mm×40mm,制备砂浆试件,并放在恒温恒湿养护室中进行养护。

按照《水泥胶砂流动度测定方法》(GB/T 2419—2005),水泥砂浆流动度采用水泥胶砂流动度测定仪进行测定,按照规范要求成型试样放置在水泥砂浆流动度振实台上,振动25次,测量砂浆底部直径最大方向和与其垂直的方向,两者取平均值作为该纤维掺量条件下的砂浆流动度。

按照《建筑砂浆基本性能试验方法标准》(JGJ/T 70—2009),水泥砂浆吸水率试验将养护28d试件置于80℃烘箱中至恒重,放入干燥器中冷却至室温,然后称量样品的质量,然后将试件浸入20℃水中48h,通过浸水前后试件的质量变化,计算砂浆的吸水率。

按照《水泥胶砂强度试验》(GB/T 17671—1999)规定,采用TEY-3000水泥胶砂抗压抗折试验机测定抗压抗折强度,参照水泥砂浆试验规程进行受力加载,分别测定聚丙烯纤维砂浆和玻璃纤维砂浆的7d、28d强度。

2 结果与讨论

2.1 纤维掺量对砂浆工作性的影响

纤维对于砂浆的工作性影响主要表现在砂浆的和易性和抗渗性。采用砂浆的流动度评价砂浆和易性和吸水率评价砂浆抗渗性。从图1、图2中可以看出,纤维用量的增加,砂浆的流动度迅速下降,水泥砂浆的吸水率逐渐下降。在0.1%掺量条件下下降趋势变缓,纤维在0.1%体积掺量条件下纤维分布均匀。在砂浆中,纤维比表面积较大大,可以吸附大量水泥浆,同时随着剂量的增加,纤维之间的间距变小,更加容易形成三维骨架结构,减少了游离水泥浆量,从而降低砂浆的流动性。同时,纤维在水泥砂浆中立体网状分布,减少了水泥砂浆的毛细孔,增强了水泥砂浆的致密性,阻碍了水分对水泥砂浆的侵入,从而降低了砂浆的吸水率。

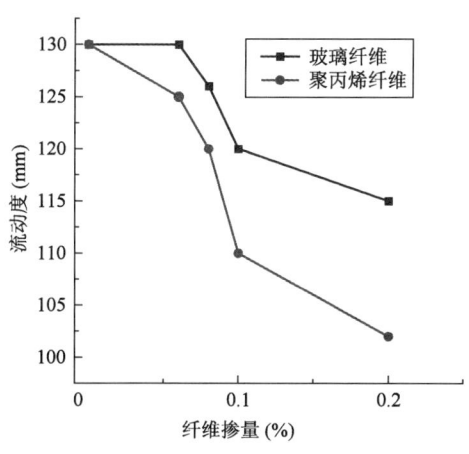
图1 纤维掺量对砂浆流动度的影响

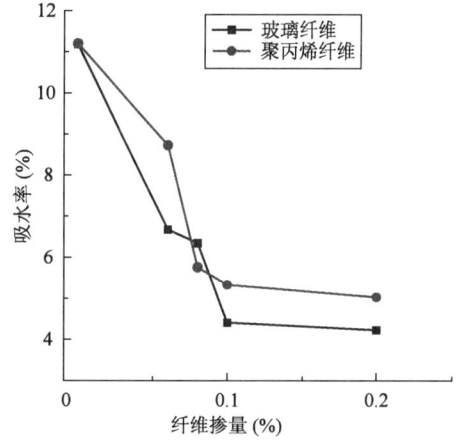
图2 纤维掺量对砂浆吸水率的影响

2.2 纤维掺量对水泥砂浆力学性能的影响

对两种纤维水泥砂浆进行7d、28d抗折强度测试,结果见图3、图4。从图中可以看出,聚丙烯纤维和玻璃纤维加入水泥砂浆,可以显著提高其抗折强度。聚丙烯纤维砂浆的7d和28d抗折强度在0.08%掺量处出现峰值,之后随纤维用量的增加,抗折强度略有降低;玻璃纤维砂浆的7d和28d抗折强度在0.06~0.1%掺量范围内快速增长。7d时在相同体积掺量条件下玻璃纤维抗折强度高于聚丙烯纤维,28d时在0.08%掺量范围内,聚丙烯纤维抗折强度高于玻璃纤维抗折强度,这是水泥水化产物对玻璃纤维产生侵蚀造成的。

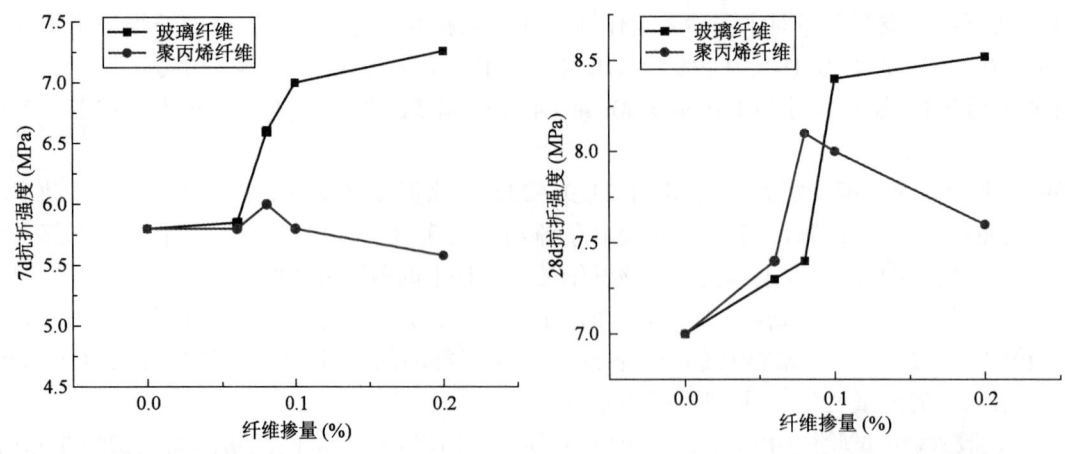

图 3　纤维掺量对 7d 抗折强度的影响　　　　　图 4　纤维掺量对 28d 抗折强度的影响

对于两种纤维砂浆进行 7d、28d 抗压强度测试,结果见图 5、图 6。从图中可以看出,聚丙烯纤维砂浆和玻璃纤维砂浆的 7d 抗压强度先降低后增加。聚丙烯纤维砂浆的 28d 抗压强度先增大后减小,且均高于空白组;玻璃纤维砂浆的 28d 抗压强度下降增强下降。早期聚丙烯纤维砂浆的抗压强度低于玻璃纤维,后期聚丙烯纤维砂浆的抗压强度高于玻璃纤维砂浆。

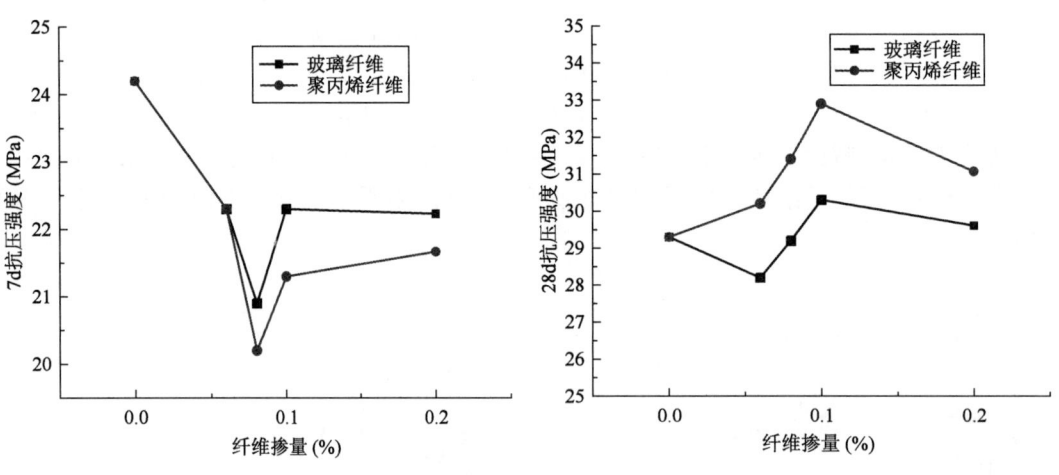

图 5　纤维掺量对 7d 抗压强度的影响　　　　　图 6　纤维掺量对 28d 抗压强度的影响

纤维在水泥砂浆存在应力集中和锚固作用,在 7d 养护,纤维掺量较少时,纤维的锚固作用较弱,纤维处应力集中明显,抗压强度较低。掺量增加,纤维在砂浆中逐渐分散均匀,锚固作用增强,抗压强度出现上升趋势。水泥砂浆 28d 养护后,随着纤维掺量的增加和水泥水化的不断进行,纤维起到的锚固作用不断增强,抗压强度提高。当纤维掺量过多时,纤维分散性较差,应力集中现象较为明显,抗压强度出现下降。

3　结　语

本文通过聚丙烯纤维砂浆和玻璃纤维砂浆的工作性和 7d、28d 强度的试验,分析了纤维对水泥砂浆性能的影响。

(1)纤维加入水泥砂浆,可以降低砂浆的吸水率,从而提高砂浆的抗渗性。水泥砂浆的流动度随纤维掺量的增加而降低,在使用过程中应注意添加减水剂保证水泥砂浆的工作性符合规范要求。

(2)纤维加入水泥砂浆可提高水泥砂浆的 7d 和 28d 抗折强度。纤维含量较少时,随着掺量的增加和水泥水化的进行,纤维在试件中分布范围增加,纤维的锚固作用增强,提高了水泥砂浆的抗折强度。纤维掺量过多时,纤维在砂浆中出现聚集,抗折强度下降。

(3)纤维加入水泥砂浆 7d 抗压强度降低,但 28d 抗压强度有所提高。早期水泥水化不完全,与纤维的锚固作用较弱,同时纤维在砂浆中的应力集中现象明显,抗压强度下降。随着水泥水化的进行,纤维的锚固作用增强,砂浆的抗压强度提高。

本文从宏观角度分析了纤维产量对水泥砂浆工作性和强度的影响,纤维的掺量在 0.1% 对于砂浆的抗渗性和强度有明显的提高,但流动性差,在使用过程中需要添加减水剂,以保证和易性。下一步将进行纤维对于砂浆性能影响的细观分析研究。

参考文献

[1] Mohammed-Rissel Khelifa, Sami Ziane, Samy Mezhoud, et al. Compared Environmental Impact Analysis of Alfa and Polypropylene Fibre-Reinforced Concrete[J]. Iranian Journal of Science and Technology, Transactions of Civil Engineering, 2021(prepublish).

[2] IBentegri O Boukendakdji E-H, Kadri T T, et al. Rheological and Tribological Behaviors of Polypropylene Fiber Reinforced Concrete[J]. Construction and Building Materials, 2020, 261.

[3] Rutger Vrijdaghs, Marco di Prisco, Lucie Vandewalle. Creep of Polymeric Fiber Reinforced Concrete: A Numerical Model with Discrete Fiber Treatment[J]. Computers and Structures, 2020, 233.

[4] 郝贠洪,刘艳晨,李永贵,等.聚丙烯纤维增强水泥复合材料抗冲蚀性能及其冲蚀机制[J].复合材料学报,2021,38:

[5] 路东,张丽哲,季涛.基于有限元的不同聚丙烯纤维掺量的纤维增强混凝土抗裂性能研究[J].硅酸盐通报,2020,39(10):3191-3195,3202.

[6] Yuan Zhu, Jia Yanmin. Mechanical properties and microstructure of glass fiber and polypropylene fiber reinforced concrete: An experimental study[J]. Construction and Building Materials, 2021, 266(PA).

[7] 李英丁,艾秀科,贾陆军,等.聚丙烯纤维对高强砂浆的性能影响研究[J].合成纤维,2020,49(06):53-55.

[8] 王来贵,陈强,潘纪伟,等.聚丙烯纤维增强水泥砂浆力学性能试验研究[J].硅酸盐通报,2017,36(03):870-877.

[9] Yan Wang, Shijie Chen, Zhengzheng Xu, et al. Damage processes of polypropylene fiber reinforced mortar in different fiber content revealed by acoustic emission behavior[J]. Wuhan University of Technology, 2018, 33(1).

[10] 方圆,陈兵.玻璃纤维对磷酸镁水泥砂浆力学性能的增强作用及机理[J].材料导报,2017,31(24):6-9,39.

[11] 刘竞怡,陈华鑫.煤矸石及纤维对 3D 打印水泥砂浆性能的影响[J].应用化工,2018,47(09):1896-1899.

[12] 高妮,喻刚强,赵亚丽,等.玻璃纤维与聚合物复掺改性水泥砂浆的研究[J].混凝土与水泥制品,2016(03):53-57.

Application Evaluation of Steel Slag in Road Base

Wuju Wei　Jinyu Xu　Bingfeng Zheng　Chao Han

(Division of Road Engineering/JSTI Group)

Abstract　In order to research the feasibility of steel slag in road base, this article analysed the differences of physical and mechanical properties for steel slag and limestone aggregates. The X-ray fluorescence spectrometer and scanning electron microscope (SEM) were employed to analyse the chemical composition, hydration products and micromorphology of steel slag. The volume soundness of steel slag was measured and the mix design of cement stabilized steel slag and crushed stone mixture was carries out. The results indicated that the percentage of flat-elongated particles of steel slag aggregates was far more smaller than that of limestone aggregates, which was beneficial to improve the friction between aggregates; More than 90% of the main components of steel slag was composed of CaO、SiO_2、Fe_2O_3、Al_2O_3 and MgO, and it fluctuates greatly with the change of batch; The immersion expansion ratio of steel slag was 2.05%, which was slight larger than the regulatory value of 2% and it was required to conduct the aging pre-treatment before the usage; The degree of hydration reaction in the early period was low, and it was required to mix with the cement in the mixture design so as to ensure the early strength of mixture; The performance of cement stabilized steel slag and crushed stone mixture designed with treated steel slag meets the specification requirements, which indicates that these steel slag can be widely applied in the relevant road base.

Keywords　Steel Slag　Road Base　Aging Process　Hydration Reaction　Mix Design

0　Introduction

Steel slag was the by-product produced during the manufacturing of steels, and its production ratio was 8%~15% of the crude steel output. In 2019, according to the data of Nation-al Bureau of Statistics, the crude steel output nationwide was 996.342 million ton with the annual steel slag output was about 100 million ton. Currently the utilization rate of steel slag in Europe, America, and Japan was close to 100%, but the comprehensive use ratio of the post-processed steel slag in China was about 25% (Huang Y, et al. 2012). A large number of steel slag has been discarded for form the slag mountain, which has seriously threatened the environmental and biological safety, as well as gradually become the bottleneck for the survival and development of steel industry. Meanwhile, the high-quality road-building resources in the field of road construction were in shortage, the steel slag has a higher density and hardness, which can be replaced with the traditional limestone crushed stone as the base material. Using steel slag as the base material of road can not only realize the waste resource recovery, dematerialization or reduction of steel slag so as to greatly save the engineering cost, but also reduce the exploitation of natural earth and stone materials, and protect the ecological environment (Shen W G, et al. 2002; Liu Y, 2014).

Since the main chemical components of both cement and steel slag are similar, the potential for steel slag to be used as a cementitious material has been the subject of consider-able research (Iacobescu et al., 2013).

Supported by the Natural Science Foundation Youth Project of Jiangsu province, China (Grant Nos. BK20170156).

Ahmed (2013) evaluated the effect of quantity of steel slag on the mechanical properties of blended mixes with crushed limestone aggregates, and results indicated that the mechanical characteristics, and the resistance factors were improved by adding steel slag to the crushed limestone. Maghool F (2016 and 2017) carried out an extensive suite of engineering characterization tests to evaluate the engineering properties of ladle furnace slag. The engineering properties of ladle furnace slag aggregates with its satisfactory geotechnical and environmental results, particularly its high CBR values, indicated that the material was ideal for usage as a construction material in road-work applications such as pavement base/subbases and engineering fills. LI X M (2017) conducted California bearing ratio and unconfined compressive strength test to analyse the feasibility of Wugang electric furnace slag for using in highway roadbed. Farshid Maghool(2019) obtained ladle furnace slag (LFS) and ladle furnace slag (LFS) 50 + Electric arc furnace slag (EAFS) 50 were well-graded and had high CBR values, which would deem them suitable for roadwork applications. Vitor A. Nunes and Paulo H. R. Borges (2021) indicated the major obstacles are the variable chemical composition of steel slag, expansion issues, and worse fresh properties when employed as aggregates. Those issues are detrimental to mechanical strength and durability.

Results show that both spherical and angular EAF slag have a positive effect on the mechanical properties of concrete. In addition, spherical EAF slag concrete showed improved fresh and durability properties.

The application feasibility of steel slag produced by Penggang Group in highway base course was analysed from the aspects of physical and mechanical properties, material composition, volume soundness and mix design of steel slag mixture in this paper.

1 Materials

Steel slag(Fig. 1) was a gray-white solidity, rough surfaces, angularity and porous surfaces produced by Penggang Group.

Limestone aggregates(Fig. 2) were produced from Jiujiang, Jiangxi Province, which demonstrate the gray-black color. The results of sieve test for Steel Slag and limestone aggregates were shown in Tab. 1 and Tab. 2 respectively.

Fig. 1 Steel Slag Aggregates

Fig. 2 Limestone Aggregates

The cement was an early-strength composite Portland cement P. C32.5R, produced in Qilian Mountains, Gansu province. The cement demonstrates the powder-like, gray without the impurity.

Results of Sieve Test for Steel Slag Aggregates Tab. 1

Steel Slag Aggregates	Mass percentage(%) through the following square mesh sieve(mm)											
	31.5	26.5	19.0	16.0	13.2	9.5	4.75	2.36	1.18	0.6	0.3	0.15	0.075
10~30mm	100	100	24.5	9.1	1.4	0.5	0.5	0.5	0.5	0.4	0.3	0.1	0.1
5~10mm	—	—	—	100	98.9	68.7	9.6	4.1	3.8	3.2	2.7	1.9	1.3
0~5mm	—	—	—	—	—	100	98.6	53.4	18.5	10.1	7.5	5.8	4.4

Results of Sieve Test for Limestone Aggregates Tab. 2

Limestone Aggregates	Mass percentage(%) through the following square mesh sieve(mm)											
	31.5	26.5	19.0	16.0	13.2	9.5	4.75	2.36	1.18	0.6	0.3	0.15	0.075
10~30mm	100	99.2	53.8	25.6	5.7	0.7	0.6	0.6	0.6	0.6	0.6	0.6	0.6
0~3mm	—	—	—	—	—	—	100	88.0	61.8	44.6	30.0	21.3	13.9

2 Test Methods

Test methods T0316, T0310, T0312 and T0307 were used to measure the crushing value, dust content below 0.075mm, flat-elongated particle content and water absorption ratio of steel slag and limestone aggregates respectively.

The chemical composition and content of steel slag were tested by X-ray fluorescence spectrometer (Fig. 3).

The hydration products and microstructure for steel slag of different ages were analysed by X-ray fluorescence spectrometer (Fig. 3) and scanning electron microscope (Fig. 4). In the test, the steel slag was mixed with water, the quality of water was 30% of the steel slag, and then cured for 7d, 28d and 58d under standard conditions (temperature was 20±2℃, relative humidity was above 95%).

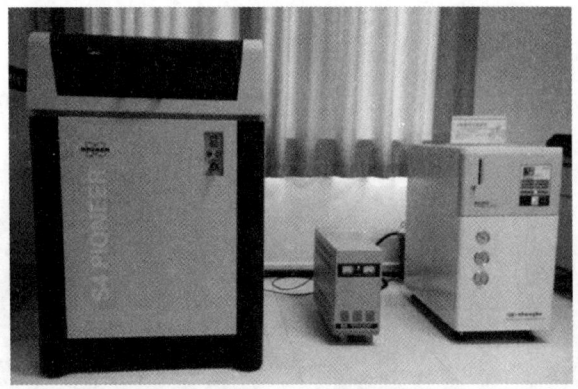
Fig. 3 Bruker S4 Pioneer

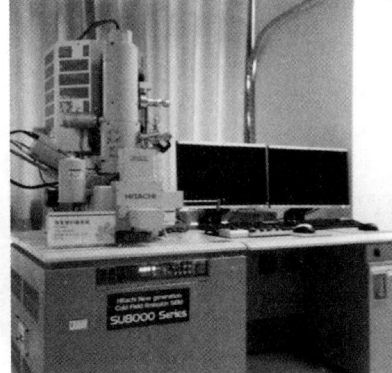
Fig. 4 Hitachi SU-8020

Due to the steel slag contained a certain amount of f-CaO and f-MgO, these components would occur the volume expansion in the presence of water. When the expansion value reached a certain degree, the tensile stress that it produced in the base would exceed the ultimate tensile strength of steel slag so as to cause the generation of crack destruction. Therefore, the volume soundness of steel slag was the key factor whether it could be applied on a large scale. Referring to the standard methods in the "Test method for stability of steel slag (GB/T 24175—2009)", we tested the immersion expansion ratio of steel slag and the expansion ratio after the hydration reaction between the steel slag and water, vapor to determine the volume soundness of steel slag (Fig. 5). The immersion expansion ratio was calculated by using Eq (1).

$$\gamma = \frac{d_{10} - d_0}{120} \times 100\% \qquad (1)$$

Where: γ——Immersion Expansion Ratio, %;

120——Original height of samples, mm;

d_{10}——Final reading of dial indicator, mm;

d_0——Initial reading of dial indicator, mm.

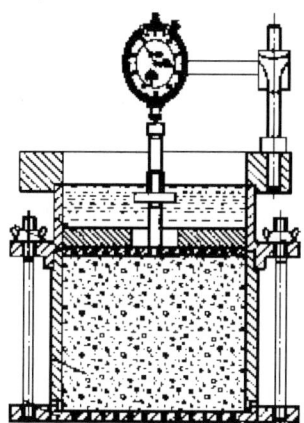

Fig. 5 Schematic Diagram for Measuring Device of Immersion Expansion Ratio

3 Results and Discussions

3.1 Physical and Mechanical Properties

Tab. 3 gave the results of physical and mechanical properties of steel slag and limestone aggregates.

Resultsof Physical and Mechanical Properties of Steel slag and Limestone Aggregates　　Tab. 3

Index	Steel slag Aggregates	Limestone Aggregates	Code Values
Crushing Value(%)	18.8	19.2	≤26
Dust Content below 0.075mm(%)	1.2	1.6	≤2
Flat-Elongated Particle Content(%)	1.5	16	≤22
Water Absorption Ratio(%)	1.52	0.87	≤2

As can be seen from the Tab. 3, the physical and mechanical properties of steel slag and limestone aggregates all meet the code values in "Technical Guidelines for construction of highway Roadbases (JTG/T F20—2015)". The crushing value, dust content below 0.075mm of steel slag were equivalent to those of limestone aggregates. Due to the porous surfaces of steel slag, its water absorption ratio was slightly larger than that of limestone. The percentage of flat-elongated particles of steel slag was far smaller than that of limestone aggregates, which helped to enhance the friction between aggregates.

3.2 Chemical Composition

Tab. 4 showed the chemical composition of steel slag.

Chemical Composition of Steel Slag　　Tab. 4

Sample	Chemical composition(%)											
	CaO	SiO_2	Fe_2O_3	Al_2O_3	MgO	MnO	P_2O_5	TiO_2	K_2O	Cr_2O_3	V_2O_5	SrO
1	45.98	18.89	19.23	2.25	6.31	3.65	2.98	1.04	0.04	0.41	0.81	0.02
2	45.28	18.42	22.54	1.79	5.99	3.82	2.48	0.89	0.02	0.43	0.41	0.03
3	35.05	26.98	15.57	9.26	6.50	3.78	0.73	1.01	0.39	0.37	0.33	0.03

As can be seen in Table 4, the chemical composition and content for the steel slag of different batches were basically consistent, which was mainly composed of $CaO, SiO_2, Fe_2O_3, Al_2O_3, MgO, MnO$ and a small amount of P_2O_5, TiO_2 and other oxides. In which, $CaO, SiO2, Fe_2O_3, Al_2O_3$ and MgO were the main components and reach above 90%. However, the content for CaO, SiO_2, Al_2O_3 fluctuates greatly, which was probably related to the additive amount of admixture during the production of steels and the later storage time. Therefore, the technical indicators of steel slag should be tested before used.

3.3 Volume Soundness

Tab. 5 showed the results of immersion expansion ratio of steel slag.

Results of Immersion Expansion Ratio of Steel Slag   Tab. 5

Sample	Reading of Dial Indicator (mm)										
	d_0	d_1	d_2	d_3	d_4	d_5	d_6	d_7	d_8	d_9	d_{10}
1	0.33	0.38	0.43	0.56	1.73	2.21	2.46	2.58	2.67	2.78	2.85
2	0.31	0.32	0.52	0.65	1.71	2.13	2.37	2.49	2.55	2.63	2.71

As the chart showed, the volume expansion of steel slag increased slowly after 1-2 days of hydration, it was increased rapidly for 3~6 days, and the accumulative expansion volume reached 1.90mm and 1.72mm respectively. The expansion amount for the steel slag samples after 6-10 days was gradually reduced, which was mainly caused by the large reduction of f-CaO, f-MgO content in steel slag. According to the calculation, the average immersion expansion ratio of steel slag was 2.05%, which was slightly larger than the regulatory value of 2% and it was required to conduct the aging pre-treatment before the usage.

3.4 Hydration Products and Microstructure

The SEM image and XRD spectrum of hydration products of steel slag at different ages shall see the Fig. 6 and Fig. 7.

Fig. 6 Scanning Electron Microscopic Image of Steel Slag at Different Ages

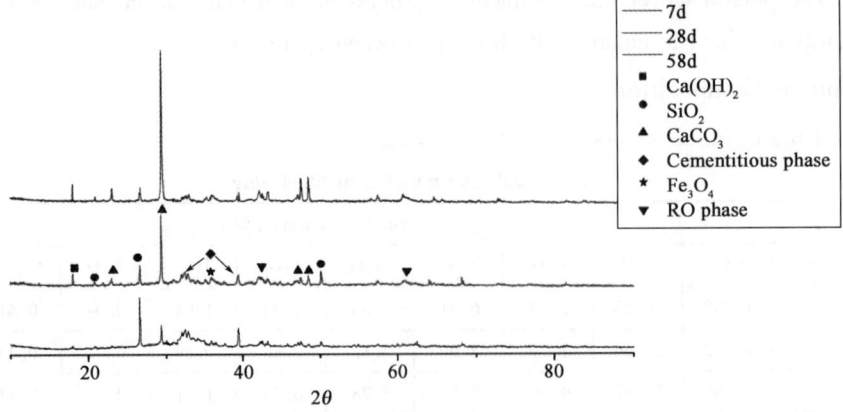

Fig. 7 XRD spectrum of hydration products of steel slag

It could be seen from the Figure 6 that a small amount of flake gelatinous substances was generated on the surface of steel slag after 7 days of hydration, which was very loose and done not bond together. After 28 days of hydration, it can be seen that the gelatinous substances attached to the surface of steel slag were thickened, and there were some crystal particles to be separated out from its surface. The gelatinous substances were loose without closely bonding together. After 58 days, the gelatinous substances on the surface of steel slag were crisscrossed, the hydration products on the surface of steel slag was significantly increased, and the structural system was more robust compared with the initial stage of hydration, which was the hydration reaction further developed with the ages.

It could be seen from the Figure 7 that, the wave crest for $Ca(OH)_2$ and $CaCO_3$ showed an obvious increasing trend, the wave crest of SiO_2 was significantly reduced, and the hydration reaction was gradually performed with the hydration length of time. Meanwhile, after 7d cured in standard condition, the wave crest for $Ca(OH)_2$ and $CaCO_3$ were not significant, which indicated that the degree of hydration reaction for steel slag in the early period was low. Therefore, cement should be added in the design of steel slag mixture to improve the early strength of the mixture.

3.5 Mix Design

The design of cement stabilized steel slag and the crushed stone mixture was carried out by using the steel slag after water aging treatment. The aggregate Grading was shown in Tab. 6 and Fig. 8.

Aggregate Grading for Cement Stabilized Steel slag and crushed stone Mixture Tab. 6

Cement Stabilized Steel Slag and Crushed Stone Mixture	Mass percentage(%) through the following square mesh sieve(mm)						
	31.5	19.0	9.5	4.75	2.36	0.6	0.075
Limestone aggregates (10 ~ 30mm): Limestone aggregates (0 ~ 3mm): Steel slag (10 ~ 30mm): Steel slag (5 ~ 10mm): Steel slag (0 ~ 5mm) = 37.0: 13.0:8.0:28.0:14.0	100.0	76.9	46.5	29.7	20.2	8.3	3.0
Upper Limit of Grading	100	86	58	32	28	15	3
Lower Limit of Grading	100	68	38	22	16	8	0

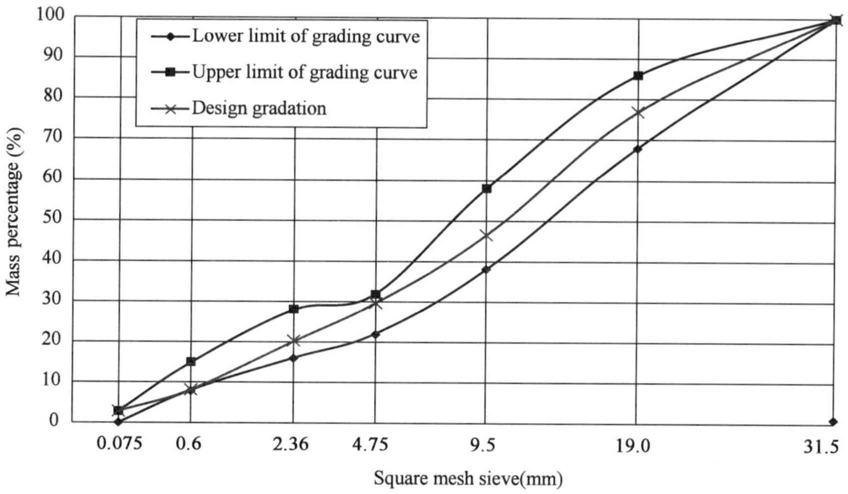

Fig. 8 Curve of Aggregate Grading

Tab. 7 showed that the optimum moisture content and the maximum dry density of cement stabilized steel slag and crushed stone mixture determined by heavy compaction method were 4.8% and 2.348g/cm³.

Results of Heavy Compaction Testing of Cement Stabilized Steel Slag and Crushed Stone Mixture Tab. 7

Cement Dosage (%)	3.0	3.5	4.0	4.5	5.0
Optimum Moisture Content (%)	4.6	4.8	4.6	5.6	4.8
Maximum Dry Density (g/cm³)	2.347	2.348	2.355	2.354	2.360

The unconfined compression strength for the cement stabilized steel slag and crushed stone mixture of 7d aging period was shown as Tab. 8. When the cement dosage was 4.5%, it meets the strength requirements under the heavy-traffic conditions of expressways and first-class highways in the "Technical Guidelines for construction of highway Roadbases (JTG/T F20—2015)".

Results of Unconfined Compression Strength test of 7d Aging Period Tab. 8

Cement Dosage (%)	3.0	3.5	4.0	4.5	5.0
Representative Value of Strength (MPa)	3.1	3.4	3.8	4.3	4.9

4 Conclusions

The main findings of this article were concluded as follows.

(1) The crushing value and dust content below 0.075mm for steel slag were comparable to that of limestone aggregates, and the water absorption ratio was slightly larger. But the percentage of flat-elongated particles was far smaller than that of limestone aggregates, which was helpful to enhance the friction between aggregates.

(2) More than 90% of the steel slag was composed of CaO, SiO_2, Fe_2O_3, Al_2O_3 and MgO, and the chemical composition content of steel slag in different batches fluctuates greatly. Therefore, it was required to perform the test to all of its indexes prior to the usage.

(3) The immersion expansion ratio for these steel slag was 2.05%, slightly larger than the regulatory value 2%, and aging pre-treatment required to perform to it prior to the usage.

(4) The degree of hydration reaction for steel slag in the early period was low, and it was required to mix with cement to enhance the early strength of the mixture.

(5) The performance of cement stabilized steel slag and crushed stone mixture designed with treated steel slag could meet the value of current design specifications, indicating that the steel slag could be promoted and applied in the relevant road base.

References

[1] Ahmed Ebrahim, Abu El-Maaty Behiry. Evaluation of Steel Slag and Crushed Limestone Mixtures as Subbase Material in Flexible Pavement[J]. Ain Shams Engineering Journal, 2013, 4, 43-53.

[2] Huang Yi, et al. An Overview of Utilization of Steel Slag[J]. Procedia Environmental Sciences, 2012, 16, 791-801.

[3] Iacobescu R I, et al. Synthesis, Characterization and Properties of Calcium Ferroaluminate Belite Cements Produced with Electric Arc Furnace Steel Slag as Raw Material[J]. Cement & Concrete Composites, 2013, 44(93), 1-8.

[4] FM A, AA A, Cs B, et al. Geotechnical properties of steel slag aggregates: Shear strength and stiffness [J]. Soils and Foundations, 2019, 59(5):1591-1601.

[5] Nunes V A, Borges P. Recent advances in the reuse of steel slags and future perspectives as binder and aggregate for alkali-activated materials [J]. Construction and Building Materials, 2021, 281:122605.

[6] Industry standards of PRC. JTG/T E42—2005 Test Methods of Aggregate for Highway Engineering[S].

[7] Industry standards of PRC. JTG/T F20—2015 Technical Guidelines for construction of highway Roadbases [S]. Beijing: People's Communications Press, 2015.
[8] LI Xinming, YIN Song, REN Kebin. Feasibility Study of Graded Electric Furnace Slag for Roadbed [J]. Highway, 2017, 62(04), 18-23. (in Chinese).
[9] Maghool F, Arulrajah A, Horpibulsuk S, et al. Laboratory Evaluation of Ladle Furnace Slag in Unbound Pavement-Base/Subbase Applications [J]. Journal of Materials in Civil Engineering, 2016.
[10] Maghool, Farshid, et al. Environmental Impacts of Utilizing Waste Steel Slag Aggregates as Recycled Road Construction Materials [J]. Clean Technologies & Environmental Policy, 2017, 19 (4), 1-10.
[11] SHEN Weiguo, ZHOU Mingkai, ZHAO Qinglin, et al. Manufacture of Steel Slag Fly-ash Road Base Material [J]. Journal of WuHan university of technology, 2002, 24 (5), 15-18. (in Chinese)
[12] Industry standards of PRC. YB/T 4184—2018 Test method for stability of steel slag [S]. Beijing: China Building Industry Press, 2019.

基于微观角度废橡胶复合材料性能研究进展

高润杰 陈玉

(长安大学公路学院)

摘 要 为了对废旧轮胎橡胶材料复合建筑材料的结构性能进行更加深入的了解。本文通过分析国内外对橡胶沥青材料和橡胶水泥复合材料的微观结构性能表现的最新研究,汇总了废橡胶复合材料的微观结构与宏观性能的相互联系。提出后续废橡胶复合材料研究重点及发展方向,为掺加废旧轮胎橡胶材料沥青混凝土及水泥混凝土的深入研究及推广应用提供参考借鉴。

关键词 道路材料 研究进展 微观结构 废橡胶复合材料

0 引 言

随着车辆数量增大,废旧轮胎也逐渐增多,废旧轮胎未妥善处置易造成环境问题。研究表明,将橡胶添加到沥青中进行改性,便得到改性沥青即橡胶沥青[1]。与基质沥青相比,橡胶沥青显示出更好的抗疲劳性和抗裂性势。水泥混凝土结构在使用过程中易产生低应力的脆断,掺入橡胶颗粒后,混凝土的多种性能得以提升,橡胶颗粒群体起微小弹簧类似的作用,会限制混凝土的微小裂纹,减缓或阻止裂缝的进一步发展[2]。橡胶颗粒水泥混凝土具有质量轻、韧性高、抗开裂好和降噪隔声等特点[3-5]。国内外对橡胶颗粒改性材料性能的研究已经相对比较成熟,现阶段主要针对材料作用机理进行研究。

1 废旧轮胎橡胶

轮胎由硫化橡胶和补强材料制成(图1),多数轮胎主要成份是天然橡胶或合成橡胶[6]。化学成分和微生物对橡胶的侵蚀会导致性能下降,从而使轮胎使用寿命缩短约50%[7]。天然橡胶受热易变形,而冷却时易碎。因为橡胶是由长聚合物链组成,聚合物链可独立移动,导致形状改变。通过硫化在聚合物链之间形成交联,施加应力时,硫化橡胶将变形;应力释放后,橡胶制品将恢复其原始形状[8]。

2 橡胶颗粒复合材料

与传统沥青相比,橡胶沥青具有更好的抗滑性能,减少裂纹并延长路面使用寿命[9]。而橡胶沥青成

图 1 轮胎结构示意图

本比传统沥青高 40%~100%。橡胶沥青混合料改性工艺技术使施工的能耗和污染排放更高[10]。郑南翔等对橡胶沥青混合料的抵抗反射裂缝提出了孔径、软化点、韧度比等多个控制指标[11];韩敏慧则针对橡胶沥青混合料的老化性能给出了抗老化性能最佳的材料组成设计[12];王凯对橡胶改性沥青混合料的性能进行了验证,在路用性能的表现与传统 SBS 改性沥青混合料几乎一致[13];Jiang Yuan 揭示了橡胶沥青混合料强度在不同温度,不同加载速率下的变化规律。创建了基于遗传算法优化的反向传播神经网络(GA-BPNN)的强度和疲劳寿命预测模型,大大提高了橡胶沥青路面结构设计的准确性[14]。

使用废橡胶的另一方法是用于水泥混凝土。研究人员将橡胶颗粒用作混凝土中的粗骨料[15],橡胶颗粒的大小、比例和表面特征显著影响橡胶混凝土的抗压强度[16]。Topçu[17]确定了韧性及橡胶混凝土的塑性和弹性变化。Toutanji[18]用废旧轮胎橡胶颗粒代替了混凝土中的粗矿物骨料,在混凝土中掺入橡胶颗粒会降低抗压强度和抗折强度。Khaloo[19]研究了含有轮胎橡胶颗粒的混凝土的物理性能,橡胶颗粒含量增加的橡胶混凝土混合物的单位重量较低,由于极限抗压强度的大幅度降低,不要超过 25% 的橡胶颗粒量。Huang[20]用硅烷混合物处理轮胎橡胶颗粒,以增加橡胶颗粒和水泥浆之间联系。处理的橡胶混凝土抗压强度有所提高,原因是水泥水化作用在橡胶颗粒周围形成了硬壳(图 2),增加了橡胶和水泥浆之间兼容性。

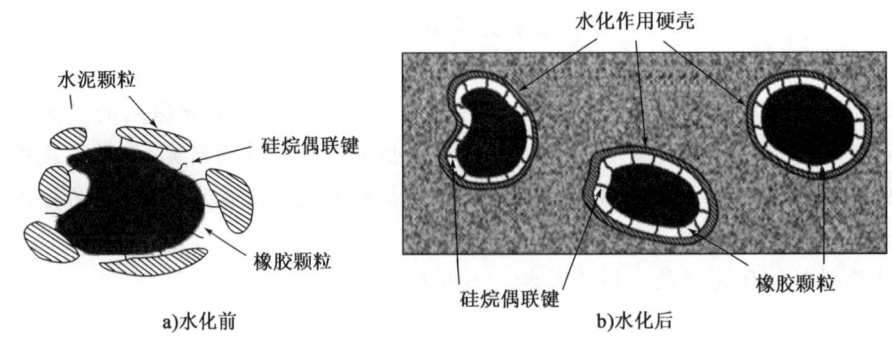

图 2 水泥水化表面处理效果[20]

3 橡胶复合材料的微观结构性能

3.1 橡胶沥青混合料微观结构

在沥青混合料中使用橡胶颗粒:一种是将橡胶颗粒用作混合料中部分矿物集料的替代物;另一种是将沥青与橡胶颗粒混合,改善沥青性能[21]。将橡胶颗粒用作沥青混合料中的材料前,应先通过磨机进行研磨。图 3 显示了不同尺寸(0.29mm 和 0.74 mm)的橡胶颗粒形状。

图 3 不同粒径橡胶颗粒扫描电子显微镜图像[20]

橡胶颗粒不是标准球形,长径比随尺寸增加而增加。Moro[22]研究了橡胶改性沥青混合料的材料内部相互作用。在荧光显微镜下,改性的橡胶改性沥青混合料比未改性的沥青混合料呈现出更深的棕色区域(图4)。橡胶中的炭黑转移到沥青中,橡胶颗粒周围呈黄色荧光区域是由于在溶胀过程中橡胶颗粒吸收了芳香族油而形成的。

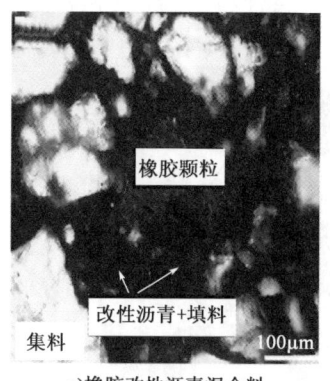 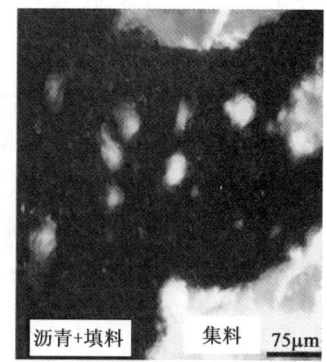

a) 橡胶改性沥青混合料　　　　b) 未改性沥青混合料

图4　混合料荧光显微镜图像[22]

Li[23]使用基质沥青作为溶胀剂并采用预混合工艺制备了样品。如图5所示,橡胶颗粒弹性体的界面是透明的,在预混工艺之前分散了许多孔隙,这表明相容性较差。经过预混工艺处理后的橡胶颗粒的界面变得模糊不清,槽孔消失,所以预混处理后相容性变好。

 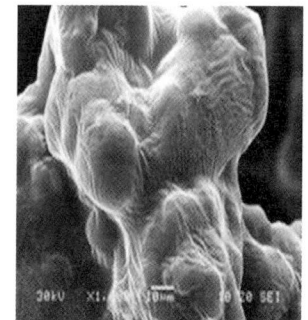

a) 未预混的橡胶粉　　　　b) 有预混的橡胶粉

图5　橡胶颗粒界面扫描电子显微镜图像[23]

Liu[24]通过添加反式聚辛烯橡胶(TOR)来研究橡胶沥青的流变特性以及TOR和橡胶颗粒改性沥青之间的改性机理。图6a)中可知在添加TOR之前,橡胶改性沥青的微观结构呈现单相连续结构,并且橡胶颗粒在沥青中分布不均。图6b)使用TOR的样品的微观结构变得更加胶粉改性沥青的单相连续结构转变为均匀的两相状态,表明TOR能促进橡胶颗粒与沥青的相容性。

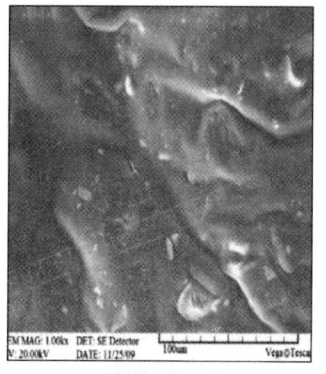 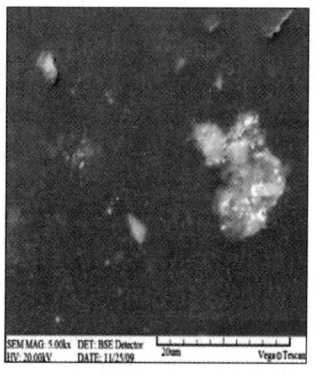

a) 橡胶改性沥青　　　　b) 添加TOR橡胶改性沥青

图6　改性沥青荧光显微镜图像[24]

3.2 橡胶水泥混合料微观结构

水泥基材料是指水泥作为胶凝材料的材料,橡胶颗粒增加会降低橡胶水泥复合材料的抗压强度,同时增加抗拉强度[25]。图7对比了水泥浆与橡胶颗粒的不良黏合及水泥浆与天然砂的紧密黏合。水泥混凝土中,水泥基质和硅集料完全黏附;在橡胶颗粒集料混合料中,橡胶颗粒集料和水泥基质之间的空隙[26],是导致抗压强度降低的一个因素。

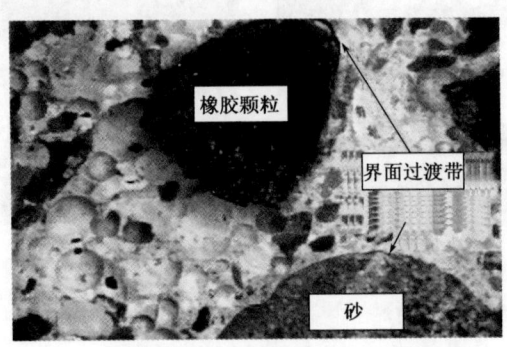

图7 水泥浆与橡胶颗粒、水泥浆与天然砂界面过渡[26]

Shen[27]使用乳胶聚合物改性剂来改善橡胶颗粒与水泥基质不良黏合。在图8a)中水泥浆和集料之间具有明显的界面过渡带,而图8b)显示了在无聚合物改性的橡胶颗粒集料混凝土中,由于疏水性导致橡胶颗粒和水泥浆之间的明显分界。橡胶和水泥浆之间的结合变弱,当聚合物改性剂加入后,橡胶颗粒聚集体和水泥浆之间的界面黏结得到了提高。

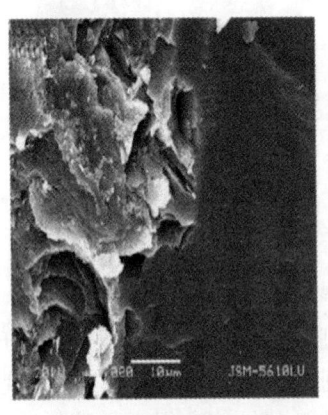 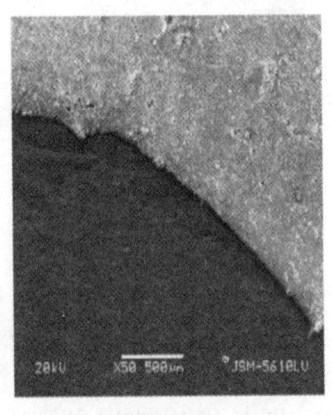

a)矿物集料　　　　　　　　　b)橡胶颗粒

图8 水泥浆的界面过渡区[27]

Segre 和 Joekes[28]通过预处理减少橡胶—水泥混凝土中粗橡胶颗粒造成的强度损失。用饱和 NaOH 溶液对橡胶颗粒进行处理。在橡胶-基质界面观察到断裂,表明橡胶对水泥浆的黏合性很差,图9a)所示。另一方面,如图9b)所示,在经 NaOH 溶液处理的橡胶颗粒和基体之间观察到黏结接头。

Chou[29]将橡胶颗粒部分氧化改变橡胶的亲水性。氧化反应保持1h,在150℃、200℃和250℃这三个温度下进行。橡胶—砂浆的抗压和抗折强度随热处理进行显著提高。如图10所示,处理过的橡胶(250℃)砂浆水合产物的晶体小,形态从长细变为短而紧凑的针状。经处理橡胶颗粒具有良好抗压强度,其拉伸强度和弯折强度也得到提高,但增加率低于抗压强度的增加。

与抗压强度特性相比,普通水泥材料的抗拉强度较低。通过在混合料中添加橡胶颗粒可以提高水泥基复合材料的拉伸强度。从图11可以看出,该结果可能是由于橡胶颗粒阻止了裂纹产生[30]。

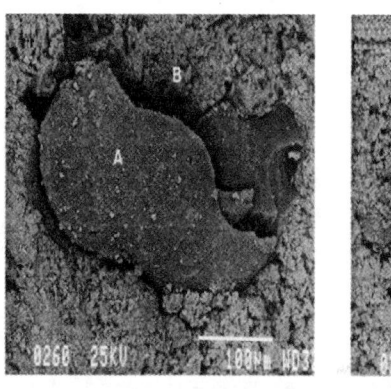 

a) 橡胶颗粒未处理　　　　　b) 橡胶颗粒由NaOH溶液处理
　　　　　　　　　　　　　　（A橡胶颗粒，B水泥浆）

图9　橡胶—水泥试样微观结构[28]

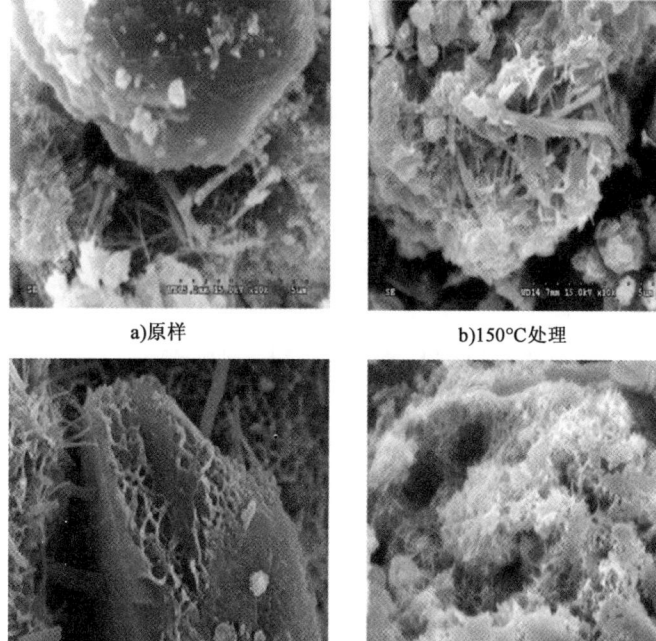

a) 原样　　　　　　　　　b) 150℃处理

c) 200℃处理　　　　　　　d) 250℃处理

图10　橡胶砂浆水合产物扫描电子显微镜图像[29]

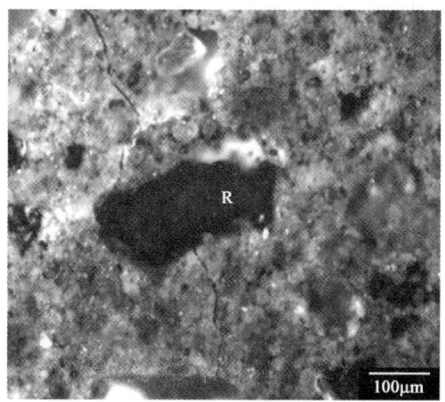

图11　橡胶—水泥中裂纹传递[30]

图12a)显示了橡胶颗粒从水泥基体中拔出后在水泥浆上的压痕,图12b)显示了橡胶颗粒附近的较多的微裂纹,图12c)显示了橡胶颗粒本身中的内部张力开裂的显微照片。表明两相复合材料之间存在应力传递,橡胶颗粒在破坏之前经历了拉伸应变[31]。

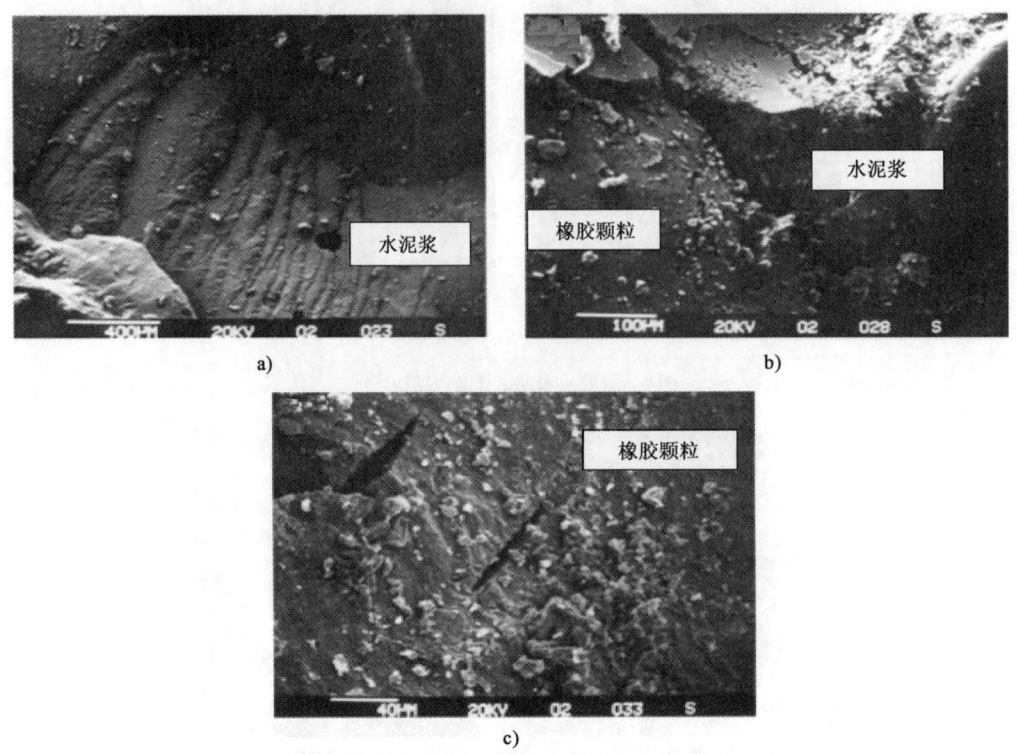

图12 橡胶颗粒在水泥基体中系列变化[31]

4 结 语

在工程材料中使用废橡胶是处理废弃物的重要方式,虽然在沥青混合料和水泥基材料中使用废橡胶颗粒对混合料性能有显著改善,但目前理技术存在不足。废轮胎橡胶颗粒复合材料的微观结构与使用性能密切相关,确定微观结构与性能之间联系具有重大意义。基于此,本文主要有以下结论:

(1)通过在沥青混合料中加入橡胶颗粒,可以显著改善结构的疲劳性能、抗开裂性能以及结构的稳定性;在加入水泥基材料之前,对橡胶颗粒进行处理后,可以改善结构的抗压强度,拉伸强度和弯折强度也得到提高。

(2)现有的微观结构研究技术已经快速发展,可以尝试多种技术相结合的研究方法,如核磁共振技术、红外光谱技术及原子力显微镜等新技术,通过多种结果整合得到准确的材料结构性能表征。

(3)针对微观结构出现的不利因素,需要寻求新的添加剂或生产工艺进行改进,力求材料的结构性能最大化,提高在实际工程应用中使用价值。

参考文献

[1] 侯德华.微波活化胶粉及其改性沥青性能研究[D].西安:长安大学,2018.
[2] 宁国芳.机场道面橡胶改性再生骨料混凝土抗弯疲劳性能试验研究[D].广州:广东工业大学,2014.
[3] 何亮,刘誉贵,牟元华.橡胶改性及其对橡胶水泥基质材料性能的影响[J].硅酸盐通报,2017,36(3):936-941.
[4] 额日德木,王海龙,王萧萧,等.表面改性废旧轮胎橡胶粉对水泥胶砂力学性能的影响[J].中国科技论文,2015,10(1):73-77.
[5] 杨晨晨,白英,田晓宇,等.掺橡胶粉与纤维混凝土力学性能研究[J].中国科技论文,2016,11(13):

1548-1550.
[6] 杨卫民.轮胎设计与制造工艺创新的发展方向[J].橡塑技术与装备,2013(02):26-33.
[7] Huynh H,Raghavan D. Durability of Simulated Shredded Rubber Tire in Highly Alkaline Environments[J]. Advanced Cement Based Materials,1997,6(3-4):138-143.
[8] Prestid L . Recycled Tyre Rubber Modified Bitumens for Road Asphalt Mixtures: A Literature Review[J]. Construction and Building Materials,2013,49(6):863-881.
[9] Wu S ,Ye Q ,Li N . Investigation of Rheological and Fatigue Properties of Asphalt Mixtures Containing Polyester Fibers[J]. Construction & Building Materials,2008,22 (10): 2111-2115.
[10] 高晶晶,樊兴华.基于桥面铺装材料的橡胶沥青反应机理研究[J].硅酸盐通报,2017(5):1582-1589.
[11] 郑南翔,李桢,焦丽亚.橡胶沥青混合料抗反射裂缝性能研究[J].中外公路,2020,40(03):268-273.
[12] 韩敏慧.橡胶沥青混合料抗老化性能分析[J].筑路机械与施工机械化,2020,37(08):9-12.
[13] 王凯,胡家波,李彬,等.基于弯沉的稳定型橡胶改性沥青混合料力学响应分析[J].公路交通科技(应用技术版),2020,16(11):107-110.
[14] Yuan J ,Lv S ,Peng X ,et al. Investigation of Strength and Fatigue Life of Rubber Asphalt Mixture[J]. Materials,2020,13(15):3325.
[15] Bravo M ,Brito J D . Concrete Made with Used Tyre Aggregate: Durability-related Performance[J]. Journal of Cleaner Production,2012,25: 42-50.
[16] Brito J D ,Saikia N . Recycled Aggregate in Concrete: Use of Industrial,Construction and Demolition Waste[M]. 2012.
[17] Ilker Bekir Topçu. Assessment of the Brittleness Index of Rubberized Concretes,[J]. Cement and Concrete Research,1997,27(2):177-183.
[18] Toutanji H A . The Use of Rubber Tire Particles in Concrete to Replace Mineral Aggregates[J]. cement & concrete composites,1996,18(2):135-139.
[19] Ali R,Khaloo M. Mechanical Properties Of Concrete Containing A High Volumern of Tire-rubber Particles[J]. Waste Management,2008,28(12):2472-2482.
[20] Huang B ,Shu X ,Cao J . A two-staged Surface Treatment to Improve Properties of Rubber Modified Cement Composites[J]. Construction and Building Materials,2013,40(Mar.):270-274.
[21] 韩丽丽,韩红红,郑木莲.低黏度Terminal Blend废胶粉改性沥青研究进展[J].中外公路,2017,037(001):271-276.
[22] Lopez-Moro F J ,Moro M C ,Hernandez-Olivares F ,et al. Microscopic Analysis of the Interaction between Crumb Rubber and Bitumen in Asphalt Mixtures Using the Dry Process[J]. Construction and Building Materials,2013,48:691-699.
[23] Xiang L ,Cheng J ,Que G . Microstructure and Performance of Crumb Rubber Modified Asphalt [J]. Construction and Building Materials,2009,23(12): 3586-3590.
[24] Liu Hongying, Chen Zhijun, Wang Wen. Investigation of the Theological Modification Mechanism of Crumb Rubber Modified Asphalt (CRMA) Containing TOR Additive [J]. Construction and Building Materials,2014,67:225-233.
[25] 张哲哲.橡胶混凝土力学性能及阻尼特性试验研究[D].郑州:河南工业大学,2016.
[26] Turki M ,Bretagne E ,Queneudec M ,et al. Microstructure,Physical and Mechanical Properties of Mortar-rubber Aggregates Mixtures[J]. Construction and Building Materials,2009,23(7):3715-3722.
[27] Shen W,Shan L,Zhang T,et al. Investigation on Polymer-rubber Aggregate Modified Porous Concrete[J]. Construction and Building Materials,2013,38(JAN.):667-674.

[28] Segre N, Joekes I. Use of Tire Rubber Particles as Addition to Cement Paste[J]. Cement & Concrete Research,2000,30(9):1421-1425.

[29] Chou L H, Yang C K, Lee M T. Effects of Partial Oxidation of Crumb Rubber on Properties of Rubberized Mortar[J]. Composites,2010,41B(8):613-616.

[30] Torgal FP, Ding Y, Jalali S. Properties and Durability of Concrete Containing Polymeric Wastes (tyre Rubber and Polyethylene Terephthalate Bottles): an Overview[J]. Construction and Building Materials, 2012,30:714-724.

[31] Holmes N, Dunne K, O'donneli J. Longitudinal Shear Resistance of Composite Slabs Containing Crumb Rubber in Concrete Toppings[J]. Construction and Building Materials,2014,55:365-378.

Effect of Humidity and Oxygen on the Weathering Aging Process of High Viscosity Modified Asphalt Using a Coupled Rheology-Morphology-Chemistry Characterization Approach

Mingjun Hu[1]　Weiwei Zhou[2]　Daquan Sun[1]　Jianmin Ma[1]

(1. Tongji University, Key Laboratory of Road and Traffic Engineering of Ministry of Education;
2. Shanghai Puxing Road and Bridge Construction Co., Ltd)

Abstract　The coupling effect of environmental factors such as heat, solar radiation, humidity and oxygen is the main external reason for the aging of high viscosity modified asphalt (HVMA) and the durability failure of the permeable asphalt pavement. Currently, many researchers are doing a systematic study on the thermal aging and solar radiation aging of HVMA, but few studies have focus on the influence of humidity and oxygen on the performance of HVMA. In this study, the accelerated weathering aging tester was used to simulate the weathering aging process of HVMA under different humidity conditions and different oxygen conditions. The dynamic shear rheometer test was conducted to study the rheological properties of HVMA under different humidity and different oxygen conditions. Then, the gel permeation chromatography test was applied to investigate the molecular weight distribution of HVMA under different weathering aging humidity and different weathering aging oxygen conditions. Afterwards, the florescence micro-scopy test was used to determine the influence of humidity and oxygen on the microscopic morphology of HVMA during weathering aging. Test results show that the changes in humidity don't have an obvious influence on the rheology-morphology-chemistry characteristics of HVMA during weathering aging. On the contrast, the participation of oxygen has a significant impact on the rheology-morphology-chemistry characteristics of HVMA during weathering aging. With the participation of oxygen, HVMA exhibits degraded polymer phase structures, severe asphalt oxidation, and apparent surface micro cracks, thus causing the deterioration of macroscopic rheological properties.

Keywords　High viscosity modified asphalt　Humidity　Oxygen　Rheological property　Molecular weight distribution　Microscopic morphology

0　Introduction

The higher noise reduction requirements, stricter safety-driving requirements, and better environmental suitability have been the substantial driving forces for the popularity and development of permeable asphalt (PA) pavements (Hu et al.,2019) (Zhang,Leng,2017). The air void content of PA pavement is generally between 18% and 25%, which helps to reduce the noise in pavement-tire contact and alleviate the spray and splash phenomenon in rainy weather significantly (Poulikakos,Partl,2012). In addition,the well-developed and connected void structures of PA pavement also helps to reduce the pavement surface temperature,thus alleviating the urban heat island effect apparently (Xie,Shen,2016). However, the open-graded characterization of PA pavement also brings some durability problems, such as the sensitivity to the environment and load, which causes a shorter service life of PA pavement in comparison with dense-graded asphalt pavement (Liu et al. 2019).

In order to reduce the sensitivity to environment/load and prolong the service life of PA pavement, it is generally recommended to use high-performance polymer modified asphalt in PA pavement, such as high-content SBS modified asphalt (HCSBSMA) and high viscosity modified asphalt (HVMA). Yan et al. (2019) recommended to use HCSBSMA (SBS content: 7.5%) in PA pavement in their studies, and found that the high-content of SBS polymers can improve the anti aging performance and extend the service life of PA pavement significantly. However, the poor storage stability and dispersion uniformity of HCSBSMA caused by high-content SBS polymers have always been the reasons for restricting its performance stability. Hence, compared with HCSBSMA,HVMA has received more extensive attention and utilization in PA pavements in Asian countries. HVMA generally contains thermoplastic rubber, resin, anti-aging agent, plasticizer and other components. The softening point of HVMA should be greater than 80°C, and the dynamic viscosity at 60°C should be higher than 20000 Pa·s. According to the research conducted by Hu et al. (2020), the storage stability of HVMA was apparently better than that of HCSBSMA. Moreover, HVMA has high viscosity, good adhesion, strong toughness and tenacity, which can improve the high-temperature performance, durability and anti-aging performance of PA pavement significantly.

Although HVMA has good rheological properties and anti-aging properties, the well-developed void structures of PA pavements also lead to obvious environmental exposures of HVMA. Some external environmental factors, such as high temperature, solar radiation, rainfall, and oxygen, have significant impacts on the performance of HVMA in PA pavement. Therefore, it needs to focus on the coupling aging problems of HVMA under complex weather conditions. Currently, many researchers have fully studied the aging effect of high temperature and solar radiation (ultraviolet radiation) on the Polymer modified asphalt during the weathering aging process. In terms of thermal aging, Hu and his coworkers (2020) investigated the rheological-chemical properties of HVMA at different weathering aging temperatures. Their findings indicated that HVMA has significant thermal oxygen aging at a temperature of 50°C under the stimulation of solar radiation. In terms of solar radiation aging, Yu et al. (2019) conducted laboratory studies on the aging effect of ultraviolet radiation on SBSMA. They found that the ultraviolet radiation damaged the crosslinked polymer networks in SBSMA severely. Continuous ultraviolet radiation increased the shrinkage stress on SBSMA surface, thus causing cracks on SBSMA surface.

Many researchers have done a systematic study on the aging of heat, ultraviolet radiation during weathering aging, and achieved fruitful results. However, few researches have focused on the effect of humidity on the performance of asphalt. Moreover, the understanding of the role of oxygen in the weathering aging process is not very clear. Therefore, this study firstly analyzed the influence of humidity on the performance of HVMA, and then investigated the role of oxygen in the weathering aging process of HVMA. The rheological properties of HVMA under different humidity and different oxygen conditions during weathering aging were studied based on a dynamic

---

Financial support of the National Natural Science Foundation of China (Grant numbers 51878500,51378393).

shear rheometer (DSR) test. Afterwards, the effect of humidity and oxygen on the molecular weight distribution of HVMA during weathering aging was analyzed using gel permeation chromatography (GPC) test. Finally, the fluorescence microscopy (FM) test was conducted to observe the microscopic morphology of HVMA at different humidity and different oxygen conditions.

1 Materials and Experiment

1.1 Materials

PEN70 base asphalt (PEN70) was provided by Sinopec Co., Ltd., and high viscosity modifiers (HVM) were supplied by Pudong Road & Bridge Co., Ltd. The preparation process of HVMA referred to Reference 7 (Hu et al., 2020). The amount of HVM was 12% wt of HVMA. The 25°C penetration, softening point, and 5°C ductility of HVMA were 39.9 (0.1 mm), 89.6°C, and 52.8 cm, respectively.

1.2 Weathering Aging Procedure

The thin film oven test (TFOT) was conducted to simulate the short-term aging of HVMA. After TFOT test, the weathering aging process of HVMA was simulated by the accelerated weathering aging tester. The accelerated weathering aging tester can simulate different weather conditions by changing the parameters of temperature, solar radiation intensity and humidity. In this study, in order to analyse the effect of humidity on the performance of HVMA, the humidity value was set as 50% RH, 70% RH, and 90% RH with unchanged parameter values of temperature (70°C) and solar radiation intensity (1000 W/m^2) during the weathering aging. The weathering aging time was set to 4 d and 12 d. Moreover, during the weathering aging of 70°C, 1000W/m^2, and 70% RH, part of HVMA samples were put into sealed bags, and vacuumed with a vacuum machine to isolate oxygen. By comparing the performance of HVMA under oxygen and no-oxygen weathering aging conditions, the effect of oxygen on the performance of HVMA during the weathering aging process was also investigated in this study.

1.3 Rheological Performance Test

1.3.1 Temperature sweep test

A temperature sweep test was conducted on HVMA under the strain-controlled mode (1.5%) with a constant frequency of 10 Hz, and the test temperature ranged from 15°C to 75°C. The storage modulus (G') and loss modulus (G") of HVMA were also recorded during the temperature sweep test. HVMA exhibited more elasticity with G' value greater than G" value, and presented more viscosity with G' value less than G" value. Hence, the temperature at the intersection of G' value and G" value was defined as the visco-elastic transition temperature of HVMA.

1.3.2 Rheological master curves

Frequency sweep test was performed on HVMA over a range of 0.1 Hz-30 Hz and 15°C-75°C in the strain-controlled mode (1.5%), which meets the visco-elastic response range of HVMA. The sigmoid model (Eq. 1) and double-logistic (DL) model (Eq. 2) were used to establish the complex modulus master curve and phase angle master curve of HVMA at a reference temperature of 45°C.

$$\log|G^*| = \nu + \frac{\alpha}{1 + e^{\beta + \gamma(\log f_r)}} \tag{1}$$

where: f_r——reduced frequency;

ν——low-frequency asymptotic value;

α——the difference between high-frequency asymptotic value and low-frequency asymptotic value;

β, γ——shape parameters.

$$\delta = \delta_P - \delta_P \cdot H(f_r - f_P) \cdot (1 - e^{-S_R(\log(f_r/f_P))^2}) + \delta_L \cdot H(f_P - f_r) \cdot (1 - e^{-S_L(\log(f_P/f_r))^2}) \quad (2)$$

where: f_r ——reduced frequency;

f_P ——the frequency at which the phase angle reaches the plateau value;

δ_P ——plateau phase angle;

S_R ——the shape parameter in the right side of plateau;

δ_L, S_L ——the shape parameters in the left side of plateau;

$H(f_P - f_r)$ and $H(f_r - f_P)$ represent Heaviside step functions.

1.4 Gel Permeation Chromatography (GPC) test

The GPC test was performed using Water Performance Liquid Chromatography System. A combination of three columns was used to separate the components of HVMA by molecular weight. The HVMA-tetrahydrofuran solution was firstly prepared with a concentration of 2 mg/mL. After standing for 24 h to fully dissolve, the HVMA-tetrahydrofuran solution was filtrated into centrifuge tubes using 0.45 μm PTFE micro-porous filters. Then, a 100 μL micro syringe was used to take the HVMA-tetrahydrofuran solution in centrifuge tubes. After removing bubbles, the solution was injected into the sampler and was passed through the columns at a flow rate of 1 mL/min for 40 minutes for testing. The GPC test results were exported and normalized using Origin software for further analysis. In GPC test, Shodex® Polystyrene standard samples were utilized to establish the calibration curve to convert retention time into molecular weight. The weight average molecular weight, number average molecular weight and dispersion of HVMA were computed using Eq. 3-Eq. 5.

$$M_w = \sum_{i=1}^{n} \frac{w_i \times M_i}{w_i} \quad (3)$$

$$M_n = \sum_{i=1}^{n} \frac{n_i \times M_i}{n_i} \quad (4)$$

$$D = \frac{M_w}{M_n} \quad (5)$$

where: M_w, M_n, D ——the weight average molecular weight, number average molecular weight, and dispersion;

M_i ——the molecular weight;

w_i, n_i ——the mass and mole number of M_i.

1.5 Fluorescence microscopy (FM) test

OLYMPUS-BX41 florescence microscopy (FM) was employed to watch the microscopic morphology of HVMA under different weathering aging conditions. The aged HVMA samples were directly placed under the objective lens for observing after different weathering aging effects. The HVMA samples were not reheated for re-sampling since it may destroy the microscopic morphology of sample surfaces due to weathering aging.

2 Results and Discussion

2.1 Rheological Performance Test Results

2.1.1 Rheological Master Curve

Fig. 1 shows the rheological master curve test results of HVMA under different humidity conditions, which can compare the complex modulus and phase angle of HVMA under a wider range of applied frequencies. As shown in Fig. 1, it can be seen that HVMA presents an increasing complex modulus and a decreasing phase angle with the increase of weathering aging days. The complex modulus master curve and phase angle modulus curve does not show significant differences under different humidity conditions. This result reveals that the changes in the rheological properties of HVMA are mainly related to the aging effect of high temperature and solar radiation, and the humidity hardly affects the rheological properties of HVMA during the weathering aging process.

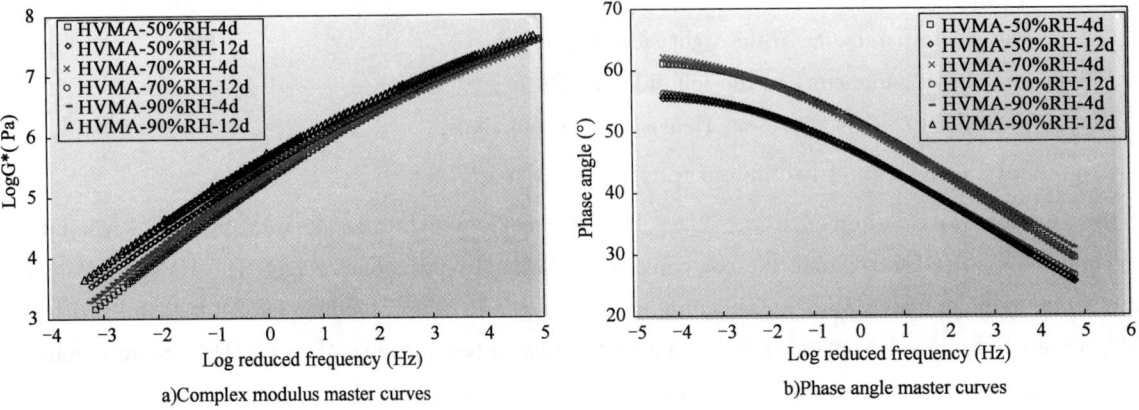

Fig.1 Rheological master curves at different humidity conditions

The rheological master curve test results of HVMA during oxygen weathering aging (OWA) and no-oxygen weathering aging (NOWA) are illustrated in Fig. 2. In order to better characterize the role of oxygen in weathering aging, the rheological master curves of virgin HVMA are also added in Fig. 2. From Fig. 2, we can see that the oxygen has a significant impact on the weathering aging process of HVMA. Under OWA condition, the complex modulus master curves of HVMA increase apparently and the phase angle master curves of HVMA decrease apparently with the increase of aging days. However, under NOWA condition, the changes of rheological master curves with aging days are not significant.

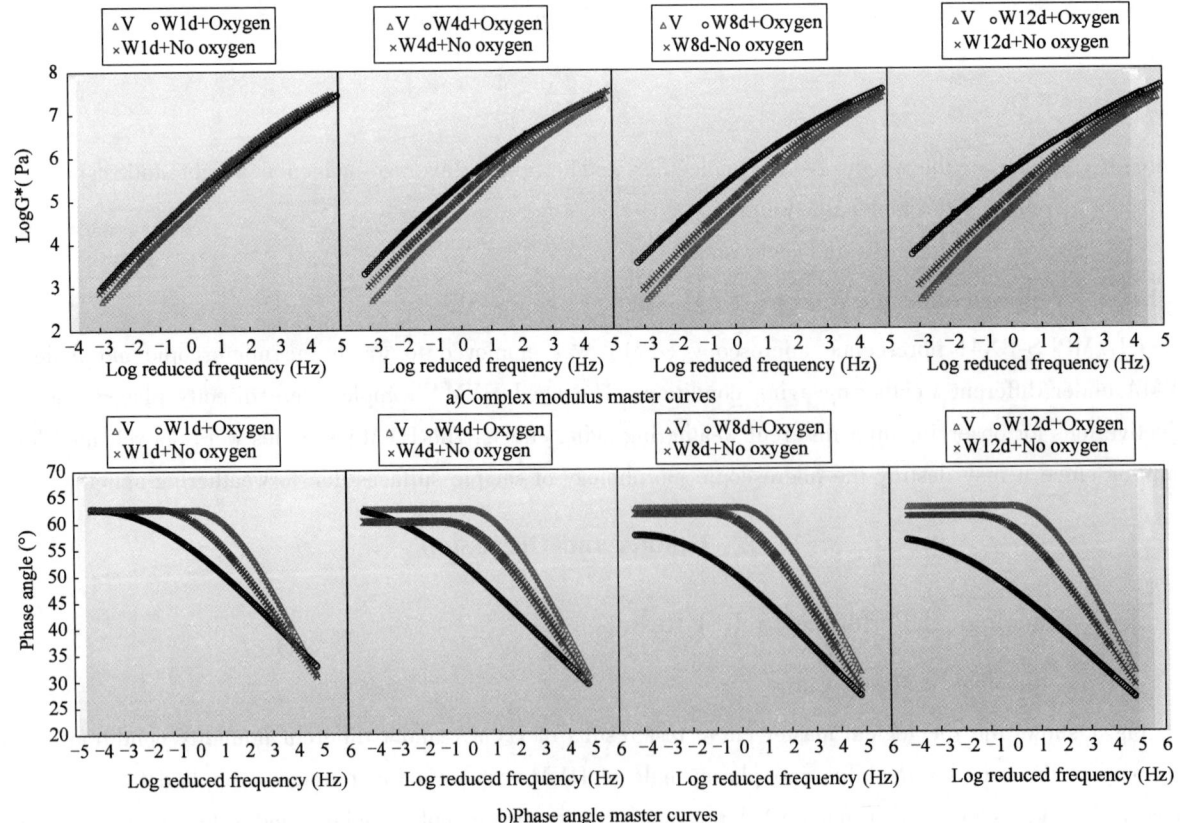

Fig.2 Rheological master curves at OWA and NOWA conditions

HVMA has a wide phase angle plateau zone in the low frequency region. In the plateau zone, the phase angle of HVMA does not change with frequency, which is because of the formation of polymer elastic networks and the winding of polymer chains. Under OWA condition, the phase angle plateau zone of HVMA disappears apparently, which shows that the participation of oxygen can cause the obvious degradation of polymer network structures during weathering aging. HVMA still has obvious phase angle plateau zone under NOWA condition. This result also reveals that the absence of oxygen delays the degradation of polymer network structures in HVMA.

2.1.2 Temperature Sweep

Fig. 3 gives the temperature sweep test results of HVMA under different humidity conditions. According to Fig. 3, it can be found that the complex modulus and phase angle of HVMA are almost the same no matter it is under 50% RH, 70% RH or 90% RH, which also proves that the changes in humidity does not have a significant impact on the rheological properties of HVMA during the weathering aging process.

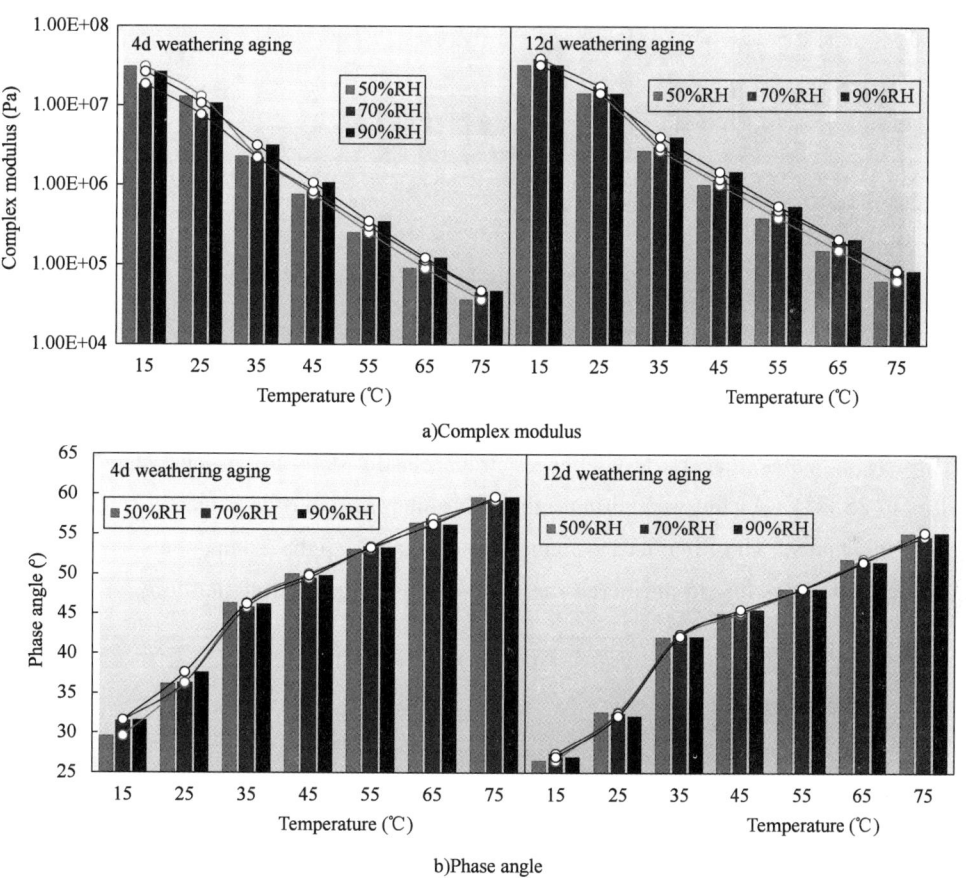

Fig. 3 Temperature sweep test results at different humidity conditions

Fig. 4 compares the temperature sweep test results of HVMA during OWA and NOWA process. As can be seen from Fig. 4, the influence of oxygen on the rheological properties of HVMA increases gradually with the extension of aging days. After 1 d of weathering aging, the differences in the complex modulus of HVMA under OWA and NOWA conditions are not significant, and the phase angle of HVMA under NOWA condition is slightly higher than that under OWA condition. When the aging days further extend, there is a significant difference in the rheological properties of HVMA between OWA condition and NOWA condition. After 12 d of weathering aging, the complex modulus of HVMA under OWA is as 1.61~3.73 times as that under NOWA, and the phase angle of HVMA under OWA is as 0.81~0.89 times as that under NOWA.

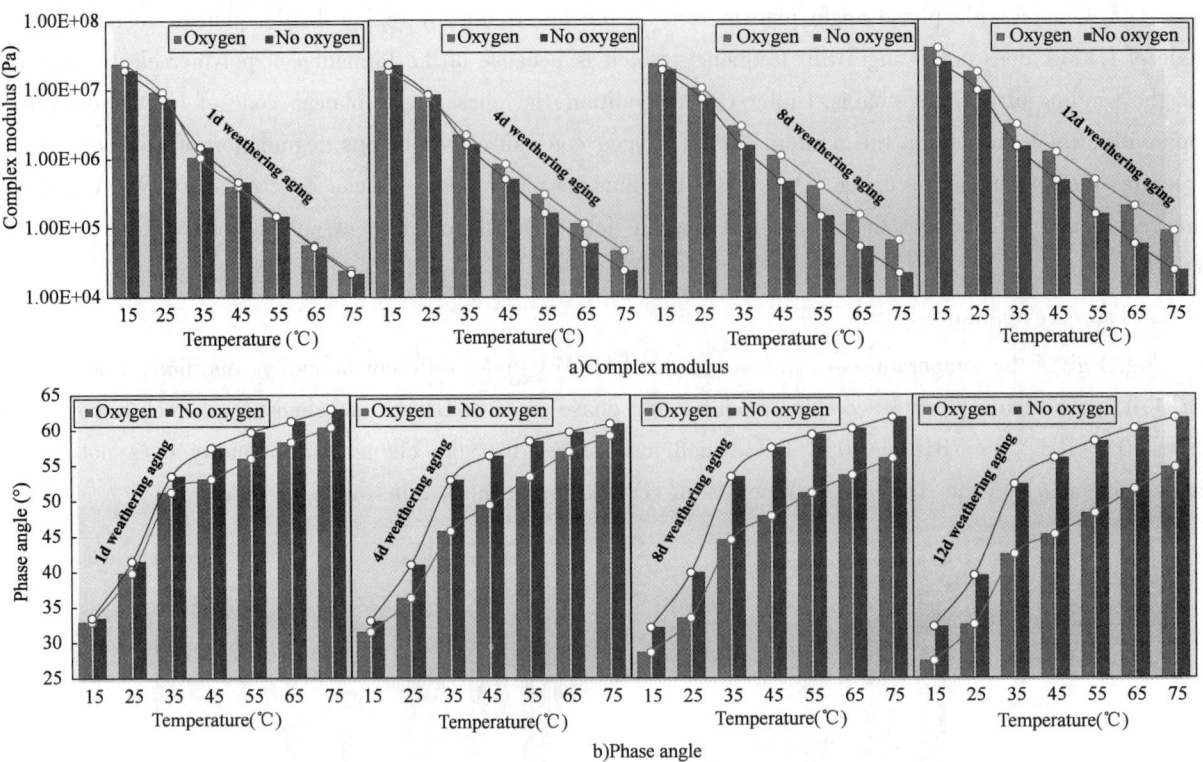

Fig. 4 Temperature sweep test results at OWA and NOWA conditions

2.1.3 Visco-elastic Transition Temperature

In the weathering aging process, the influence of oxygen and humidity on the visco-elastic transition temperature of HVMA is shown in Fig. 5. At unaged condition, the visco-elastic transition temperature of HVMA is 26.7 °C, which indicates that HVMA changes from elastic state to viscous state gradually when the temperature rises to 26.7°C. As the weathering aging days increase, the visco-elastic transition temperature of HVMA increases gradually. The weathering aging effect causes light components to transform to heavy components gradually, thus leading to an increasing visco-elastic transition temperature.

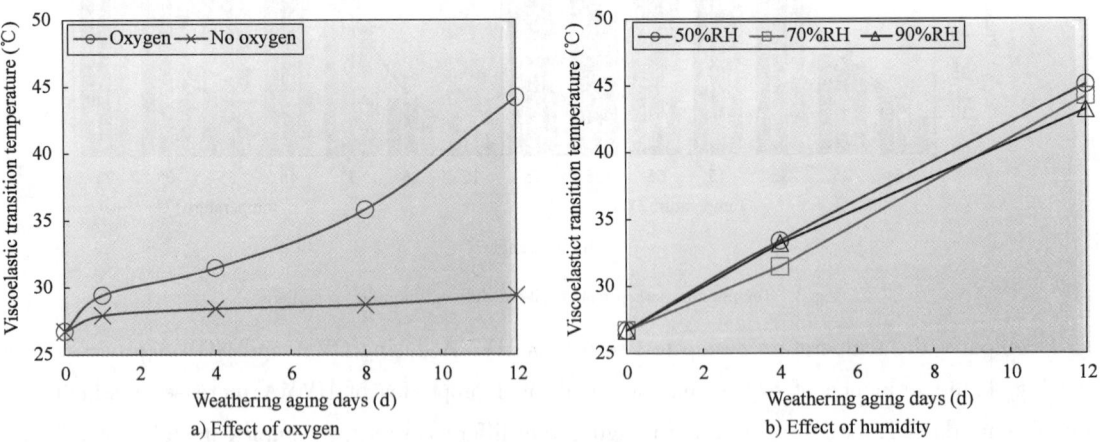

Fig. 5 Visco-elastic transition temperature results

Under different humidity conditions, there is a slight difference in the visco-elastic transition temperature of HVMA, but it does not show obvious regularity. This result show that the humidity does not have a significant effect on the visco-elastic transition temperature of HVMA during the weathering aging process. However, the presence of oxygen plays an important role in the visco-elastic transition temperature of HVMA during weathering aging process. At the condition of no-oxygen, the visco-elastic transition temperature of HVMA initially increases slightly and then almost does not changes with the increase of aging days. At the condition of oxygen, the visco-elastic transition temperature of HVMA shows a significantly increasing trend as the aging days increase. In addition, it is apparent that there is an increasing difference in the visco-elastic transition temperature between oxygen condition and no-oxygen condition with the increase of weathering aging days. After 1d, 4d, 8d, and 12d weathering aging, the difference in the visco-elastic transition temperature of HVMA is 1.5°C, 3.1°C, 7.1°C, and 14.8°C, respectively.

2.2 GPC Test Results

Fig. 6a) shows the GPC test results of HVMA under different humidity conditions during weathering aging process. It can be seen that there are three characteristic peaks in the GPC curve of HVMA, corresponding to polymer peak (about 18 min), asphaltene (about 22 min), and maltene (about 27 min). In different humidity conditions, the GPC curves of HVMA almost overlap, and no apparent difference is found in the three characteristic peaks of GPC curves. This result indicates that the changes in humidity don't have significant effects on the molecular weight composition of HVMA during the weathering aging process. Moreover, with the increase of weathering aging days, the polymer peak decreases and the asphaltene peak increases, indicating the polymer degradation and light-heavy component transition of HVMA.

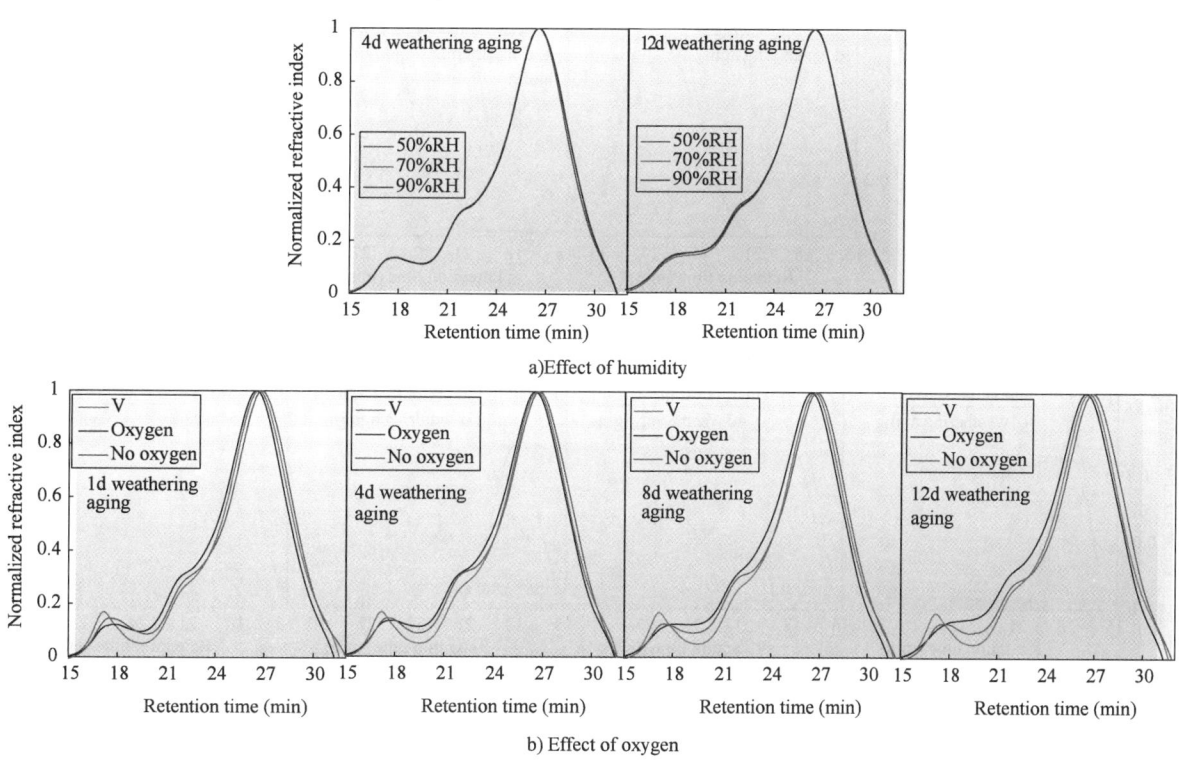

Fig. 6 GPC test results

The GPC curves of HVMA under OWA and NOWA conditions are illustrated in Fig. 6b). To better characterize the role of oxygen in weathering aging, the GPC curve of virgin HVMA is also illustrated in Fig. 6b). According to Fig. 6b), whether under OWA or NOWA conditions, the polymer peak of aged HVMA is smaller than that of virgin HVMA, and the asphaltene peak of aged HVMA is larger than that of virgin HVMA. This result can also confirm that HVMA has two behaviour process during weathering aging: polymer degradation and asphalt aging. Comparing the GPC curves of HVMA under OWA conditions and NOWA conditions, it can be found that there are apparent differences between them. Compared with OWA-HVMA, NOWA-HVMA has a higher polymer peak and a smaller asphaltene peak, which indicates that the polymer degradation and asphalt aging of HVMA under NOWA condition are both slower than those under OWA condition. The absence of oxygen delays the weathering aging process of HVMA. Under OWA conditions, the polymer peak of HVMA decreases and the asphaltene peak of HVMA increases as the aging day increases. In contrast, under NOWA conditions, the polymer peak and asphaltene peak of HVMA do not change obviously with the increase of aging days. This result also demonstrates that the presence of oxygen is an important factor in the change of molecular weight distribution of HVMA during weathering aging.

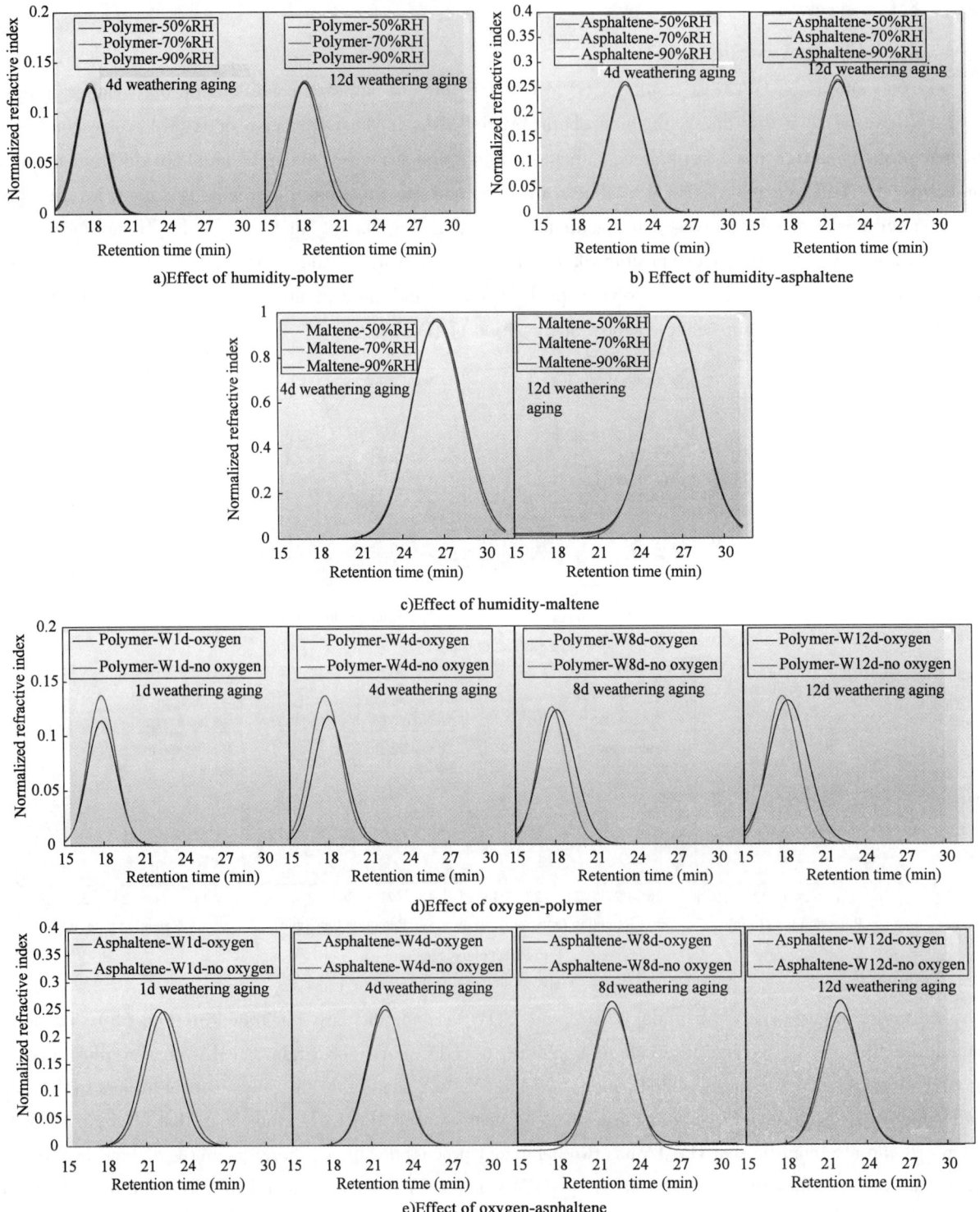

Fig.7

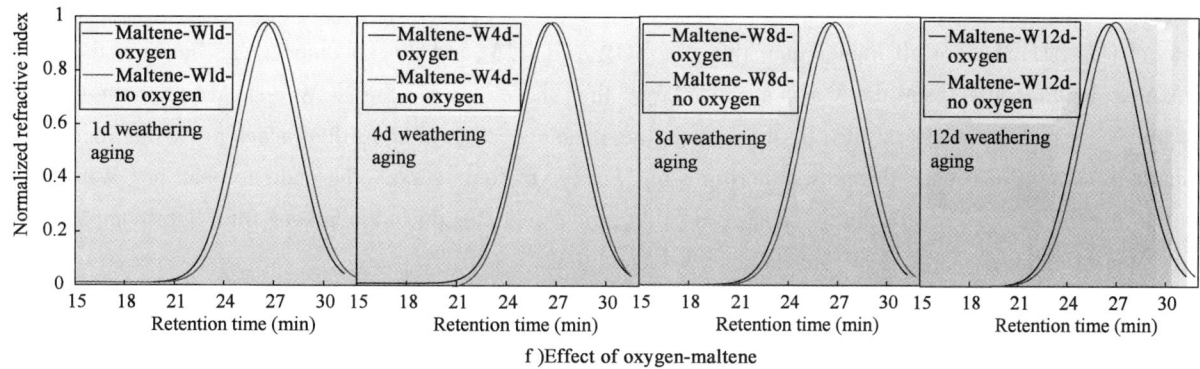

f) Effect of oxygen-maltene

Fig. 7 Asphalt component changes of HVMA under different humidity and oxygen conditions

In the process of weathering aging, HVMA has the degradation process of polymer and the oxidation process of asphalt. The degradation of polymer causes a decreased molecular weight of polymer, and the oxidation of asphalt leads to an increased molecular weight of asphalt components. This may cause the polymer peak, asphaltene peak, and maltene peak to overlap each other on the GPC curves. In order to better characterize the changes in different components of HVMA during weathering aging, a multi-peak fitting tool in Origin software was applied to perform peak splitting processing on the GPC curves of HVMA. The GPC curve is divided into polymer curve, asphaltene curve, and maltene curve, which is shown in Fig. 8.

Fig. 8a) compares the GPC peak splitting results of HVMA under different humidity conditions. As shown in Fig. 8a), the retention time of polymer, asphaltene, and maltene is about 15 ~ 23 min, 18 ~ 27 min, and 21 ~ 31.5min, respectively, which further confirms that the molecular weights of different components in HVMA do indeed overlap. The polymer curve, asphaltene curve, and maltene curve of HVMA almost coincide under different humidity conditions, which further indicates that the changes in humidity has almost no significant effect on the molecular weight distribution of HVMA during weathering aging. When the weathering aging day increases from 4 d to 12 d, the retention time of polymer changes from 15 ~ 21.46 min (molecular weight: 9457 ~ 1169326) to 15 ~ 23.18min (molecular weight: 4908 ~ 1169326), indicating the degradation of polymer molecules. In addition, the height of asphaltene curves increases slightly, and the initial retention time of asphaltene is advanced from 18 min (molecular weight: 53783) to 17.85 min (molecular weight: 59204), which indicates an increasing molecular weight of asphaltenes.

Fig. 8b) presents the peak spitting results of HVMA under OWA and NOWA conditions. According to Fig. 8b), it can be found that the height and distribution range of three characteristic peak curves (polymer, asphaltene, maltene) have apparent differences under OWA and NOWA conditions. For the polymer curves, the polymer peaks of OWA-HVMA are all smaller than those of NOWA-HVMA, and the polymer curves of OWA-HVMA shifts to the right compared with NOWA-HVMA. A slow retention time indicates a small molecular weight. Therefore, it can demonstrate that the effect of OWA causes a more significant degradation of polymer molecules compared with the effect of NOWA. When aged for 4 d, the distribution ranges of polymer curves of NOWA-HVMA and OWA-HVMA are 15 ~ 21.75 min (the minimum molecular weight: 8499), and 15 ~ 22.03 min (the minimum molecular weight: 7644), respectively. When aged for 12 d, the distribution ranges of polymer curves of NOWA-HVMA and OWA-HVMA are 15 ~ 21.52 min (the minimum molecular weight: 9261), and 15 ~ 23.18 min (the minimum molecular weight: 4908), respectively. The above analysis shows that the degradation of polymer is not apparent and the polymer molecular weight fluctuates under NOWA conditions. As a comparison, the polymer molecules degrade significantly, and the minimum of polymer molecular weight is reduced significantly under OWA conditions.

For the asphaltene curves, comparing OWA-HVMA and NOWA-HVMA, it can be found that the asphaltene peaks of OWA-HVMA are all higher than those of NOWA-HVMA, and the envelope areas between the OWA-HVMA asphaltene curves and the X axis are also larger than those between the NOWA-HVMA asphaltene curves and the X axis. This result intuitively shows that the presence of oxygen further accelerates the increase in asphaltene content of HVMA during weathering aging. For the maltene curves, the maltene peak of OWA-HVMA shifts to the left compared with that of NOWA-HVMA, which indicates that the changes from light components to heavy components are more significant under OWA conditions.

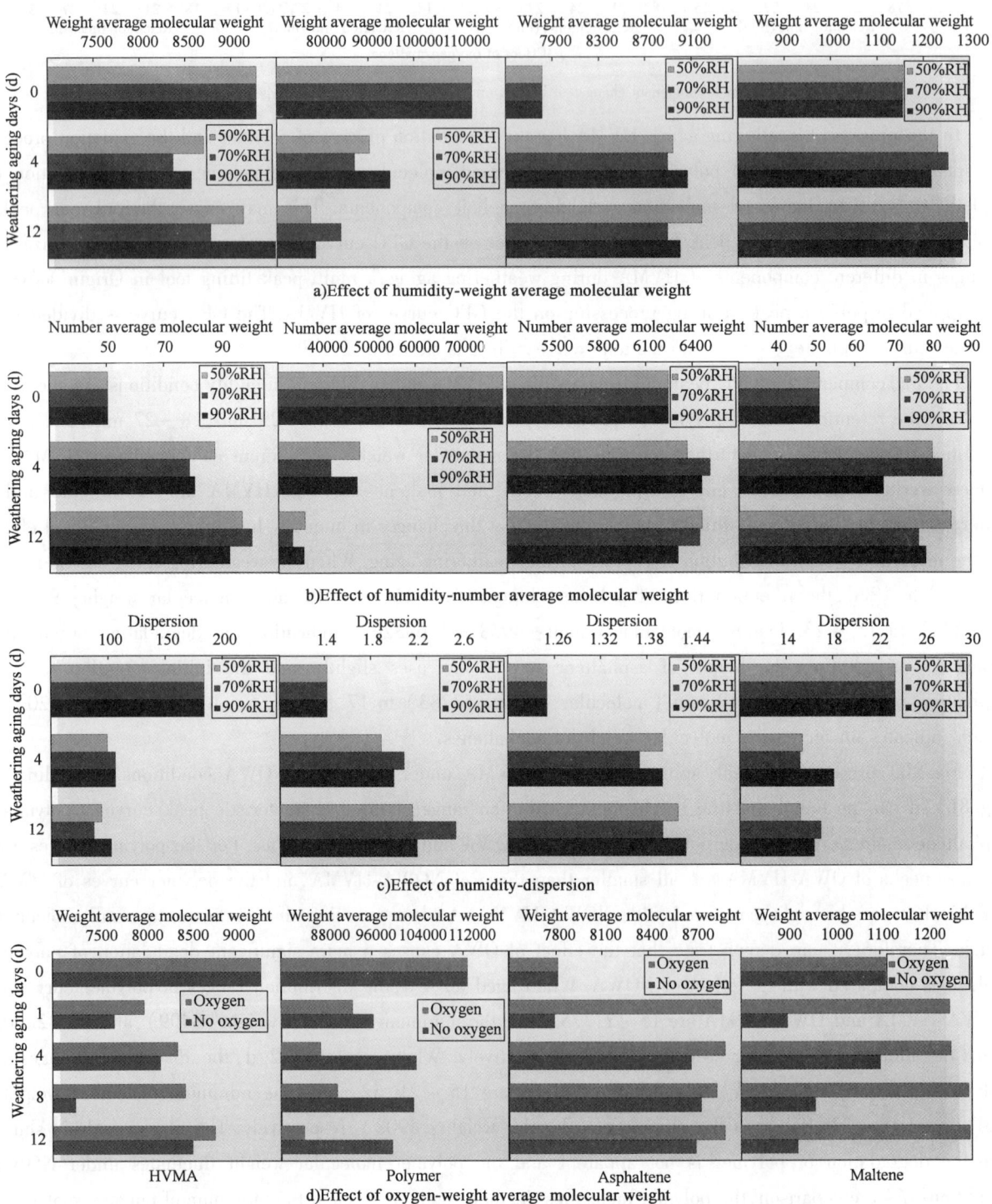

Fig. 8

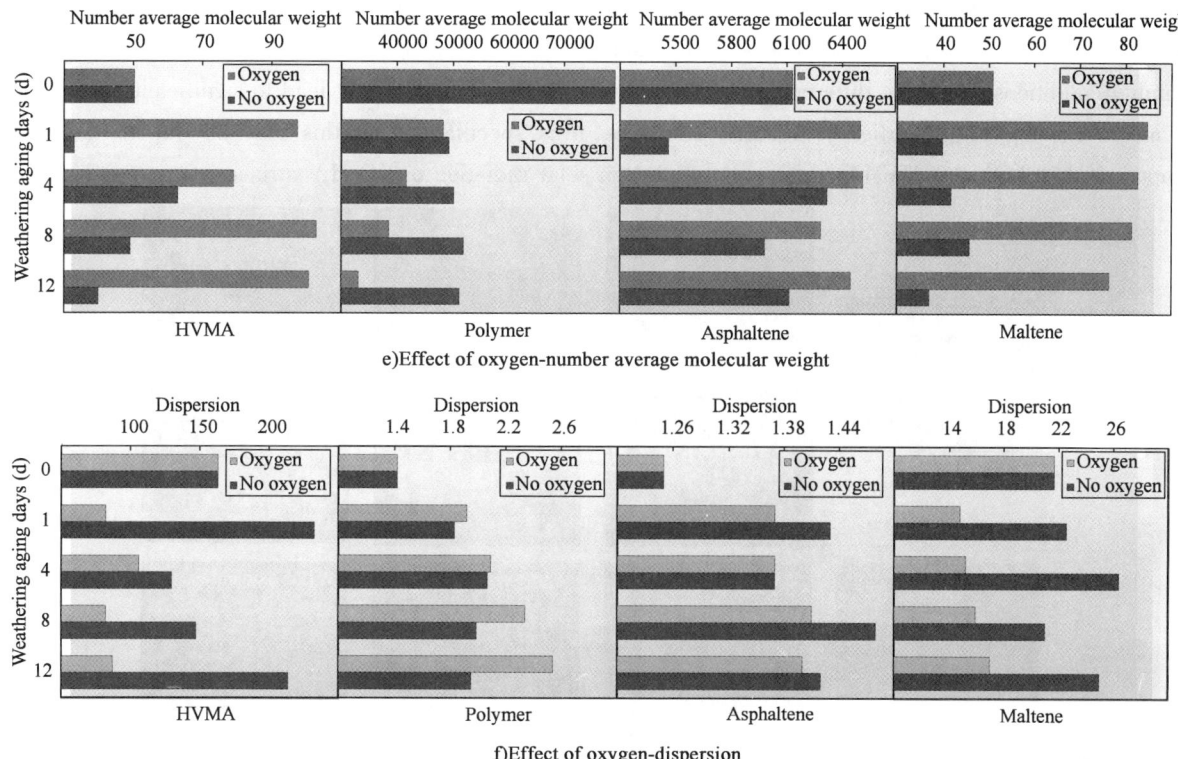

Fig. 8 Molecular weight changes of HVMA under different humidity and oxygen conditions

The results of weight average molecular weight (M_w), number average molecular weight (M_n), and dispersion (D) of HVMA under different humidity and different oxygen conditions were shown in Fig. 8. It can be seen that the distribution range of M_w value, M_n value, and D value of HVMA are 7247.57 ~ 9481.81, 32.98 ~ 102.83, and 82.14 ~ 232.64, respectively. The distribution range of M_w value, M_n value, and D value of polymer are 77463.84 ~ 112731.02, 33052.72 ~ 79128.32, and 1.42 ~ 2.54, respectively. The distribution range of M_w value, M_n value, and D value of asphaltene are 7789.45 ~ 9187.16, 5461.7 ~ 6512.51, and 1.25 ~ 1.48, respectively. The distribution range of M_w value, M_n value, and D value of maltene are 899.93 ~ 1295.73, 39.85 ~ 84.93, and 14.77 ~ 26.39, respectively. In addition, the differences in the M_w value, M_n value, and D value of HVMA are not apparent under different humidity conditions, which shows that the molecular weight distributions of HVMA under different humidity conditions are almost the same. However, there are significant differences in the molecular weight distributions of HVMA under different oxygen conditions. The M_w value and M_n value of OWA-HVMA are larger than NOWA-HVMA, and the D value of OWA-HVMA are smaller than NOWA-HVMA. The M_w value and M_n value of polymer of OWA-HVMA are smaller than the polymer of NOWA-HVMA, and the D value of polymer of OWA-HVMA are larger than the polymer of NOWA-HVMA. The M_w value and the M_n value of asphaltene and the maltene of OWA-HVMA are larger than the asphaltene and the maltene of NOWA-HVMA, and the D value of asphaltene and maltene of OWA-HVMA are smaller than the asphaltene and maltene of NOWA-HVMA.

2.3 FM Test Results

Fig. 9 illustrates the microscopic morphology of HVMA under different humidity and different oxygen conditions. In comparison with virgin HVMA, the weathering-aged HVMA has a significant degradation of polymer phase structures. There are apparent micro-cracks on the surface of HVMA samples under different weathering humidity conditions. Furthermore, the cracking phenomenon on the surface of HVMA sample becomes more serious with the increase of aging days. According to previous studies (Yu et al., 2019), these micro-cracks mainly occur when the surface shrinkage stress under strong solar radiation exceeds the allowable stress of asphalt. There are some small differences in the microscopic morphology of HVMA surfaces under different humidity conditions, but these differences in the microscopic morphology do not lead to significant differences in the macro rheological properties of HVMA. Therefore, it is speculated that this may be due to the uneven component distribution of HVMA surface or the uneven solar radiation on HVMA surface.

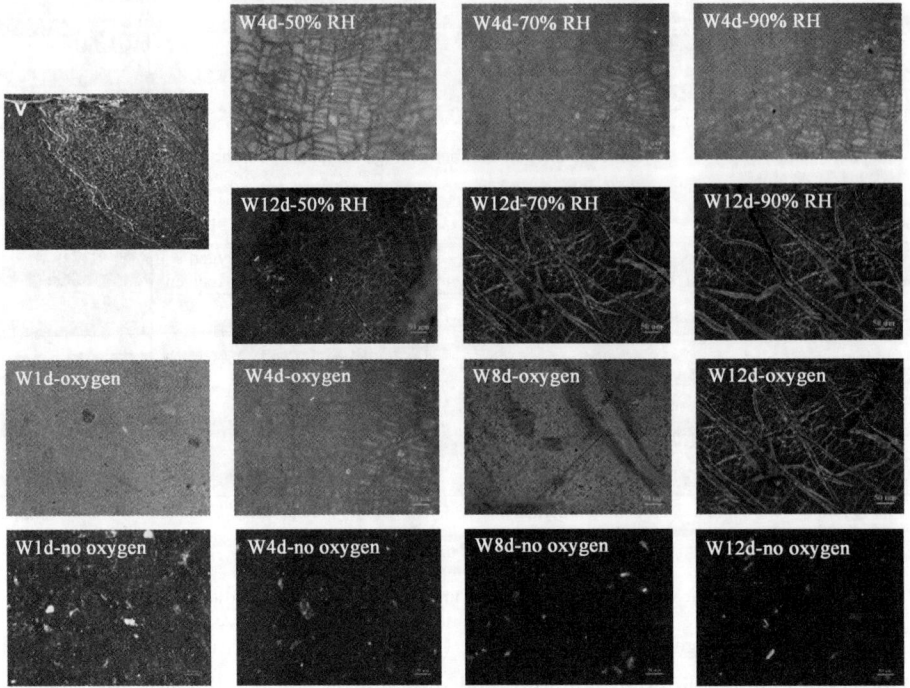

Fig. 9 Microscopic morphology of HVMA

Comparing the surface microscopic morphology of OWA-HVMA and NOWA-HVMA, it can be found that there are significant differences between them. The degradation rate of polymers under NOWA conditions is slower than that under OWA conditions. In the absence of oxygen, no cracking is found on the HVMA surface, even if it is exposed to solar radiation. In contrast, with the participation of oxygen, there are a series of microscopic morphological evolution processes on the HVMA surface, such as wrinkles, micro-crack initiation, micro-crack development, and fragment formation. Therefore, it can be concluded that the participation of oxygen is an important factor in the obvious solar-radiation aging and the formation of dense micro-cracks on the surface of HVMA during weathering aging. When oxygen is not involved, HVMA can not produce micro-cracks on the surface during weathering aging, even if the solar radiation intensity is strong (1000 W/m^2).

3 Conclusions

The objective of this study was to analyse the influence of humidity and oxygen on the rheology-morphology-chemistry performance of HVMA during weathering aging. The main conclusions were summarized as follows.

(1) The changes in humidity do not have a significant impact on the rheology-morphology-chemistry performance of HVMA during weathering aging. Under different humidity conditions, the difference in the rheological master curve, visco-elastic transition temperature, and molecular weight distribution of HVMA is not apparent.

(2) The participation of oxygen leads to a significant change in the rheological property of HVMA in the process of weathering aging. Compared with the no-oxygen-weathering aging (NOWA) condition, HVMA has a larger complex modulus, a smaller phase angle and a higher visco-elastic transition temperature under oxygen-weathering aging (OWA) condition.

(3) The molecular weight distribution of HVMA does not change significantly under NOWA conditions. In contrast, the polymer peak decreases and shifts to the right, the asphaltene peak increases, and the maltene peak shifts to the left, indicating that HVMA has apparent polymer degradation and asphalt oxidation under OWA conditions.

(4) The presence of oxygen is the main reason for the micro-cracks on the surface of HVMA during weathering aging. With the participation of oxygen, the surface shrinkage stress increases under the effect of solar radiation, thus causing significant surface cracking.

References

[1] Chuanqi Yan, Weidong Huang, et al. Chemical and Rheological Evaluation of Aging Properties of High Content SBS Polymer Modified Asphalt[J]. Fuel,2019,252:414-426.

[2] Hanbing Liu, Bing Zhu, et al. Laboratory Evaluation on the Performance of Porous Asphalt Mixture with Steel Slag for Seasonal Frozen Regions[J]. Sustainability,2019,11:6924.

[3] Huanan Yu. and Xianping Bai, et al. Impact of Ultraviolet Radiation on the Aging Properties of SBS-Modified Asphalt Binders. Polymers,2019,11:1111.

[4] L D Poulikakos, M N Partl. A multi-Scale Fundamental Investigation of Moisture Induced Deterioration of Porous Asphalt Concrete[J]. Construction and Building Materials,2012,36:1025-1035.

[5] Mingjun Hu. and Guoqiang Sun, et al. Effect of Thermal Aging on High Viscosity Modified Asphalt Binder: Rheological Property, Chemical Composition and Phase Morphology [J]. Construction and Building Materials,2020,241:118023.

[6] Mingjun Hu, Lihan Li, et al. Laboratory Investigation of OGFC-5 Porous Asphalt Ultrathin Wearing Course [J]. Construction and Building Materials,2019,219:101-110.

[7] Zhang Yuan. and Zhen Leng. Quantification of Bituminous Mortar Ageing and Its Application in Ravelling Evaluation of Porous Asphalt Wearing Courses[J]. Materials & Design,2017,119,1-11.

[8] Zhaoxing Xie. and Junan Shen. Effect of Weathering on Rubberized Porous European Mixture[J]. Journal of Materials in Civil Engineering,2016,28: 04016043.

Improving Rheological and Mechanical Performance of Epoxy Asphalt Modified with Graphene Oxide

Jingjing Si[1], Yang Li[1], Junyan Wang[1], Xiaoyong Zou[2], Xin Yu[1]

(1. Hohai University, College of Civil and Transportation Engineering;

2. Jinhua Highway and Transportation Management Center)

Abstract Graphene oxide (GO) was applied as a modifier to epoxy asphalt (EA) for GO/EA composite preparation. The influence of the GO dosage on the rheologic behavior, and mechanical performances of GO/EA

Financial support from the National Natural Science Foundation of China (Grant No. 520031811), the Fundamental Research Funds for the Central Universities (Grant No. B200202069), the Zhejiang Highway and Transportation Management Center Science and Technology Project (Grant No. 820086316).

was investigated. Results showed the GO was fully exfoliated and uniformly dispersed in the EA matrix. GO decreased the RV of EA and increased the pot life. The addition of GO improved the glass transition temperature T_g, compatibility, and stiffness of the EA. In addition, the GO/EA with 0.1 wt% GO showed excellent toughness that the elongation at break was increased by 164%, and the tensile and adhesive strength were nearly equal to that of EA.

Keywords Epoxy asphalt Graphene oxide Rheological behavior Mechanical performance

0 Introduction

As one of the most important materials for paving steel bridges, epoxy asphalt (EA) has been studied in-depth since it was first used for paving the San Mateo-Hayward Bridge. EA is a thermoplastic/thermosetting polymer composite, which is composed by thermoplastic asphalt and thermosetting epoxy resin (ER)[1,2]. When EA was cured, the asphalt was dispersed in the continuous crosslink networks of ER. This structure characteristic enables EA superior thermal and mechanical performances, and durability[3-6]. For the past few decades, EA has been extensively used as a binder and a waterproof adhesion agent to pave steel bridges[7-10].

Nano materials have been used as modifiers for developing high performance road materials. In this respect, graphene oxide (GO) has been widely studied just that it has large specific surface area, active functional groups on the surface, excellent thermal, mechanical and electrical properties[11]. It is interesting to study the GO modified asphalt materials for many research groups[12,13]. One of the main application of GO in construction materials is as modifiers to improve the strength and stiffness of asphalt materials[14]. Adnan et al.[15] has employed GO modified asphalt binder in asphalt and found that the mechanical behavior of asphalt was significantly improved. The performances of GO modified asphalt mixture were evaluated by Zhu et al.[16]. It is discovered that the mixture showed prominently high rutting resistance and compressive resilient modulus. For the GO and Sasobit modified asphalt, the mechanical performances were affected by mixing sequences of GO and Sasobit. To achieve better performance, GO should be added first in the asphalt[17]. Duan, et al.[18] found that the modified asphalt with 1.0 wt% butylated GO (C4H9-GO) showed excellent thermal stability and low stress sensitivity, in which the softening point and the ductility was increased by 11.4% and 19.3% compared with the SBS-modified asphalt (5 wt% SBS), respectively, and the penetration was decreased by 10.2%.

Based on the above literatures, GO is an effective additive to modify the mechanical performance of asphalt materials. We believe, GO will have the potential to enhance the performances of EA materials. The current study employed GO in EA for improving its rheological and mechanical performances. GO/EA composites with various GO dosages were prepared. Then the rheological behavior, glass transition temperature (T_g), dynamic mechanical properties, tensile properties and adhesive strength of the GO/EA composites were analyzed.

1 Materials and Characterizations

1.1 Materials

Epoxy monomers (E-51) were purchased from Wuxi Resin (China). The acid anhydride hardener was produced by ourselves. SBS-modified asphalt was obtained from Tongsha (China, Tab.1). GO was bought from Kaina Carbon New Material (Shenzhen, China). γ-(2,3-epoxypropoxy) propyl trimethoxysilane (KH560) with purity of 97% was bought from Aladdin Industrial Corp. (USA).

Properties of the SBS-modified asphalt Tab. 1

Property	Data	Method
SBS content (wt%)	3	—
25℃ Penetration (0.1 mm)	55.4	ASTM D 5
Softening point (℃)	66.3	ASTM D 36
5℃ Ductility (cm)	34.7	ASTM D 113
Solubility (trichloroethylene,%)	99.5	ASTM D 2042

1.2 Preparation of the GO/EA composites

Component A of the GO/EA composites was prepared by mixing E-51, KH560 (1% by mass of E-51) and a certain amount of GO. The mixture was ultrasonic dispersed at 25℃ for 20 min in an ultrasonic cleaner. Component B was composed of asphalt and hardener. The asphalt was melted at 130 ℃ for about 30 min. Then the asphalt and hardener were weighted and added in a three-necked flask with stirring rod, thermometer, and allihn condenser. The blend was heated to 130 ℃ with an agitation speed of 500 rpm for 2 h to obtain component B. Component A was added into component B at 120 ℃ for 5 min with mechanical agitation at 800 rpm to obtain GO/EA blend.

The curing condition of GO/EA blend was 120 ℃/4 h in an electric oven. The mass ratio of the epoxy monomer, hardener and asphalt was 100 : 140 : 280. The GO content was 0.02, 0.05, 0.1, and 0.2%, respectively, by the mass of epoxy resin (E-51 and curing agent), which was referred to as GO/EA0.02, GO/EA0.05, GO/EA0.1, and GO/EA0.2, respectively. The EA was prepared as a control.

1.3 Characterizations

The rheological behaviors of the blends were analyzed by a Brookfield rotational viscometer (DV-II, Brookfield Engineering Inc., USA). The rotational viscosity (RV) data at 120 ℃ were recorded every five minutes. When 60 min or the RV was higher than 5 Pa·s, the test should be terminated. The final RV value was the average of three repeated test data.

In order to acquire the E', $\tan \delta$ and T_g, T_β and T_γ, the cured EA and cured GO/EAs were measured on a dynamic mechanical analyzer (DMA/SDTA861e, Mettler Toledo, Switzerland). The strain was employed sinusoidally at a frequency of 1 Hz. The specimen was heated from −40 to 70 ℃ with a heating rate of 3℃·min^{-1} in N_2 atmosphere. The specimen diameter was 25mm×5mm×1.5mm.

The tensile properties of the cured samples were tested by a universal tester (HG-MF501, Jiangsu Zhuoheng Observation and Control Technology Co., Ltd., China) at 25 ℃. The crosshead motion speed was 10 mm·min^{-1}. The specimens were manufactured according to ASTM D638—2014 (type IV). The final value of each sample was the mean of 6 effective tests.

The adhesive strength was evaluated by a pull-off tester (PosiTest AT-A, DeFelsko Co., USA). The terminal diameter was 20 mm. The final value of each sample was the mean of 6 effective tests.

2 Results and Discussion

2.1 Rheological Properties

EA is thermoplastic/thermosetting polymer composite that will be cured as long as the component A and the component B are mixed. When the curing process happens, EA's viscosity will increase gradually with the molecular weight ER [19,20]. Meanwhile, the EA adhesive material with excessive viscosity might increase the difficulty of construction of the steel deck and concrete. As a result, the viscosity growth rate of EA should not be too quick. As applied to pave pavements and bridges, the time when EA's viscosity increases to 1 Pa·s at 120

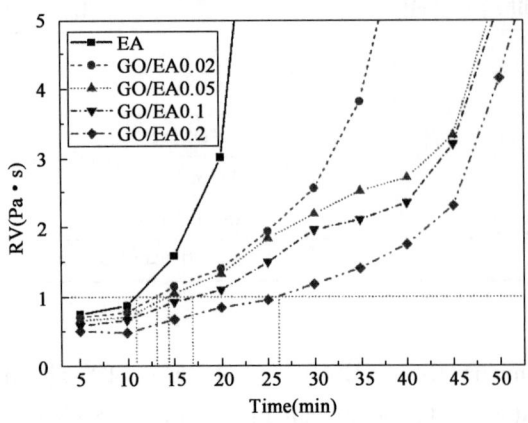

Fig. 1 RV-time curves of EA blend and GO/EA blends at 120℃

℃ is called pot life, which needs to be over 10 min as required by the general specification.

The relationship between RV and time of blends at 120℃, and the RV data are displayed in Fig. 1 and Tab. 2. Compared with EA blend, the RVs of GO/EA blends are all lower after curing for the equal time. In the meantime, with GO loading increasing, on the one hand, the RVs of GO/EA blends decreased (Tab. 2); On the other hand, the curing time need longer when the RV got the same. (Fig. 1). The factor may be that GO hinders the movement of epoxy monomers, hardener and asphalt[21]. The pot life of the EA and EA with 0.02, 0.05, 0.1 and 0.2 wt% GO is 11, 13, 14, 17 and 26 min, respectively. The results indicated there are more time for construction because of the inhibiting effect of GO nanosheets on EA. The result coincided with fibrous nanolayers[20].

RV of the EA blend and GO/EA blends at 120 ℃   Tab. 2

Sample	RV (Pa·s)		
	5 min	10 min	15 min
EA blend	0.746	0.871	1.584
GO/EA0.02 blend	0.701	0.775	1.150
GO/EA0.05 blend	0.660	0.700	1.051
GO/EA0.1 blend	0.582	0.661	0.923
GO/EA0.2 blend	0.504	0.479	0.671

2.2 Dynamic Mechanical Property

The DMA was used to evaluate the glass and secondary transition of the cured EA and cured GO/EAs and to analyze the relationship between the GO addition and the transition. The results presented in Fig. 2 and Tab. 3.

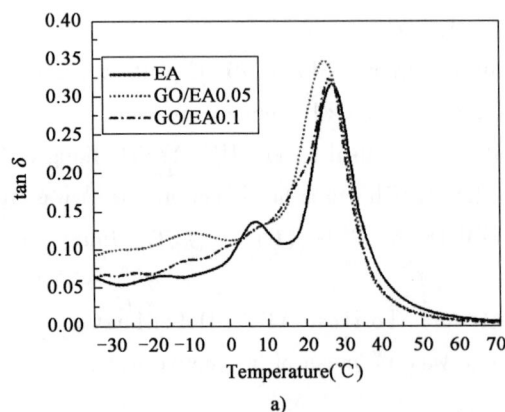
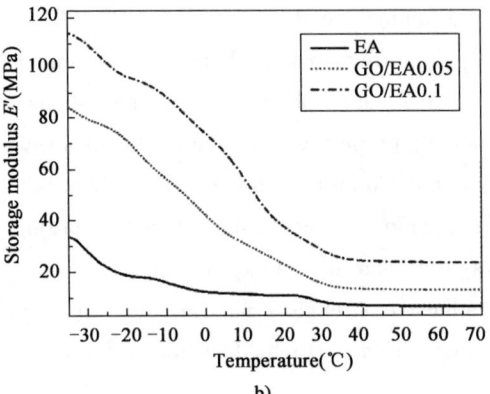

Fig. 2 Temperature dependence of tan δ for cured EA and cured GO/EAs

DMA data of cured EA and cured GO/EAs   Tab. 3

Samples	Transitions(℃)			E'(MPa)	
	T_g	T_β	T_γ	−35℃	35℃
EA	27.0	6.8	−17.9	33.85	7.02
GO/EA0.05	26.5	—	−9.7	84.55	13.50
GO/EA0.1	24.9	—	−10.1	113.98	25.04

The curve that the loss tangent ($\tan \delta$) varies with temperature is shown in Fig. 2, which is used to study the glass transition process of cured EA and cured GO/EAs. As shown in the DMA curve, there are three or two peaks for tan δ. The T_g means the temperature corresponding to the maximum peak in the glass transition process. The T_β and T_γ refers to the temperature corresponding to the other peaks in the secondary transition process. At the same time, the T_β and T_γ is from high temperature to low temperature, respectively. As presented and listed in Fig. 2 and Tab. 3, the glass transition and secondary transition of the cured EA was influenced obviously when the GO was added. EA showed three tan δ peaks, in which T_g, T_β and T_γ is 27.0 ℃, 6.8 ℃, and -17.9 ℃, respectively (black solid curve in Fig. 2, Tab. 3). The T_g and the T_β is attributed to the glass transition and local relaxation of EA, and the T_γ may accounted for the secondary transition of asphalt. Except for EA, GO/EAs have two tanδ peaks, T_g and T_γ. Moreover, the T_g s decreased while T_γ s increased with incorporating GO (Fig. 2, Tab. 3). The interaction among epoxy resin, GO and asphalt may be as follows. On the one hand, there existed epoxy groups, hydroxyl groups, and carboxyl groups on GO, which has attended curing reaction of ER. On the other hand, the π-π conjugation formed between GO and the fused ring structures in asphalt. These indicated the GO may promote the compatibility between epoxy resin and asphalt.

According to DMA analysis, the storage modulus (E')-temperature curves of the cured samples are shown in Fig. 2b). The E' value is decided by the stiffness and the energy storage capacity, which indicates the sample's elastic performance[22]. The E' values of EA and GO/EAs dropped rapidly from -35 ℃ to 35 ℃ (Fig. 2). When the temperature is lower than -35 ℃, the molecular segments were frozen; thus, the E' value of the cured EA, cured GO/EA0.05, and cured GO/EA0.1 was 33.85, 84.55, and 113.98 MPa, respectively. With the temperature increasing, the frozen molecular segments relax tardily. Above 35 ℃, the E' of EA, GO/EA0.05, and GO/EA0.1 decreased to 7.02, 13.50, and 25.04 MPa, respectively (Tab. 3), indicating that the molecular segmental relaxation increased with temperature. Compared with the E' of EA, the cured GO/EAs presented a bigger value, manifesting the GO was of promoting effect on the stiffness for the EA.

2.3 Mechanical performances

The effects of GO dosage on mechanical performance of the cured EA and cured GO/EA composites was tested and presented in Fig. 3, including tensile strength, elongation at break, and adhesive strength.

As shown in Fig. 3, GO may obviously improve the mechanical performances of EA due to GO's excellent mechanical property and specific structure. The tensile strength of GO/EA composites was decreased compared with EA (6.5MPa), which was 3.8 MPa (GO/EA0.02), 4.2 MPa (GO/EA0.05), 6.3 MPa (GO/EA0.1), 3.1 MPa (GO/EA0.2), respectively. However, the elongation at break of GO/EAs was significantly improved, which was 386.3% (GO/EA0.02), 432.7% (GO/EA0.05), 445.5% (GO/EA0.1), 352.5% (GO/EA0.2), respectively. The tensile strength as well as elongation at break increased with mass ratio of GO in EA when the GO content was lower than 0.1 wt%. Two factors may contribute to the tensile properties of GO/EA composites. One side, the GO addition inhibited the curing progress between epoxy monomer and curing agent and weakened the curing degree, which resulted in the improvement of the tensile strength while reduce of the elongation at break. What is more, the GO was of excellent strength and stiffness which resulted the tensile strength as well as elongation at break was promoted simultaneously. In addition, too much GO is

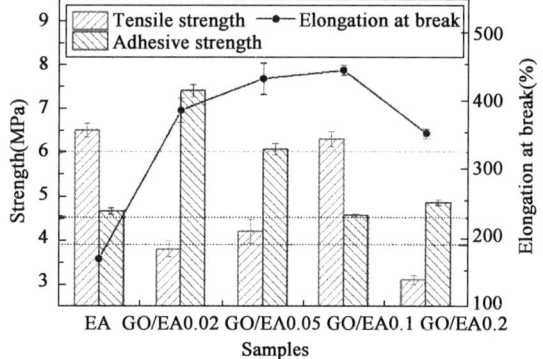

Fig.3 Mechanical performance of the cured EA and cured GO/EA composites

easy to agglomerate that might result in decreasing tensile strength and elongation at break of the GO/EA0.2.

Additionally, adhesive strength was used to characterize adhesive performance, which was required to exceed 4.5 MPa. Compared with EA (4.7 MPa), the adhesive strength of GO/EAs was promoted entirely, which was 7.4 MPa (GO/EA0.02), 6.1 MPa (GO/EA0.05), 4.6MPa (GO/EA0.1), 4.9 MPa (GO/EA0.2), respectively. As a result, the existence of the GO enhanced the adhesive strength of the EA, which be related that GO promoted the dispersion degree of system[20]. Compared with GO/EAs, the more GO dosage added, the smaller adhesive strength. The GO/EA0.02 composite (with 0.02 wt% GO) was of a biggest adhesive strength (7.4 MPa), whose adhesive strength was increased by 57% over the EA's. The reason that the curing degree of epoxy resin was restricted was why the adhesive strength decreased[23].

3 Conclusions

GO/EA composites with different content of GO were prepared, and their rheological and mechanical performances were characterized. The RV of EA blend decreased with increasing GO content during the curing process, and the pot life increased. The T_g, T_β and T_γ of the cured GO/EA composites decreased due to improved compatibility between epoxy resin and asphalt by incorporating GO. Meanwhile, the cured GO/EAs was of higher E' value compared with EA, indicating high stiffness of the GO/EA composites. Compared with EA, the adhesive strength and elongation at break of GO/EA promoted as a whole, the tensile strength reduced. As for GO/EA, the optimal addition of GO was 0.1 wt%, which was of the maximum tensile strength (6.5MPa) and elongation at break (445.5%), as well as nearly equal adhesive strength to that of EA.

References

[1] Chen L, Qian Z, Hu H. Epoxy Asphalt Concrete Protective Course Used on Steel Railway Bridge[J]. Construction and Building Materials, 2013, 41:125-130.

[2] Chen LL, Qian ZD, Hu HZ. Epoxy Asphalt Concrete Protective Course Used on Steel Railway Bridge[J]. Construction and Building Materials, 2013, 41:125-130.

[3] Jiang Y, Liu Y, Gong J. et al. Microstructures, Thermal and Mechanical Properties of Epoxy Asphalt Binder Modified by SBS Containing Various Styrene-Butadiene Structures[J]. Materials and Structures, 2018, 51.

[4] Wei J, Zhang Y. Study on the Curing Process of Epoxy Asphalt[J]. Journal of Testing and Evaluation, 2012, 40:1169-1176.

[5] Sun YF, Zhang YG, Xu K. et al. Thermal, Mechanical Properties, and Low-Temperature Performance of Fibrous Nanoclay-Reinforced Epoxy Asphalt Composites and Their Concretes[J]. Journal of Applied Polymer Science, 2015, 132:9.

[6] Luo S, Qian ZD. Preparation and Performance Evaluation of Novel High Durability Epoxy Asphalt Concrete for Bridge Deck Pavements[J]. Asian Journal of Chemistry, 2014, 26:5595-5598.

[7] Cong PL, Chen SF, Yu JY. Investigation of the Properties of Epoxy Resin-Modified Asphalt Mixtures for Application to Orthotropic Bridge Decks[J]. Journal of Applied Polymer Science, 2011, 121:2310-2316.

[8] Lu Q, Bors J. Alternate uses of Epoxy Asphalt on Bridge Decks and Roadways[J]. Construction and Building Materials, 2015, 78:18-25.

[9] Qian ZD, Liu Y, Liu CB, et al. Design and Skid Resistance Evaluation of Skeleton-Dense Epoxy Asphalt Mixture for Steel Bridge Deck Pavement[J]. Construction and Building Materials, 2016, 114:851-863.

[10] Huang W. Integrated Design Procedure for Epoxy Asphalt Concrete-Based Wearing Surface on Long-Span Orthotropic Steel Deck Bridges[J]. Journal of Materials in Civil Engineering, 2016, 28:12.

[11] Yim C, Kockerbeck ZA, Jo SB, et al. Hybrid Copper-Silver-Graphene Nanoplatelet Conductive Inks on PDMS for Oxidation Resistance Under Intensive Pulsed Light[J]. ACS Applied Materials & Interfaces,

[12] Rhee I, Lee J-S, Kim JH. et al. Thermal Performance, Freeze-and-thaw Resistance, and Bond Strength of Cement Mortar Using Rice Husk-derived Graphene[J]. Construction and Building Materials, 2017, 146: 350-359.

[13] Zhou XY, Ma B, Wei K, et al. Curing, Process and Properties of Hydrogenated Bisphenol a Epoxy Resin Particles by an Interfacial Polymerization Method for Asphalt Pavements[J]. Construction and Building Materials, 2017, 147: 448-456.

[14] Young RJ, Kinloch IA, Gong L, et al. The mechanics of Graphene Nanocomposites: A review[J]. Composites Science and Technology, 2012, 72: 1459-1476.

[15] Adnan AM, Luo X, Lu CF, et al. Improving Mechanics Behavior of Hot Mix Asphalt Using Graphene-oxide[J]. Construction and Building Materials, 2020, 254: 8.

[16] Zhu JC, Zhang K, Liu KF, et al. Performance of Hot and Warm Mix Asphalt Mixtures Enhanced by Nano-sized Graphene Oxide[J]. Construction and Building Materials, 2019, 217: 273-282.

[17] Liu KF, Zhu JC, Zhang K. et al. Effects of Mixing Sequence on Mechanical Properties of Graphene Oxide and Warm mix Additive Composite Modified Asphalt Binder[J]. Construction and Building Materials, 2019, 217: 301-309.

[18] Duan SC, Li J, Muhammad Y, et al. Synthesis and Evaluation of High-Temperature Properties of Butylated Graphene Oxide Composite Incorporated SBS (C4H9-GO/SBS)-modified Asphaltyyy[J]. Journal of Applied Polymer Science, 2019, 136: 13.

[19] Liu Y, Xi Z, Cai J, et al. Laboratory Investigation of The Properties of Epoxy Asphalt Rubber (EAR)[J]. Materials and Structures, 2017, 50.

[20] Sun YF, Liu Y, Jiang YJ, et al. Thermal and Mechanical Properties of Natural Fibrous Nanoclay Reinforced Epoxy Asphalt Adhesives[J]. International Journal of Adhesion and Adhesives, 2018, 85: 308-314.

[21] Esmizadeh E, Naderi G, Yousefi AA, et al. Investigation of Curing Kinetics of Epoxy Resin/Novel Nanoclay-Carbon Nanotube Hybrids by Non-isothermal Differential Scanning Calorimetry[J]. Journal of Thermal Analysis and Calorimetry, 2016, 126: 771-784.

[22] Gong J, Liu Y, Wang Q, et al. Performance Evaluation of Warm Mix Asphalt Additive Modified Epoxy Asphalt Rubbers[J]. Construction and Building Materials, 2019, 204: 288-295.

[23] Sun YF, Gong J, Liu Y, et al. Viscous, Damping, and Mechanical Properties of Epoxy Asphalt Adhesives Containing Different Penetration-grade Asphalts[J]. Journal of Applied Polymer Science, 2019, 136: 8.

基于果脯废糖液的公路用液态融雪剂试验研究

向 豪[1]　弥海晨[2]　陈华鑫[1]

(1. 长安大学材料科学与工程学院；2. 西安公路研究院)

摘　要　由于存在溶解电离过程，固态融雪剂融雪速率较慢，而且常用工业类融雪剂对环境危害较大，对道路设施腐蚀严重。本文以果脯废糖液为主要原料制备了液态融雪剂，以市售融雪液和环保型固态融雪剂为参照对象，分析了液态融雪剂的融冰雪性能和环保性能。研究结果表明，液态融雪剂冰点低

基金项目：陕西省交通运输厅交通科研项目(项目编号：19-26K)。

于-45℃,在融冰30min时的融冰速率是市售融雪液融冰速率的2.4倍,在融冰6h时的融冰量是市售融雪液融冰量的2.3倍,具有优良的融冰雪效果。液态融雪剂对碳钢腐蚀速率和种子受害率远小于环保型固态融雪剂,符合国家标准要求,对绿萝和三叶草的生长均没有明显影响。液态融雪剂对混凝土的腐蚀显著弱于环保型固态融雪剂。本文制备的液态融雪剂在道路除冰雪方面具有优良的应用前景。

关键词 液态融雪剂 固态融雪剂 融冰雪性能 环保性能

0 引言

路面积雪、结冰阻碍了正常的交通运输和行车安全,同时给国家或个人造成巨大的经济损失[1]。在道路除雪化冰的方法中,撒布融雪剂以其价格低廉、化雪迅速、操作简便、可提前布撒等优点成为我国道路除冰融雪的主要方式[2-3]。目前所使用的融雪剂基本上是以氯化钠为主,其优点是价格便宜,仅相当于有机类融雪剂价格的十分之一,但对环境造成污染,对道路设施腐蚀严重[4-5]。醋酸钾等有机盐类融雪剂融雪效果好、腐蚀性很小,但是价格非常昂贵,一般只适用于机场等地[6]。在融雪速率方面,固体融雪剂需要先溶解成溶液才能发挥融雪效果,颗粒状的融雪剂撒布到路面上后,需借助过往车辆的多次碾压后才能有效发挥融雪效果,融雪速率过慢,这对以保畅为主要目标的冬季高速公路除雪作业影响较大。液态融雪剂用量小、效率高,可以更好满足快速除雪保畅的需要,特别是采用雪初预洒布方式时,效果更明显。

果脯废糖液是果脯蜜饯加工后的剩余液体,其含糖量高达70%以上,直接丢不但造成了材料浪费,而且污染了环境[7]。我国废糖液每年的产量近600万t[8],目前废糖液主要用于回收糖[9],制备电容器用多孔碳球[10]等方面,利用效率不高。本文对果脯废糖液进行处理后加入乙二醇,制备出液态融雪剂,基本实现果脯废糖液的100%回收利用。然后以市售无氯液态融雪剂和某品牌的环保型固态融雪剂作为对比,测试并分析了液态融雪剂的融冰雪性能、对碳钢和水泥混凝土的腐蚀性能以及对植物的伤害性能。

1 试验

1.1 材料

将果脯加工后的废弃液经过澄清、调节pH、加入乙二醇等工序后制得液态融雪剂。市售无氯融雪液(简称市售融雪液,主要成分如表1所示,厂家提供)、环保型固态融雪剂(简称固态融雪剂,主要成分见表2)。

市售无氯液态融雪剂主要成分　　　　表1

主要成分	含量(%)	主要成分	含量(%)
丙三醇	15.0~17.0	其他醇类	6.2~11.8
Na、K等离子	16.0~24.0	水	40.0
甲酸	5.8~7.2		

环保型固态融雪剂主要成分　　　　表2

主要成分	含量(%)	测试方法
$NaCl$	48.5	GB/T 1464—1993
$CaCl_2$	32.9	GB/T 15452—2009
$MgCl_2$	15.7	GB/T 15452—2009
不溶杂质	2.9%	溶解法

1.2 试验方法

1.2.1 不同浓度液态融雪剂溶液冰点

配制不同浓度的液态融雪剂溶液,市售融雪液溶液和固态融雪剂溶液样品,按照《发动机冷却液冰点测定法》(SH/T 0090—1991)的方法测试各样品的冰点。

1.2.2 融冰速率

(1)在6个直径5cm的铁皮杯中分别加入50g去离子水,将去离子水置于-10℃的低温恒温箱中6h,使其全部冻结成冰;

(2)称取20g液态融雪剂倒入容器中,置于-10℃下1h,使样品温度与试验温度一致;

(3)将倒入铁皮杯中的冰块上;

(4)每隔10min将铁皮杯中液体倒出,称量液体的质量;以市售融雪液和固体融雪剂作为对比;

(5)液态融雪剂和市售融雪液的融冰速率按照式(1)计算,固态融雪剂的融冰速率按照式(2)计算。

$$\kappa = \frac{m_{液体} - 20}{t} \tag{1}$$

$$\kappa = \frac{m_{液体}}{t} \tag{2}$$

式中:$m_{液体}$——铁皮杯中倒出液体的质量,g;

t——融冰时间,min;

κ——融冰速率,g/min。

1.2.3 融冰量

(1)按照液态融雪剂融冰速率的试验步骤将样品倒在冰块上。

(2)每隔1h将铁皮杯中的液体倒出,称量其质量。

(3)按照式(3)计算液态融雪剂和市售融雪液的融冰量,根据式(4)计算固体融雪剂的融冰量。

$$\eta = \frac{m_{水} - 20}{m_{冰}} \times 100\% \tag{3}$$

$$\eta = \frac{m_{水}}{m_{冰}} \times 100\% \tag{4}$$

式中:$m_{水}$——铁皮杯中倒出液体的质量,g;

$m_{冰}$——冰块总质量,g;

η——融冰量,%。

1.2.4 对碳钢的腐蚀速率

根据《融雪剂》(GB/T 23851—2017)中提出的旋转挂片法测定融雪剂对碳钢的腐蚀率。刘靖等人[8]的研究表明,融雪剂在较小浓度时具有较大的腐蚀性。依据这一结论,分别配制质量分数为3.5%的液态融雪剂溶液、市售融雪液溶液和固态融雪剂溶液,同时以蒸馏水为参照,对比四种样品对碳钢的腐蚀性。碳钢腐蚀速率的计算方法如下[11]:

$$v_{corr} = \frac{8796(m - m_0) \times 10}{\rho \cdot t \cdot S}$$

式中:m——试片的失重,g;

m_0——试片酸洗空白试验的质量损失平均值的数值,g;

ρ——材料的密度,7.82g/cm³;

t——实验时间,h;

S——试样面积,cm²;

v_{corr}——平均腐蚀速率,mm/a。

1.2.5 对植物的伤害性能

(1)种子萌芽率

根据《融雪剂》(GB/T 23851—2017)中提出的植物种子相对受害率测试方法测试液态融雪剂对早熟草本禾种子发芽率的影响。

(2) 绿萝生长

将整盆绿萝用水浇灌培养,培养一个月后观察绿萝长势,绿萝未出现黄叶、枯萎现象说明绿萝培养成活。分别配置10%浓度的液态融雪剂溶液、市售融雪液溶液、固体融雪剂溶液。使用配制好的融雪液浇灌绿萝,浇灌量为每天20g,连续浇灌15d,观察绿萝生长状况,使用蒸馏水作为对比对象。

(3) 草地浇灌

选定几块三叶草生长良好的草地,将草地划分为几个明显的等面积草地块。分别配置10%浓度的液态融雪剂溶液、市售融雪液溶液和固态融雪剂溶液,使用配制好的融雪液溶液浇灌三叶草地,每次浇灌量为300g/m²,连续浇灌30d,观察并记录三叶草生长情况。

1.2.6 对水泥混凝土腐蚀

根据《普通混凝土长期性能和耐久性能试验方法》(GB/T 50082—2009)中的单面冻融法测试液态融雪剂对水泥混凝土的腐蚀性能,以市售融雪液和固体融雪剂作为对比。

2 结果与讨论

2.1 融冰雪性能

2.1.1 冰点

不同浓度的液态融雪剂、市售融雪液和固态融雪剂溶液冰点如图1所示。

由图1可知,冰点与融雪剂溶液浓度密切相关,融雪剂溶液浓度越高,冰点越低;对于相同浓度的融雪剂溶液,固态融雪剂冰点较液态融雪剂的低,液态融雪剂冰点低于市售融雪液。这是由于固态融雪剂中有效成分含量高于液态融雪剂和市售融雪液。70%的液态融雪剂冰点低于 $-45℃$,说明其可以在极低温度下发挥融雪性能,可以用于极低温度下的融雪保畅。

2.1.2 融冰速率

在液态融雪剂与冰接触面积固定的条件下,将一定时间内液态融雪剂融化冰的质量定义为液态融雪剂的融冰速率。液态融雪剂融冰速率如图2所示。

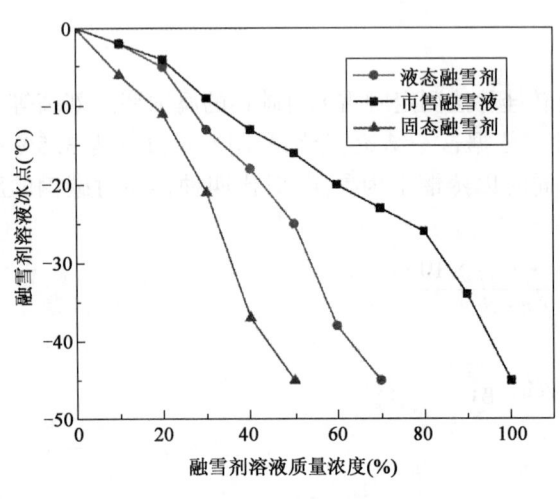

图1 不同浓度的液态融雪剂冰点

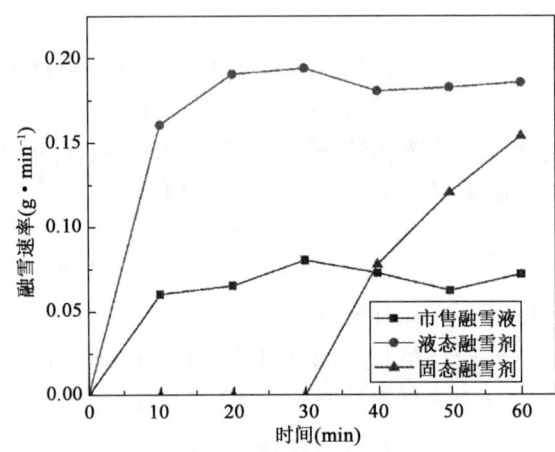

图2 液态融雪剂融冰速率

由图2可知,在 $-10℃$ 下,融雪剂与冰块接触后的30min内,放置固态融雪剂的冰层基本没有融化,表面只有少量润湿的现象。这是由于普通融雪剂是无机盐的固体状态,而发挥融冰效果的是普通融雪剂电离离解的无机离子。因此,固体融雪剂首先需要预湿,让自身溶解成离子状态,才能发挥融冰效果。液态融雪剂融雪速率显著高于市售融雪液和固态融雪剂,这对于及时清除路面冰雪,保障道路安全畅通是非常重要的。

2.1.3 融冰量

在液态融雪剂与冰接触面积固定的条件下,将一定时间内液态融雪剂融化出水的质量与冰块总质量的比值定义为该时间段内液态融雪液的融冰量。液态融雪剂融冰量如图3所示。

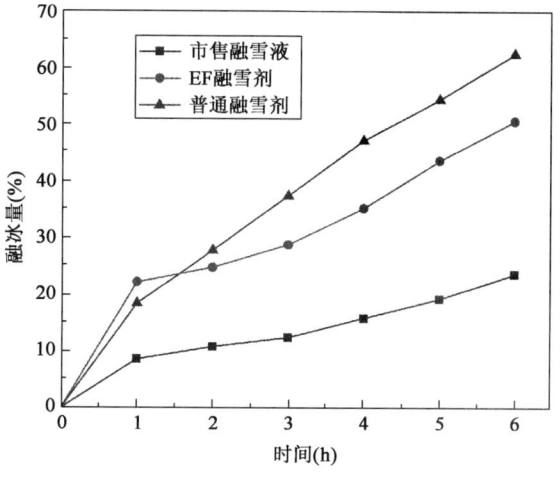

图3 液态融雪剂融冰量

由图3可知,随着融冰时间延长,融雪剂的融冰量增加。在 -10℃下,在融冰的第6h,液态融雪剂的融冰量为50.6%,与固态融雪剂62.4%的融冰量相差不大,明显大于市售融雪液23.6%的融冰量。说明液态融雪剂具有较强的融雪能力。

2.2 环保性能

2.2.1 对碳钢的腐蚀速率

不同融雪剂溶液对碳钢腐蚀程度和腐蚀速率如图4所示。

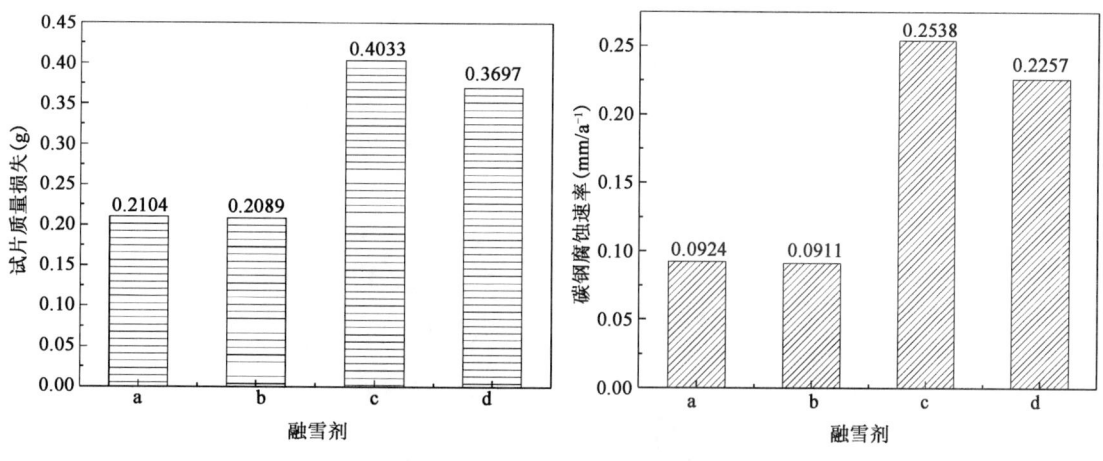

图4 不同融雪剂对碳钢的腐蚀速率

a-液态融雪剂;b-市售融雪液;c-固态融雪剂;d-蒸馏水

由图4可知,液态融雪剂溶液对碳钢的腐蚀速率为0.0924mm/a,远小于固态融雪剂和蒸馏水对碳钢的腐蚀速率,满足《融雪剂》(GB/T 23851—2017)规范要求的对碳钢腐蚀速率不大于0.11 mm/a 的要求。组成液态融雪剂的废糖液中含有表面活性类物质,这种物质同时具有极性基团与非极性基团,融雪剂与碳钢接触后,极性基团吸附在碳钢表面上,非极性基团排列在融雪液溶液中,有效地阻碍了碳钢的腐蚀。

2.2.2 对植物的伤害

(1)对种子发芽率的影响

使用不同融雪剂溶液培养的早熟草本禾种子发芽情况如图5和表3所示。

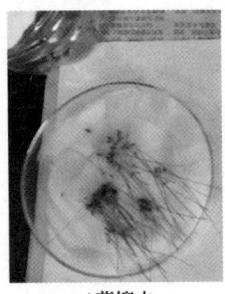 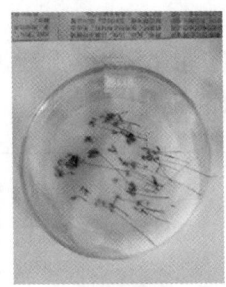 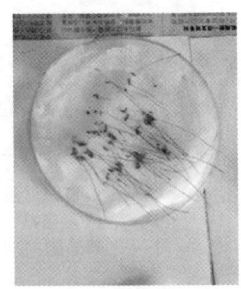 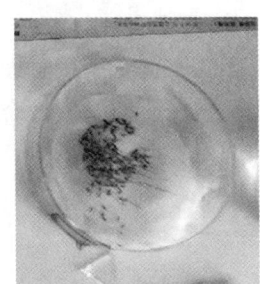

a)蒸馏水　　　　　　b)市售融雪液　　　　　　c)液态融雪剂　　　　　　d)固态融雪剂

图 5　不同融雪剂溶液对早熟草本禾种子萌芽率影响

不同融雪剂溶液处理下早熟草本禾种子的萌芽率　　　　　表 3

融雪剂样品	种子萌芽率(%)	融雪剂样品	种子萌芽率(%)
蒸馏水	96.1	液态融雪剂	73.8
市售融雪液	62.3	固态融雪剂	38.2

由图 5 和表 3 可知:蒸馏水培养的早熟草本禾种子发芽数量最多,无论是哪种融雪剂,都影响早熟草本禾种子的萌芽率。液态融雪剂培养的早熟草本禾种子萌芽率为 73%,高于市售融雪液和固态融雪剂培养的早熟草本禾种子萌芽率,满足规范(《融雪剂》(GB/T 23851—2017))早熟草本禾种子萌芽率不低于 50% 的要求。

(2)对绿萝生长的影响。

使用 10% 浓度的不同融雪剂溶液培养绿萝 15d 后,绿萝生长情况如图 6 所示。

a)液态融雪剂　　　　　　　　　　　　　　b)市售融雪液

c)固态融雪剂　　　　　　　　　　　　　　d)蒸馏水

图 6　不同融雪剂溶液浇灌对绿萝生长的影响

由图 6 可知,使用蒸馏水培养的绿萝生长旺盛,使用液态融雪剂和市售融雪液培养的绿萝生长基本没有受到影响,而使用固态融雪剂溶液培养的绿萝叶片发黄枯萎。试验结果表明液态融雪剂对绿萝生长基本没有影响。

(3)对室外三叶草生长的影响。

使用 10% 浓度的不同融雪剂溶液连续浇灌草地 30d 后,三叶草生长情况如图 7 所示。

由图 7 可知,使用液态融雪剂溶液和市售融雪液浇灌对三叶草的生长影响较小,枯萎倒伏的三叶草较少。而使用固态融雪剂溶液浇灌的三叶草倒伏程度较为严重,说明在三个融雪样品中,液态融雪剂和市售融雪液对三叶草生长影响较小,固态融雪剂严重影响三叶草的生长。

a)液态融雪剂　　　　　　b)市售融雪液　　　　　　c)固态融雪剂

图7　不同融雪剂溶液浇灌对三叶草生长的影响

2.2.3 对水泥混凝土腐蚀

使用不同浓度融雪剂溶液冻融后的水泥混凝土质量损失情况如图8所示。

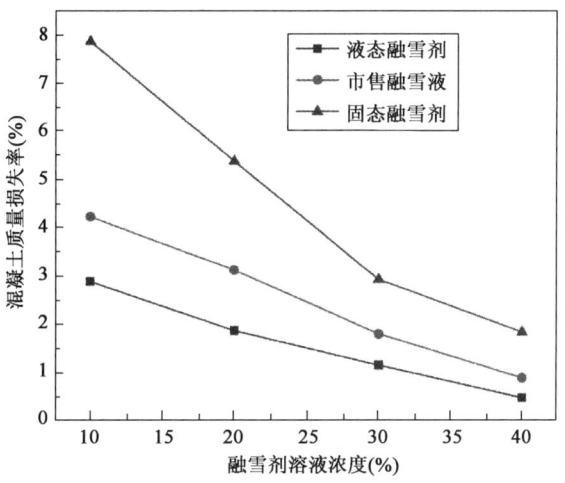

图8　不同浓度融雪剂溶液冻融后的水泥混凝土质量损失

由图8可知,随着融雪剂溶液浓度的增加,水泥混凝土质量损失降低。在同一浓度条件下,液态融雪剂浸泡的水泥混凝土质量损失最低。当融雪剂浓度为10%时,液态融雪剂浸泡的水泥混凝土质量损失为2.81%,远小于固态融雪剂浸泡的7.93%的水泥混凝土质量损失。

3　结　语

本文以果脯废糖液为主要原料制备了液态融雪剂,以市售融雪液和某品牌的环保型固态融雪剂作为对比,测试并分析了液态融雪剂的融冰雪性能和环保性能。

(1)液态融雪剂在施工后的1h内融冰速率远大于固态融雪剂和市售融雪液,在施工后的6h,其融冰量达到50.6%,是市售融雪液融冰量的2倍以上。70%浓度的液态融雪剂冰点低于-45℃,使其可以应用于极端低温地区的融冰雪。

(2)旋转挂片试验表明,液态融雪剂对碳钢的腐蚀速率为0.0924mm/a,远小于固态融雪剂和蒸馏水对碳钢的腐蚀速率,满足《融雪剂》(GB/T 23851—2017)规范的要求。

(3)早熟草本禾种子萌发试验、绿萝培养试验和草地浇灌试验表明,液态融雪剂对植物的生长影响较小,显著低于环保型固态融雪剂对植物的伤害。

(4)混凝土反复冻融试验表明,随着融雪剂溶液浓度的增加,水泥混凝土表面质量损失降低。在同一浓度条件下,液态融雪剂对水泥混凝土的腐蚀远小于环保型固体融雪剂。

参考文献

[1] 何永明,丁柏群.冰雪条件下高速公路通行能力衰减仿真研究[J].森林工程,2012,28(2):68-70.
[2] 韩志斌.中国道路融冰除雪技术发展现状及未来趋势[J].公路与汽运,2013,6:142-145.
[3] 周小鹏,黄军瑞,王腾,等.我国道路融雪剂应用现状及发展趋势[J].辽宁化工.2019,48(9):920-925.
[4] 张淑茹,赵淑华,沈宇翔,等.氯盐类融雪剂对土壤环境影响的初步调查[J].中国卫生工程学,2009,8(3):150-151.
[5] 冯守中,冒卫星,刘立湘,等.融雪剂对环境的影响和评价[J].辽宁化工,2018,47(9):947-950.
[6] 栾国颜,刘洋,王鹏,等.生物质制备环保型融雪剂的实验研究[J].吉林化工学院学报,2011,28(9):13-17.
[7] 高振鹏,岳田利,袁亚宏,等.果脯加工废糖液发酵猕猴桃酒的工艺研究[J].农产品加工学刊,2007,3(94):58-60.
[8] 林璟瑶.废燕麦糖作为污水处理厂补充碳源的高值化利用研究[D].广州:华南理工大学,2019.
[9] Pińkowska H, Krzywonos M, Wolak P, et al. Pectin and Neutral Monosaccharides Production During the Simultaneous Hydrothermal Extraction of Waste Biomass from Refining of Sugar—optimization with the Use of Doehlert Design [J]. Molecules, 2019, 24(3): 472.
[10] Wu Y, Cao J-P, Zhou Z, et al. Transforming Waste Sugar Solution into N-doped Hierarchical Porous Carbon for High Performance Supercapacitors in Aqueous Electrolytes and Ionic Liquid [J]. International Journal of Hydrogen Energy, 2020, 45(56): 31367-79.
[11] 刘靖,刘恒明,朱莹.几种融雪剂对金属材料的腐蚀性研究[J].广东化工,2015,42(23):16-18.

Research on the Carbon Materials/Polymer Self-sensing Composites for Pavement Micro-strain Detection

Xue Xin Ming Liang Linping Su Zhengmei Qiu Zhanyong Yao

(School of Qilu Transportation, Shandong University)

Abstract The monitoring of pavement structure conditions, especially the parameters of strain, stress, etc, plays a crucial rule on the design, construction, service and maintenance of asphalt road. Situ sensors with high accuracy in small strain range within 1000 and even 100 $\mu\varepsilon$, long durability and high survival rate are crucial for asphalt pavement due to the harsh environment in construction period and service life. The development of functional composites sheds a new insight for pavement strain detection with remarkable self-sensing behavior. In this paper, aligned multiwall carbon nanotubes (MWCNTs) with excellent electrical conductivity and graphene platelets were used to prepare the epoxy matrix composites. The effect of varying percent of CNT, the substitutability and synergy effect of graphene platelets with carbon nanotubes and effect of CNTs types with different specific surface areas in epoxy composites to the morphological, electrical, mechanical properties and strain-electrical resistance response peculiarity of composites were evaluated. Based on these evaluations, a well novel strain sensor that can effectively detect the strain range within 1000 and even 100$\mu\varepsilon$ with high durability, repeatability and prompt response was developed for asphalt pavement strain monitoring.

Keywords Strain sensor Nanocomposites Pavement monitoring Micro-strain Carbon nanotubes-graphene platelets-polymer

0 Introduction

As the significant part of transportation infrastructure, asphalt road pavement plays a unique role for the economic and social development worldwide (Delatte, et al., 2018; Zhang, et al., 2018). With the increasing traffic volume, heavier vehicle loads, extreme weather as well as long-term exposure to external load, temperature, humidity and other factors of the complex service environment (Liang, et al., 2015; Ji, et al., 2019), the pavement surface distresses have become key technical problems during the period of service and maintenance of pavement engineering (Afonso, et al., 2016; Ren, et al. 2018). Real-time, accurate monitoring the stress and deformation of the pavement structure has vital practical significance for the maintenance scheme design, construction quality control and early damage detection and precaution of pavement (Xue, et al., 2013).

In order to monitor the strain condition of pavement, immense efforts have been done over the past years. Researchers reported the fiber bragg grating sensor (FBG) (Barrias, et al., 2016; Meng et al., 2017), resistance strain gage, embedded vibrating wire strain gauge (Bajwa, et al., 2015) as well as theoretical analysis model for road structure monitoring (Ghauch, et al., 2013). These strain sensor or strain gage are embedded in the pavement or pasted on the surface of pavement to detect the variation of mechanical state. The changes of mechanical parameters are converted into the variation of output signals, for example, resistance or the grating reflection position. However, most of conventional strain sensors are easy to be damaged at the initial stage of embedding or in service period due to the complex environment of road pavement, which has the shortcomings of poor durability, low survival rate or insufficient accuracy on small strain monitoring (Rana, et al., 2016).

With the development of advanced materials and the improvement of testing methods, an alternative approach of polymer nanocomposites with the self-sensing function shows significant advantage for engineering structure monitoring. Polymer nanocomposites present varying electrical signals when it is loaded by strain, stress, temperature or other stimulus (Yu, et al., 2009; Yu, et al., 2012). In recent years, extensive researches on the novel carbon/polymer composites have been implemented for various purposes and applications (Spitalsky, et al., 2010), such as human-motion detection (Yamada, et al., 2011), gesture recognition (Huang, et al., 2017; Su, et al., 2017), life prediction and self-healing (Thostenson, et al., 2006). Various carbon materials with different physical and chemical properties and different polymer materials have been flexibly combined in these studies (Hu, et al., 2010). With the well-known excellent mechanical and electrical properties, carbon nanotubes (CNTs) have been widely used in the area of self-sensing composite materials as the conductive material and structural strengthening component. Furthermore, taking full advantage of high aspect ratio and tunable change in resistance, the composites with CNTs can be adapted for developing the highly sensitive strain sensors (Lin, et al., 2013; Ji, et al., 2014; Fan, et al., 2012). In principle, when at the stretching or compressing state, strain will transfer from polymer matrix to conductive network system formed by the CNTs conductive filler. The piezoresisitivity of composites is entirely provided by the deformation of conductive network system. In other words, loss or reconnection of local contact and variation of tunnel distance between the nanotubes at nano-scale or micro-scale are responsible for the resistance changes. However, these studies have not focused considerable interest on the micro-strain, especially within 1000 or even 100 microstrain where the strain range is adaptable and urgently needed for the pavement structure in service. Moreover, the sensitivity of nanocomposites need to be further illustrated.

1 Experimental Section

1.1 Materials

The polymer matrix used in this study is thermosetting epoxy resin compounded by bisphenol A and epichlorohydrin, which has the advantages of high reactivity and controllable mechanical property. The epoxy resin and polyamide curing agent were matched in a mass ratio of 100 : 30 and achieved commercially (Xingcheng Co. Ltd., Nantong, China and Xiangshan Company, Beijing, China). Three types of CNTs with different SSA and one laminar GNP were supplied by JCNANO Technology Company, China. The basic information of the conducting carbon fillers is summarized in Tab. 1.

Basic information of CNTs with different SSA and laminar GNP   Tab. 1

	CNT(SSA165)	CNT(SSA500)	CNT(SSA60)	Laminar GNP	
Purity (wt%)	95	>98	98	D50 diameter (um)	7~10
Out Diameter(nm)	10~20	4~6	>50	Stacking density (g/mL)	0.08~0.13
Length (μm)	50~100	10~20	<15	Tablet resistance (mΩ·cm)	5.6
Special surface area(m²/g)	165	~500	>60	Carbon content(wt%)	>98
Electric Conductivity (s/cm)	>100	>100	>100		
ASH (wt%)	<5	<1.5	<5		

1.2 Sample preparation of composites

In order to form a conductive network and improve the mechanical-electrical properties, aligned MWCNTs should be homogeneously dispersed in the polymer matrix (Dong, et al.,2014;Zhang, et al.,2016). However, it is difficult to disperse the MWCNTs of nano-scale to the matrix of epoxy resin with high viscosity and cohesion. So the dispersion degree and dispersion effectiveness will play a crucial role on the strain-electrical resistance response. If the dispersion of MWCNTs in the composite is not uniform or even the conductive pathway in the composite is composed by few of aggregate structure, the electric conductive ability will in a less than ideal state. So with the aim of well conductivity properties of the composite strain sensor, the dispersion of MWCNTs should be seen as the crucial steps in fabricating the composites. To overcome the van der Waals forces in case of agglomeration caused by the huge specific surface area and nanoparticle size, the aligned MWCNTs were grinded in an agate mortar for 30 min and mixed with dispersing solvent DMF. After mechanical mixing for 20 min, the DMF/CNTs suspension mixtures were subjected in an ultrasonic instrument (UH450, Oulior) for 1h. Then, the dispersed MWCNTs were added into epoxy resin and sonicated for 1h. After that, solvent evaporation was conducted in the vacuum drying oven at 80℃ for 1h. The resulting gel was added in the curing agent and poured into a polytetrafluoroethylene mould, cured at 80℃ for 2h. Samples were de-molded and further curved at 120℃ for 4h. The experimental procedures were summarized in Fig. 1. In this paper, samples were coded as CDN-xNT where x represents the content of aligned MWCNTs, from 0.80 wt.% to 1.40 wt.% with interval of 0.20 wt.% respectively.

1.3 Characterization

The electrical resistance of composites was tested by a Keithley 2100 digital multimeter under a constant voltage with the two electrode method by connecting with the copper electrode assembled at the two ends of samples. The digital multimeter with the resolution ratio of 61/2 and extremely high measurement accuracy was connected with the computer for the data record. It's worth noting that the maximum range of a resistance measurement for the instrument is 100MΩ.

Strain-electrical resistance response peculiarity was measured with a self-developed test system. To accurately measure and control strain, especially micro strain, a strain control device with the elaborate encryption screw ball screw and special clamps was assembled. By rotating the hand wheel at a constant speed of two rounds per minute, specimen will be stretched or restored and then the specimen deformation can be detected by extensometer. Electrical resistance can be obtained and recorded simultaneously by digital multimeter. In addition, cyclic stretching and recovery for 100 thousands of times were also conducted to investigate the durability and repeatability by replacing hand wheel with servo motor.

Mechanical properties were measured to evaluate the composite strength through the tensile measurement and strain-stress test, aiming to verify whether the elasticity modulus is consistent with the road materials and determine the applicability of the composites. Tests with a constant elongation rate of 2mm/min were carried out using a SANS UTM4000 universal test machine.

Dynamic mechanical tests were performed by a Discovery DMA 850 TA Instruments (Fig. 1) using the three point bending configuration with the span of 20 mm. The 25 mm × 5 mm × 2 mm dimension samples were investigated at two different scan programs, frequency sweep and temperature ramp. In the frequency sweep mode, samples were subjected from 0.1 to 100 Hz at the constant temperature of 25 °C with the controlled strain of 1%. In the temperature ramp mode, samples were subjected from room temperature to 200 °C with a heating ramp of 2 °C/min at the constant frequency of 10 Hz. The complex modulus $E*$, storage modulus E', loss modulus E'' and loss factor $tan\delta$ (calculated by the ratio of loss modulus E'' to storage modulus E') can be obtained at both scanning modes. It's worth noting that the three-point bending fixture is sensitive to the irregular degree of the sample, so all the samples should be prepared with regular shape and uniform size.

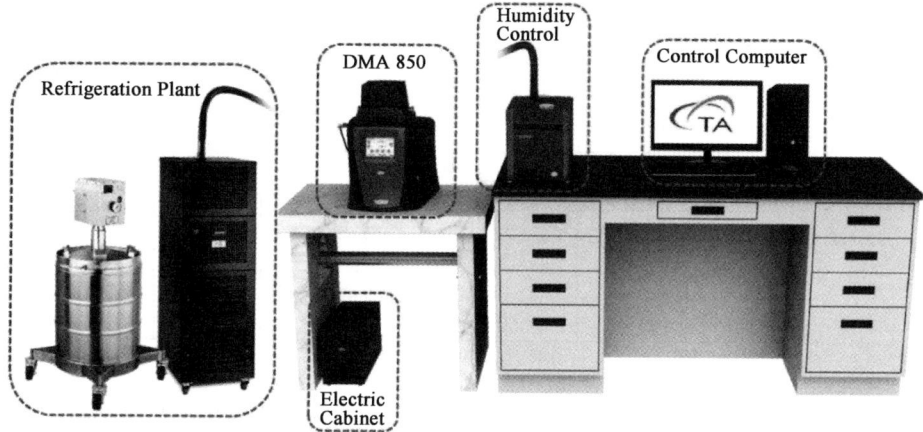

Fig. 1 DMA test equipment schematic

The cross-sectional and surface morphologies of the carbon nanotubes/polymer self-sensing composites were studied by a scanning electron microscope (SEM, Hitachi SU8010, Fig. 2) under an accelerating voltage of 10kV. To investigate the conductive network structure in the material and its transformation way at different tensile state with different CNTs content, the samples were charged to emit enriched secondary electrons to make them visible.

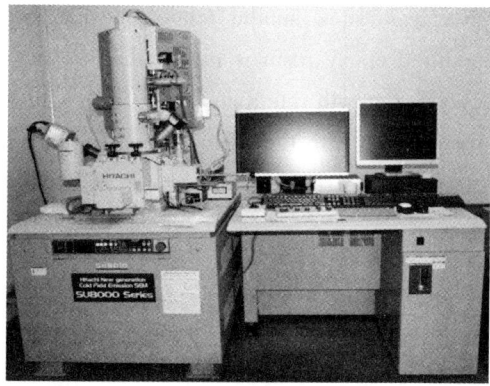

Fig. 2 SEM for morphologies investigation

2 Results and Discussions

2.1 Viscosity-time property

For different application fields, the reaction rate of the matrix epoxy resin is expected to be adjusted. For example, the matrix epoxy resin should show lower reaction rate relatively and have a certain operational time to prevent the implosion at room temperatures in the area of composites manufacturing. Whereas, the epoxy resin is expected to be cured rapidly, when is using as adhesive, healant or stuffing material. Thus, the relationship of viscosity with time of epoxy resin is a key technical parameter to evaluate the material characteristics. In this paper, the correlation between viscosity and time characteristics of the resulting epoxy resin were tested at 80 °C with the detection duration of 480 s after the initial preparation, which is performed to track the curing reaction and deduce the operable time for the practical application. Results of viscosity increment in curing time after blending with the PU modified epoxy resin were showed in Fig. 3.

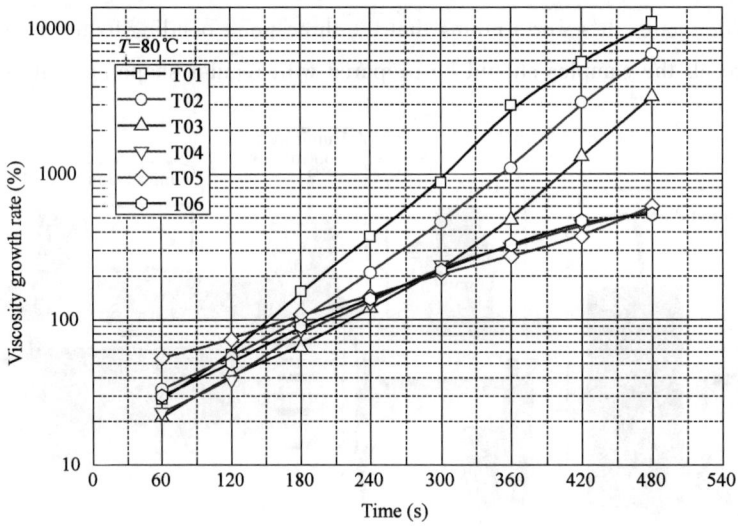

Fig. 3 Viscosity-time characteristic for the blended epoxy resin

As shown in Fig. 3, the viscosity of all samples presents the trend of similarly exponential growth with time. In other words, the viscosity increase rapidly after the preparation of blended epoxy resin, since the chemical crosslinking start to take place. However, the viscosity growth rates (the slope of the curves) present a large variation for different samples. Sample of T01 without any PU modified epoxy resin shows the fastest growth rate of viscosity, which means the cross-linking and reaction rate between bisphenol-A epoxy resin and curing agent is higher than which between PU modified epoxy resin and curing agent apparently. Samples of T02 and T03 with a certain addition of PU modified epoxy resin show similar tendencies but lower growth rate compared to T01. However, when the content of PU modified epoxy resin is higher than 60% (for T04-T06), the blended epoxy systems present significantly lower viscosity growth rate than the systems with dominant bisphenol-A epoxy resin. This is mainly attributed to the slower reaction with the curing agent and higher molecular weight of PU modified epoxy resin. Therefore, we chose T01 for the subsequent preparation of composite materials.

2.2 Morphology of conductive networks

SEM morphologies of the fracture surfaces of CNT/GNP/EP composites were investigated to measure the dispersion of CNTs-GNP fillers (displayed in Fig. 4). It can be seen that CNTs-GNP hybrid (Fig. 4 A2-C4) shows a better dispersion state. Unlike the pure CNTs with entangled each other, most of the CNTs are well dispersed in the composites when the presence of GNP and ultrasonication. The previous tortuous CNTs are separated individually and formed directional alignment in the composites. In the case of CNTs-GNP hybrid conductive structure, CNTs are arranged among the adjacently laminar GNP and the original configuration of pure CNTs or GNP are disrupted and rearranged. In most instances, the CNTs or GNP tends to aggregate because of the high Van der Waals forces. However, when the GNP was introduced into the composites, CNTs in nano scale prone easily to be dispersed homogenously and filled among GNP with micro dimensions. Thus, GNP absorbs the molecules of CNTs and prevents their aggregations. Moreover, the sandwiched CNTs among the GNP plates bridge the separated plates of GNP from nano scale to micro dimensions, which are expected to further improve the electrical conductivity and sensing the sensitivity of the composite. In addition, the approximately oriented conductive network and well dispersed CNTs and GNP fillers in the composites will promote the interaction efficiency and enhance more contact area among carbon fillers and epoxy matrix, which is further expected to lead to better electrical properties, strain-electrical resistance response and mechanical properties of the composites.

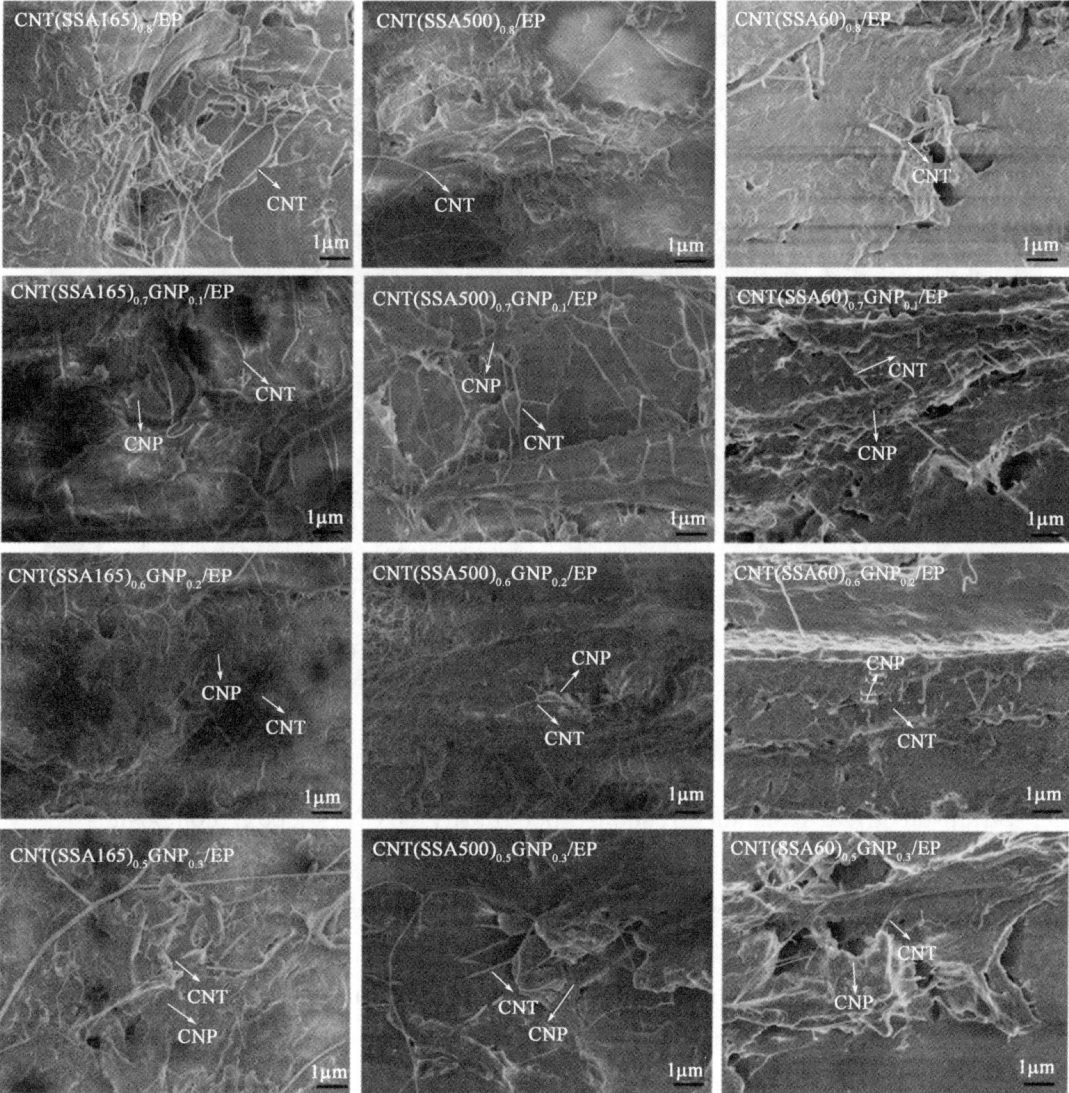

Fig. 4 SEM of the fracture surfaces for epoxy composites with different fillers

By comparing Fig. 4(A), Fig. 4(B) and Fig. 4(C), it can be found that the SSA of CNTs plays important role in the dispersion state of CNTs-GNP. Composites with CNTs (SSA500) display most amounts of CNTs and contact points within the same field of vision at the same dosage, seen in Fig. 4(B1) ~ Fig. 4(B4). Moreover, the high aspect ratio further resulted in the well-established 3D conductive network. So it is reasonable to conclude that composites with CNT(SSA500) will show the best electrical properties and strain-electrical resistance response peculiarity. To the contrary, composites with CNT(SSA60) appear the least CNT conjunction points between the laminar GNP together with the shortest tubular structure. This will lead to the poor electricity conduction, in other words, much higher dosage of CNT(SSA60) should be required if we want to achieve the same conductivity with other kinds of CNTs.

For a better understanding of the electrical response of CNTs/epoxy composite under stress, the surface morphologies of composites were studied. A typical region was choosed from the composite surface and then the surface was carried on the multiple step by step magnification, showed in Fig. 5 from (a) to (d). CNTs in the CNTs/epoxy composites present a non-directional state. Some of them are embedded into the epoxy matrix, others are fixed individually or interconnected.

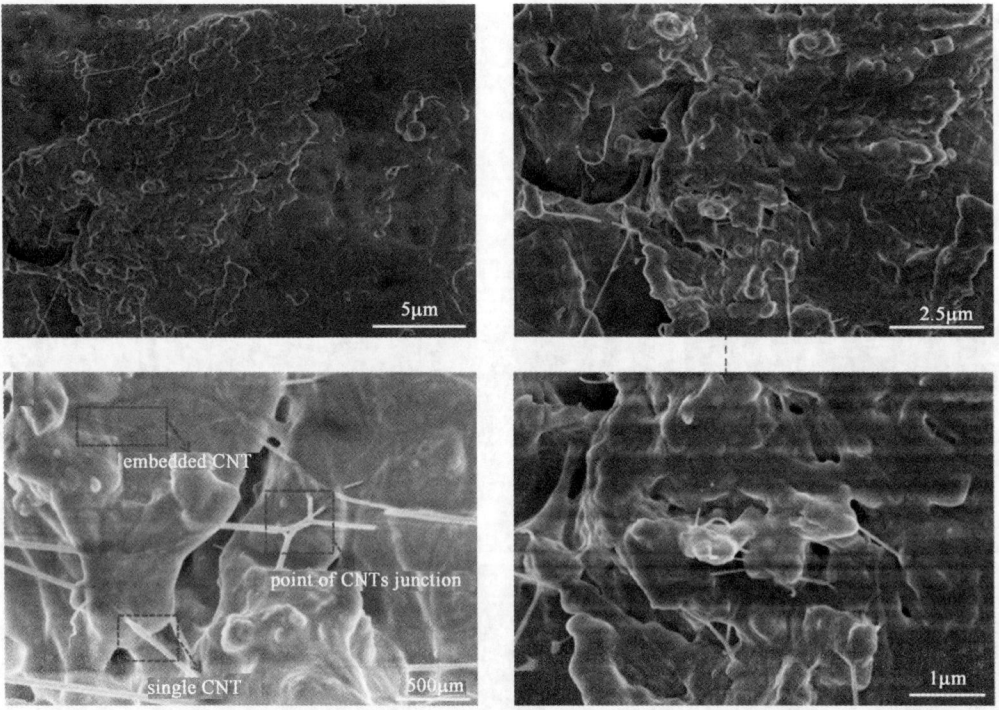

Fig. 5　SEM morphologies of composite surface at different magnification times

2.3　Strain-electrical resistance response peculiarity of CNTs/epoxy composites

With the characteristic of very high aspect ratio, CNTs are easy to form a conductive network throughout the isolating polymer matrix when appropriate methods are adopted to disperse carbon nanotubes. Thereby, it's easy to conclude that when the content of CNTs reaches a certain amount, the conductive network and the conductivity will come into being a transition from insulation to semiconductor and then to conductor, in which the critical conductivity point is defined as the conductive percolating threshold value (KovacsJ, et al., 2007). When the dosage of CNTs is lower than the conductive percolation threshold, resistance of composites is very high without forming the effective conductive structure. However, once the effective conductive structure is formed after certain CNT dosages, the conductivity ability and resistance property will be constant approximately. Even if adding more CNTs, it just increases the density inside the conductive structure without increasing the conductivity. Fig. 6 shows that the electrical resistivity of nanocomposites without strains applied, which presents a sharp decrease as

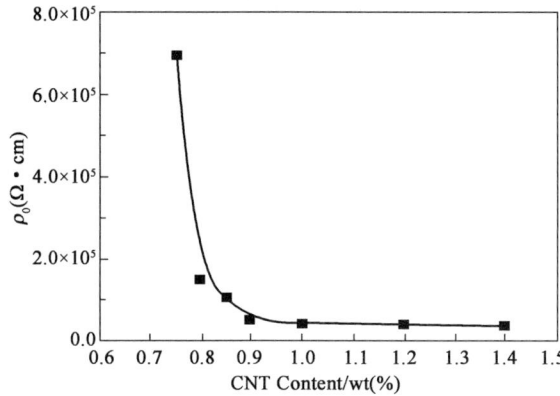

Fig. 6 Electrical resistivity of CNT/epoxy composites

the increase of CNTs content and draw towards equilibrium when exceeding 0.80 wt.% of CNTs.

Considering the small structural deformation in asphalt pavement, more emphasis is put on the strain-electrical resistance response peculiarity of the developed composites at micro strain range of $0 - 100\mu\varepsilon$. The variations of $\Delta R/R_0$ with strain were presented in Fig. 7. Apparently, the $\Delta R/R_0$ has a linear relationship with the applied strain. These linear relationships between $\Delta R/R_0$ and strain provide the core foundation for our research and development of sensors. Furthermore, the absolute value of the slope increases with GNP substitution dosage increasing. In this case, the internal structure of conductive domains consisted by CNTs and GNP are difficult to deform at such small micro strain in the effect of intense connection with the epoxy matrix and codependence between the CNTs and GNP. Deformation is transmitted to the conductive structure through the matrix material when the external force is applied to the composites, which results in less contact among conductive domains and thus the significant increment of resistance. Once the deformation occurs, the conductive domains will separate and contact less with each other. The corresponding results are the evident increase of resistance. The changes of resistance become more obvious as the increase of GNP, since more GNP in conductive domains leads to the more diminished contact under tensile. That's why sensing sensitivity improves as the substituting GNP increasing.

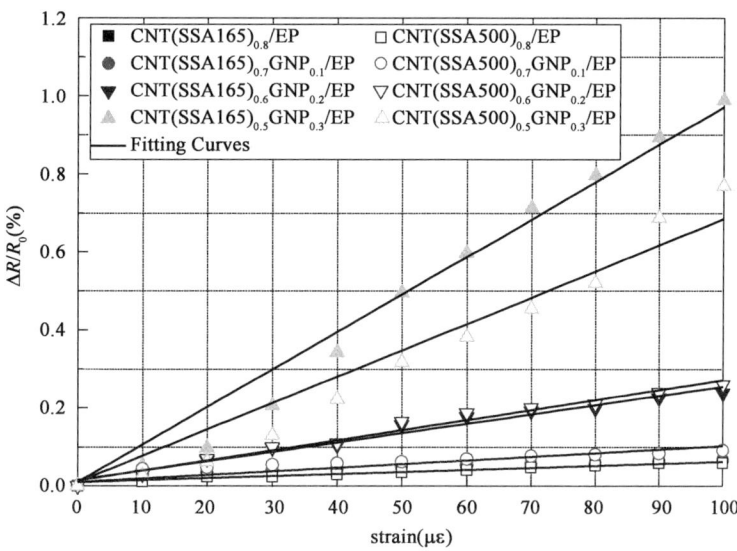

Fig. 7 Strain-electrical resistance response peculiarity at strain range of $0 - 100\mu\varepsilon$

The piezoresistive response of CNTs/epoxy composites can be mainly attributed to transform of conductive structure, including the CNTs inherent piezoresistive property and the conductive network formed by CNTs (Yu, et al., 2009; Zhang, et al., 2011). Along with the external loading and strain increasing, the epoxy matrix will deform and then deformation will transfer to nanotubes conductive network (Sumfleth, et al., 2011). In consideration of the super high strength of CNTs, deformation of CNTs themselves can be ignored comparing to the changes of contact distance among the domains of CNTs. At the beginning of deformation, dimensional change of CNTs networks and the tunneling effect cause the variation of resistance. As the strains getting higher, stress between matrix and conductive fillers will gradually concentrate, which will lead to the loss of contact between CNTs, enlargement of tunneling distance and even deformation of CNTs. The above mentioned sensing mechanisms play important and positive role in the increase of electrical resistance. It's important to note that the resistance transition and conductive morphology at the exponential growth stage is irreversible. Furthermore, lower CNT content is beneficial to the resistance increasing in comparison of the amplitude of resistance variation for different CNTs contents, which is accord with the previous studies (Li, et al. ,2004; Ma, et al. ,2010).

2.4 Mechanical properties

To identify whether the CNTs/epoxy composites can be used as strain sensors for the asphalt road, the mechanical properties were investigated, including elasticity, stiffness, elasticity modulus, tensile strength, elongation at break (Bhuiyan, et al. , 2013; Nadler, et al. , 2009). As the imposed stress increasing, the composites deform gradually and present approximately linear growth in strain. At this period, composites are in the elastic deformation stage, which means that the original condition can be restored when the stress is removed. However, when the composites deform beyond the strain that elastic deformation persists, the non-recoverable or plastic deformation occurs.

The mechanical properties of polymer curing products are closely related to the molecular weight and crosslinking density of the crosslinking points (Ma, et al. , 2015). Comparing to the neat epoxy matrix, composites with CNTs loading shows obvious and higher elongation at break and tensile strength. Furthermore, the regularity trend becomes more prominent with the increase of CNTs content. The possible reason can be explained as follows. CNTs play a similar role in reinforcing the skeleton in the epoxy resin matrix when the addition of CNTs is increased. CNTs can form a solid interface connection with the matrix through O-H chemical bond during the curing process of composites, so as to undertake the purpose of load transfer and bear the load when the strain sensor is subjected to an external force. In this case, excellent mechanical properties are developed to enhance the tensile strength and toughness of composites. However, as the content of CNTs increased further, such as to 1.4wt%, CNTs tended to agglomerate and form defects in the matrix, leading to a decline in mechanical properties. With the gradual increase of MWCNTs content, parts of MWCNTs agglomerate in the matrix and exist in the form of particles, which will not play the role of strengthening. The agglomerated particles are easy to become the defect points in the composites. So the mechanical strength of the composite strain sensor is decreased when the composite material is exposed to external forces. The tensile strength of composites with 1.4wt% CNTs (only 35 MPa) decreased significantly compared with 1.2wt%, similar to that of pure epoxy resin. This phenomenon will be reflected evidently in the microstructure of section 3.4. In addition, this is also supported by the fact that bubbles in the composites became more obvious with the increase of CNTs content during the sample preparation. It means that system will become stickier as more CNTs are added, causing certain defects in the sample. This is another key reason accounting for the significant decrease of the mechanical properties.

Based on the stress-strain characteristic curves, we can acquire the elasticity modulus of composites with various CNTs contents from the elastic deformation stage along with linear allometric growth rule, shown as Fig. 8. As can be seen from the diagram, the elasticity modulus of composites embodies a trend of increasing and then decreasing with the CNTs multiply. Comparing with the neat epoxy of 1067 MPa, the elasticity modulus of composites with 0.8wt% CNTs rises by 17% to 1250 MPa, which matches with the stiffness of surface asphalt pavement. Composite materials with different stiffness can be adjusted by mixing CNTs amount, so as to accord with the modulus range of different layer for strain monitoring.

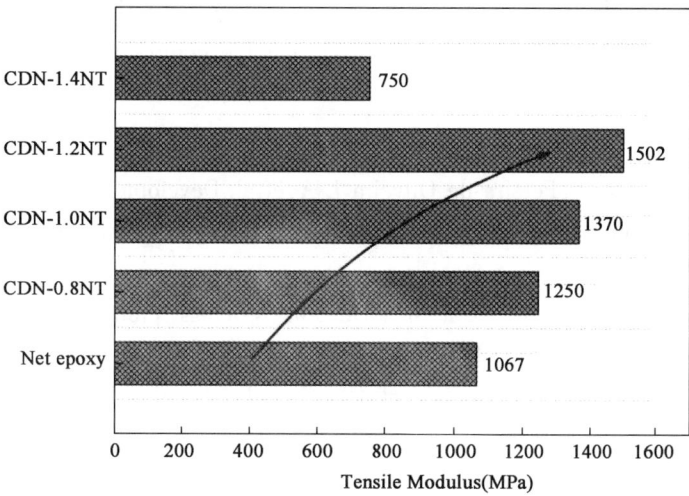

Fig. 8 Elasticity modulus of composites with various CNTs contents

3 Conclusions

This study developed a strain sensor with high sensitivity to micro-strain as well as adaptable to complex construction and working environment of asphalt pavement, the aligned MWCNTs with excellent electrical conductivity, epoxy and additional dispersants were used to prepare the composites via a serious of dispersion processes. Firstly, the resistivity-strain behaviors of sensors under $0 \sim 10000\mu\varepsilon$ were investigated, especially concerning the micro-strain range within $100\mu\varepsilon$ by the step of $10\mu\varepsilon$ respectively. It was found that the electrical resistance increased with the increase of strain and two different types of variation tendency with the tensile strain were observed. Furthermore, the composite strain sensors presented favourable sensitivity with best GF up to 26.04 and showed a linear and a slow growth trend even though at the range of $0 \sim 100\mu\varepsilon$. Besides, cyclic stretching and recovery for 100 thousands of times was also imposed on the composite and the results confirmed the excellent mechanical durability. Moreover, through the comparison of mechanical properties of composite sensors with different CNTs admixtures, elasticity modulus and tensile strength demonstrated a growing trend within a certain critical range of non-agglomerated widely among CNTs. Finally, to understand the state of CNTs dispersion in epoxy matrix and morphology evolution when subjected to external loading, SEM tests were carried out. It is observed that different conductive networks were constructed via adjusting CNTs contents. Effect of external loading on the strain-electrical response is caused by conductive structure changing in microscopy, corresponding to two stages with a different dominant mechanism respectively. CNTs-GNP hybrid in composites shows better dispersion state because of the size effect and synergetic effect comparing to the pure CNTs with entangled each other. In the case of CNTs-GNP hybrid conductive structure, CNTs are distributed among the adjacent laminar GNP and the original configuration of pure CNTs or GNP are disrupted and rearranged. Composites with CNT(SSA500) display most amounts of conductive domains within the uniform scale field of vision at the same dosage. Moreover, the higher aspect ratio will result in the well-established 3D conductive network.

The self-sensing behavior and mechanical peculiarities of the composites also present high dependence on the GNP substitution dosage and SSA of CNTs. $\triangle R/R0$ of all the epoxy composites shows an increasing trend as the increment of external tensile in the experimental range, which indicates good self-sensing property. The $\triangle R/R0$ of composites with CNT(SSA500) exhibits obvious higher than that of composites with CNT(SSA165), indicating better self-sensing behaviors. CNTs and GNP reinforced the epoxy matrix by forming three-dimensional network in the matrix. The modulus of composites sensor is accordance with that of asphalt mixture, which ensure the collaborative deformation among sensor and asphalt pavement structure, and thus the accuracy of monitoring results.

References

[1] Afonso M L, Dinis-Almeida M, Pereira-de-Oliveira L A, et al. Development of a Semi-Flexible Heavy Duty Pavement Surfacing Incorporating Recycled and Waste Aggregates-Preliminary Study[J]. Constr Build Mater, 2016 102:155-161.

[2] Bajwa R, Rajagopal R, Kavaler R, et al. In-Pavement Wireless Vibration Sensor Nodes, Networks and Systems: U. S. Patent No. 8,990,032[P]. 24 Mar. 2015.

[3] Barrias A, Casas A, Villalba S. A Review of Distributed Optical Fiber Sensors for Civil Engineering Applications[J]. Sensors-Basel, 2016, 16 (5):748.

[4] Bhuiyan M A, Pucha R V, Worthy J, Understanding the Effect of CNT Characteristics on the Tensile Modulus of CNT et al. Reinforced Polypropylene Using Finite Element Analysis[J]. Comp. Mater Sci, 2013, 79:368-76.

[5] Delatte N, Concrete Pavement Design, Construction, and Performance[M]. Crc Press, 2018.

[6] Dong L, Hou F, Li Y, Wang L, et al. Preparation of Continuous Carbon Nanotube Networks in Carbon Fiber/Epoxy Composite[J]. Compos. Pt. A-Appl. Sci. Manuf, 2014, 56:248-55.

[7] Fan Q, Qin Z, Gao S, Wu Y, The Use of a Carbon Nanotube Layer on a Polyurethane Multifilament Substrate for Monitoring Strains as Large as 400%[J]. Carbon, 2012, 50(11): 4085-92.

[8] Ghauch Z G, Abou-Jaoude G G. Strain Response of Hot-mix Asphalt Overlays in Jointed Plain Concrete Pavements due to Reflective Cracking[J]. Comput. Struct, 2013, 124 :38-46.

[9] Hu N, Karube Y, Arai M, et al. Investigation on Sensitivity of a Polymer/Carbon Nanotube Composite Strain Sensor[J]. Carbon 2010, 48 (3):680-687.

[10] Hu N, Karube Y, Yan C, et al. Tunneling Effect in a Polymer/Carbon Nanotube Nanocomposite Strain Sensor[J]. Acta. Mater. 56:2929-36.

[11] Hu N., Masuda Z., Yan C., Yamamoto G., Fukunaga H., Hashida T. (2008) Electrical properties of polymer nanocomposites with carbon nanotube fillers, Nanotechnology 19:215701.

[12] Huang Y, Gao L, Zhao Y, et al. Highly Flexible Fabric Strain Sensor Based on Graphene Nanoplatelet-Polyaniline Nanocomposites for Human Gesture Recognition [J]. Appl. Polym. Sci, 2017, 134 (39):45340.

[13] Jamal-Omidi M, ShayanMehr M. Improving the Dispersion of SWNT in Epoxy Resin through a Simple Multi-Stage Method[J]. King Saud Univ. Sci. , 2019, 31(2):202-8.

[14] Ji J, Yuan Z, Wei J, et al. Improvements of Low-Temperature Properties of Direct Coal Liquefaction Residue Modified Asphalt[J]. Journal of China University of Petroleum(Edition of Natural Science), 2019, 43(4):166-173.

[15] Ji M, Deng H, Yan D, et al. Selective Localization of Multi-Walled Carbon Nanotubes in Thermoplastic Elastomer Blends: an Effective Method for Tunable Resistivity-Strain Sensing Behavior[J]. Compos. Sci. Technol, 2014, 92 :16-26.

[16] Kovacs J Z, Velagala B S, Schulte K, et al. Two Percolation Thresholds in Carbon Nanotube Epoxy Composites[J]. Compos. Sci. Technol, 2007, 67(5): 922-8.

[17] Lachman N, Wagner H D. Correlation between Interfacial Molecular Structure and Mechanics in CNT/Epoxy Nano-Composites[J]. Compos. Pt. A-Appl. Sci. Manuf, 2010, 41(9):1093-98.

[18] Li Z, Dharap P, Nagarajaiah S, et al. Carbon Nanotube Film Sensors[J]. Adv. Mater, 2004, 16(7):640-3.

[19] Liang M, Liang P, Fan W, et al. Thermo-Rheological Behavior and Compatibility of Modified Asphalt with Various Styrene-Butadiene Structures in SBS Copolymers[J]. Mater. Des, 2015, 88: 177-185.

[20] Lin L, Liu S, Zhang Q, et al. Towards Tunable Sensitivity of Electrical Property to Strain for Conductive Polymer Composites Based on Thermoplastic Clastomer[J]. Acs. Appl. Mater. Inter, 2013, 5 (12): 5815-24.

[21] Ma C, Liu H, Du X, et al. Fracture Resistance, Thermal and Electrical Properties of Epoxy Composites Containing Aligned Carbon Nanotubes by Low Magnetic Field[J]. Compos. Sci. Technol, 2015, 114: 126-35.

[22] Ma P, Mo S, Tang B, et al. Dispersion, Interfacial Interaction and Re-Agglomeration of Functionalized Carbon Nanotubes in Epoxy Composites[J]. Carbon, 2010, 48(6): 1824-34.

[23] Martone A, Formicola C, Giordano M, et al. Reinforcement efficiency of multi-walled carbon nanotube/epoxy nano composites[J]. Compos. Sci. Technol, 2010, 70(7): 1154-60.

[24] Meng L, Wang L, Hou Y, et al. A Research on Low Modulus Distributed Fiber Optical Sensor for Pavement Material Strain Monitoring[J]. Sensors-Basel, 2017, 17 (10): 2386.

[25] Monti M, Armentano I, Faiella G, et al. Toward the Microstructure-Properties Relationship in MWCNT/Epoxy Composites: Percolation Behavior and Dielectric Spectroscopy[J]. Compos. Sci. Technol, 2014, 96: 38-46.

[26] Nadler M, Werner J, Mahrholz T, et al. Effect of CNT Surface Functionalisation on the Mechanical Properties of Multi-walled Carbon Nanotube/Epoxy-composites[J]. Compos. Pt. A-Appl. Sci. Manuf, 2009, 40(6-7): 932-7.

[27] Parveen S, Rana S, Fangueiro R. A review on Nanomaterial Dispersion, Microstructure, and Mechanical Properties of Carbon Nanotube and Nanofiber Reinforced Cementitious Composites[J]. Nanomater, 2013, 20: 13: 80.

[28] Pham G T, Park Y B, Liang Z, et al. Processing and Modeling of Conductive Thermoplastic/Carbon Nanotube Films for Strain Sensing[J]. Compos. Pt, 2008, B 39: 209-16.

[29] Rana S, Subramani P, Fangueiro R, et al. A Review on Smart Self-Sensing Composite Materials for Civil Engineering Applications[J]. Aims Mater, Sci, 2016, 357-379.

[30] Ren S, Liang M, Fan W, et al. Investigating the Effects of SBR on the Properties of Gilsonite Modified Asphalt[J]. Constr. Build. Mater, 2018, 190: 1103-1116.

[31] Spitalsky Z, Tasis D, Papagelis K, et al. Carbon Nanotube-Polymer Composites: Chemistry, Processing, Mechanical and Electrical Properties[J]. Prog. Polym. Sci, 2010, 35 (3): 357-401.

[32] Su Z, Chen H, Song Y, et al. Microsphere-Assisted Robust Epidermal Strain Gauge for Static and Dynamic Gesture Recognition[J]. Small, 2017, 13 (47): 1702108.

[33] Sumfleth J, Buschhorn S T, Schulte K. Comparison of Rheological and Electrical Percolation Phenomena in Carbon Black and Carbon Nanotube Filled Epoxy Polymers[J]. Mater. Sci, 2011, 46(3): 659-69.

[34] Thostenson E T, Chou T W. Carbon Nanotube Networks: Sensing of Distributed Strain and Damage for Life Prediction and Self-healing[J]. Adv. Mater, 2006, 18 (21): 2837-2841.

[35] Xue W, Wang L, Wang D, et al. Pavement Health Monitoring System Based on an Embedded Sensing Network[J]. Mater. Civil. Eng. 2013, 26 (10): 04014072.

[36] Yamada T, Hayamizu Y, Yamamoto Y, et al. A Stretchable Carbon Nanotube Strain Sensor for Human-Motion Detection[J]. Nat. Nanotechnol, 2011, 6 (5): 296.

[37] Yu X, Kwon E. A Carbon Nanotube/Cement Composite with Piezoresistive Properties[J]. Smart. Mater. Struct, 2009, 18 (5): 055010.

[38] Yu X, Kwon E. Carbon Nanotube Based Self-sensing Concrete for Pavement Structural Health Monitoring, Research[J]. Report-Contract Number: US DOT: DTFH61-10-C-00011, Duluth, Minnesota, 2012.

[39] Zhang J, Liu J, Zhuang R, et al. Single MWNT-Glass Fiber as Strain Sensor and Switch[J]. Adv. Mater., 2011, 23(30): 3392-7.

[40] Zhang X, Yao Z, Ge Z, et al. Piezoresistive Characterization of Polyethylene Terephthalate-Graphite Composite[J]. Test. Eval., 2016, 45(1): 303-12.

[41] Zhang X, Yao Z, Zhang S, et al. Tensile Piezoresistive Behavior of Polyethylene Terephthalate/Carbon Black Composite[J]. Mater. Civ. Eng., 2018, 30(6): 04018107.

碱激发矿渣—硅酸盐水泥复合胶凝材料性能与微观结构试验研究

丁 博　张金喜　王建刚　党海笑

（北京工业大学）

摘 要 为探究掺有硅酸盐水泥的矿渣地聚合物碱激发效应，以 Na_2SiO_3、NaOH 为激发剂，研究了不同类型碱及不同碱掺量对于矿渣—硅酸盐水泥复合胶凝材料凝结时间、抗压强度、抗折强度、收缩率的影响，并结合微观测试手段 SEM 观察水化产物微观结构。结果表明：2 种碱的加入均能显著缩短复合材料的凝结时间，加碱组初凝时间仅为未加碱组的 12.3%~19.3%；碱的添加可以使复合胶凝材料快速实现早强，与未加碱组相比，掺加 3% Na_2SiO_3 可使 3d 抗压强度提升 12.5%。SEM 分析发现，28d 强度因材料内部出现微孔与微裂缝而未能达到理想增长状态；碱激发复合胶凝材料具有较高的抗折强度，掺加 3% Na_2SiO_3 和 1.5% NaOH 可使 28d 抗折强度分别提升 20.57% 与 17.61%；与普通水泥砂浆相比，适量碱的加入会有更低的收缩率。碱激发复合胶凝材料这种快凝早强且黏结性能好的特性为矿渣部分代替水泥及用作混凝土修补等提供了新思路。

关键词 碱激发　复合胶凝材料　抗压强度　黏结性能　微观结构

0 引 言

水泥作为重要的建筑材料之一，在我国基础设施建设过程中的消耗量逐年增加。据统计，2019 年我国水泥年产量已达 23.5 亿 t[1]。由于资源的不可再生及生产环节带来的严峻环境问题，多数学者试图将矿渣、粉煤灰等存在潜在活性的物质部分或者全部代替水泥，从而减少水泥用量。但由于这些材料活性较低且水化速度较慢，传统添加方式通常会延长凝结时间，降低水泥及混凝土的早期强度。因此许多研究通过在材料中添加碱的方式激发其活性，促进辅助性胶凝材料的水化反应，并已证明经过碱活化的辅助性胶凝材料具有优异的性能[2]。

郑登登等[3]以 KOH 作为激发剂激发矿渣，当 KOH 的掺量为矿渣质量的 4% 时，其 90d 抗压强度能够达到 40MPa 以上。有研究表明，与纯粉煤灰地聚合物相比，掺加硅酸盐水泥的粉煤灰基地聚合物材料具有更优的性能。Tanakorn 等[4]研究结果表明，10% 掺量硅酸盐水泥与一定浓度的 NaOH 溶液混合可有效提升粉煤灰地聚合物砂浆的抗压强度、弹性模量与断裂韧性。此外，A. Palomo 等[5]对掺有 30% 普通硅酸盐水泥和 70% 粉煤灰的混合物进行了试验研究，依据试验结果提出：普通硅酸盐水泥的水化受 OH^- 浓度及材料中存在可溶性二氧化硅的影响而遵循不同的水化途径。在应用方面，邓新等[6]以粉煤灰、矿粉

基金项目：北京市交通行业科技项目（2016-LZJKJ-01-006）。

两种工业废料为主要原材料,水玻璃作为激发剂制备地聚合物用作混凝土修补材料,测试了在不同配合比水平下试样的流动度、凝结时间、抗压强度和拉伸黏结强度。

目前碱激发胶凝材料的相关研究主要集中于粉煤灰、矿渣等纯地聚合物的性能探究,而对于掺有硅酸盐水泥的复合胶凝材料的碱激发效应研究相对较少。与传统水泥砂浆相比,未掺加水泥的纯地聚合物材料强度相对较低,且为保证较好的激发效果往往需要添加更多的碱,造成材料收缩率大,其工程应用存在一定局限性。因此,本研究采用 Na_2SiO_3 和 NaOH 作为激发剂,对比分析不同类型激发剂及不同掺量对矿渣—硅酸盐水泥复合胶凝材料凝结时间、收缩率、抗压与抗折强度的影响,采用 SEM 试验手段观察材料的微观结构,以期为激发剂的选择及工程应用提供参考。

1 试 验

1.1 原材料

水泥为河北燕新建材有限公司生产的钻牌普通硅酸盐水泥(P·O 42.5),矿渣为北京首钢嘉华建筑材料有限公司生产的 S95 型磨细高炉矿渣粉,两者主要化学成分如表 1 所示;硅灰为北京德昌伟业建筑工程有限公司提供的优级硅灰,其技术指标如表 2 所示;砂采用的是细度模数为 2.54 的普通河砂;Na_2SiO_3 采用的是 $Na_2O:SiO_2 = 1.03 \pm 0.03$ 的固体颗粒;NaOH 采用的是纯度为 96%(分析纯)的固体颗粒;水为普通自来水。

水泥和矿渣的化学组成　　　　表1

材料	SiO_2	Al_2O_3	CaO	MgO	SO_3	Fe_2O_3	K_2O	TiO_2	Na_2O	P_2O_5
水泥(%)	21.28	4.76	59.6	3.25	3.03	2.70	0.98	0.35	0.22	0.16
矿渣(%)	33.41	14.23	38.5	9.23	2.09	0.37	0.39	0.79	0.34	0.03

硅灰的技术指标　　　　表2

烧失量(%)	氯离子(%)	二氧化硅(%)	比表面积(m^2/kg)	需水量比(%)	活性指数(%)
2.56	0.032	94.42	2.09×10^4	110	103

1.2 配合比

采用 Na_2SiO_3 和 NaOH 两种碱激发剂,其中 Na_2SiO_3 掺量(按胶凝材料计)分别为 2%、3%、4%,编号依次为 NS1、NS2、NS3;NaOH 掺量(按胶凝材料计)分别为 1%、1.5%、2%,编号依次为 NH1、NH2、NH3;水胶比固定为 0.5。编号 N0 为空白对照组,即未加入任何类型碱激发剂。配合比见表 3。

碱激发矿渣—硅酸盐水泥复合胶凝材料配合比　　　　表3

编　号	Na_2SiO_3(%)	NaOH(%)	水泥(g)	矿渣(g)	硅灰(g)	砂(g)	水(g)
N0	—	—	350	294	56	1400	350
NS1	2.0	—	350	294	56	1400	350
NS2	3.0	—	350	294	56	1400	350
NS3	4.0	—	350	294	56	1400	350
NH1	—	1.0	350	294	56	1400	350
NH2	—	1.5	350	294	56	1400	350
NH3	—	2.0	350	294	56	1400	350

1.3 试验方法

为避免 NaOH 溶于水的放热效应对试验的影响,提前 2h 制备 NaOH 溶液和 Na_2SiO_3 溶液,并冷却至室温备用。参照水泥砂浆拌和方法制备碱激发矿渣—硅酸盐水泥砂浆,首先将胶结料及砂混合搅拌均匀,然后加入碱溶液继续搅拌 5min。参考《水泥标准稠度用水量、凝结时间、安定性检验方法》(GB/T

1346—2011)测定砂浆的凝结时间。强度(抗压、抗折)参考《公路工程水泥及水泥混凝土试验规程》(JTG E30—2005)中规定的方法,将新拌砂浆材料倒入40mm×40mm×160mm的试模中,经过分层加入、振捣至密实,然后将试样放入温度20℃、湿度≥96%的标准养护室中养护3d、7d、28d。试件养护至设计龄期时,先测抗折强度,后测抗压强度,结果取每组平行试件的平均值。收缩率测试采用《水泥胶砂干缩试验方法》(GB/T 0511—2005)中规定的方法进行。利用日本电子株式会社生产的JEOL JMS 6500F型场发射扫描电子显微镜观测不同配比和不同龄期下试样的微观形貌。

2 结果与分析

2.1 凝结时间

碱激发矿渣—硅酸盐水泥复合胶凝材料的凝结时间如表4所示。由表4可知,NS和NH组初凝时间仅为N0组初凝时间的12.3%~19.3%,即两种碱激发剂的掺入均显著缩短了矿渣—硅酸盐水泥复合体系的凝结时间。其原因是碱促进了复合胶凝材料总的水化反应,在碱的作用下,矿渣中铝硅酸盐快速溶解,活性的硅氧四面体和铝氧四面体溶出并发生缩聚反应,形成硅铝酸盐凝胶相[7],表现为复合胶凝材料的凝结。

碱激发矿渣—硅酸盐水泥复合胶凝材料的凝结时间   表4

编号	N0	NS1	NS2	NS3	NH1	NH2	NH3
初凝时间(min)	300	52	45	58	50	45	37
终凝时间(min)	>420	143	122	158	118	120	104

在NaOH材料中,复合胶凝材料的凝结时间随NaOH掺量的增加而减少:NH1、NH2、NH3组初凝时间分别为50min、45min、37min。这是因为随着NaOH浓度的增加,矿渣中Si、Al的解聚和再聚合反应加快,矿渣地聚反应速率提升,促使材料中更快地形成了C—(A)—S—H。但是在Na_2SiO_3材料中未出现类似结果,随着Na_2SiO_3掺量的增加,复合体系的凝结时间呈现先减少后增加的趋势。这可能是由于硅酸钠固体本身存在结合水,在溶解的过程中部分结合水脱离,造成"实际水胶比"增大,这种效应在高掺量硅酸钠混合物中表现的更加明显:以掺量4% Na_2SiO_3为例,在硅酸钠固体溶解失去4个结晶水后,会使原水胶比从0.5上升到0.53。另一方面,较高的Si含量可能阻碍了钙的水化反应,增加了凝结时间[8]。

2.2 抗压强度

测试了碱激发矿渣—硅酸盐水泥复合胶凝材料不同龄期下的抗压强度,如图1所示。可以看出:3~7d龄期内,随着Na_2SiO_3和NaOH掺量的增加,复合体系的强度均呈现先增大后减小的趋势。在一定掺量范围内,碱的加入可以有效提升矿渣—硅酸盐水泥复合胶凝材料的早期强度。与N0相比,NS2和NH2在养护3d时的强度分别提升了12.5%、11.3%。这是因为碱中OH^-的加入促使矿渣快速溶解,Si^{4+}、Al^{3+}浓度迅速增加并又重新聚合生成C—S—H、C—A—H等,形成早期强度。与NaOH相比,Na_2SiO_3作用更明显,这可能是由于含水硅酸钠水解生成NaOH和含水硅胶,其中OH^-起到催化剂作用,而含水硅胶又继续参与了矿渣的地聚反应。两种碱掺量过多时均不利于复合材料早期强度的发展,存在一个最佳掺量范围。

与N0相比,不同类型碱激发复合胶凝材料的28d强度均出现不同程度的降低,且碱掺量越大,降低幅度越明显。从碱类型对矿渣—硅酸盐水泥复合胶凝材料的强度发展影响来看:在整个测试龄期内,Na_2SiO_3复合胶凝材料强度整体上都要高于NaOH复合胶凝材料。这可能是由于硅酸钠中游离Si的引入有利于复合体系中强度的形成和发展。与Na_2SiO_3相比,采用NaOH作为激发剂,材料中存在更高浓度的OH^-,由于矿渣过快的解聚和缩聚反应,作为中间产物的水分来不及排出,使得产物的孔隙率增加[9],从而造成强度的衰减。而Na_2SiO_3激发的矿渣—硅酸盐水泥复合体系会更密实一点。

2.3 抗折强度

碱激发矿渣—硅酸盐水泥复合胶凝材料的抗折强度试验结果如图2所示。可以看出,除NS3抗折强度有所下降以外,其余各试验组抗折强度与 N0 组相比都有不同程度的提升。其中 NS2 组较 N0 组 28d 抗折强度提升了 20.57%,NH2 组较 N0 组 28d 抗折强度提升了 17.61%。在一定掺量范围内,随着掺量的增加,碱对于矿渣—硅酸盐水泥复合体系抗折强度的提升更加明显,这可归因于碱浓度的升高促使矿渣的地聚反应加快。但对于 NS3,由于 Na_2SiO_3 掺量过多,含水硅酸钠水解后造成实际水胶比偏大,强度发展进程缓慢。

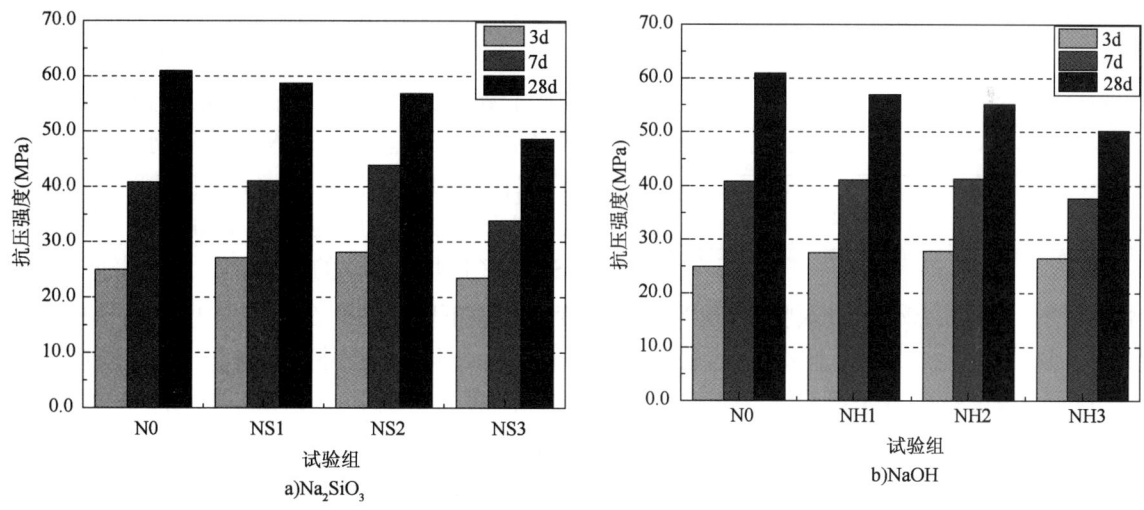

图 1 碱激发矿渣—硅酸盐水泥复合胶凝材料抗压强度

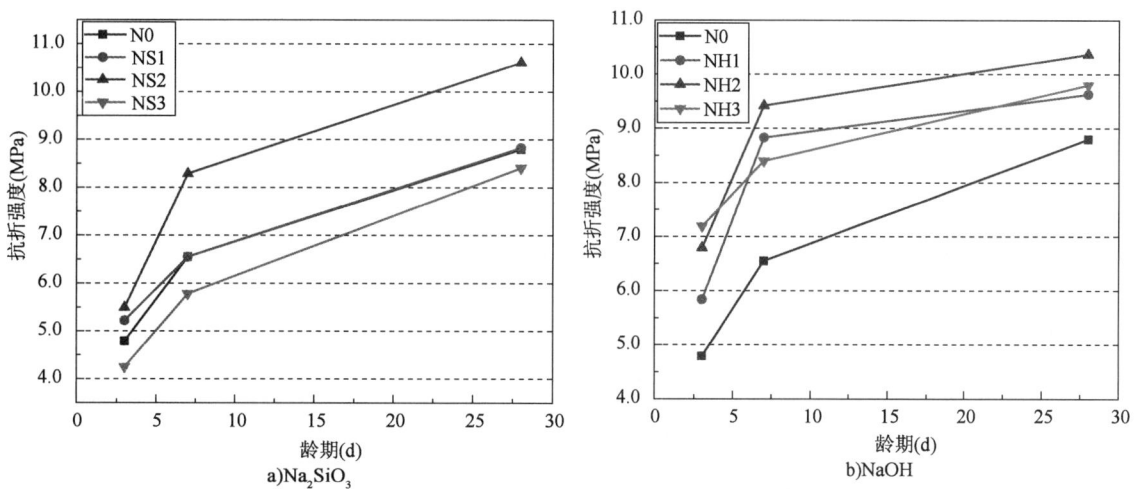

图 2 不同龄期碱激发矿渣—硅酸盐水泥复合胶凝材料抗折强度

与抗压强度变化规律不同,复合胶凝材料抗折强度在测试龄期内并没有出现先升高后降低的现象,而是持续表现优异。这可能是由于地聚反应生成的低钙硅比的 C—S—H 与正常水化反应生成物相比能够提供更好的胶结作用,与硅酸盐水泥水化产物相比,具有更好的黏结性能。Song 等[10]试验结果表明经 NaOH 激发的矿渣水化产物 C—S—H 形貌为箔片状,而硅酸盐水泥浆体中高钙硅比的 C—S—H 为纤维状。微观结构、形貌的不同是造成宏观性能差异的重要原因。

2.4 收缩率

测试了复合胶凝材料在不同龄期下的干燥收缩率,试验结果见图 3。由图 3 可以看出,与普通水泥砂浆(PC)相比,添加适量的 NaOH 或 Na_2SiO_3 会在不同程度上降低其收缩率,也从另一方面反映了碱激发过程的"微膨胀作用"[11]:在碱激发复合胶凝材料中,地聚产物在反应早期快速生成,材料内部生成了大量的硅铝酸盐凝胶造成材料微膨胀,抵消了部分因水分蒸发、化学反应等产生的收缩微应变。随着龄期

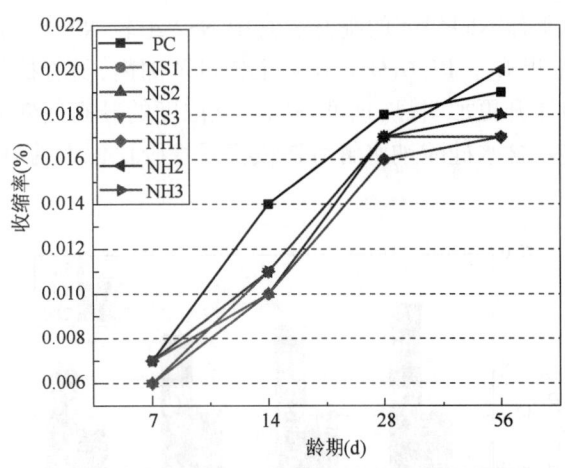

图 3 不同龄期碱激发矿渣—硅酸盐水泥复合胶凝材料收缩率

的增长,无论是 PC 还是碱激发材料,试件的收缩率都在缓慢增加并逐渐趋于稳定,所有试验组的 28 d 收缩率均小于 0.02%,满足混凝土修补工程对修补材料收缩率的相关要求。

2.5 微观结构

图 4 是 NH1、NS2、NS3 试验组的 7 d、28 d 微观形貌图。可以看出,7 d 龄期内,NH1 组有大量未反应的矿渣颗粒,表面结构疏松多孔,且出现部分"针尖状"钙矾石晶体。相对于 NH1,NS2 水化反应程度较高,水化产物呈片状连接,结构排列紧密,所以 NS2 表现出了较高的力学强度。相比之下,NS3 组是比 NS2 组多掺加了 1% 的 Na_2SiO_3,结构表面虽有一定致密性,但明显存在未水化矿渣颗粒,表现为力学强度的相对下降。28 d 龄期内,NH1、NS2、NS3 水化进一步完全,凝胶状水化产物相互联结,除了表面零散分布个别未水化颗粒外,结构趋于致密,所以与 7 d 强度相比,胶凝材料 28 d 强度呈现了较大幅度的增长。但同时表面出现了微孔以及微裂缝,正是这些微孔以及微裂缝的出现导致胶凝材料 28 d 抗压强度未能达到理想增长状态。

综上可知,碱激发矿渣—硅酸盐水泥复合胶凝材料性能表现优异,在碱的作用下可以快速实现早强并具有优异的黏结性能与较低的收缩率,揭示了矿渣部分替代水泥用作混凝土修补等工程应用的潜力。与 NaOH 相比,Na_2SiO_3 的激发效果更好。关于如何降低或者消除水化后期因出现微孔和微裂缝对复合胶凝材料抗压强度的影响需要进一步探究。

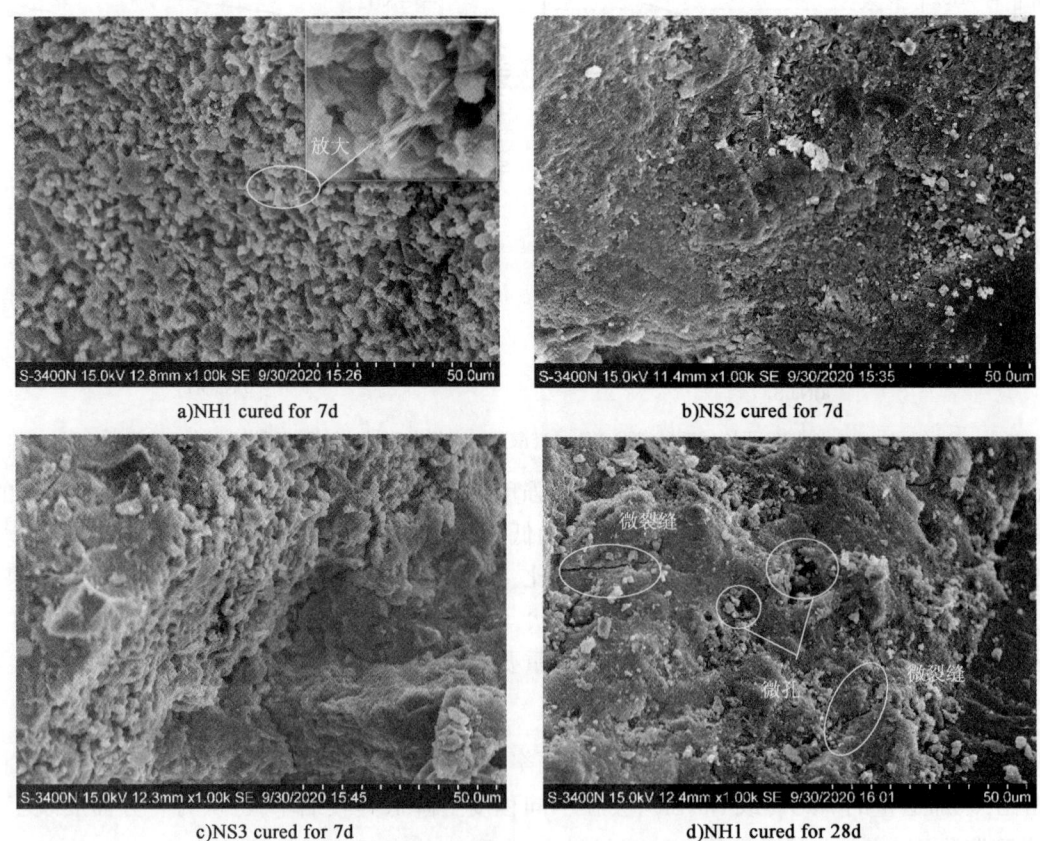

图 4

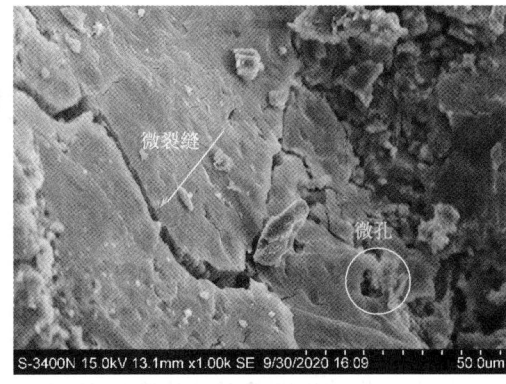

e)NS2 cured for 28d　　　　　　　　f)NS3 cured for 28d

图 4　碱激发水泥—矿渣复合胶凝材料的微观形貌

3　结　语

(1)碱的添加可以显著缩短矿渣—硅酸盐水泥复合胶凝材料的凝结时间。Na_2SiO_3 与 NaOH 的加入使得复合体系的初凝时间仅为对照组初凝时间的 12.3% ~ 19.3%。

(2)碱的加入可以使得复合胶凝材料快速实现早强,但结合 SEM 结果发现水化后期因材料内部出现微孔与微裂缝,造成 28d 强度未能达到理想增长状态。

(3)复合胶凝材料具有较高的抗折强度。与未加碱组相比,掺加 3% Na_2SiO_3 和 1.5% NaOH 可使复合胶凝材料 28d 抗折强度分别提升 20.57% 与 17.61%。

(4)与普通 PC 砂浆相比,加入适量的碱会降低收缩率。所有试验组的 28d 收缩率均小于 0.02%,满足混凝土修补工程对收缩率的相关要求。

参考文献

[1]　中华人民共和国国家统计局. 中国统计年鉴[M]. 北京:中国统计出版社,2019.

[2]　Samarakoon,M. H,Ranjith,et al. Recent Advances in Alkaline Cement Binders:A Review[J]. Journal of Cleaner Production,2019,227(AUG. 1):70-87.

[3]　郑登登,季韬,梁咏宁. 苛性碱对碱矿渣水泥砂浆抗压强度和抗折强度的影响[J]. 福州大学学报(自然科学版),2019,47(06):800-806.

[4]　Tanakorn Phoo-ngernkham,AkihiroMaegawa,NaokiMishima,et al. Effects of Sodium Hydroxide and Sodium Silicate Solutions on Compressive and Shear Bond Strengths of FA-GBFS Geopolymer[J]. Construction and Building Materials,2015,91:1-8.

[5]　Palomo A,Fernández-Jiménez,Kovalchuk G,et al. Opc-fly Ash Cementitious Systems:Study of Gel Binders Produced During Alkaline Hydration[J]. Journal of Materials Science,2007,42(9):2958-2966.

[6]　邓新,徐方,朱新,等. 粉煤灰基地聚合物修补材料的组成设计与性能[J]. 土木建筑与环境工程,2016,38(01):54-60.

[7]　朱晶. 碱矿渣胶凝材料耐高温性能及其在工程中应用基础研究[D]. 哈尔滨:哈尔滨工业大学,2014.

[8]　Malkawi A B,Nuruddin M F,Fauzi A,et al. Effects of Alkaline Solution on Properties of the HCFA Geopolymer Mortars[J]. Procedia Engineering,2016,148:710-717.

[9]　王聪. 碱激发胶凝材料的性能研究[D]. 哈尔滨:哈尔滨工业大学,2006.

[10]　Song S,Sohn D,Jennings HM,et al. Hydration of Alkali-activated Ground Granulated Blast Furnace Slag[J]. Journal of Materials Science,2000,35(1):249-257.

[11]　常利,艾涛,延西利,等. 地聚合物水泥路面快速修补材料性能研究[J]. 武汉理工大学学报,2014,36(05):49-54.

建筑垃圾在道路工程中的应用综述

李 想 毛雪松

(长安大学公路学院)

摘 要 为了解建筑垃圾在道路修筑过程中的应用情况,寻找高效利用建筑垃圾的方法,本文回顾了近年来国内外对建筑垃圾回收利用的研究进展情况,指出其中存在的问题。结果表明:建筑垃圾回收再生后,可以替代天然材料运用到道路修筑中,满足道路的使用要求。建筑垃圾再利用的价值明显,但尚未形成完善的体系。

关键词 建筑垃圾 道路工程 综述 可再生资源

0 引 言

目前由于我国限制了对天然砂石材料的开采,筑路材料变得越来越紧缺。然而,每年建筑垃圾的排放总量约为15.5亿~24亿 t[1-3],并呈现不断增长的趋势。大部分建筑垃圾未经任何处理就露天堆放或简易填埋,不仅占用大量土地,而且清运和堆放过程中引起的粉尘对周围环境造成一定的污染[4]。

而在如此巨大的储量背后,我国建筑垃圾资源化推进严重滞后,目前资源化利用率不足5%,远远低于欧盟(90%)、日本(97%)和韩国(97%)等发达国家和地区[5]。本文主要总结了近年来国内外对建筑垃圾利用于道路路基、基层以及再生混凝土方面的最新研究进展,指出其中存在的问题,并提出对建筑垃圾未来应用的展望。

1 在道路路基中的应用

由于建筑垃圾本身的成分比较冗杂,主要包括砖块、混凝土块、石块、水泥砂浆、瓷砖、木屑等,如表1[6-8]所示,因而它的物理性质十分复杂,不能直接用于路基填筑中,为保证路基的稳定与安全,国内外学者对建筑垃圾作为路基填料的可行性进行一系列研究。

建筑垃圾主要来源 表1

废料构成	废料权重	主要来源	占废料的比例(%)	说 明
混凝土砂浆	0.21	落地灰	85	该5项废料合计占总量的60%~70%
		桩头		
		余料		
		开洞和凿平		
		模板漏浆		
砖砌块	0.19	施工损坏	80	
		运输损坏		
		拆除		
木材和模板	0.16	过期产品	90	
		余料		
		异形模板		
瓦片	0.13	余料	90	
		运输损坏		
		拆除		
金属	0.13	余料	95	
		钢筋烧断		

1.1 原始的建筑材料

一些学者在不掺假任何外加剂的情况下,分析再生材料是否满足路基材料的要求。李行等[9]选用混凝土块和砖混两种再生细集料,通过对其强度性能进行研究发现当压实度满足规范要求时,两类材料的 CBR 值均能满足强度要求。刘喜等[10]发现当建筑垃圾掺量为 30%~40% 时,再生路基填料的干密度及 CBR 值均较大。张威等[11]发现压实度与建筑垃圾路基回弹模量呈现较好的线性关系,压实度越大,回弹模量越高。魏继合等[12]发现建筑垃圾掺量在 30%~40% 时,混合料的干密度值、CBR 值较大。

综上研究可知,当建筑垃圾其中不良的筑路材料被剔除后,它的 CBR 值满足路基要求;路基回弹模量与压实度呈现较好的线性关系。

1.2 改良后的建筑垃圾材料

由于不同地区的建筑垃圾成分有所不同,相应的物理力学性质不满足路用要求,因而一些学者加入一些强化材料改良。李少康等[13]发现建筑垃圾中细料的 CBR 小于 3% 时应当加入 1.5% 的水泥对其进行加固。岳爱敏等[14]发现当压实度为 96%,建筑垃圾含量为 94%,石灰、粉煤灰含量分别为 3% 时,改良后混合料的压缩系数、CBR 指标均满足规范要求。黄开正等[15]发现有 20% 碎石相对于没有碎石的建筑再生材料,CBR 值提升了 71.5%。更有学者对特殊地区的路基使用建筑垃圾材料。江思议等[16]采用建筑垃圾和灰土做成的挤密桩,可增强黄土地基的承载力。

综上研究可知,当建筑垃圾中加入一定量的碎石或水泥或二灰进行加固,建筑垃圾的 CBR 值提升较大,可进一步提高建筑垃圾的性能。

2 在道路基层中的应用

建筑垃圾中用于基层的集料可分为混凝土再生集料、砖块再生集料以及其他再生集料。

2.1 部分替代

陈朝金[17]研究了掺入砖块集料后水泥稳定碎石的多项性能,发现砖块集料可应用于公路基层或者底基层。曾梦澜等[18]发现适当掺加再生集料可以提高材料的抗压强度、回弹模量。安振源[19]研究了建筑垃圾和天然碎石按不同比例混合的力学强度,发现各项指标均满足规范要求。张自强[20]发现抗压强度、抗压回弹模量和劈裂强度随着建筑垃圾掺量的增加,先增大后减小。周新锋等[21]发现混合料的路用性能随着再生材料掺量的增加而降低,但仍能满足现行规范要求。

综上研究可知,建筑垃圾可以替代一些天然集料,虽各种强度满足基层材料的要求,但是替代率各不相同,受材料来源的影响很大。

2.2 全部替代

唐娴等[22]发现掺和比例为 100% 建筑垃圾混合料可作为良好的路面底基层或基层。崔宁等[23]发现砖混类建筑垃圾可用于路面基层中。肖田等[24]发现砖混类再生集料全部替代天然石灰岩集料制备的试件,其 7d 抗压强度均达标。

综上研究可知,建筑垃圾全部替代天然集料的技术,目前还不成熟,相关研究较少,这与材料的复杂性有很大关系。

3 在再生混凝土中的应用

再生混凝土是将废弃混凝土经过多级破碎、除尘、分档得到的再生集料,部分或全部替代天然集料制成的混凝土[25-26]。

一些学者选取建筑垃圾中的不同成分用于再生混凝土的研制,并验证了再生后的混凝土性能是否满足规范和工程实际需求。Yuwadee 等[27]发现当 RBA 和 RCA 的含量分别为 20% 和 40%~60% 时,再生混凝土具有良好的表面耐磨性和强度。乔宏霞等[28]发现陶瓷颗粒掺量为30%时,再生混凝土的抗高温损伤能力最佳。高琦等[29]通过对砖混建筑垃圾基本性能进行长期统计分析。发现取代率对砖混再生集料的强度影响最大。

综上研究可知,不同类型的材料只要采取合适的工艺和剂量,均能变废为宝应用到工程中去。

一些学者针对不同工程面临的工作环境的不同,研究了再生混凝土的特殊性能以满足工程需求。李贺等[30]发现适当减小水灰比并掺入废弃纤维可以提升再生混凝土的抗硫酸盐侵蚀性能。朱小艳等[31]发现掺加细砂可以显著提高再生混凝土的抗弯拉强度。肖建庄等[32]发现掺入纳米SiO_2能够显著改善再生混凝土抗氯离子渗透性能。

综上研究可知,选择合适的掺量,并加入合适的外加剂,可以对再生混凝土的一些性能进行强化,达到应用的要求。

4 结 语

通过国内外学者的各种研究表明,建筑垃圾通过分类分级处理,其中满足筑路要求的原材料,可以直接替代部分或全部天然材料应用到道路修筑中。但建筑垃圾还没有实现大规模、标准化的利用。今后的研究还应当从以下方面展开:

(1)对建筑垃圾材料的微细观结构进行系统的研究,进一步揭示其物理力学特性。
(2)对用建筑垃圾修筑的道路的长期路用性能进行监测,是否满足要求。
(3)制订有关建筑垃圾再生材料的配合比设计、施工、养护等方面的国家标准。

参考文献

[1] 孙岩,孙可伟,郭远臣.再生混凝土的利用现状及性能研究[J].混凝土,2010(3):105-107.

[2] Al-Mufti R L, Fried A N. The Early Age Non-destructive Testing of Concrete Made with Recycled Concrete Aggregate[J]. Construction & Building Materials, 2012, 37: 379-386.

[3] Kazemian F, RooholaminiH, Hassani A. Mechanical and Fracture Properties of Concrete Containing Treated and Untreated Recycled Concrete Aggregates[J]. Construction and Building Materials, 2019, 209(10): 690-700.

[4] 王健,李懿.建筑垃圾的处理及再生利用研究[J].环境工程,2003,21(6):49-52.

[5] 赵海英,薛俭.我国在建筑垃圾资源化中存在的问题及对策研究[J].施工技术,2010(S2):472-473.

[6] 赵翔宇,全姿宇,王璨.关于建筑垃圾回收与再生利用的分析讨论[J].山西建筑,2019,45(20):161-162.

[7] 张小燕,陈春鸣.建筑废弃物再利用综述[J].科技风,2021(02):90-91.

[8] 杨静,刘燕丽.我国城市建筑垃圾资源化现状及对策研究[J].中小企业管理与科技(中旬刊),2021(02):95-97.

[9] 李行,吴超凡,万暑.建筑垃圾在路基回填材料中的使用性能研究[J].中外公路,2019,39(01),253-256.

[10] 刘喜.建筑垃圾在公路路基中的再生应用研究[J].公路工程,2019,44(04):208-212.

[11] 张威,李哲,谢永利.建筑垃圾用作路基填料的压实性能研究路基工程[J].路基工程,2016,(04),82-85.

[12] 魏继合,李鸿运.建筑废弃物应用于路基填料的性能研究[J].低温建筑技术,2017,39(12):10-13.

[13] 李少康.建筑垃圾在公路路基中的应用研究[D].西安:长安大学,2014.

[14] 岳爱敏,李焕,坤黄.建筑垃圾再生混合料在路基工程中的应用研究[J].市政技术,2018,36(04),45-48.

[15] 黄开正,肖宏.建筑再生材料用作路基填料的CBR试验研究[J].建设科技,2012(09):70-71.

[16] 江思议,谭坦,杨炳强.建筑垃圾灰土挤密桩在黄土路基中的设计与应用[J].路基工程,2015(3):

181-183.
[17] 陈朝金.水泥稳定再生废砖块集料性能研究[D].西安:长安大学,2012.
[18] 曾梦澜,田振,肖杰.含建筑垃圾水稳碎石路面基层材料的使用性能[J].武汉理工大学学报,2016,38(01):34-38.
[19] 安振源.基于建筑垃圾再生集料的水泥稳定基层试验研究[J].城市道桥与防洪,2018(06):266-268+384-385.
[20] 张自强.建筑垃圾在城市道路基层中的再生利用研究[J].工程建设与设计,2019(16):141-143.
[21] 周新锋,徐希娟,李晓娟.水泥稳定建筑垃圾再生材料用于道路基层的性能研究[J].筑路机械与施工机械化,2016,33(08):48-51.
[22] 唐娴,王社良.城市建筑垃圾路面基层应用研究[J].科技导报,2009,27(07):88-90.
[23] 崔宁.砖混类建筑垃圾再生骨料应用前景[C].中国硅酸盐学会混凝土与水泥制品学分会,2011:297-304.
[24] 肖田,孙吉书,靳灿章.石灰粉煤灰稳定建筑垃圾的路用性能研究[J].山西建筑,2010,36(22):275-276.
[25] Al-Mufti R L, Fried A N. The Early Age Non-destructive Testing of Concrete Made with Recycled Concrete Aggregate[J]. Construction & Building Materials,2012,37:379-386.
[26] Kazemian F, RooholaminiH, Hassani A. Mechanical and Fracture Properties of Concrete Containing Treated and Untreated Recycled Concrete Aggregates[J]. Construction and Building Materials,2019,209(10):690-700.
[27] Yuwadee Zaetang, Vanchai Sata, Ampol Wongsa, et al. Properties of Pervious Concrete Containing Recycled Concrete Block Aggregate and Recycled Concrete Aggregate[J]. Construction and Building Materials,2016,111.
[28] 乔宏霞,彭宽,陈克凡.陶瓷骨料再生混凝土高温损伤研究[J].硅酸盐通报,2019,38(09):2902-2909.
[29] 高琦,柳炎,李福安.基于正交试验的砖混再生骨料混凝土配合比设计[J].中外建筑,2018(12):160-162.
[30] 李贺,刘天舒,丁向群.废弃纤维再生混凝土抗硫酸盐侵蚀性能的研究[J].混凝土,2019(10):18-21.
[31] 朱小艳,郑建军,孔德玉.灌浆预埋再生混凝土抗弯拉强度的试验研究[J].混凝土,2019(10):52-53,61.
[32] 肖建庄,李标,杨钱荣.复合改性再生混凝土抗氯离子渗透性能[J].混凝土与水泥制品,2019(10):1-5.

基于通行能力和安全性分析的集散一级公路硬路肩宽度研究

张方哲　赵一飞　杨思杰
(长安大学)

摘　要　为研究一级公路右侧硬路肩宽度指标所存在的差异,将设计速度为 80km/h 的集散一级公路作为研究对象,进行通行能力和安全性分析,分别对服务交通量和停车视距进行计算。结果表明:在发生车辆故障的情况下,1.50m的硬路肩宽度会导致外侧车道无法通行,易发生排队和拥堵状况,设计时需要将v/C值控制更加严格才能保证远景服务水平;若想满足货车的停车视距,则需要更高的圆曲线技术指标,设计时圆曲线半径值宜与纵坡大小一同考虑。然后,针对目前存在的问题,推荐了右侧硬路肩宽度值和圆曲线最小半径,为一级公路设计提供参考。

关键词 公路工程 一级公路 右侧硬路肩 通行能力 停车视距

0 引言

一级公路可以承担干线功能或集散功能,不过在技术指标的选择上两者存在着一定的差别[1]。设计速度为80km/h的一级公路,承担干线功能右侧硬路肩一般值为3.00m,承担集散功能一般值为1.50m,指标相差较大,其取值的合理性尚需研究。

国外基于交通事故统计,建立事故率与路肩宽度的关系,采用仿真等方法对路肩进行了研究。Stohner[2]基于纽约的交通数据,建立了路肩宽度与伤亡事故率的模型,结果表明硬路肩宽度为1.8~2.4m时,伤亡事故率维持在较低水平;Zegeer等[3]使用了肯塔基州的大型数据库进行了统计分析和研究,结果表明:对于更宽的车道,事故率的下降幅度不大。然而,每增加一英尺路肩宽可以使事故率下降1%;Ruimin Li等[4]采用交通仿真对拥堵状况下,路肩临时行车这种交通措施进行了研究,结果表明该措施能够提高交通运输效率。

目前,国内对于右侧硬路肩宽度的研究侧重高速公路路肩宽度。侯赛因等[5]根据事故数据研究了硬路肩宽度与安全的关系,通过相关试验统计分析了路肩宽度对车辆运行速度的影响;邢小亮等[6]以广东省实际调研资料为基础,对驾驶车辆的偏移量和速度进行了统计分析,证实了高速公路右侧硬路肩宽度会影响驾驶行为协调性;王佐等[7]基于右侧硬路肩紧急停车的功能,对其宽度进行了研究,并提出了建议值。

综上所述,国内外对右侧硬路肩宽度的研究集中于横断面几何参数与交通数据的回归分析上,缺少对通行能力和交通安全的理论分析。本文从服务水平和停车视距两个方面对集散一级公路右侧硬路肩宽度进行研究,为其右侧硬路肩宽度取值提供支撑。

1 一级公路右侧硬路肩宽度的问题

一级公路的货车比例较高,货车在通行和安全方面比小客车的影响大,所以分析时需考虑货车的影响。一级公路可以作为次要干线公路或主要集散公路,设计速度均可采用80km/h。但规范规定:干线一级公路右侧硬路肩宽度一般值为3.0m,集散一级公路右侧硬路肩宽度一般值为1.5m,两者数值相差较大,值得进行研究。

集散功能的一级公路货车混入率更高,会给通行和安全方面带来更大的压力,但规范对右侧硬路肩宽度降低了要求,会牺牲公路的部分使用性能。

2 硬路肩宽度的通行能力影响分析

2.1 服务水平分析

当硬路肩宽度为3.0m时,可供大型车辆紧急停车;硬路肩宽度为2.50m时,可供小客车紧急停靠;硬路肩宽度为1.5m时,车辆会占用最外侧行车道的部分宽度,因此车辆发生故障会导致外侧车道无法通行。

一级公路的服务水平划分以饱和度(即V/C)作为主要指标,其设计服务水平不宜低于三级,集散一级公路设计服务水平可降低一级。三、四级服务水平下,交通流均处于稳定流状态[8]。一级公路路段服务水平分级情况见表1。

一级公路路段服务水平分级表　　　　　　　　　　　　　　　　　　　　　表1

服务水平	V/C值	设计速度		
		100	80	60
		最大服务交通量[pcu/(h·ln)]	最大服务交通量[pcu/(h·ln)]	最大服务交通量[pcu/(h·ln)]
一	V/C≤0.3	600	550	480
二	0.3<V/C≤0.5	1000	900	800
三	0.5<V/C≤0.7	1400	1250	1100
四	0.7<V/C≤0.9	1800	1600	1450
五	0.9<V/C≤1.0	2000	1800	1600
六	1.0<V/C	0~2000	0~1800	0~1600

2.2 服务交通量计算

集散一级公路最不利情况是载重汽车发生故障,其总宽为2.5m。车辆临时停车与路侧护栏需要0.5m的外侧净距[9],因此故障车辆至少会占用最外侧车道1.50m的物理宽度。车辆行驶需要保持动态净空[10],会导致最外侧车道无法通车。

四级服务水平下V/C值的下限为稳定流与拥堵流的界限,所以为了保证车辆能够稳定行驶,即便在封闭外侧车道的情况下,路段服务水平等级也不应低于四级。

由于集散一级公路设计服务水平可降低一级,故本文对三、四级服务水平的服务交通量进行计算,单侧车道全部保通以及封闭最外侧车道的服务交通量计算结果见表2。

三、四级服务水平服务交通量计算表　　　　　　　　　　　　　　　　　　表2

实际的车道数	服务水平	V/C值	单侧车道全部保通		因车辆故障封闭外侧车道	
			保通可用车道数(ln)	服务交通量范围[pcu/(h·ln)]	故障可用车道数(ln)	服务交通量范围[pcu/(h·ln)]
2	三级	0.5<V/C≤0.7	2	(1800,2520]	1	(900,1260]
2	四级	0.7<V/C≤0.9	2	(2520,3240]	1	(1260,1620]
3	三级	0.5<V/C≤0.7	3	(2700,3780]	2	(1800,2520]
3	四级	0.7<V/C≤0.9	3	(3780,4860]	2	(2520,3240]
4	三级	0.5<V/C≤0.7	4	(3600,5040]	3	(2700,3780]
4	四级	0.7<V/C≤0.9	4	(5040,6480]	3	(3780,4860]

由表2可知,右侧硬路肩宽度1.50m,设计服务水平采用四级,车辆故障封闭外侧车道会导致服务水平低于四级;设计服务水平为三级,单向双车道封闭外侧车道的服务水平无法达到四级;单向三车道封闭外侧车道,设计小时交通量位于(2700,3240],则服务水平可达四级;单向四车道封闭外侧车道,设计小时交通量位于(3780,4860],则服务水平可达四级。以封闭最外侧车道状况下,四级服务水平的服务交通量上限作为最大服务交通量可计算出设计可采用的最大V/C值,计算结果见表3。

设计可采用的最大V/C计算表　　　　　　　　　　　　　　　　　　表3

车道数(ln)	最大服务交通量(pcu/h)	基准通行能力[pcu/(h·ln)]	最大V/C	设计服务水平
2	1620	1800	0.45	二级
3	3240		0.6	三级
4	4860		0.675	三级

由表3知,右侧硬路肩采用1.50m宽度,设计速度为80km/h的集散一级公路对V/C值的要求更加严格,与集散公路的设计期望不符。因此,设计速度为80km/h的一级公路右侧硬路肩取值不宜按功能

而进行区分。

3 硬路肩宽度的安全性影响分析

3.1 视距分析

视距是保证行车安全的重要设计指标,一级公路设有中央分隔带无对向车流影响,只需考虑停车视距的要求。硬路肩所影响的视距参数为横净距宽度,所以本文仅对平面停车视距进行了计算分析。停车视距计算公式如下:

$$S_c = \frac{v_{85}t}{3.6} + \frac{(v_{85}/3.6)^2}{2gf} \tag{1}$$

式中:S_c——小客车停车视距,m;
v_{85}——运行速度的计算值,km/h;
t——驾驶员反应时间,取2.5s;
g——重力加速度,取9.8m/s²;
f——纵向摩阻系数,依运行速度和路面状况而定。

将行车道中线近似作为驾驶员视点轨迹线,小客车停车视距计算中的目高和物高分别为1.2m和0.1m。一级公路中央分隔带护栏高度为70~80cm,且垂直设置,由于距内侧车道较近,易阻挡驾驶员的视线,影响停车视距,如图1所示。进行视距检查时,圆曲线半径除满足其内侧停车视距要求外,中分带的停车视距也应考虑[11]。

3.2 停车视距计算

横净距是指行车轨迹线与视距曲线间的距离,通过停车视距可以计算出不同的平曲线半径所需要的横净距[12],计算公式如下。

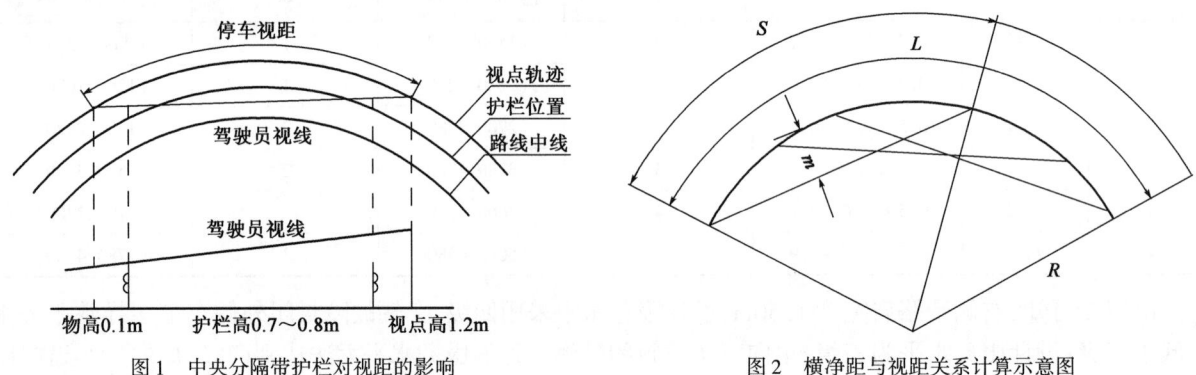

图1 中央分隔带护栏对视距的影响　　　图2 横净距与视距关系计算示意图

$$m = R\left[1 - \cos\left(\frac{28.65S}{R}\right)\right] \tag{2}$$

式中:m——所需横净距,m;
R——内车道中线处的曲线半径,m;
S——小客车或货车的相应停车视距,m。

3.2.1 小客车满足停车视距的圆曲线最小半径计算

对设计速度为80km/h一级公路的右侧硬路肩宽度进行分析,则路侧和中分带所能提供的横净距均已知,干线一级公路路侧横净距:3.75/2+3=4.875m;集散一级公路路侧横净距:3.75/2+1.50=3.375m;中分带横净距:3.75/2+0.5=2.375m。利用函数公式逆运算单变量求解的方法,可由横净距反算出所需的最小圆曲线半径,圆曲线最小半径计算结果见表4。

小客车满足停车视距最小圆曲线半径计算表　　　表4

位　置	设计速度（km/h）	横净距（m）	停车视距（m）	满足停车视距的圆曲线最小半径(m)
干线路侧	80	4.875	110	309
集散路侧		3.375		448
中分带		2.375		637

由结果知，仅考虑小客车路侧停车视距情况，路线所需最小圆曲线半径448m仍大于规范400m一般值要求，说明右侧硬路肩采用1.50m的集散一级公路对于线形指标的要求比干线一级公路更高，与期望不符。

3.2.2　货车满足停车视距的圆曲线最小半径计算

集散一级公路货车比例较高，分析时需考虑货车停车视距。公路内侧车道一般为快速车道，供小客车行驶或超车使用。货车一般于外侧车道行驶，本文在进行货车停车视距的检查时，仅对圆曲线内侧进行了计算分析，见图3、表5。

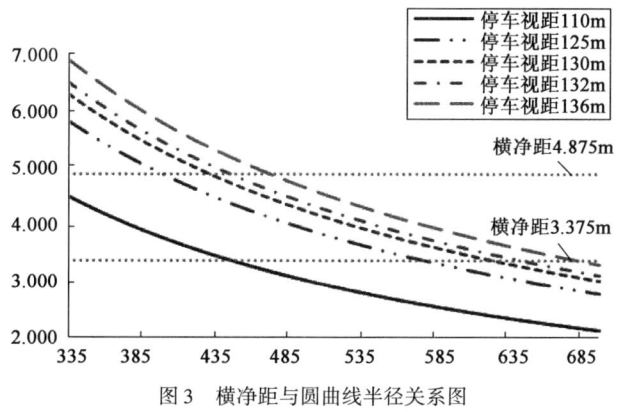

图3　横净距与圆曲线半径关系图

货车下坡满足停车视距最小圆曲线半径计算表　　　表5

公路功能	路侧横净距(m)	纵坡(%)	停车视距(m)	满足停车视距的圆曲线最小半径(m)
干线	4.875	0	125	400
		3	130	433
		4	132	446
		5	136	473
集散	3.375	0	125	578
		3	130	625
		4	132	645
		5	136	684

由结果知，右侧硬路肩宽度3.00m，货车行驶特性不受坡度影响，满足货车停车视距的最小圆曲线半径为400m；纵坡达到5%时，圆曲线半径采用473m可满足货车停车视距；右侧硬路肩宽度1.50m，货车行驶特性不受坡度影响，满足货车停车视距的最小圆曲线半径为578m；在纵坡为5%时，满足停车视距所需的圆曲线最小半径为684m。说明集散一级公路满足货车停车视距所需的技术指标要求更高，与期望不符。

4　技术指标推荐

基于通行能力和停车视距两方面计算分析，本文针对设计速度为80km/h一级公路的设计指标提出如下建议(表6)。

集散一级公路设计指标推荐值　　　　　　　　　　　　　　　　　　　　　　　　　　　表6

右侧硬路肩宽度		圆曲线最小半径		
一般值(m)	极限值(m)	一般值(m)	极限值(m)	建议值(m)
3.0	1.5	500	400	650

右侧硬路肩宽度一般值可供大型车辆紧急停车,极限值满足行车安全需要和发挥路肩基本功能。圆曲线最小半径一般值满足右侧硬路肩宽度3.0m的货车停车视距要求,极限值满足货车性能不受纵坡影响的停车视距要求,建议值为满足中央分隔带停车视距的最小半径。

当右侧硬路肩宽度取1.5m时,应设置紧急停车带以保证故障车辆尽快驶离车道;建议的圆曲线最小半径是在右侧硬路肩宽度为3.0m推荐的,若硬路肩宽度采用1.5m,圆曲线半径可参考图4取值;当受地形条件限制,圆曲线半径小于一般值要求时,其数值应大于货车停车视距所对应的最小半径。

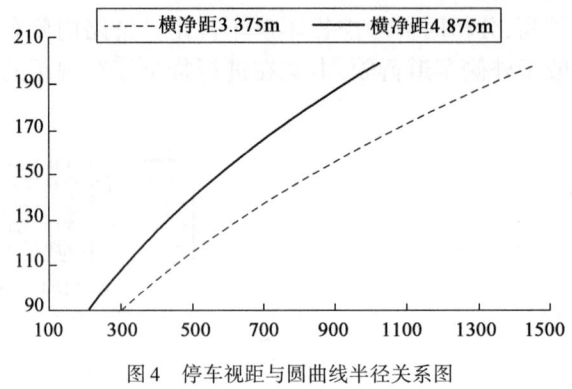

图4　停车视距与圆曲线半径关系图

5　结　语

(1)设计速度80km/h的集散一级公路,右侧硬路肩采用1.5m时,通行能力和安全性会受到影响。平面圆曲线指标较小的情况下,会存在货车停车视距不良的情况。

(2)集散一级公路的技术指标尚需提高,本文为设计者提供了建议指标,以提高安全性和通畅性。右侧硬路肩采取极限值时,应设置紧急停车带,保证故障车辆快速驶离车道。

(3)货车停车视距受纵坡大小影响,计算出不同坡度所需的最小圆曲线半径可供设计人员参考。条件允许的情况下,建议采用满足中分带停车视距的圆曲线半径值,否则应通过在局部路段增大中分带横净距、设置限速标志或减速标线等措施。

参考文献

[1] 中华人民共和国交通运输部.公路路线设计规范:JTG D20—2017[S].北京:人民交通出版社股份有限公司,2017.

[2] Stohner,W R.Relation of Highway Accidents to Shoulder width on Two-lane Rural Highways in New York State[J].Highway Research Board Proceedings.1956(35):500-504.

[3] Zegeer C V,Stewart R,Council F,et al.Accident Relationships of Roadway Width on Low-volume Roads [J].Transp Res Rec,1994(1445):160-168.

[4] Ruimin Li,Zhen YE,Bin Li,et al.Simulation of Hard Shoulder Running Combined with Queue Warning During Traffic Accident with CTM Model[J].IET Intelligent Transport Systems,2017(11):553-560.

[5] 侯赛因.横断面因素对双车道公路交通安全影响研究[D].西安:长安大学,2014.

[6] 邢小亮,崔降龙,李璨,等.高速公路右侧硬路肩宽度对驾驶行为协调性影响研究[J].交通信息与安全,2016(6):30-36.

[7] 王佐,潘兵宏,曾志刚,等.基于紧急停车功能的高速公路右侧硬路肩宽度研究[J].中外公路,2013

(3):311-315.
[8] 周荣贵,钟连德.公路通行能力手册[M].北京:人民交通出版社股份有限公司,2017:7-10.
[9] 曾志刚.高速公路硬路肩的功能与宽度值研究[D].西安:长安大学,2012.
[10] 杨智生.《公路工程技术标准》调整刍议[J].公路,2006(6):34-37.
[11] 杨帆,白浩晨,贺亚龙,等.高速公路中央分隔带停车视距评价方法研究[J].公路交通科技,2018(6).
[12] 文浩雄,钟琨,刘卓,等.高速公路中央分隔带净距问题及对策[J].公路工程,2013(6):20-23.

Study on Inspection of Highway Three-dimension Sight Distance Method Based on Civil 3D

Zhibo Liu　Tao Wu　Yuhua Peng

(University of Chang'an)

Abstract　Drivers need positive visual feedback in the process of driving. Road driving safety is closely related to the satisfaction of sight distance conditions. The traditional two-dimension sight distance inspection method analyses the influence of horizontal curve and vertical curve respectively, which is not completely consistent with the actual driving conditions. It's necessary to determine the sight distance from three-dimension level. In this paper, on the basis of existing highway projects, selecting an example curve section, and using Civil 3D to analyse the three-dimension sight distance of the section in BIM environment, the analysis results are compared with the results of two-dimension sight distance inspection, and then exploring the rationality and feasibility of Civil 3D in the application of highway three-dimension sight distance inspection.

Keywords　Road driving safety　3D sight distance　Civil 3D　Lateral clear distance

0　Introduction

With the rapid development of China's transportation industry and the arrival of the era of motorization, traffic safety is becoming more and more significant. The intervisibility of thesightline ensures the driving safety. Moreover, sufficient visual information could provide support for inspection of sight distance. There is no deny that the three-dimension characteristics of highway require to use the three-dimension method to evaluate the sight distance. The calculation of the three-dimension sight distance is more complex, which involves people, vehicles, roads and the surrounding environment.

The research of three-dimension sight distance is mainly developed from two aspects of theoretical research and practical application. The Monte Carlo method was mentioned to calculate the possible sight distance risk when horizontal curve was combined with transition curve, sag and convex vertical curve respectively (Sarhan M.; Hassan Y 2008). César De Santos-Berbel and Maria Castro (2018) evaluated stopping sight distance and passing sight distance based 3D nature of roadways and related features for a section of highway with specific sight-distance characteristics of overpasses. Ana Tsui Moreno and Vicente Ferrer (2014) calculated the sight distance profile at vertical crest curves overlapped with horizontal curves by a software application which was developed in Matlab. Zhang et al. (2009) proposed a three-dimension sight distance calculation method, which compared driver's sight line and elevation of road surface or roadside point to check the sight distance. At the same time, BIM (building information model) technology develops rapidly in the highway engineering, which gradually leads the traditional highway design from two-dimension CAD independent design to three-dimension information aided design, and brings about the change of design methods and means. Many scholars have done a lot of researches on the application of BIM Technology in inspection of 3D sight distance. Wang et al. (2020) pointed out that the use of VR (Virtual Reality Technology) and other advanced measures could further improve the performance ability of BIM, so that BIM can adapt to a variety of engineering situations. By improving users' immersive and integrated experience, BIM Technology can be applied in a wider range of infrastructure construction by building road BIM + VR model, Qi Liang et al. (2019) simulated the impact of different special weather conditions on sight distance, and then evaluated the road safety design. Chen Xiong (2019) used Civil 3D to build high-precision road and combined with solid 3D model to analyse the sight distance of the road, and obtained accurate analysis results in a short time, which improved the design efficiency and accuracy. Based on the three-dimension data model of Pu Xuan expressway, Zhao Ji (2015) used CARD/1 to check the three-dimension sight distance of bad visual road sections of Pu Xuan expressway, and put forward some improvement measures for the insufficient sight distance. Liu Xin (2017) explained the calculation principle and method of three-dimension space sight distance, checked the three-dimension space sight distance of new highway model by using Civil 3D software platform, built three-dimension visualization scene and put forward measures by checking the location of insufficient three-dimension space sight distance and occlusion. Based on Civil 3D platform, Zhang Xingyu (2017) extended the function of checking the design specifications and running speed, but 3D sight distance analysis module has been consummated. Xue Xiaojiao (2019) developed the highway 3D visibility system based on Civil 3D, which improved the functionality of the module. The traditional two-dimension design method is still used in most highway engineering design company, and the design method in BIM environment has not been unanimously recognized by all design companies. Therefore, although the above scholars combine BIM Technology with visual information or sight distance analysis, the lack of the comparison between traditional two-dimension design analysis method and three-dimension analysis method in BIM environment, so the advantages of three-dimension analysis method cannot be highlighted. This paper relies on the upgrading of a class II highway to a class I highway in Guangxi province. Due to the change of index of some sections after the reconstruction and expansion, the sight distance of special sections needs to be reverified to ensure the driving safety. It is proposed to analyse the sight distance of the road section by using the three-dimension sight distance analysis function of Civil 3D and the traditional two-dimension sight distance calculation method, and compare the results of two-dimension analysis and three-dimension sight distance analysis to illustrate the feasibility, convenience and accuracy of Civil 3D sight distance analysis function in BIM environment.

1 The Overview of 3D Sight Distance Calculation Methods

At present, the commonly used calculation methods of road sight distance are sight distance envelope diagram method and maximum lateral clear distance method. Both of them are two-dimension methods, which are not enough to reflect the real sight distance of the road. Three-dimension sight distance is proposed to solve the problem that the original sight distance inspection may ignore the influence of road terrain, horizontal and vertical alignment combination and some road ancillary structures. With the unremitting efforts of experts and scholars at home and abroad, great progress has been made in the research of 3D sight distance calculation. The specific calculation methods are mainly divided into graphic method and analytical method.

Graphic method is developed from a simple formulaabout calculating the sight distance of circular curve, the viewpoint can only act on the circular curve, so the sight distance of straight line, tangent line and reversing curve could not be calculated. However, with the deeper research and analysis of experts and scholars, the calculation formulas of straight line, tangent line and reversing curve have been worked out one after another and the graphic method has been added, which makes the application of graphic method possible. The graphic method is to express the alignment of the road in the form of mathematical parameters, and use vector function to represent a complete section of the road centreline, and combine with each other to establish the corresponding parameter expressions of the carriageway and the obstacles on both sides of the road, so as to facilitate the further calculation of the sight distance. The calculation mode as shown in Fig. 1, assuming that the distance between the starting point of the line and $X(t^*)$ is $t^* \in (0, T_{\max})$, and use vector to calculate $O_t(t^*)$ The sight distance value of the road shown in the Figure. can be obtained by iterative calculation. Because of the parameterized calculation form of the route segment, the graphic method has a large amount of calculation when the terrain of the road is complex, and the accuracy of the drawing grid division will cause errors in the calculation results. Although the above algorithm has been programmed and tested by Matlab, the degree of automation of the program is low, so it cannot be used in the actual three-dimension sight distance measurement. So the graphic calculation of complex roads is only limited to the theoretical analysis stage.

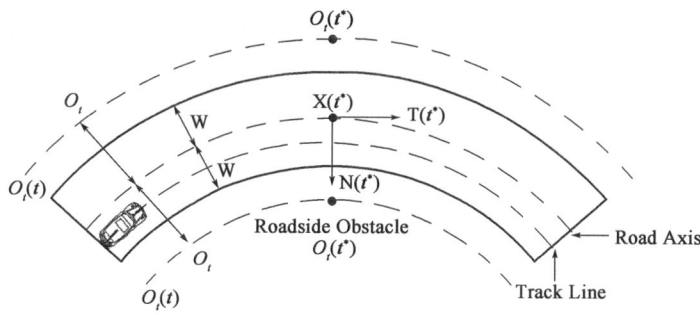

Fig. 1 The Calculation Model of Graphic Method

Analysis method is widely used in the calculation of three-dimension sight distance at present. The specific method is to calculate the sight distance value of the road when considering the horizontal, vertical and horizontal based on the driving sight distance model and considering the factors of road profile and cross section. Specifically, the finite element model is established through the parameter expression and roadside eigenvalue of the road to calculate the sight distance value. Compared with the graphic method, it is more suitable for the situation that the road alignment is more complex. However, the analysis method often simplifies some problems in the construction process of the finite element model, which may affect the three-dimension sight distance inspection results. The core of the spatial two-point intervisibility principle in the analysis method is to check whether the driver's line of sight is blocked by the road alignment or road ancillary structures, and to find the farthest road viewpoint that the driver's line of sight can reach. Using the above method, scanning point by point along the driver's view trajectory and calculating the three-dimension sight distance of the corresponding station is the main way of three-dimension sight distance inspection in this paper.

2 3D Sight Distance Inspection of Road Section Based on Civil 3D

Three-dimension sight distance inspection is different from the traditional two-dimension sight distance inspection method. Its calculation model is more complex, more factors are considered, and the data processing capacity is larger, which requires higher software computing capacity. As a platform of BIM for civil engineering, Civil 3D can establish a consistent and abundant data model, which help designers to analyze in the design stage and make changes quickly in any stage of the project for making more intelligent decisions, and finally choose the best design scheme. At present, Civil 3D is one of the few existing road design software which can achieve 3D sight distance inspection. Different from the traditional inspection of sight distance, which uses lateral clear distance method as the quantitative index, Three-dimension sight distance inspection in Civil 3D uses the principle of two-point intervisibility, and judges the intervisibility of the line of sight by judging whether there are obstacles between the driver's eye point and the object point. According to the minimum sight distance value, scan point by point along the road forward direction. When the view point is in the section with good vision such as straight line or large radius horizontal curve section, the calculated value of sight distance is far greater than the minimum sight distance value For reducing the computer calculation, the minimum sight distance value will be returned; if the sight distance calculation value is less than the minimum sight distance value, the actual sight distance value and the three-dimension coordinates of the point will be returned, as shown in Fig. 2.

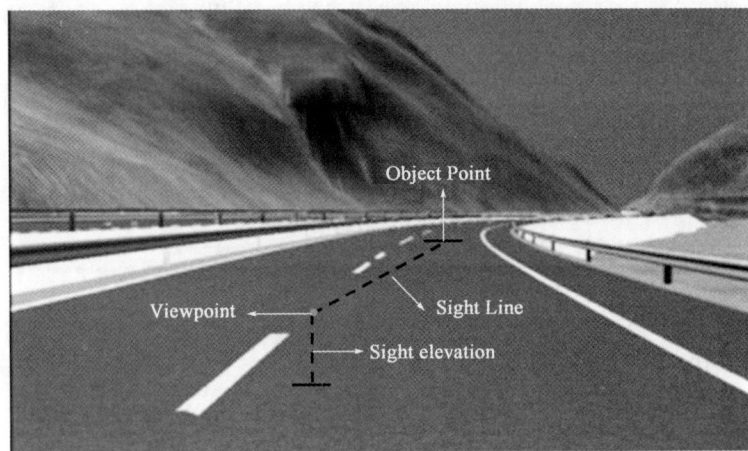

Fig. 2　Two-point Intervisibility Principle

From the above content that the calculation of 3D sight distance is heavy, and the route data of the project includes bridge section and tunnel group section, etc. the engineering technical data to be processed in the construction of the whole 3D road model after reconstruction and expansion is huge, and the implementation is relatively difficult. In order to realize the inspection of three-dimension sight distance and analyze the characteristics of three-dimension sight distance inspection method and two-dimension sight distance method, the paper selects a typical horizontal curve section to build a three-dimension road model and takes it as an example for three-dimension sight distance inspection.

2.1　Inspection of Three-dimension Sight Distance at Design Speed

According to the relevant contents of the overview research of three-dimension sight distance, the existing research of three-dimension sight distance mainly stays in the level of three-dimension sight distance model, and the research of combining three-dimension sight distance with engineering examples is relatively less. The focus of this paper is on the application and engineering popularization of three-dimension sight distance. The following parts are introductions about the steps of creating 3D road model based on Civil 3D.

2.1.1　Terrain Surface Modelling

The terrain of the project belongs to the category of mountains and hills, with more mountains and less flat land. The middle area is relatively low. The whole terrain inclines from northwest to southeast. Using the DWG topographic map as the terrain source data. Firstly, creating a new empty terrain surface in the Civil 3D, Secondly, in the surface definition, adding the contour line and elevation point data in the DWG topographic map to the empty terrain surface respectively, so as to generate the terrain surface. Finally, eliminating the surface elevation gross error, and the terrain surface model as shown in Fig. 3. The terrain surface is a triangulation surface, which is the carrier of road BIM model. It contains three-dimension coordinate terrain and other information, and is no longer the graphics object of AutoCAD.

Fig. 3 Topographic Surface Model

2.1.2 Horizontal Alignment Design

In this paper, the intersection method combined with topographic surface map is used for alignment design. The starting and ending stations are all located on the straight-line section, and there is a horizontal curve with a radius of 580m within the section. The final horizontal curve design of the sample section as shown in Fig. 4, the unit line position or modify could be adjusted dynamically by dragging its parameters by dragging, which will only affect the alignment position of adjacent units, but will not affect the whole alignment. The panoramic window of the parameters of the whole alignment unit is shown in Fig. 5. Compared with the traditional comprehensive method, this design method has greater advantages in the efficiency of horizontal alignment design.

Fig. 4 Horizontal Alignment

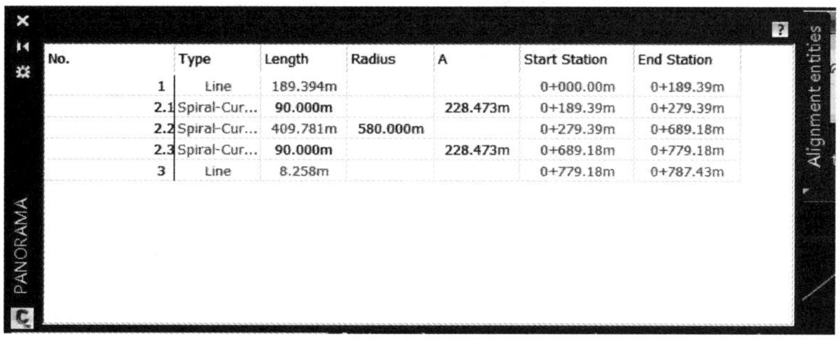

No.	Type	Length	Radius	A	Start Station	End Station
1	Line	189.394m			0+000.00m	0+189.39m
2.1	Spiral-Cur...	90.000m		228.473m	0+189.39m	0+279.39m
2.2	Spiral-Cur...	409.781m	580.000m		0+279.39m	0+689.18m
2.3	Spiral-Cur...	90.000m		228.473m	0+689.18m	0+779.18m
3	Line	8.258m			0+779.18m	0+787.43m

Fig. 5 Parameters of Horizontal Curve

2.1.3 Vertical Alignment Design

The terrain surface and alignment are selected as the data source of surface profile, which reflects the relief of the alignment and updates dynamically with the change of the alignment in real time; secondly, the slope line is determined by the way of line intersection, and then the vertical curve parameters are input to design the profile alignment, with multi-viewport in Civil 3D, the vertical alignment (lower viewport) is designed with reference to the horizontal alignment (upper viewport), which is helpful to check the combination of horizontal and vertical alignment and adjust alignment.

The design parameters of the profile of the project are shown in Fig. 6. The maximum longitudinal slope, the minimum radius of sag curve and crest curve is 5.34%, 3000m and 4500m respectively.

2.1.4 Cross Section Design Assembly

The standard cross section of subgrade in this project section as Fig. 7 shows. Slope of subgrade etc. are assembled according to the filling and excavation conditions by using Civil 3D predefined components.

2.1.5 Road BIM Model Establishment

Taking the example road section, profile design line and cross section assembly as the elements of creating road BIM model, taking the terrain surface as the surface logic target of "connecting slope to surface" component, and setting the station step spacing as 10m, the basic data of creating road BIM model is added. The road BIM model created in this paper as shown in Fig. 8, which serves as the basis for calculating the three-dimension sight distance.

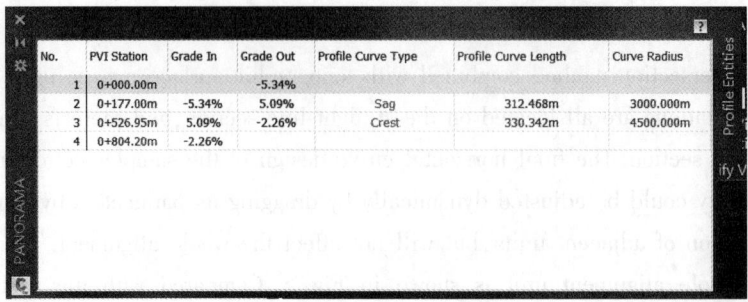

Fig. 6　Parameters of Vertical Curve

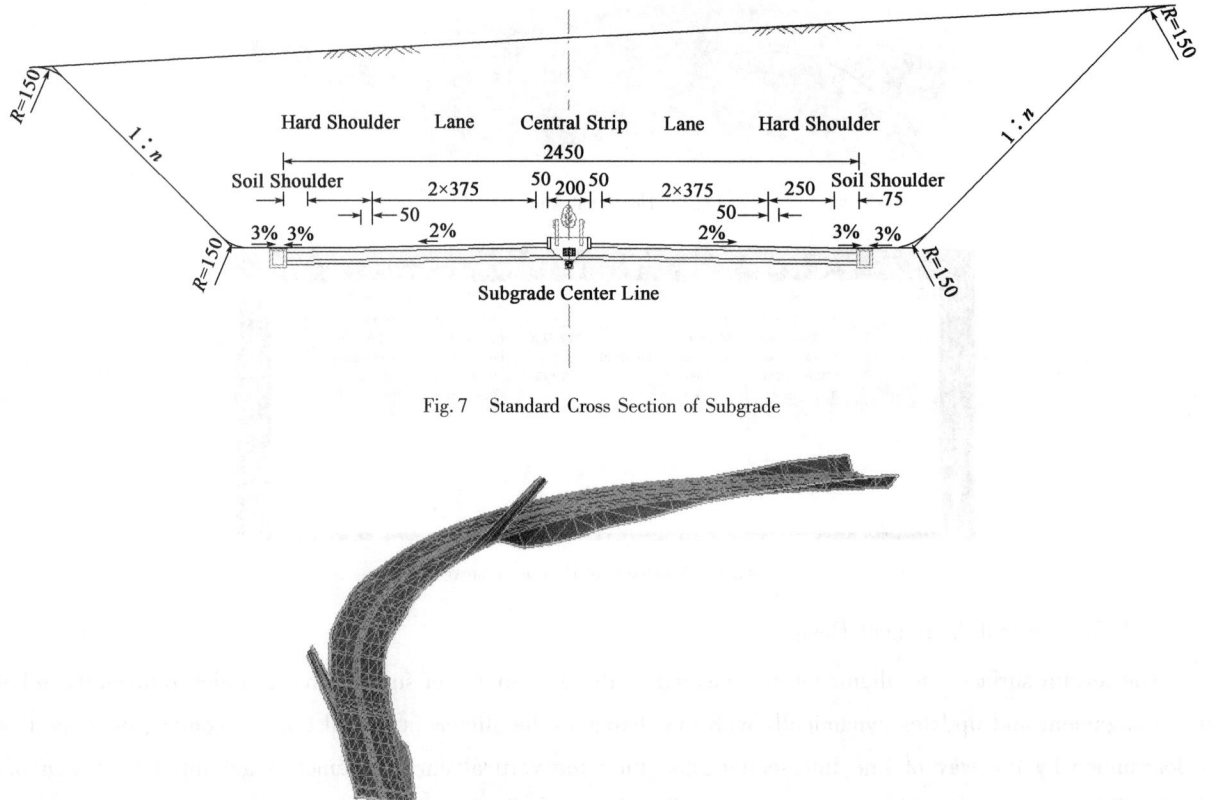

Fig. 7　Standard Cross Section of Subgrade

Fig. 8　The road BIM model

2.2　Inspection of 3D Sight Distance

Based on the three-dimension model established above, using the sight distance inspection module in Civil 3D, set the "inspection interval", the minimum sight distance required under the design speed, the viewpoint position and the object position, the three-dimension space sight distance inspection results could be obtained. The specific parameters as shown in Fig. 9.

2.3　Inspection Results Analysis

The sight distance was inspected by Civil 3D sight distance inspection module (K0 + 280m to K0 + 690m). According to the Civil 3D sight distance inspection principle, the inspection results of each station are returned to the minimum sight distance value of 110m specified in the standard, which indicates that there is no terrible 3D sight distance in the road section and meets the specification requirements.

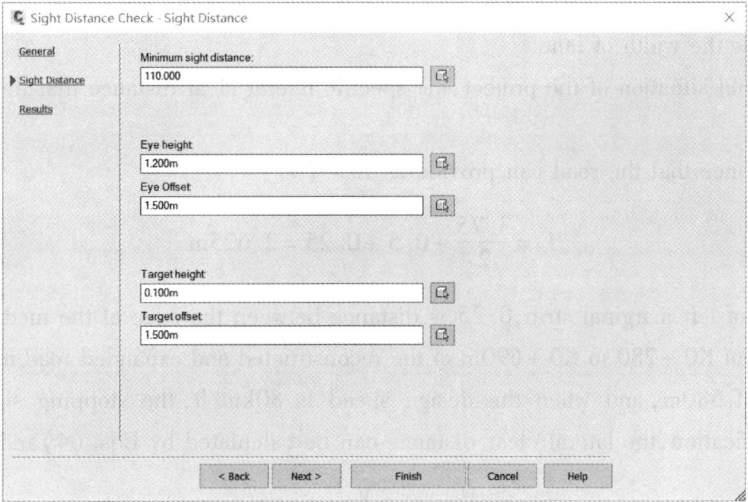

Fig. 9 Parameters setting of 3D sight distance check

3 Inspection of Stopping Sight Distance Based on Design Speed

The lateral clear distance method is selected as the quantitative index for the inspection of driving sight distance at the design speed. When the lateral clear distance provided by the road is less than the calculated lateral clear distance, the road sight distance does not meet the requirements, otherwise it meets the requirements. The calculation formula of specific lateral clear distance as shown in Eqs. (1):

$$m = R_s \left[1 - \cos\left(\frac{28.65S}{R_s}\right) \right] \tag{1}$$

Here, m is required lateral clear distance, R_s is curve radius at lane center line, S is stopping sight distance.

After reconstruction and expansion, the class of highway was improved. According to the requirements of the specification, the central divider needs to be set. Due to the setting of hard shoulder, earth shoulder, side ditch and berm at the foot of cutting slope on the inside of the curve, the horizontal clear distance of the highway is at least 4.0m, which generally will not block the line of eyesight due to the intrusion of obstacles into the clearance, and can meet the stopping sight distance at the corresponding design speed However, designers often ignore the influence of median divider on sight distance, and the three-dimension characteristics of Civil 3D software are more suitable for the description of road ancillary facilities. This paper focuses on the inspection of the sight distance of the lane outside the median divider.

3.1 Sight Distance Inspection of Median Divider

The sight distance inspection of overtaking lane outside the central divider mainly considers the influence of the central divider. Due to the high speed and the limited lateral clear distance provided by the central divider, the problem of insufficient sight distance often occurs in the overtaking lane outside the central divider According to the principle of highway lane division, the vehicles on the overtaking lane outside the central divider are mainly high-speed cars, and there are almost no trucks. It is only necessary to verify the sight distance of cars. During the specific verification, the viewpoint position of passenger cars is set at 1.2m above the center line of the overtaking lane outside the central divider, and the value of curve radius at the center line of the lane as Eqs. (2):

$$R_s = R + \frac{M}{2} + L_1 + \frac{W}{2} \tag{2}$$

R_s is curve radius at lane center line, R is curve radius, M is the width of median divider, L_1 is the width of left marginal strip, W is the width of lane.

Based on the actual situation of the project, the specific lateral clear distance that the road can provide are as follows:

Lateral clear distance that the road can provide as Eqs. (3):

$$H_c = \frac{3.75}{2} + 0.5 + 0.25 = 2.625 \text{m} \tag{3}$$

0.5 is the width of left marginal strip, 0.25 is distance between the edge of the median strip.

Within the range of K0+280 to K0+690m of the reconstructed and expanded road model, it is a horizontal curve with a radius of 580m, and when the design speed is 80km/h, the stopping sight distance is 110m according to the specification, the lateral clear distance can be calculated by Eqs. (4) and Eqs. (5).

$$R_s = R + \frac{M}{2} + L_1 + \frac{W}{2} = 583.375(\text{m}) \tag{4}$$

$$m = R_s \left[1 - \cos\left(\frac{28.65 S}{R_s}\right)\right] = 2.591(\text{m}) \tag{5}$$

Compared with the specific lateral clear distance of 2.625m < 2.591m, the sight distance based on the traditional lateral clear distance method meets the design requirements.

3.2 Comparative Analysis of Two-dimension and Three-dimension Visual Distance Detection Results

In the curve section of K0+280m to K0+690m, the inspection results of the two methods show that there is no poor sight distance in the curve range. The results of three-dimension sight distance inspection based on Civil 3D are consistent with the traditional two-dimension lateral clear distance method. The three-dimension sight distance inspection comprehensively considers the influence of horizontal and vertical alignments and surrounding conditions, so its inspection process is more perfect and the inspection results are more accurate than the traditional method.

4 Conclusions

Based on Civil 3D software under BIM platform, this paper studies the application of BIM Technology in road three-dimension sight distance evaluation from the perspective of traffic safety, the main conclusions are as follows:

(1) Through the investigation of domestic and foreign literatures, this paper analyses the main application of BIM Technology in highway engineering: three-dimension visual modelling, traffic safety evaluation, collaborative design and so on. The conclusion is that Civil 3D can make full use of the advantages of BIM, such as visual analysis and 3D sight distance evaluation.

(2) As the fact that the traditional two-dimension sight distance inspection method can't fully reflect the actual sight distance of the road, this paper introduces the three-dimension sight distance based on the two-dimension sight distance by using the principle of spatial two-point intervisibility, and uses Civil 3D realizes the three-dimension sight distance inspection of the example curve section, then compares the inspection results with the traditional two-dimension lateral clear distance inspection results, which further illustrates the feasibility and

rationality of the three-dimension sight distance inspection method.

However, as many aspects involved in the 3D sight distance inspection and the limited capacity of computer data processing, it is difficult to finish the three-dimension modelling and sight distance inspection of the whole route of highway, so the example curve section be selected for an example. Secondly, the actual space sight distance calculated in Civil 3D returns the minimum value that meets the requirements of sight distance, but the procedure does not set a maximum sight distance value which can fully ensure the safety of sight distance. The advantage of setting the maximum sight distance value is to give the maximum space sight distance value that can be provided by the road at the driver's point of view to the designer. As it's worthy to be mentioned, the results of three-dimension sight distance inspection are obtained in civil 3D, although the correctness of the inspection results has been verified, the accuracy of the results can't be determined. Therefore, it is necessary to conduct more researches on the accuracy verification method and accuracy for three-dimension sight distance inspection function of civil 3D. BIM Technology is a new product of the combination of traditional civil engineering and information technology, the application of BIM Technology in the field of traffic safety is bound to be the future development trend. Therefore, the sight distance safety of road based on BIM software needs to be further studied.

References

[1] Sarhan M, Hassan Y. Three-Dimension, Probabilistic Highway Design[J]. Transp. Res. Rec. J. Transp. Res. Board,2008,2060,10-18.

[2] César De Santos-Berbel, Maria Castro. Three-Dimensional Virtual Highway Model for Sight-Distance Evaluation of Highway Underpasses[J]. Journal of Surveying Engineering,2018,144(4).

[3] Ana Tsui Moreno, Vicente Ferrer. Evaluation of 3D Coordination to Maximize Available Stopping Sight Distance in Two-Lane Rural Highways[J]. The Baltic Journal of Road and Bridge Engineering,2014,9(2):94-100.

[4] Zhang Chi, Yang Shao-wei, et al. Methods of Three-dimension Sight Distance Inspection for Highway[J]. Journal of Chang'an University (Natural Science Edition),2009,29(3):54-57.

[5] Wang Jian-wei, Gao Chao, et al. Research Development and Prospect of Highway Infrastructure Digitalization[J]. China Journal of Highway and Transport,2020,33(11):101-124.

[6] Qi Liang, Zou Yun. Implementation Method and Application of BIM + VR Technology in Road Design, 2019,35(04):8-13.

[7] Chen Xiong. High-level Road Design based on the Application of Civil3D Sight Distance Analysis[J]. 2019(12):89.

[8] Zhao Ji. Sight Distance Security Technology Research of PuXuan Highway [D]. Xi'an: Chang'an University.

[9] Liu Xin. Highway Alignment Design and Safety Audit based on BIM[D]. Chongqing: Chongqing Jiaotong University,2017.

[10] Zhang Xing-yu. The Research on Some Problems of Highway BIM based on Civil 3D[D]. Xi'an: Chang'an University,2017.

[11] Xue Xiao-jiao. Research and Development of Highway 3D Visibility Analysis Model in BIM Environment [D]. Xi'an: Chang'an University,2019.

高速公路连续下坡路段货车追尾风险研究

马如鹏　胡　涛　王亚楠

(长安大学公路学院)

摘　要　为研究高速公路连续下坡路段货车追尾事故风险，本文利用雅西高速拖乌山北坡交通特管区长下坡路段(全长36km)的高清卡口所记录的有效货车行车数据(共78219组)，进行分析筛选后，确定车速差与车头时距为风险影响因素，定义追尾风险评价指标——碰撞减速率(Collision Reduction Rate, CRR)，并计算得到有效CRR数据3567条，通过拟合分布检验，发现CRR数据的分布规律，并以其分布的85%分位值作为危险CRR阈值。在此基础上，结合碰撞潜在指数概念(CPI)建立基于CRR的连续下坡货车追尾风险概率模型，针对特管区连续下坡路段的货车两车追尾风险问题进行了研究与分析。结果表明：所研究连续下坡路段的CRR样本服从对数正态分布，危险CRR的阈值为$0.4916 m/s^2$；在不同测点处的追尾概率风险有较为显著的差异，K2088、K2114具有较高的追尾风险水平，而不同时间段的追尾风险无明显差异；通过与事故数据的对比验证，说明基于CRR的追尾事故风险模型具有较高的适用性。

关键词　公路工程　货车追尾风险　风险概率模型　连续下坡　碰撞减速率(CRR)

0　引　言

近年来，中国提出并实行了"一带一路"倡议，在中国西南、西北地区大力建设高速公路，以适应国家经济发展的需要，但由于中国西部地区的地形与地质特点，高速公路需在较短距离上克服较大高差时，往往只能选择采用较低的设计指标，使得高速公路出现较多急弯陡坡路段，并形成连续下坡，容易引发追尾事故。据相关调查统计[1-2]，我国高速公路高速公路连续下坡路段事故频发，在事故形态中，追尾碰撞事故占有较高的比例，同时，其后果也最为严重。而连续下坡路段对大型货车的行车安全不利，更容易导致追尾事故的发生，故而提高高速公路连续下坡路段货车行驶的安全性，降低其追尾事故风险，减少我国交通事故损失与伤亡的需求是急迫的。

对于车辆追尾事故机理及其风险模型的研究方面，可以归纳为四类：

(1)对基于风险影响因素的分析：丁乃侃等[3]定义并初步界定直接和间接的追尾风险感知，并以结构方程模型探索多因素与风险的关系。刘鑫鑫[4]利用实测追尾事故数据，分别构建了追尾事故严重程度概率预测模型和追尾事故严重程度预测模型。赵杨东[5]在追尾事故的特点分析和类别界定基础上，引入高速公路追尾事故危险度的概念，提出了高速公路尾随事故和撞静止车辆危险度计算模型。Junjie Zhang等[6]探讨了驾驶行为异质性对追尾碰撞的影响，设计了模拟实验来评估跟车行为的异质性对追尾事故风险的影响。

(2)基于速度理论的追尾风险评价模型：陆斯文等[7]分析了高速公路追尾事故的机理特征，以后随车减速度临界值作为风险评价指标，计算得出了用追尾概率和能量损失来表征追尾事故风险。

(3)从空间角度建立追尾风险模型：Qiang Luo等[8]分析了安全跟车距离与各影响因素的内在关系，提出了一种改进的汽车追尾碰撞模型，然后分析了各因素与最小跟车距离的关系。史海燕[9]探讨了汽车追尾碰撞事故的各种因素及其机理，建立了安全车距的计算模型，分析了各种因素对车辆发生追尾事故的影响。陆斯[12]等研究了4种高速公路追尾碰撞情形，推理出其追尾风险量化指标，计算出高速公路跟驰追尾风险值并确定了其评价等级阈值范围。刘晓阳[10]探讨了追尾碰撞事故机理和诱发因素及其相关性，推导出了安全车距的计算模型，在此基础上建立各因素对车辆发生追尾概率的关系。

(4)从时间角度来研究追尾风险:Michiel M. Minderhoud 等[11]将碰撞时间 TTC(Time-To-Collision,TTC)概念引入道路交通安全分析,介绍了两个新的安全指标来计算总体安全指标值。同时,王佳丽[12]选取 TTC 作为风险替代指标,建立了大雾天气下的追尾事故风险传播模型。Sheng Dong 等[13]提出了一种基于红外摄像机(RLC)交叉口车辆追尾事故风险评估方法理论,建立了追尾风险模型来确定追尾概率。该方面的研究从多个角度切入,为高速公路连续下坡货车追尾风险的研究提供了众多可以借鉴的模型。

总而言之,高速公路追尾事故及风险研究中,主要从影响因素、速度、空间、时间四个角度中提取得到指标,再结合道路上车辆行车的不确定性,进一步得到汽车追尾事故风险模模型。总结以上两方面研究可以发现,现有的汽车追尾事故风险研究中缺乏针对性地研究连续下坡的货车追尾风险。为此本文提出一种基于实测车头时距与速度数据的货车追尾风险模型,将 CRR(碰撞减速率)作为车辆追尾风险指标,建立连续下坡路段货车追尾概率风险模型,希望针对性地对连续下坡路段货车的追尾事故风险做出分析,有益于山区高速公路追尾事故风险的研究。

1 连续下坡路段货车追尾事故风险分析

追尾事故按参与车辆的多少及其车辆类型可进行分类,本文针对大—大型车辆两车追尾事故进行研究,对于大型车辆的多车碰撞,由于其过程与致因复杂多样,本文暂不做研究。

由于拖乌山北坡交通特管区内实行严格的分车道分车型限速措施,管内路段实行客、货车分道行驶,左侧为客车道(限速 60~80km/h),右侧为货车道(限速 60~70km/h),使得后车无法实行超车行为,只能在单一车道上保持跟随前车行驶的状态,此时后车处于一种非自由行驶状态。有研究表明[14],从安全角度考虑,在车辆在单一车道上排队行驶时,后随车辆应当满足车速条件及间距条件,在速度离散较大的、车辆处于跟驰状态时,速差较大,前后车间距较近,有较大发生追尾事故的可能性。而高速公路各路段上,行驶车辆的速度与间距往往具有复杂性与不确定性,其影响着不利事件——追尾事故发生的可能性大小,这符合风险问题的研究特点[15],可以用通过风险分析来进行研究。

本文研究连续下坡路段货车的追尾事故风险,结合风险分析的基本原理,将此风险定义为在连续下坡路段发生两车追尾事故的可能性大小;结合安全跟车行驶的速度条件及间距条件的研究,确定以两车的速度以及后随车的车头时距作为风险影响因素,通过对两个风险影响因素分析、处理及组合,研究其不确定性,进行具体情景(连续下坡路段货车追尾事故)、不确定意义下风险的量化分析。

2 数据准备和处理

拖乌山北坡交通特管区,位于雅西高速菩萨岗服务区至石棉 51km 长下坡范围内,起于菩萨岗服务区附近(K2119),止于楠桠停车区附近(K2083),全长 36km,由于连续下坡距离较长且平均纵坡较大,且行车环境较为复杂,存在较大的交通安全隐患。

2.1 数据来源

2.1.1 高清卡口系统

高清卡口系统运用视频检测方式,通过抓拍高清图片来识别车辆行驶轨迹,并对车辆行驶轨迹进行记录,保存在服务器数据库中;然后在视频中通过照片的形式显示车辆的通过时间、行驶速度、行驶方向、车牌号码、地点等信息,为道路安全管理方法的研究与实施提供支持[16]。

2.1.2 测点信息

据不完全事故信息统计,2013—2018 年菩萨岗服务区至石棉 51km 长下坡范围内,在事故多发点安装了 4 处高清卡口系统,4 处高清卡口附近的百万车公里事故率为 0.7755 次·百万$^{-1}$·km^{-1},而 51km 内路段百万车公里事故率为 0.3594 次·百万$^{-1}$·km^{-1},前者百万车公里事故率为后者的两倍以上,可见拖乌山北坡交通特管区范围为该处连续下坡事故多发路段。

采用的数据为 2020 年 2 月 23 日—3 月 22 日期间乌托山北坡交通特管区内四处高清卡口的过车数

据,测点桩号分别为 K2084、K2088、K2110、K2114,具体布置信息见表1。

高清卡口测点位置信息　　　　　　　　　　　　　　　表1

测点桩号	纵坡(%)	平面线形	距顶坡距离(km)
K2084	-2.8	R347—R∞	35
K2088	-2.8	R560—R620—R∞	31
K2110	-3.995	R650—R∞	9
K2114	-4.003	R420—R460—R870	5

2.2 数据分析与风险指标描述

2.2.1 数据分析

本研究通过四个高清卡口测点的过车数据,共收集了 78219 组(K2084:10673 组、K2088:30932 组、K2110:20653 组、K2114:15961 组)包括货车速度、经过时间、车牌号及车辆类型等信息的有效数据,并对由南向北下坡路段大货车的速度以及通过时间进行了分析处理;结合特管区连续下坡车辆追尾风险分析,考虑其速度破坏条件及间距条件,选取大货车的速度及车头时距作为追尾风险的影响因素,并对其进行了筛选,过程如下:

由于拖乌山北坡交通特管区实行严格的分车道分车型行车管理措施,货车驾驶员们普遍采取了较慢的行驶速度,在对速度数据进行分析之后发现,四个测点的总体速度分布情况较为一致,各个时间段的分布情况变化不大,速度处于 40~70km/h 的速度数据的平均占比为 96.47%;而对于车头时距数据,当车头时距较大时,由于两车距离较远,前导车驾驶行为不对后随车辆的行驶产生影响,此时辆车处于自由驾驶状态,而非跟驰状态,车辆发生追尾事故的可能性小并且与速度和车头时距的相关性不强。对于车辆跟驰状态的判断目前研究的结论不一,部分研究得出的结论是当车头时距小于或等于 5s 时车辆处于跟驰状态[17]。综上所述,本研究对处理所得到数据的筛选条件为:

(1)车辆速度在 40~70km/h;

(2)车头时距小于或等于 5s。并以筛选出的车辆速度及车头时距数据为基础进行连续下坡货车追尾概率风险指标的定义及模型的建立。

2.2.2 风险指标描述

通过分析及筛选得到的速度以及车头时距数据及每辆车经过测点时的行驶车速,定义风险分析指标——碰撞减速率(Collision Reduction Rate,CRR):

CRR 表示了前后车辆在一个车头时距的时间间隔内(假设一车做匀速运动,另一车做匀变速运动),后车加速(或前车减速)使两车达到相等速度所需要的平均加速度,其值越大,后车(或前车)所采取的加速(或制动)操作空间就越大,对驾驶员来说操作空间越大,故而追尾事故风险越小;反之,追尾事故风险越大。CRR 能综合考虑了车速条件及间距条件的不确定性,可作为跟驰状态下表征车辆追尾风险的综合评价指标,故而选取 CRR 作为连续下坡路段货车追尾风险分析指标,其计算公式如下:

$$\mathrm{CRR} = \frac{\Delta V_i}{TH_i} \quad (1)$$

式中:CRR——碰撞减速率,m/s²;

ΔV_i——前后车速差,km/s;

TH_i——前后车车头时距,s。

在 CRR 指标的计算中,当 $\Delta V_i < 0$ 时(后车速度小于前车速度),两车间距在逐渐变大,后车没有逼近前车的趋势,因此本文只选取 $\Delta V_i > 0$ 的 CRR 数据,观测 CRR 样本个数分布信息如下:263(K2084)、2228(K2088)、225(K2110)、851(K2114)。

3 CRR 阈值及连续下坡路段追尾事故风险模型

3.1 CRR 阈值的确定

CRR 表示前后车辆在一个车头时距的时间间隔内（假设一车做匀速运动，另一车做匀变速运动），后车加速（或前车减速）使两车达到相等速度所需要的平均加速度，不同的阈值代表的危险性也不一样，故而需要先确定 CRR 的阈值（图1）。

分别采用正态分布、对数正态分布、威布尔分布对 CRR 数据的频率分布直方图进行拟合，得到各个假定分布下的分布拟合曲线，如图2所示，拟合数据结果如表2所示，当拟合优度参数 R^2 值越接近于1时，说明原数据所假定分布的拟合效果越好。通过累计比例关系图（P-P 图）（图2）进行了拟合效果的对比分析，P-P 图是根据变量的累积比例与指定分布的累积比例之间的关系所绘制的图形。通过 P-P 图可以检验数据是否符合指定的分布。当数据符合指定分布时，P-P 图中各点近似呈一条直线。分析结果如下：

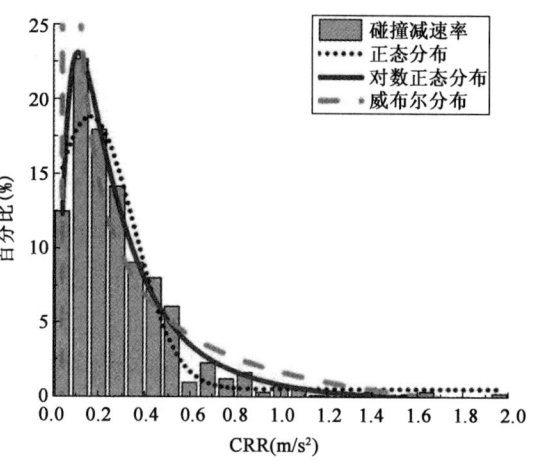

图1 CRR 直方图与拟合分布

（1）通过图2的拟合分布曲线结合表2中的拟合数据可得：数正态分布的拟合优度为0.98551，高于正态分布及威布尔分布的拟合优度（0.94461，0.92470）。

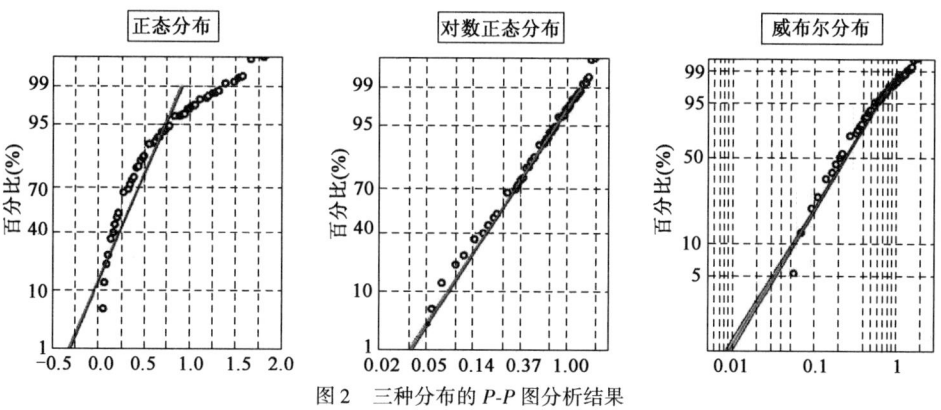

图2 三种分布的 P-P 图分析结果

CRR 数据拟合参数 表2

分布类型		参数		拟合优度 R^2
正态分布	$f(x)=\dfrac{1}{\sqrt{2\pi\sigma^2}}\exp\left(-\dfrac{(x-\mu)^2}{2\sigma^2}\right)$	μ	0.29755	0.94474
		σ	0.26399	
对数正态分布	$f(x)=\dfrac{1}{\sqrt{2\pi}}\exp\left(-\dfrac{(\ln x-\mu)^2}{2\sigma^2}\right)$	μ	−1.5212	0.98467
		σ	0.7827	
威布尔分布	$f(x)=\dfrac{b}{a}\left(\dfrac{x}{a}\right)^{b-1}\exp(-(x/a)^b)$	a	1.28569	0.92378
		b	0.3243	

注：μ 和 σ 分别为均值和标准差；a 和 b 分别为威布尔分布的比例参数和形状参数；拟合优度 R^2 的值越接近1，说明回归直线对观测值的拟合程度越好。

（2）根据拟合的对数正态分布，选取85%分位值作为追尾事故风险的 CRR 阈值（记为 CRR_{85}），其值为 0.4916 m/s² 并定义大于该阈值的 CRR 为危险 CRR 样本，危险 CRR 样本总个数为518。

3.2 基于 CRR 的追尾事故风险模型

以危险 CRR 为基础，参考碰撞潜力指数（CPI），有研究[18]表明，采用碰撞潜力指数公式（CPI）来计算后车的避免碰撞减速率(DRAC)超过最大可用减速率(MADR)的概率,能较好地识别出碰撞与非碰撞情况,且具有较高的识别精度,故而以危险 CRR 为基础,参考碰撞潜力指数(CPI)公式,提出连续下坡货车追尾事故的概率风险模型,其计算公式如下:

$$P_T = \frac{\sum_{t=0}^{N} P_r(\mathrm{CCR}_i(t) > \mathrm{CCR}_{85}) \cdot \Delta t}{T} \quad (2)$$

式中：　　　　　P_T——所取时间段 T 内的概率风险;

T——所取时间段长度$(T = N \cdot \Delta t)$, s;

$P_r(\mathrm{CCR}_i(t) > \mathrm{CCR}_{85})$——$t = i$ 时 Δt 内大于 CCR_{85} 的 CRR 样本频率。

该概率风险可以反映在连续下坡路段车辆发生追尾事故的可能性。概率风险越大,说明所取时段内,路段上逼近趋势较强的连续两车占比越大,则发生追尾事故的可能性就越大,反之则越小。

4 连续下坡路段追尾事故风险模型的应用与验证

将基于 CRR 的追尾事故模型应用于托乌山交通特管区连续下坡路段,结合所得货车 CRR 数据得出该连续下坡路段的货车追尾事故概率风险,并对结果进行显著性分析,最后以路段内事故数据对风险分析结果进行了验证。

4.1 追尾事故风险计算

根据式(4)计算得到连续下坡路段货车追尾事故概率风险,结果见表3。

追尾事故概率风险计算结果　　　　　　　　　　　　　表3

T	$P_T(\%)$				
	K2084	K2088	K2110	K2114	总体
00:00~6:00	0.000	11.163	0.000	5.556	10.889
6:00~12:00	7.094	15.327	1.515	13.492	14.850
12:00~18:00	3.421	15.541	11.301	17.178	16.103
18:00~24:00	4.167	13.994	14.502	15.147	16.198
00:00~24:00	3.670	14.006	6.830	12.843	14.510

4.2 追尾事故风险分析

追尾风险计算结果由图3所示,从图中可以看出测点 K2088 与 K2114 的追尾概率风险整体上大于其他两测点;18:00~24:00 时间段的追尾概率风险整体上最高。本文利用单因素 ANOVA 分析了四个高清卡口测点及四个时间段的概率风险是否存在差异性,结果见表4及表5。

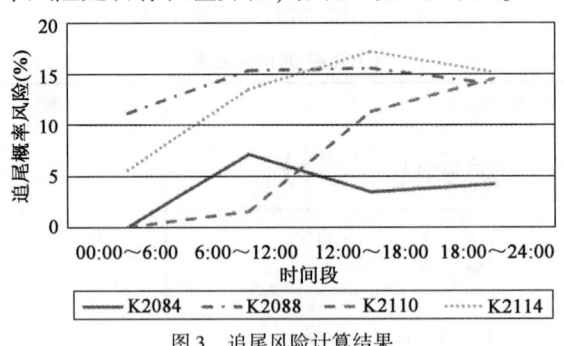

图3　追尾风险计算结果

不同时间段的追尾风险 ANOVA 结果　　　　　　　　　　　表4

时间段	追尾概率风险	
	均值	P 值
00:00~6:00	4.1798	
6:00~12:00	9.3570	0.243
12:00~18:00	11.8603	
18:00~24:00	11.9525	

不同测点的追尾风险 ANOVA 结果			表5
	追尾概率风险		
	均值	P 值	
K2084	3.6705	0.028	
K2088	14.0063		
K2110	6.8295		
K2114	12.8433		

由表4可知,12:00~18:00、18:00~24:00两时间段的概率风险均值相当,且较高,可以认为在12:00~18:00、18:00~24:00时间段内发生事故的可能性更大,但并不能说明12:00~18:00、18:00~24:00时间段的追尾风险更高。由单因素ANOVA结果可知,各个时间段下的追尾概率风险均值在显著性水平0.05下没有显著性差异($P=0.243$),及各时间段下的概率风险没有明显差异,说明四个时间段的追尾风险水平相同。

由表5可知,K2088、K2114的概率风险明显高于K2084、K2110,说明在测点K2088、K2114上发生追尾事故的可能性更大。由单因素ANOVA结果可知,各测点的追尾概率风险均值在显著性水平0.05下有显著性差异($P=0.028$),K2088、K2114具有较高的追尾风险水平。

4.3 追尾事故风险结果验证

为了验证模型计算结果的有效性,采用2013—2018年高清卡口附近追尾事故数据对其进行验证。将计算所得的追尾概率风险均值与各测点附近1km的百万车事故率进行对比验证,由计算所得各测点附近1km的百万车事故率分别为0.5288次·百万车$^{-1}$·km^{-1}、0.9518次·百万车$^{-1}$·km^{-1}、0.5640次·百万车$^{-1}$·km^{-1}、1.0575次·百万车$^{-1}$·km^{-1},对比结果如图4所示。

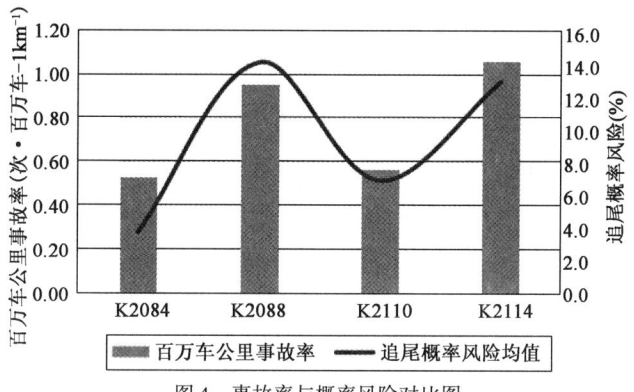

图4 事故率与概率风险对比图

由图4可以看出,测点的追尾概率风险均值与其附近百万车公里事故率的变化趋势基本相符,说明本文提出的基于CRR的追尾事故风险模型的适用性较高,能客观反映连续下坡路段追尾事故风险大小。

5 结 语

货车在连续下坡上行驶时,由于其惯性较大,刹车距离较长,容易引起追尾事故的发生,并且货车追尾事故造成的伤亡与财产损失比普通汽车追尾事故更为严重。本文利用雅西高速拖乌山北坡交通特管区长下坡路段的高清卡口所记录的大量行车数据(23205组),通过速差与车头时距计算得到碰撞减速率CRR数据,对高速公路连续下坡路段货车追尾事故风险进行研究,得到以下结论:

(1)雅西高速拖乌山北坡交通特管区长下坡路段货车CRR样本服从对数正态分布,得到85%分位值作为危险CRR阈值为0.4916m/s^2。

(2) 测点 K2088 与 K2114 的追尾概率风险整体上大于其他两测点;18:00 ~ 24:00 时间段的追尾概率风险整体上最高。

(3) 由单因素 ANOVA 结果可知,各个时间段下的追尾概率风险均值在显著性水平 0.05 下没有显著性差异,而各测点的追尾概率风险均值在显著性水平 0.05 下有显著性差异,K2088、K2114 具有较高的追尾风险水平。

(4) 通过将追尾概率风险计算结果与各测点附近的百万车公里事故率进行对比,验证说明了基于 CRR 的追尾事故风险模型具有较高的适用性,能客观反应连续下坡路段追尾事故风险大小。

本研究主要采用实测数据,分析具体路段(雅西高速拖乌山北坡交通特管区长下坡路段)的货车追尾事故风险,分析了该路段上各测点及各个时间段下的货车追尾概率风险,可为该路段交通安全管理或交安设施的设计提供参考,本文的研究方法也适用于高速公路中其他路段的行车风险研究。

同时,应用 CRR 展开风险评价存在一定的缺陷,所采用数据存在部分欠缺,在今后的研究中应采用更多测点来进行数据收集,并可对风险模型的可移植性进行研究。

参考文献

[1] 国家统计局. 中国统计年鉴 2019 [M]. 北京:中国统计出版社,2019.
[2] 公安部交通管理局. 2014 年中华人民共和国道路交通事故统计年报 [R],2015.
[3] 丁乃侃,朱顺应,王红,等. 不连续边缘标线影响追尾风险的结构方程模型[J]. 中国安全科学学报, 2017,27(03):106-110.
[4] 刘鑫鑫. 高速公路追尾事故严重程度影响因素分析及预防对策研究[D]. 长春:吉林大学,2016.
[5] 赵杨东. 高速公路追尾事故成因分析及预防对策研究[D]. 哈尔滨:哈尔滨工业大学,2007.
[6] Junjie Zhang, Yunpeng Wang, Guangquan Lu. Impact of HeteRogeneity of Car-Following Behavior on Rear-end Crash Risk[J]. Accident Analysis and Prevention,2019,125.
[7] 陆斯文,张兰芳,方守恩. 高速公路追尾机理概率分析及风险评价[J]. 同济大学学报(自然科学版),2011,39(08):1150-1154.
[8] Qiag Luo, Xiaodong Zang, Jie Yuan, et al. Research of Vehicle Rear-End Collision Model considering Multiple Factors[J]. Mathematical Problems in Engineering,2020,2020.
[9] 史海燕. 高速公路汽车追尾机理分析及仿真研究[D]. 长沙:长沙理工大学,2010.
[10] 刘晓阳. 高速公路车辆追尾概率模型及其仿真研究[D]. 长沙:长沙理工大学,2009.
[11] Michiel M. Minderhoud, Piet H. L. Bovy. Extended time-to-collision measures for road traffic safety assessment[J]. Accident Analysis and Prevention,2001,33(1).
[12] 王佳丽. 雾天高速公路连环追尾事故风险产生机理研究[D]. 北京:北京交通大学,2018.
[13] Sheng Dong, Minjie Zhang, Zhenjiang Li et al. Risk Analysis of Vehicle Rear-End Collisions at Intersections[J]. Journal of Advanced Transportation,2020,2020.
[14] 徐华中,熊和金. 汽车追尾与交通流混沌模型研究[J]. 武汉理工大学学报(交通科学与工程版), 2006(01):85-87.
[15] 黄崇福. 风险分析基本方法探讨[J]. 自然灾害学报,2011,20(05):1-10.
[16] 彭奕华. 卡口高清视频监控信息采集系统[J]. 自动化与仪器表,2017(11):84-86.
[17] 孟凡兴,张良,张伟. 驾驶员车头时距研究[J]. 工业工程与管理,2013,18(2):131-135,140.
[18] Peibo Zhao, Chris Lee. Assessing Rear-end Collision Risk of Cars and Heavy Vehicles on Freeways Using a Surrogate Safety Measure [J]. Accident Analysis and Prevention,2018,113.

公路隧道路段静态行车风险指标体系构建与评估

杨榕玮[1,2] 靳敏达[1,2] 张昆仑[1,2]

(1. 长安大学公路学院；2. 陕西省交通基础设施建设与管理数字化工程研究中心)

摘要 为减少高速公路隧道路段交通事故的发生，合理评价公路隧道行车风险程度，本文引入"静态行车风险"的概念，基于风险发生的可能性和风险事故的严重性两个方面选取了与道路、环境和管理相关的13个静态指标，构建风险评价矩阵，并提出信息量最大化/熵权法与层次分析法(AHP)—逼近理想点法(TOPSIS)—秩和比法(RSR)。首先，利用信息量最大法对定量指标定权、熵权法对定性指标定权；进而结合AHP法构建评价矩阵，引入TOPSIS法计算风险综合评价指标值以及相对接近度值；最后，将RSR法分档标准融入风险等级划分，以相对接近度值表征风险程度，进行分级评价。以西南某山区高速公路隧道为例，对提出的方法进行验证，结果表明，该公路隧道路段静态行车风险发生的可能性为Ⅲ级，严重性为Ⅲ级，综合风险等级为Ⅲ级，评价结果与2012—2018年内某山区高速隧道路段13.5%事故率相符合，评价模型可表征某山区公路隧道路段的静态行车风险状况。

关键词 道路工程 静态行车风险 风险评价 TOPSIS-RSR法

0 引言

公路隧道环境单调，行车空间封闭、安全性低，在隧道行车过程中，隧道驾驶环境(照度过渡、车道宽度、隧道壁高度、驾驶空间、视距)不断变化，越靠近隧道出入口，照度过渡越来越剧烈，车道宽度越来越小，隧道壁高度越来越高，驾驶空间越来越小，视距范围越来越小，导致风险因素具有更强的随机性、不确定性和模糊性，一旦发生交通事故，对营救和交通组织都极为不利，极易引发二次交通事故[1]。山区高速公路隧道交通运行环境直接影响着隧道所在路段整体交通状况和交通出行者的生命财产安全，因此，隧道路段静态行车风险评价具有十分重要的意义。鉴于此，本文引入"静态行车风险"以描述道路特征以及道路所构成的三维环境对行车安全的影响。

公路风险评估是以公路基础、交通基础和交通条件等为基础对交通事故发生概率和可能严重程度评估，以量化分析公路交通运行风险[2]。对于隧道路段行车风险分级评价，国内外学者在此方面展开了较多研究，但涉及高速公路隧道静态风险分级的研究较少。国外学者对隧道路段风险评价侧重于评价方法的研究，主要包括定性和定量两类方法。Helai Huang等[3]和Bassa等[4]考虑线形、驾驶行为、车辆特征和环境因素，利用分类和回归树法研究隧道内事故严重程度的交互影响，后者更着重于隧道内火灾的影响，均缺乏对隧道内行车风险的研究；Ondrej Nyvlt等[5]结合层次结构模型和模糊综合法分区段评估隧道风险，Vashitz G.等[6]考虑通风、照明、消防等因素，基于数值模拟技术和逻辑数学构建安全风险评估模型，但均缺乏对道路几何条件的考虑；Audun Borg等[7]构建定量贝叶斯网络模型评价公路隧道风险，通过试验确定隧道长度和曲率关键性影响因素，但未进行具体的风险评价分级；Xiaobo Qu等[8]基于事件树、故障树和结果估计模型，建立定量风险评估模型，对各隧道段进行风险评价。以上研究多基于既有的模型进行风险评价，对定量、定性风险影响因素的区分和综合评价欠缺层次性考虑，且所构建模型往往忽视了各指标间的相互作用对评价结果所造成的影响。

国内对隧道路段风险评价侧重于研究模型的构建，主要包括主观性高的"功能驱动"型和客观性高的"差异驱动"型。前者一般根据专家对各影响因素相对重要程度的认识来确定指标权重，进而建模。

基金项目：国家重点研发计划项目重大自然灾害监测预警与防范(2020YFC1512005)。

余鹏程等[1]基于基本指数、设计指数、施工指数和风险损失指数改进肯特指数法模型评价隧道风险等级；陈桂福[9]通过专家群策和层次分析法，得到了山区高速公路隧道风险模型；袁家伟[10]分别基于现场调查分析、层次分析、模糊综合评价和可拓综合法对四川省高速公路隧道进行了安全风险评价，以契合度分析各类方法的优劣性；于福华等[11]基于模糊数学和层次分析法，建立特长隧道风险评价体系；邓涛等[12]基于隧道路段事故的致因，应用物元分析法和集值统计模型研究隧道风险；易富君等[13]提出基于集成云模型和物元分析理论的公路隧道群运营安全性综合评价方法；贺志勇等[14]基于多级模糊综合评价模型，建立隧道结构安全状况与隧道整体结果评价之间的线性代换关系，对高速公路隧道风险进行评价。以上研究在构建隧道风险评价模型时存在两方面不足：其一，主观性较强，评价结果可能因主观偏好而偏差较大；其二，对风险影响因素的类别和相互性缺乏考虑。因此，该类模型应用局限性较大。后者主要根据数据之间的关系来确定指标权重，具有较强的数学理论依据。马跃、郑越之通过仿真试验建立了多元线性回归模型，以平均风险水平作为衡量标准建立隧道入口风险评价标准[15]；郭延永等考虑定性、定量指标的结合，构建基于灰色熵权聚类的山区高速公路隧道风险评价模型[16]；杨健等考虑评价指标的模糊性和约束性，提出基于改进 DSmT 的综合评价方法[17]。以上研究在构建隧道风险评价模型时对数据的客观性进行了考虑，但评价方法较为单一，易导致风险评价结果准确性不可靠。

在风险评价模型构建过程中，各影响因素之间可能存在一定的相关性。"功能驱动"方法主观性高，"差异驱动"方法客观性较高，两者均考虑了各个影响因素在各被评价对象间的变异程度，而对指标间的相互影响、定性和定量指标的区分定权欠缺考虑，且未对动、静态风险进行区分。因此，本文以高速公路隧道静态风险评价为目标，首先分析隧道路段的静态风险源（区别于交通流以及驾驶员驾驶行为等动态风险，静态风险一般指隧道中静态因素带来的可能风险，诸如隧道长度、曲线半径、转角、纵坡坡度、洞口朝向等几何参数），并基于风险导致交通事故的可能性和严重性构建风险评价矩阵；然后基于道路、环境、管理三方面构建评价指标体系，以信息量最大化定权归一化的方法确定定量指标的权重，以熵权 AHP 法确定定性指标权重；最后综合风险可能性和风险事故严重性并利用 TOPSIS-RSR 法进行排序和合理分档，构建隧道路段的静态风险评价模型。

1 静态风险评价指标体系构建

1.1 风险源分析

风险源是发生交通事故的必要条件，根据风险理论中危险源的分类，道路交通危险源可以分为作为载体的车辆故障与失控、能量或物质约束或限制措施被破坏（包括人的失误、物的障碍、环境因素）和管理缺陷、决策失误三类[18]。每一起交通事故在发生的过程中，三类风险源相互依存、相辅相成。分析静态风险源，可知第二类风险源（能量或物质约束或限制措施被破坏）主要包括道路缺陷、驾驶员失误和不利环境，在隧道路段中表现为小半径曲线、长大纵坡、侧向余宽不足、照明强度不足、通风不畅、交通安全标志不完善等；第三类风险源包括工作人员对交通管理缺陷和决策失误[19]，主要表现为隧道路段的救援机制、管理制度不合理等。两类风险源均可形成第一类风险源，三者与交通事故的关系如图1所示。

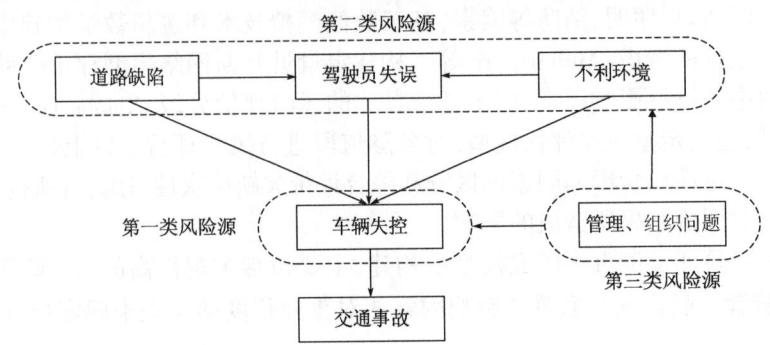

图 1　风险源与交通事故关系图

由于多种多样的因素会增加隧道风险概率,进而导致隧道内交通事故的发生,为了识别可能带来严重后果的风险源,并构建风险评价模型,本文收集并分析了 474 起某山区高速公路隧道交通事故及其静态影响因素。统计各事故发生地点的圆曲线半径、曲线转角、纵坡和坡长等道路信息以及对应隧道的长度信息。

1.1.1 隧道长度

某山区高速公路全线共 6 座短隧道,3 座中隧道,13 座长隧道,2 座特长隧道。以每公里事故数为标准,分析隧道长度与事故率的关系,如图 2 所示。

由图 2 可知,短隧道及中长隧道事故率基本一致,约为 8.3 起/km;特长隧道事故率较高,约为 11 起/km。隧道长度与事故率之间无显著变化关系,隧道长度对于事故率的区分程度较低,因此隧道长度指标不宜作为风险评价指标。

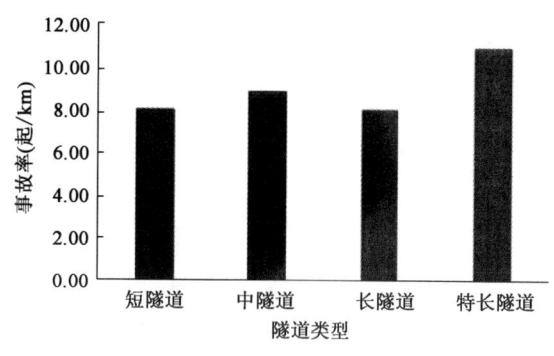

图 2　事故率与隧道类型关系图

1.1.2 圆曲线半径

依据圆曲线半径及事故数分析不同半径下该指标与公里事故数的关系,如图 3 所示。

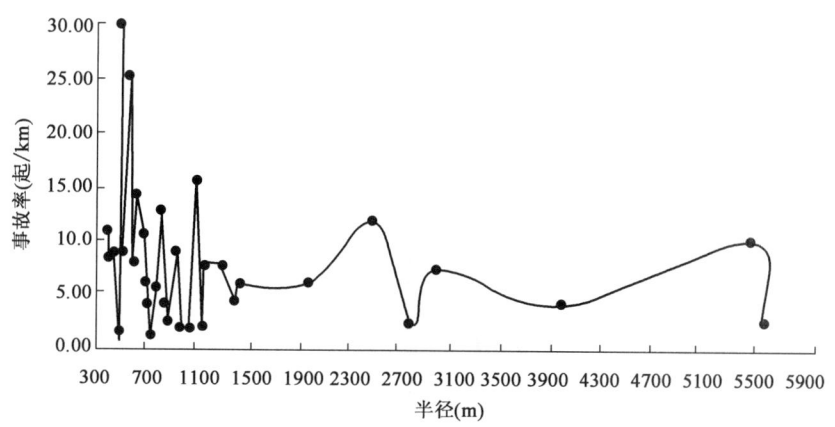

图 3　事故率与圆曲线半径关系图

易知,曲线半径对事故率影响较大。半径在 400～1100m 时,事故率波动较大,高值达 30 起/km,低值为 1 起/km;半径大于 1100m 时,事故率较低,且相对稳定。因此,曲线半径与事故率的相关性较高,可作为评价指标。

1.1.3 曲线转角

依据路线转角及事故数计算不同角度下该指标与公里事故数的关系,如图 4 所示。

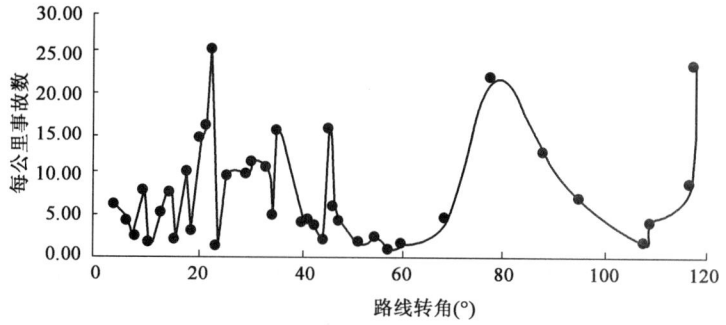

图 4　事故率与路线转角关系图

研究表明,路线转角在45°~60°为宜,该范围内事故相对率低。分析图4易知,路线转角在较大或较小时事故率较高,转角适中时,事故率较低,相关性较高。路线转角可作为风险评价指标。

1.1.4 纵坡和坡长

纵面线形对事故率的影响主要体现在纵坡和坡长的综合作用。单一指标纵坡或坡长,难以体现纵断面指标对事故的影响,上下坡事故率与纵坡、坡长关系如图5、图6所示。

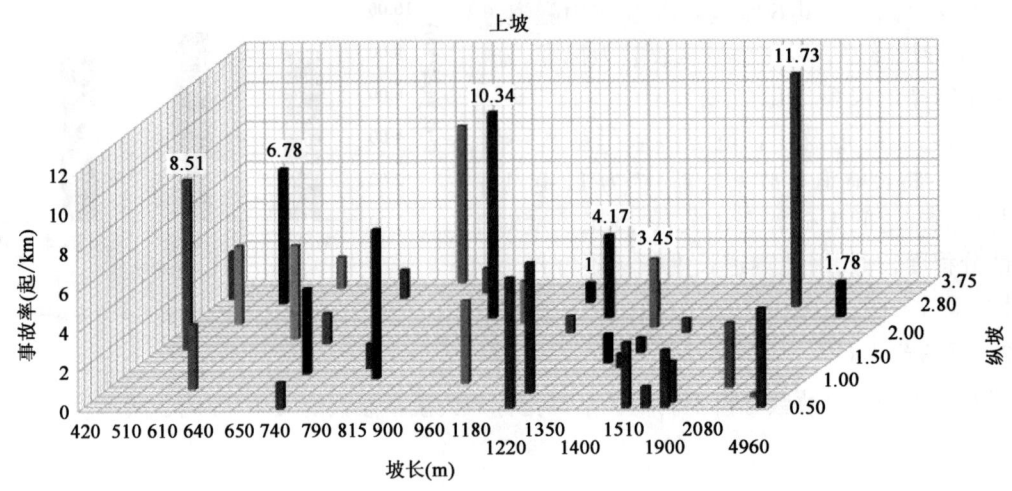

图5 上坡事故率与纵坡、坡长关系图

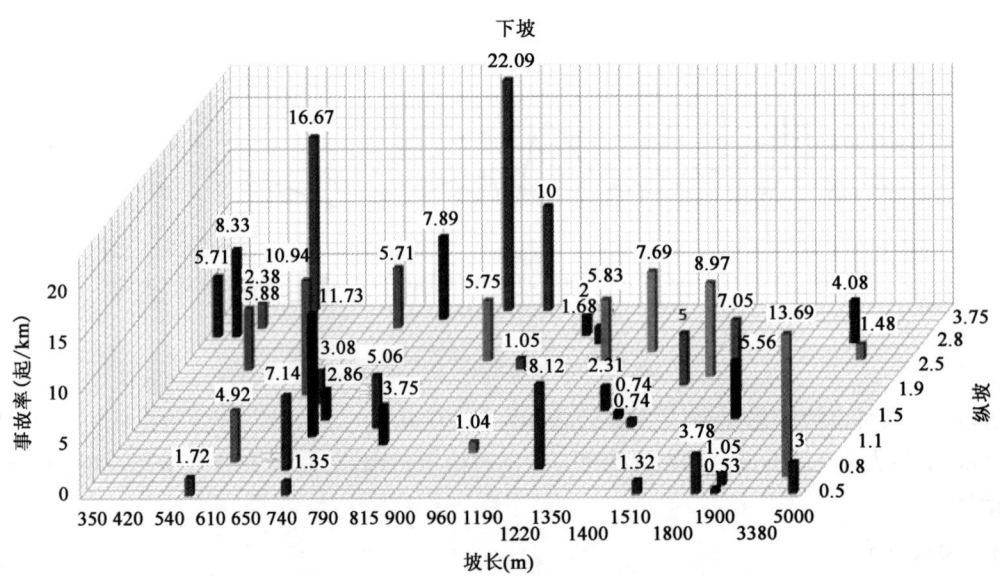

图6 下坡事故率与纵坡、坡长关系图

上下坡的事故分布趋势相差较大,下坡事故率大于上坡。事故主要集中在坡度大、坡长处,最大值达10.34起/km(纵坡3.75%、坡长1000m)。下坡时,纵坡对事故率的影响较坡长更为明显。因此,纵坡、坡长可作为风险评价指标。

1.2 风险评价体系

隧道路段静态行车风险由道路行车条件和环境决定,风险发生的概率以及风险发生后造成的影响分别取决于交通事故发生的可能性以及严重性两个方面:平纵线形等定量指标以及行车环境等定性指标均可直接造成行车风险,作为可能性指标,记为 P;隧道长度、管理制度和救援机制等因素则会加剧风险严重程度,作为严重性指标,记为 L。结合交通事故的分布特征及风险源分析选取风险影响因素的评价指标。将风险可能性和严重性轻到重分为5个等级,构建风险矩阵 R(表1)。

风 险 矩 阵 R   表1

严重性(L)	可能性(P)				
	Ⅰ级	Ⅱ级	Ⅲ级	Ⅳ级	Ⅴ级
Ⅰ级	Ⅰ级	Ⅰ级	Ⅱ级	Ⅱ级	Ⅲ级
Ⅱ级	Ⅰ级	Ⅱ级	Ⅱ级	Ⅲ级	Ⅳ级
Ⅲ级	Ⅱ级	Ⅱ级	Ⅲ级	Ⅳ级	Ⅳ级
Ⅳ级	Ⅱ级	Ⅲ级	Ⅳ级	Ⅳ级	Ⅴ级
Ⅴ级	Ⅲ级	Ⅳ级	Ⅳ级	Ⅴ级	Ⅴ级

从单维方向看,风险程度随可能性、严重性的增加而增加。从整体上看,R 矩阵可划分为5个等级,风险程度由低到高依次为Ⅰ~Ⅴ级,左上角区域风险最低,右下角区域风险最高。

1.2.1 可能性影响因素指标

研究表明,驾驶员在行驶过程中,习惯于视线平顺且合乎思维[20],且交通事故约有1/3都是发生在曲线上,其事故率明显高于直线段[21]。随着平曲线曲率增大,事故发生的频率逐渐降低[22];纵坡增大时,上坡导致车速度降低,烟雾的排放量增加,车辆废气排放量增大,易导致洞内视距降低,影响驾驶员生理,进而诱发交通事故;下坡则易影响驾驶员心理,进而导致事故。结合上文分析,圆曲线半径指标和路线转角指标与隧道事故率之间存在较高的显著性,故作为可能性影响因素指标。

路面抗滑、隧道通风、照明以及安全设施等行车环境指标易增加隧道路段的行车风险。潮湿状态下水泥路面的摩擦系数仅为正常水平的40%,极易引发交通事故。隧道照明是为减小或消除驾驶员对隧道内外道路因光线的明暗而引起视觉上的差异,通风的目的是为了把隧道内的有害气体或污染物质的浓度降至允许浓度以下,以保证汽车行驶的安全性和舒适性[23];隧道内轮廓标、反光环以及里程指示牌等指示标志也影响着行车安全,标志完善程度不足极易增加行车风险。因此,以上影响因素可作为风险评价的可能性指标。

1.2.2 严重性影响指标

严重性指交通事故发生可能导致的后果严重程度。上文分析表明,隧道类型与事故率并无明显区别,即隧道长度并不适合作为风险发生的可能性指标。考虑交通事故发生在长或特长隧道路段中间区域,道路交通疏导和受伤人员救援的难度大幅提高,加剧交通事故的严重性,故选取该指标作为严重性影响因素指标之一;隧道路段提供的侧向余宽远小于正常路段,洞内突发事故时若侧向余宽不足极易造成二次事故;安全设施是保证隧道路段车辆安全行驶的必要物质条件,是减少、减轻交通事故的有力措施,完善的管理制度和救援机制,可最大化的减轻事故损失和伤亡,降低严重程度[24]。故将隧道长度、侧向余宽、安全设施完善程度、管理制度和救援机制等作为交通事故严重性影响因素指标。构建隧道路段静态行车风险评价指标体系如图7所示。

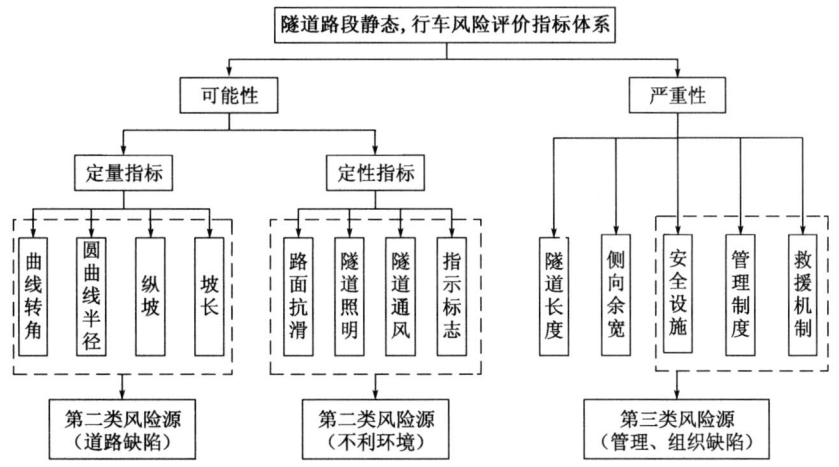

图7 隧道路段静态行车风险评价指标体系

2 静态风险评价模型构建

2.1 风险评价方法

本文结合隧道路段行车风险因素的复杂性、不确定性和综合性等特点,并考虑评价方法的适用性,提出基于信息量最大化定权和熵权 AHP 的 TOPSIS-RSR 综合方法对隧道路段的静态行车风险进行评价。具体模型框架如图 8 所示。

图8 隧道路段风险评价模型

层次分析法(AHP)的优势在于可反复统一处理决策中的定量与定性问题,综合考虑隧道路段的定量、定性评价指标对风险的影响。信息量最大化定权的方法可降低评价时主观性的影响。逼近理想点排序法(TOPSIS)是一种逼近理想解的排序方法[25],在构造初步决策矩阵并统一量纲后,找出有限方案中的最优方案和最劣方案,计算各评价对象与最优方案和最劣方案的距离,获得各评价方案与最优方案的相对接近程度并排序,以此作为评价方案优劣的依据。秩和比法(RSR)对各指标进行编秩,运用参数统计分析的概念和方法,确定 RSR 分布。基于信息量最大化定权/熵权 AHP 的 TOPSIS-RSR 综合评价法,对于定量指标采用信息量最大化与 AHP 组合定权的方式,既能考虑指标间的相关性,提高客观性,又能避免数据不合理造成权重客观性的偏离;对于定性指标,采用熵权 AHP 法可较大程度降低主观性的影响。TOPSIS 法与 RSR 法相结合,一方面可克服传统的 TOPSIS 法在确定评价指标的权重时主观因素的影响,反映各指标之间差异及优点,另一方面可利用 RSR 法来解决 TOPSIS 法不能对评价对象进行合理分级的问题[26]。

2.2 模型构建

2.2.1 评价矩阵

对量化指标,利用指标间的相互关系计算相关系数,最大化信息量确定权重。由专家打分法确定各指标的最大值、最小值以及平均值,规范化构建初始评价矩阵,进而构建规范加权矩阵。对定性指标,依据风险指标评分表,采用专家打分法,取最大值、最小值以及平均值,建立初始风险评价矩阵,规范化后利用熵权法确定指标权重,并构建加权矩阵。根据 AHP 评价指标体系,依据 Saaty 九级标度表,建立初始风险评价矩阵 X。

$$X = \begin{bmatrix} x_{11} & \cdots & x_{1n} \\ \vdots & \ddots & \vdots \\ x_{31} & \cdots & x_{3n} \end{bmatrix} \tag{1}$$

式中:x——初始评价矩阵;

x_{ij}——风险评价矩阵中第 j 个风险指标的第 i 个值,i 取值为 1、2、3。1 代表专家打分法最小值、2 代表专家打分法平均值、3 代表专家打分法最大值;评价 $j = 1, 2, \cdots, n$。

对初始评价矩阵进行量纲一化得到矩阵 Y,具体公式如下:

$$y_{ij} = \frac{x_{ij} - x_{\min}}{x_{\max} - x_{\min}} \tag{2}$$

式中:y_{ij}——矩阵 X 中对应的 x_{ij} 量纲一化后的值。

2.2.2 权重确定

从数据分析角度考虑量化指标间的相关性和冲突性,进行定权。以标准差法为基础,首先,计算第 i 个评价指标内部的对比强度,由标准差 δ_i 表示,δ_i 值越大,表明该指标在不同被评价对象之间的变异程度越大,信息量越大;然后,计算多个指标间的冲突强度,由指标间的相关系数 r_{ij} 表示,r_{ij} 值越小,代表指标

间的相关性越小,冲突强度越大,信息量越大。设第 i 个指标所包含的信息量为 E_i,其计算公式为

$$E_i = \delta_i \cdot \sum_{j=1}^{m}(1 - r_{ij}) \tag{3}$$

通过对信息量 E_i 进行归一化处理,得到各指标的风险系数值 w_i,计算公式为

$$w_i = E_i / \sum_{j=1}^{m} E_i \tag{4}$$

为了消除各指标量纲不统一的影响,首先通过线性函数变换对各指标进行标准化处理,计算公式见式(2)。根据标准化处理后的值,计算得到各指标的标准差 δ、相关系数;根据信息量最大化定权方法计算量化指标的权重 w,构造主对角权重矩阵 W_1。

对于定性指标的权重确定,为避免主观因素的影响,在 AHP 法基础上引入熵的概念。熵权法可以避免指标间的差异过小造成的分析困难的问题,其思路是评价对象在单指标上变异程度越大,则该指标相应的越重要,计算步骤为

$$a_{ij} = (1 + y_{ij}) / \sum_{k=1}^{m}(1 + y_{kj}) \tag{5}$$

$$H_j = \frac{1}{\ln(n)} \sum_{i=1}^{m} a_{ij} \ln(a_{ij}) \tag{6}$$

式中:a_{ij}——第 j 个风险指标的第 i 个值对应的影响系统熵值变化的概率;$i = 1,2,3;j = 1,2,\cdots,n$。

记第 j 个指标的数据离散程度为 g_i,则 $g_i = 1 - H_j$。若给定的指标值的差异越大,则其信息量越大,重要程度也越高。故可用熵测度来表征的第 j 个指标的权重,确定出各指标的权重后,以它们为主对角线上的元素构造主对角矩阵——指标权重矩阵[27]。各评价指标权重计算公式见式(7),权重矩阵记为 W_2。

$$\omega_j = (1 - H_j) / (n - \sum_{j=1}^{n} H_j) \tag{7}$$

2.2.3 规范化加权矩阵

根据信息量最大化定权和熵权的方法计算得到的主对角权重矩阵 W_1、W_2,与矩阵 Y 进行加权处理,得到规范化加权矩阵 V,其元素计算公式为

$$v_{ij} = y_{ij} \cdot w_j \tag{8}$$

2.2.4 确定正、负理想解

令 V^+ 表示正理想解(最优方案),由参评样本中的最大值构成;V^- 表示负理想解(最劣方案),由参评样本中的最小值构成。正、负理想解分别为

$$V^+ = (V_1^+, V_2^+, \cdots, V_n^+), V^- = (V_1^-, V_2^-, \cdots, V_n^-) \tag{9}$$

其中,$V_j^+ = \max_{1 < i < m}\{y_{ij}\}$,$V_j^- = \min_{1 < i < m}\{y_{ij}\}$。

2.2.5 计算评价体系中各指标值与正理想解和负理想解的距离 D_{i+}、D_{i-} 以及与正理想解的相对接近度 C_i[27]

距离计算见式(10),相对接近度计算见式(11)。

$$D_j^+ = \sqrt{\sum_{i=1}^{n}(V_{ij} - V_j^+)^2}, D_j^- = \sqrt{\sum_{i=1}^{n}(V_{ij} - V_j^-)^2} \tag{10}$$

$$C_j = \frac{D_j^-}{D_j^+ + D_j^-} \tag{11}$$

相对接近度可表征道路风险水平,其值越接近正理想解,则交通风险程度越低;反之,则越高。

2.2.6 计算秩和比值 R_i,确定 RSR 分布

矩阵行/列秩次的平均值称为秩和比,为非参数计量,具有 0~1 区间连续变量特征。基于秩和比法的统计分析,其基本思想是在矩阵中通过秩转换,获得量纲化 R_i 的统计量,以 R_i 值对评价对象的优劣进

行排序。TOPSIS 法用于排序的相对接近程度 C_i 值在 0~1,分布同秩和比法中的 R_i,用 C_i 值替代秩和比 R_i,并以此分档。根据 R_i 值大小进行分组,列出不同组段的频数 f、累计频数 f' 得到平均秩次 R 和 R/n 值,再求出对应概率单位值 y。

2.2.7 确定 RSR 回归方程

以 y 作为自变量,以 R_i 为因变量进行回归分析,方程为:

$$R = \alpha + \beta y$$

式中:R——秩和比的统计回归值;
y——概率单位;
α、β——回归方程相关参数。

2.2.8 RSR 值分档

按 RSR 的合理分档方法[28],根据标准正态差 μ 划分为 5 档,对评价高速公路交通安全风险水平进行归档。各档对应的百分位数及概率单位见表 2。

风险分级表　　　　表2

百分位 p	概率单位 y	风险等级	描述
3.593 以下	3.2 以下	V 级	风险程度高
3.593~27.425	3.2~4.4	IV 级	风险程度较高
27.425~72.575	4.4~5.6	III 级	风险程度一般
72.575~96.407	4.6~6.8	II 级	风险程度较低
96.407 以上	6.8 以上	I 级	风险程度低

3 案　　例

本文选取某山区高速公路 24 座隧道进行实例分析。对风险源导致风险发生的可能性指标和严重性指标分别进行风险等级的判定。对可能性影响因素指标中的定量指标和定性指标分别建立初始风险评价矩阵 X_{11} 和 X_{12},对严重性影响因素指标建立风险评价矩阵 X_2。进行量纲一化得到规范化矩阵 Y_{11}、Y_{12} 和 Y_2。

$$Y_{11} = \begin{bmatrix} 0 & 0.6 & 0 & 0 \\ 0.4 & 0.7 & 0.6 & 0.5 \\ 0.6 & 1 & 0 & 0.8 \end{bmatrix}, Y_{12} = \begin{bmatrix} 0.2 & 0.2 & 0 & 0 \\ 0.6 & 0.5 & 0.3 & 0.5 \\ 1 & 0.8 & 0.8 & 1 \end{bmatrix}$$

$$Y_2 = \begin{bmatrix} 0.2 & 0 & 0.2 & 0.2 & 0.2 \\ 0.4 & 0.2 & 0.6 & 0.4 & 0.5 \\ 1 & 0.7 & 1 & 0.7 & 0.8 \end{bmatrix}$$

结合某山区高速公路事故数据,对可能性影响因素指标中的定量指标进行权重确定,权重值依次为 0.2817、0.3200、0.1749 和 0.2233。利用熵权法对可能性影响因素指标中的定性指标和严重性指标进行权重矩阵确定,并结合初始评价矩阵计算得到规范加权矩阵。对于可能性影响因素指标中的定量与定性指标进行均权处理,即各占 0.5 的权重,修正各指标权重,计算可得规范加权矩阵 V_1 和 V_2。

$$V_1 = \begin{bmatrix} 0 & 0.0564 & 0 & 0 & 0.0181 & 0.0129 & 0 & 0 \\ 0.0693 & 0.0939 & 0.0525 & 0.0521 & 0.0604 & 0.0365 & 0.0467 & 0.0918 \\ 0.0960 & 0.1409 & 0.0875 & 0.0894 & 0.1087 & 0.0643 & 0.1168 & 0.1739 \end{bmatrix}$$

$$V_2 = \begin{bmatrix} 0.0428 & 0 & 0.0394 & 0.0179 & 0.0279 \\ 0.1069 & 0.0452 & 0.1314 & 0.0387 & 0.0835 \\ 0.2566 & 0.1550 & 0.2365 & 0.0715 & 0.1393 \end{bmatrix}$$

基于规范加权矩阵求得正理想解和负理想解,计算各评价指标与最优方案和最劣方案的距离,以及最优值的相对接近度,结合秩和比法对相对接近度进行分析,根据其值大小分布计算得出对应概率单位值,如表3所示。

相对接近度分布及概率单位值　　表3

指标类型	指标	D^+	D^-	C	f	$f(R)$	$P(R/n \times 100\%)$	y
可能性影响因素指标	曲线转角	0.0877	0.2056	0.7010	1	1	12.5	3.84
	纵坡	0.0942	0.6887	0.6887	1	2	25	4.31
	坡长	0.0969	0.1573	0.6189	1	3	37.5	4.69
	指示标志	0.1923	0.1966	0.5056	1	4	50	5.00
	路面抗滑	0.1027	0.0964	0.4843	1	5	62.5	5.36
	隧道照明	0.0765	0.0623	0.4488	1	6	75	5.70
	半径	0.1098	0.0635	0.3664	1	7	87.5	6.16
	隧道通风	0.1362	0.0603	0.2847	1	8	96.9*	7.08
严重性影响因素指标	救援机制	0.1056	0.2596	0.7108	1	1	20	4.17
	安全设施	0.1864	0.2175	0.5385	1	2	40	4.71
	管理制度	0.0628	0.0575	0.4780	1	3	60	5.31
	隧道长度	0.2610	0.1952	0.4279	1	4	80	5.82
	侧向余宽	0.1899	0.0986	0.3417	1	5	95*	6.83

* 按$[1-(1/4n)\times100\%]$校正。

以概率单位值y为自变量,C值为因变量对可能性影响因素指标和严重性影响因素指标求得回归方程分别为$R_1=-0.1349y+1.2259$和$R_2=-0.1283y+1.1882$,相关性系数r_2分别为0.9502和0.9049,F值分别为162.5和110.5,p值均远小于0.01,故两回归方程均有意义。

以各指标的均值作为风险综合指数,对某山区高速公路隧道路段总体静态风险程度进行评价。计算可得R_1值为0.5184,风险发生的可能性程度为一般;R_2值为0.4995,风险发生后的严重性程度为一般;以指标的最优值作为风险综合指数,计算可得R_1值为0.7079,R_2值为0.6532,可能性与严重性程度均为一般;以指标的最劣值作为风险综合指数,计算可得R_1值为0.2708,风险发生的可能性程度较高,R_2值为0.3120,风险发生后的严重性程度为一般。综上,该山区公路隧道路段总体风险程度为Ⅲ级,与7年内该山区高速隧道路段事故率为13.5%相符合。

通过计算风险发生的可能性与严重性两个维度的秩和比值,合理划分道路隧道的风险程度,利用风险判断矩阵标定确定隧道路段风险程度为Ⅲ级,即风险程度为一般,处于可接受状态。

4 结语

(1)综合考虑信息量最大化定权法和熵权法 AHP-TOPSIS-RSR 法对高速公路隧道路段静态行车风险进行综合评价,并基于可能性和严重性构建风险评价矩阵。综合评价法在克服各类方法不足的同时保留了其优点,拓宽了各方法的应用范围。

(2)以某山区高速公路隧道为例进行风险评价,得出该公路隧道风险等级为Ⅲ级,处于可接受范围。风险评价结果与实际情况吻合,较真实地反映了该山区高速公路隧道的行车风险情况。

(3)本文主要考虑高速公路隧道路段的静态行车风险,即第二、三类风险源中与环境、道路和管理的相关指标,考虑到风险的不确定性和多变性,未实现对隧道具体路段的风险分级评价。在后续的研究中,将基于可能性与严重性,量化各影响因子,并引入道路危险度指标,建立道路静态风险三维分级评价模型,以为道路交通安全性提升必要的理论基础。

参考文献

[1] 余鹏程,王意明,喻东.肯特指数法在高速公路隧道中的安全风险评估[J].西部交通科技,2018(8):111-114.

[2] 交通运输部公路科学研究院,贵州省交通运输厅.公路安全生命防护工程实施技术指南[M].北京:人民交通出版社股份有限公司,2015.

[3] Helai Huang, Yunying Peng, Jie Wang, et al. Interactive Risk Analysis on Crash Injury Severity at a Mountainous Freeway with Tunnel Groups in China [J]. Accident analysis and prevention, 2017, 111: 56-62.

[4] Shy Bassan. Overview of Traffic Safety Aspects and Design in Road Tunnels [J]. Elsevier Ltd, 2016, 40(1): 35-46.

[5] Ondrej Nyvlt, Samuel Prívara, Lukáš Ferkl. Probabilistic Risk Assessment of Highway Tunnels [J]. Tunnelling and Underground Space Technology, 2011, 26: 71-82.

[6] Ronchi E, Colonna P, Berloco N. Reviewing Italian Fire Safety Codes for the Analysis of Road Tunnel Evacuations: Advantages and Limitations of Using Evacuation Models[J]. Safety Science, 2013, 52: 28-36.

[7] Audun Borg, Henrik Bjelland, Ove Njå. Reflections on Bayesian Network models for road tunnel safety design: A case study from Norway [J]. Elsevier Ltd, 2014, 43: 300-314.

[8] Xiaobo Qu, Qiang Meng, Vivi Yuanita, et al. Design and implementation of a quantitative risk assessment software tool for Singapore road tunnels[J]. Expert Systems with Applications, 2011, 38: 13827-13834.

[9] 陈桂福.福建山区高速公路隧道行车安全研究[D].福州:福建农林大学,2014.

[10] 袁家伟.四川省高速公路隧道交通事故特征分析及安全风险评价研究[D].成都:西南交通大学,2018.

[11] 于福华,贺昱曜,王利民.特长高速公路隧道运营管理评价[J].武汉理工大学学报,2010,32(11):165-168.

[12] 邓涛,王武.基于物元分析的隧道路段行车安全性评价[J].公路工程,2015,40(3):245-249.

[13] 易富君,韩直,邓卫.公路隧道群运营安全性综合评价方法[J].长安大学学报:(自然科学版),2012,32(3):79-84.

[14] 贺志勇,张娟,王存宝,等.高速公路隧道安全性的综合评价[J].华南理工大学学报,2008,35(2):58-63.

[15] 马跃.郑越之.基于交通仿真的高速公路隧道入口交通流实时行车风险模型[J].城市道桥与防洪,2011(8):11,149-150,211.

[16] 郭延永,刘攀,吴瑶,等.山区高速公路隧道交通运行环境安全评价[J].武汉理工大学学报,2013,35(7):59-64.

[17] 杨健,阳富强,沈斐敏.基于改进DSmT的公路隧道行车安全综合评价方法研究[J].中国安全科学学报,2016,26(8):120-125.

[18] 田水承.第三类危险源辨识与控制研究[D].北京:北京理工大学,2001.

[19] Zhao Xuegang, Wei Lang. Research in the Model of the Area Road Traffic Security Risk Assessment[C]//Chongfu Huang, XilinLiu. Theory and Practice of Risk Analysis and Crisis Response. AMSTERDAM-PARIS: ATLANTIS PRESS, 2008: 857-861.

[20] 马璐.道路因素对道路交通安全的影响分析[D].西安:长安大学,2005.

[21] 洪英,张晓岩.影响交通安全的道路线形因素分析[J].交通标准化,2010(15):172-174.

[22] 陈斌,袁伟.交通安全的道路因素分析[J].广西交通科技,2002(4):19-22.

[23] 闫桂梅.公路隧道通风照明与行车安全关系研究[D].重庆:重庆交通大学,2008.

[24] 金治富.完善道路交通限速标准研究[J].道路交通管理,2015(1):56-57.

[25] Hwang C L, Yook K, Multiple Attribute Decision Making: Methods and Applications: a State-of-the Art Syrvey[M]. New York: Springer-verLag, 1981.

[26] 罗丽妮.加权 TOPSIS 法与 RSR 法相结合在医院综合评价中的应用[J].中国医院统计,2006,13(4):348-351.
[27] 李灿,张凤荣,朱泰峰.基于熵权 TOPSIS 模型的土地利用绩效评价及关联分析[J].农业工程学报.2013,29(5):217-227.
[28] 田凤调.RSR 法中的分档问题[J].中国卫生统计,1993,10(2):28-30.

高速公路连续下坡路段货车运行速度模型适用性分析

吕 博[1,2] 罗昱伟[1,2] 任士鹏[1,2]

(1.长安大学公路学院;2.陕西省交通基础设施建设与管理数字化工程研究中心)

摘 要 为探究高速公路连续下坡路段货车运行速度变化规律,本文以雅西高速公路拖乌山北坡交通特管区内一段 30km 连续下坡路段为研究对象,利用高清卡口系统,采集该路段 2020 年某月连续 30d 货车行车数据,分析货车在长大下坡路段运行特性,并结合现有运行速度预测模型,对预测速度与实测数据加以分析。结果表明:不同于现有运行速度预测模型预测趋势,试验路段货车速度随下坡距离增加而降低;下坡时外地牌照车辆速度降低相对较快,本地车辆总体趋于平稳。速度衰减率指标的变化情况证明了以往长大下坡运行速度预测模型没有考虑货车的频繁制动行为;驾驶员对环境的熟悉程度对长大下坡运行速度有显著影响。据此,提出了修正长大下坡路段货车运行速度预测模型的思路。

关键词 公路工程 运行速度模型 速度衰减率 连续下坡 交通安全

0 引 言

近年来,长大下坡事故率居高不下,由货车车速过高导致的制动失效是事故频发的主要原因之一[1-3]。据相关统计,2015 年公安部对全年不同地形条件的高速公路事故情况进行了统计,山区高速公路事故绝对数较少,仅占 12%,但造成的死亡人数、受伤人数和直接财产损失所占比例分别高达 18.01%、13.09% 和 16.42%。2018 年底,全国累计排查出不符合现行有关规定、平均纵坡较大且连续坡长超过极限值的长下坡危险路段达 1026 处,这些路段经自开通以来已累计发生道路交通事故 2.4 万余起,导致 6400 人死亡其中,造成了极其严重的社会经济、生命和财产损失。因此,为减少长大下坡路段交通事故,保障人民生命财产安全,需准确预测连续长下坡路段大货车运行速度变化趋势,为长下坡路段安全运行管理提供参考,提升下坡路段行车安全性。

针对长大下坡货车运行速度预测模型,国内外学者做了大量的研究。目前国内外机构、学者研究运行速度常用的方法是从实测项目中获取行车数据,经筛分处理,回归分析后得到运行速度 V_{85} 预测模型。自 20 世纪 70 年代起,美国联邦公路局(FHWA)首先提出了在平曲线车速预测模型的基础上乘以纵坡修正系数得到纵坡路段的运行速度预测模型;我国《公路项目安全性评价规范》(JTG B05—2015)[4]中沿用了此方法,但该模型在预测连续下坡路段运行速度时精度较低;廖军洪[5]等利用断面法采集了 10 段连续下坡路段的 95 个断面运行速度数据,建立了货车速度与坡长、平均纵坡 2 个参数的关系模型,但预测模型未考虑交通组成、时段及线形等因素的影响;佘明星[6]等利用断面观测法采集了汕湛高速连续下坡路段的大量行车数据,并基于多元回归分析建立了货车运行速度与平均坡度的关系模型,但该模型的显著性检验结果显示车速与坡长无关,模型预测的准确性有待观察;陈立辉[7]等利用车载 GPS 设备采集了

基金项目:国家重点研发计划项目 重大自然灾害监测预警与防范(2020YFC1512000)。

国道 G5 山西省境内一段连续下坡路段 14 个坡度的 50 组货车速度数据,引入了坡比参数,建立了基于坡度、坡长和坡比的货车运行速度预测模型,但该试验仅考虑一种车型,对于交通组成复杂的货运体系适用性有待验证。

综上所述,国内外大部分的研究仅考虑道路纵坡参数对连续下坡路段货车速度变化的影响,缺乏对驾驶员行为、道路环境、车辆性能等因素的研究。针对以上研究背景,本文通过对比实际下坡路段货车行驶速度与现有运行速度预测模型所预测速度,探究现有的运行速度预测模型应用在下坡货车速度的预测时适用性情况。并通过对实测四个点的货车速度的分析,研究货车在长下坡路段行驶时的速度特性以及速度变化趋势,以期为运行速度预测模型的改进提供一定的参考以及依据。

1 数据采集与处理

1.1 观测路段

选择雅西高速公路拖乌山北坡长下坡路段作为观测对象,拖乌山北坡长约 51 km,平均纵坡高达 2.96%,该路段具有海拔高、临崖临壁、急转弯多的特点。据不完全统计,自 2012 年 4 月至 2017 年 8 月,拖乌山北坡共发生道路交通事故 845 起,其中货车交通事故 326 起,占比 38.58%;货车失控造成交通事故 92 起,占货车事故总量的 28.22%。为有效预防和减少道路交通事故,确保人民生命财产安全,雅西高速公路在拖乌山北坡菩萨岗至楠桠之间设立"交通特管区",特管区内实行严格的客货分道行驶,特管区内路段严禁不按规定车道行驶,严禁超速行驶。

1.2 测速点分布

高清卡口系统能够详细地记录车辆轨迹等车流运行信息,该系统记录的高清卡口数据可以研究交通状态和潜在事故的内在机理[8]。大量交通监控系统的数据已经用来研究事故风险,比如线圈数据[9]、自动车辆识别系统[10]等。Xu 等人[9]使用病例对照和 Logistic 回归方法来评价交通流状态对事故风险的影响。Ahmed 等人[10]挖掘 AVI(自动车辆识别)数据,获得了 75.93% 的追尾碰撞事故预测率。Hossain 等人[11]利用贝叶斯网络将预测结果的误报率控制在 20% 以内。同济大学的研究[12]使用路段检测器的数据和爬虫天气数据预测实时事故,达到了 76.32% 的准确率,由此可见,高清卡口系统具有识别速度快、可靠性高等特点,利用高清卡口所采集的数据可用于科研分析中。

根据相关单位提供的资料,雅西高速公路共在拖乌山北坡交通特管区内布设 4 个高清卡口设备,分别位于 K2114、K2110、K2088 及 K2084,记录过往车辆信息及行驶状况。其中测点 K2114 和 K2110 位置接近坡顶,测点 K2088 和 K2084 位置接近坡底。交通特管区内各测点分布情况如图 1 所示。

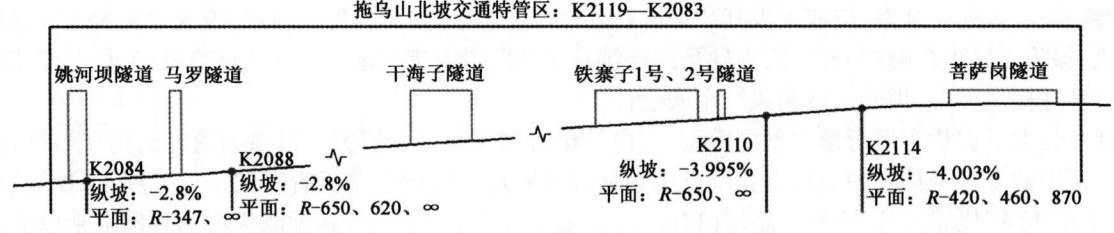

图 1 拖乌山北坡交通特管区测速点分布

1.3 数据处理

1.3.1 数据处理流程

在高清卡口设备输出数据的基础上,提取车辆车牌号、车辆类型、行驶车道、经过时间、行驶速度等相关数据,在此基础上对数据进行预处理,剔除运行速度为负值、0 等异常数据,根据车头时距与运行速度 v_{85} 的关系确定临界车头时距,进而筛选出自由流速度,提取有效的运行速度数据,再与几种常见的运行速度预测模型的预测结果进行对比分析,数据处理流程如图 2 所示。

1.3.2 自由流速度

运行速度是指在路面平整、潮湿、自由流状态下,行驶速度累计分布曲线上对应于85%分位值的速度[13],因此确定自由流速度是研究和预测运行速度的前提条件[14],相关研究[15-16]显示,车头时距可用来判别道路交通是否为自由流状态,即当车头时距大于某一临界值时,车辆速度仅取决于道路线形条件及驾驶员主观意愿,将该值定义为临界车头时距。对4个测点货车车头时距与第85分位实测车速进行统计分析,分析结果如图3所示。

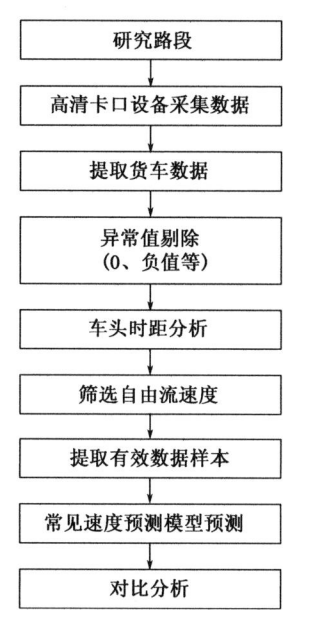
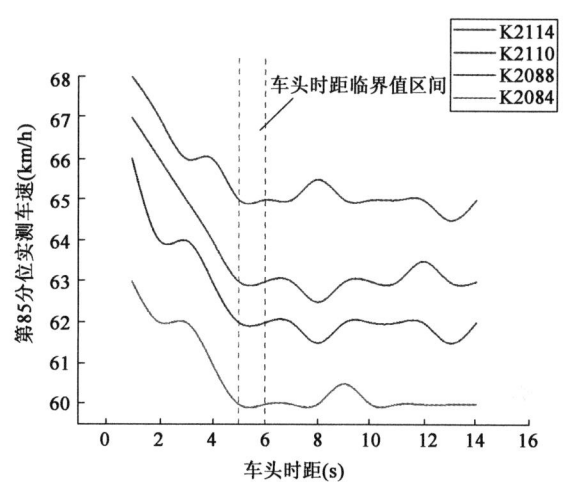

图2 长下坡货车运行速度数据处理流程　　图3 车头时距与第85分位实测车速的关系

由图3可以看出:第85分位实测车速在车头时距为5s之后趋于稳定(由于高清卡口速度数据均为整数,故v_{85}数据曲线稍显起伏),该路段临界车头时距区间为5~6s,在偏保守的情况下取6s作为货车处于自由流交通时的临界车头时距。当车头时距大于6s时,货车处于自由行驶状态,此时测点断面的实测车速可参与运行速度分析研究中。

2 对比分析

美国各州公路与运输工作者协会(AASHTO)[17]中指出长大下坡路段货车的运行速度是坡度和坡长综合作用的结果,车速随下坡距离的增加而增加,到稳定车速后保持匀速运动。据此,选取了《公路项目安全性评价规范》(JTG B05—2015)[4]中关于运行速度的预测模型和部分学者基于纵坡参数建立的速度预测模型[5-7]作为研究基础,并通过试验路段高清卡口设备采集的货车实测车速,对比分析上述所选模型的预测结果。

2.1 模型预测

2.1.1 《公路项目安全性评价规范》[4](以下简称"《规范》")

《规范》中基于下坡坡度及货车行驶距离对平曲线运行速度模型进行修正来预测长大下坡的货车运行速度,并基于此开发了运行速度预测软件,本文选取《规范》中高速公路大型车运行速度预测模型,将道路基本信息、平纵线形、构造物位置等参数输入后,可得到各测点对应货车运行速度。

2.1.2 廖军洪模型[5]

以下为该运行速度预测模型计算公式:

$$v = \exp[4.1491 + 0.1880\ln G + 0.0366 \times (\ln G)^2 0.1241\ln(L \div 1000) - 0.1129\ln(L \div 1000)\ln G]$$

2.1.3 佘明星模型[6]

以下为该运行速度预测模型计算公式:

$$v = 63.501 + 4.692G^2$$

2.1.4 陈立辉模型[7]

以下为该运行速度预测模型计算公式:

$$v = -(\log L)^3(0.016i^2 + 0.058i^2 + 1.243i \times r) + 79.592 + (48.817\log L - 111.129)i \times r$$

注:(1)陈立辉模型仅适用于坡长为12km内连续下坡。

(2)为方便对比,将不同预测模型中相同意义的参数做统一化处理。其中,v 为大货车运行速度(km/h);i 为坡度(%);G 为距坡顶平均纵坡(%);L 为累计坡长(m);r 为坡比(车辆经过的前后纵坡比值)。

分别用以上4种高速公路长大下坡路段货车运行速度预测模型对试验路段4个测点运行车速进行预测,结果如表1和图4所示。

各模型预测速度与实测速度对比 表1

桩号	平均纵坡 G (%)	坡长 L (m)	v_{85}(安评规范预测模型)(km/h)	v_{85}(廖军洪预测模型)(km/h)	v_{85}(佘明星预测模型)(km/h)	v_{85}(陈立辉预测模型)(km/h)	实测速度(km/h)
K2114	1.83	4880	64.330	78.621	79.214	88.108	65
K2110	2.06	8690	76.570	81.125	83.412	82.668	63
K2088	3.02	30500	68.277	81.391	106.294	—	62
K2084	3.04	35090	80.000	81.312	106.863	—	62

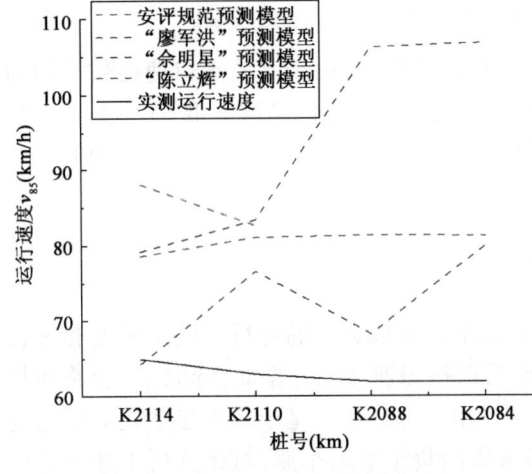

图4 各模型预测速度与实测速度对比

注:由于陈立辉模型仅适用于坡长为12km内连续下坡,故仅利用该模型预测K2114、K2110两点处运行速度。

2.2 对比分析

由模型预测结果(表1及图4)可知,《规范》运行速度预测模型所得结果虽局部路段有所降低,但整体呈升高趋势;廖军洪模型和陈立辉模型所预测的运行速度均随下坡距离的增加而增加,达到一定值后趋于稳定,这与特管区4个测点的实测车速变化趋势不符。

本文所选运行速度预测模型中廖军洪所建立模型主要影响因素为平均纵坡与累计坡长,累计坡长越长、平均纵坡越大,车辆处于加速状态的时间越长,速度增加趋势越明显;佘明星所建立模型主要影响因素为平均纵坡,平均纵坡越大,车速越快;陈立辉所建立模型主要影响因素为平均纵坡、累计坡长与坡比,车速经历坡顶处升高、坡中达某一临界值后减少,坡底稳定后略有增加,但该模型仅适用于12km内长下坡。

综上所述,以上4个运行速度预测模型在预测特管区长大下坡路段货车运行速度时偏差较大。因此,对于连续长大下坡路段,货车运行速度预测仅考虑道路纵断面指标是不够的,应综合考虑驾驶员行为、道路环境等因素对货车速度变化的影响。

3 连续下坡货车速度变化趋势

3.1 整体加减速特性分析

将试验路段四个监测点一个月内数据筛选得到1156辆车(共4624条数据)单次行程依次经过全部四个监测点的数据,对以上数据进行处理后得到测点间单车加速度及速度衰减率(同一辆车经过前后位

置时 $v_{后}/v_{前}$)等指标。但货车下坡这一过程并非匀变速运动,计算两点间的加速度并不符合物理学常识,采用速度衰减率代替加速度来描述货车运行速度变化趋势。由于测点 2 和测点 3 之间桩号相差 22km,速度差值不大的情况下速度的变化趋势不明显,故对坡顶和坡底的两段 4km 下坡路段进行分析,速度衰减率的变化趋势及累积频率曲线如图 5 所示。

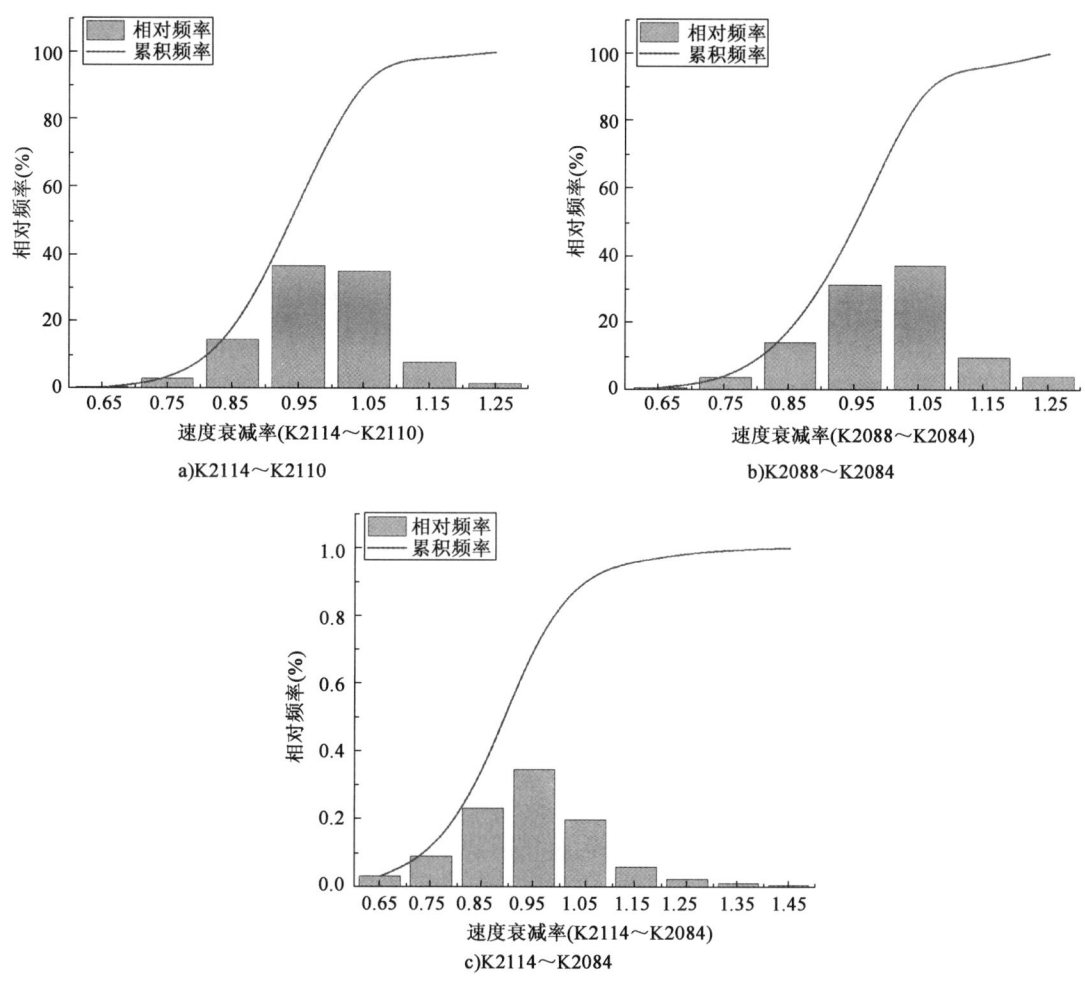

图 5 货车速度衰减率

由图 5a)、b)可知:坡顶及坡底路段有超过 60% 的车辆速度衰减率小于 1,由图 5c)可知:在 30km 长的连续下坡路段有超过 80% 的货车速度衰减率小于 1,说明大部分货车在连续长下坡时减速行驶,该结论不同于以 AASHTO[18] 为代表的研究结果,证明了以往研究方法缺乏对驾驶员频繁制动、控制车速及制动毂温度的考虑。

3.2 本地车和外地车的加减速特性对比分析

长大下坡路段货车的运行速度是人—车—路三因素耦合作用的结果[18-20],驾驶员对道路环境的熟悉程度往往会影响驾驶员的选择。对长大下坡的危险意识不够,不了解长大下坡线形指标变化时,驾驶员可能会出现紧张心理,进而影响挡位的选择及加减速的尺度大小[21]。

按照货车牌照类型将其筛分为本地车和外地车,对单车的速度衰减率指标进行分析如图 6 所示。

由图 6 可知:本地车、外地车单车速度衰减率的 70% 分位值均小于 1,说明大部分货车下坡时减速行驶;坡顶数据显示外地车单车速度衰减率率先达到 70% 分位值,且减速差值普遍偏大,说明在即将进入长大下坡时外地车司机采取了更大的制动力,操作更为谨慎;本地车与外地车在坡底的速度衰减率变化趋于一致,说明驶出长大下坡路段后,道路环境因素对货车运行速度的影响变小。

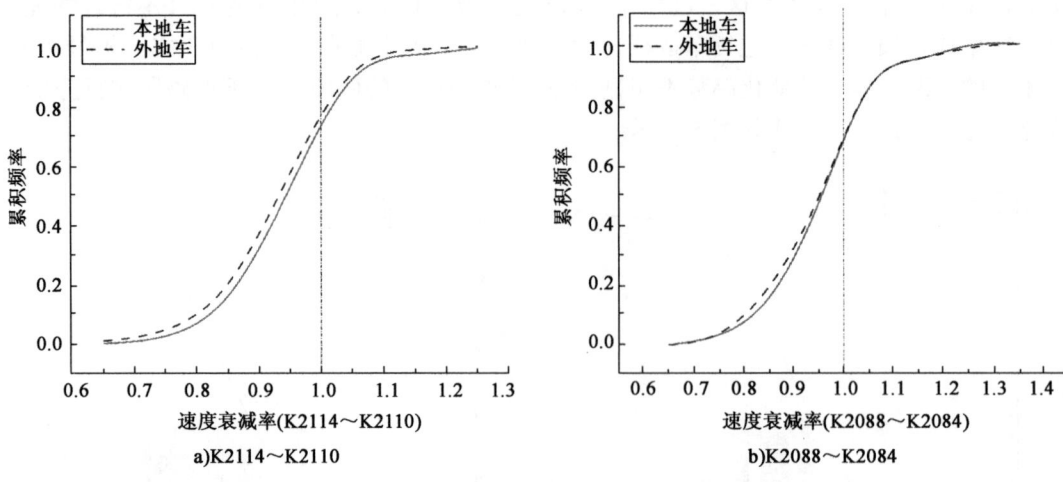

图6 货车速度衰减率

4 结 语

（1）货车在长大下坡路段运行速度变化趋势并不是单一的先增加,到稳定值时保持不变,本试验路段实测数据显示,超过80%的货车速度衰减率小于1,大部分货车在连续长下坡路段时运行速度先减小,到稳定值时保持不变。

（2）现有的长大下坡货车运行速度模型适用性不强,没有考虑连续下坡时驾驶员的频繁制动,因此,建议将驾驶员为控制车速及制动毂温度时的频繁制动因素考虑在内,将其量化后在长下坡路段运行速度预测模型中进行参数标定。

（3）连续下坡过程中货车运行速度存在一定衰减,证实了驾驶员在长下坡路段行驶时频繁刹车以控制车速。

（4）外地车的运行速度衰变相对更快,而本地车总体平稳,说明驾驶员对道路环境的熟悉程度对下坡运行速度有显著影响,建议在外地车比例较高时将该因素考虑为长大下坡货车运行速度预测模型的修正系数,提高模型的适用性。

参考文献

[1] 国家统计局.中国统计年鉴2019[M].北京:中国统计出版社,2019.

[2] 陈斌,袁伟,付锐,等.连续长大下坡路段交通事故特征分析[J].交通运输工程学报,2009,9(04):75-78,84.

[3] Roads and Traffic Authority of NSW. Speed Problem Definition and Countermeasure Summary[R]. New South Wales, Australia: Roads and Traffic Authority, 2000.

[4] 中华人民共和国交通运输部.公路项目安全性评价规范:JTG B05—2015[S].北京:人民交通出版社股份有限公司,2015.

[5] 廖军洪,邵春福,邬洪波,等.连续长大下坡路段大货车运行速度预测模型[J].北京理工大学学报,2012,32(增刊1):118-121.

[6] 佘明星.基于断面观测法的连续下坡路段车辆运行速度预测模型研究[J].公路交通科技(应用技术版),2019,15(07):310-315.

[7] 陈立辉,郭忠印.高速公路连续下坡路段大货车速度特征研究[J].重庆交通大学学报(自然科学版),2019,38(08):86-91.

[8] 游锦明,方守恩,张兰芳,等.高速公路实时事故风险研判模型及可移植性[J].同济大学学报(自然科学版),2019,47(03):347-352.

[9] C Xu, P Liu, W Wang, et al. Evaluation of the Impacts of Traffic States on Crash Risks on Freeways[J].

Accident Analysis & Prevention,2012,47:162-171.
[10] M Ahmed, M Abdel-Aty, R Yu. Bayesian Updating Approach for Real-time Safety Evaluation with Automatic Vehicle Indentification Data[J]. Transportation Research Record: Journal of the Transportation Research Board,2012,2280:60-67.
[11] M Hossain, Y Muromachi. A Bayesian Network Based Framework for Real-Time Crash Prediction on the Basic Free-Way Segments of Urban Expressway[J]. Accident Analysis & Prevention,2012,45:373-381.
[12] J You, J Wang, J Guo. Real-time Crash Prediction on Freeways Using Data Mining and Emerging Techniques[R]. Journal of modern transportation. 2017.
[13] 许金良.道路勘测设计[M].5版.北京:人民交通出版社股份有限公司,2018.
[14] 杨文臣,田毕江,胡澄宇,等.山区高速公路隧道路段运行速度分析与预测[J].中外公路,2018,38(06):308-313.
[15] Ibrahim HH. Analysis of Speed Characteristics for Rural Two-Lane Roads: A Field Study from Minoufiy a Governor-Ate,Egypt[J]. Ain Shams Engineering Journal,2011,2:43-52.
[16] 孟祥海,王丹丹,张志召.高速公路平纵组合路段运行速度分析与预测[J].交通运输系统工程与信息,2014,14(02):150-157.
[17] AASHTO. A Policy on Geometric Design of Highways and Streets[M]. 6th ed. Washington,D. C.,USA: AASHTO,2011.
[18] 郭腾峰.长大纵坡安全与车路协同矛盾探究[J].中国公路,2018(02):62-65.
[19] 刘震.基于人—车—路综合影响的运行车速预测模型研究[D].广州:华南理工大学,2010.
[20] 丁志勇,周子楚,郭忠印.运行速度预测模型在公路长大纵坡路段设计中的适用性分析及修正[J].公路工程,2016,41(05):118-122,138.
[21] 付仲才,廖军洪,邬洪波,等.山区高速公路连续下坡路段驾驶员特性分析[J].公路交通科技(应用技术版),2011,7(08):28-30.

道路行车风险评估模型综述

谢永淑　任晓玮　向宇杰　唐忠泽　杨雅钧
(长安大学公路学院)

摘　要　为比较当前各种高速公路行车风险评估模型的准确性,本文通过梳理国内外道路行车风险评估模型的研究现状,总结了其发展规律及目前研究中存在的问题。并利用美国加州交通管理系统PEMS中收集的事故数据和正常交通流数据,构建了风险评估模型,并进行算法训练。试验结果表明:基于随机森林法训练的实时风险评估模型的准确度较高,可有效实现高速公路风险的信息化管理。

关键词　道路工程　风险评价　综述　高速公路　随机森林方法

0　引　言

近年来,我国高速公路交通安全形势十分严峻,2018年发生的事故总数高达203049起,造成的直接财产损失高达121311.3万元,已经成为我国一个严重的社会问题[1]。随着道路信息化设备的完善,高速公路安全的改善方法已由传统的被动安全改善向主动安全风险防控发展[2]。主动安全防控意味着需要提前识别道路行车风险[3],道路行车风险一般来源于自然条件、线形条件以及实时交通流状况等,而这些风险的产生可能由单一的影响因素导致,也有可能是综合因素的叠加作用导致[4,6]。因此,有效选取道路行车风险评估指标并准确判断道路风险,已成为目前研究的热点。

国外对于道路行车风险的研究起步较早,主要集中在判断道路风险位置以及重点路段风险评价等方面。S. H. Park[7]、P. Senk[8]、Pradeep Kumar Agarwal[9]、S. Cafiso[10]等学者们都对行车风险有一定程度的探索。随着研究深入,驾驶员及行人的相关指标逐渐被考虑,Marciano, F. A.[11]等提出个人风险评估模型;Jonghak Lee[12]等系统分析了降雨强度对交通事故的影响。

我国在该领域的研究工作开展较晚,主要分为两个研究方向:

(1)分析某一具体路段(隧道、长大纵坡路段等)的线形、速度、驾驶员心理等相关指标,评价特征路段的道路行车风险代表方法有肯特指数法[13]、Delphi 法[14]、量化高速公路线形风险评价综合指标—线形风险指数[15]等方法。

(2)分析道路风险源[16],从道路风险识别、判断、分析到风险管理决策等环节出发,构建交通事故风险指标体系[17]和道路风险评估系统[18]。

综上,国内外学者针对道路行车风险评估模型进行了深入的研究,但目前众多的风险评估模型之间缺少对比性评价,具体选用时,找出评价精度高且便于应用的风险评估模型存在一定的困难。因此,本文通过系统梳理高速公路风险评估模型的建模方法,概述其风险理论,总结并评述相关建模方法,并基于相关数据,选取典型风险评估模型进行准确度分析,总结并分析目前道路风险评估研究中的重点问题。

1 道路风险理论概述

风险现象是指自然界和人类社会发生的与未来不利事件有关的现象。根据时间序列的划分,现象分为历史现象、当前现象和未来现象[19]。研究道路风险的主要目的是根据对当前道路交通流状态的观察,预测道路风险,提出有效降低交通事故的措施(图1)。

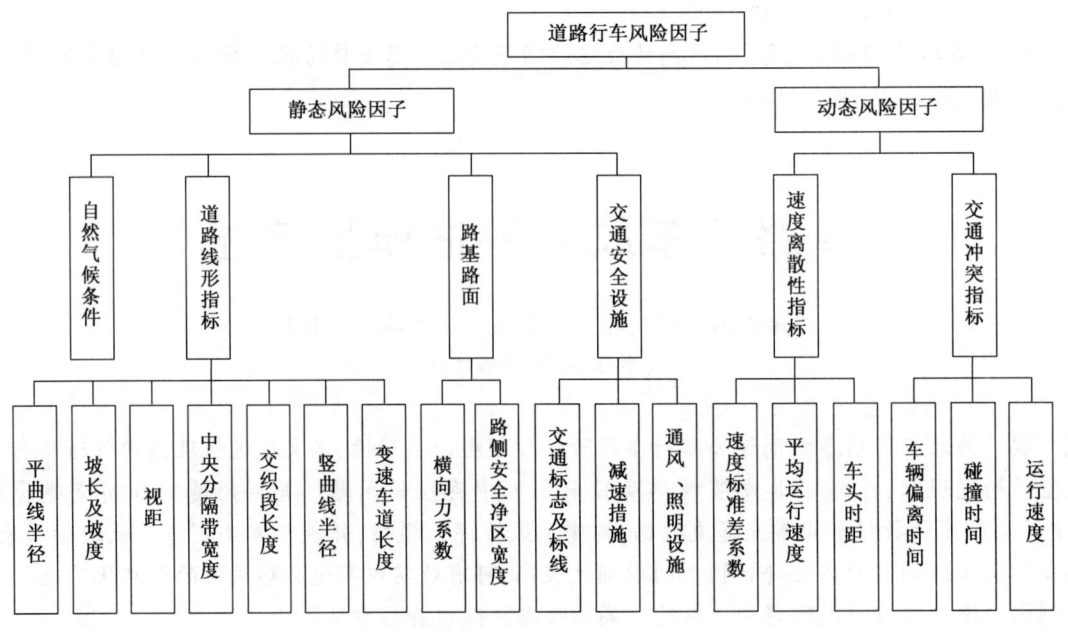

图1 道路行车风险因子

根据黄崇福[20]等学者对于风险系统的定义,风险系统通常由五部分构成:不利事件源头(道路及其周边环境[21])、源头影响场、不利事件作用对象不利事件测度空间、时间尺度。

道路风险管理分为风险识别、风险判断、风险量化与度量以及风险评价、风险管理控制五个方面。风险识别主要指道路风险管理相关人员运用相关的技术,发现道路范围内的潜在风险,目前国内风险识别的方法较为成熟,主要有:故障树分析法[22]、结构化头脑风暴风险识别法[23]、成本绩效法等[24]。为了量化风险,一般通过构建风险分析模型的方法系统的实现风险研判与分析,主要包括:模糊逻辑分析法[25]、领结分析法[26]、事故树法[27]。影响我国道路风险评估技术的主要因素为构成风险评估技术核心的评估模型,自2007年以来道路风险评估技术已经有了广泛的应用[28],但传统道路安全分析,更多是基于事故分析[29],或基于工程经验的安全评价[30]。此类方法多为被动性数据分析,难以达到事故风险预防效果。

2 道路行车风险评估模型研究综述

国内外开展道路行车风险模型研究已有十余年,主要基于应用路段、数据类型、评估过程及评估结果等方面对道路风险评估进行研究。本文将风险评估模型分为3类,即单指标控制法、多指标权重分析法以及事故模拟机器算法。各方法构建模型的流程如图2所示。

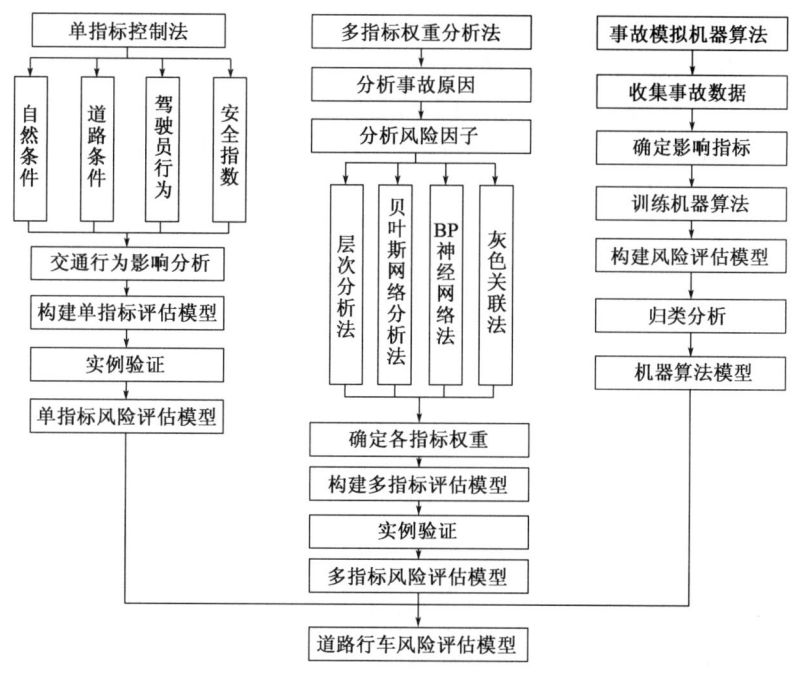

图2 道路行车风险模型构建流程

2.1 单指标控制法

国内外学者对道路行车安全的影响研究始于20世纪80年代中期,早期研究大多基于单一因素,影响因素相互结合的研究较少。主要的单一影响指标包括:道路线形条件、不良天气条件、驾驶员行为条件等。

道路线形条件主要围绕山区复杂线形路段展开研究,具体有急弯陡坡、S形曲线路段等。Yang[31]结合Dugoff利用MATLAB/SIMULINK,提出了一种基于车辆行驶安全性指标的车辆变速模型;胡江碧等[32]基于驾驶工作负荷理论,提出了驾驶员安全舒适道路条件的多因素表达;侯明瑜等[33]提出了三种基于组合决策算法的山区道路行车安全评价模型,用于评价山区道路线形的安全性。

不良天气条件主要有雾、雨、雪等,Chen[34]等人采用多元线性回归分析法研究了恶劣天气条件对感知风险的影响。Hamdar、Samer H[35]等人在以往汽车跟驰模型基础上扩展,通过对实际路段仿真,验证了模型能在不良天气条件下模拟驾驶员的行为能力。刘伟[36]等建立了基于专家打分法的不良气候交通安全预警模型,并利用ROC曲线优化BP网络预测不良天气条件下的汽车运行状态。黄冰娥[37]等构建Logit模型计算交通风险等级和相应的预警等级,并给出预警方案。

综上所述,单指标控制法主要针对影响道路行车风险的某一项具体指标进行评估,分别探究不良天气条件、道路线形条件、驾驶员行为等指标对高速公路行车安全的影响,从而达到分析道路行车风险及单一指标下交通事故致灾机理的目的。但在实际的道路环境中,行车风险发生涉及多因素综合作用。

2.2 多指标权重分析法

随着对道路行车风险等理论的深入研究,发现车辆运行过程中影响行车风险的因素错综复杂,相互耦合。因此,中外学者们开展了基于多因素对行车风险影响的研究,建立了多指标权重分析法统一评估,给各项指标分配权重以构成道路行车风险评价模型。

Gregoriades、Andreas等[38]利用贝叶斯网络法建立了道路交通事故风险评估概率模型,根据评估事故风险指数AR,识别道路网络中的事故黑点,在一定程度上量化了道路风险;赵利苹等[39]运用模糊综合评价法对风雨耦合作用下的行车风险等级进行评估,首次构建了基于DEMATEL方法的风雨耦合作用下的风险评估模型,提出了风险等级识别标志。黄晓丽等[40]结合灰色关联法和模糊评价法构建了道路交通安全风险评价指标系统,该模型在一定程度上降低了主观性。孟祥海等[41]基于三层BP神经网络的基础上结合事故率建立了能有效识别事故多发点的道路事故多发点鉴别模型。

综上所述,多指标权重分析法目前广泛应用于高速公路风险评估方法中,该方法将多种影响高速公路行车安全的指标进行综合分析,能更全面地对道路风险进行评价,体现出各影响因素之间的关系。但该方法也存在一些不足:在确定权重系数时较为依赖专家的主观经验,在建立风险预估模型时对其准确度存在影响;其评价结果多针对整个道路划分区段,无法精确到任意的道路横断面上;在适应交通流以及其他参数的变化方面也存在缺陷,仅适用于静态风险因素研究,对于动态影响因素则不能完全适应,而利用事故模拟机器算法[42]正好可以解决这些问题。

2.3 事故模拟机器算法

通过上述对单指标控制法及多指标权重分析法构建的高速公路风险评估模型的综述分析,可以看出,通过分析交通流参数与事故结果的关系进行风险评价模型的构建与分析是大多数模型常见的做法。近年来随着高速公路信息化的提高,对智能交通研究的逐步深入,道路交通安全逐渐将交通流数据分析应用于实时碰撞风险评估研究。

以往的实时碰撞风险评估研究主要采用Logistic回归和神经网络模型,以线性函数和拟合为主,随着研究深入,学者们利用分类回归树[43]、随机梯度增强技术(SGB)[44]、多层次的贝叶斯[45]、分类回归树(CART)算法[46]、Fisher判别分析法[47]、ADASYN算法、Matlab与随机森林模型结合[48]等方法进行实时交通风险评估。

通过对上述三种对高速公路风险评估模型构建方法的分类总结,可以看出:单指标控制法重点反映单一指标(如天气、线形等因素)对道路行车风险的影响;多指标控制分析法为反映多因素对风险的影响,着重通过构建多因子数学模型来实现,但确定各指标权重时存在着依赖专家经验的较为主观的方法,目前研究学者们常使用将多种方法进行结合的组合决策算法,可大大降低主观依靠性,有效避免各算法弊端;事故模拟机器算法在实际工程应用中,对道路智能化要求较高,待评价路段需配备完整的交通数据采集系统,并且要保证风险警示等交安设施的设置,但就道路行车风险评估系统的工程实用性来看,事故模拟机器算法可利用算法快速有效地判断当前交通流状态下该路段的风险程度,更加可能实现对高速公路行车风险的实时评估,并在一定程度上能实现风险量化和分级。

3 模型精度对比分析

单指标控制分析法重点研究某一具体指标对高速公路行车安全的影响,针对某一具体方面提出改善交通环境及有效降低行车风险的措施,但其应用于道路行车风险评估模型的实用性较低。对于高速公路行车风险模型,需完整考虑每一影响指标对整个行车风险的影响,故选用多指标权重分析法及事故模拟机器算法两种方法进行模型适用性对比。

3.1 数据来源

本研究从美国加州PEMS交通管理系统收集了I80-W双向四车道高速公路(事故数较高)Abs PM19.6位置处(图3),2019年1月至6月共560组事故数据(包括事故发生时间、位置、持续时间、伤亡等参数),并对事故发生前5min以内事故点上游断面(距事故点800m以内)的平均速度、流量、车道占有率、大型车比例以及VHT等参数进行收集。

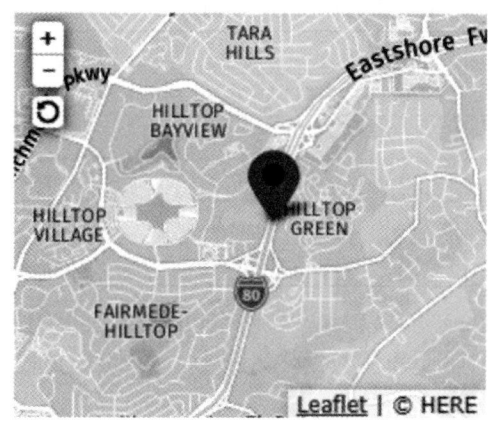

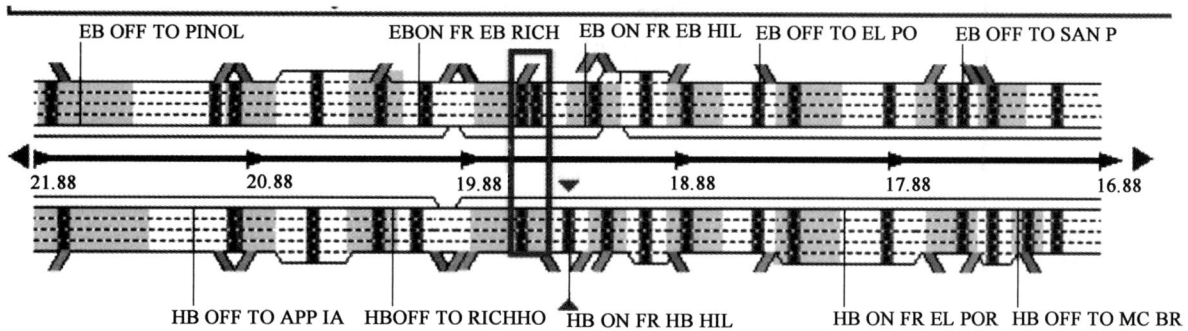

图3 PEMS中检测点及检测器位置

将收集的事故数据和相关交通流参数按照表1情况进行划分。

数据样本收集情况   表1

数据样本类型	数据时间范围	数据量	事故组与对照组比例
构建模型数据样本	2019年1—5月	440例	1:3(对照组与事故组时间地点均相同)
验证数据样本	2019年6月	120例	

根据前文中提到的相关研究,本文选取事故发生前5min内事故点上游断面交通流量[veh·(5min)$^{-1}$]、车道占有率(%)、平均速度(km·h^{-1})、大型车比例(%)、事故持续时间(Min)、行驶时间VHT(veh·h)五个指标。流量为事故发生5min内上游断面通过的车辆数;VHT代表5min内事故路段上平均交通量与通行时间的乘积,体现交通符合和交通强度;车道占有率为观测时间5min内,车辆通过某一段面的累计时间所占单位观测时间的百分比;速度为5min以内通过该断面所有车辆的平均速度。

3.2 模型选取

本文通过对比近年来应用率较高的多指标权重分析法及事故模拟机器算法,结合两种方法中各模型的适用性和完整度,选取了灰色关联及模糊综合评价法[40]、Fisher判别分析法[47]以及随机森林法[48]构建的道路风险评估模型,分别命名为模型1、模型2、模型3。

3.3 模型精度分析

本文利用上述提及的PEMS交通检测系统收集的2019年1月至5月的交通流状态数据分别进行模型1、模型2、模型3的构建,并完成机器算法的训练,得到3种高速公路风险评估模型,根据上文中的事故样本进行3种方法的模型构建。

(1)模型1——灰色关联及模糊综合评价法

首先确定参考序列和比较序列,将交通量[veh·5(min)$^{-1}$]、车道占有率(%)、平均速度(km·h^{-1})、大型车比例(%)、行驶时间 VHT(veh·h)5 个指标采用标准化法对数据进行无量纲化处理,计算关联系数后确定灰色关联度判断矩阵及各指标权重,各指标权重如表 2 所示。

各评价指标权重及不同风险等级阈值　　　　表 2

	权　重	交通量 a_1	车道占有率 a_2	行驶时间 VHTa_3	大型车比例 a_4	平均速度 a_5
		0.146	0.205	0.217	0.220	0.213
不同风险等级指标阈值	很大(20%位数)	0.318	0.434	0.519	0.598	0.318
	较大(40%位数)	0.059	0.097	0.185	0.437	0.059
	一般(60%位数)	0.046	0.089	0.137	0.267	0.046
	较小(80%位数)	0.029	0.086	0.124	0.250	0.029

将各指标风险等级指标阈值 20%位数、40%位数、60%位数、80%位数与事故发生概率 80%、60%、40%、20%相对应,将 2019 年 6 月份交通流数据代入模型 1 中,发现该模型的预测精度为 43.0%。

(2)模型 2——Fisher 判别分析法

根据 Fisher 判别分析法的原理[49],利用 SPSS 软件对多组备选变量组合执行 Fisher 判别分析,剔除产生的多个判别函数中不显著的判别函数,典则判别如图 4 所示,在多个判别函数中选取判别精度较高的判别函数建立高速公路实时风险评估模型。

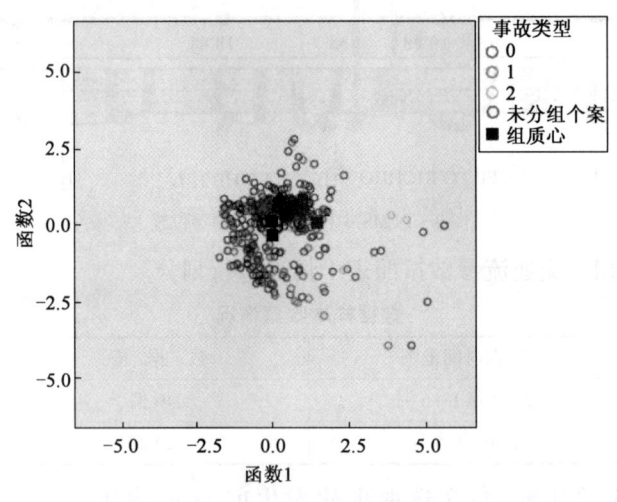

图 4　Fisher 模型典则判别图

表 3 中列出了 Fisher 判别分析法构建的风险评估模型对于样本的事故预测精度。在训练样本中,60.9%的事故样本被成功预测。66.96%的非事故样本被成功预测。这表明 Fisher 判别分析对训练样本有较好的拟合精度,在验证样本过程中,该模型在 30 个事故样本中预测了 19 个事故,预测准确率达 63.33%。

Fisher 判别法事故预测结果　　　　表 3

样　本	实际分类	预测分类	
		事故	非事故
训练样本	事故	60.9%(67)	39.1%(43)
	非事故	33.04%(109)	66.96%(221)
验证样本	事故	63.33%(19)	36.67%(11)
	非事故	34.44(31)	65.56%(59)

(3)模型 3——随机森林法

本文选用 Matlab 计算平台实现随机森林算法,由于选取的指标均为与事故安全相关性较大的指标,故本研究省略变量重要性排布。将重要性较高的指标:流量、车道占有率、平均速度、大型车比例、行驶时间 VHT 的对应数据作为训练集输入随机森林模型中,以事故数据、非事故数据以及整体数据的准确性3个标准衡量该模型的有效性。利用随机森林算法得到的事故样本准确率如表4所示。

随机森林模型分类效果表 表4

分类准确率(%)	训 练 集	测 试 集
整体	76.4	80.0
事故	76.8	74.2
非事故	80.1	79.4

表5总结了上述3种方法构建的道路行车风险评估模型的结构方程及准确率,可以看出,模型1的预测精度较低,为43.0%,模型2的预测精度为60.9%,模型3的预测精度最高,为74.2%。

典型道路行车风险模型方程 表5

模型序号	各指标系数					准确率
	交通量 a_1	车道占有率 a_2	行驶时间 VHTa_3	大型车比例 a_4	平均速度 a_5	
模型1	$Y_1 = 0.146a_1 + 0.205a_2 + 0.217a_3 + 0.220a_4 + 0.213a_5$					43.0%
模型2	$Y_2 = -2.843 + 0.004a_1 + 0.015a_2 + 0.028a_3 + 0.145a_4 - 0.076a_5$					60.9%
模型3	—					74.2%

3.4 模型精度对比结果

综上,灰色关联及模糊综合评价法因其较强的主观性,构建的风险评估模型判断事故风险较低;而 Fisher 判别分析法可以将事故样本的数据特点进行总结,对符合该特点的数据进行归类,准确度较高;采用随机森林模型得到的实时事故风险模型准确率最高,该模型不仅可以较准确的预测高速公路事故发生概率,还可以根据目前的道路交通流状况,反映实时道路风险。

4 目前研究存在的问题及研究展望

4.1 存在的问题

通过对现阶段3种风险评估方法研究过程综述,本研究认为,单指标控制法重点研究某一具体指标对道路行车风险的影响,是多指标权重分析法及事故模拟机器算法中选取指标的基础,多指标权重分析法及事故模拟机器算法均为将多种指标综合起来构建风险评估模型。而目前我国在高速公路道路行车风险的研究中主要存在以下问题:

(1)我国对于道路行车风险的研究主要基于现有的交通事故进行,针对交通事故发生前的事故数据研究较少,且缺乏交通事故发生前后与正常通行状态下的交通流数据对比分析,是否存在其他与事故发生相关性较高的指标,因此,应用以往交通事故构建的道路风险评估模型预测道路风险的精确度普遍较低。

(2)针对高速公路道路行车风险评估现有研究成果依据的样本量较少,且样本数据采集方式单一、精度不足,国内能够收集到的事故样本数据,缺乏交通流有关的指标,目前主要的交通事故样本来源,主要基于美国加州 PEMS 交通流检测系统。

(3)道路行车风险与驾驶员、行车、道路环境、不良天气等指标均有直接的关系,缺乏将人、车、路之间联系的完整考虑的风险评估模型。

(4)实际应用过程中,随着道路通行能力与交通量的短期变化,风险评估模型应进行风险更新,使之适应当前状态下道路的风险评估。

(5)目前的道路风险研究主要基于交通事故开展,但事故不能完全反映道路风险,研究方向还有待斟酌。

4.2 研究展望

当前各国学者应用不同的分析方法从各角度对道路行车风险进行了深入的研究,由于道路设施、交通流特性、交通运行环境和驾驶行为的不同,各个学者对道路行车风险的分析思路、研究方法选择、风险因子选取等方面有所不同,各种分析方法的适用性不同、模型的可移植性不强。随着智慧交通和车辆技术的不断革新,道路行车风险评估仍然是一个研究热点,今后研究方向可能从以后几个方面进行:

(1)交通事故采集。实测数据是建立或校验风险评估模型的基础,数据库的大小及其精度影响统计各模型的可信度,智慧交通是今后道路行车风险数据采集方式的一个重要的发展方向。

(2)风险评估模型研究。如何将事故模拟机器算法更好的应用于我国高速公路,也是今后一个重要的方向。

(3)风险研究指标。在今后的研究中,还应考虑其他反映道路行车风险的指标,在一定程度上,有效提高道路行车风险评估的准确度及适用性。

5 结 语

本文通过对国内外研究文献的分析,归纳出高速公路风险评估模型构建方法主要包括单指标控制法、多指标权重分析法和事故模拟机器算法,详细介绍了道路风险评估相关研究历史、现状,探讨了各种方法的特点和适用性,结合高速公路信息化发展现状和交通领域研究热点,基于PEMS交通检测系统收集的交通流状态数据,选取三种典型高速公路风险评估模型进行精度对比分析,发现随机森林算法构建的风险评估模型精度最高,更适合目前高速公路信息化的发展。

参考文献

[1] 国家统计局. 中国统计年鉴[J]. 北京:中国统计出版社,2008.

[2] 冯广刚. 基于主被动集成的汽车安全控制系统建模与仿真[D]. 长沙:湖南大学,2008.

[3] 谭金华. 道路风险管理研究[D]. 北京:清华大学,2011.

[4] 赵学刚,魏朗. 道路交通安全风险预警模糊评判模型[J]. 太原理工大学报,2009,40(04):365-368.

[5] 缪帅. 干线公路交通安全风险评估与安全保障技术研究[D]. 西安:长安大学,2018.

[6] 钟锐. 高速公路交通安全风险评价方法研究[D]. 西安:长安大学,2014.

[7] Park S H, Jang K, Kim D-K, et al. Spatial Analysis Methods for Identifying Hazardous Locations on Expressways in Korea[J]. Scientia Iranica. Transaction B, Mechanical Engineering,2015:1594-1603.

[8] P Senk, J Ambros, P Pokorny, et al. Use of Accident Prediction Models in Identifying Hazardous Road Locations[J]. Transport Research Centre, Brno, Czech Republic,2012.

[9] Pradeep Kumar Agarwal, Premit Kumar Patil, Rakesh Mehar. A Methodology for Ranking Road Safety Hazardous Locations Using Analytical Hierarchy Process[J]. Social and Behavioral Sciences,2013:1030-1037.

[10] S. Cafiso, G. La Cava. Risk Assessment for Road Safety Evaluation on Two Lane Rural Highways[J]. A Scientific and Technical Publishing Company,2011:704-043.

[11] F. A. Maricano, A. Vitetta. Risk Analysis in Road Safety: An Individual Risk Model for Drivers and Pedestrians to Support Decision Planning Processes[J]. International Journal of Safety and Security Engineering,2011:265-282.

[12] Jonghak Lee, Junghyo Chae, Taekwan Yoon, et al. Traffic Accident Severity Analysis with Rain-related Factors Using Structural Equation Modeling[J]. Accident Analysis & Prevention,2018:1-10.

[13] 余鹏程,王意明,喻东. 肯特指数法在高速公路隧道中的安全风险评估[J]. 西部交通科技,2018(08):105-108.

[14] 胡立伟,李林育,古含焱,等. 山区长大下坡路段货车行车风险因素识别[J]. 长安大学学报(自然科

学版),2019,39(01):116-126.
[15] 杨峰.基于线形风险指数的高速公路线形风险评估方法研究[J].公路交通科技,2017,34(06):71-78.
[16] 诸红.道路行车风险管理的研究与应用[J].化工管理,2014(26):77.
[17] 王恩达,石京.基于互信息理论的多风险因素下交通事故风险量化与分析[J].交通工程,2017,17(06):1-5,12.
[18] 石京,谭金华.道路风险分析与评估管理系统研究初探[J].公路工程,2011,36(04):85-88.
[19] 田静.形态发生估计及其在概率风险更新中的应用[D].北京:北京师范大学,2012.
[20] 黄崇福,杨军民,庞西磊.风险分析的主要方法[C]//中国灾害防御协会风险分析专业委员会年会,2010.
[21] Lu Jian, Cheng Zeyang. Research and Development of Road Traffic Network Security Risk Identification [J]. Journal of Southeast University (Natural Science Edition),2019:404-412.
[22] Liu B, Yan H, Zhao W. A Risk Management System of Hainan Interchange Merge Area in Maintenance Zone: Risk Analysis, Identification, Assessment and Countermeasure[C]//6th International Symposium on Life-Cycle Civil Engineering,2018.
[23] Eugene Swanepoel, Leon Pretorius. A Structured Approach to Risk Identification for Projects in a Research Environment[J]. 2015 Portland International Conference on Management of Engineering and Technology (PICMET),2015.
[24] Abhay Tawalare. Identification of Risks for Indian Highway Construction[J]. IOP Conference Series: Materials Science and Engineering,2019:471(9).
[25] Mohammad NU Mia, Theunis F P Henning, Seosamh B Costello, et al. Application of Fuzzy Logic Based Risk Analysis to Identify the Moisture Damage Potential in Flexible Road Pavements[J]. International Journal of Pavement Research and Technology,2015,8(5).
[26] Ute Christine Ehlers, Eirin Olaussen Ryeng, Edward McCormack, et al. Bowtie Analysis without Expert Acquisition for Safety Effect Assessments of Cooperative Intelligent Transport Systems[J]. ASCE-ASME Journal of Risk and Uncertainty in Engineering Systems, Part A: Civil Engineering, 2018,4(4).
[27] 施红星,闫彬.基于模糊事故树法的车辆交通安全风险识别[J].军事交通学院学报,2014,16(12):4-9.
[28] 张铁军,万娇娜.道路(路网)风险评估技术发展[J].伤害医学(电子版),2018,7(04):1-3.
[29] 王恩达.道路交通事故多因素风险的量化与分析[D].北京:清华大学,2017.
[30] 许林新,苑仁腾,王小双.基于模糊层次分析的道路交通安全评价研究[J].北方交通,2019(03):31-34,39.
[31] Jiu-ding Yang, Yi-kai Chen, Qin Shi, et al. Variable Speed Limits on Circular Curved Road Sections under Various Weather Conditions[C]//15th COTA International Conference of Transportation Professionals,2015.
[32] 胡江碧,何荷,沈康鉴.安全道路条件计算研究综述与展望[J].交通信息与安全,2015,33(01):9-15.
[33] 侯明瑜.基于组合决策算法的道路线形安全评价研究[D].重庆:重庆交通大学,2017.
[34] Chen Chen, Xiaohua Zhao, Hao Liu, et al. Influence of Adverse Weather on Drivers' Perceived Risk During Car Following Based on Driving Simulations[J]. Journal of Modern Transportation,2019.
[35] Samer H. Hamdar, Lingqiao Qin, Alireza Talebpour. Weather and Road Geometry Impact on Longitudinal Driving Behavior: Exploratory Analysis Using an Empirically Supported Acceleration Modeling Framework

[J]. Transportation Research Part C：Emerging Technologies,2016,67：193-213.
[36] 刘伟. 山区高速公路不良气候条件下行车安全保障技术研究. [D]. 西安:长安大学,2015.
[37] 黄冰娥. 恶劣天气下高速公路行车风险分析与预警管理研究[D]. 上海:上海交通大学,2012.
[38] Andreas Gregoriades, Kyriacos C. Mouskos. Black Spots Identification through a Bayesian Networks Quantification of Accident Risk Index [J]. Transportation Research Part C：Emerging Technologies, 2013,28：28-43.
[39] 赵利苹. 风雨耦合作用下高速公路交通安全与控制策略研究. [D]. 西安:长安大学,2013.
[40] 黄晓丽,刘耀龙,段锦等. 基于灰色关联及模糊综合评价法的道路交通安全风险评价[J]. 数学的实践与认识,2017,47(07):208-215.
[41] 孟祥海,盛洪飞,陈天恩. 事故多发点鉴别本质及基于BP神经网络的鉴别方法研究[J]. 公路交通科技,2008(03):124-129.
[42] 王腾辉. 基于Spark平台的短时交通流预测研究[D]. 广州:华南理工大学,2016.
[43] Rongjie Yu, Mohamed Abdel-Aty. Utilizing Support Vector Machine in Real-time Crash Risk Evaluation [J]. Accident Analysis & Prevention,2013,51：252-259.
[44] Mohamed Ahmed, Mohamed Abdel-Aty. A Data Fusion framework for Real-time Risk Assessment on Freeways. Transportation Research Part C：Emerging Technologies,2013,26：203-213.
[45] Qi Shi, Mohamed Abdel-Aty, Rongjie Yu. Multi-level Bayesian Safety Analysis with Unprocessed Automatic Vehicle Identification Data for an Urban Expressway [J]. Accident Anaiysis & Prevention, 2016,88：68-76.
[46] Jianqiang Wang, Yang Zhenga, Xiaofei Li, et al. Driving Risk Assessment Using Near-crash Database through Data Mining of Tree-based Model [J]. Accident Analysis & Prevention,2015,84：54-64.
[47] 徐铖铖,刘攀,王炜,等. 基于判别分析的高速公路交通安全实时评价指标[J]. 东南大学学报(自然科学版),2012,42(03)：555-559.
[48] 付存勇,王俊骅. 基于监控数据的高速公路实时事故风险模型[J]. 交通信息与安全,2017(05)：11-17.
[49] 张文彤. SPSS 11 统计分析教程[M]. 北京:北京希望电子出版社,2002.

高速公路同向曲线路段车辆行驶轨迹研究

李永春 李 枭 刘 斌 杨榕玮 靳敏达

(长安大学公路学院)

摘 要 为研究高速公路同向曲线路段车辆行驶轨迹特点,利用UC-win/Road开展驾驶模拟实验,得到了以80km/h、100km/h、120km/h,通过具有不同圆曲线半径或不同向曲线之间直线长度的同向曲线路段时的行车轨迹。采用多因素方差分析方法分析了行车速度、圆曲线半径以及同向曲线之间直线长度对同向曲线路段行车轨迹最大横向偏移值的影响显著性。同时对横向偏移值沿道路纵向变化情况进行分析。研究结果表明,圆曲线半径和行车速度对同向曲线路段最大横向偏移值的影响是显著的,而同向曲线之间的直线长度对其影响不显著;但同向曲线之间的直线长度对横向偏移值沿道路纵向的变化情况的影响较为明显。相关研究结果可为同向曲线路段优化设计及道路安全评价提供参考。

关键词 公路工程 行驶轨迹 驾驶仿真 同向曲线

0 引言

近年来,我国高速公路迅猛发展,并将战略重心放在"老少边穷"地区。这些地区往往由于地形崎岖复杂,在设计时会受到多方面的限制,因此在设计的过程中需要在满足规范的前提下进行设计指标的相应调整。公路平面线形由直线、圆曲线及缓和曲线3种线形单元组成,路线设计规范[1]对不同组合形式下的各基本单元作出了相应的要求。平曲线由于能够避免长直线引起的驾驶疲劳和更好适应地形的优点,成为平面设计的主要组成部分。但是平曲线也由于会增加驾驶员的操作难度而引发相关的安全问题,据有关资料表明,大部分交通事故发生在平曲线路段,在美国达到40%,在中国达到36%[2]。因此平曲线的设计对于公路平面整体的安全性具有重要的影响。平曲线路段是由圆曲线+直线+圆曲线构成的,主要包括同向曲线与反向曲线两类,本文的研究对象为同向曲线,同向曲线指的是两个转向相同的相邻圆曲线中间连以直线所形成的平面线形。同向曲线在设计时主要需要考虑曲线间的短直线长度,因为曲线间直线长度过短会引起驾驶员的视觉误判,容易从视觉上忽略,把两个曲线看成一个曲线;当直线长度不足以将两个曲线完全独立时,容易把中间的直线段看成反弯的断背曲线[3],这对车辆的安全行驶产生了严重的影响。目前国内外对于同向曲线间最短直线长度的要求都有相应规定。我国规范规定[1]两曲线间以直线径相连接时,直线的长度不宜过短,设计速度大于或等于60km/h时,同向曲线间最小直线长度(以 m 计)以不小于设计速度(以 km/h 计)的 6 倍为宜。美国对最小直线长度没有进行规定[4],而是根据不同的设计速度对平曲线长度提出不同的要求。日本对同向曲线间的短直线长度也未作出规定,而是有学者通过透视图检查,同向曲线间直线长度最好避免达 500~700m,以此认为把设计速度的 6 倍的西德经验标准是合适的数值。德国[5]作为世界上最早对最短直线长度进行规定的国家,提出了最小长度为设计速度 6 倍的要求。我国现行的规范则是主要参考了德国规范的取值,但是对于这一取值的具体意义没有进行相应的解释说明。国内学者对于同向曲线间的短直线合理长度进行了深入的研究,早期张正云和刘遵纪[6]从力学、舒适性和经济性角度对断背曲线的定量问题进行探讨,认为力学条件对定量断背曲线没有控制意义,当直线长度达到设计速度的 6s 行程以上就能满足驾驶员操作需要。从驾驶员视觉连贯性和舒适性方面考虑才有了 6V 的要求;在北京工业大学贺玉龙和郑柯的博士论文[7-8]中则分别考虑了运行速度以及驾驶员心生理反应等因素对同向曲线间的短直线长度进行了研究;张荣洁[9]认为同向曲线之间的最小直线长度,随着曲线半径的增大而减小,当半径大于一定值(约为600m)后,直线最小长度稳定在 220m 左右。

总而言之,目前的研究在考虑同向曲线间短直线长度时,主要以是否引起反弯错觉为判断依据,但是对于反弯错觉的界定标准又存在很大的主观性,因此对于同向曲线间的短直线长度进行定量化研究具有重要的意义。本文利用 UC-win/road 软件进行不同设计条件下的工况仿真模拟,得到了在不同平面设计指标和车速情况下的行车轨迹,量化分析行车速度、圆曲线半径及同向曲线之间直线长度对同向曲线路段最大横向偏移量的影响显著性,同时对比分析同向曲线之间具有不同直线长度的同向曲线路段横线偏移值沿道路纵向分布规律,从行车轨迹角度对同向曲线路段进行综合分析。

1 同向曲线行车特性

在进行同向曲线设计时,主要考虑了短直线长度不足对于驾驶员引起的视觉误判和操作困难问题。在同向曲线之间插入短直线被称为"断背曲线"。"断背曲线"不仅会破坏线形的连续性,甚至会使驾驶员产生错觉(图1),把线形看作两端同向弯曲的连续曲线中间插入一个反向弯曲线,在行车过程中,驾驶员未能注意到曲线半径的变化,不能及时调整方向及行驶速度而发生事故。此外保证驾驶员操纵转向盘不感到困难的行程长度至少有 6s 的行驶时间,这是因为往一个方向转动转向盘最少需要 3s。若直线长度过短,将会导致驾驶员操纵转向盘困难,引发交通事故[10]。

车辆在曲线路段行驶时,由于受到视距不良和线性

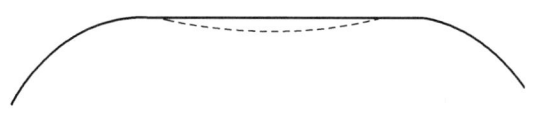

图1 断背曲线的错觉

限制的原因,驾驶员会通过不断调整车速和转向来使车辆安全通过曲线,因此车辆在通过曲线路段时很难完全沿着设计的行车道中心线进行行驶。而实际的行车轨迹也会由于车速和平面半径的不同而有所区别。在邓天民等人[11]的研究中,根据轨迹横向偏移率的聚类结果,得到山区公路曲线路段有 6 种轨迹模式,具有明显的多样性特征;而且平曲线半径越小,切弯效应越大,事故风险可控,驾驶员越倾向于采用切弯方式来通过弯道,曲线路段是否发生切弯行为的临界半径值为 200 m。由于曲线的存在,大型车和小型车驶于基本型曲线时,于弯道内侧 QZ 断面轨迹横向偏移量最小,而于弯道外侧 QZ 断面轨迹横向偏移量最大,当驾驶员对连续弯道路况较为熟悉或者行车过程逐渐适应弯道频繁转向后,倾向于靠近道路中心线行驶。在李晨[12]的硕士论文中,提出了车辆在通过曲线路段时主要有 4 种轨迹模式,并分别介绍了每一种轨迹模式所对应的条件,这四种轨迹模式分别是正常轨迹、漂移型轨迹、校正型轨迹和切弯型轨迹。一般情况而言,驾驶员会根据期望产生相应的期望速度与期望轨迹,当实际情况发生变化时,行车轨迹和速度就会做出相应调整。在邢大伟的博士论文中提出视觉作为驾驶员获取信息的主要途径,约 85%以上的信息都依靠视觉获得,因此视觉感知特性直接影响到驾驶员的操作与车辆的运行状态[13]。综上,行车轨迹能间接反映驾驶员对于路况信息的处理。

因此,为了研究车辆在通过同向曲线路段时的横向稳定性,以轨迹横向偏移值为研究对象,综合考虑车速、半径以及曲线间短直线长度的影响,本文以此为切入点,对同向曲线路段车辆进行驾驶仿真实验。通过得到的实际轨迹数据首先分析了影响行车轨迹最大横向偏移量的影响因素以及影响强弱,其次对于横向轨迹偏移量在不同设计速度和半径下的纵向分布规律进行了总结与分析。

2 驾驶仿真试验设计

目前关于车辆行车轨迹的获取方法主要可以分为实车试验法、计算机仿真法和驾驶模拟仿真法等三大类。具体如下。

实车试验法:试验者驾驶车辆在选定的实验路段行驶,通过无人机摄影,路侧安置的摄像机、传感器等来捕捉车辆运行轨迹或在特定断面的横向偏移值。例如,Fitzsimmons[14]等通过路面充气管来记录曲线路段的轨迹和速度,分析了轨迹横向偏移以及切弯行为。符锌砂、林慧等[15-16]均采用了路侧摄像来获取轨迹偏移。

计算机仿真法:应用电子计算机实现对道路、车辆、驾驶员及环境的全面模拟,相应模型均为特定的算法或程序。常见的计算机仿真法软件如 Carsim、Trucksim 等。

驾驶模拟仿真法:实验者通过操纵驾驶模拟器,在搭建的虚拟实验道路上行驶,通过软件系统自带的数据记录、输出功能获取行车轨迹数据。与计算机仿真法将特定程序作为驾驶员决策模型不同,驾驶模拟仿真法是驾驶员通过操纵驾驶模拟器来对驾驶决策进行输入,主导者仍是人。常见平台如同济大学的交通行为与交通安全模拟实验平台,长安大学的六自由度汽车性能虚拟仿真实验平台、2 自由度 UC-win/Road 运动仿真平台等。

结合上述内容,总结各方法优缺点见表 1。

行车轨迹获取方法对比　　　　　表 1

序号	试验方法	优　点	缺　点
1	实车试验法	能反映真实驾驶情况	选定试验路段困难,仅可获取有限断面数据,干扰交通,安全隐患
2	计算机仿真	可构建任意道路模型,可获取任意断面数据,车辆模型较为精确	驾驶员模型为特定算法,与实际驾驶行为相差较大
3	驾驶模拟仿真	结合了实车法和计算机仿真的优点,但与实际驾驶仍有一定差距	

驾驶仿真试验研究的目的是探讨高速公路短直线路段在不同平面设计指标及行车速度下的行车轨迹特性,在现实道路上选择具有不同平面设计指标的试验路段并开展实车试验十分困难;此外,实车试验

也仅能获取部分断面的轨迹横向偏移值,并存在一定安全隐患,因此放弃采用实车试验法。

对于计算机仿真法和驾驶模拟仿真法,两者在构建道路模型方面差别不大,计算机仿真法在车辆模型方面更为精确,而驾驶模拟仿真法在驾驶员决策方面更加贴近实车驾驶情况;在数据采集方面,因软件系统自带的数据采集、输出功能均较为强大,基本可认为能采集任意位置的行车轨迹数据,因此均可满足试验数据采集的要求。而行车轨迹可间接反映驾驶员感知道路、环境等信息,通过大脑分析处理后,并采取相应驾驶操作的结果,该过程受驾驶员影响较大。综上所述,采用驾驶模拟仿真方法获取行车轨迹数据。

2.1 道路模型

如图2所示,要确定一个短直线路段的平面线形,需要输入的指标包括两端的直线段长度 L_1 和 L_3;第一段曲线及第二段曲线之间的直线长度 L_2;第一段曲线的圆曲线半径 R_1,及其两端的回旋线参数 A_{11},A_{12};第二段曲线的圆曲线半径 R_2,及其两端的回旋线参数 A_{21},A_{22}。主要探讨短直线路段圆曲线半径(图2中 R_1 及 R_2)、同向曲线之间直线长度(图2中 L_2)以及通过短直线路段的行车速度对短直线路段行车轨迹的影响。同时采用正交试验设计试验方案。

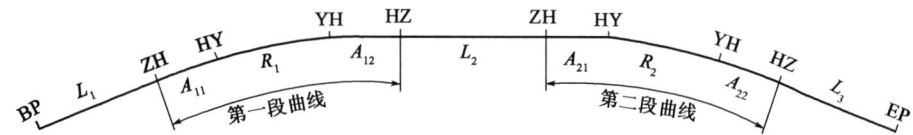

图2 短直线路段示意图

将以上三个因素均划分为三种水平。其中,通过直线路段的行车速度分别采用80km/h、100km/h、120km/h,分别与高速公路常用的设计速度相对应。短直线路段的圆曲线半径分别采用800m、1400m、2000m,分别与设计速度80km/h、100km/h、120km/h时圆曲线半径一般值相对应。根据《公路路线设计规范》(JTG D20—2017)同向曲线之间直线长度小于设计速度$6V$形成短直线路段,因此本文也将同向曲线之间的长度划分为三种水平 $0V\sim2V$,$2V\sim4V$,$4V\sim6V$,同时分别取其中值 $1V$、$3V$、$5V$ 进行道路模型构建。因素水平划分如表2所示。

因 素 水 平 表　　　　表2

水平	A 短直线路段圆曲线半径(m)	B 同向曲线之间直线长度(m)	C 通过短直线路段的行车速度(km/h)
1	800	$1V$	80
2	1400	$3V$	100
3	2000	$5V$	120

同时,选用合适的正交试验表进行实验方案设计,具体如表3所示。

正 交 试 验 方 案　　　　表3

编号	半径 A	直线长度 B	行车速度 C	空 D	试验方案
1	800	$1V$	80	1	A1B1C1
2	800	$3V$	100	2	A1B2C2
3	800	$5V$	120	3	A1B3C3
4	1400	$1V$	100	3	A2B1C2
5	1400	$3V$	120	1	A2B2C3
6	1400	$5V$	80	2	A2B3C1
7	2000	$1V$	120	2	A3B1C3
8	2000	$3V$	80	3	A3B2C1
9	2000	$5V$	100	1	A3B3C2

除了以上3个参数外,为使车辆到达曲线路段时能够达到预定的行车速度,在曲线路段两侧设置了两个直线段L_1、L_3,两段长度均为1km。缓和曲线参数A_{11}、A_{12}、A_{21}、A_{22}取值则参考《公路路线设计规范》(JTG D20—2017)相关要求,同时兼顾超高过渡长度、最小缓和曲线长度的要求。短在线试验路段具体参数如表4所示。

短直线试验路段平面参数取值 表4

设计速度 (km/h)	L_1(m)	A_{11}(m)	R_1(m)	A_{12}(m)	L_2(m)	A_{21}(m)	R_2(m)	A_{22}(m)	L_3(m)
80	1000	282.843	800	282.843	80	282.843	800	282.843	1000
	1000	282.843	800	282.843	240	282.843	800	282.843	1000
	1000	282.843	800	282.843	400	282.843	800	282.843	1000
100	1000	529.15	1400	529.15	100	529.15	1400	529.15	1000
	1000	529.15	1400	529.15	300	529.15	1400	529.15	1000
	1000	529.15	1400	529.15	500	529.15	1400	529.15	1000
120	1000	707.107	2000	707.107	120	707.107	2000	707.107	1000
	1000	707.107	2000	707.107	360	707.107	2000	707.107	1000
	1000	707.107	2000	707.107	600	707.107	2000	707.107	1000

本文主要探讨短直线路段平面设计指标及通过短直线路段的行车速度与短直线路段行车轨迹之间的关系,因此在道路建模时道路纵断面采用直坡段,未设置竖曲线。此外,为减小纵坡对实验结果的影响,本研究道路纵坡采用0.3%,道路纵断面参数标定如图3所示。

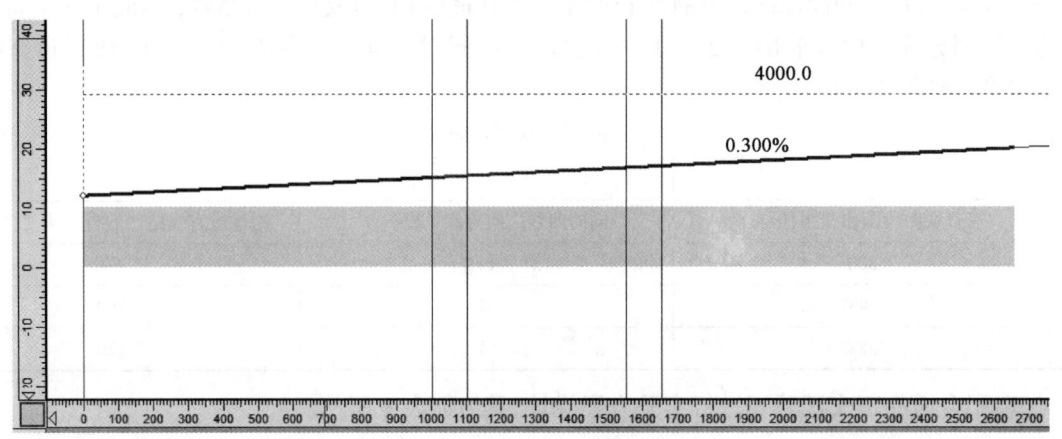

图3 道路纵断面参数标定

道路横断面采用国内双向四车道高速公路常用横断面组成,其路幅组成为:0.75m 土路肩 + 3m 硬路肩 + 2×3.75m 行车道 + 0.75m 左侧路缘带 + 2m 中央分隔带 + 0.75m 左侧路缘带 + 2×3.75m 行车道 + 3m 硬路肩 + 0.75m 土路肩 = 24.5m。道路横断面标定如图4所示,标准断面路幅宽度24.5m,行车道、硬路肩横坡均采用2%。应当注意,道路位于曲线路段时,会随着圆曲线半径、设计速度等的变化采用不同的超高值,本文对道路的超高进行标定,不同路段超高取值按照《公路路线设计规范》(JTG D20—2017)进行取值,如设计速度为80km/h,圆曲线半径为800m时道路横断面参数如图4所示,该路段行车道、硬路肩超高均采用4%。不同路段之间的超高过渡可通过添加Transition来进行设置,设置完成后其会在道路纵断面图中进行位置示意,如设计速度80km/h、圆曲线半径为800m时道路断面设置如图4所示,其对应纵断面如图3所示。某工况下UC-win/Road道路模型如图5所示。

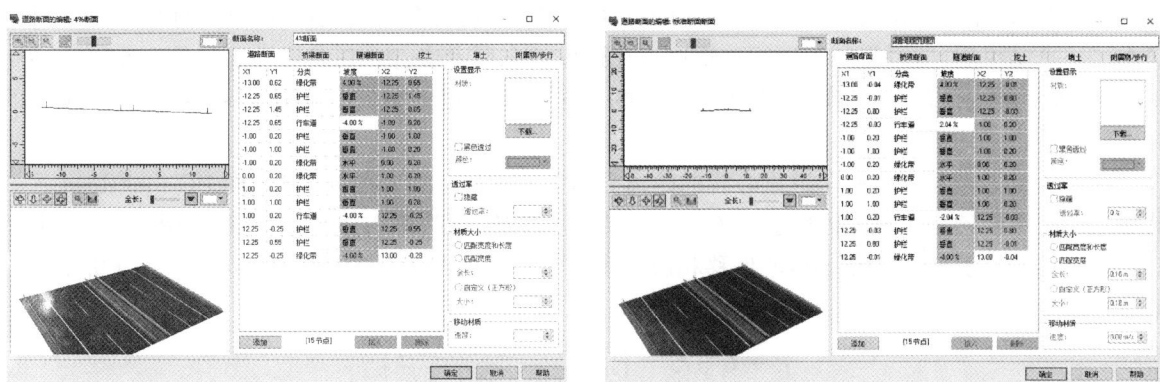

图 4 道路横断面参数标定

图 5 道路模型

2.2 车辆模型

UC-win/Road 车辆模型主要包括车辆 3D 模型及其动力学模型两部分。本研究以小型车为研究对象开展仿真实验，参考《公路工程设计标准》(JTG B01—2014)[17]中对车辆宽度、轴距等相关要求，在 UC-win/Road 中对车辆 3D 模型进行参数标定，如轴距设置为 2.5m，车辆宽度设置为 1.8m 等。相关参数设定如图 6 所示。

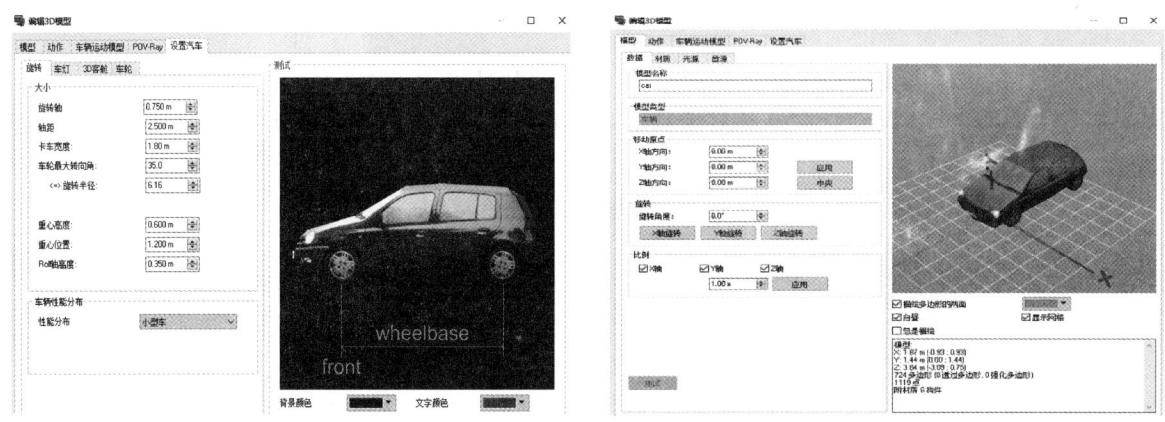

图 6 车辆参数标定

车辆动力学方面，UC-win/Road 除了可采用其自身车辆动力学外，还可采用 INNOSIMULATION 车辆动力学以及 CarSim 车辆动力学，本研究采用 UC-win/Road 车辆动力学。

2.3 试验方案

建立完仿真模型后，即可开展驾驶模型仿真试验。对于驾驶员的选取，本次驾驶试验由 15 位志愿者实际操作,在所建立的道路模型中进行无干扰的自由驾驶,平均每个驾驶次数为2次,每个工况得到约30组样本。仿真结束后,即可得到车辆行驶轨迹。在选取的志愿者中,由10名男性驾驶员和5名女性驾驶员组成,驾驶年龄主要是3~5年,具有相对充分的驾驶经验。根据得到的实验结果,对每组工况下的所有样本数据进行平均值计算。

采用车辆重心偏移相应行车道重心线的距离分析短直线路段行车轨迹特性,而UC-win/Road驾驶模拟器输出的行车轨迹为车辆左侧轮胎至左边界的距离或车辆右侧轮胎至右边界的距离(如图7中A或B所示)。因此,需要将其转化为车辆重心偏移相应行车道中心线的距离(图7中L),以便后文分析车辆的横向偏移特性。转换公式为:

$$L = 6.375 - \left(A + \frac{11.25 - A - B}{2}\right) \tag{1}$$

式中:L——车辆重心与相应行车道中心线距离,m;
A——车辆左侧轮胎至左侧边界距离,m;
B——车辆右侧轮胎至左侧边界距离,m。

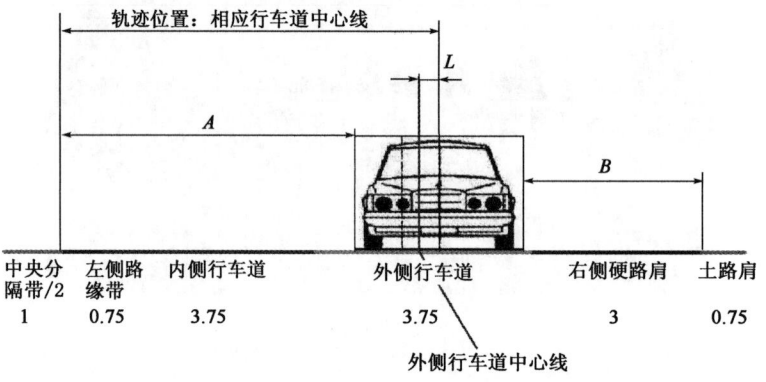

图7 L与A、B关系示意图(尺寸单位:m)

根据L定义以及图7可知,当L为负值时,表示车辆向右侧偏移;当L为正值时,表示车辆向左侧偏移。

3 仿真结果分析

3.1 最大横向偏移值

按前文所述的试验方案进行驾驶仿真实验,得到了驾驶员采用不同行车速度通过不同圆曲线半径、不同短直线长度的短直线路段时车辆的最大横向偏移值,不同试验方案下最大横向偏移值仿真结果如表5所示。

最大横向偏移值 表5

试 验 号	半径A(m)	直线长度(m)	行车速度C(km/h)	空列D	试验结果Y_i(m)
1	800	$1V$	80	1	0.465
2	800	$3V$	100	2	0.517
3	800	$5V$	120	3	0.661
4	1400	$1V$	100	3	0.450
5	1400	$3V$	120	1	0.562
6	1400	$5V$	80	2	0.407
7	2000	$1V$	120	2	0.451
8	2000	$3V$	80	3	0.308
9	2000	$5V$	100	1	0.360

对正交试验结果的分析方法主要有两种，一种是极差分析（直观分析），另一种是方差分析。极差分析原理简单，可排出影响因素的主次顺序，并确定最优水平的搭配，但无法判断考察因素对试验结果的影响是否显著，也无法确定考察因素的显著性水平；方差分析除了具有极差分析功能外，克服了极差分析的缺陷，但其分析过程较为复杂[18]。需确定行车速度、圆曲线半径以及同向曲线之间直线长度对轨迹最大横向偏移量的影响是否显著，并确定相应的显著性水平，因此对正交试验结果进行方差分析。方差分析相关原理及计算方法可参考上文提到的数理统计，同时也可借用 SPSS、MATLAB、MINITAB 等统计工具进行方差分析。

短直线路段行车轨迹最大横向偏移值方差分析结果如表6所示。

方 差 分 析 结 果　　　　表6

方差来源	离差平方和	自由度	平均离差平方和	F 值
A	0.04608	2	0.02304	133.619
B	0.00066	2	0.00033	1.922
C	0.04289	2	0.02145	124.373
误差	0.00034	2	0.00017	
总和	0.08999	8		

当给定显著水平 $\alpha = 0.05$ 时，F 分布上侧分位数，$F_{0.05}(2,2) = 19.000$。由表6可知，因素 A、C 对应 F 值分别为 133.619 和 124.373，远大于 $F_{0.05}(2,2) = 19.000$，说明圆曲线半径，以及通过短直线路段的行车速度对短直线路段行车轨迹最大横向偏移值都是非常显著的。文献[12]研究结果与本文研究结果一致，对于短直线路段而言，圆曲线半径，以及通过短直线路段的行车速度仍然是影响行车轨迹最大横向偏移值的两个关键因素。根据表6可知，因素 B 对应 F 值为 1.922，小于 $F_{0.05}(2,2) = 19.000$，说明同向曲线间直线长度对短直线路段行车轨迹横向偏移值不显著，从道路几何设计指标角度来说，其不是影响短直线路段行车轨迹最大横向偏移值的关键因素。

3.2 横向偏移值沿道路纵向分布

在圆曲线半径一定的条件下，同向圆曲线之间采用不同的短直线从而形成不同的短直线路段。本研究以设计速度 80km/h，圆曲线半径采用 800m 条件下不同的短直线路段为例，对短直线路段最大横向偏移值的位置进行分析。仿真实验时，通过短直线路段的行车速度均采用 80km/h，同向曲线间的直线长度分别取设计速度的 $1v$、$3v$、$5v$，即 80m、240m 和 500m。

本研究在分析短直线路段行车轨迹最大横向偏移值位置时，为获得一个参照标准，本研究获取了基本型曲线路段的行车轨迹数据。该基本型曲线圆曲线半径、转角、缓和曲线参数及长度与短直线路段保持一致。

通过驾驶模拟获取了驾驶员采用 80km/h 行车速度通过基本型曲线路段（直线 + 缓和曲线 + 圆曲线 + 缓和曲线 + 直线）时车辆的行车轨迹，其横向偏移值与桩号的关系如图8所示。

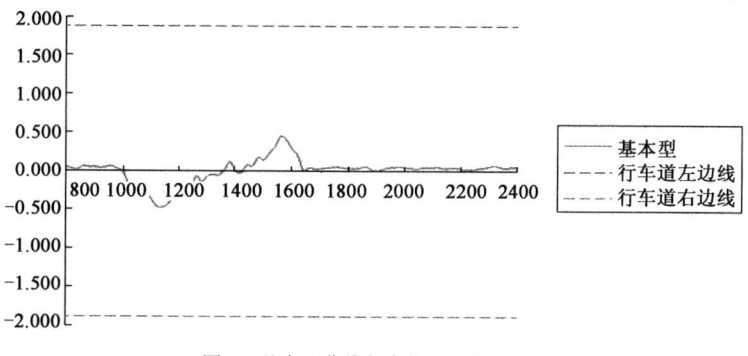

图8　基本型曲线行车轨迹（单位：m）

结合前文可知,图 7 所采用的实验路段 ZH 点桩号为 K1+000,HY 点桩号为 K1+100,YH 点桩号为 K1+555,HZ 点桩号为 K1+655。由图 7 可知,车辆进入曲线段时,行车轨迹表现为向曲线内侧偏移(向右侧偏移),车辆驶出曲线路段时,行车轨迹表现为向曲线外侧偏移(向左侧偏移)。这与文献[19]研究结果"车辆右转弯时,入弯至出弯呈现右偏—左偏"相一致。同时,由图 7 可以看出向曲线内侧的横向偏移量最大值发生在 K1+150 附近,向外侧偏移的横向偏移量最大值发生在 K1+550 附近,即分别发生在 HY 和 YH 点附近。这与文献[15]研究结果基本一致。

通过驾驶模拟获取了驾驶员采用 80km/h 行车速度通过采用不同直线长度(80m、240m、400m)的短直线路段时车辆的行车轨迹,其横向偏移值与桩号的关系如图 9 所示。

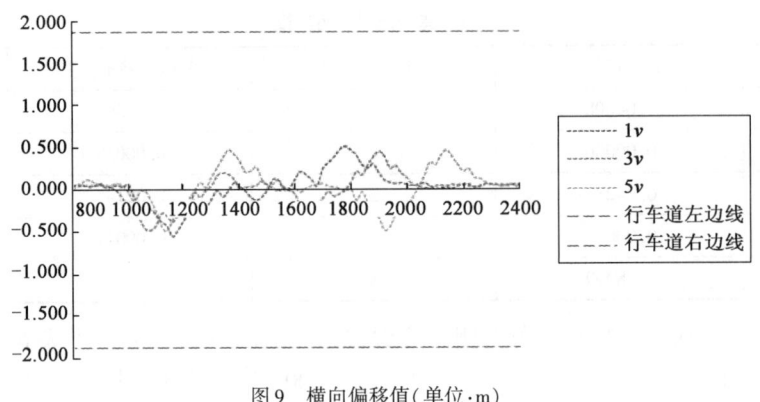

图 9　横向偏移值(单位:m)

由图 9 可知,同向曲线之间分别采用 80m、240m 和 400m 所形成的短直线路段其行车轨迹最大横向偏移值均约为 0.5m,同时与图 8 中基本型曲线路段行车轨迹最大横向偏移值也较为接近,进一步说明了同向曲线之间的直线长度不是影响短直线路段行车轨迹最大横向偏移值的主要因素。

同时,由图 9 还可发现:当同向曲线之间直线长度较短时(图 9 中的 $1v$),行车轨迹横向偏移值随桩号的变化情况与基本型曲线较为接近,这说明当同向曲线之间直线长度较小时,其往往被驾驶员误以为是曲线路段,驾驶员即使行驶在短直线上也不会将转向盘回正,而是与基本型曲线路段类似,采用一定的转向盘转角来通过短直线路段。随着同向曲线之间直线长度的增加(图 9 中的 $3v$),驶入第一段曲线和驶出第二段曲线时行车轨迹偏移值随桩号变化情况与基本型曲线类似,驾驶员均有向曲线内侧或外侧偏移的倾向,而由第一段曲线驶入短直线(驶出第一段曲线)和由短直线驶入第二段曲线(驶入第二段曲线)时,驾驶员有向曲线内侧或曲线外侧偏移的倾向,但不明显,这说明驾驶员开始意识到同向曲线之间的短直线,并具有将转向盘回正的意识,但因直线长度较短,其没有充足时间来完成操作。随着同向曲线之间直线长度的进一步增加(图 9 中的 $5v$),驶入、驶出第一段曲线,或驶入、驶出第二段曲线时行车轨迹偏移值随桩号变化情况分别与基本型曲线类似,驾驶员在驶入驶出第一段、第二段曲线时行车轨迹向内侧、外侧偏移的倾向均较为明显,说明驾驶员已经能够较为清楚的意识同向曲线之间的直线路段,并有较为充裕的时间来将转向盘回正,完成驾驶操作。

4　结　语

(1)本文分析了同向曲线路段最大横向偏移值与行车速度、圆曲线半径及同向曲线之间长度之间的相关性,发现圆曲线半径、行车速度对其影响较为显著,而同向曲线之间直线长度对其影响不显著。

(2)在 80km/h 行车速度,圆曲线半径采用 800m 条件下,对比分析了同向曲线之间长度分别采用 $1v$、$3v$、$5v$ 所构成的同向曲线路段行车轨迹横向偏移值沿道路纵向的分布规律,发现同向曲线之间直线长度的变化不影响横向偏移量的峰值(最大横向偏移量),而对横向最大横向偏移量出现的位置具有显著影响。

(3)同向曲线之间长度较短时(1v),其行车轨迹纵向变化规律与基本型曲线类似,仅在驶入第一段曲线及驶出第二段曲线时有较为明显的横向偏移;当同向曲线之间长度较大时(5v),在驶入驶出第一段曲线,驶入驶出第二段曲线时均有较为明显的横向偏移;而当同向曲线之间长度适中时(3v),在驶出第一段曲线及驶入第二段曲线时有一定的横向偏移,但不明显。

(4)仅分析了同向曲线路段最大行车轨迹偏移值与圆曲线半径、同向曲线之间直线长度、行车速度之间的相关性,后续研究中可建立同向曲线路段最大行车轨迹偏移值的预测模型。

(5)在建立道路模型时,第一段曲线半径R_1与第二段曲线半径R_2采用了同一半径,同时第一段曲线缓和曲线参数A_{11}、A_{12}与第二段曲线缓和曲线参数A_{21}、A_{22}均相等,后续可研究参数以上参数取值的变化对同向曲线路段行车轨迹的影响。

参考文献

[1] 交通运输部.公路路线设计规范:JTG D20—2017.[S].北京:人民交通出版社股份有限公司,2017.

[2] McGee H W Hanscom, Fred R. Low-Cost Treatments for Horizontal Curve Safety[M]. Washington DC, USA: Transportation Research Record(S0021-8952),2009.

[3] 覃盛科.基于运行速度的高速公路直线段最小长度取值研究[J].西部交通科技,2017(04):13-15,62.

[4] American Association of State Highway and Transportation Officials (AASHTO). A Policy on Geometric Design of Highways and Streets [M].5th Edition,Washington,D.C.2004

[5] 德国路线设计规范[M].1995.

[6] 张正云.刘遵纪.谈公路"断背曲线"[J].公路.1983(11):19-22.

[7] 贺玉龙.高速公路直线长度研究[D].北京:北京工业大学,2002.

[8] 郑柯.基于驾驶员心理生理反应的高速公路线形研究[D].北京:北京工业大学,2003.

[9] 张荣洁,程建川,凌九忠.公路最小直线长度计算[J].公路交通科技.2012,29(3):39-44.

[10] 张荣洁.公路最小直线长度计算[D].南京:东南大学,2010.

[11] 邓天民,罗晓,邵毅明,等.山区公路曲线路段汽车轨迹模式与切弯行为[J].东南大学学报,2019,49(2):388-396.

[12] 李晨.穿村镇公路小半径曲线段行车轨迹实验研究[D].北京:北京工业大学,2016.

[13] 邢大伟.驾驶人视觉感知特性及其建模研究[D].长春:吉林大学,2019.

[14] Eric J F,Shashi S N,Reginald R S,et al. Analyses of Vehicle Trajectories and Speed Profiles Along Horizontal Curves[J]. Journal of Transportation Safety & Security,2013(5):187-207.

[15] 符锌砂,何石坚,杜锦涛,等.线形空间几何突变对曲线路段车道偏移的影响[J].中国公路学报,2019,32(12):106-114.

[16] 林慧,郭建钢,陈金山,等.双车道山区公路反向连续弯道危险区域研究[J].中国安全科学学报,2017,27(8):138-143.

[17] 交通运输部.公路工程技术标准:JTG B01—2014[S].北京:人民交通出版社,2014.

[18] 汪荣鑫.数理统计[M].陕西:西安交通大学出版社,1986.

[19] 陈柳晓,唐伯明,张勃,等.二十四道拐盘山公路车辆行驶轨迹研究[J].重庆交通大学学报,2018,38:47-54.

高速公路分路段横净距评价方法与改善措施

向宇杰[1] 李丙烨[2] 谢永淑[1] 唐忠泽[1] 胡瑞来[1]

(1.长安大学公路学院；2.长安大学运输工程学院)

摘要 视距是公路设计中最基本的元素之一，是驾驶员遇到紧急情况时采取措施的安全保障，而横净距是衡量视距满足与否的重要指标。因此横净距成为公路设计中的关键控制因素，针对不同路段需提出不同的固有横净距评价方法。本文根据道路驾驶员视点位置、横断面组成形式、道路构造物的影响因素，对不同路段的固有横净距进行评价，提出符合不同路段特点的固有横净距评价方法并介绍其在实际公路工程设计中的具体运用，供设计人员参考。最后针对视距不良路段提出相应的改善措施。

关键词 横净距 视距 评价方法 路线设计 改善措施

0 引言

目前，随着经济及汽车行业的不断发展，交通安全愈发重要。公路行车安全性除受驾驶员的驾驶技术、气候条件、交通量大小、路况等因素影响外，与道路几何特征也密切相关。行车视距不良是影响交通安全的重要原因，而横净距是衡量行车视距的关键因素之一。

《公路路线设计规范》(JTG D20—2017)(以下简称《规范》)条文说明7.9.6规定："公路视距检验时，应对平曲线内侧车道、竖曲线起终点等视距最不利的车道或位置进行逐桩位的检查，并应采用对应视距的视点位置、视点高度和目标(或障碍物)的物高。视点位置应取车道宽度的1/2处(即车道中心线)；小客车视点高度取高出路面1.2m，货车取2.0m；目标(或障碍物)的位置应取路面两侧对应的车道边缘线；停车视距的物高取高出路面0.1m 识别视距的物高取0m(路面标线的高度)，超车视距的物高取对向车辆(小客车)的前灯高度0.6m。"[1] 目前《规范》中缺少对固有横净距计算的分析，并且视点的位置与我国汽车左舵驾驶的视点位置不一致，若按照《规范》规定的视点位置计算道路的固有横净距，则偏于不安全，故应采用更准确的视点位置来计算视距。

在道路设计中，曲线内侧车道旁设置硬路肩、土路肩、排水沟、碎落台等，曲线外侧超车道旁设置中央分隔带、护栏、防眩设施等，这些因素都会影响固有横净距计算。因此为提高路线设计的安全性，有必要对不同路段固有横净距进行分析。固有横净距不足的情况可分为两类：

(1)车辆左偏时中央分隔带护栏和防眩设施对中央分隔带外侧超车道的影响；

(2)车辆右偏时右侧障碍物对曲线内侧行车道的影响。本文结合不同路段对这两类情况下的固有横净距进行分析计算，并提出当横净距不足时可采取的改善措施。

1 横净距计算

在弯道各点的横断面上，驾驶员视点轨迹线与视距曲线之间的距离叫横净距，用h表示。h可根据视距S和平曲线长L、视点轨迹线半径R_s计算，如图1所示。道路视距不足的原因之一是曲线路段上障碍物导致横净距不足。对于道路横净距计算参考《道路勘测设计》(第5版)[2]。

1.1 不设置缓和曲线的横净距计算

(1)当$S<L$，如图2所示。

基金项目：国家重点研发计划项目重大自然灾害监测预警与防范(2020YFC1512000)。

$$h = R_s\left(1 - \cos\frac{\gamma}{2}\right) \tag{1}$$

式中:$\gamma = \dfrac{180° s}{\pi R_s}$。

(2)当 $S > L$,如图3所示。

$$h = h_1 + h_2$$
$$h = R_s\left(1 - \cos\frac{\alpha}{2}\right) + \frac{1}{2}(S - L)\sin\frac{\alpha}{2} \tag{2}$$

式中:$L = \dfrac{\pi}{180}\alpha R_s$。

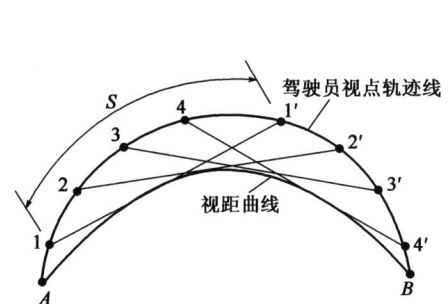

图1 横净距示图

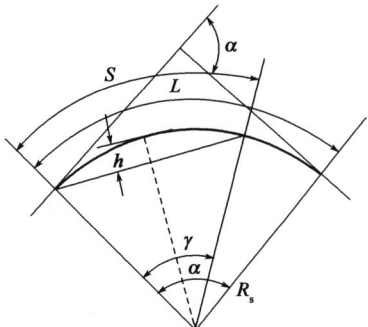

图2 无缓和曲线 $S < L$ 时计算示图

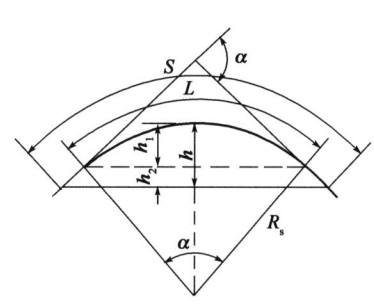

图3 无缓和曲线 $S > L$ 时计算示图

1.2 设置缓和曲线的横净距计算

(1)当 $S < L'$,同计算式(1)。

(2)当 $L' < S < L$,如图4所示。

$$h = h_1 + h_2$$
$$h = R_s\left(1 - \cos\frac{\alpha - 2\beta}{2}\right) + \sin\left(\frac{\alpha}{2} - \delta\right)(l - l') \tag{3}$$

式中:δ——$\tan^{-1}\left\{\dfrac{1}{6R_s}\left[1 + \dfrac{l'}{l} + \left(\dfrac{l'}{l}\right)^2\right]\right\}$;

$l' = \dfrac{1}{2}(L - S)$。

(3)当 $S > L$,如图5所示。

$$h = h_1 + h_2 + h_3$$

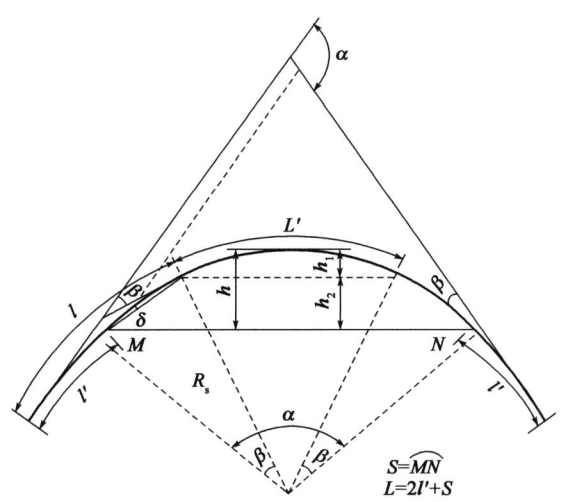

图4 设置缓和曲线 $L' < S < L$ 时计算示图

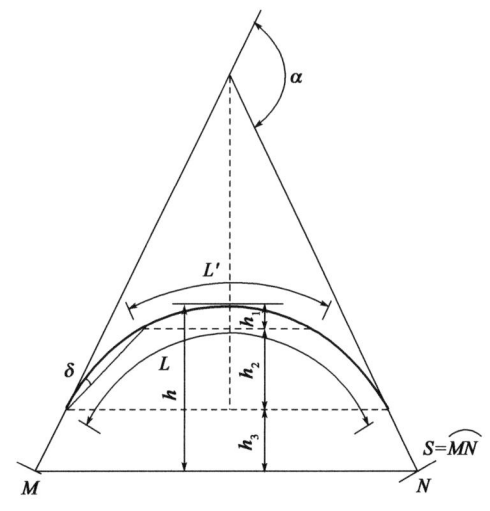

图5 设置缓和曲线 $S > L$ 时计算示图

$$h = R_s\left(1 - \cos\frac{\alpha - 2\beta}{2}\right) + \sin\left(\frac{\alpha}{2} - \delta\right)l + \frac{S - L}{2}\sin\frac{\alpha}{2} \qquad (4)$$

式中：δ——$\tan^{-1}\dfrac{l}{6R_s}$。

　　　　h——最大横净距，m；

　　　　S——视距，m；

　　　　L——平曲线长度，m；

　　　　L'——圆曲线长度，m；

　　　　l——缓和曲线长度，m；

　　　　R_s——曲线内侧视点轨迹线的半径，m；

　　　　α——曲线转角，(°)；

　　　　δ——视线所对应的圆心角，(°)；

　　　　β——道路中线缓和曲线全长所对应的回旋线角，(°)。

2 固有横净距影响因素

2.1 视点位置

《道路勘测设计》(第 5 版)以及 Dejan Gavran 等研究中将曲线内侧车道驾驶员视点的平面位置确定在距未加宽路面内侧边缘 1.5m，当设置加宽时附加加宽值[2-3]，赵永平等研究分析在中央分隔带外侧超车道上，驾驶员视点的平面位置可确定在距左侧路缘带 1.2m 处[4]。隧道断面具有特殊性，根据长安大学周海宇的调查，小客车在隧道内左侧车道行驶时视点位置在距离左侧车道左边线 1.6m 处，右侧车道视点位置在距离右侧车道左边线 0.8m 处；货车在隧道内左侧车道行驶时视点位置在距离左侧车道左边线 1.4m 处，右侧车道视点位置在距离右侧车道左边线 1m 处[5]，如图 6 和图 7 所示。由以上横净距计算公式可知，视点位置的改变对横净距计算值影响较小，但需考虑对道路固有横净距的影响。

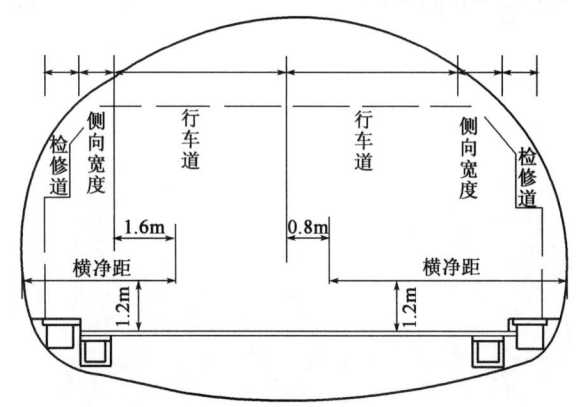

图 6　隧道段小客车视点位置示图

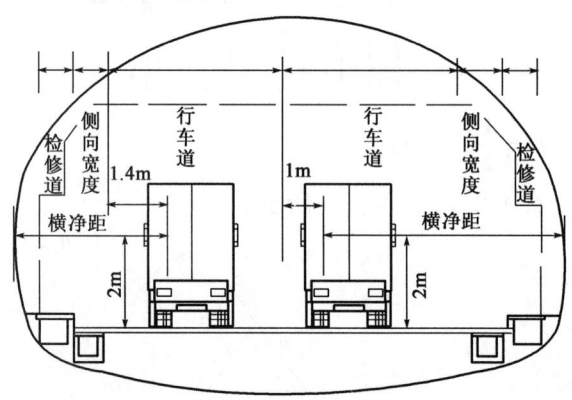

图 7　隧道段货车视点位置示图

2.2 横断面形式

道路组成形式多样，不同路段由于横断面组成不同，车辆行驶过程中视点至障碍物的距离不同，导致道路提供固有横净距的差异性。

2.3 护栏

护栏本身也是一种障碍物，护栏的布设与护栏的种类影响路段固有横净距的计算。采用波形梁护栏时，固有横净距由视点计算至护栏处，如图 8 所示；采用混凝土护栏时，固有横净距可加上护栏渐变的横向净宽值如图 9 所示；当路堑路段曲线内侧不布设护栏时，固有横净距可由视点计算至视高对应路堑边坡处，如图 10 所示。货车视高为 2m，故货车在路堑路段曲线内侧车道视线不受护栏影响，固有横净距由视点计算至视高对应路堑边坡处。

2.4 防眩板

当中央分隔带宽度较小时,要以防眩板为主进行防眩。防眩板的布设与种类影响路段固有横净距的计算。路段中央分隔带采用防眩板防眩时,在计算固有横净距时可由视点位置计算至防眩板边缘,如图11所示。

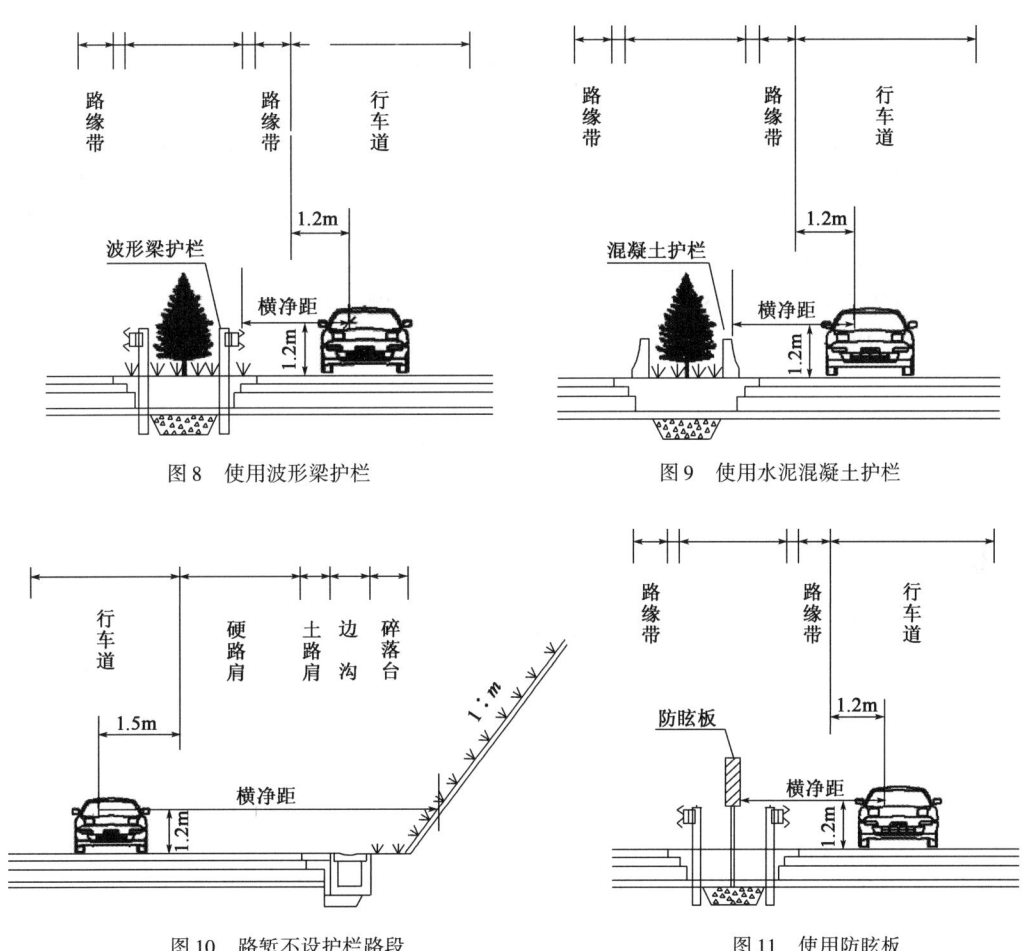

图8 使用波形梁护栏　　　　　　图9 使用水泥混凝土护栏

图10 路堑不设护栏路段　　　　　图11 使用防眩板

3 固有横净距计算方法

根据道路类型的差异性因素,结合以上固有横净距影响因素,分路段将具有普遍通用性的计算方法区分于中央分隔带外侧超车道与曲线内侧车道,见表1和表2,具体计算过程参考工程运用实例。

中央分隔带外侧超车道　　　　　　　　　　　　　　　　　　　　　表1

路段类型		固有横净距计算方法
路堤、路堑、桥梁	植物防眩	视点至行车道边缘 + 左侧路缘带宽度 + 余宽(左侧路缘带至护栏距离)
	防眩板防眩	视点至行车道边缘 + 左侧路缘带宽度 + 余宽(左侧路缘带至防眩板距离)
隧道		视点至行车道边缘 + 左侧侧向宽度 + 检修道宽度

曲线内侧车道　　　　　　　　　　　　　　　　　　　　　　　　　表2

路段类型		固有横净距计算方法
路堤		视点至行车道边缘 + 硬路肩宽度
路堑	无护栏	视点至行车道边缘 + 硬路肩宽度 + 土路肩宽度 + 边沟及护坡道宽度 + 视高×m
	布设护栏	视点至行车道边缘 + 硬路肩宽度

续上表

路 段 类 型	固有横净距计算方法
桥梁	视点至行车道边缘 + 硬路肩宽度 + 硬路肩至护栏距离
隧道	视点至行车道边缘 + 右侧侧向宽度 + 检修道宽度

注:1. 表中计算均以小客车为例。
   2. 路堑边坡坡率取 1:m。

4 工程运用实例

四川至贵州某高速公路采用设计速度 100km/h、双向六车道高速公路技术标准,路基宽度 33.5m。本项目整体式路基中央分隔带护栏和分离式路基护栏采用波形梁护栏,桥梁曲线路侧采用混凝土护栏,渐变的横向净宽值为 0.182m。本项目部分分离式路基/桥梁段左右线相距大于 9m,不用设置防眩设施,具体段落包含 K15+458.262—K15+732,其他路段采用 Gs-P-Gw1 或 Gs-P-Gw2 型防眩板。

横净距计算以道路左线 K15+458.262—K26+650.781 为例,路段曲线均未加宽,计算车型以小客车为例。各路段横断面形式如图 12 ~ 图 14 所示,计算过程如表 3 ~ 表 6 所示。

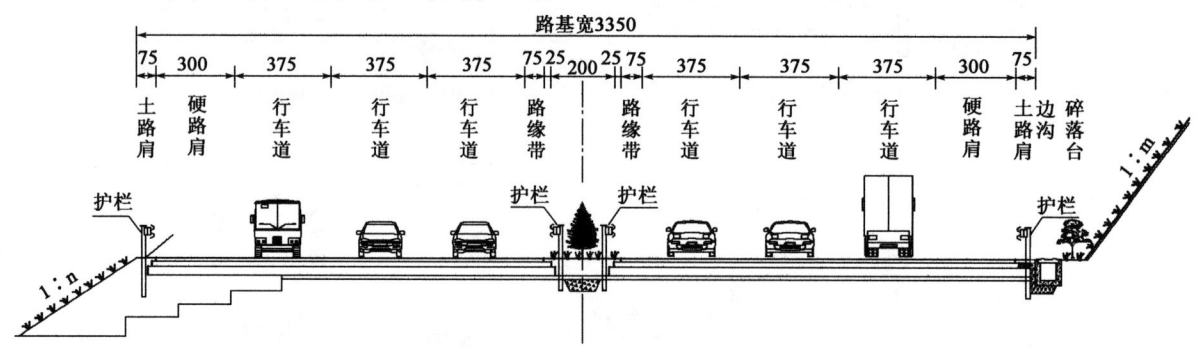

图 12 路堤、路堑横断面(尺寸单位:cm)

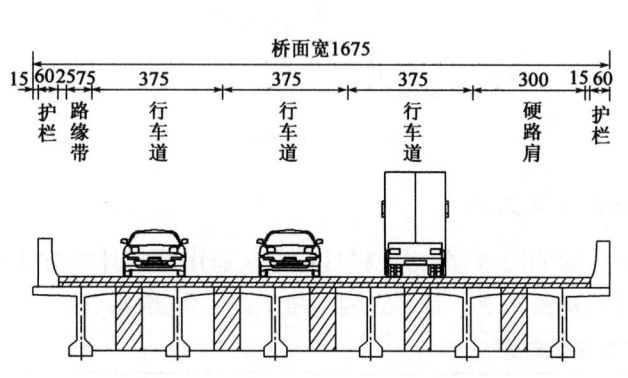

图 13 分离式桥梁横断面(尺寸单位:cm)

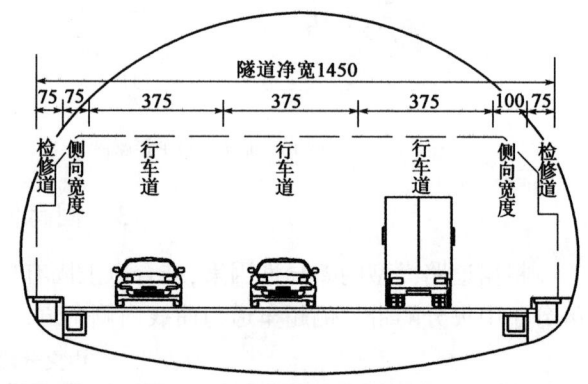

图 14 隧道横断面(尺寸单位:cm)

中央分隔带外侧超车道固有横净距(单位:m)　　　　表3

路 段 类 型	视点至行车道边缘	路缘带	余 宽	固有横净距
无防眩设施段分离式路基	1.2	0.75	0.25	2.2
无防眩设施段分离式混凝土护栏桥梁	1.2	0.75	0.25 + 0.182	2.382
采用 Gs-P-Gw1 型防眩板	1.2	0.75	0.25 + 0.3	2.5
采用 Gs-P-Gw2 型防眩板	1.2	0.75	0.25 + 0.67	2.87

注:表中 0.3m 与 0.67m 分别为护栏至 Gs-P-Gw1 型、Gs-P-Gw2 型防眩板的距离。

曲线内侧车道固有横净距(单位:m)   表4

路段类型	视点至行车道边缘	硬路肩	硬路肩至护栏	余宽	固有横净距
路堤	1.5	3	—	—	4.5
路堑路侧连续设置护栏	1.5	3	—	—	4.5
混凝土护栏桥梁	1.5	3	0.15	0.182	4.832

隧道固有横净距(单位:m)   表5

行车方向	视点至行车道边缘	侧向余宽	检修道	固有横净距
左偏	1.6	0.75	0.75	3.1
右偏	2.95	1	0.75	4.7

横净距计算   表6

交点桩号(m)	行车偏向	路段类型	设计半径(m)	速度(km/h)	计算横净距(m)	固有横净距(m)	横净距差值(m)	备注
ZK15+458.2621700	左偏	桥梁	1700	100	3.086	2.382	-0.704	分离式桥梁无防眩设施段
ZK16+510.527	左偏	路堑	1100	100	4.768	2.5	-2.268	Gs-P-Gw1防眩板
ZK18+940.932	左偏	桥梁	1999.145	100	2.625	2.87	+0.245	Gs-P-Gw2防眩板
ZK23+495.861	左偏	隧道	4000	100	1.312	3.1	+1.788	
ZK33+809.566	左偏	路堤	4000	100	1.312	2.5	+1.188	Gs-P-Gw1防眩板
ZK17+811.896	右偏	路堤	1000.72	100	5.240	4.5	-0.740	—
ZK26+650.781	右偏	桥梁	1540	100	3.407	4.832	+1.425	水泥混凝土护栏

5 横净距不足的解决措施

根据对我国高速公路交通事故分析,得出影响道路交通安全的道路因素主要包括道路几何特征、路面状况、特殊路段和交安设施四个方面。国内外赵永平、麻辉东等学者针对横净距不足问题提出了一系列解决措施[6-13],本文根据影响道路交通安全的道路因素对其进行了整理补充。

5.1 中央分隔带外侧超车道

(1)采用满足视距要求的平曲线半径。
(2)加宽中央分隔带并将护栏向曲线内侧移动,在缓和曲线上完成过渡。
(3)采用防眩板减少障碍物影响范围,必要时将防眩板偏置。
(4)采用混凝土护栏,但混凝土护栏属于刚性防护栏,交通事故损伤较大,需要谨慎使用。
(5)当平曲线转角较大时,内侧行车道和中央分隔带位置保持不变,适当减小曲线外侧行车道的平曲线半径;当中央分隔带宽度较宽且平曲线转角较小时,适当减小中央分隔带宽度,增大平曲线半径。
(6)利用交通标线重新规划行车道位置,压缩硬路肩宽度。这种方式下行车轨迹曲线与设计平曲线不一致,并且牺牲了硬路肩应急通道的功能,尽量避免采用。

5.2 曲线内侧车道

(1)清除影响视线的障碍物、开挖视距平台,以增加视线角度。
(2)加宽右侧硬路肩或者土路肩使护栏外移,挖方路段条件允许时可取消护栏。
(3)隧道纵向标线向弯道外侧偏移或隧道断面横向拓宽。

5.3 运营后路段

(1)加强中央分隔带护栏的防护等级。
(2)对该路段的路面进行局部改造,改善路面摩擦系数。

(3) 修改标线。在视距不足路段起点前200 m至终点后50 m的范围内,设置纵向减速标线,提示和引导驾驶员减速行驶,如图15所示;将路段起点前200 m至终点后100 m的行车边缘线设置为白色实线,禁止驾驶员在该路段变换车道;路面行车道外侧标线适当加宽,将标线改为振动标线。

(4) 增设标志。增设轮廓标,视线诱导标志,如图16、图17所示;对视距不足的局部路段在弯道起点前200 m设置建议速度标志如图18所示;在弯道入口前500 m增设交通监控设施预告标志,配置抓拍系统,如图19所示。

(5) 改善路面标线夜间反光可视效果;增加夜间照明设施,为在该路段上夜间行驶的车辆提供清晰的道路信息,如图20所示。

图15 纵向减速标线

图16 轮廓标

图17 视线诱导标

图18 弯道建议速度标志

图19 交通监控设施预告标志

图20 夜间照明设施

6 结 语

(1)本文通过分析驾驶员视点位置和路段横断面形式、护栏类型、防眩措施的差异性因素,提出具有普遍通用性的固有横净距计算公式,并结合四川至贵州某高速公路工程设计中的具体运用,供同行在今后公路的路线平面设计时参考。

(2)针对中央分隔带外侧超车道和曲线内侧车道横净距不足、运营后路段视距不足这三种情况提出相应的改善措施。

(3)横净距是路线设计中的关键控制因素之一,本文仅结合驾驶员与路段构造提出有关横净距的分析,未涉及驾驶环境、路段纵坡等因素对横净距需求的影响。希望有更多的学者结合工程实际对此问题展开更有意义的调查研究工作。

参考文献

[1] 交通运输部.公路路线设计规范:JTG D20—2017[S].北京:人民交通出版社股份有限公司,2017.
[2] 许金良.道路勘测设计[M].5版.北京:人民交通出版社股份有限公司,2018.
[3] Dejan Gavran, Sanja Fric, Vladan Ilić, et al. Sight Distance Analyses in Road Design Process: Serbian Practice. Transport[J]. 2016,31(2):250-259.
[4] 赵永平,杨少伟,赵一飞.具有中央分隔带公路弯道外侧超车车道的视距[J].长安大学学报(自然科学版),2004,24(5):31-34.
[5] 周海宇.山区高速公路小半径平曲线隧道交通安全保障技术研究[D].西安:长安大学,2018.
[6] 杨少伟,潘兵宏,吴华金,等.高速公路中间带型式及安全性[J].中国公路学报,2006,19(6):39-44.
[7] 麻辉东,张海忠.高速公路平面设计中的横净距计算与运用[J].公路,2011(8):129-133.
[8] 欧思嘉.高速公路视距安全保障技术研究[J].科技与创新,2019(13):101-102.
[9] 梁友哲.高等级公路平曲线外侧超车道停车视距的验算及改善措施[J].工程与建设,2018,32(4):520-522.
[10] 王晓楠,王云泽,苗慕楠,等.动态停车视距模型研究及应用[J].公路,2015,60(11):151-155.
[11] 李伟鸿.浅谈视距横净距对行车安全的影响[J].四川建材,2019,45(10):212-213.
[12] 张春发.视距辅助线在解决高速公路中央分隔带内侧横净距不足时的应用[J].交通工程,2016(29):20-25.
[13] 王永平,赵胜林,周磊.高速公路停车视距研究[J].交通运输研究,2010(17):129-138.

高速公路隧道与主线出入口小净距路段行驶特征分析

唐忠泽　翟艺阳　张昆仑　杨雅钧　谢永淑

(长安大学公路学院)

摘　要　随着我国高速公路建设步伐的加快,隧道和互通式立交、服务区等结构在建设中的使用比例逐渐上升,特别对于山区公路,小净距路段日益增多,通过竹林关小净距路段的路况与事故调研结果分析,并考虑到现有规范缺少对小净距路段明确的设计要求,引出了本文对小净距路段的专项研究。通过无人机视频拍摄,采用Kinovea、SPSS软件分析,考虑了净距长度、车辆类型、车道分布等因素,提取了陕西省内秦岭服务区、竹林关互通等七处小净距路段高精度行车数据,分析了高速公路上隧道出入口路段、车辆变道路段和减速车道前路段的车辆运行速度变化规律、车辆变道情况和断面运行速度分布规律,得到小净距路段驾驶行为特征。

关键词 交通工程 驾驶行为特征 行车数据分析 小净距路段

0 引 言

随着我国公路交通建设的发展,山区高速公路里程快速增加,地形及设计条件受限的山区高速公路极易产生隧道出口与主线出口小净距路段,已有研究及运营经验表明[1-3],隧道出口和主线出口之间小净距路段的事故发生率远高于主线其他路段,近年来已然成为高速公路营运管理的安全痛点。通过对西汉高速竹林关互通小净距路段进行专项安全性评价,发现小净距路段对驾驶员会产生负面心理,降低驾驶员的行车舒适性,严重时还将干扰驾驶员的判断和执行能力,造成行车操作失误,引发安全事故[4]。

对于净距,我国虽然多数规范标准中进行了描述,但没给出明确系统性的参数设计要求,而随着我国高速公路的发展,山区道路的日渐增多,受地形地物限制,以及对成本的考虑,小净距路段越来越多,而其会导致车辆行驶速度变化明显,实际速度与期望车速的差值越大,驾驶员在出现紧急情况时所采取的紧急措施越多,其危险性越大,越容易造成交通事故[7]。现有的规范不足以提供足够的保障,使小净距路段成为较大的安全隐患。

驾驶员作为交通环境中随机性最强的因素,在驾驶过程中由于自身驾驶习惯和驾驶偏好等原因,成为交通事故的主要诱因[5]。要准确描述隧道出入口与互通出入口小净距路段的车辆运行速度分布和驾驶行为特征,需要采集大量的实际道路工况下的交通状况数据进行分析,故本文通过现场利用无人机定点航拍,将道路交通进行细部剖析,得到驾驶行为特征,为将来系统性设计小净距路段指标提供参考。

1 现场调研方案

1.1 调研设备

目前,常用的速度等交通信息的采集方式主要有两类[6]:一是固定型检测器;二是移动型检测设备[7]。固定型检测器可全天候监测交通状况、采集交通参数,但只能获取布设点的局部交通信息[10]。移动型采集方式综合 GPS、通信和 GIS 等技术,能以交通参与者的身份动态采集交通信息,但易受 GPS 定位精度和道路交通的影响。总体而言,无论是固定型还是移动型检测器,都无法从广域的视角提供整体的时空二维交通状态。

与其他交通检测技术相比,虽然无人机有一定的作业要求,但在交通信息采集和交通监控中仍具有显著的优势,无人机可从事广域交通监控与管理、交通参数采集(密度、流量、速度、车辆轨迹等),综合考虑各方法的特点,以及本次数据采集的参数需要,最终决定采用无人机进行数据采集。本次实地调研采用的无人机为准专业无人机,如图1所示。

1.2 调研地点

针对目前已处于运营阶段的高速公路,为搜集足够的隧道出入口与互通出入口小净距路段案例,本文以西安市为中心,发散式对周边路网的京昆高速公路、延西高速公路、包茂高速公路、银百高速公路、连霍高速公路、福银高速公路、沪陕高速公路等多条高速公路隧道出入口与互通出入口小净距路段案例进行搜集。利用百度地图的测距工具模糊测量得到小净距路段的隧道长度、隧道出口与互通出口的距离,共整理得到 10 处小净距工程案例,如图2所示,其具体的距离组成见表1。

图1 Phantom 3 Advanced 大疆无人机

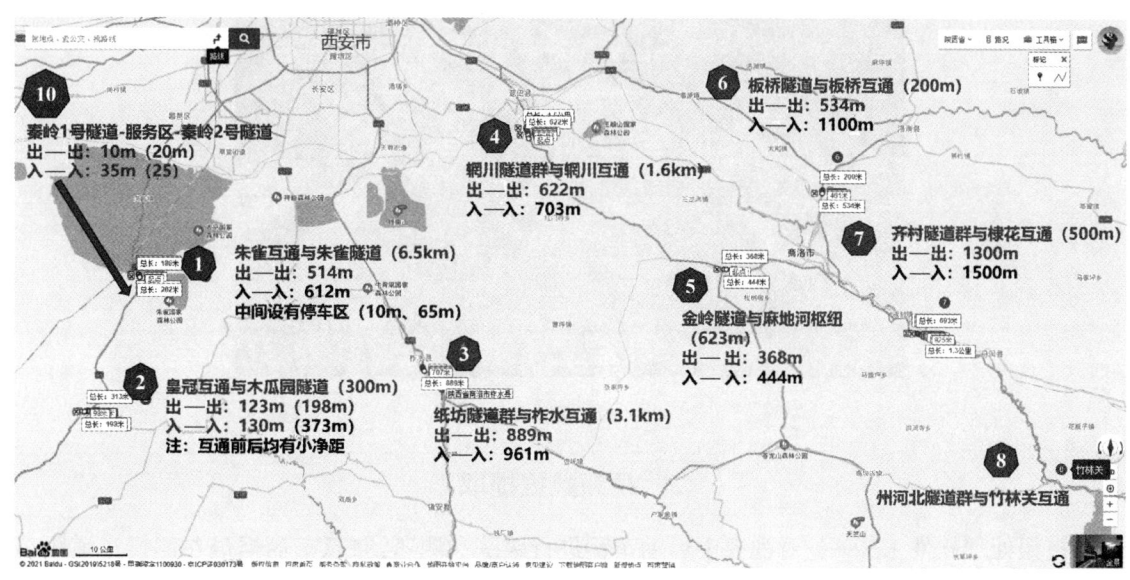

图 2　小净距工程案例分布

小净距路段概况一览表　　　　　　　　　　　　　　　　　　　　　　　　　　　　　表 1

高速公路	互通/服务区	隧道	隧道长度(m)	小净距长度(m)		是否为调研路段
				出口—出口	入口—入口	
西汉高速公路	朱雀停车区	朱雀隧道	6500	10	65	是
	秦岭服务区	秦岭 1 号隧道	6144	25	40	是
	秦岭服务区	秦岭 2、3 号隧道群	11000	28	35	是
	皇冠互通	木瓜园隧道	300	20	12	是
	皇冠互通	无名隧道	350	147	234	是
包茂高速公路	柞水互通	纸坊隧道群	3100	889	961	否
福银高速公路	铜川互通	铜川隧道群	1600	600	630	否
	麻地河枢纽	金岭隧道	623	368	444	否
沪陕高速公路	板桥互通	板桥隧道	200	534	1100	否
	棣花互通	齐村隧道群	500	1300	1500	否
	竹林关互通	州河北隧道群	1000	28	25	是

综合考虑以上小净距路段的隧道长度是否超过 1000m 以及隧道出入口与互通出入口的距离是否小净距规范要求值，本次调研选取了京昆高速(西汉段)的朱雀隧道与朱雀停车区，秦岭服务区与秦岭 1、秦岭 2、秦岭 3 号隧道等 7 处小净距路段作为本次调研的重点路段。

1.3　调研过程及数据获取

通过对天气情况的查询及车流量的初步调查，本次调研在 2021 年 1 月 10—11 日进行。根据《道路交通标志与标线　第 5 部分：限制速度》(GB 5768.5—2017)的相关要求，设计速度为 80km/h 时，断面测速样本不应少于 110 辆。为保证道路的交通流量处于一般水平，本次调研视频采集时间为 9：30—11：30 以及 14：30—17：00。每次视频拍摄时长为 30min，若车辆样本数未达到要求，相应的延长视频采集时长。具体采集实景图以朱雀停车区与朱雀隧道间的小净距路段为例，如图 3 所示。

本次调研直接获取的数据为各隧道与互通小净距路段的交通流视频数据，进一步利用 Kinovea 提取车辆的运行速度和运行轨迹以进行后续的数据分析和评价模型的构建。

图3 航拍采集实景图

2 视频数据提取

采用视频处理软件 Kinovea 对视频中运动车辆进行跟踪和测速,并以车辆据最左侧行车道距离表征车辆轨迹,提取高精度的车辆行驶数据。Kinovea 可实现对目标车辆特征点进行轨迹跟踪。在逐帧播放视频时,单击标右键选择"跟踪路径"选项,把十字光标放在特征点中心,播放下一帧图像时,软件会对该特征点进行自动跟踪。若对自动跟踪效果不满意,可手动调整位置。完成跟踪后,在视频画面的合适位置设置坐标原点,再利用"文件"中的"导出至电子表格"选项将跟踪结果(包括跟踪点的 X、Y 轴像素坐标值与对应的时间)以 Excel 的格式输出,利用这些数据就可计算出车速大小。同时,可利用软件的透视网格功能,根据道路标线,车道宽度等已知信息,对网格覆盖范围内区域进行标定,辅助测速和对车辆与车道左边线距离进行打点测量,如图4所示。

图4 Kinovea 操作界面

3 基于视频数据小净距路段驾驶行为研究

3.1 车辆变道过程运行速度变化规律

当驾驶员在驾驶车辆时,受到复杂的道路交通环境和限速管理措施等影响,实际运行速度不是简单的线形设计速度,或者各车道限制速度,本文以车辆距隧道洞口的距离为横轴,以变道车辆的平均运行速度为纵轴,绘制不同车道的车辆变道过程中的速度变化图。

隧道出口与互通出口小净距路段车辆变道速度变化

本文在分析车辆变道速度变化规律时,选取秦岭1号及2、3号隧道出口与秦岭服务区、木瓜园隧道出口与皇冠互通出口、无名隧道出口与皇冠互通出口、州河北隧道出口与竹林关互通出口5处隧道出口小净距路段,进行车辆变道时运行速度变化分析,如图5所示。

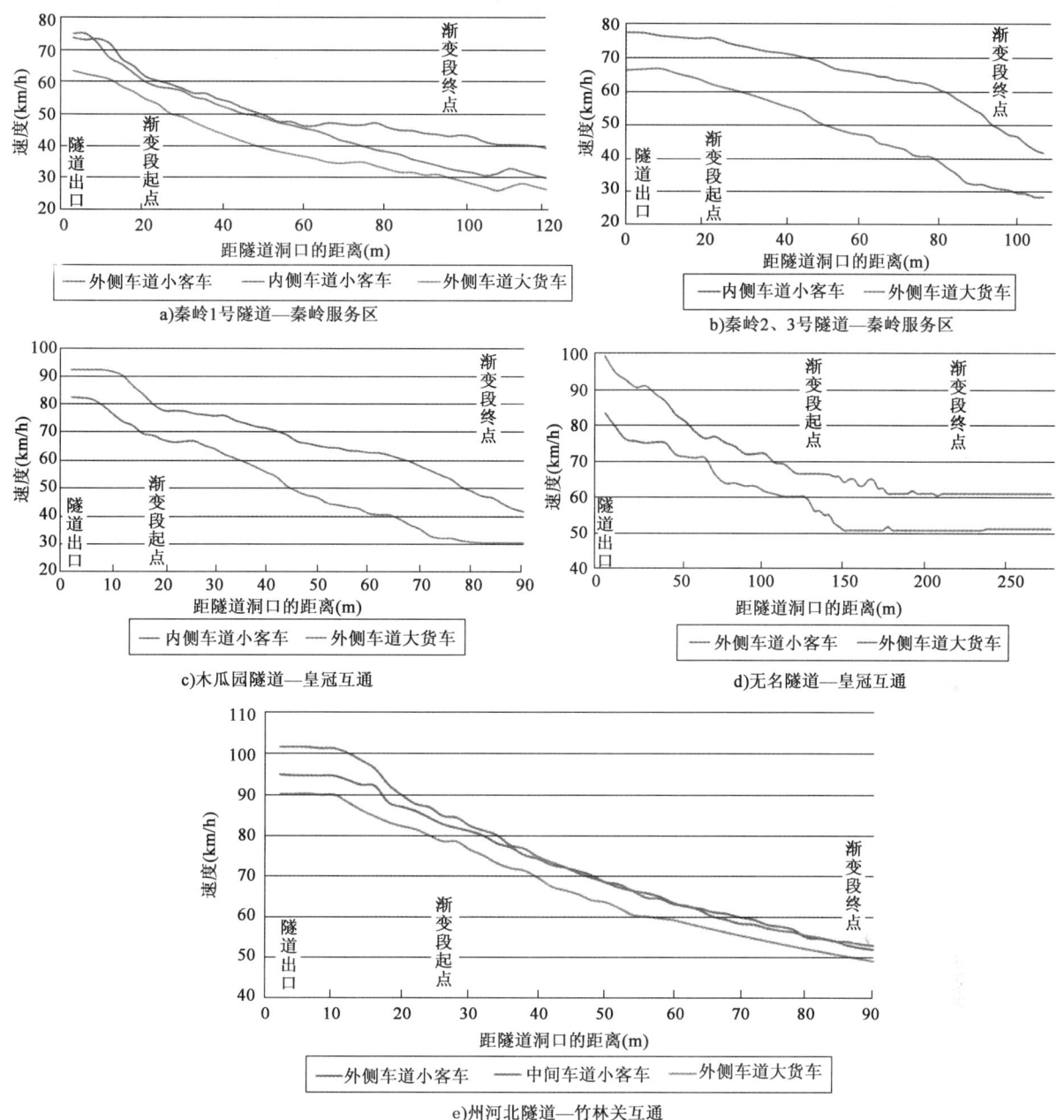

图 5 隧道出口与互通出口小净距路段车辆变道速度变化图

对各隧道出口与互通及服务区出口小净距路段变道车辆的平均速度变化进行分析可知,主要有以下特征:

(1) 在净距长度较短时,车辆在隧道出口 20m 范围内车速基本保持不变,为驾驶的识别出口时行驶的距离;在渐变段前,驶出车辆已经开始减速,至渐变段时,车速均高于 60km/h;整体上,内外侧车辆变道驶出主线的速度变化基本呈现为匀减速的趋势。

(2) 内侧车道小客车的运行速度一般高于外侧车道大货车,因此在驶出隧道后其在识别出口过程中行驶的距离大于大货车;但无名隧道出口的车辆运行速度由洞口开始减速至稳定行驶驶出主线,进一步分析,该隧道为南北朝向的短隧道且互通出口位于右偏曲线上,有利于驾驶员识别出口以及变道时保持固定的转角转动转向盘以稳定的进入出口匝道。此外,对比分析可知,小客车的减速度略大于大货车。

(3) 服务区出口与互通出口小净距路段相较于隧道出口与互通出口小净距路段,车辆变道速度变化存在较大的差异:其一,受大型车及车辆驶出比例的影响,秦岭隧道出口车辆速度均较低,比互通路段隧道出口的速度低10~20km/h,且在驶入减速车道时;其二,由于西汉高速的特殊管制,进入服务区的车辆在驶出隧道洞口前均已采取的一定程度的减速措施,识别出口要求的距离更短,与互通路段存在一定的差异。

3.2 横向轨迹变化研究

各隧道出口与互通/服务区小净距路段的车辆轨迹变化如图6所示。

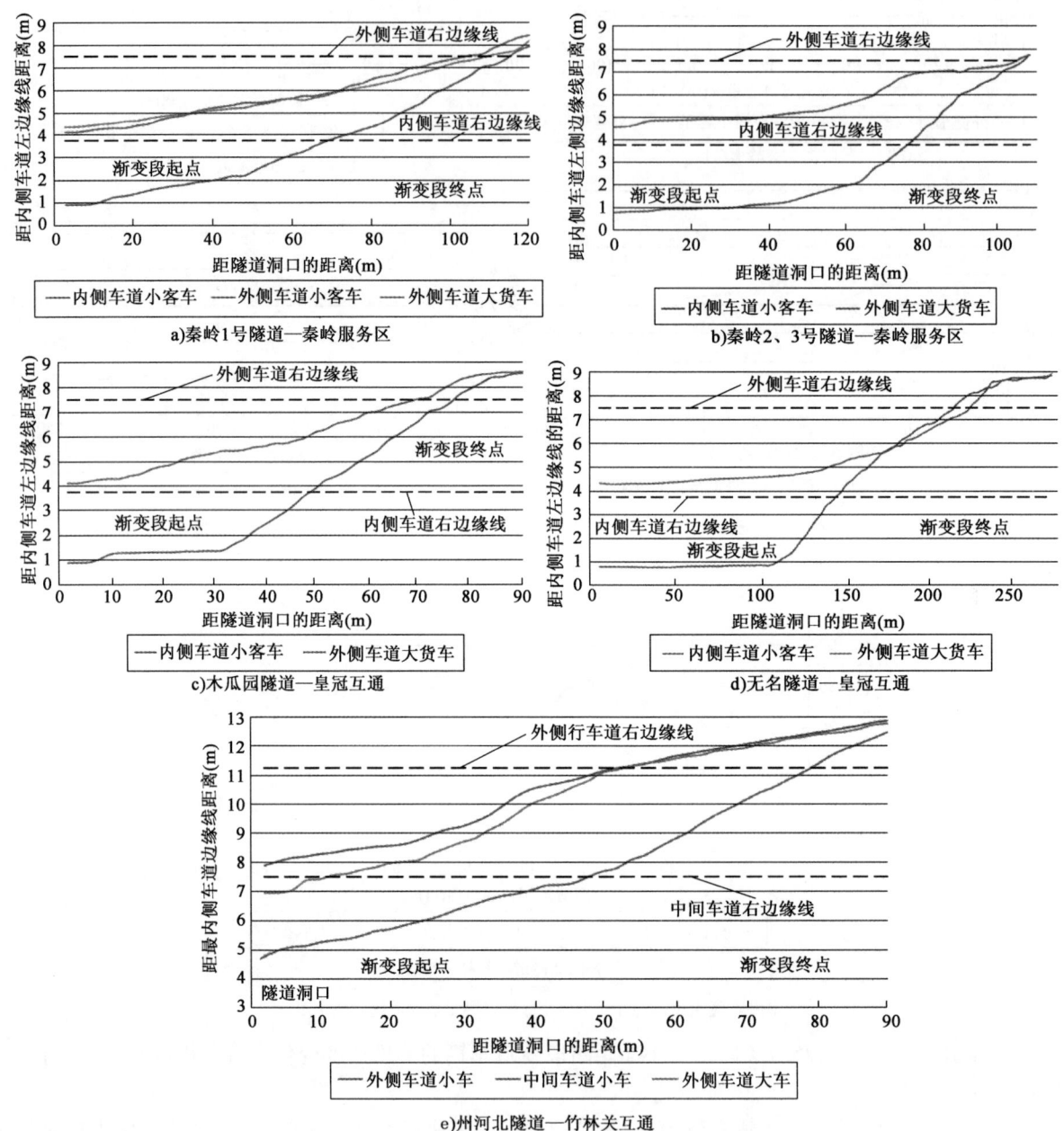

图6 隧道出口与互通出口小净距路段车辆变道轨迹变化图

结合3.1节中变道车辆速度变化规律,对于内侧车道驶出主线的车辆,在变道前,驾驶员会采取制动措施,在车辆减速过程中,驾驶员寻找换道空隙同时车辆缓慢横移,待有合适的空隙,车辆横移速度加快,驾驶员快速完成连续变道驶出主线的操作。

进一步分析可知,内侧车道小客车多靠右侧行驶,其左侧边缘距左侧车道线边缘的距离在0.7~1.0m,在渐变段前后各10m的范围内,车辆横移幅度较小或保持正常行驶;在渐变段20m后,车辆以1~1.5m/s的横向速度连续跨越外侧车道,并驶入减速车道。外侧车道大货车驶出主线时,则以较为平稳的横向速度。

结合小净距路段线形特点,可知小净距路段为直线、左偏曲线、右偏曲线时,车辆变道轨迹存在着较大的差异,主要体现在车辆横移速度上。图6a)、b)、c)均为直线,车辆横移速度约为1m/s;图6d)为右偏曲线,车辆横移速度较快,约为1.5m/s;图6e)为左偏曲线,车辆横移速度整体式较为缓慢,在0.5~0.8m/s。

3.3 断面运行速度分布特征研究

由于道路行驶条件和驾驶员个体行为差异,导致高速公路交通流断面运行车速存在随机性和不确定性[10]。我国的道路环境、车辆结构和交通管制与国外相差较大,而以往的相关研究总是基于运行车速符合正态分布的假设进行,导致计算结果与实际情况不符。因而有必要针对国内交通运行情况,结合调研的实际情况,描述我国高速公路运行车速分布特征,为互通与隧道小净距及其他研究提供理论参考。

为进一步研究断面车辆运行速度的分布特征,对调研采集的交通流数据进行综合总体分析。本文选取减速车道渐变段起点前的净距段断面、减速车道分流端小鼻点前的断面进行断面运行速度分布研究。部分隧道与互通小净距路段的运行速度频率分布直方图如图7所示,统计结果如表2所示。

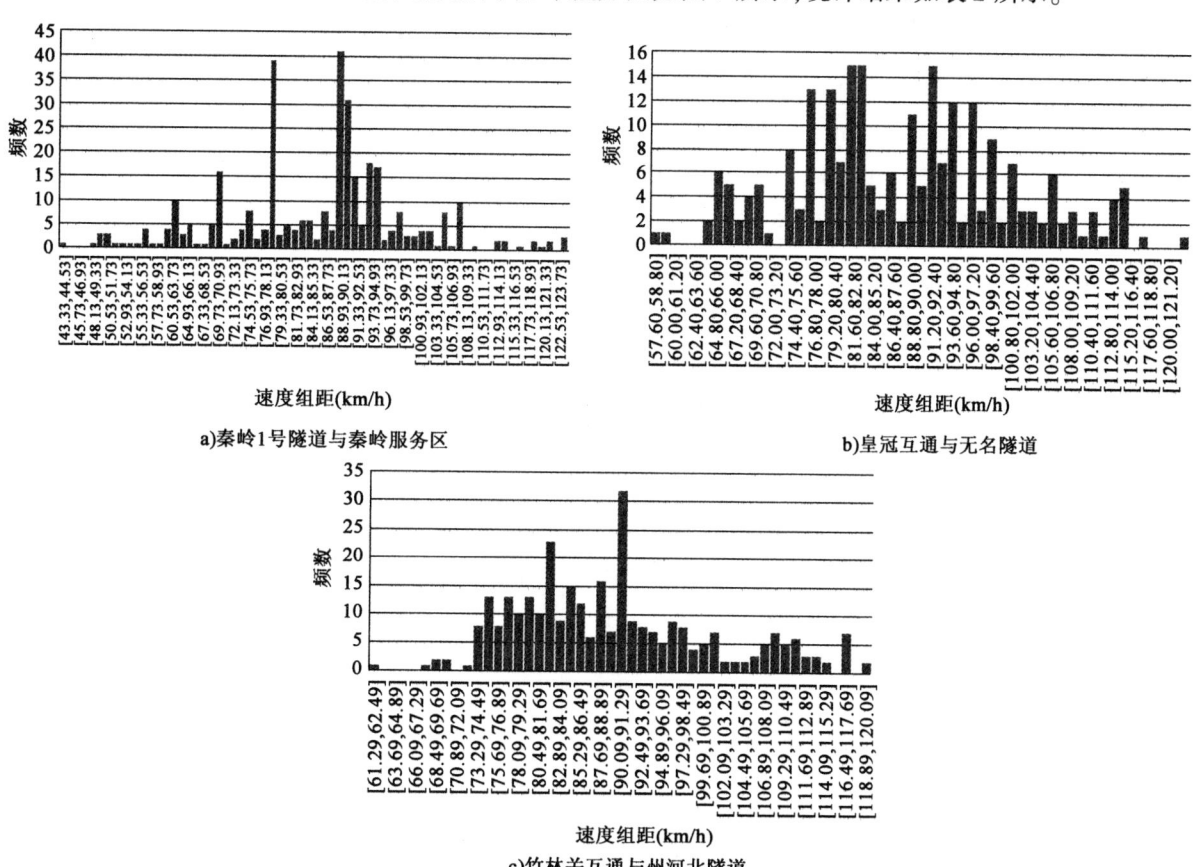

图7 部分小净距路段运行速度数据频率分布直方图

各隧道出口与互通出口小净距路段运行速度统计(单位:km/h)　　表2

统计量	均值	中位数	标准差	方差	偏度	峰度	极大值	极小值	V_{85}
隧道出口—互通出口									
秦岭1号隧道—服务区	89.94	88.4	14.79	218.77	-0.11	0.26	124.8	43.33	98.56
秦岭2、3号隧道—服务区	87.87	88.51	15.80	249.59	-0.25	-0.83	118.20	49.68	104.75
木瓜园隧道—皇冠互通	85.26	86.4	12.56	157.73	0.21	-0.45	121.6	60.63	97.92
无名隧道—皇冠互通	87.38	87.73	12.64	159.68	0.18	-0.42	120.36	57.6	101.65
辋川隧道—辋川互通	86.11	86.4	10.77	115.95	0.52	-0.16	120	62.27	97.92
州河北隧道—竹林关互通	89.78	88.31	11.63	135.27	0.60	-0.25	119.13	61.29	103.59

根据统计分析结果,可知各小净距路段速度数据的峰度均小于3,偏度均为负值,隧道出口与互通出口小净距路段的平均值与中位数有差异较小。故初步估计运行速度总体分布不具有正态分布特征。进一步运用SPSS软件采用K-S检验法进行正态性检验,如表3所示。

正态性检验结果 表3

路 段	K-S Z 值	渐近显著性(双侧)
	隧道出口—互通出口	
秦岭1号隧道—服务区	0.127	0
秦岭2、3号隧道—服务区	0.075	0.006
木瓜园隧道—皇冠互通	0.079	0
无名隧道—皇冠互通	0.083	0
辋川隧道—辋川互通	0.094	0
州河北隧道—竹林关互通	0.110	0

由图7直观分析可知,小净距路段大部分车辆的运行速度处于60～80km/h,部分车辆处于低速和高速状态。进一步分析检验结果可知,Z值与渐进显著性值均小于显著性水平0.05,故隧道出入口与互通出入口小净距路段的运行速度总体不服从正态分布。

3.4 风险影响因素关联性分析

在道路交通流运行过程中,影响其运行效率和运行安全的因素有很多,本文选取交通量、大型车比例、转向交通量比例等交通流因素及曲线半径、转角、转向、纵坡等道路几何因素两方面的风险影响因素,同时结合净距长度,分析其对小净距路段行车安全风险的影响。各小净距路段的基本信息统计如表4所示。

各小净距路段信息一览表 表4

路 段	净距长度(m)	交通量(veh/h)	大型车比例(%)	转向比例(%)	半径(m)	转角(°)	偏向	纵坡(%)
			隧道出口—互通出口					
秦岭1号隧道—服务区	25	700	25.1	14.8	直线	—	—	2
秦岭2、3号隧道—服务区	28	420	37.6	9.5	直线	—	—	2
木瓜园隧道—皇冠互通	20	710	21.7	3.5	直线	—	—	1.5
无名隧道—皇冠互通	147	478	32.2	2.3	1800	25	右偏	1.5
辋川隧道—辋川互通	600	794	19.8	5.9	1500	16	左偏	—
州河北隧道—竹林关互通	28	616	31.5	7.8	700	78	左偏	-0.65

注:仅竹林关互通与州河北隧道的主线为双向六车道,其余均为双向四车道。

基于上文的分析可知,净距长度、大型车比例以及小净距路段的线形对车辆变道轨迹存在明显的影响。速度变异系数可表征断面车速分布的离散性,用于车辆速度连续变化时,亦可说明车辆加减速过程的稳定性。因此,综合断面速度分布的离散性和车辆变道速度变化的稳定性分析交通流因素和道路几何因素对行车安全的影响。前者可表征小净距路段整体的行车安全风险,后者可从车辆驶出的稳定性方面描述驾驶行为的安全程度。各小净距路段的变道车辆速度和断面车速的离散性见表5,具体分析如下。

各小净距变道速度和断面速度离散性数据表 表5

路 段	变道速度		断面速度		变道速度		断面速度	
	平均值	速度变异系数	平均值	速度变异系数	平均值	速度变异系数	平均值	速度变异系数
	隧道出口—互通出口				互通入口—隧道入口			
秦岭1号隧道—服务区	45.99	0.34	84.94	0.17	70.55	0.26	78.77	0.17
秦岭2、3号隧道—服务区	53.96	0.27	87.27	0.18	52.73	0.23	88.03	0.13

续上表

路 段	变道速度		断面速度		变道速度		断面速度	
	平均值	速度变异系数	平均值	速度变异系数	平均值	速度变异系数	平均值	速度变异系数
	隧道出口—互通出口				互通入口—隧道入口			
木瓜园隧道—皇冠互通	60.16	0.29	85.26	0.15	67.88	0.21	80.97	0.15
无名隧道—皇冠互通	62.07	0.17	87.38	0.14	—	—	81.82	0.10
辋川隧道—辋川互通	—	—	86.11	0.13	—	—	85.85	0.12
州河北隧道—竹林关互通	69.80	0.22	89.79	0.15	68.20	0.21	89.07	0.14

3.4.1 净距长度

净距长度对变道车辆速度和断面车速分布存在明显的影响。隧道出口与出口净距长度在20~30m，变道车辆平均速度在60km/h左右，相对较低，变异系数则在0.2~0.4间，远高于净距长度为147m的情况；断面速度分布离散性同样处于较高的水平。

3.4.2 交通流因素

在交通量、大型车比例、转向交通量比例三个因素中，对小净距路段的变道车辆速度和断面车速分布的影响程度最大的为交通量，其次是大型车比例，转向交通量比例在实测数据中并无明显的影响。当交通量大于700veh/h时，隧道出口与互通出口的变道车辆的平均速度略低，变异系数约为低交通量时的1.5倍，车辆减速驶入主线的时间较短，稳定性较差。大型车比例对断面速度分布的影响相对明显，当大型车比例低于20%，断面速度分布离散程度明显低于大型车比例高于20%的路段。

3.4.3 道路几何线形因素

从理论层次分析，小净距路段的曲线偏向及转角大小直接影响着驶出车辆转向盘转动的复杂性。调研的小净距路段涉及直线、左偏和右偏曲线路段，隧道出口为左偏曲线时，其断面速度分布的离散性最高，且偏角越大，离散性越高；究其原因主要是因为互通出口以一定的流出角接入主线，出口匝道多为右偏，此刻，驾驶员需要连续反方向转动转向盘，转角越大，转动幅度越大。

结合目前道路设计的要求，隧道出口多为下坡路段，对小净距路段行车安全存在着不利的影响；隧道入口路段则为上坡，相对有利。本次调研路段的坡度均较小，对变道车辆速度的稳定性和断面车速分布的离散性并无明显影响。

4 结 语

通过用无人机对秦岭服务区、竹林关互通等处小净距路段航拍，采集道路线形、大小车辆速度变化情况、轨迹变化情况等信息数据，用SPSS软件进行描述性分析，得到一系列小净距路段的行驶特征。

因直线短，车辆进出高速横向位移大，交通标志标线识别量大等原因，高速公路隧道互通小净距路段的危险驾驶行为与高速公路一般路段存在较大差异性。位于道路内侧快速路的小车需要进匝道和外侧慢速的大货车所产生的冲突，难以在小净距路段拥有足够的时间和距离进行解决，为产生所述驾驶行为特征的主要诱因。同时，右偏曲线、小纵坡段更有利于驾驶，隧道长度与小净距段长度也是综合影响的重要因素。为进一步论证和丰富本文的结果，在后续的研究中，可以对各地更多不同小净距路段的数据进行采集，并深入考虑驾驶员的心率、瞳孔变化等表征因素，借助机器学习等技术分析，得到更高精度的驾驶行为特征。

参考文献

[1] Amundsen F H, Ranes G. Studies on Traffic Accidents in Norwegian Road Tunnels[J]. Tunneling and Underground Space Technology, 2000, 15(1): 3-11.

[2] Mcartta A T, Northrup V S, Retting R A. Types and Characteristics of Ramp-related Motorvehicle Crashes

on Urban Interstate Roadways in Northern Virgin Virginia[J]. Journal of Safety Research, 2004, 35(1): 101-114.

[3] 赵一飞,陈敏,潘兵宏. 隧道与互通式立交出口最小间距需求分析[J]. 长安大学学报(自然科学版), 2011, 31(3): 68-71.

[4] 陈云,杜志刚,焦方通,等. 小半径公路短隧道入口段不同车型视觉负荷研究[J]. 武汉理工大学学报(交通科学与工程版), 2019, 43(4): 708-711, 717.

[5] 牛敏强,周波,李堃. 高速公路隧道出口与主线出口小净距路段标志标线设计研究[J]. 交通科技, 2020(01): 92-96.

[6] 薛清文,蒋愚明,陆键. 基于轨迹数据的危险驾驶行为识别方法[J]. 中国公路学报, 2020, 33(06): 84-94.

[7] 张有节. 基于无人机视频的交通参数提取技术研究[D]. 重庆:重庆交通大学, 2017.

[8] 彭仲仁,刘晓锋,张立业,等. 无人飞机在交通信息采集中的研究进展和展望[J]. 交通运输工程学报, 2012.12(6): 119-126.

[9] Reinartz P, Lachaise M, Schmeer E, et al. Traffic Monitoring with Serial Images from Airborne Cameras[J]. ISPRS Journal of Photogrammetry & Remote Sensing. 2006, 613): 149-158.

[10] 戢晓峰,谢世坤,覃文文,等. 基于轨迹数据的山区危险性弯道路段交通事故风险动态预测[J/OL]. 中国公路学报:1-15[2021-01-31].

[11] 阎莹,王晓飞,张宇辉,等. 高速公路断面运行车速分布特征研究[J]. 中国安全科学学报, 2008(07): 171-176.

A New Method of Safety Evaluation for Sharp Bend and Steep Slope Sections of Highway Based on Braking Behavior

Yajun Yang   Hong Zhang   Bo Wang   Yongshu Xie   Yijing Zhao

(Chang'an University)

Abstract   The sharp bends and steep slopes of highways are a common part of mountainous area accidents, and the traffic safety situation is severe. This paper introduces the concept of Braking Effect Index (BEI) from the accident causes of steep slopes and sharp bends. It can improve the traffic safety environment of the sharp bend and steep slope section of the highway, reduce the traffic accidents and enhance the highway safety level. First, the concept of the Braking Effect Index (BEI) is explained, and the BEI is used as an index to evaluate the safety of the steep slope section of the highway. Then, based on the six-axle truck test, the highway alignment quality evaluation model was established and verified, and the safety of the 51km continuous downhill section of the mountainous expressway in China was analyzed. Finally, it is concluded that the steep slope sections, the sharp bend road sections, the long gentle slope and the straight sections were dangerous sections of highway. The proportion of braking action of the driver on the steep slope section with a longitudinal slope higher than 4% and the sharp section with a radius less than 400m was respectively 24% and 59%. The new method proposed in this paper to evaluate the safety of sharp bends and steep slopes of highways, and the research results can provide reference for route designers.

Keywords   Traffic safety   Safety evaluation   Sharp bend and steep slope   Braking effect index

0 Introduction

With the continuous improvement of the highway network, road construction in China gradually tends to the west. Because of its poor geological conditions, undulating terrain, the route is required to overcome a significant elevation difference within a short distance, leading to more sharp bend and steep slope sections and continuous long downhill sections. The sharp bend and steep slope sections and the continuous long downhill sections of the roads are frequent sections of mountain highway accidents due to the adverse weather conditions in mountainous areas when over the mountain. There were 29 critical sections in China that the Ministry of Public Security and the State Administration of Work Safety has studied and identified, and there were 16 hazardous sections belong to continuous long downhill sections, accounting for 55% of the total[1]. The new Design Specification for Highway Alignment put forward corresponding technical indicators for longitudinal slope and a slope length of continuous long and steep downhill sections from the point of safety and made relevant provisions for safety improvement, carrying out individual safety evaluation on sharp bend and steep slope sections and continuous long downhill sections. Thus, traffic safety problems and safety evaluation on sharp bend and steep slope sections cannot be ignored.

In recent years, many scholars have done a lot of research on traffic safety problems of sharp bend and steep slope sections and continuous long downhill sections. Lee et al.[2] consider the visual distortions in the study of the driving safety of the horizontal curved section, and list the safety standard quantitative table of the curved section with the geometric parameters of the road as a variable. Aram et al.[3] analyze the causes of traffic accidents in the curved section considering the curve length, the deflection angle, the transition curve length and the width of the shoulder et al. Agarwal et al[4] divide the potential dangerous sections into straight sections, curved sections and plane crossing sections, and find out the factors that affect their safety respectively. They use Analytic Hierarchy Process to obtain the weight of each influencing factor, and finally use the risk coefficient to rank the dangerous sections. Lill[5] introduces the concept of braking equivalent time and analyzed the maximum safe speed of downhill section, and then grades the severity of the slope according to speed. Western scholars mostly study the driving safety of horizontal curve sections, and the research results primarily evaluate the safety of the curve sections with subjectively. However, the Asian scholars primarily focus on the longitudinal slope optimal design and the identification of dangerous sections in continuous long downhill sections to improve the level of safety and security of the sharp bend and steep slope sections, but accuracy is not enough. Bo Chen[6] obtains the relationship between braking failure and slope, including slope length and slope steepness. He proposes the calculation formula of the speed, the slope length and slope steepness and analyze the brake drum temperature of the heavy truck braking on the continuous long downhill sections. Xinsha, Fu et al.[7] build on the theory of vehicle dynamics and car driving theory, using truck uphill power performance, shift behavior and downhill braking performance establish the prediction model of running speed of trucks on the highway. Lu Sun[8] considers three kinds of accident types of curve sections such as sideslip, rollover and stopping sight distance, and analyzes the driving risk in curved sections by using Monte Carlo method.

To sum up, most scholars study the driving safety of horizontal curves and longitudinal slopes separately, and most of the researchers focus on the visual analysis of vertical and horizontal combination section. There is a lack of research that associates vertical and horizontal combination section with driving behavior and verifies from a traffic accident. Moreover, few studies on traffic safety for the combined sections of the sharp bend and steep slope sections and continuous long downhill sections, the research results are subjective and lack of accuracy and such studies are mainly based on traffic accident data and brake drum temperature rise models to evaluate the quality of road alignment, lack of adequate method for assessing the safety of sharp bend and steep slope sections and continuous long downhill sections[17-18,21]. Also, the brake drum temperature rise model established based on actual vehicle test is not accurate enough, which is accidental[20]. It is quite convenient to use the traffic accident data to evaluate the road alignment quality, but the traffic accident data acquisition is difficult[9].

Therefore, a new method of vertical and horizontal combination section evaluation was proposed which combined the vertical and horizontal combination section, the driver's brake behavior and the traffic accident to quantify the three-dimensional line. Then based on the cause of accidents on the sharp bend and steep slope sections of highway, this paper introduced the concept of Braking Effect Index (BEI) as an index to evaluate the safety of sharp bend and steep slope sections. It makes up for the difficulty of traffic accident data acquisition and brake drum temperature rise model lack of accuracy, the research results can provide reference for route designers.

1 Braking Mechanism of the Truck on the Sharp Bend and Steep Slope Sections of Highway

In the process of vehicle driving, the driver is faced with a time-varying and dynamic environment. According to the stimulus-body-reaction model of human behavior and the theory of traffic conflict[9-10], the driver needs to adjust its driving conditions to keep the safety speed when the traffic environment of the road changes and the safety distance from other vehicles and roadside obstacles In the process of adjusting driving conditions, drivers usually take braking measures to reduce the speed and ensure a series of subsequent operations are timely and efficient a.

Considering the complex driving environment and the abrupt change of the traffic environment on the sharp bend and steep slope sections and continuous long downhill sections, the factors affecting braking mainly include the changes of road conditions, meteorological environment and traffic flow.

1.1 Changes of road conditions on the Sharp Curved steep slope road

During the process of continuous long downhill of the vehicle, due to the constant positive traction and the reduction of gravity potential energy into kinetic energy and heat energy, the vehicle speed will continue to increase so that the driver's psychological load increases, thus braking measures will usually be adapted to maintain a safe downhill speed. Also, due to the steep-gentle-steep longitudinal design on the steep slope and Sharp Curved road, the driver is likely to have an obvious error when driving on such a longitudinal slope and accelerate driving because the gentle slope section is regarded as an uphill section[11-12]. And the longer the length of the front ramp, the greater the slope difference between the adjacent slope sections, the more the driver is likely to have the illusion of slope, which increases the probability of the driver braking in this section thereby increasing the gradient illusion security risks of the Sharp Curved steep slope road[19].

When the vehicle is driving on the sharp bend and steep slope sections of highway, braking measures are frequently taken on the circular curve with a smaller radius due to the lateral force generated by the component of gravity and centrifugal force will make the truck unstable when driving on a flat curve. On the circular curve, the vehicle is affected by a large lateral force, and the running speed of the vehicle is small. There is a more significant impact on the speed, especially for minor radius circular curve[16].

Also, the construction of bridges and tunnels with steep slopes and continuous long downhill slopes is massive in scale. Vehicles on long high-span bridges and extra-long tunnels are affected by structures and related traffic control. In order to ensure traffic safety, braking measures will be taken to reduce the vehicle speed. Due to the "white hole" effect of the tunnel entrance of the super-long tunnel, the driver may have a more significant visual disturbance and brake measures will also be taken to ensure the safety of the vehicle in the tunnel.

1.2 Changes of the meteorological environment on the Sharp Curved steep slope road

Due to the broad span, the route sometimes needs to cross the high altitude area. The meteorological environment along the Sharp Curved steep slope section of the highway is entirely different and often accompanied by the sudden change of meteorological conditions. On the one hand, for high altitude sections, it is easy to form frozen snow sections in winter and the vehicle must slow down during the driving process. On the other hand, large structures may also change the driving behavior under changing weather conditions, for example, mission fog often occurs across bridge sections, meteoric suddenly changes in extra-large tunnel openings and brake deceleration in these cases are the driver's preferred hedging measures.[25-26]

1.3 Changes in traffic flow on the Sharp Curved steep slope road

Due to the complex driving environment of the sharp bend and steep slope sections and continuous long downhill sections, the traffic flow is often affected by the external environment. When the current traffic flow is in an abrupt change, especially in the case of unexpected traffic accidents or unexpected bad weather, the driver is affected by the overall trend of traffic flow with the running speed reducing and also needs to slow down passively.

Relevant studies show that braking failure is one of the main causes of traffic accidents on the sharp bend and steep slope sections and continuous long downhill sections[1]. When the vehicle is driving on the sharp bend and steep slope sections and continuous long downhill sections, the brake needs a long-term, intermittent, high-intensity braking to control the vehicle speed, which results in brake temperatures often above 300℃, sometimes as high as 600℃ to 700℃. When the temperature of the friction plate exceeds the maximum temperature during manufacture, the friction coefficient of the brake plate is reduced, and the deformation of the brake cylinder is enlarged and finally separated from the brake plate. This deformation causes the close engagement between the brake drum and the brake plate loose so that it can only rely on the edge of mutual linkage, which has reduced the effectiveness of the braking system and lead to braking failure.[1]

Schematic Diagram of Braking Mechanism of the Truck on the Sharp Curved Steep Slope Road is shown in Fig. 1.

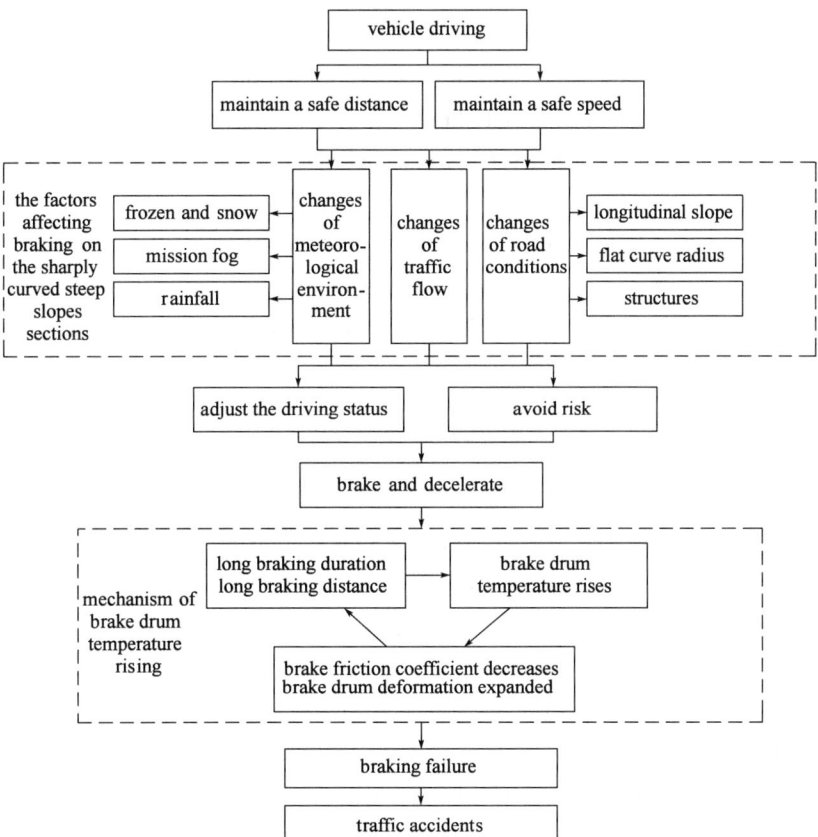

Fig. 1 Schematic Diagram of Braking Mechanism of the Truck On the Sharp Curved Steep Slope Road

To sum up, the complex driving environment of the sharp bend and steep slope sections and continuous long downhill sections can cause the driver to take frequent braking measures, resulting in the brake temperature rising and even braking failure, which seriously harms traffic safety. The temperature of the brake is directly related to the duration of a single brake, so it is also associated with the braking distance. When an individual continuous brake is applied, the brake temperature is proportional to the braking distance[13-14]. Therefore, it is reasonable and effective to evaluate the safety of road sections by analyzing the braking distance of the driver on the sharp bend and steep slope sections of highway. The braking distance can not only be obtained by using the brake signal acquisition module, but also can be achieved by using the running speed and the acceleration of the vehicle as the judgment basis, and the operation speed and acceleration of the vehicle are easy to get.

2 Quality Evaluation Model of Highway Alignment Based on Braking Effect Index

2.1 The Conception of Braking Effect Index (BEI)

To better reflect the relationship between the vertical and horizontal combination of linearity and braking distance on the Sharp Curved steep slope road sections, the conception of Braking Effect Index (BEI) was introduced. The essence is the proportion of braking distance in a specific vertical and horizontal combination section to the length of the road section. The larger BEI indicates that, the longer the braking distance of this section, the higher the accumulated temperature of the brake drum, the larger the probability of brake failure and the higher risk of driving on the road section.

2.2 The Quality Evaluation Model of Highway Alignment

The process of establishing a quality evaluation model of highway alignment based on the Braking Effect Index is shown in Fig. 2.

(1) Taking the slope change point, the intersection of straight line and transition curve, transition curve and circle curve, circle curve and transition curve, transition curve and straight line as dividing node, the section L was divided into k unit sections, and the longitudinal slope and the flat curve radius of each unit section remained unchanged. The section of each unit section that took the braking measures was considered as a subset of that unit section.

(2) The length of the unit section Lk was calculated by the reference of the Straight Curve Table and the Vertical Curve Table. The braking distance lk was calculated by using the data obtained from the braking signal acquisition module in the real vehicle test or vehicle acceleration data, and the calculation results were shown in the Eqs. (1-2).

$$L = \{L_1, L_2, L_3, \cdots, L_k\} \tag{1}$$

$$l = \{l_1, l_2, l_3, \cdots, l_k\} \tag{2}$$

$L_1, L_2, L_3, \cdots, L_k$ in the Eq. (1) were the length of the unit section which w related to the longitudinal slope (i) and the radius of the flat curve (R), $i \in [0, i_{max}]$, $R \in [R_{min}, 999]$, and the values of imax and Rmin were related to the design speed of the section.

$l_1, l_2, l_3, \cdots$, lk in the Eq. (2) were subsets of $L_1, L_2, L_3, \cdots, L_k$, which also were related to the longitudinal slope (i) and the radius of the flat curve (R).

(3) The longitudinal slope i was divided into m sections and the radius of the flat curve R were divided into n sections as shown in Eq. (3) and Eq. (4). 1% of the longitudinal interval separated the longitudinal slope section. The division of the flat curve radius section considered the minimum radius, general radius, N times ($N = 2, 3, 4, \cdots$) of general radius as well as the radius of the circular curve there was no superelevation and

the radius of a straight line as divide nodes.

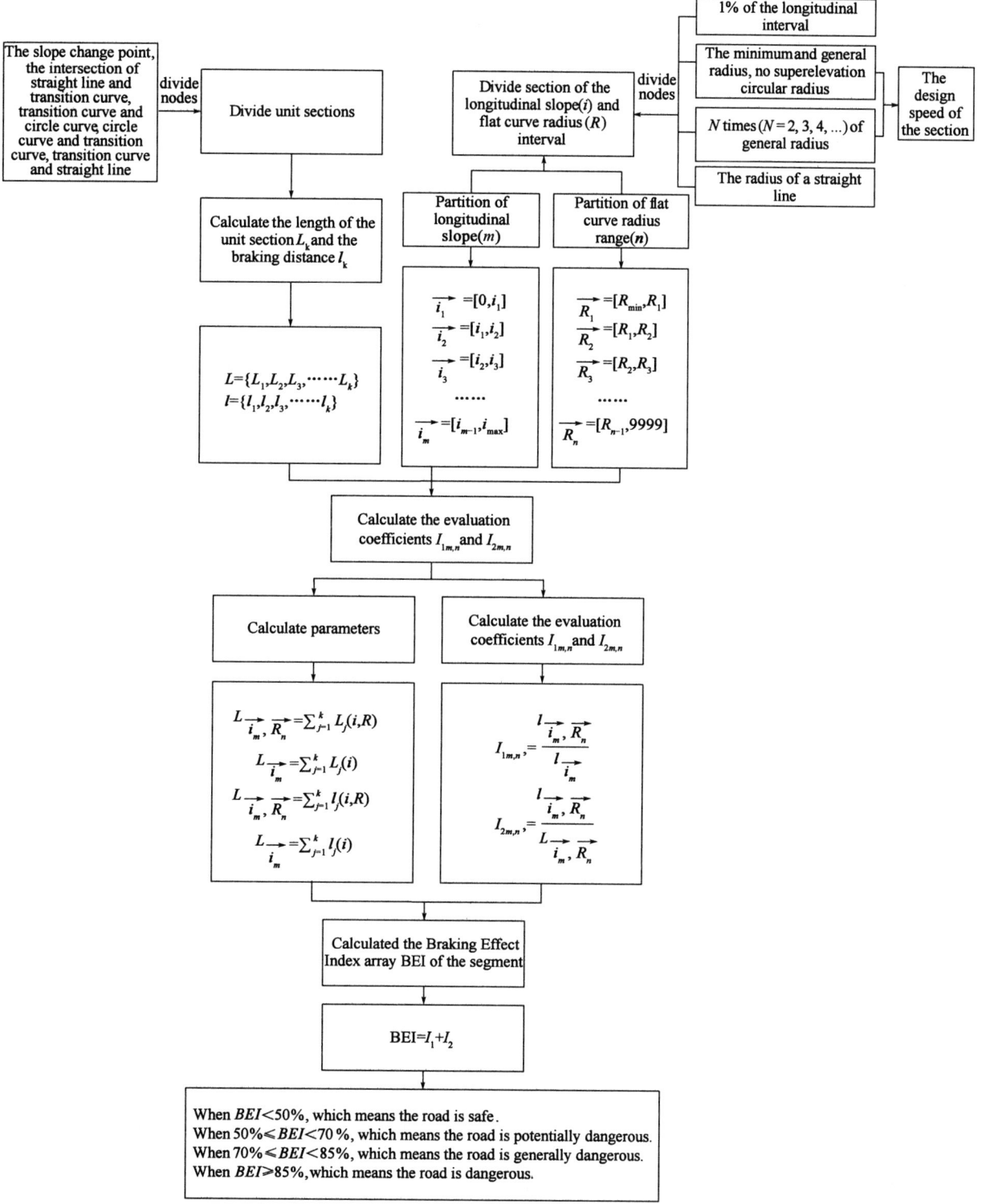

Fig. 2 The flow Chart of the Quality Evaluation Model of Highway Alignment

$$\overrightarrow{i_1} = [0, i_1)$$

$$\vec{i_2} = [i_1, i_2)$$

$$\vec{i_2} = [i_2, i_3)$$

$$\vec{i_m} = [i_{m-1}, i_{max}) \tag{3}$$

$$\vec{R_1} = [R_{min}, R_1)$$

$$\vec{R_2} = [R_1, R_2)$$

$$\vec{R_2} = [R_2, R_3)$$

$$\vec{R_n} = [R_{n-1}, 9999) \tag{4}$$

(4) According to step(3) of the partition of the longitudinal section and the radius of the curve section divided the different flat and vertical combination of sections, and calculated the evaluation coefficients I_{1m}, n and I_{2m}, n in each combination of vertical and horizontal sections as shown in Eqs. (5-10), where $i \in \vec{l_m} R \in \vec{R_n}$. I_{1m}, n represented the proportion of the braking distance in the specific vertical and horizontal combination section to the braking distance of the corresponding longitudinal slope section. I_{2m}, n represented the proportion of the braking distance in the specific vertical and horizontal combination section to the length of the section. Finally the, evaluation coefficient matrix I_1 and I_2 of the section were got.

$$L_{\vec{i_m}\vec{R_n}} = \sum_{j=1}^{k} L_j(i, R) \tag{5}$$

$$L_{\vec{i_m}} = \sum_{j=1}^{k} L_j(i) \tag{6}$$

$$L_{\vec{i_m}\vec{R_n}} = \sum_{j=1}^{k} l_j(i, R) \tag{7}$$

$$l_{\vec{i_m}} = \sum_{j=1}^{k} l_j(i) \tag{8}$$

$$I_{1mn} = \frac{l_{\vec{i_m}\vec{R_n}}}{l_{\vec{i_m}}} \tag{9}$$

$$I_{2mn} = \frac{l_{\vec{i_m}\vec{R_n}}}{l_{\vec{i_m}\vec{R_n}}} \times \frac{l_{\vec{i_m}}}{L_{\vec{i_m}}} \tag{10}$$

(5) According to step(4) calculated the coefficient of judgment array I_1 and I_2, and further calculated the Braking Effect Index(BEI) as shown in Eq. (11).

$$BEI = I_1 + I_2 \tag{11}$$

When the driver takes braking measures throughout the road indicates that the driver is very cautious, and the road section is extremely dangerous. Therefore, the road was divided into safe sections, potentially dangerous sections, generally dangerous sections and dangerous sections based on the proportion of drivers taking braking measures in the road section(the value of BEI), as shown in Tab. 1. [15,22,24]

The Relationship Among the Judgment Coefficient, the BEI and the Driving Risk Degree of the Road   Tab. 1

BEI	BEI≥85%	85%＞BEI≥70%	70%＞BEI≥50%	BEI＜50%
The Driving Risk of the Section	Safe Section	Potentially dangerous section	Generally dangerous section	Dangerous section

3 Model Verification

In traditional methods, the following indicators of steep slopes are usually evaluated.

3.1 The maximum longitudinal slope

The maximum slope of the road should not be greater than as provided in the Tab. 2.

The Maximum Longitudinal Slope   Tab. 2

Design Speed(km/h)	120	100	80	60	40	30	20
The Maximum Longitudinal Slope(%)	3	4	5	6	7	8	9

3.2 The Maximum Slope Length

The maximum length of the road slope shall comply with Tab. 3.

The Maximum Slope Length   Tab. 3

	Design Speed(km/h)	120	100	80	60	40	30	20
Longitudinal Slope(%)	3	900	1000	1100	1200	—	—	—
	4	700	800	900	1000	1100	1100	1200
	5	—	600	700	800	900	900	1000
	6	—	—	500	600	700	700	800
	7	—	—	—	—	500	500	600
	8	—	—	—	—	300	300	400
	9	—	—	—	—	—	200	300
	10	—	—	—	—	—	—	200

In addition, the length of the road section where the longitudinal slope is not less than 3% should be checked to check whether the road section meets the corresponding maximum slope length restriction requirements under the operating speed.

3.3 The Maximum Synthetic Slope

The purpose of limiting the composite slope to a certain range is to avoid the adverse effects of the combination of steep slopes and sharp bends on driving as much as possible. Prone to water slide accidents is an important research content. The Eq. (12) for the composite slope is as follows.

$$i = \sqrt{i_h^2 + i_z^2} \qquad (12)$$

i in the Eq. (12) was the composite slope. i_h in the Eq. (12) was the ultra-high slope or road cross slope. i_z in the Eq. (12) was the longitudinal slope.

Because the composite slope is a combination of longitudinal slope and lateral slope, its slope value is larger than the original longitudinal slope or super-elevated cross slope. When a car is running on a super high slope, it is not only affected by the resistance of the slope, but also by centrifugal force. When the longitudinal slope is large and the radius of the circular curve is small, the composite slope is large, which causes the car's center of gravity to shift and brings danger to the car. Therefore, on slopes with round curves, the synthetic slope should be controlled within a certain range to avoid the unfavorable combination of sharp bends and steep slopes, prevent slippage in this direction due to excessively large synthetic slopes, and ensure driving safety.

The "Design Specification for Highway Alignment" stipulates that the maximum composite slope value of the highway shall not be greater than the requirements in Tab. 4.

The Maximum Synthetic Slope of Highway   Tab. 4

Highway Class	Highway、First-class Highway				Secondary Road、Tertiary Highway、Class IV Highway				
Design Speed(km/h)	120	100	80	60	80	60	40	30	20
Synthetic Slope(%)	10	10	10.5	10.5	9	9.5	10	10	10

When a steep slope overlaps a flat curve with a small radius, a smaller composite slope should be used. When encountering one of the following conditions, the composite slope must be less than 8%.

(1) Snow and icy areas on the road in winter;
(2) The natural cross slope is steeper along the hillside section;
(3) Sections with heavy non-automotive traffic.

In this paper, a six-axle truck test was designed to get the braking data of the continuous long downhill section of 51km in the mountain expressway in China, and the safety of the section was analyzed based on traffic accidents. At the same time, the safety of different vertical and horizontal combination section in the test section was analyzed by using the above linear quality evaluation model, and the results of the two analyzes were compared.

The Six-axle Truck Vehicle Test.

Test Sections and Truck Models There are more than ten typical sharp steep slopes and continuous long downhill sections of expressways in China. Among them, the experimental expressway is extremely steep with topographical conditions, extremely complicated geological structures, extremely variable climatic conditions, extremely fragile ecological environment, extremely difficult construction conditions and safe operation. It is extremely difficult to be recognized by experts and scholars as one of the most demanding project and the highest scientific and technological content mountainous expressways with the most natural environment in China and even the whole world.

Along the edge of the Sichuan Basin, the expressway climbed up to the Hengduan Mountains. The expressway is "M" shaped and spread in the mountains with an elevation of 600m to 3200m, so it forms three continuous long downhill sections which are the northern slope of Niba Mountain, the southern slope of Niba Mountain and the northern slope of Tuowu Mountain as shown in Fig. 3. Among them, the northern slope of Tuowu Mountain is a 51km continuous long downhill section called "the devil in the devil section". The entire section of the gap is 1500m (K120 + 2020 ~ K171 + 020), and the average longitudinal slope is 2.96%. Because of the high elevation of the road section, temporary cliffs and sharp turns, the driving risk for the truck is huge. Therefore, this experiment selected the most typical 51km continuous long downhill expressway for the six-axle truck vehicle test, and then the safety of the section was evaluated based on the Braking Effect Index (BEI).

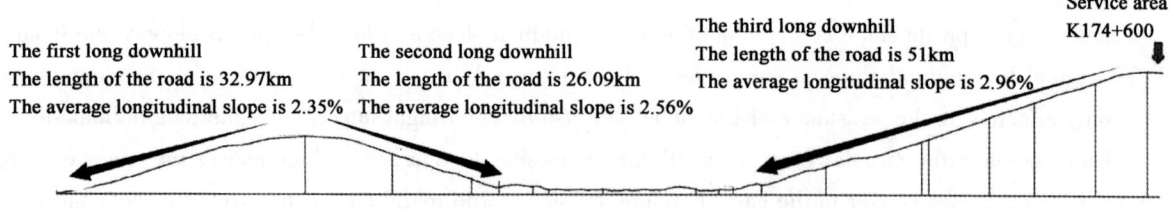

Fig. 3 The Schematic of Three Continuous Long Downhill Sections of the Experimental Expressway

Through the investigation on the type and load of trucks in the experimental expressway, the result showed that the six-axle trucks accounted for the most significant proportion, reached 61%, and its rated load was 49 tons. The trucks with a load of 30 to 40 tons accounted for the largest proportion of 41%, indicating that most of the six-axle trucks are not fully loaded as showed in Fig. 4. As the primary truck driving on the experimental expressway was a semi-linked six-axle truck with a high accident rate[20], this test selected the full load semi-trailer six-axle truck with the highest risk probability of driving, and the specific parameters of the test truck were shown in Tab. 5.

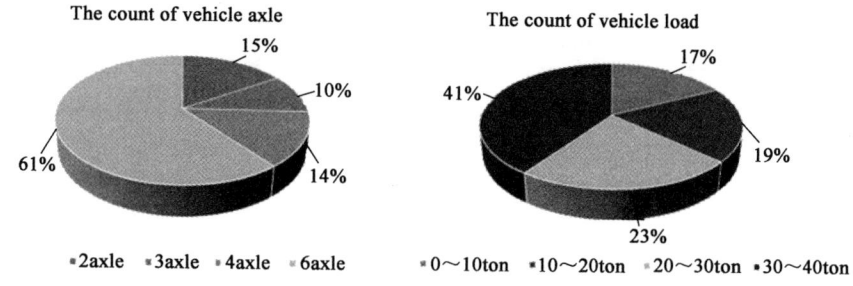

Fig. 4 Truck Axles and Load Distribution

Test Truck Models and its Parameters Tab. 5

Projects	Parameters
Truck Model	DFL4251A15
Engine Model	ISZ45041
Equipment Quality	8800kg
The Maximum Allowable Traction Quality	40000kg
Rated /Maximum Net Power	331/323kW
The Maximum Speed	90km/h
Engine Speed Range	900-1800rpm

Experimental Procedure Before the test, a data acquisition system was installed on the test truck, and the truck was weighed on the scales, as showed in Fig. 5. The collection of braking data mainly depended on the brake signal acquisition module, which consisted of a brake pedal force sensor and a data transmission line connected to it. The sensor was installed in the truck foot pedal position, wired data transmission line was connected with the VBOX data acquisition channel and the system output a brake response signals every 1s. When the driver depressed the pedal, the sensor was triggered, and the output brake response signal was 1. Otherwise the brake response signal was 0.

During the test, the truck departed from the service area and the speed ranged from 60km/h to 70km/h during the test that the truck keeps relatively constant speed. In the process of downhill, the driver controlled the speed of the vehicle by using the service brake, auxiliary brake and transmission, and the data acquisition system would record the vehicle speed, distance traveled, brake action time and other dynamic data. After the test, the braking data were derived from the data acquisition system which was shown in Tab. 6.

Test Data(part) Tab. 6

Time(s)	Speed(km/h)	Distance(m)	Height(m)	brake	Distance(km)
1	0.09	0.01	2400.00	1	0.00
2	0.21	0.07	2399.61	1	0.00
3	0.44	0.19	2399.21	1	0.00
4	0.81	0.42	2398.82	1	0.00
5	1.28	0.77	2398.43	1	0.00
6	1.8	1.27	2398.04	1	0.00
7	2.33	1.92	2397.64	1	0.00
8	2.83	2.70	2397.25	1	0.00
9	3.29	3.62	2396.86	1	0.00
10	3.72	4.65	2396.47	1	0.00

Time(s)	Speed(km/h)	Distance(m)	Height(m)	brake	continue Distance(km)
……	……	……	……	……	……
……	……	……	……	……	……
3163	0.61	49564.86	894.38	1	49.56
3164	0.2	49564.91	894.26	0	49.56
3165	0.14	49564.95	894.30	0	49.56
3166	0.13	49564.99	894.34	0	49.56
3167	0.12	49565.02	894.42	0	49.57
3168	0.11	49565.05	894.38	0	49.57
3169	0.1	49565.08	894.30	0	49.57
3170	0.11	49565.11	894.22	0	49.57
3171	0.11	49565.14	894.01	0	49.57
3172	0.11	49565.17	894.01	0	49.57

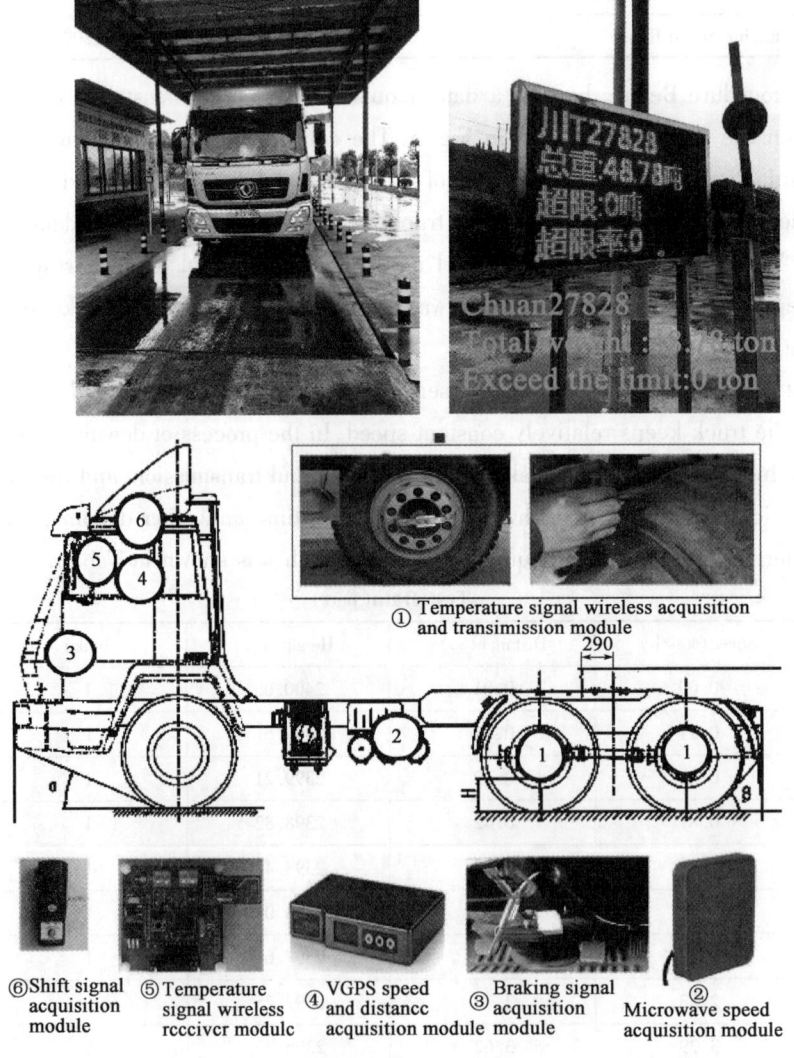

Fig. 5　Data Acquisition System and the Picture of the Test Car Weighing

3.4 The Analysis of Traffic Accidents in the Section

The traffic accidents from 2013 to 2017 were collected as shown in Table 4. An analysis of the road line of the traffic accidents occurred in the past five years was shown in Fig. 6.

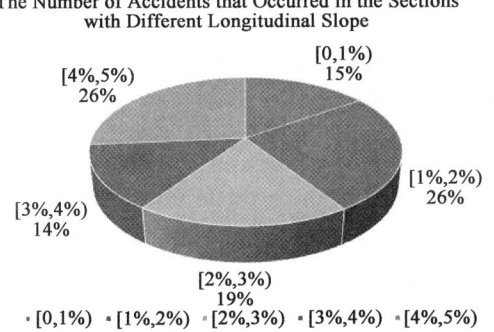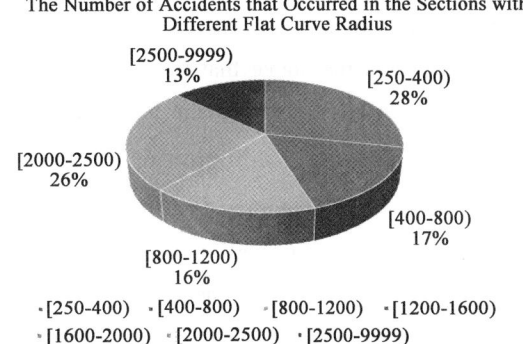

Fig. 6   The Traffic Accidents in Different Vertical and Horizontal Sections

The analysis results showed that the traffic accidents in the flat curve radius range of [2000,2500), [250,400) accounted for a high proportion, respectively accounting for 26% and 28% of the total traffic accidents. It indicated that the traffic accidents are more likely to occur in the areas with sharp curves and transition curves. The traffic accidents in the longitudinal slope range of [4%,5%), [1%,2%) accounted for a high proportion, respectively accounting for 26% and 26% of the total traffic accidents. It indicated that the traffic accidents are more likely to occur in the areas with steep slope and gentle slope.

Therefore, the accident rate per kilometer was analyzed in different vertical and horizontal combination section of K147 + 800-K172 + 340, as shown in Tab. 7. The section had a higher traffic risk and the highest elevation. There are many steep slopes and Sharp Curved road sections and flat vertical alignment is extremely complicated. Its scene photos were shown in Fig. 7.

The Accident Rate Per Kilometer in Different Vertical and Horizontal Combination Section   Tab. 7

	[250,400)	[400,800)	[800,1200)	[1200,1600)	[1600,2000)	[2000,2500)	[2500,9999]
[0,1%)	—	—	10	—	0	—	7.41
[1%,2%)	—	2.18	4.94	0	—	—	7.42
[2%,3%)	15.22	4.94	6.06	—	—	—	9.84
[3%,4%)	—	—	6.02	—	—	—	4.76
[4%,5%)	0	12.61	6.24	0	0	17.65	8.44

Fig. 7   Scene Photos of K147 +800-K172 +340

The average accident rate for this section is 7.28/ km. When the longitudinal slope interval was [0,1%), the flat curve interval where the accident rate was higher than the average accident rate were [800,1200) and [2500,9999]. When the longitudinal slope interval was [1%,2%), the flat curve interval where the accident rate was higher than the average accident rate was [2500,9999]. When the longitudinal slope interval was [2%,3%), the flat curve interval where the accident rate was higher than the average accident rate were [250, 400) and [2500,9999]. When the longitudinal slope interval was [3%,4%), the accident rate was lower than the average accident rate. When the longitudinal slope interval was [4%,5%), the flat curve interval where the accident rate was higher than the average accident rate were [400,800)、[2000,2500) and [2500,9999]. It could be seen from the above that the sections with higher traffic risk in the test section were the sharp curve sections, the steep slope sections, the long gentle slope sections and the straight sections.

3.5 The Safety Evaluation of the Section

Based on the data obtained from the brake signal acquisition module in the six-axle truck vehicle test, the safety of different vertical and horizontal combination lines of a 51km continuous downhill section of the mountain expressway in China was analyzed. The specific process was as follows.

(1) The experimental section was divided into 180 unit sections with slope change point, intersection point of straight line and transition curve, intersection point of transition curve and circle curve, intersection point of circle curve and transition curve and the intersection point of transition curve and straight line as shown in Tab. 8, and schematic of unit section division was shown in Fig. 8.

Division of Unit Section (Part) Tab. 8

Station Range		Vertical Slope (%)	Horizontal Curve (m)	Unit Section Length (m)	Braking Distance Length (m)	General Accident	Medium Accident	Serious Accident	The Total Number of Accidents
172340	171043	−0.9	9999	1297	60	1	1	0	2.2
171043	170960	−0.9	1791	83	83	0	0	0	0
170960	170260	−0.9	880	700	160	7	0	0	7
170260	170143	−1.6	880	117	117	0	0	0	0
170030	169974	−1.6	9999	56	565	0	0	0	0
169974	169585	−1.6	960	389	299	0	0	0	0
169585	169264	−1.6	9999	321	321	1	0	1	2.5
……	……	……	……	……	……	……	……	……	……
……	……	……	……	……	……	……	……	……	……
124850	124458	−3.9	1450	392	0	0	0	0	0
124458	124315	−3.9	7528	143	143	0	0	0	0
124315	124281	−3.9	9999	34	34	1	0	0	1
124281	124250	−3.9	9806	31	31	0	0	0	0
124250	124185	−2.893	3167	65	65	1	0	0	1
124185	124130	−2.893	2013	55	55	0	0	0	0
124130	124070	−2.893	1600	60	60	0	0	0	0

Notes: 1. General accident means that there was only road loss, no casualties.
2. Medium accident means that no less than five people were injured and there were no casualties.
3. Serious accident means that there were deaths or there were no casualties but more than five people were injured.
4. The total number of accidents = General accident + 1.5 * Serious accident + 1.2 * Medium accident. [23,27]

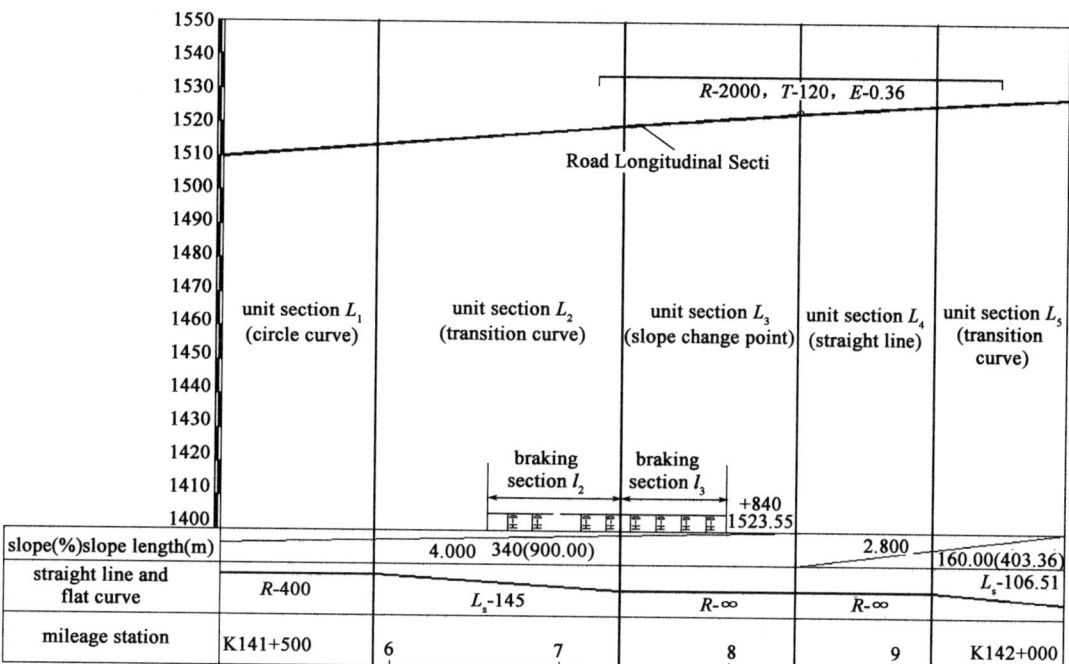

Fig. 8 Schematic of Unit Section Division

(2) The set of the length of the unit sections L_k and the length of the braking distance l_k were shown in the Eqs. (13-14).

$$L = \{1297,83,700,117,113,56,389\cdots\cdots,392,143,34,31,65,55,60\} \quad (13)$$

$$L = \{60,0,160,0,0,299,321\cdots\cdots,0,0,34,31,65,0,60\} \quad (14)$$

By analyzing the structure and line shape of the section where braking measures were taken found that the driver took frequent braking measures at the tunnel entrance and the transition curve. During the 100-300m road section which was before the tunnel entrance, the probability for a driver to take braking measures was more than 85%. The road sections the driver took braking measures accounted for 22.1% of the total test section, 53.1678% of the sections were transition curve among them.

(3) The design speed of research section is 80km/h. So the horizontal curve radius of the test section was divided into seven intervals as shown in the Eq. (15), taking the minimum radius (250m), general radius (400m), N times ($N = 2,3,4,5$) of general radius as well as the radius of the circular curve there is no superelevation (2500m) and the radius of a straight line (9999m) as divide nodes.

$$\vec{R_1} = [250,400], \vec{R_2} = [400,800), \vec{R_3} = [800,1200), \vec{R_4} = [1200,1600),$$
$$\vec{R_5} = [1600,2000), \vec{R_6} = [2000,2500), \vec{R_7} = [2500,9999] \quad (15)$$

The longitudinal slope of the test section (absolute value) was divided into 5 intervals at intervals of 1% of the longitudinal slope as showed in the Eq. (16).

$$\vec{i_1}[0,1\%), \vec{i_2}[1\%,2\%), \vec{i_3}[2\%,3\%), \vec{i_4}[3\%,4\%), \vec{i_5}[4\%,5\%) \quad (16)$$

Assuming that the average longitudinal section in different flat curve radius interval was consistent, the analysis of the braking sections in each horizontal curve radius interval showed that the probability of the driver taking braking measures in the sharp curves and the transition curves was larger than 50%. When the radius of the flat curve was less than 1600m, the probability of the driver adopting the braking measure increases as the radius of the flat curve decreases, as shown in Fig. 9a).

Assuming that the average flat curve section in different longitudinal intervals were consistent, the analysis of the braking sections in each longitudinal intervals showed that the braking distance was not only related to the longitudinal slope but also to the slope length. The probability of the driver taking braking measures on steep slopes and long gentle slopes was greater than 20%, as shown in Fig. 9b).

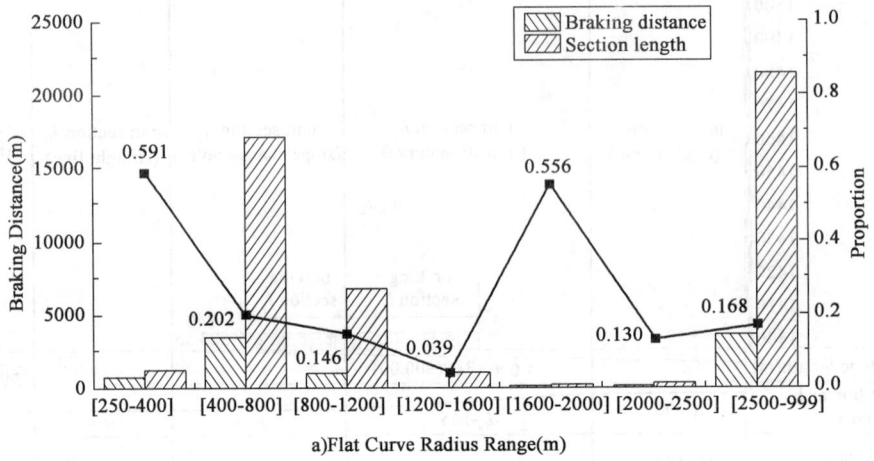

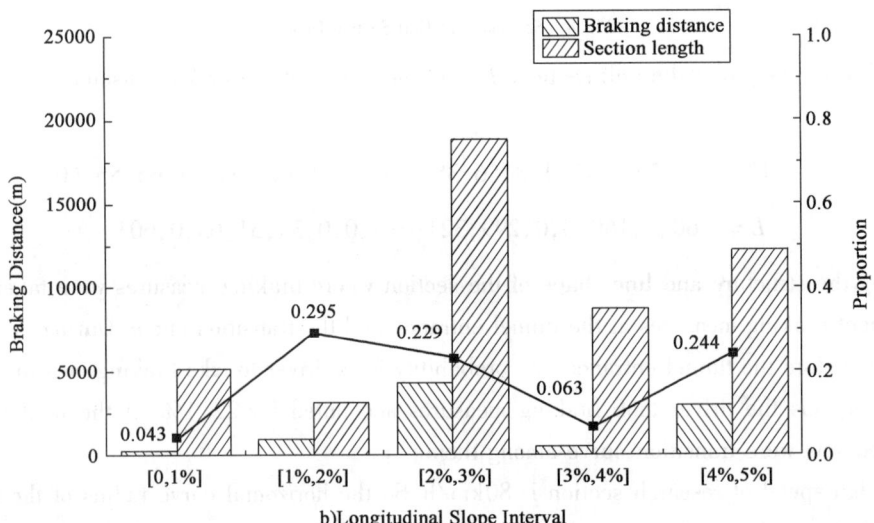

Fig. 9 The Length of Braking Distance and its Percentage in the Whole Road Sections in Different Horizontal and Vertical Intervals

(4) According to step (3) of the partition of the longitudinal section and the radius of the curve section divided the different flat and vertical combination of sections, and calculated the evaluation coefficients $I_{1m,n}$ and $I_{2m,n}$ based on the Eqs. (5-10). Finally, the evaluation coefficient matrix I_1 and I_2 of the section were got.

$$\vec{L_{i_1}} = 5150\text{m}, \vec{L_{i_2}} = 3170\text{m}, \vec{L_{i_3}} = 18892.08\text{m}, \vec{L_{i_4}} = 8790\text{m}, \vec{L_{i_5}} = 12267.92\text{m} \tag{17}$$

$$\vec{l_{i_1}} = 220\text{m}, \vec{l_{i_2}} = 935\text{m}, \vec{l_{i_3}} = 4329\text{m}, \vec{l_{i_4}} = 550\text{m}, \vec{l_{i_5}} = 2988\text{m} \tag{18}$$

$$L_{\vec{i},\vec{R}} = \begin{vmatrix} 0 & 541 & 791 & 0 & 83 & 0 & 3735 \\ 0 & 459 & 1311 & 39 & 0 & 0 & 1361 \\ 762 & 8575 & 1488 & 315 & 60 & 55 & 7637.082 \\ 424 & 1445 & 1687 & 435 & 0 & 90 & 4709 \\ 104 & 6161 & 1499 & 223 & 44 & 170 & 4066.92 \end{vmatrix}$$

$$l_{\overrightarrow{i},\overrightarrow{R}} = \begin{vmatrix} 0 & 0 & 160 & 0 & 0 & 0 & 60 \\ 0 & 84 & 299 & 39 & 0 & 0 & 513 \\ 762 & 2273 & 78 & 0 & 60 & 0 & 1156 \\ 0 & 0 & 145 & 0 & 0 & 0 & 405 \\ 0 & 1120 & 305 & 0 & 44 & 41 & 1478 \end{vmatrix}$$

$$I_1 = \begin{vmatrix} 0 & 0 & 72.7\% & 0 & 0 & 0 & 27.3\% \\ 0 & 9.0\% & 32.0\% & 4.2\% & 0 & 0 & 54.9\% \\ 17.6\% & 52.5\% & 1.8\% & 0 & 1.4\% & 0 & 26.7\% \\ 0 & 0 & 26.4\% & 0 & 0 & 0 & 73.6\% \\ 0 & 37.5\% & 10.2\% & 0 & 1.5\% & 1.4\% & 49.5\% \end{vmatrix}$$

$$I_2 = \begin{vmatrix} / & 0 & 20.23\% & / & 0 & / & 1.61\% \\ / & 18.3\% & 22.81\% & 100\% & / & / & 37.69\% \\ 100\% & 26.51\% & 5.24\% & 0 & 100\% & 0 & 15.14\% \\ 0 & 0 & 8.60\% & 0 & / & 0 & 8.60\% \\ 0 & 18.18\% & 20.35\% & 0 & 100\% & 24.12\% & 36.34\% \end{vmatrix}$$

(5) The matrix of BEI of the test section was calculated based on the Eq. (11), and then the risk of the different combination of vertical and horizontal sections could be obtained.

$$BEI = \begin{vmatrix} / & 0 & 92.95\% & / & 0 & / & 28.88\% \\ / & 27.28\% & 54.79\% & 104.17\% & / & / & 92.56\% \\ 117.6\% & 79.01\% & 7.04\% & 0 & 101.39\% & 0 & 41.84\% \\ 0 & 0 & 34.96\% & 0 & / & 0 & 82.24\% \\ 0 & 55.66\% & 30.55\% & 0 & 101.47 & 25.49\% & 85.81\% \end{vmatrix}$$

The Classification of the Driving Risk of the Test Section as shown in Tab. 9, Tab. 10.

The Classification of the Driving Risk of the Test Section(1)　　Tab. 9

	[250,400)	[400,800)	[800,1200)	[1200,1600)
[0,1%)	—	safe	dangerous	—
[1%,2%)	—	safe	potentially danger	dangerous
[2%,3%)	dangerous	generally dangerous	safe	safe
[3%,4%)	safe	safe	safe	safe
[4%,5%)	safe	potentially danger	safe	safe

The Classification of the Driving Risk of the Test Section(2)　　Tab. 10

	[1600,2000)	[2000,2500)	[2500,9999]
[0,1%)	safe	—	safe
[1%,2%)	—	—	dangerous
[2%,3%)	dangerous	safe	safe
[3%,4%)	—	safe	generally dangerous
[4%,5%)	dangerous	safe	dangerous

According to the safety of the test section evaluated by the quality evaluation model of highway alignment, found that when the longitudinal slope interval was [0,1%), the flat curve interval with higher traffic risk was [800,1200). When the longitudinal slope interval was [1%,2%), the flat curve interval with higher traffic risk were [2500,9999] and [1200,1600). When the longitudinal slope interval was [2%,3%), the flat curve interval with higher traffic risk were [250,400)、[400,800) and [1600,2000). When the longitudinal slope interval was [3%, 4%), the traffic risk was lower. When the longitudinal slope interval was [4%, 5%), the flat curve interval with higher traffic risk were [2500, 9999] and [1200, 1600].

It could be seen from the above that the sections with higher traffic risk in the test section were the sharp curve sections, the steep slope sections, the long gentle slope sections and the straight sections, which were mainly the same with the sections with higher accident rate.

4 Conclusions

In this study, the braking effect index is used as an index to evaluate the safety of the expressway sharp curves and steep slope sections. Based on the analysis of the braking effect and braking failure mechanism of the sharp curves and steep slope sections of the expressway, a six-axle truck test is selected, Established and verified the highway route quality evaluation model, which is a new method of quantitative analysis of vertical and horizontal combined sections. In this research, the conclusions are obtained.

(1) The steep slope sections、the Sharp Curved sections and the long gentle slope and the straight sections were dangerous sections of the test expressway.

(2) The sharp curve sections and the long gentle or steep slope sections with a long slope greater than 1500m had a great influence on driving safety.

(3) The proportion of taking braking of the driver on the steep slope sections with a longitudinal slope greater than 4% and the sharp sections with a radius less than 400m was respectively 24.4% and 59.1%. The longitudinal slope had more influence on the driving than the flat curve radius in the continuous long downhill section. The main factors affecting the driver to take braking measures in the gentle slope section were the flat curve radius and slope length.

However, taking into account the impact of road alignment on driving safety, the safety of sharp bends and steep slopes of the road is evaluated. Compared with the method of using traffic accident data to evaluate the linear quality, this method is convenient, simple and practical to obtain the data. This study still has some limitations to consider.

(1) Braking behavior is a very complicated driving behavior, which is not only affected by the vertical alignment of the road, but also influenced by various factors such as the environment and the driver. The model established in this paper only considered the influence of the vertical alignment of the road on braking. It has limitations and needs further study.

(2) Based on the linear quality evaluation model established in this article, the dangerous road segment only indicated that the driving risk of the section is relatively large, which cannot explain that the section must be with the high accident.

(3) There was only one type of vehicle braking data was used to determine the driving risk of the test section in instance verification. It has limitations and needs to be further judged whether the dangerous sections are consistent by using braking data of the different type of vehicle.

(4) It was difficult to obtain the braking data based on the six-axle truck test in instance verification. So it is needed to study how to use the operating speed and acceleration data to obtain the braking distance of the vehicle.

(5) Due to the difficulty of getting the data of traffic accidents, this paper only verified the driving risk of a 51km long continuous downhill section of the mountain expressway in China. The next step is to increase the test section and further amend the model.

Therefore, considering the above factors, we propose the following discussion.

(1) When the flat curve radius is less than 800m, the longitudinal slope interval with higher traffic risk is

[2%, 3%). When the longitudinal slope of the section is less than 2% or greater than 3%, the driving risk decreases instead. As longitudinal slope has more influence on the driving than the flat curve radius in the continuous long downhill section, the driver is relatively safer on the gentle slope. However, when the section is a combination of sharp curves and steep slopes, the driver will be very cautious so that driving risk is relatively low.

(2) When the flat curve radius is more than 2500m, the driver will be more vigilant when driving on this road section so that the section is with the higher accident. When there are steeper slopes, the driving risk will be higher.

(3) When the horizontal curve interval is [800, 1600), there is a higher driving risk of road sections with a longitudinal slope less than 2%, mainly due to the longer slope length of the gentle slope section where the drivers are such easy vigilance and driving fatigue that traffic accidents are easy to happen.

(4) When the horizontal curve interval is [1600, 2500), most of the sections belong to the transition curves, and the driver needs to continually change the driving state while driving on the section, so that the risk of operation errors is relatively easy to occur. When there are steeper slopes, it will increase the difficulty of driver operation, making driving risk increases.

5 Acknowledgements

The authors appreciate the National Key R&D Project [grant number 2020YFC1512005 & 2020YFC1512005].

References

[1] Bo Su. Research on Continued Braking Performance of Large Trucks and Optimum Design of Longitudinal Slope in Mountainous Expressways [J]. 2011.

[2] Lee J H, Park J J, Park S H, et al. Development of Evaluation Criteria for Curve-section Safety Level with Visual Distortions on Two-lane Rural Highways [J]. KSCE Journal of Civil Engineering, 2015:1-8.

[3] Aram A. Effective Safety Factors on Horizontal Curves of Two-lane Highways [J]. Journal of Applied Sciences(Faisalabad), 2010, 10(22):2814-2822.

[4] Agarwal P K, Patil P K, Mehar R. A Methodology for Ranking Road Safety Hazardous Locations Using Analytical Hierarchy Process[J]. Procedia-Social and Behavioral Sciences, 2013, 104:1030-1037.

[5] Lill, R. A. Development of a Grade Severity Rating System [J]. Alexandria, Vs.: American Trucking Associations, December 1975.

[6] Bo Chen. Study of Rescue Lane Design Method on the Mountainous Expressway Downhill Path [D]. Chengdu: Southwest Jiaotong University. 2007.

[7] Xinsha Fu, Jie Gao. Prediction of Running Speed of Freight Cars on Longitudinal Section of Expressway [J]. Road Traffic Technology, 2008.

[8] Lu Sun, Kesi You. Driving Risk Analysis Based on Multi-failure Mode Reliability in Curve Sections[J]. China Highway Journal, 2013.

[9] Wei Cheng. Research on the Theory Model and Method of Traffic Accidents and Traffic Conflict Technique in Urban Streets [D]. Changchun: Jilin University, 2004.

[10] Lai Zheng. Research of Safety Analysis Models Based on Extreme Statistics of Traffic Conflicts [D]. Harbin: Harbin Institute of Technology, 2014.

[11] Ana Tsui Moreno, Alfredo Garcia, Francisco Javier Camacho-Torregrosa, et al. Influence of Highway Three-dimensional Coordination on Drivers' Perception of Horizontal Curvature and Available Sight Distance[J]. IET Intell. Transp. Syst. 2013, 7(2):244-250.

[12] Wang F, Easa S M. Validation of Perspective-view Concept for Estimating Road Horizontal Curvature[J]. Journal of Transportation Engineering, 2009, 135(2):74-80.

[13] Hu Liwei, Li Linyu, Wang Miao, SHE Tian-yi. Study on Braking Risk Threshold Value for Full-loaded Medium Trucks on Continuous Long and Steep Downhill Sections Based on Bench Test[J]. Road Traffic Technology,2017,34(07):135-144,152.

[14] Jijie Ma. Study of Brake Inertia Dynamometer Measure and Control System[D]. Changchun:Jilin University,2006.

[15] Zheng Runyu. Research on the Identification Method of the Mountain Highway Accident-Prone Section[D]. Cheng chu:South China University of Technology,2013.

[16] Haynes R, Jones A, Kennedy V, et al. District Variations in Road Curvature in England and Wales and Their Association with Road-traffic Crashes[J]. Environment and Planning A,2007,39(5):1222.

[17] Su Bo, Fang Shouen, Wang Junhua. Research on Longitudinal Slope Length Limit of Mountain Expressway Based on Heavy Vehicles' Braking Ability[J]. Journal of Chongqing Jiaotong University(Natural Science Edition),2009,28(02):287-289,297.

[18] Liu Ruiguang. Theoretical Analysis of Driving Braking Behavior[J]. Journal of Shandong Normal University(Natural Science Edition),2002.

[19] Findley D J, Hummer J E, Rasdorf W, et al. Modeling the Impact of Spatial Relationships on Horizontal Curve Safety[J]. Accident Analysis & Prevention,2012,45:296-304.

[20] Wang Jianbo. A study on the Typical Truck Running Safety Tests Along 51 km-distance Downhill on Yaxi Expressway[D]. Xi'an:Chang'an university,2013.

[21] Li Duhou, Research on Accident Prevention for the Continuous Long Steep Downgrade Section Based on Vehicle Braking Performance[D]. Xi'an:Chang'an university,2010.

[22] Pei Yulong, Xing Enhui. Analysis of Slope and Slope Length Limit of High Grade Highway[J]. Journal of Harbin Institute of Technology,2005,(05):629-632,716.

[23] Khorashadi A, Niemeier D, Shankar V, et al. Differences in Rural and Urban Driver-injury Severities in Accidents Involving Large-trucks:an Exploratory Analysis[J]. Accident Analysis & Prevention,2005,37(5):910-921.

[24] Effati M, Rajabi M A, Samadzadegan F, et al. Developing a Novel Method for Road Hazardous Segment Identification Based on Fuzzy Reasoning and GIS[J]. Journal of Transportation Technologies,2012,2(1):32-40.

[25] Guo Ping. Study on Early Warning of Air-mass Fog and Security Technology of Freeway[D]. Xi'an:Chang'an University,2016.

[26] Chen Liuxiao, Liu Tangzhi, Duan Mengmeng. Deceleration Landscape Design of Tunnel Entrance Based on Visual Illusion[J]. Journal of Chongqing Jiaotong University(Natural Science Edition),2018,37(01):99-103.

[27] Wu Lina. Research on the Comparison and Improvement of Road Traffic Black-spots Identification Methods[D]. Harbin:Harbin Institute of Technology,2007.

公路运行速度模型研究综述

黄春富[1]　魏东东[1]　王亚楠[1]　马如鹏[1]　白杰[2]

(1.长安大学公路学院;2.长安大学运输工程学院)

摘　要　为明确公路运行速度模型的适用性和应用现状,对国内外公路运行速度模型研究进行了梳理。依据建模方法将现有运行速度模型分为实测回归模型、理论分析模型和软件仿真模型;重点论述了3种模型的研究进展,分别从建模方法、数据采集、模型适用性、影响因素等4个方面对模型研究现状进行分析评述,指出了目前运行速度模型存在的主要问题,最后结合运行速度分析现状和交通领域研究热点,探讨了运行速度模型研究发展方向。结果表明:车速预测研究受诸多因素制约,预测模型的适应性不强;完善数据采集方法,改进数据处理手段,改进建模方法,进一步考虑平纵组合、驾驶员行为特性及气候环境对运行速度的影响,与BIM正向设计结合,是未来运行速度研究发展的方向。

关键词 交通工程 运行速度 综述 运行速度模型

0 引 言

一直以来,交通行业的设计人员都是根据设计速度进行道路设计,但是经过多年来的实践和探索,发现这个方法存在较大的安全问题,很容易导致道路在运营过程中车辆运行速度发生较大的波动,进而诱发交通事故。为了保证道路线形的连续性,减少设计速度设计法弊端的影响,交通行业人员将设计速度和运行速度综合考虑,并应用于道路设计。

从 Federal Highway Administration(FHWA)公布的数据可以得出,车辆间的速度差绝对值不大于10km/h 时,交通事故率是 0.46(起/百万公里);而当车辆间的速度差绝对值大于 20km/h 时,交通事故率变为 2.67(起/百万公里)[1]。Solomon[2]、Cerillo[3]、West[4]、Taylor[5]、Yu R[6]等人发现不同等级公路车流平均速度与车辆运行速度相差变大时,交通事故率也相应上升,也就是说平均速度与运行速度之差和事故率符合 U 形曲线关系。因此,对道路的运行速度及其预测方法进行研究,对提高道路安全水平具有重要意义。

从1960s 开始,运行速度的研究开始进入国外学者的视线,研究重点是运行速度与经济性的关系[2]。最著名的是1970 年世界银行采取实地调查方法得到的 HDM-Ⅲ模型:模型认为,当车流处于自由流状态时,期望速度、线形平曲线、发动机制动功率和输出功率、道路平整度对车辆行驶速度有重要影响[7]。到了20 世纪80 年代,大量国外学者开始从道路几何线形指标的角度建立车辆运行速度预测模型,从而提升道路的安全性[8-9]。澳大利亚、欧洲等国在对运行速度展开了研究后,取得了很多重要成果,并开始将运行速度纳入路线设计标准中[10]。而我国构建的速度预测模型并不能完全满足需要,主要是由于我国交通数据统计工作前期没有开展,再加上研究目的、方法不同,研究人员采集到的数据存在偏向性[11-12]。近年来,随着计算机应用的发展,部分学者从算法和软件仿真等多个角度建立了较多的运行速度模型,主要包括速度影响因素、驾驶特性及建模方法[13-14]。

综上,对比国内外的研究现状,可以知道公路运行速度的研究还处于发展阶段,由于车速影响因素较多,其预测研究的观点不一,导致模型众多,但其适应性不强;而且基于不同方法和研究条件构建的模型缺少对比分析、评价,交通行业人员选用模型进行设计、评估、研究时存在一定困难,无法保障道路车辆行驶的安全性。为此,本文在系统梳理公路运行速度研究成果基础上,总结并评述其相应的建模方法,对比分析典型模型,最后对该领域研究的发展方向进行展望。

1 运行速度模型研究评述

运行车速是指在外部条件理想的条件下,在路段特征点上测得的第85 个百分位上的车速,即 V_{85} 车速[15]。从国内外开展运行速度预测研究到现在,已有40 多年的历史,通过查阅大量文献可以知道所用方法较多,本文在此基础上进行了详细的总结,按照建模方法将运行速度模型分为3 类,即实测回归模型、理论分析模型和软件仿真模型。

1.1 实测回归模型

为使模型更符合特定路段行车状况,目前国内外对基于道路线形的车速预测模型研究以实测回归法为主。该方法通常是通过选取试验路段,利用雷达等仪器,在良好的路面状况、天气和自由流交通条件下实测大量数据。采用数理统计方法建立运行速度 V_{85} 与道路线形指标、其他道路因素等变量之间的函数关系,并以此构建模型。

20 世纪 70 年代,美国 Leisch 提出了基于运行速度评价道路平面纵面几何线形一致性的方法[16]。1973 年德国提出了第一个运行速度模型,该模型将行车速度(V_{85})与平均曲线速度、车道宽度和曲率变化率联系起来,但由于实测数据有限,模型对实际没有用处[17]。1987 年美国学者 Lamm 等人基于 84 个的道路曲线,分别建立了不同车道宽度下运行速度 V_{85} 与曲率变化率、平曲线半径之间的关系[18];1990 年通过采集 322 条道路曲线数据进一步研究了 V_{85} 和平曲线的关系,发现平曲线半径是影响 V_{85} 最显著的参数,并构建了运行速度 V_{85} 与平曲线半径之间的关系[19];为了解释运行速度的可变性,1999 提出新的评价指标——单个曲线的曲线变化率 CCRS,并用 CCRS 替换平曲线曲率改进了 1994 年加拿大 Morrall 和 Talarico 运行速度模型[20],该模型可以考虑曲线的变化并可用于复合曲线[21]。但这些研究仅从平面曲线段出发。此后,国内外学者对运行速度开展了大量实测研究,研究发现运行速度与众多的道路几何设计参数有较为显著的相关性,包括平曲线半径、圆曲线长度和转角、直线段长度、纵坡坡长和坡度等。并根据这些研究分别建立了 V_{85} 与直线段[22-23]、纵断面[24-25]、平纵结合[26-27]、路侧干扰因素[28-29]等众多影响因素的运行速度预测模型。

澳大利亚通过调研大量路段、采集相应数据进行了详细的研究,根据小客车 V_{85} 与路段平曲线半径的关系建立了运行速度表,对于纵坡较大的路段则根据纵坡大小再进行车速修正。但该方法仅适用于小客车,并且将平曲线半径大于 600m 的路段按直线段考虑。我国《新理念公路设计指南》运行速度模型主要参考了澳大利亚的计算方法。《公路项目安全性评价指南》(JTG/T B05—2004)通过大量的现场调研、采集数据和回归分析,制定了划分路段单元的原则和标准以及不同线形条件下大小型车的运行速度预测模型。《公路项目安全性评价规范》JTG B05—2015 则在 04 版指南的基础上进一步完善,把公路等级划分更加具体,给出了各等级公路下的运行速度模型,并增加了高速公路隧道和立交段的运行速度模型。

随着研究的不断深入,国内外学者尝试用其他方法建立运行速度预测模型。MacFadden[30]、Taylor[31]、王栋[32]、杜锦涛[33]等人为了建立 V_{85} 与道路几何线形的关系模型,将神经网络技术应用到 V_{85} 的预测研究中。张驰建立了考虑空间视野的高速公路运行速度预测模型并提出了模型的求解方法,但仅考虑了道路平纵横和视距 4 方面指标[34]。

1.2 理论分析模型

基于行车动力学进行理论分析,推导得出了运行速度预测模型,即理论分析模型。

1.2.1 极限功率法[35]

图 1 展示了基于极限功率法的运行速度预测模型,主要是将道路线形与汽车自身动力相结合,从而实现运行速度的预测。由于汽车在换挡过程中,其离合器是顺畅无冲击地接合,所以采用极限功率法预测的运行速度能连续且平顺过渡的,但该方法考虑的是汽车在理想状态下的速度,缺少道路环境的进一步考虑。

1.2.2 可能速度预测模型

有别于运行速度,杨少伟提出了"可能速度"的概念[36]。可能速度指在良好的气候条件和交通条件下,汽车的行驶只受到公路本身线形条件影响,技术熟练的驾驶员驾驶汽车沿某条公路行驶时,可能达到的速度。事实上,可能速度和以往设计速度、运行速度的区别是很大的,它是指连续的、最大可能的运行速度,预测模型的具体流程如图 2 所示。

1.2.3 理论运行速度计算模型

符锌砂提出的理论运行速度计算模型是综合考虑了道路线形指标、车辆的动力学特性、驾驶员行为模式等,通过理论分析研究建立的基于公路线形的理论运行速度模型[35,37],但模型是假设道路交通处于良好的自由流状态。

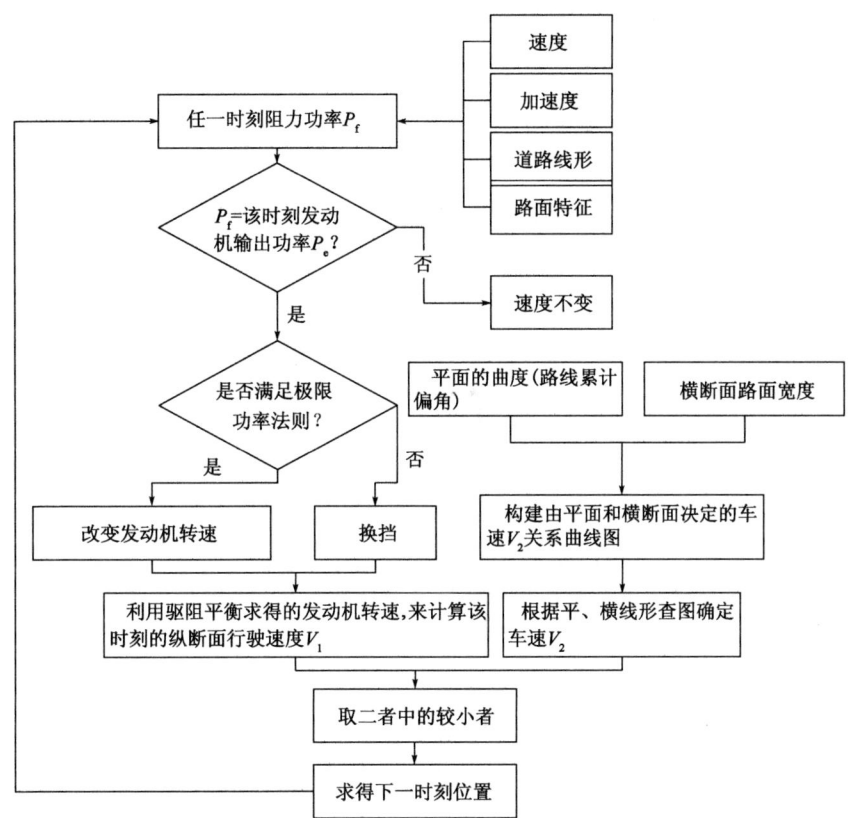

图 1 基于极限功率法的运行速度预测模型

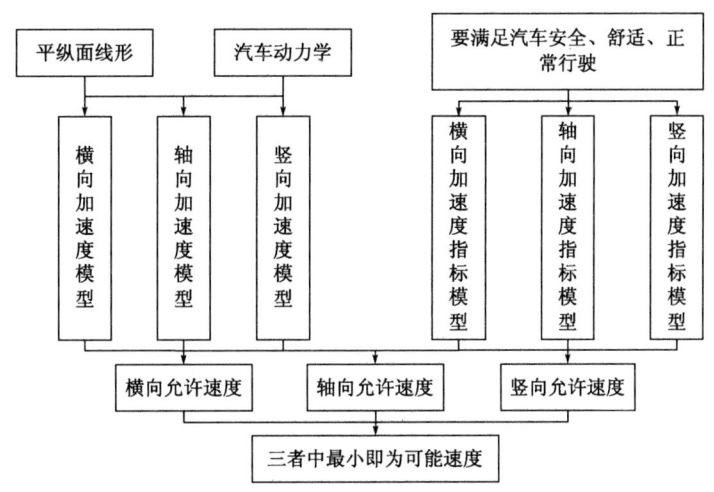

图 2 可能速度预测模型

1.3 软件仿真模型

为了解决样本有限、实现变量可控等问题,部分学者采用成熟的商业软件(如 ADAMS)构建运行速度预测模型——软件仿真模型,通过在软件中预先输入控制策略来获得运行车速,主要考虑了行车动力学和线形参数两方面,由于是在计算机中获得的数据,未能全面考虑各因素的内在关系。

陈涛等人建立了基于模糊理论的运行车速预测模型[38],并利用 Muti Gen Creator 对模糊评价因子进行了仿真,但其模糊感知集仅考虑平纵线形和[39-40]。郭启明等人基于高仿真驾驶模拟实验采集山区高速公路自由流车速,提取运行速度曲线,以当前位置上下游的坡度、曲率、超高和动态视距值为模型自变量,构建通用的运行速度预测模型,但其缺少对山区隧道路段的考虑[41]。商建伟从人—车—路系统的角度出发,综合分析了山区高速公路弯坡组合路段驾驶员的速度控制行为模式及其影响因素,并根据驾驶员行为特征建立了弯坡路段车辆运行速度的预测模型,并利用 Matlab 和 Simulink 对模型进行验证,但未进行实例验证[42]。

1.4 综合分析及评述

1.4.1 建模方法评述

综上所述,国内外大多数研究均采用实测回归模型建模,欧洲、澳大利亚、美国等国开展运行速度研究较早,其研究也相对成熟;而国内开始较晚,还处于初步探索阶段。

(1)实测回归法通过对实测数据的拟合回归进行模型构建,能综合反映众多影响因素对模型的影响,更能反映特定路段运行速度的实际变化情况,但该方法对实测数据来源要求较高。由于现场采集的数据有限且来源于已建成通车公路,加上现场环境的限制,回归出来的经验模型的普适性存在一定问题,不能完全满足拟建公路线形指标的控制、检查和评估。传统线性回归分析会造成模型简化,而文献[30]~文献[33]利用神经网络解决了这个问题,能准确表明变量间的关系,有利于运行速度的预测研究。

(2)理论分析法以汽车动力学为基础,假设在道路条件良好的自由交通流条件下进行的研究,具有一定的普适性。但忽视了驾驶员、环境因素的影响,特别是对于线形较好的路段,决定运行车速的往往会是驾驶员的主观行为。因此,需要结合道路实际情况对模型进行修正,提高模型精度。

(3)软件仿真法主要考虑了行车动力学和线形参数两方面,由于是在计算机中获得的数据,未能全面考虑各因素的内在关系,所以仿真法假设条件较多,很大程度上简化了模型,大大降低了模型的精度,且仿真数据与实际路况数据并不完全相符合,缺乏实用性。

以上 3 种建模方法的侧重点不完全相同,在工程应用中,应确定实际需求,结合个模型特点,选取建模方法,表 1 对 3 种方法构建的典型模型进行了评述。

典型运行速度模型评述　　　　　　　　　　表1

方法	模型	公式模型	评述
实测回归法	Gibreel[53]	研究平纵组合状况下车辆分别在凹形曲线和凸形曲线下车辆运行速度预测模型	(1)针对不同线形特征点,考虑线形平纵组合,采用实测回归方法进行建模,公式计算简单;(2)仅考虑双车道公路,且数据只来源于两条公路;(3)假设同类型连续线形上的速度分布是相同的,适用性有限;(4)主要考虑平纵线形指标
	《路项目安全性评价规范》JTG B05—2015	实测数据回归分析	(1)采集国内多地数据,路段单元划分按照一定原则和标准,回归出不同线形组合下大、小型车的运行速度模型;(2)数据来源广泛,但未考虑如高原等特殊地区;(3)采用系数折减法考虑道路环境因素的影响,计算过于简化;(4)假设同类型连续线形上的速度分布是相同的,忽略其他因素对同一线形路段的影响
	杜锦涛模型[33]	神经网络模型	(1)突破以"拆分—拼凑"式的二维角度进行公路运行速度预测的局限,以公路线形三维几何特征为自变量,能更精确表示变量之间的关系;(2)数据采集自珠三角平原微丘区高速公路,来源单一;(3)实现了运行速度沿桩号连续预测,避免特征断面选择对预测结果的影响;(4)主要考虑平纵线形指标
	Dharamveer Singh[54]	神经网络模型	(1)基于神经网络算法,针对是否考虑已有速度数据、事故数据分别建立模型;(2)数据来自俄克拉荷马州双车道农村公路,来源单一;(3)不仅能预测新建道路的运行速度,还能基于已建道路数据预测道路条件发生变化时的运行速度;(4)考虑了道路特性、交通流参数、事故数据、平面线形,没有考虑人、纵断面、天气等条件

续上表

方法	模型	公式模型	评述
理论分析法	极限功率法[35]	$\frac{Mn}{9549} = \frac{1}{\eta_T}\left(\frac{GfV_a}{3600} + \frac{GiV_a}{3600} + \frac{G_D AV_a^3}{76140} + \frac{\delta GV_a}{35316}\frac{dV}{dt}\right)$ $V = 0.377 \frac{nr}{i_0 i_g}$	(1)以汽车动力学为基础,推导符合车辆自身行车特性的公式;(2)能合理地解释汽车本身性能和速度之间的关系;(3)忽视了驾驶员因素及其他道路外部条件的影响
理论分析法	杨少伟可能速度模型[36]	(1)加速度模型:$a_h = \frac{V^2}{13R_p}$, $a_z = \frac{\lambda g}{\delta}(D - f - i)$, $a_s = \frac{V^2}{13R_s}$; (2)加速度模型结合加速度指标模型建立速度预测模型	考虑最理想的汽车行驶环境下的车速,不适用于实际道路运行速度的预测
软件仿真法	郭启明模型[41]	$V_j = \sum_{kB=1}^{n}\beta_{kB}X_{kB,jB} + \sum_{k}^{n}\beta_k X_{k,j} + \sum_{kA=1}^{n}\beta_{kA}(X_{kA,jA} - X_{kB,jB}) + \varepsilon_j^*$	(1)基于驾驶模拟实验,考虑上下游邻近数个路段的线形特征,进行模型构建;(2)更准确地描述车速在复杂线形路段上的连续变化情况,但模型仅针对单车;(3)仅考虑平纵线形指标
软件仿真法	商建伟模型[42]	模糊预测模型	(1)利用行车动力学和实地数据综合分析驾驶员的速度控制行为模式及影响因素,进行模型构建;(2)数据采集来自西汉高速公路,来源单一;(3)将模糊理论应用到人—车—路系统,但该模型将车辆看作刚性物体,忽略悬架、轮胎等非刚性物体的阻尼作用、车辆转弯时车辆的侧向稳定性

表中,为方便对比,将不同数学模型中相同意义的参数做了统一化处理,其中,M 为发动机有效转矩(N·m);n 为发动机转速(r/min);η_T 为机械效率;G 为汽车重力(kN);f 为滚动阻力系数;V_a 为前一时间间隔的车速(km/h);i 为道路坡度;G_D 为空气阻力系数;A 为汽车迎风面积(m²);δ 为汽车质量换算系数;V 为 t 时刻下的汽车行驶速度(km/h);r 为车轮周长(m);i_0 为变速器速比;i_g 为主传动比;a_h、a_z、a_s 为汽车横向、轴向、竖向加速度(m/s²);R_p、R_s 为圆曲线半径、竖曲线半径(m);λ 为海拔荷载修正系数;g 为当地重力加速度(m/s²);g 为动力因数;V_j 为第 j 段路的预测车速;$X_{kA,jA}$、$X_{k,j}$、$X_{kB,jB}$ 为道路几何变量(前方路段、当前位置、后方路段);β_{kB}、β_k、β_{kA} 为对应的模型系数;ε_j^* 为速度误差;n 为划分的总道路段数。

1.4.2 数据采集分析

实测回归模型最主要的影响因素就是数据来源,受道路条件、交通条件及地域等条件上的限制,研究人员在选取实测地点、样本数量、实测手段、设备布设位置等方面存在着不统一的标准,造成模型存在较大偏差和局限。Hassan 发现在安大略省东部随机选取的路段上,超过 50% 的调查曲线都带有十字路口或转弯车道[43],而 Nie、Hassan 之前开发的速度模型所选择的研究地点通常会排除一些不利条件,如存在十字路口或车道数量的变化[44]。随着大数据时代的到来,在今后研究运行速度模型时应保证数据的代表性,确定数据符合地方道路特点的基础上建模。

1.4.3 模型适用性分析

在构建模型前的前提假设也是影响模型普适性的另一大因素。1977 年 Leisch 提出的速度曲线假设加速和减速发生在水平曲线之前或之后,并且在曲线上保持恒定的运行速度[16]。Lamm 等假设同类型连续线形上的速度分布是相同的[18,45,46]。针对这些假设,提出使用相邻路段的 85% 位速度差(ΔV_{85})来评估道路的一致性,但忽视了个体驾驶员的在道路上的速度变化特性,将相邻两个路段的速度独立处理,容易低估相邻路段的速度差[47]。考虑 ΔV_{85} 的局限性,将相邻路段上每个单车最大减速或加速的第 85% 分位值(85MSR 或 85MSI)[48]、相邻路段速度差的第 85% 分位值($\Delta 85V$)[49]作为评价指标,为今后评估道路一致性提供了新的思路,但还缺少适用的相关评价标准。

大多数现有的模型具有以下形式:

$$V_i = \sum(b_k X_{ik}) + e$$

式中:V_i——第i百分位值速度;
 b_k——与变量k相关的回归参数;
 X_{ik}——影响第i百分位值速度的变量k的值;
 e——正态分布扰动项。

现有的模型估计的是一个特定的速度百分位数,大部分没有给出平均速度因子和速度离散性,这有时会导致:具有高平均速度和低速度变异性的道路可能与低平均速度但高速度变异性的道路具有相同的速度百分位值[50]。

1.4.4 影响因素分析

国外车速实测大多是针对小客车进行的,而由于纵坡对小客车的运行速度没有太大影响,因此主要以平曲线上的要素为回归变量。虽然国外有些模型及我国《指南》给出的预测模型和方法,也考虑了纵坡和组合线形的影响,实际上也是在建立平曲线要素与运行速度的关系上,然后在不同纵坡上对运行速度进行折减后得到。相关研究表明,支路密度、路侧行人、路侧停车、中央分隔形式、路侧建筑物、地区类型、标志牌的密度[29,51]及天气条件[52]均对运行速度有显著影响。如何考虑道路环境因素,构建更加全面的运行速度模型需要进一步考虑。

2 展 望

(1)从统计学的角度来看,在不同地区广泛开展数据实测,增加样本量,可以减少样本个体差异带来的误差,提高模型精度和适用性,从而促进运行车速理论的发展。

(2)在众多运行速度预测模型研究中,由于特征点间车速变化的判断是基于路段特征点运行速度和一定驾驶行为假设,为了避免这个弊端,可以采取 GPS 试验车和车联网大数据等新型的数据采集手段,获取高精度的连续车数数据。处理数据的手段可以不仅依靠线性回归,可以结合神经网络等智能算法提高预测预测模型的精确度。同时考虑平均速度因子和速度离散型。

(3)对于不同百分位的变量进行多方面考虑,不要割分影响因素来分析速度变化,要合理考虑变量间的相互影响以及它们共同对速度的作用,减少解释变量间的共性,提高变量比重的计算精度。在环境与驾驶员因素方面,可从定量角度深入研究基于行车环境及驾驶员行为特性的运行速度规律,完善目前模型多单一环境假设的缺陷;在车辆方面,应该针对不同车型的特性做进一步分析;在道路方面,应进一步考虑平纵组合对运行速度的影响。以完善目前众多模型假定车辆以恒速通过路段单元的缺陷,并引入相关区域因素修正系数,完善运行速度模型。

(4)由于 BIM 具有可视化设计、参数化设计、协同化设计、模拟分析、优化设计的特点,国内外已有学者将路线设计与 BIM 工具相互结合,实现平、纵、横设计三者之间的动态关联。以 BIM 软件为载体,利用计算机语言将运行速度模型与路线设计结合,在 BIM 平台得到运行速度的计算与路线评价信息的动态实时反馈[55],为路线设计智慧决策提供了可靠的信息支持。随着计算机的发展,未来在 BIM 平台将运行速度模型与环境、路侧干扰因素结合起来,做到设计中实时反馈,设计可视化,对于实现 BIM 正向设计、大力提升交通行业信息化水平具有重要意义。

3 结 语

(1)随着行车环境趋于复杂化和中国道路信息化水平的提高,运行速度研究的主要方向不仅仅局限于车辆和道路因素,还将涉及交通环境和驾驶员行为。

(2)通过分析、总结国内外相关文献,归纳出目前公路运行速度模型主要包括实测回归模型、理论分析模型、软件仿真模型,对比分析了各模型的优缺点,并提出了目前运行速度模型存在的主要问题:建模方法不完善,数据来源不全和存在偏差,模型适用性受限,影响因素考虑不全面等。

(3)本文提及的模型缺陷为今后研究指明了方向——基于人—车—路—环境耦合作用下的运行模型理论研究,完善数据采集方法,改进数据处理手段,改进建模方法,多方面考虑影响因素等。并指出将运行速度模型与设计相结合,有利于实现 BIM 正向设计。

参考文献

[1] 曹世理.高速公路限速区车速协调性与交通安全关系研究[D].西安:长安大学,2015.

[2] Solomon D. Accidents on Main Rural Highways Related to Speed, Driver and Vehicle[R]. Bureau of Public Roads, Washington: Federal Highway Administration, D. C. ,1964,7.

[3] Cerillo J A. Interstate System Accident Research Study II. Interim Report II[J]. Public Road,1968. 35(3):71-75.

[4] West L B, Dunn J W. Accidents, Speed Deviations and Speed Limits[J]. Traffic Engineering,1971. 41(10):52-55.

[5] Taylor W. C.. The Impact of Raising the Speed Limit on Freeways in Michigan [R]. College of Engineering, Michigan State University,2000.

[6] Yu R, Quddus M, Wang X, et al. Impact of Data Aggregation Approaches on the Relationships Between Operating Speed and Traffic Safety[J]. Accident; Analysis and Prevention,2018,(120):304-310.

[7] Watanatada T, Dhareshwar A M, Lima P R S R. Vehicle Speeds and Operating Costs: Models for Road Planning and Management[M]. Baltimore and London: The Johns Hopkins University Press,1987.

[8] Jacob A, Anjaneyulu M V L R. Operating Speed of Different Classes of Vehicles at Horizontal Curves on Two-Lane Rural Highways[J]. Journal of Transportation Engineering,2013,139(3):287-294.

[9] Camacho-Torregrosa F J, Perez-Zuriaga A M, Campoy-Ungria J M, et al. New Geometric Design Consistency Model Based on Operating Speed Profiles for Road Safety Evaluation [J]. Accident Analysis and Prevention,2013,(61):33-42.

[10] Porter Richard. Modeling Operating Speed: Synthesis Report [M]. Washington, D. C: Transportation Research E-Circular,2011.

[11] 张驰,宫权利,马向南,等.互通立交单车道入口小客车运行速度模型[J].长安大学学报(自然科学版),2018,38(04):71-79.

[12] 王丹丹.高速公路平纵组合路段运行速度预测研究[D].哈尔滨:哈尔滨工业大学,2014.

[13] 刘三兵.山区双车道公路车辆运行速度仿真[D].长春:吉林大学,2011.

[14] 刘祥敏.普通公路限速影响因素与预测模型研究[D].济南:山东建筑大学,2020.

[15] 范振宇,张剑飞.公路运行车速测算模型的研究和标定[J].中国公路学报,2002(01):110-112.

[16] Leisch J E, Leisch J P. New Concepts in Design-Speed Application[J]. Transportation Research Record Journal of the Transportation Research Board,1977(631):4-14.

[17] Dilling J. Fahrverhalten von Kraftfahrzeugen auf Kurvigen Strecken[J]. Strassenbau & Strassenverkehrstechnik,1973,(151):35-74.

[18] Lamm R, Choueiri E M. Recommendations for Evaluating Horizontal Alignment Design Consistency Based on Investigations in the State of New York [J]. Transportation Research Record Journal of the Transportation Research Board,1987,(2):68-78.

[19] Lamm R, Choueiri E M, Mailaender T. Comparison of Operating Speeds on Dry and Wet Pavements of Two-Lane Rural Highways[J]. In Transportation Research Record,1990,1280:199-207.

[20] Morrall J, Talarico R J. Side Friction Demanded and Margins of Safety on Horizontal Curves[J]. Transportation Research Record,1994,1435,145-152.

[21] Lamm R, Psarianos B, Mailaender T. Highway Design and Traffic Safety Engineering Handbook[M]. New York: McGraw Hill,1999.

[22] Polus A, Fitzpatrick K, Fambro D. Predicting Operating Speeds on Tangent Sections of Two-Lane Rural Highways[J]. Transportation Research Record Journal of the Transportation Research Board,2000,

1737:50-57.
[23] 屠书荣,姚阳,张泽良.双车道公路运行速度计算与安全性评价方法研究[J].公路交通技术,2013(02):120-124,129.
[24] Fitzpatrick K, Elefteriadou L, Harwood D, et al. Speed Prediction for Two-Lane Rural Highways[M]. Washington, D. C:Federal Highway Administration,2000.
[25] 许金良,雷斌,李诺.高速公路上坡路段载重车辆运行速度特性[J].交通运输工程学报,2013,13(06):14-19,35.
[26] Shuming Shi, Xiaodong Liu, Kangzi Cao, et. al. Study on Cloud Model of Operating Speed based on Road Alignment and Sight Distance[C]// IEEE. International Conference on Transportation, Mechanical, and Electrical Engineering. Changchun:IEEE,2011. 648-651.
[27] 徐进,邵毅明,赵军,等.山区道路弯坡组合路段重载车辆行驶速度模型[J].西安:长安大学学报(自然科学版),2015,35(02):67-74.
[28] 马向南.高速公路互通立交单车道出入口小客车运行速度模型研究[D].西安:长安大学,2017.
[29] Fitzpatrick K, Miaou S P, Brewer M A, et al. Wooldridge Exploration of the Relationships Between Operating Speed and Roadway Features on Tangent Sections[J]. Journal of Transportation Engineering, 2005,131(4):261-269.
[30] MacFadden J, Yang W T, Durrans S. Application of Artificial Neural Networks to Predict Speeds on Two-Lane Rural Highways[J]. Transportation Research Record Journal of the Transportation Research Board, 2001,1751:9-17.
[31] Taylor D R, Muthiah S, Kulakowski B T, et al. Artificial Neural Network Speed Profile Model for Construction Work Zones on High-Speed Highways[J]. Journal of Transportation Engineering,2015,133(3):198-204.
[32] 王栋,邓北川,仇建华,等.山区高速公路直线段车速预测方法[J].交通科学与工程,2014,30(03):81-86.
[33] 杜锦涛.基于公路线形三维空间几何特征的小客车运行速度预测方法研究[D].广州:华南理工大学,2020.
[34] 张驰.考虑空间视野的高速公路运行速度预测模型与应用研究[D].西安:长安大学,2010.
[35] 符锌砂.理论运行速度与公路线形设计及评价方法研究[D].西安:长安大学,2008.
[36] 杨少伟.可能速度与公路线形设计方法研究[D].西安:长安大学,2004.
[37] 符锌砂,刘震.基于平纵组合线形的理论运行速度预测模型[J].长安大学学报(自然科学版),2010,30(03):24-27.
[38] 魏朗,陈涛,高丽敏,等.汽车驾驶员车速控制模式的模拟研究[J].汽车工程,2005(06):696-701+695.
[39] 陈涛,魏朗,袁望方.运行车速认知因子虚拟仿真试验[J].交通运输工程学报,2008(02):122-126.
[40] 陈涛.人—车—路(环境)联合运行虚拟仿真理论与实现技术研究[D].西安:长安大学,2005.
[41] 郭启明,王雪松,陈志贵.基于驾驶模拟实验的山区高速公路运行速度建模[J].同济大学学报(自然科学版),2019,47(07):1004-1010.
[42] 商建伟.山区高速公路曲线路段车辆运行速度预测模型研究[D].西安:长安大学,2012.
[43] Hassan, Yasser. Highway Design Consistency: Refining the State of Knowledge and Practice[J]. Transportation Research Record Journal of the Transportation Research Board,2004,1881:63-71.
[44] Nie B, Hassan Y. Modeling Driver Speed Behavior on Horizontal Curves of Different Road Classifications[C]//Transportation Research Board 86th Annual Meeting. Washington, D. C:Transportation Research Board,2007.
[45] Krammes R A, Brackett Q, Shafer M A, et al. Horizontal Alignment Design Consistency for Rural Two-

Lane Highways [M]. Washington, D. C.: Federal Highway Administration, U. S. Department of Transportation, 1995.

[46] Fitzpatrick K, Carlson P, Brewer M, et al. Design Factors that Affect Driver Speed on Suburban Streets [J]. Texas Transportation Institute College Station Tx, 2001, 1751(1): 18-25.

[47] Hirsh M. Probabilistic Approach to Consistency in Geometric Design [J]. Journal of Transportation Engineering, 1987, 113(3): 268-276.

[48] Mcfadden J, Elefteriadou L. Evaluating Horizontal Alignment Design Consistency of Two-Lane Rural Highways: Development of New Procedure [J]. Transportation Research Record Journal of the Transportation Research Board, 2000, 1737: 9-17.

[49] Misaghi P, Hassan Y. Modeling Operating Speed and Speed Differential on Two-Lane Rural Roads [J]. Journal of Transportation Engineering, 2005, 131(6): 408-418.

[50] Fitzpatrick K, Miaou S P, Brewer M, et al. Exploration of the Relationships between Operating Speed and Roadway Features on Tangent Sections [J]. Journal of Transportation Engineering, 2005, 131(4): 261-269.

[51] Wang J, Dixon K K, Li H, et al. Operating-Speed Model for Low-Speed Urban Tangent Streets Based on In-Vehicle Global Positioning System Data [J]. Transportation Research Record Journal of the Transportation Research Board, 2006, 1961(1): 24-33.

[52] Mace D J, Porter R J. Highway Lighting Requirements for Older Drivers [M]. Washington, D. C.: Federal Highway Administration, U. S. Department of Transportation, 2004.

[53] Gibreel G. M, Easa S M, El-Dimeery I A. Prediction of Operating Speed on Three-Dimensional Highway Alignments [J]. Journal of Transportation Engineering, 2001, 127(1): 21-30.

[54] Dharamveer Singh, Musharraf Zaman, Luther White. Neural Network Modeling of 85th Percentile Speed for Two-Lane Rural Highways [J]. Transportation Research Record, 2012, 2301(1).

[55] 张兴宇, 杨宏志. 基于Civil 3D公路运行速度BIM对象模型的研发与应用[J]. 公路, 2019, 64(02): 191-195.

Study on the Influence Factors of Point Load Test by Flat Joint Model of PFC3D

Zhi He　Wuchao Yang　Peijie Yin　Changgen Yan

(Chang'an University)

Abstract　The flat joint model in three-dimensional particle flow code (PFC3D) is used to investigate the mechanical behaviours of Bentheims and stone under point load test. The micro-parameters are calibrated through the comparison between the numerical simulation and experimental results. Based on the calibrated model, the progressive failure of the point load test is captured and factors that affect point load test are systematically investigated. It is found that, the point load index decrease with size of specimen, and this index increase with the decrease of porosity, which is consistent with the experimental observations from literatures. In addition, the load eccentricity significantly affects the result of the point load test, which is explained through the failure patterns reproduced by numerical simulations. Moreover, the influence of flaw on the point load test decrease as the distance between the loading tip and flaw increases. Finally, the anisotropy behaviour of point load test is realized through the reduction of tensile strength in weak layers with specific thickness and spacing.

Keywords Point load test Influence factors Flat joint model PFC3D

0 Introduction

The point load strength test is a popular testing method in field research to classify rocks and sometimes to predict the uniaxial compression strength or tensile strength of rocks(Broch and Franklin, 1972; ISRM, 1985; Broch, 2003). Studies on point load test have been mainly reflected on the statistical information such as, the variation of the point load strength index, conversion from the point load strength to the uniaxial compression strength, and index correction due to scale effects(Bieniawski, 1975; Cargill and Shakoor, 1990; Rusnak and Mark, 2000; Heidari et al., 2012; Singh and Kainthola, 2012). Nevertheless, the proposed correlations vary because of the uncertainties in the specimen preparation and testing apparatus, e. g., the effects of the rock types, shapes, sizes, anisotropy, and loading conditions.

Relevant studies on the point load test in earlier stage include those of Brook(1980), who examined the size correction for point load testing, and Greminger(1982), who experimentally explored the effect of the rock anisotropy on the size and shape effect in the point load test. Recently, Kahraman et al. (2005) investigated the effect of the porosity on the relation between uniaxial compressive strength and point load index. They also quantified the strength anisotropy of metamorphic rock based on the point load test. Later on, Zhang et al. (2016) analysed the strength anisotropy of quartz mica schist using the point load test. More recently, Masoumi et al. (2018) performed a point load test on rocks with different sizes to study the scale effect on the point load strength index. However, most of these tests were conducted in a very short time, thus the direct monitoring of the crack propagation and failure process becomes difficult and unrealistic. In addition, these tests cannot be repeated because the rock specimens are not identical, which results in uncertainties and fluctuated results. In addition, the load-displacement relationship, crack propagation during the failure process and micro-mechanism are ignored or remain unanswered in most circumstances. Therefore, it is compulsory to conduct the research on point load test through numerical approach so as to remove the uncertainty encountered from experimental study and reveal the mechanism of point load test at the same time.

The Particle Flow Code(PFC, based on discrete element method) has been successfully used to model various aspects of rock behaviours(Ivars et al., 2011; Duan and Kwok, 2016; Hunta et al., 2003; Bahaaddini et al., 2013; Mehranpour and Kulatilake, 2017), which also provide the opportunity to systematically investigate the mechanical behaviour of rocks under point load. In PFC, the contact bond and the parallel bond are typically used to reproduce the physical behaviour of cement-like material, especially in the study of fracturing and fragmentation process in brittle rocks (Potyondy and Cundall, 2004). However, the ratio of the unconfined compressive strength to the indirect tensile strength for rock models(based on parallel bond) is unrealistically low when the sphere-shaped particles are used(Cho et al., 2007; Kazerani and Zhao, 2010; Lisjak and Grasselli, 2014). Alternatively, the flat joint model developed by Potyondy(2012) allows users to match both the direct tensile and unconfined compressive strength of rocks with less computational effort. By considering the tensile failure feature of point load test, the flat joint model would be an ideal choice comparing with the parallel bond model and the clump particle model.

Therefore, in this study, the flat joint contact model in PFC3D is used to capture the mechanical behaviour of Bentheim sandstone under axial point loads(Potyondy, 2013). Firstly, the micro-parameters are calibrated based on the uniaxial compression strength and point load strength index from available literatures. Then, the factors such as the scale effect, loading condition, existence of flaws and anisotropy, which affect the point load tests, are numerical investigated. Based on the results from numerical simulation, discussions and conclusions are provided at the end of this paper.

1 Methodology

1.1 Point Load Test

Point load test is a less expensive and useful method to estimate the strength of rocks. Currently, different types of point load tests can be adopted based on the suggestion of ISRM(1985) such as, the diametrical test on a cylindrical core, axial loading on a cylinder sample and irregular lump test. Among them, the most popular, widely used and extensively reported test is the axial point load test. The result of point load test is reflected through the point load strength index, which is expressed as

$$I_s = \frac{P}{D_e^2} \tag{1}$$

Where P is the peak load, D_e is the equivalent core diameter given by $D_e = \sqrt{4A/\pi}$ for the axial test, and A is the minimum cross-section area of a plane though the contact point.

1.2 The Flat Joint Model in PFC3D

The PFC3D based on discrete element method has been successfully used in rock mechanics, particularly in the modelling of discontinuous behaviours of rocks. In PFC3D, rock is reproduced through the collection of particles with bonds, and the interaction of these assembled particles is realized through the dynamic process with states of equilibrium development whenever the internal forces balance. The flat joint contact model in PFC3D can be used to simulate the macroscopic behaviour of a finite size, linear elastic and bonded interface subject to partial damage. Details on the fundamental principle of flat joint model such as the mechanical behaviour and force-displacement law can be found in the work by Potyondy(2012), which would not be addressed in this paper. Thus, the flat joint contact model is employed in this paper to reproduce the mechanical properties of both unconfined compression test and point load test, for its advantage in realization of high tensile to compressive strength ratio. A flat-joint contact and its corresponding flat-jointed material are shown in Fig. 1 (Potyondy, 2013). A flat-joint contact simulates the behavior of an interface between two notional surfaces, each of which is connected rigidly to a piece of a body. A flat-jointed material consists of bodies(balls, clumps, or walls) joined by flat-joint contacts such that the effective surface of each body is defined by the notional surfaces of its pieces, which interact at each flat-joint contact with the notional surface of the contacting piece. The notional surfaces are called faces, which are {lines in 2D; disks in 3D}.

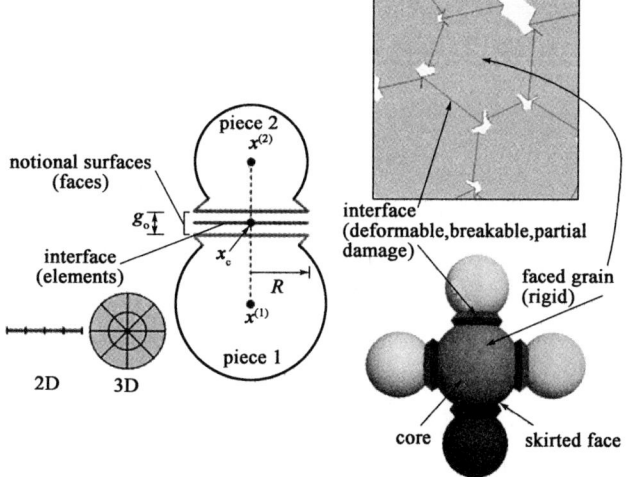

Fig.1 Flat-joint Contact(left) and Flat-jointed Material(Right) (Potyondy, 2013)

2 Numerical Calibration and Validation

Bentheim sandstone cored from Germany is used as the research material because of its relatively homogeneous microstructure. The average porosity of Bentheim sandstone in the study is 23%, and the uniaxial compressive strength (UCS, the specimen with a diameter of 50 mm and a length of 100 mm) is 41.4 MPa (Masoumi et al., 2018). The elastic modulus (E) of Bentheim sandstone varies from 8.3 GPa to 12 GPa as reported by Dubelaar and Nijl and (2014). The point load test results of Bentheim sandstone with different sizes are presented in Fig. 2.

For DEM simulations, model calibration is the first and most important step, where the micro-parameters must be calibrated to reflect the bulk property of the material (Coetzee, 2017). Thus, the uniaxial compression test is conducted on a specimen with 50 mm in diameter and 100 m in height. During the calibration process, the moderate value of 45° is set for internal friction angle, and the corresponding friction coefficient is kept constant as 1.0. The cohesion and tensile strength in the flat joint contact model is calibrated so as to reproduce both the unconfined compression test and point load test.

The parameter study conducted in this study shows that, when the tensile strength to cohesion ratio is less than 0.06, the UCS is affected slightly by the tensile strength (shown in Fig. 3). Accordingly, the cohesion is obtained as 8.7 MPa with tensile strength to cohesion ratio being kept as 0.06, where the UCS is controlled around 41.4 MPa. After that, the micro-parameters are further calibrated based on experimental study presented in Fig. 1. To numerically reproduce the point load test, the spherical loading tip is simulated by a ball with a radius of 5 mm in PFC3D, and the load is obtained from the contact force between the wall and the loading tip. The diameter of specimen varies from 19 mm to 65 mm with length to diameter ratio being as 0.5. The cohesion is kept the same as 8.7 MPa and the tensile strength varies between 0.30 MPa and 0.50 MPa to ensure roughly the same UCS.

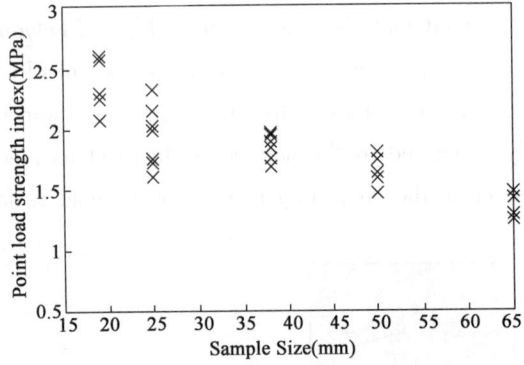

Fig. 2 Experimental Results of Point load Test for Bentheim sandstone (Masoumi et al., 2018)

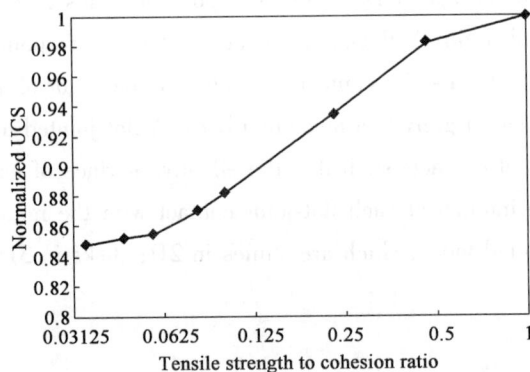

Fig. 3 Influence of Tensile Strength to Cohesion Ratio on the Unconfined Compressive Strength

The simulation results from parametric study are summarized in Fig. 4, which shows that the point strength index decrease gradually with the decrease of tensile strength for all sizes. The combination with cohesion of 8.7 MP and tensile strength of 0.35 MPa shows a good agreement for the point load strength index, which can be confirmed from the solid line in Fig. 4. The strain-stress curve of unconfined compression test with the same micro-parameters is presented in Fig. 5, which shows the similar trends as the experimental results presented by Klein and Reuschle (2003). Thus, the UCS and E are obtained as 41.4 MPa and 9.3 GPa, respectively. Based on the parametric study and numerical calibration of both unconfined compression test and point load test, the micro-parameters for the flat joint model are obtained (listed in Tab. 1).

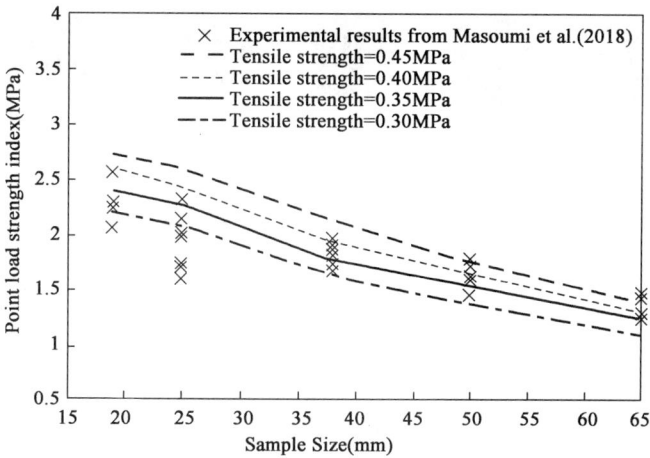

Fig. 4 Comparison Between the Experimental Results and Numerical Simulation with Different Tensile Strengths at Contacts

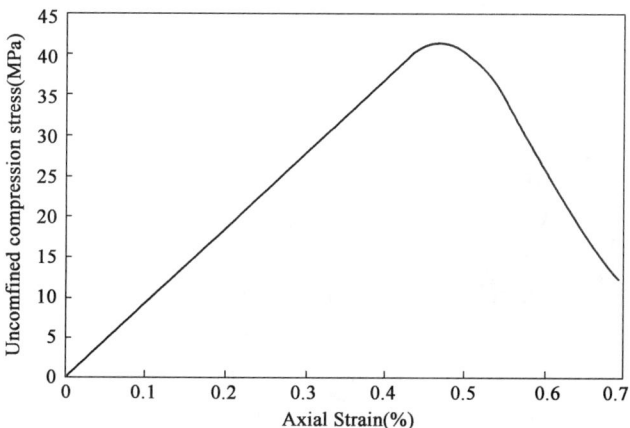

Fig. 5 Strain-stress Relationship From Unconfined Compression Test based on Flat Joint Model in PFC3D

The Micro Parameters based on Parametric Study and Model Calibration Tab. 1

Parameter	Description	Value
R_{min}	Minimum Radius	0.6mm
R_{max}	Maximum Radius	0.9mm
n	Porosity	0.23
E^*	Effective Modulus	5GPa
k_n/k_s	Stiffness Ratio	1.0
c	Cohesion	8.7MPa
σ_c	Tensile Strength	0.35MPa
ϕ	Friction Angle	45°
μ	Friction Coefficient	1.0

Based on the calibrated micro-parameters, the progressive failure of the point load test is examined. As demonstrated in Fig. 6, the failure process can be divided by five stages: ①intact stage, ②crack initiation under the loading tip, ③crack plane generation; ④crack plane propagation, and ⑤failure of specimen when crack propagate to the edge of the specimen. At the end of the test, the sample is split into two or three parts, and the failure patterns of different sizes from numerical simulation are in good agreement with the experimental results (Masoumi et al., 2018) (shown in Fig. 7).

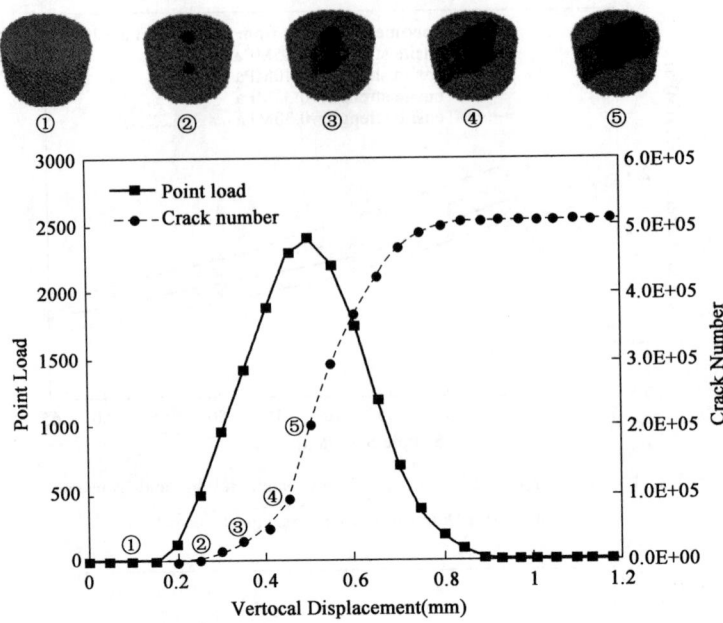

Fig. 6 The Crack Development During Point Load Test

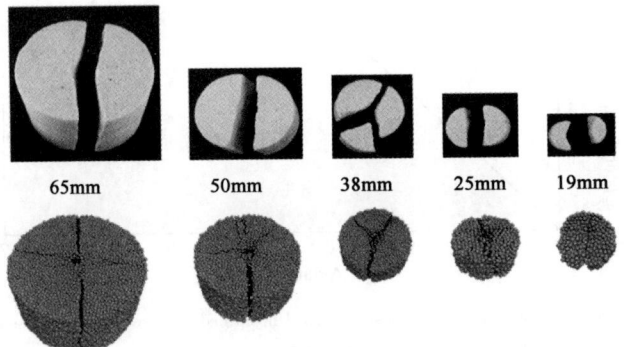

Fig. 7 Comparison of the Failure Patterns Between Numerical Simulation
and Experimental Results from Masoumi et al. (2018)

The numerical investigation on unconfined compression test and point load test indicates that, the flat joint contact model is capable to produce both UCS and Is with reasonable micro parameters, and it can be served as an effective approach to investigate the influence factors on point load test.

3　Influence Factors of Oint Lond Test

Point load test is affected by many factors, i. e. , the point load strength index varies even for rocks of identical sizes and types. However, relevant experimental studies are rarely reported because of the uncertainty in the specimen, differences in rock types and variable microstructures. In this section, the influence factors, such as scale effect, loading condition, existence of flaws and anisotropy on the point load test are systematically studied on the base of the calibrated micro parameters in Tab. 1.

3.1　Scale effect

Eq. (1) indicates that Is varies as a function of De in axial point load tests. The scale effect is investigated with rock specimens of diameter ranging from 38 mm to 65 mm and length-diameter ratio varying from 0.3 to 1.0, according to the standard of point load test (ISRM, 1985). The numerical results are presented in Fig. 8, which shows a decrease in strength with an increase in size.

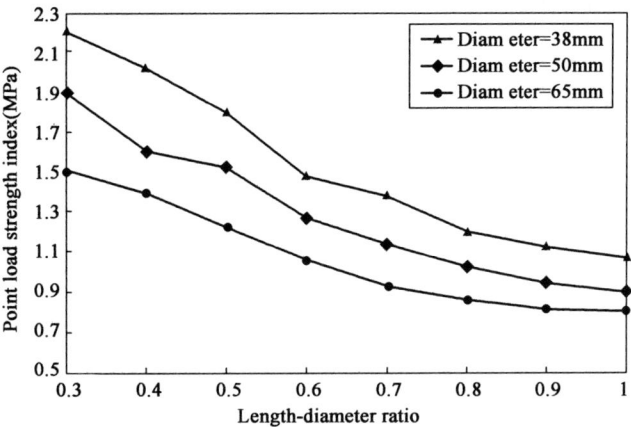

Fig. 8 Scale Effect on the Point Load Test

3.2 Effect of Load Eccentricity

The point load is required to be conducted following the way that the loading tips are at the centre of the specimen in the axial test. However, in some circumstances, the load tip moves away from the centre during the test, which causes unreliable results. Thus, a numerical simulation must be performed to find the effect of the load eccentricity. The sample was prepared with a diameter of 65 mm and a length of 37.5 mm, and the eccentricity(e) to radius(R) ratio varies from 0 to 0.8. The point load strength indexes for the test with different e/R are plotted in Fig. 9. As observed, the point load strength index decreases with the increasing eccentricity. Because the area of failure plane decreases when the load eccentricity increases, the effective area to resist the tension failure decreases accordingly, this will lead to the decrease of point load strength index.

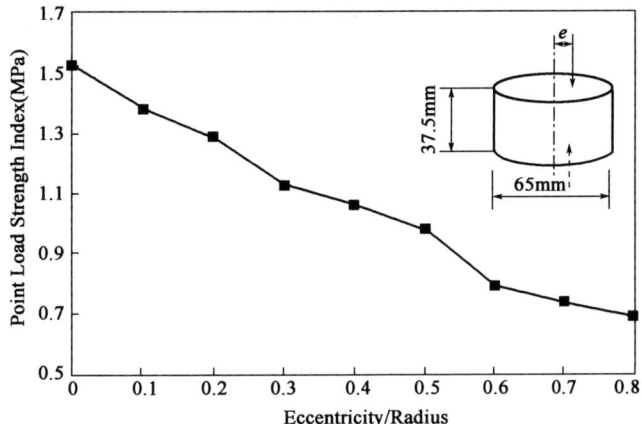

Fig. 9 Effect of Load Eccentricity(e/R) on the Point Load Test

3.3 Effect of Porosity

The porosity significantly affects the strength of rocks, which is reflected from both uniaxial compressive strength and tensile strength. However, relevant experimental works are limited to cases with the porosity varying in a small range. In addition, other factors can affect the testing results, such as the rock types and mineral components, and these effects cover the effects of the porosity in most circumstances. Therefore, the DEM-based simulation can reasonably address this problem. To this end, the micro-parameters in Table 1 are used for all simulations with porosity of 0.1 – 0.3. The corresponding results from the point load test are presented in Fig. 10, which reveals that the point load strength index decreases with the increase in porosity.

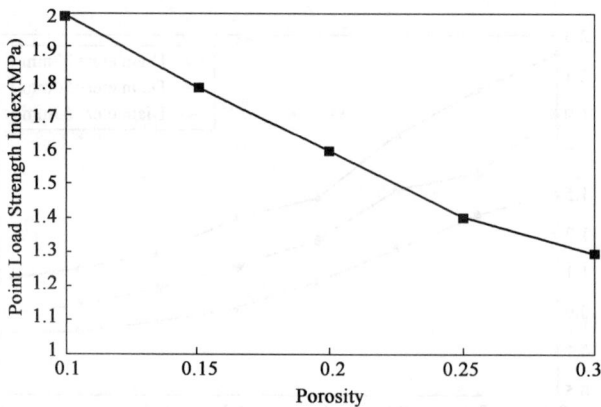

Fig. 10　Effect of Porosity on the Point Load Test

3.4　Effect of Flaw

The point load strength index varies even for the same type of rock with identical sizes, and the failure patterns change accordingly. The uncertainty may come from the difference in microstructure or the presence of flaws. In this part, the effect of flaws on the point load test is studied, where a cut-through flaw with a length of 5 mm and a width of 2 mm is put in the specimen at different locations as indicated in Fig. 11. The failure patterns obtained from the numerical simulation reveal that the crack propagates from the load tip to the predefined flaw and subsequently to the edge of the specimen for all cases. Meanwhile, the effect of the flaw decreases with the increase in distance between the flaw and the loading tip. Thus, the existence of a flaw will dominate the crack propagation direction in the point load test and control the failure pattern, and this effect will vanish if the flaw is far away from the loading tip.

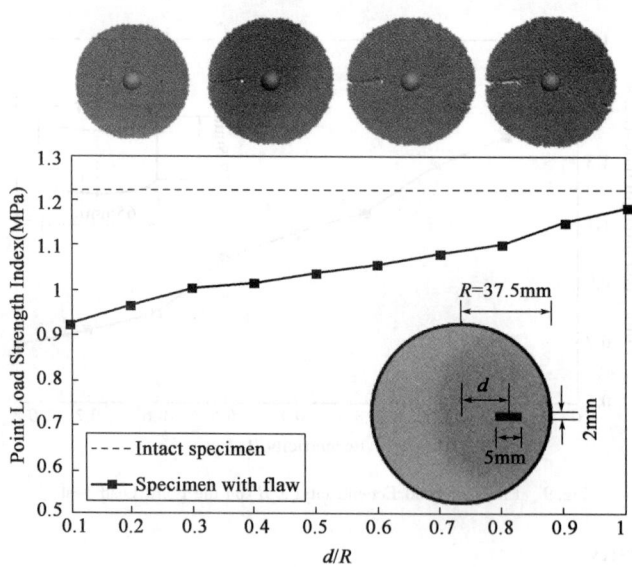

Fig. 11　Effect of a Flaw on the Point Load Test

3.5　Effect of Anisotropy

The anisotropy behaviour of rocks has been widely observed in nature, and extensive work has been conducted to investigate the anisotropy property through the uniaxial compression test or Brazilian tensile test based on experimental and numerical approaches. However, the numerical study of the effect on the point load test is rarely reported. In this part, the anisotropy behaviour of rock under a point load is numerically investigated. For simplicity, anisotropy is realized by reducing the tensile strength of the flat joint contact in the pairs of weak layers as demonstrated in Fig. 12. The anisotropy angle (β) is defined as the angle between the normal direction of the weak plane and the loading direction. The thickness of the weak layer is fixed at 2.5 mm, and the distance between weak layers is set as 5 mm. To introduce the anisotropic behaviour in strength, the tensile strength in the flat joint contact is reduced to a specified ratio of the isotropy model in Table 1 while maintaining other parameters unchanged.

The point load test was conducted on the simplified anisotropy rock model, and the simulation results with reduction ratios of 0.25, 0.01 and 0.001 are presented in Fig. 13. The point strength index gradually decreases with the anisotropy angle for both cases, and the minimum value is obtained at approximately 90°, which is consistent with the experimental works (Kahraman et al., 2005).

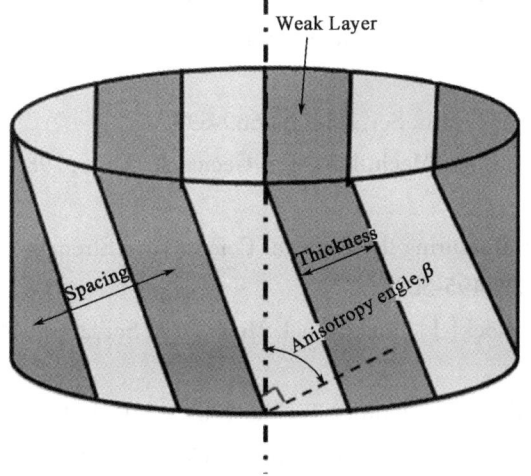

Fig. 12 Simulation of the Point Load Test on a Simplified Anisotropic Rock Model

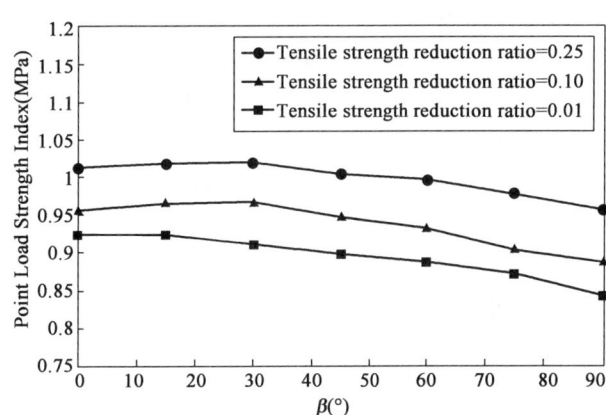

Fig. 13 Effect of the anisotropy on The Point Load Test

4 Conclusions

The micro-parameters of flat joint contact model in PFC3D were calibrated based on the bulk property from both the unconfined compression test and point load test of Bentheim sandstone. The UCS, E and Is were reasonably reproduced in the calibration and validation study. Based on the calibrated micro-parameters, the influence factors of point load test were numerically investigated and the following conclusions could be drawn.

(1) The tensile strength in flat joint model have slight influence on the UCS if the tensile strength to cohesion ratio is less than 0.06, but it still significantly affect the point load strength index. Based on this, the micro-parameter could be reasonably calibrated through experimental results from both the unconfined compression test and point load test.

(2) The scale effect on the point load test can be reasonably captured from numerical simulation, which shows a decrease of point load strength index with the increase of sample size. Meanwhile, the failure patterns with different sizes have been well reproduced by PFC3D, indicating that PFC3D is a promising numerical tool that can explicitly model the rock failure process. Numerical simulation on the eccentricity indicates that the point load test must be conducted with the load being applied at the centre of the sample; otherwise, unreliable results would be produced.

(3) The point load strength index increases when the porosity decreases, and the presence of flaws affects the crack propagation and decreases the point load index. Numerical investigation on the effect of flaw dominates that the crack propagation direction and final failure pattern in the point load test depend on the distance

between the flaw and the loading centre, and this effect can be ignored when the pre-existing crack is far away from the loading tip. Thus, it is important to check the integrity of the cored samples before performing the point load test.

(4) The effect of anisotropy on the point load test was investigated using the simplified numerical model. The point load strength index gradually decreases when the anisotropic angle increases, and the lowest value is obtained at the anisotropic angle of 90°, which shows the dramatic effect of anisotropy on point load test.

References

[1] Bahaaddini, M, Sharrock G, Hebblewhite BK. Numerical Direct Shear Tests to Model the Shear Behaviour of Rock Joints[J]. Comput. Geotech, 2013, 51: 101-115.

[2] Bieniawski ZT. The Point-load Test in Geotechnical Practice[J]. Eng. Geol, 1975, 9: 1-11.

[3] Broch E. and Franklin JA. The Point-load Strength Test[J]. Int. J. Rock Mech. Min. Sci. Geomech. Abstr, 1972, 9: 669-676.

[4] Broch E.. The Point-load Strength Test. Int. J. Rock Mech[J]. Min. Sci, 2003, 9, 669-697.

[5] Brook N. Size Correction for Point Load Testing[J]. Int. J. Rock Mech. Min. Sci. Geomech. Abstr, 1988, 17: 231-235.

[6] Cargill J S, Shakoor A. Evaluation of Empirical Methods for Measuring the Uniaxial Compressive Strength of Rock. Int. J. Rock Mech. Min. Sci. Geomech. Abstr, 1990, 27: 495-503.

[7] Cho N, Martin CD, Sego DC. A Clumped Particle Model for Rock[J]. Int. J. Rock Mech. Min. Sci, 2007, 44(7): 997-1010.

[8] Coetzee C. Review: Calibration of the Discrete Element Method[J]. Powder Technol, 2017, 310: 104-142.

[9] Duan K, Kwok CY. Discrete Element Method Modeling of Inherently Anisotropic Rocks under Uniaxial Compression Loading[J]. Int. J. Numer. Anal. Meth. Geomech, 2016, 40: 1150-1183.

[10] Dubelaar CW, Nijl and TG. The Bentheim Sandstone: Geology, Petrophysics, Varieties and Its Use as Dimension Stone[J]. Engineering Geology for Society and Territory, 2014, 8: 557-563.

[11] Greminger M. Experimental Studies of the Influence of Rock Anisotropy on Size and Shape Effects in Point-load Testing[J]. Int. J. Rock Mech. Min. Sci. Geomech. Abstr, 1982, 19: 241-246.

[12] Heidari M, Khanlari GR, kaveh MT, et al. Predicting the Uniaxial Compressive and Tensile Strengths of Gypsum Rock by Point Load Testing. [J] Rock Mech Rock Eng, 2012, 45: 265-273.

[13] Hunta SP, Meyersb AG, Louchnikovb V. Modelling the Kaiser Effect and Deformation Rate Analysis in Sandstone Using the Discrete Element Method[J]. Comput. Geotech, 2003, 30(7): 611-621.

[14] ISRM. Suggested Method for Determining Point Load Strength[J]. Int. J. Rock Mech. Min. Sci. Geomech. Abstr, 1985, 22: 51-60.

[15] Ivars DM, et al. The Synthetic Rock Mass Approach for Jointed Rock Mass Modelling[J]. Int. J. Rock Mech. Min. Sci, 2011, 48(2): 219-244.

[16] Kahraman S, Gunaydin O, Fener M. The Effect of Porosity on the Relation Between Uniaxial Compressive Strength and Point load Index[J]. Int. J. Rock Mech. Min. Sci, 2005, 42: 584-589.

[17] Kazerani T, Zhao J. Micromechanical Parameters in Bonded Particle Method for Modelling of Brittle Material Failure[J]. Int. J. Numer. Anal. Meth. Geomech, 34, 1877-1895.

[18] Klein E, Reuschle T. A Model for the Mechanical Behavior of Bentheim Sandstone in the Brittle Regime [J]. Pure Appl Geophys, 2003, 160: 833-849.

[19] Lisjak A and Grasselli G. A Review of Discrete Modeling Techniques for Fracturing Processes in Discontinuous Rock Masses[J]. J Rock Mech. Geotech. Eng, 2014, 6(4): 301-314.

[20] Masoumi H, Roshan H, Ahmadreza H. Scale-size Dependency of Intact Rock under Point-load and Indirect

Tensile Brazilian Testing[J]. Int. J. Geomech,2018,18(3):04018006.
[21] Mehranpour MH,Kulatilake P. Improvements for the Smooth Joint Contact Model of the Particle Flow Code and its Applications[J]. Comput. Geotech,2017,87:163-177.
[22] Potyondy DO,Cundall PA. A Bonded-particle Model for Rock[J]. Int. J. Rock Mech. Min. Sci,2004, 41:1329-1364.
[23] Potyondy DO. A Flat-jointed Bonded-particle Material for Hard Rock[C]. Proceedings of 46th U. S. Rock Mechanics/Geomechanics Symposium,Chicago,USA,June 24-27,2012.
[24] Potyondy DO. PFC3D Flat Joint Contact Model(version 1). Itasca Consulting Group,Inc. ,Minneapolis, MN,Technical Memorandum ICG7234-L,June 25,2013.
[25] Rusnak J,Mark C. Using the Point Load Test to Determine the Uniaxial Compressive Strength of Coal Measure Rock[C]. Proc. 19th Int. Conf. Gr. Control Mining,August 8-10,2000,Morgantown,West Virginia.
[26] Singh TN,Kainthola AAV. Correlation between Point Load Index and Uniaxial Compressive Strength for Different Rock Types[J]. Rock Mech. Rock Eng,2012,45:259-264.
[27] Zhang XP,Wu S,Afolagboye LO,et al. Using the Point Load Test to Analyze the Strength Anisotropy of Quartz Mica Schist Along an Exploration Adit[J]. Rock Mech. Rock Eng,2016,49:1967-1975.

不同击实功下黄土回弹模量变化规律分析

刘贤旺[1]　杜秦文[1]　赵伟杰[1]　程灿灿[1,2]　魏进[1]
(1. 长安大学公路学院;2. 天津市政工程设计研究院郑州分院)

摘　要　黄土高路堤常采用重锤夯实、强夯等工艺以提高施工质量。施工中采用的机具设备对填土施加的压实功能已远超标准击实试验中的规定,使得土体密实程度等状态与通常条件下的路基土体有很大不同。土基回弹模量与路基土的含水率、密实程度等有密切关系,目前针对不同击实功下黄土回弹模量的变化规律研究仍不充分。本文在4种击实功条件下,在较宽的含水率范围内对西安地区黄土进行击实试验;得到了其全压实曲线簇;沿全压实曲线测定了土样的回弹模量以分析击实功、含水率等因素对回弹模量的影响;建立了不同击实功作用下土样回弹模量变化的预估方程;该方程参数具有明确物理意义。

关键词　黄土　全压实曲线　击实功　回弹模量　预估模型

0　引　言

回弹模量能够反映路基在往复荷载作用下的弹性支撑能力,是路基承载特性的指标[1]和路面结构设计的重要参数。回弹模量受多种因素影响,如含水率、基质吸力、压实度、土的类型等。当土的类型和应力状态确定后,回弹模量主要受含水率和击实功的影响[4]。

国内外学者对回弹模量的预估进行了大量的研究。最早的模型由 Seed 等[5]提出,该模型中回弹模量与体应力相关。Davies[6]对美国多个地区的路基填土进行研究,建立了考虑气候及含水率因素的回弹模量预估模型。MR Qzel 等[7]对不同应力水平下的回弹模量进行分析,建立了回弹模量与添加剂含量、干密度、含水率等因素的关系式。林小平等[8]通过 UTM 三轴试验系统的试验分析,建立路基土回弹模量湿度调整系数预估模型。

基金项目:中央高校基本科研业务费专项资金(310821173701)。

强夯施工并不总是在填土处于最佳含水率状态时进行，且其对土体施加的击实功远大于标准击实试验中的规定。因此，在较宽含水率范围内，研究土体在不同击实功下回弹模量的变化规律具有积极的工程实用价值。

在土样能成型的前提下，对其在含水率从最低到最高的范围内进行击实试验，建立起的干密度与含水率的关系曲线，被称为"全压实曲线"[9]。本文采用4种击实功对西安地区黄土进行击实试验，建立了其"全压实曲线簇"；沿全压实曲线测定了土样的回弹模量；提出了考虑不同击实功和含水率的回弹模量预估模型；采用本文试验以及已发表文献中的数据对模型进行了验证，表明其具有较好的适用性。

1 基本试验及分析

1.1 物理指标试验

选取来自西安地区的黄土土样，按照《公路土工试验规程》(JTG E40—2007)，进行相应的室内基本试验。土样的物理性质参数见表1。

土的基本物理性质参数 表1

液限(%)	塑限(%)	塑性指数	颗粒组成(mm/%)			相对密度	土类
			>2	2~0.075	<0.075		
37.9	19.1	18.8	0	0.2	0.98	2.7	低液限粉质黏黄土

1.2 击实试验

在土样能够成型条件下，按照2%含水率间隔制样，分别采用标准轻型、标准重型，以及两种中间型击实功进行击实试验。试验结果如图1所示。

1.3 黄土全压实曲线

Faure等[10]提出的四参数方程[式(1)]，能够有效描述土体全压实曲线。Li H[10]、程灿灿[11]等通过进一步研究，实现了不同土体的全压实曲线簇预测。

$$\rho_d = \frac{G_s \times \rho_w}{1 + \dfrac{w \times G_s}{S_{r\max} - S_{r\max} \times \left(\dfrac{w_m - w}{w_m}\right)^{n+1} \times \left(\dfrac{w_m^n + p^n}{(w_m - w)^n + p^n}\right)}} \tag{1}$$

式中：ρ_d——土样干密度；

G_s——土的相对密实度；

ρ_w——4℃时水的密度；

w——含水率；

$S_{r\max}$——击实中土样的最大饱和度值；

w_m——土样的最大含水率；

n——形状控制参数；

p——有效压实区控制参数。

使用式(1)对本文四种击实功下的试验数据进行拟合，见图1。从图1可以看出，式(1)能较好地描述黄土在全含水率范围内的干密度与含水率的关系。

使用全压实曲线四参数方程，可通过在某一种击实功下进行击实试验，预测任意击实功下的全压实曲线[10-11]。现依据轻型击实功数据，预测其他击实功下黄土的全压实曲线，见图2。

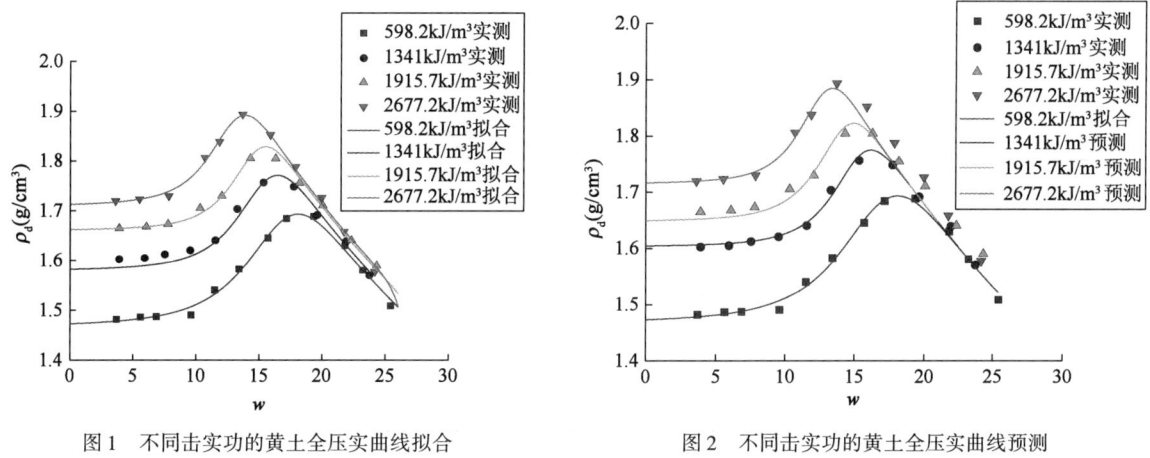

图1 不同击实功的黄土全压实曲线拟合　　　　图2 不同击实功的黄土全压实曲线预测

通过图2可以看出,使用四参数方程对不同击实功下的击实曲线进行预估,预估效果良好。

2 回弹模量预估模型

2.1 回弹模量试验

对击实后的试样采用 HM-1 型杠杆压力仪进行回弹模量 E 的测定,结果见图3。

可以看出:回弹模量随含水率的增大而减小,不同击实功下其变化规律均类似。含水率一定时,回弹模量随击实功的增大而增大。图中不同曲线的间距随着含水率的增加而减小,表明击实功对回弹模量的影响随着含水率的增加而减小。

根据特征将不同击实功下回弹模量随含水率变化的曲线划分3个区域[12]:稳定区、变化区和近饱和区,如图3所示。其中,稳定区中曲线最左端回弹模量的最大值称为"初始回弹模量"E_0。变化区和稳定区的界限含水率称为回弹模量变化阈值含水率 w_e。最佳含水率 w_{opt} 对应回弹模量均处于图3中的"变化区"内。

2.2 回弹模量预估模型建立

对图3中回弹模量随含水率变化试验数据变化规律,可采用 Slogistic 曲线表达,方程如式(2)所示。曲线拟合结果见图4。

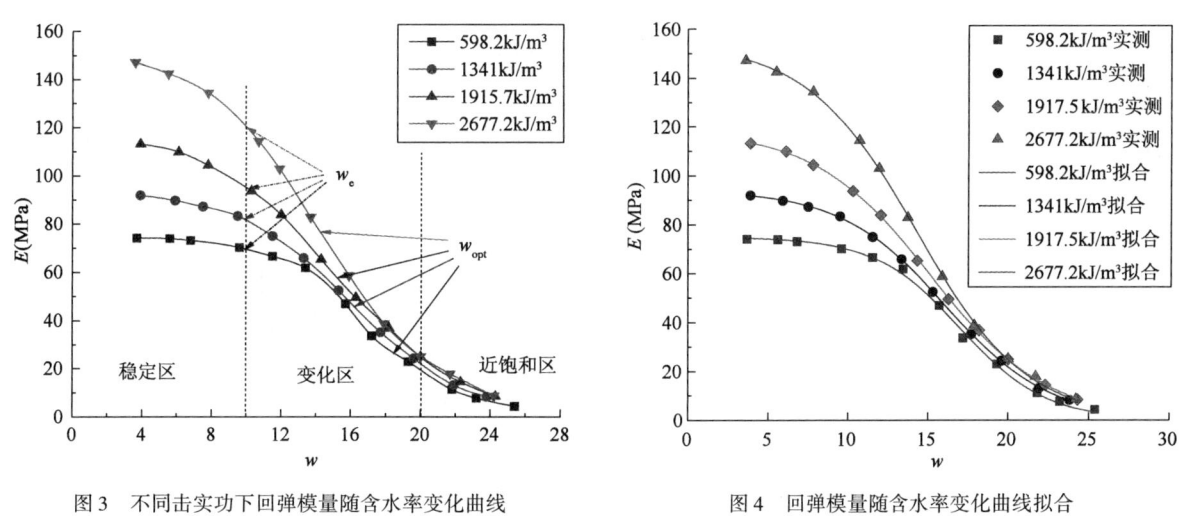

图3 不同击实功下回弹模量随水率变化曲线　　　　图4 回弹模量随水率变化曲线拟合

$$E = \frac{a}{1 + e^{k(w-b)}} \quad (2)$$

式中:E——土基回弹模量,MPa;

w——含水率,%；

a、b、k——曲线参数,见表2；

e——自然常数。

回弹模量随含水率变化曲线参数　　表2

击实功(kJ/cm^3)	曲线参数			R^2
	a	b	k	
598.2	75	17.9	0.343	0.998
1341	94	16.1	0.304	0.999
1917.5	118.7	15.1	0.273	0.999
2677.2	154.4	14.2	0.288	0.999

将参数 a、b 与试验数据进行对比分析(表3)。发现模型参数 a 与初始回弹模量 E_0 的值十分接近；参数 b 与最佳含水率 w_{opt} 在近似一致。

模型参数与试验数据对比　　表3

击实功	初始回弹模量 E_0	参数 a	最佳含水率 w_{opt}	参数 b
598.2	74.1	75	18.5	17.9
1341	92	94	16.2	16.1
1917.5	113.2	118.7	15.2	15.1
2677.2	147.2	154.4	14.3	14.2

由此,可将预估模型[式(2)]参数 a 和 b 分别取为土样的初始回弹模量 E_0 及最佳含水率 w_{opt}。模型参数 k 为曲线形状控制参数。试验中,对于同一种土在不同击实功下,其值基本不变。综上,回弹模量预估模型见式(3)：

$$E = \frac{E_0}{1 + e^{k(w - w_{opt})}} \quad (3)$$

可采用式(3)对黄土回弹模型进行预估,步骤如下：

(1)在某一击实功下进行试验,拟合确定该击实功下的 k 值(对于同一种土,其他击实功下 k 值不变)；

(2)对待预测击实功下的土样进行一组试验,确定其初始回弹模量值 E_0；

(3)通过四参数方程确定待预测击实功作用下土体的最佳含水率 w_{opt}。

2.3 预估模型验证

(1)本文试验数据

根据 598.2 kJ/m^3 击实功下的试验数据,对其他3种击实功下的回弹模量进行预估,结果如图5所示。

图5表明模型的预估效果良好。

(2)其他文献数据

由于针对黄土的相关研究较少,引用 Lee W 等[13]研究中两种黏性土的数据值,采用本文提出的预估模型进行预估。结果见图6,预估模型可以很好地对不同击实功下的回弹模量进行预估。同时也说明了本文预估模型不仅适用于所取黄土,在黏土中也具有一定的适用性。

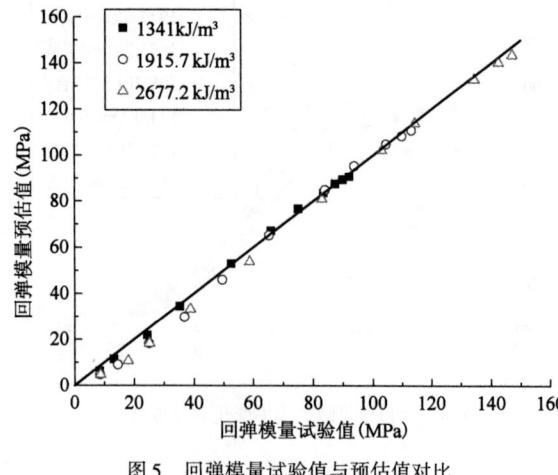

图5　回弹模量试验值与预估值对比

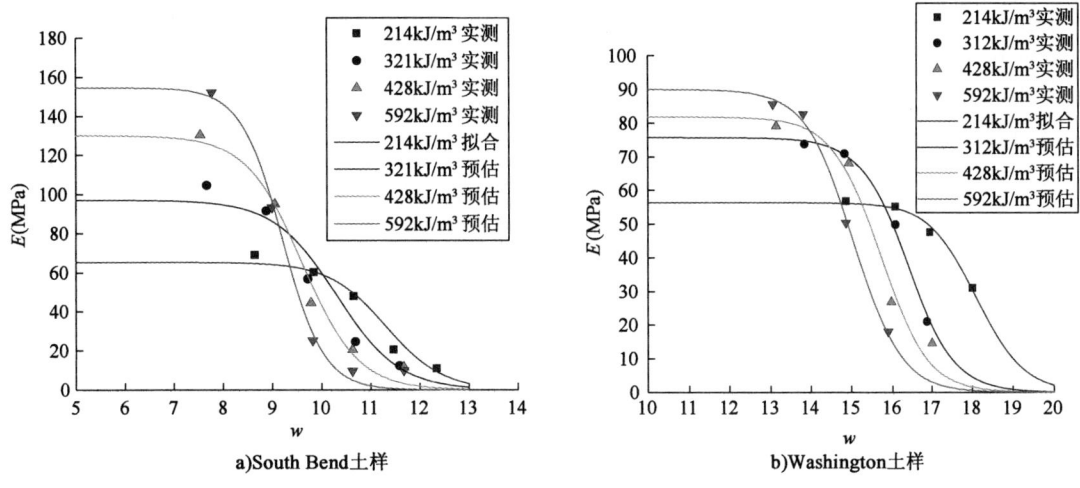

图6 两种土样的回弹模量预测

3 结 语

对西安地区黄土,在4种不同击实功下进行击实试验,得到了其"全压实曲线";沿曲线分别测定了土样的回弹模量,建立了不同击实功作用下土体回弹模量与含水率关系的预估模型。主要得到以下结果:

(1)总体上,土样回弹模量随着含水率增大而减小。随着含水率由低到高,可将回弹模量变化曲线分为3个区域:稳定区、变化区和近饱和区。在稳定区,击实功对回弹模量的影响较大;含水率增大至阈值含水率 w_e 以上后,回弹模量随含水率增大开始明显降低;近饱和区中,不同击实功下的回弹模量已比较接近。

(2)击实功对回弹模量的影响随着土样含水率的增大而降低。在"近饱和区"内,击实功的影响甚小。不同击实功作用下,土样的最佳含水率 w_{opt} 都分布在"变化区"。

(3)建立了不同击实功下土样回弹模量与含水率变化曲线的预估模型方程:

$$E = \frac{E_0}{1 + e^{k(w - w_{opt})}}$$

(4)预估方程主要参数具有明确的物理含义,据此提出了预估不同击实功下土体回弹模量的方法。采用本文试验数据和已发表文献中试验数据对预估模型进行验证,表明该模型不仅适用于黄土,在黏土中也具有一定的适用性,具有较广泛的实用价值。

参数注释见表4。

参 数 注 释 表　　表4

参　数	含　义	参　数	含　义
ρ_d	干密度	S_{rmax}、w_m、n、p	四参数方程的参数
G_s	土的相对密实度	E	回弹模量
ρ_w	4℃时水的密度	E_0	初始回弹模量
w	含水率	a、b、k	曲线参数
w_{opt}	最佳含水率	e	自然对数的底
ρ_{dd}	初始干密度		

参考文献

[1] 沙爱民.路基路面工程[M].北京:高等教育出版社.2011.
[2] 钱劲松,李嘉洋,周定,等.考虑吸力效应的非饱和黏土回弹模量预估模型[J].岩土力学,2018,39(01):123-128.

[3] Lekarp F, Isacsson U, Dawson A. State of the Art. I: Resilient Response of Unbound Aggregates[J]. Journal of Transportation Engineering, 2000, 126(1): 66-75.

[4] 李志勇,董城,邹静.湘南地区红黏土动态回弹模量试验与预估模型研究[J].岩土力学,2015,36(07):1840-1846.

[5] H. B Seed, C K Chan, C L Monismith. Effects of Repeated Loading on the Strength and Deformation of Compacted Clay[J]. HRB Proceedings, 1955, 34: 541-558.

[6] Davies, Beresford Obafemi Arnold. A Model For The Prediction Of Subgrade Soil Resilient Modulus For Flexible-Pavement Design: Influence Of Moisture Content And Climate Change[J]. 2004.

[7] Ozel M R, Mohajerani A. Resilient Modulus of a Stabilized Fine-grained Subgrade Soil[J]. Australian Geomechanics Journal, 2001, 36(3): 75-86.

[8] 林小平,李兴华,凌建明,等.路基土回弹模量湿度调整系数预估研究[J].同济大学学报(自然科学版),2011,39(10):1490-1494.

[9] Faure A G, Da Mata J D V. Penetration resistance value along compaction curves[J]. ASCE Journal of Geotechnical Engineering, 1994, (20): 46-59.

[10] LI H. The Family of Compaction Curves for Fine-Grained Soils and Their Engineering Behaviors[D]. Alberta: University of Alberta, 2001.

[11] 程灿灿.黄土压实特性及回弹模量研究[D].西安:长安大学,2019.

[12] Li D, Selig E T. Resilient Modulus for Fine-grained Subgrade Soils[J]. Journal of Geotechnical Engineering, 1994, 120(6): 939-957.

[13] Lee W, Bohra N C, Altschaeffl A G, et al. Resilient Modulus of Cohesive Soils[J]. Journal of Geotechnical and Geoenviron mental Engineering, 1997, 123(2): 131-136.

颗粒圆度对路基填料振动压实影响的离散元分析

方传峰 聂志红 刘维正 刘顺凯

(中南大学土木工程学院)

摘 要 为了研究颗粒形状对路基填料振动压实的影响,采用傅立叶变换法构建了不同圆度的二维颗粒模型,并基于离散元法从宏细观角度分析了颗粒圆度(Rd)对振动压实的影响。结果表明:随碾压遍数的增加,孔隙率及填筑厚度先急剧下降后基本不变;Rd越小的填料,孔隙率相比于初始状态下降越明显,且累积沉降量越大。细观层面,配位数随碾压遍数的增加轻微上升,Rd越小的填料其接触配位数越大,互锁效应越强,导致颗粒转动量越小;碾压过程中,填料水平向位移波动而竖向位移增加,且Rd越小的填料竖向位移越大而水平向位移越小。接触方面,竖向荷载促使填料的接触转向水平;Rd越小的填料,初始状态下接触越易于竖向集中;力链会在振动轮与填料接触处集中并呈"树根状"向填料深部延伸。

关键词 路基填料 颗粒圆度 振动压实 宏细观响应 离散元法

0 引 言

颗粒材料因取材方便、成本低、变形小等优点作为填料,在路基工程中得到广泛应用。大量研究成果表明,路基填料若无法保证良好的压实效果,常会引起道路塌陷、裂纹及坑槽等相关灾害,严重恶化路面的行驶性能,影响道路的使用寿命,造成巨大的经济损失。

基金项目:国家自然科学基金资助项目(51478481;52078500)。

振动压实是提高压实效果的常用手段。目前,大量学者采用现场试验、室内试验及数值仿真的方法探究了各类因素对压实效果的影响,包括各类工作参数[1]、摊铺厚度[2]、弹性轮胎纹理类型[3]、振动次数[4]及碎石级配[5]等。然而,这些研究极少涉及颗粒形状对振动压实效果的影响。虽然有文献初步探究了球形、扁平型和棱锥形等简单的颗粒形状与填料压实度之间的关系[10],但并没有系统地研究颗粒形状指标变化对填料振动压实效果的影响。颗粒形状是影响颗粒材料力学行为中不容忽视的因素[6-9]。因此,研究颗粒形状指标,特别是颗粒圆度的变化,对振动压实的效果的影响是至关重要的。

了解压实机理是分析压实效果的前提。离散元作为研究振动压实的一种手段,为从细观角度分析散体颗粒运动机理提供了有效的途径[1,11,12]。本研究采用傅立叶变换法构建不同圆度的二维颗粒模型,并基于离散元模拟填料的振动压实过程,分析颗粒圆度对压实效果的宏细观影响。

1 试验准备

1.1 模型准备

已有文献[2,13]研究结果表明,颗粒材料二维与三维孔隙率之间存在一一对应关系,意味着二维模拟结果反映压实效果的宏观规律是可靠的,同时,二维模型也可实现从细观角度分析颗粒运动规律的目的。因此,本文综合考虑运算效率和模拟尺寸等因素,采用PFC2D[14]进行模拟。

为确保模拟的振动轮压实效果与实际工程中具有一致性,需满足振动轮单位长度荷载一致。根据相关计算公式,具体外部荷载参数如表1所示。为确保振动轮运动过程中发生滚动而非滑动,振动轮的旋转角速度 w 和水平速度 v 之间存在式(1)所示关系。

$$v = w \times R \tag{1}$$

式中:v、w、R——振动轮的水平速度、转角速度和半径。

外部荷载参数 表1

振动轮参数	实际参数	模拟参数
振动轮质量(kg)	1×10^4	0.5×10^4
振动轮直径(mm)	1500	1500
振动轮宽度(mm)	2000	1000
振动频率(Hz)	40	40
激振力(kN)	300	150
行驶速度(m/s)	1	1
碾压遍数	12	12

模拟的填料为无黏性颗粒材料,接触模型为线弹性,该模型广泛应用于类似研究[2,11,15,16]。模拟中所采用的细观参数参考 Liu 等[2]的研究成果,见表2。需要指出的是,若颗粒间的局部阻尼过小,会发生颗粒泳动及陷碾状况,如图1a)所示,局部阻尼越大,这种现象越小,当局部阻尼为0.9时,与真实情况最为贴近,如图1所示。

模拟所用细观参数 表2

细观参数	颗 粒	振 动 轮
法向刚度(N/m)	1.5×10^7	1.0×10^9
切向刚度(N/m)	2.9×10^7	1.0×10^9
摩擦系数	0.5	0.3
局部阻尼	0.9	0.0
法向/切向阻尼	0.5	0.5
密度(kg/m³)	2600	G/V

注:G 为振动轮的质量(kg);V 为振动轮的体积(m³)。

陷碾
振动轮
泳动
a)局部阻尼=0
振动轮
堆积，挤压
b)局部阻尼=0.7
振动轮
c)局部阻尼=0.9

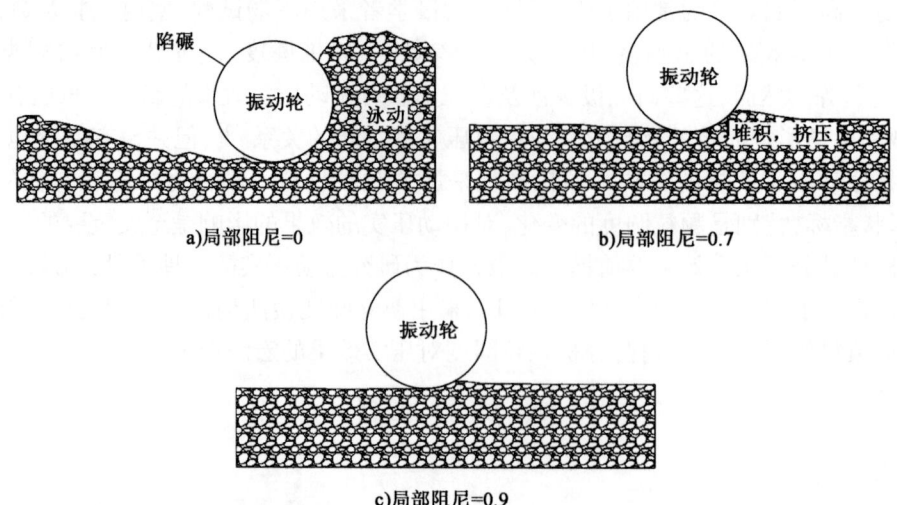

图1　不同局部阻尼对应的振动压实效果

1.2　颗粒形状生成

Barret[17]通过归纳总结众多经典的颗粒形状指标,将颗粒形状分为3个相互独立的指标:伸长度EI、圆度Rd、粗糙度Rh。其中,颗粒圆度Rd可按照图2所示定义如下:

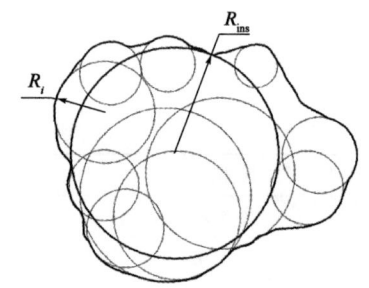

R_{ins}
R_i

图2　二维颗粒圆度计算方法示意图

$$\mathrm{Rd}=\frac{\frac{1}{n}\sum_{i=1}^{n}R_i}{R_{ins}} \tag{2}$$

式中:R_i——第i个棱角区域的局部内切圆半径;

n——棱角区域的总个数;

R_{ins}——最大内切圆的半径。

数学建模方法中,傅立叶变换法[9]和球谐函数法[8]常用于构建特定形状的不规则颗粒模型。本研究采用傅立叶变换法构建了二维颗粒模型[18-19],共生成5组不同圆度颗粒,各8个样本,如图3所示(由于Rd=1时为标准圆,故未显示)。

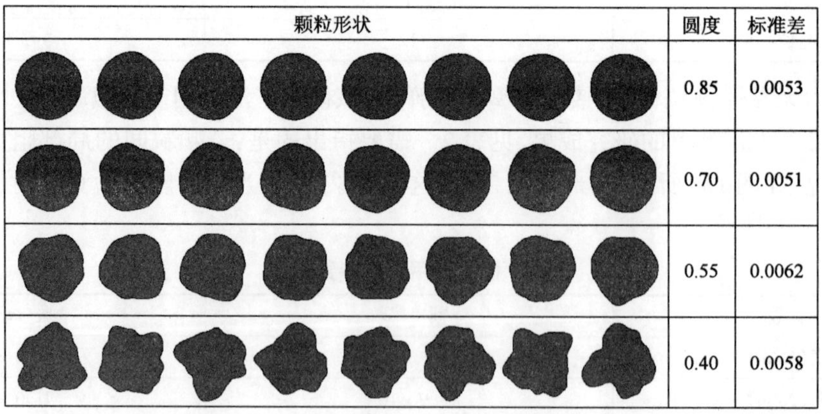

颗粒形状
圆度
标准差
0.85
0.0053
0.70
0.0051
0.55
0.0062
0.40
0.0058

图3　不同圆度的二维颗粒模型

PFC中,簇(clump)功能可实现复杂颗粒轮廓的拟合,本研究将拟合精度控制参数distance设置为162,ratio设置为0.25。图4显示一个在该指标下生成的簇(clump)模型,由该图可知,设置的两个精度值足以反映颗粒外部轮廓。

1.3 模拟过程

本次模拟采用的填料尺度分布情况如图 5 所示。

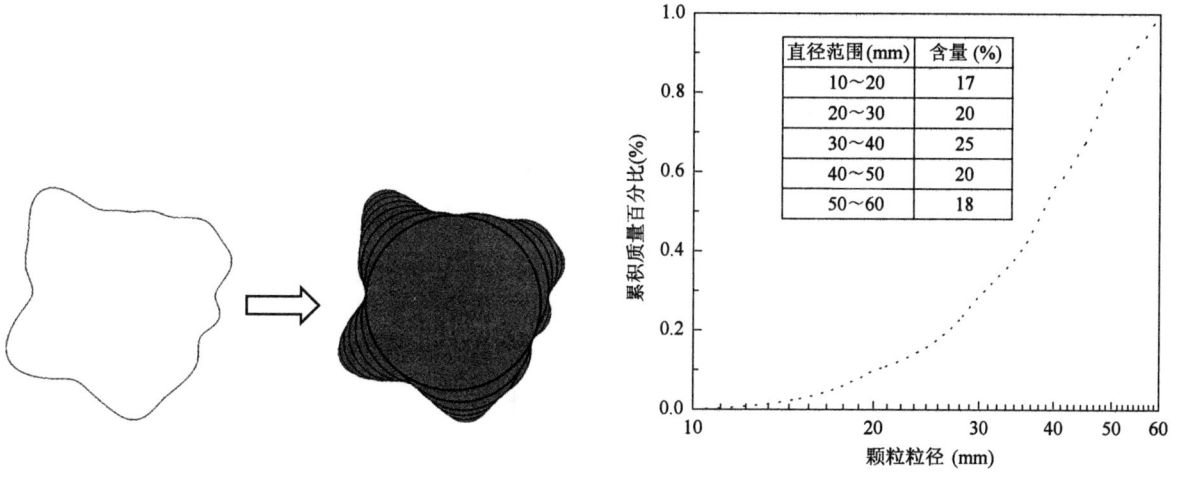

图 4　基于傅立叶的颗粒轮廓转化为 clump 模型

图 5　DEM 模拟所用的填料粒径分布

填料模型设置在高(H)×宽(W)=0.8m×8m 的范围内。初始模型通过重力沉降法生成。具体过程如下：

(1) 在 $2H×W$ 范围内按照级配曲线随机生成比目标总体积稍大的无接触颗粒体，如图 6a) 所示。

(2) 重力作用下，颗粒体自由下落，当颗粒系统的平均不平衡力与平均接触力的比值小于 $5×10^{-5}$ 时，认为颗粒系统达到准静止状态，停止运行，如图 6b) 所示。

(3) 删除指定厚度线以上多余颗粒以模拟整平过程，然后重新运行使颗粒体系再次达到平衡，整平后的填料如图 6c) 所示。

(4) 在整平的填料上方生成一个刚体圆形单元，该单元位于模型一端且紧贴填料，模拟振动轮。振动轮运动过程中对填料施加弦波振动荷载，如图 6d) 所示。碾压 12 遍停止模拟。

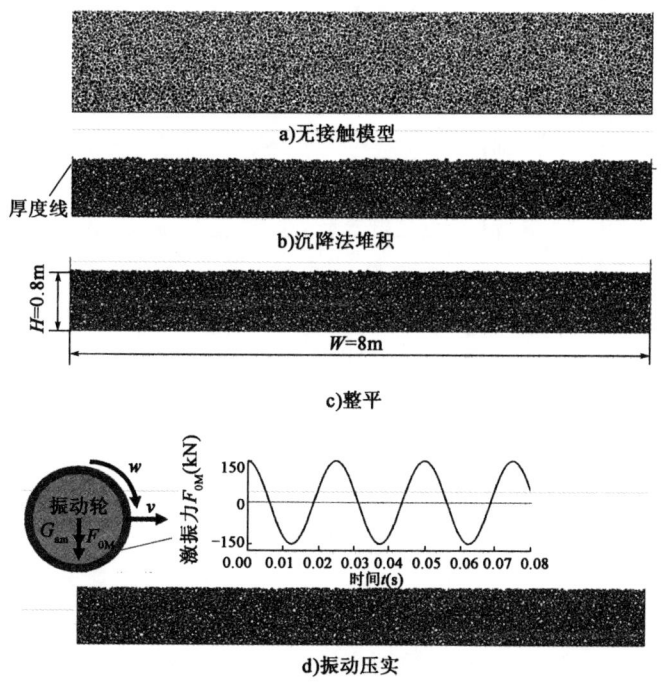

图 6　振动碾压的 PFC 模拟

2 宏观结果

图7a)表示不同圆度填料的孔隙率随碾压遍数的变化情况。很明显,随碾压遍数的增加,孔隙率先急剧降低后基本保持不变,但似乎圆度与振动压实的相关性不强。提取初始孔隙率[图7b)],发现随圆度的增加,初始孔隙率先降低后增加,这前人圆度相关的研究结果一致[7-9]。图7c)为采用式(3)换算后得到的归一化的孔隙变化率 Δn,可见圆度越小,孔隙率相比于初始状态的下降幅度越大。

$$\Delta n = \frac{n_0 - n_i}{n_0} \times 100\% \tag{3}$$

式中:n_0、n_i——初始孔隙率与碾压完成第 i 遍对应的孔隙率。

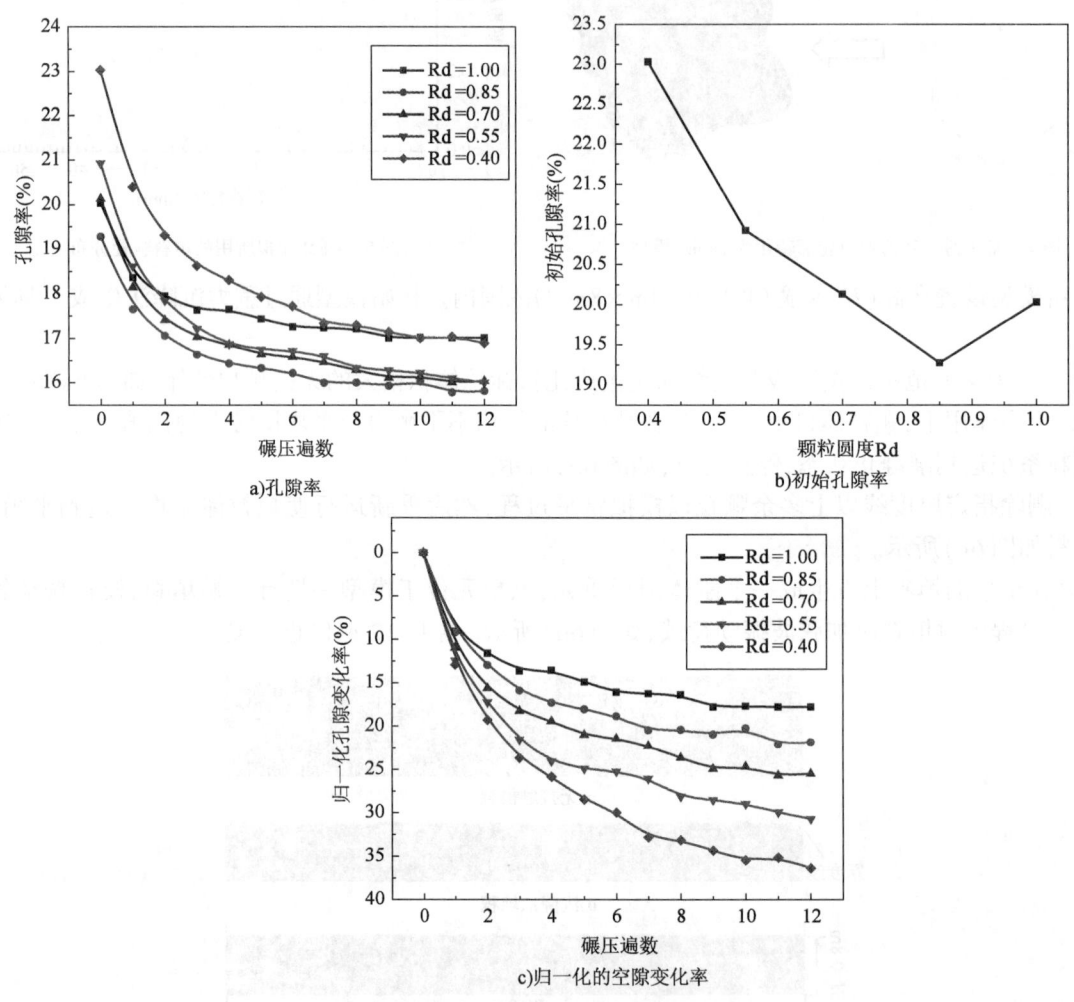

图7 不同圆度填料其碾压遍数与孔隙变化关系

图8为各碾压遍数对应的累积沉降量,与归一化的孔隙变化率有相似的趋势,即前期快速沉降,后期沉降速度放缓。该趋势与施工中实际的监测值变化情况一致[2]。另外,圆度越小,则填料的沉降量越大,且达到最大沉降量时间越晚,说明形状越不规则的填料,达到最密实状态时需要的碾压遍数越多。

3 细观结果

3.1 配位数

配位数是表征颗粒系统内部结构特征的重要指标。对于由 clump 构成的不规则颗粒模型,配位数可分为颗粒配位数和接触配位数两种类型。

图9为不同圆度的填料颗粒配位数与碾压遍数的关系。对于每种圆度情况,随碾压遍数的增加,颗

粒配位数整体上呈轻微的上升趋势,反映出随碾压遍数的增加填料的密实度变大。另外,圆度越大,颗粒配位数越大,表明越圆的颗粒越易于与多个颗粒发生接触。

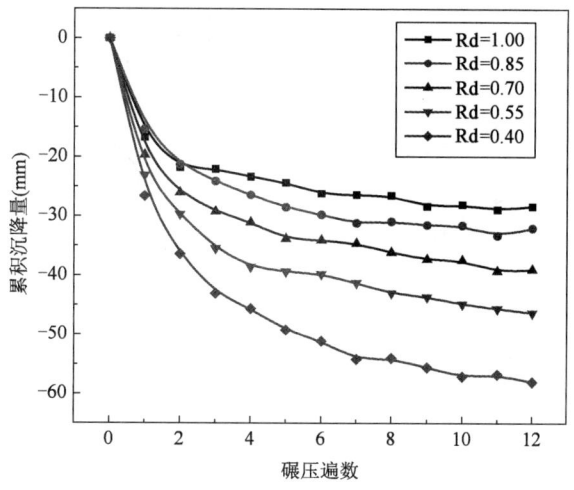

图 8　不同圆度填料其累积沉降量随碾压遍数的变化曲线

图 10 为不同圆度的填料接触配位数与碾压遍数的关系。与颗粒配位数的变化趋势类似,对某一形状颗粒,其接触配位数整体上仅发生了轻微的增加。但是,圆度越小,则颗粒的接触配位数越大,表明颗粒间的互锁现象越明显。

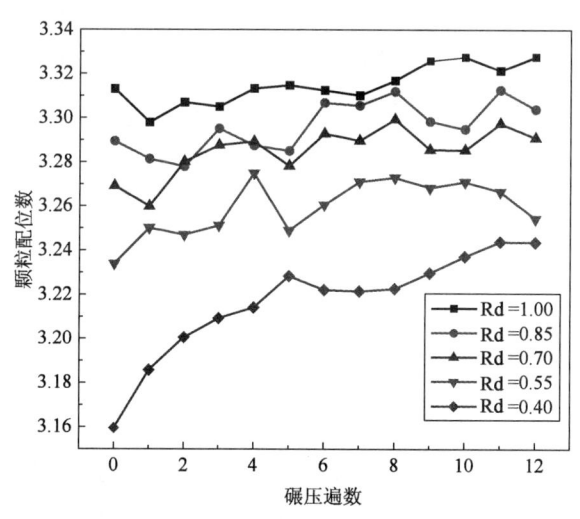

图 9　不同圆度填料碾压遍数与颗粒配位数关系

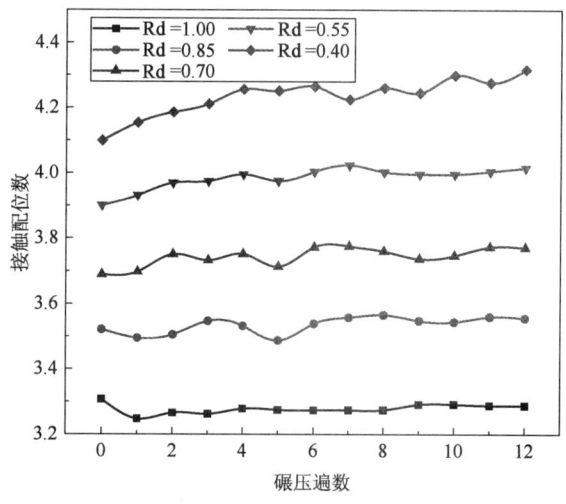

图 10　不同圆度填料接触配位数与碾压遍数关系

3.2　颗粒转动量

转动是相互接触的颗粒之间重要的相对运动。图 11 为不同圆度的填料沿顺时针和逆时针方向随碾压变化的累积转动量。由图 11 可见:填料在顺时针和逆时针方向的转动量基本相当,颗粒转动值随碾压遍数和圆度的增加而增大。原因是配位数的增加增强了颗粒间的互锁作用,阻碍了颗粒的转动。

3.3　颗粒位移量

图 12 为各压实遍数下具有不同圆度的填料在水平向和竖向的位移量。由图 12a)可见:随着碾压遍数的增加,水平向的颗粒并未出现明显的位移增减。图 12b)为填料在竖向的位移量;表现出与累积沉降量相似的变化趋势,即随着碾压遍数的增加,颗粒逐渐下沉且下降趋势逐渐放缓。另外,对于不同圆度的填料,Rd 越小,竖向的位移量越大。这是因为越不规则的颗粒越容易发生颗粒间的相对滑动[21],导致颗粒竖向位移量更大。

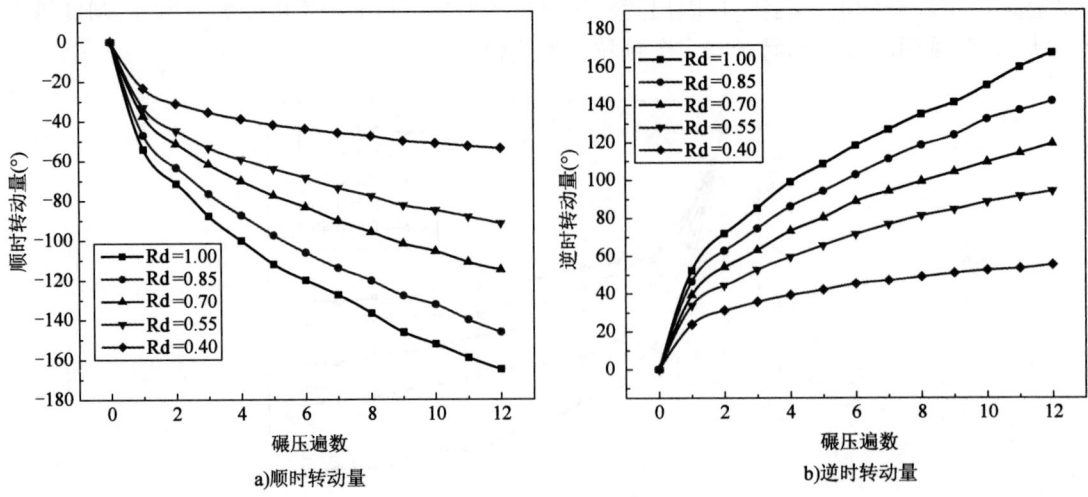

图 11　不同圆度填料在碾压条件下的转动情况

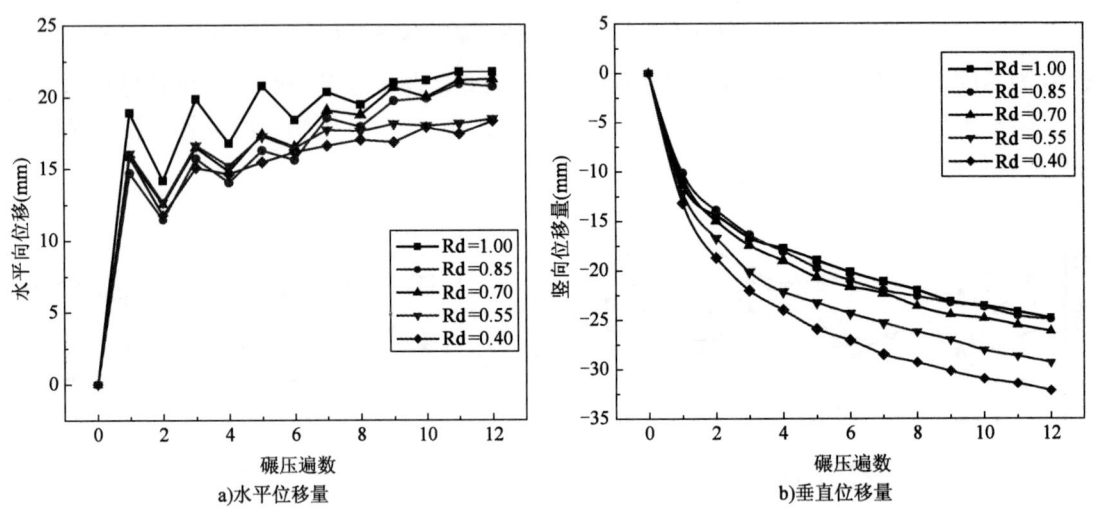

图 12　振动碾压过程中填料的各向位移分量

3.4　接触方向与力链

图 13 所示为在不同碾压遍数(0、5、12)和不同圆度情况下的填料整体的接触方向分布。对每种圆度情况,初始状态的填料各向的接触数量基本相等或偏竖向,随着碾压遍数的增加,填料在水平向的接触数量明显增加,且碾压遍数越多,差异越明显。这是因为,重力作用下平衡的初始填料其内部存在大量的非水平接触,在外部竖向激振力作用下,颗粒会发生偏移和转动,倾向于形成更稳定的偏水平方向的接触。另外,随填料圆度的减小,初始状态下的接触数量由各向接触数目基本相等向颗粒竖向接触数偏多变化,且圆度越小变化越明显。原因是因为模型生成时,颗粒在重力作用下竖向沉降,圆度更高的颗粒自然休止角更小,受到下层颗粒阻挡时更易于滑动和滚动并在与阻挡的颗粒相近的水平位置停止。

图 14 为 Rd = 1.00 的填料在未碾压状态与第一遍碾压一半时对应的接触力链分布情况,线条的粗细代表接触力的大小。由图 14a)可知,初始状态下颗粒并非均匀受力,部分颗粒承担了大部分力,这些颗粒接触相连接后构成了准直线型的强力链。由于颗粒重量的叠加,强力链随深度增加而增多。在图 14b)的碾压过程中,振动轮与填料的接触点附近力链明显且集中,并随着填料深度的增加力链逐渐减小,呈现出"树根状"的力链分布,表明振动轮位置的浅处填料承担大部分力,且形成了强力链网络。而在振动轮已碾压过的和未碾压的区域,受振动轮的影响较小,其力链分布与初始未碾压时相似。

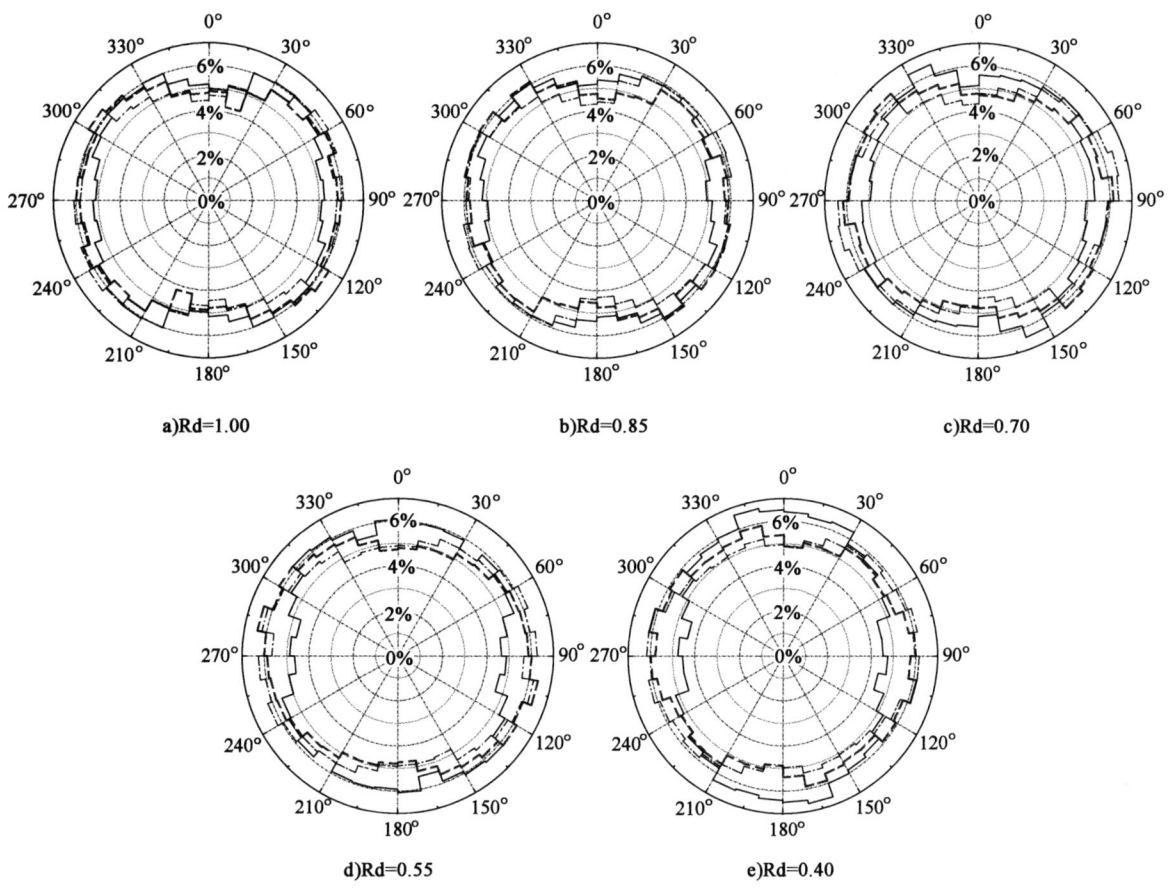

图 13　各碾压遍数后填料接触方向分布

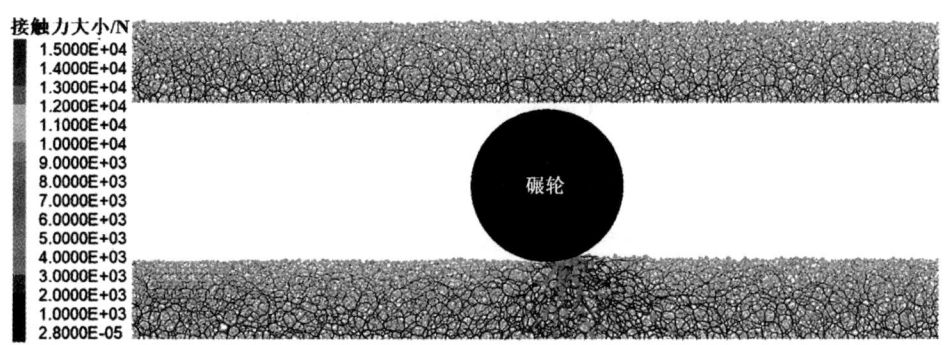

图 14　初始和碾压过程中填料接触力链分布

4　结　语

基于离散元方法,针对具有不同圆度的填料开展振动压实数值模拟研究,并从宏细观角度分析了填料圆度对振动压实的影响,结果表明:

(1)随碾压遍数的增加,填料的孔隙率逐渐减小而沉降量逐渐增加,且变化速度均为前快后慢。另外,圆度越小,填料的孔隙率相比于初始状态下降越明显且沉降量越大。

(2)在碾压荷载作用下填料的颗粒配位数和接触配位数轻微增加;圆度越小的颗粒接触配位数越大,以此增加的互锁效应阻碍了颗粒转动;颗粒在水平的位移表现出一定的波动性,而竖向位移逐渐增加;圆度越小的颗粒,其竖向位移越大而水平位移越小。

（3）各圆度的填料在振动荷载作用下，接触方向逐渐向水平方向偏移；在初始状态，圆度越小的填料，其接触方向越易于向竖向集中；碾压过程中，振动轮位置处的填料力链集中并表现出明显的"树根状"分布。

参考文献

[1] 方磊，姜在田，项伟圆.影响填石路堤压实施工因素的数值模拟[J].南京大学学报（自然科学版），2005,06:658-663.

[2] Liu D, Sun L, Ma H, et al. Process Simulation and Mesoscopic Analysis of Rockfill Dam Compaction Using Discrete Element Method[J]. International Journal of Geomechanics,2020,26(6).

[3] Nishiyama K, Nakashima H, Yoshida T, et al. 2D FE-DEM Analysis of Tractive Performance of an Elastic Wheel for Planetary Rovers[J]. Journal of Terramechanics,2016,64:23-35.

[4] 刘文劼，冷伍明，蔡德钧，等.重载铁路路基粗颗粒土循环振动试验与累积动应变研究[J].铁道学报，2015,37(02):91-97.

[5] 涂帅.基于颗粒间相互作用的高性能级配碎石基层结构与性能研究[D].西安：长安大学公路学院，2013.

[6] Gong J, Liu J. Effect of Aspect Ratio on Triaxial Compression of Multi-sphere Ellipsoid Assemblies Simulated Using a Discrete Element Method[J]. Particuology,2017,32:49-62.

[7] Nie Z, Fang C, Gong J, et al. Exploring the Effect of Particle Shape Caused by Erosion on the Shear Behaviour of Granular Materials via the DEM[J]. IJSS,2020,202:1-11.

[8] Nie Z, Fang C, Gong J, et al. DEM Study on The Effect of Roundness on the Shear Behaviour of Granular Materials[J]. Computers and Geotechnics,2020,121.

[9] Nie Z, Zhu Y, Wang X, et al. Investigating the Effects of Fourier-based Particle Shape on the Shear Behaviors of Rockfill Material via DEM[J]. Granular Matter,2019,21(2).

[10] 丁智勇，李国政，张通化，等.振动作用下填石路基压实特性的数值模拟[J].路基工程,2019,06:114-118.

[11] 刘东海，马鸿雁，孙龙飞.堆石坝离散元模拟中缩尺碾轮等效荷载确定[J].水力发电学报,2018,37(09):93-102.

[12] Smith W, Melanz D, Senatore C, et al. Comparison of Discrete Element Method and Traditional Modeling Methods for Steady-State Wheel-Terrain Interaction of Small Vehicles[J]. Journal of Terramechanics,2014,56:61-75.

[13] 何咏睿，朱晟，武利强.粗粒料二维与三维孔隙率的对应关系研究[J].水利发电,2014,40(05):27-29,47.

[14] Itasca. User's Manual for pfc3d[M]. Minneapolis, USA, Itasca Consulting Group, Inc. 2018.

[15] 刘洋，李晓柱，吴顺川.多块体形状堆石体碾压颗粒破碎数值模拟[J].岩土力学,2014,35(11):3269-3280.

[16] 李杨，佘成学，朱焕春.现场堆石体振动碾压的颗粒流模拟及验证[J].岩土力学,2018,39(S2):432-442.

[17] J BP. The shape of rock particles, a critical review[J]. Sedimentology,1980;27(3),291-303.

[18] R E, B W. An Exact Method for Characterization of Grain Shape[J]. Journal of Sedimentary Research,1970,40.

[19] Mollon G, Zhao J. Fourier-Voronoi-Based Generation of Realistic Samples for Discrete Modelling of Granular Materials[J]. Granular Matter,2012,14(5):621-638.

[20] C T. Numerical Simulations of Deviatoric Shear Deformation of Granular Media[J]. Geotechnique,2015;50(2),319-329.

[21] Estrada N, Azéma E, Radjaï F, et al. Identification of Rolling Resistance as a Shape Parameter in Sheared Granular Media[J]. Physical Review,2011,E 84(1 Pt 1):011306.

Influence of Relative Humidity on Physical Properties of Bound Water Adsorbed by Loess

Hao Zhou Xuesong Mao

(Chang'an University)

Abstract The engineering properties of loess are closely related to its internal structure and moisture content. The increase of bound water content in loess will destroy the original structure of loess, whose strength will decrease correspondingly. In this research, isotherm adsorption experiment was used to study the bound water of loess, and analyse the influence of relative humidity on the physical properties of bound water. The results of the experiment show that the bound water content of loess was 11.27-16.28%, among which the tightly bound water content was 3.59-5.07%. The bound water content was closely related to the content of clay minerals. The relative humidity of 0.9 was the critical point of tightly and loosely bound water. When the relative humidity was less than 0.9, the adsorption rate of loess was high and the adsorption capacity was small. It was monolayer adsorption and only formed tightly bound water. The density of hydrated loess was 2.52-2.60g/cm^3, and the density of bound water was around 1.23g/cm^3. When the relative humidity was greater than 0.9, the early stage of adsorption was monolayer adsorption to form tightly bound water, and the latter stage was multi-layer adsorption, with low adsorption rate and large adsorption capacity, forming loosely bound water. The density of hydrated loess was 2.2-2.33g/cm^3, and the density of bound water was around 1.12g/cm^3. The volume of bound water was 10.86-13.81cm^3, and the thickness of bound water film was around 3.98Å. Among them, the volume of tightly bound water was 2.64-4.08cm^3; and the thickness of tightly bound water film was around 1.12Å.

Keywords Bound water Loess Relative humidity Isothermal adsorption experiment

0 Introduction

The water in the soil can be divided into free water and bound water according to the activity state. The bound water refers to the water that is adsorbed on the surface of soil particles by electrostatic attraction. The distance between the bound water and the surface of soil particles is different, so the bound water can be further subdivided into tightly bound water and loosely bound water. The distance between tightly bound water and the surface of soil particles is the closest, and the gravitation is the greatest. Water molecules of tightly bound water are tightly adsorbed on the surface of soil particles, and its properties are close to solid. Outside the tightly bound water layer, the gravitation between water molecules and soil particles gradually weakens, and the bound water film thickens accordingly. Loosely bound water makes the soil plastic to a certain degree.

Loess is a special soil that is extremely sensitive to water, and its engineering properties are closely related to moisture content. Coarse particles in loess contact each other to form the skeleton structure, while fine particles attach to the surface of coarse particles to form the special loess structure with support pores as the main and inlay pores as the secondary(Xu et al. ,2007; Lei,1987). Loess is rich in binding material, which connects soil particles. Under the combined action of physical and chemical factors, cementation strength is produced between the loess particles, which forms the structural strength of loess(Tian et al. ,2005; Yan,2010). Loess is a typical unsaturated clay, which was of high matrix water absorption potential and exhibits negative pore water pressure effect, which further improves the strength of loess. Therefore, the engineering properties of loess in dry state are not bad(Xing,2001). However, when loess meets water, due to its collapsibility, large collapsible deformation will occur, resulting in significant decrease in the strength of loess(Chen et al. ,2006). From the perspective of microstructure, the pores between loess particles interact with water, and eventually form tightly and loosely bound water, which will damage the loess structure and affect the strength of loess(Luo and Zhang,2004; Chen et al. ,2015; Fang et al. ,2013; Li et al. ,2016). Studies have shown that tightly bound water affects the viscosity of loess, and the viscosity will decrease with the increase of content of tightly bound water. Loosely bound water can dissolve the binding material between particles and play a role in lubrication, reducing the friction between particles(Fang and Gu,2007; Gu and Fang,2009). As the bound water content of loess increases, the structural properties of loess weaken(Chen et al. ,2010). Cohesive force and internal friction angle of loess show decreasing trend with the increase of bound water content(Wang et al. ,2014).

Therefore, understanding the adsorption of bound water by loess is of great significance to clarify its influence on the strength of loess. A lot of research has been done on this. Water adsorption is the main cause of changes in soil moisture content, and the content of adsorbed bound water is proportional to relative humidity (Kosmas et al. ,1998; Kosmas et al. ,2001). The bound water content of loess is closely related to the particle size composition, liquid plastic limit and relative humidity. The thermal weight loss range of tightly and loosely bound water is 125-245℃ and 65-125℃ respectively. (Wang et al. ,2014; Li,2015; Zhang et al. ,2016; Zhang,2018). On the basis of previous studies, isotherm adsorption experiment was used to study the influence of relative humidity on the physical properties of loess adsorbed bound water in preparation for future research.

1 Materials and Methods

1.1 Soil Samples

The loess samples with the depths of 7.0m,8.0m,9.0m,13.0m,16.0m, and 18.0m were drilled vertically downwards from the Shichuanhe area of Fuping County, Shaanxi Province with the drill bit of Φ100mm × 180mm. The drilling process must ensure that the original loess sample was not disturbed and with no cracks. Put the loess samples taken out into the earth pressure cell quickly, marked the top and bottom of loess samples, and wrapped the sealing film outside the earth pressure cell to maintain the moisture content of the original loess samples. Put the earth pressure cell on the foam board to reduce the damage of loess samples caused by bumps during transportation and keep the original state free from disturbance.

1.2 Isothermal Absorption Experiment

The isotherm adsorption experiment refers to the relationship between the content of water adsorbed by a unit weight of solid particles with the change in humidity at a constant temperature. Therefore, the isotherm adsorption experiment can effectively measure the mass of water adsorbed by loess in different humidity environments, so that the bound water content can be quantitatively measured, and the type of bound water can be classified as well.

1.3 Experiment Procedure

The isothermal adsorption experiment was carried out on loess samples at six depths of 7.0m,8.0m,9.0m,

13.0m, 16.0m, and 18.0m. Different concentrations of sulfuric acid solutions were used to control the relative humidity in the dryer. Tab. 1 shows the relative humidity corresponding to different concentrations of sulfuric acid solutions. The experiment temperature must be controlled between 20℃ ±0.2℃, and the gap between dryer and cover must be sealed with petroleum jelly. The specific experiment procedure is as follows:

(1) Took six loess samples of different depths, put them in the high temperature oven, and dried them at 250℃ for 8 hours. Put the dried loess samples in the dryer to cool for 24 hours, and put the dried aluminium boxes in the dryer to keep them dry.

(2) Took 5-6g loess samples, and put them into an aluminium box. Three samples of each depth were set for parallel experiments in each humidity environment. Then put these aluminium boxes in a dryer, and used the same method to put the loess samples in the dryers with the other humidity.

(3) Measured the total mass of loess sample and aluminium box in the dryer every 24 hours until the difference in mass between two measurements was less than 0.0001g, indicating that the adsorption of bound water by loess had reached stable state.

Relative Humidity P/P_s Corresponding to Different Concentrations of Sulfuric Acid Solutions Tab. 1

Relative Humidity P/P_s	1.00	0.98	0.95	0.925	0.90	0.80	0.70
Mass Fraction	0.00	6.00	11.02	14.69	17.91	26.79	33.09
Relative Humidity P/P_s	0.60	0.50	0.40	0.30	0.20	0.10	0.05
Mass Fraction	38.85	43.10	45.02	47.71	52.45	57.76	64.45

1.4 Calculation of Physical Properties of Bound Water

The physical properties characterizing bound water of loess mainly include:

The bound water content w_g, which can be measured directly during isothermal adsorption experiment; the density of hydrated loess ρ_{hc} after adsorption reaching stable state, which can be measured by the neutral liquid kerosene pycnometer method.

The volume of loess V_{hc} after the adsorption of bound water reaching stable state, which can be calculated as:

$$V_{hc} = W_g/\rho_{hc} \tag{1}$$

Where, W_g is the mass of hydrated loess; and ρ_{hc} is the density of hydrated loess.

The volume of bound water V_w, which can be calculated as:

$$V_w = V_{hc} - V_c \tag{2}$$

Where, V_c is the volume of loess under drying condition.

The density of bound water ρ_w, which can be calculated as:

$$\rho_w = m_w/V_w \tag{3}$$

Where, m_w is the mass of bound water.

The thickness of bound water film h_p that is uniformly distributed around the surface of clay minerals, which can be calculated as:

$$h_p = V_w/A_{sp} \tag{4}$$

Where, A_{sp} is the specific surface area of clay minerals in loess particles.

2 Results and Discussion

2.1 Results of Isothermal Adsorption Experiment

The bound water adsorption was stable after 10-15d, indicating that the bound water content of loess had reached the maximum value. Under different relative humidity environments, the maximum bound water content adsorbed by loess at six depths took the average value of three loess samples, and the results are shown in Fig. 1.

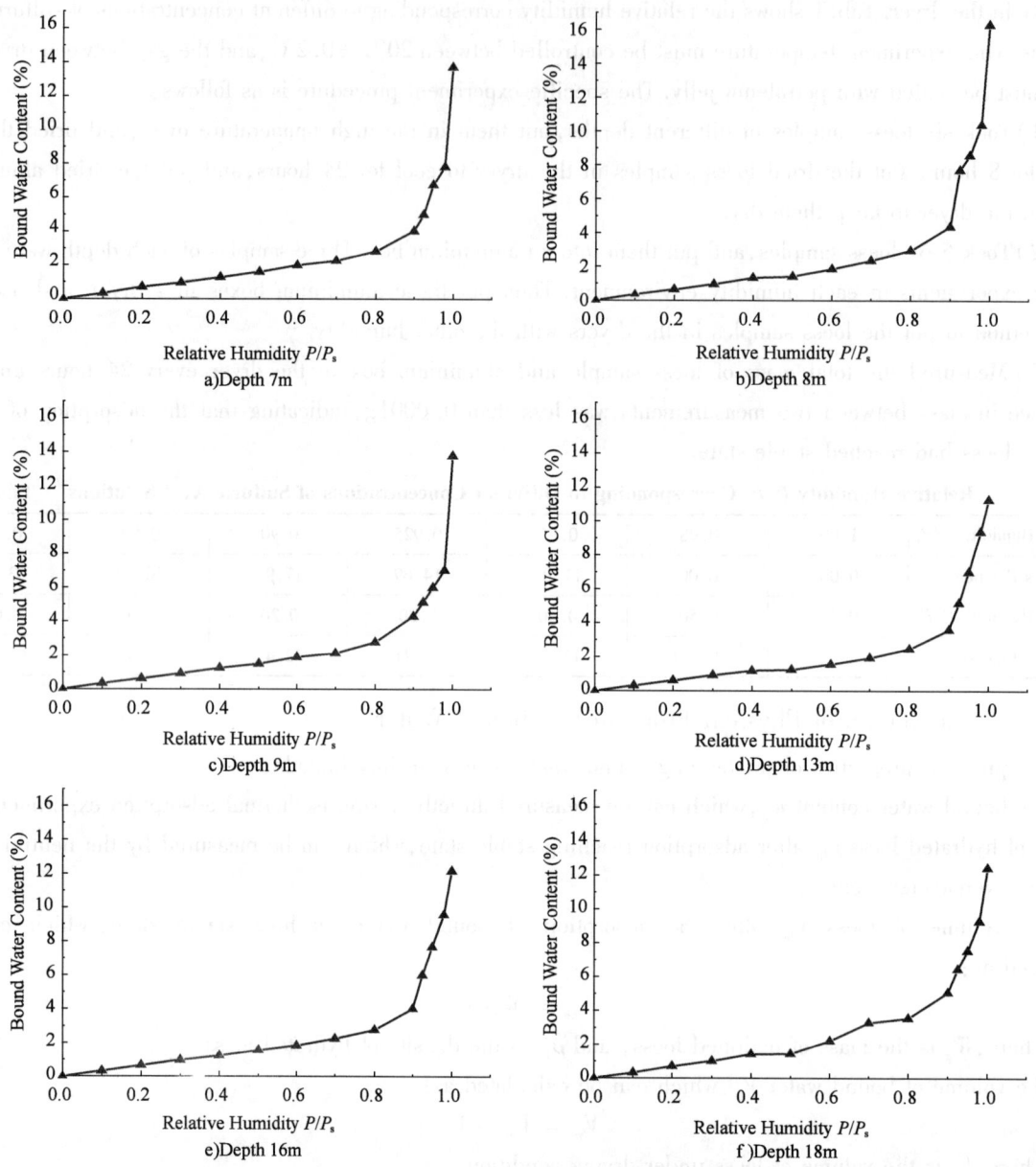

Fig. 1 Bound Water Content of Loess under Different Relative Humidity P/P_s

Results presented in Figure 1 indicate that the adsorption curves of loess at different depths were consistent, and when the relative humidity was relatively low, the loess in the dryer adsorbed water faster, but the adsorption capacity was small. The adsorption form at this stage was monolayer adsorption and the adsorption curve increased linearly. With the increase of relative humidity, the loess particles had adsorbed a layer of bound water. The adsorption form at this stage was multi-layer adsorption, and the isotherm adsorption curve increased rapidly. Therefore, it can be concluded that the formation of adsorption was complex, not only monolayer adsorption, but also multi-layer adsorption.

According to Fig. 1, it can be concluded that the adsorption of bound water by loess samples at different depths was a combination of chemical adsorption and physical adsorption during the whole stage; and the isotherm adsorption curve can be divided into three stages, namely $P/P_s = 0$-0.3, $P/P_s = 0.3$-0.9, and $P/P_s = 0.9$-1.0. The adsorption was strongest when the relative humidity was 0.0-0.9. The bound water at this stage was formed under the action of electrostatic attraction between water molecules and clay minerals of loess particles. This electrostatic attraction was the result of the interaction between cations in the medium solution in the dryer and negative charge on the surface of the loess particles. When the relative humidity was greater than 0.9, the adsorption curve increased sharply. In this stage, the dominant interaction between clay minerals and water molecules was Van der Waals force, and the formation of adsorption was multi-layer adsorption. The surface of loess particles adsorbed a large amount of bound water, which controlled the consolidation and penetration of the loess.

In addition, it can be concluded from Fig.1 that the maximum bound water content of loess with the depth of 8.0m was 16.28%; loess with the depth of 13.0m was of the smallest adsorption capacity, which was 11.27%. Among them, the tightly bound water content was 3.59-5.07%. The loess particles with the depth of 8.0m were of the largest content of clay minerals, and the loess particles with the depth of 13.0m were of the least content of clay minerals. It was verified that the more clay minerals content, the finer loess, the larger specific surface area, and the more bound water content.

2.2 Functional Relationship Between Relative Humidity and Bound Water Content

According to Figure 1, the functional relationship between relative humidity P/P_s and bound water content w_g of loess at different depths can be obtained as shown in Tab.2 below.

Functional relationship between relative humidity P/P_s and bound water content w_g of loess Tab.2

Depth (m)	Relative humidity P/P_s				0.9-1.0
	0.0-0.3		0.3-0.9		
	Fitting function	R^2	Fitting function	R^2	
7.0	$w_g = 3.184 \ (P/P_s)^{1/1.025}$	0.992	$w_g = 2.650 + 9.161 \ (P/P_s)^2$	0.979	Multi-layer Adsorption
8.0	$w_g = 2.691 \ (P/P_s)^{1/1.139}$	0.998	$w_g = 1.763 + 8.238 \ (P/P_s)^2$	0.993	Multi-layer Adsorption
9.0	$w_g = 2.567 \ (P/P_s)^{1/1.129}$	0.993	$w_g = 1.774 + 7.893 \ (P/P_s)^2$	0.971	Multi-layer Adsorption
13.0	$w_g = 3.715 \ (P/P_s)^{1/0.946}$	0.995	$w_g = 1.448 + 8.734 \ (P/P_s)^2$	0.978	Multi-layer Adsorption
16.0	$w_g = 2.051 \ (P/P_s)^{1/1.011}$	0.956	$w_g = 1.786 + 7.158 \ (P/P_s)^2$	0.987	Multi-layer Adsorption
18.0	$w_g = 3.428 \ (P/P_s)^{1/0.960}$	0.999	$w_g = 2.843 + 9.929 \ (P/P_s)^2$	0.983	Multi-layer Adsorption

From Tab.2, it can be concluded that the functional relationships are as follows:

When the relative humidity P/P_s is within 0.0-0.3, the functional relationship between the bound water content w_g and the relative humidity P/P_s is as follows, which conforms to Freundlich Equation:

$$w_g = b \ (P/P_s)^{1/n} \tag{5}$$

Where, the two constants b and n are related to the structure, surface properties and specific surface area of loess. Comparing Tab.2 and Fig.1, it can be found that b is inversely proportional to n. The greater bound water content w_g, the greater b, the smaller n.

When the relative humidity P/P_s is within 0.3-0.9, the functional relationship between the bound water content w_g and the relative humidity P/P_s is as follows:

$$w_g = a + k \ (P/P_s)^2 \tag{6}$$

Where, a and k are two constants, which are related to the type of loess, specific surface area, and activity of loess particle surface. The values of a and k are related to the particle size composition of loess, and the loess particles at these depths are finer and the specific surface area is larger.

2.3 The Influence of Relative Humidity on Density of Hydrated Loess

Accurately measure the specific gravity of loess particles is crucial for calculating the physical properties of bound water. Took specific gravity test of loess samples to obtain the relationship between the density of hydrated loess ρ_{hc} and the relative humidity P/P_s as shown in Fig. 2.

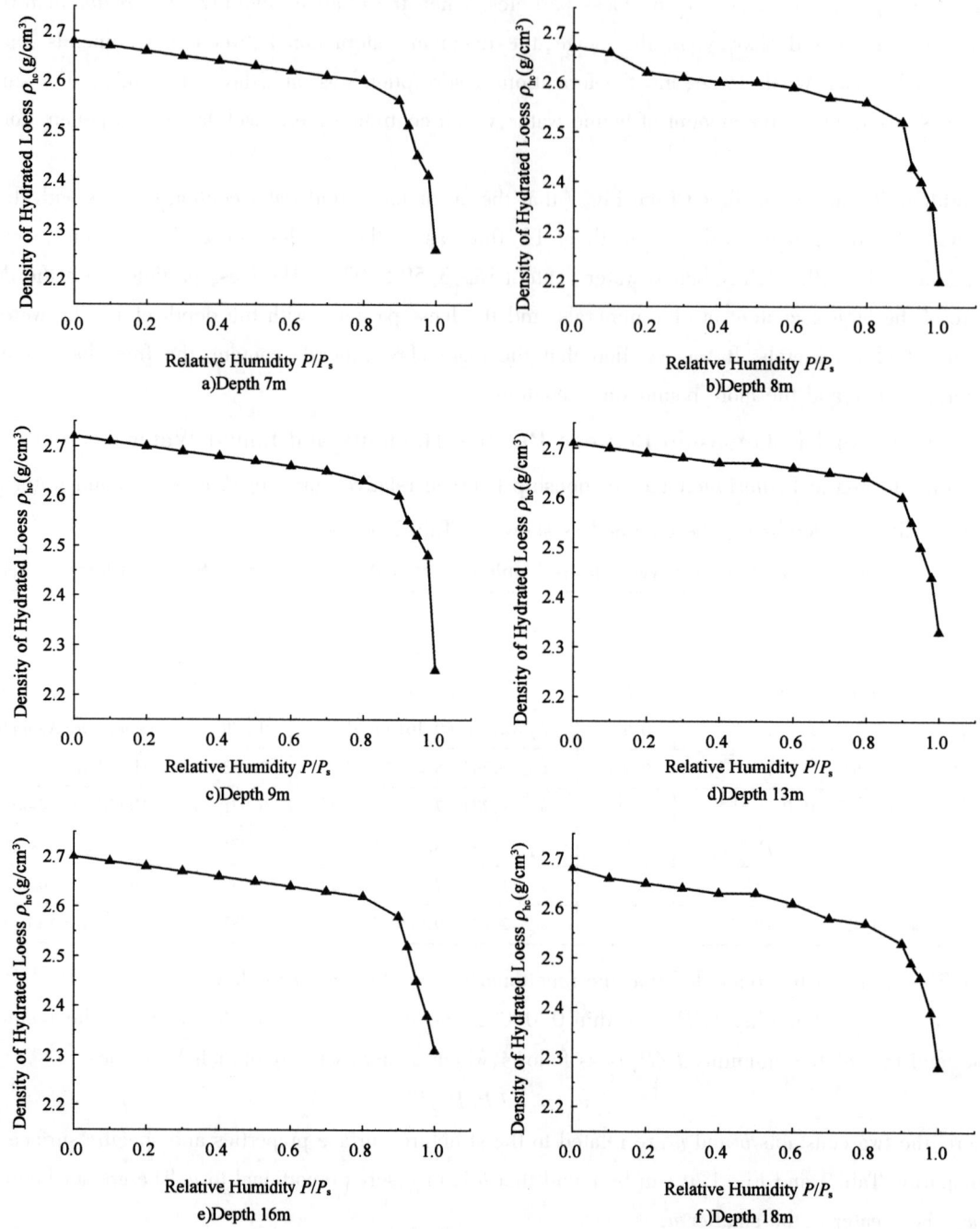

Fig. 2　Relationship between Density of Hydrated loess ρ_{hc} and Relative Humidity P/P_s

It can be analyzed from Fig. 2 that the density of loess after hydration at different depths showed the decreasing trend with the increase of relative humidity; and all of them suddenly changed when the relative humidity P/P_s was 0.9. When the relative humidity P/P_s < 0.9, the density of hydrated loess at different depths was 2.52-2.60g/cm³, an average drop of 4.77% compared with dry loess; when the relative humidity P/P_s > 0.9, the density of hydrated loess at different depths was 2.2-2.33g/cm³, an average drop of 15.66% compared with dry loess. Therefore, it can be concluded that in the tightly bound water stage, the density of hydrated loess decreased not so significantly, while in the loosely bound water stage, the density of hydrated loess decreased greatly.

2.4 The Influence of Relative Humidity on Volume of Bound Water

According to Equation (1) and (2), and combined with the data in Fig. 2, the volume of adsorbed bound water on the loess surface can be calculated. The volume of bound water per 100g loess in different humidity environments is shown in Fig. 3.

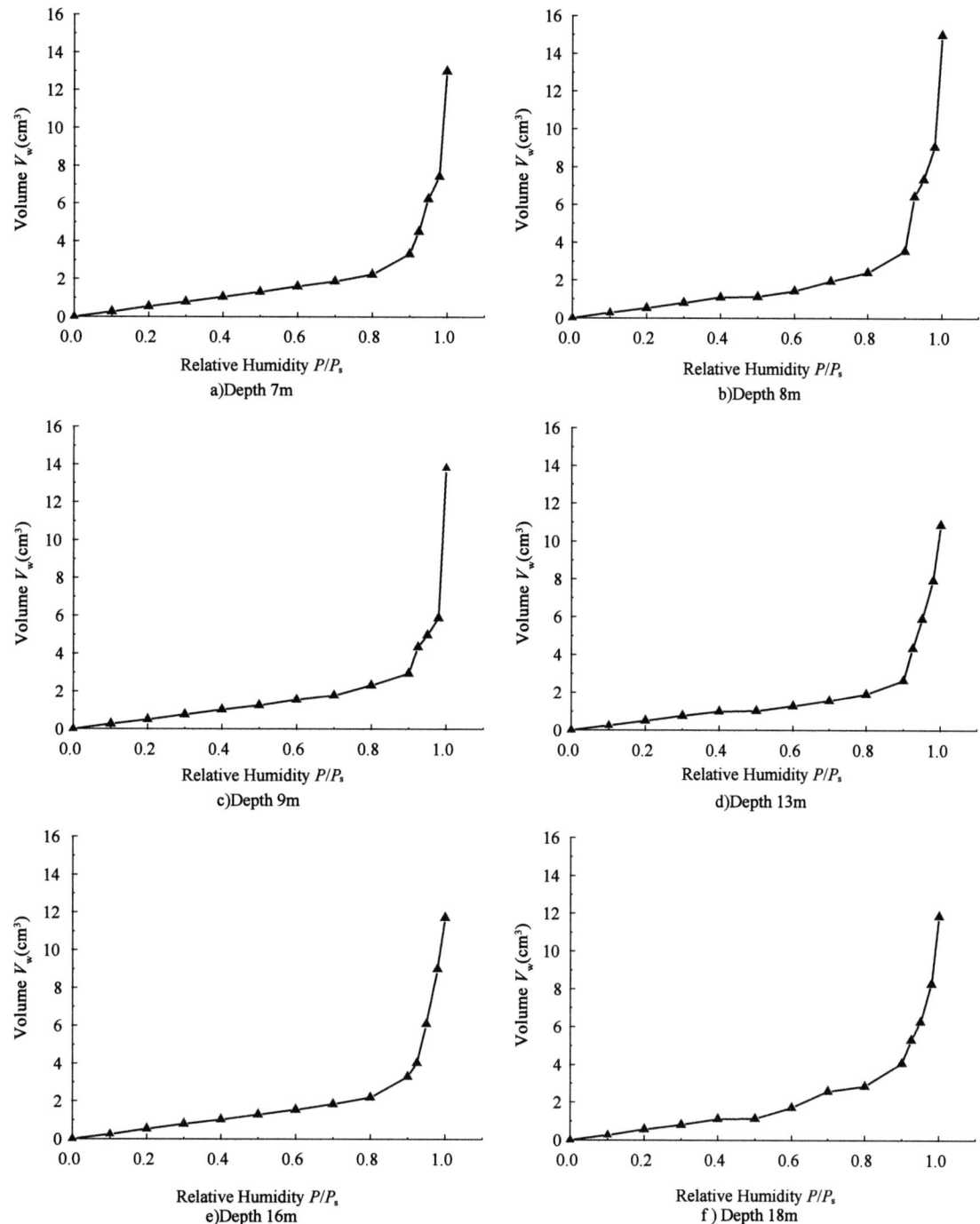

Fig. 3 Relationship between volume of bound water per 100g loess V_w and relative humidity P/P_s

Results presented in Fig. 3 indicate that the variation process of the volume of bound water per 100g loess V_w at different depths with the relative humidity P/P_s:

(1) the volume of bound water increased with the increase of relative humidity, and the volume of bound

water was 10.86-13.81cm^3, among which the volume of tightly bound water was 2.64-4.08cm^3;

(2) It can be concluded that the volume of bound water adsorbed by loess at different depths was not consistent. The loess with the largest volume of bound water was at the depth of 8.0m, and the loess with the least volume of bound water was at the depth of 13.0m. This was mainly related to the content of clay minerals in loess particles and the specific surface area of the minerals.

2.5 The Influence of Relative Humidity on Density of Bound Water

According to the above research results, the density of bound water can be calculated by Equation(3). The relationship between the density of bound water and the relative humidity is shown in Fig. 4.

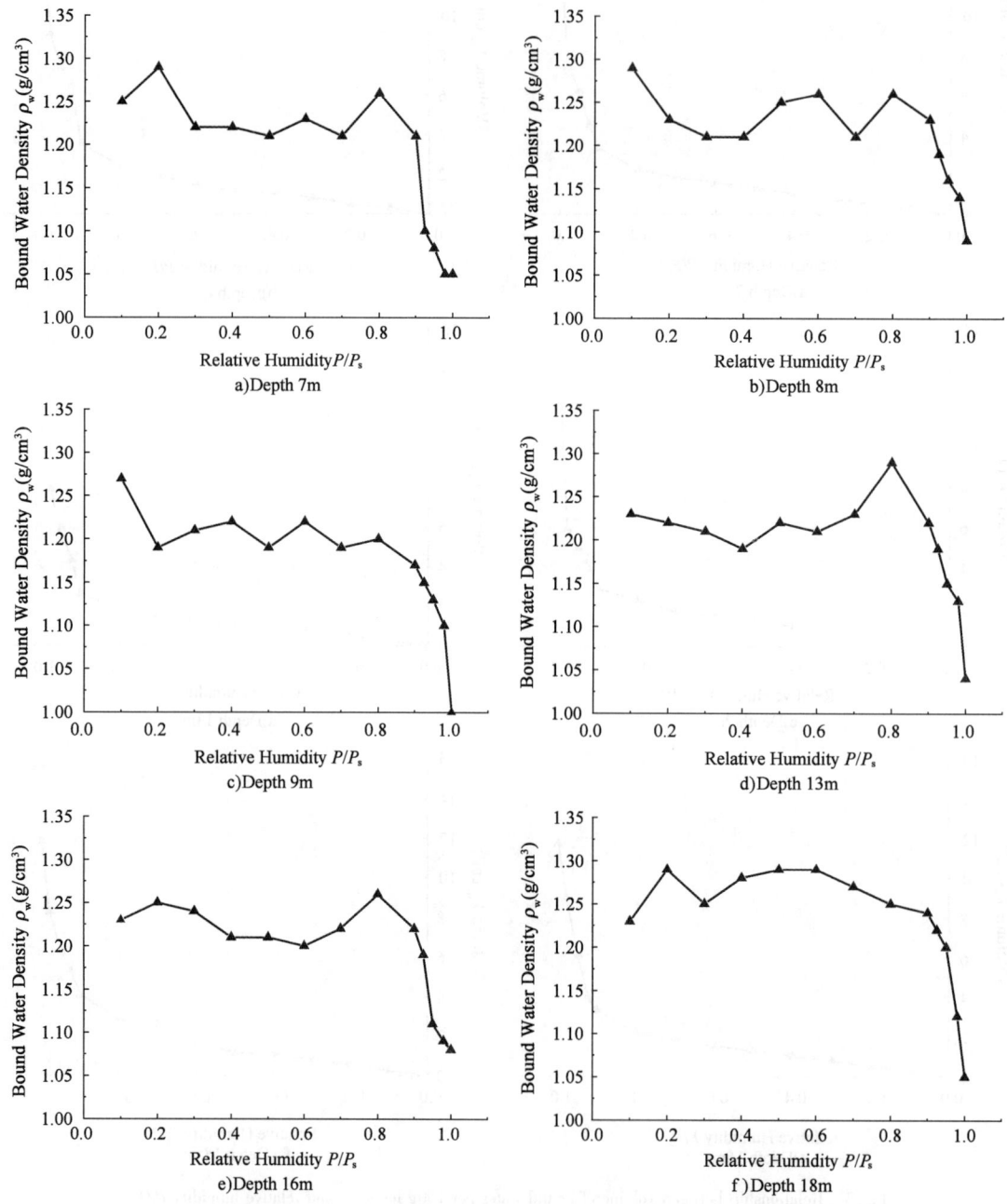

Fig. 4 Relationship between Density of Bound Water ρ_w and Relative Humidity P/P_s

It can be concluded from Fig. 4 that the density of bound water measured in this experiment can be divided into two stages. When the relative humidity $P/P_s < 0.9$, the density of bound water did not fluctuate greatly, which was around 1.23g/cm³. Because the water adsorbed at this stage was to form tightly bound water, and water molecules were closely connected, which was much denser than free water. When the relative humidity $P/P_s > 0.9$, the density of bound water decreased sharply, which was around 1.12g/cm³. Because the water adsorbed at this stage formed loosely bound water, whose density was much smaller than that of tightly bound water. Since the loosely bound water receives less gravitational force compared with tightly bound water. Because the clay minerals impose adsorption effect on loosely bound water, its density is slightly greater than that of free water.

2.6 The influence of Relative Humidity on Thickness of Bound Water Film

According to the experiment results, the bound water film thickness can be calculated by Equation(4). The specific surface area in the equation was obtained by nitrogen adsorption method, and the results are shown in Tab.3. The thickness of bound water film of loess at different depths varies with relative humidity is shown in Fig.5.

Specific Surface Area of Loess at Different Depths Tab.3

Depth(m)	7.0	8.0	9.0	13.0	16.0	18.0
Specific Surface Area(m²/g)	32.4305	36.8659	34.3538	27.9988	28.9729	29.7501

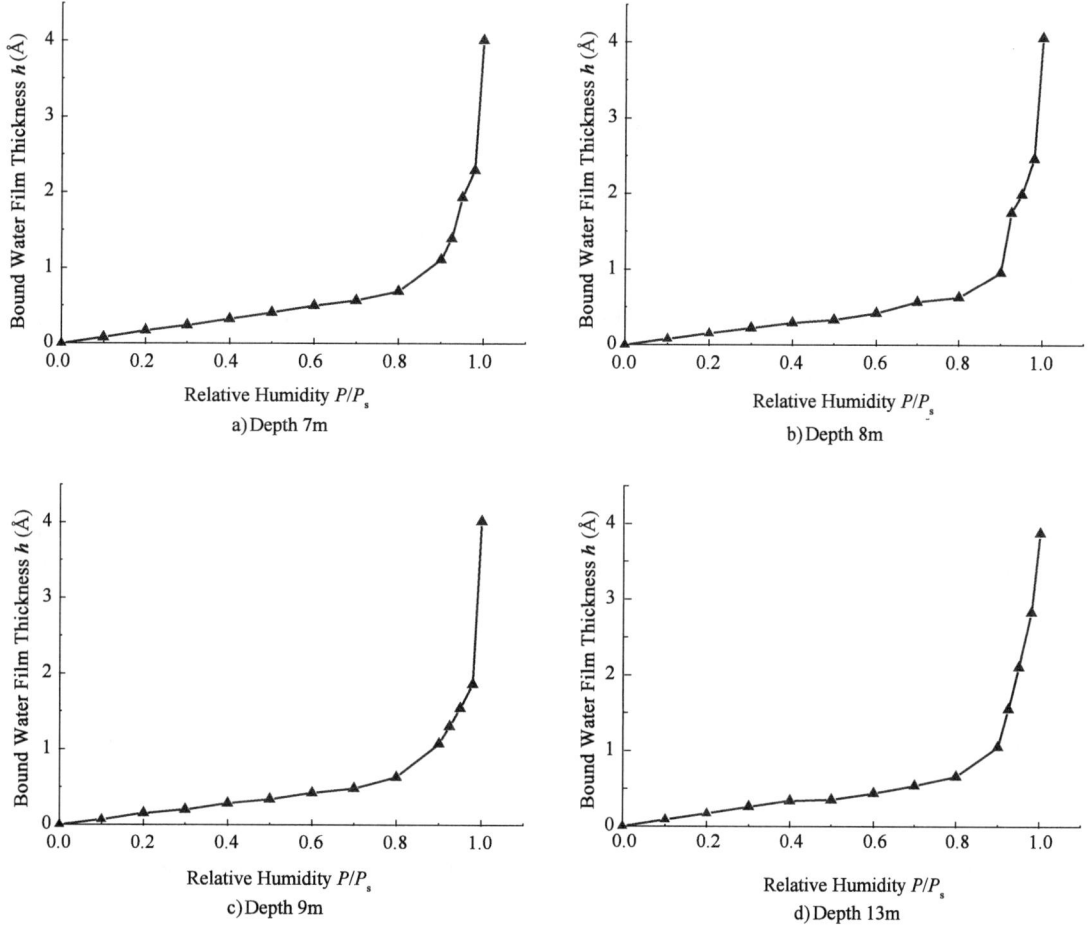

Fig.5

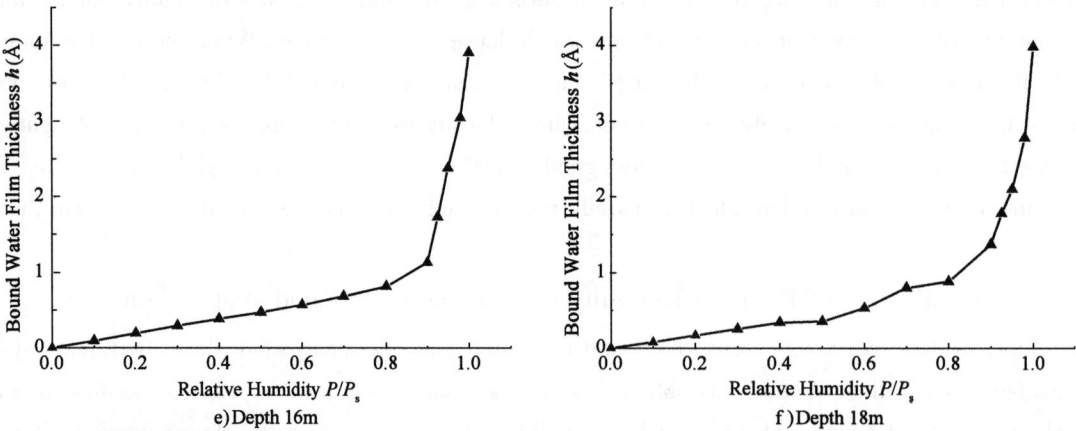

Fig. 5　Relationship between the Bound Water Film Thickness h_p and the Relative Humidity P/P_s

The thickness of bound water film increased with the relative humidity. The increase was relatively slow at first, and then the increase accelerated suddenly. When the relative humidity was 0.9, a turning change appeared. In the tightly bound water stage, the thickness of bound water film of loess at different depths did not change significantly, which was around 1.12Å; while in the loosely bound water stage, the thickness of bound water film changed greatly, which was around 3.98Å. The thickness of loosely bound water film was nearly two times that of the tightly bound water film. The curves verified that the critical point of the type of bound water was relative humidity of 0.9.

3　Conclusions

In this study, the types and contents of bound water in loess at different depths, and the relationships between physical properties of bound water and relative humidity are studied by using isotherm adsorption experiment. Our main findings are:

(1) The bound water content of loess at different depths was 11.27%-16.28%. Among them, the tightly bound water content was 3.59%-5.07%. It was verified that the more clay minerals content, the finer loess, the larger specific surface area, and the more bound water content.

(2) The critical point of tightly and loosely bound water was the relative humidity of 0.9. When the relative humidity was less than 0.9, the adsorption rate of bound water by loess was high, and the adsorption capacity was small. It was monolayer adsorption and only formed tightly bound water. When the relative humidity was greater than 0.9, the early stage of loess adsorbing bound water was monolayer adsorption to form tightly bound water. Multi-layer adsorption was in the later stage, with larger adsorption capacity and lower adsorption rate, forming loosely bound water.

(3) The bound water content and relative humidity satisfied a certain functional relationship, and the parameters in the functions were related to the specific surface area and surface properties of the loess particles, etc.

(4) The relationship between the density of hydrated loess, the density of bound water and relative humidity was similar. In the tightly bound water stage, both densities were larger, and in the loosely bound water stage, both of them decreased rapidly. This was related to the compactness of tightly and loosely bound water. When the relative humidity $P/P_s < 0.9$, the density of hydrated loess was 2.52-2.60g/cm^3, and the density of bound water was around 1.23g/cm^3; when the relative humidity $P/P_s > 0.9$, the density of hydrated loess was 2.2-2.33g/cm^3, and the density of bound water was around 1.12g/cm^3.

(5) The relationship between the volume of adsorbed bound water, the thickness of bound water film and relative humidity was similar. In the tightly bound water stage, the volume of the adsorbed bound water was smaller and the bound water film was thinner; in the loosely bound water stage, the volume of the adsorbed bound water was larger, and the bound water film was thicker. The volume of bound water was 10.86-13.81 cm^3, and the thickness of bound water film was around 3.98Å. Among them, the volume of tightly bound water was 2.64-4.08 cm^3; and the tightly bound water was around 1.12Å.

References

[1] Chen, C. L., Hu, Z. Q, Gao, P. Research on Relationship between Structure and Deformation Property of Intact Loess[J]. Rock and Soil Mechanics, 2006(11), 1891-1896.

[2] Chen, H., Liu, Z. M, Song, Z. P. Study on Structural Parameters of Disturbed Loess and Saturated Intact Loess[J]. Chinese Journal of Underground Space and Engineering, 2010.6(03):487-491, 497.

[3] Chen, Y., Li, X. A., Huang, R. Q., et al. Micro Experimental Research on Influence Factors of Loess Collapsibility[J]. Journal of Engineering Geology, 2015, 23(04):646-653.

[4] Fang, X. W., Shen, C. N., Wang L, et al. Research on Microstructure of Q_2 Loess Before and After Wetting [J]. Rock and Soil Mechanics, 2013, 34(05):1319-1324.

[5] Fang, Y. G, Gu, R. G. Experiment Study on the Effects of Adsorbed Water on Rheological Characteristics of Soft Clayey Soil[J]. Science Technology and Engineering, 2007(01), 73-78.

[6] Gu, R. G. and Fang, Y. G. Experiment Study of the Effects of Organic Matter on the Rheological Characteristics of Soft Soils[J]. China Civil Engineering Journal, 42(01), 101-106.

[7] Kosmas, C., Danalatos, N. G. and Poesen, J. The Effect of Water Vapour Adsorption on Soil Moisture Content under Mediterranean Climatic Conditions[J]. Agricultural Water Management, 36(2), 157-168.

[8] Kosmas, C., Marathianou, M., Gerontidis, S., Detsis, V., Tsara, M. and Poesen, J. Parameters Affecting Water Vapor Adsorption by the Soil under Semi-arid Climatic Conditions [J]. Agricultural Water Management, 48(1), 61-78.

[9] Lei, X. Y. (1987). Pore Types and Collapsibility of Chinese Loess[J]. Science in China, 1987(12), 1309-1318.

[10] Li, C. H., Fang, X. W., Shen, C. N. Ou, Y. X. and Zhu, Q. (2016). Wetting-induced Microstructural Change of Q_2 Loess[J]. Sichuan Building Science, 42(03), 40-45.

[11] Li, Y. L. (2015). Bound Water Properties and Moisture Migration in Unsaturated Loess[J]. Xi'an University of Architecture and Technology.

[12] Luo, Y. S. and Zhang, A. J. (2004). Outcomes on Structural Research of Loess and Its New Advance[J]. Journal of Hydroelectric Engineering, 2004(06), 66-69.

[13] Tian, K. L., Zhang, H. L., Zhang, B. P. and Luo, Y. S. (2005). Research on Structural Characteristics and Strength of Loess[J]. Journal of Hydroelectric Engineering, 2005(02), 64-67.

[14] Wang, J. J., Zhang, X. L. and Wang, T. X. (2014). The Shear Strength Research of Compacted Loess Considering the Impact of Moisture Content and Dry Density[J]. Xi'an Univ. of Arch. & Tech. (Natural Science Edition), 46(05), 687-691.

[15] Wang, T. X. Li, Y. L. and Su, L. J. (2014). Types and Boundaries of Bound Water on Loess particle surface. Chinese Journal of Geotechnical Engineering, 36(05), 942-948.

[16] Xing, Y. C. (2001). Effective Stress and Deformation-strength Characteristics of Unsaturated Soils[J]. Xi'an University of Technology.

[17] Xu, Z. J., Lin, Z. G. and Zhang, M. S. (2007). Loess in China and Loess Landslides[J]. Chinese Journal of Rock Mechanics and Engineering, 2007(07), 1297-1312.

[18] Yan, B. (2010). Research on the Structural and Mechanical Characteristics of Luochuan Loess Profile [J]. Chang'an University.

[19] Zhang, Z. H. (2018). Research on Suction of Unsaturated Loess-bonded Water[J]. Chang'an University.

[20] Zhang, Z H, Li P, Li T L. Relationship between Loess and Bound Water Content and Physical Indicators [J]. Journal of Engineering Geology, 2016.

有关硅藻土及地基处理方法研究现状分析

谢锦倩　张宏光　杨婷婷

（长安大学公路学院）

摘要 本文首先从物理、力学两个方面梳理了硅藻土的基本性质，并从微观与宏观两个尺度归纳总结了硅藻土的力学特性；其次，详细阐述了硅藻土及天然土的结构性力学特性；然后，总结了工程中常见处理软土地基的地基处理方法，着重分析了真空（堆载）预压法的作用机理；最后，对预测软土地基工后沉降的方法进行了综述，细致介绍了用于预测地基沉降的方法。综述结果表明：天然硅藻土具有与软黏土相类似的特性，应注意其结构性对工程建筑物的影响；真空联合堆载预压在处理软土地基方面具有较强的适用性，可用于硅藻土软土地基加固处理；预测地基沉降的方法较多，采取联合预测手段能够提高预测精度。

关键词 岩土工程　硅藻土　归纳分析　结构性　真空联合堆载预压　沉降预测

0 引言

作为一种生物成因的硅质沉积岩，硅藻土由硅藻的遗骸所组成，具有大孔隙、含水率较高等特点。此外，硅藻土还具有较强的结构性，结构性的存在对土的强度和变形将产生一定的影响，因此硅藻土地基应考虑结构性的影响，从而满足建筑物安全使用要求。目前对硅藻土的相关研究成果较少，主要通过室内试验对比重塑土与原状土的试验结果来进行结构性方面的研究，而有关硅藻土地基处理方法研究甚少。

鉴于此，本文对硅藻土的工程物理力学性质进行综述，详细阐释了其具有的结构性特性，总结了目前在结构性研究方面所取得的研究成果；为寻找处理硅藻土地基的方法，对国内近十年在软土地基处理方面的研究动态进行了汇总，着重分析了真空联合堆载预压方法用于软土地基处理的工作机理及所存在的问题；最后，针对备受关注的控制地基工后沉降问题，总结了相关的沉降预测方法，以期在施工过程中实现对工后沉降进行预测，进而采取相应措施对其进行加固处理。

1 硅藻土基本性质与工程性质的国内外研究现状分析

1.1 硅藻土物理指标及物质组成的研究现状

1.1.1 硅藻土物理指标研究现状

天然硅藻土是由硅藻遗体（硅藻壳）组成[1]，具有高含水率、低重度、孔隙比大、强结构性等基本性质。研究表明，不同时代的硅藻土其固结和胶结程度存在着显著的差别[2]。硅藻土多发育在古近纪、新近纪和第四纪地层中[1,3-4]，但年代的久远的硅藻土失去了土的性质，变成"硅藻岩"；仅有较近时期的硅藻土保持土的性质。现国内外按照不同形成时间和环境将硅藻土分为以下四类[5]，见表1。此外，本文总结了国内外硅藻土的基本性质及物质组成，总结如表2所示。

硅藻土的分类[5]   表1

时间和环境	举例
沉积于大陆边缘的海相硅藻土矿床	美国加州的 Lompoc 矿
沉积于湖泊、沼泽的陆相硅藻土矿床	法国中部地块和美国内华达州、加利福尼亚州东部的硅藻土
现代湖泊、沼泽、泥塘中沉积的硅藻土矿物	佛罗里达、新罕布什尔和新约克群的现代湖泊、沼泽、泥塘中的含硅藻沉积物
现代海洋沉积	—

硅藻土的基本性质   表2

地 区	含水率(%)	重度(kN/m³)	孔 隙 比	液限指数(液限)	塑限指数
浙江嵊州	44	16.9/19.72	1.330	(52.8%)	34.1
云南腾冲	38.6~107.43	11.54~17.05	2.20~2.78	0.66~2.73	18.1~66.31
纳米比亚	172.6~235.3	11.66~12.35	4.0~5.2	0.3~1.05	38~235.3
日本大阪	141.3	13.1	—	—	—

1.1.2 硅藻土物质成分研究现状

天然硅藻土的化学成分主要是无定形的 SiO_2,含有少量的 Al_2O_3、Fe_2O_3、CaO、MgO 等和有机质[6-7],另外均含有蒙脱石、伊利石和高岭石等黏土矿物。黏土矿物的含量导致硅藻土具有膨胀性;有机质具有较强的胶结作用,能够有效抑制膨胀性。研究表明有机质含量越多,硅藻土的颜色就越深,硅藻土的颜色呈绿灰至灰绿色、灰白色、土黄色和深灰色等[2,6,8-9]。

1.2 硅藻土强度和变形特性的研究现状

国内外关于硅藻土工程性质方面的研究较少,关于硅藻土的主要研究集中于工业领域,例如:吸附材料、过滤材料等。目前只能查到日本大阪关西机场项目及墨西哥地区对硅藻土工程特性研究的报告[10-13]。国内对硅藻土结构性的研究可分为微观和宏观两个方面。微观方面的研究主要观察孔隙随固结压力的变化情况,如王月香等[14]基于 SEM 图像处理技术来反映微观结构及孔隙分布随过固结压力的变化。

此外,主要通过室内试验(压缩试验及三轴试验)对宏观方面的研究,如方遥越等[1]对浙江嵊州地区初始孔隙比较接近的原状土和重塑土进行压缩试验,对比发现:原状土在达到屈服强度之后,由于结构被破坏导致其压缩性增大;而重塑图不存在结构性的影响,其压缩性就大大降低。

综上所述,天然沉积的硅藻土含水率及液限含水率均较高,一般情况下呈软塑甚至流塑状态,其透水性差、压缩性高的特点会严重影响建筑物的正常使用[4]。另外,硅藻土中细粒土的含量较高,通常引发山体滑坡等地质灾害的发生。因此,以硅藻土为地基的工程项目必须采用相应的地基处理方法来提高地基承载力,从而达到满足上部结构对地基稳定和变形的要求。

2 结构性的研究现状

土的结构性是指土颗粒、孔隙的性状和排列形式及其颗粒间的相互作用。结构性黏土会在缺乏预兆的情况下发生脆性破坏,应对黏土的结构性特点应给予充分重视[16]。目前大多数的研究均围绕重塑土展开的,沈珠江也将建立应用于岩土领域的结构性模型及相关的分析理论视为 21 世纪土力学领域的核心问题[17]。

为充分了解结构性土的力学特性及变形机理,学者们利用人工配置的结构性土进行室内试验对其进行深入研究,最常用的室内配置人工土方法就是在原料土中掺入一定量的水泥和冰粒(食盐)来人工设定化学胶结作用和大孔隙[18-19]。在研究结构性土应力—应变关系及长期变形特性方面,何森[20]等利用室内固结不排水试验来研究初始应力各向异性、各向同性及重塑土的力学特性,发现在固结应力较小的情况下,偏应力—应变曲线表现出应力软化特性;而在固结应力较大的情况下,偏应力—应变曲线表现出硬化特性。杨爱武等[21]通过室内试验来研究结构性对软黏土长期变形特性的研究,并以土体结构强度为量化参数,建立了考虑结构强度影响的长期变形预测公式。

综上所述,室内试验对结构性土的研究强度特性及变形特性方面取得的一定成果,且研究观点较为一致,伴随着软土地基工后沉降问题越来越受重视,结构性土的长期变形特性方面的研究工作将是未来的研究方向;同时,将结构性考虑在内的数值模拟方面研究也仍需进一步的研究。

3 超软地基处理方法研究现状分析

目前,国内外关于硅藻土软弱地基处理方法的研究较少,而在软土地基处理方面积累了大量的经验,因此可以借鉴软土地基的处理方法对硅藻土地基进行处理。常用于处理软弱地基的方法有:桩基处理(具体包括粉煤灰碎石桩、CFG 桩、水泥搅拌桩等)、真空预压法、堆载预压法及真空联合堆载预压法等,研究表明这些方法能够明显增强地基土的强度,减小工后沉降,有效地保证了在软土地基修筑建筑物的安全与施工质量。

目前真空(堆载)预压法在处理软土地基方面积累了深厚经验,真空联合堆载预压法是在真空预压与堆载预压的基础上发展起来的。目前对真空联合堆载预压法的研究主要集中于孔隙水压力、真空度、沉降或沉降速率、水平位移等变化规律上,另外在沉降预测及沉降计算方面也进行大量研究。

真空预压过程中,孔隙水压力的降低具体表现在两方面,一方面是在排水板与周围土体压力差的作用下,土体中的孔隙水沿着排水板排出;另一方面是随着地下水位的降低,孔隙水压力减小[22-23]。排水板与周围土体之间存在真空负压,在负压作用下周围土体中的水及细颗粒向排水板方向聚集,距离排水板较远土层中的小颗粒在渗流力的作用下也向排水板方向移动,从而导致排水板周围"土柱"的形成。为避免"土柱"现象的产生,张文彬等[25]发现分级加载可减小"土柱"厚度;另外,还应注意在真空预压法处理软土地基的初期,浅层土体中孔隙水压力先是升高,随后逐渐减小,即出现曼德尔效应,此现象的产生是由于浅层土土颗粒较小,渗透系数较低,土体中的水未被及时排出而造成孔隙水压力升高。真空预压作用仅在土体中产生球应力,在孔隙水吸力作用下,土体发生向加固区的水平运动,堆载预压法相反[26],研究真空联合堆载预压法作用下地基的水平位移问题,主要考虑其对邻近建筑物的影响及防止地基失稳。

4 沉降预测的研究现状

由于软土地基存在含水率大、压缩性高等特性,因此其施工沉降及工后沉降控制应给予高度重视,施工前后对沉降的预测环节能够地指导施工进度,有利于控制沉降。目前用于预测地基沉降的方法有很多,主要包括固结理论、数值模拟以及根据实测实验数据的反推沉降法等,本文系统性地总结了地基沉降计算或预测方法,汇总结果如表 3 所示。

地基沉降预测方法 表3

	沉降预测方法分类		特 点	
反推法	曲线拟合法	双曲线法	双曲线的预测值较实测值大,实测沉降时间至少半年以上	指数曲线模型比双曲线模型更能准确反映实际沉降变化规律
		指数曲线法	基于太沙基一维固结理论,未将次固结沉降考虑进去,因此预测值较实测值小	
		Asaoka 法	精确度与时间间隔有关	
		星野法	适合于荷载瞬时施加情况	
	系统理论法	灰色模型	需要精确的现场数据	
		神经网络法	无需建立相关的数学模型,缺乏理论基础;具有良好的非线性品质	
固结理论、本构关系及数值模拟	太沙基固结理论		由于理论假设、边界条件与参数确定较麻烦等方面的问题,理论结果较实测值误差较大;数值模拟参数的确定受室内试验影响较大,不过可以提前预测地基沉降及沉降的总体趋势	
	比奥固结理论			
	K-G 模型			
	Ducan-Chang 模型			

根据现场实测沉降数据反推沉降的方法因参数容易获取、直接明了等优点而被广泛应用于软土地基沉降预测。如赵明华等[27]观察到Gompertz成长曲线的走势与地基沉降变化的趋势相似,因此采用该方法对某滨海大道市政工程软土路基的沉降进行预测,预测效果较好。姜献东等[28]用灰色系统模型对某高级公路沉降进行预测,并采取后验差法对预测结果进行检验。检验结果表明:该方法的精度等级为一级,能够较好地预测路基沉降。

由于影响沉降的因素有很多,单一沉降预测方法所考虑到的因素不全面,其预测误差较大,因此可采取将两种或多于两种预测方法进行组合的措施来提高预测精度。如沙爱敏等[29]将Logistic模型、Gompertz模型和双曲线模型进行组合。

5 结　语

本文总结分析了天然硅藻土的物理力学性质,考虑到其压缩性高、含水率高、孔隙比大及强度低等特性,对地基处理方法及工后沉降预测进行了综述;另外,分析了土的结构性对土体变形及强度的影响。结合硅藻土基本性质及其地基处理方法研究现状及其存在的问题,提出进一步的研究方向:

(1)考虑硅藻土的蠕变变形规律,以对硅藻土的长期变形特性进行研究;

(2)在采用真空联合堆载预压法处理地基时,考虑真空度衰减(即井阻与涂抹面积)对加固效果的影响;

(3)采用有限元计算方法研究土体结构性,实现软件计算土的结构性问题的可能性。

参考文献

[1] 高华喜,殷坤龙,周春梅.硅藻土矿分布区斜坡稳定性分析与评价[J].矿业研究与开发,2006(05):14-16.

[2] Dayrb. Engineering properties of Diatomaceous Fill [J]. Journal of Geotechnical Engineers Division, American Society of Civil Engineers, 1995, 121(12):908-910.

[3] 张永双,郭长宝,曲永新,等.膨胀性硅藻土的力学性质及其灾害效应研究[J].岩土力学,2013,34(01):23-30,39.

[4] 陆浩.硅藻土资源及开发利用概况[J].浙江地质,2001,17(1):52-59.

[5] 马秋柱,何志敏,蔡泽明.纳米比亚硅藻土的工程特性[J].水运工程,2017.

[6] 洪振舜,立石义孝,邓永锋.强结构性天然沉积土的强度变形特性[J].岩土力学,2004(08):1201-1204.

[7] 胡书毅,文玲.山东临朐第三纪硅藻土的微观特征[J].电子显微镜学报,2005.

[8] 陈庸勋,贝丰,宋振亚,等.云南腾冲盆地硅藻土中有机质的初步研究[J].矿物岩石,1986.

[9] Mesri G, Rokhsar A,, Bohor B F. Composition and Compressibility of Typical Samples of Mexico City Clay [J]. Geotechnique, 1975, 11(12):527-554.

[10] Diaz Rodrijuez J, Abraham. Diatomaceous soils: Monotonic Behavior [C]//International symposium on deformation characteristics of geomaterials. Seoul, Korea, 2011.

[11] Day Robert W. Engineering Properties of Diatomaceous Fill [J]. Journal of Geotechnical Engineering, 1995, 121(12):908-910.

[12] Hiroyuki Tanaka, Locat Jacques. A Microstructural Investigation of Osaka Bay Clay [J]. Canadian Geotechnical Journal, 1999, 36(3):493-508.

[13] 王月香,吉锋,顾欢达,等.基于SEM图像处理的天然硅藻土分形特征分析[J].水利水运工程学报,2017(05):96-102.

[14] 方遥越,蒋军,姜煌辉.嵊州硅藻土的微观结构特征及其力学性质研究[J].低温建筑技术,2019,41(02):75-77,81.

[15] 张诚厚.两种结构性黏土的土工特性[J].水利水运科学研究,1983(04):65-71.

[16] 沈珠江.土体结构性的数学模型——21世纪土力学的核心问题[J].岩土工程学报,1996(01):95-97.
[17] 刘恩龙,沈珠江.结构性土压缩曲线的数学模拟[J].岩土力学,2006(04):615-620.
[18] 蒋明镜,沈珠江.结构性黏土试样人工制备方法研究[J].水利学报,1997(01):57-62.
[19] 何淼,刘恩龙,陈亚军,等.不排水条件下轴向加卸载时结构性土的力学特性探讨[J].岩石力学与工程学报,2017,36(02):466-474.
[20] 杨爱武,郑宇轩,肖敏.人工制备结构性软黏土长期变形特性试验研究[J].水文地质工程地质,2019,46(02):133-140.
[21] 龚晓南,岑仰润.真空预压加固软土地基机理探讨[J].哈尔滨建筑大学学报,2002(02):7-10.
[22] 朱建才,温晓贵,龚晓南.真空排水预压加固软基中的孔隙水压力消散规律[J].水利学报,2004(08):123-128.
[23] 雷华阳,李宸元,刘景锦,等.交替式真空预压法加固吹填超软土试验及数值模拟研究[J].岩石力学与工程学报,2019,38(10):2112-2125.
[24] 张文彬,杨建贵,彭劼,等.分级加载真空预压加固吹填流泥试验研究[J].河海大学学报(自然科学版),2019,47(06):541-547.
[25] 张青波,崔维孝,刘东,等.原状软土真空预压效果室内试验研究[J].水运工程,2017(09):192-196.
[26] 赵明华,郑焕然,刘煜.滨海软土路基最终沉降量预测研究[J].广西交通科技,2003(05):13-15,19.
[27] 姜献东,张苏俊,卢佩霞.灰色系统模型在软土路基沉降预测中的应用[J].施工技术,2016,45(05):81-83.
[28] 沙爱敏,吕凡任,尹继明,等.基于变权重组合预测模型的软土路基沉降预测研究[J].数学的实践与认识,2019,49(21):115-122.

结合水对黄土抗剪强度的影响研究

周 豪 毛雪松

(长安大学公路学院)

摘 要 为研究强、弱结合水对黄土抗剪强度的影响,本文通过配制不同结合水率的原状黄土和重塑黄土试件进行直剪试验,试验结果表明:随着黄土中结合水含量的增加,原状黄土的抗剪强度从高于重塑黄土降低到两者基本一致;黄土的黏聚力和内摩擦角减小,且下降趋势为先缓后快再缓。黏聚力主要受土颗粒之间的距离,胶结强度、结合水黏滞性和负孔隙水压力效应等因素影响。内摩擦角主要受黄土的骨架结构,土颗粒之间的咬合状态等因素的影响。两种不同形式的结合水中,弱结合水对黄土黏聚力和内摩擦角的影响更大。

关键词 黄土 抗剪强度 直剪试验 结合水 黏聚力 内摩擦角

0 引 言

干燥状态时,黄土不仅具有较高的结构强度,而且具有很高的基质吸水势,使黄土的强度进一步提高[1]。但遇水时,黄土会产生较大的湿陷变形,影响黄土的工程性质[2]。黄土结构孔隙中胶结物的赋存状态和碳酸钙等盐分的存在形式也对黄土结构体系产生重要影响。黄土对水极其敏感,其工程性质与含水率有较大关系。结合水是指受到土颗粒表面电场作用而吸附于其表面的水,结合水可进一步细分为强结合水与弱结合水。当水分进入干燥黄土时,由于受到黄土基质吸水势的强烈作用,土颗粒迅速吸收水分子形成强、弱结合水[3]。王铁行、李彦龙、张中华等[4-6]指出,黄土中结合水的形成与环境湿度有关,相对湿度小于0.59时形成强结合水,当相对湿度在0.59~0.98时形成弱结合水,并测定了强、弱结合水的热失重区间分别为125~245℃与65~125℃。湿化后,黄土结构发生了巨大变化,大孔隙逐渐减少,而中孔隙随之增加[7-10],表明黄土的原生结构发生破坏,变形也因此产生。根据学者们的大量研究[11-13]可知,含水率增加时,黄土的抗剪强度下降,对于重塑黄土的抗剪强度规律亦是如此[14-15]。但含水率增加时,黄土颗粒吸收水分形成强、弱结合水对抗剪强度的具体影响却研究甚少。因此,本文在前人研究成果的基础上,通过配制不同结合水含率的黄土深入研究结合水对黄土抗剪强度的影响,为工程实践提供参考依据。

1 直剪试验

1.1 试样采集

本试验以陕西省富平县石川河地区黄土作为研究对象,采用规格为ϕ100mm×180mm的钻头,垂直朝下钻取土样,由于取样现场上部为河床,表层黄土含砂量较高,故钻取深度为13m的黄土试样进行研究。钻取过程必须确保原状黄土试样不受扰动,保证钻取出来的试样无开裂。将钻取出来的黄土试样迅速放入土压力盒中装好,并标明土样上下面,在土压力盒外包裹密封膜,保持原状黄土试样的含水率。

1.2 试样制备

李文平[16]提出黏土中强结合水含率w_g与液塑限的关系满足公式$w_g = 0.885w_p$。黄土试样的塑限值为17.57%,故黄土试样的强结合水含率为15.55%。在试验过程中配制了三组不同结合水含率的土样,如表1所示。

原状黄土与重塑黄土含水率设置 表1

土 样	强结合水对应含水率(%)			弱结合水对应含水率(%)		饱和含水率(%)
原状黄土	10	13	15	20	25	29
重塑黄土	10	13	15	20	25	29

1.3 试验方案

本次试验采用的直剪仪器是生产于南京土壤仪器厂的ZJ型应变控制式直剪仪,采用试件的尺寸为ϕ61.8mm×20mm,分别施加50kPa、100kPa、150kPa、200kPa的垂直压力,以0.8mm/min的剪切速率,分别对六组原状黄土试件和重塑黄土试件进行直剪试验。试验过程中记录试件在不同垂直压力下的峰值位移,若没有峰值位移,则选取应力应变曲线上应变量为4mm所对应的强度作为最大值。

2 试验结果与分析

2.1 结合水对抗剪强度的影响

试验数据经过处理后,如图1、图2所示。

在相同含水率,相同垂直压力作用下,原状黄土的抗剪强度要高于重塑黄土,这是因为重塑黄土的原生骨架结构已经破坏,土颗粒间的胶结强度大部分丧失,导致其抗剪强度下降。

随着含水率的增加,原状黄土和重塑黄土试样的抗剪强度均降低,且具有相同的下降趋势。含水率小于15.55%时,黄土中的水分主要以强结合水的形式存在,强结合水具有极强的黏滞性,同时黄土中的负孔隙水压力现象依然存在,保证了黄土的抗剪强度以缓慢的速度下降。但当黄土继续吸收水分,黄土颗粒表面形成弱结合水膜后,黄土的抗剪强度急速下降。弱结合水能够大量溶解胶结物,其水膜具有一定的润滑作用,同时基质吸水势减小,破坏黄土的原生骨架结构。最后黄土的抗剪强度几乎一致,说明在高含水率作用下,原状黄土的破坏接近于将其重塑。

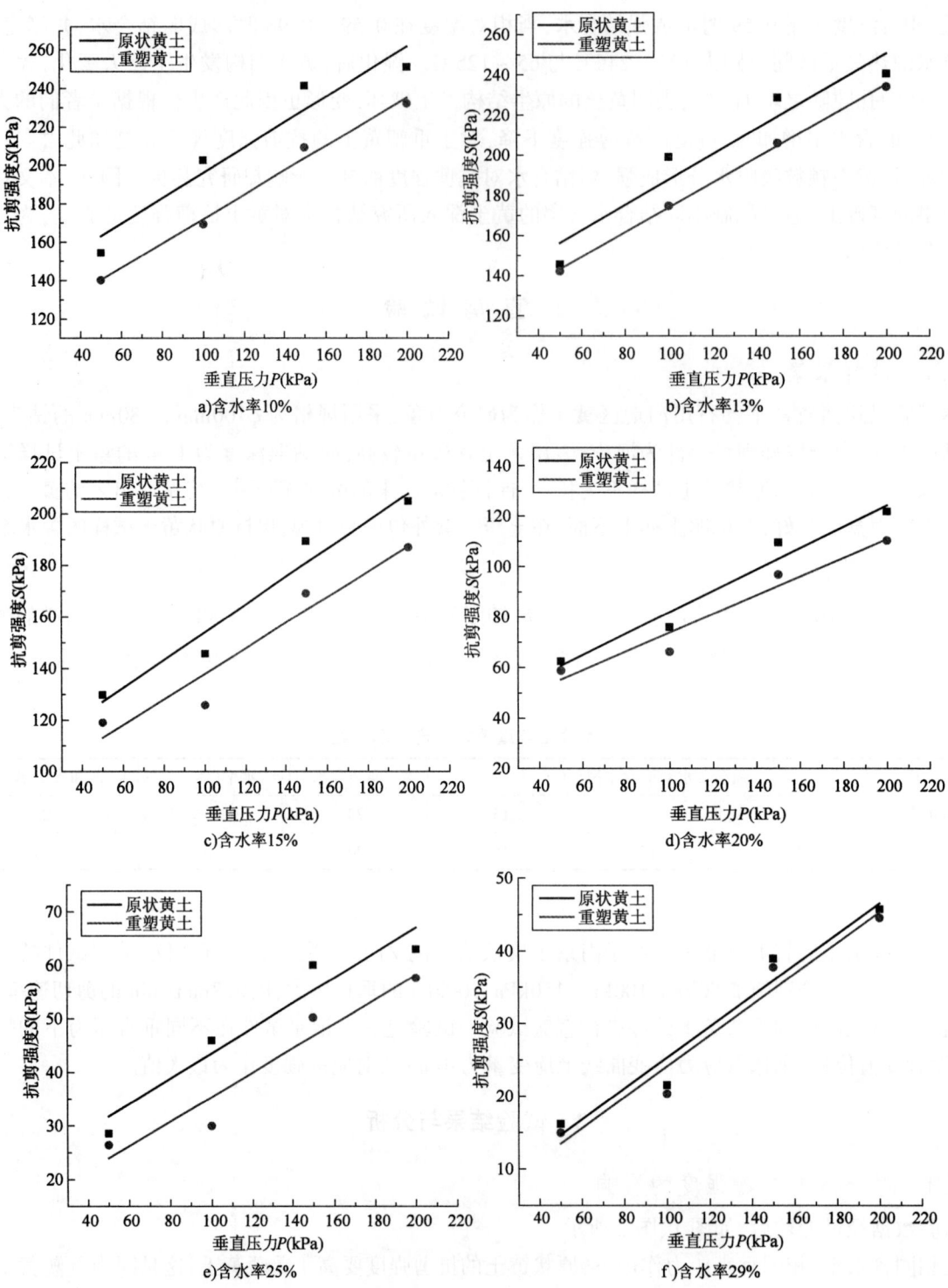

图 1 不同含水率条件下原状黄土试样和重塑黄土试样抗剪强度与垂直压力关系

2.2 结合水对黄土内摩擦角与黏聚力的影响

根据土的抗剪强度公式(1)可知,土的抗剪强度可以通过内摩擦角和黏聚力两大指标来表征。

$$\tau = c + \sigma\tan\varphi \tag{1}$$

式中:τ——土的抗剪强度;

c——土的黏聚力；
φ——土的内摩擦角。

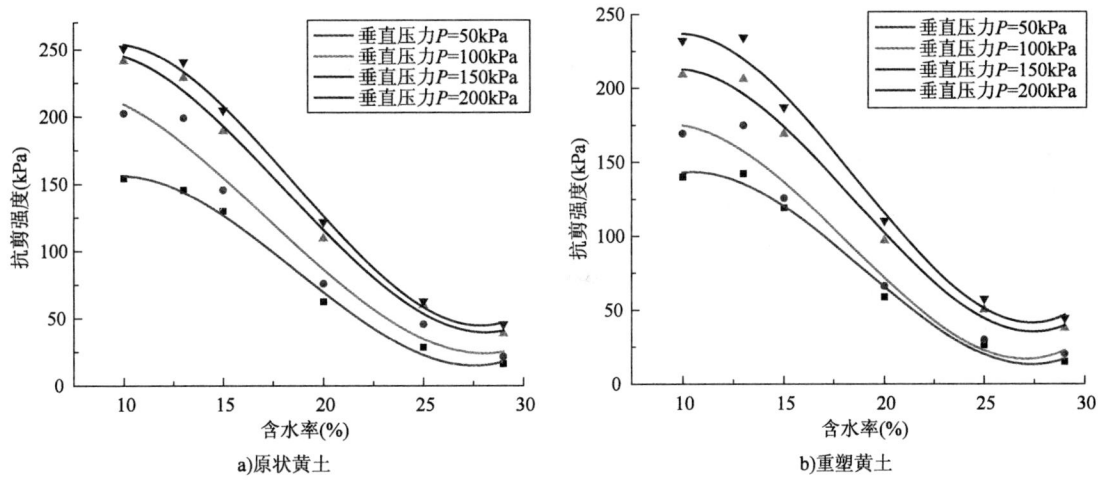

图 2　不同垂直压力条件下原状黄土试样和重塑黄土试样抗剪强度与含水率关系

不同结合水含量对黄土黏聚力和内摩擦角影响关系曲线，如图 3 所示。随着含水率的增大，无论是重塑黄土还是原状黄土，其内摩擦角和黏聚力都在减小，且趋势相同。

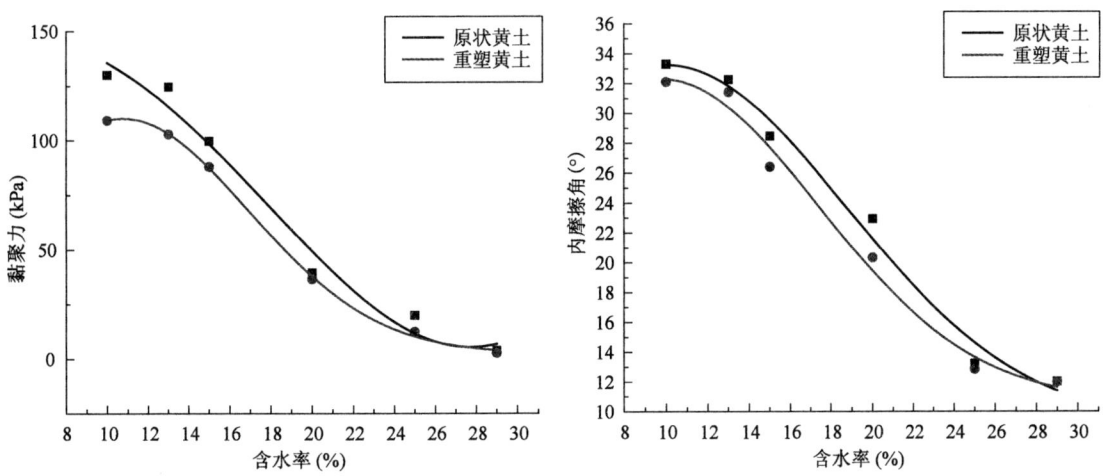

图 3　含水率对黄土黏聚力和内摩擦角影响关系曲线

通过分析可以得到，当结合水的含水率为 10%、13% 和 15%，即为强结合水状态下时，拟合曲线的斜率较小，主要原因是强结合水紧紧吸附在土颗粒周围，对内摩擦角的影响不大。强结合水含水率较低，水膜厚度薄，溶解的胶结物有限，同时其具有黏滞性，因此对黏聚力的影响也不大。此时，原状黄土的黏聚力和内摩擦角均大于重塑黄土，其根本原因在于重塑黄土破坏了黄土的原生骨架结构。

当结合水的含水率为 20% 和 25%，拟合曲线的斜率较大，此时黄土中的结合水主要是以弱结合水的形式存在。弱结合水含量较大能够大量溶解胶结物，因此土颗粒间的黏聚力会迅速降低。弱结合水具有润滑作用，黄土结构发生破坏，因此土颗粒间的内摩擦角快速降低。

当含水率超过 25% 时，黏聚力和内摩擦角的变化幅度均不大。黄土的负孔隙水压力效应基本丧失，原状黄土和重塑黄土的黏聚力和内摩擦角接近一致，说明两者的土结构在饱和状态下基本一致。

3 结 语

本文通过设置含水率为10%、13%、15%、20%、25%和29%来配制不同结合水含量的原状黄土和重塑黄土试件进行直剪试验,得出以下结论:

(1)随着黄土中结合水含量的增加,无论是原状黄土还是重塑黄土抗剪强度均不断下降。在相同条件下,原状黄土的抗剪强度要高于重塑黄土。在相同的垂直压力下,无论是原状黄土还是重塑黄土,含水率接近饱和状态时,其抗剪强度几乎一致。

(2)随着黄土中结合水含量的增加,黄土的黏聚力和内摩擦角逐渐减小,且下降趋势均为先缓后快再缓。黏聚力主要受土颗粒之间的距离,胶结强度、结合水黏滞性和负孔隙水压力效应等因素影响。内摩擦角主要受黄土的骨架结构,土颗粒之间的咬合状态等因素的影响。两种不同的结合水中,弱结合水对黄土黏聚力和内摩擦角的影响更大。

参考文献

[1] 邢义川.非饱和土的有效应力与变形——强度特性规律的研究[D].西安:西安理工大学,2001.
[2] 陈存礼,高鹏,胡再强.黄土的增湿变形特性及其与结构性的关系[J].岩石力学与工程学报,2006,25(07):1352-1360.
[3] 骆亚生,张爱军.黄土结构性的研究成果及其新发展[J].水力发电学报,2004,23(06):66-69.
[4] 李彦龙.非饱和黄土结合水特性及水分迁移问题研究[D].西安:西安建筑科技大学,2015.
[5] 王铁行,李彦龙,苏立君.黄土表面吸附结合水的类型和界限划分[J].岩土工程学报,2014,36(05):942-948.
[6] 张中华,李萍,李同录.黄土结合水含量及其与物理指标的关系研究[J].工程地质学报,2016,24(06):1004-1009.
[7] 方祥位,欧益希,李春海,等.浸湿对原状Q_2黄土微观结构与力学性质的影响研究[J].岩土力学,2015,36(S2):111-117.
[8] 李春海,方祥位,申春妮,等.浸水湿化引起的Q_2黄土微观结构变化[J].四川建筑科学研究,2016,42(03):40-45.
[9] 陈阳,李喜安,黄润秋,等.影响黄土湿陷性因素的微观试验研究[J].工程地质学报,2015,23(04):646-653.
[10] 方祥位,申春妮,汪龙,等.Q_2黄土浸水前后微观结构变化研究[J].岩土力学,2013,34(05):1319-1324.
[11] 张茂花,谢永利,刘保健.增湿时黄土的抗剪强度特性分析[J].岩土力学,2006(07):1195-1200.
[12] 申春妮,方祥位,陈正汉.Q_2黄土的非饱和直剪试验研究[J].地下空间与工程学报,2010,6(04):724-728.
[13] 王娟娟,张秀丽,王铁行.考虑含水量和密度影响的压实黄土抗剪强度特性研究[J].西安建筑科技大学学报(自然科学版),2014,46(05):687-691.
[14] 张奎,李梦姿,杨贝贝.含水率和干密度对重塑黄土抗剪强度的影响[J].安徽理工大学学报(自然科学版),2016,36(03):74-79.
[15] 朱志坤.干密度和含水量对太原重塑黄土强度及强度参数影响的研究[D].山西:太原理工大学,2018.
[16] 李生林.土中结合水译文集[M].北京:地质出版社,1982.

Stability Analysis of Cracked Loess Slope Based on Upper-bound Method

Linxuan Zhu

(University of Chang'an)

Abstract In order to study the influence of vertical cracks on the stability of loess slope, a loess slope with inclined slope top and pre-existing vertical cracks was analyzed. Formulas for the external work rates and internal energy dissipation rates of the failure mechanism were derived within the framework of limit analysis. An optimization program was developed in combination with the strength reduction method to search for the most critical failure mechanism and the corresponding upper-bound factor of safety as well as the corresponding position of vertical crack. In addition, taking one slope along Huang-Yan Expressway as example, the safety factor of the slope was calculated by the proposed method and the finite difference method respectively. And the influence of the distance between the crack on the slope top and the slope shoulder on the stability of the loess slope was discussed. The results show that the distribution of safety factor obtained by those two methods are the same. Safety factor decreases with the increase of the distance and it reaches the minimum when the threshold of the distance is reached. Thereafter factor of safety increases slowly and finally remains stable. The results of the proposed method are slightly larger than that of the finite difference method. And the relative error of the final result is 0.6%, which shows the accuracy and rationality of this method.

Keywords Loess slope Vertical tensile crack Safety factor Upper bound method Numerical simulation

0 Introduction

The presence of vertical tensile cracks on loess slope top surface is of major concern to researchers and engineers, as this phenomenon is typically considered to be an early indication of instability and potential landslides(Li et al., 2018). It is reported that more than 1000 landslides have been recorded over the past two decades(Li and Mo, 2019). Therefore, it is of great significance to study the crack and its influence on slope stability.

The effects of the cracks on the stability of slopes have been investigated using different methods, which can be generally grouped into three categories: the limit equilibrium method, limit analysis method, and numerical methods(Rao et al, 2020; Yang et al. 2020). Baker(1981) first determined the effects of tension cracks on the safety of soil slopes using the variational limit equilibrium approach and incorporated the depths of the potential tension cracks in to stability charts. Kaniraj and Abdullah(1993) studied the effects of berms and tension cracks on the stability of embankments on soft soils, but it is based on the assumption of full-height dry tension crack. Zhang et al. (2008, 2018) used the limit equilibrium method to obtain the formula of crack depth from different angles, and explained the conditions of tension crack occurrence. However, the limit equilibrium method is not rigorous, and is limited in its capacity for analysis, since it usually requires the user to assume a crack depth and location in the slope. Based on the kinematic limit analysis approach, Utili(2013) investigated the locations and depths of dry and water-filled cracks in soil slopes, and the stability factor was expressed as the upper bound to the dimensionless critical height, $\gamma h/c$, which is not commonly used in engineering practice. Xie et al(2018) analyzed the effects of crack depth and crack angle to the stability of expansive soil slope using the upper bound theory, whereas, the influence of crack location was not considered. Yang and Zhang (2020) evaluated the three-dimensional (3D) stability of soil slopes with pre-existing cracks and the reinforcement effects of pile within the strict framework of limit analysis. Over the past decades, numerical approaches have also been widely used to estimate crack generation and expansion mechanism and the influence of vertical crack on the stability of loess slope (Wang et al, 2018; Cai and Ugai, 2000; Chang et al. 2016; Wang, 2018). They found that the existence of crack reduced the safety factor, and the value of safety factor was related to the distance between the crack and the edge of the tableland, the depth of the crack, the tendency and inclination of the crack and other parameters. Generally, the existing studies have mainly focused on the existence and distribution of cracks that affect the stability of loess slopes. However, the effects of the inclination of slope top and depth of vertical tensile cracks on the stability of loess slopes have rarely been studied.

Therefore, the present work aims to investigate the stability of loess slope with pre-existing vertical tensile crack and inclined crest. An optimization program was developed in combination with the strength reduction method to search for the most critical failure mechanism and the corresponding safety factor. And the effects of distance between the crack on the slope top and the slope shoulder on the stability of the loess slope was discussed. The research results can be used to improve the accuracy of slope safety analysis and provide theoretical reference for slope protection and reinforcement.

1 Depth of a Vertical Crack

Owing to the limitations of boundary conditions, cracks beyond a certain depth cannot exist naturally. To form a reasonable and admissible failure mechanism, the depths of the cracks need to be restricted during optimization. This issue can be solved by considering an unsupported vertical cut, where the critical height of the cut is equal to the maximum depth on a vertical crack (Yang and Zhang, 2020). Following this approach, Terzaghi (1943) first proposed the depth of vertical tensile crack based on the Rankine's earth pressure theory, as follow:

$$Z = \frac{2c}{\gamma} \cdot \tan\left(45° + \frac{\varphi}{2}\right) \tag{1}$$

Where, c is cohesion, γ is soil bulk density, and φ is internal friction angle.

Spencer (1968) proposed a formula for calculating the depth of tensile crack for the arc sliding surface and found that the depth is only related to γ and c and φ. It can be expressed as follow:

$$Z = \frac{2c}{\gamma}\sqrt{\frac{1+\sin\varphi}{1-\sin\varphi}} \tag{2}$$

As shown by Zhang et al. (2008), a differential equation for right-angle slope and obtained the formula of crack depth, as follow:

$$Z = \frac{2c}{\gamma}(\tan\varphi + \sec\varphi) \tag{3}$$

In terms of the theoretical study of the crack depth, the form of Terzaghi, Spencer and Zhang-Li formulas are all $Z = A \cdot 2c/\gamma$. Although the calculation methods of the coefficient A in those formulas are different, their results are nearly the same. Therefore, Eq. (1) was selected to evaluate the depth of vertical tensile crack.

2 Derivation of Control Equation

2.1 Calculation Model of Loess Slope

The logarithmic spiral of the slope failure mode is shown in Fig 1. The length of QP is X_2, the horizontal distance of the slope surface at all levels from top to bottom are X_3 and X_1. The slope height is H and the slope height from top to bottom are H_2 and H_1. The inclination of the slope top is β, and the inclination angle of AD is $\alpha\alpha$. The slope from the top to the bottom slope of each level are $\alpha_1 = \arctan(H_1/X_1)$, $\alpha_2 = \arctan(H_2/X_3)$. The length of OA, OD, OB, OC and OQ is R_h, R_0, L_B, L_C and L_Q, The corresponding inclination angle are θ_h, θ_0, θ_B, θ_C and θ_Q, respectively. The potential tension crack CD is assumed to develop vertically from the crest of the soil slope. Assuming that the failure plane AD is a logarithmic spiral plane and the failure plane passes through the slanted leg. The sliding body $AQPBCD$ makes a rotational movement about a stable body below the rotational center O and the relative helical plane AD. AD can be expressed as:

$$R = R_0 e^{(\theta - \theta_0)\tan\varphi} \tag{4}$$

Where, R is the distance of a generic point of the spiral to its center O, θ is the angle formed by R with a reference axis (Fig. 1), and θ_0 and R_0 identifying the angle and distance of a particular point of the spiral to its center.

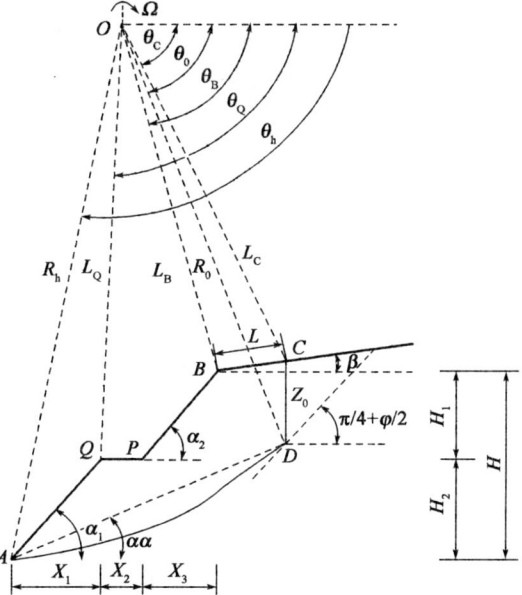

Fig. 1 Rotational Failure Mechanism for Slopes with Cracks

2.1.1 Geometric Relationship of Slope

In the vertical and horizontal direction of AD, the following equations are obtained, respectively:

$$H - Z_0 + L\sin\beta = R_h \sin\theta_h - R_0 \sin\theta_0 \tag{5}$$

$$L\cos\beta + X_1 + X_2 + X_3 = R_0 \cos\theta_0 - R_h \cos\theta_h \tag{6}$$

Combing Eq. (5) with Eq. (6), $\alpha\alpha$ is obtained as follows:

$$\alpha\alpha = \arctan\left(\frac{H - Z_0 + L\sin\beta}{L\cos\beta + X_1 + X_2 + X_3}\right) \tag{7}$$

Following the principle of the sine theorem in the triangle OAQ, R_h can be written as follows:

$$R_h = R_0 \cdot \frac{\sin(\theta_0 + \alpha\alpha)}{\sin(\theta_h + \alpha\alpha)} \tag{8}$$

According to Eq. (4), R_h can also be expressed as:

$$R_h = R_0 e^{(\theta_h - \theta_0)\tan\varphi} \tag{9}$$

Combing Eq. (8) with Eq. (9), θ_h can be obtained from solving the simultaneous equations by Newton iteration method. And combing Eq. (6) with Eq. (9), R_0 expressed as follow:

$$R_0 = \frac{H - Z_0 + L\sin\beta}{e^{(\theta_h - \theta_0)\tan\varphi}\sin\theta_h - \sin\theta_0} \tag{10}$$

θ_C and L_C can be obtained from the geometrical relationship of the slope, as follow:

$$\theta_C = \arctan\left(\frac{R_0\sin\theta_0 - Z_0}{R_0\cos\theta_0}\right) \tag{11}$$

$$L_C = \frac{R_0\cos\theta_0}{\cos\theta_C} \tag{12}$$

Following the principle of the sine theorem in the triangle OAQ and OBC, θ_h, L_Q, θ_B, L_B can be expressed as follow:

$$\frac{\sqrt{H_1^2 + X_1^2}}{\sin(\theta_h - \theta_Q)} - \frac{R_h}{\sin(\theta_Q + \alpha_1)} = 0 \tag{13}$$

$$L_Q = \frac{\sin(\theta_h + \alpha_1)}{\sin(\theta_h - \theta_Q)} \cdot \sqrt{H_1^2 + X_1^2} \tag{14}$$

$$\frac{L}{\sin(\theta_B - \theta_C)} - \frac{L_C}{\sin(\theta_B + \beta)} = 0 \tag{15}$$

$$L_B = \frac{\sin(\theta_C + \beta)}{\sin(\theta_B - \theta_C)} \cdot L \tag{16}$$

2.1.2 External Work Rate and Internal Energy Dissipation Rate

(1) External work rate of slope W_{out}

The external power of $AQPBCD$ area is also calculated by superposition method, $AQPBCD$ area = OAD area − OAQ area − OQP area − OPB area − OBC area + ODC area. The external work rate can be expressed as:

$$W_{out} = W_1 - W_2 - W_3 - W_4 - W_5 + W_6 \tag{17}$$

Where, W_1, W_2, W_3, W_4, W_5 and W_6 are the power of gravity the OAD, OAQ, OQP, OPB, OBC and ODC area, respectively. The calculation diagram of each part of the sliding body $AQPBCD$ as shown in Fig. 2. The calculation of the external work rates can be found in Chen(1975), so here only the final expressions are given.

the power of the OAD area gravity:

$$W_1 = \int dW_1 = \{(3\tan\varphi\cos\theta_h + \sin\theta_h)e^{[3(\theta_h - \theta_0)\tan\varphi]} - 3\tan\varphi\cos\theta_0 - \sin\theta_0\} \times \frac{\gamma R_0^3 \Omega}{3(1 + 9\tan^2\varphi)} \tag{18}$$

the power of the OAQ area gravity:

$$W_2 = \left[\Omega\frac{1}{3}(2R_H\cos\theta_H + X_1)\right] \cdot \left[\frac{1}{2}\gamma R_h\sin(\theta_H + \alpha_1) \cdot \sqrt{X_1^2 + H_1^2}\right] \tag{19}$$

the power of the OQP area gravity:

$$W_3 = \left[\Omega\frac{1}{3}(2L_Q\cos\theta_Q + X_2)\right] \cdot \left[\frac{1}{2}\gamma L_Q\sin(\theta_Q) \cdot X_2\right] \tag{20}$$

the power of the OPB area gravity:

$$W_4 = \left[\Omega\frac{1}{3}(2L_P\cos\theta_P - X_3)\right] \cdot \left[\frac{1}{2}\gamma L_P\sin(\theta_P + \alpha_2) \cdot \sqrt{H_2^2 + X_3^2}\right] \tag{21}$$

the power of the OBC area gravity:

$$W_5 = \left[\Omega\frac{1}{3}(2L_C\cos\theta_C - L\cos\beta)\right] \cdot \left[\frac{1}{2}\gamma L_C\sin(\theta_C + \beta) \cdot L\right] \tag{22}$$

the power of the ODC area gravity:

$$W_6 = \left(\Omega\frac{2}{3}R_0\cos\theta_0\right) \cdot \left[\frac{1}{2}\gamma R_0\cos(\theta_0) \cdot Z_0\right] \tag{23}$$

(2) Internal energy dissipation rate W_{in}

$$W_{in} = \int_{\theta_0}^{\theta_h} c(V\cos\varphi)\frac{Rd\theta}{\cos\varphi} = \frac{cR_0^2\Omega}{2\tan\varphi}\left[e^{2(\theta_h - \theta_0)\tan\varphi} - 1\right] \tag{24}$$

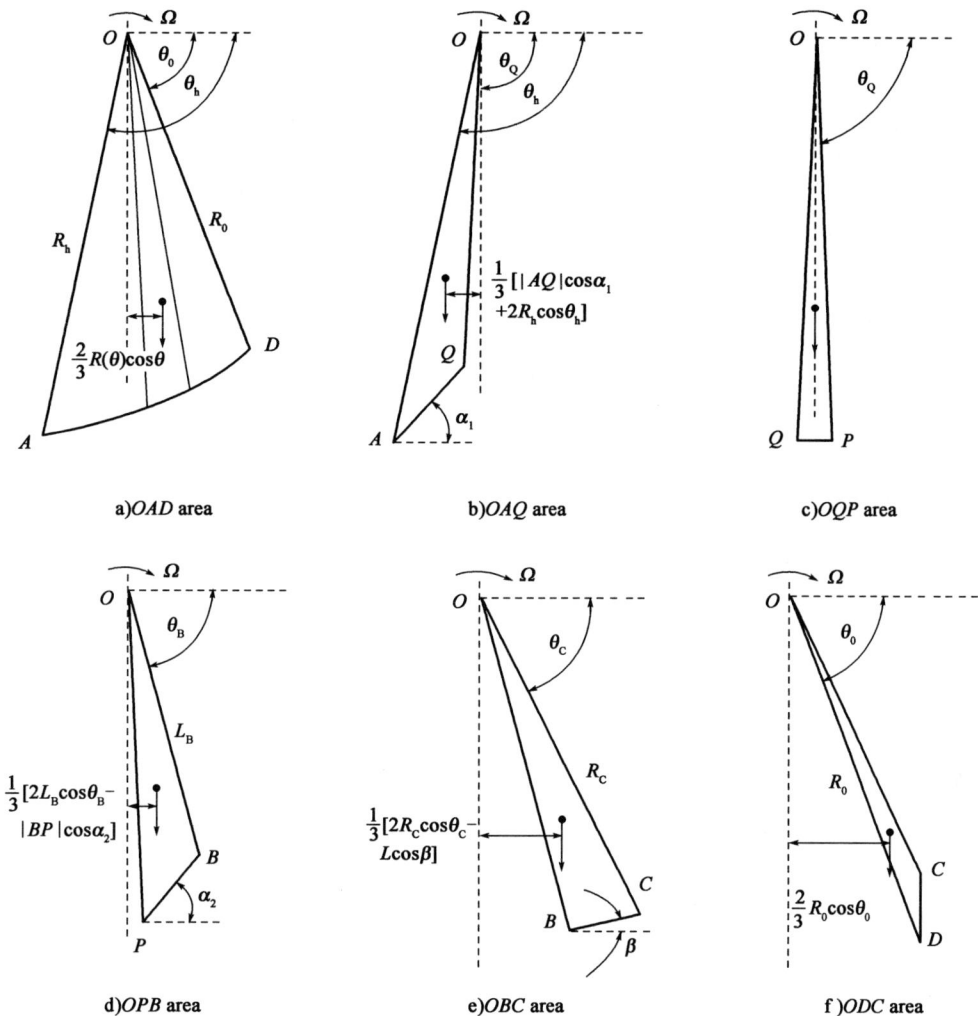

Fig. 2　Illustration of Work Dissipation on Each Part of the Slope

2.2　Slope Safety Factor Analysis

An optimization program combined with the strength reduction method was developed to search for the safety factor(K). Notably, the results of the kinematic method are upper bounds to the actual solutions, so the lowest result is the optimal solution. The problem turns out to be the optimization of an objective function with multiple variables. The K can be captured through an iteration process, by solving the implicit equation of K, as follows:

$$K = \min f(H_1, H_2, X_1, X_2, X_3, \alpha_1, \alpha_2, \beta, \gamma, \varphi, c, L_1, K_1) \tag{25}$$

Where, L_1 is the distance of the slope top, and K_1 is the upper bound of the safety factor. Flowchart of the optimization scheme as shown in Fig. 3. The accuracy of $K_{\min}$ is affected by the traversal range of L and K.

3　Verification

A four-stage loess slope along Huang-yan expressway is selected in this study, and it has been simplified to a two-stage slope as shown in Fig. 4. The material parameters of the slope are listed in Tab. 1. ψ is dilatancy angle, E is tensile modulus, μ is poisson ratio, σ_t is tensile strength of the soil.

Material Parameters of Slope　　Tab. 1

c(kPa)	γ(kN/m^3)	φ(°)	β(°)	ψ(°)	E(kN/m^2)	μ	σ_t(kN/m^2)
51.3	17.59	36.1	18.4	36.1	8.927E3	0.25	29.9

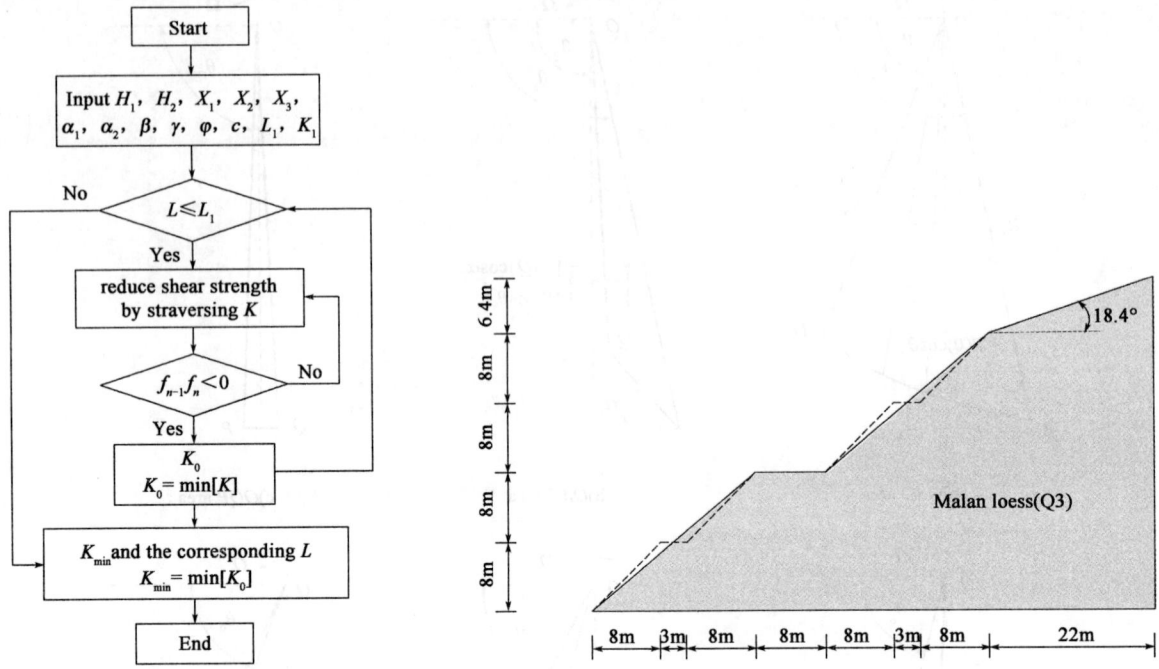

Fig. 3 Flowchart of the Optimization Scheme

Fig. 4 Simplified Geometry Dimension of Slope

The distribution rule of K-L obtained by optimization program as shown in Fig. 5. The safety factor K is influenced by the distance L between vertical crack and slope shoulder, especially when the L increases from 0 m to 15 m. K decreases significantly with the increase of L and it reduces to the minimum value (K_{min} = 2.147) when the distance L is 20 m. Thereafter the change of L has no significant effect on K, with only a small increase. And the safety factor is finally increased to 2.15.

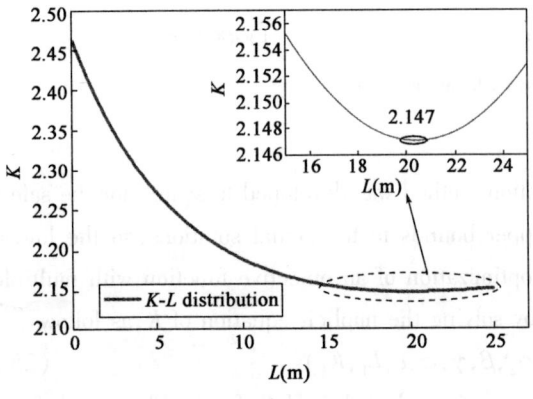

Fig. 5 K-L Distribution

Numerical Simulation Results Corresponding to Different L as shown in Fig. 6. In order to verify the effectiveness and accuracy of the proposed method, the K-L distribution law is compared with that calculated by FLAC 3D. Taking L as 0.5 m, 5 m, 10 m, 15 m, 19.2 m and 20.5 m, the corresponding slope models with a pre-existing vertical crack are established. As shown in Fig. 6, the safety factors corresponding to different L are 2.38, 2.30, 2.28, 2.26, 2.25, 2.23 respectively.

As shown in Fig. 7, the distribution of K-L can be obtained by fitting results obtained through numerical simulation. It can be founded that the value of K decreases dramatically with the increase of L. And the minimum safety factor K_{min} is 2.16 and the corresponding L is 20 m. Then with the increase of L, K slowly increases to 2.17. The reason is that the propagation path of the plastic zone is affected by the crack location. When the distance between vertical crack and slope shoulder is large, the plastic zone does not reach the position where the crack exists. Therefore, the crack has little influence on the penetration of slope sliding surface (Wang, 2018).

The results of theoretical calculation and numerical simulation are shown in Fig. 8. It can be found that the maximum error of safety factor is 0.04 when L is 8.5 m, which confirm that the theoretical calculation method in this study is reliable. And the numerical simulation results are larger than the theoretical calculation. Firstly, this is because the range of slope boundary will affect the accuracy of results when analyzing the slope stability using

FLAC3D. The larger the range of slope boundary is, the larger the safety factor of slope is. Secondly, when modeling, the left and right and bottom boundaries are bound to limit the displacement of the slope, so the safety factor is larger(Xu et al., 2019).

a)0.5m b)5m c)10m d)15m e)19.2m f)20.5m

Fig. 6 Numerical Simulation Results Corresponding to Different L

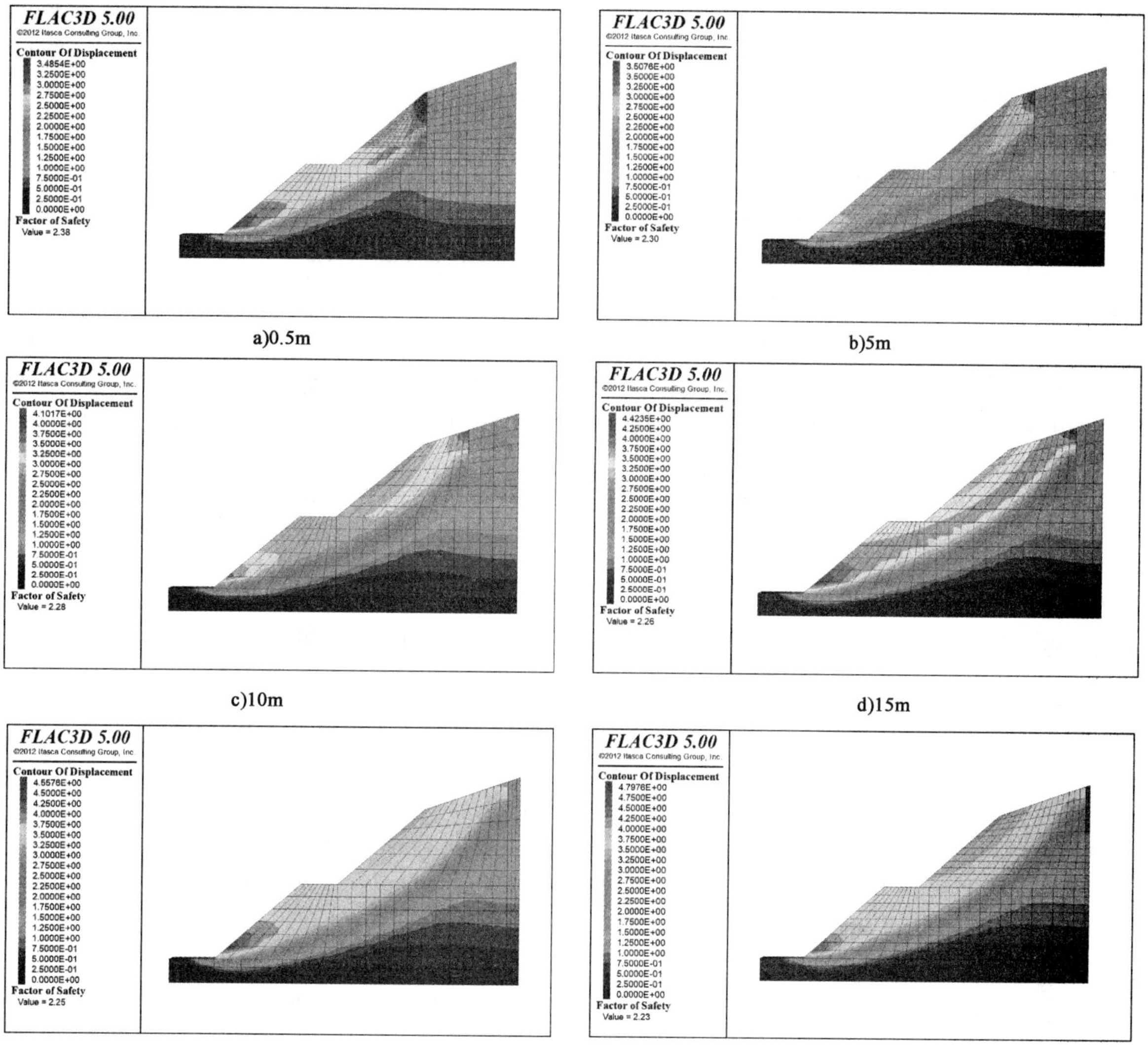

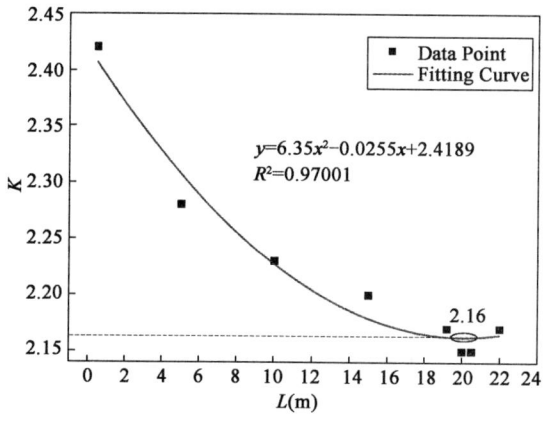

Fig. 7 K-L Distribution

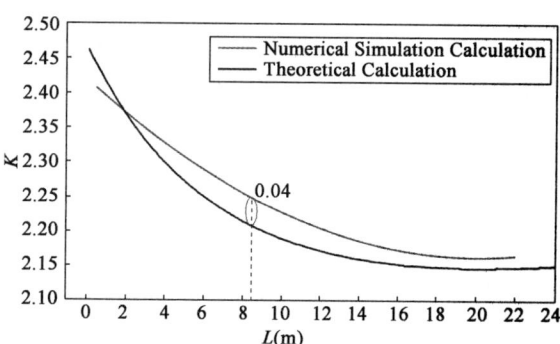

Fig. 8 K-L Distribution

4 Conclusions

This article presents a new method to estimate the factor of safety (K) of cracked loess slopes. By employing the upper-bound theorem, the formulas for the external work rates and internal energy dissipation rates of the failure mechanism is obtained. Combining with the strength reduction method, the lowest solution among all possible results and its corresponding location are sought by an optimization program developed in MATLAB. In particular, the inclination angle of slope top has been taken into account in the analysis. According to the numerical results, the main conclusions are drawn as follows.

(1) The change of the distance between the crack on the slope top and the slope shoulder affects the safety factor. Firstly, the safety factor decreases with the increase of the distance. Then it increases slowly with the increase of distance after the safety factor reduces to the minimum. Finally, the safety factor remains stable.

(2) The safety factor obtained by numerical simulation is larger than that obtained by the optimization program. The maximum error of safety factor is 0.04 when L is 8.5m. The minimum safety factor of numerical simulation is 2.147 and the final result obtained by the optimization program is 2.16, the relative error is 0.6%.

(3) The stability analysis method proposed in this paper is only applicable to the stability analysis of homogeneous loess slope. However, for the slope composed of many different soils, such as clay and rock, its applicability needs further study.

References

[1] Baker R. Tensile strength, tension cracks, and stability of slopes[J]. Soils Found, 1981, 21(2):1-17.
[2] Cai F, Ugai K. Numerical analysis of the stability of a slope reinforced with piles[J]. Soils and Foundations, 2000, 40(1):73-84.
[3] Chang J M, Song S W, Feng H P. Analysis of Loess Slope Stability Considering Cracking and Shear Failures[J]. Journal of Failure Analysis and Prevention, 2016, 16(6):982-989.
[4] Chen W F. Limit analysis and soil plasticity[M]. New York:Elsevier, 1975.
[5] Kaniraj S R, Abdullah H. Effect of berms and tension crack on the stability of embankments on soft soils[J]. Soils and Foundations, 1993, 33(4):99-107.
[6] Li Y R, Mao J R, Xiang X Q, Mo P. Factors influencing development of cracking-sliding failures of loess across the eastern Huangtu Plateau of China[J]. Nature Hazards and Earth System Sciences, 2018, 18(4):1223-1231.
[7] Li Y R, Mo P. A unified landslide classification system for loess slopes: A critical review[J]. Geomorphology, 2019, 340:67-83.
[8] Rao P P, Wu J, Mo Z H. 3D Limit Analysis of the Transient Stability of Slope during Pile Driving in Nonhomogeneous and Anisotropic Soil[R]. Advances in Civil Engineering, 2020.
[9] Spencer E. Effect of tension on stability of embankments[J]. Journal of Soil Mechanics and Foundations Div, 1968, 5(94):1159-1173.
[10] Terzaghi K. Theoretical Soil Mechanics[M]. New York:JohnWiley & Sons, 1943.
[11] Utili S. Investigation by limit analysis on the stability of slopes with cracks[J]. Geotechnique, 2013, 63(2), 140.
[12] Wang Z J, Luo J W, Pan J Y, et al. The joint strength formula and its application in disaster evaluation of loess slope[C]//2018 International Conference on Civil and Hydraulic Engineering, Qingdao, 2018, 189: 022041.
[13] Wang X P. Loess slope fissures and their influence on slope stability[D]. Xi'an:Chang'an University, 2018.

[14] Xie C R, Shen Q, Wu Z W, et al. Stability Analysis for the Expansive Soil Slope Considering the Influence of Cracks Based on the Upper Bound Method, [C]//2018 International Conference on Civil and Hydraulic Engineering, Qingdao, 2018, 022014.

[15] Xu W, Sun W F, Jiang L L, et al Discussion on the influence of slope boundary on FLAC3D numerical simulation stability calculation[J]. Highway transportation technology (Application Technology Edition), 15(03):8-9.

[16] Yang X L, Zhang S. Stability analysis of 3D cracked slope reinforced with piles[J]. Computers and Geotechnics, 2020, 122.

[17] Zhang N X, Li X. A new formula for limit equilibrium flat roof vertical slope, [C]//The 8th National Engineering Geology Congress, Shanghai, 2008, 260-265.

[18] Zhang N X, Li X, Sheng Z P. A new formula for calculating the depth of the fracture along the slope after using the principle of inflection point[J]. Journal of engineering geology, 2018, 26(01), 157-163.

Analysis of the Influence of Pipe Pile Composite Foundation on the Earth Pressure and Deformation Characteristics of Circular Pipe Culvert

Zhenyu Song[1] Weifeng Zhao[1] Zhongju Feng[1] Siqi Wang[1] Yumeng Hao[2]

(1. Chang'an University; 2. China Conmunications Construction Croup Sencond Highway Exploration Design and Research Institute Co. Ltd)

Abstract Taking the valley topography in the southern mountain area as the engineering condition, through the centrifugal model test, the influence of the length of pipe pile on the side of the culvert on earth pressure and deformation characteristics of pipe culvert under different filling height were analyzed. The results indicate that: ①when the height of equal settling surface is 5.7m to 6.5m, the length of pipe pile on the side of culvert is 10m to 20m. When the length of the pipe pile on the side of the culvert is increased, both the absolute value of the difference between internal and external settlement of the soil layer and the height of the equal settling surface will decrease. Once the length of the pipe pile on the side of the culvert exceeds 15m, the height of the equal settling surface almost does not change, and stabilizes at 5.7m in the end. ② the higher the filling height, the more obvious the influence of the length of pipe pile on the side of culvert on the variation of earth pressure at culvert top, culvert side and culvert bottom.

Keywords Pipe culvert Earth pressure Centrifugal model test Pile length High fill

0 Introduction

At present, the formula of calculating earth pressure by the settlement difference δ of pipe top as shown by Gu Anquan(1981); The variation law of strain and stress, earth pressure around pipe and culvert deformation of steel bellows culvert as shown by Feng Zhongju(2013). A method for determining the basic allowable value of bearing capacity considering strength and settlement control as indicated by Zheng Junjie(2009). The load reduction Mechanism of reinforced bridge load reduction method as illuminated by Ma Qiang(2012). A formula for calculating the vertical earth pressure at the top of the culvert, which can take time into account as illuminated by Chen Baoguo(2013).

Some international scholars have also put forward a more developed theoretical system: The vertical earth pressure of the culvert causes the uneven settlement of the soil through the theoretical analysis of the circular pipe culvert as testified by Junsuk Kang(2007). The load of the repaired culvert, measured the response at a higher load level to determine the final limit state as testified by Jacob Tetreault(2020). A discrete-continuous model which can represent positive arch and negative arch as testified by Dancygier(2003). The interaction factor of the culvert is a function of the height of the soil column above the culvert as illuminated by Abuhajar (2015); The relationship between the filling height and the pressure and internal force of the culvert as indicated by Randy Rainwater(2005).

Through centrifugal model test, this paper analyzes the influence of the length of the pipe pile on the side of culvert on the earth pressure, deformation characteristics and structural stress characteristics of pipe culvert under different filling height.

1 Centrifugal Model Test Design

1.1 Parameters of Centrifugal Model Test and Arrangement of Test Elements

1.1.1 Similarity Law of Centrifugal Model Test

The stress, strain and displacement produced during the centrifugal model test of high-filled culvert depend on the following physical quantities:

(1) geometric factors such as calculated size and buried depth of culvert.
(2) the properties of the soil around the culvert.
(3) the properties of culvert structure materials.
(4) the initial stress state of soil.

The similarity law of centrifugal model of high fill culvert as shown in Tab 1.

Similarity Law of Centrifugal Test for High-fill Culverts Tab. 1

Parameters	Prototype	Model	Similar or dissimilar
Gravity Acceleration	g	ng	Similar
Filling Material 1	v	v	Similar
	$\gamma/\rho g$	$\gamma/\rho g$	Similar
	d'/L	d'/L	Similar
Initial Stress	σ_0/C	σ_0/C	Similar
Geometry	h/L	h/L	Similar
	D/L	D/L	Similar
	d/L	d/L	Similar
Filling Material 2	φ	φ	Similar
	$\gamma L/C$	$\gamma L/C$	Similar
	E/C	E/C	Similar
Culvert Structure response	σ/C	σ/C	Similar
	ε	ε	Similar
	δ/h	δ/h	Similar

1.1.2 Design of Culvert Model and Layout of Test Elements

Plexiglass is used to replace concrete as culvert material to simulate its stress characteristics in the experiment.

The culvert model is made on a scale of 1:50, according to the prototype. The size of the large model box is 700mm × 360mm × 500mm, and the length of the culvert model is designed as 300mm so that it can be put into the model box. The design parameters of the culvert prototype and model are shown in Fig. 1a) and Fig. 1b).

In the experiment, the data are collected by the test elements and processed by computer. According to the results, the earth pressure of the culvert, the deformation of the soil around the culvert and the stress distribution of the structure are studied and analyzed.

The strain gauges and earth pressure boxes are arranged at the top and the foundation of the culvert, the back of the culvert abutment, respectively. Except for the strain gauges are arranged inside the culvert, the position of the test elements is arranged symmetrically, the test elements of the culvert model are arranged and the measuring points are numbered as shown in Fig. 1c).

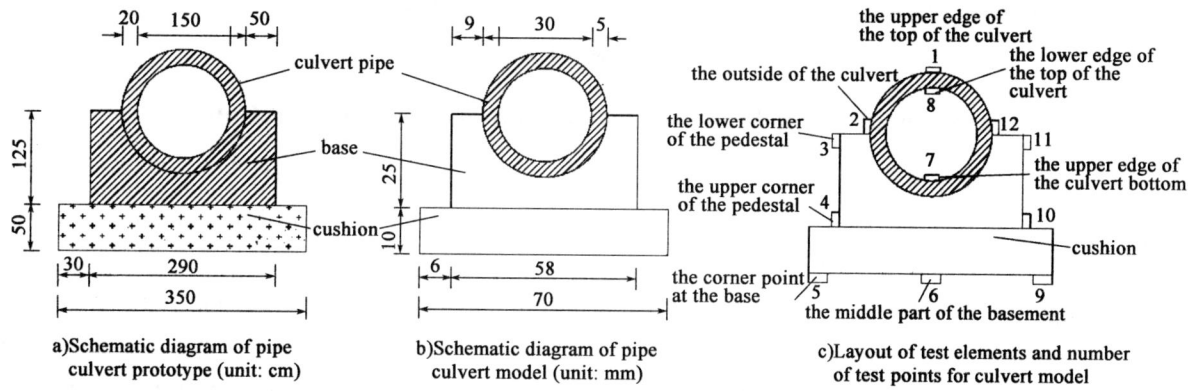

Fig. 1 Diagram of Culvert Design

1.2 Scheme Design of Centrifugal Model Test

1.2.1 Working Conditions of Changing the Height of Fill

In the high fill culvert engineering, because of the deep soft soil and high fill, the foundation bearing capacity of some sections can not meet the design requirements, so the prestressed pipe pile composite foundation is adopted in part of the high fill culvert foundation. Based on the model test, the mechanical characteristics of the culvert treated by prestressed pipe pile and the distribution of soil pressure are studied, a reasonable design methods of prestressed pipe pile foundation treatment of high fill culvert will put forward.

In the centrifugal model test, the change of filling height is simulated by changing the acceleration of centrifuge, the earth pressure of culvert and the deformation law of soil around culvert under different filling height are studied. The modulus of foundation soil is 20MPa, the width of gully is 7.5m, and the slope of gully is 45°, the height of fill is 5m, 10m, 15m, 20m, 25m, 30m, 35m, 40m, 45m, 50m respectively.

1.2.2 The Changing Working Condition of the Length of Pipe Pile

As shown in Fig. 2a), the range of width of region ① is the same as the outer diameter of the culvert, and the range of foundation on both sides are region ② and region ③. Simulated pipe piles with lengths of h_1, h_2 and h_3 are laid in area ①, ② and ③, respectively. As shown in Fig. 2b), the diameter of pipe piles is d and the distance between pipe piles is s.

In the experiment, we only changed the factor of pile length. The diameter of pipe pile is 40cm and the distance is 2m. The change of pile length can be divided into four cases. In the first case, it is $h_1 = h_3 = 5m$, $h_2 = 10m$, the second is $h_1 = h_2 = h_3 = 10m$, the third is $h_1 = h_3 = 15m$, $h_2 = 10m$, the forth is $h_1 = h_3 = 20m$, $h_2 = 10m$.

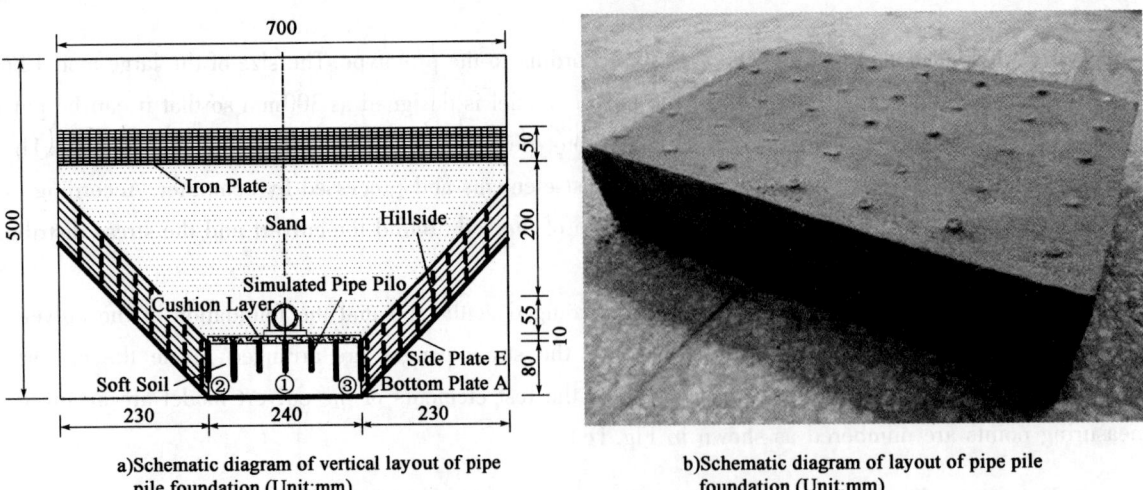

Fig. 2 The Model of Test of Pipe pile

2 Analysis of Earth Pressure Distribution of Circular Pipe Culvert

2.1 Distribution of Earth Pressure Around Culvert and Top of Culvert

As shown in Fig. 3a), the vertical earth pressure at the top of the pipe culvert is distributed in a "convex" shape. Under the condition that the filling height is constant, the earth pressure around the pipe culvert increases after conducting with pipe pile. The distribution of earth pressure around the culvert is 10m > 5m > 15m > 20m > non-pipe pile in the order from large to small. With the increase of the length of the pipe pile on the side of the culvert, the vertical earth pressure at the top of the culvert increases within the range of 0m to 10m, decreases gradually at 10m to 15m, and tends to smooth when it exceeds 15m. As shown in Fig. 4a), taking the measuring point 1 of the upper edge of the culvert top as an example, when the length of the pipe pile is within the range of 0m to 10m, the vertical earth pressure of the culvert top increases by 67.021kPa under the condition of 20m filling height, and increases by 136.217kPa under the condition of 40m filling height; When the length of pipe pile is within the range of 10m to 20m, the vertical earth pressure of culvert top is reduced by 44.681kPa under the condition of 20m filling height, and reduced by 76.596kPa under the condition of 40m filling height.

As shown in Fig. 4b), with the increase of filling height, the vertical earth pressure at the top of the culvert is more significantly affected by the length of the pipe pile on the side of the culvert. Taking the measuring point 1 in the middle of the upper edge of the culvert top as an example. Under the condition of filling height of 10m and 50m, when the length of culvert side pipe pile is 0m, 10m and 20m, the corresponding soil pressure values of culvert side pile are 90.64kPa, 106.404kPa, 89.155kPa and 266.01kPa, 327.094kPa, 261.546kPa respectively. That is to say, when the length of the pipe pile on the side of the culvert is in the range of 0m to 10m, the increment of the pile on the side of the culvert is 34.45kPa and 160.765kPa respectively. Under the condition of 10m and 50m of filling height, when the length of the pile on the side of the culvert is in the range of 10m to 20m, the reduction is 57.438kPa and 168.147kPa under the condition of 10m and 50m of filling height.

The reason for the analysis shows that the upper load and the strength of the culvert bottom foundation remain unchanged, but the strength of the culvert side foundation increases, the settlement of the culvert bottom foundation is larger than the culvert side foundation. With the increase of the length of the pipe pile on the side of the culvert, the strengthening effect of the pipe pile on the foundation on the side of the culvert is obvious, and the strength of the foundation on the side of the culvert increases, resulting in the decrease of the settlement of the outer soil column, the absolute value of the difference between the internal and external settlement of the soil at the top of the culvert, and the earth pressure on the top of the culvert.

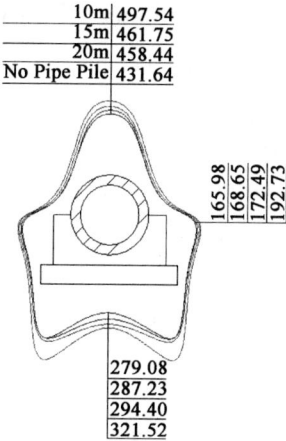

a) Schematic diagram of earth pressure distribution around culvert with different culvert side pipe pile length

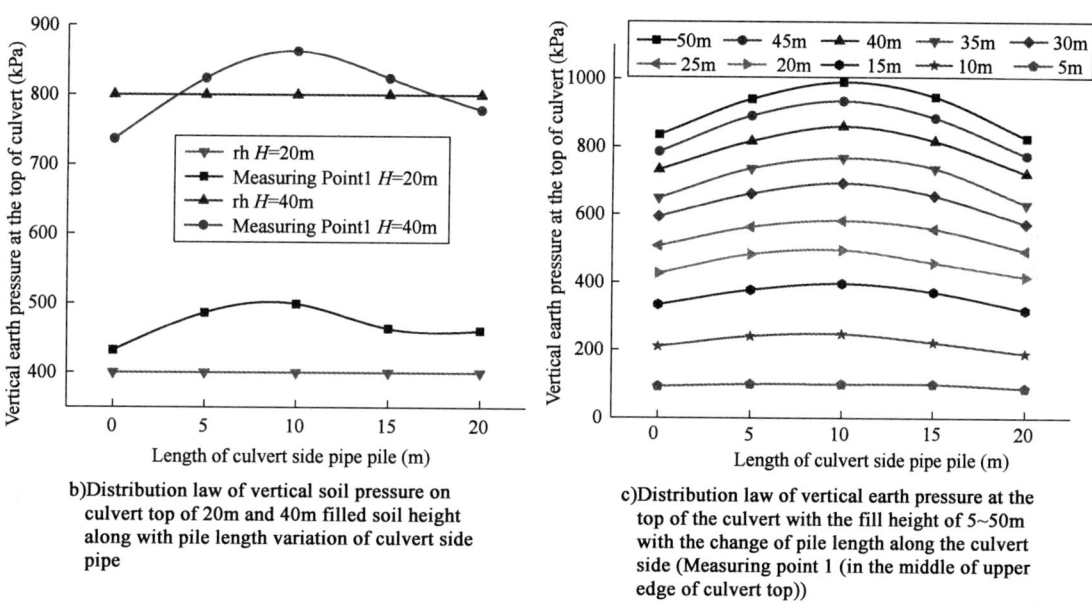

b) Distribution law of vertical soil pressure on culvert top of 20m and 40m filled soil height along with pile length variation of culvert side pipe

c) Distribution law of vertical earth pressure at the top of the culvert with the fill height of 5~50m with the change of pile length along the culvert side (Measuring point 1 (in the middle of upper edge of culvert top))

Fig. 3　Earth Pressure Distribution of Circular Pipe Culvert

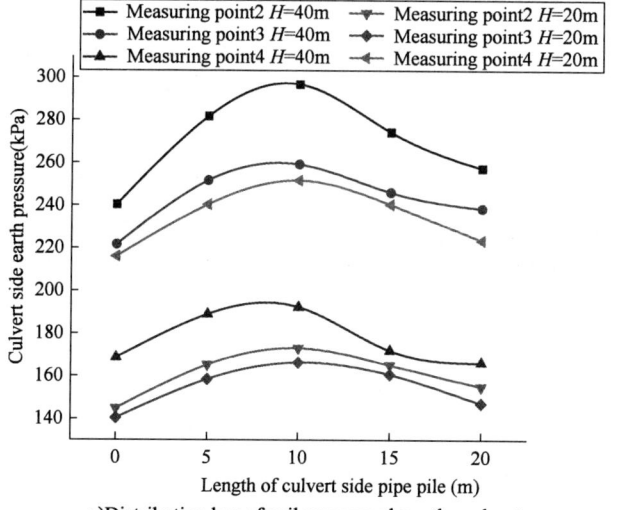

a) Distribution law of soil pressure along the culvert pipe pile length with the fill height of 20m and 40m

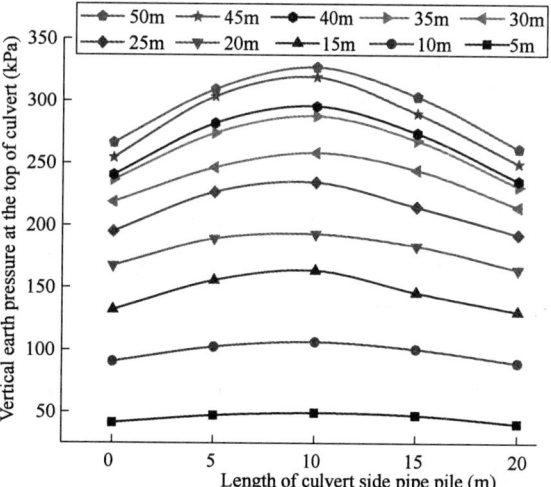

b) Distribution law of soil pressure along the culvert pipe pile length with the fill height of 5-50m (Measuring point 3 (the upper corner of the base))

Fig. 4　Distribution of earth pressure on the side of culvert

2.2 Distribution of earth pressure on the side of culvert

As shown in Fig. 4a), under the same filling height, the soil pressure on the side of the culvert pile decreases greatly when the length of the pipe pile on the side of the culvert is 10~15m. When the length of the pile is greater than 15m, the earth pressure on the side of the culvert decreases slowly and remains stable, and the higher the filling height is, the more uplift the vertical earth pressure curve of the top of the culvert is. Taking the measuring point 2 outside the culvert as an example, when the length of the pipe pile is within the range of 10m, the soil pressure on the side of the culvert increases by 23.756kPa under the condition of filling height 20m, and 56.338kPa under the condition of filling height of 40m; when the length of pipe pile is within the range of 10m 20m, the soil pressure of culvert side decreases by 19.532kPa and 23.53kPa under the condition of filling height of 40m.

As shown in Fig. 4b), the earth pressure on the side of the culvert changes more obviously with the increase of the filling height. Taking the measuring point 3 at the upper corner of the base as an example, under the condition of the filling height of 10m and 50m, when the length of the pipe pile on the side of the culvert is in the range of 0m and 10m, the increase of the pile on the side of the culvert is 15.764kPa and 61.084kPa under the condition 10m and 50m of filling height, and when the length of the pile on the side of the culvert is in the range of 10m and 20m, the reduction is 17.249kPa and 65.548kPa under the condition of 10m and 50m of filling height.

The reason for these phenomena is that the longer the culvert side pipe pile is, the greater the strength of the foundation outside the bottom of the culvert is, then the smaller the compression deformation of the fill on the side of the culvert is, the smaller the settlement difference of the soil column inside and outside the top of the culvert is. Under the condition of filling at the top of the culvert and the dead weight of the culvert, the greater the strength of the foundation at the bottom of the culvert, the greater the load that the foundation soil at the bottom of the culvert can bear.

2.3 Distribution of earth pressure on culvert foundation

As shown in Fig. 5a). At the same filling height, with the increase of the length of the pipe pile on the side of the culvert, the reaction force at the base of the culvert increases at first and then decreases. Taking the measuring point 6 in the middle of the base as an example, when the length of the pipe pile is within the range of 0m to 10m, the reaction force of the culvert base increases by 40.91kPa under the condition of the filling height of 20m, and increases by 129.465kPa under the condition of the filling height of 40m; When the length of the pipe pile is within the range of 10m to 20m, the reaction of the culvert base decreases by 37.037kPa under the condition of the filling height of 20m, and decreases by 78.534kPa under the condition of the filling height of 40m.

As shown in Fig. 5b), taking the measuring point 6 in the middle of the base as an example, under the condition of filling height of 10m and 50m, when the length of the pipe pile on the side of the culvert is in the range of 0m to 10m, the increment of the pile on the side of the culvert is 23.041kPa and 147.465kPa respectively; Under the condition of 10m and 50m of filling height, and when the length of the pile on the side of the culvert is in the range of 10m and 20m, the reduction is 24.228kPa and 151.937kPa under the condition of 10m and 50m of filling height. The longer the pipe pile on the side of the culvert is, the smaller the reaction in the middle part of the base of the culvert is, and the larger the reaction at the corner of the culvert is.

The reason for these phenomena is that the longer the pipe pile on the side of the culvert is, the greater the strength of the foundation outside the bottom of the culvert is, the smaller the compression deformation caused by the filling on the side of the culvert is, and the settlement difference between the soil columns inside and outside the top of the culvert also decreases. Under the condition that the top filling of the culvert and the dead weight of the culvert are fixed, the greater the strength of the foundation outside the bottom of the culvert, the greater the load that the foundation soil on the outside of the bottom of the culvert can bear, and the greater the reaction of the base of the corner of the culvert is.

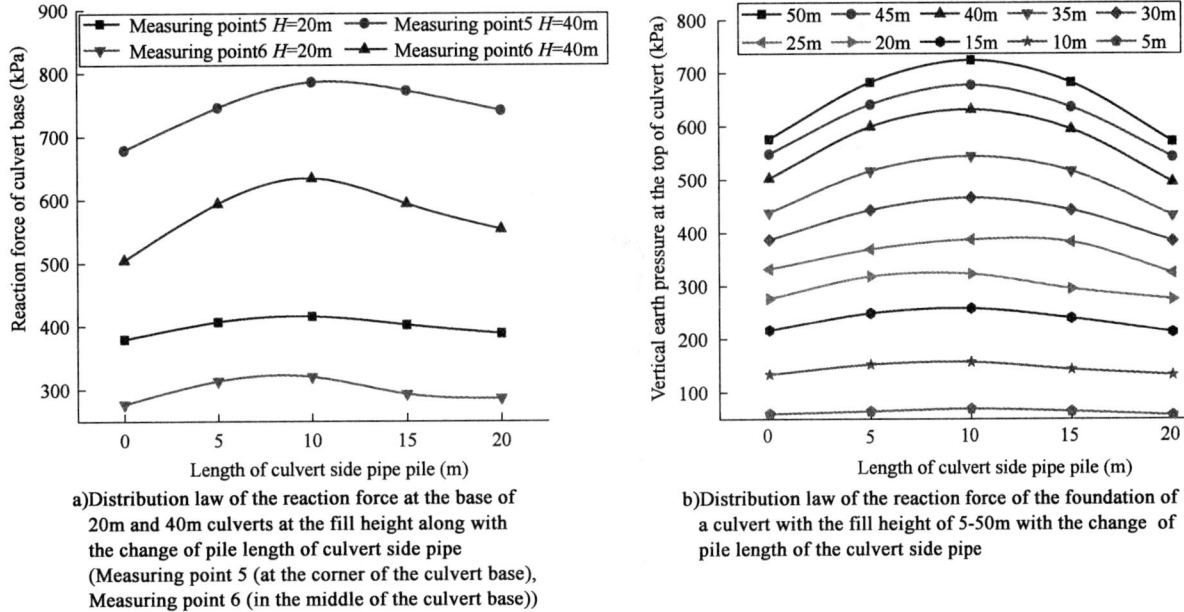

a) Distribution law of the reaction force at the base of 20m and 40m culverts at the fill height along with the change of pile length of culvert side pipe (Measuring point 5 (at the corner of the culvert base), Measuring point 6 (in the middle of the culvert base))

b) Distribution law of the reaction force of the foundation of a culvert with the fill height of 5-50m with the change of pile length of the culvert side pipe

Fig. 5 Distribution of earth pressure on culvert foundation

2.4 Analysis of the influence of vertical earth pressure concentration factor

As shown in Fig. 6a), when the pipe-pile composite foundation was adopted at the same filling height, the vertical earth pressure concentration factor K_s at the top of the culvert increases, which is almost greater than 1.

With the increase of filling height, the K_s value of vertical earth pressure concentration factor of different culvert side pipe pile length increases at first, then decreases and tends to be stable, and the maximum value appears when the filling height is 15m. When the filling height is 5m to 15m, there is no significant difference in the K_s increase of pipe pile length between non-pipe pile and different culvert side pipe pile. The increases of pipe pile length 20m, 25m, 30m and non-pipe pile in the range of filling height 0m to 15m are 0.308, 0.262, 0.212 and 0.182 respectively. Taking the 20m length of the pipe pile on the side of the culvert as an example, the vertical earth pressure concentration factor K_s of the culvert top increases from 1.006 to 1.314 under the filling height of 15m to 50m, while the vertical earth pressure concentration factor K_s of the non-pipe pile increases from 0.915 to 1.097 under the filling height of 15m to 50m, which increases by 0.262 and 0.182 respectively. When the filling height is 15m to 50m, the K_s reduction of the pipe pile without pipe pile is smaller than that of the culvert pile length 20m to 30m. The length of pipe pile on the side of culvert is 20m, 25m, 30m and the reduction of non-pipe pile in the range of filling height 15m to 50m is 0.318, 0.283, 0.272 and 0.263 respectively. Taking the 20m length of pipe pile on the side of culvert as an example, the vertical earth pressure concentration factor K_s of culvert top decreases from 1.309 to 0.991 under the condition of filling height of 150m, while the vertical earth pressure concentration factor K_s of non-pipe pile decreases from 1.097 to 0.834 under the condition of filling height of 15m to 50m, with a decrease of 0.318 and 0.263 respectively. It shows that the influence of the length of pipe pile on the vertical earth pressure concentration factor of culvert top is different under the condition of different filling height. According to Fig. 6b), when the culvert is treated with pipe pile composite foundation in the soft soil foundation of the culvert, it is suggested that the length of the pipe pile on the side of the culvert should be longer than that of the pipe pile at the bottom of the culvert, the longer the pipe pile on the side of the culvert is, the more favorable the force of the culvert structure is.

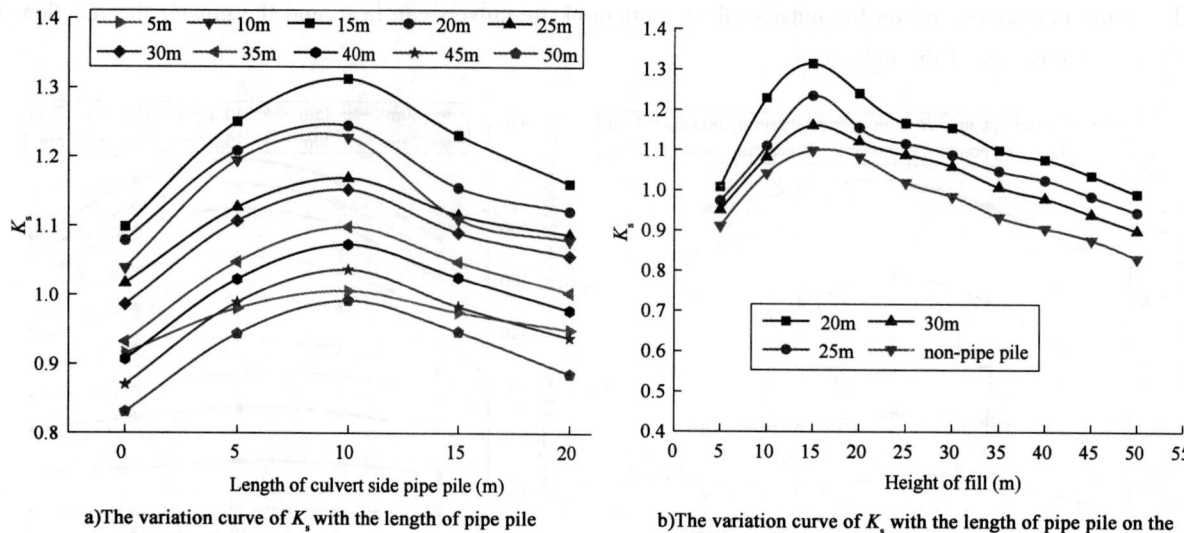

a) The variation curve of K_s with the length of pipe pile on the side of culvert

b) The variation curve of K_s with the length of pipe pile on the side of culvert

Fig. 6　Distribution law of concentration coefficient of vertical soil pressure on culvert top (pile diameter 40cm, pile distance 2.5m)

3　Settlement and Deformation Characteristics of Culvert Side Pipe Pile Length to Circular Pipe Culvert Top Fill

In order to facilitate the experimental study, when the filling height is 20m, the soil layer above the culvert top is divided into three layers, the first layer is 6.67m away from the culvert top, the second layer is 13.34m away from the culvert top, and the third layer is on the surface. As shown in Fig. 7a) and Fig. 7b), the settlement of the top of the pipe culvert is less than that of the soil outside the top of the culvert, which is larger than that of the soil column outside the upper part of the gully slope, and the settlement curve is M-shaped. Under the same length of pipe pile on the side of the culvert, along the axis of the pipe culvert, with the increase of the height of the filling soil layer, the cumulative settlement of the soil layer gradually increases, and the absolute value of the settlement difference between the inside and outside of the soil layer gradually decreases.

As shown in Fig. 7c), taking the second layer of fill as an example, the internal and external settlement difference of culvert top soil increases from −4.588cm to −5.216cm within the length of pipe pile. When the length of pipe pile is 20m, the difference of internal and external settlement of culvert top soil is −4.549cm. With the increase of the length of the pipe pile on the side of the culvert, the absolute value of the internal and external settlement difference of each test layer decreases gradually, and when the length of the pipe pile on the side of the culvert is more than 15m, the change of the internal and external settlement difference of the soil layer is basically stable. As shown in Fig. 7d), when the length of the pipe pile on the side of the culvert is within the range of 8.81m, the height of the equal settlement surface gradually increases to 6.4m. With the increase of the length of the pipe pile on the side of the culvert, the absolute value of the difference between internal and external settlement of the soil layer decreases gradually, and the height of the equal settlement surface decreases gradually. When the length of the pipe pile on the side of the culvert is more than 15m, the height of the equal settlement surface changes little, and finally stabilizes at about 5.7m.

In practical engineering, when the culvert is conducted with pipe pile composite foundation in soft soil foundation, it is suggested that the length of pipe pile on the side of culvert should be longer than that of pipe pile at the bottom of culvert, and the longer the length of pipe pile on the side of culvert is, the more favorable the force of culvert structure is.

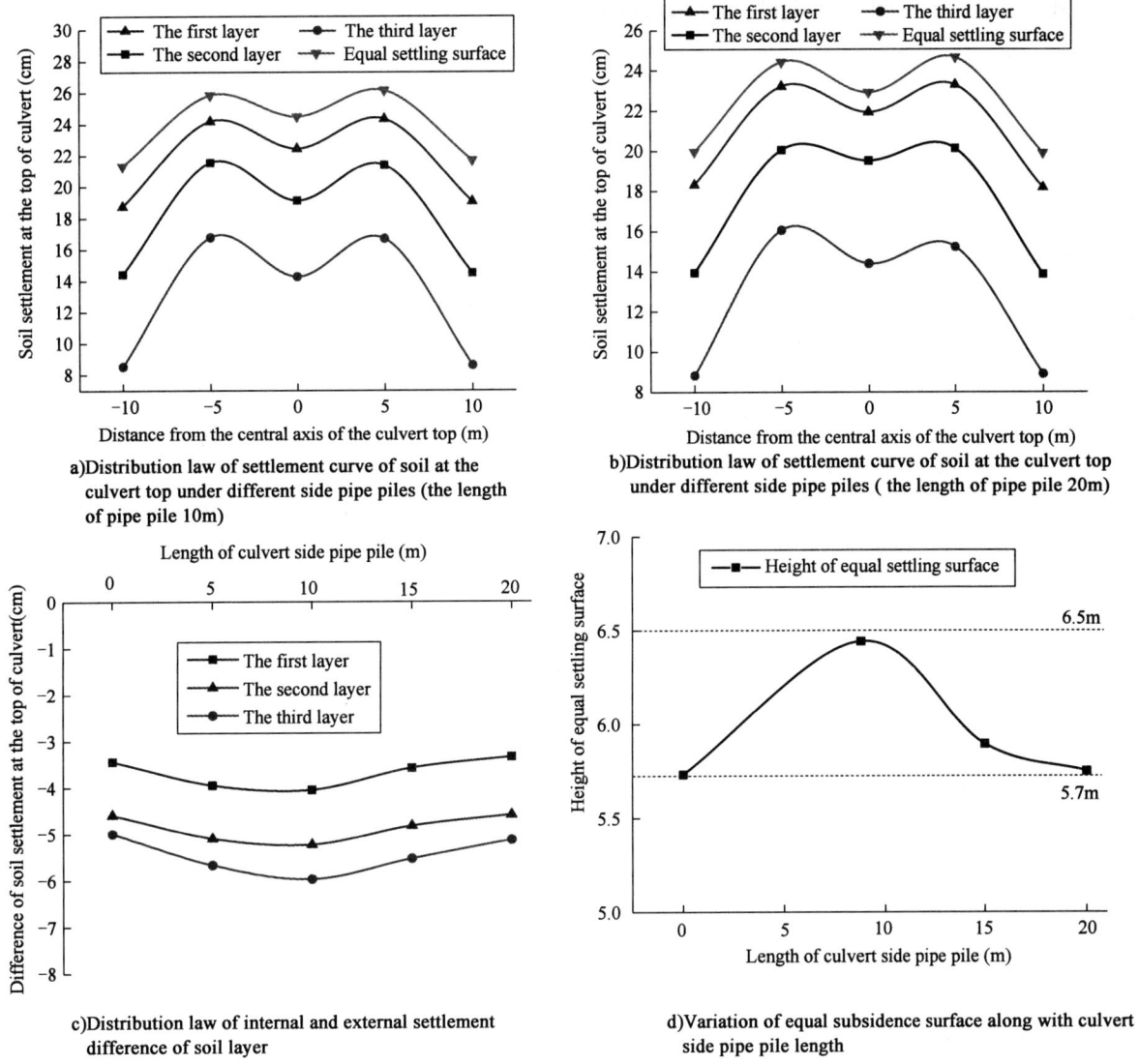

Fig. 7 Deformation characteristics of different layer in the filling above the culvert (fill height: 20m)

4 Conclusions

With the increase of the length of the pipe pile on the side of the culvert, the absolute value of the difference between internal and external settlement of the soil layer gradually decreases, and the height of the equal settlement surface decreases gradually.

The greater the filling height is, the more obvious the influence on the length of the pipe pile on the side of the culvert is, and the more obvious the variation range of the earth pressure at the top, side and bottom of the culverts.

In practical engineering, the treatment of unequal pile length should be adopted, and the length of the pipe pile on the side of the culvert should be longer than that of the pipe pile at the bottom of the culvert. Only in this way, the settlement difference between the soil columns inside and outside the soil will be smaller, and the height of the equal sinking surface will be lower.

For the culverts treated with pipe pile composite foundation in soft soil foundation, it is suggested that appropriate load reduction measures should be taken to reduce the soil pressure at the top of the culvert and prevent the concrete from cracking. For example, a small amount of steel bars should be laid on the inside of the pipe culvert to improve the bearing capacity of the culvert, or the foundation soil with insufficient bearing capacity should be replaced with rigid coarse-grained materials.

5 Acknowledgements

I would like to thank all the members of the research group for their concern and help, especially my mentor, Professor Feng Zhongju. I would like to thank the experts for taking the time to review my paper.

References

[1] A N Dancygier, I Leviathan, Y S Karinski. An analytical model to evaluate the static soil pressure on a buried structure[J]. Engineering structures, 2003, 25(1):91-101.

[2] Abuhajar Osama, El Naggar Hesham, Newson Tim. Static soil culvert interaction the effect of box culvert geometric configurations and soil properties[J]. Computers and geotechnics, 2015, 69:219-235.

[3] Chen Baoguo, Luo Ruiping, Xu Ying. Analysis of foundation bearing capacity of high fill rigid culvert on soft soil foundation [J]. Rock and soil Mechanics. 2013, 34(02):353-358.

[4] Feng Zhongju, Wu Yanling, Jia Yanwu, et al. Simulation experimental study on stress and deformation characteristics of steel bellows culvert [J]. Journal of Geotechnical Engineering, 2013, 35(1):187-192.

[5] Gu Anquan. Study on vertical earth pressure of upper buried pipeline and cavern [J]. Journal of Geotechnical Engineering, 1981(01):3-15.

[6] Jacob Tetreault, Ian D Moore, Neil A. Laboratory Study on Effect of Grout Choice on Culvert Rehabilitation Using Slip Lining[J]. Journal of Pipeline Systems Engineering and Practice, 2020, 11(1).

[7] Junsuk Kang, Frazier Parker, Chai H. Yoo. Soil-Structure Interaction and Imperfect Trench Installations for Deeply Buried Corrugated Polyvinyl Chloride Pipes[J]. Transportation Research Record, 2007(1).

[8] Lei Jinbo, Yang Kang, Zhou Xing, et al. Experimental study on pile-soil stress ratio of perforated pipe pile composite foundation with cap [J]. Journal of Rock Mechanics and Engineering, Magi, 2017, 36(S1):3607-3617.

[9] Ma Qiang, Zheng Junjie, Zhang Jun. Field experimental study on reinforcement and load reduction of high fill culvert [J]. Rock and soil Mechanics, jade, 2012, 33(08):2337-2342-2348.

[10] N. Randy Rainwater, Richard M. Bennett, Scott M. Wood, et al. Vertical Loads on Concrete Box Culverts under High Embankments[J]. Journal of Bridge Engineering, 2005, 10(6):643-649.

[11] Zhang Bo, Liu Hanlong. Analysis of vertical bearing characteristics of cast-in-place thin-wall pipe pile composite foundation [J]. Journal of Geotechnical Engineering, 2007, (08):1251-1255.

[12] Zheng Junjie, Ma Qiang, Chen Baoguo. Analysis of foundation bearing capacity of high fill culvert [J]. Journal of Huazhong University of Science and Technology(Natural Science Edition), 2009, 37(4):115-118.

路面状态对水泥磷石膏稳定土路基模量的影响研究

彭波[1] 王振生[1] 宋云峰[2] 李奕娜[1] 刘帅[1]
(1. 长安大学公路学院;2. 渭南市交通工程质量监督站)

摘 要 以水泥磷石膏稳定土为对象,利用有限元软件,研究面层温度升高、基层开裂及交通荷载加重等路面状态对路基模量的影响。结果表明:基层开裂对路基模量的影响显著,交通荷载作用影响次之,面层温度影响最小。在基层开裂状态下,建议在中等及重等、特重、极重交通荷载等级时,上路床模量不宜小于80MPa、85MPa、90MPa。研究结果有利于揭示路面状态制约路基模量的本质,为水泥磷石膏稳定土路基设计提供依据。

关键词 道路工程 路基设计 水泥磷石膏稳定土 路面状态变化 路基应力 路基回弹模量

0 引 言

路基的性能优劣决定着道路的使用寿命与服务水平。《公路路基设计规范》(JTG D30—2015)以路基顶面回弹模量作为设计指标,是以路面各结构层完好时为基础,未考虑路面状态改变对路基模量的影响,导致路基设计模量偏低。学者Pouya Salari[1]从土壤颗粒形状等角度研究了路基模量的变化情况;沙爱民、贾侃等人[2]提出水泥稳定类半刚性基层在路面的长期使用过程中,60%~75%的时间处于开裂状态,其模量大小为初始模量值的60%,模量损失较大;路鑫等人[3]指出满足路面规范要求只能说明路基回弹模量取值满足最低标准,而不能说明设计的合理性;另一方面,工业废料磷石膏在我国存量大,综合利用率还不到40%[4];而磷石膏的特性与粉煤灰类似,可用以加固路基土体,且具有较好的强度和性能[5]。综上所述,以室内试验为辅、有限元模拟为主的方式研究路面状态对水泥磷石膏稳定土路基模量的影响,有利于促进磷石膏在道路建设中的应用。

1 原材料及比例

1.1 磷石膏、水泥、黄土

磷石膏取自陕西省某化工集团磷石膏堆放场,水泥为型号P·O42.5普通硅酸盐水泥,土取自陕西省渭南市合铜高速公路取土坑,原材料性能检测结果如表1~表3所示。

磷石膏成分及含量   表1

物质成分	CaO	SO_3	SiO_2	Al_2O_3	Fe_2O_3	P_2O_5	F^-	烧失量
质量分数(%)	30.62	38.73	4.71	0.86	0.15	0.98	0.23	21.03

水泥技术指标检测结果   表2

检测项目	细度(%)	安定性(mm)	抗压强度(MPa)		抗折强度(MPa)		凝结时间(min)	
			3 d	28 d	3 d	28 d	初凝	终凝
标准值	≤10.0	<5	≥17	≥42.5	≥3.5	≥6.5	≥45	≤600
检测值	2.6	3.7	28.3	53.2	7.3	8.4	94	380

土技术指标检测结果   表3

天然含水率(%)	相对密度	塑限(%)	液限(%)	塑性指数(%)	土的类别	最佳含水率(%)	最大干密度(g/cm^3)
8.56	2.70	18.17	28.30	10.13	低液限粉质黏土	14.6	1.86

1.2 混合料比例

在室内常规试验的基础上,推荐各原材料比例为水泥4%、磷石膏6%。此时水泥磷石膏稳定路基土的性能参数如表4所示。

水泥磷石膏稳定土的性能参数   表4

密度(g/cm^3)	ω(%)	I_p(%)	压实度(%)	c(kPa)	(°)
1.92	16.40	7.2	96	15	25

基金项目:陕西省交通运输厅科技计划项目(18-04K)。

2　典型路面结构拟定

通过对我国路面结构的调查,结合施工中常用路面结构组合形式,拟定沥青路面结构如图1所示。

沥青面层	20cm
水泥稳定碎石基层	20cm
水泥稳定碎石底基层	20cm
路基	

图1　沥青路面典型结构

3　有限元模型建立

3.1　模型结构及材料参数

根据现有的有限元分析相关研究[6-7],选用X、Y方向为5m、Z方向为6.6 m的立方体三维路面结构模型,X方向为路面横断面方向,Y方向为行车方向,Z方向为路面深度方向。根据回弹模量试验及相关研究[8],确定所拟定路面结构的动态模量值,如表5所示。研究人员提出了许多描述路基土回弹模量(简称"模量")应力依赖性的应力-应变本构模型[9-10],如表6所示,路基采用AASHTO 2002模型。

路面材料参数　　表5

材　料	密度(kg/m³)	泊松比	模量(MPa)	
沥青混凝土面层	2300	0.3	5℃	10000
			25℃	6000
			50℃	1000
水泥稳定碎石基层	2000	0.25	基层完好	14000
			基层开裂	2500
			基层破裂	500

代表性路基土回弹模量本构模型　　表6

年　份	出　处	模型公式
1994	AASHTO TP46	$M_R = k_1 \theta^{k_2}$
1999	Mohammad,等	$\dfrac{M_R}{\sigma_{atm}} = k_1 \left(\dfrac{\theta}{\sigma_{atm}}\right)^{k_2} \left(\dfrac{\tau_{oct}}{\sigma_{atm}}\right)^{k_3}$
2004	AASHTO 2002	$\dfrac{M_R}{\sigma_{atm}} = k_1 \left(\dfrac{\theta}{\sigma_{atm}}\right)^{k_2} \left(\dfrac{\tau_{oct}}{\sigma_{atm}} + 1\right)^{k_3}$

注:M_R为路基土动态回弹模量;θ为体应力,$\theta = \sigma_1 + \sigma_2 + \sigma_3$;$\sigma_d$为偏应力,$\sigma_d = \sigma_1 - \sigma_3$;$\sigma_3$为围压;$\sigma_{atm}$为大气压(101.4kPa);$\sigma_{oct}$为八面体主应力;$\tau_{oct}$为八面剪应力;$J_2$为偏应力张量第二不变量;$k_1$、$k_2$、$k_3$为回归系数。

3.2　网格划分及行车荷载

面层网格为10mm×10mm,基层网格为20mm×20mm,土基网格为40cm×40cm,如图2所示。将轮胎与地面接触面等效为矩形,矩形长边为0.24 m,短边为0.16 m。交通荷载分为中等、重等、特重和极重,其对应的交通量分别为6.0×10^6辆、13.5×10^6辆、34.5×10^6辆和55×10^6辆。

图 2　模型网格划分

4　面层状态对路基模量影响分析

4.1　面层温度对路基模量的影响

沥青材料易受温度影响,考虑沥青面层的三阶段状态,以路面温度5℃、25℃及50℃来表征。不同的交通荷载下,面层温度对路基应力作用规律相似。以极重交通荷载为例,模拟结果如图3所示。

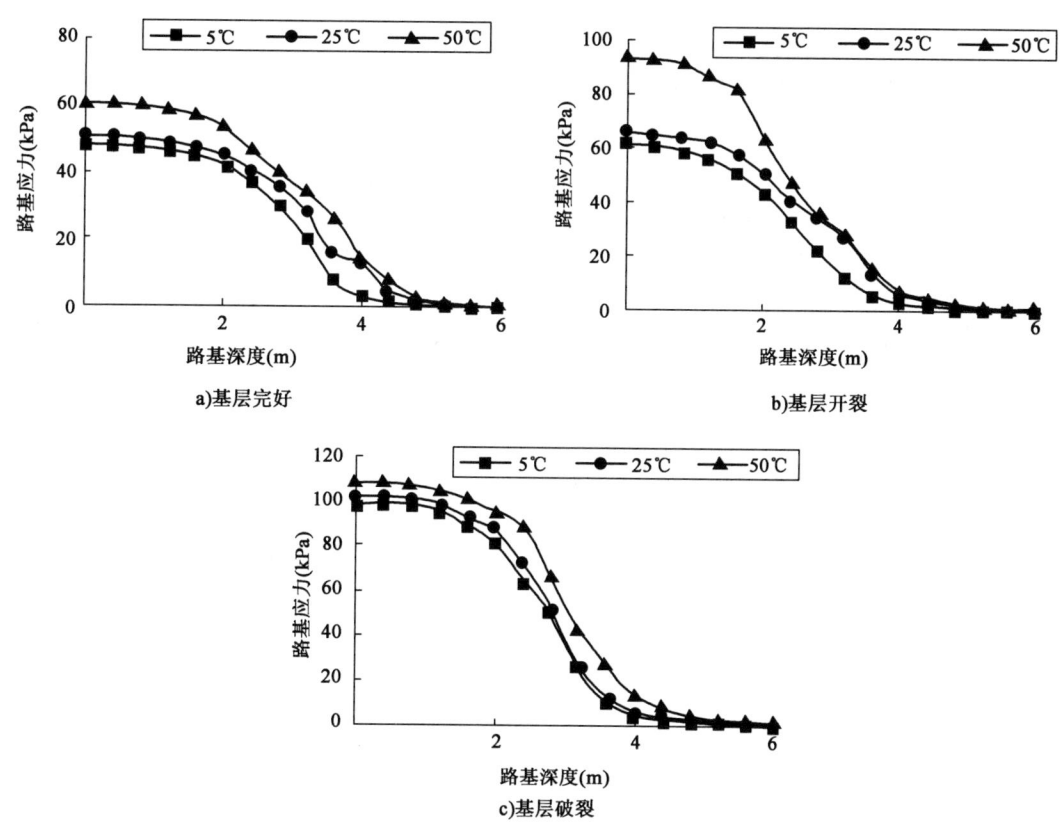

图 3　极重交通时路基应力随面层状态变化曲线

由图3可知,当交通荷载及基层状态均相同时,随着路面温度的升高,传递至路基的荷载应力增加。根据图3,利用路基土 AASHTO 2002 回弹模量本构模型,对中等交通下的路基 0~40cm 范围的模量进行计算,结果如表7和图4所示。

上路床平均模量变化情况（单位：MPa）   表7

面层温度(℃)	基层状态		
	基层完好	基层开裂	基层破裂
5	72.06	77.95	87.20
25	72.84	79.27	88.21
50	73.79	79.69	89.63

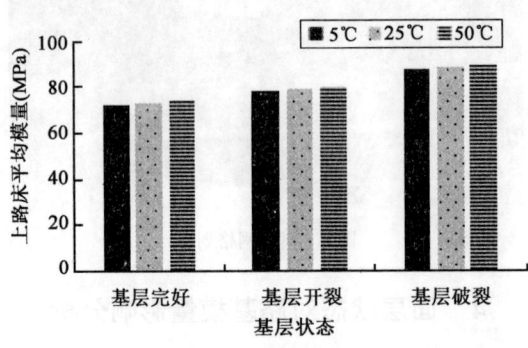

图4 路基模量随面层状态变化情况

根据表7和图4可知，随着路面温度升高，上路床平均模量要求值逐渐增大，增幅较小。在面层温度由5℃升高至25℃、50℃过程中，当基层为完好状态时，上路床平均模量增幅为1.1%、1.3%；当基层为开裂状态时，上路床平均模量增幅为1.7%、0.5%；当基层为破裂状态时，上路床平均模量增幅为1.2%、1.6%。

4.2 基层开裂对路基模量的影响

在不同的面层状态下，基层状态对路基应力的影响程度较为相近。以路面温度为25℃时的面层状态为例，模拟结果如图5所示。

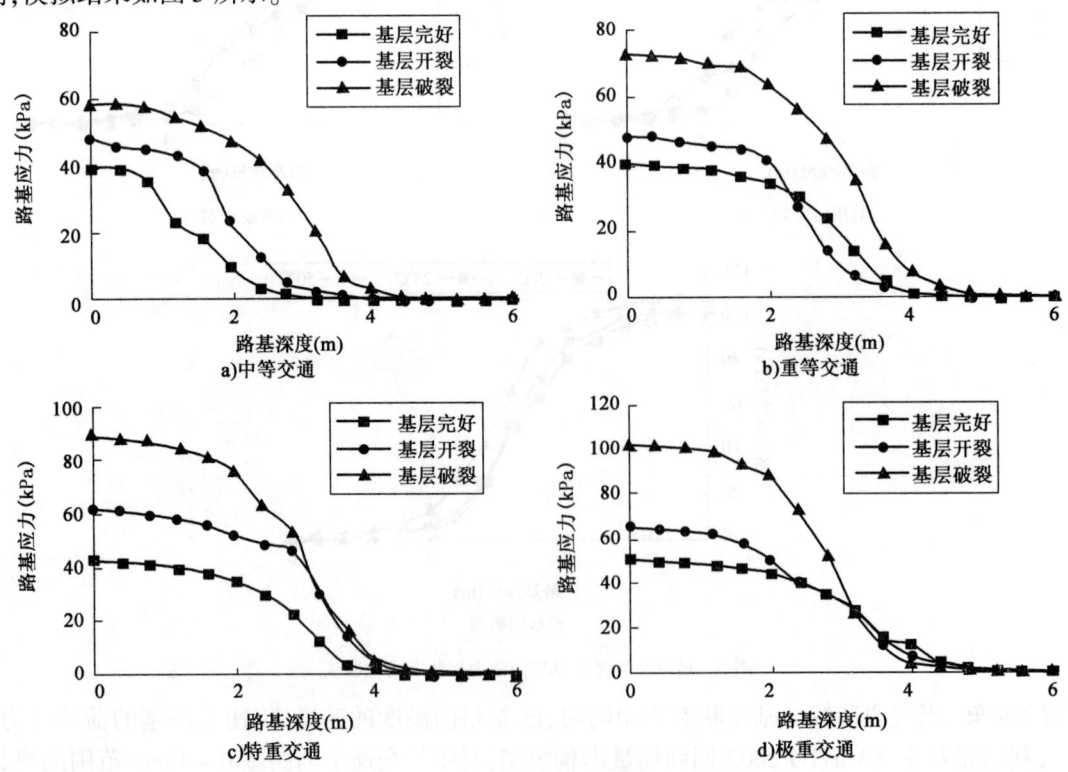

图5 面层状态为25℃时路基应力随基层状态变化曲线(kPa)

由图5可知,当面层温度及交通荷载相同时,随着基层状态的恶化,路基顶面应力增长迅速。利用路基土 AASHTO 2002 回弹模量本构模型,计算 25℃下路基 0~40 cm 范围的模量,结果如表8和图6所示。

上路床平均模量变化情况(单位:MPa)　　　　　　　　　　　　　　　　　表8

基层状态	交通荷载			
	中等	重等	特重	极重
基层完好	72.83	75.18	78.22	81.44
基层开裂	79.27	82.22	84.32	90.06
基层破裂	88.20	90.40	95.00	104.29

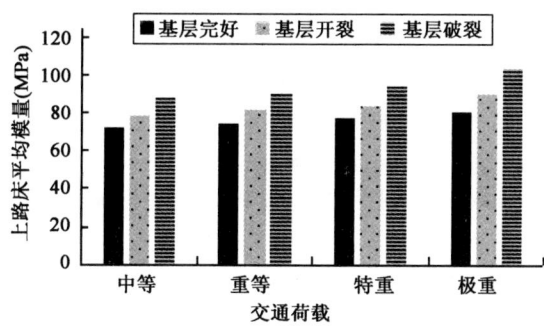

图6　路基模量随基层状态变化情况

根据表8和图6可知,随着路面基层状态的持续恶化,路基模量要求值逐渐增大。以重等交通为例,在路面基层状态由完好转变为开裂并继续恶化为破裂状态的过程中,路基模量增加幅度为9.4%、20.2%,基层开裂状态对路基模量的影响显著。

4.3　交通荷载对路基模量的影响

根据表8可知,随着交通荷载的加重,路基模量要求值逐渐增大。在基层开裂时,随着交通荷载从中等持续加重至重等、特重、极重,路基模量要求值分别为 79.27MPa、82.22MPa、84.32MPa、90.06MPa,增幅较大。由于水泥稳定类半刚性基层在路面的长期使用过程中,60%~75%的时间处于开裂状态,因此,在基层开裂状态下,对不同交通荷载的路基模量要求值进行取整与调整,作为上路床回弹模量的推荐值。

路基上路床模量推荐值见表9。

路基上路床模量推荐值　　　　　　　　　　　　　　　　　　　　　　　　表9

路面状态	基层开裂		
	中等、重等交通	特重交通	极重交通
路基上路床模量推荐值(MPa)	80	85	90

5　结　语

(1)水泥磷石膏稳定土路基回弹模量受路面状态影响较大。基层开裂是影响路基回弹模量的重要因素,交通荷载对路基回弹模量有较大的影响,面层温度对路基回弹模量影响很小。

(2)路基设计时要充分考虑使用时的路面状态。基层开裂在路面的长期使用期内所占时间长,考虑基层开裂与交通荷载的综合作用,建议在基层开裂时,水泥磷石膏上路床在中等及重等、特重、极重交通荷载等级时的回弹模量值不宜小于 80 MPa、85MPa、90MPa。

(3)研究在室内试验的基础上,通过有限元模拟理论上指明现行路基设计规范的不足,后期将加深对试验路的性能观测,将理论研究应用于工程实践。

参考文献

[1] Pouya Salari, Naser Hafezi Moghaddas, Gholam Reza Lashkaripour, et al. Evaluating the Subgrade Reaction Modulus Variations with Soil Grains Shape in Coarse-Grained Soils Using Genetic Algorithm[J]. Open Journal of Geology, 2020, 10(2):111-123.

[2] 沙爱民, 贾侃, 陆剑卿, 等. 半刚性基层材料动态模量的衰变规律[J]. 中国公路学报, 2009, 22(03):1-6.

[3] 路鑫, 毛久海, 李小刚. 路基回弹模量对路面结构力学性能影响的数值分析[J]. 路基工程, 2015(03):132-135.

[4] 马丽萍. 磷石膏资源化综合利用现状及思考[J]. 磷肥与复肥, 2019, 34(07):5-9.

[5] 丁建文, 张帅, 洪振舜, 等. 水泥-磷石膏双掺固化处理高含水率疏浚淤泥试验研究[J]. 岩土力学, 2010, 31(09):2817-2822.

[6] 王鹏. 不同轮胎花纹非均布荷载下沥青路面三维有限元分析[J]. 工程力学, 2012, 29(05):237-241.

[7] 赵孝辉. 考虑层间接触状态的路面结构有限元分析[D]. 广州:华南理工大学, 2011.

[8] 邱欣, 杨青, 钱劲松. 半刚性基层沥青路面模量参数反演的影响因素分析[J]. 交通运输工程与信息学报, 2010, 8(04):43-48.

[9] 弋晓明, 李术才, 王松根, 等. 非饱和粉土回弹模量的应力依赖性与水敏感性耦合分析[J]. 山东大学学报(工学版), 2013(02).

[10] 黄继业. 高速公路沥青路面基层材料设计与优化研究[D]. 武汉:武汉理工大学, 2003.

滨海地区地下水位动态变化对土体影响研究

程马遥 曾 洋 魏 永 杨 虹

(佛山科学技术学院)

摘 要 近年来由于滨海城市优越的地理环境，基础建设工程得到快速开展。但滨海地区由于临海的特殊性，潮汐、强降雨均会造成地下水位剧烈的波动，影响基坑变形，威胁人员生命安全。本文以珠三角地区某基坑工程为对象研究动态地下水位的土体响应和应力路径、应力状态变化影响，考虑静止水位和动态水位两种情况，以孔压边界的形式施加于基坑模型边界进行有限元计算分析。结果表明:在施加动水位后基坑内外土体的应力路径、应力状态与静水位下的土体存在较大差异。动态水位变化过程中对基坑侧壁、坑底土体带来的变形影响显著。随基坑开挖深度的加大，基坑坑外土体沉降量、支护处土体侧向位移、坑底隆起位移情况更为严重。在考虑加长支护结构长度后，基坑三处土体变形值得到不同程度的控制。故在基坑施工过程中地下水位波动时带来的影响不可忽略。

关键词 土力学 地下水位波动 有限元模拟 基坑变形

0 引 言

珠三角地区由于地理位置的优越，基础建设工作得到大力发展，而近年来诸多高层，超高层建筑更是大量出现。但由于地下水渗流对建筑基坑的变形稳定的不利影响，若处理不当将引起严重的工程事故。珠三角诸多地区地下水与海水相连接，在海水潮汐影响下地下水也表现出水位的动态变化，动态水位使得土体和基坑周围渗流场变得更加复杂。基坑工程的防护工作愈加受到重视。

基金项目:佛山市智慧型陆地与海洋土木工程材料工程技术研究开发中心;广东省科技厅粤佛联合基金项目(No. 2019A1515111100);广东省教育厅青年创新项目(No. 2019KQNCX170);佛山市科技创新项目(No. 1920001001673)。

国内外对于基坑渗流主要集中在地下水水位不变或地下水有着稳定补给的情况进行研究。M. Baligh 和 J. N. Levadoux[1]基于 Terzagh 理论对矩形波载情况下单层土的固结进行详细分析。蔡袁强和徐长节[2]针对成层饱水地基模型推导了循环荷载下地基土的一维变形及有效应力。郑刚、曾超峰[3]通过对基坑开挖前进行潜水降水处理，分析了水位下降引起的地下连续墙侧移影响。但对于地下水动态升降变化下对土体影响研究却相对匮乏。

本文通过 ABAQUS 有限元软件进行建模并对其施加水位动态荷载，分析了珠三角地区土质在地下水位变化情况下对基坑内外土体应力路径、应力状态变化影响，着重将水位上升与下降时段土体响应的不同与静水位进行比较，进一步完善了水位变化引起的土体响应研究，为后续基坑工程遭遇动态地下水进行防护时提供相应的理论支持。

1 珠三角地区基坑工程地质概况

基坑工程所处土层主要由以下几部分组成：海陆交互相沉积层（淤泥）、淤泥质土层残积层（粉质黏土）、冲积层（细砂、中粗砂层）海残积层（粉质黏土）。地质情况见表1。以上软弱砂层颗粒呈中、细砂，级配不良且强度较低，压缩性高，自稳能力差。项目地处珠江三角洲，故多呈亚热带气候环境，雨量充沛，地势开阔低平。地表水源含量多范围大。地下水主要被大气降雨，地表河流，海洋潮汐等方式影响而呈现出周期性的波动。

地 质 情 况 表　　　　表1

分　层	层序（自上而下）	土　质	土层特征
人工填土层（Q^{ml}）	1	素填土	主要为素填土，少量为杂填土、耕植土，结构松散，厚 0.5～5.0m
第四系海陆交互相沉积层（Q^{mc}）	2	淤泥、淤泥质土～淤泥质粉细砂	淤泥、淤泥质土层：淤泥质土，局部夹薄层粉砂层或含海生贝壳，层厚 1.10～14.0m。淤泥质粉细砂层：深淤泥质粉砂、中细砂层，厚度一般 0.5～7.8m
第四系冲积层（Q^{al}）	3	细砂、中粗砂～黏性土	细砂、中粗砂层：灰白色、浅黄色等细砂、中粗砂，厚度一般为 1～7m。黏性土层：土质均匀，厚度为 1～10m
第四系残积层（Q^{el}）	4	粉质黏土	为泥质粉砂岩风化残积土，广泛分布于评价区域，土质较均匀，层厚为 0.50～15.4m

2 模　型　建　立

2.1 基本假定

（1）不考虑土体渗透系数与基质吸力之间的关系，视为完全饱和土体。
（2）假定土体为均质材料，为线弹性体，参数为各向异性。
（3）由于地基顶部强透水层的渗透系数远大于下卧弱透水层的渗透系数，故不考虑强透水层的水头损失。
（4）假定地下水位变化前后强透水性土层的天然中重度和饱和重度的差异较小，成层弱透水土层中的总应力保持不变。

2.2 创建部件

不考虑地下水位动态变化的空间效应，对于大面积的地下水动态变化作用的地基问题可以视为一维问题，本文拟采用 Abquse 创建二维实体来模拟动水位作用下地基土的应力路径变化，如图1所示。

2.3 网格划分

采用 CPE4P 技术进行划分，网格划分情况如图2所示。

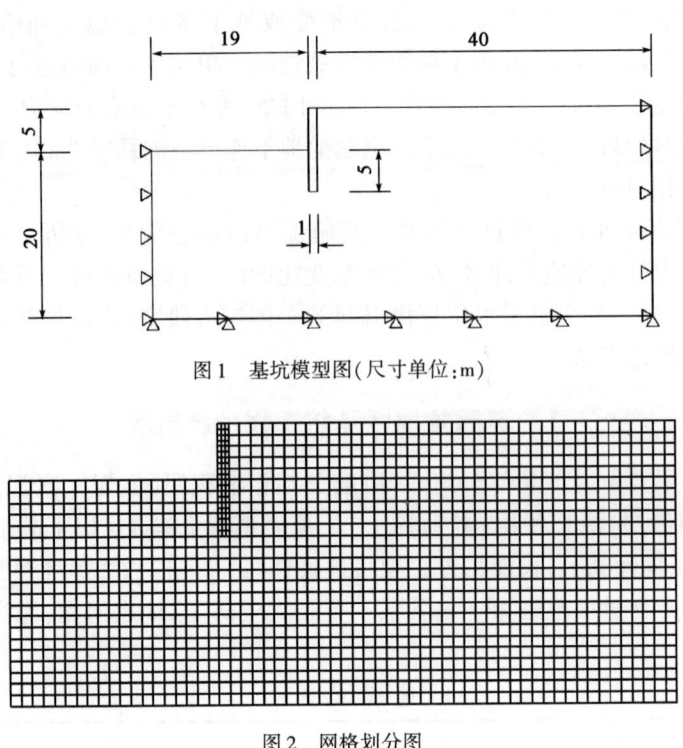

图1 基坑模型图(尺寸单位:m)

图2 网格划分图

3 结果分析

3.1 动水位周期内变化比较

3.1.1 水位上升段(0~T/4)

根据设置的动态孔压边界,在 0~T/4 时间内时,水位呈上升趋势。截取 0h、3h、6h 的孔压沿基坑深度的分布情况如图3所示。0h、3h、6h 的 σ_a 与基坑深度、σ_c 与基坑深度的关系分别如图4、图5所示。

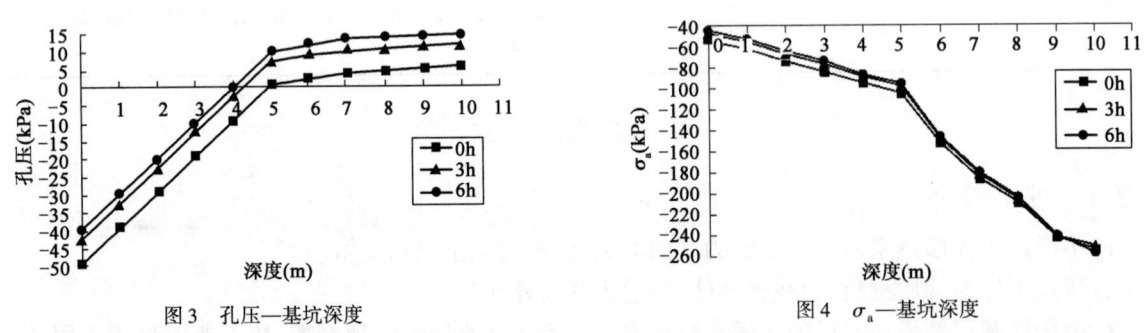

图3 孔压—基坑深度　　　　　图4 σ_a—基坑深度

设置坑外静止地下水位处于地表下5m处,同一时间点时,孔压分布情况为地下 0~5m 处呈线性增长,5m 以下土层孔压增长逐渐放缓。随水位上升,原地下水位线上的土体逐渐被水浸没,此时同一深度处孔压增加约 10kPa。由于地下水上升,浮力作用在土体上使得应力路径和应力状态发生明显变化,轴向压应力 σ_a 与围压 σ_c 在不同深度呈现出速率不一致的减小,原地下水位线上的土体应力缩减约为原地下水位线下土体的2倍。水位上升情况下基坑外土体由于应力路径和状态的改变,在图6中宏观表现为土体不同程度的沉降。并同一时间点,原水位线上的土体沉降程度略大于原水位线下土体。当水位上升达到峰值时,其沉降值达到最大 65mm。分析原因:一方面根据有效应力原理 $\sigma = \sigma' + u$,同一点处总应力不变,孔压增大,有效应力减小,土体承载力下降;另一方面由于水位的抬高,地下水侵入使得原本土体内摩擦角减小,土粒间的结合受到削弱,土体强度降低,压缩性增大。故综合影响下导致了坑外土体的沉降。

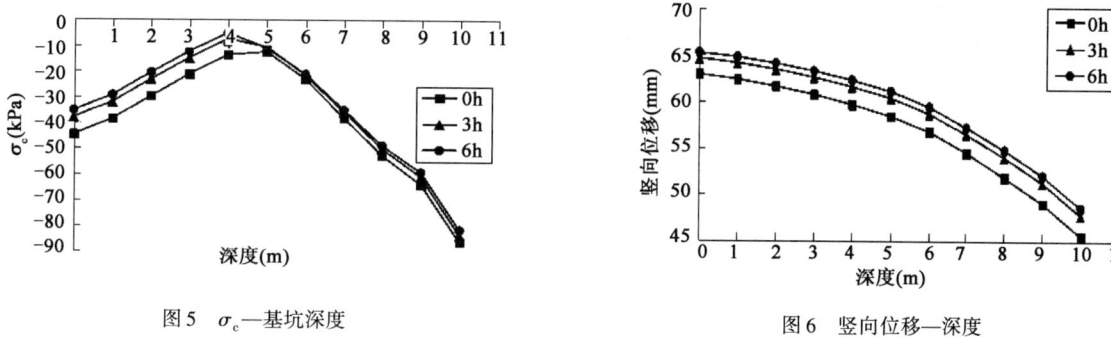

图5 σ_c—基坑深度　　图6 竖向位移—深度

3.1.2 水位下降段($T/4 \sim T/2$)

$T/4 \sim T/2$时间内时,取6.0h、9h和12h的孔压沿基坑深度的分布情况如图7所示,水位下降,孔压减低。当基坑外水位为下降情况时土中孔隙水压力开始发生转移、消散,打破了原有的力学平衡,使得土体中有效应力增加,并且降水形成坑内外水力梯度差,由此产生的渗透力将作为体积力作用在土体上,方向向下的渗流导致轴向压应力增加,此时原地下水位线上的土体应力增长约为原地下水位线下土体的10倍。而围压随水位下降逐渐减小,上部土体减小速率约为下部土体的2倍。水位下降段同一时间点各位置沉降值变化不大,此时土体表面沉降达到65mm。

6h、9h、12h的σ_a、σ_c、沉降与基坑深度的关系分别如图8、图9、图10所示。

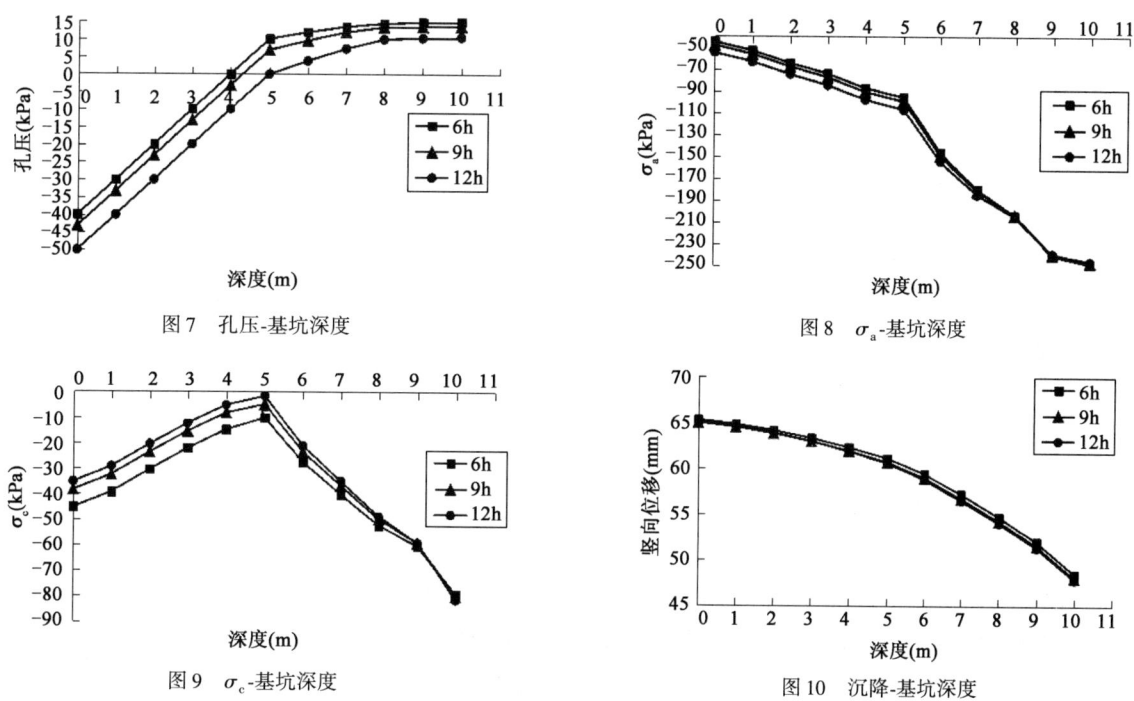

图7 孔压-基坑深度　　图8 σ_a-基坑深度

图9 σ_c-基坑深度　　图10 沉降-基坑深度

3.2 静水位与动水位下土体状态比较

通过建立不同水位下基坑模型,对静水位和动水位不同时刻下的土体进行比较。分析表明孔压响应发生了变化,由于动水位为正弦荷载的形式进行施加在基坑外上层土体,在较上层土体中孔压分布也符合正弦规律。动水位在2.5kN达到波峰,孔压随之达到最大,在2.5~7.5kN动水位持续降低至波谷,此时孔压随水位的下降而持续消散,此时段土体从饱和状态开始向非饱和状态变化。7.5~10kN时间段孔压伴随水位上涨开始回升,而在较下层土体中孔压随时间持续增加。与静水位下孔压相比,动水位孔压在周期加载完成后在不同深度略大于静水位孔压。而基坑外土体在水位条件施加后,竖向位移开始时随水位上升而逐渐加大,水位到达顶峰时,位移差值约为 3.5mm。当水位下降到最低点时沉降值也大于静水位下沉降值约 3mm。动水位周期加载后土体最终的位移相对于静水位下的位移变化不大,分析原因为原本土层在受到水浸没后土颗粒间结合度下降,当水位再次上升时土颗粒受到向上的浮力,使土层沉降值与静水位下变化不大。不同水位下孔压、沉降、测向位移与基坑关系分别如图 11 ~ 图 13 所示。

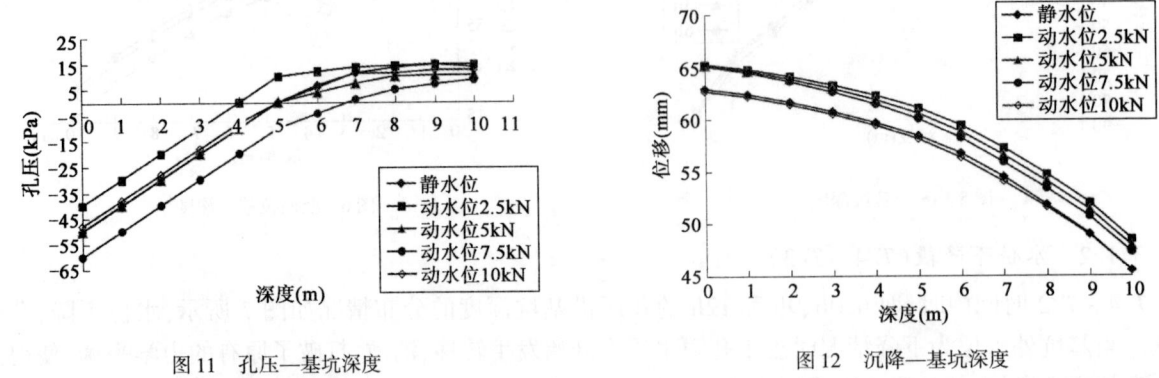

图 11　孔压—基坑深度　　　　　图 12　沉降—基坑深度

基坑挡土墙处土体侧向位移在同一时间点处沿深度表现先线性增加后逐渐减小。水位上升至顶峰时段产生的侧向位移约为静水位下的 5 倍,随水位下降侧向位移逐渐减小。水位回升至原水位后最终侧向位移与静水位相差不大。对基坑底部土体提取位移数据整理如图 14 所示,坑底土体在动水位或在静水位下所产生的竖向位移变化趋势类似,位移随距坑壁距离的增大而逐渐减小后趋于稳定。由于在坑角处流线方向发生变化故靠近坑壁处 0 ~ 8m 处流线较为密集,故仍受较大渗流力影响;而 8 ~ 19m 处流线走势趋于水平,这部分土体此时承担的竖向应力减小,故位移也趋于稳定。而在基坑外水位变化过程中,坑底土体竖向位移均大于静水位,并在动水位达到顶峰时的位移差值达到 5 ~ 7mm。

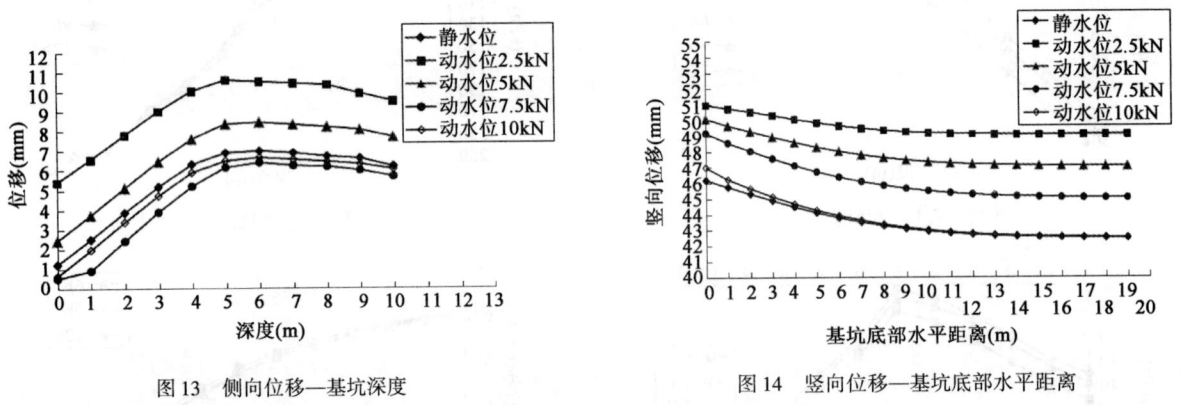

图 13　侧向位移—基坑深度　　　　　图 14　竖向位移—基坑底部水平距离

3.3　不同开挖深度、地下水位变化对基坑的影响

在其他条件一致下改变基坑的开挖深度,在开挖深度分别为 10m 和 15m 的情况下分析地下水位变化时,对基坑坑外土体、坑壁、坑底处的变形影响,如图 15 ~ 图 17 所示。

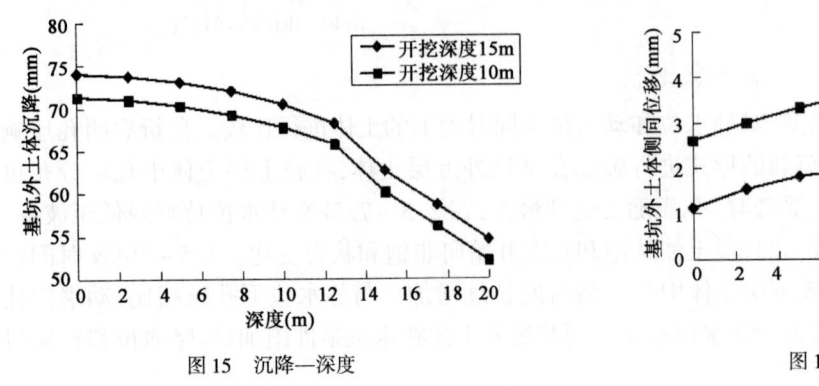

图 15　沉降—深度　　　　　图 16　侧向位移—深度

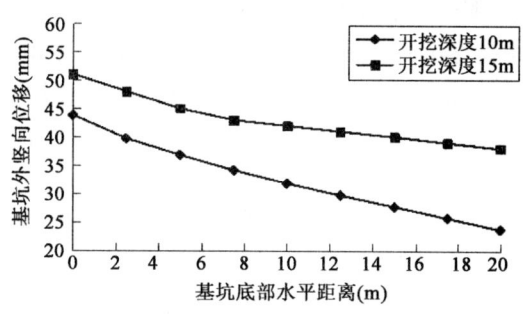

图17 竖向位移—基坑底部水平距离

在地下水位波动下随开挖深度的加大,开挖深度15m时坑外土体沉降值、侧向变形值、坑底土体隆起值均大于开挖深度为10m时的变形值。基坑深度加大情况下坑内水位与加深前相比更低,由于坑外水位并未变化,故而坑内外水头差加大,土体渗透力增强,带给坑外土体程度更为严重的沉降。侧向位移值增大约1倍,不同深度下坑底隆起值差值5~20mm。

3.4 不同支护深度、地下水位变化时对基坑的影响

考虑基坑深度为15m时,分别设置20m的支护结构和25m的支护结构,基坑沉降、侧向位移与深度关系如图18、图19所示,基坑竖向位移与基坑底部水平距离如图20所示。

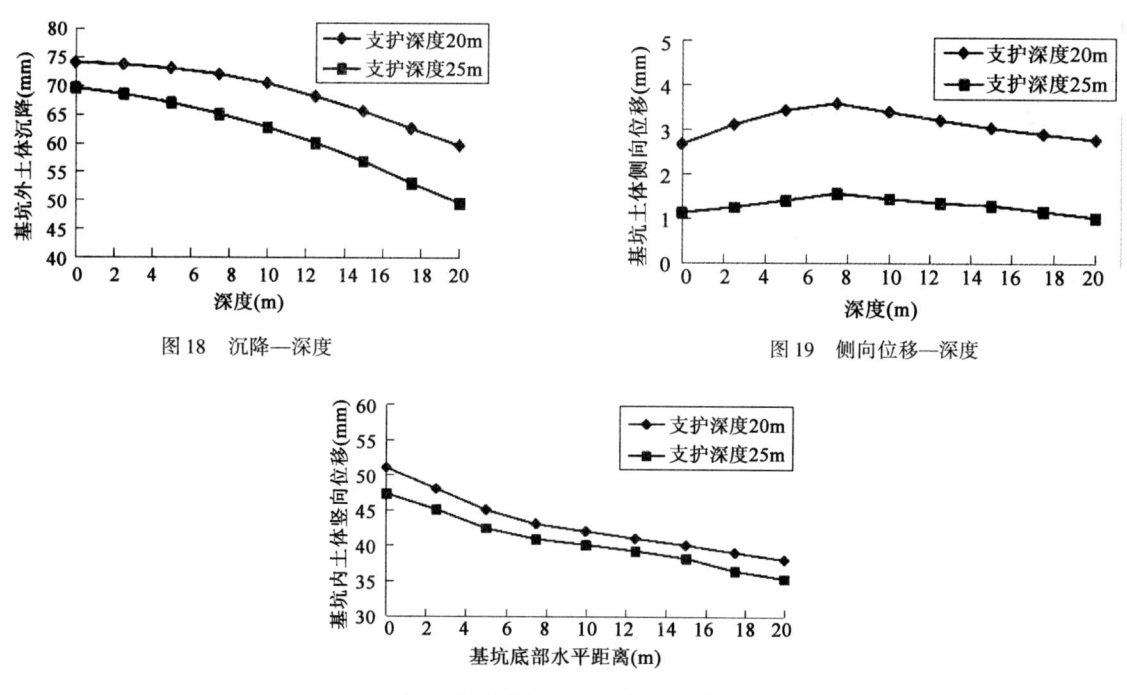

图18 沉降—深度　　　　图19 侧向位移—深度

图20 竖向位移—基坑底部水平距离

地下水位波动情况下由于支护结构深度的加大,坑底土对支护结构的约束也逐渐增加。支护25m时侧向位移值与支护20m时相比明显减小,此时坑外土体沉降值由于支护结构加强带来的侧向约束和支护结构加深随之带来的渗流路径加长影响,沉降得到了一定减小。基坑底部土体也由于渗流路径加长,能量得到有效耗散,隆起程度获得控制,减小5~10mm。

4 结　　语

通过比较静水位和动水位条件基坑土体的响应情况,本文得出以下结论:

(1)在动水位荷载上升段,周期内坑外土体应力路径、应力状态发生改变,轴向应力,围压呈减小趋势,单位土体发生压缩破坏,宏观表现为坑外土体发生沉降。在动水位荷载下降段,孔压减小,轴向应力

增大,围压减小此时土体仍保持沉降,但相对于上升段沉降变化率较小。

(2)动水位周期加载后土体最终沉降位移相对于静水位沉降位移相差不大,均为6cm左右,但动水位变化时段产生的沉降位移略大于静水位。基坑支护处土体侧向位移均大于静水位产生的侧向位移,动水位达到顶峰时产生的侧向位移约为静水位下的侧向位移的2倍。此时基坑底部土体隆起约为5cm,其位移程度略大于静水位。

(3)在动水位影响下,不同开挖深度的基坑变形值存在差异,基坑越深,基坑外土体沉降量、支护处土体侧向位移、基坑底部隆起位移呈不同程度的增大。

(4)随基坑支护结构长度的加大,地下水位波动对坑外土体沉降量、支护处土体侧向位移、坑底隆起位移的影响逐渐减小,变形得到控制。

参考文献

[1] BALIGH M, LEVADOUX J N. Consolidation theory for cyclic loading [J]. Journal of geotechnical Engineering,1978,104(2):415-431.
[2] 蔡袁强,徐长节.循环荷载下成层饱水地基的一维固结[J].振动工程学报,1998,11(2):184-193.
[3] 郑刚,曾超峰.基坑开挖前潜水降水引起的地下连续墙侧移研究[J].岩土工程学报,2013,35(12):2153-2163.
[4] 陈瑞阁,周训.潮汐引起滨海承压含水层地下水位变化的数值模拟[J].水利科技与经济,2012,18(12):4-7.
[5] 应宏伟,聂文峰,黄大中.地下水位波动引起重力式挡墙基坑周围地基土孔压变化及对挡墙稳定性的影响[J].岩石力学与工程学报,2014,33(11):2370-2376.
[6] 李广信,刘早云,温庆博.渗透对基坑水土压力的影响[J].水利学报,2002(5):75-80.
[7] 李广信.高等土力学[M].北京:清华大学出版社,2012.
[8] 章丽莎.滨海地区地下水位变化对地基及基坑渗流特性的影响研究[D].杭州:浙江大学,2017.
[9] 聂文峰.水位波动条件下基坑周围地基土的孔压响应[D].杭州:浙江大学,2013.
[10] 应宏伟,章丽莎,谢康和,等.坑外地下水位波动引起的基坑水土压力响应[J].浙江大学学报(工学版),2014,48(03):492-497.

某高速公路顺层路堑高边坡病害处治

张 魁

(深圳高速运营发展有限公司)

摘 要 某高速公路K314+680~K315+105右侧为顺层路堑高边坡,施工期受连续强降雨影响,发生整体性失稳破坏。本文结合施工实际详细描述了工点病害过程、原因分析、处治思路及处理过程,对顺层边坡防护处治有效方法进行了探讨,特别是阐述了锚杆格梁、深层泄水管对顺层边坡可起到良好的防护支挡作用。

关键词 顺层边坡 边坡防护 锚杆格梁 深层泄水管

0 引 言

某高速公路K314+680~K315+105右侧路堑高边坡,长度425m,挖方最大边坡高度24.3m。场区属于丘陵地貌,地形稍有起伏,山坡自然坡度10°~15°,倾向70°。因连续降雨,边坡在原设计防护措施已施工完成后发生了整体失稳。

K314 工点平面示意图见图 1。

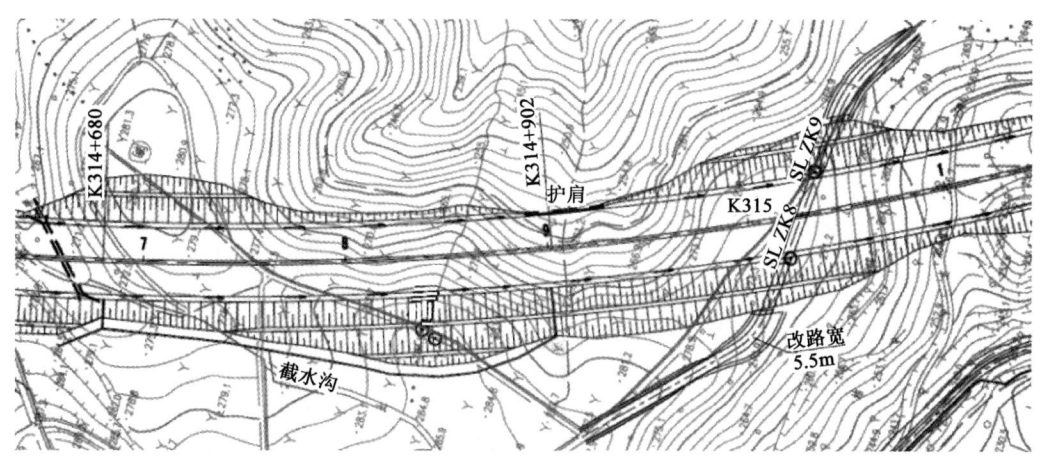

图 1　K314 工点平面示意图

1　工程地质条件

根据施工图详勘阶段地质调绘和钻探资料，场区内出露的地层为上覆第四系全新统残坡积层（Q_4^{dl+el}），下伏泥盆系上统帽子峰组（D_3m），地层特征如下：

1.1　第四系全新统残坡积层（Q_4^{dl+el}）

粉质黏土：黄褐色，硬塑，含约 5% 角砾，粒径 2～10mm，棱角状，局部夹碎石土夹层。勘察钻孔揭露层厚 14.6～16.3m。层顶高程 270.63～272.23 m，承载力基本容许值 200kPa。

碎石：灰褐色，密实，潮湿，碎石母岩成分为砂岩，粒径 20～50mm，含量约 55%，充填 45% 黏性土。勘察揭露层厚 3.1m。层顶高程 284.90 m，承载力基本容许值 400kPa。

1.2　泥盆系上统帽子峰组（D_3m）

钻探揭露路堑区下伏基岩为全风化砂岩：褐黄色，红褐色，原岩结构构造已破坏，岩芯呈砂土状，局部夹碎块状。勘察钻孔揭露层厚 23.7～36.0m，未揭穿。层顶高程 255.93～281.80 m，承载力基本容许值 300kPa。

2　治　理　工　程

2.1　原设计情况

该边坡原设计为三级坡，各级边坡坡率均为 1∶1.25，各级间平台宽均为 2m，边坡分级高度为 10.0m。坡面采用人字形骨架植草防护，该边坡变形滑塌前已经完成开挖，边坡人字形骨架植草防护也已施工完毕，正在进行边沟施工。

K314+680～K315+105 段典型断面如图 2 所示。

2.2　边坡病害调查

该路堑开挖范围内大部分为全风化砂岩，局部夹卵石土，岩体风化为土状，结构松散，孔隙比大，受设计坡口线外侧茶树农业灌溉影响，岩土体常年含水率较大，边坡开挖过程中局部出现地下水涌出。受连续强降雨影响，边坡出现大范围整体性失稳，边坡现状如图 3 所示。

经现场勘查，该边坡 K314+680～K315+040 段目前已进入全面整体失稳阶段，边坡变形几乎破坏贯彻整个工点，大部分边坡在边坡开口线附近发育大量平行于路线走向方向的裂缝，裂缝宽度 0.2～0.4m，可见深度 0.5～1.0m，局部出现地下水涌出现象，其中 2～3 处出现了整体性滑塌，边坡失稳变形破坏图如图 4 所示。

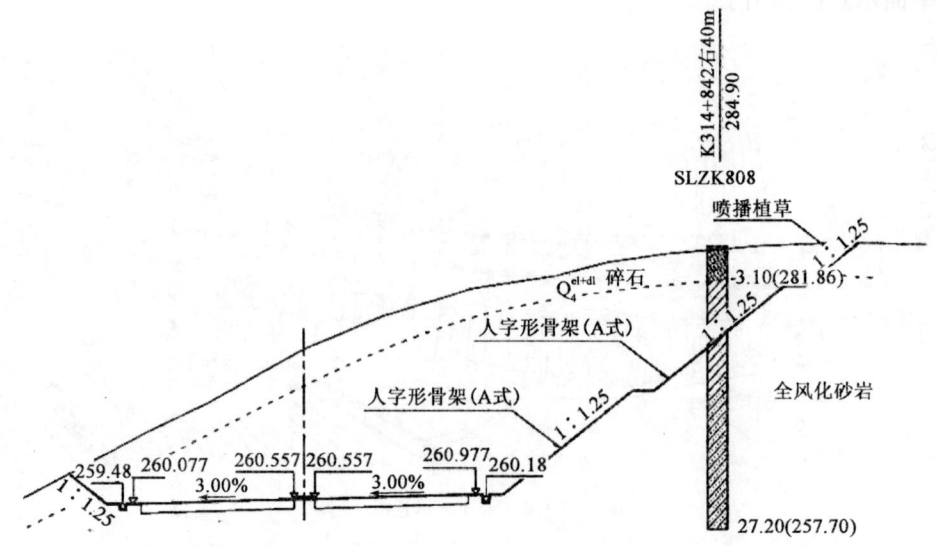

图 2　K314+680～K315+105 段典型断面图（K314+840 断面图）（单位：m）

图 3　边坡全貌图

图 4　三级平台

2.3　高边坡临时处治

2017 年 6 月，进入工点所在地雨季，大量短时强降雨是边坡发生失稳的主要原因。为防止边坡发生进一步变形破坏，降低地表雨水对边坡工点的影响，施工单位对全部坡面和坡面以后 5m 范围内的地表采用隔水薄膜覆盖；对局部地下水出露点，施打临时导水泄水孔，加快地下水的排泄；对局部存在整体性下错的边坡采用一级边坡填土反压。此外，组织人员对边坡变形进行巡查，巡查周期为每天一次。

2.4　边坡稳定性分析

2.4.1　边坡稳定性分析

经现场踏勘分析，边坡开挖范围内主要岩土体为全风化砂岩，局部夹杂较大粒径的卵石土，边坡岩土体结构松散，为地下水提供了良好的渗流通道。受此影响，边坡岩土体抗剪强度急剧下降，发生典型的圆弧形整体失稳破坏。

（1）边坡地层对边坡稳定性的影响

经现场踏勘分析，边坡开挖范围内主要岩土体为全风化砂岩，局部夹杂较大粒径的卵石土，边坡岩土体结构松散，施工开挖过程形成的临空面造成土体应力重新分布，坡体形成较大的应力松弛区，边坡发生剪切变形破坏。

（2）地表雨水渗流对边坡稳定性的影响

松散的结构为地下水的径流提供了良好的渗流通道，受雨水的动水压力作用，边坡岩土体抗剪强度急剧下降。

(3) 岩层产状对边坡稳定性的影响

边坡岩层产状为70°∠48°,边坡倾向为72°,岩层倾向和边坡倾向一致,为典型顺层边坡。全风化顺层边坡的稳定性较弱,结构面一般为泥质胶结软弱结构面,为地下水的渗透提供了良好的排泄通道,受雨水不断的侵蚀影响,易发生沿软弱结构面的层间滑动。

2.4.2 边坡稳定定量分析

由于边坡滑塌变形已出现变形裂缝,原状土体受张拉、挤压变形扰动,土体抗剪强度指标离散性较大。因此,本次稳定性定量分析拟采用反演分析并结合工程类比法确定。

地面线采用原施工图的开挖设计线,选取典型横断面K314+840为研究对象,根据现场踏勘地表裂缝分布位置限定潜在滑动面圆弧入口范围,采用简化的Bishop条分法进行搜索。

由于边坡岩土体受雨水软化作用,黏聚力一般较低,本次反演分析取$C = 20$kPa,求内摩擦角,结合相关规范及实例分析[1-8],反演分析采用的物理力学指标见表1。

岩土层设计参数建议值　　　　　　　　　　表1

地层编号	岩土名称	重度(kN/cm³)	黏聚力 C(MPa)	内摩擦角 φ(°)
1	全风化砂岩夹卵石土	19.5	20.0	18.0

经计算可知,岩土体抗剪强度参数取表1所示值时,其边坡稳定性安全系数为0.962,边坡处于极限平衡状态。其稳定性分析模型和计算显示的潜在滑动面如图5所示。

2.5 治理措施

2.5.1 边坡线

边坡放缓为二级,坡率均为1:1.5,一级坡高为10.0m,平台加宽到10m,二级边坡一坡到顶。典型断面如图6所示。

2.5.2 边坡处治加固设计

加宽平台后清除原塌方体,一级边坡K314+739~K315+050、二级边坡K314+816~K314+962均采用锚杆格梁+喷播植草进行加固,框架梁纵梁间距调整为2.5m。其余边坡坡面采用挂网客土喷播植草(8cm)进行防护。

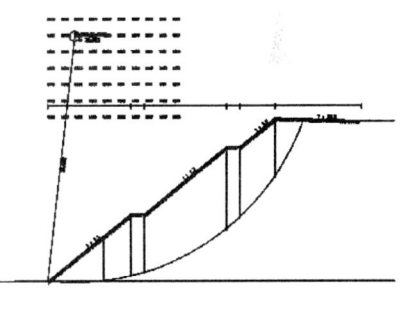

图5　反演分析结果图

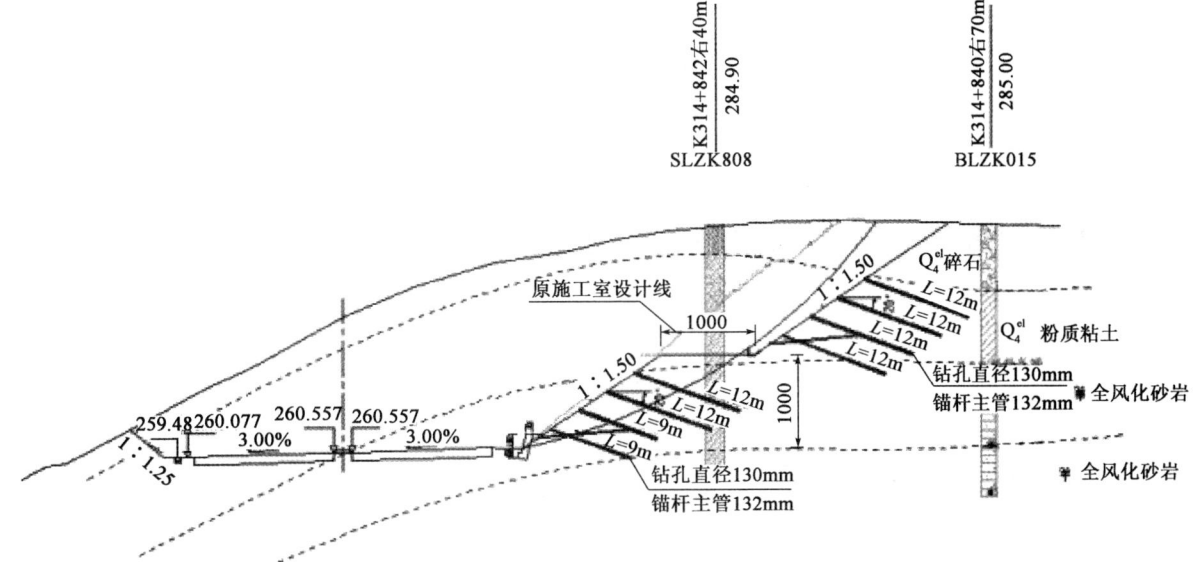

图6　典型断面图

2.5.3 边坡支挡设计

一级边坡 K314+680～K315+105 坡脚采用防护型挡土墙,加固长度为 425m,挡土墙总高度为 2.5m,其中基础埋置深度为 1.0m。

2.5.4 边坡排水设计

产生边坡不稳定重要的原因之一是地表水和地下水的作用,有效的排水设计是维护边坡稳定的措施之一。为有效排出坡体渗水,在各级边坡坡脚设置深层泄水孔,钻孔深度为 10.0m,纵向间距为 4.0m。一级平台设置 60cm×60cm 梯形截水沟。

2.5.5 边坡稳定性计算

经边坡稳定性计算,边坡稳定性安全系数为 1.211。

3 结语

K314 是顺层高路堑边坡,表层的碎石土为地下水的径流提供了良好的渗流通道,原设计防护措施较弱,受连续的强降雨影响,导致边坡整体性失稳。边坡开挖过程中局部出现过地下水涌出,施工单位并未意识到隐患,未响应增加排水措施。因此,应加强路堑高边坡施工过程中的动态管理,做到动态变更设计。

山区高速公路施工是一个破坏山体原有平衡而又支挡加固,重新建立新平衡的过程[2]。顺层地段易产生边坡病害,在路线设计中要尽量绕避,如不能绕避,应尽可能采取预加固措施,以免坡体开挖变形后再采取措施造成费用增加。锚杆格梁可适用于顺层边坡的处治,在坡脚处增加挡墙,使边坡抗剪能力加强,有效保证了边坡的稳定。

强降雨会短时间内在高边坡上形成暂时的水压力,对高边坡的稳定性会带来不利影响,对于夹杂碎石土的地层,可增加深层泄水,使渗水尽快流出坡体,降低强降雨对坡体稳定性的影响。

参考文献

[1] 国土资源部. 滑坡防治工程设计与施工技术规范:DZ/T 0219—2006[S]. 北京:中国标准出版社,2006.
[2] 马惠民,王恭先,周德培. 山区高速公路高边坡病害防治实例[M]. 北京:人民交通出版社,2006.
[3] 王恭先. 滑坡防治方案的选择与优化[J]. 岩石力学与工程学报,2006,25(2):3867-3873.
[4] 王恭先. 滑坡防治中的关键技术及处理方法[J]. 岩石力学与工程学报,2005,21(34):3818-3827.
[5] 王恭先. 滑坡学与滑坡防治技术[M]. 北京:中国铁道出版社,2004.
[6] 邵重阳. 公路工程滑坡及其防治措施研究[J]. 山西建筑,2013,39(18):120-121.
[7] 温树林. 广东云浮至罗定高速公路顺层滑坡形成机理分析及处治措施[J]. 铁道建筑,2014,86(4):86-89.
[8] 何平,邵俊江. 杭千高速公路的顺层滑坡问题及其原因分析[J]. 山西建筑,2009,35(34):286-287.

沿海地区岩溶发育区路基处治技术数值分析

伊力夏提·奥斯曼

(长安大学公路学院)

摘 要 我国沿海例如粤北以及粤西等一些地区公路工程修建常遇到岩溶灾害,同时也涌现了很多优秀的处治技术。基于汕湛高速公路实际处治工程,运用有限元软件对处治原则和处置措施进行模拟研究。结果表明:在覆盖土层较厚,顶板较薄,厚跨比为 0.27,埋深 15m 时,溶洞对于道路施工的影响较小,建议酌情考虑处理。若探明覆盖层较薄且顶板较厚时可采用混凝土盖板跨越处理,并且适当增加混凝土盖板中心区域厚度可以提升其处置效果。对覆盖层厚、塌陷风险大的段落或岩溶主要为土洞且全充填软塑、流塑状黏土的可采用高压旋喷桩处治,高压旋喷桩加固对道路路基稳定性有较大的提升。利用数值模拟技术对岩溶病害处治原则与措施进行分析,所得结果与实测数据较为相近,且对处置机理、效果进行分析,具有一定的参考作用,可供沿海岩溶地区道路工程建设参考。

关键词 道路工程 岩溶发育区 盖板跨越 高压旋喷桩 数值模拟

0 引 言

在岩溶地区修建公路工程必须考虑到岩溶对于公路本身的影响,位于地基下方的溶洞由于其自身极其不稳定的性质会直接影响土体上方的路基、路面工程的稳定性,不利于行车安全[1-2]。在国家逐步加大基础设施建设的大背景下,基础设施工程遍及全国各地,越来越多的公路运输、管道运输等线路会穿越岩溶区上方。近年来,根据岩溶区路基修建结果表明:位于岩溶发育区修建工程时,应把岩溶路基的稳定性研究放在首位,其影响因素有上方覆盖土层的厚度、跨度、强度、岩溶的发育程度及上方荷载等[3];国内学者在岩溶区域公路工程修建方面研究成果硕果累累。张永杰等[4]通过构造模糊综合评判模型,探讨多个因素对于岩溶段公路路基稳定性的影响,综合体现出不利因素对路基路面工程的影响。刘海鸿等[5]对岩溶路基突水原因进行了探讨,并对于岩溶区域地下水的勘察、施工期应注意事项提出了相关观点,这对工程施工有着良好的借鉴意义。武鑫等[6]认为岩溶上方覆盖层变形时有一种特殊的破坏类型,通过将岩溶塌陷概化为多种地质模型,从破坏模式分析其破坏类型,通过理论分析研究岩溶区的塌陷问题。以往的研究多集中在理论、公式推导、单一因素的数值模拟以及相似模型试验。针对大型工程岩溶发育区路基处治技术比选以及处治效果分析的较少。在我国沿海地区例如粤北以及粤西等一些地区,碳酸盐岩广泛分布发育,表现出强发育的特征,是高速公路建设过程中无法绕开一个重点难题。除了参考相关理论、规范之外,相邻工程经验中所使用的参数也具有极高的参考价值。依托汕湛高速公路某标段工程,根据地勘资料以及施工资料,制定岩溶处治原则及选定相应的处治措施,采用有限元的方法,对不同工程概况采取的措施以及参数进行数值模拟,并通过和监测数值进行比较,为沿海地区岩溶发育区路基处治提供一定参考。

1 工程概况

广东汕湛高速公路某标段工程经探明,有30余千米位于岩溶区域,需要采取相应的措施处理之后才能修建。该区域较为潮湿,地表杂草丛生,植被茂密。地处粤西南低纬度区域,常年受亚热带季风影响,所处新兴县最大降雨量高达400mm,年平均降雨量1680.2mm,河流较为发达,有着岩溶发育所需要的水资源。工程区域周围丘陵密布,地势高低起伏,该地区具备岩溶充分发育的条件。通过地质勘查和现场钻孔分析可知:在工程修建区域,存在大量溶洞,且溶洞具有深浅不一,厚跨比普遍较小,空洞区域较大,泥灰岩岩溶发育率相对较低等。地层组成从上到下主要依次为种植土、粉质黏土、粉细砂、圆砾土、石灰岩等。如果岩溶没有合理、妥善处置,会对工程造成较大的不良影响。常见的岩溶危害有岩溶塌陷、岩溶洞穴、地表渗出岩溶水、落水洞等,如图1所示[13]。

通过地勘探明岩溶发育区中溶洞具体分布,包括溶洞具体位置,高度、厚度、具体形状。通过钻孔探明土层分布,获知覆盖层厚度、顶板厚度,有无填充等信息。确定广东汕湛高速公路某标段道路工程下方和附近溶洞相关参数后,根据相关规范及以往的处治经验[7-12],制定处治大纲。其中主要的处置原则和手段如下:

(1)正常情况下原则上对溶洞不做处理的情形:①溶洞顶板的厚跨比大于0.8时;②溶洞顶板的厚跨比小于0.8,但其等效覆盖层厚度却远比溶洞宽度大,覆盖土层的稳定性较好且大于10m;③溶洞顶板的厚跨比小于0.8,但其等效覆盖层厚度却远比溶洞宽度大,溶洞顶板为厚度大于3m的中风化岩;④溶洞、土洞内为可塑、硬塑状全充填时。

基金项目:中央高校基本科研业务费专项资助项目(300102218408)。

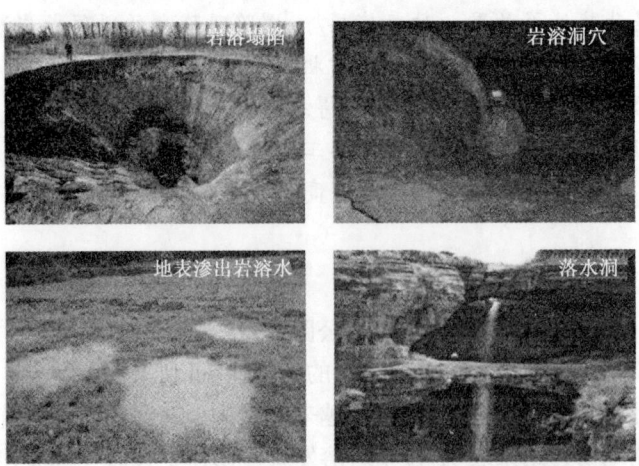

图1 浅埋偏压段岩层

(2) 不满足以上条件，根据埋深来判断是否对溶洞进行处理：处治临界深度为15m，埋深小于15m的溶洞一律处治，埋深大于15m的溶洞根据实际情况酌情处理。

(3) 对于埋深小于3m的浅层溶洞，建议开挖后根据现场实际情况回填片石、砂砾等进行处理，并保证其压实度达到相应技术标准。

(4) 对覆盖层厚、塌陷风险大的段落或岩溶主要为土洞且全充填软塑、流塑状黏土的，建议采用粉喷桩或旋喷桩对溶洞腔体内的填充物进行固结，以形成复合地基（厚跨比较小，上层覆盖土层较厚，溶洞埋深较小）。

(5) 对于挖方段岩溶，应在开挖并开展勘探后再确定具体的处置方案。如开挖后直接揭示或探明覆盖层较薄且溶洞较深的，可酌情采用混凝土盖板跨越处理（厚跨比适中，上层覆盖土层较厚，溶洞埋深较大）。

2 处治埋深界定模拟

2.1 处治埋深界定建模思路

为判断选取15m作为临界处理深度是否合理，综合考虑填方路基填土高度、路基所处区域覆盖层厚度、顶板厚度等因素，建立覆盖层厚度为15m，顶板为中风化灰岩，厚度为2m，覆盖层类型为粉土并且路堤高度较大的工况。

2.2 处治埋深界定模型概况

采用MIDAS有限元软件建立处治埋深界定模型，模型概况如图2所示：考虑边界效应选取模型尺寸为长(100m)、宽(75m)、高(50m)，土层可分为3层，依次为粉土(3m)、密实砂土(9.7m)、中风化石灰岩(35m)；溶洞位于中风化灰岩中，高7.5m，顶板厚度2.3m，厚跨比0.27；溶洞区域为流塑状粉质黏土全填充，路堤填方高度6.5m，均为三维实体单元，采用摩尔—库仑本构模型。道路按2车道设计，包括人行道宽10.5m，面层、基层和底基层厚度分别为15cm、78cm，运用板单元模拟，弹性本构关系。约束为软件自带的自动约束，荷载包括自重荷载，根据规范选取车辆荷载不利组合值为14.5 kN/m^2。

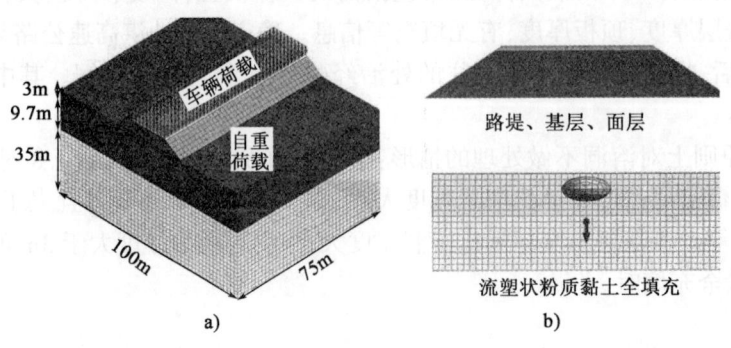

图2 处治埋深界定模型概况

2.3 模型参数选取

本次建模所使用的土体参数,路基、路面等建筑材料的参数由项目中心实验室测试所得,相关缺失数据参考相关规范和论文。具体数据见表1。

土体及结构物理及力学参数 表1

名　称	模型类型	重度(kN/m³)	弹性模量(MPa)	泊松比
粉土	摩尔—库仑	14.3	4.7	0.39
密实细砂	摩尔—库仑	17.5	8.8	0.38
中风化灰岩	摩尔—库仑	19.8	11.8	0.37
流塑状粉质黏土	摩尔—库仑	12.8	4.5	0.38
路基填土(碎石)	弹性	19.2	240	0.33
公路沥青面层	弹性	23.2	10000	0.29
公路基层及底基层	弹性	25.2	9800	0.31
混凝土盖板	弹性	25.3	12000	0.23
高压旋喷桩	弹性	23.7	9000	0.29

2.4 施工阶段模拟

道路施工模拟具体步骤如下:①初始阶段,开启土体单元组,添加边界约束,荷载组为土体自重,同时位移清零。②路堤施工,添加路堤单元组,模拟路堤的施工过程。③依次添加底基层、基层、面层模拟路面施工。④添加车辆荷载,模拟通车运营后,探究道路行车安全和行车舒适性。

2.5 结果分析

为探究选取15m作为临界处理深度是否合理,依工况建模计算,结果如下:其中模型整体沉降最大值为11.2mm,位于模型的路面中心。路基、路面施工的影响范围波及溶洞区域,溶洞顶板位置处沉降值大于周围部位沉降。可见溶洞的存在对于路基、路面的施工仍然有所影响。观察沉降数值可知:溶洞顶底沉降差异为3.7mm,埋深差距6.8m,考虑到填充物为流塑状粉质黏土,埋深差距导致的顶底沉降差异,路基、路面的施工对于溶洞顶板影响认定为微弱。观察路面云图可知:路面沉降最大区域位于路面中心,溶洞所在的正上方路面未表现出明显的差异沉降,路面中心沉降最大值为7.8mm,符合路基沉降规范所要求。可见在覆盖土层较厚,溶洞顶板较薄,溶洞厚跨比为0.27,路堤高度较大的情况,溶洞埋深15m对于道路施工的影响较小,原则上可以不处置。但是从模拟结果来看,溶洞的存在仍有影响,在其他更为恶劣的工况条件下,建议酌情考虑处理。相关模拟图如图3~图5所示。

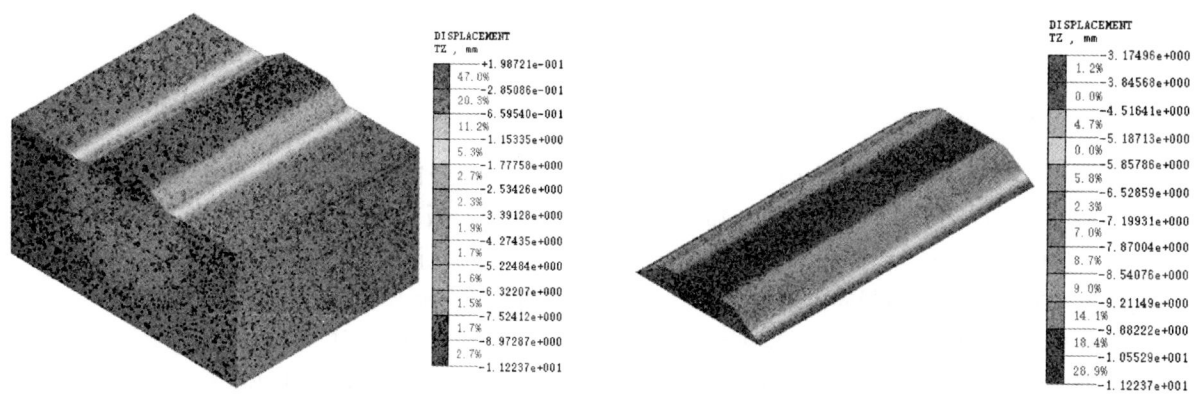

图3　处治埋深界定模型总体沉降(单位:mm)　　　　图4　处治埋深界定模型路堤沉降(单位:mm)

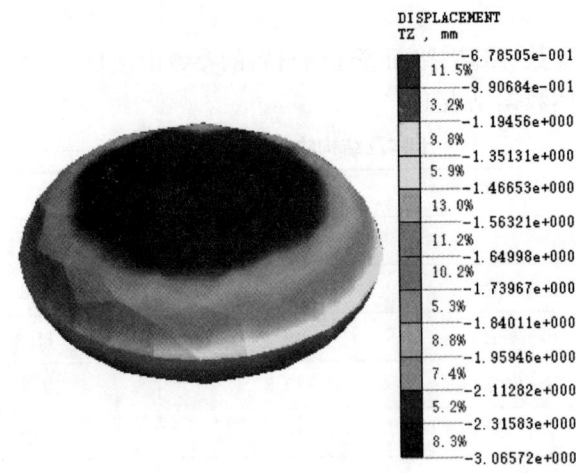

图5 处治埋深界定模型溶洞沉降(单位:mm)

3 混凝土盖板跨越模拟

3.1 模型概况

汕湛高速公路某标段岩溶路基使用了混凝土盖板跨越的处治措施,考虑边界效应模型尺寸选取长×宽×高为100m×75m×50m,具体工况为路堤高6.5m,溶洞高约5.5m,跨度15.5m,空腔无填充物,埋深8.7m,表层覆土类型粉质黏土2.5m,顶板厚度约6.2m,溶洞处于中风化灰岩之中。溶洞厚跨比为0.5,处治方案为10m×20m厚30cm盖板跨越处治。其中混凝土盖板采用2D板单元模拟,弹性本构关系,边界采用软件自带自动约束,荷载包括自重荷载,根据规范选取车辆荷载不利组合值为14.5kN/m²。模型总体如图6所示。设置对比工况,对比工况为无混凝土盖板处理。模型所设计的参数选取参考表1。其中混凝土盖板跨越阶段体现在路堤施工期,将混凝土盖板单元组添加进去,并设置对照组,对照组则无盖板跨越处治,不添加混凝土盖板。

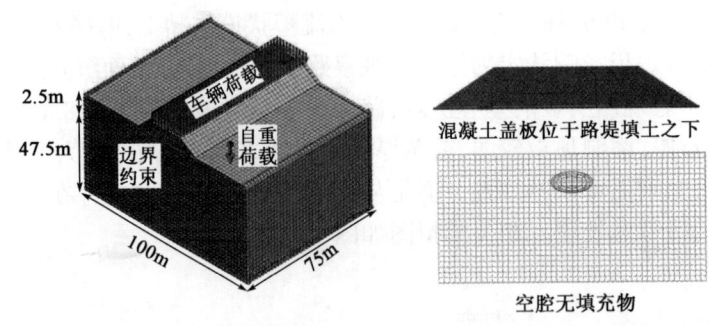

图6 模型总体图

3.2 结果分析

混凝土盖板跨越的处治措施有限元模型计算结果表明:模型竖向变形以沉降为主,其中无处治措施情况下,模型最大竖向位移达到了20.54mm,而设置混凝土盖板处治之后,最大竖向位移减小到了10.55mm。整体变形减小了48.64%,模型沉降最大值均位于溶洞所在位置的路面上方。

无处治措施运营后总体竖向位移如图7所示,混凝土盖板跨越运营后总体竖向位移如图8所示。

实际工程中需要监控测量路面的沉降值,模型中对此分析路面沉降值的变化,探究混凝土盖板跨越的实际效果。有无处治措施下模型路面沉降值分别为10.55mm、20.54mm。提取两个模型下有无处治措施道路中心线两个阶段的运营阶段沉降值,绘制分布曲线,如图9、图10所示:路面施工后路面在溶洞区域处表现出一个沉降槽,通过施加车辆荷载后模拟运营阶段,路面出现工后沉降,有无处置措施工后沉降值分别为1.25mm、2.41mm。由模型结果可知,无混凝土盖板处治措施下,路面所表现出沉降值符合规范,但是考虑到错综复杂的工程因素,安全性不高;使用混凝土盖板跨越之后,路面沉降值减小48.64%,安全性大大提升。因此在覆盖层较薄,溶洞较深的情况下使用混凝土盖板跨越对岩溶的处治效果较为显著。

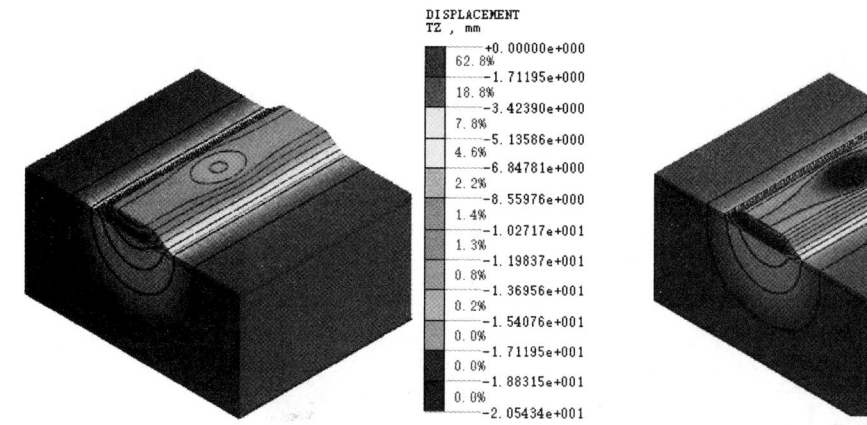
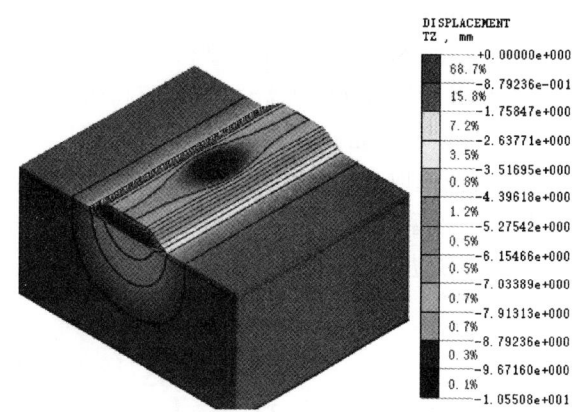

图7　无处治措施运营后总体竖向变形(单位:mm)　　　　图8　混凝土盖板跨越运营后总体竖向变形(单位:mm)

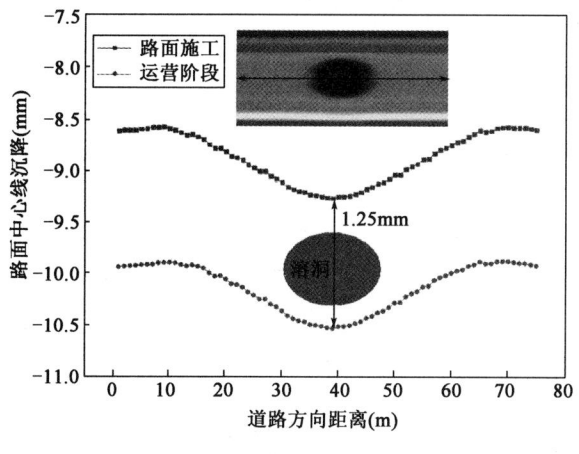
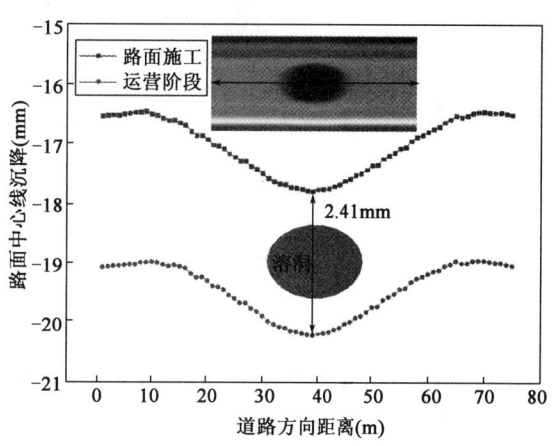

图9　无措施道路中线沉降分布　　　　　　　　图10　混凝土盖板跨越道路中线沉降分布

由混凝土盖板的竖向形变可知,由于溶洞正上方区域承载力较弱,混凝土盖板中心区域沉降值最大,为7.37mm。盖板中心部位局部变形严重,分析其自身结构的弯矩可知,其水平方向弯矩呈对称分布,值为5.45kN·m/m。混凝土板厚为30cm,即弯矩最大值为18.16kN·m。由混凝土盖板作用机理可知,适当增加混凝土盖板中心区域厚度,可以提升其处置效果。相关模拟图如图11、图12所示。

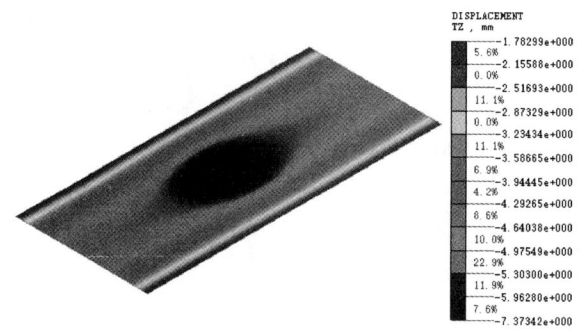
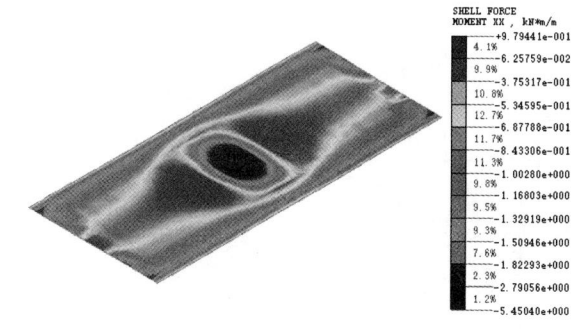

图11　混凝土盖板竖向位移(单位:mm)　　　　　　图12　混凝土盖板竖向弯矩(单位:kN·m/m)

4 高压旋喷桩加固模拟

4.1 模型概况

汕湛高速公路某标段岩溶路基使用了混凝土盖板跨越的处治措施,考虑边界效应模型尺寸选取长×宽×高为80m×50m×50m,具体工况为路堤高5m,溶洞高约10.8m,跨度3.5m,洞内全填充流塑状粉质黏土。埋深11.6m,表层覆土类型密实细砂土10.3m,顶板厚度约1.3m,溶洞处于中风化灰岩(39.7m)之中,溶洞厚跨比为0.37。处治方案采用高压旋喷桩处治,具体参数为:桩径0.8m,长度18m,旋喷桩间距为2m,处治区域20m×20m,呈梅花桩状分布,1D桩单元弹性本构。边界采用自动约束,荷载包括自重荷载,根据规范选取车辆荷载不利组合值为14.5kN/m²。如图13所示。设置对比工况,对比工况为高压旋喷桩处治。模型所设计的参数选取参考表1。其中高压旋喷桩处治阶段体现在路堤施工期,将高压旋喷桩单元组添加进去,并设置对照组,对照组则无高压旋喷桩处治。

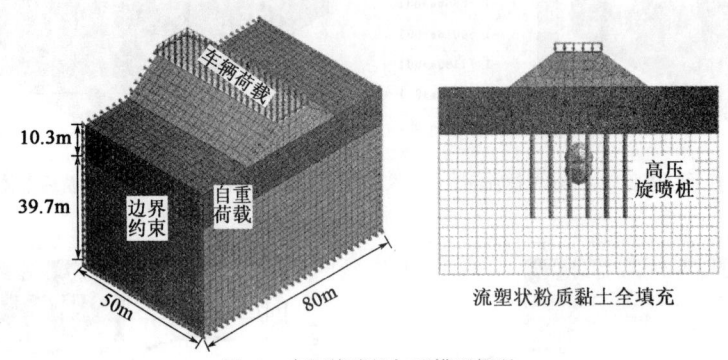

图13 高压旋喷桩加固模型概况

4.2 结果分析

高压旋喷桩加固的处治措施有限元模型计算结果表明(图14、图15):模型主要以竖向变形为主,当覆盖层较厚,溶洞顶板厚度较小时,其中无处治措施情况下,模型最大竖向位移达到32.65mm,在高压旋喷桩加固处治之后,最大竖向位移减小到16.26mm,整体变形减小50.20%。对比地基密实细砂土沉降值:无处治措施情况下最大沉降值为24.40mm,且位于在溶洞的正上方;处治后最大沉降值为10.35mm,位于溶洞附近区域。由此可知:溶洞区域在高压旋喷桩处治后,地基承载力比周围无溶洞区域地基更大。分析溶洞区域沉降值:无处治措施情况下最大沉降值为7.20mm,顶底差异4.20mm;处治后最大沉降值为3.26mm,顶底差异1.57mm,顶板稳定性有了较大的提升。分析高压旋喷桩处治机理:如图16、图17所示,桩身以竖向变形为主,竖向变形最大值为7.16mm,位于桩身顶部。桩体穿越地层密实细砂土、中风化灰岩,桩体位于密实细砂土的部分变形更大;桩体表现为承压,桩身轴力最大值为457kN,桩体位于密实细砂土的部分桩身承受轴力更大,位于中风化灰岩部位的桩身轴力较小。可见使用高压旋喷桩加固对道路路基稳定性有较大的提升,将桩体打入岩层足够深度更有利于桩身的稳定性。

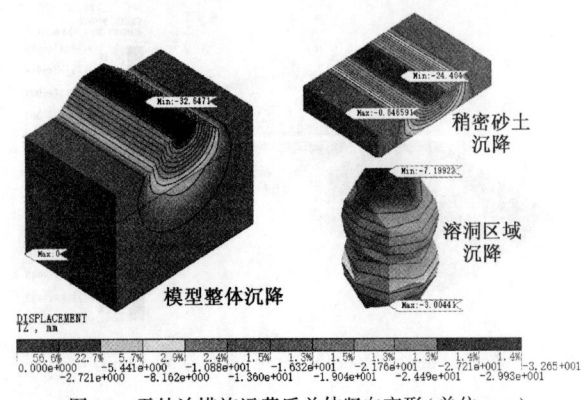

图14 无处治措施运营后总体竖向变形(单位:mm)

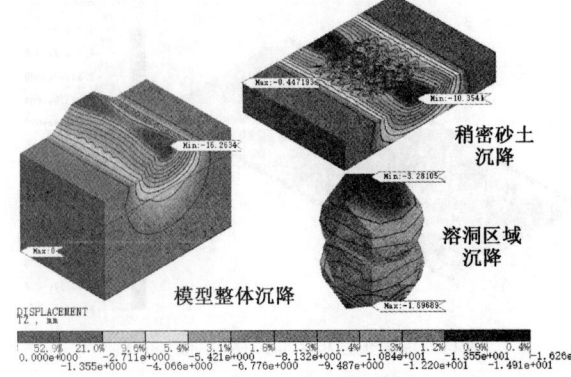

图15 高压旋喷桩运营后总体竖向变形(单位:mm)

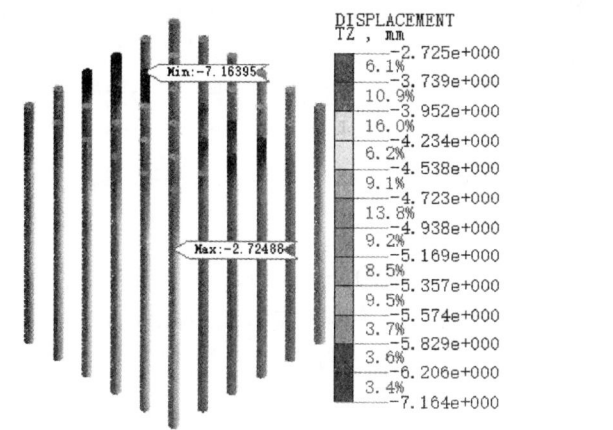 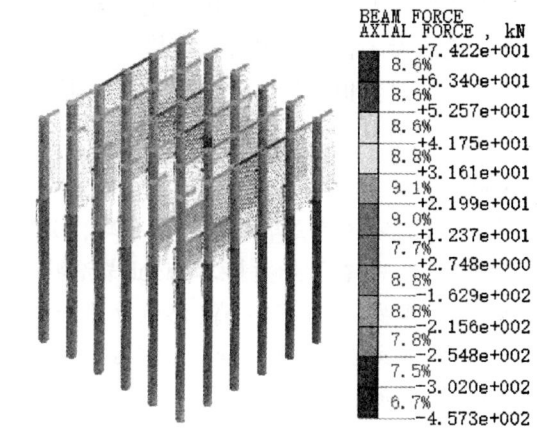

图16 高压旋喷桩处治运营后桩基础沉降(单位:mm)　　　图17 高压旋喷桩处治运营后桩基础桩身轴力(单位:kN)

5 监测数据对比分析

有限元部分选取了3个实际工况进行建模分析,从工程监测数据提取相应工况的路面沉降值,绘制时程曲线(图18)进行比较分析。其中,处治埋深界定、混凝土盖板跨越、高压旋喷桩加固数值模型最终最大沉降值分别下为11.2mm、10.55mm、16.26mm；其相对应实际工况的监测数据最终最大沉降值为13.40mm、12.67mm、16.33mm。实际工程中影响因素交互作用,数值模型难以全部都考虑进去,最终结果差距较小,数值模拟的结论有参考价值。另外,数值模型可以对处治措施的范围、效果进行定性分析。

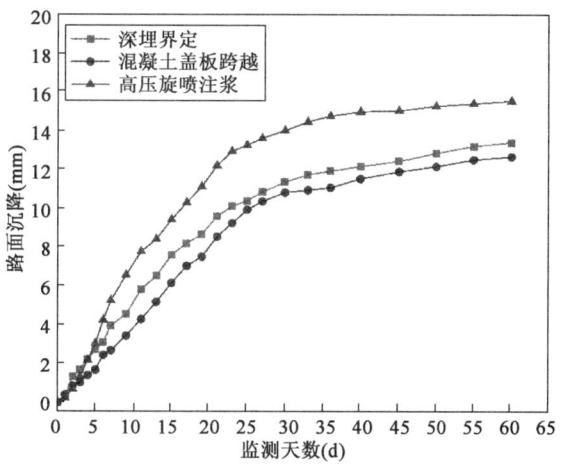

图18 相关工况路基土体竖向变形监测时程曲线

6 结　论

探究选取15m作为临界处理深度,在覆盖土层较厚、溶洞顶板较薄、溶洞厚跨比为0.27、路堤高度较大的情况下,模型整体沉降最大值为11.2mm,路面中心沉降最大值为7.8mm,符合路基沉降规范所要求。但是从模拟结果来看,溶洞的存在仍有影响,在其他更为恶劣的工况条件下,建议酌情考虑处理。

对于覆土厚度小、顶板厚度较大,等效覆盖层不及溶洞宽度大的工况,在采用混凝土盖板跨越处治之后,最大竖向位移减小到了10.55mm。整体变形减小了48.64%,由混凝土盖板作用机理可知,适当增加混凝土盖板中心区域厚度可以提升其处治效果。

对于覆土厚度大、顶板厚度较小,溶洞充填有流塑状黏土的工况,在采用高压旋喷桩处治之后,最大竖向位移减小到16.26mm,整体变形减小50.20%。从桩体作用机理可知,高压旋喷桩加固对道路路基稳定性有较大提升,将桩体打入岩层足够深度更有利于桩身的稳定。

提取相应工况的监测数据进行比对分析可知:实测数据与数值模拟结果最终沉降值差距较小,数值模拟的结论有参考价值。另外数值模拟对与处治措施的处治效果可以定性分析,对其处治机理能给出相应的解释。通过数值模拟研究工程岩溶病害的处治大纲,对其中的处治原则和手段分步建模,结论具有一定的参考价值。

参考文献

[1] 张俭.岩溶地区的公路施工[J].公路,2002(8):27-28.
[2] 谭清岚.在岩溶地区修建公路防止岩溶病害的做法[J].公路,1990(5):11-12.
[3] 姚裕春,李安洪,陈裕刚,等.洛湛铁路岩溶路基加固分析[J].铁道工程学报,2009,26(6):41-43.
[4] 张永杰,曹文贵,赵明华,等.岩溶区公路路基稳定性的区间模糊评判分析方法[J].岩土工程学报,2011(1):38-44.
[5] 刘海鸿,王跃飞,龚斌.岩溶路基突水原因分析及处治设计[J].湖南交通科技,2013,39(04):22-24.
[6] 武鑫,王艺霖,黄敬军,等.江苏徐州地区岩溶塌陷致塌力学模型及水位控制红线[J].中国地质灾害与防治学报,2019,30(02):67-77.
[7] 蒋小珍,雷明堂,李瑜,等.岩溶水作用下填石路基稳定性模型试验研究[J].中国岩溶,2005,24(2).
[8] 曾永红,丁兆锋,李楚根.确定高速铁路高填方软土及岩溶地基加固方案[J].铁道工程学报,2016,33(2):25-27.
[9] 华丽晶.芜铜铁路狮子山站岩溶塌陷路基勘察与整治研究[J].铁道工程学报,2014(1):32-36.
[10] 苏谦,黄俊杰,白皓,等.铁路站场岩溶地基加固补强技术与效果分析[J].岩土力学,2013,34(3):776-782.
[11] 叶中兵.石武客运专线路基岩溶注浆施工技术[J].铁道标准设计,2010(9):46-49.
[12] 王海艳,冯靖.岩溶注浆处理客运专线铁路软土地基施工质量控制[J].铁道标准设计,2009(s1):10-12.

地下水位变化对基坑非稳定渗流的影响研究

程马遥 魏永 曾洋 杨虹

(佛山科学技术学院土木系)

摘要 珠三角地区由于季节性强降雨,地下水位会发生突变现象。地下水位动态变化导致基坑周围渗流变得更为复杂,对基坑的安全和稳定性具有不利的影响。已有文献对稳定渗流的研究较为成熟,但对非稳定性渗流的研究较少。本文以有限元法为基础,对已有的试验模型进行渗流模拟。在进一步优化基坑渗流的数值模拟分析时,考虑了基坑土体的渗透系数、压缩模量等随深度变化,以及基坑被动区开挖卸载对坑外水位变化引起的基坑非稳定渗流的影响。结果表明,考虑土体渗透系数、压缩模量比不考虑时对基坑的非稳定渗流影响要大;随着基坑开挖的深度增加,基坑的非稳定渗流越来越强,对基坑的影响也会越来越大。

关键词 地下水位 基坑 非稳定渗流

0 引言

沿海城市的快速发展,导致了诸如超高层建筑、地下商场、地铁换乘站等重要地下工程的出现。基坑作为地下结构的重要组成部分,其安全性和稳定性尤为重要。珠三角地区强降雨导致地下水位迅速上升,且升幅大[1]。在潮位和降雨作用下,海堤长期处于饱和—非饱和非稳定渗流状态,易导致海堤失稳和滑坡[2]。滨海地区由于海床和海洋结构基础受到波浪载荷等复杂的应力[3-6],导致地下水位波动。然而,在工程实践中,受地下水影响,围护结构发生变形,进而对人们的生命财产造成损失。在建造过程中,出现各种被破坏现象,如建筑物漏水、倾斜等。应用现代技术——井点降水法和明沟排水法可减少各种破坏现象。目前施工标准往往忽略了在水头差作用下的地下水的流动,以至于没有考虑渗流场的变化[7]。本文基于ABAQUS有限元软件,结合已有的室内试验,建立基于有效应力算法的考虑渗流应力耦合作用模型。同时,考虑在不同深度下的土体渗透系数和压缩模量以及基坑被动区开挖卸荷对基坑外水位变化引起的基坑失稳渗流的影响。对基坑工程具有一定的指导意义。

1 模型试验简介

如图1所示,基坑试验模型箱前后嵌固透明钢化玻璃,水箱固定在模型箱内的侧上方,水箱与试验土用铝板隔开,铝板表面设置大量水孔,并粘贴反滤土工织物。水箱的水位通过水箱底部的阀门来调节。基坑试验模型的支护结构由挡土墙和内支撑构成。模型箱中试验砂的填筑高度为74.5cm,挡土墙采用6mm厚铝板,入土深度深为35cm。模型箱的内支撑为直径10mm的实心铝杆,用于连接挡土墙和反力板,由反力板提供支反力。基坑剖面主动侧的试验土体宽度为120cm,被动侧为40cm。基坑被动区的开挖深度为10cm。对于基坑稳定渗流试验,设定坑外水位距挡土墙主动侧试验土体的顶部距离恒为5cm;对于非稳定渗流试验,其距离变化范围设定为5~15cm。图2为坑外水位变化示意图,仅考虑水位变化为平动的形式[8]。

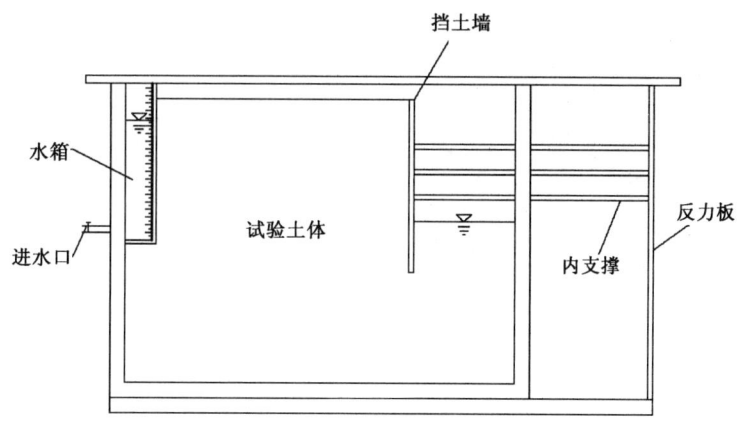

图1 模型箱示意图

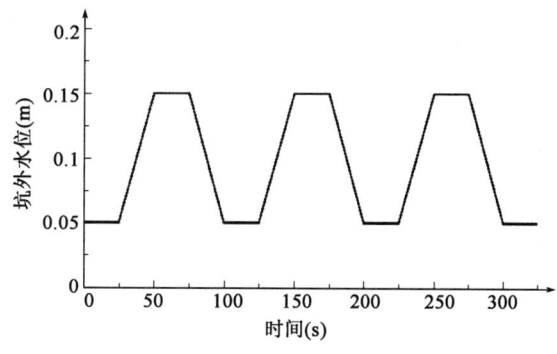

图2 坑外水位随时间变化示意图

基金项目:佛山市智慧型陆地与海洋土木工程材料工程技术研究开发中心;广东省科技厅粤佛联合基金项目(N.2019A1515111100);广东省教育厅青年创新项目(N.2019KQNCX170);佛山市科技创新项目(N.1920001001673)。

2 有限元模型的建立

2.1 基本假定

数值模拟计算过程中,为了有针对性地分析所关注的对象,将忽略掉一些次要影响因素,本文在模拟时采取一些假定,具体如下:

(1)由于试验土体采用的是标准细砂,假定土体为均质材料并取为线弹性体,力学参数各向同性。

(2)在开挖之前,土体已经达到饱和状态。

(3)初始水位处于地表,地下水渗流符合Darcy定律。

(4)设铝板为地下连续墙,为均质、连续弹性体,假定其渗透系数为0m/s。

2.2 单元类型选择及部件创建

地连墙基坑渗流问题主要部件有地连墙、土体、内支撑,本文拟分别采用ABAQUS的二维实体弹性材料单元来模拟地连墙和土体,内支撑采用施加位移约束的条件来实现,即假设支撑是刚性的。模型装配后如图3所示。

图3 模型装配

2.3 材料属性设置

地连墙和土体均采用线弹性模型,其基于广义胡克定律,为各向同性弹性。地连墙的弹性模量E为70GPa,泊松比V为0.33;土体为标准细砂,弹性模量E为120MPa,泊松比ν为0.23。

除此之外,考虑主体渗透性需要定义实体为孔压单元。严格意义上讲,孔压单元隶属于实体单元,与常规的应力位移分析中的实体单元相比,孔压单元在某些节点上增加了孔压自由度,其定义方式和常规实体单元相同,但需要添加渗透性,填入相应参数,试验所得的土体渗透系数约为5×10^{-5}m/s。

2.4 分析步设置

在ABAQUS中可通过在Step模块中选择Soils类型分析步实现流体渗透的应力耦合分析。分析步Steady-state选项为稳态渗流计算,Consolidation选项为瞬态渗流计算[9]。开挖过程中渗流作用是一直存在的,且一般情况下并不会达到最终的水头平衡值,故采用瞬态渗流进行分析。表1为开挖时的分析步设置。

分析步设置 表1

名 称	步 骤	开挖面高程(m)	备 注
Geo	地应力	0	地应力平衡
R1	土(瞬态)	-0.025	第一次开挖
A1	静力、通用	-0.025	添加第一层支撑
R2	土(瞬态)	-0.05	第二次开挖
A2	静力、通用	-0.05	添加第二层支撑

续上表

名　称	步　骤	开挖面高程(m)	备　注
R3	土(瞬态)	−0.075	第三次开挖
A3	静力、通用	−0.075	添加第三层支撑
R4	土(瞬态)	−0.01	第四次开挖

2.5 荷载模块设置和相互作用处理

2.5.1 荷载

本文荷载只考虑重力荷载，重力荷载的设置采用体力。初始应力场可在荷载模块输入，本文定义了初始孔隙比为0.794，初始孔隙压力为0.5。此处的初始应力场的数值应采用干重度γ计算的应力结果，γ取$14.6 kN/m^3$。

2.5.2 边界条件

除在相应位置创建力学边界条件约束土体位移以及在相应分析步激活和取消激活某些边界条件外，考虑渗流时需要在相应分析步创建孔隙压力的边界条件。可通过幅值设置随深度变化的孔压，并施加在土体的外围。ABAQUS默认边界为不透水边界，故土层底部可只设置力学位移约束。本文的内支撑采用限制支撑位置与地连墙交点处两个方向的位移，注意在下拉列表中选择Fixed at Current Position，这样在后续的分析中，该节点即支撑位置处就不再移动，从而模拟支撑的作用。

2.5.3 相互作用

在编辑接触属性对话框中可定义接触属性，地连墙和土体的接触本文定义切向行为为罚函数，摩擦系数为0.35。法向行为采用"硬接触"来考虑，当两个面接触时，接触面之间可以传递接触压力，当两个面之间分离时，接触压力为零。当分离后的接触面之间的间距为零时，两个面又可以重新接触。在相互作用管理器中可在相应分析步创建、修改和取消激活各个接触，以及通过创建Model Change在开挖时来"杀死"模型。

2.6 网格划分

网格划分应尽量规则，使得分析更容易收敛。单元类型选择，地连墙采用CPE8R，土体采用CPE8RP。图4为划分网格后的模型。

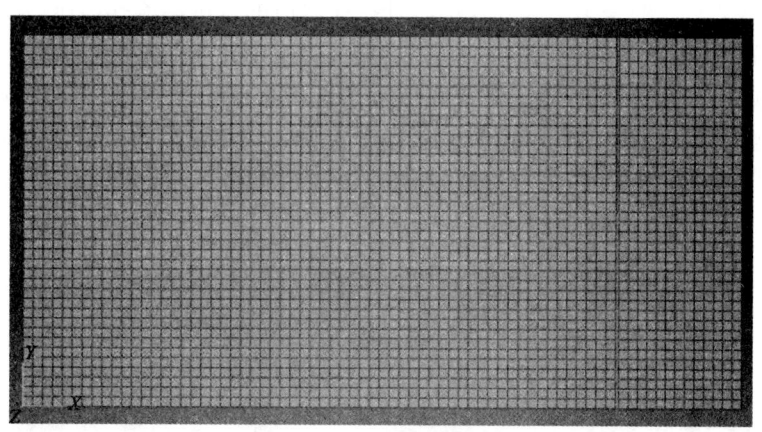

图4　网格模型

3 坑外水位变化引起的非稳定渗流分析

3.1 基坑开挖结束后渗流场分布

由图5可知，基坑底部附近主要是水平渗流，且流速随着深度的增加而减少。由于挡土墙不透水，因此在挡土墙周围,渗流主要沿竖向流动,墙趾处是渗流自下而上的转折点,此处流速较大。在基坑内部,渗透力方向往上,与土体重力方向相反,当渗透力足够大时,易发生渗透破坏,工程中应采取相关措施,如降低水力坡度,防止事故发生。

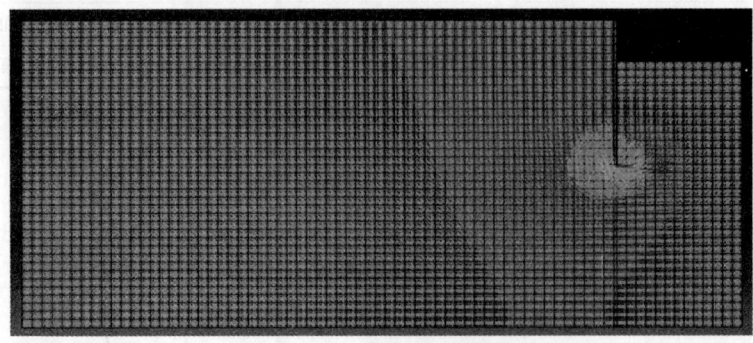

图5　基坑纵剖面流速矢量图

3.2　开挖过程孔压分析

从图6可以看出,当基坑不开挖时,地下水将处于相对稳定的状态。此时,地下水只受重力影响。基坑顶部的渗透压力为0,基坑底部的渗透压力为33.33 Pa。

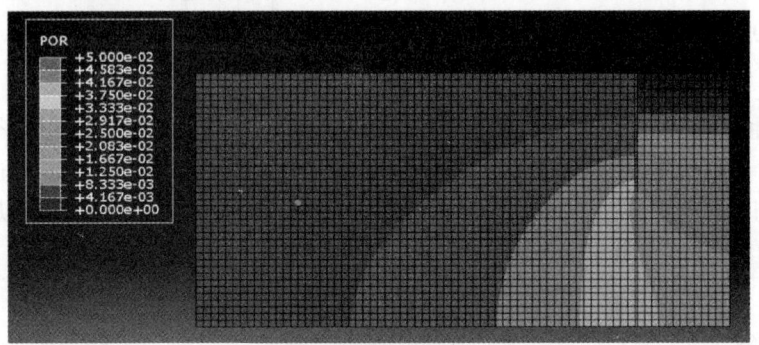

图6　开挖前孔压云图

该工程分4次开挖,由于地下水位的位置在距基坑主动区顶部0.05~0.15m处循环升降,每次开挖完的水位一样,所以本文对比的是第一次开挖中和开挖完对应的基坑渗流孔隙压力云图。如图7、图8所示,当基坑进行开挖施工时,随着地下水位增大,有效孔隙压力也会增加,地下水会发生渗流,基坑外侧的地下水会向基坑内侧渗流进而引起土体受地下水影响的区域不断变大,此时,基坑外顶部土体的一部分将从饱和状态向非饱和状态转变。在非饱和土中,孔隙水压力为负值。又如图9所示,当第四层开挖结束时,基坑底部土体的孔压值有明显上升。随着基坑开挖深度加大,基坑底部的地下水水位受到严重影响。

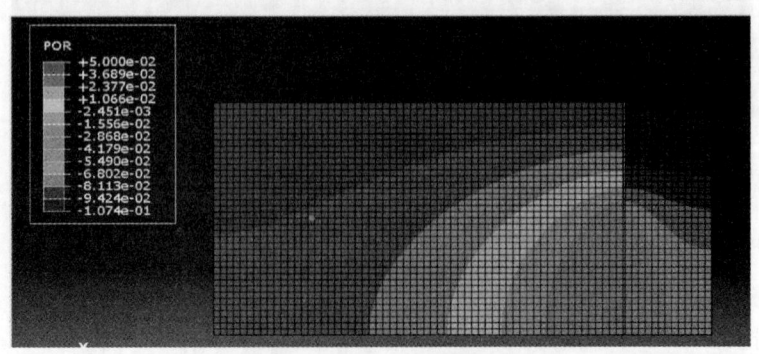

图7　第一次开挖过程中孔压云图

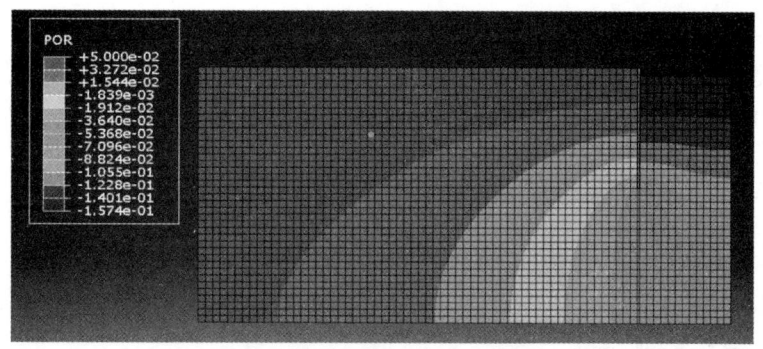

图8 第一次开挖结束时孔压云图

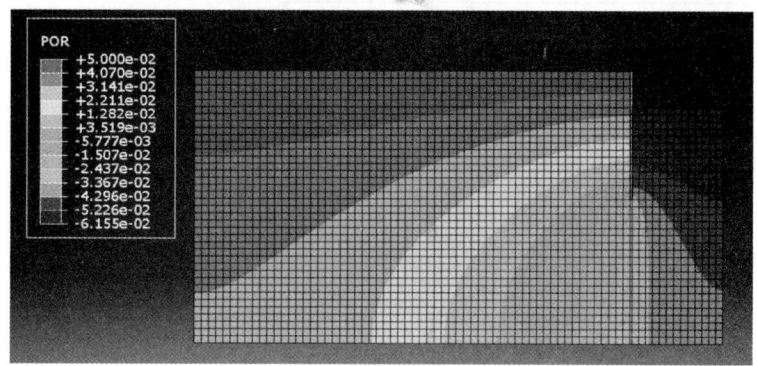

图9 第四次开挖结束时孔压云图

3.3 渗透系数随深度变化的渗流分析

土体的渗透系数是影响渗流作用大小最重要的因素之一,其数值的正确选用对渗透计算有着非常重要的意义。渗透系数大小主要取决于土体颗粒的形状、大小、不均匀系数和水的黏滞性等,通常通过试验方法来确定渗透系数 k。从文献[8]得知该试验所得的 k 为 5×10^{-5} m/s。但由于土体自重的作用,渗透系数其实是会随着深度衰减的[10],在该试验模型中用的是同一种砂,其土体的填充高度不高,所以 k 值随深度变化不会太大。取 k 值从上到下为 $1k$、$0.8k$、$0.5k$ 进行分析。

图10a)、b)分别是在 $T=25$s 和 50s 时,考虑和不考虑渗透系数随深度变化的孔压变化曲线。由图可知,虽然由于该模型是在室内试验的,土的深度不大,所以曲线相差不明显,但可以看出总体趋势就是考虑渗透系数的土受到的孔压比不考虑时的大,但随着深度更深,渗透系数减小,渗流量也随之降低,到达一定深度后孔压变化将趋于稳定。所以在实际工程中需要注意渗透系数 k 对基坑施工造成的影响。

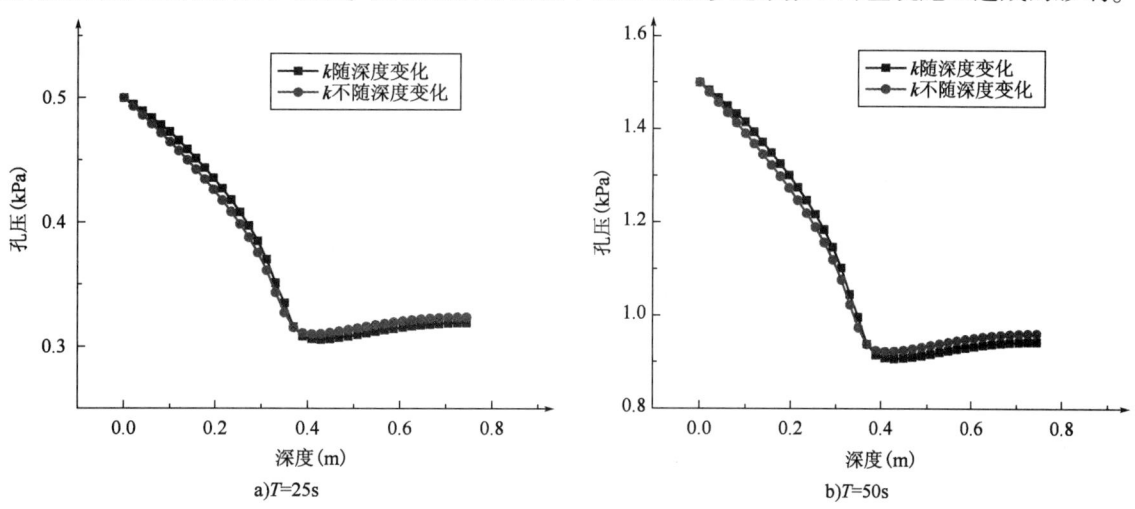

图10 渗透系数随深度变化孔压曲线

3.4 压缩模量随深度变化的渗流分析

为了探究压缩模量随深度变化对坑外水位变化引起的基坑非稳定渗流的影响,在 ABAQUS 中建立压缩模量与场变量的关系,并在【Model】/【Edit Keywords】给定场变量的初始分布。如图11所示。

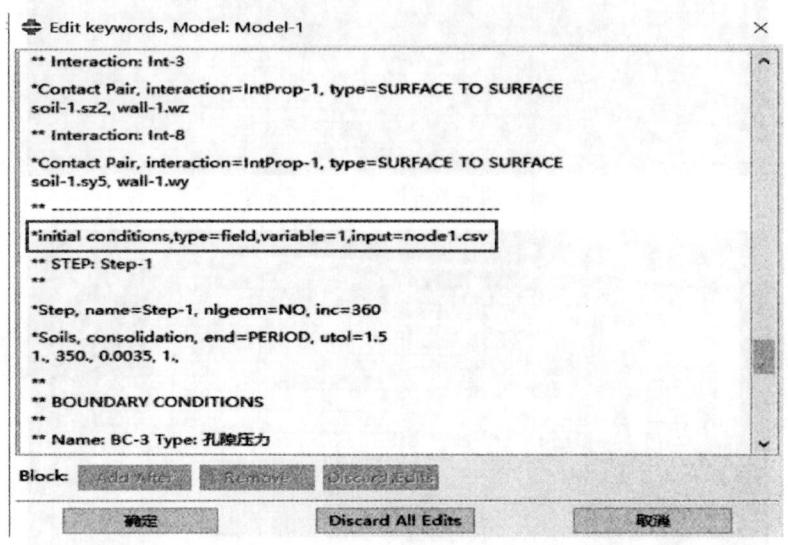

图11　编辑关键字

图12a)、b)分别选取 $T=25s$ 和 $50s$,分析压缩模量 E_s 随深度变化对坑外水位变化引起的基坑非稳定渗流的影响。由图可知,在水位逐渐上升的情况下,考虑 E_s 随深度变化的情况比不考虑的孔压要大,说明土体压缩性沿深度变化对地下水位动态变化引起的超静孔压分布具有显著影响,且随着深度增加,孔压差异会越来越明显。通过以上讨论可知,地基土体压缩性沿深度变化对地下水位动态变化引起的孔压响应问题具有明显影响。

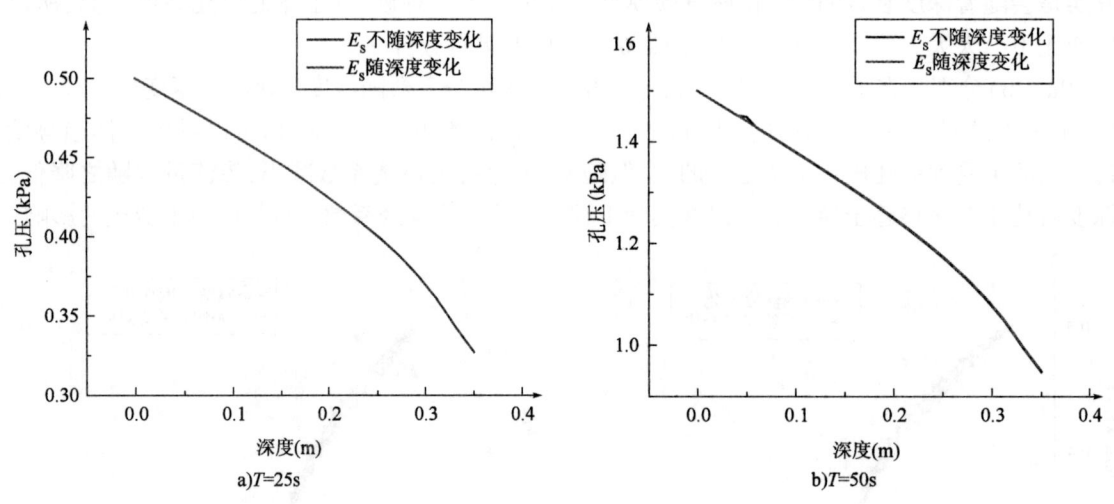

图12　孔压变化曲线图

4　结　语

本文基于 ABAQUS 有限元软件,模拟了基坑试验模型,结合不同深度下土体的渗透系数、压缩模量,考虑基坑内开挖卸荷对坑外水位变化引起的基坑非稳定渗流的影响,结论如下:

(1)在进行基坑作业时,随着挖掘深度进一步加深,基础坑底部的渗透压力增大,这表明随着挖掘深度进一步加大,基础坑底部的地下水位受到更严重的影响。

(2)考虑渗透系数的土受到的孔压比不考虑时大,但随着深度增加,渗透系数减小渗流量也随之降低,到达一定深度后孔压变化将趋于稳定,所以在实际工程中需要注意渗透系数 k 对基坑稳定性的影响。

(3)土体压缩性沿深度变化对地下水位动态变化引起的超静孔压分布具有显著影响,且随着深度增加,孔压差异会越来越明显。

参考文献

[1] 周涛,房浩.强降雨条件下北京地区地下水位动态特征——以7·21特大暴雨为例[J].地下水, 2016,38(02):81-83.

[2] 闫彭彭,黄铭,王超.降雨影响下的海堤非稳定渗流分析[J].海洋湖沼通报,2019(05):73-79.

[3] Wang Yuke, Wu Di, Qiu Yue, et al. Experimental investigation on cyclic deformation behavior of soft marine clay involved principal stress rotation[J]. Marine Georesources & Geotechnology, 2017, 35(4).

[4] Wang Yuke, Gao Yufeng, Guo Lin, et al. Cyclic response of natural soft marine clay under principal stress rotation as induced by wave loads[J]. Ocean Engineering, 2017, 129.

[5] Wang Y, Y Gao, C Zeng, et al. 2018b. Undrained cyc-lic behavior of soft marine clay involved combined principal stress rotation. Applied Ocean Research 81:141-149. doi:10.1016/j.apor.2018.10.010.

[6] Wang Y, Y Gao, B Li, et al. 2018a. Influence of initial state and intermediate principal stress on undrained behavior of soft clay during pure principal stress rotation. Acta Geotechnical, 1-23.

[7] 张小伟,姚笑青.基坑工程变形的渗流应力耦合有限元分析[J].地下空间与工程学报,2012,8(02): 339-344.

[8] 章丽莎.滨海地区地下水位变化对地基及基坑渗流特性的影响研究[D].杭州:浙江大学,2017.

[9] 黄云天.地连墙基坑开挖中渗流作用对基坑变形的影响[D].南京:东南大学,2015.

[10] 万力,蒋小伟,王旭升.含水层的一种普遍规律:渗透系数随深度衰减[J].高校地质学报,2010, 16(01):7-12.

不同击实功对黄土压实特性影响试验研究

黄鑫中[1] 杜秦文[1] 李宝江[2] 石磊[1,3] 魏进[1]

(1.长安大学公路学院;2.中国建筑第六工程局有限公司;3.中国建筑西南勘察设计研究院有限公司)

摘　要　不同击实功作用下土体压实性质及其相互之间内在联系的研究工作尚不充分。本文在较宽的含水率范围内,采用4种击实功对西安黄土进行击实,得到了相应的"全压实曲线";提出建立了"全压实曲面"方程和"压实敏感阈值曲线"方程,对比分析了最佳含水率和压实敏感阈值变化规律;指出了2种建立全压实曲面的方法。并采用已有文献中试验数据对本文研究内容进行验证。

关键词　黄土路基　全压实曲线　击实试验　击实功　压实敏感阈值

0　引　言

压实是指采用机械设备,通过碾压、夯实或振动等方法迫使土孔隙中的空气排出,使土颗粒紧密嵌合,提高土体的强度和变形性能的重要施工方法。自 Proctor 通过室内击实试验提出含水率和干密度之间的关系后,学者们针对特定的击实功,不断深化对压实曲线的认识[1],从压实机理、工艺、效果评价[2],

以及压实后土体的工程性能方面做了大量的研究[3]。但其击实曲线多采用多项式拟合,参数不具物理意义,无法同土体的性质联系起来。我国黄土分布广泛,常采用强夯的方法来压实路基填土,导致击实功超过标准击实试验标准。因此,研究击实功对土体工程性质的影响具有实际的意义。

Faure[4]、Faure 和 Da mate 等[5]对细粒土在较大含水率内进行击实,指出击实曲线上存在压实敏感阈值:当含水率小于该值时,干密度变化不大。表明土的压实性质除了受压实功影响,也与其内在的物理性质有关。在能成型的前提下,对土样在含水率从最低到最高的范围内进行击实,即可得到"全压实曲线"。Li Hua[6]针对加拿大阿尔伯塔省黏土的全压实曲线,提出了四参数方程,其中2个参数与土体物理性质直接有关。陈渊召等[7]采用该方程,对湖南低液限黏土进行了研究。

以上研究主要针对黏性土,本文取西安黄土进行4种不同击实功的击实试验,建立全压实曲线方程;提出了"全压实曲面"方程,得到了"压实敏感阈值曲线",实现根据某一击实功下击实数据,预测其他击实功下的击实曲线。采用已发表文献中黄土击实数据,对本文工作进行验证,表明其具有广泛的应用价值。

1 黄土的室内试验

1.1 基本物理指标试验

本文所用黄土取自西安地区,可塑状态,颜色为黄褐色;将风干土样过 2 mm 筛,根据现行《公路土工试验规程》(JTG 3430)进行颗粒分析、液塑限、相对密度等试验,结果见图 1 和表 1。

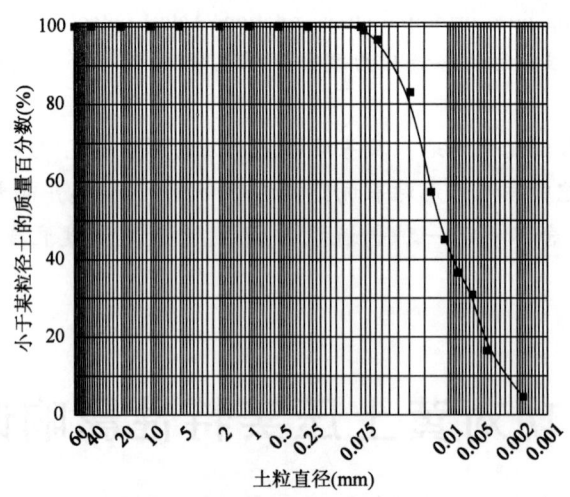

图 1 土的颗粒级配曲线

土的基本物理性质指标 表 1

土 类	液限(%)	塑限(%)	塑性指数	颗粒组成(mm)(%)			相对密度
				>2	2~0.075	<0.075	
低液限粉质黏黄土	37.9	19.1	18.8	0	0.2	0.98	2.70

1.2 击实试验

在能够成型的情况下,按2%含水率间隔从最低至最高范围进行击实。采用4种击实功,分别为598.2kJ/m³、1340.0kJ/m³、1914.3kJ/m³、2680.0kJ/m³,从小到大依次记作Ⅰ~Ⅳ型击实功。击实试验如图2所示,试验方法见表2。

基金项目:中央高校基本科研业务费专项资金(310821173701)。

a) 手动击实仪　　　　b) 击实土样

图 2　击实试验

击 实 类 型　　　　　　　　　　　　　　表 2

类　型	击实功(kJ/m^3)	锤重(kg)	落距(cm)	击实筒尺寸			层数	每层击数
				内径(cm)	高(cm)	体积(cm^3)		
Ⅰ	598.2	2.5	30	10	12.7	997	3	27
Ⅱ	1340.0	4.5	45	15.2	17	2177	3	49
Ⅲ	1914.3	4.5	45	15.2	17	2177	3	70
Ⅳ	2680.0	4.5	45	15.2	17	2177	3	98

2　黄土全压实曲线

2.1　全压实曲线分区及方程

全压实曲线可分为干燥区、过渡区及湿润区[6]。如图 3 所示。图 3 中 w_{cst} 为压实敏感阈值含水率,为干燥区与过渡区的分界点。当含水率小于 w_{cst} 时,干密度可认为是常数[6-7],称为"初始干密度",记为 ρ_{dd}。w_{opt} 为最佳含水率,为过渡区和湿润区的分界点。由三相比例指标关系,可得到四参数方程,见式(1)。

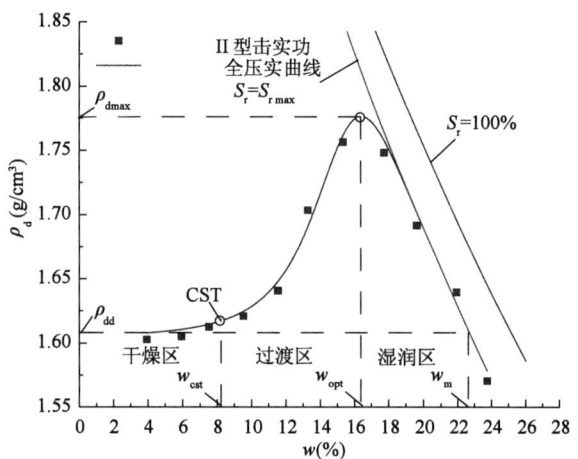

图 3　典型的全压实曲线分区

$$\rho_d = G_s \times \rho_w \bigg/ \left\{ 1 + w \times G \bigg/ \left[S_{r\,max} - S_{r\,max} \times \left(\frac{w_m - w}{w_m}\right)^{n+1} \times \left(\frac{w_m^n + p^n}{(w_m - w)^n + p^n}\right) \right] \right\} \quad (1)$$

式中,ρ_d 为干密度;G_s 为相对密实度;ρ_w 为 4℃ 时水的密度;w 为含水率。并有 4 个参数 $S_{r\,max}$、w_m、n、p。

2.2 4种击实功下试验结果

由式(1)对击实曲线进行拟合,得到4种击实功下的全压实曲线,拟合效果良好,如图4所示。图4中曲线参数如表3所示。

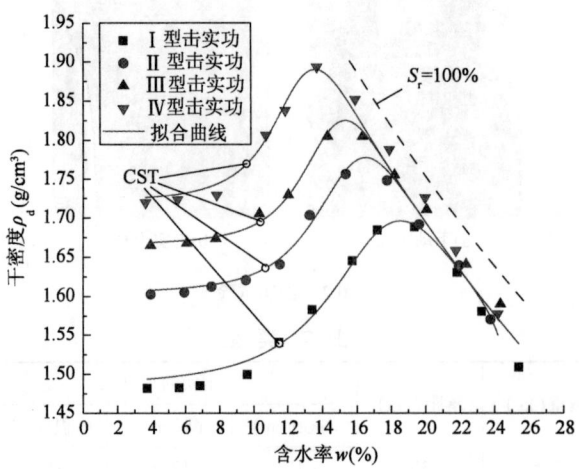

图 4　四参数方程拟合全压实曲线

全压实曲线参数　　　　　　　　　　　　　　　　　　　　表3

类　　型	$S_{r\max}$(%)	w_m(%)	n	p	R^2
Ⅰ	90.95	27.69	7.00	11.04	0.97
Ⅱ	90.95	23.06	7.00	8.02	0.98
Ⅲ	90.95	20.94	7.00	6.90	0.97
Ⅳ	90.95	19.20	7.00	6.84	0.96

2.3 全压实曲线参数

(1)参数 $S_{r\max}$

图4中击实曲线右侧平行于饱和曲线,表明其饱和度基本不变,是能击实达到的最大饱和度,记为 $S_{r\max}$。不同击实功下曲线右侧重合,表明对于同一种土,$S_{r\max}$ 为常数。

(2)参数 w_m

记曲线右侧对应 ρ_{dd} 的含水率为 w_m,该处饱和度为 $S_{r\max}$,由三项指标关系,得:

$$w_m = S_{r\max} \times \left(\frac{\rho_w}{\rho_{dd}} - \frac{1}{G_s}\right) \tag{2}$$

(3)参数 n、p

参数 n、p 为击实曲线的形状参数,对于同一土样,n 为常数,p 随击实功增大而减小。

3 黄土全压实曲面

3.1 全压实曲面方程

现对"全压实曲面"及压实敏感阈值变化规律进行分析。由前文可知,击实功对参数 w_m 和 p 具有较大影响,如图5所示。

参数 w_m 和 p 与击实功呈幂函数关系:

$$w_m = aW^b \tag{3}$$
$$p = cW^d \tag{4}$$

式中,W 为击实功;a、b、c、d 为拟合参数。

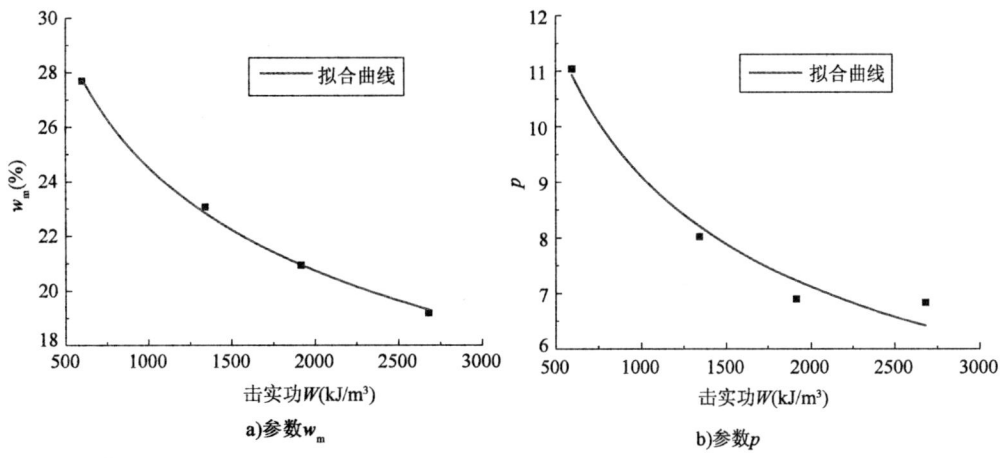

图 5 击实功对参数 w_m 和 p 的影响

将式(3)、式(4)代入式(1)可得"全压实曲面"方程,式(5)中各参数如表 4 所示。

$$\rho_d = G_s \times \rho_w / \left\{ 1 + w \times G_s / \left[S_m - S_m \times \left(1 - \frac{w}{aW^b} \right)^{n+1} \times \frac{a^n W^{b \times n} + c^n W^{d \times n}}{(aW^b - w)^n + c^n W^{d \times n}} \right] \right\} \tag{5}$$

全压实曲面参数 表 4

a	b	c	d
130.378	-0.242	105.435	-0.355

由式(5)绘制全压实曲面,如图 6 所示。

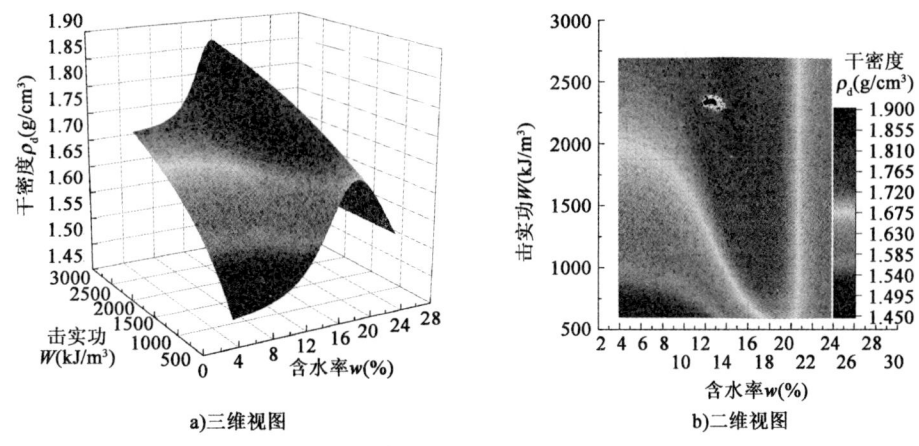

a)三维视图　　　　　　　　b)二维视图

图 6 全压实曲面

全压实曲面可分为三个区。其中,干燥区和湿润区的分界为"压实敏感阈值曲线"。该处土样的基质吸力与击实功密切相关:击实功克服基质吸力作用后,土样才能被有效击实。w_{cst} 的变化规律反映了土体内在的压实性质,对于分析压实机理具有重要作用。

3.2 压实敏感阈值曲线(CSTC)

以往研究[6-7]和本文试验均表明,对于同一种土,不同击实功下 CST 点处的饱和度 $S_{r\,cst}$ 几乎不变,可认为是常数。由饱和度表达式

$$S_r = w / \left(\frac{\rho_w}{\rho_d} - \frac{1}{G_s} \right) \tag{6}$$

绘制饱和度与含水率关系曲线。以 $(w_m, S_{r\,max})$ 点为原点建立 x-y 坐标系,如图 7 所示。饱和度与含水率曲线可表达为:

$$y = kx^{n+1}/(x^n + p^n) \tag{7}$$

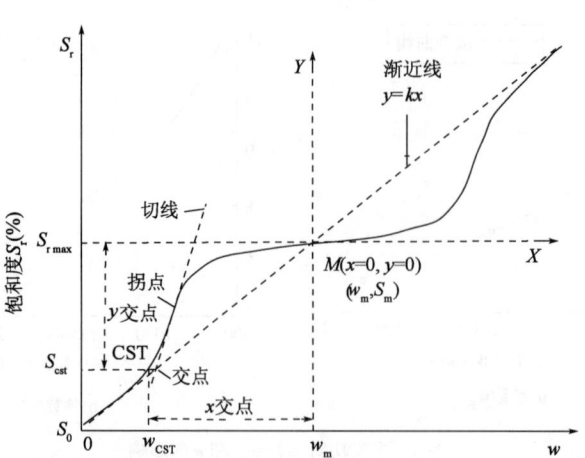

图 7 $x\text{-}y$ 坐标系上的饱和度与含水率曲线

过图 7 中"拐点"作切线与"渐近线"相交,交点坐标即为 CST 点对应的饱和度 $S_{r\,cst}$ 与含水率 w_{cst}。由图 7 中几何关系可得:

$$S_{r\,cst} = S_{r\,max} - \frac{S_{r\,max}}{w_{r\,max}} \times p \times \left(\frac{n+1}{n-1}\right)^{\frac{n+1}{n}} \tag{8}$$

将式(7)变换回 $w\text{-}S_r$ 坐标系,可得:

$$S_{r\,cst} = S_{r\,max} - \frac{S_{r\,max}}{w_m} \times \frac{(w_m - w_{cst})^{(n+1)}}{(w_m - w_{cst})^n + p^n} \tag{9}$$

将式(3)、式(4)、式(8)代入式(9),可得 W 与 w_{cst} 关系方程:

$$(aW^b - w_{cst})^{n+1}/[(aW^b - w_{cst})^n + c^n W^{d\cdot n}] - cNW^d = 0 \tag{10}$$

式中,$N = [(n+1)/(n-1)]^{(n+1)/n}$。

采用式(10)可以计算不同击实功下黄土的 w_{cst};结合式(5),可得"压实敏感阈值曲线(Compaction Sensitivity Threshold Curve,简称 CSTC)",如图 8 所示。可以看出,随击实功增加,分界含水率 w_{cst} 和 w_{opt} 均减小,且 w_{opt} 减小更多。

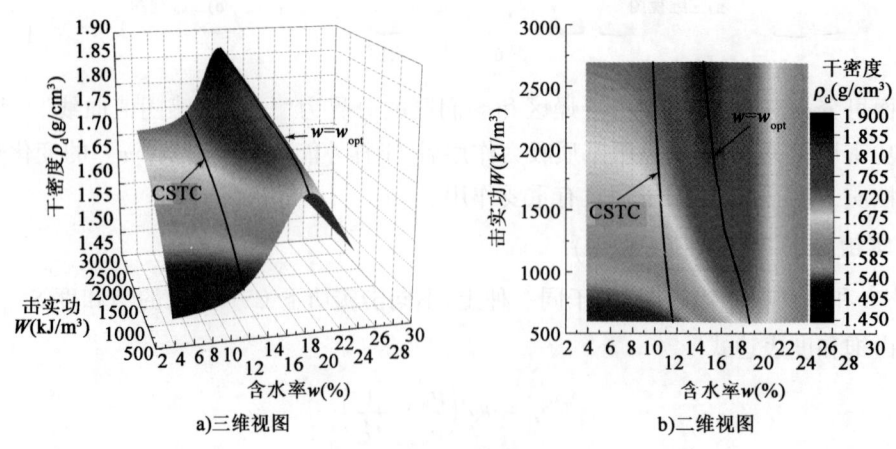

a)三维视图   b)二维视图

图 8 压实敏感阈值曲线

3.3 黄土全压实曲线的预测

已知某一击实功下的全压实曲线,可对另外的击实功下的全压实曲线进行预测,步骤如下:

①通过某一击实功下已知的全压实曲线,获得参数 $S_{r\max}$、n、w_{m0}、p_0;②对于同一黄土,不同击实功下的全压实曲线参数 $S_{r\max}$、n 是常数;③对另外击实功,在其干燥区内做一个击实样,获得此击实功下的 ρ_{dd};将其代入式(2)得到相应的 w_m;④对于同一种土,不同击实功作用下参数 $S_{r\,cst}$、$S_{r\max}$ 和 n 为常数,由②和式(8)可得关系式:

$$\frac{S_{r\max}}{w_{m0}} \times p_0 = \frac{S_{r\max}}{w_m} \times p = 常数 \tag{11}$$

则新击实功下的参数 p:

$$p = \frac{S_{r\max}/w_{m0} \times p_0}{S_{r\max}/w_m} \tag{12}$$

将新击实功下的参数 $S_{r\max}$、w_m、n、p 代入到式(1),即可得到预测击实功下的全压实曲线。此外,利用本节所述,也可得到另一种的"全压实曲面"确定方法:通过某一击实功下已知的全压实曲线;其他击实功下只需做一个击实样。通过曲面拟合即可得到"全压实曲面"。

3.4 预测验证

利用本文及文献[8-9]中黄土的击实数据,选择某种击实功下的数据,对其他击实功下的全压实曲线、全压实曲线四参数进行预测,结果如图9、表5所示,效果良好。

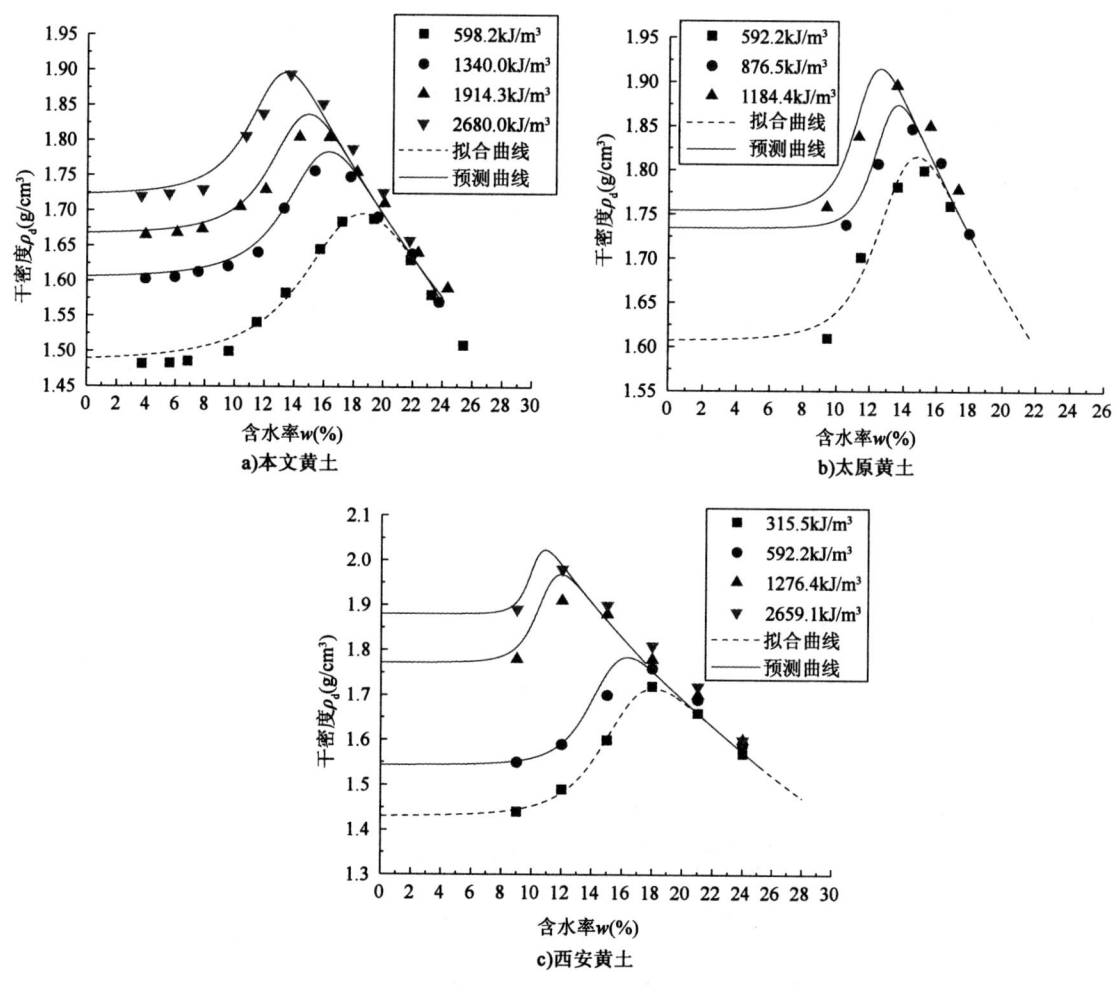

图9 全压实预测曲线

全压实曲线四参数预测值　　　　　　　　表5

土　类	击实功(kJ/m³)	$S_{r\,max}$(%)	w_m(%)	n	p
本文黄土	598.2	90.95	27.69	7.00	11.04
	1340.0	90.95	23.06	7.00	9.20
	1914.3	90.95	20.94	7.00	8.35
	2680.0	90.95	19.20	7.00	7.66
太原黄土	592.2	86.33	26.22	9.07	13.50
	876.5	86.33	17.80	9.07	6.88
	1184.4	86.33	17.24	9.07	6.66
西安黄土	315.5	90.52	29.82	10.87	13.74
	592.2	90.52	25.12	10.87	11.58
	1276.4	90.52	17.57	10.87	8.10
	2659.1	90.52	14.62	10.87	6.73

4　结　论

在4种不同击实功下对西安黄土进行击实,得到相应的全压实曲线,建立了全压实曲面和压实敏感阈值曲线方程,并用已发表文献中不同地区黄土击实数据对研究内容做了验证,得到结论如下:

(1)全压实曲线方程及其预测方法,适用于文中所涉及的黄土。

(2)提出并得到了全压实曲面方程,并指出利用本文3.3节所述,可以用少量的试验得到全压实曲面。

(3)压实敏感阈值变化规律是土体内在压实特性的反映。利用全压实曲面,得到不同击实功下压实敏感阈值变化曲线的方程,可用于压实机理研究。

(4)随着击实功的增加,压实敏感阈值含水率 w_{cst} 减小,减小程度小于对应的最佳含水率 w_{opt}。

附　表

参 数 解 释 表　　　　　　　　附表1

参数	含　义	参数	含　义
w_{cst}	压实敏感阈值含水率	$S_{r\,cst}$	压实敏感阈值点对应的饱和度
w_{opt}	最佳含水率	$S_{r\,max}$	土样在击实中能达到的最大饱和度
ρ_{dd}	当击实含水率小于 w_{cst} 时的干密度,为"初始干密度"	w_m	全压实曲线右侧干密度值等于 ρ_{dd} 的含水率
ρ_d	干密度	$n、p$	全压实曲线的形状参数
G_s	相对密实度	W	击实功
ρ_w	4℃时水的密度	$a、b、c、d$	全压实曲面拟合参数
w	含水率	N	$[(n+1)/(n-1)]^{(n+1)/n}$
S_r	饱和度	—	—

参考文献

[1] ALBADRAN Y, SCHANZ T. Modelling the Compaction Curve of Fine-Grained Soils [J]. Soils and Foundations, 2014, 54(3): 426-438.

[2] ZHANG J, PENG J, ZHENG J, et al. Prediction of Resilient Modulus of Compacted Cohesive Soils in South China [J]. International Journal of Geomechanics, 2019, 19(7): 04019068.1-04019068.11.

[3] 吴文彪,郑俊杰,曹文昭.考虑含水率影响的压实黄土路堤稳定性研究[J].岩土力学,2015,36(S1): 542-546.

[4] FAURE A G. A New Conception of The Plastic and Liquid Limits of Clay[J]. Soil and Tillage Research, 1980,1:97-105.
[5] FAURE A G, Viana D M, José D. Penetration Resistance Value Along Compaction Curves[J]. Journal of Geotechnical Engineering,1994,120(1):46-59.
[6] LI H. The Family of Compaction Curves for Fine-Grained Soils and Their Engineering Behaviors[D]. Alberta:University of Alberta,2001.
[7] 陈渊召,李振霞,付新元. 基于四参数方程的细粒土全压实特性研究[J]. 中国公路学报,2010,23(3):15-21.
[8] 朱志坤. 干密度和含水量对太原重塑黄土强度及强度参数影响的研究[D]. 太原:太原理工大学,2018.
[9] 史春燕. 击实黄土试验研究及填方地基的沉降预估[D]. 西安:西安建筑科技大学,2018.

蒸发条件下非饱和砂性土水汽迁移试验研究

张建勋 毛雪松

(长安大学公路学院)

摘 要 为了探究在蒸发条件下影响非饱和砂土汽态水迁移的因素,以及在昼夜温度变化下有、无覆盖层对路基的影响,本文做了一系列汽态水迁移试验以及一维土柱水汽迁移试验。结果表明,当非饱和砂土处于最佳含水率,更利于汽态水的迁移。汽态水的迁移与含水率梯度、水平密切相关。在昼夜温差循环的作用下,覆盖层下聚集的汽态水冷凝产生的液态水会造成上部土层的塌缩,并提高上部土层的持水能力,且与无覆盖层相比,有覆盖层时更容易造成含水量的聚集。本文阐述了影响非饱和砂土中汽态水迁移的因素,并揭示了干旱半干旱地区砂土路基水汽迁移的机理。

关键词 特殊地区路基 水汽迁移机理 一维土柱试验 非饱和砂性土 覆盖层

0 引言

近年来,因水汽迁移导致的"锅盖效应"造成了多起工程性病害,严重影响了许多公路、铁路及机场道面的工程,因此已经有许多研究学者投入水汽迁移的研究中[1-7]。滕继东等[8]将"锅盖效应"分为两类,第一类是在覆盖层下水汽遇冷凝结聚集的现象,主要是液态水的迁移;第二类是汽态水发生冻结并聚集在路基下方的现象,发生在蒸发作用强烈、地下水位较深的干旱、半干旱地区,汽态水迁移为主。通过模拟两类"锅盖效应"对比发现[9-10],第二类"锅盖效应"引起工程危害更大。而且有研究表明,产生铁路工程近地表冰的原因是汽态水的迁移[11-12]。因此对于西北干旱、半干旱地区,更应该重视汽态水迁移对本地区工程造成的破坏。王铁行等[13]根据室内试验模拟工程实际的"锅盖效应",揭示了影响汽态水迁移的主要因素是温度梯度和含水率梯度。

目前对于水汽迁移的研究主要是液态水迁移方面,对于汽态水机理的研究仍处于初步阶段。而且目前研究主要是针对低温寒旱区,对高温条件下干旱、半干旱地区的汽态水迁移研究较少。砂性土是干旱、半干旱地区常用路基填筑材料,因此本文将通过自制汽态水迁移装置来研究影响非饱和砂性土汽态水迁移的因素,并通过室内模拟一维土柱试验,研究在不同昼夜温差作用下,非饱和砂性土水汽迁移的机理。

基金项目:国家自然科学基金项目(51878064)、中央高校科研业务费专项资金项目(300102218408 和 300102218408)。

1 非饱和砂性土汽态水迁移研究

1.1 试验设计

(1) 试验装置

汽态水迁移组合装置包括2根试件管、2个封闭端口及1个中部连接环,如图1所示。

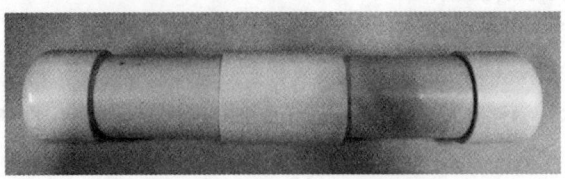

图1 汽态水迁移组合装置

(2) 试验方案

试验方案见表1。

试验方案 表1

温度	含水率差异	
45℃	含水率梯度	5%
		10%
	含水率水平	高
		低

分别配制含水率为2%、5%、10%、15%、20%的土样,根据实测土样的含水率进行设计试验,含水率梯度分布见表2,含水率水平分布见表3。

含水率梯度分布 表2

含水率梯度	干端	湿端
5%	2.1%	4.8%
	4.8%	9.2%
	9.2%	14.4%
	14.4%	20.5%
10%	2.1%	9.2%
	4.8%	14.4%
	9.2%	20.5%

含水率水平分布 表3

水平	干端	湿端
低	2.1%	4.8%
	4.8%	9.2%
	2.1%	9.2%
高	9.2%	14.4%
	14.4%	21.1%
	4.8%	14.4%
	9.2%	21.1%

将试件沿试件两端向中间按每隔3cm进行切割,利用烘干法测定不同切段的含水率,取平均值。拆样如图2所示。

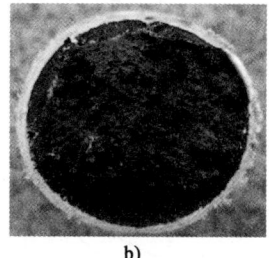

图 2 拆样

1.2 含水率差异对砂性土水汽迁移的影响

1.2.1 含水率水平对水汽迁移的影响

砂土在不同含水率梯度下 7d 后的迁移量如图 3 所示。

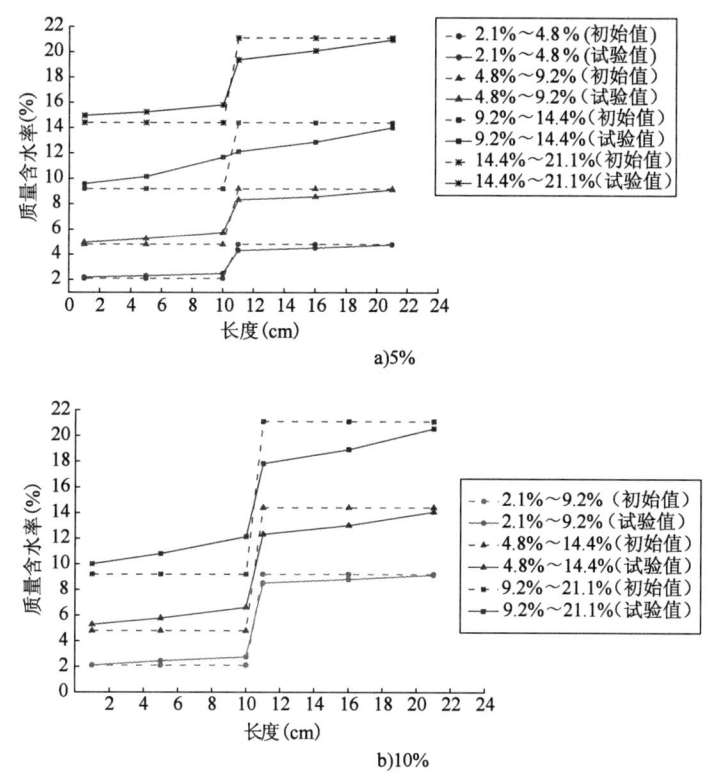

图 3 砂土在不同含水率梯度下 7d 后的迁移量

在基质势的作用下,试件内水分会发生迁移。在高温条件下,靠近空气带的湿端土样中汽态水会通过中间空气带迁移到干端,发生汽态水迁移。

通过图 4 可以发现,迁移路径越长,迁移所需能量就越大,因此远离空气带的干端水分的增加量小于靠近空气带的干端。

每条折线与水平轴包围的面积为汽态水的迁移量,在 5% 含水率梯度下,随着含水率水平的增大,迁移量呈现先增大后减小的趋势。9.2%~14.4% 的含水率水平下,迁移量最大。在最佳含水率条件下,砂性土更易形成水汽迁移的通道,更有利于水分的迁移。

1.2.2 含水率梯度对水汽迁移的影响

由图 5 看出,含水率梯度 10% 的试件的迁移量普遍大于 5% 的试件。含水率梯度越大,迁移量越大。迁移量与时间的比值为迁移速率,高含水率梯度的迁移速率要大于低含水率梯度的试件。

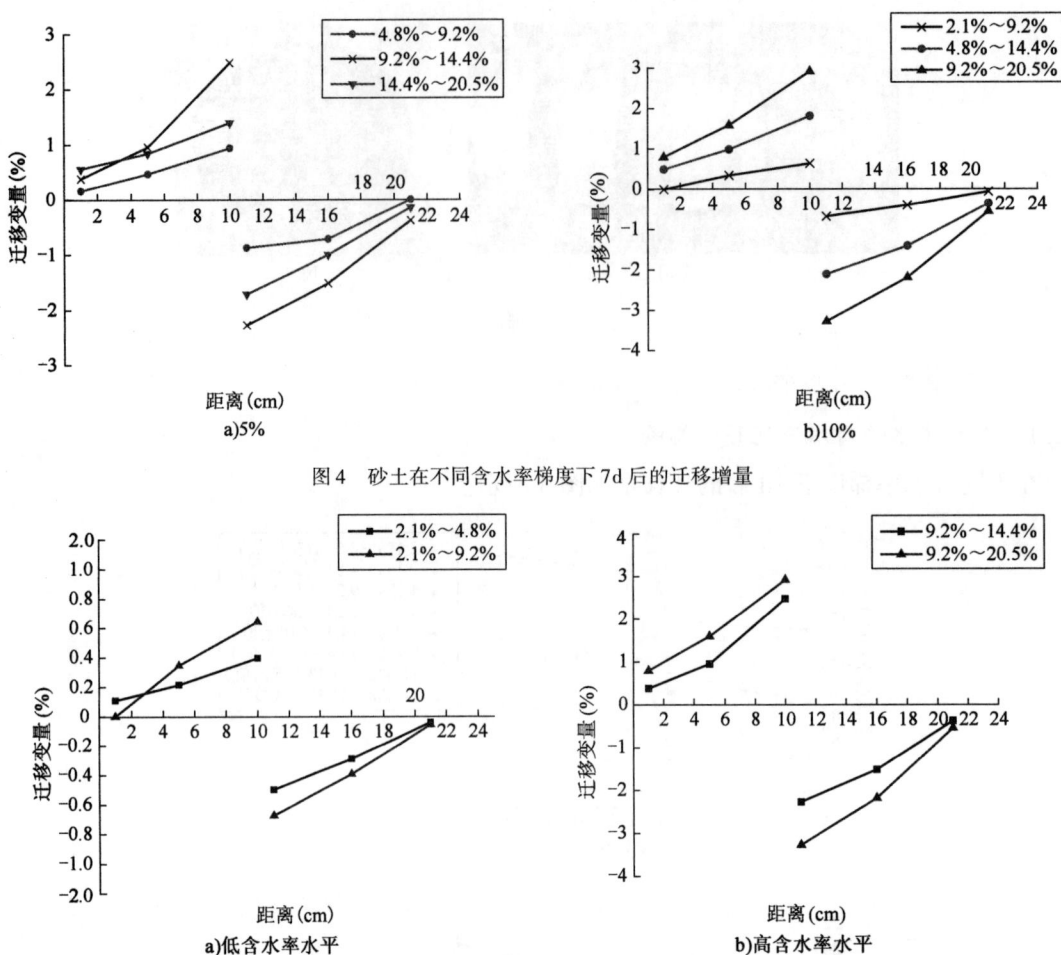

图4 砂土在不同含水率梯度下7d后的迁移增量

图5 砂土在不同含水率水平下7d的迁移增量

2 一维路基模型水汽迁移试验

2.1 试验装置

本试验装置包括土柱模型(①+②)、温控系统(③)、温度监测系统(④+⑤)及水分监测系统(⑥+⑦)等装置,如图6所示。

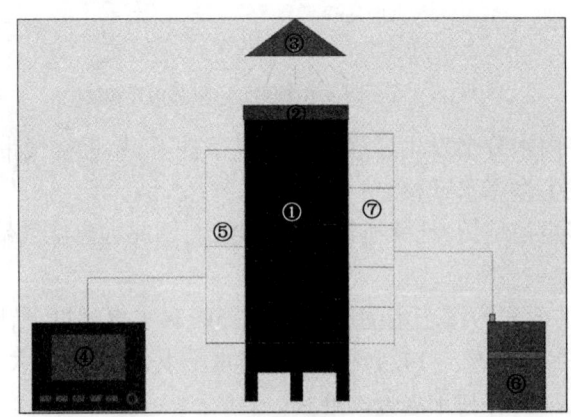

图6 一维土柱水汽迁移试验装置

2.2 试验方法

温控装置在每天8:00—22:00开灯,其余时间关闭灯光。试验周期为60 d。配制砂性土质量含水率为9%(最佳含水率),控制压实度为90%。

2.3 温度场变化规律

土柱单个周期(24h)温度的变化如图7所示。

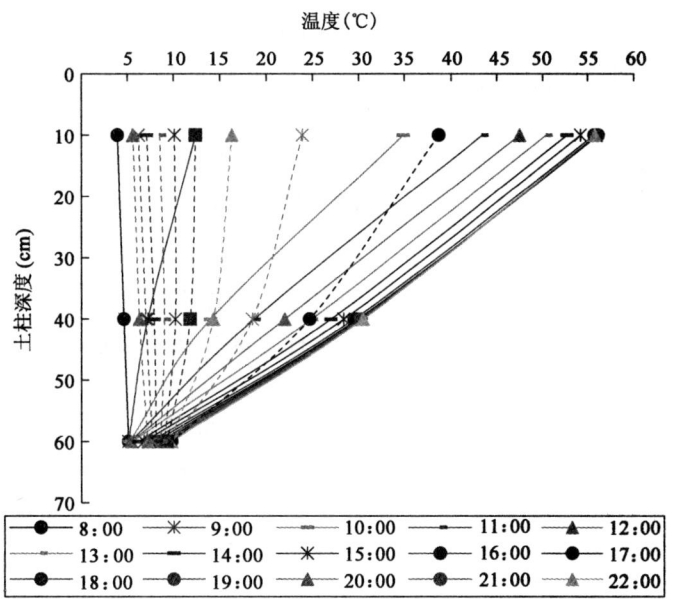

图7 土柱单个周期(24h)温度的变化

当8:00开灯之后,受到热源的影响,土柱上部温度不断升高,16:00达到最高温度,约56℃,并保持稳定。随着温度向下传递,土柱下部温度也逐渐升高,并在20:00稳定。与实际工程相似,路基深度越深,受到外界热源的影响就越小[14]。当22:00关闭热源,受到外界常温的影响,土柱温度逐渐减小,土柱上下部分温度逐渐趋向一致,约4℃。

2.4 一维土柱水分场的变化规律

2.4.1 一维土柱的水分场随时间的变化

一维土柱的水分场随时间的变化规律如图8所示。

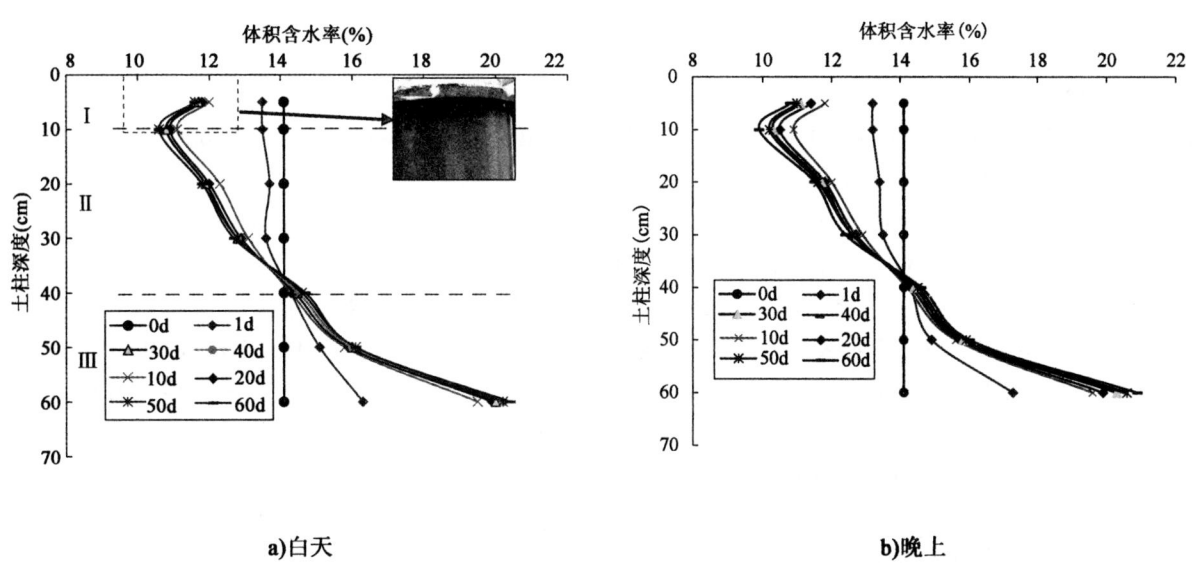

a) 白天　　　　　　　　　　　　　　　b) 晚上

图8 一维土柱的水分场随时间的变化规律

由图8可知,在整个试验周期内,Ⅰ部分和Ⅱ部分的土柱含水率在不断变小,Ⅲ部分的土柱含水率在不断变大；Ⅰ含水率减少的程度要小于Ⅱ，并逐渐趋向稳定。

在试验初期，白天土柱上部受到热源的作用，与下部土柱产生温差，土体内部液态水转化为汽态水，并在蒸气压的作用下，向气压低的方向扩散。由于砂土本身持水能力较弱，重力势占据主导地位，土柱的水分以液态水的形式向下迁移。

汽态水向上迁移，由于存在覆盖层，大量水汽便会聚集在覆盖层底。当关闭热源，大量的汽态水便会冷凝为液态水，造成上部土层含水率的增大。上部土柱水分聚集造成了Ⅰ部分砂土的塌陷现象，如图8a)所示。Ⅰ的塌陷提高了上部土体的密实度；空隙率减小，提高了砂土本身的持水能力，表现为Ⅰ含水率减少的程度要小于Ⅱ[15-16]。

2.4.2 有盖与无盖土柱水分场的差异性

有盖与无盖土柱水分场差异性对比如图9所示。

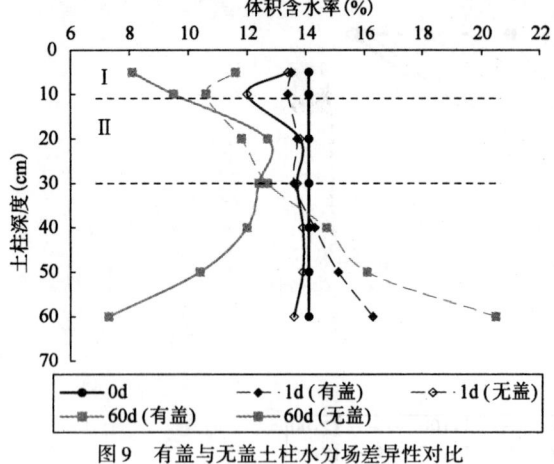

图9 有盖与无盖土柱水分场差异性对比

土柱上部存在覆盖层时，上部土柱含水率较大的部分主要分布在Ⅰ；不存在覆盖层时，上部土柱含水率较大的部分主要分布在Ⅱ，这是因为Ⅰ与外界大气发生汽态水的交换。含水率过高，会导致土体强度降低。因此，当路基上部存在覆盖层时，路基顶部聚集的水分会严重威胁工程的稳定性[17-19]。

3 结论

在本次试验研究中，可以得到以下结论：

(1)含水率差异是影响汽态水迁移的重要因素。当土体在最佳含水率时，更容易形成水汽迁移通道。高含水率梯度的土样水汽迁移量、速率均大于低含水率梯度。

(2)砂土土柱顶部有覆盖层时，汽态水在高温作用下会向上迁移，大量聚集的水分造成了上层土柱的塌缩，提高了上层土体的持水能力。

(3)有、无覆盖层土柱中的水分变化有很大不同。当存在覆盖层时，水分主要集中在0～10cm；无覆盖层时，水分主要集中在10～30cm。说明实际工程中，当土基上部存在不透气覆盖层时，对工程的影响更大。

参考文献

[1] Milly PCD. A Simulation Analysis of Thermal Effects on Evaporation From Soil, Water Resources Research [J]. 1984,20(8).

[2] Parlange M, Cahill A, Nielsen D, et al. Review of Heat and Water Movement in Field Soils, Soil and Tillage Research [J]. 1998,47(1).

[3] Nakano Y, Tice A, Oliphant J. Transport of Water in Frozen Soil: Iii[J]. Experiments on the Effects of Ice Content, Advances in Water Resources, 1984,7(1).

[4] 李强,姚仰平,韩黎明,等.土体的"锅盖效应",工业建筑[J].2014,44(2):69.

[5] 姚仰平,王琳,王乃东.干寒区锅盖效应致灾特征及案例分析,工业建筑[J].2016,46(9).

[6] 李倩.新疆地区路面覆盖下路基温湿度变化规律及力学性能研究[D].西安:长安大学,2012.

[7] 罗汀,陈含,姚仰平,等.寒区路基土锅盖效应气态水迁移试验研究[J],天津大学学报(自然科学与工程技术版)[J].2019,52(S1):29.

[8] 滕继东,贺佐跃,张升,等.非饱和土水气迁移与相变：两类"锅盖效应"的发生机理及数值再现[J].岩土工程学报,2016,38(10):1813.

[9] 贺佐跃,张升.气态水诱发高速铁路路基冻胀的潜在机理研究[J],铁道学报[J].2020,42(4):123.

[10] 张升,贺佐跃,滕继东,等.非饱和土水汽迁移与相变：两类"锅盖效应"的试验研究[J],岩土工程学

报,2017,39(5):961.

[11] Zhang S,Teng J,He Z,et al. Canopy Effect Caused By Vapour Transfer in Covered Freezing Soils[J]. Geotechnical,2016,66(11):927.

[12] Zhang S,Teng J,He Z,et al. Importance of Vapor Flow in Unsaturated Freezing Soil:a Numerical Study [J]. Cold Regions Science and Technology, 2016,126.

[13] 王铁行,贺再球,赵树德,等.非饱和土体气态水迁移试验研究[J],岩石力学与工程学报,2005 (18):3271.

[14] 冉武平,李玲.路面覆盖效应影响下的路基湿度及温度分布特性[J].武汉理工大学学报(交通科学与工程版),2015,39(4):729.

[15] Cornelis W,Corluy J,Medina H,et al. Measuring and Modelling the Soil Shrinkage Characteristic Curve [J]. Geoderma, 2006,137(1):179.

[16] Bronswijk J J B. Relation Between Vertical Soil Movements and Water-content Changes in Cracking Clays [J]. Soil Science Society of America Journal,1991,55(5):1220.

[17] Cokca E,Erol O,Armangil F. Effects of Compaction Moisture Content on the Shear Strength of an Unsaturated Clay[J]. Geotechnical & Geological Engineering, 2004,22(2):285.

[18] Tie-hang Wang, Li Ning, Ding-yi Xie. Gravitational potential, matrix suction and thermal potential of unsaturated loess soil[J]. Chinese Journal of Geotechnical Engineering,2004(5):715.

[19] Khoury CN,Khoury NN,Miller GA. Effect of Cyclic Suction History(hydraulic Hysteresis) on Resilient Modulus of Unsaturated Fine-grained Soil[J]. Transportation Research Record, 2011,2232(1):68.

Experimental Study on Strength Degradation Characteristics of Cement-improved Loess under Wetting-drying Cycles

Jiangtao Fan　Yingjun Jiang　Tian Tian　Yong Yi

(Key Laboratory for Special Area Highway Engineering of Ministry of Education,Chang'an University)

Abstract　In order to reveal the law of strength degradation of cement-improved loess under the action of wetting-drying cycles, the influence of compaction method[Vertical Vibration compaction method(VVCM), quasi-static compaction method(QSCM)], cement content, and compaction coefficient on the compressive strength of cement-improved loess under wetting-drying cycles was studied. The results show that cement-improved loess has a significant strength degradation effect under the action of wetting-drying cycles. With the increase in the number of wetting-drying cycles, the strength of the improved loess continues to attenuate. After the wetting-drying cycles exceed 15 times, the strength basically no longer attenuates, and the corresponding degradation coefficient is about 0.44; Adopting VVCM, increasing cement content and compaction coefficient to improve the strength degradation effect of improved loess, but not obvious; considering the most unfavourable conditions, the wetting-drying cycle strength degradation coefficient is taken as 0.40.

Keywords　Cement-improved Loess　Wetting-drying Cycle　Deterioration coefficient　Compressive strength

0　Introduction

Loess is widely distributed in northern China and is an inevitable road construction material for high-speed railway construction. However, due to its collapsibility, it is prone to significant subsidence after soaking[1,2]. Cement-improved loess is one of the common methods for improving subgrade. The improved strength meets the engineering requirements, but it does not consider environmental factors. The cyclical climate changes make the cement-improved loess roadbed always in a saturated and unsaturated alternate state under the action of rainfall and evaporation, and its physical and mechanical properties also vary. It is in a dynamic process of change due to continuous wetting-drying cycle action[3-5], which affects the structural stability of the cement-improved loess subgrade and reduces the strength of the subgrade.

In response to this problem, scholars have made a series of studies. Shen, et al. (2014) studied the effect of salt content on the deterioration effect of soil under wetting and drying cycles by using a non-destructive ultrasonic wave velocimeter, and estimated the deterioration degree based on the test results of mechanical properties[6]. Ye, et al. (2020) studied the structural damage evolution process of loess under the action of wetting-drying cycles, and carried out a wetting-drying cycle triaxial test considering the three influencing factors of initial water content, amplitude and number of wetting-drying cycles [7]. Duan, et al. (2009) studied the attenuation law of the mechanical strength of loess under wetting-drying cycles, and believed that wetting-drying cycles caused obvious damage to loess structures through the disturbance of soil particle size composition and internal structure [8]. Pan, et al. (2020) studied the effects of wetting-drying cycles on loess. It is believed that the wetting-drying cycles will increase the internal fissures of the loess and lead to the deterioration of the soil properties [9]. Ye, et al. (2017, 2018) studied the law of water migration in loess under the action of wetting-drying cycles, and believed that under the action of wetting-drying cycles, soil moisture is distributed radially, with high and low levels. As the number of cycles increases, the water migration speed decreases and tends stable [10,11]. Tu, et al. (2017) studied the mechanical properties of different types of soil under the action of wetting-drying cycles, and found that the strength of the soil tends to be stable as the number of dry and wet cycles increases [12].

The above research mainly involves the influence of wetting-drying cycles on the engineering properties of soil. Fang, et al. (2009) studied the change of the strength of cement-improved loess under the action of wetting-drying cycles, and believed that the cement content has little effect on the strength attenuation under the action of wetting-drying cycles [13]. However, the mechanical properties of cement-improved loess are related to the composition and structure of the material. The composition of the material depends on the nature of the loess and the cement content. The structure is manifested in the arrangement of particles and the degree of compaction. The site depends on the compaction machine and compaction process, and the indoor depends on the compaction method. In view of this, the study of different compaction methods (VVCM and QSCM) under the action of wetting-drying cycles, cement content, and compaction coefficient cement improved loess strength degradation law, the results can provide references for engineering practice.

1 Materials and Methods

1.1 Materials

1.1.1 Loess

The loess used for the test was taken from a soil sampling site in the XH-TJ01 section of the Xi'an-Hancheng intercity railway. It is bright yellow with loose soil and belongs to silty clay. The physical property indexes are shown in Tab. 1.

Supported by the Science and Technology Plan Project of Henan Provincial Department of Transportation(2020J-2-2), Science and Technology Project of Shaanxi Provincial Department of Transportation(18-02K,19-27K)。

Physical properties of loess Tab. 1

Index	Particle density (g/cm^3)	Liquid limit (%)	Plastic limit (%)	Plasticity Index	The following particle size(mm) mass fraction(%)				
					0.25~0.075	0.075~0.05	0.05~0.01	0.01~0.005	≤0.005
Test value	2.74	26.4	15.7	10.7	2.47	7.22	53.43	13.83	23.05

1.1.2 Cement

The cement is ordinary Portland cement P. O42.5 produced by Shaanxi Yao Bote Cement Co., Ltd. The technical properties are shown in Tab. 2.

Cement technical properties Tab. 2

Index	Fineness(%)	Stability	Ignition loss(%)	Initial setting time(s)	Final setting time(s)
Test value	1.2	Qualified	1.02	265	320

1.2 Methods

1.2.1 Compaction Methods

The vertical vibrator compaction equipment used in the test is shown in Fig. 1, and the working parameters are shown in Tab. 3[14,15].

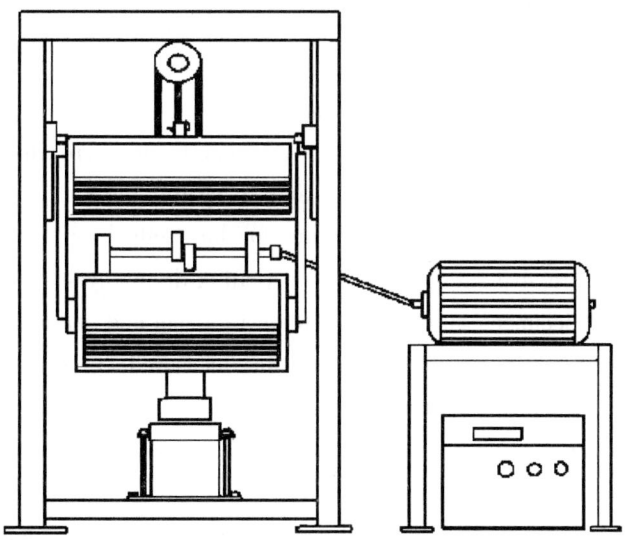

Fig. 1 Vertical vibrator compaction equipment

Working parameters Tab. 3

Working frequency(Hz)	Nominal amplitude(mm)	Working weight(kg)	
		Upper system	Lower system
35	1.2	167	275

(1) VVCM. According to the maximum dry density and the specified compaction coefficient, the cement-improved loess is vibrated to the specified height with a vertical vibration compaction equipment.

(2) QSCM. Press the cement-improved loess to the specified height in accordance with the QSCM in the "Code for Soil Test of Railway Engineering" (TB10102—2010)[16].

1.2.2 Test Methods

(1) Unconfined compressive strength. After the test piece reaches the curing age, it is taken out of the

curing room and placed in a (20 ± 2)°C water tank. After being immersed in water for 24 hours, the hydraulic servo universal testing machine WAW-100 (Fig. 2) is used to determine the cement improvement Unconfined compressive strength of the loess specimen, set the loading rate to 1mm/min, record the maximum load P when the modified loess specimen fails, and calculate the unconfined compressive strength of the specimen according to Equation(1)[16].

$$q = \frac{P}{A} \quad (1)$$

Where: q——unconfined compressive strength of specimen;
P——maximum load when the specimen fails;
A——the section area of specimen.

(2) The wetting-drying cycle test steps are as follows:

① Put the prepared specimen in an environment of 20 ± 2°C and 95% relative humidity until the prescribed curing age before 24h. The specimen was taken out and weighed its mass, which was recorded as m_0. The two groups of specimens were immersed in water at 20 ± 2°C for 24h, the water level was about 2.5cm higher than the top surface of the specimens. After the immersion, the specimens were taken out and the moisture on the surface of the specimens was wiped off with a wet cloth.

② Take one group of specimens immersed in water for 24 hours and measure the unconfined compressive strength according to the method in TB 10102—2010[16], which is recorded as the unconfined compressive strength q_u without wetting-drying cycles.

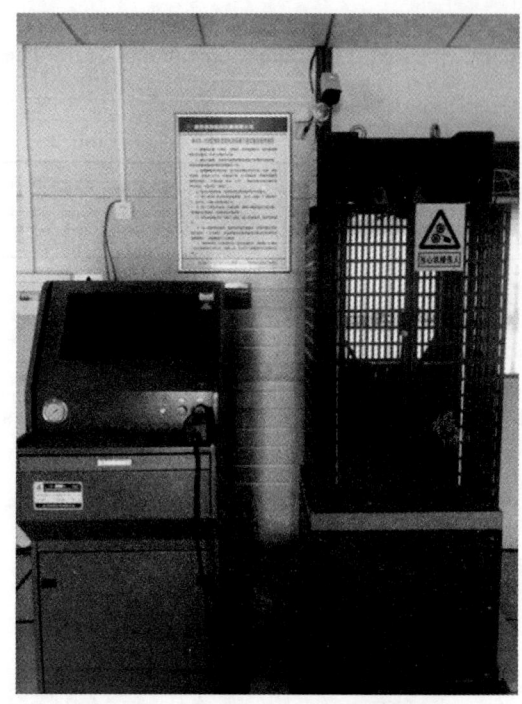

Fig. 2　Universal testing machine WAW-100

③ Place another group of specimens saturated with water in a cool and ventilated place to air dry naturally. During the air-drying process, the mass of the specimens was measured every 2h and denoted as m'. When $m' = m_0 \pm 5g$, air-drying was stopped. Then immerse the specimen in water at 20 ± 2°C for 16h, which was a wetting-drying cycle. After repeated air-drying and water-soaking processes to the specified number of times, the unconfined compressive strength is tested, denoted as q_G.

④ Wetting-drying deterioration coefficient was used to characterize the deterioration characteristics of specimens' compressive strength under wetting-drying cycles, and the deterioration coefficient was calculated according to Equation(2).

$$\eta_G = \frac{q_G}{q_u} \quad (2)$$

Where: η_G——the wetting-drying degradation coefficient;
q_u——the unconfined compressive strength of the specimen before wetting-drying cycles;
q_G——the unconfined compressive strength of the specimen after N times of wetting-drying cycles.

And the larger the deterioration coefficient is, the smaller the strength attenuation of the improved loess under the action of wetting-drying cycles is.

1.3　Test Plans

(1) To study the influence of the cement content on the strength deterioration of the improved loess under the action of wetting-drying cycles. The cement content is proposed to be 2%, 3%, 4%, 6%.

(2) The effect of the compaction coefficient on the strength deterioration of the improved loess under the action of wetting-drying cycles is studied. The compaction coefficient is proposed to be 0.92, 0.95, and 0.97.

(3) To study the influence of compaction method on the strength deterioration of the improved loess under the action of wetting-drying cycles, the compaction method is proposed to adopt VVCM and QSCM.

2 Results and Analysis

2.1 Results

The 28d compressive strength test results of cement improved loess under the action of wetting-drying cycles are shown in Tab. 4. The 28d wetting-drying degradation coefficient is shown in Tab. 5.

28d compressive strength of cement-improved loess under wetting-drying cycles　　Tab. 4

Compaction Method	P_s (%)	K	The compressive strength (MPa) of cement-improved loess under following times									
			0	1	3	5	7	9	12	15	20	25
VVCM	2	0.92	1.13	0.82	0.76	0.64	0.59	0.55	0.49	0.48	0.48	0.47
		0.95	1.53	1.22	1.06	0.93	0.86	0.80	0.70	0.67	0.67	0.67
		0.97	2.00	1.64	1.40	1.28	1.16	1.06	0.98	0.93	0.92	0.92
	3	0.92	1.47	1.18	1.01	0.93	0.79	0.74	0.66	0.65	0.65	0.64
		0.95	1.82	1.47	1.35	1.18	1.04	0.96	0.87	0.85	0.84	0.84
		0.97	2.46	2.07	1.82	1.70	1.43	1.33	1.23	1.17	1.16	1.15
	4	0.92	1.62	1.31	1.17	1.05	0.91	0.84	0.76	0.73	0.72	0.72
		0.95	2.22	1.84	1.69	1.58	1.29	1.20	1.09	1.02	1.02	1.01
		0.97	2.74	2.36	2.19	2.03	1.62	1.53	1.42	1.32	1.32	1.32
	6	0.92	1.95	1.62	1.44	1.29	1.13	1.05	0.96	0.93	0.92	0.92
		0.95	2.49	2.14	1.97	1.79	1.54	1.44	1.27	1.20	1.20	1.17
		0.97	3.02	2.63	2.48	2.30	1.93	1.78	1.60	1.48	1.48	1.45
QSCM	2	0.92	1.03	0.73	0.68	0.58	0.53	0.48	0.44	0.43	0.43	0.43
		0.95	1.34	1.06	0.91	0.80	0.72	0.66	0.60	0.58	0.58	0.56
		0.97	1.65	1.32	1.14	1.01	0.91	0.83	0.76	0.73	0.73	0.71
	3	0.92	1.30	1.03	0.88	0.75	0.69	0.64	0.57	0.55	0.55	0.55
		0.95	1.60	1.28	1.10	0.99	0.86	0.82	0.74	0.70	0.69	0.69
		0.97	2.03	1.68	1.44	1.28	1.12	1.08	0.95	0.89	0.89	0.89
	4	0.92	1.49	1.21	1.04	0.94	0.83	0.76	0.69	0.64	0.64	0.63
		0.95	1.90	1.58	1.39	1.24	1.08	0.99	0.91	0.84	0.84	0.84
		0.97	2.26	1.90	1.74	1.56	1.29	1.24	1.11	1.02	1.01	1.01
	6	0.92	2.03	1.68	1.42	1.30	1.14	1.04	0.95	0.87	0.87	0.87
		0.95	2.44	2.03	1.78	1.63	1.39	1.27	1.17	1.07	1.06	1.05
		0.97	2.80	2.38	2.18	1.96	1.62	1.60	1.34	1.26	1.25	1.25

28 days wetting-drying degradation coefficient η_G of cement-improved loess under wetting-drying cycles Tab. 5

Compaction Method	P_s (%)	K	Wetting-drying degradation coefficient η_G of cement-improved loess under following times									
			0	1	3	5	7	9	12	15	20	25
VVCM	2	0.92	1.00	0.73	0.67	0.57	0.52	0.49	0.43	0.42	0.42	0.42
		0.95	1.00	0.80	0.69	0.61	0.56	0.52	0.46	0.44	0.44	0.44
		0.97	1.00	0.82	0.70	0.64	0.58	0.53	0.49	0.46	0.46	0.46
	3	0.92	1.00	0.80	0.69	0.63	0.54	0.50	0.45	0.44	0.44	0.44
		0.95	1.00	0.81	0.74	0.65	0.57	0.53	0.48	0.46	0.46	0.46
		0.97	1.00	0.84	0.74	0.69	0.58	0.54	0.50	0.47	0.47	0.47
	4	0.92	1.00	0.81	0.72	0.65	0.56	0.52	0.47	0.45	0.45	0.45
		0.95	1.00	0.83	0.76	0.71	0.58	0.54	0.49	0.46	0.46	0.46
		0.97	1.00	0.86	0.80	0.74	0.59	0.56	0.52	0.48	0.48	0.48
	6	0.92	1.00	0.83	0.74	0.66	0.58	0.54	0.49	0.47	0.47	0.47
		0.95	1.00	0.86	0.79	0.72	0.62	0.58	0.51	0.48	0.48	0.47
		0.97	1.00	0.87	0.82	0.76	0.64	0.59	0.53	0.49	0.49	0.48
QSCM	2	0.92	1.00	0.71	0.66	0.56	0.51	0.47	0.43	0.42	0.42	0.42
		0.95	1.00	0.79	0.68	0.60	0.54	0.49	0.45	0.43	0.43	0.43
		0.97	1.00	0.80	0.69	0.61	0.55	0.50	0.46	0.44	0.44	0.43
	3	0.92	1.00	0.79	0.68	0.58	0.53	0.49	0.44	0.42	0.42	0.42
		0.95	1.00	0.80	0.69	0.62	0.54	0.51	0.46	0.43	0.43	0.43
		0.97	1.00	0.83	0.71	0.63	0.55	0.53	0.47	0.44	0.44	0.44
	4	0.92	1.00	0.81	0.70	0.63	0.56	0.51	0.46	0.43	0.43	0.42
		0.95	1.00	0.83	0.73	0.65	0.57	0.52	0.48	0.44	0.44	0.44
		0.97	1.00	0.84	0.77	0.69	0.57	0.55	0.49	0.45	0.45	0.45
	6	0.92	1.00	0.83	0.70	0.64	0.56	0.51	0.47	0.43	0.43	0.43
		0.95	1.00	0.83	0.73	0.67	0.57	0.52	0.48	0.44	0.44	0.44
		0.97	1.00	0.85	0.78	0.70	0.58	0.57	0.48	0.45	0.45	0.45

2.2 Analysis

The strength of cement-improved loess under the action of wetting-drying cycles is affected by the deterioration of internal and external factors. The internal factors mainly include compaction coefficient, cement dosage, molding method, etc., and external factors mainly include the number of wetting-drying cycles.

2.2.1 Influence of times of wetting-drying cycles

It is assumed that cement-improved loess under wetting-drying cycle conditions has a strength degradation coefficient equation, and meets the following three boundary conditions:

$$N = 0, \eta_{GN} = \eta_{G0}$$
$$N = \infty, \eta_{GN} = \eta_{G\infty}$$
$$\eta_{G0} > \eta_{G\infty}$$

Where: N —— wetting-drying cycles of cement-improved loess;

η_{GN} —— the strength degradation coefficient of cement-improved loess after N times of wetting-drying;

η_{G0} —— strength degradation coefficient of cement-improved loess without wetting-drying cycle (Which is 1);

$\eta_{G\infty}$ —— deterioration coefficient of cement-improved loess limit wetting-drying strength.

According to the above boundary conditions, the strength degradation coefficient equation of cement-improved loess after wetting-drying cycles is established:

$$\eta_{GN} = \eta_{G\infty} - \frac{\eta_{G\infty} - 1}{\zeta \cdot N^2 + 1} \tag{3}$$

Where: ζ——the regression parameters of the equation.

Equation(3) is used to fit the strength degradation equation of cement-improved loess after drying and wetting cycles, as shown in Fig. 3.

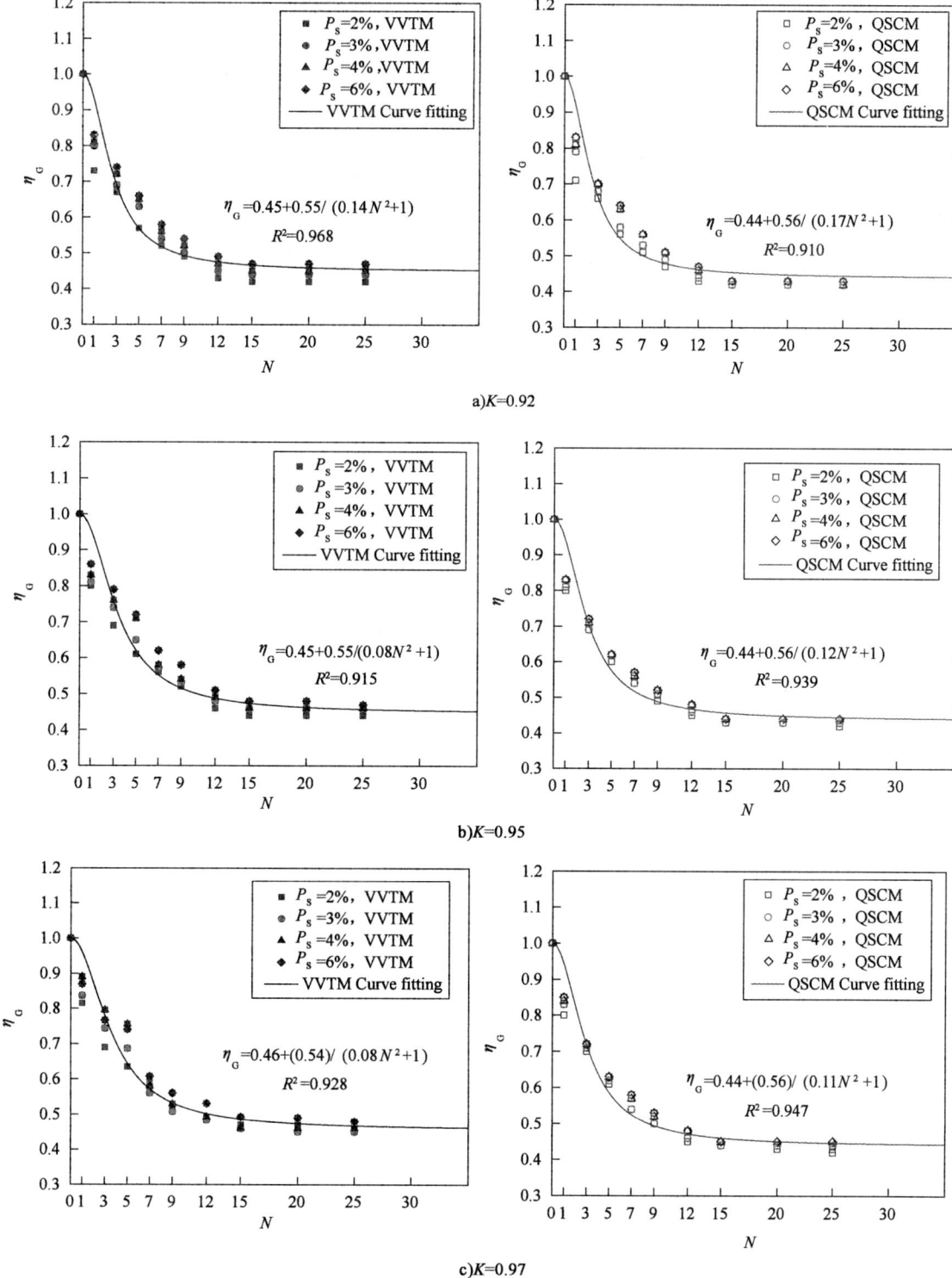

Fig. 3 The relationship between η_G and N

It can be seen from Figure 3 that as the number of wetting-drying cycle increases, the degradation coefficient of cement-improved loess gradually decreases, and the decline gradually slows down. The number of wetting-drying cycles exceeds 15 times, and the degradation coefficient stabilizes at 0.41 ~ 0.48 (VVCM) or 0.41 ~ 0.43 (QSCM). Considering the most unfavorable conditions, the deterioration coefficient of the wetting-drying cycle is taken as 0.40. The larger the coefficient ζ is, the smaller the strength deterioration coefficient of the cement-improved loess after N times of wetting-drying cycles.

The strength of cement-improved loess tends to deteriorate under the action of wetting-drying cycles, which is due to the irreversible transformation of its microstructure. There is a certain amount of soluble salt in loess, which will form salt cement on the surface of soil particles to provide a certain support for the cement-improved loess structure. The strength of cement-improved loess is mainly derived from the skeleton structure formed by the multi-faceted cementation after cement hydration. In the humidification stage, a large amount of soluble salt in the modified soil is dissolved, which leads to the increase and enlargement of pores in the cement-modified loess. At the same time, the disappearance of the reinforcing cohesive force formed by the soluble salt cementation will damage the skeleton structure formed by the cement, the improved loess appears dry shrinkage. The dry shrinkage process will promote the appearance and development of the surface and internal cracks of the improved loess. At the same time, the evaporation of water will cause the soluble salt to migrate and precipitate, resulting in the loosening of the clay particles in the cement-improved loess. Promoting cement hydration in the wet stage will restore the strength of the modified loess to some extent, but the recovery capacity is limited. Therefore, the compressive strength of the cement-modified loess is generally reduced. After a certain number of wetting-drying cycles, the soluble salt basically precipitates and the drying shrinkage phenomenon basically disappears, and the strength deterioration coefficient of cement-improved loess tends to be stable.

2.2.2 Influence of internal factors

The influence of cement content, compaction coefficient, and compaction method on the stability value of cement-improved loess after 15 times deterioration under the action of wetting-drying cycles is shown in Tab. 6.

Influence of internal factors on the wetting-drying degradation coefficient after stabilization Tab. 6

Compaction Method	K	Deterioration coefficient of cement-improved loess under following P_s			
		2	3	4	6
VVCM	0.92	0.42	0.44	0.45	0.47
	0.95	0.44	0.46	0.46	0.48
	0.97	0.46	0.47	0.48	0.49
QSCM	0.92	0.42	0.42	0.43	0.43
	0.95	0.43	0.43	0.44	0.44
	0.97	0.44	0.44	0.45	0.45

It can be seen from Tab. 6 that as the cement content increases, the compaction coefficient increases, and the stable value of the improved loess strength degradation coefficient increases, but it is not obvious. Compared with the QSCM, the strength deterioration coefficient of the improved loess specimens formed by the VVCM is slightly increased after stabilizing.

Although increasing the cement content increases the strength provided by hydration, it does not weaken the soluble salt dissolution and drying shrinkage of the cement-improved loess under the action of wetting-drying cycles. The specimen formed by VVCM and increasing the compaction coefficient can reduce the porosity of cement-improved loess and make the structure more stable. However, this cannot prevent water infiltration and loss in the process of wetting-drying cycle, and can only slightly reduce the deterioration effect in the early stage of wetting-drying cycle, thus increasing the deterioration coefficient of cement- improved loess.

3 Conclusions

(1) Using VVTM, increasing the cement content and the compaction coefficient, have improved the strength degrading effect of the improved loess, but it is not obvious.

(2) Under the action of the wetting-drying cycle, porosity, cracks and other damages of cement- improved loess develop continuously, loess voids, and the strength continues to deteriorate. After the wetting-drying cycle exceeds 15 times, the strength does not decrease. According to the most unfavorable conditions, the deterioration coefficient of wetting-drying cycle is selected as 0.40.

(3) During the wetting-drying cycle process, the soluble salt is dissolved out during the humidification process, and the shrinkage cracking during the drying process causes irreversible damage to the cement-improved loess structure, resulting in a continuous decrease in strength, until the basic precipitation of soluble salts and the drying and shrinkage disappear, the strength no longer decreases.

References

[1] Li G Y, Ma W. Effects of Freeze-Thaw Cycle on Engineering Properties of Loess Used as Road Fills in Seasonally Frozen Ground Regions[J]. North China. Journal of Mountain Science, 2017, 14(002): 356-68. DOI:10.1007/s11629-016-4005-4.

[2] Gao Y, Qian H. Effects of Lime Treatment on the Hydraulic Conductivity and Microstructure of Loess[J]. Environmental Earth Sciences, 2018, 77(14): 1-15. DOI:10.1007/s12665-018-7715-9.

[3] PIRES L, BACCHI O. Gamma Ray Computed Tomography to Evaluate Wetting/Drying Soil Structure Changes[J]. Nuclear Instruments and Methods in Physics Research Section B: Beam Interactions with Materials and Atoms, 2005, 229(3-4): 443-56. DOI:10.1016/j.nimb.2004.12.118.

[4] Tang C S, Cui Y J. Desiccation and Cracking Behaviour of Clay Layer from Slurry State under Wetting-drying Cycles[J]. Geoderma, 2011, 166(1): 111-8. DOI:10.1016/j.geoderma.2011.07.018.

[5] Xu J, Li Y F. Shear Strength and Mesoscopic Character of Undisturbed Loess with Sodium Sulfate after Dry-Wet Cycling[J]. Bulletin of Engineering Geology and the Environment, 2020, 79(3): 1523-1541. DOI:10.1007/s10064-019-01646-4.

[6] Shen X G, Chen W W. Experimental Study on Salt Deterioration of Salt Contaminated Earthen Materials under Dry-Wet Cycles [C]. 3rd International Conference on Salt Weathering of Buildings and Stone Sculptures. https://xueshu.baidu.com/usercenter/paper/show? paperid = 6bd89818f6c38354934e6a8bdd6a48ca&site = xueshu_se&hitarticle=1.

[7] Ye W, Bai Y. Deterioration of the Internal Structure of Loess under Dry-Wet Cycles[J]. Advances in Civil Engineering, 2020(2): 1-17. DOI:10.1155/2020/8881423.

[8] Duan T. The Research of Alternating Wet and Dry on the Deterioration of Loess Strength[D]. Northwest A&F University, Master's thesis, 2009. (in Chinese) http://kns-cnki-net-s.vpn.chd.edu.cn:8080/kcms/detail/detail.aspx? dbcode = CMFD&dbname = CMFD2011&filename = 2010050452.nh&v = C%25mmd2BefBPSAIoAPVgK5X8xJWRu1mzqcSp9HkmxmQCzkWyIvvpLnrBECZWhE6EM5flS4.

[9] Pan Z X, Yang G S. Study on Mechanical Properties and Microscopic Damage of Undisturbed Loess under Dry and Wet Cycles[J]. Journal of Engineering Geology, 28(06): 1186-1192. (in Chinese) DOI:10.13544/j.cnki.jeg.2019-423.

[10] Ye W J, Li C Q. Evolution of Loess Crack under Action of Dehumidification-Humidification[J]. Journal of Engineering Geology, 25(02): 376-83. (in Chinese) DOI:10.13544/j.cnki.jeg.2017.02.015.

[11] Ye W J, Liu K. Moisture Transfer Test of Remolded Loess under Drying-Wetting Cycles[J]. Journal of Xi'an University of Science and Technology, 2018, 38(06):937-44. (in Chinese) DOI:10.13800/j.cnki.xakjdxxb.2018.0609.

[12] Tu Y L, Liu X R. Experimental Study on Strength and Deformation Characteristics of Silty Clay During Wetting-Drying Cycles[J]. Rock and Soil Mechanics, 2017, 38(12):3581-9. DOI:10.16285/j.rsm.2017.12.024.

[13] Fang L F. Experimental Study on Improved Loess Using Cement for Subgrade of Zhengzhou-Xi'an Dedicated Passenger Special Line[D]. Southwest Jiaotong University, Master's Thesis, 2009. (in Chinese) http://kns-cnki-net-s.vpn.chd.edu.cn:8080/kcms/detail/detail.aspx?dbcode=CMFD&dbname=CMFD2010&filename=2009219056.nh&v=xeaviJkpZvN9lXpxsy33RezNOLRGp7ndBtxATXuz8wR8a5Iz13PPEQUZ0h0Ffr%25mmd2BP.

[14] Jiang Y J, Fan J T. Laboratory Evaluation of a Vertical Vibration Testing Method for an SMA-13 Mixture[J]. Materials, 2020, 13(19):4409. DOI:10.3390/ma13194409.

[15] Jiang Y J, Xue J S. Influence of Volumetric Property on Mechanical Properties of Vertical Vibration Compacted Asphalt Mixture[J]. Construction Build Mater, 2017, 135:612-21. DOI:10.1016/j.conbuildmat.2016.12.159.

[16] Ministry of Railways of the People's Republic of China. Code for Soil Test of Railway Engineering[M]. Beijing: China Railway Press, 2010(in Chinese).

TX-B型固化剂复配无机材料改良黄土强度特性研究

梁 燕 陈 晨 刘 霜 吴仁悠 张 婧

(长安大学公路学院)

摘 要 为研究TX-B高分子固化剂改良黄土强度的影响因素,选择不同配合比、不同养护龄期试样,通过无侧限抗压强度试验,分析不同因素对加固后黄土强度的作用强弱。试验结果表明:水泥用量对未加煤矸石的改良黄土试样强度的影响小,对加入煤矸石的改良黄土强度影响大;随养护龄期的增加,加入煤矸石的改良黄土试样强度增幅远大于未加煤矸石的改良黄土;少量TX-B固化剂就能增强改良黄土的强度,并能有效减少水泥用量。

关键词 公路工程 TX-B固化剂 无侧限抗压试验 黄土路基

0 引 言

随着"一带一路"倡议的提出,陕西、河南、甘肃等黄土地区的基础建设会极大加强,黄土地区公路和铁路的建设将会迎来高速发展。黄土作为路基材料具有高强、低压缩性等优点,但其遇水强度降低的特点,易造成路基产生变形、湿陷等破坏。因此改善其工程特性,提高黄土路基稳定性,对于保证公路质量至关重要。

其中,最常见的方法就是使用固化剂来减少水泥砂石的掺量,为此国内学者对固化剂进行了大量的研究工作,王银梅等[1]研究发现了黄土经SH高分子固化剂后,压缩性减少、湿陷性消失、后期强度很高;吴文飞等[2]通过研究固化剂改良水泥黄土,发现掺入微量固化剂能提高水泥稳定黄土的强度和水稳定性;赵瑜隆等[3]研究不同因素对复合土壤固化剂稳定碎石基层强度的影响,得出固化剂剂量能显著影响强度;李崇清等[4]利用模型试验研究了SH固化剂复配无机材料加固黄土的抗侵蚀特性,认为将SH与无机材料复合可以弥补单一固化剂的缺点。

但研究表明[5],不同地区的土壤性质存在差异,不同固化剂加固机理并不相同,同一种固化剂并不能保证在其他地区拥有相同的加固效果。因此,本文将TX-B高分子固化剂掺入不同水泥含量的黄土中,在不同龄期养护条件下,测定各试样的无侧限抗压强度,并考虑利用工业废料煤矸石,在相同试验条件下,在试样中加入一定量的煤矸石,测定固化剂复配水泥煤矸石改良黄土的无侧限抗压强度,为TX-B固化剂在黄土路基中的应用提供理论依据。

1 试验方法

1.1 试验材料

试验用土取自陕西泾阳,取土深度0.5~2m,通过基础土工试验测得其力学物理性质,如表1所示。

黄土力学物理性质 表1

天然密度 $\rho(g/cm^3)$	相对密度 G_s	天然含水率 $w(\%)$	液限 $w_l(\%)$	塑限 $w_p(\%)$	孔隙比 e	干密度 $\rho(g/cm^3)$
1.665	2.71	13.27	28.98	16.7	0.84	1.47

固化剂采用西安同鑫伟业环保科技公司生产的TX-B高分子固化剂,TX-B固化剂可以将土壤中的自由水转变为结晶水,减薄土壤团粒所吸附的双电层,使电解质浓度增加,凝聚土颗粒,体积膨胀填充土粒间的空隙,来提高土体密实度和强度等性能;试验采用普通硅酸盐水泥、黏土质煤矸石,颗粒粒径在2~5mm之间。

1.2 试验方法

将黄土碾压过筛后TX-B固化剂拌和,TX-B固化剂掺量(固化剂质量/干土质量)按实际经验设定为0.03%。试样分为两组,具体配合比见表2。

试样配合比 表2

试样编号	TX-B固化剂(%)	黄土(%)	水泥(%)	煤矸石(%)
1	0.03	96	4	0
2	0.03	94	6	0
3	0.03	92	8	0
4	0.03	90	10	0
5	0.03	20	4	76
6	0.03	20	6	74
7	0.03	20	8	72
8	0.03	20	10	70

对土样进行击实试验,测得其最佳含水率12%、最大干密度为1.9g/cm³,按相应规程制作试样并试验,试样为50mm×50mm圆柱体,采用静力压实法制备。将制备完成的试样进行标准养护,养护期龄分别为7d、14d、28d。最后对试样进行无侧限抗压试验。

2 试验结果与分析

2.1 试样的强度

通过试验得到关于不同配合比、龄期、固化剂类型的无侧限抗压强度,试验结果见图1。第一组以水泥、黄土制成的1~4号试样经TX-B固化剂加固后的强度在2.44~4.31MPa之间,第二组加入煤矸石后的5~8号试样强度在5.2~8.98MPa之间。加入煤矸石的试验组强度明显大于不加煤矸石的试验组。

2.2 分析

2.2.1 水泥含量对强度的影响

TX-B固化剂加入后,水泥含量对于改良黄土的强度影响规律如图2所示。不同龄期下,随水泥含量的增加,无侧限抗压强度增量幅度小。水泥含量从4%增到10%过程中,养护龄期分别为7d、14d、28d时,强度分别提高了5.9%、4.2%、1.7%。养护龄期越长,增加水泥含量对于强度的提高作用越小。

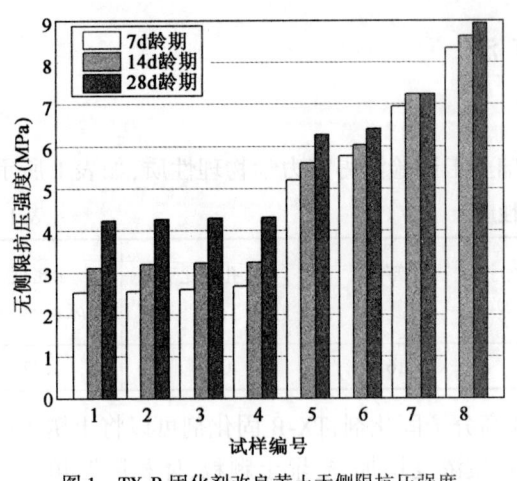

图1 TX-B固化剂改良黄土无侧限抗压强度　　　　图2 水泥含量与改良黄土强度关系

因此从工程经济角度,用TX固化剂加水泥来加固黄土路基时,当水泥含量为4%时,再增加水泥含量对强度的影响不大。

2.2.2 养护龄期对强度的影响

养护龄期对于改良黄土的强度影响较大,如图3所示。养护龄期分别为7d、14d、28d时,试样强度分别为2.5~2.7MPa、3.1~4.3MPa和4.2~4.3MPa。当养护龄期从7d增至28d,试样强度增加60%~67%。随着养护龄期的增加,水泥水化作用随着时间逐步累积。根据工程实际,应尽量增加养护龄期,以提高路基土强度。

2.2.3 煤矸石对强度的影响

煤矸石是矿产开发过程中的固体废弃物,向路基添加煤矸石,既可以一定程度解决环境问题,又可以节约细集料的用量。

加入煤矸石的试样的强度显于大于没加煤矸石的试样。由于试样加入大量煤矸石,粒径较大的煤矸石充当土样的骨架,而粒径较小的黄土填充于骨架之间,在TX-B固化剂和水泥的化学作用下,使土样形成更加致密的物理结构,极大提高土样的强度。加入煤矸石作为主骨架的试样,比未加煤矸石试样的强度提高70%~153%,并且试样养护龄期越短,其强度增幅越大。

水泥含量与加入煤矸石后改良黄土的强度关系见图4,水泥含量从4%到10%的过程中,7d、14d、28d养护龄期的试样强度分别增加了60.2%、54.1%、42.4%。这说明提升水泥含量利于增加煤矸石黄土的强度,在实际工程中可根据设计强度来选择水泥的含量。

养护龄期与改良煤矸石黄土的强度关系见图5,养护龄期对于改良煤矸石黄土的强度影响较小。随养护龄期从7d增加到28d,4%、6%、8%、10%水泥含量试样强度分别增加20%、11%、4%、7%。在0~7d内,试样强度快速增加,基本达到最大强度,7d后,强度增加幅度放缓。随着养护龄期增加,水泥的水化作用使土粒间孔隙不断减小,但由于煤矸石黄土试样比较致密,初始强度大,土粒之间初始孔隙较小,水泥水化作用随时间对强度增加有限。没加煤矸石的黄土试样初始强度低,土粒间孔隙较大,在水泥水化作用下,试样强度不断增加,增幅明显。

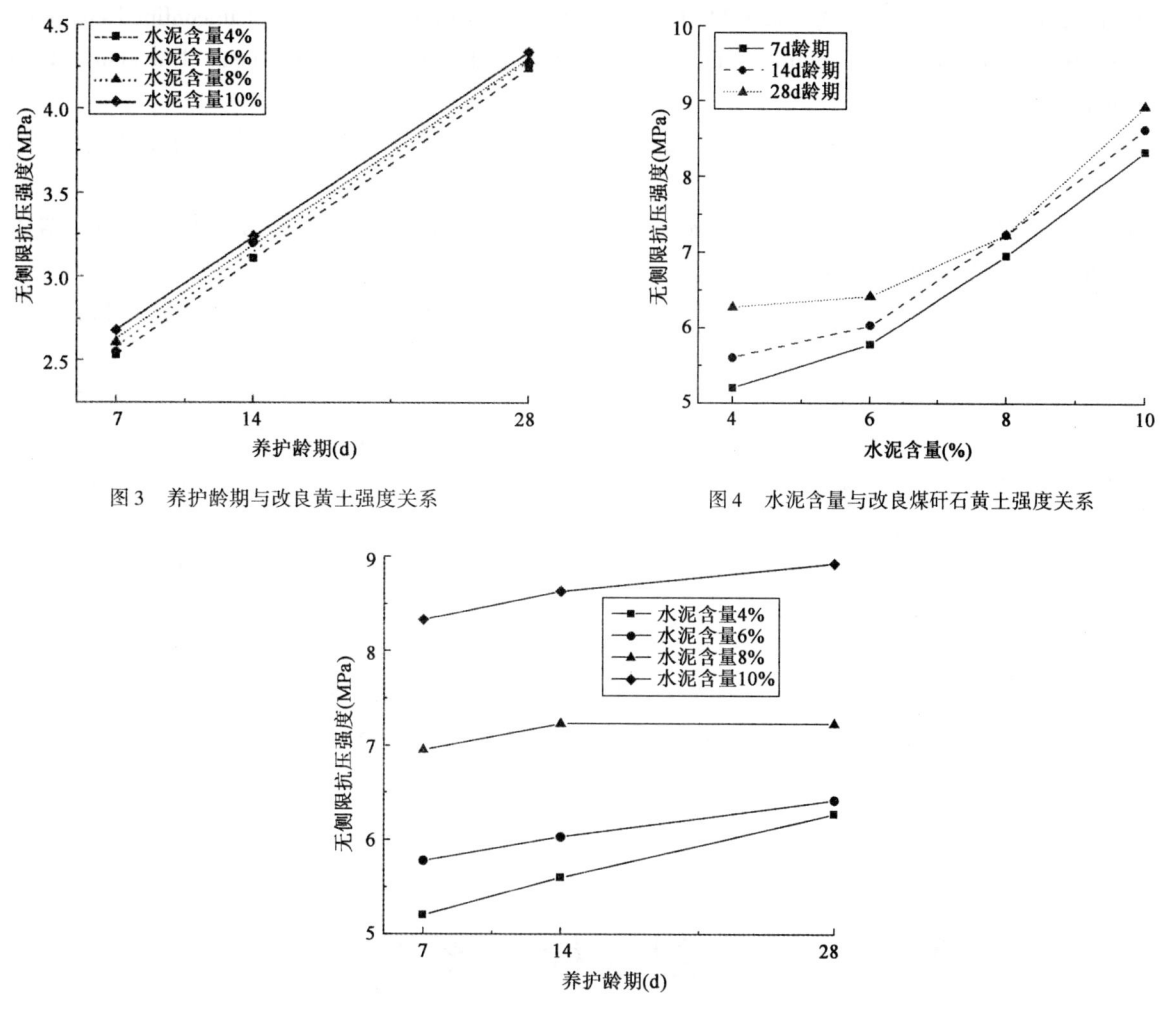

图3 养护龄期与改良黄土强度关系　　　　图4 水泥含量与改良煤矸石黄土强度关系

图5 养护龄期与改良煤矸石黄土强度关系

3 结　论

本文对 TX-B 固化剂加固黄土和煤矸石黄土的强度进行大量研究,从水泥含量、龄期分析了加固效果,得出了如下结论:

(1)TX-B 固化剂复配水泥加固黄土的强度受水泥含量的影响较小,而受养护龄期的影响较大。水泥含量从4%增加到10%,试样强度增加 1.7%~5.9%;养护龄期从 7d 增加到 28d,试样强度增加大于60%。从工程经济角度,应减少水泥含量,增加养护龄期。

(2)TX-B 固化剂复配水泥加固煤矸石黄土的强度受水泥含量影响大,受养护龄期的影响小,加入煤矸石后,土体变得更加致密,初始强度高,受养护龄期影响小,增加养护龄期,试样强度增加 4%~20%。实际工程中,应根据需要增加水泥含量,适当减少养护龄期。

(3)与其他类型固化剂相比,TX-B 固化剂加固黄土过程中所需固化剂掺量小,并能节约水泥用量,对环境影响小。

参考文献

[1] 王银梅,杨重存,谌文武,等.新型高分子材料 SH 加固黄土强度及机理探讨[J].岩石力学与工程学报,2005(14):2554-2559.
[2] 吴文飞,张纪阳,何锐,等.固化剂改良水泥稳定黄土强度及水稳性研究[J].硅酸盐通报,2016,35(07):2159-2165.

[3] Yu-long ZHAO, Ying GAO, Yi-luo ZHANG, et al. Analysis of influence factors of unconfined compressive strength for composite soil stabilizer-stabilized gravel soil[J]. Journal of Southeast University (English Edition),2017,33(04):484-489.
[4] 李崇清,刘清秉,项伟,等.SH固化剂复配无机材料加固黄土抗侵蚀试验研究[J].长江科学院院报,2018,35(08):90-94+101.
[5] 樊恒辉,高建恩,吴普特,等.基于黄土物理化学性质变化的固化土强度影响因素分析[J].岩土力学,2011,32(07):1996-2000.
[6] 田怡然,张晓然,刘俊峰,等.煤矸石作为环境材料资源化再利用研究进展[J].科技导报,2020,38(22):104-113.
[7] 潘湘辉,桂岚,李跃军.不同土壤固化剂对土质固化性能影响的对比试验研究[J].公路工程,2014,39(01):59-62.
[8] 王银梅,韩文峰,谌文武.新型高分子固化材料与水泥加固黄土力学性能对比研究[J].岩土力学,2004(11):1761-1765.
[9] 杨秀武,瞿瑜,周浩然.水泥硅微粉固化黄土的三轴试验[J].桂林理工大学学报,2017,37(04):624-628.
[10] 李沛,杨武,邓永锋,等.土壤固化剂发展现状和趋势[J].路基工程,2014(03):1-8.
[11] 徐鹏飞,李泽莹,王银梅,等.新型高分子固化剂固化黄土的冻融循环特性[J/OL].长江科学院院报,:,http://kns.cnki.net/kcms/detail/42.1171.TV.20200408.1406.014.html.
[12] 马文杰,王博林,王旭,等.改性黄土的力学特性试验研究[J].水利水电技术,2018,49(10):150-156.

混凝土结构裂缝检测系统的设计

龚 涛[1] 苏时玲[1] 廖丽琼[2]

(1.西南交通大学地球科学与环境工程学院;2.北京建筑大学测绘与城市空间信息学院)

摘 要 针对混凝土结构裂缝图像的特征,基于数字图像处理技术,研究设计了裂缝检测系统。利用互交叉双边滤波算法进行裂缝图像的有效去噪保边,对PCNN算法进行改进简化,实现裂缝图像的高效高精度分割,基于灰度相似性和方向一致性对提取裂缝达到完整连接,根据不同类型裂缝图像的投影特征进行裂缝的有效分类和相应特征参数的计算。试验验证了系统所设计算法能够提高混凝土结构表面裂缝的提取效率和准确率。

关键词 裂缝检测系统 数字图像处理 混凝土结构裂缝 算法优化 系统开发

0 引 言

裂缝是混凝土结构中最常见的病害,裂缝作为现行混凝土结构养护规范中的一个定量化指标,在混凝土结构安全性能方面具有指示作用,一般情况下混凝土结构允许带裂缝工作。但是存在裂缝的混凝土结构,其强度、耐久性和安全性都会受到影响,因此,高精度、高效率、自动化、智能化的混凝土结构体裂缝检测系统,对裂缝的全寿命周期监测、裂缝危害警示和及时修补具有重要意义。

利用混凝土结构裂缝的数字图像进行裂缝检测,具有不接触、低成本、高效率、灵活、操作简便、可进行裂缝生长状态的持续测量等特点,因而,基于数字图像处理的裂缝检测技术被广泛应用于公路、桥梁、隧道等混凝土结构裂缝检测中[1]。

混凝土结构裂缝数字图像常常受到诸如阴影、路面油污、水渍、车道线、树叶等因素的干扰,势必影响裂缝图像提取和识别的准确性和完整性;在进行裂缝图像的分割识别时,参考的裂缝特征较少则易导致误检和漏检,而参考特征过多则检测效率降低。为此,本文设计了复杂场景下,裂缝图像去噪效果较为理想的预处理算法,以提高图像质量;选取反映全面、数量适中的特征用于图像识别,以提高图像提取精度,降低裂缝误检率和漏检率;采用优化算法进行裂缝的有效分类,计算不同类型裂缝的特征参数,以准确表述裂缝的几何特征,提高裂缝的提取效率和准确率;将上述裂缝数字图像处理算法集成,设计研发了一套混凝土结构裂缝图像检测系统。

1 系统设计

本文基于混凝土结构裂缝图像的几何特征、空间分布特征、统计特征,利用数字图像处理技术,进行裂缝检测系统的研究设计。系统设计的基本思想:对普通数码摄影机采集的混凝土结构表面的裂缝图像或裂缝生长视频序列,进行数字图像处理,对提取的裂缝图像进行分析,计算不同类型裂缝的特征参数,给出裂缝图像的分析报告。系统的工作流程示于图1,系统输出的图像分析报告示于图2。

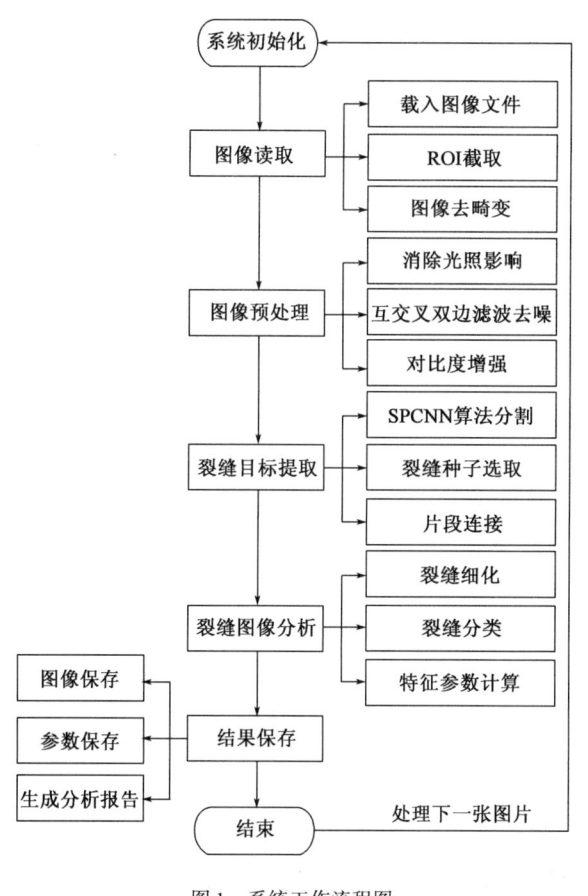

图1 系统工作流程图

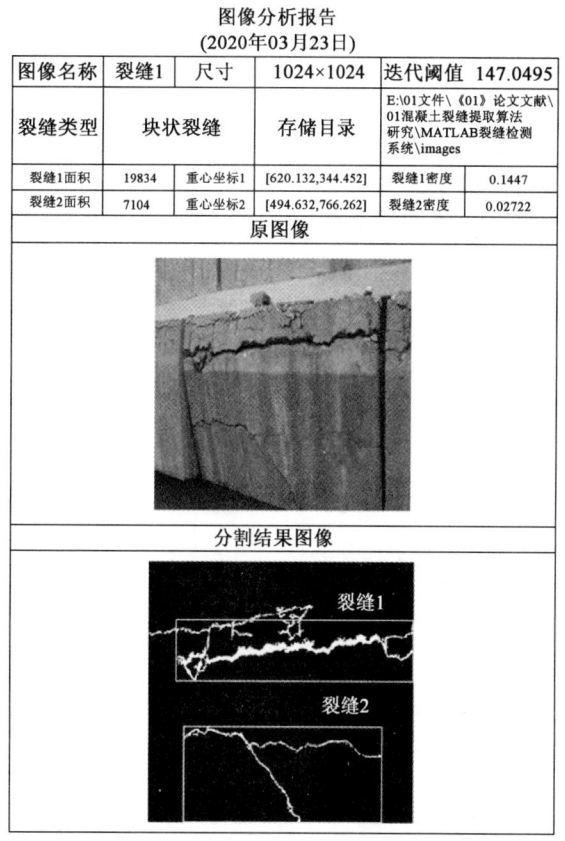

图2 系统输出的图像分析报告

2 系统实现

裂缝图像检测系统主要有5个功能模块,包括图像数据读取、图像预处理、裂缝图像目标识别与提取、裂缝分析、结果数据存储。

2.1 图像数据读取

(1)图像畸变校正。实地拍摄前,运用张正友棋盘格标定法对数码摄影机进行相机检校,获得相机参数:$c_x, c_y, f_x, f_y, k_1, k_2, p_1, p_2$。在读取裂缝图像数据时,对拍摄的裂缝图像进行去畸变校正。

(2)截取兴趣区域(ROI)。系统设计进行裂缝图像的兴趣区域(Region of interest,ROI)截取,以提高裂缝提取的精度和速度。当裂缝在整幅图像中占比小时,采取手动截取ROI;当图像中裂缝占据面积比较大时,采用顺序自动分割图像子块ROI。

2.2 图像预处理

(1)图像灰度化。系统采用符合人眼观察特性的加权平均值法,对去畸变校正的混凝土结构表面裂缝图像进行灰度化:

(2)基于小波变换的Relight增强算法消除光照不均影响。反射光$f(x,y)$等于入射光与反射系数相乘:

$$f(x,y) = i(x,y) * r(x,y) \tag{1}$$

根据式(1)可得反射函数:

$$r(x,y) = f(x,y)/i(x,y)$$

其中

$$\begin{cases} i(x,y) = 1 & i(x,y) \leqslant 1 \\ 1 < i(x,y) < +\infty & i(x,y) > 1 \end{cases} \tag{2}$$

系统设计了利用小波变换对$f(x,y)$进行频谱分析,提取其低频部分作为$i(x,y)$的近似分布,再由式(2)可得到去除光照影响的图像。

理想状态下的反射函数$r(x,y)$在(0,1)区间,但得到的是近似光照函数分布,因此将区间放宽至[0,2],大于2的值均赋值为2。最后对反射函数进行线性拉伸至[0,255]灰度范围内,即得到消除光照不均影响后的图像。

(3)去噪保边的互交叉双边滤波算法。双边滤波算法是将高斯滤波的空间距离测度与Yaroslavsky滤波的灰度测度相结合,在图像平滑时能够很好保留边缘细节。但双边滤波灰度测度计算的是两个独立像素点的灰度差,当两个相邻像素点均被噪声所污染时,中心点像素与邻域像素间的灰度测度计算的稳定性就会下降[2]。系统通过提高灰度测度权值计算的准确性,设计了将平稳小波算法(Stationary wavelet transform,SWT),作为预滤波器的互交叉双边滤波算法[3],算法框图示于图3。

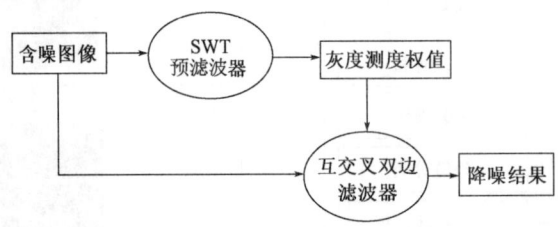

图3 互交叉双边滤波算法框图

2.3 裂缝图像识别与提取

(1)图像分割。系统结合神经元突触整合特性和图像灰度特征,通过改进传统脉冲耦合神经网络(Pulse Coupled Neural Network,PCNN)单一输入链接域和随时间指数衰减的阈值,设计基于马尔科夫网络确定的迭代灰度阈值简化PCNN裂缝图像分割算法(Simplified PCNN,SPCNN)。SPCNN算法中模型参数少且可以自适应设置,无需特定准则确定最佳分割迭代次数,可实现一次迭代即完成自动化分割。系统设计研发中,进行了4种分割算法的准确率和计算耗时的比对试验,结果示于图4,反映了系统所设计的SPCNN算法在准确率和效率上具有优于其他算法的优势[3]。

(2)裂缝连接。裂缝图像的每个像素都包含灰度和方向信息,如果裂缝种子与其周围像素具有相近的灰度值或一致的方向,则很可能属于同一条裂缝。系统综合考虑裂缝图像灰度特征和方向特征,首先根据灰度相似性进行裂缝优化连接[4],在此基础上依据方向相似性连接裂缝种子,可去除孤立噪声,得到完整形态的裂缝[3]。

图5a)、b)分别显示了纵向裂缝和网状裂缝的分割结果和连接结果,可以看出,系统的裂缝连接算法

不仅可以参照裂缝发展趋势对裂缝进行连接,而且可有效去除误提取的噪声,保证裂缝的完整性。

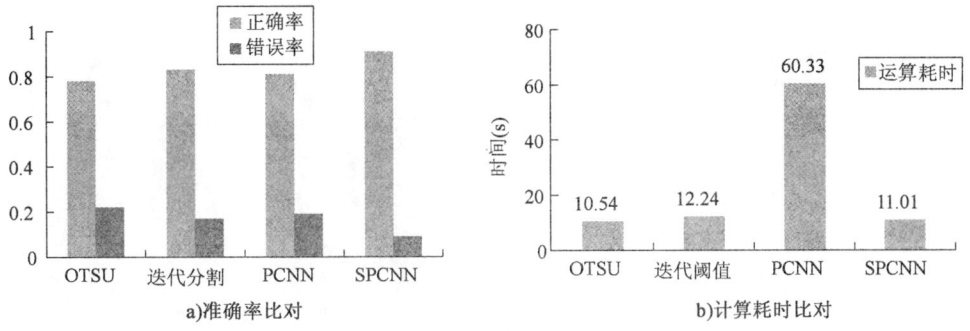

图4 4种分割算法的比对

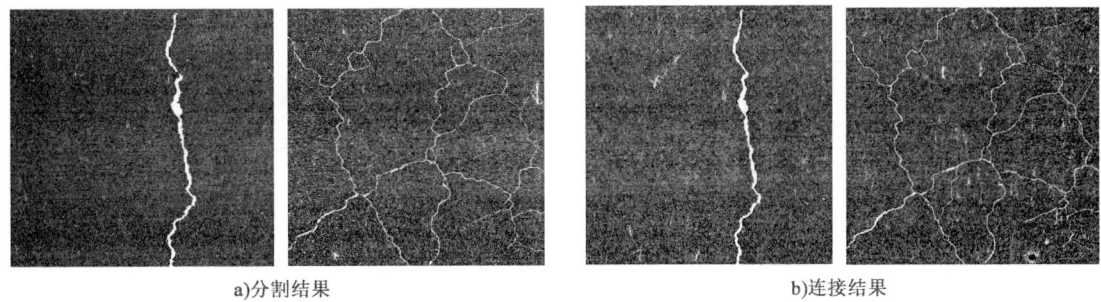

图5 不同类型裂缝图像提取结果

2.4 裂缝分类与特征参数计算

裂缝的走向对裂缝的发展至关重要,不同裂缝的破损形态造成的危害不同,比如:桥梁路面横向裂缝的发展可能会演变为横向断裂,纵向裂缝的破坏将加剧钢筋腐蚀,块状网状裂缝则会缩短建筑物的使用寿命[5]。因此混凝土结构裂缝分类在养护工作中极为重要。

依据混凝土结构裂缝的破裂走向和形态,将裂缝分为4类:横向裂缝、纵向裂缝、块状裂缝、网状裂缝。系统结合裂缝图像的几何形态和投影特征,采用简单快捷的投影法进行裂缝分类。

(1)粗分类。首先基于8方向链码编码优化后的Zhang细化算法获取裂缝骨架,并基于方向链码毛刺消除算法判定并消除细化中产生的毛刺,利用骨架节点数,将裂缝分为规则裂缝和复杂裂缝两大类,其中,横向裂缝和纵向裂缝归为规则裂缝,块状裂缝和网状裂缝归为复杂裂缝。

(2)细分类。利用投影特征对规则裂缝分类,区分横向裂缝和纵向裂缝;利用背景连通域和节点个数对复杂裂缝分类,区分块状裂缝和网状裂缝。表1对比了不同裂缝算法正确率。

不同裂缝算法正确率对比 表1

裂缝算法	横向裂缝(%)	纵向裂缝(%)	块状裂缝(%)	网状裂缝(%)
BP神经网络	89.36	84.68	50.00	50.00
SVM	96.00	94.00	88.00	92.00
投影法	80.76	80.38	—	—
本文几何特征投影法	100.00	98.00	88.00	92.00

(3)裂缝特征参数计算。裂缝分类后,为表征裂缝的损坏程度,系统选取长度、最大宽度、平均宽度作为规则裂缝的特征参数,选取面积、重心、密度作为复杂裂缝的特征参数。系统对某桥梁既有的静态裂缝图像进行处理,得到的裂缝图像特征检测结果示于图2。

图6是某桥梁加荷载时的裂缝生长图。应用检测系统对视频中截取的裂缝图像进行处理,该裂缝从开裂到结束的图像序列帧数总共109帧,帧率为29.7916帧/s,选取生长序列的第1帧、第42帧和最后一

帧(第109帧)图像进行裂缝检测,相应的裂缝提取结果示于图7,裂缝生长序列特征参数的计算结果示于表2。图7和表2充分反映了裂缝的变化情况、生长趋势和生长规律。

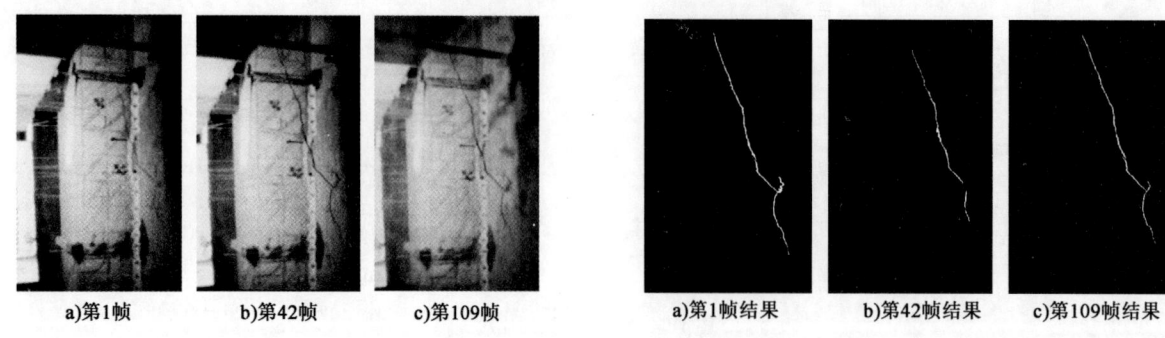

a)第1帧　　　　b)第42帧　　　　c)第109帧

图6　裂缝图像序列

a)第1帧结果　　　b)第42帧结果　　　c)第109帧结果

图7　裂缝生长序列检测结果

表2　裂缝生长序列特征参数的计算结果

第 i 帧裂缝图像($i=1,42,109$)	随生长趋势的特征参数变化		
	长度	最大宽度	平均宽度
第1帧	891.2300	14	4.0046
第42帧	1300.371	19	4.9234
第109帧	1313.572	21	5.0138

注:特征参数的单位为像素。

3　结　语

为了提高裂缝图像检测技术的时效性、准确性和裂缝特征的定量表述,本文设计了针对混凝土结构裂缝数字图像的图像处理技术,并集成所设计算法,开发了裂缝图像检测系统。该系统具备图像读取、图像预处理、裂缝目标识别、图像分析、生成分析报告、数据存储等功能,系统扩展性好、交互性强、用户可读性高。本文所设计开发的检测系统提取的裂缝特征参数仅限于图像坐标系内,对于裂缝特征参数的物理坐标系中的计算尚待后期借助摄影测量方法进一步完善。

参考文献

[1] 曹悦欣.基于方向特征的混凝土路面裂缝检测算法研究[D].重庆:重庆邮电大学,2019.
[2] 程伟,梁萍.数学形态学在旋切单板缺陷图像分割中的研究[J].林业机械与木工设备,2011,39(2):25-27.
[3] Su S L, Gong T. Bridge pavement crack detection under uneven illumination using improved PCNN algorithm[C]//International Conference on Geomatics in the Big Data Era,2019:1033-1040.
[4] 彭博,Wang K C P,陈成,等.基于1mm精度路面三维图像的裂缝种子自动识别算法[J].中国公路学报,2014,27(12):23-32.
[5] 占继刚.基于图像处理的桥梁底面裂缝检测识别方法研究[D].北京:北京交通大学,2017.

青藏公路路基不均匀变形对路面病害的影响分析

李　铭　支喜兰

(1.西安工业大学;2.长安大学公路学院特殊地区教育部重点实验室)

摘　要　青藏公路由于地处高原冻土地区,气候环境恶劣,路基易在冻融循环和重载等综合作用下产生不均匀变形,进而引发多种路面病害,导致道路使用性能受到严重制约。本文在青藏公路(格尔木—拉萨段)路面病害实地调研基础上,通过分类分级统计和PCI计算评价,开展各类病害发展机理分析,揭示路基不均匀变形对路面病害的影响。研究表明:路基不均匀变形所引发的累计折合损坏面积为路面总损坏面积的43.5%,是诱发多种路面病害的主要原因,且对纵向裂缝、坑槽、松散剥落、沉陷和车辙等影响最大。

关键词 路面评估 病害影响 病害机理分析 青藏公路 路基不均匀变形

0 引 言

青藏公路由于地处多年冻土地区,路基易在使用过程中受到冻融循环和重载等综合作用影响而产生不均匀变形,会对路面造成严重影响和危害,引发多种路面病害产生,影响公路正常使用性能。

针对这一问题,不少学者进行了相关研究。李金平[1]和穆彦虎[2]等结合现场调查结果和监测资料进行分析,得出道路80%的病害主要由路基不均匀融沉变形引起这一结论,病毒主要表现为严重的不均匀沉降变形和纵向裂缝。常艳婷[3]和窦明健[4]等通过统计研究,发现纵向裂缝、沉陷和波浪等路面病害与路基下部多年冻土融化存在直接关系。刘和平[5]等通过分析青藏公路沥青路面主要病害及其产生原因,得出沉陷变形、裂缝是多年冻土地区最主要病害的结论。

上述研究均取得了良好研究成果,但基于青藏公路路面病害分级分类划分,从不同类别角度进行路基不均匀变形对路面病害的相关影响分析研究较零散。本文在现场调研分析基础上,对青藏公路(格尔木—拉萨段)病害类型进行分类,基于路面损坏状况指数(PCI)计算评价,对各类病害发展机理分析,揭示路基不均匀变形对路面病害的影响,为病害防治措施提供理论依据。

1 青藏公路现场调研情况

1.1 路面结构形式调研

当前青藏公路所采用的是半刚性基层沥青路面结构:垫层为天然砂砾(20cm),基层为水泥稳定碎石(20cm),下面层为AC-25F沥青混凝土(6cm),上面层为AC-16F沥青混凝土(4cm)。路基填料既有工程性质良好的砂性土,也有工程性质差的红黏土和多年冻土。

1.2 路面病害调研及分级分类统计

调研基于格尔木—拉萨段路面的多种病害类型展开,内容包括其范围、分布、严重性等方面,并经过详细分析后对路面病害按照裂缝类、松散类、变形类和其他类进行分级分类统计,结果如表1所示。

青藏公路(格拉段)局部范围内沥青路面破损分类分级统计表 表1

破损类型		分级	统计量	单位
裂缝类	龟裂	轻	17689	m^2
		中	16007	
		重	11297	
	网状裂缝	轻	67746	m^2
		重	13022	
	纵向裂缝	轻	13319	m
		重	4339	
	横向裂缝	轻	21876	m
		重	6335	

1.基金项目:陕西省教育厅专项科学研究项目:19JK0410。
2.西安市碑林区科技局应用技术研发项目:GX2010。

续上表

破损类型		分级	统计量	单位
松散类	坑槽	轻	1186	m^2
		重	1146	
	松散	轻	71071	m^2
		重	37485	
变形类	车辙	轻	59339	m
		重	36226	
	沉陷(不均匀变形)	轻	12828	m^2
		重	28460	
	波浪壅包	轻	1696	m^2
		重	3783	
其他类	泛油、老化		1370	m^2
	修补损坏		10113	m^2

根据表1的调研数据分析发现，裂缝类和变形类病害是对青藏公路正常使用造成重大影响的主要病害类型。

2 路面损坏状况指数(PCI)计算评价

根据表1中所示数据，对青藏公路（格拉段）路面损坏状况指数(PCI)按照规范公式进行计算评价，计算结果如表2所示。

青藏公路（格拉段）局部范围内总体 PCI 计算结果表　　表2

破损类型		分级	累计损坏	权重	累计折合损坏面积	单位
			路段长度:1016km		路面宽度:7m	
裂缝类	龟裂	轻	17689	0.6	10614	m^2
		中	16007	0.8	12800	
		重	11297	1.0	11297	
	网状裂缝	轻	67746	0.6	40647	m^2
		重	13022	0.8	10417	
	纵向裂缝	轻	13319	0.6	7992	m
		重	4339	1.0	4340	
	横向裂缝	轻	21876	0.6	13125	m
		重	6335	1.0	6335	
松散类	坑槽	轻	1186	0.8	949	m^2
		重	1146	1.0	1146	
	松散	轻	71071	0.6	42642	m^2
		重	37485	1.0	37485	
变形类	车辙	轻	59339	0.6	35604	m
		重	36226	1.0	36226	
	沉陷(不均匀变形)	轻	12828	0.6	7697	m^2
		重	28460	1.0	28460	
	波浪壅包	轻	1696	0.6	1018	m^2
		重	3783	1.0	3783	

续上表

破损类型	分级	累计损坏	权重	累计折合损坏面积	单位
		路段长度:1016km　路面宽度:7m			
其他类	泛油、老化	1370	0.2	274	m²
	修补损坏	10113	0.1	1011	m²
评定结果		DR = 4.41%　　PCI = 72.35			

根据表2所示数据可知,PCI计算结果为72.35,破损状况为良。通过计算,得出多种路面病害的产生均与路基不均匀变形有关,累计折合损坏面积可为路面总损坏面积的43.5%。

3 路面病害发展机理分析

3.1 裂缝类病害发展机理

该类病害发展机理主要有强烈太阳辐射、温差变化、反复荷载、半刚性基层材料性能、地基处理不当、施工技术水平较低和路面老化等综合因素。具体表现形式包括 K2930+300 处和 K3213+200 处的温缩裂缝、K2980+800 等处的反射裂缝、K3174+700 处的纵向裂缝(图1)、K2996+300 处的不规则裂缝(图2)。

图1　纵向裂缝

图2　不规则裂缝

3.2 松散类病害发展机理

松散类病害(图3、图4)的发展机理是水、冻融循环和行车荷载的三重因素综合作用。如 K3122+100 处,春融时期路基底部多年冻土由于热融沉陷,会使路基产生不均匀融沉变形,造成路基强度降低,使渗水和冻融循环作用加剧,随着重载反复作用,导致坑槽、路面松散剥落等病害产生。

图3　坑槽

图4　松散剥落

3.3 变形类病害发展机理

青藏公路的变形类病害发展机理为冻土融沉、反复荷载[6]、特殊气候环境、施工技术水平较低、材料性能较差等因素的综合作用。具体表现形式有 K2996+400 等处的沉陷与不均匀变形(图5、图6);K3092+200 等处的波浪壅包(图7、图8);K2985+800 等处的车辙(图9)。

图5 沉陷

图6 不均匀变形

图7 波浪

图8 壅包

3.4 其他类病害发展机理

其他类病害主要包括泛油和路面老化。发展机理为夏季高温、反复荷载以及强紫外线辐射等因素的综合作用。如 K3030+300 等处的过早老化(图10)。

图9 车辙

图10 泛油老化

通过青藏公路四类路面病害发展机理分析可知,复杂气候环境、冻融循环导致的路基不均匀变形、较低的施工工艺水平、反复车辆荷载等因素是路面病害产生的主要原因。其中路基不均匀变形,对纵向裂缝、坑槽、松散剥落、沉陷和车辙等病害影响最大,是这些病害产生的最主要原因。在今后的青藏公路病害防治和养护工作中,可针对这些因素,开展相关措施研究。

4 结语

本文在青藏公路路面病害实地调研基础上,通过病害分类分级统计,并基于路面损坏状况指数(PCI)计算评价,开展了各类病害发展机理分析,得出以下结论:

(1)裂缝类和变形类病害是青藏公路沥青路面最常见、发生率最高的病害类型。

(2)不均匀变形所引发的累计折合损坏面积为路面总损坏面积的43.5%,其对多种路面病害的产生有直接影响,是诱发这些病害的最主要原因。

研究结论可为青藏多年冻土地区公路的养护与维修工作提供科学指导和建议,具有节约养护成本,提高使用寿命等方面的意义。

参考文献

[1] 李金平.高原冻土区既有公路病害特征和融沉变形分析[J].路基工程,2016,(04):11-16.
[2] 穆彦虎,马巍,牛富俊.多年冻土区道路工程病害类型及特征研究[J].防灾减灾工程学报,2014,34(03):259-267.
[3] 常艳婷,陈忠达,张震.青藏公路典型路基病害影响因素分析[J].中外公路,2016,36(01):19-22.
[4] 窦明健,胡长顺,多吉罗布.青藏公路路面病害成因分析[J].冰川冻土,2003,25(4):439-444.
[5] 刘和平,樊凯,吴建忠.青藏公路沥青路面病害防治技术探讨[J].中外公路,2010,(03):111-113.
[6] 张宏超,孙立军,黄进堂.沥青路面新泛油病害及机理分析[J].公路交通科技,2002,19(6):32-34.

基于惩罚型变权物元理论模型的路面使用性能评价

黄卫国[1] 张 硕[2] 胡 勇[1]

(1.江西省公路工程检测中心;2.长安大学公路学院)

摘 要 为了准确评价路面使用性能状况,针对路面使用性能在传统赋权下无法准确反映路面实际使用性能的问题,本文建立了一种基于惩罚型变权物元理论模型的路面使用性能评价模型来提高沥青路面性能评价方法的科学性和适用性,并结合某省8个普通国省道路段进行综合性能评价,结果表明:不同于规范对单项性能指标权重的规定,经过惩罚型变权处理下更能客观地反映路面实际的路用性能,在此基础上结合物元模型对路面综合性能进行评价,并发现其评价结果比由单项指标在传统权重赋权得到的综合性能等级更低,并运用此模型针对8个路段进行综合关联度排序,在养护资金限制时,为路段养护的先后顺序提供一定的参考依据。

关键词 道路工程 惩罚型变权 物元理论 使用性能 评价 养护

0 引言

截至2019年底,我国公路里程达到500万km[1],伴随着车辆荷载和气候环境条件的作用,公路路面出现了不同情况的路面病害,导致公路路网服务能力下降,也使得路面养护成为近些年研究的热点。国内外相关学者针对路面养护也开展了一系列研究,在路面使用性能评价方面,(AASHTO)提出了世界上第一个路面性能评价指标 PSI,PSI 主要包含了道路平整度、表面裂缝、路面修补、车辙深度等方面[2],日本在借鉴 PSI 的基础上提出适合本国国情的养护管理指数(MCI),主要侧重于道路表面裂缝度、车辙深度、平整度等方面,英国提出道路状况指数(RCI)来评价道路状况指标,加拿大方面更多地对道路的平整度提出更高的要求,提出了道路行驶舒适度指数(RCI)。而我国用 PQI 评价模型,它是以路面损坏指数(PCI)、路面车辙指数(RDI)、路面行驶质量指数(RQI)和路面抗滑性能(SRI)作为分项指标,以路面使用性能指数(PQI)作为综合指标,并由上述 4 项指标(PCI、RDI、RQI、SRI)按照评价等级赋予相应的百分值后加权计算得出[3-7]。

在我国的长期养护实践中发现:采用固定的权重对路面使用性能赋权进行计算评价不能有效反映路面使用状况和病害类型的影响。为此,国内外相关学者针对路面使用性能进行了一系列研究。主成分分析法计算简便且具有强大的因素降维功能,被广泛应用在路面性能评价体系中。李波等[8]、杨明等[9]采用主成分分析法对公路沥青路面使用性能的实测数据进行了评价,结合实际发现评价结果具有一定的合理性。但主成分分析法也具有一定的局限性,当采用的主成分不适当时,不能正确反映路面各因素对路面使用性能的影响,使得路面使用性能评价缺乏合理性。近些年越来越多的智能模型也被运用到路面使用性能评价方面,秦志斌等[10]基于信息熵和多目标空间理论,对沥青路面进行多目标评价,并证明了评价方法的可行性。张凯星等[11]以广云高速公路为工程实例利用 BP 神经网络,得到了最终的综合性能评价模型并确定了该高速公路路面使用性能 5 个评价指标的权重,王立国等[12]运用可拓神经网络对高速公路进行使用性能评价,并证明了可拓神经网络相比传统模型的优越性,李志刚等[13]运用灰关联分析法,针对河北省高速公路沥青路面性能进行综合评价,为路面养护决策提供了一定的决策依据。宋亮[14]提出了灰色聚类决策分析模型,丰富了旧路的评价体系,也为路面改扩建提供了一定的理论支持。谢峰[15]、张敏江等[16]采用模糊综合评价法得到了各评价检测指标对路面性能的影响权重,并对公路数据样本做出定量评价,但智能模型中缺乏对路面使用性能指标的分析,使得路面使用性能评价不够全面。

综上所述,本文针对沥青路面在路面使用性能评价中研究中的不足,并结合普通国省道的基本特点,提出了一种基于惩罚型变权的动态权重的物元理论方法,来对沥青路面使用性能进行评价,惩罚型变权的权重的确定是基于惩罚—激励型变权函数对路面各分项性能指标的客观情况综合确定而出的,在此基础上,结合物元理论可以对路面使用性能进行综合评价,并针对各路段的养护性能进行养护顺序的划分,为道路的科学决策提供一定的参考依据。

1 惩罚型变权物元理论模型的基本原理

1.1 惩罚型变权原理及方法

在路面使用性能评价中,各单项指标权重的确定方式将会影响到指标中权重的大小,进而影响到评价模型的准确性,因此选用良好适用的权重确定模型对评价模型至关重要。本文选用惩罚型变权作为客观赋予模型权重的方法,作为客观模型的一种,在权值的分配过程中,完全采用计算的形式,使数据处理更加规范、科学。采用惩罚型变权计算得到各路段各指标的权重后,根据各路段的实地状况可对整体路段和公路路网的现状进行更加准确的评价。

具体实现步骤如下:

(1)首先将检测单元段路面性能数进行归一化处理,如式(1)所示,使其值域区间落在在[0,1]的范围内。

$$x_i = \frac{A_i}{A_{\max}} \tag{1}$$

式中:x_i——归一化后路面使用性能值;

A_i——原始路面使用性能值;

$A_{\max}$——路面使用性能最大值,一般取 100。

(2)对归一化的x_i进行状态划分,看其位于惩罚—激励中的哪个区间:其中在区间$(0,a)$为惩罚阶段,在惩罚阶段中又分别分为强、中、弱3个惩罚阶段,分别对应的区间为$(0,u]$、$(u,\lambda]$、$(\lambda,a]$;$[a,b]$为函数的合格区间,在该区间内奖罚达到平衡;在区间$(b,1)$为激励区间,在此区间上对优秀的单项指标进行激励。

(3)引入了惩罚—激励型变权函数,并计算路面使用性能单项指标所对应的$S(x_i)$,$S(x_i)$为惩罚—激励状态变权向量函数,其计算如式(2)所示:

$$S(x_i) = \begin{cases} \dfrac{c_2 - c_1}{\lambda - \mu}\ln\dfrac{\mu}{x_i} + c_2 & 0 < x_i \leq \mu \\[6pt] -\dfrac{c_2 - c_1}{\lambda - \mu}x_i + \dfrac{c_2\lambda - c_1\mu}{\lambda - \mu} & \mu < x_i \leq \lambda \\[6pt] C + \dfrac{c_2 - c_1}{2(\lambda - \mu)(a - \lambda)}(a - x_i)2 & \mu < x_i \leq \lambda \\[6pt] C & \mu < x_i \leq \lambda \\[6pt] K(1 - b)\ln\dfrac{1 - b}{1 - x_i} + C & b < x_i \leq 1 \end{cases} \quad (2)$$

式中,$S(xi)$在区间$(0,1)$上具有数学意义上的连续可导性;a为惩罚水平;b为激励水平;$0 < \mu < \lambda < a < b < 1$;$0 < C < C_1 < C_2 < 1$;$C$、$c_1$、$c_2$为评价策略;$K$为调整系数。

(4)计算各检测单元路面使用性能各单项指标的权重,如式(3)所示:

$$w(x_i) = S(x_i) / \sum_{i=0}^{m} S(x_i) \quad (3)$$

式中:$w(x_i)$——各单项指标的权重。

1.2 物元分析原理及方法

物元分析方法能够定量和定性分析一些看似不相容的问题,并将其相容化,使问题得到合理解决,近些年也逐渐被应用到路面性能评价方面。其具体方法如下:

(1)普通国省道路面养护决策中有m个影响评价指标,组成特征指标集为$C = \{C_1, C_2, \cdots, C_n\}$,有$n$个养护路段,组成的路段集合$D = \{D_1, D_2, \cdots, D_n\}$,对各路段按照单项指标进行评估计算,并得到各指标的特征值规范化处理结果a_i,并将其组成一个养护路段的m维物元矩阵$\boldsymbol{R}$,如式(4)所示:

$$\boldsymbol{R} = \begin{bmatrix} & D \\ C_1 & a_1 \\ C_2 & a_2 \\ \cdots & \cdots \\ C_m & a_m \end{bmatrix} \quad (4)$$

(2)将上述路段和物元进行组合,构成$m \times n$维复合物元矩阵$\boldsymbol{R}_n$,如式(5)所示:

$$\boldsymbol{R}_n = \begin{bmatrix} & D_1 & D_2 & \cdots & D_n \\ C_1 & a_{11} & a_{12} & \cdots & a_{1n} \\ C_2 & a_{21} & a_{22} & \cdots & a_{2n} \\ \cdots & \cdots & \cdots & \cdots & \cdots \\ C_m & a_{m1} & a_{m2} & \cdots & a_{mn} \end{bmatrix} \quad (5)$$

(3)按照数值最优的原则,从$m \times n$维复合物元矩阵$\boldsymbol{R}_n$中,选取最优数值构成m维物元,并将其作为最佳路段物元,用矩阵$\boldsymbol{R}_0$表示如下:

$$R_0 = \begin{bmatrix} & D \\ C_1 & a_{10} \\ C_2 & a_{12} \\ \cdots & \cdots \\ C_m & a_{m0} \end{bmatrix} \quad (6)$$

(4)求解出各路段的单项指标与最佳路段的关联系数 L_{ij},并在此基础上构造关联系数物元矩阵 R_{Ln},如式(7)、式(8)、式(9)所示:

$$\Delta_{ij} = |a_{i0} - a_{ij}| \quad (7)$$

$$L_{ij} = \frac{\Delta_{\min} + \rho\Delta_{\max}}{\Delta_{ij} + \rho\Delta_{\max}} \quad (8)$$

$$R_{Ln} = \begin{bmatrix} & D_1 & D_2 & \cdots & D_n \\ C_1 & L_{11} & L_{12} & \cdots & L_{1n} \\ C_2 & L_{21} & L_{22} & \cdots & L_{2n} \\ \cdots & \cdots & \cdots & \cdots & \cdots \\ C_m & L_{m1} & L_{m2} & \cdots & L_{mn} \end{bmatrix} \quad (9)$$

式中:$\Delta_{\min}$——物元指标值绝对差 Δ_{ij} 的最小值;

$\Delta_{\max}$——物元指标值绝对差 Δ_{ij} 的最大值;

ρ——分辨系数,一般取0.5;

L_{ij}——第 j 个养护路段与最佳路段的第 i 项评价指标的关联系数,可按照式(8)计算。

(5)基于可拓集合理论建立关联函数,按相对重要性对每个评价指标的相关系数加权平均,获得评价 n 个路段使用性能的综合关联复合物元 R'_{Ln},如式(10)所示:

$$R'_{Ln} = W \times R_{Ln} \quad (10)$$

式中:W——评估指标的权重向量。

根据 R'_{Ln} 中综合关联度进行路面性能排序,综合关联度越小,则该路段的物元评价等级越低,路面性能越差,越优先考虑进行养护维修。将公路网沥青路面性能物元评价等级分为5个等级,如表1所示。

路面使用性能物元评价等级　　　　表1

评价等级	优	良	中	次	差
R'_{Ln}	0.9~1.0	0.6~0.9	0.4~0.6	0.2~0.4	0.1~0.2

2 物元可拓理论模型的构建

2.1 建模思路

根据公路工程相关技术状况标准的相关规定,路面使用性能各分项指标的权重已做出相关要求,但并未考虑不同地区环境气候的特点,不具有针对性。针对路面使用性能权重确定缺乏针对性的原因,根据各路段本身数据的特点,基于惩罚—激励型函数进行动态权重的确定,对各路段进行准确评价,在此基础上结合物元可拓理论对各路段进行物元评价,完善路面使用性能评价指标体系。结合物元评价体系对各路段进行排序,为养护路段的排序提供一定的参考依据。

2.2 建模过程

结合以上动态物元可拓理论的理论基础,其模型建立过程如图1所示。

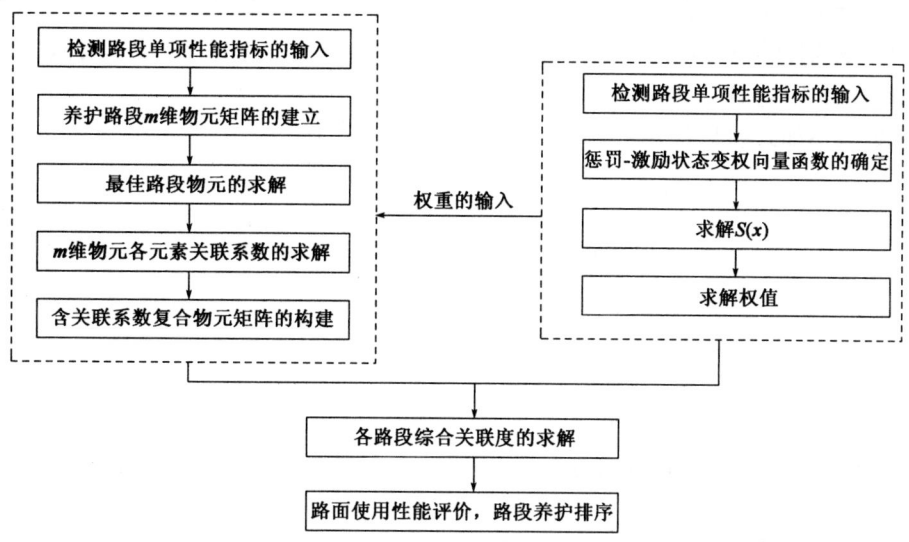

图1 惩罚型变权物元理论模型流程图

(1)惩罚型权重的确定:将各个路段的单项性能评价指标 PCI、RQI、RDI、SRI 进行归一化,在此基础上将各单项指标代入惩罚—激励状态变权向量函数进行求解变权函数值,然后将单项指标指标变权函数值与所有单项指标变权函数值之和相除,求解各单项指标的权重。

(2)物元模型的确定:将 4 个单项指标和路段组成一个向量矩阵,按照路面使用性能指标数值越大,路面使用性能更优的特点,求出最佳物元路段,然后求出各路段各个性能指标与最佳物元路段之间的关联系数,构成新的综合复合物元;将各单项性能指标的权重与综合复合物元进行矩阵相乘,得到综合关联度。

(3)根据综合关联度对路面使用性能进行评价,并结综合关联度对路段进行排序,为路面养护排序的决策提供一定的参考依据。

3 实例分析

本文选取 2019 年某省普通国省道的 8 段沥青检测路段进行分析研究。通过对 8 段沥青检测路段进行动态权重的计算,并针对相关路段进行物元分析,统计出路面养护的先后次序,为资金受限状态下路面养护的优先确定提供参考。8 段检测路段具体信息如表 2 所示。

2019 年某省普通国省道路面使用性能单项指标 表2

公路编号	起点桩号	终点桩号	PCI	RQI	RDI	SRI
1	K1662+993	K1664+940	77.05	96.13	93.01	87.91
2	K1747+000	K1753+829	86.35	89.19	92.48	72.13
3	K1672+000	K1674+430	83.77	91.65	91.18	87.91
4	K48+000	K51+446	90.17	94.22	90.87	89.85
5	K1110+495	K1111+440	96.24	96.91	98.08	95.39
6	K1726+452	K1730+500	96.30	92.00	96.18	72.90
7	K54+485	K57+200	64.70	91.87	95.10	72.90
8	K1806+84	K1810+000	85.53	84.63	91.64	87.21

3.1 惩罚型变权函数的确定

构建惩罚—激励型变权函数 $S(x_i)$ 参数的选取的构建会影响路面各分项指标权重的大小,进而影响道路评价结果的准确性。当路面使用性能单项指标小于 60 时,路面处于差的状态,这时路面需要进行大修或者补强,故此时路面应处于强惩罚阶段,故设强惩罚区间为(0,0.6];当路面使用性能单项指标小于

75时，路面使用性能需要进行一定程度的修复性养护。在此基础上，考虑到到路面使用性能在不同数值范围对路面影响的差别，设中惩罚区间为$(0.6,0.75]$，弱惩罚区间为$(0.75,0.85]$，激励区间为$(0.95,1]$，故$S(x_i)$的参数分别取值状况为$\mu=0.6, \lambda=0.75, a=0.85, b=0.95, C=0.2, c_1=0.7, c_2=0.7, K=1$，则$S(x_i)$的函数表达如式(11)所示：

$$S(x_i) = \begin{cases} 1.33\ln\frac{0.6}{x_i} + 0.7 & 0 < x_i \leq 0.6 \\ -1.33x_i + 1.7 & 0.6 < x_i \leq 0.75 \\ 0.2 + 6.67(0.85 - x_i)^2 & 0.75 < x_i \leq 0.85 \\ 0.2 & 0.85 < x_i \leq 0.95 \\ 0.05\ln\frac{1}{20(1-x_i)} + 0.2 & 0.95 < x_i \leq 1 \end{cases} \quad (11)$$

代入上式，计算各路面使用性能单项指标，并计算$S(x_i)$和$w(x_i)$，汇总如表3所示。

表3　8个路段的$S(x_i)$和$w(x_i)$

公路编号	$S(x_i)$				权重 $w(x_i)$			
	PCI	RQI	RDI	SRI	PCI	RQI	RDI	SRI
1	0.24	0.21	0.20	0.20	0.28	0.25	0.23	0.23
2	0.20	0.20	0.20	0.74	0.15	0.15	0.15	0.55
3	0.20	0.20	0.20	0.20	0.25	0.25	0.25	0.25
4	0.20	0.20	0.20	0.20	0.25	0.25	0.25	0.25
5	0.21	0.22	0.25	0.20	0.24	0.25	0.28	0.23
6	0.22	0.20	0.21	0.73	0.16	0.15	0.16	0.54
7	0.84	0.20	0.20	0.73	0.43	0.10	0.10	0.37
8	0.20	0.20	0.20	0.20	0.25	0.25	0.25	0.25

3.2　物元可拓方法的处理

将各段的路面单项指标进行输入，构建得到一个8个养护路段的4维物元矩阵：

$$\boldsymbol{R}_n = \begin{bmatrix} 77.05 & 86.35 & 83.77 & 90.17 & 96.24 & 96.30 & 64.70 & 85.53 \\ 96.13 & 89.19 & 91.65 & 94.22 & 96.91 & 92.00 & 91.87 & 84.63 \\ 93.01 & 92.48 & 91.18 & 90.87 & 98.08 & 96.18 & 95.10 & 91.64 \\ 87.91 & 72.13 & 87.91 & 89.85 & 95.39 & 72.90 & 72.90 & 87.21 \end{bmatrix}$$

从$\boldsymbol{R}_n$选取最佳物元路段：

$$\boldsymbol{R}_0 = \begin{bmatrix} & D \\ C_1 & 96.30 \\ C_2 & 96.91 \\ C_3 & 98.08 \\ C_4 & 95.39 \end{bmatrix}$$

根据所建立的路段复合物元，构造关联系数5维复合物元矩阵$\boldsymbol{R}_{Ln}$：

$$\boldsymbol{R}_{Ln} = \begin{bmatrix} & D_1 & D_2 & D_3 & D_4 & D_5 & D_6 & D_7 & D_8 \\ C_1 & 0.360 & 0.798 & 0.613 & 0.647 & 0.333 & 1.000 & 0.396 & 0.744 \\ C_2 & 1.000 & 0.890 & 1.000 & 1.000 & 1.000 & 0.696 & 0.901 & 0.683 \\ C_3 & 0.708 & 1.000 & 0.875 & 0.582 & 1.000 & 0.855 & 1.000 & 1.000 \\ C_4 & 0.608 & 0.494 & 0.838 & 0.688 & 1.000 & 0.333 & 0.490 & 0.878 \end{bmatrix}$$

基于奖罚函数确定的动态权重并与物元模型进行结合,获取各路段的综合关联度 R'_{Ln} = [0.65,0.67, 0.83,0.73,0.84,0.58,0.54,0.83]。将物元评价等级和单项指标动态赋权下所计算的 PQI 等级进行汇总,如表4所示。

PQI 评价和物元评价　　　　表4

序号	PQI	规范评价等级	R'_{Ln}	物元评价等级	物元评价排序
1	88.16	良	0.65	良	6
2	86.98	良	0.67	良	5
3	88.45	良	0.83	良	2
4	91.86	优	0.73	良	4
5	96.70	优	0.84	良	1
6	92.22	优	0.58	中	7
7	80.95	良	0.54	中	8
8	86.25	良	0.83	良	2

3.3　结果分析

(1)在《公路技术状况评定标准》(JTG 5210—2018)中权重的分配为 $w_{RQI} > w_{PCI} > w_{RDI} > w_{SRI}$,原因在于在路面技术状况评定中更看重路面的平整度、破损状况,然后是路面的车辙状况和抗滑状况,但动态权重比规范中各指标单一权重更能客观反映各单项指标的特点。基于惩罚型变权处理后,将以上动态权重进行加权平均计算,发现 w_{PCI} 为 0.25,w_{RQI} 为 0.21,w_{RDI} 为 0.21,w_{SRI} 为 0.33,4 个项目指标的权重相比权重发生明显变化,尤其是 SRI 的权重,在传统 PQI 模型中,w_{SRI} 为 0.1,这是由于在本文选用的 8 个路段中,抗滑性能 SRI 指数相比其他性能指数都要略低些,经过惩罚型变权处理,使得较低的单项性能指标权重变大,这在一方面也体现了惩罚激励型函数具有一定的"平均"特性。这样可以更好避免单一权重下存在的指标值偏大且指标权重也偏大的情况。

(2)从表4中可以看出,用传统 PQI 的评价上述 8 个路段,整体 PQI 水平都是处于良等级以上,其中序号 4、5 段路面处于优等级水平。用物元模型进行评价后 8 个养护路段的 R'_{Ln} 均在 0.5 以上,按照物元评价等级均处于中等级水平,用物元模型进行评价后发现 6、7 路段处于中级水平,其余路段处于良好等级,结合物元模型评估的路面综合性能等级比传统 PQI 模型下得到的综合性能评价等级更低,有助于更科学、合理地对路面进行养护决策管理。为防止路面病害进一步发展,有必要针对 8 个养护路段开展一定的预防性养护措施研究。

(3)在基于动态物元分析的公路网沥青路面性能评价中,R'_{Ln} 综合关联度越大,该路段的物元评价等级越高,路面性能越优。可以看出,第 5 号路段性能最优,第 7 号路段的性能最差,优先考虑对第 7 号路段进行路面养护。

4　结　　语

(1)本文通过采用基于惩罚型变权的方法确定各个单项性能指标的权重,并结合物元可拓理论对各路段进行物元评价,解决了传统路面使用性能评价体系中缺乏针对性的问题,完善了路面使用性能评价指标体系。

(2)以某省 8 段普通国省道为案例,经惩罚—激励型函数的计算发现,w_{PCI} 为 0.25,w_{RQI} 为 0.21,w_{RDI} 为 0.21,w_{SRI} 为 0.33。与传统的权重相比,经惩罚型变权方法赋权后的路面使用性能各分项指标的权重更接近,体现了惩罚—激励型函数具有一定的"平均"特性,从而更好地避免单一权重下指标值和指标权重均偏大情况。

(3)以动态权重为基础,结合物元可拓理论模型对 8 个路段进行综合关联度排序。综合关联度越大,路面使用性能评价越高。计算得到,第 5 号路段性能最优,第 7 号路段的性能最差,优先考虑对第 7 号路段进行路面养护。该排序为路段养护顺序提供了参考,有助于更科学合理地进行路面养护决策管理。

参考文献

[1] National cooperative highway research program. AASHTO guide for design of pavement structures[R]. Washington AASHTO,1993:9-22.
[2] 周岚.高速公路沥青路面使用性能评价及预测研究[D].南京:东南大学,2015.
[3] 曹慎敏.基于物元分析的高速公路沥青路面网级养护决策研究[D].西安:长安大学,2018.
[4] 李红梅.基于物元模型的网级高速公路沥青路面养护决策研究[D].南京:东南大学,2017.
[5] Li Bo,Marie Judith Kundwa,Cui Yu Jiao,et al. Pavement performance evaluation and maintenance decision-making in Rwanda[J]. International Journal of Pavement Research and Technology,2019,12(5).
[6] Md Mostaqur Rahman,M Majbah Uddin,Sarah L. Gassman. Pavement performance evaluation models for South Carolina[J]. KSCE Journal of Civil Engineering,2017,21(7).
[7] 李波,韩森,徐鸥明,等.基于主成分分析法的沥青路面使用性能评价[J].长安大学学报(自然科学版),2009,29(03):15-18.
[8] 杨明,阳亮.主成分分析法在高速公路沥青路面使用性能评价中的应用[J].中南公路工程,2006(06):55-57,89.
[9] 秦志斌,钱国平,马文彬.基于熵权的沥青路面使用性能多目标综合评价[J].中南大学学报(自然科学版),2013,44(08):3474-3478.
[10] 张凯星,王选仓,赵静,等.基于BP神经网络的广东省路面使用性能评价[J].公路,2020,65(10):309-314.
[11] 王立国,付洋.基于可拓神经网络的高速公路路面使用性能评价[J].项目管理技术,2019,17(07):25-30.
[12] 李志刚,邓学钧,顾锋.高速公路沥青路面性能综合评价模型的探讨[J].东南大学学报(自然科学版),2000(04):129-131.
[13] 宋亮.基于灰色理论的改扩建旧路路面检测与评价[J].公路,2017,62(07):88-93.
[14] 谢峰.基于GIS的高速公路路面管理智能决策模型研究[D].成都:西南交通大学,2012.
[15] 张敏江,董是,冷连志.基于模糊综合评价法的沥青路面技术状况评价与养护决策体系研究[J].沈阳建筑大学学报(自然科学版),2015,31(01):87-94.

ECA-10在预防性养护中的应用及跟踪

顾艳静

(浙江省交通规划设计研究院有限公司)

摘要 近年来预防性养护的"预防为主、防治结合"养护理念不断推行,尤以薄层罩面的养护方案最为突出。本文以G329国道路面使用状况及历年交通量等进行分析,研究了采用ECA-10作为病害处治及薄层罩面的预防性养护方案,并对相关路段进行了长期的路面性能跟踪调查、分析。根据应用情况及跟踪调查数据,ECA-10作为预防性养护方案,其处治效果较好,值得推广应用。

关键词 公路工程 预防性养护 ECA-10 PCI 车辙

0 引言

随着国省道沥青路面使用年限的不断增长,路面养护技术也在不断创新与发展,以提高路面使用性能及延长路面使用寿命为主要目的预防性养护也被更广泛应用于养护工程。

ECA-10 易密实沥青混凝土通过优化级配,同时引用温拌剂,以解决超薄沥青面层的因薄不易压实的问题,从而更适用于严重车辙、网裂等预防性养护路段。

本文以 G329 国道 2016 年养护工程为依托,对 ECA-10 在预防性养护工程中的应用进行研究,为这项技术的应用推广提供实践依据。

1 原道路状况

1.1 技术标准

G329 杭朱线上虞城区段为一级公路,设计速度为 100km/h,路基宽 60.0m,其中行车道宽度(含路缘带)为 25m,于 2009 年建成。

1.2 原路面结构形式

G329 杭朱线上虞城区段 K77+000~K81+000 于 2009 年建成为沥青混凝土路面,原路面结构形式如图 1 所示。2014 年进行中修处治,处治方案:铣刨 4cm 原沥青面层,并进行病害处理后回铺 5cm 改性 AC-16C 改性沥青混凝土,路面结构如图 2 所示。

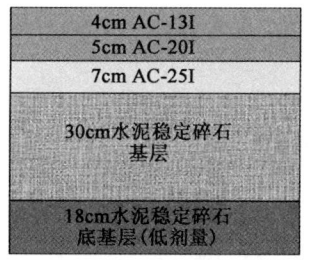

图 1　2009 年路面结构

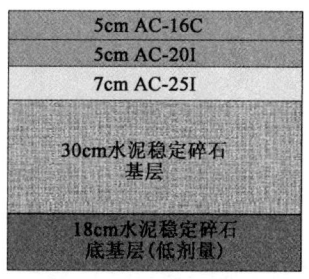

图 2　2014 年路面结构

1.3 交通量分布情况

G329 杭朱线上虞段自建成通车以来交通量迅速增长,如图 3 所示,根据 2013—2015 年的交通量观测数据,增长率为 5.3%。

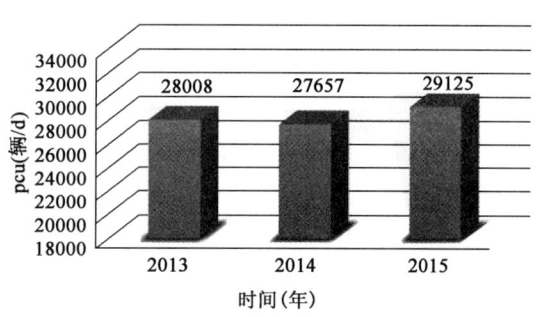

图 3　2013—2015 交通量情况

1.4 路面病害状况

路面病害以车辙病害为主,且下行全路段第二车道皆呈现重度车辙病害,第一、第三车道为纵横向裂缝、修补不良等综合性病害。部分平交口路段在距离停止线 30m 范围内出现大面积网裂、补丁等病害。

1.4.1 车辙病害

根据《公路技术状况评定标准》(JTG 5210—2018)5.2.6,将车辙深度大于 15mm 以上定义为重度车辙,深度 10~15mm 定义为轻度车辙的要求,经分析,第二车道重度车辙(深度≥20mm)占 82%,第一、第三车道重度车辙(深度≥20mm)占 15%。

车辙深度及 RDI 见表 1。

表 1 车辙深度及 RDI 一览表

起 止 桩 号	位 置	RDI	评价等级	车辙深度（mm）	评价等级
K77+000～K78+000	下行	52.2	差	21.5	重度
K78+000～K79+000		58.7	差	19.2	重度
K79+000～K80+000		67.5	次	15.7	重度
K80+000～K81+000		67.9	次	15.5	重度

1.4.2 网裂病害

网裂病害主要出现在平交口范围内距离停止线 30～50m 处，部分路段伴有纵横向裂缝及补丁等综合病害。从芯样分析，除 K80+930 出现芯样破损外其他基本完整，面层与基础之间黏结较好，下面层整体性好，病害主要集中在上面层，仅局部位置存在中、下面层松散现象。

芯样情况见图 4。

图 4 芯样情况（面层破损）

2 养护对策

2.1 养护规模决策

根据《关于加强普通国省道干线公路沥青路面预防性养护工程管理的通知》（浙公路〔2014〕29号），预防性养护原则上只安排路面使用性能指数（PQI）在 85 以上的路段，且预防性养护的路段结构强度和承载能力须满足要求，路基、基层与中下面层性能良好，仅在沥青上面层表现出简单、单一病害。

一级公路路面预防性养护技术标准见表 2。

表 2 一级公路路面预防性养护技术标准

| 公路等级 | 路况指标 | | | | |
	PCI	RQI	RDI	SRI	PSSI
一级公路	85～95	90～100	70～100	80～100	85～100

2.2 养护预防性养护方案确定

基于本项目病害类型以块状裂缝（网裂）、车辙为主，且 PCI、RQI、RDI 等指标均符合预防性养护技术标准，经综合评判选择薄层加铺 2.5cm ECA-10 易密实沥青混凝土进行路面结构补强。

公路沥青路面预防性养护对策见表 3。

公路沥青路面预防性养护对策　　　　表3

项 目		参数	预防性养护对策				
			雾封层	碎石封层	稀浆封层	微表处	薄层加铺
沥青路面病害类型及程度	裂缝类 块状裂缝	轻		√	√		√
		中		√			√
		重					√
	变形类 车辙	<5mm			√	√	√
		5~15mm				√	√
		15~25mm				√	√

注："√"表示实施预防性养护对策。

2.3 实施方案

2.3.1 路面病害处治设计方案

(1)车辙病害

轻微车辙(车辙深度<15mm):不进行病害处理,直接加铺2.5cm ECA-10。

中等车辙(15≤车辙深度<20mm):采用轨道式铣刨,一般铣刨至中面层,若铣刨过程发现下承层有松散或伴随其他病害,则铣刨至稳定部分。

重度车辙(车辙深度≥25mm或中等车辙中伴随其他病害):一般铣刨至中面层,各路段按要求铣刨后,若下承层存在松散或其他病害现象,则再铣刨至下承层稳定部分。一般采用轨道式铣刨回铺的处理方式。

(2)块状裂缝(网裂)

要求铣刨至下承层完好部分,一般铣刨两层,若基层还存在病害时,再铣刨至下承层稳定部分(铣刨厚度≥16cm),分层压实回填至上面层,面层回填采用ECA-10沥青混凝土,基层采用ATB或水稳回填(处理面积<50m时,采用ATB回填;≥50m时,采用水稳回填)。

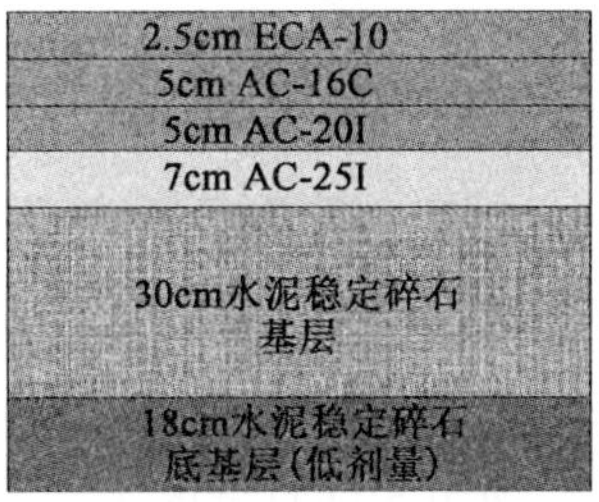

2.3.2 路面改造方案

单点病害处理+2.5cm ECA-10易密实沥青混凝土罩面(图5)。

图5　路面改造方案

3 ECA-10技术标准

3.1 材料组成及特征

ECA-10组成材料包括玄武岩集料、石灰岩矿粉、聚酯纤维、易密实添加剂、PG76-22 SBS改性沥青。粗集料约占集料总质量的50%,以提高细粒式沥青混凝土的构造深度,保证路表的抗滑性能要求;易密实添加剂的主要作用是拓宽薄层沥青混合料的可碾压温度范围,使沥青混合料易密实,保证其压实度要求。

3.2 目标配合比设计

沥青混合料的矿料级配应符合规定的设计级配范围。易密实沥青混凝土(ECA-10)有9.5mm和6.7mm两种公称最大粒径,其工程设计级配范围应满足表4的要求。

易密实沥青混凝土(ECA-10)矿料级配范围　　　　表4

级配类型		通过下列筛孔(mm)的质量百分率(%)								
		13.2	9.5	6.7	4.75	2.36	1.18	0.6	0.3	0.15	0.075
ECA-10	级配上限	100	100	50	40	36	30	25	20	12	8
	级配下限	100	80	30	20	18	14	10	7	6	4

3.3 马歇尔试验技术要求

ECA的配合比设计采用马歇尔试验方法,并采用旋转压实成型进行验证,马歇尔试验指标应符合表5的技术要求。

ECA沥青混合料马歇尔试验配合比设计技术标准 表5

检测项目	单位	技术要求
马歇尔试件尺寸	mm	$\phi 101.6mm \times 63.5mm$
马歇尔试件击实次数	—	双面击实75次
空隙率VV	%	3~6
矿料间隙率VMA	%	≥15
沥青饱和度VFA	%	70~85
稳定度MS	kN	≥8.0
流值FL	0.1mm	20~50
谢伦堡沥青析漏损失	%	≤0.2
肯塔堡飞散损失	%	≤15

4 ECA-10施工方案

4.1 原路面准备

进行ECA-10罩面前需将原有路面的病害处理彻底,清理路表的杂物和浮灰,确保施工前路表的清洁。实施罩面前应均匀撒布高黏度改性乳化沥青,撒布不均匀的局部应进行处理(有裂缝的路段应该采用聚酯玻璃纤维布处理)。

4.2 沥青混合料的摊铺

摊铺机开工前应提前0.5~1h预热烫平板不低于100℃,摊铺厚度采用非接触式平衡梁控制方式。摊铺应连续,摊铺速度应控制在2~4m/min的范围内。

易密实沥青混凝土温度控制标准见表6。

易密实沥青混凝土温度控制标准(单位:℃) 表6

矿料加热温度	145~155
沥青加热温度	160~170
沥青混合料出料温度	145~155
混合料摊铺温度	≥135
开始碾压温度	≥130
开始复压温度	≥110
碾压终了温度	≥70

4.3 混合料的碾压

易密实沥青混凝土常用的碾压工艺为:①初压2遍,第1遍前静后振,第2遍振动,压实速度宜为2~3km/h;②胶轮复压4遍,压实速度宜为2~4km/h;③终压2遍,终压钢轮收光压实速度可为3~5km/h。

5 ECA-10实施效果评价

本项目于2016年6月中旬正式开工,至2016年8月底竣工,工期两个半月。本次实施效果评价将针对2016年6月(施工前)与2018年(运营2年后)进行比较、分析。从图6可知,2016年至2018年交通量变化不大,不存在交通量偏差,具备可比性。

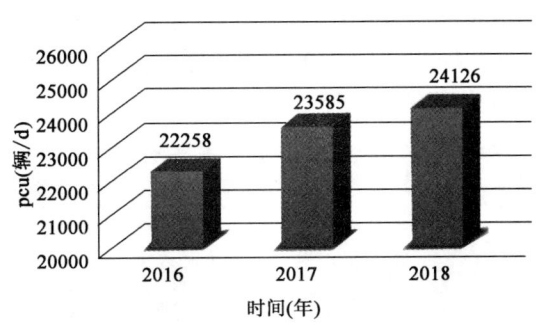

图 6　2016—2018 交通量情况

5.1　路面行驶质量指数 RQI

使用 ECA-10 薄层罩面前后路面行驶质量指数 RQI 的跟踪观测统计结果见图 7。

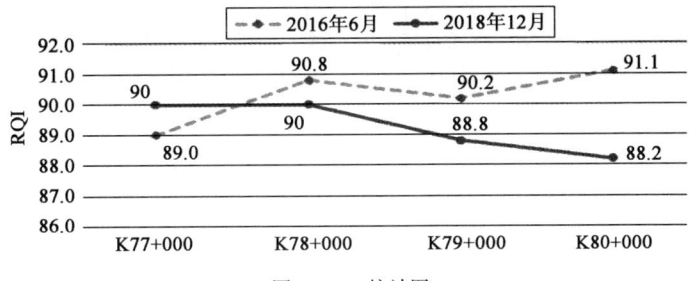

图 7　RQI 统计图

由图 7 可知,虽然 2018 年的数据相较 2016 年有明显下降,但仍处于优级、良级水平。根据现场观测,行驶质量指数下降的主要原因是沿线平交口较多,且多个平交口路段存在大面积补丁病害。

5.2　路面损坏状况指数 PCI

使用 ECA-10 薄层罩面前后路面损坏状况指数 PCI 的跟踪观测统计结果见图 8。

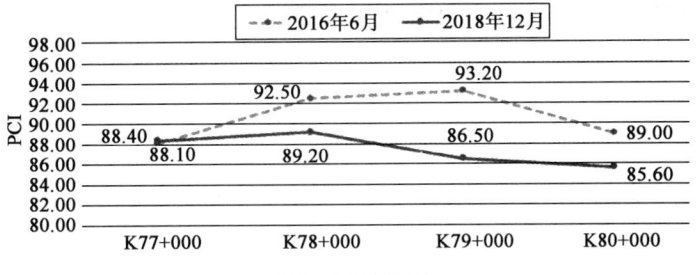

图 8　PCI 统计图

由图 8 可知,虽然 2018 年的数据与 2016 年相比有明显下降,但仍处于良级水平,且总体病害情况较好,仅存在轻微的块状裂缝、车辙病害。PCI 下降的主要原因是平交口范围内的大面积补丁病害。

5.3　路面车辙深度指数 RDI

使用 ECA-10 薄层罩面前后路面车辙深度指数 RDI 的跟踪观测统计结果见图 9。

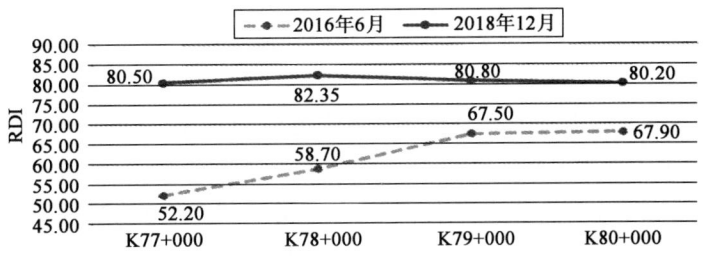

图 9　RDI 统计图

由图 9 可知,2018 年的车辙深度指数比 2016 年施工前有了大幅度提高,且经现场查勘,现场已不存在严重车辙,均为轻微车辙。根据现场芯样(图 10、图 11)分析,曾出现严重车辙的路段,经过 ECA-10 的病害处理及 2.5cm 罩面,路面结构强度有所提升。

图 10　2016 年芯样断裂

图 11　2018 年芯样完整

6　结　语

本文研究了使用 ECA-10 易密实沥青混凝土在严重车辙、块状裂缝病害路段的路面状况对比,得出以下结论:

(1)ECA-10 病害处治及罩面后,相应处治路段的损坏状况、车辙深度均得到了改善,尤其是严重车辙路段,ECA-10 的处治效果较好。

(2)ECA-10 不仅可以作为磨耗层功能层,还可作为结构补强层作用,且构造深度大,可提高路面的抗滑性能。

(3)ECA-10 高温稳定性较好,添加的易密实剂可提高沥青混合料的密实度,从而提高其压实性能。

综上所述,认为 ECA-10 易密实沥青混凝土具有较高的路用性能,能够满足预防性养护薄层罩面的使用性能要求。

参考文献

[1] 范萌,刘化学,吴昊. 苏嘉杭高速公路车辙处治方案应用研究及跟踪观测[J]. 华东公路,2014.
[2] 王朝辉,王丽君,白军华,等. 基于时段的沥青路面预防性养护时机与对策一体优化研究[J]. 中国公路学报,2010,23(5):27-34.

盲沟在泡沫沥青冷再生路面中的应用

顾艳静

(浙江省交通规划设计研究院有限公司)

摘　要　从近年来泡沫沥青冷再生路面使用情况来看,路面水的排出问题已成为冷再生技术实施与应用中的一大关键点,尤其以拼宽道路最为明显。本文以 X604 新蟠线(五四桥—山头路口段)泡沫沥青冷再生路面拼接处路面水不能外渗或排出为例,对路面渗水的原因进行分析,并提出了盲沟排水的施工工艺及防治水毁病害的效果,为泡沫沥青冷再生路面及路面拼宽等类似工程提供参考。

关键词　公路工程　泡沫沥青冷再生　盲沟　路面病害

0 引言

从近年来泡沫沥青冷再生路面使用情况来看,路面水的排出问题已成为冷再生技术实施与应用中的一大关键点,尤其以拼宽道路最为明显。因用地受限等原因,部分道路的基层拼宽部分需由老路侧分带改建而成,由于新老路面基层使用的材料不同,可造成车道拼接处有路面水无法排出的现象。如果泡沫沥青冷再生基层处,路面水不能外渗或排出,则会引起路面水毁病害,长期的积水将导致沥青路面出现不同程度的网裂或坑槽等病害,从而给公路的寿命及使用功能带来极大影响。所以,泡沫沥青冷再生路面渗水问题必须及时解决。

1 工程背景

X604新蟠线(五四桥—山头路口段)是浙江省绍兴市新昌县内的一条二级公路(兼顾城市道路),路线全长约5.03km,采用整体式路基,路幅宽度为32.5~37.0m。受公路用地限制,需通过压缩两侧侧分带来实现由四车道拓宽为六车道,但由于部分路段侧分带宽度较窄,无法采用水泥稳定碎石底基层,故采用C20素混凝土作为底基层。原老路行车道路面改造方案:30cm原老路基层(单点病害处理)+18cm泡沫沥青层厂拌冷再生基层+1cm橡胶沥青应力吸收层+加铺7cm SUP-20+4cm SMA-13。现状侧分带改造成行车道路面改造方案:30cm C20素混凝土+18cm泡沫沥青层厂拌冷再生基层+1cm橡胶沥青应力吸收层+加铺7cm SUP-20+4cm SMA-13。

2019年3月11日,在左幅第一车道、第二车道泡沫沥青冷再生基层和路面下面层施工完毕后,在第二车道、第三车道拼接缝铣刨后发现新建路面结构层有路面水渗出、外泄的现象。

2 原因分析和方案处治

2.1 路面渗水外泄原因分析

经对渗水路面情况进行现场查看,结合项目沿线气象、水文资料、施工图纸等,得出原因如下:

(1)泡沫沥青冷再生的级配、含水率等各项性能指标均符合规范要求,出现渗水现象并非冷再生工艺出现偏差。

(2)2019年2月下旬、3月初,项目所在地(新昌)大部分时间为连续阴雨天气,降水量较大。

(3)第三车道(拼宽部分)底基层材料为C20素混凝土,无渗水作用,路面水无法顺面层外渗。

(4)交通量较大,大货车、重载车等占所有通行车型4.6%。

综上所述,路面渗水主要因为泡沫沥青冷再生及下面层施工完毕后,遇强降雨天气,水和空气通过泡沫沥青的空隙进入混合料内部,水分渗入结构层内,且由于第三车道(拼宽部分)底基层材料为C20素混凝土,导致路面层间水不能顺面层外渗,一直滞留于路面结构中,从而造成路面积水。

2.2 路面渗水外泄方案处治

在第二车道、第三车道接缝处的底基层层面(即老路基层)设置40cm×16cm(宽×高)的横向排水盲沟。盲沟布置图如图1所示。

排水盲沟设计要点:

(1)采用曲纹网状PE硬式透水管作为排水盲沟,尺寸为40cm×16cm(宽×高),确保渗水能被迅速且大量排走。

(2)横向盲沟同道路方向坡率为2%,纵向盲沟的坡率一般大于3‰且夯实彻底,保证排水通畅。

(3)盲沟设置必须控制盲沟顶高程,不能超过路基顶面。

(4)横向盲沟的出水口点直接引至路基低处,或与纵向盲

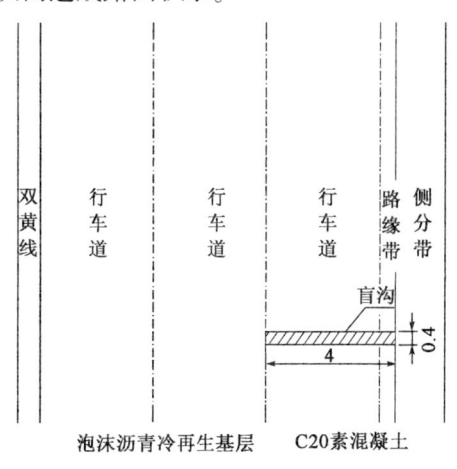

图1 盲沟布置图

沟相连接后接入侧分带雨水井,不影响路基。

3 盲沟施工流程

(1)确定横向盲沟位置。设置于第三车道底基层层面(即老路基层),盲沟同道路方向坡率为2%。

(2)盲沟开挖。在底基层层面(即老路基层)开挖出宽为400mm、高度为160mm的横向盲沟尺寸,并对盲沟内基底面清理干净。

(3)盲沟实施。放入曲纹网状PE硬式透水管,并用土工布包管,最后用碎石进行回填,且插捣夯实,避免出现空洞。

(4)泡沫沥青冷再生路面摊铺。

盲沟开挖现场如图2所示。

a)　　　　　　　　　　　　b)

图2　盲沟开挖现场

4 盲沟效果确认

X604新蟠线(五四桥—山头路口段)于2019年9月25日全线施工完毕,通过对现场路况检测和调查分析,未出现路面积水现象,无明显渗水现象,重载车驶过时,也无积水现象。经确认,设置盲沟在泡沫沥青冷再生路面应用非常成功,有效排放了再生面层与基层的层间积水,解决了渗水带来的安全隐患,进一步抑制了路面龟网裂、翻浆、坑槽等病害,同时也降低了后期道路养护成本。

5 结 语

在解决泡沫沥青冷再生路面渗水问题上,设置盲沟是一种值得选择的施工方案。该工艺施工成本低,速度快且简便,排水效果明显,后期养护方便。该工艺在X604新蟠线(五四桥—山头路口段)的成功应用,再一次验证了盲沟在再生路面排水问题中的优势,希望盲沟这一工艺能够被普及至泡沫沥青冷再生路面及路面拼宽工程中,并能引起设计单位的重视,在今后路面设计中加以考虑。

参考文献

[1] 李金,尹德龙.多雨山区公路排水施工技术[J].黑龙江交通科技,2019,42(06):21-22,24.

[2] 邹耀海.浅析公路排水施工中常见问题和对策探析[J].居舍,2019(06):8.

[3] 杨岱汶.高速公路路基路面排水系统的施工质量控制[J].黑龙江交通科技,2017,40(05):37-38.

基于红外光谱的老化沥青转移率研究

唐伟 李宁 于新 詹贺 张宇

(河海大学土木与交通学院)

摘 要 为了研究沥青路面回收料(RAP)中老化沥青的转移程度,本文基于红外光谱试验提出了转移率的计算方法。试验设计间断级配的再生沥青混合料,将拌和后的再生混合料过筛分离出新集料和RAP,并抽提出再生沥青测定羰基指数(CI);根据公式计算转移率,研究RAP粒径、拌和顺序和泡沫温拌技术对转移率的影响。结果表明,细RAP的转移率明显高于粗RAP;与热拌再生相比,采用泡沫温拌技术可以提高转移率11%以上;不同的拌和顺序下,老化沥青转移率不同,新沥青先和新集料拌和的情况下转移率最低。

关键词 再生技术 转移率 红外光谱 RAP

0 引 言

随着社会的进步,可持续发展的观念已经深入人心,由于再生技术可以回收利用废旧路面材料(RAP),在一定范围内替代沥青等资源,在路面养护行业得到了广泛的应用[1]。目前在再生混合料设计阶段,新沥青和老化沥青被认为是充分互融的[2]。但在实际工程中,老化沥青是以薄膜的形式紧密地裹覆于RAP的表层,并不能完全转移下来,与新沥青发生融合[3-4]。所以,在制备再生混合料时,RAP中老化沥青的转移量是影响混合料设计的一个重要因素。

国内外众多学者都对老化沥青的转移特性进行了研究。Zhao通过凝胶渗透色谱(GPC)发现老化沥青的大分子比例(LMSP)高于新沥青,建立了老化沥青含量和LMSP的关系,据此研究了不同RAP掺量下老化沥青的转移程度。结果表明,随着RAP掺量的提升,老化沥青转移率逐渐降低。Ding借助荧光显微镜构建了老化沥青含量与平均灰度值(MGV)的关系,然后将再生混合料颗粒直接在荧光显微镜下观察,测定MGV,再根据公式计算老化沥青转移率[5]。但该试验对样品的处理要求较高,既要保证观察面的平整度,又不能对表层的沥青造成损伤。苏卫国采用三聚氰胺作为新沥青的示踪剂,通过扫描电镜(SEM)观测示踪剂在老化沥青中的分布情况,间接反映老化沥青的转移情况。然而王勋发现三聚氰胺这种纳米颗粒材料在沥青中分散时极易发生团聚,难以保证分散均匀性[7]。杨毅文则以RAP中的矿粉标记老化沥青,将再生混合料中的RAP和新集料分离,测定转移至新集料上的矿粉质量来表征老化沥青的转移,并基于对流传质理论的特性研究了多种因素对老化沥青转移的影响[8]。杨林和杨毅文的试验思路一致,但不同的是,采用磁铁矿新集料,利用其易于分离的特性,将新集料和RAP有效分离[9]。此外,还有一些学者在开展再生剂的研究时发现,其能够有效提高老化沥青的转移程度[10-11]。

本文提出一种利用红外光谱仪来研究老化沥青转移程度的试验方法。该方法基于老化沥青和新沥青羰基指数的差异,建立老化沥青含量和再生沥青羰基指数的线性关系基准图;然后将拌和后的新集料和RAP分离,抽提再生沥青并测定羰基指数(CI);最后根据公式计算转移率。同时研究了RAP粒径、拌和顺序和泡沫温拌技术对转移率的影响。研究结果对于再生沥青混合料的性能提升和推广应用具有显著意义。

基金项目:国家自然科学基金青年基金(20175031511)。

1 老化沥青转移率检测方法

老化沥青转移是指再生沥青混合料在拌和过程中,老化沥青从 RAP 表层剥落、转移,与新添加的沥青发生融合反应生成再生沥青,然后重新分布于集料表面的现象。但许多研究表明,并非全部的老化沥青参与融合,真正再生利用的仅是外层转移的部分老化沥青,内层较硬的老化沥青仍然紧密地黏附在集料上,作为集料的一部分,即所谓的"黑石"[12],如图 1 所示。

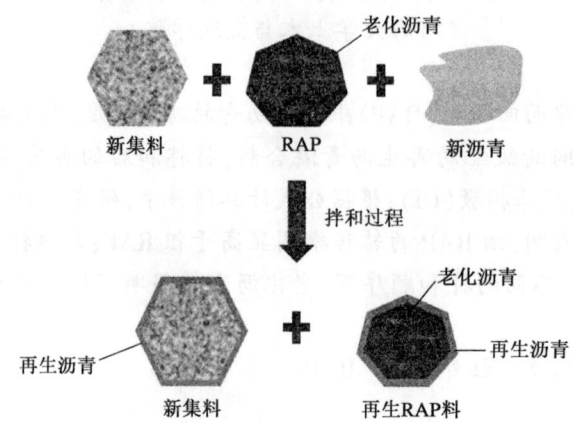

图 1 再生沥青混合料中沥青分布示意图

为量化表征老化沥青的转移状况,本文定义了老化沥青转移率(Mobilization Rate,MR)指标。转移率为实际转移并与新沥青发生融合的老化沥青质量占老化沥青总质量的百分率,计算公式见式(1)。

$$MR = \frac{W_m}{W_R} \times 100\% \tag{1}$$

式中:MR——转移率,%;
W_m——实际转移的老化沥青质量,g;
W_R——RAP 中老化沥青的总质量,g。

由于再生沥青中包含转移的老化沥青和新添加的沥青,则老化沥青所占比例可以通过式(2)计算。

$$\alpha = \frac{W_m}{W_m + W_v} = \frac{W_R \times MR}{W_R \times MR + W_v} \tag{2}$$

式中:α——再生沥青中老化沥青所占比例;
W_v——新沥青的质量,g。

将式(2)进行等式变换,可得式(3)。

$$MR = \frac{\alpha \times W_v}{(1-\alpha) \times W_R} = \frac{\alpha \times P_v}{(1-\alpha) \times P_R} \tag{3}$$

式中:P_v,P_R——再生沥青混合料中新沥青和老化沥青的质量含量。

从式(3)中可以看出,在再生混合料配合比设计完成之后,其 P_v、P_R 均为已知量。若要评估老化沥青的转移率,关键要确定融合再生沥青中转移老化沥青所占比例 α。但想要通过直接测量再生沥青的物理化学性质或者微观形态是很难确定 α 值的,因此本文提出一种间接计算的方法来确定 α 值,进而确定老化沥青的转移率 MR。

沥青的红外光谱图中,位于 $1695\ cm^{-1}$ 波数处的羰基(C=O)作为主要化学官能团之一,常用于监测沥青的氧化过程。随着沥青氧化的进行,羰基含量将逐渐增大[13]。所以老化沥青的羰基峰要明显高于新沥青,新沥青与老化沥青中羰基显著的差异性为确定 α 值提供了可行性。沥青老化前后,位于

1455cm^{-1}波数处的饱和C—C振动键基本保持不变。因此羰基含量一般采用羰基指数(Carboxyl Index,CI)来表征,计算公式见式(4)。

$$CI = \frac{A_{C=O}}{A_{C-C}} \quad (4)$$

式中:CI——羰基指数,无量纲;

　　$A_{C=O}$——沥青红外光谱中1695cm^{-1}处羰基的峰面积;

　　A_{C-C}——1455cm^{-1}饱和C—C键的峰面积。

本文确定转移率的具体步骤为:

①抽提RAP中的老化沥青,将其按照不同的比例与新沥青在室内混溶形成再生沥青,进行红外光谱试验并按式(4)计算CI;

②以老化沥青含量α为横坐标,CI为纵坐标建立坐标系,将①中测得的数据点绘制于该坐标系中,拟合老化沥青含量α与再生沥青CI的基准关系式;

③将②中α与CI的关系式代入式(3)中,从而建立MR与CI的关系式;

④拌和再生沥青混合料,抽提新集料上的沥青并通过红外光谱试验测得CI值,基于③中MR与CI的关系,最终即可算得转移率MR。

2　材料与试验

2.1　原材料及配合比

本文采用的新沥青为江苏某沥青厂生产的PG76-22SBS改性沥青。为了对比泡沫温拌技术对于老化沥青转移率的影响,采用徐工XLB10P型发泡机将新沥青发泡,沥青发泡温度为170℃,发泡用水量为3%[14]。RAP源自江苏某服役11年的高速公路上面层AC-13混合料。将其破碎筛分为粒径小于4.75mm的细颗粒和大于9.5mm的粗颗粒,分别和粒径大于4.75mm的粗新集料和粒径小于4.75mm的细新集料拌和,形成两种AC-13沥青混合料(粗新集料+细RAP,细新集料+粗RAP)。原材料性质见表1,再生混合料的配合比和集料的级配曲线分别见表2和图2。采用这种方式,既有利于新集料与RAP拌和后的分离,为新集料表层再生沥青CI的测试提供了可行性,同时又可以研究RAP的粒径对于老化沥青转移率的影响。

新集料和RAP的性质　　　　　表1

材料	级配通过率(%)										沥青含量(%)
	16	13.2	9.5	4.75	2.36	1.18	0.6	0.3	0.15	0.075	
粗新集料	100	86.5	52.6	0	0	0	0	0	0	0	—
细新集料	100	100	100	100	43.9	27.7	18.3	9.2	4.7	2.5	—
粗RAP	100	100	0	0	0	0	0	0	0	0	4.10
细RAP	100	100	100	100	51.5	22.4	9	2	0.7	0.3	6.08

注:RAP的级配通过率是未经抽提、直接筛分获得的。

再生混合料配合比　　　　　表2

混合料类型	总质量(g)	RAP掺量(%)	总沥青含量(%)	新沥青含量(%)
粗新集料+细RAP	4000	50	4.98	1.94
细新集料+粗RAP	4000	50	4.47	2.42

2.2　样品制备与试验

本文采用3种拌和顺序拌和再生沥青混合料(顺序A、B、C),以研究拌和顺序对老化沥青转移率的影响。顺序A:RAP先和新集料拌和,再和新沥青拌和。顺序B:RAP先和新沥青拌和,然后再和新集料拌和。顺序C:新集料先与新沥青拌和形成新沥青混合料,然后和RAP拌和成再生沥青混合料,每次拌和时间为90s。为了研究泡沫温拌的影响,将3种拌和顺序中的新沥青替换为泡沫沥青,普通热拌和泡沫温拌的拌和温度分别为170℃和150℃。拌和前,材料均在相应的温度下保温2h,以保证拌和时的温度均匀性。

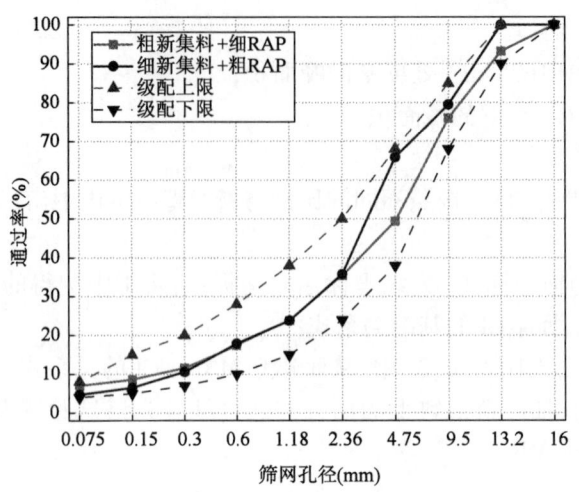

图2　再生混合料的集料级配曲线

再生沥青混合料拌和完成后,待温度降至70℃以下,将颗粒分散,然后过筛4.75mm的筛网分离出RAP和裹覆再生沥青的新集料颗粒,如图3所示。将新集料颗粒浸没于三氯乙烯中,按照《公路工程沥青及沥青混合料试验规程》(T 0727—2011)中的试验步骤将沥青抽提,并进行3次平行红光光谱测试,测试的波数范围为400~4000cm^{-1}。红外光谱试验采用的是美国Nicolet IS20红外光谱仪,按照衰减全反射法(ATR)进行[15]。通过OMINIC软件对沥青的红光光谱图进行分析并测定CI。需要说明的是,以粗新集料表层上再生沥青的羰基指数计算得到细RAP的转移率,以细新集料表层上再生沥青的羰基指数算计算得到粗RAP的转移率。

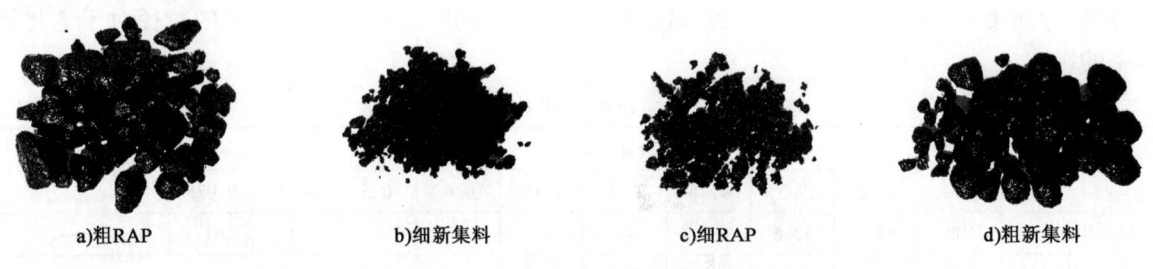

a)粗RAP　　　　b)细新集料　　　　c)细RAP　　　　d)粗新集料

图3　拌和后分离的新集料和RAP

3　试验结果与分析

3.1　羰基指数CI的计算

图4中展示了不同沥青类型的红外光谱图。从图4中可以发现,在特征频率区内,泡沫新沥青和新沥青吸收峰对应的波数的强度基本相同,这说明沥青发泡后并没有生成新的特征官能团,沥青与水的反应仅是一个物理过程。此外,与预期的结果一致,老化沥青在1695cm^{-1}波数处的羰基峰要明显高于新沥青。

采用式(4)计算再生沥青(不同老化沥青含量α)的羰基指数CI结果如图5所示。从图5中可以看出,随着老化沥青含量的增加,羰基指数CI明显增大。将图5中数据进行拟合,结果如式(5)和式(6)所示。拟合公式表明CI与α值线性正相关,相关系数R^2均大于0.95,说明结果具有较高的可靠度。

$$\text{CI} = 0.0316 \times \alpha + 4.76 \times 10^{-5}, R^2 = 0.987 \quad (\text{新沥青}) \tag{5}$$

$$CI = 0.0321 \times \alpha + 4.29 \times 10^{-4}, R^2 = 0.962 \quad (泡沫新沥青) \tag{6}$$

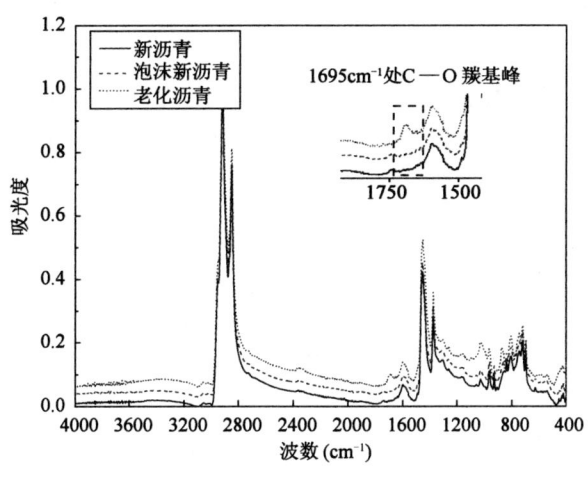

图4　不同沥青的红外光谱

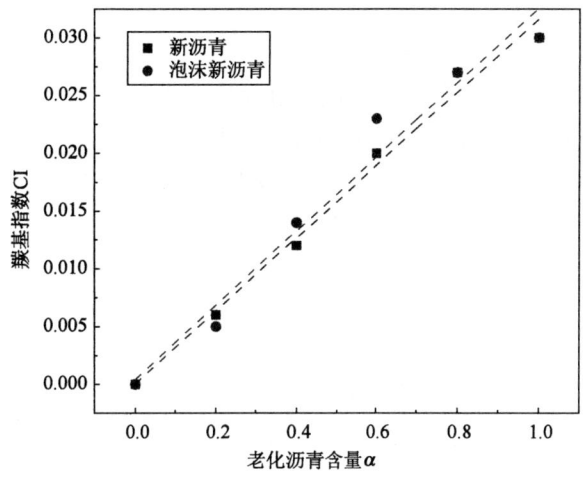

图5　再生沥青的羰基指数和老化沥青含量的关系

3.2　老化沥青转移率的计算

图5中已经得到再生沥青羰基指数CI和老化沥青含量α的关系式(5)和(6),将其带入式(3)中,分别得到对于添加新沥青和泡沫新沥青两种情况下,由新集料上再生沥青的CI测定值计算RAP中老化沥青转移率MR的公式,见式(7)和式(8)。

$$MR = \frac{P_v \times (CI - 4.76 \times 10^{-5})}{P_R \times (0.03164 - CI)} \quad (新沥青) \tag{7}$$

$$MR = \frac{P_v \times (CI - 4.29 \times 10^{-4})}{P_R \times (0.03259 - CI)} \quad (泡沫新沥青) \tag{8}$$

表3以一具体实例展示老化沥青转移率的计算,再生混合料类型为粗新集料 + 细RAP,拌和顺序为RAP先和新集料拌和,然后再和新沥青拌和,即顺序A。通过实例表明,采用本文所述方法确定老化沥青转移率是可行的。

老化沥青转移率 MR 计算实例　　表3

参　数		含　义	计算方式	数　值
P_V		新沥青含量	由配合比确定	1.94
P_R		老化沥青含量	由配合比确定	3.04
CI	（新沥青）	新集料上抽提沥青羰基指数	试验测定	0.01451
	（泡沫新沥青）			0.01600
α	（新沥青）	再生沥青中老化沥青含量	式(5)	0.458
	（泡沫新沥青）		式(6)	0.485
MR	（新沥青）	老化沥青转移率	式(7)	0.54
	（泡沫新沥青）		式(8)	0.60

3.3　不同因素对老化沥青转移率的影响

3.3.1　RAP粒径

图6展示了不同粒径RAP的老化沥青转移再生率MR(仅以拌和顺序A为例)。当使用普通新沥青时,粗RAP的MR仅为0.45,细RAP的MR为0.54,相比粗RAP高了20%。这可能是由于细RAP表层的沥青膜要厚于粗RAP,在加热和机械拌和的作用下,越厚的沥青膜越容易从RAP表面剥落,从而转移至新集料上与新沥青融合再生。在厂拌热再生实体工程中,RAP是按粒径大小分档,然后按照不同掺配

比例使用的。因此在确定细 RAP 的掺配比例时,不仅应考虑沥青含量、级配变异性等因素,还该考虑老化沥青的转移率。

3.3.2 拌和顺序

图 7 中展示了不同拌和顺序条件下的老化沥青转移率 MR(仅以细 RAP 为例)。由图 7 可以发现,不同的拌和顺序条件下,MR 也不相同。当采用普通新沥青时,拌和顺序 A 和拌和顺序 B 的 MR 基本相等,但比拌和顺序 C 高了 15% 以上;当采用泡沫沥青时,这种差距更明显,达到了 30%。这可能是因为对于拌和顺序 A 和拌和顺序 B,RAP 在拌和时接触的新沥青是可流动态的,RAP 上老化沥青受到这种流动沥青的软化作用,比较容易发生脱落、转移;而对于拌和顺序 C,新沥青先和新集料拌和之后,新沥青就以膜的形式裹覆于新集料上,仅有相对较少的新沥青对老化沥青起到软化作用。所以根据室内试验结果,实际生产建议采用拌和顺序 A 和拌和顺序 B,以保证较高比例的老化沥青能从 RAP 上转移下来,促进新沥青与老化沥青的融合再生。

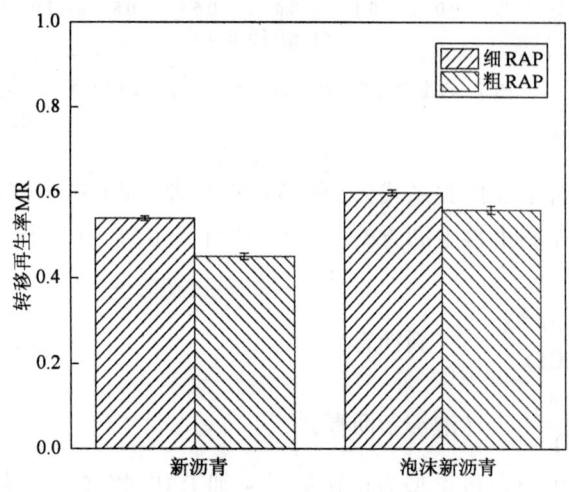

图 6 不同 RAP 粒径的老化沥青转移率(拌和顺序 A)

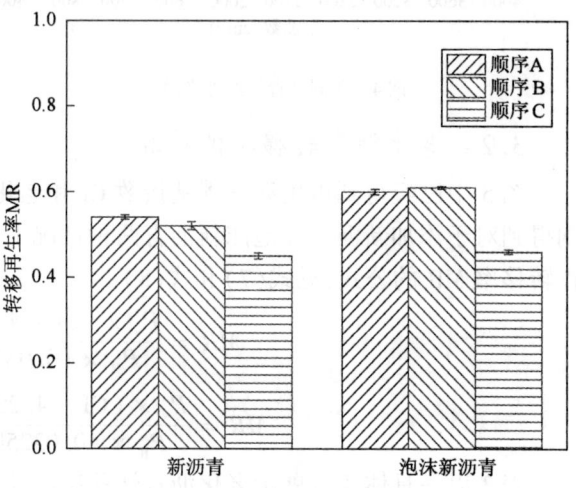

图 7 不同拌和顺序下的老化沥青转移率(细 RAP)

3.3.3 泡沫温拌技术

图 8 中展示了使用不同新沥青条件下老化沥青转移率 MR(仅以细 RAP 为例)。在使用泡沫新沥青的情况下,对于拌和顺序 A 和拌和顺序 B,MR 在 0.6 以上,与普通新沥青相比,能够提高老化沥青转移率 11%以上。这是因为沥青发泡后黏度降低,提升了对老化沥青的软化程度;而对于拌和顺序 C,泡沫沥青基本起不到促进转移再生的作用。同样,这也是因为在拌和顺序 C 的条件下,泡沫沥青先裹覆在新集料的表面。

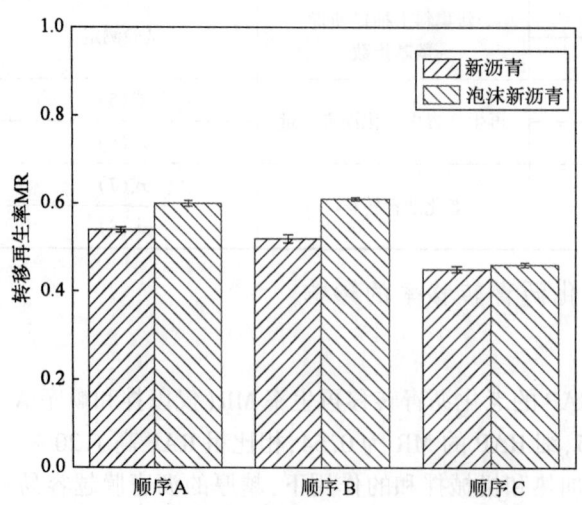

图 8 使用普通新沥青和泡沫新沥青的老化沥青转移率(细 RAP)

4 结 语

(1)基于新沥青和老化沥青羰基指数的差异,通过红外光谱试验建立了老化沥青含量与再生沥青羰基指数的线性关系图,并以其作为基准,可以研究再生沥青混合料中老化沥青的转移率。

(2)再生沥青混合料中的老化沥青并没有完全得到再生利用,其转移率只有0.4~6;通过使用泡沫沥青,转移率可以提升11%以上。

(3)由于细RAP的老化沥青转移率明显大于粗RAP,所以对于分档使用RAP的厂拌热再生技术,在确定细RAP的掺配比例时,应着重考虑其老化沥青转移率。

(4)再生沥青混合料的拌和顺序不同,老化沥青转移率也不相同。实际施工时,应选转移率高的拌和顺序,促进新沥青与老化沥青的融合再生,从而提升再生沥青混合料的性能。

参考文献

[1] SI Jing-jing, LI Yang, YU Xin. Curing Behavior and Mechanical Properties of an Eco-friendly Cold-mixed epoxy asphalt[J]. Materials and Structures, 2019, 52(4).

[2] 韦万峰,郭鹏,唐伯明.再生沥青混合料新—旧沥青扩散混合效率研究综述[J].材料导报,2017,31(11):109-114.

[3] 秦永春,黄颂昌,徐剑,等.厂拌温再生沥青混合料中新旧沥青的融合性研究[J].公路交通科技,2015,32(12):24-28.

[4] ZHAO Sheng, HUANG Bao-shan, SHU Xiang, et al. Quantitative Characterization of Binder Blending: How Much Recycled Binder is Mobilized during Blending? [J]. Transportation Research Record: Journal of the Transportation Research Board, 2015, 2506(1):72-80.

[5] DING Yong-jie, HUANG Bao-shan, SHU Xiang. Blending efficiency evaluation of plant asphalt mixtures using fluorescence microscopy[J]. Construction and Building Materials, 2018, 161(FEB. 10):461-467.

[6] 苏卫国,张旺.厂拌热再生中老化沥青有效再生率的研究[J].公路工程,2017,42(06):194-198.

[7] 王勋.高比例RAP厂拌热再生沥青混合料微观机理与性能试验研究[D].广州:华南理工大学,2014.

[8] 杨毅文,马涛,卞国剑,等.老化沥青热再生有效再生率检测方法[J].建筑材料学报,2011,14(03):418-422.

[9] 杨林,李文博.热再生沥青混合料有效再生率的影响分析[J].科学技术与工程,2019,19(5):291-296.

[10] 岳秀梅.再生剂对SBS老化沥青及热再生混合料性能的影响[J].公路工程,2016,41(03):78-84.

[11] 王子敬.再生剂及温拌剂对再生沥青混合料性能影响研究[J].公路工程,2014,39(05):315-318,355.

[12] 郭鹏,谢凤章,孟建玮,等.沥青再生过程中新-旧沥青界面混溶行为综述[J].材料导报,2020,34(13):13100-13108.

[13] DING Yong-jie, HUANG Bao-shan, SHU Xiang. Characterizing blending efficiency of plant produced asphalt paving mixtures containing high RAP[J]. Construction and Building Materials, 2016,(126):172-178.

[14] YU Xin, LIU Sheng-jie, DONG Fu-qiang. Comparative Assessment of Rheological Property Characteristics for Unfoamed and Foamed Asphalt Binder[J]. Construction and Building Materials, 2016, (122):354-361.

[15] 张德鹏,徐金枝,郝培文.基于GPC和FTIR的再生混合料新旧沥青融合程度研究[J].中外公路,2016(6):214-219.

Research on the Remaining Service Life and Rutting Deformation of Highway Pavements

Longsong Jiang Shujie Wang Huiyong Wang

(JSTI Croup Co., Ltd)

Abstract In order to study the best maintenance timing of highway asphalt pavement and formulate maintenance planning scheme in time, this paper selects accelerated loading test for continuous loading analysis of rutting specimens, and calculates the conversion relationship between indoor test axle load and actual axle load by combining the accumulated equivalent axle load times of emergency lane, and finally calculates the actual pavement equivalent axle load times by accelerated loading test results to calculate the remaining service life of asphalt pavement when it reaches the maintenance threshold. Finally, the actual pavement equivalent axle load is calculated by accelerated loading test results, and the remaining service life of the asphalt pavement when it reaches the maintenance threshold is calculated.

Keywords Accelerated loading   Remaining service life   Highways   Extreme conditions   Equivalent axle times   Timing of maintenance   Maintenance thresholds

0 Introduction

Remaining Service Interval(RSI) of pavement refers to the number of years from the current stage to the time when different maintenance strategies are implemented. Firstly, the long-term performance prediction model is established by considering the pavement maintenance history with the test results of pavement performance of highways in the past years. Based on the pavement field test results and the indoor test results of pavement materials, the RSI of the remaining service life of the structure of old roads with different opening time, pavement structure, maintenance history and traffic volume conditions are calculated and analyzed respectively, especially for the remaining service life of the pavement after the treatment of different maintenance schemes, which provides a basis for the scientific formulation of the maintenance planning of high-speed asphalt pavements.

1 Test Project

The MMLS3 quarter-scale accelerated loading equipment was mainly used to study the effect of different mix structural compositions on high-temperature stability. In view of the periodicity limitation of the road coring simulation, the maximum load of 2.7kN was used to simulate the loading in this test considering the usage condition under the most unfavourable load. The thickness of the specimen is the entire asphalt surface layer of the coring section.

A 55°C water bath heating environment was used for this test. The test reflects the high temperature deformation resistance of the mixture by recording the rutting depth of the specimens at different loading times during the loading process. The rutting depth of the specimens was recorded at different loading times(0,5000, 10000,50000,100000,150000,200000,250000,300000,etc.) to evaluate the variation of the rutting depth with the number of axial loads for each specimen. After the specimens were cut and installed in the mold, they were heated with water and loaded after the temperature of the specimens was stabilized at 55°C. When the wheel load reached a certain number of times, the middle of the specimen started to sink and rutting gradually formed, and with the increase of loading times, the rutting developed and the depth of sinking in the middle of the specimen increased.

2 Analysis of Accelerated Loading Test

2.1 Normal Asphalt Pavement

In this project, three sections with small rutting depths, K15 + 000 (Unmaintained sections), K40 + 000 (Unmaintained sections) and K91 + 000 (at the micro-meter in 2009), were selected as normal sections, and their corresponding pavement structure combination forms are as follows.

Normal asphalt pavement test parameters is shown in Tab. 1 The accelerated Loading test results of normal asphalt pavement is shown in Fig. 1.

Normal asphalt pavement test parameters Tab. 1

Mileage	K15 +000	K91 +000	K40 +000
Conservation history	Unmaintained sections	2009 micro-surfacing	Unmaintained sections
Pavement structure	Structure A	Structure B	Structure C
	4cm Sup-13	4cm SMA-13	4cm AK-13
	6cm Sup-20	6cm AC-20	
	8cm Sup-25	8cm AC-25	

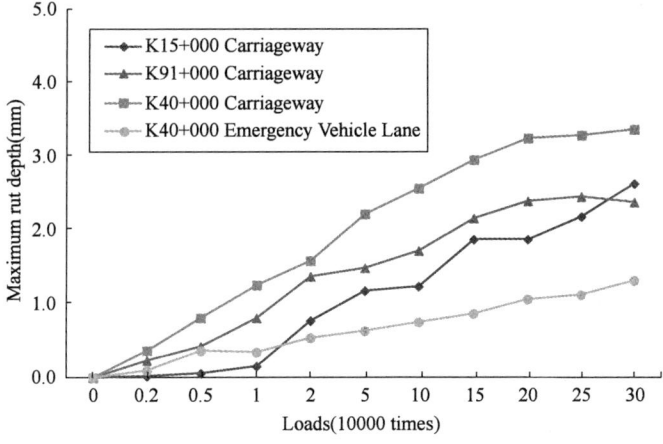

Fig. 1 The accelerated loading test results of normal asphalt pavement

2.2 Deep Rutting Asphalt Pavement

In this project, three sections with large rutting depths, K15 + 300 (Unmaintained sections), K47 + 200 (hot regeneration on site in 2010) and K91 + 800 (Unmaintained sections), were selected as rutting large sections. The section of K9 + 000 (hot regeneration on site in 2010 + milling and resurfacing in 2014) with more maintenance times is selected as the section with frequent maintenance, and its corresponding pavement structure combination form is as follows.

Deep rutting asphalt pavement test parameters is shown in Tab. 2. The accelerated loading text results of deep rutting asphalt pavement is shown in Fig. 2.

Deep rutting asphalt pavement test parameters Tab. 2

Mileage	K15 +300	K91 +800	K9 +000	K9 +000
Conservation history	Unmaintained sections	Unmaintained sections	2010 Hot In-Place Recycling	2010 Hot In-Place Recycling + 2014 Milling and resurfacing

Mileage	K15+300	K91+800	K9+000	K9+000 continue
Pavement structure	Structure A	Structure B	Structure C	Structure A
	4cm Sup-13	4cm SMA-13	4cm AK-13	4cm Sup-13
	6cm Sup-20	6cm AC-20		6cm Sup-20
	8cm Sup-25	8cm AC-25		8cm Sup-25

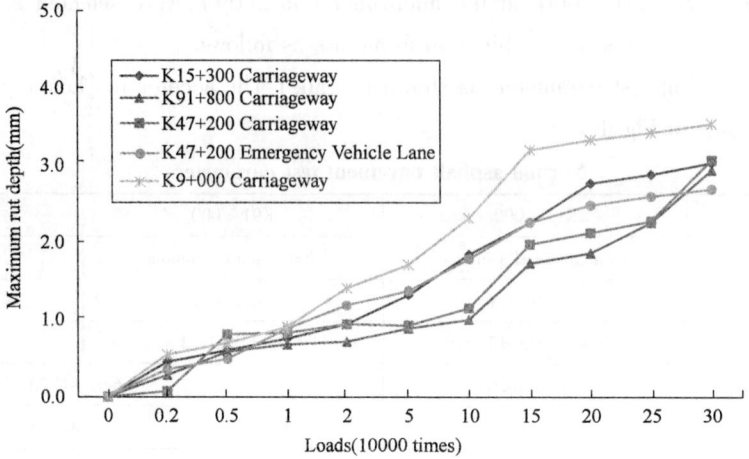

Fig. 2 The accelerated loading test results of deep rutting asphalt pavement

From the test results, it can be seen that the rutting deformation of pavement core samples in different sections within the selected loading times are basically manifested in two stages: ① before 20000 times of loading, the rutting depth develops rapidly; ② after 20000 times of loading until 300000 times, the rutting depth basically develops at an equal rate. This indicates that the current rutting depth development of this expressway is not yet stable, and will continue to develop rapidly in the short term before developing at a stable rate of equal speed.

Secondly, the accelerated loading test results in the form of different pavement structure combinations in the same section show that the overall high-temperature stability of Sup mix (structure A) is not much different from that of SMA mix (structure B), while the high-temperature stability of AK (structure C) is relatively the worst. By comparing the two pavement structures, the overall rutting depth development in the rutted larger section is greater than that in the normal section, and the rutting development trend in the rutted larger section at 10000 times loading is equivalent to 20000 times loading in the normal section rutting. 2010 on-site hot regeneration maintenance section, the rutting depth development curve shows a growing trend and has shown signs of fatigue damage.

3 Analysis of Remaining Service life

3.1 Rutting Calculation and Analysis

Based on the MMLS3 accelerated loading test, the pavement rutting development trend was predicted for normal sections and rutted sections, respectively, and the year in which the critical rutting depth occurred was discerned. According to the regression curve of the experimental results, the number of equivalent axle loads for indoor tests up to a certain rutting depth (10mm or 20mm) is calculated, and then converted into the estimated number of equivalent axle loads for the actual pavement, and finally, the total number of axle loads and the year in which the corresponding rutting occurs is calculated by considering the traffic growth rate.

Assuming that the testing base year is t_0, the base year rut depth is RD_0, the base year equivalent axle times is N_0, and the increment of rutting of the specimen after 300000 indoor loadings is ΔRD, the total rutting RD_t

reached by the pavement after 300000 indoor loadings is:

$$RD_t = RD_0 + \Delta RD \tag{1}$$

Calculate the number of equivalent axle load actions N_{10} mm or N_{20} mm for indoor tests up to a certain rutting depth (10mm or 20mm) based on the regression curve of rutting test results:

$$N_{10mm} = f_x(RD_t, RD_{10mm}, N_{300000times}) \tag{2}$$

$$N_{20mm} = f_x(RD_t, RD_{20mm}, N_{200000times}) \tag{3}$$

When the total rutting reaches 10 mm or 20 mm, the increment of the actual equivalent axle load action times is as follows:

$$\Delta N_t = \omega \times N_{10mm}(\text{or } N_{20mm}) \tag{4}$$

Where, ω is the conversion coefficient of equivalent axle number converted from accelerated loading indoor test to actual pavement equivalent axle number, which is obtained through accelerated loading test and field actual pavement.

Finally, according to the increment of the equivalent axle number and the actual pavement equivalent axle load action times when the total rutting reaches 10mm or 20mm in the test reference year, the total equivalent axle load action times of the actual pavement are calculated. Considering the traffic growth rate, the time required for the corresponding rutting (10mm or 20mm) is calculated, that is, the maintenance treatment year (t).

$$N_T = N_0 + \Delta N_t = N_0 \times (1 + \gamma)^{\Delta t} \tag{5}$$

Where, γ is the average growth rate of traffic volume, and Δt is the treatment year (t) and the detection reference year.

Since the emergency lane pavement was subjected to less traffic load during operation and no damage occurred, in the test, the emergency lane pavement was used to simulate the original pavement structure and compared with the development trend of pavement rutting disease to obtain the equivalent relationship between the number of indoor test loadings and the number of predicted pavement standard axle loads.

According to this test, the rutting loading test results of the emergency lane are shown in Fig.3, corresponding to the MMLS3 accelerated loading test number 200000 times the average depth of rutting of the emergency lane is 2.58mm. according to Fig.4 pavement rutting performance development law, it can be considered that the pavement rutting at the time of opening to traffic (opening to traffic in 2003) is 0, and the interpolation method calculates that the average rutting 2.58mm at 200000 times loading is equivalent to The rutting depth at the 2.40th year of operation in the upstream direction is equivalent to the rutting depth at the 1.14th year of operation in the downstream direction.

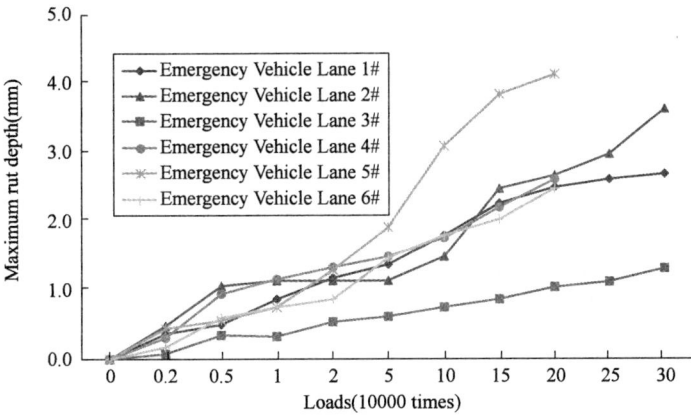

Fig.3 Test results of MMLS3 accelerated loading test for emergency Lane

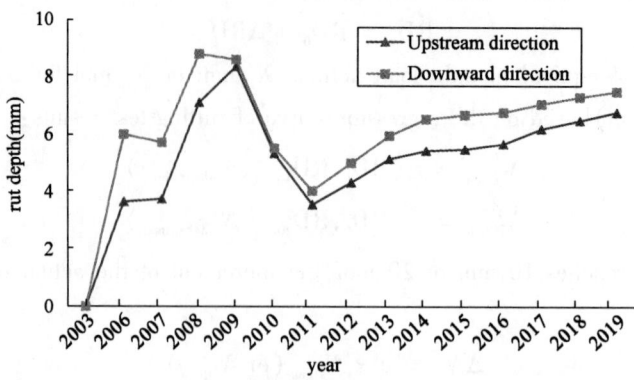

Fig. 4　The development trend of pavement rutting performance

The cumulative equivalent axle load action number(ESAL) of the freeway was obtained from the pavement management system, and the standard axle times in the upstream direction for the corresponding time were about 1.3 million based on the cumulative equivalent axle times calculation. Since the temperature used for the indoor MMLS3 accelerated loading test is 60°C, while the equivalent temperature in the field is generally about 45°C, the indoor test loading times are lower than the field axle times for producing the same size of rut. At the same time, because the emergency lane specimens have been used for more than 10 years, the rutting development rate should be lower than that of the actual pavement travel lane due to asphalt aging and other reasons, although they are less subjected to vehicle loading. Therefore, it can be considered that 60°C, 200,000 times loading in MMLS3 accelerated loading test is equivalent to 1.3 million times in actual pavement use, i.e. the conversion factor ω for converting the equivalent axle times of accelerated loading indoor test to the equivalent axle times of actual pavement is 6.5.

3.2　Analysis of Remaining Service Life

Normal road sections were judged by 10mm rutting, and rutting up to 20mm was used as the judging criterion for larger sections. The typical sections in different locations and directions were selected for calculation, and the results are shown in Tab.3 and Tab.4.

Analysis of remaining service life of normal road section　　　　　Tab.3

Parameter	Downward direction K15+000	Upstream direction K40+000	Upstream direction K91+000
Original road rut RD_0 (mm)	3.0	2.9	2.7
300000 indoor loading rut increments ΔRD (mm)	2.6	3.4	2.4
The total rut of the indoor road surface loaded with 300000 times RD_t (mm)	5.6	6.3	5.1
The total rut reaches 10mm, the equivalent number of axle loads in the indoor test N_{10mm} (10000 times)	79	179	192
The total rut reaches 10mm, the actual road equivalent axle load action times increment ΔN_t (10000 times)	513	1163	1248
Total equivalent axle load action times N_T (10000 times)	3027	2180	3793
Equivalent year t	2019	2023	2020

Analysis of remaining service life in deep rut section Tab. 4

Parameter	Downward direction K15+300	Downward direction K47+200	Downward direction K91+800
Original road rut RD_0 (mm)	13.7	14.4	14.7
300000 indoor loading rut increments ΔRD (mm)	3.0	3.1	2.9
The total rut of the indoor road surface loaded with 300000 times RD_t (mm)	16.7	17.5	17.6
The total rut reaches 10mm, the equivalent number of axle loads in the indoor test N_{10mm} (10000 times)	93	46	47
The total rut reaches 10mm, the actual road equivalent axle load action times increment ΔN_t (10000 times)	603	299	308
Total equivalent axle load action times N_T (10000 times)	3116.7	3361.5	3091
Equivalent year t	2019	2018	2018

From the results in the table, it can be seen that for normal pavement, it generally takes 2-4 years for rutting in the downstream direction to reach 10mm, which occurs in 2018—2020, and the development of rutting is accelerated when the pavement rutting is greater than 10mm, as shown by the detection data of rutting larger sections. Therefore, maintenance measures should be taken to prevent the further expansion of rutting disease in a timely manner. For rutting larger sections, it generally takes 1-2 years for rutting to reach 20mm, i. e. 2018-2019. Given that the rutting of the larger sections has now reached more than 12mm, it is recommended that maintenance measures be applied to deal with it as soon as possible.

4 Conclusions

The development of rutting depth has not been stabilized since the opening of the vehicle, and it will continue to develop rapidly in the short term, and then at a stable rate of equal speed.

The rutting depth development on the whole is greater than that on the normal section, and the rutting development trend is equivalent to 20000 times of loading on the normal section when the rutting section is loaded 10000 times. 2010 on-site hot regeneration maintenance section, the rutting depth development curve shows a growing trend and has shown signs of fatigue damage.

For normal pavement, rutting in the downstream direction up to 10mm generally takes 2-4 years, i. e. occurring in 2018—2020. For rutting larger sections, it generally takes 1-2 years for rutting to reach 20mm. in view of the rutting larger sections have now reached 12mm or more, and should be treated in time. .

References

[1] Liu Bo, Yang Tao. Analysis of asphalt pavement road construction technology[J]. People's traffic. 2018(12).

[2] Wang Lu. Water damage of highway asphalt pavement and its prevention and control measures [J]. Transportation energy saving and environmental protection. 2018(06).

[3] Ling JM, Zheng YF, Yuan Jie. Research on residual life prediction method of asphalt concrete pavement at airports[J]. Journal of Tongji University(Natural Science Edition),2004(04).

[4] E R Brown, et al. Test Method for Detemination of Draindown Characteristic in Uncompacted Asphalt Mixtures[S]. AASHTO Format Standard,1998.

[5] E R Brown, et al. Practice for Testing HMA Mortars. Standard Practice for Testing HMA Mortars[S].

AASHTO Format Standard,1998.
[6] Temperature and density differentials in asphalt concrete pavement. Kim A. Willoughby,est. 9th ISAP.
[7] Zhu Hao RAN,Cai HQ,Ren Q,et al. Experimental analysis of the development law of high temperature performance of existing asphalt pavement medium surface layer[J]. Highway,2020(08):17-22.
[8] Duan Baodong,Zhu Haoran,Cai Haiquan. Research on the evaluation method of high temperature stability of in-service highway asphalt surface layer[J]. Modern Transportation Technology,2019(06):9-13.
[9] Su Youdong. Research on highway asphalt pavement construction safety evaluation system[J]. Western Transportation Science and Technology,2019(01).
[10] Peng Wang. Overview of asphalt pavement design points[J]. Residence industry,2019(03).
[11] Wang YL. Analysis of the causes and treatment options of asphalt pavement damage on highways[J]. Traffic World,2019(11).
[12] Development and Visualization of Airport Pavement Management Information: Lessons Learned. Franz Alexander Ollerman Ⅵ,et al. 77th Annual Meeting of Transportation Research Board,1998.
[13] Dresser GB,Freeman T. Implementation of the Micro-Paver Pavement Management System on Texas Division of Aviation Airfields[R]. 1993.
[14] Dresser GB,Freeman T. Update:Implementation of Micro-Paver Pavement Management System on Texas Division of Aviation Airfields[R]. 1993.
[15] Broten M,McNeely S. Virginia Aviation Pavement Management System:A Historical Perspective[J]. Transportation Research,1995.
[16] Gonzalo R,Rada,et al. Integrated Pavement Management System for Kennedy International Airport[J]. The Journal of Transportation Engineering,1992.
[17] Liao JH,Jiang WQ,Zhang Xuan. Study on temperature field and full time domain force characteristics of asphalt pavement[J]. Highway Engineering,2017(06).
[18] Deng Xuejun,Huang Xiaoming. Principles and methods of pavement design[M]. Beijing:People's Traffic Publishing House,2001.
[19] Yang Y C. Research on the high temperature performance of asphalt pavement of trunk highway[J]. Sichuan Building Materials,2019(09):133-134.
[20] Preeda Chaturabong,Hussain U Bahia. Mechanisms of asphalt mixture rutting in the dry Hamburg Wheel Tracking test and the potential to be alternative test in measuring rutting resistance[J]. Construction and Building Materials,2017.
[21] Wu H-L. Study on rutting deformation of PAC drainage pavement based on continuous loading test[J]. Shanghai Highway,2020(03):23-26.
[22] Sheng Qingyi. Research on asphalt pavement rutting prediction based on accelerated loading test[J]. Jiangxi Building Materials,2015(01):140.
[23] Zhu Tianming. Research and numerical simulation of asphalt pavement rutting development law based on accelerated loading test[D]. Harbin:Harbin Institute of Technology,2014.
[24] Chen Qian,Wang Bo. Zhang,et al. Performance analysis of highway asphalt pavement structure based on MMLS type 3 accelerated loading test[C]//Annual Academic Conference of Road Engineering Branch of China Highway Society and the 6th(2012)International Pavement Maintenance Technology Forum,2017:475-480.

道路非开挖注浆加固材料性能研究

李 亚 张 瑜 陈先勇

(重庆重交再生资源开发股份有限公司)

摘 要 为探究不同非开挖注浆加固材料的性能,测定了水泥净浆和在水泥净浆中掺入硫铝酸盐水泥和水玻璃注浆材料的凝结时间、流动度、20min流动度、强度和收缩性能。结果表明,与水泥净浆相比,掺入硫铝酸盐水泥和水玻璃均能提高注浆材料的快硬性能,流动度降低,掺入水玻璃的降低幅度大于掺入硫铝酸盐水泥的注浆材料的幅度,二者流动度损失都较小;其1d强度都得到一定的提升,但28d强度会降低,收缩变形得到一定程度的抑制。

关键词 道路 非开挖注浆材料 加固补强 性能研究

0 引 言

在交通荷载作用和环境效应的共同作用下,道路在全寿命周期内由于路基局部承载力不足或路基脱空严重,进而导致道路表面出现反射裂缝、坑槽以及大面积的塌陷现象,对行车舒适性和道路安全性造成极大影响,现阶段国内外主要采用非开挖注浆方式对路基进行加固补强。其具有经济性高、开放交通快和工艺简单等优点,具有极好的社会效益和极高的经济价值[1-3]。非开挖注浆加固补强效果受注浆材料的影响最大,目前的注浆加固材料主要分为水泥基材料、地聚物材料、沥青类材料和高聚物材料,不同材料的特征和适用范围都不相同,如表1所示,因此需要对非开挖注浆材料进行性能对比研究,以便在实际工程应用中选择更合适的注浆材料,从而提高加固补强效率[4-6]。

不同注浆材料的优缺点和适用范围 表1

注浆材料类型	优 点	缺 点	适用范围
水泥基注浆材料	原材料来源广,成本低,注浆工艺简单	析水严重,干缩较大,凝结时间较长	可短时间内封闭交通的病害不严重路段,小裂缝路段
高聚物注浆材料	快硬早强,膨胀率高,凝结时间短	价格较高,耐久性差,施工工艺复杂,强度较低	需快速开放交通的非重载公路
地聚物注浆材料	强度高,防水抗渗,凝结时间易控制,成本低,施工工艺简单	流动度不大,材料不够密实,内部出现孔洞	适用于道路路基较大范围沉陷脱空路段
沥青注浆材料	耐水性好,与原道路黏结好,能快速开放交通	成本较高,注浆设备和工艺复杂	需快速开放交通的各等级公路以及大范围病害路段

国内外学者对注浆材料的性能研究主要包括凝结时间、流动度、强度和收缩性能等,凝结时间和流动度直接影响注浆材料的施工效率和施工设备选择,注浆材料强度和收缩性能是决定路基加固后承载力大小和耐久性的关键因素[7-9]。由于施工工艺简单和材料成本低,水泥基注浆材料和地聚物材料在实际工程中应用更广泛,有必要对二者进行深入的性能研究。本文着重对比研究了水泥净浆、内掺硫铝酸盐水泥注浆材料和掺入水玻璃注浆材料,在不同配合比情况下的凝结时间、流动度、20min流动度损失、强度和收缩性能,为非开挖注浆工程提供参考,也为以后的学者研究提供试验依据。

1 配合比设计

水泥基材料主要以水泥净浆为主,也可以在水泥净浆中加入粉煤灰、硫铝酸盐水泥、硅灰,从而提升注浆材料的性能,在水泥净浆中掺入一定掺量的水玻璃称为地聚物,其性能随水玻璃掺量的不同而不同。对水泥净浆、掺入硫铝酸盐水泥和水玻璃的水泥浆进行配合比设计,各组分掺量根据相关研究文献推荐的掺量进行确定[10-12]。通过文献可知,水泥基材料的水灰比一般为0.4~0.67,内掺硫铝酸盐水泥掺量范围为5%~30%,水玻璃掺量范围为5%~12%。本文以总水泥质量为1,硫铝酸盐水泥掺量以占总水泥量比例来计量,水玻璃掺量以占水质量比重来计算,配合比设计如表2所示。

不同注浆材料的配合比设计 表2

编号	水泥	水	硫铝酸盐水泥	水玻璃	萘系减水剂	早强剂
A1	1	0.45	—	—	1.5%	3.0%
B1	1	0.45	10%	—	1.5%	3.0%
B2	1	0.45	20%	—	1.5%	3.0%
C1	1	0.45	—	6%	1.5%	3.0%
C2	1	0.45	—	8%	1.5%	3.0%

2 原 材 料

本文水泥采用42.5R的普通硅酸盐水泥,其性能见表3,硫铝酸盐水泥为盾石牌42.5硫铝酸盐水泥;水玻璃模数为2.7,波美度为38°;萘系减水剂的减水率为18%,含气量为3%,含碱量低,早强剂技术参数满足国家相应规定,推荐掺量为2%~4%。

普通硅酸盐水泥性能 表3

80μm筛余细度(%)	比表面积(m^2/kg)	标准稠度用水量(mL)	初凝时间(min)	终凝时间(min)
0.4	360	133	184	223

3 试 验 结 果

凝结时间、流动度、20min流动度、强度和收缩性能按照《公路工程水泥及水泥混凝土试验规程》(JTG E30—2005)中的相关方法和试验步骤进行测定。

3.1 凝结时间

分别测定不同配合比的初凝时间和终凝时间,测定结果如图1所示。通过该图可知,在水灰比一定的情况下,在水泥净浆中单掺硫铝酸盐水泥和水玻璃均能极大程度缩短其凝结时间和初终凝时间间隔,缩短程度随掺量的增加而增大。

3.2 流动度和20min流动度损失

流动度的大小直接影响施工机械和注浆压力的选择,流动度是注浆材料搅拌完成后的初始流动度,20min流动度即注浆材料在搅拌完成后静置20min的流动度,二者差值即为注浆材料的20min流动度损失。

由图2可知,内掺硫铝酸盐水泥对水泥净浆的初始流动度影响不大,随掺量的增加而适当减小,20min流动度损失低于水泥净浆的流动度损失;在水泥净浆中掺入水玻璃会大幅降低其初始流动度,并随水玻璃掺量的增加而减小,其20min流动度损失非常小。

3.3 强度

本文测定了注浆材料在不同配合比下的1d和28d抗压抗折强度,试件尺寸(长×宽×高)为40mm×40mm×160mm。试验结果如表4所示。

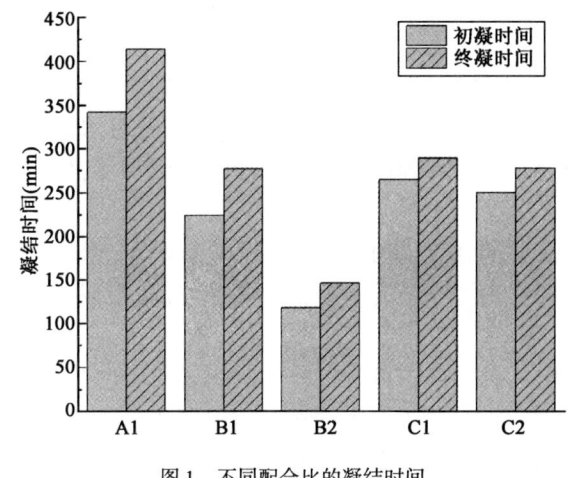

图1 不同配合比的凝结时间

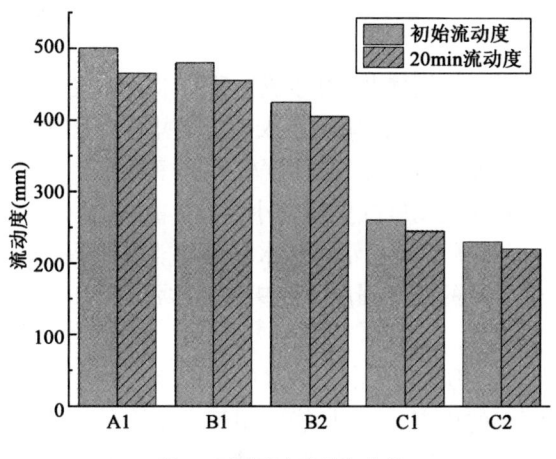

图2 不同配合比的流动度

不同配合比的强度　　　　　　　　　　　　　　　　　　　　表4

编　号	1d 抗折强度(MPa)	1d 抗压强度(MPa)	28d 抗折强度(MPa)	28d 抗压强度(MPa)
A1	3.13	12.25	9.32	48.62
B1	4.93	15.47	8.84	45.36
B2	5.28	16.72	9.45	42.77
C1	3.38	14.77	7.83	47.73
C2	4.35	24.20	6.07	40.67

由表4可知,在水泥净浆中内掺硫铝酸盐水泥和水玻璃都能有效提高其1d强度,而且提高幅度随掺量的增加而增大,但是会降低28d强度,降低幅度随掺量增加而增大,总体而言,强度对掺入水玻璃的敏感度更大。

3.4 收缩性能

本文测定注浆材料的干缩性能,试件尺寸(长×宽×高)为 25mm×25mm×280mm,测定其7d、14d、21d 和 28d 收缩率,不同配合比的注浆材料在不同龄期的收缩率如图3所示。

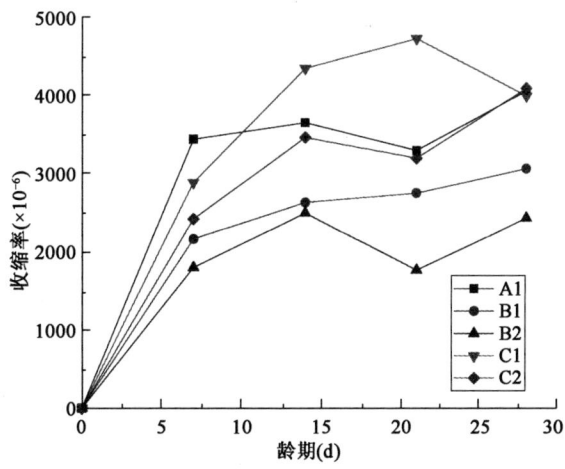

图3 不同配合比的注浆材料在不同龄期的收缩率

通过图3可知,注浆材料的收缩率随时间的增加而增大,内掺硫铝酸盐水泥和水玻璃的掺入能抑制水泥净浆的干缩,抑制效果随掺量的增加而增大,但是内掺硫铝酸盐水泥的抑制效果更好。

4 结 语

通过水泥净浆、内掺硫铝酸盐水泥注浆材料和掺入水玻璃注浆材料对比试验,可以得到以下结论:

(1)在水泥净浆中掺入硫铝酸盐水泥和水玻璃均能有效减少其凝结时间,硫铝酸盐水泥对水泥净浆的流动度影响较小,流动度较水泥净浆变化不大,水玻璃的掺入极大程度降低水泥净浆的流动度,但三者的20min流动度损失都较小。

(2)硫铝酸盐水泥和水玻璃均能有效提高水泥净浆的早期强度,并随掺量的增加而增大,但会降低注浆材料的28d强度。硫铝酸盐水泥和水玻璃的掺入能抑制水泥净浆的干缩,其中硫铝酸盐水泥的抑制效果更好。

综上所述,在水泥净浆中掺入硫铝酸盐水泥或水玻璃,二者均具有可调控凝结时间、流动度损失小和收缩小的优点,二者均能应用于需要短期开放交通的道路加固,但内掺硫铝酸盐对使用环境有一定要求,而水玻璃注浆材料的流动性较小,对加固深度有极大的影响;普通水泥净浆虽然性能偏于劣势,但是其具有取材容易和工艺简单的优点。因此,在实际工程中应根据实地情况进行注浆材料的选用。

参考文献

[1] 朱军军.高速铁路岩溶路基加固及效果检测研究[D].成都:西南交通大学,2017.
[2] 王丽娜.注浆技术在路基加固中的机理及应用研究[D].济南:山东大学,2017.
[3] 赵明华,刘汉龙.地基处理研究进展[J].土木工程学报,2016,49(1):96-115.
[4] 张磊,问鹏辉,王朝辉,等.道路非开挖注浆加固补强材料研究进展[J].材料导报,2017,31(21):98-105.
[5] 麻鹏飞,李爽,程宝军,等.碱激发矿渣水泥基材料收缩性能研究[J].无机盐工业,2020,52(10):145-150.
[6] 杨世玉,赵人达,靳贺松,等.粉煤灰地聚物砂浆早期强度的影响参数研究[J].工程科学与技术,2020:1-8.
[7] 常浩.软土路基沉降病害治理的注浆加固技术及其试验研究[J].路桥科技,2016(28).
[8] 杨新安,郭乐,王树杰.高速铁路软土路基有控注浆技术现场试验研究[J].西南交通大学学报,2018,53(01):15-22.
[9] 孙海波.非开挖注浆加固工艺在沪嘉高速公路大修工程中的应用[J].建设监理,2018(06):71-73.
[10] 邓尤东,帅建国,罗光财.快硬硫铝盐水泥单液浆性能研究及应用[J].铁道科学与工程学报,2012,9(03):99-105.
[11] 严国超,白龙剑,张志强,等.PU改性硫铝酸盐水泥注浆材料试验与应用研究[J].煤炭学报,2020:1-7.
[12] 甄泽强.水玻璃类浆材注浆性能及工程应用研究[D].太原:太原理工大学,2019.

Study on Multi-Scale Finite Element Model for Bridge Load Test

Wei Wang

(Chongqing Zhongke Constructin Quality Inspection Co., Ltd.)

Abstract The traditional beam finite element model has some shortages for bridge load test, so the multi-scale finite element model combined beam element with solid element for bridge load test is proposed. The modelling method and process of multi-scale model is introduced firstly, and then the accuracy of multi-scale model is verified by structural static and dynamic performance, the multi-scale model is applied for bridge load test finally. It can provide a more reliable basis for safe operation, management and scientific research of bridge.

Keywords Bridge engineering Load test Finite element model Multi-scale simulation Model verification

0 Introduction

Scientific decision-making for bridge maintenance during the lifetime requires accurate assessment of the technical condition and bearing capacity of bridge. The load test is the most direct and effective method to assess the bearing capacity of bridge(Wang 2017). It compares the measured value obtained from field load test with the theoretical value calculated by finite element model(FEM), and evaluates the bearing capacity of bridge. However, the traditional beam finite element model (Beam FEM) has many disadvantages, for example, the measured values of some measurement points cannot be directly compared with the theoretical values, and cannot reveal the local stiffness change and mass distribution of bridge(Yu 2012; Li et al. 2015; Chen et al. 2015). At the same time, the bridge load test not only assesses the bearing capacity of bridge, but also provides measured data for scientific research, such as shear lag effect, eccentric load effect of bridge, etc. (Zhou and Nie 2014; Zhu et al. 2014; Zhou et al. 2015; Shi and Wu 2019). In view of this, the multi-scale finite element model (Multi-Scale FEM) combined beam element with solid element for bridge load test is proposed.

1 Engineering Situation

The research object is a four-span asymmetric continuous rigid-frame bridge with the span combination of (65 + 125 + 180 + 110) m. The superstructure is a prestressed concrete single box and chamber girder. The thickness of wing plate is 28cm and the web plate is 50 ~ 70cm, the thickness of bottom plate is 32-120cm, the width of top plate and bottom plate is 15.14m and 8m respectively, and the height of box-girder is gradually changed from 3m at the mid-span to 10m at the pier-top. The substructure is reinforced concrete thin-walled box pier with bored pile foundation, No. 3 and No. 4 pier are installed artificial anti-collision island. The design load is Highway-I with bi-directional and four-lane, the crowd load is $3.5kN/m^2$. The bridge ranked the first in Asia among similar bridges when completed. The current situation of bridge is shown in Fig. 1.

Fig. 1 Current Situation of Bridge

2 Multi-Scale Finite Element Simulation

The bridge structure FEM is different according to the purpose of calculation and analysis, the modelling strategies are also different(Li et al. 2009). The FEM for the purpose of bridge design is established with the parameters specified in codes. The establishment of bridge FEM for the purpose of construction control focuses more on the simulation of construction process. The FEM establishment for the purpose of bridge load test analysis needs to consider and simulate the finished dead state correctly, and the design live load analysis should be carried out on this basis, because the bridge structure is already in the completed state at this time, the structure has already had endured a large internal force under dead loads such as structure self-weight and other dead loads.

In order to obtain both the global structural performance and local stress of bridge structure in the completed state under experiment loads and to reduce FEM size and calculation time, the Multi-Scale FEM of bridge is proposed. The core idea of this method is that we should establish a full-scale beam element FEM of bridge and calculate the internal force envelope of the structure under design live load to select the control section firstly; then we should establish small-scale solid element FEM of the control section, which selected in the previous step; finally, the two scales finite element models are coupled into one through master-slave node coupling, coupling degrees of freedom, multi-point constraint equations, etc. (Yu et al. 2012; Wang et al. 2014; Lu et al. 2019), in other words, embedding the small-scale solid element FEM into the full-scale beam element FEM so as to get both the global structural performance and local stress from Multi-Scale FEM.

2.1 Control Section Selection

The full-scale FEM is established by using all beam element and the internal force envelope of the bridge under design live load is calculated to select the most unfavorable stress section, i.e. the control section. The internal force envelope of the bridge is shown in Fig. 2.

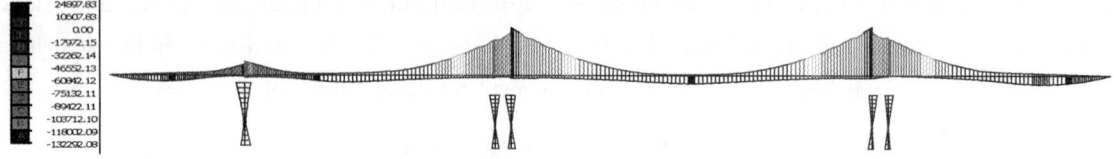

Fig. 2 The Internal Force Envelope of Bridge (Unit: kN·m)

According to the structural internal force envelope shown in Fig. 2, combined with the requirements of the code and the characteristics of the bridge (Wang et al. 2017), the 3-4# pier mid-span section, near 4# pier-top section, and 4-5# pier maximum positive bending moment section are finally selected as the control sections, as shown in Fig. 3.

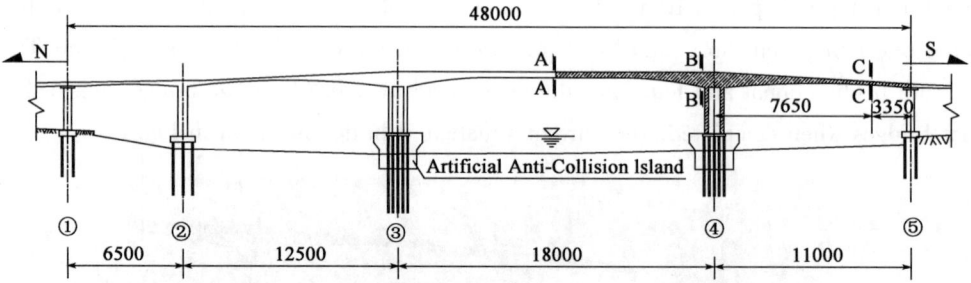

Fig. 3 Control Section Selection (Unit: cm)

2.2 Multi-Scale Model Establishment

The control sections selected in the previous step are simulated with solid element to establish the small-scale FEM, and the models of different scales are coupled into one by master-slave node method. The Multi-Scale FEM as shown in Fig. 4.

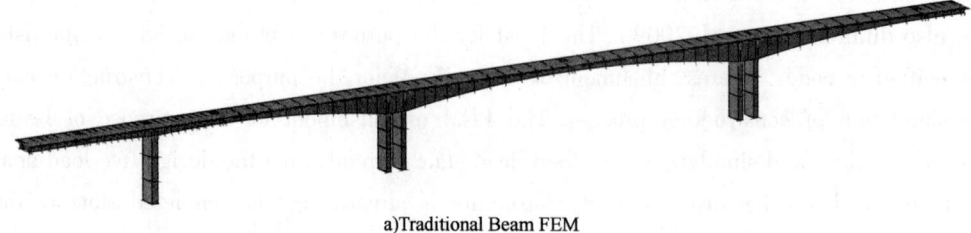

a) Traditional Beam FEM

Fig. 4

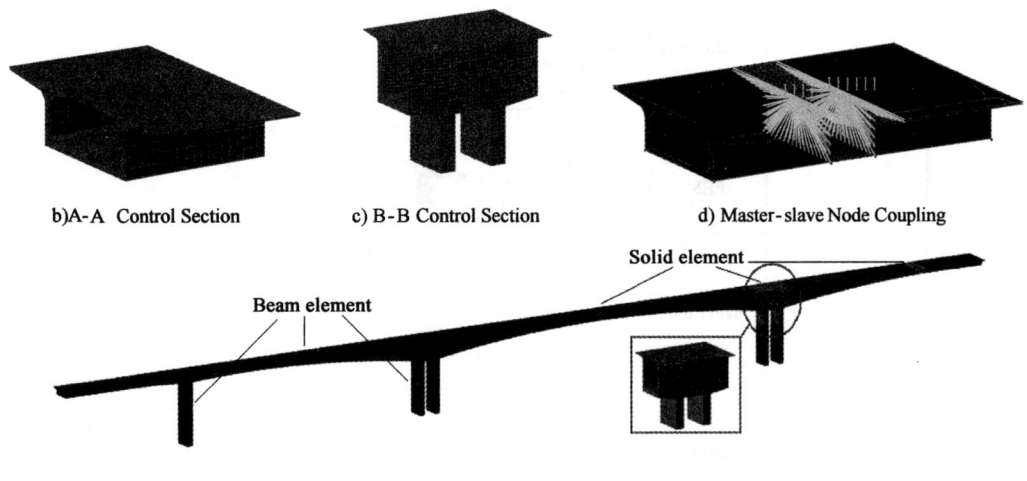

Fig. 4 Multi-Scale FEM Modelling Process

3 Multi-Scale Model Verification

A good Multi-Scale FEM can not only accurately reveal the static performance of the structure, but also be consistent with the dynamic characteristics of the actual structure. Considering that the modelling of traditional Beam FEM is mature, and it is generally used to guide design and construction, so it has the function of comparison and verification. Thus the accuracy of Multi-Scale FEM is verified by comparing both the static characteristics, mainly including the internal force, reaction force and displacement response under dead load and the dynamic characteristics, mainly including the natural frequencies and mode shapes with the traditional Beam FEM.

3.1 Dynamic Characteristics Verification

The Multi-Scale FEM has to be verified is accurate and valid before applied to practical engineering and further research. The dynamic characteristics are the inherent characteristics of structure and independent of external loads. Simultaneously, the dynamic characteristics reveal the structural global mass, stiffness distribution and structural type, so the dynamic characteristics of Multi-Scale FEM are verified firstly.

The natural frequencies comparison of the two scales finite element models are shown in Tab. 1. In the table, the error = $|(①-②)|/②$, the same below.

Comparison of the First Six Ranks Vertical Frequencies of the Structure   Tab. 1

Modal rank	Natural frequency (Hz)		Error(%)	Modal shape
	①Beam FEM	②Multi-Scale FEM		
1	0.929080	0.911705	1.87	1st Symmetric Vertical
2	1.308800	1.293541	1.17	1st Anti-symmetric Vertical
3	1.463614	1.461247	0.16	2nd Symmetric Vertical
4	2.062468	2.052839	0.47	2nd Anti-symmetric Vertical
5	2.321203	2.317838	0.14	3rd Anti-symmetric Vertical
6	3.318327	3.305159	0.40	3rd Symmetric Vertical

The first three ranks vertical modal shapes comparison of the two scales finite element models are shown in Fig. 5.

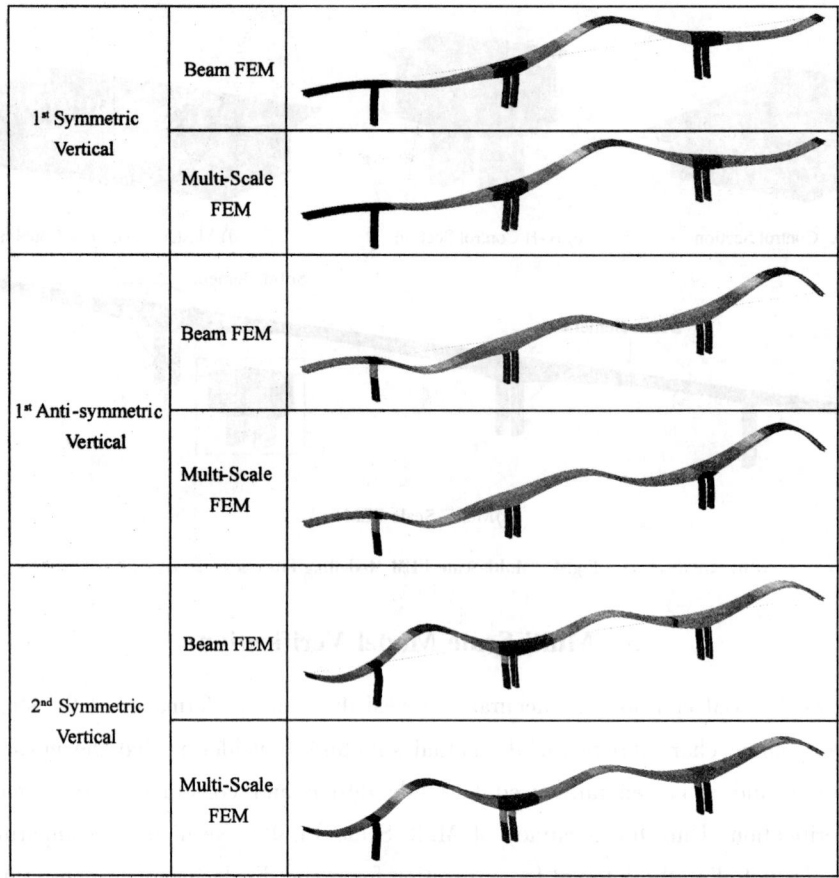

Fig. 5　Comparison of the First Three Ranks Vertical Modal Shapes of the Structure

From Tab. 1, it can be concluded that the calculated natural frequencies of the two scales models are basically the same with the maximum error of 1.87% and all within 2%. From Fig. 5, it can be concluded that the modal shapes calculated by the two scales models are also consistent. It shows that the Multi-Scale FEM can reveal the structural dynamic characteristics of the bridge accurately.

3.2　Static Performance Verification

In order to further verify the accuracy of the above-mentioned Multi-Scale FEM, the global displacement and support reaction forces of each pier under dead load are compared with the traditional Beam FEM. The global displacement comparison curve is shown in Fig. 6, and the comparison of the support reaction force at each bridge pier is shown in Tab. 2.

Comparison of Support Reaction Force at Each Pier　　Tab. 2

Pier number	Support reaction force (kN)		Error (%)
	①Beam FEM	②Multi-Scale FEM	
1#	5704.95	5663.18	0.73
2#	37445.62	37408.85	0.10
3-1#	18079.56	18682.05	3.33
3-2#	61901.79	63391.16	2.41
4-1#	57254.84	57452.73	0.34
4-2#	25971.81	25812.71	7.71
5#	7760.70	7707.81	0.68
Resultant Force	216119.27	216118.49	0

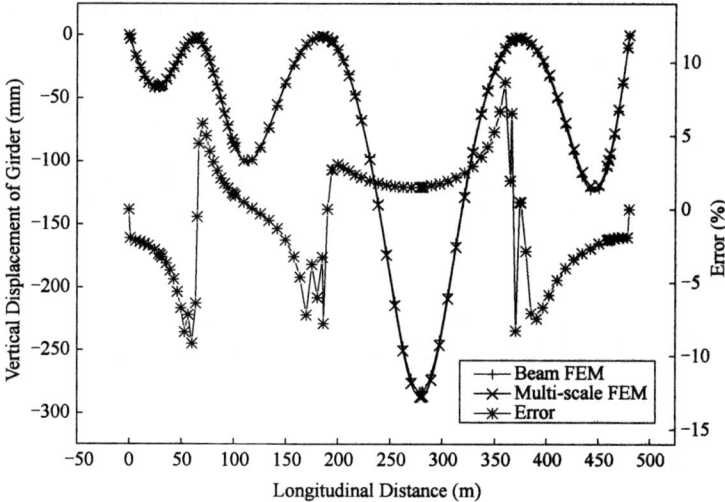

Fig. 6 Deflection Comparison of Box-girder under Dead Load

The internal force comparison of control sections of the two scales models under design live load is shown in Tab. 3.

Internal Force Comparison of Control Section under Live Load   Tab. 3

Control section	Internal force(kN · m)		Error(%)
	①Beam FEM	②Multi-Scale FEM	
A-A	23260.49	23361.94	0.43
B-B	-132300.56	-125455.12	5.17
C-C	24900.73	24730.94	0.68

As known in Fig. 6, the global displacement change trend of the two scales models is consistent and the difference is small under dead load, the errors are all below 10% with the maximum 9.14%. It can be known from Tab. 2 that the errors of the support reaction force at the piers are all below 8% with the maximum 7.71%, which occurs at the No. 4-2# pier. From Tab. 3, it can be concluded that the internal force values of control sections of the two scales models are almost the same under the design live load, the maximum error is 5.17%, which are all within 6%. The static structural response errors are all within the allowable range, that is, the accuracy of the Multi-Scale FEM meets the civil engineering requirements.

In summary, it can be concluded that the Multi-Scale FEM composed of beam elements and solid elements using master-slave node method is correct, accurate and feasible, and it can be used for bridge static and dynamic load tests.

4 Bridge Load Test Design

The bridge load test is mainly to reveal the global deformation and local stress distribution under experiment load. The global deformation of the bridge is measured by arranging deflection measurement points along the longitudinal direction of bridge deck, and at the same time, deflection measurement points are arranged on the upstream and downstream sides of bridge deck to reveal the deformation of the bridge under eccentric load. The arrangement of deflection measuring points is shown in Fig. 7.

In order to obtain the actual stress distribution of the box-girder under experiment load, five strain measuring points are respectively arranged on the top and bottom plates of the three control sections along the horizontal bridge, and five strain measuring points are respectively arranged on the upstream and downstream web plates along the height direction of box-girder. The arrangement of the strain measurement points of the B-B control section is shown in Fig. 8.

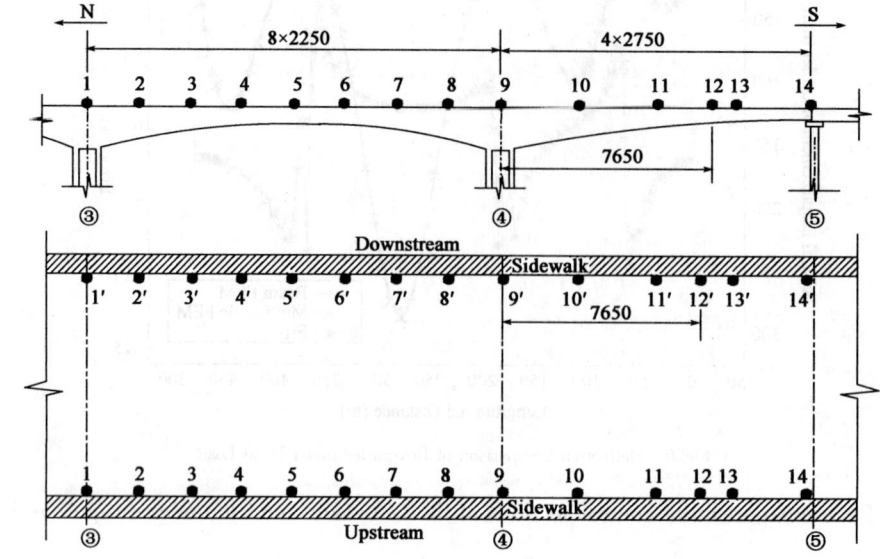

Fig. 7 The Deflection Measuring Points Arrangement(Unit:cm)

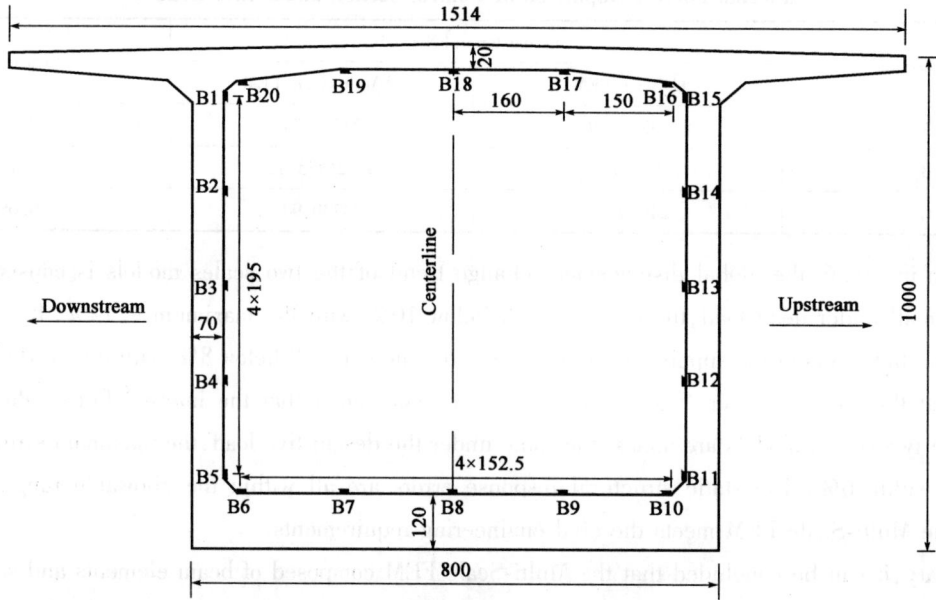

Fig. 8 The strain measurement points arrangement of B-B(Unit:cm)

5 Conclusions

In view of the shortages that the traditional Beam FEM cannot reveal the local stiffness change and mass distribution of the structure, and the time-consuming, inconvenient post-processing of the full-scale solid element FEM, the Multi-Scale FEM combined beam element with solid element for bridge load test is proposed. The accuracy of the Multi-Scale FEM is verified by comparing the structural static and dynamic performance with beam FEM, and the accuracy of Multi-Scale FEM meets the civil engineering requirements, it can not only be used for bridge static and dynamic load tests to assess the bearing capacity of bridge, but also provide measured data for scientific research, such as shear lag effect, eccentric load effect, etc. The Multi-Scale FEM can simulate the global structural performance and local stress of the bridge very well, and it is more comprehensive to obtain information, faster calculation speed and less resources occupancy, and it has higher precision and efficiency than full-scale beam element FEM or solid element FEM.

References

[1] Wang W. Cases Analysis of Bridge Load Test[M]. Beijing:China Water & Power Press,2017.
[2] Yu Y. Multi-Scale Modelling of Long-Span Bridges for Health Assessment in Structural Health Monitoring [M]. Hong Kong:Hong Kong Polytechnic University,2012.
[3] Li X F,Ni Y Q,Wong K Y,et al. Structural Health Rating(SHR)-Oriented 3D Multi-Scale Finite Element Modeling and Analysis of Stonecutters Bridge[J]. Smart Structures and Systems,2015,15(1),99-117.
[4] Chen L,Qian Z,Wang J. Multiscale Numerical Modeling of Steel Bridge Deck Pavements Considering Vehicle-pavement Interaction[J]. International Journal of Geomechanics,2015,16(1),B4015002.
[5] Zhou M,Nie J G. Multi-Scale Modeling Method for Main Cable Anchorage Zone of Self-Anchored Suspension Bridge[J]. Bridge Construction,2014,44(1),11-17.
[6] Zhu Q,Xu Y L,Xiao X. Multiscale Modeling and Model Updating of a Cable-Stayed Bridge. I:Modeling and Influence Line Analysis[J]. Journal of Bridge Engineering,2014,20(10),04014112.
[7] Zhou M,Ning X X,Nie J G. Multi-Scale FEA Modeling Method for Mechanical Behavior Analysis of Arch Feet on Tied Arch Bridge[J]. Engineering Mechanics,2015,32(11),150-159.
[8] Shi Y X,Wu X G. Research on Shear Lag Effect of Assembling Wide Continuous Box Girder Bridge[C]. // in Proceedings of the 2019 World Transport Convention. Beijing,China,2019,819-829.
[9] Li Z X,Chan T H T,Yu Y,et al. Concurrent Multi-Scale Modeling of Civil Infrastructures for Analyses on Structural Deterioration-Part I:Modeling methodology and strategy[J]. Finite Elements in Analysis and Design,2009,45(11),782-794.
[10] Yu Y,Chan T H T,Sun Z H,et al. Mixed-Dimensional Consistent Coupling by Multi-Point Constraint Equations for Efficient Multi-Scale Modeling[J]. Advances in Structural Engineering,2012,15(5),837-853.
[11] Wang F Y,Xu Y L,Qu W L. Mixed-Dimensional Finite Element Coupling for Structural Multi-Scale Simulation[J]. Finite Elements in Analysis and Design,2014,92,12-25.
[12] Lu W,Cui Y,Teng J. Mixed-Dimensional Coupling Method for Box Section Member Based on the Optimal Stress Distribution Pattern[J]. Measurement,2019,131,277-287.
[13] Wang W,Zhang Y P,Huang B,et al. Study on Static Load Test Optimization of Long-Span Continuous Rigid Frame Bridge with High Piers[J]. Journal of China & Foreign Highway,2017,37(1),98-101.

基于RAP精细化分离技术的全比例冷再生微表处技术在高速公路中的应用

高立波[1,2] 周健楠[1,2] 戴康瑜[3] 张 伟[3] 齐盛涛[3]

(1.辽宁省交通科学研究院有限责任公司;2.高速公路养护技术交通运输行业重点实验室;
3.辽宁交投公路科技养护有限责任公司)

摘 要 沥青路面再生技术的发展在道路建设中占据重要地位,微表处作为良好的预防性养护技术,使用依赖性也日益凸显。因此,本文介绍了一种基于RAP材料精细化分离技术手段的全比例冷再生微表处技术,实现了铣刨料与微表处技术的高效融合,并成功将全比例冷再生微表处技术应用在高速公路养护维修项目中。经过验证分析,该技术不仅各项路用性能指标满足规范要求,而且与全新料微表处技术相比,具有降噪、与乳化沥青配伍性好、便于施工和降低工程造价的优点。

关键词 道路工程　精细化分离技术　全比例冷再生　微表处

0　引　言

在我国高速公路陆续建成通车的情况下,根据我国高速公路设计使用年限来算,每年将会有接近12%的路面需要维修,沥青路面废料约220万t,而这一数字还将以每年15%的速度增长。废旧料不仅占用土地资源,同时还会造成生态环境的破坏与污染。

微表处作为一种预防性养护施工技术,在沥青路面出现轻微的病害或者还未出现病害的情况下使用,针对微表处技术的广阔应用前景并结合我国绿色交通发展方向,本文介绍了一种基于精细化分离技术手段的全比例冷再生微表处技术,实现了铣刨料与微表处技术的高效融合,达到了沥青路面铣刨料100%再生利用。其技术核心为采用专用聚合物改性乳化沥青、RAP粗、细集料、填料、水和添加剂等按照设计配合比拌和成稀浆混合料摊铺到原路面上,形成符合快速开放交通要求的一种薄层结构,与全新料微表处技术相比,具有降噪、与乳化沥青配伍性好、便于施工和节省工程造价的优点。

1　全比例冷再生微表处原材料

1.1　精分离后RAP

基于精细化分离技术,将RAP破碎筛分成0~3mm、3~5mm、5~10mm三档材料,用于微表处沥青混合料,相关精分离后RAP筛分数据见表1。为了保证全比例再生微表处的路用性能,还要严格控制RAP的假粒径含量。采用抽提前后筛除率偏差指标评价RAP的假粒径,试验结果如图1所示。结果表明关键筛孔假粒径含量低于10%。

精分离后RAP筛分数据　　　　　　表1

材料	粒径(mm)	沥青含量(%)	通过下列筛孔(mm)的百分率(%)								
			13.2	9.5	4.75	2.36	1.18	0.6	0.3	0.15	0.075
RAP	5~10	1.49	100.0	99.6	4.3	0.5	0.5	0.5	0.5	0.5	0.3
RAP	3~5	2.73	100.0	100.0	89.4	23.6	12.7	7.1	3.5	1.8	0.7
RAP	0~3	7.78	100.0	100.0	100.0	89.6	68.3	43.7	17.1	4.6	1.3

1.2　乳化沥青

本文所选的乳化沥青为辽宁瑞德公路科技有限公司生产的阳离子BCR产品,相关检测结果见表2。

乳化改性沥青检测结果　　　　　　表2

试验项目		技术要求	测试结果
恩格拉黏度(25℃)		3~30	6.3
1.18mm筛上剩余量(%)		≤0.1	0.0
蒸发残留物	含量(%)	≥60	63.1
	针入度(25℃,100g,5s)(0.1mm)	40~100	95
	软化点(℃)	≥53	54.0
	延度(5℃)(cm)	≥20	34
	溶解度(三氯乙烯)(%)	≥97.5	99.3
储存稳定性	1d(%)	≤1	0
	5d(%)	≤5	3

辽宁省重点研发计划项目;辽宁省科学技术计划项目(2020JH2/10300097)。

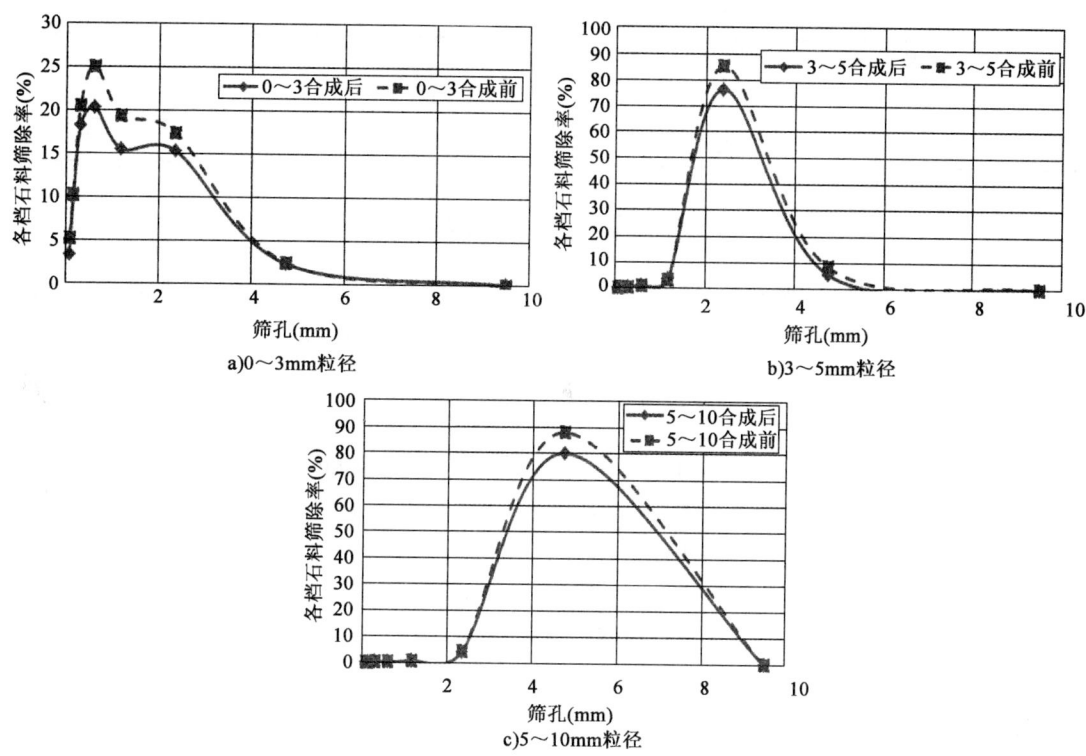

图 1　精细分离后的抽提前后各档 RAP 不同筛孔筛上筛除率(%)

1.3　再生剂

再生剂为辽宁省交通科学研究院有限责任公司研发的 LJK-Z2 型,相关检测结果见表 3。

再生剂检测结果　　　　　　　　　　　　　　　　　　　表 3

检测项目	技术要求	试验结果
闪点(℃)	≥220	240
饱和分含量(%)	≤30	15.6
芳香分含量(%)	≥60	61.8
薄膜烘箱试验前后黏度比	≤3	1.48
薄膜烘箱试验后质量变化(%)	≤4,≥-4	1.6
密度 15℃(g/m³)	实测	0.940

1.4　填料

填料选择的是 P.O42.5 水泥,生产厂家为辽宁交通水泥有限责任公司(亚泰集团),相关检测指标见表 4。

水 泥 检 测 结 果　　　　　　　　　　　　　　　　　　表 4

检测项目		技术要求	试验结果
表观密度(t/m³)		实测记录	2.979
比表面积(m²/kg)		≥300	381
凝结时间(min)	初凝	≥45	188
	终凝	≤600	421
安定性		—	无裂纹和弯曲
抗折强度(MPa)	3d	≥17	18.0
	28d	≥6.5	7.1

续上表

检测项目		技术要求	试验结果
抗压强度(MPa)	3d	≥3.5	4.3
	28d	≥42.5	44.5

2 全比例冷再生微表处混合料级配

根据各集料、水泥、矿粉、回收料RAP的筛分数据,按照设计文件中的微表处沥青混合料级配范围,经反复计算、调整,确定各材料掺配比例(表5),合成级配曲线如图2所示。

原材料信息及掺配比例　　　表5

序号	名称	规格/型号	产地/厂家	比例用量(%)
1	粗集料	碎石 5~10mm	路面现场铣刨	20
2	粗集料	碎石 3~5mm	路面现场铣刨	30
3	细集料	机制砂 0~3mm	路面现场铣刨	50
4	水泥	P.O42.5	辽宁交通水泥有限责任公司(亚泰集团)	1.5(外掺)
5	乳化沥青	阳离子BCR	辽宁瑞德公路科技有限公司	7
6	再生剂	LJK-Z2	辽宁智信公路工程技术咨询有限公司	0.4(混合料)

级配范围	通过下列筛孔(mm)的百分率(%)								
	13.2	9.5	4.75	2.36	1.18	0.6	0.3	0.15	0.075
全新料微表处级配上限	100.0	100.0	90.0	70.0	50.0	34.0	25.0	18.0	15.0
全新料微表处级配下限	100.0	100.0	70.0	45.0	28.0	19.0	12.0	7.0	5.0
全比例冷再生微表处合成级配	100.0	99.9	77.7	52.0	38.1	24.1	9.7	2.9	0.9

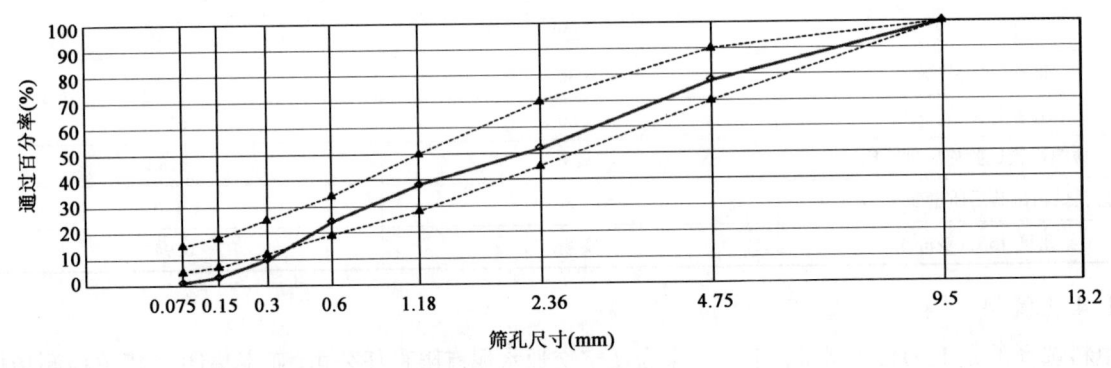

图2　精分离全比例冷再生微表处沥青混合料合成级配曲线

由于全比例冷再生微表处单挡集料采用未经过抽提的通过率,细集料被沥青裹覆,导致合成后0.3mm筛孔以下通过率较低。从图2中也可以看出,全新料微表处对0.3mm筛孔以下的级配范围要求,并不适合全比例旧料的微表混合料,此部分研究工作正在进行中。

3 全比例冷再生微表处混合料路用性能

3.1 可拌和时间试验

根据确定的全比例冷再生微表处混合料原材料比例,进行拌和试验,拌和时间满足试验要求。拌和时间试验结果见表6。

拌和时间试验结果 表6

原材料掺配比例(%)					试验结果
集料	水泥	水	添加剂	乳化沥青	
100	1.5	5	0.4	7	>180s

注:1. 集料以100%的干集料为基础。
　　2. 设计要求拌和时间大于120s。

从拌和试验得到,水泥填料对此系统的影响也比较大。如果使用或增加水泥用量,需要使用添加剂,否则会给施工带来很大困难。

3.2 黏结力试验

相容性很好的微表处混合料系统,其乳化沥青量、矿物填料、添加剂等的变化,将会影响混合料黏结力的变化。而微表处混合料在一定时间内能否具有内聚力,是通过黏结力试验考察的,同时,黏结力试验可以对微表处混合料系统能否开放交通的时间长短进行分类。本试验中黏结力试验结果见表7。

黏结力试验结果 表7

原材料掺配比例(%)					黏结力(N·m)	
集料	水泥	水	添加剂	乳化沥青	30min	60min
100	1.5	5	0.4	7	1.5	2.3

注:1. 集料以100%的干集料为基础。
　　2. 设计要求黏结力30min大于1.2N·m,60min大于2.0N·m。

3.3 湿轮磨耗试验

当乳化沥青用量变化时,混合料系统的相容能力通过湿轮磨耗试验来描述。湿轮磨耗试验结果见表8。

湿轮磨耗试验结果(25℃) 表8

原材料掺配比例(%)					磨耗损失值(g/m²)
集料	水泥	水	添加剂	乳化沥青	
100	1.5	5	0.4	7	338

注:1. 集料以100%的干集料为基础;
　　2. 设计要求磨耗损失测值不大于540g/m²(浸水1h)。

3.4 负荷轮试验

负荷轮试验的目的是控制高等级道路微表处施工时混合料沥青用量上限,当用乳化沥青过多时,施工中将会出现泛油现象,混合料产生变形。负荷轮试验结果见表9。

负荷轮试验结果 表9

原材料掺配比例(%)					宽度变化率(%)
集料	水泥	水	添加剂	乳化沥青	
100	1.5	5	0.4	7	4.66

注:1. 集料以100%的干集料为基础。
　　2. 设计要求宽度变化率不大于5%。

4 全比例冷再生微表处试验路铺筑

依据施工设计要求、施工组织设计,以及现场人员、设备准备情况,于2020年9月8日分别在桓永高速公路永陵方向K43+951和K45+514两座中桥上进行精分离、全比例冷再生微表处试验路施工。通过本次试验段的施工,验证了配合比,明确了施工参数、混合料生产控制方法及现场工艺操作等。

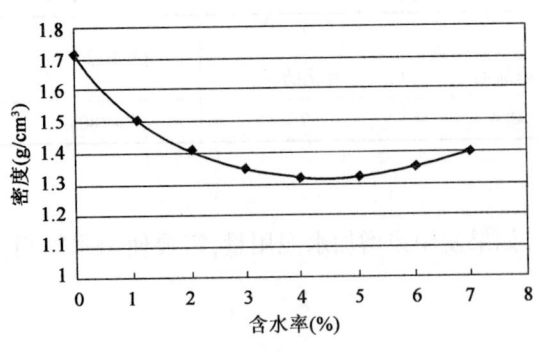

图3 全比例冷再生微表处矿料含水率曲线

4.1 用水量和稠度控制

破碎后的RAP石料与全新石料相比,其含水率较大且不稳定,因此在全比例冷再生微表处施工前需对设备进行标定,确定最佳用水量。参照《细集料紧装密度的测试方法》(T 0331—1994),检测矿料在含水率0~7%情况下的单位体积干料质量。以1%的含水率间隔,绘制矿料的"含水率-单位体积干矿料质量"的关系曲线,如图3所示。另外,需以摊铺车的标定为依据,得出摊铺车各材料出料量与泵的设定或各料门开度等的关系曲线。

4.2 超粒径及细料凝块控制

由于经过精分离破碎后,RAP集料易出现超粒径和细料凝块的现象,因此建议在微表处摊铺车内加设9.5mm筛片和振动设备,保证全比例冷再生微表处粒径的稳定性。

4.3 摊铺控制

全比例冷再生微表处采用的RAP集料中石料不含电荷,与乳化沥青配伍性好,且精分离后RAP石料形状好,这些特点很好地解决了全新料微表处摊铺过程难以控制的问题,因此全比例冷再生微表处对于摊铺的控制相对简单。

对于接缝处的摊铺控制,横向接缝处不得出现混合料堆积或缺料现象,用3m直尺测量时,接缝处的平整度应小于6mm,两幅摊铺面搭接宽度不应超过75mm。摊铺机摊铺后,应使用橡皮耙子找平摊铺过厚或不平处,并及时用稀浆修补漏补不足处。对摊铺机无法施工部分,应采取手工作业,外观尽量与机械摊铺路段一致,如需要可在施工前将手工作业路段预湿。

4.4 初期养护控制

全比例冷再生微表处的初期养护与全新料微表处相比无明显差异,在开放交通前禁止一切行人和车辆通行,且一般不需要压路机碾压。

4.5 试验路检测

施工后5d对精分离全比例冷再生微表处试验路进行检测,检测项目包括构造深度、摩擦因数及渗水,检测和观测结果见表10。

全比例冷再生微表处试验路检测、观测结果 表10

路段名称	桩号	检测位置	构造深度(mm)	摩擦因数BPN	渗水系数(mL/min)
桓永高速公路	K43+951	行车道	0.9	67	0
	K45+514	行车道	1.0	65	0
	试验路平均值		0.9	66	0
	原路面平均值		0.7	51	5.2
	设计要求		>0.6	>45	<10

从表10检测和观测结果可见,两段微表处试验路的各项指标均能够满足设计要求。与原路面相比,路面服务功能明显提高。

由于全比例冷再生微表处的集料被旧沥青层裹覆,与全新石料相比更加圆润,理论上可认为再生料微表处噪声要小于全新料微表处。对此,本文作者采用AWA6228型多功能声级计对全比例冷再生微表处试验路与全新料微表处路段进行了道路噪声振动监测对比,对比方式分别为同一车辆车速80km/h时的车内噪声和监测20min车外综合噪声。测试结果如图4所示。

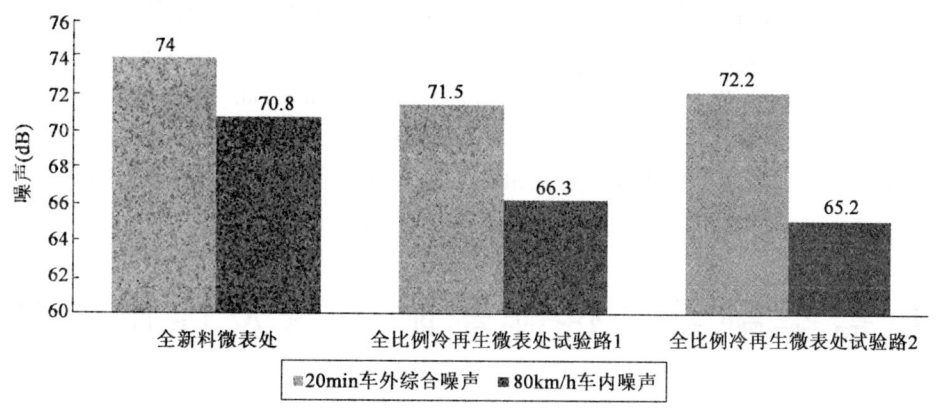

图 4　全比例冷再生微表处噪声对比图

从图中可看出,全比例冷再生微表处试验路与全新料微表处路段相比,当车速为 80km/h 时的车内噪声可降噪 4~5dB,20min 车外综合噪声可降噪 2~3dB。

5　结　语

(1)通过精细化分离技术后得到的 RAP 原材料,可以采用抽提前后筛除率偏差指标评价 RAP 的假粒径,并且试验结果证明精细化分离技术达到了关键筛孔假粒径含量低于 10%,实现 RAP 材料 100% 再生利用。

(2)由于全比例冷再生微表处单挡集料采用未经过抽提的通过率,细集料被沥青裹覆,导致合成后 0.3mm 筛孔以下通过率较低。即全新料微表处对 0.3mm 筛孔以下的级配范围要求,并不适合全比例冷再生的微表混合料。但经过合理的级配组合优化,全比例冷再生微表处的路用性能均可以满足相关技术规范要求。

(3)通过对全比例冷再生微表处的试验路的铺筑,验证了采用 100% 精分离 RAP 铺筑微表处的施工便利性、可行性及优越性,且车速为 80km/h 时的车内噪声可降噪 4~5dB,20min 车外综合噪声可降噪 2~3dB。

(4)将精分离 RAP 应用于全比例冷再生微表处,可以节省乳化沥青 35% 及 100% 石料,具有巨大的社会、经济、环境效益。

参考文献

[1] 顾建军,虞将苗,杨震. 基于加速加载试验的湖沥青微表处路用性能研究[J]. 公路,2017,62(5):221-226.
[2] 陈筑苏. 微表处技术和预防性养护在公路养护工程中的应用[J]. 公路,2012,57(6):260-264.
[3] 许秀美,丁良珉,周洁,等. 微表处稀浆混合料施工性能影响因素分析[J]. 山东交通科技,2019,(3):32-35.
[4] Xiaolong Sun,Xiao Qin,Shanqiang Li,et al. Characterization of thermal insulating micro-surfacing modinfied by inorganic insulating material[J]. Construction and Building Materials,2018,175:296-306.
[5] 樊尚志,张雅杰. 掺加 RAP 的微表处混合料性能研究[J]. 新型建筑材料,2019,46(09):19-23.
[6] 马瑞锋,王景亮,周士光,等. 回收沥青路面材料(RAP)在微表处中的应用研究[J]. 中国建材科技,2019,28(03):62-64.
[7] 张富奎. 铣刨回收沥青混合料在古永高速公路微表处中的再生应用[J]. 中国建材科技. 2017(06).
[8] 张来栋,肖鑫厚. 水泥对微表处混合料路用性能影响及其机理研究[J]. 硅酸盐通报. 2013(05).
[9] Rajesh Gujar. VinayVakharia. Prediction and validation of alternative fillers used in micro surfacing mixdesign using machine learning techniques[J]. Construction and Building Materials,2019,207:519-527.

[10] 任丽娜.再生沥青混合料在微表处技术中的应用研究[D].西安:长安大学,2017.
[11] 周洲.不同RAP料掺量热再生改性沥青混合料耐久性能研究[D].南京:东南大学,2015.
[12] Martins Zaumanis, Rajib B. Mallick. Review of very high-content reclaimed asphalt use in plant-produced pavements: state of the art[J]. International Journal of Pavement Engineering, 2015(1).
[13] 叶兴龙.沥青再生料在微表处技术中的应用[J].山西建筑,2017,43(18):91-93.

氯盐类融雪剂性能影响因素及评价方法

夏金平 韩森 张秋瑞
(长安大学公路学院)

摘要 氯盐类融雪剂会腐蚀并降低建筑物使用寿命,由此带来巨大的经济损失,但因其价格低、除冰雪效果好,在部分地区仍大量使用。基于融雪剂除冰雪、混凝土盐冻破坏及钢筋锈蚀机理,提出改善氯盐类融雪剂除冰性能及缓解建筑物损伤的方法,并简要介绍相关试验方法。

关键词 道路工程 融雪剂 凝固点 化冰率 盐冻破坏 腐蚀

0 引言

融雪剂具有价格低、高效及能有效破坏冰与路面联结的优点,大量用于冬季道路养护,常用融雪剂有氯盐类、非氯盐类及植物型环保融雪剂[1]。氯盐类融雪剂相对于其他类型融雪剂而言,具有成本低、除冰雪效果较好的优点,在部分地区仍大量应用。而在冬季氯盐融雪剂环境中,混凝土极易发生盐冻破坏及钢筋的锈蚀,进而造成结构物失效并带来巨大经济损失[2]。

当前研究主要致力于新型低温无腐蚀、环保融雪剂的研发,而对氯盐类融雪剂路用性能的系统研究较少[3]。因此,分析融雪剂除冰雪及低温氯盐环境中混凝土产生盐冻和钢筋锈蚀现象的机理及相关评价方法,提出改善氯盐类融雪剂除冰性能及缓解建筑物损伤的方案,对于提高氯盐类融雪剂性能具有重要意义。

1 机理分析

1.1 融雪化冰机理

依据稀溶液的依数性定理,稀溶液的凝固点降低和蒸气压下降只与溶质粒子数目(即浓度)有关。基于此,可从以下两方面揭示融雪剂化冰机理:一是融雪剂能降低水的凝固点,使冰雪能在负温度环境中融化;二是融雪剂被喷洒后,吸收空气及冰雪表面水分并溶解,形成溶液的蒸气压逐渐降低,为了达到固—液两相蒸气压平衡,冰块融化以稀释溶液[4]。

从融雪剂自身理化性质角度:凝固点越低,冰与溶液的化学势能差越大,化冰效果越好[5]。溶液中的溶质粒子与冰块相互接触是冰水转化的前提,化冰时冰水分界面处的溶质粒子被稀释,同时不断有新的粒子转移至分界面,转移速率与溶质粒子扩散率有关,液体融雪剂扩散率越大,化冰效果越好[6]。

1.2 盐冻破坏机理

融雪剂溶液通过细微裂缝及孔隙渗入结构物内部,混凝土及钢筋与之发生物理及化学反应后强度显著降低,最终导致结构物失效。徐港等[7]试验发现,普通水泥混凝土抗水冻次数约为抗盐冻的2.7倍,混凝土在冬季融雪剂溶液环境主要为盐冻破坏,特点为表面剥蚀和内部损伤。此外,化学侵蚀相对于盐冻

基金项目:长安大学中央高校基本科研业务费专项资金资助项目(300102219207)。

破坏对混凝土强度影响较小[8]。

静水压理论和渗透压理论是解释混凝土冻融破坏机理的经典理论[9]。静水压理论[10]认为混凝土孔隙水结冰膨胀受阻造成内部损伤,该理论仅能解释普通冻害。渗透压理论[11]认为在表面张力作用下,孔隙水的凝固点与孔径正相关,孔道中的冰块和过冷溶液间存在饱和蒸气压及盐分浓度差使溶液在孔道中迁移产生渗透压,当超过孔隙抗拉强度时即产生裂缝。渗透压理论能较好揭示融雪剂的有害作用,不能解释为什么中低浓度融雪剂的盐冻破坏最严重以及剥落现象[12]。

Valenza 等[13]的黏结—剥落理论指出,由于冰层与混凝土的热膨胀率不同,随着温度降低,冰层收缩开裂并向混凝土施加应力,外加力作用下混凝土裂缝不断发展,最终导致表层剥落。由于冰层强度与盐溶液浓度负相关,可认为中低浓度融雪剂盐冻破坏严重[14]。

杨全兵教授[15]认为黏结—剥落理论存在不合理之处,基于有限元和断裂力学理论分析,剥落物尺寸应大于碎屑,但实际与之相反,于是对常温下混凝土饱水度和 NaCl 溶液结冰压和结冰膨胀率展开研究,以揭示盐冻破坏机理。试验发现,随着溶液浓度增加,结冰压和结冰膨胀率迅速降低,这对缓解盐冻是有利的;而盐的吸湿性会增加混凝土平衡饱水度和吸水速度,且与浓度正相关,这不利于缓解盐冻。将上述两种正负效应叠加后,发现浓度为 2%~6% 的破坏力最大,较好地解释中低浓度融雪剂盐冻破坏最严重的原因。

杨全兵教授[16]进一步测试冻融循环条件下,不同浓度 NaCl 溶液对混凝土吸水量和饱水度的影响。发现混凝土吸收溶液只发生在冷冻阶段,在冷冻时,表层混凝土的饱水度高于内部,揭示了冷冻阶段混凝土表面存在的盐溶液是导致剥蚀的主要原因。

1.3 钢筋腐蚀及阻锈机理

1.3.1 钢筋腐蚀机理

在氯盐类融雪剂环境中,氯盐侵蚀是导致钢筋锈蚀的主要原因(图1)。水泥水化产生的碱性环境中,OH^- 易吸附在钢筋表面形成钝化膜保护钢筋。但 Cl^- 半径小、活性大,易透过钝化膜,降低 PH 值进而破坏钝化膜,氧气和水分进入钢筋,锈蚀开始。钝化膜破坏部位露出铁基(阳极)、钝化膜区域(阴极)及混凝土空隙中溶液(电解质),形成腐蚀电池,导致钢筋产生点状锈蚀并快速发展。

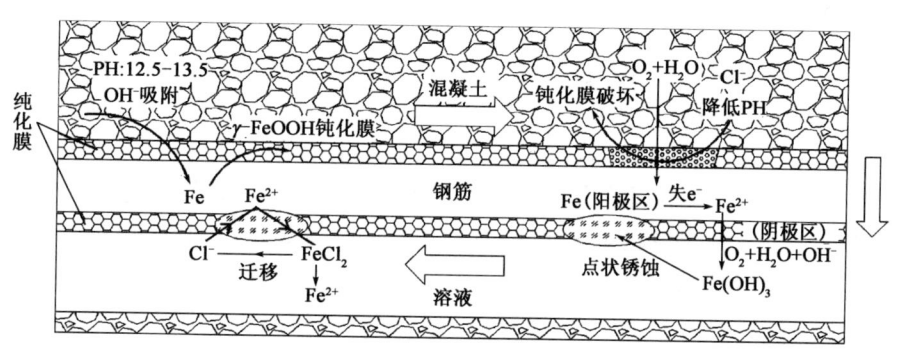

图 1 氯盐侵蚀示意图

此外,Cl^- 会加速钢筋腐蚀:阳极产生的 Fe^{2+} 与 Cl^- 反应生成 $FeCl_2$ 并向外扩散,阻止阳极的 Fe^{2+} 堆积,从而促进 Fe 失去电子(即 Cl^- 的阳极去极化作用);Cl^- 的导电性有利于腐蚀电池中阴极、阳极之间电荷转移[17]。

1.3.2 阻锈机理

常用的钢筋防护方法有涂层保护、阴极保护及使用阻锈剂,而阻锈剂与其他方法相比,用于保护建筑物结构钢筋较经济有效。阻锈剂可通过抑制腐蚀电池阴、阳极反应保护钢筋:降低腐蚀电位进而降低阴、阳极得失电子能力,或增大电荷转移电阻,降低腐蚀电流。此外,阻锈剂可在钢筋表面反应形成致密氧化膜保护钢筋[18]。

2 评价指标及方法

2.1 融冰雪性能

融雪剂的融冰雪性能一般采用凝固点和化冰率评价。一定质量融雪剂降低凝固点效果越好、短时间融冰量越大,其融冰雪性能越好。

2.1.1 凝固点

理论及实验研究表明,溶液的质量浓度与凝固点线性正相关。基于陈美婷等[19]提出的强电解质稀溶液的凝固点降低公式,推导出融雪剂凝固点降低值与质量浓度的关系式(1)。

$$\Delta T_f = \frac{v \times K_f \times C \times 1000}{M_B} \tag{1}$$

式中:ΔT_f——凝固点降低值,℃;
  v——溶液中粒子种类;
  C——质量浓度,%;
  M_B——相对分子质量。

按式(1)计算 $CaCl_2$、$NaCl$ 和 C_2H_5OH 质量浓度为5%和10%的凝固点理论值和李萍等[20]通过凝固点降低法测得的实测值,如表1所示。由表1可知,理论值与实测值在浓度为5%时差异较小,而在10%时差异较大。这是因为理论公式适用于稀溶液条件,因此实践中一般采用实测值。

融雪剂凝固点理论值与实测值(℃) 表1

质量浓度	融雪剂凝固点	$CaCl_2$	$NaCl$	C_2H_5OH
5%	理论值	-2.51	-3.18	-2.02
	实测值	-2.35	-3.10	-2.05
10%	理论值	-5.02	-6.36	-4.04
	实测值	-6.00	-7.15	-4.77

2.1.2 化冰率

采用化冰率评价融雪剂的融冰雪性能的主要有两种方法:一是,依据公路战略研究计划(SHRP)提出的融雪剂融冰试验方法,融雪剂处理冰块后,采用某一时间冰块融化质量的百分率(化冰率)评价融雪剂的融冰性能。二是,我国在SHRP计划基础上提出了相对化冰率指标,以便于融雪剂间性能对比:按使用浓度配制的融雪剂溶液与18%氯化钠溶液或29%的二水氯化钙溶液0.5h融化冰块质量之比为相对化冰率,该值大于90%时合格。融雪剂的化冰率或相对化冰率越大,融冰雪性能越好。

笔者按上述方法测量化冰率及相对化冰率,发现难以彻底分离融雪剂溶液和冰块,采用称量的方式确定融化的冰块质量导致导致结果的重复性及精确度较差,但基本满足对融雪剂性能评价的要求。

2.2 结构物损伤

2.2.1 盐冻法

氯盐环境中混凝土的抗冻性能可通过《普通混凝土长期性能和耐久性试验方法标准》(GB/T 50082—2009)中的快冻法评价。该方法主要利用单面冷冻试验箱(图2)实现冻融循环。试验时,每4个循环测试单位表面面积剥落物总质量和超声波相对动弹性模量,当单位表面面积剥落物总质量 >1500g/m² 或超声波相对动弹性模量降低到80%或达到28次冻融循环时停止试验,并用上述任意值表示混凝土抗冻性能。

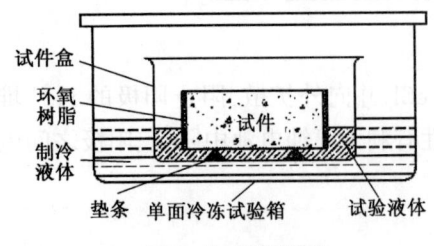

图2 快冻试验装置

2.2.2 旋转挂片法

《融雪剂》(GB/T 23851—2017)推荐采用旋转挂片法测试碳钢腐蚀率,以评价腐蚀性。具体方法为:将处理好的碳钢片置于按使用浓度配制的试液中,试验温度为40±1℃,48h后碳钢腐蚀率低于0.11mm/a为合格,新旧规范关于碳钢腐蚀率测试方法的对比如表2所示。

碳钢腐蚀试验方法对比　　　表2

标　准	融雪剂浓度	水浴温度	试验时间	通入空气否	判定指标
《道路除冰融雪剂》(GB/T 23851—2009)	50g/L	45±1℃	72h	是	0.18mm/a
《融雪剂》(GB/T 23851—2017)	使用浓度	40±1℃	48h	否	0.11mm/a

通常,低浓度溶液的碳钢腐蚀率较大。为了使结果符合实际工况,《融雪剂》(GB/T 23851—2017)规范改为按使用浓度试验。温度对结果的影响不显著,为了节约能源,将试验温度降为40℃。研究表明,48h和72h的试验结果差异并不显著,所以试验时间缩短为48h。有学者提出:发生电化学腐蚀时,Cl^-在阳极起作用而O_2在阴极起作用,当缺少O_2时腐蚀过程受阻,认为试验时通入空气更符合实际。事实上,对于48h的试验时间,是否通气的结果差异较小。此外,实际操作时较难保证通气量相同,因此《融雪剂》(GB/T 23851—2017)推荐试验时不通气[21-22]。

3　结　语

凝固点低、质量扩散率大的融雪剂,除冰雪效果较好。对于固体融雪剂,使用时撒布越均匀,除冰雪效果越好。

只要使用融雪剂就会产生盐冻破坏,避免使用低浓度融雪剂可有效减轻盐冻破坏。此外,可从改善混凝土性质入手:一是在混凝土表面使用疏水材料,减少水分进入;二是掺入硅灰,增加混凝土密实性;三是掺入引气剂,引入气泡,以切断毛细孔渗水通道,降低饱水度及缓冲静水压和渗透压[23-24]。

优化融雪剂的组配降低Cl^-含量,使用缓蚀剂、阻锈剂等外加剂能抑制氯盐类融雪剂对钢筋的腐蚀[25,26]。此外,缓解盐冻,阻止混凝土内部损伤发展也是保护结构物钢筋的有效方法。

冰雪融化伴随融雪剂溶液不断被稀释,而溶液的电导率与质量浓度相关性较好。基于上述两种化冰率测试方法,通过电导率与化冰率之间的关系间接评价融雪剂化冰性能,就能避免分离冰块和溶液,提高试验结果的准确性。

参考文献

[1] Fay L, Shi X. Environmental impacts of chemicals for snow and ice control: state of the knowledge[J]. Water, Air, & Soil Pollution, 2012, 223(5): 2751-2770.

[2] 王艳春, 白雪薇, 李芳. 氯盐融雪剂对城市道路绿化带土壤性状的影响[J]. 环境科学与技术, 2011, 34(11): 59-63.

[3] 周小鹏, 黄军瑞, 王腾, 等. 我国道路融雪剂应用现状及发展趋势[J]. 辽宁化工, 2019, 48(09): 920-922+925.

[4] Nilssen K, Klein-Paste A, Wåhlin J. Accuracy of ice melting capacity tests: Review of melting data for sodium Chloride[J]. Transportation Research Record, 2016, 2551(1): 1-9.

[5] Wåhlin J, Klein-Paste A. Chemical melting of ice: Effect of solution freezing point on the melting rate[J]. Transportation Research Record, 2016, 2551(1): 111-117.

[6] Wåhlin J, A Klein-Paste. The effect of mass diffusion on the rate of chemical ice melting using aqueous solutions[J]. Cold Regions Science and Technology, 139(2017): 11-21.

[7] 徐港, 龚朝, 刘俊, 等. 混凝土抗水冻融和盐冻融循环作用的相关性[J]. 建筑材料学报, 2020, 5: 1-10.

[8] 吴泽媚. 氯盐和冻融对混凝土破坏特征及机理研究[D]. 南京: 南京航空航天大学, 2012.

[9] 段桂珍, 方从启. 混凝土冻融破坏研究进展与新思考[J]. 混凝土, 2013(05): 16-20.

[10] Powers. A working hypothesis for further studies of frost resistance of concrete[J]. Journal of American

[11] Powers T C, Helmuth R A. Theory of volume changes in hardened cement paste during freezing[J]. Proceedings of the Highway Research Board,1953,32(5):285-297.
[12] 曹瑞实,田金亮.不同除冰盐冻融环境下对混凝土耐久性的影响[J].硅酸盐通报,2013,32(12):2632-2636.
[13] Valenza J J, Scherer G W. Mechanism for salt scaling of a cementitious surface[J]. Materials and Structures,2006,40(3):259-268.
[14] 徐亚丁,王玲,王振地.混凝土冻融/盐冻破坏现象、机理和试验方法[J].硅酸盐通报,2017,36(02):491-496,514.
[15] 杨全兵.混凝土盐冻破坏机理(Ⅰ)——毛细管饱水度和结冰压[J].建筑材料学报,2007(05):522-527.
[16] 杨全兵.混凝土盐冻破坏机理(Ⅱ):冻融饱水度和结冰压[J].建筑材料学报,2012,15(06):741-746.
[17] 陶鹏.融雪剂对碳钢腐蚀的研究[D].北京:北京化工大学,2007.
[18] 马世豪,李伟华,郑海兵,等.钢筋阻锈剂的阻锈机理及性能评价的研究进展[J].腐蚀与防护,2017,38(12):963-968.
[19] 陈美婷,顾聪,姚喆,等.强电解质稀溶液的依数性公式导出及实验验证[J].大学化学,2019,34(01):92-97.
[20] 李萍,魏西应,念腾飞,等.季节性冻土区沥青路面融雪剂凝冰点测试[J].硅酸盐通报,2019,38(05):1561-1567.
[21] 陈宗伟,张立塔,赫恩龙,等.公路融雪剂碳钢腐蚀性检测方法及缓蚀工艺研究[J].公路,2011(12):177-181.
[22] 王树轩,李宁,李波,等.氯盐型融雪剂碳钢腐蚀性的测定新方法[J].盐业与化工,2012,41(01):19-23.
[23] 杨博渊.混凝土除冰盐冻害性能退化及改善措施研究[D].北京:中国矿业大学,2016.
[24] 王瑞芳,吴永畅,程国义.水泥混凝土盐冻损害影响因素与防治措施研究[J].公路,2015,60(01):198-202.
[25] 张爱勤,贾坚,王彦敏,等.复合环保型融雪剂的优化组配试验研究[J].盐科学与化工,2018,47(11):31-34.
[26] 徐俊辉,韩俊甜,苏志俊,等.公路除冰融雪剂中添加剂的研究[J].中国井矿盐,2019,50(02):36-39.

A Mechanical Approach to Restore Road Friction Coefficient under Various Snowpack Conditions

Weixin Yang　Jinrui Shi　Xiaochen Zhang　Sirui Zhang

(SnowLion)

Abstract　Under ice and snow conditions, the road surface tends to become slippery and result in a loss of surface traction; this oftentimes is the cause to traffic accidents. This paper proposes a novel mechanical design to recovery the road friction coefficient in the snow weather. The ice-breaking & snow-removal equipment uses mechanical energy to break pavement bonded ice efficiently with minimal damage to the road surface. Experiments have been conducted to validate the proposed mechanical design. For most type of snowpack, the mechanical design can restore road access with only one-time ice-breaking & snow removal operation.

Keywords Mechanical Ice-breaking Snowpack Road friction coefficient Winter road maintenance

0 Introduction

Winter road maintenance is critically importance due to the dangers; it attributes to the winter road hazards where travellers are often confronted with snowy, slushy and icy road conditions. In order to better understand the effect of snow on traffic, we classified the snowpack into six categories according to its density, including new snow, powder snow, settled snow, slush, snow crust, and firn (Benson et al., 1962). The main determinants of density of snow are compaction degree and humidity.

The road friction coefficient (RFC) may significantly change under different type of snowpack, which results in potential risks to traffic (Wallman et al., 2001). To recover the RFC, we developed pure mechanical ice-breaking & snow-removal equipment rather than snow-melting chemicals. In recent years, mechanical ice-breaking & snow-removal equipment for breaking the bond between snowpack and ice and the pavement surface emerges as a revolutionary solution to replace traditional ice-melting chemicals for winter road maintenance. This technology use engineering designed tooth to crush and break the snowpack and bonded ice effectively that cannot be removed by regular snow shovel or salt. However, the efficiency and effectiveness of mechanical ice-breaking and snow-removal equipment under different types of snowpack conditions remains elusive. Therefore, we conducted a study aiming to investigate how much friction coefficient between road and vehicles could be recover using mechanical ice removal system for winter road management under six types of snow road conditions.

1 Snowpack Description and Effect of Snow on Rfc

Before any further discussion about the mechanical method of ice-breaking, it is crucial to understand the feature of different types of snowpack. To better understand the effect of snow on traffic, we describe the snowpack as six typical types. They are new snow, powder snow, settled snow, slush, snow crust, and firn. The snow road has a small RFC with low texture depth. Due a thin transparent film of water, snow RFC reaches the minimum around zero degree Celsius, which significantly decreases road safety. Vehicles are prone to rollover and tail swing, which may result in collisions. First, this section investigates the range of variation of RFC under six different snowpack conditions.

1.1 Type of Snow Cover

We categorized the road snowpack into six types. New snow freshly fallen snow at shallow temperature. Powder snow is dry new snow, which is composed of loose and fresh ice crystals. Settled snow that has been strongly metamorphosed and compacted. Slush is substantially melted snow with visible water in it. Snow crust indicates a layer of snow on the surface of the snowpack that is stronger than the snow below, which results from partial melting of the snow surface by direct sunlight or warm air followed by re-freezing. The firn is rounded, well-bounded snow that is older than one year and has a density higher than 550 kilograms per cubic meter. The types of snow road are shown in Fig. 1.

1.2 RFC Measurement

Different type of snowpack will have a different range of RFC, which may be an additional risk factor to the road. A Dynamic Friction (D. F.) Tester is used to measure the RFC under a different type of snow road (Henry et al. ,2000). The D. F. Tester is a portable instrument to measure the friction characteristics of paved surfaces in laboratories and on-field at roads, highways, and other areas. The D. F. Tester is able to plot the relationship between the dynamic RFC and the vehicle velocity with a single measurement. The speed associated measurement resolution could reach 0.1 miles/h, and the D. F. Tester can obtain reliable measurement results in a velocity range from 12 to 50 miles/h.

Fig.1 S6 Types of Snowpack

D. F. Tester is reliable due to its relatively simple structure and its measurement principle (Andersson et al. ,2007). A tire with load W runs on a road with speed V, and the torch surface will generate a measurable friction force F.

In this case, the governing system of equations can be written as follows:

$$\mu = \frac{F}{W} \tag{1}$$

the RFC μ is obtained. Furthermore, the friction coefficient μ has a variation of direct proportion with friction force F with a constant load of W, such that we can rewrite the equation(1) as

$$\mu = F \times k \tag{2}$$

Where, k is a proportional constant.

The D. F. Tester diagrammatic drawing is shown in Fig. 2. The D. F. Tester has a round disk. Three rubber sliders are mounted on the lower surface of the round disk that rotates with its plane parallel to the test surface. Once the spinning disc reaches the operator set and software controlled circumferential speed, the control system initiates water delivery and lowers the spinning disc to the test surface. Then rubber sliders will be pressed to the surface by the weight of the device. The torque generated by the friction between the rubber sliders and the test surface as the spinning disc is slowed down is measured. The calculated force then is divided by the weight of the disk and motor assembly to calculate the friction coefficient.

We chose to measure the RFC in a university open empty parking lot during the winter break with a speed limit of 15miles/h. The parking lot has a layer of asphalt pavement, which is similar to most highways and city roads. The experiment began with each new snowfall at a temperature of -10 degree Celsius. D. F. Tester was mounted to a vehicle that operated at a constant speed at 15miles/h. Five replicated of the experiment was performed to measure the friction on the road for various snow road conditions. It was relatively easy to measure

RFC with new snow and powder snow. In order to form settled snow on the ground, a vehicle was used to repetitively compress the snow once the snow has accumulated 4 inches. For slush, the area was irrigated with water and pressed by the vehicle. After some time has passed, the surface of the slush refreezes to form the snow crust. Firn will form after watering the road with snow crush several times.

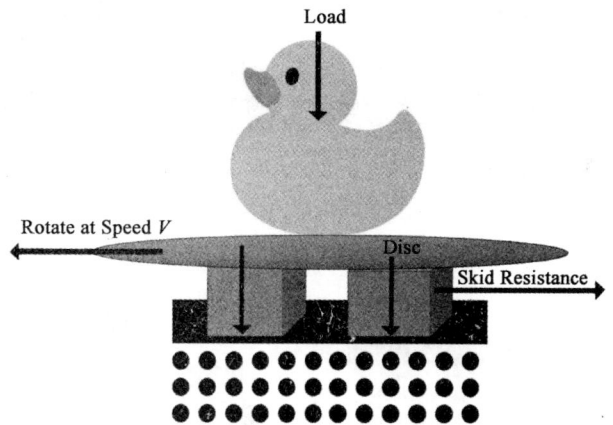

Fig. 2　D. F. Tester Diagrammatic Drawing

For each type of snow, we measured the RFC five times shown in Tab. 1.

RFC with Six Types of Snowpack　　　　Tab. 1

T RFC SP	1	2	3	4	5	Average
NewSnow	0.65	0.68	0.73	0.64	0.6	0.66
PowderSnow	0.63	0.7	0.66	0.64	0.56	0.64
Slush	0.33	0.38	0.28	0.41	0.39	0.33
SettledSnow	0.22	0.21	0.18	0.32	0.26	0.24
SnowCrust	0.11	0.09	0.11	0.10	0.08	0.10
Firn	0.08	0.08	0.09	0.10	0.07	0.09

We can conclude from the Tab. 1, before the snow crust fully covers the road, that is when the snowpack is in new snow and powder snow status, the RFC decreases in a range of 0.15. This RFC decrease will not significantly impact driving safety during new snow and powder snow stage. However, the settled snow and slush are formed after many times pressing the snow, which results in an RFC of 0.22 to 0.33. The steering force cannot keep the vehicle stable at the turning point due to the slip. The low RFC makes driving at high-risk activity. Furthermore, after the crust fully covers the road, the RFC severely decreases to around 0.10, the vehicle is no longer safe to operate at such condition.

In this section, we introduce the features of six types of snowpack. We investigate the range of variation of RFC under six different snowpack conditions with the D. F. Tester. And we conclude that the new snow and powder snow will decrease the RFC to increase the risk of driving. The driving risk will significantly increase after many layers of snow settled, and finally form the crust. It is hard to remove those risks when the snow crust and firn are formed with snow melts and regular snow removal equipment. In the next section, we will introduce a novel mechanical device to remove road risks.

2　Mechanical Ice-breaking & Snow-removal Equipment, and Comparative Experiment

Mechanical ice-breaking & snow-removal equipment has been developed and implemented in some winter road maintenance to overcome the limitations and challenges of the previous solution: chemical de-icing agents.

Fig. 3 shows various mechanical ice-breaking & snow removal equipment, where the wheel has teeth that are designed to crack the ice and compressed snow. A shovel and auger system can be added onto the unit to improve work efficiency.

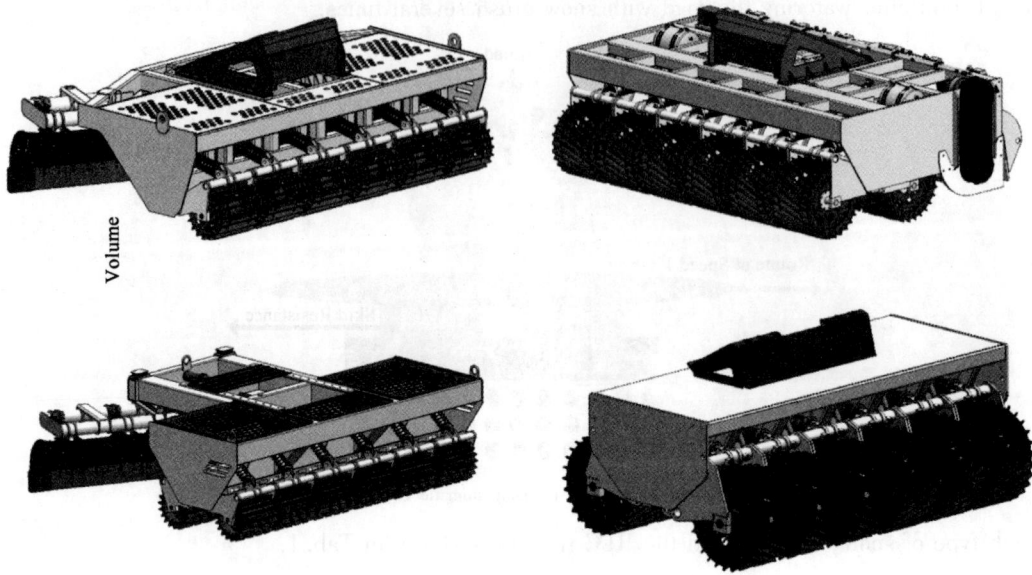

Fig. 3 Mechanical Ice-breaking and Snow-removal Equipment

The development and implementation of mechanical ice-breaking and snow-removal aim at ① maintaining winter roads safe for traveling vehicles by providing solutions for weather conditions varying from light inclement weather to severe conditions and increasing road friction for the cars in all weather conditions; and ②decreasing road chemicals and abrasives to protect the environment, reducing vehicle wear and tear, and preserving current infrastructure.

2.1 Mechanical Ice Removal Equipment Design Principles

The main design principles of the mechanical equipment are the wheels, collection shovels and hydraulic auger. The independently displaced ice-breaking wheels can be utilized to break ice and snow and can contour the road profile. The independently displaced collection shovels are an essential part of the system to gather and empty the ice and snow fragments. To re-expose the road surface, a hydraulically operated drill can be combined into the system. The independently displaced ice-breaking wheels, the independently displaced collection shovels, and the hydraulically operated auger in Fig. 4a)、Fig. 4b) and Fig. 4c), respectively.

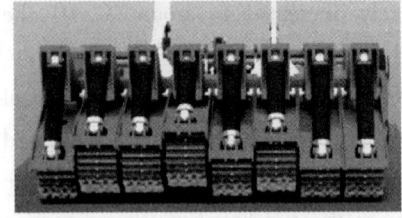 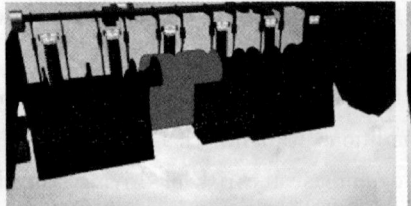 

a)Independently displaced ice-breaking wheels b)Independently displaced collection shovels c)Hydraulically operated auger

Fig. 4 Design principles of mechanical ice removal equipment

A novel and useful operation package contain three principal elements shown in Fig. 4 in the mechanical ice removal equipment with versatile functions. Nevertheless, the most crucial component of the mechanical ice removal design is the ice-breaking wheels that are employed to break the ice or the compact snow. More specifically, it is the design of engineered tooth integrated into the ice-breaking wheels. Based on the ice-breaking requirement, engineered tooth design has the following features. ① Optimize ice, and snowpack removal rate; ②Adopt a high strength/hard material to maximize the wear life; ③ Tooth profile avoids road damage; ④Account for replaceable parts to reduce cost strategies. Four types of possible engineered tooth designs are displayed in Fig. 5, which contains cutter tooth, spike tooth, straight blade, and slant blade options. The general working principle of the ice-breaking tooth is simple but efficient. The engineered ice-breaking tooth can cut the ice into pieces when it is running on the road surface, and then strip the ice from the road, finally pulverize the ice. The usage of special material ensures the minimal loss and long-time use of the ice-breaking teeth.

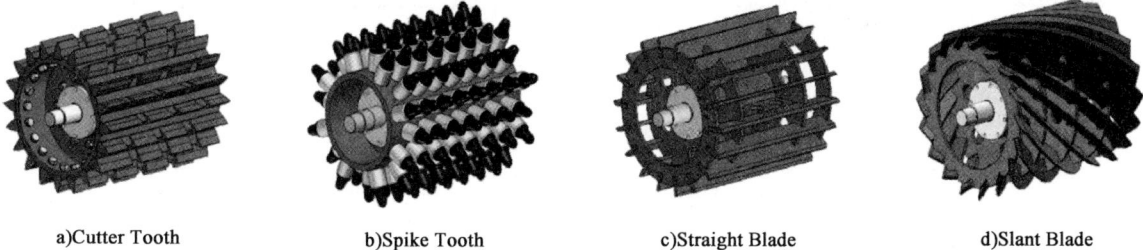

a) Cutter Tooth   b) Spike Tooth   c) Straight Blade   d) Slant Blade

Fig. 5 Four Types of Engineered Tooth Designs for Mechanical Ice-breaking & Snow-removal Equipment

2.2 Comparative Experiment

Considering the complexity of snow road conditions, we equip four types of engineered teeth to break and remove ice from the road surface. More specifically, we set up straight blade for the new snow and the powder snow; we apply cutter tooth for the settled snow; the slant blade is used to break the snow crust; finally, the spike tooth is assembled to break the hardest firn. To compare the range of variation of the RFC in a real road condition, we set up the comparative experiment in the same area with the same vehicle using the D. F. Tester. The four types above of ice-breaking tooth are used aiming to break the ice and remove six types of the snowpack. For a closer resemblance to the real road ice & snow removal requirement, we ran our device one time on the road, and then the D. F. Tester follows to collect the friction coefficient data. For each type of snowpack road, we also complete five measurements, the results are shown below in Tab. 2.

RFC After Ice-breaking & Removal Operation Tab. 2

T RFC SP	1	2	3	4	5	Average
NewSnow	0.70	0.72	0.75	0.70	0.69	0.71
PowderSnow	0.68	0.72	0.73	0.70	0.72	0.71
SettledSnow	0.40	0.39	0.41	0.42	0.39	0.40
SnowCrust	0.38	0.36	0.40	0.39	0.37	0.38
Firn	0.15	0.17	0.10	0.12	0.16	0.14

The experiment results demonstrate the high efficiency of snow removal and ice breaking. For the new snow and powder snow, the RFC is almost back to its original value, which indicates no driving risk from the snowfall. Typically, the settled snow, slush, and snow crust bring problems to the driver; however, the RFC is back to half of the normal value after one time ice-breaking and snow-removal operation. Based on the previous research on the relationship between vehicle velocity and RFC, the vehicles can have a speed of 30 miles/h after one-time ice-breaking operation using the unit. For the hardest firn, which is a more solid form of snow and ice, one pass is not sufficient to break up the pavement bounded ice.

2.3 Pavement Damage Assessment

The biggest concern for the mechanical ice-breaking and snow-removal equipment is the pavement damage. Each ice-breaking wheel is equipped with an independent suspension; this particular mechanical design will reduce the pavement damage to the minimum. To assess the pavement damage after the mechanical ice-breaking operation, we introduce the International Roughness Index (IRI) data, which is shown Fig. 6. The IRI indicates that there is no evidence of additional wear and tear of the pavement surface due to the usage of a mechanical ice breaker.

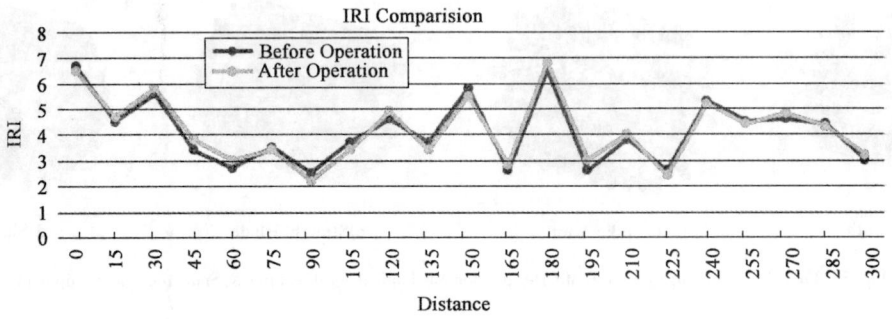

Fig. 6　Pavement Assessment

In this section, we compare the RFC variation range after the one-time ice-breaking and snow-removal operation with our ice-breaking device with engineering designed tooth. The results illustrate the high-efficiency ice-breaking effect and minimum pavement damage.

3　Conclusions

This paper proposed a novel design of ice-breaking device with engineered tooth. The ice-breaking effect and its high efficiency have been approved by the comparative experiments. The pavement is also well-protected with a special designed ice-breaking wheel. For the future work, in addition, to design more types of ice-breaking device according to different types of snowpack and develop auto-pilot ice-breaking vehicle, which is able to remove snowpack at new snow and powder snow stage.

4　Acknowledgements

Studies on mechanical ice-breaking method are fully sponsored by SNOWLION, Reno, NV, USA.

References

[1] Andersson M, Bruzelius F. Road friction estimation[R]. Saab Automobile AB, Trollhättan, Sweden, 2007.

[2] Benson Carl S. Stratigraphic studies in the snow and firn of the Greenland ice sheet[R]. Cold Regions Research and Engineering Lab Hanover NH, 1962, 74, 41-52.

[3] Henry J, Abe H. (2000). Determination of the international friction index (IFI) using the Circular Texture Meter (CTM) and the Dynamic Friction Tester (DFT) [C]. SURF 2000: Fourth International Symposium on Pavement Surface Characteristics on Roads and Airfields World Road Association-PIARC.

[4] Wallman. C. and Astrom H. Friction Measurement Methods and the Correlation Between Road Friction and Traffic Safety: A Literature Review[R]. Statens Vag-och Transport for Skning Sinstitut, 2001.

绿色理念在昌九高速公路改扩建工程中的应用实践

付凯敏[1]　黄智华[2]　曹林辉[1]

（1. 江西赣粤高速公路股份有限公司；2. 江西省交通投资集团有限责任公司）

摘　要　本文总结了江西省昌九高速公路改扩建工程绿色公路的建设实践情况。绿色理念的落实，设计是前提，创新是支撑，施工是关键，只有这样，绿色公路的建设才能得以顺利进行，目标才能得以如期实现。

关键词　高速公路改扩建　品质工程　绿色理念　应用实践

0　引　言

昌九高速公路原为南昌至九江的一条二级汽车专用道，后经多次扩建、续建，1996年成为江西省第一条高速公路。经过20多年的运营，随着沿线地区经济的快速发展，区域交通量大幅增加，道路服务水平已明显下降，难以满足通道交通量迅速增长的需求。自2012年开始，昌九高速公路进入到扩容升级的新阶段，为贯彻落实"创新、协调、绿色、开放、共享"发展新理念，昌九高速公路改扩建项目紧扣绿色公路建设要求，以资源节约、景观和谐、生态友好为核心，创新绿色建造技术，深挖资源利用途径，提升绿色设计理念，严控生态环境污染，全力打造富有"昌九特色"的绿色品质。

1　创新理念与技术

1.1　探索工业化建造模式

项目以打造构件制造中心作为理念创新、管理创新和技术创新的切入点，实行全线72%梁板、84%涵洞以及100%小型构件集中预制，实现"工厂化生产、流水化作业、智能化控制、信息化管理、装配化施工"，并集成应用拌和楼智能监控、钢筋智能加工、模板自动装拆、智能喷淋养生、机器人自动凿毛、智能张拉压浆、构件身份识别、智能安全技术交底和智能视频监控等系统，努力探索工业化建设道路，节约临时用地200余亩，减少人工投入4000余万元，节约机械设备重复性投入约3800万元，引领了江西高速公路建设管理新模式。

构件制造中心、永修服务区分别如图1、图2所示。

图1　构件制造中心

图2　永修服务区

1.2 探索服务区多元化模式

永修服务区按照复合功能型服务区规划建设。一是探索社会化服务模式。该服务区不仅给司乘人员提供服务,同时又面向地方城镇开放,吸引社会人员消费,跳出传统高速公路服务区单一经营模式。二是探索大卖场商业模式。通过规划建设综合商业体,集购物、餐饮、加油等服务为一体,打造一站式服务。三是打造新型旅游业态。结合旅游发展趋势,前瞻式设置房车营地,提供自驾游服务。

1.3 探索桥涵装配化技术

项目全线84%的盖板涵均改为预制装配式门形箱涵,通用尺寸为3m×2.5m、3m×3.5m、4m×3.5m、4m×4.5m,单节长度2~3m,节段质量20~30t,节段安装完成后现浇底板形成整体。同时,项目尝试中小跨径钢筋混凝土桥梁节段预制拼装快速建造技术。除了桩基,其他结构全部采用装配法施工,墩柱、承台、盖梁等采用套筒连接,桥台耳墙、前墙预留现浇段连接,梁板通过横向预应力形成整体,防撞墙与边梁整体预制成形。装配式技术与传统现浇方式相比,建设周期缩短约2/3,降低了施工期间的通行安全风险,为高速公路改扩建期间保持四车道通行提供了有力保证。

装配式箱涵、装配式桥梁分别如图3、图4所示。

图3 装配式箱涵

图4 装配式桥梁

1.4 探索信息化管控技术

项目以智慧工地建设为目标,先后开展了场站信息化管理平台、智能交通组织管控平台、沥青路面质量互联监控、关键工程远程视频监控、隧道健康监测系统等建设,互联网+、大数据、无人机、智能维护设施、自动控制技术、快速检测技术的应用和结合,实现视频监控、智能控制和信息管理模块的集成,做到全过程、实时、动态的管理与控制,做到科学调度和管理。

2 灵活改扩建设计

2.1 因地制宜,灵活运用技术规范

昌九高速公路老路幅存在部分路段原路基宽度仅为18m,为满足四车道通行宽度,需要对两侧山体路堑边坡进行开挖,拓宽为20.5m。项目提出了将原边沟加铺承压式盖板作为土路肩来提升路幅宽度的方案,同时采用20m路基横断面。该方案不仅节省投资800多万元,同时有效避免了路基两侧因路堑边坡开挖而出现坍塌的风险。

2.2 大胆创新,体现先行先试价值

老路幅分离路段原为双幅"人字坡",改扩建后将单幅通行,常规设计需调整为单坡。在《公路工程技术标准》(JTG B01—2014)对路面横坡没有严格规定的前提下,大胆提出了对部分路段试行"人字坡"。该方案在保证行车安全、舒适的前提下,有效减少了路面调坡的工程量,每千米节省造价200余万元,同时解决了多车道路面单坡排水不畅的问题。

2.3 道法自然,打破传统思维定式

在分离路基的老路幅起终点过渡段,原有路基宽度为24.5m,若严格按照分离式路基宽度20.5m设置,则老路基将有4m宽无法利用,造成原有路基资源的浪费。首次尝试增设左侧硬路肩和相应的标线设计,充分利用原有路基,变为五车道路幅宽度,方便应急时小车通行。

信息化综合平台、左侧硬路肩分别如图5、图6所示。

图5　信息化综合平台　　　　　　　　　图6　左侧硬路肩

3　集约与利用资源

3.1　充分减少土地资源占用

用地受限路段设置挡土墙收缩断面,结合路段填土不高(最大填土小于12m)的特点,取消填方大于8m设置的2m平台,改为折线形边坡。另外,项目驻地均租用当地民房或设施,拌和站、预制场等临时设施均利用现有场地或设于红线用地范围内,施工便道利用既有道路或设置在主线红线范围内,在互通区域营造景观微地形,有效消化主线弃土,并大量利用城市渣土作为路基填料等,从而减少临建和取弃土等临时征地500多亩。

3.2　合理循环利用旧资源

项目采用掺砂或碎石等改良措施利用沿线49万 m^3 高液限土,沥青铣刨旧料通过再生利用为路面结构层,节约用地347亩,节省费用1058万元;全线70km的中分带旧新泽西墙拆除后先作为交通隔离设施使用,最后再经过装修处理,作为改扩建后的永久中分带护栏使用,节约用地112亩、节省费用1733万元;全线拆除桥梁、涵洞等形成的旧混凝土较多,采取破碎再生形成集料,用于路基改良、台背回填、低等级路面等。清表土提前规划集中堆放,用于后续绿化种植,隧道洞渣品质好的经过破碎加工作为路面基层材料,品质相对差的用于路基填筑。

3.3　永临设施结合使用

单幅双向通行条件下的中间临时隔离设施按照"永临结合、重复利用"的原则,采取了3种方式:移动钢护栏、预制防撞墩、旧新泽西墙。施工结束后,预制防撞墩用于运营期收费站对向车道的分隔;旧新泽西墙重新作为新中分带防撞墙;移动钢护栏采取租借模式,可继续用于后续改扩建项目(图7)。另外,布置在主线范围的预制梁场地面硬化作为路面垫层或路床利用,隧道临时用电按照永久用电布设,所站监控设施、发电机等提前采购,先用于临时场站。施工便道尽量结合利用当地道路,采取费用补偿的方式,在节约成本的同时,缩短了便道的建设工期。

旧混凝土破碎再利用如图8所示。

图7　旧新泽西墙用于交通维护

图8　旧混凝土破碎再利用

4　提升绿化和景观

4.1　注重设计，追求景观效果

项目以园林景观为核心，以多彩昌北、红色共青精神、生态绿色庐山为主题，形成一片绿、处处景和引景入路、山水相融的和谐自然绿化理念。按照"一路一特色、一区一景观"思路，先后着重围绕新祺周互通打造了梯田景观，艾城互通打造具有中国风特色的山水太极图谱景观，共青南互通打造疏林草地的多彩景观。

4.2　路地协作，打造区域特色

为使高速公路绿化融入沿线自然环境，项目按照路地共建模式，从设计理念、苗木选栽、绿化施工到景观打造，与地方通力协作，全方位谋划，积极将匡庐美景引入高速公路行车环境，将高速公路景观融入沿线生态美景，倾心将昌九高速公路打造成匡庐脚下的景观绿色生态长廊。

4.3　以文塑路，传递文化名片

昌九高速公路与区域人文相融，永修和新祺周收费站以汉代海昏侯城门样式彰显厚重的历史，艾城收费站四坡顶中式民居造型韵味无穷，共青和共青南收费站的学院派形式明理辩学，德安收费站融入江州义门陈牌楼式风格，柴桑收费站一派江南田园风格。另外，沿线分布着富有诗情画意的江南文化，青砖黛瓦白墙声屏障、厚重的古城门样式挡墙、竹文化挡墙、清新的假山和赣鄱鹤文化隧道洞门等，一处处景观传递出一张张文化名片。

新祺周梯田景观、永修收费大棚分别如图9、图10所示。

图9　新祺周梯田景观

图10　永修收费大棚

5 推行节能和环保

5.1 做好文明施工

该改扩建工程路基施工做好临时排水、疏通原有水系,做到带绿施工,减少了水土流失。同时,在拌和站设置沉淀池进行施工废水的净化,有条件的进行施工废水循环利用;场站裸露的地表采取硬化、铺设草皮等进行防护。主要施工区域全部设置绿色围挡,施工便道及施工场地采取降尘措施。

5.2 有效控制污染

桥梁桩基施工推广使用旋挖钻工艺,以减少泥浆,提高效率;拌和楼采用煤改气技术,减少废气排放。服务区排污设施与市政排污系统对接,实现服务区污水零排放。饮用水源保护路段按照"先环保设施,后施工"的原则进行施工。

5.3 推广清洁能源

推广安装屋面太阳能板,提高清洁能源利用比例。具备条件的交安设施等,均采用太阳能供电。服务区配备汽车充电桩,为汽车环保出行提供保障。隧道采用节能照明技术,降低能耗。

6 结 语

昌九高速公路改扩建工程立足国家"五大"发展理念,积极打造品质工程和创建绿色公路,以建设"安全耐久、绿色环保、智慧和谐"的高速公路为目标,努力探索工业化建设道路,积极运用信息化、智能化管理手段,推行装配化施工技术;针对改扩建工程特点,敢于打破定势,在灵活设计、资源利用、节能环保新技术应用上突破传统;注重交旅融合发展,打造多元化服务区模式,并把地方历史人文作为重要元素融入高速公路建设,以景亮路、以文塑路,打造风景如画、自在如家的行车环境。相信昌九高速公路改扩建工程绿色品质的实践经验可为其他项目借鉴和推广应用。

参考文献

[1] 江西省交通设计研究院.南昌至九江高速公路改扩建施工图设计[R].2016.
[2] 中交第二公路勘察设计研究院有限公司.南昌至九江高速公路改扩建预制箱涵通用图[R].2016.
[3] 交通运输部规划研究院.南昌至九江高速公路改扩建景观绿化施工图设计[R].2017.

第二篇 桥梁工程

基于文化、生态、体验的桥梁设计实践初探
——以唐岛海湾大桥为例

李 敏

(重庆交通大学)

摘 要 本文以青岛唐岛海湾大桥的概念设计方案为例,从行人的需求出发对桥型、桥位周边环境及青岛城市特色进行分析,基于文化、生态、体验理念探求符合青岛这座城市的桥梁景观设计方法,以"虹跨海湾,魅力之都"为设计理念,将其与唐岛海湾周边环境结合进行了桥梁的整体设计,希望为其他滨海城市的桥梁景观设计提供参考。

关键词 桥梁景观 仿生学 斜拉桥 海湾 城市新地标

0 引 言

随着时代的进步和社会的发展,桥梁设计行业面对新形势、新需要,也在理论和技术方面不断做出了创新与突破。东南大学交通规划设计研究院院长丁建明教授曾提出了发展新的桥梁景观设计理念,即"基于文化、生态、体验的桥梁创新设计"。为此,借2021世界交通运输大会这次机会,以习总书记提出的"满足人民日益增长的美好生活的需要"及"传播中华优秀传统文化"为准绳,在桥梁设计竞赛当中对设计的桥梁进行了深入的研究与探讨。

这一设计理念以桥梁、建筑、艺术、历史、文化等诸多学科的交叉融合为基础,强调结构的文化创意,注重桥与自然的互动,以桥梁为媒介,讲述城市故事,从而使桥梁摆脱单一交通功能的窠臼,实现"生态功能、交通功能、文化功能、景观功能"等桥梁功能的多元化,为社会创造更多的价值。

1 前期概况

1.1 选址概况

设计选址位于山东省青岛市黄岛区的唐岛湾滨海公园。唐岛海湾周边有着得天独厚的海产资源和优越的地理环境,西北侧有中国石油大学(华东校区)、海上嘉年华摩天轮(琴岛之眼)、西海岸新区城市传媒广场、积米崖地铁站、海云游船码头、瑞港度假村等,东南侧有唐岛湾滨海公园、银沙滩、西海岸新区啤酒广场、鱼鸣嘴社区、海滋源海参养殖场等。故选择在此做一条人车两用桥,桥型也选择了大跨径的斜拉桥。

海湾两端从西北侧的地铁站到东南侧的鱼鸣嘴社区原本的陆地距离有13.6km,直线距离为1.5km。由于海湾内部的海云游船码头仅停靠一些游赏性船只,没有大型货运船只轮渡在此停靠,故唐岛海湾桥梁的高度不需考虑大型船只的通航因素。唐岛海湾大桥由西北起漓江西路,向东南接唐岛湾滨海公园园路直至银沙滩路,东西穿越唐岛约1.6km。漓江西路道路等级为城市主干路,双向八车道,道路宽度45m。唐岛海湾大桥作为漓江西路向东穿越唐岛湾公园的景观桥梁,既要满足道路通行和海域生态环境要求,又要与唐岛湾公园规划协调一致,保证唐岛湾滨海公园的景观和生态连续性。设计希望通过这座斜拉桥带动东南侧鱼鸣嘴社区的经济发展。

1.2 气候、地貌、水文概况

青岛地处北温带季风区域,属温带季风气候。市区由于海洋环境的直接调节,受来自洋面上的东南季风及海流、水团的影响,故又具有显著的海洋性气候特点。空气湿润,雨量充沛,温度适中,四季

分明。青岛为海滨丘陵城市,地势东高西低,南北两侧隆起,中间低凹。桥位区域南北纵向平行分布唐岛湾两岸,具有"一岛一湾两岸"的海湾自然环境。独特的自然地理特征为生态桥梁搭建了天然框架,是构建生态青岛的优良基础。从地形地貌看,海湾大桥桥位以两岸环绕、背靠崂山的地形特征而得天独厚。

2　功能定位

2.1　基于文化、生态、体验的设计

"文化"强调的是城市特色,青岛作为一个海滨城市,特色便是青岛人推开窗户就是山景,就是海滨。青岛是一座海岸线漫长、山脉众多、水域面积辽阔、岛屿星罗棋布的历史文化名城,被称作是"帆船之都",优越的自然条件是第一位的。这里的"山海城岛湾"可以说是青岛城市特色的彰显。

"生态"则是指注重桥梁与周边自然环境的协调设计,唐岛海湾大桥的桥端具有较为平坦的地势和现有岛屿等自然环境,在此基础上做了桥梁设计,桥梁两端倾斜延伸出来与陆上道路衔接,主塔的塔身设计在岛屿之中,做到尽量减少对自然的人为干预。

"体验"则是要求以"人"为关注焦点,提高桥梁使用者的安全度、舒适度和快乐度。设计以行人在桥梁四维空间中的感受与体验作为关注焦点,采用双索面斜拉桥加斜灯杆的整体设计提升行人的过桥体验,最终实现"人、桥、文化、自然"的和谐与统一。

2.2　桥梁功能拓展设计

2.2.1　构筑丰富的城市空间

桥梁作为唐岛湾海湾内的重要景观节点,在方案构思时重点关注桥梁与唐岛湾两岸空间的关系,充分拓展利用桥身两端平原地貌,增强桥西北侧与东南侧的沟通,为居民和游人营造舒适便捷的桥头公共景观空间。

2.2.2　与城市人文的协调

桥梁方案造型应展现城市地域文化,本方案对青岛人文、新城规划、唐岛湾海滨公园区域景观规划进行了研究,将海洋、生态、新城等文化元素融入桥梁的建筑设计之中,使得桥梁建筑与城市人文历史、区域景观规划等协调、融合。

2.2.3　扩展桥梁交通功能

桥梁功能在解决车辆和行人通行的基础上,加强桥梁与唐岛湾两岸慢性系统的沟通,提升桥梁的总体服务水平。通过桥梁方案的合理设计,利用滨海湾优美景观的优势,将人行空间与唐岛湾滨海景观空间连成一片,打造出公共、开放、多元、安全的都市交通活力空间。

2.2.4　打造城市新地标

创新是结构生命力的源泉,设计以原创景观作为桥梁景观价值的支点,因地制宜地解读场地信息和攫取场所精神,使桥梁结构更具文化张力和视觉冲击力,让桥梁成为与区域城市景观主题相契合的标志性景观建筑,打造青岛西南部滨海新城的城市新地标。

3　方案总体设计

3.1　设计理念与灵感来源

景观理念定位为"虹跨海湾,魅力之都"。围绕这一设计理念,将其与唐岛海湾周边环境结合进行了桥梁的整体设计。在原有独特桥型的基础上锦上添花,体现出结构的稳定连续、强劲力感与跨越能力,使大跨径的斜拉桥气韵生动,神形兼备,显示其不朽的生命力(图1)。

本方案桥梁设计构思主要从仿生学的角度出发,设计灵感来源于飞鱼形象(图2),其在蓝色的海面上,时隐时现、破浪前进的画面十分壮观,结合桥梁结构的受力特征,构造富有海洋特色的水上桥梁建筑[1]。

图 1　唐岛湾大桥整体效果图

图 2　飞鱼形象图

　　桥塔两端纤细的拉索,犹如飞鱼长长的胸鳍延伸到尾部,减少了行人视觉上的干扰。桥塔造型简练、流畅,塔柱曲线典雅、秀丽,富于海洋文化的浪漫气息。富有动感、充满张力的结构线条,给人一种昂扬向上的心理感受。

　　桥梁不仅在外形上体现"力"的简洁理念,还通过细腻、柔顺的局部细节处理,营造轻快、唯美的视觉感受,使桥梁建筑景观达到力与美的融合统一[2]。

　　在整个桥梁结构布置和空间分隔上,特意区分了慢行系统中非机动车道和步行道的设计。人在桥梁步道上观景,随着空间位置的不同,会带来不同的观景感受。人行道的斜灯杆设计不仅分割了行人向内的视觉空间,丰富了桥上空间层次,也意在配合斜拉索,给人以整个重心倾注于桥塔上的视觉感受,使桥梁造型更富于变化和韵味(图 3)。

图 3　斜灯杆效果图

3.2　设计重点与难点

　　目前,黄岛区属于新开发区域,现有桥梁数量不多,故唐岛湾大桥建成后在其中会占据着重要地位。根据大桥特点及桥位周边城市景观现状,将其设计的重点和难点总结如下。

3.2.1 与周边环境的协调

唐岛湾大桥所在的区域周边建筑群较多,海岸线丰富,建筑错落有致,空间感、层次感非常丰富,且海湾中间有一孤岛,自然生态环境良好。因此,在唐岛湾大桥的景观设计上与两端部分的衔接和中心岛的过渡是需要重点考虑的。

3.2.2 体现历史文化和现代人文背景

通过对青岛"帆船之都""品牌之都""海洋文化"等城市特色的提炼,对山脉一样坚忍顽强,大海一样澎湃豪爽的青岛人性格的总结,确认海湾大桥景观设计的象征精神体现在如下三方面:一是"水",体现了青岛人兼容并蓄的特征;二是"船",代表了青岛人不畏艰险,勇往直前的性格特征;三是"潮",其是新潮的意思,代表了青岛的时尚魅力。

3.2.3 与未来城市规划的结合

青岛在向现代化大都市飞速迈进的过程中,景观设计需要处理好"过去、今天和未来"的关系。桥梁景观赋予桥梁生命力的同时,需做到"内外兼修,神形兼备",因此唐岛湾大桥也应着重考虑远景设计,简洁大气,让桥梁的外观形式经受住时间的考验[3]。

3.3 桥梁结构特征

3.3.1 主塔特征分析

主塔为混凝土结构,由上塔柱、中塔柱和Y形下塔柱、塔墩组成。上塔柱高度55m,中塔柱在横桥向呈倒Y字形,高度为70m,下塔柱为分离式塔,高度为40m,四个主塔造型高度均相同。主塔横桥向将青岛开放与包容的特征融入其中,整体为帆船造型,寓意为迎风启航、无所畏惧,而塔柱向内的曲线造型意在体现青岛的包容特征。主塔外形与桥塔船型受力结构的融合是其重要特征(图4)。

图4 桥塔效果图

3.3.2 主梁特征分析

主梁采用Q355C钢材,采用正交异性钢桥面板(图5)。车道为双向四车道,两侧设人行道,横桥向布置桥面全宽为24.5m,即2×0.2m+2×2m+2×0.3m+2×9.5m+0.5m(中央分隔带)。

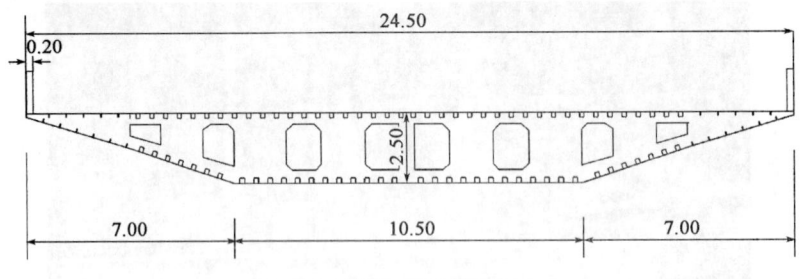

图5 主梁横截面(尺寸单位:m)

3.3.3 斜拉索特征分析

唐岛湾大桥采用了双索面密索体系,在抗风性能上有了提高和进一步的稳固。尽管为密索,但该设计的拉索数量仍尽可能有所减少,力求展现出完美的三角构图。

3.4 夜景效果展示

唐岛湾大桥主塔部分夜景照明借鉴了重庆两江大桥的景观照明处理,通过主塔内侧对夹面达到控光效果。设计希望将有效光均集中于主塔夹缝中,有效控制灯具能耗,避免能源浪费,实现最佳控光效果。针对塔柱的曲线造型,在夜景中,进行了塔柱顶端内腔控光方式和斜灯柱整体泛光照射处理两种方式的照明设计,以期展现主塔神韵,避免落入俗套(图6)。

图6 唐岛湾大桥夜景效果图

4 结 语

以唐岛湾大桥为背景,提出了双索面斜拉桥方案,并将其应用在跨海大桥当中。这种双索面斜拉桥在桥梁造型与结构之间做出了优化设计,追求力学的结构之美一直是众多桥梁设计者们努力的方向。除此之外,也在解决场地基本矛盾的基础上与场地当中现有中心岛屿做了良性结合。今后如何使桥梁这一艺术品在一泓之间被赋予独立的生命与性格,在烟波中大放异彩是桥梁设计师们在实践中应该思考的问题[4]。

参考文献

[1] 吴延辉.仿生理念在桥梁设计中的应用探析[J].城市道桥与防洪,2018(05):152-154+17.
[2] 邓文中.桥梁形态与美学[J].Engineering,2018,4(02):221-242.
[3] 王国彬."美学四性"桥梁设计策略探究——以北京城市副中心北关大道跨北运河大桥为例[J].艺术教育,2018(04):78-80.
[4] 王大海,崔永彬.城市桥梁造型及景观设计思考[J].交通世界(运输·车辆),2010(09):108-110.
[5] 仇福林.柴埠大桥斜拉桥设计方案分析[J].公路交通科技(应用技术版),2014,10(04):185-189.
[6] 李彬.桥梁结构选型与构造设计的建筑艺术研究[D].兰州:兰州交通大学,2015.

Effects of Complex Temperature Actions on the Dynamic Response of High-Speed Railway Trains

Hongye Gou Tianqi Zhao Rui Yang Liang Li

(Southwest Jiaotong University)

Abstract To study the additional rail deformation of high-speed railway bridge under complex temperature actions and the influences of deformation on vehicle dynamic response, a coupled finite element model of high-speed railway simply supported bridge and CRTS III unballasted track was established by ABAQUS. The additional deformation of the rail was calculated. Then the additional rail deformation and the track random irregularity spectrum were superimposed as the excitation source of the vehicle-bridge coupling system, the variation law of the dynamic response of the train under different temperature conditions was analyzed by SIMPACK. The results indicate that the vertical temperature gradient has more impacts on the vertical rail deformation while the lateral temperature gradient mainly affects the gauge of the rail. the amplitude and the fluctuation range of the vertical vehicle acceleration become larger with the in-crease of the temperature gradient amplitude. the wheel unloading rates and wheel-rail vertical force are not sensitive to the change of temperature gradient amplitude.

Keywords Additional rail deformation High-speed railway Vehicle dynamic response Vehicle-bridge coupling system Temperature gradient

0 Introduction

Unballasted track, as the most important track structure of high-speed railway in China, has the advantages of good ride, long service life and less maintenance work. With the development of high-speed railway construction in China, the high-speed railway has been widely applied in the complex natural environment such as the alpine mountain area and the severe cold area. The bridge track of high-speed railway will generate additional deformation under the combined action of train cyclic and complex temperature, which will cause the track geometric irregularity and eventually threaten the running safety of high speed railway(Gou et al. ,2018).

In recent years, the research on unballasted track deformation under the action of temperature has been widely developed. Liu(2016) analyzed the mechanical properties of unballasted track under complex temperature action by establishing a CRTS I unballasted track model. Liu et al. (2015) analyzed the temperature gradient characteristics of CRTs III based on the measured temperature data of CRTs III, taking into account the actual factors such as the total amount of daily solar radiation and the maximum daily temperature, and fitted the fitting formula of the maximum positive temperature gradient. Xie et al. (2015) established a rail-bridge-piers calculation model, studied the effect of vertical temperature difference load(TDL) of a simply supported beam bridge section on the track vertical irregularity. Zhu and Cai. (2014) established a three-dimensional coupled dynamic model of a vehicle and the slab track, studied the interface damage evolution under the joint action of temperature and vehicle load and its influence on the dynamic response of the slab track. Song et al. (2014) established the finite element simulation model of CRTs II unballasted track with complete and partial bond deterioration, and analyzed the influence of temperature deformation on the dynamic properties of the track.

Many scholars have analyzed the influence of temperature on the safety of high-speed railways. Yang et al. (2016) simulated the temperature field of the track slab through the loading mode of node temperature load, studied the running safety of high-speed train passing through the warped section of the track slab. Based on Xijiang bridge, Zhu et al. (2019) calculated the track irregularity under the action of temperature, and then analyzed the dynamic response of high-speed train. Sung et al. (2018) analyzed the influence of the long wavelength irregularity caused by the temperature change on the running dynamic index and proposed the relevant control measures. Based on coupling vibration analysis, Li et al. (2012) studied the effect on a rigid frame-continuous bridge induced by track irregularities, temperature and creep.

At present, CRTS III unballasted track has been used in many high-speed railway lines in China. The CRTS III unballasted track is significantly different in structure from the previous track, therefore, it is necessary to conduct the thorough research on the influence of temperature deformation of CRTS III unballasted track on running safety. In this paper, based on the Zhengzhou to Xuzhou section of Xulan high speed railway, the additional rail deformation under different temperature actions and the influences of deformation on vehicle dynamic response are analyzed by using ABAQUS and SIMPACK. The research results can be used to ensure the safe operation of high-speed railway during its service period and improve the standard system of infrastructure safety maintenance.

1 Research Content

1.1 32m Simply Supported Girder Bridge-CRTS III Unballasted Track System

CRTS III ballastless track system consists of rail, track slab, self-compacting concrete layer and base plate. The specification of the rail is 60kg/m. P5600 and P4925 track slab models are used for analysis, the dimension of the two models are 5.6m × 2.5m × 0.2m and 4.925m × 2.5m × 0.2m. The center distance of the bearing platform on the track slab is 0.65m. The thickness of the base plate concrete is 200mm, the section width is 2.9m, and the strength grade is C40. 90mm thick self-compacting concrete is laid between the track slab and the base plate.

1.2 ABAQUS Finite Element Model of Bridge and Unballasted Track

The bridge model is built by the SOLID element, the WIRE element is used to simulate the prestressing tendons, the EMBED constraint is set between the prestressing tendons and the concrete. At the same time, the "cooling method" is used to apply prestress. The track slab, self-compacting concrete layer, base plate, bearing platform and rail are both built by the SOLID element. The fastener and base plate between rail and bearing platform are simulated by the CARTESIAN spring element with the COUPLING constraint, the stiffness of the fasteners is 30kN/mm.

According to the actual situation, the Tie constraint is used to simulate the reinforcement between track slab and self-compacting concrete layer. The Tie constraint is arranged between the boss of the self-compacting concrete and the groove of the base plate, friction is considered for the contact between the base plate and self-compacting concrete, and the penalty function coefficient is 0.5. Because the pavement on the box girder forms a firm lateral constraint on the base plate, the Tie constraint is set between the base plate and the box girder. The track-bridge coupling model is shown in Fig. 1, and the material parameters are shown in Tab. 1.

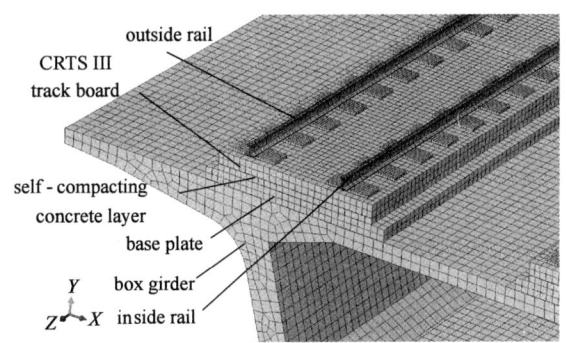

Fig. 1 Track-Bridge Coupling Model

Material Parameters Tab. 1

Component	Elastic modulus(MPa)	Poisson ratio	linear expansion coefficient(/℃)
rail	2.06×10^5	0.3	1.18×10^{-5}
track slab	3.6×10^4	0.2	1.0×10^{-5}
self-compacting concrete layer	3.25×10^4	0.2	$1.0e \times 10^{-5}$
base plate	$3.25e \times 10^4$	0.2	$1.0e \times 10^{-5}$
box girder	3.55×10^4	0.2	1.0×10^{-5}
prestressing tendons	1.95×10^5	0.3	1.15×10^{-5}

1.3 Vehicle-Track-Bridge Model Based on SIMPACK

Under the action of temperature gradient, the simply supported beam bridge will produce vertical deformation, which will cause rail deformation. In this paper, a CRH380 train model is established by SIMPACK, and the four-span simply supported girder bridge-track model established in ABAQUS is imported into SIMPACK through the FEMBS interface to simulate vehicle-bridge coupling, and the initial track irregularity (German low power spectral density function) is superimposed in SIMPACK. The hertz elasticity contact theory is used for normal contact between wheel and rail, and the kalker creep theory is used for tangent contact. Then, the dynamic safety indexes of the CRH380 train running at 350km/h under different temperature conditions are analyzed by SIMPACK.

1.4 Working Conditions

The temperature gradient is simulated with reference to China's railway bridge design code. Three different temperature conditions are selected. In the first condition, a vertical maximum positive temperature gradient is applied to the box girder and CRTS III track; In the second condition, a vertical maximum negative temperature gradient is applied to the box girder and CRTS III track; In the third working condition, the vertical positive temperature gradient and the lateral temperature gradient are applied to the box girder, the vertical maximum positive temperature gradient is applied to the CRTS III track.

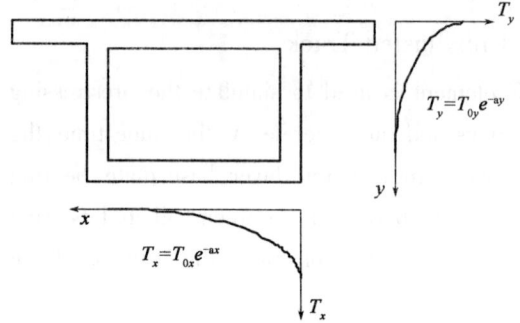

Fig. 2 Temperature Gradient Action Diagram

The temperature gradient amplitude of the box girder is calculated according to the "Code for Design of Concrete Structures of Railway Bridges and Culvert" (TB 10092—2017). The form of temperature gradient load is shown in Fig. 2.

The maximum positive temperature gradient of the track slab is calculated according to the actual situation, as shown in Eq. (1):

$$T_g = 0.018Q + 0.003T_{max} + 0.015 \tag{1}$$

where denotes the maximum positive temperature gradient in °C, denotes the total daily solar radiation in MJ/(m² · d), denotes the maximum daily temperature in °C.

The maximum negative temperature gradient of the track slab is taken as -0.35°C/cm. The temperature gradient amplitudes of the box girder and the track slab are shown in Tab. 2.

Temperature Gradient Amplitudes of Each Working Condition   Tab. 2

Working condition/part	Box girder		Track slab(cm)
	vertical	lateral	
condition 1	$20e^{-5y}$	—	0.4325
condition 2	$-10e^{-14y}$	—	-0.35
condition 3	$16e^{-7y}$	$16e^{-7x}$	0.4325

2 Calculation Results and Discussion

2.1 TheAdditional Rail Deformation under Different Temperature Actions

The vertical deformations of the rails are shown in Fig. 3, in the picture, the vertical deformations of the rails have four layers of peak curves from top to bottom, which respectively represent the calculation results of the first condition, the third condition, only prestressing and the second condition. Each layer includes the vertical deformation of the inside rail and the outside rail. The lateral deformations of the rails are shown in Fig. 4 to Fig. 6.

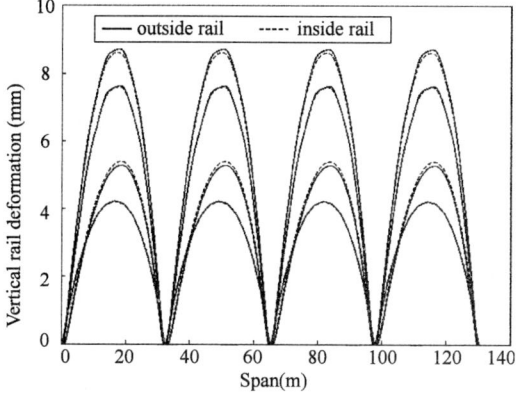

Fig. 3 Vertical Rail Displacement under Different Working Conditions

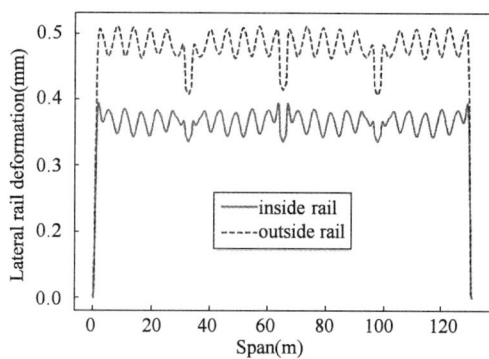

Fig. 4 Lateral Rail Displacement under Working Condition1

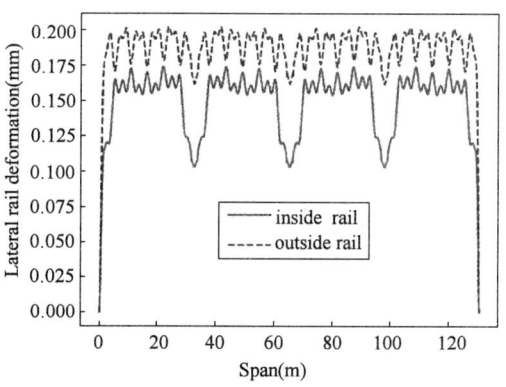

Fig. 5 Lateral Rail Displacement under Working Condition2

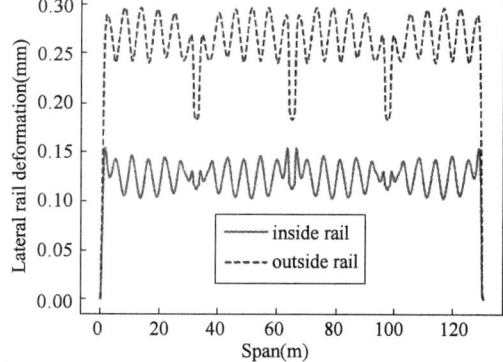

Fig. 6 Lateral Rail Displacement under Working Condition3

As can be seen from the figure, the rail will produce camber deformation under the action of prestress. The positive temperature gradient will increase the camber deformation, while the negative temperature gradient will reduce the camber deformation of the rail. The deformation value is positively related to the temperature gradient. When the structure is only prestressed, the maximum vertical displacement of the outside rail is larger than that of the inside rail, because there are more prestressed tendons in the web and the outer rail is closer to the web. Under the action of temperature gradient, the box girder appears camber deformation in the horizontal plane and the vertical plane along the length of the bridge, resulting in the height difference between the inside rail and the outside rail, and the high difference value increases with the increase of the positive temperature gradient.

It can be seen from Fig. 4 to Fig. 6 that the lateral displacement of the rail is also positively related to the magnitude of the temperature gradient amplitude. The lateral displacement of the outside rail is greater than the inside rail under the vertical temperature gradient, in addition, the lateral temperature gradient will increase the displacement difference between the outside rail and the inside rail.

2.2 The Additional Rail Deformation under Different Temperature Actions

When the train passes the bridge at a speed of 350km/h, the safety of the train under three working conditions is analyzed. Because the vertical deformation of the rail under temperature gradient is much larger than the lateral deformation, this paper evaluates the safety of train operation by the parameters of the vertical vehicle acceleration, the wheel unloading rates and the wheel-rail vertical force. Running safety parameters under various operating conditions are shown in the Fig. 7 to Fig. 15. According to Chinese "Code for Design of High Speed Railway", the wheel unloading rates must not be greater than 0.6 and the wheel-rail vertical force must not be greater than 170kN.

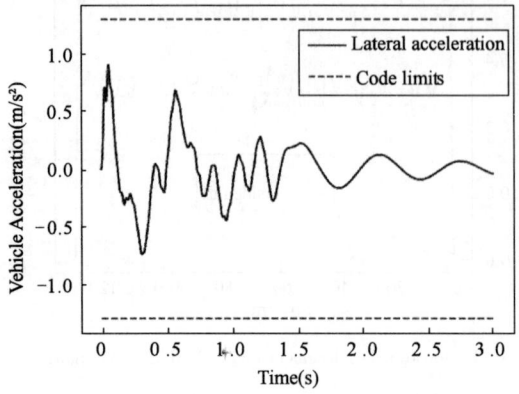

Fig. 7　Lateral Vehicle Acceleration under Working Condition1

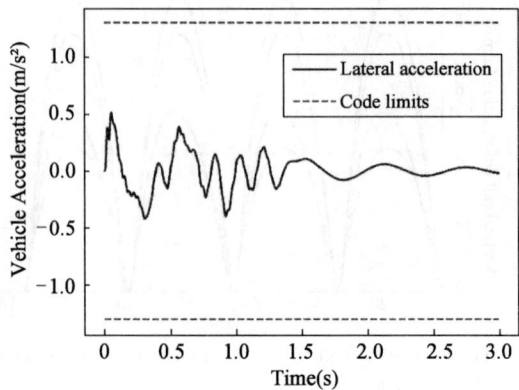

Fig. 8　Lateral Vehicle Acceleration under Working Condition2

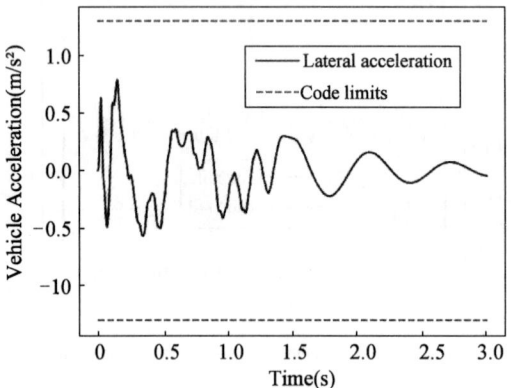

Fig. 9　Lateral Vehicle Acceleration under Working Condition3

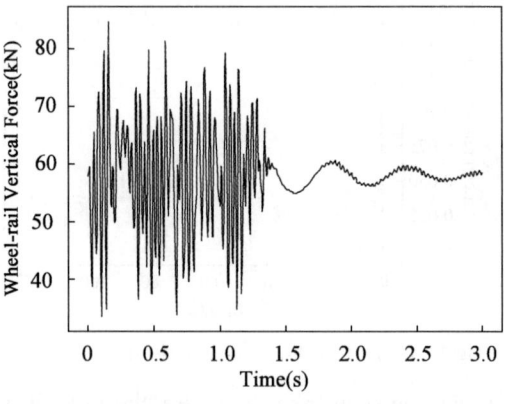

Fig. 10　The Wheel-Rail Vertical Force under Working Condition1

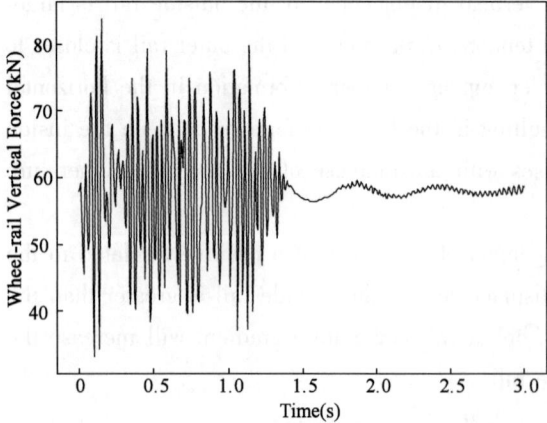

Fig. 11　The Wheel-Rail Vertical Force under Working Condition2

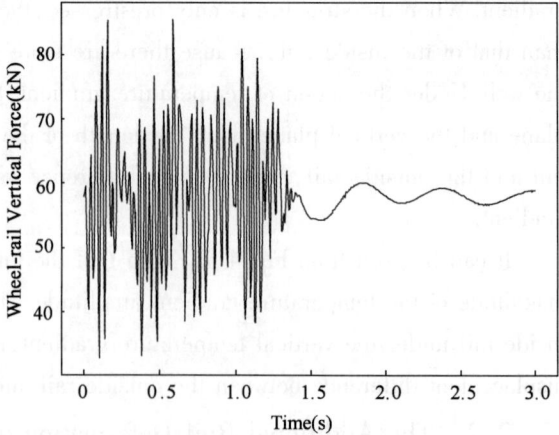

Fig. 12　The Wheel-Rail Vertical Force under Working Condition3

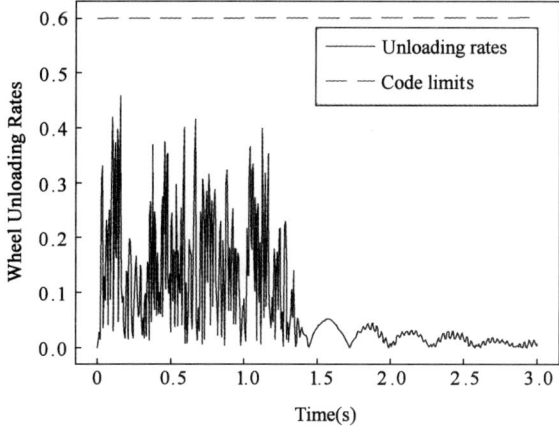
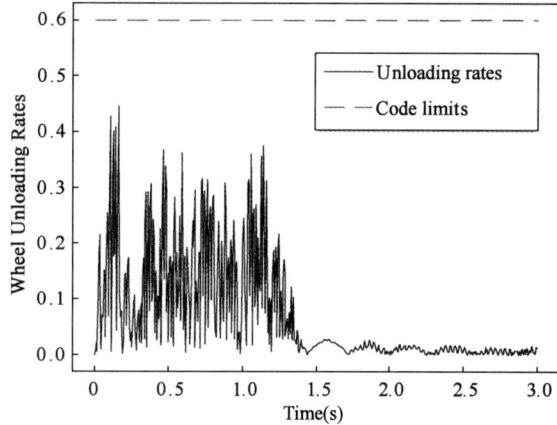

Fig. 13 The Wheel Unloading Rates under Working Condition1

Fig. 14 The Wheel Unloading Rates under Working Condition2

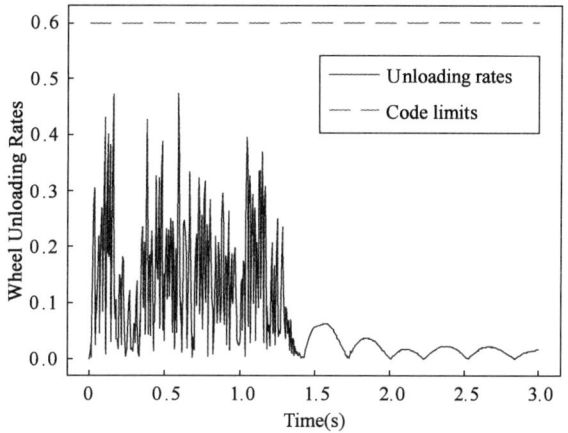

Fig. 15 The Wheel Unloading Rates under Working Condition3

From the picture, it can be seen that the running safety parameters of train under the three extreme temperature gradient conditions meet standard requirements. From the Fig. 7 to Fig. 9, it can be seen that with the increase of the amplitude of temperature gradient, the greater the peak value of vertical acceleration, the greater the fluctuation of vertical acceleration. The difference in the wheel-rail vertical forces under different temperature conditions is small. The wheel unloading rates do not differ significantly under different temperature conditions.

3 Conclusions

Based on the above investigations, the key findings can be summarized:

As the amplitude of temperature gradient action increases, rails' lateral deformation and vertical deformation increase as well.

Vertical temperature gradients mainly deform rail in vertical plane and have little effects in lateral plane while lateral temperature gradients mainly influence track gauge in lateral plane.

All above conditions considered, higher amplitude of temperature gradients can cause higher vertical acceleration of car-body and greater fluctuation but they are all covered by the limit values in the code.

Wheel-rail vertical force and wheel unloading rates don't seem to have obvious correlation with amplitudes of temperature gradients.

The research achievements can provide reference for the design of high-speed railway and the running safety estimation of train on bridges.

References

[1] Ho Hwang S, et al. Effects of Long-Wavelength Track Irregularities Due to Thermal Deformation of Railway Bridge on Dynamic Response of Running Train[J]. Applied Sciences, 2018(12), 2549.

[2] Hong-ye G, et al. Study on the Influence Factors of Vertical Deformation of High-speed Railway Bridge on the Track Geometry[J]. Journal of Railway Engineering Society, 201835(11), 41-47.

[3] Jingjing Y, et al. Temperature Warping and It's Impact On Train-Track Dynamic Response of CRTS II Ballastless Track[J]. Engineering Mechanics, 201623(04), 210-217.

[4] Kaize X. Effect of Temperature Difference Load of 32m Simply Supported Box Beam Bridge on Track Vertical Irregularity[J]. Journal of Modern Transportation, 201523(04), 262-271.

[5] Kexu L. Study on Relation Between CWR on Bridge and CRTS I Slab Ballastless Track Under Complex Temperature[D]. Beijing: Beijing Jiaotong University, 2016.

[6] Shengyang Z, Chengbiao C. Interface Damage and Its Effect on Vibrations of Slab Track Under Temperature and Vehicle Dynamic Loads[J]. International Journal of Non-Linear Mechanics, 2014, 58, 222-232.

[7] Weibin L, et al. Experimental Study On Temperature Gradient For CRTS III Slab-Type Ballastless Track On High Speed Railway[J]. Railway Engineering, 2015(3), 103-106.

[8] Wen Qiu L, et al. Dynamic Response of Bridges to Moving Trains: A Study on Effects of Concrete Creep and Temperature Deformation[J]. Applied Mechanics and Materials, 2012: 193-194, 1179-1182.

[9] Xiaolin S, et al. Temperature-induced Deformation of CRTS II Slab Track and Its Effect on Track Dynamical Properties[J]. Science China Technological Sciences, 2014(10), 1917-1924.

[10] Zhihui Z, et al. Driving Dynamic Response Analysis of Long-span Arch Bridge Considering Temperature Deformation[J]. Journal of Railway Engineering Society, 2019: 036(003), 26-31, 44.

装配式箱涵在公路中的应用实践及思考

付凯敏[1]　黄智华[2]　聂建春[1]　曹林辉[1]

(1. 江西赣粤高速公路股份有限公司; 2. 江西省交通投资集团有限责任公司)

摘　要　本文结合预制装配式箱涵在江西省昌九高速公路改扩建工程中的应用状况对其进行了分析，对该项技术的施工工艺及方法进行了总结。实践证实，采用预制装配技术，可以实现对机械设备、模板、人工高效利用，实现了工厂化、标准化、机械化，减少了外部因素对涵洞施工作业的影响，从而有效提高施工效率和质量，降低工程全寿命成本，同时还节能环保。

关键词　高速公路　应用实践　装配式箱涵　预制装配

0　引　言

昌九高速公路改扩建采用"边施工边通车、不分流、维持四车道通行"的交通组织方式，施工作业面受到严重的限制，且存在较大的通行安全风险，加上征地拆迁难度巨大，有效的施工工期较短，必须采用"短平快"的施工工艺。从工期、质量、安全等方面综合考虑，全线涵洞采用预制装配式建造技术。

我国除了装配式圆形管涵大量使用外，其他形式的装配式结构研究起步相对较晚，最早于1963年用于京广铁路立交桥上，随后在上海世博园综合管廊工程，2010年以后在安徽高速公路上得到了一定的推广应用。目前，装配式拱形、方形涵洞施工技术在国内工程建设中已逐步开始推广使用。

1 涵洞形式

结合昌九高速公路改扩建工程项目特点及建设和工期的要求,本项目采用预制门式整体箱形涵洞,如图1所示。此方案箱涵断面分段少,接缝少,连接可靠,施工简便,且箱涵的整体性较好。

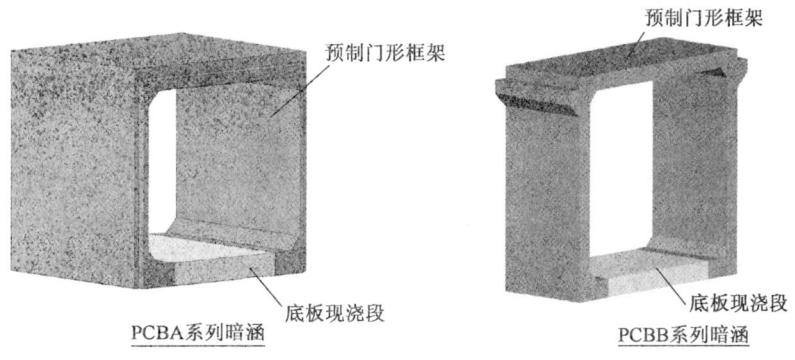

图1 预制装配式箱涵

通过对原涵尺寸进行归纳,采用通用的 3m×2.5m、3m×3.5m、4m×3.5m、4m×4.5m 明、暗涵各4类[1],考虑吊装质量,单节长度2~3m,底板镂空,节段质量为200~300kg。

2 施工要点

2.1 箱涵预制

2.1.1 预制厂布置

涵洞预制件应全线集中预制或者单独招预制标,为了发挥预制场站使用效率,集梁板、小构等为一体,打造综合性、智慧型预制厂,有条件的按照永久性、服务型预制工厂建设,做到永临结合。以昌九高速公路改扩建项目为例,预制场占地面积约20万 m^2,如图2所示。箱涵预制采用短链式流水线作业,如图3所示。

图2 构件制造中心

图3 箱涵预制流水线

2.1.2 构件预制

(1)预制方式

根据节段形式,综合考虑到预制外观质量、混凝土浇筑难易程度、移运的便利性以及最后收光面对拼装的影响等因素,最终采用立式预制方式。

(2)预制模板

箱涵预制采用定制液压连杆式自拼装大面钢模板(由底模、侧模、内模、端模等组成),模板厚12mm,底模通过轨道式桁车进行周转,侧模采用C20混凝土,将左右各2根液压连杆一端浇筑固定在制作区两侧,内模拼装在轨道式自动桁走框架上,凸面端头模板与芯模一起连接在轨道式自动桁走框架上,凹面端头模板在钢筋入模后采用龙门吊进行拼装,如图4所示。

(3)钢筋制安

为提高钢筋加工精度,钢筋从调直、切割、输送、弯曲等各个生产环节采用自动化、数字化控制,同时引进机械手替代人工进行重复性、高强度的劳动,半成品尺寸合格率达到100%,质量优良率100%。预制箱涵钢筋骨架采用井字式钢筋绑扎工作平台(胎架)制作,对横竖向钢筋的间距及垂直度进行严格控制。

(4)构件浇筑

钢筋骨架成型后安装好高强度砂浆垫块,采用门式起重机提吊至模板底座上进行下道工序,提吊前钢筋骨架需做好内支撑,并采用多点吊方式,防止提吊过程中钢筋发生受力形变。混凝土浇筑前,检查模板、支架、钢筋的正确性。构件采用逐步分层浇筑,浇筑顺序是由下至上。用插入式的振动棒配合高频附着式振动器进行振捣。

(5)构件养生

浇筑完毕混凝土硬结后,待混凝土强度达到脱模要求,拆除侧模、芯模、端模,用平板小车顶起底模及构件至养生区,进行自动喷淋养生,如图5所示。为保证混凝土有适宜的硬化条件和防止发生不正常的收缩,需使混凝土经常保持潮湿状态,预设参数为温度36.8℃、湿度73%。

图4 箱涵构件预制

图5 预制箱涵养生

(6)成品存放

箱涵存放采用立式存放,由60t门式起重机直接吊装至存放区进行存放。在吊装前需通过试验室进行混凝土强度试验,确定混凝土强度大于36MPa。存放时必须采用橡胶垫片垫放在箱涵存放区台座上。在吊转前需进行混凝土强度检测,吊运时需安装H型钢临时支撑。

2.2 箱涵安装

2.2.1 基础施工

箱涵基坑开挖后,检测地基承载力,符合要求的铺筑40cm砂砾垫层,压实后浇筑10cm厚C25混凝土基层,要求基础平整度控制在3mm以内、高程控制在10mm以内。

2.2.2 预制件运输

箱涵节段采用平板车通过高速公路运往施工点,受道路限高,除3m×2.5m节段采用立式运输,其他需要在预制场翻转后运输。

(1)预制件翻转

工厂预制好涵洞构件后,在预留孔内穿入高强螺栓,并将开孔钢板拧紧在结构两侧墙上,然后利用开孔板上的吊耳及顶板吊环将构件翻转至水平地面,以备装车,为防止翻转过程侧墙与地面接触破损,应在水平地面预铺设柔软材料或垫松软沙土。构件翻转至水平地面后,采用平衡梁起吊系统,将构件水平吊至平板车上,如图6所示。

(2) 预制件运输

涵洞节段运输的关键点在于运输的安全以及构件的保护。由于构件属于超宽运输,运输过程中主要占用行车道与应急车道,运输车队前后请交警或者路政车辆引导或者断后,对整个运输过程进行严密监控,如图7所示。

图6 预制件翻转

图7 预制箱涵运输

2.2.3 预制件安装

(1) 交通布控

箱涵安装应做好交通组织和管控,设置交通导行标识牌,临时封闭硬路肩及行车道作为运输车辆的停靠区,专职安全员配合交警在布控区段全程指挥交通,确保社会车辆正常慢速安全的通过施工区域。

(2) 现场吊装

箱涵安装采用吊车吊装、人工辅助定位的方式,如图8所示。每安装一节,立即核对高程,对于高程达不到设计要求的,采用钢板铺设钢板调节,同时校对中线、外侧边线后再进行下一个节段安装。

2.2.4 底板浇筑

涵洞安装到位后,对底部预留钢筋进行除锈处理,侧面墙角部位进行凿毛处理,按照设计要求安装钢筋,进行底部现浇段施工,将箱涵预制件连接为一体。现浇段混凝土强度与预制结构相同。

2.2.5 防水处理

涵洞安装完毕后要对构件和节段间接缝进行防水处理。先用沥青麻絮填充,然后对于内侧接缝填塞M10水泥砂浆,配合硅酮胶嵌缝,保证接缝内实外美;接缝外侧采用具备黏结功能的防水卷材张贴牢固,如图9所示。

图8 预制箱涵安装

图9 预制箱涵防水处理

3　效益分析

传统现浇涵洞施工需在现场搭设支架、拼装模板等,受现场环境、天气、征地拆迁等影响较大,施工周期长(一般在2个月左右),质量安全管理难度大、现场隐患多。而预制装配式涵洞具有如下特点和显著效益:

(1)项目工期得到保障。构件预制不受天气制约,不受现场用地交付影响,后场构件预制和现场基础施工可平行进行,甚至可提前预制完成,再择机安装,极大地缩短了工期。

(2)质量得到大幅提升。因采用工厂化生产、标准化设计,产品得以准确实现。特别是互联网+科技成果的应用,大大节省人力资源,提高了管理和生产效率。

(3)安全隐患大幅减少。生产方式、作业方式和环境、监管手段和范围都发生了根本性的改变,安全生产得到保障。特别是装配式结构施工工序简化,大大缩短现场施工周期,减少既有交通干扰,降低通行安全风险。

(4)社会经济效益显著。装配式相比现浇混凝土涵洞建设费用节省约20%~30%,工作效率提高5~7倍。另外,各工点技术特点突出,施工设备集中,最大限度地降低了业主、监理、施工管理人员投入和工作难度。

4　改进之处

(1)目前实践中斜交涵洞和新老涵洞拼接过渡段采用工地现浇方式,虽然工程量小,但各项工序均需按部就班开展,消耗了不少人力、物力,削弱了装配式涵洞快速高效施工的优点,后续可以尝试将斜交的非标准节段也进行工厂化定制。

(2)后续应结合现场运输条件情况,因地制宜、有选择性地采用半预制半现浇(山区公路涵洞可预制盖板、台车现浇墙身)、分块预制拼装式结构(铰接体系适用抗震要求低、填土高度小的路段;现浇湿接缝体系整体性好,但施工周期长)。

5　结　语

预制装配式箱涵的应用有效地解决了公路改扩建涵洞有效施工时间短、通行安全隐患大、现场施工条件差等难题,并实现了全部构件工厂集中预制,提升涵洞品质,缩短施工周期,预制拼装工艺适应于机械化施工作业,符合公路建设集约化、工业化要求和发展趋势,有着广阔的应用前景。目前也还存在非标节段预制率低、市场化程度不高、配套技术和装备不完善等问题,需要下一步进行解决。

参考文献

[1] 宋林,吴大健,段宝山.昌九高速改扩建项目装配式箱涵设计研究[J].公路,2020(04):150-156.
[2] 董杰.预制装配式箱涵设计计算与试验研究[D].武汉:武汉理工大学,2017.

Disease Mechanism and Influence Analysis on Force-bearing Members of Composite Beam Cable-stayed Bridge

Chi Wang　Hanhao Zhang　Linhao Zhu

(Chang'an University)

Abstract　With the increase of steel-concrete composite beam cable-stayed bridges, the disease problem during the operation period became prominent gradually. This paper summarizes the possible diseases that may occur during the operation of the steel-concrete composite beam cable-stayed bridge, analyzes the disease mechanism on the main stressed members of the steel-concrete composite beam cable-stayed bridge and studies the disease consequences. Finally, the finite element program is built to simulate the corrosion of the cable-stayed members, and analyze the corrosion influence of each stay cable on the bridge stress. The results of this paper clarify the disease characteristics of the main stressed members on the steel-concrete composite beam cable-stayed bridge, and provide reference and help for this type of bridge to formulate corresponding maintenance measures.

Keywords Steel-concrete composite beam cable-stayed bridge　Main stressed members　Disease mechanism　Corrosion of stay cables

0　Introduction

The composite beam cable-stayed bridge takes the structural advantages of the cable-stayed bridge and the composite beam bridge into account, so it has been more and more widely used in bridge construction at this stage. At the same time, the harmful erosion factors in the environment, the substantial increase in traffic on the bridge, and various unfavorable factors have accelerated the deterioration of the bridge's structural performance, resulting in various diseases of the composite beam cable-stayed bridge. Besides, the diseases of the main load-bearing components have a serious impact on the mechanical performance of the bridge, and cause great hidden dangers to the durability of the bridge structure and even the safety of operation.

At present, the research on the disease phenomenon of cable-stayed bridges and composite beam bridges has been reported, but there arestill few studies on the disease mechanism of composite beam cable-stayed bridges and their effects extent on the structural forces. Therefore, based on the research results, this article summarizes the disease characteristics of the main stressed components(cable stays, bridge decks, steel beams, and shear connector), and analyzes the disease mechanism of the main stress members in detail. At the same time, a simulation calculation of the corrosion of the stay cable was carried out for the stress-bearing component, which is the most affected by the disease. The degree of change to the stress was quantitatively analyzed. The research results of this paper provide guidance for the prevention and treatment of this type of bridge's major diseases. The research have strong engineering practical value.

1　Analysis on Main Diseases of Steel-Concrete Composite Beam Cable-stayed Bridge

The diseases of the main stressed members are mainly divided into the diseases on the stay cable, the main girder concrete deck, the main girder steel box girder, and the shear connector.

1.1　Stay Cable Disease

Due to the inadequate protection of stay cables during construction and service periods, sheath defects are prone to occur, which results in the loss of the protection of stay cables and the occurrence of stay cable diseases. The diseases of stay cables are mainly focused on stay cable diseases and anchorage system diseases.

The disease of stay cable is mainly caused by the external corrosive medium entering the interior from the damaged part of the sheath, which results in the cable body wire deterioration and severely weakens the effective force performance of the stay cable. Eventually, the stay cable cannot meet the load requirements and it is easy to trigger the bridge safety accident. The anchors at the main beam end are easily eroded by rain and other corrosive media. The anchorages of the cable are prone to fatigue damage under the action of vibration and sunlight during operation. These problems will cause the failure of the force transmission function between the main beam and the pylon, thereby affecting the structural bearing capacity and durability (Fig. 1、Fig. 2).

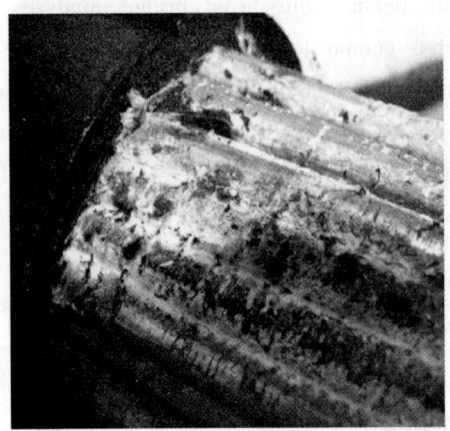
Fig. 1　Corrosion of Cable Body

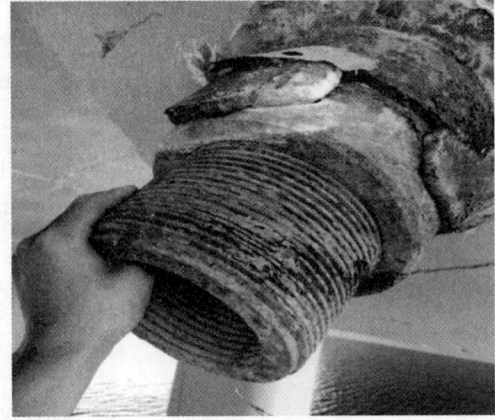
Fig. 2　Corrosion of Stay Cable Anchor Head

1.2　Concrete Bridge Deck Diseases

The disease on the concrete bridge deck mainly affects the service level and durability of the bridge structure. The main factors affecting the durability of concrete bridge decks are concrete carbonation and steel corrosion.

Concrete carbonation is caused by the reaction of $Ca(OH)_2$ and CO_2 inside the concrete to form water and $CaCO_3$. As the concrete carbonization causes the internal PH value of the concrete to decrease, the passive film on the steel bars will gradually be destroyed, which will lead to corrosion and deterioration of the steel bars. The corrosion of reinforcement in concrete is mainly caused by the intrusion of concrete carbonation and Cl-anions. During the service phase, it must be ensured that the rebar passivation film will not be damaged prematurely (Fig. 3).

 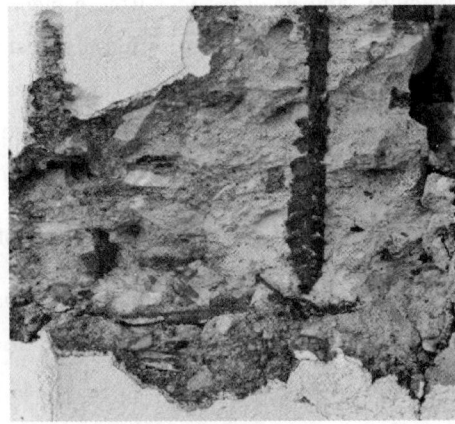
Fig. 3　Reinforcement Corrosion

1.3　Steel Beam Disease

Steel beams in steel-concrete beam cable-stayed bridges are subject to corrosion and fatigue damage, which are the main pathogenic factors of concrete-steel beams in the current operation.

When concrete-steel beam bridges are under cyclic stress for a long time, the steel beams may fail due to fatigue over time. The main reasons for fatigue failure of steel beams are material defects and local stress concentration of steel. Fatigue failure is low stress, suddenly brittle failure at the ultimate strength, which will cause irreparable losses once it occurs (Fig. 4).

Fig. 4 Steel Beam Corrosion

1.4 Analysis of Shear Connector Disease

The roots of shearstuds are easily affected by welding. Under the action of overweight vehicle loads and corrosive media, fatigue cracks are prone to appear at the roots of shear studs, which will eventually lead to corrosion and fatigue fracture of the studs.

The huge horizontal shear force and fatigue stress amplitude from heavy and overloaded vehicles acted on the shear connector will cause the shear connector to crack and shear failure. Thus, the steel-concrete composite beam will lose its overall working performance. At the same time, the force connector also bears the lifting force between the concrete slab and the steel beam which is mainly related to the external load. Lifting will not only greatly reduce the overall mechanical performance of the steel-concrete composite beam, but also result in bulging, cracks, and breakage of the concrete bridge deck pavement, which will seriously affect the durability of the main beam.

2 Response Analysis of Bridge Structures Under Cable Damage

The disease and damage of cable-stayed bridges have a greater impact on the mechanical performance. The contribution rate of the cable-stayed components to the overall structural stiffness of the bridge system is much greater than that of the steel-concrete composite beams. Therefore, the stay cables play a significant role in the safe operation and normal service of steel-concrete composite beam cable-stayed bridge structure. Therefore, it is necessary to analyze the corrosion damage by numerical method.

2.1 Analysis of the Importance of Stay Cables

Combined with the actual disease situation of the stayed cables, the importance evaluation index based on the generalized stiffness of the structure is used to analyze the importance of each stayed cable. It is necessary to use MIDAS CIVIL to perform finite element simulation and force analysis on the bridge structure. When calculating the importance, it is necessary to carry out the most unfavorable load of the lane load according to the influence line of the stay cable, so as to calculate the mechanical behavior of the bridge structure before and after the cable break under the determined load. Then calculate the strain energy of the bridge structure before and after the cable break to get the importance coefficient of the stay cable.

The applied project (LI Zhi-gang, 2020) in this paper is a double-tower and three-span cable-stayed bridge, whose span composition is 30m + 95m + 305m + 110m + 30m. The stay cables are finished with parallel steel wire bundles. The main tower is an inverted Y-typepylon, and the main beam is a separated double-sided box composite beam. MIDAS CIVIL is used to establish a finite element simulation analysis model for the steel-concrete composite beam cable-stayed bridge. The material parameters of each element are shown in the table. The full bridge model diagram and cable number diagram are as follows (Tab. 1、Fig. 5)

Material Parameter Table of Full bridge Model Element   Tab. 1

Component name	Unit type	Material	Elastic modulus ($\times 10^4$ MPa)
Steel-concrete composite beam	Beam element	Q345 steel + C60 concrete	steel:20.6 concrete:3.6
Stay cable	Truss element	$\phi 7$ high-strength steel wire	19.5
cable tower	Beam element	C50 concrete	3.45
pier	Beam element	C40 concrete	3.25
pile	Beam element	C35 concrete	3.15

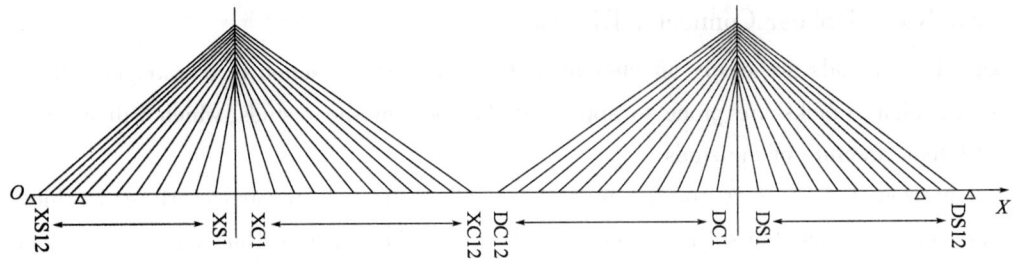

Fig. 5 Model and Cable Number

According to the axial force influence line of the stay cable member, the loading condition is determined according to the most unfavorable conditions. Take XC3 stay cable as an example, the axial force influence line of this cable is shown in the Fig. 6.

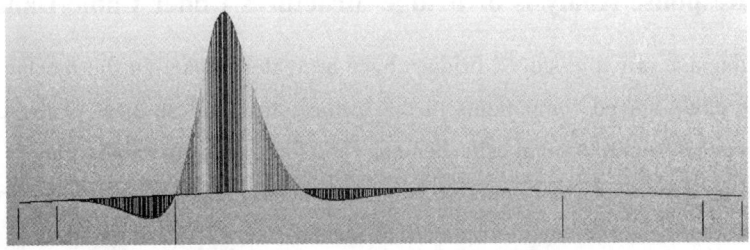

Fig. 6 Axial force influence line of stay cable XC3

According to the XC3 stay cable axial force influence line, load according to the most unfavorable load conditions.

After the load form is determined, the corresponding load forms of each stay cable are respectively applied to the complete bridge structure model and the broken cable bridge structure model. The stress state of the bridge before and after the cable break occurs under the determined load form is calculated. The internal force diagram before and after the XC3 stay cable is broken under the corresponding loading conditions is shown in Fig. 7.

According to the internal force of the bridge, use the formula (LI Zhi-gang, 2020; YE Lie-ping et al., 2010) to calculate the strain energy of the bridge structure before and after the cable break. The importance coefficient of the stay cable determined according to the generalized structural stiffness theory is calculated. The calculation results are shown in Tab. 2.

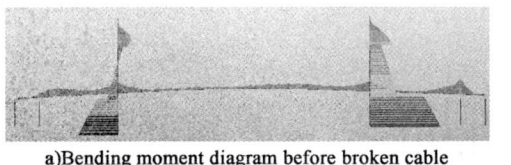
a) Bending moment diagram before broken cable

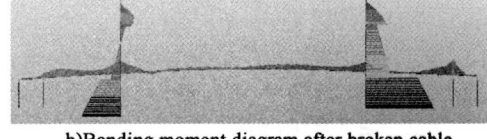
b) Bending moment diagram after broken cable

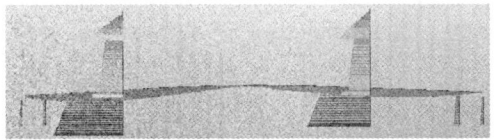
c) Axle force diagram before broken cable

d) Axle force diagram after broken cable

Fig. 7 The internal force diagram of the bridge before and after the cable break

Result of Importance Coefficient of Full Bridge Cable Members Tab. 2

Cable number	Total strain energy of intact structure (kJ)	Total strain energy of broken cable structure (kJ)	Importance coefficient	Cable number	Total strain energy of intact structure (kJ)	Total strain energy of broken cable structure (kJ)	Importance coefficient
XS12	44457.1	46092.2	0.035	DC12	42376.5	43868.0	0.034
XS11	43489.4	45159.5	0.037	DC11	43089.4	44978.5	0.042
XS10	42579.1	44238.5	0.038	DC10	43614.6	45574.3	0.043
XS9	42240.4	43532.6	0.030	DC9	43702.9	45382.1	0.037
XS8	42042.3	43241.6	0.028	DC8	40199.1	41787.0	0.038
XS7	41896.4	42745.6	0.020	DC7	38541.3	39692.4	0.029
XS6	39511.6	40335.4	0.020	DC6	37079.8	38148.0	0.028
XS5	39327.9	40037.5	0.018	DC5	35973.8	36708.0	0.020
XS4	38689.7	39384.8	0.018	DC4	34819.1	35529.7	0.020
XS3	36156.8	36571.1	0.011	DC3	35979.7	36527.6	0.015
XS2	30856.5	31062.2	0.007	DC2	35840.6	36020.7	0.005
XS1	30822.6	30796.8	−0.001	DC1	36685.3	36685.3	0.000
XC1	36687.2	36637.6	−0.001	DS1	30820.8	30790.0	−0.001
XC2	35846.0	35996.5	0.004	DS2	30856.4	31042.6	0.006
XC3	35984.0	36506.1	0.014	DS3	36148.7	36587.7	0.012
XC4	34827.0	35520.3	0.020	DS4	38684.0	39393.1	0.018
XC5	35979.2	36766.9	0.021	DS5	39324.6	40086.2	0.019
XC6	37087.2	38143.1	0.028	DS6	39506.8	40354.3	0.021
XC7	38549.0	39672.0	0.028	DS7	41889.2	42831.5	0.022
XC8	40202.7	41741.1	0.037	DS8	42040.3	43206.9	0.027
XC9	43709.5	45305.7	0.035	DS9	42238.1	43634.4	0.032
XC10	43615.5	45595.7	0.043	DS10	42572.8	44300.5	0.039
XC11	43095.3	45009.1	0.043	DS11	43483.5	45201.1	0.038
XC12	42382.0	43964.0	0.036	DS12	44452.9	46065.2	0.035

In the above calculation results, the importance coefficient of some stay cable has a negative value. They should be directly taken as 0. It does not mean that the stayed cable has no effect on the structure. Instead, it still bears the load directly acting on the stayed cable.

The distributionabout the importance of cable stays along the longitudinal direction is shown in Fig. 8.

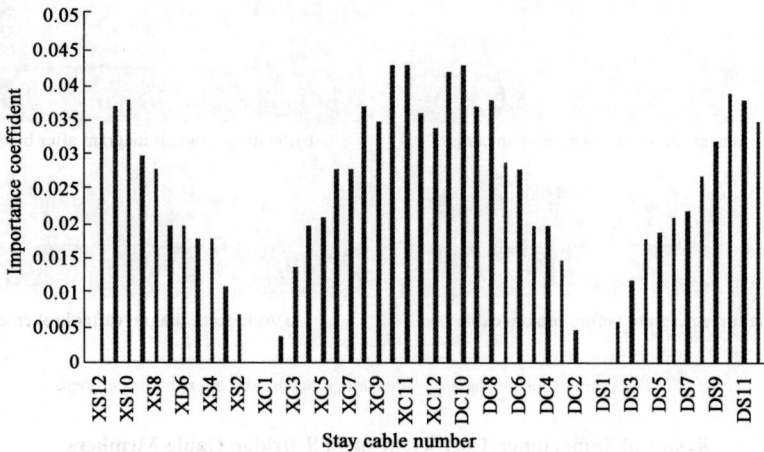

Fig. 8 Relation chart of cable importance coefficient

2.2 Response Analysis

According to 2.1, the importance of stay cables S10 and C10 of the bridge is relatively high. Theirs damage will have a greater impact on the overall performance of the bridge. The following mainly calculates and analyzes the corrosion damage of S10, C10 stay cables (add rust area to the tail to distinguish, such as "working condition 1%-2.5%" means that the stay cable corrosion rate in S10 is 2.5%, working condition 3%-2.5% means that the stay cable corrosion rate in C10 is 2.5%), the results are as follows (Fig. 9-Fig. 13)

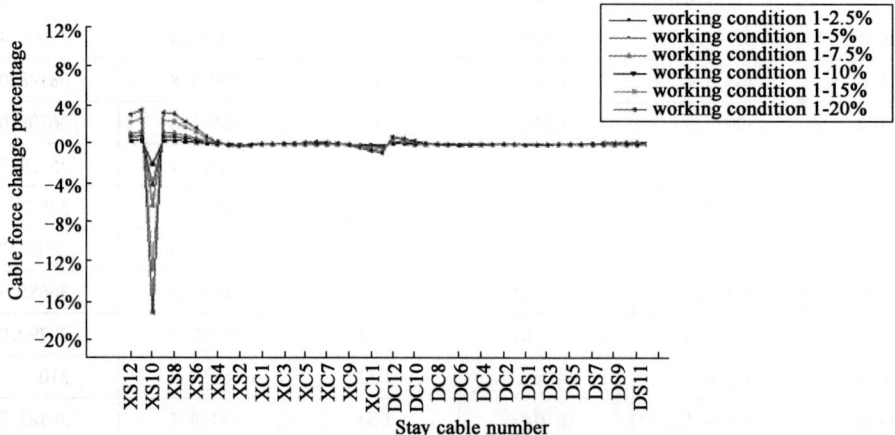

Fig. 9 The influence of S10 Cable Corrosion on the Cable Force

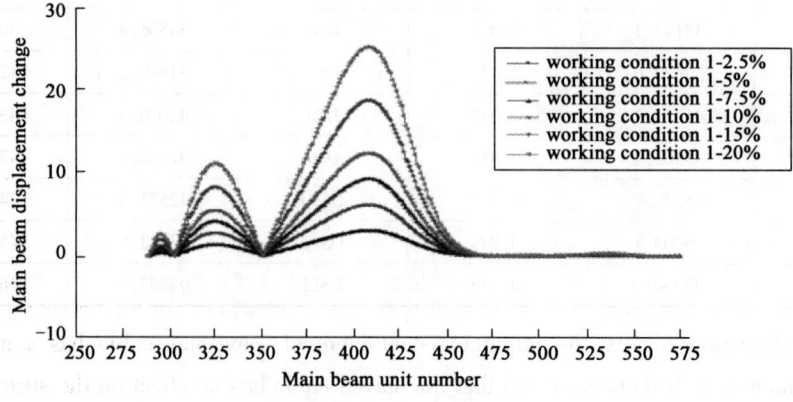

Fig. 10 Influence of S10 Cable Corrosion on Displacement of Main Girder

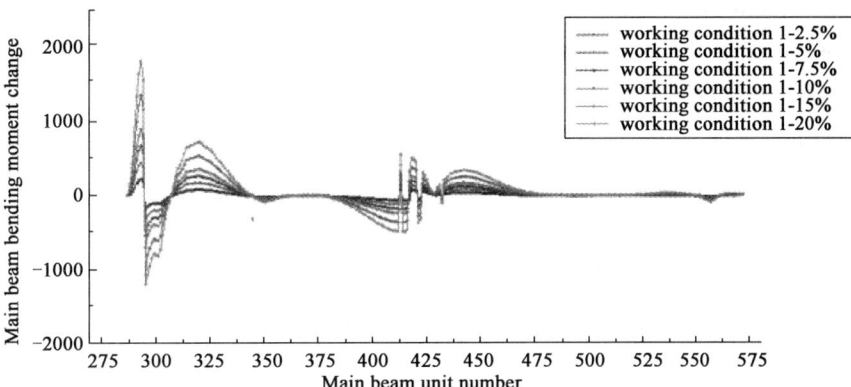

Fig. 11 Influence of S10 Cable Corrosion on Bending Moment of main Girder

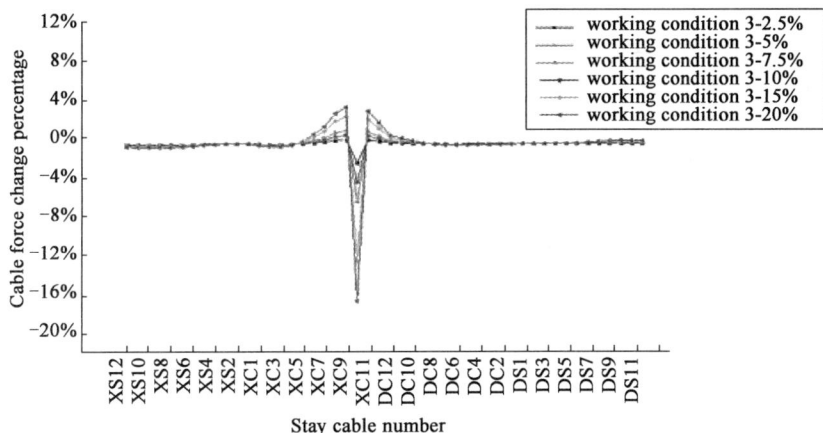

Fig. 12 Influence of Corrosion of C10 Cable on Bending Moment of Main Girder

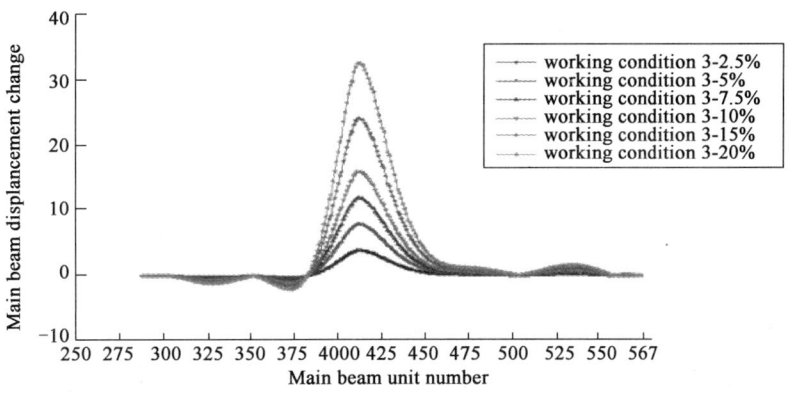

Fig. 13 Influence of Corrosion of C10 Cable on Displacement of Main Girder

It can be seen from the above variation figure that the rust of the stay cable will cause decrease of the cable force and corresponding changes in the cable force of the remainingstay cables. The rust of the stay cable has a greater influence on the cable force in the adjacent area, which cable force decrease more than 16%, while the variation amplitude of the remaining cable force is not more than 5% of the original cable force. The corrosion of stay cables will have the greatest impact on the deformation of the mid-span main girder. The maximum deformation increment of the main girder caused by the corrosion of the stay cables in the S10 cable zone is 27mm. The maximum deformation increment of the main girder caused by the corrosion of the stay cables in the C10 cable zone is 32mm. The bending moment of the main girder will change with the corrosion of stay cables.

Among them, the area where the bending moment changes the most is the area of corroded stay cables located. The maximum increment of the bending moment of the main beam caused by the corrosion of the stay cables in C10 and S10 cable areas is 1747kN·m(Fig. 14).

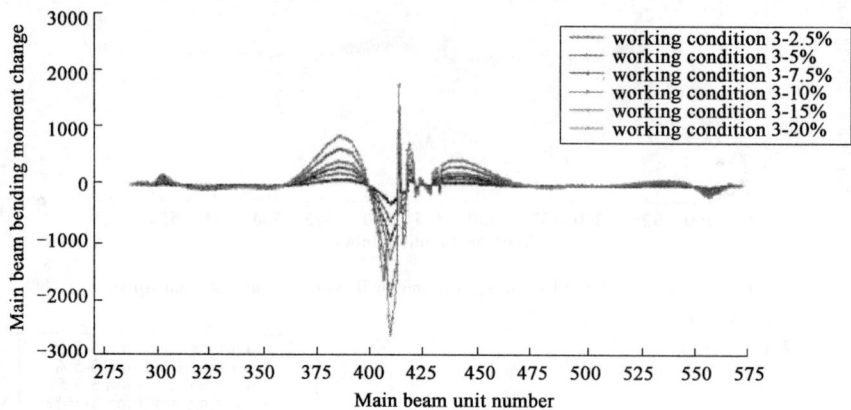

Fig. 14 Influence of Corrosion of C10 Cable on Bending Moment of Main Girder

3 Conclusions

This paper combines investigation and numerical simulation. The main conclusions drawn based on the analysis of the disease mechanism and the disease impact of the composite beam cable-stayed bridge are as follows:

(1) The steel-concrete composite girder cable-stayed bridge combines the disease characteristics of the composite girder bridge and the cable-stayed bridge. The disease of the main force-bearing members will cause the failure on original working performance of each component, or affect the overall performance of the coordinated work and joint bearing of each part.

(2) Cable-stayed bridge diseases (corrosion damage) have a greater impact on the mechanical performance of the bridge structure, while the greater the number of rust failures of stay cables, the greater the impact on its internal force characteristics. The important cable areas are shown below. Therefore, the maintenance level of stay cable components should be improved during the operation phase (Fig. 15).

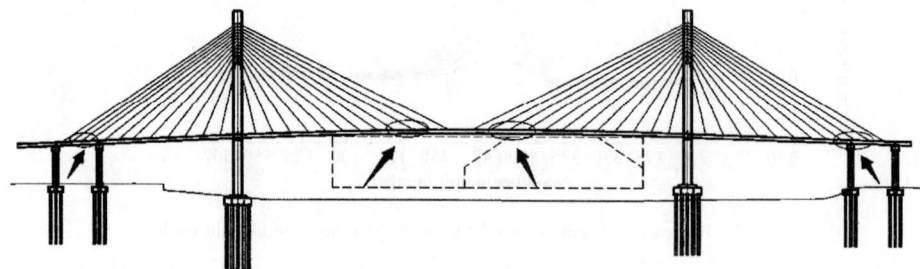

Fig. 15 Important cable areas

References

[1] Zongquan Gao, Qiang Zhang, Yingliang Wang. (2007). Evolution of Design on Hybrid Beam Cable-Stayed Bridge with Combined Structure. Railway Investigation and Surveying, 2007(zl), 50-53.

[2] Gharaibeh E S, Frangopol D M, Onoufriou T. (2002). Reliability-based Importance Assessment of Structural Members with Applications to Complex Structures. Computers and Structures, 80(12), 1113-1131.

[3] Weiliang Jin, Yuxi Zhao. (2002). Concrete structure durability. Beijing: Science Press, 2002.

[4] Zhigang Li. (2020). Research on Preventive Maintenance Method of Long-span Steel-Concrete Composite Beam Cable-stayed Bridge. Changan University.

[5] Baolian Luo. (2011). Common diseases and protection of steel structure bridges. Engineering and Construction. 25(03), 426-427.

[6] Maes M A, Fritzsons K E, GlowienJca S. (2006). Structural robustness in the light of risk and consequence analysis[J]. Structural engineering international, 16(2), 101-107.

[7] Lieping Ye, Xuchuan Lin, Zhe Qu, et al. (2010) Evaluating Method of Element Importance of Structural System Based on Generalized Structural Stiffness. Journal of Architecture and Civil Engineering, 27(01), 1-6+20.

[8] Zhao Zhao. (2018). Theoretical and Experimental study on damage Identification of Shear joints of Steel-Concrete Composite Beams. Jilin University.

[9] XiaoQiang Zhou, Wei Zhao, Juanli Cao. (2015). Development of long-span steel structure cable-stayed bridge and description of cable-stayed diseases. Technology Wind, 2015(16), 166.

A New Model for Slender Columns Retrofitted with CFRP

Zhengpu Yang   Peiwen He   Peng Wang

(Chang'an University, School of Highway)

Abstract This paper develops a model to predict the behavior of concentrically loaded slender circular section columns retrofitting carbon fiber reinforced polymer(CFRP) sheets. Columns deflection curves for linear elasticity conditions containing imperfection are derived to aid in developing the subsequent model. The model predicts the deflection curve of specimens, accounting for the plasticity of steel, FRP failure, and imperfection (initial out-of-straightness, initial eccentricity, and residual stress). An experiment verified the model. The results show that CFRP sheets could increase the columns' stiffness and decrease the lateral displacement corresponding to the maximum load. When the sum of the values of initial eccentricity and initial out-of-straightness is equal, their respective values have a limited effect on the deflection curve. The effect of imperfection on the response of the columns will diminish as displacement increases.

Keywords Retrofitting Steel columns Buckling Imperfection Composite material

0 Introduction

To overcome the limitations of durability, construction ability, and self-weight in the traditional retrofitting methods for steel structures by bolt connections, welding, and steel reinforcements, the carbonfiber reinforced polymer(CFRP), as a preferred solution to upgrade and repair the steel structures due to its good durability (Yuanqing et al., 2017), lightweight(Lu et al., 2010) and high tensile strength(Mohammed et al., 2020), is adopted. At present, the research of retrofitting steel structures focus mainly on the flexural(Linghoff et al., 2010) and fatigue analysis of beam(Huawen et al., 2010), axial compression short column(Ghaemdoust et al., 2016), and interface performance between the FRP and steel (Fernando et al., 2014), research work on strengthening of elongate tubular steel member with compression force is, however, minimal. Therefore, it is necessary to study the CFRP reinforced long tubular steel member further, especially the axial compression stability, compression failure mechanism, and maximum bearing capacity prediction approach.

An experimental study was carried by (Gao et al., 2013) to analyze the behavior of the circular-section columns bonded by CFRP sheets, and a numerical model has been developed to predict the axial load capacity, lateral and axial displacements. However, this study did not address the involvement of other influences on column behavior such as imperfection, nor could the information be analyzed further for the column's entire length.

This research paper is a complementary work for the numerical model presented by (Gao et al., 2013). To perfect the model, imperfection, including initial eccentricity, initial out-of-straightness, and residual stress, is introduced. The deflection curve containing the initial deflection and initial eccentricity under the linear elasticity condition is derived to obtain more information about the column response. A model that considers steel yielding, FRP failure, and residual stresses can also be established based on this equation. Further, this study analyses the effect of the above parameters on the columns' behavior.

1 Experiment Investigation

A summary of the experimental study is presented, and more details can be found elsewhere (Gao et al., 2013). There are seven hot finished hollow section steel braces ($D = 88.9$mm, $t = 4$mm) in the experiment. A slenderness ratio of 80 is accepted to ensure overall buckling failure. High-modulus carbon-fiber sheets (MBRACE CF 130) was bonded to the steel braces in the longitudinal direction using a wet lay-up procedure. A GFRP sheet (MBRACE ED 900) is installed between the CFRP layers and steel braces to simulate field practice to prevent galvanic corrosion. MBRACE SATURANT epoxy is applied to bond the sheet to another sheet or steel brace. The mechanical properties given by the manufacture are listed in Tab. 1.

Mechanical properties of materials Tab. 1

	Steel	CFRP	GFRP	Epoxy resin
Thinness (mm)	—	0.56	1.10	—
(Tensile) Strength (MPa)	490	3000	500	39
(Tensile) Modules (GPa)	206	230	28	2.4
Elongation (%)	3.0	1.5	2	—

Two hot finished hollow section steel braces without CFRP retrofitted is set as the control specimens. The rest of the experiments were conducted on CFRP retrofitted specimens with two, four, six, and eight layers, respectively. Two specimens retrofitted with four CFRP sheets due to the strain gauge failure happen in the first specimen. Only the second specimens are discussed in this research.

Test setup and instrumentation for specimens are shown in Fig. 1. A 1000kN hydraulic universal testing machine was used to apply compression. Fig. 2 shows the lubricated roller bearing used at the bottom end of a specimen to free for rotation. Eight linear variable displacement transducers (LVDTs), settled at the end of the specimen, record net axial measure. The longitudinal strains at mid-length were measured with 10-mm electric resistance strain gauges (S1-S4) attached directly on two opposite sides of the specimens.

There are 4 LVDTs settled at the midpoint of the specimen to record lateral displacement, which can only measure the lateral displacement in a single direction. The record data need to be processed to get the maximum lateral displacement of the specimen. Calculate the maximum lateral displacement (δ) using the larger displacement value in two mutually perpendicular directions by the Pythagorean theorem.

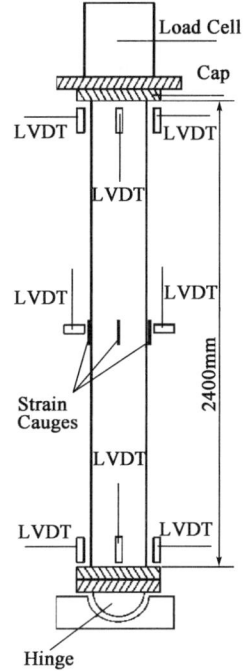

Fig. 1 Test setup and instrumentation for specimens   Fig. 2 Lubricated cylindrical bearing

The steel specimen fails due to overall buckling. Overall buckling leads to massive lateral displacement, which results in the dramatically increasing bending moment. Part of the steel specimen starts under tensile stress, while the other part withstands more compression stress, and the final result is that local buckling happens in the compression side. Overall buckling also occurs in CFRP-retrofitted specimens, but the CFRP sheet partly counteracts the local buckling. The failure mode in this condition is a combination of delamination and crushing of the CFRP sheets.

2 linear Elasticity Analysis

A linear elasticity model is developed to predict the deflection curve of slender columns. Equilibrium at any cross-section of the steel brace can be expressed using differential equation(1) and the solution to it is(2).

$$y'' + k^2(y + e + y_0) = 0 \tag{1}$$

$$y(x) = A\sin kx + B\cos kx - e - a\frac{k^2}{k^2 - \left(\frac{\pi}{l}\right)^2}\sin\left(\frac{\pi}{l}x\right) \tag{2}$$

Where, y is the deflection curve of the steel brace, e is the initial eccentricity, x is the distance of the section from the top. l is the length of the steel brace. A and B is undetermined coefficients of solutions of differential equations. k and y_0 is defined as follows:

$$k^2 = \frac{P}{EI(x)} \tag{3}$$

$$y_0 = a\sin\left(\frac{\pi}{l}x\right) \tag{4}$$

Where, P is the axial force; EI is the flexural rigidity of steel brace, the function of Young's modulus E and moment of inertia I of the column's cross section.

The boundary of the steel brace is simplified as pin-pin at the end. In this context, the undetermined coefficients can be solved by:

$$\begin{pmatrix} 0 & 1 \\ \sin kl & \cos kl \end{pmatrix} \begin{pmatrix} A \\ B \end{pmatrix} = \begin{pmatrix} e \\ e \end{pmatrix} \tag{5}$$

It follows that the initial eccentricity and the out-of-straightness determine the deflection curve. The deflection curve is Eq(5).

$$y(x) = e\left[\sqrt{1 + \left(\frac{1-\cos kl}{\sin kl}\right)^2} \sin(kx + \alpha) - 1\right] + \frac{ak^2}{k^2 - \left(\frac{\pi}{l}\right)^2}\sin\left(\frac{\pi}{l}x\right) \tag{6a}$$

$$2\alpha + kl = \pi \tag{6b}$$

Therefore, the range of values of $(kx + \alpha)$ is symmetric about $\pi/2$. The deflection curve is equal to the superposition of a portion of a half-wave sinusoidal curve caused by the initial eccentricity and a half-wave sinusoidal curve determined by the out-of-straightness. It is important to note that Eqs. (4) and (5) assume a constant flexural stiffness and that residual stress and FRP effects are not accounted for in these expressions. In the following sections, approaches are proposed to account for residual stress, material nonlinearity, and the FRP contribution.

3 Nonlinearity Analytical Model

A nonlinearity analytical model is developed to predict the deflection curve of the CFRP-retrofitted steel columns. The model accounts for material nonlinearities and imperfection (out-of-straightness, initial eccentricity, and residual stress). An increment approach is used, where the concepts of equilibrium and strain compatibility are satisfied at each loading step. An elastic-perfectly plastic model is applied in the stress-strain curve of steel, combined with the effect of residual stresses, as discussed next. The FRP sheet's stress-strain curve is assumed to follow an elastic-perfectly model, and the experimental results determine the failure strain of the FRP sheet.

3.1 Residual Stress

Residual stress is an essential factor for deflection curve analysis. It causes the steelfiber to yield at lower loads and reduces the flexural rigidity, which ultimately leads to a lower buckling strength. The first yielding happens in the cross-section with massive compressive residual stress in columns performed Davison and Birkemo(1983) and Key and Hancock(1985). The ratio of maximum residual stress to yielding stress varies from 22% to 88%. In this approach, the maximum residual stress will be analyzed as a parameter.

3.2 Initial Eccentricity and Out-of-straightness

It is unavoidable that the force loaded on the specimen does not coincide with its geometriccenter due to the specimen's imperfect layout. The distance between the center of the geometry and the force is called the initial eccentricity. The initial eccentricity causes a reduction in the specimen's strength, allowing yielding to occur sooner due to the more massive lateral displacement of the specimen under the same load. For simplicity, in this approach, the initial eccentricity and the axial direction of the specimen from the XY plane and the out-of-straightness discussed later are also in this plane.

Due to manufacturing errors, the steel column is not guaranteed to be perfectly straight. Allen and Bulson (1980) reported that the deflected shape could be represented by a Fourier series, which can be reduced to its first term to account for the first mode of buckling.

3.3 Meshing System

In this research, the nominal thickness of the CFRP and GFRP section is 0.56mm and 1.10mm. Therefore, the steel section (A1) is divided into eight strips, the GFRP section (A2) is divided into two strips, and every layer of CFRP does not divide through the thickness so that there is little difference in the size of each element.

The different circumferential division is applied, and the 180 strips along the circumference are dense enough to get accurate axial force and displacement. The centroid of each element is located at its mid-thickness, and the stress is assumed constant within the element area. After calculating the coordinate of elements, the strain of every element is determined as follows:

$$\varepsilon_i = \varepsilon\left(1 - \frac{y_i}{c}\right) \tag{7}$$

Where, y_i is the distance between the element i and the element with maximum strain. The stress in the elements σ_i is calculated as $\sigma_i = E_i\varepsilon_i + \sigma_r$, where E_i is Young's modulus of element i and σ_r is the residual stress. c is the depth of the neutral axis. By introducing the failure criteria, stress values for subsequent analysis are determined following. For the steel element, if the stress is larger than 355MPa, and the effective stress is selected as 355MPa. For the FRP element, if the stress is larger than the failure criteria, the effective stress is zero. Therefore, the total axial load and the corresponding moment is

$$P = \sum \sigma_{ei} A_i \tag{8}$$

$$M = \sum \sigma_{ei} A_i y_i \tag{9}$$

Where, σ_{ei} is the stress by considering failure criteria.

3.4 Nonlinear Analysis

First yielding will typically occur in the maximum residual stress of the buckled brace atmidheight. As the axial load and corresponding lateral deflection increase, yielding spreads within the cross-section and in the brace's longitudinal direction. Therefore, the moment of inertia varies longitudinally within the yielded length. In this study, the moment of inertia of the composite brace is assumed to vary in a parabolic manner over a distance of ± 0.2L from the mid height with a value at the mid-length and at ± 0.2L from the mid-length, where is the gross moment of inertia of the cross section. In this study, the brace is evenly divided into 100 segments, and the geometric coordination equations are shown as:

$$y_i(x_i) = y_{i+1}(x_{i+1}) \tag{10}$$

$$y'_i(x_i) = y'_{i+1}(x_{i+1}) \tag{11}$$

$$y_i(x_i) = A_i \sin k_i x_i + B_i \cos k_i x_i - e - a \frac{k_i}{k_i - \left(\frac{\pi}{l}\right)^2} \sin\left(\frac{\pi x_i}{l}\right) \tag{12}$$

$$y'_i(x_i) = A_i k_i \cos k_i x_i - B_i k_i \sin k_i x_i - a\left(\frac{\pi}{l}\right) \frac{k_i}{k_i - \left(\frac{\pi}{l}\right)^2} \cos\left(\frac{\pi x_i}{l}\right) \tag{13}$$

Where, $y_i(x_i)$ is the deflection curve for a composite brace, the definition field of $y_i(x_i)$ is (x_{i-1}, x_i) and x_0 is equal to zero. Due to steel elements yielding and the failure of FRP elements, the value $k(x)$ varies with x. To simplified the analysis, it is assumed that the value of $k(x)$ in a segment is constants and $k_i = \frac{1}{(x_i - x_{i-1})} \int_{x_{i-1}}^{x_i} \sqrt{\frac{P}{EI(x)}}$.

The axial displacement Δ is the sum of two components, Δ_a and Δ_b, as shown in Eq s(14).

$$\Delta = \Delta_a + \Delta_b \tag{14}$$

Where, Δ_a is the axial displacement caused by axial shortening and Δ_b is the axial displacement due to curvature. They can be approximated as following:

$$\Delta_a = \sum_{\text{whole length}} \frac{PL_i}{EA_i} \tag{15}$$

$$\Delta_b = l - \Delta_a - S \tag{16}$$

Where, S is the chord of length of the deformed column and is calculated based on the deflection curve.

3.5 Convergent analysis

In the complete analysis, the presumption of the neutral axis depth c is presented at the beginning of the approach. In order to verify this assumption, the eccentricity $e' = \dfrac{M}{P}$ should be equal to $(y + e)$. If the ratio of e' to $(y + e)$ is larger than 1, it can be explained that the preconfigured curvature at the mid-height section is too large and the neutral axis depth c should be larger, vice versa. Change in the amount of c could be adjusted according to the value of the ratio of e' to $(y + e)$.

3.6 Generation of Full Responses

To obtain the deflection curve of the composite brace and the axial-displacement response, the procedure can be summarized as follows:

(1) Mesh the section and calculate the area A_i and coordinate y_i of every element, the point has the maximum compressive strain it the origin of this one-dimensional coordinate system, and the y-axis direction coincides with the direction of maximum displacement.

(2) Select a value for the maximum compressive strain ε.

(3) Select a value for the neutral axial depth c.

(4) Calculate the strain ε_i of each element.

(5) Calculate the axial stress of each element σ_i according to the material constitution.

(6) Get the axial force P and bending moment M for the cross-section and calculate the eccentricity e'.

(7) Calculate the lateral displacement at this section δ by the deflection curve.

(8) Compare the eccentricity e from step 5 with the value $(\delta + e)$. If e' is larger than $(\delta + e)$, increase the value of c and repeat the steps from 3 to 7 until the ratio of the two value equal to 1 (convergence $= 10^{-4}$), vice versa.

(9) Check if failure happens and stop the procedure if it does.

(10) Increase the maximum compressive strain ε and repeat the steps from 3 to 10.

4 Model Verification and Parametric Study

The analysis model included several features: residual stress, the plasticity of steel, failure of FRP, initial eccentricity, and initial out-of-straightness. To analyze the effect of those features, the load-lateral displacement curve of steel with two CFRP layers has been predicted by four different cases. The initial eccentricity and initial out-of-straightness are assumed as $e = a = 0.3$. The maximum residual stress is considered as $0.7\sigma_y$. In case 1, the failure of elements (Steel yielding and failure of FRP sheets) is ignored, and the residual stress is also equal to zero. In case 2, the steel yielding is considered based on case 1. In case 3, the failure of FRP sheets is considered based on case 2. In case 4, the residual is also considered.

Fig. 3 shows the analytical responses for the four cases. The figure clearly shows that the axial load-lateral displacement does not significantly decrease if the steel plasticity and the FRP failure are ignored. The introduction of steel material yielding causes the load-lateral displacement curve to stagnate over a while. The introduction of residual stresses had a large effect on the axial load-axial displacement curve.

To verify the model, lateral displacement at the mid-height point, and the axial displacement is calculated by the deflection curve. The test results were reported by (Gao et al., 2013). The load versus lateral displacement and axial displacements of the specimens retrofitting with four CFRP layers are predicted and presents in Fig. 3. According to the figure, it is easy to find that for the load-lateral displacement curves, the analytical values are more consistent with the experimental results, except near the maximum load, while for load-axial displacement curves, the analytical results are an excellent fit to the test results. The effect of CFRP layers, the initial out-of-straightness, initial curve, and the residual stress is discussed in this section.

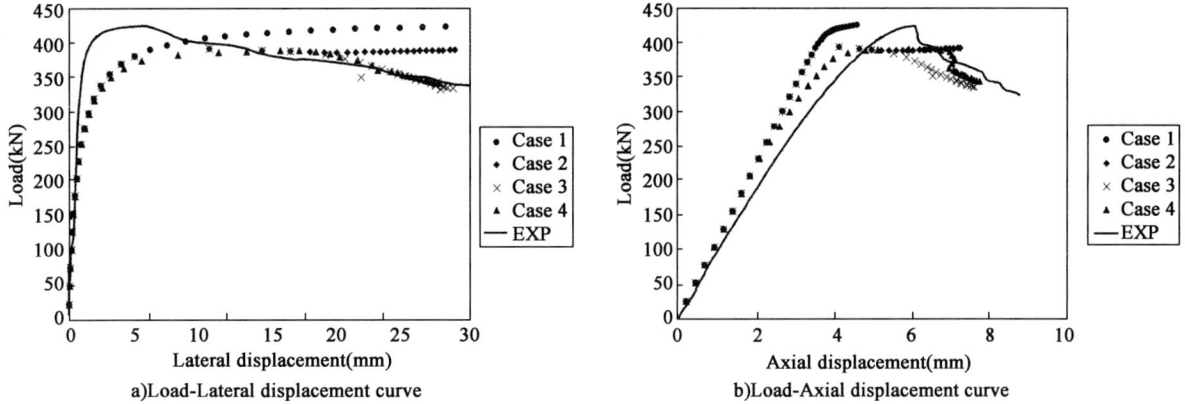

Fig. 3　Illustration of the significance of various features of the analytical model. Case 1: Linear elasticity analysis, Case 2: Same as Case 1 and plasticity of steel, Case 3: Same as case 2 and residual stresses, Case 4: Same as Case 3 and FRP failure.

4.1　Effect of CFRP layers

Fig. 4 show that bonding CFRP sheets to slender steel columns can increase their axial stiffness. The lateral displacement corresponding to the maximum load gradually decreases while the axial displacement increases as the number of CFRP sheets increases. For example, Fig. 4 shows that the lateral displacement corresponding to the maximum load with two, four, six, and eight CFRP layers are 16%, 29%, 29%, and 53% for specimens with $e = a = 0.3$mm respectively. As for the axial displacement corresponding to the maximum load, the ratio of specimens with two, four, six, and eight CFRP layers to steel specimens are 95%, 91%, 104%, and 77%. On the other hand, the percentage increase in axial stiffness is in order of 13%, 24%, 34%, and 44% for specimens retrofitted with 2, 4, 6, and 8 layers.

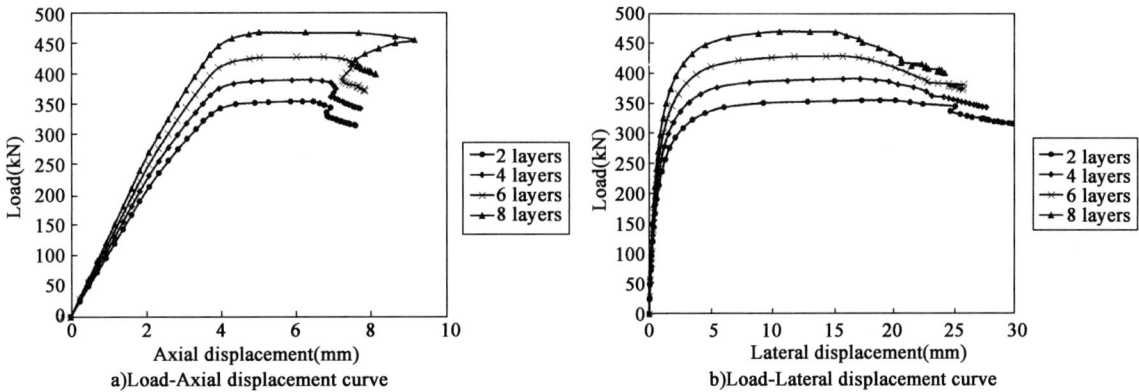

Fig. 4　Effect of number of CFRP layers on the behavior of specimens

4.2　Effect of Initial Out-of-straightness and Initial Eccentricity

The effect for initial out-of-straightness and initial eccentricity consists of two components: sum equivalence of the two values and equality of the two values. Fig. 5a) and Fig. 5b) show the load-displacement curve of the sum of the values of initial out-of-straightness, and initial eccentricity is equal to 0.6mm, and four CFRP sheets layers are retrofitted. As the value of an increase from 0.1mm to 0.5mm, the maximum load on the specimen increases from

389.15kN to 391.50kN. The axial displacement and the mid-height lateral displacement corresponding to the maximum load change from 17.25mm to 17.28mm and 6.34mm to 6.44mm, respectively. The difference is so small that it is negligible in engineering. Similar findings were also obtained under numerical experiments where the sum of the values of initial out-of-straightness and initial eccentricity was equal to 6mm. Fig.5c) and Fig.5d) show the load-displacement curve of values of initial out-of-straightness and initial eccentricity is similar and vary from 0.1mm to 0.6mm. As the value of imperfection increases, the lateral displacement of the specimen is more massive for the same load condition before the maximum load is reached. However, as the load-lateral displacement curve enters the descending section, the curves show a tendency to converge. However, for load-axial displacement curves, the curves at different imperfection values overlap highly until a specific load. The load corresponding to the branch point of the curve decreases with an increasing degree of imperfection.

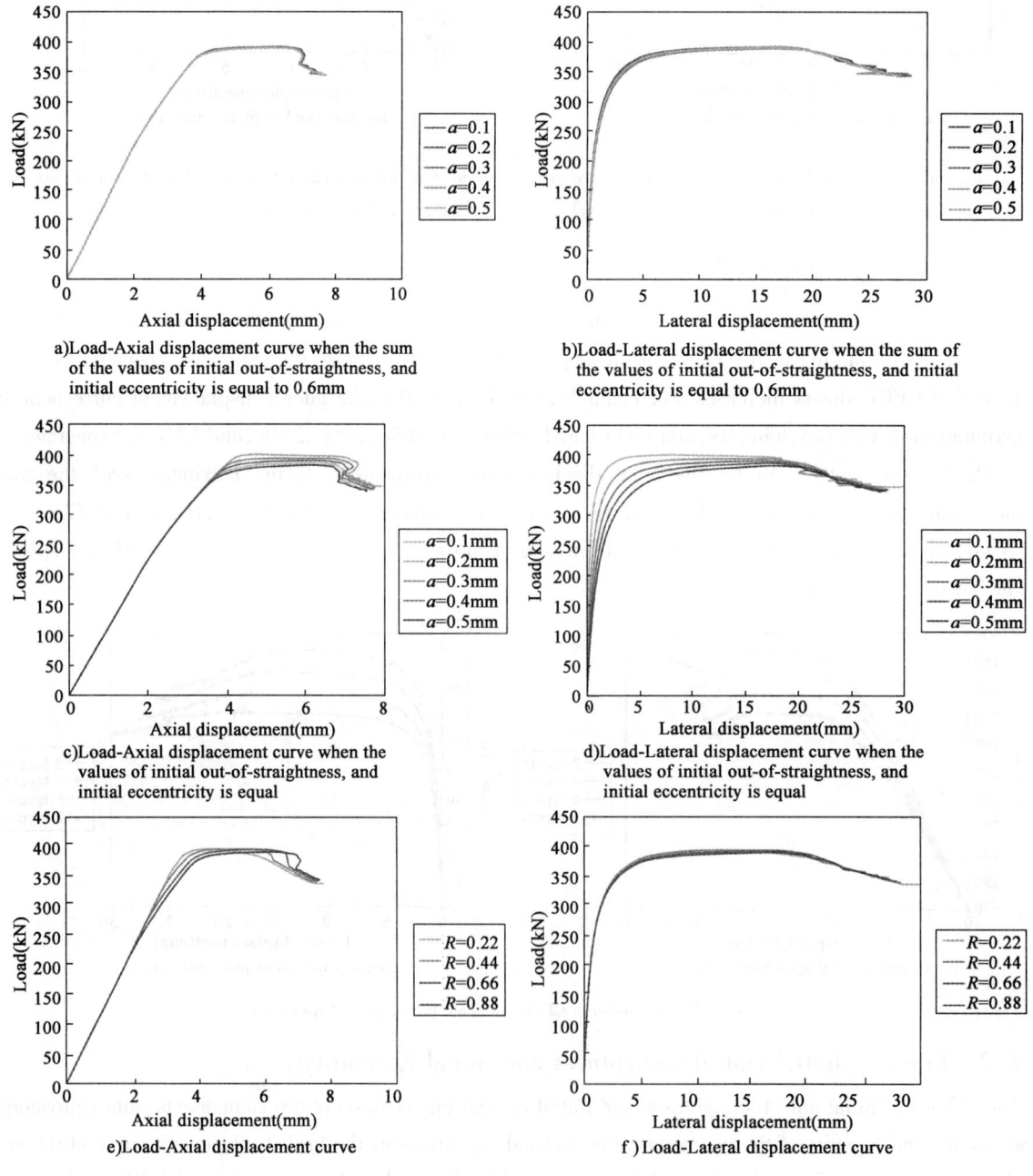

Fig.5 Summary of Results of Parametric Study

4.3 Effect of residual stress

The residual stress on the specimen response is mainly reflected in the decrease in strength and the load-axial displacement curve. Form the Fig. 5e) and f), it is shown that as the residual stress increases, the strength of the specimen gradually decreases from 394.71kN to 390.45kN, and the corresponding axial displacement increase from 4.63mm to 5.90mm. The slope of the initial segment of the load-axial displacement curve was not affected by residual stresses. Still, the specimens with higher residual stresses showed earlier changes in axial stiffness. However, a specimen with more significant residual stress after the maximum load is present will withstand greater axial forces for the same axial displacement. As for the load-lateral displacement curves, the residual stresses have less influence on them.

5 Conclusions

A nonlinear model based on the concepts of equilibrium and strain compatibility has been developed to predict the deflection curve of slender circular-section columns retrofitted with CFRP sheets. The columns' imperfection(out-of-straightness, initial eccentricity and residual), material and geometric nonlinearities, and CFRP reinforcement ratio are accounting. The model was verified using experimental results and showed good agreement. The following conclusions are drawn:

(1) Externally bonded longitudinal CFRP sheetseffectively increase the stiffness of slender circular-section columns, and the lateral displacement corresponding to the maximum load is reduced. The percentage increase in stiffness between 13% to 44%, depending on the number of CFRP layers. The lateral displacement corresponding to the maximum load decrease between 19% to 53%.

(2) The two various values have less influence on the maximum lateral deflection and axial displacement, provided that the initial deflection and initial eccentricity are constant and unchanged. The effect of strength, axial and lateral displacements corresponding to the maximum load does not exceed 2 percent in the case of a change in the initial out-of-straightness value from 0.1mm to 0.5mm.

(3) The effect of residual stresses on lateral displacement at the mid-height position exists only near the maximum load. The load-displacement curves of the different residual stresses overlap highly when the load on the member is too small or when a large buckling of the steel or FRP failure has already occurred. Greater residual stresses will cause the axial load-displacement curve to inflect earlier. However, after the occurrence of the maximum load, the specimen with greater residual stresses instead takes on a greater amount of the same axial displacement for the same axial displacement.

In this study, the boundary condition is simplified, assumed as pin-pin columns. Further research is needed to examine the other boundary conditions. What's more, the compression elastic modulus of the CFRP sheets is considered as equal to the tensile compression modulus. The correct selection of the compressive modulus of elasticity for CFRP materials also needs further study.

References

[1] Davison T A, Birkemoe P C. Column behaviour of cold-formed hollow structural steel shapes[J]. Canadian Journal of Civil Engineering, 1983, 10(1), 125-141.

[2] Fernando D, Yu T, Teng J G. Behavior of CFRP laminates bonded to a steel substrate using a ductile adhesive[J]. Journal of Composites for Construction, 2014, 18(2), 04013040.

[3] Gao X Y, Balendra T, Koh C G. Buckling strength of slender circular tubular steel braces strengthened by CFRP[J]. Engineering structures, 2013, 46, 547-556.

[4] Ghaemdoust M R, Narmashiri K, Yousefi O. Structural behaviors of deficient steel SHS short columns

strengthened using CFRP[J]. Construction and Building Materials,2016,126,1002-1011.
[5] Huawen Y, König C, Ummenhofer T, et. al Fatigue performance of tension steel plates strengthened with prestressed CFRP laminates. Journal of Composites for Construction,2010,14(5),609-615.
[6] Key B W, Hancock G J. An experimental investigation of the columnbehaviour of cold formed square hollow sections[R]. 1985.
[7] Linghoff D, Al-Emrani M, Kliger, R. Performance of steel beams strengthened with CFRP laminate-Part 1: Laboratory tests[J]. Composites Part B:Engineering,2010,41(7),509-515.
[8] Lu X, Lu M, Zhou L M, et. al. (2010). Evaluation of welding damage in welded tubular steel structures using guided waves and a probability-based imaging approach[J]. Smart materials and structures,2010,20(1),015018.
[9] Mohammed Ali A, Allan C Manalo, Wahid Ferdous, et al. State-of-the-art of prefabricated FRP composite jackets for structural repair[J]. Engineering Science and Technology,2020.
[10] Yuanqing W, Liang Z, Gang S, et al. Application research on new strengthening technologies for steel structures[J]. Industrial Construction,2017. (In Chinese)

Force Analysis of T-beam from Simple Support to Continuous

Liuyu Zhang Qichen Wang Xinyue Chen Peiqi He Zhiguo Wang Guitong Zhang

(College of highway, Chang'an University)

Abstract In view of the large area of continuous T-beam bridges where the main body of the beam is cracked, the finite element software is used to carry out refined mechanical analysis from three main aspects: time-varying effect, prestress effect and live load effect. The results show that: The greater the age difference, the greater the axial force produced by uneven shrinkage, and an increase in assembly time can effectively reduce the shrinkage axial tension due to the age difference. ; The shorter the concrete loading age, the greater the loss of bending moment and axial force in the span. ; The loss of positive moment prestress is proportional to the reduction of compressive stress at the bottom of the beam, and the loss of positive moment prestress has a greater effect on the stress reserve of the beam than the loss of negative moment prestress; in the actual construction of continuous T-beams, the bridge should be prevented from carrying the beam in the simple support state.

Keywords Continuous T-beam Beam crack Time-varying effect Prestress effect Live load effect

0 Introduction

At present, China has conducted a lot of research and put into use of simple support trans-continuous beam bridge[1-2], The reasonableness of the force and design of the simple variable continuous structure, the convenience and reliability of construction, the continuous bridge of this construction process has become the main bridge type in China[3-4]. However, after testing, it is found that the continuous T-beam bridge has widespread diseases mainly caused by cracks in the girders, such as vertical (partly oblique) cracks and horseshoe cracks distributed symmetrically on both sides of the web of the T-beam bridge. The cracks will reduce the effective section of the girder and the stiffness of the girder, and air and moisture will enter the concrete through the cracks and cause the internal steel corrosion, which may reduce the bearing capacity of the girder.

For prestressed reinforced concrete girders under high stress, severe corrosion of the prestressing reinforcement may lead to brittle fracture of the girder, which is extremely dangerous[5]. Early cracks in concrete are considered by some domestic scholars to be stress cracks caused by external forces or deformations[6-10]. Based on the previous research, this paper mainly carries out the fine mechanical analysis of the relying project bridges in terms of the three main influences, namely, time-varying effect, prestressing effect and constant-load live-load effect, and studies the influence of these three types of effects on the cracks of T-beams.

1 Rely on Engineering

The project is located on a highway in a mountainous area, with a total length of about 42km, 32 bridges of various types, and a total length of 1.1km, accounting for about 27% of the total route length, from which a three-span, one-linked, simple-support T-beam bridge with a single beam length of 30m, a height of 2m, a test length of 90m, a total width of 12.25m, and five post-tensioned sections is selected for experimental study. The pre-stressed concrete T-beams consist of a fully prestressed concrete design.

2 Finite Element Modeling

The bridge structural parameters refer to the drawing of the 30m T-beam of the relying project, with a beam height of 2.0m and 10cm pavement layers of cast-in-place concrete and asphalt concrete at the top of each beam. The calculated parameters for the model are taken as the reference design parameters.

(1) The gravitational density of concrete concretes, modulus of elasticity.

(2) Prestressed strand: nominal diameter, modulus of elasticity, relaxation coefficient, relaxation rate; the use of two tensile way.

(3) Pipeline friction coefficient, coefficient of deviation, considering the end of the anchor deformation, beam retraction deformation, the sum of the two taken 12mm.

(4) The vehicle load is highway-I grade; the design speed is 120km/h.

(5) The common steel bar is hot-rolled HPB300 and HRB400.

(6) The reinforcement ratio of hot-rolled HPB300 and HRB400 bars is 0.92%, 0.28% and 3.23% respectively for the roof, web and horseshoe of the common steel.

(7) The round Teflon sliding rubber bearing with specification GYZF4ϕ450 × 101mm is used at the simple support end and the round plate rubber bearing with specification GYZϕ600 × 110mm is used at the continuous end.

(8) Ambient humidity: According to on-site data monitoring, the ambient humidity is 60% during the daytime and 71% at night.

ADINA and Midas FEA finite element software were used to build the solid model, 3D-SOLID unit was used for the concrete beam, and Rebar was used for the steel reinforcement and steel technique. Midas FEA was used for the analysis of the T-beam erection, prestressing tensioning, bridge deck concrete pavement and the gun carriage crossing, which was loaded with concentrated forces at the corresponding positions of the T-beam at the actual wheel spacing in the field. The finite element model is shown in Fig. 1.

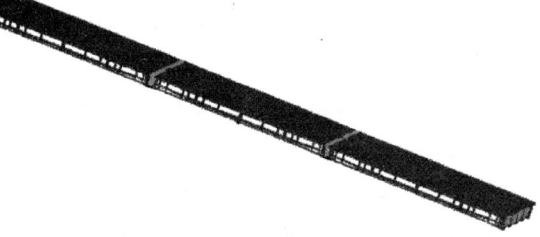

Fig. 1 Finite element model diagram

3 Refinement Analysis of Force on Continuous T-beam After First Simple Support

3.1 Analysis of the Time-varying Effect of the Continuous Structure after the first Simple Support

3.1.1 Analysis of the Effects of Contraction

(1) Effect of uneven cross-sectional shrinkage on webs

According to the definition in the *Design Specification for Highway Reinforced Concrete and Prestressed Reinforced Concrete Bridge Culverts* (JTG 3362—2018)[11]: the theoretical thickness of the member $h = 2A/\mu$, three test intercepts were taken for the theoretical thickness calculation, and the sections taken are shown in Fig. 2.

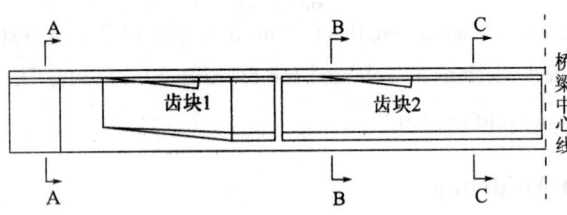

Fig. 2 Body-to-surface Ratio of Different T-beam Sections

Ordinary steel reinforcement plays an effective role in blocking the uneven shrinkage of the cross-section of T-beams, therefore, the study of the shrinkage effect of concrete in this paper considers the role of ordinary steel reinforcement, and analyses the self-shrinkage effect of T-beam cross-section from two aspects: with bridge deck pavement and without bridge deck pavement.

①No bridge deck paving

It can be seen from Fig. 3 that the influence of horseshoe and flange plate on the web of T-beam is larger, and the influence of horseshoe on the web of T-beam is larger than that of flange plate; the tensile stress of the web of T-beam as a whole shows a gradual decrease with the increase of the height of the web of T-beam; in the first 1460 days of the beam, the tensile stress of the web of T-beam caused by the uneven contraction of the cross-section increases with the increase of time, and the tensile stress at the bottom of the web of T-beam at 2 years. The tensile stress in the middle of the web reaches 1.3 MPa, and the uneven shrinkage of the cross-section has an obvious influence on the stress of the web of the T-beam.

②With bridge deck pavement

It can be seen from Fig. 4 that after considering the bridge deck pavement, the web is still in the overall tensile state, and the tensile stress in the web increases, but the rule is different from that without bridge deck pavement, showing the phenomenon of tensile stress gradually increasing with the increase of the height of the web of T-beam; this is because the bridge deck pavement increases the thickness of the beam body flange plate, increases the stiffness of the flange plate section, so that the influence of the flange plate on the web is greater than that of the horseshoe, and the beam body is still in the overall tensile state. In the first 1460 days, the tensile stresses in the webs due to the uneven shrinkage of the cross-section increased with time, and at 2 years the tensile stresses at the top position of the webs reached 1.9 MPa, the tensile stresses at the middle position of the webs reached 2.4 MPa, and the tensile stresses at the bottom position of the webs reached 2.3 MPa, and the extent of the influence of the uneven shrinkage of the cross-section on the force of the T-beam webs was more obvious.

(2) Age differential shrinkage effect of concrete

①Average of age difference on the force on each main beam

In this paper, three working conditions (10d, 20d and 30d) are selected to study the influence of age difference on the force of T-beam, and three beams of side span and three beams of middle span are taken for the study. The project is composed of three spans with five T-beams in each span. Due to the symmetry of the structure, only the left side span is studied for the side span. The numbering of each T-beam is shown in Fig. 5.

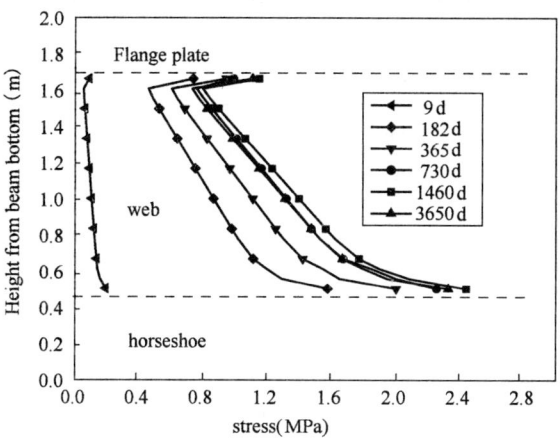
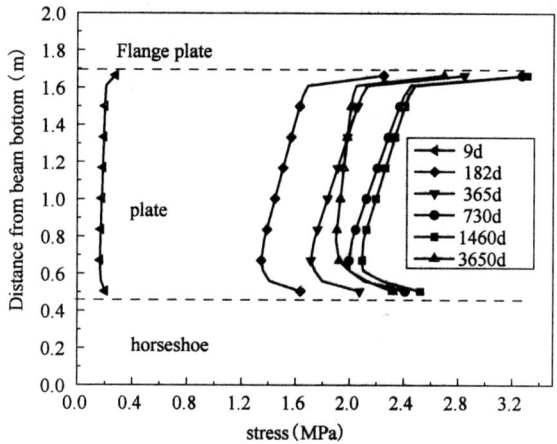

Fig. 3 Change of Shrinkage Stress with Time at Different Moments   Fig. 4 Contraction Stress Changes with time at Different Moments

It can be seen from Fig. 6 and Tab. 1 that the larger the age difference is, the larger the axial force produced by uneven shrinkage; when the age difference is the same, the axial tension produced by shrinkage difference in the middle beam is larger than that in the side beam; when the age difference reaches 30d, the axial tension in the middle beam of the middle span is the largest, reaching 771 kN, and after calculation, the tensile stress in the beam reaches 0.9 MPa; this has obviously affected the force performance of the T-beam. The shrinkage effect is obvious.

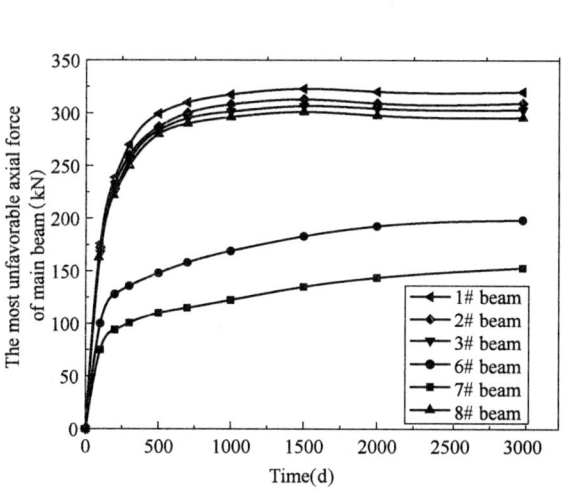
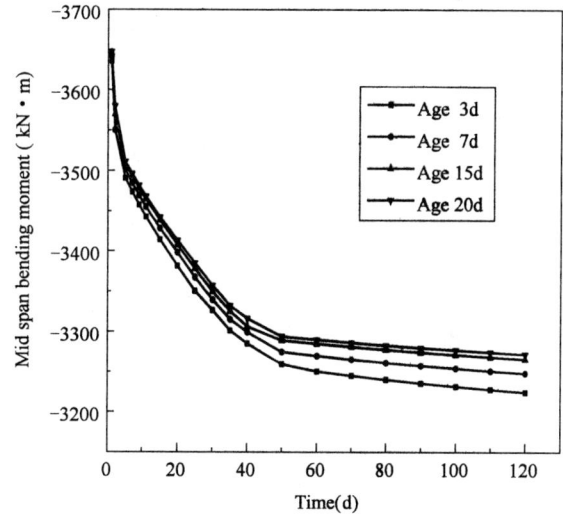

Fig. 5 Relationship between Axial Force and Time ($\Delta t_0 = 10d$)   Fig. 6 Variation of Mid-span Bending Moment with Time for Different Loading Ages

T-beam main Beam Number   Tab. 1

Left span	Mid span	Right span
①	⑥	
②	⑦	
③	⑧	
④	⑨	
⑤	⑩	

②Effect of assembly time on force on each main beam

Since the T-beam may not only have different pouring times, but also different assembly times, the paper takes several cases of age differences of 10d, 20d, 30d, and assembly time differences of 10d, 30d, 60d, and 90d for analysis. The most unfavourable shrinkage differential axial forces are shown in Tab. 2.

The most Unfavourable Shrinkage Differential Axial Force　　　　　Tab. 2

Beam number	Axial force(pull;kN)		
Age difference	10d	20d	30d
1#	154	331	491
2#	296	510	703
3#	303	527	729
6#	199	404	588
7#	309	541	750
8#	320	558	771

When the age difference is 30d, the assembly time is 10d, the axial tensile force is 1195kN, the cross-sectional tensile stress can reach 14MPa, its shrinkage effect has been more obvious(Tab. 3).

The most Unfavorable Shrinkage Differential Axial Force(tension;kN)　　　　　Tab. 3

Beam number	Age difference 10d	Age difference 20d			Age difference 30d
Assembly time difference	10d	10d	30d	60d	90d	10d
1#	284	540	331	240	195	753
2#	490	799	510	367	294	1057
3#	505	830	527	381	304	1099
6#	356	655	404	296	241	902
7#	518	852	541	389	311	1129
8#	532	876	558	402	321	1159

3.1.2　Analysis of the Impact of Creeping Effects

The creep effect has an important influence on the mechanical properties of concrete structure, especially during the construction of bridges, the influence of creep effect is more obvious [12], like shrinkage, creep is an inherent property of concrete materials, the creep of concrete will reduce the prestressing steel pretension, reduce the compressive stress reserve at the bottom of the beam, and increase the deflection deformation of the beam.

(1) Effect of loading age on creep effect

T-beams are in the precast stage, and the prestressing tension may be 3-5 days after the beam is poured, or 10-20 days after it is poured. Therefore, this paper mainly investigates the effects of the creep effect on the bending moment and axial force in the beam span under different loading ages of concrete, and analyses the effects of the creep effect on the internal force of the structure under four cases of concrete loading ages of 3d, 7d, 15d and 20d.

It can be seen from Fig. 6 and Fig. 7 that the shorter the concrete loading age, the greater the loss of span moment and axial force, and when the storage beam time reaches 2 months, the span moment is only 90% of the starting value, and the axial force is only 77% of the starting value, indicating that the effect of creeping on the axial force is greater than that on the moment; and the reduction of axial force is mainly in the first 60d of concrete, and the reduction of axial force indicates the reduction of pre-stress, and the first 60d is the pre-stress of The loss value is 94% of the first 120d prestressing loss value.

(2) Analysis of the creep effect after considering ordinary steel reinforcement bars

In this section, the equivalent elastic modulus method is used to analyse the effect of creeping effect.

According to Fig. 8, the common steel reinforcement increases the compressive stress at the top of the T-beam by 18% and gradually increases it with time, while the compressive stress at the bottom of the T-beam decreases by 20% and gradually decreases it with time.

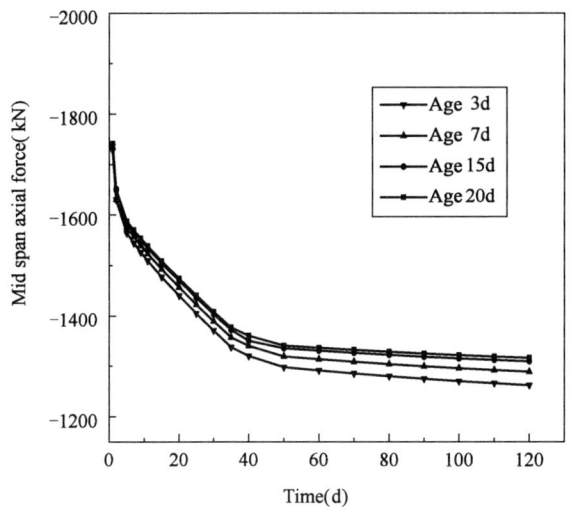

Fig. 7 Variation of Cross-axial Force with Time in Different Loading Ages

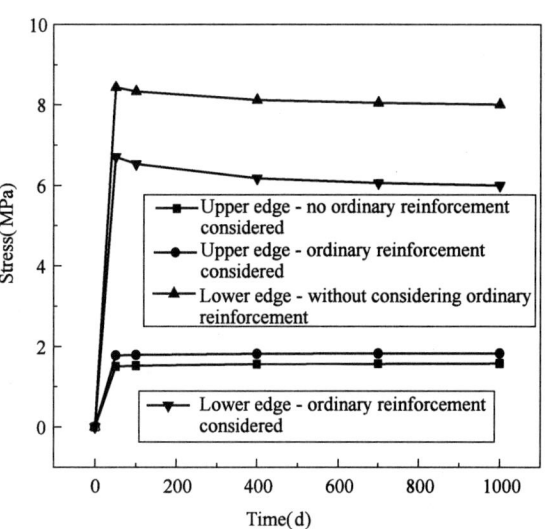

Fig. 8 Axial Force vs. Time Diagram ($\Delta t_0 = 10d$)

3.2 Analysis of the Effects of Prestressing

3.2.1 Prestressing Tensile Stage

Tensioning of prestressing reinforcement is an extremely important process in the prefabrication of T-beams, and the quality of its construction will affect the performance of the beam in subsequent use. Therefore, the structural forces of T-beams after tensioning of prestressing reinforcement are studied.

From Fig. 9 to Fig. 11, it can be seen that the beam body shows a nearly linear variation relationship along the height direction in the tensioning stage.

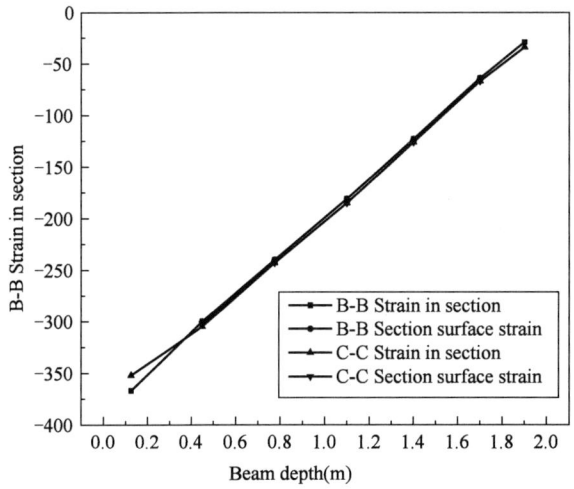

Fig. 9 Strain Diagram of Side-span Beam

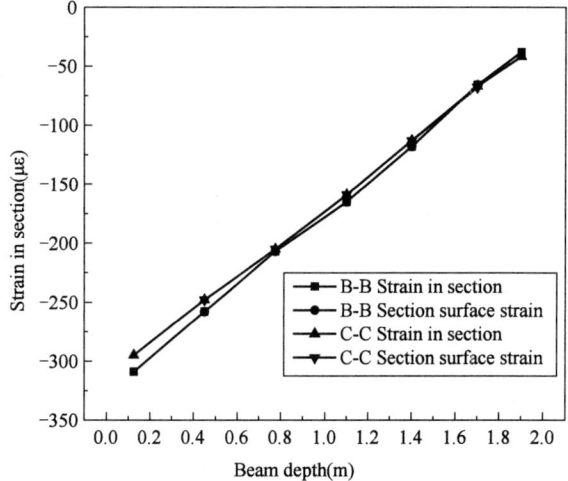

Fig. 10 Mid-span Side Beam Strain Diagram

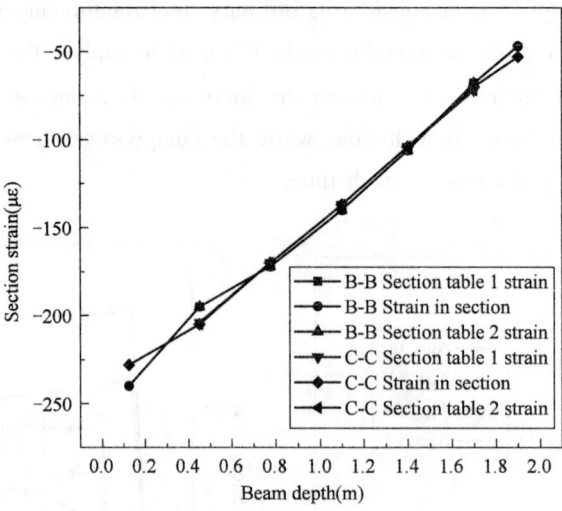

Fig. 11 Mid-span strain diagram

3.2.2 Effects of Insufficient Prestressing Tension on the Structure

Insufficient prestressing tensioning still exists in the actual project, which is due to the differences in the technical level, construction experience and responsibility of the field operators, resulting in the pre-stressing reinforcement not being in place during the tensioning process, the pre-stressing pipe not being grouted, and even the clips and anchor holes being separated and the strand being cut. The failure of pre-stress tensioning in place directly leads to a big difference between the actual load state of the beam body and the design load state, and the construction space of the continuous T-beam after simple support is large because the beam body is manufactured in the prefabricated beam yard. In this section, three scenarios are analysed with the tensile values of 100%, 90% and 80% of the design value, and the construction of prestressing reinforcement in the negative moment area is more complicated because the tensile stage is at the corresponding bridge site, differences in the technical level of the construction personnel resulting in large discrepancies between the actual tensile values and the design values, Therefore, this paper simulates three scenarios with the values of 100%, 75% and 50%, so this section is mainly about the coupling analysis of the failure of the prestressing reinforcement tensile at the positive and negative moments of the beam body. The effective tensile values of T-beam prestressing are shown in Tab.4.

T-beam Prestress Effective Tension Value Table (%) Tab.4

Condition number	Effective tension value of prestress in positive bending moment area	Negative pre bending moment region
1	100	100
2	100	75
3	100	50
4	90	100
5	90	75
6	90	50
7	80	100
8	80	75
9	80	50

Comparing Process 2 to Process 8 with Process 1, the stress reduction in the B-B and C-C sections are shown in Fig. 12 and Fig. 13, where the tensile stress is positive.

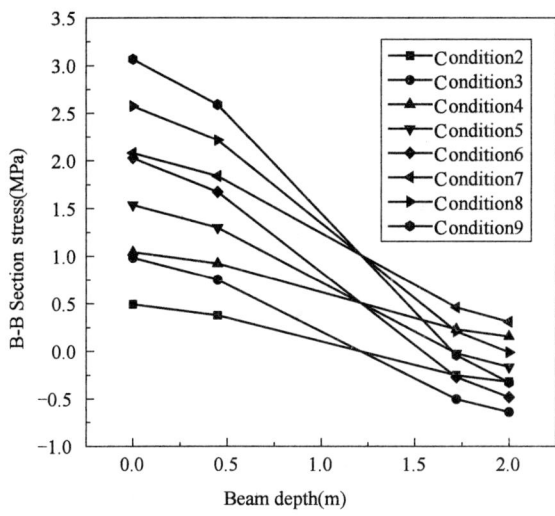
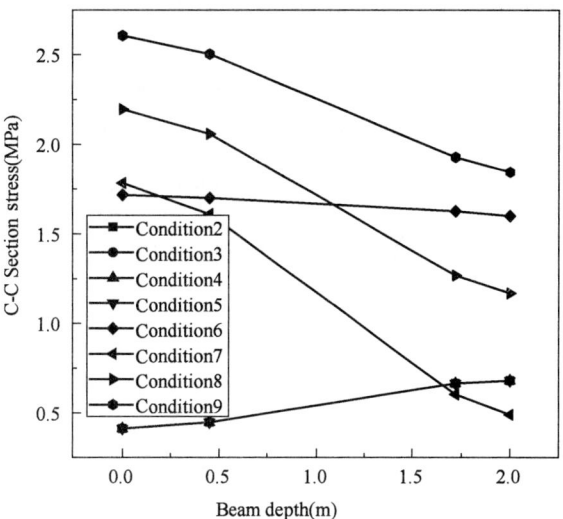

Fig. 12 Diagram of the Stress Reduction Status of the 1B-B Section of the Relative Working Condition under Each Working Condition

Fig. 13 The Stress Reduction Situation of the 1C-C Section of the Relative Working Condition under each Working Condition

According to Fig. 12 and Fig. 13, by comparing working conditions 1, 4 and 7, it is found that the loss of prestress at positive bending moment is proportional to the decrease of compressive stress at the bottom of the beam body, and the stress at the bottom of the C-C section web decreases by 1.8MPa at working condition 7; By comparing working conditions 1 and 2 with working conditions 3, the amount of prestress loss in the negative moment area has a great influence on the reduction of compressive stress of the roof of B-B section. In working condition 3, the stress at the bottom of the C-C section web decreases by 0.8MPa; The effect of the loss of positive moment prestress on the stress reserve is greater than that of the loss of negative moment prestress. At 9 working conditions, the compressive stress at the bottom of C-C section and B-B section web decreased by 2.7MPa and 2.6MPa, respectively.

3.3 Impact Analysis of Live Load Effect

3.3.1 Effect of the Vehicle Transporting the Beam on the Forces on the Beam Webs

According to the actual situation, the girder transport vehicle is usually in the process of transportation of the beam body walking along the middle part of the whole bridge, namely the majority to walk along the centre sill, sometimes is still in a state of simply supported beam body or only the longitudinal connection, at this point, combined with the weight of the girder transporting girder vehicle driving on the beam body effect will be close to or even greater than that of beam body serviceability limit state, Usually T girder bridge across the centre sill minimum reinforcement ratio, so the camion when transporting girder span centre sill in the danger, therefore this paper studies centre sill in camion bridge beam body force of the critical section, divided into three working condition, working condition 1: simply supported state, condition 2: only the longitudinal connection status, working condition of three concrete pavement shop to complete cases, the most unfavorable conditions for transportation of the transportation T-beam 40 m side beams, 40 m side beam are calculated by about 101t, 10t camion, impact coefficient of 0.3.

Fig. 14 and Fig. 15 show that under the joint action of the cannon and beam body, the compressive stress reserve of C-C section in the simply supported state decreases gradually from top to bottom, and the tensile stress at the lower part of the horseshoe is close to 4MPa, Exceeds the tensile strength of concrete, the web stress value between 7.71MPa to 0.6MPa, in the condition of simply supported, B-B section in the compression state, almost no compressive stress reserves, but the lower part of the girder web compressive stress values between 2.1-6MPa, and the longitudinal continuous state and concrete pavement completion status under the section stress, compressive stress value between 4-8MPa, so the actual construction of continuous T bridge to avoid beam body under the state of simply supported girder transporting girder vehicle.

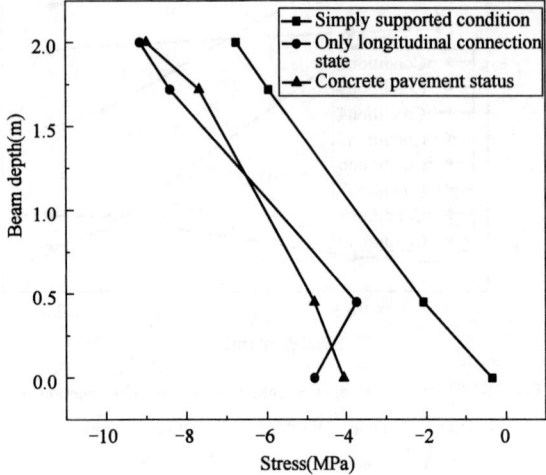 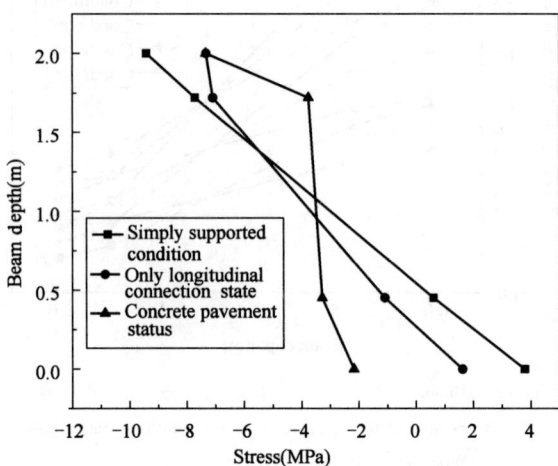

Fig. 14　Stress Distribution of the Middle Beam B-B Section　　　Fig. 15　Stress Distribution of the C-C Section of the Middle Beam

3.3.2　Influence of Highway I-load on Web Stress

Because the prestressed tendon is the least laid in the middle beam of the middle span, this section only analyzes the impact of the highway I-class load on the middle beam, to understand the web mechanical properties of the middle beam under the action of the highway I-class load. The Midas civil determines the position of the most unfavourable vehicle load M_{max} and M_{min}, and then obtains the stress characteristics of the beam body at this time.

It can be seen from Fig. 16 and Fig. 17 that, under the action of M_{max} vehicle load, the compressive stress reserve at the lower part of the beam body is reduced greatly. The compressive stress of B-B and CC sections is only about 4MPa, and the compressive strain of c-C section roof is small, only about 2MPa, under the action of M_{min} load.

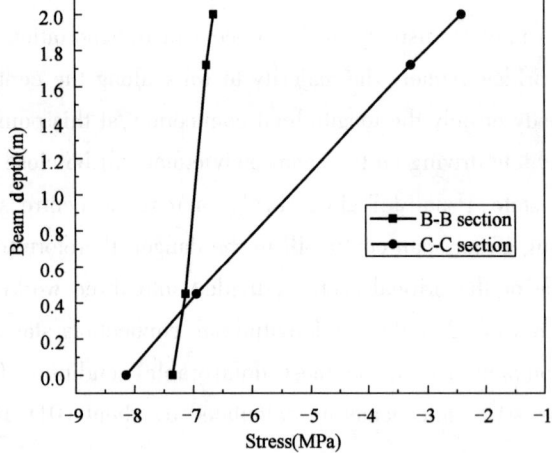 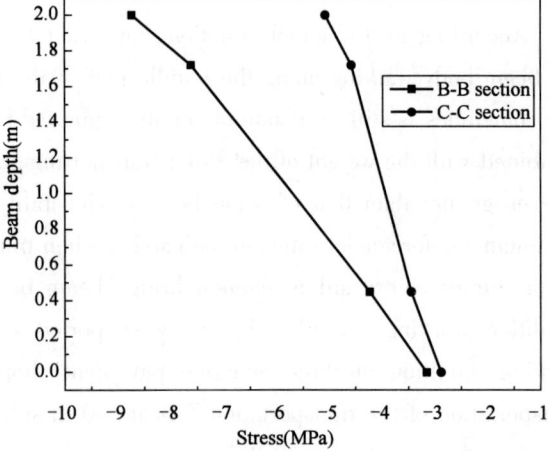

Fig. 16　Stress Distribution at Each Position of the Center Beam under the Action of Vehicle Load M_{min} (impact coefficient 0.3)　　　Fig. 17　The Stress Distribution at Each position of the Center Beam under Vehicle Load M_{max} (impact coefficient 0.3)

4 Conclusions

In this chapter, Modeling analysis is carried out to analyse the failure causes of the T-beam webs that are first briefly supported and then continuous from a theoretical level, taking into account the actual site conditions. The mechanical properties of the T-beam web and other parts are analysed in detail from the three main aspects of time-varying effect, prestressing effect and live load effect of the structure, and the following conclusions are drawn.

(1) The shrinkage effect of the beam is analysed. When there is no bridge deck pavement, the overall tension of the Web of T beam is basically reduced with the increase of the height of the Web of T-beam. After considering the pavement of the bridge deck, the web is still in the overall tensile state, and the tensile stress of the web increases to some extent, presenting a phenomenon that the tensile stress increases gradually with the increase of the height of the Web of the T-beam. In addition, the larger the phase difference, the greater the axial force generated by uneven shrinkage. When the phase difference is the same, the axial force generated by shrinkage difference in the middle beam is greater than that generated by the side beam. The increase of assembly time can effectively reduce the axial tension of shrinkage due to age difference.

(2) For creep effect, the shorter the loading age of concrete, the greater the mid-span bending moment and axial force loss. Ordinary steel bars increase the compressive stress at the top of T-beam by 18%, and the compressive stress increases gradually with the increase of time, while the compressive stress at the bottom of T-beam decreases by 20%, and the compressive stress decreases gradually with the decrease of time.

(3) In this paper, positive moment prestressing under tension is combined with negative moment prestressing under tensioning. It is found that the loss of the positive moment prestress is proportional to the decrease of the compressive stress at the bottom of the beam. The effect of the loss of positive moment prestress on the stress reserve is greater than that of the loss of negative moment prestress.

(4) In the actual construction, continuous T-beam bridge should avoid beam carriage and beam carriage under the state of simple support. The impact analysis of highway class I load on the mid-span and mid-beam shows that the compressive stress reserve at the lower part of the beam body is greatly reduced under the action of vehicle load M max.

References

[1] Jiasheng Zhang. Theoretical design and construction of simply supported continuous beam bridge [D]. Changchun: Jilin University, 2010.

[2] Jian Li. The development and engineering practice of prestressed concrete continuous beam bridges in China. [C]. Proceedings of the 2000 academic annual meeting of the municipal engineering branch of the Chinese Civil Engineering Society, 2000: 272-279.

[3] Fengmin Chen, Lijuan Zhang. Design and application of "simply supported and then continuous" girder bridge [J]. Highway traffic technology, 2006(01), 55-56+62.

[4] Min Chen. Spatial stress analysis of simply supported continuous T-beam bridge in Expressway [D]. Chongqing: Chongqing Jiaotong University, 2014.

[5] Shengqian Huang. Research on deformation mechanism of cracking of long span prestressed concrete box girder bridge [D]. Chengdu: Southwest Jiaotong University, 2014.

[6] Junyan Wang, Junyuan Guo, Rucheng Xiao, et al. Crack control mechanism and research of high strain strengthened ultra high performance concrete [J]. Acta Civil Engineering, 2017(11), 10-17.

[7] Calculation of stiffness and cracks in reinforced concrete members [J]. Journal of Nanjing Institute of Technology (02), 29-41.

[8] Shaowei Hu, Zhengxiang Mi. Numerical simulation of concrete crack propagation process based on extended finite element method[J]. Acta hydrologica Sinica, 2014(S1), 51-56.

[9] Dajun Ding, Defu Huang, Zhisheng Jin. Experimental study on stiffness and crack of reinforced concrete members and suggestions for calculation. Acta civil engineering Sinica(04), 1-13.

[10] Dajun Ding. On the mechanical mechanism of cracks in reinforced concrete members[J]. Acta Civil Engineering(01), 41-48.

[11] Industry standard of the people's Republic of China. Code for design of highway reinforced concrete and prestressed reinforced concrete bridges and culverts: JTG 3362—2018 [S]. Beijing: People's Communications Press, 2018.

[12] Feng Xiong, Shangmin Zheng. Influence of shear deformation on creep effect of PC continuous beam bridge with corrugated steel webs[J]. Highway Engineering, 2019, (05), 9-13 + 24.

Analysis of Mechanical Capacity of Continuous Rigid Frame Bridge under the Climate of Chloride Erosion

Lei Hao[1] Feng Chen[1] Bin Zha[2]

(1. Chang'an University, School of Highway; 2. State Key Laboratory of Safety and Health for In-service Long Span Bridges)

Abstract In the chloride erosion environment, the continuous rigid frame bridge is subjected to the coupling effect of chloride erosion and stress. The structure should concern the problems of concrete deterioration, corrosion of steel bars and prestressed steel bars. That could lead to the gradual declination of the mechanical capacity of the structure, and affect the state of service also. According to the characteristics of chloride erosion, this paper modifies the time-history variation of relevant parameters in prestressed concrete beam bridge. Then, the calculation model of structural bearing capacity in chloride environment is summed up. Based on the actual project in service, the study establishes the finite element model using the time-induced parameters, which could calculate the bearing capacity of the structure in the chloride environment during the whole service period, and the deterioration law could be obtained. The research finds that the main factor of the ultimate bending capacity deterioration is corrosion of the steel bars, and the main reason of the ultimate shear capacity deterioration is the decrease of the bond performance of the concrete and steel bars. Once the initial corrosion of steel bar occurs, the corrosion will develop rapidly until it causes the corrosion and cracking of concrete covering layer. This study provides some references for the assessment of bearing capacity, structural safety and durability, for the in-serviced prestressed concrete beam bridges in chloride erosion environment.

Keywords Chlorine salt erosion Corrosion Continuous rigid frame bridge Bearing capacity

0 Introduction

In the offshore environment, with the increase of service life, there will be various corrosion effects such as aging, cracking, reduction of bearing capacity and so on, which lead to the decline of structural mechanical properties. Whether the degraded bridge owns sufficient bearing capacity and performance, and whether it can continue to serve, has aroused widespread concern among scholars.

Ditao Niu (2002), Jianren Zhang (2006), Lei Wang (2011) and others have studied the mechanical properties of reinforced concrete beams after corrosion, and all proposed the modified calculation model for bearing capacity degradation of corroded reinforced concrete beams. In terms of layout and material properties, there is a big difference between prestressed tendons and steel bars, and the research results on the mechanical properties of corroded reinforced concrete members may not be applicable to corroded prestressed members. Fumin Li (2008, 2011) has carried out bending tests on prestressed concrete beams corroded by steel strands and found that wire breakage caused by corrosion will reduce the ultimate bearing capacity and deformation capacity of the beams. Rinaldi (2010) has found that steel strand corrosion can significantly reduce the flexural bearing capacity of prestressed concrete beams. With the increase of corrosion degree, the members change from ductile failure to brittle failure. Huilin Lu (2014) has proposed a model of chloride ion diffusion coefficient of prestressed concrete structures considering the influence of multiple factors, and calculated the bearing capacity of corroded prestressed concrete beam bridges on the basis of the current code.

The above researches of domestic and foreign scholars on the mechanical properties of corroded components mainly start from the material and the natural environment (such as temperature, humidity, chloride concentration, etc.). The actual bridge is subjected to a variety of combined actions in the process of operation, and the complex stress environment of the members could also affect the change of structural mechanical properties. And the study of prestressed concrete structures usually only considered the corrosion of tendons. In fact, the deterioration of concrete and the corrosion of steel bars also have a significant impact on the mechanical properties of prestressed concrete structures.

By summarizing the previous research results, this paper modifies tendons and steel bar parameters and concrete compressive strength of prestressed continuous rigid frame bridge under chloride erosion environment. According to the finite element model, the time-varying law of structural bearing capacity and service performance is calculated and analysed. It could provide decision-making basis for the evaluation and reinforcement of existing operational bridges and also could provide a reference for the durability design and research of newly-built bridges.

1 Study on Mechanical Property Deterioration of Continuous Rigid Frame Bridge

The mechanical properties of concrete structures are often affected by the coupling of many factors. In this paper, the deterioration of mechanical properties of continuous rigid frame bridges is studied from the aspects of natural environment and structure.

1.1 Natural Environmental Factors

On the basis of summarizing the previous studies, Pengfei Xue (2009) found that when the water-cement ratio is low and the environmental humidity is high, it could be considered that the chloride ion erosion is not affected by carbonation and the coupling effect is not obvious. Therefore, the structural corrosion caused by chloride ion erosion can be regarded as the main factor for the performance deterioration of concrete structures in offshore areas.

The entry of chloride ion into concrete is the result of a variety of erosion modes. It has been generally believed that the diffusion of chloride ion in concrete obeys Fick's law (Mangat and Molloy 1994). The chloride ion diffusion coefficient model under multiple influence factors such as Eq. (1).

$$C_{x,t} = C_0 + (C_s - C_0)\left(1 - \mathrm{erf}\frac{x}{2\sqrt{\dfrac{\dfrac{1}{1+R} \cdot k_T \cdot k_{rh} \cdot k_\sigma \cdot k_K \cdot D_0 \left(\dfrac{t_0}{t}\right)^m \cdot t}{1-m}}}\right) \quad (1)$$

Guoping Li(2011) has carried out salt solution immersion erosion tests on C50 concrete members with the water-cement ratio of 0.35, 0.40 and 0.45 under different stress states, and fitted the coefficient of stress state, such as Eq. (2).

$$\begin{cases} k_{\sigma c} = 1 - 0.0542\sigma_c + 0.00297\sigma_c^2 \\ k_{\sigma t} = 1 + 0.3027\sigma_t - 0.0933\sigma_t^2 \end{cases} \quad (2)$$

Thomas (1999) has considered that the maximum influence time of chloride ion diffusion coefficient deterioration is about 25~30 years, and the established decay index model of chloride ion diffusion coefficient is as follows Eq. (3).

$$D_t = D_0 \left(\frac{t_0}{t}\right)^m \quad (3)$$

Amey (1998) has proposed a method for calculating diffusion coefficient considering the effect of temperature, such as Eq. (4).

$$D_T = D_{T_0}\left(\frac{T}{T_0}\right)\exp\left[q\left(\frac{1}{T_0} - \frac{1}{T}\right)\right] \quad (4)$$

Where, D_t and D_{T_0} are the diffusion coefficients when the absolute temperature is T and T_0.

The humidity of concrete will affect the diffusion ability of chloride ion in concrete. Ruobing Wang(2018) has modified coefficient expression considering the influence factors of humidity, such as Eq. (5).

$$k_{rh} = \left[1 + \frac{(1+RH)^4}{(1-RH_c)^4}\right]^{-1} \quad (5)$$

Where, k_{rh} is the humidity influence correction coefficient; RH is the relative humidity of the concrete member; RH_c is the critical relative humidity of the concrete member.

The relationship among the total value of chloride ion, the value of bound chloride ion and free chloride ion in concrete is: $C_t = C_b + C_f = C_f(1 + R)$. Hongfa Yu(2002) has presented out the law of R value is: ordinary concrete, $R = 2~4$; high performance concrete, $R = 3~15$.

Hongfa Yu(2002) has summarized the basic law of the value of cracking effect coefficient k_K: for ordinary cement concrete, $k_K = 1~14$; for high performance cement concrete, $k_K \geq 6$.

1.2 Structural Factors

The continuous rigid frame bridge can be composed of steel bars, prestressed tendons and concrete. In the whole life cycle of the bridge operation, the performance of these three parts will deteriorate under the chloride erosion, resulting the deterioration of the mechanical properties of the concrete bridge.

1.2.1 Concrete Degradation Model

On the basis of summarizing and analysing the long-term exposure test of concrete and the measured results of buildings at home and abroad, Ditao Niu(1995) has analysed the time-varying law of concrete compressive strength in the service environment of marine environment, such as Eq. (6).

$$f_c(t) = 1.2488\exp[-0.0347(\ln t - 0.3468)^2]f_c(0) \quad (6)$$

1.2.2 Corrosion Model of Steel Bar

When the chloride ion concentration on the surface of steel bar reaches the critical value, the passivation film on the surface of steel bar is gradually destroyed and loses its protective effect on steel bar. Under the condition of air and water, steel bar corrosion would occur. According to the calculation model of chloride ion diffusion coefficient, the initial corrosion time of steel bar can be obtained, such as Eq. (7).

$$t_i = \left\{ \frac{(1+R)(1-m)}{4k_T \cdot k_{rh} \cdot k_\sigma \cdot k_K \cdot D_0 t_o^m} \left[\frac{c}{\text{erf}^{-1}\left(1 - \frac{C_{cr}}{C_s}\right)} \right]^2 \right\}^{\frac{1}{1-m}} \qquad (7)$$

Where, t_i is the time when the steel bar begins to corrode, year; c is the thickness of the concrete cover, (mm); C_{cr} is the critical chloride concentration; erf^{-1} is the inverse function of the error function $\text{erf}(u)$.

According to the experimental data under the chloride ion erosion, Demeng Jiang (2004) has obtained the current density model of steel bar corrosion, such as Eq. (8).

$$i_{corr}(t) = \eta_T \cdot \eta_{RH} \cdot 37.8(1 - w/c)^{-1.64}/c \times 0.85(t - t_i)^{-0.29} \qquad (8)$$

The quantitative relationship between corrosion current density and temperature and humidity is as follows: $\eta_T = e^{1.0512 \times (T/20 - 1)}$; $\eta_{RH} = e^{0.0361 \times [(RH - 75\%)/45\%]}$.

Chloride ion erosion is easy to cause local pit corrosion of steel bar. Huilin Lu (2014) has proposed a model for calculating the effective diameter of corroded steel bars, which considering the obvious acceleration of steel bar corrosion rate after cracking, such as Eq. (9).

$$D(t) = \begin{cases} D_0 & t \leq t_i \\ D_0 - 2\lambda_1(t - t_1) & t_i < t \leq t_{cr} \\ D_0 - 2\lambda_1(t - t_i) - 2\lambda_2(t - t_{cr}) & t > t_{cr} \end{cases} \qquad (9)$$

Where, before the cracking of the protective layer, $\lambda_1 = 11.6 \times 10^{-3} \cdot i_{corr}(t)$, after the cracking of the protective layer, $\lambda_2 = (4.5 - 2.6\lambda_1) \cdot \lambda_1$, when $\lambda_2 < 1.8\lambda_1$, $\lambda_2 = 1.8\lambda_1$.

As estimating and predicting the bearing capacity of newly-built or bridges in service during the whole service period, the formula of coordination coefficient [Eq. (10)] given by Ditao Niu (2003) can be used to calculate the corrosion depth of steel bars.

$$k_{bi} \begin{cases} 1 & \delta_{ei}(t) \leq \delta_{cri} \\ 1 - 0.85[\delta_{ei}(t) - \delta_{cri}] & \delta_{cri} < \delta_{ei}(t) \leq 0.3 \\ 0.745 + 0.7\delta_{cri} & \delta_{ei}(t) > 0.3 \end{cases} \qquad (10)$$

Where, δ_{cri} is the corrosion depth of the steel bar corresponding to the cracking of the cover of the steel bar (mm).

1.2.3 Corrosion Model of Prestressed Tendons

The calculation of the initial corrosion time of prestressed tendons can refer to the corresponding formula of steel bars. However, the existence of metal pipeline delays the corrosion time of prestressed tendons. The time from corrosion to cracking of metal bellows can be calculated according to the principle of electrochemical corrosion of steel. Assuming that the steel is corroded uniformly, the relationship between the corrosion amount of steel and the corrosion current density can be obtained, such as Eq. (11) (Huilin Lu, 2014).

$$\Delta D = \int v_{corr} dt = 11.6 \times 10^{-3} \int i_{corr}(t) dt \qquad (11)$$

Strands are twisted from several high-strength steel wires, and their corrosion patterns are different from steel bars. Huilin Lu (2014) has assumed that the electrochemical corrosion of all steel wire could be uniform, regardless of the difference of corrosion time between the near side and the far side. Determine the corrosion number of strands, such as Eq. (12).

$$\Delta D(t) = \begin{cases} 0 & t \leq t_i \\ \lambda_1(t - t_i) & t_i < t \leq t_{cr} \\ \delta_{cr} + \lambda_2(t - t_{cr}) & t > t_{cr} \end{cases} \qquad (12)$$

2 Finite Element Model Establishment and Parameter Correction

2.1 Engineering Background

In the offshore environment, a three-span prestressed concrete continuous rigid frame bridge is in service. And the span composition is 50m + 90m + 50m. The beam structure adopts the form of variable cross-section continuous box girder, and the substructure adopts hollow thin-walled pier.

The superstructure of the bridge adopts C50 concrete, the water-cement ratio is not more than 0.40. The main beam adopts a single box section with straight web, the height of the beam is 2.2-5.5m, according to quadratic parabola, and the standard section is shown in Fig.1.

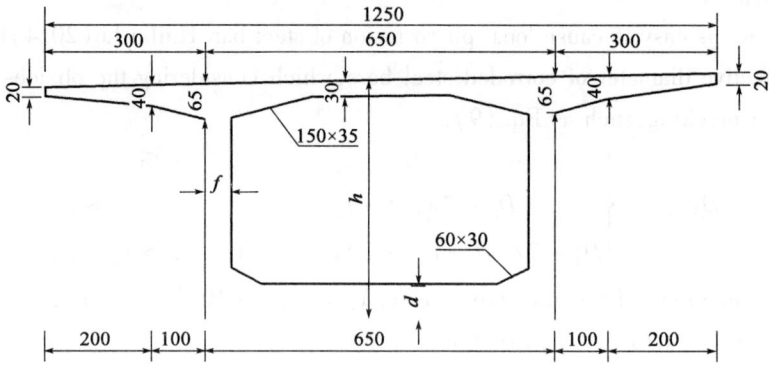

Fig.1 Section of main beam (unit: m)

2.2 Parameter Correction

According to the time-varying model of structural parameters in the theory we have mentioned at section 2, the corrosion number of tendons and steel bars and the time nodes of concrete strength degradation are modified in the finite element model during the life cycle.

For post-tensioned prestressed concrete beam, the bond between tendons and concrete has no significant effect. Therefore, this study uses the reduction of cross-sectional area to reflect the corrosion of strands. The loss of cross-sectional area of partially strands is shown in Tab.1.

Lost cross-sectional area of strands and steel bar Tab.1

Steel bundle	Strands of pier roof		Strands of side span		Steel bar of pier top		Steel bar of middle span	
Time (year)	Lost area (mm^2)	Corrosion rate (%)	Lost area (mm^2)	Corrosion rate (%)	Lost area (mm^2)	Corrosion rate (%)	Lost area (mm^2)	Corrosion rate (%)
0	2380.00	0.00	2100.00	0.00	0.00	0.00	0.00	0.00
40	2124.36	10.74	1953.35	6.98	59.36	29.52	54.65	27.17
60	1847.70	22.37	1704.55	18.83	79.84	39.70	76.57	38.07
80	1559.95	34.46	1459.01	30.52	95.47	47.47	92.83	46.16
100	1332.11	44.03	1265.77	39.73	108.45	53.93	106.21	52.81

In this paper, we could consider the influence of the reduction of coordination coefficient through reducing the cross-sectional area. According to the Eq.(10), considering the stress environment of steel bars at different locations, the loss of cross-sectional area of several steel bars is shown in Tab.1.

The decrease of concrete compressive strength directly affects the mechanical properties of the structure. In this paper, according to the method we have mentioned at section 2, it is calculated that the concrete decreases by one label from C50 to C30, and the operating time is 18 years, 28 years, 44 years and 75 years respectively.

2.3 Finite Element Model

In this paper, the finite element analysis software Midas is used for structural analysis. Among, the beam structure adopts the box section beam element. There are 115 beam elements in the model. The width of the bridge deck is 12.5m, of which the width of the carriageway is 3.75m. The calculation model is shown in Fig. 2. At the same time, the relevant parameters in the calculation model at different operating times are modified according to the calculation results at section 3.2.

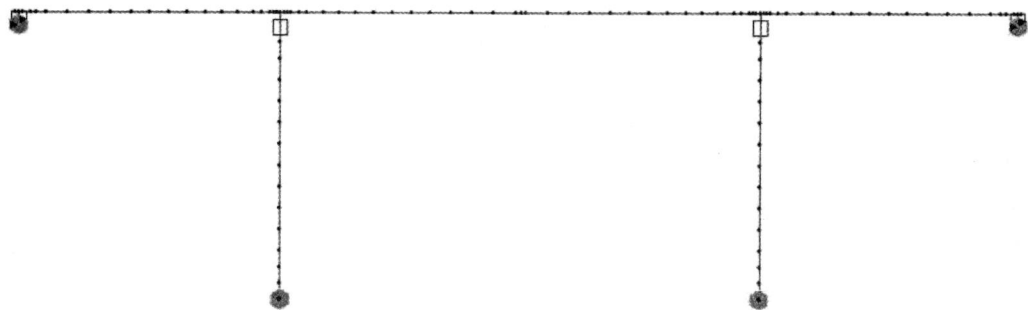

Fig.2 Finite element model of the whole bridge

3 Performance Deterioration of Bearing Capacity

The ultimate bearing capacity is an important index to judge whether the bridge can bear the expected design or not, and it is also the key parameter for the design of new bridge and the evaluation of old bridge. The finite element method is used to analyse the degradation of bearing capacity under the chloride erosion, which is a powerful basis for bridge condition evaluation.

3.1 Change of Bending Bearing Capacity

For the beam structure system, the internal force is mainly bending moment and shear force, and the flexural bearing capacity is an important bearing capacity control condition. Usually, the main sections concerned about the bending bearing capacity include pier top section, 1/4 of span section, 3/4 of span section and middle of span section. The change trend of the flexural bearing capacity of the main section of the structure with time is shown in Fig. 3.

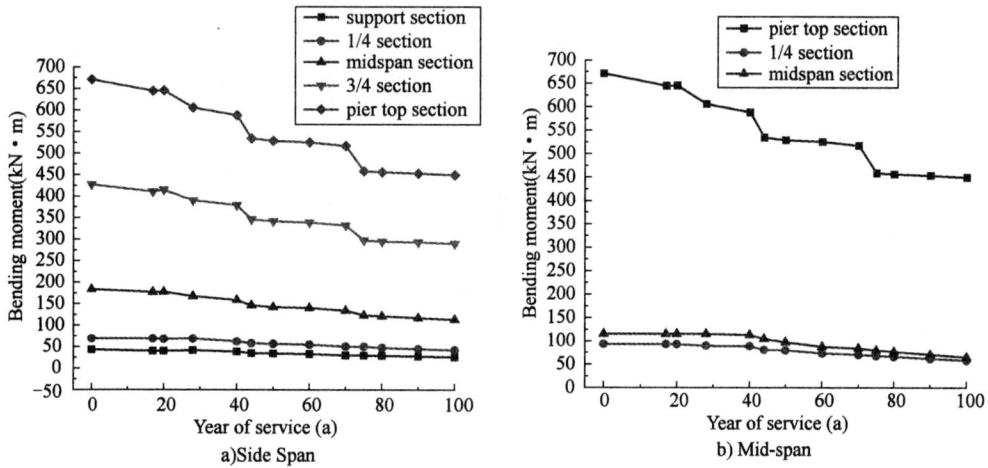

Fig.3 The change trend of the flexural bearing capacity

The ultimate bending bearing capacity of the main sections decrease with the increase of time, and it decreases slowly within initial 40 years of operation, which are showing the obvious platform trend. Then the rate of decline accelerates significantly. At the end of the bridge service, the ultimate bending bearing capacity on the main control sections decrease, the decreased values are 39.81%, 39.32%, 38.24%, 32.09%, 32.97%, 32.97%, 37.65% and 43.55%, respectively. The overall change shows a significant double broken line form. Among them, the ultimate bending bearing capacity of the middle of span section at Mid-span is the most significant reduction of the whole bridge.

3.2 Change of Shear Bearing Capacity

The beam structure system bears a huge shear force in the range of bending-shear. Sometimes, the shear capacity in this section may also become the control index of the bearing capacity of the structure. It is also mainly concerned about the changes of shear bearing capacity of each span bearing sections, including pier top section, 1/4 of span section, 3/4 of span section. In addition, the middle span section also has the possibility of shear failure under the action of the vehicle load, so it also needs to be concerned. The change trend of the shear capacity of these sections of the structure with time is shown in Fig. 4.

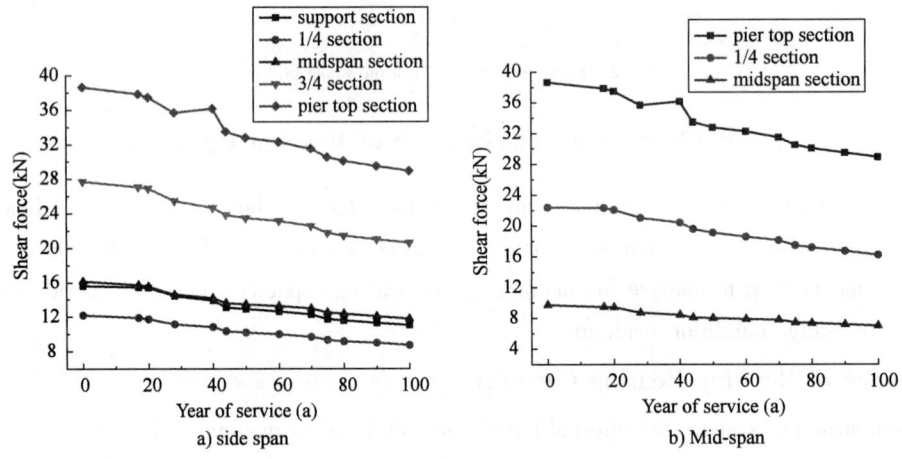

Fig. 4 The change trend of the shear capacity

The shear ultimate bearing capacity of the main sections decreases with time. It has almost no deterioration in the first 20 years of service, and then it decreases slowly in the subsequent service life. The shear ultimate bearing capacity of these control sections decrease at the values as follows: 29.39%, 28.44%, 27.15%, 25.59%, 25.18%, 25.18%, 27.50% and 27.82%. Each section decreases sharply during the period of 20-40 years of operation, and the decline rate is much higher than that of other time periods. The main reason for the analysis is that the initial rust time of steel bars is mostly concentrated in about 20 years, while tendons is mainly concentrated in about 40 years. When the characteristics of the main tendons are deteriorated, the shear capacity will be greatly reduced, and then the decline rate of shear capacity tends to slow down. Compared with the change of bending bearing capacity, the deterioration degree of shear bearing capacity is obviously being less degree.

4 Time-varying Law of Structural Performance

4.1 Corrosion Time

Ignoring the difference of temperature and relative humidity in different spatial locations, it is assumed that the whole bridge is in the same environment which's temperature is 20℃ and relative humidity is 80%. According to the finite element model at section 2, the initial rust time and the concrete cracking time of steel bar and tendons are calculated under the coupling action of natural environment and stress environment, as shown in Tab. 2.

Corrosion Time of Steel Bars and Tendons   Tab. 2

Position	Time(year)	Roof reinforcement	Floor reinforcement	Stirrups	Tendons	
Pier top	Initial corrosion	21.24	26.28	18.68	36.79	36.48
	Concrete cracking	27.08	33.12	23.84	39.16	38.86
Mid-span 1/4L	Initial corrosion	23.44	25.42	19.26	48.06	44.5
	Concrete cracking	29.28	32.26	24.42	50.54	46.39
Middle span	Initial corrosion	25.01	35.37	20.13	42.12	41.92
	Concrete cracking	30.85	44.79	25.29	45.58	45.38

From the analysis of the above tables, it can be seen that the initial rust time of stirrups is much earlier than torsional bars at the position of web, due to the minimum thickness of concrete protective layer(47mm). Because of the thick protective layer of tendons, it takes a long time for initial rust. No matter where the steel bar is, once the initial corrosion occurs, the corrosion will develop rapidly in a short period of 5 years. And then it will cause cracking of the cover concrete. The initial rust time of steel bars under different stress conditions are different, but the difference is less than 5 years. It can be seen that the speed and development of steel bar corrosion is very rapid in the chloride corrosion environment, so the timeliness of bridge maintenance in coastal corrosion environment will be very urgent.

4.2 Time-varying Law of Natural Frequency

The natural frequency of the bridge directly reflects the dynamic characteristics of structure and the relationship between the impact coefficient of vehicle load and the structure. The calculation results of natural frequencies corresponding to the 1st and 10th modes of continuous rigid frame bridges with different service life are shown in Tab. 3.

Natural frequency of continuous rigid frame bridge under different operating years (Hz)   Tab. 3

Mode	0 year	20 year	40 year	50 year	60 year	70 year	80 year	90 year	100 year
1	4.42	4.36	4.36	4.30	4.29	4.23	4.22	4.22	4.22
2	7.26	7.15	7.15	7.04	7.02	6.92	6.91	6.91	6.92
3	11.63	11.47	11.47	11.31	11.29	11.11	11.10	11.09	11.08
4	15.75	15.53	15.53	15.29	15.25	15.01	15.00	15.00	15.02
5	20.40	20.12	20.13	19.85	19.80	19.49	19.48	19.46	19.43
6	24.70	24.35	24.37	24.03	23.96	23.59	23.57	23.56	23.52
7	30.68	30.25	30.24	29.78	29.70	29.24	29.22	29.21	29.25
8	32.26	31.82	31.84	31.40	31.31	30.83	30.80	30.78	30.73
9	39.25	38.69	38.70	38.13	38.09	37.51	37.49	37.48	37.46
10	44.70	44.06	44.07	43.42	43.38	42.72	42.71	42.70	42.68

The natural frequencies corresponding to the 1st and 10th modes of continuous rigid frame bridges decrease with the increase of service years. After 100 years of operation, the reduction rates are 7.40%, 7.71%, 7.66%, 7.72%, 7.70%, 7.70%, 7.73%, 7.71%, 7.41%, 7.36%, respectively. The natural frequency of the structure can also reflect the characteristics of structural stiffness to a certain extent. Under the influence of steel bar corrosion and concrete strengthdeterioration, the structural stiffness is decreasing continuously, and the decline degree of stiffness should be a uniform value in the whole bridge.

5 Conclusions

In this paper, based on the continuous rigid frame bridge under the climate of chloride erosion, the change rules of ultimate bearing capacity and service performance of the structure under chloride erosion environment are analysed. Through the research of this paper, the main conclusions are as follows:

(1) The corrosion of steel bar is affected by the coupling action of concrete cover thickness and stress state. No matter where the steel bar occurs, once the initial corrosion occurs, the corrosion will develop rapidly in a short period of 5 years. Therefore, the timeliness of bridge maintenance under chloride erosion environment will be very urgent.

(2) The study shows that the initial rust time of ordinary steel bar is mostly about 20 years, which the prestressed tendons are about 40 years. The stress state of the structure will change during these two periods. The bearing capacity and shear bearing capacity of bridge show a significant double-broken line trend before and after 40 years of operation.

(3) After 50 years of operation, the flexural bearing capacity of the bridge reduced value up to about 17%, and the shear bearing capacity is reduced by about 10%. The research results can be combined with the field test results, which can provide a reference basis for the decision-making of bridge performance maintenance, reinforcement.

(4) The corrosion of prestressed tendons and steel bars has little effect on the stiffness of structural section. The cracking of concrete is the main reason for the stiffness degradation of bridge section.

References

[1] Ditao N, Lumei, Qinglin W. Research on calculation method of flexural bearing capacity of corroded reinforced concrete beam[J]. Building structure, 2002; 14-17.

[2] Jianren Z, Lei W. Estimated Approach to Carrying Capacity of Existing Reinforced Concrete Bridge Member [J]. Journal of China Highway, 2006, 49-55.

[3] Lei W, Wei D, Yafei M, et al, Probabilistic model of shear resistance degradation for corroded reinforced concrete beam[J]. Journal of Changsha University of Science and Technology (Natural Science Edition), 2011, 8, 34-41.

[4] Fumin L. Effect of steel strands corrosion on prestressed concrete structures under chloride environment [D]. Xuzhou: China University of Mining and Techndogg, 2008.

[5] Fumin L, Yingshu Y, Bo W et al. Evaluation on flexural strength of Prestressed concrete beams with corroded steel strands[J]. Journal of Building Structures, 2011, 32, 10-16.

[6] Rinaldi Z, Imperatore S, Valente C. Experimental evaluation of the flexural behavior of corroded P/C beams [J]. 2010, 24, 2267-2278.

[7] Huilin L. Research of the Degeneration of Bearing Capacity of Prestressed Concrete Bridges [D]. Zhengzhou: Zhengzhou University, 2014.

[8] Pengfei X. Prediction and Assessment of behavior degeneration of P. C. continuous rigid farm bridge[D]. Hangzhou: Zhejiang University.

[9] Mangat P S, Molloy B T. Prediction of long-term chloride concentration in concrete[J]. 1994, 27, 338-346.

[10] Guoping L, Fangjian H, Yongxian W. Chloride ion corrosion test of concrete specimens under stress[J]. Prestress technology, 2011, 19-25.

[11] Thomas M D A, Bamforth P B. Modelling chloride diffusion in concrete effect of fly ash and slag[J]. 1999, 29, 487-495.

[12] Amey S L, Johnson D A, Miltenberger M A et al. Predicting the service life of concrete marine structures:

An environmental methodology[J]. 1998,95,205-214.
[13] Ruobing W. Study on Prestressed Concrete Continuous Box Girder Bridge under The Influence of Steel Strand Corrosion[D]. Chongqing:Chongqing Jiaotong University,2018.
[14] Hongfa Y,Wei S,Lianghui Y et al. Study on Prediction of Concrete Service Life I-Theoretical Model[J]. Journal of The Chinese Ceramic Society,2002,686-690.
[15] Ditao N. Changing models of concrete strength along with time in marine environment[J]. Journal of Xi'an University of Architecture & Technology,1995,49-52.
[16] Dewen J,Lin L,Yingshu Y. Effect of Temperature and Humidity on the Rebar Corrosion Rate[J]. Journal of Huaihai Institute of Technology(Natural Science Edition),2004,59-62.
[17] Ditao N. Durability and Life Forecast of Reinforced Concrete Structure[M]. Beijing:Science Press,2003.

基于海外设计实践的桥梁汽车荷载对比研究

商雪枫　潘竺兰

(浙江数智交院科技股份有限公司)

摘　要　本文对汽车荷载在中国规范《公路桥涵设计通用规范》(JTG D60—2015)和英国规范《BS5400-2,2006》之间进行对比,着重比较汽车移动荷载在荷载取值、跨径影响和横向、纵向车道折减三方面的异同。经研究发现:英国规范HA和HB荷载比我国汽车荷载取值灵活,且大于我国汽车荷载值;中、英规范汽车荷载效应针对不同跨径所对应的差别变化较大;英国规范中汽车的荷载效应大于我国车道荷载效应。

关键词　桥梁工程　汽车荷载　对比研究　中、英规范

0　引　言

在"交通强国"的引领下,我国交通建设实力不断增强,更多企业把基建市场的"全球化"竞争列入了企业未来发展的目标。"一带一路"沿线有较多属于英联邦的发展中国家,延续着英国规范设计体系,对英标的熟练掌握成为海外工程师们新的挑战。由于中国规范和英国规范各自成系统,涵盖范围广泛,内容多,文化和技术上的差异使得很多方面同中有异。本文对汽车荷载在英国规范《BS5400-2,2006》和我国《公路桥涵设计通用规范》(JTG D60—2015)(以下简称《通规》)进行对比,通过荷载取值、跨径影响和横向、纵向车道折减三方面的分析研究,为海外设计项目设计或在海外推行我国桥梁设计规范提供借鉴与参考。

1　公路桥梁汽车荷载值的比较

我国《通规》表明:公路桥梁的汽车荷载分为车道荷载和车辆荷载,其中车辆荷载用于桥梁的局部加载、涵洞等计算,车道荷载用于桥梁结构的整体计算,且两者不进行叠加作用,汽车冲击作用根据结构基频计算得到。英国《BS5400》规定桥梁的标准荷载分为HA和HB荷载两种,即HA荷载代表正常运营车辆荷载,HB是特殊车辆荷载,大小采用若干个单位荷载表示,两者均已计入车辆冲击作用。经对比发现:HA荷载与车道荷载相似,HB荷载与车辆荷载相似,且均采用影响线加载,即集中荷载作用于影响线峰值处,均布荷载满布于最不利效应的同号影响线上。

1.1　车道荷载与HA荷载对比分析

中国规范的车道荷载包括了均布荷载和集中荷载,如图1所示。公路-Ⅰ级的荷载标准值为:计算跨

径不大于5m,集中荷载标准值$P_k=270$kN;计算跨径不小于50m,集中荷载标准值$P_k=360$kN;计算跨径在5~50m之间,采用直线内插法求得集中荷载值。如需计算剪力效应时,采用上述集中荷载标准值乘以系数1.2。均布荷载标准值为定值,$q_k=10.5$kN/m。

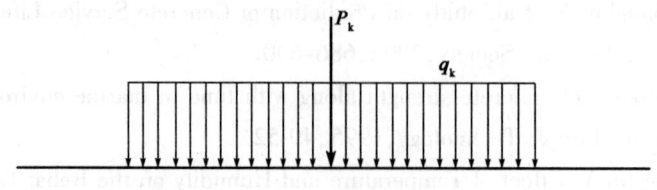

图1 车道荷载加载示意图

在BS5400中,HA荷载由均布荷载(UDL)和集中荷载(KEL)组成,均布荷载为变值,跟随加载长度变化,集中荷载取120kN,其加载方式如图2所示。

当加载长度不大于50m时,均布荷载UDL由式(1)得出:

$$W = 336\left(\frac{1}{L}\right)^{0.67} \tag{1}$$

当加载长度大于50m且小于1600m时,均布荷载UDL由式(2)得出:

$$W = 36\left(\frac{1}{L}\right)^{0.1} \tag{2}$$

式中:L——加载长度;

W——均布荷载。

L和W关系曲线如图3所示。

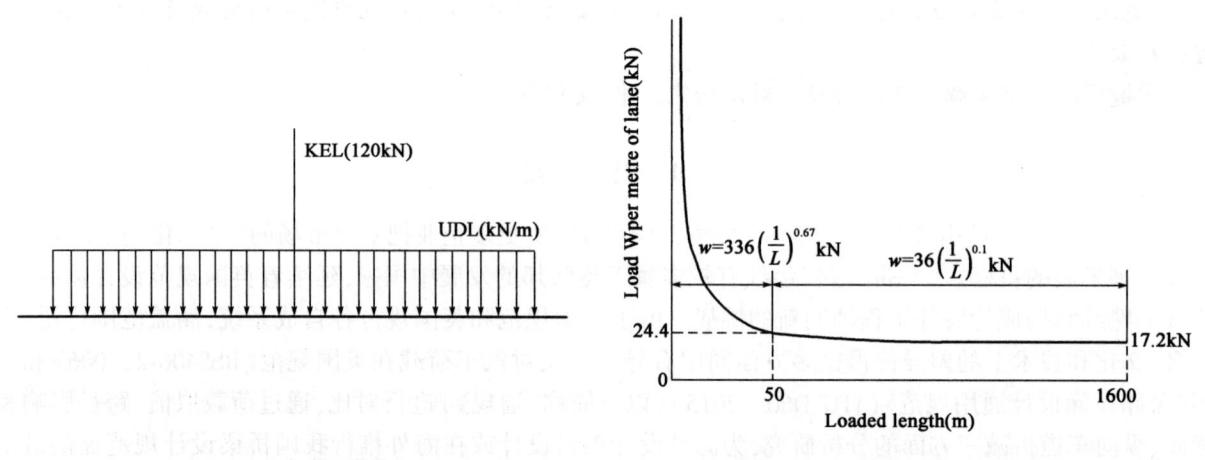

图2 HA加载示意图 图3 HA荷载均布荷载(UDL)曲线

根据上述对比可知:英标BS5400中的HA荷载与中国规范的车道荷载有相似之处,但取值的方式和大小均不同。英标规定中小跨径桥梁车道均布荷载(UDL)数值在22.7~211.2kN/m,大跨径桥梁的UDL取值在17.5~22.5kN/m。中规的公路—Ⅰ级的均布荷载为$q_k=10.5$kN/m。由此可见,英规的车道均布荷载大于我国规范规定的值。

1.2 车辆荷载与HB荷载对比研究

在《公路桥涵设计通用规范》(JTG D60—2015)中,车辆荷载重力标准值为550kN,其立面、平面尺寸如图4所示。

在BS5400中,"HB车辆"一般为四轴,轴间距为:1.8m+(6.0~26.0)m+1.8m,一个单位HB荷载每轴重10kN,即每轮重2.5kN。一般情况,HB荷载的最小单位数是30个,如有特殊指示,单位数可增加到45个。HB荷载的平面和车轮位置如图5所示。

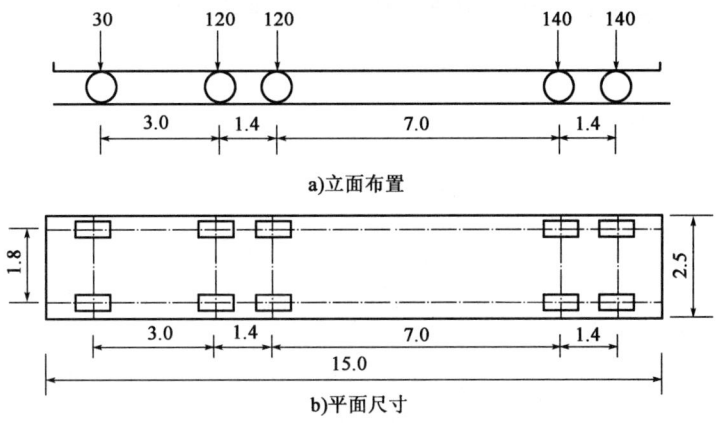

图4 车辆荷载尺寸图（尺寸单位：m）

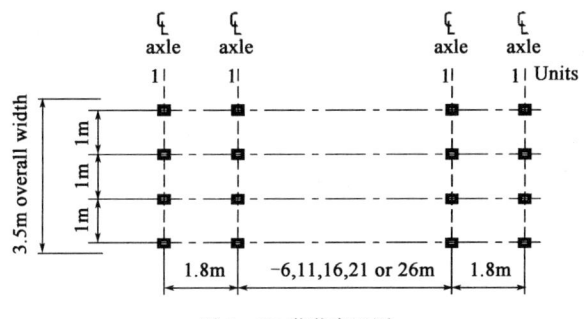

图5 HB荷载布置图

车辆荷载方面，中、英规范有较大差别。仅仅从两者数值比较，有30个基本单位的HB荷载轴重为300kN，车辆总重120t，但是中规的车辆荷载单轴重量最大只有140kN，车辆总重55t。因此，英国规范考虑车辆荷载的重载效应明显大于中国规范。另外，HB车辆的内轴距需根据加载长度和荷载影响线灵活变动，中规显示车长为15m，是一个定值。英国规范BS5400规定的HB车辆长度比中国规范更符合实际运营状态。

2 公路桥梁汽车荷载效应与跨径影响比较

根据汽车荷载取值比较可知，中、英桥梁设计规范的荷载取值都与跨径相关。需特别引起注意的是，在BS5400中，"L"代表的是影响线最不利面积的加载长度，而非跨径长度。因此，对于简支梁，加载长度L与跨径相等，但是对于连续梁来说，加载长度L随着验算截面的影响线不同而变化。本文以等截面简支梁为例，推导出跨中弯矩、支座剪力效应与跨径的函数关系，并对结果通过曲线图进行对比分析。

假设计算跨径为L，以影响线加载可得不同跨径下相应汽车荷载标准值的效应谱。汽车荷载在影响线加载后得荷载效应影响线函数为跨中弯矩$M(L)$、支座剪力$Q(L)$：

$$M(L) = \frac{1}{8}L^2 \times q_{udl} + \frac{1}{4}LP_{kel} \tag{3}$$

$$Q(L) = \frac{1}{2}L \times q_{udl} + P_{kel} \tag{4}$$

假设公路—Ⅰ级车道荷载与跨径关系函数为$F(L)$，则

$$F_C(L) = q_k + P_k \tag{5}$$

式中：
$$P_k = \begin{cases} 270 & L \leqslant 5\text{m} \\ 2L + 260 & 5\text{m} < L < 50\text{m} \\ 360 & L \geqslant 50\text{m} \end{cases}$$

推导出弯矩、剪力分段函数表达式,计算剪力时,集中荷载乘以 1.2 的系数。

$$M_c(L) = \begin{cases} 1.3125 L^2 + 67.5L & L \leq 5\text{m} \\ 1.8125 L^2 + 65L & 5\text{m} < L < 50\text{m} \\ 1.3125 L^2 + 90L & L \geq 50\text{m} \end{cases} \quad (6)$$

$$Q_c(L) = \begin{cases} 5.25L + 324 & L \leq 5\text{m} \\ 7.25L + 312 & 5\text{m} < L < 50\text{m} \\ 5.25L + 432 & L \geq 50\text{m} \end{cases} \quad (7)$$

同理,英国规范 HA 荷载产生的弯矩和剪力效应与跨径的相关函数表达式:

$$M_{bs}(L) = \begin{cases} 42 L^{1.33} + 30L & L \leq 50\text{m} \\ 4.5 L^{1.9} + 30L & 50\text{m} < L \leq 1600\text{m} \end{cases} \quad (8)$$

$$Q_{bs}(L) = \begin{cases} 168 L^{0.33} + 120 & L \leq 50\text{m} \\ 18 L^{0.9} + 120 & 50\text{m} < L \leq 1600\text{m} \end{cases} \quad (9)$$

结合上述式(6)~式(9)可得到任意跨径下两种规范对应的简支梁弯矩和剪力标准值效应谱。为了更明显地展现变化趋势,取不同跨径的 L 值得出效应结果,相关规律曲线如图 6~图 8 所示。

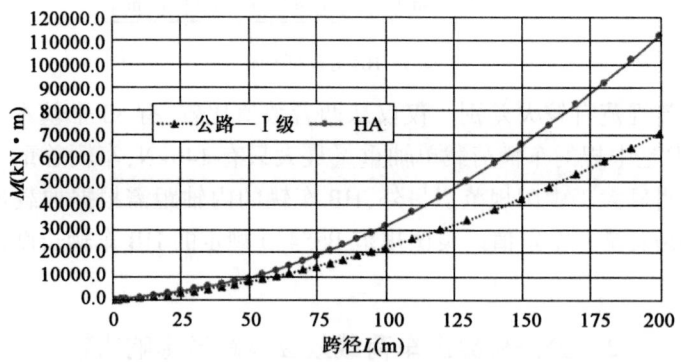

图 6 跨中弯矩效应对比

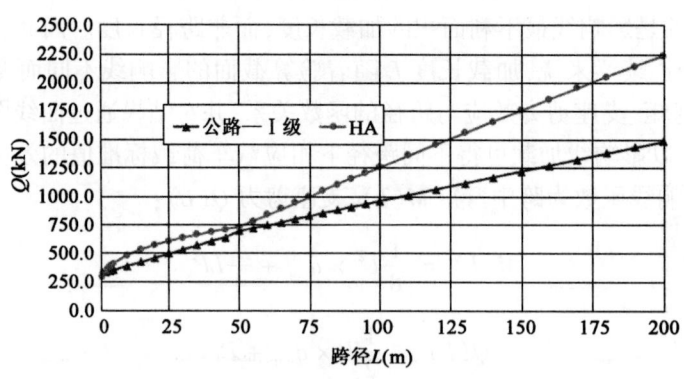

图 7 支座剪力效应对比

图 6 和图 7 表明,HA 荷载加载的弯矩和剪力标准值效应均大于公路—Ⅰ级产生的效应。图 8 是针对简支梁加载,中英规范荷载标准值效应的比值系数。综合来说,纵观整个曲线变化过程,效应比值随跨径的增加呈阶段性变化。当 $L < 50\text{m}$ 时,比值呈凸形曲线,先增大后减小;当 $L \geq 50\text{m}$ 时,比值逐渐增长,后趋于稳定,稳定后对应弯矩比值为 1.6,剪力比值为 1.5。

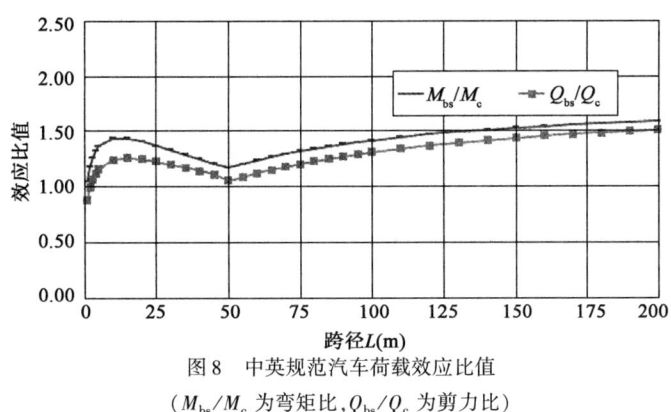

图8 中英规范汽车荷载效应比值

(M_{bs}/M_c 为弯矩比,Q_{bs}/Q_c 为剪力比)

3 公路桥梁汽车荷载横、纵向折减系数比较

3.1 横向折减系数

对于布载多车道的横向折减系数,中英规范采用不同的形式。中规采用等量折减,即在总活载效应的基础上乘以一个相应的折减系数,而英国规范则是以一个或者两个车道的标准荷载为基础,其余其他车道上的荷载乘以与其最大车道荷载的比值 β。

中国《通规》(JTG D60—2015)在考虑多车道折减时引入一个"多车道加载横向折减系数",引用规范表1,如表1所示。

中国规范横向车道折减系数 表1

横向布载道路数(条)	1	2	3	4	5	6	7	8
横向车道布载系数	1.20	1.00	0.78	0.67	0.60	0.55	0.52	0.50

英国规范是使各车道分别乘以系数 β_1、$\beta_2 \cdots \beta_n$。当 $\beta=1$,则该车道为满载;当 $\beta<1$,则该线荷载按相应系数折减效应。在多车道加载的情况下,为使不同构件分别承受最不利效应,各车道的 β 值可以互换。由于 β 值针对车道数的不同而变化,在车道布载组合的同时,也考虑了车道的偏载效应。如图9所示。

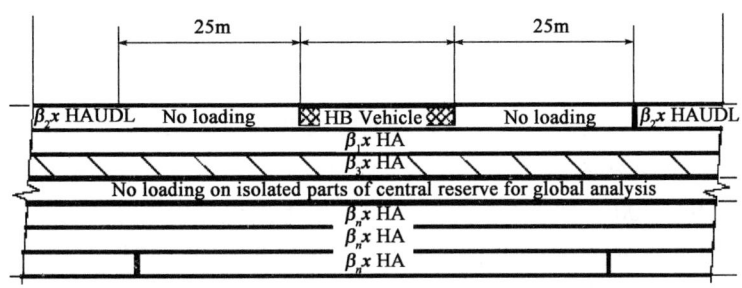

Loaded length L (m)	First lane factor β_1	Second lane factor β_2	Third lane factor β_3	Fourth and subsequent lane factor β_n
$0<L\leqslant20$	α_1	α_1	0.6	$0.6\alpha_1$
$20<L\leqslant40$	α_2	α_2	0.6	$0.6\alpha_2$
$40<L\leqslant50$	1.0	1.0	0.6	0.6
$50<L\leqslant112$ $N<6$	1.0	7.1/L	0.6	0.6
$50<L\leqslant112$ $N\geqslant6$	1.0	1.0	0.6	0.6
$L>112$ $N\geqslant6$	1.0	0.67	0.6	0.6
$L>112$ $N\geqslant6$	1.0	1.0	0.6	0.6

图9 英国规范 HA 和 HB 组合及多车道系数 β 示意图

根据以上分析对比显示,英标的多车道横向折减系数相比于中国规范考虑得更具体、全面。

3.2 纵向折减系数

大跨径桥梁的汽车荷载应考虑纵向折减。英国规范 BS5400 在确定 HA 均布荷载 UDL 取值时已考虑根据跨径变化,对大跨径桥梁上的汽车荷载值已进行纵向折减,故在设计时不需折减效应。中国《通规》(JTG D60—2015)仍以列表的形式提出了纵向折减,引用规范表2,如表2所示。

中国规范纵向车道折减系数　　　　　　　　　　　　　　　　表2

计算跨径 L_0(m)	纵向折减系数	计算跨径 L_0(m)	纵向折减系数
$150 < L_0 < 400$	0.97	$800 \leq L_0 < 1000$	0.94
$400 \leq L_0 < 600$	0.96	$L_0 \geq 1000$	0.93
$600 \leq L_0 < 800$	0.95	—	—

4 结 语

本文将英国荷载规范《BS5400-2,2006》和中国《公路桥涵设计通用规范》(JTG D60—2015)中的汽车荷载进行了比较研究。主要差异体现在以下几方面:

(1)计算桥梁整体受力时,中国规范仅仅考虑车道荷载,活载效应的计算模式比英国规范更为简单,有利于手算验证,便于检查。而英标的 HA 和 HB 荷载共同组合方式较多,尤其 HA 荷载的值是根据加载长度决定的,采用影响线加载的计算方式较为复杂,对于一些连续梁等复杂结构,手算很难实现。

(2)中、英桥梁设计规范的汽车荷载效应都与跨径相关,但从荷载数值、计算方式和加载方式均不同。总体来说,英标的汽车荷载效应比我国汽车荷载大。因此,在海外工程中推行我国桥梁设计理念时,应根据具体跨径配置来分析荷载效应的差别,选择适当的安全系数,保证结构安全,确保工程顺利实施。

(3)随着我国工业的迅速发展,从收集桥梁垮塌事故资料可知,绝大部分事故都是超载、重车偏载导致的。从大型重载车超载来看,中国规范的车辆荷载总重为 550kN,而英国规范一辆 HB 车的总重在 1200~1800kN 之间,是中国车辆荷载的3倍左右。因此,中国规范可参照英国规范(BS5400-2,2006)关于汽车活载的相关规定,适当提高荷载等级,来减少因超、重载引起的安全事故,提高桥梁的使用寿命,保护生命和财产安全。

参考文献

[1] 肖小艳.中英规范汽车荷载效应与桥梁跨径的比较分析[J].交通科技,2016.
[2] 吴腾,葛耀君,熊沽.现行国内外公路桥梁汽车荷载及其相应的比较[J].结构工程师,2008(10).
[3] 余顺新.欧洲规范与英国公路设计[J].中外公路,2010.
[4] 吴雪亮.英国规范 BS 5400 与欧洲规范在预应力混凝土梁设计中的异同[J].中外公路,2014(6).
[5] 周勇军,梁玉照,贺拴海.公路桥梁汽车荷载标准值对比分析[J].建筑科学与工程学报,2010(9).
[6] 施迪.基于空心板标准图的中外桥梁规范比较研究[D].重庆:重庆交通大学,2016.
[7] Bridges Mark Hanselman. Brand Cross. Long term investigation of live load on illions[J]. ASCE. 2007.
[8] Steel, concrete and composite bridges-Prat 2: Specification for loads[S]. British Standard Institution, England, 2006.

系杆拱桥吊杆更换关键技术研究

商雪枫

(浙江数智交院科技股份有限公司)

摘　要　系杆拱桥以其结构受力稳定、外形美观、施工成熟等特点得到了广泛应用。但早期建成运营的系杆拱由于吊杆在防腐设计方面考虑不足,引起钢丝锈蚀,降低了吊杆的安全性,更严重的还导致了安全事故。本文基于某大桥吊杆更换实例,结合精细建模计算,对吊杆更换施工动态模拟分析,阐述更换吊杆的关键技术,实现对系杆拱桥的快速可靠加固,为其他类似工程提供参考和借鉴。

关键词 桥梁工程 系杆拱 吊杆锈蚀 更换吊杆 加固

0 引 言

吊杆是系杆拱桥的"生命之索"。受早期施工工艺、设计条件等因素的制约,部分已运营的桥梁存在吊杆防腐性能低、防腐工艺落后、未考虑吊杆可更换性等系统性缺陷,吊杆内部锈蚀成为影响结构使用寿命和运营安全的重要因素之一。在长期疲劳作用下,越来越多的系杆拱桥进入了吊杆更换周期。如何合理选择吊杆更换方案、精确分析各个步骤的应力分布情况,确保施工过程结构受力的平稳、安全,成为目前吊杆更换技术面临的一个共性问题。

1 吊杆病害及成因分析

1.1 吊杆防护套破坏

结合对系杆拱桥的调研,吊杆 PE 护套发生开裂现象普遍,最短不到 1 年,最长 10 年出现开裂,防护套破损开裂原因为:

(1)吊杆拉索松弛、受交变荷载和温度变化导致防护材料变形开裂。
(2)在紫外线作用下,聚乙烯护套发生老化进而出现裂缝。
(3)吊杆内泥浆在固结中会逐渐收缩,使套管收缩开裂(图1)。
(4)施工和运营中聚乙烯管表面被划伤、磨损,加剧套管内应力分布的不均匀,引起开裂(图2)。

图 1 吊杆护套老化破损

图 2 吊杆护套破损开裂

1.2 吊杆钢丝锈蚀

钢丝腐蚀是影响吊杆安全的重大威胁。吊杆内部锈蚀的主要原因有:

(1)防护套开裂失效,导致水、氧气及其他有害物质与钢丝直接接触引起锈蚀。
(2)吊杆下锚头上部防水罩失效,使积水渗入内部导管内,吊杆钢丝及下锚头长期处于潮湿受腐环境中,导致吊杆钢丝及锚头锈蚀。
(3)吊杆上下锚头盖板焊接质量不满足要求,水汽沿焊缝渗入,导致锚头锈蚀。如图3~图6所示。

图 3　PE 剥开后钢丝锈蚀(一)　　　　　　　图 4　PE 剥开后钢丝锈蚀(二)

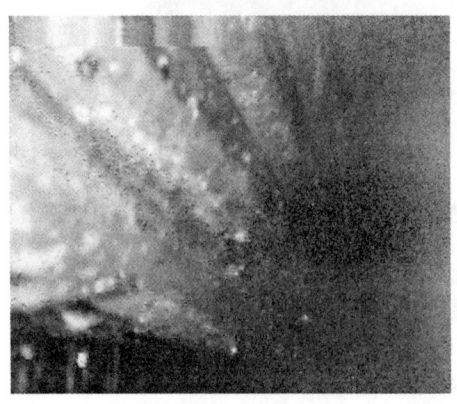 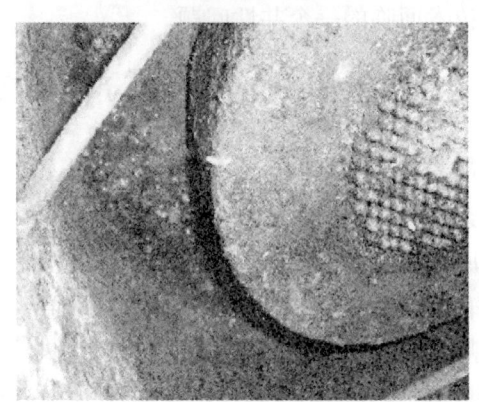

图 5　内窥镜下钢丝锈蚀　　　　　　　　　图 6　吊杆锚头锈蚀

2　吊杆更换技术

2.1　吊杆更换原则

吊杆更换应遵守以下原则：
(1)施工时确保桥梁的结构安全,吊杆更换后桥梁满足设计要求和今后的运营要求。
(2)吊杆更换后索力和桥面线形满足设计要求,并采用调索等方式使结构实际内力与更换前内力相近。
(3)新吊杆和锚具应改进设计,保证新吊杆耐久适用和便于二次更换。
(4)吊杆更换方案具有可操作性、安全性和较好的经济性。

2.2　吊杆更换方法

合理的施工方案是吊杆顺利更换和结构安全的重要保障。目前,更换吊杆可采用临时替代换索方法,且已在较多桥梁上得到了成功的应用。根据替代方式可分为临时吊杆法和兜吊法。

2.2.1　临时兜掉法

采用贝雷架拼装成提升支撑梁,固定在需换吊杆两侧的横梁上,并在横梁底部设置短纵梁,在待更换吊杆附近的桥面上打洞,支撑梁上安装 2 台千斤顶,临时吊杆穿过桥面孔洞,与横梁底纵梁相连。通过千斤顶提升横梁,使吊杆松弛,当索力为零时,迅速换下吊杆。临时兜掉布置如图 7、图 8 所示。

2.2.2　临时吊杆法

在拱顶和系梁底固定临时横梁,每根钢横梁上安装 2 台千斤顶,每台千斤顶向下穿数根预应力粗钢筋(或钢绞线),可采用打孔或拆除吊杆四周桥面板的方法穿过桥面,锚固于桥下横梁底。通过千斤顶逐级张拉临时吊杆,使更换吊杆松弛,进行体系转换后,换下旧吊杆。临时吊杆布置如图 9、图 10 所示。

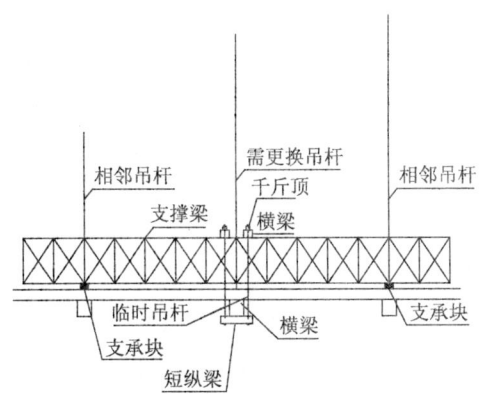

图 7 临时兜掉立面图

图 8 临时兜掉实体图

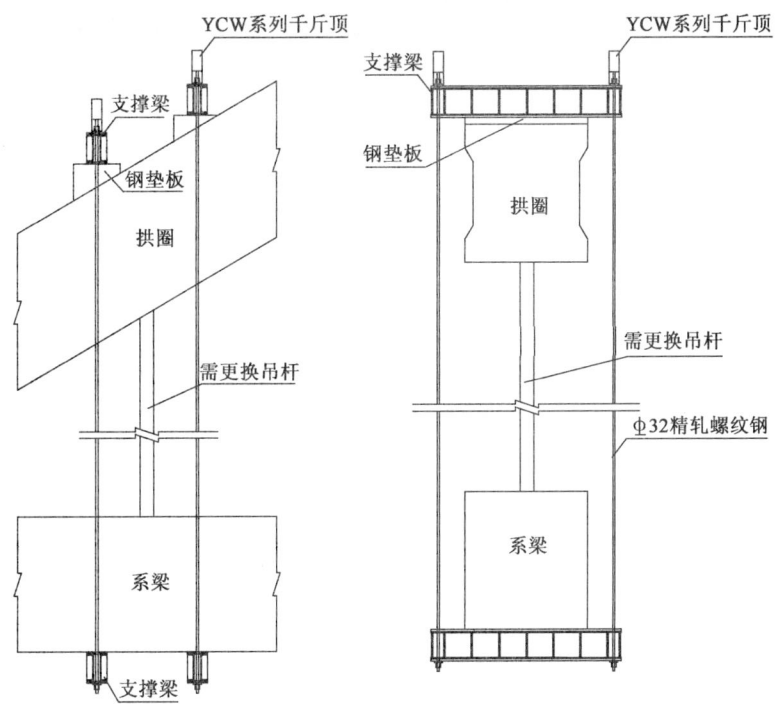

图 9 临时吊杆布置图

图 10 临时吊杆实体图

对拱桥更换吊杆方案主要从方案的安全性、可操作性、经济性、工期等几方面进行比选。推荐采用临时吊杆法,实施过程不损坏原结构、对交通影响小、安全性高。

3 工程实例

某大桥营运至今近15年,根据检测报告及吊杆计算结果,部分吊杆考虑检算系数后不满足规范要求,从安全考虑,对全桥吊杆进行更换。如图11、图12所示。

图11 某大桥整体照

图12 某大桥主桥系杆拱

3.1 计算分析

本文通过对某系杆拱成桥阶段现状模拟,吊杆更换最不利情况模拟以及临时吊杆构件分析,为吊杆更换提供可靠的理论依据。

3.1.1 桥梁现状及施工动态模拟验算

首先,应用有限元软件建立系杆拱模型,通过计算索力与实测索力对比,使模型更换前的内力状态逼近结构目前的内力状态。

其次,按照施工流程模拟实际卸除过程,临时吊杆张拉力采用等差变化,并依据张拉力数值建立相应的工况。另外,验算最不利工况(不使用临时吊杆,完全拆除一根吊杆)下,对其他吊杆的最大索力、拱肋最大内力影响。

最后,得到吊杆更换完工后的实测索力和线形,与计算的完工索力及线形比较,确保桥梁的受力状态接近理想的设计状态。

主要验算结果截图如图13~图18所示。

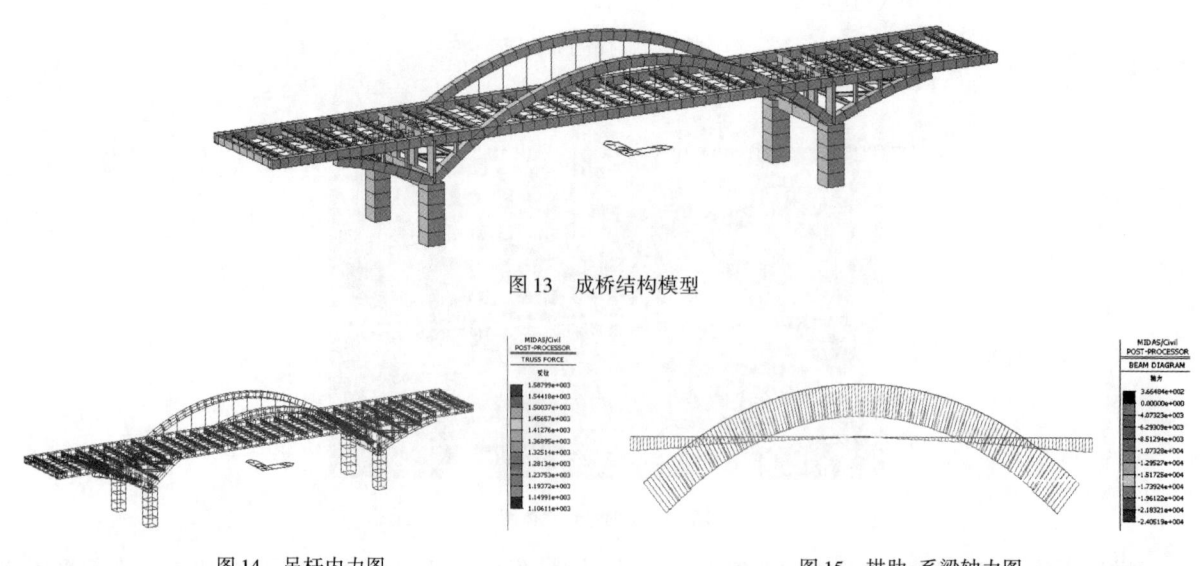

图13 成桥结构模型

图14 吊杆内力图　　图15 拱肋、系梁轴力图

根据图13~图18计算结果,桥梁原结构验算和吊杆更换过程中杆件受力状态均满足规范要求。

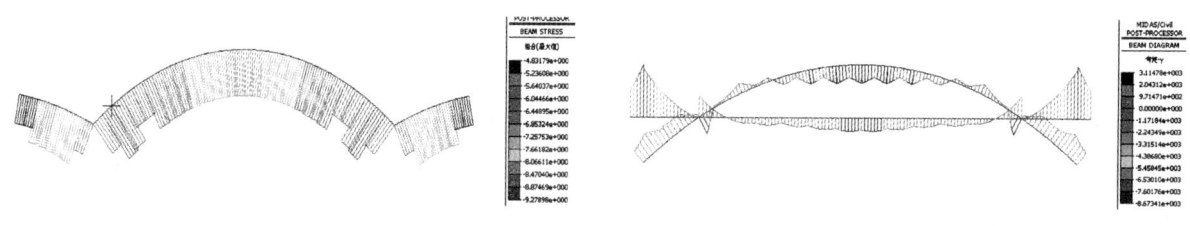

图 16　拱肋应力图　　　　　　　　　　　图 17　拱肋、系梁弯矩力图

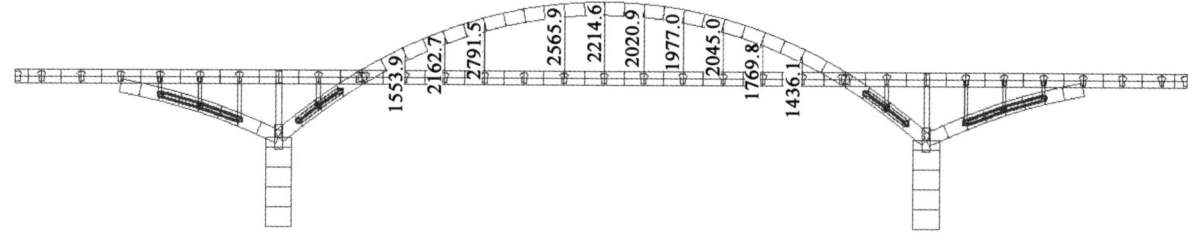

图 18　完全拆除一对吊杆后吊杆内力图

3.1.2　临时吊杆的设计验算

在拱肋顶和系梁底放置临时横梁,作为临时吊杆张拉的工作平台。每个横梁两端的钢垫板设置两个可以穿过临时吊杆的孔以安装、固定和张拉临时吊杆。验算主要包括临时吊杆、临时横梁和垫板垫块的验算。如图 19、图 20 所示。

图 19　临时吊杆上端　　　　　　　　　　　图 20　临时吊杆下端

3.1.2.1　临时吊杆的计算

临时吊杆一般采用高强钢筋,假定截面面积为 A,设计抗拉强度为 f_{pd},承载极限为 F_u,则有:

$$F_u = Af_{pd}$$

在恒载状态下,假设中吊杆的索力设计值为 $T_{中}$,则每根临时吊杆上施加的张拉分别为称 $T_{中}/4$,此时,临时吊杆的安全系数 $k=4F_u/T_{中}$,为了确保施工安全可靠,临时吊杆的安全系数须满足规范要求。

3.1.2.2　临时横梁的计算

钢横梁的计算图式如图 21 所示,图中 A 点和 D 点为吊点,F_1 和 F_2 是临时吊杆的张拉力,B 点和 D 点为三角垫块对钢横梁的支点,F_3 和 F_4 是三角垫块对钢横梁的支承力,$l_1 = l_2 = l_4 = l_5$,l_3 表示拱肋的宽度。根据平衡原则,必然有 $F_1 = F_2 = F_3 = F_4$。

为确保安全,钢横梁应满足强度要求。AB、CD 段承受弯矩和剪力,而 BC 段则仅承受弯矩,处于纯弯曲状态,整个梁的最大弯矩出现在两支点之间。取支点处进行验算,设支点处的弯矩为 $M_{支}$,钢横梁的截面惯性矩为 $I_{支}$,危险点到支点截面中性轴的最大距离为 $y_{支}$,则有 $M_{支} = F_1 l_2$。

梁的最大应力需满足:

$$\sigma_{\max} = \frac{M_{支}}{I_{支}} y_{支} \leq [\sigma] \tag{1}$$

3.1.2.3 三角垫块摩擦系数计算

在上吊点与拱肋之间设置三角垫块,保证上吊点为水平状态,同时为临时吊杆张拉提供平台。三角垫块采用配筋混凝土块,也可用钢板预制,拱肋同宽。三角垫块的计算图式如图22所示,图中 P 为千斤顶的压力,N 为拱肋对于垫块的支撑力,F 为静摩擦力,α 为拱肋的倾角。

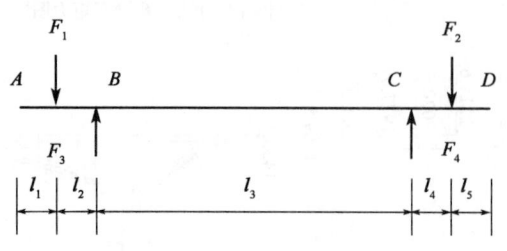

图21 临时横梁的计算图式

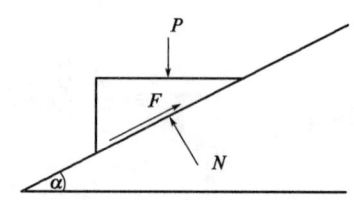

图22 三角垫块的计算简图

为了不使垫块滑落,必须满足下列关系:

$$P\sin\alpha < F \tag{2}$$

静摩擦力即将产生滑动时临界关系式为

$$F = \mu P\cos\alpha \tag{3}$$

将式(3)代入式(2),化简后可得到:

$$\mu > \tan\alpha \tag{4}$$

3.2 施工关键流程

替代法吊杆更换最重要的是完成两次体系转换,即索力从旧吊杆和临时吊杆相互转移。施工过程主要分为旧吊杆卸除、新吊杆安装张拉和后续防护。

3.2.1 旧吊杆拆除

系杆拱桥吊杆更换采用等步长张拉临时吊杆,再按比例割断相应钢丝,直到将被更换吊杆拆除。如图23~图26所示。

图23 钢管切割

图24 钢丝逐级切割

3.2.2 新吊杆安装张拉

新吊杆采用卷扬机或吊机配合人工进行下料,锚垫板安装后,再进行体系转换。过程中需监测吊杆处桥面的高程,使其变化在设计控制范围内,并且全程进行新吊杆应力的监控。如图27~图30所示。

3.2.3 后续防护

新吊杆张拉到位之后,拆除上下吊点,外部加装防水罩和锚头罩(图31、图32)。

图 25 钢丝逐级切割

图 26 吊杆拆除

图 27 新吊杆吊装

图 28 新吊杆锚头紧固

图 29 新吊杆张拉

图 30 新吊杆索力检测

图 31 吊杆防水罩安装

图 32 吊杆防腐涂料涂装

4 吊杆更换施工注意事项

(1) 保持原结构的应力状态，尽量减小施工引起的内力和线形偏差。

(2) 施工时，临时吊杆和旧吊杆、临时吊杆和新吊杆之间的荷载体系转换要平稳，即要对临时吊杆分级均匀加载，对旧吊杆要分级割断和新吊杆分级张拉等，加、卸载过程中千斤顶泵油量应相等以保持临时吊杆均衡受力。

(3) 吊杆更换应选择温度变化小的时段进行，减弱温差对索力和挠度测量的不利影响，且对交通影响小。

(4) 需采用第三方施工监控，及时了解拱结构的应力、变形及桥面线形状态，保证系杆拱桥吊杆更换结构安全和稳定。

5 结 语

吊杆是系杆拱桥的"生命之索"，为养护之重点。以全面、精细的理论计算为基础的临时吊杆法更换技术，保证了吊杆更换过程安全、可控，确保桥梁的受力状态接近理想的设计状态。实现了对系杆拱桥的快速可靠加固，形成了一套精确有效的系杆拱桥吊杆更换工艺技术，具有广泛的工程意义和应用前景。

参考文献

[1] 傅斌,许晓锋,黄福伟.对钢管混凝土拱桥病害的调研及分类[J].交通标准化,2008(4).

[2] 杨敏.钢管混凝土系杆拱桥的常见病害及处治方法[J].城市道桥与防洪,2008(7).

[3] 徐建伟,李飞泉,彭卫.中承式拱桥的吊杆损伤识别[J].公路,2007(12).

[4] 鹿建阁.钢管混凝土拱桥吊杆的破损行为分析[D].天津:天津大学,2005.

[5] 中华人民共和国交通部.公路桥涵养护规范:JTG H11—2004[S].北京:人民交通出版社,2004.

[6] 赵洋.系杆拱桥吊杆更换研究[D].杭州:浙江大学,2006.

[7] Zui H,Shinke T. Namita Y. Practical formulas for estimation of cable tension by vibration method[J]. J Struct Eng 1996.122(6):651-665.

曲线钢箱组合梁桥空间受力特征及简化设计方法研究

朱 钊 贺拴海 宋一凡 李 源 沈传东

(长安大学)

摘 要 钢箱组合梁桥因其线形适应性强、施工速度快等特点，已广泛应用于公路及城市曲线桥梁建设中。目前，多梁式曲线钢箱组合梁桥设计多采用梁格模型进行分析验算，难以准确考虑空间变形特征、桥面板及钢梁的三维应力分布，往往获得偏保守或不安全的设计。本研究进行了曲线半径为50~600m多梁式钢箱组合梁桥的三维精细化模型及梁格模型分析，探讨了梁格模型对于曲线组合梁桥空间变形及应力分布的适用性。分析结果表明:曲线钢箱组合梁桥结构变形呈现明显的弯扭耦合特征，应结合工程需求进行曲面预拱度设置。因弯扭耦合效应的影响，曲线钢箱组合梁桥负弯矩桥面板拉应力分布区域呈现内侧大于外侧的特点，应区别于直桥进行特殊设计。由于曲线钢混组合梁桥桥面板及钢箱梁的应力分布的不均匀性，负弯矩区采用梁格模型设计偏于不安全,本研究中建议应力放大值分别为1.41和1.81。正弯矩区梁格模型应力计算结果与三维精细化模型计算结果比值为0.99~1.07,表明梁格模型在曲线钢箱组合梁桥正弯矩区应力分析中具有较好的适用性。

关键词 桥梁工程 曲线钢箱组合梁 空间受力特征 简化设计方法

0 引言

随着我国城市化进程的推进,由于既有建筑及建设用地的限制,城市立交桥梁成为缓解城市交通拥堵的有效方案之一。城市立交桥建设过程中,为使得桥梁适应设计线形,不可避免地会产生大量曲线梁桥。同时,为加快城市桥梁建设速度,减少施工围挡引起的交通拥堵,采用预制拼装技术的曲线钢混组合桥梁已大量应用于城市桥梁建设过程中。

随着我国钢混组合桥梁的快速发展,大量学者开始了钢混组合梁桥设计方法、剪力键连接性能、钢梁精确应力及混凝土桥面板抗裂性能等方面的研究[1-5]。我国《公路钢混组合梁桥设计与施工规范》(JTG/T D64-01—2015)的颁布,标志着我国直线钢混组合梁桥设计施工的相对成熟。目前,多梁式曲线钢箱组合梁桥设计多采用空间梁格模型进行分析验算,难以准确考虑空间变形特征、桥面板及钢梁的三维应力分布,往往获得偏保守或不安全的设计。本研究通过不同曲线半径(50~600m)多梁式钢箱组合梁桥的三维精细化模型及梁格模型分析,进行了结构三维变形及钢箱梁、桥面板应力状态对比,建立了不同弯曲半径时,钢箱组合梁桥正负弯矩区剪力滞系数量值及发展规律,曲面预拱度及曲梁变形的梁格计算方法。本研究对于推进小半径钢箱组合梁桥梁格法设计中模型建立,钢箱梁精细化应力分析,桥面板抗裂性准确评估具有重要的意义。

1 数值分析模型

1.1 结构设计参数

本研究分析模型中,除曲线半径外,其他设计参数与依托工程保持一致。其中桥梁设计宽度9.8m,设计车道为双向两车道。桥梁跨径为25m,桥梁全长50m,结构形式为两跨连续梁。钢箱梁材料为Q345钢,桥面板采用C50混凝土。主梁采用两梁式钢箱组合梁,梁高1.5m,其中钢箱梁高度1.1m,桥面板厚度为0.25~0.4m。钢箱梁顶板厚度25mm,底板厚度20mm,腹板厚度16mm,其他设计参数如图1、图2所示。

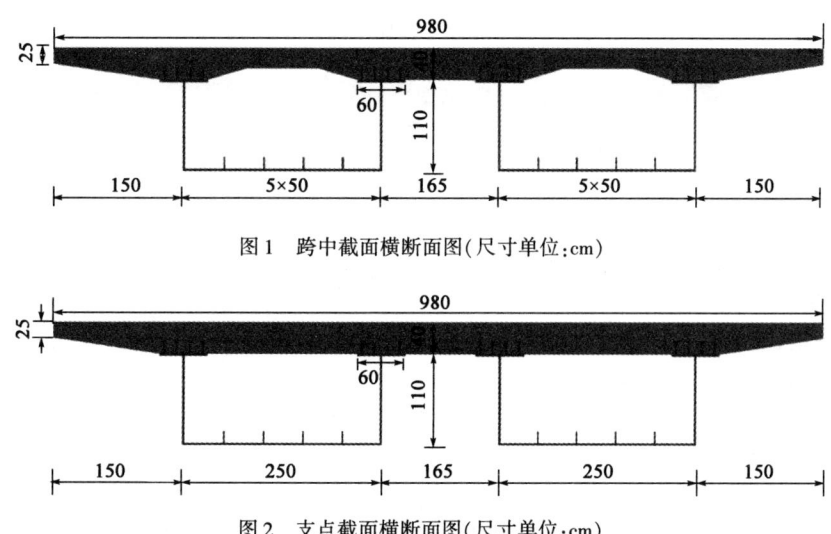

图1 跨中截面横断面图(尺寸单位:cm)

图2 支点截面横断面图(尺寸单位:cm)

1.2 三维精细化模型

曲线钢箱组合梁桥三维精细化分析模型中,桥面板采用块单元,桥面板与钢箱梁连接以实际剪力键位置耦合平动自由度模拟,不考虑桥面板与钢梁间可能发生的黏结滑移,三维精细化模型节段如图3所示。

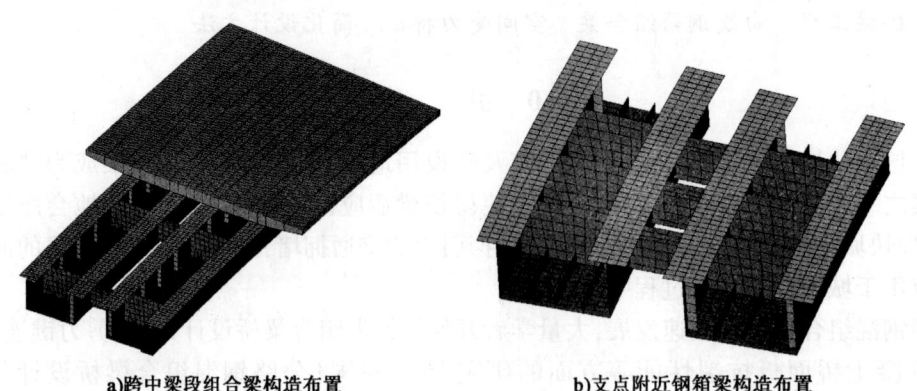

a) 跨中梁段组合梁构造布置   b) 支点附近钢箱梁构造布置

图3 三维精细化模型图

1.3 梁格模型刚度取值方法

采用梁格模型分析时,虚拟横梁采用矩形截面,宽度1m,厚度以桥面板等效变形相等计算得到,计算示意如图4所示。计算原理为简支梁跨中作用单位集中力时跨中变形相等,推导过程如式(1)~式(4)所示。其中,式中L为钢梁内腹板间桥面板跨度,h为桥面板厚度;L_1为虚拟横梁桥面板跨度,h_1为虚拟横梁桥面板厚度。E为桥面板混凝土弹性模量,I为桥面板抗弯刚度,I_1为虚拟横梁抗弯刚度,b和b_1均为桥面板单位宽度。本研究中L为165cm,L_1为440cm,h为40cm,计算得到虚拟横梁厚度h_1为107cm。

$$\frac{PL^3}{48EI} = \frac{PL_1^3}{48EI_1} \tag{1}$$

$$\frac{L^3}{I} = \frac{L_1^3}{I_1} \tag{2}$$

$$\frac{L^3}{1/12bh^3} = \frac{L_1^3}{1/12b_1h_1^3} \tag{3}$$

$$\frac{L}{L_1} = \frac{h}{h_1} \tag{4}$$

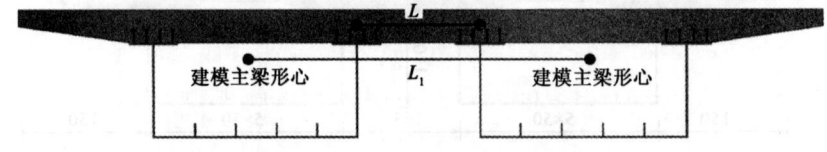

图4 虚拟横梁刚度计算示意图

1.4 分析位置及测点布置

维应力状态分析以边跨$0.4L$正弯矩及支点负弯矩截面应力分布为重点研究对象。横截面上,变形及应力分析点位置相同,如图5所示。

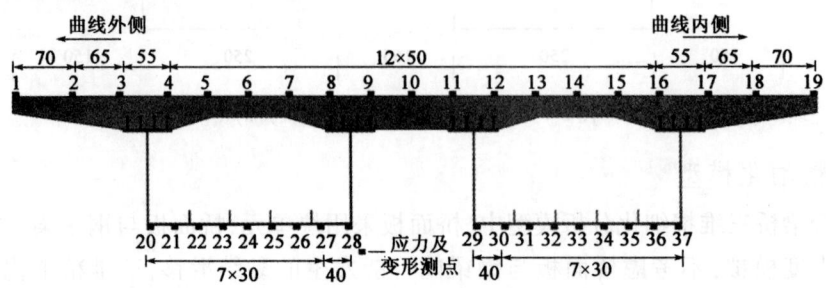

图5 应力及变形测点布置图

2 空间受力特征分析及简化设计方法讨论

2.1 弯扭耦合变形

因本研究旨在研究曲线钢箱组合梁的空间受力特征,本文分析中荷载仅考虑结构自重,且不考虑预应力布束对结构受力的影响。曲线梁桥三维分析结果表现出明显的弯扭耦合特征,边跨四分点附近主梁变形呈现外侧大、内侧小的特点,如图6所示。随着曲线半径从50m增大到600m,桥面板及钢箱梁的弯扭耦合变形特征逐渐减弱,如图7、图8所示。采用梁格模型计算得到的不同半径主梁变形范围为4.5~4.8mm,可见采用梁格模型计算的主梁变形明显小于板单元计算值,且难以考虑变形的空间分布特征。采用梁格模型计算的曲线钢箱组合梁桥预拱度适用性较差,该结构的预拱度设置应该为曲面预拱度。

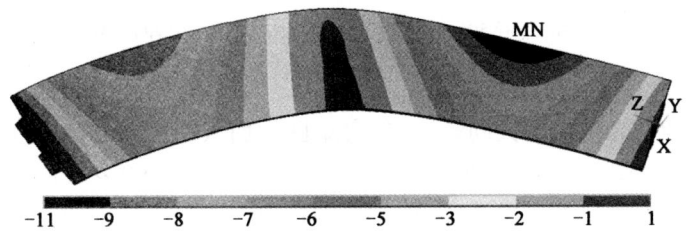

图6 曲线半径50m时主梁变形图(尺寸单位:mm)

注:负号表示变形向下。

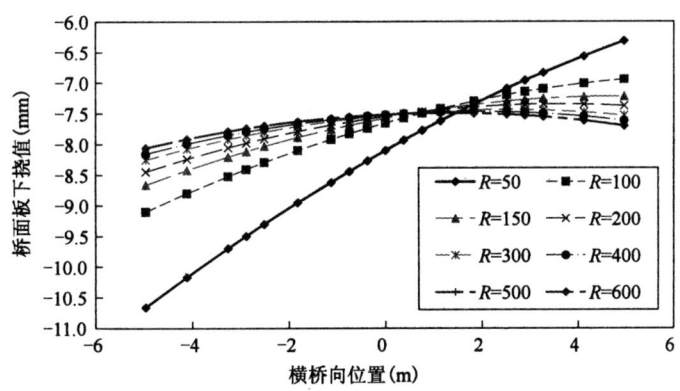

图7 半径变化时四分点桥面板变形分布图(负号表示变形向下)

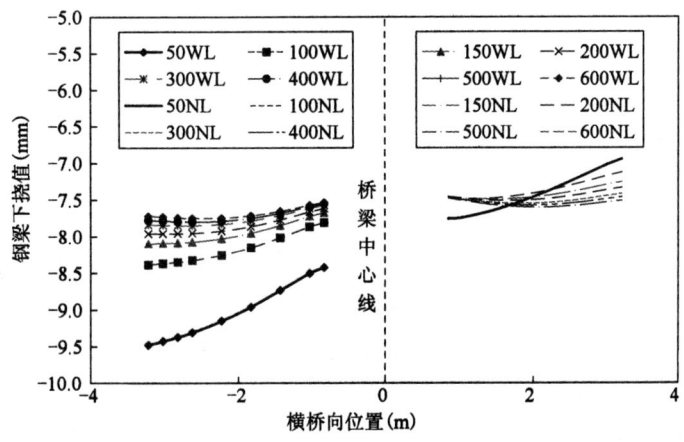

图8 半径变化时四分点钢箱梁变形分布图(负号表示变形向下)

2.2 负弯矩区应力状态分析

精细化三维模型分析结果表明,因弯扭耦合效应的影响,曲线内外侧拉应力分布长度表现为外侧短、内侧长的特点,应区别于直桥进行负弯矩区特殊设计,其中负弯矩区主拉应力分布如图9所示。

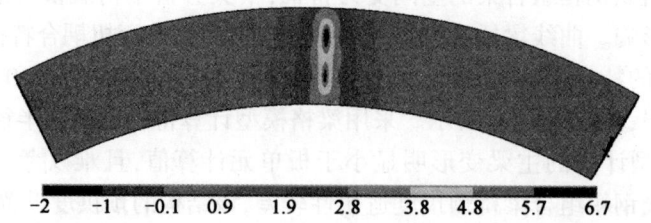

图9 曲线半径50m时负弯矩区桥面板主应力云图(单位:MPa)
注:受拉为正,受压为负。

因剪力滞效应和弯扭耦合效应的共同影响,负弯矩区桥面板应力分布表现为显著的不均匀性,与梁格模型计算值差别较大,如图10所示。但桥面板应力平均值为3.90~4.89MPa,与梁格模型计算值4.42~4.71MPa接近。负弯矩区剪力滞效应最大值1.41,剪力滞效应最小值为0.46,可见采用梁格模型进行曲线钢箱连续梁桥桥面拉应力分析时,将导致安全系数的不均衡,设计偏于不安全。

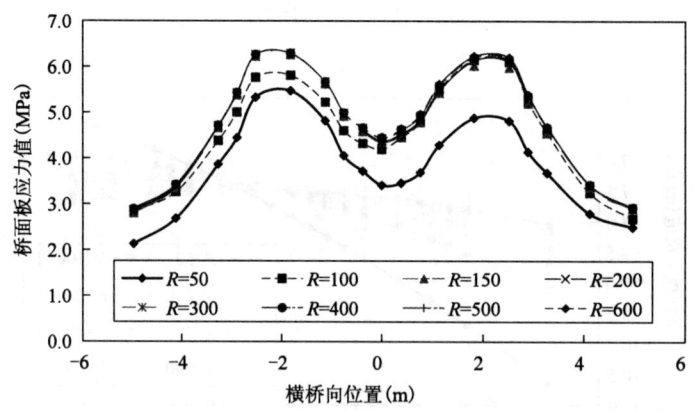

图10 半径变化时负弯矩区桥面板正应力分布图(受拉为正)

板单元模型分析结果表明,负弯矩区钢梁应力呈现明显的不均匀性,由于支座约束的影响,最小压应力为0,但接近腹板位置钢箱梁压应力达到62.1MPa。负弯矩区钢梁平均压应力为30.4~35.6MPa,与梁格模型计算值34.3~36.0MPa接近。负弯矩区钢梁剪力滞系数最大值为1.81,剪力滞系数最小值为0。曲线半径为50~100m时,曲线半径对钢梁应力分布影响较大;大于100m时,曲线半径对受压区钢梁应力分布影响逐渐减小,如图11所示。

2.3 正弯矩区应力状态分析

除考虑负弯矩区应力分析的准确性外,正弯矩区应力分析准确性同样重要。分析结果表明,相比负弯矩区桥面应力分布的不均匀性,正弯矩区桥面板应力分布均匀性较好,应力水平为1.5~1.9MPa,梁单元分析值为1.7~1.9MPa,表明梁格模型对于钢箱梁桥正弯矩区设计适用性较好。因扭矩引起的桥面板内侧上翘影响,正弯矩区桥面板应力分布呈现为内侧小、外侧大的特点,如图12所示。

与正弯矩区桥面板应力分布均匀性相比,钢箱梁应力分布不均匀程度轻微增强,应力分布范围为24.4~27.9MPa,如图13所示。梁格模型分析值为26.1~27.5MPa,与板单元分析结果比值为0.99~1.07,表明梁格模型分析准确性优异。

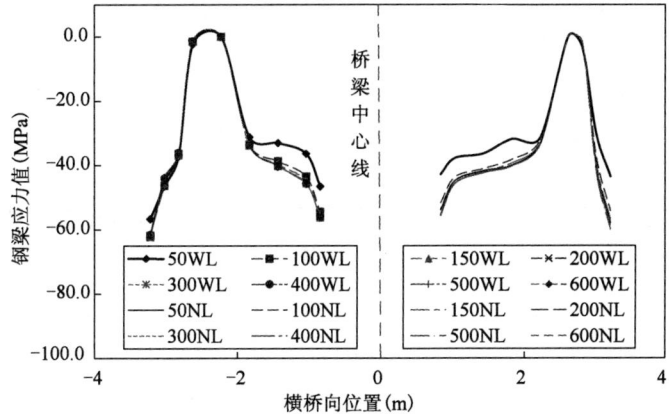

图 11 半径变化时负弯矩区钢箱梁正应力分布图(受拉为正)

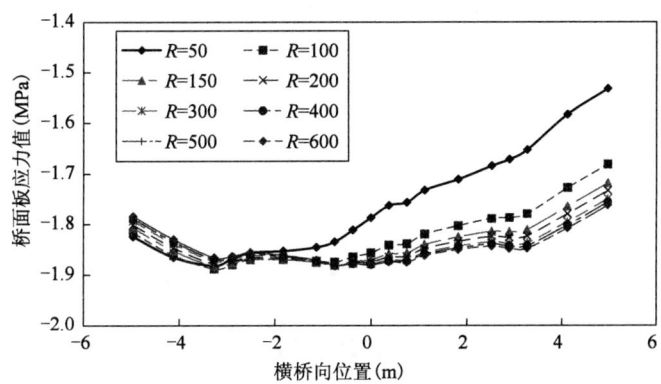

图 12 半径变化时正弯矩区桥面板正应力分布图(受拉为正)

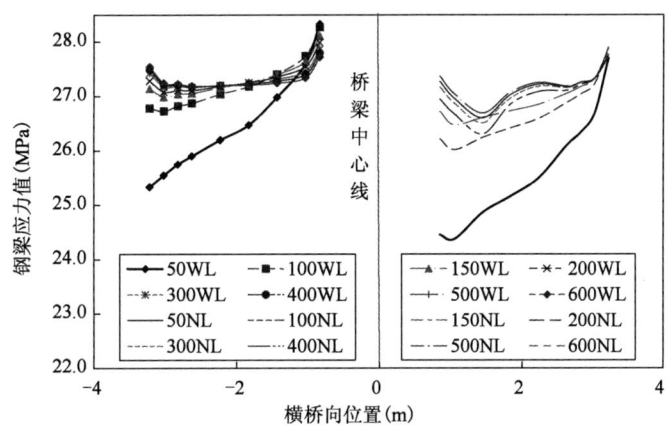

图 13 半径变化时正弯矩区桥面板正应力分布图(受拉为正)

3 结 语

本研究采用三维精细化模型与空间梁格模型进行了不同曲线半径的钢箱组合梁桥受力性能分析,分析结果揭示了曲线钢箱组合梁桥的空间受力特征,并以结构变形、负弯矩区应力分布及正弯矩区应力分布验证了梁格模型设计钢箱组合梁桥的合理性。

对于采用梁格模型进行空间受力特征分析及简化设计方面主要研究结果有:

(1)采用梁格模型难以精确考虑弯扭耦合效应引起的结构空间变形分布特征,导致预拱度设置与结构实际变形不相符。曲线钢箱组合梁桥预拱度设置时,应采用三维精细化模型分析其变形规律,并结合工程需求,必要时需设置曲面预拱度。曲线半径为 50~100m 时,结构变形呈现明显的弯扭耦合特征;半径为100～600m时,弯扭耦合特征逐渐减弱;半径大于600m时,内外侧变形差值仅为0.6mm,可按照直桥设计。

(2)曲线半径引起负弯矩桥面板拉应力内外侧分布的不均匀性,应区别于直桥进行特殊设计。曲线钢混组合梁桥负弯矩区采用梁格模型设计时,应采用剪力滞系数考虑桥面板及钢箱梁的应力分布不均匀性,本研究中建议值分别为1.41和1.81。

(3)由于正弯矩区桥面板厚度较大,压应力水平较低,且该位置构造相对支点位置简单,其应力不均匀性明显减弱,采用梁格模型进行应力分析准确性高,适用性好。

参考文献

[1] 项贻强,竺盛,赵阳.快速施工桥梁的研究进展[J].中国公路学报,2018,31(12):1-27.
[2] 刘永健,高诣民,周绪红,等.中小跨径钢-混凝土组合梁桥技术经济性分析[J].中国公路学报,2017,30(3):1-13.
[3] 吴冲,曾明根,翟慧娜.我国公路简支钢混组合梁合理截面研究[J].桥梁建设,2007,5:30-33.
[4] 赵建,郑舟军.大跨度钢-混组合梁桥剪力钉群受力分析研究[J].桥梁建设,2011,43(3):48-53.
[5] 沈传东,宋一凡,马小伟.考虑剪力滞与约束扭转影响的曲线双工字钢板组合梁耦合效应分析[C].全国结构工程学术会议,2019:85-92.

Modal Frequency Analysis of Suspension Bridge under the Action of Temperature

Qichen Wang   Xiaoyue Gao

(School of Highway, Chang'an University)

Abstract   The mechanism of modal frequency change of suspension bridges under the effect of temperature is discussed. In this study, long-span steel truss suspension bridges are used to analyze the effects of material changes, temperature secondary stresses and boundary condition changes on the natural vibration frequency of suspension bridges. Firstly, a simple influence mechanism is given through the analysis of simply supported beams. Then, the degree of influence of different factors and temperature variations of different members on the natural vibration frequency of suspension bridges is discussed by ANSYS software modeling with the control variable method. The results show that, among the three factors, the temperature stress has the greatest influence, while the boundary conditions have the least influence. The range of natural vibration frequencies influenced by temperature should be considered during bridge health monitoring for more accurate identification of structural damage.

Keywords   Temperature   Bridge modal frequency   Finite element Analysis

0   Introduction

Bridge structures are exposed to nature for long periods of time and are subjected to the complex effects of various air-temperature variations, and a non-uniform temperature distribution is formed inside the structure, which has a significant effect on the structural characteristics of the bridge such as the self-oscillation frequency[1]. The natural frequency is sensitive to the variation of temperature, which often disturbs the frequency-based identification and even results in the false evaluation of the structural health condition[2].

Ambient temperature influences the modal frequency of the bridge structure mainly in three ways, namely, changing the structural size, producing internal force in the statically indeterminate structure and changing the mechanical properties of the structural material, and the influence of structure size change on the modal frequency can be neglected [3].

Christian, C. found that temperature difference has caused the natural frequencies of the bridge to vary up to 3.63%, by modeling the structure in Finite Element(FE) Model and performing vibration testing [4]. Meng, Q.'s study shows that an overall decrease in modal frequency is occurred with increasing temperature, and for long-span suspension bridges, the time-varying dynamic properties are mainly caused by a thermal stress stiffening effect [5]. Cheynet, E. used the approach of full-scale ambient vibration testing to study the temperature effects on the modal parameters of a suspension bridge across a Norwegian fjord [6]. Jang, J. used two approaches to model the temperature effects on natural frequencies(thermal prestress imposed at an element level and temperature-dependent Young's modulus) in the FE model [7]. In the research by Zolghadri, N., two models were used to identify natural frequencies of the structure from ambient vibration data, these were Natural Excitation Technique (NExT) and the Eigen System Realization(ERA) algorithm [8].

In recent years, with the development of calculation methods and theories, more and more new methods have been used to identify the influence of temperature on the dynamic characteristics of bridges. He, H. adopted the co-integration theory with the ability to quantify the long term balance relationship among multiple non-stationary sequences to study the comprehensive effects of temperature and humidity on the bridge's frequencies [9]. Furtmueller, t employed A time series model that captures the impact of the environmental temperature on the frequency and simultaneously describes the dynamic behaviour of the underlying complex process properly [10]. Hong P. developed a framework for data-driven structural diagnosis and damage detection using a support vector machine(SVM) integrated with enhanced feature extraction techniques for rapid condition assessment for large-scale cable-stayed bridges [11]. Tan, G. Proposed a new method for temperature effect analysis of natural frequency of bridge based on the particle swarm optimized (PSO) neural network. The PSO neural network algorithm was adopted to analyze the measured data, and the relationship between temperature and natural frequency was established, then the method on eliminating temperature effect was derived [12]. Jiao, Y. proposed a fuzzy neural network-based damage assessment method which can distinguish the damage from temperature effect [13].

The objective of this study is to discuss the influence mechanism of temperature, and the change of bearing stiffness is considered. Setting out to three factors of internal force change, material change and bearing change, this research took the temperature difference among the components into consideration, and discussed their influence on the natural vibration frequency of the bridge.

1 Influence Mechanism

Undamped free vibration equation of structures [14]:

$$[M]\{\ddot{u}\} + [K]\{u\} = 0 \quad (1)$$

$$[K] = [K_0] + [S] \quad (2)$$

Where: $[M]$——Mass matrix;
$[K]$——Stiffness matrix;
$\{\ddot{u}\}$——Node acceleration vector;
$\{u\}$——Node displacement vector;
$[K_0]$——Initial stiffness matrix;
$[S]$——Initial stress stiffness matrix.

Under the action of temperature, the change of material, stress state and boundary conditions will affect the structural stiffness matrix, and then affect the natural vibration characteristics of bridge structure.

1.1 Material Properties

Temperature mainly affects the elastic modulus and linear expansion coefficient of the material. The elastic modulus is an important parameter to form the initial stiffness matrix of the structure, and the linear expansion coefficient affects the size and distribution of the temperature stress, thus affecting the initial stress stiffness matrix.

The results[15] show that in the normal temperature range, the variation law of them with temperature is as follows::

Steel:

$$E = E_0\left[1 - \frac{13(T - T_0)}{33000}\right] \quad (3)$$

$$\alpha_s = (0.004T + 12) \times 10^{-6} [\text{m/(m} \cdot ℃)] \quad (4)$$

Concrete:

$$E = E_0\left(1.06 - \frac{0.003T}{T_1}\right) \quad (5)$$

$$\alpha_s = (0.008T + 10) \times 10^{-6} [\text{m/(m} \cdot ℃)] \quad (6)$$

Where: E——Elasticity modulus of materials at $T℃$;

T_1——1℃;

T_0——20℃;

E_0——Elasticity modulus of materials at 20℃;

α_s——Linear expansion coefficient of materials at T℃.

1.2 Structural Stress

The temperature stress has obvious time and non-linearity. Temperature stress is divided into two types, one is temperature self-stress, the other is temperature secondary stress[16]. When the temperature changes, the temperature stress is added to the stiffness matrix as a part of the initial stress of the structure, and then affects the natural vibration characteristics of the bridge.

1.3 Boundary Conditions

1.3.1 Torsional Frequency

The bearing is the force transfer component between the superstructure and the substructure of the bridge. At present, rubber bearings are mostly used. Relevant studies show that the vertical stiffness of rubber bearing is affected by temperature, and the stiffness decreases by about 0.2% for every 1℃ increase in temperature[17].

Assuming that the transverse stiffness of the girder was infinite and the displacement of the axis was not considered. The spring vertical support can be used to simulate the rubber bearings at both ends of the simply supported girder. The following can be obtained according to the undamped vibration of the single-degree-of-freedom system[18]:

$$\omega = \sqrt{\frac{Wh + (k_1 + k_2)\frac{B^2}{4}}{J}} \quad (7)$$

$$k_1 = k_{T_0}[1 - (T_1 - 20) \times 0.2\%] \quad (8)$$

$$k_2 = k_{T_0}[1 - (T_2 - 20) \times 0.2\%] \quad (9)$$

Where: ω ——Natural frequency of structure;
  W ——Weight of structure;
  h ——The distance from the center of mass to the bottom of the beam;
  k_1 ——Stiffness of left bearing;
  k_2 ——Stiffness of right bearing;
  B ——The width of the beam;
  J ——The moment of inertia of a beam around its axis;
  k_{T_0} ——Stiffness of bearing at 20℃;
  T_1 ——Temperature of left bearing;
  T_2 ——Temperature of right bearing.

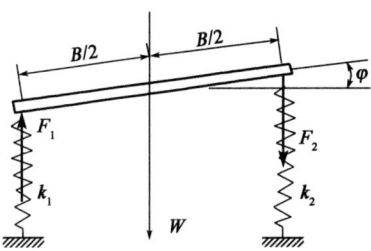

Fig. 1 Torsional Frequency Calculation Model of Simply Supported Girder

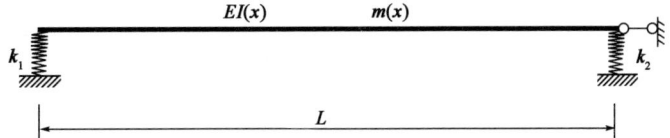

Fig. 2 Bending frequency calculation model of simply supported girder

1.3.2 Bending Frequency

The centralized mass method was adopted to simplify the calculation. The relationship between the first-set natural frequency and the temperature of the structure is approximately obtained as follows:

$$\omega = \sqrt{\frac{k_1 + k_2}{ml^3} \cdot \frac{1}{Il^3 + \frac{5(k_1 + k_2)}{486EI}}} \tag{10}$$

Where: ω ——Natural frequency of structure;
  k_1 ——Stiffness of left bearing;
  k_2 ——Stiffness of right bearing;
  m ——Beam's mass per meter;
  l ——The span of the beam;
  E ——Elasticity modulus of materials;
  I ——Moment of rotational inertia.

1.3.3 Finite Element Model

A finite element model of a simply supported girder was designed considering the stiffness of the bearing, which was presented as a numerical example. By using ANSYS software to calculate the dynamic characteristics in different boundary conditions, there were some quantitative analysis of the influence of temperature on the natural frequency of bridge structures by changing the boundary conditions. The working conditions are as follows (Tab. 1, Fig. 3):

Simply Supported Girder Working Condition Tab. 1

Temperature change(℃)	Bearing1	Bearing2	Bearing3	Bearing4	Remark
1	-20	-20	-20	-20	Uniform temperature change
2	-15	-15	-15	-15	
3	-10	-10	-10	-10	
4	-5	-5	-5	-5	
5	5	5	5	5	

Temperature change(℃)	Bearing1	Bearing2	Bearing3	Bearing4	Remark
6	10	10	10	10	Uniform temperature change
7	15	15	15	15	
8	20	20	20	20	
9	−20	0	−20	0	Transverse temperature difference
10	20	0	20	0	
11	−20	−20	0	0	Longitudinal temperature difference
12	20	20	0	0	
13	0	0	−20	−20	
14	0	0	20	20	

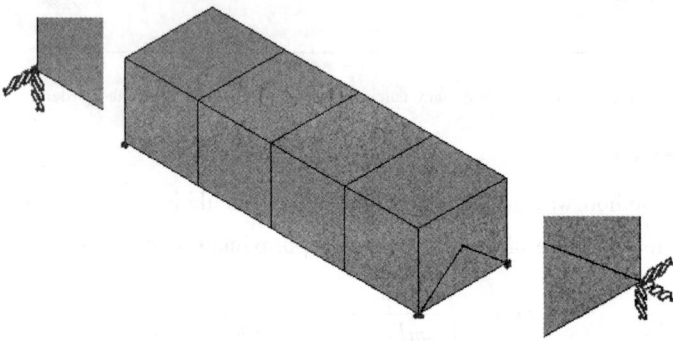

Fig. 3 Model of Simply Supported Beam with Temperature-induced Change in Support Stiffness

(1) Uniform Temperature Change

When the temperature of each bearing changed at the same time, the results can be obtained as shown in the Fig. 4. When the temperature goes up, the frequency goes down, and vice versa. The effects of temperature rise and temperature fall were largely symmetrical. The maximum frequency change caused by uniform change of bearing temperature was about 1.6%, while vertical bending and torsion were the most affected.

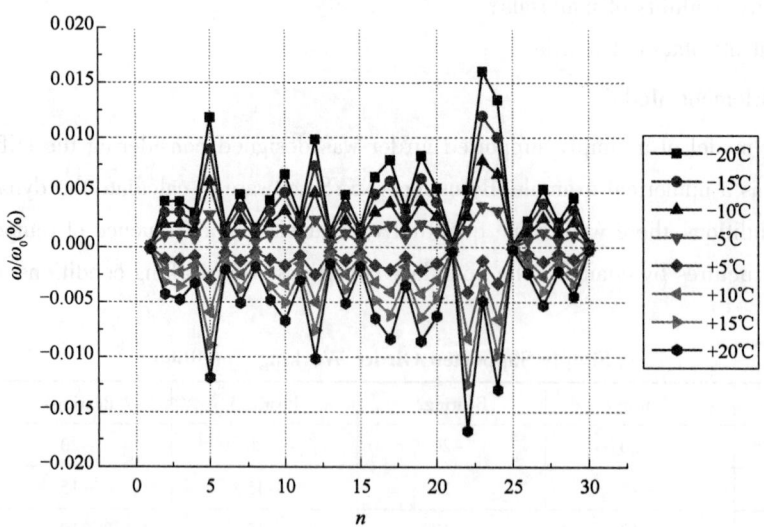

Fig. 4 Frequency Change of Simply Supported Girder in Different Temperature

(2) Transverse Temperature Difference

When the bearing temperature at both sides of the girder was different, the results can be obtained as shown in the Fig. 5. The effects of temperature rise and temperature fall were largely symmetrical. The maximum frequency change caused by uniform change of bearing temperature was about 0.8%, while torsion was the most affected.

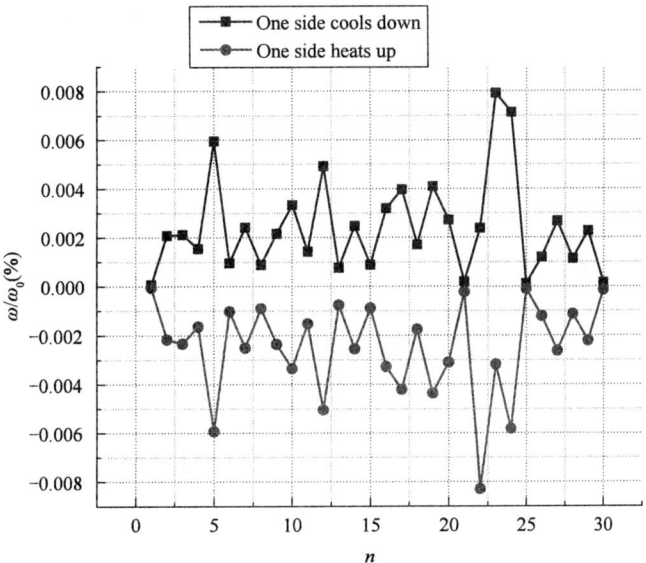

Fig. 5 Influence of Transverse Temperature Difference on the Frequency of Simply Supported Girder

(3) Longitudinal Temperature Difference

When the bearing temperature at both ends of the girder was different, the results can be obtained as shown in the Fig. 6 The effects of temperature rise and temperature fall were largely symmetrical. The maximum frequency change caused by uniform change of bearing temperature was about 1.2%, while vertical bending was the most affected. In addition, for individual sets, the frequency variation caused by articulated supports was greater.

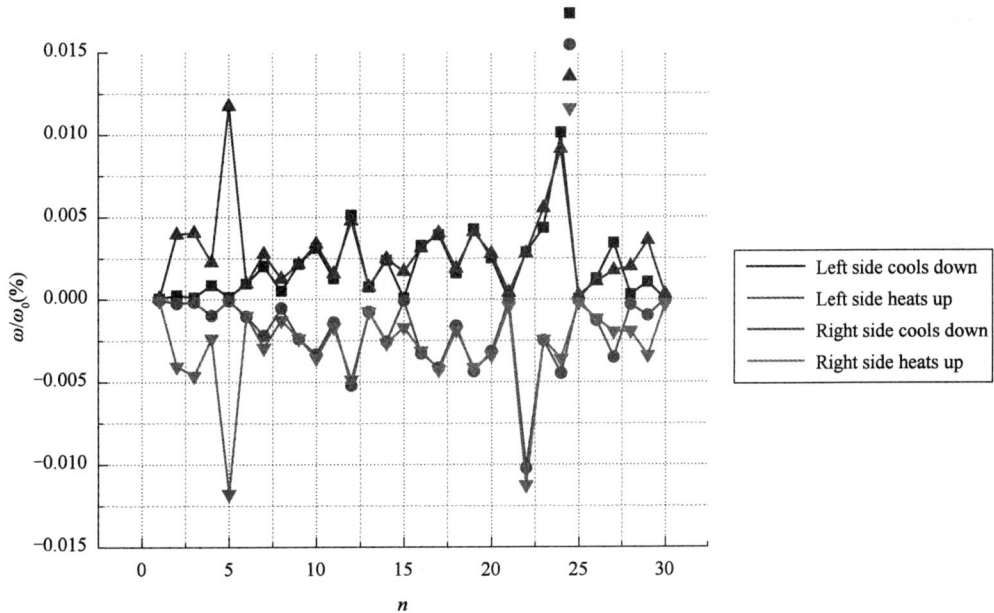

Fig. 6 Influence of Longitudinal Temperature Difference on the Frequency of Simply Supported Girder

2 Finite Element Analysis Modelling of a Project

2.1 Basic Information of the Model

This bridge is a suspension bridge with 1366 meters main span, which is composed of the main cable of steel strand, steel hanger, concrete bridge tower and steel truss girder. This research adopted ANSYS structural analysis software for modeling. According to the structural characteristics of the bridge, a certain simplification was made on the premise that its quality and stiffness were consistent with the actual structure(Fig. 7).

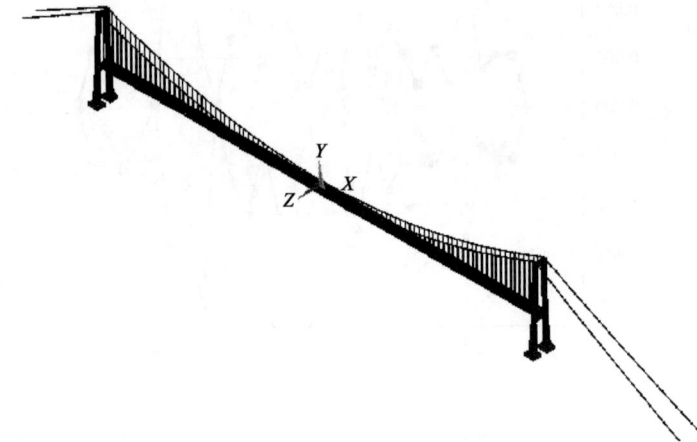

Fig. 7 Finite Element Model of this Bridge

In this paper, Beam4 was used to simulate the steel truss girder, longitudinal girder, bridge tower and yoke of suspension bridge; Link10 was used to simulate the main cable and hanger; Shell63 was used to simulate the bridge panel; MASS21 was used to simulate the mass and moment of mass inertia of guardrail, bridge deck pavement, cable clamp, etc; COMBIN14 was used to simulate the bearings.

The BlockLanczos method is used for solving in the analysis of structural dynamic properties. This method is an improvement of the classical Lanczos for solving the eigenvalue problem of the system.

2.2 Representative Working Conditions

In order to explore the influence mechanism of temperature on bridge natural frequency quantitatively, the influence of material, stress and boundary condition under the action of uniform temperature change is considered. The bridge has a large number of components and the temperature distribution is complex. Therefore, the temperature difference of each component was also taken into account for calculation. Control variable method was adopted and the working conditions were as follows:

(1) Uniform temperature field: Let the temperature of a single factor increase from −20 degrees to 20 degrees, 5 degrees at an interval, holding all other factors constant.

(2) Non-uniform temperature field: Let the temperature of a single component increase from −20 degrees to 20 degrees, 5 degrees at an interval, holding all other factors constant.

2.3 Results and Discussions

2.3.1 Uniform Temperature Change

In practical engineering, we mainly focus on the first-order frequency corresponding to various vibration modes. Therefore, taking the temperature change value as the abscissa and the frequency change rate(taking the frequency at 20 ℃ as the standard) as the ordinate, the change of the main order frequency with temperature was drawn.

As shown in Fig. 8, the natural frequency of bridge changes linearly with the change of material. With the increase of temperature, the elastic modulus of material decreases, the linear expansion coefficient increases and the natural frequency decreases. Among them, the frequency of the order corresponding to the positive symmetric torsion is the most affected, which can reach 3.332% in the normal temperature range, and the frequency corresponding to the longitudinal drift is the least affected, generally within 0.3%. Furthermore, it is found that the coefficient of linear expansion has little effect on the natural frequency of the bridge, and the elastic modulus is the main material parameter affecting the natural frequency of the bridge.

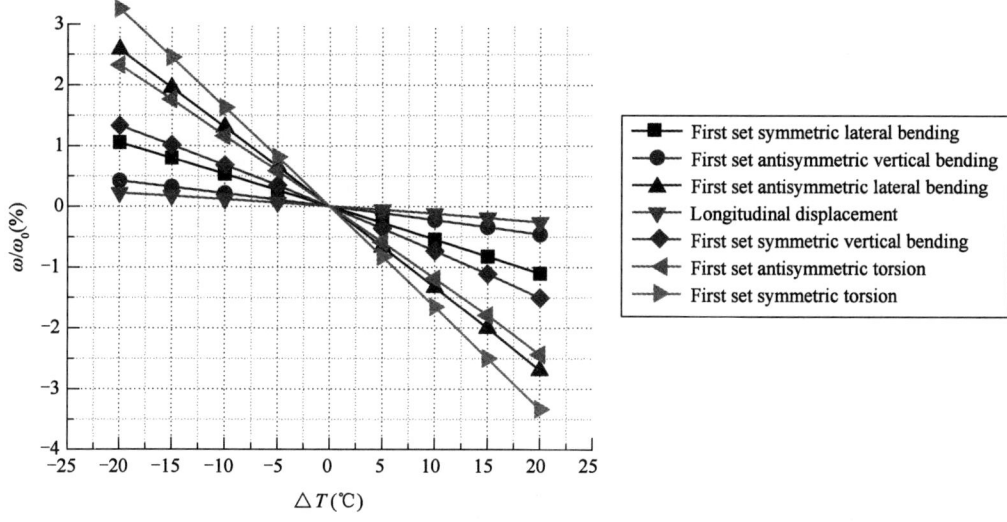

Fig. 8 Influence of Material Change

The influence of temperature stress on the natural frequency of bridge is more complex, which mainly affects the order of torsional mode, and has little influence on the order of other modes. When the temperature decreases, the torsional mode appears ahead of time, and when the temperature rises, the torsional mode appears later, which can be changed by more than 2 orders at most. In order to show the influence law of temperature stress more clearly, the frequency corresponding to other main modes except torsion mode was given in the figure. As shown in Fig. 9, the basic trend is that the temperature increases and the frequency increases, but there are fluctuations in some orders.

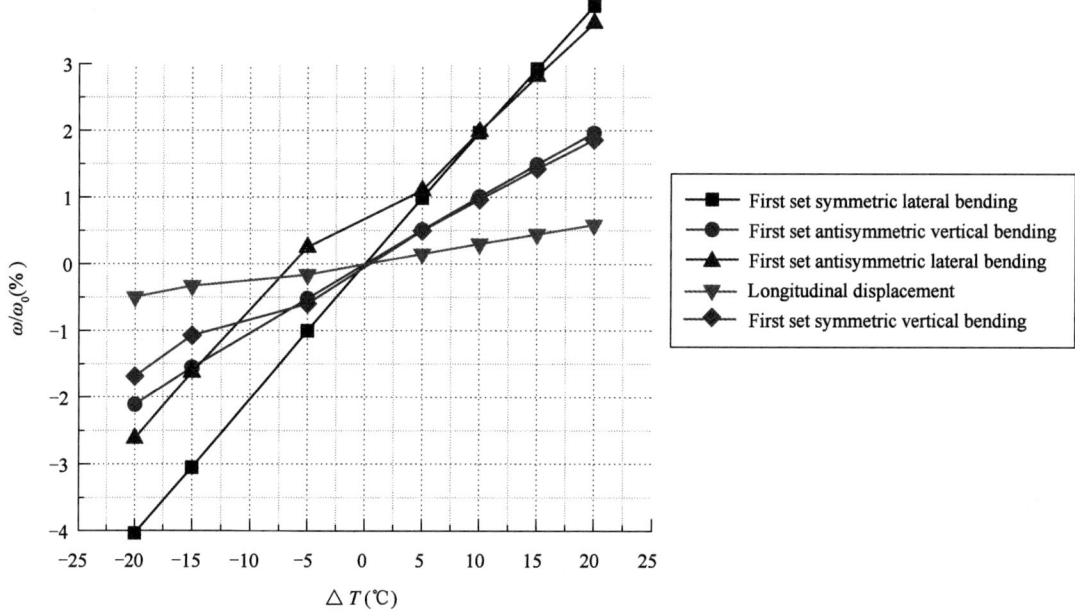

Fig. 9 Influence of Temperature Stress

As shown in Fig. 10, the change of support stiffness has little effect on the natural frequency of suspension bridge, which can be explained as: the main girder of suspension bridge mainly relies on hanger for direct support, and the role of support is very small.

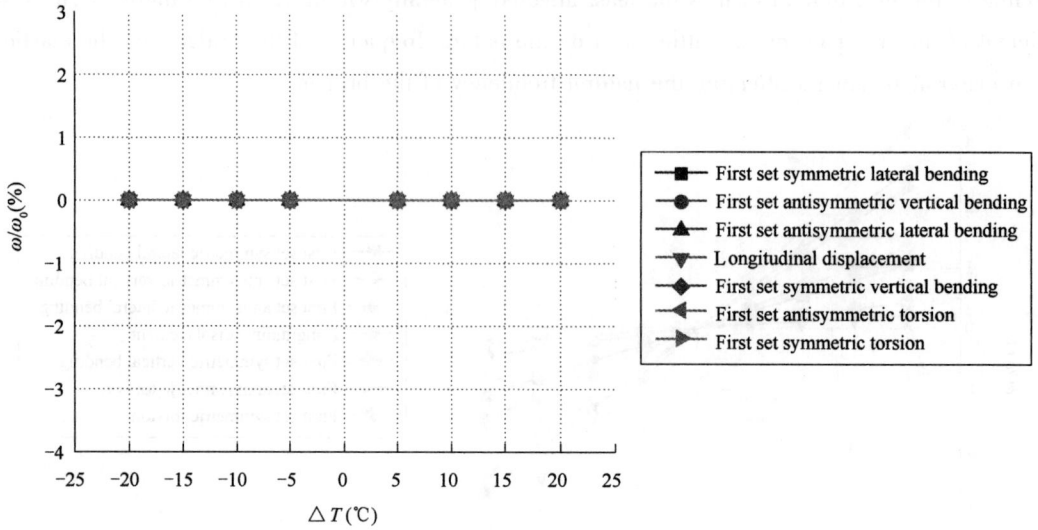

Fig. 10 Influence of Boundary Conditions

As shown in Fig. 11, when all kinds of factors act at the same time, the natural frequency of the bridge fluctuates with the change of temperature. It can be inferred that the fluctuation is mainly caused by temperature stress. It should be noted that the sum of frequency changes caused by various factors acting alone is not the same as that caused by simultaneous action of all factors, because the temperature stress changes with the change of material and boundary conditions, and the influence is complex.

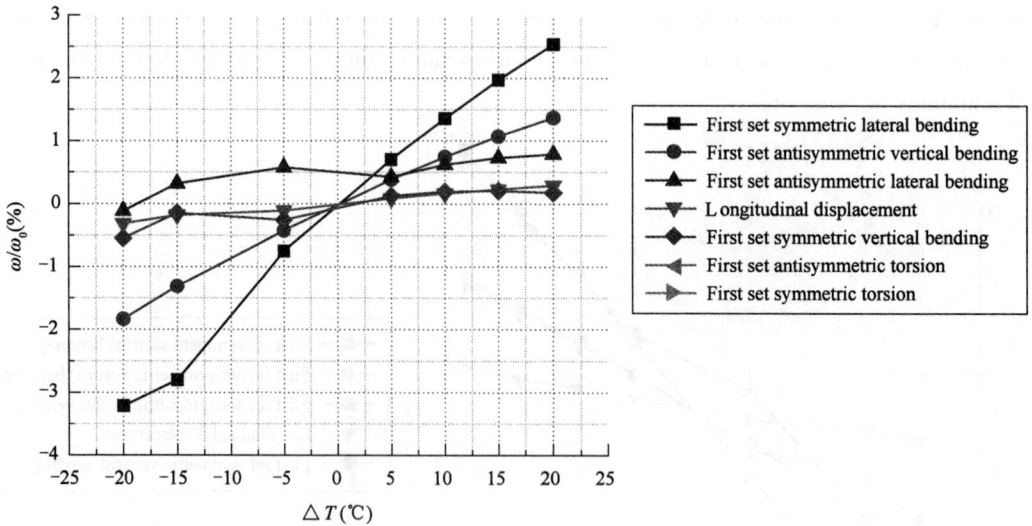

Fig. 11 Comprehensive Effect of Multiple Factors Caused by Temperature

As shown in Fig. 12, for the fundamental frequency, the frequency change caused by stress is the largest, which can reach 2% in the normal temperature range. And the influence of material is the second, generally within 0.5%. In addition, the boundary conditions have almost no effect. Due to the opposite influence of material and stress, the influence range of comprehensive action of various factors is between the material and temperature stress.

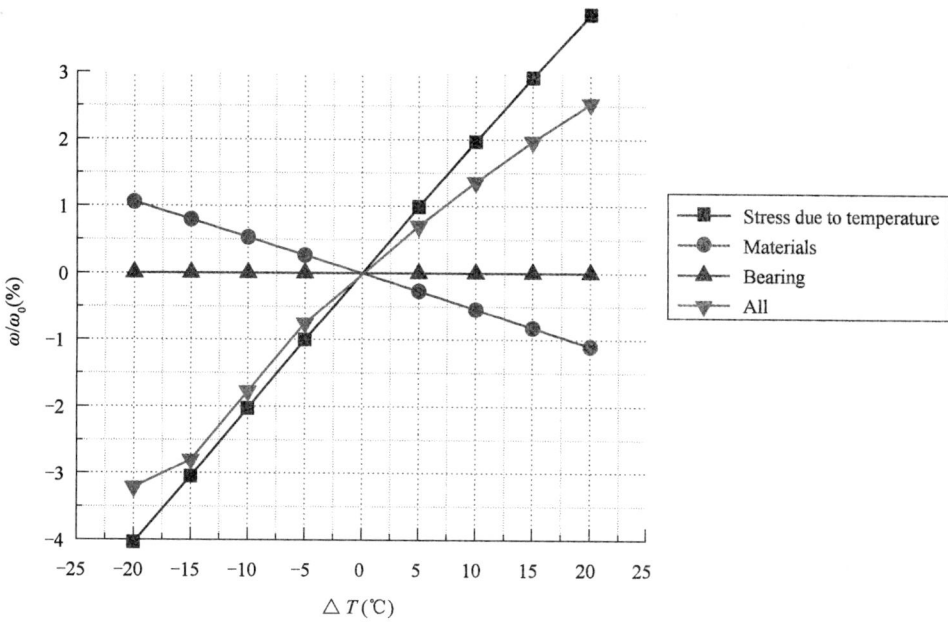

Fig. 12 Influence Comparison of Different Factors on Fundamental Frequency

Taking the frequency corresponding to the main mode as group 1 and temperature change as group 2, the significance level is $a < 0.05$, that is, there is a significant positive correlation between temperature and frequency, which is consistent with the results in Tab. 2.

Typical Correlations Tab. 2

Relevance		Characteristic value	Wilke statistics	F	Numerator degrees of freedom	Denominator degrees of freedom	Significance
1	1.000	65931.153	0.000	26372.461	5.000	2.000	0.000

The H_0 for Wilks test means that the correlation between the current row and the subsequent row is zero.

2.3.2 Components Temperature Difference

In practical engineering, due to the influence of many factors, such as sunshine, wind and so on, the non-uniform temperature field inside the bridge is often formed. For the sake of convenience, this study discusses the extreme cases of single component temperature change, and the actual frequency distribution is within the envelope range of these extreme cases.

As shown in Fig. 13, the natural frequency of the bridge changes linearly with the temperature of the main cable. When the temperature increases, the natural frequency decreases. Among them, the frequency of the order corresponding to the positive symmetric torsion is the most affected, reaching 2.379% in the normal temperature range. Followed by the positive symmetric vertical bending, reaching 1.413% in the normal temperature range. And the frequency corresponding to other vibration modes is less affected, within 0.55%.

As shown in Fig. 14, the influence of girder temperature change on the natural vibration frequency of the bridge is relatively complex. It can be inferred that the temperature change of the girder is the main factor causing the nonlinear change of the natural frequency of the whole bridge with temperature. The temperature change of the girder will change the order of the torsional vibration mode, the temperature of the girder will decrease, and the torsional mode will appear in advance, otherwise it will be delayed. Generally speaking, the girder temperature increases, the frequency increases, but there are also some fluctuations.

As shown in Fig. 15, the temperature change of suspender has little influence on the natural frequency of bridge, and the frequency increases when temperature decreases, with strong linear correlation. And the variation range is within 0.3%. Among them, the frequency of the first-order antisymmetric torsion is most affected, and the others are less than 0.05.

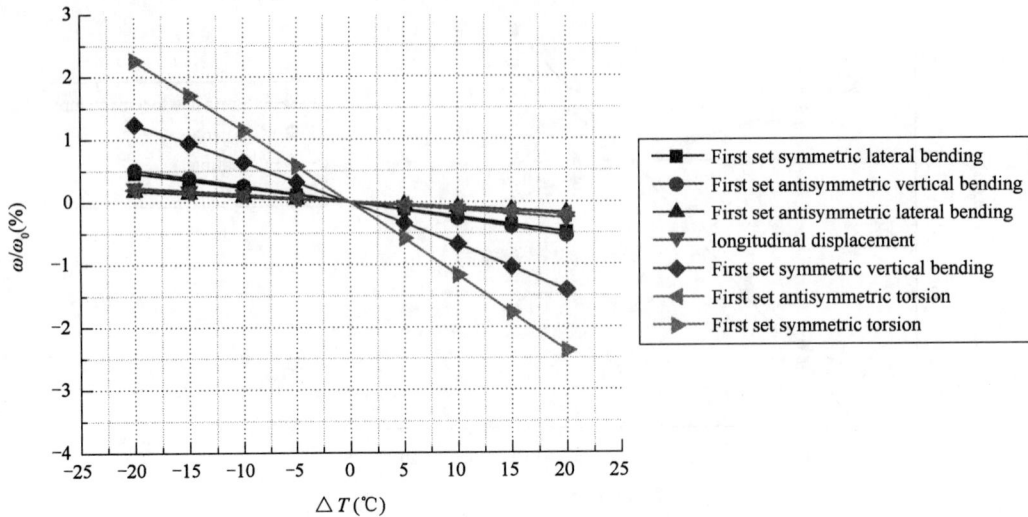

Fig. 13 Influence of Main Cable Temperature Change

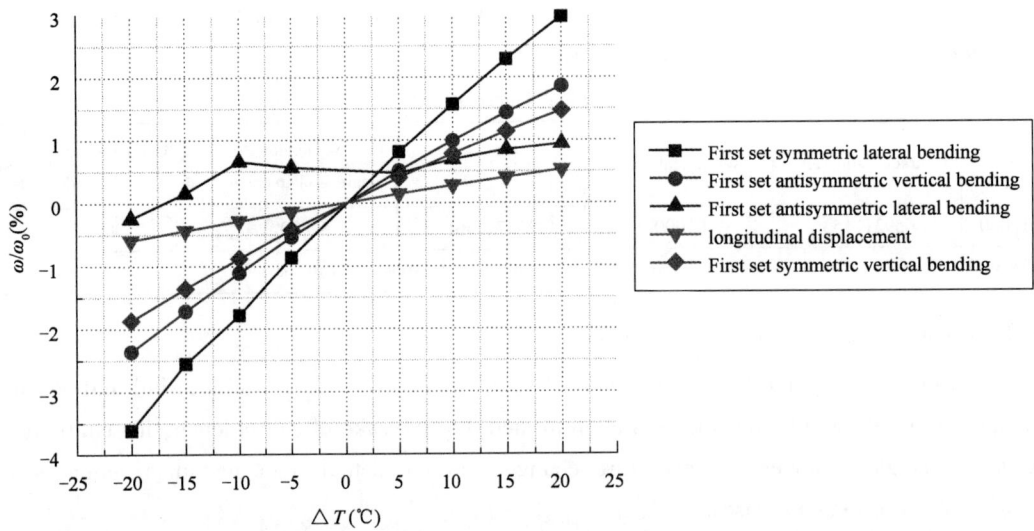

Fig. 14 Influence of Main Girder Temperature Change

As shown in Fig. 16, the influence of temperature change of bridge tower on natural vibration frequency of bridge is also very small, which is less than 0.06%. It is worth noting that the influence law of bridge tower on different order frequencies is different, some frequencies are positively correlated with temperature change, and others are negatively correlated. In addition, the influence of positive and negative temperature changes is also asymmetric. The linear correlation between the temperature change of bridge tower and the change of bridge natural frequency is weak. It can be inferred that the temperature change of bridge tower also contributes to the nonlinear change of natural frequency with temperature.

As shown in Fig. 17, for the fundamental frequency, the frequency change caused by the temperature change of the girder is the largest, which can reach 3.6% in the normal temperature range, while the influence of the main cable temperature change is less than 0.5%. Other components have almost no effect. Due to the opposite effect of the main girder and the main cable, the influence amplitude of the simultaneous temperature change of all components is between the temperature of the girder and the main cable, and it is basically linear and positive correlation.

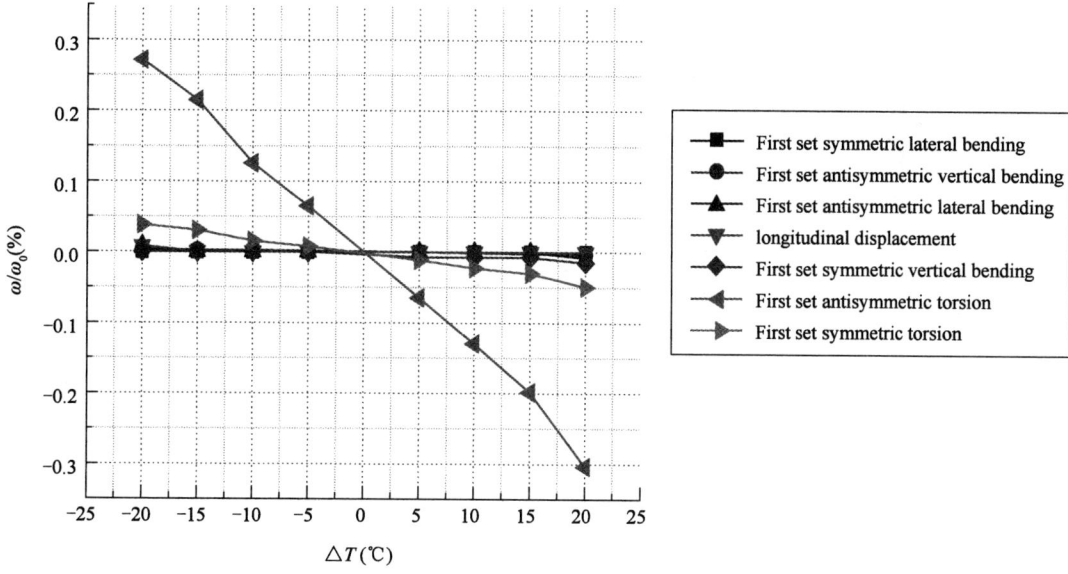

Fig. 15 Influence of Hanger Temperature Change

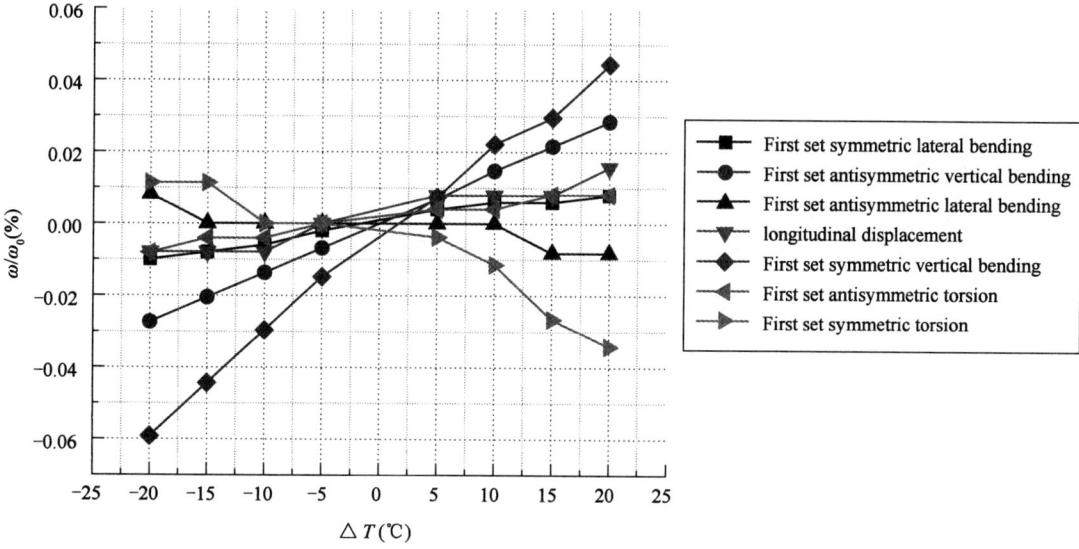

Fig. 16 Influence of Bridge Tower Temperature Change

2.3.3 Influence of Temperature Variation in Normal Temperature Range

Tab. 3 Influence range of temperature on main frequency shows the frequency variation amplitude of each major set. It can be seen that the influence of temperature on the lateral bending mode is the greatest, followed by the vertical bending and the longitudinal floating. The temperature field of the actual bridge is complex, so it is difficult to calculate directly, but the influence range is generally within the range given in this study. When a similar type of bridge needs to take the temperature influence of frequency into account, the value can be taken from this study on the basis of considering a certain safety factor.

In practical engineering, there are some uncertainties in bridge structural parameters, which will directly affect the natural frequency. However, they can be described by probability distribution[20]. On the basis of the research on the statistical characteristics of natural frequency made by other scholars, considering the influence of temperature will make the results more realistic.

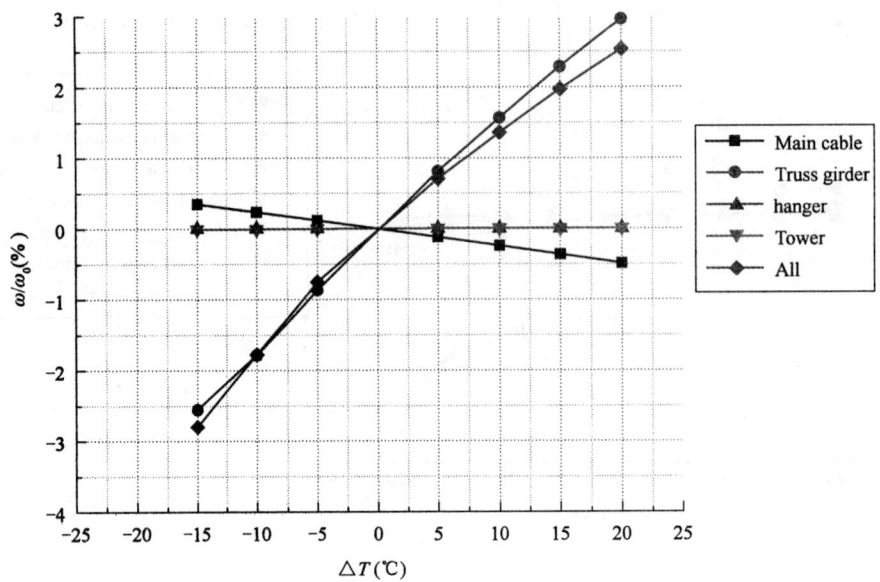

Fig. 17 Influence Comparison of Different Component Temperature Changes

Influence Range of Temperature on Main Frequency(%)   Tab. 3

	First set symmetric lateral bending	First set antisymmetric vertical bending	First set antisymmetric lateral bending	longitudinal displacement	First set symmetric vertical bending
Min	−4.038955607	−2.364195422	−2.691613327	−0.59246386	−1.871994081
Max	3.871661588	1.962191094	3.610700804	0.584564342	1.857195708

3 Conclusions

(1) In order to explore the mechanism of temperature influence on the structural frequency of the bridge, both theoretical derivation and numerical simulation were used in this study. The results show that the effect of temperature stresses on suspension bridges is slightly greater than that of materials. In addition, the modal frequencies of bridges are positively correlated with temperature stresses and negatively correlated with material changes.

(2) The results show that the elastic modulus of the material and the temperature secondary stress have approximately linear effects on the structure frequency. For suspension bridge, the influence of support is very small, even can be ignored. The temperature stress will change the order of torsional modes, but the material will not.

(3) In this study, the influence of temperature on three factors including boundary conditions was considered, and the influence range of main frequency under temperature was given, which provides reference for bridge health monitoring.

References

[1] 刘永健,刘江,张宁.桥梁结构日照温度作用研究综[J].土木工程学报,2019,52(05):59-78.
[2] Yabin Liang, Dongsheng Li, Gangbing Song, et al. Frequency Co-integration-based damage detection for

bridges under the influence of environmental temperature variation, Measurement[J]. 2018,125:163-175.

[3] 李小年,陈艾荣,马如进. 温度对桥梁模态参数的影响[J]. 华南理工大学学报(自然科学版),2012, 40(04):138-143.

[4] C. Christian, J. I. Rastandi, Y. Lase. Temperature Changes Effects to Dynamics Performances of a Pinned-supported Steel-arch-bridge, IOP Conference Series-Materials Science and Engineering[C]. 2018, 473:27.

[5] Qingling Meng, Jinsong Zhu. Fine Temperature Effect Analysis-Based Time-Varying Dynamic Properties Evaluation of Long-Span Suspension Bridges in Natural Environments, Journal of Bridge Engineering[J]. 2018,23(10).

[6] Cheynet, Etienne. Temperature Effects on the Modal Properties of a Suspension Bridge, Dynamics of Civil Structures[J]. 2017:87-93.

[7] Jinwoo Jang, Andrew W. Smyth. Data-driven models for temperature distribution effects on natural frequencies and thermal prestress modeling, Structural Control and Health Monitoring[J]. 2020,27(2).

[8] Zolghadri, Halling, Barr. Effects of Temperature Variations on Structural Vibration Properties, Geotechnical and Structural Engineering Congress2016[C]. 2016:1032-43.

[9] Haoxiang He, Xiaofu Zhang, Xiaobing Wang. Frequency modification of continuous beam bridges based on co-integration theory under effects of temperature and humidity, Journal of Vibration and Shock[J]. 2018, 37(07):23-31+61.

[10] Furtmueller, Adam, Veit-Egerer. Temperature and mass loading compensation for long-term bridge monitoring, Bauingenieur[J]. 2017,92:528-536.

[11] Hong Pan, MohsenAzimi, Fei Yan, Zhibin Lin. Time-Frequency-Based Data-Driven Structural Diagnosis and Damage Detection for Cable-Stayed Bridges, Journal of Bridge Engineering[J]. 2018,23(6).

[12] Guo-jin Tan, Zi-yu Liu, Ieee. Temperature Effect Analysis of Bridge Natural Frequency Based on Particle Swarm Optimized Neural Network, IEEE Annual International Conference on Cyber Technology in Automation Control and Intelligent Systems[C]. 2017,903-907.

[13] Yubo Jiao, Hanbing Liu, Yongchun Cheng, Xianqiang Wang, Yafeng Gong, Gang Song. Fuzzy Neural Network-Based Damage Assessment of Bridge under Temperature Effect, Mathematical Problems in Engineering[J]. 2014.

[14] 王新敏. ANSYS 工程结构数值分析[M]. 北京:人民交通出版社,2007.

[15] Yu, M. Fire Responses and Resistance of Concrete-filled Steel Tubular Frame Structures, International Journal of Structural Stability and Dynamics[J]. 2010,10(02):253-271.

[16] 贺栓海. 桥梁结构理论与计算方法[M]. 北京:人民交通出版社,2003.

[17] 庄学真,周福霖,徐丽,等. 大直径建筑叠层橡胶隔震装置温度相关性及老化性能研究[J]. 西安建筑科技大学学报(自然科学版),2009,41(06):791-798.

[18] 宋一凡. 公路桥梁动力学[M]. 北京:人民交通出版社,2000.

[19] 邓敬良. 大跨度钢箱梁悬索桥温度所致力学响应的数值分析[D]. 广州:华南理工大学,2019.

[20] 万华平,任伟新,钟剑. 桥梁结构固有频率不确定性量化的高斯过程模型方法[J]. 中国科学:技术科学,2016,46(09):919-925.

钢筋混凝土桥梁用融雪剂的探讨

吴玉辉[1]　蒋明伟[2]

(1.辽宁省交通科学研究院有限责任公司;2.辽宁省沈阳市第十中学)

摘　要　本文从钢筋混凝土桥融雪化需要和腐蚀机理出发,重点研究了钢筋混凝土桥梁用融雪剂技术要点,提出科学选用融雪剂、减轻融雪剂对钢筋混凝土桥梁的腐蚀破坏影响的建议。

关键词　融雪剂　钢筋　混凝土　桥梁　腐蚀

0　引　言

除雪防滑是北方及寒冷地区冬季公路桥梁养护的重点。为了消除冬季桥面上的冰雪,使用融雪剂是保障桥梁安全通行必不可少的措施。虽然氯盐类融雪剂资源丰富、价格便宜、效果好,大量使用,但被公认是对钢筋混凝土桥梁腐蚀破坏严重、影响公路养桥梁使用安全和使用寿命的材料,会造成巨大经济损失[1-2]。

融雪剂对混凝土保护层的破坏是循环渐近、长久多次且不断深入的。在融雪化冰过程中,含融雪剂的水溶液,逐渐渗透到混凝土内部,直至钢筋与混凝土接触的界面。这个过程不是一次完成的,而经历多次冻融,循环往复,同时存在水结冰融化及盐结晶再溶解的物理过程。正是结冰和盐结晶产生的胀力,不断加剧了混凝土的物理破坏[3]。当融雪剂的水溶液抵达钢筋表面即开始对钢筋产生电化学腐蚀作用,消耗钢筋成分,降低混凝土与钢筋的黏结力和握裹力,减小钢筋的有效半径,降低钢筋的抗拉强度,严重影响钢筋混凝土整体强度、耐久性和结构安全[4-5]。本文重点从选用融雪剂的角度讨论减轻融雪剂对钢筋混凝土桥梁的腐蚀破坏影响,提出钢筋混凝土桥梁用融雪剂使用建议,为冬季钢筋混凝土桥梁养护提供技术参考。

1　融雪剂融雪化冰性能研究

物理化学理论表明相对于比纯溶剂凝固点,稀溶液凝固点降低是重要的依数性之一。对于水来说,凝固点即冰点。那么以水为溶剂的融雪剂水溶液的冰点(凝固点)是低于纯水的冰点的,融雪剂融雪化冰就是利用该原理[6]。

1.1　融雪剂融雪化冰能力

冰点是评价融雪剂融雪化冰能力的重要指标。本研究参照我国标准《融雪剂》(GB/T 23851—2017)[7]中融雪剂冰点测试方法,测试一定浓度的融雪剂溶液在冷却介质中缓慢冷却过程中,冷却溶液开始结晶的温度;或在过冷的情况下,冷却溶液最初形成结晶后迅速回升所达到的最高温度,即该溶液的冰点。本研究选用了工业盐、WD、LB-1、LB-2四种代表性融雪剂作为研究对象。其中,工业盐是最普遍使用的融雪剂;WD是从市面购买的氯盐类融雪剂;LB-1自行研制的含缓蚀剂的复合氯盐类融雪剂、LB-2为自行研制的非氯盐有机融雪剂。项目对以上融雪剂在不同浓度下进行了冰点测试,本研究中浓度(C)以融雪剂的质量占水质量(Q)的百分比计,测试数据汇总如表1所示。

基金项目:辽宁省自然科学基金项目(2019-ZD-0863)。

融雪剂冰点测试结果(单位:℃) 表1

融雪剂名称	不同质量分数下的冰点			
	10%	20%	30%	40%
工业盐	-3.9	-12.0	-21.6	-21.8
WD	-4.1	-10.1	-16.4	-24.8
LB-1	-4.2	-11.8	-23.5	-36.2
LB-2	-4.9	-11.6	-20.2	-33.0

结论如下:

(1)同一种融雪剂水浓度越高,用量越大,相应的冰点越低。气温越低,融雪剂施用量越多,才能发挥融雪剂融雪化冰的功能;

(2)同一浓度的不同融雪剂的冰点是有差异的,但浓度较低时(如浓度低于20%),不同融雪剂的冰点差距不大0~2℃,仅从融雪化冰能力方面考虑在不是很低的气温下,选用其中任一融雪剂均可;但是当融雪剂浓度较高(30%~40%)时,溶液的冰点差异增大,冰点越低,融雪化冰能力越强。以上四种融雪剂,30%浓度时,冰点从低到高的排序(即融雪化冰能力从优到劣的排序):LB-1 < 工业盐 < LB-2 < WD;40%时,冰点从低到高的排序:LB-1 < LB-2 < WD < 工业盐。

(3)一定温度下,融雪剂在水中的溶解度是定值。溶解度是一定温度下,100g水中所能溶解的溶质的最大克数。工业盐(主要成分氯化钠)溶解度随温度升高变化十分微小,20℃溶解度为36g,0℃溶解度35.7g。常温下配制36%的工业盐溶液,测试其冰点在-22℃左右,这是工业盐作为融雪剂使用的最低温度。因此,低于该温度下,无论使用再多的工业盐,也不能实现融雪化冰。如表1中工业盐40%的溶液是无法配制成功的,最多能配制浓度约36%,对对应的冰点是36%对应的冰点,也是工业盐融雪化冰的极限温度。在更低的温度下,工业盐是无效的。

1.2 融雪剂施用量测算

某一浓度溶液的冰点(T)是该溶液由液态变为固态,即结冰的温度,当温度低于溶液的冰点时,溶液则结冰。因此,融雪剂的施用量(q)是由气温和待融化的冰雪数量决定的。一定的温度下,融化一定数量的冰雪所需用的某种融雪剂的数量是可以计量的。这是由该温度下对应的融雪剂溶液的浓度决定的。已知融雪剂的浓度$C(\%)$和现场单位面积冰雪的数量Q(实质上是溶剂的数量),它们之间的关系如下式所示:$C = q/Q$。由此可以换算出单位面积所需要融雪剂的数量$q = C \times Q$。

实践中,选定融雪剂后,配制浓度由低到高的融雪剂溶液,然后分别测试不同浓度融雪剂溶液的冰点,接下来绘制融雪剂冰点—浓度工作曲线,如图1是融雪剂WD的冰点-浓度工作曲线。假设除雪现场气温-20℃,从工作曲线上找出-20℃对应的融雪剂浓度为$C = 34\%$,再根据除雪现场测量或估算单位面积,按式$q = C \times Q$可以计算出需要融雪的质量q,即得到现场单位面积上融雪剂的施用量。除雪实践中,现场气温有一个变化范围,那么在温度变化范围的高温、低温则分别对应测算出融雪剂撒布的最小量q_{min}和最大量q_{max},实操过程中融雪剂的使用量宜控制在$q_{min} \sim q_{max}$之间。

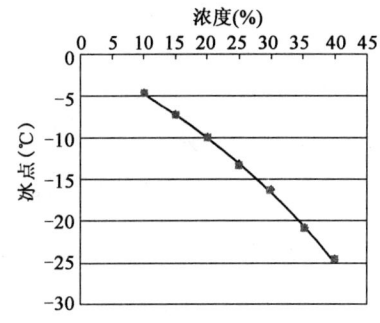

图1 融雪剂WD冰点—浓度工作曲线

2 融雪剂对混凝土桥梁的腐蚀影响研究

融雪剂对钢筋混凝土桥梁的腐蚀主要包括两个方面,一方面是对水泥混凝土的腐蚀,另一方面是对钢筋的腐蚀。腐蚀与混凝土、钢筋材料的性能、环境条件、防护措施等多种因素有关。但融雪剂对钢筋混凝土桥梁的腐蚀有其特殊性,除去其他因素的影响,本研究从使用融雪剂的桥梁处于的融雪剂溶液冻融环境下的腐蚀进行试验研究。

2.1 融雪剂对水泥混凝土的腐蚀机理

在冰冻地区,混凝土受冻融循环作用及融雪剂腐蚀作用下,早期使混凝土表皮脱落,进而造成混凝土的抗压强度、抗拉强度及冻弹模量降低,严重影响水泥混凝土的抗冻性和抗盐冻剥蚀性能,这也是融雪剂的应用对混凝土耐久性影响最大因素之一[8]。融雪剂将桥面上的冰雪融化过程中形成含有融雪剂的水溶液,经由混凝土表面及内部的孔隙和裂缝不断渗透到混凝土中。由于冻融及干湿交替,同时发生水结冰和盐结晶,使体积增大,对围限它孔隙和裂隙产生膨胀压力,且不断扩大加深,造成加剧混凝土破坏。作为选择融雪剂的参考指标之一应该简便快捷,融雪剂对混凝土的腐蚀首先表现为混凝土表面剥落。因此以混凝土在融雪剂溶液作用下进行冻融循环试验后,测试混凝土剥落量可以用来快速评价融雪剂对混凝土的腐蚀作用。

2.2 融雪剂对水泥混凝土的腐蚀的试验研究

2.2.1 原材料

本研究采用本试验采用铁新水泥厂的 P.O42.5 普通硅酸盐水泥,营顺石场 16.5~31.5mm、5~20mm 碎石,房木砂场河砂(中砂),大连融合硅粉拌制成型的水泥混凝土试件。所有材料均能满足《公路水泥混凝土路面施工技术细则》(JTG F30—2014)的要求。混凝土抗盐冻性试验中采用的配合比见表2。

水泥混凝土配合比　　表2

配合比 (kg/m^3)					含气量 (%)	坍落度 (mm)	抗压强度 (MPa)	抗折强度 (MPa)
水泥	水	砂	石	硅粉			28d	
458	182	660	1135	25	2.6	40	48.7	5.8

2.2.2 冻融试验设计

本研究推荐采用水泥混凝土试件单面浸在融雪剂溶液中进行冻融试验,模拟融雪剂对混凝土的腐蚀破坏实际情况,以中低浓度的盐溶液对混凝土剥蚀破坏影响最大,选择3%融雪剂溶液为冻融介质,测试水泥混凝土表面剥落量来比较不同融雪剂对水泥混凝土腐蚀程度。本研究按现行《公路工程水泥及水泥混凝土试验规程》(JTG E30—2005)将 $15×15×15cm^3$ 的立方体试件水泥混凝土试件单面浸在5mm深试液中(图2),在 -18℃~5℃经30次冻融循环试验后,测试混凝土试件表皮剥落量,分析评价不同融雪剂对水泥混凝土的影响。

图2　水泥混凝土冻融试验

2.2.3 融雪剂对混凝土剥蚀影响测试结果

不同融雪剂环境条件下,水泥混凝土表面剥落量测试结果如表3所示。

融雪剂种类对混凝土剥落量的影响　　表3

浸湿状态	剥落质量(g)	单位面积剥落量(g/m^2)
未浸湿	0	0
蒸馏水	0.2357	0.01
3%工业盐	157.2	6.99
3%LB-1	36.9	1.61
3%WD	71.9	3.19
3%LB-2	98.2	4.36

2.2.4 融雪剂对水泥混凝土抗冻融剥蚀性结论

(1) 相比于浸湿状态,蒸馏水中也存在冻融破坏,表明仅有水存在也会发生冻融破坏。

(2) 混凝土单位面积剥落量由大到小排序:工业盐 > LB-2 > WD > LB-1 > 蒸馏水 > 未浸湿,所有融雪剂均具有腐蚀破坏作用,不同融雪剂对水泥混凝土冻剥蚀破坏程度不同,工业盐对混凝土剥蚀破坏最严重。

(3) 蒸馏水和融雪剂中均也存在冻融破坏,但相对于单纯水的冻融破坏比融雪剂要轻,表明融雪剂加剧了混凝土的破坏。

(4) 减轻融雪剂对混凝土的冻融破坏程度也是选用融雪剂要考虑的重要依据之一。

3 融雪剂对钢筋腐蚀影响研究

3.1 水泥混凝土中钢筋腐蚀机理

水泥混凝土内部是碱性环境,钢筋锈蚀实质是钢筋中的主要成分铁(Fe),铁中有碳等杂质。铁生锈的本质也就是铁与铁中的少许碳形成了一个个微小的原电池,氧气、水、电解质溶液缺一不可。Fe、氧气、水参与了电化学反应,含融雪剂的电解质溶液中氯离子破坏钝化膜、形成原电池、去极化和导电作用是其腐蚀钢筋的机理。融雪剂的电解质溶液参与原电池将化学能转为电能的闭合回路的一部分,且具有转移输送阴阳离子产生电流的作用,提供电化学反应的介质环境,加速了电子和离子的转移,加速腐蚀速度和程度。发生的电化学吸氧腐蚀过程如下[13]:

负极:$Fe - 2e^- = Fe^{2+}$

正极:$O_2 + 4e^- + 2H_2O = 4OH^-$

总式:$2Fe^{2+} + O_2 + 2H_2O = 2Fe(OH)_2$

$Fe(OH)_2$ 化学性质不稳定,极易被 O_2 氧化,发生反应:

$4Fe(OH)_2 + O_2 + 2H_2O = 4Fe(OH)_3$

最后 $Fe(OH)_3$ 分解,生成铁锈(Fe_2O_3):

$2Fe(OH)_3 = Fe_2O_3 + 3H_2O$

3.2 融雪剂对钢筋腐蚀影响研究

3.2.1 融雪剂对碳钢腐蚀试验研究

本研究参照我国标准《融雪剂》(GB/T 23851—2017)中规定的旋转挂片法《水处理剂缓蚀性能的测定 旋转挂片法》(GB/T 18175—2000)开展融雪剂对金属腐蚀的影响研究测试,如图 3 所示。符合 GB/T 699 要求的 20 号碳钢试片,温度控制在 40℃,在浓度 3% 融雪剂溶液中浸泡 7d 后,称量碳钢片质量损失,并计算出不同融雪剂的腐蚀速度、腐蚀深度和相对氯化钠腐蚀的比率,如表 4 所示。

图 3 旋转挂片法金属腐蚀测试

融雪剂对碳钢的腐蚀速率和相对工业盐的缓蚀率 表 4

融雪剂	腐蚀速度 $V(g/m^2 \cdot h)$	年腐蚀深度 $K_e(mm/a)$	相对工业盐的比率(%)
蒸馏水	0.2042	0.2608	45.17
工业盐	0.4521	0.5774	100
WD	0.5716	0.730	126.43
LB-1	0.0041	0.0053	0.91
LB-2	0.0158	0.0185	3.20

3.2.2 融雪剂对碳钢腐蚀试验研究结论

从以上试验结果可以得出如下结论：

(1) 金属在水会发生金属锈蚀，但比工业盐和市面所售的 WD 对金属的腐蚀程度低许多，普通氯盐融雪剂会加剧金属锈蚀。

(2) 不同融雪剂对碳钢腐蚀程度明显不同，按腐蚀严重程度从高到低的次序排序：WD > 工业盐 > 蒸馏水 > LB-2 > LB-1。普通氯盐类融雪剂能加剧对金属腐蚀。

(3) 选用钢筋混凝土桥梁用融雪剂时，应当考虑融雪剂对钢筋的加剧腐蚀作用，两种途径可以大幅减缓普通氯盐类融雪剂对金属的腐蚀，一是在氯盐类融雪剂中掺配有效的缓蚀剂，二是选用非氯盐类融雪剂。

4 结 语

除了提高钢筋混凝土桥梁自身的防护能力外，如提高混凝土密实性、抗冻性、做好表面防护和钢筋除锈、防护层保护等措施外，从钢筋混凝土桥梁用融雪剂的选用方面考虑，应该注意以下几点：

(1) 融雪化冰能力需要满足工程所在地区气候条件。

(2) 尽量选择对钢筋和混凝土腐蚀破坏作用小的融雪剂，如有效缓蚀作用的复合氯盐类融雪剂和非氯盐类融雪剂。

(3) 融雪剂使用量应当结合气温和桥面单位面积冰雪数量，进行科学计算确定。

(4) 经济性也是融雪剂的选用时需要考虑的重要因素，非氯盐融雪剂成本高，推荐选用具有缓蚀作用的环保型复合氯盐类融雪剂。

参考文献

[1] 康曼楠.钢筋混凝土的钢筋腐蚀现状调查与原因探究[J].工程技术,2013(08):146-147.
[2] 姚艺,姚乐.含氯融雪剂(盐)对交通基础设施的影响研究进展[J].当代化工,2015(6):1359-1360.
[3] 何文.混凝土耐盐结晶膨胀腐蚀性能研究[D].长沙:湖南大学,2001.
[4] 陈梦成,杨超,谢国强.氯盐环境下钢筋混凝土梁的黏结试验研究[J].铁道学报2019,8:84-93.
[5] 朱绩超.氯离子环境下钢筋混凝土桥梁耐久性研究[D].长沙:湖南大学,2008.
[6] 邓崇海,胡寒梅,邵国泉.稀溶液依数性的相图解析与应用[J].合肥学院学报(自然科学版),2013,23(1):70-73.
[7] 全国化学标准化技术委员会无机化工分会.融雪剂:GB/T 23851—2017[S].北京:中国标准出版社,2017.
[8] 程波.寒区钢筋混凝土盐冻损伤机理及耐久性研究[J].公路交通科技,2018,3:160-162.

基于机器视觉技术和深度学习算法的桥梁荷载时空分布识别系统

易雨时　乔可鑫　张路

(长安大学公路学院)

摘　要　准确的车辆荷载信息对保证桥梁结构安全起着重要作用。然而，目前确定荷载的方法往往耗时且不够精确。因此，有必要开发一种有效的、低成本的技术来识别桥梁的车辆荷载。针对这种情况，本文提出了一种基于机器视觉技术和深度学习算法的车辆识别方法，首先建立了基于深度关联度量的车辆检测与跟踪网络，通过监控摄像机系统采集的视频对多辆车辆进行跟踪。通过对深度网络的预先训练和调整,可以获得桥梁上行驶车辆的时空信息,且处理时间短。同时,利用动态称重系统(WIMs)获取车辆荷载信息。在此基础上,提出了将这两部分信息进行信息融合的方法来生成车辆荷载信息。车辆类型、位置和运动轨迹等信息可以很方便地从监控摄像头获取,建立了一个包含4000多张车辆图像的数据集,用于训练深度神经网络,其中包含6种车辆分类,以增强网络的泛化性。为提高网络在车型识别中的精度,进行了优化分析。随机选取了某桥梁,通过两个监控摄像头和一个WIMs系统采集交通视频和车辆荷载信息,在本次测试中,交通荷载谱均能达到97.6%的检测率。检测速度、精度和可靠性均能满足实际要求。

关键词 桥梁工程 荷载识别 深度学习 机器视觉 车辆识别 动态称重系统

0 引　言

车辆荷载是公路桥梁的主要可变荷载,随着经济与交通运输业的快速发展,车辆荷载与设计时期已经有了很大差异[1]。超载等异常行为会影响桥梁的结构性能,缩短桥梁的使用寿命,甚至可能导致桥梁倒塌。因此,识别桥面上移动荷载的值和位置是至关重要的,这对在役桥梁的性能评估、剩余使用寿命预测、耐久性分析和维修等方面很有帮助。

车辆荷载的值可以通过动态称重系统(WIMs)进行测量,它通过安装一组传感器和电子仪器,测量动态轮胎力和车辆通过时间并提供轮重、轴重、总重等数据。对桥梁进行实时分析时,应测量桥梁上的横向和纵向车辆荷载分布。在许多研究中,已经使用WIMs的车辆重量和速度数据建立交通荷载的统计模型,研究桥梁的荷载效应[2-3]。

移动荷载识别作为桥梁健康监测领域的关键问题之一,近几十年来得到了广泛的研究。现有的识别方法可以分为两类:基于结构响应的间接方法[4-5]和基于称重传感器测量的直接方法[6-7]。这些方法也可以总体分为四类:解释方法I(IMI)、解释方法II(IMII)、时域方法(TDM)及频域-时域方法(FTDM)[8]。由于这些方法是基于梁的基本理论,其应用仅限于一维荷载识别信息,为了识别二维桥面上的车辆信息,开发一种有效的车辆荷载空间分布信息获取技术至关重要。

机器视觉技术提供了一种直接监测整个桥面车辆荷载的方法,作为一种识别桥梁车辆荷载信息的新方法,已被广泛采用。许多学者通过对高清摄像机获取的图像序列进行处理,对桥梁上车辆的空间分布进行了研究。动态称重系统(WIMs)和摄像头已广泛应用于交通监控。动态称重系统(WIMs)可以获取车辆荷载信息,而摄像头则提供桥梁上的交通流图像。对于车辆位置的识别,Chen等使用摄像机捕捉车辆,通过单台摄像机计算移动荷载在图像中的位置,统计分析移动荷载的横向分布[9]。Ryan和Al提出将背景-前景分割方法应用于桥梁健康监测系统,并通过动画仿真讨论了车辆位置识别的准确性[10]。虽然这两项研究很好地利用了图像信息,但荷载信息仍未合并。

神经网络可以通过训练来学习执行特定的任务,特别是卷积神经网络(CNN)由于其良好性能,在计算机视觉领域得到了广泛应用。这提供了一种直接的方式,通过桥梁上的监控摄像头拍摄的视频,智能地监控整个桥面的交通负荷。Zhang等基于计算机视觉技术,提出了一种通过基于区域的更快卷积神经网络(FASTER R-CNN)获取车辆时空信息的方法[11]。虽然这项研究已经很好地用于获取车辆的位置,但关于车辆重量的信息仍然是未知的。现在可以通过多源信息融合来识别整个桥梁跨度上的交通荷载。

在本研究中,提出一种基于深度学习算法的机器视觉技术来检测桥梁上的车辆荷载。利用已建立的车辆图像数据集对神经网络模型进行训练,并进行一系列优化分析,以提高网络对车辆分类的准确性,利用YOLO-v4和卡尔曼滤波分别实现对目标车辆的实时检测和跟踪,将车辆识别与动态称重系统进行融合生成车辆荷载与时空信息。本文的第一章主要介绍移动荷载识别系统,第二章介绍从图像坐标到桥梁坐标的转换方法,第三章介绍系统的实际工程应用,最后在第四章给出结论。

1 移动荷载识别

1.1 系统框架

桥梁上车辆荷载信息主要包括重量信息和时空信息,分别由桥梁 WIMs 系统和监控摄像头捕获,实时输出指定区域的交通荷载分布。如图 1 所示,在桥头安装 WIMs 系统,压电线圈埋在路面中,获取轴重、轴距、轴数等信息。在桥梁入口附近的摄像头视图中必须能看到 WIMs 线圈,且在桥梁纵向方向上相邻摄像头之间存在重叠监控区域,并在现场设置了信息采集和传输系统,将数据传输到远程云系统。

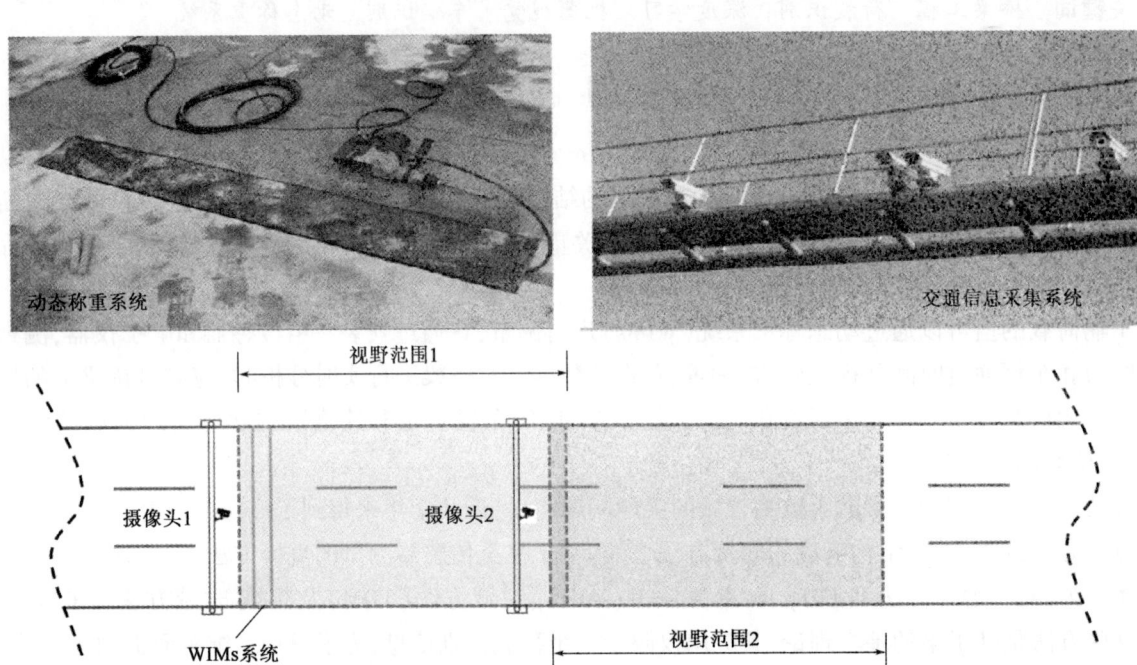

图 1 动态称重系统与交通信息采集系统

车辆时空信息的获取主要包括车辆动态检测、多车辆跟踪和图像标定。基于深度学习,建立了检测速度快、检测精度高的车辆检测网络。监控视频中的多车辆跟踪是基于深度关联度量的跟踪方法,然后将车辆的像素坐标转换为世界坐标系中的坐标。通过在车辆所处横截面上相同的行驶时间和车辆的横向位置,将车辆与监控摄像头获取的信息进行融合,从而实现车辆的重量信息和时空信息的精确匹配,同时形成了流量负荷谱。

1.2 基于 YOLO-v4 的车辆目标检测

在图像中定位车辆是计算桥面上车辆位置的先决条件,这本质上是目标检验问题,卷积神经网络已经成为解决目标检测问题的主要方法。在目标检测中,两阶段检测算法包括古典的目标识别、R-CNN、SPPNET、FAST R-CNN、R-FCN 等,一阶段检测则包括 YOLO、SSD、RETINANET 等。

YOLO-v4 是在 YOLO、YOLO-v2、YOLO-v3 基础上改进的单级深度检测卷积神经网络,与其他目标检测方法不同,YOLO-v4 直接通过回归得到预测框的坐标和各类目标预测的概率,因此检测模型的计算速度大大提高,能够更加适应实时检测的要求。

如图 2 所示,YOLO-v4 将一幅图像分为 $S \times S$ 个网格,如果某个物体的中心落在这个网格中,则这个网格就负责预测这个物体。每个网格要预测 B 个边界框,每个边界框除了要回归自身的位置外,还要预测一个置信度值(confidence),这个置信度值代表了所预测的边界框中含有物体的置信度和边框预测的准确度两重信息,置信度定义如下:

$$\text{Confidence} = p_r(\text{Object}) \times \text{IOU}_{\text{pred}}^{\text{truth}}, p_r(\text{Object}) \in [0,1] \tag{1}$$

$\text{Pr}(\text{Object})$ 代表边界框中存在对象的概率,当物体在该网格中时,$\text{Pr}(\text{Object}) = 1$,否则 $\text{Pr}(\text{Object}) = 0$。

IOU_{pred}^{truth}是预测边界框与真实包含物体边界框的交并比,体现了预测的边界框与真实包含物体的边界框的接近程度,本研究将其定义为0.6,这表明IOU重叠率大于0.6的预测区域将被区分为正标签。在进行目标检测时,每一个预测边界框会对应一个种类置信度(CSCS),定义如下:

$$CSCS = Pr(Class_i | Object) \times Pr(Object) \times IOU_{pred}^{truth} = Pr(Class_i) \times IOU_{pred}^{truth} \tag{2}$$

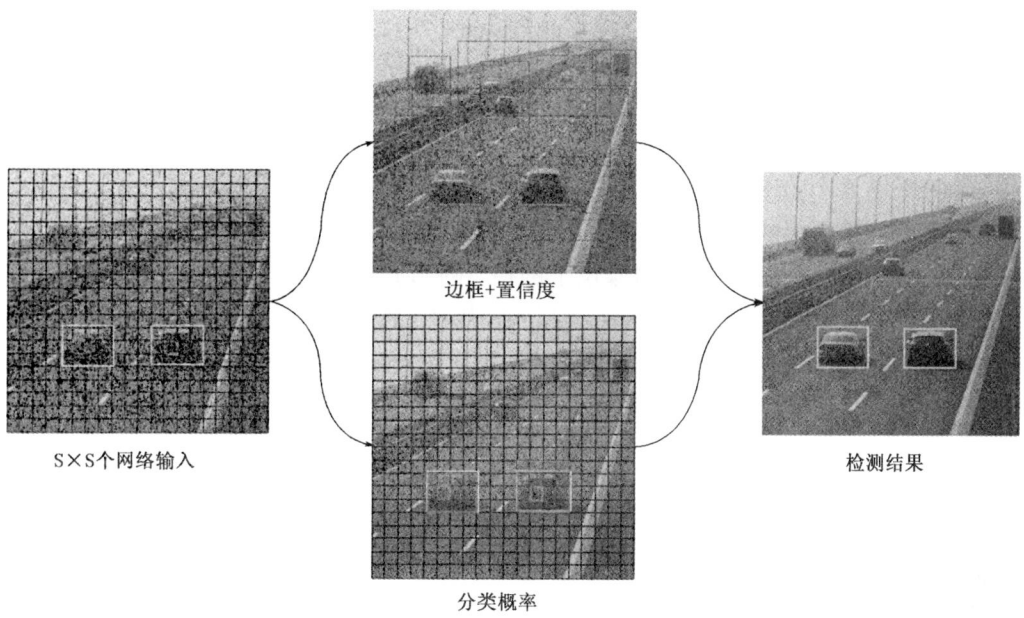

图2 YOLO-v4检测原理

将CSCS应用于目标分类和定位的精度评估。如果多个边界盒同时检测同一个目标,可以使用非最大抑制获得最优边界盒,每个网格通过k-means方法聚类确定9个预先选择的边界盒,提高检测速度。

YOLO-v4的结构图如图3所示,图中的CBM代表卷积+正则化+Mish激活函数,CBL代表卷积+正则化+Leakyrelu激活函数。首先将输入到网络的图像大小调整为416×416,在经过了全过程的特征提取与分类之后,会得到三个不同尺寸的特征图,分别为76×76、38×38、13×13,分别用于小目标检测、中目标检测与大目标检测。将三幅特征图融合后,在检测层计算边界盒的损失函数值,从而实现最佳边界盒的分类定位。在模型训练过程中,将边界盒的损失函数值进行反向传播,以优化网络参数。

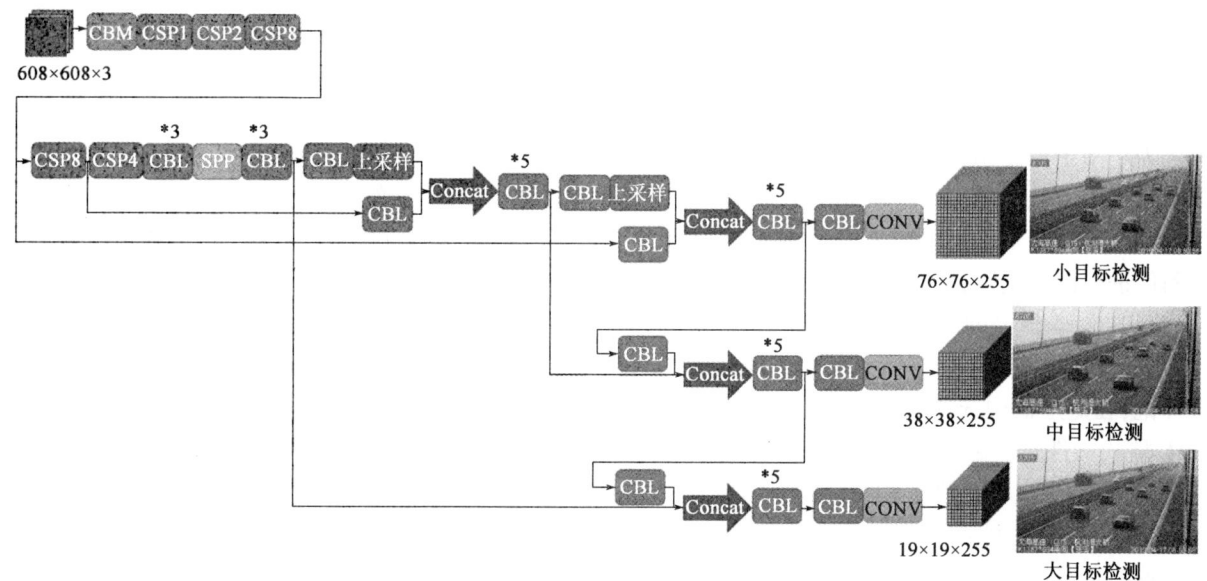

图3 YOLO-v4结构图

YOLO-v4 的损失函数定义如下：

$$Loss = Error_{coord} + Error_{IOU} + Error_{cls} \tag{3}$$

在上式中，坐标预测误差 $Error_{coord}$ 定义为：

$$Error_{coord} = \lambda_{coord} \sum_{i=1}^{S^2} \sum_{j=1}^{B} 1_{ij}^{obj} [(\hat{u}_i - u_i)^2 + (\hat{v}_i - v_i)^2] +$$

$$\lambda_{coord} \sum_{i=1}^{S^2} \sum_{j=1}^{B} 1_{ij}^{obj} [(\sqrt{w_i} - \sqrt{\hat{w}_i})^2 + (\sqrt{h_i} - \sqrt{\hat{h}_i})] \tag{4}$$

式中：λ_{coord}——坐标误差的权值；

S^2——输入图像中的网格数；

B——每个网格生成的边界框个数。

在本研究中，模型的参数设置为：当对象位于网格 i 的第 j 个边界框时，表示 $1_{ij}^{obj} = 1$；否则，$1_{ij}^{obj} = 0$。$(\hat{u}_i, \hat{v}_i, \hat{w}_i, \hat{h}_i)$ 表示预测的边界框的中心坐标、宽度和长度，(u_i, v_i, w_i, h_i) 代表真实框的中心坐标、宽度和长度。

IOU 误差 $Error_{IOU}$ 定义为：

$$Error_{IOU} = \sum_{i=1}^{S^2} \sum_{j=1}^{B} 1_{ij}^{obj} (C_i - \hat{C}_i)^2 + \lambda_{noobj} \sum_{i=1}^{S^2} \sum_{j=1}^{B} 1_{ij}^{obj} (C_i - \hat{C}_i)^2 \tag{5}$$

式中：λ_{noobj}——IOU 误差的权值，本研究中取 $\lambda_{coord} = 0.5$；

$\hat{C}_i$——预测的置信度；

C_i——真实的置信度。

分类误差 $Error_{cls}$ 定义为：

$$Error_{cls} = \sum_{i=1}^{S^2} \sum_{j=1}^{B} 1_{ij}^{obj} \sum_{c \in classes} [p_{ri}(c) - \hat{p}_{ri}(c)]^2 \tag{6}$$

式中：c——检测对象所分种类；

$p_{ri}(c)$——以网格 i 为中心的对象属于 c 类的真实概率；

$\hat{p}_{ri}(c)$——预测概率；

$Error_{cls}$——指以网格 i 为中心的所有对象的分类误差之和。

1.3 建立数据集

一些开源的图像数据集可以用来有效地训练 YOLO-v4 模型，但是共享的图像数据库很少包含实际的车辆。同时，对于常用的车辆数据集，如 KITTI、BDD100K、TME 高速公路数据集，主要用于自动驾驶仪研究，采用车载摄像头多视角采集图像，Cars 数据集和 CompCars 主要研究小型汽车的细粒度分类。

为了基于深度学习方法有效区分车辆荷载，在 YOLO-v4 模型训练任务中需要建立具有不同车辆类型的车辆图像数据集。这项研究使用了 4000 多张图像的数据集，建立的数据集的车辆图像主要是通过安装在桥梁上的现场摄像头采集的，或者是从网站上采集的，并包含了 6 种分类后的车辆类型，对采集到的图像进行图像增强，包括旋转、镜像、颜色和亮度调整、模糊等，以提高检测模型的泛化能力，增强训练好的 YOLO-v4 模型的可泛化性。

在对每幅图像进行编号后，使用 LabelImg 标注工具对图像数据集进行标注，每辆车使用 2D 边框进行标记，在矩形框中选择完整的目标车辆，同时获取相应的背景信息，这对于后续的车辆预测非常重要。XML 格式文件然后由标记数据集生成，该数据集被表示为 $[x, y, w, h]$，表格中分别包含了所选目标区域的边界坐标、宽度和高度等相关信息。随机选取其中 90% 作为训练集，10% 作为测试集。为了提高网络的泛化能力，减少网络的训练时间，在图像中简单地将车辆分为三组（Truck，Bus，Car），并对这些车辆的前部或后部进行标记，以区分不同行驶方向的车辆。如图 4 所示，将车辆分为六种类型：CarA、CarB、BusA、BusB、TruckA 及 TruckB。

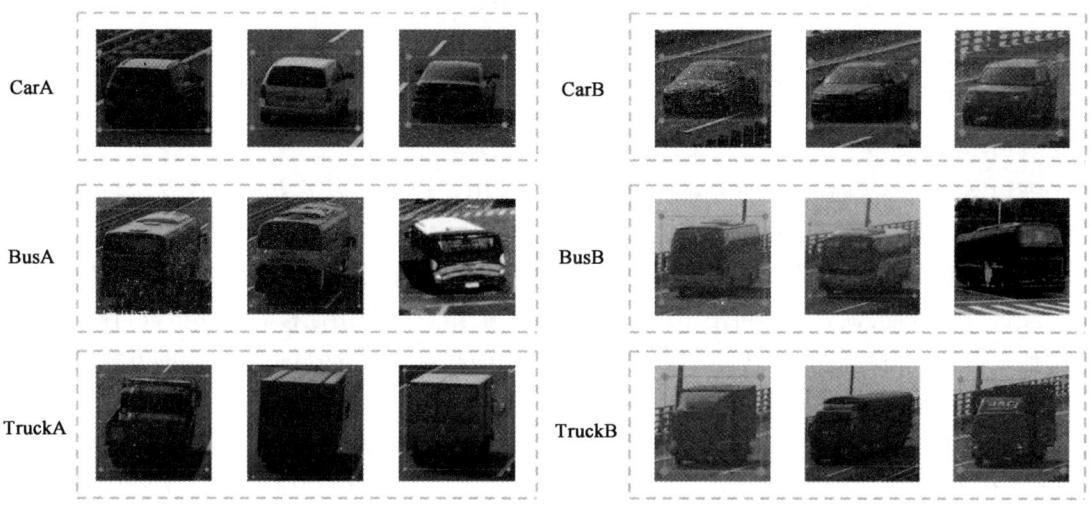

图 4 六种车辆类型

1.4 卡尔曼滤波跟踪理论

为了从监控视频中自动实现车辆载荷的时空定位,开展运动车辆的实时跟踪研究是十分必要的。卡尔曼滤波跟踪算法是一种递推滤波方法,利用贝叶斯理论和线性最小方差理论建立目标运动估计模型,利用该模型可以获取目标物体的实时时空位置。本节采用卡尔曼滤波方法进行车辆跟踪研究。

卡尔曼滤波跟踪算法一般包括由目标状态转移函数计算得到的状态预测模型和由目标状态测量函数计算得到的状态更新模型。当下时刻的状态变量会在最后一刻发现预测的目标,经过特征提取过程周围的邻近地区预测位置,然后利用获得的测量向量将迭代更新最优状态估计的状态向量,直到当前时刻。对象状态转换函数 K_i 描述如下:

$$K_i = AK_{i-1} + \xi_{i-1} \tag{7}$$

式中:A——从最后时刻转移到现在时刻的转移矩阵。

同时,目标状态测量函数 L_i 计算如下:

$$L_i = HK_i + \eta_i \tag{8}$$

式中:H——度量矩阵;

ξ_{i-1}、η_i——服从正态分布的系统高斯噪声和观测高斯噪声。

然而,由于矢量 K_i 不能直接测量,当前时刻的状态,包括状态变量和协方差误差,都是由目标对象在下一时刻的运动状态来估计的。状态测量函数 L_i 用于更新位置矢量 K_i 给定时刻状态变量的预测方程可以表示为:

$$\hat{K}_i^- = A \hat{K}_{i-1} + \xi_{i-1} \tag{9}$$

给定时刻协方差函数误差的预测方程可以表示为:

$$P_i^- = AP_{i-1}A^T + Q_i \tag{10}$$

式中:Q_i——系统高斯噪声的协方差函数。

状态更新模型包括对卡尔曼权值的更新过程和对状态变量及协方差误差的优化过程。卡尔曼权值的增益方程可以表示为:

$$\omega_i = P_i^- H^T (HP_i^- H^T + R_i)^{-1} \tag{11}$$

式中:R_i——高斯噪声观测值的协方差。

同时,更新状态变量的优化方程可计算如下:

$$\hat{K}_i = \hat{K}_{i-1}^- + \omega_i (L_i - H\hat{K}_{i-1}^-) \tag{12}$$

进一步可得用于更新协方差误差的优化方程为:

$$P_i = (1 - \omega_i H)P_i^- \tag{13}$$

在实际的车辆监控视频中,一旦确定了状态转换函数和状态测量函数,就可以通过卡尔曼滤波得到下一帧目标车辆的位置,得到目标物体的运动轨迹。

1.5 训练与测试

为了缩短网络的训练时间,改进基本特征提取器,采用了迁移学习的方法。迁移学习是一种机器学习的方法,指的是一个预训练的模型被重新用在另一个任务中。通过 YOLO-v4 的框架对丰富的数据集进行预训练,得到训练好的网络参数,然后将训练好的网络参数迁移到基本网络进行初始化,生成迁移后的模型。经过上述过程,训练集不再使用进行特征提取,而是直接使用迁移后的模型进行特征提取,改进了基本特征提取器。在转移学习中的旧权值是初始训练的起点,而不必从一个复杂的方程重新开始梯度下降,从而缩短了网络训练时间。

本训练设置了三个不同学习率(Learning rate)进行训练,分别为 1×10^{-2}、1×10^{-3}、1×10^{-4},如图 5 所示,显示了在不同学习率下经过迭代后的损失函数曲线。对于学习率为 1×10^{-2}、1×10^{-3} 的情况,损失函数的值能够在几个循环后达到平稳状态,且精确度能分别达到 97.9% 与 96.8%。而对于学习率为 1×10^{-4} 的情况而言,需要更多的迭代次数才能稳定,并且损失函数的值要明显高于另外两种学习率,且精确度较低,为 92.3%。

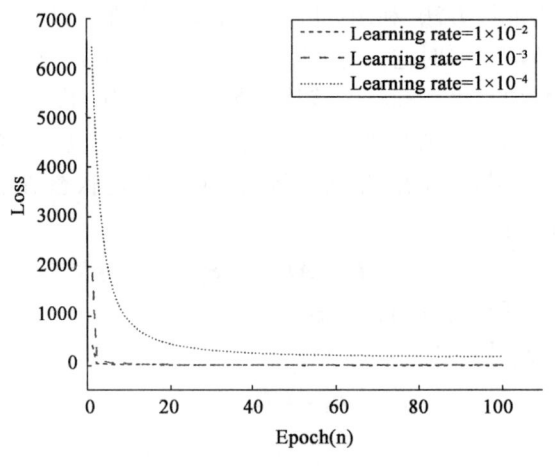

图 5 损失函数曲线

较大的学习率能够提高训练的速度,但是容易造成损失函数值爆炸,较小的学习率会导致训练速度慢,且容易出现过拟合的现象,收敛速度慢,在综合考虑各种训练成本后,选择 1×10^{-3} 的学习率作为最终训练的学习率,该学习率下能取得较快的训练速度,并且取得较高精度。

2 从图像坐标到桥梁坐标的转换

从视频流计算出的车辆坐标在图像坐标系中。为了确定车辆在桥面上的位置,必须建立图像坐标系与桥面坐标系之间的投影变换矩阵。图像坐标与桥梁坐标之间的变换关系如图 6 所示。确定像素平面坐标系 (u, v)、图像坐标系 (x, y)、相机坐标系 (X_c, Y_c, Z_c) 和世界坐标系 (X_w, Y_w, Z_w) 之间的关系。数字图像在计算机中以 $M \times N$ 的数组形式展示,M 和 N 表示行和列中的像素个数。直角坐标系 uO_0v 定义在成像面上,(u, v) 对应表示像素所在的数组的行数和列数。建立了以物理单位表示的图像坐标系 xO_1y,$O1(u0, v0)$ 代表相机光轴与图像平面的交点,dx 与 dy 分别表示每个像素在横轴 x 和纵轴 y 上的物理尺寸,则图像中的每个像素在 $u-v$ 坐标系中的坐标和在 $x-y$ 坐标系中的坐标之间都存在如下关系:

$$\begin{cases} u = \dfrac{x}{\mathrm{d}x} + u_0 \\ v = \dfrac{y}{\mathrm{d}y} + v_0 \end{cases} \tag{14}$$

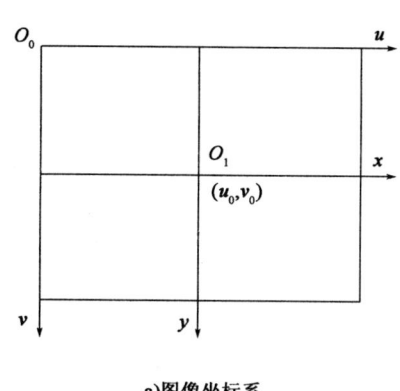
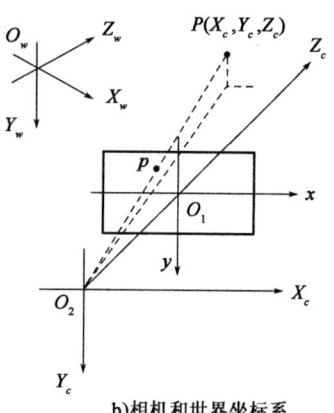

a) 图像坐标系   b) 相机和世界坐标系

图 6 坐标系

用矩阵形式表示为:

$$\begin{bmatrix} u \\ v \\ 1 \end{bmatrix} = \begin{bmatrix} \dfrac{1}{\mathrm{d}x} & 0 & u_0 \\ 0 & \dfrac{1}{\mathrm{d}y} & v_0 \\ 0 & 0 & 1 \end{bmatrix} \begin{bmatrix} x \\ y \\ 1 \end{bmatrix} \tag{15}$$

相机坐标系与图像坐标系的关系如图 6b) 所示,$O_2 X_c Y_c Z_c$ 为相机坐标系,$O_3 X_w Y_w Z_w$ 为世界坐标系,平面 $X_c O_2 Y_c$ 平行于 $x O_1 y$。假设空间点 P 在世界坐标系下的齐次坐标是 $(X_w, Y_w, Z_w, 1)^T$,在相机坐标下的齐次坐标是 $(X_c, Y_c, Z_c, 1)^T$,则存在如下关系:

$$\begin{bmatrix} X_c \\ Y_c \\ Z_c \\ 1 \end{bmatrix} = \begin{bmatrix} \boldsymbol{R} & \boldsymbol{t} \\ 0^T & 1 \end{bmatrix} \begin{bmatrix} X_w \\ Y_w \\ Z_w \\ 1 \end{bmatrix} \tag{16}$$

式中:$\boldsymbol{R}$——3×3 旋转矩;

$\boldsymbol{t}$——3×1 平移矢量。

图像平面上任意点 P 的位置都可以用针孔模型表示。如果 f 是相机的焦距,则其图像坐标 (x,y) 可以通过将其与相机坐标系中的坐标联系起来:

$$\begin{cases} x = f\dfrac{X_c}{Z_c} \\ y = f\dfrac{Y_c}{Z_c} \end{cases} \tag{17}$$

用矩阵表示为:

$$Z_c \begin{bmatrix} x \\ y \\ 1 \end{bmatrix} = \begin{bmatrix} f & 0 & 0 & 0 \\ 0 & f & 0 & 0 \\ 0 & 0 & 1 & 0 \end{bmatrix} \begin{bmatrix} X_c \\ Y_c \\ Z_c \\ 1 \end{bmatrix} \tag{18}$$

通过式(14)~式(18),可以得到世界坐标系到像素平面坐标系的变换公式:

$$Z_c \begin{bmatrix} x \\ y \\ 1 \end{bmatrix} = \begin{bmatrix} \dfrac{1}{dx} & 0 & u_0 \\ 0 & \dfrac{1}{dy} & v_0 \\ 0 & 0 & 1 \end{bmatrix} \begin{bmatrix} f & 0 & 0 & 0 \\ 0 & f & 0 & 0 \\ 0 & 0 & 1 & 0 \end{bmatrix} \begin{bmatrix} \boldsymbol{R} & \boldsymbol{t} \\ \boldsymbol{0}^T & 1 \end{bmatrix} \begin{bmatrix} X_w \\ Y_w \\ Z_w \\ 1 \end{bmatrix}$$

$$= \begin{bmatrix} m_{11} & m_{12} & m_{13} & m_{14} \\ m_{21} & m_{22} & m_{23} & m_{24} \\ m_{31} & m_{32} & m_{33} & m_{34} \end{bmatrix} = \boldsymbol{M} \boldsymbol{X}_w \tag{19}$$

式中:$\boldsymbol{M}$——3×4矩阵,如果摄像机的参数未知,则需要通过图像坐标和参考点的世界坐标来计算矩阵$\boldsymbol{M}$。

对于n个参考点,可以得到$2n$个线性方程,其中有11个独立的未知变量。该变换矩阵可由至少6对参考点的坐标确定。由于桥面高度不变,因此Z_w可以看作一个常量,若$Z_w=0$,则独立未知变量个数由11变为8,则至少需要4对参考点来确定$\boldsymbol{m}$,矩阵$\boldsymbol{m}$为:

$$\boldsymbol{m} = \begin{bmatrix} m_{11} & m_{12} & m_{14} \\ m_{21} & m_{22} & m_{24} \\ m_{31} & m_{32} & m_{34} \end{bmatrix} \tag{20}$$

如图7所示,P1、P2、P3、P7、P8、P9用于计算投影变换矩阵$\boldsymbol{m}$,P4、P5、P6用于验证变换矩阵$\boldsymbol{m}$的准确性。

a)位于桥面坐标系　　　　　　　　　　　b)位于图像坐标系

图7　参考点

利用桥梁视频监控的实测数据,求解了坐标变换问题。如图7所示,在桥面上标注了9个参考点,定义了桥面坐标系。这9个参考点的图像坐标由图像得到,桥面坐标可由设计文件确定。计算中参考点越多,表中的结果越准确。但是,从下面的讨论可以发现,该精度对于本文的应用是足够的。误差可能来源于以下两个原因:参考点图像坐标的选取是像素精度的问题,造成了读取误差;由于相机结构、制造工艺等原因造成镜头畸变,图像坐标存在偏差。如表1所示,展示了参考点在两个坐标系中的坐标值。

如表2所示,一旦矩阵$\boldsymbol{m}$确定,桥面上某一点的坐标(X_w, Y_w)可以唯一地由其图像坐标(u,v)计算出来。如表3所示,P4、P5、P6的计算坐标与实测坐标的最大误差为$0.239m$。这说明$\boldsymbol{m}$是可靠的,通过这个$\boldsymbol{m}$,就可以准确地得到车辆在桥面坐标系中的位置。

两个坐标系中的坐标 表1

参 考 点	u(pixel)	v(pixel)	x(m)	y(m)
P1	422	736	0	0
P2	955	768	5.25	0
P3	1481	808	10.5	0
P4	723	597	0	15
P5	1131	629	5.25	15
P6	1538	665	10.5	15
P7	899	514	0	30
P8	1250	531	5.25	30
P9	1594	549	10.5	30

投影变换矩阵的值 表2

m_{11}	m_{12}	m_{14}	m_{21}	m_{22}	m_{24}	m_{31}	m_{32}	m_{34}
1.31×10^{-3}	1.29	30.6	-0.12	-8.3×10^{-8}	-5.6×10^{-6}	-4.3×10^{-5}	-5.2×10^{-6}	9.9×10^{-8}

验证点坐标的误差值 表3

参 考 点	x(m)	y(m)	x 计算值(m)	y 计算值(m)	x 误差	y 误差
P4	0	15	0.032	14.780	0.032	0.22
P5	5.25	15	5.011	15.230	0.239	0.23
P6	10.5	15	10.690	15.130	0.19	0.13

3 工程应用

通过现场实验验证了该方法的可靠性,选取了某大桥作为测试路段,该桥为双向六车道,视频监控视野可以覆盖该桥某一路段,在桥头安装有WIMs系统。如图所示,目标车辆的识别与跟踪能够较好地实现,跟踪车辆得到的轨迹是连续的,保证了车辆时空信息的完整性。

建立的数据集的车辆图像被调整到416×416个像素块的尺寸进行网络训练,最终得到的平均精确度(AP)值为97.6%。这是一个可以接受的精度范围,可以通过增加数据集的数量或改善神经网络结构等方法继续提高精度。如图8所示,6种车型的预测精度均在90%以上,其中小轿车的精度较高,客车与货车的精度相对较低,这是由于路面行驶的车辆中小轿车的数量占大多数,这导致数据集中小轿车的相关数据最多,而客车与货车的数据相对较少,可以通过增加客车与货车的数据集数量来提高精度。

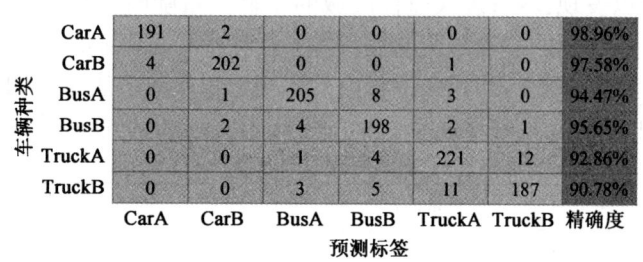

图8 车辆种类预测精度

如图9所示,跟踪车辆得到的轨迹是连续的,保证了车辆时空信息的完整性。在视频中的一些帧中,车辆检测网络得到的车辆边界框与实际车辆边界存在偏差,这会导致不应该出现在车辆轨迹中的弯角,这些错误的车辆边框可以在以后通过误差分析予以删除。通过本研究提出的方法,可以识别车辆在桥面任意位置的横向和纵向位置。

采用WIMs系统和桥梁图像监控系统,交通负荷分布已被成功识别,2019年4月17日上午9点的一些典型结果如图10所示。在图10中,这里的桥面坐标仍然基于图7中的坐标系统,每一列表示车辆的总重量。此外,为了证明权重信息是否正确附加,确定的权重与WIMs测量的权重的比较如表4所示。

图9 车辆轨迹追踪

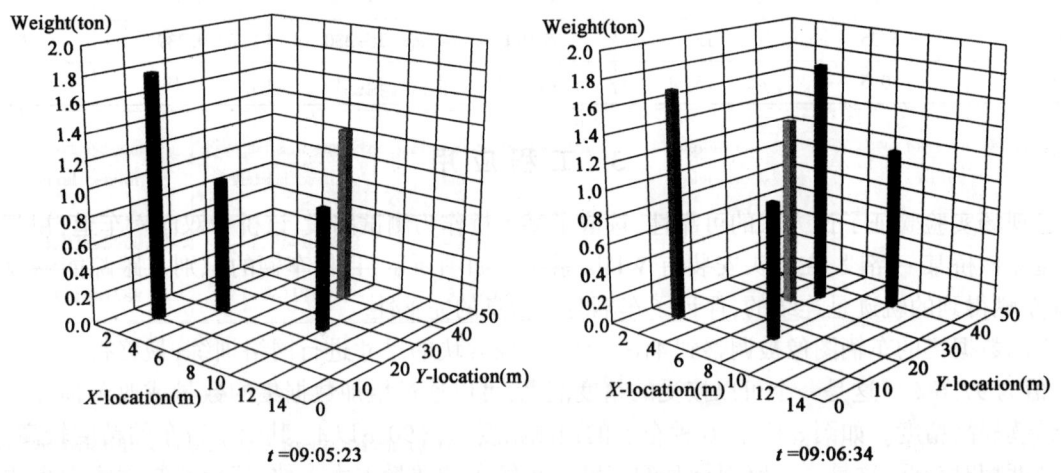

图10 交通荷载识别结果

对比图和监控视频可以发现,尽管进入监控区域的车辆数量随时间变化较大,本文方法仍然可以成功同时识别出所有车辆。所识别的移动载荷的数量等于视频中可见车辆的数量,不存在虚假车辆的遗漏或增加。所识别的移动荷载的位置也与视频中相应的车辆位置一致。表4中的数据表明,该方法成功地将重量信息附加到正确的车辆上,即在多运动目标的情况下,荷载值仍能正确识别。

交通荷载识别结果　　　　表4

时间	编号	重量(t)	x(m)	y(m)	车辆类型
09:05:23	4	1.8	2.11	10.11	Truck B
09:05:23	5	1.0	3.89	20.20	Bus B
09:05:23	6	1.3	8.01	39.91	Bus B
09:05:23	7	0.9	10.21	24.53	Car B
09:06:34	190	1.7	2.03	9.85	Truck B
09:06:34	191	1.4	4.99	29.90	Truck B

续上表

时间	编号	重量(t)	x(m)	y(m)	车辆类型
09:06:34	192	1.8	6.33	34.80	Truck B
09:06:34	193	1.2	9.98	41.45	Bus B
09:06:34	194	1.0	7.89	13.56	Car B

4 结 语

本文提出一种基于深度学习算法和机器视觉技术的桥梁车辆载荷自动辨识方法，该方案能够实时提供全桥交通荷载的空间分布，有望应用于桥梁结构的实时力学分析，车辆信息通过路边交通监控摄像机拍摄的监控视频获取。为评估系统的可靠性，进行了现场试验，主要结论如下：

（1）为了快速、准确地识别车辆的时空信息，首先建立了基于深度关联度量的车辆深度检测与跟踪网络，利用监控摄像机系统采集的视频对多辆车辆进行跟踪。

（2）WIMs系统与第一摄像机的位置可能会影响车辆与其重量信息的匹配精度，该确保WIMs系统在第一个摄像头视野范围内。

（3）通过卡尔曼滤波对运动车辆进行实时跟踪研究，对一帧对应的参数进行更新。即使车辆颜色与背景相似，在监控视频中车辆的运动状态也能被有效跟踪。

（4）图像坐标与桥面坐标转换关系的精度由参考点个数决定，选择的参考点越多，变换越精确。

（5）该方法具有良好的适用性，不仅适用于各种桥梁上的车辆荷载识别，也适用于各种道路上的车辆荷载识别。然而，该方法的准确性仍然受到光照条件的影响。

未来可以从二维图像中重建出车辆的三维信息，获得更准确的车辆荷载时空信息。可以继续提高车辆检测网络的泛化能力，从而实现在恶劣光照条件下对车辆的准确识别。表5所示为参数解释。

参 数 解 释 表 表5

Confidence	置信度	A	最后时刻转移到现在时刻的转移矩阵
Pr(Object)	边界框中存在对象的概率	L_i	目标状态测量函数
IOU_{pred}^{truth}	预测边界框与真实包含物体边界框的交并比	H	度量矩阵
CSCS	种类置信度	ξ_{i-1}	系统高斯噪声
LOSS	损失函数	η_i	观测高斯噪声
$Error_{coord}$	坐标预测误差	Q_i	系统高斯噪声协方差函数
$Error_{IOU}$	IOU误差	R_i	高斯噪声观测值的协方差
$Error_{cls}$	分类误差	P_i	协方差函数误差的预测值
λ_{coord}	坐标误差的权值	(u,v)	像素平面坐标系
λ_{noobj}	IOU误差的权值	(x,y)	图像坐标系
$P_r(c)$	真实概率	(X_c,Y_c,Z_c)	相机坐标系
$\hat{p}_r(c)$	预测概率	(X_w,Y_w,Z_w)	世界坐标系
M, m	变换矩阵	R	转换矩阵
K_i	对象转换函数	t	平移矢量

参考文献

[1] M. Lydon, S. E. Taylor, D. Robinson, et al.. Recent developments in bridge weigh in motion(B-WIM)[J]. Civil Struct. Health Monitor. 2015, 6:69-81.

[2] C Cremona. Optimal extrapolation of traffic load effects[J]. Struct. Saf. 2001,23:31-46.

[3] E J OBrien, B Enright. Using weigh-in-motion data to determine aggressiveness of traffic for bridge loading [J]. Bridge Eng. 2013,18:232-239.

[4] Yu Y,Cai CS,Deng L. State-of-the-art review on bridge weigh-in-motion technology[J]. Adv Struct Eng. 2016,19(9):1514-1530.

[5] Lydon M,Taylor SE,Robinson D,Mufti A,Brien EJO. Recent developments in bridge weigh in motion(B-WIM)[J]. Journal of Civil Struc-tural Health Monitoring. 2016,6(1):69-81.

[6] OBrien EJ,Enright B. Using weigh-in-motion data to determine aggressiveness of traffic for bridge loading [J]. Journal of Bridge Engineering. 2012,18(3):232-239.

[7] Han W, Liu X, Gao G, et al. Site-specific extra-heavy truck load characteristics and bridge safety assessment. Journal of Aero-space Engineering. 2018,31(6):04018098.

[8] L Yu T. H. T. Chan, Recent research on identification of moving loads on bridges[J]. Sound Vib. 2007, 305:3-21.

[9] 陈艾荣,马如进,许艳梅. 苏通大桥运营阶段车辆荷载识别及其特性[J]. 重庆交通大学学报,2013, 32(1):729-733.

[10] Ryan Brown, Al Wicks. Vehicle tracking for bridge load dynamics using vision techniques, in: Al Wicks, Christopher Niezrecki[J]. Structural Health Monitoring, Damage Detection & Mechatronics, 2016, 7: 83-90.

[11] Zhang B. ,Zhou L,Zhang J. A methodology for obtaining spatiotemporal information of the vehicles on bridges based on computer vision[J]. Computer-aided Civil and Infrastructure Engineering, (2019),34 (6):471-487.

Safety Evaluation of Continuous Beam Bridges under Heavy Load

Yushi Yi Lu Zhang

(Highway College,Chang'an University)

Abstract CTV(customized transport vehicle)load limit standards directly affect the actual load level and distribution characteristics of vehicles and the service performance of Bridges and other infrastructure. In order to analyse the CTV load limit of medium and small-span Bridges, this paper firstly establishes the CTV load limit analysis model based on the reliability theory. Secondly, based on WIM(Weigh in Motion) data recorded for a long time,the CTV load characteristics of typical highway sections in China were analysed and the heavy-duty CTV models that needed to be studied were determined, and the bridge structure type that controlled the CTV load limit was selected according to the current situation of medium and small-span Bridges in China. Finally, to establish a structure of key section flexural functions, select multi-level target reliability index, the various types of CTV load limit reverse iterative analysis, based on the results of the analysis respectively to discuss the target reliability index, regional load characteristics influence on CTV load limit, and the current highway grade will cure for small and medium-sized vehicle bridge models the applicability of the limit load. The analysis results show that the load limit of each type of CTV decreases linearly with the increase of target reliability index. The difference of regional CTV load characteristics has a significant influence on CTV load limit. The current national over-regulation standards have good applicability to the vehicle load limitation of medium and small-span Bridges.

Keywords Bridge engineering Safety evaluation PCB bridge CTV load WIM

0 Introduction

Automobile load is a kind of social load. Compared with wind, earthquake and other natural loads, environmental protection requirements, national or regional macro-transport policies, freight demand and the relationship between supply and demand of freight capacity, and carriers' pursuit of profits may affect the actual level and distribution characteristics of automobile load. The comprehensive external manifestation of the influence of the above factors on vehicle load is that the number of heavy trucks and their load levels are increasing year by year. In 2002, the number of heavy trucks in China was 1482800, and by 2011, the number had reached 4605800. Meanwhile, truck load levels in various regions have also increased to different degrees (Li, W. J 2009). The above changes not only improve the logistics efficiency, but also transfer the consequent conflicts to the environment, citizens and highway infrastructure (Huang, S. et al. 2012). For long-span Bridges with a small live constant load ratio, their sensitivity to the above problems is relatively low. In contrast, the service performance of medium and small-span Bridges with a high live constant load ratio is more sensitive to the evolution of vehicle load. In order to ensure the long life and healthy operation of such structures, it is widely adopted in various countries to limit vehicle load level through legally effective provisions (Ruan, X. 2017). There are a large number of middle and small-span girder Bridges in China, and the study of truck load limit of middle and small-span Bridges based on the reliability theory is of great significance for the further improvement of vehicle load regulation under the condition that the probabilistic limit state design has been used.

Firstly, this paper establishes a truck load limit analysis model based on probability theory, which mainly includes the determination of truck load information, bridge structure information and the iterative analysis of truck load limit based on reliability theory. Secondly, based on the long-term vehicle load monitoring data, the model of heavy-duty truck and its probabilistic characteristics that need to be studied are determined, and the bridge structure information that plays a controlling role in truck load limit is obtained according to the construction status of medium and small-span Bridges in China. Thirdly, based on the established analysis model and the reliability analysis theory, the truck load effect threshold corresponding to different target reliability indexes is obtained. Furthermore, the truck load limit is set through on-site traffic flow observation for analysis of working conditions, and the load limit of each type of truck is determined by ANSYS. Finally, based on the analysis results, this paper discusses the selection of target reliability index, the influence of regional load characteristic difference on truck load limit, and the applicability of the current over-regulation standard to vehicle load limit of medium and small-span Bridges, and puts forward some Suggestions for further optimization of the current standard.

1 Analysis Method of Truck Load Limit Based on Reliability Theory

Similar to the probabilistic limit state design of the structure, the truck load limit analysis based on the reliability theory should first determine the target reliability index, and then select the multi-level target reliability index for analysis according to the reliability design level of highway Bridges in China, which is 5.0, 4.7, 4.5, 4.3, 4.0 and 3.7 respectively. Secondly, the target models for truck load limit analysis should be determined according to the high-frequency heavy-duty models in actual road transportation. This work can be expanded based on the vehicle load data recorded in the dynamic weighing (WIM) system for a long time. Middle and small-span beam Bridges are widely used in China. According to the actual construction conditions, the structure types controlling the analysis results can be determined, which can simplify the analysis process to a large extent. Medium and small span Bridges in highway engineering practice in our country is more bending beam structure is built, and the flexural bearing capacity of the structure's allowance(Han, W. S., Li Y. W. and Ma L. et al. 2016), much lower than the shear bearing capacity by is bending effect into a truck load limit analysis of the characteristics of the response of building structure close section flexural functions, using the JC method iteration is bending effect under different target reliability index threshold. Finally, by observing the traffic flow on site, the most unfavourable driving condition of truck crossing the bridge is set, and then the limit of truck load is searched and calculated. Based on the above analysis, the truck load limit analysis method based on reliability theory is established, as shown in Fig. 1.

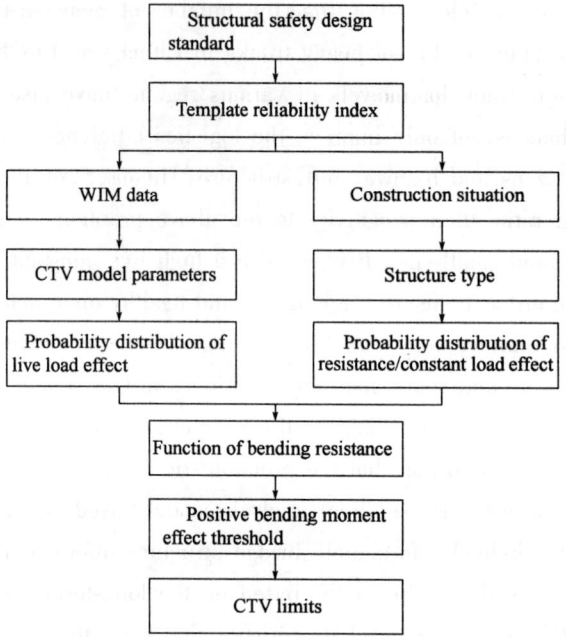

Fig. 1 Analysis method of truck load limitation based on probabilistic theory

2 Truck Load Information Based on Wim

The dynamic weighing system(WIM) can record the number of shafts, shaft quality, wheelbase and other information of passing vehicles. The equipment has been put into use on roads of different grades in many parts of China. Based on the long-term WIM data of national highway G104 in Zhejiang province, Xuanda expressway in Hebei province and Shanghai-Shaanxi expressway, this paper analyzes the composition and probability distribution characteristics of heavy-duty truck models in each section. Highway G104 for first-class highway, traffic flow measuring point is located in Shaoxing bell bay flyover, xuan big highway is located in Hebei province, based on coal transportation as the main function of mountainous expressway, the Shanghai-Shaanxi expressway transport features can represent China's enormous quantity wide ordinary highway, traffic flow measuring point choose Shanghai, the above three sections also covers the traffic load characteristics of the north-south differences, function, etc.

The three periods of traffic flow monitoring were from April 2013 to January 2014, January 2011 to June 2012, and December 2011 to May 2012. Due to the large number of cars in each section but the small impact on the structure, only truck load data are retained in the probability analysis of vehicle load. The overall distribution histogram of truck mass in each section is shown in Fig. 2.

Through the classification of WIM data statistical analysis, found that each section of high frequency overloaded truck models focused on four axis and 5 axis, six axis trucks, four axis is presented, five axis and six axis trucks in each section of overall percentage of the number. (Han, W. S. 2017). It shows that 4 axis and 5 axis, six axis trucks combined occupy three sections respectively 50.3%, 96.7%, 56.2% of the total, including G104 national highway, the Shanghai-Shaanxi expressway are in the majority with four axis truck number, truck followed six axis, Xuan big six axis high speed truck number occupies absolute advantage, the truck number of sections of 91%. Based on the wheelbase and shaft quality information in WIM data, the diagram of heavy-duty truck models in each section is shown in table 1 (Yuan, Y. G. 2015). In Tab. 1, the values of shaft mass and wheelbase of each model are taken from the mean values of various parameters of WIM data corresponding to each model.

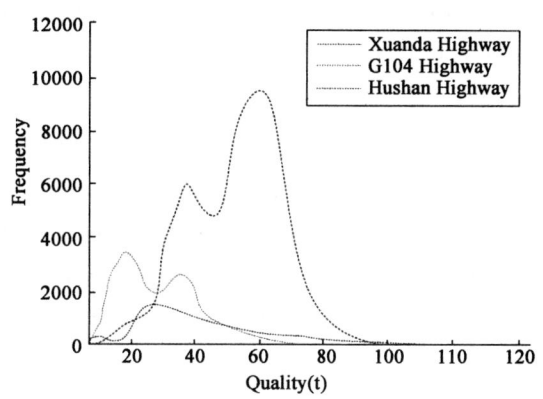

Fig. 2 Truck Weight Distribution of the Three Routes

CTV Model of the Three Routes Tab. 1

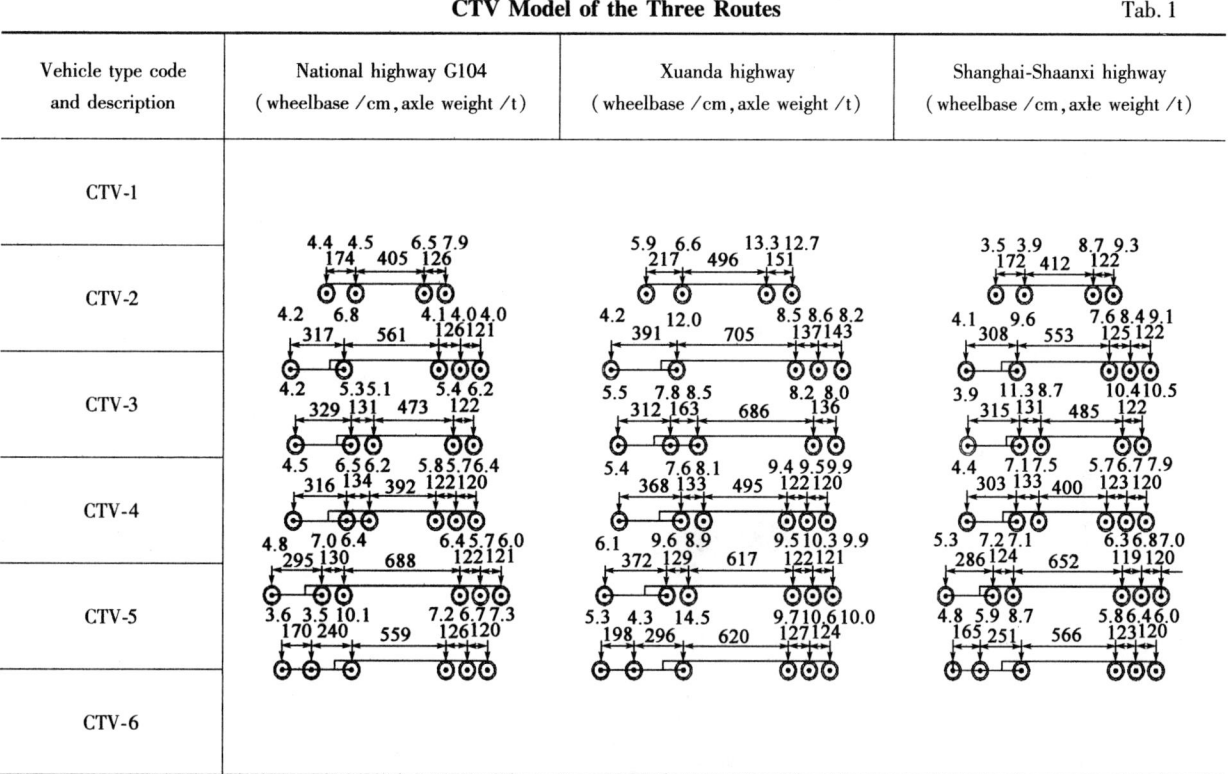

3 Typical Medium and Small Span Bridges and Analysis Models

3.1 Superstructure Type Screening

In the process of bridge construction, economy is often one of the important factors influencing the selection of superstructure. Combined with the research of Bao Weigang and li Xuemei Bao, (W. G. 2003), the hollow slab bridge, t-beam bridge and box girder bridge with standardized design are more likely to meet the requirements of economy in the construction of medium and small-span Bridges (Han, W. S. 2018).

According to the study of li sung-hui et al. (Li, S. H. 2013), the load limiting coefficient of a bridge of the same superstructure increases with the increase of the ratio of live and constant load, that is, the load limiting coefficient of the same superstructure increases with the increase of the ratio of live and constant load. In the superstructure type of bridge, the bridge with smaller span controls the load limiting result. Therefore, the final selection of bridge structure is as follows: rcs-6m, pcs-10m, pct-20m, and pcb-4 ×20m.

3.2 Analysis Model of Bridge Superstructure

The four Bridges selected are prefabricated structures, and the correctness of the transverse distribution of internal forces is the key to ensure the accuracy of the study on truck load limit (Li, S. H. 2014). Here, in order to satisfy the calculation efficiency and the transverse distribution correctness of internal force at the same time, ANSYS solid finite element model was used to modify the relatively simplified beam lattice model, and the elastic modulus and mass density of the beam were selected. In the process of building the solid model, the main girder and crash-proof guardrail were simulated by Solid65 unit. Beam4 was selected as the main girder and beam unit type in the grillage model. Due to the low girder height of the four Bridges, the concrete pavement of the bridge deck was considered as part of the roof, but the influence of asphalt abrasion layer was not considered.

Fig. 3 PCS to 10m, PCT - 20m as an example, gives the corresponding correction girder model and entity finite element model of Fig. 4 PCS to 10m, for example, further shows the 1000kN under the action of concentrated force in the middle of the bridge deck and fixed grillage model and the real model across the cross section of the various pieces of the beam deflection, the Fig. 4 shows that modified features of transverse distribution of the grillage model and the real model fits, maximum error is not more than 6%. The modified grillage model will be used to carry out the analysis below.

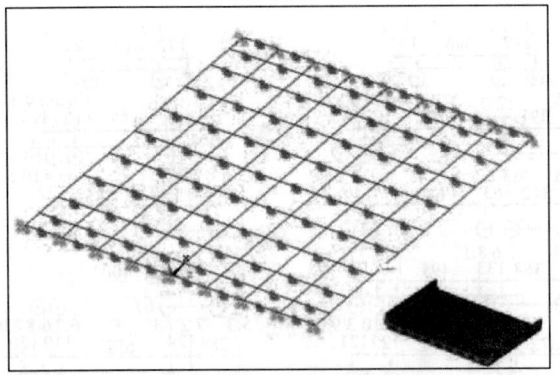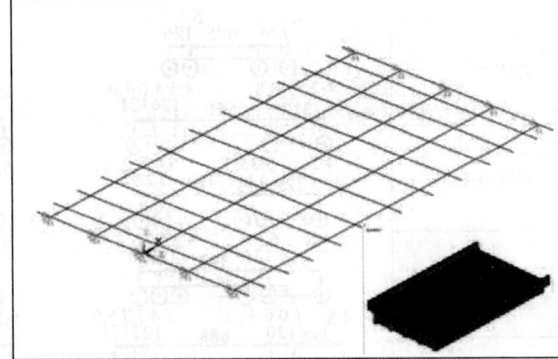

Fig. 3 Modified Grillage Model and Corresponding Solid Model

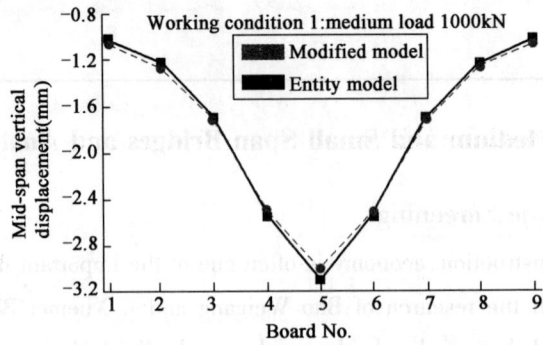

Fig. 4 Modified Transverse Distribution of PSC-10m

4 Truck Load Effect Threshold is Determined

4.1 Bending Resistance Function and Variable Parameters

As the selected Bridges are prefabricated structures, the bending resistance function is established for the section internal beam with the most unfavorable force, as shown in Eq. (1). By default, if the section internal beam of the superstructure fails, the structure fails. The function mainly aims at the bending resistance performance of the section internal beam with the most unfavorable force under the limit state of bearing capacity.

$$Z = R - G - Q - m \tag{1}$$

In Eqs. (1), R, G, Q and m are respectively section resistance, constant load effect, automobile load effect and other load effects. In order to simplify the analysis process and ignore secondary factors, R, G and Q are only taken as random variables, while other load effects are taken as constants. For statically indeterminate structural systems, $m = 0$, and for statically indeterminate structural systems, such as pcb-4 × 20 m, other load effects should also be considered.

According to the study of Yanghai Li et al. (Li, Y. H., Bao, W. G. and Guo, X. W. et al. 1997), structural resistance and constant load effect can be treated as logarithmic normal distribution and normal distribution random variable respectively. The distribution parameters are shown in Tab. 2 (Sykora, M. 2017).

Distribution Parameters of Resistance and Dead Load Effect Tab. 2

Bridge types	R_K	G_K	K_R/δ_R	K_G/δ_R
RCS-6 m	414.8	52	1.2262/0.1414	1.0148/0.0431
PCS-10 m	995.1	169.6		
PCS-20 m	4803.4	1539.9		
PCB-4 ×20 m	6345.4	1610.9		

JC method in reliability analysis, the non-normal random variables in the checking point equivalent normal into a normal random variable, so in the process of truck load limit analysis, can ignore the first random variable Q specific distribution types, in the condition of known coefficient of variation, using the JC method reverse iteration the equivalent normal distribution of the mean.

5 Positive Bending Moment Effect Threshold

According to the research of the Wenjie Li, etc, even in the case of strict control, truck overloading transfinite will still exist, so from the perspective of the theory of probability can be thought of, successful truck load regulation behavior is not strict with all quality must be smaller than the limit of heavy truck in the actual standard, just after the limit load of the truck load peak near the weight standard, and its variability is small, the size of the variability can use all sorts of economic leverage or law enforcement measures to control. The mean value of the equivalent normal distribution of vehicle load effect corresponding to each target reliability index is selected as the threshold of truck load effect. With the aid of MATLAB preparation of JC method backward iteration, in turn, get the corresponding target reliability index is bending effect of threshold value, the result is shown in Fig. 5, visible threshold is increased as the target reliability index is reduced, and because of national highway G104 coefficient of variation of maximum load effect, the sections of the corresponding target reliability index of the threshold value is less than the Xuan large high speed and the Shanghai-Shaanxi expressway.

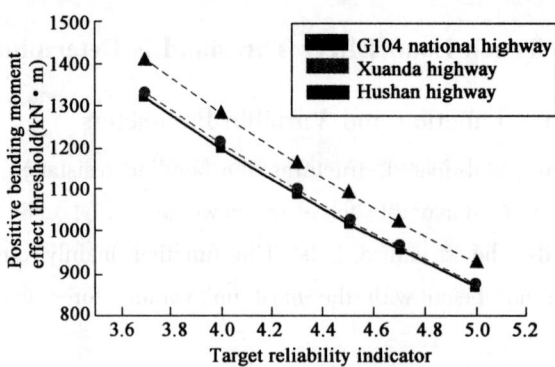

Fig. 5 PCB-4×20m Positive Bending Moment Effect Threshold

6 Truck Load Limit and Analysis

6.1 Condition Setting and Reverse Calculation of Vehicle Mass

When determining the load limit of each type of truck based on the positive bending moment effect threshold, it is necessary to identify the actual possible truck driving conditions across the bridge, and control the inverse calculation of the load limit of truck by the most unfavorable principle. Four typical truck crossing conditions observed through field traffic survey, respectively, one truck passing the bridge alone, two trucks passing along the bridge in different lanes, two trucks following the bridge along the same lane, and two trucks crossing the bridge in parallel.

The video data recorded by the camera can be used to calculate the occurrence probability of four working conditions, and the results are shown in Fig. 6. Visible, bike across the bridge is the most common, but this kind of condition on the structure effects of load level is relatively low, the parallel across the bridge in the actual probability is small, only occupy 1.3% of the total condition, but the structure of the load effect level obviously higher than the previous three kinds of condition, in this based on the principle of the most unfavorable loading choose parallel calculation the working condition of the bridge truck cars of the same quality of load limit.

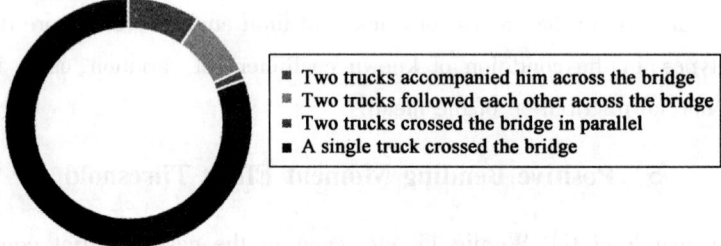

Fig. 6 Scenarios of moving trucks

6.2 Analysis of Truck Load Limit and Its Influencing Factors

Fig. 7a), Fig. 7b) and Fig. 7c) respectively give the analysis results of load limits of different types of trucks corresponding to different target reliability indexes in three sections. First of all, can be seen from the diagram, along with the rising of the target reliability index, the truck load limit is on the decline, further to the G104 national highway as an example, various types of truck load limit is given with the change of target reliability index, visible each type truck load limit approximate linearly increases with the target reliability index decline.

In order to analyse the influence of regional load characteristics on truck load limit. The load limit of each type of truck when the target reliability index is 4.5. It can be seen that the corresponding analysis results of different sections are not the same, mainly because of the differences in load variability in different regions and truck types (size, shaft mass distribution).

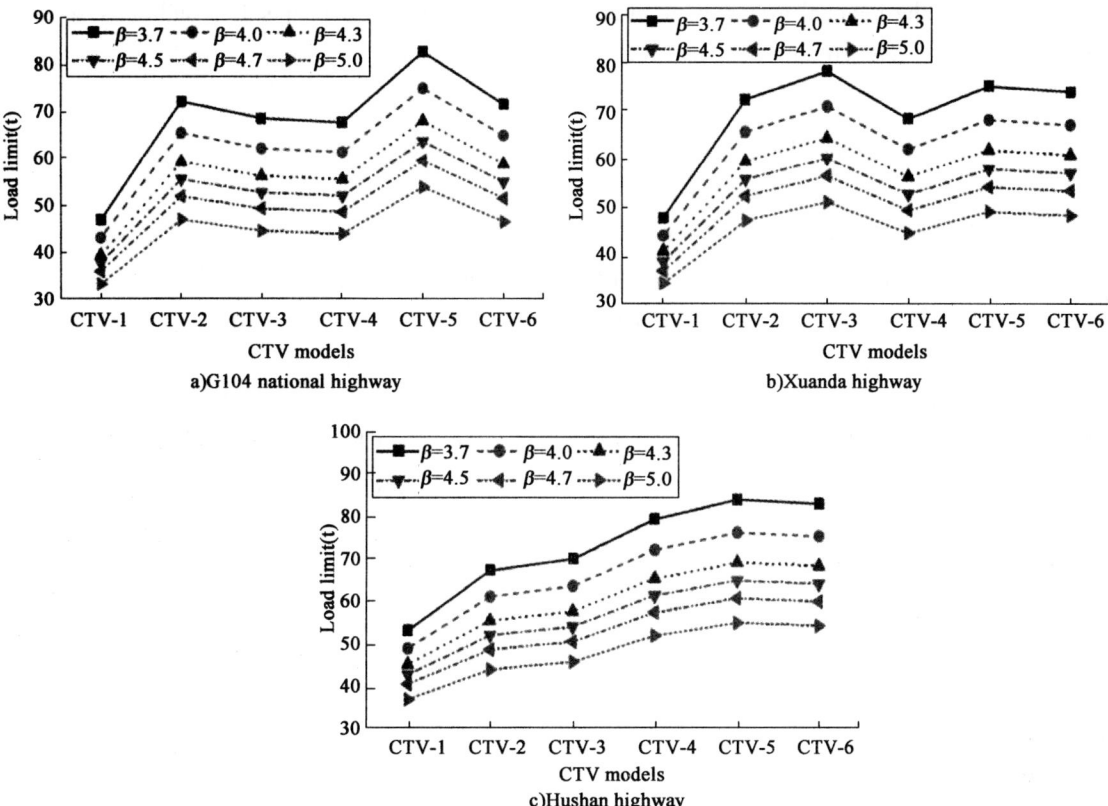

Fig. 7　Analysis Results of Truck Load Limitation

7　Conclusions

Based on the probabilistic analysis model of truck load limit, this paper discusses the limit of heavy truck load in three typical sections of G104 national highway, Xuanda expressway and Shanghai-Shaanxi expressway. First, the truck load characteristics were analysed based on WIM data, and the heavy-duty truck models needed to study load limit were extracted. Secondly, according to the current construction status of medium and small span Bridges in China, the Bridges that control the truck load limit are selected. Thirdly, through the establishment of the function of the critical section of the structure and the determination of the distribution parameters of each random variable, the JC method is adopted to iteratively solve the threshold of positive bending moment effect. Finally, based on the actual traffic flow observation, truck loading condition was selected, and the load limit of each truck type was searched and calculated with the help of ANSYS, and the results were analysed, and the following conclusions were obtained:

(1) The composition of heavy-duty truck models in different sections and load variability are different, but the variation coefficient of positive moment effect of truck load on small and medium-span simply supported beams has a small floating range. When the bridge span exceeds 20m, the truck load effect variability and truck load variability show a strong linear correlation.

(2) The threshold of positive bending moment effect of truck load and load limit value of each vehicle model show a linear decline trend with the increase of target reliability index.

(3) The difference of regional load characteristics has a non-negligible impact on the analysis result of truck load limit, mainly due to the difference of truck model composition and load variability.

(4) The current national highway over-regulation standards still have good applicability to the truck load limitation of medium and small-span Bridges, but it is suggested that different regions should make fine

adjustments based on the national over-regulation standards according to their specific conditions, so as to seek the optimal balance between structural safety and cargo turnover efficiency.

Refernces

[1] Li, W. J. (2009). Research on vehicle load of highway bridge. Dalian university of technology. (in Chinese).

[2] Huang, S. et al. (2012). Failure simulation of reinforced concrete arch bridge collapse caused by overload. Engineering mechanics, 29(S2), 122-127+138. (in Chinese).

[3] Han, W. S., Li Y. W. and Ma L. et al. (2016). Visual simulation of dynamic bridge crossing of heavy load traffic and structural safety evaluation. Beijing: people's communications press, 34-38. (in Chinese).

[4] Yuan, Y. G. (2015). Study on response characteristics, safety evaluation and load limitation of medium and small-span Bridges under heavy loads. Chang'an university. (in Chinese).

[5] Bao, W. G. (2003). Collected works of Bao Wei-Gang. Beijing: people's communications press, 1-20. (in Chinese).

[6] Li, S. H. (2013). Reliability analysis model research on load limit value of highway bridge. Journal of civil engineering, 46(09), 83-90. (in Chinese).

[7] Li, S. H. (2014). Analysis method of bridge load limitation based on vehicle load effect truncated distribution [J]. Engineering mechanics, 31(02), 117-124. (in Chinese).

[8] Li, Y. H., Bao, W. G. and Guo, X. W. et al. (1997). Reliability and probabilistic limit state design of highway and bridge structures. Beijing: people's communications press, 78-87, 148-170. (in Chinese).

[9] Han, W. S., Y. G. Yuan, et al. (2017). Dynamic impact of heavy traffic load on typical T-beam bridges based on WIM data[J]. Perform. Constr. Facil. 31(3): 04017001.

[10] Han, W. S., Y. G. Yuan, et al. (2018). Reliability-based truck weight regulation of small-to medium-span bridges[J]. Bridge Engineering. 23(1): 04017109.

[11] Ruan, X., J. Y. Zhou, et al. (2017). A site-specific traffic load model for long-span multi-pylon cable-stayed bridges[J]. Structure Infrastructure Engineering. 13(4): 494-504.

[12] Sykora, M., D. Diamantidis, et al. (2017) Target reliability for existing structures considering economic and societal aspects[J]. Structure Infrastructure Engineering. 13(1): 181-194.

Research on Non-stationary Characteristics of Wind Field at Bridge Site Based on Multiresolution Analysis

Huan Zhang   Zufeng Liu   Cong Li   Yang Wang

(Chang'an University)

Abstract In order to investigate the non-stationary characteristics of the wind field at the bridge under strong wind conditions, a multiresolution analysis model suitable for non-stationary wind speed is established. Firstly, the non-stationary wind speed model based on wavelet transform is analysed and improved, and the multiresolution analysis model is introduced to the non-stationary wind speed model. Then, in order to verify the reliability of the method, take the typhoon Rumbia at the bridge site detected by the health monitoring system of a cable-stayed bridge along the coast as the research object. Extract the time-varying average wind at the bridge location under the typhoon environment. On this basis, the non-stationary wind characteristics including turbulence intensity, gust factor and power spectral density are calculated and further studied. The results show that there are differences between the stationary wind speed model and the non-stationary wind speed model. The steady wind speed model overestimates the statistical parameters of the relevant wind field, especially in a strong typhoon environment. Therefore, it is necessary to consider the non-stationary characteristics of the wind field. At the same time, the non-stationary wind speed model based on the multiresolution analysis method can better reflect the statistical characteristics of the wind field, and can provide a new idea for the study of non-stationary characteristics in strong wind environments.

Keywords Strong wind   Multiresolution analysis   Non-stationary wind speed model   Wind characteristics   Bridge health monitoring

0 Introduction

Wind field characteristics are the basic and key data for bridge wind resistance design, which affects the bridge's wind resistance safety, driving safety and comfort. Field measurement is the first method to obtain the characteristics of the wind field, followed by physical simulation (wind tunnel test) and numerical simulation (CFD) (Chen 2005).

For the analysis of the statistical characteristics of the measured wind, traditionally mostly based on the assumption of a stable random process, it is believed that the average wind in the basic time interval is a constant wind and the fluctuating wind obeys a Gaussian distribution with a mean value of 0 (Yim and Chou 2001). However, the measured wind records in recent years show that the measured wind speed under strong wind conditions is mostly a non-stationary random process, and the non-stationary characteristics are significant. Research on typhoon characteristics based on the assumption of stability will cause certain deviations in the analysis results (Liao et al. 2019).

For this reason, many scholars at home and abroad have begun to study the characteristics of the wind field based on the assumption of non-stationarity. Xu and Chen (2004) used empirical mode decomposition (EMD) to decompose the wind speed series into time-varying average wind speed and zero mean steady pulsating wind speed, and found that the non-Gaussian characteristic of pulsating wind speed after excluding the time-varying wind speed was significantly weakened. However, the non-stationary characteristics of pulsating wind speed are not discussed. Sun et al (2006) extracted time-varying mean wind by empirical model method and redefined the calculation formula of wind characteristic parameters. Shen et al (2008) used wavelet transform (WT) method and EMD method to extract non-stationary wind speed and time-varying trend terms. The comparative analysis results show that the WT method is more efficient and accurate than the EMD method, and the EMD method has obvious advantages. The end effect of this requires further research and improvement. He et al (2011) conducted a study on the non-stationary wind characteristics of strong winds based on the wavelet transform method for the wind-rain-vibration problem of stay cables of the Dongting Lake Bridge. Wang et al (2016, 2017) used the wavelet transform method to study the long-term wind characteristics of the bridge site based on the structural health monitoring system (SHMS) of Sutong Bridge and Runyang Yangtze River Bridge.

Although scholars at home and abroad have done a lot of work on non-stationary characteristics under strong wind conditions, in general, compared with the research of wind field stability, non-stationary research has not been in-depth and systematic. In addition, the study of wind field monitoring data for the bridge health monitoring system is still in the exploratory stage, and it is of great significance to carry out research on the non-stationary wind characteristics of the measured typhoon.

1 Non-Stationary Wind Speed Model

1.1 Traditional Steady Wind Speed Model

In the steady wind speed model, the downwind wind speed $U(t)$ at a given height in the boundary layer is assumed to be a random process experienced by each state, and it is composed of constant average wind $\overline{U}$ and fluctuating wind $u(t)$. The average wind means that the wind speed and direction do not change with time in a long period, while the pulsating wind changes randomly with time. It should be considered as a random process for analysis.

$$U(t) = \overline{U} + u(t) \tag{1}$$

The first step of wind characteristics analysis is to extract the average wind from the wind downwind time history curve. Then, after removing the average wind, the corresponding pulsating wind is obtained. At present, the extraction of average wind is generally approximate, and natural wind is regarded as a steady Gaussian process experienced by various states, which assumes that the statistical characteristics of the wind field within the basic time interval do not change with the passage of time.

$$E[X(t)] = \overline{x(t)} = \mu_X = \lim_{T \to \infty} \frac{1}{2T} \int_{-T}^{T} x(t) \, dt = \mu_X \tag{2}$$

$$E\{[X(t)X(t+\tau)]\} = \phi_X(\tau) = \lim_{T \to \infty} \frac{1}{2T} \int_{-T}^{T} x(t) x(t+\tau) \, dt = \phi_X(\tau) \tag{3}$$

Based on the steady Gaussian process, as shown in the formula, the average wind speed $\overline{U}$ is synthesized by the vector of wind speed time history $\overline{U}_x$ and $\overline{U}_y$ along two orthogonal directions in the horizontal rectangular coordinate system, and then the forward pulsating wind $u(t)$ and the lateral pulsating wind $v(t)$ are obtained after removing the average wind.

$$\overline{U} = \sqrt{(\overline{U}_x)^2 + (\overline{U}_y)^2} \tag{4}$$

$$\cos\alpha_x = \frac{\overline{U}_x}{\overline{U}}, \cos\alpha_y = \frac{\overline{U}_y}{\overline{U}} \tag{5}$$

$$\begin{aligned} u(t) &= U_x(t) \cdot \cos\alpha_x + U_y(t) \cdot \cos\alpha_y - \overline{U} \\ v(t) &= -U_x(t) \cdot \cos\alpha_y + U_y(t) \cdot \cos\alpha_x \end{aligned} \tag{6}$$

Therefore, the statistical characteristics of the wind field, such as turbulence intensity, gust coefficient, etc., can be obtained in turn according to the average wind speed, forward pulsating wind and lateral pulsating wind.

1.2 Non-stationary Wind Speed Model

In the non-stationary wind speed model, the downwind wind speed $U(t)$ can be expressed as the deterministic time-varying average wind speed part $\overline{U}^*$ and the zero mean fluctuating wind speed part $u^*(t)$, as shown in Eq(7).

$$U(t) = \overline{U}^*(t) + u^*(t) \tag{7}$$

The difference from the steady wind speed model is that $\overline{U}^*(t)$ is the time-varying average wind speed, which also changes with time in the basic time interval, while $\overline{U}$ is a constant value in the basic time interval. For strictly stationary random processes, the non-stationary wind speed model will degenerate into a stationary wind speed model, that is $\overline{U}^*(t) = \overline{U}$.

After the time-varying average wind speed is calculated, the forward pulsating wind u and the lateral pulsating wind v can be calculated in the same way as the steady wind speed model. The calculation method is shown in Eq(8):

$$u^*(t) = U_x^*(t) \cdot \cos\alpha_x^* + U_y^*(t) \cdot \cos\alpha_y^* - \overline{U}^*$$
$$v^*(t) = -U_x^*(t) \cdot \cos\alpha_y^* + U_y^*(t) \cdot \cos\alpha_x^* \tag{8}$$

Therefore, the statistical characteristics of the wind field, such as turbulence intensity and gust coefficient, can also be calculated and derived.

1.3 Non-stationary Model Based on multiresolution Analysis

The main difference between the steady wind speed model and the non-stationary wind speed model is the calculation method of the time-varying average wind speed. The stationary wind speed model regards the time-varying average wind speed as a stationary random process, so it is a definite value. For non-stationary wind speed models, the time-varying average wind speed is regarded as a time-varying value. Commonly used to extract the time-varying average wind speed calculation methods in the non-stationary wind speed time history include moving average(MA), empirical mode decomposition(EMD) and wavelet transform(Wavelet transform, WT).

Among them, the wavelet transforms(Wavelet transform, WT) is a powerful tool for extracting the time-varying average wind due to the fixed and invariable window area. It can analyse the signal from both time and scale at the same time, and has the characteristics of multiresolution.

In order to more effectively extract the time-varying average wind speed of non-stationary wind speed, this paper uses the multiresolution Analysis proposed by S. Mallat to extract the time-varying average wind speed.

The main ideas of the signal decomposition and reconstruction algorithm based on the multiresolution analysis method are shown in Fig. 1. Assume that $S_j f$ is the approximate coefficient of the energy-limited signal at resolution 2^j, then $S_j f$ can be further decomposed into the approximate coefficient ($S_{j-1} f$) of f at the resolution of 0 to 2^{j-1} and the detail coefficient ($D_{j-1} f$) between the resolution of 2^{j-1} to 2^j.

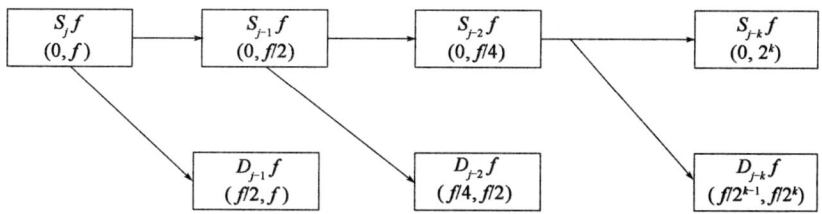

Fig. 1 Wavelet tree decomposition diagram of multiresolution analysis

In this way, the space L is decomposed into subspace sequences with different resolutions, and a signal is represented as a low frequency component and high frequency components at different resolutions.

The specific algorithm is as follows:

Step1: According to the idea of multiresolution analysis, decompose the $S_j f$ signal into two parts: the low-frequency signal $S_{j-1} f$ and the high-frequency signal $D_{j-1} f$.

Step2: Decompose the low-frequency part $S_{j-1} f$ that was previously decomposed again to obtain the new low-frequency signal $S_{j-2} f$ and high-frequency signal $D_{j-2} f$.

Step3: Repeat Step2 until the resolution of the decomposition meets the preset resolution, and finally construct a set of orthogonal wavelet bases that are highly close to the space $L^2(R)$ in frequency.

Step4: Reconstruct a single branch of the wavelet decomposition approximate coefficients obtained in Step3, and remove the detail coefficients to obtain the time-varying average wind.

2 Analysis of Non-stationary Characteristics of Measured Wind at Bridge Location

2.1 Project Overview

The wind field at the location of a cable-stayed bridge is selected as the research object. The main span of the bridge is 580m, and the bridge deck width is 27.6m. The bridge span layout of 48m + 48m + 50m + 580m + 50m + 48m + 48m, and the bridge is a hybrid cable-stayed bridge with two towers and two cable planes and a semi-floating system. The bridge is located in the coastal area, which is a typical monsoon climate area with frequent typhoons and the wind field at the bridge site is more complicated.

In order to monitor the wind environment at the bridge site in real time, the bridge health monitoring system is equipped with a special wind environment monitoring subsystem. The monitoring system includes a propeller anemometer and a three-way ultrasonic anemometer. The propeller anemometer is installed on the top of the tower and the three-way ultrasonic anemometer is installed in the middle of the main beam, as shown in Fig. 2.

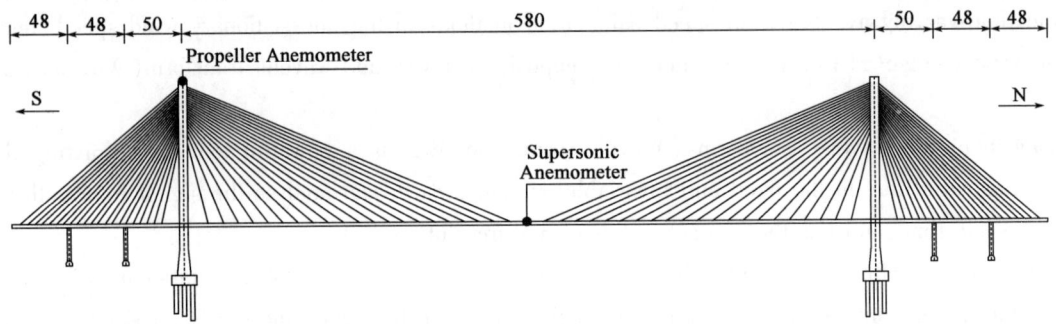

Fig. 2 Anemometer of a Cable-stayed Bridge Health Monitoring System (Unit: m)

Taking the typhoon Rumbia which occurred 30 km away from the bridge site on August 16, 2018 as the object, the non-stationary characteristics of its strong wind environment are studied. Fig. 3 shows the wind speed recorded by the health monitoring system before and after typhoon Rumbia. It can be seen from Fig. 3 that the main impact time of typhoon Rumbia is from 12:00 on the 16th to 6:00 on the 17th, and the time period with the highest wind speed at the bridge location are 15:00-20:00 on the 16th and 2:00-6:00 on the 17th.

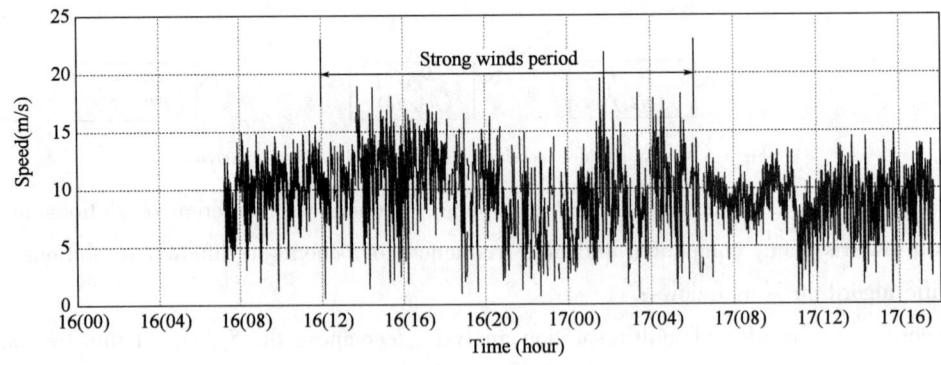

Fig. 3 Wind speed during Typhoon Rumbia

2.2 Time-varying Average Wind Speed

The time-varying trend item included in the non-stationary wind speed model can reflect the time-varying characteristics of non-stationary wind speed. This paper takes the basic time interval of 10 min recommended by the "Wind-resistant Design Specification for Highway Bridges" (Tongji 2019) as a single sample duration. The multiresolution analysis method (Multiscale) was used to extract the time-varying average wind in the measured typhoon, and the results were compared with the constant average wind (Constant) in the steady wind speed model and the empirical mode decomposition (EMD) extraction effect in the non-stationary wind speed model. In the multiresolution analysis, wavelet decomposition is performed by using coif-5 wavelet and the time history of the time-varying average wind in some time periods after extraction is shown in Fig. 4.

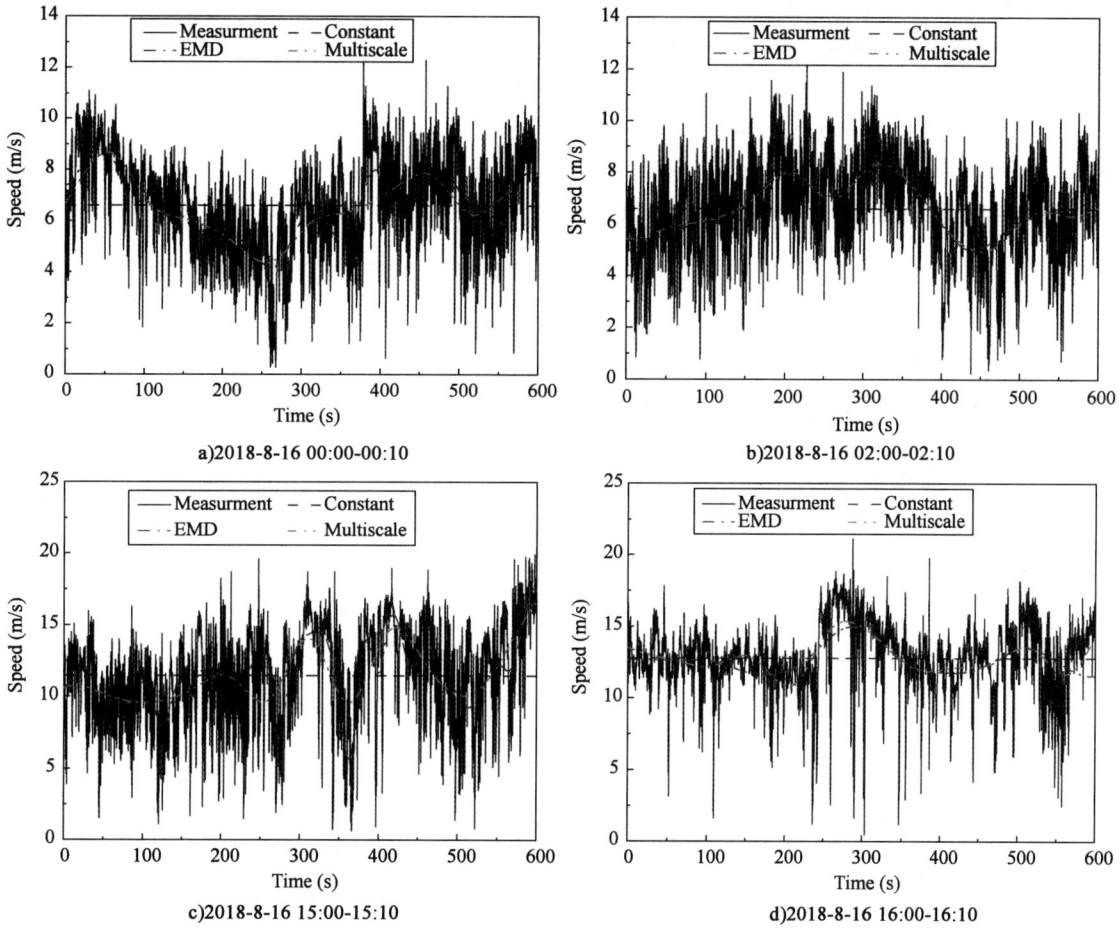

Fig. 4 Time-varying Average Wind during Typhoon Rumbia

It can be seen from Fig. 4 that the non-stationary wind speed model decomposes the measured wind into time-varying average wind and fluctuating wind. Compared with the steady wind speed model, the time-varying average wind has a time-varying effect on the basis of the constant wind, which fluctuates up and down. On the other hand, compared with the empirical mode decomposition (EMD) method, the time-varying average wind extracted based on the multiresolution analysis can better reflect the non-stationary characteristics of the measured wind speed in the strong wind environment, and has the characteristics of multiresolution, which is more adaptable in strong wind environment. Compared with the wavelet transform, the EMD method has obvious end effect, and there is an overfitting effect in some areas (Fig. 4c), and the fluctuation is severe. In a comprehensive comparison, the time-varying wind speed extracted from the non-stationary wind speed model based on multiresolution analysis performs better.

2.3 Turbulence Intensity and Gust Factor

2.3.1 Turbulence Intensity

The intensity of turbulence can be used to characterize the average variation amplitude of the pulsation component. The turbulence intensity corresponding to the downwind and crosswind directions based on the non-stationary wind speed model is represented by I_u^* and I_v^* respectively, and the calculation formula is as shown in Equation(9).

$$I_a^* = \frac{\sigma_a^*}{\overline{U}^*} \quad (a = u, v) \quad (9)$$

In the Equation(9), σ_a^* is the pulsating wind variance in the non-stationary model; $\overline{U}^*$ is the time-varying average wind speed in the non-stationary model; u and v represent the downwind and crosswind directions, respectively.

In order to study the influence of non-stationary characteristics on the intensity of turbulence, the turbulence intensity of the measured typhoon Rumbia was calculated based on the steady wind speed model and the non-stationary wind speed model. The calculation results are shown in Fig. 5 and Fig. 6.

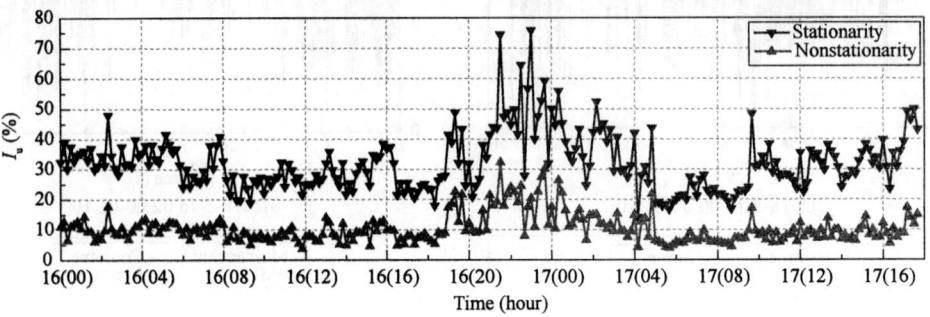

Fig. 5   Change of longitudinal direction turbulence intensity(I_u)

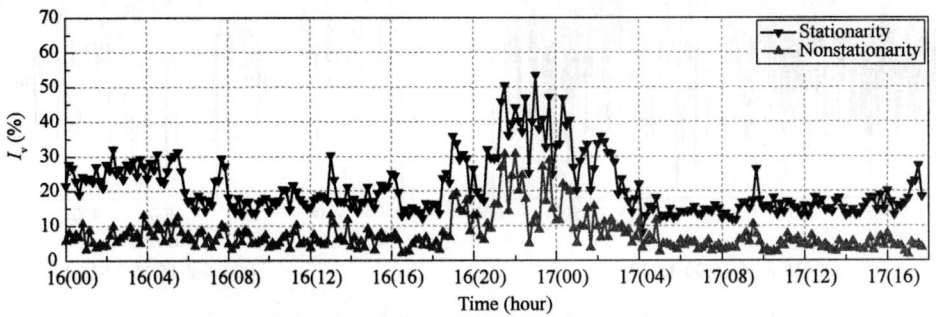

Fig. 6   Change of lateral direction turbulence intensity(I_v)

It can be seen from Fig. 5 and Fig. 6: ①The typhoon turbulence intensity and its variation range based on the non-stationary wind speed model are generally smaller than the results based on the stationary model; ②In a strong wind environment, the non-stationary characteristics of the wind field are enhanced. The calculation result of the stationary model overestimates the intensity of turbulence. At this time, the analysis result based on the non-stationary wind speed model is more reasonable.

2.3.2   Gust factor

The gust factor can be used to characterize the short-term variation range of pulsating wind, and it is defined as the proportional coefficient between the instantaneous wind speed with a time interval of 1-3s and the average wind speed with a time interval of 10min. In order to study the influence of non-stationary characteristics on the gust coefficients, the gust coefficients of the measured typhoon Rumbia are calculated based on the non-stationary wind speed model. And the calculation results of the gust factor are shown in Fig. 7.

It can be seen from Fig. 7: the gust factor based on the non-stationary wind speed model has a strong correlation with the wind field environment. During the period of strong wind(2018-8-16 16:00-2018-8-16 04:00), the non-stationary characteristics of the wind field increase, and the gust factor changes drastically. At this time, the analysis result based on the non-stationary wind speed model is more reasonable.

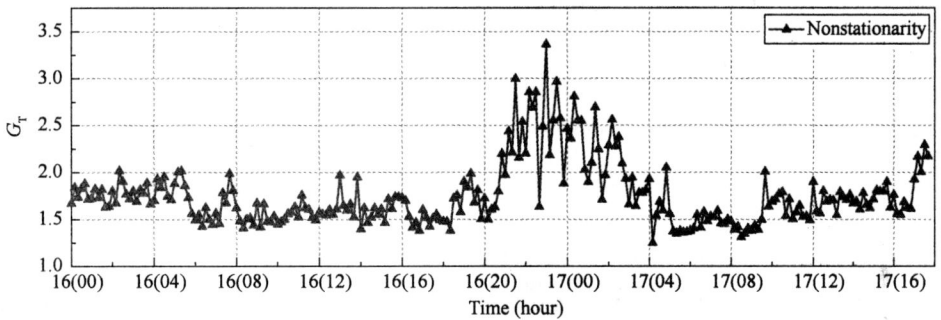

Fig. 7 Change of gust factor during typhoon Rumbia

2.3.3 Correlation between turbulence intensity and gust factor

For turbulence intensity and gust factor, it can be seen from the figure that there is a strong correlation. At the same time, Ishizaki(1983) Choi(1983) and Cao et al(2009) studied the correlation between the turbulence intensity and the gust factor based on the measured wind speed and proposed a mathematical model between the turbulence intensity and the gust factor in the downwind direction, as shown in Equation(10):

$$G_u = 1 + k_1 I_u^{k_2} \ln \frac{T}{t_g} \tag{10}$$

In order to study the correlation between turbulence intensity and gust factor at the bridge site, regression fitting was performed on the measured turbulence intensity and gust factor based on the stationary model and the non-stationary model. The regression fitting results are shown in Fig. 8.

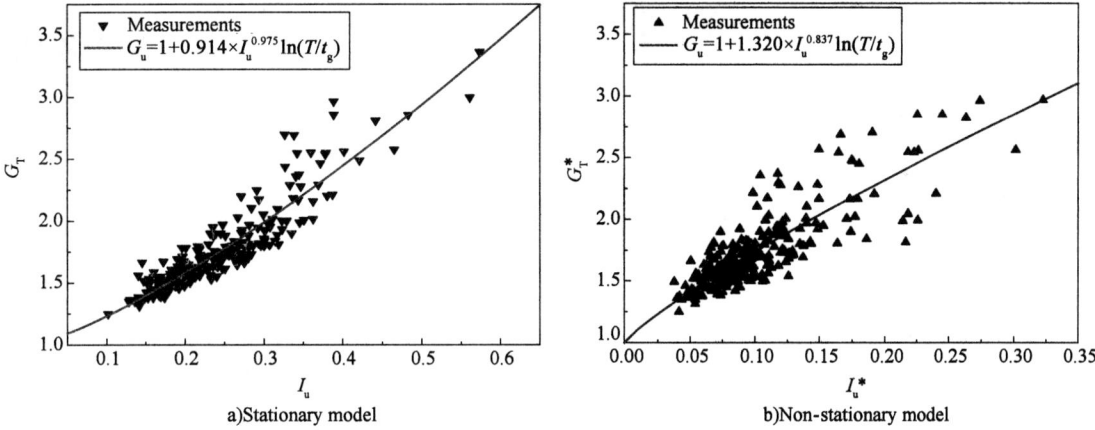

a) Stationary model   b) Non-stationary model

Fig. 8 The Correlation between Turbulence and Gust Factors of Typhoon Rumbia

It can be seen from Fig. 8 that whether it is a stationary model or a non-stationary model, the gust factor of pulsating wind generally increases with the increase of turbulence intensity. This indicates that there is a close relationship between the gust factor and turbulence intensity of pulsating wind, and the two are generally consistent in characterizing the turbulence characteristics of pulsating wind.

However, the relationship between gust factor and turbulence intensity is basically the same in different wind speed models, but the results of different wind speed models are still different. The parameter k1 calculated by the non-stationary model is larger than that of the stationary model, and k2 is smaller than that of the stationary model.

2.4 Wind Speed Power Spectrum

In order to obtain the pulsating wind spectrum characteristics of the measured temperature of the typhoon, the steady wind speed model and the non-stationary wind speed model were used to calculate the pulsating wind of the measured typhoon, and the corresponding power spectral density function (PSD) was obtained. And compare it with commonly used wind spectrum such as Davenport spectrum, Simiu spectrum and Karman spectrum. The calculation results of longitudinal fluctuating wind power spectral density and transverse fluctuating wind power spectral density are shown in Fig. 9 and Fig. 10.

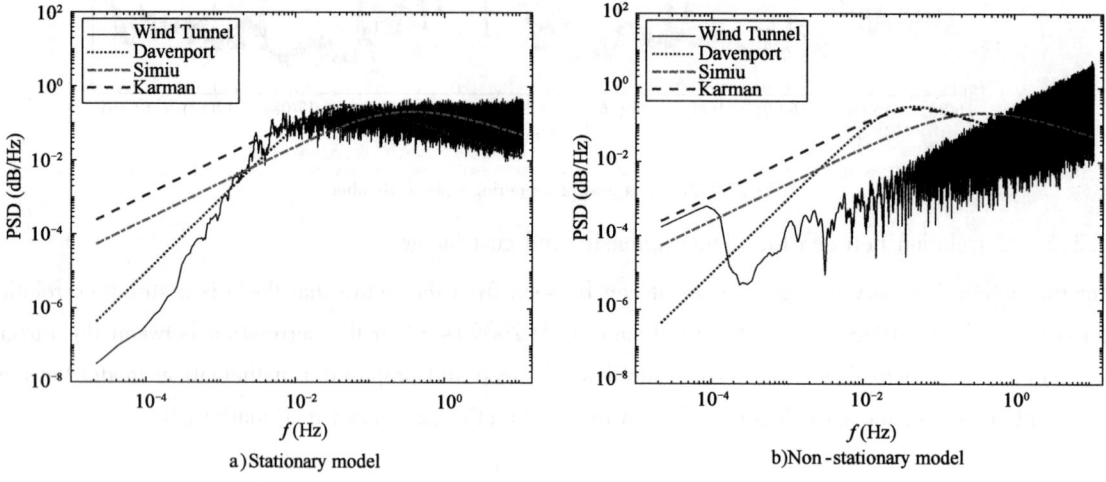

Fig. 9　The power spectral (Longitudinal direction)

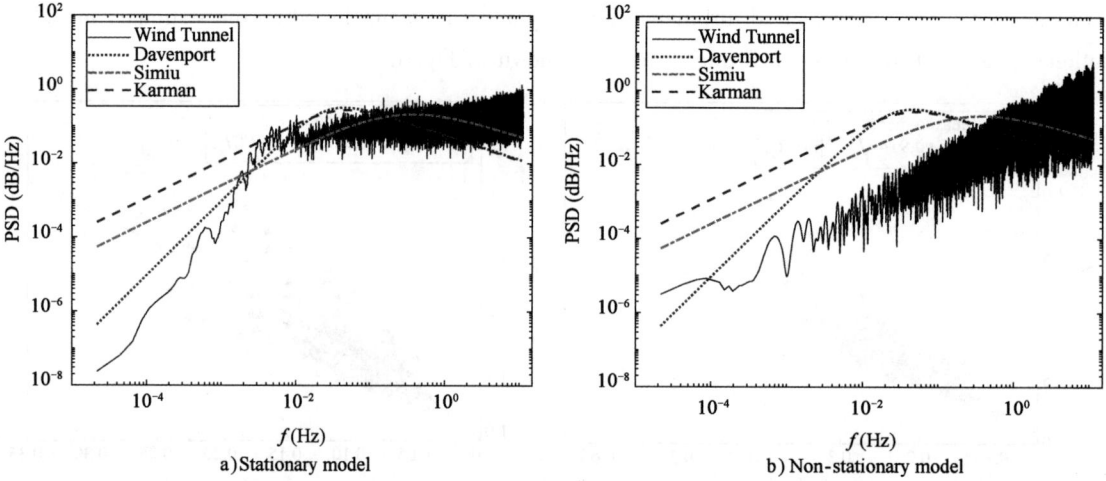

Fig. 10　The power spectral density (Lateral direction)

It can be seen from Fig. 9 and Fig. 10 that the power spectrum density:

(1) For the stationary model, the measured downwind and crosswind power spectrum and the Simiu spectrum recommended by the specification have a good fit in the high frequency region, but the Simiu spectrum in the low frequency region cannot It is a good representation of the power spectrum of the measured typhoon. For the non-stationary model, the measured power spectral density in the downwind direction and the crosswind direction are difficult to express with three existing turbulent wind spectra. Explain that if the non-stationary characteristics of typhoons are considered, the wind spectrum needs to be further studied based on the measured wind.

(2) For the stationary wind speed model and the non-stationary wind speed model, the measured wind spectrum and the recommended wind spectrum have common characteristics. In other words, these three suggested spectra overestimate the fluctuating wind energy in the low frequency region, but underestimate the fluctuating wind energy in the high frequency region.

(3) Compared with the fluctuating wind spectrum model that does not consider the non-stationary characteristics, since the time-varying average wind containing low-frequency components is excluded, the wind spectrum of the non-stationary wind speed model and the wind spectrum of the stationary wind speed model are basically the same in the high frequency region. But there is a big difference between the low frequency area and the middle frequency area.

3 Conclusions

In order to study the non-stationary characteristics of wind field under strong wind environment, the non-stationary wind speed model established by the multiresolution analysis method is adopted. An analysis of the non-stationary characteristics of the measured wind field at the site of a cable-stayed bridge along the coast was carried out, and the following conclusions were obtained:

(1) Compared with the empirical mode decomposition method (EMD), the time-varying average wind speed extracted based on the multiresolution analysis method can effectively eliminate the end effect, and the time-varying average wind extracted by the multiresolution analysis method is better.

(2) The typhoon turbulence intensity, gust factor and their variation range obtained based on the non-stationary wind speed model are generally smaller than those obtained from the stationary model. The stationary wind speed model overestimates the turbulence intensity, and the analysis result based on the non-stationary wind speed model is more reasonable.

(3) Compared with the fluctuating wind spectrum model that does not consider stationarity, the wind spectrum of the non-stationary model and the wind spectrum of the stationary model are basically the same in the high-frequency region, but there are big differences in the low-frequency and middle-frequency regions.

(4) For strong wind conditions, especially typhoons, it is necessary to consider the non-stationarity of the wind field. The non-stationary wind speed model established based on the multiresolution analysis method can better reflect the statistical characteristics of the wind field and it can provide a basis for the bridge wind resistance design.

References

[1] Cao, S., Tamura, Y., Kikuchi, N., et al. (2009) Wind characteristics of a strong typhoon. Journal of Wind Engineering & Industrial Aerodynamics, 97, 11-21.

[2] Chen, Z. 2005. Bridge wind engineering. : China Communications Press.

[3] Choi, E. C. C. (1983) Gradient Height and Velocity Profile during Typhoons. Journal of Wind Engineering and Industrial Aerodynamics, 13, 31-41.

[4] He, X., Chen, Z., Li, C, et al. (2011) Nonstationary wind characteristics analysis for wind-rain induced vibration of stay cables. Zhendong yu Chongji/Journal of Vibration and Shock, 30, 54-60.

[5] Ishizaki, H. (1983) Wind profiles, turbulence intensities and gust factors for design in typhoon-prone regions. Journal of Wind Engineering and Industrial Aerodynamics, .

[6] Liao, H., Li, M., Ma, C., et al. (2019) State-of-the-art review of bridge wind engineering in 2019. Journal of Civil and Environmental Engineering, 1-11.

[7] Shen, J. H., Li, C. X. and Li, J. H. (2008) Extracting Time-varying Mean of The Non-stationary Wind Speeds Based on Wavelet Transform (WT) and EMD. Zhendong yu Chongji/Journal of Vibration and Shock, 27, 126-130.

[8] Sun, H., Chen, W. and Chen, J. (2006) Nonstatioanry Wind Speed Model and Its Application in Strong Winds. Journal of Disaster Prevention and Mitigation Engineering, 52-57.

[9] Tongji, U. 2019. Wind-resistant Design Specification for Highway Bridges. : China Communications Press

[10] Wang, H., Yang, M., Tao, T., et al. (2017) Analysis on non-stationary wind characteristics of measured strong winds at the site of Sutong Bridge. Zhendong Gongcheng Xuebao/Journal of Vibration Engineering, 30, 312-318.

[11] Wang, H., Mao, J., Yang, M., et al. (2016) Study on non-stationary characteristics of measured typhoons at Runyang Suspension Bridge site. Zhendong Gongcheng Xuebao/Journal of Vibration Engineering, 29, 298-304.

[12] Xu, Y. L. and Chen, J. (2004) Characterizing nonstationary wind speed using empirical mode decomposition[J]. Journal of Structural Engineering, 130, 912-920.

[13] Yim, J. Z. and Chou, C. R. (2001) A study of the characteristic structures of strong wind[J]. Atmospheric Research, 57, 151-170.

基于有限元的钢围堰施工阶段分析

朱豪杰 张谢东 汪 威 李志锋 潘靖勃

(武汉理工大学交通学院)

摘 要 为了确保河谷汉江大桥23号主墩钢板桩围堰施工顺利进行，依据此钢围堰工程的设计施工方案，采用有限元软件Midas/Civil建立钢围堰空间有限元模型，将施工过程划分为六个施工阶段，进行有限元施工阶段分析，计算了六个工况下各构件的最大应力与变形。采用理正软件建立平面有限元模型，对基坑的稳定性进行计算与复核。计算结果表明，此钢板桩围堰内力与变形均满足要求。

关键词 钢板桩围堰 施工阶段分析 有限元 稳定性

0 引 言

钢围堰在水中施工时，钢板桩在土体、腰梁及内支撑的约束下需承受复杂的外部荷载。为了确保施工安全，钢围堰结构分析尤为重要[1]。通过查阅文献可知，围堰的结构分析可采用等值梁法或平面有限元等简化方法[2-3]。为了提高计算精度以及计算结果可视化，采用有限单元法建立空间模型计算更具优越性[4]。本文结合空间有限元法和平面有限元法，对汉江河谷大桥23号主墩围堰进行施工阶段分析。

1 工程概况

1.1 围堰信息

此大桥主桥跨径为110m+200m+110m的双塔单索面预应力混凝土部分斜拉桥。23号主墩承台位于河道中，河床高程72.261m，承台尺寸为24m×19m×5.5m，承台下有20根80m桩长、2m桩径的钻孔灌注桩。23号墩承台围堰设计参数如表1所示。钢围堰立面图见图1，平面布置图见图2。

23号墩承台围堰设计参数　　　　　表1

项 目	参 数	备 注
钢板桩底、顶高程	+61m、+79m	钢板桩长18m
承台底、顶高程	+66.5m、+72m	基坑底面高程+66.3m
设计高水位	+78m	
最大水头差	11.7m	

续上表

项　目	参　数	备　注
设计水流速度	2.23m/s	
设计风速	6级	
封底混凝土厚度	0.2m	

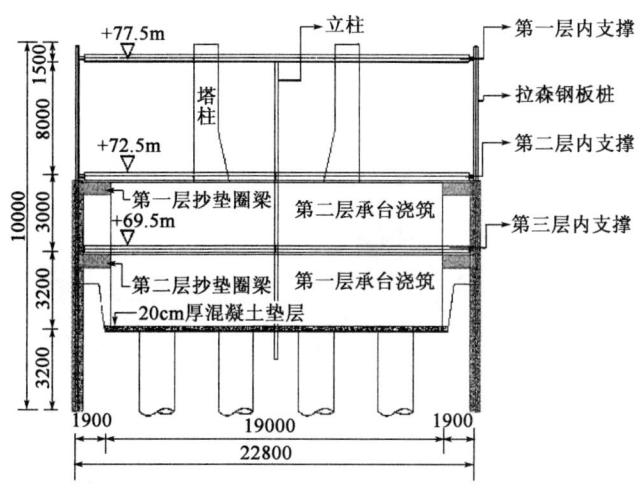

图1　钢围堰立面图(尺寸单位:m)　　　　　图2　内支撑平面图(尺寸单位:m)

1.2　材料特性与土体参数

（1）拉森Ⅳ$_w$型钢板桩材质 Q295bz，设计允许应力$[\sigma]=230$MPa。支撑体系材质为钢材 Q235B，抗拉、抗压与抗弯强度设计值均为 215MPa，抗剪强度设计值为 125MPa。

（2）河床至钢板桩底间存在卵石、强风化细砂岩，土体参数如表2所示。

土 体 参 数 表　　　　表2

岩层名称	土层厚度(m)	饱和重度(kN/m³)	浮重度(kN/m³)	快剪试验	
				内摩擦角φ(°)	黏聚力c(kPa)
卵石	3.6	20	10	36	0
强风化泥质粉砂岩	7.5	20	10	40	20

2　有限元施工阶段分析

钢板桩、内支撑、腰梁、立柱均用梁单元进行模拟，封底混凝土用实体单元模拟。空间模型共12166个节点，11416个单元。钢板桩围堰有限元空间模型如图3所示，钢板桩围堰有限元局部详图如图4所示。

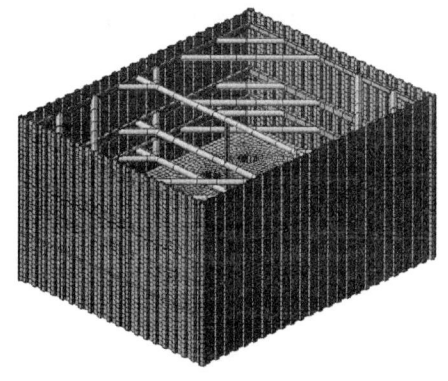

图3　钢板桩围堰有限元模型

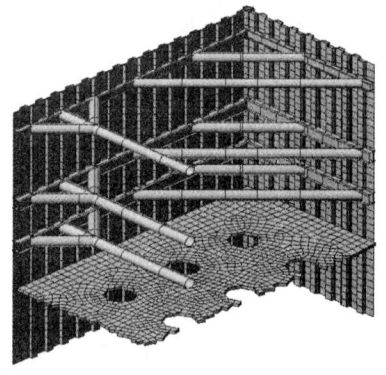

图4　钢板桩围堰有限元局部详图

2.1 计算工况划分

在围堰的施工进程中选取6个代表工况。

第一工况:拼装第一层腰梁与内支撑,围堰内抽水至设计高程+72m;

第二工况:设置第二层腰梁与内支撑,围堰内抽水开挖至设计高程+69m;

第三工况:装配第三层腰梁与内支撑,围堰内抽水开挖至设计高程+66.3m;

第四工况:第一层承台顶部浇筑50cm厚混凝土圈梁,拆除第三层腰梁与内支撑;

第五工况:第二层承台顶部浇筑50cm厚混凝土圈梁,拆除第二层腰梁与内支撑;

第六工况:围堰内回水至设计高程+77m,拆除第一层腰梁与内支撑。

如图5、图6所示。

图5 安装腰梁内支撑

图6 插打钢板桩

2.2 荷载计算

土压力计算基本假定:围堰外侧所受土压力视为主动土压力,围堰内侧所受土压力视为被动土压力。根据W.J.M郎金(RanKing)理论可求得各个施工阶段土压力[5]。静水压力随水深线性增加,流动水压力根据《港口荷载规范》(JTS 144-1—2010)[6]计算,采用如下公式:

$$F_w = C_w \frac{\rho}{2} v^2 A \tag{1}$$

式中:F_w——水流力标准值(kN);

C_w——水流阻力系数;

ρ——水密度(t/m³),淡水取1.0;

v——水流设计流速(m/s);

A——计算构件在与流向垂直平面上的投影面积(m²)。

计算$F_w=21.56$kN,流水压力随着水深线性减小,假定为倒三角形分布,其合力的作用点位于水位线以下1/3水深处。

2.3 边界条件计算

钢板桩在考虑桩土效应时土弹簧刚度计算如下:假定土体是线弹性的连续介质,等代土弹簧刚度由"m法"计算[7],其公式为:

$$K_s = a \times b_p \times m \times z \tag{2}$$

式中:a——土层的厚度(m);

b_p——该土层在垂直于计算模型所在平面的方向上的宽度(m);

m——非岩石地基水平向抗力系数的比例系数(kN/m⁴);

z——土层的深度(m)。

桩的计算宽度 $b_p = 1.2$m。由地勘报告,$m_{卵石层} = 100000$kN/m^4,$m_{强风风化层} = 20000$kN/m^4,将两层土的比例系数换算成一个 m 值,$m = 53440$kN/m^4。

2.4 有限元分析结果

各工况下钢围堰各构件应力及变形结果汇总见表3。工况二各构件应力变形情况如图7所示。

钢围堰各构件应力及变形结果(应力:MPa;变形:mm)　　　表3

名称	应力与变形	工况一	工况二	工况三	工况四	工况五	工况六
钢板桩	最大应力	58.830	64.290	77.460	117.430	83.910	33.740
	最大变形	13.301	14.396	25.432	20.832	9.359	9.749
第一层围檩	最大应力	141.210	145.080	199.490	182.510	10.2.830	
	最大变形	12.692	13.600	24.222	19.863	9.145	
第二层内支撑	最大应力	45.630	44.350	56.390	48.10	42.560	
	最大变形	29.553	29.574	29.659	29.545	29.491	
第二层围檩	最大应力		52.790	166.830	132.110		
	最大变形		8.419	14.118	10.827		
第二层内支撑	最大应力		46.290	84.900	77.330		
	最大变形		22.970	23.015	22.905		
第三层围檩	最大应力			60.780			
	最大变形			8.440			
第三层围檩	最大应力			50.080			
	最大变形			22.641			
立柱	最大应力			4.130			
	最大变形			23.015			

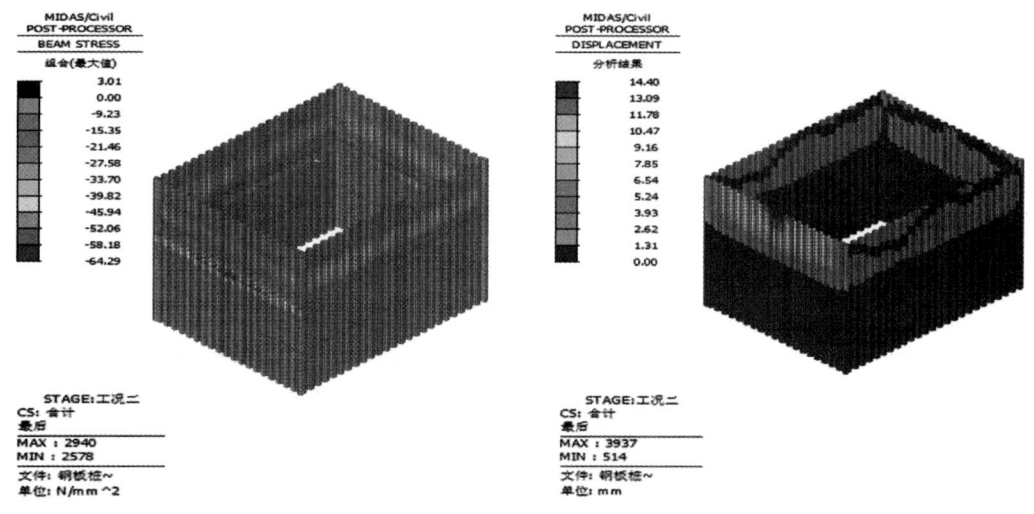

a)钢板桩的应力　　　　　　　　b)钢板桩的变形

图 7

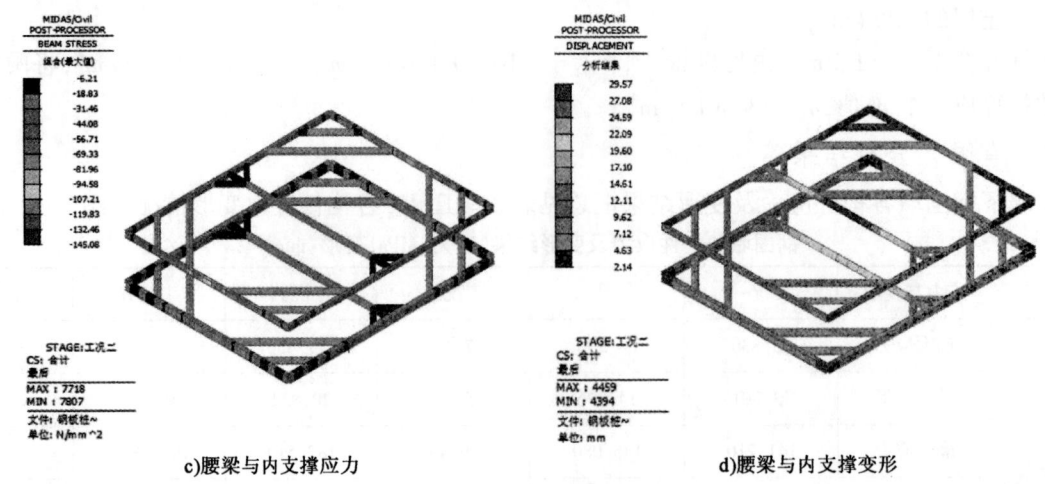

c) 腰梁与内支撑应力　　　　　　d) 腰梁与内支撑变形

图7　工况2计算结果

3　基坑稳定性分析

3.1　内支撑稳定性验算

在第一层内支撑中,八字撑最大轴力为117.8kN,角撑最大轴力391.2kN,对撑最大轴力328.8kN。在第二、三层内支撑中,八字撑最大轴力为552.9kN,角撑最大轴力1369.4kN,对撑最大轴力1400.1kN。根据《钢结构设计标准》(GB 50017—2017)5.1.2实腹式轴心受压构件的稳定性计算公式[8]为:

$$\sigma = \frac{N}{\varphi A} < f \tag{3}$$

式中:σ——实际应力(MPa);

N——受压构件所受轴力(N);

φ——折减系数;

A——受压构件的截面面积(mm);

f——材料容许应力(MPa)。

经过计算各层内支撑的稳定性均满足规范要求。

3.2　基坑底部隆起验算

根据《建筑基坑支护技术规程》(JGJ 120—2012)4.2.4条,支撑式支挡结构,其嵌固深度应满足坑底抗隆起稳定性要求[9]。抗隆起稳定性可按下式计算:

$$\frac{\gamma_{m2}DN_q + cN_c}{\gamma_{m1}(h+D) + q_0} \geqslant K_{he} \tag{4}$$

式中:K_{he}——抗隆起安全系数,此围堰安全等级为一级,K_{he}不应小于1.8;

γ_{m1}——围堰外桩底以上土的重度(kN/m³);

γ_{m2}——围堰内桩底以上土的重度(kN/m³);

D——桩体入土深度(m);

h——围堰开挖深度(m);

N_c、N_q——承载力系数,钢板桩底为强风化细砂岩,由桩底土层的内摩擦角计算得$N_q = 64.11$,$N_c = 75.21$。

计算式(4)等号左边等于28.84,大于抗隆起安全系数规定下限值1.8,钢板桩坑底抗隆起稳定性满足要求。

3.3　基坑整体抗倾覆稳定性验算

取单位宽度进行计算,流水压力$P = 21.56$kN。对钢板桩底部取矩,流水压力产生的力矩$M_w = 345.82$kN·m,主动土压力产生的力矩$M_{Ka} = 152.8$kN·m,被动土压力产生的力矩$M_{Kp} = 2345.89$kN·m,

稳定安全系数 K 计算如下：

$$K = \frac{M_{K_p}}{M_{K_a} + M_w} \tag{5}$$

稳定安全系数 $K=4.70$，大于稳定安全系数下限值 2，基坑整体抗倾覆稳定性满足要求。

3.4 围堰坑底涌砂验算

若围堰底存在砂土，桩侧水头差过大可能引起涌砂的危险，避免引起坑底涌砂的条件是紧靠钢板桩土体的垂直向上渗透力不超过土的浮重度。其计算公式如下：

$$K = \frac{\gamma'}{j} \tag{6}$$

$$j = i\gamma_w \tag{7}$$

式中：K——抗管涌安全系数，取 1.5；

γ'——土的浮重度（kN/m^3）；

j——最大渗流力（kN/m^3）；

i——水头梯度；

γ_w——水的重度，取 $10kN/m^3$。

围堰内抽水开挖最大水头差 11.7m，施工时浇筑封底混凝土后抽水无涌砂现象，故涌砂验算仅考虑封底前。

当基坑开挖至底面且未浇筑封底混凝土时为最不利工况，计算得抗管涌安全系数为 1.91，大于抗管涌安全系数下限 1.5，基坑坑底抗涌砂安全系数满足要求。

3.5 钢板桩最小入土深度的计算

首先确定钢板桩桩体反弯点的位置，计算反弯点至封底混凝土底面距离 l_1 与桩体反弯点截面的剪力 R_p，建立反弯点至桩底的钢板桩有限元模型，找出钢板桩在剪力 R_p 和土压力共同作用下的弯矩零点位置，求得反弯点距离弯矩零点的距离 l_2，从而得到封底混凝土底面至弯矩零点的距离 $t_0 = l_1 + l_2$，最后按 $t = Kt_0$ 计算桩体的入土深度，其中 K 为经验系数，取 $K=1.2$。

计算钢板桩最小入土深度的最不利工况为工况四，此时钢板桩入土深度为 5.3m。由于主动土压力存在负值区，且其值相对于静水压力较小，故可忽略主动土压力，计算时只取水压力为最不利外侧压力，计算得到最小入土深度 $t_0 = 3.216m$，满足钢板桩最小入土深度要求。

4 基坑稳定性验算

利用理正深基坑软件建立平面有限元模型。计算依据为《建筑基坑支护技术规程》[9]（JGJ 120—2012），内力计算采用增量法，支护结构安全等级为一级，支护结构重要性系数为 1.0，基坑深度为 12.7m，嵌固深度为 5.3m，钢板桩截面参数见表 2，无冠梁与防水帷幕，无放坡无超载。

（1）基坑抗隆起验算

基坑底部抗隆起安全系数 $K_{s1} = 29.576 \geqslant 1.800$，抗隆起稳定性满足要求。

（2）抗倾覆稳定性验算

最小安全系数 $K_{ov} = 4.669 \geqslant 1.250$，满足抗倾覆要求。

（3）整体稳定验算

整体稳定安全系数 $K_{s2} = 3.660 \geqslant 1.35$，满足整体稳定要求。

（4）嵌固深度构造验算

嵌固构造深度等于嵌固构造深度系数与基坑深度的乘积，计算得最小嵌固构造深度为 2.540m，满足钢板桩最小入土深度的要求。

平面有限元模型求解与空间有限元模型求解相符，复核基坑稳定性满足要求。

5 结语

经过有限元施工阶段分析,各工况下各构件的强度、刚度、稳定性均满足规范要求,基坑稳定性也满足要求。施工阶段的危险点如下:①工况一至工况五,最大应力均出现在第一层腰梁处,应力最大值为199.490MPa。②工况一至工况五,最大变形均出现在第一层内支撑对撑处,挠度最大值为29.659mm。③在各个工况下,钢板桩产生的最大位移均发生在迎水面钢板桩顶部。

针对可能存在的安全隐患,通过适当调整各层腰梁与内支撑的竖向间距,增加内支撑与竖支撑,在钢板桩顶部设置一层冠梁等措施,增加结构安全储备。

参考文献

[1] Khee-Kwong Han, Meen-Wah Gui. An investigation on a failed double-wall cofferdam during construction[J]. Engineering failure analysis, 2009, 16(1): 421-432.
[2] 张骏. 深水基础钢板桩围堰最小入土深度分析[J]. 石家庄铁道大学学报(自然科学版), 2013, 26(3): 37-42.
[3] 李劲松. 某大桥7号墩钢板桩围堰方案设计及计算[J]. 中外建筑, 2019(09): 160-161.
[4] 杜闯, 丁红岩, 张浦阳, 等. 钢板桩围堰有限元分析[J]. 岩土工程学报, 2014, 36(S2): 159-164.
[5] 钱建固, 袁聚云. 土质学与土力学[M]. 北京: 浙江大学出版社, 2015.
[6] 中国港湾工程有限责任公司. 港口工程荷载规范[M]. 北京: 人民交通出版社股份有限公司, 2016.
[7] 李国豪. 桥梁结构稳定与振动[M]. 北京: 中国铁道出版社, 1996.
[8] 中华人民共和国国家标准. 钢结构设计规范: GB 50017—2017[S]. 北京: 中国建筑工业出版社, 2017.
[9] 中华人民共和国住房和城乡建设部. 建筑基坑支护技术规程: JGJ 120—2012[S]. 北京: 中国建筑工业出版社, 2012.

The Effect of Ernst Equation on the Dynamic Characteristics of Double-Tower Cable-Stayed Bridge with Different Heights of Towers

Lu Wang

(School of Highway, Chang'an University)

Abstract In order to study the influence of Ernst equation on the dynamic characteristics of double-tower cable-stayed bridges with different heights of towers, taking a double-tower cable-stayed bridges with different heights of towers as a research background, considering the Ernst equation and not considering the Ernst equation, an ANSYS model is established for dynamic analysis. The analysis results show that there is error between the double-tower cable-stayed bridges with different heights of towers without considering the Ernst equation and with considering the Ernst equation, so when constructing a double-tower cable-stayed bridges with different heights of towers, the Ernst equation should be considered.

Keywords Ernst equation Double-tower cable-stayed bridges with different heights of towers Dynamic characteristics Error

0 Introduction

With the development of society and the advancement of technology, the application of cable-stayed bridges is increasing at home and abroad[1-11]. During the construction of the cable-stayed bridge model[12-17], the sag effect of the cable affects the quality of the model and also affects the safety of the actual bridge. With considering Ernst equation and not considering Ernst equation, this paper take a double-tower cable-stayed bridge with different heights of towers as the research background, and according to the actual situation, an ANSYS model is established to perform dynamic analysis, and at the same time, deepen the understanding of the Ernst equation.

1 Ansys Model

1.1 Parameters Definition

According to the actual situation, define the material parameters of the cable-stayed bridge(Tab. 1).
Where, Mass density(kg/m^3) = Unit weight(N/m^3)/ acceleration of gravity(9.806N/kg)

Material Parameters Tab. 1

Parts	Elastic Modulus(Pa)	Mass density(kg/m^3)	Poisson's ratio
Concrete of Tower	3.45×10^{10}	2651.44	0.2
Steel girder	2.06×10^{11}	7850.30	0.3
Concrete girder	3.45×10^{10}	2549.46	0.2
Cable	2.05×10^{11}	8005.30	0.3
Pier	3.35×10^{10}	2549.46	0.2
Rigid arm	2.06×10^{14}	0	0.3

1.2 Define and Assign Real Constants

Define cable real constant without considering Ernst equation:

In ANSYS software, the real constant of the cable is defined as "R, real constant number, cross-sectional area of the cable, initial strain of the cable".

Where, The initial strain of the cable = Stress / Elastic modulus

According to the actual situation, the elastic modulus of the cable is 2.05×10^{11} Pa without considering the Ernst equation(without considering the sag effect of the cable).

Define cable real constant with considering Ernst equation:

In the modeling process, if the Ernst equation(considering the sag effect of the cable) is considered, the cable stress should be calculated one by one according to the initial tension and the cross-sectional area of the cable. And then modify the elastic modulus of the cable according to the Ernst equation. The equations are as follows[18]:

$$\sigma(i) = F(i) \div A(i) \quad (1)$$

$$t(i) = [\text{DEN} \times 9.806 \times \text{Cable length}(i)^2 \div [12 \times \sigma(i)^3]] \quad (2)$$

$$E(i) = Ea \div [1 + Ea \times t(i)] \quad (3)$$

Where: $\sigma(i)$——the stress of the i-th cable;
$F(i)$——the tension of the i-th cable;

$A(i)$——the cross-sectional area of the i-th cable;
$t(i)$——the i-th correction coefficient of the cable;
DEN——the mass density of the cable material;
9.806——the acceleration of gravity;
Cable length(i)——the horizontal projection length of the i-th cable;
$E(i)$——the elastic modulus of the i-th cable after modification;
Ea——the elastic modulus when the cable is not modified.

A part of the table for modifying elastic modulus is as follows (Tab.2).

A Part of the Modified Elastic Modulus Tab. 2

No.	Tension (N)	Area(m²)	Stress(Pa)	DEN(kg/m³)	Projection length(m)	correction coefficient	Ea(Pa)	Modified E (Pa)
1	5748630	0.011584	4.96×10^8	8005.3	116.5	5.70×10^{14}	2.05×10^{11}	2.03×10^{11}
2	4889485	0.009275	5.27×10^8	8005.3	109.0	4.16×10^{14}	2.05×10^{11}	2.03×10^{11}
3	5123004	0.009275	5.52×10^8	8005.3	101.5	3.14×10^{14}	2.05×10^{11}	2.04×10^{11}
4	4930041	0.009737	5.06×10^8	8005.3	94.0	3.50×10^{14}	2.05×10^{11}	2.04×10^{11}
5	5030900	0.009737	5.17×10^8	8005.3	86.5	2.79×10^{14}	2.05×10^{11}	2.04×10^{11}
6	4841157	0.009275	5.22×10^8	8005.3	79.0	2.25×10^{14}	2.05×10^{11}	2.04×10^{11}
7	4960279	0.009275	5.35×10^8	8005.3	71.5	1.72×10^{14}	2.05×10^{11}	2.04×10^{11}
8	4661377	0.008582	5.43×10^8	8005.3	64.0	1.31×10^{14}	2.05×10^{11}	2.04×10^{11}
9	4813436	0.008582	5.61×10^8	8005.3	56.5	9.29×10^{15}	2.05×10^{11}	2.05×10^{11}
10	4958768	0.008582	5.78×10^8	8005.3	49.0	6.39×10^{15}	2.05×10^{11}	2.05×10^{11}

A part of the real constants table of the modified cables is as follows (Tab.3).

A part of Modified Cable Constant Real Table Tab. 3

Command	No.	Area(m²)	Modified strain
R	185	0.011584	0.00245
R	186	0.009275	0.002595
R	187	0.009275	0.002713
R	188	0.009737	0.002488
R	189	0.009737	0.002535
R	190	0.009275	0.002558
R	191	0.009275	0.002618
R	192	0.008582	0.002657
R	193	0.008582	0.002741
R	194	0.008582	0.002822

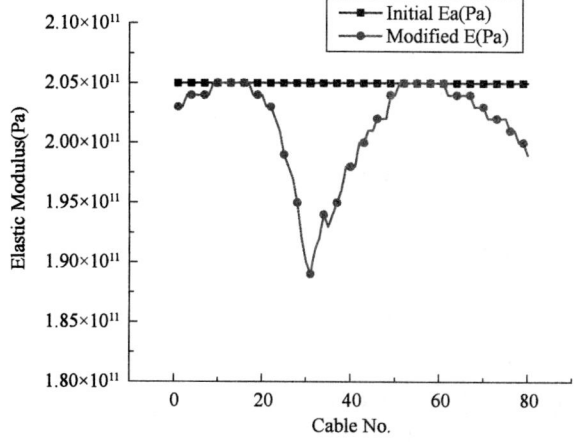

Fig. 1 Comparison of Initial E_a and Modified E

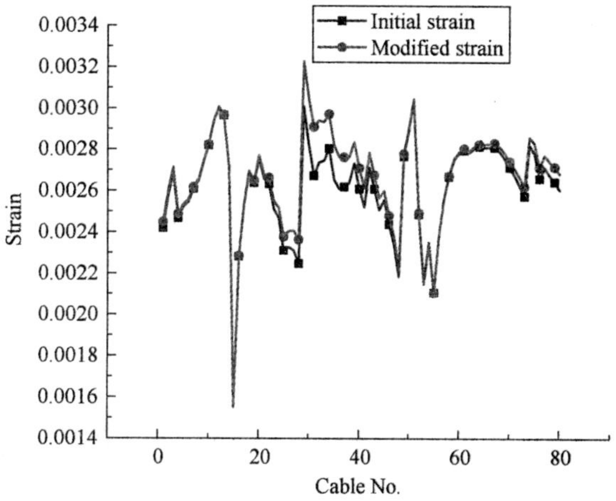

Fig. 2 Initial Strain and Modified Strain

2 Dynamic Analysis

Run the ANSYS models without considering Ernst equation and considering Ernst equation successively. Perform post-processing in ANSYS software, and the top 50th order frequency are gotten.

A part of the Top 50th Order Frequency Tab. 4

Order	without considering Ernst equation	With considering Ernst equation
1	0.09510	0.09509
2	0.28089	0.28086
3	0.36129	0.36128
4	0.38978	0.38979
5	0.40093	0.40080
6	0.49792	0.49792
7	0.52624	0.52609
8	0.62675	0.62675
9	0.68682	0.68663
10	0.86606	0.86589
11	0.93773	0.93771
12	0.95017	0.95015
13	0.96588	0.96583
14	0.96985	0.96975
15	1.00980	1.00970
16	1.13550	1.13540
17	1.13950	1.13940
18	1.17990	1.17990
19	1.23900	1.23900
20	1.25630	1.25620

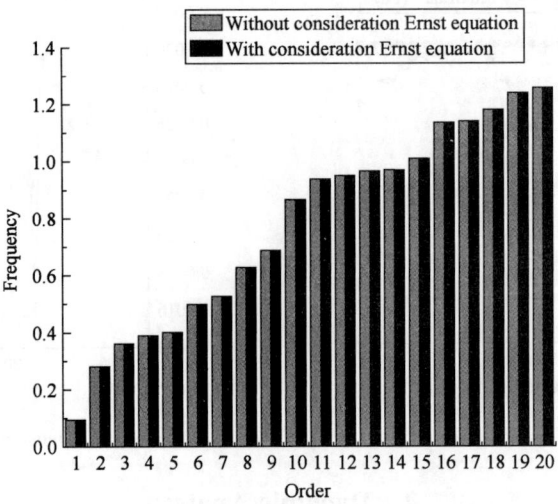

Fig. 3 The top 20 Frequency

In ANSYS software, observe the real-time deformation status of the model through the PlotCtrls / Animate / Mode Shape command[19], and determine the respective key vibration mode frequencies (Tab. 5).

Key Mode Frequency Tab. 5

Type	Order	without considering Ernst equation	with considering Ernst equation
First-order positive symmetric vertical bend	2	0.28089	0.28086
First order antisymmetric side bend	3	0.36129	0.36128
First-order positive symmetrical side bend	4	0.38978	0.38979
First order antisymmetric vertical bend	5	0.40093	0.40080
First order positive symmetric torsion	8	0.62675	0.62675
First order antisymmetric torsion	11	0.93773	0.93771

By comparing the frequencies of key mode shapes, the errors without considering Ernst equation and considering Ernst equation are obtained (Tab. 6).

Key Mode Frequency and Error Tab. 6

Type	Order	without considering Ernst equation	With considering Ernst equation	Error%
First-order positive symmetric vertical bend	2	0.28089	0.28086	−0.0107
First order antisymmetric side bend	3	0.36129	0.36128	−0.0028
First-order positive symmetrical side bend	4	0.38978	0.38979	0.0026
First order antisymmetric vertical bend	5	0.40093	0.40080	−0.0324
First order positive symmetric torsion	8	0.62675	0.62675	0
First order antisymmetric torsion	11	0.93773	0.93771	−0.0021

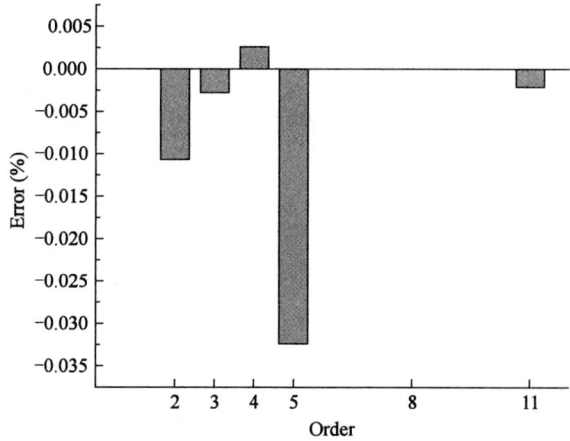

Fig. 4 The Errors of Key Mode Frequency

3　Conclusions

(1) Through the analysis of ANSYS dynamic characteristics, the six key mode frequency errors (first-order positive symmetric vertical bending, first-order antisymmetric side bending, first-order positive symmetric side bending, first-order antisymmetric vertical bending, first-order positive symmetric torsion, first-order antisymmetric torsion) of with considering Ernst equation and without considering Ernst equation are: -0.0107%, -0.0028%, 0.0026%, -0.0324%, 0, -0.0021%.

(2) Limitations of this paper: Only double-tower cable-stayed bridges with different tower heights were analyzed. The obtained conclusions cannot be guaranteed to be universal.

(3) In the actual construction process, the sag effect of the cable should be considered (that is, the Ernst equation must be considered in the modeling process).

References

[1] 郭攀. 边中跨比对双塔双索面混凝土斜拉桥动力特性影响分析[J]. 河南科技, 2018(07):104-105.
[2] 曹少辉, 谢勇. 砼双塔斜拉桥的动力特性研究[J]. 公路与汽运, 2014(02):159-161.
[3] 刘立红. 双塔双索面斜拉桥动力特性分析[J]. 中外建筑, 2012(06):149-150.
[4] 赵越, 黄平明. 高低塔斜拉桥辅助墩的优化分析[J]. 深圳大学学报(理工版):1-8[2020-07-07].
[5] 张鹏. 预应力混凝土斜拉桥调索设计新方法[J]. 城市道桥与防洪, 2020(04):68-71+13.
[6] Kaiqi Lin, You-Lin Xu. Cluster computing-aided model updating for a high-fidelity finite element model of a long-span cable-stayed bridge[J]. Earthquake Engineering & Structural Dynamics, 2020, 49(9).
[7] Kaize Xie, Weigang Zhao. Interaction between Track and Long-Span Cable-Stayed Bridge: Recommendations for Calculation. 2020.
[8] Hongjiang Li. Assessment of a Concrete Cable-stayed Bridge after Replacement of Closure Segment. 2020: 1-11.
[9] Yu Zhang, Zhi Fang. Static Performance of a Long-Span Concrete Cable-Stayed Bridge Subjected to Multiple-Cable Loss during Construction. 2020, 25(3).
[10] Min Liu, Liangfu Zheng. Stability and Dynamics Analysis of In-Plane Parametric Vibration of Stay Cables in a Cable-Stayed Bridge with Superlong Spans Subjected to Axial Excitation. 2020, 33(1).
[11] O. BenMekki, F. Auricchio. Performance evaluation of shape-memory-alloy superelastic behavior to control a stay cable in cable-stayed bridges[J]. International Journal of Non-Linear Mechanics, 2010, 46(2).
[12] 赵海霞, 张文明. 基于悬链线的斜拉索垂度效应等效弹性模量计算方法[J]. 中外公路, 2020, 40

(02):62-66.
[13] 梁立农,韩大建.索的非线性有限元与调索方法研究[J].工程力学,2007,24(11):146-152. DOI:10.3969/j.issn.1000-4750.2007.11.025.
[14] 杨佑发,白文轩.采用Ernst公式计算斜拉桥拉索振动特性的精度分析[J].世界地震工程,2008 (02):50-53.
[15] N. Hajdin, G. T. Michaltsos. Konstantakopoulos. About the Equivalent Modulus of Elasticity of Cables of Cable-stayed Bridges[J]. 1998,(5).
[16] W. Pakos, Z. Wójcicki. Experimental research of cable tension tuning of a scaled model of cable stayed bridge[J]. Archives of Civil and Mechanical Engineering,2016,16(1).
[17] M. H. Koryem, M. Yousefzadeh. Dynamic Modeling and Feedback Linearization Control of Wheeled Mobile Cable-Driven Parallel Robot Considering Cable Sag[J]. Arabian Journal for Science and Engineering, 2017,42(11):4779-4788.
[18] Wei Miao, Ping Liu. Vertical Effects of Large Cable-Stayed Bridges[J]. 2017,11(1):38-41.
[19] 王新敏. ANSYS工程结构数值分析[M]. 北京:人民交通出版社,2007.

Shear Behavior of Joints in Precast Concrete Segmental Bridges

Hao Chen   Liang Xie   Gao Cheng   Zhiheng Zhang   Kaiqiang Wang

(School of Highway, Chang'an University)

Abstract   In this paper, a full-scale direct shear test of shear keys is carried out considering the joint form and the number of shear keys. According to the test results, the failure modes of the specimens are observed, the ultimate shear loads and vertical relative slips are recorded, the normalized shear stress-vertical relative slip curves are studied, and the errors of the existing formulas for calculating the shear capacity of epoxy joints are compared and analyzed. The results show that compared with flat epoxy joints and integral joints, the shear capacity, normalized shear stress and plastic deformation capacity of single-keyed epoxy joints are improved; the shear capacity of double-keyed epoxy joints is higher than that of single-keyed epoxy joints, and its plastic deformation capacity is better than that of single-keyed epoxy joints. When the thickness of epoxy resin is 1mm, Xueshuai Sun's formula has the best prediction effect on the shear capacity of single-keyed epoxy joints and double-keyed epoxy joints.

Keywords   Joints   Direct shear   Shear capacity   Plastic deformation capacity

0 Introduction

Due to the need for economical and safe design, externally prestressed precast concrete segment bridges have become more and more popular in construction [1]. In this kind of bridge, the common steel bars are broken at the joints, and the precast concrete segments are assembled together by prestressed tendons [2]. The mechanical properties of joints are complex, and the joints are also weak parts, which have a significant impact on the mechanical properties of precast concrete segmental bridges.

Many scholars have carried out a series of experimental studies on the shear strength and shear behavior of shear key. Kuranishi S et al. [3] pointed out that the shear capacity of epoxy joints with rough surfaces is greater than that of epoxy joints with smooth surfaces. ISSA MA [4] proved that the shear failure of single-keyed epoxy joints occurs at the root of the shear keys, and epoxy resin can improve the shear capacity of the joints. Jiang [5] et al. found that the shear strength of steel fiber reinforced concrete single-keyed joints is 20.1% higher than that of ordinary concrete single-keyed joints. Yuan Aimin et al. [2,6] carried out shear tests on segmental epoxy joints, and proved that the shear capacity of joints has little relationship with the depth and distance of keys. The reinforcement of shear keys and the arrangement of prestressed tendons in the body of shear keys can obviously improve the ductility of shear keys and reduce the ratio of cracking load to ultimate load.

At present, the number of shear keys has little research on the shear resistance of keyed epoxy joints. In this paper, the number of shear keys is the key factor, and the joint form is considered in order to verify the related research results of previous scholars. There are 2 factors in total. The failure modes, ultimate shear loads and vertical relative slips of the specimens under direct shear are studied, and a comparative evaluation of the calculation formulas for the shear capacity of the keyed joints proposed by some domestic and foreign scholars.

1 Experiment Program

1.1 Test Specimens

In this paper, Z-shaped specimens are used to test the shear performance of joints. Since the influence of the lateral pressure on the performance of the shear key at the joint has been extensively studied[5,7], the experiment will no longer consider the lateral pressure as an influencing factor. The initial lateral pressure applied by all specimens in this paper is 0.1 MPa. In order not to damage the other parts of the specimens before the joint surface, it is reinforced by arranging structural steel bars. The type of steel bar is HPB300 and the diameter is 12mm. Fig. 1 and Tab. 1 respectively list the geometric dimensions and structure of the Z-type specimens.

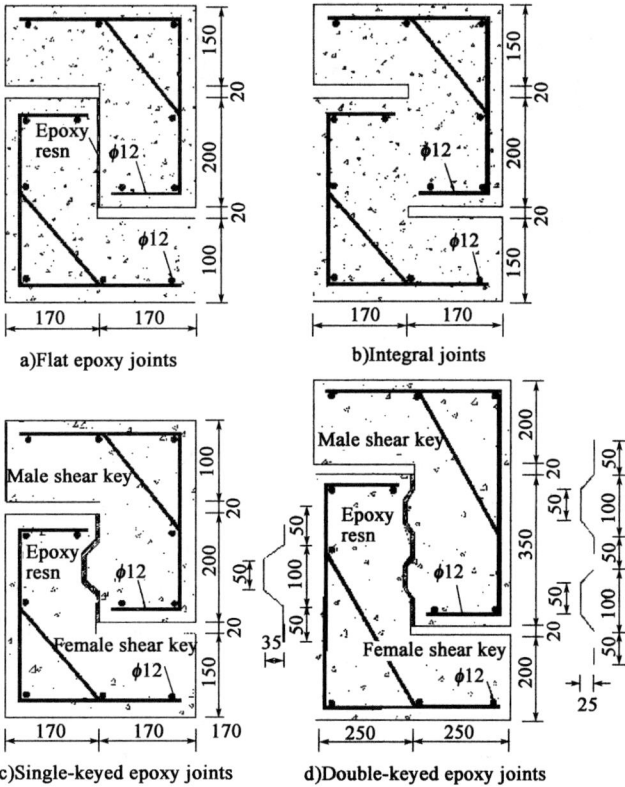

Fig. 1 Specimen Dimension and Configurations (unit: mm)

Design Parameters of Each specimen				Tab. 1
Specimen	Type	Epoxied resin thickness (mm)	Dimensions (mm)	
BP	Flat epoxy joints	1.0	540 × 340 × 150	
BU	integral joints	—	540 × 340 × 150	
BD	single-keyed epoxy joints	1.0	540 × 340 × 150	
BS	double-keyed epoxy joints	1.0	790 × 500 × 150	

1.2 Material Performance

The design strength grade of the concrete in this test is C50, and the mass ratio of cement, sand, fly ash, medium stone, small stone, water, and water reducing agent is 358 : 768 : 63 : 815 : 203 : 169 : 1. The integral specimens are poured at one time, and the epoxy specimens are divided into female key and male key. The specimens are divided into two parts by using wooden formwork and prefabricated steel partition. After the concrete strength reaches 80% of the design strength, the epoxy resin is evenly coated on the joint surface of the specimens, and the assembled specimens are placed at 20-40℃ for 24 hours before being tested. The detailed production process of the specimens is shown in Fig. 2.

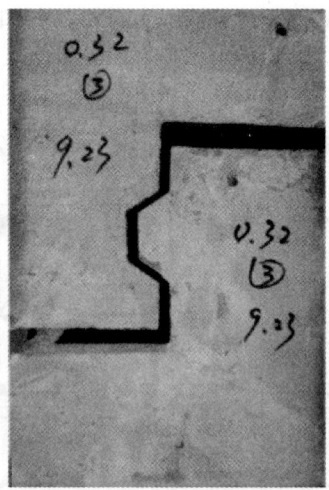

Fig. 2 The Production Process of Specimen

1.3 Setup and Instrumentation

The test loading device for this test is shown in Fig. 3. The loading end of the pressure cylinder and the base of the test piece are respectively placed with a linear displacement meter to collect the vertical relative slip. A sensor is placed at the loading end of the vertical load pressure head, and a steel plate is placed under the sensor to evenly transmit force. In order to simulate the prestress effect between the precast segmental concrete bridge segments, horizontal loading devices are arranged on both sides of the specimen. The vertical load is divided into two parts: pre-loading and formal loading. The pre-loading part adopts load control. After pre-loading, it can be unloaded slowly to enter the formal loading test. The formal loading part adopts displacement control, and the loading rate is 0.5mm/min until the component is crushed. As all the tests are destructive tests, there is no need to measure the residual stress and deformation of the components after the test, so the unloading process is not graded, and the unloading is directly and slowly to zero.

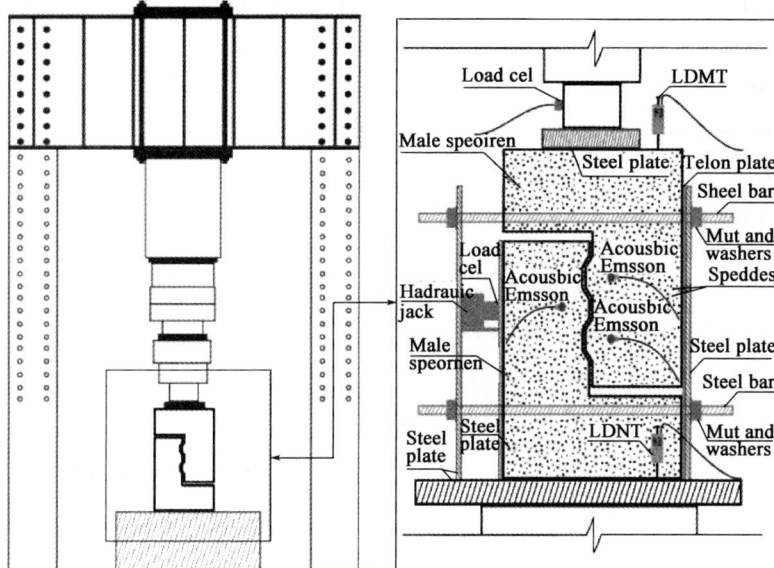

Fig. 3 Test Setup

2 Experimental Results and Discussion

2.1 Summary of Test Results

In order to ensure the accuracy of the test results, two identical specimens were made for each specimen, and two tests with the same loading conditions were carried out. The test results were compared with each other, and the test data of the two specimens were averaged to fit into a curve. The summary of test results in this paper is shown in Tab. 2.

Summary of Test Results of Specimens Under Monotonic Loading　　Tab. 2

Specimen	Ultimate shear load(kN)	Shear area(m^2)	Relative vertical slip(mm)	Ultimate shear stress(MPa)	Normalized shear stress	Mean normalized shear stress
BP-1	115.26	0.03	0.37	3.84	0.56	0.58
BP-2	123.42	0.03	0.33	4.11	0.60	
BU-1	145.38	0.03	0.41	4.85	0.70	0.68
BU-2	136.66	0.03	0.39	4.56	0.66	
BD-1	150.98	0.03	0.46	5.03	0.73	0.75
BD-2	157.22	0.03	0.47	5.24	0.76	
BS-1	255.99	0.0525	1.03	4.88	0.71	0.72
BS-2	263.19	0.0525	1.06	5.01	0.73	

2.2 Failure Modes

This article described and analyzed the experimental phenomenon of some representative specimens in this test, and the fracture damage pattern was shown in Fig. 4. For the specimen BP-1, when the load was loaded in the early stage, no cracks appeared in the joint area of the specimen. When the vertical load reached 115.26kN, a main crack was produced, and a small amount of micro cracks were produced near the main crack. At this time, the vertical relative slip was 0.37mm. For the specimen BU-1, when the vertical load reached 145.38kN, a main crack was produced, and a large number of micro cracks were produced near the main crack. After the shear load reached the shear bearing capacity, the relative slip was about 0.41mm. For the specimen BD-1, when the vertical load reached 150.98kN, a main crack was generated, and a small amount of micro cracks were generated near the main crack. After the shear load reached the shear bearing capacity, the relative slip at this time was about 0.46mm. For the specimen BS-1, When the vertical load reached 255.99kN, a main crack was generated, and a few micro cracks were generated near the main crack. After the shear load reached the shear bearing capacity, the relative slip at this time was about 1.03mm.

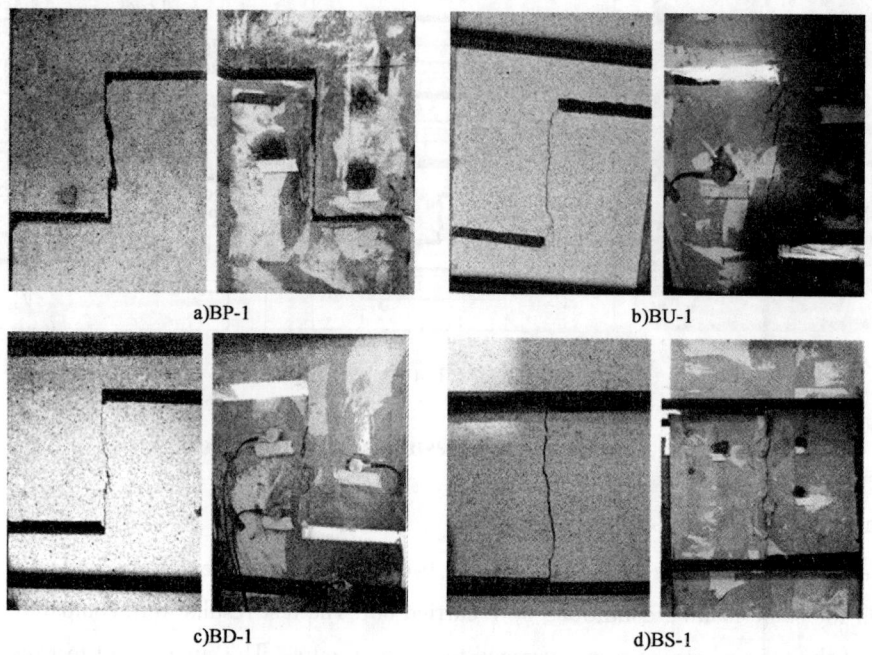

Fig. 4 Failure Mode of the Specimens

All specimens eventually experienced shear slip, and a small amount of concrete peeled off on the surface of the joint area. The other areas of the specimen were crushed and cracked during the test. The failure process of the specimen was rapid without obvious signs, and the sound was loud when it was broken, which belonged to the brittle failure type.

2.3 Analysis of Experimental Parameters

In order to eliminate the influence of concrete strength factors on the shear performance, the concept of standardized shear stress widely used by AASHTO and ACI is introduced when processing experimental data, $\tau_n = \tau / \sqrt{f'_c}$ is the shear stress τ and the concrete cylinder The ratio of the arithmetic square root of the cubic compressive strength f'_c. When the concrete strength grade of this test is C50, the compressive strength f'_c of the concrete cylinder can be approximately converted from 0.79 times the cubic compressive strength f_{cu}, and the shear stress τ is defined as the shear force divided by the shear area.

2.3.1 Form of Joints

In Tab. 2, BP-1, BP-2, BU-1, BU-2, BD-1 and BD-2 are used to study the influence of joint forms on the shear performance of specimens. It can be seen from the data in the table that the average shear capacity of BD-1 and BD-2 has increased by 29.1% compared with that of BP-1 and BP-2, and the average shear capacity of BD-1 and BD-2 has increased by 9.3% compared with that of BU-1 and BU-2. Compared with the average vertical relative slip of BP-1 and BP-2, the average vertical relative slip of BD-1 and BD-2 is increased by 32.9%, and that of BU-1 and BU-2 is increased by 16.3%. Comparing the test results, it can be concluded that the shear capacity and plastic deformation ability of single-keyed epoxy joints are higher than those of flat epoxy joints and integral joints.

Fig. 5 shows the normalized shear stress-vertical relative slip curves of BP, BU and BD. It can be seen from Fig. 5 that the normalized shear stress-vertical relative slip curves of BP, BU and BD have similar slopes. After shear failure, the curves no longer rise and remain horizontal, the slope is approximately zero, and the vertical relative slip continues to increase. The normalized shear stress and vertical relative slip of BD are the largest, followed by BU, and the normalized shear stress and vertical relative slip of BP are the smallest. In summary, compared with the flat epoxy joints and the integral joints, single-keyed epoxy joints have the largest normalized shear stress.

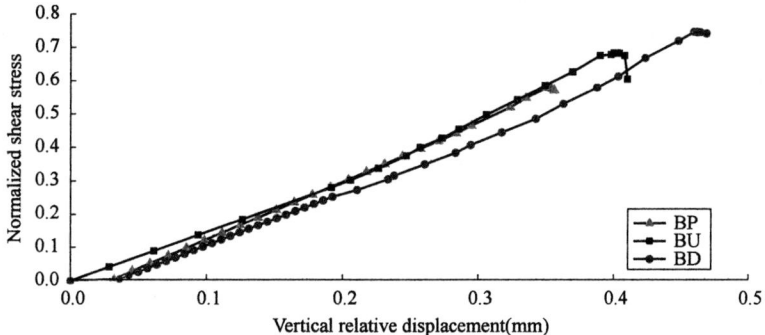

Fig. 5 Normalized Shear Stress-vertical Relative Slip Curves for Form of Joints

2.3.2 Number of Shear Keys

BD-1, BD-2, BS-1 and BS-2 in Tab. 2 are used to study the influence of the number of shear keys on the shear performance of specimens. It can be seen from the data in the table that the average shear capacity of BS-1 and BS-2 is increased by 68.5% compared with that of BD-1 and BD-2, and the average vertical relative slip of BS-1 and BS-2 is increased by 114.7% compared with that of BD-1 and BD-2. Comparing the test results, it can be concluded that the shear bearing capacity of the specimens with double-keyed epoxy joints is higher than that of the specimens with single-keyed epoxy joints, and its plastic deformation ability is better than that of the specimens with single-keyed epoxy joints.

Fig. 6 shows the normalized shear stress-vertical relative slip curves of BD and BS. It can be seen from Figure 6 that the failure modes of specimens of BD and BS are the same. The normalized shear stress-vertical relative slip curve changes linearly before reaching the ultimate shear strength. the slope of the normalized shear stress-vertical relative slip curve of BS is much smaller than that of BS, while the normalized shear stress of BS is slightly smaller than that of BD. This is because the number of shear key keys increases, and the assembly error between the female shear keys and the male shear keys increases, and stress concentration is more likely to occur, so that each shear key cannot simultaneously exert a shear resistance effect.

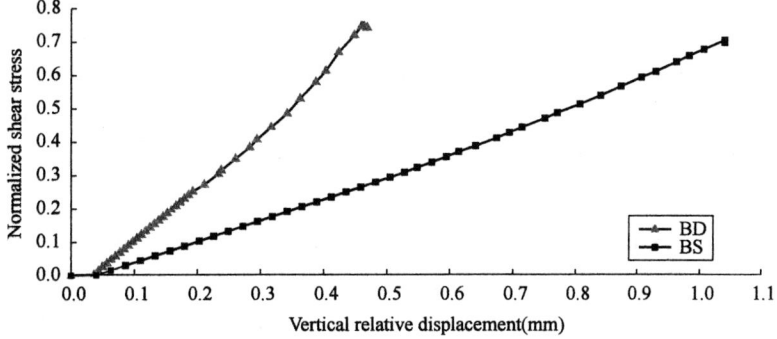

Fig. 6 Normalized Shear Stress-vertical Relative Slip Curves for Number of Shear Keys

3 Comparisons of Existing Formula

Scholars have studied the shear performance of epoxy resin joints and put forward some calculation formulas for epoxy resin joints under direct shear. This article will compare and analyze the calculated values of the formulas proposed by some scholars. The calculation formula proposed by BUYUKOZTURK O[7] et al. is a formula obtained by regression analysis using mathematical statistics; the calculation formula proposed by Lu Wenliang [8] is based on the joint shear capacity is determined by the friction resistance and shear resistance of full-section concrete; The calculation formula proposed by Xueshuai Sun[9] is based on the theory of joint shear resistance, and the direct shear failure mechanism and the calculation method of bearing capacity of the joint are studied; the calculation formula proposed by Aimin Yuan[2] is based on Mohr-Coulomb friction failure criterion evaluates the shear strength of epoxy resin joints. The calculation results of the calculation formula proposed by the above-mentioned scholars are shown in Tab. 3.

Comparisons of Existing Formula   Tab. 3

Specimen	f_c(MPa)	V_u(kN)	V_a(kN)	V_u/V_a	V_b(kN)	V_u/V_b	V_c(kN)	V_u/V_c	V_d(kN)	V_u/V_d
BD-1	47.30	150.98	193.62	0.78	126.28	1.20	146.87	1.03	131.05	1.15
BD-2	47.30	157.22	193.62	0.81	126.28	1.25	146.87	1.07	131.05	1.20
Average				0.795		1.225		1.05		1.175
BS-1	47.30	255.99	338.84	0.76	221.00	1.16	257.02	1.00	187.65	1.36
BS-2	47.30	263.19	338.84	0.78	221.00	1.19	257.02	1.02	187.65	1.40
Average				0.77		1.17		1.01		1.38

The formula proposed by BUYUKOZTURK O et al. is:

$$V_a = A_j(0.921\sqrt{f_c} + 1.20\sigma_n) \tag{1}$$

Where, σ_n is the normal stress of the jointed surface (MPa); A_j is the shear area of the jointed surface of shear keys (mm^2).

The formula proposed by BUYUKOZTURK O et al. is:

$$V_b = A_j(0.6\sqrt{f'_c} + 0.83\sigma_n) \tag{2}$$

The calculation formula proposed by Xueshuai Sun is:

$$V_c = \alpha_1 \alpha A_j(0.39 f_{cu}^{2/3} + 1.51\sigma_n) \tag{3}$$

Where, α_1 is the direct shear reduction factor, and it is recommended to take 0.8; α is the multi-bond reduction factor, and when the number of key teeth is 1-2, α is 1.00.

The calculation formula proposed by Aimin Yuan is:

$$V_d = \alpha A_{joint}^{eq}(0.56\sqrt{f'_c} + 1.2\sigma_n) \tag{4}$$

Where, α is the coefficient considering the number of shear keys, the α of single shear key and multi-shear key are 1.1 and 0.9 respectively; A_{joint}^{eq} is the converted cross-sectional area, $A_{joint}^{eq} = A_j + (n-1)A_s$, where A_s It is the area of reinforcement (mm^2). Since the shear key tested in this paper is plain concrete, A_s is 0.

For single-keyed epoxy joints, the average values of the ratios of the experimental ultimate shear load values to the calculated values of formulas (1)-(4) are 0.795, 1.225, 1.05, and 1.175, respectively. It shows that formula (1) overestimates the shear capacity of the single-keyed epoxy joints, and the formulas (2)-(4) underestimate the shear capacity of the single-keyed epoxy joints.

For double-keyed epoxy joints, the average values of the ratios of the experimental ultimate shear load values to the calculated values of formulas (1)-(4) are 0.77, 1.17, 1.01, and 1.38, respectively, It shows that equation (1) overestimates the shear capacity of the double-keyed epoxy joints is calculated, and formulas (2)-(4) underestimate the shear capacity of the double-keyed epoxy joints.

4 Conclusions

By studying the shear resistance of the prefabricated segmented joints under direct shear, considering two factors, the form of joints and the number of shear keys, the following conclusions are drawn:

(1) Compared with flat epoxy joints and integral joints, the shear capacity, standardized shear stress and plastic deformation capacity of the single-keyed epoxy joints are improved.

(2) The shear capacity of the double-keyed epoxy joints is higher than that of the single-keyed epoxy joints, and its plastic deformation capacity is better than that of the single-keyed epoxy joints.

(3) When the thickness of the epoxy resin is 1mm, Xueshuai Sun's formula has the best prediction effect on the shear capacity of single-keyed epoxy joints and double-keyed epoxy joints.

References

[1] SHAMASS R, X Zhou, ALFANO G. Finite-Element Analysis of Shear-Off Failure of Keyed Dry Joints in Precast Concrete Segmental Bridges[J]. Journal of Bridge Engineering, 2014, 20(6): 04014084.

[2] Aimin Yuan, Jundong Fu, Leike Cheng, et al. Experiment of Shear Performance of Epoxied Resin Joints with Reinforced Keys in Precast Concrete Segmental bridge [J]. China Journal of Highway and Transport. 2018, 31(12): 81-87.

[3] Kuranishi S, Naganuma F, Nakazawa M, et al. Mechanical behavior of metal contact joint[J]. Journal of Structural Engineering, 1994, 120(7): 1977-1990.

[4] ISSA M A, ABDALLA H A. Structural Behavior of Single Key Joints in Precast Concrete Segmental Bridges [J]. Journal of Bridge Engineering, 2007, 12(3): 315-324.

[5] Jing H, Chen L, Ma ZJ, et al. Shear Behavior of Dry Joints with Castellated Keys in Precast Concrete Segmental Bridges [J]. Journal of Bridge Engineering, 2015, 20(2): 04014062.

[6] Aimin Yuan, Yu He, Leike Cheng, et al. Study on Shear Behavior of Glued Joint Structure in Segmental Precast Concrete Beam [J]. journal of chongqing jiaotong university (natural science). 2014, 33(6): 22-26, 33.

[7] BUYUKOZTURK O, BAKHOUM MM, BEATTIE S M. Shear Behavior of Joints in Precast Concrete Segmental Bridges[J]. Journal of Structural Engineering, 1990, 116(12): 3380-3401.

[8] Wenliang Lu. Theoretical Research on the Design of Segmental Precast Externally Prestressed Concrete Beam [D]. Beijing: Beijing Jiaotong University, 2004.

[9] Xueshuai Sun. Experimental Study on Shear Behavior of Joints in Precast Segment Bridges [D]. Nanjing: Southeast University. 2015.

Study on Boundaries Between Straight Bridges and Curved Bridges with Box Section in Cantilever Construction

Liang Xie　Hao Chen　Gao Cheng　Zhiheng Zhang　Bohua Wen

(School of Highway, Chang'an University)

Abstract　In order to obtain the calculation limit of straight bridge and curved bridge with medium span length in cantilever pouring construction, this paper studies the mechanical performance of curved bridge and straight bridge with equal cross-section with span distribution of 62 + 105 + 62m. The finite element model adopts box section, the construction method is cantilever casting construction, and the element is beam element. Under the premise of the same load, shear, bending moment, torque and deflection under the second stage of load are taken as the research indicators, and a comparative study is carried out between the constant-section box girder model and the straight bridge model with a radius of 115m, 500m, 1000m and 1500m. The results of comparative analysis show that the finite element analysis of curved bridge can be replaced by finite element analysis of straight bridge when the radius of curvature is greater than 500m. Finally, in order to verify the validity of the boundary, a fine finite model with a radius of curvature of 900m and its straight bridge model are established. The verification results show that the boundary value obtained is correct.

Keywords Cantilever pouring Curved bridge Continuous beam Calculation boundary The finite element

0 Introduction

With the construction of expressways and urban overpasses, curved girder bridges have become a very common type of bridges. Because the box section has good torsion resistance and beautiful shape, it has become the preferred section of curved girder bridge(Zhang et al., 2006).

Because of its unique plane alignment, the curved girder bridge will produce the torsional effect, which will be coupled with the bending moment of the beam(Zhang and Lyons, 1984). And the shear lag effect caused by the wide deck of the box girder, and the cumulative effect of the construction process should be considered in the cantilever construction(Chen et al., 2019). Especially the cantilever construction is a long period. Due to creep, the vertical displacement of the beam will change with time(Malm and Sundquist, 2010). And the monitoring personnel need to consider that after 10 years of shrinkage and creep, the bridge alignment can reach the design alignment under the action of 1/2 vehicle load. Designers or monitoring personnel need to consider many of the above factors when calculating, and the use of manual calculation brings a lot of inconvenience, and the calculation efficiency is low, so the use of finite element software calculation has become the preferred method of calculation(Wang et al., 2020). The common finite element software are ABAQUS and ANSYS, although the simulation of components is accurate enough, but it is difficult to master it, and the modeling process is complex and prone to bug, so designers generally use Midas Civil, a special finite element calculation software for civil engineering, in bridge design, which is accurate enough for engineering(ZHANG et al., 2012). Generally speaking, the curved box girder bridge should be analyzed and calculated by three-dimensional space model, but in the actual design process, in order to save the design time, for the curved bridge with large plane radius, the beam element is used to establish the calculation and analysis model according to the straight bridge. It is proved that when the radius of curvature is large enough, the internal force and deflection of straight bending and curved bridge are similar, and the difference between them can be ignored(Gouda, 2013). However, the boundary of calculation and analysis of curved box girder according to straight-line bridge is not clear enough. This paper will study the law of the middle span cantilever cast curved box girder bridge changing with the radius, and give the analysis limit of the curved bridge according to the straight bridge, and use the actual engineering case to verify the correctness of the limit.

1 Finite Element Model

In order to obtain the law that the internal force and deflection of the curved bridge vary with the radius of curvature, the finite element software Midas, is used to compare and analyze the straight bridge and the curved bridge under the action of dead weight, prestress, construction load and so on. The span distribution of the bridge is 62m + 105m + 62m, the width of the bridge is 16.25m, and the bridge type is a continuous beam bridge. In order to simplify the modeling process, the analytical model is simplified to be arranged in the equal section of the whole bridge, and the arrangement of prestressed steel strands is simplified to standard steel strands and a small amount in each cantilever cast-in-place segment. In order to obtain the effect of constant load and temporary load accumulation in the cantilever pouring process, the construction process is established strictly according to the cantilever pouring process. The cast-in-place support is used in the 0# block, the cantilever casting construction is used in the 2# block, and the support cast-in-place is used in the rest of the block. The construction process of each cast-in-place section of the box girder is established according to the forward movement of the hanging basket, the application of wet weight load and the tension prestress. The boundary constraints are arranged according to the continuous beam. Without changing the constraint conditions and block length, the radius of curvature is 115m, 500m, 1000m and 1500m respectively. The finite element model established in the corresponding construction stage according to the actual cantilever pouring process is shown in Fig. 1.

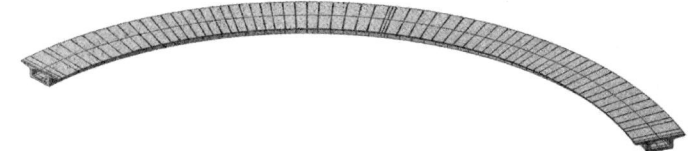

Fig. 1 Simplified Finite Element Model

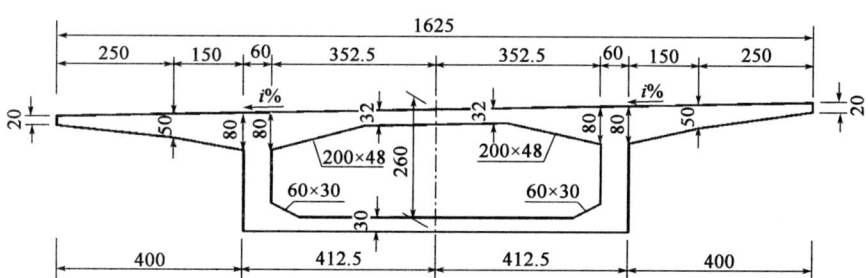

Fig. 2 Cross section dimension (unit: m)

2 The Influence of Curvature Radius on the Mechanical Performance of Bridges under the Second Stage Load

2.1 Influence on Longitudinal Bending Moment

Fig. 3 reflects the change of the longitudinal bending moment of the curved bridge in the length direction of the curved bridge obtained by changing the curvature radius of the cantilever pouring continuous beam bridge under the premise of considering the cumulative effect in the process of cantilever construction in the second stage of load. In the picture, the Abscissa origin is the left end of the beam, the Abscissa value is the distance between the section position on the centerline of the curved beam and the origin, and the ordinate is the longitudinal bending moment along the beam. It can be seen from Fig. 3 that when the radius of curvature changes, the longitudinal bending moment has the same distribution under dead load. The maximum positive bending moment is produced in the side span and the middle span, and the maximum negative bending moment is produced at the fulcrum, and the absolute value of the negative bending moment is obviously larger than that of the positive bending moment. With the increase of the radius of curvature, the positive bending moment at the side span increases, while the positive bending moment at the middle span and the negative bending moment at the support decrease. However, when the radius of curvature changes from 115m to 1500m, the change of longitudinal moment is not obvious, indicating that the radius of curvature has little effect on the longitudinal moment.

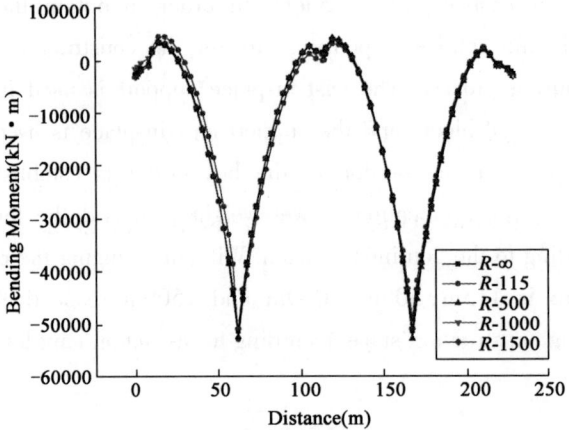

Fig. 3　Distribution of Longitudinal Bending Moment along Span

2.2　Influence on Torque

Fig. 4 reflects the distribution of torque along the whole bridge under each radius of curvature when considering the cumulative effect of cantilever construction in the second stage of load. As shown in Fig. 4, the maximum torque is generated at the mid-span support, gradually decreases with the increase of the distance from the mid-span support, and decreases to 0 at the middle of the mid-span. With the increase of the radius, the visible torque decreases gradually. In order to obtain the variation law of torque with radius, Fig. 5 is drawn for the variation of torque with radius at the support in the middle of the span. As shown in Fig. 5, when the radius changes from 115m to 500m, the torque at the support changes most obviously, reducing by 78.70%. When the radius is more than 500m, the decreasing trend of torque slows down obviously, and it can be considered that when the radius is greater than 500m, the influence of radius on torque weakens.

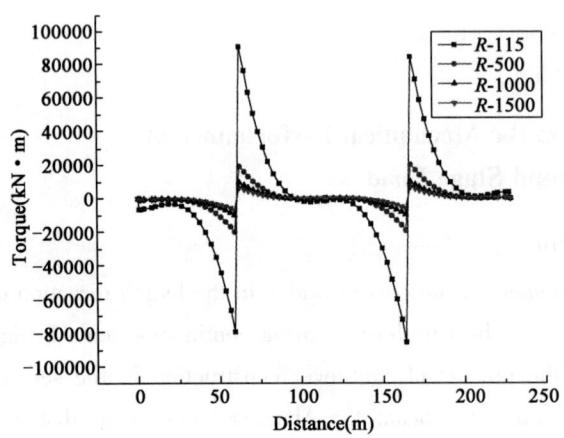

Fig. 4　Torque Distribution along Span

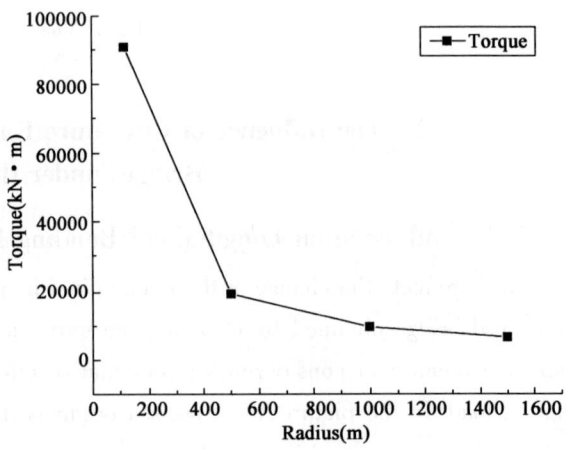

Fig. 5　Maximum Torque Varies with Radius

2.3　Influence on Shear Force

Fig. 6 reflects the distribution of vertical shear force along the whole bridge under each radius of curvature when considering the cumulative effect of cantilever construction in the second stage of load. From Fig. 6, it can be seen that the maximum shear stress occurs near the mid-span support, and as the vertical shear force decreases away from the mid-span support, the shear force decreases to 0 in the middle span. When the radius changes from 115m to a straight line, the vertical shear force distribution of the whole bridge is almost unchanged, so it can be considered that the effect of radius on shear force can be ignored.

2.4 Influence on Deflection

Fig. 7 reflects the distribution of vertical cumulative displacement along the whole bridge under each curvature radius when considering the cumulative effect of cantilever construction in the second stage of load. As shown in Fig. 7, the maximum vertical cumulative displacement occurs in the middle of the side span and near the middle of the middle span, the cumulative displacement of the middle span is relatively small due to the use of hangers, and the vertical cumulative displacement of the side span near the side span is relatively small due to the use of support cast-in-place vertical displacement. Due to the removal of the temporary bearing, the radius of the curved bridge with a radius of 115m has a large upward movement near the middle span. Generally speaking, the cumulative displacement of the vertical bar decreases with the increase of the radius. When the radius is greater than 500m, the change of the radius of the curved bridge can only bring about a small change of displacement. Therefore, it is considered that when the radius is greater than 500, the radius has little influence on the vertical cumulative displacement.

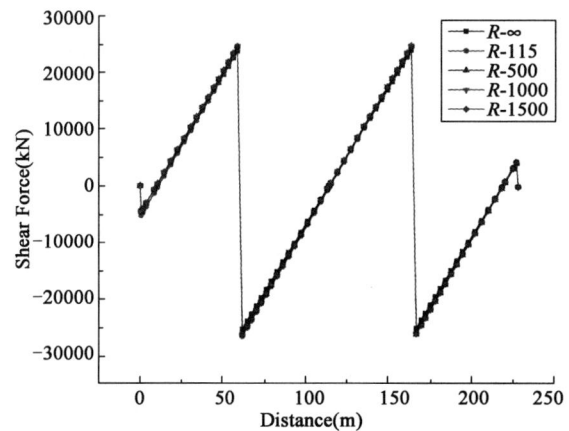

Fig.6　Shear Force Distribution along Span

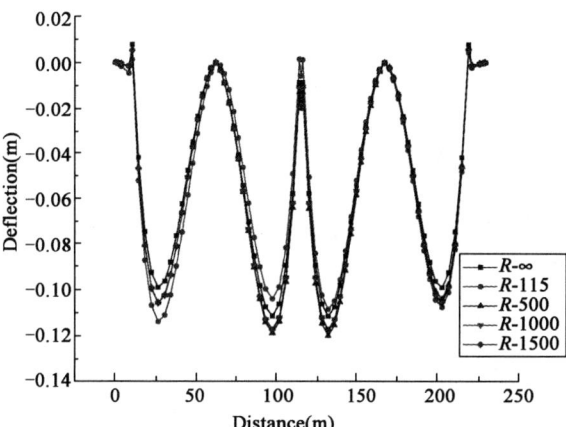

Fig.7　Cumulative Deflection Distribution with Span

2.5 Research Conclusion of Simplified Model

In summary, the shear force and longitudinal bending moment have no obvious change with the change of radius. The torque and deflection decrease with the increase of the radius, and the decreasing rate slows down obviously when the radius is more than 500m, and there is little difference between the straight bridge and the straight bridge. It can be considered that there is no big error when the radius of the curved bridge is greater than 500m.

3 Engineering Example Verification

This project is a continuous box section beam with span distribution of 62m + 105m + 62m under construction. The construction method is to use hanging basket cantilever casting, and support cast-in-place casting is adopted for the segment of the side span close to the side support. The Midas finite element model was established by beam element, and the bottom surface of the beam was a quadratic parabolic curve. The construction stage of each casting section is divided into hanging basket moving forward, applying wet heavy load and tensioned prestressed steel beam. The order of closing is to first close the edge span and then close the middle span. The prestressed steel beam shall be considered as both horizontal and vertical bending according to the design drawing. Under the same condition, the linear model and the model with a radius of 900m are established, and the schematic diagram of the model is shown in Fig. 8.

Fig. 8 Engineering Finite Element Model

The bending moment, torque, shear force and deflection of the actual engineering model are shown in Fig. 9 to Fig. 12. It can be seen from the above several internal forces and deflection diagrams that when the radius is 900m, the internal forces and deflection of the finite element model of a curved bridge are not much different from those of the finite element model of a straight bridge. Therefore, it can be verified that the boundary value proposed in the previous section is an effective value.

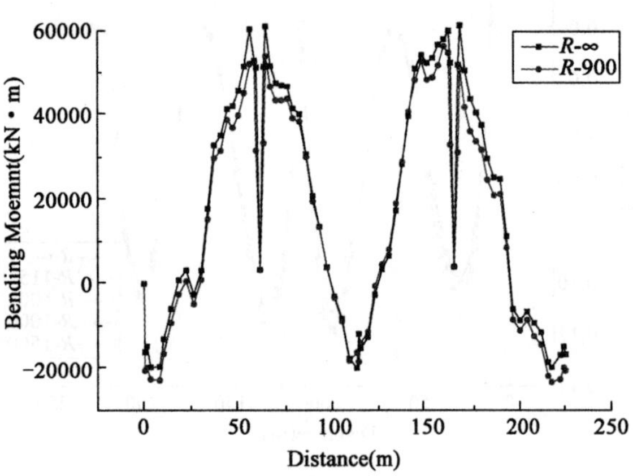

Fig. 9 Longitudinal Bending Moment

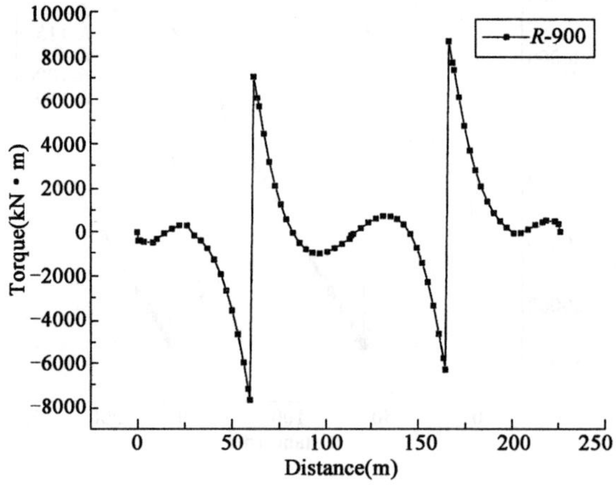

Fig. 10 Torque Distribution

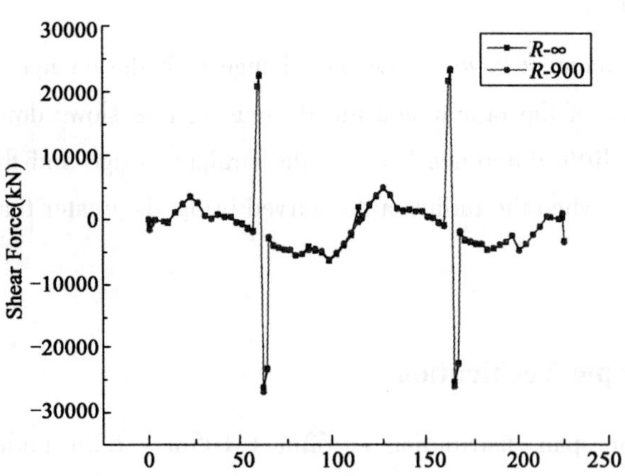

Fig. 11 Shear Force

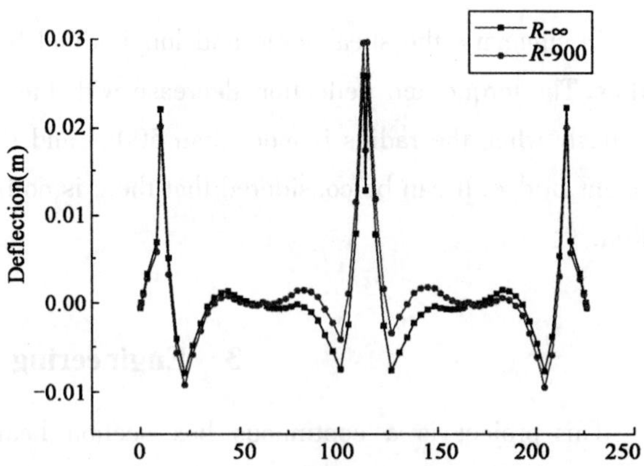

Fig. 12 Cumulative Deflection

4 Conclusions

In this paper, simplified models of curved bridges with radius 115m, 500m, 1000m and 1500m as well as simplified models of straight Bridges are established to conduct comparative analysis of internal forces and deflections. The decrease of the radius of curvature has the greatest adverse effect on the torque and will increase the cumulative displacement in the construction process, but has almost no effect on the shear force. It is concluded that when the radius is greater than 500m, the straight bridge finite element model can be used to replace the curved bridge finite element model. Then the internal forces and deflects between the unsimplified 900m curved bridge finite element model and the straight bridge finite element model are compared. The above boundary value is verified to be correct. When the finite element model of curved box girder is established, the limit value can be used as the basis for design and monitoring personnel. When the radius is more than 500m, the straight bridge model established by the standard steel cable can be used instead of the curved bridge model established by the curved steel cable, which greatly saves the modeling time of designers and monitors and improves the efficiency of calculation and analysis.

References

[1] Chen, K., Wang, L., & Zhang, W. (2019). Research on Shear Lag Effect of Three-span Continuous Curved Steel Box Girder Bridge. in "IOP Conference Series: Materials Science and Engineering," Wuhan, Hubei, China, July, 2019, p. 012050.

[2] Gouda, L. P. (2013). Study on parametric behaviour of single cell box girder under different radius of curvature(Doctoral dissertation).

[3] Malm, R., & Sundquist, H. (2010). Time-dependent analyses of segmentally constructed balanced cantilever bridges. Engineering Structures, 32(4), 1038-1045.

[4] Wang, D., Wang, L., Liu, Y., Tan, B., & Liu, Y. (2020). Failure mechanism investigation of bottom plate in concrete box girder bridges. Engineering Failure Analysis, 116, 104711.

[5] Zhang, S. H., & Lyons, L. P. R. (1984). A thin-walled box beam finite element for curved bridge analysis. Computers & structures, 18(6), 1035-1046.

[6] ZHANG, Y. X., HUANG, S. F., & YANG, G. (2012). Nonlinear Analysis on Reinforced Concrete Based on ABAQUS and ANSYS. Hongshui River, 4.

[7] ZHANG, Y., Zhao-tong, H. U., & Run-zhong, J. I. A. (2006). Temperature gradient of RC continuous curved box girder bridge. Journal of Changpan University: Natural Science Edition, 26(4), 58-62.

桩径变化对不同剥落厚度下桩基横轴向承载特性影响

冯忠居　全超文　李　铁　白少奋
（长安大学公路学院）

摘　要　依托青海省德香高速公路盐沼泽区桥梁工程，以MARC有限元软件为平台，采用室内腐蚀测试参数，构建盐沼泽区桥梁桩基础受腐蚀的有限元模型，分析了不同桩径情况下，桩基在腐蚀后脱落厚度对桩基横轴向承载特性的影响。研究结果显示，桩基受腐蚀后，其横轴向极限承载力呈现降低趋势，桩身剥落厚度小于6.0cm时，其横轴向承载力不会显著下降，当剥落厚度超过6.0cm时，其横轴向承载力大幅下降。全文通过对受腐后的桥梁单桩横轴向承载特性的研究，为评估位于盐沼泽地的公路桥梁桩基础长期服役状态提供了参考依据。

关键词　桥梁工程　极限承载力　数值模拟　桩基础腐蚀　盐沼泽区

0 引言

桩基础的承载特性是桩基础设计中最重要的设计参数[1-5]。桥梁桩基因受腐蚀发生桩身混凝土剥落后,横轴向承载力会显著降低,桥梁结构的正常使用及安全性能也会受到严重影响。余发红等调查发现,普通混凝土在盐渍土环境下,3年左右就开始出现粉化,桥梁在滨海地区仅能使用7~8年,就开始出现墩柱钢筋严重腐蚀、桩身混凝土剥落的现象[6-7]。蒋卫东等研究发现,腐蚀严重处的柱顶与立柱接头会发生严重脱落破坏[8]。马希和等通过数值模拟的方法研究了桥梁桩基中的钢筋混凝土在海洋环境中的耐久性[9]。

桥梁桩基横轴向极限承载力的确定方法一般为分析计算法和水平静载试验。郭朋鑫等研究了高应变水平受荷桩的各种分析方法,并将其划分为四类:非线性连续体法、非线性地基反力法、极限状态法和应变楔法[10]。戴自航等针对现行多层地基中水平荷载桩计算 m 法存在的问题,提出了用有限差分法和弹性地基杆系有限元法计算桩的位移和内力作为实际成层地基强度系数的函数的方法[11]。刘晋超、朱斌等通过离心模型试验获得了干砂和饱和沙的大直径单桩水平荷载 p-y 曲线,提出了砂土海床中大直径单桩基础的合理数值分析模型及参数取值方法[12-13]。冯忠居等采用理论分析和数值模拟相结合的方法,建立了深厚软基区桥梁基础三维模型,分析了不同工况下桩基的横轴向承载能力容许值[14]。祝彦知等基于黏弹性理论,考虑横向受荷桩基础周围土体的黏弹性,研究了横向荷载作用下桩基础与周围土体共同作用问题[15]。

众多专家学者对横轴向荷载作用下单桩的力学特性进行了相关研究[16-20],但对于受腐蚀后的单桩横轴向极限承载力的确定研究较少,理论计算还不成熟;水平静载试验耗时长、费用高、破坏性大。本文以有限元分析作为研究手段,以青海省盐沼泽区德香高速公路工程为依托,研究桥梁桩基受腐蚀后桩径变化对其横轴向承载特性的影响,为评估位于盐沼泽地的公路桥梁桩基础长期服役状态提供了参考依据。

1 有限元假定与计算模型

1.1 假定

桥梁桩基础采用混凝土材料,桩采用理想弹性本构模型,微风化岩采用弹性模型进行分析,地基土采用弹塑性模型分析,采用 Mohr-Coulomb 屈服准则。进行有限元分析时,有以下假定。

(1)假定桩和土为均质、各向同性的。
(2)假定岩体满足均质、各向同性和完全连续这三个条件。
(3)假定土体在水平方向为无限。
(4)不考虑钢筋锈蚀和混凝土黏结的影响。

1.2 计算模型

依据圣维南原理,考虑地基土对桩基承载力的影响,结合混凝土桩基础实际受力的特点,在满足有限元分析软件 MARC 对计算资源需求的基础上,经多次试算,桩基础底部以下取 20m 土层厚度,桩侧土层厚度取 $8D$(D 为桩径)。

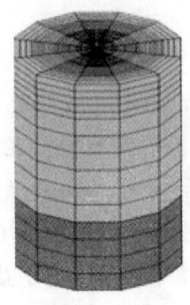 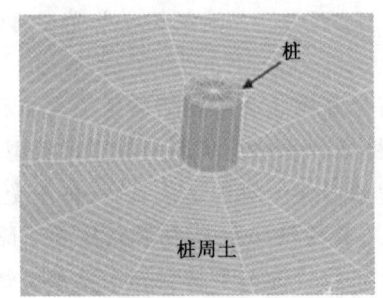

a)整体单元划分　　b)模型局部放大

图 1　有限元计算模型

2 有限元计算工况的确定及参数选取

2.1 计算工况

由于桥梁桩基础受盐沼泽中腐蚀性离子腐蚀的影响，桩基下部桩身混凝土会发生剥蚀、脱落的现象，腐蚀严重时会进一步加重桩基础的损坏程度。

桩身混凝土剥落厚度能够直观体现桩基所受腐蚀的严重程度，通过对青海省桩基础腐蚀病害的调查研究，发现桩基础下部桩身腐蚀主要发生在地面以上1m至地下水位之间。德香高速公路所处路域环境中质粉土和饱水细砂主要集中于地表以下8.0m，因此在进行工况选定时考虑受腐深度为1.5m、5.0m、8.0m。

依据青海腐蚀性工程中桥梁桩基础桩径大小，选取桩径为1.2m，1.6m，1.8m，2.0m。最终得到桩的计算工况如表1所示。

计 算 工 况　　　　　　　　　　　　　　　　　表1

受腐深度 H(m)	桩径 D(m)	桩长(m)	剥落厚度 δ(cm)
1.5	1.2、1.6、1.8、2.0	40	0.0、3.0、6.0、9.0、12.0、15.0
5.0			
8.0			

2.2 参数选取

桩基受腐蚀后，其桩身混凝土不仅会在质量上发生衰减，强度也会随之下降，进行有限元模拟时主要通过弹性模量的衰减来对腐蚀状况进行模拟。

室内测试数据表明，当混凝土试件出现剥落现象时，随试件的损伤程度，其相对动弹性模量衰减为原来70%~90%，由此类比桩的弹性模量衰减，在进行数值模拟分析时，桩基材料的弹性模量按照变为原来的90%、85%、80%、75%与70%选取。最终得到桩的有限元分析模型材料参数如表2所示。

有限元计算参数　　　　　　　　　　　　　　　　　表2

材料名称	弹性模量 E (MPa)	泊松比 N	黏聚力 c (kPa)	内摩擦角 φ (°)	容重 γ (kN/m³)
桩	3.0×10^4	0.20	—	—	25.0
粉细砂	12.5	0.33	10.8	30	18.4
粉质黏土	5.6	0.30	20	20	18.3
剥落混凝土	2.40×10^4	0.20	—	—	25.0
剥落3.0cm	2.16×10^4	0.20	—	—	25.0
剥落6.0cm	2.04×10^4	0.20	—	—	25.0
剥落9.0cm	1.92×10^4	0.20	—	—	25.0
剥落12cm	1.80×10^4	0.20	—	—	25.0
剥落15cm	1.68×10^4	0.20	—	—	25.0

3 桩径变化对不同剥落厚度下桩基水平向位移的影响

如图2所示，桩长不变，桩基受腐深度为1.5m时，不同剥落厚度情况下，桩径相同的桩基础，其横向位移变化与第一零点位置大致相同。以桩径1.2m的桩基础为例，桩基剥落厚度为0.0cm时，桩基第一位移零点距桩底 26.354m,其距桩底距离占桩长 65.9%;桩基剥落厚度为 3.0cm 时,桩基第一位移零点距桩底 26.537m,其距桩底距离占桩长 66.3%;桩基剥落厚度分别为 6.0cm 时,桩基第一位移零点距桩底 26.539m,其距桩底距离占桩长 66.3%;桩基剥落厚度为 9.0cm 时,桩基第一位移零点距桩底 26.532m,其距桩底距离占桩长 66.3%;桩基剥落厚度为 12.0cm 时,桩基第一位移零点距桩底 26.532m,其距桩底距离占桩长 66.3%;桩基剥落厚度为 15.0cm 时,桩基第一位移零点距桩底 26.529m,其距桩底距离占桩长 66.3%。对于桩径为 1.6m、1.8m、2.0m 的桩基有相同变化趋势。说明桩基受腐深度为 1.5m 时,剥落厚度的增加对桩基横向位移以及第一零点影响不大,对桩基横向稳定并无太大影响。

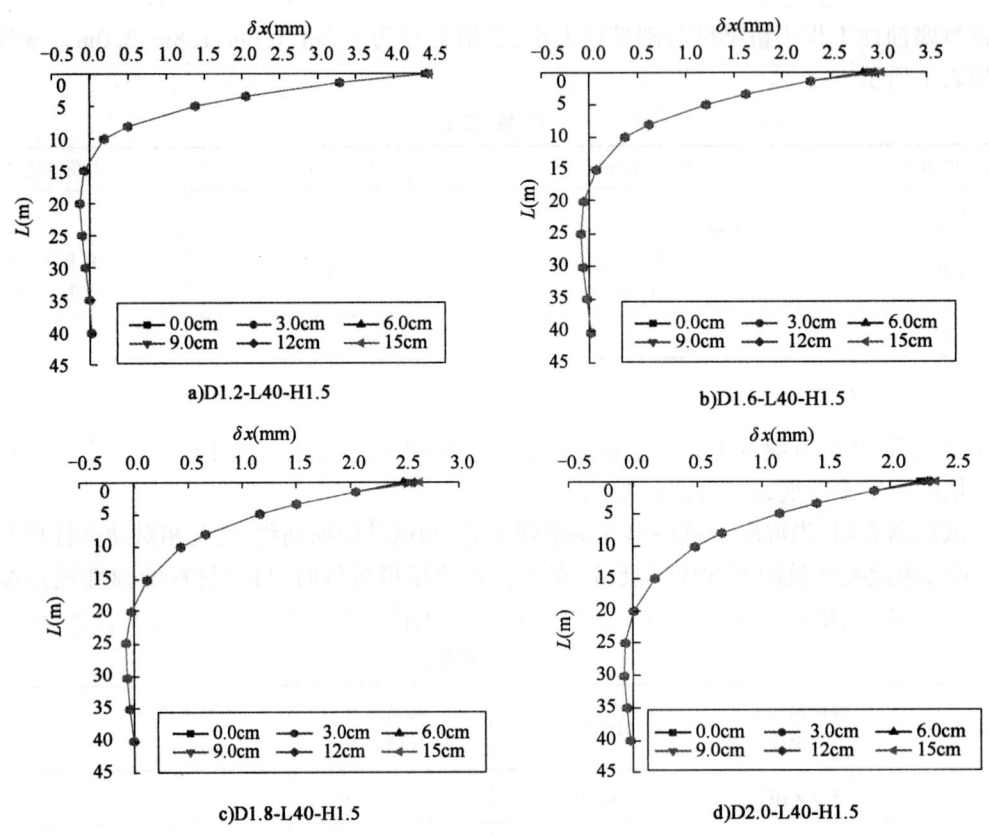

图 2 沿桩身方向桩基水平位移变化曲线 1

如图 3 所示,桩长不变,受腐深度为 5.0m 时,同一桩径的桩基础随剥落厚度的增加,其第一位移零点逐渐上移。以桩径 1.2m 的桩基础为例,桩基剥落厚度为 0.0cm 时,桩基第一位移零点距桩底 26.354m,其距桩底距离占桩长 65.9%;桩基剥落厚度为 3.0cm 时,桩基第一位移零点距桩底 26.534m,其距桩底距离占桩长 66.3%;桩基剥落厚度分别为 6.0cm 时,桩基第一位移零点距桩底 26.534m,其距桩底距离占桩长 66.3%;桩基剥落厚度为 9.0cm 时,桩基第一位移零点距桩底 26.739m,其距桩底距离占桩长 66.8%;桩基剥落厚度为 12.0cm 时,桩基第一位移零点距桩底 26.792m,其距桩底距离占桩长 67.0%;桩基剥落厚度为 15.0cm 时,桩基第一位移零点距桩底 26.980m,其距桩底距离占桩长 67.4%。说明桩基受腐深度为 5.0m 时,随着剥落厚度的增加,桩基第一位移零点不断上移,桩基稳定性下降,这是因为桩身混凝土剥落导致桩基总体弹性模量减弱,桩的刚度不断降低。如图 4 所示,桩基受腐深度为 8.0m 时,其规律与桩基受腐深度 5.0m 时相似。

如图 5 所示,桩径相同,受腐深度为 1.5m 时,随剥落厚度的逐渐增加,横向承载力的变化不大。说明在受腐深度 1.5m 时,剥落厚度对桥梁桩基影响较小,其横向承载力不会发生显著下降。

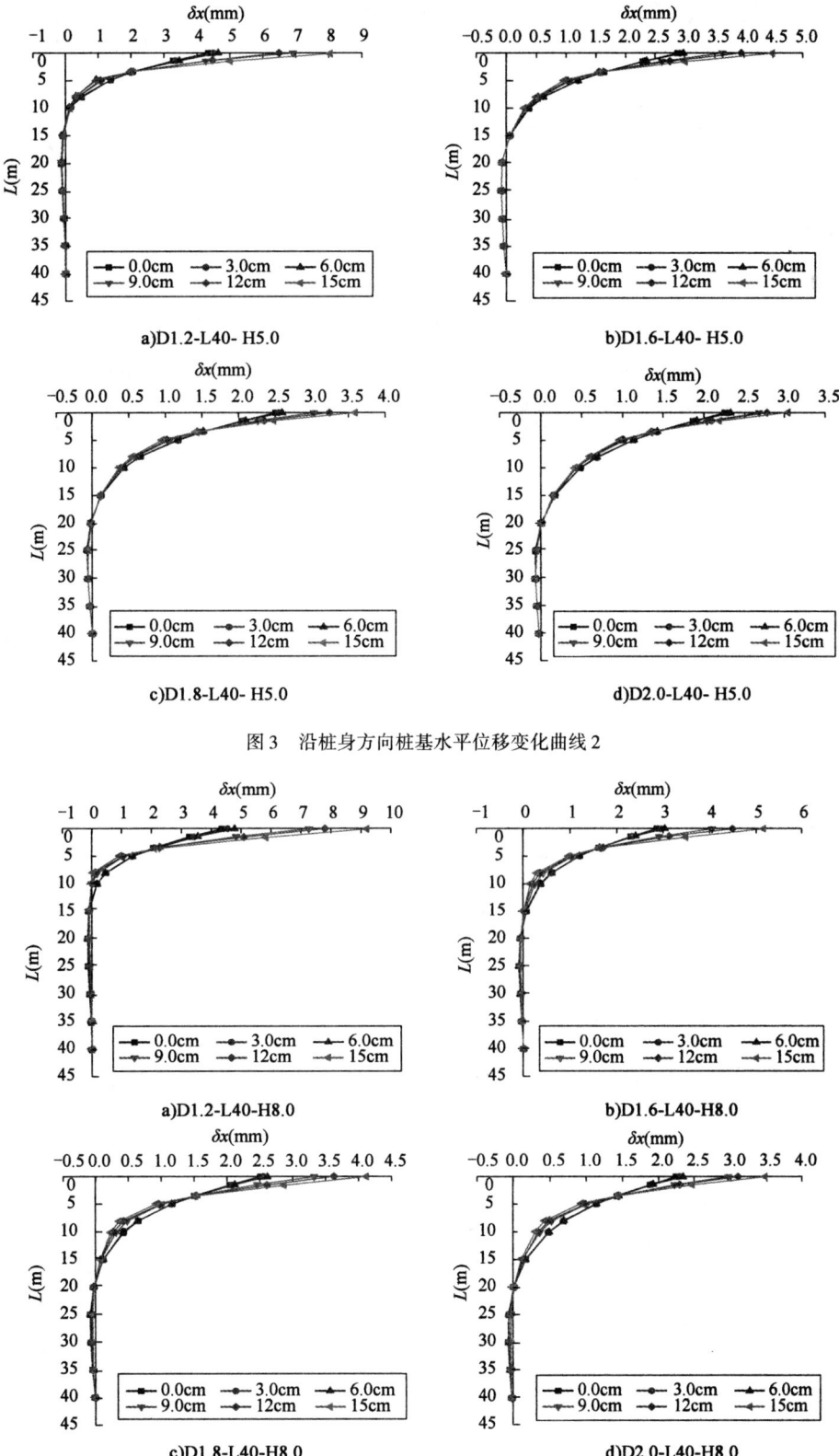

图3 沿桩身方向桩基水平位移变化曲线2

图4 沿桩身方向桩基水平位移变化曲线3

如图6所示,当桩径相同,桩基受腐深度为5.0m时,随桩基剥落厚度的逐渐增加,发生相同横向位移所需的横向荷载逐渐减小,即桩基稳定性逐渐下降。说明随着受腐深度的增加,剥落厚度对于桩基稳定性的影响逐渐增大。如图7所示,桩基受腐深度为8.0m时,其规律与受腐深度5.0m时大致相同。

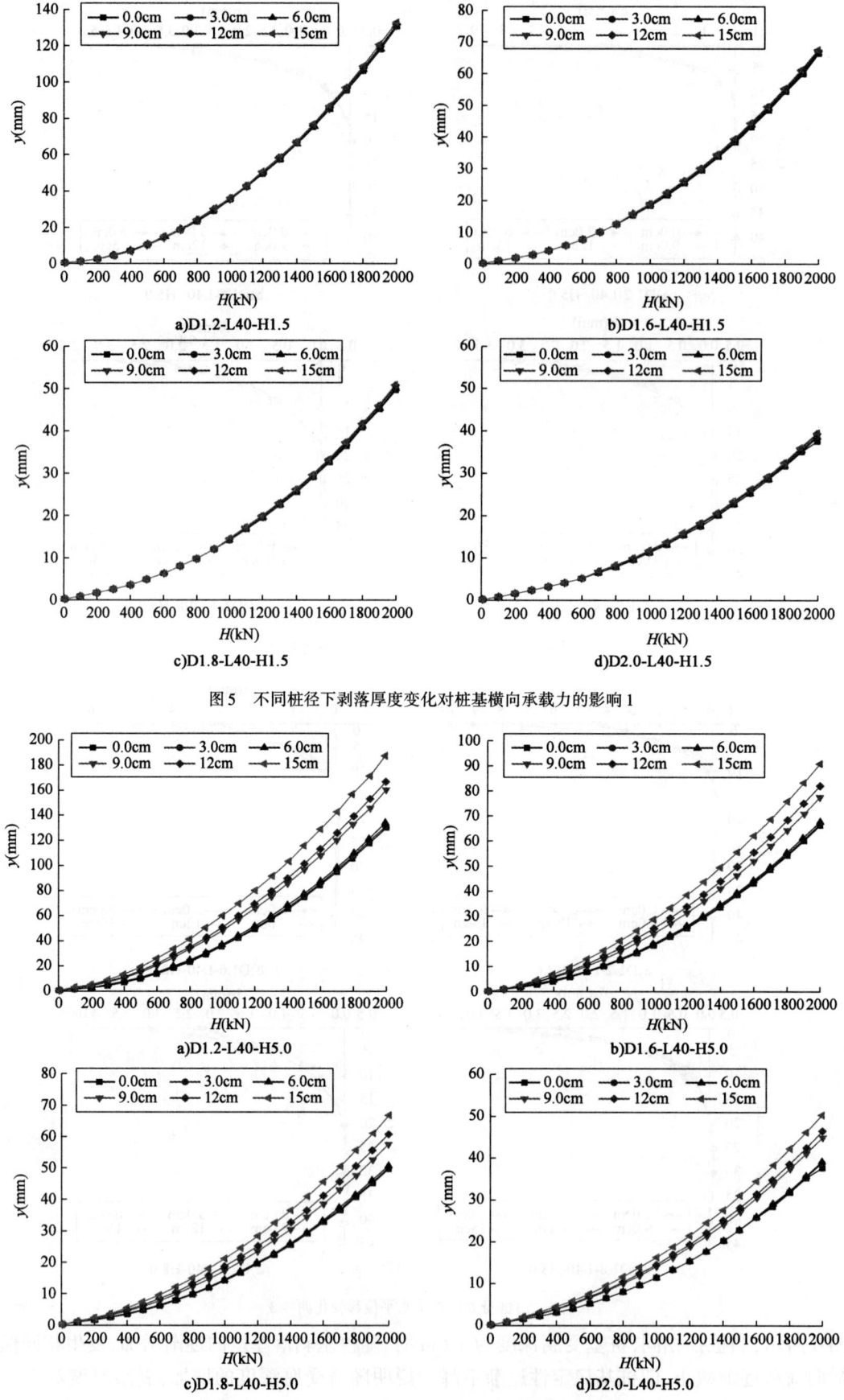

图5 不同桩径下剥落厚度变化对桩基横向承载力的影响1

图6 不同桩径下剥落厚度变化对桩基横向承载力的影响2

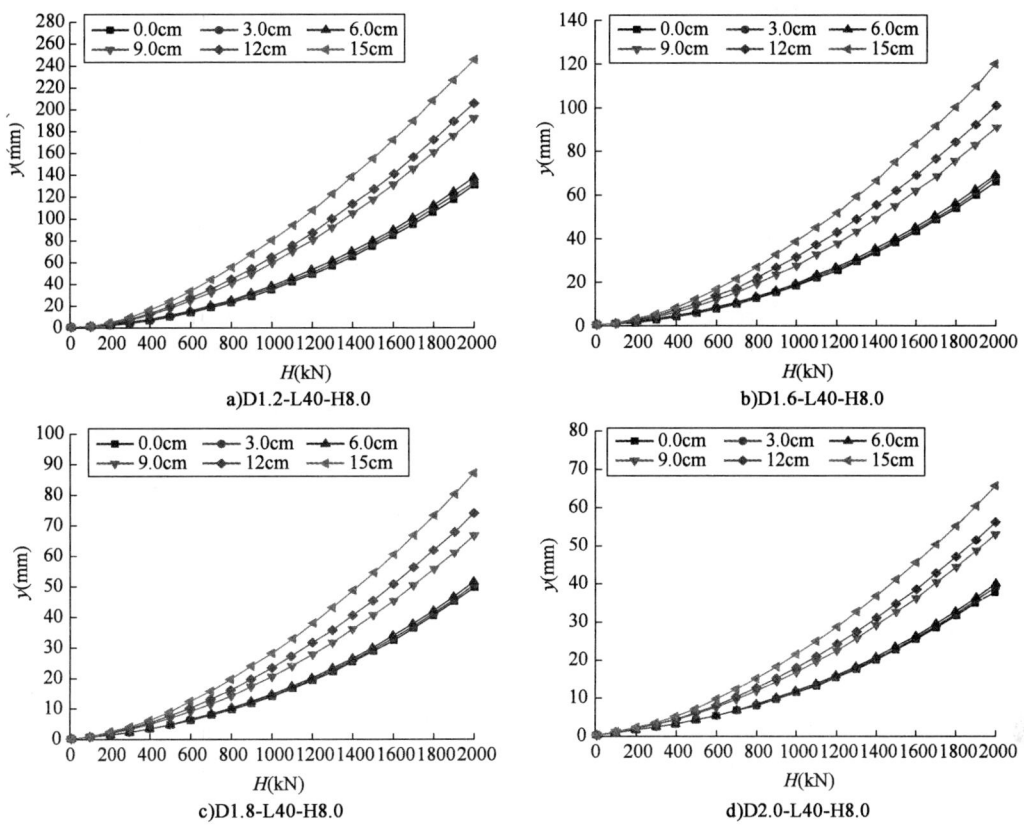

图7 不同桩径下剥落厚度变化对桩基横向承载力的影响3

如图8所示，桩基受腐深度为1.5m时，随着剥落厚度的不断增加，桩基的横向承载力降低幅度也随之降低。桩基受腐深度为5.0m和8.0m，剥落厚度小于6cm时，桩基的横向承载力不会发生显著降低，当桩基剥落厚度大于6cm时，其横向承载力发生显著下降。以桩径1.6m的桩基为例，当受腐深度为1.5m，桩身混凝土未发生剥落时，其横向承载力为511.03KN；当桩身混凝土出现3.0cm的剥落厚度时，其横向承载力为510.58KN，承载力降幅0.1%；桩身混凝土剥落厚度为6.0cm时，其横向承载力为510.08kN，承载力降幅0.2%；桩身混凝土剥落厚度为9.0cm时，其横向承载力为504.28kN，承载力降幅1.3%；桩身混凝土剥落厚度为12.0cm时，其横向承载力为501.52kN，承载力降幅1.9%；桩身混凝土剥落厚度为15.0cm时，其横向承载力为485.70kN，承载力降幅5.0%。

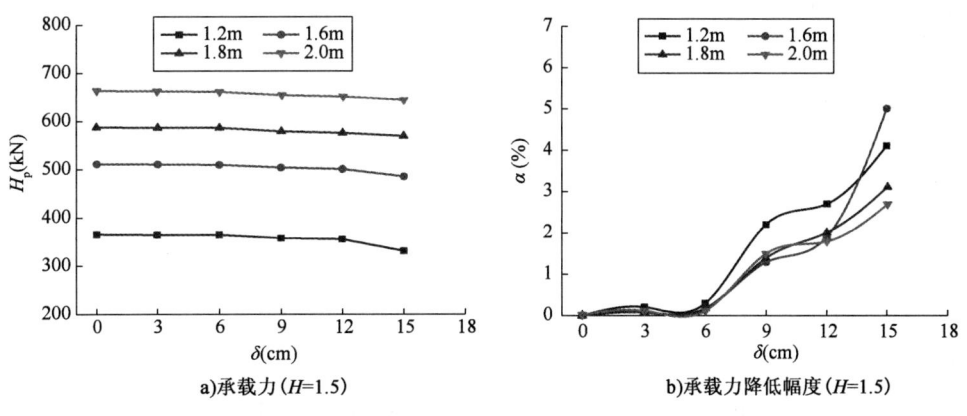

图 8

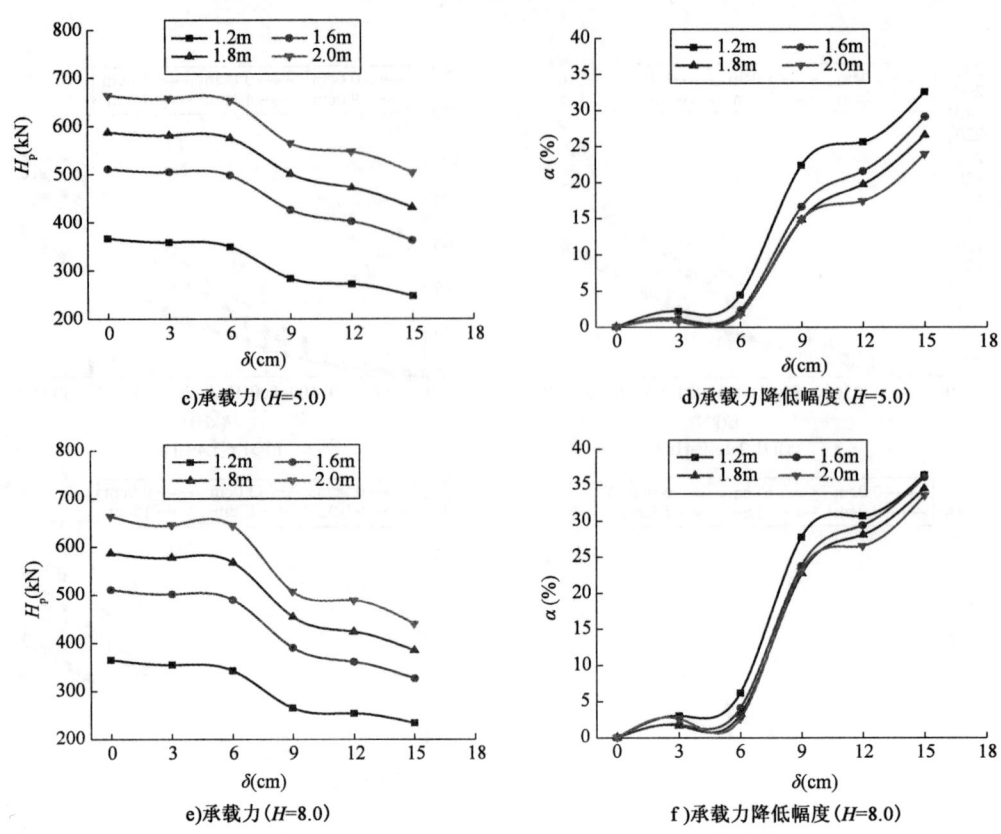

图8 不同腐蚀深度下不同桩径桩基承载力随剥落厚度变化规律

当受腐深度为5.0m,桩身混凝土未发生剥落时,其横向承载力为511.03kN;桩身混凝土剥落厚度为3.0cm时,其横向承载力为505.35KN,承载力降幅1.1%;当桩身混凝土出现6.0cm的剥落厚度时,其横向承载力为498.79kN,承载力降幅2.4%;当桩身混凝土出现9.0cm的剥落厚度时,其横向承载力为424.93kN,承载力降幅16.6%;当桩身混凝土出现12.0cm的剥落厚度时,其横向承载力为400.70kN,承载力降幅21.6%;当桩身混凝土出现的剥落厚度时,其横向承载力为362.28KN,承载力降幅29.1%。

4 结 语

(1)桩基桩身混凝土剥落厚度6.0cm,受腐深度8.0m的情况下,桩径1.2m的单桩,其横轴向极限承载力由366.20kN降为343.50kN,降幅仅为6.2%;剥落厚度9.0cm,受腐深度为8.0m的情况下,桩径2.0m的单桩,其横轴向极限承载力由663.57vN降为509.99kN,降幅达到22.8%。由此可以看出桩身混凝土剥落厚度超过6.0cm时,其承载力大幅下降。因此桩基服役时间达到八年时,应及时进行桩基横轴向稳定性检测。

(2)在受腐深度8.0m,桩身混凝土剥落厚度15cm的情况下,桩径1.2m的单桩其横轴向极限承载力为233.34kN,桩径1.6m、1.8m、2.0m的单桩其横轴向极限承载力分别为326.53kN、385.12kN、440.28kN,与桩径为1.2m的单桩横轴向极限承载力相比较,增幅分别为39.9%、65.1%、88.7%。因此,提高盐沼泽区桩基础横轴向承载能力的有效方法是增大桩径。

参考文献

[1] 冯忠居,冯瑞玲,赵占厂,等.黄土湿陷性对桥梁桩基承载力的影响[J].交通运输工程学报,2005(03):60-63.

[2] Fan Zhenhui, Wang Yonghe, Xiao Hongbin. Analytical method of load-transfe-rof single pile under expansive soil swelling[J]. J Cent South Univ Technol,2007,14(4):575-579.

[3] 崔强,鲁先龙,冯自霞.水平荷载作用下加翼掏挖基础承载特性研究[J].地下空间与工程学报,2011,7(03)457-463.
[4] 冯忠居,王航,魏进,等.黄土冲沟斜坡桥梁桩基竖向承载特性模型试验研究[J].岩土工程学报,2015,37(12):2308-2314.
[5] 王富春,姚贤华,冯忠居,等.盐沼泽腐蚀对公路桥梁桩基础竖向极限承载力影响的数值模拟研究[J].公路,2017,62(01):60-66.
[6] 余红发,刘连新,曹敬党,等.东西部氯盐环境中混凝土的耐久性和服役寿命[J].沈阳建筑大学学报(自然科学版),2005(02):125-129.
[7] 余红发,孙伟,王甲春,等.盐湖地区的环境条件与混凝土和钢筋混凝土结构的耐久性[J].工业建筑,2003(03):1-4+10.
[8] 蒋卫东,尹正风,闫俊,等.宁夏盐渍地区混凝土破坏模式与防治研究[J].混凝土,2006(06):18-21+25.
[9] 马希和,平树江,蔡长松,等.海水环境中钢筋混凝土桥桩耐久性数值模拟研究[J].混凝土,2004(07):19-23.
[10] 郭朋鑫,肖岩,Kunnath S K.大变形水平受荷桩静力分析方法综述[J].自然灾害学报,2015,24(03):132-142.
[11] 戴自航,陈林靖.多层地基中水平荷载桩计算m法的两种数值解[J].岩土工程学报,2007(05):690-696.
[12] 刘晋超,熊根,朱斌,等.砂土海床中大直径单桩水平承载与变形特性[J].岩土力学,2015,36(02):591-599.
[13] 朱斌,熊根,刘晋超,等.砂土中大直径单桩水平受荷离心模型试验[J].岩土工程学报,2013,35(10):1807-1815.
[14] 冯忠居,李孝雄,苏航州,等.深厚软基区桥梁桩基横轴向承载特性研究[J].中外公路,2018,38(01):123-127.
[15] 祝彦知,程楠.横向受荷桩基-土体共同作用黏弹性分析[J].工业建筑,2009,39(06):74-78.
[16] 冯忠居,乌延玲,成超,等.板块状盐渍土的盐溶和盐胀特性研究[J].岩土工程学报,2010,32(09):1439-1442.
[17] 李晋,谢永利,冯忠居.桩身设计参数对大直径空心桩承载性状影响的仿真分析[J].公路交通科技,2005(09):102-105.
[18] Masouleh S F, Fakharian K. Application of a continu-um numerical model for pile driving analysis and comparison with a real case[J]. Computers and Geotechnics,2008,35(3):406-418.
[19] 王梅,楼志刚,李建乡,等.水平荷载作用下单桩非线性m法试验研究[J].岩土力学,2002(01):23-26+30.
[20] 武星,王志新,张小明.软土地基摩擦桩承载特性的有限元方法研究[J].公路,2013(06):105-111.

Construction Technology of Pile Foundation of Bridge passing through Extra-large Karst Cave

Shaofen Bai[1]　Junhua Cai[2]　Zhongju Feng[1]　Chenming Xia[2]　Huiyun Chen[1]

(1. Chang'an University, School of Highway; 2. Fujian Provincial Bureau of Quality and Safety Supervision of Traffic Construction)

Abstract　In order to solve the problems encountered in the construction of highway bridge pile in karst area, the method of combining theoretical method with on-site construction is adopted, on the basis of systematically summarizing the common problems and treatment measures in the construction process of bridge pile passing through extra-large karst cave in karst development area. Combined with the specific problems encountered in the construction of 0a#-3 pile of FujianPuyan expressway crossing 25.7m extra-large karst cave, comprehensively considering the size, location and filling of karst cave as well as many factors such as project safety, quality, construction period and cost, and comparing the influence of different treatment measures on the construction and cost of bridge pile, the optimal treatment scheme of karst cave is adopted. Ensure the pile quality of pile and meet the actual engineering needs of Puyan highway, and provide a reference basis for bridge pile construction in similar areas.

Keywords Bridge engineering Pile foundation Extra-large karst cave Construction technology

0 Introduction

The karst area in China is very broad, and it is mainly concentrated in the southwest. With the acceleration of highway construction in southwest China, in order to meet the needs of route selection, extra-large karst caves are encountered in the process of bridge pile foundation construction from time to time. In view of the problems and corresponding treatment measures in the construction process of bridge pile foundation passing through extra-large karst cave in karst development area, there have been a lot of research at home and abroad. Zhongju Feng and others made a systematic study on the bearing capacity of bridge pile foundation in special soil area [1]. Aiming at the problems encountered in the construction of karst area, such as hole collapse, slurry leakage, pile subsidence and so on, some effective measures are put forward, such as slurry backfilling method, cast-in-place concrete wall secondary hole drilling method and steel casing follow-up method [2]. Yunxiu Dong et al carried out the test of bearing capacity of pile foundation in karst area and put forward a reasonable calculation method of rock-socketed depth [3]. Zhenming Shi systematically summarized the influence of karst cave on pile foundation, the general principles of karst cave treatment and the selection basis of treatment methods, and combined with engineering practice, put forward the pile foundation construction methods and matters needing attention in karst area [4]. Guowei Liu and others analyze the influence of karst cave on pile foundation construction and its treatment methods, and comprehensively consider many factors such as pile foundation safety, quality, construction period, cost and so on. Backfilling sheet stone, backfilling clay and steel casing follow up construction technology under different geological conditions in karst area to solve the technical problems of pile foundation construction of single-layer or multi-layer karst cave [5-6]. According to the actual construction situation, Yong Liu and others summarized the construction technology and construction quality control points suitable for bored cast-in-place pile of bridge in karst area. the treatment methods of different types of karst caves, the economic benefits and construction time of various methods are compared and analyzed [7-8]. Zhongju Feng et al studied the influence of surface water on pile foundation in loess area [9-11] and found that the ultimate bearing capacity of bridge pile foundation will be greatly reduced after loess flooding [12-13]. Through shaking table test, it is found that the buried depth of liquefied layer has a great influence on the seismic design of pile foundation [14]. Shaohui Wang et al adopted the method of combining theory with site, comprehensively considered the characteristics and treatment difficulties of super-large karst cave, established the construction method of bottom-up cross construction treatment structure based on backfilling, and studied the settlement mechanism of backfill body. the pile quality of pile foundation is ensured [15-18].

Although a series of karst cave treatment measures have been put forward in the above research, there is a relative lack of research on the construction technology of the pile foundation of the bridge passing through the extra-large karst cave, especially for the karst cave treatment measures and effects under the actual situation.

Based on the construction situation of the 0a#-3 pile foundation of the provincial highway from Youxi Zhongxian to Jianning Lixin section of Puyan Expressway, from the point of view of the construction period, the project cost and the overall stability of the structure after construction, this paper fully compares the differences of bridge pile foundation construction and cost under different karst cave treatment measures, and studies the construction technology of bridge pile foundation through extra-large karst cave. It is expected to provide a reference basis for the construction of bridge pile foundation in similar areas.

1 Distribution Characteristics of Extra-large Karst Caves at Pile Position

The No. 0 pier of the provincial highway 204 separation overpass is located in the karst area, and the central mileage of pile 0a#-3 is YK281 + 572.45, which belongs to the end-bearing pile. The designed pile length and diameter are 61m and 1.5m respectively, and the actual construction pile length is 64m. The depth of the roof and bottom of the cave is 35.50m and 61.20m, with a height of 25.7m. According to the classification standard of karst cave type in Tab.1, the height of the karst cave is much more than 4m, so it can be judged to be a super large karst cave. Combined with the results of previous drilling, in-hole electromagnetic wave CT exploration and ground penetrating radar exploration, the specific location, size and filling state of the karst cave at the pile site are determined. The specific size and location of the cave are shown in Fig. 1.

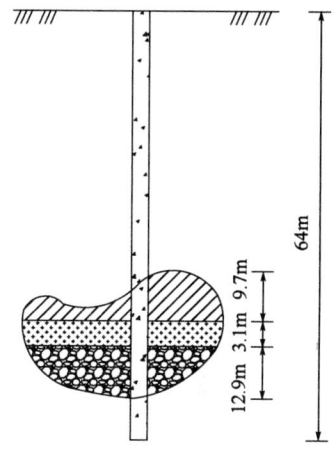

Fig. 1 Schematic Diagram of Karst of Pile 0a#-3

The filling state and characteristics of karst cave are as follows: large karst cave, ①35.50-45.20m is yellow brown and grayish brown gravel clayey soil filling, wet, plastic, gravel particle size is 0.3-3cm, limestone, filling is dense; ②45.2-48.30m is grayish brown fine sand filling, slightly dense, saturated, high mud content, poor separability, dense filling. ③48.30-61.20m is filled with grayish brown pebble, slightly dense, saturated, with a particle size of 2-7 cm, full filling.

Classification of Karst Cave Types   Tab. 1

Serial Number	Species	Remarks
1	Karst fissures and small karst caves	$h \leq 0.5m$
2	General karst cave	$h \leq 4m$
3	Large karst cave	$h > 4m$
4	Other karst caves	—
5	Incomplete karst cave	The rock surface shows complex conditions such as slope, scarp, stalagmite, solution ditch, solution trough and so on
6	String of slurry and holes in karst channel	The connected hole means that due to the development of karst fissures in the site, abundant groundwater and the existence of karst caves with good connectivity, the adjacent pile holes are penetrated by karst caves in some part of the pile body
7	Deep and large solution trough	The bedrock surface at the bottom of the solution trough is uneven, and karst caves and fissures are developed
8	Fully filled karst cave	The cave is completely filled with coarse gravel, sand, fine gravel and clay, and most of the fillings are hard plastic, soft plastic and flow plastic
9	Semi-filled karst cave	There are fillers at the bottom of the cave and a cavity at the top of the cave
10	Unfilled karst cave	—

2　Treatment Technology and Parameters of Pile Foundation in Extra-large Karst Cave Area

There are mainly some problems in the construction of pile foundation in karst development area, such as slurry leakage, sticking, drill drop, buried drill, hole collapse, drilling deviation and so on. the reason is that the soil(rock) around the pile is missing or the soil around the pile can not provide stable resistance because of the karst cave near the side or bottom of the pile. When the pile foundation is constructed, the disturbance of the upper construction load to the original rock and soil leads to the collapse of the karst cave, which leads to the ground subsidence or the collapse or deviation of the pile hole. Therefore, the reasonable treatment technology of karst cave is of great significance to the quality and safe operation of the whole bridge project.

2.1　Grouting Consolidation Method

The grouting consolidation method is to use all kinds of plugging slurry to inject into the leakage zone to block the leakage passageway. This method is generally consolidation hardening. When the karst cave rock mass is broken, cracks are developed, and there are flow plastic fillers in the cave, the grouting consolidation method can be used. First, explore the specific conditions of the rock surface of the pile hole location, and then use the geological drilling rig to drill grouting, the plane layout should be basically uniform, but for the trenches, grooves and the lower parts of the rock surface can be relatively dense, and the hole depth should be determined according to the rock surface conditions and the required consolidation thickness. The consolidation thickness range is controlled from 50cm above the casing blade foot to the lowest point of the rock surface, and the peripheral width is controlled within the range of 1.0-1.5cm larger than the pile diameter. After the consolidation of rock surface sand and clay layer is completed and reaches a certain strength, the drilling construction of pile foundation can be started. The advantage of this method is that after consolidation is completed, drilling can be carried out according to ordinary formation conditions, sand leakage is not easy to occur, hole cleaning is easy, and quality is easy to be guaranteed, but the construction period is relatively long and the cost is high.

2.2　Steel Casing Follow-up Method

When a very large empty karst cave or semi-filled karst cave is encountered, in order to prevent the hole wall from collapsing caused by slurry leakage, the method of pre-drilling and then burying steel protective tube to isolate the upper soft cover is used to deal with it. When passing through large empty karst caves or semi-filled karst caves, the protective tube follow-up method can achieve better results. That is, first, the larger diameter bit is used to impact to the top of the karst cave, the inner protective tube is lowered to the bottom of the hole after 1.0m, and the small bit continues to smash until it breaks through the karst cave, then the mixture of clay and sheet stone is backfilled, and the hole is compacted by repeated impact, and then transferred to normal drilling. The key points of this scheme are: ①the position of the inner casing must be accurate; ②the inner casing must have sufficient stiffness; ③the mixture of clay and sheet stone should be backfilled in time after breaking through the karst cave. In general, the steel casing follow-up method should be combined with the backfilling sheet stone in the karst cave and the plugging treatment between the bottom of the karst cave and the protective tube foot, otherwise the treatment effect may be greatly reduced.

3　The Treatment Technology and Parameters of Bead-shaped Karst Cave in Solid Engineering

When the pile foundation construction is carried out in the solid project, the safety and rationality of the pile foundation construction should be ensured firstly, and then the construction difficulty should be reduced as much as possible and the engineering materials should be saved so as to reduce the project cost. Therefore, considering the actual geological conditions and other factors of the pier and combining with the existing actual cases of karst cave treatment technology, the treatment scheme of "backfilling and plugging slurry" is determined. This scheme can effectively treat super-large karst caves, multi-layer karst caves, semi-filled and fully filled karst caves, at the same time, the treatment technology is more mature, the construction difficulty is low, and the goal of economy and reliability can be achieved.

There is a 25.7m karst cave at the pile 0a#-3 of the provincial highway 204. The bridge pile foundation construction needs to pass through the karst cave, and the main method is backfilling and plugging slurry leakage treatment measures. When you encounter an extra-large karst cave, especially the semi-filled karst cave where there is a leakage source at the bottom of the cave, the silt and pebbles that have been filled in the process of the formation of the cave will block the source of leakage, and the filling material will slip or be reopened in the process of punching, resulting in re-leakage. In order to stop the source of the leakage, after the leakage is found, the centralized pump replenishes water into the hole to maintain the water head, and immediately throws cement into the hole, and then puts a mixture of clay and flake stone 3m thick into the hole, and then punches the hole again after the slurry leakage stops. The time from punching to the leakage site should be controlled before the cement final setting time, and then stop for 6 ~ 10 hours. This is done repeatedly until the solidified cement clay slurry blocks the source of the leakage.

The detailed construction process of 0a#-3 pile foundation of YA1 section of provincial highway 204 separation overpass is shown in Tab. 2.

General Situation of Treatment of Karst Cave at Station 0a#-3 of Provincial Highway 204 in YA1 Bid Section　　Tab. 2

Date	Hole Depth During Slurry Leakage(m)	Backfill Hole Depth (m)	Backfill Earthwork (m^3)	Backfill Stone Square (m^3)	Backfill Cement (ton)
2019.03.09	33	3.2	—	5	—
2019.03.15	37.8	27.8	72	24	4
2019.03.17	44.8	38.8	101	34	5
2019.03.18	45	43	110	37	6
2019.03.19	53	47	122	41	7
2019.03.21	56	35	91	30	5
2019.03.24	57	38	99	33	6
2019.03.26	57.7	41	107	36	7
2019.03.28	57.9	51	133	44	8
2019.04.01	62	59	153	51	9
2019.04.03	62.3	59.3	154	51	9.5
2019.04.06	62.5	58.2	151	48	9
Total	—	501.3	1293	434	75.5

As can be seen from Tab. 2, backfilling and plugging slurry was carried out for 29 days and 12 times, with a total of 1293m^3 of backfill, 434m^3 of stone and 75.5 tons of cement. After the quality inspection of pile foundation, pile No.3 of Pier 0 is Class I pile, which shows that this scheme can effectively solve all kinds of problems occurred in the process of hole formation, ensure the normal construction of pile foundation, and greatly reduce the construction difficulty and project cost.

4　Comparative Analysis

Compared with the steel protective tube follow-up method to treat the karst cave, the backfilling method used in the solid project has the following advantages:

(1) Using the backfilling method to treat the karst cave, the construction difficulty is small and the construction period is short. The steel casing follow-up method not only needs to customize the steel casing according to the actual situation, but also needs to lower the auxiliary steel casing for the backfilling of the karst cave, so the construction is difficult. The project is located in the mountain area, and the backfilling method requires more earth and stone and other raw materials, which can save a lot of manpower and material resources. Combined with the on-site situation, it is more appropriate to use the backfilling method to treat the karst cave.

(2) The cost of karst cave treatment by backfilling method is lower than that by steel casing follow-up method. According to the actual investigation, if the steel casing follow-up method is used for karst cave treatment, the total cost is about 430000 yuan, while the backfilling method is only about 130000 yuan, which greatly saves the material cost. The cost of materials required for different treatment methods is shown in Tab. 3.

Material Costs for Different Treatment Methods　　　　Tab. 3

Treatment Method	Materials	Material Consumption	Unit Price (yuan)	Total Cost (ten thousand yuan)
Backfilling method	Earthwork(m^3)	1293	45	12.85
	Stone(m^3)	434	70	
	Cement(ton)	75.5	500	
Steel casing follow-up method	Steel casing(m)	64	6700	42.88

(3) Because the pile foundation passes through the extra-large karst cave in the process of construction, after the pile is treated by the backfilling method, the backfill can provide a certain side friction resistance for the pile foundation, and then increase the bearing capacity of the pile foundation, while the steel tube follow-up method is adopted. then the lack of soil around the pile and the existence of steel casing affect the exertion of the lateral friction of the pile foundation, so it is more reasonable to choose the construction method actually used in the project.

5　Conclusions

The main results are as follows:

(1) The influence of karst cave on pile foundation mainly includes slurry leakage, sticking, drill drop, buried drill, hole collapse, drilling deviation and so on. Try to avoid the above problems and reduce unnecessary losses in the actual project.

(2) The main treatment methods of large karst cave in pile foundation construction are backfilling method and steel casing follow-up method. In the actual treatment process, the treatment measures should be comprehensively selected according to the factors such as the location, size, filling and construction period of the cave, in order to achieve the principles of rationality, economy and safety.

(3) There is a strong development of karst caves in the area where the No. 0 pier of the separation interchange of Puyan highway YA1 section is located. Combined with the actual construction requirements of the project, the engineering geological conditions and the principle of economic rationality are comprehensively considered. The scheme of backfilling and plugging leakage is adopted to treat the karst cave, which achieves good results, ensures the quality of the pile, and provides a reference basis for the subsequent construction of pile

foundation crossing of similar super-large karst cave bridge.

References

[1] Zhongju Feng. Infrastructure projects in special areas [M]. Beijing: People's Communications Publishing House, 2008.

[2] Hongsheng Yao, Zhongju Feng, Zhan Yuan, et al. Study on construction technology of pile foundation of extra-large bridge in karst development area [J]. Construction Technology, 2017, 46(19): 130-133.

[3] Yunxiu Dong, Zhongju Feng, Yumeng Hao, et al. Bearing capacity test and reasonable rock-socketed depth of bridge pile foundation in karst area [J]. Journal of Traffic and Transportation Engineering, 2018, 18(06): 27-Qing.

[4] Zhenming Shi, Danfu Shen, Ming Peng, et al. Karst cave treatment technology for pile foundation construction in karst area- taking the pile foundation construction of Ji'an Yonghe bridge as an example [J]. Journal of Engineering Geology, 2015, 23(06): 1160-1167.

[5] Guowei Liu, Zhi Yang, Haibo Zhang, et al. Study on construction technology of bored cast-in-place pile in karst area [J]. Construction Technology, 2018, 47(S4): 116-119.

[6] Guowei Liu, Haibo Zhang, Zhi Yang, et al. Study on treatment technology of collapse cavity of large cross-section deep-buried karst tunnel [J]. Construction Technology, 2018 4. 47(S4): 1406-1409.

[7] Yong Liu, Rao Fu, Long Chang, et al. Construction technology of pile foundation in karst cave development area [J]. Construction Technology, 2017, 46(14): 10-12.

[8] Yong Liu. A brief discussion on the construction technology of pile foundation in karst cave [J]. Green Building Materials, 2018(06): 144, 145.

[9] Zhongju Feng, Fuchun Wang, Hangzhou Suzhou, et al. Centrifugal model test on the influence of loess cave on vertical bearing characteristics of bridge pile foundation [J]. Journal of Chang'an University (Natural Science Edition), 2017, 37(02): 35-44.

[10] Zhongju Feng, Hang Wang, Jin Wei, et al. Model experimental study on vertical bearing characteristics of pile foundation of loess gully slope bridge [J]. Journal of Geotechnical Engineering, 2015, 37(12): 2308-2314.

[11] Zhongju Feng, Ruiling Feng, Zhanchang Zhao, et al. Influence of collapsibility of loess on bearing capacity of bridge pile foundation [J]. Journal of Transportation Engineering, 2005(03): 60-63.

[12] Zhongju Feng, Yongli Xie, Hongguang Zhang, et al. Experimental study on the influence of surface water on the bearing capacity of bridge pile foundation in loess area [J]. Journal of Rock Mechanics and Engineering, 2005(10): 1758-1765.

[13] Zhongju Feng, Yongli Xie, Hongguang Zhang, et al. Comprehensive study on influencing factors of pile foundation bearing capacity of large diameter bridge in "West Yunnan Red bed" area [J]. Journal of Geotechnical Engineering, 2005(05): 540-544.

[14] Zhongju Feng, Xiqing Wang, Xiaoxiong Li, et al. Influence of sand liquefaction on mechanical properties of pile foundation under strong earthquake [J]. Journal of Traffic and Transportation Engineering, 2019, 19(01): 71-84.

[15] Shaohui Wang, Zhao Chen, Chong Jiang, et al. Comprehensive treatment scheme and construction technology of super large karst cave tunnel [J]. Tunnel Construction, 2017, 37(06): 748-752.

[16] Xiguo Chen, Zhao Chen, Lin Liu, et al. Study on construction technology of steep slope backfill pile foundation in extra-large karst goaf [J]. Construction Technology, 2018, 47(07): 119-123.

[17] Cinnamon Chrome, Shatze, Liu Lin. Study on construction technology of backfilled karst tunnel based on numerical analysis [J]. Mining and Metallurgical Engineering, 2018, 38 (03): 20-25.

[18] Wujun Jiang, Dingyuan Kui, Mingming Wang, et al. Study on load-settlement law and calculation of foundation pile of extra-large karst cave backfill [J]. Journal of Geotechnical Engineering, 2017, 39 (S2): 67-70.

V形峡谷地区空间Y形钢箱拱桥缆索吊装系统设计

黄骞 邬晓光 胡科坚 徐宁

(长安大学公路学院)

摘 要 V形峡谷地区中承式空间Y形钢箱拱桥结构新颖,施工工艺复杂。本文以缆索吊装系统为工程背景,阐述了针对中承式空间Y形钢箱拱桥施工所用缆索吊装系统的横向及纵向设计方案。基于弹性变形理论,根据静力平衡原理,运用解析法对主索、工作索及牵引索的垂度、张力、作用在塔架上的荷载进行设计,计算其设计参数及安全系数,并与规范限值作比较;以有限元理论为基础,运用容许应力法,利用通用结构分析与设计软件SAP2000对主要结构构件的力学特性进行分析,给出了总体设计思路与设计建议,为峡谷地区同类型桥梁无支架缆索吊装设计提供参考。

关键词 异形拱桥 索力 容许应力法 缆索吊装 受力特性

0 引 言

在景观桥梁的建造中,异形拱桥由于具有较好的美学效果而被广泛采用[1-4]。现有异形拱桥多为斜靠拱桥,蝴蝶拱桥和斜跨拱桥等一系列新型拱桥,而中承式空间Y形拱桥较少见,由于桥梁空间上呈Y形,主副拱协同作用,结构受力复杂,为无支架缆索吊装施工增加了难度。根据可查文献,文献[5]介绍了横移式缆索吊机的设计与施工。文献[6]提出"零弯矩法",可计算任意多段扣索在临时铰接及固结情况下的索力。文献[7]从公式推导和计算实例方面说明了运用"零弯矩法"计算扣索索力会出现负值和不均衡的情况,并指出了"零弯矩法"的适用范围。文献[8]应用零弯矩法、零位移法计算扣索索力并比较计算方法的优缺点。国外也有文献[2]对缆索吊装系统的基本组成及其发展现状,以及在桥梁工程中的应用进行研究。

目前尚未有文献对空间Y形钢箱拱桥无支架缆索吊装系统的设计与受力特性进行研究。本文对中承式空间Y形钢箱拱桥施工所用缆索吊装系统及主要构件进行设计与受力分析,给出总体设计思路与设计建议。

1 工程概况

中承式空间Y形钢箱拱桥是景观桥梁,桥梁全长284m,跨径布置为19.5m+220m+19.5m。立面投影上,主拱净跨径220m,净矢高62.5m,矢跨比为1/3.52,副拱净跨径为183.21m,净矢高42.8m,矢跨比为1/4.28,副拱绕其轴线起终点的连线外倾5°。主跨主梁采用π形扁平钢箱梁,标准断面宽18m,观景平台处宽36m。主拱采用变高矩形钢箱结构,主梁边、主跨采用悬吊式连续梁结构,墩台及拱上横梁处设竖向支座,计算跨径为2×19.5m+197m(14.5m+28×6m+14.5m)+2×19.5m。吊杆为柔性吊杆,布置间距6m,共29对,吊杆两端采用钢锚箱分别与梁、拱连接,拱端张拉,梁端锚固。总体布置图如图1所示。

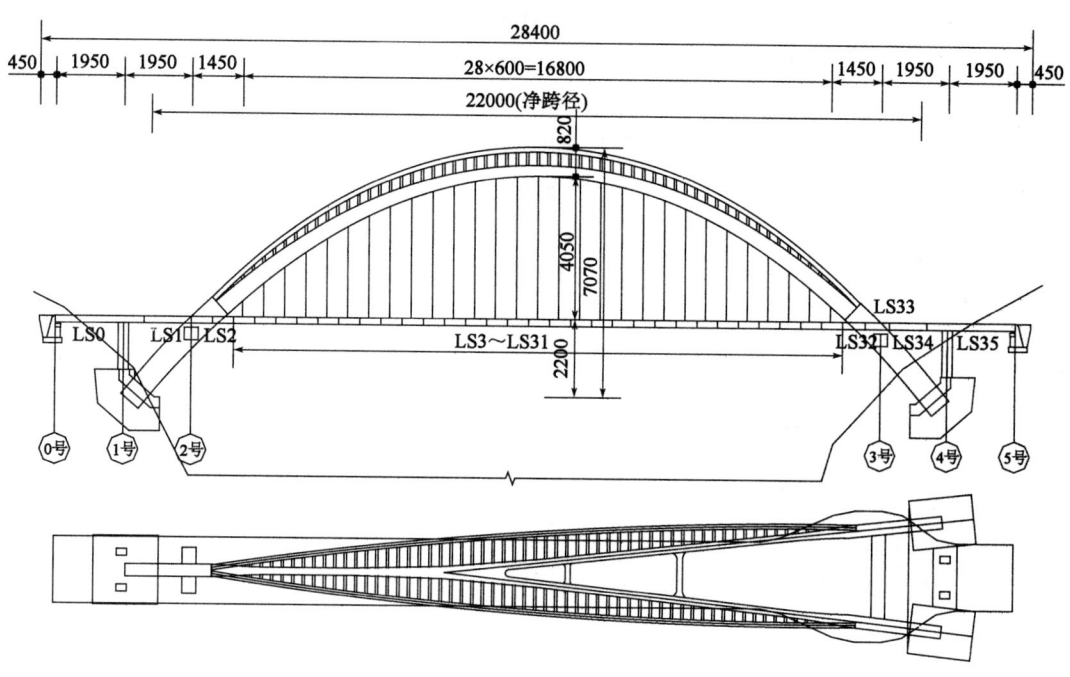

图 1 中承式空间 Y 型钢箱拱桥总体布置图(尺寸单位:mm)

2 总体设计

缆索吊机设计以满足钢箱、拱肋、横梁、吊杆及桥面主梁等安装需要为目的,根据桥梁跨径布置,桥位处地形、地质情况,并结合现场已施工完成的临时设施及桥梁基础开挖等情况,考虑两岸塔架皆设置在桥台后方山坡上,缆索运输系统主索跨径设计为430m。根据现场地形条件,同时根据主索后拉索水平倾角要求,两岸主、扣索锚碇皆设置在同一位置,淳化岸主锚碇距离塔架65m,礼泉岸主锚碇距离塔架68m,如图2所示。每岸主锚碇设置3个分离式锚碇,并相对于桥轴线对称布置,礼泉岸为单拱肋,扣锚索锚固在中间锚碇上;淳化岸为双拱肋,扣锚索分别锚固在上下游锚碇上。

缆索吊机在上、下游(距离桥轴线18m)及桥轴线上共设置3组每组额定起吊能力为135t的承重索,每组承重索不同时承载额定荷载。每组承重索设置前后2个吊点,单个吊点额定起重量67.5t。承重索总体布置跨度为68m+430m+65m,礼泉岸主索后拉索与水平面间的夹角为23.0°,淳化岸由于施工便道影响,锚碇位置不能再往后移,主索后拉索与水平面间的夹角为34.1°,相对较大,缆索系统对塔架产生的较大的水平推力只有通过加强前后风缆来克服。缆索吊机系统由主索、起重索、牵引索、通风缆、后风缆、天跑车及起吊滑车组、索鞍、塔架、锚碇和卷扬机等组成,如图2所示。另在上下游承重索内侧各设置1组额定起吊能力10t的工作索,作为小型机具运输、设备检修、扣索及拱肋、桥面系钢梁等安装辅助。

2.1 总体纵向设计

每段悬拼拱箱对应设置1道钢绞线扣索,每道扣索为2束钢绞线索,每道扣索对应一道锚索,礼泉岸第7道锚索为双束钢绞线索,其余锚索为单束钢绞线索。分叉岸扣锚索分别锚固在扣塔上下游侧塔柱顶部,单肋岸扣锚索皆锚固在扣塔中部塔柱顶部,扣索对应平衡锚索锚固在主锚碇上。扣锚索张拉端皆设置于扣塔上,锚固端分别设置在与拱肋连接处及主锚碇上。扣锚索对称张拉,前后水平力互相平衡,并以扣锚索张拉力及扣塔位移进行双控,扣塔位移为主要控制指标。

两岸塔架采用吊、扣塔合一的构造形式,三柱门式结构,扣塔与基础固结,吊塔与扣塔顶铰接,扣塔每肢立柱平面尺寸2×2.4m(横)×2.4m(纵),每肢立柱采用6φ630×14mm钢管并通过法兰盘接长,以确保扣塔的强度和刚度,腹杆采用万能杆件并通过螺栓与立柱钢管上焊接的缀板连接,扣塔顶横向全宽47.6m,扣塔顶设置H型钢分配梁来支撑扣锚索锚箱及吊塔,扣锚索锚箱梁皆设置在扣塔顶部。吊塔下部铰座分配梁采用钢箱梁,吊塔高21.5m,淳化岸为21.9m,纵向万能杆件设双柱脚,纵向宽2.56m,顶部横向宽44m,吊塔采用钢桁架结构,每肢立柱2.56m(纵)×4m(横),塔顶设置钢箱分配梁来支撑运输主索鞍座滑轮,吊塔通过塔后风缆及跨间通风缆来约束塔顶纵向位移,扣塔前后设置斜风缆,同时吊塔每侧设置2组横向风缆,扣塔每侧设置1组横向风缆,如图3所示。

主锚碇采用钢筋混凝土桩基承台结构,每岸设置3个分离式主锚碇。主锚碇分为Ⅰ类、Ⅱ类两种结构,Ⅰ类用于承重主索、工作索、锚索及塔架后风缆等的锚固,Ⅱ类仅用于承重主索、工作索及塔架后风缆等的锚固。主锚碇部分桩基露出承台并设置横向水平锚梁锚固钢索,Ⅰ类主锚碇承台内根据每束锚索方向预埋锚索管及锚垫板,通过固定端锚具来锚固锚索,如图2所示。

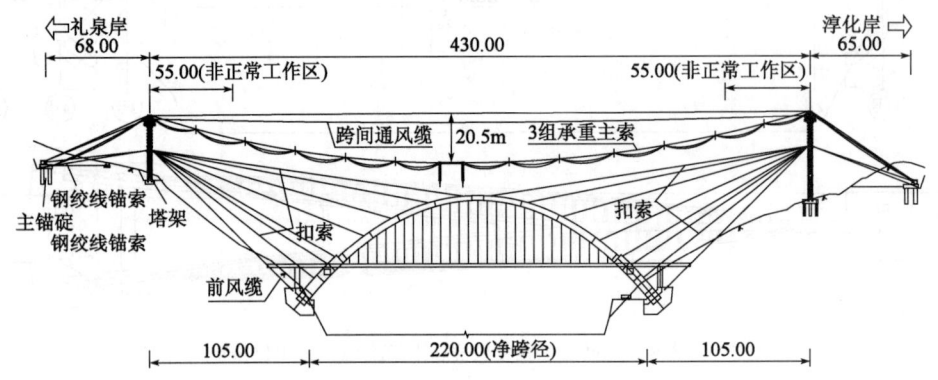

图2 缆索吊机总体立面布置图(尺寸单位:m)

2.2 总体横向设计

每安装一段拱肋,皆在上下游各设置一道2ϕ22mm拱肋风缆索,防止拱肋横向失稳,同时方便拱肋横向位置的调整,分叉段由于拱肋横向倾斜,除拱肋风撑外,另设置一道临时横撑来确保拱肋空间位置和保持拱肋的横向稳定,临时横撑及拱肋风缆索、扣锚索在拱肋合拢、接头焊接完成、桥面横梁安装焊接完成后拆除。全桥共设置10个拱肋风缆锚碇。

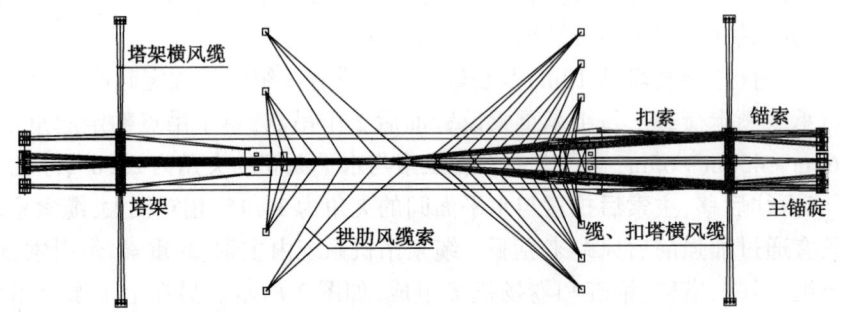

图3 主拱扣、锚索系统平面布置图

2.3 总体吊装方案

主副拱肋节段、肋间横梁、风撑、主副拱间连系梁、桥面主梁等皆采用缆索吊装安装。单拱肋及双拱肋节段安装采用两岸及上下游对称悬拼,每一悬拼节段为一个扣段,每段各设一道(两束)扣索,每道扣索对应一道背索。节段为单肋安装,分叉岸待上下游同一节段吊装就位后,安装节段间连接风撑、横撑或临时横撑,即完成一个双肋节段,单肋节段安装就位后,设置侧向浪风索。为确保合龙前拱肋的横向稳定,在淳化岸第五节段,另增设临时横撑。为确保安装精度,副拱肋采用小节段安装,先在主拱肋上定位焊接主副拱间连接肋,然后再焊接一段副拱肋,两岸及上下游对称安装、焊接,拱顶合龙,副拱安装不设扣索,利用主拱支承安装。

桥面主梁先在支架上安装两岸引桥LS0、LS1、LS35段,预留LS34段作为主梁下放缺口,然后从淳化岸向礼泉岸安装,安装顺序为从LS33段至LS2段,LS2段为礼泉岸合龙段,最后在支架上安装LS34段,最终主梁合龙。LS33 段需与拱肋横梁临时固结,LS32 段需在拱肋上设置临时吊杆。最后安装、拼接淳化岸观光平台段,完成全桥主梁安装。

主副拱肋及肋间连系梁皆由两组主索四个吊点抬吊出台及就位。待拱肋合龙、接头及风撑焊接完毕,灌筑拱脚钢箱内微膨胀混凝土,浇筑拱座二期混凝土后可拆除扣索、风缆及临时横撑。桥面主梁利用上下游两组主索四个吊点抬吊进行。

3 缆索设计计算

3.1 缆索设计计算原理

基于弹性变形理论,根据静力平衡原理进行缆索计算。先假定主索初始垂度,根据经验可在 $L/30 \sim L/20$ 之间取值,计算重索垂度。初始(空索)垂度 F_0 设定以后,空索长度 S_0 为:

$$S = L_3/\cos\alpha_1 + L_4/\cos\alpha_2 + Q^2 L_3^3/24 T_{10}^2 \cos^4\alpha_1 + Q^2 L_4^3/24 T_{20}^2 \cos^4\alpha_2 + L + DH^2/2L + 8F_0^2/3L - 32F_0^4/5L^3 \tag{1}$$

空索长度为定值,荷载作用产生弹性伸长,受载后的总长度 S 为空索长度 S_0 与荷载引起的弹性伸长值 ΔS 之和,即 $S = S_0 + \Delta S$。重索长度 S 计算按假设重索垂度,以几何关系求得。

$$\begin{aligned} S = &\, L_3/\cos\alpha_1 + \sqrt{(F_1 - \Delta H L_1/L)^2 + L_1^2} + \sqrt{(F_2 - F_1 - DH L_2/L)^2 + L_2^2} + \\ &\, \sqrt{[F_2 + DH(L - L_1 - L_2)/L]^2 + (L - L_1 - L_2)^2} + \\ &\, L_4/\cos^4\alpha_2 + Q^2 L_3^3/24 T_1^2 \cos^4\alpha_1 + Q^2 L_1 S_2^2/24 H^2 + Q^2 L_2 S_3^2/24 H^2 + \\ &\, Q^2 (L - L_1 - L_2) S_4^2/24 H^2 + Q^2 L_4^3/24 T_3^2 \cos^4\alpha_2 \end{aligned} \tag{2}$$

按假设重索垂度,以计算主索内张力得到弹性伸长值 ΔS,算得重索长度 $S' = S_0 + \Delta S$。在要求的精度内,当 $S \approx S'$ 时,则假设重索垂度为所求解,其他需要值即可解出,如表1、表2所示。

$$\begin{aligned} \Delta S = &\, \{[L_3/\cos\alpha_1 + \sqrt{(F_1 - DH \times L_1/L)^2 + L_1^2} + Q^2 L_3^3/24 T_1^2 \cos^4\alpha_1 + Q^2 L_1 S_2^2/24 H^2](T_1 - T_{10}) + \\ &\, [Q^2 L_2 S_3^2/24 H^2 + \sqrt{(F_2 - F_1 - DH \times L_2/L)^2 + L_2^2}](T_2 - H_0) + \\ &\, \{\sqrt{[F_2 + DH(L - L_1 - L_2)/L]^2 + (L - L_1 - L_2)^2} + L_4/\cos^4\alpha_2 + \\ &\, Q^2 (L - L_1 - L_2) S_4^2/24 H^2 + Q^2 L_4^3/24 T_3^2 \cos^4\alpha_2\}(T_3 - T_{30})\}/EA \end{aligned} \tag{3}$$

式中:A——主索截面面积;

E——弹性模量;

α_1——起吊岸主索后拉索与水平面夹角;

α_2——非起吊岸主索后拉索与水平面夹角;

DH——两岸塔顶高差;

DS——主索弹性伸长量;

F_0——跨中安装垂度;

F_1——后吊点吊重垂度;

F_2——前吊点吊重垂度;

H_{10}——起吊岸塔顶空索水平力差;

H_{20}——非起吊岸塔顶空索水平力差;

H_1——起吊岸塔顶重索水平力差;

H_2——非起吊岸塔顶重索水平力差;

L——吊装跨径;

L_1——后吊点距起吊岸塔顶水平距离;

L_2——前后两吊点间水平距离;

L_3——起吊岸主锚碇距塔架水平距离;
L_4——非起吊岸主锚碇距塔架水平距离;
Q——主索单位重量;
P——起吊重量;
S_0——初始索长;
S——吊重索长;
V_{10}——起吊岸塔顶空索竖直力;
V_{20}——非起吊岸塔顶空索竖直力;
V_1——起吊岸塔顶重索竖直力;
V_2——非起吊岸塔顶重索竖直力。

如图4、图5所示。

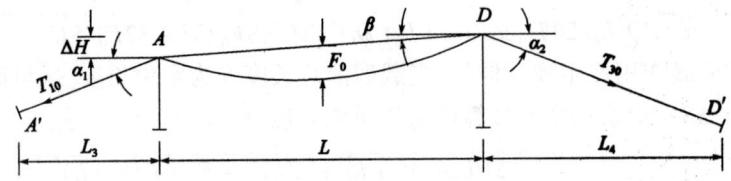

图4 空索索跨布置示意图

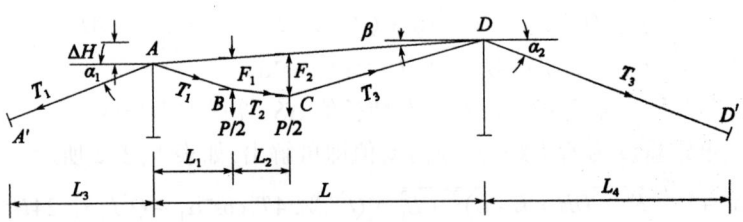

图5 吊重索跨布置示意图

主索计算表 表1

状 态	跨间竖直力		塔顶水平力差		塔顶竖直力	
	R_{10}(A岸)	R_{20}(D岸)	H_{10}(A岸)	H_{20}(D岸)	V_{10}(A岸)	V_{20}(D岸)
空索	$Q\sqrt{L^2+DH^2}/2 - H_0DH/L$	$Q\sqrt{L^2+DH^2}/2 - H_0DH/L$	$H_0 - T_{10}\cos\alpha_1$	$H_0 - T_{30}\cos\alpha_2$	$R_{10} + T_{10}\sin\alpha_1$	$R_{20} + T_{20}\sin\alpha_2$
	R_1(A岸)	R_2(D岸)	H_1(A岸)	H_2(D岸)	V_1(A岸)	V_2(D岸)
重索	$P[1-(2L_1+L_2)/2L] + Q\sqrt{L^2+DH^2}/2 - DH/L$	$P(L_1+L_2/2)/L + Q\sqrt{L^2+DH^2}/2 + HDH/L$	$H - T_1\cos\alpha_1$	$H - T_3\cos\alpha_2$	$R_1 + T_1\sin\alpha_1$	$R_2 + T_3\sin\alpha_2$

各阶段承重主索计算成果表(一组主索) 表2

阶 段	运输位置	承重索张力 T (kN)	安全系数 K	承重索垂度 f (m)	对礼泉岸塔架作用力(kN)	对淳化岸塔架作用力(kN)
空索状态	仅有承重索自重	1546.583		20.5	$H = 92.789$ $V = 873.646$	$H = 239.929$ $V = 1169.757$
空载状态	起重小车等位于跨中	2527.485		$f_1 = 23.700$ $f_2 = 23.700$	$H = 157.294$ $V = 1396.352$	$H = 398.077$ $V = 1880.204$

续上表

阶 段	运输位置	承重索张力 T (kN)	安全系数 K	承重索垂度 f (m)	对礼泉岸塔架作用力(kN)	对淳化岸塔架作用力(kN)
额定荷载状态	至礼泉岸塔前 55m	5787.919		$f_1 = 18.873$ $f_2 = 21.319$	$H = 128.059$ $V = 4111.709$	$H = 921.730$ $V = 3732.743$
	至淳化岸塔前 55m	5802.021		$f_1 = 21.348$ $f_2 = 18.898$	$H = 392.647$ $V = 2676.569$	$H = 671.114$ $V = 5220.608$
		7355.262	3.15	$f_1 = 31.551$ $f_2 = 31.551$	$H = 462.258$ $V = 4037.225$	$H = 1163.234$ $V = 5445.233$
	至索跨跨中	考虑弯曲作用应力 $\sigma_{max} = 0.849$MPa,安全系数 $K = 2.37 > [2]$ 考虑接触作用应力 $\sigma_{max} = 0.577$MPa,安全系数 $K = 3.40 > [2]$				

3.2 主索设计

每组承重索额定承载力1350kN,每组承重索设置前后2个吊点,每个吊点设置一台8门100t起吊滑车组。起吊卷扬机布置于礼泉岸锚碇前缘40m左右位置。考虑吊具、配重、起吊牵引绳和冲击系数后,单组承重索最大集中荷载为1863.772kN,则每个吊点起吊重量 G_1 为931.886kN。每台起吊滑车走16线布置,动头绕过礼泉岸塔顶及锚碇位置导向滑轮后进入起重卷扬机,如图6所示。跑头拉力为:

$$F = G_1/(\eta^3 + \eta^4 + \eta^5 + \eta^6 + \eta^7 + \eta^8 + \eta^9 + \eta^{10} + \eta^{11} + \eta^{12} + \eta^{13} + \eta^{14} + \eta^{15} + \eta^{16} + \eta^{17} + \eta^{18})$$
$$= 931.886/12.998 = 71.695\text{kN} < [0.7 \times 120\text{kN}] = [84\text{kN}] \tag{4}$$

式中:η——起重滑轮效率系数,取值0.98;

0.7——卷扬机效率系数。

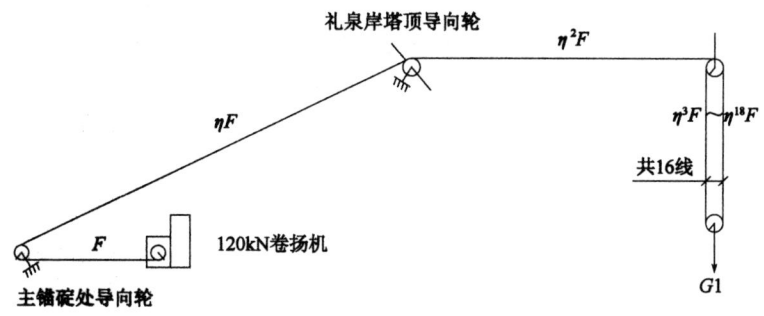

图6 一台起吊滑车走线布置示意图

采用120kN卷扬机起吊满足要求。运输至跨中时主索张力最大,主索应力安全系数按此阶段控制计算。主索弯曲作用应力为:

$$s = T_{max}/A_n + V_{max}\sqrt{E/T_{max}A_n}/n \tag{5}$$

式中:T_{max}——单组钢索最大张力,其值为355.262kN;

V_{max}——运输至索跨跨中时索鞍处有最大支反力,其值为5445.233kN;

A_n——钢索截面积,其值为14878.4mm^2;

E——钢索弹性模量,其值为105kN/mm^2;

n——支撑轮数量,其值为16。

主索接触作用应力为:

$$\sigma = T_{max}/A_n + C_e Ed/D \tag{6}$$

式中：d——钢丝直径，其值为3.45mm；
　　　D——滑轮直径，其值为500mm；
　　　C_e——钢索弹性模量折减系数，$C_e = 0.104 + 0.04 \times 2d/D$；
　　　d——钢索直径，其值为60mm。

主索安全系数为：

$$K = s_{max}/s \tag{7}$$

式中：s_{max}——主索钢丝公称抗拉强度，其值为1.96kN/mm^2。

主索考虑弯曲作用应力及接触作用应力计算结果如表2所示，安全系数参考《缆索起重机》(GB/T 28756—2012)取值，主索在额定荷载作用下的各运输工况，其张力安全系数及应力安全系数皆满足规范要求，主索受力安全。

3.3 工作索计算

在每组主索旁各布置了1根φ56mm的工作索，工作索距主索中心距离1.8m。工作索公称抗拉强度1770MPa，弹性模量为75.6kN/mm^2，单根钢绳钢丝截面积为1233.79mm^2，单根钢绳单位长度重量为11.6kg/m，索安装垂度为18.0m，每根工作索额定承载力按100kN设计。工作索按吊篮位于两岸塔架前50m及索跨跨中3种受力工况计算，计算原理和方法与主索相同，计算结果如表3所示。由计算结果知，吊篮位于跨中时工作索张力最大，工作索应力安全系数按此阶段控制。工作索弯曲作用应力为：

$$s = T_{max}/A_n + G_{max}\sqrt{E/T_{max}A_n}/n \tag{8}$$

式中：G_{max}——计算重量，其值为355.262kN；
　　　n——支撑轮数量，其值为4。

主索接触作用应力及安全系数分别按式(6)、式(7)计算，主索弯曲作用应力及接触作用应力计算结果如表3所示，安全系数参考《缆索起重机》(GB/T 28756—2012)取值，工作索在各运输工况下，其张力安全系数及应力安全系数皆满足规范要求，工作索受力安全。

各阶段工作索计算成果表　　表3

计算工况	工作索张力 T (kN)	安全系数 K	工作索垂度 f (m)	对礼泉岸塔架作用力(kN)	对淳化岸塔架作用力(kN)
空索状态	148.171		18	$H = 9.462$ $V = 80.431$	$H = 23.592$ $V = 108.793$
礼泉岸塔前50m	434.512		17.888	$H = 7.824$ $V = 313.760$	$H = 69.238$ $V = 274.983$
淳化岸塔前50m	435.572		17.915	$H = 29.688$ $V = 196.109$	$H = 48.539$ $V = 396.987$
至索跨跨中	570.289	3.21	31.683	$H = 36.267$ $V = 310.481$	$H = 90.643$ $V = 419.645$
	考虑弯曲作用应力 $\sigma_{max} = 0.828$MPa，安全系数 $K = 2.14 > [2]$ 考虑接触作用应力 $\sigma_{max} = 0.519$MPa，安全系数 $K = 3.41 > [2]$				

起吊卷扬机布置在礼泉岸,起吊绳动头过礼泉岸塔顶及主锚碇处导向轮后进入起吊卷扬机,定头锚固于定滑车轴上,因而起吊索仅对礼泉岸塔架及锚碇产生作用力。按运输至两岸塔前55m及索跨跨中3种运输状态分别计算起吊索对礼泉岸塔架及锚碇的作用力,计算示意图如图7所示。计算原理和方法与主索相同,计算结果表4表明,起吊索对礼泉岸塔架及锚碇的作用力不大,两岸锚碇设计过程中更应关注扣、锚索系统对其作用力的大小。

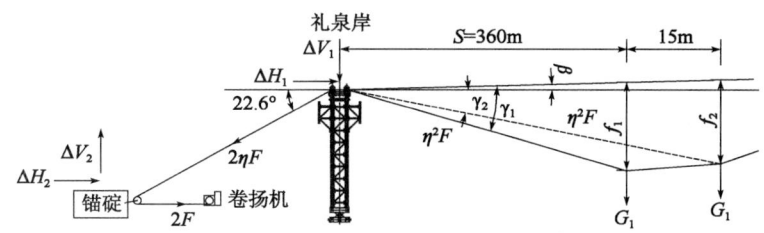

图7 起吊索对礼泉岸塔架力作用示意图

各阶段起吊索对礼泉岸塔架作用荷载汇总表(一组承重索作用荷载) 表4

运输位置	卷扬机最大拉力 F (kN)	礼泉岸塔架		礼泉岸锚碇	
		水平力 ΔH_1 (kN)	竖直力 ΔV_1 (kN)	水平力 ΔH_2 (kN)	上拔力 ΔV_2 (kN)
淳化岸塔前55m		7.829	60.389	273.122	54.002
索跨跨中	71.695	6.628	73.244	273.122	54.002
礼泉岸塔前55m		1.487	95.720	273.122	54.002

3.4 牵引索计算

牵引卷扬机布置于礼泉岸,牵引跑头通过礼泉岸塔顶及锚碇位置的导向滑轮后进入15t的牵引卷扬机,两岸牵引定滑车组皆通过连接绳连接后,连接绳再经过塔顶座滑轮导向并进入主锚碇锚固。按运输至两岸塔前55m及索跨跨中3种运输状态分别计算牵引索单组主索的牵引力。牵引索转向滑轮为球轴承,滑轮效率系数 $\eta=0.98$,跑车运行阻力系数为0.012。牵引力由跑车运行阻力 W_1、起重索运行阻力 W_2 和后牵引松弛张力 W_3 三部分组成。三种运输位置处的单组牵引索牵引力计算结果如表5所示。结果表明,运输至淳化岸塔前55m牵引力最大,单组主索最大牵引力 W_{max} 为603.190kN。

各阶段牵引力汇总表 表5

运输位置	W_1(kN)	W_2(kN)	W_3(kN)	W(kN)
礼泉岸塔前55m	311.438	-137.712	132.300	306.026
至索跨跨中	11.598	137.712	76.256	225.566
淳华岸塔前55m	333.178	137.712	132.300	603.190

牵引索安全系数计算参考图8,运输至淳化岸塔前55m处时牵引力最大。由图8得 $W_{max}=\eta^3 F+\eta^4 F+\eta^5 F+\eta^6 F+\eta^7 F+\eta^8 F$,则卷扬机动头力为:

$$F = W_{max}/(\eta^3+\eta^4+\eta^5+\eta^6+\eta^7+\eta^8) \quad (9)$$

三种运输位置下的卷扬机动头力如表6所示,因而选用额定牵引力150kN的卷扬机牵引较合适。牵引索采用 ϕ30mm 纤维芯钢绳,其安全系数为:

$$K = T_p/F \quad (10)$$

式中:T_p——破断拉力,其值为526kN。

安全系数参考《缆索起重机》(GB/T 28756—2012)取值,安全系数计算结果如表6所示,满足规范要求。

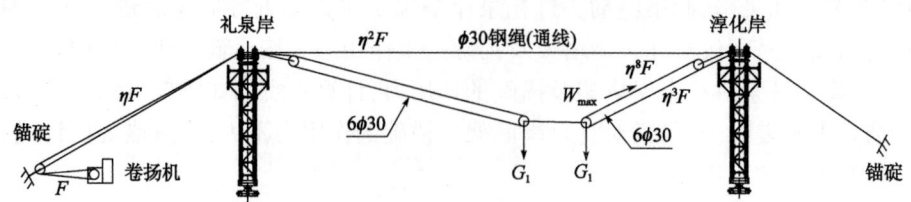

图 8　运输至淳化岸塔前 55m 时牵力示意图

各阶段总牵引力、卷扬机动头力及张力安全系数　　表6

运输位置	牵引力 W(kN)	卷扬机动头力 F(kN)	张力安全系数 K	备 注
礼泉岸塔前 55m	306.026	55.825		单组牵引力
至索跨跨中	225.566	41.988		单组牵引力
淳华岸塔前 55m	603.19	112.280	4.68 > [4.5]	单组牵引力

4　主要设备构件设计

4.1　钢锚箱设计

礼泉岸第 7 道扣锚索采用 2 束 $10\phi15.2$mm 钢绞线,在扣塔顶设置两根锚箱承载,其余扣锚索为 1 道(2 束),扣索对应一束锚索,在扣塔顶设置 1 根锚箱承载,钢锚箱构造示意图如图 9 所示。因而淳化岸第 7 道扣锚索作用在单个钢锚箱耳板上的荷载最大,作为锚梁控制设计荷载。

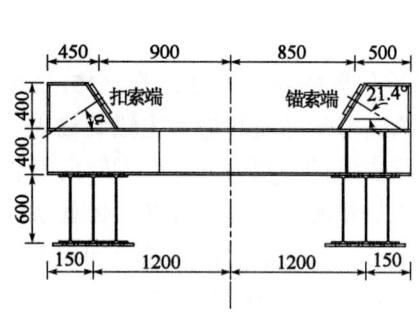

图 9　钢锚箱构造图(尺寸单位:mm)

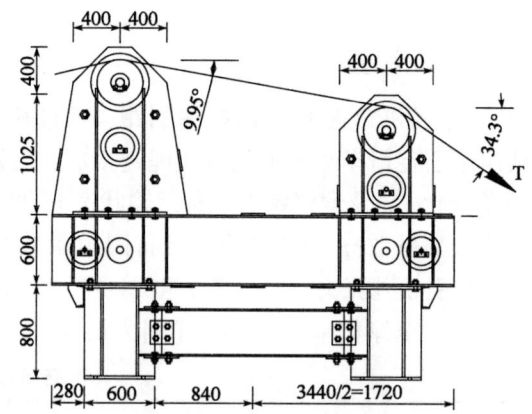

图 10　索鞍构造图(尺寸单位:mm)

钢锚箱扣锚索张拉端支承在扣塔分配梁支点上方,钢锚箱自身弯矩、剪力皆很小,不需进行强度计算,现仅对牛腿抗剪强度进行计算。淳化岸第七段锚索力最大,单束锚索力 T'_{max} 为 1554.519kN,则对牛腿的最大剪力 $Q = T'_{max}\cos21.4° = 1447.344$kN。

钢锚箱由 Q345 钢板焊接而成,扣索端牛腿为 4 块 16mm 厚肋板,锚索段为 2 块 20mm 厚肋板,仅对截面较弱的锚索端进行计算,顶底板仍为 20mm 厚的钢板。截面惯性矩为:

$$I = 2 \times 20 \times 460^3/12 + 2 \times 360 \times 20^3/12 + 2 \times 360 \times 20 \times 240^2 = 1.1544 \times 10^9 (\text{mm}^4)$$

中性轴以外截面对中性轴的静矩为:

$$S = 360 \times 20 \times 240 + 230 \times 20 \times 2 \times 230/2 = 2.786 \times 10^6 (\text{mm}^3)$$

则最大剪应力为:

$$\tau = \frac{QS}{Ib} = \frac{1447344 \times 2.786 \times 10^6}{1.1544 \times 10^9 \times 20 \times 2} = 87.325(\text{MPa}) < [\tau] = 120(\text{MPa})$$

可见,钢锚箱受力满足要求。

4.2 锚固缆索的钢筋混凝土锚梁设计

锚梁直径2.2m,跨度3m,按两端固结梁采用通用结构分析与设计软件SAP2000进行计算。锚梁材料为C40钢筋混凝土,周边均匀配置32根直径25mm的HRB400钢筋,保护层厚度6cm,箍筋为直径16mm的HRB400钢筋,箍筋间距12cm。锚梁承受缆索系统荷载,礼泉岸缆索系统荷载较大,最大荷载为10854.855kN,由两根锚梁承受,单根锚梁受力为5427.428kN。近似按集中荷载作用在锚梁跨中及$L/3$偏载进行计算,实际作用为锚梁一定范围内线荷载,按集中力计计算偏安全。锚梁按两端固结建模,荷载工况按集中荷载作用在跨中及$L/3$处考虑,配筋设计按2个工况的最大弯矩及剪力控制,计算模型与结果如图11所示。

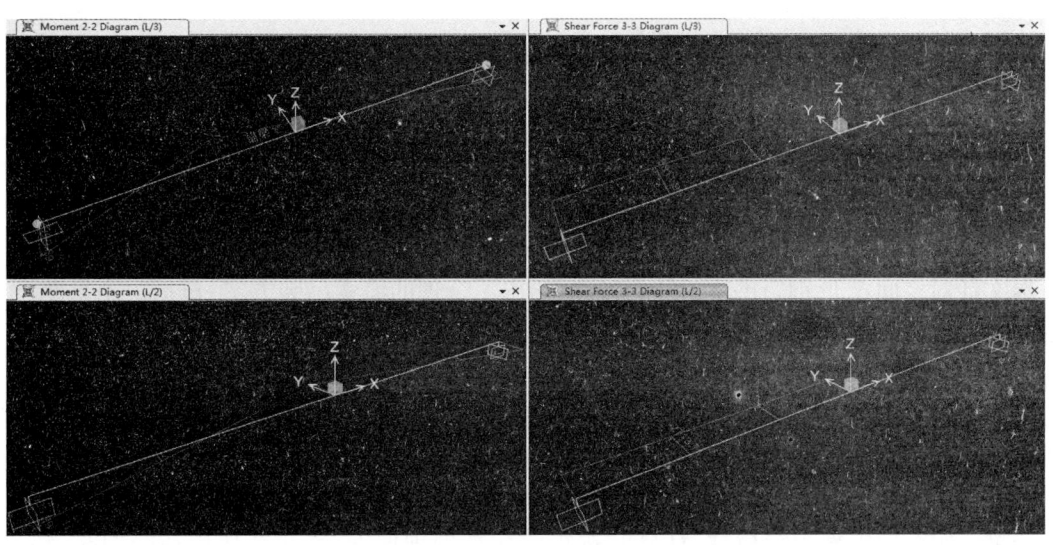

图11 锚梁有限元计算

荷载作用在跨中时,锚梁弯矩最大,荷载作用在$L/3$时剪力最大,如图11所示。最大弯矩M_{max}为2099.690kN·m,最大剪力Q_{max}为3811.984kN。根据《混凝土结构设计规范》(GB 50010—2010),锚梁截面设计为直径D为220cm的圆截面,将圆截面等截面、等刚度换算成矩形截,矩形截面宽高分别为$b_0 = 0.88D = 193.6$cm,$h_0 = 0.8D = 176$cm。锚梁抗剪承载力:

$$V_{cs} = 0.7f_t bh_0 + \frac{f_{yv}A_{sv}}{s}h_0 = 0.7 \times 1.71 \times 1936 \times 1760 + \frac{360 \times 402.124}{120} \times 1760 = 6201824.64(\text{N})$$

$$= 6201.825(\text{kN}) > 1.2Q_{max} = 1.2 \times 3811.984 = 4574.381(\text{kN})$$

式中:f_t——C40混凝土抗压强度设计值,取值1.71N/mm²;

f_{yv}——HRB400钢筋抗拉强度设计值,取值360N/mm²;

A_{sv}——箍筋面积,取值402.124mm²(2肢ϕ16mm HRB400箍筋);

s——箍筋间距,取值120mm。

锚梁抗剪承载能力满足要求。

4.3 索鞍设计

主索鞍为8门座滑轮,索鞍下部设置起吊索及牵引索的导向滑轮,滑轮采用前后两组。每组正对缆塔顶前后钢箱分配梁布置。礼泉岸前后座滑轮等高布置;淳化岸由于承重索后倾角较大,为使前后座滑轮数值压力相差不太大,将前部座滑轮高度提高40cm,具体见图10。索鞍轮轴采用直径为ϕ80mm的40Cr销轴,墙板及底板皆为25mm厚的钢板,外侧撑板为16mm厚的钢板,所有钢板材质为Q345B。

承重索对索鞍总的作用荷载随构件运输位置的不同而变化,同时总荷载在前后索鞍上作用力的分配比例也是变化的。淳化岸索鞍受力较大,按运输至淳化岸塔前 55m 及运输至索跨跨中分别计算淳化岸前后座滑轮受力。计算结果显示,在运输至跨中阶段,后侧索鞍受力最大,对单个索鞍总的作用力最大值为 3102.299kN。每组索鞍 8 个滑轮,单个滑轮受力为 387.787kN。

墙板为 $\delta 25$mm 钢板,轮轴直径 d 为 80mm,则墙板孔壁挤压应力:

$$\sigma_j = \frac{N_1}{d\delta} = \frac{387.787}{0.08 \times 0.025} = 193893.5(\text{kPa}) = 193.894(\text{MPa}) < [\sigma_j] = 300(\text{MPa})$$

轮轴剪应力为:

$$\tau_{max} = \frac{4}{3} \times \frac{N_1}{2\frac{\pi \times d^2}{4}} = \frac{8 \times 387.787}{3 \times \pi \times 0.080^2} = 51431.848\text{kPa} = 51.432(\text{MPa}) < [\sigma_j] = 260\text{MPa}$$

墙板孔壁抗压、轮轴抗剪满足要求。

5 结 语

(1)本文针对空间 Y 形钢箱拱桥的结构特点,给出了合理的缆索吊装方案,包括主副拱肋、主梁及观景平台的吊装次序,有效避免了交叉作业对吊装施工的影响,详细阐述了缆索吊装系统的组成及合理设计参数。为确保合龙前拱肋的横向稳定,建议吊装施工过程中增设临时横撑。

(2)吊篮运输至跨中时主索、工作索张力最大,此时主索与工作索考虑弯曲作用应力安全系数、考虑接触作用应力安全系数皆大于 2;吊篮运输至淳化岸塔前 55m 处牵引索牵引力最大,牵引索张力安全系数大于 4.5。

(3)锚梁一定范围内承受线荷载,计算时按集中荷载处理偏安全,荷载作用在跨中时,锚梁弯矩最大,荷载作用在锚梁长度的 1/3 处时,剪力最大。当承重索后倾角较大时,为使索鞍前后座滑轮数值压力相差不太大,可将前部座滑轮高度提高。

参考文献

[1] 王玮瑶,李生智,陈科昌.异型系杆拱桥[J].中国公路学报,1996(01):45-50.
[2] Huili Wang, Rongbin Jiang, Zhe Pan. Design and Analysis of Slanting Cross Special-Shaped Arch Bridge. 2011, 1279:786-791.
[3] Xuejin Huo, Lizhong Han. Analysis of Geometric Nonlinearity of Special-Shaped Arch Bridges. 2014, 8(3):37-45.
[4] Changhuan Kou, Chinsheng Kao, Mingchang Yang, et al. An Investigation into the Dynamic Mechanical Behaviors of Special-Shaped Arch Bridges. 2012, 1802:2260-2263.
[5] 王令侠.新建南广铁路西江特大桥 4200kN 横移式缆索吊机设计[J].铁道标准设计,2014,58(03):59-62.
[6] 周水兴,江礼忠,曾忠,等.拱桥节段施工斜拉扣挂索力仿真计算研究[J].重庆交通学院学报,2000(03):8-12.
[7] 张玉平,李传习,董创文."零弯矩法"应用于斜拉扣挂索力确定的讨论[J].长沙交通学院学报,2004(01):15-18.
[8] 肖伟.超大跨度钢管混凝土拱桥施工过程中扣索索力计算方法研究[D].重庆交通大学,2011.
[9] Xiaoli YAN. Cable Hoisting Technology Development and Application in Bridge Engineering. 2016, 5(4).

Automatic Modal Identification Based on Graph Clustering and Outlier Detection

Shengyu Liu   Xin Sun

(School of Highway, Chang'an University)

Abstract Bridge modal parameters are important parameters for damage identification and performance evaluation of bridge structures, which play a significance role in bridge health monitoring systems. In order to solve the problem of automatic identification of a large number of modal parameters and the accuracy of identification result, this paper proposes the stochastic subspace identification based on graph clustering and outlier detection method, which realizes accurate automatic modal identification. Firstly, the modal parameters are identified by the stochastic subspace identification method. Secondly, the graph clustering method is used to initially cluster the recognition results, which eliminates some spurious modes, and then the K-means clustering is used to eliminate the clusters with fewer modes. Finally, outlier detection algorithm based on box plot is used for identified results, which detects the outliers of stale axes for detection indicators and eliminates the outliers. So that the identification results are accurate and stable on all indicators. The proposed method is applied to the measured data of a cable-stayed bridge. The results show that the proposed modal automatic identification method based on graph clustering can realize the automatic identification of stable axes. The outlier detection method based on box plot can eliminate outliers in stable axes without predicting distribution of data and obtain accurate identification results.

Keywords Bridge engineering   Modal recognition   Graph clustering   Abnormal diagnosis

0 Introduction

In order to understand the operation status of the bridge in time, the structure health monitoring (SHM) of the bridge is particularly important, which can detect diseases of bridge and user can make reinforcement and repair schemes. However, the premise of structure health monitoring is to obtain accurate and true modal parameters, so operational modal analysis(OMA) is the key to structure health monitoring(Min and Sun et al., 2009; Mao and Wang et al., 2018).

The operational modal analysis of bridge is to convert the structural acceleration signals obtained by the sensors in the health monitoring system into the frequency, damping and modal shape parameters that present the dynamic characteristics of structures with modal identification technology(Khatibi and Akbar et al., 2017). Then, the clustering method is used to remove the spurious modes of the structure, and the physical modes of the structure is retained(Ren and Zong, 2004; Du and Zhu et al., 2018).

The traditional power spectrum method such as Peak-picking method (PP), Frequency Domain Decomposition method (FDD) is to identify the mode by picking up the peak of the power spectrum. It is difficult to identify the mode of the structure due to the close proximity of the high-order modal peaks and the influence of damping errors. In recent years, Stochastic subspace identification method (SSI) (Deraemaeker and Reynders et al., 2008) is well developed, which can be implemented in two classic forms: covariance driven (SSI-cov) and data driver (SSI-cov). Stochastic subspace identification method does not need conduct dynamical test to obtain vibration information and identify modal parameters. The method is based on time domain data, so it has no error of frequency resolution Stochastic subspace identification method can not only accurately identify the frequency of the system, but also can well identify the modal shape and damping of the structure.

The accuracy of the identified modal parameters has always been a concern of many researchers. In order to obtain the real modal parameters, many researchers had introduced the clustering method into the automatic identification process of the stability diagram(Wu and Liu et al., 2013; Liang and Song et al., 2018), which overcomes the shortcoming of manual selecting modal parameters(Zheng and Lin et al., 2017). In common, clustering methods include hierarchical clustering, K-means clustering, pedigree clustering and so on. However, these two clustering methods spend much time in calculating and require prior manual intervention. In graph clustering, mode date is mapped as undirected graph, and clustering is completed by cutting undirected edges, which is straightforward and simple.

In order to solve the precision of the existing modal parameter identification results and realize the precise and automatic modal identification, this work proposes a stochastic subspace modal parameter identification method based on graph clustering. First, the stochastic subspace identification method is used to identify the modal parameters, and then the graph clustering method is used to preliminarily cluster, to eliminate the spurious modes, and then K-means clustering(Roeck, 2012) is used to reject the groups with a small number of modes, finally the outlier detection algorithm based on the box plot is introduced into the modal parameter identification, to detect the outliers in the stable axes and get accurate modal parameter identification results.

1 Methodology

1.1 Stochastic Subspace Modal Identification Method

The stochastic subspace method is based on the state equation of the structure. And modal parameter of the structure is obtained by calculating the state equation. Firstly, the vibration response information of the structure is obtained by the vibration data acquisition system of the structure, and then the vibration response of the structure is discretized into time random output data. The state matrix of the structure is calculated by the state equation. Finally, the state matrix is decomposed to obtain the frequency, damping and mode shapes of the structure, and modal parameter identification is finished.

In operation state, the equation of motion of the structure is as:

$$M\ddot{q}(t) + C\dot{q}(t) + Kq(t) = Bu(t) \quad (1)$$

Where, M, C and $K \in R^{n \times n}$ is respectively mass matrix, damping matrix and stiffness matrix and n is degree of freedom of structure. $\ddot{q}(t), \dot{q}(t)$ and $q(t) \in R^n$ is respectively acceleration vector, velocity vector and displacement vector. $B \in R^{n \times m}$ is input matrix and $u(t) \in R^{m \times 1}$ is time input matrix. m is number of channel.

The discrete-time stochastic state-space model corresponding to Eq(1) is as:

$$\begin{aligned} x_{k+1} &= Ax_k + w_k \\ y_k &= Cx_k + v_k \end{aligned} \quad (2)$$

Where, k is sampling instance; is state vector of the k-th sampling; is input vector of the k-th sampling; is state matrix of structure; is output matrix of structure; denote unknown input of system which are modelling inaccuracies and measurement noise.

The stochastic subspace method includes covariance-driven Stochastic subspace identification method (SSI-cov) and data-driven Stochastic subspace identification method (SSI-data). In this paper, covariance-driven

Stochastic subspace identification method is used and the basic flow and calculation process are as follows:

1.1.1 Build Hankel matrix

Using dynamic response data of structure to build a hankel matrix. The Hankel matrix is defined as follows: the matrix is made up with $2i$ rows and j columns. The Hankel matrix is divided tow block, and each block is made up with rows that indicate number of output channel.

Using dynamic response data of structure to build a Hankel matrix. The Hankel matrix is defined as follows: the matrix is made up with $2i$ rows and j columns. The Hankel matrix is divided tow block, and each block is made up with rows that indicate number of output channel.

$$H_{0/2i-1} = \frac{1}{\sqrt{j}} \begin{pmatrix} Y_0 & Y_1 & \cdots & Y_{j-1} \\ Y_1 & Y_2 & \cdots & Y_j \\ \cdots & \cdots & \cdots & \cdots \\ Y_{j-1} & Y_j & \cdots & Y_{i+j-2} \\ Y_i & Y_{i+1} & \cdots & Y_{j-1} \\ Y_{i+1} & Y_{i+2} & \cdots & Y_{i+j} \\ \cdots & \cdots & \cdots & \cdots \\ Y_{2i-1} & Y_{2i} & \cdots & Y_{2i+j-2} \end{pmatrix} = \begin{pmatrix} H_{0/i-1} \\ H_{0/2i-1} \end{pmatrix} = \begin{pmatrix} H_{past} \\ H_{future} \end{pmatrix} \quad (3)$$

Where, $2i$ and j are quantities of representing the number of output block rows and columns of H respectively. $Y_k \in M^{l \times dl}$, $H_{0/2i-1} \in M^{(2l \times i) \times (j \times dl)}$, dl is the Signal intercept length.

1.1.2 Calculate the covariance matrix

Covariance matrix R_i of dynamic response is calculated as:

$$R_i = E[\{Y_{k+i}\}\{Y_k^T\}] = \lim \frac{1}{j} \sum_{k=0}^{j-1} [\{Y_{k+i}\}\{Y_k^T\}] \quad (4)$$

Block Toeplitz matrix is made up with covariance matrix and j is assumed to infinite, so the T matric is as:

$$T_{1/i} = H_f H_p^T = \begin{pmatrix} R_i & R_{i-1} & \cdots & R_1 \\ R_{i+1} & R_i & \cdots & R_2 \\ \cdots & \cdots & \cdots & \cdots \\ R_{2i-1} & R_{2i-2} & \cdots & R_i \end{pmatrix} \quad (5)$$

Where, $R_i \in M^{l \times l}$, $T_{1/i} \in M^{(l \times i) \times (l \times i)}$.

1.1.3 Singular Value Decomposition is conducted for Toeplitz matric

$$T_{1/i} = US V^T = (U_1 \quad U_2) \begin{pmatrix} S_1 & 0 \\ 0 & S_2 = 0 \end{pmatrix} (V_1^T \quad V_2^T) = U_1 S_1 V_1^T \quad (6)$$

1.1.4 Modal parameter is identified

$$T_{2/i+1} = O_i A \Gamma_i \quad (7)$$

$$O_i = US_1^{1/2}$$

$$\Gamma_i = S_1^{1/2} V_1^T \quad (8)$$

Then

$$A = O_i^\dagger T_{2/i+1} \Gamma_i^\dagger = S_1^{1/2} U_1^T T_{2/i+1} V_1 S_1^{1/2}$$

$$A = \Psi_c \Lambda_c \Psi_c^{-1} \quad (9)$$

Where, "†" represents generalized inverses of a matrix. Λ_c is a diagonal matrix and $\Lambda_c = \text{diag}[\mu_i]$.

So, the eigenvalue of mode shape matric and mode shape is equaled to as:

$$\sigma_i = \frac{\ln \mu}{\Delta t} \quad (10)$$

$$\boldsymbol{\Phi} = \boldsymbol{C}\boldsymbol{\Psi} \tag{11}$$

1.2 Graph Clustering Method

The modes of the structure identified are usually presented in terms of stability diagram which are many poles in stability diagram. However, there are not only real modes of the structure but also spurious modes generated by external environment. Therefore, the clustering needs to be conducted to eliminate spurious modes and obtain physical modes in stability diagram.

In the graph, two points are connected by a series of points and edges. The sequence of alternating points and edges is called a path between the two points, which is recorded as. A graph in which any tow points are connected by edge is called as connected graph and the connected graph without loop is called as tree. If a tree that contains all vertexs of graph G, the tree T is spanning tree of G.

The graph clustering method was originally a clustering algorithm proposed by Zahn, also known as the minimum support tree clustering method. In the graph clustering algorithm, firstly the data are transformed into a weighted undirected graph, which is a geometric graph composed of nodes and edges connected adjacent nodes. In graph clustering, a line without arrows between two nodes constitutes an undirected edge, and a graph composed of nodes and undirected edges is an undirected graph, which is recorded as:

$$G = (P, E)$$

Where, P is the set of nodes of undirected graph which is all data. E is the set of edge of undirected graph. For each edge of the undirected graph, there is a corresponding weight $w(e_i)$ representing the similarity of adjacent nodes, and the weight function can be defined according to the actual situation. After the undirected edge is weighted, a minimum support tree can be found. The minimum support tree satisfies the following conditions:

$$w(\text{MST}) = \min_i \left\{ \sum_{e \in E} w(e_i) \right\} \tag{12}$$

The process of graph clustering is as follow:

(1) Construct Minimum Spanning Tree (MST) with prim algorithm in undirected graph.

$$G = (P, E), \text{MST} = \{(U, T) \mid U = P, T = \{e_1, e_2, \cdots, e_{k-1}\}\}$$

(2) Define a threshold as d and delete the edges of MST weight value of which is lager than threshold d. So, the forest F is produced which is made up with many trees.

$$F = \{(P, E') \mid E' = T - \{e' \mid w(e') > d\}\}$$

(3) Search every tree in the forest F. $\{(P_i, T_i) \mid i = 1, 2, \cdots q\}$

(4) Clustering is finished and every tree is a cluster.

From the process of graph clustering, it can be seen that graph clustering does not need to set the number of clusters and cluster center in advance. What's more, computational complexity is small and the division is simple.

1.3 Clustering Criterion

Clustering criterion is a very important factor in the clustering process. It will accurately eliminate spurious modes and make the clustering result more accurate to accurately and reasonably set clustering criterion. According to the characteristics of the structural mode, the clustering criterion is get by calculating the similarity of every physical parameter which contains similarity of frequency, damping and vibration mode. Verboven et al. used the maximum likelihood estimation method to identify the structural modes, and proposed to use the "polar-zero pair" as an indicator to eliminate the spurious modes. In 2011, Reynders et al. proposed a three-stage modal identification method and used multiple indicators to eliminate spurious modes. He divided those indicators into two categories, namely the hard validation criteria and the soft validation criteria. Common indicators are shown in the Tab. 1 (Peeters and Roeck, 1999). Detail introduction is in literature (Peeters and Roeck, 1999) and will not be repeated here.

Clustering criteria Tab. 1

Criterion	Ideal value	Spurious
$d(\lambda_i, \lambda_j)$	0	1
$MAC(\Phi_i, \Phi_j)$	1	0
$MTN_{\infty i}^d$	1	0
$MTN_{\infty i}^s$	1	0
$d(MTN_{\infty i}^d, MTN_{\infty j}^d)$	0	1
$d(MTN_{\infty i}^s, MTN_{\infty j}^s)$	0	1
$MPC(\Phi_i)$	1	0
$MPD(\Phi_i)/90$	0	1
d_{ij}	<1	>1
$\xi_i > 0$	1	0
$\xi_i < 20\%$	1	0
Conjugate pair	1	0

2 Automatic Modal Parameter Identification Based on Graph Clustering and Outlier Detection

2.1 Graph Clustering Method and Process of Clustering

Clustering is a process of classifying data based on the similarity between the data. In this process, by reasonable setting criterion, the spurious modes of the structure can be eliminated, and the true modes that reflects the structural characteristics is retained. In graph clustering, the data is mapped into an undirected graph, and clustering is completed by cutting off the undirected edges, which is not affected by the number of clusters; no one is involved in clustering; and the calculation amount is small. In this paper, graph clustering is adapted. In the process of clustering, weight function of edge equals to the sum of the frequency difference ( ) and the MAC difference ( ). Then the initial clustering is finished by cutting MST according to threshold d set. Finally, K-means clustering is adapted to eliminate the clusters that contain a few modes. The detail process of clustering is as follow

In this case, the governing system of equations can be written as follows:

(1) Define weight function of edge and calculate distance matrix of modes

$$w(p_i, p_j) = \frac{|f_i - f_j|}{\max(f_i, f_j)} + 1 - MAC \tag{13}$$

(2) Use the Prim algorithm to construct a minimum spanning tree (MST) by traversing the search on an undirected graph $G = (P, E)$.

(3) Threshold d is set as 1% then the edges of which weight is larger than threshold is deleted so that frost F is produced $F = \{(P, E') \mid E' = T - \{e' \mid w(e') > d\}\}$.

(4) Get all the trees in the forest $F\{(P_i, T_i) \mid i = 1, 2, \cdots, q\}$ and initial clustering is finished.

(5) For initial result, K-means clustering is adapted in which the number of clusters is $K = 2$. so, clusters with fewer modes are eliminated and finial clustering is completed.

In the clustering process, the MAC reflects the similarity of adjacent modes. When the two adjacent modes are similar, the closer the MAC value is to 1, the more it can be said to belong to the same cluster. Smaller the relative distance of frequency is, the better the similarity of the two modes is. Therefore, the threshold is set to

1%, according to the accuracy of clustering and experience of actual engineering. After the initial clustering, a large number of spurious modes have been eliminated and only fewer spurious modes is contained in real modes. So, in the K-means clustering, the spurious modes are clustered into a cluster that contains few modes.

2.2 Outlier Detection Based on Box Plot

After the modes are clustered, many axises are presented in the stable graph, but the stable axes of different orders have different data discrete characteristics. And there is phenomenon in which a small amount of data deviates from the stable axis. Existing clustering algorithms (including the methods in this paper) all uses fixed clustering indicators for stable axis recognition, which generates some outliers in the recognition results.

In order to accurately evaluate the rationality of the identification results and obtain more accurate modal parameters, the iterative outlier culling process based on the box plot method is introduced in this paper. In process of outliers detection, frequency, MAC, damping ratio, MTN, MPC and MPD are successively as indicators to eliminate outlier. The traditional clustering process which only uses frequency and MAC index does not consider the physical characteristics such as damping ratio and mode phase angle. Because the rationality of physical parameters such as damping ratio can't be judged, it is easy to mix outliers of which damp or other physical parameters are spurious into real modes. The box plot outlier detection method can detect the rationality of any physical index and ensure the accuracy of the recognition result.

MTN is modal transfer norm which is defined as follow:

$$\text{MTN}_{\infty i} = \max_w \sigma [S_{V,j}^+(w)] = \max \sigma \left(\left. \frac{\phi_i g_{di}^T}{z - \lambda_{di}} \right|_{z = e^{iw_i T}} + \frac{\phi_i g_{di}^T}{2\lambda_{di}} \right) \quad (14)$$

MPC is a physical quantity which describes the collinearity between the real part and the imaginary part of the mode, and its value is 0~1. when the value of MPC is closer to 1, the more likely the modes are to be the real modes. On the contrary, the more likely the mode is to be the spurious modes. It is defined as follow:

$$\text{MPC}(\Phi_i) = \frac{\|\text{Re}(\tilde{\phi}_i)\|_2^2 + \frac{1}{\zeta_{\text{MPC}}} \text{Re}(\tilde{\phi}_i^T) \text{Im}(\tilde{\phi}_i) [2(\zeta_{\text{MPC}}^2 + 1)\sin^2(\zeta_{\text{MPC}} - 1)]}{\|\text{Re}(\tilde{\phi}_i)\|_2^2 + \|\text{Im}(\tilde{\phi}_i)\|_2^2} \quad (15)$$

MPD is a physical quantity used to characterize the average phase deviation of the mode vector, which is defined as:

$$\text{MPD}(\phi_i) = \frac{\sum_{o=1}^{n} w_o \arccos \left| \frac{\text{Re}(\phi_i)V_{22} - \text{Im}(\phi_i)V_{12}}{\sqrt{V_{12}^2 + V_{22}^2}|\phi_i|} \right|}{\sum_{o=1}^{n} w_o} \quad (16)$$

Process of outlier detection based on box plot is as follow:

(1) Calculate quartiles and diagnostic threshold of frequency, MAC, damping, MTN, MPC and MPD of identification result.

(2) Eliminate outliers outside the box plot.

(3) With the remaining recognition results as samples, repeat (1) (2) until no outliers are detected and stop the calculation

2.3 Process of automatic modal parameter identification based graph clustering and outlier detection

The process of automatic SSI modal identification based on graph clustering is as follow:

(1) SSI-cov method is used to identify the modal parameter of the structures and stability graph is obtained.

(2) Use modal parameter to construct MST based on graph clustering, then according to threshold set by

user, cut MST to eliminate spurious modes. This step is initial clustering.

(3) K-means clustering is adapted for initial clustering result to eliminate the clusters which contains few modes.

(4) The box plot outlier detection method is used to detect the outliers for each index, and the final modal parameters are obtained.

3 Application

3.1 Introduction of Example Bridge

In order to verify the feasibility and applicability of the automatic modal parameter identification method based on graph clustering proposed in this paper, a single-pylon double-cable planes cable-stayed bridge was used as a study. The bridge was constructed in 2008 with length of 578m and span of 100 + 160 + 318m. The pylon is A type pylon and the main beam is steel box gird. The bridge is equipped with a complete health monitoring system, which mainly monitored the vehicle load, cable tension, main beam strain, structural acceleration response, wind speed and direction, and temperature and humidity. 10 vertical acceleration sensors were arranged on the main beam to monitor the dynamic response of the main beam. The numbers of sensor were 1, 3, 5, 7, 20, 22, 23, 25, 26, 28, and the acceleration sensor is arranged as shown in Fig. 1.

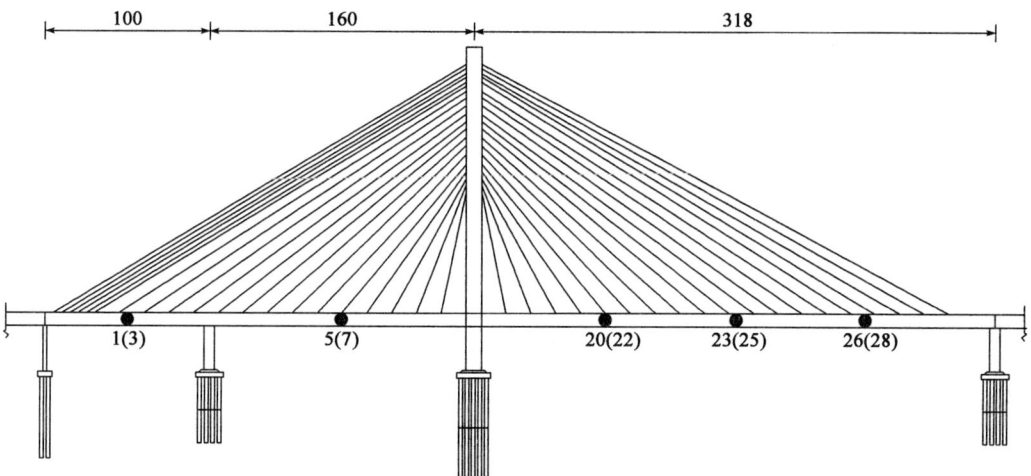

Fig. 1 Layout of sensors(unit:m)

3.2 Automatic Identifying Mode

In this work, firstly, based on the acceleration response data collected by the bridge health monitoring system, the covariance-driven stochastic subspace identification method was used to identify modal parameter with modal order 2-100. The identified modal parameters are shown in Fig. 2. As is shown in Fig. 2, the stable axis can be seen in the stability graph, but there are also a large number of unstable points which responses the real modes contain a large number of spurious modes.

Then, the graph clustering method is used to perform initial clustering in stabilization diagram based on the identified modal parameters. Using the Prim algorithm, a minimum spanning tree (MST) is created as shown in Fig. 3. In prim algorithm, weight

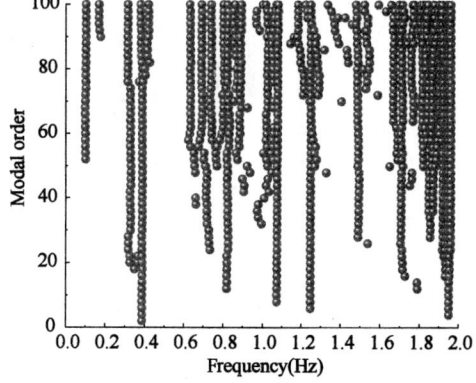

Fig. 2 Stabilization diagram of identification results

function is defined as shown in Section 2.1. The stable points in the figure represent the vertices of the undirected graph, and the dashed lines connecting the stable points represent the undirected edges between the vertices. According to the threshold set, the edges larger than the threshold in the minimum spanning tree are deleted, and the forest F as shown in Fig. 4 is obtained. Each tree in the forest F is obtain, and the tree with the number of stable points less than 6 is deleted. So, the initial clustering is completed, and the stable graph is as shown in Fig. 5.

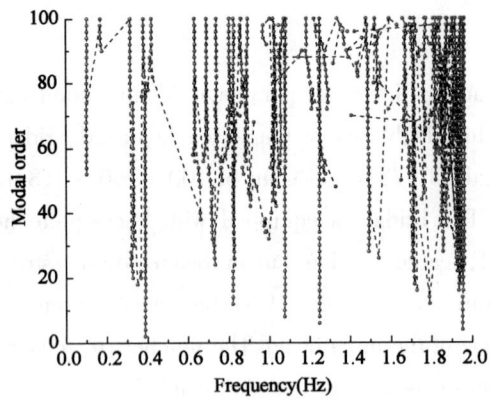 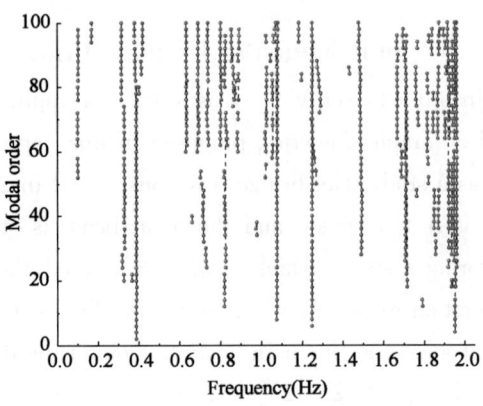

Fig. 3　Minimum spanning tree (MST)　　　　　　　　Fig. 4　Forest F

As is shown in Fig. 3, the graph clustering is to connect the stable points closest to each other into a tree, which is to connect the stable points with high similarity to each other. it is consistent with the principle of clustering.

As is shown in Fig. 3, after the MST is cut, the stable points in each tree are basically on the same stable axis, which indicates each tree is a cluster. As is shown in Fig. 5 compared with Fig. 2, it can be seen that a large number of unstable points (spurious modes) have been eliminated by using the graph clustering method, and clear visible stable axes are obtained, which illustrates the feasibility of the graph clustering method. And it can be seen from the graph clustering process that the graph clustering method is efficient.

After initial clustering, the K-means clustering method is used to divide the modes into two groups: real modes and spurious modes. Then, the clusters with fewer stable points is removed, and the final real modes are obtained, which is as shown in Fig. 6. As is shown in Fig. 6 compared with Fig. 5, more spurious modes are eliminated in the step and stable axes with a large number of stable points are obtained, which ensures the authenticity of the obtained modes.

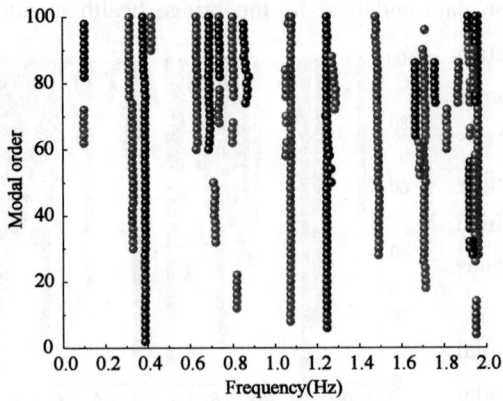 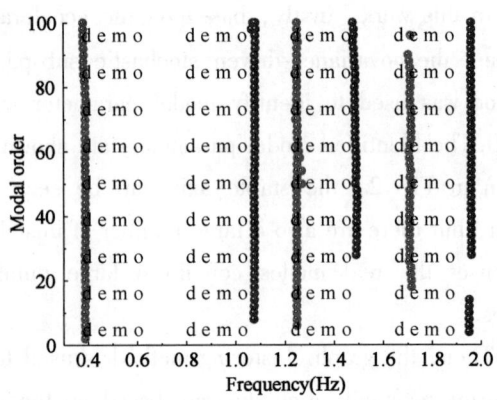

Fig. 5　Stabilization diagram of initial clustering　　　　Fig. 6　Stabilization diagram of final clustering

3.3 Outlier Detection of Modes

It can be seen from the box plot detection result that with the iterative box plot outlier elimination process, the modes of the structure have been not detected outliers on each index, which indicates that the modes are stable and accurate. As is shown in Fig. 7 compared with Fig. 6, with the process of outlier detection, the abnormal stability points near the stable axes are eliminated, more stable and accurate stale axes are obtained.

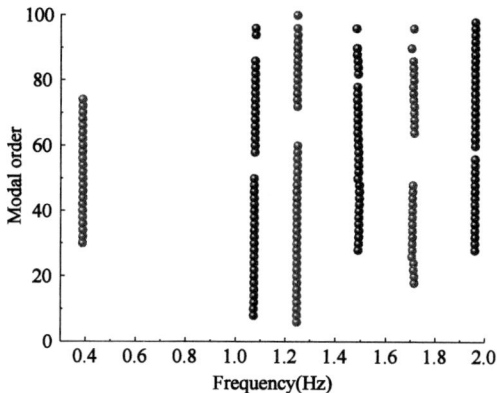

Fig. 7 Stabilization diagram after the outliers are removed

From the whole modal recognition process, it can be seen that graph clustering and outlier diagnosis can realize automatic recognition of stable axes. Compared with other clustering algorithms, more accurate structural modes can be identified in the method.

4 Conclusions

This paper proposes a automatic modal identification based on graph clustering and outlier diagnosis method and it is used for modal identification of a cable-stayed bridge. The following conclusions are drawn:

(1) The graph theory clustering method can automatically and efficiently identify the stable axis based on the frequency and MAC index, and the clustering results are clearly classified.

(2) On the basis of graph theory clustering, K-means clustering method can be used to eliminate spurious modes with small number modes, and the real structural mode is obtained.

(3) The box plot outlier diagnosis method can identify the outliers of frequency, MAC, damping ratio, MTN, MPC, MPD indicators without predicting distribution of mode parameters which solves the shortcoming that the traditional clustering algorithm cannot discriminate the accuracy of the recognition results.

(4) The box plot outlier detection method can combine multiple indicators to identify and eliminate the outliers in the stable axes, so that the recognition results are accurate and stable on multiple indicators.

References

[1] Deraemaeker, A. and E. Reynders, et al. (2008). "Vibration-based structural health monitoring using output-only measurements under changing environment." Mechanical Systems & Signal Processing 22 (1): 34-56.

[2] Du, Y. and Q. Zhu, et al. (2018). "Analysis of the Abnormal Change of Isolated Structure Modal Parameters Under Healthy Condition Based on Long-Term Monitoring Data." Zhendong Ceshi Yu Zhenduan/Journal of Vibration, Measurement and Diagnosis 38 (3): 517-525.

[3] Khatibi and Akbar, et al. (2017). "Fully Automated Operational Modal Analysis using multi-stage clustering." Mechanical Systems & Signal Processing.

[4] Liang, S. U. and M. Song, et al. (2018). "Automatic analysis of stabilization diagrams using a convolutional

neural network." Journal of Vibration and Shock.

[5] Mao, J. X. and H. Wang, et al. (2018). "Investigation of dynamic properties of long-span cable-stayed bridges based on one-year monitoring data under normal operating condition." Structural Control and Health Monitoring: e2146.

[6] Min, Z. H. and L. M. Sun, et al. (2009). "Effect analysis of environmental factors on structural modal parameters of a cable-stayed bridge." Journal of Vibration & Shock.

[7] Peeters, B. and G. D. Roeck (1999). "REFERENCE-BASED STOCHASTIC SUBSPACE IDENTIFICATION FOR OUTPUT-ONLY MODAL ANALYSIS." Mechanical Systems and Signal Processing 13 (6): 855-878.

Ren, W. X. and Z. H. Zong (2004). "Output-only modal parameter identification of civil engineering structures." Structural Engineering & Mechanics 17 (3_4): 429-444.

[8] Roeck, H. (2012). "Fully automated (operational) modal analysis." Mechanical Systems and Signal Processing.

Wu, C. L. and H. B. Liu, et al. (2013). "Parameter identification of a bridge structure based on a stabilization diagram with fuzzy clustering method." Journal of Vibration and Shock 32 (4): 121-126.

[9] Zheng, P. and D. Lin, et al. (2017). "Automatic stochastic subspace identification of modal parameters based on graph clustering." Dongnan Daxue Xuebao (Ziran Kexue Ban)/Journal of Southeast University (Natural Science Edition) 47 (4): 710-716.

不同中小跨径梁桥动态称重算法对比研究

乔可鑫 韩万水 陈适之 易雨时
(长安大学)

摘要 为工程中桥梁动态称重(Bridge Weigh-in-Motion,BWIM)算法的选取提供参考,现以中小跨径装配式混凝土T形梁桥为研究对象展开BWIM识别精度研究,对比当下各代表性BWIM算法的适用性。首先建立不同跨径装配式T形梁桥有限元模型,基于车-桥耦合模拟获取桥梁动力响应,然后代入Moses算法、应变面积法、支座反力法、虚拟简支梁法4种代表性BWIM技术方法进行待测车辆的总重和轴重识别,最后对比在桥梁跨径、汽车速度、路面平整度等因素影响下各方法的识别效果。结果表明:大部分工况下,4种方法均能保持较为可靠的精度,其中虚拟简支梁法在50m跨径桥梁仍能保持较高的识别精度,应变面积法受各个参数影响较小,但只能进行总重识别,对于可识别轴重的3种方法,支座反力法识别精度最优。此外,随着桥梁跨径减小,方法的识别精度均会升高;而车速升高会导致识别精度下降;路面平整度恶化会导致识别误差增大,所以工程中维护路面平整和控制车速等对动态称重的精度维持有着重要意义。

关键词 桥梁工程 动态称重 车-桥耦合模拟 中小桥 对比研究

0 引 言

随着我国交通行业的不断发展,交通量和轴载的增加使得超载频发,加速路面恶化,甚至造成桥梁垮塌,对桥梁的安全运营造成极大危害。因此,快速准确地识别桥上车辆荷载,对超载车辆进行控制十分必要。桥梁动态称重系统(Bridge Weight-in-Motion,BWIM)将采集仪器安装在桥梁底部,通过测量车辆过桥时的结构响应来反解车辆信息,系统安装维护方便,稳定性强,测量精度高,具有广泛适用性。

1979年,Moses[1]首次提出桥梁动态称重的概念及算法,在车重识别方面具有较高精度。朱全军等[2]提出基于支座反力的动态称重方法,进一步提高识别精度。Ojio 等[3]提出应变面积法,摆脱 Moses 算法中复杂的影响线标定过程,但仅能适用于小跨径桥梁。邓露等[4]提出虚拟简支梁法,不受跨径限制,可适用于大跨径的桥梁。

装配式中小跨径混凝土梁桥又在中小跨径桥梁中占有很大比重,对其上的车辆荷载进行高效准确地采集有着十分重要的现实意义,但现有 BWIM 算法种类繁多,特点各异,在工程应用时难以选取。因此本文通过建立4种不同跨径装配式混凝土 T 梁桥,基于车-桥耦合数值模拟考察各方法在不同参数工况下的识别精度表现,得出各 BWIM 方法的适用范围。

1 既有桥梁动态称重方法

1.1 Moses 算法

Moses 算法是大多数桥梁动态称重算法的基础,通过使桥梁实测响应与理论响应之间差值最小化来计算车辆轴重。

其基本原理如图1所示,当车辆以匀速 v 在桥梁上行驶,梁上某一测点处的实测弯矩 M_q^M 可以表示为:

$$M_q^M = EW\varepsilon_q^M \tag{1}$$

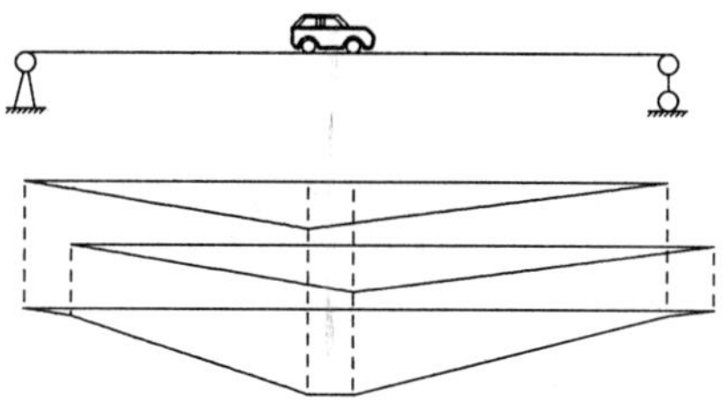

式中:E——主梁弹性模量;

W——主梁截面抗弯系数;

ε_q^M——q 时刻测点处的实测应变。

图1 车辆荷载下跨中应变时程曲线

根据结构力学,可得相应的理论静态应变 ε^T 为:

$$\{\varepsilon^T\}_{Q\times 1} = [I]_{Q\times N}\{P\}_{N\times 1} \tag{2}$$

$$[I] = \frac{1}{EW}\begin{bmatrix} I_1 & I_{1-C_2} & \cdots & I_{1-C_N} \\ I_2 & I_{2-C_2} & \cdots & I_{2-C_N} \\ \vdots & \vdots & \ddots & \vdots \\ I_Q & I_{Q-C_2} & \cdots & I_{Q-C_N} \end{bmatrix}, \{P\} = \begin{Bmatrix} P_1 \\ P_2 \\ \vdots \\ P_N \end{Bmatrix}, Q \text{ 为测量的应变时程数据点数}, N \text{ 为车轴数量}, P_i$$

为车辆的第 i 根轴重,I_{q-Ci} 为 q 时刻第 i 根车轴所对应的影响线值。

由于实际车辆作用下桥梁将产生动态响应,与理论静态响应间存在偏差,这里建立误差函数 $E = [\{\varepsilon^M\} - \{\varepsilon^T\}]^2$,取 E 的极值得到轴重表达式为:

$$\{P\} = ([I]^T[I])^{-1}[I]^T\{\varepsilon^M\} \tag{3}$$

1.2 应变面积法

应变面积法利用响应面积等于车辆总重与影响线面积乘积的关系,通过车辆标定实现动态称重。具体理论如下:

车辆通过桥梁时,产生的响应面积 A 可表示为:

$$A = \int_0^{l+L}\sum_{i=1}^N P_i \times I_{q-C_i}\mathrm{d}x = \sum_{i=1}^N P_i \times \int_0^l I_q\mathrm{d}x = G \times \int_0^l I_q\mathrm{d}x \tag{4}$$

式中:G——车辆总重;

　l——桥长;

　L——车辆长。

由公式(4)可知,车重与响应面积成正比,则待测车辆的轴重 G_t 可以表示为:

$$G_{t} = G_{c}\frac{A_{t}}{A_{c}} \tag{5}$$

式中:G_c——已知轴重的标定车重;

A_c、A_t——待测车辆和标定车辆匀速通过桥梁的应变面积。

1.3 支座反力法

支座反力法思路和 Moses 算法相同,利用任意时刻各个车轴轴重与其对应支座反力影响线值乘积作为理论值,建立实测与理论支反力的误差函数并取极值,反算轴重,表达式为:

$$\{P\} = ([I]^{T}[I])^{-1}[I]^{T}\{F^{M}\} \tag{6}$$

式中:$[I]$——桥梁入口端支座反力影响线矩阵;

$\{F^M\}$——桥梁入口端支座反力的实测值。

1.4 虚拟简支梁法

虚拟简支梁法采用桥梁上隔离体响应计算车辆轴重和总重。对于一根具有任意边界条件的线弹性梁 mn,假设 i、o、j 分别为 mn 上三个连续点,其位置和距离关系如图3所示。

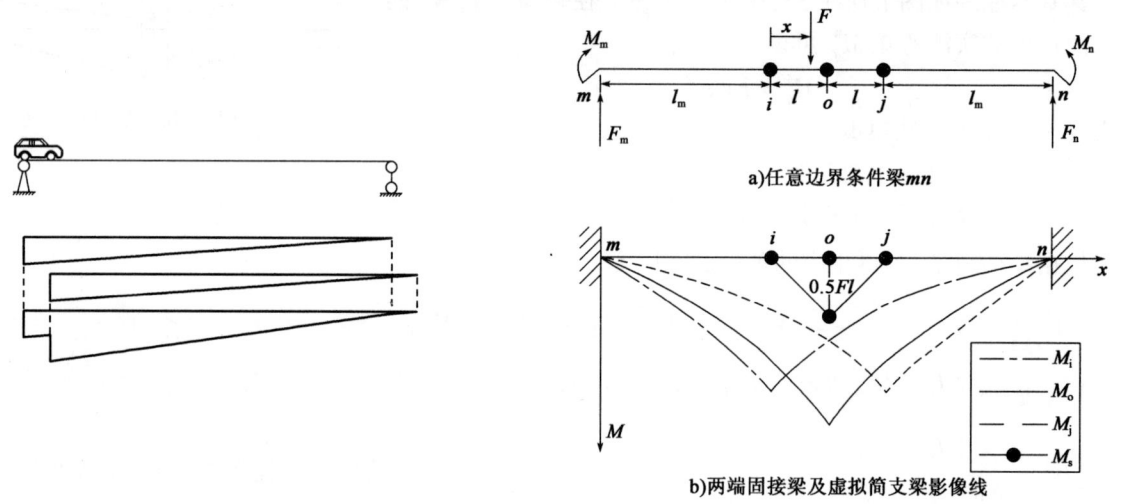

图2 车辆荷载下支座反力时程曲线　　图3 虚拟简支梁法原理图

当梁 mn 上距离 i 点 x 位置处施加一个集中力 F 时,支反力为 F_m、F_n、M_m、M_n,i、o、j 三点的弯矩 M_v 可以表示为支反力和集中力 F 在相应位置引起的弯矩 M_v^R、M_v^F 之和:

$$M_{v} = M_{v}^{R} + M_{v}^{F} \tag{7}$$

由结构力学可得 i、o、j 三点处支反力和集中力弯矩:

$$\begin{cases} M_{i}^{R} = M_{m}(x) + F_{m}(x)l_{m} \\ M_{o}^{R} = M_{m}(x) + F_{m}(x)(l_{m} + l) \\ M_{j}^{R} = M_{m}(x) + F_{m}(x)(l_{m} + 2l) \end{cases} \quad \begin{cases} M_{i}^{F} = \begin{cases} Fx & x < 0 \\ 0 & x \geqslant 0 \end{cases} \\ M_{o}^{F} = \begin{cases} F(x-l) & x < l \\ 0 & x \geqslant l \end{cases} \\ M_{j}^{F} = \begin{cases} F(x-2l) & x < 2l \\ 0 & x \geqslant 2l \end{cases} \end{cases} \tag{8}$$

可发现:

$$M_{o}^{R} = \frac{1}{2}(M_{i}^{R} + M_{j}^{R}) \tag{9}$$

因此,定义 M_s 为 $M_s = M_o - (M_i + M_j)/2$:

$$M_s = \begin{cases} 0 & x < 0 \text{ 或 } x \geq 2l \\ \dfrac{1}{2}Fx & 0 \leq x < l \\ \dfrac{1}{2}F(2l - x) & l \leq x < 2l \end{cases} \quad (10)$$

M_s 仅与 i、o、j 三点之间距离和集中力 F 加载位置有关,与 ij 隔离体之外的因素无关。得到 ij 段的隔离弯矩影响线后,即可根据 Moses 算法进行称重求解。

2 车-桥耦合振动模拟

为真实模拟桥梁结构在车辆荷载作用下的动力响应特性,利用课题组自行研发的车-桥耦合动力分析程序 BDANS(Bridge Dynamic Analysis System)进行分析,该程序框架如图4所示。

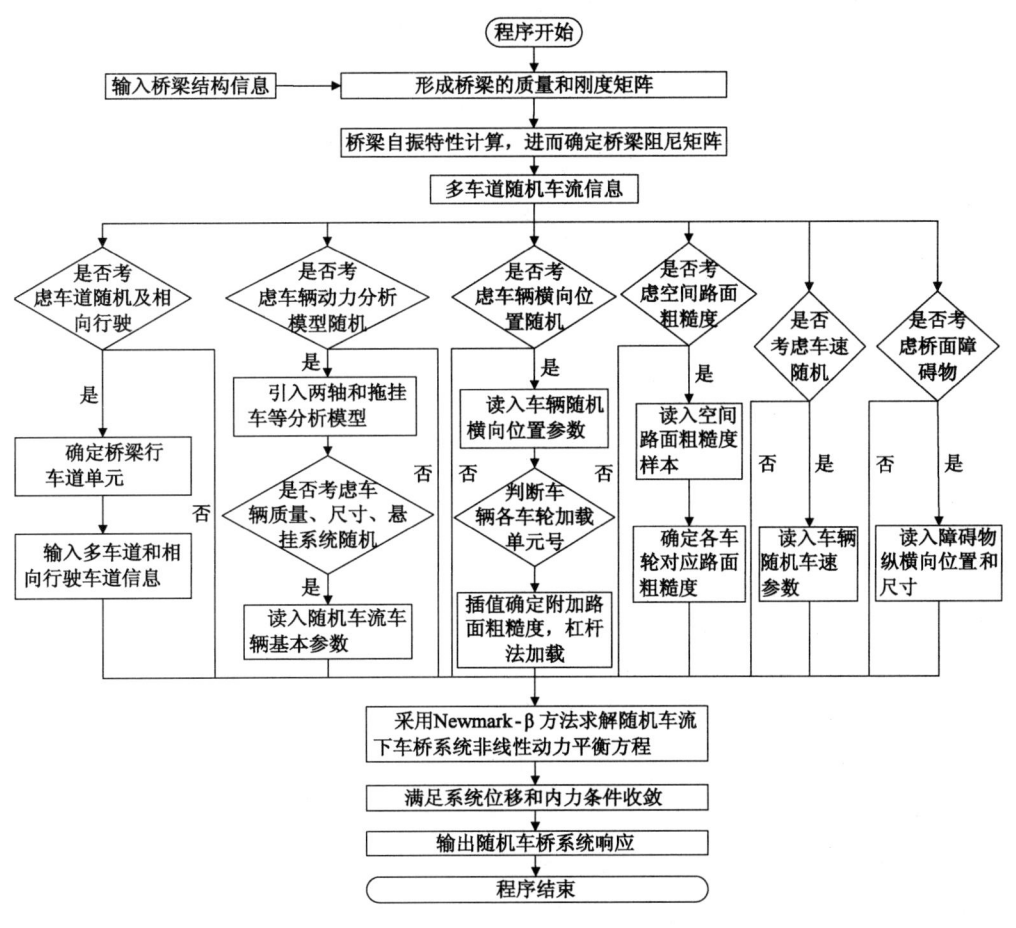

图4 BDANS 程序框架

在模拟中,选择了代表性车型作为标定车辆及待测车辆,如图5所示。

2.1 桥梁模型

选取了四座跨径分别为 13m、16m、20m、50m 的简支 T 形梁桥有限元模型用于检验各方法(图6)。

基于4座装配式 T 形梁桥有限元模型,采用 BDANS 进行不同工况下的车桥耦合模拟,分析频率为 1kHz。对于 Moses 方法和应变面积法,测点布置在跨中位置;对于支座反力法,测点布置在支座位置;对于虚拟简支梁法,测点布置在 16m 梁桥 4m、8m、12m 位置和 50m 梁桥 20m、25m、30m 位置。各参数工况如表1所示,相应桥梁应变如图7和图8所示。

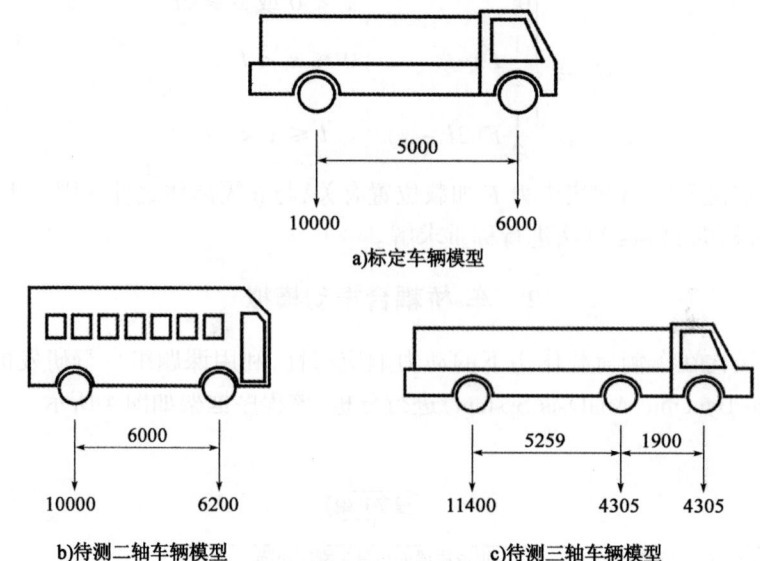

图5 车辆模型轴距(尺寸单位:mm)及轴重(kg)

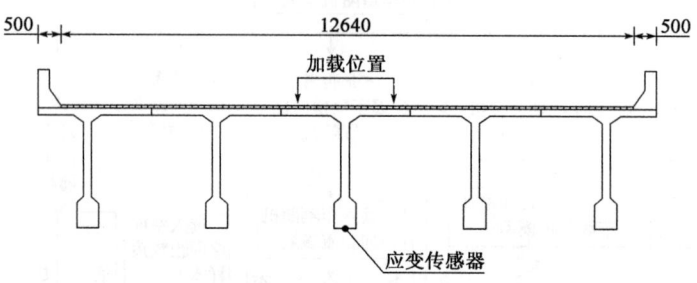

图6 桥梁跨中截面横断面图(尺寸单位:mm)

数值模拟工况 表1

参 数	设置工况
桥梁跨径(m)	13、16、20、50
车辆速度(m·s^{-1})	10、20、30
路面平整度	非常好、好、一般
输入噪声	0、1%、5%

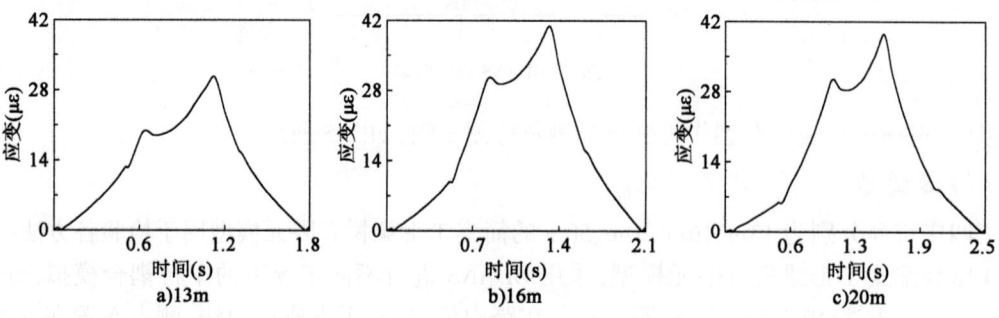

图7 不同桥梁跨径下跨中应变时程曲线图

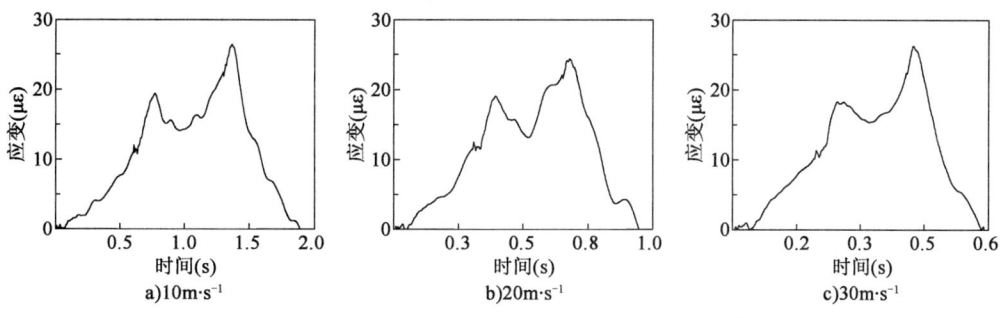

图 8 不同车速下跨中应变时程曲线图

3 模拟结果分析

3.1 桥梁跨径对识别结果的影响

图 9 和图 10 给出了 4 种动态称重方法针对不同跨径桥梁的总重和轴重识别误差。图中,"MA"表示传统 Moses 算法,"IA"表示应变面积法,"SRF"表示支座反力法,"VSSB"表示虚拟简支梁法,跟随的数字 i 表示各方法下的第 i 根轴的识别误差。

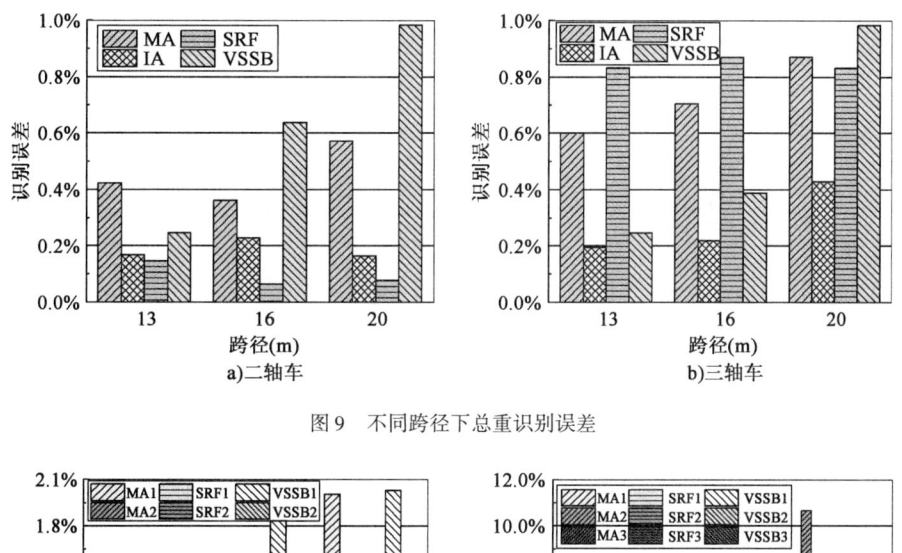

图 9 不同跨径下总重识别误差

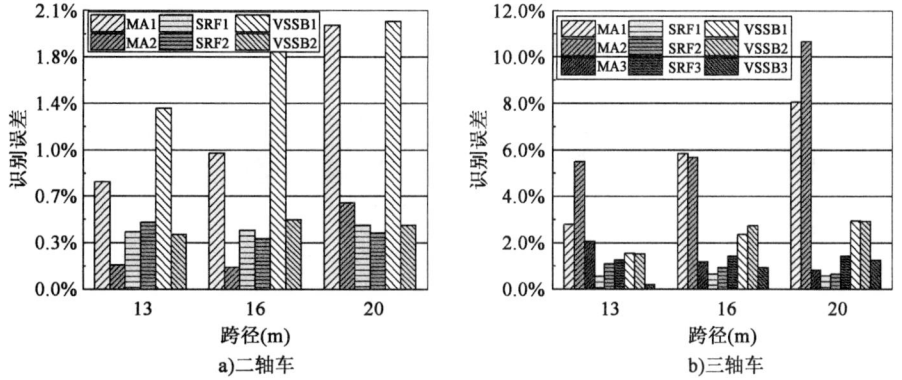

图 10 不同跨径下轴重识别误差

对于总重识别,4 种方法识别误差均能保持在 1% 以下。由于 IA 法仅能进行总重识别,所以本文仅对另外 3 种方法进行轴重识别误差统计,3 种方法在 20m 以内跨径 T 梁均能保持较好的识别精度,较轻的前轴识别误差普遍大于较重的后轴。当跨径达到 20m 时,MA 法的轴重识别误差超过 10%,而 SRF 法和 VSSB 法的轴重识别误差仍在 3% 以下,并且 SRF 法的识别效果相对更优。图 11 为 50m T 梁桥下 MA 算法和 VSSB 法的总重和轴重识别误差。对于 50m T 梁,MA 法轴重识别误差已经超过 20%;而 VSSB 法总重和轴重都有较好的识别精度,体现其不受桥梁跨径限制的优点。

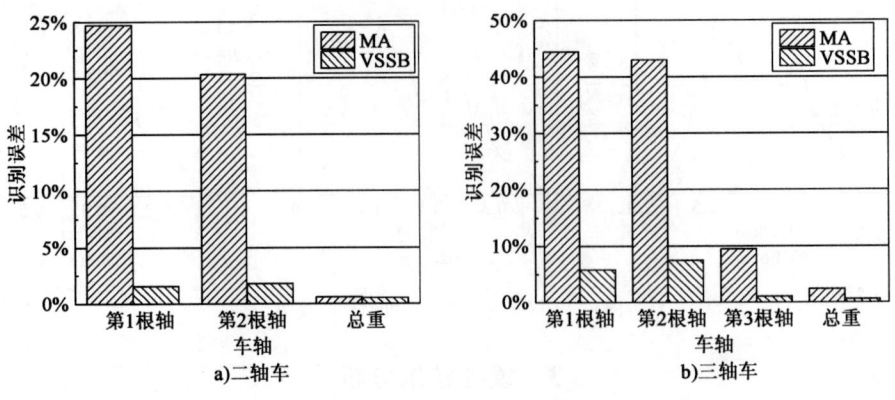

图 11　50mT 梁总重和轴重识别误差

3.2　车辆速度对识别结果的影响

图 12 和图 13 分别为 4 种动态称重方法在不同车辆行驶速度下两种待测车辆总重和轴重识别误差。观察可知:车辆总重和轴重识别误差有随车速增加而增大的趋势。当车速达到 30 m·s^{-1} 时,SRF 法总重识别误差达到 3.8%,识别精度略低于其他三种方法;轴重识别误差最高达到 15% 左右,所以为了获取较高的识别精度,应该适当控制待测车辆的行驶速度。总体而言,4 种方法针对不同车速的车辆轴重识别精度相当。

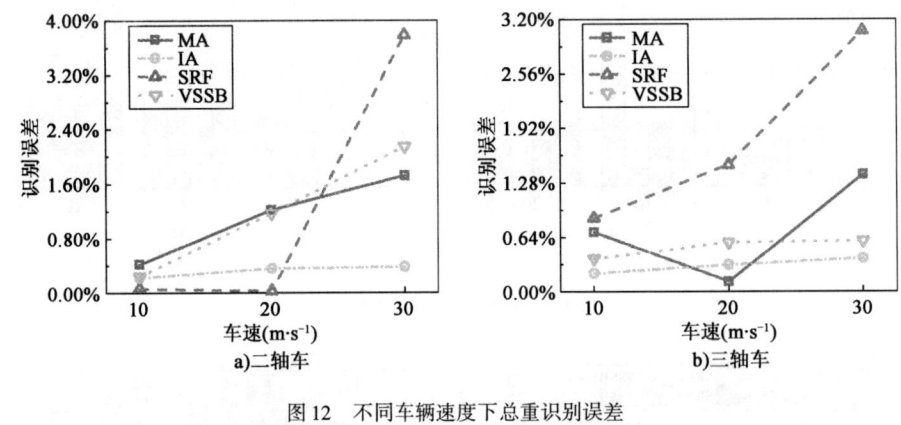

图 12　不同车辆速度下总重识别误差

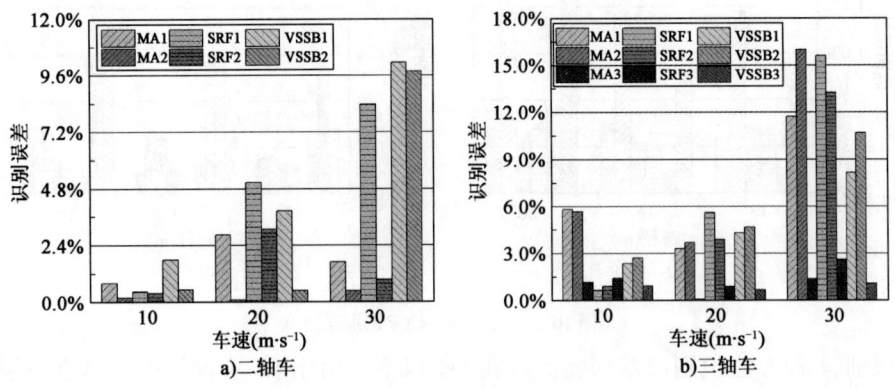

图 13　不同车辆速度下轴重识别误差

3.3　路面平整度对识别结果的影响

图 14 和图 15 分别为 4 种动态称重方法在不同路面平整度下的车辆总重和轴重识别误差。图中,VG 代表非常好,G 代表好,A 代表一般路面平整度。可以看出路面平整度越差,总重和轴重识别误差也越

大。在路面平整度为一般时,待测车辆总重识别误差不超过5.1%,MA法和IA法的识别效果相对较优。轴重识别误差随路面平整度降低而快速增加,SRF法甚至达到20%以上,说明维护桥面平整对保证识别精度有重要意义。

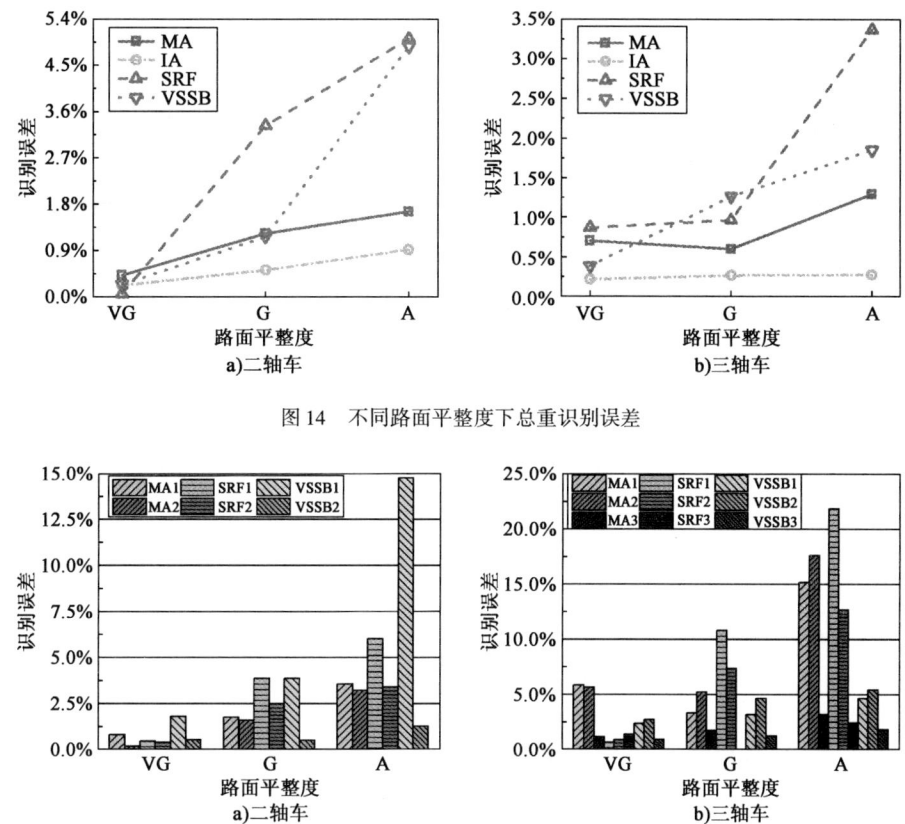

图14 不同路面平整度下总重识别误差

图15 不同路面平整度下轴重识别误差

4 结　语

本文基于车桥耦合数值模拟,针对Moses算法、应变面积法、支座反力法和虚拟简支梁法4种典型桥梁动态称重方法在中小桥上的表现开展对比研究,结论如下:

(1)对于小跨径梁桥,4种方法均能达到较为理想的车辆总重和轴重识别精度,且较重轴的识别精度普遍高于较轻轴。对于50mT梁,Moses算法轴重识别误差较大,失去可靠性;虚拟简支梁方法在较大跨径的桥梁动态称重中具有可靠性。

(2)随着车辆行驶速度的增加,各方法对于车辆总重和轴重的识别精度均有所下降。当车速控制在$10\sim30\,\text{m}\cdot\text{s}^{-1}$范围内时,车辆总重识别精度还较为理想,但超出这个范围的车速会严重降低轴重识别精度。实际应用时应采用车速控制手段,提升动态称重精度。

(3)随着路面平整度恶化,4种方法在总重和轴重方面的识别精度均会相应减小。因此,为了保证实际使用中方法的识别精度,需要长期维持桥面平整度水平。

参考文献

[1] Moses F. Weigh-in-motion System using Instrumented Bridges[J]. Transportation Engineering Journal,1979,105(3):233-249.

[2] 朱全军,肖强,邓露.基于支座反力的桥梁动态称重方法[J].中外公路,2019,39(1):87-94.

[3] Ojio T, Yamada K. Bridge Weigh-in-motion Systems using Stringers of Plate Girder Bridges[C]. Proceedings of the 3rd International Conference on Weigh-in Motion. Orlando,2002:209-218.

[4] 邓露,施海,何维,等.基于虚拟简支梁法的桥梁动态称重研究[J].振动与冲击,2019,37(15):210-215.
[5] 邓露,李树征,淡丹辉,等.桥梁动态称重技术在中小跨径混凝土梁桥上的适用性研究[J].湖南大学学报(自然科学版),2020,47(3):89-96.

Structural Safety Assessment of Steel-concrete Composite Girder Cable-stayed Bridge Exposed to Fires on Deck

Linhao Zhu Haoyun Yuan Chi Wang Zhi Liu

(Chang'an University)

Abstract Aimed at the structural safety of long-span steel-concrete composite girder cable-stayed bridges exposed to fires on deck, this paper proposed a simplified calculation process and took a large-span cable-stayed bridge as the research object to conduct structural safety analysis. Firstly, FDS (Fire Dynamics Simulator) was used to simulate two typical fire scenarios and the heating curves of different fire types were obtained. Then used ABAQUS to analyze the temperature of the stay cable in the FDS temperature field. The temperature curve of stay cables at different heights in a tanker fire was given. Thus, the failure analysis was carried out based on the yield strength variation of stay cable under fire, and the failure numbers of stay cables under three unfavorable conditions were obtained. Finally, the strength analysis of the main girder and bridge deck of the steel-concrete composite beam was carried out, and the most unfavorable position of fire was determined. The results show that the cables lose their effective strength quickly in the fire; under the most unfavorable conditions, that is, when the fire occurs in the middle of span, 3 stayed cables will break, which will affect the safety performance of the cable-stayed bridge structure. Therefore, necessary preventive measures should be taken.

Keywords Steel-concrete composite gird cable-stayed bridge Deck fire Fire dynamics simulator Failure of stay cables Structural safety assessment

0 Introduction

Steel-concrete composite beam is a new type of structure developed on the basis of steel structure and reinforced concrete structure. With the rapid growth of traffic volume, bridge fire accidents have become more frequent. For bridges, especially long-span cable-stayed bridges, fire will not only cause damage to the bridge structure, but also cause huge economic losses. Therefore, the fire safety of long-span bridges has been a research hotspot in the field of bridge engineering in recent years (Garlock M et al., 2012).

In recent years, scholars all over the world have conducted a lot of research on bridge fires. Kodur V et al. (2013) proposed the important coefficient of bridge fire resistance according to the importance of the bridge and the load level. Zhang Gang et al. (2018) gave a numerical calculation method for the entire fire process of thermal coupling analysis and proposed an equivalent calculation method for the strength zoning. Scholars have also done a lot of work on the fire resistance research of cable-stayed bridges. Chen Qi-feng et al. (2016) simulated the temperature field of the stay cable with time, and obtained the damage degree of the stay cable's elastic modulus. Ningbo et al. (2012) calculated the ultimate bearing capacity and fire resistance time of steel cables by simplifying the section.

In summary, the current research is mainly focused on small and medium span bridge types such as simply supported beams and continuous beams. There are few studies on long span bridges, especially steel-concrete composite beam cable-stayed bridges. Steel-concrete composite beam bridges are very different from traditional prestressed concrete cable-stayed bridges or steel cable-stayed bridges in terms of structural forces due to their structural particularities. In addition, for the cable-stayed bridge, most scholars only put forward the adverse effect of fire on the stay cable, but there is little research on the safety performance of the whole bridge structure after the cable fracture. Therefore, on the basis of previous studies, this paper put forward a simplified calculation method for the deck fire problem of steel-concrete composite girder cable-stayed bridge, and gave the curve of environmental temperature varying with height in different fire scenarios. It also analyzed the fire temperature curves and cable failures of stayed cables under different fire types. Taking a large-span steel-concrete composite beam cable-stayed bridge as the research object, the structural safety assessment of steel beams and bridge decks at different fire positions was carried out, and the most unfavorable fire position was obtained. It can provide a basis for the fire resistance design method and post-disaster assessment of steel-concrete composite beam cable-stayed bridges.

1 Simulation of Fire Scenarios on bridge deck

1.1 Simulation of Fire Scenarios

In the analysis of bridge fires, the occurrence and development of fires can generally be considered as two stages, the rising stage and the stable stage. In a fire, the heat release rate (HRR) Q is considered to be an important factor in determining the size of the fire (Heskestad., 2015). For different vehicles on the bridge, research institutions such as NFPA502 in the United States, CETU in France, and BD78/99 in the United Kingdom have done a lot of experiments and have given their respective recommended values for the HRR. The fire parameters of different types of vehicles are shown in Tab. 1 (Ma Ming-lei et al., 2015).

It can be seen from Tab. 1 that for a tanker carrying dangerous goods, the heat release rate, combustion duration and area of action after a fire are larger than other vehicles. At the same time, small cars are the most numerous models on bridge roads, so this paper selects the most common cars and the most serious tanker and heavy truck fire types for analysis.

Parameters of Common Vehicle Fires in Bridges   Tab. 1

Type of Fire	Type of fire Traffic Volume	Heat Release Rate (MW)	Fire duration (s)	Area (m^2)
F-1	Small cars	5	1800	2×2.5
F-2	Medium-sized cars	20	3600	4×5
F-3	Tanker and heavy truck	100	7200	4×6

1.2 Fire Heating Curve

FDS (Fire Dynamics Simulator) is a computational fluid dynamics software developed by the Building Fire Research Laboratory of the National Institute of Standards and Technology to simulate fluid movement in a fire. The focus of the calculation is on the heat transfer process in a fire. The software divides the setting space into multiple small three-dimensional rectangular control bodies or calculation units. Using finite volume technology on the same grid to calculate heat radiation, turbulence in fluid flow, and calculate the growth and spread of fire. The mathematical model for solving the FDS fire temperature field was proposed by McGrattan K B et al. (2014).

The fire on the bridge deck is in an open environment with sufficient oxygen supply. In this paper, the size of the fire is defined by HRR. The temperature rise curve above the center of the fire source with height changes is shown in Fig. 1. For the F-1 fire type, the maximum temperature of the fire temperature field dropped from about 810℃ to about 320℃ within 1 to 6m from the bridge deck, and dropped to below 100℃ at about 26m from the bridge deck. For the F-3 fire type, in the range of 0-6m, the temperature drops relatively slowly, from about 1080℃ to 970℃. At 26m from the bridge deck, the temperature drops to about 300℃, and the temperature field temperature is significantly higher than F-1 fire. Through comparison, it can be found that the F-3 fire is much higher than the F-1 fire type in terms of burning duration and temperature value. Therefore, the F-3 fire type is selected for subsequent analysis.

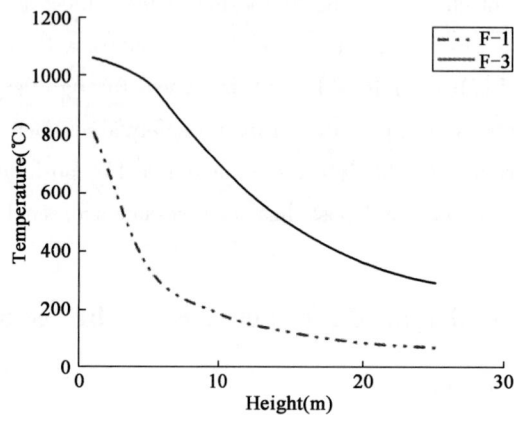

Fig. 1　Temperature Curve of Fire Field

2　Force Analysis of Stay Cables Under Fire

When a fire occurs on the deck of a cable-stayed bridge, the main girder is located under the flame, and the bridge deck pavement has a thermal insulation effect, which is less affected by the fire. The fire mainly affects the components above the flame, such as cables and bridge towers. The cable-stayed bridge tower in this paper is a reinforced concrete structure, which has good fire resistance and limited fire impact. Stayed cables are steel components, and their mechanical properties degrade significantly at high temperatures. Therefore, this paper focuses on analyzing the impact of fire on the cables and derives the most unfavorable fire position.

2.1　Selected Research Objects

In this paper, a steel-concrete composite beam cable-stayed bridge is taken as the research object. The span layout is 30m + 95m + 305m + 110m + 30m, and the structure adopts a double-tower double-cable composite beam cable-stayed bridge. The horizontal bridge is divided into left and right double widths, a single width of 14.5m, and one-way three lanes. A five-span continuous semi-floating system is adopted, and the space is densely cable-shaped. The elevation is shown in Fig. 2.

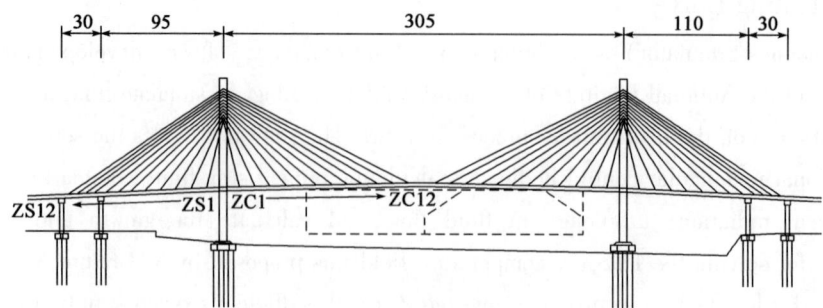

Fig. 2　Elevation View of Cable-stayed Bridge(unit:m)

The main girder is composed of steel girder and concrete bridge deck, which are combined by shear nails. The steel beam part consists of longitudinal beams, cross beams and small longitudinal beams to form a steel girder grid system. A single main bridge is equipped with two box-shaped longitudinal beams. The thickness of the web is 14-24mm, the thickness of the top is 16mm, and the thickness of the bottom is 24mm. The main girder structure adopts Q345qD steel grade with a design strength of 270MPa. The concrete strength grade of the main beam bridge deck is C60, the thickness is 250mm, the compressive design strength is 26.5MPa, and the tensile design strength is 1.96MPa. The cross section of the composite beam is shown in Fig.3.

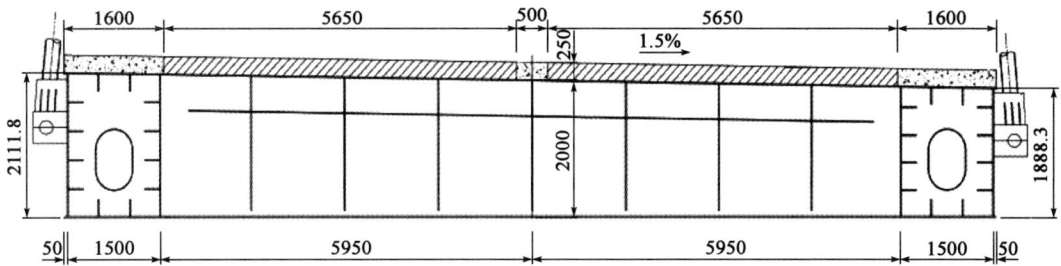

Fig.3 Cross Section of Composite Beam(unit:m)

The stay cable adopts parallel steel wire stay cable. The basic cable spacing of stay cables on the main girder is 12m, and the bridge has 48 (24 × 2) stay cables in total, with a design strength of 1770MPa. The number of stay cables is shown in Fig.2. The bridge is a major urban road with a large traffic volume, so there is a greater possibility of bridge deck fires.

2.2 Material Properties of Steel Cables at High Temperatures

The diameter of the cable is relatively small relative to the length, so in the temperature analysis, it can be approximated that the heat transfer on the surface of the cable is the same. The thermal differential equation of the cable can be expressed by the following formula(Kodur V K et al.,2017):

$$\frac{\rho_s c \partial \theta_s}{\lambda_s \partial t} = \frac{\partial^2 \theta_s}{\partial r^2} + \frac{1}{r}\frac{\partial \theta_s}{\partial r} + \frac{\partial^2 \theta_s}{\partial z^2} \tag{1}$$

Where: θ_s ——temperature of the cable;

λ_s ——thermal conductivity of the cable, which decreases with the increase of temperature;

c ——specific heat capacity of the cable;

ρ_s ——bulk density of the cable, taking 7850kg/m³;

z ——diameter of the cable;

s ——length of the cable.

The thermal conductivity of the stay cable adopts the thermal conductivity of the steel given by the research by Yulian Jia(2010). Fig.4 shows the thermal conductivity versus temperature curve.

The specific heat capacity of the cable adopts the method proposed by Lie and Chabot(1992) to consider the specific heat capacity and bulk density of steel together. Fig.5 is the curve of the specific heat capacity with temperature.

The effects of fire include surface heat exchange conditions and surface radiation(Yang Y et al.,2018). The temperature field boundary conditions of the cable are shown in Eq(2).

$$\begin{cases} \dfrac{\partial \theta_s}{\partial r} = 0, r = 0 \\ \lambda \dfrac{\partial \theta_s}{\partial r} = \varphi \sigma \varepsilon [(\theta + 273)^4 - (\theta_s + 273)^4] + h(\theta - \theta_s), r = r_s \end{cases} \tag{2}$$

Where: r_s —— cable radius;

m; φ —— angle coefficient;

σ —— Stefan-Boltzmann constant;

h —— the surface heat transfer coefficient, which is 45;

ε —— the system emissivity, which is 0.7.

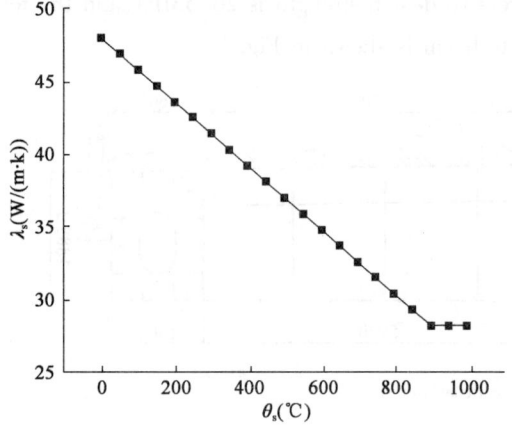

Fig. 4 Thermal Conductivity Curve with Temperature

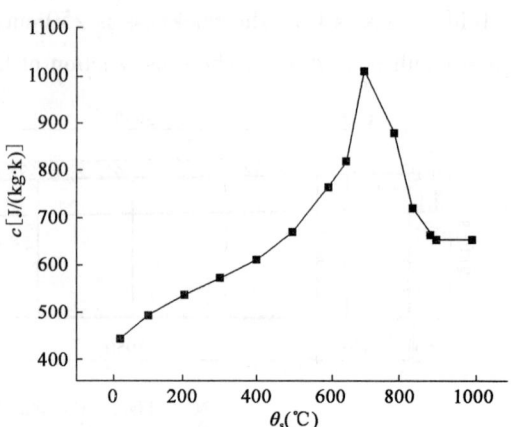

Fig. 5 Curve of Specific Heat Capacity with Temperature

2.3 Stay Cables Failure Analysis

In a fire, the yield strength of stay cables will decrease as the temperature increases. When the temperature rises to the point where the reduced yield strength is lower than the actual stress, the cable is considered to have failed and disconnected for safety reasons.

Using Abaqus CAE finite element software, The convective heat transfer coefficient is 25W/(m·℃), the comprehensive radiation coefficient is 0.7. The temperature of typical stay cables at different heights of 1m, 5m, 10m, 15m, 25m from the bridge deck is calculated and analyzed, and the highest values of stay cables of different heights under the action of F-3 type fire are obtained. The temperature is shown in Fig. 6 below.

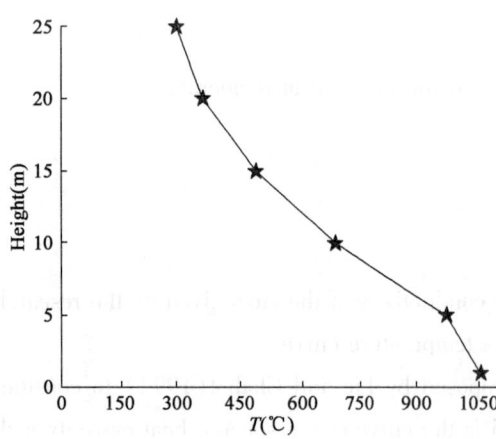

Fig. 6 Maximum Temperature of Stay Cables of Different Heights Under F-3 Fire

The variation of the yield strength of the cable with temperature is as follows:

$$\begin{cases} f_\theta/f_y = 1.0, 0 \leqslant \theta_s \leqslant 150 \\ f_\theta/f_y = (700-\theta_s)/550, 150 < \theta_s \leqslant 700 \end{cases} \quad (3)$$

Where: f_θ —— cable yield strength at high temperature;

f_y —— cable yield strength at normal temperature.

Fire is a kind of accidental effect, and the effect design value of its combination of effects can be calculated according to the following formula according to the relevant content of the "General Specifications for Design of Highway Bridges and Culverts":

$$S_{ad} = S(\sum_m^{i=1} G_{ik}, A_d, \psi_{q1}Q_{1k}, \sum_n^{j=2} \psi_{qj}Q_{jk}) \quad (4)$$

Where: S_{ad} —— design value of the effect under the limit state of the bearing capacity under fire;

G_{ik} —— the standard value of the permanent effect;

A_d —— the design value of the accidental effect of the fire;

$\psi_{q1}Q_{1k}$ —— frequency value of the car load, selected according to the actual lane layout and the coefficient is 0.7;

$\psi_{qj}Q_{jk}$——quasi-permanent value of the j-th variable effect.

In this paper, the stay cable adopts parallel steel wire stay cable with a yield stress of 1770MPa. Under the action of F-3 type fire, when the cable temperature reaches 532℃, The yield strength of the stay cable drops to 563MPa below the stress borne by the stay cable, causing failure and fracture. In order to find the most unfavorable fire position, assuming that the bridge deck fire occurs near the cable stays, the cable failure analysis is carried out on the fire position of the whole bridge. This paper takes the left side span for analysis (the same on the right side). Fig. 7 shows the number of cable breaks above different fire positions.

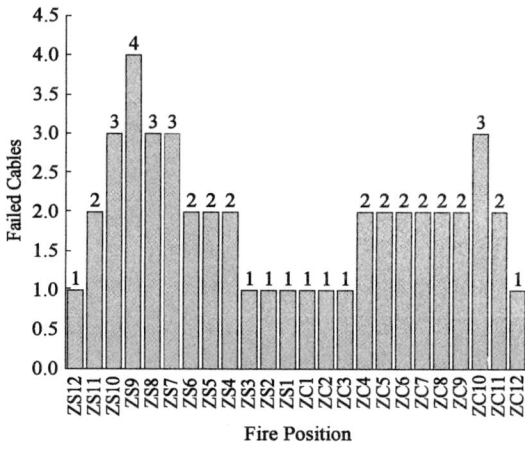

Fig. 7 Number of Cable Breaks Caused by Fire in Different Fire Locations

Perform finite element analysis on all fire conditions. According to the side span fire, the fire near the bridge tower and the mid-span fire, there are 24 categories in total. The most unfavorable fire location conditions for each category are as follows (Tab. 2, Fig. 8).

Parameters of Common Vehicle Fires in Bridges Tab. 2

Working Condition	Feature	Fire Position	Failed Cable
FP-1	Maximum number of side span failure cables	ZS9	ZS9、ZS10、ZS11、ZS12
FP-2	Maximum number of tower failure cables	ZC1	ZC1
FP-3	Maximum number of middle span failure cables	ZC10	ZC10、ZC11、ZC12

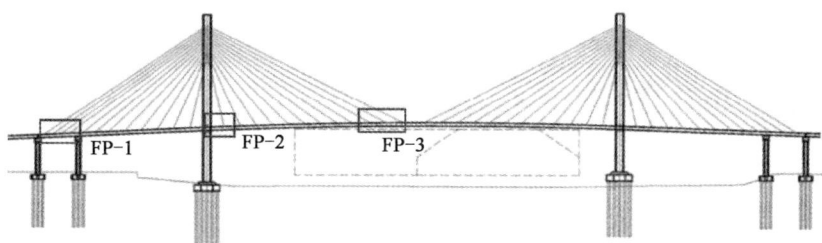

Fig. 8 Schematic Diagram of the Most Unfavorable Fire Position

3 Safety Analysis of Whole Bridge Structure

From the above analysis, it is known that the effect of fire will cause the breakage of the bridge cable, which will cause the stress of the main girder section to increase. Because the concrete bridge deck has a good thermal insulation effect and poor thermal conductivity, this paper does not consider the effect of high temperature on the loss of prestress of the concrete deck. It is conservative that the elastic modulus of concrete is not reduced due to the thermal insulation effect of the bridge deck pavement. According to the cable failure, the finite element software is used to calculate the stress value of the main girder and the bridge deck section and the displacement of the control section under the three most unfavorable fire conditions. It is worth putting out that there are two ways to simulate the failure of stayed cables at high temperatures in the full bridge model. One is to reduce the elastic modulus of the cable material, and the other is to passivate the effect of the stay cable. For safety reasons, this article uses the second method to simulate. The finite element model is shown in Fig. 9.

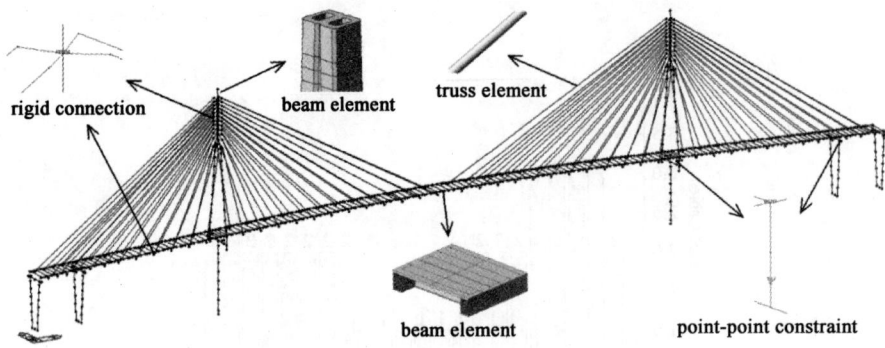

Fig. 9 Finite Element Model

3.1 Strength Analysis of main Girder Section

Fig. 10 shows the stress values of the top and bottom points of the steel main beam in the steel-concrete composite beam under the three most unfavorable fire conditions of FP-1, FP-2, and FP-3.

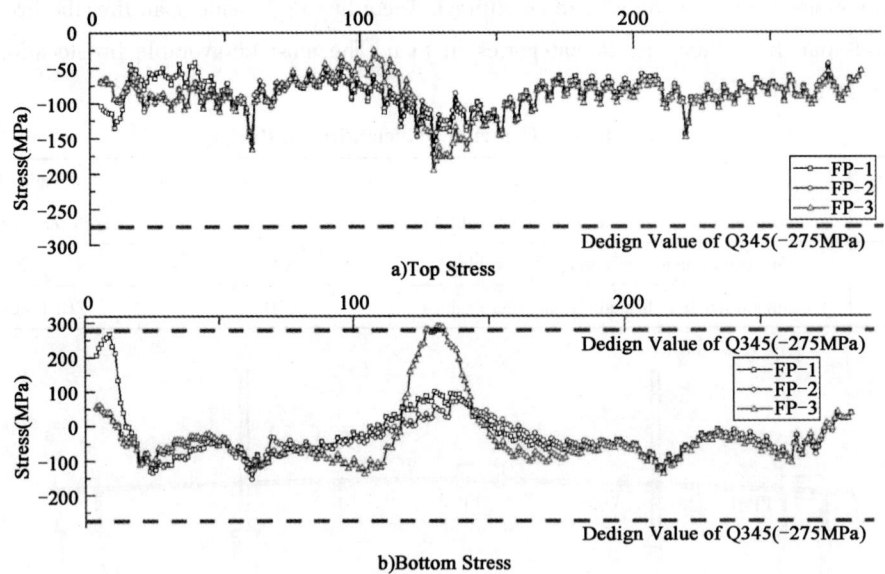

Fig. 10 Strength of Steel Main Beam Section

It can be seen from the above figure that under the action of the F-3 type fire, in the FP-3 working condition, that is, when the fire occurs at the ZC10 stay cable, a total of 3 cables ZC10, ZC11, ZC12 fractured and failed. The compressive stress of the steel main girder of Unit 124, where the FP-3 fire occurred, reached the maximum value of 195.98 MPa, which did not exceed the design strength of 270MPa specified by the specification, and there was still a 27.4% margin. But for the section tensile stress, under the FP-3 working condition, the tensile stress of the steel main girder at the fire location reaches 290.05MPa, which exceeds the design strength by 7.43%. In addition, under FP-1 and FP-2 working conditions, the fire has a limited effect on the section strength of the steel main girder.

Fig. 11 shows the stress values of the top and bottom of the concrete bridge deck in the steel-concrete composite girder under the three most unfavorable fire conditions of FP-1, FP-2 and FP-3.

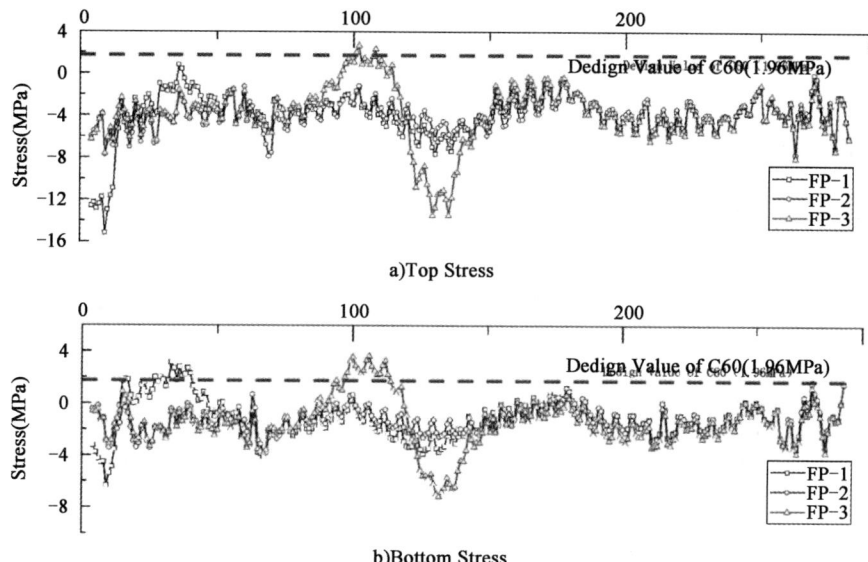

Fig. 11 Strength of Concrete Bridge Deck

It can be seen from the above figure that under the action of F-3 type fire, when the compressive stress of concrete bridge deck is under FP-1 working condition, that is, when the fire occurs at the ZS9 stay cable, a total of 4 cables ZS9, ZS10, ZS11, and ZS12 fracture and fail. The maximum compressive stress of the concrete bridge slab occurred at the No.6 unit, the stay cable ZS10, which was 15.18MPa. There is a margin of 42.72% from the design value of the standard compressive stress strength. For the section tensile stress, under the FP-1 working condition, The maximum tensile stress reaches 3.15MPa, which is 60.71% higher than the design strength of 1.96MPa. In the FP-2 working condition, the maximum tensile stress of the concrete bridge deck reaches 1.6MPa. Under the FP-3 working condition, the maximum tensile stress of the concrete bridge deck reaches 3.64MPa, which exceeds the limit by 85.71%.

It can be seen that the fire has little influence on the compressive stress intensity of the bridge deck, and has a serious influence on the tensile stress intensity.

3.2 Displacement analysis

The vertical displacement of the key section of the main beam after the fire is shown in Fig. 12.

The maximum vertical displacement occurred at the mid-span position. The maximum displacement reached 1031.39mm, and the torsion-span ratio was about 1/296, which was greater than the prescribed limit of 1/400, indicating that the performance of the bridge structure was greatly affected by the fire.

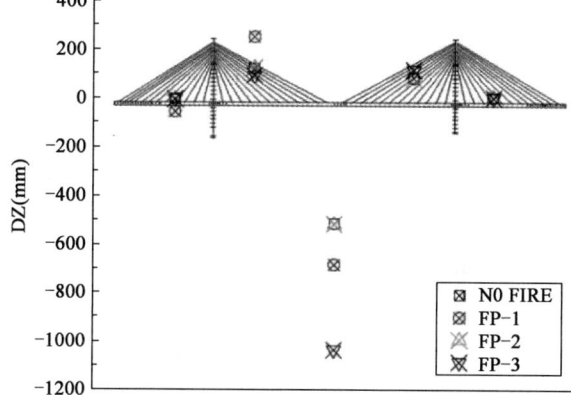

Fig. 12 Displacement of Control Section under fire

4 Conclusions

Aimed at the deck fire of steel-concrete composite beam cable-stayed bridge, this paper proposes a simplified calculation method. The heating curve of the fire scenarios of the bridge deck is calculated by FDS software. The fire temperature curve of the stayed cable is given and the failure of the stayed cable is analyzed. Finally, the safety analysis of the main girder and bridge deck of the steel-concrete composite beam is carried out.

The results show that under the action of F-3 type fire, when the temperature of the stay cable reaches 532℃, the yield strength of the stay cable drops to lower than the stress that the stay cable bears, and fracture occur. When the fire occurs near the mid-span cable of the main span, the steel-concrete composite beam is greatly affected by the fire, especially the concrete deck part exceeds the standard design value by more than 80%.

Therefore, it is recommended to set up a complete set of fire extinguishing devices every 10 meters in the middle-span cable area and side-span cable area of the bridge deck to ensure that effective fire extinguishing measures can be taken in the first time when a fire occurs, and the time and scope of the fire action can be reduced. To reduce the impact of fire.

References

[1] Cheng Qifeng, Li Lilin, Hao Tianzhi, et al. (2016). Study on Stayed Cable Thermal Analysis Temperature Field Simulation Methods of Cable-stayed Bridges. Bridge and Tunnel Engineering,09,59-63.

[2] Garlock M, PayaZaforteza I, Kodur V, et al. (2012). Fire Hazard in Bridges: Review, Assessment and Repair Strategies. Engineering Structures,35,89-98.

[3] Heskestad G. (1983) Luminous Heights of Turbulent Diffusion Flames. Fire Safety Journal,5(2). 103-108.

[4] Jia Yu-lian. (2010). Numerical simulation of oil tanker fire. North University of China.

[5] Kodur V and Naser M. (2013). Importance Factor for Design of Bridges against Fire Hazard. Engineering Structures,54,207-220.

[6] Kodur V K, Aziz E M, Naser M Z. (2017) Strategies for enhancing fire performance of steel bridges. Engineering Structures,2017,131.

[7] Lie. T, Chabot M. Experimental Studies on the Fire Resistance of Hollow Steel Columns Filled with Plain Concrete. NRC-CNRC Internal Report,.573.

[8] Ma Minglei, Ma Rujin, Cheng Airong. (2014). Safety of Cables and Full Structure of a Cable-Stayed bridge Exposed to Fires on Deck, Journal of South China University of Technology (Natural Science Edition),42(10).117-124.

[9] McGrattan K B. Hostikka S. Floyd J E et al. (2014) Fire dynamics simulator (version 5) technical reference guide [CP/OL]..http:/www.fire.nist.gov/fds/download/.

[10] Ning Bo, Liu Yongjun, Yu Baoyang, et al. (2012). Numerical Simulation of Ultimate Bearing Capacity of Cables for A Cable-Stayed Bridge under Tanker Fire. Steel Construction,27(02),68-72.

[11] Yang Y, Yang B, Bing Z. (2018) The Study on Influence of Water Mist Particle Size on Fire Smoke Migration with Longitudinal Ventilation in Road Tunnel. Procedia Engineering,211.917-924.

[12] Zhang Gang, Zong Huanru, Huang Qiao, et al. (2018). Degradation Mechanism of Simply Supported Steel-concrete Composite Box Girder under Tanker Fire Condition. Journal of Chang'an University (Natural Science Edition),38(06),31-39.

刚构-连续结构体系梁桥组合式桥墩力学性能分析

杨 光 徐 岳

(长安大学)

摘 要 为了研究组合式桥墩在刚构-连续组合梁桥使用阶段的力学性能,通过结构稳定理论中的能量法,推导了墩底固结墩顶的组合式桥墩纵向失稳临界荷载公式,依托工程实例将公式计算结果与桥墩有限元模型计算结果进行对比。通过建立不同分界点的全桥有限元模型,分析了分界点变化对刚构-连续组合梁桥运营使用阶段力学性能的影响,最后给出组合式桥墩工程设计中合理分界点的建议值和桥梁在使用阶段需要关注的力学性能问题。

关键词 桥梁工程 力学性能分析 瑞利-里兹法 组合式桥墩 刚构-连续结构体系梁桥 桥梁稳定性

0 引 言

连续梁桥的桥墩结构形式有独墩、双薄壁墩和上部为双肢墩下部为独墩的组合式桥墩。其中组合式桥墩将双薄壁墩与单薄壁墩的优点结合,又能在设计时通过分界点的调整获得理想的刚度适应需求,适合在高墩大跨的连续刚构体系桥梁中使用。对于组合式桥墩形式的刚构-连续体系桥梁在设计施工上仍缺乏完善的理论作为参考,所以对组合式桥墩刚构-连续组合梁桥的研究很有意义。

欧阳青以瓦窑堡特大桥为工程实例对空心薄壁墩、双薄壁墩、组合式桥墩三种不同形式的桥墩展开稳定性分析,认为组合式桥墩在经济性、稳定性上对比另外两种桥墩有一定优势。[1] 2012年,李璐、周水兴等人利用有限元法对某组合式桥墩刚构桥进行稳定分析,结果表明组合式桥墩变刚度位置就其工程实例而言在0.5~1之内较优。[2] 周水兴、满泽联等人利用里兹法,推导出了组合式桥墩面外屈曲临界荷载计算公式,最后认为桥墩变截面位置在0.4~0.65之间比较合理。[3] 王俏等人基于能量法研究了组合式桥墩稳定系数的计算方法,并利用此计算方法分析得到组合式桥墩理想变截面位置为0.61。[4] 2017年,刘东用有限元模型法对某组合式桥墩连续刚构桥的力学性能展开分析研究,总结出了组合式桥墩各因素对桥梁结构力学性能的影响。[5]

目前对组合式桥墩临界荷载公式研究多为对桥墩构件进行施工阶段的自体稳定分析以给出建议的分界点位置,缺少刚构-连续组合梁桥的组合式桥墩分界点位置对成桥阶段桥梁整体力学性能的影响分析。本文基于瑞利里兹法,推导墩底固结墩顶铰接的组合式桥墩面外屈曲临界公式;依托弘农涧特大桥工程建立有限元模型,将公式计算结果与有限元计算结果进行对比,并分析组合式桥墩分界点位置对刚构-连续组合梁桥使用阶段力学性能的影响。

1 组合式桥墩失稳临界荷载

1.1 组合式桥墩临界荷载分析的能量法

对于高度较大的组合式桥墩,能量法中的瑞利里兹法是稳定性计算的常用方法。

能量法计算的基本思想为能量守恒原理和势能驻值原理。能量守恒原理为在整个结构体系中,外力所做的功始终等于结构体系内的应变能,即$\Delta U = \Delta V$。势能驻值原理为当外力作用时,结构有小位移二结构的总势能Π不变,结构体系处于平衡状态,即总势能有驻值,表达式为$\delta \Pi = 0$,其中$\Pi = U + V$。

瑞利里兹法是在势能驻值原理的基础上,用变形函数$y(x)$来表示结构体系的总势能,并把$y(x)$用多个函数的线性组合来表示,即将无限自由度化为有限自由度。

1.2 基本假定

(1)组合式桥墩采用弹性结构的计算方法。
(2)组合式桥墩采用杆件结构计算。
(3)忽略初始缺陷和非线性因素的影响。
(4)瑞利里兹法可以基于大位移小变形假定进行临界荷载推导。
(5)变形函数取满足边界条件的函数表达式。

1.3 临界荷载公式

对于刚构-连续组合梁桥成桥阶段的组合式桥墩,可将桥墩视为底端固结顶端铰接的结构进行公式推导,结构为第一类失稳的轴心受压构件,失稳方向为y轴方向的纵向失稳。

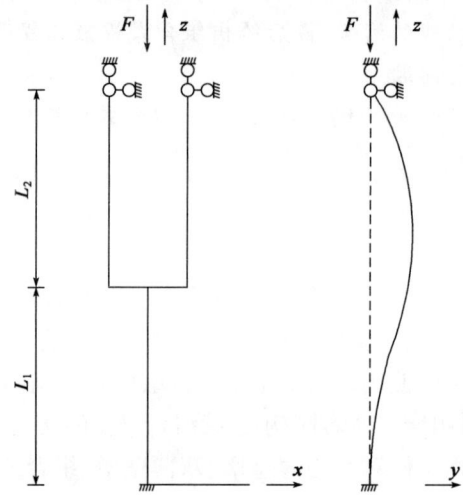

图1 组合式桥墩失稳分析

对于组合式桥墩,在轴心力N的作用下,应变能:

$$U = \frac{1}{2}\int_0^l \frac{M^2}{EI}dx = \frac{1}{2}\int_0^l EI(y'')^2 dx \tag{1}$$

其中独墩部分应变能:

$$U_1 = \frac{1}{2}\int_0^{\beta l} EI_1 (y'')^2 dx \tag{2}$$

双肢墩部分应变能:

$$U_2 = \frac{1}{2}\int_{\beta l}^l EI_2 (y'')^2 dx \tag{3}$$

外力势能为:

$$V = -\frac{1}{2}N\int_0^l (y')^2 dx \tag{4}$$

总势能为:

$$\Pi = U_1 + U_2 + V = \frac{1}{2}\int_0^{\beta l} EI_1 (y'')^2 dx + \frac{1}{2}\int_{\beta l}^l EI_2 (y'')^2 dx - N\int_0^l (y')^2 dx \tag{5}$$

设变形函数$y(x)$为:

$$y(x) = \alpha_1 f_1(x) + \alpha_2 f_2(x) + \alpha_3 f_3(x) + \cdots + \alpha_n f_n(x) \tag{6}$$

对一端固定一端铰接的变截面杆件,满足边界条件的变形函数[6]可以取:

$$y(x) = \alpha_1(l-x)x^2 + \alpha_2(l-x)x^3 \quad (7)$$

代入相关数据得:

$$U = j_1\alpha_1^2 + j_2\alpha_1\alpha_2 + j_3\alpha_2^2 \quad (8)$$

$$V = k_1\alpha_1^2 + k_2\alpha_1\alpha_2 + k_3\alpha_2^2 \quad (9)$$

其中

$$j_1 = 2El^3(I_1\beta^3 + I_2 - I_2\beta^3)$$
$$j_2 = 4El^4(I_1\beta^4 + I_2 - I_2\beta^4)$$
$$j_3 = 2.4El^5(I_1\beta^5 + I_2 - I_2\beta^5)$$
$$k_1 = -0.0667l^5 N$$
$$k_2 = -0.1Nl^6$$
$$k_3 = -0.04285Nl^5$$

式中:l——墩高;
E——弹性模量;
I_1——独墩纵向失稳方向惯性矩;
I_2——双肢墩纵向失稳方向的惯性矩之和;
N——竖向力;
β——桥墩分界点位置,即 $\beta = l_1/l$。

用 α_1、α_2 来表示总势能:

$$\Pi = (j_1 - k_1)\alpha_1^2 + (j_2 - k_2)\alpha_1\alpha_2 + (j_3 - k_3)\alpha_2^2 \quad (10)$$

由势能驻值原理 $\delta\Pi = 0$,瑞利里兹法将问题转化为求 α_1、α_2 的偏导:

$$\begin{cases} \dfrac{\partial \Pi}{\partial \alpha_1} = 0 \\ \dfrac{\partial \Pi}{\partial \alpha_2} = 0 \end{cases} \quad (11)$$

$$\frac{\partial \Pi}{\partial \alpha_1} = 2(j_1 - k_1)\alpha_1 + (j_2 - k_2)\alpha_2 = 0 \quad (12)$$

$$\frac{\partial \Pi}{\partial \alpha_2} = (j_2 - k_2)\alpha_1 + 2(j_3 - k_3)\alpha_2 = 0 \quad (13)$$

$$[A]\{x\} = \begin{pmatrix} 2(j_1 - k_1) & (j_2 - k_2) \\ (j_2 - k_2) & 2(j_3 - k_3) \end{pmatrix} \begin{Bmatrix} \alpha_1 \\ \alpha_2 \end{Bmatrix} = 0 \quad (14)$$

当行列式 $[A]$ 的值为 0 时,方程组有非零解,求解此方程式得面外屈曲临界公式:

$$N_{cr} = \frac{-C \pm \sqrt{C^2 - 0.00576l^{12}(4j_1j_3 - j_2^2)}}{0.00288l^{12}} \quad (15)$$

其中 $C = 0.1714j_1l^7 + 0.267j_3l^5 - 0.2j_2l^6$。

2 工程应用及分析

弘农涧特大桥主桥为 87m + 160×6m + 87m 刚构-连续组合梁桥,7 号~12 号桥墩采用 C50 混凝土变截面空心墩形式,其中 7 号墩、11 号墩、12 号墩处为连续梁,8 号~10 号墩处为连续刚构。空心墩上部 65m 横向采用双肢形式,单肢宽度为 6.5m,空心墩壁厚 0.8m,竖向每 20m 设置一道横隔板,横隔板壁厚 0.8m。空心墩下部采用整体式单箱三室结构,壁厚均为 0.8m,墩高为 125m。

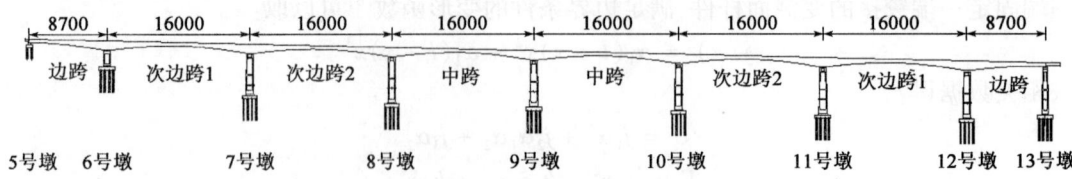

图2 泓农涧特大桥主桥总体布置(尺寸单位:mm)

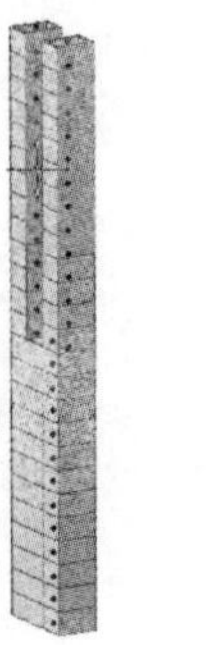

C50混凝土弹性模量 $E=3.45\times10^4 MPa$；
独墩惯性矩 $I_1=659.68(m^4)$；
双肢墩惯性矩 $I_2=235.46\times2=470.92(m^4)$；
9号墩 $\beta=65/125=0.52$；
代入式(15)，得9号墩 $N_{cr}=7206138 kN$。

同时建立如图3所示的9号墩的Midas civil有限元模型，将有限元计算结果与式(15)计算的结果进行对比，结果如表1所示。

从表(1)可以看出式(15)计算结果模型计算结果差值较小，分别为3.6%，误差主要来源于瑞利里兹法所选取变形函数，得到的计算值为近似值。

图3 桥墩模型

临界荷载计算值(kN) 表1

桥 墩	公式(15)	模型计算
9号墩	7206138	6946717

3 分界点对桥梁力学性能的影响分析

结合弘农涧特大桥，建立如图4所示的组合式桥墩分界点不同情况下的全桥有限元模型进行力学性能分析，主要分析桥墩的墩底弯矩以及全桥的稳定安全系数。有限元模型中用梁单元的形式模拟主梁和桥墩结构，其中8号~10号墩处墩梁固结，7号、11号、12号墩处设置支座，墩底固结，上部双肢墩与下部独墩刚性连接，除分界点位置外，模型其余参数均不变。

图4 全桥有限元模型

3.1 分界点对桥墩静力性能的影响

桥梁使用阶段荷载有自重、二期恒载、基础变位荷载、温度荷载、汽车荷载。不同分界点墩底弯矩分析见表2。

桥墩墩底最大弯矩值(kN·m) 表2

β	0.28	0.4	0.52	0.64
7号墩	306.2	307.1	305	305
8号墩	−286137	−299047	−306454	−309522
9号墩	−15995	−16038	−15856	−15616
10号墩	285998	298887	306480	309738
11号墩	226.3	226	224	224
12号墩	308.4	307.9	303	303

从表 3 可以看出,当分界点的高度提高,刚构部位的 8 号墩与 10 号墩墩底弯矩值逐渐变大。以 8 号墩为例,8 号墩的 β 从 0.28 到 0.4 时,弯矩增加 12910kN·m;β 从 0.4 到 0.52 时,弯矩增加 7407kN·m;β 从 0.52 到 0.64 时,弯矩增加 3068kN·m。分界点位置 β 从 0.28 提高到 0.4,弯矩增幅最大,从 0.52 提高到 0.64 时增幅最小。

3.2 分界点对桥梁稳定性的影响

3.2.1 成桥阶段全桥稳定性

对全桥进行使用阶段屈曲稳定分析,以自重、二期、基础变位作用为不变荷载,温度荷载、车道荷载为可变荷载,桥梁使用阶段全桥稳定特征值如表 3 和图 5 所示。

全桥使用阶段稳定特征值　　　　表 3

稳定特征值	分界点位置			
	0.28	0.4	0.52	0.68
1 阶	5.61	8.01	12.31	17.03
2 阶	6.01	8.94	13.06	17.83
3 阶	7.36	9.02	14.58	19.41
4 阶	7.78	9.89	15.12	19.99

从表 3 和图 5 可以看出,随着分界点位置的提高,全桥的稳定安全系数明显增大,当分界点 β 从 0.28 增大到 0.68,一阶稳定系数增大 11.42,增大近两倍,说明对于纵向双幅形式的刚构-连续组合梁桥来说,分界点位置对全桥稳定性影响较大,提高分界点的位置有利于桥梁使用阶段的稳定性。

3.2.2 成桥阶段桥墩稳定性

建立不同分界点情况下 7 号墩和 8 号墩的桥墩模型,7 号墩墩顶为铰接,8 号墩墩顶为刚接,以自重为不变荷载,主梁与桥墩连接处单元的全桥静力计算结果作为可变荷载施加于墩顶,成桥阶段桥墩 1 阶稳定特征值如表 4 所示,桥墩与全桥的一阶稳定特征值见图 6。

桥墩使用阶段稳定特征值　　　　表 4

β	0.32	0.4	0.52	0.6
7 号墩	14.02	15.38	16.82	17.58
8 号墩	72.61	77.17	82.42	88.31

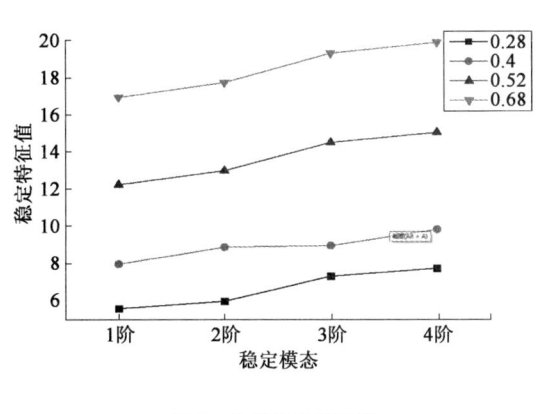

图 5　全桥稳定特征值

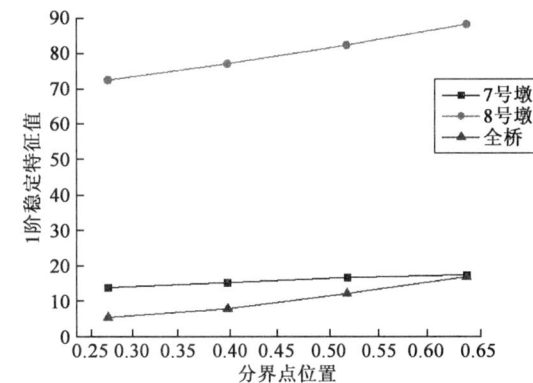

图 6　桥墩与全桥稳定特征值

从表 4 可以看出,成桥运营阶段 8 号墩的稳定特征值远大于 7 号墩,说明成桥阶段连续梁处的桥墩先于墩梁固结处的桥墩发生失稳破坏。从图 6 可以看出,当分界点位置为 0.28、0.4 和 0.52 时,全桥结构体系失稳先于桥墩构件失稳,当分界点位置为 0.64 时,全桥体系失稳与连续梁处桥墩构件失稳几乎同时发生。

4 结语

根据结构稳定理论推导了一端固结一端铰接的组合式桥墩面外失稳临界荷载公式,并应用于实桥算例,与有限元模型计算结果进行对比,两者差值较小,可将公式作为临界荷载估算使用。建立有限元模型分析了分界点位置对桥梁力学性能的影响,结果表明,提高分界点位置会增大桥墩的墩底弯矩,但能提高桥墩和全桥结构运营阶段的稳定性,且分界点低于0.64时应优先对全桥结构体系进行稳定性控制。分界点高度0.4以后全桥结构已经有足够的稳定系数,考虑到对经济层面的影响,就文中所用工程实例模型而言,在刚构-连续结构体系梁桥组合式桥墩设计中分界点位置取0.4~0.5范围内较优,桥梁在运营阶段需要关注整桥结构体系的失稳问题。

参考文献

[1] 欧阳青,王艳,王艳华.高墩大跨连续刚构桥墩形式研究[J].中外公路,2008(01):153-155.

[2] 李璐,周水兴,江雄飞.双薄壁-独墩组合型桥墩合理构造形式研究[J].重庆交通大学学报(自然科学版),2012,31(01):19-21+153.

[3] 周水兴,满泽联,周光强.连续刚构桥组合式桥墩临界荷载分析[J].重庆交通大学学报(自然科学版),2014,33(01):17-20+138.

[4] 王俏,李彪,杨美良.连续刚构桥组合式桥墩合理分界点研究[J].湖南交通科技,2017,43(02):130-134+144.

[5] 刘东.组合式桥墩连续刚构桥力学性能分析[D].长沙:长沙理工大学,2017.

[6] 周绪红.结构稳定理论[M].北京:高等教育出版社,2010.

高墩超多跨连续刚构桥合龙方案与顶推控制研究

朱军生[1] 陆泽磊[1] 牛六喜[2] 王少鹏[2]

(1.长安大学公路学院;2.中铁二十一局三公司)

摘要 为确定某高墩超多跨连续刚构桥的最优合龙方案及其不同合龙温度情况下的顶推力,基于不同合龙方案建立不进行顶推的数值分析模型,并对结构进行详细的仿真分析和计算,以完全消除连续刚构桥各墩顶在成桥10年后由于混凝土收缩与徐变等因素所引起的纵向位移为目标,确定各合龙方案的顶推力理论值。在确定最优合龙方案后,计算并确定合龙温差值与顶推力之间的拟合公式。本文为此座高墩超多跨连续刚构桥以及同类型桥梁的合龙顶推施工提供参考。

关键词 高墩超多跨连续刚构桥 数值分析模型 合龙顺序 顶推力 合龙温差

0 引言

高墩超多跨连续刚构桥因其强大的跨越能力和地形适应能力成为我国西部山区桥梁建设中的主要桥型。随着跨数增多的同时,合龙段的数目也在增多,合龙顺序会影响顶推力的大小和结构整体的受力情况。实际合龙温度若高于设计合龙温度,在运营阶段环境温度下降至较低时,桥梁结构将会收缩,产生不利于结构安全的水平变位。因此,合龙施工应选择在低温浇筑,并施加抵抗温差效应的顶推力。

众多学者对连续刚构桥合龙方案和顶推控制展开了大量研究[1-6]。本文以某高墩多跨连续刚构桥为工程背景,采用Midas-Civil建立不同合龙方案的有限元模型,计算不同合龙方案的顶推位移和顶推力,确定最优合龙方案,得出不同合龙温度下的顶推力公式。

1 工程概况与有限元模型

桥梁全长1398.2m,主桥最大墩高94.5m,设计荷载为公路Ⅰ级。主桥上部结构为65m+120×5m+65m预应力混凝土连续刚构,下部结构为单、双薄壁式空心墩,主桥立面见图1。主梁采用单箱单室截面,支点处梁高7.2m,跨中处梁高2.8m,箱梁高度按1.8次抛物线变化。箱梁顶板宽度为12.9m,底板宽度为7.0m。主桥箱梁采用C55混凝土,主桥墩身采用C40混凝土。全桥共计275个单元,294个节点,有限元模型见图2。

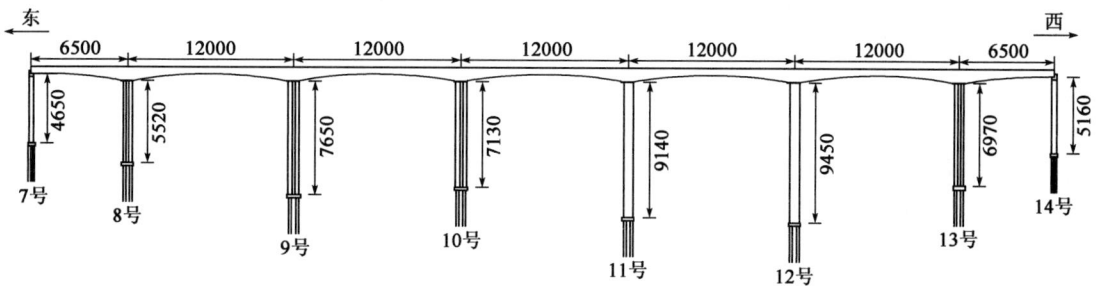

图1 主桥立面图(尺寸单位:cm)

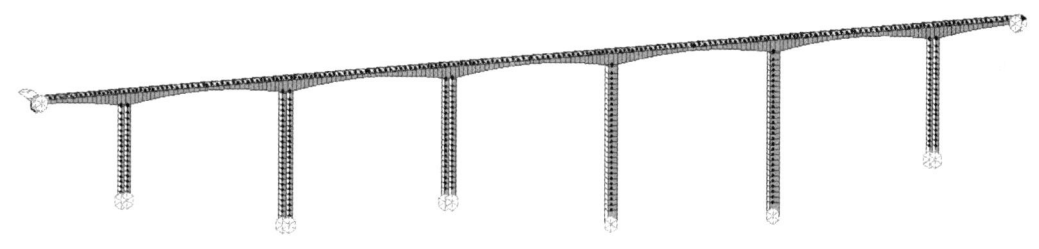

图2 有限元模型

2 最优合龙方案的确定

本文提出以下三种合龙方案,并均在次边跨合龙前、次中跨合龙前对主梁悬臂端施加一次水平顶推力,合龙位置见图3。

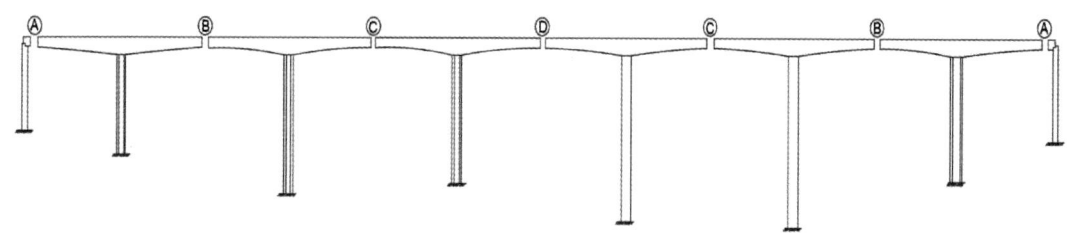

图3 合龙位置示意图

方案一:(ABCD)先边跨A,再次边跨B,之后次中跨C,最后中跨D合龙。
方案二:(DCBA)先中跨D,再次中跨C,之后次边跨B,最后边跨A合龙。
方案三:(DCAB)先中跨D,再次中跨C,之后边跨A,最后次边跨B合龙。

2.1 顶推位移计算

假定以上三个合龙方案均按设计温度合龙,计算得到各合龙方案主桥成桥10年后因混凝土收缩徐变产生的墩顶水平位移,如表1所示,其中双肢薄壁式主墩墩顶水平位移取其位移平均数。本文中理想顶推即以完全抵消成桥10年后的墩顶水平位移为目标,故下文中以完全消除墩顶水平位移为目标,确定边跨及次中跨的顶推力。

不顶推合龙时主桥成桥10年后墩顶水平位移(mm) 表1

桥墩编号	方案一	方案二	方案三
8号	66.05	65.88	65.93
9号	40.02	39.67	39.43
10号	12.36	12.11	11.94
11号	-13.95	-13.84	-13.95
12号	-40.24	-40.06	-40.12
13号	-68.78	-68.65	-69.01

注:偏向小里程方向为正,偏向大里程方向为负。下同。

2.2 顶推力计算

为了确定顶推力的大小,将100kN水平合龙顶推力分别施加到主梁次边跨、次中跨的最大悬臂端节点,并增加平衡力以保持"T"构平衡,得到三个方案下的位移水平增量,如表2所示。

100kN顶推力作用下各墩墩顶的纵桥向位移(mm) 表2

方案编号	施工阶段	8号	9号	10号	11号	12号	13号
方案一	次边跨顶推	-3.35	0.00	0.00	0.00	0.00	4.60
	次中跨顶推	-1.92	-2.20	0.00	0.00	2.21	2.00
方案二	次边跨顶推	-4.47	0.00	0.00	0.00	0.00	5.80
	次中跨顶推	0.00	-6.54	0.00	0.00	6.79	0.00
方案三	次边跨顶推	-3.36	0.00	0.00	0.00	0.00	3.41
	次中跨顶推	0.00	-6.54	0.00	0.00	6.79	0.00

本文对合龙口处施加100kN的初始顶推力,再根据顶推位移求得总顶推力,考虑实际合龙过程的方便性,取同一工况两顶推力的平均值。该算法形式简单,能够迅速求得顶推力的数值。联立表1、2的数据,根据水平顶推力与顶推位移成正比,进行各方案合龙顶推力计算。计算结果统计于表3。

各合龙方案顶推力(kN) 表3

预推力	方案一	方案二	方案三
次边跨顶推力	817	1328	1993
次中跨顶推力	1820	598	597

方案一次中跨顶推力为1819kN(9号墩)和1821kN(12号墩),为满足对称顶推施工的要求,取顶推力1820kN为次中跨顶推力;方案一次边跨顶推力受限于次中跨顶推力,次中跨顶推力1820kN已对8号墩和13号墩分别产生-34.94mm和-36.4mm的纵桥向位移,综合计算得次边跨顶推力为929kN(8号墩)和704kN(13号墩),取次边跨顶推力为817kN。

方案二次边跨顶推力为1473kN(8号墩)和1183kN(13号墩),取顶推力1328kN为次边跨顶推力;方案二的次中跨顶推力为606kN(9号墩)和590kN(12号墩),取顶推力598kN为次中跨顶推力。

方案三次边跨顶推力为1962kN(8号墩)和2024kN(13号墩),取顶推力1993kN为次边跨顶推力;方案三的次中跨顶推力为603kN(9号墩)和591kN(12号墩),取顶推力597kN为次中跨顶推力。

2.3 方案分析比较

本文中方案选取指标是选取最优顶推效果的方案。因而,将表3中顶推力施加到各合龙方案的有限元模型中,得到各方案施加顶推力合龙10年后的墩顶水平位移,如表4所示。

顶推后主桥成桥 10 年后墩顶水平位移（mm）　　表4

桥墩编号	方案一	方案二	方案三
8 号	-0.26	6.53	-4.17
9 号	2.10	-4.58	-4.67
10 号	12.36	12.64	12.30
11 号	-13.95	-14.37	-14.14
12 号	-3.64	8.45	8.17
13 号	3.30	8.20	11.19

从表4与表1的数据可知，次边跨和次中跨顶推合龙后，8号、9号、12号和13号墩的墩顶水平位移显著改善，各合龙方案主桥成桥10年后墩顶水平位移柱状图见图4。因未顶推中跨，10号和11号墩墩顶水平位移几乎不变。方案一和方案二的部分桥墩成桥10年后墩顶水平位移为不利于桥梁的纵向变形。再者方案一从边跨依次向中跨合龙，每次顶推须额外增加顶推力以保持"T"构平衡。方案三墩顶水平位移方向背离主桥中跨，优于方案一和方案二。综上，确定方案三为该桥最优合龙方案，即先中跨，再次中跨，之后边跨，最后次边跨合龙。

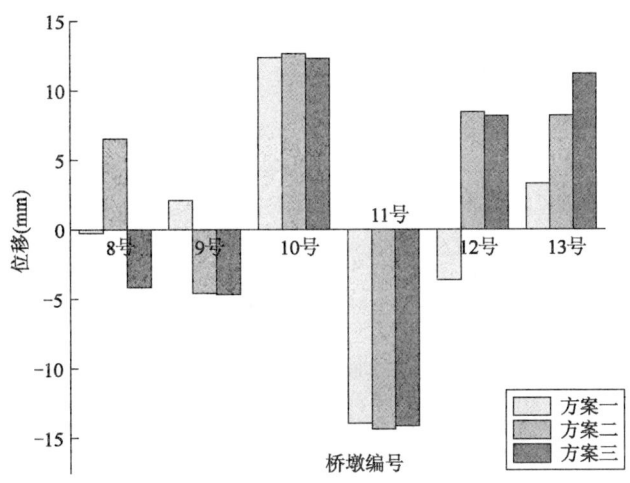

图4　各合龙方案主桥成桥 10 年后墩顶水平位移（尺寸单位：mm）

3　高温合龙的顶推力计算

3.1　温度与墩顶水平位移

该桥根据实际施工计划，合龙时的温度将会大于设计温度。该桥应选择在低温下合龙，并根据实际温差增大顶推力，以抵抗温差效应。在确定方案三为最优方案后，为分析该桥高温合龙状态下顶推力，计算该桥在设计温度合龙后，升温 10℃ 对成桥状态下各墩墩顶水平位移的影响，得到各墩墩顶水平位移见表5、图5。

升温对成桥状态下各墩墩顶水平位移的影响（mm）　　表5

升温(℃)	桥墩编号					
	8 号	9 号	10 号	11 号	12 号	13 号
1	-2.80	-1.69	-0.53	0.60	1.71	2.91
2	-5.59	-3.39	-1.06	1.20	3.41	5.83
3	-8.39	-5.08	-1.59	1.79	5.12	8.74
4	-11.19	-6.77	-2.11	2.39	6.83	11.65
5	-13.99	-8.47	-2.64	2.99	8.53	14.57

续上表

升温(℃)	桥墩编号					
	8号	9号	10号	11号	12号	13号
6	−16.78	−10.16	−3.17	3.59	10.24	17.48
7	−19.58	−11.85	−3.70	4.19	11.95	20.39
8	−22.38	−13.55	−4.23	4.79	13.65	23.31
9	−25.18	−15.24	−4.76	5.38	15.36	26.22
10	−27.97	−16.93	−5.28	5.98	17.04	29.13

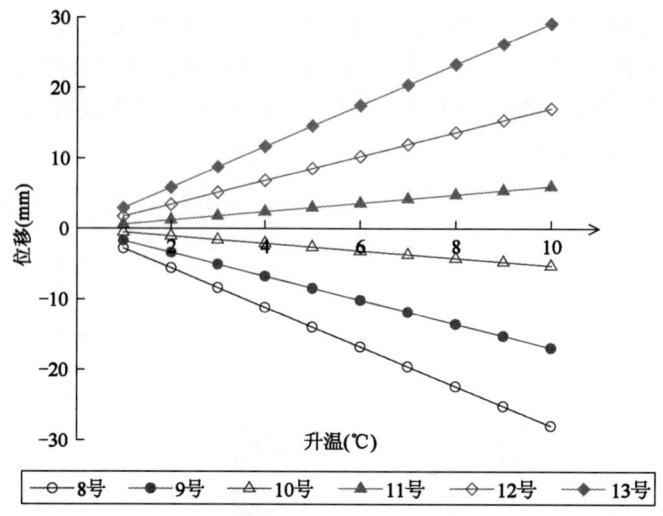

图5 升温对成桥状态下各墩墩顶水平位移的影响(单位:mm)

从上述图表中可知,随着温度的升高,主桥各墩墩顶在成桥状态下的纵向位移越来越大,位移方向均背离中跨跨中。当实际合龙温度上升10℃时,13号墩墩顶水平位移达到最大为29.13mm。

3.2 计算与公式拟合

由上一节中确定的随温度升高所需额外顶推的位移量,调整模型中顶推力的大小,经过不断的试算,在设计温度且选择方案三合龙的前提下,统计升温10℃的顶推力见表6。

不同合龙温度顶推力(kN)　　　　表6

升温(℃)	0	1	2	3	4	5	6	7	8	9	10
次边跨(kN)	1993	2044	2121	2249	2419	2631	2886	3183	3523	3907	4332
次中跨(kN)	597	617	661	722	804	908	1033	1178	1344	1530	1737

根据表6中的数据绘出散点图,对其进行线性拟合和二次多项式拟合,拟合结果见图6、图7。

上述两图中,X轴为10℃的升温值,Y轴为顶推力,固定截距分别为在设计合龙温度下的次中跨顶推力597kN和次边跨顶推力1993kN。

顶推力的线性拟合方程为$y=a+bx$,式中y为顶推力,a为设计合龙温度的顶推力,x为升温值。其中,次中跨的系数b为91.85,拟合程度R^2为0.98;次边跨的系数b为788.35,拟合程度R^2为0.99。

顶推力的二次多项式拟合方程为$y=a+b_2x+b_2x^2$,式中y为顶推力,a为固定截距即设计合龙温度的顶推力,x为升温值。其中,次中跨的系数b_2为10.58,系数b_2为10.34,拟合程度R^2为1.00;次边跨的系数b_2为21.68,系数b_2为21.21,拟合程度R^2为1.00。

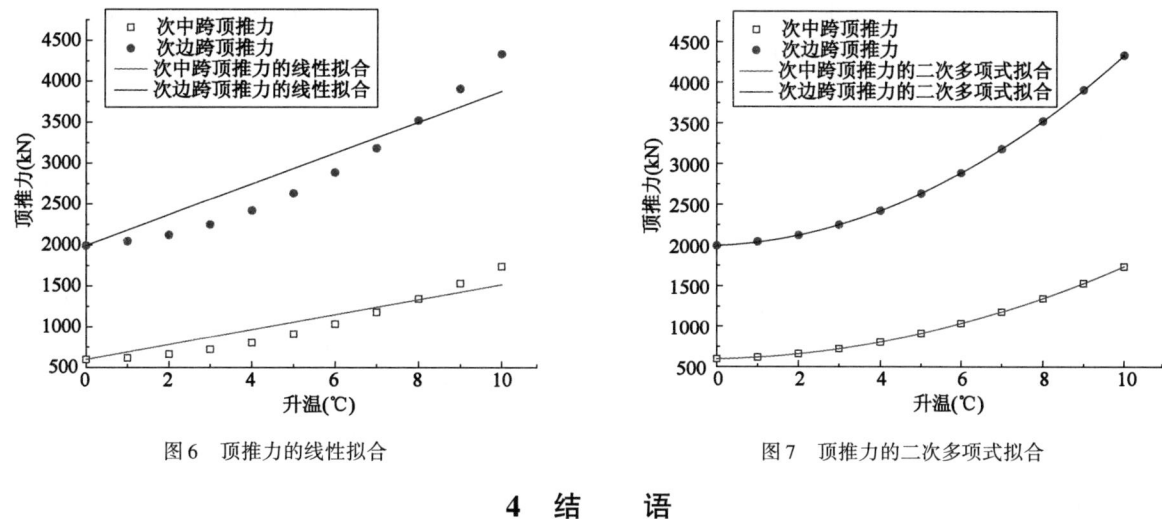

图6 顶推力的线性拟合　　　　　图7 顶推力的二次多项式拟合

4 结 语

本文研究了某高墩超多跨连续刚构桥的合龙方案与顶推控制,提出了三个合龙方案并进行比较分析,以完全抵消成桥10年后墩顶水平位移为理想顶推结果,确定了最优合龙方案,即先中跨,再次中跨,之后边跨,最后次边跨合龙。

在最优合龙方案下,随着合龙温度的上升,所需顶推力越大,升温10℃所需顶推力最大值达4332kN。本文拟合了不同合龙温度的顶推力计算公式,线性方程与二次多项式方程相互参照对比,可为今后的工程实际顶推提供参考。

由于时间与能力的有限,本文的研究尚存不足之处,如:本文提出了三种合龙方案,确定的最优合龙方案也仅是所列三种之间的最优者,而该桥为七跨连续刚构桥,有更多的合龙顺序及顶推方案可计算分析。

参考文献

[1] 陈金盛.多跨连续刚构桥合龙顶推力计算及分析控制[J].公路,2019,64(02):121-124.
[2] 耿永魁.高墩大跨预应力混凝土连续刚构桥合龙施工分析与控制[D].西安:长安大学,2016.
[3] 梁勇旗.高墩多跨连续刚构桥合龙方案及合龙顶推力计算研究[J].公路,2016,61(08):116-119.
[4] 杨超,赵艳艳.大跨径连续刚构桥合龙顶推控制浅析[J].公路交通科技(应用技术版),2017,13(09):34-35.
[5] 陈熹,鞠丹,张文明,等.高墩大跨连续刚构桥合龙方案选择与顶推控制研究[J].现代交通技术,2018,15(03):23-26,44.
[6] 杨国俊,郝宪武,段瑞芳,等.高墩大跨连续刚构桥中跨合龙顶推力计算方法[J].科技导报,2016,34(02):271-276.

Component Importance Analysis of Composite Girder Cable-stayed Bridge Based on Generalized Structural Stiffness

Binxian Wang　Hanhao Zhang　Zhi Liu　Huishuang Xiao

(Chang'an University)

Abstract The steel-concrete composite girder cable-stayed bridge has complex structure and large volume, so it is difficult to manage and maintain it comprehensively. In order to improve the efficiency of daily management and maintenance, it is necessary to analyze the importance of each component of composite girder cable-stayed bridge to determine the key areas of daily management and maintenance of the bridge. In this paper, the importance evaluation method based on generalized structural stiffness is used to analyze the importance of each stay cable and girder segment. In this method, the ratio of generalized structural stiffness change before and after failure is taken as the evaluation index of component importance. The results show that: from the pylon to both sides, the importance coefficient of stay cable increases gradually, and the importance coefficient of stay cable near auxiliary pier and mid-span is the highest; the importance coefficient of main girder is higher at the middle of each span, auxiliary pier and pylon, but it is far lower than that of stay cable. Based on this method, the component importance analysis can effectively determine the important areas of stay cables and main girders of composite girder cable-stayed bridges, and provide important reference for the daily management and maintenance of bridges.

Keywords Composite girder cable-stayed bridge　　Bridge management and maintenance　　Component importance analysis　　Structural important areas

0　Introduction

For long-span steel-concrete composite girder cable-stayed bridge, the health status of stay cables, girders and pylons is crucial to the safe and economic operation of bridges. With the extension of service time, each component is bound to produce a certain degree of structural performance degradation, so as to reduce the durability of the bridge structure, and even safety accidents, causing huge losses of personnel and property to the society. In recent years, many cable-stayed bridges due to corrosion and deterioration of stay cables lead to the occurrence of cable-breaking events, which has attracted great attention of the majority of bridge management and maintenance departments. In order to master the actual health status of the bridge, the maintenance personnel will regularly inspect the bridge components. Due to the large volume of long-span steel-concrete composite girder cable-stayed bridge, and many diseases occur in the hidden place, it is difficult to carry out a comprehensive and detailed inspection of each component in the actual detection process. However, the real health status information of bridge, especially the key parts, is the key to accurate preventive maintenance decision. Therefore, combined with the actual performance degradation of each component, the influence of the performance degradation of different components in service period on the overall stress state of the bridge structure system is studied and analysed, so as to obtain the importance degree of each bridge component, which is of great significance for bridge maintenance personnel to make preventive maintenance decisions.

The importance of structural components refers to the influence of performance degradation of structural components on the overall structural system (Hunley et al., 2012). After a large number of targeted studies, scholars in China and abroad have given the corresponding evaluation methods and indicators of component importance. At present, the proposed important evaluation indexes of various structural components have certain differences in the evaluation results of the importance of components due to the different key objects. LIU Cheng-mao believed that the damage and deterioration of components will weaken the stiffness of components in the principal axis direction, so a balance force system along the principal axis can be applied; the sum of axial force, shear force and bending moment under the balance force system can be used as the evaluation index of component importance (LIU et al., 2005). However, the sum of the three internal force values as important indicator of the component is still lack of corresponding theoretical basis. Nafday proposed to use the determinant ratio of the structural stiffness matrix before and after deterioration as the evaluation index of component importance (Nafday et al., 2008). Luo Li-sheng et al. puts forward a calculation method suitable for determining the importance of structural members from the perspective of structural stiffness and member resistance to external load (LUO et al. ,2017). Gharaibeh et al. put forward a reliability-based evaluation method to evaluate the importance of structural components, and the ratio of the reliability variation of the structure after deterioration to that of the original structure is used as an indicator to evaluate the importance of structural components (Gharaibeh et al. ,2002). But the reliability theory still stays at the theoretical level. Baker used the ratio of direct risk to total risk as an evaluation index to assess the importance of the structural components (Baker et al. ,2006). However, it is more difficult to collect a large number of statistical data when analysing the importance of engineering structure. Based on the research of risk analysis theory and consequence analysis theory, Maes proposed the importance index of structural components based on risk (Maes et al. ,2006). Based on the theory of strain energy, Li Yun-song et al. introduced the concept of total strain energy at critical point, and proposed that the total strain energy at critical point should be used as the evaluation index to analyse the influence of local component damage on the overall bearing capacity of the structure, so as to determine the importance of the component (LI et al. ,2020). Zhang Lei-ming et al. proposed from the perspective of energy flow to determine the ratio of the strain energy of the degraded structure after the removal of the evaluation component under load to the strain energy of the intact structure before the removal as the component importance evaluation index (ZHANG et al. ,2007). ZHU Nan-hai et al. proposed a component importance evaluation method suitable for frame and spatial grid structure by establishing component redundancy and vulnerability evaluation indicators (ZHU et al. ,2020). Based on the redundancy theory, Jiang Shu-hui et al. proposed a quantitative method to evaluate the importance of hinged members (JIANG et al. ,2018). YE Lie-ping et al. analysed the importance of structural members from the generalized structural stiffness of the structural system under certain load, and put forward the ratio of the generalized structural stiffness difference before and after the failure of members to the generalized structural stiffness of the intact structure as the component importance evaluation index (YE et al. ,2010).

The evaluatio nindexes of component importance mentioned by the former scholars have the shortcomings of lack of theoretical basis, high difficulty in operation and large uncertainty of evaluation results in the application of composite girder cable-stayed bridge. The evaluation index of component importance based on generalized structural stiffness proposed by Ye Lie-ping et al. comprehensively considered the influence of structural system's own attributes and load conditions, and incorporated the load action factor into the component importance evaluation method. This method has the advantages of comprehensive evaluation, simple operation and accurate results, which is suitable for the daily management and maintenance units of bridges to determine the key management and maintenance areas of bridges. In this paper, the evaluation index is used to analyse the importance of composite girder cable-stayed bridge.

1 Basic Principles

The generalized structural stiffness is used to evaluate the importance of components. The ratio of the difference between the generalized structural stiffness before and after component failure and the generalized structural stiffness of intact structure is taken as the evaluation index of component importance. The specific expression is as follows:

$$\gamma_i = \frac{K_0 - K'_i}{K_0} = 1 - \frac{K'_i}{K_0} \tag{1}$$

Where, K'_i is the generalized structural stiffness of the structure after the member I is deteriorated or removed under the action of determined load; K_0 is the generalized structural stiffness of intact structure under load.

The value range of the importance evaluation index γ is $[0,1]$. When $\gamma = 0$, it means that the generalized structural stiffness of the structural system will not be affected by the deterioration or failure of the evaluated component; when $\gamma = 1$, it means that the generalized structural stiffness of the structural system will be completely lost after the degradation or failure of the evaluated component, which means that the component is extremely important. Therefore, it can be seen from the above that the physical meaning of the importance evaluation index γ refers to the contribution of the evaluation component to the generalized structural stiffness of the structural system.

The work done by external load in the conservative structural system is equal to the increment of structural strain energy. Therefore, in the linear elastic structure analysis, the strain energy of the structure under load is determined as follows:

$$U = \frac{1}{2} F_{stru} D_{stru} \tag{2}$$

Where, F_{stru} is the generalized force and represents the load distribution on the structure; D_{stru} is the generalized displacement, which represents the structural displacement under the generalized force.

The generalized stiffness of the structure is as follows:

$$K = \frac{F_{stru}}{D_{stru}} \tag{3}$$

By substituting formula (3) into equation (1), we can get the following results:

$$\gamma_i = 1 - \frac{U_0}{U'_i} \tag{4}$$

That is to say, the formula is the expression of structural strain energy to calculate the importance index of members based on generalized structural stiffness. The formula is simple in structure and convenient in calculation, which is more conducive to the practical application in engineering.

The upper structure of cable-stayed bridge is mainly composed of cable towers, main girders and stay cables. The cable towers and main girders are mainly subjected to compression and bending, and the bending is supplemented. Cables bear strong axial tension without bending moment. Therefore, when calculating the structural strain energy of cable-stayed bridge, the tension, compression and bending strain energy of cable towers and girders and the tension and compression strain energy of stay cable are mainly considered. In addition, because the shear strain energy of each component is relatively small, it can be ignored. Combined with the above-mentioned structural strain energy analysis of the cable-stayed bridge, the strain energy calculation formula of the whole bridge is given for the steel-concrete composite beam cable-stayed bridge:

$$U = \int \frac{M_t(x)^2}{2E_t I_t} dx + \int \frac{N_t(x)^2}{2E_t A_t} dx + \int \frac{M_b(x)^2}{2E_b I_b} dx + \int \frac{N_b(x)^2}{2E_b A_b} dx + \int \frac{N_c(x)^2}{2E_c A_c} dx \tag{5}$$

Where, $M_t(x), M_b(x)$ are the section bending moment of cable tower and main beam under load; $N_t(x), N_b(x), N_c(x)$ are the section axial force of cable tower, main beam and stay cable under load; E_t, E_b, E_c are the material elastic modulus of cable tower, main beam and stay cable; I_t, I_b are the bending moment of inertia of the cable tower and main beam respectively; A_t, A_b, A_c are the sectional area of cable tower, main beam and stay cable respectively.

2 Component Importance Analysis

The importance of stay cables and steel-concrete composite girders is analysed by using the component importance evaluation index based on generalized structural stiffness.

2.1 Brief Introduction of Calculation Example

In this paper, a steel-concrete composite girder cable-stayed bridge is taken as an example for analysis. The structure system of the bridge adopts five span continuous semi-floating system with dense cable layout. The total length of the main bridge is 570m; the span layout is 30m + 95m + 305m + 110m + 30m; the side to middle span ratio is 0.46 and 0.41 respectively. The facade layout is shown in Fig. 1. The main girder adopts the steel-concrete composite beam which is connected by shear studs, and the section diagram of the main beam is shown in Fig. 2. The steel beam is composed of box girder, cross beam and small longitudinal beam. The concrete bridge deck is constructed by block prefabrication and cast-in-place wet joint connection. The stay cable is made of parallel steel wire. The basic cable distance of stay cables on the main girder is 12m, and the basic spacing of stay cables in the tail cable area of side spans are 6.3m and 9.6m respectively. The cable distance on tower is 2.0m. There are 96 stay cables in the whole bridge, and the longest stay cable is 160.6m.

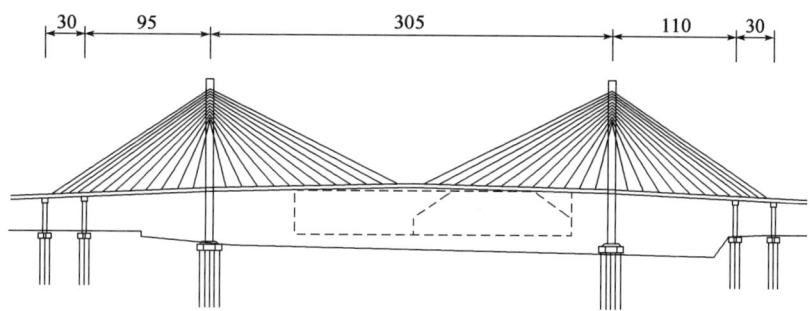

Fig. 1 Facade layout of cable-stayed bridge(unit:m)

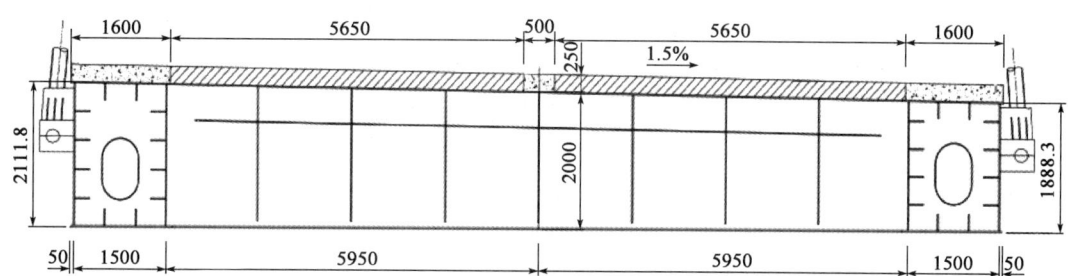

Fig. 2 Cross section of main girder(unit:m)

Using the importance evaluation index based on the generalized stiffness of the structure to analyse the importance of each component, the finite element simulation and stress analysis of the bridge structure need to be carried out with Midas civil. When calculating the importance of each component, it is necessary to load the most unfavourable lane load according to the influence line of the component, so as to calculate the mechanical behaviour of the bridge structure before and after the failure of the component under the load.

Midas civil is used to establish the finite element simulation analysis model for the steel-concrete composite girder cable-stayed bridge. There are 2091 nodes and 2016 elements in total. The material parameters of each element are shown in Tab. 1. The truss element is used to simulate the stay cables, and the beam element is used to simulate other members. The whole bridge model is established as shown in Fig. 3.

Material parameters table of full bridge model elements Tab. 1

Component name	Unit type	Material	Elastic modulus($\times 10^4$ MPa)
Steel-concrete composite beam	Beam element	Q345 steel + C60 concrete	steel:20.6 concrete:3.6
Stay cable	Truss element	Φ7 high-strength steel wire	19.5
cable tower	Beam element	C50 concrete	3.45
pier	Beam element	C40 concrete	3.25
pile	Beam element	C35 concrete	3.15

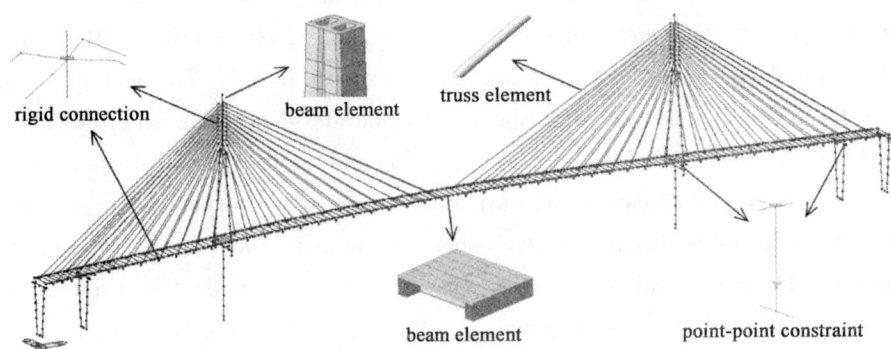

Fig. 3 Finite element model of the whole bridge

2.2 Importance Analysis of Stay Cables

As the core components of cable-stayed bridge, the stay cables in good condition are the basis to ensure the normal operation of cable-stayed bridge. However, under the action of long-term fatigue load, the sheath of stay cable exposed to natural environment is prone to aging and cracking. When the steel wire is exposed to moisture and corrosive medium in the atmosphere, a series of complex corrosion effects will occur, which will reduce the effective section product of cable body steel wire, reduce the rigidity of cable body, and even break the cable. Therefore, combined with the actual cable diseases, the importance index based on generalized structural stiffness is used to analyse the influence of cable breaking on bridge structure, so as to determine the importance of each stay cable. It is worth noting that, for safety reasons, when considering the cable fracture, this paper directly considers the cable failure and passivates its role in the model.

The load is applied to the complete bridge structure model and the broken cable bridge structure model respectively to calculate the stress state of the bridge structure before and after the cable breaking under the determined load form. According to the internal force of the bridge structure before and after the cable breaking, the strain energy of the bridge structure before and after the cable breaking is calculated, and then the importance coefficient of stay cable determined by the generalized structural stiffness theory is calculated. The distribution of the importance of stay cables along the longitudinal direction of the bridge is shown in Fig. 4.

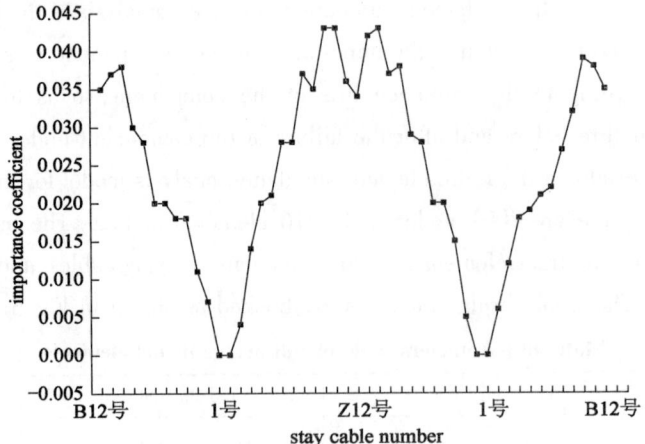

Fig. 4 Importance diagram of stay cable

In the calculation results of the importance index of stay cable components, the importance index of individual stay cable components appears negative value, in this case, the importance index of the stay cable should be directly taken as 0. For the stay cable with a value of 0, it does not mean that the stay cable has no effect on the structure and is a redundant component. Although the stay cable is of low importance to the bridge system, it still has the importance to the cable itself, that is, bearing the load directly acting on the stay cable belongs to the safety problem of the component itself.

It can be seen from the calculation results of cable importance that the importance of side-span stay cables increase first and then decrease from the outside to the cable tower. The importance index of B10 stay cable near the auxiliary pier is the highest, and the importance indexes of B10 cables across left and right sides are 0.038 and 0.039 respectively. The importance of mid-span stay cables increase gradually from near the pylon to the middle of the span, and then decrease after Z10 cable. The cable with the highest importance coefficient of mid-span is Z10 cable, and the importance indexes of two Z10 cables are 0.043. It can be concluded that the cable areas near B10 and Z10 should be the focus areas in the process of cable force monitoring, daily detection and maintenance, as shown in Fig. 5.

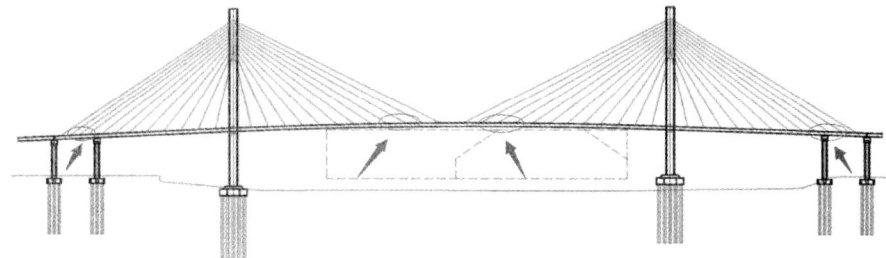

Fig. 5 Important cable area of stay cable

2.3 Importance Analysis of Steel-concrete Composite Girder

When using generalized structural stiffness to evaluate the importance of main girders in each region, the degradation degree of steel-concrete composite girder stiffness should be determined. According to the most unfavourable principle, this paper considers that the degradation of the main girder stiffness is that the concrete deck of the steel-concrete composite girder is cracked and broken in the evaluation area, and the residual stiffness of the main girder only considers steel beam and the longitudinal reinforcement in concrete. After calculation, the residual stiffness of the main beam after degradation is 0.5 times of the original stiffness.

With Midas civil, the corresponding intact model and the stiffness degradation model of the main girder segment are established respectively for stress analysis. On the basis of finite element simulation analysis and calculation, the strain energy of bridge structure is calculated according to the principle of strain energy calculation. Then the importance evaluation index of each section of the main girder is calculated based on the generalized structural stiffness to analyse and evaluate. The distribution of the importance of each segment of the steel-concrete composite girder along the longitudinal direction of the bridge is shown in Fig. 6.

From the above calculation results of the steel-concrete composite girder segment importance, it can be seen that the importance of the mid-span girder segment is obviously higher than that of the non-mid-span girder segment. The importance coefficient of the mid-span girder segment of the side span is 0.001, and that of the mid-span segment is 0.0045. In addition to the girder section near the bearer, the importance of each girder segment shows a general change rule, which is gradually increasing from the bearer to the mid-span; the importance of the main girder section at the auxiliary pier and pylon increase sharply compared with other girder sections. The importance coefficient of the auxiliary pier and pylon are 0.0012 and 0.003 respectively. According to the above distribution law of the importance of main girder segments, the importance of auxiliary pier, pylon and mid-span girder sections are high. Therefore, the auxiliary pier, pylon and mid-span girder sections should be the key areas of attention in the process of girder inspection and maintenance, as shown in Fig. 7.

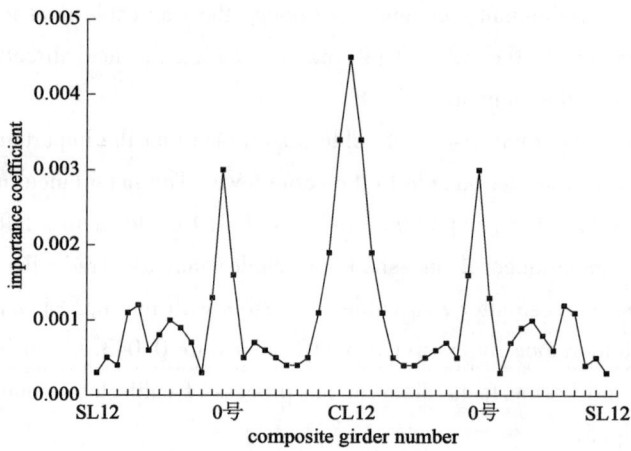

Fig. 6　Importance diagram of each girder segment

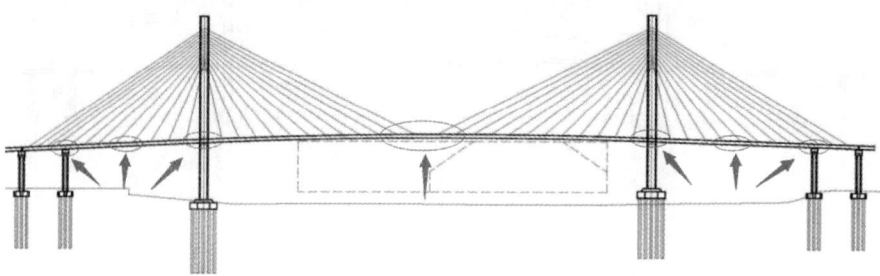

Fig. 7　Important area of steel-concrete composite beam

3　Conclusions

In this paper, using reasonable and scientific evaluation index of bridge components, with the help of finite element analysis and calculation software, the importance analysis of stay cables and main girder segments of long-span steel-concrete composite girder cable-stayed bridge is carried out. According to the results of importance analysis, it can effectively determine the important cable areas and main girder areas, and divide the important level of bridge management and maintenance areas. In the process of daily bridge management and maintenance, strengthening the inspection, detection and maintenance of components in such areas can significantly improve the level of bridge management, maintenance and service level, and reduce the cost of bridge management and maintenance.

(1) The importance coefficients of stay cables increase gradually from the pylon to both ends, and reach the maximum value in the mid-span of main span and near the auxiliary pier.

(2) The importance coefficients of steel-concrete composite girder sections increase gradually from the end of the span to the middle of the span, and the importance of the main girder sections at the auxiliary pier and pylon will increase sharply. Therefore, the important areas of steel-concrete composite girder are the beam section at the middle span, auxiliary pier and pylon.

(3) By comparing the results of the importance of stay cable and steel-concrete composite girder segments, it can be found that the importance of stay cable components is far greater than that of steel-concrete composite girders. Therefore, the maintenance level of stay cables should be better than that of steel-concrete composite girders.

(4) Using this method to analyse the component importance of composite girder cable-stayed bridge can effectively determine the important areas of stay cables and main girders, and provide important reference for the daily management and maintenance of the bridge.

References

[1] Baker J W., Schubert M., Faber M H. (2006). On the Assessment of Robustness. Structural Safety, 30(3), 253-267.

[2] Gharaibeh E S., Frangopol D M., Onoufriou T. (2002). Reliability-based Importance Assessment of Structural Members with Applications to Complex Structures. Computers and Structures, 80(12), 1113-1131.

[3] Hunley C. T., Harik I E. (2012). Structural Redundancy Evaluation of Steel Tub Girder Bridges. Journal of Bridge Engineering, 17(3), 481-489.

[4] Jiang Shu-hui, YUAN Xing-fei, MA Shuo. (2018). An Evaluation for Component Importance of Pin-jointed Structures Considering Structural Redundancy. Journal of Harbin Institute of Technology, 50(12), 187-192.

[5] Li Yun-song, Nie Qi, Luo Yong-feng, et al. (2020). Classification Method of Member Importance Based on Strain Energy Theory for Lattice Shell Structure. Journal of South University of Technology, 48(05), 22-31.

[6] Liu Cheng-mao, Liu Xi-la. (2005). Stiffness-Based Evaluation Component Importance and Its Relationship with Redundancy. Journal of Shanghai Jiaotong University, 39(5), 746-750.

[7] Luo Li-sheng, Luo Yong-feng. (2017). A Practical for Evaluation of Member Importances of Existing Spatial Structures. Structural Engineers, 33(02), 109-114.

[8] Maes, Marc A., Fritzsons, Kathleen E., et al. (2006). Structural robustness in the light of risk and consequence analysis. Structural Engineering International, 16(2), 101-107.

[9] Nafday, Avinash M. (2008). System safety performance metrics for skeletal structures. Journal of Structural Engineering, 134(3), 499-504.

[10] Ye Lie-ping, Lin Xu-chuan, Qu Zhe, et al. (2010). Evaluating Method of Element Importance of Structural System Based on Generalized Structural Stiffness. Journal of Architecture and Civil Engineering, 27(1), 1-6.

[11] Zhang Lei-ming, Liu Xi-la. (2007). Network of Energy Transfer in Frame Structures and Its Preliminary Application. China Civil Engineering Journal, 03, 45-49.

[12] Zhu Nan-hai, Li Jie-ming, He Xiao-ling, et al. (2020). The Importance Evaluation of Structural Components Based on The Analysis of Vulnerability and Redundancy. Chinese Journal of Computational Mechanics, 37(05), 608-615.

Study on Construction Control Parameters of Pile Foundation of Highway Bridge passing through Beaded Karst Cave

Junhua Cai[1]　Zhongju Feng[2]　Jie Cai[1]　Huiyun Chen[2]　Shaofen Bai[2]

(1. Fujian Provincial Bureau of quality and Safety Supervision of Traffic Construction;
2. Chang'an University, School of Highway)

Abstract　In order to explore the construction technology and treatment methods of bridge pile foundation of beaded karst cave in karst development area, and to solve the problems in the construction process of bridge pile foundation passing through beaded karst cave in karst area, this paper makes a theoretical analysis on the construction of pile foundation of Puyan expressway bridge in Fujian Province, which is located in the area of beaded karst cave. Combined with the specific problems encountered during the construction of 6.4m, 4.9m and 1.7m karst caves of the separated overpass of provincial highway 204m, the construction schemes of steel tube follow-up method and backfilling method for the treatment of beaded karst caves are compared and analyzed, and the optimal treatment scheme of karst caves is adopted considering the influence of construction period and construction cost of bridge pile foundation. It ensures the pile quality of the pile foundation and meets the actual engineering needs of Puyan highway, and provides a reference basis for the construction of bridge pile foundation in similar areas.

Keywords Bridge engineering Beaded cave Pile foundation Backfilling method

0 Introduction

Karst landform is widely distributed in China, with an area of about 3.44 million square kilometers, accounting for 1/3 of China's land area. the existence of karst area increases the difficulty for the construction of bridge pile foundation, and the treatment technology of karst cave has a great influence on the pile quality of pile foundation. In recent years, many scholars at home and abroad have done a lot of research on the bearing characteristics of bridge pile foundation in special areas [1]. Aiming at the problems of slurry leakage, sticking, buried drill and hole collapse in the construction of pile foundation in karst development area, Yao Hongsheng and others put forward that in practical engineering, a variety of treatment measures such as schist cement soil grouting method, cast-in-place concrete wall secondary hole drilling method and steel casing follow-up method can be used to treat the karst cave [2]. Dong Yunxiu and others carried out the vertical static load test of the bridge pile foundation based on the actual project in the karst area, and put forward a method for calculating the rock-socketed depth of the bridge pile foundation in the karst area, which can reduce the rock-socketed depth of the pile foundation by 2.4 m [3]. In order to avoid the problems of slurry leakage and hole collapse when the pile foundation passes through the karst cave, Zhang Kun and others take the actual project as an example, study the pre-grouting construction technology, and introduce the construction method of pre-grouting construction technology in detail [4]. In view of the specific problems in the construction of karst cave pile foundation near the existing highway, Shi Aidong put forward some treatment schemes such as high-pressure rotary jet grouting pile pretreatment combined with schist clay backfilling method [5]. Zhang Guangwu et al studied the causes of the formation of beaded karst caves, classified them, and put forward the treatment methods of different types of karst caves [6]. Zhu Mingzhun et al analyzed the treatment methods of karst caves in karst development area based on the actual bridge pile foundation engineering, and made corresponding treatment schemes for different types of karst caves [7]. Feng Zhongju et al studied the bearing characteristics of bridge pile foundation after water immersion in loess region, and found that the ultimate bearing capacity of pile foundation decreased obviously and the settlement deformation of soil around pile increased significantly after loess flooding [8]. Then, the bearing characteristics of bridge pile foundation in loess gully region were studied through model test, and it was concluded that the bearing capacity of pile foundation in loess gully area decreased with the increase of slope [9]. In the salt swamp area, Yao Xianhua and others carried out corrosion resistance tests on bridge pile foundation materials in salt swamp environment, and proposed that reasonable matching of mineral admixtures can effectively improve the corrosion resistance of bridge pile foundations. the addition of rust inhibitor will reduce the corrosion resistance of concrete [10]. Feng Zhongju et al studied the damage mechanism of bridge pile foundation under dry-wet cycle and freeze-thaw cycle through field simulation test, and obtained the regression curve of anti-erosion coefficient of pile foundation concrete. it is considered that the invasion of corrosive ions will lead to internal damage of bridge pile foundation [11]. Feng Zhongju and others investigated and collected the data on the geometric size, corrosion resistance and anti-collision performance of the bridge pile foundation of the sea-crossing bridge in China, and analyzed the application status of the large-diameter deep-long pile foundation of the bridge in the marine environment [12]. Combined with karst geological conditions, Tu Wen et al analyzed the problems of karst cracks and leakage of karst cave in the construction of bridge pile foundation in karst development area. a variety of hole-forming measures for pile foundation are put forward, such as conventional pile foundation hole-forming method, clay, sheet stone wall protection method, steel tube follow-up method and advance grouting method [13]. Chen Jie and others explored the construction technology of bridge pile foundation under different karst cave layers in karst area, and considered that the multi-layer karst cave can be treated by filling clay bags and gravel materials [14]. Hou Xibiao and others compared and analyzed the karst cave treatment methods such as pre-treatment method, steel casing follow-up method and flake-filled clay method, and summarized the advantages, disadvantages and applicability of different treatment methods [15]. Xu Yongchun and others discussed and summarized the matters needing attention in karst cave treatment by backfilling wall construction method, protective tube method and karst grouting method [16]. Li Qiang and others studied the treatment techniques of different forms of karst caves, and compared and analyzed the rationality, advantages and disadvantages of throwing and filling clay sheet stone wall construction method, steel casing follow-up method and the combination of the two methods [17].

Most of the above research results are aimed at the construction technology and treatment methods of a single karst cave in the construction of pile foundation, and few experts study the treatment methods of beaded karst caves. Through the practical application of the string-shaped karst cave treatment method in the 0b#-2 pile construction of Fujian Puyan expressway YA1 section crossing provincial highway 204 separation overpass, this paper compares and analyzes the advantages and disadvantages of steel tube follow-up method and backfilling method in the treatment of string-shaped karst cave, and summarizes the technical essentials of bridge pile foundation construction of string-shaped karst cave, which provides a reference basis for bridge pile foundation construction in similar areas.

1 Distribution Characteristics of Beaded Karst Caves at Pile Position

The 0b#-2 pile of crossing provincial highway 204 separation overpass passes through the karst cave with a height of 6.4m, 4.9m and 1.7m respectively, and is supported in the lower rock stratum. It belongs to the end-bearing pile. The design pile length is 58m, the design pile diameter is 1.5m, and the actual construction pile length is 61m.

According to the standard table of cave type classification (Tab. 1), it is known that the first layer cave with a height of 6.4m is a large cave, the second layer cave with a height of 4.9m is a large cave, and the third layer cave with a height of 1.9m is a general cave. Combined with the results of previous drilling, in-hole electromagnetic wave CT exploration and ground penetrating radar exploration, the specific location, size and filling state of the karst cave at the pile site are determined. The specific size and location of the cave are shown in Fig. 1.

Classification of karst cave types Tab. 1

Serial Number	Species	Remarks
1	Karst fissures and small karst caves	$h \leqslant 0.5m$
2	General karst cave	$h \leqslant 4m$

continue

Serial Number	Species	Remarks
3	Large karst cave	$h > 4m$
4	Other karst caves	—
5	Incomplete karst cave	The rock surface shows complex conditions such as slope, scarp, stalagmite, solution ditch, solution trough and so on
6	String of slurry and holes in karst channel	The connected hole means that due to the development of karst fissures in the site, abundant groundwater and the existence of karst caves with good connectivity, the adjacent pile holes are penetrated by karst caves in some part of the pile body
7	Deep and large solution trough	The bedrock surface at the bottom of the solution trough is uneven, and karst caves and fissures are developed
8	Fully filled karst cave	The cave is completely filled with coarse gravel, sand, fine gravel and clay, and most of the fillings are hard plastic, soft plastic and flow plastic
9	Semi-filled karst cave	There are fillers at the bottom of the cave and a cavity at the top of the cave
10	Unfilled karst cave	—

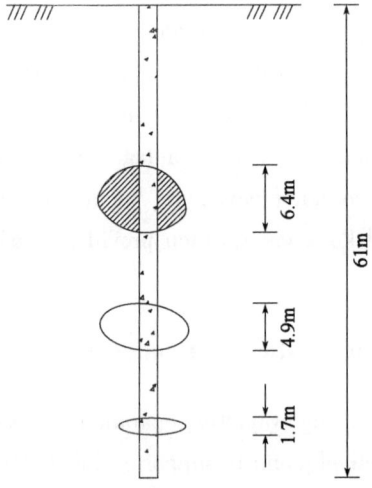

Fig. 1 Schematic Diagram of Karst of Pile 0b#-2

The filling state and characteristics of the karst cave are as follows: ①the first layer karst cave below the ground is filled with grayish brown and grayish black gravelly clayey soil, showing a soft plastic shape, wet and containing some gravel, in which the filling material of the karst cave 44.2-45.0 m below the ground is block stone, and the original rock is composed of sand-conglomerate, which is compacted and fully filled; ②the second layer karst cave below 50.8-55.7 m below the ground, no filling, drilling while drilling, cavity. ③the third layer karst cave of 56.1-57.8m below the ground is filled with clay filled with sand and gravel, saturated, slightly dense, loose and half-filled.

2 Construction Treatment Technology and Parameters of Pile Foundation in Beaded Karst Cave Area

When passing through three or more beaded karst caves, the steel casing follow-up method is generally adopted. That is, first, the larger diameter bit is used to impact to the top of the karst cave, the inner protective tube is lowered to the bottom of the hole after 1.0m, and the small bit continues to smash until it breaks through the karst cave, then the mixture of clay and sheet stone is backfilled, and the hole is compacted by repeated impact, and then transferred to normal drilling. The key to this solution is:

(1) The inner casing must be positioned accurately.

(2) The inner casing must have sufficient stiffness.

(3) Backfill the mixture of clay and schist in time after breaking through the karst cave.

When the pile foundation passes through the cavity with large karst cave height, the treatment scheme of steel protective tube is adopted. After the percussion drill penetrates the karst cave, the steel protective tube is inserted into the steel protective tube which is slightly smaller than the orifice protective tube, and the steel protective tube is vibrated to the rock surface at the bottom of the karst cave with a guide hammer. In general, the steel casing follow-up method must be combined with the backfilling sheet stone in the karst cave and the plugging treatment between the bottom of the karst cave and the protective tube foot, otherwise the treatment effect may be greatly reduced.

3 Treatment Technology and Parameters of Beaded Karst Cave in Solid Engineering

During the construction of pile foundation crossing of beaded karst cave bridge, the key point of construction lies in the treatment of engineering disasters such as slurry leakage, hole collapse, buried drilling and ground collapse. The underground karst pole of 0b#-2 pile in the separated interchange of trans-provincial highway 204 is well developed. the geological prospecting data show that there are three layers of karst caves, the first layer is full-filled karst cave, and the second and third layers are unfilled cavities. In order to ensure the safety and rationality of pile foundation construction, reduce the difficulty of pile foundation construction and save construction materials, shorten the construction period, reduce the cost, comprehensively consider the actual geological conditions and other factors, combined with the existing beaded cave treatment technology, determine to use the backfilling method for karst cave treatment. When large beaded karst caves are encountered during the construction of 0b#-2 piles in the separated interchange of provincial highway 204, especially the semi-filled karst caves with leakage source at the bottom of the cave, the filled silt and pebbles will block the leakage source in the process of cave formation, but the filling material will slip or be reopened in the process of punching, resulting in re-leakage. After the slurry leakage is found in the process of drilling, the centralized pump replenishes water into the hole to maintain the water head, and immediately throws cement into the hole, and then puts a mixture of clay and sheet stone with a thickness of 3~5m into the hole, and then punches the hole again after the slurry leakage stops. the time from punching to the leakage site should be controlled before the cement final setting time, and then stop for 6~10hours. This is done repeatedly until the solidified cement clay slurry blocks the source of the leakage.

The construction material parameters and cost of 0b#-2 pile in YA1 section are shown in Tab. 2. It can be seen from Tab. 2 that the total construction time of the pile foundation is 66 days, with a total of 3253m^3 of backfill earth, 1116m^3 of backfill rock and 151t of backfill cement, with a total cost of about 300000 yuan. After the completion of the pile, the quality inspection of the pile foundation shows that the pile is a type I pile, which shows that the scheme effectively prevents the occurrence of slurry leakage and hole collapse, and ensures the normal construction of the pile foundation. At the same time, the application of this method to the treatment of karst cave reduces the difficulty of construction, speeds up the construction speed and reduces the project cost.

General Situation Table of Karst Cave Treatment in 0b#-2 Station of YA1 Section Cross-Provincial Highway 204 Separator Interchange   Tab. 2

Date	Hole Depth During Slurry Leakage (m)	Backfill Hole Depth (m)	Backfill Earthwork (m³)	Backfill Stone Square (m³)	Backfill Cement (ton)
2019.05.24	46.2	41	148	48	7
2019.06.03	48.8	34	120	38	5
2019.06.06	50	38.3	137	44	6
2019.06.08	53	43.7	160	52	7
2019.06.12	53.6	42.8	156	41	7
2019.06.13	54	44.8	164	43	7
2019.06.15	54	45	165	44	7
2019.06.17	54	44.8	164	43	7
2019.06.19	54	51	189	52	9
2019.07.02	54.3	46.4	171	46	7
2019.07.04	54.3	44.2	162	43	6
2019.07.06	54.3	43.8	160	42	5
2019.07.09	54.3	43.2	157	41	8
2019.07.13	54.2	42	153	39	7
2019.07.16	56.2	43.5	159	42	7
2019.07.20	59.2	44	160	38	7
2019.07.24	59.2	45.2	166	44	7
2019.07.29	59.2	54	202	56	8
Total	—	791.7	2893	756	97

4 Comparative Analysis

In the actual construction, the backfilling method is adopted to treat the karst cave of the 0b#-2 pile in the separation interchange of the provincial highway 204. compared with the steel casing follow-up method, it has the following advantages:

The main results are as follows:

(1) The treatment of karst cave by backfilling method can shorten the construction period and facilitate the construction; the follow-up law of steel casing should be customized according to the actual situation, and the backfilling method should be used to assist the lowering of steel casing, so the construction process is complex and the construction period is long. The project is located in the mountain area, and the backfilling method requires more earth and stone and other raw materials, which can save a lot of manpower and material resources. combined with the on-site situation, it can be seen that it is more appropriate to use the backfilling method to deal with beaded karst caves.

(2) The cost of using backfilling method to treat karst cave is lower than that of steel casing follow-up method. according to the actual investigation, the total cost of using steel cover follow-up method is about 400000 yuan, while the total cost of backfilling method is only about 240000 yuan. Greatly reduce the construction cost. The cost of materials required for different treatment methods is shown in Tab. 3.

Material Costs for Different Treatment Methods   Tab. 3

Treatment Method	Materials	Material Consumption	Unit Price (yuan)	Total Cost (ten thousand yuan)
Backfilling method	Earthwork (m^3)	2893	45	23.84
	Stone (m^3)	796	70	
	Cement (ton)	97	500	
Steel casing follow-up method	Steel casing (m)	60	6700	40.20

(3) The pile foundation passes through the bead-shaped karst cave in the process of construction, if the backfilling method is used to treat the karst cave, it can provide a certain side friction resistance, and then increase the bearing capacity of the pile foundation, while the steel tube follow-up method is adopted, after the pile is formed, the lateral friction resistance of the pile foundation is affected because of the lack of soil around the pile and the smooth surface of the steel tube, so the backfilling method can ensure the bearing capacity of the pile foundation.

5 Conclusions

The main results are as follows:

(1) Engineering diseases such as slurry leakage, hole collapse, sticking and ground collapse are easy to occur during the construction of beaded karst cave bridge pile foundation, so we should comprehensively consider the economic conditions of the project location and formulate a detailed construction plan. make adequate preparations to deal with the occurrence of engineering diseases.

(2) If the beaded karst cave encountered in the actual bridge pile foundation construction process is not combined with the karst cave situation and the construction period and other factors are analyzed, and the conventional treatment measures steel protective tube follow-up method is blindly adopted, the construction difficulty and project cost will be increased. It is suggested that the corresponding construction technology should be selected according to the actual situation on the site.

(3) The 0b#-2 pile of crossing provincial highway 204 separation overpass passes through the beaded karst cave. Combined with the engineering practice and the principle of economic rationality, the pile adopts the method of backfilling sheet stone clay and plain concrete to treat the karst cave according to the filling situation of the karst cave in different positions and the different fillers in the construction process, and a better effect is obtained. Compared with the steel casing follow-up method, the cost is saved. It provides a reference for bridge pile foundation construction in similar areas.

References

[1] Feng Zhongju. Infrastructure Projects in Special Areas[M]. Beijing: People's Communications Publishing House, 2008.

[2] Yao Hongsheng, Feng Zhongju, Yuan Zhan, et al. Study on Construction Technology of Pile Foundation of Extra-large Bridge in Karst Development Area [J]. Construction Technology, 2017, 46 (19): 130-133.

[3] Dong Yunxiu, Feng Zhongju, Hao Yumeng, et al. Bearing Capacity Test and Reasonable Rock-socketed Depth of Bridge Pile Foundation in Karst Area [J]. Journal of Traffic and Transportation Engineering, 2018 Ji 18 (06): 27-Qing.

[4] Zhang Kun, Liu Jianmin, Wu Huan, et al. Construction Technology of Pre-grouting for Pile Foundation of Urban Bridge through Karst Cave [J]. Construction Technology, 2011, 40 (01): 77-79.

[5] Shi Aidong. Discussion on Karst Cave Treatment Technology of Bridge Pile Foundation near Expressway [J]. Engineering and Technical Research,2020,5(07):68-69.

[6] Zhang Guangwu, Fu Junjie, Huang Ming. Analysis of the Morphology, Evolution Mechanism and Engineering Treatment Methods of Beaded Cave [J]. Subgrade Engineering,2016(01):159162.

[7] Zhu Mingjun. Treatment Method of Karst Cave in Bridge Pile Foundation Construction [J]. Engineering Construction and Design,2019(15):241-242-257.

[8] Feng Zhongju, Xie Yongli, Zhang Hongguang, et al. Experimental Study on the Influence of Surface Water on the Bearing Capacity of Bridge Pile Foundation in Loess Area [J]. Journal of Rock Mechanics and Engineering,2005(10):1758-1765.

[9] Feng Zhongju, Wang Hang, Wei Jin, et al. Model Experimental Study on Vertical Bearing Characteristics of Pile Foundation of Loess Gully Slope Bridge [J]. Journal of Geotechnical Engineering,2015 Ji 37(12):2308-2314.

[10] YaoXianhua, Feng Zhongju, Wang Fuchun, et al. Corrosion Resistance Test of Highway Bridge Pile Foundation Materials in Salt Swamp Environment [J]. Journal of Chang'an University (Natural Science Edition),2018.38(01):49-58.

[11] Feng Zhongju, Hu Haibo, Wang Fuchun, et al. Field Simulation Test of Bridge Pile Foundation Damage in High Altitude Strong Salt Swamp Area [J]. Journal of Traffic and Transportation Engineering,2019(13) 19(03):46-57.

[12] Feng Zhongju, Chen Huiyun, Yuan Fengbin, et al. Analysis on the Application Status of Steel Protective Sleeve in Marine Environment [J]. Road Construction Machinery and Mechanization of Construction, 2017 Journal 34(05):27-32.

[13] Tu Wen. Discussion on Construction Technology of Pile Foundation in Karst Area [J]. Technology and Market,20205,27(05):128-129.

[14] Chen Jie. On the Construction Technology of Bridge Pile Foundation in Karst Geomorphology Area [J]. Building Materials and Decoration,2020(13):274-275.

[15] Hou Xibiao. Application of Karst Cave Treatment Method in Bridge Pile Foundation Construction in Karst area [J]. Transportation World,2020(Z1):186188.

[16] Xu Yongchun. Karst Cave Treatment Method of Bridge Bored Cast-in-place Pile [J]. Transportation World,2020(11):93-94.

[17] Li Qiang, Qin Yushun. Construction Technology of Karst Treatment of Pile Foundation of Chinese-Laos Railway Bridge [J]. Sichuan Hydropower,2019,581.38(05):111-114.

Analysis of Long-term Deformation Sensitive Parameters of Extradosed Cable-stayed Bridge

Guang Yang Lingzhu Yang Yue Zhao

(Chang'an University)

Abstract Based on aextradosed cable-stayed bridge in Yunnan Province, combined with the design data, through the finite element simulation, the initial tension of stay cable, the control of the tension prestress, the wet weight of concrete and the atmospheric humidity are selected as the influencing parameters, and the sensitivity analysis of the completed bridge alignment and long-term deformation characteristics of the main girder is carried out, and the main parameters affecting the bridge alignment and long-term deformation of the main girder are obtained, which are the bridge construction of this kind Provide effective suggestions for construction and operation maintenance management.

Keywords Extradosed cable-stayed bridge Sensitivity analysis Completed bridge alignment Long-term deformation characteristics

0 Introduction

The extradosed cable-stayed bridge was proposed by Jacques mathivat, a French engineer, and then popularized. Japan built the world's first extradosed cable-stayed bridge in 1994 (YAN et al. ,1996). Extradosed cable-stayed bridge is a bridge type between continuous beam bridge and cable-stayed bridge. The stay cable can be regarded as external prestressed tendons arranged on continuous beam or continuous rigid frame.

Yingji Bao et al. based on Hongxi super large bridge project studied the variation law of various parameters on the main beam stress and displacement in the operation stage through parameter sensitivity analysis(Bao et al. ,2020); Kou Jing analyzed the shape and stress of the completed bridge state by taking the main beam and cable materials as parameters (Kou,2020); Yongjun Zhou et al. divided the parameters into three sensitivity levels, and studied the influence of each parameter on the completed bridge line the influence of shape (Zhou et al. ,2020); Based on the Xijiang bridge, Mu-yu Liu et al. studied the influence of main design parameters such as tower height and side to middle span ratio on the load response of main girder control section (Liu et al. , 2009); Lifeng Wang et al. carried out parameter sensitivity analysis on extradosed cable-stayed bridge with corrugated rigid webs and long-span hybrid girder cable-stayed bridges (Wang et al. ,2015); According to various mechanical parameters of self anchored double pylon cable-stayed bridge, Wanzhong Wu et al. studied the influence of mechanical parameters of self anchored double pylon cable-stayed bridge on mechanical properties of structural system (Wu et al. ,2014); By selecting some sensitive parameters, Wu Wenfang et al. compared the influence of the design parameters on the main beam deflection, cable force and main beam stress (Wu et al. ,2009); Taking Ma'anshan Yangtze River Highway Bridge as an example, Yuping Zhang et al. selected the cable-stayed force, the thickness of concrete box girder slab and the thickness of deck pavement as sensitive parameters to study the construction control standard of three tower cable-stayed bridge (Zhang et al. , 2015).

This paper will select the cable initial tension, control tension prestress, concrete wet weight, atmospheric humidity as the influencing parameters, and carry out sensitivity analysis on the completed bridge alignment and long-term deformation characteristics of the main girder of the extradosed cable-stayed bridge, study the main parameters affecting the bridge alignment and long-term deformation, and provide effective suggestions for the construction, operation and maintenance management of this kind of bridge.

1 Engineering Background and Finite Element Model

1.1 Project Overview

The project example is a three span double tower prestressed concrete extradosed cable-stayed bridge in Yunnan. The bridge adopts the complete consolidation system of tower pier beam, and the main bridge layout is 108m + 180m + 108m. The main girder section is a single box three chamber inclined web box girder, and the top plate width of the box girder is 27.3m. The beam height at the top of the main beam pier is 5.8m, and the thickness of the bottom plate is 1.1m. The mid span beam is 3m high and the bottom plate is 0.32m thick. The height of pier top to mid span beam is in quadratic parabola transition, and the thickness of bottom slab is linear transition. Each tower is provided with 9 pairs of stay cables, the spacing between the main beam ends is 7m, and the spacing between the bridge tower ends is 1.2m. The layout of the bridge type of the example project is shown in Fig. 1.

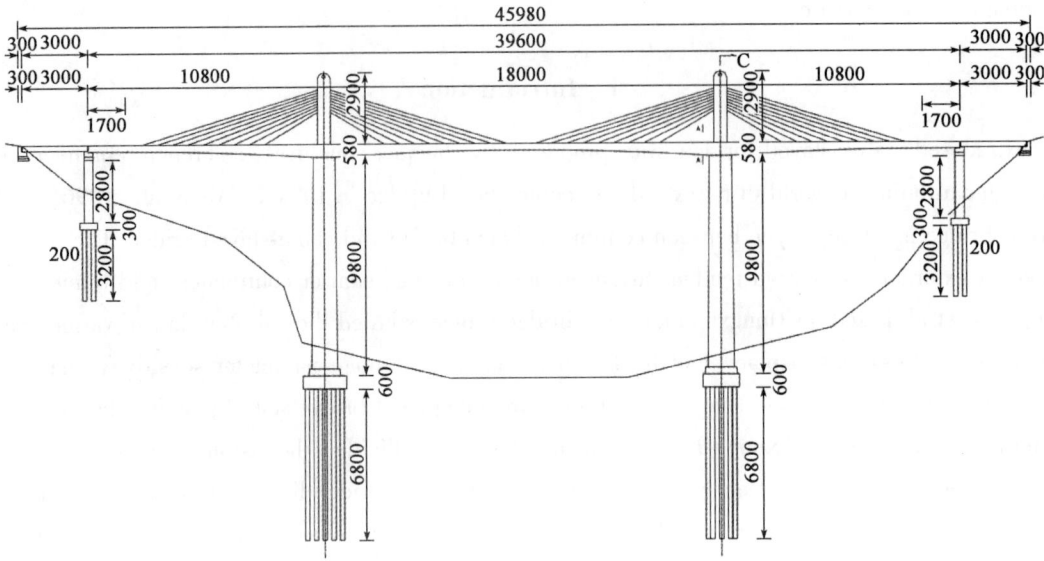

Fig. 1 layout of bridge type (unit: m)

1.2 Finite element model

Through the finite element software MIDAS/civil, the numerical analysis model of extradosed cable-stayed bridge is established. The whole bridge is divided into 303 nodes and 253 elements. The cable and truss elements are used to simulate the initial tension of the bridge. The finite element analysis model is shown in Fig. 2.

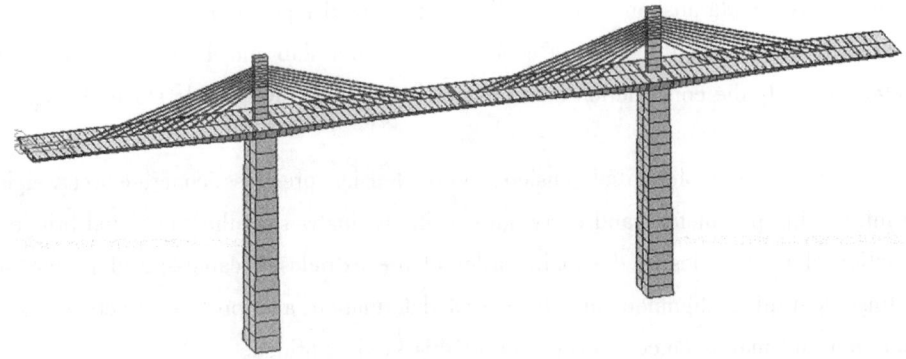

Fig. 2 finite element model

1.3 Structural parameters and their variation amplitudes

The structural parameters studied in this paper are the initial tension of stay cable, the controlled tension prestress, the wet weight of concrete and the atmospheric humidity. The design value and variation amplitude are shown in Tab. 1. In the case of keeping other parameters unchanged, by changing a certain parameter, the bridge alignment and long-term deformation characteristics of the structure are analyzed, and the main parameters affecting the bridge alignment and long-term deformation are studied.

design Value and Variation Amplitude of Parameters			Tab. 1
Structural parameters	Design value	Condition 1	Condition 2
Controlled tension prestress (MPa)	1395	-5%	+5%
Atmospheric humidity (%)	70	65	75
Initial tension of stay cable (kN)	5600	-5%	+5%
Wet weight of concrete (kN)	Add according to the weight of each cantilever block	-5%	+5%

2 Linear and Long Term Deformation Characteristics of Main Girder of Completed Bridge

After analysis according to the original parameters, the linear shape of the bridge and the deflection change of the main girder in eight years are obtained. Fig. 3 shows the alignment of the main girder of the completed bridge, and Fig. 4 shows the annual change of the main beam relative to the previous year in the eight years after completion of the bridge.

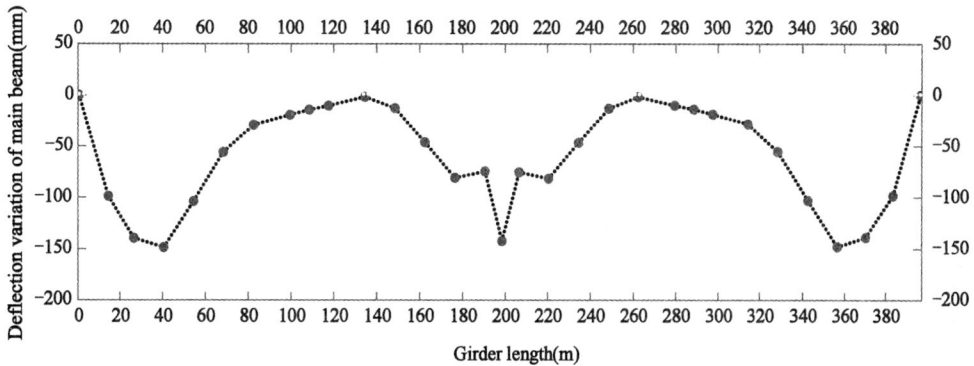

Fig. 3　Alignment of main girder of completed bridge

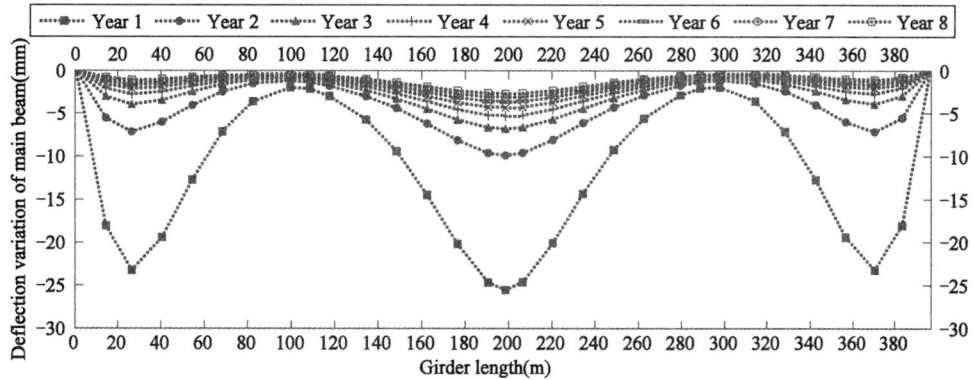

Fig. 4　Alignment of main girder of completed bridge and its change in eight years

As shown in Fig. 3, the deflection of the whole bridge at the completion stage is downward deflection, the mid span deflection is -142.20mm, and the maximum deflection of side span is -148.46mm.

As shown in Fig. 4, in the first year, the change is the most obvious in the first year, the midspan deflection changes by -25.56mm, and the maximum deflection of the side span changes by -19.40mm. After that, the annual variation of the main beam decreases year by year, and the mid span deflection changes by -2.69mm in the eighth year, which is only 10.52% of the first year; the maximum deflection of the side span changes -0.98mm, which is only 5.08% of the first year.

3 Sensitivity Analysis of Structural Parameters

Stay cable and prestress are important parts of extradosed cable-stayed bridge, which have an important impact on bridge alignment and long-term deformation. Due to the influence of various site factors, deviation may occur during construction. Therefore, the initial tension of stay cable and control tension prestress are selected as the influencing parameters. The wet weight of concrete is the construction load, which will be affected by the pouring deviation in the construction process. Therefore, the wet weight of concrete is selected as the influencing parameter to analyze the linear and long-term deformation of the main beam. Due to the long construction period of the bridge, with the seasonal changes, the environmental humidity will change, which will have a certain impact on the creep of the bridge. Therefore, the atmospheric humidity is also taken as the influence parameter to analyze the linear and long-term deformation of the main girder.

Therefore, the initial tension of stay cable, control of tension prestress, wet weight of concrete and atmospheric humidity are selected for parameter sensitivity analysis of girder deformation.

3.1 Linear Analysis of Girder Bridge under two Conditions

Fig. 5 shows the difference between the completed bridge alignment and the original parameters under condition 1 with the original parameters as the reference. Fig. 6 shows the difference between the completed bridge alignment and the original parameters under condition 2 with the original parameters as the reference.

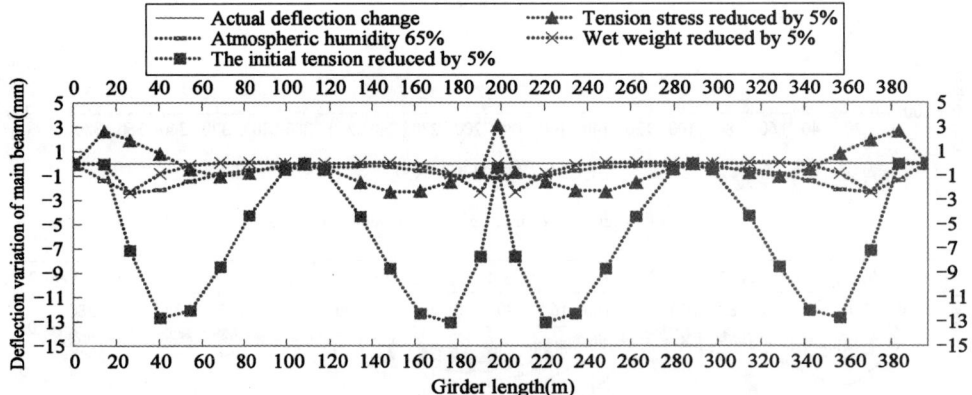

Fig.5 Linear difference diagram of completed bridge under condition 1

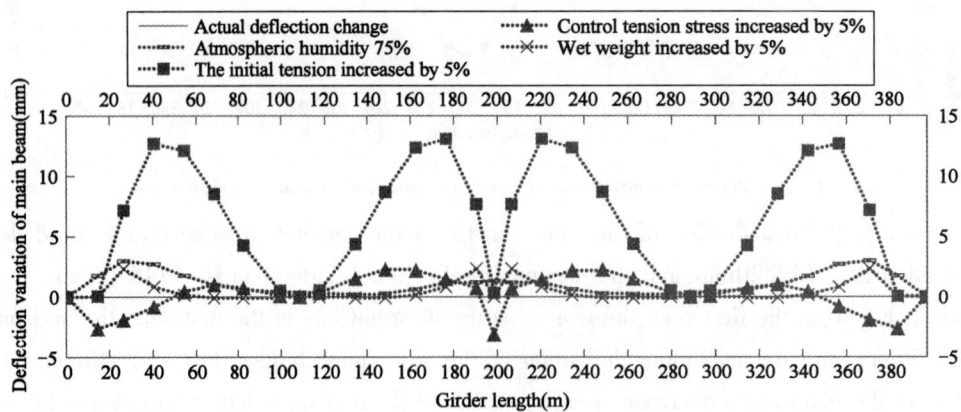

Fig.6 Linear difference diagram of completed bridge under condition 2

As shown in Fig. 5, the initial tension of stay cable causes the most obvious change of the bridge alignment, and the maximum difference of side span and middle span is 12.70mm and 13.08mm respectively; the maximum difference of side span and middle span caused by tension stress is 2.67 and 3.15mm respectively; the maximum difference of side span and middle span caused by concrete wet weight is -2.34mm and -2.34mm respectively; the maximum difference of side span and midspan caused by atmospheric humidity is -2.36mm and -2.34mm respectively 20mm.

As shown in Fig. 6, the initial tension of stay cable causes the most obvious change of the bridge alignment, and the maximum difference of side span and middle span is 12.70mm and 13.08mm respectively; the maximum difference of side span and middle span caused by tension stress is -2.63mm and -3.11mm respectively; the maximum difference of side span and midspan caused by concrete wet weight is 2.34mm and 2.34mm; the maximum difference of side span and midspan caused by atmospheric humidity is 3.00mm and 1.33mm respectively.

3.2 Long Term Deformation Analysis of Main Girder Bridge under two Working Conditions

Fig. 7 shows the difference between the midspan deflection of the main beam and the original midspan deflection of the main beam caused by the change of various parameters within 8 years from the completion of the bridge (the initial deflection value is 0). Fig. 8 shows the difference between the midspan deflection of the main beam and the original midspan deflection of the main beam caused by the change of various parameters within 8 years from the completion of the bridge (the initial deflection value is calculated from 0).

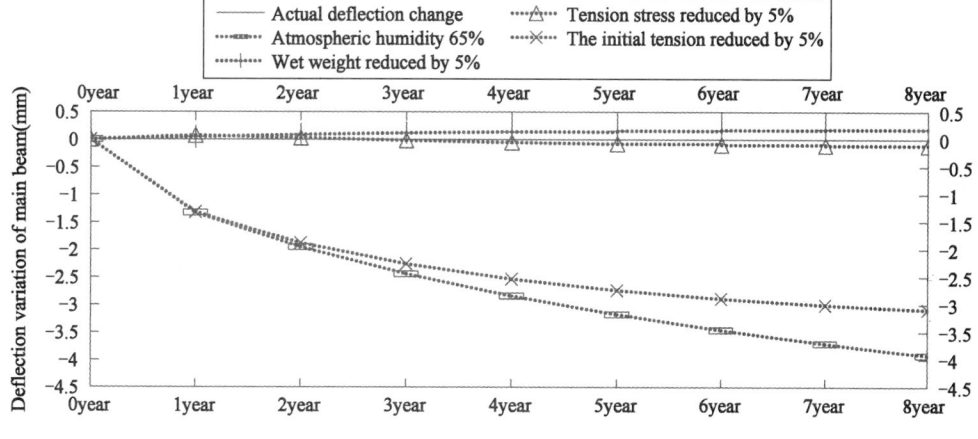

Fig. 7 Deflection difference diagram of midspan under condition 1

As shown in Fig. 7, under condition 1, the long-term deformation caused by atmospheric humidity is the most obvious, and the difference between it and the original parameters at the midspan deflection in the eighth year is −4.11mm; the difference between the initial tension of the cable-stayed lock and the original parameters at the midspan deflection in the eighth year is -3.16mm; the difference between the wet weight of concrete and the original parameters at the midspan deflection in the eighth year is 0.19mm; The difference between the control tension stress and the original parameters at the mid span deflection in the eighth year is −0.12mm.

As shown in Fig. 8, under condition 2, the long-term deformation caused by atmospheric humidity is the most obvious, and the difference between it and the original parameters at the midspan deflection in the eighth year is 4.30mm; the difference between the initial tension of the cable-stayed lock and the original parameters at the midspan deflection in the eighth year is 3.16mm; the difference between the wet weight of concrete and the original parameters at the midspan deflection in the eighth year is −0.19mm; The difference between the control tension stress and the original parameters at the mid span deflection in the eighth year is 0.13mm.

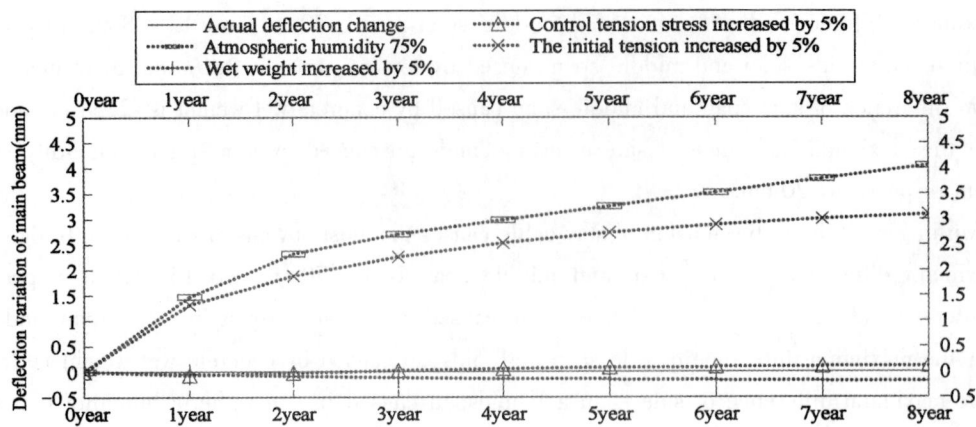

Fig. 8 Deflection difference diagram of midspan under condition 2

4 Conclusions

Based on a extradosed cable-stayed bridge in Yunnan Province, this paper selects the initial tension of stay cable, control tension stress, wet weight of concrete and atmospheric humidity as the influencing parameters to carry out sensitivity analysis on the linear and long-term deformation characteristics of the main girder of the extradosed cable-stayed bridge:

(1) Analysis on the influence parameters of the finished girder alignment: the initial tension of stay cable is the main sensitive parameter affecting the finished girder alignment, and the control tension stress, wet weight of concrete and atmospheric humidity are the secondary sensitive factors.

(2) Analysis of long-term deformation parameters of main girder: atmospheric humidity and initial tension of stay cables are the main sensitive parameters affecting the linear change of main girder bridge, and the control of tensile stress and concrete wet weight are secondary sensitive factors.

(3) The results of structural sensitivity analysis of extradosed cable-stayed bridge can provide effective reference for the construction, operation and maintenance management of this kind of bridge.

References

[1] Yingji Bao. Binsong Jiang, Wenbin Li. (2020). Sensitivity Analysis of Pylon Cable-stayed Bridge in Operation-stage. HIGHWAY, 8, 217-221.

[2] Jing Kou. (2020). Sensitivity Analysis of Structural Parameters of Extradosed Cable-stayed Bridge, 3, 159-162.

[3] Muyu Liu, Xiangdong Sun, Kaizhi Tu, et al. (2009). Sensitivity Analysis for the Structural Design Parameters of Four-tower Extradosed Cable-stayed Bridge with Singlepla. J of hust (Urban Science Edition), 26(4), 10-14.

[4] Lifeng Wang, Hongwei Jiang, Hailong Cui. (2015). Analysis of Parameters Sensitivity of Extradosed Cable-stayed Bridge with Corrugated Steel Webs. Highway Engineering, 40(2), 117-121.

[5] Wenfang Wu, Lei Zhao. (2009). Analysis of Sensibility of Constructional Mechanical Behavior of Large-span Cable-stayed Bridges to Constructional Parameters. Journal of Lanzhou University of Technology, 35(6), 124-130.

[6] Wanzhong Wu, Yangyong Zhang, Bin Syn, et al. (2014). Study on Mechanical Parameters of Self-anchored Double-tower Cable-stayed Bridges. Journal of Tongji University (Natural Science Edition), 42(1), 19-24.

[7] Guo-min YAN. (1996). On "partially cable-stayed bridge"—South Bridge, North Bridge and Haragawa Bridge in Japan. Bridge Abroad,1,47-50.//
[8] Yuping Zhang, Wenchang Xie, Chuanxi Li. (2015). Parameter Analysis and Construction Control of Ma'anshan 3-tower Cable-stayed Bridge. Journal of Changsha University of Science and Technology (Natural Science Edition),12(2),38-42.//
[9] Yongjun Zhou, Lingling Wu, Jang Liu, et al. (2020). Research on Geometry Sensitive Parameters for PC Extradosed Cable-stayed Bridge. HIGHWAY,3,87-91.

连续刚构桥施工中大悬臂停工的分析研究

陆泽磊 张永飞 朱军生

(长安大学公路学院)

摘 要 连续刚构桥悬臂施工周期较长,在北方易受冬季环境影响,导致在大悬臂状态下被迫停工。为研究桥梁悬臂施工过程中出现的大悬臂停工对桥梁线形和应力的影响,以某连续刚构桥作为研究对象,运用有限元分析软件计算分析,对大悬臂T构在不同停工块段和不同停工时间产生的挠度变化值和应力变化值进行分析。结果表明:不同停工块段和不同停工时间产生的挠度变化值有较大差异,但应力变化值差异不大且数值较小。因此,在实际施工过程中需要根据施工进度,停工时间,环境状况等对最佳停工块段提出建议,并对实际停工块段的预拱度做出相应的调整,控制桥梁线形,达到顺利施工,保证连续刚构桥合理应力和线形的目的。

关键词 连续刚构桥 停工 有限元 大悬臂 挠度

0 引 言

连续刚构桥受力性能良好,跨越能力强,在山区得到了快速的发展,但其工作周期长,尤其是在西北地区,易受到冬季环境因素的影响,导致工程无法在连续的施工周期内合龙,迫使已完成的大悬臂T构需要经历冬季停工。在经历停工之后,桥梁大悬臂的线形与应力均会发生变化,对后续合龙过程造成影响。目前,许多学者对连续刚构桥的冬季停工进行了研究[1-3]。袁广学等[4]计算分析了悬臂施工过程中停工阶段截面挠度实测值和理论值的差异。陈黎明[5]分析了连续刚构桥悬臂过冬期间对结构施工监控产生的影响。李向旺等[6]对长悬臂停工期间连续刚构线形影响进行了分析研究。因此,本文依托某连续刚构桥,针对不同停工时间和不同停工块段分析停工对大悬臂的影响,计算冬季停工后其线形和应力的变化值,分析影响悬臂挠度的主要因素,以此对调整立模高程,进而控制桥梁线形和应力。

1 桥梁概况

某在建桥梁位于西北山区,主桥为65m+3×120m+65m连续刚构桥,有四个桥墩,分别为6号~9号墩,上部结构为预应力混凝土变截面连续刚构,采用单箱单室直腹板箱形断面,采用悬臂浇筑施工,悬臂划分为16个节段,各墩同步施工。0号、1号块在墩旁的托架上浇筑,其余梁段采用挂篮浇筑,采用先边跨再次边跨后中跨的顺序进行合龙段施工。

在实际施工中,由于新冠疫情、施工设备故障等各种不利因素,大桥很难在年内完成合龙,依据相关规定即将进入冬季停工阶段,为了掌握冬季停工对连续刚构桥的影响,分析了该桥不同停工块段和不同停工时间对大悬臂结构的影响,进而对施工提出合理建议。

2 有限元模型的建立

采用有限元分析软件Midas建立该连续刚构桥的有限元模型,成桥有限元模型见图1。

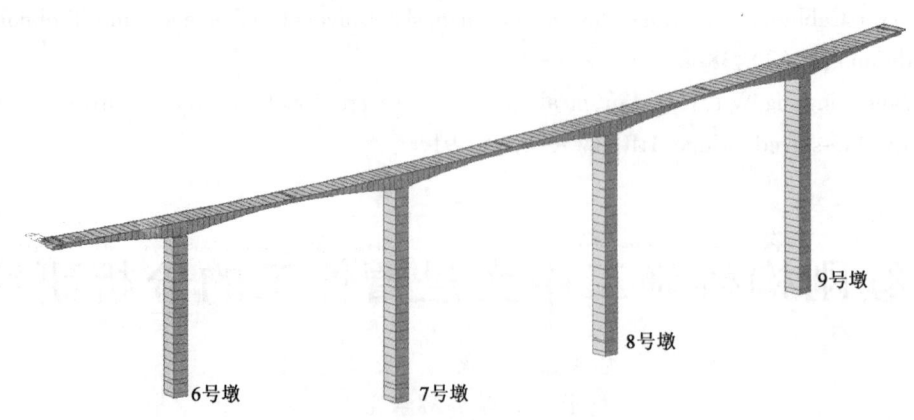

图1 成桥有限元模型示意图

针对该成桥有限元模型,分析各个桥墩分别施工至10号~16号块开始停工30d、60d、90d和120d的情况下,其主梁大悬臂各节段关键截面的挠度变化和应力变化,并分析影响这些变化的因素。

3 停工对桥梁大悬臂结构的影响

本文依托在建工程,各墩施工现场的复杂性等原因导致不同墩的悬臂施工进度不同,但由于各墩主梁的截面参数、钢束参数基本一致,经过对各墩施工至10号块时开始停工120d后的悬臂线形分析可知,各墩大悬臂阶段的线形变化基本一致,因此,以6号墩为例,对桥梁大悬臂结构进行分析。图2为各墩施工至10号块时开始停工120d后悬臂挠度变化量。

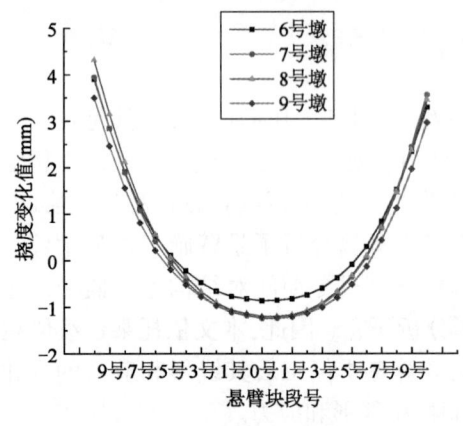

图2 各墩挠度变化值

3.1 不同停工时间下挠度对比分析

停工时间的不同导致在停工时间段内T构的悬臂的挠度变化不同,为研究不同停工时间对各悬臂挠度的影响,取T构悬臂浇筑至10号块、11号块、15号块和16号块停工,对冬季停工时间取30d、60d、90d和120d四种工况进行分析,计算各个工况下的悬臂各块段的挠度变化量。图3a)~d)分别为6号墩分别施工至10号块、11号块、15号块和16号块时开始停工不同时间后T构悬臂挠度变化量。

由图3可以看到,在不同停工时间下,T构悬臂挠度变化量呈抛物线,悬臂端截面挠度随着停工时间的增加而增大,但各停工时间之间的相对挠度在逐渐减小。同时可以看到,0号块附近的挠度变化量随着停工时间的增大而减小,这说明挠度变化量不仅包括T构主梁的挠度变化量,还包括桥墩的挠度变化量,且在0号块附近的主梁挠度变化量小于桥墩的挠度变化量,主梁的上挠无法抵消桥墩的收缩徐变影响。

3.2 不同停工块段下挠度对比分析

为了进一步研究停工时悬臂长度的影响,现分别模拟当主梁施工至10号至16号块时开始停工的7种工况进行分析,停工时间按120d计算。计算结果如下所示,图4为6号墩分别施工至10号~16号块时开始停工120d后T构悬臂挠度变化量,图5为6号墩分别施工至10号~16号块时开始停工120d后悬臂端截面挠度变化量。

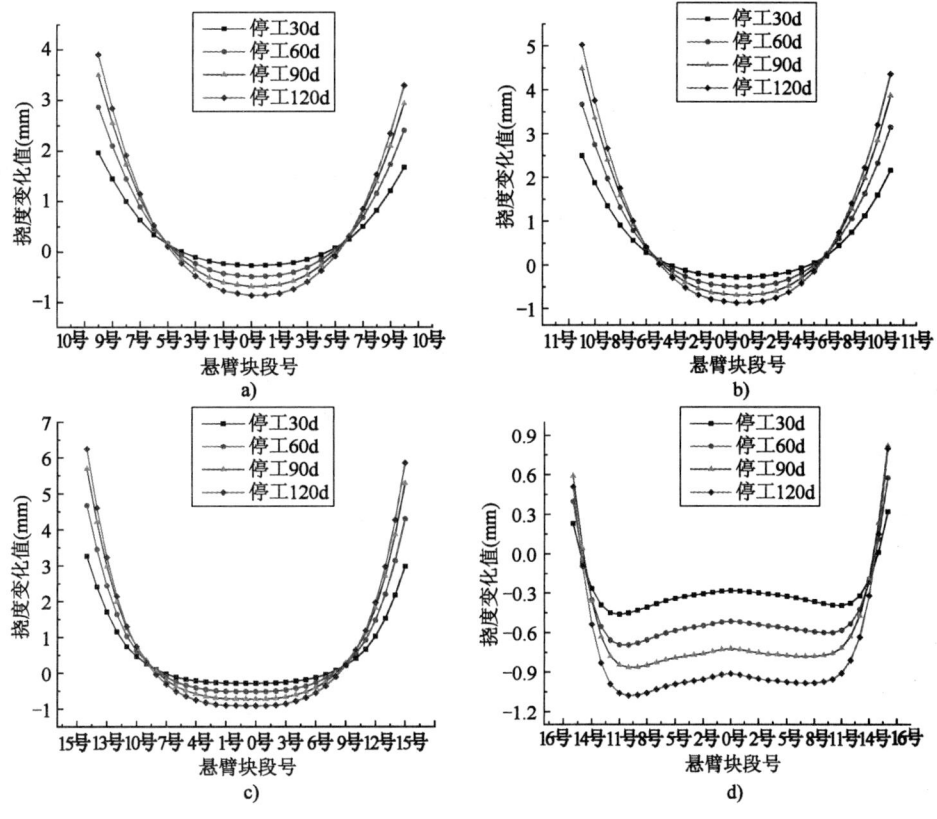

图3 不同停工时间下悬臂挠度变化量

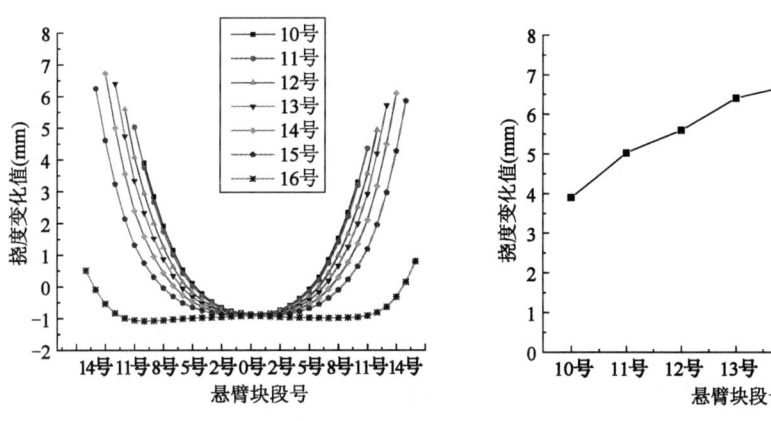

图4 不同停工块段下悬臂挠度变化量

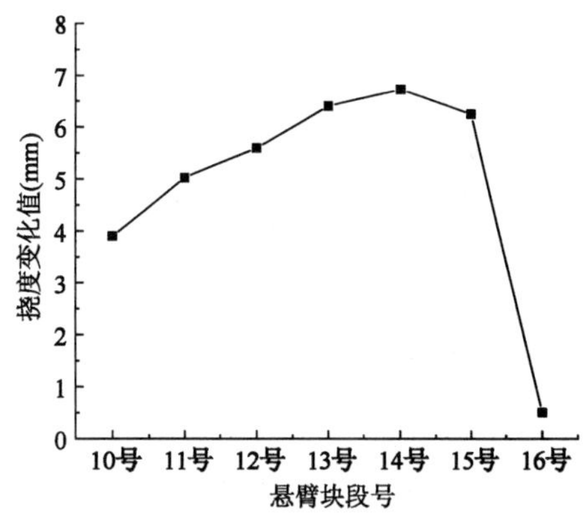

图5 悬臂端截面挠度变化量

由图4可以看到，不同停工块段对T构悬臂挠度变化量的影响较大，当主梁悬臂施工至10号~15号块时开始停工，在停工期间各悬臂节段的变形呈上挠趋势，当主梁悬臂施工至16号块时开始停工，在停工期间各悬臂节段的变形呈先下挠后上挠趋势。由图5可知，悬臂端的挠度变化量在14号块达到峰值，当主梁悬臂施工至10号~14号块时开始停工，随着悬臂长度的增加，停工期间悬臂端挠度变化量增大；当主梁悬臂施工至15号、16号块时开始停工，随着悬臂长度的增加，停工期间悬臂端挠度变化量减小，建议将14号块作为最佳停工块段，以避免连续刚构桥在大悬臂停工期间出现下挠的现象。

总体来看，T构在大悬臂停工期间挠度变形均处于-2~7mm，相比规范要求的允许施工误差10mm小，但仍需要重视。在大悬臂施工期间应考虑停工对悬臂挠度产生的影响，根据实际情况计算其变化值，

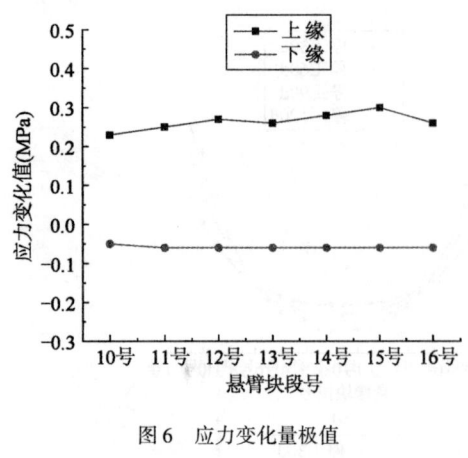

图6 应力变化量极值

对其立模高程做出相应的调整,以保证接下来的桥梁线形符合预期。

3.3 应力对比分析

对不同停工块段悬臂端截面的应力变化量进行比较,分析当主梁施工至10号~16号块时开始停工的7种工况,停工时间按120d计算。计算结果如下图所示,图6为6号墩施工至16号块时开始停工120d后悬臂上下缘应力变化量绝对值的最大值。

由图6可知,在停工阶段,T构悬臂端截面上缘压应力增大,下缘压应力减小,但不同工况下应力变化量的极值基本一致,上缘压应力变化量的最大值均在0.26MPa左右,而下缘压应力变化量的最小值均在-0.06MPa左右,各截面的应力变化量较小。T构悬臂在停工期间的影响较小。

4 影响因素分析

从图4、图5可知,虽然不同停工块段下的T构悬臂端的挠度变化都为上挠,但是挠度变化量并非只随着停工长度和停工时间的增加而增大,而是出现了转折,可以分析得到随着停工时间增加,在结构自重、预应力等作用下,主梁混凝土出现了收缩徐变,同时收缩徐变又会导致预应力损失,这些因素都会影响停工期间悬臂端挠度变化量,为了进一步研究影响悬臂端截面挠度大小的因素,分别计算在不同停工块段和不同停工时间下混凝土收缩、徐变和预应力损失3种效应的挠度变化量,计算结果如下图所示,图7a)为6号墩分别施工至10号~16号块时开始停工120d后受不同效应的悬臂挠度变化量,图7b)为6号墩施工至14号块时开始停工30d、60d、90d和120d后受不同效应的悬臂挠度变化量。

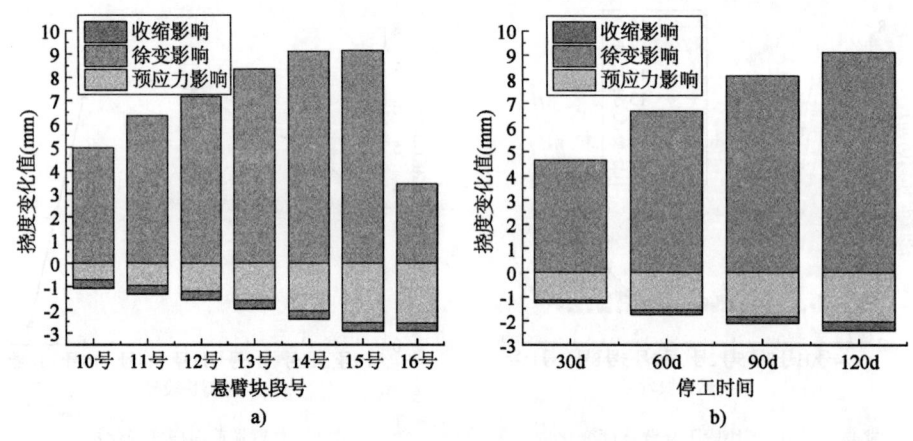

图7 不同效应的悬臂挠度变化量

由图7a)可知,在不同效应影响下,混凝土徐变导致悬臂出现上挠,混凝土收缩和预应力损失导致悬臂出现下挠。其中混凝土徐变的上挠影响占比较大,超过了混凝土收缩和预应力损失的下挠影响,导致在总体情况下悬臂呈现上挠趋势。且混凝土徐变的上挠影响与图5中悬臂端挠度变化趋势相符,在14号块的停工位置出现了挠度的峰值。混凝土收缩的影响在不同停工块段处基本一致,且占比最小,均在3%左右。

由图7b)可知,不同效应的悬臂挠度变化量均随停工时间的增加而增大,且各个效应导致的挠度变化量的占比基本保持不变。在施工至14号块时开始停工后,混凝土徐变的上挠影响占挠度变化量的79%左右,预应力损失的下挠影响占挠度变化量的18%左右,凝土收缩的下挠影响占挠度变化量的3%左右。

5 结 语

(1)在不同停工时间下,T构的悬臂线形呈抛物线线形,悬臂端挠度变化量随着停工时间的增加而增大,但停工时间越长,增加幅度越少,0号块附近的挠度变化量受桥墩的收缩徐变而逐渐减小。

(2)不同停工块段下,T构悬臂线形总体保持上挠趋势,16号块作为停工块段时会使挠度变化量出现先下挠再上挠的趋势;T构悬臂端挠度在14号块作为停工块段时出现峰值,在14号块之前或之后出现停工导致的悬臂端挠度变化量均较小,可将14号块作为最佳停工块段,以避免连续刚构桥在大悬臂停工期间出现下挠的现象。

(3)随着停工时间的增加,T构悬臂端截面上缘压应力在不断增大,下缘压应力在不断减小,但应力变化量较小,对T构悬臂在停工期间的影响较小。

(4)混凝土徐变效应导致T构悬臂出现上挠,混凝土收缩效应、预应力损失导致T构悬臂出现下挠,其中混凝土徐变效应产生的挠度变化量占比较大。不同效应影响下的悬臂挠度变化量均随停工时间的增加而增大,且各个效应导致的挠度变化量的占比基本保持不变。

参考文献

[1] 韦正茂.连续刚构桥梁冬季长悬臂停工的结构影响分析[J].甘肃科技纵横,2019,48(10):33-39+6.

[2] 杨晋文.连续刚构桥跨中下挠的影响因素分析[J].石家庄铁道大学学报(自然科学版),2015,28(02):17-20.

[3] 刘欣欣.大跨度连续刚构施工控制及停工对结构的影响分析[D].西南科技大学,2016.

[4] 袁广学,孙延飞,秦冰冰.连续刚构桥悬臂浇筑施工中停工对截面挠度影响研究[J].公路,2018,63(03):101-107.

[5] 陈黎明.温泉特大桥大悬臂过冬施工监控影响性分析[J].公路交通科技(应用技术版),2019,15(03):124-126.

[6] 李向旺,康新章,张君健,等.长悬臂过冬对连续刚构桥线形影响的分析研究[J].交通科技,2017(05):32-34.

Research on Preventive Maintenance Timing of Steel-Concrete Composite Beam Cable-stayed Bridge

Zhi Liu　Hanhao Zhang　Binxin Wang　Linhao Zhu

(Chang'an University)

Abstract　In recent years, as the number of steel-concrete composite girder cable-stayed bridges has increased, the problems in the operation process have become more prominent. In particular, the usage status of the main load-bearing components affects the durability of the bridge structure. Therefore, it is necessary to carry out preventive maintenance planning for each main force-bearing component in order to reduce the maintenance cost of the structure and extend the service life of the structure. In preventive maintenance planning, the choice of preventive maintenance timing is very important, and inappropriate maintenance timing is difficult to achieve the expected effect of preventive maintenance. Based on investigation and calculation analysis, this paper clearly puts forward a calculation method for the preventive maintenance time of the main stressed components of a steel-concrete composite beam cable-stayed bridge, and applies this method to a new bridge. The method proposed in this paper has important guiding significance for the management of actual projects.

Keywords Steel-concrete composite beam cable-stayed bridge   Preventive maintenance   Optimal curing time   Durability

0 Introduction

With the developing of long-span bridge management technology research, the concept of preventive maintenance has been throughout the life of the bridge. Preventive maintenance planning includes maintenance timing, maintenance location and maintenance measures. Among them, preventive maintenance focuses on the determination of the maintenance time: corresponding maintenance measures should be taken to treat the structure when there is no disease or the disease is very slight. Excessive advancement of the maintenance time will result in excessive maintenance of the bridge structure during its service life, resulting in a substantial increase in maintenance costs.

The steel-concrete composite girder cable-stayed bridge is a space-complex stress-bearing system composed of main stress-bearing components such as stay cables, bridge decks and steel main girder. The component diseases caused by delayed maintenance will seriously affect the safety and durability of the bridge structure. At present, there are still few studies on the preventive maintenance timing of the main stressed components of steel-concrete composite beam cable-stayed bridges, and the existing results are relatively general, which is difficult to directly use in the actual engineering management process. Therefore, the research on the optimal preventive maintenance timing of the main stressed components in this paper is practical and innovative.

1 Bridge Structure Performance Degradation Prediction Model

Whether preventive maintenance can achieve the expected results depends on the control of the degradation process of the bridge structure. Therefore, in order to establish a suitable bridge structure performance degradation prediction model on the basis of as close as possible to the real performance degradation of the bridge structure[1], it is very necessary to simulate and predict the performance degradation of the in-service bridge structure.

At this stage, the methods for predicting the performance degradation of bridge structures can be roughly divided into two categories: one is to use mathematical methods such as probability statistics to predict the performance degradation of the bridge structure on the basis of certain historical performance degradation statistics of the bridge structure; The other is to obtain the law of structural degradation by studying the time-varying relationship between the main influencing factors of structural performance degradation and the degradation of bridge structural performance, so as to predict bridge degradation.

This paper combines the above two methods to establish a performance degradation prediction model for the main stressed members of a steel-concrete composite beam cable-stayed bridge.

2 Engineering Background

The supporting project of this paper is a double-tower five-span cable-plane composite beam cable-stayed bridge, which adopts a semi-floating system. Its span is composed of: 30m + 95m + 305m + 110m + 30m. The stay cables are finished cables with parallel steel wire bundles, the main tower is an inverted Y-type pylon, and the main beam is a separated double-sided box composite beam. The bridge span layout is shown in Fig. 1.

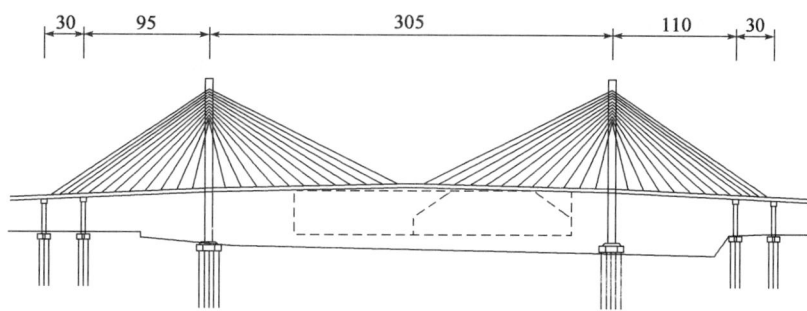

Fig. 1 Bridge span layout drawing 1(unit:m)

3 Method for Determining Preventive Maintenance Timing of Each Component

3.1 Method for Determining the Timing of Preventive Maintenance of stay Cables

At present, the flexible stay cable system used in most cable-stayed bridges usually adopts galvanized steel wire heating and extruding HDPE sheath for protection. For this type of stay cable, the degradation process is divided into three stages: sheath aging and cracking, galvanized layer corrosion, and steel wire iron matrix corrosion.[2]

When the sheath is damaged, different repair methods can be used to repair it, but when the galvanized layer is damaged by corrosion, it is difficult to repair with current technology and means at a lower cost with the current technical means. Therefore, preventive maintenance is appropriate when the cable HDPE sheath is damaged.

Establishment of HDPE sheath degradation prediction model: In order to predict the cracking time of the stay cable HDPE sheath, the performance degradation prediction model of the stay cable HDPE sheath must be established. Take relying on a bridge as an example to illustrate the method of establishing the prediction model. Relying on the bridge is located in the southeast coastal area, subtropical maritime monsoon climate zone, with strong sunlight, high ultraviolet radiation, high temperature, high humidity, and frequent acid rain. It is a coastal typhoon area. The natural environment is similar to the natural environment of Wanning area[3]. Use the measured data to draw the change curve of the nominal strain retention rate at fracture with time during the aging process of HDPE in the natural environment, and use the exponential regression method in the least square method to regression fit the curve, The result is shown in Fig. 2.

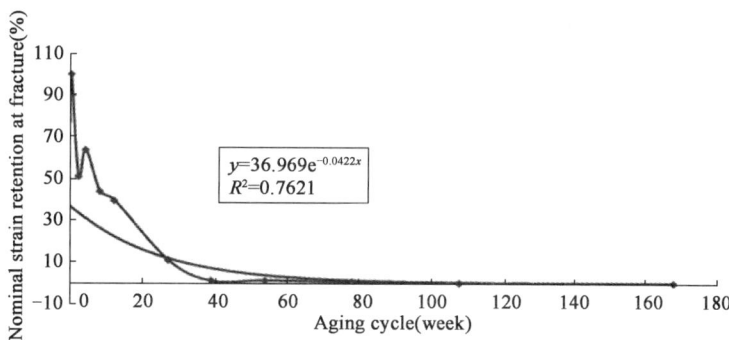

Fig. 2 HDPE aging curve in Wanning area

That is, the degradation model of the nominal strain retention rate of HDPE jacket fracture over time is:
$$\zeta(t) = 36.969 e^{-0.0422t} \tag{1}$$
The nominal breaking strain e1 of the stay cable HDPE sheath before degradation can be measured

according to the standard test, here according to the relevant regulations, the lower limit is taken for the limit requirements for the nominal strain of the cable sheath material when the material is not aging $e_1 = 600\%$, substituting the values of formula (1) and e_1 into the formula $xe_1 = \dfrac{T}{EA}$, we can get:

$$36.969e^{-0.0422t} \times 600\% = \dfrac{T}{EA} \tag{2}$$

Relying on the cable force T of the bridge stayed cable under dead load and vehicle live load can be calculated by establishing a bridge finite element simulation model, E and A are the material characteristics and geometric characteristics of the stay cable, respectively. Substituting the parameters T, E, and A of each stay cable of the supporting bridge into the formula (2), the aging and cracking time of the sheath can be calculated. Since the stay cable is protected by a double-layer HDPE sheath, the aging and cracking time of each stay cable HDPE sheath can be calculated by multiplying the calculation result by 2. Based on the analysis of the calculation results, the stay cables of the bridge will face the risk of aging and cracking after being exposed to the atmosphere for about 10 years. At this time, preventive maintenance is carried out on the stay cables.

3.2 Method for Determining the Timing of Preventive Maintenance of Bridge Deck

Establish a bridge degradation prediction model based on Markov chain for concrete deck[4], Selected to rely on the historical inspection data of 5 bridge concrete decks in the bridge engineering area[5], the test results are evaluated and sorted according to the five levels of component technical status. Among them, the evaluation period of concrete bridge deck is 1 year, and every 5 years is a degradation stage. The results of the inspection and evaluation of the technical condition of the reinforced concrete deck of each bridge over the years are shown in Tab. 1.

Test and evaluation results of bridge deck technical condition[6]   Tab. 1

Degradation	Degradation					Degradation					Degradation stage				
Age	1	2	3	4	5	6	7	8	9	10	11	12	13	14	15
Bridge1	1	1	1	1	1	1	2	2	2	2	2	2	2	2	3
Bridge 2	1	1	1	1	1	1	1	1	2	2	2	2	2	3	3
Bridge 3	1	1	1	1	2	2	2	2	2	2	2	3	3	3	3
Bridge 4	1	1	1	2	2	2	2	2	2	3	3	3	3	3	4
Bridge 5	1	1	1	1	1	1	2	2	2	2	2	3	3	3	3

According to the statistical data of the above-mentioned concrete bridge slab over the years, the one-step transition probability matrix can be calculated for each degradation stage:

$$P(1) = \begin{bmatrix} 0.9167 & 0.0833 & 0 & 0 & 0 \\ 0 & 1 & 0 & 0 & 0 \\ 0 & 0 & 1 & 0 & 0 \\ 0 & 0 & 0 & 1 & 0 \\ 0 & 0 & 0 & 0 & 1 \end{bmatrix}$$

$$P(2) = \begin{bmatrix} 0.625 & 0.375 & 0 & 0 & 0 \\ 0 & 0.9412 & 0.0588 & 0 & 0 \\ 0 & 0 & 1 & 0 & 0 \\ 0 & 0 & 0 & 1 & 0 \\ 0 & 0 & 0 & 0 & 1 \end{bmatrix}$$

$$P(3) = \begin{bmatrix} 1 & 0 & 0 & 0 & 0 \\ 0 & 0.6923 & 0.3077 & 0 & 0 \\ 0 & 0 & 0.9167 & 0.0833 & 0 \\ 0 & 0 & 0 & 1 & 0 \\ 0 & 0 & 0 & 0 & 1 \end{bmatrix}$$

The state transition probability matrix of each degradation stage of the component is calculated from the inspection and evaluation data of the concrete bridge deck over the years. It can be concluded that the state degradation law of concrete bridge deck in this area[7]. In the known case, the distribution vector of the initial technical condition of the concrete deck of the bridge is $P_0 = (1,0,0,0,0)$, then the technical status distribution and expectations of the concrete bridge slab in each degradation can be predicted. The prediction results are as follows:

In the 5th year,
$$P_5 = P_0 \cdot P(1)_5$$
$$E(5) = P_5 \cdot E^T = (0.6473, 0.3527, 0, 0, 0) \cdot (1, 2, 3, 4, 5)^T = 1.3527$$

In the 10th year,
$$P_{10} = P_0 \cdot P(1)_5 \cdot P(2)_5$$
$$E(10) = P_{10} \cdot E^T = (0.0617, 0.7543, 0.1840, 0, 0) \cdot (1, 2, 3, 4, 5)^T = 2.1222$$

In the 15th year,
$$P_{15} = P_0 \cdot P(1)_5 \cdot P(2)_5 \cdot P(3)_5 = P_{10} \cdot P(3)_5$$
$$E(15) = P_{15} \cdot E^T = (0.0617, 0.1200, 0.6242, 0.1942, 0) \cdot (1, 2.3, 4, 5)^T = 2.9507$$

The degradation curve of the technical status of the concrete bridge deck over time is shown in Fig. 3.

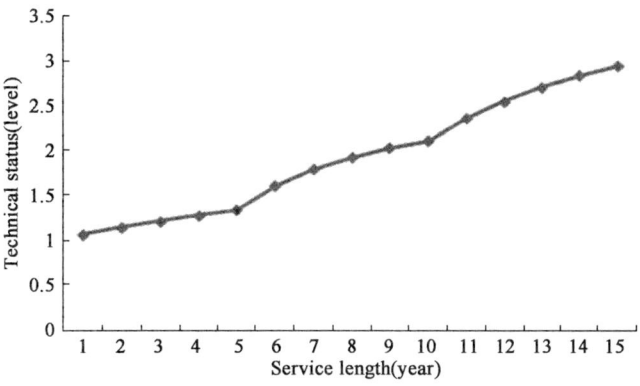

Fig. 3

In engineering applications, an 85% guarantee rate is usually used to judge whether the bridge components reach the allowable state[8]. The preventive maintenance of concrete bridge slab requires that the technical status of the component should not be lower than level 2 during preventive maintenance. That is, the probability of the technical status of the concrete bridge slab at the first or second level during preventive maintenance should not be less than 85%.

The grade distribution vector of the technical condition of concrete bridge deck in the 9th year is:
$$P_9 = P_0 \cdot P(1)_5 \cdot P(2)_4 = (0.0988, 0.7621, 0.1392, 0, 0)$$
$$R(I_1 = 1, I_2 = 2) = 0.0988 + 0.7621 = 0.8609 > 85\%$$

The grade distribution vector of the technical condition of the concrete bridge deck in the 10th year is:
$$P_{10} = (0.0617, 0.7543, 0.1840, 0, 0)$$
$$R(I_1 = 1, I_2 = 2) = 0.0617 + 0.7543 = 0.816 < 85\%$$

The preventive maintenance time of the concrete deck of the bridge should be 9-10 years.

3.3 Method for Determining the Timing of Preventive Maintenance of Bridge Deck

Due to the corrosion characteristics of metal materials, in order to prevent the corrosion of metal components, which will affect the safety of use and extend the service life, certain anti-corrosion measures must be taken when the steel beam is used.

From the perspective of in-service bridges, the corrosion degradation process of steel beams is mainly divided into two stages: Coating deterioration corrosion stage and iron matrix corrosion stage. Combining the current status and research results of steel bridge maintenance[9], it can be seen that: The preventive maintenance of steel beams should be at the stage when the anti-corrosion measures of the steel beams are about to fail and the steel beams have not undergone major corrosion damage.

Using Grey System Method to Establish a Prediction Model for Degradation of Anticorrosive Coating on Steel Beams of Bridge Engineering[10]. Relying on bridge engineering to use epoxy zinc-rich primer, epoxy mica paint and epoxy paint heavy anti-corrosion coating system for steel beam anti-corrosion. From the third year of service of the bridge steel girders, regular inspections of the coating corrosion of the steel girders have been carried out, once a year, and a total of 6 consecutive years of coating corrosion inspection data have been obtained as shown in Tab. 2.

Corrosion test results of steel beam coating   Tab. 2

Detection time	3	4	5	6	7	8	9
Coating corrosion ratio	0.8	1.2	1.5	1.8	2.2	2.7	3.4

The corrosion prediction model is established by taking the coating corrosion test data from the 3rd to 7th years after the steel beam has been in service, and the corrosion prediction accuracy is verified by using the 8th and 9th years of steel beam coating corrosion detection information. The corrosion area ratio of the steel beam coating service for t years is $x_{(t)}^{(0)}$, then the original sequence is:

$$X_{(t)}^{(0)} = \{0.8, 1.2, 1.5, 1.8, 2.2\}$$

Accumulate the original sequence to get a new sequence:

$$X_{(t)}^{(1)} = \{x_{(3)}^{(1)}, \cdots x_{(k)}^{(1)}\} = \{0.8, 2, 3.5, 5.3, 7.5\}$$

among them, $X_{(k)}^{(1)} = \sum_{t}^{k} = 3 x_{(t)}^{(0)}$

Construct data array B and data column Y_n and bring in data:

$$B = \begin{bmatrix} -[X_{(3)}^{(1)} + X_{(4)}^{(1)}]/2 & 1 \\ -[X_{(4)}^{(1)} + X_{(5)}^{(1)}]/2 & 1 \\ -[X_{(5)}^{(1)} + X_{(6)}^{(1)}]/2 & 1 \\ -[X_{(6)}^{(1)} + X_{(7)}^{(1)}]/2 & 1 \end{bmatrix} = \begin{bmatrix} -1.4 & 1 \\ -2.75 & 1 \\ -4.4 & 1 \\ -6.4 & 1 \end{bmatrix}$$

$$Y_n = [X_{(4)}^{(0)}, X_{(5)}^{(0)}, X_{(6)}^{(0)}, X_{(7)}^{(0)}]^T = [1.2, 1.5, 1.8, 2.2]^T$$

Solve the parameter sequence in the GM(1,1) model:

$$[a, u]^T = (B^T B)^{-1} \cdot B^T Y_n = [-0.1979, 0.9354]^T$$

Then, $A = X_{(3)}^{(0)} - u/a = 0.8 - 0.9354/(-0.1979) = 5.5266$

Establish the prediction formula for the corrosion area of the steel beam coating on the bridge:

$$t = N\left[1 + \frac{\ln(1 - e^a) - \ln\frac{S}{A}}{a}\right] + t_o = \frac{\ln(1 - e^{-0.1979}) - \ln\frac{S}{5.5266}}{-0.1979} + 3$$

Use this formula to predict the corrosion area of the coating and compare it with the measured value. The results are shown in Tab. 3.

Corrosion prediction results of steel beam coating　　　　Tab. 3

Service time(a)	Measured corrosion area(%)	Forecast corrosion area(%)	Relative deviation(%)
3	0.8	0.89	11.5
4	1.2	1.21	0.8
5	1.5	1.47	−1.7
6	1.8	1.80	−0.2
7	2.2	2.19	−0.5
8	2.7	2.67	−1.1
9	3.4	3.25	−4.3

It can be seen from the results of the above table that the prediction results of steel beam coating corrosion are in good agreement with the actual measurement results, that is, the gray system method to establish a steel beam coating corrosion prediction model can meet the requirements of engineering applications.

The well-known anticorrosion scholar Takashi Yamamoto believes that the coating reaches the end of its life when the opening area rate of the coating reaches 5%. Therefore, it can be considered that when the corrosion area of the coating of the steel beam reaches 5%, preventive maintenance measures can be taken on the steel beam to prevent steel The beam suffers from greater corrosion. Using the steel beam coating corrosion prediction formula to calculate the service life of the coating when the corrosion rate is 5%:

$$t = \frac{\ln(1 - e^{-0.1979}) - \ln\frac{S}{5.5266}}{-0.1979} + 3 = \frac{\ln(1 - e^{-0.1979}) - \ln\frac{5}{5.5266}}{-0.1979} + 3 = 11.2$$

That is, when the service life of the steel beam coating on the bridge engineering exceeds 11 years, preventive maintenance measures can be considered for the steel beam.

4　Conclusions

(1) In view of the durability problems of each component of the long-span steel-concrete composite beam cable-stayed bridge in service, a suitable prediction model of bridge structural performance degradation was established, and a reasonable preventive maintenance decision was made.

(2) This article starts from the performance degradation prediction model of bridge components. According to the respective degradation characteristics of its main components, comprehensively considers the economics and state of the preventive maintenance of bridge components. For long-span steel-concrete composite beam cable-stayed bridges Typical components such as stay cables, reinforced concrete bridge decks, and steel beams propose simple, applicable and reliable methods for determining the best preventive maintenance timing.

(3) Taking a long-span steel-concrete composite beam cable-stayed bridge as an example, according to the steel-concrete composite beam preventive maintenance timing determination method given in this paper, the degradation model of each cable-stayed bridge member is established to determine The best time for preventive maintenance of each component of the steel-concrete composite girder cable-stayed bridge was established.

References

[1] Dai Y, Han D. Development of Bridge Deterioration Model in Bridge Management System [J]. Port & Waterway Engineering, 2005(9):78-82. (in Chinese).

[2] Wang Y, Ye H, Duan X. Hydrogen Embrittlement and Corrosion Fatigue of Corroded Bridge Wires [J]. Journal of China & Foreign Highway, 2014, 34(06):110-116. (in Chinese).

[3] Liu Y, Li H, Wei X. Study on the Mechanical Property of the Nature Aging HDPE Specimens [J]. Shandong Chemical Industry, 2007(08):5-7. (in Chinese).

[4] Lu Y, He S. Prediction of Markov fuzzy reliability for existing bridge[J]. Journal of Chang'an University (Natural Science Edition), 2005, 25(4):41-43. (in Chinese).

[5] Sun M, Liu Q, Xiang C. Comprehensive Evaluation Index System of Bridge Preventive Maintenance [J]. Journal of Chongqing Jiaotong University(Natural Science), 2013, 32(S1):899-902. (in Chinese).

[6] Huang Yinghua, Adams T M, Pincheira J A. Analysis of Life-cycle Maintenance Strategies for Concrete Bridge Decks [J]. Journal of Bridge Engineering, 2004, 9 (3): 250-258..

[7] Pang L. Fatigue Cumulative Damage Detection and Fatigue Life Prediction on Reinforced Concrete Slabs. [D]. Southeast University, 2004..

[8] JTG H10—2009. Technical Specifications of Maintenance for Highway: JTJ 073—96 [S]. China Communications Press, 1996.

[9] Zhang B, Li Y, Fu H. Methods of Corrosion Protection for Steel Structure Bridges[J]. World Bridges, 2006 (03):67-70.

[10] Lu Y, Yin J. Evaluation Method for Bridge Distress Condition [J]. China Journal of Highway and Transport, 1996, 9(3):55-61.

[11] Li Z. Study on preventive maintenance methods of long-span steel-concrete composite beam cable-stayed bridge. [D]. Chang'an University, 2020.

Finite Element Analysis of Pile-Soil Interaction under Scouring

Haofei Guo   Wenliang Hu   Huishuang Xiao   Haoyun Yuan

(Chang'an University)

Abstract This paper analyzes the effect of pile-soil interaction under the scouring action and calculates the load-displacement curve of the pile groups, discusses the stress changes and soil displacement of the piles. The calculation results show that the stress of piles and the displacement of soil have increased significantly after platform is scoured deeper than its height, which is very likely to accelerate the damage of the structure. These results acquired in this paper lay a foundation for further research on this kind of design, and also have a certain guiding significance for the design of disaster reduction in practical engineering.

Keywords Pile group foundation   Scouring action   Load displacement curve   Pile stress   Soil displacement

0 Introduction

Bridge water damage accidents are serious natural disasters faced by all countries, which can cause heavy casualties and economic losses. The National Bridge Annual Report issued by the Federal Highway Administration points out that 153871 of the 596808 existing bridges in the United States have structural or functional defects [1]. In other words, a quarter of the bridges are unqualified. Under normal circumstances, most bridges can operate normally, but unqualified bridges will suffer greater damage when they continue to be scoured by water for a long time, which can easily lead to serious accidents. Wardhana and hadipriono studied 503 bridge damage accidents in the United States from 1989 to 2000, of which 243 were related to water erosion [2]. Lagasse et al. mentioned in a report published in 2007 that bridge damage caused by scouring accounted for about 60% [2]. In summary, water erosion is one of the most important causes of bridge damage and collapse [3-5].

The pile group foundation is a very widely used foundation form, but people have not done enough research on the settlement of pile groups under the action of scouring. At present, the method of calculating the settlement of pile groups include equal-generation pier foundation method [6-9], in-situ test estimation method [9-10], settlement ratio method [11-12], elastic theory method [13-14], finite element method [15], mixed method [16], etc. Among them, the equal-generation pier foundation method is easy to calculate and is most used in engineering practice.

Lee[16] used the hyperbolic model to study the settlement of pile groups in layered soil. Randolph et al. [17] proposed a settlement calculation method for pile groups considering the settlement interaction of pile groups based on an iterative method. Mylonakis et al. [18] proposed a simple calculation method for the settlement of pile groups in layered soil based on the shear displacement method. Zhang et al. [19] assumed that the soil at the pile side and the pile end satisfies the hyperbolic and bifold line load transfer models respectively, obtained the load-sinking curve of a single pile, and used the influence coefficient to propose the load of the pile group-calculation method of settlement curve.

Most of the above-mentioned researches focus on the load-settlement relationship of piles with uniform cross-section, and there are few studies on the load-settlement relationship of pile groups under scouring. Based on the current research status, this paper assumes that the pile body adopts a homogeneous isotropic linear elastic material model, the soil body is an elastoplastic material, adopts a modified Mohr-Coulomb constitutive model, and considers the pile-soil interaction. The finite element software ABAQUS is used to analyze the load settlement and pile stress of the pile group under scouring. The results of this paper have a certain reference value for practical engineering.

1 Numerical Simulation

1.1 Basic Assumptions

The numerical model established in this chapter is based on the following basic assumptions:

(1) The pile adopts a homogeneous isotropic linear elastic material model.

(2) The soil is made of elastoplastic material, using a modified Mohr-Coulomb constitutive model.

(3) Considering the pile-soil interaction, the normal direction of the contact surface between the pile and the soil is hard contact, and the tangential direction uses the Coulomb friction model;

(4) The normal direction of the contact surface between the pile and the soil at the end of the pile adopts hard contact, and the tangential direction adopts the frictionless free sliding mode. The pile loading process is regarded as quasi-static and simulated by the static loading method.

1.2 Numerical analysis-parameters

The material parameters of the piles and soil are shown in Tab. 1, and the model size is shown in Fig. 1 to Fig. 2.

Model material parameters Tab. 1

Category	E(MPa)	ν	γ(kN/m^3)	C(kPa)	φ(°)
Pile	300000	0.2	25	—	—
Soft clay	8	0.2	18	10	30
Sand	50	0.2	18	10	30

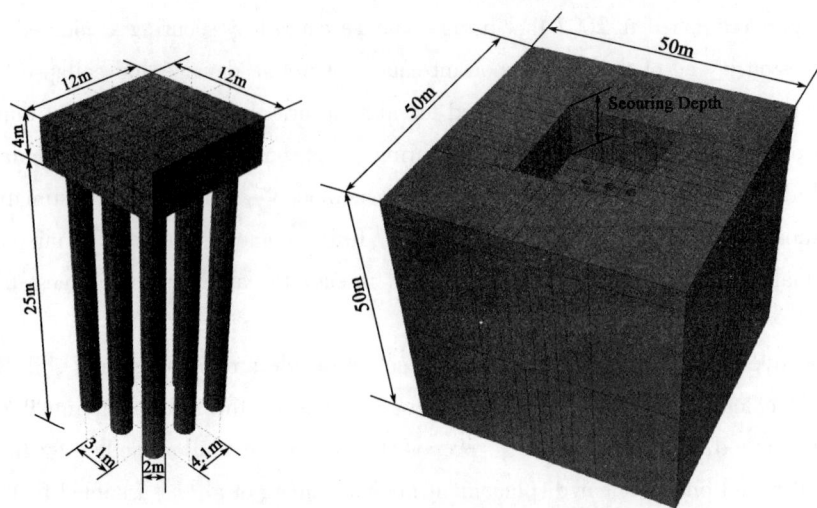

Fig. 1 Dimensions of piles and platform and soil

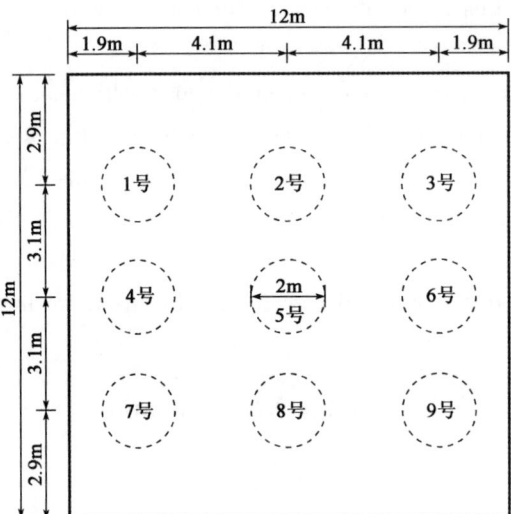

Fig. 2 Diagram of pile location

1.3 Boundary Conditions and Loading Methods

The specific boundary conditions of the model are as follows: the bottom boundary of the model Z-direction is a fixed constraint to limit all displacements; a roller support constraint is set on the radial outer boundary to limit the displacement of the soil in the corresponding radial direction. The soil gravity load is applied by force, and the value is the effective weight of the soil.

The initial ground stress adopts the method imported by ODB for balance calculation. Firstly, the model calculates the initial ground stress under a larger displacement threshold, and then imports the resulting ground stress ODB file into the model for calculation again, until the pile sinking value meets the convergence after the ground stress is balanced.

1.4 Simulation of Scouring Process

Consider(s)ing that the erosion effect is consistent with the mechanism of soil excavation in foundation pits. This paper uses ABAQUS to simulate the scour problem of the existing bridge pile foundation, and the method of excavating the soil layer around the pile is adopted to excavate the soil layer corresponding to the depth of the erosion soil layer to simulate the situation of water erosion when studying the influence mechanism of water erosion on the static bearing characteristics of pile foundations

1.5 Working Condition Design

This paper analyzes the influence law of scouring depth on the bearing capacity of bridge pile foundations, and formulates a calculation and analysis plan for each scouring 2m as a working condition. Taking into account the actual situation of scouring, the maximum scouring depth considered in this paper is 10m, and a total of 6 working conditions are designed.

2 Result Analysis

2.1 Q-S curve Results

The Q-S curve of the pile foundation structure in different soil types is drawn as shown in Fig. 3-Fig. 4 by applying force on the top surface of the platform through the coupling node. It can be seen from the figures that the Q-S curve of the pile foundation structure is different under different scouring depths, and there are obvious differences before and after the scouring to the platform. For the Q-S curves in the two soils, the changing trends are basically the same. When the soil layer is not washed under the platform, as the load on the top of the platform increases, the displacement of the structure also increases. With the increase of the scouring depth, the law of change becomes more obvious, but the amplitude of the change with different scouring depths is smaller. In soft clay and dense sand, when the load is 1×10^5 kN, the maximum variation is 74.8mm and 12.0mm, respectively. When the soil is washed under the platform, the maximum variation is 108.0mm and 18.5mm respectively. Compared with these two cases, the values of the maximum change amount increased by 44.4% and 54.2%, respectively. This is because after scouring under the platform, the soil at the bottom of the platform no longer bears the load, and is completely borne by the pile foundation itself, so the settlement will have such a large change under the external load.

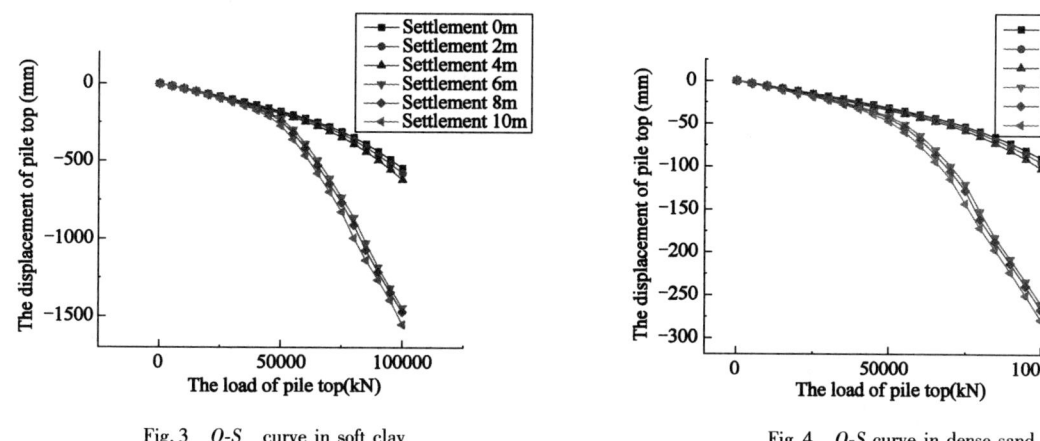

Fig. 3 Q-S curve in soft clay   Fig. 4 Q-S curve in dense sand

Based on the response surface analysis of the Q-S curves under the two soil qualities, the Q-S results of the soil strength at 15MPa, 22MPa, 29MPa, 36MPa, and 43MPa are obtained, as shown in Fig. 5.

2.2 Pile Stress Results

It can be seen from the above analysis that when the scouring stage is analyzed, the changes in the mechanical properties of the structure before and after the scouring depth exceeds the height of the platform are quite different. The paper analyzes the pile body stress under different scouring depths, and the results are shown in Fig. 6-Fig. 12. It can be seen from the diagram that the stress distribution of pile 1#, pile 2# and pile 5# is different when the soil is not completely washed under the platform. The stress of 1# pile is relatively large, the maximum stress is 16.5MPa, which occurs on the side close to the pile 5#, and the pile 2# is 8.6MPa, which also occurs on the side close to the pile 5#, and the pile 5# is 5.2MPa, which occurs less than 1m from the pile top. In comparison, after the soil is washed under the platform, the stress of three parts of pile foundation increases obviously, and the maximum stress of pile 1#, pile 2# and pile 5# is 19.7 MPa, 11.2 MPa and 8.7 MPa respectively, which is similar to that before scouring for location. This is because the soil at the bottom of the pile platform plays a role in sharing the force when the pile platform is not completely washed out. After continuous scouring, when the pile foundation drops to the point where the force is fully shared by the soil at the bottom of the pile and the side friction, the stress of the pile itself increases greatly, and the increase is about 36.1% of the former.

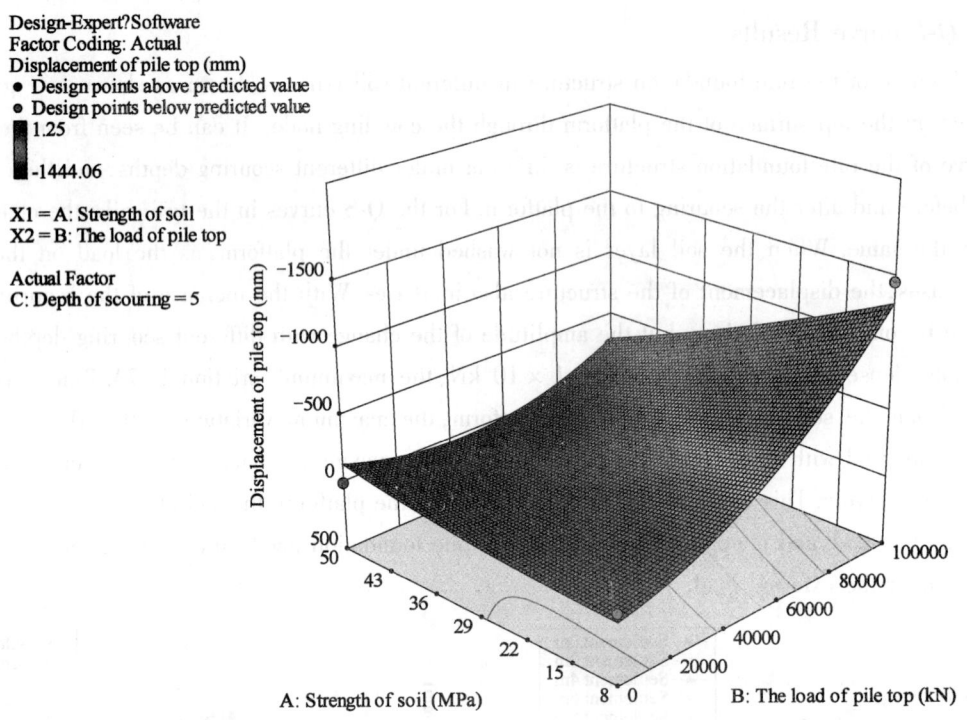

Fig. 5 Response surface analysis

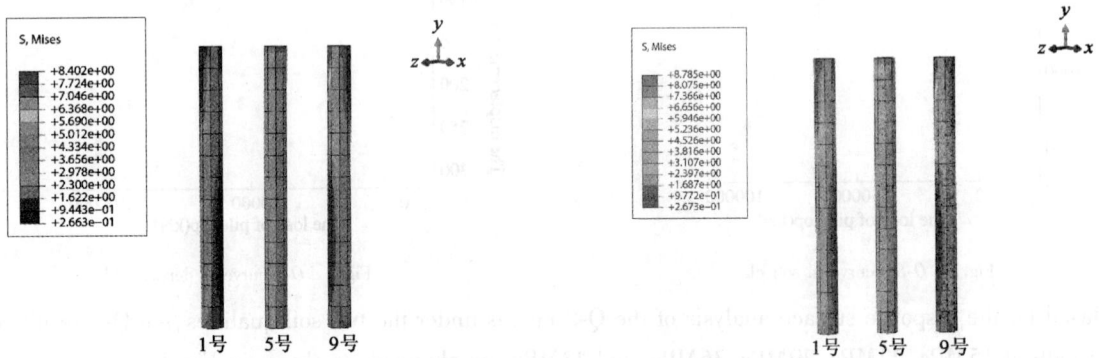

Fig. 6 Pile stress diagram at 0m scouring   Fig. 7 Pile stress diagram at 2m scouring

2.3 Soil displacement results

The soil displacement results of the two different states described can be seen from Fig. 13 to Fig. 18. The change trend of soil displacement at different scouring depths is basically the same, the closer the soil is to the pile, the greater the displacement. With the continuous increase of scouring depth, especially after the scouring depth exceeds the height of the platform, the soil displacement increment near the bottom of the platform increases obviously, and the soil displacement value when scouring to 10m is about three times that of scouring to 4m.

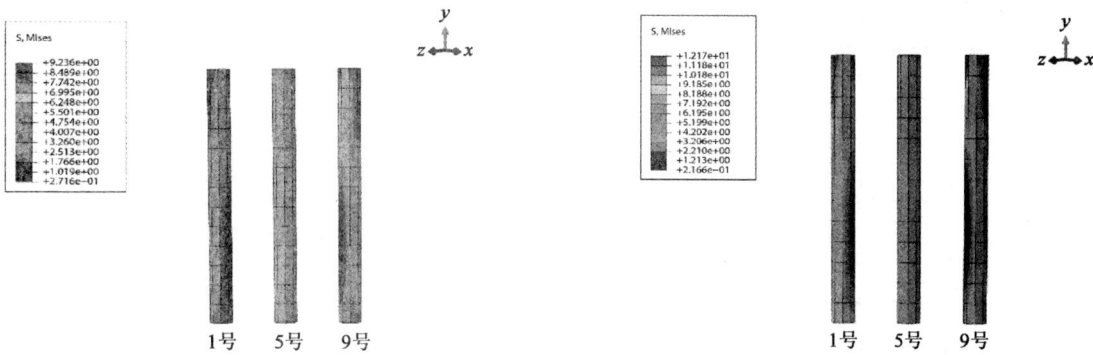

Fig. 8　Pile stress diagram at 4m scouring　　　　Fig. 9　Pile stress diagram at 6m scouring

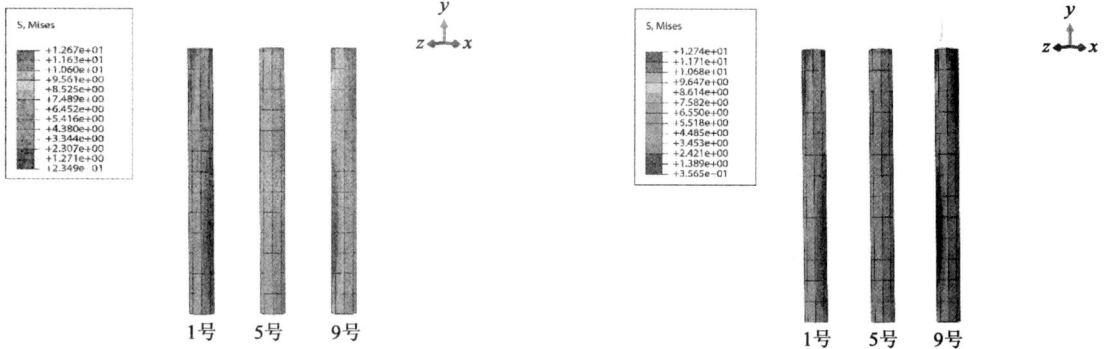

Fig. 10　Pile stress diagram at 8m scouring　　　　Fig. 11　Pile stress diagram at 10m scouring

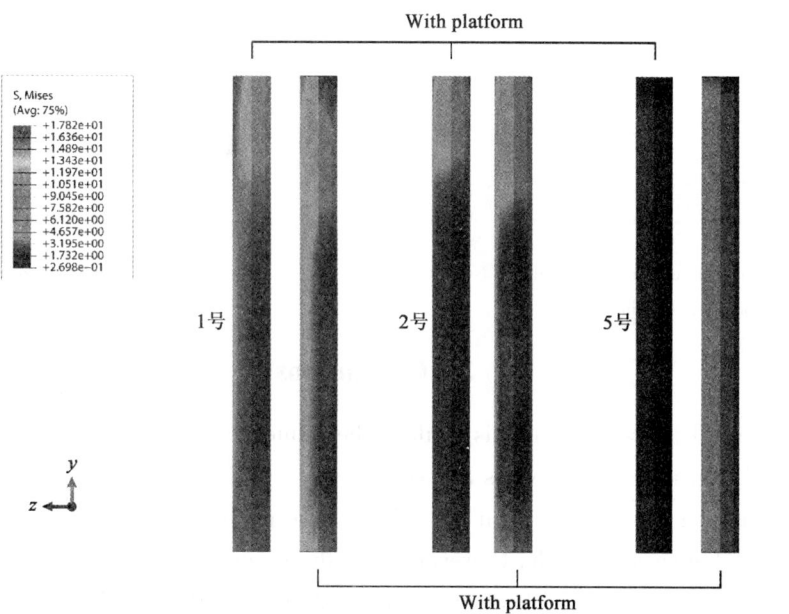

Fig. 12　Comparison of pile stress before and after scouring to the platform

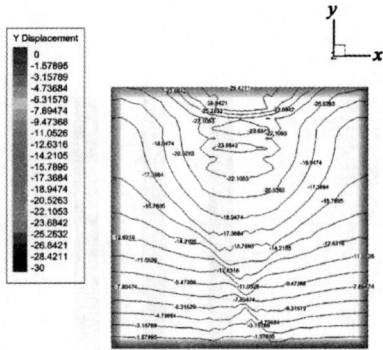

Fig. 13　Displacement contour map of soil in Y direction when scouring 0m

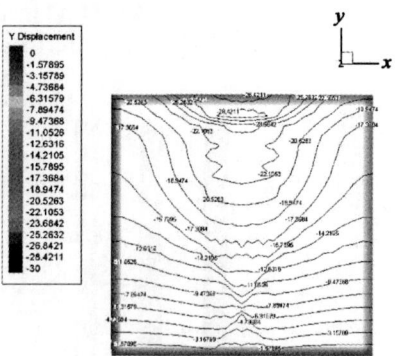

Fig. 14　Displacement contour map of soil in Y direction when scouring 2m

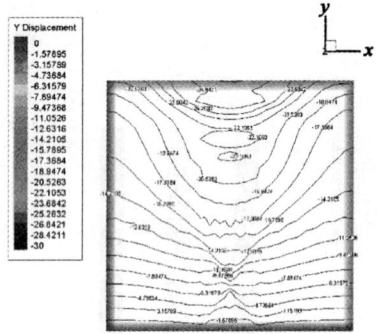

Fig. 15　Displacement contour map of soil in Y direction when scouring 4m

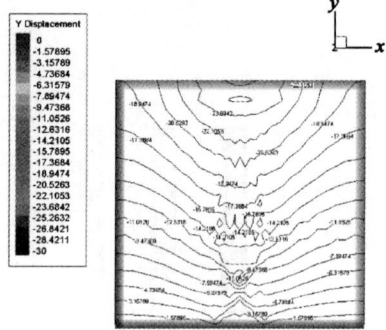

Fig. 16　Displacement contour map of soil in Y direction when scouring 6m

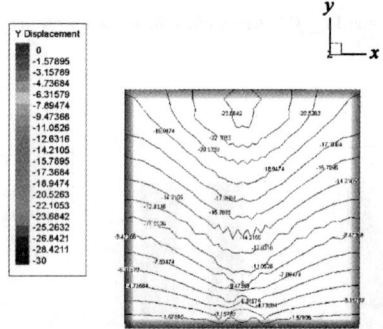

Fig. 17　Displacement contour map of soil in Y direction when scouring 8m

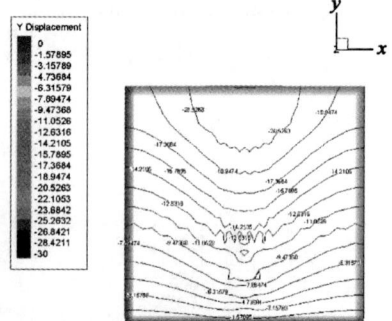

Fig. 18　Displacement contour map of soil in Y direction when scouring 10m

3　Conclusions

Based on the pile-soil interaction analysis method, the influence of the pile foundation under the scouring action is considered. The research conclusions are as follows:

(1) When the scouring depth is less than the height of the platform, the settlement of the pile top and the load show a linear distribution as a whole. However, when the scouring depth is greater than the height of the platform, with the gradually increase of load, the settlement of the pile top shows nonlinear characteristics. Therefore, in actual projects, it is necessary to prevent the adverse effects of running water erosion in special areas.

(2) Under different scouring depths, the position where the maximum stress of the piles body occurs is

basically the same, but when the scouring depth exceeds the height of the platform, the stress of the pile body has a substantial increase.

(3) The change trend of soil displacement is similar to that of piles stress, after the scouring depth exceeds the height of the platform, the displacement of soil increases obviously with the increase of scour depth. This kind of phenomenon may accelerate the destruction of the concrete pile, and it is necessary to prevent this kind of phenomenon from occurring in the actual project.

References

[1] Fayun Liang. A Literature Review on Behavior of Scoured Piles under Bridges[J]. International Foundation Congress and Equipment Expo,2009:482-488.

[2] Lagasse. Countermeasures to protect bridge piers from scour[J]. NCHRP Report 593. Washington DC: Transportation research Board.

[3] Jin Yuquan, pan Jun. summary of bridge accidents [J]. Shanxi architecture,2008,27:334-335.

[4] Ma Lei. Research on bridge foundation safety protection technology [D]. Xi'an: Chang'an University,2009.

[5] Cheng Lanyan. Experimental study on local scour protection of ring wing piers [D]. Inner Mongolia: Inner Mongolia Agricultural University,2012.

[6] Terzaghi K, Peck R B. Soil mechanics in engineering practice[M]. 2nd ed. New York: John Wiley & Sons Inc,1967.

[7] LIU Jin-li, HUANG Qiang, LI Hua, et al. Deformation behaviour and settlement calculation of pile group under vertical load[J]. Chinese Journal of Geotechnical Engineering,1995,17(6): 1-13.

[8] ZAI Jing-ming, ZAI Jing-zhang. Analysis and design of foundation of tall building[M]. Beijing: China Architecture & Building Press,1993.

[9] Clancy P, Randolph M F. Simple design tools for piled raft foundations[J]. Geotechnique,1996,46(2): 313-328.

[10] Meyerhof G G. Bearing platformacity and settlement of pile foundation [J]. Journal of Geotechnical Engineering, ASCE,1976,102(3): 531-537.

[11] Skempton A W, Northey R D. The sensitibity of clays [J]. Geotechnique,1953,39(1): 30-53.

[12] Castelli F, Maugeri M. Simplified nonlinear analysis for settlement prediction of pile groups [J]. Journal of Geotechnical and Geoenvironmental Engineering,2002(1): 76-84.

[13] Poulos H G, Davis E H. Pile foundation analysis and design [M]. New York: Wiley,1980.

[14] Shen W Y, Chow Y K, Yong K Y. Practical method for settlement analysis of pile groups [J]. Journal of Geotechnical and Geoenvironmental Engineering,2000(11): 890-897.

[15] Polo J M, Clemente J L M. Pile-group settlement using independent shaft and point load[J]. Journal of Geotechnical Engineering, ASCE,1988,114(4): 469-487.

[16] Lee C Y. Pile group settlement analysis by hybrid layer approach [J]. Journal of Geotechnical Engineering, ASCE,1993,119(6): 984-997.

[17] RANDOLPHMF, WROTHCP. An analysis of the vertical deformation of pile-groups[J]. Géotechnique, 1979,29(4):423-439.

[18] MYLONAKISG, GAZETASG. Settle mentand addition alinternal forces of grouped pile sinlayered soil[J]. Géotechnique,1998,48(1):55-72.

[19] Zhang GQQ, Zhang ZM. A simplified calculation approach for settlement of single pile and pilegroups[J]. Journal of Computing in Civil Engineering,2012,26(6):750-758.

中等跨径钢-混凝土组合箱梁桥负弯矩区力学性能研究

姬子田[1]　张之恒[1]　程高[1,2,3]　谢亮[1]　王鹏琪[1]

(1.长安大学公路学院；2.陕西省公路桥梁与隧道重点实验室；
3.旧桥检测与加固技术交通行业重点实验室(西安))

摘要　为研究墩顶横梁内充填混凝土对中等跨径钢箱组合梁桥负弯矩区受力性能的影响,基于对K146+177.763阜城村G211分离立交桥进行的前期实时数据采集,建立有限元数值分析模型,其有效性得到理论与试验数据的验证。运用有限元方法对模型计算结果进行对比分析,并以填充混凝土的强度等级作为变量进行参数分析。研究结果表明:墩顶填充混凝土可以有效地降低负弯矩区钢梁下翼缘的应力;考虑墩顶横梁内充填混凝土作用后,桥梁的结构刚度略有提高,中跨跨中挠度及底板受力略有减少;改大横梁内混凝土强度等级,对钢箱组合梁桥内力及变形的变化幅度影响不大,最大变化幅度不超过4%。由有限元模型计算得到的结构特征内力和位移与理论、实测结果吻合较好,可为中等跨径钢-混凝土组合箱梁桥负弯矩区的设计与研究提供参考。

关键词　桥梁工程　力学性能　现场实测试验　钢-混凝土组合箱梁　负弯矩区　有限元分析

0 引言

钢-混凝土组合梁因其材料的优点即混凝土受压性能好,钢材可以承受较大拉力,并且结构轻巧,厂内可实现快速预制和装配,施工便捷,缩短工期,在桥梁工程领域得以广泛使用。组合梁桥按照受力通常可以分为简支组合梁桥和连续组合梁桥。与简支组合梁桥相比,连续组合梁桥正负弯矩分配合理,使跨中正弯矩大幅度减少,结构跨越能力增强、提高了其刚度和结构整体性能[1]。箱型截面是一种薄壁闭口截面,抗弯抗扭性能得到改善,可抵抗正负弯矩,广泛应用于连续梁桥。然而,连续梁在中间支点位置附近不可避免的会产生负弯矩使这部分桥面板受拉多发生混凝土开裂,中性轴以下钢箱梁下翼缘受到压力会发生局部失稳现象,减少结构的使用年限,限制了钢-混凝土组合箱梁桥的发展,也使得研究组合梁桥负弯矩区力学性能成为一种趋势。

针对负弯矩附近截面中性轴以上桥面板多发生混凝土开裂问题,近些年来国内外学者投入了大量的试验与理论研究。聂建国等[2]提出一种新型的抗拔不抗剪连接件新技术,研发连接件的构造形式,并进行大量的性能对比试验,表明这种新型连接件具有很好的力学性能,在不削弱负弯矩区结构的极限抗弯承载力和刚度的同时,可以显著降低桥面板混凝土的开裂。刘永健等[3]提出了在负弯矩区的混凝土桥面板里面布置预应力钢筋并使用抗拔不抗剪的连接件形成组合桁梁结构,通过在跨中位置施加反向的集中荷载来模拟连续梁中间支点的受力,对2榀矩形钢管混凝土组合桁梁结构进行试验加载,表明采用在混凝土桥面板内置预应力钢筋与局部释放剪切作用的连接件形成的组合桁梁结构可以显著降低桥面板混凝土的开裂,但对结构抗弯承载力影响不明显。欧阳政[4]分析了正负弯矩区不同的混凝土强度等级、不同抗剪连接程度、不同混凝土翼板处横向配筋率对连续组合梁结构承载能力、界面黏结滑移、挠度、负弯矩开裂荷载的影响。桥面板采取钢纤维混凝土的方法[5-7]、合理变换施工阶段、改进施工工艺[8-10]或分析对比不同连接件力学性能[11]等改善结构负弯矩区桥面板混凝土开裂。目前,钢-混凝土组合结构桥面板混凝土防开裂的方法总体可以归纳为:纵向配置预应力钢筋、群钉技术、梁底填筑混凝土形成双层组合梁、改进施工方法等[2]。周安等[12]在负弯矩下对5根简支梁依照文献[13]提出的临界高厚比的要求进行承载能力试验,钢箱梁发生局部屈曲。刘洋等[14]对钢-混凝土组合梁结构在负弯矩区易发生畸变屈曲现象进行参数分析。Xu 等[15]对两跨钢箱组合梁的双层组合效应进行试验,表明双层组合可以缓解桥面板混凝土开裂,并且可以有效改善钢箱梁的局部稳定性能。聂建国等[16]进行相关实桥试验,表明双层组合对钢箱梁稳定性能影响是有利的,并且提高了结构刚度。

既有文献在解决钢-混凝土组合箱梁结构负弯矩区桥面板混凝土易开裂和钢梁易屈曲问题方面虽取得了一定的效果,但仍然存在一些不足,目前尚未形成优势突出的解决方案。本文以 K146 + 177.763 阜城村 G211 分离立交桥为工程背景,通过现场实桥试验,进行实时数据采集并建立非线性有限元全桥模型,对比分析了有限元计算结果与理论、实测结果,以墩顶填充混凝土的常用强度等级为变量进行参数分析,探讨墩顶横梁内充填混凝土对组合梁负弯矩区力学性能的影响。

1 工程案例分析

1.1 工程概况

K146 + 177.763 阜城村 G211 分离立交桥位于甘肃省庆城县马岭镇下午旗与卅铺镇阜城村交界处,桥跨设计是 30m + 40m + 30m,不含桥台侧墙在内,桥梁全长 100m,三跨一联等截面钢-混凝土组合梁桥(图1)。主梁采用多箱单室等高连续组合梁,截面中心处组合梁高 2m,全桥混凝土板厚 25/40cm,钢箱梁采用斜腹式开口截面,钢箱梁之间设小纵梁,增加混凝土板刚度,主梁横截面尺寸如图 2 所示,结构体系是连续体系。钢箱梁横隔板分为支点横隔板和跨中横隔板,均采用实腹式横隔板形式,横隔板间距按照 3.5m 或者 4m 一道布置,局部位置稍作调整,横隔板间腹板每隔 1m 设置一道竖向加劲肋,箱梁上翼缘宽度是 60cm,厚度是 2.5cm,斜腹板厚度是 1.6cm,底板厚为 2cm。桥面板与钢箱梁通过焊钉形成组合结构,共同受力。桥墩台均设置 GPZ(Ⅱ)支座,所有 DX 型支座均应顺桥向放置,桥墩墩顶横梁内填充 C50 无收缩混凝土,C50 无收缩混凝土应符合现行国家标准《混凝土结构设计规范》的规定。无收缩混凝土水胶比不宜大于 0.5,最小胶凝材料用量 360kg/m³,混凝土膨胀剂用量 30-50kg/m³,桥面板限制膨胀率设计值不小于 0.02%,无收缩混凝土的配合比设计,应该满足设计所需要的强度、膨胀性能、抗渗性、耐久性等技术指标和施工工作性能要求。施工方法简便、快捷,填充的混凝土与横隔梁、箱梁底板形成组合形式,参与结构受力。

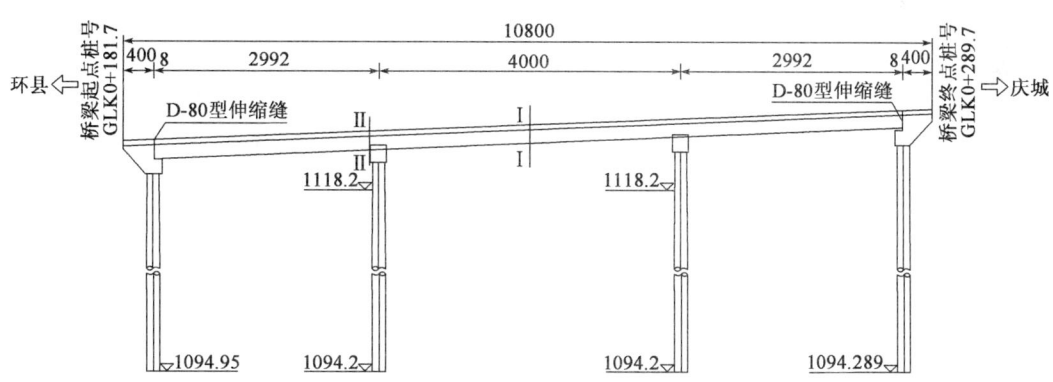

图 1 K146 + 177.763 阜城村 G211 分离立交总体布置图(尺寸单位:cm)

1.2 数据采集

依据连续组合箱梁桥的受力特点,对桥梁施工阶段全过程进行实时数据收集。主要的施工阶段有:现场拼装钢箱梁、绑扎桥面板钢筋并浇筑正弯矩区混凝土、预压堆载、拆除临时支架、浇筑负弯矩区混凝土、卸除预压堆载、桥面二期铺装等附属设施。主要测试项目有:全桥挠度变化,中跨跨中截面(Ⅰ-Ⅰ)截面应变,中支点截面(Ⅱ-Ⅱ)截面应变,主桥挠度变化采集使用精密水准仪,测点沿纵桥向平均布置,充分保证精度要求。控制截面应变采用 JMZX-3001L 智能弦式数码应变计。挠度及应变各测点布置如图 2 所示。

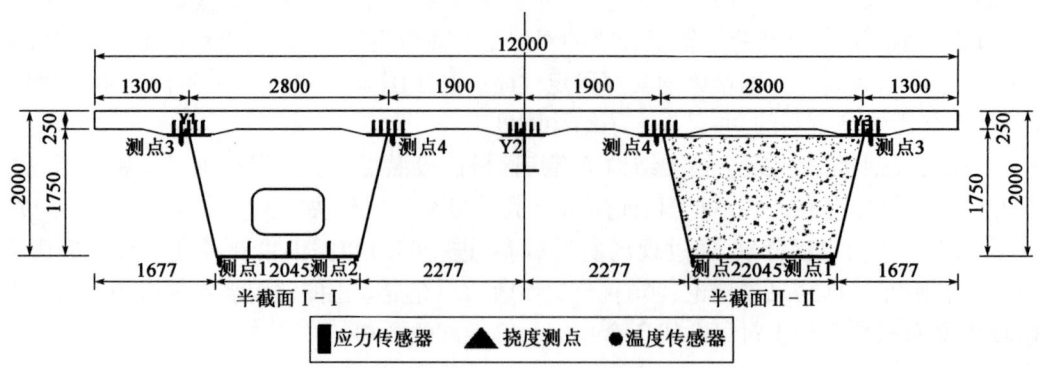

图 2 K146+177.763 阜城村 G211 分离立交横断面图(尺寸单位:mm)

2 有限元数值分析

2.1 有限元模型的建立

采用有限元软件 ABAQUS 建立实桥模型,保证满足计算精度的前提下,简化模型仅对单片主梁进行模拟,如图 3 所示。为探讨墩顶填充混凝土的作用,按照横梁内是否考虑填充混凝土作为主要变量分别建立模型,钢-混凝土组合梁桥有限元仿真模型共有 8 部分组成,即混凝土桥面板、钢筋网、钢梁、底板加劲肋、腹板加劲肋、填充混凝土块、横隔板、支座。钢材与混凝土的力学性能如表 1、表 2 所示。

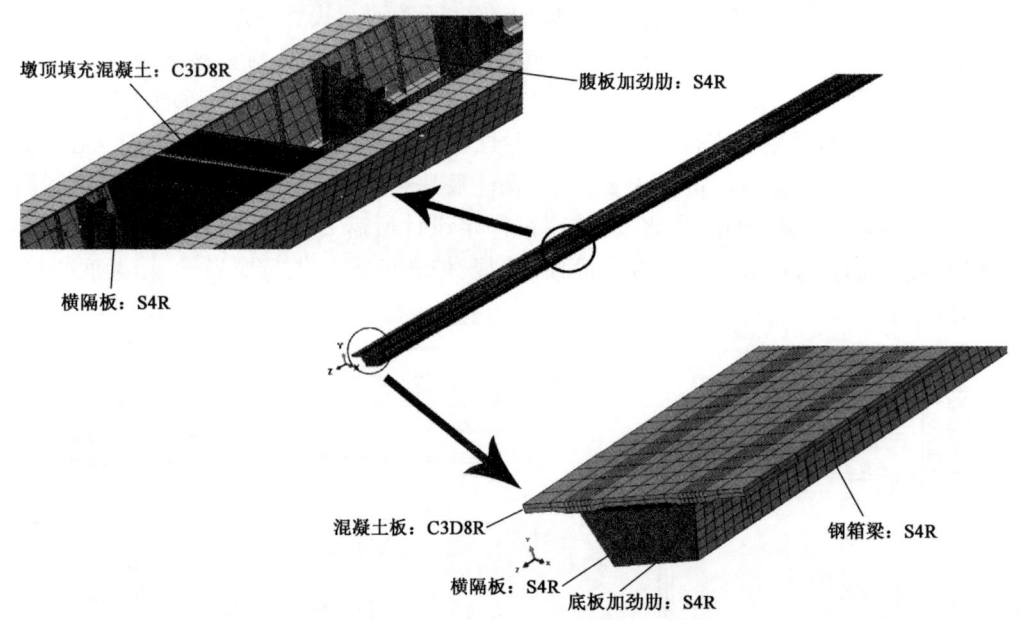

图 3 有限元模型

有限元分析模型采用的钢材力学性能   表 1

名 称	f_y(MPa)	f_u/f_y	E(MPa)	v	ρ(t/mm³)
钢梁	345	1.42	2.06×10^5	0.25~0.3	7.85×10^{-9}
钢筋	400	1.35	2×10^5	0.3	7.85×10^{-9}
加劲肋	345	1.42	2.06×10^5	0.25~0.3	7.85×10^{-9}
横隔板	345	1.42	2.06×10^5	0.25~0.3	7.85×10^{-9}
支座	345	1.42	2.06×10^5	0.25~0.3	—

注:f_y-屈服强度;f_u-抗拉强度;E-弹性模量;v-泊松比;ρ-质量密度。

有限元分析模型采用的混凝土力学性能 表2

名 称	f_c(MPa)	f_t(MPa)	E(MPa)	v	ρ(t/mm)^3
混凝土桥面板	32.4	2.65	3.45×10^4	0.2	2.6×10^{-9}
填充混凝土块	32.4	2.65	3.45×10^4	0.2	2.6×10^{-9}

注:f_c-混凝土轴心抗压强度;f_t-混凝土抗拉强度;E-弹性模量;v-泊松比;ρ-质量密度。

混凝土桥面板、支座、填充混凝土块用实体单元C3D8R;钢筋选用桁架单元T3D2;钢箱梁、加劲肋、横隔板采用减缩积分壳单元S4R。满足计算精度的要求下,忽略混凝土板内钢筋及钢梁翼缘与混凝土板的剪切-滑移作用,钢筋网与混凝土板之间用Embedded方式,将钢筋嵌入混凝土中,两者协同工作。混凝土填充块体与钢梁、钢梁底板与临时支架之间用面面接触;支座与钢梁底板,加劲肋、横隔板与钢梁之间采用Tie命令,使它们相互绑定在一起。

2.2 结果验证与分析

三跨连续钢-混组合箱梁桥,依照结构力学的力法方法,通过简化结构形式,求解支座反力得出的理论结果与有限元计算结果对比如表3所示。Z1-Z4表示图1中所示从左至右的支座编号,工况一表示浇筑负弯矩区混凝土施工阶段,工况二表示桥面二期铺装施工阶段。

支座反力理论计算与有限元计算的比较 表3

编号	工 况 一			工 况 二		
	RT1/N	RT2/N	RT2/RT1	RT1/N	RT2/N	RT2/RT1
Z1	677164.04	722553	1.07	967537.94	1051230	1.09
Z2	2207168.22	2106940	0.95	3371794.32	3260800	0.97
Z3	2207168.22	2110600	0.96	3371794.32	3264690	0.97
Z4	677164.04	721288	1.07	967537.94	1049900	1.09

注:RT1为支座反力理论结果;RT2为支座反力有限元计算结果。

表3是理论解与数值解获得的支反力大小比较,可见,两者吻合较好,相差在10%以内。

图4依次为工况一和工况二两个施工阶段主梁实测挠度与有限元计算结果对比,计算值1代表考虑墩顶填充混凝土作用的有限元计算结果,计算值2代表未考虑墩顶填充混凝土的有限元计算结果。

由桥长-变形值折线图可见,两种工况下主桥的刚度实测值与有限元计算结果图形变化趋势相同,大小也基本一致。随着结构恒载加大,主梁的实测变形与有限元变形值逐渐增加。其中,从计算值1与计算值2结果可以看出,墩顶考虑填充混凝土效应可以提高桥梁的结构刚度,降低了负弯矩区内结构的向上挠曲变形,但对主梁刚度的贡献并不明显。

图5和图6依次是截面Ⅰ-Ⅰ及截面Ⅱ-Ⅱ钢箱梁底板有限元计算结果所得应变对比情况,横坐标分别表示现场拼装钢箱梁、绑扎桥面板钢筋并浇筑正弯矩区混凝土、预压堆载、拆除临时支架、浇筑负弯矩区混凝土、卸除预压堆载、施工桥面二期铺装7个施工阶段。从图中不难看出,箱梁底板应变随施工阶段的不同呈现不断累积的过程,拆除临时支架后应变会有很大增加,施工过程中应该注意该阶段结构产生不合理变形;考虑墩顶填充混凝土时,中跨跨中截面底板应变略有减小,但是影响不大;截面Ⅱ-Ⅱ箱梁底板应变由有限元计算结果对比可知,两个计算值相差较大,桥面二期铺装等附属设施完成时,两种模型计算得到的钢箱梁底板应变相差47%。表明在墩顶箱内填充混凝土后,可以显著限制钢箱截面的变形,混凝土代替钢梁参与受压,有效地降低钢箱梁下翼缘的应力,提高其局部稳定性,在实际设计过程中不用在负弯矩区专门设计厚钢板,减少了用钢量,为现场施工带来方便。

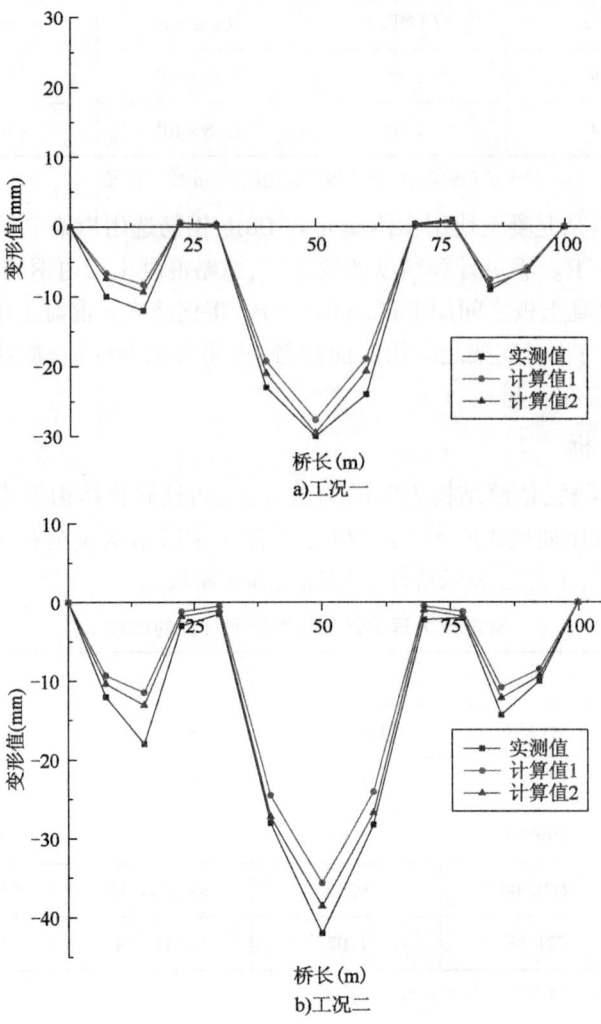

a) 工况一

b) 工况二

图4 不同工况作用下全桥变形对比

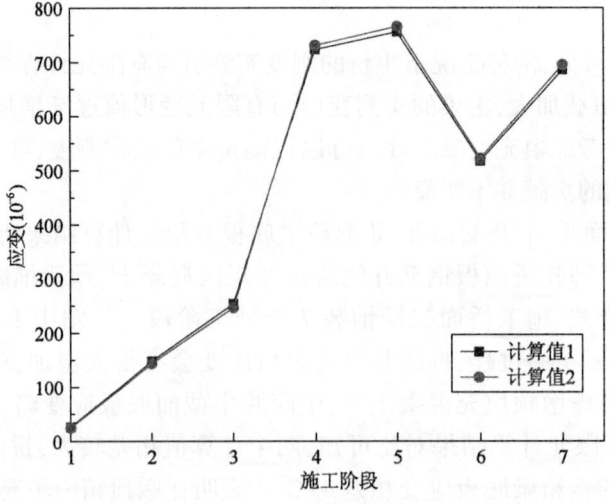

图5 截面Ⅰ-Ⅰ钢箱梁底板应变

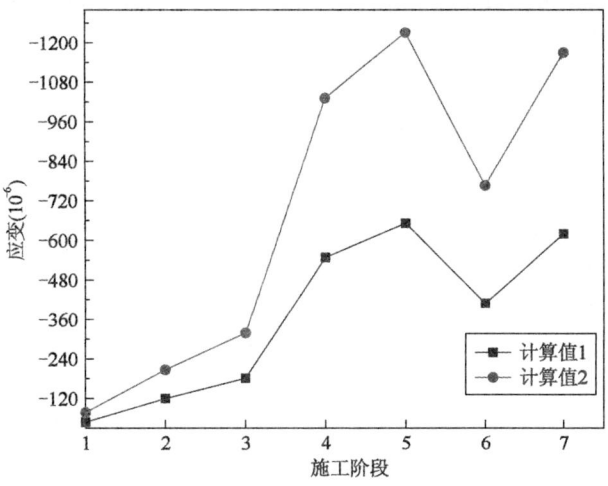

图 6　截面 Ⅱ-Ⅱ 钢箱梁底板应变

3　参数分析

为考察墩顶充填混凝土对钢-混凝土组合箱梁桥整体力学行为的影响,对 K146+177.763 阜城村 G211 分离立交桥建立有限元全桥模型,以填充混凝土的强度等级为变量进行参数分析。依据已建成的桥梁实例,常用混凝土的强度等级范围是 C30～C60,图 7 给出钢-混凝土组合连续梁桥内力及变形随混凝土强度等级的变化情况。图中 S_0 和 U_0 表示未考虑填充混凝土作用时对应截面的应变与变形;从图 7 可以看出,考虑填充混凝土作用后,连续梁支点底板应变明显减少,中跨挠度略有减小。混凝土强度等级由 C30 加大到 C60,上述作用有所提高,但是变化幅度不大,并呈逐渐放缓趋势,最大变化幅度不超过 4%。综合墩顶填充混凝土对钢箱组合连续梁桥的影响,考虑到施工便捷性,墩顶填充混凝土宜与混凝土桥面板强度等级保持一致。

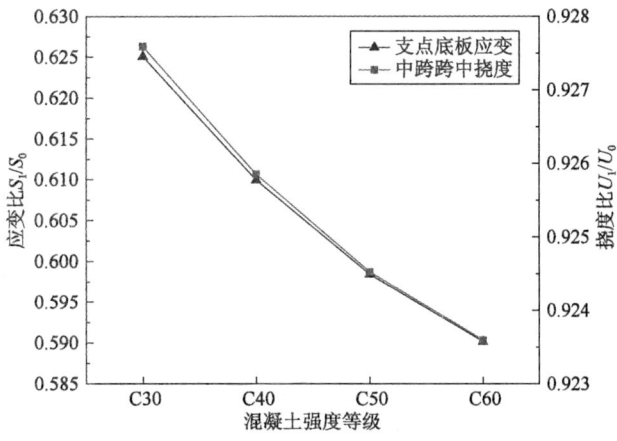

图 7　钢箱组合梁桥内力及变形随混凝土强度等级变化

4　结　语

本文基于对 K146+177.763 阜城村 G211 分离立交桥进行实桥实时数据采集,建立考虑施工阶段的有限元全桥模型,通过有限元仿真计算与理论、实测结果对比分析,并对墩顶横梁内充填混凝土的重要变量混凝土强度等级进行参数分析,得出以下几点结论:

(1)中等跨径钢-混凝土组合箱梁桥中支点处充填混凝土,可以参与结构受力,提高桥梁的整体刚度,降低了负弯矩区内结构的向上挠曲变形,但对主梁刚度的贡献并不明显。

(2)考虑墩顶填充混凝土效应对负弯矩区钢梁受力影响较大,可以有效的降低钢箱梁下翼缘的应力,提高钢箱梁的结构稳定性。

(3)改变墩顶横梁内混凝土强度等级,对钢箱组合梁桥内力及变形的影响幅度不大,考虑到施工的便捷性,墩顶填充混凝土宜与混凝土桥面板强度等级保持一致。

参考文献

[1] 羊海林,郑艳,莫时旭.负弯矩区部分充填混凝土对窄幅钢箱-混凝土组合梁受力性能影响试验研究[J].建筑结构学报,2019,40(11):131-139.

[2] 聂建国,陶慕轩,聂鑫,等.抗拔不抗剪连接新技术及其应用[J].土木工程学报,2015,48(04):7-14.

[3] 刘永健,王康宁,刘彬,等.矩形钢管混凝土组合桁梁负弯矩区受力性能试验研究[J].建筑结构学报,2019,40(09):74-83.

[4] 欧阳政.钢-混凝土连续组合梁受力性能及负弯矩区开裂分析[D].长沙:长沙理工大学,2017.

[5] HAMODA A, HOSSAIN K M A, SENNAH K, et al. Behaviour of composite high performance concrete slab on steel I-beams subjected to static hogging moment [J]. Engineering Structures, 2017, 140:51-65.

[6] Lin W, YODA T, TANIGUCHI N. Application of SFRC in steel-concrete composite beams subjected to hogging moment [J]. J Constr Steel Res (UK), 2014, 101:175-183.

[7] 周安,戴航,刘其伟.体内预应力钢纤维混凝土-钢组合梁负弯矩区抗裂及裂缝宽度试验研究[J].建筑结构学报,2007,28(03):82-90.

[8] 梁心普.中支点顶升法控制钢混组合梁桥面板裂缝[J].科技创新与应用,2019,(09):115-117.

[9] 朱家海.连续组合梁桥负弯矩区支点顶升施工受力研究[J].中外公路,2014,34(03):110-113.

[10] 郑和晖,巫兴发,黄跃,等.钢-混组合连续梁负弯矩区桥面板抗裂措施[J].中外公路,2014,34(05):152-155.

[11] 彭元诚,刘玉擎.大宁河特大桥钢-混组合连续梁负弯矩区受力特性模型试验研究[J].世界桥梁,2012,40(01):28-31.

[12] 周安,戴航,刘其伟.钢箱-预应力混凝土组合梁负弯矩区结构性能试验研究[J].土木工程学报,2009,42(12):69-75.

[13] 樊健生,聂建国,吴道闻.钢-混凝土组合梁弹性屈曲的力学性能[J].清华大学学报(自然科学版),2004,44(06):786-788.

[14] 刘洋,童乐为,孙波,等.负弯矩作用下钢-混凝土组合梁受力性能有限元分析及受弯承载力计算[J].建筑结构学报,2014,35(10):10-20.

[15] XU C, SU Q, WU C, et al. Experimental study on double composite action in the negative flexural region of two-span continuous composite box girder [J]. J Constr Steel Res (UK), 2011, 67(10):1636-1648.

[16] 聂建国,李法雄,樊健生,等.大跨钢-混凝土连续组合箱梁桥双重组合作用[J].清华大学学报(自然科学版),2012,52(02):133-138.

Study on Shrinkage of Concrete with Multi Row Stud Connectors in Steel-concrete Composite Beams

Shuaishuai Zhang   Laijun Liu   Changjiang Yu   Peiqi He

(School of Highway, Chang'an University)

Abstract To study the shrinkage performance of high strength concrete confined by studs, based on the engineering background, a single row of high-strength concrete confined by single row of studs was designed by experimental research and numerical method. The model was established and analyzed. The results were compared with the experimental results to prove the feasibility of the model. The model of high-strength concrete with multiple rows of studs is established and analyzed, and the results are compared with that of single row of studs. The results show that: no matter single row or multi row, the maximum stress of high-strength concrete is located at the root of the stud; Compared with the single row of studs, the multi row studs have a certain inhibitory effect on the stress range of high-strength concrete; For the maximum stress of the structure, the multi row studs do not effectively reduce the maximum stress of the composite structure. The research results of this paper provide a reference for crack control of steel-concrete composite structure under stud restraint during construction.

Keywords Steel-concrete composite structure   Shrinkage of concrete   Experimental study   Finite element analysis   Stud connector

0 Introduction

Steel concrete composite structure is widely used in buildings and bridges because it can give full play to the high tensile strength and ductility of steel, high compressive strength and low heat transfer rate of concrete. The types of steel-concrete composite structure are generally divided into four types: stud connector, PBL shear connector, PZ shear connector and embedded corrugated steel plate shear connector. The composite structure of stud and concrete is more used. However, in a large number of practical projects, the composite structure of stud and concrete is seriously cracked. This is because high-strength concrete is widely used in the composite structure of stud and concrete. The stud has a certain restraint effect on the shrinkage deformation of concrete, and there is a high constraint stress inside, which leads to the early crack of high-strength and high-performance concrete in the use process. When the composite structure of stud and high strength concrete has serious concrete cracking, it not only affects the applicable function of the structure, but also reduces the bearing capacity and durability of the structure.

In previous studies, scholars mainly focus on the structural performance of steel-concrete composite structure[1-7]. In 2010, Nie Jianguo et al. Carried out the research on the shear bearing capacity of stud connectors in steel-concrete composite beams through push-out test[1]. In 2014, Ding faxing et al. Studied the influence of stud diameter and stud yield strength on the shear bearing capacity of three groups of stud shear connectors [7]. Some scholars [8-12] have studied the shrinkage of reinforced concrete. In 2003, West et al. Measured the drying shrinkage of high-strength concrete under different internal constraints and made a comparative study[8]. In 2004, Wang Jiyue studied the influence of concrete shrinkage stress under steel bar restraint[9], and Sivakumar in 2007 In 2006, Li Yue and others studied the influence of admixtures and admixtures on the early shrinkage performance of concrete under the constraint of reinforcement[11]. In 2009, Pan zuofeng et al. Studied the general law of the influence of reinforcement on the shrinkage and creep of high-strength concrete [12].

Throughout the research of domestic and foreign scholars, the research of steel plate concrete composite wall focuses on its structure, but little on its durability. Due to its complex coupling constraint, some scholars only study the shrinkage of high-strength concrete under the constraint of steel bars, and lack of relevant research on the shrinkage cracking of high-strength concrete under bolt restraint, only a few studies have been carried out on the effect of single row studs on the shrinkage of high strength concrete[13]. Therefore, this paper studies the influence of multi row studs on the shrinkage performance of high-strength concrete, and compares the shrinkage performance of high-strength concrete confined by single row of studs, so as to provide some reference for the influence of stud and high-strength concrete structure in steel-concrete composite structure.

1 Experimental Model Design

1.1 Research object

The engineering background of this study is a steel-concrete composite structure cable-stayed bridge. The superstructure of the cable-stayed bridge is composed of multiple rows of studs and high-strength concrete, which are welded on the upper plate of I-steel beam. Through the combination of studs and cast-in-situ high-strength concrete of wet joint, the wet joint high-strength concrete and precast bridge deck are connected together, which makes the precast prestressed concrete slab and steel beam bear the force together. Therefore, the structure of stud and high strength concrete is particularly important in the whole bridge. The site drawing of stud connector model is shown in Fig. 1.

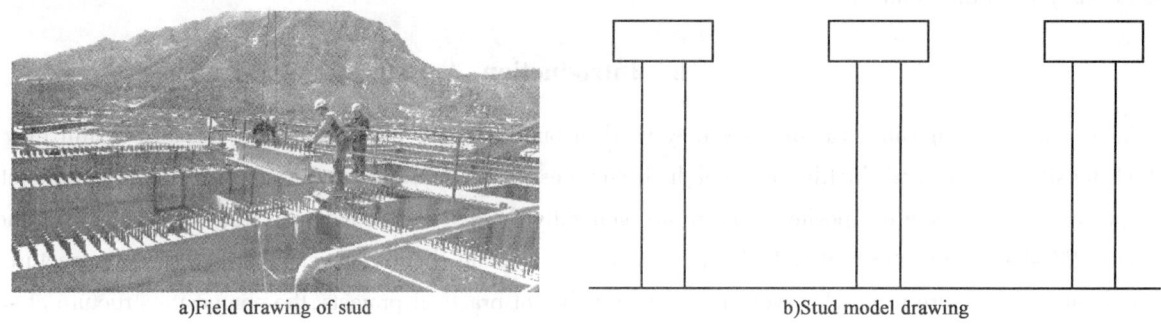

a) Field drawing of stud   b) Stud model drawing

Fig. 1 Structural Diagram of Stud

1.2 Model Design

1.2.1 Mix proportion design of high strength concrete

According to the engineering background test of this paper, based on the material mix proportion and strength of high-strength concrete, the model is established and the actual results are obtained. C60 high strength concrete is used in the test. Based on the engineering background, the concrete grinding tools are made, and the following C60 high-strength concrete model blocks are obtained, as shown in Fig. 2. The stud mold with various layout methods is welded in the steel welding plant, and the stud mold with one arrangement method is shown in Fig. 3.

Fig. 2 High Strength Concrete Test Bloc   Fig. 3 Stud Specimen

1.2.2 Experimental study on basic mechanical properties of high strength concrete

The basic mechanical property test of this test includes the test of compressive strength and elastic modulus of high-strength concrete, as shown in Fig. 4. The specification of compressive strength test block is 150mm ×

150mm, and the test time is 3d, 7 d, 14 d, 21 d and 28 d, with 3 blocks in each group; the elastic modulus test block is 150 mm × 150 mm × 300 mm, and the test time is also 3 d, 7 d, 14 d, 21 d and 28 d groups, with 3 test blocks in each group.

1.3 Test Results

In the test, all the test blocks are cured under the same conditions, and the main stress of concrete depends on the compressive capacity of concrete, so the compressive strength of concrete is one of the most important indexes to measure the basic mechanical properties of concrete. The compressive strength of concrete increases with the age of concrete. Elastic modulus is also one of the important indicators of concrete, which is a measure of the strength of concrete plasticity. In construction, the concrete often reaches the compressive strength, and the elastic modulus does not reach the standard or the compressive strength does not reach the index, so the elastic modulus of concrete needs to be paid more attention in the construction. The results of compressive strength and elastic modulus of high strength concrete at different ages are shown in Tab. 1.

Compressive Strength and Elastic Modulus of Concrete at Different Ages Tab. 1

Age	3d	7d	14d	21d	28d
Compressive strength (MPa)	40.1	52.5	56.33	61.66	67.2
Modulus of elasticity (GPa)	32.2	34.5	35.8	37.5	38.8

a) Compressive strength test   b) Elastic modulus test

Fig. 4 Mechanical Property Test

The line chart of compressive strength and elastic modulus results is shown in Fig. 5、Fig. 6.

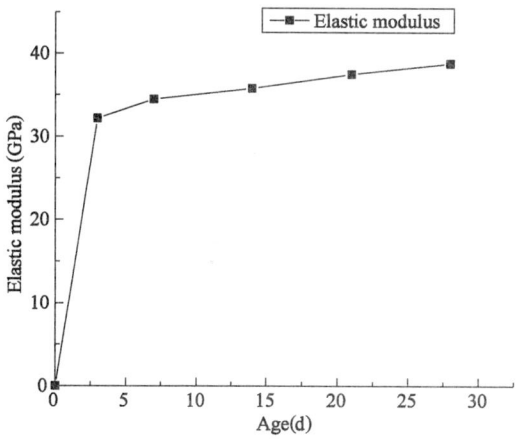
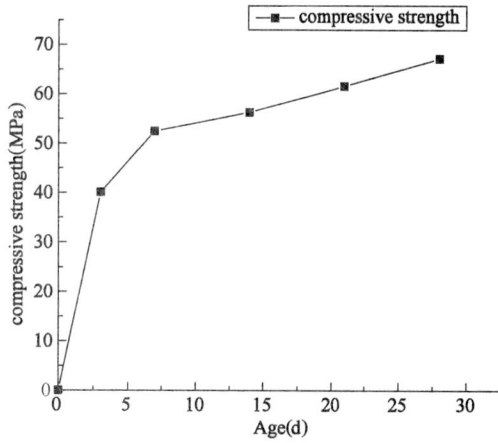

Fig. 5 Line Chart of Compressive Strength and Age of Concrete

Fig. 6 Line Chart of Elastic Modulus and Age of Concrete

In order to compare and analyze the reliability of the simulation results of finite element software, the test results of single row studs with diameter of 22, height of 80 and spacing of 200 were compared with the results of finite element numerical simulation. The comparison results are shown in Tab. 2.

Tab. 2 Results and Test Results of Group 9 High Strength Concrete Restrained by Studs

Age (d)	3	7	14	21	28
Test shrinkage deformation (10^{-6})	75.53	203.63	200.36	277.37	310.71
Model shrinkage deformation (10^{-6})	68.61	227.39	195.22	270.00	319.13
Error between model and test (%)	-9.16%	11.67%	-2.57%	-2.66%	2.71%

It can be seen from the above table that the maximum absolute error of the model and the test is 11.67%, the minimum is 2.57%, and the average absolute error is 5.754%. The results are in good agreement, which shows that the high-strength concrete structure under the restraint of single row studs established by ANSYS finite element analysis software is reliable. Therefore, this method can be used to further analyze the shrinkage of high-strength concrete and the stress of high-strength concrete under the restraint of multiple rows of studs.

2 Finite Element Analysis

2.1 Model Establishment

2.1.1 Geometric model

The finite element analysis software ANSYS is used to analyze the influence of high-strength concrete shrinkage under the restraint of single row and multiple rows of studs. The simulation elements of stud and high-strength concrete are solid elements, and the unit number is SOLID65, which has the performance of tensile cracking and crushing. The contact relationship between high-strength concrete and stud adopts the point-to-point non slip connection mode. Since the stud is a cylinder and the high-strength concrete is a cuboid, the free mesh generation technology is used to mesh the model. The geometric model is shown in Fig. 7. The mesh generation is shown in Fig. 8.

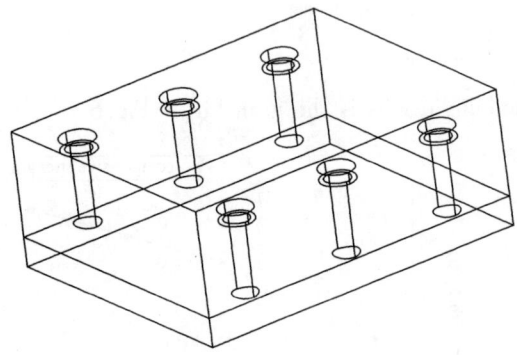
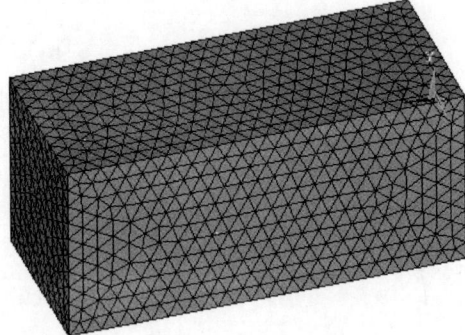

Fig. 7 Geometric Model   Fig. 8 Model Meshing

2.1.2 Structural parameters

There are four factors influencing the constraint of different types of studs, which are diameter of studs, height of studs, spacing of studs, and rows of studs. The analysis and design method adopted is the control variable method, with other factors as the constant value, and the row number of studs as variables, which are single row, three rows and six rows respectively. The specific geometric parameters of the model are shown in Tab. 3, and the material parameters are shown in Tab. 4.

Geometric Parameters of the Model   Tab. 3

number	Diameter (mm)	Height (mm)	Spacing (mm)	Row number
1	22(30)	80	200	1
2	22(30)	80	200	3
3	22(30)	80	200	6

Calculation Parameters of Two Materials   Tab. 4

Parameter name	Elastic modulus(MPa)	Density(kg/m^3)	Efficient of linear expansion	Poisson's ratio
concrete	1.3	2368.4	1×10^{-5}	0.2
Stud	2.06×10^5	7850	1.2×10^{-5}	0.3

2.1.3 Load cases

In order to better simulate the actual situation, this paper uses the temperature method to convert the shrinkage of plain concrete into temperature load. The calculation of temperature method is shown in formula (1).

$$T_{(T)} = \varepsilon_{(T)} / \alpha_C \tag{1}$$

Where: $T_{(T)}$——shrinkage temperature;

$\varepsilon_{(T)}$——early shrinkage strain of concrete;

α_C——thermal expansion coefficient of concrete, value.

According to the above formula, the equivalent shrinkage temperature of concrete can be obtained as shown in Tab. 5.

Temperature and Shrinkage Strain   Tab. 5

Age(d)	0	3	7	14	21	28
Shrinkage strain(10^{-6})	0	117	246	275	380	404
Temperature(℃)	0	-11.7	-24.6	-27.5	-38.0	-40.4

2.2 Discussion

ANSYS software is used to establish single row, three row and six row stud models to analyze the influence of studs on concrete shrinkage deformation and stress results, focusing on the analysis of concrete stress and deformation under the influence of multiple rows of studs, and comparing with the results of single row of studs, so as to discuss the influence of different rows of studs on the overall structure.

2.2.1 Analysis of shrinkage deformation results of multi row studs

The structural models of single row, three row and six row studs are established respectively, and the axial displacements of the models at 3D, 7d, 14d, 21d and 28d are analyzed. Due to the space, the deformation diagram of high-strength concrete model under the constraint of studs at 28d is only shown here, as shown in Fig. 9-Fig. 11.

From the front view, it can be seen that the shrinkage deformation of high-strength concrete under the restraint of multiple rows of studs is symmetrical laterally, and the shrinkage from the middle to both sides is increasing. From the same section, it can be seen that except for a small part of the middle part, the shrinkage of the bottom and the top is the same, and the shrinkage of the rest parts is greater than that of the bottom.

From the side view, it can be seen that the simulated shrinkage deformation of high-strength concrete under the restraint of multiple rows of studs shows a wave line trend, and the section at the stud is upward convex. This is because of the restraint effect of the stud, the shrinkage of high-strength concrete at the stud is less than that between the stud and the stud.

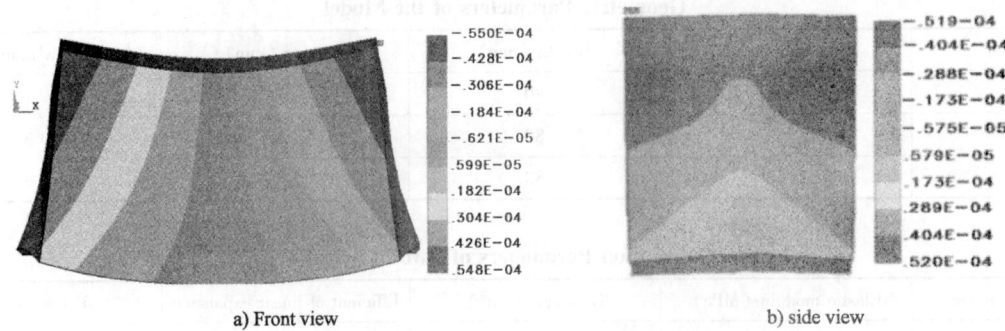

Fig. 9　Deformation Diagram of Single Row Studs

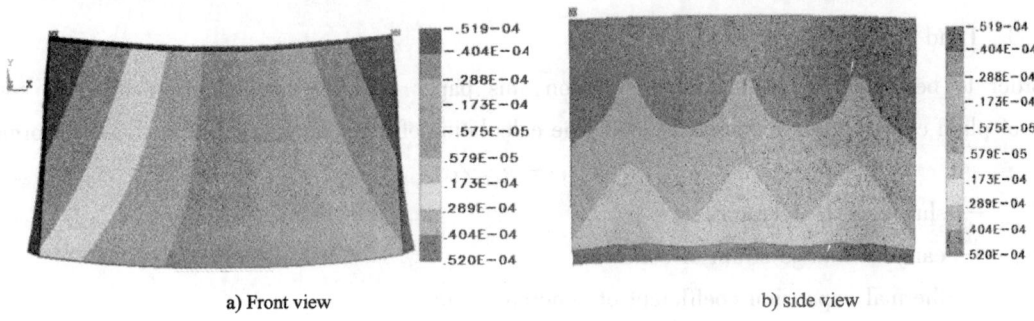

Fig. 10　Deformation Diagram of 3 Rows of Studs

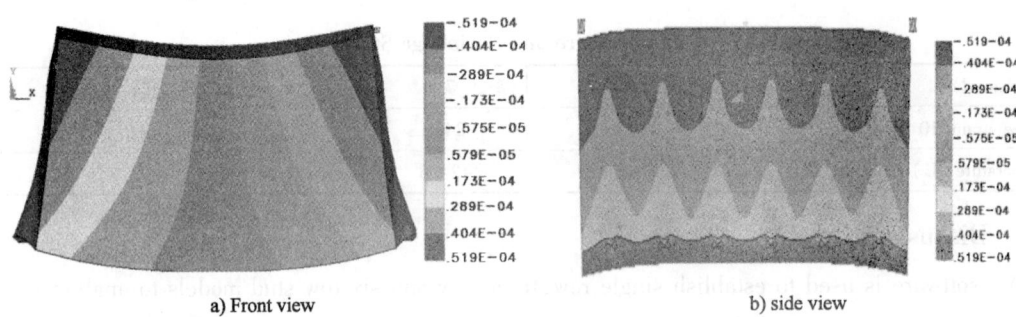

Fig. 11　Deformation Diagram of 6 Rows of Studs

On the other hand, it can be seen that the high-strength concrete shrinkage between the bottom of the stud and the bottom of the stud is smaller than that of the high-strength concrete at the bottom of the edge stud, which indicates that the binding effect of multiple rows of studs on the high-strength concrete between the studs is greater than that of the edge high-strength concrete. The deformation values of concrete under the restraint of multi row studs and single row studs are shown in Tab. 6.

Comparison of Overall Shrinkage of Test Blocks at Different Ages　　　　Tab. 6

Age(d)	3	7	14	21	28
Shrinkage of single row stud concrete(10^{-6})	68.61	227.39	195.22	270.00	319.13
Concrete shrinkage of 3 rows of studs(10^{-6})	70.22	206.52	219.13	251.30	300.87
Concrete shrinkage of 6 rows of studs(10^{-6})	63.30	206.48	219.14	251.31	301.30
Ratio of difference between 3 rows and single row in single row(%)	2.35%	-9.18%	12.25%	-6.93%	-5.72%
Ratio of difference between 6 rows and single row in single row(%)	-7.74%	-9.20%	12.25%	-6.92%	-5.59%

In order to better compare the constraints of single row and multi row studs on the shrinkage deformation of concrete, the deformation values of concrete with different ages and rows are plotted as shown in Fig. 12.

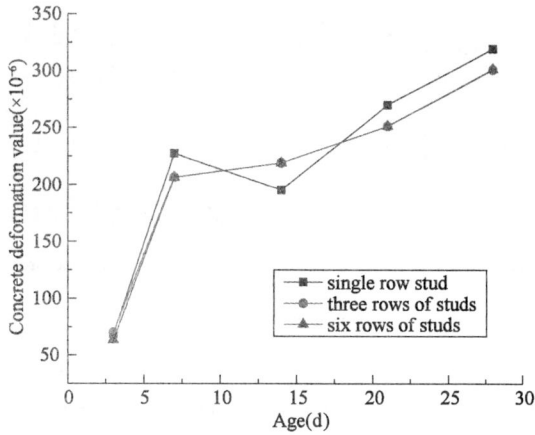

Fig. 12 Deformation Value of Concrete at Different Ages

It can be seen from the chart that the overall shrinkage of high-strength concrete under the restraint of multiple rows of studs is almost less than that of high-strength concrete under the restraint of single row of studs at the age of 0-28 days. In general, multi row studs can better restrain the overall shrinkage of high-strength concrete than single row studs, and it has better inhibition effect on the shrinkage ratio of high-strength concrete between studs and studs and edge of high-strength concrete.

2.2.2 Result analysis of shrinkage stress under multi row studs

When the plain high strength concrete shrinks freely, it will not produce large stress because it is not restrained. However, the high-strength concrete under the restraint of the stud can not freely shrink due to the restraint of the stud, which will produce large stress. When the stress exceeds the ultimate tensile bearing capacity of the high-strength concrete, cracks will occur. Therefore, in this paper, the model of high-strength concrete under the restraint of single row of studs and the model of high-strength concrete with multiple rows of studs (3 rows, 6 rows) are analyzed and compared. Only the stress diagram of the stud structure at 28d age is shown here, as shown in Fig. 13-Fig. 15.

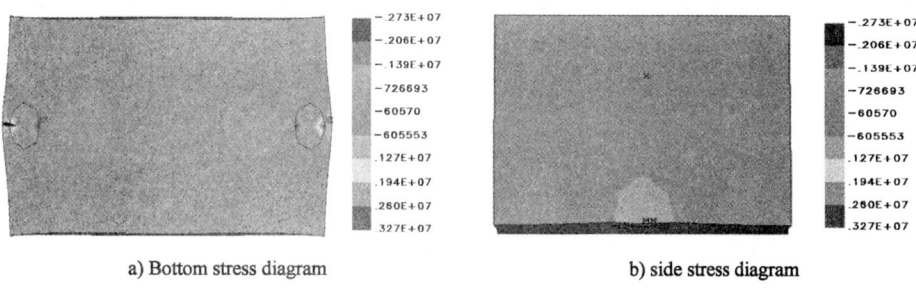

Fig. 13 Stress Diagram of Single Row Studs

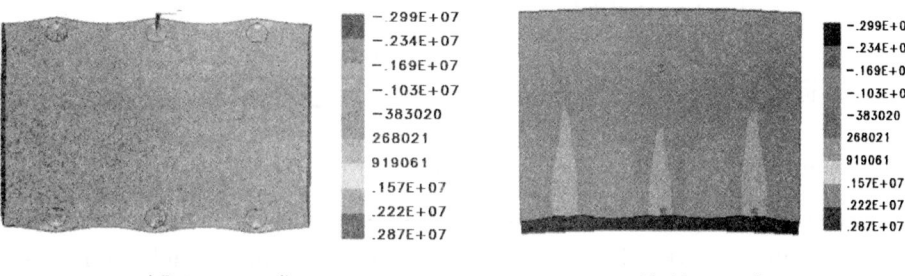

Fig. 14 Stress Diagram of 3 Rows of Studs

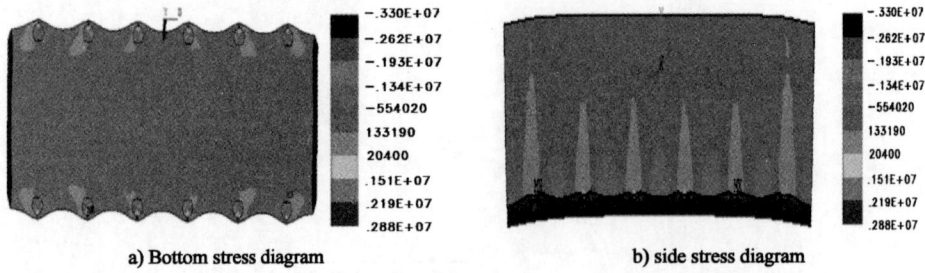

a) Bottom stress diagram b) side stress diagram

Fig. 15　Stress Diagram of 6 Rows of Studs

By comparing the stress diagrams of high-strength concrete under the restraint of single row of studs, three rows of studs and six rows of studs, it can be seen that in the bottom stress diagram, the maximum stress of high-strength concrete under the restraint of single row of studs, three rows of studs and six rows of studs is at the root of studs, and the phenomenon of stress concentration appears at the bottom of studs. Compared with the high-strength concrete confined by single row of studs, the edge high-strength concrete between the bottom of stud and the bottom of stud does not produce local edge stress after 28 days of age, and the inward high-strength concrete does not produce large stress.

In order to quantitatively compare and analyze the concrete stress under the restraint of single row and multi row studs, the summary of concrete stress at different ages is shown in Tab. 7.

Comparison of Maximum Stress Values at Different Ages (MPa)　　Tab. 7

Age	Single row	3 rows	Difference between three row and single row	6 rows	Difference between six row and single row
3d	0.80	0.74	-0.06	0.27	-0.53
7d	2.15	2.00	-0.15	2.91	0.76
14d	2.24	2.07	-0.17	2.27	0.03
21d	2.88	2.64	-0.24	2.91	0.03
28d	3.27	2.99	-0.28	3.30	0.03

The broken line diagram is shown in Fig. 16、Fig. 17.

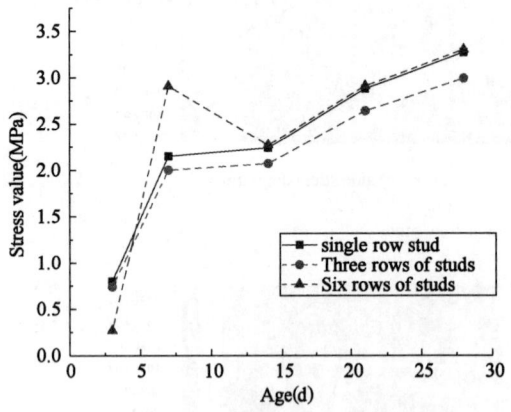
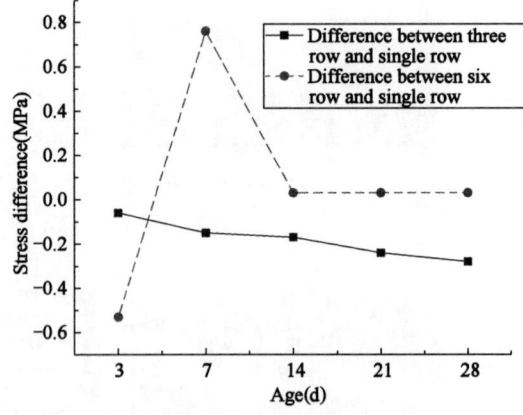

Fig. 16　Maximum Stress Diagram at Different Ages　　Fig. 17　Stress Difference between Single Row and Multi Row Studs

It can be seen from the above chart that the maximum stress of high-strength concrete under three rows of constraints is slightly less than that of high-strength concrete under single row of studs during 0-28 days, and that of high-strength concrete under 6-Row constraints is slightly greater than that of high-strength concrete under single row of studs during 3-28 days. The minimum value of the difference in the table is 0.03MPa, and the maximum value is 0.76MPa. For the stud reinforcement, the difference can be ignored. From the point of view of maximum stress value, compared with single row of studs, multi row studs do not effectively reduce the maximum stress value of stud and high strength concrete composite structure. Therefore, in practical engineering, the maximum stress value of components can not be ignored because of the increase of the number of stud rows.

The stress value of high-strength concrete at the root of stud and between stud and stud in side view is analyzed. The stress values of high-strength concrete confined by single row of studs and high-strength concrete with multiple rows of studs (3 rows and 6 rows) during 0-28 days are compared with the stress values of high-strength concrete at the root of studs and between the roots of studs, as shown in Tab. 8-Tab. 9.

Comparison of Maximum Stress Values at the Root of Studs (MPa)　　　Tab. 8

Age(d)	3	7	14	21	28
Single row stress value	0.22	0.60	0.63	0.82	0.94
3 rows of stress values	0.15	0.39	0.41	0.52	0.59
6 row stress value	0.13	0.32	0.33	0.42	0.48

Comparison of Maximum Stress Values of Concrete between Stud Roots (MPa)　　　Tab. 9

Age(d)	3	7	14	21	28
Single row stress value	0.11	0.28	0.29	0.36	0.39
3 rows of stress values	0.18	0.48	0.49	0.63	0.71
6 row stress value	0.22	0.59	0.62	0.79	0.90

The line chart is shown in Fig. 18、Fig. 19.

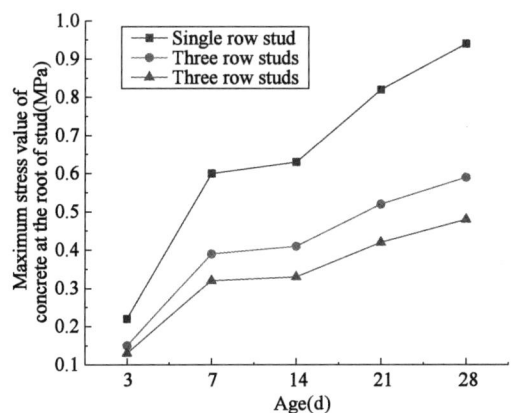

Fig. 18　Maximum Stress of Concrete At the Root of Stud at Different Ages

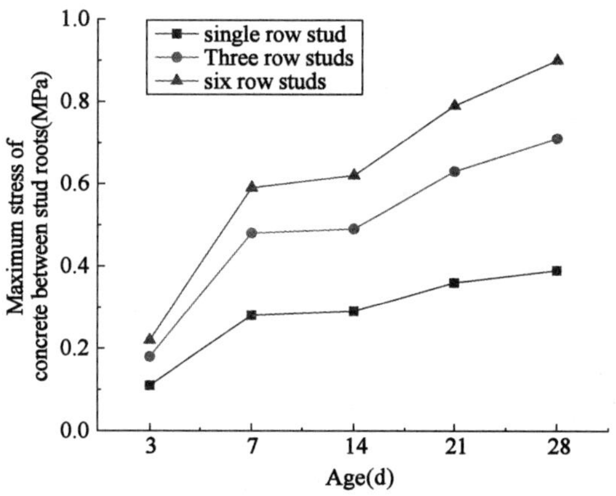

Fig. 19　Maximum Stress of Concrete between Studs at Different Ages

From the stress difference, it can be seen that the difference between the stress value of high-strength concrete under the restraint of six rows of studs and that of high-strength concrete under the restraint of single row of studs is greater than that of the stress value of high-strength concrete under the restraint of three rows of studs and that of single row of studs at the age of 0-28 days. It can be concluded that with the increase of the number of stud rows, the unloading effect on the stud root and the loading effect of high-strength concrete between the stud roots also increase.

3　Conclusion

(1) The x-direction deformation and shrinkage of high-strength concrete under the restraint of stud is left

and right symmetrical, and the shrinkage is basically the same. The shrinkage of the left and right ends of the test block bottom is much smaller than that of the top of the test block. From the analysis of the same section, except for the middle, the shrinkage of the bottom is smaller than that of the top.

(2) From the bottom stress diagram, compared with the high-strength concrete confined by single row of studs, the edge high-strength concrete between the bottom of the stud and the bottom of the stud does not produce local edge stress after 28 days of age, and the inward high-strength concrete does not produce large stress.

(3) The stress height of the stud increases with the increase of the number of stud rows, and the stress height of high-strength concrete between the stud and the stud decreases with the increase of the number of stud rows. With the increase of the number of stud rows, the stress height at the edge of the stud is significantly higher than that at the root of the middle stud. It can be concluded that, compared with the single row of studs, the multi row studs have a certain inhibitory effect on the stress range of high strength concrete.

(4) From the point of view of maximum stress value, compared with single row of studs, multi row studs do not effectively reduce the maximum stress value of stud and high strength concrete composite structure. Therefore, in practical engineering, the maximum stress value of the whole component cannot be ignored because of the increase of the number of stud rows.

References

[1] Jianguo Nie, Jiansheng Fan, et al. Experimental study on steel plate shear wall [J]. Journal of building structure,2010,09:1-8.

[2] Jianguo Nie. and Jie Zhao. Experimental study on steel plate concrete composite simply supported beams [J]. Acta civil engineering,2008,41:28-34.

[3] Xiaodong Ji,Xiangfu Jia,Jiaru Qian. Experimental study on shear performance of steel plate concrete shear wall [J]. Journal of building structure,2015,(11):46-55.

[4] Lanhui Guo, Qin Rong, Bing Qu,et al. Testing of steel plate shear walls with composite columns and infill plates connected to beams only [J]. Engineering Structures,2007,136:165-179.

[5] MuWang Wei, J Y Richard Liew, Du Yong et al. Experimental and numerical investigation of novel partially connected steel plate shear walls[J]. Journal of Constructional Steel Research,2017,132:1-15.

[6] Yuntian Wu, Daoyang Kang, YeongBin Yang. Seismic performance of steel and concrete composite shear walls with embedded steel truss for use in high-rise buildings [J]. Engineering Structures,2016,125:39-53.

[7] Faxing Ding,Ming Ni,Yongzhi Gong, et al. Experimental study on slip behavior of stud shear connectors and calculation of shear capacity [J]. Journal of building structures,2014,35(9):98-106.

[8] Jiyue Wang,Xiaoqian Qian. Effect of reinforcement on shrinkage stress of concrete [J]. Concrete,2004.

[9] Sivakumar A. and Manu S. A quantitative study on the plastic shrinkage cracking in high strength hybrid fibre reinforced concrete[J]. Cement and Concrete Composites,2007,29(7):575-581.

[10] Yue Li, Da Huo, Xiuli Du. Study on early shrinkage characteristics of reinforced concrete [J]. Journal of Beijing University of technology,2004,32(11):1002-1006.

[11] Zhuangfeng Pan, Zhitao Lv, Shaoping Meng. Experimental study on effect of reinforcement on shrinkage and creep of high strength concrete [J]. Acta civil engineering,2009,42(2):11-23.

[12] Chao Feng. Experimental study on influence of stud on shrinkage of high strength concrete. Chongqing University,2007.

[13] Tiemeng Wang. Crack control of engineering structures [M]. China Construction Industry Press,62-64,1997.

[14] Deng renyun. Research on early temperature crack control of steel plate concrete composite shear wall [D]. Chongqing University, 2014.

Research on Slender Column with Circular Cross-section Considering Boundary Condition and Imperfection

Peng Wang   Zhengpu Yang   Peiwen He   Jiawei Niu   Runxiang He

(Chang'an University, School of Highway)

Abstract   In this paper, the boundary condition and imperfection in numerical simulation of axial compression members are studied. Using ABAQUS to establish a finite element model and considering the effects of initial eccentricity and initial out-of-straightness, an analysis is carried out based on the slender column with a circular cross-section, and the accuracy of the model is verified based on the experiment. Furthermore, a parametric analysis of the boundary condition and imperfection set in the finite element model is carried out. The results show that the finite element model's different boundary conditions have a significant impact on the bearing capacity and deformation at failure. The effect of boundary conditions should be considered in the numerical simulation to set reasonable boundary conditions. The numerical simulation results also show that the boundary conditions and the initial imperfection mainly affect the lateral displacement of the axial compression member. In contrast, the axial displacement is not as sensitive as the previous one. Therefore, lateral displacement can be used as one of the indicators to evaluate whether the initial imperfection and boundary conditions set in the FEM model are reasonable.

Keywords   Axial compression member   Numerical simulation   Boundary condition   Imperfection

0 Introduction

Because of the excellent performance of steel structure, scholars have done a large number of research on the steel column under axial compression from various aspects, such as imperfection, the material's constitutive law and retrofitting. The impact of initial imperfection on the structure's strength and deformation can not be ignored(Wei, L and Ganping, S, 2019). The change of material properties has little effect on the bearing capacity of stainless steel axial compression members, and the slenderness ratio only affects the bearing capacity of members with a small slenderness ratio(Yang, S et al., 2020). As for retrofitting, because carbon fiber reinforced polymer(CFRP) were involved in civil engineering, it has become a more competitive method to improve the performance of steel structure compared with traditional method. CFRP layers could increase the strength of both short column (Hongyuan, T et al., 2019) and slender column (Gao et al., 2013), and longitudinal layers were suitable for slender column while transverse layers appropriate for short column (Shaat et al., 2006).

To sum up, there are many studies on the axially compressed column. Also, experts have conducted a large number of experiments and corresponding numerical simulations. Still, the previous research mainly focused on the impact of the material's constitutive law, the influence of different reinforcement methods, and other factors on a member's performance. However, the boundary conditions, which directly impact the bearing capacity and failure mode of a column, were somehow ignored. To get a further study about the influence of the boundary conditions on numerical simulation results, this paper studies the boundary conditions based on the experimental results and numerical simulation.

1　Finite Element Model

The experimental data used in this paper to compare the results of the numerical simulation comes from (Gao et al., 2013).

1.1　Meshing

ABAQUS is used to simulate the slender column's experiment, and the C3D8R element is selected to model and mesh. When meshing, the number of elements divided along the radius has a significant impact on the results. Fig. 1 and Fig. 2 shows the different meshing and calculation results in ABAQUS when a spring with a stiffness of 8×10^5 N/rad was set at the upper end of the column. When the model is divided into one layer and two layers along the radius, the calculation results represent a high dispersion degree. When dividing it into three or more layers, the calculation results reach convergence. Therefore, to ensure the accuracy of the simulation while considering the ability of the computer, the model was meshed into three layers along the radius. 2 reference point were set at the center of both the bottom and top of the column, which were coupled to the end sections so that they have the same displacements and rotations.

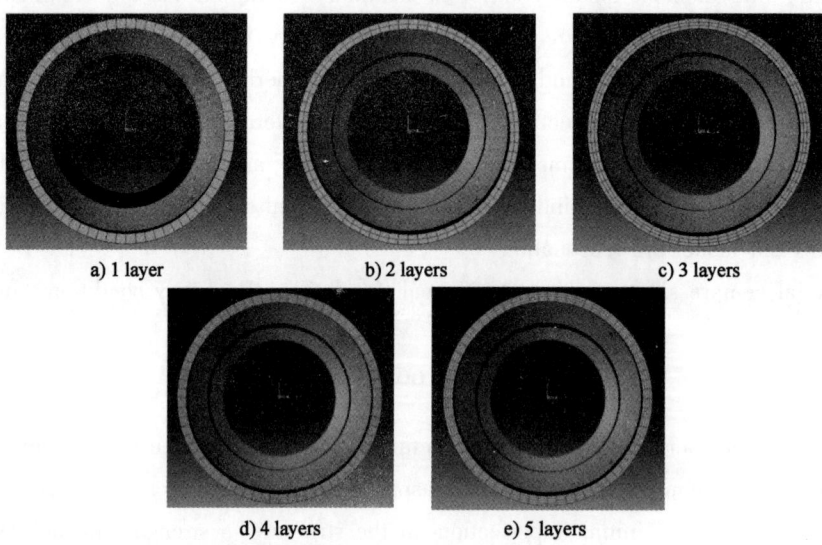

Fig. 1　Meshing along radius

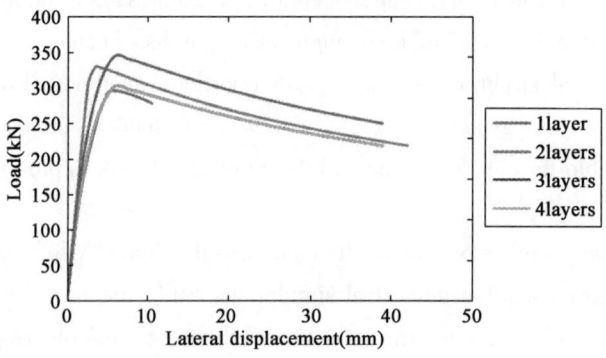

Fig. 2　Load-lateral displacement curve under different meshing

1.2 Imperfection

According to the Chinese standard of steel structure design (GB 50017—2017), the structure's initial out-of-straightness can be adopted as the first buckling mode with an amplitude of 2.4mm The imperfection of the model is applied by the method of editing keywords. The initial eccentricity is simulated by applying a bending moment to the end of the column, and the eccentricity $e = 2.4$mm.

2 Parametric Analysis

2.1 Boundary Conditions

After establishing finite element models with different boundary conditions, this paper studies the influence of boundary conditions on the slender column under axial compression. Tab. 1 shows the experimental and numerical simulation results. EXP represents the experimental result, P-P represented that the top and bottom of the component were hinged, P-T represented the bottom of the member was hinged while the top was fixed, P-1 represented the bottom of the column was hinged, the top was connected with a spring, which was with a stiffness of 1×10^5 N/rad, and the rest were named as the same as P-1. It can be seen that the different boundary conditions in the numerical simulation have a great influence on the bearing capacity. In the numerical simulation, the bearing capacity obtained by using P-P boundary condition was much smaller than the bearing capacity obtained in the experiment. With the gradual increase of the spring stiffness at the top, the member's bearing capacity increased significantly at first. When the stiffness of spring at top was 8×10^5 N/rad, the bearing capacity was almost equal to that in the experiment, but when the stiffness increased to 32×10^5 N/rad, the improvement was no longer obvious. Finally, the rod's bearing capacity converged to the simulation result, which was hinged at the bottom while fixed at the top. From the perspective of the elastic buckling of the column under axial compression, changing the boundary conditions directly result in the change of the effective length of column, which affects the critical load of the column. The slender column works within the elastic stage (Yudong, Y, and Zhiqian, W, 1991), so it is greatly affected by the boundary conditions.

Bearing capacity Tab. 1

Boundary condition	Bearing capacity(kN)	Deviation
EXP	296.09	—
P-P	223.69	-24.72%
P-T	314.74	6.30%
P-1	253.19	-14.49%
P-2	269.57	-8.96%
P-4	287.03	-3.06%
P-8	299.93	1.30%
P-16	307.76	3.94%
P-32	311.45	5.19%
P-64	312.93	5.69%
P-128	313.95	6.03%

Fig. 3 shows parts of the load-lateral displacement curve. Compared with the experimental results, it can be seen that the lateral displacement at mid-span that reached the peak load in the numerical simulation results is more significant and gradually went down with the increase of the stiffness of the boundary conditions. Finally, it converges to the result of P-T. The reason for the significant displacement in the simulation results may be that the initial imperfection set in the model is larger than that in the experiment.

Fig. 4 shows the load-top axial displacement curve. As is shown, compared with the experimental results, the value of the axial displacement that reached the peak load calculated by the numerical simulation is larger. Simultaneously, it can be found that under the same imperfection, the axial displacement of the member at the initial stage was less affected by the applied boundary conditions. However, the boundary conditions had a greater impact on the bearing capacity. Before the peak load was reached, there was a linear relationship between the load and the axial displacement in the numerical simulation. While in the experiment, before reaching the peak load, the load-axial displacement curve has already been significantly curved. This may be because the residual stress was not considered in the finite element model, which may cause the member to yield in advance.

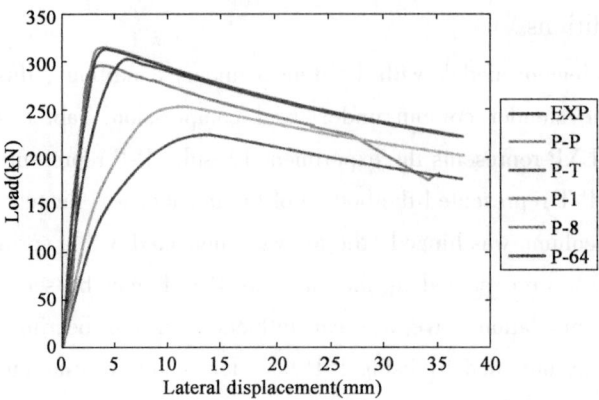

Fig. 3 Load-lateral displacement curve

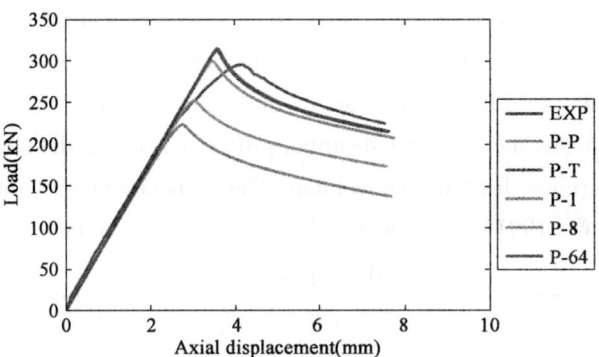

Fig. 4 Load-lateral displacement curve

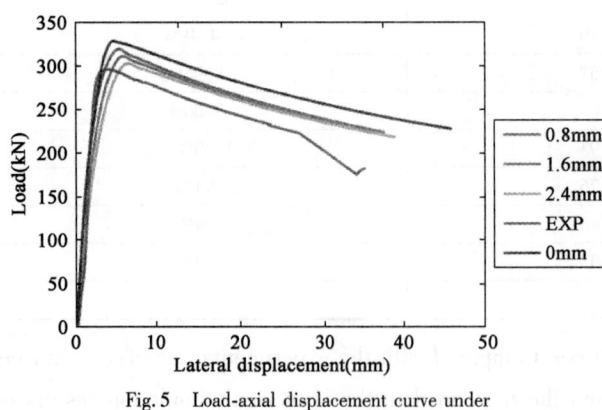

Fig. 5 Load-axial displacement curve under different initia(eccentricity)

2.2 Initial Eccentricity

Fig. 5 shows the load-lateral displacement curve obtained by setting different initial eccentricities to the finite element model under the boundary conditions of P-8. It can be seen that the initial eccentricity not only affects the bearing capacity of the member but also has a greater impact on the lateral displacement when the structure reaches the bearing capacity. The greater the eccentricity set in the model, the smaller the bearing capacity and the greater the lateral displacement. When the initial eccentricity set in the numerical model was zero, the lateral displacement at the peak load was close to the experimental result. As is shown Fig. 5, the load-axial displacement curves corresponding to different initial eccentricities almost coincided with that of the experiment before reaching a certain load, indicating that the initial eccentricity had little effect on the axial displacement of the member.

2.3 Initial out of Straightness

According to the Chinese standard of seamless steel tubes for structural purposes (GB/T 8162—2018), the degree of bending for the steel tube is less than 1.5mm/m. For the specimens used in this paper, the maximum initial out-of-straightness should be 3.6mm. Fig. 6 and Fig. 7 are the calculation results of setting different initial out-of-straightness for the model with the boundary condition of P-8. It can be seen that the initial out-of-straightness set in the numerical model not only affects the bearing capacity of the column, but also has a greater impact on the lateral displacement. It can be seen from Fig. 7, as the same as Fig. 5, the initial out-of-straightness has little effect on the axial displacement of the member.

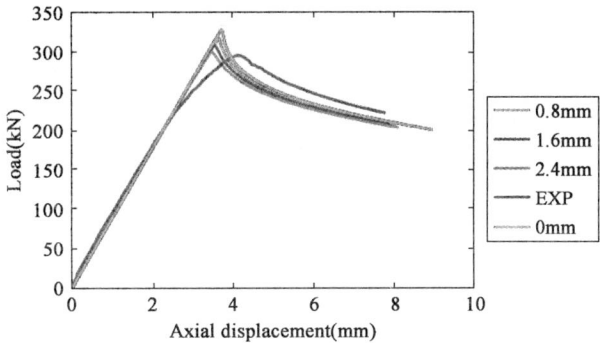

Fig. 6 Load-axial displacement curve under different initial eccentricity

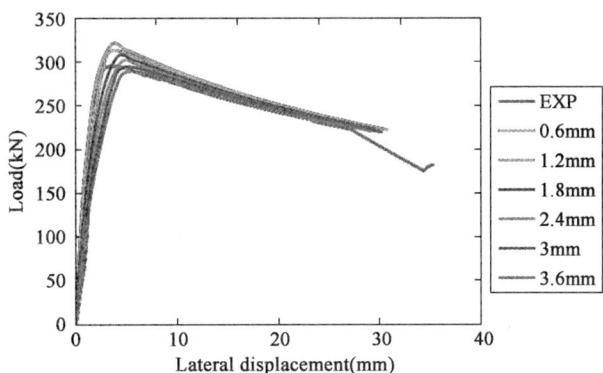

Fig. 7 Load-lateral displacement curve under different out of straightness

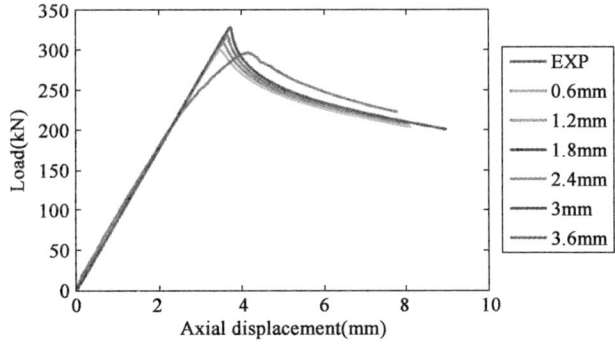

Fig. 8 Load-axial displacement curve under different out of straightness

3 Conclusion

By comparing the results of the numerical simulation with the experimental data, it can be found that:

(1) The test specimen's bearing capacity is different from that in the FEM model with the boundary condition of P-T. The bearing capacity increases with the increase of the spring stiffness set at the top of the column. The bearing capacity of the experimental specimen is almost equal to that in the model with the boundary condition of P-8.

(2) According to the experiment, the axial displacement curve slope went up when the column was going to buckle. In contrast, the axial displacement of FEM models had a linear increase until a specific load. One possible reason is that the residual stress is not considered in the FEM model.

(3) The lateral displacement that peaked in the FEM model is larger than that in the experiment. According to the above discussion, the reason can be that the initial imperfection set in the FEM model was too large.

(4) The lateral displacement of a column under axial compression is greatly affected by the initial imperfection (initial deflection and initial out-of-straightness are considered) and boundary conditions. In contrast, the axial displacement is not sensitive. Therefore, it is recommended to use the lateral displacement of the numerical simulation as one of the indexes for judging whether the initial imperfection and boundary conditions set in the FEM model are reasonable.

References

[1] Gao X Y, Balendra T, Koh C G. Buckling strength of slender circular tubular steel braces strengthened by CFRP[J]. Engineering structures, 2013, 46, 547-556.

[2] Hongyuan T, Huan Z, Chunmei P, et al. Experiment on bearing capacity of cold-formed stainless steel square pipe under axial compression[J]. Journal of Lanzhou University of Technology, 2019.

[3] Sen Y, Yongquan Z, Jiachang W, et al. Numerical Study of Bearing Capacity of Cold-formed Duplex Stainless Steel Columns[J]. Journal of Taiyuan University of Technology, 2020.

[4] Shaat A, Fam, A. Axial loading tests on short and long hollow structural steel columns retrofitted using carbon fibre reinforced polymers[J]. Canadian Journal of Civil Engineering, 2006, 33(4), 458-470.

[5] Wei L, Ganping S. Research on equivalent initial imperfections of compression members in direct analysis design method[J]. Journal of Building Structures, 2019.

[6] Yudong Y, Zhiqian W. Principle of Steel Structure Stability Theory[J]. Xi'an Jiaotong University Press, 1991.

小半径曲线简支叠合梁桥设计分析

张茜

（招商局重庆交通科研设计院有限公司）

摘要 近年高速公路互通内处于小半径平曲线段的匝道跨线桥屡见不鲜，为减少对运营道路干扰，加快施工进度，采用钢-混凝土叠合梁桥成为常见的桥梁构造形式。本桥从方便跨线曲线桥施工角度考虑，通过可靠的计算分析提出了可行的构造优化设计方案，为同类型桥梁的设计提供参考。

关键词 小半径曲线梁桥　双箱叠合梁　有限元分析　设计方案

0 引言

受高速公路用地及运营道路的限制，互通跨线桥采用小半径大跨曲线桥已成为一种典型桥梁方案。而匝道曲线桥因宽度较小、半径较小的原因而采用单箱单室钢箱梁构造居多。但钢箱梁因钢桥面铺装规模小、单价高、施工工艺要求高等特点,应用具有一定局限性。而钢-混凝土叠合梁综合了钢结构桥和混凝土结构桥的优点,既充分利用了钢材的拉伸性能,又较好发挥了混凝土的受压性能,并具有兼做施工辅助构件的优势,被广泛应用于大跨曲线梁桥设计中。[1-3]

本文以一跨简支双箱叠合梁为例,从施工便利及运营安全角度分析桥梁受力特点,提出可行的优化设计方案,为此类桥梁提供合理的设计及施工参考依据。

1 项目介绍

1.1 桥跨拟定

某高速路互通枢纽立交位于连接市区与近郊县城高速路的起点段,该互通B匝道上跨运营期京藏高速公路,大桥平面布置图参见图1。本项目桥跨设计主要受以下制约因素影响:

(1)平曲线半径小。虽桥梁位于圆曲线半径仅85m的匝道缓和曲线段,桥位处拟合圆曲线半径约174m,属于较小曲线半径段。

(2)桥梁纵坡较大。桥梁位于纵断面单向坡段,纵坡坡率达3.5%。

(3)跨运营高速。本段桥梁跨越运营期的京藏高速公路整体式路基段桥梁,高速桥宽26m,分幅布置,左右幅桥梁净距0.5m,施工期要求不中断高速交通。

为减少对高速公路影响,本桥设计拟采用一跨跨越京藏高速公路;从降低工程投资,后期维护工作量上考虑,采用一跨36m简支叠合梁桥较为合理。

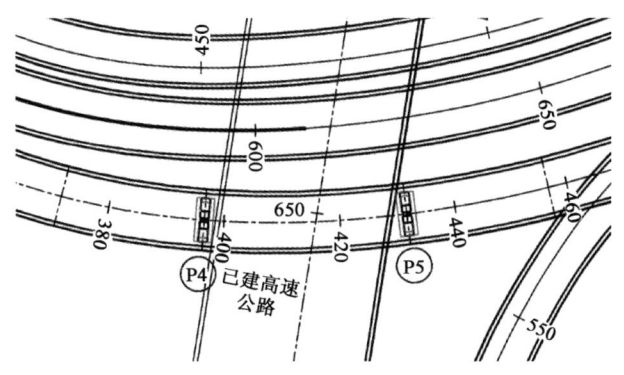

图1 桥位平面布置图

1.2 横断面比选

宽10.5m的36m跨叠合梁断面可选用以下三种形式[图2a)、b)、c)],[4]即单箱双室箱形断面、肋式断面、双箱单室箱形断面。

因本桥处于较小平曲线半径段,曲线梁桥特点是:内外侧腹板长度不等,所以结构在荷载作用下外侧力大于内侧,使得主梁产生背离圆心方向的扭转效应,且半径越小扭转效果越大。在曲线桥中,箱形断面因其底板连续,抗扭性能强,所以底板应力分布较均匀;而肋式断面受"扭转效应"和"曲梁效应"的影响,内外侧应力差别明显,各肋板受力严重不均;因此,针对曲线桥扭矩较大的特点,采用箱形断面是理想方案。

再则,本桥桥宽10.5m,箱形断面中钢结构部分若采用整体吊装,则吊装重量约120000kg,在减小对京藏高速公路影响的前提下,需对箱梁进行节段划分,并在高速公路内设置临时支墩。而临时墩及分段吊装均增加了施工工期及投资,存在临时墩碰撞风险,因而单箱单室断面不适用本桥。

综合肋式断面分部拼装、吊装重量小的特点,以及箱形断面抗扭性能强的特点,本桥采用窄双箱单箱室断面是更为合理的方案。本方案单个箱室钢结构整体吊装重量约70000kg,较整箱断面减少近半,可节省为分段拼装而设的临时支墩。

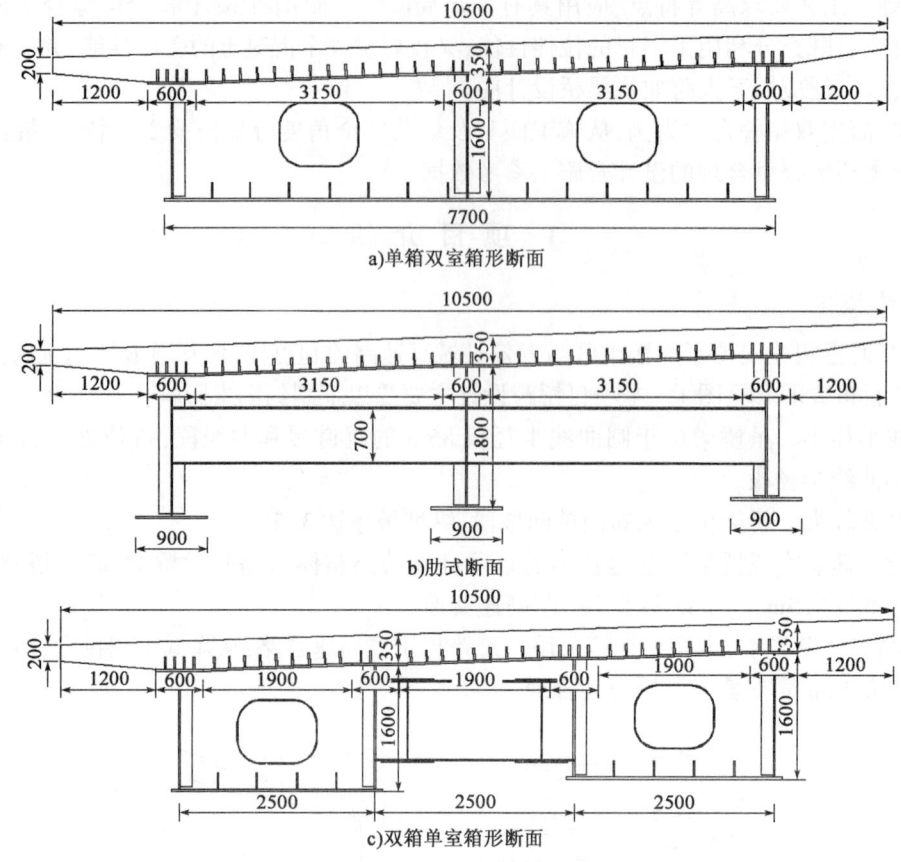

图2 主梁典型横断面图(尺寸单位:mm)

1.3 结构简述

主梁采用分离式双箱单室普通钢筋混凝土钢-混凝土组合梁桥,梁高1.95m,其中钢结构高1.6m,现浇桥面板厚0.35m。桥面全宽10.5m,悬臂1.2m。钢箱底板水平,桥面横坡由腹板高度变化形成。

钢梁采用Q345D钢材,翼板厚25mm;腹板厚20mm;底板除跨中段厚30mm外,其余段为40mm。钢箱内纵向沿设计道路中心线设置3道横梁;为了抵抗钢梁的畸变,每隔4m设置一道横隔板。

2 设计优化分析

本桥双箱断面,在施工阶段需分开架设单箱,再通过横梁连接为整体,而单箱的支座间距仅1.5m,自重下的扭转效应极有可能造成单个箱室侧翻,给运营高速造成危险。一般情况下,施工可考虑通过运营高速公路中分带处设置的临时支墩来防止单箱侧翻。临时支墩还能在钢梁兼做施工支架和模板的时候起到增加支点,减弱钢梁受力的优点。但临时墩设置在高速中,存在较大的碰撞风险,并增加了工程投资。因而,笔者对临时墩在施工中的作用进行了计算分析。[5-6]

2.1 计算模型

采用MIDS/Civil软件建立如图3所示空间模型,采用梁格法加双单元模拟:将组合梁分为两个单箱,单箱之间用钢横梁连接;采用双单元法模拟将桥面板与钢梁分开建模,刚性连接桥面板与钢梁,使两者共同承受荷载。

两个单钢箱底部中心处分别布置支座,一端采用固定支座+横向活动支座,另一端采用顺桥向活动支座+双向活动支座。

2.2 施工阶段支点受力分析

本桥因处于小半径曲线段,防止施工架梁阶段梁体侧翻是本桥研究的重点。本桥架设主要考虑五个施工步骤:①整体吊装单个钢梁;②连接钢横梁;③将单梁临时双支座更换为单支座;④现浇桥面板;⑤施工二期恒载。从设置临时支墩和不设临时支墩两种架梁方案进行计算模拟。因不设临时支墩,在现浇桥面板后,跨中产生较大的弯矩,导致跨中截面应力超标,在加大钢结构梁高至1.8m后受力得到改善,所以不设临时支墩,需增加钢结构段梁高。现从施工阶段架梁分析得到如下支点最大反力结果,见表1。

从表1、表2可知:①曲线桥施工阶段外侧受力大于内侧;②临时支墩在施工架梁阶段分担大部分支点受力;③虽然加大了梁高,但不设临时支墩的各阶段反力比设置的要增加约3倍。

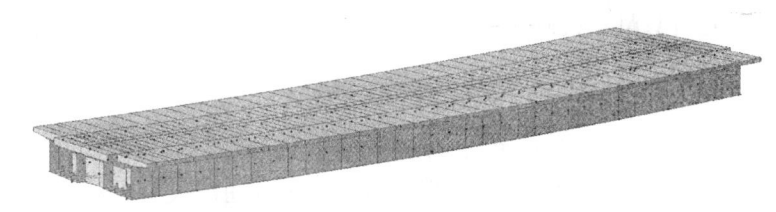

图3 计算模型

设置临时支墩支点最大反力(单位:kN)　　表1

项目	步骤1	步骤2	步骤3	步骤4	步骤5
外侧支点	68.5	78.2	144.4	556.9	2093.9
临时墩支点	356.1	370.2	370.1	1304	0
内侧支点	58.5	69.3	134.7	521.3	1355.1

不设临时支墩支点最大反力(单位:kN)　　表2

项目	步骤1	步骤2	步骤3	步骤4	步骤5
外侧支点	263.7	274.7	419.1	1453.6	2116.4
临时墩支点	—	—	—	—	—
内侧支点	65.6	84.2	273.6	956.9	1368.5

2.3 施工阶段抗弯验算

按照《公路钢混组合桥梁设计与施工规范》(JTG/T D64-01—2015)第7.2.1条进行施工阶段组合梁的强度验算,根据有限元计算结果,提取了施工阶段钢梁与混凝土桥面板的应力结果,见表3。

施工阶段强度验算结果(单位:MPa)　　表3

项目	钢梁最大拉应力	钢梁最大压应力	混凝土桥面板最大拉应力	混凝土桥面板最大压应力
1.6m高钢梁	74.1	95.6	1.62	7.14
1.8m高钢梁	87.2	167.1	1.73	2.45

从表3可以看出:

(1)施工阶段钢梁最大拉应力出现在下缘,最大压应力出现在上缘;不设临时支墩最大压应力较设置临时支墩增加约75%。

(2)钢梁截面加高后承受了较多的压应力,降低了混凝土桥面板受压。

(3)混凝土桥面板产生的拉应力可通过配置钢筋控制混凝土的裂缝。[7-8]

2.4 施工方案结论

通过以上计算对比分析,得出以下结论:

(1)不设临时墩需增加梁高,钢结构部分较设临时墩主梁用钢量增加约5%;

(2)设置临时支墩,在施工架梁阶段能较好地发挥钢受拉和混凝土受压的特性;

(3)从经济上考虑,不设临时支墩可节约造价以及较大地缩减工期;

(4)临时支墩取消,亦可减少运营高速施工期车撞风险。

2.5 运营阶段抗倾覆验算

曲线小半径桥梁运营阶段应特别考虑桥梁抗倾覆的能力。本桥将常规窄箱下两个小支座更换为一个支座的设计具有如下优势：

(1)减少了支点数量,使桥梁受力更明确。

(2)方便调节支座间距或偏心,优化主梁受力,提高抗倾覆能力。[9]

参照《公路钢筋混凝土及预应力混凝土桥涵设计规范》(JTG 3362—2018)第4.1.8条规定进行曲线桥抗倾覆计算,本桥抗倾覆计算最小抗倾覆稳定系数为 $8.57 > K = 2.5$,满足规范要求。

3 结 语

钢-混凝土叠合梁具有自重轻、跨度大、施工周期短、能较好发挥材料特性的特点,在曲线小半径桥梁上钢混凝土叠合梁的优势更为明显。因跨越限制条件较多,布置曲线段叠合梁,其施工方案直接影响设计尺寸的拟定。通过以上分析,主要得出以下结论:[10]

(1)分离钢箱叠合梁断面具有分部拼装、吊装重量小的优点,施工便利,且占道少。

(2)设置临时支墩可节约主梁用钢量,较好地发挥钢和混凝土的特性,受力合理。

(3)桥下运营道路限制条件较多且桥下净空富裕的情况下,采用不设临时支墩的架梁方案具有缩短工期、减少车撞墩风险的优点,是可行的设计方案。

(4)单个窄钢箱下设一个支点,不仅使结构受力更明确,也加大了支座间距及预偏移动的空间,提高了曲线桥抗倾覆能力。

本桥从方便跨线曲线桥施工角度考虑,通过可靠的计算分析提出了可行的设计方案和优化方法,为同类型桥梁的设计提供参考。

参考文献

[1] 徐君兰,孙淑红.钢桥[M].2版.北京:人民交通出版社,2011.
[2] 陈海滨.梁格法在异性钢箱梁桥计算分析中的应用[J].上海公路,2009.
[3] 王礼友,史金伟.城市立交曲线箱梁设计分析[J].路桥科技,2012,12.
[4] 曾礼.关于曲线钢混叠合梁设计的一些讨论[J].山西建筑,2017,43(5).
[5] 王伟臣,城市立交匝道小半径曲线钢混叠合梁设计关键技术[J].城市道桥与防洪,2018.
[6] 于长皓,宋文学,李永,等.双箱单室曲线钢箱梁桥的不同建模方法计算结果对比分析[J].公路交通技术,2018.
[7] 徐建清.钢-混凝土简支叠合梁的设计与计算[J].华东公路,2011.
[8] 王明明.浅论城市立交曲线箱梁设计[J].黑龙江交通科技,2013(9).
[9] 黎海堤.小半径曲线叠合钢箱梁桥的支座受力分析[J].中外公路,2009,4.
[10] 李泉彬.曲线钢-混叠合梁架设及顶升分析[J].工程与建设,2016,30(3).

Prediction of Effective Width of Varying Depth Box-girder Bridge Using Artificial Neural Network

Kejian Hu　Xiaoguang Wu

(Chang'an University, Highway School)

Abstract Effective flange width is widely used to consider shear lag effects in bridge design. The existing simplified formulas for effective flange width of varying depth box-girder bridge in codes and researches may be unconservative while accurate methods such as finite element method are time-consuming. The aim of this study is to develop a method to predict effective width of varying depth box-girder bridge using artificial neural network (ANN). Four different neural networks which take bridge parameters as input and output effective width are created. These models were trained, validated and tested on the dataset produced by thousands of finite element models. The lower errors in test set demonstrate that the ANN models can be used to predict the effective width. Moreover, the influence of different architecture is also studied. The proposed approach makes real-time analysis possible and has wide application in the analysis and design of varying depth box-girder bridges.

Keywords Effective width　Box girder　Varying depth　Artificial neural network

0 Introduction

The shear lag effect, a phenomenon of non-uniform distribution of normal stress, exits in various civil engineering structures, such as box girder bridges. This phenomenon can lead to an misestimate of the displacements and stresses at the extreme fibers based on beam bending theory(Amadio and Fragiacomo, 2002; Aref et al., 2007; Masoudnia et al., 2018) and this misestimation increase with the width of box girder(Křístek and Bažant, 1987). Thence, the shear lag is essential to be studied as part of bridge designs, especially under the trance of increasing bridge deck width.

Since the shear lag effect was recognized in engineering field, a lot of analyze methods were proposed, such as finite-stringer method(EVANS and TAHERIAN, 1977), energy-variational method(Chen et al., 2013; Chen et al., 2014), finite beam element method(Zhou, 2010) and so on. Those methods are too complex to be applied in engineering despite higher accuracy. So, the concept of the effective width was introduced to simplify the calculation and analysis. The effective width is a reduced width of the section with a uniform distribution of normal stress. It is used to replace the actual width in a simplified analysis based on elementary beam theory and the normal stress within the effective flange width must be the maximum normal stress, which likely occurs near the web-flange interaction at the critical sections with peak moments to satisfy strength-design requirements(Lin and Zhao, 2011). This concept is recommended by various codes and standards, including the AASHTO LRFD Bridge Design Specifications, British Standards Institution (BSI)BS 5400 and so on. Those codes provide some formulas and empirical curves for different support conditions to simplify calculations by considering only the section width(b) and the width over the girder span(L). For example take the AASHTO LRD Bride Design Specifications as representative of these, it provide two empirical curves of the effective flange width coefficients, which is equal to the effective width divided by the physical width, for the given values of the ratio of width to the notional girder span(b/l_i)(American Association of State Highway and Transportation Officials, 2007).

Similar situation is reflected in some researches. Huang Yuan et al. (Yuan et al., 2016) found out the width of the concrete slab(b), the span of the beam(L) and the thickness of the floor slab(h_c) are the most relevant parameter, and proposed design formulas based on it. Gara F, Ranzi G & Leoni G(Gara et al., 2011) proposed several effective width expressions for composite continue bridge obtained by linear and second polynomial regressions. These expressions are functions of the girder span(L), slab width(B) and beam spacing (B_1)including at least 5 coefficients for each expression. Qin X & Liu H. (Qin and Liu, 2010) obtained the closed polynomial effective width expression under uniform loads based on the Symplectic Elasticity method. In the expression, the Poisson's ratio (μ) is considered as well as the flange slab width(b).

It is easily found that almost existing codes and researches only consider girder span (L) and slab width (B). However, the shear lag effect can be significantly affected by load type, boundary conditions and the geometry properties such as web dimensions, flange thickness and so on. Thus, the result produced by these formulas may be unconservative (Lin and Zhao, 2011). Besides, these formulas and empirical curves was proposed by taking the constant depth box girder as the research object, so that it can be imprecise for varying depth girders using these formulas directly.

Over the last couple of decades, deep learning, a specific machine learning method based on artificial neural networks, has made remarkable achievement in many fields, especially in computer vision and language modeling (Voulodimos et al., 2018; Sorin et al., 2020). And many researchers have proved that the neural networks are able to discover non-linear mappings between the input and the desired output (Goodfellow et al., 2016). Thus, some researches use the neural networks to learning the relationship between the structural design variables and performances recently. Nguyen et al. predicted the maximum horizontal deformation of structures subjected to an earthquake using ANN instead of finite element method (FEM) (Nguyen et al., 2020). ANN was adopted by Wu to predicted the acceleration response for a box section under a turbulent wind flow (Wu and Kareem, 2011). Liang et al. developed a deep learning (DL) model witch was designed and trained to take the input of FEM and directly output the aortic wall stress distributions, bypassing the FEM calculation process (Liang et al., 2018). All these studies showed the ANN approach have enough acutance compared with FEM and were advanced in computation time and consumptions.

Given above these, the aim of this paper was to predict the effective width of varying depth girder bridge through ANN with less computing time and high accuracy compared with FEM. Firstly, a parameter dataset was established to modeling thousands of finite element models which provide the effective width and effective width effective coefficient. Then, those result combined with the parameter dataset form a dataset which is further divided into three parts: training set, validation set and test set. Four ANN models with different architecture were created to study the influence of architecture. Afterwards all models were trained in training and validation set, and tested in test set. The lower error shows the ANN models are able to predict effective width with high accuracy. Further, diving the network into subnets do have effect in improving accuracy. The novelty of this approach is that the trained ANN models can predict effective width within 1 second, so that a real-time preliminary analysis can be realized. Since ANN is a data driven approach, it is considered as a 'black box' model. Therefore, the ANN models can't replace the FEM for the final analysis, but can make the design process more efficient. To the best of author's knowledge, this approach has not been presented before.

1 Method

1.1 Bridge Parameters Dataset

The foundation of accurate prediction via ANN is a mass of data about varying depth girder bridge. The amount of the data depends on the size of the ANN model, and is thousands of pieces of data in general. Using real bridge data is the optimist option, but it is hard to collect such amount of data. Another option is generating dataset based on real bridge data. In literature (Wang et al., 2019), authors evaluated 349 continuous rigid-frame bridges and analyzed the design parameters. Based on these data, a dataset was created in this paper.

Before created the dataset, there is one thing to do. As depicted in Fig. 1, a simplifying assumption is made, that the haunch of box girder was ignored. Besides, the prestressed tendons and rebars are also ignored. The design parameters analyzed in (Wang et al., 2019) include span, girder bottom curve parameter, span-to-height ratio at piers and midspan, thickness of the bottom slab and top slab, but the width of top slab and bottom slab are missing. The width of top slab is slightly greater than the width of pavement, and the continuous rigid-frame bridges are mostly constructed in high-grade highways. So, width range of top slab is assumed to be 10m to 20m. The width of bottom slab depends on the flange width. According to design experience, flange width is generally more than 5m, and less than half of the girder width. All the parameters used in this paper are listed in Tab. 1.

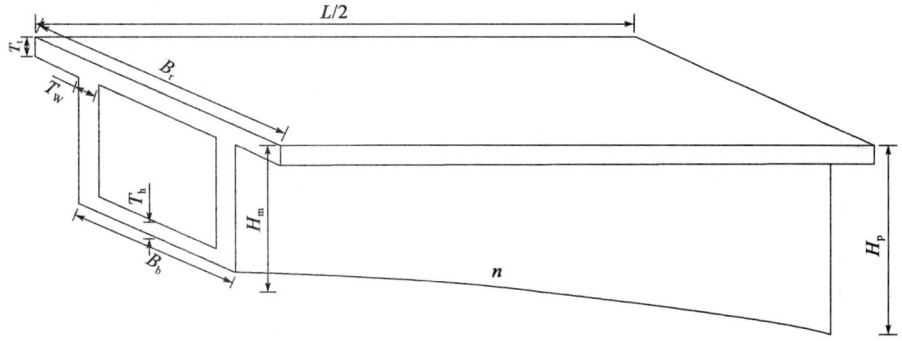

Fig. 1　Simplified box girder and design parameters

Parameters and its value of the bridge parameters dataset　　Tab. 1

Parameter	Symbol	Value	Unit
Span	L	$U(100,300)$	m
Girder bottom curve parameter	n	$U(1.5,2.0)$	—
Span-to-height ratio at piers	R_p	$U(1/18,1/16)$	—
Span-to-height ratio at midspan	R_m	$U(1/50,1/40)$	—
Girder height in piers	H_p	$R_p \times L$	m
Girder height in midspan	H_m	$R_m \times L$	m
Thickness of the bottom slab	T_b	$U(25,35)$	cm
Thickness of the top slab	T_t	$U(25,35)$	cm
Thickness of the web	T_w	$U(30,80)$	cm
Width of top slab	B_t	$U(10,20)$	m
Width of bottom slab	B_b	$U(B_g-5, B_g/2)$	m

Note: U denote a uniform distribution. Value of girder bottom curve parameter keeps 1 decimal place, and values of R_p and R_m keep 3 decimal places, the rest values keep integer.

1.2 Finite Element Method Model

It is a common practice to analyze accurate effective width using finite element method. There are two ways to implement finite model, two-dimensional or three-dimensional (Tenchev, 1996). Two-dimensional way models web and flange respectively via introducing some assumptions. But the less the assumptions imposed on the analysis are, the closer to a reality the analysis model becomes, and the better stress concentration factor would be obtained (Lertsima et al., 2004). So, two thousand finite element models with 3D shell elements of the varying depth girder are created based on parameters in the dataset. In order to simplify model and reduce computer effort, only one single girder of main span is modeled and piers are ignored as same as foundations. Hence, fixed boundaries are applied on both ends of the girder to simulate the effect of the piers. Besides the geometrical parameters and support condition, how the load is applied is also crucial factors. Different load types, such as concentrated load and uniformly distributed load, leads to different stress distribution, and lead to different effective width finally. In the present study, the main aim is to explore a way to predict the effective width through neural network rather than the parameters analysis, so only gravity is applied in the models. For specific load or load combination, the way presented in this paper can be modified and create the neural network model corresponded to the load. Besides, the rebar and prestressed tendons are also ignored based on the reason mentioned in Section 2.1.

All these finite element models mentioned above are implemented by ANSYS software, and a script in python was written to assist finish the job. Shell 63 elements is used for the concrete, and the elasticity modulus, Poisson's ratio and density of concrete are set to 3.45×10^4 MPa, 0.2 and 2500kg/m³ respectively. Mesh generation also plays an important role in finite element modeling. The sparser the mesh is, the lower the computing precision is. On the other hand, the denser mesh can improve the accuracy while more computing time is consumed. The element size is set to 0.5m after lots of tries.

Fig. 2 shows the stress distribution of the girder along the Z direction or longitudinal direction. It is easily found that the stress distribution is not uniform, the stress at rib is the greatest, and the further from the web, the less stress is. According to the definition, the effective width can be expressed as follow:

$$b_e = \frac{t\int_0^b \sigma(x,y)\mathrm{d}y}{t\,\sigma_{\max}} \tag{1}$$

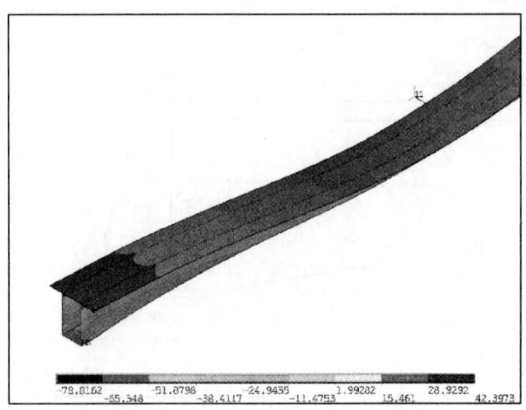

Fig. 2 Stress distribution along the Z direction

in which $\sigma(x,y)$ is the function of the normal stress along the girder width, $\sigma_{\max}$ means the maximum normal stress in the top slab, y is the position along the top slab, and b is width of the top slab. Besides, a coefficient of the effective width (η) is defined which is equal to the effective width divided by width, as follow:

$$\eta = \frac{b_e}{b} \tag{2}$$

1.3 Neural Network Model

1.3.1 Network Architecture Description

The ANN is one of the forms of machine learning composed by a lot of interconnected nodes called neurons. Those connected neurons enable the ANN to serve as universal approximators for complex functions (Hornik et al., 1989), so it can be used to formed a model from a large dataset in order to make predictions.

It is atrial-and-error process to form an ANN model. An ANN with little nodes or layers may have poor performance in prediction. Increasing number of hidden layer and neurons in each layer will improve the prediction accuracy, and improve the difference of training and the size of the dataset meantime. Furthermore, too much nodes and layers may lead to overfit, thereby decreasing the accuracy. In this paper, there are four different model architectures formed and tested to find out which is the best one. Those models are graphically summarized in Fig. 3.

Model One is a typical multiple layer ANN, including one input layer, 5 hidden layers with 30 neurons in each hidden layer and one output layer in total. This model takes all the design parameters as input and predict one value. This value can be effective width or effective width factor depending the training data. Since there is only one output in this model architecture, two models are needed for effective width (or effective width coefficient) on pier and midspan respectively.

Model Two has the same input and output as Model, but architecture is like the wide & deep model (Cheng et al., 2016), consisted of wide component and deep component. The wide component is a generalized linear model of the form $y = W^T X + b$. y is the prediction, X means inputs data, W means the model parameters and b is the bias. The deep component is a feed-forward neural network, contains 5 hidden layers and 30 neurons in each hidden layer. Accordingly, the inputs are divided inputs into two group, section parameters group and non-section parameters group. Section parameters group includes Span (L) and Girder bottom curve parameter (n), the rest parameters belongs to non-section parameters group. The section parameters group flow through the deep component and combined with non-section parameters group to calculate the final predict values. As same as Model One, two models must be produced.

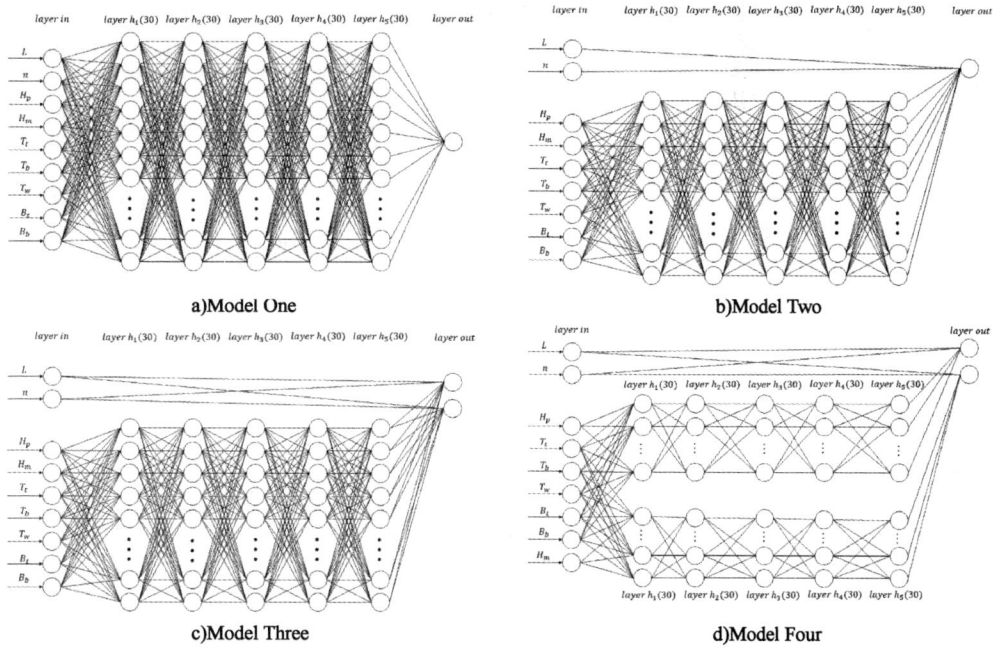

Fig. 3 Schematic of ANNs to predict effect width

Model Three has improved a little in the basis of the Model Two. In this architecture, the model train and predict the effective width (or effective width coefficient) on pier and midspan at same time.

Model Four takes the same inputs and predict same final values like Model Three, but is different in hidden layers. There are two subnets in hidden layers, one for section on pier and another for section on midspan. Certainly, the inputs are reorganized into two groups to ensure each subnet have the right information. Each subnet has the 5 hidden layers and 30 neurons in each hidden layer.

1.3.2 Data preprocessing

Once the model architecture is set, the next step is training the model. From the dataset of bridge parameters and the finite models' simulations, the input space including 9 bridge design parameters and the output space including the effective width (b_e) or effective width coefficients (λ) can be got. Before transferring these data in to the model, it is necessary to preprocess the data in order to accelerate model training speed and improve the accuracy. Standardization is one of the wildly adopted preprocess method, which rescales the input space into a distribution with $\mu = 1$ and $\sigma = 0$. All the inputs are calculated as follows:

$$z = \frac{x - \mu}{\sigma} \tag{3}$$

Where: μ is the mean of the of the samples and σ is the standard deviation from the mean. By doing this, all inputs are centered around 0 with a standard deviation of 1, and bias due to large magnitude of some variables can be avoided.

The next step is dividing the dataset into training set, test set and validation set. The training set is used to fitting model. The validation can be used to adjust the hyperparameter of the model and to make a preliminary assessment of the model's capability. And the test set is to evaluate the generalization ability of the final model. Firstly, the dataset is divided into training set and test set with a ratio of 8∶2. Then, the training data is further split by sampling 20% of the training data for the validation set. So, in the end, the training, validation and test set has 1200, 400 and 400 samples, respectively, and all these samples are divided randomly.

1.3.3 Training of the Models

The parameters of the neural network model are learned from the training data. And the network training process is a data-sensitive process, which means different dataset leads to different predict accuracy. On this account, all models are trained 5 times to reduce error, and the training, validation and test dataset for each model are randomly generated each time, thereby reducing the error due to the dataset, and enabling a more objective evaluation of the models.

During the training process, two performance metrics are used to evaluate the predict accuracy: mean absolute error (MAE) and mean absolute percentage error (MAPE). For each model, the MAE and the MAPE are defined as follows respectively:

$$\text{MAE} = \frac{1}{n}\sum_{i=1}^{n} |y_i - y'_i| \tag{4}$$

$$\text{MAPE} = \frac{1}{n}\sum_{i=1}^{n} \frac{|y_i - y'_i|}{y_i} \tag{5}$$

where: y_i is the effective width or effective width coefficient from finite element models while y'_i is prediction from the network.

2 Result and Discussion

The proposed models in Section 2.3 were trained on the dataset of 1600 bridge parameters, effective width, and effective width coefficient for 5 times independently. All the learning curves of those 4 models had the same trend with different values. Firstly, the curves stared in a very high value, and decreased sharply in first 2 or 3 epoch. Whereafter, the rate of decline began to slow. After around 25 epochs of slow descent, the metrics hold steady around 0 and keep it until the end of training.

From the curves, a lot of information can be obtained. First, the dramatically change in first few epochs showed that the network learned effectively from the training dataset. On the contrary, the curves changed slightly after the 25th epoch, which indicated that the network had achieved the optimal state after 25 epochs and were fully trained. In addition, the steady trend proved these models are not over-fitting as well, because it is a common phenomenon for the over-fitting network that the curves bounced back at the end of training. Besides, the same trend of the curves in training set and validation set also prove these models had well generalization ability, which means these models could also work well in strange dataset.

Similarly, these models were tested in the test dataset for 5 times independently after trained. As the effective width and effective width coefficient have different magnitude, different dimension, it is impossible to discuss their accuracy directly by comparing the difference between predict value and test value. So, percentage error was chosen, and for effective width and effective width coefficient the percentage error is define as follow:

$$\delta_{b_e} = \frac{b_{e_{\text{pred}}} - b_{e_{\text{test}}}}{b_{e_{\text{test}}}} \times 100\% = \frac{\eta_{\text{pred}} \times b - \eta_{\text{test}} \times b}{\eta_{\text{test}} \times b} \times 100\% = \frac{\eta_{\text{pred}} - \eta_{\text{test}}}{\eta_{\text{test}}} \times 100\% = \delta_{\eta} \tag{6}$$

Then, some statistical parameter of the four models' percentage error, including mean percentage error, max percentage error and variance of percentage error, were calculated and list in Tab. 2.

Statistical parameters of 4 models   Tab. 2

Model	Position	Mean Percentage Error (%)		Max Percentage Error (%)		Variance of Percentage Error (%)	
		b_e	η	b_e	η	b_e	η
Model One	Pier	0.619	0.393	4.190	1.977	0.329	0.096
	Midspan	0.710	0.327	6.263	1.841	0.403	0.081
Model Two	Pier	0.630	0.233	5.169	1.804	0.405	0.041
	Midspan	0.472	0.194	1.919	1.036	0.138	0.028
Model Three	Pier	0.898	0.345	5.051	1.796	0.569	0.076
	Midspan	0.777	0.351	5.195	1.529	0.662	0.095
Model Four	Pier	0.850	0.290	7.157	1.415	0.508	0.053
	Midspan	0.541	0.206	4.382	0.930	0.213	0.031

Tab. 2 showed the mean percentage error of 4 models in different position with different output. It can be easily found that all these models had lower error, the maximum value was only 0.898 of Model Three on pier with effective width as output. In other words, all these models had high accuracy, about 99%. Especially, the mean percentage of models with effective width coefficient as output were below 0.5%. Meanwhile, all mean percentage error reduced when the models use the effective width coefficient as output rather than effective width, although drops were different for different models. The maximum decline was 65.9%, happened in Model Four on pier. The reason for the decrease is that effective width coefficient was a series of numbers between 0 and 1. So, replacing the effective width (b_e) with effective width coefficient (η) reduced the error caused by the different magnitudes of effective width, like the standardization in the preprocess. Furthermore, the larger the error, the greater the reduce.

Model One and Four with effective width as output had the greatest max percentage error, 6.263 and 7.15% respectively. Except for these two models, all the rest models' max errors were around 5%, which is acceptable in the engineering field. Particularly, all models with effective width coefficient as output had errors below 2%.

As for variance of percentage error, all variances were less than 1. It implied that the error distribution was centered around the mean percentage error, and the models had stable predictive accuracy. The same rules like the mean percentage error can also be found from Tab. 2: the max percentage error and variance of percentage reduced when the effective width coefficient was used instead of the effective width. Especially on variance of Model Four, the decrease reached up to 89.7% and 85.6%.

Comparing the mean percentage error of all 4 models with effective width coefficient as output, it could be found that Model Two has the lowest percentage error. The decreased error between Model One and Mode Two showed that dividing the network into deep part and wide part is effective. The had fallen by roughly 15%. But increasing the number of outputs from 1 to 2 would lead to a rise in error, about 48% and 81% for different position. This may be caused by that penultimate layer of the deep part was sharing by two outputs, so the weighs and bias of this layer were controlled by both outputs. In order to avoid a big difference of error between outputs, weights and bias were decided eclectically and produce a greater error, and that was why error reduced 16% and 41% when deep component was divided 2 subnets like Model four. Since the purpose of establishing 4 models is to study the influence of different architecture on the results, Model Two, Three and Four only change the architecture, and some hyper-parameter, such as number of layer number of neurons in each layer, remained the same as Model One. So, it's not immediately clear that Model Two was the optimal model because Model Two, Three and Four didn't have the optimal hyper-parameter. Further research is needed.

All these model were implemented using Tensorflow. Given design parameters, the models can output the effective width coefficient within 1s. As a comparison, it took approximately 30 min for FEA to obtain the effective width coefficient for the same input. It was much more faster using the models to predict the effective width, although training the models was an time-consuming process. But, once the models learned the relationship between the output and input of FEM, there were no training process required anymore. Compared to the existing effective width formulas, the models took into account more factors, thus predicted more accurate results.

As a feasibility study, the bridge design parameters were generated based on a survey of continuous reinforced concrete rigid-frame bridges in China and some design experience. Therefore, it is possible that inputs which are significantly different from those of the training data may lead to great error to the models. This problem can be solved by using larger training dataset according a study about the relationship between deep-learning model and training data (Sun et al., 2017). Besides, some factors are not considered in finite element modeling, such as prestress, re-bra and so on. This problem can be sivled by using more elaborate models or test data in real bridge.

This approach will make a huge impact on bridge design. As the varying depth box-girder bridge geometrise are similar, the range of design parameters is cinfined. So this approach can be appiled in most statiuation. For the other bridge type, similar models can be created and trained like this approach to predict the effective width. What is more important is that this approach will enable a real-time effective width analysis, thereby accelerating the design of safe and economical bridges. Futhermore, this approach can be combined with some optimization algorithms to optimum design of bridge. No longer requires designers to spend a lot of time trying. After the preliminary design is determined, the finite element model is used to carry out accurate calculation. Or it can be combined with some BIM software to provided real-time effective width display, so that designers will have an intuitive understanding.

3 Conclusions

In this paper, an approach were presented to predict effective width of varying depth box-girder bridge utilizing advantages of ANN. Four multi-layer feed-forward ANN models with different architecture were created. A bridge design parameters dataset and finite element dataset were established to train, verify and test the models. Those models used bridge design parameters as inputs to predict effective width which showed a good agreement in general.

The lower errors in test set demonstrates that the ANN models can be used to predict effective width. In addition, it can be founded that using effective width coefficient as output rather than effective width will improve accuracy effectively by comparing the prediction errors of each model. Besides, diving the network into several subnet depend on the number of outputs can also achieve the same effect while predicting both effective widths of different position will lead to greater errors.

The proposed ANN models provide much more efficient calcuations with same accuracy as compared to finite element models. This approach will enable real-time analysis of effective width and play a bigger role combine with other technologies such as optimization algorithms.

The paper has shown the advantages of ANN in predicting effective width. However, the proposed models needs sufficient data for proper ANN training before using it for the prediction. It will be unreliable when the input data is beyond the training set data range. Moreover, the accuracy of finite element models is also an important factors, but some simplifications were made in this paper.

References

[1] Amadio C, Fragiacomo M. Effective width evaluation for steel-concrete composite beams[J]. Journal of Constructional Steel Research,2002,58(3),373-388, DOI:10. 1016/S0143-974X(01)00058-X.

[2] American Association of State Highway and Transportation Officials. AASHTO LRFD Bridge Design Specifications,2007.

[3] Aref A J, Chiewanichakorn M, Chen S S. Effective slab width definition for negative moment regions of composite bridges[J]. Journal of Bridge Engineering,2007,12(3),329-349, DOI:10. 1061/(ASCE)1084-0702(2007)12:3(339).

[4] Chen J, Shen S. L, et atl. Closed-form solution for shear lag with derived flange deformation function[J]. Journal of Constructional Steel Research,2014,102,104-110, DOI:10. 1016/j. jcsr. 2014. 07. 003.

[5] Chen H S, Zhao, Q L. Gu Y, et al. Shear Lag in Fiber-Reinforced Plastics Composite Simply Supported II-Beams[J]. Mechanics of Advanced Materials and Structures,2013,20(7),564-570, DOI:10. 1080/15376494. 2011. 643277.

[6] Cheng H T, Koc. et al. Wide & Deep Learning for Recommender Systems[J]. Proceedings of the Eleventh ACM Conference on Recommender Systems,2016. 396-397, DOI:10. 1145/3109859. 3109933.

[7] EVANS H, TAHERIAN A. The prediction of the shear lag effect in box girders[J]. Proceedings of the Institution of Civil Engineers. 1977,63(1), 69-92, DOI:10. 1680/iicep. 3294.

[8] Gara F, Ranzi G, Leoni G. Simplified method of analysis accounting for shear-lag effects in composite bridge decks[J]. Journal of Constructional Steel Research,2011,67(10),1684-1697, DOI:10. 1016/j. jcsr. 2011. 04. 013.

[9] Goodfellow I, Bengio Y, Courville A. Deep Learning[M]. MIT Press,2016.

[10] Hornik K, Stinchcombe M, White H. et al Multilayer feedforward networks are universal approximators [J]. Neural Networks,1989,2(5),359-366, DOI:10. 1016/0893-6080(89)90020-8.

[11] Křístek V, Bažant Z. P. Shear Lag Effect and Uncertainty in Concrete Box Girder Creep[J]. Journal of Structural Engineering,1987,113(3),557-574, DOI:10. 1061/(ASCE)0733-9445(1987)113:3(557).

[12] Lertsima C, Chaisomphob T, Yamaguchi E. Stress concentration due to shear lag in simply supported box girders[J]. Engineering Structures. 2004,26(8),1093-1101, DOI:10. 1016/j. engstruct. 2004. 03. 010.

[13] Liang L, Liu, M, Martin C, et al. A deep learning approach to estimate stress distribution: a fast and accurate surrogate of finite-element analysis[J]. Journal of the Royal Society Interface,2018,15(138), DOI:10. 1098/rsif. 2017. 0844.

[14] Lin Z, Zhao J. Revisit of AASHTO effective flange-width provisions for box girders[J]. Journal of Bridge

[15] Masoudnia R, Hashemi, A, Quenneville P. Predicting the Effective Flange Width of a CLT Slab in Timber Composite Beams[J]. Journal of Structural Engineering (United States), 2018.144(7), 1-18, DOI:10.1061/(ASCE)ST.1943-541X.0001979.

[16] Nguyen H, Moayedi, H, Foong L K, et al. Optimizing ANN models with PSO for predicting short building seismic response[J]. Engineering with Computers, 2020, 36(3), 823-837, DOI:10.1007/s00366-019-00733-0.

[17] Qin X, Liu H. Effective flange width of simply supported box girder under uniform load[J]. Acta Mechanica Solida Sinica, 2010, 23(1), 57-65, DOI:10.1016/S0894-9166(10)60007-9.

[18] Sorin V, Barash Y, Konen E, et al. Deep Learning for Natural Language Processing in Radiology—Fundamentals and a Systematic Review[J]. Journal of the American College of Radiology, 2020, 17(5), 639-648, DOI:10.1016/j.jacr.2019.12.026.

[19] Sun C, Shrivastava A, Singh, S, et al. Revisiting Unreasonable Effectiveness of Data in Deep Learning Era[C]. 2017 IEEE International Conference on Computer Vision (ICCV), IEEE, 2017, 843-852.

[20] Tenchev R T. Shear lag in orthotropic beam flanges and plates with stiffeners[J]. International Journal of Solids and Structures, 1996, 33(9), 1317-1334, DOI:10.1016/0020-7683(95)00093-3.

[21] Voulodimos A, Doulamis N, Doulamis A, et al. Deep Learning for Computer Vision: A Brief Review[J]. Computational Intelligence and Neuroscience, 2018, DOI:10.1155/2018/7068349.

[22] Wang H, Xie C, Liu, D., et al. Continuous Reinforced Concrete Rigid-Frame Bridges in China[J]. Practice Periodical on Structural Design and Construction, 2019, 24(2), 05019002, DOI:10.1061/(ASCE)SC.1943-5576,0000421.

[23] Wu T, Kareem A. Modeling hysteretic nonlinear behavior of bridge aerodynamics via cellular automata nested neural network[J]. Journal of Wind Engineering and Industrial Aerodynamics, 2011, 99(4), 378-388, DOI:10.1016/j.jweia.2010.12,011.

[24] Yuan H, Deng, H, Yang Y, et al. Element-based effective width for deflection calculation of steel-concrete composite beams[J]. Journal of Constructional Steel Research, 2016.121, 163-172, DOI:10.1016/j.jcsr.2016,02,010.

[25] Zhou S. J. Finite Beam Element Considering Shear-Lag Effect in Box Girder[J]. Journal of Engineering Mechanics, 2010, 136(9), 1115-1122, DOI:10.1061/(ASCE)EM.1943-7889,0000156.

箱形截面独柱墩连续弯桥倾覆稳定性分析

肖慧双[1] 李 源[1] 宋一凡[1] 边旭辉[2]
(1.长安大学;2.陕西省高速公路建设集团)

摘 要 随着车辆超载问题愈加严重,箱形截面独柱墩连续弯桥在车辆荷载作用下的抗倾覆性能也愈加引起学者们的重视。为探讨影响箱形截面独柱墩连续弯桥抗倾覆性能的因素,同时提出增强该类桥型抗倾覆性能的措施,本文基于《公路钢筋混凝土及预应力混凝土桥涵设计规范》(JTG 3362—2018),以

基金项目:陕西省自然科学基础研究计划资助项目(2020JQ-377)。

工程中应用最为广泛的四跨独柱墩连续弯箱梁桥为研究对象,分析弯桥曲率半径,支座布置数量和支座偏移距离对桥梁抗倾覆性能的影响。主要研究结果表明:随着桥梁曲率半径的增大,支座脱空的情况逐渐得到改善,抗倾覆系数也随之增大;弯箱梁桥曲率半径相同时影响最不利支座的支反力和桥梁抗倾覆系数的因素不同;增加支座数量对弯桥抗倾覆系数有明显的正面影响,而对最不利支座的支反力几乎没有影响;弯桥抗倾覆性能随支座偏移增大而增大,支座偏移距离较小时,弯桥抗倾覆性能急剧下降;弯桥曲率半径越大,要使弯桥抗倾覆性能满足规范要求所需偏移支座的距离越短;在特殊情况下采用小曲率半径设计方案时,应增加支座数量或合理设置独柱墩支座偏移量。本文研究成果对四跨独柱墩连续弯箱梁桥的设计,施工和管养都具有较强的指导意义。

关键词 独柱墩连续弯箱梁桥 抗倾覆性能 曲率半径 支座布置数量 支座偏移距离

0 引 言

随着社会经济的发展,货车超载现象愈加严重,独柱墩连续梁桥在车辆荷载作用下更容易发生倾覆现象[1-2]。目前,学者们对桥梁抗倾覆性能的研究已取得一定成果:早在1984年,GT Michaltsos[3]等对桥梁倾覆问题进行了研究,提出稳定性安全系数法,并给出了安全限值;焦驰宇[4]等建立了北京某曲线桥梁数值模型,探讨了恒载、活载、混凝土收缩徐变、温度、预应力等荷载作用下结构的受力特点;宫亚峰[5]等选取三跨曲线梁桥的倾覆轴,研究了不同曲率半径下弯桥的稳定系数;万世成[6]等通过研究认为横截面形式、主梁线形和加载条件是影响独柱墩连续梁桥抗倾覆的主要因素;魏霞[7]以长岭高架桥的第五联为例,对独柱墩桥梁进行抗倾覆验算,并提出相应措施;施颖[8]等研究了钢混叠合梁桥和钢筋混凝土梁桥的抗倾覆性能,结果表明钢混叠合梁桥抗倾覆性能弱于钢筋混凝土桥弱,支座布置间距可以有效提高抗倾覆能力。虢玉标[9]等采用《公路钢筋混凝土及预应力混凝土桥涵设计规范》(JTG 3362—2018)(以下简称《新混规》)提出的方法探究曲线半径、支座横向间距和边跨比对独柱墩连续弯箱梁桥抗倾覆稳定性的影响。彭卫兵[10-11]指出刚体与变形体转动的耦合是倾覆破坏的实质,表示《新混规》提出的倾覆计算方法未考虑刚体转动和自重的有利影响,可较保守地计算梁桥倾覆承载力。

综上可知:当前主要基于《公路钢筋混凝土及预应力混凝土桥涵设计规范》(JTG D62—2004)(以下简称《旧混规》)对曲线连续梁桥进行抗倾覆稳定性研究。《旧混规》中关于桥梁倾覆问题未考虑到梁体的扭转,也没给出确切的验算方式。因此,基于《旧混规》进行曲线连续梁桥抗倾覆研究存在一定的不合理性;当前对城市桥梁应用最为广泛的四跨独柱墩连续弯箱梁桥在活载下的抗倾覆性能研究较少。

本文对《新混规》中提出的抗倾覆验算方法进行总结,并以工程中常见的四跨连续弯箱梁桥为例,通过有限元模拟分析,探究曲率半径、支座布置数量以及支座偏移距离对桥梁抗倾覆性能的影响,最后提出四跨连续弯箱梁桥的抗倾覆措施。

1 抗倾覆稳定性分析验算方法

《新混规》对事故桥梁的破坏过程进行分析得出两个明确的特征状态:特征状态1,某一单向受压支座脱空;特征状态2,主梁的扭转支承全部失效。采用两种特征状态作为抗倾覆验算工况:

(1)作用基本组合下单向受压支座反力不出现拉力,即支座不脱空。满足下式:

$$k = 1.0R_{Gki} + 1.4R_{Qki} \geq 0 \tag{1}$$

(2)上部结构的抗倾覆稳定系数大于等于2.5,即应满足下式要求:

$$K = \frac{S_{bk}}{S_{sk}} \geq 2.5 \tag{2}$$

式中:K——抗倾覆稳定系数;

S_{bk}——使上部结构倾覆的汽车荷载(含冲击作用)标准值效应;

S_{sk}——使上部结构稳定的作用效应标准组合。

在桥梁倾覆处于特征状态2时稳定效应和失稳效应按照失效支座对有效支座的力矩计算:

稳定效应

$$\sum S_{\text{bk},i} = \sum (R_{\text{G}ki} \cdot l_i) \tag{3}$$

失稳效应

$$\sum S_{\text{sk},i} = \sum (R_{\text{Q}ki} \cdot l_i) \tag{4}$$

式中：l_i——第 R 个桥墩处失效支座与有效支座的支座中心间距；

$R_{\text{G}ki}$——永久作用标准值效应；

$R_{\text{Q}ki}$——失效支座对应最不利汽车荷载的标准值效应。

所以式(2)等效于式(5)：

$$K = \frac{\sum (R_{\text{G}ki} \cdot l_i)}{\sum (R_{\text{Q}ki} \cdot l_i)} \geq 2.5 \tag{5}$$

两种特征状态均满足要求的情况下，该箱梁才满足抗倾覆性能验算要求。另外需要注意的是，《新规范》中所提出的方法的验算对象是整体式箱梁。

2 工程概况

以某市匝道桥为例，该匝道桥为四跨独柱墩连续弯箱梁桥。主梁采用 C50 混凝土，横断面尺寸如图 1 所示。桥梁跨径布置为 4×20 m。下部结构采用独柱墩，支座采用单支座布设情况：桥台处采用双支座，支座间距为 3.8 m，其余三个桥墩处都采用单支座，具体如图 2 所示。MIDAS 三维模型如图 3 所示。

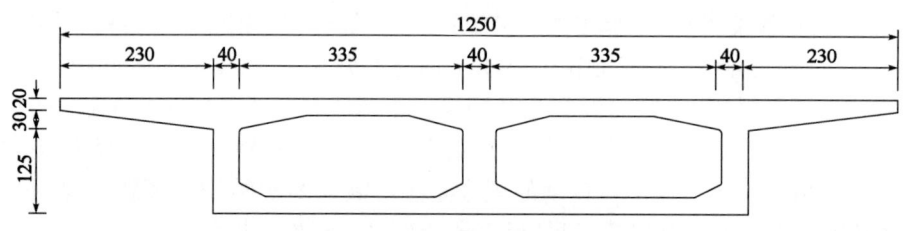

图 1 桥梁横断面示意(尺寸单位：mm)

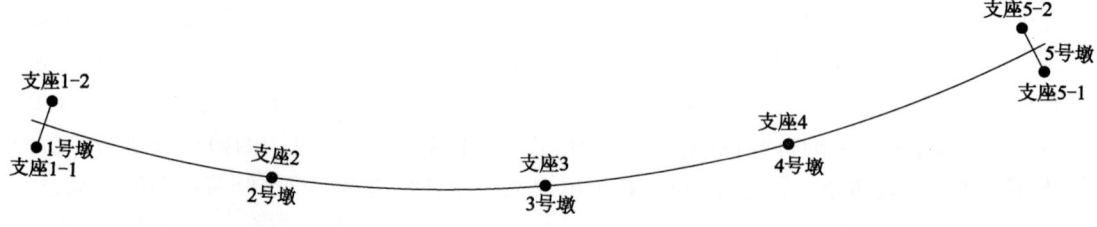

图 2 单支座布设情况

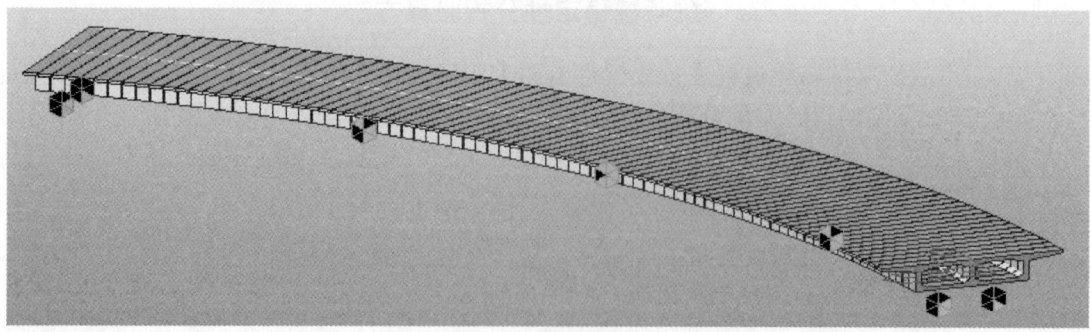

图 3 MIDAS 三维模型

本文采用 Midas Civil 进行有限元模拟。分别布置不同车道数并进行验算，选择抗倾覆系数值最小的车道布置情况下的车道荷载偏载作用作为最不利车道荷载偏载作用。以恒载 + 公路 Ⅰ 级车道荷载（$q_k = 10.5$ kN/m，$p_k = 270 \sim 360$ kN）为荷载工况进行抗倾覆验算。

3 抗倾覆性能影响因素研究

3.1 曲率半径对弯箱梁抗倾覆性能的影响

通过改变弯桥的曲率半径,分析不同曲率半径对桥梁倾覆性能的影响。联系实际工程情况,选择较为常见的曲率半径 R 为:50m、100m、150m、200m、300m、400m、500m。

通过 Midas Civil 导出自重下的支座反力 R_{Gki},以及支座 1-2 和 5-2 分别处于最不利情况时所有支座的支座反力 $R_{Qki,12}$ 和 $R_{Qki,52}$。根据公式(1)和公式(5)进行计算判断,验算结果汇总于表 1 中。

不同曲率半径独柱墩梁桥特征状态 1、2 验算结果　　　表1

R (m)	特征状态					
	特征状态 1			特征状态 2		
	K_{12}	K_{52}	验证结果	k_1	k_5	验证结果
50	−184	−184	不满足要求	1.81	1.81	不满足要求
100	−107	−107	不满足要求	2.10	2.10	不满足要求
150	−82	−82	不满足要求	2.19	2.19	不满足要求
200	51	51	满足要求	2.44	2.44	不满足要求
300	60	60	满足要求	2.49	2.49	不满足要求
400	70	70	满足要求	2.53	2.53	满足要求
500	85	85	满足要求	2.57	2.57	满足要求

由于模型结构、支座情况对称,故得出的结果 $K_{12}=K_{52}$,$k_1=k_5$。根据表格结果分析:①随着曲率半径 R 的增大支座脱空的情况逐渐得到改善;②抗倾覆系数 k 值随着曲率半径 R 的增大而增大;③特征状态 1 在曲率半径 $R\geqslant 200$m 时支座不再脱空,特征状态 2 在曲率半径 $R\geqslant 400$m 时抗倾覆系数 $k\geqslant 2.5$,特征状态 1 和特征状态 2 首次满足要求时桥梁曲率半径不同,说明在弯箱梁桥曲率半径相同时影响特征状态 1 和特征状态 2 的因素不同。

3.2 支座数量对弯箱梁抗倾覆性能的影响

四跨弯桥的支座数量布设情况可分为三种:单支座布设,1 号和 5 号桥墩上布设两个支座,其余三个桥墩上均布设一个支座,如图 2 所示;单双支座间接布设,1 号、3 号和 5 号桥墩上布设两个支座,2 号和 4 号桥墩上布设一个支座,如图 4a)所示;双支座布设,所有桥墩上都布设两个支座,如图 4b)所示。

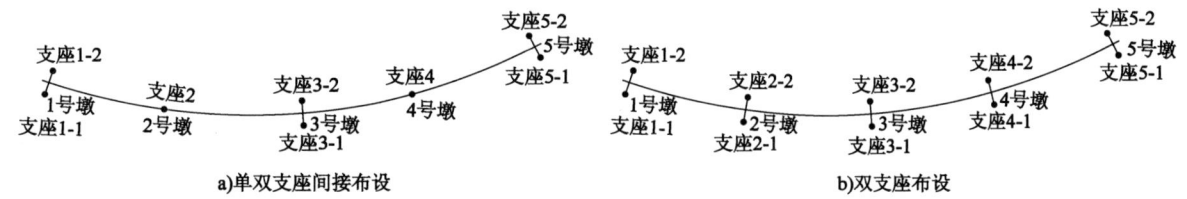

图 4　支座布设情况

若小跨径桥梁在每根桥墩上都设双支座,不仅大大提高成本,而且不能充分利用支座的作用,造成浪费,所以工程上通常不会将每个桥墩上都布置两个支座。因此本文只讨论比较常用的单双支座间接布设情况。采用上述桥梁的上部结构,支座选用图 4a)的单双支座间接布设情况,1 号、3 号和 5 号桥墩上两个支座之间的距离为 3.8m。弯桥曲率半径选用上一节中抗倾覆验算结果不满足要求的半径值,即 R 为 50m、100m、150m、200m、300m。

通过 Midas Civil 导出自重下的支座反力 R_{Gki} 以及支座 1-2、3-2 和 5-2 处于最不利情况时所有支座的支座反力 $R_{Qki,12}$、$R_{Qki,32}$ 和 $R_{Qki,52}$。根据公式(1)和公式(5)进行计算判断,验算结果汇总于表 2 中。

调整支座数量后独柱墩梁桥特征状态 1、2 验算结果　　　　表 2

R (m)	特征状态				
	特征状态 1	特征状态 2			
	验证结果	k_1	k_3	k_5	验证结果
50	不满足要求	3.65	3.35	3.65	满足要求
100	不满足要求	3.95	3.58	3.95	满足要求
150	不满足要求	4.02	3.79	4.02	满足要求
200	满足要求	4.44	3.95	4.44	满足要求
300	满足要求	4.51	4.16	4.51	满足要求

比较表 1 和表 2 结果：①增加 3 号桥墩上的支座数量很大程度上能够提高弯箱梁桥抗倾覆系数，其中曲率半径 R 为 50m、100m、150m、200m、300m 弯桥的抗倾覆系数 k 值分别增加 85.08%、71.29%、63.93%、62.55%、59.04%；②增加 3 号桥墩上的支座数量使得所有曲率半径弯桥的特征状态 2 都满足要求；③增加 3 号桥墩上支座数量对特征状态 1 的验算结果几乎没有影响，原因是同一桥墩上支座的反力主要受车辆荷载在纵桥向位置的影响，增加支座数量只能起到分担反力的作用。

3.3 支座偏移距离对弯箱梁桥抗倾覆性能的影响

选择单支座布设情况中不满足规范要求的曲率半径为 50m、100m、150m、200m 的弯桥进行支座偏移距离对弯箱梁桥抗倾覆性能影响的研究。调整各弯桥 2 号、3 号、4 号桥墩处支座向外侧的偏移量，以 0.1m 为偏移增量，直到弯桥特征状态 1 和特征状态 2 均满足规范要求。支座偏移前后弯桥特征状态 1 和特征状态 2 计算值随偏移量 D 变化情况以折线图展示，如图 5 ~ 图 8 所示。

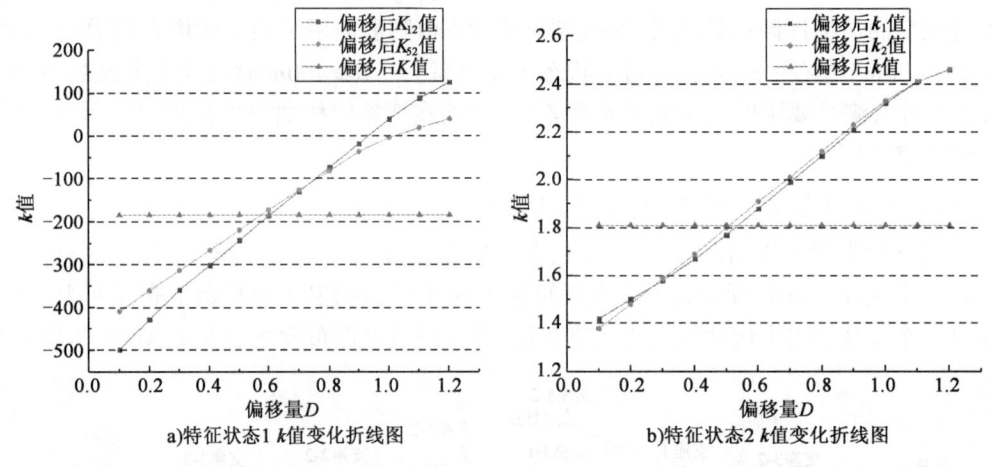

图 5　曲率半径 $R=50$m 弯桥计算值随偏移量 D 变化折线图

曲率半径 $R=50$m 弯桥在偏移量逐渐增大的过程中，K_{12} 和 K_{52} 的变化曲线在 $D=0.7$m 时出现交点，支座反力最小值从支座 1-2 处转变到支座 5-2 处，即在偏移量增大的过程中桥梁在荷载作用下最先脱空的支座位置发生了转变。这是由于曲率半径小，单位长度弯箱梁内外侧的重量差较大，支座偏移距离对支座反力的变化影响大。在 3 号、4 号、5 号桥墩处支座向外偏移的量很小时，弯桥特征状态 1 和特征状态 2 的系数值均急剧降低，弯桥抗倾覆性能急剧下降。弯桥系数 K 值和 k 值随着偏移量的增大逐渐增大，并且均在偏移量 $D=0.6$m 时，首次大于偏移前的 K 值和 k 值。在偏移量 D 为 1.2m、0.9m、0.8m、0.6m 时曲率半径 R 为 50m、100m、150m、200m 的弯桥抗倾覆性能分别满足规范要求，即弯桥曲率半径越大，要使弯桥抗倾覆性能满足规范要求，所需偏移支座的距离越短。

对支座进行适量的偏移能够有效地提高弯桥抗倾覆性能，与增加支座数量影响不同的是，偏移支座不仅对特征状态 2 的抗倾覆系数 k 值有影响，对特征状态 1 的支座反力同样有着较大的影响。

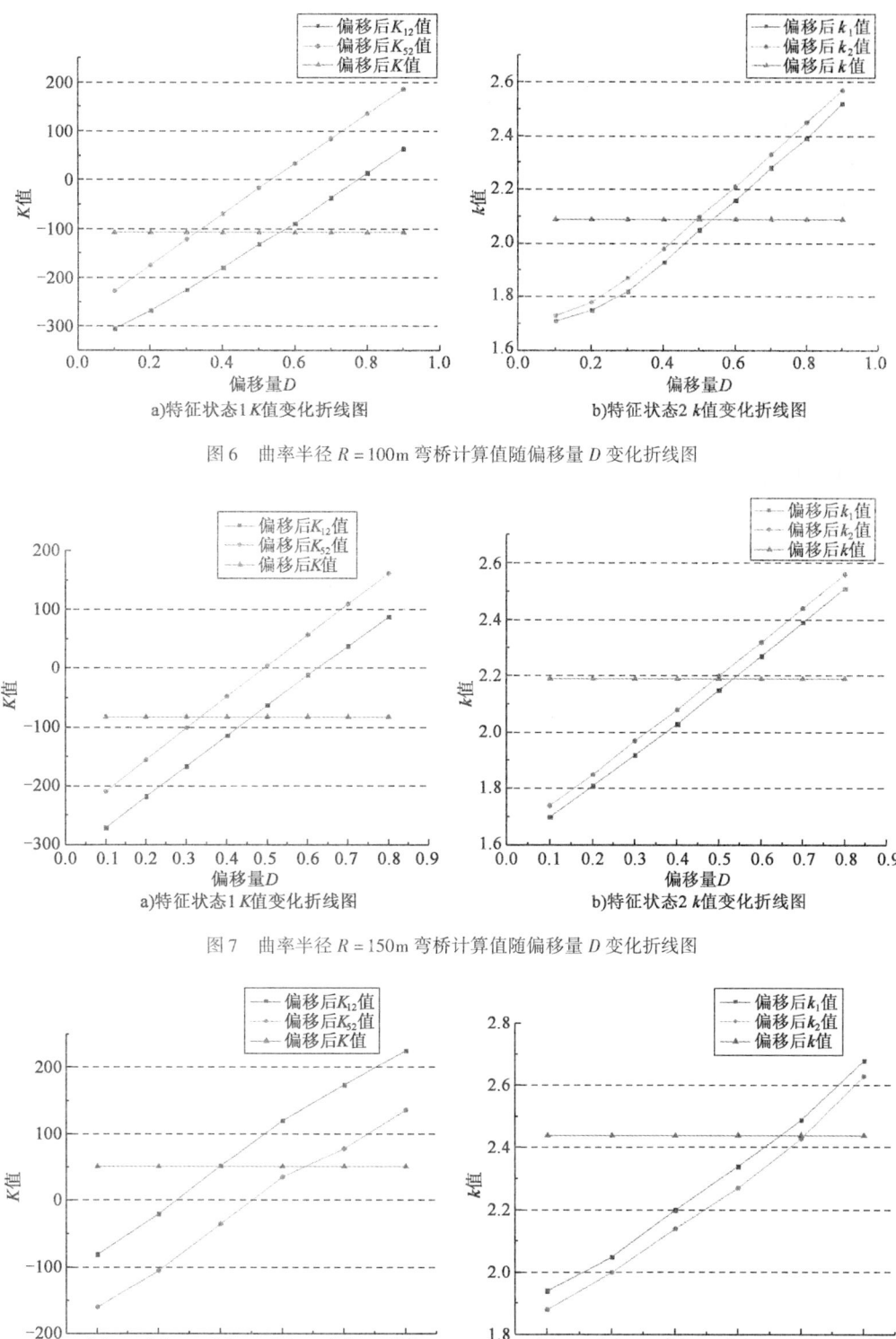

图6 曲率半径 $R=100\mathrm{m}$ 弯桥计算值随偏移量 D 变化折线图

图7 曲率半径 $R=150\mathrm{m}$ 弯桥计算值随偏移量 D 变化折线图

图8 曲率半径 $R=200\mathrm{m}$ 弯桥计算值随偏移量 D 变化折线图

4 结 语

本文选取工程中最常见的四跨独柱墩连续弯箱梁桥,具体分析了曲率半径、支座布置数量及支座偏移距离对独柱弯箱梁桥抗倾覆性能的影响,主要得出的结论如下:

(1) 随着桥梁曲率半径的增大支座脱空的情况逐渐得到改善;抗倾覆系数随着桥梁曲率半径的增大而增大。

(2) 增加支座数量很大程度上能够提高弯箱梁桥抗倾覆系数,对弯桥的抗倾覆系数有明显的正面影响,而对防止支座脱空几乎没有影响。

(3) 支座偏移距离很小时,弯桥抗倾覆性能急剧下降。弯桥曲率半径越大,要使弯桥抗倾覆性能满足规范要求,所需偏移支座的距离越短。

(4) 在独柱墩弯箱梁桥设计时,应尽量选择较大的曲率半径。在特殊情况下采用小曲率半径设计方案时,应增加支座数量或合理设置独柱墩支座偏移量。

参考文献

[1] 薛爱新,李志勇,王洁光,等.特殊荷载作用下独柱墩匝道桥抗倾覆稳定性研究[J].公路工程,2018,43(04):140-144+179.

[2] 肖光术,冯玉龙,岳彬,等.公路独柱桥梁抗倾覆设计与钢结构支撑加固改造施工研究[J].公路工程,2020,45(03):111-116.

[3] Michaltsos G T, Raftoyiannis I G. A mathematical model for the rocking, overturning and shifting proble in bridge[J]. Engineering Structures,2008,30(12):3587-3594.

[4] 焦驰宇,刘陆宇,龙佩恒,等.城市曲线梁桥爬移现象及解决措施研究[J].工程力学,2015,32(S1):177-183.

[5] 宫亚峰,何钰龙,谭国金,等.三跨独柱连续曲线梁桥抗倾覆稳定性分析[J].吉林大学学报(工学版),2018,48(01):113-120.

[6] 万世成,黄侨.独柱墩连续梁桥偏载下的抗倾覆稳定性研究综述[J].中外公路,2015,35(04):156-161.

[7] 魏霞,曹猛.独柱墩弯桥抗倾覆稳定性分析[J].公路交通科技(应用技术版),2018,14(05):236-237+270.

[8] 施颖,林龙,陈国永,等.独柱墩匝道桥抗倾覆能力分析和构造措施研究[J].科技通报,2015,31(07):63-68+72.

[9] 虢玉标,南吉锋,唐焱,等.独柱墩连续弯梁桥抗倾覆稳定性分析[J].工程建设,2020,52(03):28-32.

[10] 彭卫兵,徐文涛,陈光军,等.独柱墩梁桥抗倾覆承载力计算方法[J].中国公路学报,2015,28(03):66-72.

[11] 彭卫兵,朱志翔,陈光军,等.梁桥倾覆机理、破坏模式与计算方法研究[J].土木工程学报,2019,52(12):104-113.

Force Analysis of Frame Abutment

Kunkun Jiang Huishuang Xiao Fujun Li

(Chang'an University)

Abstract Based on the overpass in the railway bridge, this paper analyzed the mechanical characteristics of the traditional frame abutment, and focused on the influence of the unilateral thickening on the traditional structure. Combined with the actual project, the entity finite element is used for analysis and calculation, and engineering measures to improve the mechanical performance of this type of structure are proposed.

Keywords Prestressed concrete structure   Frame structure   Structural analysis   Design considerations

0 Introduction

When the railway crosses the highway, it is often necessary to set up a frame structure abutment to meet the requirements of the cross-line. However, the calculation of the cross-line structure generally uses a frame structure with equal thickness on both sides. But in actual situations, a frame structure with a significantly increased thickness on one side is often used. As a result, the thickening of one side of the frame will greatly increase the stiffness of the thickened side section, and these situations may occur:

(1) The increase of stiffness results an increase in the bending moment of the thickened side, which could cause some adverse effects.

(2) The size of the cross section is increased to improve the mechanical properties of the frame abutment and enhance the resistance of the thickened side, which is benefit for the structure.

In this engineering context, detailed calculations are needed to tell the difference between the frame abutment and the conventional frame structure, and then optimize the calculation method and design plan to guide the subsequent design of similar projects. In reinforced concrete structures, the stress state of steel bars, the stress distribution of concrete, and the cracking of concrete are important indicators to evaluate the structural bearing capacity and serviceability limit state. This calculation will focus on the above contents.

In order to ensure the accuracy of the calculation results, the research plan is as follows:

(1) Use commonly frame structure design calculation software to obtain the reinforcement condition, steel bar and concrete stress state calculated by conventional frame structure.

(2) Establish the entity finite element model of the frame structure and the frame abutment with two reinforcement conditions, and load according to the worst case.

(3) Compare and analysis the calculation results of the four models, get a general conclusion, and give design suggestions.

Based on this research plan, the following conclusions are obtained:

The calculated results using the frame structure method are relatively consistent with the actual calculation results of the frame structure; the actual calculation results of the frame abutment structure show that the frame structure with one thickening side will improve the mechanical performance of the overall structure. The specific manifestations are as follows:

(1) The maximum principal stress of the steel bar is reduced in the middle of the span.

(2) The frame structure cracked in a large area in the middle of the span and cracked under tension with the rigid connection position on both sides, and the frame type abutment structure only had cracks in the middle of the span.

(3) The main tensile stress in the mid-span and rigid connection position of the frame structure exceeds the limit, the main tensile stress in the mid-span position of the frame abutment and the top of the abutment is relatively large, and the mid-span position exceeds the limit.

After calculation and analysis, it is believed that the single-sided thickening of the frame abutment will increase the tensile stress of the concrete at the top of the thickened side. It is worth noting in the design and should be set according to the actual situation.

1 Model Calculation

1.1 Entity Finite Element Calculation

The material constitutive relations, boundary conditions, element types, etc. need to be carefully selected to ensure the accuracy of the calculation results.

1.2 Material Constitutive Relationship

1.2.1 Concrete Compression Constitutive Model

The frame abutment is a reinforced concrete structure, and cracks may exist during operation, so the damage plasticity model (referred to as the CDP model) is selected as the constitutive model of concrete. The damage plasticity model (CDP model) in ABAQUS is one of many concrete material performance constitutive models. It uses the damage factor as a scalar parameter to consider the failure characteristics of the material. It can be applied to the tension and compression of the material. It is a more typical constitutive model that cananalyze the performance of concrete materials (Fig. 1).

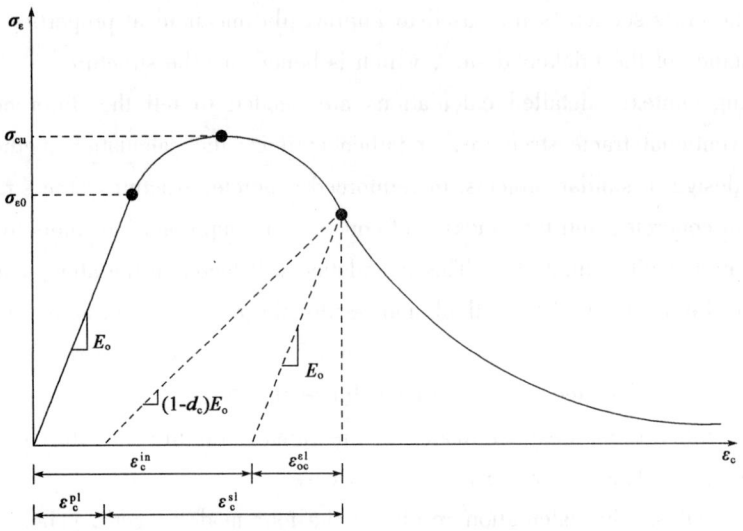

Fig. 1 Constitutive diagram of concrete compression damage

$$\varepsilon_{0c}^{el} = \frac{\sigma_c}{E_o} \tag{1}$$

Where ε_{0c}^{el} is the elastic compressive strain of concrete; σ_c is the elastic compressive stress of concrete; E_o is the modulus of elasticity of concrete.

$$\varepsilon_c^{in} = \varepsilon_c - \varepsilon_{0c}^{el} \tag{2}$$

Where ε_c^{in} is the inelastic compressive strain of concrete; ε_c is the compressive strain of concrete.

$$\varepsilon_c^{pl} = \varepsilon_c^{in} - \frac{d_c}{1-d_c} \cdot \frac{\sigma_c}{E_o} \tag{3}$$

Where ε_c^{pl} is the compression damage strain of concrete; d_c is the compression damage factor of concrete.

Combining formula (1) to formula (3), the relationship between the stress of concrete and the elastic deformation and plastic deformation can be obtained:

$$\sigma_c = (1 - d_c) E_o (\varepsilon_c - \varepsilon_c^{pl}) \tag{4}$$

Introduce constant coefficient $b_c (0 < b_c < 1)$:

$$b_c = \frac{\varepsilon_c^{pl}}{\varepsilon_c^{in}} \tag{5}$$

From this, the expression of the compression damage factor d_c can be obtained:

$$d_c = 1 - \frac{\sigma_c E_o^{-1}}{\varepsilon_c^{pl}(1/b_c - 1) + \sigma_c E_o^{-1}} \tag{6}$$

1.2.2 Concrete tensile damage constitutive (Fig. 2)

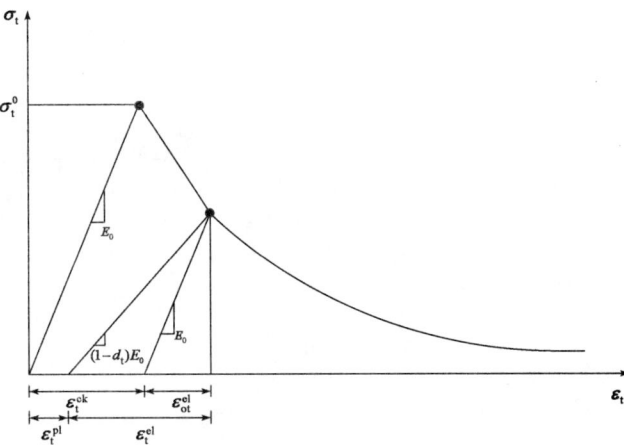

Fig. 2 Concrete tensile damage constitutive diagram

$$\varepsilon_{ot}^{el} = \frac{\sigma_t}{E_o} \quad (7)$$

Where ε_{0t}^{el} is the elastic tensile strain of concrete; σ_t is the tensile stress of concrete; E_o is the modulus of elasticity of concrete.

$$\varepsilon_t^{ck} = \varepsilon_t - \varepsilon_{ot}^{el} \quad (8)$$

Where ε_t^{ck} is the inelastic tensile strain of concrete; ε_t is the tensile strain of concrete.

$$\varepsilon_t^{pl} = \varepsilon_c^{ck} - \frac{d_c}{1 - d_c} \cdot \frac{\sigma_t}{E_o} \quad (9)$$

Where ε_t^{pl} is the tensile damage strain of concrete; d_t is the tensile damage factor of concrete.

Combining formula (1) to formula (3), the relationship between the stress of concrete and the elastic deformation and plastic deformation can be obtained:

$$\sigma_t = (1 - d_t)E_o(\varepsilon_t - \varepsilon_t^{pl}) \quad (10)$$

Introduce constant coefficient $b_t (0 < b_t < 1)$:

$$b_t = \frac{\varepsilon_t^{pl}}{\varepsilon_t^{ck}} \quad (11)$$

From this, the expression of the compression damage factor d_t can be obtained:

$$d_t = 1 - \frac{\sigma_t E_o^{-1}}{\varepsilon_t^{pl}(1/b_t - 1) + \sigma_t E_o^{-1}} \quad (12)$$

The concrete material of the supporting project is C35, referring to the C35 tension-compression constitutive relationship in the 《Specification for Design of Concrete Structures》(GB 50010—2010) and the method of selecting damage factors in related papers, the concrete parameters explored this time are as follows (Tab. 1).

Concrete plastic constitutive parameters (Unit: N, mm, t) Tab. 1

Expansion angle	Eccentricity	f_{b0}/f_{c0}	k	Stickiness parameter	Density	E_o	μ
38	0.1	1.16	0.66667	1.00×10^{-5}	2.39×10^{-9}	31500	0.2

In the initial design stage, the selected steel bar is marked HRB400. According to the specification, the steel bar cannot yield during use, so the steel bar adopts the elastic constitutive, the elastic modulus is 200000 MPa, and the Poisson's ratio is 0.3.

1.3 Build Entity Finite Element Model

This calculation includes the frame structure finite element model and the frame type abutment entity finite element model. The element type is C3D8R (eight-node linear hexahedral element, reduced integral, hourglass control). Reinforcing bars include skeleton main bars and transverse bridge bars. The finite element models were established based on design drawings. The element type is T3D2 truss element. It should be noted that the cantilever section is calculated separately here for stress and strain analysis (Fig. 3-Fig. 5).

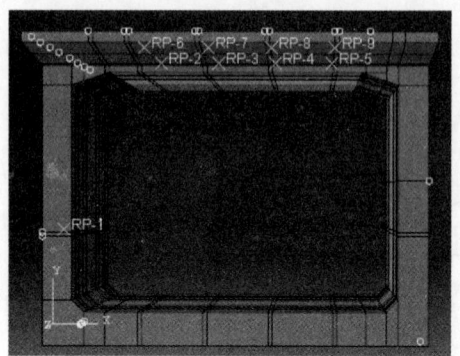 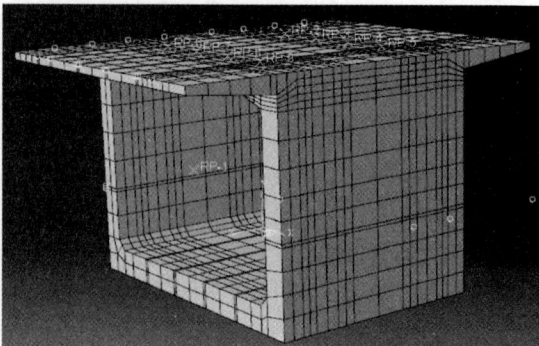

Fig. 3　Finite element model of traditional frame structure

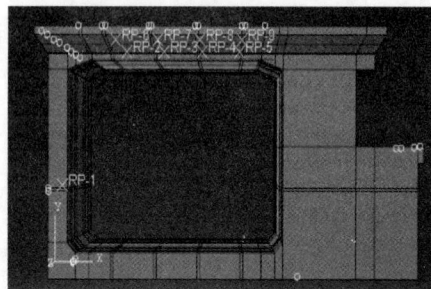 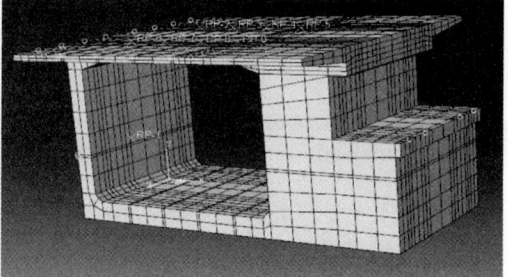

Fig. 4　Finite element model of bridge-type frame structure

Fig. 5　Rebar finite element model

1.4　Loads and Boundary Conditions

In the actual project, the bottom of the abutment directly acts on the foundation, similar to the cap, so the bottom of the frame structure is fixed to simulate.

The external loads acting on the structure include the self-weight of the structure, the second-stage dead load (190.3kN/m), the vehicle load below the structure (ZKH; including the impact coefficient 1.23), the support reaction force and the active earth pressure.

The main purpose of this investigation is the difference in force and deformation of two different structures under the action of structural weight and live load, so other loads such as temperature and settlement are not considered (Fig. 6).

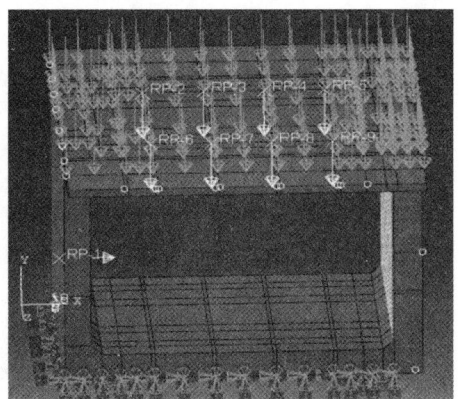
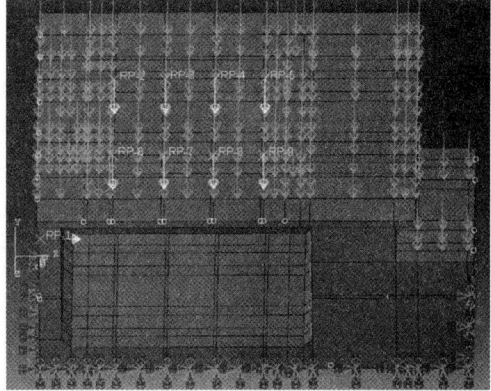

Fig. 6 Schematic diagram of frame structure(left) and Schematic diagram of frame type abutment structure(right)

2 Results and Analysis

2.1 Calculation Result of Frame Abutment

There are two types of commonly used steel bars, namely d16 and d20, which are calculated separately here

2.1.1 Frame Abutment with Steel Bar Number d16

For the frame abutment with d16 steel reinforcement, the maximum tensile stress of concrete appears at the top of the abutment (the thickened side of the frame structure; Fig. 7), which is 2.163MPa; the maximum compressive stress appears at the junction of the abutment and the roof, which is 1.84MPa; the tensile stress in the middle of the frame part is 2.04MPa.

It can be seen from Figure 9 that the mid-span position has cracked under tension, and the cracking stress has been reached during the loading process. However, the E_0 of concrete is reduced due to cracking during finite element calculation, resulting in a certain degree of stress reduction. The concrete of the frame abutment has no compression damage except for stress concentration locations (Fig. 8).

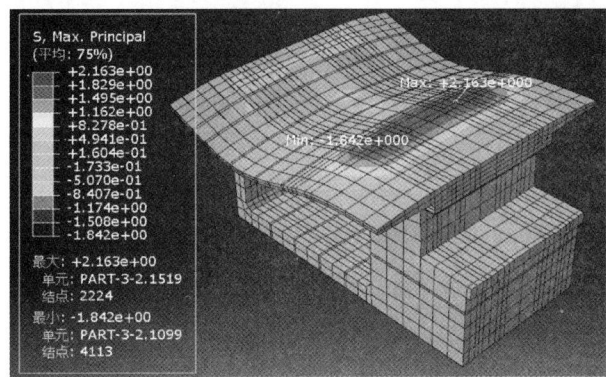
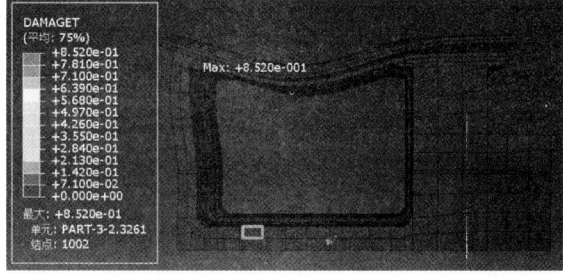

Fig. 7 Concrete principal stress cloud diagram (MPa)　　Fig. 8 Concrete principal stress cloud diagram (MPa)

The maximum principal stress of the steel bar is 34.4MPa, which appears at the mid-span position of the frame abutment (Fig. 9). During operation, the maximum vertical displacement of the frame abutment is 2.75mm, which appears at the edge of the cantilever in the middle of the span (Fig. 9).

2.1.2 Frame Abutment with Steel Bar Number d20

For the frame abutment with d20 reinforcement, the maximum tensile stress of concrete appears at the top of the abutment (the thickened side of the frame structure; Fig. 10), which is 2.119MPa; the maximum compressive stress appears at the junction of the abutment and the roof, which is 1.77MPa; the tensile stress in the middle of the frame part is 1.91MPa.

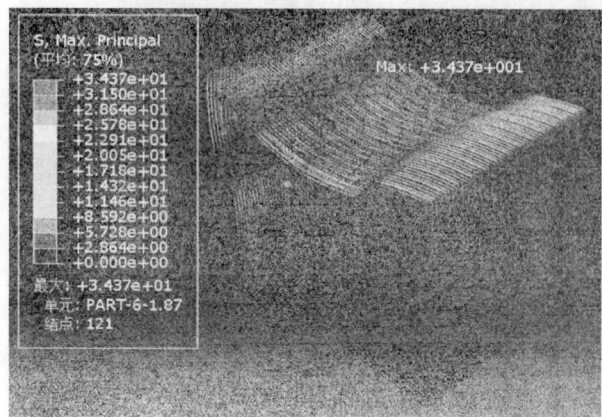

Fig.9 Rebar principal stress cloud diagram (MPa)

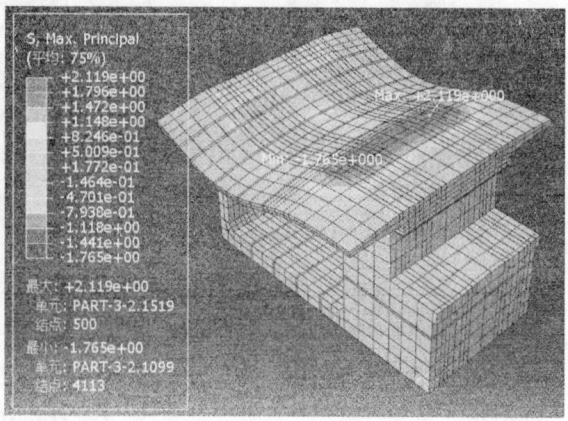

Fig.10 Concrete principal stress cloud diagram (MPa)

It can be seen from Fig. 11 that the mid-span position has been pulled and cracked. The concrete of the frame abutment has no compression damage except for stress concentration locations (Fig. 11).

The maximum principal stress of the steel bar is 31.4MPa, which appears at the mid-span position of the frame abutment (Fig. 12). During operation, the maximum vertical displacement of the frame abutment is 2.69mm, which appears at the edge of the mid-span cantilever.

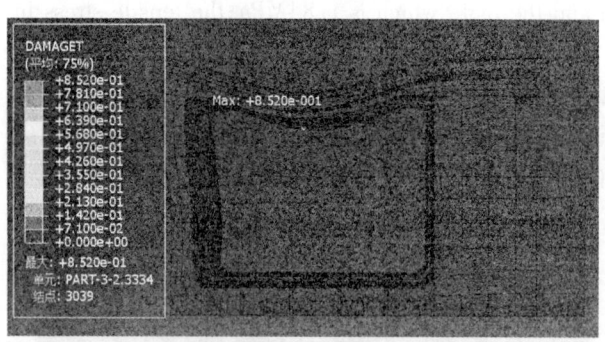

Fig. 11 Concrete tensile damage cloud diagram (MPa)

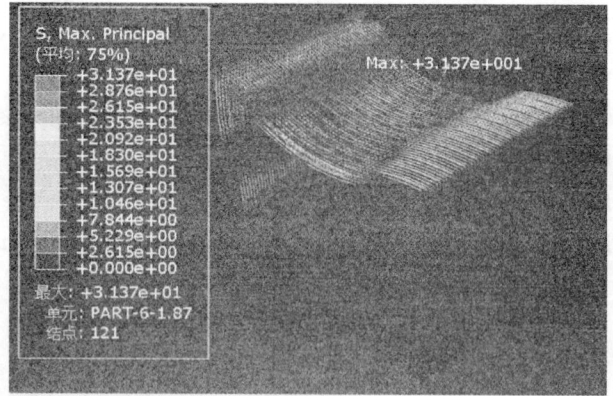

Fig. 12 Rebar principal stress cloud diagram (MPa)

2.2 Frame Structure Calculation Results

2.2.1 Frame Structure with Steel Bar Number d16

For the frame structure with d16 steel bars, the maximum tensile stress of concrete appears at the top of the left side of the frame structure (Fig. 13), which is 2.104MPa; the maximum compressive stress appears at the junction of the right side and the roof, which is 1.77MPa; The tensile stress in is 0.55MPa.

It can be seen from Fig. 14 that the middle-span and left outer positions have been tensile and cracked, and the stresses corresponding to these positions have exceeded the limit during the loading process, which in turn causes damage to reduce the elastic modulus, and the stress reduction is greater. Too much meaning. The concrete of the frame abutment has no compression damage except the stress concentration location (Fig. 14).

The maximum principal stress of the steel bars is 270.3 MPa. At the outer position of the frame structure (Fig. 15), the maximum tensile stress of the steel bars in the middle of the span is 204 MPa. During operation, the maximum vertical displacement of the frame abutment is 36.5mm, which appears at the edge of the cantilever in the middle of the span (Fig.16).

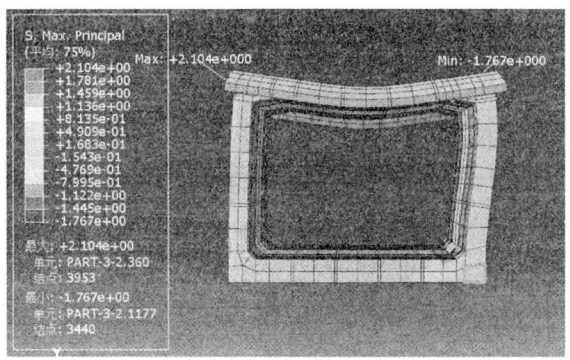

Fig. 13 Concrete principal stress cloud diagram (MPa)

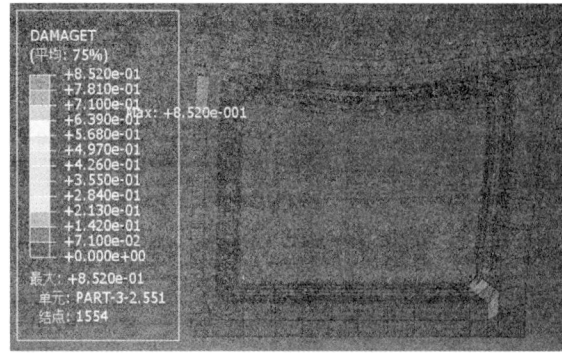

Fig. 14 Concrete tensile damage cloud diagram (MPa)

2.2.2 Frame Structure with Steel Bar Number d20

For the frame structure with d20 steel bars, the maximum tensile stress of concrete appears at the top of the left side of the frame structure (Fig. 16), which is 2.33MPa; the maximum compressive stress appears at the junction of the right side and the roof, which is 1.49MPa; The tensile stress in is 0.65MPa.

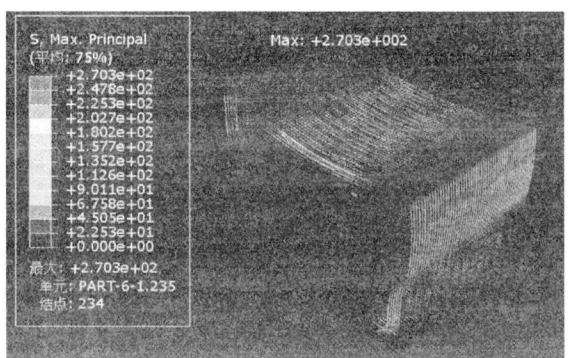

Fig. 15 Rebar principal stress cloud diagram (MPa)

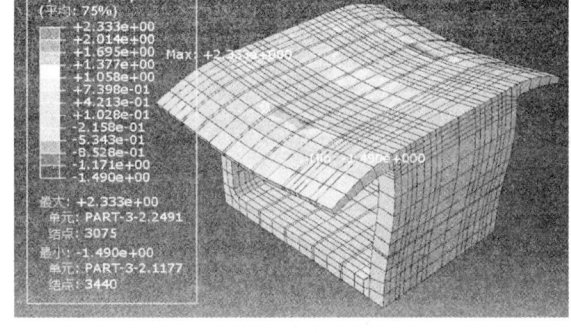

Fig. 16 Concrete principal stress cloud diagram (MPa)

From Fig. 17, it can be seen that the middle-span and left outer positions have been tensile and cracked. The stresses corresponding to these positions have exceeded the limit during the loading process, resulting in damage, resulting in a decrease in elastic modulus and a large reduction in stress. Too much meaning. The concrete of the frame abutment has no compression damage except for stress concentration locations (Fig. 18).

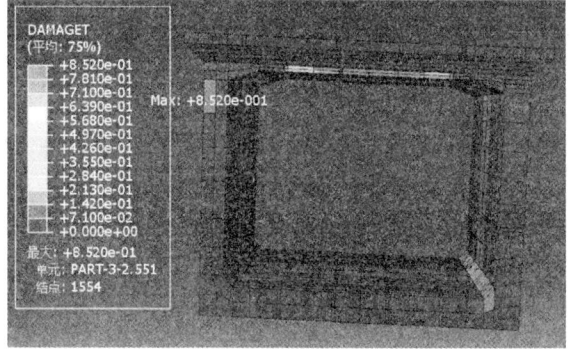

Fig. 17 Concrete tensile damage cloud diagram (MPa)

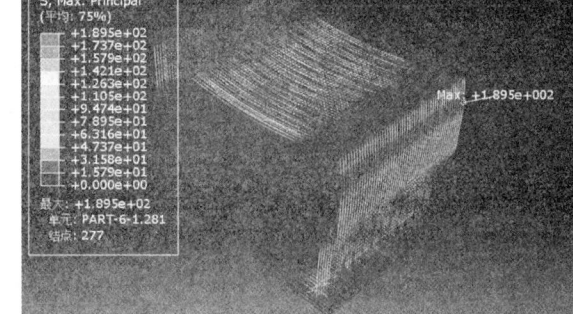

Fig. 18 Rebar principal stress cloud diagram (MPa)

The maximum principal stress of the steel bars is 189.5 MPa. At the outer position of the 1 frame structure (Fig. 18), the maximum tensile stress of the steel bars at the mid-span position is 162.5 MPa. During operation, the maximum vertical displacement of the frame abutment is 32.8mm, which appears at the edge of the mid-span cantilever.

3 Comparasion of Results and Conclusions

Comparing the calculation results of the frame structure and the entity finite element, the main concern is the stress state of the steel bar, the cracking of the concrete and the stress distribution of the concrete (Tab. 2).

Comparison of results Tab. 2

Project	Calculation plan			
	Frame structure with d16 steel bar	Frame structure with d20 steel bar	Frame abutment with d16 steel bar	Frame abutment with d20 steel bar
Rebar principal stress	Maximum stress on the outside: 270.4MPa Mid-span position: 204MPa	Maximum stress on the outside: 270.4MPa Mid-span position: 204MPa	Mid-span position: 33.4 MPa	Mid-span position: 31.4MPa
Concrete cracking	Large area cracks in the middle of the span and cracks under tension at the rigid connection position	Large area cracks in the middle of the span and cracks under tension at the rigid connection position	Cracking in mid-span	Cracking in mid-span
Concrete tensile stress	Stress overrun in the mid-span and rigid connection position, causing cracks	Stress overrun in the mid-span and rigid connection position, causing cracks	The mid-span position exceeds the limit, and the top of the abutment is 2.16MPa	The mid-span position exceeds the limit, and the top of the abutment is 2.12MPa

The calculation results show that the calculation results obtained by using the frame structure method are relatively consistent with the actual calculation results of the frame structure. Therefore, the following conclusions can be obtained:

(1) When designing a single-side thickened frame abutment, the frame model can be used for calculation.

(2) When the frame abutment cannot meet the design requirements, a single-sided thickening design can be used.

(3) If a single-sided thickened frame abutment is used, the concrete at the top of the thickened side will have a large tensile stress, and the tensile steel bars should be dense.

References

[1] Jiang Yu, Jian Guo. Design and Research of Large-span Frame Piers of Expressway [J]. Journal of Highway and Transportation Research and Development, 2011, 7(06): 203-205.

[2] Ming Wan. The influence of stiffness in the calculation of frame pier [J]. Railway Investigation and Surveying, 2010, 36(05): 88-89.

[3] WanJun Tian. Research on Design of Prestressed Concrete Frame Pier [J]. Railway Standard Design, 2003 (08): 67-69.

[4] ChangHui Tang, ZhengYu Yin. Analysis of seismic performance of partially prestressed concrete frame [J] Highway Engineering, 2020, 45(04): 67-73.

[5] YaoZhao Shang. Design of steel beam frame piers of Tianjin Southwest Loop Railway [J]. Railway Engineering, 2013(01): 14-16.

[6] Ouyang ZhangZhi, DongQuan Wang, GuangYun Yu, et al. Finite element analysis of mechanical properties

of hollow box frame bridges[J]. Railway Construction, 2011(04):9-12.
[7] HongYan Liang. Design of top-entry under-passing railway frame bridge[J]. Railway Construction, 2009(06):25-27.

大跨度斜交框架式地道桥空间有限元分析研究

范香艳 刘来君 丁昊 王鑫

(长安大学公路学院)

摘 要 采用Midas/FEA实体有限元分析软件建立实体单元模型,模拟自重作用下单孔、两孔、三孔斜交框架地道桥的受力情况,探讨结构随斜交角度、宽度、斜跨度、垂直跨度变化时的应力和变形规律。研究结果表明:自重作用下,地道桥加腋位置的应力随斜角角度的增大成先增大后减小的趋势,斜角角度在20°左右时的应力取得最大值;正交地道桥宽度的变化对结构的影响较小,斜交框架地道桥随着宽度的增大结构顶板跨中和钝角加腋位置处的应力数值都不断减小;保持斜角角度不变时,单孔和两孔斜交框架地道桥顶板中心线跨中位置的应力基本上与ls^2成正比例关系。实体有限元分析为此类结构的设计和施工提供思路。

关键词 大跨度 斜交 框架式 地道桥 有限元分析

0 引言

斜交地道桥与正交地道桥相比其受力情况更为复杂,不仅有弯矩、剪力、轴向力的作用,还有扭矩的存在,且扭矩随斜交角度的增大而变得不可忽略[1]。此外影响斜交框架地道桥的力学性能因素也较多,结构的力学性能因结构的不同而表现不同。潘文怡[2]采用薄板单元对斜交框架地道桥的结构进行空间受力分析,重点研究随着斜交角度的减小,框架桥顶板、底板各单元弯矩的变化,为斜交框架地道桥的结构设计,特别是顶板、底板的配筋设计提供参考依据。尤广杰[3]以实际工程为背景,运用Midas civil软件建立厚板单元的三维空间模型,分析常见斜交结构形式和改进的斜交结构的受力特征。聂利英,吴鸿庆[4]采用组合板单元对多种地道桥结构进行空间有限元分析,通过大量的计算分析提出了斜交地道桥简化为正交地道桥的计算模型,以便于设计施工单位直接采用规范方便地计算。王庆贵[5]基于平面杆系模型和空间板壳模型,对斜交框架双孔地道桥进行受力特性分析,探讨了两种计算模型的适用性。大多专家学者采用厚板单元理论模拟分析和地道桥的力学性能,但是采用实体单元模型的比较少,结构力学性能与结构形状是否有联系没有明确的界定,本文采用MIDAS/FEA空间实体有限单元软件,建立实体单元模型,所选结构参数与文献[6]中结构的尺寸相同。将建立的实体单元模型计算结果与文献[6]中所建的板单元计算模型相比较,分析不同宽度、不同斜交角度、垂直跨度和斜跨度的不同对结构受力的影响,为同类型的结构分析提供思路。

1 结构尺寸与模型类型

1.1 结构尺寸

探讨结构在自重作用下的受力随宽度、角度、跨度的变化情况[4]。现作出如下规定:l_s为斜跨度、l_t为垂直跨度、B为宽度、B_s为斜宽度、θ为斜交角,斜交地道桥的宽度、角度和跨度示意图见图1。两孔、三孔斜交框架地道桥尺寸详图见图2和图3。

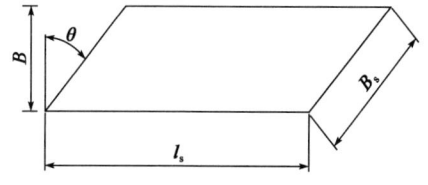

图1 斜交地道桥的宽度、角度和跨度示意图

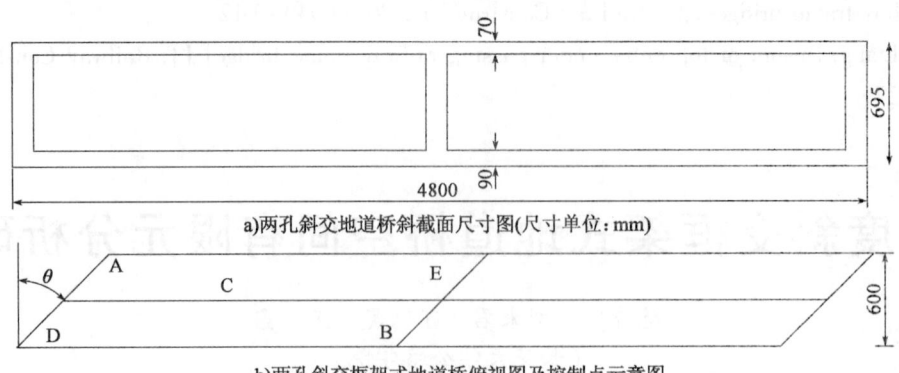

图 2 两孔斜交框架式地道桥尺寸图(尺寸单位:mm)

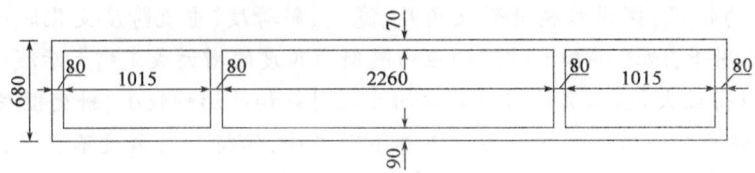

图 3 三孔斜交框架式地道桥斜截面尺寸图(尺寸单位:mm)

1.2 模型类型

采用 Midas/FEA 软件建立三维实体单元模型。结构主体采用 C35 混凝土,抗渗等级为 P8。钢筋混凝土重度 $\gamma = 25 \text{kN/m}^3$、弹性模量 $E = 3.3 \times 10^4 \text{kN/m}$、泊松比 $\mu = 0.2$、线膨胀系数 $\alpha = 0.00001$。只考虑和分析框架主体在自重作用下结构的力学特性。以主要控制点的应力数值变化来考察结构的力学特性。

2 计算参数

(1)保持跨度 L_s 和宽度不变,改变斜交角度 θ。θ 取值分别为 10°、20°、30°、40°、50°、60°、0°,分别建立三孔和两孔斜交框架式地道桥模型,分析结构在自身重力作用下结构应力变化情况。

(2)分别建立斜交角度为 45°和 0°的三孔斜交框架式地道桥模型,改变结构宽度,分别取宽度 $B = 6 \sim 10 \text{m}$,取顶板中心线处跨中的 von-Mises-Stress 应力数值来分析结构应力随宽度变化的情况。

(3)保持斜交角度 θ 和宽度 B 不变,改变斜跨度 L_s,分别建立单孔跨度为 5m、10m、15m、20m 和斜跨度分别为 20m、25m、30m、35m、40m 两孔斜交角度地道桥,斜交角度为 30°,宽度分别为 6m 和 5m。比较单孔、两孔斜交框架式地道桥自重作用下顶板应力变化情况。

3 计算结果分析

3.1 斜交角度变化对结构应力影响

保持斜跨度和宽度不变的情况下,用 MIDAS/FEA 软件分别建立两孔和三孔斜交角度分别为 0°、10°、20°、30°、40°、50°、60°的框架地道桥实体单元模型。斜交角度为 0°和 30°时结构应力云图分别见图 4 和图 5。

由计算结果云图 4 和图 5a)可知正交框架地道桥应力分布较均匀,应力最大值分布在与中墙相交的顶板上,三孔顶板跨中位置的应力以及两孔边孔跨中位置的应力数值向四周呈带状扩散;斜交框架式地道桥随着斜交角度的增大顶板与中墙相交位置处的应力集中现象越来越明显,应力数值分布也是从顶板跨中位置处和中墙顶面同时向四周不均匀扩散;由于结构刚度很大,结构底板与边墙的应力数值所占比例最大达到 47%,应力变化不明显,所以在考虑自重作用下框架式地道桥的力学性能时重点分析结构顶板应力应变变化。

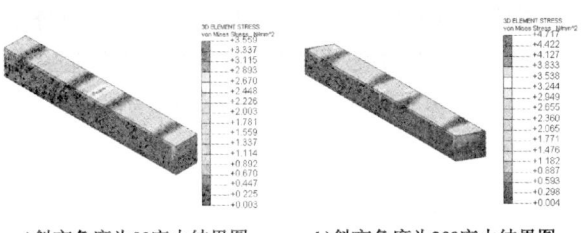

a) 斜交角度为0°应力结果图　　　　b) 斜交角度为30°应力结果图

图4　两孔斜交地道桥应力结果云图

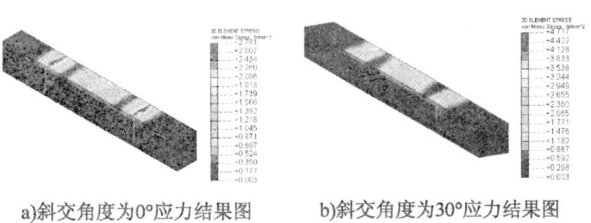

a) 斜交角度为0°应力结果图　　　　b) 斜交角度为30°应力结果图

图5　三孔斜交地道桥应力结果云图

3.2　宽度变化对结构的影响

保持斜跨度和斜交角度分别为0°和45°不变的情况下改变宽度。宽度取值为6m、7m、8m、9m、10m分别建立结构实体单元模型。模型离散图见图6。

图6　三孔框架地道桥模型离散图

选取计算模型中顶板中心线处跨中的von-Mises-Stress应力值作为控制数值,来考察宽度变化对结构的影响。以宽度作为横坐标,以von-Mises-Stress应力作为纵坐标,顶板中心线跨中位置应力数值变化曲线见图7。在斜交角度为45°时顶板与中墙相交钝角位置处的应力数值变化曲线见图8。

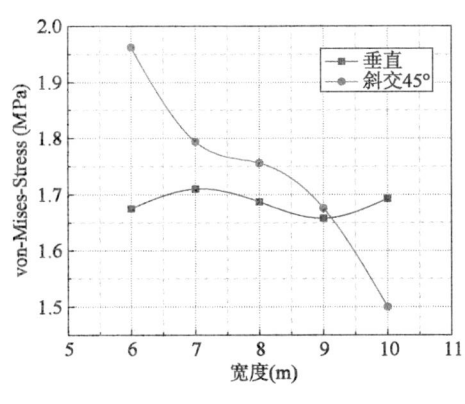

图7　跨中位置应力随宽度变化的曲线

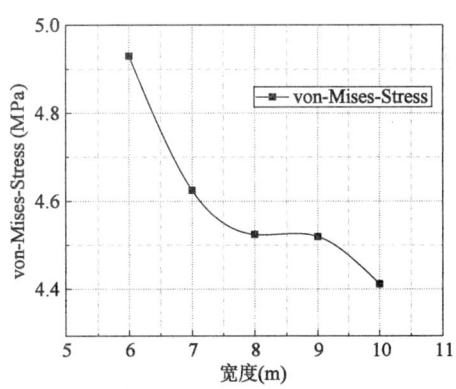

图8　钝角位置处应力随宽度变化曲线

由图7可以看出,斜交角度和跨度不变,宽度改变时:斜交角度为0°即正交的地道桥在自重荷载也即均布荷载作用下的应力数值变化较小,没有明显的改变;对于斜交框架地道桥,自重作用下随着宽度的增大,顶板中心线处跨中位置应力不断减小。由图8可以看出斜交地道桥中孔顶板与中墙相交钝角位置处应力随宽度的增加而减小,钝角位置存在应力集中现象且随宽度的增大这种现象逐渐减弱。

3.3　斜跨度和垂直跨度对结构影响

单孔、两孔地道桥的结构尺寸见表1、表2,尺寸详图见图9。其中保持顶板与底板的厚度、结构高度、中隔墙和边墙的厚度不变,不计顶板加腋处的尺寸,通过改变单孔的跨径来改变结构的总跨度。规定L_s为斜跨度,B为宽度,θ为斜交角。L_1为边孔的净跨径。单孔斜交地道桥的顶底板厚分别是0.5m和0.9m,边墙厚0.6m,框架高6.8m,宽度B为6m。两孔斜交地道桥顶底板厚分别为0.7m和0.9m,中墙厚0.8m,框架高6.8m,宽度B为10m。

单孔斜交地道桥尺寸表单位(m)　　　　　　　　　　　　　　　　　表1

L_s	5	10	15	20
L_1	3.8	8.8	13.8	18.8

两孔斜交框架地道桥尺寸表单位(m)　　　　　　　　　　　　　　表2

L_s	20	25	30	35	40
L_1	8.8	11.3	13.8	16.3	18.8

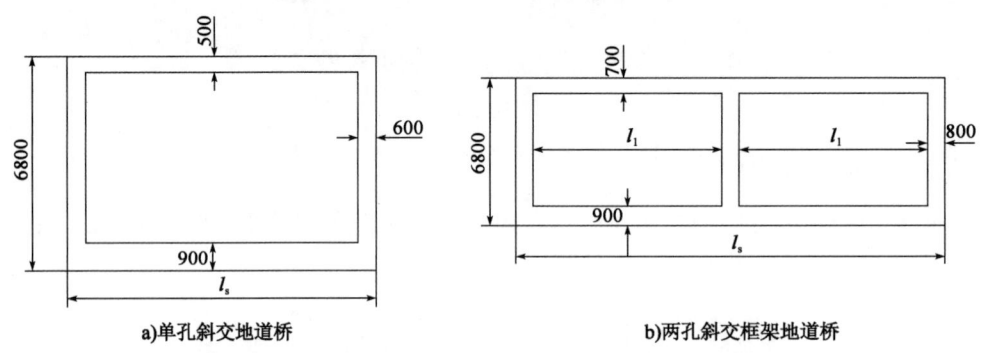

图9　框架地道桥尺寸详图(尺寸单位:mm)

分别建立实体单元模型,对于单孔和两孔斜交地道桥,取顶板中心线跨中位置的应力变化来考虑结构的特性。应力随跨度变化的曲线分别见图10和图11。

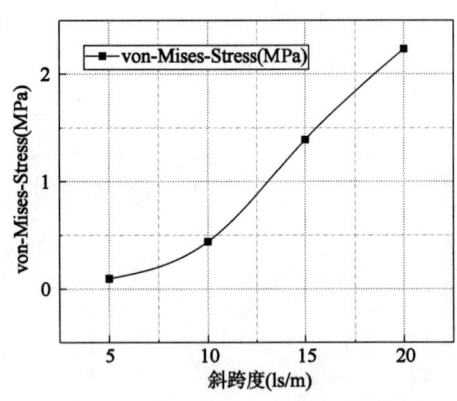
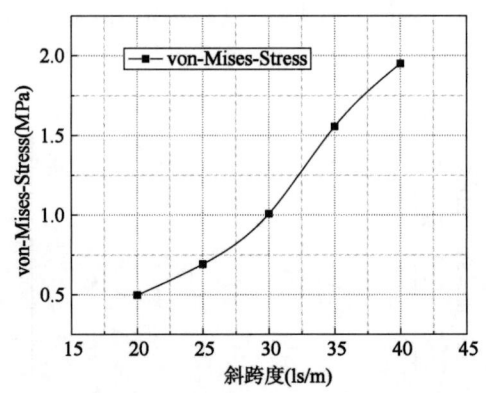

图10　单孔顶板跨中Mises屈服应力曲线图　　　图11　两孔顶板跨中Mises屈服应力曲线图

由以上计算结果图我们可以看出在保持宽度和斜交角度不变的情况下,无论B/ls的比值为多少,顶板中心线跨中位置的应力基本上与ls^2成正比关系,基本上与文献[6]结论相同。

4　结　语

建立三维实体单元模型,分析在自身重力作用下斜交框架地道桥在不同斜交角度、不同宽度、不同跨度作用下结构的力学性能,得出以下结论:

(1)保持跨度和宽度不变的情况下:随着斜交角度的增大,地道桥顶板加腋位置以及顶板各孔跨中心线处的应力均先增大后减小,在斜交角度为20°左右时应力数值达到最大。各孔跨中心线位置处的位移变化与应力数值变化基本一致,这说明斜交角度为20°时结构是最易损坏,所以在工程实践中尽量避免使斜交角度在20°左右,特殊情况下斜交角度为20°时采取一些有效的保护措施。

(2)保持斜交角度和跨度不变的情况下:宽度对正交框架地道桥的应力影响小;斜交框架地道桥随着宽度的增大结构顶板跨中和钝角加腋位置处的应力数值都不断减小。

(3)保持斜交角度和斜跨度不变的情况下:单孔和两孔斜交框架地道桥顶板中心线跨中位置的应力基本上与ls^2成正比例关系;三孔斜交地道桥因为中孔与边孔的尺寸大小比例不同以及跨度的不同中墙与顶板相交钝角位置处的应力也不尽相同,在中孔与边孔比例相同的情况下,跨度越大,钝角位置处应力数值也就越大。

(4)斜交框架地道桥力学特性较正交地道桥复杂,尤其是加腋位置的应力较大,结构设计可以采用加强钢筋增加加腋位置的强度,避免因斜交角度过大而导致结构损坏。

参考文献

[1] 伍振宇.大跨度多孔斜交框架桥的设计与力学分析[J].低碳世界,2017(04):217-218.
[2] 潘文怡.斜交框架地道桥的设计探讨[J].铁道标准设计,2009(06):79-81.
[3] 尤广杰.下穿既有铁路大斜交框架桥结构分析[J].铁道勘察,2016,42(05):98-101.
[4] 聂利英,吴鸿庆.钢筋混凝土地道桥力学特性的研究[J].兰州铁道学院学报,2001(03):19-24.
[5] 王庆贵.斜交框架地道桥的参数分析[J].盐城工学院学报(自然科学版),2013,26(01):75-78.
[6] 朱尔玉,王恒栋,谢灵.框架式地道桥设计理论与应用[M].北京:北京交通大学出版社.2017:86-90.

矩形空心钢筋混凝土高墩延性抗震性能分析

廖泳华 张谢东

(武汉理工大学交通学院)

摘 要 空心高墩是墩身为空腔体,墩高40m以上的桥墩,其由于自重小、节省圬工材料,并具有良好的结构强度和刚度,在大跨高墩桥梁中得到了广泛的应用。本文从全长649m的长虫沟大桥矩形空心高墩模型出发,采用OpenSees有限元软件进行建模,计算并分析了在不同轴压比、配筋率的情况下屈服曲率、极限曲率以及曲率延性系数的变化特性,为矩形空心高墩延性抗震研究提供经验。

关键词 矩形空心高墩 延性抗震性能 有限元 曲率延性系数

0 引 言

随着社会的不断发展,人民生活越来越聚集,桥梁作为交通生命线上的枢纽工程,一旦遭受地震破坏[1],不仅会造成巨大的经济损失,还会给震后的救援工作带来极大的困难。桥墩作为桥梁的主要承重构件,主要负责将作用在桥梁上部的恒、活载传递给地基,是桥梁结构中首先受到地震作用的构件。由于空心桥墩自重小,刚度和强度性能良好,减轻了墩柱质量对桥梁地震反应的影响,因此适应于桥梁工程向大跨径、高墩方向发展的趋势,在我国西部大跨高墩桥梁中得到广泛应用。有关研究表明,采用相同材料的空心桥墩与实心桥墩相比,刚度差异不大,但能节省1/3的圬工材料,且当桥墩越高,节省材料也越多,经济效果越好,而其自重较轻,又有利于地基的处理[2]。空心桥墩内部呈中空形态,是实心墩体轻型化发展的主流思路,当墩体高度超过40m时,实心墩墩体往往因设计尺寸较大,混凝土用量较多,在各类工程实践中显得十分不适应,而钢筋混凝土空心墩却表现出极大的优越性[3]。因此,为减少地震对桥梁的破坏,应对空心高墩的抗震性能进行相关的研究[4-7]。

1 计算模型以及实例

1.1 背景项目概况

长虫沟大桥是准格尔至兴和运煤高速公路上的一座重要桥梁,桥梁原设计起点桩号 K166+825.5(耳墙尾),设计终点桩号 K167+474.5(耳墙尾),桥梁全长 649.0m。桥梁上部结构为先简支后连续预应力混凝土连续 T 梁,桥跨布置为 4×40m(第一联)+4×40m(第二联)+4×40m(第三联)+4×40m(第四联)。桥梁下部结构为钢筋混凝土桩柱式桥墩,桩柱式桥台。

原设计方案全桥上部结构均采用预制预应力混凝土 T 梁,下部结构均采用桩柱式桥梁,当桥墩高度较大时,宜加大桥梁跨度以减少高墩数量来提升抗震性能,宜采用整体性较好的、自重较轻的结构形式,为之本设计将原设计桥跨布置变更为:3×40m(装配式 T 梁)+(43m+77m+80m+77m+43m)(波形钢腹板预应力混凝土箱型梁刚构桥)+4×40m(装配式 T 梁)。主桥上部结构采用波形钢腹板预应力混凝土箱型梁,刚构体系,下部结构采用箱型桥墩,群桩基础。

1.2 钢筋混凝土矩形空心高墩模型

本文研究的钢筋混凝土矩形空心高墩模型是墩底固结,墩顶自由的矩形空心截面墩,截面钢筋按照外侧选用 32mm,内测选用 28mm 配置,且截面内侧倒角去掉换为直角。墩柱截面各项具体参数和图形如图1、表1所示。

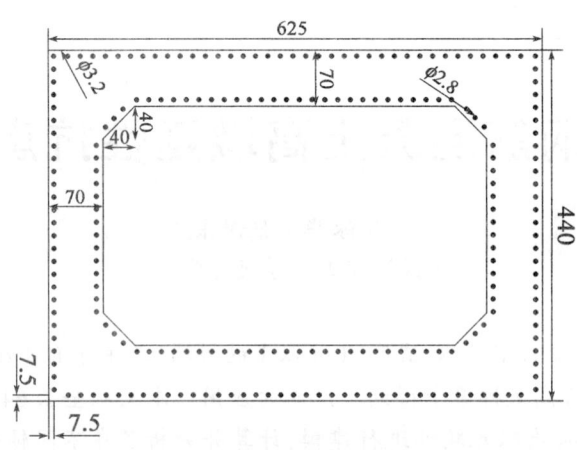

图1 桥墩模型横截面(尺寸单位:m)

空心矩形截面墩基本参数 表1

基本信息	
墩高	46m
截面长	6.25m
截面宽	4.4m
沿截面长方向壁厚	0.7m
沿截面宽方向壁厚	0.7m
纵筋类型	HRB400
纵筋配筋率	2.633%
混凝土类型	C40
保护层厚度	0.075m

2 确定墩高下不同因素对桥墩模型延性抗震性能影响的分析

2.1 轴压比的影响分析

我国桥梁抗震设计规范对桥墩的轴压比进行了规定限制,其目的是为了保证墩柱的塑性变形能力,使得其在破坏时尽量发生弯曲破坏而不是剪切破坏。桥墩的轴压比是指墩柱的轴压力设计值与混凝土轴心抗压强度设计值和墩身截面面积的比值,即

$$u = \frac{N}{A \cdot f_c} \tag{1}$$

式中:u——轴压比;

N——轴压力设计值;

A——墩身截面面积;

f_c——混凝土轴心抗压强度设计值。

本节在确定墩高为46m以及桥墩的其余参数不变的条件下,采用OpenSees有限元软件对矩形空心截面钢筋混凝土桥墩模型的抗震性能进行研究[8],计算在不同轴压比情况下截面的屈服弯矩、极限弯矩等系数,并通过绘图对比分析其对桥墩延性抗震性能的影响。

上述各项结果均列于表2中。

桥墩模型在不同轴压比下的各项参数结果　　　　表2

轴力(N)	轴压比μ	M_y(kN·m)	M_u(kN·m)	f_y(m^{-1})	f_u(m^{-1})	u_f
0	0	95216	117549	5.84×10^{-4}	1.08×10^{-2}	18.4003
2473450	0.01	99512	122174	5.91×10^{-4}	1.02×10^{-2}	17.2322
7420350	0.03	108057	131378	6.05×10^{-4}	8.98×10^{-3}	14.8389
12367250	0.05	116568	140078	6.20×10^{-4}	7.98×10^{-3}	12.8777
24734500	0.1	137341	161332	6.55×10^{-4}	6.52×10^{-3}	9.9665
37101750	0.15	157489	181887	6.92×10^{-4}	5.46×10^{-3}	7.8987
49469000	0.2	177156	201612	7.31×10^{-4}	4.64×10^{-3}	6.3434
74203500	0.3	214514	237220	8.19×10^{-4}	2.92×10^{-3}	3.5613
98938000	0.4	245398	256937	9.43×10^{-4}	1.76×10^{-3}	1.8647
123672500	0.5	257038	257704	1.22×10^{-3}	1.26×10^{-3}	1.0326

将上表不同轴压比情况下所得到的各类系数绘成关系图,如图2~图4所示。

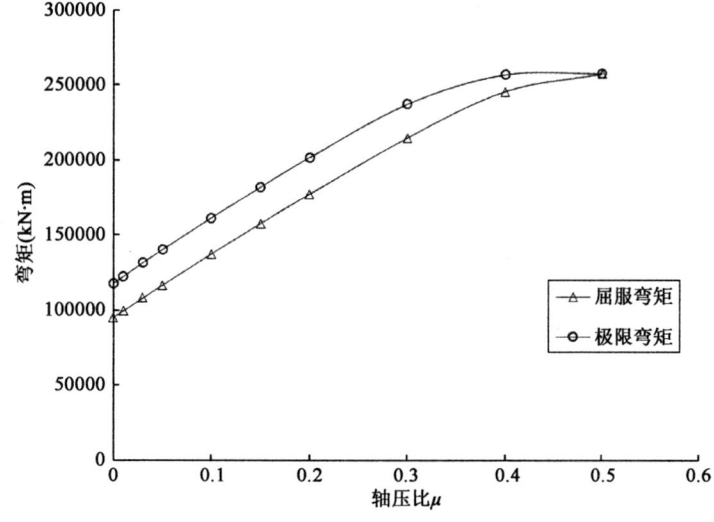

图2　弯矩-轴压比关系图

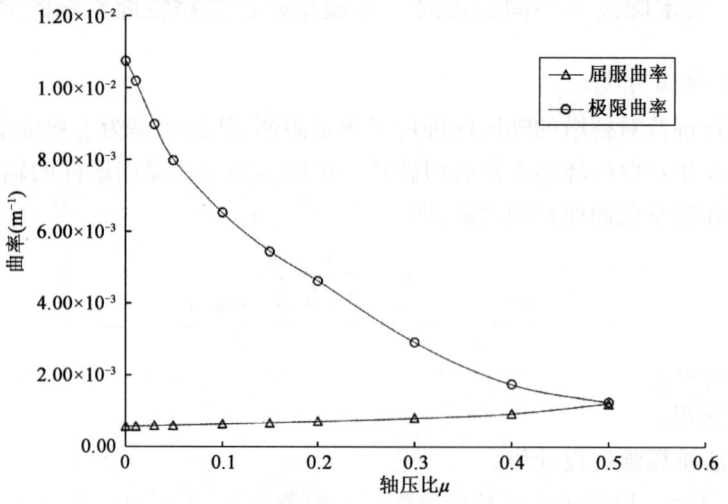

图3 曲率-轴压比关系图

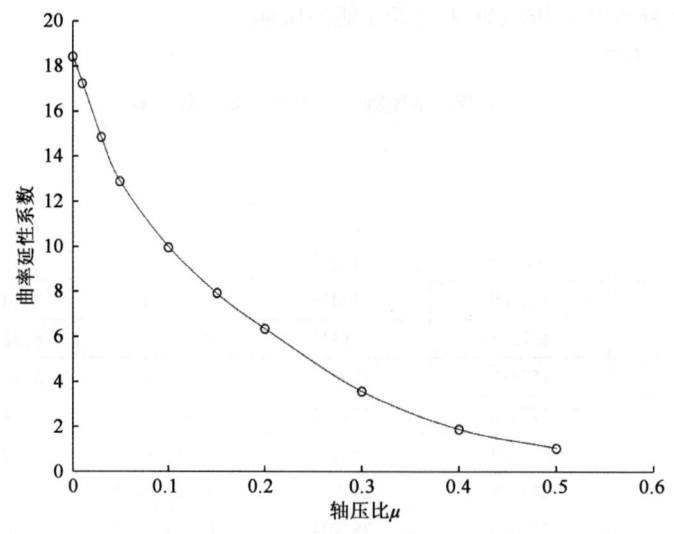

图4 曲率延性系数-轴压比关系图

对表中数据以及关系图进行分析可知：

（1）随着轴压比的增大，截面的屈服弯矩与极限弯矩缓慢增大，在轴压比为0-0.3范围内，二者增速近似正相关；当轴压比进一步增大时，极限弯矩增速降低，直到到达峰值，桥墩的屈服弯矩也同理，此时屈服弯矩与极限弯矩重合，原因是纵筋屈服时混凝土也正好达到极限压应变；若继续增大轴压比，此时截面的极限弯矩与屈服弯矩均会下降，由此可见，轴压比并非越大越好，而是要选定一个合适的值。

（2）从图3可以看出，截面的屈服曲率在轴压比的影响下变动很小，以一个很缓慢的速度增加，而极限曲率随着轴压比的增大下降较为显著，且减小的速率是由大到小的。

（3）曲率延性系数随着轴压比的增大而迅速下降，由此可见，增大轴压比会降低桥墩的曲率延性系数，也就降低了钢筋混凝土桥墩的非弹性变形能力。

2.2 配筋率的影响分析

上节讨论了在不同轴压比的情况下对桥墩延性抗震性能的影响，本节以配筋率为研究对象，固定轴压比为0.15，讨论在不同配筋率情况下桥墩延性抗震性能会产生什么变化。

钢筋混凝土桥墩的配筋率是指钢筋混凝土桥墩中纵向受力钢筋的面积与墩身截面有效面积的比值，即：

$$\rho = \frac{A_s}{A_c} \tag{2}$$

式中:A_s——纵向受力钢筋的面积;

A_c——墩身截面有效面积。

本节在确定墩高为46m以及桥墩的其余参数不变的条件下,计算在不同配筋率情况下截面的屈服弯矩、极限弯矩等系数,并通过对比绘图分析其对桥墩延性抗震性能的影响。

上述各项结果均列于表3中。

桥墩模型在不同配筋率下的各项参数结果 表3

配筋率 ρ	M_y(kN·m)	M_u(kN·m)	f_y(m^{-1})	f_u(m^{-1})	u_f
0.00658	91888	102906	6.50×10^{-4}	7.71×10^{-3}	11.8673
0.00843	98104	110399	6.55×10^{-4}	7.41×10^{-3}	11.3080
0.0105	104972	118778	6.59×10^{-4}	7.09×10^{-3}	10.7584
0.0128	112630	128026	6.65×10^{-4}	6.73×10^{-3}	10.1185
0.01614	123854	141518	6.71×10^{-4}	6.31×10^{-3}	9.3945
0.02045	138047	158546	6.80×10^{-4}	5.93×10^{-3}	8.7176
0.02633	157489	181887	6.92×10^{-4}	5.46×10^{-3}	7.8987
0.0337	181373	210401	7.05×10^{-4}	5.05×10^{-3}	7.1584
0.04198	207892	242199	7.18×10^{-4}	4.63×10^{-3}	6.4552
0.06057	269819	315438	7.41×10^{-4}	3.97×10^{-3}	5.3544

将上表不同配筋率情况下所得的屈服弯矩、极限弯矩绘成弯矩-配筋率关系图;屈服曲率、极限曲率绘成曲率-配筋率关系图;曲率延性系数绘成曲率延性系数-配筋率关系图,如图5~图7所示。

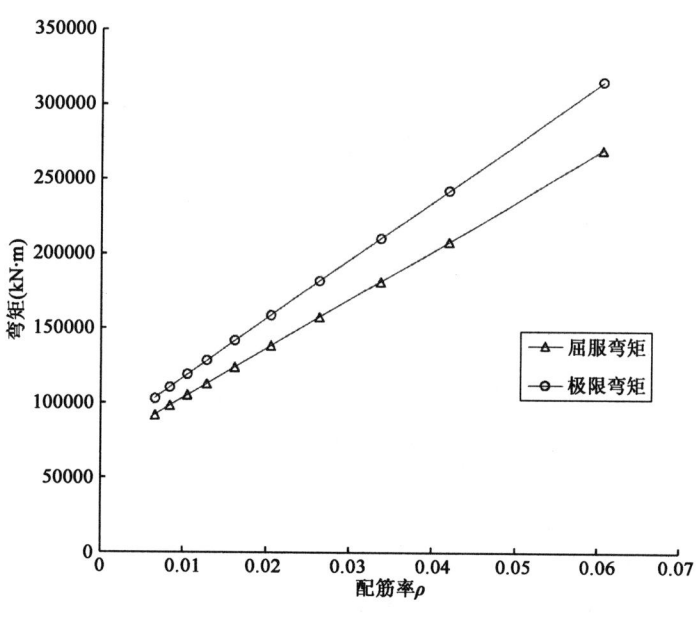

图5　弯矩-配筋率关系图

对表中数据以及关系图进行分析可知:

(1)随着配筋率的增大,截面的屈服弯矩与极限弯矩均增大,两者呈近似线性正相关。

(2)随着配筋率的增大,截面的屈服曲率缓慢增大,而极限曲率却逐渐减小,且减小的速率逐渐放缓。

(3)曲率延性系数随着配筋率的增大而逐渐减小,变化趋势和截面的极限曲率类似,由此可见,配筋率不宜过低。

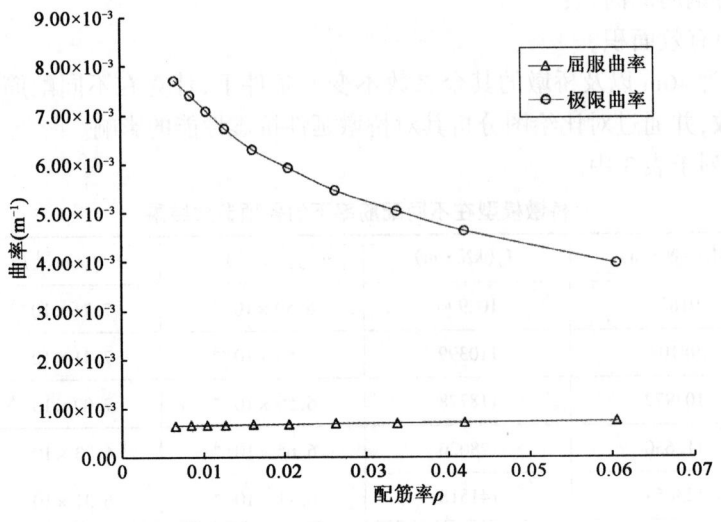

图6 曲率-配筋率关系图

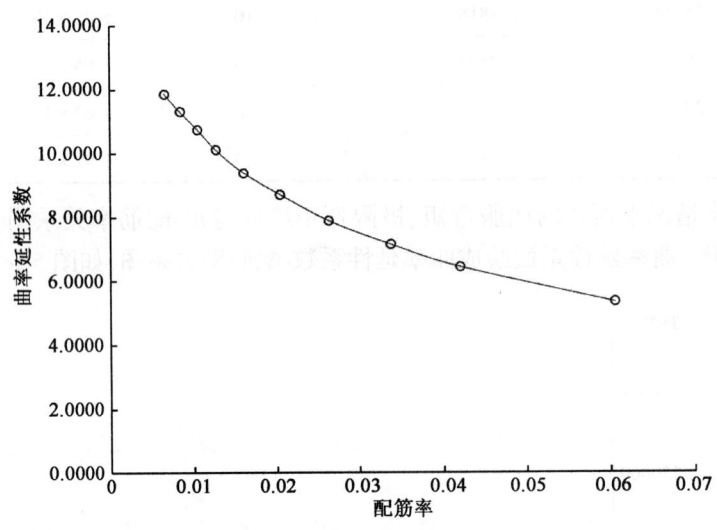

图7 曲率延性系数-配筋率关系图

3 结 语

本文采用OpenSees对矩形空心截面钢筋混凝土桥墩模型的抗震性能进行研究,结论如下。

(1)如图8所示,该图为不同轴力下压弯构件的截面应变分布图,a点表示受压区边缘混凝土压应变,b、c、d等表示纵向受力钢筋的应变,当墩柱轴心受压时,全截面均匀受压,由于平截面假定,压应变呈一条竖直线分布,即$a''h$虚线。当墩柱大偏心受压时,压应变不再为一竖直线,而是变成一条斜线,即ab、ac线;随着轴压比或纵筋配筋率的增大,截面的应变分布图逐渐过渡到ad线。在大多数情况下,受压区边缘混凝土都达到了极限压应变,即上图中的a点,若受拉钢筋也正好屈服(ad),此时为界限状态。若轴压比或配筋率继续增大,截面将会进入全截面受压状态,此时混凝土边缘的压应变会逐渐减小,而应变分布直线与截面的夹角也会逐渐减小,即截面的极限曲率会随着轴压比或配筋率的增大而逐渐减小;同理,当全截面受压时,纵筋的屈服应变随着轴压比的增大而增大,即屈服曲率随之增大。

(2)增大轴压比会导致曲率延性系数降低,也就降低了钢筋混凝土桥墩的非弹性变形能力和塑性铰区截面的延性,这对于结构是不利的,但是这种降低会随着轴压比的增大而逐渐趋于平缓。因此,在进行桥梁抗震设计的过程中,应根据实际情况合理考虑轴压比的大小。

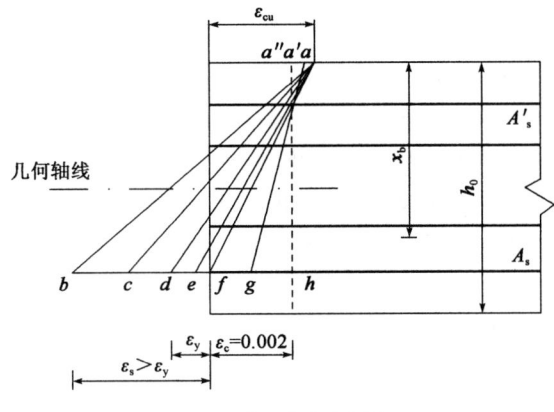

图8 截面应变分布图

(3)与轴压比类似,增大配筋率也会导致曲率延性系数的降低,也就降低了钢筋混凝土桥墩的延性抗震性能,但是这并不意味着配筋率越低越好,配筋率太低时构件容易发生少筋破坏,而少筋破坏为脆性破坏,应尽量避免;同时配筋率太高时又会降低钢筋混凝土桥墩的非弹性变形能力,导致桥墩的延性抗震能力下降,因此,应尽量将配筋率设置在一个合适的范围,这样才能最好地发挥桥墩的延性抗震性能。

参考文献

[1] 余方亮.基于汶川地震的桥梁震害评估模型研究[D].哈尔滨:中国地震局工程力学研究所,2018.
[2] 杜修力,陈明琪,韩强.钢筋混凝土空心桥墩抗震性能试验研究[J].振动与冲击,2011,11(30):254-259.
[3] 宗周红,夏坚,徐绰然.桥梁高墩抗震研究现状及展望[J].东南大学学报,2013,43(2):445-452.
[4] 中华人民共和国交通运输部.JTG 3362—2018.公路钢筋混凝土及预应力混凝土桥涵设计规范[S].北京:人民交通出版社股份有限公司,2018.
[5] 曾纪华.基于OpenSees的柱板式空心高墩抗震性能分析[J].兰州工业学院学报,2020,27(02):24-27.
[6] Paolino Cassese, Paolo Ricci, Gerardo M. Verderame. Experimental study on the seismic performance of existing reinforced concrete bridge piers with hollow rectangular section[J]. Engineering Structures,2017,144.
[7] 房麟.钢筋混凝土空心墩抗震性能试验研究[D].成都:西南交通大学,2016.
[8] 杨洒.基于OpenSEES的钢筋混凝土空心桥墩抗震性能的研究[D].邯郸:河北工程大学,2015.

Research on the Technology of Lag Pouring of Wet-joint Used in Composite Girder Cable-stayed Bridge

Tianrui Gao Zhenbei Liu Haijing Ning

(Chang'an University)

Abstract In order to improve the construction efficiency of the main girder of composite girder cable-stayed bridge and ensure that the whole project can be completed on schedule under adverse weather conditions, some scholars have proposed a new technology of lag pouring wet-joint of bridge deck. Under the condition of the original prestressed system unchanged, this technology can save the construction period and ensure the reasonable stress of the bridge deck structure by regrouping and tensioning. In this paper, finite element method is used to simulate the construction of main girder of composite girder cable-stayed bridge. By comparing the results of stress analysis of main beam deck and steel beam under different construction procedures and working conditions, the rationality of mechanics and the advantages of construction period of wet-joint concrete of bridge deck slab are verified. On the basis of the analysis of the finite element simulation results above, the comparison and prediction of the effect on lag wet-joint concrete pouring of main girder bridge deck slab in more segments are compared and predicted, which provides guidance for accelerating the construction of composite girder cable-stayed bridge in special areas in the future.

Keywords Composite girder cable-stayed bridge   Construction stage   Deck cracking   Construction optimization   Lagging concrete wet-joint

0 Introduction

The steel-concrete composite beam promotes the development of the construction and design of long-span cable-stayed bridges because of the advantages of the two materials and good economy. The main girder of composite beam is used in many domestic sea and river crossing bridges. But once the concrete bridge deck cracks, under the influence of load and surrounding environment, it will affect the combination of steel and concrete, destroy the durability of the structure, and further endanger the safety of the bridge structure. Therefore, in the construction of bridge deck, tensioning prestressed steel tendons are widely used, which can effectively increase the compressive stress reserve of the section and avoid the possibility of deck cracking. Some scholars have studied the sequence of prestressed tendon tension and wet-joint pouring in the corresponding position during the prefabrication of concrete bridge deck. The results show that the process sequence of lag combination of main longitudinal beam, cross beam and bridge deck can achieve the highest prestress application efficiency, as shown by Cai et al. (2019)

Due to the complex construction process and various contents of composite beam cable-stayed bridge, the final completed bridge structure and alignment are closely related to the construction process. Different construction technology and the sequence of tensioning stay cable and prestressed tendon will affect the internal force distribution of main beam. Once not fully considered, the bridge deck concrete will be subject to greater tensile stress, resulting in cracking in the process of operation and construction. In the project of Yueqing Bay No. 2 bridge, Qi et. al. (2017) put forward the construction technology of multi segment continuous hoisting of composite beam cable-stayed bridge, which effectively improves the construction efficiency of composite beam cable-stayed bridge, shortens the maintenance time of the whole bridge deck joint, and saves the construction period. In the study of cantilever matching construction of long-span composite beam cable-stayed bridge, the technology of lag pouring wet-joint of bridge deck is also mentioned, as shown by Sun et al. (2018)

For the Jiaojiang Second Bridge, the construction technology of two segments cyclic installation of main girder of cable-stayed bridge is put forward, by Hong et al. (2013), which reasonably avoids the situation that the upper structure enters into the high incidence period of typhoon with the dangerous state of large cantilever before closure. It can be seen that, different from the standard single segment construction process of pouring wet-joint concrete between segments, the main beam construction of multi segment cable-stayed bridge lags behind the pouring of wet-joint concrete, that is, after the steel beam installation is completed, the wet-joint between the segment and the previous beam segment is not poured, but the wet-joint of the installed beam segment is poured at a time after hoisting multiple beam segments, which can greatly reduce the construction cycle and also bring good economic benefits.

However, in terms of stress, whether this multi segment construction technology can meet the safety of bridge deck during the whole construction stage is less studied by domestic scholars, which needs further analysis and verification. In this paper, based on the background of the construction of bridge girder segments, the finite element model of lag pouring wet-joint of different segments is established. The efficiency of the process is analysed from the perspective of lagging pouring process, and the rationality of multi segment lagging construction technology is analysed from the perspective of bridge deck and steel beam stress.

1 Project Overview

A sea crossing bridge is a cable-stayed bridge with double pylons, double cable planes and steel-concrete composite beams as its main girder. The span arrangement is 85m + 145m + 488m + 145m + 85m. The total length of the main bridge is 948m, the side span ratio is 0.471, and the side span is equipped with auxiliary piers. The spatial double cable plane layout is adopted for the stay cables. The standard cable spacing at the beam end is 10.5m, and the cable spacing in the side span near the tail cable area is 8.4m, as shown in Fig. 1.

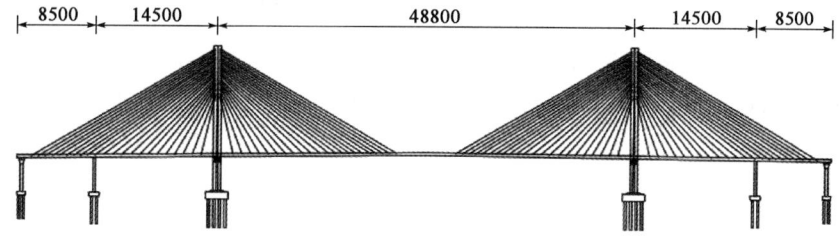

Fig.1 General layout of main bridge of a sea crossing bridge (structural dimension unit:cm)

Its structure system adopts five span continuous semi floating system. The main beam at the cable tower is provided with vertical support and transverse wind bearing, auxiliary pier top is set with vertical support, and transition pier top is set with vertical bearing and transverse wind bearing. Four longitudinal viscous dampers are installed at each pylon to improve the mechanical performance of the structure under static wind load and earthquake load along the bridge direction. Under the earthquake condition, the device can reduce the vibration and bear the longitudinal horizontal force.

The main beam adopts PK streamline flat steel box composite beam, and the air nozzle is set at the outside of the steel beam. The width of the main beam is 38.5m (excluding the width of the air nozzle is 34m); the height of the center beam is 3.5m, of which the height of the center line of the steel beam is 3.1m, as shown in Fig. 2. Precast concrete slab is used for bridge deck. The standard segment of the main span is 10.5m long, with a solid web diaphragm every 3.5m, and four straight webs inside and outside the box girder. The standard thickness of bridge deck is 28cm, which is thickened to 40cm at the top plate and diaphragm plate of steel beam; in order to reduce the weight of side span box, the bridge deck of small side span is 40cm thick. To increase the compressive stress reserve of the bridge deck in the operation stage, 30 15-12 prestressed steel strands are arranged in the mid span and side span areas respectively.

Q345D steel is used for main beam steel beam, and Q235B steel is used for air nozzle. C55 concrete is used for bridge deck, and C55 micro expansion concrete is used for cast-in-place wet joint.

The stay cable adopts parallel steel wire stayed cable with standard tensile strength of 1770MPa. Five specifications of cables, lpes7-151, lpes7-199, lpes7-241, lpes7-283 and lpes7-301, are used respectively. The maximum length of stay cable is 200.755m (M22 cable, model lpes7-283), and the maximum weight of single cable is 16072kg (S22 cable, model les7-301). There are 176 stay cables in the whole bridge, which are anchored by steel anchor box on the main beam, anchored by steel anchor beam structure on the cable tower, and the tension end is set at the tower end.

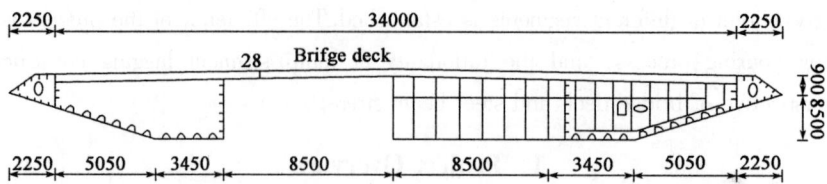

Fig.2 Cross Section Layout of Main Bridge (structural dimension unit:cm)

All text paragraphs should be single spaced, with first line intended by 10 mm. Double spacing should only be used before and after headings and subheadings as shown in this example. Position and style of headings and subheadings should follow this example. No spaces should be placed between paragraphs.

2 Finite Element Simulation

The Midas finite element software is mainly used to simulate the whole bridge span construction process, to analyze the mechanical characteristics of bridge deck concrete and steel beam under different working conditions of lag pouring wet-joint process.

The whole bridge has 2659 nodes and 2293 units. The finite element model is shown in Fig.3.

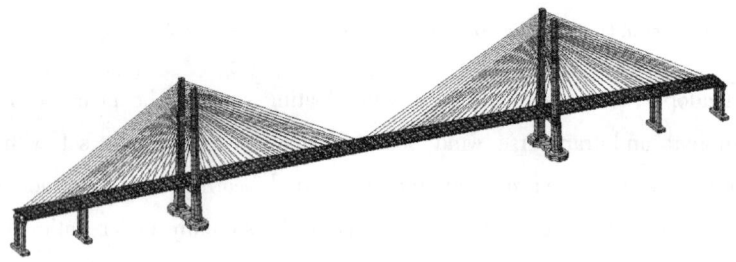

Fig.3 Full span finite element model

The main beam is a streamlined flat steel box composite beam with double side box, and the air nozzle is set outside the steel beam. The precast concrete bridge deck forms a composite beam through the joint force of shear studs and steel beams, which plays the synergistic effect of the two materials. The main girder is simulated by two elements, and the rigid connection between the bridge deck and the steel beam is taken as the boundary condition to simulate the composite section under the action of shear stud. In the model of cable simulation without considering the construction stage, the truss element is used to simulate the cable without considering the deformation, while the truss element is used to simulate the nonlinear problem in the construction stage.

As for the boundary conditions, the consolidation of general supports is considered at the bottom of tower, Auxiliary Pier and transition pier. The general elastic connection is considered in the support simulation at the bridge tower, transition pier and auxiliary pier, and a certain support stiffness is given in each direction.

The rigid connection in elastic connection is adopted for the connection between bridge deck and steel beam, so is the temporary consolidation of tower and beam. The other positions were simulated by rigid connection.

The deck crane is shown in Fig.4. The deck crane load is simulated by the vertical force of two node loads. In the construction condition of lifting load, a vertical concentrated force and a bending moment are used to simulate the effect of the bridge deck crane on the main beam during the process of lifting and installing the steel beam and bridge deck. The forward movement of the bridge deck crane is realized through the activation and passivation steps in the model.

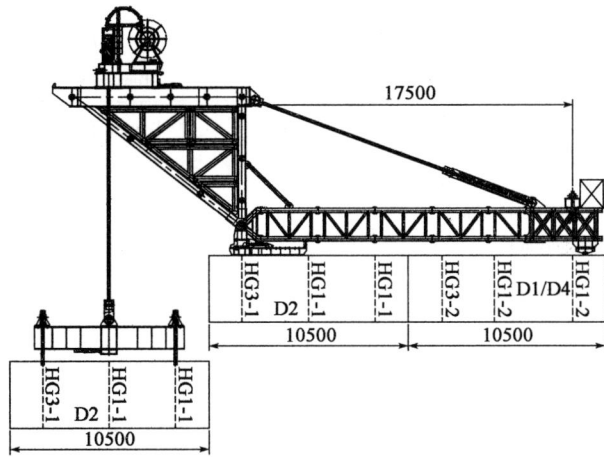

Fig. 4 Diagram of deck crane(structural dimension unit:m)

The following three kinds of girder installation process are simulated. In the first scheme, the wet-joints of main beam segments are poured immediately and the prestressed steel tendons are tensioned. The second scheme is to lag the wet-joints of the main beams in two segments, then the wet joint is poured at one time and the prestressed steel tendons are tensioned. The third scheme is to lag the wet-joints of three main girder segments, and then to cast and tension the prestressed steel tendons at one time. In the different construction schemes based on simulating the wet-joint of segment lagging pouring, the main beam, cable and other elements used are unchanged, and the boundary conditions remain unchanged except for the temporary support installed near Block 0. The prestressing tendons of bridge deck in the design drawing of main girder are not changed, and the prestressing force is lengthened and tensioned by changing the groups of tendons to simulate the delayed activation of prestressed tendon grouping.

The construction scheme of the bridge tower remains unchanged, and the construction time is recorded as n days. The main beams of the three schemes are constructed with supports at the bridge tower, and the number of beam segments is 3, 5 and 7 respectively. In the process of cantilever pouring standard beam segment, the construction stage of single segment construction is divided into the installation of the nth unstressed segment, the first tensioning of the nth cable, the second tensioning of the nth cable, pouring the corresponding wet joint and tensioning the prestressed steel bundle. The second tensioning of the nth cable also includes the process steps of crane moving forward and lifting the next segment, so as to complete the construction of the remaining beam segments and cables. The standard cantilever segment construction of the other two schemes only delays the pouring of wet-joint, that is, the wet-joint is poured once after one or two segments and the corresponding prestressed steel tendon is tensioned. In the three schemes, the 13th and 14th beam segments at the auxiliary pier are all constructed on the support, the 21st and 22nd beam segments are installed by single segment, the 23rd beam segment of side span is constructed by bracket, and the closure construction of side and mid span and the corresponding prestressed tensioning scheme are also the same.

3 Time Effect Comparison and Economic Analysis of Construction Technology for Wet Joint Concrete of Main Beam Withlag Pouring

The time spent in each working condition of standard segment construction with different construction schemes is statistically sorted out, and a detailed list of construction period comparison of standard section is obtained, which is listed in Tab. 1.

Construction period comparison of standard beam segment   Tab.1

Serial number	Construction steps (Single segment)	Time spent (Day)	Serial number	Construction steps (Two segments)	Time spent (Day)
1	The nth unstressed segment	2	1	The nth unstressed segment	2
2	Tension the nth cable for the first time	0.5	2	Tension the nth cable for the first time	0.5
3	The nth wet joint and tension prestress	7	3	Tension the nth cable for the second time and move the crane forward	1
4	Tension the nth cable for the second time and move the crane forward	1	4	Lifting weight [lifting the $(n+1)$th segment]	1
5	Lifting weight (lifting the next segment)	1	5	The $(n+1)$th unstressed segment	2
—	—	—	6	Tension the $(n+1)$th cable for the first time	0.5
—	—	—	7	The nth and the $(n+1)$th wet joint tension prestress	7
—	—	—	8	Tension the $(n+1)$th cable for the second time and move the crane forward	1
—	—	—	9	Lifting weight [lifting the $(n+2)$th segment]	1
Total	—	11.5	—	—	16

The technological process of different pouring wet joints from left to right is single segment, double segment and three segment pouring, as shown in Fig. 5. The position of the blackened wet joint indicates that it has been poured.

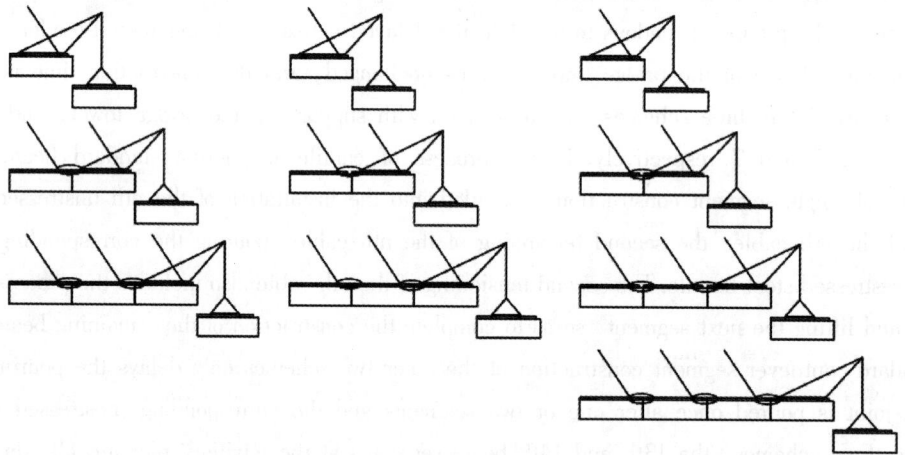

Fig. 5 Flow chart of three different pouring wet joint processes

The above table only shows the comparison chart of single segment and double segments construction period. According to the results of the table, the construction time of single segment girder is 11.5 days, while the construction time of pouring wet-joint after two beam segments is 16 days, and the average single segment construction time is 8 days, which is greatly shortened by one third of the original. It is obvious that the pouring wet-joint scheme with more segments lagging behind can shorten the construction period. The construction period of the whole bridge is calculated according to the above three construction technologies. The accumulated wet-joint pouring time of single section is $n+396$ days, that of two segments lagging behind is $n+328.5$ days, and that of three segments lagging behind is $n+304.5$ days.

The shortening of construction period means that the expenses of workers' wages, the cost of machine operation on the construction site and the cost of site use are reduced by day, which facilitates the organization and management of construction and reduces the total cost of construction. In the construction stage, with the change of construction scheme, the effect of prestressed steel tendon tension scheme on the main beam needs to be analyzed and verified by simulation results.

4 Comparative Analysis of Mechanical Behavior of Steel Beam and Bridge Deck Under the Condition of Lagging Behind Wet Joint Pouring of Different Segments

Through the establishment of the standard single segment instant pouring wet-joint, lagging two segments pouring wet-joint, lagging three segments pouring wet-joint process model, the stress state of bridge deck and steel girder under each construction condition is analyzed. The regularity is found to verify the rationality of multi segment lagging wet-joint pouring, and the feasibility of construction technology for lagging pouring more segments of wet-joint is predicted.

A part of the main girder segment of the whole bridge model in many construction stages is analyzed.

4.1 Comparison and Analysis of the Stress for the Main Beam in the Scheme of Single Segment Immediate Pouring Wet-joint and Lagging two Segment Pouring Wet-joint

Based on the analysis of the simulation results of the construction process of 3# and 4# beam segments, the distribution of stress results for bridge deck and steel girder under different working conditions of 3# and 4# beam segments under the single segment pouring bridge deck wet-joint process is shown in Fig. 6-Fig. 9.

The following distal end refers to the side of the cantilever construction girder segment away from the bridge tower, and the proximal end refers to the side close to the bridge tower.

Among them, the node numbers of the wet-joint unit at the distal end of the 3# beam segment are 1455 and 1456, and the corresponding steel beam unit node numbers are 584 and 585. The wet-joint unit nodes between 3# and 4# beam segments are 1446, 1447 and 1448, and the corresponding steel beam unit node numbers are 575, 576 and 577.

During the construction of single section, there is a small tensile stress on the upper edge for the deck of 3# beam segment without pouring wet-joint, and the maximum tensile stress is at the proximal end, reaching 0.162 MPa, as shown in Fig.8a). At this stage, the composite beam section is not formed, and only the upper edge of the steel beam bears the corresponding tensile stress. The tensile stress level is relatively high, reaching 4 MPa, as shown in Fig.8a). After pouring the wet-joint, a composite section is formed at the original wet-joint position, and the concrete part shares the stress. The stress level of the steel beam at this place is greatly reduced and no tensile stress occurs. At the same time, the prestressed steel bundle is tensioned, and the stress level for the upper edge in the bridge deck of the whole beam section is reduced, which is in the compressive stress state, reaching 0.4 MPa. Under the conditions of crane moving, the second tensioning and the subsequent lifting of the new segment, the stress on the upper edge of the steel beam experienced a rise and fall, which was in the range of compressive stress. At the wet-joint position, the compressive stress level for the upper edge of the deck was higher, reaching 1.6 MPa. Under the condition of 4# segment lifting load, that is, lifting 5# beam segment, the stress level for the upper edge of the bridge deck rises to the tensile stress level as a whole, but the value is relatively low. In the process of 4# beam segment installation, the stress level of bridge deck and upper edge of steel beam is the same as that of the previous stage, but the stress levels of different beam segments are different.

Under the construction conditions of 4# beam segment, the stress level for the upper edge of 3# beam deck is much lower than that of 4# beam segment. The maximum tensile stress for the upper edge of 4# beam deck reaches 0.426 MPa, which is also at the position where the wet-joint is not poured the proximal end. The tensile stress for the upper edge of the proximal end steel beam reaches 4 MPa. For the steel beam stress, the upper edge of the proximal end also reached 4 MPa, but after pouring wet-joint concrete, the stress for the upper edge of the steel beam also experienced a rise and fall, and the maximum compressive stress reached 4 MPa. At this moment, the upper edge for the steel beam of the last 3# beam segment is in the range of compressive stress, and the overall level is higher than that of the 3# beam segment during construction.

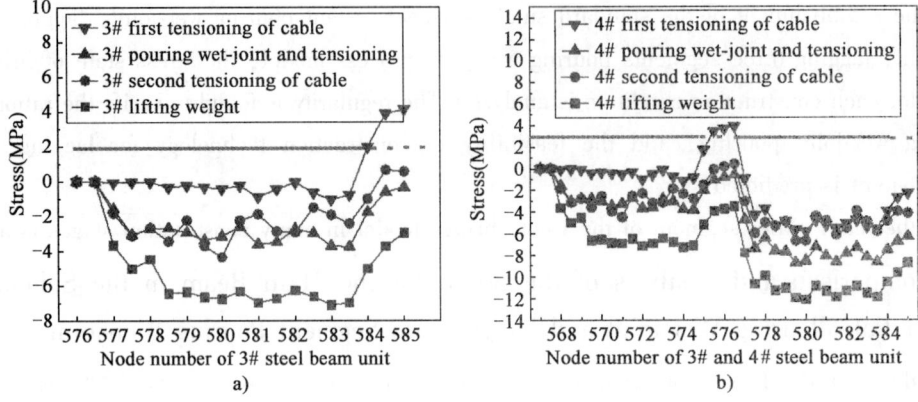

Fig. 6　Stress distribution on the upper edge of steel girder in single segment scheme

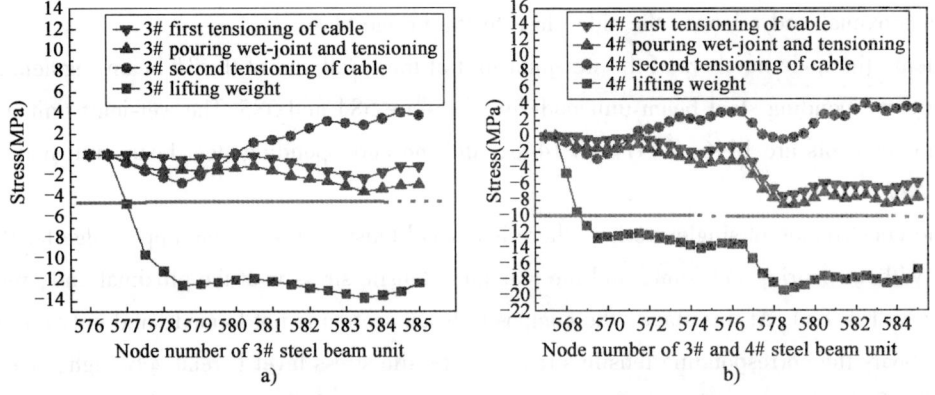

Fig. 7　Stress distribution of lower edge of steel beam in single segment scheme

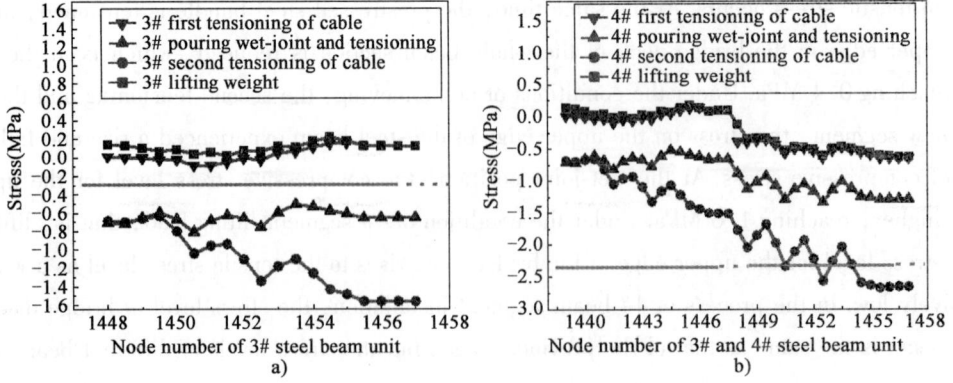

Fig. 8　Stress distribution on the upper edge of single segment deck

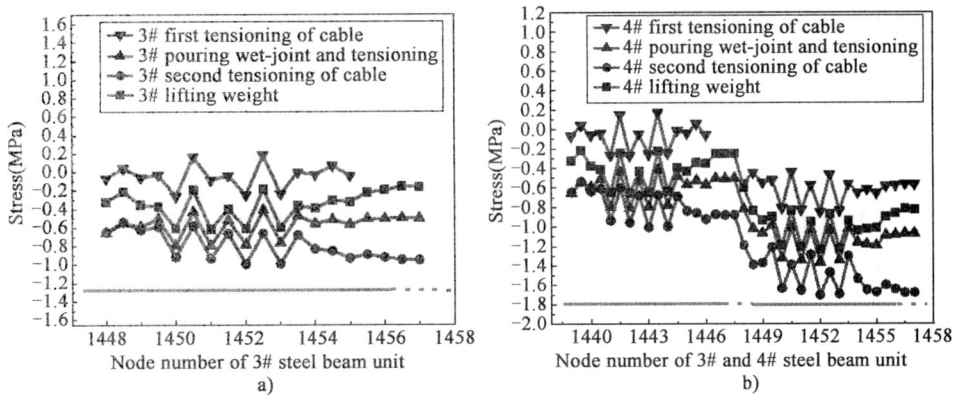

Fig. 9 Stress distribution on the lower edge of single segment deck

Prestressed tension can effectively solve the problem of large tensile stress in the deck during the installation of main girder, especially in the position of wet-joint at the proximal end, where the tensile stress level is high. After the prestressing tendon is tensioned, the stress level drops obviously, which ensures the safety of the structure. The tensile stress level for the lower edge of the bridge deck is generally not high, which is basically in the range of compressive stress, and does not exceed the strength limit of the material. The stress level of the lower edge of the steel beam fluctuates with the change of working conditions, but the law is similar.

Under the scheme of lagging two segments of wet-joint pouring, 3# and 4# beam segments are still selected. The stress results of bridge deck and steel beam under different working conditions in construction stage are extracted, and draw the results, as shown in in Fig. 10-Fig. 12.

During the construction of 3# beam segment, the stress of the upper edge of the steel beam is basically near 0 when the cable is tensioned for the first time, and at the wet joint is relatively large. However, the tensile stress level of the upper edge of the bridge deck is generally low, which is below 0.2 MPa. When the crane moves forward to the far end of the beam section, the stress of the steel beam decreases to the compressive stress level at this wet-joint position. Then the new beam section is lifted, and the unit at the same wet-joint position is subjected to the negative bending moment caused by the concentrated force at the distal end. At this time, the wet joint has not been poured and no composite section has been formed, so the stress level of the upper edge of the steel beam at the corresponding position is very high. The tensile stress on the upper edge of 3# beam segment at the wet joint to be poured is relatively large, reaching 1.2 MPa. Due to the absence of prestressed steel tendons, the tensile stress on the upper edge of the deck at the proximal end of the beam segment is continuously accumulated.

The results of stress distribution shown in Fig. 12b) show that the upper edge of the bridge deck is in tension when the cables are tensioned for the first time. The stress level is lower than that of the previous 3# segment. When the prestressed tendons of two segments are tensioned at one time and the wet joint is poured, the stress at the upper edge of the two segments of bridge deck is significantly decreased, especially the tensile stress of the deck slab at the position of wet-joint to be poured in 3# segment is significantly reduced, which timely improves the possibility of the upper edge of the bridge deck being cracked during construction. The stress at the lower edge of the bridge deck is within the strength range of the material, so it is safe under all construction conditions.

As shown in Fig. 6 to Fig. 12, the red solid line indicates the beam section where the bridge deck is located, and the red dotted line indicates the position of concrete corresponding to wet joint.

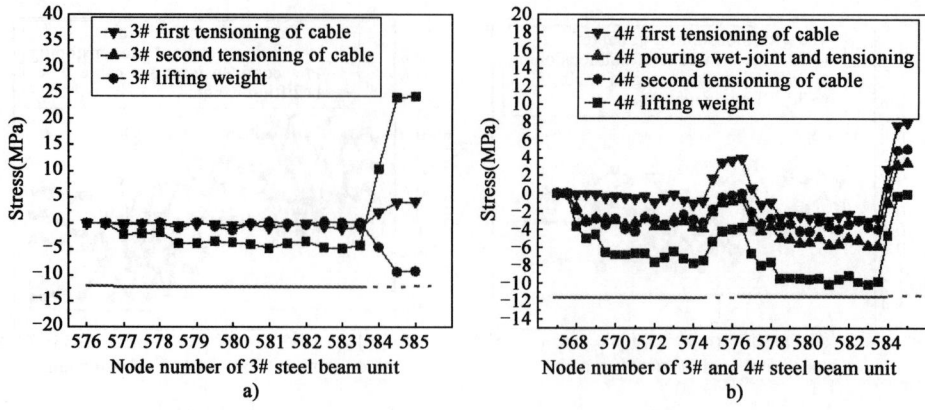

Fig. 10 Stress distribution on the upper edge of steel girder with wet joint poured by two segments lagging behind

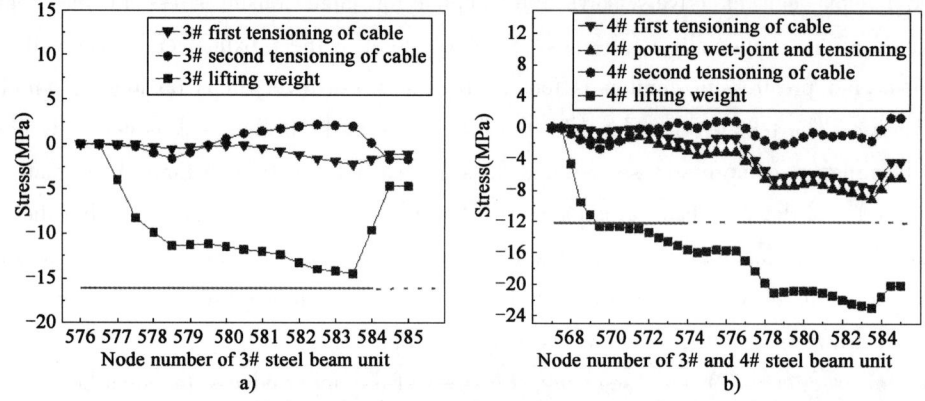

Fig. 11 Stress distribution on the lower edge of steel girder with wet joint poured by two segments lagging behind

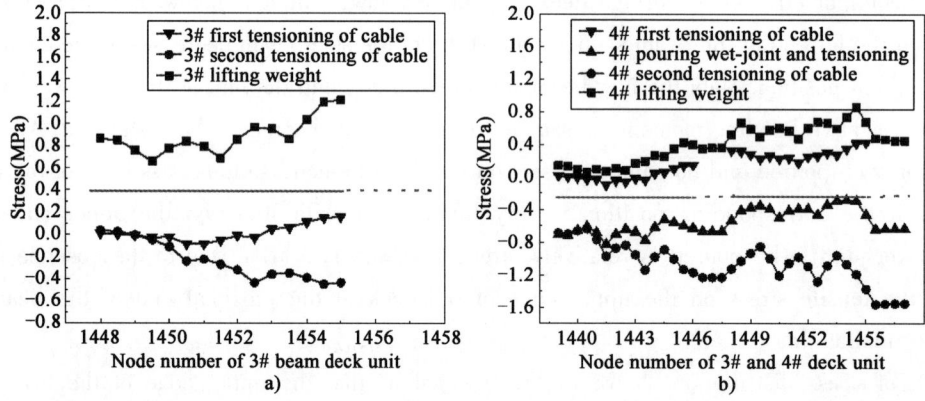

Fig. 12 The stress distribution of the upper edge of the deck slab with wet joint poured by two segments lagging behind

4.2 Analysis on stress results of main girder in the scheme for lagging three segment pouring wet-joint

The construction scheme of delaying the pouring of wet-joint in three segments, that is, when the three beam segments are installed, the wet-joint of adjacent main beam segments is not poured in time. After the steel beam is installed and connected, the wet-joint of bridge deck is poured at one time. The stress results of bridge deck and steel beam under different working conditions in 3 beam segments of 4#-6# are taken for analysis.

In the scheme of lagging three segments pouring wet-joint, the upper edge for the first two sections of steel girder has the peak value of tensile stress level except the position of the wet-joint, and the other positions are relatively low, basically in the range of compressive stress. The lower edge of the steel beam is compressed, and the compressive stress level at the wet joint is lower than that at other positions. Overall, all parts of the steel beam are safe.

The variation trend of the stress results at the edge of the bridge deck is the same as that in the scheme of lagging two segments pouring wet-joint.

When lifting the next beam segment, the upper edge of the deck in the installed segments is tensioned, and the stress at the proximal end reaches a peak value near 1.0 MPa. During the construction of the second beam segment, when the cables are tensioned for the first time, the lifting effect of the previous working condition is removed, and the tensile stress for the upper edge of the bridge deck is reduced, which in the 4# beam segment is slightly higher than that of the 5# beam segment, but the whole is in a safe state. When lifting the next 6# beam segment, the tensile stress of the bridge deck has a protruding peak at the wet-joint position near the 4# and 5# beam segments, which reaches 1.2 MPa at the 5# beam segment and 1.8 MPa at the 4# beam segment. The safety redundancy of the structure is insufficient, and the bridge deck may crack. During the construction of the third beam segment, the wet-joints and prestressed steel tendons of the previous beam segment are poured and tensioned. The tensile stress for the upper edge of the deck decreases after the first tensioning of the cables of the beam segment, and the upper edge is basically compressed after the second tensioning. The stress level of the lower edge of the bridge deck is basically $-0.5\text{MPa} \sim +0.5\text{MPa}$, which can ensure the safety in construction. However, in the process of lifting the 7# beam segment, the tensile stress for the upper edge of the bridge deck in the three installed beam segments is larger, and the value of the proximal end is higher, which endangers the structural safety in the construction. It can be seen that this construction scheme is not suitable.

5 Conclusions

Shortening the time of concrete strength increase, that is, changing the original strength growth time of adjacent segments in different periods of pouring joint concrete into a period of strength growth time in the same period of pouring, can effectively shorten the construction period and avoid bad weather. As a result, the construction efficiency is significantly improved, and the construction cost is reduced economically.

The project lags one segment to pour wet-joint, that is, two segments are constructed circularly and tendons are tensioned in batches. The tensile stress of the upper edge of the concrete bridge deck can be ensured not to exceed the limit through the re adjustment of group tension and cable force without changing the arrangement of prestressed steel tendons in the original design scheme.

The comparison between single segment construction and lag multi segment pouring wet-joint construction scheme in main girder of cable-stayed bridge shows that in single segment construction, the cast-in-place joint is completed segment by segment and the prestressed tendon is tensioned. The tensile stress of flange is almost reduced to zero under the condition of the cable for the first tensioning. Compared with the single segment, the construction technology of lagging two segments pouring wet-joint produces the same tensile stress at the flange during the first tension of the cable. The lagging pouring wet-joint leads to the continuous accumulation and increase of the stress at the proximal end, but it does not exceed the limit for the time being. In general, the tensile stress for the lower edge of the bridge deck is lower than that of the upper edge, even the value is 0 in the single segment construction scheme.

The main girder of cable-stayed bridge is constructed by the scheme of lagging three segments pouring wet-joint, which leads to the accumulation of large tensile stress at the proximal end of each beam segment. However, after pouring the wet-joint and tensioning the prestressed tendon, the tensile stress for the upper edge immediately decreases a lot because of the combined effect of the bridge deck and the steel beam. In the whole construction process, the lifting load is the main factor leading to the excessive tensile stress for the whole bridge deck, especially the upper edge of the concrete slab at the proximal end. With the increase of the cantilever construction section, the tensile stress for the upper edge of the bridge deck will become larger, which may exceed the strength index of the material. As a result, the improvement effect of prestressed steel bundle is not obvious, so it is necessary to control the number of segments lagging behind in the actual construction, and it is not allowed to blindly delay more segments casting wet joints in order to speed up the construction progress.

References

[1] Cai Bangguo, Qiu Guoyang, Tan Huashun. Study on longitudinal crack resistance measures of composite girder cable stayed bridge deck [J]. World bridge, 2019, 3, 44-48. (in Chinese)

[2] Hong Lijuan, Zhou Xiantong, Guo Jiexin, Double segment cyclic installation technology of composite girder cable stayed bridge [J]. World bridge, 2013, 05, 46-49. (in Chinese)

[3] Qi Tiedong, Zhang Jin, Yang Zhiyong. Research on multi segment continuous hoisting construction technology of composite girder cable stayed bridge [J]. Highway, 2017, 062 (011), 99-104. (in Chinese)

[4] Sun Lipeng, Liu Yongjian, Yang Yuehua. Study on key problems of suspension assembly for Navigation Span Bridge of Taizhou Bay Bridge [J]. Bridge construction, 2018, 048 (006), 116-121. (in Chinese)

双向压弯下空心矩形截面桥墩承载力分析

孟宪聪　张谢东

（武汉理工大学交通学院）

摘　要　本文使用 OpenSEES 有限元软件对双向压弯状态下的桥墩抗弯承载力进行了分析，讨论了大偏心受压和小偏心受压两种不同工况的影响，探究了双向弯矩的耦合作用，最后对混凝土强度和钢筋强度在截面承载力方面的影响进行研究。结果表明双向压弯对截面承载力有着削弱作用，混凝土强度对小偏心受压的情况影响很大，对于大偏心受压的情况影响甚微，钢筋强度则对于两种受压状态下的桥墩承载力都有着较大的影响。单向压弯时抗弯承载力相等的同一构件，大偏心受压工况要比小偏心受压工况抵抗双向弯矩的能力更强。

关键词　桥墩　空心矩形截面　双向压弯　承载力

0　引　言

目前桥墩高度达到 40m 以上的桥梁普遍选用空心桥墩，空心截面桥墩同实心截面桥墩相比更能减少混凝土的用量，由于孔径的存在利于散热，因此减少了水化热的影响，且钢筋混凝土桥墩空心截面的收缩裂缝较小，也确保了更好的构件质量，所以空心截面桥墩对于高墩大跨径钢筋混凝土桥梁来说是十分适用的。目前我国规范[1]对空心桥墩的设计大多采用现行实心桥墩的设计理论，而空心桥墩的截面特性、细部构造及不同受力状态下的破坏特征与实心钢筋混凝土截面有较大的差异。矩形空心柱中段的空隙会使混凝土向内膨胀，从而会降低了约束效果，大量试验也表明双向压弯状态下矩形空心桥墩的刚度和强度会发生退化[2-5]。随着空心截面桥墩的不断应用，对其截面承载力的精确分析显得尤为重要，所以需要对空心矩形截面压弯构件的承载力进行进一步的分析研究。

1　基于 OpenSEES 建立模型

本文主要目的是探究双向压弯下桥墩的受压状态和材料强度对于抗弯承载力的影响，使用

OpenSEES 有限元软件对某钢筋混凝土连续刚构桥的空心矩形主墩进行计算研究,桥墩高程为 17.5m,是单箱双室空心矩形截面,截面尺寸如图 1 所示,原桥墩采用 C40 强度的混凝土,HRB400 的钢筋,外圈钢筋公称直径为 32mm,内圈钢筋公称直径为 25mm。使用 OpenSEES 对截面进行划分并规定坐标轴方向,如图 2 所示,加入高程,建立桥墩模型。

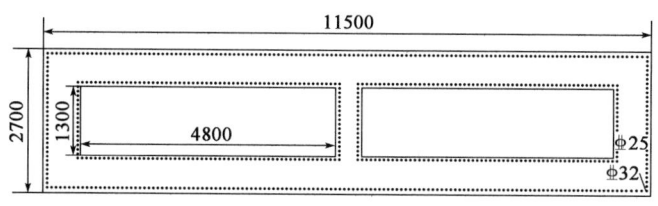

图 1 桥墩截面(尺寸单位:mm)

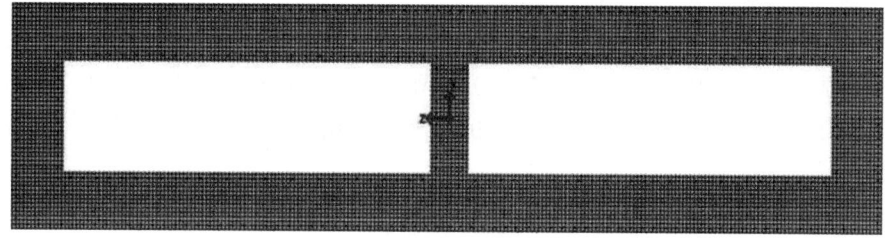

图 2 桥墩截面划分模型

2 双向压弯对桥墩承载力的影响

2.1 不同受压状态对桥墩的承载力的影响

对桥墩模型单向压弯作用时的抗弯承载力进行分析,绘制桥墩 Y 轴和 Z 轴的 P-M 曲线图,如图 3 和图 4 所示。对桥墩模型双向压弯作用时的抗弯承载力进行分析,绘制 M_y-M_z 曲线[6],如图 5 所示。

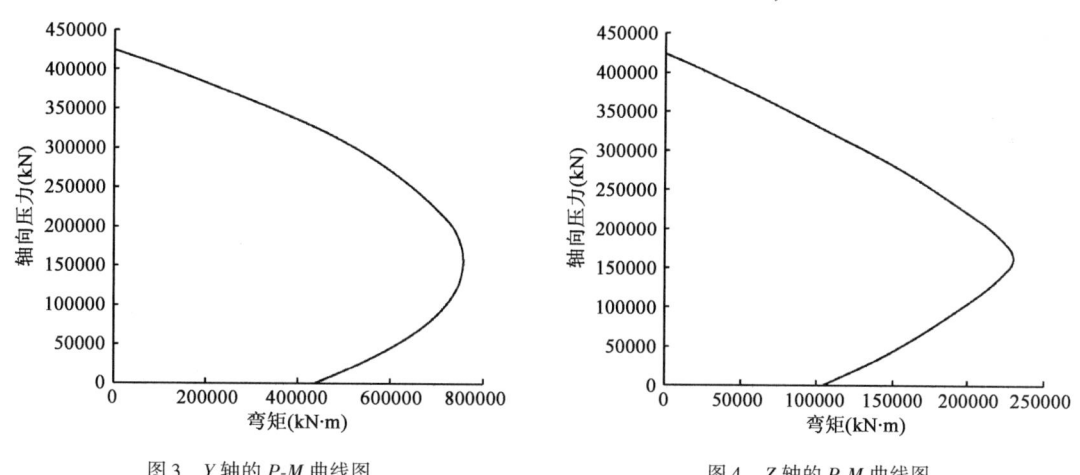

图 3 Y 轴的 P-M 曲线图   图 4 Z 轴的 P-M 曲线图

图 5 中 100000kN(大偏心受压)和 200000kN(小偏心受压)的曲线,在 P-M 曲线图中关于大小偏心的分界点大致对称,两者曲线呈现出先分后合再分的形态,曲线在中间段比较相近。同样 50000kN(大偏心受压)和 250000kN(小偏心受压)的曲线也是这样的形态。对比 100000kN 和 200000kN 的曲线在坐标轴交点的位置,可以看出曲线关于偏心分界点对称的大偏心受压和小偏心受压构件,接近单向受弯时,大偏心受压要比小偏心受压下降得更快,所以推测单向压弯下抗弯能力相同的构件,大偏心受压工况对双向弯矩的抵抗能力更强。

为验证推测,从两个方向的 P-M 曲线图中各选取一对单向承弯能力相近的大偏心受压和小偏心受压工况进行对比分析。取 Y 轴曲线中轴向压力 75000kN 和 237500kN 的工况,取 Z 轴曲线中轴向压力 75000kN 和 250000kN 的工况,绘制 M_y-M_z 曲线图,如图 6 所示。

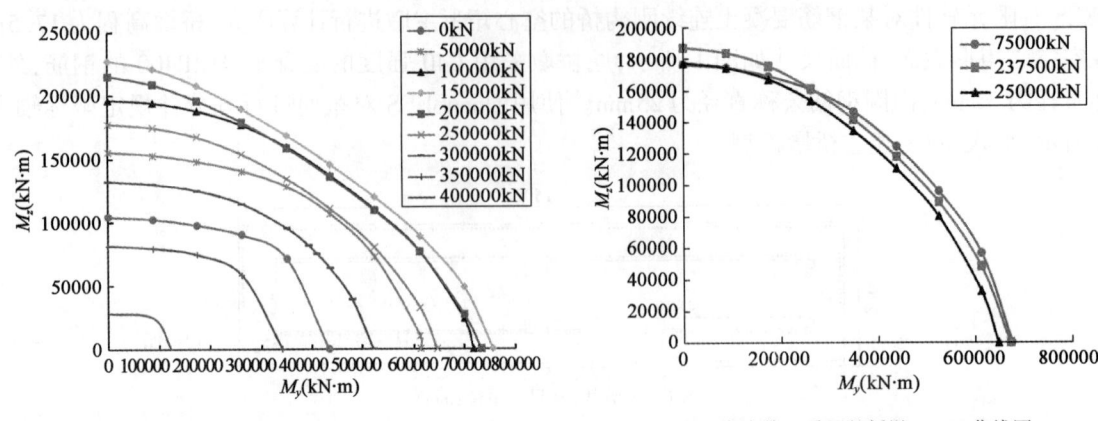

图 5 不同轴力下的 M_y-M_z 图　　　　图 6 大小偏心受压的桥墩 M_y-M_z 曲线图

图6中75000kN和250000kN两条曲线Z轴的单向抗弯承载力相同,受到双向弯矩作用时,75000kN的曲线在中间段明显高于250000kN的曲线,75000kN和237500kN这两条曲线的对比说明了桥墩抗弯承载力在Y轴方向也有这个特点。因此构件在单向抗弯承载力相同的情况下,抵抗双向受弯的能力大偏心受压工况要强于小偏心受压。

2.2 双向弯矩耦合作用对于桥墩承载力的影响

为比较单向压弯和双向压弯作用的不同,取两种不同的荷载工况进行对比,并分别用"■"和"▲"表示,"■"点的 P、M_y、M_z 分别为250000kN、150000kN·m、500000kN·m;"▲"点的则为50000kN、100000kN·m、500000kN·m,将其坐标表示于图7和图8中。

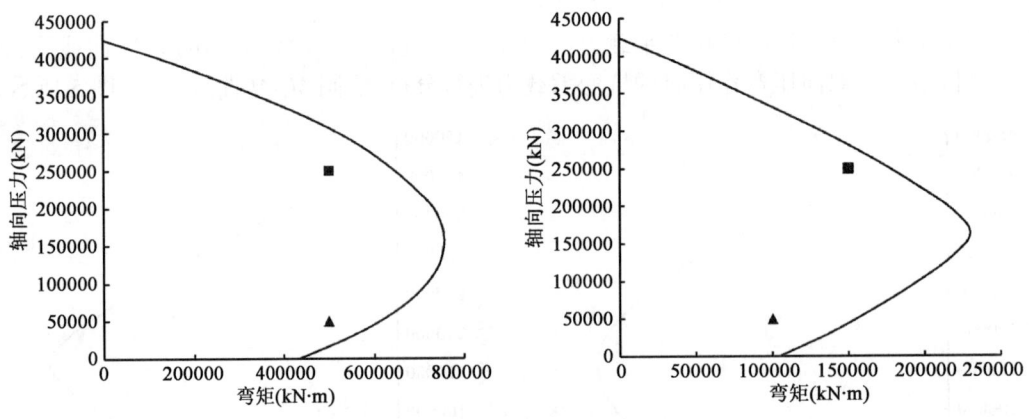

图 7 P-M 曲线图中两种工况的位置

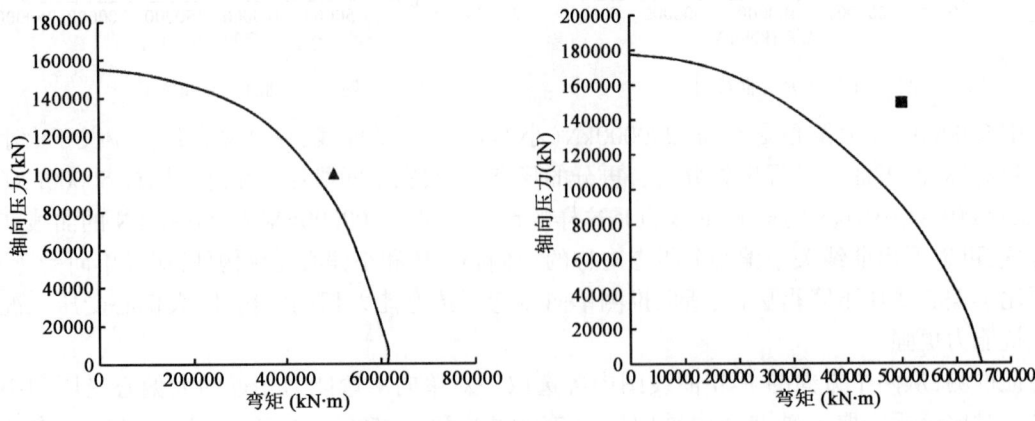

图 8 M_y-M_z 曲线图中两种工况的位置

在 P-M 曲线图中,两种荷载工况都位于曲线内,当受到双向弯矩的联合作用时,均超出了 M_y-M_z 曲线的包络范围。桥墩在处于这两种工况时,单向压弯的情况下都满足承载力要求,但受到双向弯矩的耦合作用就发生了破坏,所以弯矩耦合对桥墩的承载力会有削弱,截面设计时只考虑单向压弯作用对结构是不安全的。

3 材料强度等级对桥墩承载力的影响

3.1 双向压弯下混凝土强度等级对桥墩承载力的影响

选取双向压弯作用下轴向压力 50000kN(大偏心受压)和 250000kN(小偏心受压)的两种受力工况,分别将混凝土强度等级设为 C40、C45、C50,其余条件不变,绘制 M_y-M_z 曲线图,如图 9 和图 10 所示。

由图 9 可知,三条曲线呈现两边窄、中间略宽的形态,桥墩处于单向压弯大偏心受压工况时,提升混凝土强度等级对于承载力的提升十分微小,当桥墩两个方向都存在较大弯矩时,提升混凝土强度等级对承载力的提高有了些许效果,因此双向承弯的构件,在大偏心受压工况下,提升混凝土的强度等级对于承载力的提升较小。

由图 10 可知,小偏心情况下,三条曲线呈现两端宽、中间窄的形态,说明提升混凝土强度等级对单向压弯作用下的桥墩承载力有着显著的增强,但是受到双向压弯时,增强效果受到了减弱。图中两条相近曲线间的距离相差不大,说明双向压弯小偏心受压工况下,混凝土强度等级的提高带来抗弯承载力的提升是均匀的。

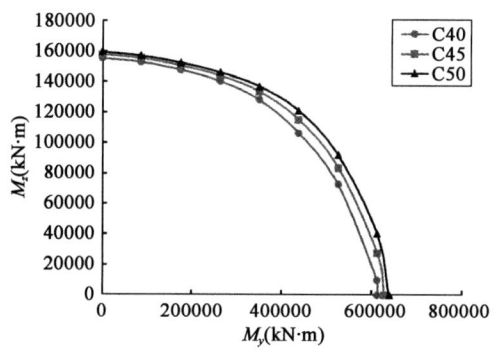

图 9 轴力 50000kN 下使用不同强度等级混凝土的桥墩 M_y-M_z 曲线图

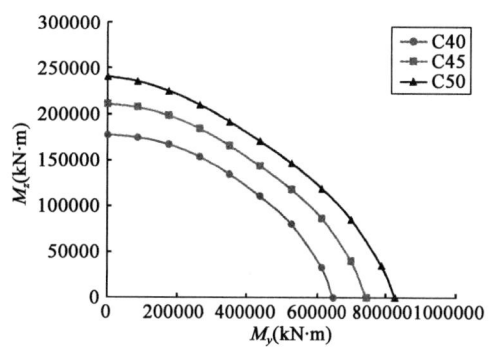

图 10 轴力 250000kN 下使用不同强度等级混凝土的桥墩 M_y-M_z 曲线图

3.2 双向压弯下钢筋强度等级对桥墩承载力的影响

选取双向压弯作用下轴向压力 50000kN 和 250000kN 的两种受力工况,分别将钢筋种类设为 HRB300、HRB400、HRB500,其余条件不变,绘制 M_y-M_z 曲线图,如图 11 和图 12 所示。

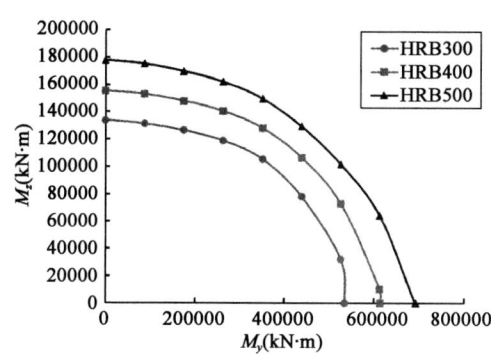

图 11 轴力 50000kN 下使用不同强度等级钢筋的桥墩 M_y-M_z 曲线图

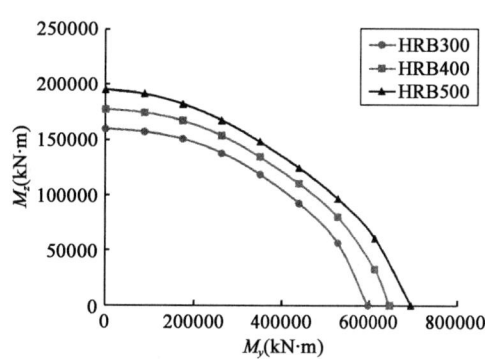

图 12 轴力 250000kN 下使用不同强度钢筋的桥墩 M_y-M_z 曲线图

图11中是大偏心受压情况,三条曲线各处的间距都比较均匀,说明提升钢筋强度等级对受到单向和双向压弯作用的桥墩承载力都有着不错的增强效果。当桥墩接近只承受Y轴方向的弯矩时,曲线存在断崖式的下降,随着钢筋等级的提高,这种现象出现了减弱。图中两条相近曲线间的距离也近似相等,说明大偏心受压工况下,无论是单向压弯还是双向压弯,增大钢筋的强度,带来桥墩承载力的提高是均匀的。

由12图可知,小偏心受压下,三条曲线呈现出两边宽、中间窄的形态,说明提升钢筋强度对单向压弯作用下的桥墩承载力有着较好的增强效果,但对于双向压弯,这种增强效果受到了减弱。图中两条相近曲线间的距离也近似相同,说明在小偏心受压工况下,随着钢筋强度等级的提高,桥墩承载力的增长也是较为均匀的。

3.3 双向压弯下材料强度等级对桥墩承载力的影响特点

分别计算轴向压力50000kN和250000kN下使用C50混凝土和HRB500钢筋的桥墩抗弯承载力,加入上文中相同轴力的曲线,绘制M_y-M_z曲线图,如图13和图14所示,比较钢筋和混凝土的强度对于桥墩承载力影响的特点。

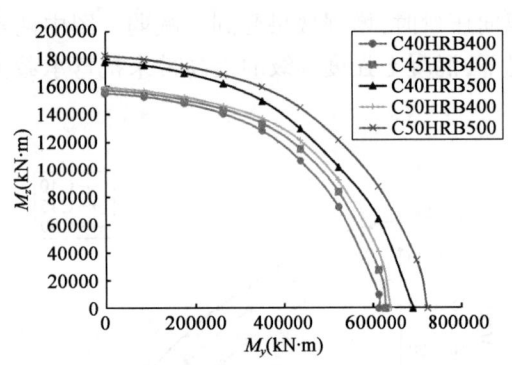

图13 轴力50000kN下使用不同强度混凝土和钢筋的桥墩M_y-M_z曲线图

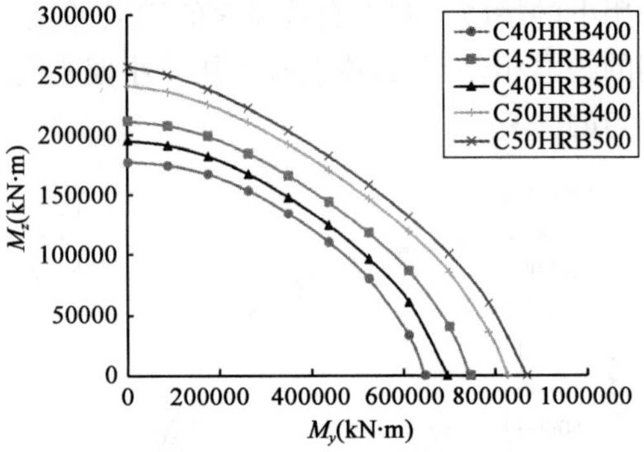

图14 轴力250000kN下使用不同混凝土和钢筋的桥墩M_y-M_z曲线图

图13中改变混凝土强度等级的曲线差距不大,而改变钢筋的强度等级使得曲线升高,所以提升钢筋的强度,对双向压弯下大偏心受压的桥墩承载力有着较大的提高。图14中所有曲线分布较为均匀,没有出现较大的间隔,双向压弯小偏心受压下,增加混凝土和钢筋的强度等级都可以提高桥墩的抗弯承载力,但是提升混凝土的强度更加有效。

4 结 语

双向弯矩作用对于截面的承载力会有削弱,要在工程中考虑到双向弯矩的耦合作用。单向压弯抗弯承载力相同的情况下,同一构件受到双向弯矩作用,大偏心受压工况要比小偏心受压工况的抗弯能力更强。相较单向压弯,双向压弯下提升混凝土的强度等级使得大偏心受压的桥墩承载力有了些许提高,但两者都不显著,对小偏心受压的桥墩,无论单向压弯还是双向压弯,提升混凝土的强度等级对承载力的提升都有着良好的效果。双向压弯下,提升钢筋强度等级对两种受压状态的桥墩承载力都有着显著地提高,但提升的幅度较单向压弯会有一定的削弱。

参考文献

[1] 中华人民共和国交通部.公路钢筋混凝土及预应力混凝土桥涵设计规范:JTG D62—2018[S].北京:人民交通出版社股份有限公司,2018.

[2] Xiao Liang,Sritharan. Effect of Confinement in Square Hollow Concrete Column Sections[J]. Journal of Structural Engineering, 2019, 191:526-535.

[3] 韩强,杜修力,赵彦,等.双向压弯状态下矩形空心桥墩循环试验[J].中国公路学报,2013,26(01):58-66.

[4] 董振华,韩强,杜修力.双向压弯下 RC 矩形空心截面桥墩承载能力评估[J].中国公路学报,2014,27(2):77-83.

[5] 邵长江,漆启明,韦旺,等.矩形混凝土空心墩延性抗震性能试验研究[J/OL].西南交通大学学报:1-9[2021-01-09].

[6] 许紫刚,贾俊峰,韩强,等.双轴压弯作用下 RC 桥墩矩形空心截面性能评价[J].工程力学,2015,32(01):17-25.

基于挠度影响线导数的连续梁桥损伤识别

王康迪 生尧文

(长安大学公路学院)

摘 要 提出了适用于连续梁的挠度影响线差值导数识别损伤的方法,并研究了局部损伤位置与程度对主梁挠度影响线的影响。采用 ANSYS 有限元软件建立连续梁模型识别挠度影响线,并验证损伤识别效果。结果表明:该方法在基于静力测试数据的结构损伤识别上效果显著。挠度影响线的二阶导数是比较合适的损伤指标,可以用来识别结构的损伤位置和损伤程度。位置识别较为准确,而程度识别有一定的误差。该方法有一定的理论与应用意义。

关键词 桥梁工程 损伤识别 连续梁桥 挠度影响线 有限元分析

0 引 言

损伤识别作为中小跨径桥梁的健康监测系统的核心内容近年来受到了大量研究人员的关注[1]。针对中小跨径桥梁健康监测系统传感器少、结构构件参数未知、车辆荷载信息未知的特点,学者[2-4]从多种方向对桥梁结构损伤识别进行了研究,并指出选取合适的识别指标是正确识别桥梁结构损伤的前提和保障。挠度影响线因其包括较多的结构信息和数据精度较高的特点逐渐被学者关注,并取得了一定的进展[5-8]。本文关注于连续梁的损伤识别及影响线方法在损伤识别中的应用,在已有研究的基础上提出了基于挠度影响线差值的损伤识别方法,经数值算例模拟和验证认为该方法具有一定的理论和实践意义。

1 影响线力学分析

1.1 影响线基本理论

影响线是表示沿结构跨度移动的单位集中载荷作用下各观测截面的受力效果曲线,在桥梁结构承载能力计算和结构最不利截面确定等方面具有重要价值。常用的影响线有位移影响线、内力影响线、应变影响线等,每种影响线各有其应用特点,基于现场测量的难易程度,各种的影响线有其适用的情境。

在力学课程当中,一般都探讨了简支梁挠度影响线解法,可参见各结构力学教材如。而连续梁作为超静定结构,其挠度影响线的求解则稍显复杂,需要借助超静定问题的力法或者位移法去求解,下面以工程中常见的三跨连续梁的力学模型为例,说明三跨连续梁的挠度影响线的求解。下面的推导有符合以下假定,结构处于弹性阶段。

根据变形体的虚功原理,在荷载作用下任一点的弹性位移可表示为:

$$\Delta = \sum \int \frac{\overline{M} M_P}{EI} ds + \sum \int \frac{\overline{F}_N F_{NP}}{EA} ds + \sum \int \frac{k \overline{F}_Q F_{QP}}{GA} ds \tag{1}$$

在以弯曲变形为主的梁结构分析中,通常可以略去轴力项和剪力项的影响,所以公式可简化为:

$$\Delta = \sum \int \frac{\overline{M}M_P}{EI} ds \tag{2}$$

在正常无损伤的情况下,推导连续梁的挠度影响线方程。

由于连续梁是超静定结构,需要用力法或者位移法来求解,此处应用力法求解。

取基本体系,力法方程为:

$$\begin{cases} \delta_{11}X_1 + \delta_{12}X_2 + \Delta_{1p} = 0 \\ \delta_{21}X_1 + \delta_{22}X_2 + \Delta_{2p} = 0 \end{cases} \tag{3}$$

分别做出三个弯矩图,利用图乘法可得:

$$\delta_{11} = \delta_{22} = \frac{4l^3}{9EI} \tag{4}$$

$$\delta_{12} = \delta_{21} = \frac{7l^3}{18EI} \tag{5}$$

$$\Delta_{1p} = \Delta_{2p} = -\frac{23l^3}{48EI} \tag{6}$$

解得:

$$X_1 = X_2 = \frac{23}{40}$$

并可以做出其中跨跨中作用力时的弯矩图。

然后,使一个单位力在梁上面移动,用以推导连续梁的挠度影响线,当其分别作用在第一跨、第二跨和第三跨时,可以得到单位力作用下的弯矩图,再依据图乘法,可以得到挠度影响线的解析表达式,如:

$$\Delta H = \begin{cases} \dfrac{x_0(x_0-l)(x_0+l)}{80EI}, & 0 \leq x_0 \leq l \\[2mm] \dfrac{-20x_0^3 + 69l \cdot x_0^2 - 72l^2 x_0 + 23l^3}{240EI}, & l \leq x_0 \leq \dfrac{3l}{2} \\[2mm] \dfrac{20x_0^3 - 111lx_0^2 + 198l^2 x_0 - 112l^3}{240EI}, & \dfrac{3l}{2} \leq x_0 \leq 2l \\[2mm] \dfrac{(x_0-2l)(x_0-3l)(4l-x_0)}{80EI}, & 2l \leq x_0 \leq 3l \end{cases} \tag{7}$$

并且可以做出挠度影响线的图形。

当连续梁上出现损伤时,假设损伤区段位于中跨,损伤后的抗弯刚度折减为 EI',利用同样的方法来研究连续梁损伤状况下的挠度影响线。

可以由结果推论出,挠度影响线在识别连续梁桥损伤方面具有积极作用。

1.2 影响线用于损伤识别

结构的损伤是指在环境和荷载的作用下材料和结构的劣化。对于钢筋混凝土结构来说,混凝土开裂、钢筋锈蚀、预应力损失等都可视为损伤,出现各种不利于继续承载的情况,为了避免安全事故发生,及时有效的识别出结构的损伤,有必要对结构进行损伤识别和运营状态的评估。[9] 相比于其他方法,基于挠度影响线识别结构损伤不需要布设大量测点[10],仅仅需要测量移动荷载作用下主梁的挠度,计算截面曲率变化即可推算梁截面刚度改变情况,即实现损伤识别。

然而工程中的实际桥梁模型并非和理想力学模型完全一致,其在材料性质、边界连接等方面都有不同的地方,所以在实际分析过程中二者还是有一定的差距,这是工程科学基本都具有的一个特点,利用有限元方法建立模型来分析结构的力学特性时,也是对实际结构有一定的简化,满足一定的力学前提条件,这样也会导致实际结构和有限元模型之间存在着一定的差距,所以有必要对这一问题进行分析。

三跨连续梁的挠度影响线为三次曲线,解析式也为三次曲线,若对其进行求导,可以更加清楚地反映曲线的局部特性,也可以借以识别结构的特性。挠度影响线二阶导数会出现突变,可以反映结构的位置,其中$\dfrac{EI'}{EI}$的值可以反映结构的损伤程度。

2 影响线识别损伤数值算例分析

2.1 模型建立

本文以一三跨连续梁数值算例,以单元刚度的降低模拟损伤,验证所提方法的可行性。该模型利用通用有限元软件 ANSYS 建立,其跨度为 40m、60m、40m,采用 BEAM3 单元建立模型,弹性模量为 3.3×10^{10} Pa,泊松比为 0.2,截面面积为 7.5×10^{-3} m³,绕 z 轴、y 轴的惯性矩为 7×10^{-3} m⁴,2.4×10^{-3} m⁴。

模型如图 1 所示。

可以得到未损伤状态下的跨中的挠度影响线和弯矩影响线,然而实际工程中较难直接得到桥梁结构的内力值,故利用挠度影响线进行分析。

损伤工况如下,分别对此进行分析(表 1)。

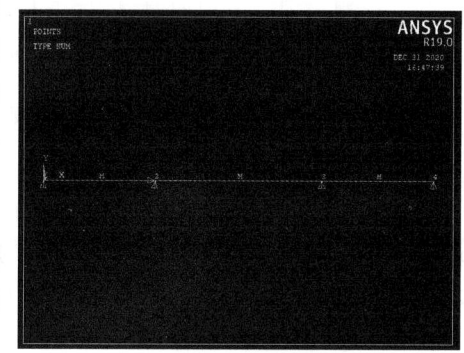

图 1 有限元模型

损伤工况表 表1

损伤工况	Ⅰ	Ⅱ	Ⅲ
损伤单元	25、26	60、61	80、81
损伤程度	10%	10%	10%
	20%	20%	20%
	50%	50%	50%

2.2 未损伤影响线及损伤影响线

提取中跨跨中的位移影响线,可以看出,其符合基本力学原理,各点的值也可以由结果导出,并用来绘制影响线,该线为光滑曲线,反映了结构的静力特性和准静力特性,区别于频率、振型等动力指标。下对各个可能的指标子在无损状况及损伤状况的条件下图线进行分析和对比探讨影响线用于损伤识别的可能性(图 2、图 3)。

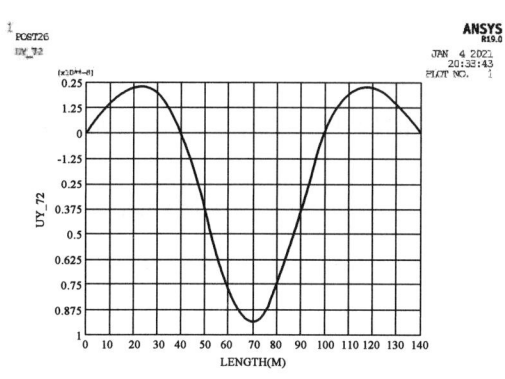

图 2 未损伤状况下影响线

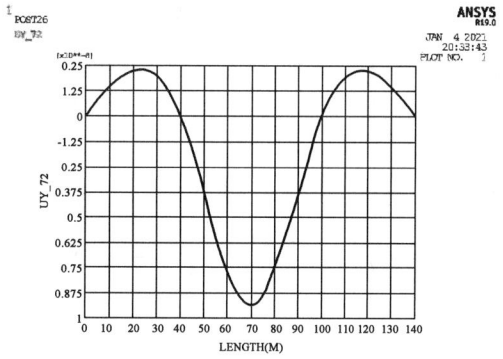

图 3 第一跨跨中损伤状况下影响线

由图 2 和图 3 看出,未损伤和损伤状况下的影响线形状类似,几乎无差别,并不能通过影响线本身来识别出损伤是否存在,所以对原始得到的数据进行处理,寻求新的损伤指标。

导数可以反映曲线的局部特征和单调性,考虑对影响线曲线求导来寻找其他信息(图 4、图 5)。

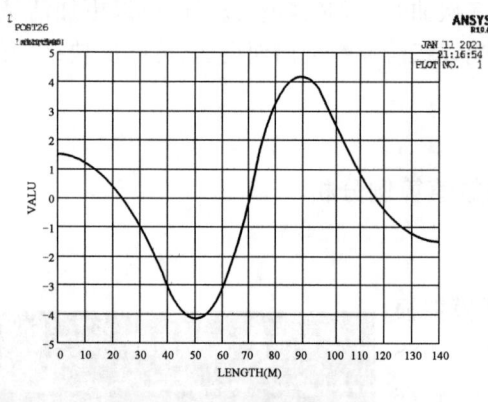
图4 未损伤状况下影响线导数

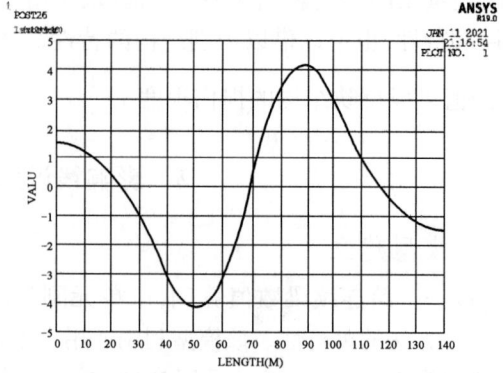
图5 第一跨跨中损伤状况下影响线导数

挠度差值影响线指的是挠度影响线对应位置的值做差,我们可以看到其存在明显的尖点(此处是否可以用连续不可导来描述),尖点对应的就是损伤发生的位置,此处说明了挠度影响线差值可以用来识别损伤是否存在,而且可以判定损伤发生的位置,是一个比较好的损伤指标,但是它不能识别出损伤的程度,更不能对结构的剩余寿命进行预测,所以还需要寻找其他的损伤指标。

从力学上看,挠度曲线的微分方程忽略高阶项之后,便得到了挠曲线近似微分方程,对挠曲线方程二阶求导,可得到反映截面刚度的是截面曲率方程,即用以模拟损伤的量。从几何上看,一阶导数反映曲线的单调性,二阶导数反映曲线的凹凸性,都可以反映出曲线的特性,从理论上来讲,都可以用来借以判断包含力学意义的曲线的性质。

挠度影响线二阶导数,如图6、图7所示,可以反映一定的力学特性,可以很好地说明结构的特点。

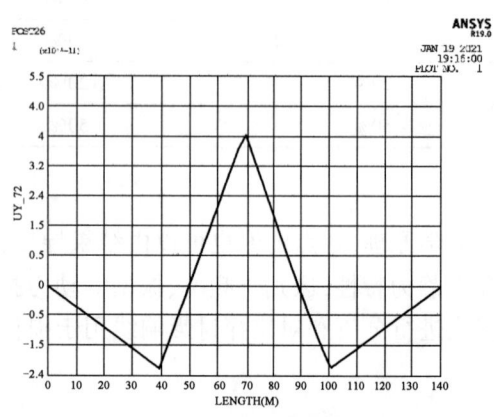
图6 未损伤状况下影响线二阶导数

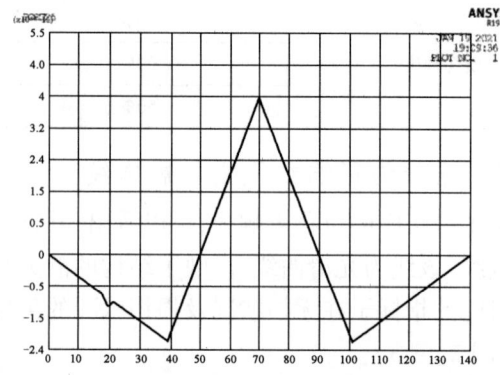
图7 第一跨跨中损伤状况下影响线二阶导数

由挠度影响线二阶导数的对比可知,损伤状况下的挠度影响线存在突变,且该突变位置正位于损伤单元处,由此证明挠度影响线的二阶导数可以用来识别连续梁的损伤位置,具有不依赖原始数据识别单处损伤的能力。

对于损伤程度的判定,此处算例采用30%损伤,拟合得到损伤和未损伤区域的斜率二者作一个比值,可以得到 $\alpha = \dfrac{EI'}{EI} = \dfrac{-4.56 \times 10^{-13}}{-1.63 \times 10^{-12}} = 0.2808$,接近于30%,有一定的误差,说明该方法也可以识别结构的损伤程度。

挠度影响线曲线作差,可以得到挠度影响线差值曲线。挠度影响线的差值能够显现出一定的规律和有效的信息,与原始信息不同。将损伤前后同一点的影响线量值作差,横坐标依然为各个单元的位置,纵坐标为计算所得的差值,便可以得到挠度影响线差值的图线,该图便显示出了一定的规律和信息。

不同损伤程度下的挠度差值影响线如所示,可以借助比值来判断损伤程度的大小,如损伤30%和损伤50%的情况下,尖点绝对值的比值即为其损伤程度之比(图8)。

2.3 结果讨论

利用单元刚度降低来模拟损伤,在不同的损伤工况下,利用有限元分析得到第一跨跨中损伤后的挠度影响线,不同的损伤工况具有不同的结果,将影响线绘制于如所示。由图可以看出,挠度影响线可以识别出部分的损伤,但是部分情况下识别的效果并不好,实际工程中由于环境干扰和噪声影响,会导致识别的效果不好,鲁棒性不好,所以拟采用其他的方法解决这一问题。以30%损伤程度为例,说明了该方法在损伤位置和损伤程度的识别上具有一定的意义。

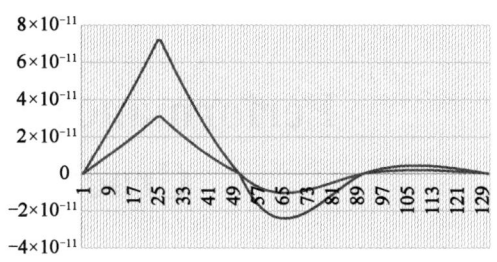

图8 不同工况影响线差值

挠度差值影响线是挠度影响线的数据初步处理后得到的数据,得到的方法为有损伤下挠度影响线的大小,减去无损伤下挠度影响线的大小,可以得到二者的差值,此值可以用来判断结构是否有损伤,损伤的位置和损伤的程度,是一种可以用来判断损伤的指标。

结构的刚度下降,对应于实际的梁桥可能产生的病害为跨中下挠,出现竖向、斜向裂缝,整体性较差横向连接失效等,这些病害在梁桥中都可能会出现,故此项研究在后续工程应用中也具有一定的意义。然而实际环境干扰较多,如何排除实际噪声干扰仍然是值得研究的工作。

3 结 语

本文研究了基于DIL的中小跨径桥梁损伤是识别方法。首先分析影响线的力学特性确定其可以用于结构的损伤识别,而后建立有限元模型,作数值算例分析影响线的获取,及其用于损伤识别的可行性,然后分析指标对于损伤的敏感程度,说明挠度影响线可以用于损伤识别。

本文未针对多损伤模式进行进一步的检验,所以后续在此方面还需要进一步的研究和探讨;本文暂未进行实际桥梁数据试验,故所提方法是否适用于实际桥梁还有待于进一步检验;剩余寿命预测等方面并不能通过此种方法显示,相关的研究还可以继续进行。

参考文献

[1] 单德山,罗凌峰,李乔.桥梁健康监测2019年度研究进展[J].土木与环境工程学报(中英文),2020,42(5):115-125.

[2] Xu Zheng, DongHui Yang, TingHua Yi, et al. Development of Bridge Influence Line Identification Methods Based on Direct Measurement Data: A Comprehensive Review and Comparison[J]. Elsevier Ltd, 2019, 198(2):100-107.

[3] Alamdari MM, Kildashti K, Samali B, et al. Damage Diagnosis in Bridge Structures Using Rotation Influence Line: Validation on a Cable-stayed Bridge[J]. Engineering Structures, 2019, 185.

[4] 刘苏文.考虑荷载横向分布的影响线损伤识别研究[D].青岛:青岛理工大学,2016.

[5] 史文军.基于准静态影响线的桥梁承载能力评估方法研究[D].天津:河北工业大学,2012.

[6] 牛杰.基于模型确认的桥梁结构概率损伤识别方法研究[D].南京:东南大学,2018.

[7] 杨维彪.基于稀疏正则化的桥梁影响线识别方法及其工程应用[D].厦门:厦门大学,2018.

[8] 杜永峰,刘云帅,王晓琴.基于挠度差值影响线曲率的简支梁桥损伤识别[J].桥梁建设,2009,(4):80-83.

[9] 徐勇华.基于挠度影响线的变截面梁损伤识别研究[D].广州:广州大学,2015.

[10] 王艺霖.基于影响线二次差值的桥梁损伤识别方法[D].上海:上海交通大学,2011.

Performance Evaluation of Bridge with Cracks under Heavy Load

Yushi Yi Kexin Qiao

(Highway College, Chang'an University)

Abstract Depth and width of the crack have a significant impact on the deterioration performance of steel and concrete. Calculating and analyzing the crack performance of concrete bridge under heavy load is necessary. Firstly, based on Bazant size effect law and double-K fracture criterion of concrete, crack toughness K_{IC}^{ini} and instability toughness K_{IC}^{un} of medium and small span bridges are calculated. Secondly, the heavy truck model, typical medium and small span bridge finite element model and dynamic stress intensity factor calculation program are integrated to form a calculation system. Calculating the crack tip stress intensity factor time history and substituted into the double-K fracture criterion. Finally, the control moment of concrete bridges is deduced according to the fracture parameters. The results show that the cracks of reinforced concrete bridge will propagate and the cracks of prestressed reinforced concrete bridge will not propagate under the action of heavy truck. The crack performance of different types of bridge is controlled by different types of heavy truck. Crack initiation moment of reinforced concrete hollow slab bridge is 0.32 ~ 0.39 times of the design vehicle load effect, critical moment of reinforced concrete hollow slab bridge is 1.02 ~ 1.25 times of the design vehicle load effect.

Keywords Bridge engineering Duble-K fracture criterion Stress intensity factor Performance evaluation

0 Introduction

During the service period of concrete bridges, due to the external load, the initial defects of the materials, the adverse factors in the environment and other reasons, there will inevitably be some cracks on the surface and inside. Especially for the bridges that have been built and operated for many years or have more heavy loads in the regional sections. The cracks are often structural, which have adverse effects on the durability and bearing capacity of the bridges. Double-K fracture criterion is proposed by combining the stress intensity factor with the virtual fracture model, and took the stress intensity factor as the standard parameter (Xu et al., 1992). Crack toughness K_{IC}^{ini} and instability toughness K_{IC}^{un} are combined to represent the crack growth state. When $K < K_{IC}^{ini}$, there is no crack growth. When $K_{IC}^{ini} < K < K_{IC}^{un}$, the crack propagates steadily. When $K > K_{IC}^{un}$, the crack propagates unsteadily. When $K = K_{IC}^{ini}$ and $K = K_{IC}^{un}$, the crack is in critical state. Sinusoidal and linear loads are applied on the finite element model of three-point bending specimen to calculate the dynamic stress intensity factor at the crack tip. The results show that the dynamic crack toughness can be directly determined by the crack initiation time measured by experiments (Zhong et al., 2004). Crack propagation law of cracked beam under the action of moving vehicle load is studied (Zhu Jinsong et al., 2018). The influence of vehicle weight, vehicle speed and road roughness on the crack propagation performance are researched, which provided ideas for the safety evaluation of bridge vehicle induced vibration based on fracture mechanics.

The remaining of the paper is organized as follows. First, calculating crack toughness and instability toughness of concrete bridges. Second, calculating crack tip stress intensity factor and substituted into double-K fracture criterion. Finally, according to fracture parameters, calculating the control moment of concrete bridges.

1 Size Effect of Concrete Fracture Parameters

Size effect is one of the basic characteristics of concrete, which is caused by the distribution of aggregate in concrete, component size, crack propagation speed and other factors. There are obvious differences between the fracture parameters of large scale components and those of small scale components. Size effect is caused by the strain energy consumed during the macro crack propagation, and embodies the size effect law in the nominal stress expression (Bazant, 1984). Based on the viewpoint of energy method, the formula derived by Bazant is simple in form and high in accuracy. It can be combined with the fracture process zone theory and double-K fracture criterion, and can also be applied to non geometrically similar components, so it is widely used.

Bazant derived the size effect rate of non geometrically similar members by means of progressive analysis method (Bazant, 1995):

$$\sigma_N = c_n \sqrt{\frac{EG_f}{c'_f g(\alpha_0) + g(\alpha_0) h}} \tag{1}$$

$$g(\alpha) = \pi a c_n^2 f^2(\alpha) \tag{2}$$

$$g'(\alpha) = 2\pi a c_n^2 f(\alpha) f'(\alpha) \tag{3}$$

Where: E is the elastic modulus of the material; G_f is the fracture energy; c_f, is the equivalent crack length; h is the height of large scale components; $g(\alpha)$ is the dimensionless energy release rate; $g'(\alpha)$ is the derivative function of $g(\alpha)$; a is the crack length; c_n is any constant; α is the ratio of crack length to beam height (Chinese Aeronautical Establishment, 1981).

$$f(\alpha) = 2.9\alpha^{1/2} - 4.6\alpha^{3/2} + 21.8\alpha^{5/2} - 37.6\alpha^{7/2} + 38.7\alpha^{9/2} \tag{4}$$

If the geometry of the specimen is given, Eq. (1) can be transformed into a linear expression:

$$Y = AX + C \tag{5}$$

Where: $X = \frac{g(\alpha_0)}{g'(\alpha_0)} d$; $EG_f = \frac{1}{A}$; $c_f = \frac{C}{A}$; $Y = \frac{c_n^2}{g'(\alpha_0)\sigma_n^2}$, for a three-point bending beam, the value in the formula can be obtained from the formula of mechanics of materials:

$$\sigma_n = 1.5 \frac{PS}{td^2(1-\alpha)^2} \tag{6}$$

Where: P is the external load imposed on the specimen, when the crack toughness is solved, the cracking load P_{ini} is substituted. When the instability toughness is solved, the limit load P_u is substituted; S is the distance between two supports of the specimen; t is the width of the specimen; d is the height of the specimen.

The calculation formula of stress intensity factor at crack tip of three-point bending beam given in *handbook of stress intensity factors* is as follows:

$$K_I = \frac{PS}{4td^{3/2}} f(\alpha) \tag{7}$$

Substituting Eq. (6) into Eq. (7), getting the following results:

$$K_I = \frac{\sigma_n (1-\alpha)^2 \sqrt{h}}{6} f(\alpha) \tag{8}$$

The linear equation of Eq. (5) can be regressed by transforming the test data under crack initiation load and unstable fracture load respectively, A and C can be obtained. Then the nominal stress value σ_n considering the size effect can be obtained according to Eq. (1), the crack toughness value and instability toughness value of large size components can be obtained by substituting Eq. (8).

2 Calculation of Fracture Parameters

Due to the high degree of standardization, industrialization and mechanization of design and construction. Medium and small span bridges are widely used in China's highway construction. The reinforced concrete hollow slab bridge, prestressed concrete hollow slab bridge, prestressed concrete T-beam bridge and prestressed concrete box girder bridge in the general drawing of bridge superstructure are selected as the research objects (Ministry of Transport of People's Republic of China, 2008). The design load level is highway grade I, and the integral subgrade width is 24.5m.

According to the Eq. (8), the crack toughness K_{IC}^{ini} and instability toughness K_{IC}^{un} of each bridge type are calculated, as shown in Tab. 1.

Calculation Results of Crack Parameters   Tab. 1

No.	Cross section	Span (m)	Height (m)	Crack parameter (MPa·m$^{1/2}$)	
				K_{IC}^{ini}	K_{IC}^{un}
1		6	0.32	0.24453	0.77989
		8	0.42	0.25713	0.82371
		10	0.50	0.26440	0.84917
2		10	0.60	0.27129	0.87354
		13	0.70	0.27654	0.89226
		16	0.80	0.28070	0.90713
		20	0.95	0.28551	0.92445
3		20	1.58	0.29663	0.96487
		25	1.78	0.29865	0.97224
		30	2.08	0.30100	0.98088
		35	2.38	0.30279	0.98748
		40	2.58	0.30377	0.99110
4		20	1.20	0.29117	0.94493
		25	1.40	0.29438	0.95660
		30	1.60	0.29684	0.96569
		35	1.80	0.29882	0.97292
		40	2.00	0.30042	0.97880

3 Bridge and Vehicle Model

Based on the statistical analysis of the traffic load data of heavy truck on three expressways, five typical heavy truck models have been selected (Han et al., 2018) as shown in Tab. 2, in which the wheelbase and axle load parameters of each model are listed. The speed of heavy truck crossing the bridge is set at 5km/h.

Typical Heavy Truck   Tab. 2

Type	Schematic Diagram	Wheelbase and Axle Load Information
CI		7t 7t 11t 9×11t 180 270 345 8×160 2075

Type	Schematic Diagram	Wheelbase and Axle Load Information
C II		10t 10t 10t 5×20t; 345 135 1275 4×160; 2395
C III		9.4t 9.4t 9.3t 9.3t 9×15.7t 9×15.7t; 180 345 180 345 8×160 1000 8×160; 4610
C IV		9.6t 9.6t 9.6t 9.5t 31×14.7t 9.5t 9.5t 9.5t; 180 345 180 345 30×160 345 345 180; 6720
C V		9.4t 9.4t 9.4t 9.5t 14×14.7t 17×14.7t 9.4t 9.4t 9.4t 9.4t; 180 345 180 345 13×160 4540 16×160 345 180 345 180; 11120

In the general drawing of bridge superstructure, the beam height of typical medium and small span bridges increases with the span, and the dimensions of other parts is similar. Therefore, the parametric modeling in ANSYS can be used to establish the finite element models of reinforced concrete hollow slab bridge, prestressed concrete hollow slab bridge, prestressed concrete T-beam bridge and prestressed concrete box girder bridge conveniently and quickly. The model is shown in Fig. 1. Solid65 is used to built the bridge model, elastic modulus is 3.45×10^4 MPa, poisson's ratio is 0.2, bulk density is 2.5×10^{-5} N/mm^3.

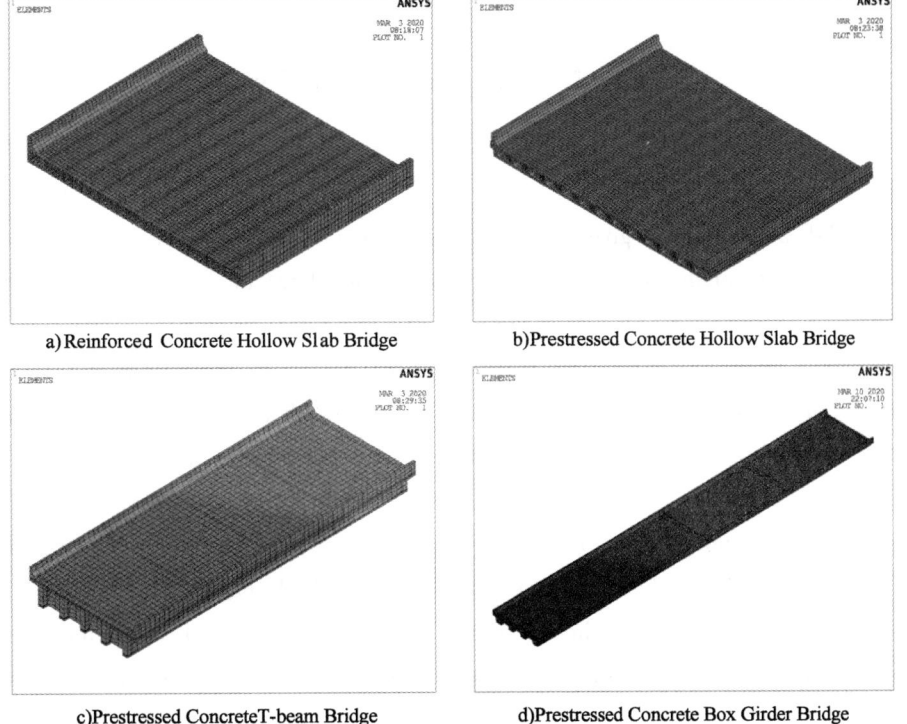

a) Reinforced Concrete Slab Bridge   b) Prestressed Concrete Hollow Slab Bridge

c) Prestressed Concrete T-beam Bridge   d) Prestressed Concrete Box Girder Bridge

Fig. 1 Finite Element Model of Typical Medium and Small Span Bridges

Large cargo transportation has higher requirements for road smoothness. Generally, pits and unevenness are not allowed. When selecting the route for vehicles, the expressway with better road condition should be selected. Therefore, the road roughness condition is taken as "good". On the premise of generality and engineering applicability, the simplified treatment is adopted for cracks. A crack is only established at the bottom of the middle span of middle beam. The width of the crack is equal to the width of the lower edge of the beam, the direction is assumed perpendicular to the longitudinal direction of the bridge. The critical crack depth is used as the crack depth, 70% of the protective layer thickness is recommended (Salah El-Din A. S. et al., 1975). It should be pointed out that although the tensile stress is not allowed at the lower edge of the beam or does not exceed the limit value in the design of prestressed concrete structure, some cracks will appear due to construction defects, temperature effect, vehicle impact or vehicle load exceeding the design load.

The convergence of nonlinear calculation in finite element software is related to the accuracy of mesh, algorithm, load step, convergence criterion and other factors. Reasonable setting of these factors is related to the speed and accuracy of calculation. If the load step is too small, the calculation amount is too large. If the load step is too large, the calculation results are difficult to converge. In order to improve the calculation speed and ensure the calculation accuracy, it is necessary to ensure that all the grids are hexahedron in the modeling. In the area near the crack, the grid size should be appropriately smaller, but not too small, to prevent the sudden damage caused by serious stress concentration. Other areas, such as near the bearing and the bridge deck, are not the key research areas, the grid size should be larger. The specific grid size and load step size are determined according to the trial calculation.

Compared with the general numerical calculation method of homogeneous continuum mechanics, the calculation of reinforced concrete structure with non-uniform characteristics is more simple and stable. On the basis of ensuring the engineering requirements, the accuracy requirements can be appropriately relaxed. It is suggested that the convergence tolerance should be 2%-3% (Jiang Jianjing et al., 2005), and 2% in this study.

4 Stress Intensity Factor Time History

The stress intensity factor time history of four types bridges under the action of five kinds of heavy trucks are calculated. The stress intensity factor time history of 6 m span reinforced concrete slab bridge and 30 m prestressed concrete T-beam bridge are given, and the laws contained in the former are expounded. As shown in Fig. 2 and Fig. 3, the values of the upper and lower blue dashed lines in the figure represent the instability toughness K_{IC}^{un} and crack toughness K_{IC}^{ini} of the bridge respectively.

In Fig. 2, the stress intensity factors at the crack tip under the action of five kinds of heavy trucks all reach the crack toughness value. CIII, CIV and CV heavy trucks soon reach this value when they just drive on the bridge deck, which indicates that the original cracks at the bottom of 6 m slab bridge will crack under the action of heavy trucks and enter the stable expansion stage. The stress intensity factor at the crack tip of the bridge is 0 when some heavy trucks are running, such as CII, CIV and CV heavy trucks, which is caused by the length of the middle concave beam or hanging beam exceeding the length of the bridge.

Under the action of CII heavy truck, the stress intensity factor at the crack tip in the middle span of 6m slab bridge is close to the value of instability toughness. It shows that the decisive parameter in the process of crack propagation is not the total vehicle weight, but the wheel load and its distribution on the bridge deck. Among the five kinds of heavy truck, CII heavy truck plays a controlling role.

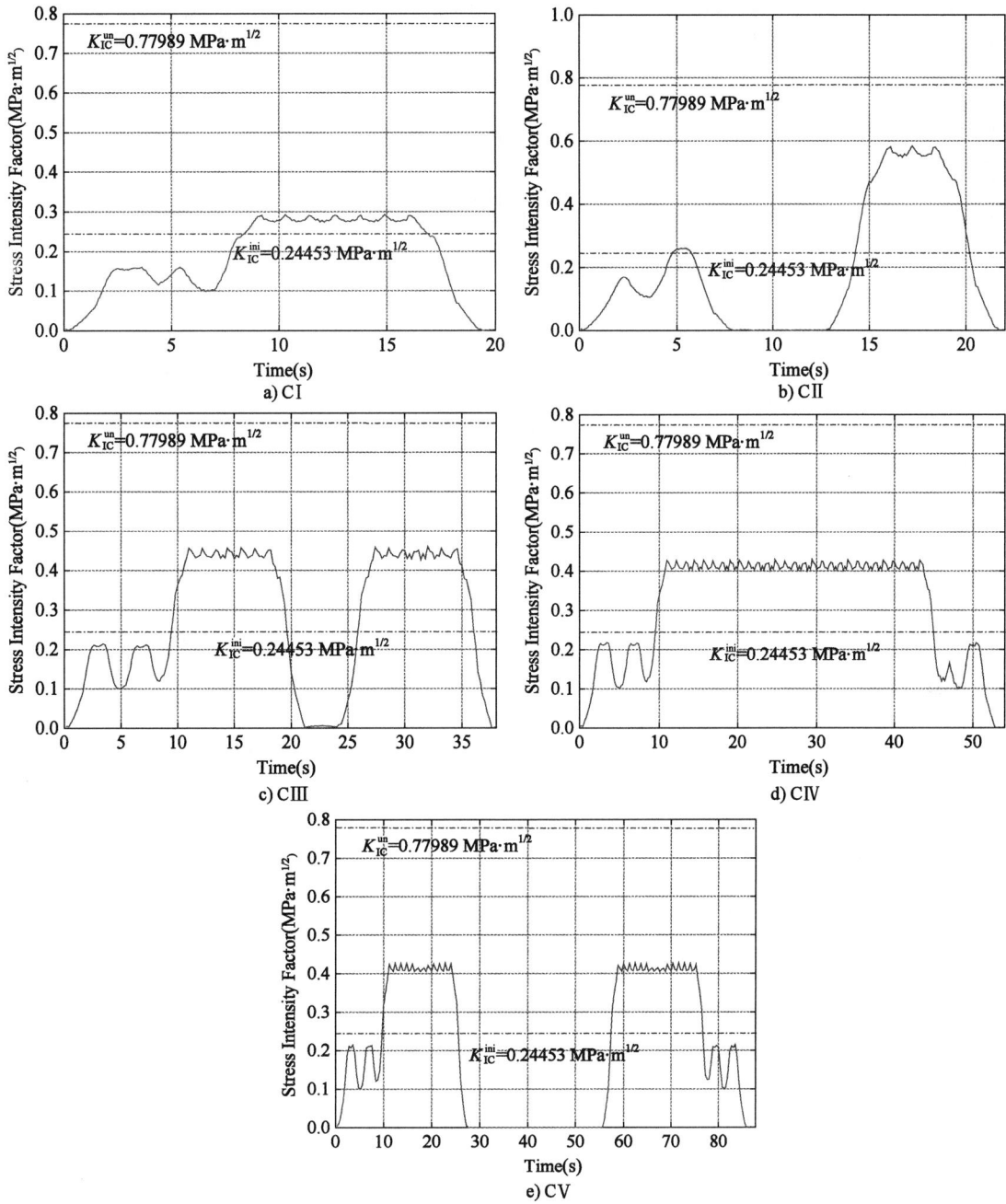

Fig. 2 Stress Intensity Factor Time History of 6m Slab Bridge

For a 30m span prestressed concrete T-beam bridge, the cracks are basically closed due to the existence of prestress. If the value of stress intensity factor is less than 0, it is meaningless, so the value less than 0 is taken as 0.

When CII heavy truck runs on 30m prestressed concrete T-beam bridge, Fig. 4a) and Fig. 4b) respectively show the stress distribution of the web of the center beam when the stress intensity factor at the crack tip of the mid span reaches the maximum due to the tractor part and the trailer part.

It can be seen from Fig. 4 that there is stress concentration at the connection between web and diaphragm. Due to the existence of cracks at the bottom edge of the middle span, the stress on both sides of the cracks is significantly lower than that in other nearby areas. There is a serious stress concentration near the crack tip. This once again verified the accuracy of solid finite element modeling calculation.

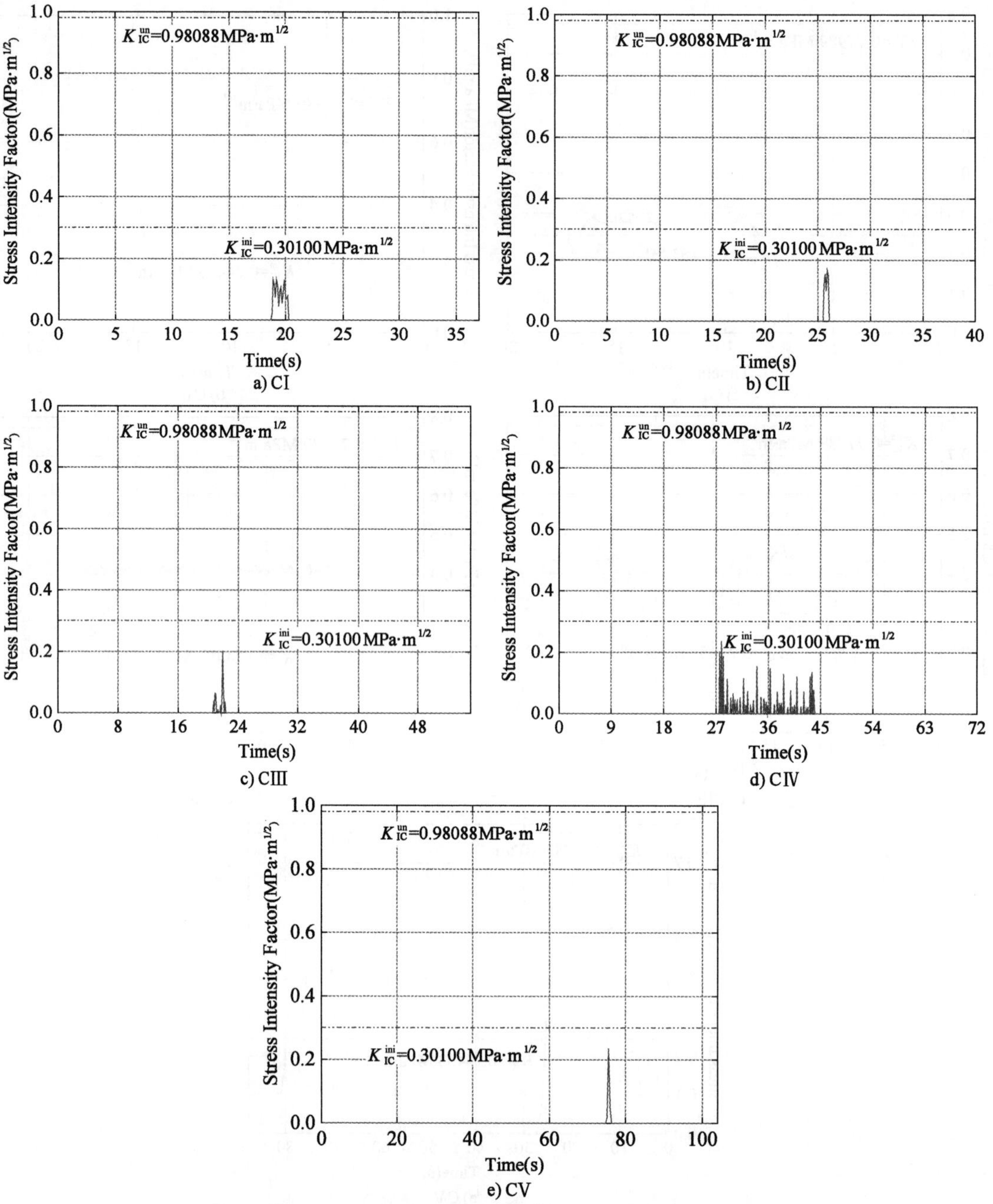

Fig. 3 Stress Intensity Factor Time History of 30m Prestressed T-Beam Bridge

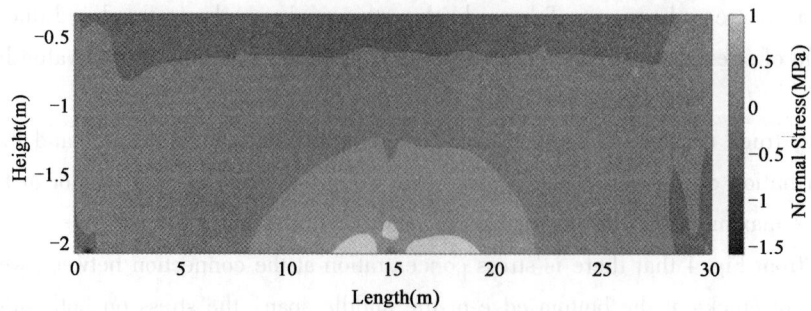

a) Maximum Stress Intensity Factor Caused by Tractor Part

Fig. 4

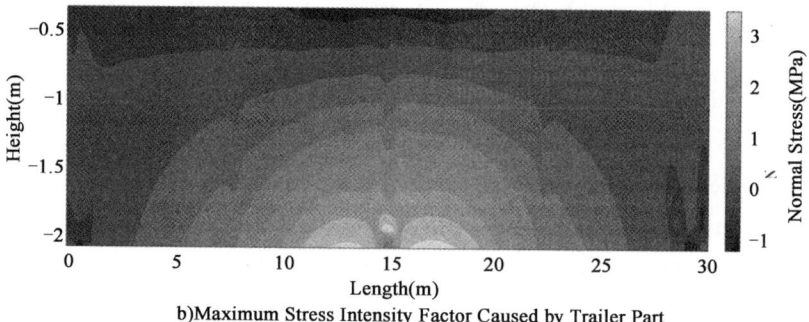
b) Maximum Stress Intensity Factor Caused by Trailer Part

Fig. 4　Web Stress Distribution of 30m Prestressed T-Beam Bridge

5　Stress Intensity Factors Comparison

The maximum value of stress intensity factor of different span bridges in each bridge type under the action of five kinds of heavy trucks is extracted, as shown in Fig. 5a)、Fig. 5d), in which the span number of prestressed concrete box girder bridge is taken as 4. The focus is on the section with the largest positive bending moment of side span.

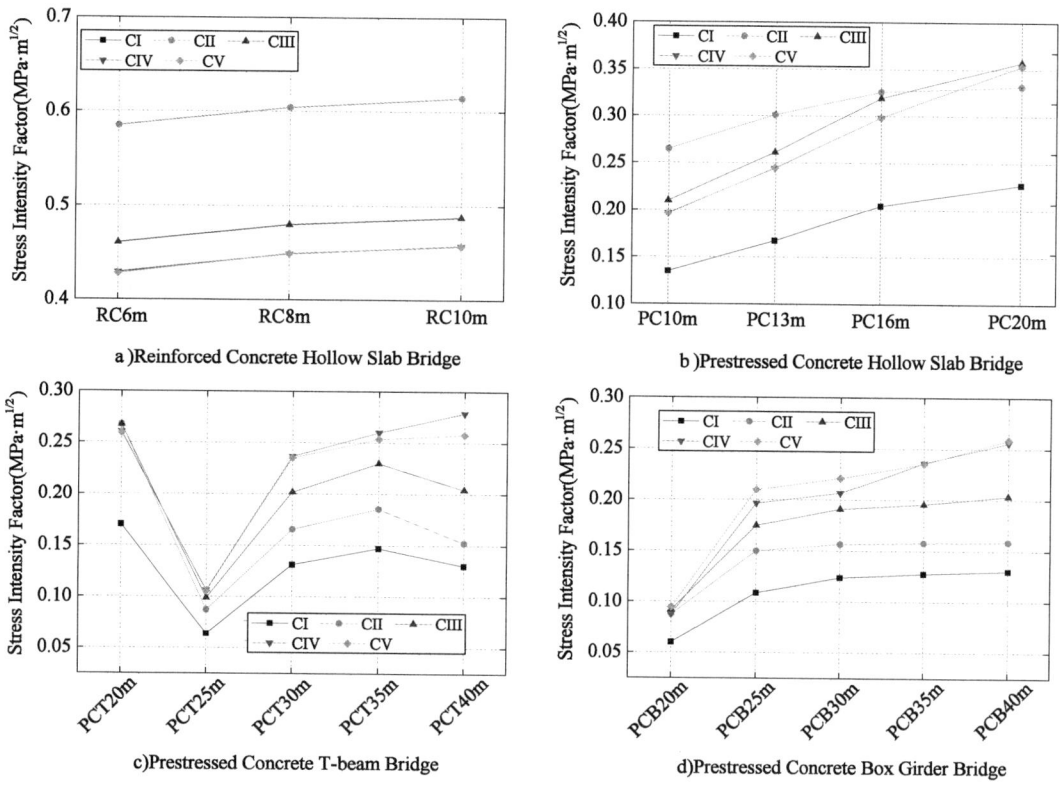

Fig. 5　Stress Intensity Factors of Different Bridge Types

The following conclusions can be drawn from Fig. 5:

(1) The stress intensity factor K of reinforced concrete bridge under the action of five kinds of heavy truck exceeds the crack toughness, and some of them reach about 75% of the instability toughness. The stress intensity factor K of prestressed reinforced concrete bridge under the action of five kinds of heavy truck mostly does not reach the crack toughness, and the value of K of some bridges that exceed the crack toughness is also less than the instability toughness, and there is a lot of surplus.

(2) The initial cracks of concrete hollow slab bridge will crack under the action of heavy truck, and the

stress intensity factor at the crack tip is the largest under the action of CII heavy truck.

(3) In the prestressed concrete hollow slab bridge, the cracks of 10m, 13m and 16m span bridges are controlled by CII truck, and the cracks of 20m span bridges are controlled by CIII truck.

(4) The stress intensity factors at the crack tip of prestressed concrete T-beam bridge do not reach the crack toughness, and the crack performance is basically controlled by CIV truck.

(5) The stress intensity factors at the crack tip at the maximum positive moment effect of prestressed concrete box girder bridge do not reach the crack toughness, and the crack performance is controlled by CV truck.

6 Research on Load Effect Based on Fracture Parameters

For the problem of single-edge crack, the stress intensity factor can be calculated according to Eq. (9):

$$K_\mathrm{I} = g_\mathrm{m} \sigma_\mathrm{n} \sqrt{\pi a} \tag{9}$$

Where: σ_n it is the nominal stress calculated according to the state of no crack at the crack position; a is the crack size; g_m is a shape factor, which is related to the geometric shape, load form, crack size and location of the component.

Shape factor g_m can be calculated with following formula:

$$g_\mathrm{m} = 1.122 - 1.4 \frac{a}{h} + 7.33 \left(\frac{a}{h}\right)^2 - 13.08 \left(\frac{a}{h}\right)^3 + 14 \left(\frac{a}{h}\right)^4 \tag{10}$$

According to the formula in mechanics of materials:

$$M_\mathrm{cr} = \frac{W_0}{g_\mathrm{m} \sqrt{\pi a}} K_\mathrm{IC} \tag{11}$$

K_IC is the fracture parameter of concrete, which can be taken as the crack toughness $K_\mathrm{IC}^\mathrm{ini}$ or safety factor η_K multiplied by the instability toughness $K_\mathrm{IC}^\mathrm{un}$. For the sake of simplification, the crack depth is 70% of the thickness of protective layer, W_0 is the elastic moment of resistance at the crack edge of the converted section.

Substituting the crack toughness of reinforced concrete hollow slab into Eq. (11), the crack initiation bending moment M_ini of the section with cracks is calculated as shown in Tab. 3. The calculated value of the positive bending moment effect of each bridge design vehicle load is listed in Tab. 3.

Crack Initiation Moment of Hollow Slab Bridge   Tab. 3

Span (m)	Design Vehicle Load Effect (kN·m)	g_m	W_0 (m^3)	a (m)	$K_\mathrm{IC}^\mathrm{ini}$ (MPa·m$^{1/2}$)	M_ini (kN·m)	Ratio
6	92.73	1.06753	0.03379	0.0217	0.24453	29.64	0.32
8	127.60	1.07543	0.05017	0.0217	0.25713	45.94	0.36
10	166.21	1.08036	0.06918	0.0217	0.26440	64.84	0.39

Notes: "Ratio" is the ratio crack initiation moment to design vehicle load effect.

As shown in Tab. 3, the crack initiation bending moment values are small and less than the design vehicle load effect, which indicates that although the mid span bending moment of the bridge with cracks under the action of heavy truck does not reach the design value, the existing cracks in the beam have entered into a state of slow propagation. After the determination of the crack initiation moment, it can provide suggestions for the durability evaluation, route planning and bridges reinforcement under heavy truck. For example, if a heavy truck is about to pass the reinforced concrete bridge, the most unfavorable moment in mid span calculated is less than the crack initiation moment, it can be considered that the vehicle passing the bridge has no effect on the existing crack state. If the most unfavorable moment in mid span calculated is greater than the crack initiation moment, it indicates that the crack will propagate.

Substituting the durability control toughness $\eta_K K_{IC}^{un}$ of reinforced concrete hollow slab bridge into Eq. (11), the crack initiation bending moment M_{un} of the section with cracks is calculated as shown in Tab. 4.

Critical Moment of Hollow Slab Bridge Tab. 4

Span (m)	Design Vehicle Load Effect (kN·m)	g_m	W_0 (m³)	a (m)	K_{IC}^{ini} (MPa·m^{1/2})	M_{ini} (kN·m)	Ratio
6	92.73	1.06753	0.03379	0.0217	0.77989	94.54	1.02
8	127.60	1.07543	0.05017	0.0217	0.82371	147.17	1.15
10	166.21	1.08036	0.06918	0.0217	0.84917	208.26	1.25

Notes: "Ratio" is the ratio crack initiation moment to design vehicle load effect.

If the most unfavorable bending moment in midspan is greater than the critical bending moment, it can be considered that the vehicle crossing the bridge has a great impact on the existing crack state, there may be obvious cracking phenomenon. If it is not controlled, the durability of the bridge will be seriously affected, and then the service life of the bridge structure and the driving safety will be adversely affected.

7 Conclusion

Firstly, the vehicle model, bridge model and calculation method are integrated to establish the evaluation system of heavy truck crossing the bridge. Secondly, the stress intensity factor time history of crack tip of typical medium and small span bridge with cracks is calculated to analyze and evaluate the crack performance. Finally, the crack initiation moment and critical moment are calculated according to the crack toughness and durability control toughness.

(1) The cracks of reinforced concrete bridge will propagate under the action of heavy truck, but it will not reach the unstable fracture state. The cracks of prestressed reinforced concrete bridge will not propagate under the action of heavy truck.

(2) The crack performance of different types of bridge is controlled by different types of heavy truck. The concrete hollow slab bridge is controlled by CII heavy truck. The prestressed concrete hollow slab bridge is controlled by CIII heavy truck except the 20m span. The prestressed concrete T-beam bridge is basically controlled by CIV heavy truck. The prestressed concrete continuous small box girder bridge is controlled by CV heavy truck.

(3) The crack initiation moment of reinforced concrete hollow slab bridge is 0.32 ~ 0.39 times of the design vehicle load effect, and the critical moment of reinforced concrete hollow slab bridge is 1.02 ~ 1.25 times of the design vehicle load effect.

References

[1] Xu Shilang, Zhao Guofan. A Double-K Fracture Criterion for the Crack Propagation in Concrete Structures [J]. China Civil Engineering Journal, 1992, 25(2): 32-38.

[2] Zhong Weizhou, Luo Jingrun. Finite Element Analysis on Three-point Bending Sample Loaded by Impact Loading[J]. Environmental Technology, 2004, 27(1): 147-165.

[3] Zhu Jinsong, Zhang Yifeng, Chen Xingda. Crack Propogation of Concrete Beams under Moving Vehicle Loads[J]. Journal of Southeast University, 2018, 48(04): 678-686.

[4] Bažant Z. P. Size Effect in Blunt Fracture: Concrete, Rock, Metal[J]. Journal of Engineering Mechanics, 1984, 110(4): 518-535.

[5] Bažant Z. P. Scaling of Quasi-Brittle Fracture and the Fractal Question[J]. Journal of Engineering Materials

and Technology,1995,117(4): 361-367.
[6] Chinese Aeronautical Establishment. Handbook of Stress Intensity Factors[M]. Beijing: Science Press,1981.
[7] Ministry of Transport of the People's Republic of China. General Drawings of Bridges and Culverts for Transportation Industry of the People's Republic Of China[M]. Beijing: China Communication Press,2018.
[8] Han W. S., Yuan, Y. G., Chen, X., et al. Safety Assessment of Continuous Beam Bridges under Overloaded Customized Transport Vehicle Load[J]. Journal of Bridge Engineering 2018, 23(6), 04018030.
[9] Salah El-Din A. S., El-Adawy Nassef M. M. A Modified Approach for Estimating Craching Moment of Reinforced Concrete Beams[J]. 1975,ACI. J.72(7):356-360.
[10] Jiang Jianjing, Lu Xinzheng, Ye Lieping. Finite Element Analysis of Concrete Structures[M]. Beijing: Tsinghua University Press,2005.

Dynamic Analysis for Hanger Fracture of Network Arch Bridge

Ruixuan Li Xianwu Hao Teng Xu Xinke Cao

(University of Chang'an, Department of Highway)

Abstract In order to study the influence of hanger fracture on dynamic performance of network arch bridge. Taking a network arch bridge with a calculated span of 96m as the study object, the finite element model is established by using ANSYS software. By simulating the short hanger fracture near arch foot and the long hanger fracture in the middle of the span, the internal force changes of other hangers and the displacement response of arch rib and tie girder after the hanger fracture are analyzed. The analysis results show that the adjacent hangers with similar inclination angle of the broken hanger suffer the largest impact, and the short hanger fracture has more obvious impact on the internal forces of the other hangers. When the hanger fractures, attention should be paid to the stress of the adjacent hangers. After the hanger is broken, the longitudinal and vertical displacement of tie girder is larger, and the displacement of arch rib is smaller, and the long hanger fracture has a greater impact on the displacement response of arch rib and tie girder.

Keywords Network arch bridge Hanger Fracture Finite element method Transient dynamic analysis

0 Introduction

Tied arch bridge is mainly composed of arch rib, hanger, tie girder and other components. According to the relative stiffness of arch rib and ties, it can be divided into flexible tied rigid arch, rigid tied flexible arch (Langer arch) and rigid tied rigid arch (Lohse arch). According to the layout of hangers, it can be divided into vertical hanger system, Nielsen system and network system[1]. Compared with the vertical hanger system, the inclined hanger system of Nielsen system and network system can greatly reduce the bending moment of arch bridge, and the mechanical performance of long-span arch bridge with inclined hanger system will be better. The actual network arch bridge is a kind of arch bridge structure which increases the number of hangers on the basis of Nielsen arch bridge. This arrangement can reduce the bending moment in the arch rib and tie girder to a greater extent, and make the structural mechanical performance more reasonable. At the same time, the network arch bridge also has the advantages of simple structure, strong integrity, economy, durability and applicability.

As the main stress component of tied arch bridge, hangers play the role of connecting arch rib and bridge channel system by transferring the dead load and live load of bridge deck to arch rib. Therefore, the reliability of hanger is directly related to the safety and serviceability of tied arch bridge. The cable structure of hanger is more sensitive to the external damage. When the hanger is subjected to explosion, impact, fire, lightning and other emergencies, or under the action of corrosion and fatigue damage, it is very likely to fracture. The sudden fracture of hanger may lead to the collapse of bridge system, even the local or overall damage of the arch rib[2-3]. In recent years, arch bridge collapse accidents due to vehicle overload are common, which cause serious casualties and property losses. The hangers, as the main stress component of arch bridge structure, should be paid more attention. On November 7, 2001, the Xiaonanmen bridge on Jinsha River in Yibin, Sichuan Province, collapsed due to the broken hangers. On April 12, 2011, the main girder of Kongque River Bridge in Korla, Xinjiang Province, fell into the river owing to the broken hangers, the bridge deck about 10m long and 12m wide collapsed. On October 1, 2019, the south Macao across Hong Kong bridge in Ilan, Taiwan Province, collapsed due to a broken hanger.

Aiming at the problem of hanger fracture in arch bridge, Yao Xiang[4] studied the influence of different hanger parameters on the hanger fatigue failure of tied arch bridge, and put forward suggestions on how to reduce hanger fatigue damage from the perspective of structural design. Wu Qingxiong et al.[5] used the finite element software to simulate the hanger fracture process of a concrete-filled steel tube tied arch bridge by selecting two working conditions of short suspender fracture and long suspender fracture, which provided reference for the safety and reliability design of concrete-filled steel tube arch bridge. Taking the Baoguo Jinshajiang bridge in Panzhihua as the background, Wu Wenqing et al.[6] studied the damage safety design method of hangers of tied arch bridge. and proposed the method of asymmetric parallel suspension system. The finite element model is established to verify the safety of the asymmetric parallel double boom system. Yang Bingnan et al.[7] analyzed the influence of long and short hangers fracture on the dynamic performance of a tied arch bridge, and found that the dynamic response generated at the moment of hanger fracture can not be ignored. The above research on the related arch bridge is aimed at the ordinary vertical hanger arch bridge, the research on the arch bridge with network system is less, and the research on the phenomenon of hanger fracture in the network arch bridge is also less involved.

In this paper, a network arch bridge is taken as the object. The "life and death element" function of ANSYS finite element software is used to simulate the sudden fracture process of long and short hangers. The mechanical characteristics of the remaining hangers and the displacement response of the arch rib and tie girder after the hanger fracture are analyzed, which provides a reference for the design of the network arch bridge considering the fracture load.

1 Project Introduction and finite Element Model

1.1 Project Introduction

The project background is a 96 m span concrete-filled steel tube arch bridge with rise span ratio of $f/l = 1/5$, $l = 96$m, $f = 19.2$m, and a deck width of 14.8m, the arch axis is a quadratic parabola. The two arch rings are of concrete-filled steel tube structure and arranged in parallel. The arch ring adopts dumbbell shaped section, the steel tube material is Q235QE, with an outer diameter of 1m and a wall thickness of 1.4cm. There are 32 pairs of hangers in the whole bridge, which are arranged symmetrically. The finished hangers are PES (FD)7-61 low stress anti-corrosion cables. There are 7 cross braces in the whole bridge, including 5 straight cross braces and two K-shaped cross braces. The diameter of the main cross brace is 0.7m. Due to the overall symmetry of the bridge, Fig.1 only shows the number of hangers and lower lifting points of half span. The tie girder is a prestressed concrete box girder structure, which is 2m high and 1.2m wide. A tie girder is set under each arch rib, and the tie girders are connected by transverse connection to form a spatial stable structure.

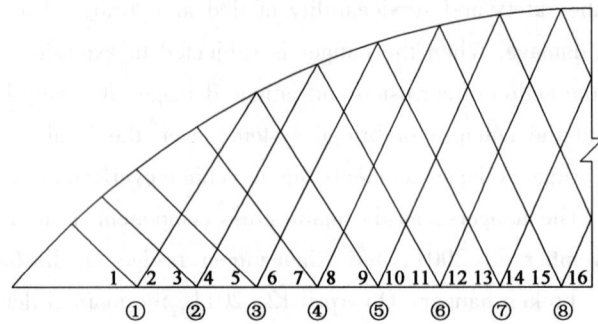

Fig.1 Hangers and Lower Lifting Points Number

1.2 Finite Element Model

This paper mainly studies the influence of hanger sudden fracture on the network arch bridge. The process of hanger fracture is equivalent to removing the hanger in the structure in a very short time. From the aspect of stress, the internal force is suddenly transformed into a pair of external force with equal size and opposite direction. In order to simulate the sudden fracture process of the hanger, the element with birth and death capability in ANSYS is used to "kill" the broken hanger by setting instantaneous load step, that is to do a transient dynamic analysis starting with static analysis. This simulation process is "static" first and then "dynamic", so it is called semi-dynamic simulation method[8]. The element with birth and death capability of ANSYS is equivalent to multiplying the elastic modulus matrix (or other characteristic matrix) of the element by a very small coefficient, thus "killing" the element and leaving a pair of hanger internal forces caused by the most unfavorable load. The arch rib, tie girder, transverse brace and cross girder are simulated by beam188 element, the hanger is simulated by link8 tension element with birth and death capability. There are 2058 elements in the whole bridge, including 68 link8 elements. The structures which have no influence on the overall calculation, such as the bridge deck and the secondary loads, are loaded on the cross girder in the form of concentrated load. Hanger and cross girder are connected by master-slave coupling, and the boundary conditions are arranged according to the actual situation, Fig.2 shows the finite element model of the whole bridge established by ANSYS.

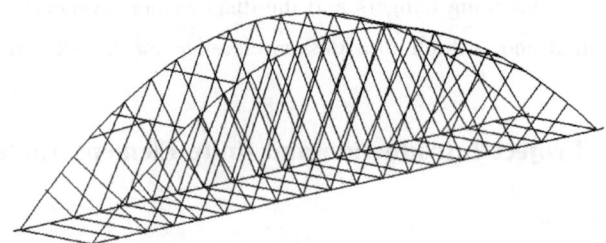

Fig.2 Finite Element Model of The Whole Bridge

The influence of Rayleigh damping should be considered in the dynamic analysis. The damping matrix $[C]$ in ANSYS is the combination of mass matrix and stiffness matrix, that is, $[C] = \alpha[M] + \beta[K]$, the damping ratio of concrete structure is 0.05[9]. The coefficients α and β of stiffness matrix and mass matrix are obtained by calculation, from which the basic equation of structure motion can be obtained:

$$[M]\{\ddot{x}\} + [C]\{\dot{x}\} + [K]\{x\} = \{F(t)\} \tag{1}$$

As shown in formula (1), $[M]$, $[C]$, $[K]$ are the mass matrix, damping matrix and stiffness matrix of the structure respectively, $\{\ddot{x}\}$, $\{\dot{x}\}$ and $\{x\}$ are the acceleration, velocity and displacement vectors of the structural node respectively, and $F(t)$ is the external load vector. Therefore, the transient dynamic analysis of ANSYS is the problem of solving the equation[10].

Hanger fracture is a kind of brittle failure in the actual situation, which will be completed in a very short time. The shorter the time is, the greater the impact on the arch bridge will be. In dynamic analysis, the local failure time of the structure is generally less than 1/10 of the main vibration period of the structure, and the failure time is about 0.016 seconds when taking 1/100 of the fundamental frequency[11]. In this paper, No. 1 hanger at the arch foot and No. 16 hanger in the middle of the span are selected as the research objects, the internal force change and displacement response of the rest parts of the bridge after hanger fracture are mainly considered.

2 Calculation Results

2.1 The Short Hanger Fracture

In order to study the influence of hanger fracture on the internal force of other hangers. No. 2 hanger at the same hanging point as No. 1 broken suspender, adjacent No. 3 and No. 4 hangers, No. 15 and No. 16 hangers at midspan, No. 31 and No. 32 hangers farthest from the broken hanger are selected as research objects.

2.1.1 Impact on Other Hangers

Fig. 3 shows the axial force increment time history curve of the short hanger (No. 1 hanger) when it fractures and the adjacent No. 2, No. 3, No. 4 hangers. Fig. 4 shows the time history curve of axial force increment of No. 15, No. 16, No. 31 and No. 32 hangers which are far away from No. 1 hanger. It can be seen from the figures that the axial force of the hangers adjacent to No. 1 hanger increase rapidly after the fracture, sharing the axial force of the broken hanger, and then the axial force of the hangers tend to be stable, in which the axial force variation amplitude of No. 3 hanger is the largest. The farther the hangers are from No. 1 hanger, the smaller the increment of axial force and the longer the time to reach the maximum value of axial force, the axial force increment of No. 31 and No. 32 hangers which are farthest from No. 1 hanger is the smallest. The axial force increment of No. 3 hanger reaches the maximum value of 894.21kN in 0.19 seconds after the short hanger fracture, which is 1.85 times of the hanger axial force under the most unfavorable load combination.

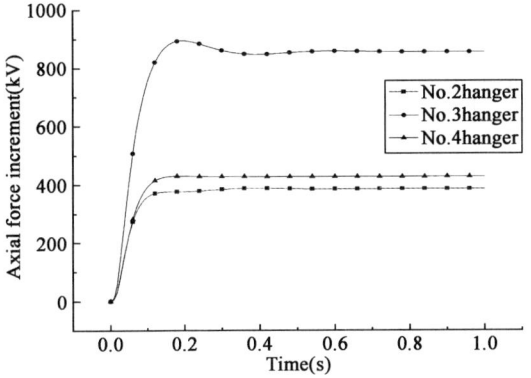

Fig. 3　Time History Curve of Hanger Axial Force Increment Near Fracture

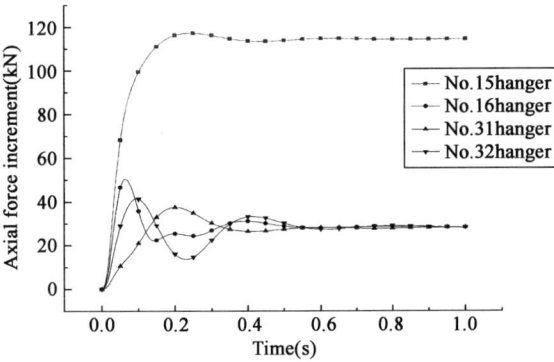

Fig. 4　Time History Curve of Axial Force Increment of Hanger Far Away From Fracture

2.1.2 Along Bridge Displacement Response of Tie Girder and Arch Rib

In order to understand the influence of short hanger fracture on the displacement of network arch bridge along the bridge direction, No. 1, No. 2, No. 4, No. 8, No. 12 and No. 16 lower lifting points are selected as the research objects to observe the displacement of tie beam, the upper hanging points corresponding to the lower lifting points are selected as the observation points of arch rib, the location of each observation point is shown in Fig. 1. In order to compare the displacement along the bridge between arch rib and tie girder, the displacement increment along the bridge direction is obtained by subtracting the displacement under static action from the exciting displacement caused by fracture, and the time history curve of the displacement increment along the bridge direction at each observation point of tie girder and arch rib is drawn.

Fig. 5 is the incremental displacement time history curve of tie girder observation points along the bridge direction when the short hanger fractures. From the displacement increment. time history curves of these lower lifting points, it can be concluded that at the moment of hanger fracture, due to the potential energy of tie girder itself, the displacement increases rapidly and reaches the maximum value within 0.2 seconds, then decreases gradually, and tends to be stable within 0.8 seconds after short time fluctuation. The absolute value of the displacement along the bridge from the lower lifting point at the hanger fracture to the lower lifting point far away from the fracture increases gradually, and the maximum displacement along the bridge generally occurs within 0.19 seconds after the hanger fracture.

Fig. 6 shows the time history curve of displacement increment along the bridge direction of each part of arch rib when the short hanger fractures, which is similar to the displacement variation trend of tie girder. The displacement of each observation point on arch rib increases rapidly after hanger fracture and reaches the peak within 0.2 seconds. It can be seen from the figure that the displacement increment of arch rib caused by hanger fracture is larger than that of tie girder, and the corresponding internal force of arch rib is also larger than that of tie girder. It should be noted that after the hanger fracture, the upper hanging point on the arch rib has a negative displacement in a very short time. After the negative displacement reaches the peak, the displacement increases positively, and the fluctuation range of this displacement is more severe than that of tie girder. Different from the displacement response along the bridge of tie girder, the displacement increment of arch rib is smaller at arch foot and mid span, larger at 1/4 span.

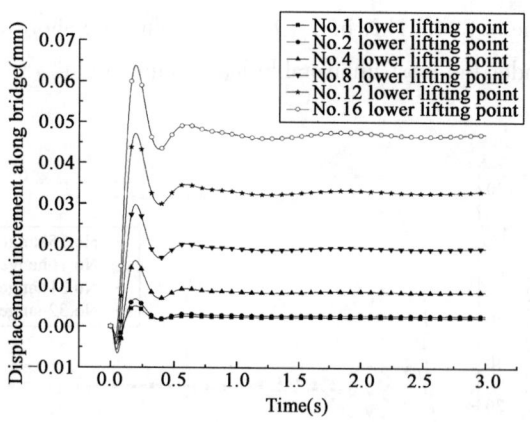

Fig. 5 Time History Curve of Incremental Displacement along Bridge Direction of Tie Girder

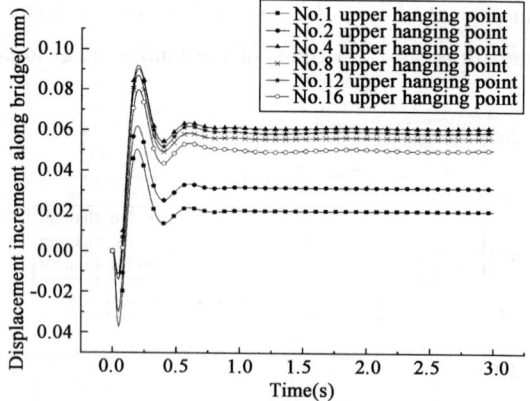

Fig. 6 Time History Curve of Displacement Increment along Bridge Direction of Arch Rib

2.1.3 Vertical Displacement Response of Tie Beam and Arch Rib

Fig. 7 shows the time history curve of vertical displacement increment of each observation point of tie girder when the short hanger fractures. The vertical displacement increment of lower lifting points near the fractured hanger in tie girder is larger than that of lower lifting points far from the fracture. When the lower lifting points of tie girder reach the maximum vertical displacement in 0.2 seconds, it will produce diaplacement rebound. After a period of fluctuation, it is basically stable in 0.8 seconds, and the vertical displacement increment at No. 2 lower lifting point is the largest, the peak value is −0.95mm in 0.19 seconds after fractur.

Fig. 8 shows the time history curve of the vertical displacement increment of upper hanging points on arch rib when the short hanger fractures, which is similar to the vertical displacement response of tie girder. The vertical displacement increment at arch foot is smaller, and the vertical displacement increment of No. 4 lower lifting point on arch rib is the largest at 1/4 span. Through comparison, it is found that the vertical displacement response of tie girder and arch rib caused by the short hanger fracture is much larger than the corresponding displacement response along bridge direction. The reason is that the inclination of hangers in the network arch bridge is relatively small, and the hanger is mainly used as the medium to transfer the vertical load of bridge deck system to arch rib, and the vertical displacement excitation of the whole bridge is mainly caused by hanger fracture.

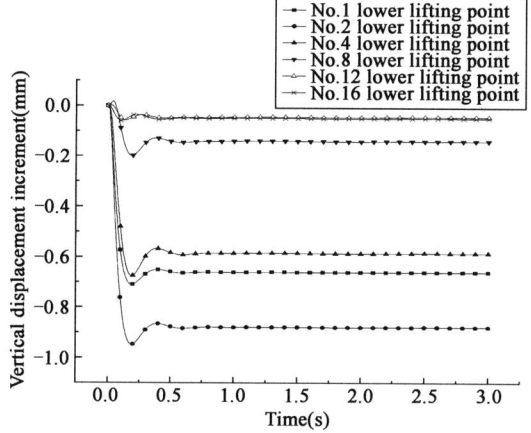 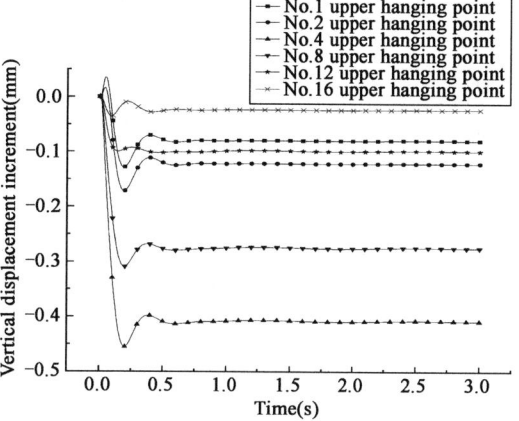

Fig. 7 Time History Curve of Vertical Displacement Increment of Tie Girder

Fig. 8 Time History Curve of Vertical Displacement Increment of Arch Rib

2.2 The Long Hanger Fracture

No. 16 hanger is selected as the fracture hanger to study the influence of long hanger fracture on the internal force of other hangers. No. 13, No. 14, No. 15, No. 17 and No. 18 hangers near the No. 16 hanger are selected respectively, and No. 1, No. 2, No. 31, No. 32 hangers far away from the No. 16 hanger are selected as the research objects.

2.2.1 Impact on Other Hangers

The time history curves of hangers axial force increment after fracture are drawn, as shown in Fig. 9 and Fig. 10. Similar to the internal force change of hangers after the short hanger fracture, the hangers with larger internal force change after No. 16 hanger fracture are No. 14 and No. 18 hangers adjacent to it, the maximum internal force increment of No. 18 hanger reaches 582.30kN in about 0.2 seconds, which is 1.02 times of the most unfavorable load combination. It is different from the internal force change of the other hangers cased by the short hanger fracture, the long suspender fracture has a more uniform influence on the internal force of the other hangers, and there is no sharp increase in the axial force of a certain hanger.

2.2.2 Along Bridge Displacement Response of Tie Girder and Arch Rib

No. 16 hanger in the middle span is the broken hanger, when the long hanger fractures, the selection principle of observation points is similar to that when the short hanger fractures. Fig. 11 and Fig. 12 are the time history curves of displacement increment along the bridge direction at each observation point of the tie girder and arch rib. From the displacement response along the bridge direction of tie girder, it can be seen that the displacement of each observation point reaches the maximum value in about 0.06 seconds, the displacement rebounds within 0.2 seconds, and the displacements of all observation points no longer fluctuate after the fracture occurs for 1 second, The maximum absolute value of displacement increment at No.16 lower lifting point is 0.18mm, which is about three times of the maximum absolute value of the tie girder when the short hanger fractures. The peak value of the displacement along the bridge at each observation point on the arch rib is about 0.2 seconds, which is similar to the displacement change trend of short hanger fracture. The displacement increment of No.4 upper hanging point is the largest, and the displacement increment of arch foot is smaller. The peak displacement increment of No.4 upper hanging point is 1.22mm, which is larger than the maximum displacement increment of the upper hanging point when the short hanger fractures.

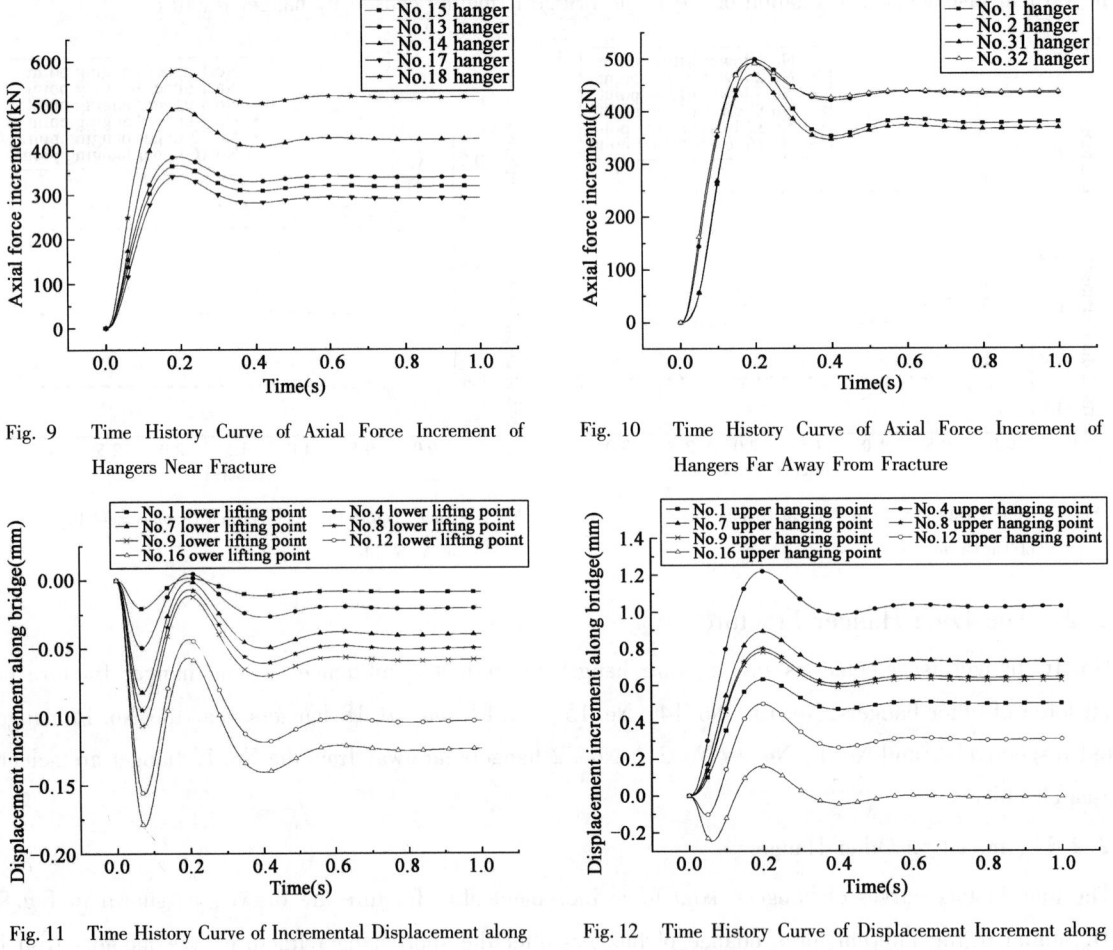

Fig. 9　Time History Curve of Axial Force Increment of Hangers Near Fracture

Fig. 10　Time History Curve of Axial Force Increment of Hangers Far Away From Fracture

Fig. 11　Time History Curve of Incremental Displacement along Bridge Direction of Tie Girder

Fig. 12　Time History Curve of Displacement Increment along Bridge Direction of Arch Rib

2.2.3　Vertical Displacement Response of Tie Beam and Arch Rib

Fig. 13 and Fig. 14 are the time history curves of vertical displacement increment at each observation point of tie girder and arch rib respectively. The overall vertical displacement change curve of tie girder shows that the vertical displacement excitation at No.7, No.8 and No.9 lower lifting points adjacent to the hanger fracture point is larger, while the direction of vertical displacement increment at No.12 and No.16 lifting points is opposite to that of other observation points, and the excitation is smaller. The vertical displacement increment of tie girder at No. 7 lower lifting point is the largest, reaching the peak value of -3.42mm within 0.2 seconds after the long hanger fracture. From the time history curve of vertical displacement increment of arch rib, it can be concluded that the vertical displacement increment of No. 8 and No. 16 upper hanging points is small and positive, and the vertical displacement increment of No. 4 upper hanging point is larger, which is similar to the change trend of vertical displacement of arch rib when the short hanger fractures.

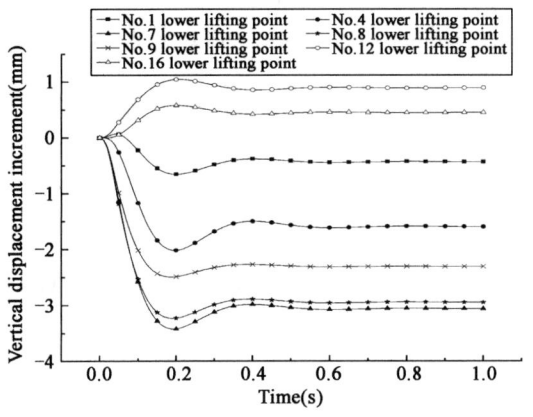

Fig. 13 Time History Curve of Vertical Displacement Increment of Tie Girder

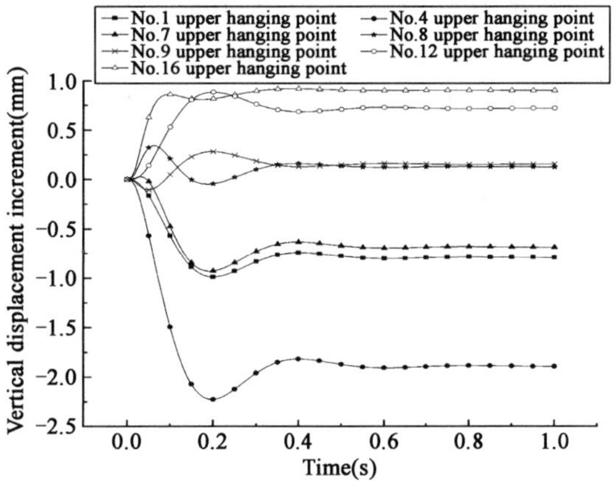

Fig. 14 Time History Curve of Vertical Displacement Increment of Arch Rib

3 Conclusion

In this paper, the transient analysis module of ANSYS is used to simulate the dynamic response of the bridge when the long hanger or short hanger of the network arch bridge fractures. When the hanger fractures, the internal force changes of the other hangers and the displacement response of arch rib and tie girder are analyzed, the following conclusions are obtained.

(1) When the hanger fractures, it will have a certain impact effect on the whole bridge components, such as the rest of the hangers. The action time of this impact effect on the arch bridge is short. The axial force of the hanger will reach the maximum value within 0.2 seconds, and then this impact effect will rapidly decay. By comparing the axial force changes of the other hangers after the long and short hangers are broken, it is found that the internal force of the hangers adjacent to the broken hanger change more obviously. Therefore, when the hanger of the network arch bridge fractures, it is necessary to control the internal force of the hangers adjacent to the broken hanger to prevent secondary fracture.

(2) Because the hangers are arranged obliquely, there will be a horizontal disturbance and a vertical disturbance to the arch bridge when the hanger is broken. By analyzing the excitation displacement of tie girder and arch rib when the long and short hangers fracture, the vertical displacement increment of tie girder near the broken hanger is larger, The potential energy released when the mid span hanger fractures makes the tie girder and arch rib produce vertical displacement in the opposite direction, and spreads outward from the place where the fracture occurs, the exciting displacement of the tie girder is larger. The vertical force produced by short hanger fracture is smaller than that produced by long hanger fracture, and the impact effect caused by long hanger fracture is closer to that of vertical hanger system.

References

[1] Xingxing Liu. Research on Mechanical Behavior and Ultimate Bearing Capacity of Network Arch Bridge [D]. Huazhong University of Science and Technology, 2019.

[2] Zhiliang Guo. Analyse on the Process of Suspender's Fracture and Research on the Safty Countermeasure

[3] Huitao Duan. Dynamic Response Analysis of Suspender's Fracture in Half Through or Through Arch Bridge [D]. Zhengzhou University, 2017.
[4] Xiang Yao. Influence Factors on Fatigue of Hangers of Tied Arch Bridge [J]. Highway, 2007, 12, 38-44.
[5] Qingxiong Wu, et al. Dynamic Analysis for Cable Loss of a Rigid-frame Tied Through Concret-filled Steel Tubular Arch Bridge [J]. Journal of Vibration and Shock, 2014, 15, 144-149.
[6] Wenqing Wu, Jiangyu Yu. Study of Failure Safety Design Method for Hangers of Tied Arch Bridge [J]. Bridge Construction, 2010, 1, 35-39.
[7] Bingnan Yang, et al. Influence of Suspender Fracture on Dynamic Performance of Tied Arch Bridge [J]. Northern Communications, 2019, 9, 31-34.
[8] Zhaole Qu, et al. Research on Dynamic Simulation Methodology for Cable Loss of Cable-stayed Bridge [J]. Stuctural Engineers, 2009, 6, 89-92.
[9] British Standard Institute. Structural Use of Concrete: (Part1): Code of Practice for Design and Construction [S], 1997.
[10] General Service Administration. Progressive Collapse Analysis and Design Guidelines for New Federal Office Buildings and Major Modernization Projects [S], 2008.
[11] Jun Tu. Study on Failure-safety of Arch Bridge Suspender [D]. Harbin Institute of Technology, 2008.

基于 CFD 数值模拟研究扁平流线型钢箱梁流场和三分力系数

王 路

（长安大学）

摘 要 扁平流线型钢箱梁在桥梁设计中应用十分广泛。通过 CFD 数值模拟，采用对钝体外部扰流模拟结果较好的 SST k-ω 湍流模型，使用定常流计算，研究了高宽比为 1∶11 的扁平流线型钢箱梁在不同风攻角下的三分力系数。得到了不同风攻角下钢箱梁的三分力系数，同时可以得到高宽比为 1∶11 的钢箱梁断面的周围流场特性，实现流场可视化研究。为提取钢箱梁断面的气动三分力参数和风荷载设计提供参考。

关键词 桥梁工程 三分力系数 CFD 数值模拟 钢箱梁

0 引 言

三分力系数是在桥梁抗风领域中最基本的无量纲气动参数，用于表征桥梁风荷载，是桥梁静风荷载、驰振响应分析、抖振响应分析和稳定性分析的基础。许多研究者对各类主梁断面的三分力系数进行了大量研究，结果表明：通过风洞试验或者数值分析的方法可以得到有效的三分力系数，并将研究成果并应用于桥梁建设中，对桥梁建设起到推动作用。

李加武[1]研究了不同高宽比下两类典型桥梁断面的三分力；高宇琦[2]通过 CFD 数值模拟识别了高铁连续梁桥钝体箱梁断面的三分力系数；白桦[3]通过频域分析法确定了颤振导数和三分力系数的关系，并通过三分力系数研究颤振失稳问题；刘昊苏[4]结合风洞试验和 CFD 数值模拟方法确定了双层桁架梁的三分力系数，并发现两种方法的结果吻合程度较高；王锋[5]以 CFD 数值模拟的方法分析了大跨径连续梁桥的抗风性能，得到的三分力系数与风洞试验结果变化趋势非常接近；王旭[6]基于计算流体力学

(CFD)方法得到的钢箱梁三分力系数与风洞试验结果较为温和,表明CFD在流体运动方面极大的优越性。王志鹏[7]通过CFD方法计算钢箱梁典型断面的三分力系数,研究了涡振和颤振流场驱动机理。

由众多学者的研究可知,目前通过CFD数值模拟和风洞试验方法得到的三分力系数吻合程度较高,同时,可以了解到对高宽比较小的扁平流线型钢箱梁进行数值模拟,计算得到三分力系数的研究相对较少。本文针对高宽比为1:11的扁平流线型钢箱梁,通过CFD数值模拟的方法,采用对钝体外部扰流模拟结果较好的SST k-ω 湍流模型,对该钢箱梁断面进行三分力系数的计算。得到了在风攻角为0°、±2°、±4°、±6°下的三分力系数,同时,对该钢箱梁断面进行流场特性分析,进行简单的可视化研究。

1 计算原理

扁平流线型钢箱梁结构在来流风荷载的作用下,可以分解为三个方向的力:升力、阻力和升力矩。按风轴和体轴这两类坐标系的划分,其气动力方向不同。扁平流线型钢箱梁断面所受的三分力示意图如图1。

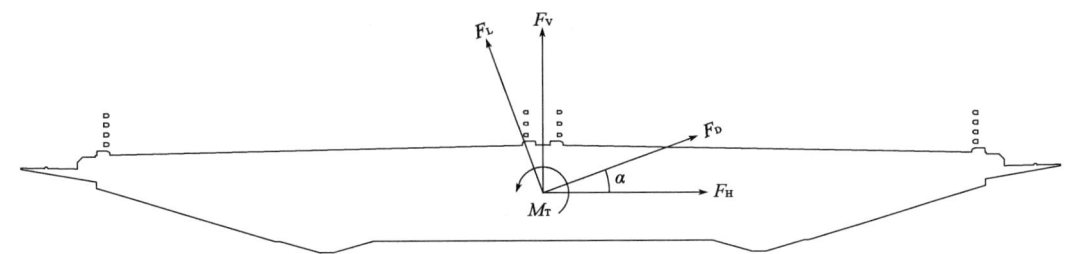

图1 风轴和体轴坐标系以及气动力方向

F_D、F_L、M_T-在风轴坐标系下的扁平流线型钢箱梁断面受到的阻力、升力和扭转力矩;F_H、F_V 和 M_T-体轴坐标系下扁平流线型钢箱梁断面受到的横向气动力、竖向气动力和扭转力矩

风轴气动力参数和体轴气动力参数的数学关系式如下:

$$C_H = C_D \times \cos\alpha - C_L \times \sin\alpha \times \frac{B}{H} \tag{1}$$

$$C_V = C_D \times \sin\alpha \times \frac{H}{B} + C_L \times \cos\alpha \tag{2}$$

式中:B——扁平流线型钢箱梁断面的特征宽度;

H——扁平流线型钢箱梁断面的特征高度;

α——风攻角。

2 网格设计

2.1 设计方法

计算域外风场宽度为21倍梁宽,高度为12倍梁宽,内风场宽度为4.5倍梁宽,高度为2倍梁宽。速度入口设置为Velocity inlet,出口设置为Outflow,上边边界设置为Symmetry,内部边界设置为Interior,模型壁面边界设置为Wall。采用SST k-ω 湍流模型,利用定常流计算。方程求解使用SIMPILEC算法。计算模型的尺寸采用实际尺寸。使用对形状适应性良好的三角形网格对计算域网格进行划分。加密主梁断面周围网格,提高精确度,同时以一定渐变率向四周发散,使得远离主梁断面位置的网格逐渐渐疏,从而提升计算效率。为了使得网格设计更加合理,使数值模拟计算结果更加精确,对网格进行了无关性检查。

2.2 设计结果

该扁平流线型钢箱梁断面尺寸如表1所示。

模型尺寸 表1

	成 桥		成 桥
宽(m)	38.5	高(m)	3.5

网格划分如图2所示。

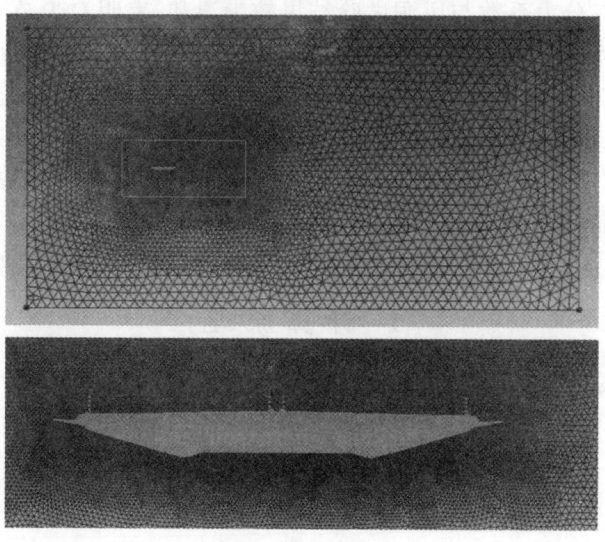

图 2 网格划分图

3 设计工况

风攻角为:-6°、-4°、-2°、0°、+2°、+4°、+6°,共 7 个攻角变化。来流风速设为 10m/s。

4 数值模拟

4.1 结果

以 Fluent 为计算平台,使用 SST k-ω 湍流模型,通过定常流计算。方程求解采用 SIMPILEC 算法,迭代 3000 步。得到三分力系数计算结果见表 2,风轴坐标系下三分力系数—风攻角图如图 3 所示。

三分力系数　　　　　　　　　　表 2

风攻角	C_D	C_L	C_M
-6°	0.78097	-0.67198	0.13782
-4°	0.63287	-0.68712	0.10786
-2°	0.63011	-0.69339	0.108785
0°	0.514378	-0.52024	0.02410
+2°	0.58293	-0.35355	-0.01232
+4°	0.65823	-0.18904	-0.04853
+6°	0.77821	0.07019	-0.07268

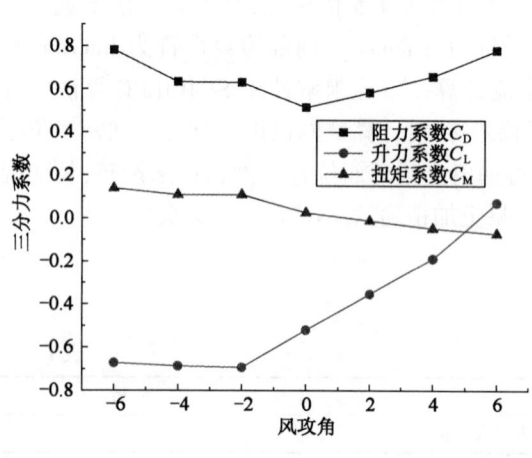

图 3 三分力系数—风攻角图

通过对上述三分力系数的数值模拟结果进行分析,可以得到以下结论:

高宽比为 1:11 的扁平流线型钢箱梁的阻力系数 C_D 随着风攻角的增大先减小,在 0°风攻角达到最小时,又开始逐渐增大;升力系数 C_L 在负风攻角时数值变化不大,对负风攻角变化不敏感,在正风攻角时随着风攻角的增加而逐渐增大;扭矩系数 C_M 随着风攻角的增大而缓慢降低,总体数值在 0 附近波动。

4.2 流场可视化结果

在 Fluent 计算平台中,得到各个风攻角下扁平流线型钢箱梁断面的速度流线图(图 4)和压力云图(图 5)如下。

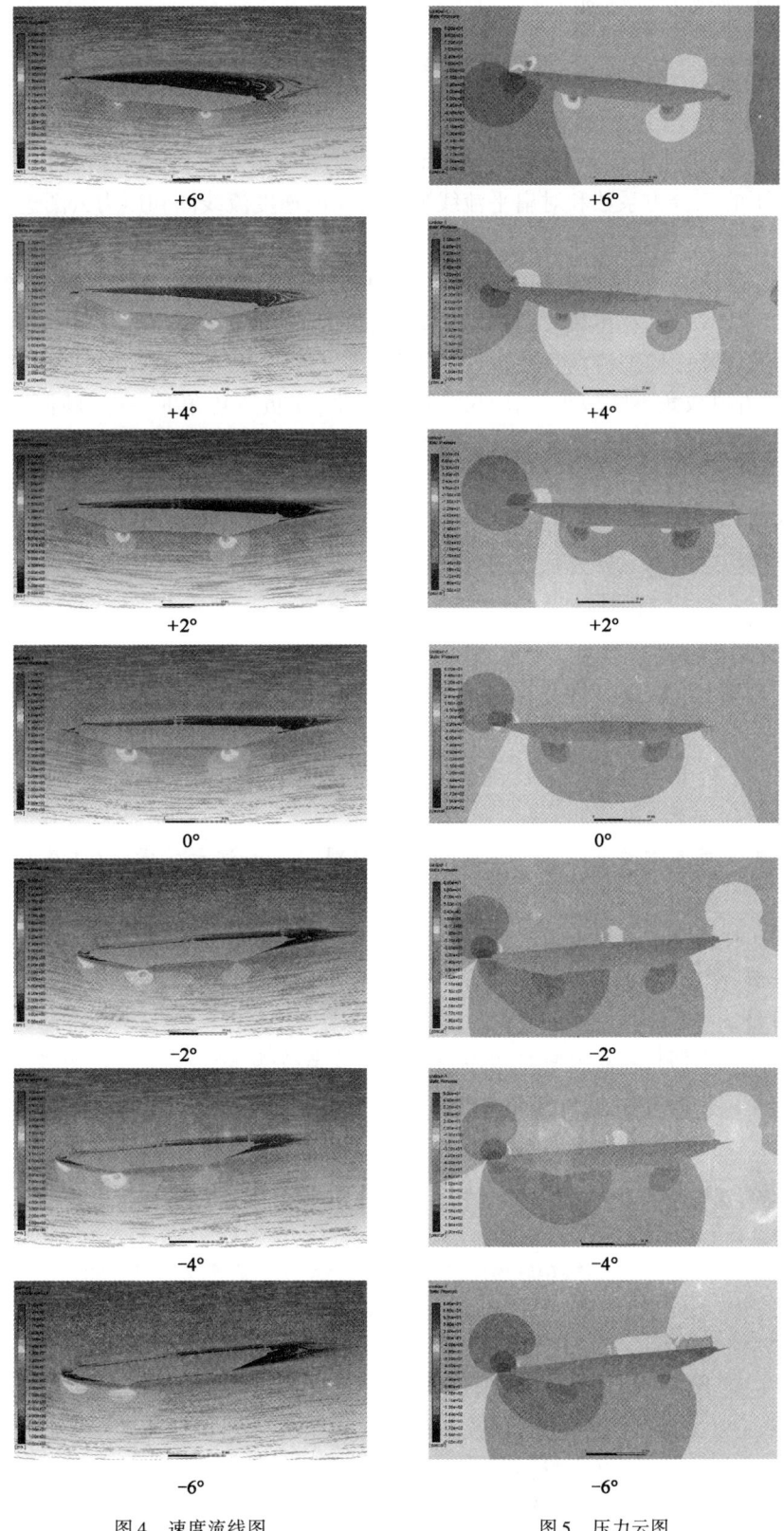

图4 速度流线图　　图5 压力云图

通过分析上述速度流线图和压力云图,可以得到如下结论:

高宽比为1:11的扁平流线型钢箱梁的周围流场特性较好;在正风攻角时,在梁断面上缘存在一个尺寸较大的涡旋,随着风攻角不断减小,涡旋尺寸逐渐变小;在负风攻角时,在梁断面尾流区存在一个涡旋,随着风攻角不断减小,涡旋尺寸逐渐变大。

5 结语

本文通过对高宽比为 1∶11 的扁平流线型钢箱梁断面进行 CFD 数值模拟计算,得到了该断面在不同风攻角下的三分力系数,为桥梁设计、提取钢箱梁断面的气动三分力参数和风荷载设计提供了参考。通过对比不同风攻角下的三分力系数和对扁平流线型钢箱梁的速度流线图和压力云图进行分析,可以得到如下结论:

阻力系数 C_D 随着风攻角的增大先减小后增大,存在一个最小值;升力系数 C_L 在负风攻角时数值变化不大,对负风攻角变化不敏感,在正风攻角时随着风攻角的增加而逐渐增大;扭矩系数 C_M 随着风攻角的增大而缓慢降低。对该断面周围流场特性进行分析时,可以得到:在正风攻角时,在梁断面上缘存在一个尺寸较大的涡旋,随着风攻角不断减小,涡旋尺寸逐渐变小;在负风攻角时,在梁断面尾流区存在一个涡旋,随着风攻角不断减小,涡旋尺寸逐渐变大。同时,本文风攻角取 0°、±2°、±4°、±6°,丰富了《公路桥梁抗风设计规范》中三分力系数的风攻角只有 0°、±3°、±5°的情况。

后续工作的展望:可以在本文的基础上,研究不同高宽比下钢箱梁断面的三分力系数,比较其结果,得到不同高宽比下钢箱梁断面三分力系数的变化规律。

参考文献

[1] 李加武.桥梁断面雷诺数效应及其控制研究[D].上海:同济大学,2003.
[2] 高宇琦,王浩,徐梓栋,等.大跨度高铁连续梁桥箱梁断面静力三分力系数的数值模拟[J].南京工业大学学报(自然科学版),2020,42(03):358-365.
[3] 白桦,方成,王峰,等.桥梁颤振稳定性快速评价参数及其应用[J].中国公路学报,2016,29(08):92-98+133.
[4] 刘昊苏,雷俊卿.大跨度双层桁架主梁三分力系数识别[J].浙江大学学报(工学版),2019,53(06):1092-1100.
[5] 王锋.基于 CFD 对大跨度连续桥梁抗风性能分析[J].公路工程,2018,43(03):83-86+167.
[6] 王旭,袁波,陈耀,等.桥梁断面三分力系数的数值风洞研究[J].贵州大学学报(自然科学版),2017,34(02):128-133.
[7] 王志鹏.基于 CFD 的钢箱梁典型断面涡振和颤振流场驱动机理研究[D].东南大学,2019.

中承式钢桁架拱桥设计参数敏感性分析

许汉铮 任浪博 韦 辉 唐署博

(长安大学公路学院)

摘 要 为了研究中承式钢桁架拱桥拱肋线形和系梁线形对设计参数的敏感性,以及各设计参数对拱肋内力的影响,本文以温泉河主桥为例,以设计理想状态下有限元模型为基准,研究了结构刚度、结构自重和环境温度对成桥状态下拱肋线形、系梁线形和拱肋内力的影响。结果表明,在结构刚度中,拱肋线形和系梁线形对拱肋刚度最为敏感;在结构自重中,拱肋线形和系梁线形对桥面系自重最为敏感;对比结构刚度和结构自重,发现拱肋线形对结构刚度更加敏感;系梁线形对结构自重更加敏感。此外环境温度对拱肋线形和系梁线形的影响尤其显著;结构各参数对拱肋内力影响较小,但环境温度的改变会使拱脚处产生较大的附加内力。

关键词 钢桁架拱桥 敏感性分析 拱肋线形 系梁线形 拱肋内力

0 引言

钢桁架拱桥具有外形美观、跨越能力大、承载能力高、耐久形能好等优点[1],在大跨径桥梁选型中具有较强的竞争力。近年来,许多学者对此类问题进行了研究,康俊涛以苏岭山大桥主桥为例,分析了不同施工阶段,结构刚度、结构自重和环境温度对拱肋线形的影响,康俊涛等[2]的研究表明,拱肋线形对结构温度和自重比较敏感;卢伟升等[3]对大跨度钢管混凝土拱桥拱肋施工误差进行了分析,其着重分析了拱肋多种典型的误差对结构受力的影响;刘宇飞等[4]对大跨拱桥拱肋拼接温差效应进行了分析,并提出来了相应的控制方法;周彦文等[5]对大跨度钢管混凝土拱桥成拱线形进行了研究,提出来通过现场监控、对比分析、动态调整等技术手段,使主拱成桥线形和桥面标高满足设计要求;袁晓燕等[6]在梁拱组合体系桥梁设计中分析了结构自重、可变荷载以及温度效应对结构的影响;郭玉龙[7]在大跨度钢桁架拱桥施工控制技术研究中,分析了杆件制作、安装等方面的误差对拱肋线形的影响;梁茂然等[8]分析指出支承体系和矢跨比对拱桥结构受力和施工有较大影响,税静[9]分析了体系参数对结构受力的影响,其指出体系参数会对结构不同部分内力造成不同程度的影响;王高新等[10]通过对京沪铁路钢桁架拱桥温差特性进行长期观测和分析,为钢桁架拱桥温差效应的计算提供了参考。

目前,对于中承式钢桁架拱桥成桥状态下的拱肋线形和系梁线形以及拱肋受力的敏感形因素分析较少,本文以温泉河主桥设计理想状态为基准,研究结构刚度、结构自重和环境温度对拱肋线形、系梁线形和结构受力的影响,并对比分析了拱肋线形和系梁线形对结构刚度和结构重度的敏感形。

1 工程背景及计算模型

1.1 工程背景

温泉河主桥为三跨中承式钢桁架系杆拱桥,跨径布置为 50m + 120m + 50m,桥面全宽为 41.0m。桥梁整体布置图见图 1。

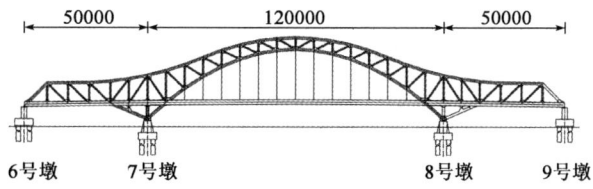

图 1 桥梁整体布置图(尺寸单位:mm)

拱肋由上、下弦杆及其腹杆组成,上、下弦杆采用箱形截面,中跨腹杆采用"H"形截面,中支点附近以及边跨腹杆采用箱形截面,上、下弦杆与腹杆之间采用高强螺栓连接。主桁由两片桁架与平联组成,两片桁架横向中心间距 24m。中跨桁架拱顶至中支点高度为 35.1m,下弦线形采用二次抛物线,矢高为 30.1m,下弦线与系梁的两个交点间的水平距离为 105m,桥面以下部分水平长度为 7.5m,中跨跨径为 120m,矢跨比为 1/4。上弦部分线形也采用二次抛物线,上弦拱轴线与边跨平弦轴线采用圆曲线平顺过渡,圆曲线半径为 $R = 122.659$m。

两拱脚之间设置钢系梁,以承受拱肋产生的巨大水平力。中跨拱肋与系梁之间采用吊杆连接。桥面系由横梁、系梁、纵梁组成的整体格构体系。

主跨中墩采用棱柱形墩柱,横向布置两个墩柱,每个墩柱底部为八边形,尺寸为 8m×5.5m,按线形变化到顶部四边形,顶部尺寸为 4m×3m。

此中承式钢桁架拱桥采用支架法施工,临时支架分为 2 个节段施工,第 1 阶段施工桥面系临时支架,第 2 阶段施工拱肋临时支架,在拱肋合龙以后拆除拱肋临时支架;在吊杆张拉完成以后拆除桥面系支架。全桥临时支架立面布置图见图 2。

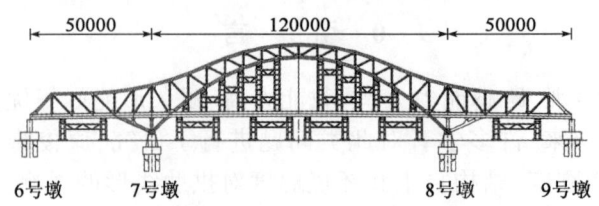

图2 全桥临时支架立面布置图(尺寸单位:mm)

1.2 有限元模型

采用有限元软件 Midas civil 建立设计理想状态有限元模型,如图3所示。

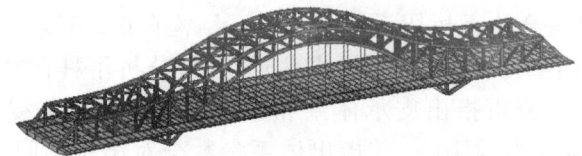

图3 有限元模型图

模型中拱肋、纵梁、横梁采用梁单元模拟,吊杆采用桁架单元模拟,桥面板采用板单元模拟.全桥共划分为3170个单元,1309个节点,各主要构件材料特性见表1。

主要材料特性表　　表1

材　料	部　位	重度(kN/m³)	弹性模量(MPa)	线膨胀系数(℃$^{-1}$)	抗拉强度(MPa)
Q345	弦杆	78	2.06×10^5	1.20×10^{-5}	345
	腹杆				
	纵梁				
	桥面板				
	平联				
钢绞线	吊杆	78.5	1.95×10^5	1.20×10^{-5}	1860

2 敏感性设计参数的确定

设计参数是引起施工控制误差的主要原因,但由于结构设计参数众多,不可能对每个参数都进行分析,因此需要找到施工过程中对结构状态影响较大的参数即设计主要参数进行敏感性分析。考虑本桥采用支架法施工,其设计参数敏感性分析就是研究设计参数的调整对结构成桥状态的影响程度。采用结构计算来对设计参数进行敏感性分析,具体的做法是:在设计参数发生一定幅度的变化后,引起结构控制部位的位移和内力变化幅度的大小,以此确定出各参数对结构状态影响的敏感程度。本文设计参数敏感性分析选取拱肋和桥面系八分点成桥后的位移以及拱肋的内力作为控制目标。设计理想状态下,拱肋和系梁控制截面变形值如图4所示。

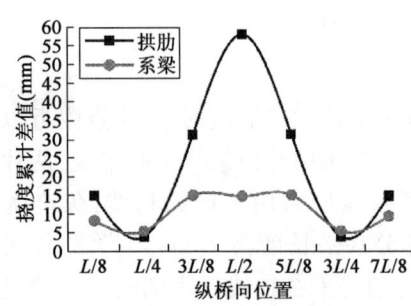

图4 设计理想状态下拱肋和系梁变形图

3 设计参数敏感性分析

3.1 结构刚度敏感性分析

本文主要通过改变材料的弹性模量来实现结构刚度的改变,主要分析了拱肋弹性模量、桥面系弹性模量和吊杆弹性模量的敏感性效应。

3.1.1 拱肋弹性模量敏感性分析

将拱肋弹性模量增大10%、增大5%、减小5%、减小10%带入有限元模型进行计算,成桥后拱肋和系梁累计挠度差值如图5、图6所示。

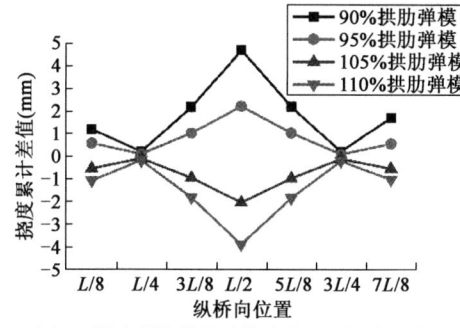
图5 拱肋弹性模量对拱肋线形的敏感性效应

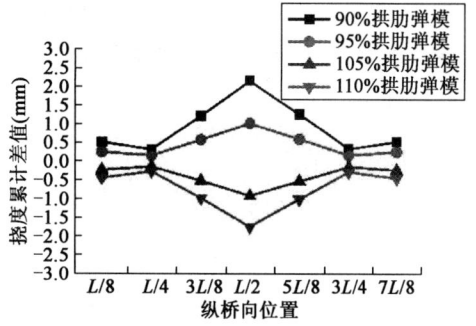
图6 拱肋弹性模量对系梁线形的敏感性效应

由图5所示,随着拱肋弹性模量的削弱,拱肋的挠度在不断增大,在90%拱肋弹性模量的情况下,其中$L/8$处拱肋挠度增大8.1%,$L/2$处拱肋挠度增大8.1%,$7L/8$处拱肋挠度增大11.67%,其相应位置挠度增大值分别为1.21mm、4.72mm、1.736mm。在四种不同拱肋弹性模量的情况下,$2/L$处拱肋累计挠度变形值分别为-3.884mm、-2.032mm、2.24mm、4.72mm。

由图6所示,随着拱肋弹性模量的改变,控制截面处系梁挠度累计差值变化较为均匀,从边跨到主跨跨中,系梁挠度变化幅度越来越大,在90%拱肋弹模时,在$L/2$处变化14.6%。

3.1.2 桥面系弹性模量敏感性分析

将系梁、横梁、桥面板的弹形模量增大10%、增大5%、减小5%、减小10%带入有限元模型进行计算,成桥后拱肋和系梁挠度累计差值如图7、图8所示。

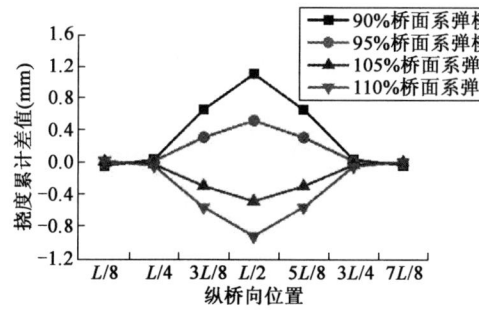
图7 桥面系弹性模量对拱肋线形的敏感性效应

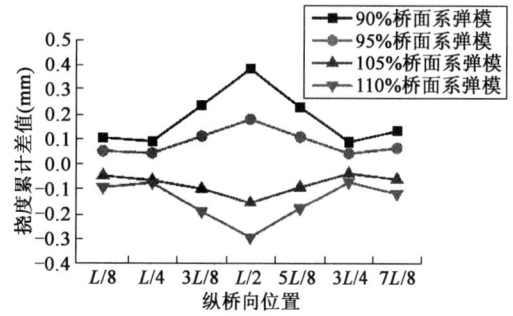
图8 桥面系弹性模量对系梁线形的敏感性效应

如图7所示,在桥面系弹性模量发生一定变化的条件下,拱肋挠度累计差值较小,拱肋挠度累计差值在2.1%以内;如图8所示,在桥面系弹性模量发生一定变化的条件下,系梁挠度累计差值变化幅度很小,变化范围在2.6%以内。

3.1.3 吊杆弹性模量敏感性分析

将吊杆的弹性模量增大10%、增大5%、减小5%、减小10%带入有限元模型进行计算,成桥后的拱肋和系梁挠度累计差值如图9、图10所示。

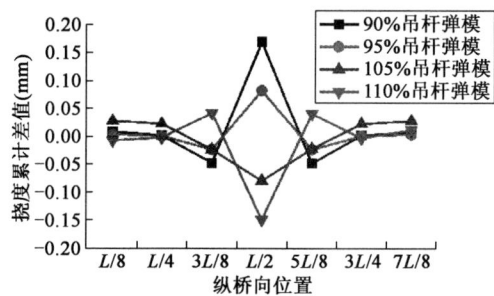
图9 吊杆弹性模量对拱肋线形的敏感性效应

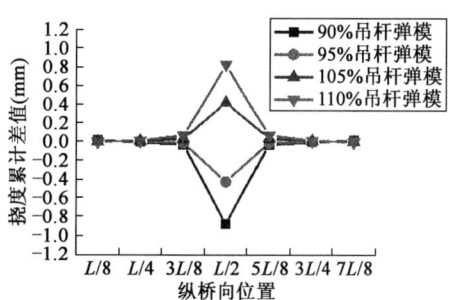
图10 吊杆弹性模量对系梁线形的敏感性效应

如图9所示,吊杆弹性模量在一定范围内变化时,对拱肋挠度的影响很小,拱肋最大挠度累计差值为0.19mm;如图10所示,随着吊杆弹性模量的减小,系梁的挠度也在减小,在90%吊杆弹模情况下,在 $L/2$ 处下令挠度变化幅度最大,$L/2$ 处系梁挠度减小0.89mm,变化了6.0%。

3.2 结构重度敏感性分析

3.2.1 拱肋重度敏感性分析

将拱肋重度增大10%、增大5%、减小5%、减小10%带入有限元模型进行计算,成桥后的拱肋和系梁挠度累计差值如图11、图12所示。

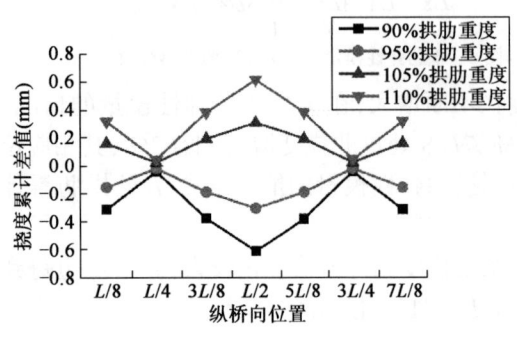

图11 拱肋重度对拱肋线形的敏感性效应　　图12 拱肋重度对拱肋线形的敏感性效应

如图11、图12所示,随着拱肋重度的变化,拱肋挠度和系梁挠度变化均很小。两者变化幅度均在2%以内。

3.2.2 桥面系重度敏感性分析

将桥面系的重度增大10%、增大5%、减5%、减小10%带入有限元模型进行计算,成桥后的拱肋和系梁挠度累计差值如图13、图14所示。

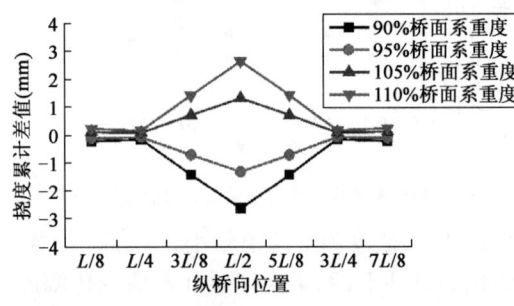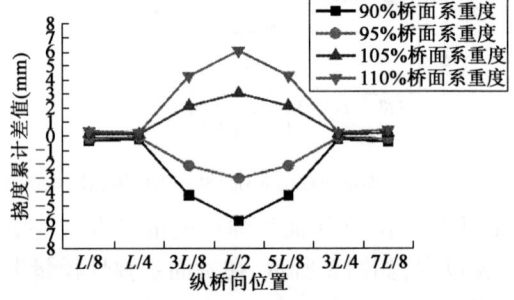

图13 桥面系重度对拱肋线形的敏感性效应　　图14 桥面系重度对系梁线形的敏感性效应

如图13所示,随着桥面系重度的变化,拱肋挠度变化幅度较小,在90%桥面系重度下,拱肋挠度变化最大,挠度减小2.6mm,变化了4.5%;由图14所示,在桥面系重度发生变化时,系梁挠度变化幅度很大,在105%桥面系重度下,$3L/8$ 处,系梁挠度增大2.1mm,变化14.2%,在 $L/2$ 处,系梁挠度增大3.0mm,变化20.5%;在110%桥面系重度下,$3L/8$ 处,系梁挠度增大4.3mm,变化28.5%,在 $L/2$ 处,系梁挠度增大6.1mm,变化41.3%。

3.3 环境温度敏感性分析

钢材的导热性能相对于混凝土来说较好,其线膨胀系数也较大。而且桥梁结构所处周边环境状况都很复杂,从施工到投入运行一般都要经历寒来暑往的变化。本桥研究季节性温差引起的系统温差对线形的影响。本文分别研究结构在整体升温10℃、整体升温20℃、整体降温10℃、整体降温20℃情形下结构的线形变化,见图15、图16。

如图15所示,随着环境温度的改变,拱肋挠度整体变化较为均匀,在结构整体升温10℃情况下,$L/2$

处拱肋挠度增大4.7mm,变化8.0%,除L/2处外,其他位置处,挠度变化幅度均超过10%;在结构整体升温20℃,L/2处拱肋挠度增大9.4mm,变化16.2%,除L/2处外,其他位置处,挠度变化幅度均超过20%;在结构整体降温时,结构产生与升温时反向的挠度;

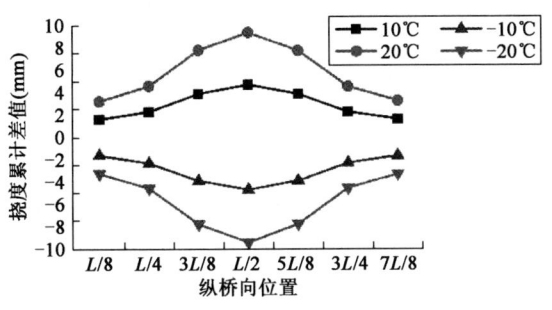

图15　环境温度对拱肋线形的敏感性效应

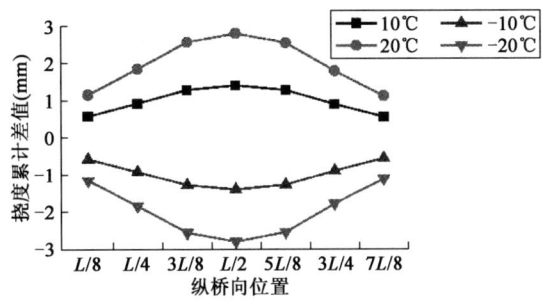

图16　环境温度对系梁线形的敏感性效应

如图16所示,随着结构整体温度的改变,系梁的挠度发生明显的改变,系梁挠度变化幅度较拱肋挠度变化幅度较小,在结构整体升温10℃情况下,L/2处拱肋挠度增大1.4mm,变化9.5%,L/4处变化16.9%,挠度增大0.92mm、3L/4变化16.2%,挠度增大0.89mm其他位置处,挠度变化幅度均小于9%;在结构整体升温20℃,L/2处拱肋挠度增大2.8mm,变化18.9%,L/4处变化16.9%,挠度增大1.84mm、3L/4变化16.2%,挠度增大1.78mm其他位置处,挠度变化幅度均小于18%。

经有限元软件分析,随着环境温度的改变,7号墩拱脚处产生明显的附加压应力。在结构整体升温10℃、整体升温20℃、整体降温10℃、整体降温20℃情况下,拱脚分别产生25.47MPa、50.96MPa、19.99MPa、39.98MPa的压应力。

3.4　结构刚度与结构自重对比分析

将结构整体刚度提高10%、降低10%;将结构整体重量增大10%、减小10%带入有限元模型中,成桥后的拱肋和系梁挠度累计差值如图17、图18所示。

由图17所示,当结构刚度和结构自重变化时,拱肋挠度累计差值变化幅度,结构整体刚度比结构自重变化幅度大;由图18所示,当结构刚度和结构强度变化时,系梁挠度累计差值变化幅度,结构整体自重比结构刚度变化幅度大。

如图19所示,当结构设计参数在一定范围内变化时,拱肋截面内力和结构设计参数基本呈线性关系;在结构各参数中,桥面系重度的敏感性效应最高,在110%桥面系重度条件下,拱肋截面内力增大了5.73MPa,变化率4.5%。

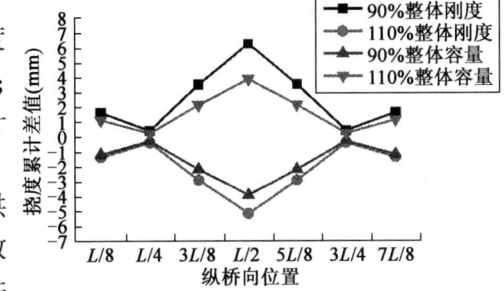

图17　结构刚度和结构自重对拱肋线形的敏感性效应

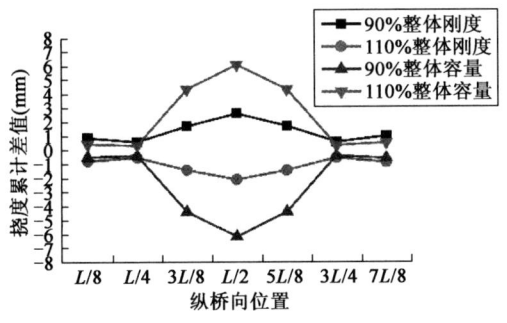

图18　结构刚度和结构自重对系梁线形的敏感性效应

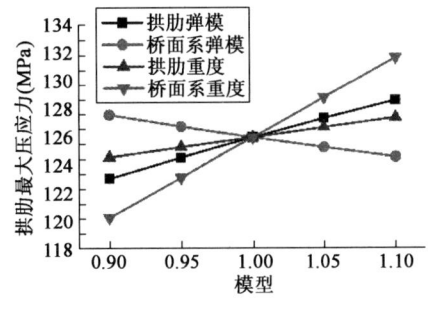

图19　拱肋内力变化图

4　结　语

(1)从上述对拱肋弹性模量、桥面系弹性模量和吊杆弹性模量的敏感性分析可知,各参数对拱肋线形和系梁线形均有影响,拱肋弹性模量对拱肋线形的影响较系梁更加敏感;桥面系弹形模量对拱肋线形和系梁线形的影响相当;吊杆弹性模量对系梁线形和拱肋线形的影响都很小。

(2)从对拱肋重度、桥面系重度的分析中发现:拱肋重度对拱肋线形和系梁线形的影响都不敏感;桥面系重度对系梁线形和拱肋线形的影响都很敏感,桥面系重度对系梁线形较拱肋的影响更加敏感。

(3)从对结构整体刚度和整体重度对比分析中发现,结构刚度对拱肋线形的影响较结构自重更加敏感;结构自重对系梁线形的影响较结构刚度更加敏感;在对比结构各设计参数发现,桥面系重度对拱肋内力的影响较大。

(4)分析表明,环境温度对拱肋线形和系梁线形的影响都很敏感,说明结构对环境温度变化很敏感;环境温度对拱肋线形较系梁线形的影响更加敏感;在分析环境温度对结构内力的影响时发现,随着环境温度的改变,在拱脚处产生较大的附加内力。

参考文献

[1] 孙海涛.大跨度钢桁架拱桥关键问题研究[D].上海:同济大学,2007.
[2] 康俊涛,胡杰,等.大跨度钢桁架拱桥施工误差敏感性分析[J].武汉理工大学学报(交通科学与工程版),2017,41(06):900-904.
[3] 卢伟升,颜东煌.大跨度钢管混凝土拱桥拱肋施工误差影响分析[J].中外公路,2015,35(03):84-88.
[4] 刘宇飞,李传习,于孟生,等.大跨拱桥拱肋拼装温差效应分析及控制方法[J].交通科学与工程,2020,36(01):63-69.
[5] 周彦文,李书兵,唐剑.大跨度钢管混凝土拱桥成拱线形控制技术研究[J].施工技术,2020,49(02):55-60+98.
[6] 袁晓燕,童金虎 等.梁拱组合体系钢桥结构设计[J].中国市政工程,2020(02):29-31+35+127.
[7] 郭玉龙.大跨度钢桁架拱桥施工控制技术研究[D].成都:西南交通大学,2015.
[8] 梁茂然,邢乔山,齐铁东.大跨度钢桁架拱桥关键设计参数研究[J].公路交通科技(应用技术版),2016,12(05):260-262.
[9] 税静.大跨度钢桁架拱桥结构参数影响分析[D].成都:西南交通大学,2017.
[10] 王高新,丁幼亮.京沪铁路钢桁拱桥温差特性的长期监测与分析[J].中南大学学报(自然科学版),2018,49(12):3040-3050.

大跨径桥梁风致振动和抗风措施研究

王 路

(长安大学)

摘 要 大跨径桥梁的重量相对较低、阻尼较小、频率较低,风致振动现象较为明显。由风引起的桥梁封闭、受损甚至垮塌的例子不在少数。查阅桥梁风毁案例及当前抗风设计的研究现状,对大跨径桥梁风致振动的原因进行概述,并从空气动力学措施、机械减振措施和结构措施阐述了大跨径桥梁抗风措施。为工程实践和后续研究提供依据。

关键词 桥梁工程 风致振动 抗风措施 文献综述 大跨径桥梁

0 引 言

随着科技的发展和社会的进步,我国桥梁事业飞速发展,大跨径桥梁的应用越来越多。由于大跨径桥梁的重量相对较低、阻尼较小、频率较低,风致振动现象较为明显。而桥梁又是社会科技技术水平和人民生活安定的一个侧面表现,一旦出现桥梁风致振动振幅过大甚至风毁事故,在社会上影响极其恶劣。

李加武[1]利用非线性理论和混沌时间序列分析方法,建立了桥梁风致振动的数学模型,研究了桥梁风致振动的混沌特性;刘智虎[2]通过静力作用和动力作用(颤振、驰振、涡振、抖振)对大跨度桥梁风振动问题进行文献综述;郑元勋[3]基于统计分析研究了桥梁坍塌事故原机及预防措施;《中国公路学报》编辑部[4]通过桥梁防灾减灾和桥梁监测等方面对中国桥梁工程学术研究进行文献综述;李允[5]查阅概述了当前抗风设计研究现状,对桥梁抗风设计有一定研究;陈羽[6]介绍了三种桥梁抗风方法(理论分析、风洞试验和数值模拟)及其研究现状;兰华华[7]从风特性、风浪和风沙形成条件对桥梁风灾及对策进行了研究。

通过查阅大跨度桥梁风致振动的研究文献,对桥梁风毁、风致振动进行研究,并从气动外形方面、阻尼方面和结构方面阐述了大跨径桥梁的抗风措施。

1 大跨径桥梁的风致振动

1.1 桥梁风毁

历史上,第一次有明确文字记载的桥梁风毁事故发生在1818年,主跨为260m的英国德莱堡修道院桥(Drburgh Abbey Bridge)风毁[8]。最著名的风毁事故发生在1840年,美国旧塔科马海湾悬索桥(Tacoma Narrows Bridge)风毁。自此,人们开始认识到了风对桥梁结构的另外一种不同于静力效应的作用——风致振动。从1818年起,在世界上桥梁风毁事故多次发生,部分桥梁风毁事件如表1所示。

桥梁风毁事件　　　　　　　　　　　　　　表1

年　份	桥梁名称	主跨(m)	国　家
1818年	Drburgh Abbey Bridge	260	英国
1839年	Brighton Chair Pier Bridge	180	英国
1852年	Roche-BernardBrideg	195	法国
1854年	Wheeling Bridge	310	美国
1879年	Firth of Tay Bridge	74	英国
1889年	Niagara-Clifton Bridge	380	美国
1940年	Tacoma Narrows Bridge	853	美国

桥梁风毁事故古而有之,每次出现都会对社会产生不利的影响,严重影响了人民的生命财产安全和交通出行,所以对大跨径桥梁风致振动和抑振措施的分析是十分必要的。

1.2 风致振动的类型

1.2.1 涡激共振

流经结构表面的风会在结构上产生周期性的漩涡脱落,从而在结构表面产生周期性变化的涡激力,迫使结构产生大幅度的振动,而结构的振动又会对漩涡脱落产生影响,这种典型的流固耦合现象称为涡激振动[9]。涡激共振是一种限幅振动,由强迫力和自激力引起[10]。主梁的形状为钝体时,在主梁背面会产生漩涡交替脱落。初期为漩涡从大跨径桥梁上脱落产生的涡激力强迫作用引起的共振,随着涡激共振振幅不断地增加,大跨径桥梁的运动对漩涡脱落和涡激力产生了影响,使涡激振动具有了自激特性。涡激共振一般不会导致桥梁垮塌,但由于大跨径桥梁频率低,涡激共振发生的风速较低,在常遇风速下就有可能发生涡击共振,从而容易造成大跨径桥梁构件疲劳和行车舒适度降低等不良影响。

1.2.2 抖振

抖振一种随机强迫限幅振动,由来流紊流和特征紊流产生的随机脉动风荷载引起。结构的抖振现象主要可以分为三类:结构物自身尾流引起的、其他结构物特征紊流引起的、自然风中的脉动成分引起的[11]。抖振一般由较低的风速引起,连续的抖振会导致桥梁构件的疲劳,降低桥梁的寿命。

1.2.3 颤振

在过去的一个多世纪里,大跨度桥梁的建设举世瞩目,随着跨径的不断增加,颤振问题也给大跨径桥梁带来了考验[12]。跨径增加的颤振是一种发散振动,分为扭转颤振和弯扭耦合颤振。扭转颤振由扭转振动产生的气动负阻尼引起;弯扭耦合颤振由弯扭耦合振动产生的气动负阻尼引起。当达到颤振临界风速时,大跨径桥梁会不断地从大风中吸收能量,由于大跨径桥梁自身的阻尼无法消耗这些能量,桥梁振动会越发剧烈,由于颤振的发散性,一旦大跨径桥梁发生颤振,则桥梁风毁,对人民生活安全和社会安定会造成极其不利的影响。

1.2.4 驰振

驰振是一种气动自激力驱动的发散振动,其振动形式通常为大幅弯曲振动[13]。驰振分为横风向驰振和尾流驰振。横风向驰振由横风向振动产生的气动负阻尼引起;尾流驰振由尾流的气动不稳定性引起。驰振一般发生在桥塔、裹冰输电线、吊杆、拉索等具有棱角的方形截面中,由于桥塔等构件自身频率较高,驰振发生概率较低。

2 大跨径桥梁的抗风措施

在大跨径桥梁设计阶段,就可以通过理论分析、风洞试验和CFD数值模拟和神经网络预测[14]等方法对其风致振动进行分析考虑,一旦发现桥梁出现了风致振动病害,可以采取各种抗风措施[9],抗风措施主要分为三大类。

2.1 空气动力学措施

大跨径桥梁结构的外形与桥梁风致振动有着十分密切的关系,在不改变桥梁结构性能的前提下,适当增加一部分导流装置来改变桥梁的外形,对桥梁风致振动有着积极影响。通过加装风嘴、导流板、稳定板的方式,对风进行导流,使主梁断面趋近于流线型,增强大跨径桥梁的抗风稳定性。通过对主梁中央开槽,选择双幅桥的形式,改变主梁断面的气动外形,提高主梁的抗风性能。通过选择桁架形式的主梁,桁架主梁的透风率相对较高,对风的阻挡较小,受到风的影响也较小。通过调整防撞栏杆、人行道栏杆和检修车轨道的外形和位置,来改善主梁的气动性能,从而提高主梁的抗风稳定性。

2.2 机械减振措施

由于在大跨径桥梁主梁的宽度方向上比高度方向上有更多的安装空间,可以选择控制装置的范围也较大,可以在大跨径桥梁的宽度方向上安装被动调质阻尼器TMD,也可以使用控制水平振动的调谐液体类阻尼器TLD等[15]。通过加装各类机械阻尼器,把主梁从风中吸收的能量通过机械阻尼来耗散,从而加快主梁对能量的耗散速度,降低主梁的振幅,提高大跨径桥梁的稳定性。

2.3 结构措施

通过对主梁进行加固,并适当提高主梁的高度,从而提高大跨径桥梁的结构刚度和扭转刚度,减小风致振动对大跨径桥梁的影响。

3 结 语

随着跨越障碍的需求和理论、材料、计算机技术的进步,大跨径桥梁有着更为广阔的发展舞台,同时也面临着更严峻的技术挑战,更拥有无限美好的想象空间[16]。

本文概述了部分桥梁风毁的案例、大跨径桥梁的风致振动和抗风措施,为工程实践和后续研究提供理论依据。

参考文献

[1] 李加武,王新,张悦等.桥梁风致振动的混沌特性[J].交通运输工程学报,2014,14(03):34-42.
[2] 刘智虎.大跨度桥梁风振问题综述[J].山西建筑,2007(24):319-320.

[3] 郑元勋,郭慧吉,谢宁.基于统计分析的桥梁坍塌事故原因剖析及预防措施研究[J].中外公路,2017,37(06):125-133.
[4] 《中国公路学报》编辑部.中国桥梁工程学术研究综述·2014[J].中国公路学报,2014,27(05):1-96.
[5] 李允.桥梁抗风设计[J].科学技术创新,2020(20):133-134.
[6] 陈羽,张亮亮.桥梁抗风研究方法综述[J].四川建筑,2010,30(06):145-146.
[7] 兰华华.风灾对桥梁安全的影响及对策研究[D].成都:西南交通大学,2016.
[8] 陈强.π型断面斜拉桥涡激振动特性及气动抑制措施研究[D].成都:西南交通大学,2019.
[9] 王阳.双边箱式Ⅱ型断面涡振抑振试验与机理研究[D].西安:长安大学,2020.
[10] 陈政清.桥梁风工程[M].北京:人民交通出版社股份有限公司,2005.
[11] 方成.基于静三分力系数的大跨径桥梁气动稳定性的评价及其应用[D].西安:长安大学,2014.
[12] 葛耀君.大跨度桥梁抗风的技术挑战与精细化研究[J].工程力学,2011,28(S2):11-23.
[13] 段永锋.典型桥塔断面非定常与非线性驰振力的数值模拟研究[D].西安:长安大学,2018.
[14] 李加武,党嘉敏,吴拓,等.径向基神经网络用于钢-混Ⅱ型梁原始断面涡振性能的预测[J].振动工程学报,2021,34(01):1-8.
[15] 陈艾荣,陈伟,项海帆.大跨斜拉桥的侧向弯曲抖振及其控制[J].振动与冲击,1995(02):35-39.
[16] 肖汝诚.桥梁结构体系[M].北京:人民交通出版社,2013.

高强钢丝及缆索体抗火性能研究进展

厉 萱 沈锐利 陈 巍

(西南交通大学土木工程学院)

摘 要 缆索承重桥梁主要用于大跨度桥梁结构,多数属于重大工程项目,设计施工和管养方面都比较重视,但是到目前为止,针对其抗火防火方面的研究较少,桥上或桥下一旦发生火灾,会对桥梁结构的安全造成极大的威胁。由高强钢丝组成的缆索体作为缆索承重桥梁的关键构件,其抗火性能对火灾下及灾后缆索承重桥梁的结构安全性能影响巨大。通过分析国内外学者在高强钢丝及缆索体抗火领域的研究成果,包括高强钢丝及索体火灾高温下的力学性能退化、索体火灾高温下温度场分布、缆索构件抗火性能数值分析方法等内容,对高强钢丝及缆索体抗火性能研究进展进行了总结和分析,并阐述今后可供研究的方向。

关键词 缆索承重桥梁 抗火性能 研究进展 高强钢丝 缆索体

0 引 言

近年来,桥梁火灾事故频发。根据纽约交通厅进行的桥梁损毁事故调查,每1000座桥梁损毁就有52座是火灾造成。美国高速公路年平均火灾次数为376000次,导致12.8亿美元损失[1]。

目前对于桥梁火灾研究大多是借鉴建筑火灾的研究成果,缺乏系统性和针对性的研究,尤其是对于缆索承重为主的斜拉、悬索或协作体系桥梁,缺少相应的研究。由高强钢丝组成的缆索体作为缆索承重桥梁的关键构件,当其遭受到火灾后,力学性能会大幅度降低。研究表明,火灾高温下钢丝温度能在30min内上升至800℃以上。而200℃高温时钢材强度开始退化,达到600℃时退化十分严重,此时钢材的弹性模量只有常温下的0.4倍左右,抗拉强度只有常温下的0.2倍左右,火灾作用下缆索体构件具有很高的断索风险。2014年施工中的湖南赤石特大桥发生火灾事故,短时间内9根斜拉索发生不同程度的火致破坏,使施工中的混凝土主梁严重变形、大范围开裂;2016年泰州长江公路大桥上一车辆起火,危及吊索安全;2017年苏通长江大桥主桥斜拉索附近发生大型车辆火灾。这些事故的发生,敲响了缆索承重抗火设计的警钟。

通过收集国内外科研人员在高强钢丝及缆索体抗火领域研究成果,本文对高强钢丝高温下力学性能进行了归纳总结,分析了目前缆索体火灾高温下力学性能及温度场研究现状,介绍了缆索构件抗火性能数值仿真研究方法及其中的不足。

1 高强钢丝及索体高温力学性能研究

结构的抗火设计应立足于其组成材料,高强钢丝作为缆索构件的主要组成材料,其火灾高温下的力学性能退化值得重点关注。吕志涛等[2-5]对各型号预应力高强钢丝进行了一系列的高温力学性能试验,得到了各型号高强钢丝在高温下的力学性能指标。卢杰[6]对1670、1770、1860和1960级预应力钢丝进行了一系列的火灾灾后力学性能试验,建立了包含不同冷却方法影响的预测方程来评估钢丝的灾后力学性能。Francisco[7]开展了高强钢丝在不同高温及加载速率下的拉伸试验,得到了在不同温度及加载速率下的应力-应变曲线。各型号高强钢丝高温下及高温后力学性能折减整理见图1~图6。

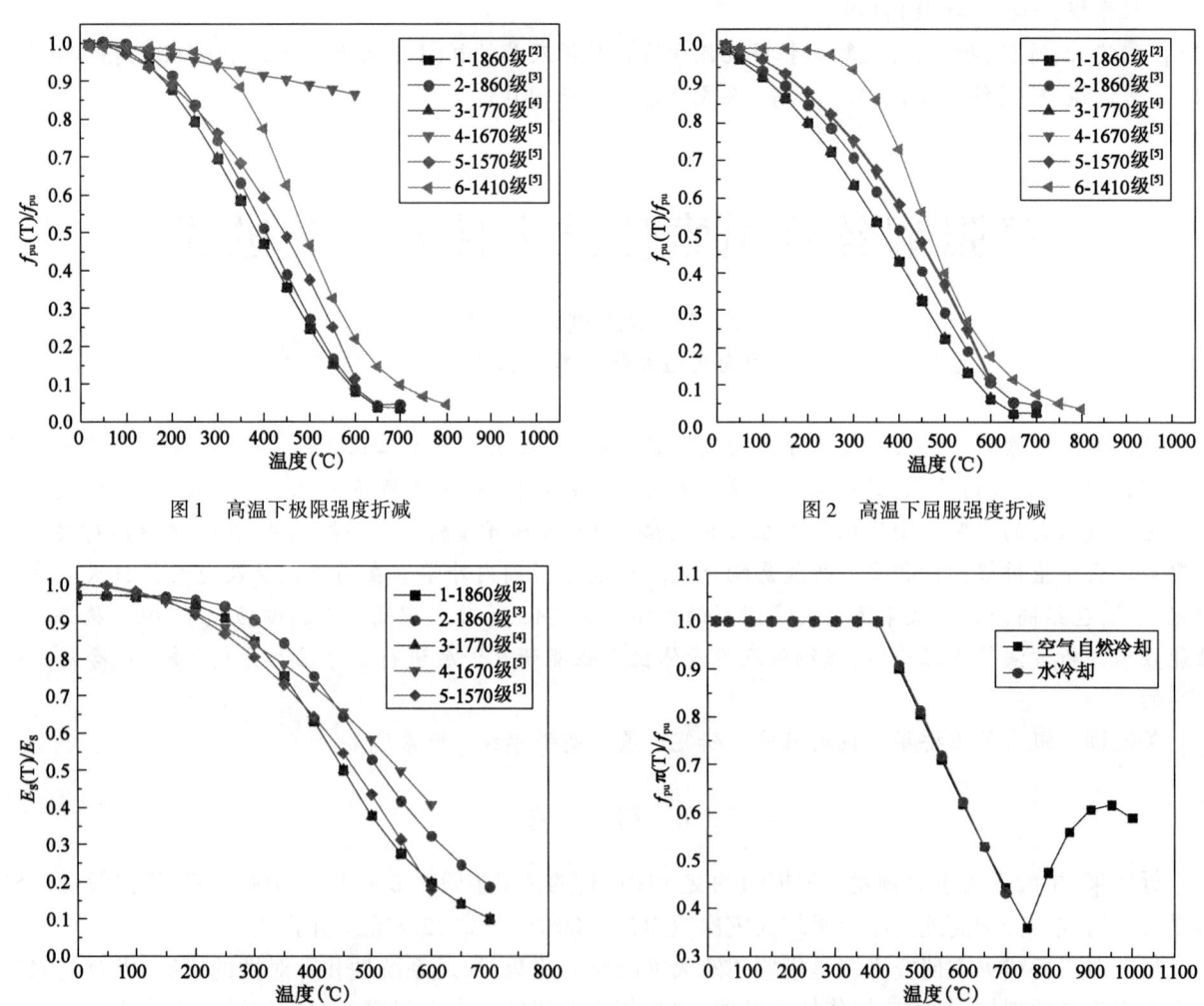

图1 高温下极限强度折减

图2 高温下屈服强度折减

图3 高温下弹性模量折减

图4 高温后极限强度折减

有研究表明钢索高温下力学性能指标退化比单根钢丝更为严重[8]。Benedett等[9]测定了不同直径钢丝高温下的应力-应变曲线,并将其应用到钢丝绳索股精细化有限元模型中,得到了钢丝绳索股高温下力学性能演变规律。Ataei等[10]建立了7丝钢绞线精细化有限元模型,得出了其在20~800℃温度范围内力学性能指标。杜咏等[12]采用非接触式应变视频测量系统,对1670级7×7平行钢丝束进行了高温力学性能试验研究,得出了平行钢丝束力学性能的高温折减系数以及高温应力—应变函数关系。

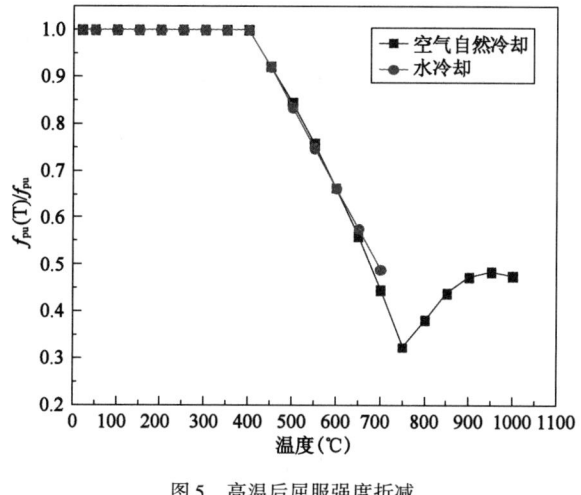

图5 高温后屈服强度折减

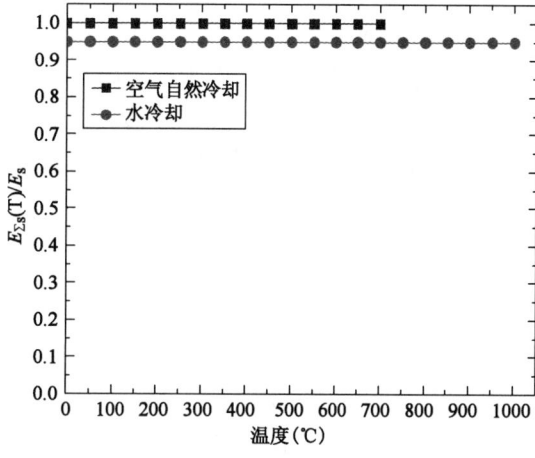

图6 高温后弹性模量折减

从目前研究进展来看,现阶段国内外学者通过试验研究,得到了各型号高强钢丝高温力学性能指标。但是,由于试验方法的不同,对于同一型号高强钢丝各学者测试结果也存在差异,缺乏对其系统归纳与总结。另外,诸如1960级乃至更高强度的高强钢丝已逐步应用于缆索承重桥梁中,目前该类型高强钢丝的相关试验研究较少。现阶段对高强钢丝索体高温力学性能的研究主要是针对钢丝绳及预应力钢绞线,力学试验主要是针对预应力混凝土结构用7丝钢索开展的,针对大跨桥梁用的大直径钢索热力学试验测试均未涉及。

2 缆索体高温下截面温度场研究

缆索体截面温度场研究是评估缆索构件火灾安全性的前提。Lugaresi[14]通过在19丝平行钢丝索股截面内埋置热电偶,实测得到了不同位置处钢丝的升温规律。Zou等[15]利用火灾动力学仿真软件,将悬索桥缆索简化为匀质同性体钢圆棒模型建立有限元分析,分析了燃料尺寸、横向偏移距离及风效应对缆索体温度场的影响。Kotsovinos等[16]通过文献综述,对缆索体火灾下的截面传热机理进行了归纳总结。

对于火灾下缆索体截面温度理论分析,少数学者基于集总热质量法及能量守恒定理提出了一些简化计算模型。Bennetts等[17]基于集总热质量法及能量守恒定理,进行了索体截面传热计算的推导。杜咏等[18]基于集总热质量法计算理论推导了钢索截面中心钢丝升温的理论计算公式,并研究了在ISO834标准火灾升温曲线下,考虑了钢索截面空腔辐射传热的影响,不同丝数钢丝索股截面与圆钢截面的温度场分布差异。

从目前研究成果来看,针对钢索截面温度场研究主要以试验研究和数值模拟为主,有少数学者建立了考虑截面空隙的钢索截面精细化有限元模型。有关钢索截面温度场理论研究开展很少,少数学者基于能量守恒定理或集总热质量法提出了一些简化计算模型。因此,有必要开展具备一定尺寸规模的索体高温下温度场试验研究,测试火灾高温下缆索截面的温度场分布,明确实际索体截面传热机理。

3 缆索构件抗火性能研究

针对缆索构件抗火性能的研究,大多采用数值模拟的方法进行研究。从目前抗火模拟计算的研究进展来看,针对简单体系,采用板壳、实体精细化有限元模型作为分析手段对结构的抗火性能进行研究;对于缆索承重桥梁结构,构件类型组合较多,索、杆、梁及板等均有涉及,此时一般均偏向于易于前后处理的杆系模型,人为进行大量的简化。

对于缆索构件抗火方面的研究,王莹等[19]采用热-结构耦合分析法,构建了武汉鹦鹉洲长江大桥多尺度有限元模型,研究了油罐车火灾引起主缆、吊索力学性能随受火时间变化的规律,得到了吊索的破坏时间。李利军等[20]采用火灾动力学模拟软件FDS对公路火灾下缆索承重桥梁瞬态空间温度场进行数值模拟,给出了悬索桥主缆、吊索表面温度及热流密度随火灾的发展过程变化的计算公式,确定了吊索及不同直径主缆的受火安全距离。Gong[21]等对缆索体构件火致损伤机理展开了研究。

从目前研究成果来看,针对缆索构件抗火性能的研究主要以数值模拟为主,所建立的数值计算模型以杆系模型为主,而杆系模型由于自身固有的基本力学假定使结构分析过程过于简化。因此,迫切需要开展新的桥梁体系数值模拟方法的研究,平衡计算精度与效率,建立能真实反映缆索构件抗火性能的数值计算模型,满足缆索承重用缆索构件抗火设计需求。

4 结 语

对高强钢丝及缆索体抗火领域的研究成果总结分析得到以下结论,并指出需进一步开展的研究工作:

(1)现阶段国内外学者通过试验研究,针对高强钢丝高温力学性能的研究成果较为丰富,但缺乏对不同强度等级、不同直径的高强钢丝高温力学性能指标的系统归纳与总结;对于诸如1960级乃至更高强度的高强钢丝开展的相关试验研究较少;对于高强钢丝索体高温下的力学性能研究,缺乏大直径钢索热力学试验测试。

(2)目前对于钢索截面温度场研究多以小直径钢索为主,针对大跨度缆索承重桥用钢索的抗火试验研究十分缺乏,对于钢索截面温度场理论研究及传热机理缺乏试验数据的验证。因此,有必要开展具备一定尺寸规模的索体火灾高温下温度场试验研究,明确实际索体截面的温度场分布及传热机理。

(3)目前针对缆索构件抗火性能的研究主要以数值模拟为主。数值计算模型以杆系模型为主,忽略了索体截面空隙对截面升温传热的影响,不能真实地反映缆索构件抗火性能。需兼顾计算精度与效率,开展缆索构件抗火性能数值计算模型的研究。

参考文献

[1] Raouffard M M, Nishiyama M. Fire resistance of reinforced concrete frames subjected to service load: Part 1. Experimental study[J]. Journal of Advanced Concrete Technology, 2015, 13(12):554-563.

[2] 张昊宇,郑文忠.1860级低松弛钢绞线高温下力学性能[J].哈尔滨工业大学学报,2007,39(6):861-865.

[3] 宗钟凌,张晋,蒋德稳,等.高温下1860级钢绞线钢丝力学性能试验研究[J].建筑科学,2016,32(1):43-47.

[4] 郑文忠,胡琼,张昊宇,等.高温下及高温后1770级$\phi P5$低松弛预应力钢丝力学性能试验研究[J].建筑结构学报,2006,27(2):120-128.

[5] 华毅杰.预应力混凝土结构火灾反应及抗火性能研究[D].上海:同济大学,2000.

[6] Lu J, Liu H, Chen Z. Post-fire mechanical properties of low-relaxation hot-dip galvanized prestressed steel wires[J]. Journal of Constructional Steel Research, 2017, 136:110-127.

[7] Galvez F, Atienza J M, Elices M. Behaviour of steel prestressing wires under extreme conditions of strain rate and temperature[J]. Structural concrete: Journal of the FIB, 2011, 12(4):255-261.

[8] Wang Ye-hua, Shen Zu-yan, Li Yuan-qi. Experimental Study of the Mechanical Properties of Prestressed Steel Wire at Elevated Temperatures[C]. Structures in Fire. 2010:711-718.

[9] Fontanari V, Benedetti M, Monelli B D. Elasto-plastic behavior of a Warrington-Seale rope: Experimental analysis and finite element modeling[J]. Engineering Structures, 2015, 82:113-120.

[10] Ataei H, Mamaghani M, Aboutaha R S. Finite Element Analysis of Cable-Stayed Strands Failure due to Fire[C]// Asce Forensic Engineering, Congress, 2015.

[11] A. M. Shakya, V. K. R. Kodur. Effect of temperature on the mechanical properties of low relaxation seven-wire prestressing strand[J]. Construction and Building Materials, 2016, 124.

[12] 汪贤聪,杜咏,周浩.火灾高温下材料力学性能测试技术试验研究[J].建筑钢结构进展,2018,20(06):39-45.

[13] 杜咏,肖丽萍,李国强,等.预应力平行钢丝束高温力学性能[J].建筑材料学报,2020,23(01):114-121.

[14] Lugaresi F. Thermal response of structural spiral strands subject to fire[D]. The University of Edinburgh, 2017, UK.

[15] Qiling Zou, Kavi Pool, Suren Chen. Performance of suspension bridge hangers exposed to hazardous material fires considering wind effects[J]. Advances in Bridge Engineering,2020,1(1).

[16] Kotsovinos P, Atalioti A, Mcswiney N, et al. Analysis of the Thermomechanical Response of Structural Cables Subject to Fire[J]. Fire Technology, 2019, 56(3).

[17] Bennetts I, Moinuddin K. Evaluation of the Impact of Potential Fire Scenarios on Structural Elements of a Cable-Stayed Bridge[J]. Journal of Fire Protection Engineering, 2009, 19(2):85-106.

[18] Du Y, Sun Y K, Jiang J, et al. Effect of cavity radiation on transient temperature distribution in steel cables under ISO834 fire[J]. Fire Safety Journal, 2019.

[19] Liu M Y, Tian W, Wang Y, et al. Risk Prevention Measures for Three-Tower and Four-Span Suspension Bridge under Vehicle Fire[J]. Advanced Materials Research, 2014, 919-921:590-597.

[20] 李利军,董晓明,胡兆同.大跨径悬索桥承重构件公路火灾安全距离研究[J].广西大学学报,2014, 39(04):886-893.

[21] Xu Gong, Anil K. Agrawal. Safety of Cable-Supported Bridges during Fire Hazards[J]. Journal of Bridge Engineering,2016.

[22] Eva Kragh, Harikrishna N, Jakob L. Fire Protection of Bridge Cables [J]. Structural Engineering International,2020.

The Formulation of the Error Control Range of Composite Beam Section Size Based on Monte Carlo Method

Liuyu Zhang Xingyue Chen Xiaochuan Shi Qichen Wang

(The University of Chang'an, Department of Highway School)

Abstract The geometric parameters of the bridge section are an essential factor that affects the limit state of the bridge. Therefore, a reasonable control range of construction errors is very important to ensure the safety of the bridge. In this paper, by changing the control section size parameters of the composite beam, the sensitivity of the section stress and mid-span deflection of the composite beam to the change of the section geometric parameters is analysed. Preliminarily formulate the control range of the section size construction error, and give inspection method for construction applicability. the paper concludes that the error control range of the existing cross-sectional dimensions is already strict, and the reliability of the corresponding control index calculated by using the smallest error control range in each specification is greater than 99.0%. By comparing the coefficient of variation of the control index corresponding to the error control range and the coefficient of variation of the material, it is found that the variability of material quality has a greater impact on construction reliability. The error control range of the width of the concrete slab and the height of the steel beam web is stricter and can be relaxed first. The error control range of the thickness of the concrete slab and the width of the steel beam bottom plate is moderate and can be adjusted appropriately. The error control range of the steel plate thickness should be strictly controlled.

Keywords   Monte carlo   Composite beam   Reliability   Control index

0 Introduction

The geometric parameters of the bridge section are anessential factor affecting the limit state of the bridge. A reasonable control range of construction errors can not only ensure the requirements of construction safety, but also ensure the operability and economic needs of construction. After sorting out the relevant specifications of existing beam bridges, it is found that different specifications (Ministry of Construction of the People's Republic of Chian, 2001; M. o. C. o. t. P. s. R. o. China, 2011; Ministry of Communications of the People's Republic of China, 2015b; Ministry of Communications of the People's Republic of China, 2017; M. o. H. a. U. -R. D. o. t. P. s. R. o. China, 2008, 2011) have inconsistencies in the section size error control range. In this paper, combined with the actual construction process, by calculating the degree of influence of the change of single section size on the limit state of the main beam, the control index of the section size is determined. Then through the influence of different construction error control ranges on construction reliability, the control ranges that meet the reliability of the limit state of the bridge are initially formulated.

1 Composite Beam Calculation Method

The research is based on the general drawing of a 30m steel-concrete composite beam of a specific expressway in Yunnan. The bridge deck is made of C50 concrete. The steel beam is made of Q345qD steel. The I-beam height is 1.42m. The upper flange is 400mm wide and 16mm thick; the lower flange is 650mm wide, the side beam thicknesses are 24mm and 36mm, and the middle beam thickness is 24mm and 32mm. The web thickness is 16mm. This paper takes the middle beam as the calculation object.

MATLAB programming is used to calculate the effect of different loads on the bridge. The specification (Ministry of Communications of the People's Republic of China, 2015a) stipulates that the bearing capacity of composite beam bridges should be calculated by elastic theory. The normal stress and shear stress of composite beam section under dead load and live load should use the theory provided by the specification. Since the supporting project is a simply supported beam, the temperature gradient can be calculated by the average temperature difference between the steel beam and the concrete slab according to the specification (Ministry of Communications of the People's Republic of China, 2012).

According to the calculation method provided by the specification (Ministry of Communications of the People's Republic of China, 2012), the cooling method is used to equivalent the shrinkage of the concrete. The 90-day precast age of the concrete slab is considered in the calculation.

According to the specification (Ministry of Communications of the People's Republic of China, 2012), the effective elastic modulus method is used to simplify the calculation of the influence of creep effect on the internal force of the composite beam.

Since the supporting project is a simply supported beam, according to the specification, the deflection calculation adopts the reduced stiffness method considering the slip effect. The calculation formula adopts the theoretical formula given in the specification for calculation. The result of the ultimate state check of the composite beam.

1.1 Checking calculation of bearing capacity limit state

The following Fig. 1 is a schematic diagram of each check point of the main beam mid-span and fulcrum section.

Tab. 1 is the theoretical formula for calculating the stress at the checkpoint of each working condition. In the table, except F and D' are section shear stresses, the rest are normal section stresses. According to the calculation results, it is not difficult to obtain the most unfavorable combination of the cross-section. The four points A, D, E, and F, are found to be the cross-section stress control points. The maximum compressive stress at point A is 11.15MPa. Because the normal stress at point D is larger and the shear stress is smaller, the calculated stress at the mid-span is the largest. Tab. 1.1 only shows the normal stress and shear stress at point D at the mid-span section. The converted stress is 173.24 MPa, the normal stress at point E is 180.46 MPa, and the shear stress at point F is 77.70MPa.

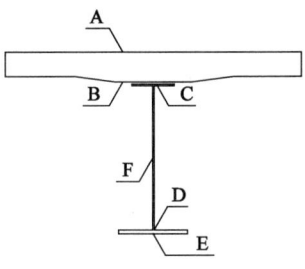

Fig.1 I-beam position number diagram

Sectional Stress Data (unit: MPa) Tab. 1

Load	Location						
	A	B	C	D	E	F	D'
Self-weight + pavement	−4.90	−1.91	−10.12	76.99	79.29	28.11	0
Vehicle load	−5.40	−2.10	−11.15	84.79	87.31	49.59	12.92
Positive temperature gradient	1.70	0.81	−14.58	2.83	3.43	—	—
Negative temperature gradient	−0.85	−0.41	7.29	−1.41	−1.71	—	—
shrink	2.55	1.22	−21.87	4.24	5.14	—	—
Creep	3.25	0.78	−13.80	4.39	5.29	—	—

1.2 Checking Calculation of Serviceability Limit State

Since the project is a simply supported beam, and there is no prestress, the compressed concrete deck of a simply supported composite beam bridge generally does not produce lateral cracks. (Nie, 2011b) Therefore, the serviceability limit state only pays attention to the deflection limit of the structure. After calculation, the vertical deflection of the simply supported beam under vehicle load is 22.84mm.

2 The Influence of Section Geometry on the Limit State of Main Beam

Domestic and foreign experimental studies (Nie, 2011a) have found that when the simply-supported beam adopts full shear connection, the bending failure of the simply-supported beam is caused by the failure of the concrete slab. In the shear design, the shear effect of the steel beam web is mainly considered. According to the specification (Ministry of Communications of the People's Republic of China, 2012), when the concrete and steel beams are effectively connected as a whole, the positive bending moment section of the composite beam may not be checked for overall stability. Therefore, in the process of analysing the changes of cross-section geometric dimensions, the main attention is paid to the normal stress value of the lower edge of the steel beam, the compressive stress value of the upper edge of the bridge deck, the maximum converted stress of the web, the shear stress value of the steel beam web, and the change of beam deflection.

In the following, by controlling the change of section size parameters, the sensitivity of the control factors of the composite beam to the change of section geometric parameters is analysed. In order to facilitate comparative analysis, the change of cross-section parameters adopts equal proportion changes.

2.1 Concrete Slab Stress Change

It can be seen from Tab. 2 that the stress on the upper edge of the concrete is most sensitive to the change of the web height, followed by the change of the width of the concrete slab, and then the change of the thickness of the concrete slab. The change of the width and thickness of the lower flange of the steel beam also has a certain influence on the stress on the upper edge of the concrete slab. The changes in the thickness and width of the upper flange of the steel beam and the thickness of the web have little effect on the stress on the upper edge of the concrete slab. Except for the thickness of the web, the stress on the edge of the concrete slab increases with the decrease of the geometric size, and when the percentage of change is the same, the decrease has a greater impact than the increase.

Stress Change Table of the A Control Point (unit: %)　　　　Tab. 2

parameters	Change ratio							
	-10	-7	-4	-1	1	4	7	10
Concrete slab thickness	3.36	2.26	1.24	0.30	-0.29	-1.13	-1.90	-2.62
Concrete slab width	4.96	3.37	1.87	0.45	-0.45	-1.74	-2.97	-4.13
Upper flange thickness	0.13	0.09	0.05	0.01	-0.01	-0.05	-0.09	-0.13
Upper flange width	0.02	0.02	0.01	0.00	0.00	-0.01	-0.02	-0.02
Web thickness	-0.40	-0.28	-0.16	-0.04	0.04	0.16	0.27	0.39
Web height	10.88	7.35	4.06	0.98	-0.96	-3.72	-6.31	-8.75
Lower flange thickness	1.78	1.21	0.67	0.16	-0.16	-0.62	-1.06	-1.48
Lower flange width	1.66	1.13	0.63	0.15	-0.15	-0.58	-0.98	-1.37

2.2 Steel Beam Stress Change

It can be seen from Tab. 3 that the stress on the lower edge of the steel beam is more sensitive to the change of the web height. The stress at the lower edge of the steel beam is also more sensitive to the change in the thickness of the bottom plate of the steel beam and the width of the bottom plate. The influence of web thickness change on the stress on the lower edge of the steel beam is improved compared with the influence of the stress on the upper edge of the concrete slab.

Stress Change Table of the E Control Point (unit: %)　　　　Tab. 3

Parameters	Change ratio							
	-10	-7	-4	-1	1	4	7	10
Concrete slab thickness	-1.15	-0.80	-0.45	-0.11	0.11	0.44	0.77	1.09
Concrete slab width	-2.09	-1.47	-0.84	-0.21	0.21	0.85	1.49	2.13
Upper flange thickness	-0.05	-0.03	-0.02	0.00	0.00	0.02	0.03	0.05
Upper flange width	-0.16	-0.11	-0.06	-0.02	0.02	0.06	0.11	0.16
Web thickness	1.31	0.91	0.51	0.13	-0.13	-0.50	-0.88	-1.24
Web height	10.27	6.99	3.88	0.94	-0.93	-3.62	-6.17	-8.59
Lower flange thickness	7.46	5.10	2.85	0.70	-0.69	-2.68	-4.59	-6.43
Lower flange width	7.63	5.21	2.91	0.71	-0.70	-2.74	-4.70	-6.57

2.3 Change of Shear Stress of Support Web

It can be seen from Tab. 4 that the support point shear stress is more sensitive to the variation of web thickness and web height, and the variation of concrete slab thickness and concrete slab width has a certain influence on the fulcrum shear stress. The support point shear force is less sensitive to the variation of the geometric dimensions of the remaining sections.

Stress Change Table of the F Control Point (unit: %) Tab. 4

Parameters	Change ratio							
	-10	-7	-4	-1	1	4	7	10
Concrete slab thickness	2.09	1.46	0.83	0.20	-0.21	-0.84	-1.47	-2.10
Concrete slab width	2.09	1.46	0.83	0.20	-0.21	-0.84	-1.47	-2.10
Upper flange thickness	0.06	0.04	0.02	0.00	-0.01	-0.03	-0.05	-0.07
Upper flange width	0.06	0.04	0.02	0.00	-0.01	-0.03	-0.05	-0.07
Web thickness	10.88	7.37	4.08	0.99	-0.97	-3.77	-6.41	-8.90
Web height	10.88	7.37	4.08	0.99	-0.97	-3.77	-6.41	-8.90
Lower flange thickness	0.22	0.15	0.09	0.02	-0.03	-0.09	-0.16	-0.23
Lower flange width	0.22	0.15	0.09	0.02	-0.03	-0.09	-0.16	-0.23

2.4 Maximum Converted Stress Change of Steel Beam Web

It can be seen from Tab. 5 that the sensitivity of the web converted stress is similar to that of the lower flange stress of the steel beam.

Conversion Stress Change Table of the D Control Point (unit: %) Tab. 5

Parameters	Change Ratio							
	-10	-7	-4	-1	1	4	7	10
Concrete slab thickness	1.01	0.91	0.81	0.71	0.61	0.51	0.41	0.31
Concrete slab width	1.97	1.78	1.58	1.38	1.18	0.98	0.79	0.59
Upper flange thickness	0.05	0.04	0.04	0.03	0.03	0.02	0.02	0.01
Upper flange width	0.15	0.13	0.12	0.10	0.09	0.07	0.06	0.04
Web thickness	-1.80	-1.63	-1.46	-1.28	-1.11	-0.93	-0.75	-0.56
Web height	-8.63	-7.83	-7.02	-6.19	-5.35	-4.50	-3.63	-2.75
Lower flange thickness	-5.94	-5.38	-4.82	-4.25	-3.67	-3.08	-2.48	-1.88
Lower flange width	-6.07	-5.51	-4.93	-4.34	-3.75	-3.15	-2.54	-1.92

2.5 Deflection Changes of Main Beam Mid-span

It is found from Tab. 6 that the change of the web height has the greatest influence on the deflection of the main beam. The variation of concrete slab thickness, concrete slab width, lower flange thickness, lower flange width, and web thickness has a certain influence on the mid-span deflection of the main beam, and the sensitivity of the mid-span deflection to the variation of the upper flange thickness and the upper flange width Lower.

Deflection Change Table of Main Beam Mid-span (unit: %) Tab. 6

Parameters	Change Ratio							
	-10	-7	-4	-1	1	4	7	10
Concrete slab thickness	4.73	3.25	1.83	0.45	-0.44	-1.74	-3.00	-4.22
Concrete slab width	3.26	2.22	1.24	0.30	-0.30	-1.16	-1.99	-2.78
Upper flange thickness	0.36	0.25	0.14	0.04	-0.04	-0.14	-0.25	-0.36
Upper flange width	0.15	0.11	0.06	0.02	-0.02	-0.06	-0.11	-0.15
Web thickness	1.24	0.86	0.49	0.12	-0.12	-0.48	-0.84	-1.19
Web height	21.29	14.27	7.82	1.88	-1.83	-7.03	-11.84	-16.30
Lower flange thickness	5.86	4.01	2.24	0.55	-0.54	-2.11	-3.62	-5.06
Lower flange width	5.67	3.87	2.16	0.53	-0.52	-2.04	-3.49	-4.88

Through the above analysis, for the thickness and width of concrete, the normal stress of control point A is the most sensitive. For the width and thickness of the upper flange of the steel beam, the mid-span deflection is the most sensitive, but the sensitivity is low. The most sensitive index for the height of the web is the mid-span deflection. The most sensitive index for the thickness of the web is the shear stress at the control point F. The most sensitive index for the variation of the thickness and width of the lower flange is the normal stress at the control point E. When the error between the thickness and width of the concrete slab is positive, it is beneficial to control the stress of point A, but is not conducive to the normal stress of point E. The control point A and the control point E restrict each other.

3 Reliability-based Construction Error Control Range of Section Geometry

3.1 Reliability Calculation Method

Monte Carlo method (P, 2011; Zou, 1998) is a method that uses numerical simulation technology to solve practical engineering problems related to random variables. In the reliability analysis, it can directly obtain the failure probability of the structure or component, and then obtain the reliability index by $P_f = \varphi(-\beta)$. According to the reference (He, 2014), the concept of construction reliability is used to measure the rationality of the error control range. Construction reliability refers to the probability that the structure will reach the limit state of the design target after construction is completed.

In the analysis of the reliability of bridge structure, the resistance of structural members is an extremely important basic variable. Structural resistance is the result of many factors acting simultaneously, so it is difficult to accurately analyse many factors for resistance calculation. Therefore, the calculation of resistance in the design specification generally only considers the structural geometry and material properties. Therefore, when calculating resistance, the following three factors should be used to calculate the statistical parameters:

(1) Uncertainty of component material performance.
(2) Uncertainty of component geometric parameters.
(3) Uncertainty of component calculation mode.

3.2 Selection of Section Geometric Statistical Parameters and Material Statistical Parameters

The cross-section geometric statistical parameters and member material statistical parameters of the steel-concrete composite structure are obtained through the literature (Li, 2007) and the specification (Ministry of Communications of the People's Republic of China, 1999). Tab. 7 and Tab. 8 show the statistical characteristics of each random variable.

Statistical Characteristics of Section Geometry Tab. 7

Random Variables	Distribution type	Measured average value/ standard value	Coefficient of Variation
Concrete slab thickness	Normal distribution	1.0121	0.0835
Concrete slab width	Normal distribution	1.0019	0.0076
Steel plate thickness	Normal distribution	0.979	0.022
Steel flange width	Normal distribution	1.005	0.011
Steel beam web height	Normal distribution	1.003	0.011

Statistical Properties of Material Strength Tab. 8

Random Variables	Distribution Type	Measured average value/ standard value	Coefficient of Variation
Concrete C50	Normal distribution	1.3877	0.0942
Q345 Yield Strength	Normal distribution	1.132	0.032

Since the statistical characteristics of the elastic modulus of materials are not given in the specification (Ministry of Communications of the People's Republic of China, 1999), the statistical characteristics of the elastic modulus of concrete in Tab. 9 are selected by literature (Wang, 2004), and the statistical characteristics of the elastic modulus of steel are selected by literature Bin,2018;Gao,2012;Yan,2015;zhao,2011.

Statistical Properties of Material Elastic Modulus   Tab. 9

Random variables	Distribution type	Measured average value/ standard value	Coefficient of variation
C50 Concrete Elastic Modulus	Normal distribution	1.1962	0.051
Q345 Steel Elastic Modulus	Normal distribution	1.0621	0.0267

3.3 Preliminary Limitation of the Control Range of Section Size error

Now there are relevant specifications(M. o. C. o. t. P. s. R. o. China. 2011; Ministry of Communications of the People's Republic of China,2015b; Ministry of Communications of the People's Republic of China,2017; M. o. H. a. U. -R. D. o. t. P. s. R. o. China,2008) to take values for the control limits of construction errors in component section dimensions. Refer to these specifications and according to the main control indicators of steel-concrete composite beams, and take the error control range that is more favourable to the control indicators as the initial value of the calculation according to the sensitivity analysis in section 3. See Tab. 10 for specific values.

Initial Value of Cross-section Size Error Control Range   Tab. 10

Item	Change size	Allowable deviation(mm)
1	Concrete beam flange width	(-3, +3)
2	Concrete beam flange thickness	(0, +5)
3	Steel beam flange width	(-3, +3)
4	Steel beam web height	(-2, +2)
5	Overall height of beam	(-2, +2)
6	Steel plate thickness 16mm	(-0.65, +0.65)

According to the provisions of the construction inspection standards, the general control index construction error must meet the pass rate of 80%, and the important index must meet the pass rate of 95%. Then, since the distribution of section size and material properties obey normal distribution, and normal distribution parameters are only two unknowns of mean and standard deviation, a normal distribution can be determined according to the qualified rate and error control range. Therefore, it is necessary to assume a normal distribution to calculate the mean and variance of the section size distribution parameters.

According to the principle of reliability, increasing the standard deviation will reduce the reliability. Therefore, when the standard deviation is assumed, the largest standard deviation that satisfies the qualification rate is selected safely to calculate the structural construction reliability corresponding to different construction error control ranges.

Based on the above assumptions, the standard deviation of the section size corresponding to the different cross-section size error control ranges is shown in the Tab. 11.

The Standard Deviation of the Section Size Corresponding to the Different Cross-section Size Error Control Range   Tab. 11

Varible	Allowable deviation(mm)	Standard deviation
Width of concrete beam flange and slab	(-3, +3)	2.340912
Thickness of concrete beam flange and slab	(0, +5)	1.275533

continue

Varible	Allowable deviation(mm)	Standard deviation
Steel beam flange width	(−3, +3)	2.340912
Steel beam web height	(−2, +2)	1.560608
Beam height	(−2, +2)	1.560608
Steel plate thickness 16mm	(−0.65, +0.65)	0.331638

3.4 Calculation of Normal Stress Reliability

It can be seen from the specification that the flexural bearing capacity should meet the following Eq. (1):

$$\gamma_0 \sigma \leqslant f \tag{1}$$

Where, γ_0 is the bridge importance factor; σ is the section normal stress; f is the design value of steel bar, steel beam or concrete strength.

Therefore, the performance function can be written as Eq. (2):

$$g(R,S) = \gamma_0 \sigma - f \tag{2}$$

When the error control range are all within the range of Tab. 10, the number of times of Monte Carlo simulation is taken as 100 million. The probability that the normal stress of the lower flange of the I-beam is less than 0 is 0.99906; the probability that the normal stress of the upper flange of the concrete is less than 0 is 0.99998. It shows that the error control range of the thickness and width of the concrete slab have met the requirements of the flexural bearing capacity of the section.

3.5 Calculation of Shear Stress Reliability

It can be seen from the specification that the shear capacity should meet the requirements of the Eq. (3):

$$\gamma_0 \tau \leqslant f \tag{3}$$

Where, γ_0 is the bridge importance factor; σ is the Section shear stress; f is the design value of steel bar, steel beam or concrete strength.

Therefore, the performance function can be written as the Eq. (4):

$$g(R,S) = \gamma_0 \tau - f \tag{4}$$

When the error control range are all within the range of Tab. 10, the reliability of the limit equation 4 is solved by the Monte Carlo method, and the number of simulations is 100 million times, and the probability that the performance function is less than 0 is 0.99587. It shows that the error control range of web thickness and web width meet the requirements of shear capacity.

3.6 Calculation of Reliability of Construction Deflection

For the deflection, the construction error control range of the section size should be determined to ensure that the construction quality should meet the design requirements, that is, the structure deflection after construction is less than the design deflection, so the performance function can be written as the Eq. (5):

$$g(f_{construction}, f_{design}) = f_{construction} - f_{design} \tag{5}$$

When the error control range are in the range of Tab. 10, the reliability of the limit equation 5 is solved by the Monte Carlo method, and the number of simulations is 100 million times, and the probability that the performance function is less than 0 is 0.99890. It shows that the error control range of the web height meets the requirements of the serviceability limit state. It can be seen from the above analysis that the error control range of the web height is already strict for the reliability of the serviceability limit state of this project.

4 Conclusion

Based on the above analysis, without considering factors such as the difficulty of construction, only considering the influence of the geometrical dimension error of the cross-section on the ultimate state and serviceability limit state of the bridge's bearing capacity, the construction error control range of the simple-supported I-shaped composite beam section size is initially used Tab. 12 shows the error control range.

The Construction Error Control Range of the Simple-supported I-shaped Composite Beam　　Tab. 12

Item	Variable	Error control range(mm)
1	Width of concrete beam flange and slab	(−3, +3)
2	Thickness of concrete beam flange and slab	(0, +5)
3	Steel beam flange width	(−3, +3)
4	Steel beam web height	(−2, +2)
5	Beam height	(−2, +2)
6	Steel plate thickness	Meet the requirements of specification (The General Administration of Quality Supervision, 2006)

The paper analyses the sensitivity of the cross-section stress and mid-span deflection of the main beam to changes in cross-section dimensions, and obtains the control indicators of the geometric dimensions of each cross-section. Then, through the analysis of the influence of the error control range of different cross-section dimensions on the reliability of the control indicators, the error control range of the construction of the cross-section dimensions are preliminarily formulated. Finally, the following conclusions are reached in this chapter:

(1) The error control range of the existing cross-sectional dimensions has been stricter, and the reliability of the corresponding control index calculated by using the minimum error control range in each specification is greater than 99.0%.

(2) Comparison of the coefficient of variation of the control index of the error control range corresponding to the section size and the coefficient of variation of the material found that the variability of material quality has a greater impact on construction reliability.

(3) Through analysis, the construction error control range of the simple-supported I-shaped composite beam section size as shown in Tab. 12 is initially formulated. The error control range of the concrete slab width and the steel beam web height in the table is strict and can be relaxed first; the error control range of the concrete slab thickness and the steel beam bottom plate width is moderate and can be adjusted appropriately; the error control range of the steel plate thickness should be strictly controlled.

The deficiency of this paper is that only simply supported beams are considered. Whether this criterion is equally applicable to continuous beams remains to be studied. Besides, due to the limitation of the length of the paper, the wheel load effects and cross beams are not included to check the response of concrete slabs. A further explanation is needed.

References

[1] Bin, T. X. Z. H. D. Reliability analysis of bridge static deflection of prestressed concrete simply supported beams[J]. Journal of Lanzhou University of Technology, 2018, 44(01), 128-132.

[2] China, M. o. C. o. t. P. s. R. o. GB/T 50283—1999. Unified Standard for Structural Reliability Design of Highway Engineering[S]. China Planning Press, 1999.

[3] China, M. o. C. o. t. P. s. R. o. GB 50205—2001 Steel Structure Engineering Construction Quality Acceptance Standard[S]. Beijing: China Standards Press, 2001.

[4] China, M. o. C. o. t. P. s. R. o. JTGT F50—2011 Technical Specification for Construction of Highway Bridges and Culverts[S]. Beijing: People's Communications Publishing House, 2011.

[5] China, M. o. C. o. t. P. s. R. o. JTG D62—2012 Specification for Design of Highway Reinforced Concrete and Prestressed Concrete Bridges and Culverts[S]. Beijing: People's Communications Press,2012.

[6] China, M. o. C. o. t. P. s. R. o. JTG D64—2015 Design Specification for Highway Steel Structure Bridges [S]. Beijing: People's Communications Press,2015.

[7] China, M. o. C. o. t. P. s. R. o. JTG/T D64-01—2015 Specification for Design and Construction of Highway Steel-Concrete Composite Bridges[S]. Beijing: People's Communications Press,2015.

[8] China, M. o. C. o. t. P. s. R. o. JTG F80/1—2017 Highway Engineering Quality Inspection and Evaluation Standard[S]. Beijing: People's Communications Press,2017.

[9] China, M. o. H. a. U.-R. D. o. t. P. s. R. o. CJJ 2—2008 Specification for Construction and Quality Acceptance of Urban Bridge Engineering[S]. Beijing: China Building Industry Press,2008.

[10] China, M. o. H. a. U.-R. D. o. t. P. s. R. o. GB 50661—2011 Steel Structure Welding Specification[S]. Beijing: China Construction Industry Press,2011.

[11] Gao, G. Research on seismic probability risk assessment of single-layer spherical reticulated shell structure[D]. Harbin:Harbin Institute of Technology,2012.

[12] He, H. Construction reliability analysis and parameter control of bearing capacity of highway prestressed concrete bridges[D]. Shanghai:Tongji University,2014.

[13] Li, K. Research on Probabilistic Limit State Design Method of Highway Steel Bridge Based on Reliability Theory[D]. Shanghai:Tongji University,2007.

[14] Nie, J. Steel-concrete composite structure[M]. Beijing: China Building Industry Press,2011.

[15] Nie, J. Steel-concrete composite structure bridge[M]. Beijing:People's Communications Press,2011.

[16] P, R. R. Y. K. D. Simulation and the Monte Carlo method[M]. John Wiley&Sons,2011.

[17] The General Administration of Quality Supervision, I. a. Q. o. t. P. s. R. o. C. Hot-rolled steel plate and steel strip size, shape, weight and allowable deviation:GB T709—2006. Beijing: China Standard Press,2006.

[18] Wang, W. Research on probability model of resistance of concrete cable-stayed bridge during construction period[D]. Changsha:Changsha University of Science and Technology,2004.

[19] Yan, S. Experimental study on high temperature creep properties of steel[D]. Chongqing:Chongqing University,2015.

[20] Zhao, G. Research on the stability performance of Q345GJ steel H-section axial compression members [D]. Chongqing:Chongqing University,2011.

[21] Zou, T. Structural reliability[M]. Beijing: People's Communications Press,1998.

Study on Shrinkage Properties of Stud Connectors for Steel-composite Beams

Changjiang Yu　Laijun Liu　Jie Zhang

(Highway College,Chang'an University)

Abstract　Aiming at the problem of insufficient mechanical properties of high-strength concrete under the constraint of a single row of studs, stud connectors of different sizes were designed through orthogonal experiments, and the shrinkage test of high-strength concrete under restraint was carried out to obtain the sensitive factors to the shrinkage of high-strength concrete. According to the test results, the relationship between the shrinkage performance of the high-strength concrete and the design parameters of the stud connectors is analyzed. A finite element model is established based on the test specimens and compared with the test results. Research indicates: The influence of the design parameters of a single row of studs on the shrinkage of high-strength concrete is as follows: the height of the studs > the spacing of the studs > the diameter of the studs; there is a stress concentration phenomenon at the junction of the concrete and the root of the stud, which is also the place where the concrete is prone to cracks.

Keywords Steel-concrete composite structure   High-strength concrete shrinkage   Stud connector

0 Introduction

The steel-concrete composite structure has excellent mechanical properties and is widely used in the construction of long-span bridges. Shear connectors are a key element to ensure the coordinated work of steel and concrete. In the field construction, the stud connector is widely used because of its convenient construction, economical application and good stress performance, as described by Luo [1] (2008) and Nie(1999)[2].

At present, domestic and foreign scholars have mostly studied the shear resistance or fatigue performance of shear connectors in steel-concrete combinations, and the results are quite fruitful. For example, Song et al.[3] (2019) explored the shear performance and failure mechanism of corrugated steel plate shear connectors in steel-concrete composite structures through push out tests of two types of shear connectors with and without holes; Liu et al.[4] (2017) studied the insufficient fatigue performance of the stud connectors in the steel-concrete composite bridge deck system. According to the results of the finite element model and the model fatigue test, the fatigue performance of the stud connector is evaluated, and the fatigue stress characteristics of the stud are analyzed; Li et al.[5] (2017) studied the shear resistance mechanism and bearing capacity of shear studs in prefabricated steel-concrete composite bridges on the basis of the introduction test.

The steel-concrete composite structure has a significant disease, and the shrinkage of the concrete causes the pavement to crack and damage. There are two main factors affecting the shrinkage performance of concrete. One important reason is the shrinkage stress of the concrete itself, and the other is the influence of internal constraints such as studs on its shrinkage. So far, no effective solutions have been found for crack control of concrete slabs of steel-concrete composite structures. The analysis of the crack resistance of the steel-concrete composite structure is still based on the research results of reinforced concrete. Kang[6] (2010) selected the actual concrete mix ratio of the project, studied the difference in shrinkage between plain concrete and reinforced concrete, and gave an estimation formula for early restrained shrinkage after concrete reinforcement. Zhang et al.[7] (2014) compared the shrinkage of reinforced concrete and plain concrete through experiments and obtained the influence of steel bars on the shrinkage strain of concrete columns. This leads to the conclusion that reinforced concrete is not necessarily applicable to steel-concrete composite structures.

This paper is based on the actual background project: a steel-concrete composite structure cable-stayed bridge. The superstructure of the bridge is mostly composed of studs and high-strength concrete. The studs are welded on the upper plate of the I-beam steel beam. Through the combination of studs and cast-in-place wet-joint high-strength concrete, the wet-joint high-strength concrete and the precast bridge deck are connected together. The precast prestressed concrete slab and steel beam are stressed together. It is particularly important to study the effect of studs on the shrinkage of high strength concrete in the whole bridge.

Therefore, this paper analyzes the complex constraints and characteristics of steel-concrete composite structure through experiments and finite element simulation. The influence of stud restraint on shrinkage of high strength concrete was studied. It provides a reference for the influence of stud and high strength concrete on the shrinkage performance of steel-concrete composite structure.

1 Experimental Study on shrinkage Properties of High Strength Concrete Specimens with Single Row Studs

1.1 Experimental Design and Implementation

1.1.1 Experimental Study on basic Mechanical Properties of high Strength Concrete

The basic mechanical property test includes the compressive strength and elastic modulus of high-strength concrete. C60 high-strength concrete was used in the test, and the mix proportion was described by Feng[8] (2017). The test blocks were cube blocks with 150mm side length, and there were 3 test blocks in each group. The test time was 3d, 7d, 14d, 21d and 28d, respectively. The test block specification for testing compressive strength is a rectangular test block with 150mm × 150mm × 300mm side length, with 3 test blocks in each group. The test time was also 3d, 7d, 14d, 21d, and 28d.

1.1.2 Test on the Factors Influencing the Shrinkage of High Strength Concrete by Studs

The orthogonal experimental design method described by Chen[9] (2005) was used in the experiment. Nine test schemes are obtained through the intersection of three different factors. In addition, test block No. 0 is plain concrete, and test block No. 10 is the control group of stud No. 9 after oil brushing treatment, which is used to simulate the non friction state between stud covered with paint and high strength concrete in the construction site, as shown in Tab. 1 below.

Types of Test Blocks for Orthogonal design Experiment Tab. 1

Numbering	Stud Diameter(mm)	Stud Height(mm)	Stud Spacing(mm)
0(Plain Concrete)	—	—	—
1	14(18)	40	150
2	14(18)	60	200
3	14(18)	80	250
4	18(24)	40	200
5	18(24)	60	250
6	18(24)	80	150
7	22(30)	40	250
8	22(30)	60	150
9	22(30)	80	200
10(Brushing Treatment)	22(30)	80	200

2 Test Results and Analysis

2.1 Results and Analysis of Basic Mechanical Properties of High-strength Concrete

In the experiment, all the test blocks were cured under the same conditions, and the tests of the compressive strength and elastic modulus of the high concrete test blocks were counted.

（1）The compressive strength data (The denominator represents the relative value of the 28-day compressive strength) of high-strength concrete is shown in Tab. 2. The compressive strength of concrete increases monotonously with age. The growth rate slows down and tends to converge. The early strength development accounts for the largest proportion, and the hydration reaction is the most active. Therefore, in actual projects, the pre-maintenance of concrete is particularly important to avoid early cracking of high-strength concrete.

(2) The compressive strength data (the denominator represents the value of the relative 28-day compressive strength) of high-strength concrete is shown in Tab. 3. The compressive strength of concrete increases monotonously with age. The growth rate slows down and tends to converge. And the development of early elastic modulus accounts for the largest proportion. The higher the elastic modulus is, the higher shrinkage and deformation stress will appear in the high strength concrete, which is unfavorable to the prevention and treatment of early age cracks.

Types of Test Blocks in Orthogonal Design Test Tab. 2

Compressive strength (MPa)					
Curing Time	3d	7d	14d	21d	28d
Mean Compressive Strength	40.1/59.7	52.5/78.1	56.33/83.8	61.66/91.7	67.2/100

Elastic Modulus of Concrete at Different Ages Tab. 3

Modulus of elasticity (GPa)					
Curing Time	3d	7d	14d	21d	28d
Modulus of elasticity	32.2/83.0	34.5/88.9	35.8/92.3	37.5/96.6	38.8/100

2.2 Orthogonal Test Results of Restraining High Strength Concrete by Studs

2.2.1 Influence of The Presence or Absence of Studs on The Shrinkage Value of High-strength Concrete

The specimens were cured for 28 days at 20 ± 2 (℃) and 60 ± 5 (%) relative humidity. According to the shrinkage strain of each age, draw the broken line chart as shown in Fig. 1.

(1) As can be seen from Fig. 1, the 7d shrinkage value of high strength concrete under the constraint of studs is less than that of plain high strength concrete. The shrinkage value of 10 groups of test blocks can reach 60% of the peak shrinkage value on 28 days, so the early shrinkage of high-strength concrete is serious. In order to reduce the shrinkage in engineering practice, it is necessary to set reasonable reinforcement.

(2) It can be seen from the broken line diagram in Fig. 1 that the shrinkage trend of high-strength concrete (No. 1-9) under stud restraint is roughly the same as that of plain high-strength concrete (No. 0) within 28 days. The

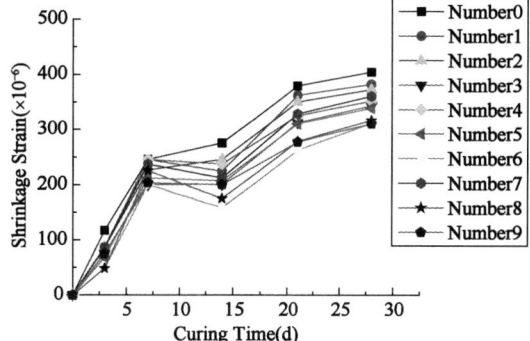

Fig. 1 Broken Line Diagram of Shrinkage of Concrete at Different Ages

shrinkage rate is the fastest in the first 7 days, and reaches the peak in 7 days. After that, it begins to expand slightly in 7 days. After 14 days, the high-strength concrete begins to shrink further, which is the main reason After 28 days, the shrinkage of high strength concrete reaches the maximum. The shrinkage value of high-strength concrete restrained by studs is always less than that of plain high-strength concrete, and the studs always have inhibitory effect on the shrinkage of high-strength concrete. The shrinkage value of high-strength concrete in each age stage is different with the diameter, height and spacing of studs, which can be roughly divided into: the shrinkage value of high-strength concrete in groups 1, 2 and 7 is larger, the shrinkage value of high-strength concrete in groups 3, 4 and 5 is moderate, and the shrinkage value of high-strength concrete in groups 6, 8 and 9 is smaller.

2.2.2 Influence of Stud Design Parameters on Shrinkage Value of High Strength Concrete

According to the data of groups 4 and 7 in Tab. 4, the influence of stud spacing on shrinkage of high strength concrete is greater than that of stud diameter on shrinkage of high strength concrete. From the data of the first group and the third group, the effect of stud spacing on the shrinkage of high-strength concrete is less than that of stud height on the shrinkage of high-strength concrete. Among the three influencing factors of stud diameter, height and spacing, the influence on high strength concrete is as follows: stud height > stud spacing > stud diameter.

Types and 28d Shrinkage of Four Groups of Test Blocks Tab. 4

Numbering	Diameter(mm)	Height(mm)	Spacing(mm)	Shrinkage strain(ε_{st}) $\times 10^{-6}$
1	14(18)	40	150	382.35
3	14(18)	80	250	343.48
4	18(24)	40	200	352.17
7	22(30)	40	250	360.87

2.2.3 Relationship between Stud Restraint Rate and Shrinkage of High Strength Concrete

Feng (2017) gave the calculation formula of constraint rate:

$$C = \frac{\varepsilon_t}{\varepsilon_f} \times 100\% \tag{1}$$

In the formula: ε_t ——The strain value of concrete which can't contract freely after being restrained;

ε_f ——The shrinkage strain of concrete in free state.

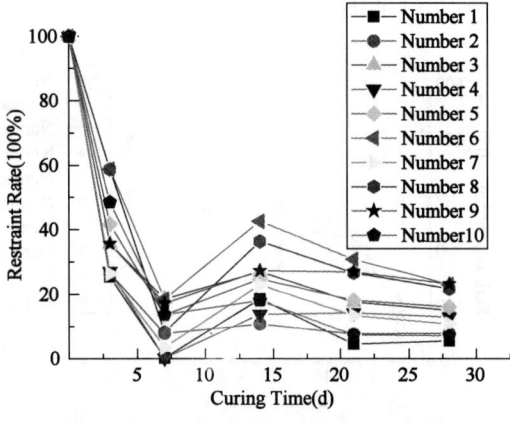

Fig. 2 Line Chart of Constraint Degree of Each Test Block at Different Ages

The constraint rate of each test block at different ages was obtained by using the constraint rate calculation formula, as shown in Fig. 2. Within the 28d age, the constraint of the pin on concrete firstly decreased, then increased, and finally tended to be stable and reached the state of convergence. In the first 7 days of age, the restraint effect of studs on high-strength concrete decreases rapidly. From 7d to 21d, the restraint effect of stud on high-strength concrete fluctuates in a certain range. From 7d to 14d, it can be seen that the restraint rate has an upward trend, which is that the concrete has entered the expansion period. Finally, it reached a stable state between 21d and 28d. It can be known that the best inhibition effect of single row studs on the shrinkage performance of high-strength concrete is in the first three days, and then the inhibition effect decreases and tends to be stable. In actual construction, the restraint rate of studs on concrete can be enhanced by changing the spacing, diameter and length of studs.

2.2.4 Influence of Stud Bond on Shrinkage Value of High Strength Concrete

In the test, oil painting was used to simulate the stud situation in the actual construction. According to the shrinkage strain values of groups 0, 9 and 10, the broken line Fig. 3 was drawn. According to the shrinkage rates of groups 9 and 10 at different ages, the broken line Fig. 4 was drawn..

(1) It can be seen from Fig. 3 that the shrinkage value after 28d of No. 9 (stud without painting) is 76.84% of that after 28d of No. 0 (plain high-strength concrete), and the shrinkage value after 28d of No. 10 (stud painting) is 92.92% of that after 28d of No. 0 (plain high-strength concrete). The results show that the stud has a great influence on the shrinkage of high strength concrete after 28 days.

(2) It can be seen from Fig. 3 that from 0d to 7d, the shrinkage value curves of No. 9 (unpainted stud) and No. 10 (stud painting) are close to each other, while from 7d to 28d, the shrinkage strain of No. 10 (stud painting) is significantly higher than that of No. 9 (unpainted stud). This shows that there is almost no influence on the shrinkage of high strength concrete in the early age, and the inhibition effect of oil painting is enhanced in the later age.

(3) It can be seen from Fig. 4 that there is no significant difference in the restraint rate of stud for high-strength concrete between No. 9 (unpainted stud) and No. 10 (stud painting) from 0 to 7 days. From 7d to 28d, the restraint rate of No. 9 was significantly different from that of No. 10, and gradually increased. At 28d, the restraint rate of No. 9 was 16.08% higher than that of No. 10.

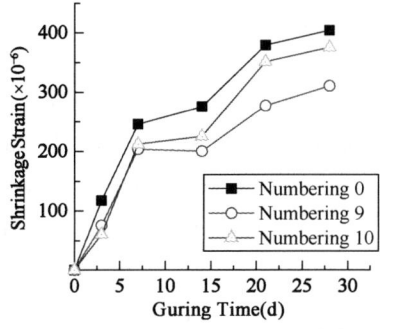

Fig. 3 Broken Line Diagram of Shrinkage of Three Groups of High Strength Concrete

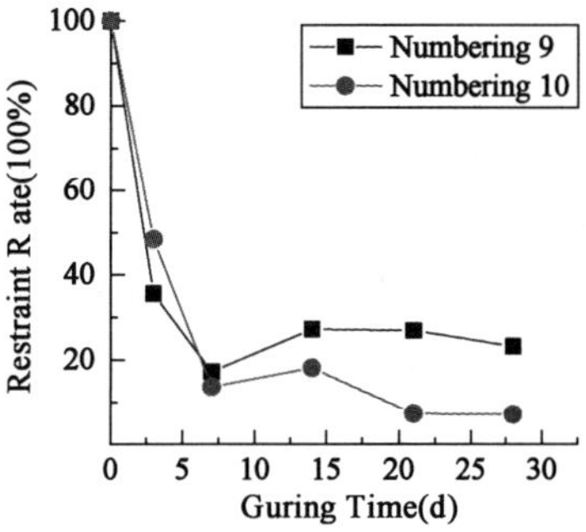

Fig. 4 Line Chart of Restraint Degree of Two Groups of High Strength Concrete

Through the comparison of the above test results, it can be concluded that the shrinkage inhibition and restraint rate of high strength concrete are significantly reduced. Before pouring concrete on site, the surface of stud should be painted to reduce the cracking of high strength concrete.

2.2.5 Influence of different Stud Restraint Ratio on Shrinkage Value of Middle and End of High Strength Concrete

The shrinkage data of the middle and end of high-strength concrete under different stud types are analyzed and sorted out, and Tab. 5 and Tab. 6 are obtained, and the broken line Fig. 5-Fig. 8 is drawn.

(1) According to Fig. 5, the development trend of shrinkage strain of middle and end concrete of plain high-strength concrete is roughly the same, and the end shrinkage at 28d is slightly more than 1.24% of the middle shrinkage, which can be ignored. That is to say, in high-strength concrete constrained by different stud types, the difference of middle shrinkage and end shrinkage caused by the thickness of high-strength concrete itself can be ignored.

(2) According to the broken line Fig. 5-Fig. 8, the development trend of the shrinkage curve of the middle part and the end part of the specimen is consistent, and the shrinkage of the middle part is generally lower than that of the end part, which indicates that the restraint effect of the restraint strip is strong.

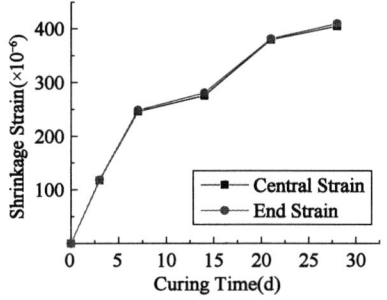 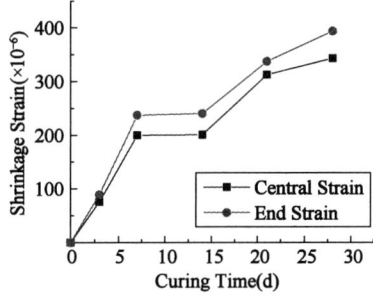

Fig. 5 Central and End Shrinkage Line Diagram of Group No. 0

Fig. 6 Central and End Shrinkage Line Diagrams of Group No. 3

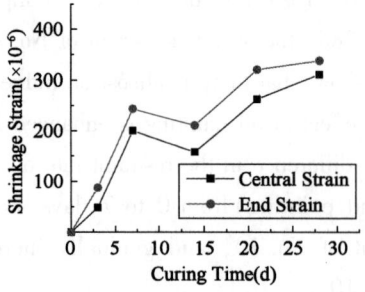
Fig. 7 Central and End Shrinkage Line Diagram of Group No. 6

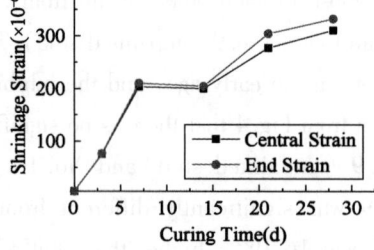
Fig. 8 Central and End Shrinkage Line Diagrams of Group No. 9

(3) According to the analysis in Tab. 6, with the increase of stud restraint effect, the middle and end contractions of the corresponding 28 day age decreased, and the mutual decreasing amplitude was also smaller, and the ratio of the difference to the middle was also smaller and smaller. The results showed that with the increase of the restraint effect of the stud, the restraint effect of the restraint band (the middle contraction zone) increased.

Comparison of Shrinkage at Middle and End of High Strength Concrete under Different Restraint Degrees   Tab. 5

Numbering	Place	Shrinkage strain(ε_{st}) $\times 10^{-6}$				
		3d	7d	14d	21d	28d
0	Central Strain	117.38	245.97	275.49	379.52	404.49
	End Strain	118.43	248.63	280.58	381.37	409.52
3	Central Strain	75.65	200.34	201.25	312.63	343.48
	End Strain	89.36	237.74	240.63	337.52	393.82
6	Central Strain	48.35	200.46	158.25	262.59	311.11
	End strain	87.63	243.74	210.98	320.63	338.35
9	Central Strain	75.53	203.63	200.36	277.37	310.71
	End Strain	76.36	210.32	204.72	304.25	332.46

Comparison of Shrinkage at Middle and End of Three Groups of Test Bocks   Tab. 6

Numbering	Central Shrinkage Strain (ε_{st}) $\times 10^{-6}$	End Contraction Strain (ε_{st}) $\times 10^{-6}$	Difference between end and middle (ε_{st}) $\times 10^{-6}$	Ratio of difference to middle (%)
3	343.48	393.82	50.34	14.7
6	311.11	338.35	27.24	8.76
9	310.71	332.46	21.25	6.84

3 Finite Element Analysis

3.1 Finite Element Model

3.1.1 Mechanical and Geometric Parameters of Materials

The mechanical properties of materials are shown in Tab. 7. The size of the finite element model is Group 9 in the test scheme. Geometric parameters are shown in Tab. 11, and other geometric dimensions are shown in Fig. 9.

Material Mechanical Property Parameters Tab. 7

Parameter Name	High-strength Concrete	Stud
Elastic Modulus(MPa)	experimental data	2.06×10^5
Density(kg/m³)	2368.4	7850
Coefficient of Linear Expansion	1×10^{-5}	1.2×10^{-5}
Poisson'sRatio	0.2	0.3

3.2 Finite Element Model Establishment

The finite element model was established by ANSYS. Solid65 solid element was used for both the pin and the high-strength concrete. It was assumed that the material of the high-strength concrete was uniform and the contact relationship between the isotropic pin and the pin was point-to-point non-slip connection, both of which were ideal elastic materials. The bottom surface of the thin steel plate under the boundary condition is set as completely fixed, and the free mesh division technology is used to mesh the model.

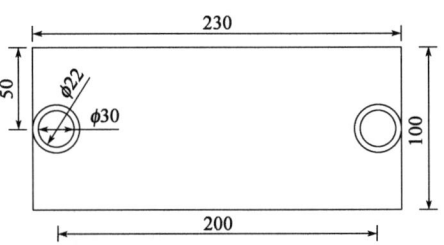

Fig. 9 Top View of No.9 Test Block (unit: mm)

In order to better simulate the actual situation, this paper uses the temperature method to convert the shrinkage of plain concrete in the test into temperature load. The calculation of the temperature method is shown in Eq. (2).

$$T(t) = \frac{\varepsilon_t}{\alpha_c} \quad (2)$$

In the formula: $T(t)$——Shrinkage temperature;

ε_t——Early shrinkage strain of concrete;

α_c——Coefficient of thermal expansion of concrete, value: 1×10^{-5}.

According to the above formula, concrete temperature load parameters can be set as shown in Tab. 8.

Temperature and Shrinkage Strain Tab. 8

Curing Time(d)	0	3	7	14	21	28
Shrinkage strain($\times 10^{-6}$)	0	117	246	275	380	404
Temperature(℃)	0	-11.7	-24.6	-27.5	-38.0	-40.4

3.3 Finite Element Analysis Results

3.3.1 Comparison and Analysis of Finite Element Simulation Results and Test Results

The axial displacement of this model at 0-28d age is shown in Tab. 9. Fig. 10 shows the ninth group of 28d age X-direction deformation schematic diagram.

(1) It can be seen from the Fig. 10 that the deformation and shrinkage of the 9th group in the X direction are symmetrical and the same size. This is because the studs at the bottom are in a consolidated state and the top is high-strength concrete in a free state, which also conforms to the theory of mechanics. The contraction of the left and right ends of the bottom of the test block is much smaller than that of the top ends of the test block. This is because the studs at the bottom are in a consolidated state and the top is in a free state of high-strength concrete, which is also in line with the theory of mechanics. From the analysis of the same section, except the middle part, it can be seen that the contraction at the bottom is smaller than that at the top. This is because the bottom surface of the studs at the bottom and the bottom surface of the high strength concrete are constrained, resulting in the effect of lag constraint, which is also consistent with the hypothesis of simulation.

(2) The contraction of the left and right center parts of the model was taken as the contraction result of the

simulation test and compared with the test result, as shown in Tab. 8. As can be seen from the table, the maximum absolute value error of the model and the test is 11.67%, the minimum is 2.57%, and the average absolute value error is 5.754%. The results are in good agreement, indicating that the model established in this paper is reliable. Therefore, it can be used to further analyze the stress of high-strength concrete under the restraints of studs in the 9th group test block.

Results and Test Results of High-strength Concrete under the Constraint of Studs in Group 9   Tab. 9

Curing Time(d)	3	7	14	21	28
Test shrinkage deformation($\times 10^{-6}$)	75.53	203.63	200.36	277.37	310.71
Model shrinkage deformation($\times 10^{-6}$)	68.61	227.39	195.22	270.00	319.13
Model error(%)	-9.16%	11.67%	-2.57%	-2.66%	2.71%

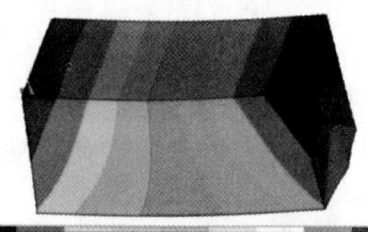

-.550E-04 -.306E-04 -.621E-05 -.182E-04 -.426E-04
-.428E-04 -.184E-04 -.599E-05 -.304E-04 -.548E-04

Fig. 10 *X*-direction Deformation Map of Group 9 at 28 Days of Age

3.3.2 Single Row Shrinkage Stress Analysis

The following is the stress of high strength concrete under the restraint of group 9 stud, as shown in Fig. 11 (unit: Pa). It can be seen from the bottom stress diagram that the maximum stress of high-strength concrete under the single row of studs is at the bottom of the studs, and the stress concentration occurs at the bottom of the studs. High stress also appears at the edge of the same side at the bottom of the single row of studs, which indicates that the restraint of the single row of studs has a certain range of restraint effect on the high strength concrete at the edge of the same side of the studs, which will produce large stress. It can also be seen that when the age develops from 0d to 28d, the stress at the bottom of the model is gradually approaching to the middle of the high-strength concrete from the bottom of the stud, and the range is larger and larger, which shows that with the increase of age, the stress effect of the single row of stud restraint on the high-strength concrete is more and more obvious, which verifies the correctness of the previous test conclusion.

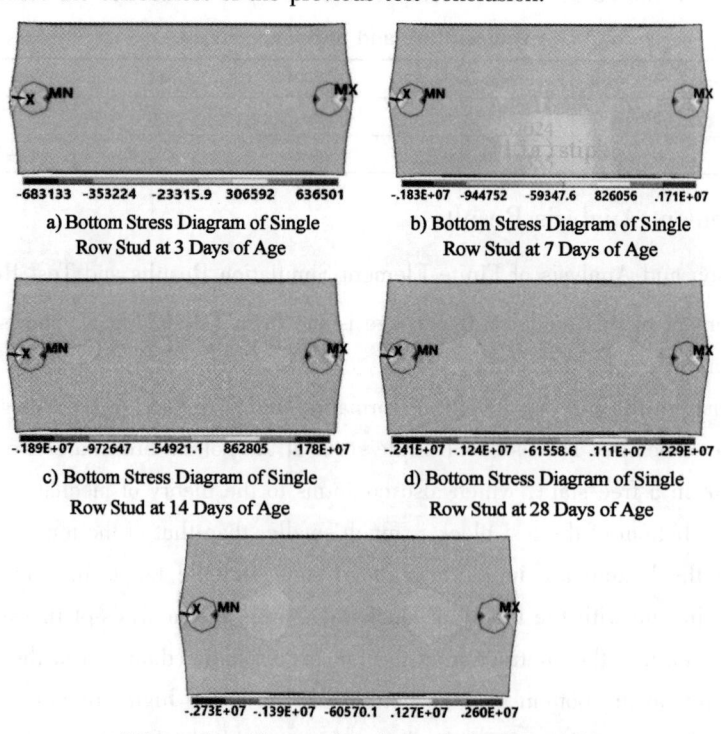

Fig. 11 Stress Diagram of Model No. 9 at Different Ages

4　Conclusion

In this study, the shrinkage behavior of high-strength concrete confined by studs is studied through the combination of experiment and finite element simulation:

(1) In the whole curing process of high strength concrete, the shrinkage of high strength concrete is restrained by studs. The shrinkage of any stud type of high-strength concrete and plain high-strength concrete at the age of 7 days (early stage) accounts for more than 60% of the shrinkage at 28 days, so the early shrinkage of high-strength concrete is more serious. The influence of stud on high strength concrete is as follows: stud height > stud spacing > stud diameter. With the increase of the restraint rate of the stud, the corresponding contraction of the middle and the end decreases, and the smaller the mutual reduction is, the stronger the restraint effect is.

(2) The results of finite element analysis show that the maximum stress of high-strength concrete under stud restraint is at the bottom of stud, and the stress concentration occurs at the bottom of stud. The deformation and shrinkage of high-strength concrete in X direction under stud restraint are symmetrical, and the shrinkage is basically the same. The shrinkage of the left and right ends at the bottom of the test block is much smaller than that at the top of the test block. From the same section, except for the middle, the shrinkage of the bottom is also smaller than that of the top, which indicates that there is a certain lag between the stud consolidation at the bottom and the concrete symmetric axis consolidation Bundle effect.

(3) In this paper, the model is simplified and the division of temperature difference is not detailed enough, so the temperature field can be used for calculation.

References

[1] Luo Yingzhang. Study on Stud Shear Connectors of Steel-concrete Composite Beams [D]. Central South University, 2008.

[2] Nie Jianguo, Tan Ying. Design and Calculation of Stud Shear Connectors in Steel High Strength Concrete Composite Beams [J]. Journal of Tsinghua University, 1999, 39, 94-97.

[3] Song Ruinian, Zhan Yulin. Push out Test and Numerical Analysis of Embedded Corrugated Steel Plate Shear Key [J]. Journal of China Highway, 2019, 32, 88-99.

[4] Liu Cheng, Fan Jiansheng. Fatigue Behavior of Stud Connectors in Steel Ultra High Performance Concrete Composite Bridge Deck System [J]. Journal of China Highway, 2019, 30, 139-146.

[5] Li Chengjun, Zhou Zhixiang. Study on Shear Capacity of Shear Studs in Fabricated Composite Beams [J]. Journal of China Highway, 2017, 30, 264-270.

[6] Kang Ming. Research on Restrained Shrinkage Deformation of Reinforced Concrete Members during Construction [D]. Chongqing University.

[7] Zhang Kai Cao Guohui. Experimental Study on Effect of Reinforcement on Long Term Shrinkage Strain of Concrete [J]. Highway Transportation Technology, 2014, 31, 78-81.

[8] Feng Chao. Experimental Study on Effect of Stud on Shrinkage of High Strength Concrete [D]. Chongqing University, 2017.

[9] Chen Kui. Experimental Design and Analysis[H]. Tsinghua University Press. 2005.

单向流及往复流作用下桩基局部冲刷研究

翁博文 郭 健 吴继熠

(浙江工业大学土木工程学院)

摘 要 局部冲刷是导致桥梁水毁的主要原因,研究桥梁桩基在单向流及往复流作用下局部冲刷特征具有重要意义。本文将通用数值模拟方法的结果与 Melville 经典冲刷试验的结果进行了比较,以验证该方法的有效性。基于实测数据和有效的数值模拟方法,建立了一座实桥的群桩模型,对单向流和潮流作用下桩周流场和冲刷特性进行了对比分析。研究发现:①单向流条件下冲刷坑表现出前冲后淤,往复流作用下冲刷坑的前后区域均表现出冲刷,且冲刷坑的范围大于单向流。②往复流条件下最大冲刷深度较单向流缩减了 20%~30%。

关键词 群桩 局部冲刷 数值仿真 单向流 往复流

0 引 言

桥梁是公路铁路交通的枢纽,桥梁的健康运营对交通运行安全、人民群众生活、社会经济效益有巨大的促进作用。涉水桥梁桩基础的阻水效应,会导致水流与泥沙相互作用发生变化,打破床面原有的泥沙运动平衡,在桥桩周围造成冲淤变化。桥桩局部冲刷的发生,不仅影响到桥梁所在水域床面的演变趋势,而且还威胁到桥梁结构本身的安全与稳定。虽然大部分跨海大桥建于近十几年,但由于跨海大桥一般跨度大,跨海桥梁基础所处的海域往往具有水深、浪高、潮大等水动力条件复杂的特点,涉及桥墩的局部冲刷相当频繁,冲刷现象更为严重,具有严重的安全隐患。

Shirhole 和 Holt[1]曾对截至 1991 年美国境内已毁的 823 座桥梁的毁坏原因及类型进行分析和统计,被冲刷毁坏的桥梁占毁坏桥梁总数的 60%。1966 年至 2005 年,美国交通安全委员会统计的 1502 座倒塌桥梁中[2],58% 的桥梁破坏是由桥梁基础结构冲刷病害及相关水力学作用引起的,每年因为桥梁冲刷破坏造成的经济损失高达 3000 万美元。Wardhana[3]对 1989 年至 2000 年间的 500 多起桥毁事故的原因进行统计分析,发现有 53% 的桥毁事故是由冲刷造成的。

自 20 世纪 90 年代起,学者们逐步开展桩基冲刷的相关研究[4-8],基于大量的试验及现场观测研究成果[9-10],得到了较为一致的结论,以圆柱形单桩为例,将桩周的流场特征分为以下四类:①桩前壅水;②桩前向下射流;③桩底马蹄形漩涡;④桩后尾流漩涡。Kwan 和 Melville[11]通过试验测量桩周的三维流场发现,桥桩上游存在下降水流及马蹄形漩涡,这两者是造成桩前局部冲刷的主要原因,除此以外,马蹄形漩涡附近还存在二次涡,旋转方向与马蹄形漩涡相反,削弱马蹄形漩涡的冲刷能力,桥桩下游由于边界层的分离存在向下游传播的尾涡体系。Dey 和 Barbhuiya[12]通过固化达到冲刷平衡的冲坑床面,测量得到冲坑内的三维流场,水流在桥桩上游侧发生离散,在竖直方向产生动水压力梯度,形成向下射流,旋转进入冲刷坑形成主漩涡流,研究表明马蹄形漩涡及下降水流是局部冲刷坑形成的主要原因,且局部冲刷坑的发展会导致马蹄形漩涡在冲坑内扩散。Melville[13]和 Ettema[14]将局部冲刷过程分为三个阶段:①冲刷起始阶段,桩底周围泥沙在马蹄形漩涡的作用下被水流吸收带走;②主要冲刷阶段,桩周上游的输沙率小于下游的输沙率,形成局部冲刷坑并不断发展③冲刷平衡阶段,随着冲刷深度的增加,桩底马蹄形漩涡强度下降,桩周上下游输沙率达到平衡,局部冲刷坑不再发展。国际上开展了大量桩基在单向流作用的冲刷

基金项目:浙江省交通科技计划项目(2020062);浙江省重点研发计划项目(2019C03098);国家自然科学基金项目(52078461,U1709207)。

研究,但对往复流作用下的桩基冲刷研究较少。

本文在上述研究基础上开展群桩在单向流及往复流作用下的冲刷研究,通过 FLOW-3D 模拟分析单向流及往复流作用下的桩周流场分布、局部冲刷深度、局部冲刷坑分布形态。

1 数值模型验证

1.1 泥沙输运方程

FLOW-3D 中的 sediment scour 模块通过计算泥沙的侵蚀、输送、沉积来预测泥沙运动,具体包括:计算水流中悬移质泥沙的输送;计算重力引起的泥沙沉降;计算床面剪切及水流紊动引起的泥沙挟带;计算推移质泥沙的输送,包括泥沙颗粒沿床面底部的滚动。

FLOW-3D 提供基于 Mastbergen 和 Van den Berg[15] 的经验输沙模型,包括推移质输沙率方程和悬移质输沙方程。

推移质输沙率方程:

$$g_b = \rho_n \beta \left[\frac{\tau - \tau_{cr}}{gd(\rho_n - \rho)} \right]^{3/2} \left[g\left(\frac{\rho_n - \rho}{\rho}\right) d^3 \right]^{1/2} \tag{1}$$

悬移质输沙方程:

$$\frac{\partial C_s}{\partial t} + \nabla \left\{ C_s \left[\bar{u} + \frac{g}{\|g\|} \left\{ (10.36^2 + 1.046 d_*^3)^{1/2} - 10.36 \right\} \frac{v_f}{d} c_s \right] \right\} = \nabla \cdot \nabla(DC_s) \tag{2}$$

式中:g_b——床面单宽推移质输沙率;

ρ_n——泥沙密度;

β——推移质系数;

d——泥沙直径;

d_*——泥沙无量纲颗粒直径;

C_s——悬沙质量密度;

$\bar{u}$——水沙混合物速度;

c_s——悬沙体积浓度;

D——扩散系数;

τ——床面剪切力;

τ_{cr}——临界床面剪切力。

冲刷模块根据 Soulsby-Whitehouse 公式计算临界 Shields 数,并考虑泥沙休止角对临界 Shields 数进坡度调整:

$$D_* = [g(s-1)/v^2]^{1/3} d \tag{3}$$

$$\theta_{cr} = \frac{0.30}{1 + 1.2 D_*} + 0.055[1 - \exp(-0.020 D_*)] \tag{4}$$

$$\theta'_{cr} = \theta_{cr} \frac{\cos\psi\sin\beta + \sqrt{\cos^2\beta\tan^2\varphi - \sin^2\psi\sin^2\beta}}{\tan\varphi} \tag{5}$$

式中:θ_{cr}——临界 Shields 数;

θ'_{cr}——修正后临界 Shields 数;

D_*——无量纲直径;

g——重力加速度;

s——泥沙相对密度；
υ——流体的黏性系数；
d——泥沙颗粒直径；
ψ——水流方向与逆坡方向的夹角；
β——床面坡度；
φ——泥沙休止角。

1.2 模型设置

本节采用 Melville 经典冲刷试验模型,进行数值模型的验证。试验水槽长 19m,宽 45.6cm,在水槽中间放置直径 5.08cm 的圆柱桩模型,床面铺设泥沙粒径为 0.385mm,具体试验布置见图 1,工况参数设置见表 1。按照试验模型尺寸建立与模型水槽同比尺的试验段数值模型,具体如下。

工 况 参 数 设 置　　　　　　　　　　表1

桩　　型	来流量($m^3 \cdot s^{-1}$)	水深(m)	来流平均流速($m \cdot s^{-1}$)	泥沙粒径(mm)
单桩圆柱形	0.01712	0.15	0.25	0.385

数值模型的边界条件设置如图 2 所示,入流边界设置为速度边界(specified velocity),保证来流以 0.25m/s 的流速均匀入流,出流边界设置为压力边界(specified pressure),控制出流边界处的水深防止边界处出现水位骤降现象,两侧边界设置为对称边界(symmetry),对称边界条件下水流流通量为零,流体剪切应力为零,保证水流不受两侧壁面的挤压,避免壁面效应的影响,底面边界设为壁面边界条件(wall),边界处流体的法向流速为零。

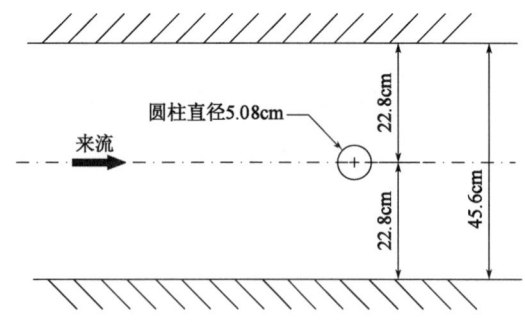
图1　Melville 冲刷试验模型布置图

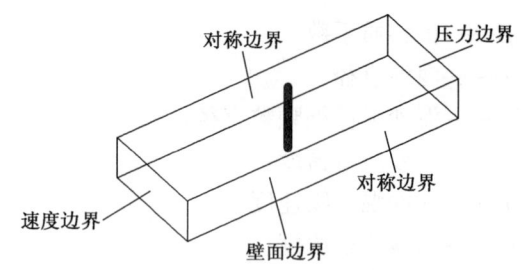
图2　模型边界条件设置

数值模型的计算域大小及网格划分如图 3 所示,计算域总宽度 9D,总长度 20D,圆柱形单桩位于计算域中心,距入流边界 6D,距出流边界 14D,网格划分采取嵌套网格的方法,对桩周进行局部加密,在保证计算精度的同时节省计算量,该验证数值模型共设置三层不同大小的网格块,相邻网格块之间网格尺度的比值为 1:2,网格密度由外向内逐渐增大,网格类型均为正六面体,网格总数为 1120392 个。

该验证数值模型初始时间步长取 0.001s,最小时间步长取 1×10^{-12} s,模拟总时长 1800s,采用二阶动量对流方程。

1.3 验证结果

数值模型的计算结果如图 4、图 5 所示,局部冲刷最大冲刷深度点出现在桩前,冲刷坑的范围不断增大,并逐渐延伸至桩后,在 25~30min,冲刷深度逐渐达到平衡冲刷深度 4.2cm,这与 Melville 室内试验冲刷深度 4cm 很接近。模拟所得局部冲刷坑的形态也与 Melville 室内试验所得结果大致吻合,局部冲刷最大值点出现在桩前。

综上对模拟结果与试验结果得对比分析,可见无论是局部冲刷坑的最大冲刷深度或是冲刷坑的分布形态,模拟结果与试验结果都有较高的吻合度,因此,该数值模型对局部冲刷的模拟具有较高的精度,所得计算结果是可靠的。

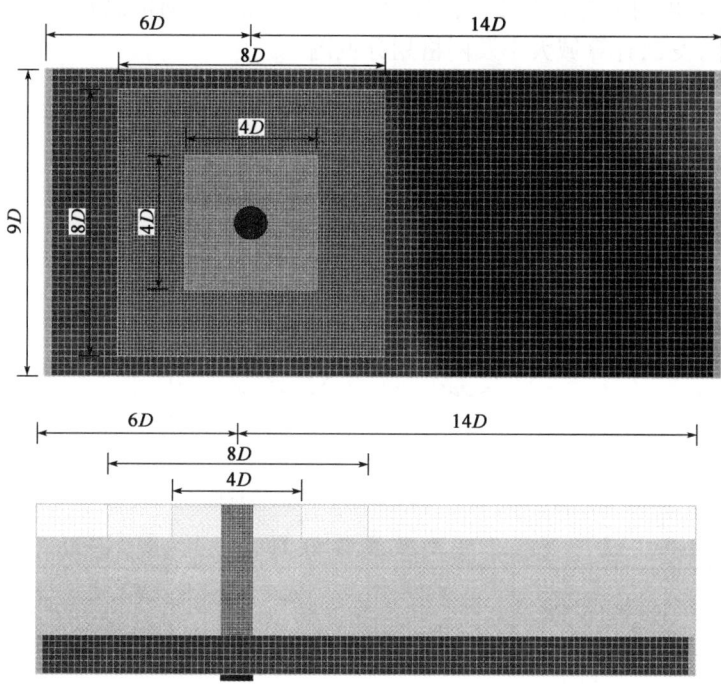

图 3 模型计算域大小及网格划分

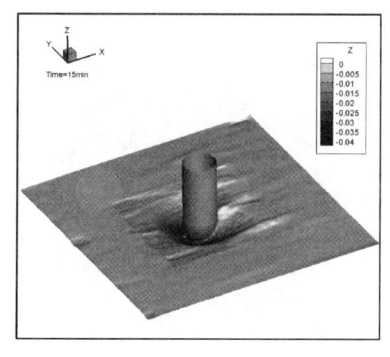
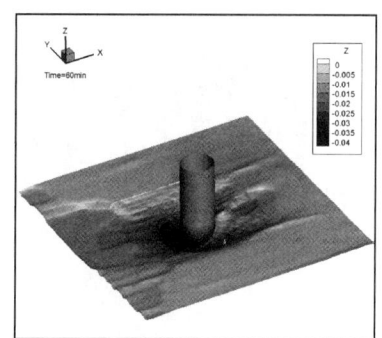

图 4 局部冲刷坑发展过程

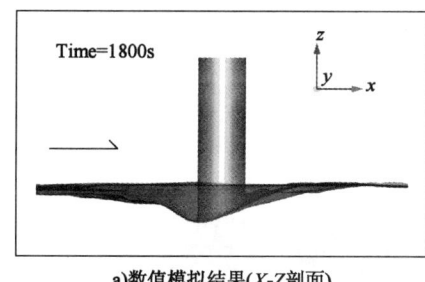
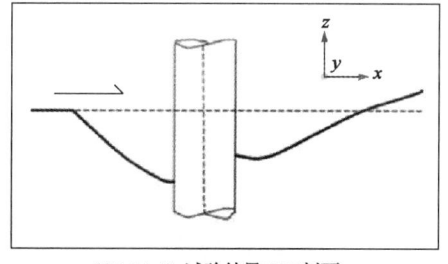

a) 数值模拟结果(X-Z剖面)   b) Melville试验结果(X-Z剖面)

图 5 冲刷坑形态对比

2 群桩局部冲刷数值模型建立

在模型验证的基础上，基于实桥群桩参数建立冲刷数值模型。群桩布置形式如图 6 所示。

模型设置如下：圆柱形单圆桩桩径为 2.5m，水深为 11m，水体动力黏滞系数为 0.001Pa·s，床面泥沙选用均匀沙，泥沙中值粒径为 0.049mm，泥沙相对密度为 2.71，泥沙休止角为 30°，泥沙表面粗糙高度为 $2.5d_{50}$，即 2.5 倍泥沙中值粒径，整个计算域长 40 倍桩径、宽 20 倍桩径，网格设置与 3.2 节中验证模型类似,采用三层嵌套网格对桩周进行局部加密,网格类型为正六面体,网格总数1473000。群桩基础局部冲刷模拟具体参数设置见表2,计算域大小及网格划分见图7。

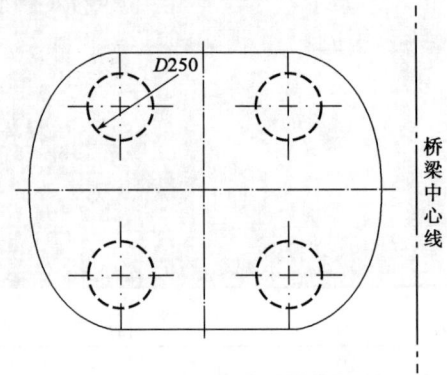

图6 典型群桩布置形式平面图(多桩梅花形)

工况参数设置 表2

工况	桩型	流向	直径(m)	水深(m)	来流平均流速(m·s^{-1})	泥沙粒径(mm)	泥沙相对密度
1	四桩串列	单向流	2.5	11	2.3	0.049	2.71
2	四桩串列	往复流	2.5	11	—	0.049	2.71

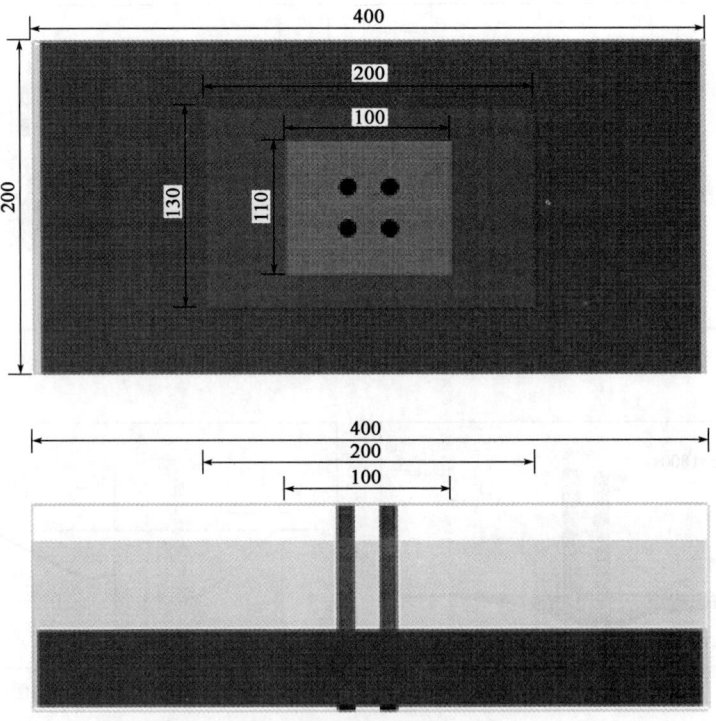

图7 模型计算域大小及网格划分:四桩串列型

本次模拟分为单向流及往复流两个工况:单向流条件下,来流平均流速为2.3m/s;往复流条件下,模型设置时变来流如图8所示,剩余包括数值虚拟水槽的边界条件设置、湍流模型选择等均与第1节验证模型保持一致。

该模型初始时间步长取0.001s,最小时间步长取1×10^{-12}s,模拟总时长60min,采用二阶动量对流方程,满足模型稳定性要求。

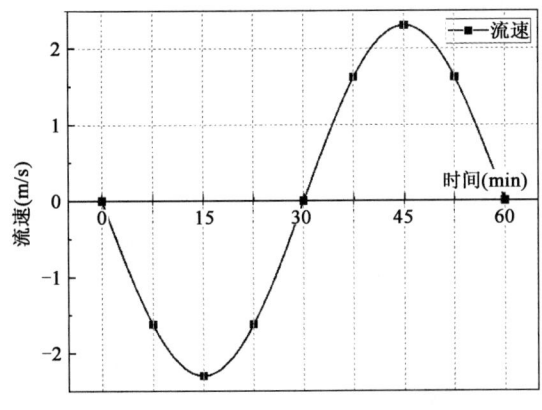

图 8　往复流条件下时变来流流速

3　单向流及往复流作用下局部冲刷数值分析

图 9 为单向流条件下冲刷起始阶段近床面纵向流速分布平面图。前排桩迎水面的流速分布与单桩类似,同样出现桩前水流减速,且由于桩径增大,阻水效应更加明显,桩侧水流出现绕流加速,前排双桩之间水流加速带出现重叠,桩间最大流速达到 2.45m/s;受前排桩的遮蔽效应影响,后排桩的桩前流速接近于零,桩侧水流同样出现绕流加速现象,然而加速水流的范围及流速大小都不及前排桩。

图 10 为单向流条件下冲刷起始阶段桩周流速分布纵剖面图。由图 10a)可知,桩前 2 倍桩径范围内出现阻水效应,上游来流流速自 1.75m/s 递减至 0.35m/s,前排桩与后排桩之间沿水深高度方向出现多个漩涡,包括最靠近床面的正流速漩涡,内涡流速达到 1.05m/s;由图 10b)可知,前排桩桩前 1.5 倍桩径范围内存在一个较大的马蹄形漩涡,内涡负流速达到 -0.6m/s,后排桩桩前 0.5 倍桩径范围内存在一个尺寸相对偏小的马蹄涡,然而内涡负流速同样达到了 -0.6m/s。

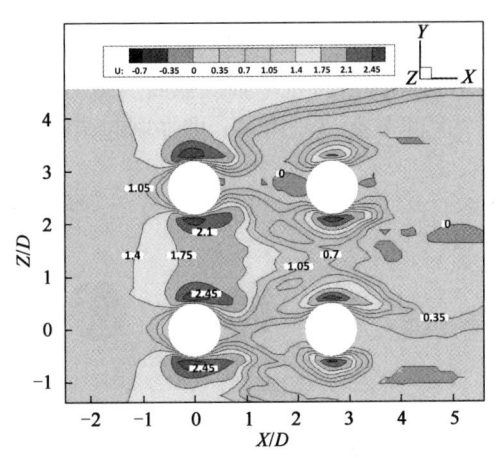

图 9　桩周流速分布平面图

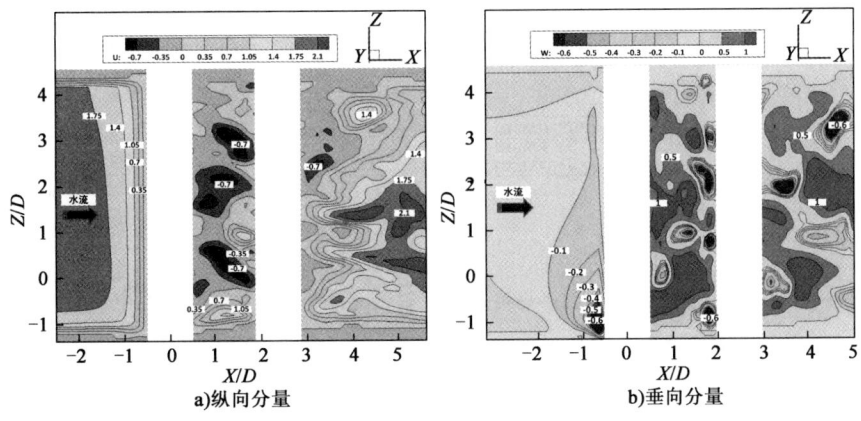

图 10　桩周流速分布纵剖面图

图 11a)为单向流条件下冲刷 10min 局部冲刷地形等高线图,桩侧泥沙先被带走,冲刷深度可以达到 1.5m,由图 11b)可知,冲刷 60min 后,基本达到冲淤平衡,最大冲刷深度位置出现在前排桩的迎水面,最大冲刷深度为 -2.23m,前排桩冲刷坑的发展范围延伸至桩前 2 倍桩径,桩侧 1.5 倍桩径处,后排桩的冲刷坑范围及深度均小于前排桩,后排桩桩间内侧冲刷量大于外侧,冲刷深度达到 -1m,结合图 11 的流

速平面图分析,这是由于受前排桩挤压加速的桩间水流流经后排桩桩间,继续冲刷后排桩桩间泥沙,而前排桩桩外侧绕流水流则向外侧扩散分离,难以继续冲刷后排桩外侧泥沙,故后排桩桩间泥沙冲刷量大于桩外侧。

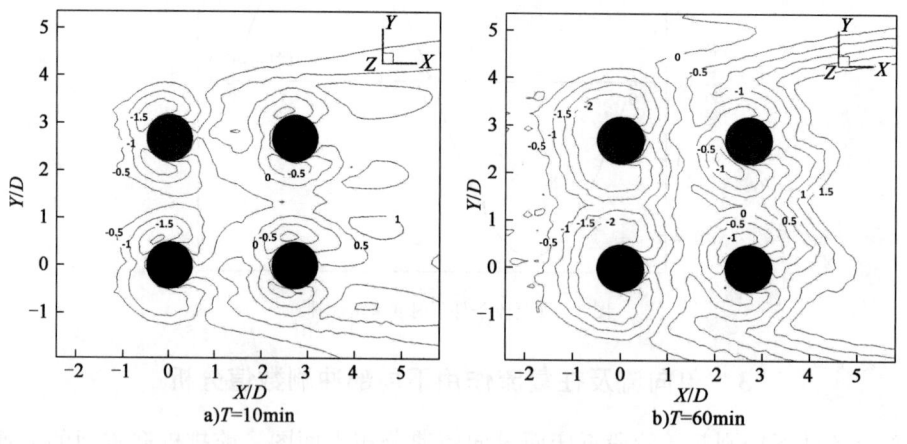

图11 局部冲刷坑分布形态等高线图

为便于观察四桩串列型群桩在冲刷过程中各个阶段的冲刷坑截面形态发展演变规律,分别沿纵向及横向对计算模型进行切片,共得到 A、B、C 三个剖面:A 为纵向桥桩中轴线截面;B 为横向前排桩中轴线截面;C 为横向后排桩中轴线截面。图12a)为剖面示意图。从时间尺度分析桩周床面高程的变化,共选取三个时间节点:$T=10\text{min}$,即冲刷起始阶段;$T=30\text{min}$,即主要冲刷阶段;$T=60\text{min}$,即冲淤平衡阶段。

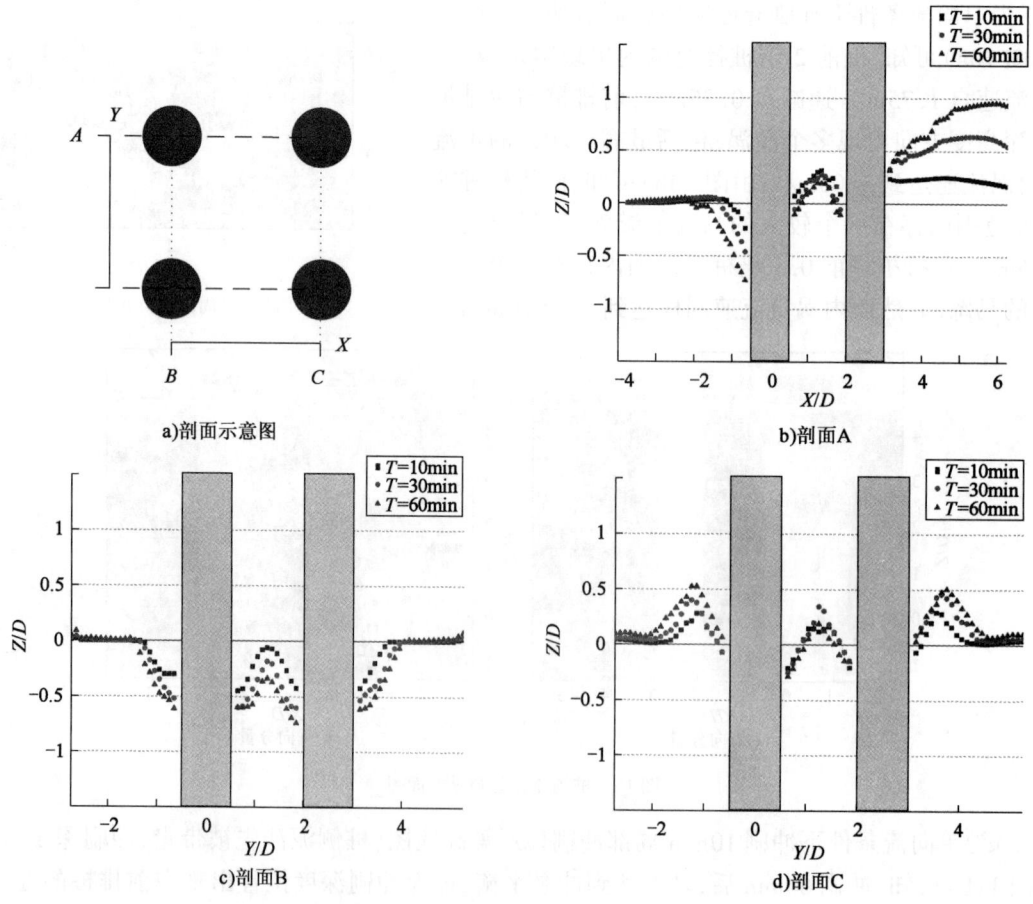

图12 桩周地形随时间变化图

由图 12b)可知,各时间节点的冲刷坑纵向截面特征均保持一致:前排桩前缘出现剧烈冲刷,床面高程下降,从 $T=10\min$ 至 $T=60\min$,前排桩前缘冲刷范围从桩前 1 倍桩径延伸至 2 倍桩径,冲深从 0.25 倍桩径增幅至 0.75 倍桩径;前排桩与后排桩之间出现淤积,淤积高度增长缓慢,三个时间节点的淤积高度均接近于 0.3 倍桩径;后排桩后缘淤积现象更为严重,$T=10\min$ 时,淤积高度变化较为平缓,约为 0.25 倍桩径,$T=30\min$ 时,随着远离后排桩,淤积高度先增大后减小,最大达到 0.6 倍桩径,$T=60\min$ 时,淤积高度达到 1 倍桩径。

由图 12c),前排桩横向截面冲刷现象明显,随着时间推移,横向截面的高程呈整体下降,最大冲深从 0.5 倍桩径上升至 0.75 倍桩径,但前排桩桩侧冲刷范围基本稳定在 1.5 倍桩径不变。值得注意的是,前排桩桩间存在一个冲刷量较小的隔离带。

由图 12d),不同于前排桩,相较于冲刷,后排桩横向截面的淤积现象更为明显,随着时间推移,淤积高程呈整体上升,从 0.25 倍桩径升高至 0.5 倍桩径,且淤积范围也逐渐横向发展延伸至 2 倍桩径,后排桩桩间同样存在一个隔离带。

保持同样的切片剖面 A、B、C,对比分析单向流条件下及往复流条件下四桩串列型群桩冲淤平衡阶段($T=60\min$)的冲刷坑截面形态。

由图 13b),往复流条件下前排桩前缘及后排桩后缘均出现冲刷,前排桩与后排桩之间存在淤积。往复流条件下前排桩前缘冲深约为 0.25 倍桩径,远小于单向流条件下的 0.75 倍桩径,前缘冲坑范围约为 1.5 倍桩径,略小于单向流;往复流条件下前排桩与后排桩之间淤积高度约为 0.3 倍桩径,略大于单向流;往复流条件下后排桩后缘由于流向的改变,同样出现范围为 1.5 倍桩径,深度为 0.25 倍桩径的冲刷。

由图 13c),相较于单向流,往复流条件下前排桩横向截面的高程整体上升,桩侧最大冲深回弹至 0.5 倍桩径,冲刷范围侧向发展至 2 倍桩径。

由图 13d),后排桩横向截面表现出整体冲刷,最大冲深大于 0.5 倍桩径,桩侧冲刷范围为 2 倍桩径。

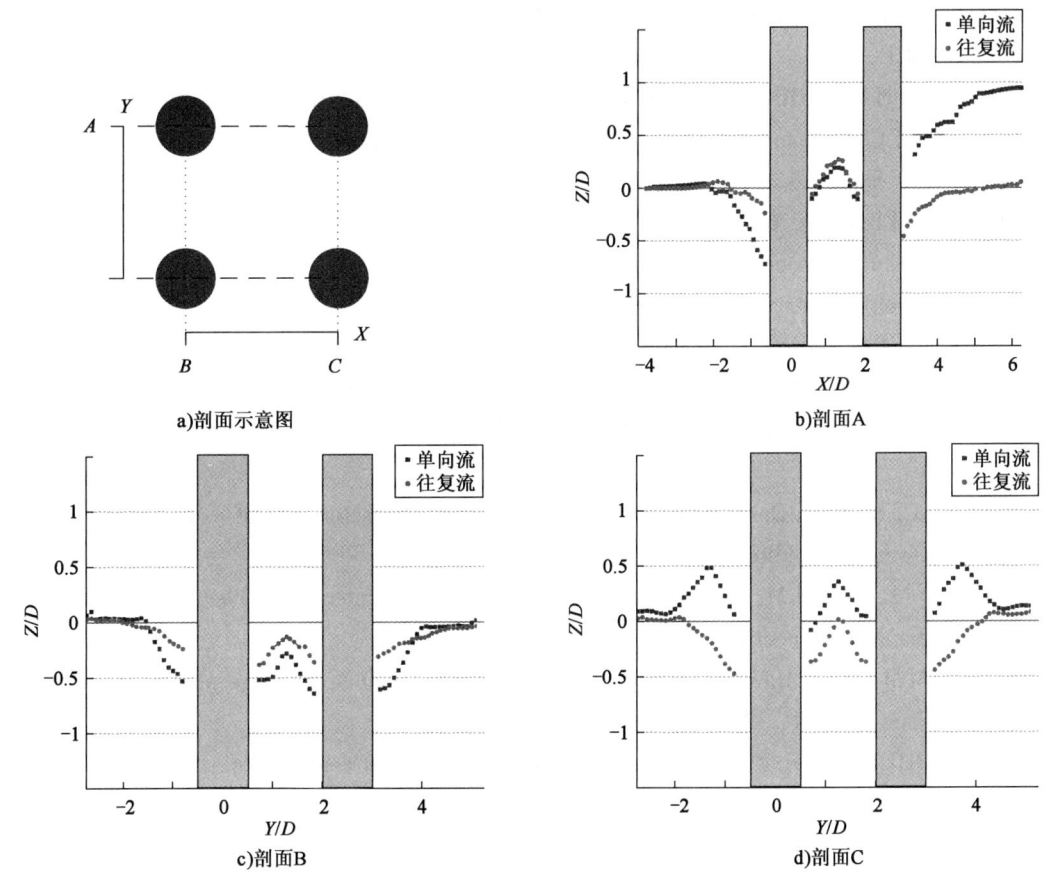

图 13 桩周地形对比图

4 结　语

本章选取 FLOW-3D 软件建立局部冲刷的三维数值模型,首先采用 Melville 经典冲刷试验模型,进行数值模型的验证,得到的结果无论从最大冲刷深度或是冲刷坑的分布形态来看,均与试验结果有较高的吻合度。其次,建立实桥群桩基础局部冲刷模型,模拟分析了在单向流及往复流作用下的桩周流场分布、局部冲刷深度、局部冲刷坑分布形态。单向流冲刷坑与往复流冲刷坑的主要差异可以归纳为以下几点:

(1)单向流条件下冲刷坑表现出前冲后淤,往复流作用下冲刷坑的前后区域均表现出冲刷,且冲刷坑的范围大于单向流。

(2)往复流条件下最大冲刷深度较单向流缩减了 20%~30%。

针对上述单向流冲刷坑与往复流冲刷坑形态的差异,结合桩周流场结构及流速分布进行分析,其中的原因可以归纳为以下几点:

(1)往复流条件下,由于流向的改变,后排桩后缘淤积区域转而成为冲刷区域,故后排桩后缘同样表现为冲刷。

(2)后排桩后缘淤积泥沙被反向水流带走回填至局部冲刷坑,故往复流冲坑整体高程低于单向流冲坑。

(3)单向流的水流流速始终为 2.3m/s,往复流的水流流速仅部分时间维持在接近 2.3m/s 的大流速条件下,在流向改变时,在短时间内流速接近于 0,故往复流的有效冲刷时间低于单向流,往复流冲坑的整体冲刷量同样低于单向流冲坑。

参考文献

[1] SHIROLE A M, HOLT R C. Planning for a comprehensive bridge safety assurance program [J]. Transportation Research Record, 1991, 1(01): 39-50.

[2] HARRISON L J, DENSMORE D H. Bridge Inspections Related to Bridge Scour [C]. Hydraulic Engineering. ASCE, 2015.

[3] WARDHANA K, HADIPRIONO F C. Analysis of Recent Bridge Failures in the United States [J]. Journal of Performance of Constructed Facilities, 2003, 17(03): 144-150.

[4] 郭健,蒋兵.近30年桥梁基础冲刷研究进展及关键问题[J].中国公路学报,2020,33(07):1-16.

[5] MA Li-li, Wang LI-zhong, GUO Zhen, et al. Time Development of Scour Around Pile Groups in Tidal Currents[J]. Ocean Engineering,2018, 163: 400-418.

[6] Han Haiqian, Chen Yifan, Sun Zhilin. Estimation of Maximum Local Scour Depths at Multiple Piles of Sea/Bay-crossing Bridges[J]. Ksce Journal of Civil Engineering,2019, 23(2): 567-575.

[7] 郭健.跨海大桥建设的主要技术现状与面临的挑战[J].桥梁建设,2010(06):66-69.

[8] 郭健,汪涛,王金权,等.基于能量平衡的跨海桥梁钢管桩局部冲深计算[J].海洋工程,2020,38(06):96-106.

[9] UNGER J, HAGER W H. Down-flow and horseshoe vortex characteristics of sediment embedded bridge piers [J]. Experiments in Fluids, 2006, 42(01): 1-19.

[10] SHEPPARD D M, ODEH M, GLASSER T. Large Scale Clear-Water Local Pier Scour Experiments [J]. Journal of Hydraulic Engineering, 2004, 130(10): 957-963.

[11] KWAN T F, MELVILLE B W. Local scour and flow measurements at bridge abutments [J]. Journal of Hydraulic Research, 1994, 32(05): 661-673.

[12] DEY S, BARBHUIYA A K. Turbulent flow field in a scour hole at a semicircular abutment [J]. Canadian Journal of Civil Engineering, 32(01): 213-232.

[13] MELVILLE B. Local scour of bridge sites [D]. Auckland:University of Auckland, 1975.

[14] ETTEMA R. Scour at bridge piers [D]. Auckland:University of Auckland, 1980.

[15] MASTBERGEN D R, BERG J H V D. Breaching in fine sands and the generation of sustained turbidity currents in submarine canyons[J]. Sedimentology, 2003, 50(4): 625-637.

准设计状态下简支梁桥冲击系数研究

赵洋[1] 曹群[2]

(1. 长安大学公路学院;2. 呼和浩特市市政工程管理局)

摘要 为对中小跨径简支梁桥冲击系数进行评价。运用空间有限元程序 ANSYS 建立了标准跨径的公路简支 T 形梁桥,选用五自由度三轴平面车辆模型,基于车-桥耦合振动理论建立车桥耦合振动方程,采用 ANSYS 的二次开发语言 APDL 进行数值分析。首先,通过荷载等效原理,建立了准设计状态的概念,对准设计状态进行冲击系数分析,分析速度、平整度等因素对简支梁桥冲击系数的影响规律;其次,将准设计状态下冲击系数的结果与规范取值进行对比分析;最后探究不同桥梁响应冲击系数之间的关系。结果表明:在本文研究对象及准设计状态的研究方法的基础上,简直梁桥冲击系数随平整度情况变差而增大,速度对冲击系数的影响规律不明显;我国现行规范取值的冲击系数偏不安全,在桥面状况良好和低速行驶时安全性较高;弯矩冲击系数小于挠度冲击系数,且冲击系数的比值随着平整度的变化而改变。研究结论可为新的桥梁规范修编提供参考。

关键词 桥梁工程 简支梁桥 冲击系数 准设计状态

0 引言

动载作用下的桥梁在空间横竖纵三向都产生动力效应,其中竖向产生的动力效应被称作冲击效应。通常把移动荷载的总竖向荷载效应定义为竖向静力效应乘以与之相应的动力放大系数$(1+\mu)$,μ 为冲击系数,引入冲击系数的概念可以有效地将桥梁结构复杂得动力问题静力化[1],但冲击系数存在很大的随机性[2],且受众多因素的影响。

桥梁结构冲击系数与桥梁的特性和车辆的特性以及行驶速度等影响因素有关,且不同响应的冲击系数大小不同[3]。然而《公路桥涵设计通用规范》(JTG D60—2015)在冲击系数计算上仍然采用《公路桥涵设计通用规范》(JTG D60—2004)的规定,用桥梁基频这个单一参数来表达冲击系数。其依据是 2 座钢筋混凝土矩形板、4 座钢筋混凝土 T 梁及 1 座预应力混凝土箱梁桥的现场实测数据,桥梁样本较少且均为简支梁桥,部分学者对规范的适用性进行探究[4]。

桥面平整度是影响车-桥耦合系统振动的敏感因素之一[5-6],且众多研究表明冲击系数随着桥面平整度情况变差而显著增加[7-8]。在不同效应冲击系数研究方面,研究表明桥梁的弯矩或者应变冲击系数小于桥梁的挠矩冲击系数[3],一些研究发现挠度冲击系数与弯矩或应变冲击系数的比值关系与平整度等影响因素有关[9]。

规范中规定的动力放大系数应是汽车荷载标准值的放大系数,而不是只有少数车辆荷载的作用时的动力放大系数[10],研究表明,冲击系数随车辆重量的增加而减小[11-12],车辆载重较小时,会获得更大的冲击系数,但载重较小的车辆产生的静载效应也相对较小,虽然得到较大的动力放大系数,但将轻载车得到的较大的冲击系数与规范值对比,会造成规范值偏小,没有实际意义。

若要研究设计荷载作用的冲击系数,应采用与 15 规范规定的设计荷载标准值相近的车辆荷载来进行研究。规范中规定的车道荷载为均布力和一个集中力,通过三轴重车荷载等效还原规范中规定的车道

基金项目:国家自然科学基金项目(51978063)。

荷载,进行准设计状态研究。

基于此,首先进行准设计状态下的冲击系数研究,将现行《公路桥涵设计通用规范》(JTG D60)中规定车道荷载还原为与设计荷载等效的三轴重车荷载,考虑跨径、桥面不平整度、速度、加载位置等因素的影响,建立车桥耦合振动方程,进行准设计状态下的冲击系数计算,得出冲击系数结果,进行参数分析,并将冲击系数计算结果与相关规范值进行对比,其次进行不同响应冲击系数对比分析,分析不同效应冲击系数的差别。

1 公路桥梁冲击系数分析理论

本文采用的最大动力效应由车辆过桥时的挠度时程曲线获得,最大静力效应为车辆准静态过桥时结构的最大效应值。

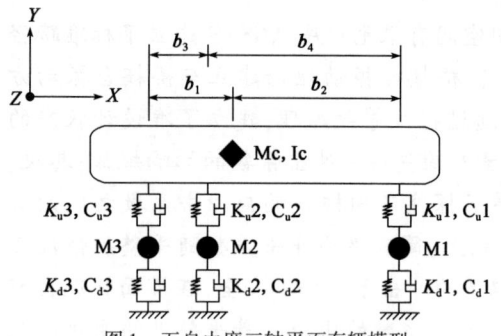

图1 五自由度三轴平面车辆模型
M_c-车体质量;α-仰俯旋转自由度;z-竖向位移;构架与轮对质量之和 M_1、M_2、M_3 竖向位移自由度 z_1、z_2、z_3,悬挂刚度、阻尼 K_u、C_u、K_d、C_d

1.1 车辆模型及振动方程

本文选用五自由度三轴平面车型,车辆模型如图1所示,所采用车辆模型参数见表1。

由车桥耦合振动理论可得车辆模型振动方程:

$$[M_v]\{\ddot{Z}_v\} + [C_v]\{\dot{Z}_v\} + [K_v]\{Z_v\} = \{G_v\} + \{F_{bv}\} \quad (1)$$

式中:$[M_v]$、$[C_v]$、$[K_v]$——质量、矩阵、刚度矩阵;
$\{F_{bv}\}$——瞬时耦合荷载向量;
$\{G_v\}$——重力荷载向量。

车辆模型参数   表1

参 数	数 值	参 数	数 值
车体质量(kg)	—	前轴上层悬挂系统刚度系数(kN·m^{-1})	1200
每个前、中、后轮质量(kg)	500	中后轴上层悬挂系统刚度系数(kN·m^{-1})	2400
车体仰俯惯性矩(kg·m^2)	40000	前轴上层悬挂系统阻尼系数(kN·s·m^{-1})	5
前轴到车体重心的水平距离(m)	3.4	中后轴上层悬挂系统刚度系数(kN·s·m^{-1})	10
中轴到车体重心的水平距离(m)	1.6	前轴下层悬挂系统刚度系数(kN·m^{-1})	2400
中后轴之间的水平距离(m)	1.5	中后轴下层悬挂系统刚度系数(kN·m^{-1})	4800
轮距(m)	1.8	前轴下层悬挂系统阻尼系数(kN·s·m^{-1})	6
		中后轴下层悬挂系统刚度系数(kN·s·m^{-1})	12

注:其中车体质量参数根据具体的分析需要而调整。

1.2 桥梁模型及桥面不平整度模型

本文以20m、30m、40m跨径的简支T形梁桥为研究对象,桥面净宽为11m,横向分布5片梁,20m跨径桥梁横断面尺寸如图2所示,运用ANSYS有限元程序建立空间梁格模型如图3所示。

采用傅里叶变逆换法方法生成桥名不平整度样本,且生成10次不同的桥梁不平整度样本,计算时取平均值,桥面不平整度状况如图4所示。

1.3 不同响应动力放大系数理论推导

对单个集中力匀速通过简支梁的冲击系数分析。

跨中截面竖向静挠度和静弯矩最大值为:

$$y_{j,\max}\left(\frac{L}{2}\right) = \frac{PL^3}{48EI} \tag{2}$$

$$M_{j,\max}\left(\frac{L}{2}\right) = \frac{PL}{4} \tag{3}$$

其竖向动挠度为：

$$y_d(x,t) = \sum_{n=1}^{N} \varphi_n(x) q_n(t) \qquad n=1,2,3,\cdots \tag{4}$$

简支梁振型函数为：

$$\varphi(x) = \sin\frac{n\pi x}{L} \qquad n=1,2,3,\cdots \tag{5}$$

竖向动挠度为：

$$y_d(x,t) = \sum_{n=1}^{N} \varphi_n(x) q_n(t) = \sum_{n=1}^{N} q_n(t) \sin\frac{n\pi x}{L} \tag{6}$$

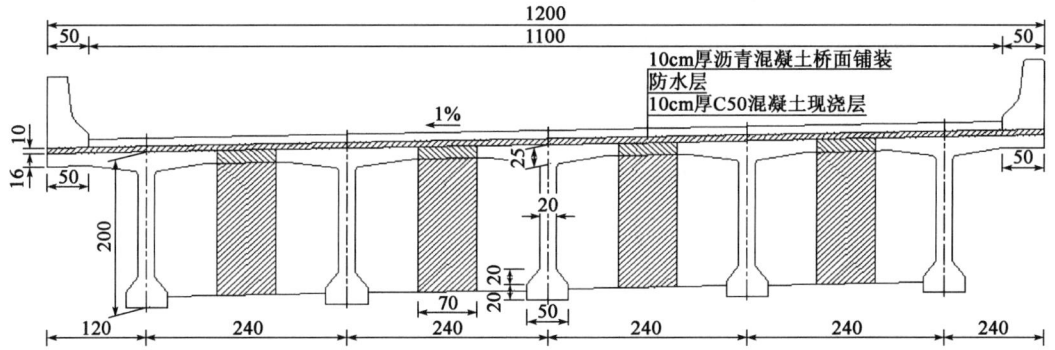

图2 简支T形梁桥横断面图(尺寸单位:cm)

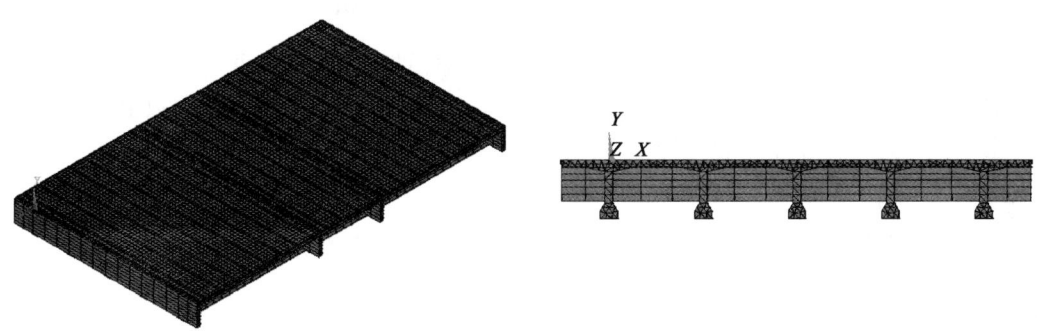

图3 简支T梁桥模型示意图

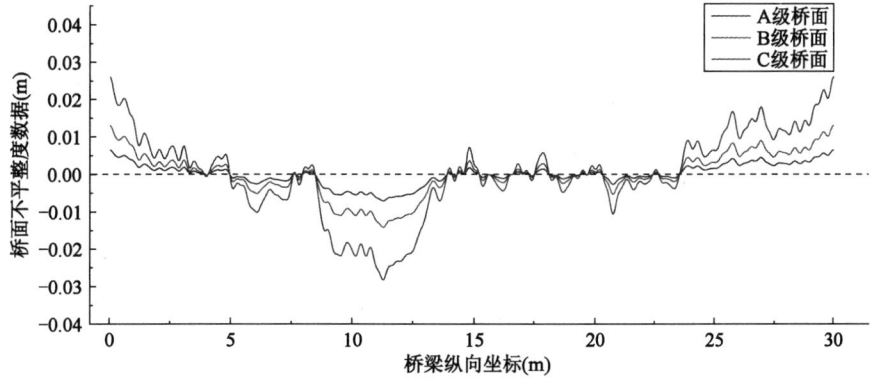

图4 桥面不平整度曲线

竖向动弯矩为：

$$M_d(x,t) = -EI\frac{\partial^2 y(x,t)}{\partial x^2} = EI\left(\frac{\pi}{L}\right)^2 \sum_{n=1}^{N} n^2 q_n(t)\sin\frac{n\pi x}{L} \qquad (7)$$

不同响应的跨中冲击系数分别表示为：

$$\mu_y = \frac{\sum_{n=1}^{N} q_n(t_y)\sin\frac{n\pi}{2}}{\frac{PL^3}{48EI}} - 1 \qquad (8)$$

$$\mu_M = \frac{EI\left(\frac{\pi}{L}\right)^2 \sum_{n=1}^{N} n^2 q_n(t_M)\sin\frac{n\pi}{2}}{\frac{PL}{4}} - 1 \qquad (9)$$

式中：t_y、t_M——挠度值、弯矩值最大对应的时刻。

定义弯矩冲击系数 μ_M 与挠度冲击系数 μ_y 的比值为 ε_{My}，有：

$$\varepsilon_{My} = \frac{\mu_M}{\mu_y} = \frac{\pi^2}{12} \times \frac{\sum_{n=1}^{N} n^2 q_n(t_M)\sin\frac{n\pi}{2} - 1}{\sum_{n=1}^{N} q_n(t_y)\sin\frac{n\pi}{2} - 1} \qquad (10)$$

若只考虑第一阶模态振型，则：

$$\varepsilon_{My} = \frac{1+\mu_M}{1+\mu_y} = \frac{\pi^2}{12} = 0.822 \qquad (11)$$

2 准设计状态下冲击系数分析

本文采用公路桥梁车桥耦合振动响应分析系统进行数值模拟仿真分析，通过将有限元计算值与实桥实测值进行对比[11]发现吻合度较好，验证了分析系统的正确性，表明本文冲击系数数值计算结果的准确性。计算冲击系数时选取十组不平整度样本，冲击系数取十次计算值的平均值。

2.1 准设计状态的概念

参考相关规范，当使用荷载试验常用的三轴加载车加载时，且荷载效应等效比介于0.95~1.05，则认为试验车辆荷载与设计荷载标准值等效，此时称为准设计状态。

荷载效应等效比计算式为：

$$\eta = \frac{S_s}{S} \qquad (12)$$

式中：S_s——静载作用下，某一加载试验项目对应的加载控制截面内力或位移的最大计算效应值；

S——控制荷载产生的同一加载控制截面内力或位移的最不利效应计算值（不计冲击效应）；

η——荷载效应等效比。

2.2 准设计状态的车辆布载

选择1号、2号、3号主梁分析。车辆布载参照相关规范，纵向车间距为5m，纵向车辆首尾衔接。根据各主梁的荷载横向分布影响线，分析1号和2号梁时所对应的车辆空间布载位方式如图5a)所示，分析3号梁时所对应的车辆空间布载方式如图6所示。

2.3 准设计状态的等效计算

计算各跨径简支T形梁桥在公路I级设计汽车荷载（不计冲击系数）作用下跨中控制截面的效应值，然后将车辆按图5布载，通过调整车辆载重，使等效比 η 等于或接近1，达到准设计状态，计算结果见表2。

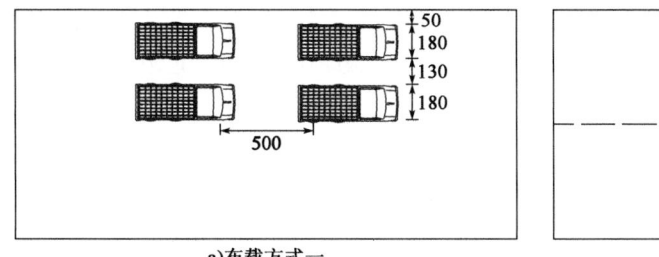
a) 布载方式一

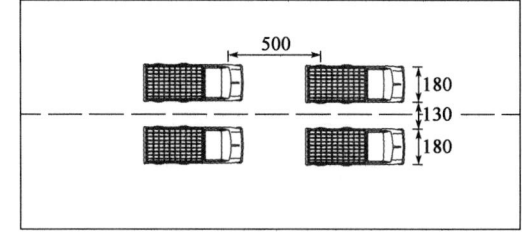
b) 布载方式二

图 5 简支 T 梁桥的车辆空间布载方式（尺寸单位：cm）

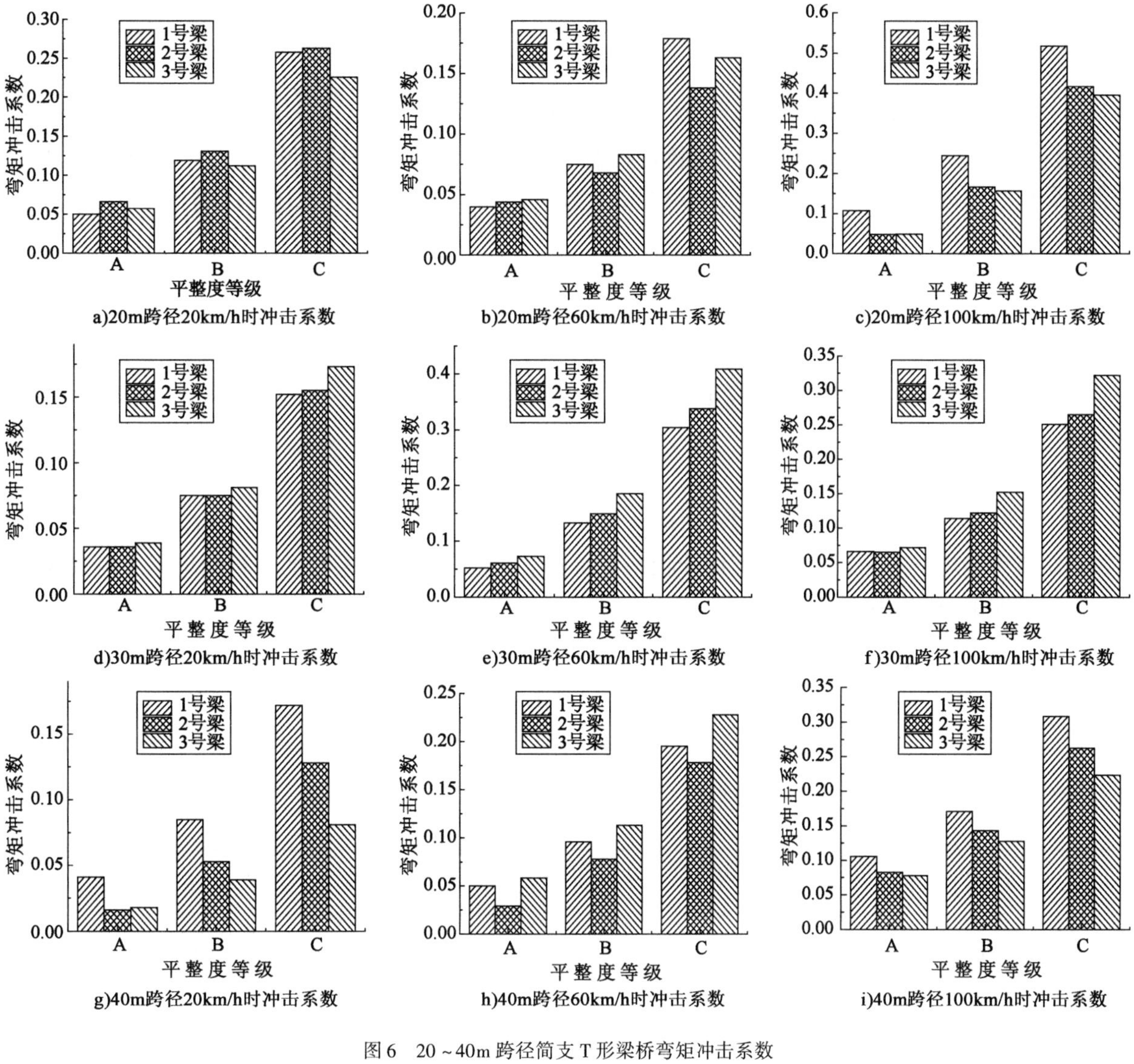

a) 20m 跨径 20km/h 时冲击系数
b) 20m 跨径 60km/h 时冲击系数
c) 20m 跨径 100km/h 时冲击系数
d) 30m 跨径 20km/h 时冲击系数
e) 30m 跨径 60km/h 时冲击系数
f) 30m 跨径 100km/h 时冲击系数
g) 40m 跨径 20km/h 时冲击系数
h) 40m 跨径 60km/h 时冲击系数
i) 40m 跨径 100km/h 时冲击系数

图 6　20~40m 跨径简支 T 形梁桥弯矩冲击系数

简支梁桥跨中弯矩效应等效计算结果　　　　　　　　　　　　　　　表 2

跨径 (m)	主梁编号	布载方式	车重 (t)	设计效应① (kN·m)	等效弯矩效应② (kN·m)	等效比 ②/①
20	1号	方式一	35	1388.6	1400.5	1.01
	2号	方式一	35	1135.4	1100.2	0.97
	3号	方式二	41	1003.1	963.4	0.96

续上表

跨径(m)	主梁编号	布载方式	车重(t)	设计效应①(kN·m)	等效弯矩效应②(kN·m)	等效比②/①
30	1号	方式一	35	2524.8	2606.6	1.03
	2号	方式一	35	2014.4	2041.0	1.01
	3号	方式二	41	1728.4	1696.3	0.98
40	1号	方式一	35	3750.3	3842.5	1.02
	2号	方式一	35	3027.9	3081.0	1.02
	3号	方式二	41	2636.0	2626.2	0.99

2.4 准设计状态冲击系数计算结果分析

考虑常见的A、B、C三个桥面平整度等级,同时选取行驶速度20km/h、60km/h、100km/h来代表低、中、高速行驶状态。对各跨径简支T形梁桥进行准设计状态下车桥耦合振动分析。对共18个工况的车桥耦合振动问题进行计算,将各工况的弯矩冲击系数计算结果按照不同行驶速度汇总于图7。

由图6分机可知:

(1)总体来看,1号、2号、3号梁间冲击系数差值随桥面不平整度等级变低而增大。

(2)速度对1号、2号、3号梁间弯矩冲击系数的差值影响较大,但速度对各片梁间弯矩冲击系数差值的影响无明显规律。

(3)随着桥面平整度情况变差,弯矩冲击系数明显增大,尤其C级不平整度桥面的冲击系数增大速率较快。

2.5 与我国规范进行对比分析

为了进一步分析我国冲击系数规范值的适用性,定义冲击系数计算值超过规范值的工况数与总的工况数的比值为超规范工况百分比。准设计状态下简支T梁桥弯矩冲击系数的分析结果汇总见表3,进一步分析我国冲击系数规范值的适应性。

简支T梁桥弯矩冲击系数超规范工况统计　　表3

规范	跨径(m)	基频(Hz)	规范值	超规范工况百分比	对应速度(km/h)	对应平整度等级
15规范	20	4.28	0.278	9.7%	100	C
	30	3.40	0.201	18.4%	60、100	C
	40	2.59	0.152	25.1%	60、100	B、C

由表3可得,在准设计状态下,随着桥梁跨径的增大,冲击系数超规范工况百分比增大;低、中、高速行驶时均出现超规范工况,速度对冲击系数影响规律不明显;超规范工况对应的平整度等级为B、C级,可见桥面平整度对冲击系数影响较大。对于各跨径简支T梁,按15规范取值冲击系数偏不安全,但桥面状况良好和低速行驶时较安全。

3 不同响应冲击系数的对比分析

本节采用于数值模拟对简支梁桥两种冲击系数的关系进行分析,并进行影响参数分析。

3.1 车辆荷载作用方式

车辆行驶车道宽度取值3.5m,且车辆始终行驶在车道中间,具体布载方式如图7所示。

3.2 不同响应冲击系数分析

考虑桥面不平整度,选取行驶速度20km/h、60km/h、100km/h模拟低、中、高速行驶状态,车重选择25t、30t、35t、40t,对各跨径简支T形梁桥进行分析,挠度冲击系数与弯矩冲击系数的比值见表4。

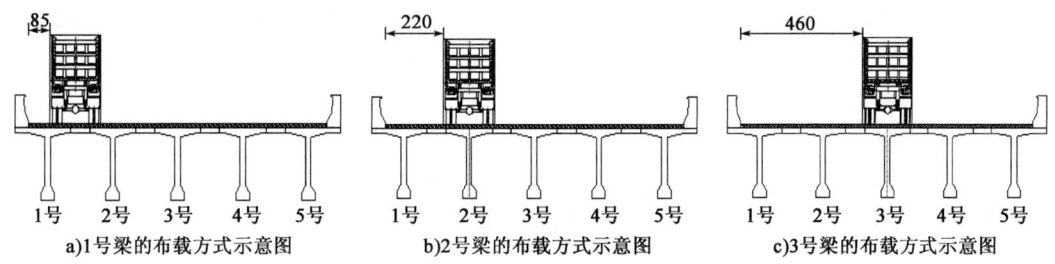

a) 1号梁的布载方式示意图　　b) 2号梁的布载方式示意图　　c) 3号梁的布载方式示意图

图 7　简支 T 梁桥单辆车横向布载示意图(尺寸单位:cm)

冲击系数比值的平均值　　　　　　　　　　　　　　　　表 4

梁 号	20 ~ 40m 跨径		
	A	B	C
1 号	0.97	0.96	0.95
2 号	0.97	0.96	0.94
3 号	0.97	0.95	0.93

由表 4 数据可得,弯矩与挠度冲击系数的比值的平均值位于 0.93 ~ 0.97,挠度动力放大系数大于弯矩动力放大系数。

由图 8 可看出,冲击系数比值基本随着平整度变差而减小,分析原因是弯矩和挠度放大系数均随平整度变差而增大,但弯矩放大系数增大的速度小于挠度放大系数增大的速度,所以导致动力放大系数的比值随平整度的变差而减小。

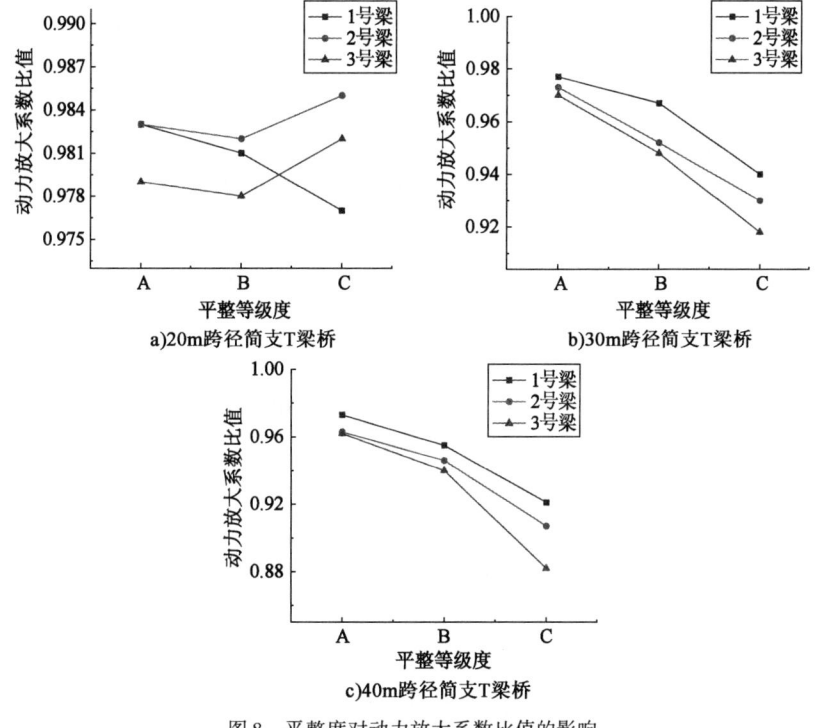

a) 20m 跨径简支 T 梁桥　　b) 30m 跨径简支 T 梁桥

c) 40m 跨径简支 T 梁桥

图 8　平整度对动力放大系数比值的影响

4　结　语

本文以标准跨径的简支 T 形梁桥为研究对象,采用 1/2 五自由度三轴平面车型,考虑了平整度、速度、跨径等因素的影响,进行了准设计状态下冲击系数的分析,并将准设计状态下的冲击系数与规范值进行对比,并分析了不同响应冲击系数间的关系,在本文的研究对象及准设计状态的研究方法基础上得出以下主要结论:

（1）将规范的设计荷载的车道荷载还原为两排两列三轴重车荷载,进行准设计状态下的车桥耦合振动分析。结果表明,桥面平整度等级对冲击系数的影响较大,随着桥面平整度等级变低,冲击系数明显增大；桥面平整度等级越高,不同主梁间的冲击系数差值越小；速度对不同主梁间冲击系数的差值影响较大,但影响无明显规律。

（2）将准设计状态下冲击系数的计算值与规范取值进行对比,结果表明规范取值偏不安全,且随着跨径增大安全储备降低,但在桥面状况良好时且低速行驶时取值较为安全。

（3）桥梁挠度冲击系数大于弯矩冲击系数,弯矩冲击系数与挠度冲击系数的比值,基本随桥面不平整度情况变差而减小,随桥梁跨径增大而减小,即两者差值随不平整度情况变差与桥梁跨径增大而增大。

参考文献

[1] 施尚伟,杜松,李莹雪.桥梁冲击系数随机性分析[J].重庆交通大学学报(自然科学版),2012,31(3):377-379.

[2] 朱劲松,香超,祁海东.大跨度悬索桥冲击系数影响因素研究[J].天津大学学报(自然科学与工程技术版),2019,052(4):413-422.

[3] 邓露,段林利,邹启令.桥梁应变与挠度动力放大系数的大小关系研究[J].工程力学,2018,35(01):126-135.

[4] 陈洪彬,谭平荣,赵国虎.公路桥梁冲击系数适应性研究[J].公路,2014,059(008):259-262.

[5] 周勇军,赵煜,贺栓海,等.刚构-连续组合桥梁冲击系数多因素灵敏度分析[J].振动与冲击,2012,31(03):97-101.

[6] REZAIGUIA A, OUELAA N, LAEFER D F, et, al. Dynamic Amplification of A Multi-span, Continuous Orthotropic Bridge Deck under Vehicular Movement[J]. Engineering Structures, 2015, 100 (OCT. 1): 718-730.

[7] 邓露,陈雅仙,韩万水,等.中小跨径公路混凝土简支梁桥冲击系数研究及建议取值[J].中国公路学报,2020,33(1):69-78.

[8] 刘晨光,王宗林,高庆飞.考虑桥面不平整度退化的简支梁桥冲击系数检测方法研究[J].振动与冲击,2019,38(1):206-214.

[9] 周勇军,蔡军哲,石雄伟,等.基于加权法的桥梁冲击系数计算方法[J].交通运输工程学报,2013,13(04):29-36.

[10] 袁向荣,吴晶.极限荷载作用下简支梁桥冲击系数研究[J].世界桥梁,2014,42(1):55-59.

[11] Broquet C, Bailey SF, Fafard M, et al. Dynamic Behavior of Deck Slabs of Concrete Road Bridges[J]. Journal of Bridge Engineering, 2004,9(2):137-146.

[12] Huang D. Vehicle-Induced Vibration of Steel Deck Arch Bridges and Analytical Methodology[J]. Journal of Bridge Engineering, 2012,17(2):241-248.

[13] 蒋培文.公路大跨径连续体系桥梁车桥耦合振动研究[D].西安:长安大学,2012.

基于模糊综合评价法的桥梁火灾脆弱性评价

李 洁 徐 峰

(长安大学公路学院)

摘 要 近年来,我国交通网络不断发展和完善,桥梁火灾事故数量逐年上升。为了预防桥梁火灾的发生,本文将脆弱性理论引入桥梁火灾风险评价,提出桥梁火灾脆弱性的概念,从敏感度、暴露度以及抗逆度三方面分析影响桥梁火灾脆弱性的因素,构建桥梁火灾脆弱性评价体系,根据模糊数学理论对桥梁火灾脆弱性进行评价。该方法应用于泰州大桥的桥梁火灾脆弱性评价,结果表明,泰州大桥的火灾脆弱性等级为Ⅲ级,与工程实际情况相符,证明了模糊综合评价法可用于桥梁火灾脆弱性评价中。

关键词 桥梁火灾 脆弱性评价 模糊综合评价法 指标体系

0 引 言

近几年来,工程火灾研究备受关注,但火灾风险研究主要集中在建筑和隧道等方面。周红波[1]通过建立深基坑的模糊综合评判模型,评估深基坑工程以及相关风险事件的风险等级。徐坚强等[2]通过引入贝叶斯网络方法对建筑火灾风险进行实时监测和动态评估。在桥梁火灾研究中,主要集中在火灾对桥梁力学性能的影响方面。秦智源等[3]通过建立有限元模型,得到火灾下钢-混组合连续箱梁极限承载力的衰减规律。在桥梁脆弱性研究中,主要集中研究桥梁的结构上的脆弱性。张凯等[4]通过纤维监测模拟桥墩在地震中的破坏过程,并通过FEMA440能力谱方法确定桥墩的脆弱性损伤界限状态。本文尝试将脆弱性理论引入桥梁火灾风险分析,构建桥梁火灾脆弱性评价体系,运用模糊综合评价法评价桥梁火灾脆弱性,为桥梁设计和运营阶段的火灾风险防控提供依据。

1 桥梁火灾脆弱性评价

1.1 桥梁火灾脆弱性

目前,脆弱性研究已成为一门科学,广泛运用于灾害学、生态学等研究领域。从自然灾害角度[5-6],脆弱性是暴露于环境或社会变化中的系统,不具备足够高的适应能力应对变化,而造成的损害。从灾害学来看[7],脆弱性指系统在自然灾害冲击作用下发生损害的程度。结合不同领域对脆弱性的定义,本文将桥梁火灾脆弱性定义为:环境中存在着多种火灾不确定性因子,根据桥梁系统对外部扰动的敏感性和适应能力,桥梁发生火灾的可能性和受损程度。则桥梁火灾脆弱性评价框架如图1所示。

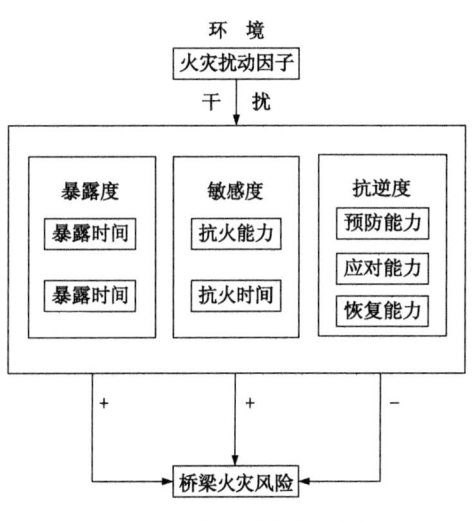

图1 桥梁火灾脆弱性评价框架

1.2 桥梁火灾脆弱性指标体系的构建

结合桥梁自身结构、周围环境等特点,从敏感度、暴露度、抗逆度三个方面分析桥梁火灾的原因,构建桥梁火灾脆弱性评价体系,如图2所示。为了便于评价,根据划分标准将桥梁火灾脆弱性分为五个等级,如表1所示。

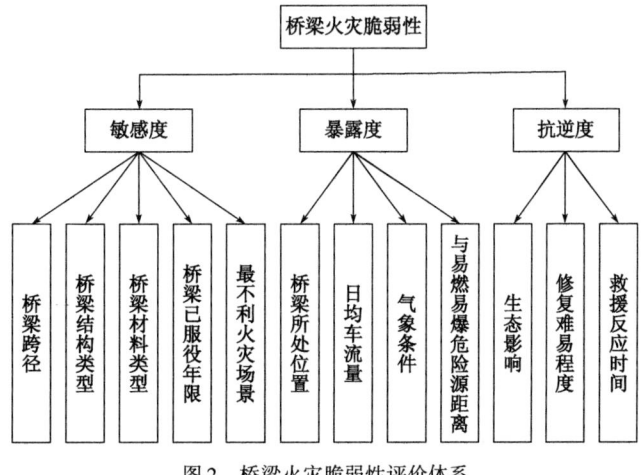

图2 桥梁火灾脆弱性评价体系

桥梁火灾脆弱性分级描述 表1

一级指标	二级指标	Ⅰ级	Ⅱ级	Ⅲ级	Ⅳ级	Ⅴ级
敏感度	桥梁跨径(m)	<30	30~100	100~500	500~1000	>1000
	桥梁结构类型	桁架等组合桥	拱式桥	梁式桥	斜拉桥	悬索桥
	桥梁材料类型	钢筋混凝土桥	预应力钢筋混凝土桥	钢-混组合桥	钢桥	木桥
	桥梁已服役年限(年)	<25	25~50	50~75	75~100	>100
	最不利火灾场景	桥面下方或桥下净空区域车、船起火	桥面或桥面附近电气、车以及雷电起火	拉索、拉杆、钢架等构件或桥面与桥塔柱电气、车辆或雷电起火	桥塔内部电气起火	—
暴露度	桥梁所处位置	山区	农村	郊区	城区	—
	日均车流量(辆)	<1000	1000~5000	5000~10000	10000~50000	>50000
	气象条件	气象条件良好(风力≤3级,相对湿度≥75%)	气象条件良好(3级<风力≤5级,55%≤相对湿度<75%)	气象条件差(5级<风力≤7级,30%≤相对湿度<55%)	气象条件恶劣(5级<风力≤7级,30%≤相对湿度<55%)	—
	与易燃易爆危险源距离	附近无危险源	满足安全距离	不满足安全距离	—	—
抗逆度	生态影响	区域内生态功能基本无影响	区域内生态功能影响较小	区域内生态功能部分丧失	区域内生态功能丧失严重	区域内生态功能丧失并对周边生态功能产生影响
	修复难易程度	一般困难	次要困难	中等困难	困难	很困难,需重建
	救援反应时间(min)	<15	15~25	25~35	35~45	>45

2 桥梁火灾脆弱性评价流程

桥梁火灾事故的因素众多且关系复杂、具有不确定性,并且桥梁火灾属于小概率事件。根据桥梁火灾的特点,本文选取层次分析法与模糊综合评价法相结合的方法,满足脆弱性评价的层次化和数量化需求。

2.1 层次分析法主观权重计算

(1)建立各级判断矩阵

本文采用的是1~9模糊标度法,由专家对同一层次不同指标因素下的桥梁火灾脆弱性的重要性进行比较分析。

$$A = (a_{ij})_{n \times n} = \begin{bmatrix} a_{11} & a_{12} & \cdots & a_{1n} \\ a_{21} & a_{22} & \cdots & a_{2n} \\ \vdots & \vdots & \ddots & \vdots \\ a_{n1} & a_{n2} & \cdots & a_{nn} \end{bmatrix} \quad (1)$$

式中:A——判断矩阵;

a_{ij}——指标i相对指标j的元素重要性赋值。

其中$a_{ij} = 1/a_{ji}$,当$i = j$时,$a_{ij} = 1$;n为指标总数。

(2)判断矩阵归一化

通过归一化处理判断矩阵,得到评价指标的相对权重。公式如下:

$$w_i = \frac{w'_{ij}}{\sum_{j=1}^{n} w'_{ij}}, i = 1,2,3,\cdots,n \tag{2}$$

式中，$w'_{ij} = \sqrt[n]{\prod_{j=1}^{n} a_{ij}}, i = 1,2,3,\cdots,n$，$w_i$ 表示第 i 个指标的相对权重。

可得相对权重向量 $W = [w_1, w_2, \cdots, w_n]^T$。

(3) 判断矩阵一致性检验

由于层次分析法具有人为主观性和偏好性。因此，通过 CR 检验判断矩阵是否有一致性。当 CR < 0.1 时，A 的不一致性满足要求。

$$CR = \frac{(\lambda_{max} - n)/(n-1)}{RI} \tag{3}$$

式中：λ_{max}——矩阵最大特征根，$\lambda_{max} = \sum_{i=1}^{n} \frac{(AW)_i}{nW_i}$；

RI——一致性指标，取值参照表2。

平均随机一致性指标　　　　　　　　　表2

阶数	1	2	3	4	5	6
RI	0	0	0.52	0.89	1.12	1.26

2.2 熵权法客观权重确定

(1) 初始矩阵标准化处理

将 a_{ij} 按照公式(4)进行无量纲化处理，得到无量纲矩阵 $A' = (a'_{ij})n \times m$。

$$a'_{ij} = \frac{a_{ij} - a_{i\min}}{a_{i\max} - a_{i\min}} \tag{4}$$

式中：A'、a'_{ij}——经过无量纲处理后的矩阵和指标值；

$X_{i\max}$、$X_{i\min}$——指标属性值的最大值和最小值。

(2) 计算指标熵值和信息效用值

$$H_j = -\frac{\sum_{i=1}^{m} k_{ij} \ln k_{ij}}{\ln m} \tag{5}$$

$$D_j = 1 - H_j \tag{6}$$

式中：$k_{ij} = \frac{1 + a_{ij}}{\sum_{i=1}^{m}(1 + a_{ij})}$；

H_j、D_j——第 j 项指标的信息熵和信息效用值。

(3) 计算指标熵值

$$W_2 = \frac{D_j}{\sum_{j=1}^{n} D_j} \tag{7}$$

2.3 综合权重计算

层次分析法具较大的主观性和个人的偏好性，会对权重产生不可忽略的影响，通过引入熵权法，进行客观赋权，可降低人为因素的影响。综合权重为主观权重 W_1 和客观权重 W_2 的线性组合。

$$W = \beta W_1 + (1-\beta)W_2 \tag{8}$$

式中：β——主观权重占综合权重的比例，通常取0.5。

2.4 桥梁火灾脆弱性评价等级划分

根据风险评估相关规定，划分桥梁火灾脆弱性评价集为：$V = (Ⅰ级，Ⅱ级，Ⅲ级，Ⅳ级，Ⅴ级)$，如表3

所示。其中,等级越高代表桥梁火灾脆弱性水平越高,即桥梁发生火灾的风险越高。

桥梁火灾脆弱性判定等级划分 表3

火灾脆弱性判定等级	Ⅰ级	Ⅱ级	Ⅲ级	Ⅳ级	Ⅴ级
脆弱性评分值	80~100	60~80	40~60	20~40	0~20

2.5 确定三级指标隶属度矩阵

根据评价对象的实际情况,参考评价标准表1确定隶属度矩阵。

$$P_{ij} = \begin{bmatrix} p_{11} & p_{12} & \cdots & p_{1n} \\ p_{21} & p_{22} & \cdots & p_{2n} \\ \vdots & \vdots & \ddots & \vdots \\ p_{n1} & p_{n2} & \cdots & p_{nn} \end{bmatrix} \quad (9)$$

式中:$p_{ij}(i=1,2,3,\cdots,n;j=1,2,3,\cdots,k)$——第 i 个指标在第 j 个评价等级的隶属度;

P_{ij}——第 i 个指标的隶属度矩阵。

2.6 多层次模糊综合评价

(1)二级指标评价

由三级指标隶属度矩阵 P_{ij} 和三级指标权重集 W_{ij},可得到二级指标评价矩阵。

$$P'_i = W_{ij} P_{ij} \quad (10)$$

式中:$W_{ij} = (w_{i1}, w_{i2}, \cdots, w_{in})$,$P'_i$——二级评价结果。

(2)一级指标评价

在完成二级指标评价的基础上,可由二级指标评价矩阵和二级指标权重集 W_i,计算得到一级指标评价结果。

$$B = W_i P'_i = (b_1, b_2, b_3, b_4, b_5) \quad (11)$$

式中:$W_i = (w_1, w_2, w_3)$;

$P'_i = (P'_1, P'_2, \cdots P'_n)$;

B——一级评价结果。

(3)目标指标综合评价

根据表3的各影响因子赋值和一级指标评价结果,可得桥梁火灾脆弱性评分。

$$B_0 = BV^T = (b_1, b_2, b_3, b_4, b_5) \cdot (v_1, v_2, v_3, v_4, v_5)^T \quad (12)$$

3 工程应用

3.1 工程概况

泰州大桥位于江苏省的泰州市和扬中市之间,采用双向六车道高速公路标准,设计速度为100km/h,主桥采用三塔双跨钢箱梁悬索桥,跨径布置为 2×1080m,是世界上三塔悬索桥最大跨径。

3.2 各级指标权重计算

根据"1~9标度法"对因素集内各指标进行主观权重赋值,获得判断矩阵如下:

$$A_1 = \begin{bmatrix} 1 & \frac{1}{4} & \frac{1}{6} & \frac{1}{2} & \frac{1}{3} \\ 4 & 1 & \frac{1}{2} & 3 & 2 \\ 6 & 2 & 1 & 4 & 2 \\ 2 & \frac{1}{3} & \frac{1}{4} & 1 & \frac{1}{3} \\ 3 & \frac{1}{2} & \frac{1}{2} & 3 & 1 \end{bmatrix}, A_2 = \begin{bmatrix} 1 & \frac{1}{6} & \frac{1}{2} & \frac{1}{8} \\ 6 & 1 & 3 & \frac{1}{2} \\ 2 & \frac{1}{3} & 1 & \frac{1}{3} \\ 8 & 2 & 3 & 1 \end{bmatrix}$$

$$A_3 = \begin{bmatrix} 1 & 5 & 2 \\ \frac{1}{5} & 1 & \frac{1}{3} \\ \frac{1}{2} & 3 & 1 \end{bmatrix}, A_4 = \begin{bmatrix} 1 & \frac{1}{2} & 2 \\ 2 & 1 & 2 \\ \frac{1}{2} & \frac{1}{2} & 1 \end{bmatrix}$$

用 Matlab 程序按照上述的层次分析法和熵权法计算步骤，按照公式(1)~公式(8)，分别得出各级指标的主观权重、客观权重以及综合权重，计算结果如表 4 所示。

各向指标因子权重计算结果 表 4

评 价 指 标	层次分析法权重	熵权法权重	综 合 权 重
桥梁跨径	0.0588	0.1621	0.1104
桥梁结构类型	0.2648	0.2091	0.2370
桥梁材料类型	0.3965	0.1759	0.2862
桥梁已服役年限	0.0900	0.1864	0.1382
最不利火灾场景	0.1899	0.2665	0.2282
桥梁所处位置	0.0588	0.2528	0.1558
日均车流量	0.3221	0.2488	0.2854
气象条件	0.1276	0.2857	0.2067
与易燃易爆危险源距离	0.4915	0.2127	0.3521
生态影响	0.5815	0.3403	0.4609
修复难易程度	0.1095	0.3239	0.2167
救援反应时间	0.3090	0.3358	0.3224
敏感度	0.3108	0.2841	0.2974
暴露度	0.4934	0.4110	0.4522
抗逆度	0.1958	0.3049	0.2504

3.3 多层次模糊综合评价

(1) 二级评价

根据泰州大桥工程概况，并依据表 1 中的桥梁火灾脆弱性评价等级标准，得到隶属度矩阵 P_i，按照公式(10)计算，得到二级评价结果。

$$A_1' = (0.1104, 0.2370, 0.2862, 0.1382, 0.2282) \times \begin{bmatrix} 0 & 0 & 0 & 0 & 1 \\ 0 & 0 & 0 & 1 & 0 \\ 0 & 0 & 0 & 1 & 0 \\ 1 & 0 & 0 & 0 & 0 \\ 0.20 & 0.33 & 0.28 & 0.19 & 0 \end{bmatrix}$$

$$= (0.1838, 0.0753, 0.0639, 0.5665, 0.1104)$$

$$A_2' = (0.1558, 0.2854, 0.2067, 0.3521) \times \begin{bmatrix} 1 & 0 & 0 & 0 & 0 \\ 0 & 0 & 0 & 0 & 1 \\ 1 & 0 & 0 & 0 & 0 \\ 0 & 1 & 0 & 0 & 0 \end{bmatrix}$$

$$= (0.3625, 0.3521, 0, 0, 0.2854)$$

$$A_3' = (0.4609, 0.2167, 0.3224) \times \begin{bmatrix} 0.28 & 0.41 & 0.18 & 0.09 & 0.04 \\ 0.42 & 0.35 & 0.14 & 0.07 & 0.02 \\ 0.23 & 0.43 & 0.28 & 0.05 & 0.01 \end{bmatrix}$$

$$= (0.2942, 0.4034, 0.2036, 0.0728, 0.0260)$$

(2) 一级评价

在二级评价计算结果的基础上,根据公式(11),可得一级评价结果。

$$B = (0.2975, 0.2504, 0.4522) \times \begin{bmatrix} 0.1838 & 0.0753 & 0.0639 & 0.5665 & 0.1104 \\ 0.3625 & 0.3521 & 0 & 0 & 0.2854 \\ 0.2942 & 0.4034 & 0.2036 & 0.0728 & 0.0260 \end{bmatrix}$$

$$= (0.3049, 0.2780, 0.0617, 0.1866, 0.1684)$$

(3) 综合评价

根据公式(12),可得到泰州大桥火灾脆弱性评分值。

$$B_0 = BV^T = (b_1, b_2, b_3, b_4, b_5) \cdot (v_1, v_2, v_3, v_4, v_5)^T$$

$$= (0.3049, 0.2780, 0.0617, 0.1866, 0.1684) \times (90, 70, 50, 30, 10) = 57.2847$$

该桥火灾脆弱性评分值为57.2847,由表3可知其火灾脆弱性等级为Ⅲ级,处于火灾风险较严重的等级。根据相关资料显示,自泰州大桥投入运营以来,发生两起火灾事故,与文中脆弱性等级结果相吻合。

4 结 语

(1) 根据前人对脆弱性理论的相关研究,提出桥梁火灾脆弱性概念,并从敏感度、暴露度及抗逆度三个方面,提出了12个评价指标,建立桥梁火灾脆弱性评价体系。

(2) 结合层次分析法和熵权法各自的优点,运用模糊数学理论,对桥梁火灾脆弱性进行评价,确定桥梁火灾脆弱性等级,为更好地在规划设计阶段防范桥梁火灾事故的发生,在运营阶段合理设置防火措施提供理论依据,降低桥梁火灾脆弱性。

(3) 根据泰州大桥实际情况,将模糊综合层次法运用到泰州大桥火灾脆弱性评价中。结果表明,泰州大桥的火灾脆弱性等级为Ⅲ级,与实际情况相符;该方法有效、可行,为桥梁火灾风险评估提供新的方向。

参考文献

[1] 周红波. 基于贝叶斯网络的深基坑风险模糊综合评估方法[J]. 上海交通大学学报, 2009, 43(09): 1473-1479.

[2] 徐坚强, 刘小勇, 苏燕飞, 等. 基于贝叶斯网络的建筑火灾动态风险评估方法研究[J]. 中国安全生产科学技术, 2019, 15(02): 138-144.

[3] 秦智源, 张岗, 王高峰, 等. 油罐车火灾下钢-混组合连续箱梁性能及失效机理[J]. 长安大学学报(自然科学版), 2018, 38(06): 98-108.

[4] 张凯. 桥梁结构基于性能的地震风险评估方法研究[D]. 北京: 北京交通大学, 2017.

[5] White G F. Natural Hazards[M]. Oxford: Oxford University Press, 1974.

[6] Cutter S L. Living with risk: The Geography of Technologi-cal Hazards [M]. London: Edward Arnold, 1993.

[7] Walter J. Ammann, StefanieDannenmann, Laurent Vulliet. Coping with Risks due to Natural Hazards in the 21st Century[M]. AK Leiden, The Netherlands: Taylor and Francis/Balkema, 2006.

承托设置对钢混组合箱梁桥面板
横向预应力效应的影响

杨领柱 杨 光

(长安大学)

摘 要 基于abaqus大型有限元通用分析软件研究承托设置对钢混组合箱梁桥面板横向预应力效应的影响。分别对承托设置前后单箱单室及单箱双室钢混组合箱梁桥面板横向应力结果进行对比,发现承托设置对桥面板横向预应力效应的影响不可忽略。增加承托竖向加腋高度和降低横向预加力对顶板上缘横向受力的影响一致,均使得桥面板上缘横向压应力减小。承托的设置还可增加桥面板刚度,降低活载产生的应力。

关键词 桥梁工程 组合梁 桥面板 承托 横向应力

0 引 言

箱型截面钢混组合桥梁,为使力线过渡平缓通常在顶板与钢腹板结合处设置承托,已有研究表明承托的设置能提高截面抗弯刚度和抗扭刚度,减小扭转剪应力和畸变应力同时还能提高腹板对桥面板的支承刚度,可以吸收负弯矩,从而减少了桥面板的跨中正弯矩。

承托对箱梁截面桥面板横向受力的影响已有一定研究,赵品、荣学亮等分析了承托对波形钢腹板桥面板横向内力的影响,研究了在竖向荷载下加设承托对桥梁挠度、横向应力以及桥面板有效分布宽度的影响,但未考虑承托设置对桥面板横向预应力效应的影响。彭亚军、王宗林等研究发现预应力混凝土箱梁桥承托纵向裂缝的产生主要与横向预应力有关,但缺乏对钢混组合型桥梁的研究。

为了解承托设置对钢混组合箱型截面横向预应力效应的影响,本文通过有限元软件abaqus建立桥梁空间三维实体模型,对比分析了单箱单室和单箱双室钢混组合桥梁在承托设置前后桥面板的横向应力分布情况以及承托尺寸变化对横向预应力效应影响的参数分析,同时还进一步分析了承托设置对活载效应的影响,从而为钢混组合箱型截面桥梁承托设置提供一定理论参考。

1 建模分析

采用abaqus有限元分析软件建立结构实体模型,箱梁全长45m,梁高3.5m,桥面宽度:单箱单室桥宽为13.5m,单箱双室桥宽为19.5m,桥面板采用C50混凝土材料,钢材用Q345材料,横向预应力筋采用 $\phi15.2\times3$ 钢绞线。横向采用直线布束,钢束距桥面板顶缘0.1m,钢束纵向间距为0.8m,不考虑预应力筋与混凝土之间的黏结滑移,将预应力筋内置到混凝土桥面板中并采用降温法施加预应力。组合梁截面形式及模型分别如图1和图2所示。

1.1 承托设置对桥面板横向预应力效应的影响

本节就单室组合箱梁和双室组合箱梁讨论承托设置对桥面板横向预应力效应的影响。在横向预应力作用下通过对比承托设置前后桥面板上缘和桥面板下缘横向应力结果展开讨论。在横向预应力作用下,各分析模型跨中截面桥面板上下缘横向应力分布情况分别如图3和图4所示。

1.1.1 承托设置对桥面板上缘横向应力的影响

通过图3和图4中桥面板上缘横向应力分布对比可知,承托设置对单室组合箱梁和双室组合箱梁顶板上缘预应力效应的影响一致,承托的设置不会影响桥面板上缘横向压应力分布规律,但对横向应力值的大小将产生一定影响。设置承托后,位于承托之间的桥面板,其上缘横向预压应力明显减小,而承托附近处桥面板上缘的横向压应力有所增大。悬臂板上缘离承托较远处横向应力受承托影响较小。

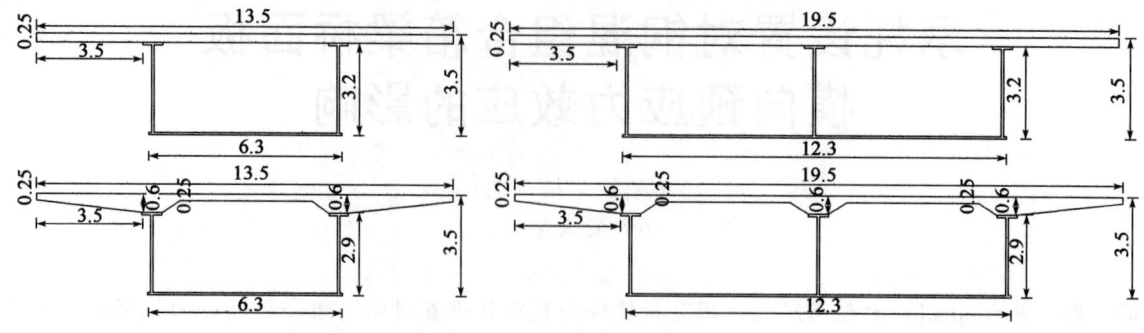

图1 加承托与不加承托的组合梁截面形式(尺寸单位:m)

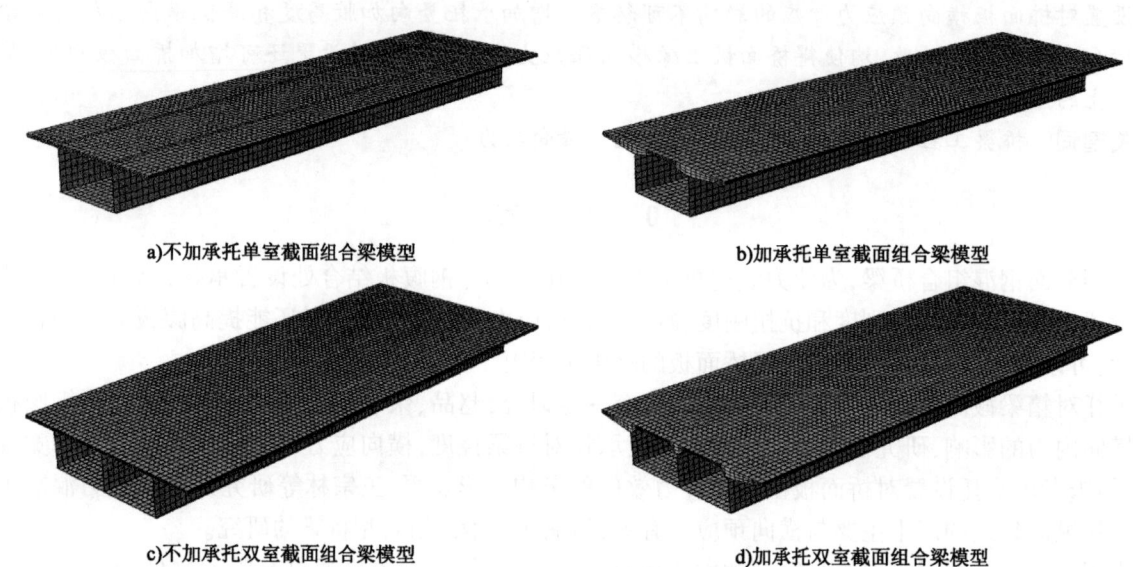

a)不加承托单室截面组合梁模型　　b)加承托单室截面组合梁模型

c)不加承托双室截面组合梁模型　　d)加承托双室截面组合梁模型

图2 加承托与不加承托的组合梁实体模型

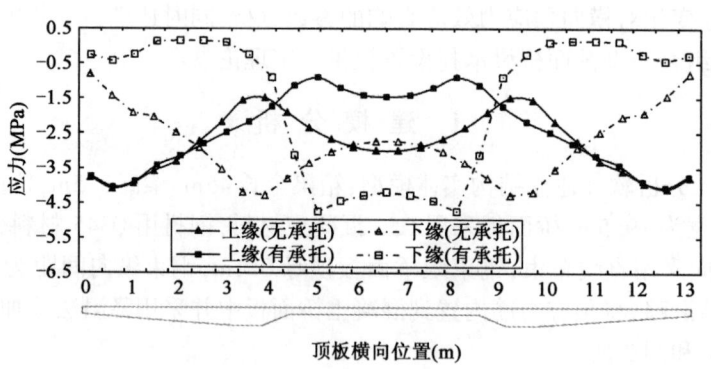

图3 单室组合梁桥面板横向应力分布图

1.1.2 承托设置对桥面板下缘横向应力的影响

通过图3和图4中桥面板下缘横向应力分布对比可知,承托设置对单室组合箱梁和双室组合箱梁顶板下缘预应力效应的影响也是一致的,且桥面板下缘横向应力受承托影响较上缘要大。设置承托后,位于承托之间的桥面板,其下缘的横向压应力明显增大,悬臂部分及承托附近的桥面板其下缘的横向压应力明显减小。此外,对于双室组合箱梁而言,设置承托后,中承托处,桥面板下缘的横向压应力明显减小。产生该现象的主要原因在于,设置承托后承托位置处桥面板厚度增加,预应力作用的截面积增大,钢束距桥面板下缘的偏移量也增大,而距桥面板上缘的距离却没有改变,两者相互叠加,从而使得桥面板下缘的横向预压应力减小明显。

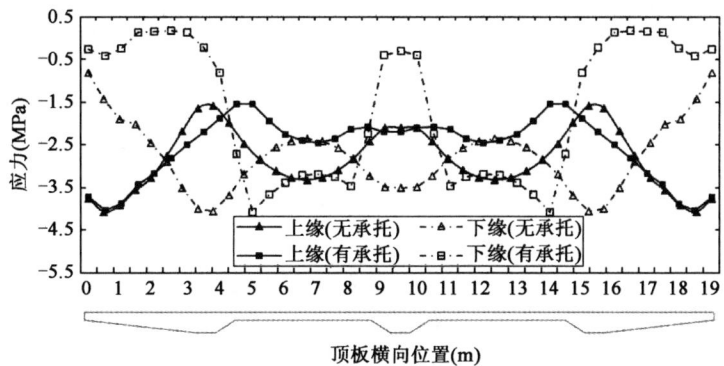

图 4　双室组合梁桥面板横向应力分布图

可见承托的设置对桥面板横向预应力效应将产生一定影响且其对单室截面和双室截面组合梁的影响是一致的,不可忽视。为定量研究承托设置所带来的桥面板横应力值改变情况,下面将讨论承托尺寸大小与桥面板横向应力值变化的相互关系。

1.2　承托尺寸对桥面板横向预应力的影响

由上述分析可知单室和双室截面组合梁桥面板横向预应力效应受承托影响一致,以下仅以双室截面组合梁为例进行分析。承托一般构造如图 5 所示,承托处竖向加腋为 h,水平加腋为 b,通过改变 h 与 b 值的大小分析承托尺寸对桥面板横向预应力效应的影响。承托一般构造如图 5 所示,图中 t 为桥面板厚度,w 为承托底部水平宽度。

1.2.1　承托水平加腋宽度对桥面板横向应力的影响

在保证承托其他参数一致的情况下,仅改变承托水平加腋 b 值的大小,分析承托水平加腋宽度对桥面板横向预应力效应的影响。b 取值分别为 $1.5h$、$2h$、$3h$。三种参数下桥面板横向应力分布如图 6 所示。

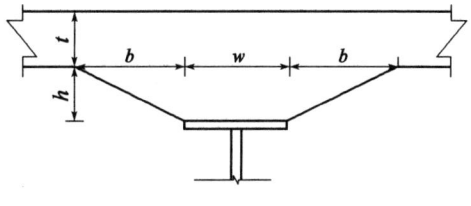

图 5　承托一般构造图

由图 6 可知,三种情况下,桥面板上缘及下缘的横向应力分布规律保持一致,随着承托水平加腋宽度 b 值的增大,在承托处顶板上缘及下缘的横向应力逐渐减小但幅度较小,且应力值的过渡也逐渐趋于平缓。悬臂板及各箱室中间位置处顶板的横向应力受承托宽度 b 值的影响很小,可以忽略不记。

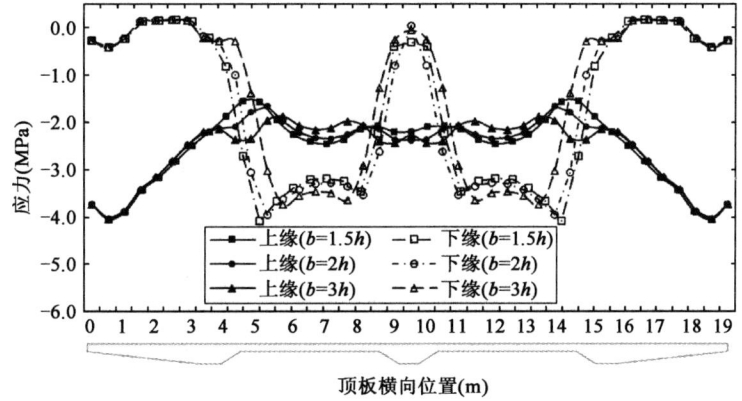

图 6　桥面板横向应力分布图

因此,承托水平加腋主要使的腹板处桥面板横向应力过渡平缓,从而改善钢混结合处桥面板的受力特性,而对桥面横向预应力作用效应的影响较小。在满足构造要求的情况下可适当加宽承托水平加腋,改善承托受力。

1.2.2 承托竖向加腋高度对桥面板横向应力的影响

在保证承托其他参数一致的情况下,仅改变承托竖向加腋 h 值的大小,分析承托竖向加腋高度对桥面板横向预应力效应的影响。h 取值分别为 t、$1.5t$、$2t$。三种参数下桥面板横向应力分布如图7所示。

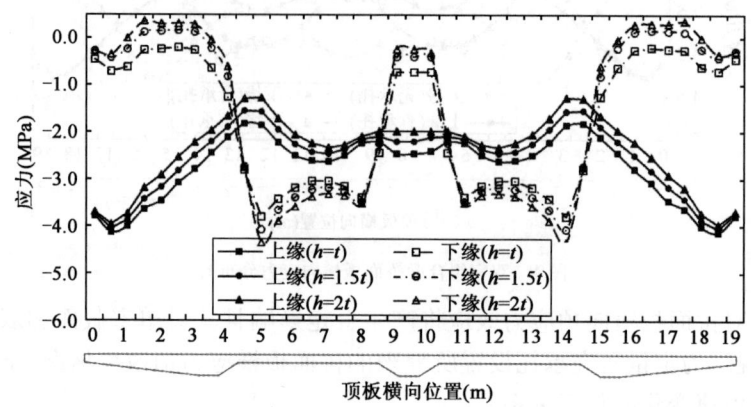

图7 桥面板横向应力分布图

由图7可知,三种情况下,桥面板上缘及下缘的横向应力分布规律保持一致,承托竖向加腋高度 h 的变化对顶板横向预应力效应的影响相对于承托水平加腋来说较大。对于顶板上缘而言,随着承托高度 h 的增加,顶板上缘的横向应力逐渐减小;对于顶板下缘而言,悬臂板和中腹板处,顶板下缘横向应力随着承托高度 h 的增加逐渐减小,而各承托之间位置处顶板下缘的横向应力随着承托高度 h 的增加逐渐增大。

这主要是因为承托竖向加腋增高导致承托处桥面板刚度增大,从而分配较大的横向负弯矩,而两箱室横向跨中位置桥面板分配的正弯矩减小,同时,在承托处由于承托加高带来的预应力作用截面增大,使得顶板预压应力随之减小。两者效应叠加,使得顶板上缘横向压应力减小。

1.3 预加力增减引起的桥面板横向应力变化

通过上述分析发现承托竖向加腋增高使得桥面板上缘横向压应力减小,这相当于减小了桥面板的横向预应力效应。为验证这一点,现统一将钢束预加力同时增加5%或减小5%,分析在横向预加力正常以及分别增加和减少5%这三种情况下,桥面板横向应力分布情况。三种预加力下桥面板上缘及下缘横向应力分布如图8所示。

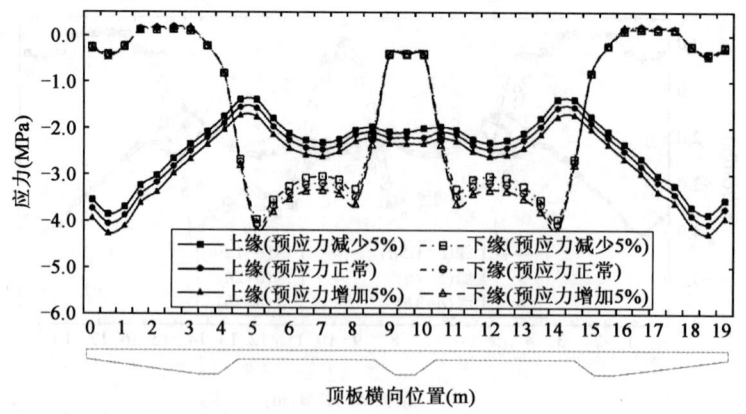

图8 桥面板横向应力分布图

由图8中不同横向预加力下桥面板横向应力分析可知,随着预加力的减小,顶板上缘的横向应力也随之减小；对于顶板下缘而言，随着钢束预加力的减小，除各箱室中间位置处顶板下缘的横向应力有所增加，其余位置处顶板下缘的横向应力变化较小。

由图7与图8对比可知，增加承托竖向加腋高度和降低横向预加力对顶板上缘横向受力的影响一致，承托高度的增加会降低顶板的横向预应力效应，因此承托高度不宜设置过高，以免过多降低横向钢束的预应力效应，使得桥面板抗裂性能降低。

1.4 车辆荷载效应

按图9所示两种工况进行车辆荷载的加载，分析承托设置对桥面板活载效应的影响。分析结果如图10所示，由于活载下桥面板下缘的横向应力与上缘正好相反，因此仅给出桥面板上缘结果进行说明。

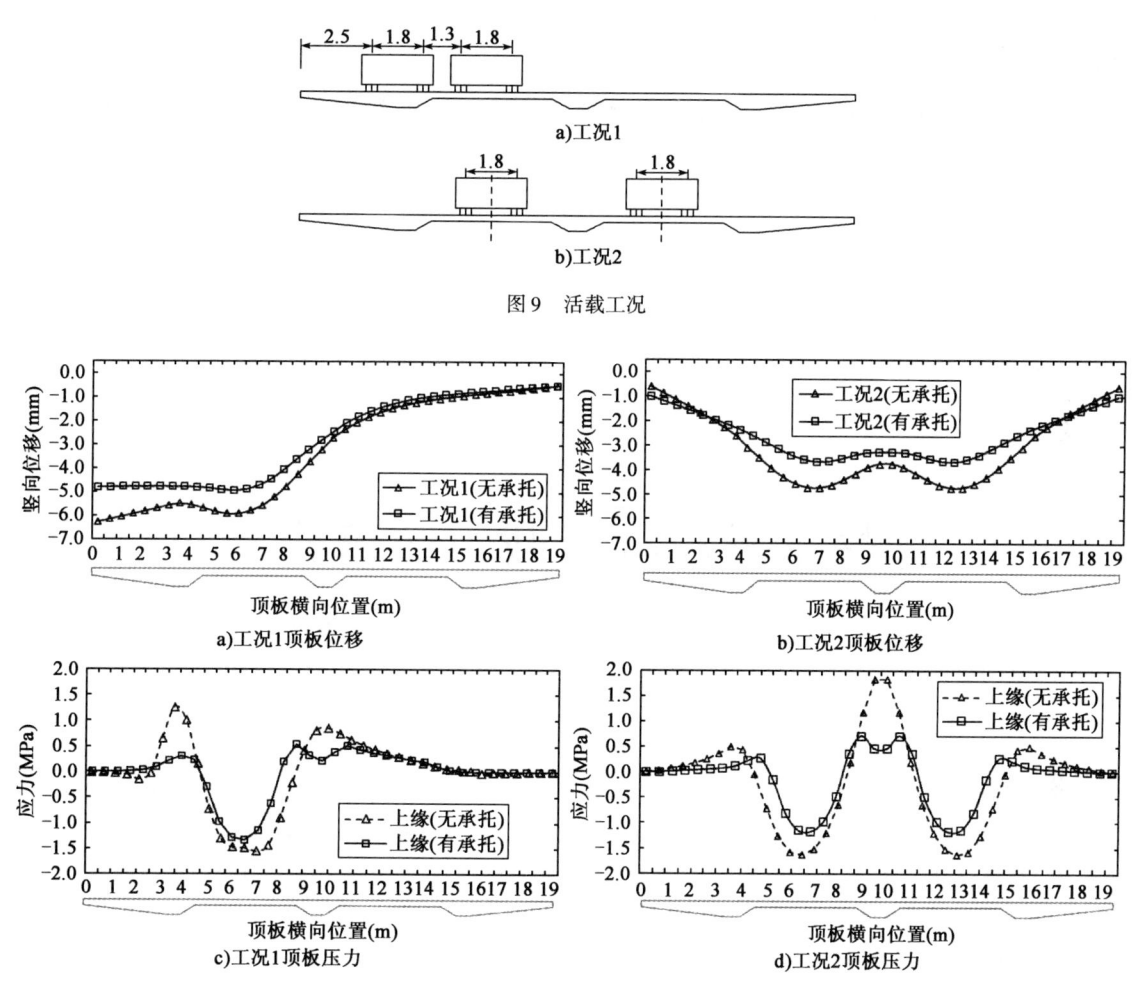

图9 活载工况

图10 活载效应

从图10a)、b)可知，设置承托后顶板竖向位移有一定程度减小。两种工况下设置承托前后桥面板横向应力分布规律相同，只是后者数值较前者有所减小，特别使得腹板位置处桥面板拉应力有较大程度减小。因为在车辆荷载作用下腹板处桥面板主要承受横向负弯矩，增加承托后使得该位置处刚度增大从而降低了横向应力。

由此可见，在组合梁腹板处增设承托，可使桥面板刚度增大，减小了活载作用下顶板的挠度，降低了活载产生的横向应力。

2 结　语

承托设置对钢混组合梁桥面板横向预应力效应有一定影响，且对单室和双室钢混组合梁桥面板横向预应力效应的影响一致，设置承托还可增加桥面板刚度降低活载应力。合理地设置承托能改善组合梁桥面板的横向受力特性。承托水平加腋宽度对桥面板横向预应力效应影响较小且能使承托处桥面板横向应力过渡平缓,增加承托竖向加腋高度和降低横向预加力对顶板上缘横向受力的影响一致,均使得桥面板上缘横向压应力减小,因此承托竖向加腋不宜设置过高,一般不超过2倍桥面板厚度,以免降低桥面板抗裂性能而导致开裂。

在实际工程中通过调整承托尺寸来改善桥面板横向受力是有限的,为兼顾纵向预应力布束要求、横向预压应力储备以及经济效应,承托竖向加腋高度 h 建议取 $1.2t \sim 1.5t$,为使桥面板横向应力过渡平缓,水平加腋宽度 b 可适当加宽,建议取 $3h$。

由于条件有限,本文分析主要基于有限元模拟结果难免存在一定的不足,有条件的读者可以根据试验加以完善,为组合梁桥面板承托的设置提供一定参考。

参考文献

[1] 赵品,荣学亮,叶见曙.承托设置对波形钢腹板箱梁桥面板横向内力的影响[J].公路交通科技,2020,37(08):41-47.
[2] 赵品,荣学亮,叶见曙.波形钢腹板箱梁桥面板横向内力计算方法[J].同济大学学报(自然科学版),2019,47(04):467-474.
[3] 朱颖杰.钢-混凝土组合箱梁桥横向受力性能与设计方法研究[D].北京:清华大学,2018.
[4] 钟新谷,舒小娟,张昊宇.预应力混凝土箱梁横向框架效应有限元分析[J].计算力学学报,2013,30(04):549-553.
[5] 朱聘儒.钢-混凝土组合梁设计原理[M].北京:中国建筑工业出版社,2006.

弹性支承压杆承载力数值分析

何培文 杨正朴 王 鹏 贺润祥 牛家伟
(长安大学公路学院)

摘 要 从目前已有的长杆弹性失稳分析研究出发,根据已知的弹性支承边界条件,建立了以失稳荷载水平为根的方程。在此基础上,进一步引入了新的无量纲参数,实现了对端部弹簧铰的刚度和临界失稳荷载水平的无量纲化。此外,以二分法作为方程解的方法,得到临界荷载与无量纲参数之间的关系。其研究成果,可避免量纲不统一导致的繁琐运算,有利于借助无量纲参数进行数据比较,对工程中失稳荷载的批量计算具有一定的参考价值。

关键词 材料力学 压杆稳定 解析法 边界条件 无量纲化

0 引 言

受压杆件能否正常工作,不仅依赖于其材料强度,且与其压曲失稳密切相关。1729 年,荷兰物理学教授穆欣布罗克(Musschenbroek P van)通过木杆的受压试验,得出"压曲荷载与杆长的平方成反比"的结论[1]。欧拉(L. Euler)于 1744 年提出了压杆失稳的临界荷载[2]。此后,众多学者依据欧拉公式进行了深入研究,广泛讨论了压杆在实际工程中的应用方法[3],进行了在不同边界条件下压杆的失稳分析[4]。

已有的研究通过研究杆件失稳临界状态[5],推导出长杆在边界弹性支承下的欧拉公式。但该欧拉公式的计算需要考虑量纲的统一,在工程应用中需要对不同的量纲进行转化,使计算复杂化,且没有给出具体的求解过程;此外,其推导出的欧拉公式,并不能体现在端部边界条件、杆件属性的改变下临界荷载的变化规律。因此,基于现有研究,引入新的无量纲参数进行合理优化,并对求解方法和参数规律进行探讨显得尤为重要。

1 长杆失稳临界力

1.1 建立微分方程

工程中常应用的两端焊接杆件在转化为分析模型时,杆件两端并非完全无法转动,但也不能够自由转动。这类杆件可以视作两端受到弹性支承,其特性与杆件两端焊接的其他部件材料属性相关。因此,对于一根两端受到弹簧铰约束的长杆,可作如图1所示的受力分析。

已知等截面直梁的挠曲线近似微分方程为:

$$y'' = -\frac{M(x)}{EI} \quad (1)$$

截取杆件的下部分,根据图1中受力分析图建立平衡方程,并代入式(1)可得:

$$M_A + P_A x = EIy'' + Py \quad (2)$$

式中:M_A——杆件A端弹簧铰支座提供的弯矩(N·m);

P_A——杆件A端提供的水平支反力(N);

x——沿杆件方向截取的长度(m);

EI——杆件的抗弯刚度(N·m²);

y——杆件的侧向挠曲(m);

P——杆件受到的轴向力(N)。

M_A、M_B为假设杆件两端受到与其他构件相连的弹性约束[5]。使得杆件沿水平方向不能移动,但端部可有微小转动,因此其提供的弯矩为杆件端部弹簧铰的刚度与转角之积:$M = Cy'$。

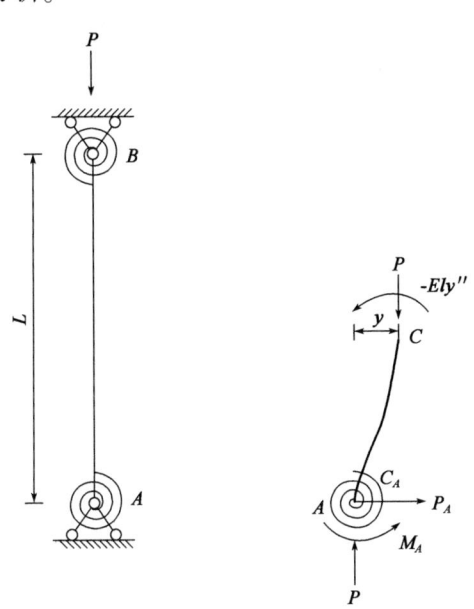

图1 两端受弹簧铰约束受力分析

引进参数 $k^2 = \dfrac{P}{EI}$,并将其代入式(2),简化可得:

$$y'' + k^2 y = \frac{P_A}{EI}x + \frac{M_A}{EI} \quad (3)$$

对该微分方程进行求解,可得:

$$y = A\sin kx + B\cos kx + \frac{P_A x}{P} + \frac{M_A}{P} \quad (4)$$

1.2 引入边界条件

杆件的A端和B端均有支反力为杆件平衡弹簧铰提供的弯矩,两支反力值分别如下:

$$P_A = \frac{M_B - M_A}{L} \quad (5)$$

$$P_B = \frac{M_B - M_A}{L} \quad (6)$$

式中:P_A、P_B——杆件A端和B端提供的水平支反力(N);

M_A、M_B——A端和B端弹簧铰支座提供的弯矩(N·m);

L——杆件的长度(m)。

对于两端采用弹簧铰支承的受压长杆,令C_A、C_B为A、B两端的弹簧铰的刚度(N·m),引入以下边界条件:

杆件A端无侧向挠曲(1-7:$x=0$, $y=0$);杆件B端无侧向挠曲(1-8:$x=L$, $y=0$);杆件A端弹簧铰提供的弯矩为该弹簧铰的刚度与转角之积(1-9:$M_A = C_A y'_A$);杆件B端弹簧铰提供的弯矩为该弹簧铰的刚度与转角之积(1-10:$M_B = C_B y'_B$)。

$$B + \frac{1}{P}M_A = 0 \tag{7}$$

$$\sin kLA + \cos kLB + \frac{1}{P}M_B = 0 \tag{8}$$

$$kC_A A - \left(\frac{C_A}{PL} + 1\right)M_A + \frac{C_A}{PL}M_B = 0 \tag{9}$$

$$C_B k\cos kLA + C_B k\sin kLB - \frac{C_B}{PL}M_A + \left(\frac{C_B}{PL} - 1\right)M_B = 0 \tag{10}$$

为使 M_A、M_B、A 和 B 具有非零解，可得方程组对应行列式为零。
简化行列式可得式(11)：

$$\left(\frac{\sin kL}{kL} - \cos kL\right)\left(\frac{1}{C_A} + \frac{1}{C_B}\right) + \frac{1}{C_A C_B}\frac{P^2}{kL}\sin kL + \frac{1}{L}(2 - 2\cos kL - kL\sin kL) = 0 \tag{11}$$

在式中，P 以外的其他参数均与构件自身材料属性相关，k 可通过 P 确定。故式(11)为单变量方程，变量为 P。

1.3 公式无量纲化

为了便于对方程求解，以下进行方程的无量纲化处理。定义临界荷载水平 $\chi = \sqrt{\frac{PL^2}{EI}}$；$A$ 端弹簧铰无量纲刚度 $\overline{C_A} = \frac{C_A L}{EI}$；$B$ 端弹簧铰无量纲刚度 $\overline{C_B} = \frac{C_B L}{EI}$。

并将以上参数代入式(11)简化可得：

$$\chi^3 \frac{\sin\chi}{C_A C_B} - \chi^2 \cos\chi\left(\frac{1}{C_A} + \frac{1}{C_B}\right) + \chi\sin\chi\left(\frac{1}{C_A} + \frac{1}{C_B}\right) + (2 - 2\cos\chi - \chi\sin\chi) = 0 \tag{12}$$

假定以下函数并求该函数的 χ 根，各参数适用范围也将在接下来进行讨论。

$$f(\chi) = \chi^3 \frac{\sin\chi}{C_A C_B} - \chi^2 \cos\chi\left(\frac{1}{C_A} + \frac{1}{C_B}\right) + \chi\sin\chi\left(\frac{1}{C_A} + \frac{1}{C_B}\right) + (2 - 2\cos\chi - \chi\sin\chi) \tag{13}$$

经无量纲处理，发现临界荷载水平和杆件两端的弹簧铰无量纲刚度之间有以下规律：
①定义的临界荷载水平、端部弹簧铰无量纲刚度均和杆件的长度成正比。
②对于弹簧铰无量纲刚度，在已知一种临界荷载水平和相关参数的情况下，若不改变材料刚度 EI，通过保持杆件长度 L 和端部提供的弹簧铰刚度 C 之积不变，则得到的临界荷载水平也不变，从而可确定临界荷载大小。
③对于临界荷载水平，在杆件刚度 EI 和长度 L 比例保持不变的情况下，通过调整两个端部弹簧铰刚度的关系，同样可以使得临界荷载水平保持不变，即要求 $(C_A + C_B)$ 和 $C_A C_B$ 的值为定值。
④同理，保持 χ、$\overline{C_A}$、$\overline{C_B}$ 或 $\left(\frac{1}{C_A} + \frac{1}{C_B}\right)$、$\frac{1}{C_A C_B}$ 的值恒定的情况下，可通过调整 C_A、C_B、EI 和 L 中部分参数，求得其他参数。

1.4 参数适用范围

目前已有的研究[5]表明，在杆端弯矩为该弹簧铰刚度与转角之积的情况下，两端铰接的弹簧铰的刚度可视作 $C = 0$，函数中 χ 的根能取得的最小非零解为 π；而两端固结的弹簧铰的刚度则可视作 $C = \infty$，函数中 χ 能取得的最小非零解为 2π；对一端固结一端铰接的杆件，函数中 χ 能取得的最小非零解约为 1.43π。在式(13)中，使得 $\overline{C} \to 0^+$ 和 $\overline{C} \to +\infty$ 可以分别近似模拟端部支承为铰接和固结的情况。

经分析，当 $\overline{C_A} > 10^3$ 且 $\overline{C_B} > 10^3$ 时 $\chi > 1.99\pi$，边界条件非常接近于两端固结；当 $\overline{C_A} < 10^{-2}$ 且 $\overline{C_B} < 10^{-2}$ 时 $\chi < 1.01\pi$，边界条件非常接近于两端铰接。当 $\overline{C_A} = 10^{-2}$ 且 $\overline{C_B} = 10^3$ 时 $\chi = 1.431\pi$，与一端铰接一端固结的边界条件下的预期值一致。因此，本函数适用无量纲刚度等于 10^{-2} 和 10^3 铰接边界条件与固结边界

条件,$\overline{C_A},\overline{C_B} \in [10^{-2}, 10^3]$。

2 公式求解讨论

本文推导出的式(13)中自变量为χ,包含于三角函数中,因此该方程属于超越方程,解析解很难求得。因此采用数值方法进行计算,为了取得较快的解算效率,通常采用的方法有具有较快收敛速度的牛顿(Newton)迭代法和二分法。

2.1 Newton迭代法可行性讨论

为求得近似数值解,将牛顿(Newton)迭代法纳入考虑范围,构造无限循环的迭代函数,使得函数值向方程根收敛,进行其可行性的讨论。

该方法是否适用,需要讨论迭代式是否在相应区间内收敛。因此,首先求出式(13)对χ的两阶导数如下:

$$f'(\chi) = \chi(-1 - B + A\chi^2)\cos\chi + (1 + B + 3A\chi^2 + B\chi^2)\sin\chi \tag{14}$$

$$f''(\chi) = \chi\{(6A + B)\chi\cos\chi + [1 + 3B - A(-6 + \chi^2)]\sin\chi\} \tag{15}$$

$f'(\chi), f''(\chi)$在区间$[\pi, 2\pi]$上连续,构造迭代函数:

$$\chi_{k+1} = \chi_k - \frac{f(\chi_k)}{f'(\chi_k)} = \chi_k - \frac{2 - (2 + B\chi^2)\cos\chi + \chi(-1 + B + A\chi^2)\sin\chi}{\chi(-1 - B + A\chi^2)\cos\chi + (1 + B + 3A\chi^2 + B\chi^2)\sin\chi} \tag{16}$$

此时可以考虑迭代的收敛性如下:

(1)$f(\pi) = 4 + B\pi^2, f(2\pi) = -4B\pi^2, f(\pi)f(2\pi) < 0$;

(2)$f'(\pi) = \pi + B\pi - A\pi^3, f'(2\pi) = -2\pi - 2B\pi + 8A\pi^3$,在$A$和$B$未确定的情况下$f'(\pi)$和$f'(2\pi)$可能异号,因此,$f'(\chi) \neq 0$的条件不能保证成立;同时,$f''(\pi) = -6A\pi^2 - B\pi^2 < 0, f''(2\pi) = 24A\pi^2 + 4B\pi^2 > 0$,因此在区间$[\pi, 2\pi]$存在$f''(\chi) = 0$,牛顿迭代法在该区间内不收敛。

故可知构造迭代法时,牛顿迭代法不适用于本方程。

2.2 二分法

根据该函数的适用范围,χ在区间$[\pi, 2\pi]$上连续不断,且$f(\pi) \cdot f(2\pi) < 0$。结合其物理含义,在区间上,函数有且仅有一个零点,符合二分法的适用条件[7]。

令$A = \dfrac{1}{C_A C_B}, B = \left(\dfrac{1}{C_A} + \dfrac{1}{C_B}\right)$,可将式(13)简化为下式:

$$f(\chi) = 2 - (2 + B\chi^2)\cos\chi + \chi(-1 + B + A\chi^2)\sin\chi \tag{17}$$

下面给出利用二分法求函数根的计算过程。

(1)首先确定$f(\chi) = 0$的根的存在区间为$[a, b]$,计算端点值$f(a)$和$f(b)$,若端点值为0则终止计算,根即位于该端点。

(2)计算区间的中点值$f\left(\dfrac{a+b}{2}\right)$,并进行如下判断:若$f\left(\dfrac{a+b}{2}\right) = 0$,终止计算,根即为$\dfrac{a+b}{2}$;若$f\left(\dfrac{a+b}{2}\right) \cdot f(a) < 0$,则根属于区间$\left(a, \dfrac{a+b}{2}\right)$,以新的区间$\left(a, \dfrac{a+b}{2}\right)$代替原区间;若$f\left(\dfrac{a+b}{2}\right) \cdot f(b) < 0$,则根属于区间$\left(\dfrac{a+b}{2}, b\right)$,以新的区间$\left(\dfrac{a+b}{2}, b\right)$代替原区间。

(3)重复步骤②直到区间缩小至不大于0.01,此时区间中点$\dfrac{a+b}{2}$即为根。

经验证,二分法能够有效取得方程根,并满足误差要求。相关算例将于后文中体现。

3 算例分析

3.1 算例

一等截面长杆长度为 $L=3\text{m}$,采用 10 号热轧工字钢(GB/T 706—2016),其高度 $h=100\text{mm}$,腿宽度 $b=68\text{mm}$,腰厚度 $d=4.5\text{mm}$,截面积为 14.3cm^2,惯性矩为 $I=2.45\times10^{-6}\text{m}^4$,材料刚度采用 $E=215\text{GPa}$,A 端的弹簧铰刚度 $C_A=1404667\text{N}\cdot\text{m}$,B 端的弹簧铰刚度 $C_B=1404667\text{N}\cdot\text{m}$,求解杆件的临界失稳荷载。

3.2 结果分析

通过提供的弹簧铰的刚度,将其转化为本文定义的弹簧铰无量纲刚度如下:

$$\overline{C_A}=\frac{C_A L}{EI}=1.139$$

$$\overline{C_B}=\frac{C_B L}{EI}=1.139$$

引入 $A=\dfrac{1}{C_A C_B}=0.77074, B=\left(\dfrac{1}{C_A}+\dfrac{1}{C_B}\right)=1.75583$,代入式(17)求根。

首先,$f(\pi)=21.329>0, f(2\pi)=-69.318$,且 $f(\chi)$ 在区间内是一个连续函数,故 $[\pi,2\pi]$ 是该函数的有根区间。将 $[\pi,2\pi]$ 等分为两个区间 $[\pi,1.5\pi]$、$[1.5\pi,2\pi]$,并计算 $f(1.5\pi)=-518.065$,可知 $[1.5\pi,2\pi]$ 将替换原有根区间。以此类推,直至符合所求根的误差要求。具体过程见表1。

二分法计算过程　　　　表1

χ	$f(\chi)$	有根区间
π	21.329	—
2π	−69.318	$[\pi,2\pi]$
1.5π	−82.217	$[\pi,1.5\pi]$
1.25π	−12.542	$[\pi,1.25\pi]$
1.125π	10.067	$[1.125\pi,1.25\pi]$
1.1875π	0.182	$[1.1875\pi,1.25\pi]$
1.21875π	−5.837	$[1.1875\pi,1.21875\pi]$
1.203125π	−2.740	$[1.078125\pi,1.203125\pi]$

$x^*=(1.078125\pi+1.203125\pi)/2=1.1953125\pi$,即所求的根,误差不超过 1%。

根据 $\chi=\sqrt{\dfrac{PL^2}{EI}}$ 可求得临界失稳荷载 $P=113.786\text{ kN}$。

4 结 论

本文采用解析法,分析了杆端弹簧铰支承下长杆的临界力,并引入新的无量纲参数,导出了便于求解的无量纲压杆失稳函数。经分析,可以得到以下结论:

(1)本文基于已有的研究和假设,考虑长杆端部受到弹簧铰约束的影响,推导建立以失稳荷载水平为根的方程。

(2)推导得到的方程实现了参数无量纲处理,在进行批量计算时,可避免不同数据中量纲不统一带来的繁琐计算。同时,在改变边界条件和材料属性的情况下,本文提出的无量纲参数失稳荷载水平和端部弹簧铰的刚度,可通过其代数关系实现相互转化。

(3)针对建立的方程,通过算例,验证了二分法相较于牛顿迭代法具有计算的可行性。若进行其他迭代函数的构造,则需要进行多次求导,计算不如二分法求解简便。

(4)本文提出的公式适用于具有端部弹性支承的等截面长杆。杆件受压作用下端部的荷载偏心、杆件初始挠曲等其余缺陷造成的影响,还需要进一步的研究讨论。

参考文献

[1] Luis A. Godoy, Isaac Elishakoff. The Experimental Contribution of Petrus Van Musschenbroek to the Discovery of a Buckling Formula in the Early 18th Century[J]. International Journal of Structural Stability and Dynamics, 2020, 20(05).
[2] EULER LEONHARD. Sur la force de colonnes[J]. Memoires de l'Academie de Berlin, 1759.
[3] 王立军. 轴心受压杆件的弯曲屈曲[J]. 建筑结构, 2019, 49(19):126-135.4.
[4] 尤明庆. 端部切向载荷作用下的压杆失稳分析及其应用[J]. 力学季刊, 2019, 40(01):160-166.
[5] 孙训方,方孝淑,关来泰. 材料力学(II)[M]. 5版. 北京:高等教育出版社, 2009.
[6] 封建湖,车刚明. 数值分析原理[M]. 北京:科学出版社, 2001.
[7] 何天荣. 非线性方程的数值解法中的二分法[J]. 科技风, 2016(13):28.

提高铁路悬索桥竖向刚度的结构措施研究

陈 鑫[1] 沈锐利[1] 童登国[2]

(1. 西南交通大学土木工程学院; 2. 中铁二院工程集团有限责任公司)

摘 要 铁路行车对桥梁刚度要求严格,需要足够的线路平顺度;采取结构措施提高大跨度铁路悬索桥的结构刚度,有利于铁路悬索桥向更高运营速度发展。以1000m级双线铁路悬索桥为背景,通过有限元计算比较了不同梁高下的结构竖向刚度指标;为提高结构竖向刚度,增设连接主缆与桥塔下横梁的斜拉索,计算分析表明:通过布置斜拉索可以有效减小加劲梁的上挠值,下挠值虽没有明显降低,但其最大值会由主跨1/4位置向跨中靠近;竖向刚度的改善程度与布置斜拉索的对数成正比。

关键词 铁路悬索桥 桥梁刚度 有限元分析 斜拉索

0 引 言

随着铁路技术标准的提高,铁路选线的自由度受到比较大的制约,客观上需要铁路桥梁向更大跨度发展。悬索桥跨越能力强,是大跨度桥梁的首选桥型之一[1]。铁路悬索桥恒活比相对较小、活载作用下竖向变形大,然而铁路行车对桥梁变形均匀性等要求很严格,正是这一矛盾限制了1000m级铁路悬索桥的应用。因此,研究提高铁路悬索桥竖向刚度的结构改善措施,对铁路建设意义重大。

大跨度铁路悬索桥结构柔性较大,控制结构设计的往往是桥梁刚度。李迎九[2]系统阐述了千米跨度铁路悬索桥的建造关键技术、技术难点,认为悬索桥的合理刚度及其结构构造是设计必须解决的首要问题。铁路悬索桥充分考虑了列车运行平稳性,加劲梁设计为多跨连续结构[3]。因此从科学角度考虑,刚度标准的确定应与列车运营速度相关[4]。五峰山长江大桥属于高速铁路范畴,其单独列车作用、列车+汽车作用竖向挠跨比限值分别为1/450、1/400[5],在建的丽香铁路金沙江大桥为主跨660m的铁路悬索桥,为双线普速铁路,竖向挠跨比限值为1/350[5]。五峰山长江大桥和金沙江大桥的竖向挠跨比均考虑了列车运营速度的要求[6],2座大桥的设计标准不同,具体采用的刚度限值也不同。

为提高悬索桥的刚度,从总体布置方面主要考虑改变加劲梁的边中跨比、高跨比、宽跨比以及设置辅助墩等措施,从结构方面主要可以采用斜拉-悬吊组合体系及双链式悬索桥体系等[7]。2016年建成通车的土耳其博斯普鲁斯海峡三桥就采用了斜拉-悬索协作体系,以增加桥梁刚度[8]。

本文针对铁路悬索桥竖向刚度问题,以一主跨1060m的铁路悬索桥为基础,计算了不同桁高下结构的竖向指标,研究了增设连接主缆与桥塔下横梁的斜拉索的措施对竖向刚度的提高效果。

1 方案及计算说明

以一主跨1060m的单跨悬吊钢桁梁悬索桥为基本模型,结构总体布置如图1所示。为比较桁高影响,确立了以下方案分别命名为A方案、B方案、C方案及D方案。各方案的梁宽都取30m,梁高则分别为10m(A方案)、和12m(B方案),在A方案的基础上增设一对连接桥塔下横梁和主跨1/8位置的1号索为方案D,增设连接桥塔下横梁和主跨1/8位置的1号索和连接到主跨1/4位置的2号索为E方案。调整主缆线型保证各矢跨比都为1/9。

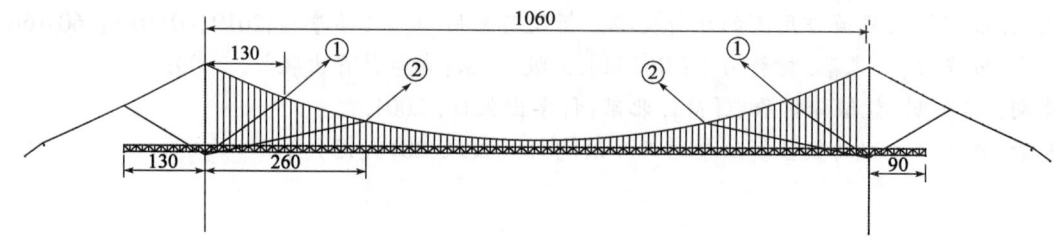

图1 添加斜索方案图(尺寸单位:m)

本桥拟服务于某一级客货共线铁路,故参照客货共线铁路的荷载图示施加列车荷载。计算中对列车荷载的处理除常规的影响线加载外,为反映列车在加劲梁各位置时结构的竖向变形,把列车作为一定长度的静荷载,按前进方向依次向前推进。通过计算每个工况下结构的变形指标并连成曲线作图,更真实地反映列车在桥上各位置时的结构变形。

2 竖向刚度对比分析

悬索桥的竖向刚度指标国内外规范主要包括挠跨比和梁端转角,日本在新干线网设计标准中对结构物的相对位移和转动容许值做了要求,本文主要关心桥台位置处的相对竖向位移即桥台错位。从本质上来说,桥梁刚度问题就是要使轨道具有满足要求的平顺度以保证列车运行的爬坡性能及连接可靠性,进行列车走行性计算时,考虑将最新版的《铁路线路规范》中[9]最大坡度限值及相邻坡度差作为计算指标。

2.1 影响线加载计算分析

对上文拟定的五个方案分别建立BNLAS有限元模型,为与后文列车走行指标对应,取单列列车按影响线加载的方式计算加劲梁各节点的位移转角,作位移包络及变形比较图如图2所示,将最大坡度及相邻坡度见表1。

坡 度 对 比 表1

方 案	坡度限值(‰rad)	相邻坡度差(‰rad)
A	7.81	0.495
B	6.55	0.46
C	6.32	0.5
D	5.50	0.5

分析位移包络图的计算结果可知:

(1)比较A、B方案,梁高是影响铁路悬索桥竖向刚度的重要因素,增加梁高可明显减小竖向挠跨比和桥台错位,并能有效改善列车走行过程中的最大坡度值及相邻坡度差。

(2)比较A、C方案,增设斜拉索后加劲梁整体位移减小,活载作用下加劲梁的上挠值减小约50%,下挠最大值出现的位置由1/4主跨位置向跨中改变,位移包络图呈现向跨中收拢的趋势。

(3)比较C、D方案,增设的斜拉索对数越多,位移包络图收拢得越明显,增设两对斜拉索相比于一对,最大上挠值减小0.189m,最大下挠值略微增大0.007m。

（4）比较 B、C 方案，在桁高 10m 的基础上增设一对斜拉索后，相较于桁高为 12m 的 B 方案，最大挠度减小为 0.026m，桥台错位减小为 2.778mm。增设连接桥塔下横梁与主缆的斜拉索可以在不增加梁高的前提下有效提高竖向刚度，且斜拉索的对数越多，效果越好。

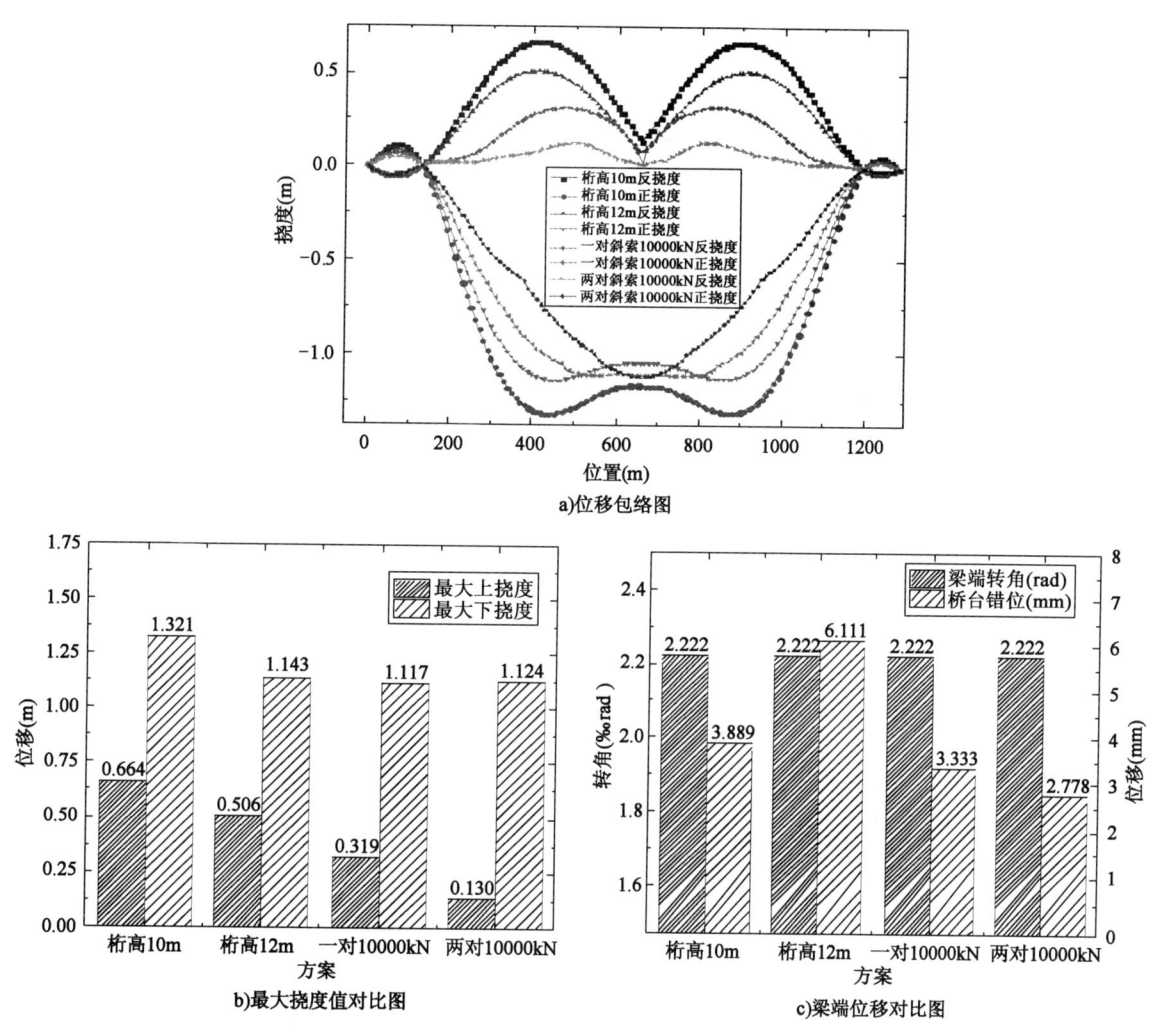

图 2　加斜索方案比较图

2.2　列车走行性计算分析

将列车作为一定长度的静荷载（文中取单列列车长度为 242m），按前进方向依次向前推进进行走行性刚度计算。为记录列车所在的位置，记车头从桥左端上桥为工况①，列车每前进 50m 分别作为工况②、③、④、…、㉗，直到车尾从桥右端下桥，共 27 个工况。计算列车在各个位置的位移及转角并连线作图，以车中为例可做图如图 3，车头及车尾的规律与车中一致，此处不做赘述。

分析各方案车中走行过程的竖向位移及转角图可以发现：

（1）列车过桥的过程中，车中的最大位移位置出现在约主跨 1/4 位置处，车头或车尾通过点的转角最大，最大转角出现在主跨靠近桥塔的位置。

（2）比较 A、B 方案，桁高越大，列车走行至加劲梁各位置处的竖向位移和转角越小，列车走行的平顺度越好。

（3）比较 A、C 方案，增设斜拉索后，车中过桥过程中在加劲梁各位置的位移和转角都有减小，最大位移减小为 0.217m，最大转角减小 1.37‰rad，列车过桥位移图向跨中收拢，最大位移出现的位置由 1/4 主跨趋近于跨中位置。

（4）比较 C、D 方案，增设斜拉索的对数越多，列车过桥的位移和转角图的收拢趋势越明显，但最大位移值有所增大。斜拉索由一对增加至两对后,最大位移值略增大 0.013m,但最大转角值减小 0.79‰rad。

(5)比较 B、C 方案,与桁高 12m 方案对比,在桁高 10m 的基础上增设一对斜拉索后,车中在过桥过程中的最大挠度减小 0.024m,最大转角减小 0.54‰rad,通过增设连接桥塔下横梁与主缆的斜拉索,可在不增加梁高的前提下有效减小列车过桥过程的位移和转角。

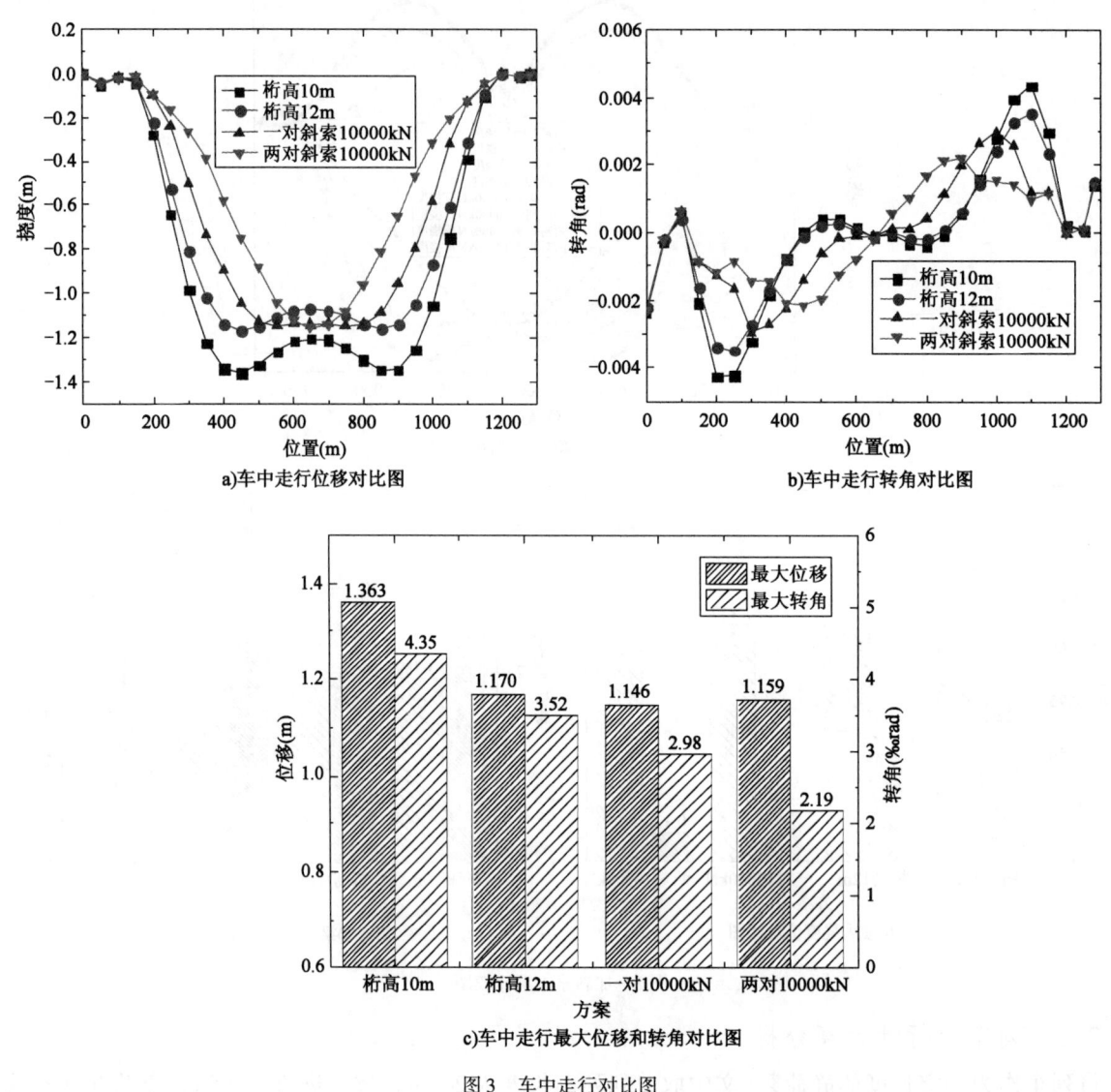

图 3　车中走行对比图

3　结　语

本文以一1000m 级铁路悬索桥为背景,计算了不同桁高和设置斜拉索结构的竖向刚度指标,研究的主要结论如下:

(1)结构的竖向刚度与桁高成正相关,增设主缆和桥塔下横梁之间的斜拉索,可以在不增大桁高的前提下有效提高铁路悬索桥的竖向刚度指标。其中活载作用下的上挠值减小明显,最大下挠位置由 1/4 主跨位置向跨中靠近,桥台错位值随之减小。

(2)考虑列车走行过程,在主缆和桥塔下横梁之间增设斜拉索后,列车在加劲梁上各点的位移值整体减小,各位置处的转角同样也呈现减小趋势,最大位移及转角值向跨中靠近。

(3)增设斜拉索对铁路悬索桥竖向刚度的提高效果与斜拉索对数及张拉力成正比,增设主缆到桥塔下横梁处的斜拉索,对提高列车运营条件下加劲梁竖向刚度有较好的效果。

参考文献

[1] 肖海珠,张晓勇,徐恭义.武汉杨泗港长江大桥主桥静动力特性研究[J].世界桥梁,2019,047(06):70-73.
[2] 李迎九.千米跨度高速铁路悬索桥建造技术现状与展望[J].中国铁路,2019(09):1-8.
[3] 唐贺强,徐恭义,刘汉顺.悬索桥用于铁路桥梁的可行性分析[J].桥梁设计,2017,47(02):13-18.
[4] 李永乐,蔡宪棠,安伟胜,等.大跨度铁路悬索桥结构刚度敏感性研究[J].中国铁道科学,2011,032(04):24-30.
[5] 辛杰.铁路悬索桥设计活载模式与结构合理刚度标准研究[J].铁道建筑,2020,60(12):1-4.
[6] 陈岳剑.车辆轨道耦合建模与轨道不平顺在线惯性监测研究[D].南京理工大学,2015.
[7] 沈锐利,张东,唐茂林.大跨度铁路悬索桥合理刚度指标值的探讨[A].中国土木工程学会桥梁及结构工程分会.第二十届全国桥梁学术会议论文集(上册)[C]//中国土木工程学会桥梁及结构工程分会:中国土木工程学会,2012:8.
[8] 王志平.主跨1500 m公铁合建悬索桥结构参数研究[J].铁道标准设计,2020,64(S1):69-73+109.
[9] 铁路线路设计规范:TB 10098—2017[S].2017.

变权理论在桥梁评定中的应用

张亚博 陈峰 彭文锋 曹黎明 查斌

(1.长安大学;2.在役长大桥梁安全与健康国家重点实验室)

摘　要　根据现行技术状况评定标准,结合桥梁检测实践分析,提出了桥梁一般状态和特殊状态的相关定义,分析了变权理论对特殊状态下的桥梁进行技术状况评定时的适用性;以变权理论中均衡系数 α 为核心研究指标,对 α 的取值进行了探究,推导了基于变权理论的桥梁技术评定新方法,完成了相关的工程验证。

关键词　桥梁工程　变权理论　均衡系数　程度分析法　桥梁技术状况评定

0　引　言

现行《公路桥梁技术状况评定标准》(JTG/T H21—2011)对桥梁检测工作给出了规范化的流程和方法,标准的实行实现了桥梁检测工作的标准化和规范化,同时保证了检测结果对桥梁真实技术状态的客观反映。

但考虑到桥梁技术状况评定规范的普适性,标准中给出的结构权值均为固定值,谓之"常权",而常权显然只能以桥梁的一般状态为基础进行确定,这就造成了对部分特殊状态的桥梁,标准适应性略有不足的情况。

相对于常权理论,变权理论能够更好地考虑指标间的均衡性及差异性,被广泛应用于多目标决策领域,多位学者[1-2]尝试将变权理论引入桥梁技术状况评定工作中。本文变权理论在桥梁评定中的适用性进行了较为全面的分析,并推导了基于变权理论的桥梁评定修正方法。

1　桥梁的一般性状态与特殊状态

以某省干线公路桥梁定期检查项目为依托,选取了总体技术状况评定等级在3类及3类以下的桥梁共计153座,提取其上部结构,下部结构及桥面系的技术状况评定等级,定义结构评定等级3级及以下为损伤状态,分析各部位损伤的差异性。

由于上部结构与桥面系为主要承重结构和车辆荷载的直接作用结构,故损概率较大。这与如图1所示规律一致,为表述方便,我们将这一状态定义为桥梁结构在服役过程中的"一般性状态"。但并非所有桥梁的状态均符合这种"一般性状态"。

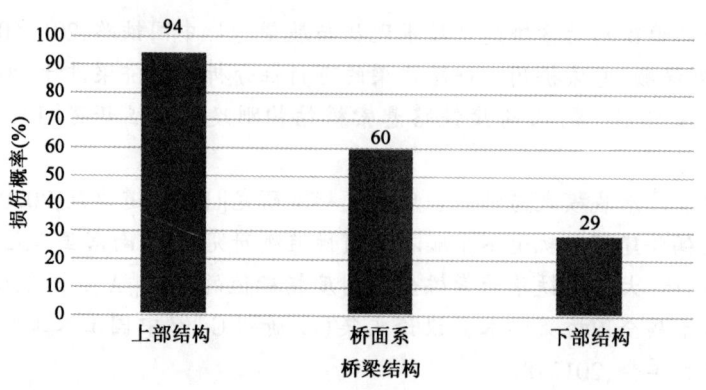

图1 结构损伤概率图

将收集到的153座3类桥按其评定等级在3类及3类以下的结构数量分为不同的桥梁状态,汇总各状态桥梁的数量及占比如表1所示。

不同状态的桥梁占比　　　　　　　　　　　　　　　　　　　表1

评定等级为3类及以下的结构	桥梁数量	占比(%)
仅上部结构	39	26
仅下部结构	2	1
仅桥面系	2	1
上部结构,下部结构,桥面系	18	12
上部结构,桥面系	66	43
上部结构,下部结构	20	13
桥面系,下部结构	6	4

可以看到,与上述的"一般状态"有所不同的是,小部分评定等级较低桥梁,处于仅单一结构状态情况,对该状态下的桥梁,当受损结构的权重值较低时,则会出现受损结构病害严重而总体状况评定等级较好的结果。这显然与结构的真实状态存在差异;我们将这种部分结构病害严重而整体技术状态良好的情况称为"特殊状态"。

为真实客观评价这类特殊状态的桥梁,本文在桥梁评定过程中引入变权理论,以期使桥梁技术状况评定的结果更好地反映桥梁的真实状态。

2　变权理论在桥梁评估中的应用

2.1　变权理论

变权理论本质上是对常权的修正理论,其核心在于评估目标的过程中构造一组能够表征各指标的实际状态以及相对均衡性的状态变权向量,对已经确定的权值进行调整,从而实现在评定过程中对结构实际状态的考虑。李洪兴教授引入了均衡函数的概念,提出通过构造均衡函数来获得状态变权向量的理论方法,并给出了一系列构造均衡函数的方法[3-4]。按照工程经验,均衡函数按下式取值:

$$B(x_1,\cdots,x_n) = \sum_{j=1}^{n} x_j^{\alpha} \quad (0 < \alpha \leq 1) \tag{1}$$

在已知均衡函数的前提下,变权计算公式如下:

$$w_j[x_1,\cdots,x_n,\omega_1^{(0)},\cdots,\omega_n^{(0)}] = \frac{\omega_j^{(0)}\dfrac{\partial B(x_1,\cdots,x_n)}{\partial x_j}}{\sum_{k=1}^{n}\dfrac{\partial B(x_1,\cdots,x_n)}{\partial x_k}} \qquad (2)$$

式中：B——均衡函数；

$\omega_j^{(0)}$——第 j 个指标的初始权值；

D_j——指标评估值；

ω_j——第 j 个指标的变权后权值；

x_j——D_j 的百分数；

α——均衡函数。

将式(1)代入式(2)，得到常用的变权公式如下：

$$w_j[x_1,\cdots,x_n,\omega_1^{(0)},\cdots,\omega_n^{(0)}] = \frac{\omega_j^{(0)} x_j^{\alpha-1}}{\sum_{k=1}^{n}\omega_k^{(0)} x_k^{\alpha-1}} \qquad (3)$$

显然，在已知各指标值初始权重 $\omega_j^{(0)}$ 和指标评估值 D_j 的情况下，确定均衡系数后即可按照变权公式求解新的权重。当前，对均衡系数如何取值的问题尚缺乏理论研究，故多按工程经验取 0.2～0.5 之间的值[1]，但这样必然导致盲目性，因此有必要对均衡系数的取值问题进行探究。

2.2 均衡系数 α 取值特性分析

为分析均衡系数的取值特性，现假设某桥下部结构为主要缺损结构，以受损结构的缺损程度和个结构间的均衡状态为变量设置了 4 组有代表性的桥梁状态，按变权公式对桥梁下部结构的分别进行变权计算，并计算不同均衡系数取值下经变权后的下部结构权重值，见表 2。

桥梁状态取值 表 2

桥梁状态编号	结构评估值			均衡函数取值				
	桥面系	上部结构	下部结构	0	0.2	0.5	0.7	1
				下部结构计算权重值				
1	90	90	60	0.50	0.48	0.45	0.43	0.4
2			50	0.55	0.52	0.47	0.44	0.4
3			40	0.60	0.56	0.50	0.46	0.4
4			30	0.67	0.62	0.54	0.48	0.4

显然，均衡系数取值越低，则结构经变权计算后的权值改变越大，且被变权结构的损伤度越大，各结构间损伤程度越不均衡，均衡系数的取值对变权结果的影响越大。

显然，均衡系数直接反映了需变权结构的自身状态及各结构状态之间的均衡性。

3 确定均衡系数的程度分析法

模糊数学中提供了将程度这一概念性的判断转化为具体量值的方法，本文将均衡系数赋予"接受程度"这一概念，以均衡系数作为度量决策者对现有权值的接受程度的指标，其相互关系为：接受程度越低，均衡系数取值越小，接受程度越高，均衡系数越大。接受程度的量化可采用程度分析法进行。

程度分析法则是将集值统计法中的指标值按区间划分为不同的程度[5-6]，这样，在桥梁技术状况评定实践中，采用程度分析法将专业工程师对桥梁现行权重的接受程度量化为数值，再以该数值作为均衡系数，从而达到满足均衡系数特性的基础上实现桥梁权重科学的再分配。

本文采用多级估量法完成接受程度的量化分析。

3.1 多级估量法

多级估量法的实质是以集值统计为目的的实验方法。设计满意程度调查表格进行分析(表3),表中第一行为预设的调查结果,一、二列则表示被调查人对预设调查结果的接受程度,每一个预设的调查结果为一次试验。对每个预设的调查结果,可选择一位专业工作者给出对该预设结果的接受程度。

满意程度调查表　　　　　　　　　　　表3

项	目	很不满意	较不满意	中等	较满意	很满意
赞成	坚决		√			
	基本	√		√		
中立					√	
反对	基本					
	坚决					√

考虑到均衡系数的取值在 0~1,因此我们将预设的五级满意程度量化为 5 个数值:0,0.25,0.5,0.75,1;对应上述表中五个接受程度.则如表3所示的试验结果即对应坐标平面上的五个点:这5个点连成的折线表示[0,1]上的一个模糊集,其中蕴含了五位专业工作者对于判断目标的接受程度信息(图2)。

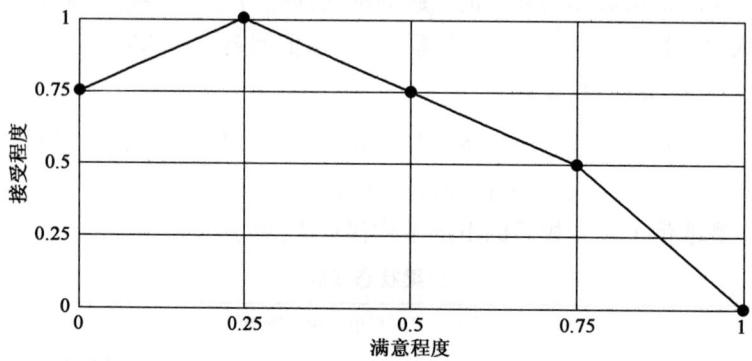

图2 接受程度的模糊分布统计图

3.2 均衡系数计算

得到模糊分布图后,我们进一步引入一个度量决策者均衡倾向的量——均衡标度:考虑[0,1]上的连续函数 $A:[0,1] \rightarrow [0,1]$,称 A 为均衡标度,定义域[0,1]表示均衡强度,值域表示决策人的均衡要求,A 实质上是[0,1]上的模糊集,按式4将 A 清晰化:

$$\alpha = \frac{\int_0^1 xA(x)\,\mathrm{d}x}{\int_0^1 A(x)\,\mathrm{d}x} \tag{4}$$

即可得到均衡系数 α 的值,这样就可使用前述变权公式实现变权计算。

4 变权理论的工程应用

以某大桥为工程背景,采用变权分析法进行桥梁技术状况的客观评定。原始桥梁技术状况评定表见表4。

桥梁技术状况评定表　　　　　　　　　　　表4

桥梁结构	桥梁技术状况评分	桥梁结构组成	桥梁总体技术状况评分
上部结构	80.8	0.4	
下部结构	79.47	0.4	76
桥面系	59.46	0.2	

使用以变权理论基础的修正评定方法,流程如下:

(1)将标准中给定的权重值确定为初始权重。
(2)应用多级估量法对该结构权值进行满意程度调查(表5)。

满意程度调查表 表5

项目		很不满意	较不满意	中等	较满意	很满意
赞成	坚决					
	基本	√				
中立			√	√		
反对	基本				√	
	坚决					√

据此给出模糊分布图,如图3所示。

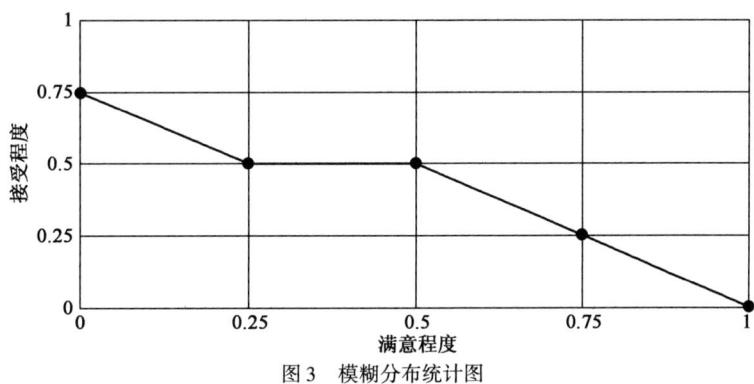

图3 模糊分布统计图

(3)根据模糊分布图计算均衡系数。

分布图对应函数关系为:$\begin{cases} y = -x + 0.75 & 0 \leq x \leq 0.5 \\ y = 0.5 & 0.5 < x \leq 0.75 \\ y = -x + 1 & 0.75 < x \leq 1 \end{cases}$

由公式(3)计算得 $\alpha = \dfrac{\int_0^{0.25}(-x+0.75)x\mathrm{d}x + \int_{0.25}^{0.5}0.5x\mathrm{d}x + \int_{0.5}^{1}(-x+1)x\mathrm{d}x}{\int_0^{0.25}(-x+0.75)\mathrm{d}x + \int_{0.25}^{0.5}0.5\mathrm{d}x + \int_{0.5}^{1}(-x+1)\mathrm{d}x}$

得 $\alpha = 0.365$。

(4)按变权公式进行变权。

桥梁初始评分及权重如下所示。

根据已得的均衡系数 α 和变权公式可对上部承重结构进行变权得到合理的权重:

$$w_j = \frac{w_j^{(0)} x^{\alpha-1}}{\sum_{k=1}^{m} w_k^{(0)} x^{\alpha-1}} = 0.278/1.12 = 0.232$$

变权后的权重 $w = 0.232$,将上部结构降低的权重值按比例分配到桥面系中,得到变权后桥梁各结构权重值如表6所示。

变权后桥梁技术状况评分表 表6

桥梁结构	桥梁部件技术状况评分	桥梁结构组成权重	桥梁总体技术状况评分
上部结构	80.8	0.384	75.3
下部结构	79.47	0.384	
桥面系	59.46	0.232	

可以看出,变权后桥梁总体技术状况评分有所降低,当采用变权评估法时,通过适当调整各部分结构的权重值,能够在结构出现不均衡的严重缺陷时,将这种缺陷状态反映在总体的评估结果中,使得桥梁技

术状况评定结果更加真实地反映桥梁的实际状态。

5 结语

5.1 本文的主要研究结论
（1）根据现行技术状况评定标准，结合桥梁检测实践分析，提出了一般状态和特殊状态的相关定义。
（2）探索了变权理论在对"特殊状态"（各部分结构技术状况不均衡）桥梁进行评定时的适用性。
（3）探讨了均衡系数 α 的含义并进一步给出了确定 α 取值的程度分析法。
（4）以实际工程为案例论证了评定新方法的可行性。

5.2 研究存在的不足
选用程度分析法结合专业工作者的判断来确定均衡系数，减小了均衡系数取值的盲目性，但如何进一步减小主观性仍待探索。

参考文献

[1] 胡铁明,汪子龙,韩基刚.基于变权层次分析法的桥梁状态评估[J].沈阳大学学报(自然科学版),2018,30(05):395-400.

[2] 钟恒,杨玲,刘益豪.基于变权理论的山区公路在役桥梁功能性综合评价修正[J].北方交通,2016(05):1-4+8.

[3] 王永.变权综合评估法在桥梁状况评定中的应用[J].铁道建筑技术,2010(S2):241-243.

[4] 唐鹏,宫赛.基于层次分析——模糊理论桥梁网养护中的应用[J].公路工程,2020,45(06):86-90+154.

[5] 汪培庄.模糊数学及其应用[J].河南师大学报(自然科学版),1983(02):1-20.

[6] 汪培庄,李洪兴.模糊信息与模糊决策[J].天津纺织工学院学报,1986(Z1):107-111.

Seismic Hazard Analysis Study for the Panama Canal Fourth Bridge

Jun Wu[1]　Jun Ji[1]　Yun Liao[1]　Jiaer Wu[1]　Penglin Li[2]

(1. CHEC (USA) Inc; 2. China Harbour Engineering Company Ltd.)

Abstract　Seismic hazard assessment is essential to analyze the earthquake risks and provide reliable design parameters to engineering projects located in seismic zones. As widely accepted by the literature, Probabilistic Seismic Hazard Assessment (PSHA) method is the dominant technique to evaluate seismic risks. The fundamental factors of PSHA include seismic source characterization (SSC) and ground motion characterization (GMC), logic tree modelling, uniform hazard spectra (UHS) derivations, seed earthquake record selection and scaling for final ground motion data, etc.

Panama Canal Fourth Bridge (P4B), a new long-span cable-stayed bridge, is among the largest infrastructure projects in Panama, crossing the Panama Canal at the Pacific Ocean side. Due to its significance and high seismic risks in its vicinity, the project team conducted a sophisticated PSHA for all concerned sites in the region, and recommended ground motion time histories for use in dynamic structural analyses of the project.

This study employed the latest and innovative PSHA modelling methods and parametric research techniques, also reviewed and critically incorporated the previously available seismic hazard and seismicity of the Panama Canal region. Further, its results have now been acknowledged by the Panama's largest government agency, Panama Canal Authority (ACP).

Keywords Seismic hazard PSHA P4B SSC GMC UHS Ground motion

0 Introduction

The Panama Canal FourthBridge (P4B) is a new high quality, durable cable-stayed bridge with a design life of 100 years. For the fourth bridge over the Panama Canal, the Main Bridge consists of a dual traffic road of 3 lanes in each direction and will allow an expansion to 4 lanes in each direction in the future. The navigation clearance required for the Panama Canal waterway below the bridge is of 350m wide by 75m high, requiring the minimum length of 485m for main span of the main bridge. The illustration of the cable-stayed main bridge is shown inside the Fig. 1.

Based on the Owner's requirements, the P4B main structures need to resist seismic loads with following two earthquake levels for design criteria:

(1) Earthquake Functional Evaluation (FEE) is for a seismic of 10% exceedance probability in 50 years, which corresponds to a return period of 475 years.

(2) Earthquake Safety Evaluation (SEE) is for a seismic risk of 2% exceedance probability in 50 years, which corresponds to a return period of 2475 years.

The project team will need to conduct the state-of-the-art seismic analyses corresponding to all design earthquake levels. The first essential task is to accurately evaluate the project-specific seismic hazard and provide reliable earthquake data for both geotechnical and structural analyses.

During the tendering phase, the Owner involved TY Lin-Langan team to perform a preliminary seismic hazard assessment for the project site to create the hazard spectra data and three sets of ground motion time histories for selected project locations. The Design-Build contractor's seismic study team contracted with JL Donahue Engineering (JLD) and advisor Norman Abrahamson to conduct the comprehensive re-evaluation of seismic risks using more advanced Probabilistic Seismic Hazard Assessment (PSHA) technique, reviewed and critically incorporated available seismicity information of the Panama Canal region previously done by others.

1 Psha Methodology and Sites

1.1 Psha Methodology

The new PSHA followed the methodology with the key procedure as stated below:

(1) Build Seismic Source Characterization (SSC) Model.

(2) Develop Ground Motion Characterization (GMC) Model.

(3) Perform PSHA for the interested project sites including representative locations of Main Bridge, Access Viaducts, and Interchanges. Create the Uniform Hazard Spectra (UHS).

(4) Carry out the deaggregation work at the appropriate return period(s) for the given sites.

(5) Select seed ground motions, then scale and match for final design ground motion data.

1.2 Geology Conditions and Interested Sites

The Panama Canal Fourth Bridge is located in the complex geological basin called Panama Canal Basin. The Canal Zone is further divided into 6 different geological formation zones, and the P4B project is within Zone 6 - Pacific Coast.

Overall, the project area is located in a transitional zone between a small hill of volcanic rocks (Sosa Hill) on the eastern side and a low region of coastal plain on the western side. The eastern side of the main bridge and part of the east approach viaduct adjacent to the Sosa Hill are underlain by Basalt (Tb) formation consisting of basalt of middle and late Miocene age, while the western side of the main bridge and the west approach viaduct are located on an alluvial plain underlain by La Boca (Tl) formation consisting mainly of sedimentary rocks of siltstone, sandstone, conglomerate of early Miocene age.

The hazard assessment are performed for total 25 sites, among which eight are labeled 1 to 8, nine are labeled 101 through 109, and the remaining eight are labeled 201 to 208. The specific locations, were selected based on the major bridge segments such as main bridge, east and west access viaducts, east and west interchanges, together with associated V_{s30} (i.e., average shear-wave velocity of the upper 30 m of material) for these sites. The Vs_{30} values for all the sites are based on the latest geotechnical investigation results and geologic variability of the region as described in the paragraphs above.

2 Seismic Source Characterization Development

2.1 Crustal Faults in Canal Zone

Several strike-slip faults within the Canal Zone were considered as potential seismic sources for this study. The crustal faults include the Rio Gatun, Rio Limon (Limon), Pedro Miguel, and Azota faults. The URS (2008) Report provided a comprehensive study of the shallow crustal, background, and subduction faults coincidental within the Panama Canal region.

In this study, the Baseline crustal fault seismic source model was developed with the characterizations as shown in Tab. 1 Logic trees for the Azota fault, Rio Gatun fault, and Pedro Miguel-Limon Fault system were replicated from figures in the URS (2008) report. Similar to the URS (2008) report, the fault width for each fault was assumed to be 15 km. The Baseline model also uses the same M_{max} magnitude model using the Wells and Coppersmith (1994) magnitude / area relation. At the meantime, several key aspects of the Seismic Source Characterization (SSC) are missing, such as fault locations, fault geometries, and background area regions. To supplement the data, the Global Earthquake Model Foundation's Global Active Faults project (GEM-GAF) was consulted to provide fault locations and geometries, to include latitude and longitude of the surface traces of the faults. The program EZ-FRISK 8.00 (Fugro Consultants, 2016) was consulted for background region dimensions. Where information was not available from the GEM-GAF or EZ-FRISK models, fault geometries were digitized from the URS report. Tab. 1 shows the faults nearest to the sites greatly contributing to the hazard.

Summary of Crustal Fault Characteristics and Weighting from URS (2008) Tab. 1

Fault	Slip Type	Length	Magnitude	Segmentation	Slip Rate	Dip
Pedro Miguel Fault	Strike Slip	48 km	Preferred: 6.9	Rupture with Limon (0.85) Rupture Separately (0.15)	Preferred: 6.3 mm/yr (0.5) Maximum: 9.0 mm/yr (0.25) Minimum: 3.6 mm/yr (0.25)	Preferred: 90 (0.6) Maximum: 70 west (0.2) Minimum: 80 east (0.2)
Limon Fault	Strike Slip	28 km	Preferred: 6.7	Rupture with Pedro Miguel (0.85) Rupture Separately (0.15)	Preferred: 3.54 mm/yr (0.5) Maximum: 5.91 mm/yr (0.3) Minimum: 1.77 mm/yr (0.2)	Preferred: 75 (0.6) Maximum: 60 west (0.2) Minimum: 90 (east) (0.2)

continue

Fault	Slip Type	Length	Magnitude	Segmentation	Slip Rate	Dip
Pedro Miguel -Limon Fault System	Strike Slip	70 km	Preferred: 7.1 (0.53) Maximum: 7.3 (0.18) Minimum: 7.2 (0.29)	Rupture together (0.85) Rupture Separately (0.15)	Preferred: 6.3 mm/yr (0.5) Maximum: 9.0 mm/yr (0.25) Minimum: 3.6 mm/yr (0.25)	Preferred: 90 (0.6) Maximum: 70 west (0.2) Minimum: 80 (east) (0.2)
Rio Gatun Fault	Strike Slip	41 to 50 km	Preferred: 6.8 (0.6) Maximum: 7.2 (0.2) Minimum: 6.8 (0.2)	None	Preferred: 3.0 mm/yr (0.6) Max: 8.0 mm/yr (0.2) Minimum: 1.0 mm/yr (0.2)	Preferred: 80 (0.6) Maximum: 90 (0.2) Minimum: 70 (0.2)
Azota Fault	Strike Slip	28 km	Preferred: 6.7 (1.0)	None	Preferred: 1.8 mm/yr (0.4) Max: 3.6 mm/yr (0.2) Minimum: 0.9 mm/yr (0.4)	Preferred: 80 (0.6) Maximum: 90 (0.2) Minimum: 70 (0.2)

Note: * weighting shown in parentheses.

2.2 Background Seismicity

The URS (2008) report provides basic guidance into the development of the background seismicity. For this Baseline model, the same deep background characteristics were used to develop the background seismicity model inputs:

(1) Fault Type: Background.

(2) Sense of Slip: Strike Slip.

(3) Depth: 35 km.

(4) Magnitude: 5.0 ~ 7.5.

(5) b-value: 0.6.

(6) Estimated Activity Rate: 0.36 based on the hazard for the New-Pacific-Locks-site.

The studies indicated that the hazard is controlled by nearby faults instead of background seismicity. The activity rate of the controlling faults is based on geologic estimates of the slip rate, not on the historical seismicity and Gutenberg-Richter models. The background zones are included in this study for completeness, but not contributing much to the hazard at the interested return periods.

3 Ground Motion Characterization Development

The Ground Motion Characterization (GMC) model has two types of seismic sources: shallow crustal earthquakes and deep background areal zones. The GMC model relies heavily on the evaluations in the most recent Senior Seismic Hazard Analysis Committee (SSHAC) Level 3 studies for GMC: the 2015 Southwest United States (SWUS) study for crustal earthquakes (GeoPentech, 2015). Logic trees were implemented to decide GMC models with justifications for the model selection and the weights on the logic trees described herein.

3.1 Ground Motion Attenuation for the Median

The Next Generation Attenuation (NGA) Ground Motion Prediction Equations (GMPEs) were primary used for shallow crustal events. The GMC model for this study was established using the most recent attenuation models, the Next Generation Attenuation-West 2 (NGA-W2) GMPEs. While some GMPEs also provide regional estimations, such as for California or Japan, the "Global" GMPEs were used for this study. In the PSHA model, two GMC logic trees were utilized in this study for both shallow crustal and deep background sources. The Tab. 2 shows the attenuation relations and weighting for the shallow crustal faults and the deep background seismicity, respectively.

Attenuation Relations Used in PSHA Study   Tab. 2

Types of Sources	Ground Motion Predication Equation	Weight
Shallow Crustal Faults	Abrahamson, Silva, and Kamai (2014)	0.25
	Boore, Stewart, Seyhan, and Atkinson (2014)	0.25
	Campbell and Bozorgnia (2014)	0.25
	Chiou and Youngs (2014)	0.25
Deep Background Seismicity	Abrahamson, Silva, and Kamai (2014)	0.34
	Boore, Stewart, Seyhan, and Atkinson (2014)	0.33
	Chiou and Youngs (2014)	0.33

3.2 Additional Epistemic Uncertainty for Median

The NGA-W2 models may not capture the full epistemic uncertainty due to the limited data set size during the development. Al-Atik and Youngs (2013) evaluated potential statistical uncertainties and developed additional uncertainty factors applicable to each of the NGA-W2 models.

Also given the lack of historic strong-motion data in Panama, there exists larger epistemic uncertainty for NGA-W2 GMPEs to be applied here. Such larger epistemic uncertainty was considered adopting and increasing the standard deviation for the additional epistemic uncertainty (σ_u) given Al-Atik and Youngs (2013) model from 0.07 to 0.18 natural log units. Also, in the logic tree, $\pm 1.65 \sigma_u$ was used corresponding to a change in the constant term of ± 0.3 natural log units. This range of constant values captures the range of median crustal ground-motion models seen in different regions of the world.

3.3 Form of the Distribution

The 2015 SWUS study for crustal earthquakes (GeoPentech, 2015) showed that the ground-motion distribution deviated from lognormal at an epsilon value of 2.5. In the SWUS study, this fat-tailed distribution was modeled using a mixture model consisting of a sum of two lognormal distributions: mean(μ) = 0, sigma(σ) = 0.8ϕss, weight = 0.5 for distribution 1; and $\mu = 0$, $\sigma = 1.2\phi$ss, weight = 0.5 for distribution 2. For this GMC model, the SWUS model is simplified to use only the mixture model with a weight of 1.0.

4 Sensitivity Studies and Results

Considering both URS (2008) report and additional research thereafter near the project Sites., following sensitivity analyses were performed to warrant the validity of the final hazard results.

4.1 Background Seismicity

The GEM's research stated that the hazard model for Central America uses a single source for in-slab seismicity that covers the whole western coast of Mexico and Central America, however not extending to Panama. They have recommended a b-value of 0.97, as opposed to the b-value of 0.6 used by URS (2008). In this study an alternate b-value of 0.8 was chosen, acknowledging both the GEM suggestion and the crustal value of 0.8 given in the URS (2008) report. The comparison of hazard results for this sensitivity change leads to a slight decrease in hazard for all sites.

4.2 Slip Rates

Slip rates on faults near the project sites have also been extensively researched such as the recommended values by the URS (2008) Report. Rockwell et al. (2010) concluded that collectively, the Limon - Pedro Miguel fault zone appears to be a major, high - rate dextral fault with a rate in the same range as the Rio Gatun fault. The following Tab. 3 listed the changes of slip rate ranges and recommendations from URS (2008) to Rockwell (2010).

Researched Slip Rates and Recommendations   Tab. 3

Researches	Fault	Preferred (mm/yr)	Range (mm/yr)
URS (2008) Report	Rio Gatun	3	1-8
	Pedro Miguel	7	4-10
	Limon	6	3-10
Rockwell (2010) Report	Rio Gatun	5	3-8
	Pedro Miguel - Limon	5	4-7

The comparison of hazard results for this sensitivity indicated that this slip rate change results in a slight decrease in overall hazard.

4.3 Location of Pedro Miguel Fault

The location of the fault trace near the project sites has also been studied for years. Work by Schug et al (2018), Bennett et al (2014), and Gath and Gonzalez (2011) position the fault at varying locations. This epistemic uncertainty in the fault location created the requirement to test varying locations of the fault trace. Two alternate traces were selected to move the fault 0.3 km and 0.5 km to the west, respectively. The comparison of hazard results for this sensitivity result in no hazard change from the baseline for each successive trace westward.

4.4 Final SSC Model Development

Based on the previous sensitivity results, the following was implemented into final SSC model through a modified logic tree for the Limon-Pedro Miguel fault system, as shown in Fig. 1 This figure combines the uncertainty on the fault traces as well as the slip rates.

4.5 Inclusion of Single Station Sigma

With increased knowledge such as a site's Vs profile with depth and/or ground motion observations from past events, the uncertainty in the prediction of site response can be reduced. When the ergodic assumption is applied to ground motions both epistemic uncertainty, and aleatory variability are contributing to the standard deviation, σ, of a model. Aleatory variability has a great influence on predicted mean hazard (Abrahamson and Bommer 2006). The SWUS study evaluated global datasets to develop updated single-station sigma models for application to shallow crustal earthquakes and is the most up-to-date evaluation. The SWUS report provides three alternative single-station sigma models that capture the epistemic uncertainty, all of which are adopted for an alternative GMC model in this study for better accuracy in this significant project.

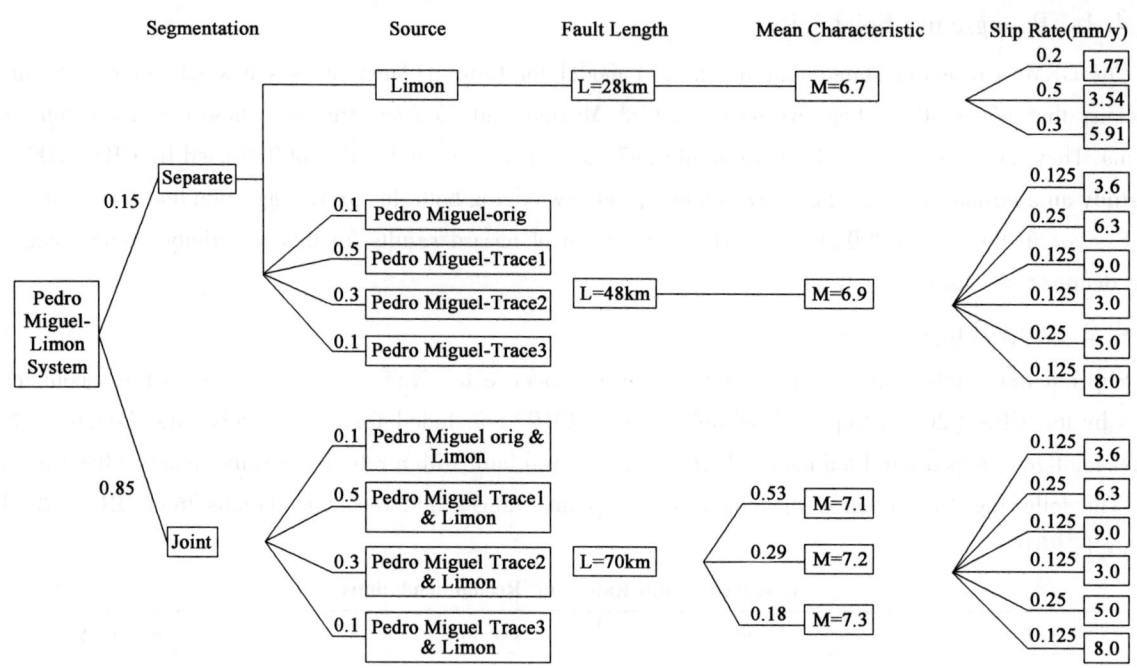

Fig. 1 Revised Logic Tree for the Pedro Miguel - Limon Fault System

5 PSHA Study Results

The PSHA was performed on the interested project sites using the SSC and GMC models described above. The ground motions are calculated for the horizontal components of motion in terms of peak ground acceleration (PGA) and response spectral acceleration (SA) at 5% damping for periods between 0.01 and 10 seconds. The PSHA calculates the annual frequency of exceeding a specified ground motion level and creates plot of these results for a given period as a hazard curve. The hazard curves for PGA and SA are used to develop equal-hazard acceleration response spectra for selected average return periods. Using the logic-tree framework, the hazard curves and response spectra are shown for the mean estimates. The hazard at a given site is also deaggregated to determine which sources (or faults) and which magnitudes, distances and epsilon combinations are the strongest contributors to the hazard at a particular oscillator period and a particular return period.

5.1 Uniform Hazard Spectra

The uniform hazard horizontal acceleration response spectra were calculated for the 25 selected sites: Sites 1~8, 101~109 and 201~208, at three return periods: 475, 1034, and 2475 years. With the field-verified Vs_{30} information, the alternative single-station sigma ground motion model were used. The uniform hazard spectra (UHS) are generated for all selected sites, among which Fig. 2 displays the UHS calculated at Sites 1 and 2 as examples for all three return periods. Based on the analyzed results, due to the close proximity of the site, the UHS are essentially in narrow ranges, and decrease in value as the distance from the Pedro-Miguel fault increases.

5.2 Deaggregation

The hazard for a given return period and ground motion parameter at each site was disaggregated first as a function of magnitude, distance and epsilon. These results are plotted in Fig. 3 for the first two sites 1 and 2 as example, at return periods of 475 years, 1034 years, and 2475 years. For each return period at each site, six ground motion parameters (spectral acceleration at 0.01 sec, 0.2 sec, 1 sec, 2 sec, 3 sec, and 5 sec) were analyzed. Due to the close proximity of the sites, the deaggregation results are essentially similar across the region.

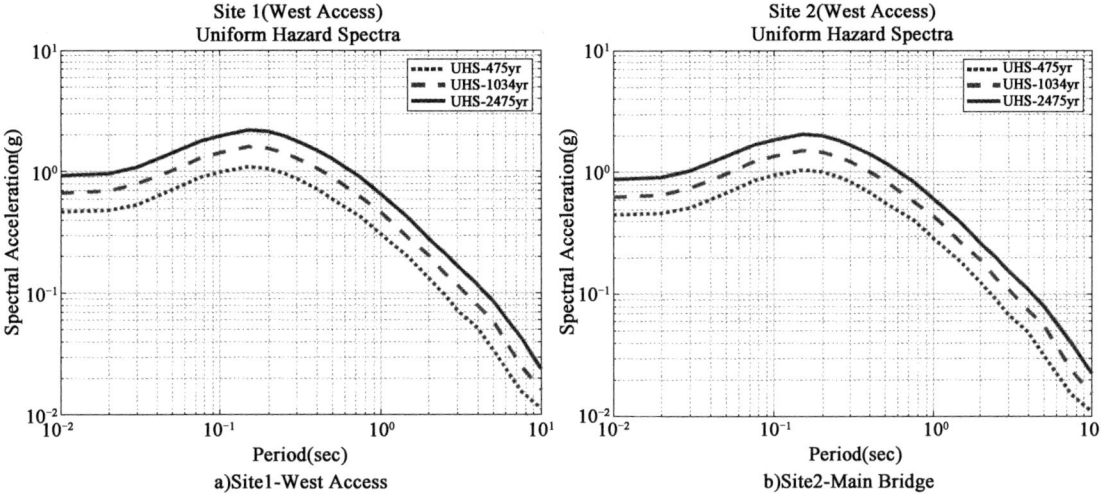

Fig. 2 UHS Plots for Site 1-West Access and Site 2-Main Bridge

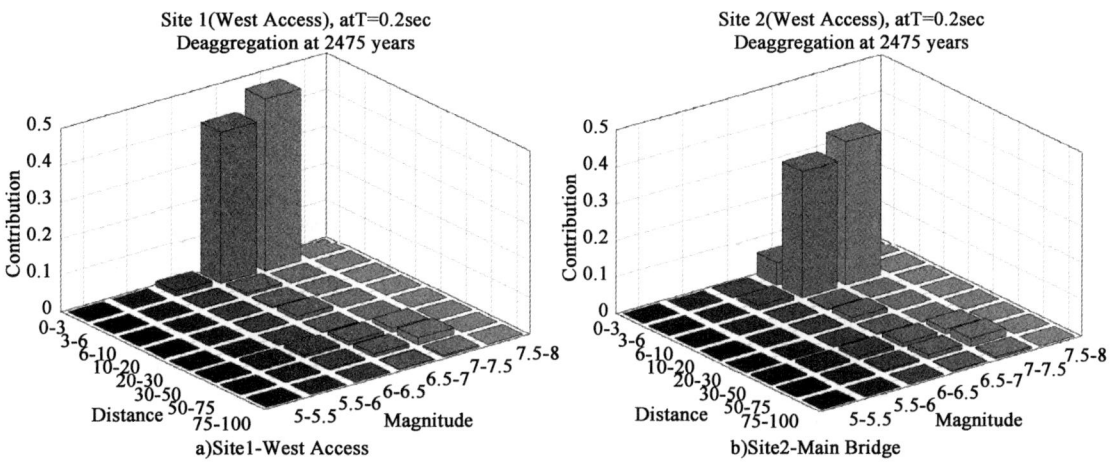

Fig. 3 Deaggregation for Site 1-West Access and Site 2-Main Bridge -2475 Years

6 Ground Motion Selection and Scaling

Based on the needs of seismic design and analysis, ground motion data including acceleration time histories are required. Considering both locations and seismic design criteria for different structures, the design ground motions were developed for all sites based on the UHS developed in the preceding section.

6.1 Definition of Groups and Target Spectra Selection

Ground motion analysis was carried out for the all the sites. To begin the analysis, first the UHS were normalized at 1 sec (or 1 Hertz). At both the 475-year return period and the 2475-year return period, it was found the spectral shapes fell into three categories. Considering the site locations and measured representing Vs30 values, the interested sites were further categorized into three groups for ease of seed motion and scaling:

(1) Group 1 represents the mid-range V_{s30} (700 ~ 900m/s) sites, such as West Access Separate (101), Main Bridge -V_{s_2} (103), West Access Full (104), etc.

(2) Group 2 represents the higher V_{s30} (higher than 900m/s), such as Main Bridge-V_{s_1} (102), East Access (105), East Access Part 1-V_{s_1} (106), etc.

(3) Group 3 represents the lower V_{s30} (less than 700m/s), including East Interchange-2 (EI-2) (202), West Interchange-6 (WI-6)-V_{s_2} (207) and West Interchange-7 (WI-7) (208).

Further, when the 475-year and 2475-year return period normalized response spectra are compared, the shapes are found very similar. Hence, one target spectrum can be used per Group for both the 475-year return period and the 2475-year return period, and specific scale factors were computed for other sites and return periods.

6.2 Seed Ground Motion Selection

Once the target spectra were identified, sets of seed ground motions (two horizontal and one vertical) are required per Group. The results of the deaggregation were used to identify the controlling scenarios. In addition to the response spectrum shape, other factors considered consist of the Peak Ground Velocity (PGV), Arias Intensity (AI), Durations (D5-95%) and the presence of a velocity pulse in selecting time histories. The PGV conditional ground-motion models (GMM) developed by Abrahamson and Bhasin (2018) and AI GMM developed by Abrahamson et al (2016) were adopted using the SA, M and distance as input parameters to ensure that target PGV and AI values be consistent with the design spectrum. The duration model given by Abrahamson and Silva (1996) was also used. Finally, the GMM developed by Hayden et al (2014) was adopted using the standard deviations above the median ground motion from the hazard analysis at $T = 1s$ and the distance to determine the fraction of the ground motions that will have near-fault velocity pulses (Tab. 4).

Selected Seven Seed Motions and their Characteristics　　Tab. 4

Earthquake Name	Station Name	5-95% Duration (s)	AI-Unscaled (m/sec)	Year	M	Distance (km)
Loma Prieta	Gilroy Array #3	11.4	2.1	1989	6.93	13
Loma Prieta	Santa Teresa Hills	10.1	1.3	1989	6.93	15
Northridge-01	LA-Sepulveda VA Hospital	8.5	7.0	1994	6.69	8
Hector Mine	Hector	11.7	1.9	1999	7.13	12
Cape Mendocino	Centerville Beach, Naval Fac	10.6	1.6	1992	7.01	18
Niigata, Japan	NIGH11	12.2	2.2	2004	6.63	18
Duzce, Turkey	Bolu	9.0	3.7	1999	7.14	12

An initial set of 14 candidate seed records were selected from the PEER NGA-W2 data set based on the spectral shape and the distance and magnitude. From this set, the 7 sets were selected based on how well they matched other secondary parameters after scaling. The targets range of the secondary parameters for the Seed Records for the design spectra were also studied. Table 4 above provides the final seed records and their original characteristics.

6.3 Scaling and Matching for Final Ground Motion Data

Prior to matching, horizontal motions were first rotated to Fault Normal (FN) and Fault Parallel (FP). The spectral matching was performed using the program RSPMatch. For each set of horizontal components, the geometric mean of the two horizontal components was matched to the target spectrum. The variability between the FN and FP components was maintained. This is consistent with the definition of the ground motion (RotD50) used in the GMPEs.

Vertical component design spectra were developed for Group 1, Group 2 and Group 3 for 475-yr and 2475-yr return periods by scaling the horizontal spectrum by a V/H ratio. The median V/H ratio given by Gülerce and Abrahamson (2011) for the design scenario for the 475-yr and 2475-yr UHS was used to such scaling. For simplicity, to estimate the vertical spectrum at other locations, the same scale factors developed for the horizontal spectrum can be applied to the vertical spectrum.

The spectral matching was performed for the seed motion data for all Groups and verified for compatibility with the target spectra. Two sample plots from the horizontal motion time histories are presented here as Fig. 4a) and b) to indicate the levels of consistency between the key parameters of matched motion data and those of the target spectra, through UHS and Arias Intensity (AI) graphics. The Fig. 6c) also shows the characteristics of the sample spectrally matched ground motions with 2475-yr return period.

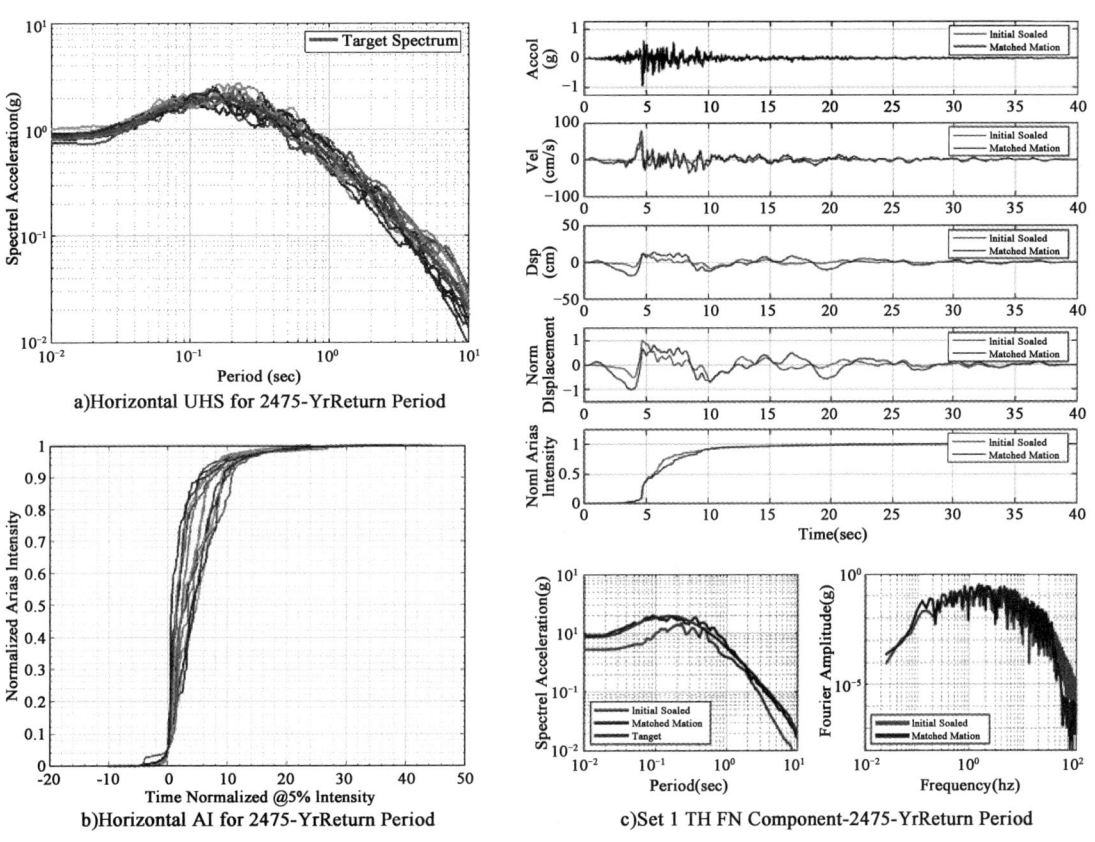

Fig. 4　Final Matched Ground Motion Data Sample (2475-Year Return Period)

7　Conclusions

Based on the state-of-the-art PSHA technique and the latest comprehensive seismic source data, the research team completed the seismic hazard study specifically for the Panama Canal 4th Bridge Project. Intensive sensitivity analyses were conducted to optimize the SSC and GMC models through logic trees. This paper summarizes the entire PSHA process and results, consisting of identifying seismic sources near the site and developing site-specific hazard curves and uniform hazard spectra based on probabilistic and final seismic hazard analyses, as well as the final seed earthquake records selection and matching for design ground motion data.

Compared to all previous studies in Panama, this study incorporated quite a few major changes with most advanced and innovative models, such as the inclusion of additional estimates for the slip rate, additional epistemic uncertainty for the deep background seismicity, quantification of epistemic uncertainty in the location of the Pedro Miguel-Limon fault system, and the use of NGA-West 2 ground motion relations for the crustal earthquake sources with the additional epistemic uncertainties, etc. Such changes significantly enhance the hazard assessment accuracy and lead to more robust seismic design data for one of the largest essential infrastructures in Panama. Also, this research work is now acknowledged by Panama Canal Authority for its future consideration, which indicates this study's ultimate contribution to one of the most important infrastructures of worldwide transportation.

8 Acknowledgements

It should be recognized that the PSHA study, conclusions, and recommendations contained in this paper are primarily based on information provided andwork conducted by CHEC (USA) Inc and JL Donahue Engineering, Inc. team with the consultation and guidance from Dr. Norman Abrahamson. The research team acknowledge and appreciate the sponsorship and supports provided by the Design-Build Contractor CPCP for Panama Canal Fourth Bridge Project and China Harbour Engineering Company Ltd.

References

[1] Abrahamson C, Shi H-J M, Yang B. Ground-Motion Prediction Equations for Arias Intensity Consistent with the NGA-West2 Ground-Motion Models[C]. PEER Report 2016/05, Pacific Earthquake Engineering Research Center, Berkeley, CA.

[2] Abrahamson N A. HAZ45 Software, version 45. 2, released Jan 2, 2017. https://github.com/abrahamson/HAZ/releases.

[3] Abrahamson N A, Bhasin S. Conditional Ground-Motion Models for Peak Ground Velocity.

[4] Abrahamson N A, Silva W J, Empirical Ground Motion Models[R]. Report to Brookhaven National Laboratory.

[5] Abrahamson N A, Silva W J, Kamai R. Summary of the ASK14 Ground Motion Relation for Active Crustal Regions[J]. Earthquake Spectra, 2014, 30(3), 1025-1055.

[6] Al Atik L, Youngs R R, Epistemic Uncertainty for NGA-West2 Models[C]. PEER Report No. 2013/11, Pacific Earthquake Engineering Research Center, University of California, Berkeley, 59.

[7] Bayless JR, Somerville P G. Chapter 2: Bayless and Somerville model, in Final Report of the NGA-West2 Directivity Working Group[C]. PEER Report 2013/09, Pacific Earthquake Engineering Research Center, Berkeley, CA.

[8] Bennett R A, Spinler J C. Compton K, et al. Global Positioning System Constraints on Active Crustal Deformation in Central Panama[EB/OL] Seismological Research Letters, 85(2), March/April 2014. doi: 10. 1785/0220130177, 278-283.

[9] Boore D M, Stewart J P, Seyhan E, et al. NGA-West2 Equations for Predicting PGA, PGV, and 5% Damped PSA for Shallow Crustal Earthquakes[J]. Earthquake Spectra, 2014, 30(3), 1057-1085.

[10] Campbell K W, Bozorgnia Y. NGA-West2 Ground Motion Model for the Average Horizontal Components of PGA, PGV, and 5% Damped Linear Acceleration Response Spectra[J]. Earthquake Spectra, 2014, 30 (3), 1087-1115.

[11] Chiou B S J, Youngs, R R. Update of the Chiou and Youngs NGA Model for the Average Horizontal Component of Peak Ground Motion and Response Spectra[J]. Earthquake Spectra, 2014, 30(3), 1117-1153.

[12] Gath E M, Gonzalez, T. Three-dimensional Investigation of the AD 1621 Pedro Miguel Fault Rupture for Design of the Panama Canal's Borinquen Dam [C]. 2nd INQUA-IGCP-567 International Workshop on Active Tectonics, Earthquake Geology, Archaeology and Engineering, Corinth, Greece.

[13] GeoPentech. Southwestern United States Ground Motion Characterization SSHAC Level 3-Technical Report Rev 2, 2015, 4.

[14] Gulerce Z. Abrahamson A. Site-Specific Design Spectra for Vertical Ground Motion[J]. Earthquake

Spectra,2011,27(4),1023-1047.
[15] Hale C, Abrahamson N, Bozorgnia Y. Probabilistic Seismic Hazard Analysis Code Verification[R]. PEER Report 2018/03, Pacific Earthquake Engineering Research Center, Berkeley, CA.
[16] Hayden P C, Bray J D, Abrahamson N. Selection of Near-Fault Pulse Motions[J]. Journal of Geotechnical and Geoenvironmental Engineering, 2014.
[17] Rockwell T K, Bennet R A, Gath E,et al. Unhinging an indenter: A new tectonic model for the internal deformation of Panama[J]. American Geophysical Union, Tectonic,2010(29):1-10.
[18] Schug D L, Salter P, Goetz C, et al. [J] Pedro Miguel Fault Investigations: Borinquen Dam 1E Construction and the Panama Canal Expansion[J]. Geological Society of America Environmental & Engineering Geoscience, 2018(1):39-53.
[19] Shahi S K. Baker J W. An empirically calibrated framework for including the effects of near-fault directivity in probabilistic seismic hazard analysis[J]. Bulletin of the Seismological Society of America 2011,(0112):742-755.
[20] TY Lin-Langan. Asistencia Tecnica A Gerencia Del Cuarto Puente Sobre El Canal De Panama, Informde de Estudio de Riesgo Sismico Especifico Del Sitio para Estructuras Criticas. December 02, 2016.
[21] TY Lin-Langan. Asistencia Tecnica A Gerencia Del Cuarto Puente Sobre El Canal De Panama, Estudio Sismico Especifico Para Estrcturas Regulares. January 26, 2017.
[22] URS Probabilistic Seismic Hazard Analysis for Six Sites in Panama. Final Report Prepared for the Panama Canal Authority, September.
[23] URS. ACP Geotechnical Services Contract, Task Orders 1 and 5: Seismic Design Criteria for ACP Critical Structures, Contract N CMC-172538, Tas A: Development of Design Earthquake Ground Motions, Final Report, Prepared for: Panama Canal Authority, February 2008.
[24] Wells D L, Coppersmith J K. New Empirical Relationships among Magnitude, Rupture Length, Rupture Width, Rupture Area, and Surface Displacement, Bulletin of the Seismological Society of America, 1994, 84: 974-1002.

纵向约束体系对公铁两用三塔斜拉桥静力特性影响的分析

刘 喆 沈锐利 马政辉
(西南交通大学土木工程学院)

摘 要 不同纵向约束体系的公铁两用三塔斜拉桥静力特性差异较大,不同跨度三塔斜拉桥的适宜约束体系也不同,利用有限元非线性分析软件建立了主跨300~1300m的六座公铁两用三塔斜拉桥模型,比较分析了半飘浮体系、三塔纵向全约束体系、中塔纵向约束体系与中塔弹性索约束体系在纵风荷载、温度荷载与活载下的作用效应。结果表明,主梁与桥塔间有纵向约束的体系会改变纵风荷载的传力路径,降低纵向风力在桥塔上的作用高度,将有效减小结构纵向位移和桥塔顺桥向内力;纵向约束体系对结构的力学行为影响程度随主跨跨度的增大而增大,中小跨度的公铁两用三塔斜拉桥可选择半飘浮体系、中塔纵向约束体系和中塔弹性索约束体系,但是半飘浮体系不适用于大跨度三塔斜拉桥;跨度超过900m及以上的公铁两用桥,弹性索约束方式比支座约束方式更容易实现。

关键词 公铁两用三塔斜拉桥 不同跨度 约束体系 纵风荷载 力学行为

0 引言

世界上最早的多塔斜拉桥是1962年意大利教授Ricardo Morandi设计的马拉开波桥[1],我国1998年修建了第一座多塔斜拉桥——香港汀九大桥[2]。与单一功能桥梁相比,公铁两用桥更能合理利用土地和山川河流以及海洋的自然空间,具有良好的环保性、经济性、安全性和可持续发展性[3]。如何提高多塔斜拉桥整体刚度,有效控制中塔变位,是多塔斜拉桥发展中必须解决的问题[4]。约束体系是影响多塔斜拉桥整体刚度的重要因素之一,适宜的约束体系[5]可有效控制多塔斜拉桥的结构位移[6],改善结构受力[7]。

斜拉桥的梁塔约束体系形式主要有飘浮体系、支承体系、固结体系和刚构体系等[3]。香港汀九大桥[8]采用塔墩固结,连续梁支撑于墩上的约束体系;岳阳洞庭湖大桥[9]采用塔墩固结,主梁全漂浮的约束体系;武汉二七长江大桥[10]采用中塔塔梁固结,边塔半漂浮的约束体系;英国昆斯费里大桥[11-12]将中塔和主梁固结提供纵向约束。

国内外对多塔斜拉桥约束体系的研究,大多以某一固定跨度为研究对象,对跨度的变化是否会对结构体系产生影响这一问题没有详细研究。本文依据已有文献资料,建立六座不同跨度的公铁两用三塔斜拉桥模型,计算分析不同跨度不同约束体系在纵风荷载、温度荷载及活载下的作用效应,研究纵向约束对不同跨度公铁两用三塔斜拉桥的影响。

1 结构体系与模型建立

为研究不同跨度公铁两用三塔斜拉桥适宜的纵向约束体系,本文建立了主跨为300~1300m的三塔双索面双层公铁两用斜拉桥基本模型,如图1所示。

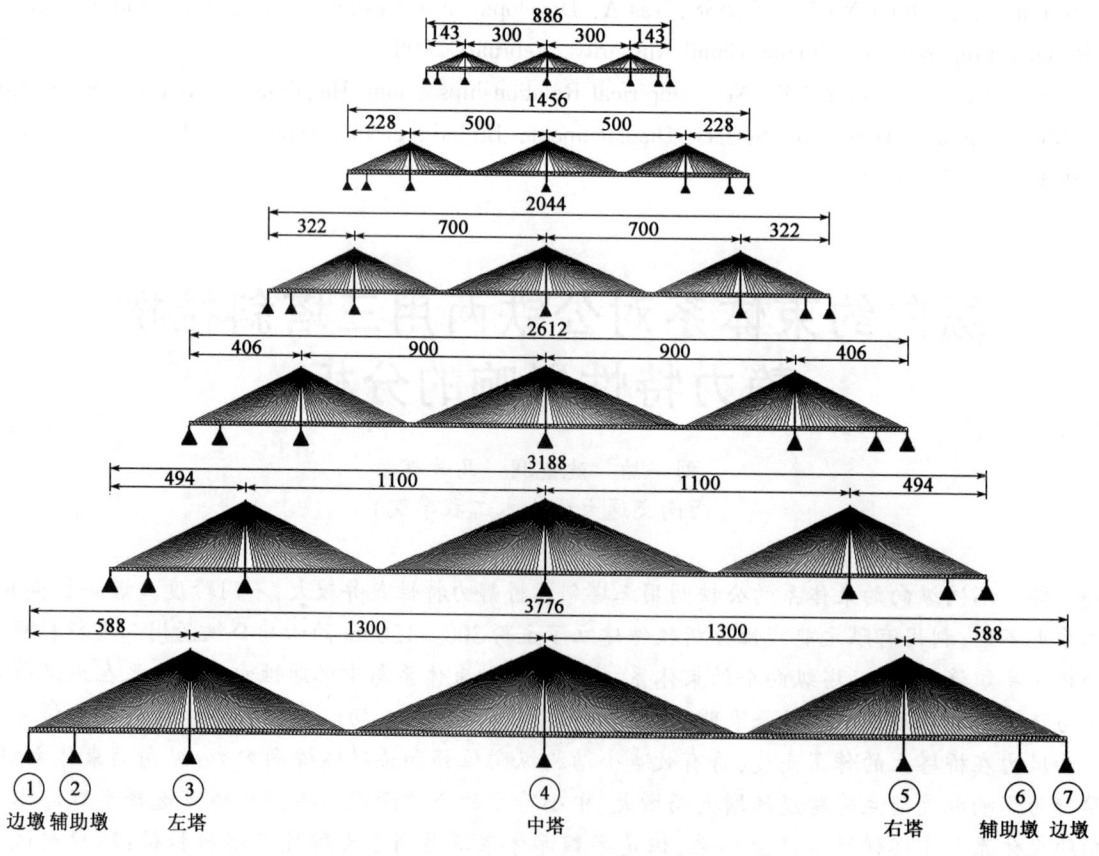

图1 主跨300~1300m三塔斜拉桥桥跨布置图(尺寸单位:m)

本文共比较4种塔梁纵向约束体系:①半飘浮体系(塔梁间不设纵向约束);②三个桥塔塔梁间均设

纵向约束体系;③中塔处纵向约束体系;④中塔纵向弹性索体系(中塔塔梁间设置纵向水平弹性索),接下来将以体系1～体系4依次对其命名。顺桥向共七个位置设置支承,以支座1～支座7进行编号。四种体系所有支承位置均对主梁竖向位移进行约束,仅纵向约束存在差异,各体系纵向约束见表1。

主梁支座纵向约束 表1

约束体系	支座1	支座2	支座3	支座4	支座5	支座6	支座7
体系1	0	0	0	0	0	0	0
体系2	0	0	1	1	1	0	0
体系3	0	0	0	1	0	0	0
体系4	0	0	0	▲	0	0	0

注:0表示纵向不设约束,1表示约束纵向位移,▲表示采用弹性拉索约束。

本文基于"桥梁结构静动力非线性分析系统BNLAS"建立不同跨度公铁两用三塔斜拉桥模型进行计算。模型中纵向风荷载依据《公路桥梁抗风设计规范》(JTG/T 3360-01—2018)计算,温度荷载:桥塔混凝土部分升降温18℃,桥塔钢材部分、主梁及斜拉索升温33℃,降温34℃。活载按照双层考虑:上层双向6车道市政快速路,下层双线高速铁路和双线城际铁路。

2 不同约束体系结构内力

本文主要研究不同跨度不同纵向约束体系下主塔、主梁、弹性索或支座的作用效应,通过对比纵向极限风荷载、温度荷载及活载作用下的结构受力响应,分析不同约束体系对于不同跨度的适用性。由于所建模型关于中塔完全对称,边塔计算结果取左塔塔柱结果。

2.1 主塔塔底弯矩

在纵向极限风荷载作用下,各约束体系主塔塔底弯矩计算结果如图2所示。

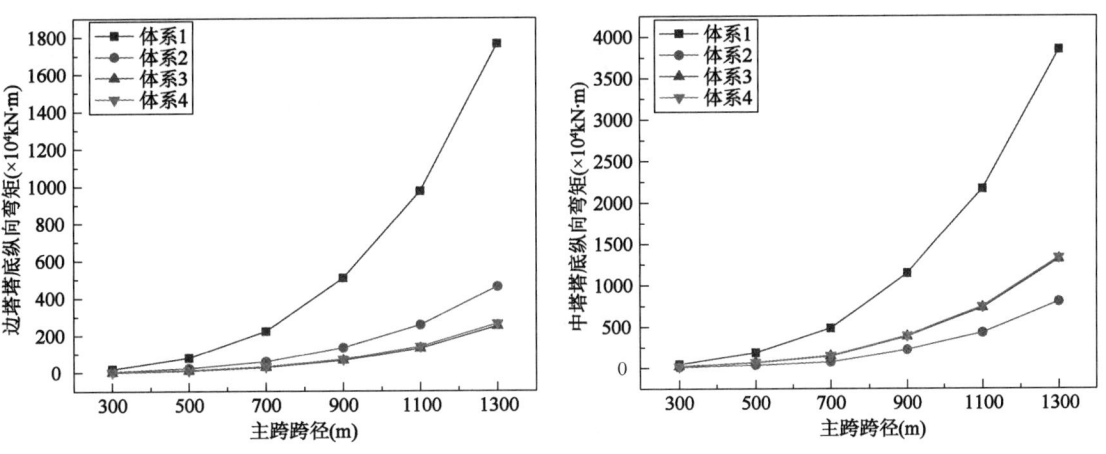

图2 纵风荷载下边塔、中塔塔底弯矩

从图2可见,在纵向极限风荷载作用下,体系1边中塔产生的塔底弯矩均大于其他体系,且随跨度增大,体系1的塔底弯矩将远大于其他体系;体系2的边塔塔底弯矩介于体系1与体系3、4之间,中塔塔底弯矩最小;体系3和体系4的边中塔塔底弯矩值基本相同。以上结果说明,在体系1的基础上增加额外的纵向约束会改变纵风荷载的传力路径,纵向风力通过纵向约束传递至桥塔下塔柱,可有效降低塔底弯矩。

在温度荷载作用下,由于结构关于中塔完全对称,整体升降温在中塔塔底处将不产生弯矩,整体升温下边塔塔底弯矩如图3所示。体系2的三个主塔均设纵向约束,主梁在边塔处的纵向变形受到限制,将产生较大的边塔塔底弯矩,且随跨度增大,弯矩呈线性增大趋势。

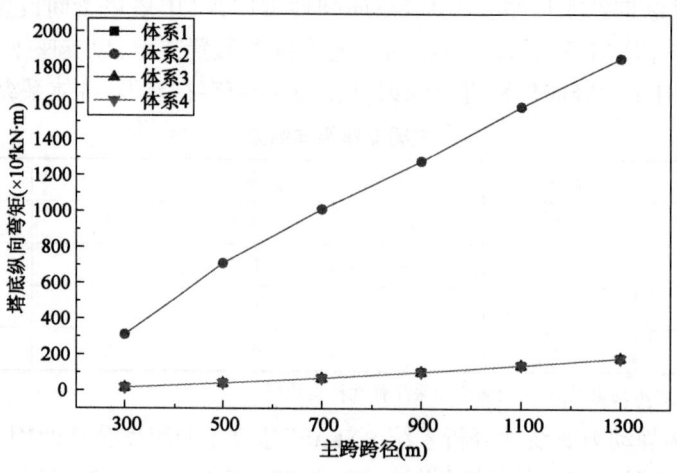

图3 整体升温下边塔塔底弯矩

2.2 主塔处纵向约束反力

纵向极限风荷载作用下,不同跨度不同约束体系中塔处纵向约束反力如图4所示,活载作用下,中塔处约束反力如图5所示。

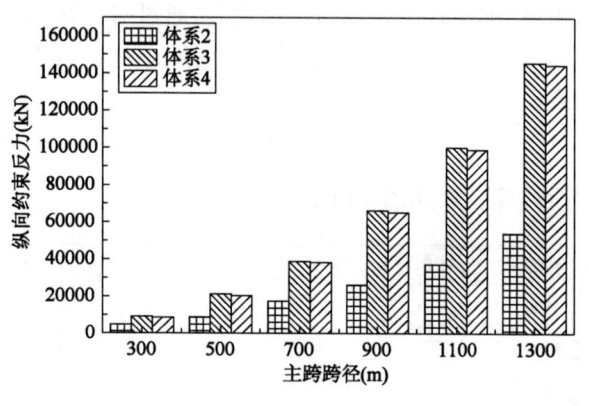

图4 纵风下中塔处纵向约束反力

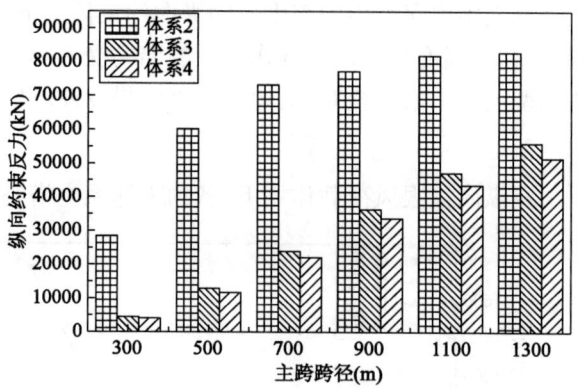

图5 活载下中塔处纵向约束反力

从图4和图5可见,在纵风荷载和活载作用下,体系2和体系3、4的纵向约束反力差异明显,且受主跨跨度影响较大,各约束体系的约束反力均随跨度的增大而增大。活载作用下,体系3在中塔支座处的纵向约束反力,从300m跨度时的4450kN增大到1300m跨度时的5.6万kN;体系4的纵向约束反力略小于体系3。

3 不同约束体系结构位移

3.1 主塔纵向位移

在纵向极限风荷载作用下,各约束体系主塔塔顶水平位移计算结果如图6所示。

从图6可见,体系1在纵风作用下边中塔水平位移远大于其他体系,且随跨度增大,位移大幅度增大;体系2由于三个塔柱主梁处均设置了纵向约束,其各跨度边中塔塔顶水平位移均最小,但与体系3和体系4边中塔位移差距不大。以上结果表明,主梁上设置约束体系后,可大幅度减小桥塔顶的纵向变形,仅在中塔位置设计约束体系,与在三个主塔处都设计约束体系效果相当。

3.2 主梁竖向挠度

在活载作用下,各跨度不同约束体系主梁挠度结果见图7所示;四种体系的竖向挠度比如图8所示,图中以体系3计算结果为参照,将其他约束体系换算为它的倍数。

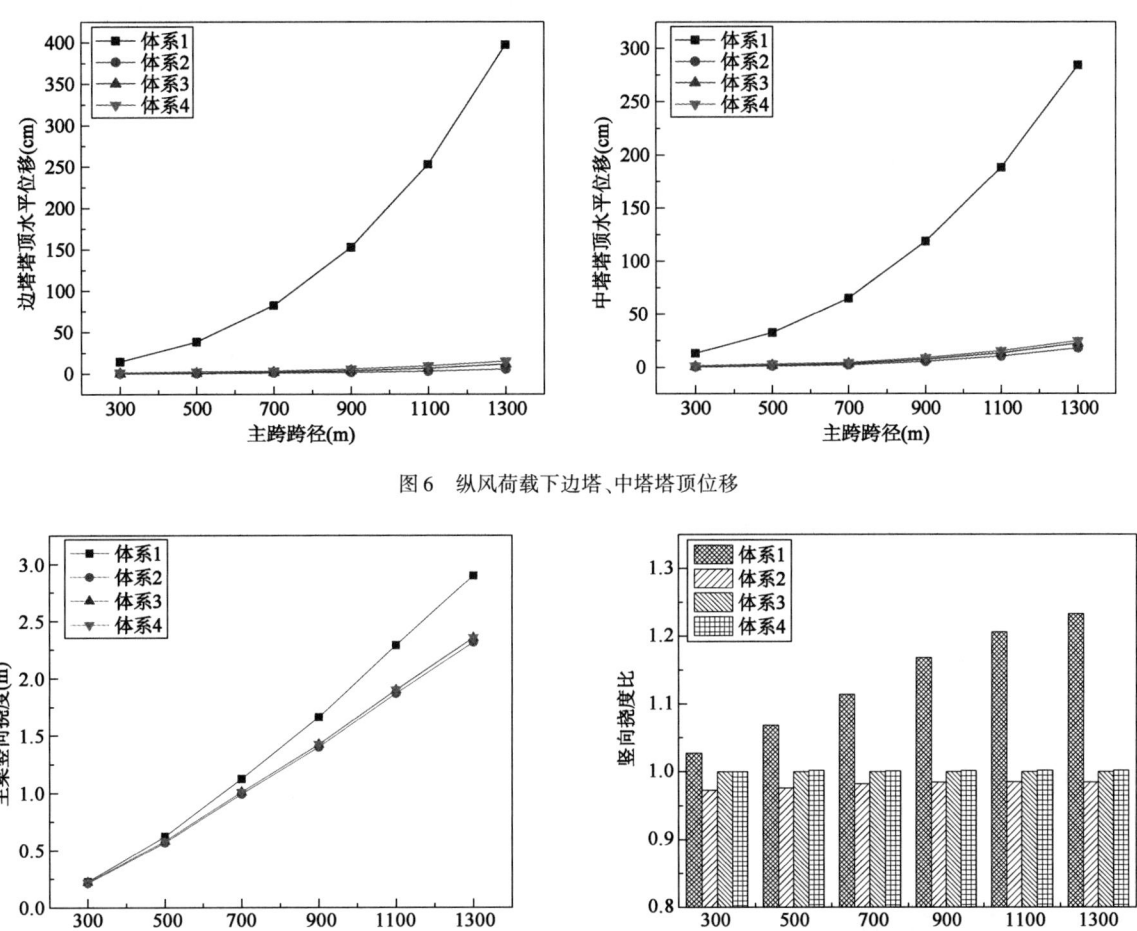

图6 纵风荷载下边塔、中塔塔顶位移

图7 活载下主梁竖向挠度

图8 不同约束体系竖向挠度对比

从图7和图8可见，体系1由于塔柱主梁处无纵向约束，其结构竖向挠度最大，体系3和体系4挠度曲线基本重合，且介于体系1和体系2之间；随着主跨跨度的增大，塔梁间的连接形式对结构刚度的影响越来越显著。三塔斜拉桥在中塔塔柱主梁处设置纵向约束对结构竖向刚度的提高有较好的效果，主跨跨度越大，提高效果越显著。

4 结　语

本文以不同主跨跨度的公铁两用三塔斜拉桥为分析对象，研究了半飘浮体系、三塔纵向全约束体系、中塔纵向约束体系和中塔弹性索约束体系在纵向极限风荷载、温度荷载与活载下的结构受力响应，主要结论有：

（1）缺少纵向约束的半飘浮体系，抵抗纵向荷载的能力较差，随跨度的增大，索塔的高耸，作用于斜拉索和主梁上的纵风荷载，通过斜拉索传递至主塔上塔柱，增大了力臂，此时纵向极限风荷载将控制设计，因此半飘浮体系不适用于跨度大于300m的公铁两用三塔斜拉桥。

（2）设置纵向约束可将主梁与主塔下塔柱联系在一起，将原本通过斜拉索作用在上塔柱的力通过纵向约束传递至下塔柱，作用点高度显著降低，一定程度上减小了桥塔纵向位移和顺桥向内力；在中塔设置纵向约束的体系更适用于公铁两用三塔斜拉桥，300m及以下跨度可比较半飘浮体系。

（3）三塔纵向全约束体系的整体刚度最大，但在温度荷载作用下主梁纵向变形受约束会产生较大的温度内力，因此，不适用于常规墩高公铁两用三塔斜拉桥。

（4）随跨度的增大，中塔纵向约束体系的中塔支座处将产生较大的纵向力，会提高支座的设计难度；

相比于设计能够抵抗较大纵向力的支座,通过水平弹性索将主梁与索塔约束在一起的设计方法更容易实现。

参考文献

[1] Wilson J C, Gravelle W. Modelling of a cable-stayed bridge for dynamic analysis[J]. 1991, 20(8):707-721.

[2] 华有恒.试论香港汀九斜拉桥设计构思的特色和探讨[J].桥梁建设,1997,000(003):27-33.

[3] 雷俊卿,黄祖慰,曹珊珊,等.大跨度公铁两用斜拉桥研究进展[J].科技导报,2016(34):33.

[4] 喻梅,廖海黎,李乔,等.多塔斜拉桥的结构体系研究[J].铁道建筑,2015,000(003):12-15.

[5] 徐利平.超大跨径斜拉桥的结构体系分析[J].同济大学学报:自然科学版(4):400-403.

[6] 喻梅,李乔,廖海黎.多塔斜拉桥的刚度配置[J].四川建筑科学研究,2010(04):67-71.

[7] 朱斌,林道锦.大跨径斜拉桥结构体系研究[J].公路,2006,000(006):97-100.

[8] 李忠三.基于静动力特性的多塔长跨斜拉桥结构体系刚度研究[D].北京:北京交通大学,2014.

[9] 廖建宏,胡建华.岳阳洞庭湖大桥多塔斜拉桥新技术研究[C]// 中国公路学会桥梁和结构工程学会全国桥梁学术会议.2002.

[10] 陈炜,张德平.武汉二七长江大桥结构体系方案研究[J].桥梁建设,2011(01):1-4.

[11] Carter M, Kite S, Hussain N, et al. Forth Replacement Crossing: Scheme design of the bridge[J]. Iabse Symposium Report, 2009, 96(6):107-116.

[12] Alastair A S, Colford B R. Forth Road Bridge-maintenance challenges[J]. Advances in Cable-Supported Bridges,2017.

Two-Dimensional Site Response Analysis for the Panama Canal Forth Bridge

Yun Liao[1]　Jiaer Wu[1]　Jun Ji[2]　JunWu[2]　Han Xiao[2]

(1. CHEC (USA)Inc.；2. China Harbour Engineering Company USA Inc)

Abstract　A cable-stayed bridge with a main span of 510m is proposed for the new and 4th crossing of the Panama Canal. Due to its close proximity to active faults in the canal area, the structural design of the bridge is mainly controlled by the seismic hazard. It is well known that the local soil condition is an important factor in modifying the ground motion parameters during earthquakes. This paper presents a study of the site-specific site response analysis on characterizing the effects of the local soil condition on the parameters of ground motions.

In the study, two-dimensional soil models were created in PLAXIS 2D to evaluate the effects of the non-horizontal ground surface and stratigraphy on the ground motions. The models were developed to match in-situ measurements of shear wave velocity at different pier locations, and nonlinear modulus reduction and damping curves were used to characterize the dynamic behaviours of the soils. Compliant base boundary condition and free-field vertical boundary conditions were applied to the models to simulate continued wave propagation into the half-space and the far field.

The study results indicated that ①ground motions within shallow soils are generally de-amplified from the bedrock input for period ranges of less than about 0.7 second. For periods ranging from about 0.7 to 2 seconds, ground motions could be either amplified or de-amplified. For longer periods greater than 2 seconds, there is nearly no significant de-amplification/amplification; ② site amplifications at different pier locations are noticeably different. In general, the thicker the overburden soils, the more the de-amplification for short to intermediate periods.

Keywords Site response analysis Panama canal 4th bridge Plaxis numerical modelling Dynamic modulus reduction Ground motion

0 Introduction

It is well known that the local soil condition is an important factor in modifying the ground motion parameters during earthquakes (Idriss, 1991; Bollina et al., 1997; Rathje et al., 2000). Site response analysis has long been used to characterize the effects of the local soil condition on changing ground motion parameters (Hashash et al., 2010). In many cases, one-dimensional site response analysis is performed to assess the effect of the local soil condition on ground shaking because vertically propagating and horizontally polarized shear waves dominate the earthquake ground motion wave field. One key assumption associated with performing one-dimensional site response analysis is that soil layers could be simplified as one-dimensional soil columns (i.e., no thickness variations in the horizontal direction). However, it is usually found that the ground surface and soil stratigraphy could vary significantly in the horizontal direction. As such, the influence of the non-horizontal ground surface and soil layer contacts could be pronounced on the propagation of ground motions. Panama Canal 4th Bridge site has a very complex geological condition due to its regional geological settings. Therefore, a study of two-dimensional site-specific site response analysis was carried out to investigate the effects of the local soil condition on changing ground motion parameters.

The computer program PLAXIS 2D (Bentley, 2021) adopted in this study is a commercial finite element code that allows performing stress-strain analyses for various types of geotechnical systems. An earthquake analysis can be performed by imposing an acceleration time-history at the base of the finite element model and solving the equations of motion in the time domain by adopting a Newmark type implicit time integration scheme. This program has been successfully used for performing dynamic site response analysis in both research and engineering practice. The main objective of the study was to provide displacement time histories in FN, FP and vertical orientations and at different elevations for each bridge pier for use in soil-structural interaction analysis of the Main Bridge. Due to the limitation on paper length, this paper presents only the analysis of the western half of the Main Bridge.

1 Geologic and Subsurface Conditions at the West Main Bridge

The new 4th Bridge Crossing is located in Pacific Coast Zone of the Panama Canal Basin, which is a structurally complex and consists of six different geological zones. Fig. 1 shows the layout of the Main Bridge structure. The overall project area is located in a transitional area between volcanic rocks on the eastern side and coastal plain on the western side. While the eastern half of the Main Bridge is underlain by Basalt (T_b) formation of middle and late Miocene age, the western half of the Main Bridge is located on an alluvial plain underlain by La Boca (T_l) formation consisting mainly of sedimentary rocks of siltstone, sandstone, conglomerate of early Miocene age.

Fig. 2 illustrates the profile of subsurface conditions along the longitudinal direction of the West Main Bridge. The subsurface conditions consist of Pacific Muck (Qml and Qmk) underlain by residual soil (Ov). Pacific Muck consists of Holocene sediments of very soft clay (Qmk) and shelly sand (Qml) and the residual soil is typically cohesive sandy materials. The overburden soil is underlain by weathered La Boca bedrock. The thickness of the weathered bedrock (T_{lw}) varied from just a few meters near the canal to several tens of meters towards the western shore. The sound bedrock (T_{ls}) that underlies the weathered bedrock is located about 15 m below the ground surface near the pier M6 and more than 50 m below the ground surface at other piers. As it can be seen, while the ground surface gently slopes towards the canal, the contacts between soil/rock layers are highly variable in the horizontal direction. Thus simplification of subsurface conditions using one-dimensional models may significantly overlook the effects of the soil stratigraphy on the ground motion parameters. Fig. 2 also shows the approximate locations of the five piers of the West Main Bridge (M6 through M10).

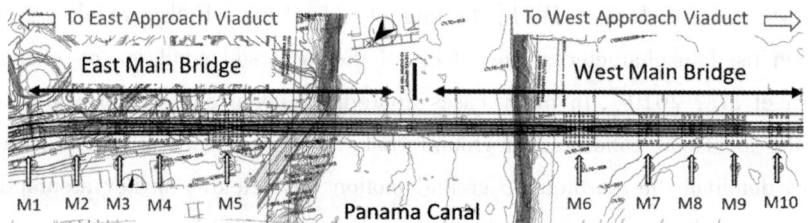

Fig. 1　Layout of the Main Bridge Structure

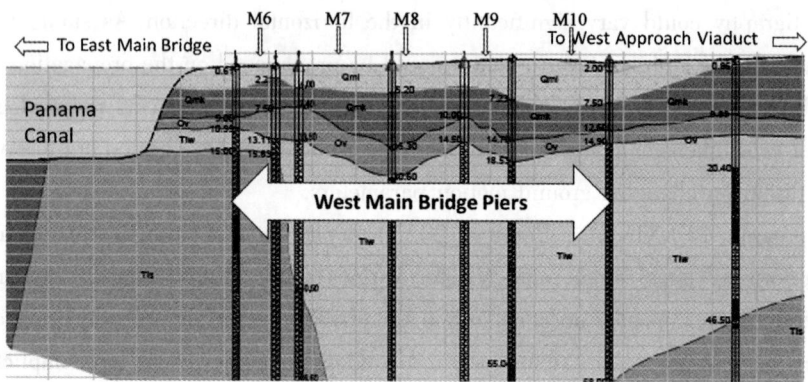

Fig. 2　Soil Profile Along Longitudinal Direction of the West Main Bridge

A summary of plasticity index values of Qmk and Ov soils tested for the West Main Bridge is as plotted in Fig. 3 A representative PI value of 30 was chosen for Qmk and 15 for Ov, respectively. The Qml soils are primarily non-plastic so that a representative PI of 0 was assumed. These representative values were used to determine the modulus reduction curves and damping curves.

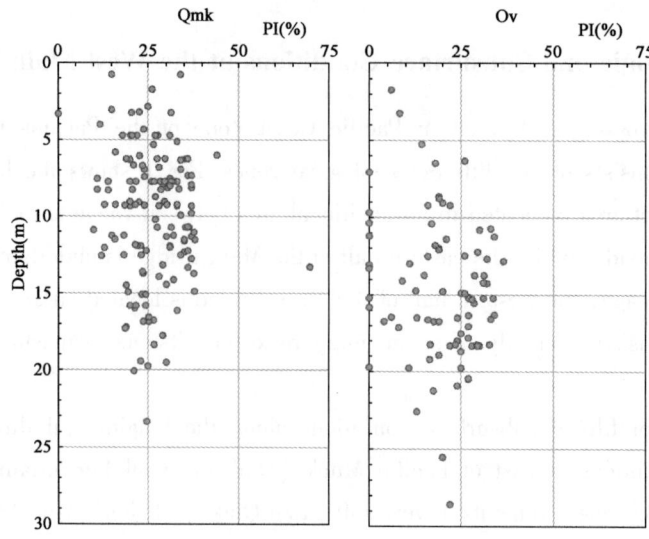

Fig. 3　Summary of Plasticity Index Values for Qmk and Ov Soils

2 Soil Properties

2.1 Shear Wave Velocity Profiles

A total of three shear wave velocity (V_s) profiles (M6-BH3, M7-BH1, and RM9-BH3) were measured for the West Main Bridge using seismic down-hole and/or cross-hole testing methods. These measured V_s profiles were carefully reviewed and idealized for site response analysis. The V_s measurements were first cross-checked against boring logs and laboratory testing results for quality insurance, the as-measured shear wave velocity profiles were then idealized with some fine adjustments to match the final geological profiles. As an example, Fig. 4 illustrates the shear wave velocity profile modeled in PLAXIS at the location of M7-BH1 in comparison to the field measured shear wave velocity profile. A shear wave velocity of 800 m/s was adopted for the sound bedrock, which matches the shear wave velocity of the bedrock used in the seismic hazard analysis.

2.2 Modulus Reduction Curves

Based on their representative PI values of each soil layer, Darendeli (2001) modulus reduction curves were chosen for each soil layer. PLAXIS does not allow direct inputs of the dynamic modulus reduction curves. Instead, it utilizes Santos and Correia (2001) formulation for producing modulus reduction curves. Santos and Correia (2001) formulation uses a parameter $\gamma_{0.7}$ to control the shape of the dynamic modulus reduction curve. The parameter $\gamma_{0.7}$ can be adjusted to match target modulus reduction curves. It should be noted that the Santos and Correia (2001) formulation cannot simulate the shape of the Schnabel (1973) curve well. However, the weathered rock is anticipated to subject to a much smaller shear strain compared to overburden soils. Therefore, it was intended to match the Schnabel (1973) curve as much as possible in small strain levels which are likely to occur for rock layers. Fig. 5 show the matching of Santos and Correia (2001) formulation in PLAXIS to selected Darendeli (2001) modulus reduction curve for soils and Schnabel (1973) curve for weathered rocks. A summary of the parameter $\gamma_{0.7}$ obtained for each layer is listed in Tab. 1.

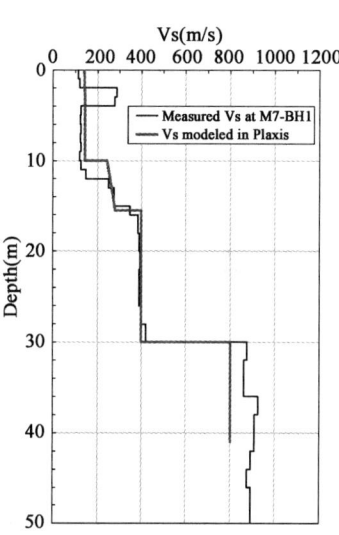

Fig. 4 Comparison between Measured and Idealized Vs Prfofiles at M7-BH1

Soil Parameters for PLAXIS Modelling Tab. 1

Soil/Rock Type	Model	Unit Weight (kN/m³)	E_5^r (kPa)	Cohesion (kPa)	Friction Angle (degree)	Dilation Angle (degree)
Qml	HSsmall	18	3.0E3	5	28	0
Qmk	HSsmall	17	5.0E3	25	0	0
Ov	HSsmall	18	2.0E4	20	37	7
Weathered Rock 1	HSsmall	20	3.0E4	250	0	0

2.3 Summary of Soil Properties

A summary of soil parameters for PLAXIS modelling is shown in Tab. 1. Soil layers Qml, Qmk, Ov and top weathered rock 1 are all modelled with the HSsmall model built in PLAXIS with other related parameters listed in Tab. 2. Slightly weather bedrock and sound bedrock are modelled with a linear elastic model. A shear wave velocity of 600 m/s was used for slightly weathered bedrock and 800 m/s was used for sound bedrock. It should be noted that while the loose saturated Qml soils are considered susceptible to liquefaction during strong earthquakes, they were not modelled as liquefiable soils in the site response analysis in order to obtain ground motions corresponding to non-liquefaction, as-constructed conditions around the piers.

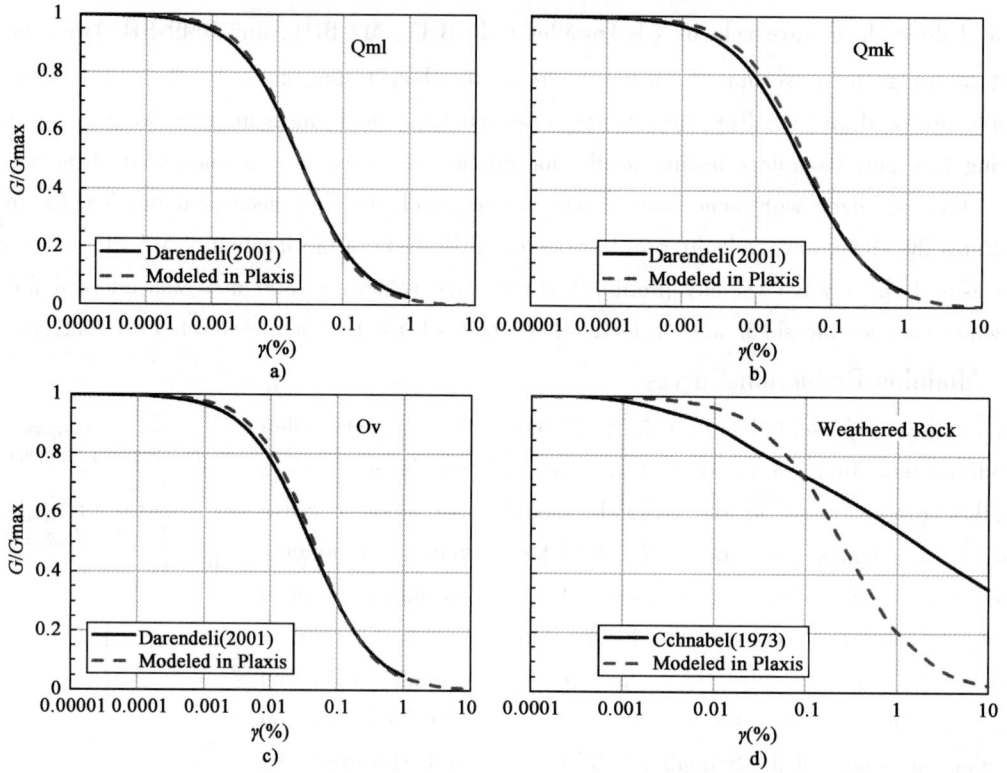

Fig. 5 Matching of Modulus Reduction Curve for Soils and Weathered Rock

Soil Parameters for PLAXIS Modelling (continued) Tab. 2

Soil/Rock Type	Rayleigh Damping		Q (kPa)	l	$\gamma_{\text{cut-off}}$
	α	β			
Qml	0.5712	1.45×10^{-3}	4.0×10^{-4}	8.5×10^{-5}	0.5×10^{-3}
Qmk	0.5712	1.45×10^{-3}	3.5×10^{-4}	2.0×10^{-4}	1.0×10^{-3}
Ov	0.2285	5.79×10^{-4}	2.2×10^{-5}	1.7×10^{-4}	9.0×10^{-4}
Weathered Rock 1	0.1142	2.89×10^{-4}	3.3×10^{-5}	8.0×10^{-4}	4.0×10^{-3}

3 Plaxis Finite Element Model

Fig. 6 shows the PLAXIS finite element model for the West Main Bridge. The model includes the pier locations M6 through M10 and is approximately 580 m in the horizontal (X) direction. In the vertical (Y) direction, the model was extended to the depth where the sound bedrock is defined as in the probabilistic seismic hazard analysis. For numerical modeling purpose, a few meters of sound bedrock were included in the model. The mode extended down to an elevation of -50 m. Also shown in the figure are actual station numbers and elevations.

The model was meshed with about 16000 6-node triangular elements. For each soil layer, the average element size is calculated using the formular recommended by PLAXIS:

$$\text{AverageElementSize} \leq V_s / (8 f_{\max}) \qquad (1)$$

Where, V_s is the shear wave velocity; $f_{\max}$ is the maximum frequency of the input ground motion. For soil layers, this AverageElementSize is usually less than 3 m calculated with a $f_{\max}$ of 20 to 30 Hz.

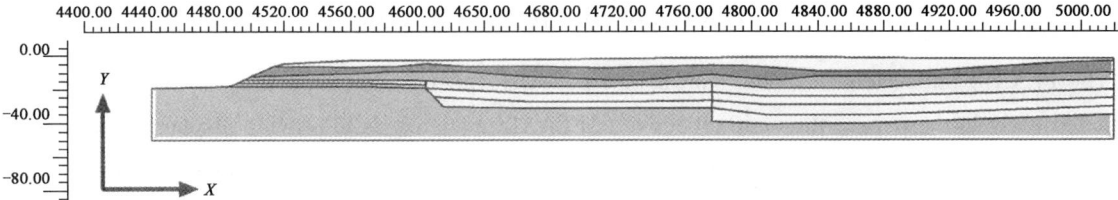

Fig. 6 Idealized PLAXIS Finite Element Model

A compliant base boundary condition (Lysmer and Kuhlemeyer, 1969) was applied to the bottom boundary of the models. The Lysmer-Kuhlemeyer boundary allows downward propagating waves that have been reflected off the surface or at impedance contrasts within the profile to be partially absorbed by the dashpot, thereby emulating continued downward propagation of the wave into the half-space. For two vertical boundaries on the sides of the model, a free-field boundary condition was applied, which simulates the propagation of waves into the far field with minimum reflection at the boundary.

4 Input Ground Motions

In accordance with the design criteria, the seismic design of the bridge structure should meet two levels of earthquake events, the safety evaluation event (return period of 2475 years) and function evaluation event (return period of 475 years). For each level, three sets of ground motion time histories including two horizontal and one vertical component were selected, spectrally matched to the target response spectra developed in the probabilistic seismic hazard analysis. The two horizontal components were rotated to fault normal and fault parallel directions. Each component of ground motions was converted into a displacement time history as the input ground motion for PLAXIS modeling. As an example, Fig. 7 shows the acceleration time history, displacement time history, and acceleration response spectra for the ground motion RSN1602. It should be pointed out that only half amplitude of the input displacement time history was applied to the PLAXIS model since a compliant based boundary condition was used.

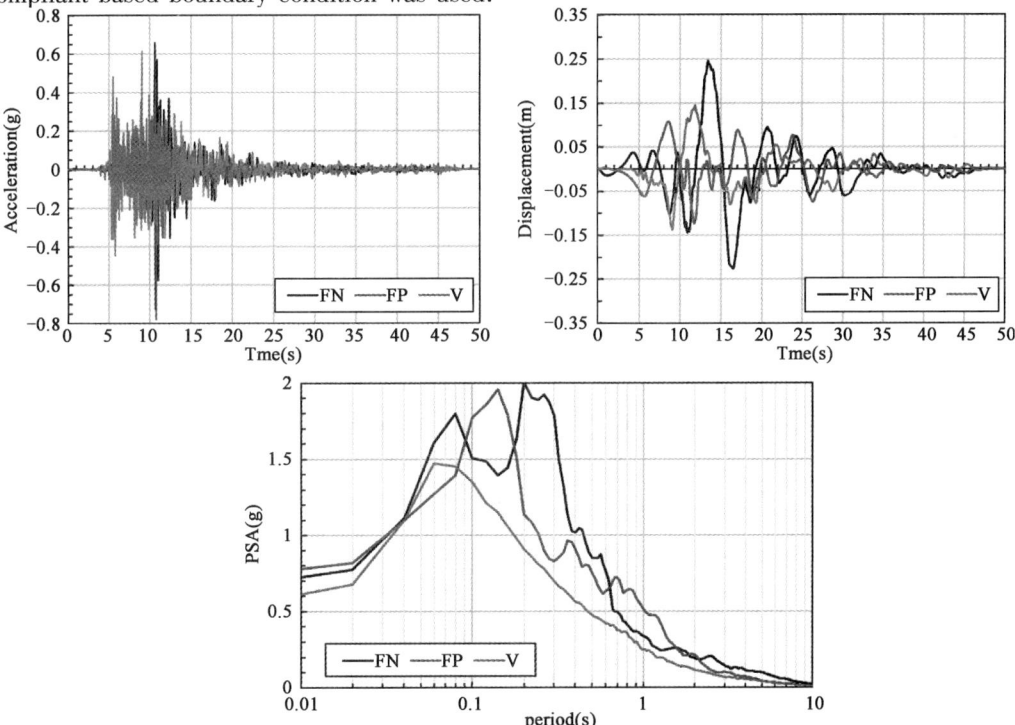

Fig. 7 Acceleration, Displacement Time Histories and Accleration Response Spectra for RSN1602

5 Results of Site Response Analysis

The PLAXIS finite element model shown in Fig. 5 was run for each input displacement time history. As mentioned early in the paper, the main objective of PLAXIS modeling is to provide displacement time histories at different elevations for piers M6 through M10 for soil-structure interaction analysis. A query point was predefined in the PLAXIS model for each output location as requested by structural engineers. Due to the limited space, only the results of pier M9 for the ground motion RSN1602 FN component are presented herein.

Fig. 8 shows the distribution of the computed maximum horizontal acceleration within the model. As it can be seen, the maximum acceleration in general occurred within top of the bedrock where a soil/rock stiffness contrast exits. Fig. 9 presents the distribution of the maximum horizontal displacements during the shaking within the model. Fig. 10 illustrates the distribution of residual horizontal displacements after the shaking within the model. It is observed that due to the presence of the canal slope, the maximum soil movement towards the canal is about 1m; meanwhile, in the vicinity of Station 4 + 850 the shallow soil moved towards the right side following the sloping ground surface. It is worth noting that the maximum displacements shown in Fig. 9 are not consistent with the residual displacements shown in Fig. 10, which suggested that soil plastic failure in the canal slope area and near Station 4 + 850 occurred during the shaking. Because the site response model does not include the effects of potential soil liquefaction, the as-calculated maximum transient and residual displacements distribution should not be used directly for design purposes.

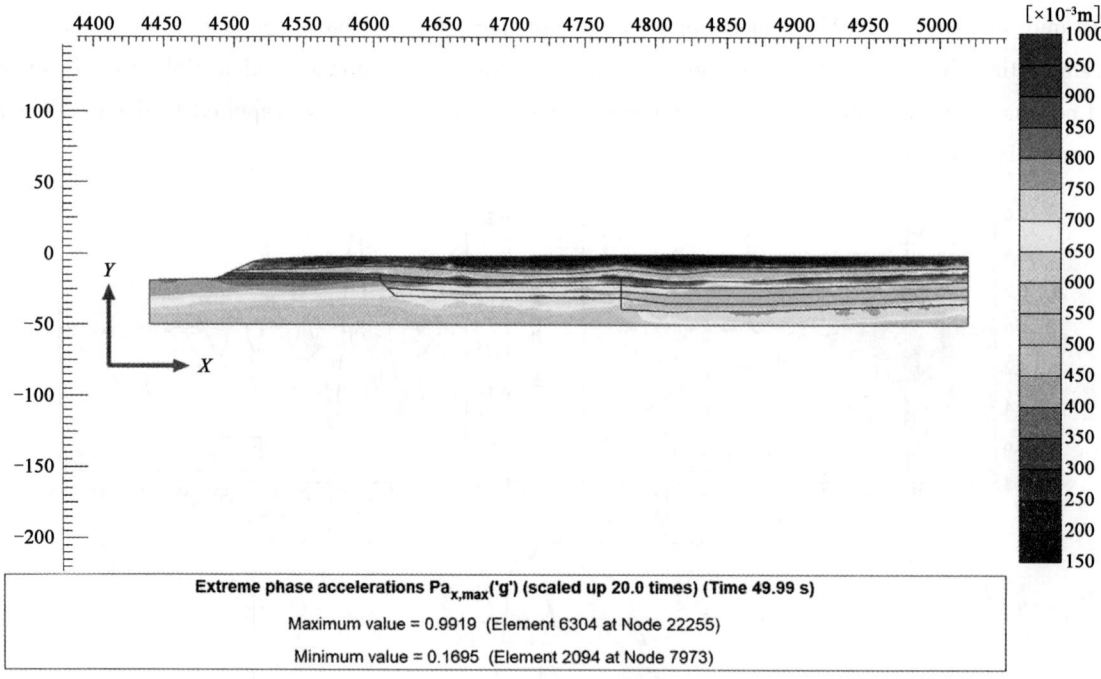

Fig. 8 Contour of Maximum Horizontal Acceleration for RSN1602 FN

Fig. 11 shows the computed acceleration response spectra at 12 different depths at Pier M9 location. The line M900 represents the computed acceleration response spectra at the shallowest depth within the top layer and the line M911 represents the computed acceleration response spectra within the weathered bedrock that is modelled as a linear elastic material with a shear wave velocity of 600 m/s. The depths increase with the line numbers from 900 to 911. Fig. 12 shows the computed horizontal displacement time histories at the corresponding depths. The results indicated that the shear strain within the soil increased with a decrease in the depth, which led to a greater residual displacement.

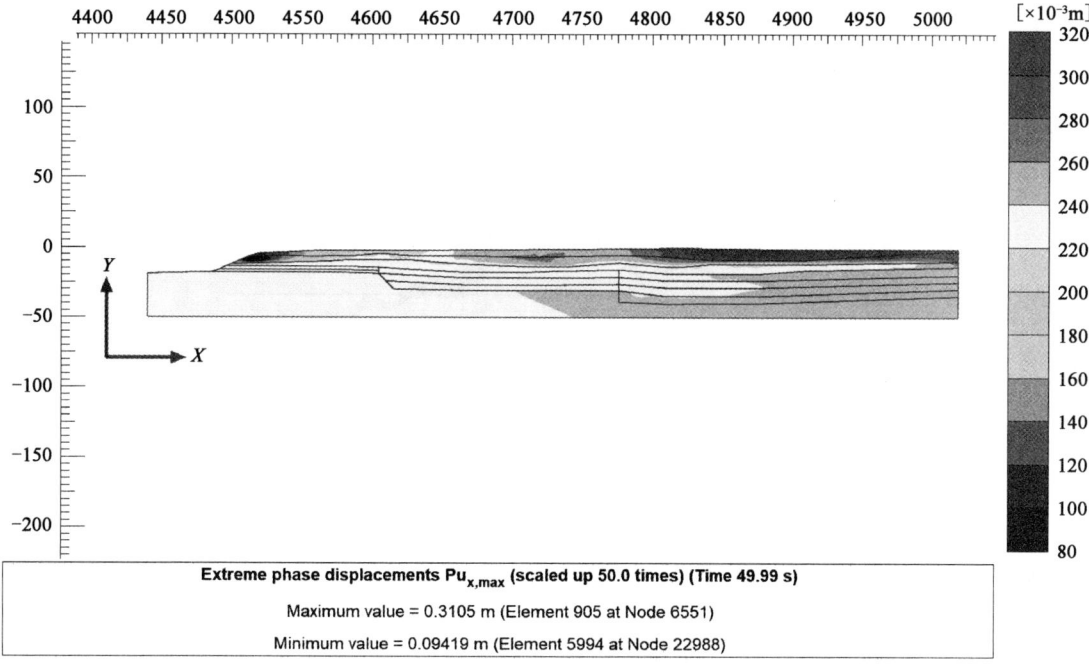

Fig. 9 Contour of Maximum Horizontal Displacement for RSN1602 FN

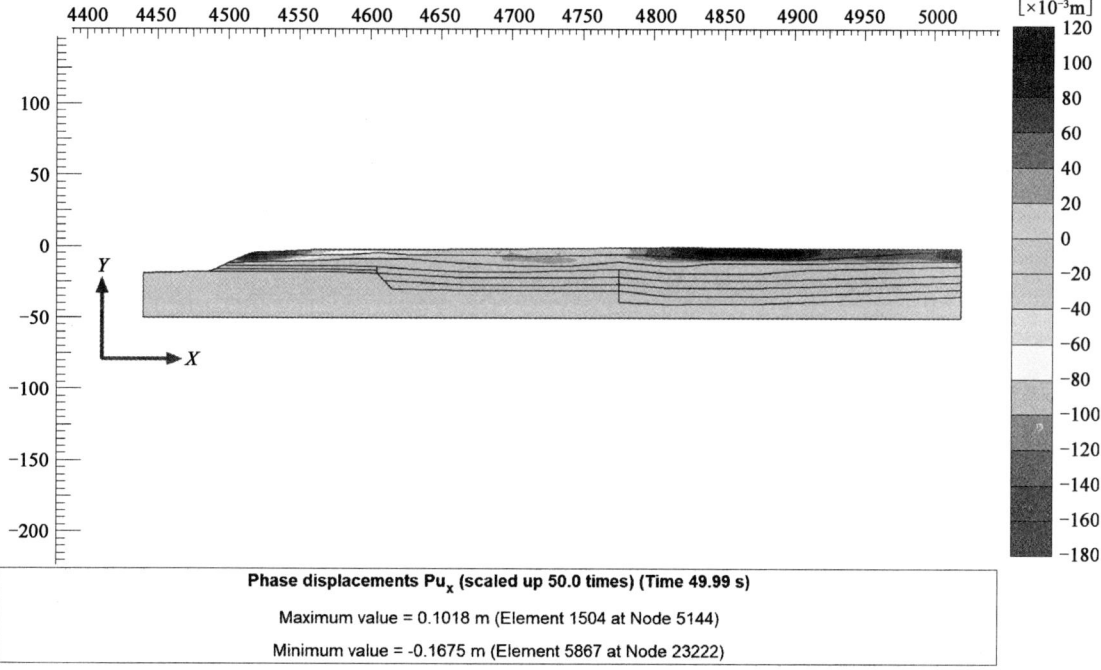

Fig. 10 Contour of Residual Horizontal Displacements for RSN1602 FN

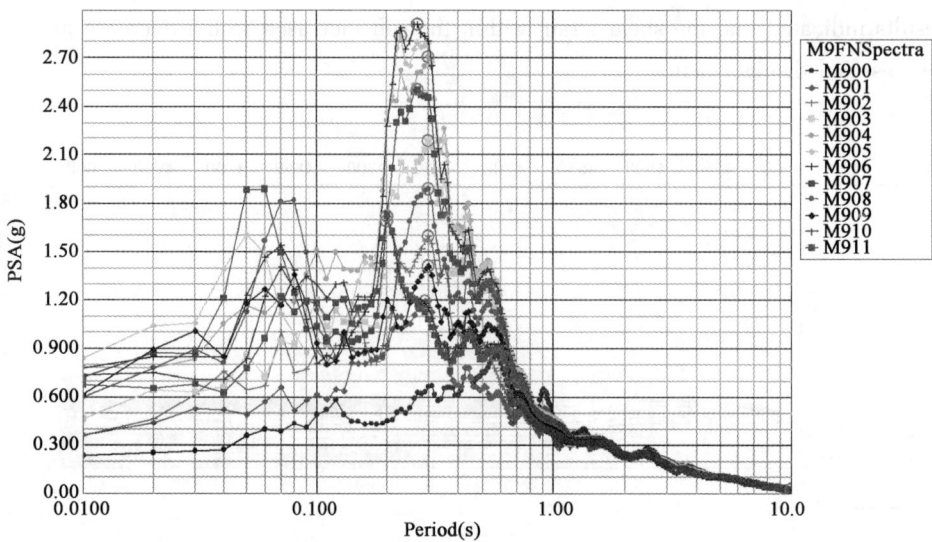

Fig. 11 Acceleration Response Spectra for Pier M9 for RSN1602 FN

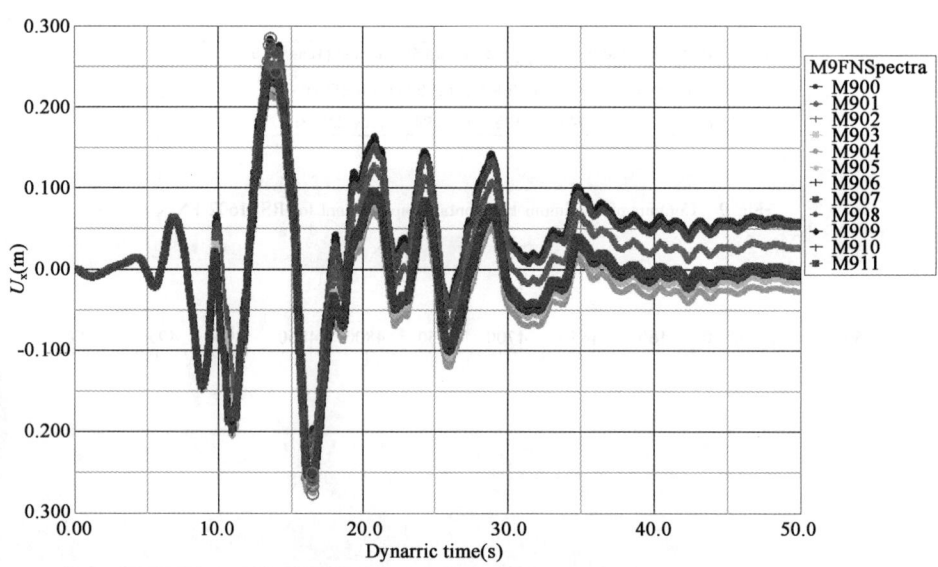

Fig. 12 Horizontal Displacement Time Histories for Pier M9 for RSN1602 FN

6　Conclusions

In this study, a two-dimensional site-specific site response analysis was performed to characterize the effects of the local soil condition on changing ground motion parameters. The results of site response analysis in the format of the displacement time histories are provided for soil-structural interaction. The following conclusions can be reached:

(1) Horizontal ground motions at shallow soils, especially the Qmk layer, are generally de-amplified from the bedrock input ground motions for the period range of less than about 0.7 second. For the period range from about 0.7 to 2 seconds, ground motions could be either amplified or de-amplified. For periods longer than 2 seconds, no significant de-amplification/amplification was observed.

(2) For deeper residual soil layers, the horizontal ground motion amplifications within short to intermediate period range (< 1s) are likely to happen, while either negligible amplification or attenuation typically happen for longer period range.

(3) For vertical ground motions, short period amplification is the dominating behaviour for the period range less than 0.5s, while no significant amplification or attenuation was observed beyond 0.5s period.

(4) At different pier locations, the calculated site amplifications are slightly different, but in general, the de-amplification effect within short to intermediate periods increases with thicker overlying soil layers.

(5) According to the displacement time histories, peak horizontal soil displacements among the 5 piers are similar. However, residual permanent displacements at the end of shaking are significantly different. They were most affected by the thickness of the soil layers and the sloping of the ground surface.

It becomes clear from this study that two-dimensional site-specific site response analysis can provide significant benefits for design/evaluation of critical structures located in seismically active regions when the following two conditions present: 1) soft overburden soils play an important role in changing ground motions parameters that needs to be considered in the structural design, 2) non-horizontal ground surface and soil stratigraphy have a significant effect on the calculated site response including transient and permanent residual soil displacements, which cannot be captured in typical one-dimensional site response analysis.

References

[1] Bonilla L. F., Steidl J. H., Lindley G. T., et al. Site Amplification in the San Fernando Valley, California: Variability of Site-Effect Estimation Using the S-wave, Coda, and H/V methods, Bulletin of the Seismological Society of America, 1997, 87 (3): 710-730.

[2] Rathje E., Idriss I. M., Somerville P., et al. Strong Ground Motions and Site Effects[J]. Earthquake Spectra, 2000, 16: 65-96.

[3] Idriss I. M. Earthquake Ground Motions at Soft Soil Sites, Second International Conference on Recent Advances in Geotechnical Earthquake Engineering and Soil Dynamics, 1991, MissouriUniversity of Science and Technology, March 11-15, St. Louis, Missouri,1991.

[4] Hashash Y., Phillips C., and Groholski D. R. Recent Advances in Non-Linear Site Response Analysis, 5th International Conference on Recent Advances in Geotechnical Earthquake Engineering and Soil Dynamics, Missouri University of Science and Technology, May 24-29, San Diego, California,2010.

[5] Darendeli, M. B. Development of a New Family of Normalized Modulus Reduction and Material Damping Curves. Ph. D. thesis, University of Texasat Austin, Austin, TX,2001.

[6] Santos J. A., and Correia A. G. Reference Threshold Shear Strain of Soil: Its Application to Obtain a Unique Strain-Dependent Shear Modulus Curve for Soil. Proceedings of 15th International Conference on Soil Mechanics and Geotechnical Engineering,2001,Vol 1: 267-270, Istanbul, Turkey.

[7] Schnabel, P. B. Effects of Local Geology and Distance from the Earthquake Ground Movement Source. Ph. D. Thesis, University of California, Berkeley, California,1973.

[8] Lysmer, J., and Kuhlemeyer R. L. Finite Dynamic Model for Infinite Media, J. Eng. Mech. Div., ASCE 95 EM4, 859-877,1969.

不同高宽比下钢箱梁三分力系数变化规律研究

王 路

(长安大学)

摘 要 三分力系数是评价大跨径桥梁抗风稳定性的重要参数。以CFD软件Fluent为计算平台,采用对钝体外部扰流模拟结果较好的SST k-ω湍流模型,使用定常流计算,研究了流线型钢箱梁三分力系数随高宽比的变化规律,得到了在不同风攻角、高宽比下流线型钢箱梁的三分力系数,为提取流线型钢箱梁断面的三分力系数和工程实践提供设计参考。

关键词 桥梁工程 变化规律 CFD数值模拟 流线型钢箱梁 高宽比 三分力系数

0 引 言

三分力系数是一组无量纲参数,它用于表征桥梁风荷载,是分析桥梁气动问题的基础。许多研究者通过风洞试验或者数值分析的方法对各类主梁断面进行了大量研究,得到了许多研究成果并应用于桥梁建设中。

李加武[1]通过静三分力与颤振导数的关系对颤振控制特性进行了研究;汪家继[2]分别对加拿大国家试验中心NRCC试验和昂船洲大桥试验进行三分力计算,分析了雷诺数、来流湍流强度、中央开槽宽度等对桥梁断面三分力系数的影响;刘小兵[3]现针对分离双主梁桥中的双钝体箱梁,在15个不同的间距下进行了三分力的风洞测试,详细地分析了三分力系数的气动干扰效应;杨阳[4]通过风洞试验和数值模拟的方法对宽高比为12的宽体钢箱梁的气动力特性和涡振性能进行了研究;白桦[5]基于频域分析法确定了三分力系数与颤振导数的关系,并通过典型工程案例加以验证;邓南忠[6]通过CFD软件对大跨度变截面连续钢箱梁空气静力特性进行了研究;王志鹏[7]基于CFD软件计算三分力系数,研究了钢箱梁典型断面涡振和颤振流场驱动机理;M. W. Sarwar[8]通过Fluent数值模拟研究了箱梁断面的气动措施,发现了导流板可以改变箱梁断面的涡脱形态;张亮亮[9]通过Overset Mesh网格技术,利用SST k-ω湍流模型对Π型主梁断面涡激振动进行了数值模拟研究。

由众多学者的研究可知,目前通过CFD软件Fluent计算平台对不同高宽比下流线型钢箱梁进行数值模拟,计算得到三分力系数随高宽比的变化规律的研究相对较少。本文针对高宽比为1:7、1:9、1:11、1:13、1:15的流线型钢箱梁,通过CFD软件Fluent计算平台,采用对钝体外部扰流模拟结果较好的k-ω湍流模型,对该钢箱梁断面进行三分力系数的计算。得到了在风攻角为0°、±3°、±5°下的三分力系数,并进行比较分析。

1 计算原理

流线型钢箱梁结构在来流风荷载的作用下,可以分解为三个方向的力:升力、阻力和升力矩。按照风轴和体轴这两类坐标系的划分,其气动力方向不同。流线型钢箱梁断面所受的三分力示意图如图1所示。

其中,F_H、F_V、M_T为体轴坐标系下流线型钢箱梁断面受到的横向气动力、竖向气动力和扭转力矩;F_D、F_L、M_T为在风轴坐标系下的流线型钢箱梁断面受到的阻力、升力和扭转力矩。

体轴气动力参数和风轴气动力参数的数学关系式如下:

$$C_H = C_D \times \cos\alpha - C_L \times \sin\alpha \times \frac{B}{H}$$

$$C_V = C_D \times \sin\alpha \times \frac{H}{B} + C_L \times \cos\alpha$$

式中：H——流线型钢箱梁断面的特征高度；
　　　B——流线型钢箱梁断面的特征宽度；
　　　α——风攻角。

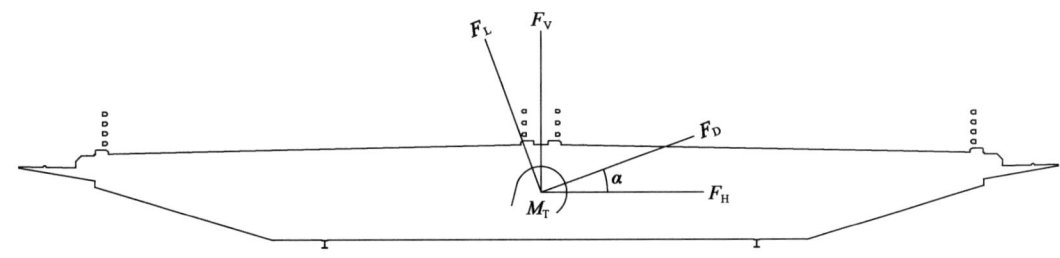

图 1　风轴和体轴坐标系以及气动力方向

2　CFD 网格设计

2.1　CFD 网格设计方法

网格划分的质量对于数值模拟得到的结果起到至关重要的作用，并且影响计算效率。如果网格划分过于稀疏，那么不能保证得到的计算结果的准确性；如果网格划分的过于密实，虽然计算精度有所提高，但是计算量也随之增大，会降低计算效率，资源和时间的消耗量也会大幅增加。计算模型采用实际尺寸。计算域的网格划分采用对形状适应性较好的三角形网格。在主梁断面周围网格节点密集，以一定的渐变率向四周发散，远离主梁断面位置的网格逐渐渐疏。

2.2　CFD 网格设计结果

为了保证设计的网格的可靠性、合理性，对网格进行了无关性检查。计算域的来流一侧为速度入口，其边界采用 Velocity inlet，上边界和下边界采用 Symmetry，出口边界采用 Outflow，计算域内部边界采用 Interior，模型壁面边界采用 Wall。该扁平流线型钢箱梁断面尺寸如表 1 所示。

模　型　尺　寸　　　　　　　　　表 1

高 宽 比	高（m）	宽（m）
1∶7	5.50	38.5
1∶9	4.28	38.5
1∶11	3.50	38.5
1∶13	2.96	38.5
1∶15	2.57	38.5

计算模型与网格划分如图 2 所示。

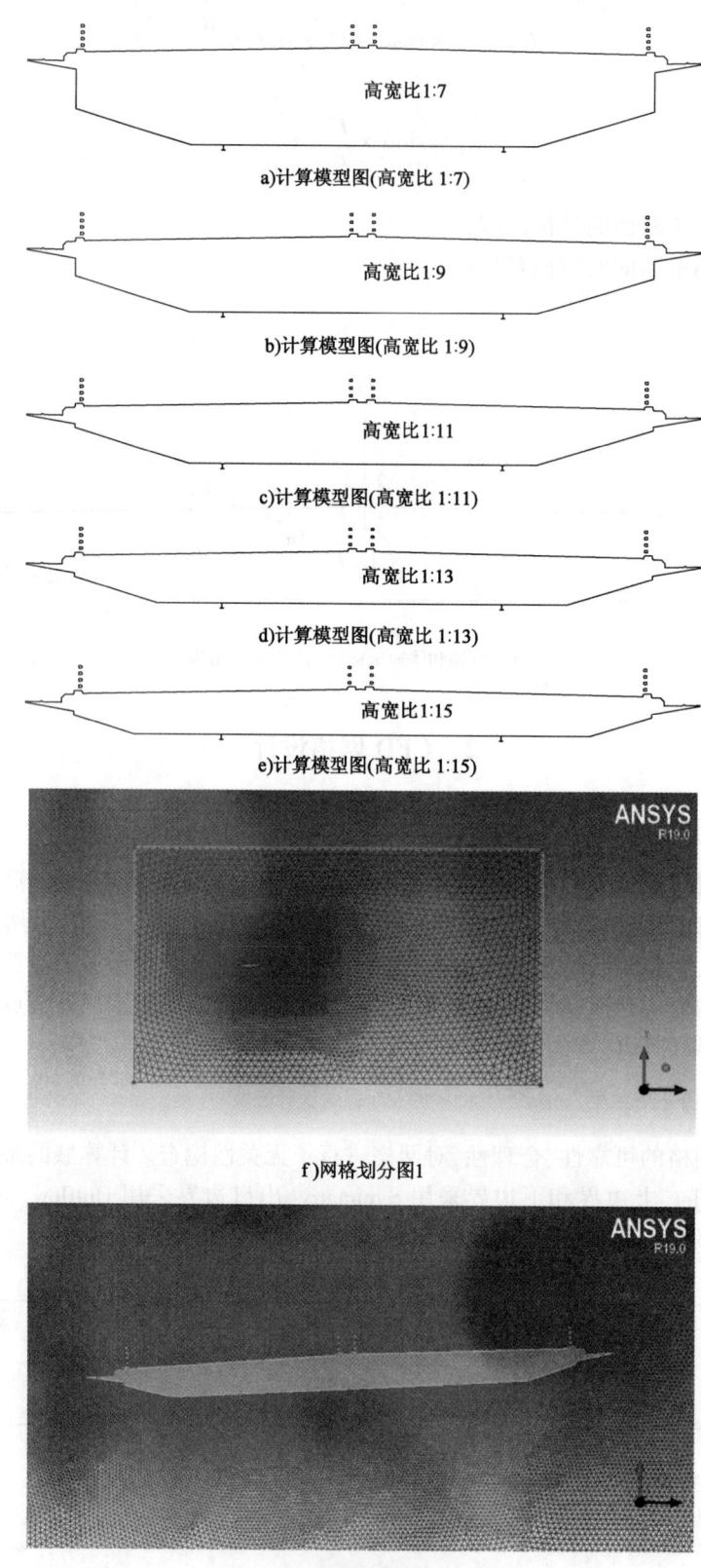

图 2 计算模型及网格划分

3 设 计 工 况

风攻角为：$-5°$、$-3°$、$0°$、$+3°$、$+5°$，共 5 个攻角变化。来流风速设为 10m/s。

4 数值模拟结果

4.1 从风攻角的角度

为了更好地进行数值模拟,以 Fluent 为计算平台,采用对钝体外部扰流模拟结果较好的 SST k-ω 湍流模型,使用定常流计算。方程求解采用 SIMPILEC 算法。得到三分力系数计算结果(表2),风轴坐标系下三分力系数-风攻角图如图3所示。

三 分 力 系 数 表2

高宽比	1:7		
风攻角	C_D	C_L	C_M
+5°	0.911247	0.409333	-0.095567
+3°	0.675621	0.238136	-0.096987
0°	0.711929	-0.040241	-0.027496
-3°	0.730644	-0.284811	0.033151
-5°	0.748705	-0.442108	0.071083
高宽比	1:9		
风攻角	C_D	C_L	C_M
+5°	0.867874	0.372555	-0.129495
+3°	0.843610	0.112719	-0.068580
0°	0.810458	-0.040653	-0.021484
-3°	0.776789	-0.308359	0.039269
-5°	0.798354	-0.505162	0.082087
高宽比	1:11		
风攻角	C_D	C_L	C_M
+5°	0.961504	0.132795	-0.074616
+3°	0.996945	0.065073	-0.063702
0°	0.909843	-0.077567	-0.013566
-3°	1.029841	-0.352788	0.050233
-5°	0.935935	-0.495549	0.089292
高宽比	1:13		
风攻角	C_D	C_L	C_M
+5°	0.977041	-0.027338	-0.067305
+3°	0.951693	-0.079313	-0.043798
0°	0.897209	-0.159869	0.003840
-3°	0.828855	-0.432987	0.077288
-5°	0.970381	-0.530835	0.110537
高宽比	1:15		
风攻角	C_D	C_L	C_M
+5°	1.060497	0.028195	-0.071808
+3°	1.019296	-0.086212	-0.039121
0°	0.955726	-0.236660	0.014468
-3°	0.947584	-0.440526	0.079263
-5°	1.056358	-0.554498	0.122712

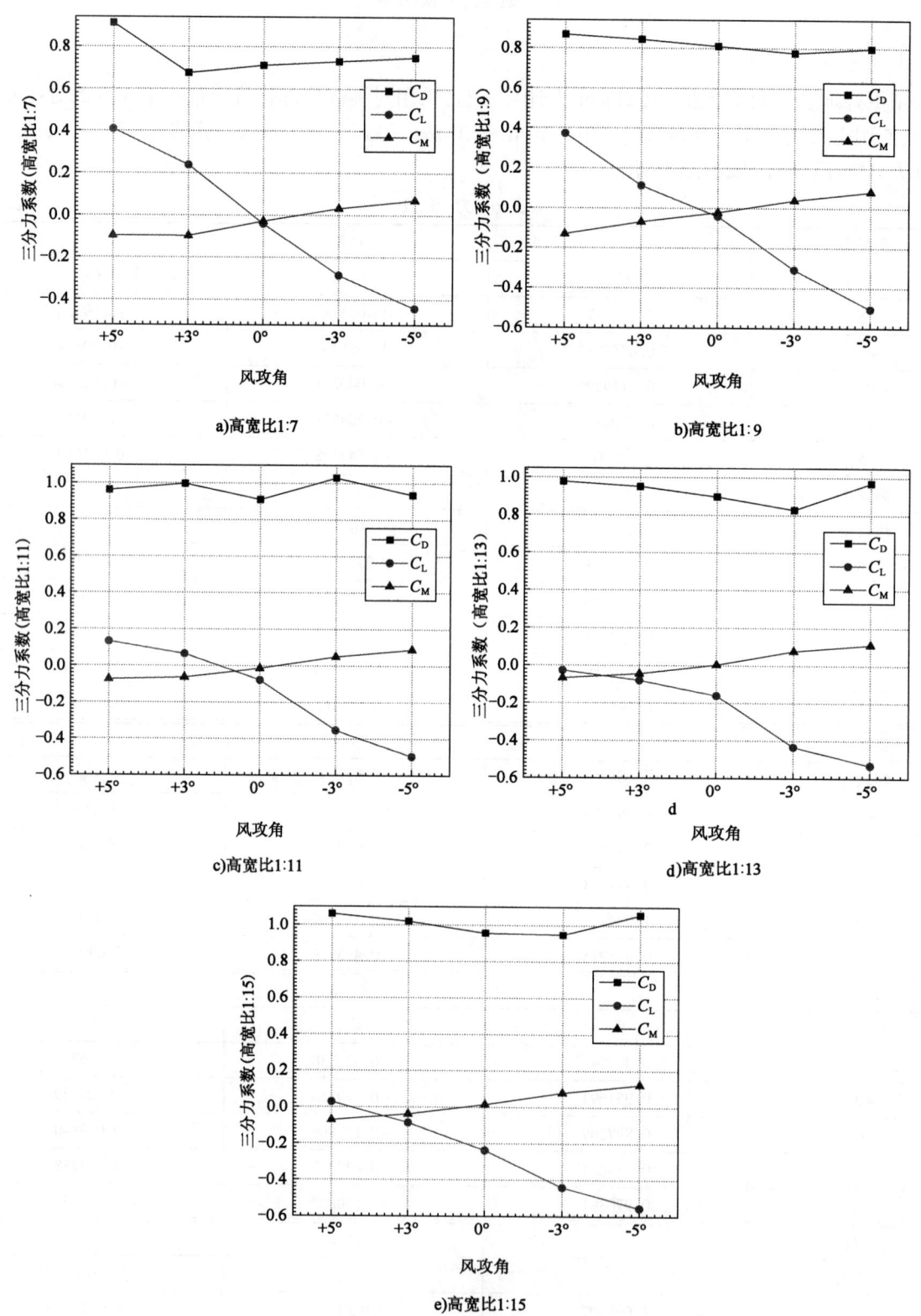

图 3 三分力系数-风攻角图

通过数值模拟得到上述三分力系数结果,分析上述结果,可以得到如下结论:随着高宽比从 1∶7 到 1∶15 不断变化,从总体上可以得到,阻力系数 C_D 逐渐上升;升力系数 C_L 逐渐下降;升力矩系数 C_M 变化对高宽比不敏感。

4.2 从高宽比的角度

在同一风攻角下,对不同宽高比的流线型钢箱梁三分力系数进行比较,得到结果如表3和图4所示。

三分力系数比较表　　表3

风攻角	+5°				
高宽比	1:7	1:9	1:11	1:13	1:15
C_D	0.911247	0.867874	0.961504	0.977041	1.060497
C_L	0.409333	0.372555	0.132795	-0.027338	0.028195
C_M	-0.095567	-0.129495	-0.074616	-0.067305	-0.071808
风攻角	+3°				
高宽比	1:7	1:9	1:11	1:13	1:15
C_D	0.675621	0.843610	0.996945	0.951693	1.019296
C_L	0.238136	0.112719	0.065073	-0.079313	-0.086212
C_M	-0.096987	-0.068580	-0.063702	-0.043798	-0.039121
风攻角	0°				
高宽比	1:7	1:9	1:11	1:13	1:15
C_D	0.711929	0.810458	0.961504	0.897209	0.955726
C_L	-0.040241	-0.040653	0.132795	-0.159869	-0.236660
C_M	-0.027496	-0.021484	-0.074616	0.003840	0.014468
风攻角	-3°				
高宽比	1:7	1:9	1:11	1:13	1:15
C_D	0.730644	0.776789	1.029841	0.828855	0.947584
C_L	-0.284811	-0.308359	-0.352788	-0.432987	-0.440526
C_M	0.033151	0.039269	0.050233	0.077288	0.079263
风攻角	-5°				
高宽比	1:7	1:9	1:11	1:13	1:15
C_D	0.748705	0.798354	0.935935	0.970381	1.056358
C_L	-0.442108	-0.505162	-0.495549	-0.530835	-0.554498
C_M	0.071083	0.082087	0.089292	0.110537	0.122712

通过分析上述在同一风攻角时,流线型钢箱梁三分力系数的结果,可以得到如下结论:

在各个风攻角时,阻力系数C_D随着高宽比逐渐降低(从1:7到1:15)而逐渐上升;升力系数C_L在0°风攻角时,随着高宽比逐渐降低(从1:7到1:15)先上升后下降,在±3°和±5°风攻角时,随着高宽比逐渐降低(从1:7到1:15)而下降;升力矩系数C_M变化幅值相对较小,对高宽比的变化不敏感。

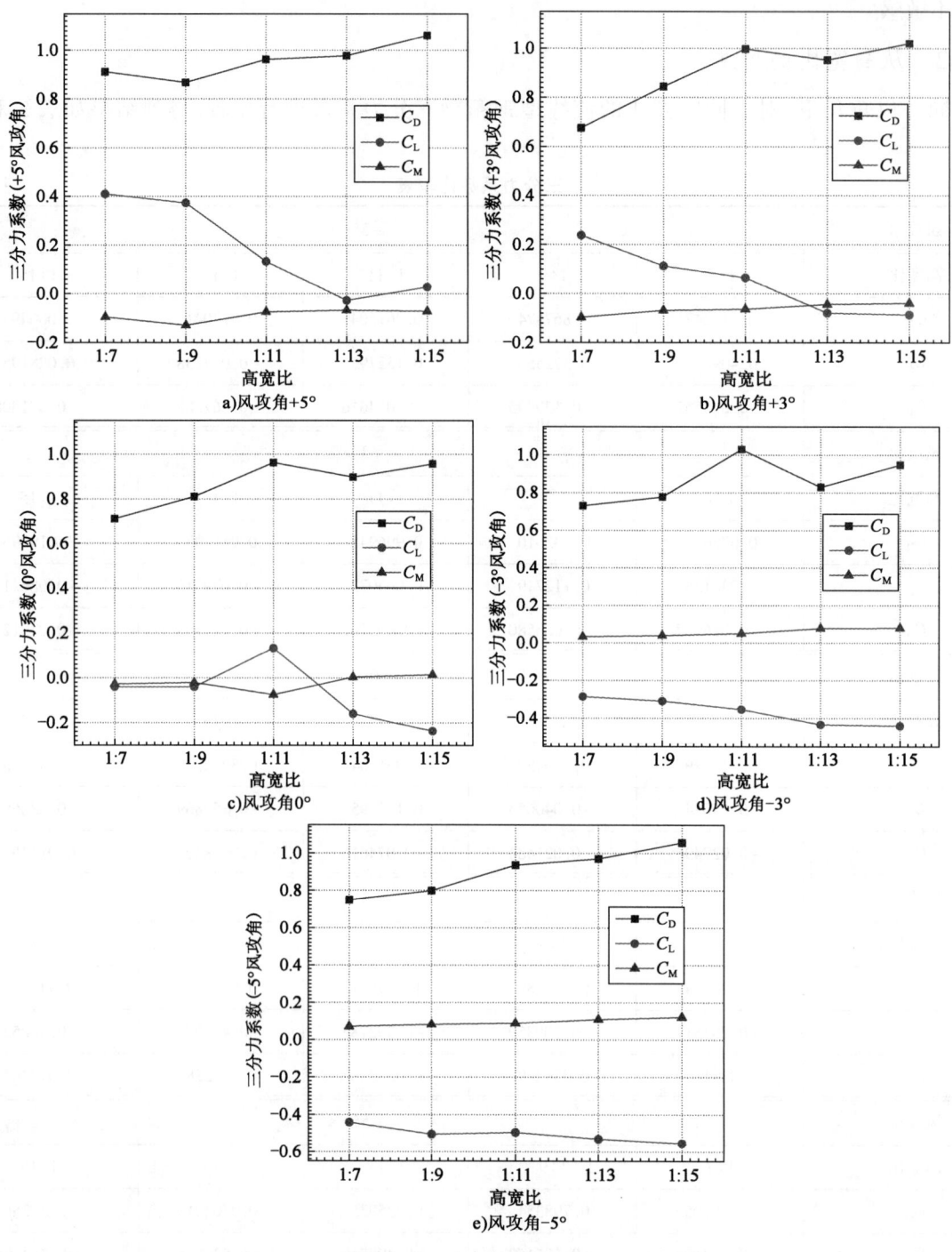

图 4 三分力系数比较图

5 结 语

通过对高宽比为 1:7、1:9、1:11、1:13、1:15 的流线型钢箱梁断面进行 CFD 网格设计、Fluent 数值模拟计算,得到了不同高宽比的流线型钢箱梁在不同风攻角下的三分力系数,为提取钢箱梁断面的气动三分力系数和工程实践提供设计参考。通过分析,可以得到如下结论:

阻力系数 C_D 在各个风攻角时,随着高宽比逐渐降低(从 1:7 到 1:15)而逐渐上升;升力系数 C_L 在 0°风攻角时,随着高宽比逐渐降低(从 1:7 到 1:15)先上升后下降,在 ±3°和 ±5°风攻角时,随着高宽比逐渐降低(从 1:7 到 1:15)而下降;升力矩系数 C_M 变化幅值相对较小,对高宽比的变化不敏感。

参考文献

[1] 李加武,潘辉,高广中,等.扁平钢箱梁颤振气动措施试验研究[J].公路交通科技,2021,38(01):69-78.
[2] 汪家继,樊健生,聂建国,等.大跨度桥梁箱梁的三分力系数识别研究[J].工程力学,2016,33(01):95-104.
[3] 刘小兵,李少杰,杨群,等.并列双钝体箱梁三分力系数的气动干扰效应[J].石家庄铁道大学学报(自然科学版),2018,31(01):1-5.
[4] 杨阳,张亮亮,吴波,等.宽体扁平钢箱梁气动力特性及涡振性能研究[J].桥梁建设,2016,46(01):70-75.
[5] 白桦,方成,王峰,等.桥梁颤振稳定性快速评价参数及其应用[J].中国公路学报,2016,29(08):92-98+133.
[6] 邓南忠.大跨度变截面连续钢箱梁空气静力特性研究[D].重庆大学,2018.
[7] 王志鹏.基于CFD的钢箱梁典型断面涡振和颤振流场驱动机理研究[D].东南大学,2019.
[8] SARWAR M W, ISHIHARA T. Numerical study on suppression of vortex-induced vibrations of box girder bridge section by aerodynamic countermeasures [J]. Journal of Wind Engineering & Industrial Aerodynamics, 2010, 98(12): 701-711.
[9] 张亮亮.基于Overset Mesh典型桥梁断面涡激振动数值模拟[D].西安:长安大学,2018.

独柱墩微弯梁桥横向抗倾覆稳定性研究

王业路[1,2] 闫强[3] 郑东[4]

(1.长安大学公路学院;2.旧桥检测与加固技术交通行业重点实验室;
3.北京首发公路养护工程有限公司;4.安徽省交通规划设计研究总院股份有限公司)

摘 要 桥梁的横向倾覆稳定系数与抗倾覆计算方法有关,还与所采用的车列模型联系密切。为研究独柱墩微弯梁桥横向抗倾覆稳定性,采用国内外规范典型汽车荷载和抗倾覆的计算方法,得到桥梁的抗倾覆稳定系数。结果表明:对于微弯梁桥,桥台外侧支座连线并非结构的最不利倾覆轴;支座的最小支反力与最不利汽车荷载加载总量均可作为易脱空支座的判定标准;55t车队与公路-Ⅰ级的汽车荷载加载总量相同的情况下,推荐在同类桥梁的抗倾覆验算中采用7m间距的55t密集车队荷载。

关键词 微弯梁桥 抗倾覆验算 设计规范 汽车荷载 独柱墩 倾覆轴

0 引 言

独柱墩桥梁因结构轻巧、通透度好和占地量小等优点在城市立交桥和高架桥得到应用[1]。独柱墩桥梁常采用小间距支座或单支座,偏载情况下支座容易出现脱空,结构抗倾覆能力较弱[2]。近些年来,因重车过桥导致独柱墩梁桥倾覆的事故屡有报道,造成人力、物力和财力的巨大损失[3]。在上述桥梁倾覆事故中,超载是诱发主因,桥梁设计亦存在先天不足[4]。

事实上,由设计缺陷带来的桥梁倾覆问题已经引起了各国的关注[5]。我国《公路桥涵设计通用规范》(JTG D60—2004)、《铁路桥涵钢筋混凝土和预应力混凝土结构设计规范》(TB 10002.3—2005)和《公路钢筋混凝土及预应力混凝土桥涵设计规范》(JTG 3362—2018,以下简称18混规)等先后给出了抗倾覆的计算方法。AASHTO LRFD Bridge Design Specifications 2017(以下简称美国规范)对于独柱墩支座最小竖向反力与支座承载力的比值进行了限定,日本道路桥示方书·同解说2002(共通编,以下简称日本规范)中考虑活载与恒载组合后的最小反力作为横向抗倾覆的控制依据[6]。

基金项目:中央高校基本科研业务费资助项目(300102218506)。

国内外学者曾对不同国家规范中有关汽车荷载做过研究,尚未对倾覆效应进行深入探讨[7-8]。桥梁的倾覆安全系数除与抗倾覆计算方法有关,还与所采用的荷载加载模式联系密切[9]。因此,浙江省、广东省和上海市等先后给出了抗倾覆计算的汽车荷载标准,通过采用55t密集车队荷载或调整车道系数保证桥梁结构横向稳定的安全冗余度[10]。

现有规范汽车荷载大多根据对结构弯矩、剪力效应的统计归纳得出,其对验算桥梁倾覆效应的适用性值得商榷[7]。不同的计算理论和方法会得到不同的抗倾覆冗余度,微弯梁桥尤为显著[11]。本文以高速路某匝道微弯桥为工程背景,以现有规范或规定的汽车荷载为代表,基于各规范和典型车辆荷载研究其抗倾覆稳定性。

1 各国荷载及抗倾覆规定

1.1 中国规范

1.1.1 荷载

《公路桥涵设计通用规范》(JTG D60—2004)采用汽车—超20级作为汽车荷载标准,见图1。《公路桥涵设计通用规范》(JTG D60—2015)规定,汽车荷载由车道荷载和车辆荷载组成,车道荷载如图2所示,车辆荷载如图3所示。

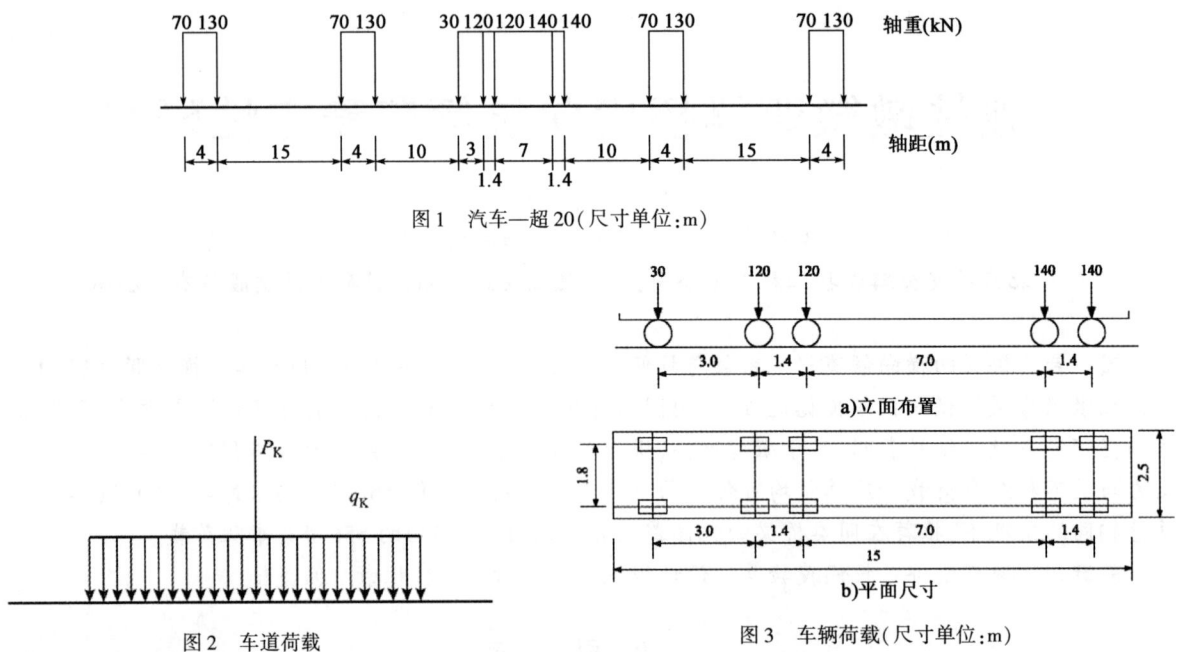

图1 汽车—超20(尺寸单位:m)

图2 车道荷载

图3 车辆荷载(尺寸单位:m)

1.1.2 倾覆规定

2012年征求意见稿中明确了一种抗倾覆的验算方法:对于弯桥,当跨中桥墩全部支座位于桥台外侧支座连线内侧时,倾覆轴线为桥台外侧支座连线;当跨中桥墩全部支座位于桥台外侧支座连线外侧时,倾覆轴线取为一桥台外侧支座和跨中桥墩支座连线。独柱墩连续梁桥倾覆轴示意图如图4所示。

当梁桥整联仅采用单向受压支座支撑时,上部结构的抗倾覆性能应满足要求:

$$\gamma_{qf} = \frac{\sum S_{bk,i}}{\sum S_{Sk,i}} \geq k_{qf} \tag{1}$$

式中:$\sum S_{bk,i}$——使上部结构稳定的作用效应标准组合;

$\sum S_{Sk,i}$——使上部结构失稳的作用效应标准组合;

γ_{qf}——抗倾覆稳定系数;

k_{qf}——横桥向抗倾覆稳定系数限值,取2.5。

对于弯桥,为使以上结论具有可操作性,采用等效公式(2):

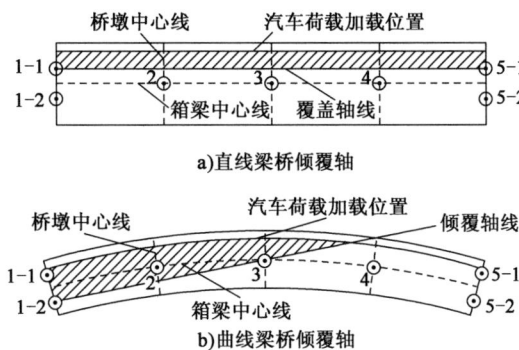

a) 直线梁桥倾覆轴

b) 曲线梁桥倾覆轴

图 4 独柱墩连续梁桥倾覆轴示意图

$$\gamma_{qf} = \frac{\sum R_{Gi} x_i}{(1+\mu)(q_k \Omega + P_k e)} \geqslant 2.5 \tag{2}$$

式中：q_k——车道荷载中的均布荷载；

P_k——车道荷载中的集中荷载；

e——横向最不利车道位置到倾覆轴线的垂直距离；

μ——冲击系数；

R_{Gi}——成桥状态时各个支座的支反力；

x_i——各个支座到倾覆轴线的垂直距离；

Ω——倾覆轴线与横向加载车道围成的面积。

18 混规中规定：在持久状况，公路独柱墩桥梁的结构体系不应发生改变；在作用基本组合下单向受压支座始终保持受压状态；在作用标准值组合下，整体式截面简支梁和连续梁的作用效应符合式(1)的要求。

1.2 美国规范

1.2.1 荷载

美国 AASHTO 规范规定美国桥规规定作用在桥梁或其附属结构上的汽车荷载取以下两项组合中的较大者：①设计货车荷载＋设计车道荷载；②设计双轴荷载＋设计车道荷载。其中，车道荷载如图 5 所示，设计货车荷载和设计双轴荷载如图 6、图 7 所示。

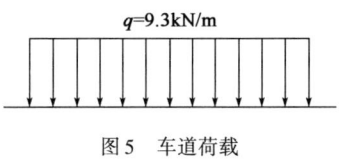

图 5 车道荷载

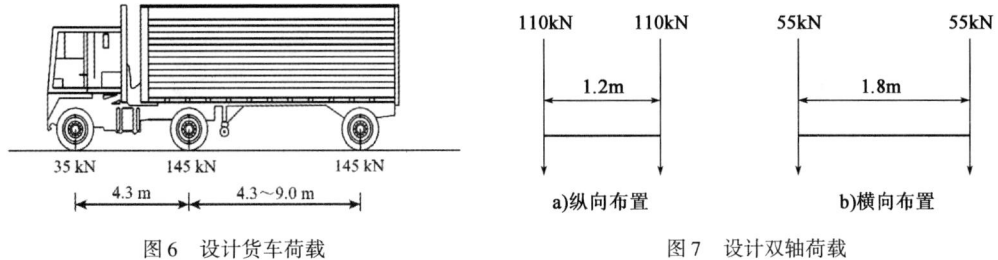

图 6 设计货车荷载　　　　　　图 7 设计双轴荷载

1.2.2 倾覆规定

美国 AASHTO 规范中指出：结构作为一个整体或者其构件，都应设计成能抵抗滑动、倾覆、提离或压曲，分析和设计中应考虑荷载偏心距的影响，并对连续结构的最小支座数量进行限制。

具体规定表现为：

(1) 在任何极限状态下，有发生脱空倾向的支座应采用拉杆或锚具约束住。

(2) 多向活动支座不适用于竖向支反力小于支座竖向承载能力 20% 的位置。

(3) 支反力小于竖向承载能力 20% 的支座要求特殊设计。

1.3 日本规范

1.3.1 荷载

日本规范中规定了 A 类活荷载和 B 类活荷载(以下简称 A 类活载和 B 类活载),类似于我国规范的公路—Ⅰ级和公路Ⅱ级;其中,A 类活荷载和 B 类活荷载如图 8 所示。

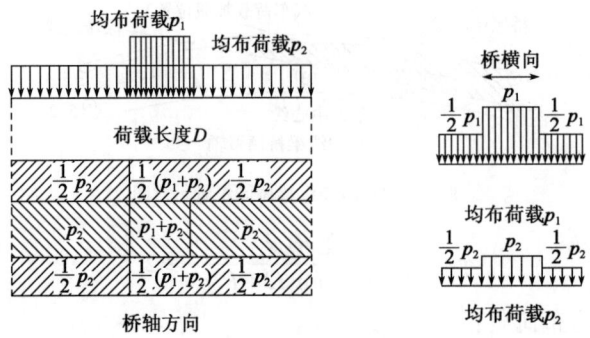

图 8 汽车荷载布置图

1.3.2 倾覆规定

日本规范规定在计算支座负反力时活载效应取用 2 倍的系数。

支座负反力 R_U 采用下式计算,如下式所示:

$$R_U = 2R_{L+1} + R_D \text{ 或 } R_U = R_D + R_W \tag{3}$$

式中:R_D——恒载反力;

R_{L+1}——活载最大负反力;

R_W——风荷载最大负反力。

2 不同规范抗倾覆分析

2.1 工程背景

某高速路一座 35m + 28m + 35m 跨线匝道桥,为预应力混凝土支架现浇连续箱梁,桥型图如图 9 所示,横断面见图 10;考虑斜向被交路的影响,桥墩均采用独柱墩并设置单支座。桥台设置双支座,两支座总间距为 8.05m。该桥位于左偏($A=435$)和右偏($A=159$)的缓和曲线上,属于典型的微弯梁桥;根据不同的位置需求分别布置单向、双向及固定支座三种类型。

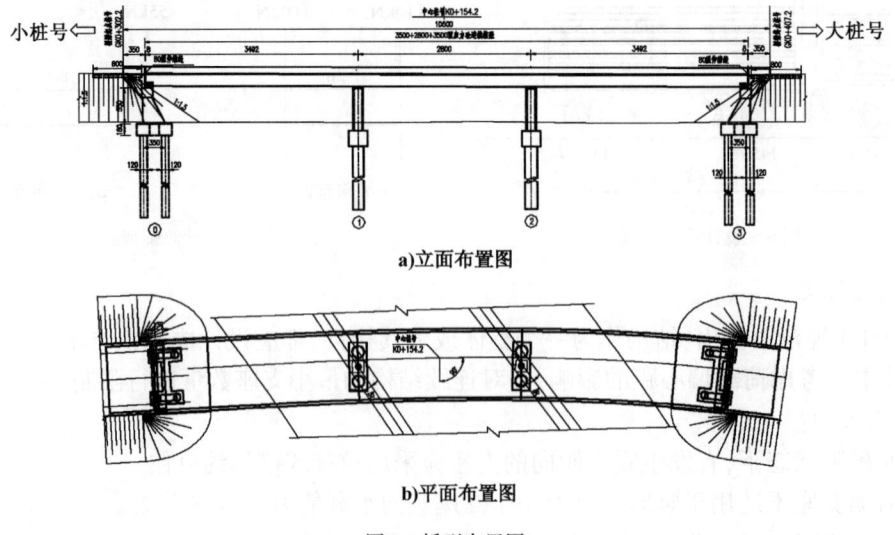

图 9 桥型布置图

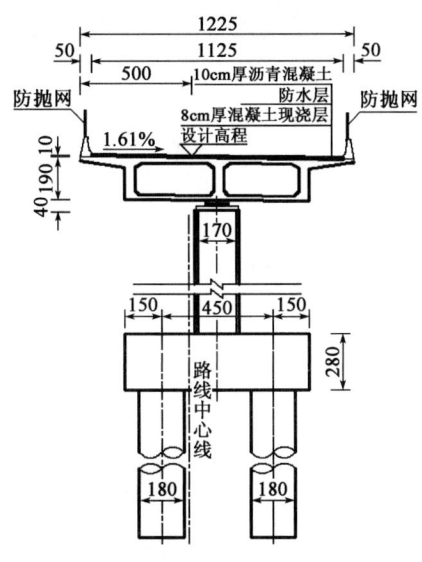

图 10 典型横断面图

2.2 2012 征求意见稿

根据 2012 征求意见稿要求,2 号和 3 号支座位于桥台外侧支座连线内侧,确定两桥台外侧支座连线作为倾覆轴 1,如图 11 所示。然而,当外侧桥台支座失效后,结构应考虑沿倾覆轴 2 和倾覆轴 3 翻转落梁的可能性。按倾覆轴内外侧的不同在"Ω"区域内进行加载,得到倾覆力矩和抗倾覆力矩如表 1 所示。结构沿倾覆轴 1 失稳,抗倾覆稳定系数为 8.8,安全冗余度较大。若考虑倾覆轴 2 的横向失稳,结构的稳定系数为 3.3,小于倾覆轴 1 的结果;若 4-1 支座失效后,主梁也有可能绕倾覆轴 3 转动,因倾覆轴与支座失效侧桥台边缘直线距离较远,形成事实上的刚性支撑以弥补 4-1 支座脱空的影响,虽不致落梁,亦不可避免造成局部构件的损坏;且该情况发生概率极低,需 10.4 倍的上述活载作用才能发生。上述结果进一步说明 2012 征求意见稿的计算方法除未考虑柔性体箱梁扭转变形的影响,还存在倾覆轴选择不合理的规定。

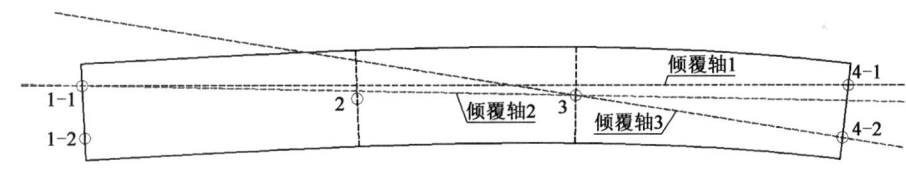

图 11 倾覆轴线示意

抗倾覆计算结果(2012 征求意见稿)　　表 1

轴　号	Ω(m²)	e(m)	稳定效应 $\sum S_{bk,i}$(kN·m)	失稳效应 $\sum S_{Sk,i}$(kN·m)	稳定系数 γ_{qf}
倾覆轴 1	407.233	2.99	54700	6232	8.8
倾覆轴 2	503.899	4.23	26272	7919	3.3
倾覆轴 3	396.459	7.59	82415	7896	10.4

2.3 18 混规

根据 18 混规的规定考虑两种状态进行抗倾覆分析。表 2 中,1-2 支座的最小支反力为 1118KN,所有支座均未出现负反力,支座不脱空。在状态 2 下考虑 1-1、1-2、4-1 和 4-2 支座的失效,出现左倾和右倾两种情况;图 12 中,结构的稳定效应与失稳效应的比值介于 3.65~5 之间,均大于 2.5 的限值,不会发生倾覆失稳破坏。其中 1-2 支座和 4-2 支座失效后结构的横向稳定系数较小,1-1 和 4-1 支座失效后结构的横向抗倾覆能力相对较高。

标准组合支座竖向反力　　　　　表2

支反力 (kN)	支座编号					
	1-1	1-2	2	3	4-1	4-2
	2249	1119	8889	8839	2083	1294

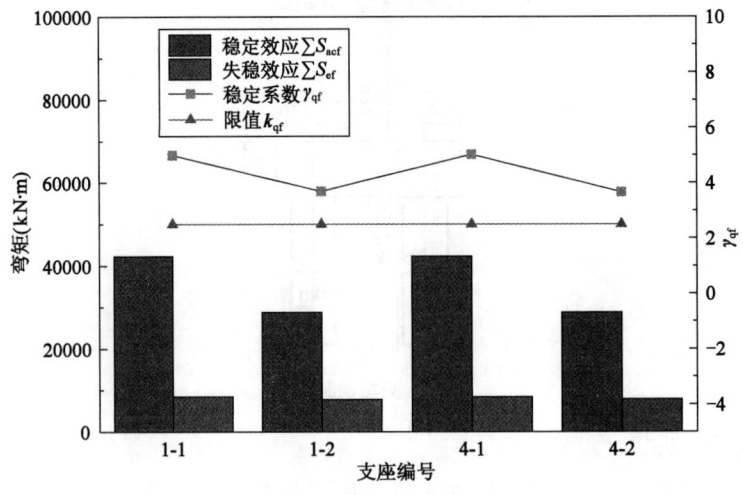

图12 稳定系数(中国规范)

2.4 美国规范

根据 AASHTO 规范规定,经计算,设计货车荷载和设计车道荷载组合(下同简称 AASHTO 活载)支座竖向支反力更为不利,计算结果如图13所示。图13表明,基于 AASHTO 活载加载模式下,1-2 支座竖向反力最小,4-2 支座的次之,1-1 和 4-1 相对较大。1-2 最小竖向反力为 1355kN,占竖向承载力的 15%,小于 20% 限值的要求。4-2 最小竖向反力为 1453kN,占竖向承载力的 16%。1-2 支座和 4-2 支座中的双向活动型需要特殊设计才能满足使用要求。所有支座均不出现负反力,无须设置拉杆等冗余设施。

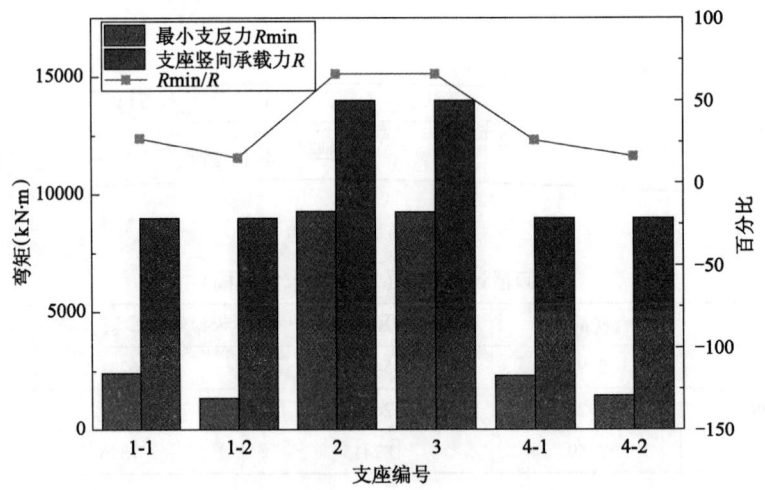

图13 AASHTO 活载支座最不利反力

2.5 日本规范

根据日本规范规定,采用 B 类活荷载进行影响面加载,考虑汽车荷载和风荷载的最不利组合,结果如图14所示。风荷载(R_W)对倾覆的贡献很小,在中小跨径桥梁中并不控制结构横向抗倾覆稳定性。2倍汽车荷载(R_{L+1})与恒载(R_D)组合后,1-2 支座反力最小,为 819kN。两种工况下支座均未出现脱空现象,结构处于稳定状态,满足规范要求。

基于各国规范荷载及抗倾覆规定对预应力混凝土现浇连续箱梁进行了横向抗倾覆分析。结果表明：日本规范对支座脱空验算要求更为严格，AASHTO 规范规定了支座的最小反力要求，并对超限支座采取特殊设计或其他构造措施，两种规范并未给出倾覆力矩的计算方法，仅以限制支座反力作为安全储备。18 混规限制了支座脱空状态并给出了抗倾覆的安全系数。1-2 支座和 4-2 支座的竖向反力冗余度相对较小，随着荷载增大，最容易出现脱空现象，故将其定义为易脱空支座，将其余各支座（即 1-1、2、3 和 4-1 支座）定义为非脱空支座，以便开展进一步研究。

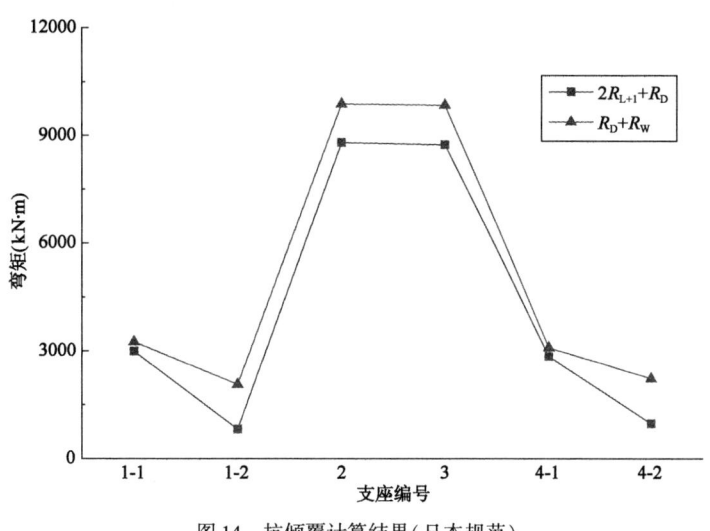

图 14　抗倾覆计算结果（日本规范）

3　不同加载模式抗倾覆分析

3.1　汽车荷载加载总量

综合考虑实际拥堵情况下的车辆间距[11-12]及浙江省公路管理局[10]关于抗倾覆汽车荷载的要求，提出考虑 7m 间距的 55t 车队作为抗倾覆分析的汽车荷载车辆模型之一。针对倾覆问题，以现有汽车—超 20、公路—Ⅰ级、7 间距 55t 车队、B 类活载和 AASHTO 活载为典型活载加载模式，研究不同汽车荷载模式下桥梁的横向抗倾覆稳定性。

汽车荷载加载总量是指作用在桥梁结构上的汽车荷载总重量，该值倾覆效应随着关系密切。不同规范及荷载模式作用下，各支座最不利汽车荷载加载总量如图 15 所示。易脱空支座（1-2 和 4-2 支座）不同加载模式下汽车荷载加载总量大小关系为：公路—Ⅰ级≈55t 车队＞汽车—超 20＞AASHTO 活载＞B 类活载＞挂车—120。由 2.1 节可知，易脱空支座，在除挂车—120 外的各活载作用下，荷载加载总量明显大于其他支座。公路—Ⅰ级荷载与汽车—超 20 的荷载总量与趋势接近。AASHTO 规范采用车辆荷载与车道荷载组合的方式，类似汽车—超 20 级荷载，汽车荷载加载总量比汽车—超 20 级略小，最大差异 7.7%。两端支座最大加载量由 55t 车队引起，中墩支座的最大加载量由挂车—120 引起。

3.2　支座竖向反力

由图 16 可知，易脱空支座（1-2 和 4-2 支座）在不同加载模式引起的最不利竖向负反力大小关系为：55t 车队＞公路—Ⅰ级＞汽车—超 20＞B 类活载＞挂车—120＞AASHTO 活载。加载总量相同的情况下，55t 车队比公路—Ⅰ级更容易引发易脱空支座的竖向脱空倾向；AASHTO 活载作用下易脱空支座的负反力最小，为 −602kN 和 −593kN。公路—Ⅰ级、汽车—超 20、挂车—120、B 类活载引起的支座负反力量值和变化规律接近。桥墩处非脱空支座（2 号和 3 号支座），公路—Ⅰ级汽车荷载加载总量均小于挂车—120 和 55t 车队，却能得到更大的支座负反力。桥台处非脱空支座（1-1 和 4-1 支座），除 B 类活载外，其他荷载模式所引起的最不利负反力差异不大，说明其对荷载加载模式的影响并不敏感。

3.3　抗倾覆稳定系数

从图 17 和图 18 可以看出，易脱空支座在不同加载模式的横向抗倾覆稳定系数大小关系为：挂车—

120＞AASHTO 活载＞B 类活载＞汽车—超 20＞公路—Ⅰ级＞55t 车队。在加载总量相同的情况下，55t 车队比公路—Ⅰ级更容易引起桥梁失稳；AASHTO 活载、B 类活载和汽车—超 20 的加载总量相近，其抗倾覆稳定系数相差不大，说明这几类活载的荷载模式更为接近。易脱空支座在挂车—120 作用下的加载总量与其他活载模式相比最小，由此引起的稳定系数最大。

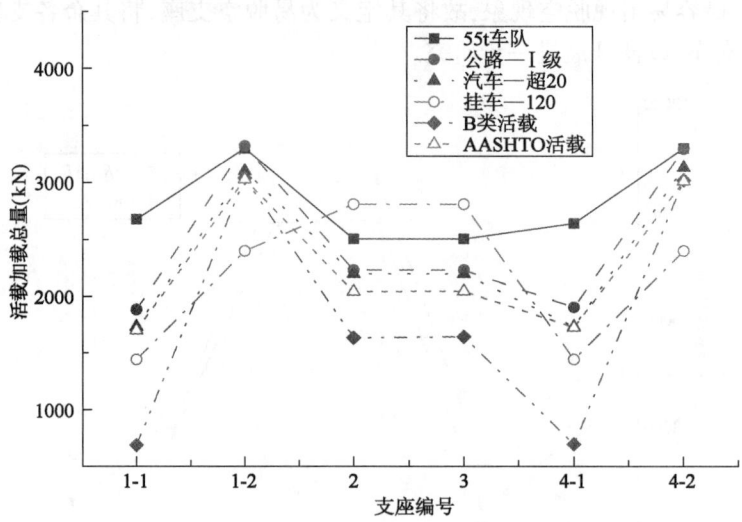

图 15　各支座最不利反力汽车荷载加载总量

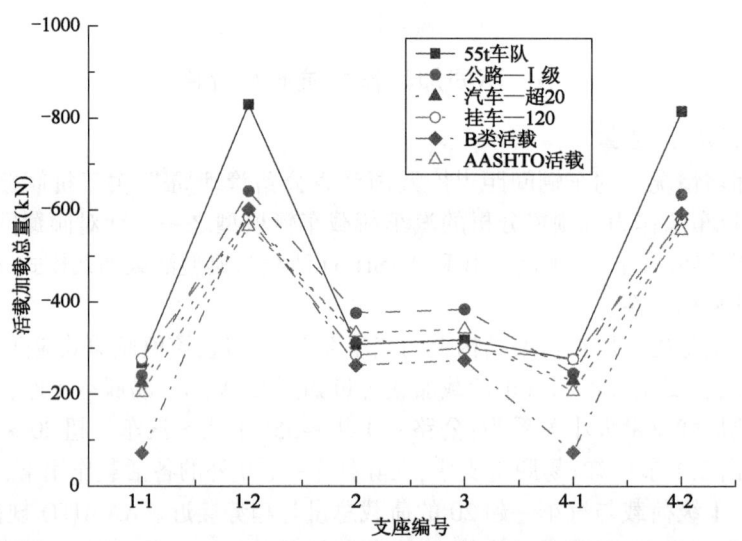

图 16　各支座最不利竖向支反力

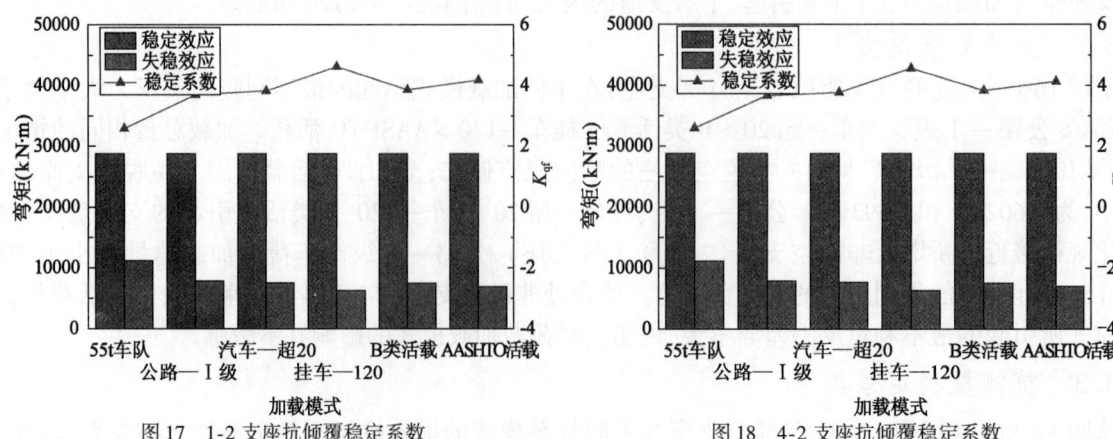

图 17　1-2 支座抗倾覆稳定系数　　　　　　　　图 18　4-2 支座抗倾覆稳定系数

4 结 语

桥梁倾覆破坏为"脆性"破坏,结构的失稳属于第二类稳定问题,即极值点失稳。本文以高速公路某一微弯匝道桥为例,进行横向抗倾覆稳定性研究并得到以下结论:

(1)对于微弯桥,桥墩支座位于全部位于桥台外侧支座连线内侧,桥台外侧支座连线并非结构的最不利倾覆轴;2012征求意见稿的计算方法除存在未考虑柔性体箱梁扭转变形的影响,还存在倾覆轴选择不合理的规定。

(2)日本规范对支座脱空验算要求更为严格,事实上从结构体系方面对抗倾覆稳定性进行了限制;美国AASHTO规范规定了支座的最小反力,但双向活动型支座均需要特殊设计才能满足使用要求;虽然桥梁抗倾覆稳定性满足中国18混规的要求,与其他规范相比缺少相应的构造措施规定。

(3)支座的最大负反力与最不利汽车荷载加载总量均可作为易脱空支座的判定标准。55t车队和公路—I级的汽车荷载加载总量相同,55t车队作用下支座的竖向负反力最大,抗倾覆稳定系数最小;故推荐在同类桥梁的抗倾覆验算中采用7m间距的55t密集车队荷载。

参考文献

[1] 姜爱国,杨志.独柱墩曲线梁桥倾覆轴线研究[J].世界桥梁,2013,41(04):58-61.
[2] 李盼到,张京,王美.独柱支承梁式桥倾覆稳定性验算方法研究[J].世界桥梁,2012,40(06):52-6.
[3] 彭卫兵,朱志翔,陈光军,等.梁桥倾覆机理、破坏模式与计算方法研究[J].土木工程学报,2019,52(12):104-13.
[4] 彭卫兵,沈佳栋,唐翔,等.近期典型桥梁事故回顾、分析与启示[J].中国公路学报,2019,32(12):132-44.
[5] Deng L, Wang W, Yu Y. State-of-the-Art Review on the Causes and Mechanisms of Bridge Collapse[J]. Journal of Performance of Constructed Facilities, 2015, 20(5): 04014080.
[6] 庄冬利.偏载作用下箱梁桥抗倾覆稳定问题的探讨[J].桥梁建设,2014,44(02):27-31.
[7] 张喜刚.公路桥梁汽车荷载标准研究[M].北京:人民交通出版社股份有限公司,2014.
[8] 彭卫兵,潘若丹,马俊,等.独柱墩梁桥倾覆破坏模式与计算方法研究[J].桥梁建设,2016,46(02):25-30.
[9] 李盼到,马利君.独柱支撑匝道桥抗倾覆验算汽车荷载研究[J].桥梁建设,2012,42(03):14-8.
[10] 浙公路[2009]102号,桥梁上部结构抗倾覆验算荷载的规定[S].
[11] 曹景,刘志才,冯希训.箱形截面直线桥及曲线桥抗倾覆稳定性分析[J].桥梁建设,2014,44(03):69-74.
[12] 梅刚,林道锦,秦权.现状车载下旧桥承载力评定和可靠度有限元分析[J].中国铁道科学[J].2004,26(06):72-77.

循环荷载下高强螺栓受剪连接状态声发射监测

吕世文 李丹 任伟新

(合肥工业大学)

摘 要 本文利用声发射技术对受剪连接的高强螺栓在循环荷载作用下加载直至破坏的整个过程进行监测,分析高强螺栓连接的试件在摩擦阶段、相对滑移阶段、螺杆传力弹性阶段和塑性阶段四个受力阶段的声发射源,对各阶段的声发射信号进行参数和频谱分析。结果表明:每个受力阶段的声发射机制有所不同，产生的声发射信号不尽相同，信号的特征参数之间存在差异；各阶段声发射信号的频谱能量分布呈现不同的特征，可以有效地识别高强螺栓摩擦失效和螺杆断裂。

关键词 高强螺栓 循环荷载 受力阶段 声发射 参数分析 频谱分析

0 引 言

钢结构桥梁、工业厂房、大跨径结构等都是由工厂预制的型钢等基本构件通过必要的连接所组成的结构，除了必要的基本构件之外还需要螺栓连接等连接方式才使结构完整从而承受荷载。结构中由螺栓连接的部位往往是结构承载能力较弱的区域，许多钢结构设施往往都是螺栓连接部位的损伤或破坏导致的构件丧失稳定或者引起结构整体的破坏，因此对螺栓连接部位要着重考虑。相比普通螺栓，高强螺栓连接的结构能够承受动力荷载，而且连接强度高，几乎不会对构件的强度造成影响，此外高强螺栓便于更换，因此在实际工程中高强螺栓连接在结构的大部分位置逐渐取代了铆钉连接，甚至有些部位采用螺栓连接比焊接表现得更加出色。在钢结构桥梁及钢结构建筑中使用的螺栓大多数为高强度螺栓，在结构服役的过程中，高强螺栓连接部位会承受荷载特别是地震作用和汽车荷载等反复荷载作用以及外界环境等因素的影响，会使高强螺栓出现预应力损失而出现松动等损伤情况。对这些损伤情况需要及时发现并采取相对的措施，否则有可能导致结构产生局部失效或者整体破坏。因此，需要对循环荷载作用下高强螺栓的连接状态进行监测。

在结构健康监测领域研究越来越多人关注螺栓连接的损伤识别和状态监测。目前主要有超声法、时间反演法、声发射检测方法等。基于超声波能量散射原理的螺栓状态检测是通过超声仪器发出激励信号，发出的超声波沿着介质进行传播，若物体有损伤，波的传播方向或特征会发生变化，这样超声波的能量由于这些变化而产生损耗，采集并分析这些改变的信息来对结构的损伤进行识别，该方法在螺栓松动等类型的损伤方面有着大量研究[1-3]。但该方法在检测的过程中容易受噪声的影响，且需要主动激发装置成本高，此外检测范围有限，不宜检测出早期的螺栓松动。基于时间反演法的螺栓状态检测在压电阻抗方法的基础上利用时间反演技术的自适应聚焦效果及能有效提高信号信噪比的特性，将首次采集的响应信号在时域上进行反演，将反演信号作为激励信号对试件或者结构再次进行激励，之后采集再次激励后的聚焦信号，建立聚焦信号与螺栓预紧力之间的关系[4-6]。但该方法需要二次激励，过程比较繁琐，现场条件复杂不易实现，且对群栓结构的分析存在困难。

声发射是指材料受外力或者内力作用发生变形或断裂时快速释放能量而随之向外释放弹性波的现象。声发射弹性波能够反映出材料的部分性质，所以对声发射信号进行检测可以判断结构的状态。声发射检测技术不同于其他几种无损检测方法，基于声发射技术的监测方法可以实现长时间实时监测，而且不需要主动激励，只需要采集材料或者部件自身所发出的信号即可，可以实现在工程现场进行结构的实时损伤监测，在土木工程领域有着大量科研工作者对该方法进行了的研究和应用[7-12]。目前利用声发射检测法对结构普通螺栓连接状态、高强螺栓连接的复合材料构件状态和高强螺栓静力作用下的监测和损伤识别有了初步研究[13-18]。循环荷载作为动力荷载的一种，该技术应用于循环荷载作用下的高强螺栓连接件状态监测的研究甚少，因此对高强度螺栓连接结构或试件在循环荷载作用下的受力状态进行监测具有重要的意义和工程实用价值。本文对钢结构高强螺栓受剪连接在循环荷载下的连接状态进行实时监测，对高强螺栓在分级加载多次循环受力情况下直至高强螺栓螺杆剪切破坏全过程的声发射信号进行采集，对声发射信号进行参数分析与频谱分析，为高强螺栓在承受循环荷载等动力荷载作用下受剪连接状态的监测提供参考。

1 实验与数据采集

为了确定螺杆剪切断裂破坏模式下各受力阶段的声发射信号特征，对此破坏模式设计了三组单栓搭接试件进行实验研究，研究螺栓受剪连接承受循环荷载下的力学行为，发现各受力阶段与声发射信号的关系,在结构实验室进行试件的循环加载,将试件编号为 Specimen-01、Specimen-02 及 Specimen-03。此次加载的试件均采用高强螺栓搭接连接的形式,试件尺寸如图 1 所示,选用 8.8 级 M12 的高强螺栓,盖板的厚度为 10mm,芯板的厚度为 20mm,板材为 Q345 等级,这是为了确保螺栓剪切断裂的破坏形态,板件采取的螺栓孔径大小为 13.5mm,高强螺栓施加的预紧力为 45kN。

实验采用分级加载形式,每级荷载循环三次之后再进行下一荷载等级的加载,加载速率为 3mm/min,每个加载等级的峰值荷载为 20kN、40kN、60kN、80kN、100kN 等,加载直至试件破坏。安装位移计测量盖板相对于芯板之间的位移,为了防止试件之间产生不要的位移误差利用磁性表座将位移计固定在试件上,位移计和磁性表座的底座分别固定在盖板和芯板上。之后进行声发射传感器的安装,为了不影响声发射数据的采集,安装时使用耦合剂将传感器和试件表面进行耦合,为了防止在加载的过程中传感器出现移动或者掉落,利用磁夹将其固定。声发射传感器的布置位置为:3 个传感器处于试件纵向中心线上,自上而下依次为通道 1、通道 2、通道 3。将各个传感器与相应的采集仪器进行连接。试件安装好之后的示意图如图 2 所示。采用 SHT4106-G 液压伺服万能实验机对连接好的试件进行循环加载实验,声发射信号由 Express8 声发射系统完成采集,前置放大器的增益、采样阈值均设置为 40dB,采样频率设置为 5MHz。利用 G5299N 动态数据采集仪实时采集盖板与芯板之间的相对位移。

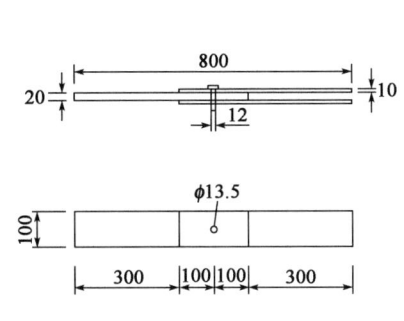
图 1　试件尺寸示意图(尺寸单位:mm)

图 2　试件加载示意图

2　高强螺栓受力分析

通过分析三组试件的结果发现它们的受力情况相近,在循环荷载作用下试件的荷载-位移曲线与静力作用下的受力阶段大致相同,由于循环荷载的作用,结构受力性能小于静力作用下的受力性能。以 Specimen-02 为代表进行分析,从加载实验得到的荷载与位移的关系中可以看出,高强螺栓在分级循环加载作用下的受力过程可以分为四个阶段,如图 3 所示。0-a 为摩擦阶段,此阶段试件没有任何变化。荷载与位移呈线性关系增加,材料处于弹性受力范围,在此阶段施加的外荷载主要克服板件之间的静摩擦力。由于板件表面并非绝对光滑,材料微观表面是凹凸不平的情况,在荷载作用下板件上凹凸不平的表面之间发生接触,并产生塑性变形[19]。a-b 为相对滑移阶段,可以发现随着加载的进行,相对位移增加的同时荷载几乎不变。该阶段板间产生动摩擦滑移,表明上个阶段高强螺栓发生摩擦失效。板件凹凸不平的表面发生微观突起的断裂,板件进一步磨损。b-c 为螺杆传力弹性阶段,这个阶段荷载进一步增加导致高强螺栓的螺杆与板件的孔壁之间相互接触,盖板与芯板之间的相对位移进一步增加,可以发现荷载-位移之间的关系基本上为线性关系。相互接触的部位由于压力的作用使得材料发生弹性形变。c-d 为螺杆传力塑性阶段,这个阶段外荷载比较大,螺杆材料开始发生塑性变形,板件之间的位移增加迅速,相比之下荷载的增速缓慢,甚至之后出现荷载下降的情况,最后出现砰的一声,螺杆断裂,板件孔壁未见明显挤压痕迹。螺栓杆材料在受力的过程中内部会有微裂纹的产生,随着外荷载的增加使得裂纹扩展成宏观裂缝,宏观裂纹的继续增加最终导致螺杆脆性断裂。

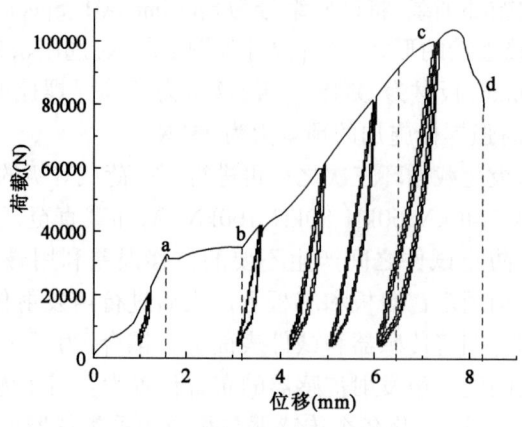

图3 Specimen-02 荷载-位移图

3 声发射参数分析

高强螺栓试件破坏过程中各受力阶段的声发射信号的参数表现出不同的特征,据此对试件 Specimen-02 通道 2 的声发射数据进行单参数和多参数分析[20]。高强螺栓受剪连接构件的循环荷载实验中,声发射特征参数与试件破坏过程表现出良好的对应关系,图 4 给出了循环加载工况下声发射特征参数撞击幅值随时间与荷载变化的对应关系。可以看出,在荷载接近或超过上一循环峰值荷载时,会出现大量声发射撞击事件,并且对应的声发射特征参数值在不同程度上出现了较高的数值,可以较好地反映高强螺栓受剪连接构件在循环荷载作用下的损伤演化过程,在图中能清晰地看出当试件在循环加载过程中临近破坏时,具有较高声发射特征参数值的撞击事件,可以为高强螺栓受剪连接构件的临界破坏状态提供预警。

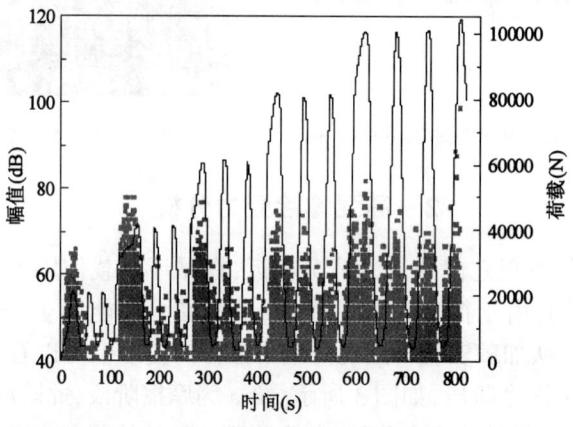

图4 幅值-荷载-时间分布

(1)0~130s 为摩擦阶段,这个阶段的主要声发射源为板件微观下材料凹凸不平的表面发生相互接触并产生一定的塑性变形。该阶段幅值信号均维持在较低水平。

(2)130~150s 为相对滑移阶段,这个阶段的主要声发射源为盖板与芯板之间产生的相对滑动引起材料表面上的微凸体发生断裂和磨损。板件材料表面大量微凸体的变形和断裂释放的大量高幅值的声发射信号。这个阶段持续时间较短,但是该阶段高幅值事件明显增多,幅值达到 80dB。

(3)第三个受力阶段(螺杆传力弹性阶段)为 150~800s,此阶段的主要声发射源为板间相对位移增加引起的微凸体进一步的断裂及磨损,但较上一阶段有所减少。因此,该阶段声高幅值事件逐渐减少且伴随超过 80dB 很少的高幅值事件。

(4)800~850s 为螺杆传力塑性阶段,这个阶段的声发射源较之前阶段有所变化,包含螺杆弹塑性变形、螺杆断裂。螺栓杆材料在受力的过程中内部产生微裂纹,随着荷载的施加使微裂纹扩展成宏观裂缝,宏观裂纹的继续增加最终导致螺杆脆性断裂。从裂纹的出现和扩展到螺杆的断裂整个过程的持续时间比较短。该阶段虽然声发射事件有所减少,但幅值在螺杆断裂时显著增加,出现很大程度的很高的峰值事件,此时发生螺栓杆断裂。

为了进一步研究各受力阶段声发射信号的特征,对声发射信号进行持续时间与幅值两个参数间的关联分析。图 5 展示了这两个参数的关联分析结果。可以发现,四个阶段的持续时间与幅值散点图具有较大程度的差异,摩擦阶段大部分幅值都在 70dB 以下,且该阶段低幅值事件密集,和上面分析对应,且该阶段持续时间分布集中。相对滑移阶段大部分幅值都在 70dB 以下,但是这个阶段的持续时间分布十分不集中,此外声发射事件明显少于其他阶段。螺杆传力弹性阶段的声发射事件最多,幅值集中在 50~80dB 之间,持续时间不集中。螺杆传力弹性阶段幅值集中在 50~70dB 之间,持续时间分布集中。由上面的分析得出,高强螺栓承受循环荷载下的各受力阶段声发射参数有所区别,但不足以建立直观的参数指标进行连接状态的监测。

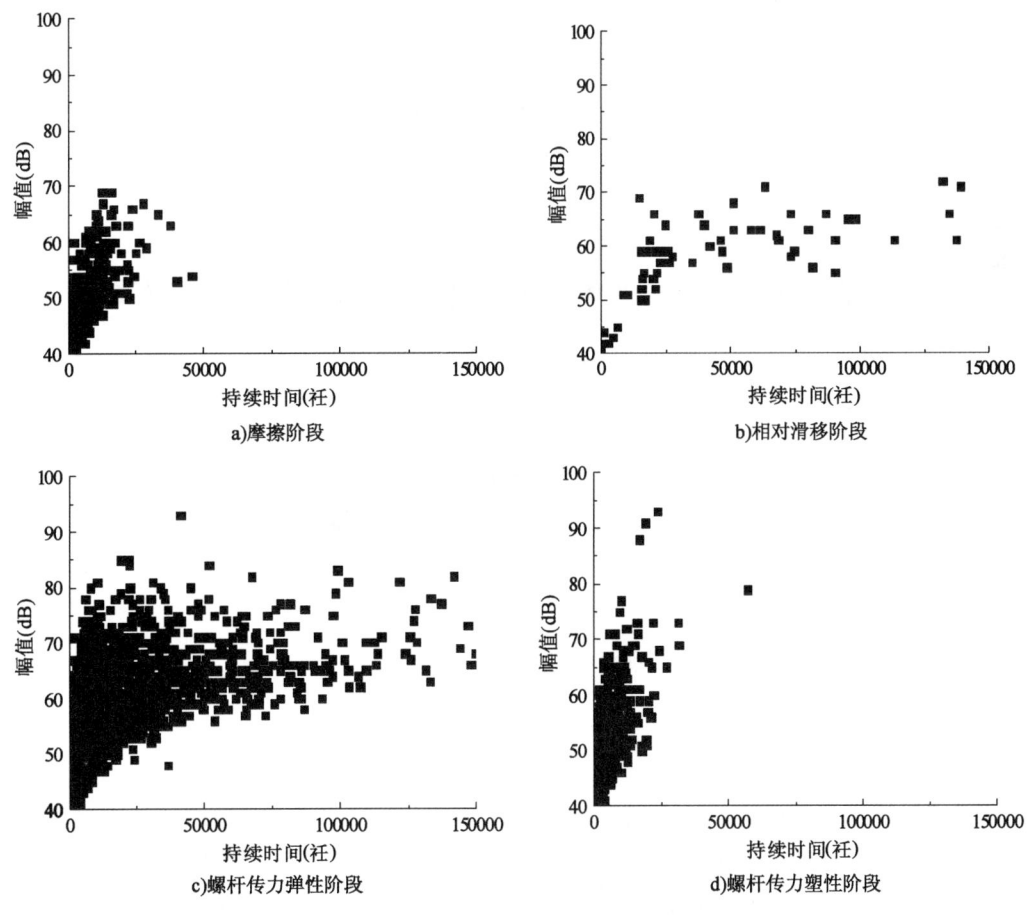

图 5　Specimen-02 持续时间-幅值关联图

4　声发射信号频谱分析

每个受力阶段的声发射机制不相同,不同的声发射机制会产生含有不同频率成分的声发射信号。对试件四个受力阶段的声发射信号利用快速傅立叶变换处理之后进行频谱分析,图 6 展示了各阶段具有代表性的声发射特征波形。由图 6 可知,高强螺栓受剪连接试件在循环荷载作用下的四个受力阶段的频率范围分布较广,在 50~700kHz 频段内均有声发射信号频率分布,但每个阶段声发射信号的峰值频率分布特征呈现出不同的情况。在摩擦阶段,声发射源的峰值频率主要集中在 100~150kHz 频段。在相对滑移阶段的峰值频率主要分布在100~130kHz、250kHz左右和300kHz左右。第三个受力阶段声发射信号的峰值频率主要分布在两个频段:100~130kHz、300kHz左右两个频段。在螺杆传力塑性阶段,这个阶段的声发射源引起的声发射信号峰值频率分布在100~150kHz、300kHz两个频段,但100~150kHz频段的峰值近似为300kHz左右峰值的一半。由分析结果可知,当信号在快速傅立叶变换之后出现三个频段的峰值频率且主要分布在100~130kHz、250kHz左右和300kHz左右时,可判断高强螺栓连接试件发生摩擦失效开始滑移。之后,当声发射信号再次出现幅度十分接近的100~150kHz、300kHz左右两个频段且100~150kHz频段的峰值近似为300kHz左右峰值的一半时螺杆开始塑性变形,之后将发生螺栓杆断裂,可以为试件失效作出预警。

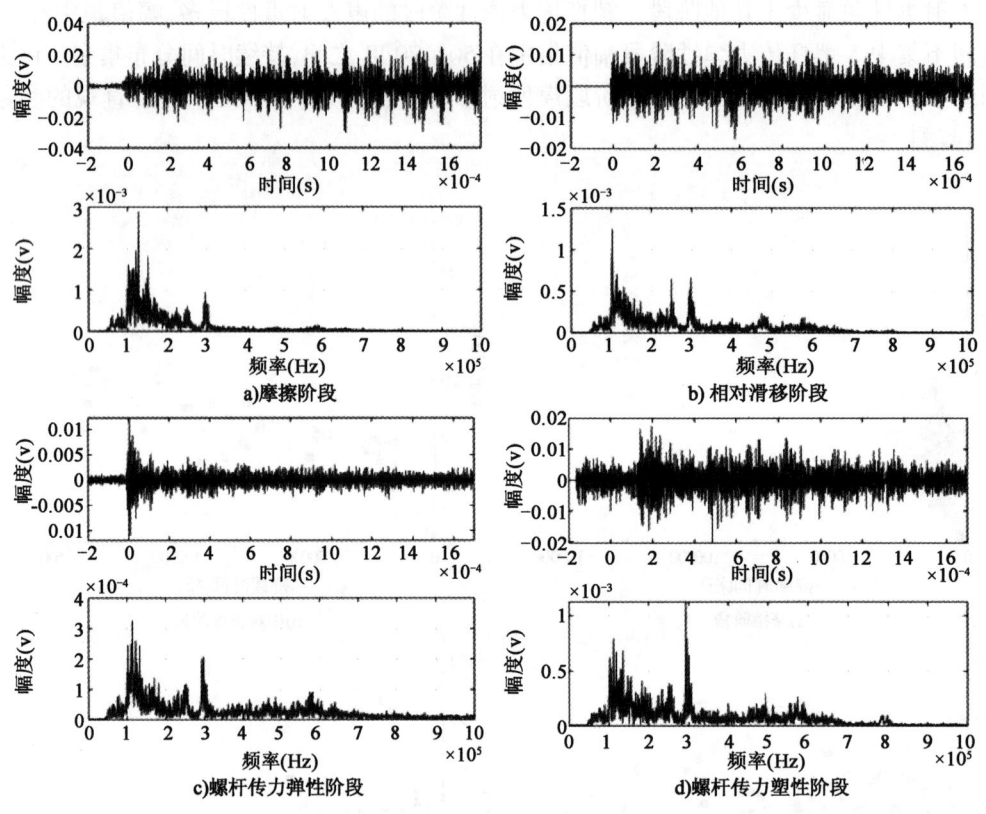

图6 Specimen-02声发射信号频谱图

5 结　语

本文利用声发射技术对受剪连接的高强螺栓在循环荷载作用下加载直至破坏的整个过程进行监测,对摩擦阶段、相对滑移阶段、螺杆传力弹性阶段和螺杆传力塑性阶段四个受力阶段的声发射信号进行参数和频谱分析。结果发现:各受力阶段的声发射机制不尽相同,声发射信号特征参数之间同样存在一定的差别,只从特征参数分析不足以确定直观的指标用于区分螺栓的受力状态;每个阶段声发射信号的峰值频率分布特征呈现出不同的情况,当信号的峰值频率出现三个频段且主要分布在100~130kHz、250kHz左右和300kHz左右时,可判断高强螺栓连接试件发生摩擦失效开始滑移。之后,当声发射信号再次出现幅度十分接近的100~150kHz、300kHz左右两个频段且100~150kHz频段的峰值近似为300kHz左右峰值的一半时螺杆开始塑性变形,之后将发生螺栓杆断裂,可以为试件失效作出预警。以后可对各受力阶段的声发射信号进一步分析处理从而建立可靠的参数指标来直观地对各受力阶段进行识别,进而实现高强螺栓连接状态的精确监测。

参考文献

[1] JR Wait, G Park, CR Farrar. Integrated structural health assessment using piezoelectric active sensors[J]. Shock and Vibration, 2005, 12(6): 389-405.

[2] Yang J Y, Chang F K. Detection of bolt looseness in C-C composite thermal protection: diagnosis principle [J]. Smart Mater Structure, 2006, 15(2): 581-590.

[3] MillerD, Das S, Chattopadhyay A, et al. Wave scattering analysis of bolted joints [C]. Nondestructive Evaluation and Health Monitoring of Aerospace Materials, Composites, and Civil Infrastructure V. International Society for Optics and Photonics, 2006, 6176: 617603.

[4] Furui Wang, Gangbing Song. Bolt early looseness monitoring using modified vibro-acoustic [J]. Mechanical Systems and Signal Processing, 2019, 130: 349-360.

[5] DuFei, Xu Chao, Wu Guannan, et al. Preload Monitoring of Bolted L-Shaped Lap Joints Using Virtual Time Reversal Method. [J]. Sensors (Basel, Switzerland), 2018, 18(6).

[6] 王涛,李桥,邵俊华,等.基于时间反演法的螺栓健康监测研究[J].科学技术与工程,2014,14(19):20-24.

[7] 王岩,路桂娟,王瑶,等.声发射技术在土木工程中的应用研究综述[J].水利水电科技进展,2012,32(04):89-94.

[8] Mc KEEFRY J, SHIELD C. Acoustic emission monitoring of fatigue cracks in steel bridge girders[R]. St Paul: University of Minnesota, 1999.

[9] Dan Li, Kevin Sze ChiangKuang, Chan Ghee Koh. Rail crack monitoring based on Tsallis synchrosqueezed wavelet entropy of acoustic emission signals: a field study [J]. Structural Health Monitoring, 2018, 17(6): 1410-1424.

[10] SUZUKI T, OBTSU M. Quantitative damage evaluation of structural concrete by a compression test based on AE rate process analysis core test of concrete[J]. Construction and Building Materials, 2004, 18(3): 197-202.

[11] A. Carpinteri, G. Lacidogna, N. Pugno. Structural damage diagnosis and life-time assessment by acoustic emission monitoring[J]. Engineering Fracture Mechanics, 2006, 74(1).

[12] KrzysztofJemielniak. Some aspects of AE application in tool condition monitoring[J]. Ultrasonics, 2000, 38(1).

[13] Yicheng Du, Jilei Zhang. Acoustic emission of bolt-bearing testing on structural composite lumbers [J]. Wood and Fiber Science, 2014, 46(1): 118-126.

[14] Gang Wang, Yongzheng Zhang. Shear behaviour and acoustic emission characteristics of bolted rock joints with different roughnesses [J]. Rock Mechanics and Rock Engineering, 2018, 51(6): 1885-1906.

[15] Zhen Zhang, Yi Xiao, Zhongqing Su, et al. Continuous monitoring of tightening condition of single-lap bolted composite joints using intrinsic mode functions of acoustic emission signals: a proof-of-concept study [J]. Structural Health Monitoring, 2019, 18(4): 1219-1234.

[16] T. Dang Hoang, C. Herbelot, A. Imad. Rupture and damage mechanism analysis of a bolted assembly using coupling techniques between A. E. and D. I. C. [J]. Engineering Structures, 2010, 32(9): 2793-2803.

[17] 王怡,王宁,卢萍,等.基于声发射原理的螺栓连接状态辨识方法研究[J].声学技术, 2010, 29(5): 453-456.

[18] 姚舜,李丹,任伟新.基于声发射的高强螺栓受剪连接状态监测[C]//第29届全国结构工程学术会议, 2020. 122-127

[19] 何思明,吴永,沈均.切向荷载下弹塑性材料的微观位移特性[J].工程力学, 2010, 27(2): 73-77.

[20] 许中林,李国禄,董天顺,等.声发射信号分析与处理方法研究进展[J].材料导报,2014,28(09):56-60+73.

疲劳裂纹止裂孔与高强螺栓复合止裂方法研究

杨羿[1] 刘朵[1,2] 陈春霖[2] 王贤强[1] 张建东[1]

(1. 苏交科集团股份有限公司;2. 河海大学)

摘 要 钻孔止裂后疲劳裂纹常穿过止裂孔继续扩展,使止裂孔失效,为提高钻孔止裂的止裂效果,本文提出了止裂孔与高强螺栓复合止裂方法。通过模型试验验证了该方法的有效性,分析了止裂孔与螺栓直径对止裂效果的影响。结果表明:增加高强螺栓后,裂纹扩展路径上的应变下降20%以上;直径16mm止裂孔+M14高强螺栓的止裂效果最优,相对于直径14mm止裂孔+M12高强螺栓的止裂效果提高2倍以上。

关键词 钢桥 疲劳裂纹 高强螺栓 钻孔止裂

0 引 言

正交异性钢桥面板具有自重轻、承载力高、适用范围广等优点,在我国从20世纪末开始得到广泛应用。但正交异性钢桥面板构造复杂,焊缝较多,应力集中问题突出,再加上局部往复轮载作用,疲劳问题非常显著[1],虎门大桥与江阴大桥分别在建成7年和12年后发现疲劳裂纹[2]。国内外统计结果表明:超过30%的疲劳裂纹在横隔板与U肋连接焊缝底部受拉区产生,沿着焊缝或斜向上发展[3-4]。这类裂纹通常扩展速度很快,如果不进行处理,有可能影响桥梁运营及结构安全。

目前,针对该类疲劳裂纹的处置方法主要有钻孔止裂[5]、粘贴CFRP、栓接钢板等。陈卓异[6]提出了"改善弧形开孔+补强钢板"的长裂纹加固方法,计算结果表明最大拉应力降幅达到54.6%,李传习[7]通过试验证明经CFRP加固的弧形开孔试件疲劳寿命达到未加固试件的14.5倍以上。粘贴CFRP与栓接钢板加固技术在工程应用与试验测试中取得了很好的加固效果,但是这两种加固方法施工工艺复杂、时间长,对路面交通影响大。

钻孔止裂法操作简便,但在实际应用中发现许多裂纹穿过止裂孔继续向前发展[3]。姚悦[8]针优化了钻孔止裂的位置与直径,但疲劳寿命提升效果并不明显。袁周致远[9]与M.Fanni[10]对止裂孔形状进行了优化,提高了止裂效果,但异形孔实施比较困难。刘天箫[11]提出了钻孔止裂技术的多孔布置方法,但并没有明显减小应力集中现象。国外学者在裂纹路径上附加高强螺栓取得了良好的加固效果。T.N.Chakherlou[13]采用高强螺栓加固了含中心裂纹的试板,有效降低了裂尖应力强度因子。T.Ishikawa[14]通过在长裂纹路径上设置高强螺栓,阻止裂缝张开,有效减小了止裂孔周围的应力。但是,裂纹路径上可钻孔空间有限,目前对于止裂孔与高强螺栓参数的选择也未明确。

本文首先分别采用钻孔止裂、高强螺栓与止裂孔复合止裂方法对带预制裂纹钢板进行处置,并通过疲劳试验对比了两种止裂方法的疲劳寿命。并且研究了止裂孔与螺栓直径的合理取值,为钢桥疲劳裂纹处置与维修提高借鉴。

1 止裂孔与高强螺栓复合止裂试验

1.1 试件设计与制作

参照现行《金属材料 疲劳试验 疲劳裂纹扩展方法》(GB/T 6398)[15]制作了单边缺口试件,试件具体尺寸为680mm×120mm×10mm,在长边一侧开20mm长的缺口(图1)。钢板材料为Q345低碳钢,加固使用的螺栓采用10.9级高强螺栓。

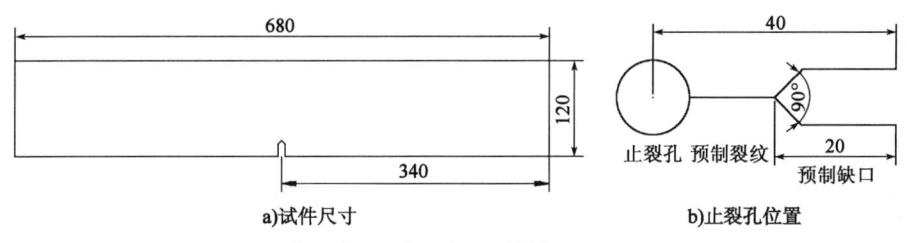

图 1 模型基本尺寸(尺寸单位:mm)

1.2 试件加载与测试

试验加载装置采用 MTS 疲劳试验机(图2),荷载采用大小为 72kN ± 48kN、频率为 8Hz 的拉力。首先进行疲劳裂纹预制,待裂纹扩展了 20mm 后,进行钻孔处理(图3),圆心布置在距离试件边缘 40mm 处(图4)。试件 JGS1~JGS3 采用的止裂孔直径、高强螺栓直径及预紧力如表1所示,然后采用相同的荷载直至试件断裂。

图 2 试件加载图

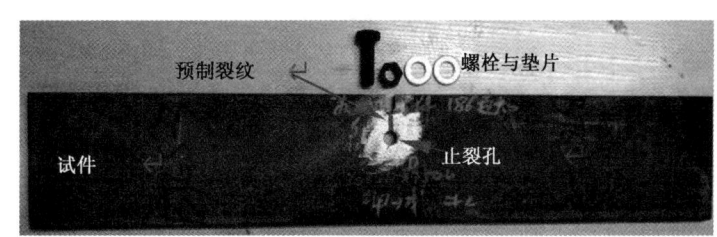

图 3 试件加固处理

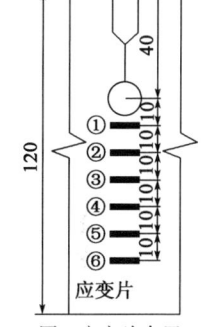

图 4 应变片布置

试验过程中主要测试内容包括:最大静载作用下裂纹扩展路径上的应变;裂纹扩展至不同位置的循环次数,应变片布置位置见图4,其中试件 JGS2、JGS3 在①号应变片处因布置了高强螺栓无法布置应变片。

试 验 模 型 参 数 表1

试件编号	止裂孔直径(mm)	螺栓直径(mm)	预紧力(kN)
JGS1	14	无螺栓	—
JGS2	14	M12	56.5
JGS3	16	M14	77.5

2 试 验 结 果

表2给出了在 72kN 静载作用下三个试件裂纹扩展路径上的应变测试结果,可以看出,JGS1 试件①号应变显著大于其他应变片,表现出明显的应力集中现象;JGS2 与 JGS3 试件②号应变比试件 JGS1 小 20%,说明高强螺栓复合止裂提升了止裂效果;JGS2 与 JGS3 试件②~⑥号应变相差不大,从应变角度无法判断哪个试件加固效果更好。

静载作用应变测试结果 表2

应 变 片	JGS1	JGS2	JGS3
①	3624	—	—
②	1017	814	837
③	612	513	516
④	432	347	362
⑤	257	259	261
⑥	112	188	178

表3给出了各组试件裂纹扩展到不同位置的荷载循环次数。试件JGS1在钻孔止裂后,未采用高强螺栓复合加固,仅仅1.8万次荷载循环之后试件再次开裂,2.9万次荷载循环之后试件完全破坏。试件JGS2与JGS3采用止裂孔与高强螺栓复合止裂方法,采用了不同的止裂孔与螺栓直径,均在荷载循环次数达到20万次后,发现高强螺栓垫片开裂(图5)。对比试件JGS1~JGS3的疲劳寿命,采用M12的高强螺栓相对于JGS1疲劳寿命提升了7.69倍,从垫片开裂至试件发现裂纹经历1.2万次循环;采用M14的高强螺栓疲劳寿命提升了15.76倍,从垫片开裂至试件发现裂纹经历了22.9万次循环。因此,采用止裂孔与高强螺栓复合止裂方法明显提高了止裂效果,试件JGS2在垫片开裂之后,高强螺栓复合止裂效果失效,试件JGS3在垫片开裂之后,高强螺栓还可以起到较好的复合止裂效果,垫片开裂之后存在一段时间较长的"预警期",可以对垫片进行更换。因此,在实际工程中保护母材及止裂孔尽量小的原则,采用M14的高强螺栓+16mm止裂孔加固效果最好。

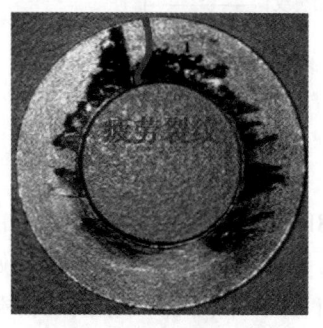

图5 垫片疲劳开裂

疲劳寿命对比(万次) 表3

裂纹长度	JGS-1	JGS-2	JGS-3
垫片开裂	—	20	22
发现裂纹	1.8	21.2	44.9
60mm	2.4	21.5	45
70mm	2.75	22	45.5
断开	2.9	22.3	45.7

3 结 语

(1)采用止裂孔与高强螺栓复合止裂,相比于普通止裂孔,测试得到裂纹扩展路径应变下降20%,明显降低了止裂孔周围应力集中。

(2)三个试件的疲劳寿命,试件JGS2是JGS1的7.69倍,试件JGS3是JGS1的15.76倍,采用止裂孔与高强螺栓复合止裂,试件疲劳寿命明显提升。

(3)相比于试件JGS2,试件JGS3在垫片开裂之后,仍能保持较好的复合止裂效果,M14的高强螺栓+16mm止裂孔是10mm钢板止裂孔与高强螺栓复合止裂方法的推荐止裂参数。

参考文献

[1] 张清华,卜一之,李乔.正交异性钢桥面板疲劳问题的研究进展[J].中国公路学报,2017(3):14-39.
[2] 张丽芳,艾军,张鹏飞,等.大跨度钢箱梁病害及成因分析[J].公路与汽运,2013(03):203-206.
[3] 张允士,李法雄,熊锋,等.正交异性钢桥面板疲劳裂纹成因分析及控制[J].公路交通科技,2013,30(08):75-80.
[4] 陈卓异,熊永明,李传习.正交异性钢桥面板横隔板弧形切口切割残余应力分析[J].桥梁建设,2020,50(06):46-52.
[5] 谢曙辉,吉伯海,傅中秋,等.钢桥面板疲劳裂纹钻孔止裂分析及实验验证[J].河南大学学报(自然科学版),2016,46(06):732-738.
[6] 李传习,柯璐,陈卓异,等.正交异性钢桥面板弧形切口及其CFRP补强的疲劳性能[J/OL].中国公路学报,2020,12(09):1-14.
[7] 陈卓异,李传习,柯璐,等.某悬索桥钢箱梁疲劳病害及处治方法研究[J].土木工程学报,2017,50

(03):91-100.
[8] Yue Yao, Bohai Ji, Zhongqiu Fu, et al. Optimization of stop-hole parameters for cracks at diaphragm-to-rib weld in steel bridges. 2019, 162.
[9] 袁周致远,吉伯海,傅中秋,等.钢结构疲劳裂纹合理止裂孔形状研究[J].南京理工大学学报,2017,05(v.41;No.216):16-21.
[10] Mohamed Fanni, N Fouda, N shabare, et al. New crack stop hole shape using structural optimizing technique[J]. Ain Shams Engineering Journal, 2015, 6(3):987-999.
[11] 刘天笳,吉伯海,傅中秋,等.钢桥疲劳裂纹钻孔止裂技术多孔布置方法研究[J].合肥工业大学学报(自然科学版),2016,39(10):1376-1380.
[12] Dexter Robert J, Justin M Ocel. Manual for repair and retrofit of fatigue cracks in steel bridges[S]. No. FHWA-IF-13-020. United States. Federal Highway Administration, 2013.
[13] T. N. Chakherlou, B. Abazadeh, J. Vogwell. The effect of bolt clamping force on the fracture strength and the stress intensity factor of a plate containing a fastener hole with edge cracks. 2008, 16(1):242-253.
[14] 全国钢标准化技术委员会.金属材料 疲劳试验 疲劳裂纹扩展方法:GB/T 6398—2017[S].北京:中国标准出版社,2017.

循环荷载下高强螺栓抗剪模型

曹燕飞　李　丹　任伟新
(合肥工业大学)

摘　要　在循环荷载等动力荷载作用下,高强螺栓连接表现出强非线性,对结构整体的动力响应影响显著,具有重要的研究意义。循环荷载下螺栓连接有限元建模收敛困难,需要考虑接触非线性,计算效率较低。本文根据循环荷载作用下高强螺栓连接节点的试验研究结果,在Iwan模型的基础上,提出了循环荷载下高强螺栓抗剪破坏的力学模型,准确地描述螺栓抗剪破坏全过程的各个受力阶段,反映不同阶段的能量耗散特性。

关键词　高强螺栓　循环荷载　抗剪破坏　力学模型　能量耗散

0　引　言

高强螺栓连接具有连接紧密、耐疲劳、可拆换以及在循环荷载、地震荷载等动力荷载作用下不容易松动等优点,在大跨桥梁、工业与民用建筑中应用广泛[1]。高强螺栓连接结构在循环荷载、地震荷载等动力荷载的作用下,结构的非线性特性明显[2-3]。基于螺栓连接的有限元模型和实验研究表明,螺栓连接结合面在外荷载的作用下,结合面的状态有黏结、微滑移、宏观滑移三种状态[4],具有代表性的接触本构模型有库伦摩擦模型[5]、Dahl模型[6]、剪切层模型[7]以及Iwan模型。库伦摩擦模型是一种准静态摩擦模型,不能描述速度为零时的摩擦力,模型的摩擦力只与运动方向有关,与摩擦接触的实际受力情况偏差较大;Dahl模型不能描述Stribeck效应;剪切层模型的虚拟材料参数识别复杂。

Iwan模型是W. D. Iwan通过将连接界面假设由一系列理想弹塑性单元组成,而提出的接触非线性滞回模型[8,9],Iwan模型由一系列Jenkins单元组成,每个Jenkins单元中包括一个弹簧单元和一个滑块单元,都是理想的弹塑性单元[10],根据Jenkins单元的不同组合形式,Iwan模型又可以分为并联—串联型和串联—串联型两种类型[11]。

本文基于Iwan模型[12-17]建立了循环荷载下高强螺栓抗剪破坏模型的简化力-位移和能量-力分段线性表达式。分析了高强螺栓连接在螺栓抗剪破坏形态下的力-位移曲线,将高强螺栓抗剪破坏分为摩擦阶段、滑移阶段、螺杆受力阶段。通过高强螺栓抗剪破坏试验,分析并识别了模型参数,结果证明模型能很好描述循环荷载作用下高强螺栓连接破坏的力学性质,能准确区分高强螺栓连接在各级循环荷载下的能量耗散,验证了模型的正确性。

1 螺栓连接力学模型

1.1 高强螺栓受力分析

高强螺栓连接分为摩擦型和承压型两种,承压型高强度螺栓连接承载力的计算方法与普通螺栓连接承载力的计算相同,根据破坏形态的不同分为螺栓抗剪和孔壁承压两种,两种破坏形态如图1所示,具体的承载力计算公式如下:

螺栓抗剪承载力计算:

$$N_v^b = n_v f_v^b \pi d^2 / 4 \tag{1}$$

孔壁承压承载力计算:

$$N_c^b = d \sum t f_c^b \tag{2}$$

式中:n_v——受剪面数目;

d——螺栓杆直径;

$\sum t$——在不同受力方向中一个受力方向承压构件总厚度的较小值;

f_v^b, f_c^b——螺栓抗剪强度设计值和孔壁承压强度设计值。

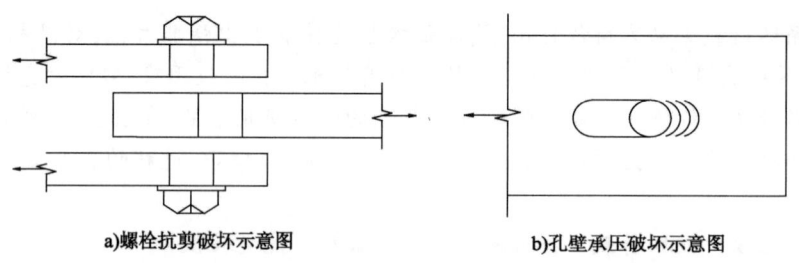

a)螺栓抗剪破坏示意图　　　　　　　　b)孔壁承压破坏示意图

图1　高强螺栓连接的两种破坏模式示意图

1.2 连接接触Iwan模型

Iwan模型由一系列Jenkins单元组成,每个Jenkins单元由串联的线性弹簧和摩擦阻尼滑块组成,可以描述拉压两个方向的非线性行为,Jenkins单元的力-位移关系如图2所示,图中f_i为摩擦阻尼滑块的屈服力,k_i为线性弹簧的刚度,φ_i为Jenkins单元的屈服位移。

$$f(x) = \begin{cases} k_i x & 0 < x \leq \varphi_i \\ f_i & x > \varphi_i \end{cases} \tag{3}$$

六参数Iwan模型[14,15]基于Segalman[16]提出的四参数含截断幂律分布和单脉冲的非均匀密度函数,提出了含截断幂律分布和双脉冲的非均匀密度函数,能同时描述微观滑移、宏观滑移以及宏观滑移时接触界面存在残余刚度的现象,Iwan模型侧重于对连接界面的非线性特性进行分析,没有对外荷载克服接触界面摩擦力发生宏观滑移后,螺栓与孔壁接触,螺栓连接节点在极限荷载下破坏时的非线性力学行为进行描述。

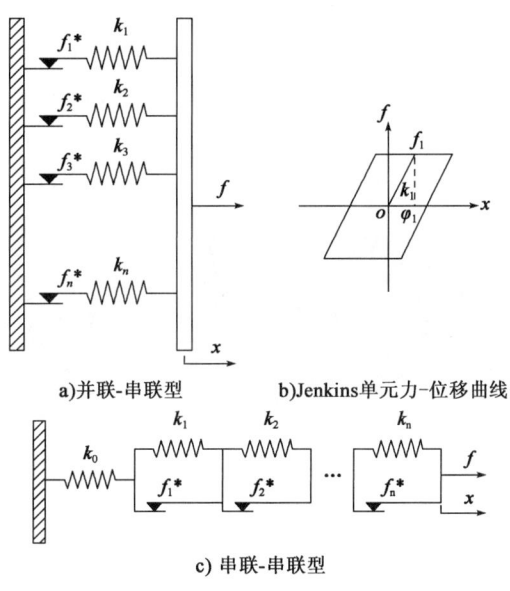

图 2 Iwan 模型示意图

2 循环荷载下高强螺栓连接螺栓抗剪破坏模型

2.1 循环荷载下高强螺栓连接抗剪破坏试验

为研究高强螺栓连接的螺栓抗剪破坏设计了三组试件(图 3),螺栓采用 8.8 级 M12 高强螺栓,通过扭力扳手施加预紧力 45kN;盖板厚度 10mm,芯板厚度 20mm,螺栓孔的直径比螺栓的直径大 1.5mm;板的宽度 100mm,长度 500mm,材料为 Q345 钢材,抗滑移系数为 0.35。8.8 级高强螺栓的屈服强度 f_y 为 660MPa,抗拉强度 f_u 为 830MPa;Q345 钢材的屈服强度 f_y 为 345MPa,抗拉强度 f_u 为 470MPa。

试验装置包括 100tSHT4106-6 电液伺服万能实验机,XITE 预置可调式扭力扳手,YHD 型位移计,DH5922N-GD 动态信号分析系统。试验的加载制度为以 20kN 为一级,逐级往上加载,每一级荷载内经历三次加载和卸载的循环,试验时采用力控制的加载方式,加载过程中采用位移加载(图 4),加载速率为 3mm/min,直至高强螺栓被剪断。

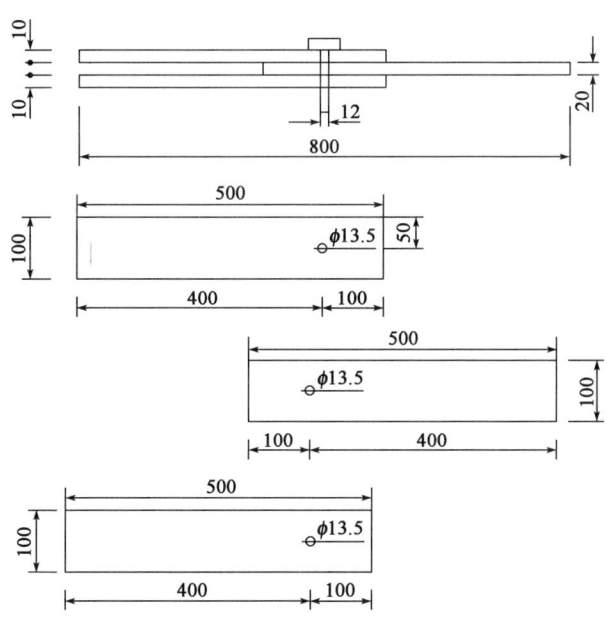

图 3 试件尺寸示意图 (尺寸单位:mm)

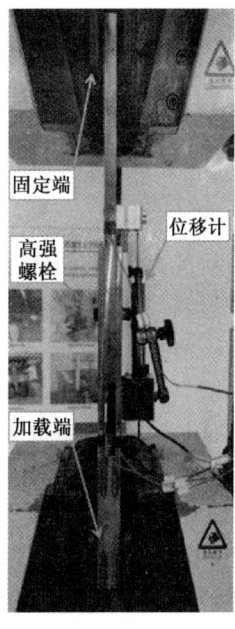

图 4 试件加载示意图

在试验加载的初期,螺栓连接节点主要靠连接界面间的摩擦力抵抗荷载,试件外观无明显变化。随着荷载的增加,对比试验过程中的力-位移曲线,发现在实验过程中,力-位移曲线出现水平趋势时,试件会出现金属摩擦的声音,此时连接板之间的摩擦力被克服,连接界面发生宏观滑移,在试件发生宏观滑移后,螺栓与孔壁接触,螺栓开始受切向剪力,力-位移曲线的整体趋势成线性增加。直至试件出现"砰"的一声,螺栓被突然剪断,试验结束。试验完成后螺栓和螺栓孔的变形如图5所示。

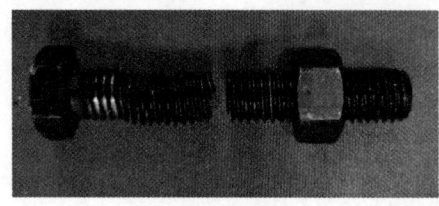
a)试件1 螺栓

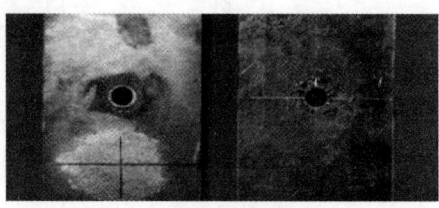
b)试件1 螺栓孔

图5 螺栓连接试件破坏形态

2.2 高强螺栓连接螺栓抗剪破坏全过程模型

通过循环荷载下高强螺栓连接抗剪破坏的试验研究,结合 Iwan 模型中不同阶段的力—位移和能量耗散—力方程呈分段线性的特性,本文建立了循环荷载下高强螺栓连接螺栓抗剪破坏的分析模型:

$$F(x) = \begin{cases} k_1 x & 0 < x < \varphi_1 \\ k_1 \varphi_1 & \varphi_1, x < \varphi_2 \\ k_1 \varphi_1 + k_2(x - \varphi_2) & \varphi_2, x \end{cases} \quad (4)$$

$$D(F) = \begin{cases} \eta_1 F & 0 < F < F_1 \\ \eta_1 F + \eta_2 (F - F_1) & F_1, F \end{cases} \quad (5)$$

式中:F——螺栓连接的受力;

D——螺栓连接的能量耗散;

x——螺栓连接的位移;

φ_1——宏观滑移起点;

φ_2——螺栓抗剪起点;

k_1——摩擦阶段力—位移曲线的斜率;

k_2——螺杆受力阶段力—位移曲线的斜率;

η——能量耗散与力之间的系数。

3 结果与分析

通过对试验获得的力-位移曲线图的分析,在加载的初期,荷载较小,螺栓连接主要由接触界面间的摩擦力抵抗外荷载,接触界面未发生宏观滑移,力—位移曲线的整体趋势是线性增加;随着荷载的增加,连接界面在发生宏观滑移后,螺栓与孔壁接触,力-位移曲线的整体趋势呈不同斜率的线性增加,螺栓的破坏是突然的脆性断裂,螺栓孔的变形很小,不考虑连接板的塑性变形,试件的极限承载力主要由螺栓的抗剪承载力决定;三组螺栓抗剪破坏试件的力—位移曲线都表明,螺栓抗剪破坏没有明显的塑性变形阶段,验证了本文提出的高强螺栓抗剪破坏力-位移方程的正确性。

图6结合试件1的力-位移曲线,给出了循环荷载下螺栓抗剪破坏模型中力-位移表达式的拟合曲线;图7给出了循环荷载作用下螺栓抗剪破坏模型中能量耗散-力表达式的拟合曲线。三组试件的力—位移表达式参数识别结果如表1所示,最后求出各组试件参数识别结果的均值,利用均值确定力—位移表达式的参数。

力-位移表达式的参数识别

表1

试 件	φ_1 (mm)	φ_2 (mm)	k_1 (N/m)	k_2 (N/m)
试件1	1.58	3.20	2.09×10^7	1.87×10^6
试件2	1.62	2.95	1.99×10^7	1.90×10^6
试件3	1.60	3.10	1.99×10^7	1.94×10^6
均 值	1.60	3..08	2.02×10^7	1.90×10^6

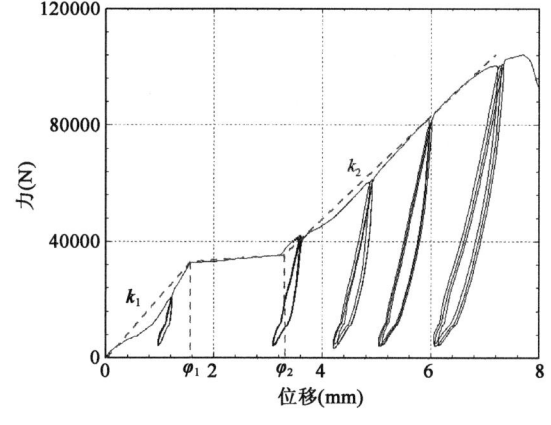

图6 螺栓抗剪力—位移表达式的参数识别　　　　图7 螺栓抗剪能量耗散—力表达式的参数识别

将表1识别的参数,代入模型的力-位移表达式,可以计算出能量耗散—力表达式中的 F_1 和 F_2。再根据试验的力—位移曲线,分别求出各级荷载中每次循环荷载的滞回曲线面积,再求取三次循环荷载滞回曲线面积的均值,利用求取的均值绘制能量耗散—力的散点图,通过散点图与螺栓抗剪破坏各阶段的划分,以及对模型力—位移表达式各参数的确定,可以绘制能量耗散—力的折线图,确定循环荷载下高强螺栓抗剪破坏分析模型中,能量耗散—力表达式的参数 η_1 和 η_2,完成能量耗散—力表达式的参数识别。

根据高强螺栓连接节点,螺栓抗剪破坏试件1-3的力-位移曲线求得各级荷载中,每次循环荷载的滞回曲线面积,和三次循环荷载滞回曲线面积的均值,由滞回曲线面积确定的能量耗散见表2～表4。

试件1 各级荷载不同循环下的能量耗散

表2

荷 载	第一次循环(J)	第二次循环(J)	第三次循环(J)	均值(J)
20kN	0.93	0.86	0.84	0.88
40kN	3.84	3.96	3.93	3.91
60kN	9.43	9.37	9.61	9.47
80kN	15.58	15.94	16.36	15.96
100kN	21.47	21.43	21.69	21.53

试件2 各级荷载不同循环下的能量耗散

表3

荷 载	第一次循环(J)	第二次循环(J)	第三次循环(J)	均值(J)
20kN	0.84	0.77	0.82	0.81
40kN	4.46	4.56	4.60	4.54
60kN	9.73	9.77	9.50	9.74
80kN	15.58	15.94	15.58	15.70

试件3各级荷载不同循环下的能量耗散　　　　　　表4

荷　　载	第一次循环(J)	第二次循环(J)	第三次循环(J)	均值(J)
20kN	0.74	0.77	0.77	0.76
40kN	3.86	3.93	3.94	3.91
60kN	8.98	9.47	9.60	9.35
80kN	15.28	15.25	15.37	15.30

将各级循环荷载下滞回曲线面积的均值绘制成散点图,通过力—位移表达式计算出的F_1,结合循环荷载下螺栓抗剪破坏不同受力阶段的划分,确定能量耗散折线图中不同阶段分界点的横坐标,将零荷载零能量耗散的默认起点与加载力幅值为20kN下的能量耗散值进行线性拟合,即确定能量耗散折线图的第一阶段,根据第一阶段确定的能量耗散—力的关系,可以确定能量耗散折线图中,不同阶段分界点横坐标F_1对应的纵坐标的能量耗散值。再结合求得的分界点坐标与40kN、60kN、80kN和100kN加载力幅值下的能量耗散,进行线性拟合,即可确定能量耗散折线图的第二阶段,由此便可以绘制出能量耗散-力的折线图,根据折线图中各阶段的能量耗散-力的斜率,即可确定循环荷载下高强螺栓连接螺栓抗剪破坏模型中能量耗散-力表达式的参数η。三组试件能量耗散-力表达式参数识别的结果如表5所示,最后求出各组试件参数识别结果的均值,利用均值确定能量耗散-力表达式的参数。

能量耗散-力表达式的参数识别　　　　　　表5

试　　件	F_1(kN)	η_1	η_2
试件1	32.8	4.08×10^{-5}	2.10×10^{-4}
试件2	32.56	4.10×10^{-5}	2.07×10^{-4}
试件3	31.84	4.12×10^{-5}	2.13×10^{-4}
均值	32.40	4.10×10^{-5}	2.10×10^{-4}

三组试件参数拟合的结果表明,模型中的能量耗散-力表达式,能准确地反映循环荷载下高强螺栓连接螺栓抗剪破坏,不同阶段的能量耗散特性。

4　结　　语

本文基于Iwan模型建立的循环荷载下高强螺栓抗剪破坏模型,将高强螺栓抗剪破坏分为摩擦阶段、滑移阶段和螺杆受力阶段。通过高强螺栓抗剪破坏试验,识别了模型的参数,证明了模型的准确性。通过对高强螺栓抗剪破坏的能量耗散-力折线图进行分析可知,在加载的初期,主要靠接触界面的摩擦力抵抗荷载,试件的耗能能力较弱;当外荷载克服接触界面摩擦力,接触界面发生宏观滑移后,螺栓与孔壁接触,主要靠螺栓抗剪抵抗荷载时,试件的耗能能力增强,因此,在设计高强螺栓连接时,可以适当考虑螺栓与孔壁接触后的受力,以此来提升高强螺栓连接节点的耗能能力。

参考文献

[1] 张耀春,周绪红.钢结构设计原理[M].北京:高等教育出版社,2010.

[2] 刘冰.螺栓连接结合面非线性特性分析及动态响应[D].上海:上海交通大学,2019.

[3] 黄楠,任伟新.高强度螺栓连接抗剪非线性简化模型[A].天津大学、天津市钢结构学会.第十九届全国现代结构工程学术研讨会论文集[C].天津大学、天津市钢结构学会:全国现代结构工程学术研讨会学术委员会,2019:7.

[4] Jamia N,Jalali H,Taghipour J,et al. An equivalent model of a nonlinear bolted flange joint[J]. Mechanical system and Signal Processing,2021,153.

[5] Karnopp D. Computer Simulation of Stick-Slip Friction in Mechanical Dynamic Systems[J]. Journal of Dynamic Systems Measurement and Control,1985,107(1):100-103.

[6] Dahl,Philip R. Solid Friction Damping of Mechanical Vibrations[J]. AIAA Journal,1976,14(12):

1675-1682.

[7] Tian H, Li B, Liu H, et al. A new method of virtual material hypothesis-based dynamic modeling on fixed joint interface in machine tools[J]. International Journal of Machine Tools and Manufacture, 2011, 51(3): 239-249.

[8] Iwan W D. A Distributed-Element Model for Hysteresis and Its Steady-State Dynamic Response[J]. Journal of Applied Mechanics, 1966, 33(4):893.

[9] Iwan W D. On a Class of Models for the Yielding Behavior of Continuous and Composite Systems[J]. Journal of Applied Mechanics, 1967, 34(3).

[10] Y song, C J Hartwigson, D M McFarland, et al. Simulation of dynamics of beam structures with bolted joints using adjusted Iwan beam elements[J]. Journal of Sound & Vibration, 2004, 273(1-2):249-276.

[11] Segalman D J, Gregory D L, Starr M J, et al. Handbook on dynamics of jointed structures[J]. Sandia National Laboratories, 2002.

[12] 张相盟, 王本利, 卫洪涛. Iwan 模型非线性恢复力及能量耗散计算研究[J]. 工程力学, 2012, 29(011):33-39.

[13] Yikun Li, Zhiming Hao. A six-parameter Iwan model and its application. 2016, 68-69:354-365.

[14] 李一堃, 郝志明, 章定国. 基于六参数非均匀密度函数的伊万模型研究[J]. 力学学报, 2015.

[15] 李一堃. 预紧连接结构非线性力学模型研究[D]. 2017.

[16] Segalman D J. A Four-Parameter Iwan Model for Lap-Type Joints[J]. Journal of Applied Mechanics, 2002, 72(5).

[17] Biswas S, Chatterjee A. A two-state hysteresis model for bolted joints, with minor loops from partial unloading-ScienceDirect[J]. International Journal of Mechanical Sciences, 2018, 140:506-520.

基于 LSTM 的子结构试验模型更新方法

于长江[1] 郑艺炜[2]

(1.长安大学公路学院;2.哈尔科夫汽车道路大学交通学院)

摘 要 子结构试验是一种将真实物理加载试验和有限元数值模拟进行耦合的试验方法。其中非线性构件的数值模型精度是研究热点,神经网络能够对无法用确定数值模型描述的本构模型进行在线辨识以及更新。为了提高传统神经网络算法的自适应性,本文提出了一种基于长短期记忆(Long Short-Term Memory, LSTM)的在线模型更新方法,将长短时记忆神经网络模型作为识别模型,且采用滑动样本窗口实现了数值子结构本构模型的在线识别更新,以及同步预测恢复力。针对两个自由度非线性系统,分别进行了基于传统神经网络和 LSTM 神经网络的子结构试验数值仿真。研究表明:数值单元恢复力预测值的最大相对误差仅为 4.4%,与传统神经网络算法相比,LSTM 神经网络算法具有更好的自适应性、恢复力预测精度。

关键词 子结构试验 模型更新 LSTM 神经网络 恢复力预测

0 引 言

子结构试验[1]是一种将物理加载试验与有限元数值模拟耦合联动的一种试验方法,在大型复杂结构抗震试验中具有重要的应用前景。一般将首先发生非线性变形的关键构件作为试验子结构进行物理试验,其余构件采用假定的数值模型进行计算机模拟。一般来说,大型复杂结构的许多关键构件或部件在强地震动作用下都可能进入非线性,如消能支撑、框架节点、桥墩或阻尼器等。由于试验室场地或设备限制,一般在试验室中只对一个或多个可能首先经历非线性的关键构件进行物理试验,而其余具有相似滞回性能的构件被放入数值子结构中进行模拟仿真。然而,对于可能已进入非线性但无法进行加载试验的关键构件,其假定的数值模型可能存在较大的模型误差。第一类误差来源于数值模型过于简化所造成的模型缺陷;第二类误差来源于数值模型参数的不确定性。当这些非线性单元所占比例较大时,模型误差会累积到不可忽略的程度,进而导致结构的动力响应失真。为了减少模型误差、提高子结构试验的精度,各种模型更新技术已被有效地应用到子结构试验中,即利用试验子结构的实测数据在线辨识其滞回模型,然后同步更新数值子结构中具有相似材料特性和非线性行为的相应本构模型。

在线模型更新技术大致可分为两类:基于数值模型的参数更新方法和基于智能算法的非参数更新方法。在参数修正方法中,假设构件的本构模型是一个具有特定参数的数值模型,通过参数识别技术优化估计数值模型参数,对于减小第二类模型误差有重要作用。目前,参数辨识方法主要有非线性多变量优化算法(梯度法[2]、Nelder-Mead 单纯形法[3]、目标函数优化算法[4])、最小二乘法[5]、无迹 Kalman 滤波法[6-10](UKF)和约束无迹 Kalman 滤波法[11-12](CUKF)。对于参数识别技术,当没有足够的参数来表示构件的具体非线性行为时,无法从根本上避免由数值模型缺陷引起的结构响应失真的风险。

对于基于智能算法的非参数更新方法,不需要预先指定构件的数值模型。利用神经网络、支持向量机等智能算法对滞回模型进行精确拟合。神经网络能够通过不断调整各层神经元之间的连接权值来逼近任意非线性函数,在非线性动态系统辨识领域得到了广泛的应用。神经网络可用于对不能用确定的数学模型来描述的系统进行建模,学习到假定数值模型中不存在的滞回信息,进一步提高子结构试验精度。因此,神经网络方法对于准确揭示非线性构件或结构的抗震性能、提高子结构试验的精度具有重要的工程应用价值。

近几十年来,神经网络方法逐渐被人们所探索。2005 年,Yang 等[13]利用神经网络识别试验子结构的本构模型,并更新了数值子结构中的相应部分。2008 年,Yun 等人[14]在静态往复加载试验中,应用了五个输入变量的神经网络来拟合滞回模型。根据输入变量在滞回曲线不同位置的正负符号,初步证明了该方法在模型辨识中的可行性。2016 年,Elanwar 等[15]使用离线 ANN 方法识别了两跨钢框架的双线性模型,该模型不符合子结构试验中逐步加载的事实。2017 年,Wang 等人[16]提出了一种基于在线神经网络算法的更新方法,只使用当前加载步骤的实验数据来训练神经网络模型,并通过数值模拟验证了该方法的可行性。Wang 等[17]提出了一种带遗忘因子的在线神经网络方法,采用带遗忘因子的滑动窗口样本在线训练神经网络模型,提高了传统神经网络方法的自适应性。数值研究表明,当初始数值模型存在固有缺陷的情况下,带遗忘因子的在线神经网络方法比 UKF 方法具有更高的模型更新精度。

但是,在线系统辨识为动态建模问题,传统神经网络算法仍是一种基于前馈型的静态神经网络。为了进一步提高神经网络算法的自适应性和模型更新精度,本研究采用动态神经网络中较为常用的 LSTM 神经网络[18]进行在线模型识别,以此实现本构模型的滚动优化。通过对两自由度非线性结构进行数值仿真,验证 LSTM 神经网络算法的模型更新效果、恢复力预测精度。

1 LSTM 神经网络原理

1.1 循环神经网络

目前神经网络方法(NN,Neural Network)已经广泛应用于非线性动力系统识别领域,具备强大的自学习能力和非线性映射能力。对于在线模型更新,恢复力模型的力-位移可看为时间序列数据,且当前步恢复力与之前历史时刻的恢复力是有关联的。而传统神经网络基本难以对时间序列数据进行建模以及预测。循环神经网络(RNN,Recurrent Neural Network)对传统神经网络进行了改进,增加了一个反馈层,将神经元的输出在下一时刻传递给自身,将信息从上一时间步传递到另一个时间步,达到保留之前学习内容的目的。图 1a)为 t 时刻的单个 RNN,A 为一个 RNN 单元,x_t 为输入,h_t 为输出。

1.2 LSTM 神经网络

在 RNN 训练期间,由于 RNN 信息不断地循环往复反馈,RNN 的权重更新非常大,累积了错误梯度,容易发生梯度爆炸、梯度消失和长期记忆能力不足的问题,可能会影响 RNN 对时间序列的预测效果。基于此,LSTM 是一种在 RNN 基础上改进的循环神经网络,已经被广泛用于语音识别,语言建模和时序预测等领域,LSTM 在 RNN 基础上改进了以下两点:

(1)增加单元记忆状态 C_t,实现神经网络模型的长期记忆;

(2)设置多个"门",克服梯度消失和梯度爆炸的问题。

其中,添加了"遗忘门",可以忘记不必要的信息,并决定从旧输出中删除哪些部分;添加了"输入门",决定并存储记忆单元新的输入信息;添加了"输出门",决定要输出的内容;Tanh 层根据新的输入创建所有可能的值的向量;Sigmoid 函数输出 0 到 1 之间的值,决定遗忘或保留信息的百分比。

图 1b)是一个 LSTM 单元,左侧输入为 $t-1$ 时刻的单元记忆状态 C_{t-1} 和输出 h_{t-1},输出为当前时刻 t 的单元记忆状态 C_t 和输出 h_t,W_1,W_2,W_3,W_4 分别为不同的权重系数矩阵,σ 和 Tanh 分别为 Sigmoid 和 Tanh 激活函数。

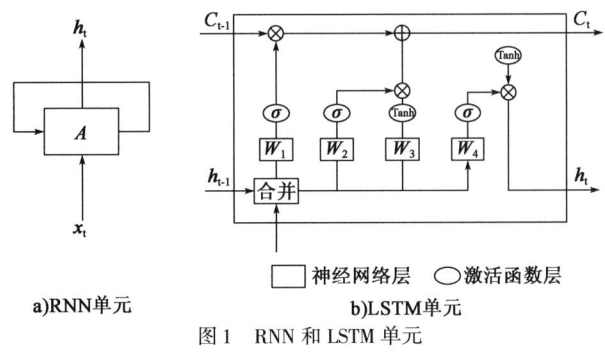

图 1 RNN 和 LSTM 单元

2 子结构试验的模型更新原理

图 2 展示了子结构试验的模型更新方法框架,重要的是在传统子结构试验中添加了模型更新模块。在传统的子结构试验中,将整体结构划分为物理子结构和数值子结构。取整体结构中较为复杂、非线性较强或具有代表性的部分作进行真实物理试验,将此部分结构称为试验子结构,其他部分设置为数值子结构进行数值模拟。根据数值子结构中与物理子结构的相似程度,将数值子结构区分为两类,即数值子结(可更新)和数值子结构(不更新)。数值子结构(可更新)与物理子结构具有相似的力学特性,可用相同的本构模型描述,但不要求其与物理子结构具有相同的加载路径。这类数值子结构可以充分利用试验子结构的试验数据在线校正其选用的本构模型。不更新的数值子结构与物理子结构的力学特性差异明显,通常来讲其所经历的非线性较弱,根据经验选用数学模型带来的模拟误差在可接受的范围之内。

关于在线模型更新混合试验的运行,具体试验流程:首先,把当前加载步试验子结构的预测位移 d_E 发送给作动器加载并测量反力 F_E。接着,把试验子结构的位移 d_E 和测量反力 F_E 发送到模型更新模块,运用模型更新方法对试验子结构的本构模型进行在线识别,且利用识别到的本构模型同步更新数值子结构(可更新)的不精确本构模型。然后,把预测位移 d_{N1} 和 d_{N2} 各自发送到数值子结构(可更新)和数值子结构(不更新),分别计算出各部分的内力 F_{N1} 和 F_{N2}。最后,将各个数值子结构的内力返回到数值积分模块中,迭代预测下一步的结构位移。重复上述步骤直到地震动输入完毕。模型更新混合试验采用以下基本假定:①假定试验子结构和数值子结构(可更新)具有相同的恢复力模型;②假定最先进入非线性的构件作为试验子结构。

需要注意的是,将神经网络应用于子结构试验的在线模型更新时,神经网络可能会出现错误的累积传播和夸大。在线训练样本的选取和新旧样本训练权重的设置对在线神经网络算法的自适应性有着重要的影响。因此,一般采用带有遗忘因子的滑动窗口样本[17]作为每时步的在线训练样本,其中新加入的样本被赋予较大的训练权值,而早期历史样本的训练权值较小,增强了在线辨识系统的适应性。一个固定数量 L 的滑动窗口如图 3 所示,将当前加载步骤中最近的一个试验子结构样本放入后,同时移除最早的历史样本。具有 L 个样本的滑动窗口可以表示如下:

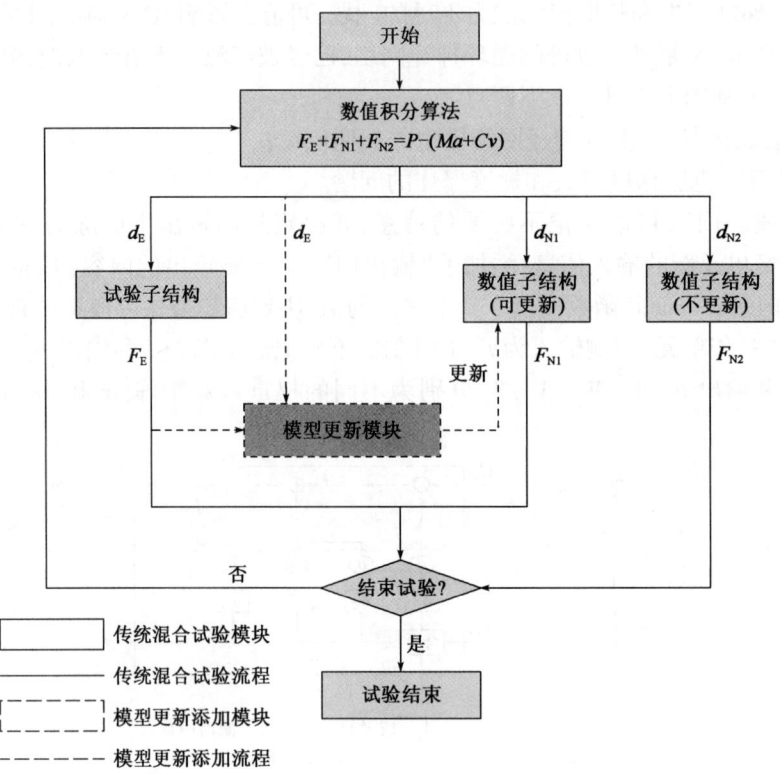

图 2 子结构试验的模型更新方法框架

$$\text{window} = [(X_1, Y_1), \cdots, (X_L, Y_L)] \tag{1}$$

式中：(X_L, Y_L)——最新添加的试验样本；

(X_1, Y_1)——窗口中最早的历史样本。

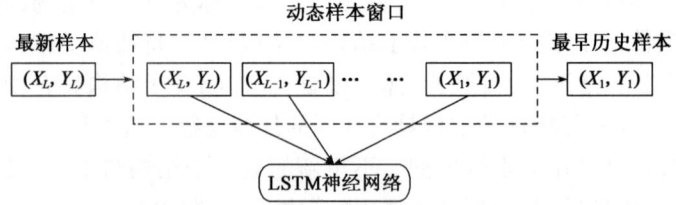

图 3 带遗忘因子的动态样本窗口

λ_i 是动态窗口中第 i 个样本的训练权重，由指数遗忘法确定，如下所示，其中 μ 表示遗忘因子。

$$\lambda_i = \frac{1-\mu}{1-\mu^L}\mu^{L-i} \tag{2}$$

$$\sum_{i=1}^{L}\lambda_i = 1 \tag{3}$$

3 数值仿真算例

3.1 结构模型

针对一个两自由度的非线性结构进行模型更新子结构试验数值仿真，以验证本文提出的基于神经网络模型更新的混合试验方法在相似加载路径下的有效性，如图 4 所示。整体结构模型在 MATLAB 软件中进行建模计算，神经网络调用 MATLAB 内置的神经网络工具箱进行计算。将第一自由度的部分作为试验子结构，将第二自由度对应的部分作为数值子结构。试验子结构和数值子结构的位移分别为 d_E 和 d_N，恢复力分别为 F_E 和 F_N。试验子结构和数值子结构的质量为 $M_1 = M_2 = 2500t$，初始刚度为 $K_1 = K_2 = $

394785kN/m,结构阻尼系数为 $C_1 = C_2 = 5026.5$ kN/(m·s^{-1})。地震动采用 1994 年 1 月 17 日 Northridge 地震 SimiValley-Katherine Rd 台站所记录得到的地震波记录,地震加速度峰值为 1000cm/s^2。数值积分算法选取显式 Newmark-β 算法,积分步长设置 0.01s。

混合试验数值仿真中,试验子结构和数值子结构具有相同的恢复力模型,均选取为 Bouc-Wen 模型:

$$\left.\begin{array}{l} \dot{z} = A\dot{d} - \beta |\dot{d}||z|^{n-1}z - \gamma \dot{d}|z|^n \\ F = \alpha Kd + (1-\alpha)Kz \end{array}\right\} \quad (4)$$

式中:F——结构恢复力;

d——结构的位移;

z——结构的滞回位移;

K——结构的初始刚度;

α——后屈服刚度系数;

A、β、γ、n——控制滞回环形状的参数。

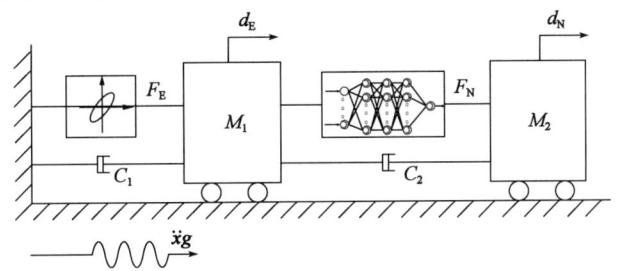

图 4　子结构试验模型示意图

Bouc-Wen 模型参数的真实值和基于经验设定的有误差的初始值如表 1 所示。

Bouc-Wen 模型参数的真实值和有误差的初始值　　表 1

模型参数	K(kN/m)	α	A	β	γ	n
真实值	394785	0.01	1	0.3	0.08	1
有误差的初始值	350000	0.02	1	1.2	1.96	2

为了验证基于 LSTM 神经网络模型更新方法的可行性和有效性,进行了四种工况下的数值仿真和对比分析,如表 2 所示。其中,基于神经网络离线校正的子结构试验和基于神经网络模型更新的子结构试验中,将数值子结构的初始恢复力模型设置为离线数据预训练的 ANN 模型。

四种子结构试验模拟工况　　表 2

序号	工况标记	子结构试验类型	试验子结构恢复力模型	数值子结构初始恢复力模型	模型更新方法
1	Reference	真实子结构试验	Bouc-Wen 真实值	Bouc-Wen 真实值	不更新
2	Traditional	传统子结构试验	Bouc-Wen 真实值	Bouc-Wen 有误差的初始值	不更新
3	Updated with ANN	基于传统神经网络在线模型更新的子结构试验	Bouc-Wen 真实值	离线数据预训练的 ANN 神经网络模型	传统神经网络算法
4	Updated with LSTM	基于 LSTM 神经网络模型更新的子结构试验	Bouc-Wen 真实值	离线数据预训练的 LSTM 神经网络模型	LSTM 神经网络算法

3.2　LSTM 神经网络设置

3.2.1　LSTM 神经网络结构参数设置

本文数值模拟采用的 LSTM 网络模型含有 2 个隐藏层,每个隐藏层有 10 个神经元,其模型结构如图 5 所示。当本构模型在非线性情况下,需要采用足够的状态变量来描述恢复力。在本次数值验证中,

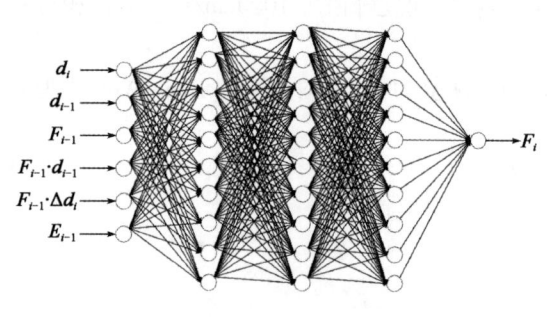

输入层使用六个输入变量 $[d_i, d_{i-1}, F_{i-1}, F_{i-1}d_{i-1}, F_{i-1}\Delta d_i, E_{i-1}]$[20]，输出层使用一个输出变量 $[F_i]$。d_i 和 F_i 分别表示第 i 步中的位移和恢复力。E_{i-1} 表示到第 $(i-1)$ 步的累积能量耗散，$E_{i-1} = E_{i-2} + |F_{i-1}d_{i-1}|$。

3.2.2 LSTM 神经网络初始权值、阈值确定

训练初始化的 LSTM 神经网络模型，本次数值模拟中将神经网络模型的初始权值、阈值设置为离线数据预训练得到的神经网络模型，离线数据来源于初始有误差的 Bouc-Wen 模型。

图 5 LSTM 神经网络模型结构图

3.2.3 LSTM 神经网络训练算法参数设置

本次数值模拟中，LSTM 神经网络模型的遗忘门的初始阈值设为 1.0，输入门和输出门的初始值设为 $[0,1]$ 区间上的随机浮点数。采用 Mini-Batch 随机梯度下降训练网络，学习率为 0.001，衰减因子为 0.95。采用均方误差 MSE 作为目标函数。训练次数设为 50，并在 12 轮之后，学习率在每一轮乘以衰减因子 0.95。选择 75% 作为训练集，其余数据作为测试集。此外，滑动窗口样本个数选为 200，遗忘因子 λ 设置为经验值 0.79。

4 结果分析

本文数值算例进行了四种子结构试验工况的数值仿真，如表 2 所示，每种工况模拟进行 10 次，取 10 次结果的平均值作为最终的模拟结果。观察数值子结构的位移响应和恢复力响应，评价数值子结构的恢复力预测精度。利用预测恢复力的相对误差作为误差指标进行精度评价，对比分析数值子结构的预测滞回曲线和预测恢复力相对误差曲线，如图 6 ~ 图 9 所示。其中，恢复力的相对误差定义如下：

$$|R_i| = \frac{|F_{p,i} - F_{e,i}|}{|F_e|_{max}} \tag{5}$$

其中 $|R_i|$ 表示第 i 时步下恢复力的相对误差，$F_{p,i}$ 与 $F_{e,i}$ 分别表示第 i 时步下的预测恢复力与真实恢复力，$|F_e|_{max}$ 表示在时程范围内真实恢复力的绝对值最大值。

从图 6 ~ 图 8 中可以看出，同一测试地震波的同一时步下，对于数值子结构的预测位移、预测恢复力以及滞回曲线，LSTM 神经网络方法相对于传统神经网络算法具有更高的模型更新精度。具体比较地震波下预测恢复力的最大相对误差，如图 9 所示，通过传统神经网络方法预测得到的恢复力最大相对误差为 17.8%，而通过 LSTM 神经网络方法进行在线校正后，最大相对误差控制在 4.4% 以下，说明动态神经网络模型对于在线模型更新具有较高的适用性和有效性。

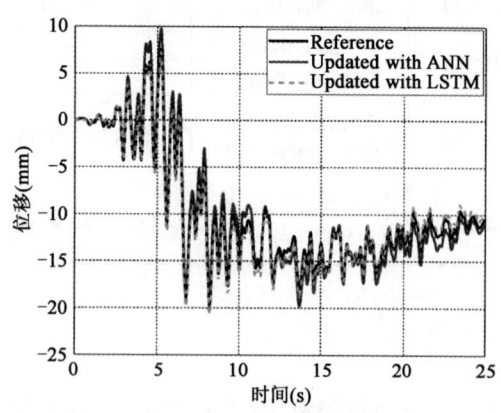

图 6 数值子结构位移时程曲线图

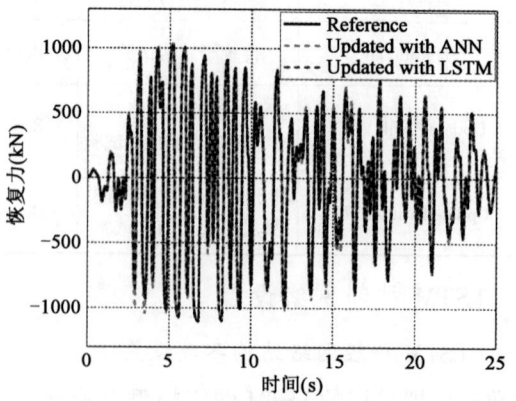

图 7 数值子结构恢复力时程曲线图

另外,LSTM 神经网络方法和传统神经网络方法的仿真均步耗时在 0.12~0.15s 范围内,基本满足慢速子结构试验的时间要求。

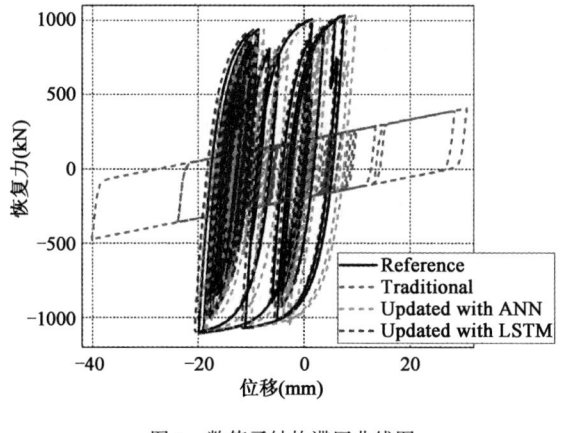

图 8　数值子结构滞回曲线图　　　　图 9　预测恢复力相对误差时程图

5　结　语

本文提出了一种基于 LSTM 神经网络的子结构试验模型更新方法,采用动态神经网络模型对数值子结构的本构模型进行辨识和更新,使得模型随着时间推移进行滚动优化,极大提高了数值子结构的模型精度。最后,对一个两自由度非线性结构进行了数值验证,结果表明了本文方法的有效性。结论如下:

(1)将 LSTM 神经网络方法应用于两个自由度结构的数值模拟,验证了该方法的可行性和有效性。

(2)相对传统神经网络算法,LSTM 神经网络方法具有更好的自适应性,极大提高了数值子结构的模型精度。

(3)从算法的计算效率来讲,虽然 LSTM 神经网络方法满足慢速拟动力子结构试验的要求,但是仍需要进一步研究提高神经网络算法计算效率的方案。

参考文献

[1] Nakashima M, Kato H, Takaoka E. Development of real-time pseudo dynamic testing[J]. Earthq Eng Struct Dyn, 1992, 21(1): 79-92.

[2] Chuang MC, Hsieh SH, Tsai KC, et al. Parameter identification for on-line model updating in hybrid simulations using a gradient-based method[J]. Earthq Eng Struct Dyn, 2018, 47(2): 269-293.

[3] Yang YS, Tsai KC, Elnashai AS, et al. An online optimization method for bridge dynamic hybrid simulations[J]. Simul Model Pract Th, 2012, 28: 42-54.

[4] Kwon O, Kammula V. Model updating method for substructure pseudo-dynamic hybrid simulation[J]. Earthq Eng Struct Dyn, 2013, 42(13): 1971-1984.

[5] Wang T, Wu B, Zhang J. Adaptive pseudo-dynamic substructure testing based on least square method[J]. Structural Engineers, 2011, 27(S1): 57-62. (in Chinese)

[6] Wang T, Wu B. Hybrid testing method based on model updating with constrained unscented Kalman Filter [J]. Earthq Eng Eng Vib, 2013, 33(5): 100-109. (in Chinese)

[7] Hashemi MJ, Masroor A, Mosqueda G. Implementation of online model updating in hybrid simulation[J]. Earthq Eng Struct Dyn, 2014, 43(3): 395-412.

[8] Shao X, Mueller A, Mohammed BA. Real-Time Hybrid Simulation with Online Model Updating: Methodology and Implementation[J]. J Eng Mech, 2016, 142(2): 04015074.

[9] Wu B, Chen Y, Xu G, et al. Hybrid simulation of steel frame structures with sectional model updating[J].

Earthq Eng Struct Dyn,2016,45(8):1251-1269.
[10] Wu B, Ning X, Xu G, et al. Online numerical simulation: A hybrid simulation method for incomplete boundary conditions[J]. Earthq Eng Struct Dyn,2018,47(4):889-905.
[11] Wu B, Wang T. Model updating with constrained unscented kalman filter for hybrid testing[J]. Smart Struct Syst,2014,14(6):1105-1129.
[12] Ou G, Dyke SJ, Prakash A. Real time hybrid simulation with online model updating: An analysis of accuracy[J]. Mech Syst Signal Proc,2017,(84):223-240.
[13] Wang YH, Lv J, Wu J, et al. ANN based on forgetting factor for online model updating in substructure pseudo-dynamic hybrid simulation[J]. Smart Struct Syst,2020,26(1):63-75.
[14] Yun GJ, Ghaboussi J, Elnashai AS. A new neural network-based model for hysteresis behavior of materials[J]. Int J Numer Meth Eng,2008,73(4):447-469.
[15] Elanwar HH, Elnashai AS. Framework for online model updating in earthquake hybrid simulations[J]. J Earthqu Eng,2016,20(1):80-100.
[16] Wang T, Zhai XH, Meng LY, et al. Hybrid testing method based on an online neural network algorithm[J]. Journal of Vibration and Shock,2017,36(14):1-8. (in Chinese)
[17] Wang YH, Lv J, Wu J, et al. ANN based on forgetting factor for online model updating in substructure pseudo-dynamic hybrid simulation[J]. Smart Struct Syst,2020,26(1):63-75.
[18] Hochreiter S, Schmidhuber J. Long Short-Term Memory[J]. Neural Computation,1997,9(8):1735-1780.
[19] Ma F, Zhang H, Bockstedte A, et al. Parameter analysis of the differential model of hysteresis[J]. Journal of Applied Mechanics,2004,71(3):342-349.
[20] Kim J, Ghaboussi J, Elnashai AS. Hysteresis mechanical-informational modeling of bolted steel frame connections[J]. Eng Struct,2012,45:1-11.

基于锁相红外热成像的钢桥涂层厚度检测

王贤强[1] 杨羿[1] 刘朵[1] 张建东[1,2]

(1. 苏交科集团股份有限公司；2. 南京工业大学)

摘 要 钢结构桥梁防腐涂层厚度是施工质量重点检测指标，一般采用磁性测厚仪进行检测，是一种随机抽检的点测量方式，测试结果受人为因素和测试条件影响显著，数据离散性大，亟须探索新的检测技术提高钢桥涂层厚度检测精度和检测效率。红外热成像具有非接触、面测量、快速扫查的特点，在涂敷材料的检测中具有明显优势。为验证红外热成像技术在钢桥涂层厚度检测中的有效性，本文采用锁相红外热成像技术对环氧富锌漆涂层厚度进行了试验测试。结果表明：不同激励频率作用下，锁相相位差与涂层厚度的相关性存在明显差异，0.1Hz激励频率作用下相位差与涂层厚度线性相关性最优；建立了相位差与涂层厚度定量关系曲线，通过锁相相位差评估涂层厚度，与磁性测厚结果的偏差仅为7.88%，具有良好的测试精度。

关键词 钢桥 涂层厚度 红外热成像 锁相 相位差

基金项目：江苏省交通运输科技项目(2019Y69)；中国博士后基金面上项目(2018M642300)；江苏省博士后科研资助计划项目(2018K136C)。

0 引　言

防腐涂装是钢结构桥梁防止锈蚀、延长寿命的主要措施，能够有效隔绝腐蚀介质，使钢材保持良好的耐久性。防腐涂层的重要作用决定了其在施工过程中需对涂装质量进行检测，涂层厚度成为控制涂装质量的关键控制指标[1]。其中，涂层厚度常用的检测方法有磁性测厚法、涡流测厚法、超声波测厚法[2]，这些方法仅能得到测点涂层厚度，检测结果与测点选择相关性大。

红外热成像检测技术具有非接触、大面积检测等优点，逐渐被人们所重视。目前，国内外学者针对红外热成像涂层厚度检测进行了研究与应用[3-5]，Ranjit Shrestha[6-7]针对锁相与脉冲两种技术对热障涂层厚度的检测效果进行了对比分析，结果表明两种技术均能有效测量热障涂层厚度。马晔[8]将该技术应用到混凝土结构内部缺陷检测，在试验构件和实体工程上验证了其有效性；孙杰[9]采用红外热成像技术对涂层下锈蚀、剥离等缺陷进行识别，取得了良好效果。随着红外热成像技术在涂装性能检测领域的研究和应用，探索红外热成像对涂层厚度的大范围快速检测和客观评价具有重要的工程意义和应用价值。

本文选取钢结构桥梁常用的环氧富锌漆为研究对象，采用锁相红外热成像技术对涂层厚度进行了试验测试，对比了不同激励频率对检测结果的影响，确定了最优激励频率，制定了环氧富锌漆涂层厚度与相位差的定量表征关系曲线，对涂层厚度的评估误差仅为7.88%。

1 试件设计与制作

为了研究锁相红外热成像对于钢结构桥梁环氧富锌涂层的适用性，设计并制作了1块变厚度涂层试件，7块均匀厚度涂层试件，试件基底采用Q345qD钢材，按照现行《公路桥梁钢结构防腐涂装技术条件》（JT/T 722）进行喷砂处理，试件尺寸为$180mm \times 60mm \times 8mm$。变厚度涂层试件喷涂过程中，喷头移动速度逐渐减慢，涂层厚度也因此逐渐增加，如图1所示。

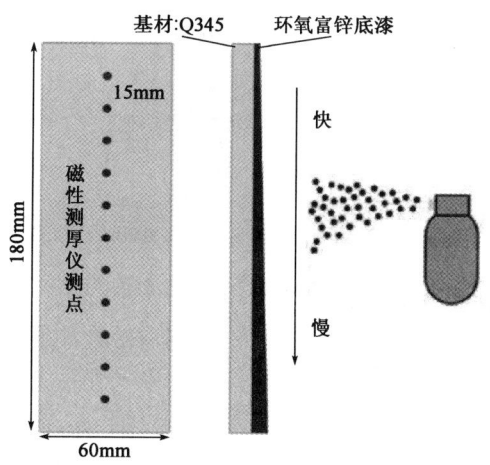

图1　变厚度涂层试件制作

针对每块试件，在其中线上选取11个测点，采用磁性测厚仪进行测试，试件编号及7块均匀厚度涂层试件11个测点的平均值如表1所示。

试　件　编　号　　　　　　　　　　　　　　　　表1

试件编号	平均厚度(μm)	试件编号	平均厚度(μm)
T-LIT-B0	变厚度	T-LIT-B4	159.5
T-LIT-B1	55.6	T-LIT-B5	214.2
T-LIT-B2	88.9	T-LIT-B6	254.5
T-LIT-B3	112.5	T-LIT-B7	278.5

2 试验测试

锁相红外涂层检测试验,采用锁相热波成像无损检测系统,热激励源总功率为400W,图像分辨率为640像素×512像素,帧频选用20Hz。为了研究锁相红外热成像对环氧富锌漆的最优检测频率,针对变厚度涂层分别采用了0.1Hz、0.2Hz、0.4Hz、0.6Hz、0.8Hz、1.0Hz共6种不同激励频率开展了试验。

3 试验结果分析

不同激励频率作用下试件T-LIT-B0的锁相红外热成像结果如图2所示,可以看出,锁相红外热成像可以实现对检测区域内每个像素点的涂层厚度测试,更直观地显示了涂层厚度变化。根据试件中线11个测点位置的测试数据变化趋势,随着激励频率的增加,磁性测厚仪的测试结果与锁相红外相位差的变化趋势偏差越来越大,说明激励频率是涂层厚度红外检测的重要影响因素。

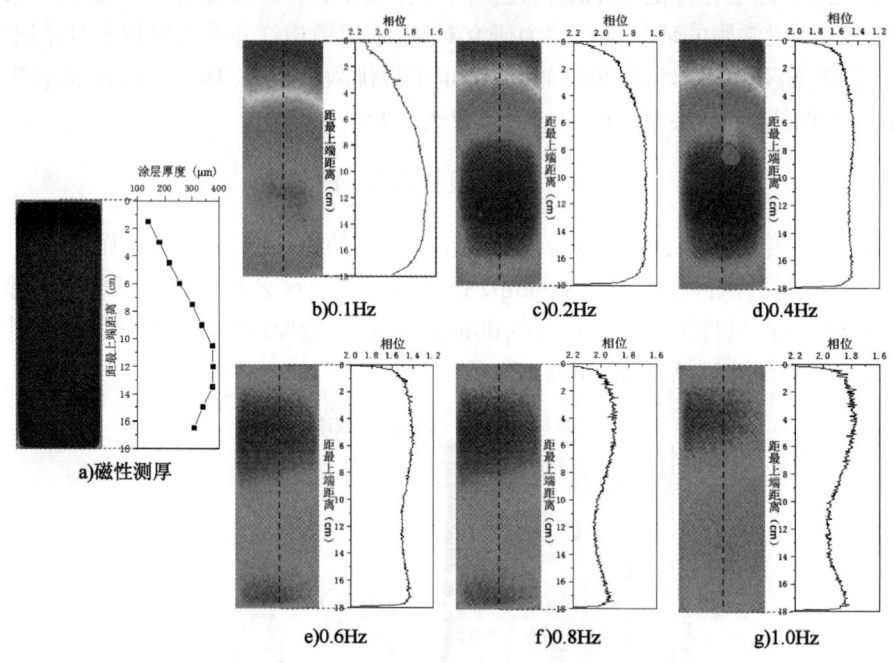

图2 试件T-LIT-B0磁性测厚与红外测试结果

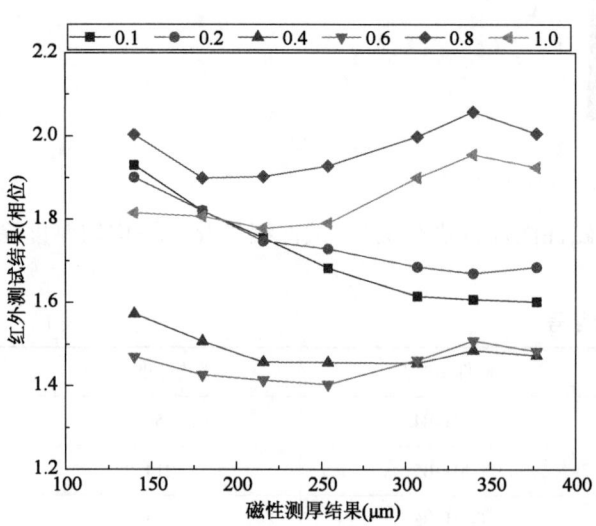

图3 磁性测厚与锁相相位差关系

选取磁性测厚仪测点位置对应的相位差,得到涂层厚度与相位差关系曲线,如图3所示。激励频率0.1Hz时,对于试件T-LIT-B0涂层厚度相位差关系曲线单调递减,斜率较为均匀,具有足够分辨率;激励频率为0.2Hz、0.4Hz、0.6Hz、0.8Hz、1.0Hz时,相位差先减小后增大,这是因为频率较高时,热波波长较短,无法检测厚度较大涂层的内部信息,环氧富锌漆锁相热成像涂层厚度检测激励频率建议采用0.1Hz。

4 涂层厚度评估

试件T-LIT-B1~T-LIT-B7测点涂层厚度磁性测厚平均值与0.1Hz激励频率下相位差平均值的关系如图4所示,分别进行线性和二次多项式拟合。线性拟合见式(1),拟合度 $R^2=0.988$;二次多项式拟合见式(2),整体拟合度 $R^2=0.993$。

$$T = 979 - 402\phi \qquad (1)$$

$$T = 1000(1.59 - 1.02\phi + 0.15\phi^2) \qquad (2)$$

式中:T——涂层厚度;

ϕ——锁相红外热成像相位差。

根据拟合结果,线性拟合与二次多项式拟合的拟合度接近,从简化操作角度出发,采用线性拟合作为涂层厚度与相位差的表征关系曲线。采用T-LIT-B0的检测结果进行了对比验证,去除涂层厚度大于300μm的部分,由相位差评估得到的涂层厚度与磁性测厚结果如表2所示,环氧富锌涂层锁相红外热成像涂层厚度检测结果与磁性测厚结果最大偏差仅为7.88%,验证了锁相红外热成像技术在钢桥涂层厚度检测上的可行性,以及建立的环氧富锌漆和涂层厚度表征关系的准确性。

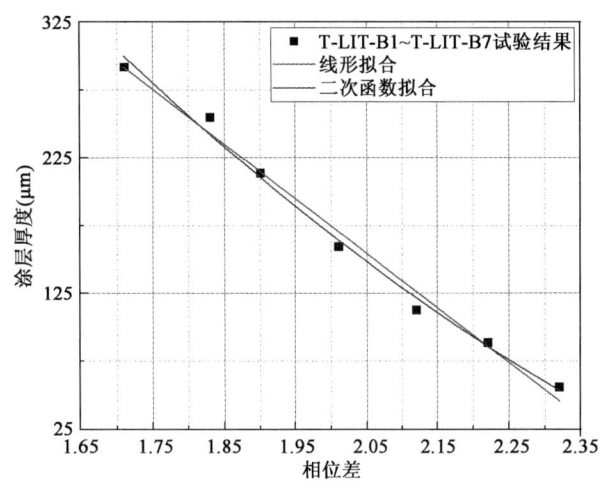

图4 环氧富锌漆涂层厚度与锁相相位差拟合曲线

T-LIT-B0 检测结果对比分析　　　　表2

项　目	测　点				
	1	2	3	4	5
磁性测厚值(μm)	140	180	216	254	300
锁相相位差	2.04	1.94	1.86	1.79	1.73
红外测厚值(μm)	159	199	232	261	285
误差(μm)	18.9	19.1	16.1	6.8	-15.2
百分比误差(%)	13.5%	10.6%	7.5%	2.7%	-5.1%
百分比误差均值	7.88%				

5　结　语

本文采用锁相红外热成像技术对环氧富锌漆涂层厚度进行了试验测试,分析了激励频率的影响,以磁性测厚检测结果为基准,构建了涂层厚度与相位差的关系曲线,实现了钢桥涂层厚度红外热成像检测评估。具体得到以下结论:

(1)不同激励频率作用下,锁相相位差与涂层厚度的相关性存在明显差异,0.1Hz激励频率作用下相位差与涂层厚度线性相关性最优;

(2)建立了相位差与涂层厚度定量关系表征曲线 $T=979-402\phi$,通过锁相相位差评估变厚度涂层试件关键测点的涂层厚度,与磁性测厚结果的偏差仅为7.88%,具有较高检测精度。

参考文献

[1] 中华人民共和国交通运输部.公路工程质量检验评定标准　第一册　土建工种:JTG F80/1—2017[S].北京:人民交通出版社股份有限公司,2017.

[2] 杨华,董世运,徐滨士.涂镀层厚度检测方法的发展现状及展望[J].材料保护,2008,358(11):34-37,71.

[3] 何棱云.基于红外无损检测技术的涂层厚度检测方法研究[D].成都:电子科技大学,2018.

[4] 江海军,陈力.锁相热波成像技术对涂层厚度的测量[J].无损检测,2017,39(4):38-41,48.
[5] 江海军,陈力.激光扫描热波成像技术及在航空领域的应用[J].红外技术,2018,40(6):618-623.
[6] ShresthaRanjit,Kim Wontae. Evaluation of coating thickness by thermal wave imaging:A comparative study of pulsed and lock-in infrared thermography-Part I:Simulation[J]. Infrared Physics and Technology,2017,83(2):124-131.
[7] ShresthaRanjit,Kim Wontae. Evaluation of coating thickness by thermal wave imaging:A comparative study of pulsed and lock-in infrared thermography-Part II:Experimental investigation[J]. Infrared Physics and Technology,2018,92(2):24-29.
[8] 马晔.混凝土结构缺陷的红外热成像检测识别技术[J].公路交通科技,2017,34(12):59-65.
[9] 孙杰,甄宗标.红外热成像技术在桥梁钢结构涂装检测中的应用[J].世界桥梁,2019,47(5):69-73.